OSBORNE'S

ORIGINAL
RECORD COLLECTORS PRICE GUIDE

Popular & Rock PRICE GUIDE FOR 45's

The little record with the big hole.

by Jerry Osborne

associate
Bruce Hamilton

3rd Edition

Published by
O'SULLIVAN
WOODSIDE
& CO.
Phoenix, Arizona

Printed in the United States of America.

Third Edition.

First Printing.

Manufactured in the United States of America.

Library of Congress Cataloging in Publication Data

Osborne, Jerry.
Popular & rock price guide for 45's.

(Osborne & Hamilton's original record collectors
price guide)
Second ed. published in 1978 under title: Popular
& rock records, 1948-1978.
1. Sound recordings--Prices. I. Title. II. Series:
Osborne, Jerry. Osborne & Hamilton's original record
collectors price guide.
ML156.4.P608 1981 789.9'1245'0029473 80-28568
ISBN 0-89019-075-5

FOLLETT: T 1594

Distributed to Booksellers by:
Follett Publishing Company
1010 West Washington Blvd.
Chicago, Illinois, 60607

TABLE OF CONTENTS

INTRODUCTION

UNPRECEDENTED GROWTH!

The most drastic and immediately noticable change in this book, compared to the others in our *Record Collector's Price Guide Series,* is our graduation to a three column format. This was, of course, made necessary by the leaps and bounds increase in the number of record listings contained within this volume.

We are quite proud of the fact that this guide contains about 50% more individual and separate listings than its second edition, bringing the total number of records documented to around 50,000!

The greatest area of expansion for this edition was in the area of late sixties and seventies bands. As you also would expect, we have made many new additions in the earlier years and all record pricing reviewed and revised. There's no question that this will be a valuable reference work to all who use it.

Most major sections of this guide (the most collectible artists and labels) have been carefully scrutinized by the most knowledgeable dealers and collectors available; people who are currently active in the mainstream of the hobby, attend the conventions and regularly participate in buying, selling and trading.

Specialization always has and probably always will raise some eyebrows. Collectors of one type of music will gasp in disbelief that records outside their area of interest can command collector prices. It's important, however, to remember that we are not putting together guides and data for the ones who don't desire the records. If you collect the Beach Boys and cannot understand how on earth an early Frank Sinatra record could be worth ten dollars, it probably means that you are just simply not in touch with the Sinatra collector's market. Don't be a bit surprised if running a list of his (or any of dozens of 'pop' artists) records in a rock oriented fan publication netted poor results. In all probability that's exactly what would happen, and it doesn't mean that the guide is wrong for listing them as worthwhile records. It's all a matter of reaching the right market, and with a little preparation and planning that's not so difficult to do...at least not with any of the records listed in our guides.

Expanding our record guides is, as our acknowledgments page clearly demonstrates, a team effort. Never before have we been blessed with so many specialists in the hobby; people who collect primarily one artist or label. It is this type of expert input that we eagerly solicit more of. The expanse of useful information in such sections as Bob Dylan, the Beatles, the Beach Boys, Elvis Presley, the Rolling Stones, Alice Cooper, the 4 Seasons, John Denver and many others will serve to point out what we hope all important artists' sections will soon look like.

WHAT CAN YOU DO ?

If you possess a great deal of expertise in an area of music that is not yet adequately covered in this guide, there is a great deal you can do about it!

Outline as much information about each artist as known, keeping in mind that too much is better than too little. There are four primary areas of collecting a specific artist that should be covered and used as a foundation.

1) Commercial or store stock releases:
These are the records pressed and prepared for retail sales.

2) Promotional releases:
Specially produced and/or labeled copies, destined for the broadcast and printed media. Often promotional pieces are done separately for retail record locations; usually referred to as "in store" samplers.

3) Oddities and variations:
Releases in this catagory can be either commercial or promotional, but in one way or another they're unique. Special boxed sets, compact 33 singles, fifties and early sixties stereo singles, custom pressings, advertising premiums, limited edition runs, colored plastic pressings, production errors and foreign releases are the most common oddities and variations.

4) Picture sleeves:
Paper collectibles, most often thought of but certainly not limited to picture sleeves, truly have a place in record collecting. In addition to those attractive sleeves, this section may also include paper inserts or materials which may offer anything from a brief biography of the artist to the printed song lyrics.

Many collectors enjoy physically flipping through their records,one at a time, comparing the information on the labels to that in the guide, and noting any discrepencies. That is one of the most reliable sources of corrections and additions for us. Others have made photocopies of labels and sent those along to us, letting us copy as needed directly from the discs.

Regardless of your method, additional listings on any artist in this guide, or who isn't but should be in this guide, are both encouraged and appreciated.

The Jellyroll address appears at the conclusion of this introduction and elsewhere in this book.

PICTURE SLEEVES

We have finally arrived at a sensible solution to our age-old problem of how to handle the listings of picture sleeves. Since most picture sleeves can accurately be valued the same as the disc for which they were made, using identical grading standards, we need not try to list every picture sleeve ever manufactured. What is needed is a separate listing for every sleeve that has a value that differs greatly from the disc itself, whether higher or lower.

We have taken great strides in this guide, particularly with the most prolific and collectible artists, to list those sleeves individually that merit same. Naturally, we want to expand our sleeve coverage to cover every popular and rock artist, keeping in mind that only those with values beyond the discs themselves need separate pricing.

We feel that separate pricing will make the guide more useful, since it is quite common to find either the record or the sleeve being offered sans its counterpart.

78RPM SINGLES

At one time, we thought it would be possible to combine the 78rpm singles with the ones listed in this guide. The staggering number of 45s now included (and still to come in future editions) make this an impossibility. As a rule of thumb,though, it should again be pointed out that 78s from the late fifties and early sixties, especially those by widely collectible artists, stand a good chance of being as valuable as the 45 issue...or more so. Nothing that we can put into a few sentences will begin to cover all the possibilities and we would recommend consulting a reliable dealer for specifics.

STEREO SINGLES

The introductory article by Mike Callahan on the subject of stereo singles covers much of the ground in this area. As far as the listings in this guide, anytime a separate listing appears for a stereo single it designates a release that appeared at a time when issuing stereo singles was the exception rather than the rule. These late fifties and early sixties stereo singles usually bring at least twice as much as the monaural issues...sometimes much, much more.

From the more recent years, when stereo singles were no longer unique, there is no special notation other than an occasional promotional release that has one side in stereo and one side in mono.

COMPACT 33 SINGLES

The compact 7″ single has been with us since around 1951, and the number of those listings has greatly increased with this edition. Even so, there are still hundreds of compact 33 singles that we have yet to discover, document and price. Additions in this area are actively solicited.

REISSUES AND REISSUE LABELS

Most of the hits of our time have been reissued in one form or another. Our position is to list reissues only when it is deemed as essential to the collectors of that material, such as Bob Dylan's Columbia "Hall Of Fame" reissues. We are ready, willing and able to list those reissues that are sought after and command collector prices.

Once in awhile, we receive an inquiry about an odd or unlisted label's release of a well known tune. In most cases, these are simply reissues with very little value. They are only a convenience to the record buyer, enabling one to own a copy of an otherwise unavailable (without paying collector prices for an original label) favorite.

COLORED PLASTIC

All records listed in this guide are on standard black plastic (either vinyl or polystyrene) unless otherwise indicated. Naturally, we want to expand our coverage of colored plastic originals and would be grateful for any contributions in this area.

FAKES & COUNTERFEITS

In every case where we know of a counterfeit issue's existence, we will pass on all of the details available to us to assist in identifying the fake from the original. Collectors who send us this important data are truly appreciated by all of fandom. Please continue to do so, as there are still many counterfeit issues floating around that may be passed off as originals.

THE NECESSARY MINIMUM

Records in this guide that are quite recent and are listed more for discographical purposes than for their current value are, nevertheless, priced at our two dollar minimum for near-mint condition copies. Even though it may be easy to obtain a copy for less at this time, it is also likely that when the disc is deleted from the company's catalog, it will be impossible to order a copy from an "oldies" outlet for much less than two bucks. While the two dollar minimum may be merely symbolic in some cases, it may be quite factual in others.

Keeping in mind the underlying truth about price guides in general; that they are only a guide and not necessarily a bible, the two dollar minimum should be acceptable. Regardless, it can't be more than a dollar off!

PRICES MAY VARY!

Since our very first guide, we've stressed the point that prices will sometimes vary greatly from those in the guide. Even with our planned annual updates, there will be changes in the marketplace that will cause price changes, some perhaps only weeks after this edition hits the streets.

One individual who's willing to pay handsomely for an ultra-rare item can surely jolt the market sending prices spiraling upward, often to the chagrin of others who have yet to locate a copy.

KEEPING TRACK OF THE STARS

As pop music personnel shifts from group to group, band to band, group to solo and solo to group, keeping track of who's on first can be a problem. But with value directly related to the importance and collectibility of the performers, we feel it's in your best interest for the price guides to note key individuals when known. You can help in this fact-finding mission, by sending along to us the names of group personnel, guest performers, lead singers and pseudonyms not listed in this edition. LP covers and liner notes are an excellent source of this information.

PARTIAL DISCOGRAPHIES

The transition to a country music style has been made by several pop & rock singers of the fifties and sixties. The pop & rock releases by these artists will appear in this guide, while the country music releases will be listed in our guides covering that field of music.

Likewise, your favorite soul and rhythm & blues artists that are not covered in this guide are—or will soon be—included in our Blues-Rhythm & Blues-Soul Price Guide.

YOUR NUMBER PLEASE?

When writing Jellyroll, particularly if you're an authority on one specific artist(s) or label, remember to include your phone number so that we can call you and review the material within your area of interest.

Another point to remember is that our production schedule requires us to proceed from this guide immediately to another, probably covering an entirely different area of the hobby. Therefore, the need to contact you in regard to the fourth edition of this guide would not arise for perhaps several months.

CAN YOU PICTURE THAT?

If you have a nice black and white photo of either a record or an artist that you would like to see in one of our guides, we'd like to see it. We'll try to use as many as we can in each new edition. Don't forget though, print or stamp your name and address on the back of each one if you'd like them returned.

THE BEST IS YET TO COME!

As of this writing, we've been in the business of putting out the Record Collector's Price Guide Series for over five years. We couldn't have done it without each and every one of you! Thanks so very much...and here's to the next five years. The best is yet to come!

STEREO SINGLES

By Mike Callahan

We take it for granted today that when we go down to the local record store and buy one of the latest hit singles, the record will be in stereo. As trivial as it may seem, it took the record industry the better part of 15 years to get stereo onto singles on a routine basis. The history of stereo singles is a fascinating one, full of false starts and bad judgements. From the collector's point of view, however, this history has left us with many interesting and unusual collector's items.

Stereo itself has an interesting history. After the many attempts and failures of the early twentieth century, the early 1950s finally saw a genuine breakthrough; stereophonic reel-to-reel tape. During the period 1952-1954 this subject was discussed occasionally in the trade papers, but the general public scarcely heard of it. In 1955, there were finally some reel-to-reel tape catalogs available, but the cost of the stereo recorder was prohibitive to all but the hi-fi fanatic. During the mid-fifties, some songs were recorded in stereo, but these tended to be movie soundtracks and not rock and roll.

The big break came in late 1957, when Audio Fidelity demonstrated the first workable stereo record, using a new Westrex stereo cartridge. The demonstration caused immediate action within the industry, as the various labels began gearing up for stereo. By the next summer, the major record labels had all introduced new catalogs of stereophonic albums. To some, it must have seemed logical that stereo singles would be next.

In the summer of 1958, however, there were two major drawbacks to putting stereo on singles. First, stereo and mono records were not compatable, which meant stereo singles could only be played on stereo phonographs, and in 1958 stereo phonographs were not exactly a household item. The other problem with stereo singles was that the best selling singles were usually rock and roll, and as the common wisdom went, "the kids don't care if it's stereo or not." Actually, there were very few good reasons *for putting stereo onto singles.*

On August 28, 1958, things changed in a hurry. Wurlitzer announced in New York that they were going to market the first stereo juke box, and they had entered into an arrangement with RCA Records to ship ten stereo EPs with each new stereo juke box. Up until that time, stereo singles were oddities nobody seemed to know what to do with. The first known stereo single was issued as a demonstration disc for dealers by Ben Canto, a west coast stereo tape label. Now stereo singles had a customer.

A week after the Wurlitzer announcement, RCA announced that they would also release all of their major hits on stereo singles. The other major labels, not having RCA's interest in seeing the stereo juke box experiment succeed, took a "wait and see" attitude. By late 1958, RCA, MGM, and a few smaller labels were regularly releasing stereo singles; with many other labels preparing to test the commercial market.

In the Spring of 1959, a flurry of stereo singles hit the market from dozens of labels. Major labels like Decca, Capitol, and Mercury released stereo singles, but so did small independents like Abner, Big Top, King, Ace, and Laurie. The Summer of 1959 was the heyday of the original stereo single craze. At any given time, about half the top 25 was available on stereo 45s. But by September, sales were not looking very good. The juke box companies were buying; the general public wasn't.

Columbia Records, which had been the most conservative label of all, decided to try an experiment of their own near the end of 1959. With the sales of stereo 45s not doing well, they introduced the 33 1/3 rpm single in both mono and stereo. After a few other labels followed Columbia's lead, 1960 became the year when the record buyer had the greatest variety of speeds and formats to choose from in buying the hit of their choice. There were mono and stereo 45s, mono and stereo compact 33s, mono and stereo EPs, mono and stereo albums, and even a rare stereo 78. Trade papers were carrying stories which spoke of a "one-speed industry standard," 33 1/3 rpm, with the 45 rpm record on the way out.

Again, the public wasn't buying. The popular large-hole 45s maintained a substantial lead in sales over the poor-selling 33s. Stereo 45s and stereo 33s managed to hang on until early 1961, but at that point, the industry gave up on stereo singles. The mono compact 33 singles managed to last a little longer, going under in mid-1963. The idea of stereo singles was before its time, killed as much by the incompatability of mono and stereo as by consumer apathy. The idea of replacing 45s with 33s was a bad one all around, and probably would be unsuccessful today.

The stereo juke box companies saw the writing on the wall long before the eventual demise of the stereo single. As early as 1960, they began making special arrangements with labels to press custom juke box singles. When the commercial stereo single died in 1961, the juke boxes carried on with their own 33 1/3 rpm juke box singles. These normally were not the same as the hits of the day, but were usually album cuts. From 1961 to 1968, these were essentially the only stereo singles being made.

In 1968, however, things began to change once more. The reason that the early stereo records were incompatable with mono actually was not the fault of the disc itself, but rather that the mono phonograph cartridges of the time had inflexible styli which would eventually damage the stereo records. By 1968, even monaural cartridges were being made which would allow vertical motion of the stylus, so the compatability problem had been solved. Buddah Records announced in early 1968 that henceforth all its 45s would be "Dual 45s," that is, playable on both mono and stereo players. "Rice Is Nice" by The Lemon Pipers (Buddah 31) was issued this way, but Buddah for some reason temporarily reverted back to mono 45s soon after. Elektra picked up the ball by releasing the Doors' "Hello I Love You" as a Dual 45 in mid-1968, as did MGM with "Can't Find The Time" by Orpheus and "Sky Pilot" by Eric Burdon and the Animals. More and more labels then started releasing their singles in compatable stereo until 1975, when the mono single vanished from the hit record charts altogether.

For record collectors, the early stereo singles from the 1958-61 period are interesting items. Since most of them were used in juke boxes and worn out, the remaining pieces usually bring at least twice the price of a comparable monaural single. In certain cases, such as several Duane Eddy singles and "The Shape I'm In" by Johnny Restivo, the stereo version of the song has never appeared on any other record other than the stereo single, so asking prices increase considerably. Many of the early stereo singles are true rarities. It is only lack of demand, perhaps due to general unawareness of their existance, that keeps the prices of these records reasonable.

The juke box singles from the 1960-68 period are also usually quite reasonably priced due to low demand. The exceptions here are records by certain highly collectible artists such as the Beach Boys, Bob Dylan, etc. whose more scarce records generally are at a premium.

A few words here about numbering systems may benefit the collector buying records through auction lists. In general, the catalog numbers of the stereo singles from 1958-61 correspond to the numbers of the mono singles, except that usually there is an "S" added either before or after the mono number. For example, Fabian's "Turn Me Loose" on a mono 45 is Chancellor C-1033, while the stereo single is S-C-1033.

Mercury, MGM, and Dot, however, used a completely different series. The stereo series for Mercury was the SS-10000 series, for MGM the SK-5000 series, and for Dot the 200 series. For these three labels, there is no correspondence whatsoever between the stereo and the monaural single numbers.

In this edition of *Popular & Rock Records*, we have tried to list as many stereo singles as possible. Should you have any additional information on stereo singles, particularly any not listed, please send it to us for inclusion in the next edition. You may write to me at the address below:

Mike Callahan
Box 384
Vienna, Virginia 22180

We would also appreciate a carbon or photocopy being sent to the author at the address below:

Jellyroll Productions
Box 3017
Scottsdale, Arizona 85257

Mike Callahan is a regular columnist for Goldmine Magazine. His column appears monthly under the title: "Both Sides Now: The Story of Stereo Rock and Roll."

Acknowledgments

We would like to gratefully acknowledge the contributions of the following people, each of whom provided some degree of expertise in this third edition. Also listed are some of the fine publications serving record fandom, whose pages may have been consulted in cross-checking data.

In addition, the following individuals deserve an extra special *thank you,* for their assistance was absolutely invaluable to the finished product: Mike Tiefenbacher, Mark Crocker, Jon McAuliffe, Tim Jenson, Len Eisenstein, Dick Haggett, Bob Snyder, Thomas R. Grosh, Mitch McGeary, Joe Williams, Rex Woodard, Larry Ray and Peter Reum.

Amato, Jim
Antonicello, Louis
Arthur, Billy, Jr.
Asheim, Tore
Bancroft, Dave
Barth, Mitch
Beaudoin, Robert
Belich, Gary
Bennett, Randall
Bernhardt, Clete
Black, Frank
Blair, John
Blaise, Marty
Bland, Stephen
Blauvelt, Doug
Block, Dave
Brown, Edward
Brown, Kip
Bryan, Walter R.
Buddy Holly Memorial Society
Bunting, Paul
Burchill, Mark
Caldwell, Patty
Callahan, Michael A.
Childress, Marty
Clee, Ken
Clemmons, Richard
Cole, Bill
Collins, Jeff
Collona, Don
Cooper, James A.
Cotten, Lee
Dalley, Robert
David, John S.
Davis, Barry
DeWitt, J. Ralph
Dilella, Paul
Doolittle, Robert R.
Doughty, Earl
Dungan, Mike
Edelson, Bruce
Engel, Ed
Fiscante, Dale
Flechtner, Jim
Fodor, Frank
Gasperecz, Stephen R.
Gengaro, Frank
Gilson, Bruce R.
Golden Oldies Times
Goldmine
Goodstein, Paul
Gregoire, Denise M.
Griggs, William
Hafeman, Buck
Hatcher, Norm
Herr, Edwin S.
Hickey, Dennis
Hitch, Tom
Humphreys, Bill
Jakimiak, Mark
Johnson, Bill
Johnson, William
Jordan, William C.
Kasenetz, Jerry
Katz, Jeff
Khalil, Charles G.
Kielhau, Lars
Kurze, Bolker
Lapata, George J.
Lay, Rip
Leary, Thomas A.
Lego, Don
Leonard, Wayne
Lepri, Paul
Lewis, Mike
Lindquist, John
London, Wayne
Lowe, Leonard
Loyd, Warren
Makima, Mrs. G.
Marchand, Dale
Marien, James E.
Martin, Scott S.
Matheney, Louis
Mazza, Joseph A.
Mighty John
Miller, Vincent P.
Moody, Wilton, Jr.
Mull, George
Music World
Myers, Derek J.
New Haven Sound
Orsini, James
Osborne, Geri-Anne
Pawlowski, Gareth
Pearlin, Victor
Penn, Don
Petryszyn, Steve
Pewter, Jim
Pimper, Steve
Pulsipher, Lynn
Radloff, Toby
Record Research
Robertson, Terry D.
Rocky
Rudy, Jeff
Sayers, Scott
Schell, John
Seip, Lindy
Self, Bob
Shane's Record Finding
Siebler, Bill
Silverstone, Dean
Sindel, D.C.
Smith, Bill R.
Smith, Ed
Smith, Spencer
Sinatra Sessions
Solid Smoke Records
Spangler, Jerry
Squyres, Chris
Stidom, Larry
Swank, Craig
Taylor, Cheryl H.
Tebblorr, Springfield Bear
Time Barrier Express
Towe, Ric
Tucker, Mark
Valois, Diana
Vaughan, Michael J.
Very English & Rolling Stone
Vignes, Sidney
Watts, Ken
Weaver, Bruce
Weaver, Jim
Whitburn, Joel
White & Still Alright
Witten, Dwayne
Wiur, D.
Yates, Leonard, Jr.

CONDITION: YOU NEED TO KNOW WHAT SHAPE YOUR RECORDS ARE IN

Just because a record is old does not necessarily make it valuable. There *has* to be a demand for it. For the value to continue to rise, the demand must always be greater than the supply. Another factor is condition. The most accurate grading system and the easiest one to explain and understand is as follows:

M - MINT

Mint means the record must be in perfect condition. There can be no compromise. If you have two mint records, but can tell a slight difference between the two, one is not mint. It is for this reason that the term "near mint" appears as the highest grade listed in our books. Label defects—such as stickers, writing, rubbing, fading, or warping and wrinkling—will detract from its value. If a record is, indeed, perfect in every way, it will bring somewhat more than the near mint listing.

VG - VERY GOOD

The halfway mark between good and near mint. The disc should have only a minimum amount of foreign, or surface noise and it should not detract at all from the recorded sound. A VG record may show some label wear, but as with audio, it would be minimal.

G - GOOD

The most misunderstood of all grades. Good should not mean bad! A record in good condition will show signs of wear, with an audible amount of foreign noises. There may be scratches and it may be obvious it was never properly cared for (such as being stacked with other records not in sleeves). Nevertheless, it still plays "good" enough to enjoy.

F - FAIR

Fair is the beginning of bad. A fair record will play all the way through without skips, but will contain a distracting amount of noises.

A

A DATE WITH SOUL

TITLE/FLIP	LABEL & NO.	GOOD	NEAR MINT	YR.
YES SIR, THAT'S MY BABY/Bee Side Soul	(York 408)	3.75	15.00	67

(This record was previously issued as by Hale & the Hushabyes but was actually performed by a star studed group assembled by Jack Nitzsche, featuring: Brian Wilson, Sonny & Cher, Darlene Love & the Blossoms, Jackie DeShannon, Edna Wright and Albert Stone.)
Also see Honey Cone, The
Also see Shacklefords, The

A PAIR OF KINGS (Featuring Jerry Vance)

TITLE/FLIP	LABEL & NO.	GOOD	NEAR MINT	YR.
EV'RY TIME/Just Two Guys	(Warwick 647)	1.25	5.00	61
I WONDER WHERE MY BABY IS TONIGHT/ Just Two Guys	(Warwick 608)	1.25	5.00	61
MONSTER/Once	(RCA Victor 47-7659)	1.50	6.00	59

ABBA

TITLE/FLIP	LABEL & NO.	GOOD	NEAR MINT	YR.
CHIQUITITA/Lovelight	(Atlantic 3629)	.50	2.00	79
DANCING QUEEN/That's Me	(Atlantic 3372)	.50	2.00	76
DOES YOUR MOTHER KNOW/Kisses Of Fire	(Atlantic 3574)	.50	2.00	79
FERNANDO/Rock Me	(Atlantic 3346)	.50	2.00	76
GIMME, GIMME (A MAN AFTER MIDNIGHT)/	(Atlantic 3652)	.50	2.00	80
HONEY HONEY/Dance While The Music Still Goes On	(Atlantic 3209)	.50	2.00	75
I DO, I DO, I DO, I DO, I DO/Bang A Boomerang	(Atlantic 3310)	.50	2.00	76
KNOWING ME, KNOWING YOU/Happy Hawaii	(Atlantic 3387)	.50	2.00	77
MAMMA MIA/Tropical Loveland	(Atlantic 3315)	.50	2.00	76
MONEY, MONEY, MONEY/Crazy World	(Atlantic 3434)	.50	2.00	77
NAME OF THE GAME, THE/I Wonder (Departure)	(Atlantic 3449)	.50	2.00	77
RING RING/Hasta Manana	(Atlantic 3240)	.50	2.00	75
SOS/Man In The Middle	(Atlantic 3265)	.50	2.00	75
TAKE A CHANCE ON ME/I'm A Marionette	(Atlantic 3457)	.50	2.00	78
VOULEZ-VOUS/Angeleyes	(Atlantic 3609)	.50	2.00	79
WATERLOO/Watch out	(Atlantic 3035)	.50	2.00	74

The Name ABBA is simply the first initial of each of the group's first names: Anni-frid Lyngstad, Bjorn Ulvaeus, Benny Andersson, Agnetha Flatskog.
Also see "Bjorn and Benny"

ABACO DREAM

TITLE/FLIP	LABEL & NO.	GOOD	NEAR MINT	YR.
ANOTHER NIGHT OF LOVE/Chocolate Pudding	(A&M 1160)	.50	2.00	70
LIFE & DEATH IN G & A/Cat Woman	(A&M 1081)	.50	2.00	69

ABBEY TAVERN SINGERS, The

TITLE/FLIP	LABEL & NO.	GOOD	NEAR MINT	YR.
OFF TO DUBLIN IN THE GREEN/Gallant Forty TWA	(HBR 489)	.75	3.00	66

ABBOT SISTERS, The

TITLE/FLIP	LABEL & NO.	GOOD	NEAR MINT	YR.
WE'RE GONNA BOP/My Heart Has A Conscience	(Fabor 4003)	1.00	4.00	59

ABBOTT & COSTELLO (Bud Abbott & Lou Costello)

TITLE/FLIP	LABEL & NO.	GOOD	NEAR MINT	YR.
JACK & THE BEANSTALK (PART 1)/ Jack & The Beanstalk (Part 2)	(Decca 88096)	1.25	5.00	55
WHO'S ON FOIST (PART 1)/Who's On Foist (Part 2)	(Campbell 1001)	.75	3.00	60

Comedy

ABBOTT, Billy, & The Jewels

TITLE/FLIP	LABEL & NO.	GOOD	NEAR MINT	YR.
GROOVY BABY/C'mon & Dance With Me	(Parkway 874)	.75	3.00	63
HEY GOOD LOOKIN'/It Isn't Fine	(Parkway 905)	.75	3.00	64

ACADEMICS, The

TITLE/FLIP	LABEL & NO.	GOOD	NEAR MINT	YR.
DARLA MY DARLIN'/At My Front Door	(Ancho 100)	3.00	12.00	
DRIVE-IN MOVIE/Something Cool	(Elmont 1001/2)	2.00	8.00	
HEAVENLY LOVE/Too Good To Be True	(Ancho 101)	3.00	12.00	

ACCENTS, The

TITLE/FLIP	LABEL & NO.	GOOD	NEAR MINT	YR.
LITTLE BOY BLUE/Movin' Along	(Matt 0001)	1.25	5.00	62
OUR WONDERFUL LOVE/A Hundred Wailin' Cats	(Vee Jay 484)	1.25	5.00	62
OUR WONDERFUL LOVE/A Hundred Wailin' Cats	(Jive 888)	5.00	20.00	62

ACCENTS, The (Featuring Robert Draper Jr.)

TITLE/FLIP	LABEL & NO.	GOOD	NEAR MINT	YR.
ANYTHING YOU WANT ME TO BE/Autumn Leaves	(Brunswick 9-55151)	2.50	10.00	59
I GIVE MY HEART TO YOU/Ching-a-ling	(Brunswick 9-55123)	2.50	10.00	59
WIGGLE WIGGLE/Dreamin' & Schemin'	(Brunswick 9-55100)	1.00	4.00	58

ACCENTS, The (Featuring Sandi)

TITLE/FLIP	LABEL & NO.	GOOD	NEAR MINT	YR.
BETTER WATCH OUT BOY/ Tell Me (What's On Your Mind)	(Commerce 5012)	1.00	4.00	64
BETTER WATCH OUT BOY/Tell Me	(Challenge 1112)	.75	3.00	64
HE'S THE ONE/On The Run	(Karate 529)	.75	3.00	
I'VE GOT BETTER THINGS TO DO/Then He Starts To Cry	(Charter 1017)	.75	3.00	64

ACCIDENTALS, The

TITLE/FLIP	LABEL & NO.	GOOD	NEAR MINT	YR.
TWANGIN MACHINE/No Reason	(Beau Monde 1933)	1.00	4.00	62

AC/DC (Featuring Bon Scott)

TITLE/FLIP	LABEL & NO.	GOOD	NEAR MINT	YR.
HIGHWAY TO HELL/Night Prowler	(Atlantic 3617)	.50	2.00	79
IT'S A LONG WAY TO THE TOP (IF YOU WANT TO ROCK & ROLL)/	(Atco 7068)	.50	2.00	77
PROBLEM CHILD/	(Atco 7086)	.50	2.00	77
ROCK 'N' ROLL DAMNATION/Kicked In The Teeth	(Atlantic 3499)	.50	2.00	78

Angus Young, brother of the Easybeats' George Young, was a member of this group.

ACE

TITLE/FLIP	LABEL & NO.	GOOD	NEAR MINT	YR.
HOW LONG/Sniffin' About	(Anchor 21000)	.50	2.00	75
NO FUTURE IN YOUR EYES/I'm A Man	(Anchor 21001)	.50	2.00	75
ROCK & ROLL RUNAWAY/Know How It Feels	(Anchor 21002)	.50	2.00	75
YOU'RE ALL THAT I NEED/	(Anchor 21004)	.50	2.00	77

ACE SPECTRUM

TITLE/FLIP	LABEL & NO.	GOOD	NEAR MINT	YR.
DON'T SEND NOBODY ELSE/ Don't Let Me Be Lonely Tonight	(Atlantic 3012)	.50	2.00	74
KEEP HOLDING ON/	(Atlantic 3296)	.50	2.00	75

ACORNS, The

TITLE/FLIP	LABEL & NO.	GOOD	NEAR MINT	YR.
ANGEL/I'm Going To Stick To You	(Unart 2006)	1.50	6.00	58
PLEASE COME BACK/Your Name & Mine	(Unart 2015)	1.50	6.00	59

ACTION

TITLE/FLIP	LABEL & NO.	GOOD	NEAR MINT	YR.
NEVER EVER/24th Hour	(Capitol 5949)	.75	3.00	67

AD LIBS, The

TITLE/FLIP	LABEL & NO.	GOOD	NEAR MINT	YR.
BOY FROM NEW YORK CITY, THE/Kicked Around	(Blue Cat 102)	.75	3.00	65
HE AIN'T NO ANGEL/Ask Anybody	(Blue Cat 114)	.75	3.00	65
JUST A DOWN HOME GIRL/Johnny My Boy	(Blue Cat 123)	.75	3.00	65
ON THE CORNER/Oo-wee Oh Me Oh My	(Blue Cat 119)	.75	3.00	65

ADAM, MIKE & TIM

TITLE/FLIP	LABEL & NO.	GOOD	NEAR MINT	YR.
LITTLE BABY/You're The Reason	(Press 9728)	.75	3.00	64

ADAMS, Billy, & The Rock-a-teers

TITLE/FLIP	LABEL & NO.	GOOD	NEAR MINT	YR.
BLUE EYED ELLA/Fun House	(Nau Voo 808)	2.50	10.00	59
CAN'T GET ENOUGH/The Gods Were Angry With Me	(Capitol F-4373)	1.50	6.00	60
COUNT EVERY STAR/Peggy's Party	(Capitol F-4308)	1.50	6.00	59
DARLING, TAKE MY HAND/Tender Years	(Fern 807)	2.50	10.00	60
RETURN OF THE ALL AMERICAN BOY/That's My Baby	(Nau Voo 805)	6.25	25.00	59
TATTLE TALE/Born To Be A Loser (With Georgia & The Teens)	(Fern 808)	2.50	10.00	61
YOU GOTTA HAVE A DUCK TAIL/Walking Star	(Nau Voo 802)	6.25	25.00	58
YOU HEARD ME KNOCKIN'/ (Answer song)	(Dot 15689)	1.00	4.00	58

ADAMS, Link

TITLE/FLIP	LABEL & NO.	GOOD	NEAR MINT	YR.
ANGEL OR NOT/Lonely Teen	(A-Okay 111)	2.50	10.00	

ADAMS, Nick

TITLE/FLIP	LABEL & NO.	GOOD	NEAR MINT	YR.
BORN A REBEL/Bull Run	(Mercury 71579)	1.25	5.00	60
JOHNNY YUMA, THE REBEL/Ballad Of Scatter Gun Hill	(Mercury 71607)	1.25	5.00	60

ADAMS, Ray

TITLE/FLIP	LABEL & NO.	GOOD	NEAR MINT	YR.
VIOLETTA/You Belong To My Heart	(Laurie 3118)	.75	3.00	62

ADAMS, Richie (Of The Fireflies)

TITLE/FLIP	LABEL & NO.	GOOD	NEAR MINT	YR.
BACK TO SCHOOL/Don't Go My Love, Don't Go	(Ribbon 6913)	1.00	4.00	60
I AIN'T GONNA MAKE IT WITHOUT YOU/ Every Window In The City	(Congress 248)	.75	3.00	65
I GOT EYES/Something Inside Me Died	(Imperial 5806)	1.00	4.00	62
WHAT AM I (WITHOUT YOU)/Slippin' Away	(Congress 232)	.75	3.00	65
WHAT TOOK YOU SO LONG/Two Initials	(Beltone 1011)	1.00	4.00	61

ADAMS, Tim

TITLE/FLIP	LABEL & NO.	GOOD	NEAR MINT	YR.
EL PUSO/Big Bad Mary (Parodies)	(Twi-lite)	.75	3.00	62

ADDEO, Nicky, & The Darchaes

TITLE/FLIP	LABEL & NO.	GOOD	NEAR MINT	YR.
GLORIA/Bring Back Your Heart (Green Plastic)	(Savoy 200)	6.25	25.00	
GLORIA/Bring Back Your Heart	(Savoy 200)	3.75	15.00	
GLORIA/Bring Back Your Heart	(Earls 1533)	1.00	4.00	
OVER THE RAINBOW/Fool #2 (Shown as by Nicky Addeo & The Uniques)	(Selsom 104)	6.25	25.00	
WHERE THERE IS LOVE/You Can Depend On Me	(Melody 1417)	2.00	8.00	

Also see Barbaroso & The Historians

ADDRISI BROTHERS, The (Dick & Don)

TITLE/FLIP	LABEL & NO.	GOOD	NEAR MINT	YR.
AS LONG AS THE MUSIC KEEPS PLAYING/	(Scotti Bros. 506)	.50	2.00	79
CHERRYSTONE/Lilies Grow High	(Del Fi 4116)	.75	3.00	59
DANCE IS OVER, THE/Sleeping Beauty	(Warner Bros. 5268)	.75	3.00	62
DANCE IS OVER, THE/Socialite	(Pom Pom 4160)	1.00	4.00	62
DOES SHE DO IT LIKE SHE DANCES/ Baby, Love Is A Two Way Street	(Buddah 579)	.50	2.00	77
EVERYBODY HAPPY/I'll Be True	(Brad 003/4)	1.50	6.00	58
FOUR LITTLE GIRLS/What A Night For Love	(Imperial 5715)	1.00	4.00	60
GHOST DANCER/Ghost Dancer (Part 2)	(Scotti Bros. 500)	.50	2.00	79
I CAN COUNT ON YOU/	(Columbia 4-45705)	.50	2.00	73
GONNA SEE MY BABY/Ven Ami	(Del Fi 4130)	.75	3.00	59
IT'S LOVE/Old Salt Mine	(Del Fi 4125)	.75	3.00	59
LITTLE MISS SAD/C'mon Home Baby	(Valiant 6158)	.75	3.00	64
NEVER MY LOVE/Emergency	(Buddah 587)	.50	2.00	77
ONE LAST TIME/I Can Feel You	(Columbia 4-45610)	.50	2.00	72
SAVING MY KISSES/Un Jarro	(Del Fi 4120)	.75	3.00	59
SIDE BY SIDE/Mr. Love	(Valiant 720)	.75	3.00	65
SLOW DANCIN' DON'T TURN ME ON/	(Buddah 566)	.50	2.00	77
TIME TO LOVE/Good News	(Warner Bros. 7249)	.75	3.00	68
WAY YOU LOOK AT HIM, THE/Love Me Baby	(Valiant 6047)	.75	3.00	64
WE'VE GOT TO GET IT ON AGAIN/ You Make It All Worth While	(Columbia 4-45521)	.50	2.00	72

ADELPHIS, The

TITLE/FLIP	LABEL & NO.	GOOD	NEAR MINT	YR.
DARLING IT'S YOU/Kathleen	(Rim 2020)	1.25	5.00	58
KISS-A-KISS/Shine Again	(Rim 2022)	1.25	5.00	58

ADLIBS, The

TITLE/FLIP	LABEL & NO.	GOOD	NEAR MINT	YR.
NEIGHBOR, NEIGHBOR/Lovely Ladies	(Interphon 7717)	1.00	4.00	66

ADMIRATIONS, The (Featuring Joseph Lorello)

TITLE/FLIP	LABEL & NO.	GOOD	NEAR MINT	YR.
BELLS OF ROSA RITA, THE/Little Bo-Peep	(Mercury 71521)	2.50	10.00	59
OVER THE RAINBOW/In My Younger Days	(Kellway 108)	1.00	4.00	
TO THE AISLE/Hey Senorita	(Mercury 71883)	5.00	20.00	61

ADRIAN & THE SUNSETS

TITLE/FLIP	LABEL & NO.	GOOD	NEAR MINT	YR.
BREAKTHROUGH (Instrumental)/Cherry Pie	(Sunset 63-602)	1.00	4.00	63

Also see Rumblers, The

ADRIAN, Lee

TITLE/FLIP	LABEL & NO.	GOOD	NEAR MINT	YR.
BARBARA, LET'S GO STEADY/I'm So Lonely	(Richcraft 5006)	1.25	5.00	
26 MEN/ Love Theme From The Brothers Karamazov	(RCA Victor 47-7201)	.75	3.00	58

ADVENTURERS, The

TITLE/FLIP	LABEL & NO.	GOOD	NEAR MINT	YR.
IT'S ALRIGHT/I Don't Mind	(Ran-Dee 106)	1.25	5.00	62
RIP VAN WINKLE/Trail Blazer	(Capitol 4292)	1.25	5.00	59
ROCK & ROLL UPRISING/My Mama Done Told Me (Compact 33 single)	(Columbia 3-42227)	6.25	25.00	61
ROCK & ROLL UPRISING/My Mama Done Told Me	(Columbia 4-42227)	3.00	12.00	61
2 O'CLOCK EXPRESS/Shaggin'	(Mecca 11)	1.25	5.00	60

AERIAL

TITLE/FLIP	LABEL & NO.	GOOD	NEAR MINT	YR.
EASY LOVE/Race For The Sun	(Capitol 4617)	.50	2.00	78

AEROSMITH (Featuring Steve Tyler)

TITLE/FLIP	LABEL & NO.	GOOD	NEAR MINT	YR.
BACK IN THE SADDLE/Nobody's Fault	(Columbia 3-10516)	.50	2.00	77
CHIP AWAY THE STONE (Studio Track)/ Medley: S.O.S.-Chip Away The Stone (Recorded live)	(Columbia 3-10880)	.50	2.00	79
COME TOGETHER/Kings & Queens	(Columbia 3-10802)	.50	2.00	78
DRAW THE LINE/Bright, Light, Fright	(Columbia 3-10637)	.50	2.00	77
DREAM ON/Somebody	(Columbia 3-10278)	.50	2.00	76
DREAM ON/Somebody	(Columbia 4-45894)	.50	2.00	73
GET IT UP/Milk Cow Blues	(Columbia 3-10727)	.50	2.00	78
HOME TONIGHT/Pandora's Box	(Columbia 3-10407)	.50	2.00	76
KINGS & QUEENS/Critical Mass	(Columbia 3-10699)	.50	2.00	78
LAST CHILD/Combination	(Columbia 3-10359)	.50	2.00	76
REMEMBER (WALKING IN THE SAND)/ Bone To Bone (Coney Island White Fish Boy)	(Columbia 1-11181)	.50	2.00	79
SAME OLD SONG & DANCE/	(Columbia 4-46029)	.50	2.00	74
S.O.S./Lord Of The Thighs	(Columbia 3-10105)	.50	2.00	74
SWEET EMOTION/Uncle Salty	(Columbia 3-10155)	.50	2.00	75
TRAIN KEEP A ROLLIN'/Spaced	(Columbia 3-10034)	.50	2.00	74
UNCLE SALTY/Walk This Way	(Columbia 3-10449)	.50	2.00	76
WALK THIS WAY/Round & Round	(Columbia 3-10206)	.50	2.00	75
YOU SEE ME CRYING/Toys In The Attic	(Columbia 3-10253)	.50	2.00	75

AFRIQUE

TITLE/FLIP	LABEL & NO.	GOOD	NEAR MINT	YR.
KUMBO COMIN'/	(Mainstream 5547)	.50	2.00	73
SOUL MAKOSSA/Hot Mud	(Mainstream 5542)	.50	2.00	73

AINLEY, Charlie

TITLE/FLIP	LABEL & NO.	GOOD	NEAR MINT	YR.
(YOU TELL ME) LIES/Walk A Mile	(Nemperor 7517)	.50	2.00	78

AIRWAVES

TITLE/FLIP	LABEL & NO.	GOOD	NEAR MINT	YR.
DOIN' THE BEST/Next Stop	(A&M 2171)	.50	2.00	79
LOVE STOP/Hideaway	(A&M 2056)	.50	2.00	78
SO HARD LIVING WITHOUT YOU/Hope You Won't	(A&M 2032)	.50	2.00	78

A-JACKS, The

TITLE/FLIP	LABEL & NO.	GOOD	NEAR MINT	YR.
KNIGHT RIDE/Fury (Instrumentals)	(Valiant 6048)	.75	3.00	64

AKENS, Jewel

TITLE/FLIP	LABEL & NO.	GOOD	NEAR MINT	YR.
BIRDS & THE BEES, THE/Tic Tac Toe	(Era 3141)	.75	3.00	65
DANCING JENNY/Wee Bit More Of Your Lovin'	(Minasa 6716)	.75	3.00	65
(DANCING) MASHED POTATOES, THE/ Wee Bit More Of Your Lovin'	(Capehart 5007)	1.00	4.00	61
GEORGIE PORGIE/Around The Corner	(Era 3142)	.75	3.00	65
OVER & OVER/Music Box	(RTV 2005)	1.00	4.00	

Also see Jewel & Eddie

AKI: see Aleong, Aki

AKINS, Jim

TITLE/FLIP	LABEL & NO.	GOOD	NEAR MINT	YR.
FLOATING ON A CLOUD/One Little Girl & One Little Boy	(Marlo 1517)	1.50	6.00	

ALADDIN, Johnny

TITLE/FLIP	LABEL & NO.	GOOD	NEAR MINT	YR.
WHY DID YOU GO/Happy Together (With the Passions)	(Chip 1001)	2.00	8.00	

ALADDINS, The

TITLE/FLIP	LABEL & NO.	GOOD	NEAR MINT	YR.
DOT, MY LOVE/My Charlene	(Frankie 6)	10.00	40.00	61

ALAIMO, Chuck, Quartet

TITLE/FLIP	LABEL & NO.	GOOD	NEAR MINT	YR.
LEAP FROG/That's My Desire	(Ken 311)	2.00	8.00	57
LEAP FROG/That's My Desire	(MGM 12449)	1.00	4.00	57

ALAIMO, Steve

TITLE/FLIP	LABEL & NO.	GOOD	NEAR MINT	YR.
ALL NIGHT LONG/I'm Thankful	(Checker 989)	.75	3.00	61
AMERIKAN MUSIC/Nobody's Fool	(Entrance 7507)	.75	3.00	72
BIG BAD BEULAH/I Cried All The Way Home	(Checker 981)	.75	3.00	61
BLOWIN' IN THE WIND/Lady Of The House	(ABC-Paramount 10712)	.75	3.00	65
BLUE FIRE/My Heart Never Said Goodbye (With the Red Coats)	(Dickson 6445)	2.00	8.00	60
BLUE FIRE/I Want You To Love Me (With the Red Coats)	(Imperial 5699)	1.00	4.00	60
BRIGHT LIGHTS, BIG CITY/	(ABC-Paramount 10764)	.75	3.00	66
CAST YOUR FATE TO THE WIND/Mais Oui	(ABC-Paramount 10680)	.75	3.00	65
CRY MYSELF TO SLEEP/One Good Reason	(Checker 1024)	.75	3.00	62
DENVER/I Do	(Atco 6561)	.75	3.00	68
DON'T LET THE SUN CATCH YOU CRYIN'/I Told You So	(Checker 1047)	.75	3.00	63
EVERY DAY I HAVE TO CRY/Little Girl	(Checker 1032)	.75	3.00	63
EVERYBODY KNOWS BUT HER/Happy	(ABC-Paramount 10605)	.75	3.00	64
FADE OUT, FADE IN/ Love Is A Many Splendored Thing	(ABC-Paramount 10553)	.75	3.00	64
GOTTA LOTTA LOVE/Happy Pappy	(Imperial 66003)	.75	3.00	63
HAPPY/On The Beach	(ABC-Paramount 10833)	.75	3.00	66
I DON'T KNOW/That's What Love Will Do	(ABC-Paramount 10580)	.75	3.00	64
I WANT YOU TO LOVE ME/Blue Fire (With the Red Coats)	(Marlin 6064)	3.00	12.00	59
LIFETIME OF LONELINESS/ It's A Long Way To Happiness	(Checker 1042)	.75	3.00	63
MASHED POTATOES (PART 1)/Mashed Potatoes (Part 2)	(Checker 1006)	.75	3.00	62
MICHAEL (PART 1)/Michael (Part 2)	(Checker 1054)	.75	3.00	63
MY FRIENDS/Goin' Back To Marty	(Checker 1018)	.75	3.00	62
NOBODY'S FOOL/Thorn In Our Roses	(Entrance 7503)	.50	2.00	71
PARDON ME (IT'S MY FIRST DAY ALONE)/ Savin' All My Love	(ABC-Paramount 10873)	.75	3.00	66
REAL LIVE GIRL/Need You	(ABC-Paramount 10620)	.75	3.00	65
SHE'S MY BABY/Should I Care (With the Red Coats)	(Marlin 6067)	1.50	6.00	59
SO MUCH LOVE/Truer Than True	(ABC-Paramount 10805)	.75	3.00	66
UNCHAINED MELODY/It Happens Ev'ry Time	(Imperial 5717)	.75	3.00	61
WHEN MY LITTLE GIRL IS SMILING/	(Entrance 7501)	.50	2.00	71

ALAN, Lee

TITLE/FLIP	LABEL & NO.	GOOD	NEAR MINT	YR.
TRIP TO MIAMI, A (PART 1)/ A Trip To Miami (Part 2) (Lee Alan interviews the Beatles)	(Lee Alan Presents - No number given)	3.75	15.00	64
Special Paper Insert Sheet For The Above Record		2.50	10.00	64

ALBANO, Frankie

TITLE/FLIP	LABEL & NO.	GOOD	NEAR MINT	YR.
SHE'LL NEVER KNOW/Forgetful One	(Tower 153)	.75	3.00	65

ALBEE & FRIENDS

TITLE/FLIP	LABEL & NO.	GOOD	NEAR MINT	YR.
HEXORCIST-WORLD PREMIERE (Novelty/Break-In)/ Shall We Walk Or Take A Dog (By Freddie & The Flea)	(Nik Nik 74)	.75	3.00	74

ALBERGHETTI, Anna Marie

TITLE/FLIP	LABEL & NO.	GOOD	NEAR MINT	YR.
KISS, KISS, KISS/Song From Desiree	(Mercury 70478)	1.00	4.00	54

ALBERT, Eddie

TITLE/FLIP	LABEL & NO.	GOOD	NEAR MINT	YR.
JUST WAITIN'/Fall Away	(Hickory 1278)	.50	2.00	68
LITTLE CHILD/Jenny Kissed Me (With Sondra Lee)	(Kapp 134)	1.00	4.00	56

ALBERT, Morris

TITLE/FLIP	LABEL & NO.	GOOD	NEAR MINT	YR.
CONVERSATION/	(RCA PB-10958)	.50	2.00	77
DIME (FEELINGS) (Spanish Language)/Christine	(Audio Latino 577)	.50	2.00	75
FEELINGS/This World Today Is A Mess	(RCA PB-10279)	.50	2.00	75
SOMEONE, SOMEWHERE/	(RCA PB-11089)	.50	2.00	77
SWEET LOVING MAN/Christine	(RCA PB-10437)	.50	2.00	76

ALBERTI, Willy

TITLE/FLIP	LABEL & NO.	GOOD	NEAR MINT	YR.
MARINA/Cerasella	(London 1888)	1.00	4.00	59

ALBERTINE, Charles

TITLE/FLIP	LABEL & NO.	GOOD	NEAR MINT	YR.
LONG SHIPS, THE (PART 1)/The Long Ships (Part 2) (Instrumentals)	(Colpix 726)	.75	3.00	64

ALCOVES, The

TITLE/FLIP	LABEL & NO.	GOOD	NEAR MINT	YR.
BALLAD OF CASSIUS CLAY, THE/Heaven	(Carlton 602)	2.00	8.00	64

TITLE/FLIP	LABEL & NO.	GOOD	NEAR MINT	YR.
ALDA, Alex (Nick Massi)				
LITTLE PONY/	(Topix 6007)	7.50	35.00	
(In all probability this record was never released commercially. Only promotional copies have been found, accounting for the lack of a flip side.)				
Also see 4 Seasons, The				
ALEONG, Aki				
BODY SURF/Mary Ann	(Vee Jay 520)	.75	3.00	63
(With The Nobles)				
FALL IN LOVE WITH ME/Voodoo Drums	(Reprise 20006)	.75	3.00	61
(Shown as by Aki)				
GIVING UP ON LOVE/Love Is Funny	(Vee Jay 527)	.75	3.00	63
MAGIC LOVER MAN/How Long?	(Reprise 20050)	.75	3.00	62
MOON RIVER TWIST/Tonight Twist	(Reprise 20042)	.75	3.00	62
TRADE WINDS, TRADE WINDS/Without Your Love	(Reprise 20021)	.75	3.00	61
ALEXANDER & THE GREATS				
HOT DANG MUSTANG/Do The Mustang	(Limelight 3040)	1.00	4.00	64
ALEXANDER & THE HAMILTONS				
OVER THE RAINBOW/I Don't Need You	(Warner Bros. 5844)	2.50	10.00	66
ALEXANDER, Arthur				
ANNA/I Hang My Head & Cry	(Dot 16387)	.75	3.00	62
BYE BYE LOVE/	("Sound Stage 7" 2626)	.50	2.00	71
BLACK KNIGHT/Ole John Amos	(Dot 16616)	.75	3.00	64
DREAM GIRL/I Wonder Where You Are Tonight	(Dot 16454)	.75	3.00	63
EVERYDAY I HAVE TO CRY SOME/ Everybody Needs Somebody To Love	(Buddah 492)	.50	2.00	75
HOUND DOG MAN'S GONE HOME/So Long Baby	(Music Mill 1012)	.50	2.00	77
KEEP HER GUESSIN'/Where Did Sally Go	(Dot 16554)	.75	3.00	63
LOVER PLEASE/They'll Do It Every Time	(Warner Bros. 7676)	.50	2.00	73
PRETTY GIRLS EVERYWHERE/Baby Baby	(Dot 16509)	.75	3.00	63
SHARING THE NIGHT TOGETHER/ She'll Throw Stones At You	(Buddah 522)	.50	2.00	76
SHARING THE NIGHT TOGETHER/ She'll Throw Stones At You	(Buddah 602)	.50	2.00	78
TURN AROUND (AND TRY ME)/ Show Me The Road	("Sound Stage 7" 2572)	.75	3.00	66
WHERE HAVE YOU BEEN/Soldier Of Love	(Dot 16357)	.75	3.00	62
YOU BETTER MOVE ON/Shot Of Rhythm & Blues	(Dot 16309)	.75	3.00	62
YOU'RE THE REASON/Go Home Girl	(Dot 16425)	.75	3.00	63
ALEXANDER, Jeff, Quartet				
DR. GEEK/I'll Pay As I Go	(Aardell 001)	3.75	15.00	
ALEXANDER, Max				
ROCK, ROCK, ROCK EVERYBODY/Little Rome	(Caprock 116)	1.00	4.00	59
ALEXANDER, Willie, & The Boom Boom Band				
YOU'VE LOST THAT LOVIN' FEELIN'/You Beat Me To It	(MCA 40861)	.50	2.00	78
ALEXANDER'S TIMELESS BLUES BAND				
LOVE SO STRONG/Horn Song	(Matamat 101)	1.25	5.00	
MAYBE BABY/Power Of Your Love	(Kapp 967)	1.00	4.00	
ALFI & HARRY (David Seville)				
PERSIAN ON EXCURSION/Word Game Song	(Liberty 55016)	1.25	5.00	56
SAFARI/Closing Time	(Liberty 55066)	1.25	5.00	57
TROUBLE WITH HARRY, THE/Little Beauty	(Liberty 55008)	1.25	5.00	55
ALHONA, Richie				
YOUNG BOY, YOUNG GIRL/One Desire	(Fantasy 553)	.75	3.00	62
ALICE COOPER: see Cooper, Alice				
ALICE WONDER LAND				
HE'S MINE (I LOVE HIM, I LOVE HIM, I LOVE HIM)/ Cha Linde	(Bardell 774)	.75	3.00	63
ALICIA & THE ROCKAWAYS				
WHY CAN'T I BE LOVED/Never Coming Back	(Epic 9191)	1.25	5.00	56
ALIVE & KICKING				
JUST LET IT COME/Mother Carey's Chicken	(Roulette 7087)	.50	2.00	70
TIGHTER, TIGHTER/Sunday Morning	(Roulette 7078)	.50	2.00	70
ALL NIGHT WORKERS, The				
DON'T PUT ALL YOUR EGGS IN ONE BASKET/ Why Don't You Smile	(Round Sound 1)	1.00	4.00	
ALL STARS, The (Featuring Alex Hodge)				
HONEY BABY/2 AM On Mulholland Dr.	(Starla 3)	.75	3.00	60
ALLAN & THE FLAMES				
WINTER WONDERLAND/Till The End Of Time	(Colonial 7006)	.75	3.00	60
ALLAN, Davie				
WAR PATH/Beyond The Blue	(Marc 3223)	1.25	5.00	63
(Instrumentals)				
Also see Arrows, The				
ALLEN, Blinky				
BATTLE OF BEATNIK BAY, THE/Make Me Your Leader	(Personality 3502)	.75	3.00	61
ALLEN, Chad				
THROUGH THE LOOKING GLASS/Ramona's Hourglass	(Mala 12033)	.75	3.00	70
TRIBUTE TO BUDDY HOLLY/Back & Forth	(Canadian American 802)	3.00	12.00	64
(Shown as by Chad Allen & The Reflections)				
Also see Guess Who				
ALLEN, Chad				
LITTLE LONELY/Domino	(Lama 7779)	1.25	5.00	61
LITTLE LONELY/Domino	(Smash 1720)	.75	3.00	61
WHO INVENTED THE TWIST/Come On Linda	(Radiant 1508)	.75	3.00	62
ALLEN, Dean				
ROCK ME TO SLEEP/Oooh Ooh Baby Baby	(Argo 5272)	1.00	4.00	57
ALLEN, Duane				
SURF AROUND THE WORLD/The World Stands Still	(Keynote 25)	1.25	5.00	
ALLEN, Jimmy				
MY GIRL IS A PEARL/Forgive Me My Darling	(Al-Brite 1200)	7.50	30.00	60
(With the Two Jays)				
WHEN SANTA COMES OVER THE BROOKLYN BRIDGE/ What Would You Like To Have For Xmas	(Al-Brite 1300)	1.00	4.00	59
(With Tommy Bartella)				
ALLEN, Lee, & His Band				
JIM JAM/Funky	(Ember 1047)	1.00	4.00	59
STROLLIN' WITH MR. LEE/Boppin' At The Hop	(Ember 1031)	1.00	4.00	58
TIC TOC/Chuggin'	(Ember 1039)	1.00	4.00	58
WALKIN' WITH MR. LEE/Promenade	(Ember 1027)	1.00	4.00	58
Instrumentals				
ALLEN, Michael				
BIG PARADE, THE/Rosemary Blue	(Slipped Disc 45288)	.50	2.00	77
ALLEN, Milton				
JAMBORIE/Don't Bug Me Baby	(RCA Victor 47-7116)	6.25	25.00	58
ALLEN, Ray, & The Upbeats				
LET THEM TALK/Sweet Lorraine	(Sinclair 1004)	1.25	5.00	
PEGGY SUE/La Bamba	(Blast 204)	3.00	12.00	
ALLEN, Richie (Richard Podolor)				
BALLAD OF THE SURF/The Quiet Surf	(Imperial 5984)	1.00	4.00	63
BUTTERSCOTCH/Sunday Picnic	(Imperial 5917)	1.00	4.00	63
CAVEMAN/Room 304	(Imperial 5872)	1.00	4.00	62
COMIN BACK TO YOU/Mr. Hobbs (Theme)	(Imperial 5846)	1.00	4.00	62
FOOT STOMP U.S.A./Skeg Along Pete	(Imperial 5929)	1.00	4.00	63
STRANGER FROM DURANGO/Redskin	(Imperial 5683)	1.00	4.00	60
SURF BEATER/Rising Surf	(Imperial 5941)	1.00	4.00	63
TOUCH OF BLUE, A/Not So Quiet	(Imperial 5865)	1.00	4.00	62
UNDERCURRENT/Kick Off	(Imperial 5885)	1.00	4.00	62
ALLEN, Ronnie				
JUVENILE DELINQUINT/River Of Love	(San 208)	1.00	4.00	59
ALLEN, Steve				
AUTUMN LEAVES/High & Dry (By George Cates)	(Coral 61485)	1.00	4.00	55
("Autum Leaves" has Steve Allen on piano, with the George Cates Orchestra)				
CUANDO CALIENTA EL SOL/Leave It To Me	(Dot 16507)	.75	3.00	63
(With The Copacabana Quartet)				
GRAVY WALTZ/Preacherman	(Dot 16457)	.75	3.00	63
I AM THE GREATEST/Mouth To Mouth Resuscitation	(Dot 16613)	.75	3.00	64
SNOW WHITE & THE SEVEN DWARFS/ Jack & The Beanstalk	(Brunswick 86003)	1.00	4.00	
ST. LOUIS BLUES/Ida, Sweet As Apple Cider	(Dot 15891)	.75	3.00	59
WHAT IS A WIFE/Memories Of You	(Coral 61542)	1.00	4.00	55
WHAT IS A WIFE/What Is a Husband	(Coral 61554)	1.00	4.00	55
Also see Freed, Alan, Steve Allen, Al "Jazbo" Collins & The Modernaires				
ALLEN, Stu				
JORDON BLOOPER (Novelty/Break-in)/ Bloopers Morse Code (By the Bloopers)	(Rowax 803)	1.25	5.00	
ALLENS, The				
SHE'D RATHER BE WITH ME/ I Can Only Give You Love	(Mercury 73975)	.50	2.00	78
ALLENS, Arvee (Ritchie Valens)				
FAST FREIGHT/Big Baby Blues	(Del Fi 4111)	2.50	10.00	59
ALLEY CATS, The				
PUDDIN' N' TAIN/Feel So Good	(Philles 108)	1.25	5.00	62
ALLIE OOP'S GROUP				
BLOOP, BLOOP/Dinosaur	(Caprice 102)	.75	3.00	60
ALLISON, Jerry: see Ivan				
ALLISONS, The				
LESSONS IN LOVE/Oh, My Love	(Smash 1749)	.75	3.00	62
ALLISONS, The				
SURFER STREET/Money	(Tip 1011)	1.00	4.00	63
ALLMAN & WOMAN (Gregg Allman & Cher)				
LOVE ME/Move Me	(Warner Bros. 8504)	.50	2.00	77
ALLMAN BROTHERS BAND, The (Featuring Duane & Gregg Allman)				
AIN'T WASTIN' TIME NO MORE/Melissa	(Capricorn 0003)	.50	2.00	72
BLACK HEARTED WOMAN/Every Hungry Woman	(Capricorn 8003)	.50	2.00	70
BLUE SKY/Melissa	(Capricorn 0007)	.50	2.00	72
CAN'T TAKE IT WITH YOU/Sail Away	(Capricorn 0326)	.50	2.00	79
COME & GO BLUES/Jessica	(Capricorn 0036)	.50	2.00	73
CRAZY LOVE/Just Ain't Easy	(Capricorn 0320)	.50	2.00	79
DON'T MESS UP A GOOD THING/Midnight Rider	(Capricorn 0053)	.50	2.00	75
I STILL WANT YOUR LOVE/Power Of Love	(Liberty 56002)	2.00	8.00	68
(Shown as by Hour Glass)				
JESSICA/Come & Go Blues	(Capricorn 0036)	.50	2.00	73
MELISSA/Blue Sky	(Capricorn 0007)	.50	2.00	72
MIDNIGHT RIDER/Whipping Post	(Capricorn 8014)	.50	2.00	71
NEVERTHELESS/Louisianna Lou & Three Card Monty John	(Capricorn 0246)	.50	2.00	75
NOTHING BUT TEARS/Heartbeat	(Liberty 56002)	2.00	8.00	68
(Shown as by Hour Glass)				
ONE WAY OUT/Stand Back	(Capricorn 0014)	.50	2.00	72
RAMBLIN' MAN/Pony Boy	(Capricorn 0027)	.50	2.00	73
REVIVAL (LOVE IS EVERYWHERE)/	(Capricorn 8011)	.50	2.00	71
ALLMAN, Duane & Gregg				
MORNING DEW/Morning Dew	(Bold 200)	1.00	4.00	73
Also see Allman Joys, The				
Also see 31st Of February, The				
ALLMAN, Gregg (Of The Allman Brothers Band)				
DON'T MESS UP A GOOD THING/Please Call Home	(Capricorn 0042)	.50	2.00	74
CRYIN' SHAME/One More Try	(Capricorn 0279)	.50	2.00	
MIDNIGHT RIDER/Multi-Colored Lady	(Capricorn 0035)	.50	2.00	73
ALLMAN, Gregg, & Hour Glass				
D-I-V-O-R-C-E/Changing Of The Guard	(Liberty 56053)	1.25	5.00	68
I'VE BEEN TRYING/Silently	(Liberty 56091)	1.25	5.00	69
NOTHING BUT TEARS/Heartbeat	(Liberty 56002)	1.25	5.00	67
POWER OF LOVE/I Still Want Your Love	(Liberty 56029)	1.25	5.00	68
ALLMAN JOYS, The (Duane & Gregg Allman)				
SPOONFUL/You Deserve Each Other	(Dial 4046)	2.50	10.00	66
(This was the first record by the Allman Brothers)				
ALMOND, Herschel				
GREAT TRAGEDY, THE/Let's Get It On	(Ace 558)	1.50	6.00	59
("The Great Tragedy" is a tribute to Buddy Holly, Ritchie Valens, & the Big Bopper.)				
AL-NETTIE				
NOW YOU KNOW/San Francisco Twist	(Gendinson's 6159)	.75	3.00	62
NOW YOU KNOW/Now You Know (Part 2)	(Art Tone 829)	.75	3.00	62
ALPERT, Dore				
DINA/You're Doin' What You Did With Me With Him	(A&M 714)	.75	3.00	63
LITTLE LOST LOVER/Won't You Be My Valentine	(RCA Victor 47-7988)	.75	3.00	62
TELL IT TO THE BIRDS/Fall Out Shelter	(Carnival 701)	.75	3.00	62
TELL IT TO THE BIRDS/Fall Out Shelter	(Dot 16396)	.50	2.00	62
Dore Albert is Herb Alpert's brother.				
ALPERT, Herb, & The Tijuana Brass				
A BANDA/Miss Frenchy Brown	(A&M 870)	.75	3.00	67
AFRICAN MELODY/	(A&M 1688)	.50	2.00	75
ALL MY LOVING/El Presidente	(A&M 751)	.75	3.00	64
BELL THAT COULDN'T JINGLE, THE/Las Mananitas	(A&M 1237)	.50	2.00	70
CABARET/Slick	(A&M 925)	.75	3.00	68
CARMEN/Love So Fine	(A&M 890)	.75	3.00	68
CASINO ROYALE/The Wall Street Rag	(A&M 850)	.75	3.00	67
FLAMINGO/So What's New?	(A&M 813)	.75	3.00	66
FOX HUNT/	(A&M 1526)	.50	2.00	74
HAPPENING, THE/Town Without Pity	(A&M 860)	.75	3.00	67
HULLY GULLY/Summer School	(Andex 1-4036)	1.00	4.00	59
(Shown as by Herbie Alpert & His Sextet)				
JERUSELUM/Strike Up The Band	(A&M 1225)	.50	2.00	70
LAST TANGO IN PARIS/Fire & Rain	(A&M 1420)	.50	2.00	73
LONELY BULL, THE/Ride Ride Ride (Script Label)	(A&M 703)	.75	3.00	62
LONELY BULL, THE/Acapulco 1922	(A&M 703)	.75	3.00	62
MAE/El Garbanzo	(A&M 767)	.75	3.00	65
MALTESE MELODY, THE/Country Lake	(A&M 1159)	.50	2.00	70
MAME/Our Day Will Come	(A&M 823)	.75	3.00	66
MARCHING THROUGH MADRID/Struttin' With Maria	(A&M 706)	.75	3.00	63
MEXICAN DRUMMER MAN/Great Manolete	(A&M 732)	.75	3.00	64
MEXICAN SHUFFLE, THE/Numero Cinco	(A&M 742)	.75	3.00	64
MY FAVORITE THINGS/The Christmas Song	(A&M 1001)	.75	3.00	68
OB-LA-DI, OB-LA-DA/Marjorine	(A&M 1102)	.75	3.00	69
RISE/Aranjuez (Mon Amour)	(A&M 2151)	.50	2.00	79
(Shown as by Herb Alpert)				
ROTATION/Angelina	(A&M 2202)	.50	2.00	79
(Shown as by Herb Alpert)				
SAVE THE SUNLIGHT/	(A&M 1542)	.50	2.00	74
SHE TOUCHED ME/My Favorite Things	(A&M 1015)	.75	3.00	69
SPANISH FLEA/What Now My Love	(A&M 792)	.75	3.00	66
SPANISH HARLEM/A-me-ri-ca	(A&M 721)	.75	3.00	63
SPANISH HARLEM/A-me-ri-ca	(A&M 1586)	.75	3.00	63
SWEET GEORGIA BROWN/Viper's Blues	(Carol 700)	1.00	4.00	59
(Shown as by Herbie Alpert & His Quartet)				
TASTE OF HONEY/3rd Man Theme	(A&M 775)	.75	3.00	65
THIS GUY'S IN LOVE WITH YOU/Quiet Tear (Lagrima Quieta)	(A&M 929)	.75	3.00	68
(Shown as by Herb Alpert)				
TO WAIT FOR LOVE/Bud	(A&M 964)	.75	3.00	68
(Shown as by Herb Alpert)				
WADE IN THE WATER/Mexican Road Race	(A&M 840)	.75	3.00	67
WHIPPED CREAM/Las Mananitas	(A&M 760)	.75	3.00	65
WITHOUT HER/Sandbox	(A&M 1065)	.75	3.00	69
(Shown as by Herb Alpert)				
WORK SONG, THE/Plucky	(A&M 805)	.75	3.00	66
YOU ARE MY LIFE/Good Morning Mr. Starshine	(A&M 1143)	.75	3.00	69
ZAZAUEIRA/Treasure Of San Miguel	(A&M 1043)	.75	3.00	69
ZORBA THE GREEK/Tijuana Taxi	(A&M 787)	.75	3.00	65
Also see Herb B, Lou				
ALPERT, Herb, & Hugh Masekela				
SKOKIAN/African Summer	(Horizon 115)	.50	2.00	78
ALPHA BAND, The				
YOU ANGEL YOU/	(Arista 0292)	.50	2.00	77
This group toured as back-up band with Bob Dylan				
ALPINES, The				
SHUSH-BOOMER/Skier's Melody	(Challenge 59230)	.75	3.00	61
(Instrumentals)				
ALTAIRS, The				
IF YOU LOVE ME/Groovie Time	(Amy 803)	2.50	10.00	60
ALTECS, The				
EASY/Recess	(Felsted 45-8618)	.75	3.00	60
YOK YOK YOK/Tweeda	(Cloister 6201)	1.25	5.00	
ALVANS, The				
LOVE IS A GAME/What Can It Be	(May 102)	3.75	15.00	61
ALZO				
SUNDAY KIND OF LOVE/Everybody Knows	(A&M 1719)	.75	3.00	75
AMATO, Larry				
WE'RE GONNA HAVE A PARTY/He Made A Miracle	(RCA Victor 47-7411)	1.25	5.00	58
AMATO, Tony				
BRENDA (IS HER NAME)/I Could Love You So	(Peddy 1003)	1.25	5.00	
AMAZING RHYTHM ACES, The				
AMAZING GRACE (USED TO BE HER FAVORITE SONG)/ Beautiful Lie	(ABC 12142)	.50	2.00	75
ASHES OF LOVE/All That I Had Left (With You)	(ABC 12369)	.50	2.00	78
BURNING THE BALLROOM DOWN/ All That I Had Left (With You)	(ABC 12359)	.50	2.00	78
DANCING THE NIGHT AWAY/If I Just Knew What To Say	(ABC 12242)	.50	2.00	76
LIPSTICK TRACES (ON A CIGARETTE)/	(ABC 12454)	.50	2.00	79
LOVE & HAPPINESS/	(Columbia 10983)	.50	2.00	79
NEVER BEEN TO THE ISLANDS/	(ABC 12287)	.50	2.00	77
THIRD RATE ROMANCE/Mystery Train	(ABC 12078)	.50	2.00	75
TWO CAN DO IT TOO/Living In A World Unknown	(ABC 12272)	.50	2.00	77
AMBASSADORS, The				
CAN'T TAKE MY EYES OFF YOU/A.W.O.L.	(Artic 156)	1.25	5.00	
AMBASSADORS, The				
I CAN'T BELIEVE YOU LOVE ME/I Really Love You	(Mercury 73975)	.50	2.00	78
AMBASSADORS, The				
BIG BREAKER/Surfin' John Brown	(Dot 16528)	1.00	4.00	63
AMBER, Jan				
LITTLE MARTIAN MAN/Waiting	(Clef-Tone 157/8)	1.00	4.00	59
AMBERS, The				
LISTEN TO YOUR HEART (CAROLINE)/Loving Tree	(Greezie 501)	2.00	8.00	
AMBERS, The				
BLUE BIRDS/Baby (I Need You)	(New Art 104)	1.00	4.00	
AMBERS, The (Featuring Ralph Mathis)				
ALL OF MY DARLING/So Glad	(Todd 1042)	2.00	8.00	60
NEVER LET YOU GO/I'll Make A Bet	(Ebb 142)	2.50	10.00	58
Ralph is Johnny Mathis' brother.				
AMBERTONES, The				
CHARLENA/Bandido	(GNP Crescendo 329)	.75	3.00	64
AMBOY DUKES, The (Featuring Ted Nugent)				
AIN'T IT THE TRUTH/Sweet Revenge	(Disc Reet 1199)	.50	2.00	74
BABY PLEASE DON'T GO/Psalms of Aftermath	(Mainstream 676)	.75	3.00	67
FOR HIS NAMESAKE/Loaded For Bear	(Mainstream 703)	.75	3.00	69
JOURNEY TO THE CENTER OF THE MIND/ Mississippi Murderer	(Mainstream 684)	.75	3.00	68
YOU TALK SUNSHINE I BREATHE FIRE/Scottish Tea	(Mainstream 693)	.75	3.00	68
SWEET REVENGE/Ain't It The Truth	(DiscReet 1199)	.50	2.00	74
AMBROSIA				
CAN'T LET A WOMAN/The Brunt	(20th Century 2310)	.50	2.00	76
HOLDIN' ON TO YESTERDAY/Make Us All Aware	(20th Century 2207)	.50	2.00	75
HOW MUCH I FEEL/Ready For Camarillo	(Warner Bros. 8640)	.50	2.00	78
IF HEAVEN COULD FIND ME/Apothecary	(Warner Bros. 8817)	.50	2.00	79
LIFE BEYOND L.A./Angola	(Warner Bros. 8699)	.50	2.00	79
MAGICAL MYSTERY TOUR/Cowboy Star	(20th Century 2327)	.50	2.00	77
NICE, NICE, VERY NICE/Lover Arrive	(20th Century 2244)	.50	2.00	75
AMEN CORNER (With Andy Fairwether Low)				
HALF AS NICE/Hey Hey Girl	(Immediate 5013)	.75	3.00	69
HIGH IN THE SKY/Run Run Run	(Deram 5013)	.75	3.00	67
AMERICA (Gerry Beckley, Dan Peek, Dewey Bunnell)				
ALL MY LIFE/	(Capitol 4777)	.50	2.00	79
AMBER CASCADES/Who Loves You	(Warner Bros. 8238)	.50	2.00	76
CALIFORNIA DREAMIN'/See It My Way (By F.D.R.)	(American Int'l. 700)	.50	2.00	79
DAISY JANE/Tomorrow	(Warner Bros. 8118)	.50	2.00	75
DON'T CROSS THE RIVER/To Each His Own	(Warner Bros. 7670)	.50	2.00	73
DON'T CRY BABY/Monster	(Warner Bros. 8397)	.50	2.00	77
GOD OF THE SUN/Down To The Water	(Warner Bros. 8373)	.50	2.00	77
HORSE WITH NO NAME, A/ Everyone I Meet Is From California	(Warner Bros. 7555)	.50	2.00	72
HORSE WITH NO NAME, A/I Need You	(Warner Bros. 7650)	.50	2.00	72

TITLE/FLIP	LABEL & NO.	GOOD	NEAR MINT	YR.
I NEED YOU/Riverside	(Warner Bros. 7580)	.50	2.00	72
LONELY PEOPLE/Mad Dog	(Warner Bros. 8048)	.50	2.00	75
MUSKRAT LOVE/Cornwall Bank	(Warner Bros. 7725)	.50	2.00	73
ONLY IN YOUR HEART/Moon Song	(Warner Bros. 7694)	.50	2.00	73
RAINBOW SONG/Willow Tree Lullabye	(Warner Bros. 7760)	.50	2.00	73
SHE'S A LIAR/She's Beside You	(Warner Bros. 8285)	.50	2.00	76
SHE'S GONNA LET YOU DOWN/Green Monkey	(Warner Bros. 7785)	.50	2.00	74
SISTER GOLDEN HAIR/Midnight	(Warner Bros. 8086)	.50	2.00	75
TIN MAN/In The Country	(Warner Bros. 7839)	.50	2.00	74
TODAY'S THE DAY/Hideaway, (Part 2)	(Warner Bros. 8212)	.50	2.00	76
VENTURA HIGHWAY/Saturn Nights	(Warner Bros. 7641)	.50	2.00	72
WOMAN TONIGHT/Bell Tree	(Warner Bros. 8157)	.50	2.00	76
AMERICAN BEETLES, The (The American Beatles)				
DON'T BE UNKIND/You Did It To Me	(Roulette 4550)	1.00	4.00	64
IT'S MY LAST NIGHT IN TOWN/You're Getting To Me	(BYP 101)	1.00	4.00	64
IT'S MY LAST NIGHT IN TOWN/You're Getting To Me	(BYP 102)	1.25	5.00	64
SCHOOL DAYS/Hey Hey Girl	(Roulette 4559)	1.00	4.00	64
SHE'S MINE/Theme Of The American Beatles	(BYP 1001)	1.00	4.00	64
AMERICAN BREED, The (Formerly Gary & the Nite Lites)				
ANYWAY THAT YOU WANT ME/Master Of My Fate	(Acta 827)	.75	3.00	68
BEND ME, SHAPE ME/Mindrocker	(Acta 811)	.75	3.00	67
BRAIN, THE/Cool It (We're Not Alone)	(Acta 837)	.75	3.00	69
DON'T FORGET ABOUT ME/Short Skirts	(Acta 808)	.75	3.00	67
GIVE TWO YOUNG LOVERS A CHANCE/ I Don't Think You Know Me	(Acta 802)	.75	3.00	67
GREEN LIGHT/Don't It Make You Cry	(Acta 821)	.75	3.00	68
HUNKY FUNKY/Enter Her Majesty	(Acta 833)	.75	3.00	68
KEEP THE FAITH/Private Zoo	(Acta 830)	.75	3.00	68
READY WILLING & ABLE/Take Me If You Want Me	(Acta 824)	.75	3.00	68
ROOM AT THE TOP/Walls	(Acta 836)	.75	3.00	68
STEP OUT OF YOUR MIND/Same Old Thing	(Acta 804)	.75	3.00	67
Also see Rufus				
AMERICAN FLYER				
BACK IN '57/Light Of Your Love	(United Artists UA-XW916-Y)	.50	2.00	77
DEAR CARMEN/Flyer	(United Artists UA-XW1029)	.50	2.00	77
LET ME DOWN EASY/Queen Of All My Days	(United Artists UA-XW874-Y)	.50	2.00	76
SPIRIT OF A WOMAN/	(United Artists UA-XW984-Y)	.50	2.00	77
Included in this band was: Eric Kaz of Blues Magoos/Blues Project; Steve Katz of Blues Magoos; Craig Fuller of Pure Prairie League and Doug Yule of Velvet Underground; produced by George Martin.				
AMERICAN REBELS, The				
REBEL SONG/Rebel Theme	(Super 106)	1.25	5.00	
AMERICAN ROCK REVIVAL, The				
OH HAPPY DAY/Stompin' (Instrumental)	(Bell 788)	.75	3.00	69
AMERICAN SPRING (Spring)				
SHYIN' AWAY/Fallin' In Love	(Columbia 45834)	5.00	20.00	73
AMERICAN ZOO				
WHAT AM I/Back Street Thoughts	(Reena 1030)	1.25	5.00	
AMES BROTHERS, The (With Ed Ames)				
CAN ANYONE EXPLAIN?/Sittin' Starin' & Rockin'	(Coral 60253)	1.25	5.00	50
FOREVER DARLING/I'm Gonna Love You	(RCA Victor 47-6400)	1.00	4.00	56
49 SHADES OF GREEN/Summer Sweetheart	(RCA Victor 47-6608)	1.00	4.00	56
HAWAIIAN WAR CHANT/Sweet Lelani	(Coral 60510)	1.25	5.00	51
I SAW ESAU/Game Of Love	(RCA Victor 47-6720)	1.00	4.00	56
IT ONLY HURTS FOR A LITTLE WHILE/ If You Wanna See Mamie Tonight	(RCA Victor 47-6481)	1.00	4.00	56
I WANNA LOVE YOU/I Still Love You	(Coral 60617)	1.25	5.00	51
LITTLE GYPSY/In Love	(RCA Victor 47-7142)	1.00	4.00	58
LONELY WINE/Can't I	(Coral 9-60926)	1.25	5.00	53
MAN WITH THE BANJO, THE/ Man, Man Is For The Woman Made	(RCA Victor 47-5644)	1.00	4.00	54
MELODIE D'AMOUR/So Little Time	(RCA Victor 47-7046)	1.00	4.00	57
MORE THAN I CARE TO REMEMBER/ 3 Dollars & Ninety Cents	(Coral 60363)	1.25	5.00	51
MUSIC! MUSIC! MUSIC!/I Love Her Oh, Oh, Oh	(Coral 60153)	1.25	5.00	50
MY BONNIE LASSIE/So Will I	(RCA Victor 47-6208)	1.00	4.00	55
NAUGHTY LADY OF SHADY LANE, THE/Addio	(RCA Victor 47-5897)	1.00	4.00	54
RED RIVER ROSE/When The Summer Comes Again	(RCA Victor 47-7413)	1.00	4.00	58
SENTIMENTAL ME/Blue Prelude	(Coral 60173)	1.25	5.00	50
TAMMY/Rockin' Shoes	(RCA Victor 47-6930)	1.00	4.00	57
THING, THE/Music By The Angels	(Coral 60333)	1.25	5.00	51
UNDECIDED/Sentimental Journey	(Coral 60566)	1.25	5.00	51
VERY PRECIOUS LOVE, A/Don't Leave Me Now	(RCA Victor 47-7167)	1.00	4.00	58
WANG WANG BLUES/Who'll Take My Place	(Coral 60489)	1.25	5.00	51
WE'LL BE HONEYMOONING/Barroom Polka	(Coral 60052)	1.50	6.00	49
WINTER WONDERLAND/White Christmas	(Coral 60113)	1.50	6.00	49
YOU YOU YOU/Everything's Gonna Be Alrite	(Coral 60549)	1.25	5.00	51
YOU, YOU, YOU/Once Upon A Time	(RCA Victor 47-5325)	1.00	4.00	53
AMES, Ed (Of The Ames Brothers)				
APOLOGIZE/The Wind Will Change Tomorrow	(RCA Victor 47-9517)	.75	3.00	68
MY CUP RUNNETH OVER/ It Seems A Long Long Time	(RCA Victor 47-9002)	.75	3.00	66
SON OF A TRAVELIN' MAN/2001	(RCA 74-0156)	.75	3.00	69
TIME, TIME/Ballad Of "The War Wagon"	(RCA Victor 47-9249)	.75	3.00	67
TIME, TIME/One Little Girl At A Time	(RCA Victor 47-9178)	.75	3.00	67
TIMELESS LOVE/Two For The Road	(RCA Victor 47-9255)	.75	3.00	67
TRY TO REMEMBER/Love Is Here To Stay	(RCA Victor 47-8483)	.75	3.00	64
WHEN THE SNOW IS ON THE ROSES/ Let Me So Love	(RCA Victor 47-9319)	.75	3.00	67
WHO WILL ANSWER?/My Love Is Gone From Me	(RCA Victor 47-9400)	.75	3.00	68
AMES, Nancy				
HE WORE THE GREEN BERET (Answer song)/ War Is A Card Game	(Epic 10003)	.75	3.00	66
AMES, Stacey				
CALENDAR BOY (Answer song)/Look Out	(Random 604)	1.25	5.00	61
AMOS & ANDY				
LITTLE BITTY BABY/The Lord's Prayer	(Columbia 40002)	2.00	8.00	53
LITTLE BITTY BABY/The Lord's Prayer	(Columbia 42623)	.75	3.00	62
AMSTERDAM, Morey				
MY WIFE DOES THE CUTEST THINGS/True Mon True	(Decca 28212)	1.00	4.00	52
ANDERS, Peter (Peter Andriola)				
REMEMBER ME/I'm Your Slave	(Corvair 903)	1.25	5.00	
SUNRISE HIGHWAY/Baby Baby	(Buddah 3)	.75	3.00	67
VIRGIN OF THE NIGHT/So It Goes	(Kama Sutra 240)	1.00	4.00	67
(With Vinnie Poncia)				
Also see Innocence, The				
Also see Pete & Vinnie				
Also see Tradewinds, The				
Also see Treasures, The				
Also see Videls, The				
ANDERSEN, Eric				
BORN AGAIN/Rocky Mountain Red	(Warner Bros. 7459)	.50	2.00	70
CAN'T GET YOU OUT OF MY LIFE/Ol' 55	(Arista 0121)	.50	2.00	75
SO HARD TO FALL/Think About It	(Warner Bros. 7231)	.50	2.00	69
ANDERSON, Elliot "Suitcase"				
SADDLE & BOOT FACTORY THAT FADED AWAY IN THE LAND OF L.B.J., THE/I Can't Get Started With You	(Poverty Record Co. 001)	1.00	4.00	
Comedy				

TITLE/FLIP	LABEL & NO.	GOOD	NEAR MINT	YR.
ANDERSON, Elton				
SECRET OF LOVE, THE/Cool Down Baby	(Mercury 71542)	.75	3.00	59
ANDERSON, Ernestine				
LOVER'S QUESTION, A/That's All I Want From You	(Mercury 71772)	.75	3.00	61
ANDERSON, Jon (Of Yes)				
FLIGHT OF THE MOORGLADE/To The Runner	(Atlantic 3356)	.50	2.00	75
ANDERSON, Lale				
EIN SCHIFF WIRD KOMMEN (A SHIP WILL COME)/Manchmal Traum-Ich Von Kornfeld (I Dream About The Cornfield)	(King 5478)	.75	3.00	61
ANDERSON, Leroy				
BLUE TANGO/Belle Of The Ball	(Decca 27875)	1.00	4.00	51
SELIGH RIDE/Promeade	(Decca 16000)	1.25	5.00	50
SELIGH RIDE/Saraband	(Decca 28429)	1.00	4.00	52
SYNCOPATED CLOCK, THE/The Waltzing Cat	(Decca 16005)	1.00	4.00	51
Instrumentals				
ANDERSON, Miller (Of Savoy Brown)				
GREY BROKEN MORNING/Bright City	(Deram 85084)	.50	2.00	72
ANDREWS, Chris				
YESTERDAY MAN/Too Bad You Don't Want Me	(Atco 6385)	.75	3.00	66
ANDREWS, Gene				
LINDA LINDA/Lonely Room	(Rust 5054)	1.00	4.00	63
ANDREWS, Julie				
SUPER-CALI-FRAGIL-ISTIC-EXPI-ALI-DOCIOUS/ Spoonfull Of Sugar	(Buena Vista 434)	.75	3.00	65
(With Dick Van Dyke)				
THOROUGHLY MODERN MILLIE/Jimmy	(Decca 32102)	.75	3.00	65
ANDREWS, Patty (Of the Andrews Sisters)				
FRIENDSHIP RING/Music Drives Me Crazy	(Capitol 3403)	1.00	4.00	56
SUDDENLY THERE'S A VALLEY/Booga Do Woog	(Capitol 3228)	1.00	4.00	55
TOO OLD TO ROCK & ROLL/Broken	(Capitol 3495)	1.00	4.00	56
TOO YOUNG/Gotta Find Somebody To Love	(Decca 27569)	1.25	5.00	51
ANDY & THE LIVE WIRES				
MAGGIE/You've Done It Again	(Applause 1249)	2.00	8.00	60
ANDY & THE MARGLOWS				
JUST ONE LOOK/Symphony	(Liberty 55570)	1.00	4.00	63
SUPERMAN LOVER/I'll Get By	(Liberty 55623)	1.00	4.00	63
ANGEL				
AIN'T GONNA EAT OUT MY HEART ANYMORE/ Flying With Broken Wings (Without You)	(Casablanca 914)	.50	2.00	78
(Casablanca 914 was also the catalog number on "Flying With Broken Wings"/"Under Suspicion")				
DON'T LEAVE ME LONELY/Stick Like Glue	(Casablanca 933)	.50	2.00	78
DON'T TAKE YOUR LOVE/	(Casablanca 963)	.50	2.00	79
FLYING WITH BROKEN WINGS (WITHOUT YOU)/ Under Suspicion	(Casablanca 914)	.50	2.00	78
(Also see "Ain't Gonna Eat Out My Heart Anymore")				
THAT MAGIC TOUCH/Big Boy (Let's Do It Again)	(Casablanca 878)	.50	2.00	77
WINTER SONG/Can You Feel It	(Casablanca 903)	.50	2.00	77
ANGEL & THE DEVINES				
BIG MOUTH/The Octopus	(Siana 720)	.75	3.00	
ANGEL, Bobby, & The Hillsiders				
BABY-O/That's The Way I Want To Go	(Rhum 101)	.75	3.00	61
HEARTBREAK HOTEL/Submarine Races	(Astra 300)	.75	3.00	62
ANGEL, Johnny				
BABY, YOU GOT SOUL/All Night Party	(Gardena 117)	1.00	4.00	61
DOUBT/Falling Teardrops	(Imperial 5673)	1.25	5.00	60
FEVER, THE/A Day Late & A Dollar Short	(Parliament 778)	1.00	4.00	
LOOKING FOR A FOOL/Roller-Motion	(Felsted 8659)	1.00	4.00	62
LONELY NIGHTS/Seven Words	(JAF 2024)	1.00	4.00	61
MASHED POTATO STOMP/One More Tomorrow	(Felsted 8646)	1.00	4.00	62
TEENAGE WEDDING/Baby, It's Love	(Vin 1004)	2.00	8.00	
TELL LAURA I LOVE HER/The Way I Feel Tonight	(Bell 472)	1.00	4.00	
WITHOUT HER HEART/Lady Of Spain	(Felsted 8633)	1.00	4.00	61
(With the Halos)				
ANGEL, Ronnie				
THAT'S ALRIGHT/	(Rita 1011)	1.25	5.00	60
ANGELENOS, The				
AS LONG AS I HAVE YOU/Don't Cry Baby	(Peppers P-2824-45)	1.00	4.00	

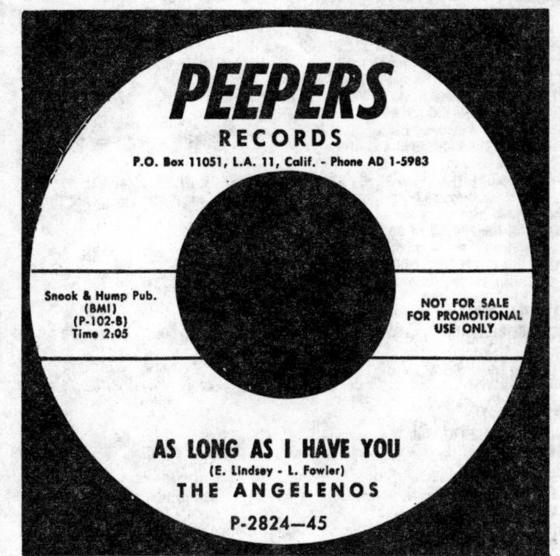

TITLE/FLIP	LABEL & NO.	GOOD	NEAR MINT	YR.
ANGELETTES, The				
DON'T LET HIM TOUCH YOU/Rainy Day	(London 1040)	.50	2.00	71
ANGELO, Bonnie				
ELVIS MAGIC/The Ballad Of Sam Diamond	(Bonny T.S.S. 3253)	.75	3.00	78
ANGELO & THE INITIALS				
SOMEDAY SHE'LL LOVE ME/I Should Have Listened	(Congress 229)	1.25	5.00	64
ANGELOS, The				
BAD MOTORCYCLE/Backfield In Motion	(Tollie 9003)	.75	3.00	64
JUST LIKE TAKIN' CANDY FROM A BABY/Lonely Hours	(Vee Jay 531)	1.00	4.00	63
YOU TURN ME ON/Raining Teardrops	(Cameo 250)	.75	3.00	63

TITLE/FLIP	LABEL & NO.	GOOD	NEAR MINT	YR.
ANGELO'S ANGELS				
DIRTY SHIRT/Mach 9	(Tabb 3230)	.75	3.00	63
I DON'T BELIEVE/Shimmy Jimmy	(Ermine 59)	.75	3.00	64
SPRING CLEANING/Tomorrow	(Ermine 55)	.75	3.00	64
ANGELS, The (The Safaris)				
LOVER'S POEM (TO HER), A/A Lover's Poem (To Him)	(Tawny 101)	2.50	10.00	59
ANGELS, The				
BOY WITH THE GREEN EYES, THE/But For Love	(RCA Victor 47-9612)	1.00	4.00	68
COTTON FIELDS/A Moment Ago	(Caprice 121)	1.25	5.00	62
COTTON FIELDS/Irresistible	(Ascot 2139)	.75	3.00	63
CRY BABY CRY/That's All I Ask Of You	(Caprice 112)	1.00	4.00	62
(With Linda Jansen)				
DREAM BOY/Jamaica Joe	(Smash 1915)	.75	3.00	64
EVERYBODY LOVES A LOVER/Blow Joe	(Caprice 116)	1.00	4.00	62
I ADORE HIM/Thank You & Goodnight	(Smash 1854)	.75	3.00	63
LITTLE BEATLE BOY/Java	(Smash 1885)	.75	3.00	64
MERRY GO ROUND/So Nice	(RCA Victor 47-9681)	1.00	4.00	68
MODLEY, THE/If I Didn't Love You	(RCA Victor 47-9541)	1.00	4.00	68
MY BOYFRIEND'S BACK/(Love Me) Now	(Smash 1834)	.75	3.00	63
PAPA'S SIDE OF THE BED/You're All I Need To Get By	(Polydor 14222)	.50	2.00	74
P.S. I LOVE YOU/Where Is My Love Tonight	(Astro AS202-1)	3.75	15.00	60
'TIL/A Moment Ago	(Caprice 107)	1.00	4.00	61
(With Linda Jansen)				
WHAT TO DO/I Had A Dream I Lost You	(RCA Victor 47-9129)	1.00	4.00	67
WITH LOVE/You're The Cause Of It	(RCA Victor 47-9404)	1.00	4.00	67
WORLD WITHOUT LOVE, A/The Boy From Cross Town	(Smash 1931)	.75	3.00	64
WOW WOW WEE (HE'S THE BOY FOR ME)/ Snowflakes & Teardrops	(Smash 1870)	.75	3.00	63
YOU'LL NEVER GET TO HEAVEN/Go Out & Play	(RCA Victor 47-9246)	1.00	4.00	67
YOU SHOULD HAVE TOLD ME/I'd Be Good For You	(Caprice 118)	1.00	4.00	62
Also see Starlets, The				
ANGIE (With Pete Townshend)				
PEPPERMINT LUMP/Breakfast In Naples (By Angie's Orchestra)	(Stiff-Epic 50793)	.50	2.00	79
ANGIE & THE CHICKLETTES				
TREAT HIM TENDER, MAUREEN (NOW THAT RINGO BELONGS TO YOU)/Tommy	(Apt 25080)	2.00	8.00	65
ANGLOS				
INCENSE/Stepping Stone	(Orbit 201)	.75	3.00	65
ANGLOS				
SMALL TOWN BOY/Since You've Been Gone	(Scepter 12204)	1.25	5.00	68
ANIMALS The (Featuring Eric Burdon)				
ANYTHING/It's All Meat	(MGM K-13917)	.75	3.00	68
BOOM BOOM/Blue Feeling	(MGM K-13298)	.75	3.00	64
BRIDGE OF LIFE/Electronic Magnetism	(MGM K-14221)	.50	2.00	71
BRING IT ON HOME TO ME/For Miss Caulker	(MGM K-13339)	.75	3.00	65
DON'T BRING ME DOWN/Cheating	(MGM K-13514)	.75	3.00	66
DON'T LET ME BE MISUNDERSTOOD/Club A-Go-Go	(MGM K-13311)	.75	3.00	65
FIRE ON THE SUN/Riverside County	(Jet JT XW-1070)	.50	2.00	77
GONNA SEND YOU BACK TO WALKER/ Baby Let Me Take You Home	(MGM K-13242)	.75	3.00	64
HELP ME GIRL/That Ain't Where It's At	(MGM K-13636)	.75	3.00	66
HOUSE OF THE RISING SUN, THE/Talking About You	(MGM K-13264)	1.00	4.00	64
I'M CRYING/Take It Easy Baby	(MGM K-13274)	.75	3.00	64
INSIDE LOOKING OUT/You're On My Mind	(MGM K-13468)	.75	3.00	66
IT'S MY LIFE/I'm Going To Change The World	(MGM K-13414)	.75	3.00	65
MONTEREY/Ain't It So	(MGM K-13868)	.75	3.00	66
SAN FRANCISCAN NIGHTS/Good Times	(MGM K-13769)	.75	3.00	67
SEE SEE RIDER/She'll Return It	(MGM K-13582)	.75	3.00	66
SKY PILOT/Sky Pilot (Part 2)	(MGM K-13939)	.75	3.00	68
SKY PILOT (Long Version)/ Sky Pilot (Short Version)	(MGM K-13939-SS)	1.00	4.00	68
WE GOTTA GET OUT OF THIS PLACE/I Can't Believe It	(MGM K-13352)	.75	3.00	65
WHEN I WAS YOUNG/Girl Named Sandoz	(MGM K-13721)	.75	3.00	67
WHITE HOUSES/River Deep, Mountain High	(MGM K-14013)	.75	3.00	68
ANITA & THE SO-AND-SO'S (The Anita Kerr Singers)				
JOEY BABY/Rinky Tinky Rhythm	(RCA Victor 47-7974)	1.50	3.00	62
TO EACH HIS OWN/Tell Tale	(RCA Victor 47-8050)	1.00	2.00	62
ANKA, Paul				
(ALL OF A SUDDEN) MY HEART SINGS/ That's Love	(ABC-Paramount 9987)	1.00	4.00	58
(ALL OF A SUDDEN) MY HEART SINGS/ That's Love	(ABC-Paramount S-9987)	2.00	8.00	58
(Stereo single)				
ANYTIME (I'LL BE THERE)/	(United Artists UA-XW789-Y)	.50	2.00	76
AS LONG AS WE KEEP BELIEVING/	(RCA PB-11662)	.50	2.00	79
CRAZY LOVE/Let The Bells Keep Ringing	(ABC-Paramount 9907)	1.00	4.00	58
DANCE ON, LITTLE GIRL/I Talk To You	(ABC-Paramount 10220)	.75	3.00	61
DIANA/Don't Gamble With Love	(ABC-Paramount 9831)	1.00	4.00	57
DID YOU HAVE A HAPPY BIRTHDAY/ For No Good Reason At All	(RCA Victor 47-8272)	.75	3.00	63
DO I LOVE YOU/	(Buddah 252)	.50	2.00	78
ESO BESO/Give Me Back My Heart	(RCA Victor 47-8097)	.75	3.00	62
EVERY NIGHT/There You Go	(RCA Victor 47-8068)	.75	3.00	62
FOOLS HALL OF FAME/ Far From The Lights Of Town	(ABC-Paramount 10282)	.75	3.00	62
FROM ROCKING HORSE TO ROCKING CHAIR/ Cheer Up	(RCA Victor 47-8311)	.75	3.00	64
GOODNIGHT MY LOVE/This Crazy World	(RCA Victor 47-9648)	.50	2.00	69
HAPPIER/Closing Doors	(United Artists UA-XW911-Y)	.50	2.00	76
HAPPY/Can't Get You Out Of My Mind	(RCA Victor 47-9767)	.50	2.00	69
HELLO JIM/You've Got The Nerve To Call This Love	(RCA Victor 47-8195)	.75	3.00	63
HELLO YOUNG LOVERS/ I Love You In The Same Old Way	(ABC-Paramount 10132)	.75	3.00	60
HELLO YOUNG LOVERS/ I Love You In The Same Old Way	(ABC-Paramount S-10132)	1.50	6.00	60
(Stereo single)				
HEY GIRL/	(Buddah 349)	.75	3.00	73
HURRY UP & TELL ME/ Wondrous Are The Ways Of Love	(RCA Victor 47-8237)	.75	3.00	63
(I BELIEVE) THERE'S NOTHING STRONGER THAN OUR LOVE/ Today I Became A Fool	(United Artists UA-XW685-Y)	.50	2.00	75
(With Odia Coates)				
I CAN'T HELP LOVING YOU/ Can't Get Along Very Well Without Her	(RCA Victor 47-8893)	.75	3.00	66
I CONFESS/Blau-Wile Deveest Fontaine	(RPM 472)	5.00	20.00	56
(Vocal backing by either the Jacks or the Flairs)				
I CONFESS/Blau-Wile Deveest Fontaine	(RPM 499)	5.00	20.00	56
(Vocal backing by either the Jacks or the Flairs)				
I DON'T LIKE TO SLEEP ALONE/ How Can Anything Be Beautiful, After	(United Artists UA-XW615-X)	.50	2.00	75
I LOVE YOU, BABY/Tell Me That You Love Me	(ABC-Paramount 9855)	1.00	4.00	57
I MISS YOU SO/Late Last Night	(ABC-Paramount 10011)	1.00	4.00	59
I MISS YOU SO/Late Last Night	(ABC-Paramount S-10011)	2.00	8.00	59
(Stereo single)				
I WENT TO YOUR WEDDING/I Wish	(RCA Victor 47-8839)	.75	3.00	66
IN MY IMAGINATION/It's Easy To Say	(RCA Victor 47-8396)	.75	3.00	64
IN THE STILL OF THE NIGHT/Pickin' Up The Pieces	(RCA 74-0126)	.50	2.00	69
I'D NEVER FIND ANOTHER YOU/Uh Huh	(ABC-Paramount 10311)	.75	3.00	62
I'D RATHER BE A STRANGER/Poor Old World	(RCA Victor 47-9228)	.75	3.00	67
I'LL HELP YOU/Never Gonna Fall In Love Again (Like I Fell In Love With You)	(United Artists UA-XW945-Y)	.50	2.00	77
I'M COMING HOME/Cry	(ABC-Paramount 10338)	.75	3.00	62
IT'S CHRISTMAS EVERYWHERE/ Rudolph The Red Nosed Raindeer	(ABC-Paramount 10169)	1.25	5.00	60

TITLE/FLIP	LABEL & NO.	GOOD	NEAR MINT	YR.
IT'S TIME TO CRY/Something Has Changed Me	(ABC-Paramount 10064)	1.00	4.00	59
IT'S TIME TO CRY/Something Has Changed Me (Stereo single)	(ABC-Paramount S-10064)	2.00	8.00	59
JUBILATION/Everything's Been Changed	(Buddah 294)	.75	3.00	72
JUST YOUNG/So It's Goodbye	(ABC-Paramount 9956)	1.00	4.00	58
KISSIN' ON THE PHONE/Cinderella	(ABC-Paramount 10239)	.75	3.00	61
LET ME GET TO KNOW YOU/Fame	(FM-XW345-W)	.50	2.00	73
LIFE SONG/	(Buddah 314)	.75	3.00	72
LONELIEST BOY IN THE WORLD, THE/ Dream Me Happy	(RCA Victor 47-8595)	.75	3.00	65
LONELY BOY/Your Love	(ABC-Paramount 10022)	1.00	4.00	59
LONELY BOY/Your Love (Stereo single)	(ABC-Paramount S-10022)	2.00	8.00	59
LOVE (MAKES THE WORLD GO ROUND)/ Crying In The Wind	(RCA Victor 47-8115)	.75	3.00	62
LOVE ME LADY/Brought Up In New York	(RCA PB-11351)	.50	2.00	78
LOVE ME WARM & TENDER/I'd Like To Know	(RCA Victor 47-7977)	.75	3.00	62
LOVELAND/The Bells At My Wedding	(ABC-Paramount 10279)	.75	3.00	61
MAKE IT UP TO ME IN LOVE/You (With Odia Coates)	(Epic 8-50298)	.50	2.00	76
MAKE IT UP TO ME IN LOVE/ (12" single issue, with Odia Coates)	(Epic 28-50353)	1.25	5.00	77
MIDNIGHT/Verboten	(ABC-Paramount 9937)	1.00	4.00	58
MIDNIGHT MISTRESS-BEFORE IT'S TOO LATE/ This Land Is Your Land	(RCA 47-9746)	.75	3.00	70
MY BABY'S COMIN' HOME/No, No	(RCA Victor 47-8349)	.75	3.00	64
MY BEST FRIEND'S WIFE/	(United Artists UA-XW972-Y)	.50	2.00	77
MY HOME TOWN/Something Happened	(ABC-Paramount 10106)	.75	3.00	60
ONE MAN WOMAN-ONE WOMAN MAN/ Let Me Get To Know You (With Odia Coates)	(United Artists UA-XW569-X)	.50	2.00	74
PUPPY LOVE/Adam & Eve	(ABC-Paramount 10082)	.75	3.00	60
PUPPY LOVE/Adam & Eve (Stereo single)	(ABC-Paramount S-10082)	1.50	6.00	60
PUT YOUR HEAD ON MY SHOULDER/ Don't Ever Leave Me	(ABC-Paramount 10040)	1.00	4.00	59
PUT YOUR HEAD ON MY SHOULDER/ Don't Ever Leave Me (Stereo single)	(ABC-Paramount S-10040)	2.00	8.00	59
REMEMBER DIANA/At Night	(RCA Victor 47-8170)	.75	3.00	63
SINCERELY/Next Year	(RCA 74-0164)	.50	2.00	69
STEEL GUITAR & A GLASS OF WINE, A/ I Never Knew Your Name	(RCA Victor 47-8030)	.75	3.00	62
STORY OF MY LOVE, THE/ Don't Say You're Sorry	(ABC-Paramount 10168)	.75	3.00	60
STORY OF MY LOVE, THE/ Don't Say You're Sorry (Stereo single)	(ABC-Paramount S-10168)	1.50	6.00	60
SUMMER'S GONE/I'd Have To Share	(ABC-Paramount 10147)	.75	3.00	60
SUMMER'S GONE/I'd Have To Share (Stereo single)	(ABC-Paramount S-10147)	1.50	6.00	60
SYLVIA/Behind My Smile	(RCA Victor 47-8493)	.75	3.00	65
THAT'S HOW LOVE GOES/ A Woman Is A Sentimental Thing	(RCA Victor 47-9228)	.75	3.00	67
THIS IS LOVE/	(RCA PB-11395)	.50	2.00	78
TIMES OF YOUR LIFE/Water Runs Deep	(United Artists UA-XW737-Y)	.50	2.00	75
TONIGHT/Everybody Ought To Be In Love	(United Artists UA-XW1018)	.50	2.00	77
TONIGHT, MY LOVE, TONIGHT/ I'm Just Your Fool Anyway	(ABC-Paramount 10194)	.75	3.00	61
TRULY YOURS/Oh, Such A Stranger	(RCA Victor 47-8764)	.75	3.00	66
UNTIL IT'S TIME FOR YOU TO GO/ Would You Still Be My Baby	(RCA Victor 47-9128)	.75	3.00	67
WHEN WE GET THERE/ Can't Get You Out Of My Mind	(RCA Victor 47-9457)	.75	3.00	68
WHILE WE'RE STILL YOUNG/	(Buddah 337)	.75	3.00	73
WHY ARE YOU LEANING ON ME, SIR/ You're Some Kind Of Friend	(Barnaby ZS72027)	.75	3.00	71
YOU ARE MY DESTINY/When I Stop Loving You	(ABC-Paramount 9880)	1.00	4.00	57
(YOU CAN) SHARE YOUR LOVE/ (Special Product-Fan Club Item)	(ABC-Paramount PRO 104)	2.50	10.00	
(YOU'RE) HAVING MY BABY (With Odia Coates)	(United Artists UA-XW454-W)	.50	2.00	74

ANKA, Paul, George Hamilton IV, Johnny Nash

TITLE/FLIP	LABEL & NO.	GOOD	NEAR MINT	YR.
TEEN COMMANDMENTS, THE/ If You Learn To Pray	(ABC-Paramount 9974)	1.50	6.00	58

ANN, Cheryl

TITLE/FLIP	LABEL & NO.	GOOD	NEAR MINT	YR.
I CAN'T LET HIM/Goodbye Baby (Group Sound)	(Patty 52)	2.00	8.00	

ANNETTE (Funicello)

TITLE/FLIP	LABEL & NO.	GOOD	NEAR MINT	YR.
BABY NEEDS ME NOW/Moment Of Silence	(Epic 9828)	1.00	4.00	65
BELLA BELLA FLORENCE/Canzone D' Amore (With Marzocchi)	(Buena Vista 407)	1.25	5.00	62
BIKINI BEACH PARTY/The Clyde	(Buena Vista 436)	1.25	5.00	64
BOY TO LOVE/No One Could Be Prouder	(Buena Vista 442)	1.25	5.00	65
CUSTOM CITY/Rebel Rider	(Buena Vista 432)	1.25	5.00	64
DREAM BOY/Please, Please Signore	(Buena Vista 374)	1.25	5.00	61
DREAMIN' ABOUT YOU/Strummin' Song (Shown as by Annette & The Vonnair Sisters)	(Buena Vista 388)	1.25	5.00	61
FIRST NAME INITIAL/My Heart Became Of Age	(Buena Vista 349)	1.00	4.00	59
HAWAIIAN LOVE TALK/Blue Muu Muu	(Buena Vista 384)	1.25	5.00	61
HOW WILL I KNOW MY LOVE/ Something Borrowed, Something Blue	(Buena Vista 438)	1.25	5.00	65
HOW WILL I KNOW MY LOVE/ Annette (By Jimmie Dodd)	(Disneyland LG-758)	2.50	10.00	57
HOW WILL I KNOW MY LOVE/ Don't Jump To Conclusions	(Disneyland 102)	2.00	8.00	58
HUKILAU SONG/My Little Grass Shack	(Buena Vista 400)	1.25	5.00	62
INDIAN GIVER/Mama, Mama Rosa (Shown as by Annette with the Upbeats)	(Buena Vista 375)	1.25	5.00	61
JO-JO THE DOG FACED BOY/Lonely Guitar	(Buena Vista 336)	3.00	12.00	59
JO-JO THE DOG FACED BOY/Love Me Forever	(Buena Vista 336)	1.25	5.00	59
LONELY GUITAR/Wild Willy	(Buena Vista 339)	1.00	4.00	59
MERLIN JONES (With The Wellingtons)/ Scrambled Egghead (With Tommy Kirk)	(Buena Vista 431)	1.25	5.00	64
MONKEYS UNCLE, THE (With The Beach Boys)/ How Will I Know My Love (Counterfeit copies exist of this release)	(Buena Vista 440)	2.50	10.00	65
MR. PIANO MAN/He's My Ideal	(Buena Vista 405)	1.25	5.00	62
MUSCLE BEACH PARTY/I Dream About Frankie	(Buena Vista 433)	1.25	5.00	62
NO WAY TO GO BUT UP/Crystal Ball	(Buena Vista 450)	1.25	5.00	66
O DIO MIO/It Took Dreams	(Buena Vista 354)	1.00	4.00	60
PARENT TRAP, THE/ Let's Get Together (With Tommy Sands)	(Buena Vista 802)	1.25	5.00	61
PINEAPPLE PRINCESS/Luau Cha-cha-cha	(Buena Vista 362)	1.00	4.00	60
PROMISE ME ANYTHING/Treat Him Nicely	(Buena Vista 427)	1.25	5.00	63
TALK TO ME BABY/I Love You Baby	(Buena Vista 369)	1.25	5.00	60
TALL PAUL/Ma He's Makin' Eyes At Me	(Disneyland 118)	1.50	6.00	59
TEENAGE WEDDING/Walkin' & Talkin'	(Buena Vista 414)	1.25	5.00	63
THAT CRAZY PLACE FROM OUTER SPACE/ Gold Doubloons & Pieces Of Eight	(Disneyland 114)	1.50	6.00	
THAT CRAZY PLACE FROM OUTER SPACE/ Seven Moon	(Buena Vista 392)	1.25	5.00	62
TRAIN OF LOVE/Tell Me Who's The Girl	(Buena Vista 359)	1.25	5.00	60
TRUTH ABOUT YOUTH/I Can't Do The Sum	(Buena Vista 394)	1.25	5.00	62
WAH-WATUSI/The Clyde	(Buena Vista 437)	1.25	5.00	64
WHAT'S A GIRL TO DO/When You Get What You Want	(Tower 326)	1.25	5.00	

Also see Fred MacMurray

ANNIE & THE ORPHANS

TITLE/FLIP	LABEL & NO.	GOOD	NEAR MINT	YR.
MY GIRL'S BEEN BITTEN BY THE BEATLE BUG/ A Place Called Happiness	(Capitol 5144)	1.25	5.00	64

ANN-MARGRET

TITLE/FLIP	LABEL & NO.	GOOD	NEAR MINT	YR.
BEAUTY & THE BEARD (With Al Hirt) (A set of five compact 33 singles from the "Beauty & The Beard" LP. Complete set includes two color inserts and juke box title strips.)	(RCA Victor VP-2690-1,2,3,4,5)	10.00	40.00	64
BILL BAILEY/ My Baby Just Cares For Me: see "Beauty & The Beard"				
BYE BYE BIRDIE/Take All The Kisses	(RCA Victor 47-8168)	.75	3.00	63
BYE BYE BIRDIE/Take All The Kisses (Picture sleeve)	(RCA Victor 47-8168)	2.00	8.00	63
CHICO/Sleep In The Grass (With Lee Hazlewood)	(LHI-2)	.50	2.00	69
FOR YOU/Love Rush	(MCA 41186)	.50	2.00	80
FOR YOU/Midnight Message	(MCA 41223)	.50	2.00	80
HANGIN' ON/Walk On Out Of My Mind (With Lee Hazlewood)	(LHI-11)	.50	2.00	69
HEY LITTLE STAR/Man's Favorite Sport	(RCA Victor 47-8295)	.75	3.00	63
I JUST DON'T UNDERSTAND/I Don't Hurt Anymore	(RCA Victor 47-7894)	.75	3.00	61
I JUST DON'T UNDERSTAND/I Don't Hurt Anymore (Compact 33 single)	(RCA Victor 37-7894)	2.50	10.00	61
I JUST DON'T UNDERSTAND/I Don't Hurt Anymore (Picture sleeve)	(RCA Victor 47-7894)	2.00	8.00	61
IT DO ME SO GOOD/Gimmie Love	(RCA Victor 47-7952)	.75	3.00	61
IT DO ME SO GOOD/Gimmie Love (Compact 33 single)	(RCA Victor 37-7952)	2.50	10.00	61
IT DO ME SO GOOD/Gimmie Love (Picture sleeve)	(RCA Victor 47-7952)	2.00	8.00	61
IT'S A NICE WORLD TO VISIT/Turned My Head Around (With Lee Hazlewood)	(LHI-1)	.50	2.00	68
JIM DANDY/I Was Only Kidding	(RCA Victor 47-8061)	.75	3.00	62
JIM DANDY/I Was Only Kidding (Picture sleeve)	(RCA Victor 47-8061)	3.00	12.00	62
JIM DANDY/Thirteen Men: see "Vivacious One, The"				
JUST BECAUSE/ Baby, It's Cold Outside: see "Beauty & The Beard"				
LITTLE BOY, LITTLE GIRL/ Everybody Loves My Baby: see "Beauty & The Beard"				
LOST LOVE/I Ain't Got Nobody	(RCA Victor 47-7857)	.75	3.00	61
LOST LOVE/I Ain't Got Nobody (Compact 33 single)	(RCA Victor 37-7857)	2.50	10.00	61
MR. WONDERFUL/Paradise (Compact 33 single from the "Bachelor's Paradise" LP.)	(RCA Victor VP-2659)	2.50	10.00	63
NO MORE/So Did I	(RCA Victor 47-8130)	.75	3.00	63
PLEASE DON'T TALK ABOUT ME WHEN I'M GONE/ C'est Sin Bon: see "Vivacious One, The"				
ROW, ROW, ROW/The Best Man: see "Beauty & The Beard"				
SLOWLY/Row, Row, Row (With Al Hirt)	(RCA Victor 47-9524)	.75	3.00	64
SOMEDAY SOON/He's My Man	(RCA Victor 47-8446)	.75	3.00	64
SOMEDAY SOON/He's My Man (Picture sleeve)	(RCA Victor 47-8446)	2.00	8.00	64
SWINGER, THE/ You Came A Long Way From St. Louis	(RCA Victor 47-9013)	.75	3.00	66
T'AINT WHAT YOU DO/Personality: see "Beauty & The Beard"				
TELL ME, TELL ME/Make Love To Me: see "Vivacious One, The"				
THERE'LL BE SOME CHANGES MADE/ Rock & Roll Waltz: see "Vivacious One, The"				
VICTIMS OF THE NIGHT/Dark End Of The Street (With Lee Hazlewood)	(LHI-5)	.50	2.00	69
VIVACIOUS ONE, THE (A set of five compact 33 singles from "The Vivacious One" LP. Complete set includes two color inserts and juke box title strips.)	(RCA Victor VP-2551-1,2,3,4)	10.00	40.00	62
WHAT AM I SUPPOSED TO DO/ Let's Stop Kidding Each Other	(RCA Victor 47-7986)	.75	3.00	62
WHAT DID I HAVE THAT I DON'T HAVE/ Mr. Kiss Kiss Bang Bang	(RCA Victor 47-8734)	.75	3.00	65

ANN-MICHAEL

TITLE/FLIP	LABEL & NO.	GOOD	NEAR MINT	YR.
TEENAGE CLEOPATRA/Nine Out Of Ten	(Kip 0067)	.75	3.00	63

ANNONYMOUS

TITLE/FLIP	LABEL & NO.	GOOD	NEAR MINT	YR.
WHERE'S ELVIS/	(Planet 1001)	3.75	15.00	58

ANSWER, The

TITLE/FLIP	LABEL & NO.	GOOD	NEAR MINT	YR.
DIS-ADVANTAGES OF YOU, THE/Legacy	(Columbia 43992)	.75	3.00	67
SWEET, SOUR, BITTER/The Girl From Breadsticks	(Columbia 44190)	.75	3.00	67

ANTELL, Pete

TITLE/FLIP	LABEL & NO.	GOOD	NEAR MINT	YR.
KEEP IT UP/You In Disguise	(Cameo 264)	1.00	4.00	63
LAND OF LOVE/	(Bounty 101)	1.00	4.00	65
NIGHT TIME/Something About You	(Cameo 234)	1.00	4.00	62
YESTERDAY & TOMORROW/ The Times They Are A-Changing	(Bounty 103)	1.50	6.00	65

ANTHONY & THE SOPHMORES

TITLE/FLIP	LABEL & NO.	GOOD	NEAR MINT	YR.
BETTER LATE THAN NEVER/Swingin At Chariot	(Mercury 72168)	1.25	5.00	63
EMBRACEABLE YOU/Beautiful Dreamer	(Grand 4562)	2.00	8.00	
GEE (BUT I'D GIVE THE WORLD)/ It Depends On You	(ABC-Paramount 10073)	1.50	6.00	59
HEARTBREAK/I'll Go Through Life Loving You	(ABC 10844)	1.50	6.00	66
IT DEPENDS ON YOU/Gee	(ABC-Paramount 10737)	2.00	8.00	65
ONE SUMMER NIGHT/Workout (Instrumental)	(Jamie 1340)	2.00	8.00	65
PLAY THOSE OLDIES MR. D.J./Clap Your Hands	(Mercury 72103)	3.75	15.00	63
WILD FOR HER/Get Back To You	(ABC-Paramount 10770)	2.00	8.00	66
WORKOUT/Serenade	(Jamie 1330)	1.50	6.00	65

Also See Dynamics, The
Also See Tony & The Twilights

ANTHONY, Frankie

TITLE/FLIP	LABEL & NO.	GOOD	NEAR MINT	YR.
GOIN TO THE RIVER/Brenda	(Joey 101)	1.25	5.00	62
GOIN TO THE RIVER/Brenda	(Paradise 1003)	1.00	4.00	63
LITTLE GIRLS HAVE BIG EARS/I'm A New Personality	(DRA 329)	.75	3.00	63

ANTHONY, Mark

TITLE/FLIP	LABEL & NO.	GOOD	NEAR MINT	YR.
MAMA'S TWISTIN' WITH SANTA/Music From Studio "D"	(La Belle 779)	.75	3.00	61

Also see Hollywood Stars, The

ANTHONY, Paul

TITLE/FLIP	LABEL & NO.	GOOD	NEAR MINT	YR.
BOP BOP BOP/My Promise To You	(Roulette 4099)	2.00	8.00	58
HELLO TEARDROPS, GOODBYE LOVE/Angel Face	(Gambit 1103)	5.00	20.00	
STEP UP/Look At Me Now	(Metro International 1003)	5.00	20.00	

ANTHONY, Ray

TITLE/FLIP	LABEL & NO.	GOOD	NEAR MINT	YR.
AT LAST/I'll See You In My Dreams	(Capitol 1912)	1.00	4.00	52
BUNNY HOP (Vocal)/Blow Man, Blow	(Capitol 2251)	1.00	4.00	52
BUNNY HOP/Hokey Pokey	(Capitol 2427)	1.00	4.00	53
CAN ANYONE EXPLAIN/Sky Coach	(Capitol 1131)	1.00	4.00	50
COUNT EVERY STAR/Bamboo	(Capitol 859)	1.00	4.00	50
COUNT EVERY STAR/Darktown Strutters Ball	(Capitol 979)	1.00	4.00	50
DRAGNET/Dancing In The Dark	(Capitol 1912)	1.00	4.00	53
LET ME ENTERTAIN YOU/Wishing Star	(Capitol 4876)	.75	3.00	62
NEVERTHELESS/Harbor Lights	(Capitol 1190)	1.00	4.00	50
PETER GUNN/Tango For Two	(Capitol 4041)	1.00	4.00	58
SENTIMENTAL ME/	(Capitol 923)	1.00	4.00	50
SKOKIAAN/Say Hey	(Capitol 2896)	1.00	4.00	54
WALKIN' TO MOTHER'S/Bunny Hop	(Capitol 4176)	1.00	4.00	59
WORRIED MIND/Al di la	(Capitol 4742)	.75	3.00	62

ANTOINETTS, The

TITLE/FLIP	LABEL & NO.	GOOD	NEAR MINT	YR.
RONNY BOY/Double Timing Lover	(Karen 318)	1.00	4.00	

ANTON, Susan

TITLE/FLIP	LABEL & NO.	GOOD	NEAR MINT	YR.
LISTEN TO MY SMILE/My Baby	(Columbia 10740)	.50	2.00	78

ANTRELL, Dave

TITLE/FLIP	LABEL & NO.	GOOD	NEAR MINT	YR.
LOOKIN' FOR LOVE/ Friends (Give Me The Strength To Carry On)	(Amaret 144)	.50	2.00	71
MIDNIGHT SUNSHINE/I'm Taking No Chances	(Amaret 124)	.50	2.00	70
STRAIGHT FROM A RAINBOW/The Clock Strikes Twelve	(Amaret 122)	.50	2.00	70

APES, The

TITLE/FLIP	LABEL & NO.	GOOD	NEAR MINT	YR.
DON'T MONKEY WITH THE PONY/Tarzan's Monkey	(Mercury 72219)	.75	3.00	64

APRHODITE'S CHILD (With Demis Roussos & Vangelis)

TITLE/FLIP	LABEL & NO.	GOOD	NEAR MINT	YR.
BABYLON/Break	(Vertigo 107)	.75	3.00	71

APOSTLES, The

TITLE/FLIP	LABEL & NO.	GOOD	NEAR MINT	YR.
STRANDED IN THE JUNGLE/Tired Of Waiting	(A-Square 401)	2.00	8.00	

APPALACHIANS, The

TITLE/FLIP	LABEL & NO.	GOOD	NEAR MINT	YR.
BIG BETTY/Hill-Billy-Ding-Dong-Choo-Choo	(ABC-Paramount 10464)	.75	3.00	63
BONY MORONIE/It Takes A Man	(ABC-Paramount 10419)	.75	3.00	63

APPLE, The

TITLE/FLIP	LABEL & NO.	GOOD	NEAR MINT	YR.
THANK U VERY MUCH/ Your Heart Is Free Just Like The Wind	(Smash 2143)	.75	3.00	68

APPLEJACKS, The

TITLE/FLIP	LABEL & NO.	GOOD	NEAR MINT	YR.
LIKE DREAMERS DO/Everybody Fall Down	(London 9681)	.75	3.00	64
SEND ME LOVE/You're The One	(London 9709)	.75	3.00	64
THREE LITTLE WORDS/You're The One For Me	(London 9709)	.75	3.00	64
TELL ME/Baby Jane	(London 9658)	.75	3.00	64

APPLEJACKS, The (With Dave Appell)

TITLE/FLIP	LABEL & NO.	GOOD	NEAR MINT	YR.
BACK IN SIXTY SECONDS/Hippies Waltz	(Cameo 248)	.75	3.00	63
BROTHER BILL/Sugar Baby (Shown as by the Dave Appell Trio)	(London 30107)	1.25	5.00	50
BUNNY HOP/Night Train Stroll	(Cameo 158)	.75	3.00	59
DINNER WITH DRAC/No Name Theme	(Cameo 132)	.75	3.00	58
HONEY BUNCH/Ookey Ook	(Tone-Craft 200)	1.00	4.00	55
LOVE IN THE JUNGLE/Chitter Chatter Baby	(Cameo 110)	.75	3.00	57
LOVE SCENE/Circle Dance	(Cameo 170)	.75	3.00	59
MEXICAN HAT ROCK/Sophisticated Swing	(Cameo 149)	1.00	4.00	58
MEXICAN HAT ROCK/Stop! Red Light (Second pressing)	(Cameo 149)	.75	3.00	58
MEXICAN HAT TWIST/Cherry Valley	(Cameo 203)	.75	3.00	61
MOONLIGHT SERENADE/Walk On	(Cameo 138)	.75	3.00	58
RING AROUND MY BABY/Love Express	(President 1005)	1.00	4.00	56
ROCKA CONGA/Am I Blue	(Cameo 155)	.75	3.00	58
ROCK & ROLL STORY, THE/Rainbow Of Love	(President 1011)	1.00	4.00	56
SHE LOVES YOU/Bongo Beach	(Cameo 321)	.75	3.00	64
SMARTER/My Heart Will Wait For You	(Decca 29218)	1.00	4.00	54
STRUTTIN' IN THE SUMMERTIME/Anytime	(Cameo 222)	.75	3.00	62
SWEET PATOOTIE/Reunion	(Decca 29330)	1.25	5.00	54
TEEN AGE MEETING/Ooh Baby, Ooh	(President 1006)	1.00	4.00	56
THEME FROM "THE YOUNG ONES"/September Song	(Cameo 184)	.75	3.00	60
UNTOUCHABLES, THE/Memories (Instrumentals)	(Cameo 177)	.75	3.00	60

APRIL WINE

TITLE/FLIP	LABEL & NO.	GOOD	NEAR MINT	YR.
BAD SIDE OF THE MOON/Believe In Me	(Big Tree 142)	.75	3.00	72
GET READY FOR LOVE/ Comin' Right Down On Top Of Me	(Capitol 4728)	.50	2.00	79
I'M ON FIRE FOR YOU BABY/	(Big Tree 15006)	.75	3.00	73
OOWATANITE/	(Big Tree 16036)	.75	3.00	74
ROLLER/Right Down To It	(Capitol 4660)	.50	2.00	78
SAY HELLO/Before The Dawn	(Capitol 4802)	.50	2.00	79
YOU COULD HAVE BEEN A LADY/Teacher	(Big Tree 133)	.75	3.00	72

AQUANAUTS, The

TITLE/FLIP	LABEL & NO.	GOOD	NEAR MINT	YR.
RUMBLE ON THE DOCKS/Bombora (Instrumentals)	(Safari 1005)	1.00	4.00	63
SWIM ALL DAY/Highdivin'	(Sande 104)	1.00	4.00	64

AQUA-NITES, The

TITLE/FLIP	LABEL & NO.	GOOD	NEAR MINT	YR.
CARIOCA/Lover Don't You Weep	(Astra 1000)	6.25	25.00	
CHRISTIE/Lover Don't You Weep	(Astra 2001)	5.00	20.00	

AQUATONES, The

TITLE/FLIP	LABEL & NO.	GOOD	NEAR MINT	YR.
CRAZY FOR YOU/Wanted	(Fargo 1016)	1.25	5.00	60
EVERY TIME/There's A Long Long Trail	(Fargo 1015)	1.25	5.00	59
MY DARLING/For You, For You	(Fargo 1111)	1.25	5.00	59
MY TREASURE/My One Desire	(Fargo 1005)	1.25	5.00	59
OUR FIRST KISS/The Drive-In	(Fargo 1003)	1.25	5.00	58
SAY YOU'LL BE MINE/So Fine	(Fargo 1002)	1.25	5.00	58
YOU/She's The One For Me	(Fargo 1001)	1.25	5.00	58

AQUAVIVA

TITLE/FLIP	LABEL & NO.	GOOD	NEAR MINT	YR.
CURTAIN TIME/That's All (Instrumentals)	(MGM 12761)	1.00	4.00	59

ARBOGAST & ROSS (With Bob Arbogast)

TITLE/FLIP	LABEL & NO.	GOOD	NEAR MINT	YR.
CHAOS (PART 1)/Chaos (Part 2) (Novelty)	(Liberty 55197)	1.50	6.00	59

ARBORS, The

TITLE/FLIP	LABEL & NO.	GOOD	NEAR MINT	YR.
GRADUATION DAY/I Win The Whole Wide World	(Date 1561)	.75	3.00	67
I CAN'T QUIT HER/Lovin' Tonight (Maybe Tonight)	(Date 1645)	.75	3.00	69
JUST LET IT HAPPEN/Dreamer Girl	(Date 1546)	.75	3.00	67
LETTER, THE/Most Of All	(Date 1638)	.75	3.00	69
SYMPHONY FOR SUSAN, A/Love Is The Light	(Date 1529)	.75	3.00	66
TOUCH ME/Motet-Overture	(Date 1651)	.75	3.00	69
VALLEY OF THE DOLLS/You Are The Music	(Date 1581)	.75	3.00	67
WITH YOU GIRL/Love For All Seasons	(Date 1570)	.75	3.00	67

Paul Anka

Ann-Margret

Steve Allen

The Andrews Sisters

TITLE/FLIP	LABEL & NO.	GOOD	NEAR MINT	YR.
ARCADES, The				
BLACKMAIL/June Was The End Of August	(Guyden 2015)	1.50	6.00	62
FINE LITTLE GIRL/My Love	(Johnson 116)	1.50	6.00	62
OUR LOVE/The Pal	(Julia 1100)	2.00	8.00	
ARCHER, Con				
ELVIS IS GONE (BUT NOT FORGOTTEN)/ Let's Start A New Tomorrow	(QCA 463)	.75	3.00	78
(Orginally issued with paper insert)				
ARCHIBALD PLAYERS, The				
MR. GRILLON/The Big Nothing	(Arch 1606)	1.00	4.00	58
(Comedy)				
ARCHIE & EDITH: see O'Connor, Carroll, & Jean Stapleton				
ARCHIES, The (Featuring Ron Dante)				
BANG-SHANG-A-LANG/Truck Driver	(Calendar 1006)	.50	2.00	68
FEELING SO GOOD/Love Light	(Calendar 1007)	.50	2.00	68
JINGLE JANGLE/Justine	(Kirshner 5002)	.50	2.00	69
LOVE IS LIVING IN YOU/Hold On To Lovin'	(Kirshner 5018)	.50	2.00	71
STRANGERS IN THE MORNING/	(Kirshner 5021)	.50	2.00	72
SUGAR SUGAR/Melody Hill	(Calendar 1008)	.50	2.00	69
SUNSHINE/Over & Over	(Kirshner 1009)	.50	2.00	70
THIS IS LOVE/Throw A Little Love My Way	(Kirshner 5011)	.50	2.00	71
TOGETHER WE ARE TWO/Everything's Alright	(Kirshner 5009)	.50	2.00	71
WHO'S YOUR BABY/Senorita Rita	(Kirshner 5003)	.50	2.00	70
ARDELLS, The				
EEFENANNY/Lonely Valley	(Epic 9621)	1.00	4.00	63
EVERY DAY OF THE WEEK/Roll On	(Marco 102)	2.00	8.00	
SEVEN LONELY NIGHTS/You Can Fall In Love	(Selma 4001)	2.50	10.00	
ARDEN, Toni				
ARE YOU SATISFIED/ I Forgot To Remember To Forget	(RCA Victor 47-6346)	1.00	4.00	55
KISS OF FIRE/I'm Yours	(Columbia 39737)	1.00	4.00	52
PADRE/All At Once	(Decca 30628)	1.00	4.00	58
ARGENT (Featuring Rod Argent)				
GOD GAVE ROCK & ROLL TO YOU/Christmas For The Free	(Epic 10972)	.50	2.00	72
HOLD YOUR HEAD UP/Closer To Heaven	(Epic 10852)	.50	2.00	72
IT'S ONLY MONEY (PART 2)/	(Epic 11014)	.50	2.00	73
MAN FOR ALL REASONS/Music From The Spheres	(Epic 11137)	.50	2.00	74
SWEET MARY/Rejoice	(Epic 10718)	.50	2.00	71
THUNDER & LIGHTNING/Coming Off Kahoutek	(Epic 50025)	.50	2.00	74
TRAGEDY/He's A Dynamo	(Epic 10919)	.50	2.00	72
Group member Chris White, like Rod Argent, was previously with the Zombies.				
ARGYLES, The				
EVERYTIME YOU SMILE/Moonbeam	(Bally 7004)	2.00	8.00	57
VACATION DAYS ARE OVER/It Takes Time	(Brent 7004)	2.00	8.00	59
ARIEL				
I LOVE YOU/It Feels Like I'm Crying	(Brent 7060)	1.25	5.00	
ARISTOCRATS, The (Featuring Lee Raymond)				
BELIEVE ME/I'm Waiting For The Ships	(Essex 366)	1.25	5.00	54
ARK				
NAM MYO HO RENGE KYO/Times Like This	(Sentinel 501)	1.25	5.00	
ARKADE				
MORNING OF OUR LIVES, THE/Rhythm Of The People	(Dunhill 4268)	.50	2.00	71
ARLIN, Bob (Of The Leaves)				
707/708	(Olympia 500)	.75	3.00	
ARMAGGEDDON				
GET YOURSELF TOGETHER/Get Yourself Together (Part 2)	(Capitol 3142)	1.00	4.00	72
ARMAND, Renee				
RAINING IN L.A./	(A&M 1390)	.50	2.00	73
(WE'RE) DANCING IN THE DARK/ The Bitter Taste Of Wild Things	(Windsong 11290)	.50	2.00	78
ARMATRADING, Joan				
BOTTOM TO THE TOP/Your Letter	(A&M 2102)	.50	2.00	78
DOWN TO ZERO/Like Fire	(A&M 1898)	.50	2.00	77
LONELY LADY/Together In Words & Music	(A&M 1452)	.50	2.00	74
LOVE & AFFECTION/Help Yourself	(A&M 1865)	.50	2.00	76
ROSIE/	(A&M 2210)	.50	2.00	79
SHOW SOME AFFECTION/No Way Out	(A&M 1994)	.50	2.00	77
WATER WITH THE WINE/People	(A&M 1914)	.50	2.00	77
ARMEN, Kay				
HA! HA! HA!/Till	(Decca 30474)	.75	3.00	57
ARMENIAN JAZZ SEXTET, The				
HAREM DANCE/Pretty Girl	(Kapp 181)	.75	3.00	57
(Instrumental)				
ARMS, Russell				
CINCO ROBLES/The World Is Made Of Lisa	(Era 1026)	1.00	4.00	56
I SAW A STAR/Is There A Heaven	(Era 1018)	1.00	4.00	56
ARMSTRONG, Jimmy				
RISE SALLY, COME TO ME/	(Zell's 1009)	.75	3.00	63
(Answer song)				
ARNAU, B.J.				
LIVE & LET DIE/	(RCA 74-0014)	.50	2.00	73
ARNAZ, Desi				
STRAW HAT SONG/Forever Darling	(MGM 12144)	1.00	4.00	56
THERE'S A BRAND NEW BABY AT OUR HOUSE/ I Love Lucy	(Columbia 39937)	1.50	6.00	52
ARNAZ, Lucie				
JUST FOR TONIGHT/I Still Believe In Love	(Casablanca 970)	.50	2.00	79
Lucie is the daughter of Lucille Ball & Desi Arnaz.				
ARNDT, Bill				
BREAKING UP IS HARD TO DO/	(Hit 21)	.75	3.00	
ARNELL, Ginny				
BRAND NEW/Mister Saxophone	(Decca 31033)	1.00	4.00	60
CARNIVAL/We	(Decca 31104)	1.00	4.00	60
DUMB HEAD/How Many Times Can One Heart Break	(MGM 13177)	.75	3.00	63
FAITHFUL OUR LOVE/Classical Rock & Roll	(Decca 30934)	2.50	10.00	59
(With Gene Pitney, shown as by Jamie & Jane)				
I WISH I KNEW WHAT DRESS TO WEAR/He's My Little Devil	(MGM 13226)	.75	3.00	64
I'M CRYING TOO/Trouble's Back In Town	(MGM 13146)	.75	3.00	63
JUST LIKE A BOY/Portrait Of A Fool	(MGM 13309)	.75	3.00	65
LET ME MAKE YOU SMILE AGAIN/Yesterday's Memories	(MGM 13248)	.75	3.00	64
LITTLE BIT OF LOVE CAN HURT, A/Billy Why	(MGM 13362)	.75	3.00	65
LOOK WHO'S TALKIN'/Tell Me What He Said	(Decca 31190)	1.00	4.00	60
MARRIED TO YOU/He Likes Rock & Roll Better Than Me	(Warwick 680)	.75	3.00	62
STROLLING (THRU' THE PARK)/Snuggle Up Baby	(Decca 30862)	2.50	10.00	59
(With Gene Pitney, shown as by Jamie & Jane)				
TRIBUTE TO YOU/No One Cares	(Warwick 671)	.75	3.00	61
ARNO, Audrey				
LA PACHANGA/Believe	(Decca 31238)	.75	3.00	61
ARNOLD, Jerry				
RACE FOR TIME/Let's Take A Ride	(Cameo 120)	1.00	4.00	58
ARNOLD, P.P.				
FIRST CUT IS THE DEEPEST/Speak To Me	(Immediate 1901)	1.50	6.00	67
THOUGH IT HURTS ME BADLY/ (If You Think Your) Groovy	(Immediate 257-5006)	1.50	6.00	68
ARNOLD, Vance, & The Avengers (Joe Cocker)				
I'LL CRY INSTEAD/Those Precious Words	(Philips 40255)	1.25	5.00	64
ARPEGGIO				
LOVE & DESIRE (PART 1)/Love & Desire (Part 2)	(Polydor 14564)	.50	2.00	79
RUNNAWAY/Spellbound	(Polydor 14564)	.50	2.00	79
ARROGANTS, The (Featuring Ray Morrow)				
MIRROR MIRROR/Canadian Sunset	(Lute 6226)	2.50	10.00	
TAKE LIFE EASY/Stone Broke	(Vaness 200)	2.00	8.00	
TOM BOY/Make Up Your Mind	(Big A 12184)	2.00	8.00	60
ARROWS, The (Featuring Davie Allan)				
APACHE '65/Blue Guitar	(Sidewalk 1)	1.25	5.00	65
APACHE '65/Blue Guitar	(Tower 116)	.75	3.00	65
BABY RUTH/I'm Looking Over A Four Leaf Clover	(Tower 142)	.75	3.00	65
BLUE RIDES AGAIN/Cycle-delic	(Tower 381)	.75	3.00	68
BLUES THEME/Bongo Party	(Tower 295)	.75	3.00	67
DEVIL'S ANGELS/Cody's Theme	(Tower 341)	.75	3.00	67
GRANNY GOOSE/Space Hop	(Tower 158)	.75	3.00	65
MOON DAWG '65/Dance The Freddie	(Tower 133)	.75	3.00	65
WILD ANGELS THEME, THE/U.F.O.	(Tower 267)	.75	3.00	66
Instrumentals				
ARROWS, The				
RUN LIKE THE WIND/When You Were Sweet 16	(Cupid 105)	1.00	4.00	
ARTFUL DODGER				
CAN'T STOP PRETENDING/	(Columbia 10603)	.50	2.00	77
SCREAM/Keep Me Happy	(Columbia 10431)	.50	2.00	76
THINK THINK/Follow Me	(Columbia 10339)	.50	2.00	76
ARTHUR, Jay				
LONELY GIRL ON SWEETHEART MOUNTAIN/Psychology	(Smash 1805)	.75	3.00	63
ARTIE & LINDA WITH THE PREMERES				
BLUEBERRY HILL/Laughing On The Outside	(Chancellor 1147)	.75	3.00	63
ARTIS, Ray				
ART OF LOVE/That's All I Want From You	("A" A-111)	2.00	8.00	61
(With Bob & Joe)				
DEAR LIZ/Wella-Wella	(Bundy 222)	2.50	10.00	61
ARVON, Bobby				
FROM NOW ON/Drift Away	(First Artists 41003)	.50	2.00	78
ROCK & ROLL MUSIC MAN/Early Misty Morning	(Ariola American 7612)	.50	2.00	76
UNTIL NOW/Stay A Little Longer	(First Artists 41000)	.50	2.00	77
A'S, The				
AFTER LAST NIGHT/Teenage Jerk Off	(Arista 0452)	.50	2.00	79
ASCOTS, The				
MIDNIGHT HOUR/Midnight Hour (Part 2)	(Super 103)	1.00	4.00	
MONKEY SEE-MONKEY DO/You Can't Do That	(Super 102)	1.00	4.00	
PUT YOUR ARMS AROUND ME/Sookie Sookie	(Super 104)	1.00	4.00	
ASCOTS, The				
ACAPULCO RUN/The Gladiator	(Dual-Tone DT-1120)	1.25	5.00	63
DARLING I'LL SEE YOU TONIGHT/I Don't Care One Bit	(King 5679)	2.00	8.00	62
PERFECT LOVE/I'm Touched	(Ace 650)	2.00	8.00	62
SHE DID/Hip Talk	(Bethlehem 3046)	1.25	5.00	
WHAT LOVE CAN DO/Everything Will Be All Right	(J&S 1628)	1.50	6.00	56
Even though all of these releases are shown as being by a group using the same name, the possibility exists that they are not all by the same group.				
ASHBY, Irving				
LOCO-MOTION/Night Winds	(Imperial 5426)	1.00	4.00	57
(Instrumentals)				
ASHE, Clarence				
TROUBLE I'VE HAD, THE/Dancing In A Dream World	(Chess 1896)	.75	3.00	64
TROUBLE I'VE HAD, THE/Dancing In A Dream World	(J&S 1466)	1.25	5.00	56
ASHES, The				
HOMEWARD BOUND/Homeward Bound	(Vault 972)	1.00	4.00	65
IS THERE ANYTHING I CAN DO/Every Little Prayer	(Vault 924)	1.00	4.00	64
ASHLEY, Del: see David Gates				
ASHMAN, Charles				
AN AMERICAN'S ANSWER (Answer Record)/ Middle Class Is In The Middle Now	(Dot 17507)	.75	3.00	74
ASHTON, GARDNER & DYKE (With Tony Ashton)				
RESURRECTION SHUFFLE/I'm Your Spiritual Breadman (Featuring George Harrison on Guitar)	(Capitol 3060)	.75	3.00	71
Also see Deep Purple				
ASSOCIATION, The				
ALONG COMES MARY/Your Own Love	(Valiant 741)	.75	3.00	66
ALONG THE WAY/	(Warner Bros. 7429)	.50	2.00	70
ARE YOU READY/Dubuque Blues	(Warner Bros. 7349)	.50	2.00	70
BABY I'M GONNA LEAVE YOU/ Baby, Can't You Hear Me Call Your Name	(Jubilee 5505)	1.00	4.00	65
BRING YOURSELF HOME/It's Gotta Be Real	(Warner Bros. 7515)	.50	2.00	71
CHERRISH/Don't Blame The Rain	(Valiant 747)	.75	3.00	66
COME THE FALL/Kicking The Gong Around	(Columbia 45654)	.50	2.00	72
DARLING BE HOME SOON/Indian Wells Woman	(Columbia 45602)	.50	2.00	72
EVERYTHING THAT TOUCHES YOU/We Love Us	(Warner Bros. 7163)	.50	2.00	68
FORTY TIMES/One Too Many Mornings	(Valiant 730)	1.00	4.00	66
GOODBYE COLUMBUS/The Time It Is Today	(Warner Bros. 7267)	.50	2.00	69
JUST ABOUT THE SAME/Look At Me, Look At You	(Warner Bros. 7372)	.50	2.00	70
NAMES, TAGS, NUMBERS & LABELS/Rainbows Bent	(Mums 6061)	.50	2.00	73
NEVER MY LOVE/Requiem For The Masses	(Warner Bros. 7074)	.50	2.00	67
NO FAIR AT ALL/Looking Glass	(Valiant 758)	.75	3.00	66
PANDORA'S GOLDEN HEEBIE JEEBIES/Standing Still	(Valiant 755)	.75	3.00	66
P.F. SLOAN/Traveler's Guide	(Warner Bros. 7471)	.50	2.00	71
SIX MAN BAND/Like Always	(Warner Bros. 7229)	.50	2.00	68
THAT'S RACIN'/Makes Me Cry	(Warner Bros. 7524)	.50	2.00	71
TIME FOR LIVING/Birthday Morning	(Warner Bros. 7195)	.50	2.00	68
UNDER BRANCHES/Hear In Here	(Warner Bros. 7277)	.50	2.00	69
WINDY/Sometime	(Warner Bros. 7041)	.75	3.00	67
YES, I WILL/I Am Up For Europe	(Warner Bros. 7305)	.50	2.00	70
Mark Hamilton, of the Electric Prunes, and Ray Gillman, of Paul Revere & the Raiders, were, for awhile, members of this group.				
ASTRA-LITES, The				
SPACE HOP/Lonely	(Tribute 101)	1.00	4.00	62
ASTRO JETS, The				
BOOM A LAY/Hide & Seek	(Imperial 5760)	1.00	4.00	61
(Instrumentals)				
ASTRONAUTS, The				
FAREWELL/Chili Charlie	(Trial 3521)	3.75	15.00	
ASTRONAUTS, The				
COME ALONG BABY/Tryin' To Get To You	(Palladium 610)	3.75	15.00	61
ASTRONAUTS, The (With Stormy Patterson)				
ALMOST GROWN/My Sin is Pride	(RCA Victor 47-8499)	1.00	4.00	65
BAJA (Instrumental)/Kuk	(RCA Victor 47-8194)	1.00	4.00	63
BLUES BEAT/Ski Lift	(Vanruss 1000)	1.00	4.00	
CAN'T YOU SEE I DO/I'm A Fool	(RCA Victor 47-8463)	1.00	4.00	64
COMPETITION COUPE/Surf Party	(RCA Victor 47-8298)	1.00	4.00	64
GENEVA TWIST/Take 17	(Jan Ell 459)	1.00	4.00	62
GO FIGHT FOR HER/Swim Little Mermaid	(RCA Victor 47-8364)	1.00	4.00	64
HOT DOGGIN' (Instrumental)/Everyone But Me	(RCA Victor 47-8224)	1.00	4.00	63
IT DOESN'T MATTER ANYMORE/La La La Song	(RCA Victor 47-8628)	1.00	4.00	65
MAIN STREET/In My Car	(RCA Victor 47-8885)	1.00	4.00	
RIDGE ROUTE/Blast Off	(Luney 100)	1.00	4.00	
THEME FROM 'RIDE THE WILD SURF' (Instrumental)/ Around & Around	(RCA Victor 47-8419)	1.00	4.00	64
ASTRO-NOTES, The				
MONKEY WORKOUT/Teenage Blues	(Dot 16621)	.75	3.00	64
ASYLUM CHOIR, The (With Leon Russell & Marc Benno)				
TRYIN' TO STAY/Straight Brother	(Shelter 7313)	.50	2.00	71
AT LAST-THE 1958 ROCK & ROLL SHOW				
I CAN'T DRIVE/Working On The Railroad	(Epic 10344)	.75	3.00	68
ATKINS, Dave, & His Offbeats				
SHAKE-KUM-DOWN/	(Viv 106)	.75	3.00	63
ATLANTA RHYTHM SECTION, The				
ALL IN YOUR MIND/Can't Stand It No More	(Decca 32928)	.75	3.00	72
ANGEL (WHAT IN THE WORLD'S COME OVER US)/ Help Yourself	(Polydor 14262)	.50	2.00	75
BACK UP AGAINST THE WALL/It Must Be Done	(Decca 33051)	.75	3.00	72
BACK UP AGAINST THE WALL/Large Time	(Polydor 2039)	.50	2.00	79
CHAMPAGNE JAM/The Great Escape	(Polydor 14504)	.50	2.00	78
CONVERSATION/Cold Turkey, Tenn.	(MCA 40059)	.50	2.00	73
CRAZY/	(Polydor 14289)	.50	2.00	75
DOG DAYS/Cuban Crisis	(Polydor 14411)	.50	2.00	77
DO IT OR DIE/My Song	(Polydor 14568)	.50	2.00	79
DORAVILLE/Who You Gonna Run To	(Polydor 14248)	.50	2.00	74
EARNESTINE/	(Decca 32948)	.75	3.00	72
FREE SPIRIT/Police! Police!	(Polydor 14339)	.50	2.00	76
GEORGIA RHYTHM/Hitch Hicker's Hero	(Polydor 14432)	.50	2.00	77
GET YOUR HEAD OUT OF YOUR HEART/	(Polydor 14273)	.50	2.00	75
IMAGINARY LOVER/Silent Treatment	(Polydor 14459)	.50	2.00	78
I'M NOT GONNA LET IT BOTHER ME TONIGHT/ The Ballad Of Lois Malone	(Polydor 14484)	.50	2.00	78
JUNKIN'/Beautiful Dreamer	(Polydor 14323)	.50	2.00	76
NEON NITES/Don't Miss The Message	(Polydor 14397)	.50	2.00	77
SO IN TO YOU/Everybody Gotta Go	(Polydor 14373)	.50	2.00	77
SPOOKY/It's Only Music	(Polydor 2001)	.50	2.00	79
This band contains members of the Candymen & the Classics IV.				
ATLANTICS, The				
BOO-HOO-HOO/Everything Is Gonna Be All Right	(Linda 103)	.75	3.00	61
REMEMBER THE NIGHT/Flame Of Love	(Linda 107)	1.00	4.00	62
ATLANTICS, The				
BEAVER SHOT/Fine Fine Fine	(Rampart 643)	.75	3.00	65
BOMBORA/Greensleeves	(Columbia 42877)	.75	3.00	63
HEART BURN/Monkey Tree	(Amon 90590)	1.00	4.00	
SONNY & CHER/Sloop Dance	(Rampart 647)	.75	3.00	65
ATLANTICS, The				
ONE LAST NIGHT/Television Girl	(MCA 41037)	.50	2.00	79
ATOMIC ROOSTER				
TOMORROW NIGHT/Play The Game	(Elektra 45727)	.50	2.00	71
ATTILA & THE HUNS				
CHERYL/Lonely Huns	(Sara 65111)	.75	3.00	66
ATTITUDES, The (Danny Kortchmar, David Foster, Jim Keltner)				
AIN'T LOVE ENOUGH/The Whole World's Crazy	(Dark Horse 10004)	.50	2.00	75
HONEY DON'T LEAVE L.A./Lend A Hand	(Dark Horse 10008)	.50	2.00	76
IN A STRANGER'S ARMS/Good News	(Dark Horse 8452)	.50	2.00	75
SWEET SUMMER MUSIC/If We Want To	(Dark Horse 10011)	.50	2.00	76
Also see Flying Machine				
Also see Skylark				
Also see Lewis, Gary, & The Playboys				
ATTITUDES, The (Featuring Randy Silverman)				
THAT OLD BLACK MAGIC/Mama's Doing The Jerk	(Times Square 110)	1.00	4.00	
AU GO-GO'S, The				
WAITED FOR YOU/All Over Town	(Jest 1)	1.25	5.00	
AUDIENCE (With Howard Werth)				
INDIAN SUMMER/It Brings A Tear	(Elektra 45732)	.50	2.00	71
AUDREY				
DEAR ELVIS (PAGE 1)/Dear Elvis (Page 2)	(Plus 104)	3.75	15.00	56
(Novelty/Break-in. Shown As "With Love From Audrey")				
AUGER, Brian, & The Trinity (With Julie Driscoll)				
BUMPIN' ON SUNSET/A Day In The Life	(Atco 6656)	.50	2.00	69
HAPPINESS IS JUST AROUND THE BEND/ Inner City Blues	(RCA 74-0085)	.50	2.00	
(Shown as by Brian Auger's Oblivion Express.)				
LISTEN HERE/I Wanna Take You Higher	(RCA 74-0381)	.50	2.00	70
SAVE THE COUNTRY/	(Atco 6685)	.50	2.00	69
THIS WHEEL'S ON FIRE/Kind Of Love-In	(Atco 6593)	.50	2.00	68
AUGUST (Featuring G.W. Kenny)				
CHARLIE BOY/404 (Carry On)	(Buddah BDA-358)	1.00	4.00	73
Group members Howie Blauvelt and James Santoro later joined Ram Jam.				
AUGUST, Jan				
BEWITCHED/Blue Prelude	(Mercury 5399)	1.00	4.00	50
AUGUST, June				
HIP KITTY TO THE BOPPER/	(Groovie 101)	1.25	5.00	
AUM				
AUM/Little Brown Hen	(Fillmore 7001)	1.00	4.00	
BYE BYE BABY/Resurrection	(Fillmore 7000)	1.00	4.00	
AUSTIN, Gene				
RAMONA/Carolina Moon	(RCA Victor 47-0015)	1.25	5.00	49
TOO LATE/That's Love	(RCA Victor 47-6880)	1.00	4.00	57
AUSTIN, Sil				
BIRTHDAY PARTY/The Last Time	(Mercury 71027)	1.00	4.00	57
DANNY BOY/Hungry Eye	(Mercury 71442)	1.00	4.00	59
SLOW WALK/Wildwood	(Mercury 70963)	1.00	4.00	56
Instrumentals				
AUSTIN, Tom, & The Healeys				
SUMMER'S OVER/Maybe You'll Be There	(Old Town 1147)	2.00	8.00	62
AUTOMATIC MAN				
MY PEARL/Newspapers	(Island 063)	.50	2.00	77

TITLE/FLIP	LABEL & NO.	GOOD	NEAR MINT	YR.
AUTUMNS, The				
DEAREST LITTLE ANGEL/Maureen	(Medieval 208)	1.00	4.00	
NEVER/Exodus	(Amber 856)	.75	3.00	
AVALON, Frankie				
AFTER YOU'VE GONE/If You Don't Think I'm Leaving	(Chancellor C1101)	.75	3.00	62
AGAIN/Don't Make Fun Of Me	(United Artists 728)	.75	3.00	64
ALL OF EVERYTHING/Call Me Anytime	(Chancellor C1071)	.75	3.00	61
BEACH PARTY/Don't Stop Now	(Chancellor C1139)	.75	3.00	63
BOBBY SOX TO STOCKINGS/A Boy Without A Girl	(Chancellor C1036)	1.00	4.00	59
BOBBY SOX TO STOCKINGS/A Boy Without A Girl (Stereo single)	(Chancellor S-C1036)	2.00	8.00	59
BUT I DO/Dancing On The Stars	(Reprise 697)	.75	3.00	68
CLEOPATRA/Heartbeats	(Chancellor C1135)	.75	3.00	63
COME FLY WITH ME/Girl Back Home	(Chancellor C1134)	.75	3.00	63
COME ON BACK TO ME BABY/Empty	(Metromedia 181)	.50	2.00	70
CUPID/Jivin' With The Saints	(Chancellor C1004)	2.00	8.00	57
DEDE DINAH/Ooh La La	(Chancellor C1011)	1.00	4.00	57
DON'T MAKE FUN OF ME/Again	(United Artists 728)	.75	3.00	64
DON'T THROW AWAY ALL THOSE TEARDROPS/ Talk, Talk, Talk	(Chancellor C1048)	.75	3.00	60
DON'T YOU DO IT/It's Over	(Reprise 796)	.75	3.00	68
EVERY GIRL SHOULD GET MARRIED/Moon River	(United Artists 800)	.75	3.00	65
FIRST LOVE NEVER DIES/My Ex-Best Friend	(Chancellor C1131)	.75	3.00	63
GINGER BREAD/Blue Betty	(Chancellor C1021)	1.00	4.00	58
GIRL BACK HOME/Heartbeats	(Chancellor C1134)	.75	3.00	63
I'LL WAIT FOR YOU/What Little Girl	(Chancellor C1026)	1.00	4.00	58
I'M IN THE MOOD FOR LOVE/It's The Same Old Dream	(Regalia 5508)	.50	2.00	72
IT'S HIS GAME/Thank You For That Extra Sunrise	(De Lite 1582)	.50	2.00	76
JUST ASK YOUR HEART/Too Fools	(Chancellor C1040)	1.00	4.00	59
JUST ASK YOUR HEART/Too Fools (Stereo single)	(Chancellor S-C1040)	2.00	8.00	59
MIRACLE, A/Don't Let Me Stand In Your Way	(Chancellor C1115)	.75	3.00	62
MY LOVE IS HERE TO STAY/New Fangled Jingle Jangle Swimming Suit From Paris	(United Artists 748)	.75	3.00	64
PERFECT LOVE, A/The Puppet Song	(Chancellor C1065)	.75	3.00	60
SLEEPING BEAUTY/The Lonely Bit	(Chancellor C1095)	.75	3.00	61
TEACHER'S PET/Shy Guy	(Chancellor C1006)	2.00	8.00	57
TOGETHERNESS/Don't Let Love Pass Me By	(Chancellor C1056)	.75	3.00	60
TOGETHERNESS/Don't Let Love Pass Me By (Stereo single)	(Chancellor S-C1056)	1.50	6.00	60
TRUE, TRUE LOVE/Married	(Chancellor C1087)	.75	3.00	61
TRUMPET SORRENTO/The Book	("X" 0006)	2.50	10.00	54
TRUMPET TARANTELLA/Dormi Dormi	("X" 0026)	2.50	10.00	54
(Shown as by 11 Year Old Frankie Avalon on both of the above records on "X". Both are instrumentals with Frankie on the trumpet.)				
VENUS/I'm Broke	(Chancellor C1031)	1.00	4.00	59
VENUS/I'm Broke (Stereo single)	(Chancellor S-C1031)	2.00	8.00	59
VENUS (PART 1)/Venus (Part 2) (A newly recorded version of the Chancellor hit.)	(De Lite 1578)	.50	2.00	76
VOYAGE TO THE BOTTOM OF THE SEA/ Summer Of '61	(Chancellor C1081)	.75	3.00	61
WELCOME HOME/Dance Bossa Nova	(Chancellor C1125)	.75	3.00	62
WHERE ARE YOU/Tuxedo Juction	(Chancellor C1052)	.75	3.00	60
WHO ELSE BUT YOU/Gotta Get A Girl	(Chancellor C1077)	.75	3.00	61
WHY/Swinging On A Rainbow	(Chancellor C1045)	1.00	4.00	59
WHY/Swinging On A Rainbow (Stereo single)	(Chancellor S-C1045)	2.00	8.00	59
WHY DON'T THEY UNDERSTAND/	(Reprise 826)	.75	3.00	69
WOMAN CRYING/The Star	(Amos 127)	.75	3.00	69
YOU ARE MINE/Ponchinello	(Chancellor C1107)	.75	3.00	62
YOU EXCITE ME/Darlin'	(Chancellor C1016)	1.00	4.00	58
AVANT-GARDE, The				
FLY WITH ME/Revelations Revelations	(Columbia 4-44701)	.75	3.00	68
NATURALLY STONED/Honey & Gall	(Columbia 4-44590)	.75	3.00	68
YELLOW BEADS/Honey & Gall	(Columbia 4-44388)	.75	3.00	67
AVANTIS, The				
KEEP ON DANCING/I Wanna Dance	(Argo 5436)	.75	3.00	63
AVANTIS, The				
PHANTOM SURFER/Lucille	(Regency 110)	1.00	4.00	64
TOO MUCH/Mid-Night Blues	(Ikon 115)	1.00	4.00	
WAX 'EM DOWN/Gypsy Surfer	(Chancellor 1144)	1.00	4.00	63
Instrumentals				
AVENGERS, The				
BATMAN THEME/Back Side Blues (Instrumental)	(MGM 13465)	.75	3.00	66
AVERAGE WHITE BAND, The (AWB)				
CLOUDY/Love Your Life	(Atlantic 3388)	.50	2.00	77
CUT THE CAKE/Person To Person	(Atlantic 3261)	.50	2.00	75
HOW CAN YOU GO HOME/	(MCA 40196)	.50	2.00	74
IF I EVER LOSE THIS HEAVEN/High Flyin' Woman	(Atlantic 3285)	.50	2.00	75
LOVE OF YOUR OWN, A/Soul Searching	(Atlantic 3363)	.50	2.00	76
ONE LOOK OVER MY SHOULDER (IS THIS REALLY GOODBYE?)/ Your Love Is A Miracle	(Atlantic 3481)	.50	2.00	78
PICK UP THE PIECES/Work To Do	(Atlantic 3229)	.50	2.00	74
QUEEN OF MY SOUL/Would You Stay	(Atlantic 3354)	.50	2.00	76
SCHOOL BOY CRUSH/Groovin' The Night Away	(Atlantic 3304)	.50	2.00	75
SHE'S A DREAM/Big City Lights	(Atlantic 3500)	.50	2.00	78
WALK ON BY/Too Late To Cry	(Atlantic 3563)	.50	2.00	79
AXTON, Hoyt				
BONEY FINGERS/Life Machine	(A&M 1607)	.50	2.00	75
DELLA & THE DEALER/In A Young Girl's Mind	(Jeremiah 1000)	.50	2.00	79
FLASH OF FIRE/Paid In Advance	(A&M 1811)	.50	2.00	76
GREENBACK DOLLAR/Crawdad Song	(Horizon 351)	.75	3.00	
L.A. TOWN/Double, Double Done	(Vee Jay 604)	.75	3.00	64
LION IN THE WINTER/No No Song (With Linda Ronstadt)	(A&M 1683)	.50	2.00	75
LITTLE WHITE MOON/Funeral Of The King	(MCA 40731)	.50	2.00	77
NASHVILLE/Speed Trap	(A&M 1657)	.50	2.00	75
RUSTY OLD HALO, A/Gotta Keep Rollin'	(Jeremiah 1001)	.50	2.00	79
WHEN THE MORNING COMES/Billie's Theme (With Linda Ronstadt)	(A&M 1497)	.50	2.00	74
YOU'RE THE HANGNAIL OF MY LIFE/ Never Been To Spain	(MCA 40711)	.50	2.00	77
AYERS, Kevin				
MR. COOL/	(ABC 12303)	.50	2.00	77
AZALEAS, The				
HANDS OFF/Our Drummer Can't Keep Time	(Romulus 3001)	.75	3.00	63
AZTECS, The				
SUMMERTIME BLUES/What'cha Gonna Do 'Bout It	(GNP Crescendo 346)	1.00	4.00	65
Also see Thorpe, Billy, & The Aztecs				
AZTECS, The				
DA DOO RON RON/Hi-Heel Sneekers	(World Artists 1029)	1.00	4.00	64
TEENAGE HALL OF FAME/Traffic Jam	(Card 901)	1.00	4.00	
AZTECS, The				
REGULATION THREE PUFF/ Most People I Know Think I'm Crazy	(RAK 4510)	.50	2.00	73
AZTEC TWO-STEP, The				
BAKING/	(Elektra 45794)	.50	2.00	73
I WONDER IF WE TRIED/Hurting	(RCA 11221)	.50	2.00	78
ONE THING I FORGOT TO TELL YOU/	(RCA 11313)	.50	2.00	78
ON THE ROAD (THE PERSECUTION & RESTORATION OF DEAN MORIARTY)/	(Elektra 45814)	.50	2.00	73
SO WE DANCED/	(RCA 10850)	.50	2.00	76

B

TITLE/FLIP	LABEL & NO.	GOOD	NEAR MINT	YR.
BABE RUTH				
ELUSIVE/	(Capitol 4219)	.50	2.00	76
WELLS FARGO/Theme From "For A Few Dollars More"	(Harvest 3553)	.50	2.00	73
BABS TINO				
MY HONEYBUN/Sweet Cakes	(Cameo 114)	1.00	4.00	57
TOO LATE TO WORRY/My Heart Just Can't Say Goodbye	(Kapp 458)	.75	3.00	62
BABY BUGS, The				
BINGO/Bingo's Bongo Bingo Party	(Vee Jay 594)	1.25	5.00	64
BINGO/Bingo's Bongo Bingo Party (Promotional picture sleeve)	(Vee Jay 594)	2.50	10.00	64
BABY DOLLS, The (With Bill Baker)				
HEY BABY/Quiet	(Warner Bros. 5086)	1.00	4.00	59
I WILL DO IT (CAUSE HE WANTS ME TO)/ Now That I've Lost You	(Boom 60002)	.75	3.00	66
I'M LONELY/Go Away Baby	(Maske 103)	1.25	5.00	58
IS THIS THE END/Boyfriend	(Elgin 021)	3.00	12.00	
THANKS MR. DEE JAY/What A Wonderful Love	(Maske 701)	1.50	6.00	61
TUTTI FRUTTI/Cause I'm In Love	(RCA Victor 47-7296)	1.00	4.00	58
Even though all of these releases are shown as being by a group using the same name, the possibility exists that they are not all by the same group.				
BABY GRAND				
ALL NIGHT LONG/	(Arista 0394)	.50	2.00	79
BRING ME YOUR BROKEN HEART/Lady Of My Dreams	(Arista 0293)	.50	2.00	78
NEVER ENOUGH/	(Arista 0312)	.50	2.00	78
BABY JANE & THE ROCKABYES				
GET ME TO THE CHURCH ON TIME/ Half Deserted Street	(Spokane 4004)	1.00	4.00	63
HICKORY DICKORY DOCK/Half Deserted Street	(Spokane 4001)	1.00	4.00	62
HOW MUCH IS THAT DOGGIE IN THE WINDOW/ My Boy John	(United Artists 560)	1.00	4.00	62
BABY RAY & THE FERNS (Featuring Frank Zappa)				
HOW'S YOUR BIRD/World's Greatest Sinner	(Donna 1378)	2.50	10.00	63
BABYS, The				
EVERY TIME I THINK OF YOU/Head First	(Chrysalis 2279)	.50	2.00	78
HEAD FIRST/California	(Chrysalis 2323)	.50	2.00	79
IF YOU'VE GOT THE TIME/Head Above The Waves	(Chrysalis 2132)	.50	2.00	77
ISN'T IT TIME/Give Me Your Love	(Chrysalis 2173)	.50	2.00	77
SILVER DREAMS/And If You Could See Me Fly	(Chrysalis 2201)	.50	2.00	78
BACHARACH, Burt				
ALL KINDS OF PEOPLE/She's Gone Away	(A&M 1241)	.50	2.00	72
I'LL NEVER FALL IN LOVE AGAIN/	(A&M 1064)	.50	2.00	69
LOOK OF LOVE, THE/Reach Out For Me	(A&M 888)	.50	2.00	67
SATURDAY SUNSHINE/And So Goodbye My Love	(Kapp 532)	.50	2.00	63
BACHELORS, The				
CAN I TRUST YOU/Who Can I Turn To	(London 20010)	.75	3.00	66
CHAPEL IN THE MOONLIGHT/Old Wishing Well	(London 9793)	.75	3.00	65
CHARMAINE/Old Bill	(London 9584)	.75	3.00	62
DIANE/Happy Land	(London 9639)	.75	3.00	64
FARAWAY PLACES/Is There A Chance	(London 9623)	.75	3.00	63
I BELIEVE/Sweet Lullaby	(London 9672)	.75	3.00	64
I WOULDN'T TRADE YOU FOR THE WORLD/ Beneath The Willow Tree	(London 9693)	.75	3.00	64
LEARN TO LIVE WITHOUT YOU/ 3 O'clock Flamingo Street	(London 20033)	.75	3.00	67
LOVE ME WITH ALL YOUR HEART/ There's No Room In My Heart	(London 9828)	.75	3.00	66
MARIE/You Can Tell	(London 9762)	.75	3.00	65
NO ARMS CAN EVER HOLD YOU/Oh Samuel Don't Die	(London 9724)	.75	3.00	64
OH HOW I MISS YOU/Martha	(London 20027)	.75	3.00	67
WALK WITH FAITH IN YOUR HEART/Molly Malone	(London 20018)	.75	3.00	66
WHISPERING/No Light In The Window	(London 9623)	.75	3.00	63
BACHMAN, Randy (Of Bachman-Turner Overdrive)				
IS THE NIGHT TOO COLD FOR DANCING/	(Polydor 14478)	.50	2.00	78
Also see Guess Who, The				
Also see Iron Horse				
BACHMAN-TURNER OVERDRIVE (Randy Bachman & C.F. Turner)				
BLUE COLLAR/	(Mercury 73417)	.50	2.00	73
DOWN TO THE LINE/She's A Devil	(Mercury 73724)	.50	2.00	75
GIMME YOUR MONEY PLEASE/Little Gandy Dance	(Mercury 73383)	.50	2.00	73
HEARTACHES/	(Mercury 74046)	.50	2.00	79
HEY, YOU/Flat Broke Love	(Mercury 73683)	.50	2.00	75
JAMAICA/	(Mercury 74062)	.50	2.00	79
JUST FOR YOU/Life Still Goes On (I'm Lonely)	(Mercury 73951)	.50	2.00	77
LET IT RIDE/Tramp	(Mercury 73457)	.50	2.00	74
LOOKIN' OUT FOR #1/Find Out About Love	(Mercury 73784)	.50	2.00	76
MY WHEELS WON'T TURN/Freeways	(Mercury 73903)	.50	2.00	77
ROLL ON DOWN THE HIGHWAY/Sledgehammer	(Mercury 73656)	.50	2.00	75
SHOTGUN RIDER/Down, Down	(Mercury 73926)	.50	2.00	77
TAKE IT LIKE A MAN/Woncha Take Me For A While	(Mercury 73766)	.50	2.00	76
TAKIN' CARE OF BUSINESS/Stonegates	(Mercury 73487)	.50	2.00	74
YOU AIN'T SEEN NOTHIN' YET/Free Wheelin'	(Mercury 73662)	.50	2.00	74
After Randy Bachman left (1978) the band became known as BTO.				
BACK STREET CRAWLER: see Crawler				
BACK-BEAT PHILHARMONIC, The				
ROCK & ROLL SYMPHONY/Rock & Roll Symphony (Part 2)	(Laurie 3092)	.75	3.00	61
BACK PORCH MAJORITY, The (With Randy Sparks & Kim Vassy)				
FRIENDS/Hand-me-down Things	(Epic 5-9689)	.75	3.00	64
HONEY & WINE/Brother John	(Epic 5-10036)	.75	3.00	66
JACK O' DIAMONDS/Smash Flops	(Epic 5-9769)	.75	3.00	64
MIGHTY MISSISSIPPI/Song Of Hope	(Epic 5-9850)	.75	3.00	65
OL' DAN TUCKER/Hey Nelly, Nelly	(Epic 5-9754)	.75	3.00	65
ONCE AGAIN/Slippery Sal & Dirty Dan, The Oyster Man	(Epic 5-10079)	.75	3.00	66
RAMBLIN' MAN/Good-time Joe	(Epic 5-9809)	.75	3.00	65
SOUTHTOWN U.S.A./This Little Light	(Epic 5-10129)	.75	3.00	67
THAT'S THE WAY IT'S GONNA BE/Second Hand Man	(Epic 5-9879)	.75	3.00	66
Also see New Christy Minstrels, The				
Also see Eddy, Duane				
BACKUS, Jim				
CAVE MAN/Rocks On The Roof	(Jubilee 5361)	1.25	5.00	59
CAVEMAN/Why Don't You Go Home For Christmas	(Jubilee 5351)	1.25	5.00	58
DELICIOUS/I Need A Vacation (Shown as by Jim Backus & Friend)	(Jubilee 5330)	1.25	5.00	58
OFFICE PARTY/I Was A Teenage Reindeer	(Dico 101)	1.25	5.00	59
Comedy				
BAD BOY				
DISCO/I've Had Enough	(United Artists 1118)	.50	2.00	78
THINKING OF YOU/Shake Me Up	(United Artists 1063)	.50	2.00	77
BAD BOYS, The				
OWL & THE PUSSYCAT, THE/That's What I'll Do	(Warner Bros. 5605)	.50	2.00	65
BAD COMPANY (Featuring Paul Rodgers)				
BURNIN' SKY/Everything I Need	(Swan Song 70112)	.50	2.00	77
CAN'T GET ENOUGH/Little Miss Fortune	(Swan Song 70015)	.50	2.00	74
FEEL LIKE MAKIN' LOVE/Wild Fire Woman	(Swan Song 70103)	.50	2.00	75
GONE, GONE, GONE/Take The Time	(Swan Song 71000)	.50	2.00	79
HONEY CHILD/Fade Away	(Swan Song 70109)	.50	2.00	76
MOVIN' ON/Easy On My Soul	(Swan Song 70101)	.50	2.00	75
ROCK 'N' ROLL FANTASY/Crazy Circles	(Swan Song 70119)	.50	2.00	79
YOUNGBLOOD/Do Right By Your Woman	(Swan Song 70108)	.50	2.00	76
Group also includes Simon Kirke (of Free) & Mike Ralphs (of Mott The Hoople).				
BAD HABITS, The (Delaney & Bonnie Bramlett)				
I DON'T WANT TO DISCUSS IT/ If The Whole World Stopped Loving	(Paula 342)	.75	3.00	71
IT'S BEEN A LONG TIME COMING/Night Owl	(Paula 327)	.75	3.00	70
MY BABY SPECIALIZES/	(Paula 333)	.75	3.00	70
THANK YOU FOR THE LOVE/My Days Are Numbered	(Paula 353)	.75	3.00	71
BADFINGER (Formerly the Iveys)				
APPLE OF MY EYE/Blind Owl	(Apple 1864)	.50	2.00	73
BABY BLUE/Flying	(Apple 1844)	.50	2.00	72
COME & GET IT/Rock Of All Ages	(Apple 1815)	.50	2.00	70
DAY AFTER DAY/Money	(Apple 1841)	.50	2.00	71
I MISS YOU/Shine On	(Warner Bros. 7801)	.50	2.00	74
LOVE IS GONNA COME AT LAST/Sail Away	(Elektra 46025)	.50	2.00	79
LOST INSIDE YOUR LOVE/Come Down Hard	(Elektra 46002)	.50	2.00	79
NO MATTER WHAT/Carry On Till Tomorrow	(Apple 1822)	.50	2.00	70
BADMAN, Hickey: see Creep, The				
BAD SEEDS, The				
ALL NIGHT LONG/	(J. Beck 1005)	1.00	4.00	
BAEZ, Joan				
BANKS OF THE OHIO/Old Blue	(Vanguard 35012)	1.00	4.00	61
BEST OF FRIENDS/Mary Call	(A&M 1454)	.50	2.00	73
BLUE SKY/Dida	(A&M 1703)	.50	2.00	75
CARUSO/Time is Passing Us By	(A&M 1884)	.50	2.00	76
DIAMONDS & RUST/Winds Of The Old Days	(A&M 1737)	.50	2.00	75
FOREVER YOUNG/Guantanamera	(A&M 1516)	.50	2.00	74
HERE'S TO YOU/The Ballad Of Sacco & Vanzetti (Part 2)	(RCA 74-0568)	.50	2.00	71
HONEST LULLABY/Michael	(Portrait 70032)	.50	2.00	79
I'M BLOWIN' AWAY/Altar Boy & The Thief	(Portrait 70006)	.50	2.00	77
IN THE QUIET MORNING (For Janis Joplin)/To Bobby	(A&M 1362)	.50	2.00	72
LET IT BE/Poor Wayfaring Stranger	(Vanguard 35145)	.50	2.00	71
LITTLE DRUMMER BOY, THE/Cantique de Noel	(Vanguard 35046)	.75	3.00	66
LOVE IS JUST A FOUR LETTER WORD/ Love Minus Zero-No Limit	(Vanguard 35088)	.50	2.00	69
MARIA DELORES/Plane Wreck At Los Gatos (Deportee)	(Vanguard SPV-6)	.50	2.00	70
MIRACLES/Time Rag	(Portrait 6-70009)	.50	2.00	77
NEVER DREAMED YOU'D LEAVE IN SUMMER/ Children & All That Jazz	(A&M 1820)	.50	2.00	76
NIGHT THEY DROVE OLD DIXIE DOWN, THE/ When Time Is Stolen	(Vanguard 35138)	.50	2.00	71
NO EXPECTATIONS/One Day At A Time	(Vanguard 35092)	.50	2.00	69
NORTH/Be Not Too Hard	(Vanguard 35055)	.75	3.00	67
O BROHER/Still Waters At Night	(A&M 1906)	.50	2.00	77
PAL OF MINE/Lonesome Road	(Vanguard 35013)	1.00	4.00	62
PICK UP YOUR SORROWS/Swallow Song	(Vanguard 35040)	.75	3.00	66
PLEASE COME TO BOSTON/Love Song To A Stranger	(A&M 1802)	.50	2.00	76
REJOICE IN THE SUN/Silent Running	(Decca 32890)	.50	2.00	72
ROCK SALT & NAILS/If I Knew	(Vanguard 35092)	.50	2.00	69
SONG OF BANGLA DESH/Prison Trilogy (Bill Rose)	(A&M 1334)	.50	2.00	72
THERE BUT FOR FORTUNE/ Daddy You Been On My Mind	(Vanguard 35031)	.75	3.00	65
TIME RAG/Miracles	(Portrait 70009)	.50	2.00	77
TUMBLEWEED/Love Song To A Stranger	(A&M 1393)	.50	2.00	72
WE SHALL OVERCOME/ What Have They Done To The Rain	(Vanguard 35023)	.75	3.00	63
WILL THE CIRCLE BE UNBROKEN/ Just A Closer Walk With Thee	(Vanguard 35148)	.50	2.00	72
BAG (Featuring Jimmy Curtiss)				
RED PURPLE & BLUE/I Want You By My Side	(Decca 32463)	1.00	4.00	69
UP IN THE MORNING/Down & Out	(Decca 32409)	1.25	5.00	69
BAG, The				
INCUBATIN' MIDDLE OF THE NIGHT GYRATIN' BLUES/ Face It	(Jerden 769)	.75	3.00	
BAGBY, Doc				
DUMPLIN'S/Sylvia's Calling (Instrumental)	(Okeh 7089)	1.00	4.00	57
BAGDASARIAN, Ross (David Seville)				
BOLD & THE BRAVE, THE/See A Teardrop Fall	(Liberty 55013)	1.00	4.00	56
COME ON-A-MY HOUSE/Gotta Get To Your House	(Liberty 55837)	.75	3.00	65
GOTTA GET TO YOUR HOUSE/Cecelia	(Liberty 55557)	.75	3.00	63
LAZY LOVERS/One Finger Waltz	(Mercury 70254)	1.25	5.00	54
LUCY, LUCY/Scallywags	(Liberty 55619)	.75	3.00	63
SPANISH PIZZA/Jone Cone Phone	(Imperial 66379)	.75	3.00	69
WALKING BIRDS OF CARNABY/Red Wine	(Liberty 56004)	.75	3.00	67
WHEN I LOOK IN YOUR EYES/The Winds Of Time	(Liberty 56048)	.75	3.00	67
BAGELS, The				
I WANNA HOLD YOUR HAIR/ Yeah, Yeah, Yeah, Yeah	(Warner Bros. 5420)	1.25	5.00	64
BAGGYS, The				
EL SURFER/El Seagull	(Pipeline 501)	1.25	5.00	63
BAILEY, Pearl				
FIVE POUND BOX OF MONEY/Jingle Bells Cha Cha Cha	(Roulette 4206)	1.00	4.00	59
TAKES TWO TO TANGO/Let There Be Love	(Coral 60817)	1.25	5.00	52
BAIN, Babette				
GRADUATION NIGHT/That's It	(Rendezvous 108)	1.00	4.00	59
BAJA MARIMBA BAND, The (With Julius Wechter)				
ACAPULCO 1922/Moonglow & Theme From "Picnic"	(Almo 203)	.75	3.00	64
COMIN' IN THE BACK DOOR/December's Child	(Almo 201)	.75	3.00	63
UP CHERRY STREET/The Woody Woodpecker Song	(Almo 207)	.75	3.00	64
BAKER, Abie				
MOCCASIN ROCK/The Web	(Laurel 1010)	1.00	4.00	59

TITLE/FLIP	LABEL & NO.	GOOD	NEAR MINT	YR.
BAKER, Bill				
BLEEDING HEARTS/There's A Small Hotel	(ETC. 227)	.75	3.00	63
IS IT A DREAM/I Want To Know	(Avdicon 115)	1.25	5.00	62
PRICE OF LOVE, THE/Thank Heaven	(VIM 515)	1.00	4.00	60
TEENAGE TRIANGLE/Why Did Summer Have To End	(Music Tone 119)	1.00	4.00	62
TO THE AISLE/Just To Be Near You	(Avdicon 118)	1.25	5.00	62
TO THE AISLE/Just To Be Near You	(Music Tone 1108)	1.00	4.00	
TWITCHIN'/Big Top (With The Twitchers)	(Dore 606)	.75	3.00	61
WONDERFUL GIRL/Chit Chat	(Coral 9-62171)	1.00	4.00	60
BAKER, Bobbi (Joan Rivers)				
MY NEIGHBORS/	(Tiffany 4001)	.75	3.00	
BAKER, George, Selection				
DEAR ANN/Fly	(Colossus 117)	.75	3.00	70
I WANNA LOVE YOU/	(Colossus 124)	.75	3.00	70
LITTLE GREEN BAG/Pretty Little Dreamer	(Colossus 112)	.75	3.00	70
MORNING SKY/Baby Blue	(Warner Bros. 8207)	.50	2.00	76
PALOMA BLANCA/Dreamboat	(Warner Bros. 8115)	.50	2.00	75
BAKER, Ginger (Of Cream)				
ATTUNDE (PART 1)/Attunde (Part 2) (Shown as by the Ginger Baker Drum Choir)	(Atco 6816)	.75	3.00	70
MAN OF CONSTANT SORROW.Doin' It (Shown as by Ginger Bakers' Air Force)	(Atco 6750)	.75	3.00	70
BAKER, Kenny				
GOODBYE LITTLE STAR/I'M Gonna Love You	(Orbit 541)	3.00	12.00	
BAKER, Penny, & The Pillows				
BRING BACK THE BEATLES/Gonna Win Him	(Witch 123)	1.50	6.00	64
BAKER, Rodney, & The Chantiers				
TEENAGE WEDDING SONG/Graduation	(Jan Ell 8)	2.50	10.00	61
BAKER, Ronnie (Of The Bell-Tones)				
GLORY BE/This Big Wide World (With The Bell-Tones)	(Jell 200)	1.00	4.00	
I LOVE YOU MY DARLING/Merngue	(Scatt 1609)	1.25	5.00	
I LOVE YOU MY DARLING/Merngue	(J&S 1609)	1.25	5.00	
MY STORY/I Want To Be Loved (With The Deltones)	(Laurie 3128)	5.00	20.00	62
SEE YOU IN SEPTEMBER/Young At Heart	(Laurie 3250)	1.00	4.00	64
BAKER-GURVITZ ARMY, The (Ginger Baker & Adrian Gurvitz)				
PEOPLE/	(Atco 7043)	.50	2.00	74
Also see Gun				
BALBOA				
JIMMY & JANIS/Your Love's All Mine	(Event 200)	1.00	4.00	
BALCOM, Bill				
CORRIDO ROCK (PART 1)/Corrido Rock (Part 2)	(Starla 7)	1.25	5.00	58
CORRIDO ROCK (PART 1)/Corrido Rock (Part 2) (Instrumentals)	(Dot 15711)	.75	3.00	58
On some issues this artist was shown as "Handsome" Jim Balcom.				
BALDASSARE, J.F.				
WAY ABOUT HER, A/It All Works Out	(Magna-Glide MGR-330)	.50	2.00	77
BALDRY, Long John				
DON'T TRY TO LAY NO BOOGIE-WOOGIE ON THE KING OF ROCK & & ROLL/Mr. Rubin	(Warner Bros. 7506)	.50	2.00	71
DON'T TRY TO LAY NO BOOGIE-WOOGIE ON THE KING OF ROCK & & ROLL (PART 1)/Don't Try To Lay No Boogie-Woogie On The King Of Rock & Roll (Part 2)	(Warner Bros. 7516)	.50	2.00	71
HOLD BACK THE DAYBREAK/Since I Lost You Baby	(Warner Bros. 7184)	.50	2.00	69
IKO IKO/You Can't Judge A Book By Its Cover	(Warner Bros. 7597)	.50	2.00	72
LET THE HEARTACHES BEGIN/Hey Lord, You Made The Night Too Long	(Warner Bros. 7098)	.50	2.00	68
MOTHER AIN'T DEAD/	(Warner Bros. 7617)	.50	2.00	72
WHEN THE SUN COMES SHININ' THRU/Wise To The Ways Of The World	(A&M 974)	.75	3.00	68
YOU'VE LOST THAT LOVING FEELING (With Kathi McDonald)/Baldry's Out	(EMI American 8018)	.50	2.00	79
BALESTRIERI, Brian (Of The Sidewalk Skipper Band)				
WORKIN MY BAR/Sad Eyed Lady	(Desmond 102)	.50	2.00	78
BALIN, Marty				
I SPECIALIZE IN LOVE/You Alive With Love	(Challenge 9156)	5.00	20.00	62
YOU MADE ME FALL/Nobody But You	(Challenge 9146)	5.00	20.00	62
Also see Jefferson Airplane				
Also see Jefferson Starship				
BALLADEERS, The (Fred Darian, Al Delory, Joe Van Winkle)				
HURTIN' (FOR THE LOVE OF YOU)/Roll Call Company "J"	(Del Fi 4138)	1.00	4.00	60
MORNING STAR/Tom Get's The Last Laugh (Answer song)	(Del Fi 4123)	1.00	4.00	59
TURTLE DOVE/Durant Jail	(Del Fi 4127)	1.00	4.00	59
BALLADIERS, The (Featuring Rod Barton)				
THERE THEY GO/When Our Love Is Locked In Lovelock	(Love Lock 115)	.75	3.00	
BALLADS, The				
BEFORE YOU FALL IN LOVE/Broke	(Franwil 5028)	3.00	12.00	
BALLARD, Russ (Of the Unit 4 + 2)				
TREAT HER RIGHT/What Does It Take	(Epic 50542)	.50	2.00	78
WINNING/Here I Am	(Epic 50211)	.50	2.00	76
YOU CAN DO VOODOO/	(Epic 50085)	.50	2.00	74
Also see Argent				
BALL BROTHERS, The				
GOODNIGHT SURPRISE/Underground Railroad	(Easy 101)	1.25	5.00	
BALL, Kenny				
GREEN LEAVES OF SUMMER, THE/I Shall Not Be Moved	(Kapp 460)	.75	3.00	62
MARCH OF THE SIAMESE CHILDREN/Villia	(Kapp 451)	.75	3.00	62
MIDNIGHT IN MOSCOW/American Patrol (Instrumentals)	(Kapp 442)	.75	3.00	62
BALLOON FARM, The				
HURRY UP SUNDOWN/	(Laurie 3445)	.75	3.00	68
QUESTION OF TEMPERATURE, A/Hurtin' For Your Love	(Laurie 3405)	.75	3.00	68
BALTIMORE & OHIO MARCHING BAND, The				
LAPLAND/Condition Red (Instrumental)	(Jubilee 5592)	.75	3.00	67
BANANA & THE BUNCH (With Jesse Colin Young)				
BACK IN THE U.S.A./Back In The U.S.A.	(Warner Bros. 7626)	.50	2.00	72
MY TRUE LIFE BLUES/Vanderbilt's Lament	(Warner Bros. 7621)	.50	2.00	72
BANANA SPLITS, The				
LONG LIVE LOVE/Pretty Painted Carousel	(Decca 32536)	.75	3.00	69
TRA LA LA SONG, THE/	(Decca 32429)	.75	3.00	69
WAIT TIL' TOMORROW/We're The Banana Splits	(Decca 32391)	.75	3.00	68
BANANA'S BUNCH				
KING KONG GOES APE/Ape Stomp (Novelty/Break-in)	(Fun-e-bone 320)	.75	3.00	76

TITLE/FLIP	LABEL & NO.	GOOD	NEAR MINT	YR.
BAND The (With Levon Helm)				
AIN'T GOT NO HOME/Get Up Jake	(Capitol 3758)	.50	2.00	73
AIN'T GOT NO HOME/Don't Do It	(Capitol 6246)	.50	2.00	77
CALEDONIA MISSION/Hang Up My Rock N' Roll Shoes	(Capitol 3500)	.50	2.00	72
DON'T DO IT/Rag Mama Rag	(Capitol 3433)	.50	2.00	72
GEORGIA ON MY MIND/Night They Drove Old Dixie Down	(Capitol 4361)	.50	2.00	76
JABBERWOCKY/Never Too Much Love	(Capitol 2041)	.75	3.00	67
LIFE IS A CARNIVAL/Moon Struck One	(Capitol 3199)	.50	2.00	71
OPHELIA/Hobo Jungle	(Capitol 4230)	.50	2.00	76
RAG MAMA RAG/Unfaithful Servant	(Capitol 2705)	.50	2.00	70
THIRD MAN THEME/W.S. Walcott Medicine Show	(Capitol 3828)	.50	2.00	74
TIME TO KILL/Shape I'm In	(Capitol 2870)	.50	2.00	70
TWILIGHT/Acadian Driftwood	(Capitol 4316)	.50	2.00	76
UP ON CRIPPLE CREEK/The Night They Drove Old Dixie Down	(Capitol 2635)	.75	3.00	69
UP ON CRIPPLE CREEK/The Night They Drove Old Dixie Down	(Capitol 6188)	.50	2.00	72
WEIGHT, THE/I Shall Be Released	(Capitol 2269)	.75	3.00	68
WELL, THE/Out Of The Blue	(Warner Bros. 8592)	.50	2.00	78
WHEN I PAINT MY MASTERPIECE/Where Do We Go From Here	(Capitol 3249)	.50	2.00	71
Also see Dylan, Bob				
Also see Hawkins, Ronnie & The Hawks				
Also see Levon & The Hawks				
BAND WITHOUT A NAME, The				
THEME FROM THUNDER ALLEY/Time After Time (I Keep Loving You)	(Sidewalk 913)	.75	3.00	67
TURN ON YOUR LOVELIGHT/A Perfect Girl	(Tower 246)	.75	3.00	66
BANDANA (Bandanna)				
JUKEBOX SATURDAY NIGHT/	(Haven 807)	.50	2.00	76
TIME WILL EQUALIZE/Here Comes The Sun	(Paramount 0026)	.50	2.00	73
Also see Player				
BANDIT				
ONE WAY LOVE/I'm A Rocker	(Ariola 7731)	.50	2.00	79
BANDITS				
NOTHING CAN CHANGE MY LOVE FOR YOU/	(Emjay 1935)	2.50	10.00	
BANKS, Bessie				
GO NOW/It Sounds Like My Baby	(Tiger 102)	1.00	4.00	64
BANKS, Tony (Of Genesis)				
FOR A WHILE/	(Charisma 3503)	.50	2.00	79
BANNED				
IT COULDN'T HAPPEN HERE/It Couldn't Happen Here	(Fontana 1616)	.75	3.00	68
BANNERS, The				
FORTUNE TELLER/Sales Talk	(MGM K-12862)	.75	3.00	60
BARAKAT, Johnny, & The Vestells				
HAPPY TIME/Long Ride	(Dell-Star 103)	1.00	4.00	64
BARBARA & BRENDA (With Brenda Holloway)				
LET'S GET TOGETHER/Shame	(Avanti 1600)	1.00	4.00	63
BARBARA & THE BELIEVERS				
WHEN YOU WISH UPON A STAR/What Can Happen To Me Now	(Capitol 5866)	2.50	10.00	67
BARBARA & THE BOYS				
HOOTY SAPPERTICKER/Cobra	(Dot 45-15798)	1.00	4.00	58

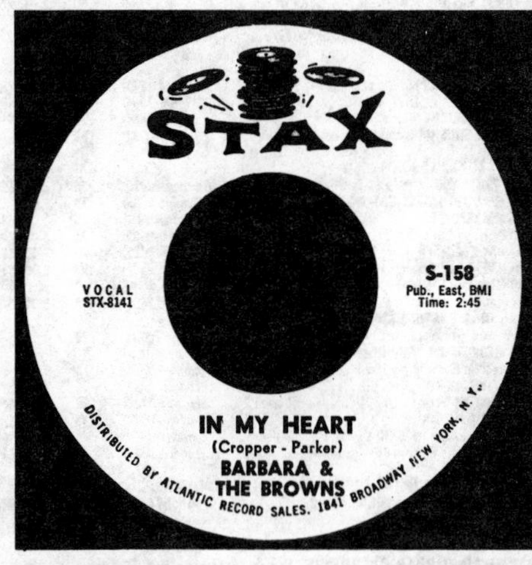

TITLE/FLIP	LABEL & NO.	GOOD	NEAR MINT	YR.
BARBARA & THE BROWNS				
BIG PARTY/You Belong To Her	(Stax 150)	.75	3.00	64
IN MY HEART/Please Be Honest With Me	(Stax 158)	.75	3.00	64
BARBARIANS, The				
ARE YOU A BOY OR A GIRL/Take It Or Leave It	(Laurie 3308)	1.25	5.00	65
MOULTY/I'll Keep On Seeing You (With backing by the Elegants)	(Laurie 3326)	1.00	4.00	66
SUSIE Q/What The New Breed Say	(Laurie 3321)	1.00	4.00	65
YOU'VE GOT TO UNDERSTAND/Hey Little Bird	(Joy 290)	2.00	8.00	64
BARBAROSO & THE HISTORIANS (Featuring Nick Addeo)				
ZOOM/When I Fall In Love	(Jade 110)	2.50	10.00	
BARBER, Chris: see Chris Barber's Jazz Band				
BARBOUR, Dave				
MAMBO JAMBO/Dave's Boogie	(Capitol 973)	1.25	5.00	50
BARBOUR, Keith				
ECHO PARK/Here I Am Losing You	(Epic 10486)	.75	3.00	69
BARCLAY, James Harvest				
CHILD OF THE UNIVERSE/Crazy City	(Polydor 15104)	.50	2.00	75
HYMN/Our Kid's Kid	(MCA 40795)	.50	2.00	77
ROCK 'N' ROLL STAR/	(MCA 40690)	.50	2.00	76
THANK YOU/Medicine Man	(Harvest 3501)	.50	2.00	72
TITLES/	(Polydor 15118)	.50	2.00	75
BARCLAY, Nickey (Of Fanny)				
BAD BOY/That's The Kind Of Love I've Got For You	(Ariola America 7642)	.50	2.00	76
LONELY DAYS/Fairweather Friend	(Ariola America 7622)	.50	2.00	75

TITLE/FLIP	LABEL & NO.	GOOD	NEAR MINT	YR.
BARD, Annette (Of the Teddy Bears)				
ALIBI/What Difference Does It Make	(Imperial 5643)	3.00	12.00	60
BARDOT, Brigitte				
SIDONIE/A Very Private Affair (Theme)	(MGM K-13099)	.75	3.00	62
BARE, Bobby				
BOOK OF LOVE/Lorena	(Fraternity 878)	.75	3.00	61
BROOKLYN BRIDGE/Zig Zag (Twist)	(Fraternity 890)	1.50	6.00	61
I'M HANGING UP MY RIFLE (Answer Song)/That's Where I Want To Be	(Fraternity 861)	1.50	6.00	59
ISLAND OF LOVE/Sailor Man	(Fraternity 885)	.75	3.00	61
LYNCHIN' PARTY/No Letter From My Baby	(Fraternity 871)	1.00	4.00	60
MORE THAN A POOR BOY COULD GIVE/Sweet Singin' Sam	(Fraternity 867)	1.00	4.00	60
THAT MEAN OLD CLOCK/The Day My Rainbow Fell	(Fraternity 892)	.75	3.00	61
In 1958 Bobby Bare, in Cincinnati, Ohio, had just recorded "All American Boy" — a novelty tune about Elvis being drafted — when, because of a label error, the record was released showing the artist as Bill Parsons, another singer for Fraternity. Rather than re-do the stock they decided to go ahead and give Bobby the name of Bill Parsons .. for awhile anyway. See Bill Parsons for that listing.				
BARE FAT				
YOU CAN ALL JOIN IN/Soft	(Bang 573)	.75	3.00	70
BAREFOOT, Spencer				
HOLD ON/Shine On	(Magna-Glide MGR-335)	.50	2.00	77
BARIN, Pete (With the Belmonts)				
LONELIEST GUY IN THE WORLD, THE/Look For Cindy	(Sabrina 512)	3.00	12.00	63
SO WRONG/Broken Heart	(Sabrina 504)	5.00	20.00	62
BARITONES, The				
AFTER SCHOOL ROCK/Sentimental Baby	(Dore 501)	5.00	20.00	58
BARKLE, Al				
MUSCLE BEACH/Graduation Party	(Frantic 108)	1.00	4.00	
BARNES, Benny, & The Echoes				
LONELY STREET/Moon Over My Shoulder	(Mercury 71284)	1.50	6.00	58
BARNES, Jimmy				
NO REGRETS/Keep Your Love Handy	(Gibraltar 101)	1.00	4.00	59
BARNSTORMERS, The				
BIG STOMP/Bug Stompin' (Instrumentals)	(Capitol 4692)	.75	3.00	62
BARNUM, H.B.				
LOST LOVE/Hallelujah	(Eldo 111)	.75	3.00	60
RENTED TUXEDO/Backstage	(Imperial 66011)	.75	3.00	63
BARONETS, The				
MINE ALL MINE/That's The Way Love Happens	(Vee Jay 701)	2.00	8.00	65
BARON, Steve				
TELL ME/California Friends	(Bell 45129)	.50	2.00	71
BARONS, The (With Larry Chance)				
BANDIT, THE/Wanderin'	(Bellaire 103)	.75	3.00	63
DRAWBRIDGE/	(Tender 1011)	.75	3.00	
(I JUST GO) WILD INSIDE/Silence	(Imperial 66057)	1.25	5.00	64
LULA MAE/Lovely Loretta	(Dart 126)	1.00	4.00	62
PERFECT LOVE/Until The 13th Chime	(Dart 134)	1.50	6.00	63
PLEDGE OF A FOOL/Don't Go Away (Pretty Little Girl) (Answer song)	(Epic 9586)	2.00	8.00	63
PLEDGE OF A FOOL/Don't Go Away (Pretty Little Girl)	(Epic 10093)	1.25	5.00	66
REMEMBER RITA/Lucky Star	(Epic 9747)	2.50	10.00	64
Also see Earls, The				
BAROQUES, The				
MARY JANE/Iowa, A Girl's Name	(Chess 2001)	.75	3.00	67
BARRACUDAS, The				
HOT ROD USA/Boss Barracuda	(Canjo 104)	1.25	5.00	64
BARRACUDAS, The				
IT'S BEEN SO LONG/Affection	(MFI 102)	1.00	4.00	
BARRAN, Rob				
TOM TOM ROCK/Mother Goose Hop (Instrumentals)	(Silver Streak 311)	1.25	5.00	60
BARRETT, Hugh, & The Victors				
GOT THE BULL BY THE HORNS/There Was A Fungus Among Us	(Madison 164)	2.50	10.00	61
BARRETTO, Ray				
EL WATUSI/Ritmo Sabroso	(Tico 419)	.75	3.00	63
BARRI, Steve				
DOWN AROUND THE CORNER/Please Let It Be You	(Rona 1003)	2.00	8.00	61
NEVER BEFORE/Whenever You Kiss Me	(Rona 1006)	1.50	6.00	62
STORY OF THE RING/I Want Your Love	(Rona 1004)	2.00	8.00	61
TWO DIFFERENT WORLDS/Don't Run Away From Love	(Rona 1005)	1.50	6.00	62
Also see Fantastic Baggies, The				
BARRIES, The				
TONIGHT TONIGHT/Mary-Ann	(Ember 1101)	2.50	10.00	62
WHY DON'T YOU WRITE ME/Mary-Ann	(Vernon 102)	5.00	20.00	
BARRIES, The				
WHEN YOU'RE OUT OF SCHOOL/Loneliest Man In Town	(Di-Nan 101)	1.50	6.00	
BARRON-KNIGHTS, The				
LAZY FAT PEOPLE/In The Night	(Decca 32160)	1.25	5.00	67
POP GO THE WORKERS (PART 1)/Pop Go The Workers (Part 2)	(Epic 9835)	1.25	5.00	65
TOPICAL SONG, THE/The Big V-Asectomy	(Epic 50755)	.50	2.00	79
YOU'RE ALL I NEED/Nothin' Doing	(Mercury 73302)	.50	2.00	72
BARRY & THE DEANS				
ROCK WITH ME BABY/	(Zirkon 1001)	1.00	4.00	60
BARRY & THE TAMERLANES (Featuring Barry De Vorzon)				
DATE WITH JUDY, A/Pretty Things	(Valiant 6050)	1.00	4.00	64
GEE/Don't Cry Cindy	(Valiant 6059)	1.00	4.00	65
I DON'T WANT TO BE YOUR CLOWN/Lucky Guy	(Valiant 6046)	1.00	4.00	64
I WONDER WHAT SHE'S DOING TONIGHT/Don't Go	(Valiant 6034)	1.00	4.00	63
ROBERTA/Butterfly	(Valiant 6040)	1.00	4.00	64
BARRY, Dave, & Sara Berner				
OUT OF THIS WORLD WITH FLYING SAUCERS/Out Of This World With Flying Saucers (Part 2) (Novelty/Break-in - Using Cover Versions)	(RPM 469)	1.50	6.00	56
BARRY, Jack, & Winky Dink				
WINKY DINK & YOU/	(Decca 88174)	2.50	10.00	55
BARRY, Jan: see Berry, Jan				

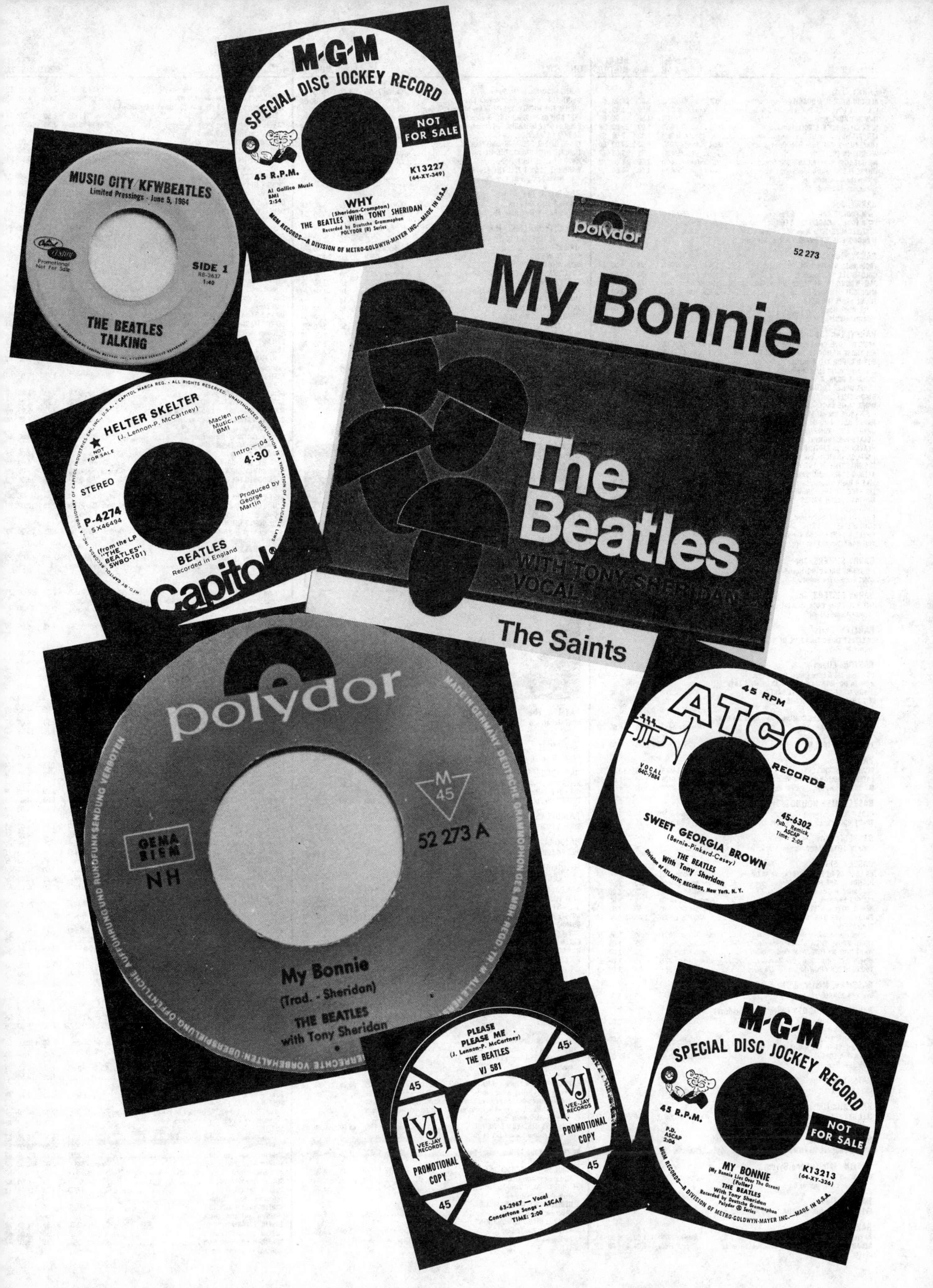

MUSIC CITY/KFWBEATLES
Limited Pressings - June 5, 1964
Promotional Not For Sale
SIDE 1
THE BEATLES TALKING
M-G-M
SPECIAL DISC JOCKEY RECORD
NOT FOR SALE
45 R.P.M.
K13227
(64-XY-349)
Al Gallico Music BMI 2:54
WHY
(Sheridan-Crompton)
THE BEATLES With TONY SHERIDAN
Recorded by Deutsche Grammophon POLYDOR (R) Series
MGM RECORDS—A DIVISION OF METRO-GOLDWYN-MAYER INC.—MADE IN U.S.A.
polydor
52 273
My Bonnie
The Beatles
WITH TONY SHERIDAN
VOCAL
The Saints
HELTER SKELTER
(J. Lennon-P. McCartney)
Maclen Music, Inc. BMI
NOT FOR SALE
Intro.—:04
4:30
STEREO
Produced by George Martin
P-4274
SX46494
(from the LP "THE BEATLES" SWBO-101)
BEATLES
Recorded in England
Capitol
polydor
GEMA BIEM
NH
M 45
52 273 A
My Bonnie
(Trad. - Sheridan)
THE BEATLES
with Tony Sheridan
45 RPM
ATCO
RECORDS
VOCAL
45-6302
Pub., Remick, ASCAP
Time: 2:05
SWEET GEORGIA BROWN
(Bernie-Pinkard-Casey)
THE BEATLES
With Tony Sheridan
Division of ATLANTIC RECORDS, New York, N.Y.
PLEASE PLEASE ME
(J. Lennon-P. McCartney)
THE BEATLES
VJ 581
45
VJ
VEE-JAY RECORDS
PROMOTIONAL COPY
63-2967 — Vocal
Concertone Songs - ASCAP
TIME: 2:00
M-G-M
SPECIAL DISC JOCKEY RECORD
45 R.P.M.
NOT FOR SALE
P.D. ASCAP 2:06
MY BONNIE
(My Bonnie Lies Over The Ocean)
(Fuller)
THE BEATLES
With Tony Sheridan
Recorded by Deutsche Grammophon Polydor ® Series
K13213
(64-XY-326)
MGM RECORDS—A DIVISION OF METRO-GOLDWYN-MAYER INC.—MADE IN U.S.A.

TITLE/FLIP	LABEL & NO.	GOOD	NEAR MINT	YR.
BARRY, Jeff				
ALL YOU NEED IS A QUARTER/Teen Quartet	(RCA Victor 47-7821)	5.00	20.00	60
I'LL STILL LOVE YOU/Our Love Can Still Be Saved	(Red Bird 026)	1.00	4.00	65
IT WON'T HURT/Never, Never	(Decca 31037)	1.50	6.00	60
IT'S CALLED ROCK & ROLL/Hip Couple	(RCA Victor 47-7477)	5.00	20.00	58
LENORE/Why Doesn't This Feeling Go Away	(Decca 31089)	2.00	8.00	60
LONELY LIPS, THE/Face From Outer Space	(RCA Victor 47-7797)	5.00	20.00	60
WALKIN' IN THE SUN/	(A&M 1422)	.75	3.00	73
WE GOT LOVE MONEY CAN'T BUY/Welcome Home	(United Artists 440)	2.00	8.00	62
WHERE IT'S AT/Much Too Young	(United Artists 50529)	1.00	4.00	69
Also see Raindrops, The				
Also see Redwoods, The				
BARRY, Joe				
I'M A FOOL TO CARE/I Got A Feeling	(JIN 144)	1.50	6.00	61
I'M A FOOL TO CARE/I Got A Feeling	(Smash 1702)	.75	3.00	61
JUST BECAUSE/Little Jewel Of The Veaux Carre	(Smash 1762)	.75	3.00	62
TEARDROPS IN MY HEART/For You, Sunshine	(Smash 1710)	.75	3.00	61
BARRY, John				
FROM RUSSIA WITH LOVE/007	(Mercury 72261)	.75	3.00	64
GOLDFINGER/Troubadour	(United Artists 791)	.75	3.00	65
JAMES BOND THEME/March Of The Mandarians	(United Artists 581)	.75	3.00	63
MIDNIGHT COWBOY/	(Columbia 44891)	.75	3.00	68
THEME FROM THE DEEP/ The White House Years	(Casablanca 987)	.50	2.00	77
Instrumentals				
BARRY, Len (Of The Dovells)				
ABC'S OF LOVE/Come Rain Or Shine	(RCA Victor 47-9348)	1.00	4.00	67
ALL THOSE MEMORIES/Rainy Side Of The Street	(RCA Victor 47-9275)	1.00	4.00	67
BOB & CAROL, TED & ALICE/ In My Present State Of Mind	(Scepter 12284)	.75	3.00	70
CHILD IS BORN, A/Wouldn't It Be Beautiful	(Amy 11047)	.75	3.00	69
CHRISTOPHER COLUMBUS/You're My Picasso Baby	(Amy 11037)	.75	3.00	69
DIGGIN' LIFE/Just The Two Of Us	(Buddah 284)	.50	2.00	72
DON'T COME BACK/Jim Dandy	(Cameo 303)	.75	3.00	64
4-5-6 (NOW I'M ALONE)/Funky Night	(Amy 11026)	1.25	5.00	68
HAPPY DAYS/Let's Do It Again	(Mercury 72299)	1.00	4.00	64
HEARTS ARE TRUMP/Little White House	(Cameo 318)	1.00	4.00	64
HEARTS ARE TRUMP/Little White House	(Parkway 969)	1.00	4.00	65
HEAVEN PLUS EARTH/I'm Marching To The Music	(Paramount 206)	.75	3.00	
I STRUCK IT RICH/Love Is	(Decca 32011)	.75	3.00	66
IT'S THAT TIME OF THE YEAR/Happily Ever After	(Decca 31969)	.75	3.00	66
KEEM-O-SABE/This Old World	(Scepter 12263)	.75	3.00	69
LIKE A BABY/Happiness (Is A Girl Like You)	(Decca 31889)	.75	3.00	66
LIP SYNC (TO THE TONGUE TWISTERS)/At The Hop "65"	(Decca 31788)	.75	3.00	65
MOVING FINGER WRITES, THE/Our Love	(RCA Victor 47-9150)	1.00	4.00	67
1-2-3/Bullseye	(Decca 31827)	.75	3.00	65
PUT OUT THE FIRE/Spread It On Like Butter	(Scepter 12251)	.75	3.00	69
SOMEWHERE/It's A Cryin' Shame	(Decca 31923)	.75	3.00	66
SWEET & FUNKY/I Like The Way	(RCA Victor 47-9464)	1.00	4.00	68
YOU BABY/Would I Love You	(Decca 32054)	1.00	4.00	66
BARRY SISTERS, The				
I MUST BE DREAMING/Nobody's Asking Questions	(Colpix 722)	.75	3.00	64
SOMEWHERE/Too Smart	(Colpix 706)	.75	3.00	63
BARRY SISTERS, The				
TILL YOU COME BACK TO ME/Intrigue	(Cadence 1295)	1.00	4.00	56
(With Archie Bleyer)				
BARTLEY, Chris				
SWEETEST THING THIS SIDE OF HEAVEN, THE/ Love Me Baby	(Vando 101)	.75	3.00	67
BARTON, Eileen				
CRY/Hold Me A Little Longer Daddy	(Coral 60592)	1.25	5.00	51
HOW-JA DO, HOW-JA DO, HOW-JA DO (IF I KNEW YOU WERE COMING I'D'VE BAKED A CAKE)/	(Coral 61377)	.75	3.00	55
IF I KNEW YOU WERE COMIN'/ When Love Happens To You	(MGM 12758)	.75	3.00	59
IF I KNEW YOU WERE COMING I'D'VE BAKED A CAKE/ Poco Loco In The Coco	(Mercury 5392)	1.00	4.00	50
(Reissue of the National single)				
YOU SAY YOU LOVE ME/Oh! Love	(Crest 1107)	.75	3.00	62
BASH, Otto				
ELVIS BLUES, THE/Later	(RCA Victor 47-6585)	2.50	10.00	56
LATER ALLIGATOR/Lookout Mountain	(RCA Victor 47-6426)	1.00	4.00	56
MY BABE/Straighten Up & Fly Right	(HDS 2008)	1.00	4.00	56
BASKERVILLE HOUNDS, The				
DEBBIE/Jackie's Theme	(Dot 45-17017)	.75	3.00	67
SPACE ROCK/Space Rock (Part 2)	(Dot 45-17004)	.75	3.00	67
BASSETT, Tony				
ROCKIN' LITTLE MAMA/Tonight & Always	(Orchid 873)	.75	3.00	61
BASSEY, Shirley				
AS LONG AS HE NEEDS ME/Above All Others	(United Artists 511)	.75	3.00	62
DIAMONDS ARE FOREVER/For The Love Of Him	(United Artists 50845)	.50	2.00	72
GOLDFINGER/Strange How Love Can Be	(United Artists 790)	.75	3.00	64
I'LL GET BY/Climb Ev'ry Mountain	(United Artists 404)	.75	3.00	62
NEVER, NEVER, NEVER/Day By Day	(United Artists UA-XW211-W)	.50	2.00	73
PARTY'S OVER, THE/'S Wonderful	(MGM K-12919)	1.00	4.00	60
SOMETHING/ What Are You Doing The Rest Of Your Life	(United Artists 50698)	.50	2.00	70
THEME FROM "THE VICTORS"/How Can You Tell	(United Artists 681)	.75	3.00	64
WHAT NOW MY LOVE/What Kind Of Fool Am I	(United Artists 503)	.75	3.00	62
WHERE ARE YOU/Climb Ev'ry Mountain	(United Artists 421)	.75	3.00	62
YOU'LL NEVER KNOW/Reach For The Stars	(United Artists 363)	.75	3.00	61
BASSMAN, Mister, & The Symbols				
RIP VAN WINKLE/You're The One	(Graphic Arts 1000)	2.00	8.00	
BATDORF & RODNEY (With Joan Batdorf)				
CAN YOU SEE HIM/	(Atlantic 2863)	.50	2.00	71
HOME AGAIN/	(Asylum 11012)	.50	2.00	72
OH MY SURPRISE/	(Atlantic 2880)	.50	2.00	72
SOMEWHERE IN THE NIGHT/Ain't It Like Home	(Arista 0159)	.50	2.00	75
YOU ARE A SONG/	(Arista 0132)	.50	2.00	75
Also see Silver				
BATS, The				
BIG BRIGHT EYES/Nothing Atall	(HBR 445)	.75	3.00	65
BATTEAUX (David Batteaux)				
TELL HER SHE'S LOVELY/Wishing My Father	(Columbia 45783)	.50	2.00	73
Also see Pierce Arrow				
BATTEN, Cecelia				
MY BIG BROTHER'S FRIEND/Before	(Colonial 431)	.75	3.00	
BATTIN, Skip (Of the Byrds)				
BALLAD OF DICK CLARK/	(Signpost 70010)	.50	2.00	73
Also see Flying Burrito Brothers, The				
BAXTER, Duke				
EVERYBODY KNOWS MATILDA/I Ain't No School Boy	(VMC 740)	.75	3.00	69
BAXTER, Les				
APRIL IN PORTUGAL/Suddenly	(Capitol 2374)	1.00	4.00	53
BECAUSE OF YOU/Somewhere, Somehow, Someday	(Capitol 1760)	1.00	4.00	51

TITLE/FLIP	LABEL & NO.	GOOD	NEAR MINT	YR.
BLUE TANGO/Please Mr. Sun	(Capitol 1966)	1.00	4.00	52
GIANT/There's Never Been Anyone Else	(Capitol 3526)	1.00	4.00	56
HIGH & THE MIGHTY, THE/More Love Than Your Love	(Capitol 2845)	1.00	4.00	54
LEFT ARM OF BUDDHA, THE/Buenos Aires	(Capitol 3573)	1.00	4.00	56
POOR PEOPLE OF PARIS, THE/Theme From Helen Of Troy	(Capitol 3336)	1.00	4.00	56
RUBY/A Little Love	(Capitol 2457)	1.00	4.00	53
TANGO OF THE DRUMS/Simmer Man	(Capitol 3404)	1.00	4.00	56
TROUBLE WITH HARRY, THE/Havana	(Capitol 3291)	1.00	4.00	56
UNCHAINED MELODY/(Theme From) "Medic"	(Capitol 3055)	1.00	4.00	55
WAKE THE TOWN & TELL THE PEOPLE/ I'll Never Stop Loving You	(Capitol 3120)	1.00	4.00	55
BAY BOPS, The				
JOANIE/Follow The Rock	(Coral 61975)	1.25	5.00	58
TO THE PARTY/My Darling My Sweet	(Coral 62004)	1.50	6.00	58
BAY CITY ROLLERS, The				
ALL OF ME LOVES ALL OF YOU/	(Bell 45618)	.50	2.00	75
ALRIGHT/Keep On Dancing	(Bell 45169)	.50	2.00	72
BYE BYE BABY/It's For You	(Arista 0120)	.50	2.00	75
DEDICATION/Rock N' Roller	(Arista 0233)	.50	2.00	77
I ONLY WANT TO BE WITH YOU/Write A Letter	(Arista 0205)	.50	2.00	76
MONEY HONEY/Mary Anne	(Arista 0170)	.50	2.00	76
ROCK & ROLL LOVE LETTER/Shanghai'd In Love	(Arista 0185)	.50	2.00	76
SHANG A LANG/	(Bell 45481)	.50	2.00	74
SATURDAY NIGHT/Marlina	(Arista 0149)	.50	2.00	75
SUMMERLOVE SENSATION/	(Bell 45607)	.50	2.00	75
WAY I FEEL TONIGHT, THE/Love Power	(Arista 0272)	.50	2.00	77
WHERE WILL I BE NOW/If You Were My Woman	(Arista 0383)	.50	2.00	78
YESTERDAY'S HERO/My Lisa	(Arista 0216)	.50	2.00	76
YOU MADE ME BELIEVE IN MAGIC/Dance Dance Dance	(Arista 0256)	.50	2.00	77
Also see Rollers, The				
BAYER, Carole: see Sager, Carole Bayer				
BAYLANDERS, The				
SURFERS RULE/Surfer's Blues	(Iona 1115)	1.00	4.00	63

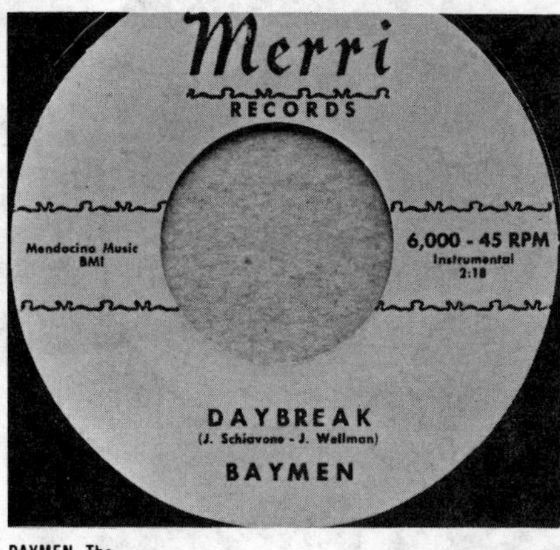

TITLE/FLIP	LABEL & NO.	GOOD	NEAR MINT	YR.
BAYMEN, The				
BONZAI/Daybreak	(Merri 6000)	.75	3.00	63
(Instrumentals)				
BAY RIDGE				
BACK TRACK/I Can't Get Her Out Of My Mind	(Atlantic 2431)	.75	3.00	67
BAYSIDERS, The				
BELLS OF ST. MARYS/Comin' Thru The Rye	(Everest 19393)	1.00	4.00	60
OVER THE RAINBOW/My Bonnie	(Everest 19366)	1.00	4.00	60
TREES/Look For The Silver Lining	(Everest 19386)	1.00	4.00	60
BAYTOVENS, The				
SUCH A FOOL/Waiting For You	(Belfast 1001)	2.00	8.00	
BAZOOKA				
BOO ON YOU/The Deal	(Bang 559)	.75	3.00	68
B. BUMBLE & THE STINGERS (Billy Brumble, Ron Brady, Fred Richard)				
APPLE KNOCKER/The Moon & The Sea	(Rendezvous 179)	.75	3.00	62
BABY MASH/Night Time Madness	(Rendezvous 192)	.75	3.00	63
BEE HIVE/Caravan	(Rendezvous 160)	.75	3.00	62
BOOGIE WOOGIE/Near You	(Rendezvous 151)	1.00	4.00	61
BUMBLE BOOGIE/School Day Blues	(Rendezvous 140)	.75	3.00	61
DAWN CRACKER/Scales	(Rendezvous 182)	.75	3.00	63
GREEN HORNET THEME/Flight Of The Hornet	(Mercury 72614)	.75	3.00	66
NUT ROCKER/Nautilus	(Rendezvous 166)	.75	3.00	62
ROCKIN-ON-'N'-OFF/Mashed #5	(Rendezvous 174)	.75	3.00	62
(Instrumentals)				
BEACH BOYS, The (Brian Wilson, Carl Wilson, Dennis Wilson, Mike Love, Al Jardine)				
ADD SOME MUSIC TO YOUR DAY/Susie Cincinnati	(Reprise 0894)	2.00	8.00	70
BARBARA ANN/Girl Don't Tell Me	(Capitol 5561)	.75	3.00	65
BARBARA ANN/Girl Don't Tell Me	(Capitol 5561)	10.00	40.00	65
(Picture sleeve)				
BARBARA ANN/Little Honda	(Capitol 4110)	.75	3.00	75
(Lead Vocal on "Barbara Ann" shared by Dean Torrence)				
BARBEE/What Is A Young Girl Made Of	(Randy 422)	87.50	350.00	61
(Red & yellow plastic)				
(Shown as by Kenny & the Cadets)				
BARBEE/What Is A Young Girl Made Of	(Randy 422)	56.25	225.00	61
(Shown as by Kenny & the Cadets)				
Both the black plastic and colored plastic orginals of "Barbee" were issued with a pink label. Counterfeit versions exist of this record, but are easily identified by their white label.				
BEACH BOYS' SINGLES '63-'70, THE/	(Capitol PSR-436)	25.00	100.00	79
(English release, Boxed Set of 26 singles, including the bonus record "Pamela Jean"/"After The Game".)				
BE TRUE TO YOUR SCHOOL/In My Room	(Capitol 5069)	1.50	6.00	63
(With the Honeys)				
BE TRUE TO YOUR SCHOOL/In My Room	(Capitol 6059)	1.25	5.00	64
(Green swirl label reissue)				
BE TRUE TO YOUR SCHOOL/Graduation Day	(Capitol 4334)	.75	3.00	76
(With the Honeys)				
BLUEBIRDS OVER THE MOUNTAIN/ Never Learn Not To Love	(Capitol 2360)	2.00	8.00	68
BLUEBIRDS OVER THE MOUNTAIN/ Never Learn Not To Love	(Capitol HF-300)	5.00	20.00	68
(Netherlands release, contains a alternate of "Bluebirds Over The Mountain".)				

TITLE/FLIP	LABEL & NO.	GOOD	NEAR MINT	YR.
_____BREAK AWAY/Celebrate The News	(Capitol 2530)	2.50	10.00	69
CALIFORNIA GIRLS/Let Him Run Wild	(Capitol 5464)	1.00	4.00	65
CALIFORNIA SAGE (ON MY WAY TO SUNNY CALIFORN-I-A)/ Funky Pretty	(Reprise REP-1156)	2.50	10.00	73
CAROLINE NO/Summer Means New Love	(Capitol 5610)	2.50	10.00	66
(Shown as by Brian Wilson)				
CHILD OF WINTER/Susie Cincinnati	(Reprise RPS-1321)	8.75	35.00	74
COOL, COOL WATER/Forever	(Reprise 0998)	20.00	80.00	71
COOL, COOL WATER/Forever	(Reprise 0998)	12.50	50.00	71
(Promotional issue)				
COTTONFIELDS/Nearest Faraway Place	(Capitol 2765)	3.75	15.00	70
CUDDLE UP/ You Need A Mess Of Help To Stand Alone	(Reprise REP-1091)	8.75	35.00	72
DANCE, DANCE, DANCE/The Warmth Of The Sun	(Capitol 5306)	1.00	4.00	64
DANCE, DANCE, DANCE/The Warmth Of The Sun	(Capitol 5306)	3.75	15.00	64
(Picture sleeve)				
DARLIN'/Here Today	(Capitol 2068)	1.25	5.00	67
DARLIN'/Here Today	(Capitol 2068)	2.00	8.00	67
(Picture sleeve)				
DO IT AGAIN/Wake The World	(Capitol 2239)	1.25	5.00	68
DON'T GO NEAR THE WATER/ Student Demonstration Time	(Stateside SR-2944)	15.00	60.00	71
(Japanese issue, red plastic edition.)				
Most Beach Boys' singles were pressed on red plastic, as well as black, in Japan. U.S. collectors value these red plastic editions at $20-$40 for near-mint copies.				
DO YOU WANNA DANCE?/Please Let Me Wonder	(Capitol 5372)	1.50	6.00	65
DO YOU WANNA DANCE?/Help Me Rhonda	(Capitol 6081)	1.25	5.00	66
(Green swirl label reissue)				
FRIENDS/Little Bird	(Capitol 2160)	1.25	5.00	68
FUN, FUN, FUN/Why Do Fools Fall In Love	(Capitol 5118)	1.25	5.00	64
FUN, FUN, FUN/Why Do Fools Fall In Love	(Capitol 5118)	2.00	8.00	64
(Picture sleeve)				
GETTIN' HUNGRY/Devoted To You	(Brother 1002)	3.75	15.00	67
(Shown as by Brian Wilson & Mike Love)				
GOIN' ON/Endless Harmony	(Caribou ZS9-9032)	.75	3.00	80
GOOD TIMIN'/Love Surrounds Me	(Caribou ZS8-9029)	.75	3.00	79
GOOD VIBRATIONS/Let's Go Away For Awhile	(Capitol 5676)	1.25	5.00	66
GOOD VIBRATIONS/Let's Go Away For Awhile	(Capitol 5676)	2.00	8.00	66
(Picture sleeve)				
GOOD VIBRATIONS/Barbara Ann	(Capitol 6132)	1.50	6.00	68
(Red & white "Target" label reissue)				
HAWAII/Little Honda	(Capitol 4093)	.75	3.00	75
HELP ME, RHONDA/Kiss Me Baby	(Capitol 5395)	1.00	4.00	65
HERE COMES THE NIGHT (4:28)/Baby Blue	(Caribou ZS8-9026)	.75	3.00	79
HERE COMES THE NIGHT (10:57)/Baby Blue	(Caribou CRB-7204)	6.25	25.00	79
(Netherlands 12" single issue, on blue plastic.)				
HERE COMES THE NIGHT (3:18)/ Here Comes The Night (4:28)	(Caribou ZS8-9026)	2.50	10.00	79
(Promotional issue)				
HERE COMES THE NIGHT (10:36)/ Here Comes The Night (4:28)	(Caribou CRB-7204)	6.25	25.00	71
(English 12" single issue, on blue plastic.)				
HERE COMES THE NIGHT (10:36)/ Here Comes The Night (Instrumental)	(Caribou AS-557)	12.50	50.00	79
(Promotional blue plastic issue. This listing is for any of the 100 copies autographed by the Beach Boys.)				
HERE COMES THE NIGHT (10:36)/ Here Comes The Night (Instrumental)	(Caribou AS-557)	2.50	10.00	79
(Promotional blue plastic issue. This listing is for copies not autographed by the Beach Boys.)				
HERE COMES THE NIGHT (10:36)/ Here Comes The Night (Instrumental)	(Caribou 2Z8-9028)	1.25	5.00	79
(12" single issue)				
HERE COMES THE NIGHT (10:36)/ Here Comes The Night (Instrumental)	(Caribou 9028)	10.00	40.00	79
(Canadian 12" single issue, pressed on three different, equally valuable, colors of plastic.)				
HERE COMES THE NIGHT (6:44)/ Here Comes The Night (10:36)	(Caribou 2Z8-9028)	6.25	25.00	79
(Promotional 12" single issue)				
To aid in identification and separation of the various vocal releases of "Here Comes The Night," we have indicated the time of each track in parenthesis.				
HEROES & VILLAINS/You're Welcome	(Brother 1001)	1.50	6.00	67
HEROES & VILLAINS/You're Welcome	(Brother 1001)	3.75	15.00	67
(Picture sleeve)				
HONKIN' DOWN THE HIGHWAY/Solar System	(Reprise RPS-1389)	1.00	4.00	77
I CAN HEAR MUSIC/All I Want To Do	(Capitol 2432)	1.50	6.00	69
I CAN HEAR MUSIC/Let The Wind Blow	(Reprise RPS-1310)	1.25	5.00	74
I GET AROUND/Don't Worry Baby	(Capitol 5174)	1.00	4.00	64
I GET AROUND/Don't Worry Baby	(Capitol 5174)	1.50	6.00	64
IT'S A BEAUTIFUL DAY/Sumahama	(Caribou-Lorimar ZS8-9031)	1.00	4.00	79
IT'S O.K./Had To Phone Ya	(Reprise RPS-1368)	1.00	4.00	76
LADY LYNDA/Full Sail	(Caribou ZS9-9030)	1.00	4.00	79
LITTLE GIRL I ONCE KNEW, THE/ There's No Other (Like My Baby)	(Capitol 5540)	1.50	6.00	65
LITTLE SAINT NICK/The Lord's Prayer	(Capitol 5096)	2.50	10.00	63
LIVIN' WITH A HEARTACHE/Santa Ana Winds	(Caribou ZS9-9033)	.75	3.00	80
LONG PROMISED ROAD/Deirdre	(Reprise 1015)	6.25	25.00	71
LONG PROMISED ROAD/Til I Die	(Reprise 1047)	6.25	25.00	71
MAN WITH ALL THE TOYS, THE/Blue Christmas	(Capitol 5312)	3.00	12.00	64
MARCELLA/Hold On Dear Brother	(Reprise REP-1101)	6.25	25.00	72
PAMELA JEAN/After The Game	(Capitol 5102)	25.00	100.00	63
(Shown as by The Survivors)				
PAMELA JEAN/After The Game	(Capitol PSR-436)	6.25	25.00	79
(Bonus single, offered with the English Box Set "The Beach Boys' singles '63-'70.")				
PEGGY SUE/Hey Little Tomboy	(Reprise RPS-1394)	.75	3.00	78
ROCK & ROLL MUSIC/The TM Song	(Reprise RPS-1354)	.75	3.00	76
SAIL ON SAILOR/The Trader	(Reprise PRO-557-2)	25.00	100.00	73
(Promotional issue only)				
SAIL ON SAILOR/Only With You	(Reprise REP-1138)	3.00	12.00	73
SAIL ON SAILOR/Only With You	(Reprise RPS-1325)	1.50	6.00	75
SALT LAKE CITY/Amusement Parks U.S.A.	(Capitol PRO-2936)	50.00	200.00	65
(Special giveaway item, produced for Salt Lake City downtown merchants to distribute free during one of their promotions.)				
SLIP ON THROUGH/This Whole World	(Reprise 0929)	2.00	8.00	70
SLOOP JOHN B./You're So Good To Me	(Capitol 5602)	1.00	4.00	66
SLOOP JOHN B./You're So Good To Me	(Capitol 5602)	2.00	8.00	66
(Picture sleeve)				
SPIRIT OF AMERICA/Boogie Woogie (Instrumental)	(Capitol Custom)	37.50	150.00	63
(Special giveaway item, produced in conjunction with KFWB radio & Wallichs Music City to enhance a record store grand opening.)				
SURFER GIRL/Little Deuce Coupe	(Capitol 5009)	1.50	6.00	63
SURFER GIRL/Little Deuce Coupe	(Capitol 6107)	1.00	4.00	
(Green label reissue, true stereo version of "Surfer Girl")				
SURFER GIRL/The Freeze (By Tony & Joe)	(Era 042)	.50	2.00	70
SURFIN'/ Luau (Doesn't show "Distributed by Era Record Sales Inc.")	(Candix 301)	20.00	80.00	61
(Distributed only in the Los Angeles area.)				
SURFIN'/ Luau (Shows "Distributed by Era Record Sales Inc.")	(Candix 301)	15.00	60.00	61
SURFIN'/Luau	("X" 301)	30.00	120.00	62
SURFIN'/Luau	(Candix 331)	18.75	75.00	62
SURFIN' SAFARI/Luau	(Ariola 45441)	50.00	200.00	64
(German release, contains an early alternate take of "Surfin' Safari".)				
SURFIN' SAFARI/409	(Capitol 4777)	1.50	6.00	62
SURFIN' SAFARI/409	(Capitol 4777)	3.75	15.00	62
(Picture sleeve)				
SURFIN' SAFARI/409	(Capitol 6095)	1.25	5.00	67
(Green swirl label reissue)				
SURFIN' SAFARI/Surfin'	(Era 043)	.50	2.00	70
SURFIN' U.S.A./Shut Down	(Capitol 4932)	1.50	6.00	63
SURFIN' U.S.A./Shut Down	(Capitol 6094)	1.25	5.00	67
(Green swirl label reissue)				

TITLE/FLIP	LABEL & NO.	GOOD	NEAR MINT	YR.
SURFIN' U.S.A./The Warmth Of The Sun	(Capitol 3924)	.75	3.00	74
SURF'S UP/Don't Go Near The Water	(Reprise 1058)	12.50	50.00	71
SUSIE CINCINNATI/Everyone's In Love With You	(Reprise RPS-1375)	1.00	4.00	76
TEARS IN THE MORNING/It's About Time	(Reprise 0957)	3.75	15.00	70
TEN LITTLE INDIANS/County Fair	(Capitol 4880)	3.75	15.00	62
TEN LITTLE INDIANS/County Fair (Picture sleeve)	(Capitol 4880)	15.00	60.00	62
TEN LITTLE INDIANS/She Knows Too Well (Green swirl label reissue)	(Capitol 6060)	1.50	6.00	64
WHAT'S IT ALL ABOUT (THE BEACH BOYS)/ What's It All About (The Rolling Stones) (Public service disc, Bill Hule interviews Mike Love & Dennis Wilson.)	(Program #508/507)	5.00	20.00	
WHAT'S IT ALL ABOUT (THE BEACH BOYS)/ What's It All About (Dr. Hook)	(Program #450/449)	5.00	20.00	
WHEN I GROW UP (TO BE A MAN)/ She Knows Me Too Well	(Capitol 5245)	1.00	4.00	64
WHEN I GROW UP (TO BE A MAN)/ She Knows Me Too Well	(Capitol 5245)	1.50	6.00	64
WILD HONEY/Wind Chimes	(Capitol 2028)	1.50	6.00	67
WOULDN'T IT BE NICE/Caroline No	(Reprise RPS-1336)	1.50	6.00	75
WOULDN'T IT BE NICE/God Only Knows	(Capitol 5706)	1.25	5.00	66
WOULDN'T IT BE NICE (Live Version)/ The Times They Are A-Changin' (By Merry Clayton)	(ODE 66016)	3.75	15.00	71
WOULDN'T IT BE NICE (Live Version)/ The Times They Are A-Changin' (By Merry Clayton) (Promotional issue)	(ODE '70 S-66016)	10.00	40.00	71

Also see Blossoms, The
Also see Bob & Sheri
Also see California Music
Also see Four Speeds, The
Also see Hondells, The

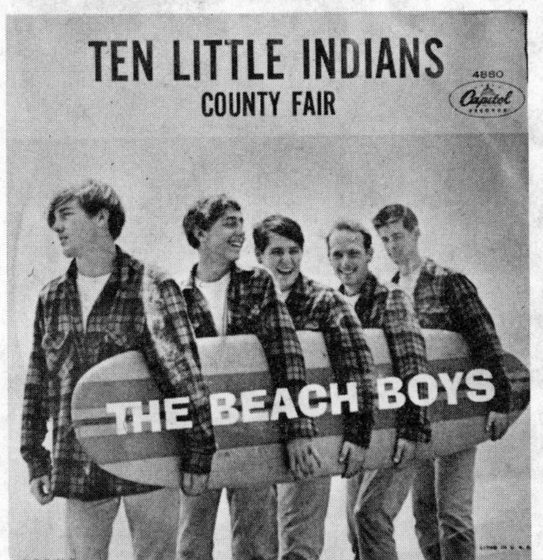

TEN LITTLE INDIANS
COUNTY FAIR
4880
Capitol
THE BEACH BOYS

BEACH BOYS, The

TITLE/FLIP	LABEL & NO.	GOOD	NEAR MINT	YR.
BATHING BEAUTY/On The Beach At Sunset	(Kapp 289)	1.00	4.00	59

BEACH BUMS, The (With Bob Seger)

TITLE/FLIP	LABEL & NO.	GOOD	NEAR MINT	YR.
BALLAD OF THE YELLOW BERET/ Florida Time (Novelty)	(Are You Kidding Me? 1010)	1.50	6.00	66

BEACH GIRLS, The

TITLE/FLIP	LABEL & NO.	GOOD	NEAR MINT	YR.
HE'S MY SURFIN' GUY/Bobby's The Boy	(Vault 905)	1.25	5.00	63
SKIING IN THE SNOW/Goin' Places	(Dyno Vox 202)	1.25	5.00	65

BEACH NUTS, The

TITLE/FLIP	LABEL & NO.	GOOD	NEAR MINT	YR.
OUT IN THE SUN (HEY-O)/Someday So On	(Bang 504)	1.00	4.00	65
SURF BEAT '65/The Last Ride	(Coronado 131)	1.25	5.00	65

BEACH, Scott

TITLE/FLIP	LABEL & NO.	GOOD	NEAR MINT	YR.
RELIGION & POLITICS (Uncensored)/ Religion & Politics (Censored)	(Captain SAC-160)	1.25	5.00	

BEACHCOMBERS, The

TITLE/FLIP	LABEL & NO.	GOOD	NEAR MINT	YR.
DAYTONA DARLIN'/Daytona Darlin' (Part 2)	(Spar 760)	1.00	4.00	65
LONE SURVIVOR/Samoa	(Dot 16354)	2.00	8.00	62
THIS IS MY LOVE/Surfin' The Summer Away	(Diamond 168)	2.00	8.00	64

BEACH-NIKS, The

TITLE/FLIP	LABEL & NO.	GOOD	NEAR MINT	YR.
LAST NIGHT I CRIED/It Was A Nightmare	(MMC 008)	.75	3.00	65
LIKE STONED/Good Things	(MMC 007)	.75	3.00	65

BEACON STREET IRREGULARS, The

TITLE/FLIP	LABEL & NO.	GOOD	NEAR MINT	YR.
MOCKING BIRD/I'm Not So Certian Anymore	(Simper Fi 2002)	1.00	4.00	

BEACON STREET UNION

TITLE/FLIP	LABEL & NO.	GOOD	NEAR MINT	YR.
BLUE SUEDE SHOES/Four Hundred & Five	(MGM 13935)	.75	3.00	68
KICKIN' IT BACK TO YOU/	(Janus 113)	.75	3.00	70
LORD WHY IS IT SO HARD/Can't Find My Fingers	(RTP 10011)	.75	3.00	69
MAYOLA/May I Light Your Cigarette	(MGM 14012)	.75	3.00	69
SOUTH END INCIDENT/Speed Kills	(MGM 13865)	.75	3.00	67

BEAD GAME

TITLE/FLIP	LABEL & NO.	GOOD	NEAR MINT	YR.
SWEET MEDUSA/	(Avco-Embassy 4539)	1.00	4.00	70

BEAM, Tommy Jim

TITLE/FLIP	LABEL & NO.	GOOD	NEAR MINT	YR.
BAYOU/My Little Jewel (With the 4-Flights)	(100 Proof Records 101)	18.75	50.00	58

BEANO

TITLE/FLIP	LABEL & NO.	GOOD	NEAR MINT	YR.
CANDY BABY/Rock & Roll (Gonna Save Your Soul)	(Deram 424)	2.00	8.00	
LITTLE CINDERELLA/Bye & Bye	(Deram 427)	2.00	8.00	

BEAR (With Eric Kaz)

TITLE/FLIP	LABEL & NO.	GOOD	NEAR MINT	YR.
GREETINGS/Don't Say A Word	(Verve Forecast 5096)	.50	2.00	69

Also see Blues Magoos, The
Also see Blues Project, The
Also see American Flyer

BEAR, Edward: see Edward Bear

BEAR, Richard T.

TITLE/FLIP	LABEL & NO.	GOOD	NEAR MINT	YR.
BRING ON THE NIGHT/Lay Your Head Against My Pillow	(RCA 11430)	.50	2.00	78
UNDER THE BOARDWALK/When I Really Get To You	(RCA 11289)	.50	2.00	78

BEAT

TITLE/FLIP	LABEL & NO.	GOOD	NEAR MINT	YR.
LET ME INTO YOUR LIFE/	(Columbia 11161)	.50	2.00	79

BEAT BROTHERS, The

TITLE/FLIP	LABEL & NO.	GOOD	NEAR MINT	YR.
NICK NACK HULLY GULLY/Laternen Hully Gully	(MGM 13201)	.75	3.00	61

BEAT BROTHERS, The (With Tony Sheridan): see Beatles, The

BEATIN' PATH, The

TITLE/FLIP	LABEL & NO.	GOOD	NEAR MINT	YR.
ORIGINAL NOTHING PEOPLE, THE/I Waited So Long	(Fontana 1583)	1.00	4.00	68

BEATLES, The (John Lennon, Paul McCartney, George Harrison, Ringo Starr)

TITLE/FLIP	LABEL & NO.	GOOD	NEAR MINT	YR.
AIN'T SHE SWEET/Nobody's Child	(Atco 6308)	1.25	5.00	64
AIN'T SHE SWEET/Nobody's Child (Promotional issue)	(Atco 6308)	12.50	50.00	64
AIN'T SHE SWEET/Nobody's Child (Picture sleeve)	(Atco 6308)	18.75	75.00	64
AIN'T SHE SWEET/If You Love Me Baby (Released in Germany on Polydor's red label.)	(Polydor 52 317)	12.50	50.00	64
AIN'T SHE SWEET/If You Love Me Baby (Blue picture sleeve, released in Germany.)	(Polydor 52 317)	25.00	100.00	64
AIN'T SHE SWEET/Take Out Some Insurance On Me Baby (Released in Germany on Polydor's red label.)	(Polydor 52 317)	12.50	50.00	64
AIN'T SHE SWEET/Take Out Some Insurance On Me Baby (Red picture sleeve, released in Germany.)	(Polydor 52 317)	25.00	100.00	64
ALL YOU NEED IS LOVE/ Baby You're A Rich Man (Red/orange target label)	(Capitol 5964)	2.00	8.00	
ALL YOU NEED IS LOVE/ Baby You're A Rich Man (Orange/yellow swirl label)	(Capitol 5964)	1.00	4.00	67
ALL YOU NEED IS LOVE/Baby You're A Rich Man	(Apple 5964)	.50	2.00	
ALL YOU NEED IS LOVE/ Baby You're A Rich Man (Orangel label)	(Capitol 5964)	.50	2.00	
ALL YOU NEED IS LOVE/Baby You're A Rich Man (Promotional issue)	(Capitol 5964)	15.00	60.00	67
ALL YOU NEED IS LOVE/Baby You're A Rich Man (Picture sleeve)	(Capitol 5964)	1.50	6.00	67
AND I LOVE HER/If I Fell (Red/orange target label)	(Capitol 5235)	2.00	8.00	
AND I LOVE HER/If I Fell (Orange/yellow swirl label)	(Capitol 5235)	1.00	4.00	64
AND I LOVE HER/If I Fell	(Apple 5235)	.75	3.00	
AND I LOVE HER/If I Fell (Orange label)	(Capitol 5235)	.50	2.00	
AND I LOVE HER/If I Fell (Picture sleeve)	(Capitol 5235)	3.75	15.00	64
BALLAD OF JOHN & YOKO/ Old Brown Shoe (With Capitol logo)	(Apple 2531)	1.50	6.00	69
BALLAD OF JOHN & YOKO/ Old Brown Shoe (Without Capitol logo)	(Apple 2531)	.75	3.00	69
BALLAD OF JOHN & YOKO/ Old Brown Shoe (Orange label)	(Apple 2531)	.50	2.00	
BALLAD OF JOHN & YOKO/Old Brown Shoe (Picture sleeve)	(Apple 2531)	2.50	10.00	69
CAN'T BUY ME LOVE/ You Can't Do That (Red/orange target label)	(Capitol 5150)	2.00	8.00	
CAN'T BUY ME LOVE/ You Can't Do That (Orange/yellow swirl label)	(Capitol 5150)	2.00	8.00	64
CAN'T BUY ME LOVE/ You Can't Do That	(Apple 5150)	.75	3.00	
CAN'T BUY ME LOVE/ You Can't Do That (Orange label)	(Capitol 5150)	.50	2.00	
CAN'T BUY ME LOVE/You Can't Do That (Picture sleeve)	(Capitol 5150)	31.25	125.00	64
CAN'T BUY ME LOVE/Beatle Interviews (Picture sleeve for the KFWB custom pressing.)	(KFW-Beatles RB-2637)	250.00	1000.00	64
DO YOU WANT TO KNOW A SECRET/ Thank You Girl (Green swirl label)	(Capitol Starline 6064)	3.75	15.00	65
DO YOU WANT TO KNOW A SECRET/ Thank You Girl (Green swirl label)	(Capitol Starline 6064)	3.75	15.00	65
DO YOU WANT TO KNOW A SECRET/ Thank You Girl (With oval logo)	(Vee Jay 587)	3.00	12.00	64
DO YOU WANT TO KNOW A SECRET/ Thank You Girl (With brackets logo)	(Vee Jay 587)	2.50	10.00	64
DO YOU WANT TO KNOW A SECRET/ Thank You Girl	(Oldies 149)	1.50	6.00	64
DO YOU WANT TO KNOW A SECRET/ Thank You Girl (Promotional issue)	(Vee Jay 587)	8.75	35.00	64
DO YOU WANT TO KNOW A SECRET/ Thank You Girl (Picture sleeve)	(Vee Jay 587)	7.50	30.00	64
EIGHT DAYS A WEEK/I Don't Want To Spoil The Party (Red/orange target label)	(Capitol 5371)	2.00	8.00	
EIGHT DAYS A WEEK/I Don't Want To Spoil The Party (Orange/yellow swirl label)	(Capitol 5371)	1.00	4.00	65
EIGHT DAYS A WEEK/I Don't Want To Spoil The Party	(Apple 5371)	.75	3.00	
EIGHT DAYS A WEEK/I Don't Want To Spoil The Party (Orange label)	(Capitol 5371)	.50	2.00	
EIGHT DAYS A WEEK/I Don't Want To Spoil The Party (Picture sleeve)	(Capitol 5371)	1.50	6.00	65
FROM ME TO YOU/Thank You Girl (With oval logo)	(Vee Jay 522)	3.75	15.00	64
FROM ME TO YOU/Thank You Girl (With brackets logo)	(Vee Jay 522)	2.00	8.00	64
FROM ME TO YOU/Thank You Girl (Promotional issue)	(Vee Jay 522)	10.00	40.00	64
GET BACK/Don't Let Me Down (With Capitol logo)	(Apple 2490)	1.50	6.00	69
GET BACK/Don't Let Me Down (Without Capitol logo)	(Apple 2490)	1.00	4.00	69
GET BACK/Don't Let Me Down (Orange label)	(Capitol 2490)	.50	2.00	
GIRL/You're Gonna Loose That Girl (Promotional issue)	(Capitol 4506)	12.50	50.00	77
GIRL/You're Gonna Loose That Girl (Picture sleeve)	(Capitol 4506)	3.00	12.00	77
HARD DAY'S NIGHT, A/ I Should Have Known Better (Red/orange target label)	(Capitol 5222)	2.00	8.00	
HARD DAY'S NIGHT, A/ I Should Have Known Better (Orange/yellow swirl label)	(Capitol 5222)	1.25	5.00	64
HARD DAY'S NIGHT, A/ I Should Have Known Better	(Apple 5222)	.75	3.00	
HARD DAY'S NIGHT, A/ I Should Have Known Better (Orange label)	(Capitol 5222)	.50	2.00	
HARD DAY'S NIGHT, A/ I Should Have Known Better (Picture sleeve)	(Capitol 5222)	3.00	12.00	64
HELLO GOODBYE/ I Am The Walrus (Red/orange target label)	(Capitol 2056)	2.00	8.00	
HELLO GOODBYE/ I Am The Walrus (Orange/yellow swirl label)	(Capitol 2056)	1.00	4.00	67
HELLO GOODBYE/I Am The Walrus	(Apple 2056)	.75	3.00	
HELLO GOODBYE/ I Am The Walrus (Orange label)	(Capitol 2056)	.50	2.00	
HELLO GOODBYE/I Am The Walrus (Promotional issue)	(Capitol 2056)	15.00	60.00	67
HELLO GOODBYE/I Am The Walrus (Picture sleeve)	(Capitol 2056)	3.00	12.00	67
HELP!/I'm Down (Red/orange target label)	(Capitol 5476)	1.00	8.00	
HELP!/I'm Down (Orange/yellow swirl label)	(Capitol 5476)	1.00	4.00	65
HELP!/I'm Down	(Apple 5476)	.75	3.00	
HELP!/I'm Down (Orange label)	(Capitol 5476)	.50	2.00	
HELP!/I'm Down (Picture sleeve)	(Capitol 5476)	2.50	10.00	65
HELTER SKELTER/Got To Get You Into My Life	(Capitol 4274)	.50	2.00	76
HELTER SKELTER/Got To Get You Into My Life (Promotional issue)	(Capitol 4274)	3.00	12.00	76
HELTER SKELTER/Helter Skelter (Promotional issue only)	(Capitol 4274)	3.00	12.00	76
HEY JUDE/Revolution (With Capitol logo)	(Apple 2276)	1.50	6.00	68
HEY JUDE/Revolution (Without Capitol logo)	(Apple 2276)	1.00	4.00	
HEY JUDE/Revolution (Orange label)	(Capitol 2276)	.50	2.00	
I FEEL FINE/She's A Woman (Red/orange target label)	(Capitol 5327)	2.00	8.00	
I FEEL FINE/She's A Woman (Orange/yellow swirl label)	(Capitol 5327)	1.00	4.00	64
I FEEL FINE/She's A Woman	(Apple 5327)	.75	3.00	
I FEEL FINE/She's A Woman (Orange label)	(Capitol 5327)	.50	2.00	
I FEEL FINE/She's A Woman (Picture sleeve)	(Capitol 5327)	2.50	10.00	64
I WANT TO HOLD YOUR HAND/ I Saw Her Standing There (Red/orange target label)	(Capitol 5112)	2.00	8.00	
I WANT TO HOLD YOUR HAND/ I Saw Her Standing There (Orange/yellow swirl label)	(Capitol 5112)	1.25	5.00	64
I WANT TO HOLD YOUR HAND/ I Saw Her Standing There	(Apple 5112)	.75	3.00	
I WANT TO HOLD YOUR HAND/ I Saw Her Standing There (Orange label)	(Capitol 5112)	.50	2.00	
I WANT TO HOLD YOUR HAND/ I Saw Her Standing There (Picture sleeve)	(Capitol 5112)	5.00	20.00	64
I WANT TO HOLD YOUR HAND/ I Saw Her Standing There (WMCA promotional picture sleeve issue. Identical to commercial release on front, but with WMCA dee jays pictured on back.)	(Capitol 5112)	200.00	800.00	64
IF I FELL/And I Love Her (Red/orange target label)	(Capitol 5235)	2.00	8.00	
IF I FELL/And I Love Her (Orange/yellow swirl label)	(Capitol 5235)	1.25	5.00	64
IF I FELL/And I Love Her	(Apple 5235)	.75	3.00	
IF I FELL/And I Love Her (Orange label)	(Capitol 5235)	.50	2.00	
IF I FELL/And I Love Her (Picture sleeve)	(Capitol 5235)	3.75	15.00	64
I'LL CRY INSTEAD/I'm Happy Just To Dance With You (Red/orange target label)	(Capitol 5234)	2.00	4.00	
I'LL CRY INSTEAD/I'm Happy Just To Dance With You (Orange/yellow swirl label)	(Capitol 5234)	1.00	4.00	64
I'LL CRY INSTEAD/ I'm Happy Just To Dance With You	(Apple 5234)	.75	3.00	
I'LL CRY INSTEAD/ I'm Happy Just To Dance With You (Orange label)	(Capitol 5234)	.50	2.00	
I'LL CRY INSTEAD/ I'm Happy Just To Dance With You (Picture sleeve)	(Capitol 5234)	3.75	15.00	64
I'LL GET YOU/ (One-sided promotional issue only)	(Swan 4152-1)	37.50	150.00	64
KANSAS CITY/Boys (Green swirl label)	(Capitol Starline 6066)	3.75	15.00	65
KANSAS CITY/Boys (Red/orange target label)	(Capitol Starline 6066)	2.50	10.00	
KFWB (KFW-BEATLES): see "Can't Buy Me Love"				
LADY MADONNA/The Inner Light (Red/orange target label)	(Capitol 2138)	2.00	8.00	
LADY MADONNA/The Inner Light (Orange/yellow swirl label)	(Capitol 2138)	1.25	5.00	68
LADY MADONNA/The Inner Light	(Apple 2138)	.75	3.00	
LADY MADONNA/The Inner Light (Orange label)	(Capitol 2138)	.50	2.00	
LADY MADONNA/The Inner Light (Promotional issue)	(Capitol 2138)	15.00	60.00	68
LADY MADONNA/The Inner Light (Picture sleeve)	(Capitol 2138)	3.00	12.00	68
LADY MADONNA/The Inner Light (Beatles fan club flyer; orginally issued with the Capitol 2138 picture sleeve. Price is for flyer only.)	(Capitol 2138)	2.00	8.00	68
LET IT BE/You Know My Name (Look Up The Number) (With Capitol logo)	(Apple 2764)	1.50	6.00	70
LET IT BE/You Know My Name (Look Up The Number) (Without Capitol logo)	(Apple 2764)	.75	3.00	70
LET IT BE/You Know My Name (Look Up The Number) (Orange label)	(Capitol 2764)	.50	2.00	
LET IT BE/You Know My Name (Look Up The Number) (Picture sleeve)	(Apple 2764)	3.00	12.00	70
LONG & WINDING ROAD/For You Blue (With Capitol logo)	(Apple 2832)	1.50	6.00	70
LONG & WINDING ROAD/For You Blue (Without Capitol logo)	(Apple 2832)	.75	3.00	70
LONG & WINDING ROAD/For You Blue (Orange label)	(Capitol 2832)	.50	2.00	
LONG & WINDING ROAD/For You Blue (Picture sleeve)	(Apple 2832)	3.00	12.00	70
LOVE ME DO/ P.S. I Love You (Green swirl label)	(Capitol Starline 9008)	3.75	15.00	65
LOVE ME DO/P.S. I Love You	(Oldies 151)	1.50	6.00	64
LOVE ME DO/P.S. I Love You	(Tollie 9008)	1.25	5.00	64
LOVE ME DO/P.S. I Love You (Promotional issue)	(Tollie 9008)	12.50	60.00	64
LOVE ME DO/P.S. I Love You (Picture sleeve)	(Tollie 9008)	5.00	20.00	64
MADISON KID/Let's Dance (Released in Germany. Shown as by Tony Sheridan & the Beat Brothers.)	(Polydor 24 948)	125.00	500.00	61
MADISON KID/Let's Dance (Picture sleeve, released in Germany. Shown as by Tony Sheridan & the Beat Brothers.)	(Polydor 24 948)	250.00	1000.00	61
MISERY/Roll Over Beethoven (Green swirl label)	(Capitol Starline 6065)	3.75	15.00	65
MISERY/Roll Over Beethoven (Red/orange target label)	(Capitol Starline 6065)	2.50	10.00	

The transition to a country music style has been made by several pop & rock singers of the fifties and sixties. The pop & rock releases by these artists will appear in this guide, while the country music releases will be listed in our guides covering that field of music.

Likewise, your favorite soul and rhythm & blues artists that are not covered in this guide are—or will soon be—included in our Blues-Rhythm & Blues-Soul Price Guide.

David Bowie
RCA
PB-12078
Ashes to ashes
(Edited Version)
B/W
It's No Game
(Part 1)
From the
Scary Monsters
Album
AQL1-3647
Ashes to ashes
CUSTOM
SOUND
Stereo
SC-164-A
Rogan Pub. Co.
EMI:230
P.O. Box 136
Dickens, Texas
Produced By
Bill Brown
Arranged
By
RON DIIULIO
Tight Levis & Boots
(Bill Brown)
Bill Brown
Recorded At
SOUND CITY
Shreveport La.
D
45-1008
Glad Music
1017 BMI
Vocal
Time 2:20
CHANTILLY LACE
(J. P. Richardson)
BIG BOPPER
The Bachelors

Johnny Burnette

TITLE/FLIP	LABEL & NO.	GOOD	NEAR MINT	YR.
MY BONNIE/The Saints	(Decca 9-31382)	650.00	2500.00	62
(Shown as by Tony Sheridan & the Beat Brothers.)				
MY BONNIE/The Saints	(Decca 31382)	175.00	700.00	62
(Promotional issue, pink label. Shown as by Tony Sheridan & the Beat Brothers.)				
MY BONNIE/The Saints	(MGM K-13213)	2.50	10.00	64
(Does not show the MGM "My Bonnie" LP number on the label. Shown as by the Beatles with Tony Sheridan.)				
MY BONNIE/The Saints	(MGM K-13213)	1.50	6.00	64
(Shows the MGM "My Bonnie" LP number on the label. Shown as by the Beatles with Tony Sheridan.)				
MY BONNIE/The Saints	(MGM K-13213)	15.00	60.00	64
(Promotional issue, shown as by the Beatles with Tony Sheridan.)				
MY BONNIE/The Saints	(MGM K-13213)	5.00	20.00	64
(Picture sleeve)				
MY BONNIE (MEIN HERZ IST BEI DIR NUR)/ The Saints	(Polydor 24 673)	200.00	800.00	62
(Released in Germany and the first few lines are sung in the German language. Shown as by Tony Sheridan & the Beat Brothers.)				
MY BONNIE (MEIN HERZ IST BEI DIR NUR)/ The Saints	(Polydor 24 673)	250.00	1000.00	62
(Picture sleeve, released in Germany. Although shown on the label as by Tony Sheridan & the Beat Brothers, the sleeve credits only Tony Sheridan.)				
MY BONNIE (TWIST)/The Saints	(Polydor 24 673)	100.00	400.00	62
(Released in Germany, sung in the English language. Shown as by Tony Sheridan & the Beat Brothers.)				
MY BONNIE (TWIST)/The Saints	(Polydor 24 673)	125.00	500.00	62
(Picture sleeve, released in Germany. The word "Twist" appears at the bottom of the sleeve's front side, on the left.)				
MY BONNIE/The Saints	(Polydor 52 273)	12.50	50.00	64
(Released in Germany on Polydor's red label.)				
MY BONNIE/The Saints	(Polydor 52 273)	25.00	100.00	64
(Picture sleeve for Polydor's red label reissue, released in Germany.)				
MY BONNIE/The Saints	(Polydor NH 66-833)	625.00	2500.00	62
(Released in England. Some label printing is thin and curved. On the reissue, that same printing is in a thicker type style and not curved. Shown as by Tony Sheridan & the BEATLES, thus becoming the world's first record release showing the group as the Beatles.)				
MY BONNIE/The Saints	(Polydor NH 66-833)	25.00	100.00	63
(Released in England. This reissue does not have the thin and curved printing, as described above. Shown as by Tony Sheridan & the Beatles.)				
MY BONNIE/The Saints	(Decca 31382)	300.00	1200.00	62
(Canadian commercial issue, black and silver label)				
NOWHERE MAN/What Goes On (Red/orange target label)	(Capitol 5587)	2.00	8.00	
NOWHERE MAN/What Goes On (Orange/yellow swirl label)	(Capitol 5587)	1.00	4.00	66
NOWHERE MAN/What Goes On	(Apple 5587)	.50	2.00	
NOWHERE MAN/What Goes On (Orange label)	(Capitol 5587)	.50	2.00	
NOWHERE MAN/What Goes On	(Capitol 5587)	2.00	8.00	66
(Picture sleeve)				
OB-LA-DI OB-LA-DA/Julia	(Capitol 4347)	.75	3.00	76
OB-LA-DI OB-LA-DA/Julia	(Capitol 4347)	2.50	10.00	76
(Promotional issue)				
OB-LA-DI OB-LA-DA/Julia	(Capitol 4347)	.75	3.00	76
(Picture sleeve)				
PAPERBACK WRITER/Rain (Red/orange target label)	(Capitol 5651)	2.00	8.00	
PAPERBACK WRITER/Rain (Orange/yellow swirl label)	(Capitol 5651)	1.00	4.00	66
PAPERBACK WRITER/Rain	(Apple 5651)	.50	2.00	
PAPERBACK WRITER/Rain (Orange label)	(Capitol 5651)	.50	2.00	
PAPERBACK WRITER/Rain	(Capitol 5651)	2.50	10.00	66
(Picture sleeve)				
PENNY LANE/Strawberry Fields Forever (Red/orange target label)	(Capitol 5810)	2.00	8.00	
PENNY LANE/Strawberry Fields Forever (Orange/yellow swirl label)	(Capitol 5810)	1.00	4.00	67
PENNY LANE/Strawberry Fields Forever	(Apple 5810)	.50	2.00	
PENNY LANE/Strawberry Fields Forever (Orange label)	(Capitol 5810)	.50	2.00	
PENNY LANE/Strawberry Fields Forever	(Capitol 5810)	20.00	80.00	67
(Promotional issue)				
PENNY LANE/Strawberry Fields Forever	(Capitol 5810)	5.00	20.00	67
(Picture sleeve)				
PLEASE PLEASE ME/Ask Me Why (With oval logo)	(Vee Jay 498)	62.50	250.00	63
PLEASE PLEASE ME/Ask Me Why (With brackets logo)	(Vee Jay 498)	50.00	200.00	63
PLEASE PLEASE ME/Ask Me Why (With oval logo)	(Vee Jay 498)	300.00	1200.00	63
(Shown as by the BEATTLES. Label printing uses thin style lettering similiar to that which is used on the promotional issue.)				
PLEASE PLEASE ME/Ask Me Why (With oval logo)	(Vee Jay 498)	50.00	200.00	63
(Shown as by the BEATTLES. This is the more common varation, using the thicker style lettering.)				
PLEASE PLEASE ME/Ask Me Why (With oval logo)	(Vee Jay 498)	62.50	250.00	63
(Promotional issue, shown as by the BEATTLES.)				
PLEASE PLEASE ME/From Me To You (With oval logo)	(Vee Jay 581)	5.00	20.00	64
PLEASE PLEASE ME/From Me To You (With brackets logo)	(Vee Jay 581)	2.50	10.00	64
PLEASE PLEASE ME/From Me To You	(Vee Jay 581)	15.00	60.00	64
(Promotional issue)				
PLEASE PLEASE ME/From Me To You	(Vee Jay 581)	20.00	80.00	64
(Picture sleeve)				
PLEASE PLEASE ME/From Me To You	(Oldies 150)	1.50	6.00	64
PLEASE PLEASE ME/ From Me To You (Green swirl label)	(Capitol Starline 6063)	3.75	15.00	
RUBY BABY/What'd I'd Say	(Polydor 52 025)	125.00	500.00	60
(Released in Germany. Shown as by Tony Sheridan & the Beat Brothers.)				
RUBY BABY/What'd I'd Say	(Polydor 52 025)	250.00	1000.00	60
(Picture sleeve, released in Germany. Shown as by Tony Sheridan & the Beat Brothers.)				
SGT. PEPPER'S LONELY HEARTS CLUB BAND (WITH A LITTLE HELP FROM MY FRIENDS)/A Day In The Life	(Capitol 4612)	.50	2.00	78
SGT. PEPPER'S LONELY HEARTS CLUB BAND (WITH A LITTLE HELP FROM MY FRIENDS)/A Day In The Life	(Capitol 4612)	.75	3.00	78
(Picture sleeve)				
SHE LOVES YOU/I'll Get You	(Swan 4152)	25.00	100.00	63
(First pressing: white label with red printing. Does not have "Don't Drop Out" on the label.)				
SHE LOVES YOU/I'll Get You	(Swan 4152)	7.50	30.00	64
(Second pressing: white label with red printing. Label reads "Don't Drop Out.")				
SHE LOVES YOU/I'll Get You	(Swan 4152)	2.00	8.00	64
(Third pressing: black label with silver printing.)				
SHE LOVES YOU/I'll Get You	(Swan 4152)	37.50	150.00	64
(Promotional issue)				
SHE LOVES YOU/I'll Get You	(Swan 4152)	6.25	25.00	64
(Picture sleeve)				
SIE LIEBT DICH (SHE LOVES YOU)/I'll Get You	(Swan 4182)	6.25	25.00	64
(With the German title and English translation on the same line.)				
SIE LIEBT DICH (SHE LOVES YOU)/I'll Get You	(Swan 4182)	2.50	10.00	64
(With the English translation "She Love You" on a separate line, directly below the German title.)				
SLOW DOWN/Matchbox (Red/orange target label)	(Capitol 5255)	2.00	8.00	
SLOW DOWN/Matchbox (Orange/yellow swirl label)	(Capitol 5255)	1.00	4.00	64
SLOW DOWN/Matchbox	(Apple 5255)	.50	2.00	
SLOW DOWN/Matchbox (Orange label)	(Capitol 5255)	.50	2.00	
SLOW DOWN/Matchbox	(Capitol 5255)	8.75	35.00	64
(Picture sleeve)				
SOMETHING/Come Together (With Capitol logo)	(Apple 2654)	1.50	6.00	69
SOMETHING/Come Together (Without Capitol logo)	(Apple 2654)	.75	3.00	69
SWEET GEORGIA BROWN/Skinny Minny	(Polydor 52 324)	12.50	50.00	64
(Released in Germany on Polydor's red label.)				
SWEET GEORGIA BROWN/Skinny Minny	(Polydor 52 324)	25.00	100.00	64
(Picture sleeve for Polydor's red label reissue, released in Germany.)				
SWEET GEORGIA BROWN/ Take Out Some Insurance On Me Baby	(Atco 6302)	3.00	12.00	64
SWEET GEORGIA BROWN/ Take Out Some Insurance On Me Baby	(Atco 6302)	12.50	50.00	64
(Promotional issue)				
TICKET TO RIDE/Yes It Is (Red/orange target label)	(Capitol 5407)	2.00	8.00	
TICKET TO RIDE/Yes It Is (Orange/yellow swirl label)	(Capitol 5407)	1.00	4.00	65
TICKET TO RIDE/Yes It Is	(Apple 5407)	.75	3.00	
TICKET TO RIDE/Yes It Is (Orange label)	(Capitol 5407)	.50	2.00	
TICKET TO RIDE/Yes It Is	(Capitol 5407)	3.75	15.00	65
(Picture sleeve)				
TWIST & SHOUT/ There's A Place (Green swirl label)	(Capitol Starline 6061)	3.75	15.00	65
TWIST & SHOUT/There's A Place	(Tollie 9001)	1.50	6.00	64
TWIST & SHOUT/There's A Place	(Oldies 152)	1.50	6.00	64
VEE JAY RECORDS SPECIAL CHRISTMAS SLEEVE/		6.25	25.00	64
(This picture sleeve is listed separately since it often turns up without an accompanying disc.)				
WE CAN WORK IT OUT/ Day Tripper (Red & white label)	(Capitol Starline 5555)	25.00	100.00	65
(This was the only Beatles single issued on the red and white Starline label. Reportedly, this was an error in production.)				
WE CAN WORK IT OUT/ Day Tripper (Red/orange target label)	(Capitol 5555)	2.00	8.00	
WE CAN WORK IT OUT/ Day Tripper (Orange/yellow swirl label)	(Capitol 5555)	1.00	4.00	65
WE CAN WORK IT OUT/Day Tripper	(Apple 5555)	.75	3.00	
WE CAN WORK IT OUT/Day Tripper (Orange label)	(Capitol 5555)	.50	2.00	
WE CAN WORK IT OUT/Day Tripper	(Capitol 5555)	3.75	15.00	65
(Picture sleeve)				
WHAT'D I SAY/Ya Ya	(Polydor 0462)	200.00	800.00	63
(Released in Mexico)				
WHAT'S IT ALL ABOUT (BEATLES PART 1)/ What's It All About (Beatles Part 2)	(Program 386/386)	5.00	20.00	77
(Public service disc, with interviews by Bill Huie)				
WHY/Cry For A Shadow	(MGM K-13227)	2.50	10.00	64
(Shown as by the Beatles with Tony Sheridan.)				
WHY/Cry For A Shadow	(MGM K-13227)	15.00	60.00	64
(Promotional issue, shown as by the Beatles with Tony Sheridan.)				
WHY/Cry For A Shadow	(MGM K-13227)	10.00	40.00	64
(Picture sleeve)				
WHY/Cry For A Shadow	(MGM K-13227)	12.50	50.00	64
(Released in Germany on Polydor's red label.)				
WHY/Cry For A Shadow	(MGM K-13227)	25.00	100.00	64
(Picture sleeve for Polydor's red label reissue, released in Germany.)				
YELLOW SUBMARINE/ Eleanor Rigby (Red/orange target label)	(Capitol 5715)	2.00	8.00	
YELLOW SUBMARINE/ Eleanor Rigby (Orange/yellow swirl label)	(Capitol 5715)	1.00	4.00	66
YELLOW SUBMARINE/Eleanor Rigby	(Apple 5715)	.75	3.00	
YELLOW SUBMARINE/ Eleanor Rigby (Orange label)	(Capitol 5715)	.50	2.00	
YELLOW SUBMARINE/Eleanor Rigby	(Capitol 5715)	3.00	12.00	66
(Picture sleeve)				
YESTERDAY/Act Naturally (Red/orange target label)	(Capitol 5498)	2.00	8.00	
YESTERDAY/Act Naturally (Orange/yellow swirl label)	(Capitol 5498)	1.00	4.00	65
YESTERDAY/Act Naturally	(Apple 5498)	.75	3.00	
YESTERDAY/Act Naturally (Orange label)	(Capitol 5498)	.50	2.00	
YESTERDAY/Act Naturally	(Capitol 5498)	2.50	10.00	65
(Picture sleeve)				
YOU ARE MY SUNSHINE/Swanee	(Polydor 24 849)	125.00	500.00	61
(Released in Germany. Shown as by Tony Sheridan & the Beat Brothers.)				
YOU ARE MY SUNSHINE/Swanee	(Polydor 24 849)	250.00	1000.00	61
(Picture sleeve, released in Germany. Shown as by Tony Sheridan & the Beat Brothers.)				

All Capitol singles prior to 1970 exist in at least four label configurations: orange/yellow swirl, red/orange target, Apple, and orange Capitol. In most cases, the orange Capitol would be of lesser value than the Apple release of the same single, however with our established two dollar minimum on both they will appear with identical pricing in this edition.

As with any of the more exotic collectibles in this book, Beatle collectors should keep in mind that prices do vary widely. If there are only one or two known copies of a certain record or sleeve and the only documented sale is $2500.00 for a near mint copy, it's conceivable that the next copy that is sold will have a similar asking price, even though the record may be in lesser condition. On the other hand, if several copies surface and are offered for sale, the actual sales price could be only a fraction of what the first copy brought.

One final note on the Beatles section. Many of their rare records and sleeves have been counterfeited. Always consult with a reputable dealer or knowledgable collector before spending big money for a "rare treasure."

BEATLES COSTELLO, The (With Andy Paley)

TITLE/FLIP	LABEL & NO.	GOOD	NEAR MINT	YR.
WASHING THE DEFECTIVES: SOLDIER OF LOVE/ I Feel Fine-Theme From A Summer Place-Out Of Limits	(Pious 310)	.50	2.00	78

Also see Paley Brothers, The

BEATLETTES, The

TITLE/FLIP	LABEL & NO.	GOOD	NEAR MINT	YR.
ONLY SEVENTEEN/Now We're Together	(Jubilee 5472)	.75	3.00	65
YES, YOU CAN HOLD MY HAND/ Yes You Can Hold My Hand (Part 2)	(Assault 1893)	1.50	6.00	64
(Answer song)				

BEAT MERCHANTS, The

TITLE/FLIP	LABEL & NO.	GOOD	NEAR MINT	YR.
SO FINE/You Were Made For Me (By Freddie & the Dreamers)	(Tower 127)	.75	3.00	65

BEATNIKS, The

TITLE/FLIP	LABEL & NO.	GOOD	NEAR MINT	YR.
BEAT GENERATION/Get Yourself-A-Ready	(Performance 500)	1.00	4.00	59

BEATS, The

TITLE/FLIP	LABEL & NO.	GOOD	NEAR MINT	YR.
BEATNIK BOUNCE/Beatnik Bounce (Part 2)	(Columbia 41781)	.75	3.00	60

BEATSTALKERS, The

TITLE/FLIP	LABEL & NO.	GOOD	NEAR MINT	YR.
YOU BETTER GET A HOLD ON/Left Hand Right	(Press 5001)	1.00	4.00	66

BEATTY, E.C.

TITLE/FLIP	LABEL & NO.	GOOD	NEAR MINT	YR.
SKI KING/I'm A Lucky Man	(Colonial 7003)	1.00	4.00	59

BEAU-BELLS, The

TITLE/FLIP	LABEL & NO.	GOOD	NEAR MINT	YR.
KISSING CHA CHA A PEEZEE KEELA/Promise Me	(Colpix 109)	1.00	4.00	59

BEAU BRUMMELS, The

TITLE/FLIP	LABEL & NO.	GOOD	NEAR MINT	YR.
ARE YOU HAPPY/Lift Me	(Warner Bros. 7204)	.75	3.00	68
CHEROKEE GIRL/Deep Water	(Warner Bros. 7260)	.75	3.00	68
DON'T TALK TO STRANGERS/In Good Time	(Autumn 20)	1.00	4.00	65
FINE WITH ME/Here We Are Again	(Warner Bros. 5848)	.75	3.00	66
GOOD TIME MUSIC/Sad Little Girl	(Autumn 24)	1.25	5.00	65
I'M A SLEEPER/Long Walk Down To Misery	(Warner Bros. 7218)	.75	3.00	68
JUST A LITTLE/They'll Make You Cry	(Autumn 10)	1.50	6.00	65
LAUGH, LAUGH/Still In Love With You Baby	(Autumn 8)	1.50	6.00	64
MAGIC HOLLOW/Lower Level	(Warner Bros. 7079)	.75	3.00	67
ONE TOO MANY MORNINGS/She Reigns	(Warner Bros. 5813)	.75	3.00	66
TWO DAYS 'TIL TOMORROW/Don't Make Promises	(Warner Bros. 7014)	1.25	5.00	67
YOU TELL ME WHY/I Want You	(Autumn 16)	1.00	4.00	65
YOU TELL ME WHY/Down To The Bottom	(Warner Bros. 8119)	.50	2.00	75

Also see Valentino, Sal

BEAUCHEMINS, The

TITLE/FLIP	LABEL & NO.	GOOD	NEAR MINT	YR.
MY LOVIN' BABY/Shenandoah	(Mustang 3015)	.75	3.00	66

BEAU-MARKS, The

TITLE/FLIP	LABEL & NO.	GOOD	NEAR MINT	YR.
'CAUSE WE'RE IN LOVE/Billy Went A-Walking	(Shad 5021)	.75	3.00	60
CLAP YOUR HANDS/Daddy Said	(Shad 5017)	.75	3.00	60
CLASSMATE/School Is Out	(Rust 5035)	1.00	4.00	63
LOVELY LITTLE LADY/Little Miss Twist	(Port 70029)	.75	3.00	62
OH JOAN/Rockin' Blues	(Time 1032)	1.00	4.00	59
TENDER YEARS/I'll Never Be The Same	(Rust 5050)	.75	3.00	63

BEAUMONT, Jimmy (Of the Skyliners)

TITLE/FLIP	LABEL & NO.	GOOD	NEAR MINT	YR.
END OF A STORY, THE/Baion Rhythms	(Colpix 607)	1.50	6.00	61
EVERYBODY'S CRYING/Camera	(May 112)	.75	3.00	61
I NEVER LOVED HER ANYWAY/ You Got Too Much Going For You	(Bang 525)	1.50	6.00	66
I SHOULDA LISTENED TO MAMA/Juarez	(May 115)	1.50	6.00	62
I'LL ALWAYS BE IN LOVE WITH YOU/Give Her My Best	(May 136)	1.00	4.00	62
NEVER SAY GOODBYE/I'm Gonna Try My Wings	(May 120)	1.50	6.00	62
PLEASE SEND ME SOMEONE TO LOVE/ There Is No Other Love	(Gallant 3007)	1.00	4.00	
TELL ME/I Feel I'm Falling In Love	(Bang 510)	1.50	6.00	66

BEAVERS, The

TITLE/FLIP	LABEL & NO.	GOOD	NEAR MINT	YR.
LOW AS I CAN BE/	(Capitol 4015)	1.00	4.00	58
ROCKIN' AT THE DRIVE IN/Sack Dress	(Capitol 3956)	1.00	4.00	58

BE-BOP DELUXE (With Bill Nelson)

TITLE/FLIP	LABEL & NO.	GOOD	NEAR MINT	YR.
MAID IN HEAVEN/Sister Seagull	(Harvest 4151)	.50	2.00	75
PANIC IN THE WORLD/Blue As A Jewel	(Harvest 4571)	.50	2.00	78
SHIPS IN THE NIGHT/	(Harvest 4244)	.50	2.00	76

BECK, Becky Lee

TITLE/FLIP	LABEL & NO.	GOOD	NEAR MINT	YR.
I WANTA BEATLE FOR CHRISTMAS/Puppy Dog	(Challenge 9372)	1.25	5.00	64

BECK, BOGART & APPICE (Jeff Beck, Neil Bogart, Carmine Appice)

TITLE/FLIP	LABEL & NO.	GOOD	NEAR MINT	YR.
I'M SO PROUD/Oh To Love You	(Epic 10998)	.50	2.00	72

Also see Vanilla Fudge

BECKETT QUINTET, The

TITLE/FLIP	LABEL & NO.	GOOD	NEAR MINT	YR.
BABY BLUE/No Correspondence	(Gemcor 5003)	1.25	5.00	65
BABY BLUE/No Correspondence	(A&M 782)	.75	3.00	65

BECK, Jeff (Of the Yardbirds)

TITLE/FLIP	LABEL & NO.	GOOD	NEAR MINT	YR.
COME DANCING/Head For Backstage Pass	(Epic 50276)	1.00	4.00	76
HI HO SILVER LINING/Beck's Bolero	(Epic 10157)	1.25	5.00	67
JAILHOUSE ROCK/Plynth (Water Down The Drain)	(Epic 10484)	1.25	5.00	69
TALLY MAN/Rock My Plimsoul	(Epic 10218)	1.25	5.00	67
YOU KNOW WHAT I MEAN/Constipated Duck	(Epic 50112)	1.00	4.00	75
(Shown as by the Jeff Beck Group)				

BECK, Jimmy

TITLE/FLIP	LABEL & NO.	GOOD	NEAR MINT	YR.
PIPE DREAMS/Blue Night	(Champion 1002)	1.00	4.00	59

BECKHAM, Bob

TITLE/FLIP	LABEL & NO.	GOOD	NEAR MINT	YR.
CRAZY ARMS/Beloved	(Decca 31029)	.75	3.00	59
JUST AS MUCH AS EVER/Your Sweet Love	(Decca 30861)	.75	3.00	59

BECKMEIER BROTHERS (Fred & Steve)

TITLE/FLIP	LABEL & NO.	GOOD	NEAR MINT	YR.
ROCK & ROLL DANCIN'/You Can Love	(Casablanca 1000)	.50	2.00	79

BECKY & THE LOLLIPOPS

TITLE/FLIP	LABEL & NO.	GOOD	NEAR MINT	YR.
I DON'T CARE (WHAT THEY SAY)/Come On Home	(Troy 6493)	1.00	4.00	64
I DON'T CARE (WHAT THEY SAY)/Come On Home	(Epic 9736)	.75	3.00	64

BED OF ROSES

TITLE/FLIP	LABEL & NO.	GOOD	NEAR MINT	YR.
I DON'T BELIEVE YOU/Hate	(Deltron 813)	1.25	5.00	

BEDBUGS, The

TITLE/FLIP	LABEL & NO.	GOOD	NEAR MINT	YR.
YEAH YEAH/Lucy Lucy	(Liberty 55679)	1.25	5.00	64

BEDWELLS, The

TITLE/FLIP	LABEL & NO.	GOOD	NEAR MINT	YR.
KARATE/Karate Again	(Del Fi 4230)	.75	3.00	63

BEEDS, The

TITLE/FLIP	LABEL & NO.	GOOD	NEAR MINT	YR.
YOU DON'T HAVE TO/Run To Her	(Team TM-519)	.75	3.00	68

BEE GEES, The (Barry Gibb, Maurice Gibb, Robin Gibb)

TITLE/FLIP	LABEL & NO.	GOOD	NEAR MINT	YR.
ALIVE/Paper Mache, Cabbages & Kings	(Atco 6909)	.50	2.00	72
BOOGIE CHILD/Lovers	(RSO 867)	.50	2.00	77
CHARADE/Heavy Breathing	(RSO 501)	.50	2.00	74
DON'T FORGET TO REMEMBER/I Lay Down & Die	(Atco 6702)	.50	2.00	69
DON'T WANNA LIVE INSIDE MYSELF/ Walking Back To Waterloo	(Atco 6847)	.50	2.00	71
EDGE OF THE UNIVERSE/Words	(RSO 880)	.50	2.00	77
FANNY (BE TENDER WITH MY LOVE)/Country Lanes	(RSO 519)	.50	2.00	75
FIRST OF MAY/Lamplight	(Atco 6657)	.50	2.00	69
HOLIDAY/Every Christian, Lion-Hearted Man Will Show You	(Atco 6521)	.75	3.00	67
HOW CAN YOU MEND A BROKEN HEART/Country Woman	(Atco 6824)	.50	2.00	71
HOW DEEP IS YOUR LOVE/Can't Keep A Good Man Down	(RSO 882)	.50	2.00	77
I CAN'T LET YOU GO/Throw A Penny	(RSO 410)	.50	2.00	73
IF I ONLY HAD MY MIND ON SOMETHING ELSE/Sweetheart	(Atco 6741)	.50	2.00	70
I.O.I.O./Then You Left Me	(Atco 6752)	.50	2.00	70
I STARTED A JOKE/Kilburn Towers	(Atco 6639)	.75	3.00	68
I'VE GOTTA GET A MESSAGE TO YOU/Kitty Can	(Atco 6603)	.75	3.00	68
JIVE TALKIN'/Wind Of Change	(RSO 510)	.50	2.00	75
JUMBO/The Singer Sang His Song	(Atco 6570)	.75	3.00	68
(LIGHTS WENT OUT IN) MASSACHUSETTS, THE/ Sir Geoffrey Saved The World	(Atco 6532)	.75	3.00	67
LONELY DAYS/A Man For All Seasons	(Atco 6795)	.50	2.00	70
LOVE SO RIGHT/You Should Be Dancing	(RSO 8806)	.50	2.00	77
LOVE SO RIGHT/You Stepped Into My Life	(RSO 859)	.50	2.00	76
LOVE YOU INSIDE OUT/I'm Satisfied	(RSO 925)	.50	2.00	79
MASSACHUSETTS/Sir Geoffrey Saved The World	(Atco 6532)	.75	3.00	67
MR. NATURAL/It Doesn't Matter Much To Me	(RSO 408)	.50	2.00	74
MY WORLD/On Time	(Atco 6871)	.50	2.00	72
NEW YORK MINING DISASTER 1941 (HAVE YOU SEEN MY WIFE, MR. JONES)/I Can't See Nobody	(Atco 6487)	.75	3.00	67
NIGHT FEVER/Down The Road	(RSO 889)	.50	2.00	78
NIGHTS ON BROADWAY/Edge Of The Universe	(RSO 515)	.50	2.00	75
RUN TO ME/Road To Alaska	(Atco 6896)	.50	2.00	72
SAW A NEW MORNING/My Life Has Been A Song	(RSO 401)	.50	2.00	73
SHE'S LEAVING HOME/Oh! Darling (By Robin Gibb)	(RSO 907)	.50	2.00	78
STAYIN' ALIVE/If I Can't Have You	(RSO 885)	.50	2.00	77
TO LOVE SOMEBODY/Close Another Door	(Atco 6503)	.75	3.00	67
TOMORROW TOMORROW/Sun In The Morning	(Atco 6682)	.75	3.00	69
TOMORROW TOMORROW (Long version)/ Tomorrow Tomorrow (Short version)	(Atco 6682)	1.25	5.00	69
(Promotional issue only)				
TOO MUCH HEAVEN/Rest Your Love On Me	(RSO 913)	.50	2.00	78
TRAGEDY/Until	(RSO 918)	.50	2.00	79
WORDS/Sinking Ships	(Atco 6548)	.75	3.00	68
WORDS/Edge Of The Universe	(RSO 880)	.50	2.00	77
WOULDN'T I BE SOMEONE/Elisa	(RSO 404)	.50	2.00	73
YOU SHOULD BE DANCING/Subway	(RSO 853)	.50	2.00	76
YOU SHOULD BE DANCING/Love So Right	(RSO 8003)	.50	2.00	77

Also see Gibb, Andy
Also see Sang, Samantha

BEE JAY

TITLE/FLIP	LABEL & NO.	GOOD	NEAR MINT	YR.
THERE'S NO ONE FOR ME/I'll Go On	(Clock 1743)	2.00	8.00	

BEE, Joe

TITLE/FLIP	LABEL & NO.	GOOD	NEAR MINT	YR.
TRIP TO MOSCOW/Trip To Moscow (Part 2)	(Stop 402)	1.25	5.00	71
(Novelty/Break-in)				

BEE, Molly

TITLE/FLIP	LABEL & NO.	GOOD	NEAR MINT	YR.
I WAS ONLY KIDDIN'/He's My True Love	(Liberty 55569)	.75	3.00	63
JUST FOR THE RECORD/Lyin' Again	(Liberty 55438)	.75	3.00	62
SHE'S NEW TO YOU/All My Love, All My Life	(Liberty 55543)	.75	3.00	63

BEECHER, Johnny

TITLE/FLIP	LABEL & NO.	GOOD	NEAR MINT	YR.
SAX FIFTH AVENUE/Jack Saks The City	(Omega OM-116)	1.25	5.00	63
SAX FIFTH AVENUE/Jack Saks The City	(Warner Bros. 5341)	.75	3.00	63
(Instrumentals)				

BEECHWOODS, The

TITLE/FLIP	LABEL & NO.	GOOD	NEAR MINT	YR.
I'M NOT A KID ANYMORE/Place	(Smash 1843)	.75	3.00	63

BEEFCAKE

TITLE/FLIP	LABEL & NO.	GOOD	NEAR MINT	YR.
DON'T YOU KNOW/There You Go Again	(Deram 85064)	.75	3.00	70

BEEFEATERS, The

TITLE/FLIP	LABEL & NO.	GOOD	NEAR MINT	YR.
PLEASE LET ME LOVE YOU/Don't Be Long	(Elektra 45013)	7.50	30.00	65

Also see Byrds, The

BEEHIVES, The

TITLE/FLIP	LABEL & NO.	GOOD	NEAR MINT	YR.
I WANT TO HOLD YOUR HAND/She Loves You	(King 5881)	1.50	6.00	64

BEES, The

TITLE/FLIP	LABEL & NO.	GOOD	NEAR MINT	YR.
VOICES GREEN & PURPLE/Trip To New Orleans	(Liverpool 62225)	1.50	6.00	66

BEETLES, The

TITLE/FLIP	LABEL & NO.	GOOD	NEAR MINT	YR.
AIN'T THAT LOVE/Welcome To My Heart	(Blue Car 115)	1.00	4.00	65

BEGINNING OF THE END, The

TITLE/FLIP	LABEL & NO.	GOOD	NEAR MINT	YR.
FUNKY NASSAU (PART 1)/Funky Nassau (Part 2)	(Alston 4595)	.50	2.00	71

BEHAN, Dominic

TITLE/FLIP	LABEL & NO.	GOOD	NEAR MINT	YR.
LOVE IS WHERE YOU'LL FIND IT/Liverpool Lou	(Hickory 1263)	.75	3.00	64

BELAFONTE, Harry

TITLE/FLIP	LABEL & NO.	GOOD	NEAR MINT	YR.
BANANA BOAT/Star-O	(RCA Victor 47-6771)	.75	3.00	56
BLUE MAN IS, THE (PART 1)/ Blue Man Is, The (Part 2)	(RCA Victor 47-6458)	.75	3.00	56
COME BACK LIZA/Brown Skin Girl	(RCA Victor 47-6788)	.75	3.00	56
DANNY BOY/Take My Mother Home	(RCA Victor 47-6790)	.75	3.00	56
HOLD 'EM JOE/I'm Just A Country Boy	(RCA Victor 47-0322)	.75	3.00	57
HOSANNA/I Do Adore Her	(RCA Victor 47-6787)	.75	3.00	56
IN THAT GREAT GETTIN' UP MORNIN'/ Jump Down, Spin Around	(RCA Victor 47-6785)	.75	3.00	56
ISLAND IN THE SUN/Cocoanut Woman	(RCA Victor 47-6885)	.75	3.00	57
JAMAICA FAREWELL/Once Was	(RCA Victor 47-6663)	.75	3.00	56
JOHN HENRY/Tol' My Captain	(RCA Victor 47-6780)	.75	3.00	56
MAMA LOOK AT BUBU/Don't Ever Love Me	(RCA Victor 47-6830)	.75	3.00	57
MAN PIABA/The Fox	(RCA Victor 47-6782)	.75	3.00	56
MAN SMART/Chimney Smoke	(RCA Victor 47-6783)	.75	3.00	56
MARY'S BOY CHILD/Venezuela	(RCA Victor 47-6735)	.75	3.00	56
NO MARY/Lord Randall	(RCA Victor 47-6781)	.75	3.00	56
PRETTY AS A RAINBOW/Acorn In The Meadow	(RCA Victor 47-5722)	.75	3.00	54
SCARLET RIBBONS/Shenandoah	(RCA Victor 47-0321)	.75	3.00	56
SLEEP LATE MY LADY FRIEND/ By The Time I Get To Phoenix	(RCA Victor 47-9542)	.50	2.00	68
SUZANNE/Matilda! Matilda!	(RCA Victor 47-0320)	.75	3.00	56
TROUBLES/Hello Everybody	(RCA Victor 47-6249)	.75	3.00	55
UNCHAINED MELODY/A Roving	(RCA Victor 47-6784)	.75	3.00	56
WATER BOY/Noah	(RCA Victor 47-6789)	.75	3.00	56
WILL HIS LOVE BE LIKE HIS RUM?/Dolly Dawn	(RCA Victor 47-6786)	.75	3.00	56

BEL-AIRES, The

TITLE/FLIP	LABEL & NO.	GOOD	NEAR MINT	YR.
MY YEARBOOK/Rockin' & Strollin'	(Decca 30631)	1.50	6.00	58

Vocal Group

BELAIRS, The (With Richard Delvy)

TITLE/FLIP	LABEL & NO.	GOOD	NEAR MINT	YR.
BAGGIES/Charlie Chan	(Lucky Token 107)	1.00	4.00	64
KAMI-KAZE/Vampire	(Triumph 54)	1.00	4.00	63
PONY ROCK/Palmeras	(Nu Sound 1022)	1.00	4.00	62
MR. MOTO/Little Brown Jug	(Arvee 5034)	1.25	5.00	61

Instrumental group - may also be shown as the Belaires.
Also see Challengers, The

BELFAST GYPSYS, The

TITLE/FLIP	LABEL & NO.	GOOD	NEAR MINT	YR.
GLORIA'S DREAM (ROUND & ROUND)/Secret Police	(Loma 2051)	.75	3.00	66
PEOPLE, LET'S FREAK OUT/Portland Town	(Loma 2050)	.75	3.00	66

BELL, Benny

TITLE/FLIP	LABEL & NO.	GOOD	NEAR MINT	YR.
EVERYBODY LIKES MY FANNY/	(Vanguard 35185)	.75	3.00	75
SHAVING CREAM/The Girl From Chicago	(Vanguard 35183)	.75	3.00	75

Novelties

BELL, Eddie, & The Rock-a-fellas

TITLE/FLIP	LABEL & NO.	GOOD	NEAR MINT	YR.
COUNTIN' THE DAYS/Night Party	(Coed 512)	1.25	5.00	59

BELL, Eddy & The Bel-Aires

TITLE/FLIP	LABEL & NO.	GOOD	NEAR MINT	YR.
ANYTIME/The Masked Man (Hi-Yo Silver)	(Mercury 71677X45)	1.00	4.00	60

BELL, Freddie, & The Bell Boys

TITLE/FLIP	LABEL & NO.	GOOD	NEAR MINT	YR.
DING DONG/I Said It & I'm Glad (Also known as "Giddy Up A Ding Dong")	(Wing 90066)	1.50	6.00	56
5-10-15 HOURS/Old Town Hall	(Teen 103)	3.75	15.00	55
HOUND DOG/Move Me Baby	(Teen 101)	3.75	15.00	55
ROMPIN' & STOMPIN'/The Hucklebuck	(Wing 90082)	1.50	6.00	56
STAY LOOSE, MOTHER GOOSE/All Right, Ok, You Win	(Mercury 70919)	1.50	6.00	56

BELL HOPS, The

TITLE/FLIP	LABEL & NO.	GOOD	NEAR MINT	YR.
ANGELLA/Ring Dang Doo Ting A Ling	(Barb 100)	2.00	8.00	
TEENAGE YEARS/Carmella	(Barb 101/102)	2.00	8.00	

BELL, Jessica

TITLE/FLIP	LABEL & NO.	GOOD	NEAR MINT	YR.
ODE TO FOUR/Follow My Star (Beatle novelty)	(Fire-Sign 74501)	1.50	6.00	77

BELL, Johnny

TITLE/FLIP	LABEL & NO.	GOOD	NEAR MINT	YR.
THIRD DEGREE, THE/Flip, Flop & Fly	(Brunswick 9-55142)	12.50	50.00	59

BELL, Kay & The Tuffs

TITLE/FLIP	LABEL & NO.	GOOD	NEAR MINT	YR.
SURFER STOMP (PART 1)/Surfer Stomp (Part 2) (Instrumental)	(Dot 16304)	.75	3.00	

BELL, Madeline (Of Blue Mink)

TITLE/FLIP	LABEL & NO.	GOOD	NEAR MINT	YR.
DOING THINGS TOGETHER WITH YOU/ Finding You Loving You	(Philips 40539)	.75	3.00	67
DON'T CRY MY HEART/Daytime	(Ascot 2180)	.75	3.00	65
I'M GONNA MAKE YOU LOVE ME/Picture Me Gone	(Mod 1007)	.75	3.00	67
I'M GONNA MAKE YOU LOVE ME/Picture Me Gone	(Philips 40517)	.75	3.00	68

BELL, Maggie (Of Stone The Crows)

TITLE/FLIP	LABEL & NO.	GOOD	NEAR MINT	YR.
AFTER MIDNIGHT/	(Atlantic 3013)	.75	3.00	73
CADDO QUEEN/Oh My My	(Atlantic 3040)	.50	2.00	74
SOUVENIRS/	(Atlantic 3018)	.75	3.00	73
WISHING WELL/Comin' On Strong	(Swan Song 70105)	.50	2.00	76

BELL NOTES, The (Carl Bonura, Ray Ceroni, Lenny Giambalvo, Pete Kane, John Casey)

TITLE/FLIP	LABEL & NO.	GOOD	NEAR MINT	YR.
BETTY DEAR/That's Right	(Time 1013)	1.00	4.00	59
FRIENDLY STAR/	(Madison 141)	1.00	4.00	60
I'VE HAD IT/Be Mine (Red Label)	(Time 1004)	1.00	4.00	59
I'VE HAD IT/Be Mine (Blue Label)	(Time 1004)	1.25	5.00	59
LITTLE GIRL IN BLUE/Too Young Or Too Old	(Autograph 204)	1.00	4.00	60
NO DICE/ White Buckskin Sneakers & Checkerboard Socks	(Time 1017)	1.00	4.00	60
OLD SPANISH TOWN/She Went That-a-way	(Time 1010)	1.00	4.00	59
SHORTNIN' BREAD/To Each His Own	(Madison 136)	1.00	4.00	60
YOU'RE A BIG GIRL NOW/Don't Ask Me Why	(Time 1015)	1.00	4.00	59

BELL SISTERS, The

TITLE/FLIP	LABEL & NO.	GOOD	NEAR MINT	YR.
BERMUDA/June Night	(RCA Victor 47-4422)	1.25	5.00	51
BOOM BOOM MY HONEY (Gonna Get Along Without You Now)/ Baby, Count Ten	(Bermuda 1000)	1.25	5.00	56

BELLTONES, The

TITLE/FLIP	LABEL & NO.	GOOD	NEAR MINT	YR.
(PLEASE TRY) TO UNDERSTAND ME/ Swing Little Chickie	(Olympic 1068)	1.25	5.00	62
(PLEASE TRY) TO UNDERSTAND ME/Swinging Little Chickie	(Itzy 1)	1.00	4.00	62

BELL, Vincent

TITLE/FLIP	LABEL & NO.	GOOD	NEAR MINT	YR.
GOIN' OUT OF MY HEAD/Eleanor Rigby	(Decca 32224)	1.00	4.00	67
QUICKSAND/Lead Guitar	(Independent 102)	1.00	4.00	

BELL-TONES, The: see Baker, Ronnie

BELLAMY, David (Of The Bellamy Brothers)

TITLE/FLIP	LABEL & NO.	GOOD	NEAR MINT	YR.
NOTHIN' HEAVY/Baby, You're Not A Legend	(Warner Bros. 8123)	.50	2.00	75

BELLAMY BROTHERS, The

TITLE/FLIP	LABEL & NO.	GOOD	NEAR MINT	YR.
BIRD DOG/Make Me Over	(Warner Bros 8521)	.50	2.00	78
CROSSFIRE/Tiger Lily Lover	(Warner Bros 8350)	.50	2.00	77
HELL CAT/I'm The Only Sane Man Left Alive	(Warner Bros. 8220)	.50	2.00	76
HIGHWAY 2-18/Livin' In The West	(Warner Bros. 8284)	.50	2.00	77
I COULD BE MAKIN' LOVE TO YOU/Sugar Daddy	(Warner Bros. 49160)	.50	2.00	80
IF I SAID YOU HAD A BEAUTIFUL BODY WOULD YOU HOLD IT AGAINST ME?/	(Warner Bros. 8790)	.50	2.00	79
LET YOUR LOVE FLOW/Inside Of My Guitar	(Warner Bros. 8169)	.50	2.00	76
LOVIN' ON/My Shy Anne	(Warner Bros. 8692)	.50	2.00	78
MEMORBILIA/You Made Me	(Warner Bros. 8401)	.75	3.00	77
SATIN SHEETS/ Rainy, Windy, Sunshine (Roder Road)	(Warner Bros. 8248)	.50	2.00	76
SLIPIN' AWAY/Let's Give Love A Go	(Warner Bros. 8558)	.50	2.00	78
WILD HONEY/Tumbleweed & Rosalee	(Warner Bros. 8637)	.50	2.00	78
YOU AIN'T JUST WHISTLIN' DIXIE/ Blue Ribbons	(Warner Bros. 49032)	.50	2.00	79

BELLINO, Johnny

TITLE/FLIP	LABEL & NO.	GOOD	NEAR MINT	YR.
ANGEL GIRL/I Keep Telling Myself	(Decca 31753)	1.25	5.00	65

BELLS, The (With Frank Mills)

TITLE/FLIP	LABEL & NO.	GOOD	NEAR MINT	YR.
FLY LITTLE WHITE DOVE, FLY/Follow The Sun	(Polydor 15016)	.50	2.00	71
I LOVE YOU LADY DAWN/Rain	(Polydor 15027)	.50	2.00	71
KRIS KRISTOFFERSON MEDLEY/	(Polydor 15063)	.50	2.00	72
OH MY LOVE/You You You	(Polydor 15036)	.50	2.00	71
SHE'S A LADY/Sweet Sounds Of Music	(Polydor 15029)	.50	2.00	71
STAY AWHILE/Sing A Song Of Freedom	(Polydor 15023)	1.50	6.00	71
TO KNOW YOU IS TO LOVE YOU/For Better Or Worse	(Polydor 15031)	.50	2.00	71

BELLUS, Tony

TITLE/FLIP	LABEL & NO.	GOOD	NEAR MINT	YR.
END OF MY LOVE, THE/The Echo Of An Old Song	(NRC 051)	1.00	4.00	60
HEY LITTLE DARLIN'/Only Your Heart	(NRC 035)	1.25	5.00	59
ROBBIN' THE CRADLE/Valentine Girl	(NRC 023)	1.25	5.00	59
YOUNG GIRLS/	(NRC 040)	1.00	4.00	60

BELMONTS, The

TITLE/FLIP	LABEL & NO.	GOOD	NEAR MINT	YR.
ANN-MARIE/Ac-cent-tchu-ate The Positive	(Sabrina 509)	1.00	4.00	63
C'MON EVERYBODY/Why	(Sabrina 519)	4.00	12.00	64
COME ON LITTLE ANGEL/How About Me	(Sabrina 505)	1.50	6.00	62
COME WITH ME/You're Like A Mystery	(United Artists 507)	3.00	12.00	62
DIDDLE-DEE-DUM/Farewell	(Sabrina 507)	1.00	4.00	62
DON'T GET AROUND MUCH ANYMORE/ Searching For A New Love	(Sabrina 501)	1.50	6.00	61
HAVE YOU HEARD-WORST THAT COULD HAPPEN/ Answer Me My Love	(Dot 17257)	1.00	4.00	69
HOMBRE/I Confess	(Sabrina 503)	1.25	5.00	62
I DON'T KNOW WHY/Wintertime	(United Artists 809)	1.50	5.00	65
I GOT A FEELING/To Be With You	(United Artists 966)	1.50	6.00	65
I NEED SOMEONE/American Dance	(Sabrina 502)	2.00	8.00	61
I WALKED AWAY/Today My Heart Has Gone Away	(United Artists 904)	1.50	6.00	65
LET'S CALL IT A DAY/Walk On By	(Sabrina 513)	3.00	12.00	63
MORE IMPORTANT THINGS TO DO/Walk On By	(Sabrina 517)	2.00	8.00	64
NOTHING IN RETURN/Summertime	(Sabrina 521)	5.00	20.00	64
SHE ONLY WANTS TO DO HER THING/Reminiscing	(Dot 17173)	2.00	8.00	68
TEENAGE CLEMENTINE/Santa Margerita	(Mohawk 106)	5.00	20.00	57
TELL ME WHY/Smoke From Your Cigarette	(Sabrina 500)	2.50	10.00	61
TELL ME WHY/Smoke From Your Cigarette	(Suprise 1000)	6.25	25.00	61
WE BELONG TOGETHER/Such A Long Way	(Laurie 3080)	2.50	10.00	61

Also see Barin, Pete
Also see Carlo
Also see Dion & The Belmonts
Also see Sheppard, Buddy & The Holidays
Also see Strange Brothers Show, The
Also see Tony & The Holidays

BEL-TONES, The

TITLE/FLIP	LABEL & NO.	GOOD	NEAR MINT	YR.
BACK DOWN/Breaktime (Instrumental)	(Del Amo 4647)	1.00	4.00	

BELUSHI, John (Of The Blues Brothers)

TITLE/FLIP	LABEL & NO.	GOOD	NEAR MINT	YR.
LOUIE, LOUIE/Money (That's What I Want)	(MCA 40950)	.50	2.00	78

BELVEDERES, The

TITLE/FLIP	LABEL & NO.	GOOD	NEAR MINT	YR.
COME TO ME BABY/	(Baton 214)	2.50	10.00	55
LET'S GET MARRIED/Wow Wow, Mary Mary	(Trend 009)	2.00	8.00	58
LOST LOVE/Why Do You Treat Me This Way	(Poplar 114)	1.25	5.00	62
MCCOY, THE/Tired Out	(Rhapsody 5163)	.75	3.00	
PEPPER HOT BABY/Come To Me Baby	(Baton 217)	2.50	10.00	55
SUZANNE/Hey Honey	(Dot 15852)	1.25	5.00	58
WALKIN' IN THE GARDEN/Buona Sera	(Jopz 45-1771)	.75	3.00	

Even though all of these releases are shown as being by a group using the same name, the possibility exists that they are not all by the same group.

BEN & BEA

TITLE/FLIP	LABEL & NO.	GOOD	NEAR MINT	YR.
GEE BABY/Let The Good Times Roll	(Philips 40000)	.75	3.00	62

BENATAR, Pat

TITLE/FLIP	LABEL & NO.	GOOD	NEAR MINT	YR.
HEARTBREAKER/My Clone Sleeps Alone	(Chrysalis 2395)	.50	2.00	79
IF YOU THINK YOU KNOW HOW TO LOVE ME/	(Chrysalis 2373)	.50	2.00	79

BENNETT, Boyd

TITLE/FLIP	LABEL & NO.	GOOD	NEAR MINT	YR.
BLUE SUEDE SHOES/Mumbles Blues	(King 4903)	1.00	4.00	56
BIG JUNIOR/Hershey Bar	(Mercury 71724)	.75	3.00	60
BOOGIE BEAR/A Boy Can Tell	(Mercury 71479)	1.00	4.00	59
BRAIN, THE/Coffee Break	(Mercury 71813)	.75	3.00	61
COOL DISC JOCKEY/High School Hop	(King 5282)	1.00	4.00	59
EVERLOVIN'/Boogie At Midnight	(King 1443)	2.50	10.00	55
GROOVY AGE, THE/Let Me Love You	(King 4925)	1.25	5.00	56
HIT THAT JIVE, JACK/Rabbit-eye Pink & Charcoal Black	(King 4953)	1.00	4.00	56
I'M WASTING MY TIME/Prescious Sweetheart	(King 1201)	3.75	15.00	53
IT'S WONDERFUL/Amo, Amas, Amat	(Mercury 71605)	.75	3.00	60
MOST, THE/Desperately	(King 4853)	1.00	4.00	56
MY BOY-FLAT TOP/Banjo Rock & Roll	(King 1494)	2.50	10.00	55
NAUGHTY ROCK & ROLL/Lover's Night	(Mercury 71537)	1.00	4.00	59
POISON IVY/You Upset Me Baby	(King 1432)	2.50	10.00	55
RIGHT AROUND THE CORNER/Partners For Life	(King 4874)	1.25	5.00	56
ROCKIN' UP A STORM/A Lock Of Your Hair	(King 4985)	1.25	5.00	57
SEVENTEEN/Little Old You All (Maroon label)	(King 1470)	3.75	15.00	55
SEVENTEEN/Sarasota (Blue label)	(Mercury 71648)	2.00	8.00	60
TEAR IT UP/Tight Tights	(Mercury 71409)	1.00	4.00	60
TENNESSEE ROCK & ROLL/Oo-oo-oo	(King 1475)	2.50	10.00	55
WATERLOO/I've Had Enough (Shown as by Boyd Bennett & His Southlanders)	(King 1413)	3.00	12.00	54

BENNETT, Cliff & The Rebel Rousers

TITLE/FLIP	LABEL & NO.	GOOD	NEAR MINT	YR.
EVERYBODY LOVES A LOVER/My Old Standby	(Ascot 2146)	.75	3.00	64
GOT TO GET YOU INTO MY LIFE/Baby Each Day	(ABC 10842)	.75	3.00	66
ONE WAY LOVE/I'm In Love With You	(Capitol 5309)	.75	3.00	64
IF ONLY YOU'D REPLY/Three Rooms With Running Water	(Amy 930)	.75	3.00	65

BENNETT, Jerry

TITLE/FLIP	LABEL & NO.	GOOD	NEAR MINT	YR.
REPORT FROM OUTER-SPACE/ (Novelty/Break-in)	(Arch 1617)	3.75	15.00	

BENNETT, Joe & The Sparkletones

TITLE/FLIP	LABEL & NO.	GOOD	NEAR MINT	YR.
ARE YOU FROM DIXIE/Beautiful One	(Paris 542)	1.00	4.00	60
BAYOU ROCK/Beautiful One (Shown as by Joe Bennett)	(Paris 530)	1.25	5.00	59
BLACK SLACKS/Boppin Rock Boogie	(ABC-Paramount 9837)	1.25	5.00	57
BOYS DO CRY/What The Heck	(Paris 537)	1.00	4.00	59
COTTON PICKIN' ROCKER/I Dig You Baby	(ABC-Paramount 9885)	1.00	4.00	58
DO THE STOP/Late Again	(ABC-Paramount 9959)	1.00	4.00	58
PENNY LOAFERS & BOBBY SOX/Rocket	(ABC-Paramount 9885)	1.25	5.00	57
RUN RABBIT RUN/Well Dressed Man	(ABC-Paramount 10659)	.75	3.00	65
WE'VE HAD IT/Little Turtle	(ABC-Paramount 9929)	1.00	4.00	58

BENNETT, Pete, & The Embers

TITLE/FLIP	LABEL & NO.	GOOD	NEAR MINT	YR.
FEVER/Soft	(Sunset 1002)	.75	3.00	63
TRANTELLA ROCK/Bunny Hop	(Cupid 1212)	1.00	4.00	59

Instrumentals

BENNETT, Ron

TITLE/FLIP	LABEL & NO.	GOOD	NEAR MINT	YR.
DINGLE DANGLE DOLL/My Only Girl	(Ta-Rah 1)	2.00	8.00	

BENNETT, Tony (Anthony Dominick Benedetto)

TITLE/FLIP	LABEL & NO.	GOOD	NEAR MINT	YR.
AUTUMN WALTZ, THE/Just In Time	(Columbia 40770)	.75	3.00	56
BECAUSE OF YOU/I Won't Cry Anymore	(Columbia 39362)	1.00	4.00	51
BLUE VELVET/Solitaire	(Columbia 39555)	1.00	4.00	51
CAN YOU FIND IT IN YOUR HEART/Forget Her	(Columbia 40667)	.75	3.00	56
COLD, COLD HEART/While We're Young	(Columbia 39449)	1.00	4.00	51
FIREFLY/The Night That Heaven Fell	(Columbia 41237)	.75	3.00	58
FROM THE CANDY STORE ON THE CORNER/ Happiness Street	(Columbia 40726)	.75	3.00	56
GOOD LIFE, THE/Spring In Manhattan	(Columbia 42779)	.50	2.00	63
HAVE A GOOD TIME/Please My Love	(Columbia 39764)	1.00	4.00	52
HERE IN MY HEART/I'm Lost Again	(Columbia 39745)	1.00	4.00	52
I LEFT MY HEART IN SAN FRANCISCO/ Once Upon A Time	(Columbia 42332)	.50	2.00	62
I WANNA BE AROUND/I Will Live My Life For You	(Columbia 42634)	.50	2.00	62
IF I RULED THE WORLD/Take The Moment	(Columbia 43220)	.50	2.00	65
IN THE MIDDLE OF AN ISLAND/I Am	(Columbia 40965)	.75	3.00	57
ONE FOR MY BABY/No Hard Feelings	(Columbia 40907)	.75	3.00	57
RAGS TO RICHES/Here Comes That Heartache Again	(Columbia 40048)	1.00	4.00	53
SMILE/You Can't	(Columbia 41434)	.75	3.00	59
STRANGER IN PARADISE/Why Does It Have To Be Me	(Columbia 40121)	1.00	4.00	53
THIS IS ALL I ASK/True Blue Lou	(Columbia 42820)	.50	2.00	63
YOUNG & WARM & WONDERFUL/ Now I Lay Me Down To Sleep	(Columbia 41172)	.75	3.00	58

BENNO, Marc (Of The Asylum Choir)

TITLE/FLIP	LABEL & NO.	GOOD	NEAR MINT	YR.
CHASIN' RAINBOWS/	(A&M 2184)	.50	2.00	79
SOUTHERN WOMAN/Jive Fade Jive	(A&M 1387)	.50	2.00	73

BENNY & THE BEDBUGS

TITLE/FLIP	LABEL & NO.	GOOD	NEAR MINT	YR.
ROLL OVER BEETHOVEN/The Beatle Beat	(DCP 1008)	1.25	5.00	64

BENSON, Jane

TITLE/FLIP	LABEL & NO.	GOOD	NEAR MINT	YR.
GROWING UP/Surrendering	(Atco 6151)	.75	3.00	59

TITLE/FLIP	LABEL & NO.	GOOD	NEAR MINT	YR.
BENTLEY, Jay, & The Jet Set				
COME ON-ON/Everybody's Got A Dancing Partner	(GNP Crescendo 347)	.75	3.00	65
WATUSI '64/I'll Get You	(GNP Crescendo 332)	.75	3.00	64
BENTLEYS, The				
SHE'S MY HOT ROD QUEEN/ Why Does Everybody Want To Hold My Baby	(Smash 1967)	.75	3.00	65
WHY DIDN'T I LISTEN TO MOTHER/Lose A Tear	(Smash 1988)	2.50	10.00	
BENTON, Barbie				
BRASS BUCKLES/Put A Little Bit On Me	(Playboy 6032)	.75	3.00	75
MOVIE MAGAZINE, STARS IN HER EYES/ He Looks Just Like His Daddy	(Playboy 6043)	.75	3.00	75
NOW I LAY ME DOWN TO SLEEP WITH YOU/ If You Can't Do It, That's All Right	(Playboy 6018)	.75	3.00	74
REVEREND BOB, THE/ Ain't That Just The Way (That Life Goes Down)	(Playboy 6058)	.75	3.00	75
STAYING POWER/San Diego Serenade	(Playboy 6078)	.75	3.00	76
(With members of Elton John's Band & Linda Ronstadt's Band)				
WELCOME STRANGER/That Country Boy Of Mine	(Playboy 6008)	.75	3.00	74
BERGEN, Polly				
COME PRIMA/Au Revoir Again	(Columbia 41275)	.75	3.00	58
BERMUDAS, The (Featuring Rickie Page)				
BLUE DREAMER/Seeing Is Believing	(Era 3133)	.75	3.00	64
DONNIE/Chu Sen Ling	(Era 3125)	.75	3.00	64
BERNADETTE & THE SWINGING BEARS				
CRAZY YOGI/When You're Dancing With Me	(Beach 1001)	1.25	5.00	61
BERNARD, Rod				
COLINDA/Who's Gonna Rock	(Hall 1902)	.75	3.00	62
FORGIVE/I Want Somebody	(Hall 1915)	.75	3.00	62
ONE MORE CHANCE/Shedding Teardrops Over You	(Mercury 71507)	.75	3.00	59
THIS SHOULD GO ON FOREVER/Pardon Mr. Gordon	(Argo 5327)	.75	3.00	59
THIS SHOULD GO ON FOREVER/ Pardon, Mr. Gordon (With the Twisters)	(Jin 105)	3.00	12.00	59
WEDDING BELLS/I Had A Girl	(Hall way 1806)	.75	3.00	61
BERNIE & LEE				
SOLDIER BOY/Johnny's Girl	(Todd 1041)	1.00	4.00	59
BERNSTEIN, Elmer				
MAN WITH THE GOLDEN ARM/Clark Street	(Decca 29869)	.75	3.00	56
WALK ON THE WILD SIDE/Walk On The Wild Side Jazz	(Choreo 101)	.75	3.00	61
Instrumentals				
BERRY, Dave				
MEMPHIS, TENN./My Baby Left Me	(London 9666)	.75	3.00	64
BERRY, Dorothy				
FALLING IN LOVE ALL OVER AGAIN/	(Tangerine 1020)	.50	2.00	71
GIRL WHO STOPPED THE DUKE OF EARL, THE/	(Little Star [illegible])			
(Answer song)				
YOU BETTER WATCH OUT/Ain't That Love	(Planetary 101)	2.00	8.00	
BERRY, Huckle				
DRIFTWOOD/Life Is A Heartache	(MGM 11362)	1.25	5.00	52
BERRY, Jan (Of Jan & Dean)				
DON'T YOU JUST KNOW IT (With Brian Wilson)/ Blue Moon Shuffle (Vocal)	(Ode 66034)	7.50	30.00	73
(Shown as by Jan)				
LITTLE QUEENIE/That's The Way It Is	(A&M 1975)	1.00	4.00	77
MOTHER EARTH/Blue Moon Shuffle (Instrumental)	(Ode 66023)	3.75	15.00	72
SING SANG A SONG/Sing Sang A Song (Singalong Version)	(Ode 66120)	2.50	10.00	76
SKATEBOARD SURFIN' U.S.A. (SIDEWALK SURFIN' WITH ME)/ How, How I Love Her	(A&M 2020)	1.00	4.00	78
TINSEL TOWN/Blow Up Music	(Ode 66034)	2.50	10.00	73
(Shown as by Jan)				
TOMORROWS TEARDROPS/My Midsummer Nights Dream	(Ripple 6101)	6.25	25.00	61
(Shown as by Jan)				
UNIVERSAL COWARD, THE (Answer Song)/ I Can't Wait To Love You	(Liberty 55845)	1.25	5.00	66
Also see Jan & Arnie				
BERRY, Lou, & The Bel Raves				
HOT ROD/What A Dolly	(Dreem 1001)	15.00	60.00	59
BERRY, Mike				
I AM A ROCKER/Boogaloo Dues	(Epic 9-50748)	.50	2.00	79
ONE BY ONE/	(Epic 9-50913)	.50	2.00	79
TRIBUTE TO BUDDY HOLLY/Every Little Kiss	(Coral 62341)	3.75	15.00	62
(With the Outlaws)				
BERT (Of TV's Sesame Street)				
CLINK, CLANK/	(Columbia 45718)	.50	2.00	71
BERWICK, Brad				
I'M BETTER THAN THE BEATLES/ Walkin' Down Easy Street	(Clinton 1012)	1.50	6.00	64
BEST, Peter				
BOYS/Kansas City	(Cameo 391)	2.00	8.00	66
BOYS/Kansas City (With Picture Sleeve)	(Cameo 391)	7.50	30.00	66
CAROUSEL OF LOVE/The Way I Feel About You	(Capitol P-2092)	2.00	8.00	
CASTING MY SPELL/I'm Blue	(Mr. Maestro 712)	3.00	12.00	
I CAN'T GO WITHOUT YOU/Keys To My Heart	(Mr. Maestro 711)	3.00	12.00	
IF YOU CAN'T GET HER/The Way I Feel About You	(Happening 1118)	2.00	8.00	
(I'LL TRY) ANYWAY/I Wanna Be There	(Beatles 800)	3.75	15.00	64
Pete Best was the drummer for the Beatles prior to their 1964 rise to fame.				
BETHLEHEM EXIT				
WALK ME OUT/Blues Concerning My Girl	(Jabberwock 110)	2.50	10.00	
BETTS, Richard (Of The Allman Brothers)				
BOUGAINVILLEA/	(Arista 0269)	.50	2.00	77
RAIN/	(Capricorn 0221)	.50	2.00	76
This artist was later known as Dickey Betts & Great Southern.				
BEVERLY HILLS BLUES BAND, The (Deno Martin, Jr., Desi Arnaz, Jr. & Tony Martin, Jr.)				
IF I CAN JUST GET THROUGH TONIGHT/ Just Because	(Warner Bros. 8191)	.50	2.00	75
BEVERLEY SISTERS, The				
GREENSLEEVES/I'll See You In My Dreams	(London 1703)	1.00	4.00	56
BEVIS, Rita, & California Gold				
BALLAD OF ELVIS PRESLEY, THE/Wind In The Pines	(Larupin 100)	.50	2.00	77
BHANG				
BLACK EYED PEAS/Mellow Day	(Monster 0003)	1.00	4.00	
BICENTENNIAL NEWS TEAM, The				
FLASHBACK '76/	(St. Johns-No Number)	1.00	4.00	76
BIG BEATS, The				
CLARK'S EXPEDITION/Big Boy	(Columbia 41072)	1.00	4.00	58
SAX APPEAL (Instrumental)/	(Tel 1012)	.75	3.00	
BIG BO				
BIG BO'S TWIST/Hully Gully Now	(Duchess 1013)	.75	3.00	62
BIG BOB				
WOWSVILLE/Wowsville (Part 2)	(Stacy 952)	.75	3.00	62
BIG BOPPER (Jape Richardson)				
BIG BOPPER'S WEDDING/Little Red Riding Hood	(Mercury 71375)	1.00	4.00	58
CHANTILLY LACE/ The Purple People Eater Meets The Witch Doctor	(D 1008)	10.00	40.00	58
(Counterfeit copies exist of this record, but are most easily identified by the thin plastic disc used. Original pressings were on thicker plastic.)				
CHANTILLY LACE/ The Purple People Eater Meets The Witch Doctor	(Mercury 71343)	1.00	4.00	58
IT'S THE TRUTH RUTH/That's What I'm Talking About	(Mercury 71451)	2.50	10.00	59
PINK PETTICOATS/The Clock	(Mercury 71482)	2.50	10.00	59
WALKING THROUGH MY DREAMS/ Someone Watching Over You	(Mercury 71416)	2.50	10.00	59
BIG BROTHER & THE HOLDING COMPANY (Featuring Janis Joplin)				
ALL IS LONELINESS/Blindman	(Mainstream 657)	1.25	5.00	66
BLACK WIDOW SPIDER/Nu Boogaloo Jam	(Columbia 45502)	.75	3.00	69
(Without Janis Joplin)				
BYE BYE BABY/Intruder	(Mainstream 666)	1.25	5.00	67
COO COO/Last Time	(Mainstream 678)	1.25	5.00	68
DOWN ON ME/Call On Me	(Mainstream 662)	1.25	5.00	68
KEEP ON/Home On The Stranger	(Columbia 45284)	1.00	4.00	69
PIECE OF MY HEART/Turtle Blues	(Columbia 44626)	1.00	4.00	68
WOMEN IS LOSERS/Light Is Faster Than Sound	(Mainstream 675)	1.25	5.00	67
BIG DADDY				
TEACHER, THE/Teacher, The (Part 2)	(Crakerjack 4002)	.75	3.00	61
WALKING HER HOME/Where In The World	(Gee 1051)	1.00	4.00	57
BIG DADDY WITH THE LITTLE SISTERS				
DADDY FROG/Bus Ride (By D.H. & The Down Beats)	(Royal 1004)	1.50	6.00	59
BIG FRAMUS				
CHANGE YOUR LUCK/Put Some Color In Your Life	(Shoreline 2131)	2.50	10.00	65
BIG GUYS, The				
MR. CUPID/Hang My Head (& Cry)	(Warner Bros. 7047)	.75	3.00	67
BIG JIVE				
BLUE EYES/Stardust In Her Eyes	(Shad 5019)	1.50	6.00	
BIG JOHN'S SWING CARAVAN				
TOSSING MY HEART AROUND/	(J.F.J. 600)	1.50	6.00	
BIG SAMBO				
RAINS CAME, THE/At The Party	(Eric 7003)	.75	3.00	62
(Label reads "Distributed by London")				
RAINS CAME, THE/At The Party	(Eric 7003)	1.00	4.00	62
(Label does not read "Distributed by London")				
BIG STAR (With Alex Chilton)				
DON'T LIE TO ME/Watch'd Sunrise	(Ardent 2904)	.75	3.00	
SEPTEMBER GURLS/September Gurls	(Ardent 2912)	.75	3.00	
SEPTEMBER GURLS/September Gurls	(Privilege 7003)	1.00	4.00	
WHEN MY BABY'S BESIDE ME/In The Street	(Ardent 2902)	.75	3.00	
Also see Box Tops, The				
BIG WALTER				
WATUSIE FREEZE/Watusie Freeze (Part 2)	(Myrl 409)	.75	3.00	62
WATUSIE FREEZE/Watusie Freeze (Part 2)	(Global 409)	.75	3.00	62
BIG WHEELIE & THE HUBCAPS				
ELVIS PRESLEY MEDLEY/Chuck Berry Medley	(Scepter 12375)	.75	3.00	73
BIG-BITE & MAC				
DROP TOOTH/The Big Bite	(Fun-E-Bone 4322)	1.00	4.00	
(Novelty/Break-in)				
BIGGS, Kenny				
SWINGIN' SWANEE RIVER/There's No Excuse	(B/W 616)	.75	3.00	61
SWINGIN' SWANEE ROCK/There's No Excuse	(B/W 615)	.75	3.00	61
BIKINIS, The				
CRAZY VIBRATIONS/Spunky	(Top Rank 2032)	.75	3.00	60
BILK, Mr. Acker				
ABOVE THE STARS/Soft Sands	(Atco 6230)	.50	2.00	62
LIMELIGHT/Lonely	(Atco 6238)	.50	2.00	62
STRANGER ON THE SHORE/Cielito Lindo	(Atco 6217)	.50	2.00	62
SUMMER SET/Acker's Way	(Atco 6160)	.75	3.00	60
UNDERNEATH THE ARCHES/Lady Of The Lake	(Atco 6264)	.75	3.00	63
Instrumentals				
BILL & TAFFY (Bill & Taffy Danoff)				
HOW LUCKY CAN YOU BE/Maybe	(RCA 10009)	.75	3.00	74
Also see Fat City				
Also see Starland Vocal Band, The				
BILL BLACK'S COMBO				
BLUE TANGO/Willie	(Hi 2027)	.75	3.00	60
COMIN' ON/Soft Winds	(Hi 2072)	.75	3.00	64
DO IT-RAT NOW/Little Jasper	(Hi 2064)	.75	3.00	63
DON'T BE CRUEL/Rollin'	(Hi 2026)	.75	3.00	60
HEARTS OF STONE/Royal Blue	(Hi 2028)	.75	3.00	61
JOEY'S SONG/Hot Taco	(Hi 2059)	.75	3.00	65
JOSEPHINE/Dry Bones	(Hi 2022)	.75	3.00	60
LITTLE QUEENIE/Boo Ray	(Hi 2079)	.75	3.00	64
MONKEY SHINE/Long Gone	(Hi 2069)	.75	3.00	63
MOVIN'/Honky Train	(Hi 2038)	.75	3.00	61
OLE BUTTERMILK SKY/Yogi	(Hi 2036)	.75	3.00	61
SMOKIE (PART 2)/Smokie (Part 1)	(Hi 2018)	.75	3.00	59
SO WHAT/Blues For The Red Boy	(Hi 2055)	.75	3.00	62
TEQUILA/Raunchy	(Hi 2077)	.75	3.00	64
TWIST-HER/My Girl Josephine	(Hi 2042)	.75	3.00	61
TWISTIN' WHITE SILVER SANDS/My Babe	(Hi 2052)	.75	3.00	62
WHITE SILVER SANDS/The Wheel	(Hi 2021)	.75	3.00	60
Bill Black's bass fiddle playing can be heard on many of Elvis Presley's early recordings.				
Instrumentals				
BILLIE & MARK				
DEEP DOWN/Just So You Love Me	(Demon 1513)	1.00	4.00	59
BILLIE & RICKY				
BABY DOLL/Mama Papa Please	(Sue 711)	1.00	4.00	59
BILLIE & THE MOONLIGHTERS				
YOU MADE ME CRY/Little Indian Girl	(Crystal Ball 101)	.75	3.00	
YOU MADE ME CRY/Little Indian Girl (Red Plastic)	(Crystal Ball 101)	1.00	4.00	
YOU MADE ME CRY/ Little Indian Girl (Multi-color Plastic)	(Crystal Ball 101)	3.00	12.00	
BILLION DOLLAR BABIES, The				
ROCK 'N' ROLL RADIO/Wasn't I The One	(Polydor 14394)	.75	3.00	77
ROCK 'N' ROLL RADIO/Wasn't I The One	(Polydor 14394)	1.25	5.00	77
(Promotional issue)				
TOO YOUNG (Stereo)/Too Young (Mono)	(Polydor 14406)	2.50	10.00	77
(Promotional issue, may not have been issued commercially)				
This group was formerly Alice Cooper's Band.				
BILLY & EDDIE				
KING IS COMING BACK, THE/Come Back, Baby	(Top Rank 2017)	3.75	15.00	59
BILLY & LILLIE (Billy Ford & Lillie Bryant)				
AIN'T COMING BACK/Bananas	(Swan 4069)	3.75	15.00	61
BELLS, BELLS, BELLS/Honeymoonin'	(Swan 4036)	3.75	15.00	59
CARRY ME ACROSS THE THRESHOLD/ Why I Love Billy (By Lillie)	(ABC-Paramount 10489)	1.25	5.00	63
FREE FOR ALL/The Ins & Outs (Of Love)	(Swan 4051)	.75	3.00	60
HANGING ON TO YOU/The Greasy Spoon	(Swan 4011)	.75	3.00	58
HAPPINESS/Creepin' Crawlin' Cryin'	(Swan 4005)	.75	3.00	58
LA DEE DAH/The Monster	(Swan 4002)	1.00	4.00	57
LOVE ME SINCERELY/Whip It To Me Baby	(ABC-Paramount 10421)	.75	3.00	63
LUCKY LADYBUG/I Promise You	(Swan 4020)	1.00	4.00	58
OVER THE MOUNTAIN, ACROSS THE SEA/ That's The Way The Cookie Crumbles	(Swan 4058)	.75	3.00	60
TUMBLED DOWN/Alloysius Horatio Thomas, The Cat	(Swan 4030)	.75	3.00	59
TWO OF US/Nothing Moves	(Cameo 412)	.75	3.00	65
BILLY & SUE (William Oliver Swofford & Lesley Gore)				
COME SOFTLY TO ME/Billy & Sue's Love Scene	(Crew 343)	1.00	4.00	70
Also see Oliver				
BILLY & THE ECHOES				
BODACIOUS TWIST/Come Softly	(Gala 121)	.75	3.00	62
BILLY & THE ESSENTIALS				
BARALU'S WEDDING DAY/My Way Of Saying	(Smash 2045)	1.25	5.00	66
DANCE IS OVER, THE/Steady Girl	(Landa 691)	2.50	10.00	62
DON'T CRY (SING ALONG WITH THE MUSIC)/ Baby Go Away	(Smash 2071)	1.50	6.00	66
I WROTE THE SONG/	(SSS International 706)	1.50	6.00	67
REMEMBER ME BABY/The Actor	(Cameo 344)	2.50	10.00	65
LAST DANCE/Yes Sir, That's My Baby	(Mercury 72210)	2.50	10.00	63
LONELY WEEKEND/Young At Heart	(Mercury 72127)	2.50	10.00	63
OVER THE WEEKEND/Maybe You'll Be There	(Jamie 1239)	2.50	10.00	62
STEADY GIRL/Dance Is Over, The	(Jamie 1229)	1.50	6.00	62
Also see Heatwaves, The				
BILLY & THE FLEET				
POWER SHIFT (Instrumental)/ Nobody Wants To Give Me What I Want	(Arlen 514)	1.00	4.00	63
BILLY & THE KIDS				
TAKE A CHANCE ON LOVE/The Way It Used To Be	(Lute 312)	3.75	15.00	
THE WAY IT USED TO BE/Take A Chance On Love	(Lute 6016)	3.75	15.00	61
BILLY & THE PATIOS				
LOVE IS A STORY/You Name It	(Lite 9002)	3.75	15.00	
BILLY FALCON'S BURNING ROSE				
SAIL AWAY/Reachin'	(Manhattan 1232)	.50	2.00	78
BILLY JOE & THE CHECKMATES (Featuring Billy Joe Hunter)				
PERCOLATOR (TWIST)/Round & Round & Round & Round	(Dore 620)	.75	3.00	61
ROCKY'S THEME/Twist That Thing	(Dore 636)	.75	3.00	62
BILLY JOE & THE CHESSMEN				
HAPPY JACK/The Loaf	(Wolfie 102)	.75	3.00	63
BIRDMEN, The				
DANCE THE JAYBIRD (PART 1)/ Dance The Jaybird (Part 2)	(Rock-It 1003)	1.25	5.00	61
BIRDS, The				
MOTIVATIONS/Motivate (The Motivations)	(Pride 301)	1.00	4.00	
BIRDS OF A FEATHER (With Caleb Quaye)				
COUNTRY COMFORD/One More Time	(Page One 21037)	.50	2.00	70
ELVIS, HOW COULD I RESIST/Elvis, How Could I Resist	(Armour 8426)	.50	2.00	77
Caleb Quaye was formerly with Elton John's Band.				
BIRKIN, Jane, & Serge Gainsbourg				
JE T'AIME...MOI NON PLUS/Jan B.	(Fontana 1665)	.75	3.00	69
BISCAYNE BAY SURFERS, The				
SURFIN IS A SIGHT TO SEE/ Surfin' On A Swinging Soiree	(Mayhams 214)	1.25	5.00	64
BISCAYNES, The				
CHURCH KEY (Instrumental)/ Moment Of Truth (By the Surfaris)	(Reprise 20180)	1.25	5.00	63
CHURCH KEY (Instrumental)/ Moment Of Truth (By the Surfaris)	(Northridge 1001)	2.00	8.00	63
Also see Walker Brothers, The				
BISHOP, Elvin (Of Paul Butterfield's Blues Band)				
DON'T FIGHT IT FEEL IT/Don't Fight It Feel It	(Fillmore 7003)	.75	3.00	
FOOLED AROUND & FELL IN LOVE/Slick Titty Boom	(Capricorn 0252)	.75	3.00	76
FOOLED AROUND & FELL IN LOVE/Have A Good Time	(Capricorn 0252)	.50	2.00	76
(Alternate flip side, for any who objected to "Slick Titty Boom")				
HOLLER & SHOUT/	(Epic 10926)	.50	2.00	73
I JUST CAN'T GO ON/I Just Can't Go On	(Fillmore 7005)	.75	3.00	
IT'S A FEELIN'/	(Capricorn 0313)	.50	2.00	79
JUKE JOINT JUMP/Calling All Cows	(Capricorn 0243)	.50	2.00	75
KEEP IT COOL/	(Capricorn 0269)	.50	2.00	77
ROCK MY SOUL/Yes Sir	(Capricorn 0285)	.50	2.00	78
SO FINE/So Fine	(Fillmore 7002)	.75	3.00	
SPEND SOME TIME/	(Capricorn 0266)	.50	2.00	76
STRUTTIN' MY STUFF/Grab All The Love	(Capricorn 0256)	.50	2.00	76
SURE FEELS GOOD/Arkansas Line	(Capricorn 0237)	.50	2.00	75
TRAVELIN' SHOES/	(Capricorn 0202)	.50	2.00	74
BISHOP, Stephen				
ANIMAL HOUSE/Dream Girl	(ABC 12435)	.50	2.00	78
EVERYBODY NEEDS LOVE/Only The Heart Within You	(ABC 12406)	.50	2.00	78
ON & ON/Little Italy	(ABC 12260)	.50	2.00	77
SAVE IT FOR A RAINY DAY/Careless	(ABC 12232)	.50	2.00	77
BITTER SWEETS, The				
ANOTHER CHANCE/In The West	(Original 70)	1.50	6.00	
WHAT A LONELY WAY TO START THE SUMMERTIME/ Mark My Words	(Cameo 368)	1.00	4.00	65
BJORN & BENNY (Bjorn Ulvaeus & Benny Anderson)				
PEOPLE NEED LOVE/Merry-go-Round	(Playboy 50014)	1.25	5.00	73
(With Anna & Frieda)				
ROCK'N ROLL BAND/Another Town, Another Train	(Playboy 50025)	1.25	5.00	73
(With Anna & Frieda)				
Also see Hep Stars				
Also see Abba				
BLACK, Bill: see Bill Black's Combo				
BLACK, Cilla				
ALFIE/Night Time Is Here	(Capitol 5674)	.75	3.00	66
ACROSS THE UNIVERSE/	(DJM 018)	.50	2.00	74
DON'T ANSWER ME/The Right One Is Left	(Capitol 5763)	.75	3.00	67
FANTASY/	(Private Stock 45077)	.50	2.00	75
FOR NO ONE/	(Capitol 5783)	.75	3.00	67
HE WAS A WRITER/	(EMI 4003)	.50	2.00	74
IF YOU SHOULD EVER/It Feels So Good	(DJM 015)	.50	2.00	73
I'LL TAKE A TANGO/	(Private Stock 45040)	.50	2.00	75
I'VE BEEN WRONG BEFORE/My Love Come Home	(Capitol 5414)	.75	3.00	65
IS IT LOVE/One Little Voice	(Capitol 5373)	.75	3.00	65
IT'S FOR YOU/He Won't Ask Me	(Capitol 5258)	1.25	5.00	64
ONLY FOREVER WILL DO/What The World Needs Now	(DJM 007)	.50	2.00	73

The Beatles

Debbie Boone & Pat Boone

J.F. Baldassare

The Byrds

TITLE/FLIP	LABEL & NO.	GOOD	NEAR MINT	YR.
STEP INSIDE LOVE/ I Couldn't Take My Eyes Off You (Answer song)	(Bell 726)	1.25	5.00	68
YOU'RE MY WORLD/Suffer Now I Must	(Capitol 5196)	.75	3.00	64
YESTERDAY/Love's Just A Broken Heart	(Capitol 5595)	.75	3.00	66
"It's For You" & "Step Inside Love" are Lennon-McCartney originals written for Cilla Black.				
BLACK, Jay (Of Jay & The Americans)				
ONE NIGHT AFFAIR/	(Roulette 20499)	.50	2.00	76
RUNNING SCARED/	(Atlantic-Migration 3273)	.50	2.00	75
BLACK, Jeanne				
HE'LL HAVE TO STAY (Answer song)/ Under Your Spell Again	(Capitol 4368)	.75	3.00	60
OH, HOW I MISS YOU TONIGHT (Answer song)/ Little Bit Lonely	(Capitol 4492)	.75	3.00	60
LETTER TO ANYA/Guessin' Again	(Capitol 4685)	.75	3.00	61
LISA/Journey Of Love	(Capitol 4396)	.75	3.00	60
BLACK, Jimmy Carl (Of The Mothers Of Invention)				
JIMMY CARL BLACK RAPS ABOUT GERONIMO BLACK (PART 1)/ Jimmy Carl Black Raps About Geronimo Black (Part 2)	(MCA 1914)	1.00	4.00	71
(Promotional 33 single issue)				
BLACK OAK ARKANSAS (Featuring "Jim Dandy")				
FISTFUL OF LOVE/Storm Of Passion	(MCA 40586)	.50	2.00	76
GREAT BALLS OF FIRE/Highway Pirate	(MCA 40536)	.50	2.00	76
HOT & NASTY/Singing The Blues	(Atco 6849)	.50	2.00	72
JIM DANDY/Red Hot Lovin'	(Atco 6948)	.50	2.00	73
LORD HAVE MERCY ON MY SOUL/	(Atco 6829)	.50	2.00	
NOT FADE AWAY/Feels So Good	(Capricorn 0285)	.50	2.00	78
RIDE WITH ME/	(Capricorn 0305)	.50	2.00	78
STRONG ENOUGH TO BE GENTLE/Ace In The Hole	(MCA 40496)	.50	2.00	76
WHEN THE BAND WAS SINGIN' "SHAKIN' ALL OVER"/ Bad Boy's Back In School	(MCA 40621)	.50	2.00	77
BLACK SABBATH				
ELECTRIC FUNERAL/Iron Man	(Warner Bros. 7764)	.50	2.00	74
IRON MAN/Electric Funeral	(Warner Bros. 7530)	.50	2.00	72
IRON MAN/Electric Funeral	(Warner Bros. 7802)	.50	2.00	75
IT'S ALRIGHT/Rock 'N' Roll Doctor	(Warner Bros. 8315)	.50	2.00	76
PARANOID/	(Warner Bros. 7437)	.50	2.00	70
PARANOID/Iron Man	(Warner Bros. 0312)	.50	2.00	74
SABBATH, BLOODY SABBATH/Changes	(Warner Bros. 7764)	.50	2.00	74
TOMORROW'S DREAM/Laguna Sunrise	(Warner Bros. 7625)	.50	2.00	72
BLACK, Sharon				
MOTHER DEAR YOU'VE GOT A SILLY DAUGHTER (Answer Song)/ Under The Smile Of Love	(Philips 40290)	.75	3.00	65
BLACK SHEEP (With Lou Gramm)				
BROKEN PROMISES/A Little Or A Lot	(Capitol 4012)	.50	2.00	75
STICK AROUND/	(Chrysalis 2038)	.50	2.00	73
Also see Foreigner				
BLACK SOCIETY				
SHERRY/I Feel	(MCA 40068)	1.00	4.00	73
BLACK, Terry				
HOW MANY GUYS/Only Sixteen	(Dunhill 4005)	.75	3.00	65
UNLESS YOU CARE/Can't We Go Somewhere	(Tollie 026)	.75	3.00	64
BLACK, Terry & Laurel Ward				
GOIN' DOWN (ON THE ROAD TO L.A.)/	(Kama Sutra 540)	.50	2.00	72
WARM DAYS, WARM NIGHTS/	(Kama Sutra 559)	.50	2.00	72
BLACK WATCH				
LEFT BEHIND/I Wish I Had The Verve	(Fenton 2508)	1.00	4.00	
BLACKBURN & SNOW				
STRANGER IN A STRANGE LAND/Uptown-Downtown	(Verve 10478)	1.25	5.00	67
TIME/Postwar Baby	(Verve 10563)	1.25	5.00	67
BLACKBYRDS, The				
DO IT, FLUID/Summer Love	(Fantasy 729)	.50	2.00	74
FLYING HIGH/All I Ask	(Fantasy 747)	.50	2.00	75
HAPPY MUSIC/Love So Fine	(Fantasy 762)	.50	2.00	76
PARTY LAND/You've Got That Something	(Fantasy 794)	.50	2.00	77
PARTY LAND/In Life	(Fantasy 794)	.50	2.00	77
ROCK CREEK PARK/Thankful 'Bout Yourself	(Fantasy 771)	.50	2.00	
SOFT & EASY/Something Special	(Fantasy 809)	.50	2.00	77
SUPERNATURAL FEELING/Looking Ahead	(Fantasy 819)	.50	2.00	78
TIME IS MOVIN'/Lady	(Fantasy 787)	.50	2.00	77
WALKING IN RHYTHM/The Baby	(Fantasy 736)	.50	2.00	75
BLACKFOOT				
HIGHWAY SONG/Road Fever	(Atco 7104)	.50	2.00	79
TRAIN, TRAIN/Baby Blue	(Atco 7207)	.50	2.00	79
BLACKHOLES				
WARREN SPAHN/Captain Payday	(Blackhole 0604)	.50	2.00	79
BLACKJACK				
FOR YOU/	(Polydor 2026)	.50	2.00	79
LOVE ME TONIGHT/Heart Of Mine	(Polydor 14572)	.50	2.00	79
BLACKMORE'S RAINBOW (With Richie Blackmore, Roger Glover, & Ronnie Dio)				
LONG LIVE ROCK 'N' ROLL/Sensitive To Light	(Polydor 14481)	.50	2.00	78
MAN ON THE SILVER MOUNTAIN/	(Polydor 14290)	.50	2.00	75
SINCE YOU'VE BEEN GONE/Bad Girls	(Polydor 2041)	.50	2.00	79
(Shown as by Rainbow)				
STARSTRUCK/Run With The Wolf	(Oyster 701)	.50	2.00	76
Blackmore & Glover were with Deep Purple, Ronnie Dio was in Elf.				
BLACKSHEEP				
I TOLD YOU/Baa-Baa	(Bellcor 102)	.75	3.00	
BLACKWELL				
WONDERFUL/	(Astro 1000)	.75	3.00	69
BLACKWELL, Charlie				
GIRL OF MY BEST FRIEND/Choppin' Mountains	(Warner Bros. 5132)	.75	3.00	59
MIDNIGHT OIL/None Of 'Em Glow Like You	(Warner Bros. 5031)	.75	3.00	59
BLACKWELLS, The				
ALWAYS IT'S YOU/Honey, Honey	(Jamie 1150)	.75	3.00	60
CHRISTMAS HOLIDAY/Little Match Girl	(Jamie 1173)	.75	3.00	60
HERE'S THE QUESTION/Please Don't Come Crying	(G&G 126)	1.25	5.00	59
HOLEY SOMBRERO/Oh, My Love	(G&G 131)	1.25	5.00	59
HOLEY SOMBRERO/Oh, My Love	(Guyden 2020)	.75	3.00	59
LOVE OR MONEY/Big Daddy & The Cat	(Jamie 1179)	1.00	4.00	61
MANSION ON THE HILL/Unchained Melody	(Jamie 1157)	.75	3.00	60
YOU ARE FREE/Depot	(Jamie 1141)	.75	3.00	59
YOU TOOK ADVANTAGE OF ME/I	(Jamie 1199)	.75	3.00	61
BLADES OF GRASS, The				
BABY YOU'RE A REAL GOOD FRIEND OF MINE/ Just Another Face	(Jubilee 5590)	.75	3.00	67
HAPPY/That's What A Boy Likes	(Jubilee 5582)	.75	3.00	67
HELP/Just Ah	(Jubilee 5605)	.75	3.00	67
YOU WON'T FIND THAT GIRL/Charlie & Fred	(Jubilee 5616)	.75	3.00	68

TITLE/FLIP	LABEL & NO.	GOOD	NEAR MINT	YR.
BLAINE, Hal, & The Young Cougars				
(DANCE WITH THE) SURFIN' BAND/ The Drummer Plays For Me	(RCA Victor 47-8223)	1.00	4.00	63
BLAKE, Buddy				
YOU PASSED ME BY/Please Convince Me	(Phillips International 3516)	2.50	10.00	58
BLAKELY, Ronee (Of Bob Dylan's Rolling Thunder Review)				
BLUEBIRD/	(Elektra 45786)	.50	2.00	73
BLANCHARD, Red				
CAPTAIN HIDEOUS/Dig That Crazy Mised-Up Kid	(Columbia 40280)	1.25	5.00	54
OPEN THE DOOR, RICHARD/Open The Door Richard (Part 2)	(Dot 15901)	.75	3.00	59
Also see Nervous Norvus				
BLANC, Mel				
HAT I GOT FOR CHRISTMAS IS TOO BEGG, THE/ Pancho's Christmas	(Capitol 3902)	1.00	4.00	58
I DESS I DOTTA DOE/Lady Bird Song	(Capitol 2718)	1.50	6.00	54
I LOVE ME/Somebody Stole My Gal	(Capitol 2470)	2.00	8.00	53
I TAN'T WAIT 'TILL QUITHMUTH/Xmas Chopsticks	(Capitol 1853)	2.50	10.00	51
I TAN'T WAIT 'TILL QUITHMUTH/Christmas Tree	(Capitol 2169)	2.00	8.00	52
I TAUT I TAW A PUDDY TAT/Yosemite Sam	(Capitol 1360)	2.50	10.00	51
K-K-KATY/Flying Saucers	(Capitol 1441)	2.00	8.00	52
LITTLE RED MONKEY/Tia Juana	(Capitol 2430)	2.00	8.00	53
MISSUS WOULDN'T APPROVE/I Tell My Troubles	(Capitol 2261)	2.00	8.00	54
MONEY/Polly, Pretty Polly	(Capitol 2764)	1.50	6.00	55
MORRIS/The Lord Bless His Soul	(Capitol 2048)	2.00	8.00	52
PUSSY CAT PARADE/Little Red Monkey	(Capitol 3170)	1.50	6.00	55
10 LITTLE BOTTLES ON THE SINK/O-K-M-N-X	(Capitol 1727)	2.50	10.00	51
THAT'S ALL FOLKS/Wontcha Ever	(Capitol 1948)	2.50	10.00	51
(With Pee Wee Hunt)				
WOODY WOODPECKER/Trixie & The Piano Pixie	(Capitol 1330)	2.50	10.00	51
Novelties				
BLANDERS, The				
JITTERBUG/Desert Sands	(Smash 2005)	3.75	15.00	65
BLANE, Marcie				
BOBBY DID/After The Laughter	(Seville 133)	.75	3.00	63
BOBBY'S GIRL/Time To Dream	(Seville 120)	.75	3.00	62
LITTLE MISS FOOL/Ragtime Sound	(Seville 126)	.75	3.00	63
SHE'LL BREAK THE STRING/The Hurtin' King	(Seville 137)	.75	3.00	64
WHAT DOES A GIRL DO?/How Can I Tell Him	(Seville 123)	.75	3.00	63
YOU GAVE MY NUMBER TO BILLY/Told You So	(Seville 128)	.75	3.00	63
BLAZE				
JAIME/	(Fraternity 237)	.50	2.00	76
LIKE A FALLING STAR/	(Epic-Sweet City 50472)	.50	2.00	77
SILVER HEELS/Rock N' Roll Madness	(Epic-Sweet City 50292)	.50	2.00	77
BLAZERS, The				
BANGALORE/Sound Of Mecca	(Acree 102)	1.00	4.00	
(Instrumentals)				
HULA HOP PARTY/Vive La Compagnie	(Golden Crest 552)	1.00	4.00	
SHORE BREAK/Beaver Patrol	(Acree 101)	1.00	4.00	63
(Instrumentals)				
BLAZONS, The				
MAGIC LAMP/Little Girl	(Baravura 5001)	3.75	15.00	
BLEND				
I'M GONNA MAKE YOU LOVE ME/ I Hope You Find Somethin'	(MCA 40961)	.50	2.00	78
BLENDAIRS, The				
MY LOVE IS JUST FOR YOU/Repetition	(Tin Pan Alley 252)	2.50	10.00	

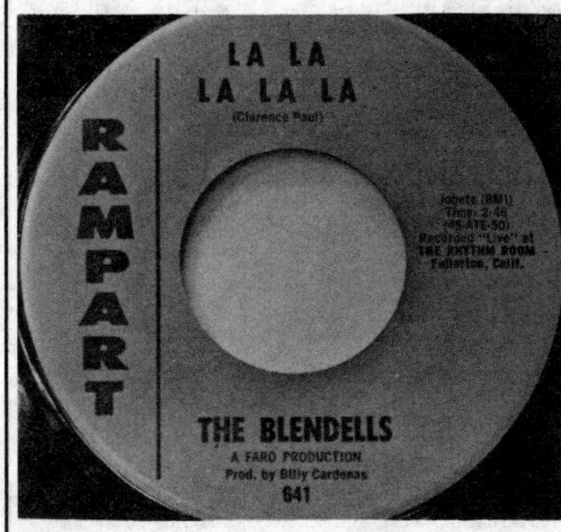

TITLE/FLIP	LABEL & NO.	GOOD	NEAR MINT	YR.
BLENDELLS, The				
LA LA LA LA LA/Huggie's Bunnies	(Rampart 641)	1.25	5.00	64
LA LA LA LA LA/Huggie's Bunnies	(Reprise 0291)	.75	3.00	64
BLEN-DELLS, The				
FOREVER/Say You're Mine	(Bella 608)	3.75	15.00	
BLENDERS, The				
BOYS THINK (EVERY GIRL'S THE SAME)/ Squat & Squirm	(Witch 117)	1.00	4.00	63
DAUGHTER/Everybody's Got A Right	(Witch 114)	1.00	4.00	63
BLENDS, The				
MUSIC MAESTRO PLEASE/1000 Miles Away	(Casa Grande 5000)	3.75	15.00	
NOW IT'S YOUR TURN/Someone To Care	(Casa Grande 5037)	3.75	15.00	
BLESSING, Michael (Michael Nesmith)				
NEW RECRUIT, THE/A Journey With Michael Blessing	(Colpix 787)	1.50	6.00	65
UNTIL IT'S TIME FOR YOU TO GO/ What Seems To Be The Trouble, Officer?	(Colpix 792)	1.50	6.00	65
BLEYER, Archie				
HERNANDO'S HIDEAWAY/S'il Vous Plait	(Candence 1241)	1.00	4.00	54
(With Maria Alba)				
HERNANDO'S HIDEAWAY/S'il Vous Plait	(Archie Bleyer 1241)	1.50	6.00	54
(With Maria Alba)				
NAUGHTY LADY OF SHADY LANE, THE/ While The Vesper Bells Were Ringing	(Candence 1254)	1.00	4.00	54
ROCKIN' GHOST, THE/Sleep Sleep Daughter	(Candence 1293)	.75	3.00	56

TITLE/FLIP	LABEL & NO.	GOOD	NEAR MINT	YR.
BLIND DATE				
I'LL TAKE YOU ANYWHERE/Twin Engines	(Windsong 11722)	.50	2.00	79
BLIND FAITH (Eric Clapton, Ginger Baker, Dave Mason, Rick Gretch)				
CAN'T FIND MY WAY BACK HOME/Presence Of The Lord	(RSO 873)	.50	2.00	77
BLISS BAND, The (Featuring Peter Bliss)				
SLIPAWAY/Take It If You Need It	(Columbia 10857)	.50	2.00	78
BLISS, Peter (Of The Bliss Band)				
TONIGHT (THERE'LL BE JUST THE TWO OF US)/	(United Artists 1019)	.50	2.00	77
BLISTERS, The				
50 MILE HIKE/Recitation	(Titanic 5005)	1.00	4.00	
(Novelties)				
BLOCKBUSTERS, The				
HI HON (Novelty)/Boogie Bop (Instrumental)	(Crystalette 725)	2.50	10.00	59
BLOCKBUSTERS, The				
GOODBYE SQUARESVILLE/Muddy (Part 1)	(Rockin' 500)	.75	3.00	68
BLODWYN PIG (With Mick Abrahams)				
DEAR JILL/Summer Day	(A&M 1158)	.75	3.00	70
Also see Jethro Tull				
BLOND				
DEEP INSIDE MY HEART/ I Will Bring You Flowers In The Morning	(Fontana F-1673)	1.25	5.00	68

TITLE/FLIP	LABEL & NO.	GOOD	NEAR MINT	YR.
BLONDIE (Featuring Deborah Harry)				
ATOMIC/	(Chrysalis 2410)	.50	2.00	80
CALL ME (THEME FROM "THE AMERICAN GIGOLO")/ Call Me (Instrumental)	(Chrysalis 2414)	.50	2.00	80
DENIS/I'm On E	(Chrysalis 2220)	.75	3.00	77
DREAMING/Living In The Real World	(Chrysalis 2379)	.50	2.00	79
HANGING ON THE TELEPHONE/Fade Away & Radiate	(Chrysalis 2271)	.50	2.00	78
HARDEST PART, THE/	(Chrysalis 2408)	.50	2.00	80
HEART OF GLASS/Heart Of Glass (Instrumental)	(Chrysalis 2275)	1.00	4.00	78
(12" single issue)				
HEART OF GLASS/11:59	(Chrysalis 2295)	.50	2.00	79
I'M GONNA LOVE YOU TOO/Just Go Away	(Chrysalis 2251)	.50	2.00	78
IN THE FLESH/	(Private Stock 45141)	.75	3.00	77
ONE WAY OR ANOTHER/Just Go Away	(Chrysalis 2336)	.50	2.00	79
X OFFENDER/	(Private Stock 45097)	.75	3.00	76
BLOOD, SWEAT & TEARS (Featuring David Clayton Thomas)				
AND WHEN I DIE/Sometimes In Winter	(Columbia 45008)	.50	2.00	69
BLUE STREET/ Somebody I Trusted (Put Out The Light)	(ABC 12310)	.50	2.00	78
GO DOWN GAMBLIN'/Valentine's Day	(Columbia 45427)	.50	2.00	71
GOT TO GET YOU INTO MY LIFE/Naked Man	(Columbia 10151)	.50	2.00	75
HI-DE-HO/The Battle	(Columbia 45204)	.50	2.00	70
I CAN'T QUIT HER/House In The Country	(Columbia 44559)	.75	3.00	68
LISA, LISTEN TO ME/Cowboys & Indians	(Columbia 45477)	.50	2.00	71
LUCRETIA MACEVIL/Lucretia's Reprise	(Columbia 45235)	.50	2.00	70
SAVE OUR SHIP/Song For John	(Columbia 45965)	.50	2.00	73
SO LONG DIXIE/Alone	(Columbia 45661)	.50	2.00	72
SPINNING WHEEL/More & More	(Columbia 44871)	.50	2.00	69
TELL ME THAT I'M WRONG/	(Columbia 46059)	.50	2.00	74
YOU'RE THE ONE/Heavy Blue	(Columbia 10400)	.50	2.00	77
YOU'VE MADE ME SO VERY HAPPY/ Blues (Part 2)	(Columbia 44776)	.50	2.00	69
Also see Kooper, Al				
BLOODROCK				
CERTAIN KIND, A/	(Capitol 3089)	.50	2.00	71
D.O.A./Children's Heritage	(Capitol 3009)	.50	2.00	71
BLOOM, Bobby				
ALL I WANNA DO IS DANCE/Taggin' Along	(White Whale WW-285)	.75	3.00	69
MAKE ME HAPPY/	(MGM 14212)	.50	2.00	71
MONTEGO BAY/Try A Little Harder	(L&R 157)	.50	2.00	70
WE'RE ALL GOIN' HOME/Careful Not To Break The Spell	(MGM 14246)	.50	2.00	71
WHERE ARE WE GOING/Of Yesterday	(Roulette 7095)	.50	2.00	71
Also see Capt. Groovey & His Bubblegum Army.				
Also see Music Explosion, The				
BLOOMFIELD, Mike, Al Kooper & Steve Stills				
SEASON OF THE WITCH/Albert Shuffle	(Columbia 44657)	.75	3.00	68
WEIGHT, THE/Man's Temptation	(Columbia 44678)	.75	3.00	68
BLOSSOMS, The				
BABY DADDY-O/No Other Love	(Capitol 4072)	1.00	4.00	58
BIG TALKIN' JIM/The Search Is Over	(Challenge 9138)	.75	3.00	62
HE PROMISED ME/Move On	(Capitol 3822)	1.00	4.00	57
LITTLE LOUIE/Have Faith In Me	(Capitol 3878)	1.00	4.00	58
SON-IN-LAW (Answer Song)/I'll Wait	(Challenge 59109)	.75	3.00	61
THINGS ARE CHANGING/Things Are Changing	(EEOC-8472)	12.50	50.00	65
(The instrumental track for this song, produced by Phil Spector, was originally intended for "Don't Hurt My Little Sister," a Beach Boy tune. Brian Wilson plays piano on this track.)				
THINGS ARE CHANGING/Things Are Changing	(EEOC-8472)	15.00	60.00	65
(Picture sleeve)				
WHAT MAKES LOVE/I'm In Love	(Okeh 7162)	.75	3.00	63

TITLE/FLIP	LABEL & NO.	GOOD	NEAR MINT	YR.
WRITE ME A LETTER/Hard To Get	(Challenge 9122)	.75	3.00	61
Also see Eddy, Duane				
Also see Soxx, Bob B & Blue Jeans				
Also see Wildcats				
Also See Love, Darlene				
BLUE (With Ian McMillan, Hugh Nicholson, & Dave Nicholson)				
ANOTHER NIGHT TIME FLIGHT/	(Rocket 40762)	.50	2.00	77
BRING BACK THE LOVE/Falling	(Rocket 40801)	.50	2.00	77
CAPTURE YOUR HEART/The Shepherd	(Rocket 40706)	.50	2.00	77
COOKIE IN A JAR/	(RSO 508)	.50	2.00	75
LITTLE JODY/	(RSO 405)	.50	2.00	74
This group was known in England as the Poets. Ian McMillan & Hugh Nicholson were in Marmalade, Dave Nicholson was in the Mob.				
BLUE ASH				
ANYTIME AT ALL/She's So Nice	(Mercury 73455)	.50	2.00	73
BLUE BARRON, The				
ARE YOU LONESOME TONIGHT?/ Penny Wise & Love Foolish	(MGM 10628)	1.25	5.00	50
CRUSING DOWN THE RIVER/ Powder Your Face With Sunshine	(MGM 8013)	1.25	5.00	49
BLUE BELLS, The				
ATLANTIS/Moccasin	(Last Chance 1)	.75	3.00	
BLUE CHEER				
FEATHERS FROM YOUR TREE/Sun Cycle	(Philips 40561)	1.00	4.00	68
FEATHERS FROM YOUR TREE/Sun Cycle (With Picture Sleeve)	(Philips 40561)	3.00	12.00	68
FOOL/Ain't That The Way	(Philips 40682)	1.00	4.00	70
JUST A LITTLE BIT/Gypsy Ball	(Philips 40541)	1.00	4.00	68
PILOT/Babaji	(Philips 40691)	1.00	4.00	70
SUMMERTIME BLUES/Out Of Focus	(Philips 40516)	.75	3.00	68
BLUE CRYSTALS, The				
BROKE UP/Queen Of All The Girls	(Mercury 71455)	1.00	4.00	59
BLUE, David				
ANOTHER ONE LIKE ME/	(Asylum 11001)	.50	2.00	73
OUTLAW MAN/Troubadour Song	(Asylum 11015)	.50	2.00	73
David is the brother of Leonard Cohen.				
BLUE DIAMONDS, The				
LITTLE SHIP/Carmen My Love	(London 10006)	.75	3.00	62
RAMONA/All Of Me	(London 1954)	.75	3.00	60
BLUE ECHOES, The				
BLUE BELLE BOUNCE/Tiger Talk	(Itzy 11)	1.25	5.00	
BLUE EYED SOUL (With Billy Vera)				
SHADOW OF YOUR LOVE, THE/Look Gently At The Rain	(Cameo 401)	1.25	5.00	66
TONIGHT I AM KING/Something New	(Cameo 423)	1.25	5.00	66
BLUE HAZE				
SMOKE GETS IN YOUR EYES/Anna Rosanna	(A&M 1357)	.50	2.00	72
BLUE JAYS, The				
CAVE-MAN LOVE/	(Roulette 4264)	1.00	4.00	60
PRACTICAL JOKER/Barbara	(Roulette 4169)	1.00	4.00	59
SWEET GEORGIA BROWN/	(Laurie 3037)	1.00	4.00	59
BLUE LITES, The				
FOREVER/They Don't Know My Heart	(Bay Sound 67003)	5.00	20.00	
LONELY MAN'S PRAYER, A/Bony Marony	(Bay Sound 67007)	3.75	15.00	
BLUE MINK (With Roger Cook & Madeline Bell)				
BY THE DEVIL I WAS TEMPTED/	(MCA 40031)	.50	2.00	73
MELTING POT/But Not Forever	(Philips 40658)	.75	3.00	69
OUR WORLD/Respect To Mr. Jones	(Philips 40686)	.75	3.00	70
Also see David & Jonathan				
BLUE MOONS, The				
SUNDAY KIND OF LOVE, A/Peace Of Mind	(Jaguar 1001)	1.50	6.00	
BLUE OYSTER CULT				
BORN TO BE WILD/Born To Be Wild (Live)	(Columbia 10169)	.50	2.00	75
CAREER OF EVIL/Dominance & Submission	(Columbia 10046)	.50	2.00	74
(DON'T FEAR) THE REAPER/Tattoo Vampire	(Columbia 10384)	.50	2.00	76
GODZILLA/Nosferatu	(Columbia 10697)	.50	2.00	78
GOIN' THROUGH THE MOTIONS/Searchin' For Celine	(Columbia 10659)	.50	2.00	77
IN THEE/Lonely Teardrops	(Columbia 11055)	.50	2.00	79
THIS AIN'T THE SUMMER OF LOVE/Debbie Denise	(Columbia 10560)	.50	2.00	77
WE GOTTA GET OUT OF THIS PLACE/ E.T.I. (Extra Terrestrial Intelligence)	(Columbia 10841)	.50	2.00	78
YOU'RE NOT THE ONE (I WAS LOOKING FOR)/	(Columbia 11145)	.50	2.00	79
BLUE RAYS, The				
WHO (WILL IT BE TODAY)/Come On Baby	(Phillips 40186)	2.00	8.00	64
BLUE RIDGE RANGERS, The (Featuring John Fogerty)				
BACK IN THE HILLS/You Don't Owe Me	(Fantasy 710)	.50	2.00	73
BACK IN THE HILLS/You Don't Owe Me	(Fantasy 711)	.50	2.00	73
(These songs were issued on both Fantasy 710 & 711)				
BLUE RIDGE MOUNTAIN BLUES/ Have Thine Own Way, Lord	(Fantasy 683)	.50	2.00	72
HEARTS OF STONE/Somewhere Listening	(Fantasy 700)	.50	2.00	73
JAMBALAYA/Workin' On A Building	(Fantasy 689)	.50	2.00	72

TITLE/FLIP	LABEL & NO.	GOOD	NEAR MINT	YR.
BLUE RONDOS, The				
LITTLE BABY/I Go For You	(Parkway 937)	.75	3.00	64

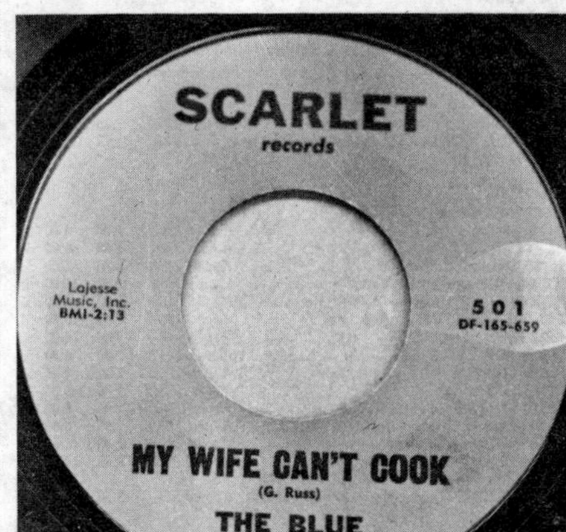

TITLE/FLIP	LABEL & NO.	GOOD	NEAR MINT	YR.
BLUE SATINS, The				
MY WIFE CAN'T COOK/You Don't Know Me	(Scarlet 501)	1.25	5.00	
BLUE SKY BOYS, The				
CHERIE/Just Another One In Love With You	(Blue Sky 101)	.75	3.00	
BLUE SONNETS, The				
THANK YOU MR. MOON/It's Never Too Late	(Columbia 42793)	2.50	10.00	63
BLUE STARS, The				
LULLABY OF BIRDLAND/That's My Girl	(Mercury 70742)	1.00	4.00	55
BLUE STARS, The				
ERLENE/My Love Will Never Die	(Arcade 3/4)	.50	2.00	
I ONLY HAVE EYES FOR YOU/Hey Pretty Baby	(Arcade 5/6)	.50	2.00	
BLUE STEEL				
NO MORE LONELY NIGHTS/Twist One Up	(Infinity 50029)	.50	2.00	79
SHARK/	(Infinity 50044)	.50	2.00	79
BLUE SWEDE				
DR. ROCK & ROLL/	(EMI-Capitol 4065)	.50	2.00	75
HOOKED ON A FEELING/Gotta Have Your Love	(Capitol 3627)	.75	3.00	74
HOOKED ON A FEELING/Gotta Have Your Love	(EMI-Capitol 3627)	.50	2.00	73
HUSH-I'M ALIVE/Lonely Sunday Afternoon	(EMI-Capitol 4029)	.50	2.00	75
NEVER MY LOVE/Pinewood Rally	(EMI 3938)	.50	2.00	74
SILLY MILLY/Lonely Sunday Afternoon	(EMI 3893)	.50	2.00	74
BLUE WOOD				
TURN AROUND/Happy Jack Mine	(Jet Set 4)	1.00	4.00	
BLUENOTES, The				
I DON'T KNOW WHAT IT IS/Summer Love	(Brooke 111)	1.00	4.00	59
I'M GONNA FIND OUT/Forever On My Mind	(Brooke 116)	.75	3.00	60
BLUES BROTHERS, The (Dan Aykroyd & John Belushi)				
(I GOT EVERYTHING I NEED)/Hey Bartender	(Atlantic 3576)	.50	2.00	79
JAILHOUSE ROCK/	(Atlantic 3758)	.50	2.00	80
RUBBER BISCUIT/"B" Movie Box Car Blues	(Atlantic 3564)	.50	2.00	79
SOUL MAN/Excusez Moi Mon Cherie	(Atlantic 3545)	.50	2.00	78
BLUES IMAGE				
GAS LAMPS & CLAY/Running The Water	(Atco 6777)	.50	2.00	70
LAY YOUR SWEET LOVE ON ME/Outside Was Night	(Atco 6718)	.50	2.00	69
RIDE CAPTAIN RIDE/Pay My Dues	(Atco 6746)	.50	2.00	70
RISE UP/Take Me Back	(Atco 6798)	.50	2.00	71
BLUES MAGOOS, The				
I CAN HEAR THE GRASS GROW/Yellow Rose	(Mercury 72838)	1.00	4.00	68
I WANNA BE THERE/Summer Is The Man	(Mercury 72707)	1.00	4.00	67
NEVER GOIN' BACK TO GEORGIA/ Feelin' Time (I Can Feel It)	(ABC 11250)	.75	3.00	68
ONE BY ONE/Dante's Inferno	(Mercury 72692)	1.00	4.00	67
PIPE DREAM/There's A Chance We Can Make It	(Mercury 72660)	1.00	4.00	67
SO I'M WRONG & YOU ARE RIGHT/ People Had No Faces	(Verve Folkways 5006)	2.00	8.00	66
SO I'M WRONG & YOU ARE RIGHT/ People Had No Faces	(Verve Folkways 5044)	1.25	5.00	67
THERE SHE GOES/ Life Is Just A Cher O' Bowlies	(Mercury 72729)	1.00	4.00	67
TOBACCO ROAD/Sometimes	(Mercury 72590)	1.00	4.00	66
(WE AIN'T GOT) NOTHING YET/Gotta Get Away	(Mercury 72622)	1.00	4.00	66
WHO DO YOU LOVE/Let Your Love Ride	(Ganim 1000)	2.50	10.00	66
Also see Kaz, Eric				
Also see American Flyer				
Also see Blues Project, The				
BLUES PROJECT, The				
BACK DOOR MAN/Violets Of Dawn	(Verve Folkways 5004)	1.25	5.00	66
CATCH THE WIND/I Want To Be Your Drive	(Verve Folkways 5013)	1.25	5.00	66
GENTLE DREAMS/Lost In The Shuffle	(Verve Folkways 5063)	1.25	5.00	67
I CAN'T KEEP FROM CRYING/ The Way My Baby Walks	(Verve Folkways 5032)	1.25	5.00	66
NO TIME LIKE THE RIGHT TIME/Steve's Song	(Verve Folkways 5040)	1.25	5.00	67
WHERE THERE'S SMOKE THERE'S FIRE/ Goin' Down Louisiana	(Verve Folkways 5019)	1.25	5.00	67
Also see Bear				
Also see Blues Magoos, The				
BLUESVILLE				
DON'T THINK TWICE, IT'S ALRIGHT/As Tears Go By (Instrumentals)	(Jerden 788)	.75	3.00	66
BLUNSTONE, Colin (Of The Zombies)				
ANDORRA/	(Epic 11004)	.50	2.00	73
CAROLINE GOODBYE/Misty Roses	(Epic 10826)	.50	2.00	71
I DON'T BELIEVE IN MIRACLES/	(Epic 10948)	.50	2.00	73
I'LL NEVER FORGET YOU/You Are The Way For Me	(Rocket 11356)	.50	2.00	78
I WANT SOME MORE/	(Epic 10981)	.50	2.00	73
PHOTOGRAPH/	(Rocket 11412)	.50	2.00	78
SAY YOU DON'T MIND/	(Epic 10868)	.50	2.00	72
BLUR, Ben				
CHARIOT RACE/The Flight (by Aaron Plane) (Novelty/Break-in)	(Mark X 8007)	1.25	5.00	60

TITLE/FLIP	LABEL & NO.	GOOD	NEAR MINT	YR.
BO, Eddie				
DINKY DOO/Everybody, Everything Needs Love	(Capitol 4617)	.75	3.00	61
DINKY DOO/Everybody, Everything Needs Love	(Ric 981)	1.00	4.00	61
I LOVE TO ROCK & ROLL/I'll Keep On Trying	(Ace 555)	.75	3.00	59
BOATZ				
IT WAS ONLY THE RADIO/Blame It On The Future	(Capricorn 0319)	.50	2.00	79
BOB & JERRY (Bob Feldman & Jerry Goldstein)				
CHUBBY/Nursery Rhyme Folk	(Musicor 1018)	1.00	4.00	62
(The complete title "Chubby (Isn't Chubby Anymore)" appears on promotional copies only.)				
WE'RE THE GUYS (Answer song)/Dreamy Eyes	(Columbia 42162)	1.50	6.00	61
BOB & LUCILLE (With Lucille Starr)				
EENY-MEENY-MINEY-MOE/Demon Lover	(Ditto 121)	6.25	25.00	59
EENY-MEENY-MINEY-MOE/Big Kiss	(King 5631)	2.00	8.00	62
Also see Canadian Sweethearts, The				
BOB & MARCIA				
PIED PIPER/Save Me	(A&M 1294)	.50	2.00	72
BOB & RAY				
MAMA LOVE/Go Home Ginny, Ginny	(Modern Sound 6906)	2.00	8.00	
BOB & SHERI				
SURFER MOON, THE/Humpty Dumpty	(Safari 101)	150.00	600.00	61
(Brian Wilson's first record production. Original commercial copies were on a light blue label; promotional copies on a white label.)				
BOB & THE AVERONES				
PLEASE SAY YOU WANT ME/Patti	(Brent 7054)	1.50	6.00	64
BOB & THE MESSENGERS				
SPLASH DOWN/Bob's Groove	(Rust 5069)	1.00	4.00	63
BOB B. SOXX & THE BLUE JEANS (Bobby Sheen with the Blossoms)				
NOT TOO YOUNG TO GET MARRIED/Annette	(Philles 113)	1.00	4.00	63
WHY DO LOVERS BREAK EACH OTHER'S HEARTS/ Dr. Kaplan's	(Philles 110)	1.00	4.00	63
ZIP-A-DEE DOO-DAH/Flip & Nitty	(Philles 107)	1.00	4.00	62
BOBBIE & THE BEAUS				
LOSING GAME/Melvin	(Unart 2009)	1.00	4.00	59
BOBBIE & THE PLEASERS				
MONSTER, THE/The Switch	(Jamie 1118)	1.25	5.00	59
BOBBIES, The				
(SHE) PUT ME DOWN (PART 1)/ (She) Put Me Down (Part 2)	(Sonny 1001)	.75	3.00	66
BOBBY & THE CONSOLES (Featuring Bobby Pedrick Jr.)				
MY JELLY BEAN/Nita	(Diamond 141)	6.25	25.00	63
BOBBY & THE ORBITS				
TEEN AGE LOVE/What Do I Say	(Seeco 6030)	1.25	5.00	59
BOBBY & THE VELVETS (With Bobby Sanders)				
I PROMISE/Now We Know	(Rason 501)	3.75	15.00	59
BOBBY-PINS, The				
DARLING, DON'T LEAVE ME/I Want You	(Okeh 4-7110)	1.00	4.00	59
WHY DID YOU GO/I Wanna Love	(Mercury 72193)	.75	3.00	63
BOBOLINKS, The				
CHOCOLATE ICE CREAM/Mechanical Man	(Key 575)	1.00	4.00	59
ELVIS PRESLEY'S SERGEANT/Your Cotton Pickin' Heart	(Key 573)	2.50	10.00	59
LONESOME WIND/Message From Me	(Tune 226)	1.00	4.00	61
BOB-O-LINKS, The				
I PROMISED/Now We Know	(Rason 501)	3.75	15.00	62
I PROMISE/Mr. Grog	(Hi-Ho 101)	2.00	8.00	62
BOBSLED & THE TOBAGGANS (With Bruce Johnston)				
HERE WE GO/Sea & Ski	(Cameo 400)	1.50	6.00	66
BODNER, Phil, Sextet				
HIGH LIFE, THE/Hanky Panky (Instrumentals)	(RCA Victor 47-8220)	.75	3.00	63
BOENZEE CRYQUE				
SKY GONE GRAY/Still In Love With You Baby	(Chicory 406)	2.00	8.00	67
Group members Rusty Young & George Grantham later joined Buffalo Springfield. Shortly thereafter they formed Poco.				
BOGIE, Col. Doug				
AWAY IN THE MANGER/Cokey Cokey	(ABC 12148)	.50	2.00	75
BOLGER, Ray				
I SAID MY PAJAMAS (& PUT ON MY PRAYERS)/ Dearie (With Ethel Merman)	(Decca 24873)	1.25	5.00	50
BOLIN, Tommy (Of Deep Purple)				
GRIND, THE/Homeward Strut	(Nemperor 004)	.50	2.00	76
SAVANNAH WOMAN/	(Nemperor 005)	.50	2.00	76
Also see James Gang, The				
BOLL WEEVIL				
FREE-DUMB RIDERS/Free-Dumb Riders (Part 2) (Novelty/Break-in)	(Funn 1001)	3.75	15.00	
BOMPERS, The (Featuring Carol Connors)				
DO THE BOMP/Early Bird	(HBR 441)	1.25	5.00	65
BON BONS, The				
EVERYBODY WANTS MY BOYFRIEND/Each Time	(Coral 62435)	1.50	6.00	64
WHAT'S WRONG WITH RINGO/Come On Baby	(Coral 62402)	2.00	8.00	64
Also see Shangra-Las, The				
BON-AIRES, The				
BLUE BEAT/	(Rust TR3)	5.00	20.00	62
BYE BYE/My Love My Love	(Rust 5077)	2.50	10.00	62
SHRINE OF ST. CECILIA, THE/Jeanie Baby	(Rust 5097)	2.50	10.00	62
BOND				
DANCIN' (ON A SATURDAY NIGHT)/Mardi Gras	(Columbia 10101)	.50	2.00	75
BOND, Bobby (With the Bandits)				
LIVIN' DOLL/Sweet Love	(Danceland 1000)	.75	3.00	61
BONDS, Gary "U.S." (Gary Anderson)				
COPY CAT/I'll Change To That Too	(Legrand 1020)	.75	3.00	62
DEAR LADY/Havin So Much Fun	(Legrand 1015)	1.00	4.00	62
DEAR LADY TWIST/Havin So Much Fun	(Legrand 1015)	.75	3.00	62
(Second pressing with "Twist" added to title.)				
DO THE BUMPSIE/Beaches U.S.A.	(Legrand 1039)	.75	3.00	65
DO THE LIMBO WITH ME/ Where Did The Naughty Little Girl Go	(Legrand 1025)	.75	3.00	63
I DIG THIS STATION/Mixed Up Faculty	(Legrand 1022)	.75	3.00	62
KING KONG'S MONKEY/My Sweet Ruby Rose	(Legrand 1031)	.75	3.00	64
NEW ORLEANS/Please Forgive Me	(Legrand 1003)	.75	3.00	60
(Shown as by U.S. Bonds)				

TITLE/FLIP	LABEL & NO.	GOOD	NEAR MINT	YR.
NO MORE HOMEWORK/She's Alright	(Legrand 1029)	.75	3.00	63
NOT ME/Give Me One More Chance	(Legrand 1005)	.75	3.00	61
(Shown as by U.S. Bonds)				
PERDIDO (Part 1)/Perdido (Part 2)	(Legrand 1030)	.75	3.00	64
QUARTER TO THREE/Time Ole' Story	(Legrand, 1008)	.75	3.00	61
(Shown as by U.S. Bonds)				
SCHOOL IS IN/Trip To The Moon	(Legrand 1012)	.75	3.00	61
SCHOOL IS OUT/One Million Tears	(Legrand 1009)	.75	3.00	61
SEVEN DAY WEEKEND/Gettin' A Groove	(Legrand 1019)	.75	3.00	62
TAKE ME BACK TO NEW ORLEANS/I'm That Kind Of Guy	(Legrand 1040)	.75	3.00	65
TWIST, TWIST SENORA/Food Of Love	(Legrand 1018)	.75	3.00	62
WHAT A DREAM/I Don't Wanna Wait	(Legrand 1027)	.75	3.00	63

Also see Church Street Five, The
Also see Facenda, Tommy

BONDSMEN, The

TITLE/FLIP	LABEL & NO.	GOOD	NEAR MINT	YR.
Wipe Out '66/People Say	(Dawn 303)	.75	3.00	66

BONNER, Garry (Of The Magicians)

TITLE/FLIP	LABEL & NO.	GOOD	NEAR MINT	YR.
HEART OF JULIET JONES/Me About You	(Columbia 44306)	.50	2.00	67
I CAN'T TAKE IT/	(Atlantic-Migration 3275)	.50	2.00	75
JUG OF WINE/Saddest	(Columbia 44703)	.75	3.00	68
SHOULD ANYBODY ASK/	(Atlantic-Migration 3234)	.50	2.00	74

BONNEVILLES, The

TITLE/FLIP	LABEL & NO.	GOOD	NEAR MINT	YR.
BONNEVILLES STOMP/Knock Around	(Question Mark 103)	1.00	4.00	
DIRTY HERB/High Noon Stomp (Instrumental)	(Question Mark 101)	1.00	4.00	

BONNEVILLES, The

TITLE/FLIP	LABEL & NO.	GOOD	NEAR MINT	YR.
GIVE ME YOUR LOVE/Until You Say We're Through	(Capri 102)	1.25	5.00	
LORRAINE/Zu Zu	(Barry 104)	1.50	6.00	62
LORRAINE/Zu Zu	(Munich 103)	5.00	20.00	62

BONNIE & THE BUTTERFLYS

TITLE/FLIP	LABEL & NO.	GOOD	NEAR MINT	YR.
I SAW HIM STANDING THERE (Answer Song)/Dust Storm	(Smash 1878)	1.50	6.00	64

BONNIE & THE DENIMS

TITLE/FLIP	LABEL & NO.	GOOD	NEAR MINT	YR.
CLASS REUNION/Time Will Tell	(LLP 101)	.75	3.00	65

BONNIE & THE TREASURES

TITLE/FLIP	LABEL & NO.	GOOD	NEAR MINT	YR.
HOME OF THE BRAVE/Our Song	(Phi Dan 5005)	3.75	15.00	65

Bonnie is Veronica of the Ronettes, also known as Ronnie Spector.

BONNIE FLOYD & THE ORIGINAL UNTOUCHABLES

TITLE/FLIP	LABEL & NO.	GOOD	NEAR MINT	YR.
I'M JUST A POOR BOY/	(Bright Yellow 1067)	1.25	5.00	

BONNIE SISTERS, The

TITLE/FLIP	LABEL & NO.	GOOD	NEAR MINT	YR.
CRY BABY/				
I Saw Mommy Cha Cha Cha With You Know Who	(Rainbow 328)	1.00	4.00	55
DO YOU KNOW/Little Bo Peep	(Rainbow 336)	1.00	4.00	56
TRACK THAT CAT/Wandering Heart	(Rainbow 333)	1.00	4.00	56

BONNY, Billy

TITLE/FLIP	LABEL & NO.	GOOD	NEAR MINT	YR.
BOBBY JEAN/Bootleg Rock	(Mark '56 830)	1.00	4.00	59

BONO, Sonny: see Sonny

BONOFF, Karla

TITLE/FLIP	LABEL & NO.	GOOD	NEAR MINT	YR.
I CAN'T HOLD ON/Falling Star	(Columbia 10618)	.50	2.00	77
ISN'T IT ALWAYS LOVE/Rose In The Garden	(Columbia 10710)	.50	2.00	78
SOMEONE TO SAY DOWN BESIDE ME/				
Rose In The Garden	(Columbia 10751)	.50	2.00	78
TROUBLE AGAIN/If He's Ever Near	(Columbia 11041)	.50	2.00	79

Also see Bryndle

BONQUETS, Tootie

TITLE/FLIP	LABEL & NO.	GOOD	NEAR MINT	YR.
YOU DONE ME WRONG/The Conquer	(Parkway 887)	5.00	20.00	

BONUS, Jack

TITLE/FLIP	LABEL & NO.	GOOD	NEAR MINT	YR.
ST. LOUIS MISSOURI BOY/Sweet Mahidabelle	(Grunt 0504)	.50	2.00	72

BONZO DOG BAND, The (With Neil Innes & Viv Stanshall)

TITLE/FLIP	LABEL & NO.	GOOD	NEAR MINT	YR.
I'M THE URBAN SPACEMAN/Canyons Of Your Mind	(Liberty 66345)	1.00	4.00	68
I'M THE URBAN SPACEMAN/				
Canyons Of Your Mind	(United Artists 50809)	.50	2.00	71
SLUSH/	(United Artists 50943)	.50	2.00	72

This group may also be shown as The Bonzo Dog Doo-Dah Band. The producer, Apollo C. Vermouth, shown on some of their records is actually Paul McCartney.

BOO BOO & BUNKIE

TITLE/FLIP	LABEL & NO.	GOOD	NEAR MINT	YR.
TURN AROUND/This Old Town	(Brent 7045)	1.00	4.00	63

BOOK ENDS, The

TITLE/FLIP	LABEL & NO.	GOOD	NEAR MINT	YR.
MINNOWS, CRICKETS, WORMS, BEER/All Night Ride	(Virginia 3002)	1.25	5.00	60

BOOKER, James

TITLE/FLIP	LABEL & NO.	GOOD	NEAR MINT	YR.
GONZO/Cool Turkey	(Peacock 1697)	.75	3.00	60

BOOKER T. & PRISCILLA (Booker T. Jones & Priscilla Coolidge-Jones)

TITLE/FLIP	LABEL & NO.	GOOD	NEAR MINT	YR.
SHE/The Wedding Song	(A&M 1298)	.50	2.00	72

Priscilla is Rita Coolidge's sister.

BOOKER T. & THE MG's (Featuring Booket T. Jones)

TITLE/FLIP	LABEL & NO.	GOOD	NEAR MINT	YR.
BOOT-LEG/Outrage	(Stax 169)	.75	3.00	65
CHINESE CHECKERS/Plum Nellie	(Stax 137)	.75	3.00	63
GREEN ONIONS/Behave Yourself	(Stax 127)	.75	3.00	62
JELLYBREAD/'Aw Mercy	(Stax 131)	.75	3.00	62
MO-ONIONS/Fannie Mae	(Stax 142)	.75	3.00	64
SILVER BELLS/Winter Show	(Stax 236)	.75	3.00	67
SOUL DRESSING/MG Party	(Stax 153)	.75	3.00	64
Instrumentals				

BOOKWORMS, The

TITLE/FLIP	LABEL & NO.	GOOD	NEAR MINT	YR.
DITCHIN'/Just Cruisin' Around	(Titan 1714)	1.00	4.00	61

BOOMTOWN RATS, The

TITLE/FLIP	LABEL & NO.	GOOD	NEAR MINT	YR.
I DON'T LIKE MONDAYS/It's All The Rage	(Columbia 11117)	.50	2.00	79
RAT TRAP/Do The Rat	(Columbia 10960)	.50	2.00	79

BOONE, Daniel

TITLE/FLIP	LABEL & NO.	GOOD	NEAR MINT	YR.
ANNABELLE/Sleepyhead	(Mercury 73339)	.50	2.00	72
BEAUTIFUL SUNDAY/Truly Julie	(Mercury 73281)	.50	2.00	72
DADDY DON'T YOU WALK SO FAST/Tiger Woman	(Epic 10787)	.50	2.00	72
LOVE SPELL/Lelly I Love You	(Mercury 73461)	.50	2.00	74
SKY DIVER/Do You Thank The Lord	(Mercury 73428)	.50	2.00	74
SUNSHINE LOVER/Crying	(Mercury 73357)	.50	2.00	73

BOONE, Len

TITLE/FLIP	LABEL & NO.	GOOD	NEAR MINT	YR.
LOVE WON'T BE DENIED/	(Chrysalis 2227)	.50	2.00	78
THERE'S NO ME WITHOUT YOU (With Holly Sherwood)/	(Chrysalis 2317)	.50	2.00	79

BOONE, Pat

TITLE/FLIP	LABEL & NO.	GOOD	NEAR MINT	YR.
AIN'T THAT A SHAME?/Tennessee Saturday Night	(Dot 15377)	1.25	5.00	55
APRIL LOVE/When The Swallows Come Back To Capistrano	(Dot 15660)	1.00	4.00	57
AT MY FRONT DOOR (CRAZY LITTLE MAMA)/				
No Other Arms	(Dot 15422)	1.25	5.00	55
BEACH GIRL/Little Honda	(Dot 16658)	1.00	4.00	64
BEYOND THE SUNSET/My Faithful Heart	(Dot 16006)	.75	3.00	59
DEAR JOHN/Alabam	(Dot 16152)	.75	3.00	60
DELIA GONE/Candy Sweet	(Dot 16122)	.75	3.00	60
DON'T FORBID ME/Anastasia	(Dot 15521)	1.00	4.00	56
FOOL'S HALL OF FAME/Brightest Wishing Star	(Dot 15982)	.75	3.00	59
FOR A PENNY/The Wang Dang Taffy-Apple Tango	(Dot 15914)	.75	3.00	59
FOR MY GOOD FORTUNE/Gee But It's Lonely	(Dot 15825)	.75	3.00	58
FRIENDLY PERSUASION/Chains Of Love	(Dot 15490)	1.00	4.00	56
GEE WHITTAKERS!/Take The Time	(Dot 15435)	1.25	5.00	55
I ALMOST LOST MY MIND/I'm In Love With You	(Dot 15472)	1.00	4.00	56
I NEED SOMEONE/Loving You Madly	(Republic 7084)	2.50	10.00	54
I NEED SOMEONE/My Heart Belongs To You	(Republic 7119)	2.00	8.00	55
IF DREAMS CAME TRUE/That's How Much I Love You	(Dot 15785)	.75	3.00	58
I'LL BE HOME/Tutti' Frutti	(Dot 15443)	1.25	5.00	58
I'LL REMEMBER TONIGHT/The Mardi Gras March	(Dot 15840)	.75	3.00	58
I'LL SEE YOU IN MY DREAMS/Pictures In The Fire	(Dot 16312)	.75	3.00	61
JOHNNY WILL/Just Let Me Dream	(Dot 16284)	.75	3.00	61
LONG TALL SALLY/Just As Long As I'm With You	(Dot 15457)	1.25	5.00	56
LOVE LETTERS IN THE SAND/Bernadine	(Dot 15570)	1.00	4.00	57
MOODY RIVER/A Thousand Years	(Dot 16209)	.75	3.00	61
QUANDO, QUANDO, QUANDO/Willing & Eager	(Dot 16349)	.75	3.00	62
REMEMBER TO BE MINE/Half Way Chance With You	(Republic 7062)	2.50	10.00	53
REMEMBER YOU'RE MINE/				
There's A Gold Mine In The Sky	(Dot 15602)	1.00	4.00	57
SPEEDY GONZALES/The Locket	(Dot 16368)	.75	3.00	62
SUGAR MOON/Cherie, I Love You	(Dot 15750)	.75	3.00	58
THERE'S A MOON OUT TONIGHT/Exodus Song, The	(Dot 16176)	.75	3.00	60
TWIXT TWELVE & TWENTY/Rock Boll Weevil	(Dot 15955)	.75	3.00	59
TWO HEARTS/Tra La La	(Dot 15338)	1.25	5.00	55
UNTIL YOU TELL ME SO/My Heart Belongs To You	(Republic 7049)	2.50	10.00	54
WALKING THE FLOOR OVER YOU/Spring Rain	(Dot 16073)	.75	3.00	60
(WELCOME) NEW LOVERS/Words	(Dot 16048)	.75	3.00	60
(WELCOME) NEW LOVERS/Words	(Dot S-220)	1.50	6.00	60
(Stereo single issue)				
WHY BABY WHY/I'm Waiting Just For You	(Dot 15545)	1.00	4.00	57
WITH THE WIND & THE RAIN IN YOUR HAIR/				
Good Rockin' Tonight	(Dot 15888)	.75	3.00	58
WITH THE WIND & THE RAIN IN YOUR HAIR/				
Good Rockin' Tonight	(Dot S-200)	1.25	5.00	59
(Stereo single issue)				
WONDERFUL TIME UP THERE, A/It's Too Soon To Know	(Dot 15690)	.75	3.00	58

Also see Fontane Sisters, The

BOONES FARM

TITLE/FLIP	LABEL & NO.	GOOD	NEAR MINT	YR.
GOOD OLD FEELIN'/	(Columbia 45713)	.50	2.00	73
IF YOU CAN'T BE MY WOMAN/	(Columbia 45623)	.50	2.00	73

BOOT, Joe, & The Winds

TITLE/FLIP	LABEL & NO.	GOOD	NEAR MINT	YR.
ROCK & ROLL RADIO/	(Celestial 111)	.50	2.00	

BOOTLES, The

TITLE/FLIP	LABEL & NO.	GOOD	NEAR MINT	YR.
I'LL LET YOU HOLD MY HAND/Never Till Now	(GNP Crescendo 311)	1.25	5.00	64
(Answer Song)				

BOP SHOP, The

TITLE/FLIP	LABEL & NO.	GOOD	NEAR MINT	YR.
DON'T SAY GOODNIGHT/7 Wonders Of The World	(Kelway 105)	.50	2.00	
NUT'S N' SPRINKLES/Cry Baby Cry	(Larric 7301)	.50	2.00	
STARS, THE/That's How I Feel	(Horizon Ent. Ltd.)	.50	2.00	

BOPTONES, The

TITLE/FLIP	LABEL & NO.	GOOD	NEAR MINT	YR.
BY MY PUSSY CAT/I Had A Love	(Ember 1043)	1.25	5.00	59

BORESON, Stan, & Doug Setterberg

TITLE/FLIP	LABEL & NO.	GOOD	NEAR MINT	YR.
TELEPHONE, THE/Swanson, Swenson, Jenson	(Kapp 198)	1.00	4.00	57

BOSMAN, Millie

TITLE/FLIP	LABEL & NO.	GOOD	NEAR MINT	YR.
REALLY SATISFIED/Your Good Doin'	(Cat 107)	.75	3.00	

BOSS FIVE, The

TITLE/FLIP	LABEL & NO.	GOOD	NEAR MINT	YR.
PLEASE MR. PRESIDENT/You Cheat Too Much	(Impact 1003)	1.00	4.00	

BOSSMEN, The

TITLE/FLIP	LABEL & NO.	GOOD	NEAR MINT	YR.
BABY BOY/You & I	(Lucky Eleven 231)	1.25	5.00	66
BAD GIRL/A Rainy Day	(Date 1577)	1.00	4.00	67
HELP ME BABY/Thanks To You	(M&L 1809)	1.25	5.00	
HERE'S CONGRATULATIONS/Bad Girl	(Dicto 1001)	1.25	5.00	
LITTLE GIRL/Sunshine	(Date 1596)	1.00	4.00	68
TAKE A LOOK/It's A Shame	(Soft 121)	1.50	6.00	
TINA MARIA/On The Road	(Lucky Eleven 001)	1.25	5.00	
WAIT & SEE/You're The Girl For Me	(Lucky Eleven 227)	1.25	5.00	66
WAIT & SEE/You're The Girl For Me	(Dicto 1002)	1.50	6.00	

BOSTON

TITLE/FLIP	LABEL & NO.	GOOD	NEAR MINT	YR.
DON'T LOOK BACK/The Journey	(Epic 50590)	.50	2.00	78
FEELIN' SATISFIED/Used To Bad News	(Epic 50677)	.50	2.00	79
LONG TIME/Let Me Take You Home Tonight	(Epic 50329)	.50	2.00	77
MAN I'LL NEVER BE, A/Don't Be Afraid	(Epic 50638)	.50	2.00	78
PEACE OF MIND/Foreplay	(Epic 50381)	.50	2.00	77
MORE THAN A FEELING/Smokin'	(Epic 50266)	.50	2.00	76

BOSTON CRABS, The

TITLE/FLIP	LABEL & NO.	GOOD	NEAR MINT	YR.
DOWN IN MEXICO/Who	(Capitol 5493)	.75	3.00	64
GIN HOUSE/You Didn't Have To Be So Nice	(Tower 368)	.75	3.00	66

BOSTON POPS ORCHESTRA, The

TITLE/FLIP	LABEL & NO.	GOOD	NEAR MINT	YR.
I WANT TO HOLD YOUR HAND/Hello Dolly	(RCA Victor 47-8378)	.75	3.00	64
SYNCOPATED CLOCK, THE/Classical Juke Box	(RCA Victor 47-3044)	1.00	4.00	51
Instrumentals				

BOSTON TEA PARTY, The

TITLE/FLIP	LABEL & NO.	GOOD	NEAR MINT	YR.
FREE SERVICE/I'm Tellin' You	(Flick-Disc 900)	1.00	4.00	
WORDS/Spinach	(Challenge 59368)	1.00	4.00	66

BOSWELL, Bolliver

TITLE/FLIP	LABEL & NO.	GOOD	NEAR MINT	YR.
CENTER CITY SEX EDUCATION SEMINAR/	(Pyro 55)	.75	3.00	

BOSWELL, Connie

TITLE/FLIP	LABEL & NO.	GOOD	NEAR MINT	YR.
IF I GIVE MY HEART TO YOU/Tennessee	(Decca 29148)	1.00	4.00	54

BOTTLES, The

TITLE/FLIP	LABEL & NO.	GOOD	NEAR MINT	YR.
I DON'T WANNA BE YOUR MAN/Broken Apart	(MCA 41108)	.50	2.00	79
TOO LATE TO DANCE/	(MCA 41145)	.50	2.00	79

BOULEVARDS

TITLE/FLIP	LABEL & NO.	GOOD	NEAR MINT	YR.
DELORES/Chop Chop Hole In The Wall	(Everest 19316)	2.50	10.00	59

BO-WEEVILS

TITLE/FLIP	LABEL & NO.	GOOD	NEAR MINT	YR.
BEATLES WILL GETCHA, THE/	(United States 1934)	2.00	8.00	64

BOWEN, Jimmy

TITLE/FLIP	LABEL & NO.	GOOD	NEAR MINT	YR.
BY THE LIGHT OF THE SILVERY MOON/The Two Step	(Roulette 4083)	1.00	4.00	58
CROSS OVER/It's Shameful	(Roulette 4023)	1.00	4.00	57
DON'T DROP IT/Someone To Love	(Crest 1085)	.75	3.00	61
DON'T TELL ME YOUR TROUBLES/				
Ever Since That Night	(Roulette 4017)	1.00	4.00	57
I'M STICKIN' WITH YOU/Party Doll (By Buddy Knox)	(Triple-D 797)	37.50	150.00	57
(Shown as by Jim Bowen with the Orchids)				
I'M STICKIN' WITH YOU/Ever Lovin' Fingers	(Roulette 4001)	1.00	4.00	57
(I NEED) YOUR LOVING ARMS/Oh Yeah! Mm Mm	(Roulette 4224)	1.00	4.00	60
MY KIND OF WOMAN/Blue Moon	(Roulette 4102)	1.00	4.00	58
TEENAGE DREAMWORLD/It's Against The Law	(Capehart 5005)	.75	3.00	62
WARM UP TO ME BABY/I Trusted You	(Roulette 4010)	1.00	4.00	57
WISH I WERE TIED TO YOU/Always Faithful	(Roulette 4122)	1.00	4.00	59
YOU'RE JUST WASTING YOUR TIME/Walkin On Air	(Roulette 4175)	1.00	4.00	59
YOUR LOVING ARMS/Oh Yeah, Oh Yeah	(Roulette 4224)	1.00	4.00	60

BOWERS, Bob

TITLE/FLIP	LABEL & NO.	GOOD	NEAR MINT	YR.
SANDY/Teenage Loneliness	(Dart 120)	.75	3.00	60

BOWERY BOYS, The

TITLE/FLIP	LABEL & NO.	GOOD	NEAR MINT	YR.
IT'S FOR YOU/Duck	(Hemisphere 102)	.75	3.00	69

BOWIE, David

TITLE/FLIP	LABEL & NO.	GOOD	NEAR MINT	YR.
ALL THE MADMEN/All The Madmen	(Mercury DJ-311)	6.25	25.00	70
(Promotional issue only, both sides mono)				
ASHES TO ASHES/It's No Game (Part 1)	(RCA PB-12078)	.50	2.00	80
ASHES TO ASHES/It's No Game (Part 1)	(RCA PB-12078)	.75	3.00	80
(Picture sleeve)				
ASHES TO ASHES (Stereo)/Ashes To Ashes (Mono)	(RCA JH-12078)	.75	3.00	80
(Promotional issue)				
ASHES TO ASHES (Stereo)/Ashes To Ashes (Mono)	(RCA JH-12078)	1.00	4.00	80
(Promotional picture sleeve)				
ASHES TO ASHES/Ashes To Ashes-Space Oddity	(RCA DJL1-3795)	3.00	12.00	80
(Promotional 12" single)				
BEAUTY & THE BEAST/Sense Of Doubt	(RCA PB-11190)	.50	2.00	78
BEAUTY & THE BEAST (Stereo)/				
Beauty & The Beast (Mono)	(RCA PB-11190)	.75	3.00	78
(Promotional issue)				
BEAUTY & THE BEAST/Fame	(RCA JD-11204)	2.00	8.00	77
(Promotional 12" single.)				
BEAUTY & THE BEAST/Fame	(RCA JD-11204)	2.50	10.00	77
(Promotional 12" single picture sleeve.)				
BE MY WIFE/Speed Of Life	(RCA PB-11017)	.50	2.00	77
BE MY WIFE (Stereo)/Be My Wife (Mono)	(RCA JH-11017)	.75	3.00	77
(Promotional issue)				
BOYS KEEP SWINGING/Fantastic Voyage	(RCA PB-)	.50	2.00	79
BOYS KEEP SWINGING (Stereo)/Boys Keep Swinging (Mono)	(RCA JH-)	.75	3.00	79
(Promotional issue)				
BOYS KEEP SWINGING/Fantastic Voyage	(RCA PD-1585)	37.50	150.00	79
(Promotional issue only, released in Spain.)				
CAN'T HELP THINKING ABOUT ME/				
And I Say To Myself	(Warner Bros. 5818)	8.75	35.00	66
(Shown as by David Bowie & With the Lower Third)				
CAN'T HELP THINKING ABOUT ME/				
And I Say To Myself	(Warner Bros. 5815)	8.75	35.00	66
(Shown as by David Bowie & With the Lower Third)				
(Promotional issue only; note earlier catalog number)				
CHANGES/Andy Warhol	(RCA 74-0605)	.50	2.00	71
CHANGES/Andy Warhol	(RCA 74-0605)	1.00	4.00	71
(Promotional issue)				
CRYSTAL JAPAN/Alabama Song	(RCA SS-3270)	5.00	20.00	80
(Issued only in Japan, "Crystal Japan" was an instrumental done specifically for that country. Price includes picture sleeve.)				
D.J./Fantastic Voyage	(RCA PB-11661)	.50	2.00	79
D.J. (Stereo)/D.J. (Mono)	(RCA JH-11661)	.75	3.00	79
(Promotional issue)				
DO ANYTHING YOU SAY/Good Morning Girl	(Pye 17079)	37.50	150.00	66
(Released only in England)				
FAME/Right	(RCA PB-10320)	.50	2.00	75
FAME (Stereo)/Fame (Mono)	(RCA JH-10320)	.75	3.00	75
(Promotional issue)				
FASHION/Scream Like A Baby	(RCA PB-12134)	.50	2.00	80
FASHION/Scream Like A Baby	(RCA PB-12134)	.75	3.00	80
(Picture sleeve)				
FASHION (Stereo)/Fashion (Mono)	(RCA JH-12134)	.75	3.00	80
(Promotional issue)				
FASHION/Scream Like A Baby	(RCA PD-12145)	1.00	4.00	80
(12" single issue)				
FASHION (Long Version)/Fashion (Short Version)	(RCA JD-12140)	2.00	8.00	80
(Promotional 12" single)				
GOLDEN YEARS/Can You Hear Me	(RCA PB-10441)	.50	2.00	75
GOLDEN YEARS (Stereo)/Golden Years (Mono)	(RCA JHB-10441)	.75	3.00	75
(Promotional issue)				
HELDEN/V-2 Schneider	(RCA PB-9168)	1.25	5.00	77
(German language "Heroes," price includes record and picture sleeve.)				
HEROES/V-2 Schneider	(RCA PB-11121)	.50	2.00	77
HEROES (Stereo)/Heroes (Mono)	(RCA JH-11121)	.75	3.00	77
(Promotional issue)				
HEROES/V-2 Schneider	(RCA PB-91667)	1.50	6.00	77
(French language issue, price includes record and picture sleeve.)				
HEROES (Long Version)/Heroes (Short Version)	(RCA JD-11151)	3.00	12.00	77
(Promotional 12" single)				
HOLY, HOLY/Black Country Rock	(Mercury 6052-049)	5.00	20.00	70
(European release)				
HOLY, HOLY/Black Country Rock	(Mercury 6052-049)	7.50	30.00	70
(Picture sleeve, European release)				
I PITY THE FOOL/Take My Tip	(Parlophone R5250)	25.00	100.00	65
(Shown as by the Manish Boys)				
JEAN GENIE, THE/Hang On To Yourself	(RCA 74-0838)	.50	2.00	72
JEAN GENIE, THE/Hang On To Yourself	(RCA 74-0838)	.75	3.00	72
(Promotional issue)				
JOHN, I'M ONLY DANCING, 1972/Joe The Lion	(RCA PB-11887)	.50	2.00	80
JOHN, I'M ONLY DANCING, 1972 (Stereo)/				
John, I'm Only Dancing, 1972 (Mono)	(RCA JH-11887)	.75	3.00	80
(Promotional issue)				
JOHN, I'M ONLY DANCING, AGAIN/				
John, I'm Only Dancing, 1972	(RCA PD-11886)	1.00	4.00	79
(12" single issue)				
JOHN, I'M ONLY DANCING, AGAIN/Golden Years	(RCA JD-11886)	3.00	12.00	79
(Promotional 12" single)				
LAUGHING GNOME, THE/				
The Gospel According To Tony Day	(London 20079)	1.50	6.00	74
LET'S SPEND THE NIGHT TOGETHER/				
Lady Grinning Soul	(RCA APBO-0028)	.50	2.00	73
LET'S SPEND THE NIGHT TOGETHER (Long Version)/				
Let's Spend The Night Together (Short Version)	(RCA APBO-0028)	.75	3.00	73
(Promotional issue)				
LIZA JANE/Louie Louie Go Home	(Vocalion 9221)	37.50	150.00	64
(Shown as by Davie Jones & the King Bees)				

TITLE/FLIP	LABEL & NO.	GOOD	NEAR MINT	YR.
LOOK BACK IN ANGER/Move On	(RCA PB-11724)	.50	2.00	79
LOOK BACK IN ANGER (Stereo)/ Look Back In Anger (Mono)	(RCA JH-11724)	.75	3.00	79
(Promotional issue)				
LOVE YOU TILL TUESDAY/Did You Ever Have A Dream...	(Deram 85016)	3.00	12.00	67
LOVE YOU TILL TUESDAY/Did You Ever Have A Dream...	(Deram 85016)	3.75	15.00	67
(Promotional issue)				
MEMORY OF A FREE FESTIVAL (PART 1)/ Memory Of A Free Festival (Part 2)	(Mercury 73075)	5.00	20.00	70
MEMORY OF A FREE FESTIVAL (PART 1)/ Memory Of A Free Festival (Part 2)	(Mercury 73075)	6.25	25.00	70
(Promotional issue)				
MEMORY OF A FREE FESTIVAL (PART 1)/ Memory Of A Free Festival (Part 2)	(Mercury 6052-026)	7.50	30.00	70
(European release)				
MEMORY OF A FREE FESTIVAL (PART 1)/ Memory Of A Free Festival (Part 2)	(Mercury 6052-026)	10.00	40.00	70
(Picture sleeve, European release)				
1984/Queen Bitch	(RCA PB-10026)	.50	2.00	74
1984 (Stereo)/1984 (Mono)	(RCA JH-10026)	.75	3.00	74
(Promotional issue)				
PETER & THE WOLF/	(RCA JD-11306)	2.50	10.00	78
(Promotional 12" single)				
PRETTIEST STAR, THE/Conversation Piece	(Mercury 1135)	6.25	25.00	70
(Released in England)				
PRETTIEST STAR, THE/Conversation Piece	(Mercury 1135)	6.25	25.00	70
(Picture sleeve, released in England)				
PRETTIEST STAR, THE/Conversation Piece	(Mercury 6052-011)	6.25	25.00	70
(Released in Germany and Holland)				
PRETTIEST STAR, THE/Conversation Piece	(Mercury 6052-011)	8.75	35.00	70
(Picture sleeve, released in Germany and Holland)				
RAGAZZA SOLA, RAGAZZA SOLO/ Wild Eyed Boy From Freecloud	(Philips BW-704-208)	25.00	100.00	69
(Released in Italy only)				
RAGAZZA SOLA, RAGAZZA SOLO/ Wild Eyed Boy From Freecloud	(Philips BW-704-208)	20.00	80.00	69
(Picture sleeve, released in Italy only)				
REBEL REBEL/Lady Grinning Soul	(RCA APBO-0287)	.50	2.00	74
REBEL REBEL (Stereo)/Rebel Rebel (Mono)	(RCA APBO-0287)	.75	3.00	74
(Promotional issue)				
REBEL REBEL/Queen Bitch	(RCA LPBO-5009)	.75	3.00	74
(Released in England only.)				
REBEL REBEL/Queen Bitch	(RCA LPBO-5009)	2.00	8.00	74
(Promotional issue, released in England only.)				
ROCK 'N' ROLL SUICIDE/Quicksand	(RCA APBO-5021)	.50	2.00	74
ROCK 'N' ROLL SUICIDE (Stereo)/ Rock 'N' Roll Suicide (Mono)	(RCA APBO-5021)	.75	3.00	74
(Promotional issue)				
ROCK 'N' ROLL WITH ME/Panic In New York	(RCA PB-10105)	1.00	4.00	74
ROCK 'N' ROLL WITH ME (Stereo)/ Rock 'N' Roll With Me (Mono)	(RCA PB-10105)	1.00	4.00	74
(Promotional issue)				
RUBBER BAND/There Is A Happy Land	(Deram 85009)	3.75	15.00	67
RUBBER BAND/There Is A Happy Land	(Deram 85009)	5.00	20.00	67
(Promotional issue)				
SORROW (Stereo)/Sorrow (Mono)	(RCA DJHO-0160)			73
(Promotional issue)				
SORROW/Amsterdam	(RCA APBO-0160)	.75	3.00	73
SORROW (Stereo)/Sorrow (Mono)	(RCA APBO-0160)	.75	3.00	73
(Promotional issue)				
SOUND & VISION/A New Career In A New Town	(RCA PB-10905)	.50	2.00	77
SOUND & VISION (Stereo)/Sound & Vision (Mono)	(RCA JH-10905)	.75	3.00	77
(Promotional issue)				
SOUND & VISION-SISTER MIDNIGHT (Stereo)/ Sound & Vision-Sister Midnight (Mono)	(RCA JT-10965)	7.50	30.00	77
(Issued as a part of RCA's 'Segue Series,' this 12" promotional issue combined David Bowie's "Sound & Vision" with Iggy Pop's "Sister Midnight.")				
SPACE ODDITY/ Wild Eye Boy From Freecloud	(Mercury 72949)	3.75	15.00	69
SPACE ODDITY (Stereo)/Space Oddity (Mono)	(Mercury 72949)	6.25	25.00	69
(Promotional issue)				
SPACE ODDITY/The Man Who Sold The World	(RCA 74-0876)	.50	2.00	73
SPACE ODDITY/The Man Who Sold The World	(RCA 74-0876)	.75	3.00	73
(Promotional issue)				
SPACE ODDITY/The Man Who Sold The World	(RCA 74-0876)	1.25	5.00	73
(Picture sleeve)				
STARMAN/Suffragette City	(RCA 74-0719)	.50	2.00	72
STARMAN/Suffragette City	(RCA 74-0719)	.75	3.00	72
(Promotional issue)				
STARMAN/Suffragette City	(RCA 74-0719)	1.25	5.00	72
(Picture sleeve)				
STAY/Word On A Wing	(RCA PB-10736)	.50	2.00	76
TIME/The Prettiest Star	(RCA 0001)	.50	2.00	73
TIME (Long version)/Time (Short version)	(RCA APBO-0001)	1.00	4.00	73
(Promotional issue)				
TIME/The Prettiest Star	(RCA ESP-540)	8.75	35.00	73
(Promotional issue, released in Spain only. Price includes both record and sleeve.)				
TVC 15/We Are The Dead	(RCA PB-10664)	.50	2.00	76
YOUNG AMERICANS/Knock On Wood	(RCA PB-10152)	.50	2.00	75
YOUNG AMERICANS (Stereo)/Young Americans (Mono)	(RCA JH-10152)	.75	3.00	75
(Promotional issue)				
YOU'VE GOT A HABIT OF LEAVING/ Baby Loves That Way	(Parlophone R-5315)	31.25	125.00	65
(Shown as by Davy Jones)				

There are dozens of David Bowie releases from around the world that would be of interest to his followers. We have tried to limit those foreign pressings listed here to a sampling of the more interesting and unusual ones, but should point out that any foreign Bowie single could be valued at between five and ten dollars mininum.

BOWLEGS, The

TITLE/FLIP	LABEL & NO.	GOOD	NEAR MINT	YR.
ONE MORE TIME (PART 1)/One More Time (Part 2)	(Zab 101)	1.25	5.00	61
ONE MORE TIME (PART 1)/One More Time (Part 2)	(Vee Jay 400)	.75	3.00	61

BOWN, ALAN

TITLE/FLIP	LABEL & NO.	GOOD	NEAR MINT	YR.
STORY BOOK/Little Leslie	(Music Factory 406)	.50	2.00	71
TOYLAND/Technicolor Dream	(Music Factory 402)	.50	2.00	71
Also see Robert Palmer				

BOWS & ARROWS, The

TITLE/FLIP	LABEL & NO.	GOOD	NEAR MINT	YR.
I DON'T BELIEVE YOU/ You Know What You Can Do	(GNP Crescendo 356)	.75	3.00	65

BOX, David (Of The Crickets)

TITLE/FLIP	LABEL & NO.	GOOD	NEAR MINT	YR.
I'VE HAD MY MOMENTS/If You Can't Say Something Nice	(Candix 339)	1.25	5.00	62

BOX, Euel

TITLE/FLIP	LABEL & NO.	GOOD	NEAR MINT	YR.
FRITOS PRESENTS THE FRITO TWIST/ How To Twist	(Pams Productions)	.75	3.00	62
(Advertising preimum)				

BOX TOPS, The (With Alex Chilton)

TITLE/FLIP	LABEL & NO.	GOOD	NEAR MINT	YR.
ANGEL/Hold On Girl	(Hi 2242)	.75	3.00	71
CHOO CHOO TRAIN/Fields Of Clover	(Mala 12005)	.75	3.00	68
CRY LIKE A BABY/The Door You Closed To Me	(Mala 593)	.75	3.00	68
I MET HER IN CHURCH/People Gonna Talk	(Mala 12107)	.75	3.00	68
I SHALL BE RELEASED/I Must Be The Devil	(Mala 12038)	.75	3.00	69
KING'S HIGHWAY/Since I Been Gone	(Bell 981)	.50	2.00	71
LETTER, THE/Happy Times	(Mala 565)	.75	3.00	67
NEON RAINBOW/Everything I Am	(Mala 580)	.75	3.00	67
SOUL DEEP/(The) Happy Song	(Mala 12040)	.75	3.00	69
SUGAR CREEK WOMAN/It's All Over	(Hi 2228)	.75	3.00	71
SWEET CREAM LADIES, FORWARD MARCH/ I See Only Sunshine	(Mala 12035)	.75	3.00	68
TURN ON A DREAM/Together	(Mala 12042)	.75	3.00	69
YOU KEEP TIGHTENING UP ON ME/Come On Honey	(Bell 865)	.75	3.00	70
Also see Carson, Wayne				

BOXER

TITLE/FLIP	LABEL & NO.	GOOD	NEAR MINT	YR.
ALL THE TIME IN THE WORLD/Save Me	(Virgin 9506)	.50	2.00	76
HEY BULLDOG/Loony Ali	(Virgin 9509)	.50	2.00	77

BOYCE, Tommy

TITLE/FLIP	LABEL & NO.	GOOD	NEAR MINT	YR.
ALONG CAME LINDA/You Look So Lonely	(RCA Victor 47-7975)	2.50	10.00	61
BETTY JEAN/I'M Not Sure	(R-Dell 111)	1.50	6.00	
CHANGE OF HEART/Sweet Little Baby	(RCA Victor 47-8126)	1.25	5.00	62
COME HERE JO ANNE/The Way I Used To Do	(RCA Victor 47-8025)	1.50	6.00	62
DON'T BE AFRAID/A Million Things To Say	(RCA Victor 47-8208)	1.50	6.00	63
GIVE ME THE CLUE/Gypsy Song	(Dot 16117)	2.00	8.00	60
HAVE YOU HAD A CHANGE OF HEART/ Sweet Little Baby	(RCA Victor 47-8126)	1.00	4.00	63
I DON'T HAVE TO WORRY ('BOUT YOU)/ Pretty Thing (You're Out Of Sight)	(MGM 13400)	1.50	6.00	65
I'LL REMEMBER CAROL/Too Late For Tears	(RCA Victor 47-8074)	1.25	5.00	62
IN CASE THE WIND SHOULD BLOW/Simon Smith	(A&M 826)	3.00	12.00	66
IS IT TRUE/Little One	(Wow 345)	1.50	6.00	
LET'S GO WHERE THE ACTION IS (Vocal)/ Let's Go Where The Action Is (Instrumental)	(Colpix 794)	2.00	8.00	65
LITTLE SUZIE SOMETHIN'/Pee's N Que's	(MGM 13429)	1.50	6.00	65
SUNDAY, THE DAY BEFORE MONDAY/ Green Grass (Is Turning Brown)	(A&M 809)	.75	3.00	66
THANK GOD FOR ROCK & ROLL/ Thank God For Rock & Roll	(Chelsea 78-0101)	.75	3.00	72
(Shown as by Christopher Cloud)				
ZIP A DEE DOO DAH/	(Chelsea 78-0118)	.75	3.00	73
(Shown as by Christopher Cloud)				

BOYCE, Tommy & Bobby Hart

TITLE/FLIP	LABEL & NO.	GOOD	NEAR MINT	YR.
ALICE LONG (YOU'RE STILL MY FAVORITE GIRLFRIEND)/ P.O. Box 9847	(A&M 948)	.75	3.00	68
BLOW A KISS IN THE WIND/	(Aquarian 380)	.75	3.00	68
GOODBYE BABY (I DON'T WANT TO SEE YOU CRY)/ Where Angels Go (Trouble Follows)	(A&M 919)	.75	3.00	68
I WONDER WHAT SHE'S DOING TONIGHT/The Ambushers	(A&M 893)	.75	3.00	67
IT'S ALL HAPPENING ON THE INSIDE/ Maybe Somebody Heard	(A&M 1017)	.75	3.00	68
L.U.V. (LET US VOTE)/I Wanna Be Free	(A&M 1031)	.75	3.00	68
OUT & ABOUT/My Little Chickadee	(A&M 858)	.75	3.00	67
SOMETIMES SHE'S A LITTLE GIRL/Love Every Day	(A&M 874)	.75	3.00	67
WE'RE ALL GOING TO THE SAME PLACE/Six + Six	(A&M 993)	.75	3.00	68
Also see Hart, Bobby				
Also see Dolenz, Jones, Boyce & Hart				

BOYD, Jimmy

TITLE/FLIP	LABEL & NO.	GOOD	NEAR MINT	YR.
DAY DREAMER/I've Got It Made	(Capitol 4967)	.75	3.00	63
DENNIS THE MENNACE (With Rosemary Clooney)/ Little Josey	(Columbia 39988)	1.25	5.00	53
DENNIS THE MENACE (With Rosemary Clooney)/ I Only Saw Him Once (By Rosemary Clooney)	(Columbia 41547)	1.00	4.00	60
I SAW MOMMY DO THE MAMBO/Santa Claus Blues	(Columbia 40365)	1.25	5.00	54
I SAW MOMMY KISSING SANTA CLAUS/Thumbelina	(Columbia 39871)	1.25	5.00	52
I WANNA GO STEADY/ Gonna Take My Baby On A Hayride	(Columbia 40881)	1.00	4.00	57
I WANNA HAIRCUT WITH A MOON ON TOP/ How Come	(Columbia 40504)	1.25	5.00	55
I WOULD NEVER DO THAT/Lazy Me	(Imperial 66166)	.75	3.00	66
I WOULD NEVER DO THAT/So Young & So Fine	(Imperial 66233)	.75	3.00	67
I'LL STAY IN THE HOUSE/Early Bird	(Columbia 39927)	1.25	5.00	53
I'M SO GLAD (I'M A LITTLE BOY & YOU'RE A LITTLE GIRL)/ Kitty In The Basket	(Columbia 40218)	1.25	5.00	54
I'VE GOT THOSE "WAKE UP, SEVEN-THIRTY, WASH YOUR EARS THEY'RE DIRTY, EAT YOUR EGGS & OATMEAL, RUSH TO SCHOOL" BLUES/Jelly On My Head	(Columbia 40138)	1.25	5.00	54
LITTLE BONNIE BUNNY/Jimmy, Roll Me Gently	(Columbia 40181)	1.25	5.00	54
LITTLE DOG/Don't Forget To Say Your Prayers	(Columbia 40756)	1.25	5.00	56
LITTLE SIR ECHO/Little White Duck	(Columbia 40304)	1.25	5.00	54
LITTLE TRAIN/Needle In, Needle Out	(Columbia 39733)	1.25	5.00	52
MA, I MISS YOUR APPLE PIE/Shepherd Boy	(Columbia 40253)	1.25	5.00	54
MY BUNNY & MY SISTER/2 Easter Sweethearts	(Columbia 39955)	1.25	5.00	53
OWL LULLABY/God's Little Candles	(Columbia 39696)	1.25	5.00	52
PLAYMATES/Shoo-Fly Pie & Apple Pan Dowdy	(Columbia 40007)	1.25	5.00	53
POOR LITTLE PIGGY BANK/Let's Go Fishin'	(Columbia 40069)	1.25	5.00	53
REINDEER ROCK/A Kiss For Christmas	(Columbia 40601)	1.25	5.00	55
SANTA GOT STUCK IN THE CHIMNEY/ I Said A Prayer For Santa Claus	(Columbia 40080)	1.25	5.00	53
Also see Laine, Frankie & Jimmy Boyd				

BOYD, William (As Hopalong Cassidy)

TITLE/FLIP	LABEL & NO.	GOOD	NEAR MINT	YR.
HOPALONG CASSIDY & THE HAUNTED GOLD MINE/	(Capitol 3166)	2.00	8.00	55
HOPALONG CASSIDY & THE MAIL ROBBERY/	(Capitol 3164)	2.00	8.00	55
HOPALONG CASSIDY & THE SINGING BANDIT/	(Capitol 3058)	2.00	8.00	55
HOPALONG CASSIDY & THE SQUARE DANCE HOLDUP/	(Capitol 3075)	2.00	8.00	55
HOPALONG CASSIDY & THE STORY OF TOPPER/	(Capitol 3110)	2.00	8.00	55
HOPPY'S HAPPY BIRTHDAY/	(Capitol 3114)	2.00	8.00	55
All of these were two part stories & adventures.				

BOYE, Franny

TITLE/FLIP	LABEL & NO.	GOOD	NEAR MINT	YR.
ROCK AROUND THE CLOCK/I Know That We're In Love	(Gone 5095)	.75	3.00	61

BOY FRIENDS, The

TITLE/FLIP	LABEL & NO.	GOOD	NEAR MINT	YR.
SHY BOY/Snake In The Grass	(Glaser 1000)	.75	3.00	61

BOYFRIENDS, The

TITLE/FLIP	LABEL & NO.	GOOD	NEAR MINT	YR.
LET'S FALL IN LOVE/Oh Lana	(Kapp 569)	6.25	25.00	63
(Small print used on label)				
LET'S FALL IN LOVE/Oh Lana	(Kapp 569)	5.00	20.00	63
(Large print used on label)				
Also see Five Discs, The				

BOYS, The

TITLE/FLIP	LABEL & NO.	GOOD	NEAR MINT	YR.
IT'S HOPELESS/How Do You Do With Me	(SVR 1002)	1.00	4.00	
I WANNA KNOW/Angel Of Mine	(SVR 1001)	1.00	4.00	

BOYS BLUE, The

TITLE/FLIP	LABEL & NO.	GOOD	NEAR MINT	YR.
TAKE A HEART/You Got What I Want	(ABC-Paramount 10658)	.75	3.00	65

BOYS FROM NEW YORK CITY, The

TITLE/FLIP	LABEL & NO.	GOOD	NEAR MINT	YR.
GOIN' TO CALIFORNIA/A Little Bit Harder	(Laurie 3443)	.75	3.00	68
MARY & JOHN/I'm Down Girl	(Laurie 3434)	.75	3.00	68
TAKE IT OR LEAVE IT/These Are The Things	(Laurie 3412)	.75	3.00	67

BOYS NEXT DOOR, The

TITLE/FLIP	LABEL & NO.	GOOD	NEAR MINT	YR.
MANDY/One Face In The Crowd	(Atco 6443)	1.50	6.00	66
SEE THE WAY SHE'S MINE/Be Gone Girl	(Atco 6477)	.75	3.00	67
SWEET LOVE OF MINE/You Talk Too Much	(Vik 0207)	2.00	8.00	56
THERE'S NO GREATER SIN/ I Could See Me Dancing With You	(Cameo 394)	.75	3.00	66
WE GO TOGETHER/Now You're Talkin' Baby	(Rainbow 349)	3.75	15.00	55

BOYZZ, The

TITLE/FLIP	LABEL & NO.	GOOD	NEAR MINT	YR.
SHADY LADY/Dianne (Part 2)	(Epic-Cleveland Int'l 50685)	.50	2.00	79
WAKE IT UP, SHAKE IT UP/Hoochie Koochie	(Epic-Cleveland Int'l 50610)	.50	2.00	78

BRACELETS, The

TITLE/FLIP	LABEL & NO.	GOOD	NEAR MINT	YR.
WADDLE, WADDLE/I'll Play Around	(Congress 104)	.75	3.00	62
YOU'RE JUST FOOLING YOURSELF/You Better Move On	(20th Fox 539)	.75	3.80	64

BRADFORD, Keith

TITLE/FLIP	LABEL & NO.	GOOD	NEAR MINT	YR.
SOMEWHERE ELVIS IS SMILING/Somewhere Elvis Is Smiling	(Nu-Sound)	.50	2.00	77

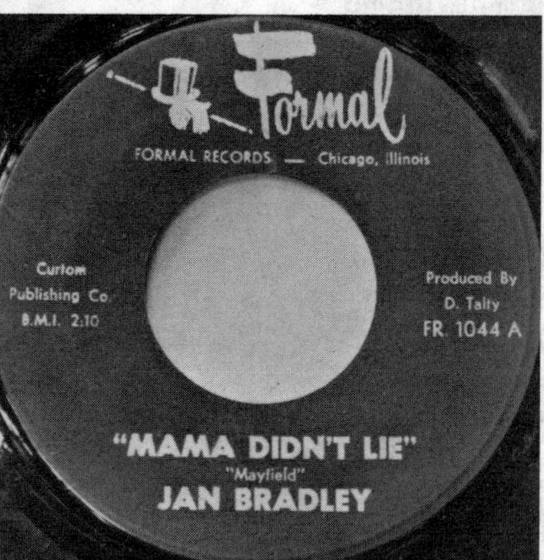

BRADLEY, Jan

TITLE/FLIP	LABEL & NO.	GOOD	NEAR MINT	YR.
BACK IN CIRCULATION/Love Is The Answer	(Sound Spectrum 36002)	1.00	4.00	
CURFEW BLUES/We Girls	(Formal 1015)	1.25	5.00	64
CURFEW BLUES/We Girls	(Chess 1884)	.75	3.00	64
I'M OVER YOU/The Brush Off	(Chess 1919)	.75	3.00	65
MAMA DIDN'T LIE/Lovers Like Me	(Formal FR-1044)	1.50	6.00	62
MAMA DIDN'T LIE/Lovers Like Me	(Chess 1845)	.75	3.00	62
PLEASE MR. D.J./Two Of A Kind	(Chess 1897)	.75	3.00	64

BRADLEY, Owen, Quintet

TITLE/FLIP	LABEL & NO.	GOOD	NEAR MINT	YR.
BEYOND THE BORDER/I Will Still Love You	(Coral 60892)	1.00	4.00	53
BIG GUITAR/Sentimental Dream	(Decca 30564)	.75	3.00	58
BLUES, STAY AWAY FROM ME/Fairy Tales	(Coral 60107)	1.00	4.00	50
I'LL NEVER BE FREE/Is There Somebody Else	(Coral 60293)	1.25	5.00	50
MY HEART'S DESIRE/Baby I'm Lost Without You	(Coral 60908)	1.00	4.00	53
PLINK, PLANK, PLUNK/The Penny Whistle Song	(Coral 60735)	1.00	4.00	52
WHITE SILVER SANDS/Midnight Blues	(Decca 30363)	.75	3.00	57

BRAGG, Doug, & Cheri Robbins

TITLE/FLIP	LABEL & NO.	GOOD	NEAR MINT	YR.
TEENAGE FEELING/Juvenile Baby	(Skippy 106)	1.00	4.00	59

BRAMLETT, Bonnie (Of Delaney & Bonnie)

TITLE/FLIP	LABEL & NO.	GOOD	NEAR MINT	YR.
I'VE JUST SEEN A FACE/Except For Real	(Capricorn 0306)	.50	2.00	78
NEVER GONNA GIVE YOU UP/	(Capricorn 0262)	.50	2.00	76

BRAMLETT, Delaney

TITLE/FLIP	LABEL & NO.	GOOD	NEAR MINT	YR.
HEARTBREAK HOTEL/You Never Looked Sweeter	(GNP-Cresendo 328)	1.00	4.00	64
LIVERPOOL LOU/You Have No Choice	(GNP-Crescendo 339)	1.00	4.00	65
WITHOUT YOUR LOVE/Better Man Than Me	(GNP Crescendo 363)	1.00	4.00	66
(Shown as by Delaney)				
Also see Delaney & Bonnie				

BRAND, Jack

TITLE/FLIP	LABEL & NO.	GOOD	NEAR MINT	YR.
ELVIS, WE'RE SORRY WE FENCED YOU IN/ Elvis We're Sorry We Fenced You In	(Shane 7101)	.50	2.00	77

BRANDO, Marlon (With Jean Simmons)

TITLE/FLIP	LABEL & NO.	GOOD	NEAR MINT	YR.
LUCK BE A LADY/If I Were A Bell	(Decca 29782)	1.25	5.00	55
WOMAN IN LOVE, A/I'll Know	(Decca 29783)	1.25	5.00	55

BRANDON, Johnny

TITLE/FLIP	LABEL & NO.	GOOD	NEAR MINT	YR.
SANTA CLAUS JR./ Theme From Santa Claus Jr. (Instrumental)	(Laurie 3042)	1.00	4.00	59

BRANDON, Kathy

TITLE/FLIP	LABEL & NO.	GOOD	NEAR MINT	YR.
SURFIN' DOLL/A Boy To Love Me	(Crystalette 759)	1.00	4.00	61

BRASHER, Cathy (Of The Murmaids)

TITLE/FLIP	LABEL & NO.	GOOD	NEAR MINT	YR.
I'LL REMEMBER JIMMY/Too Late To Be Lovers	(Era 3129)	.75	3.00	64
SH....LISTEN/He Told Me He Loved Me	(Chattahochee 690)	.75	3.00	65
(Shown as by Miss Cathy Brasher)				

BRASS RING, The

TITLE/FLIP	LABEL & NO.	GOOD	NEAR MINT	YR.
DIS-ADVANTAGES OF YOU, THE/The Dating Game	(Dunhill 4065)	.75	3.00	67
I'LL NEVER FALL IN LOVE/(Theme From) Last Summer	(Itco SS 101)	.75	3.00	
PHOENIX LOVE THEME, THE/Lightning Bug	(Dunhill 4023)	.75	3.00	66
Instrumentals				

B.R.A.T.T.S., The (Brotherhood for the Re-establishment of American Top Ten Supremacy)

TITLE/FLIP	LABEL & NO.	GOOD	NEAR MINT	YR.
SECRET WEAPON (THE BRITISH ARE COMING)/ Jealous Kind A Woman	(Tollie 9024)	1.50	6.00	64

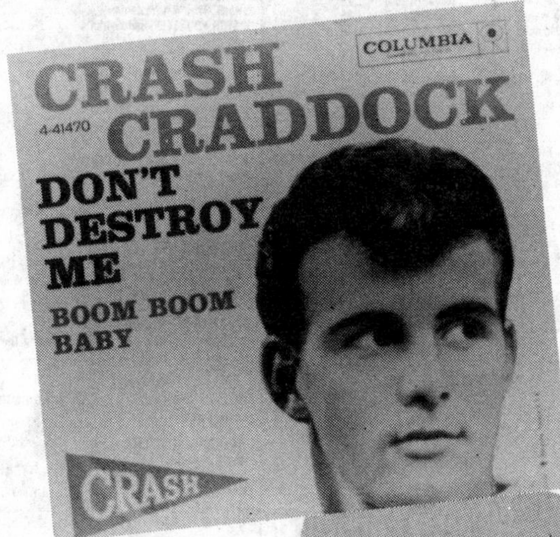

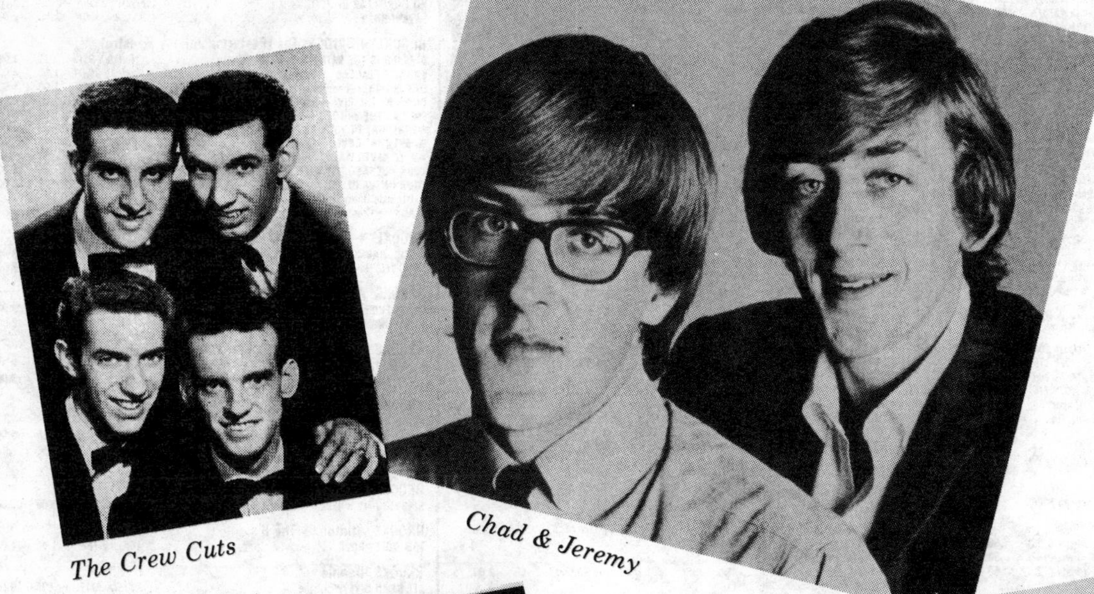

The Crew Cuts

Chad & Jeremy

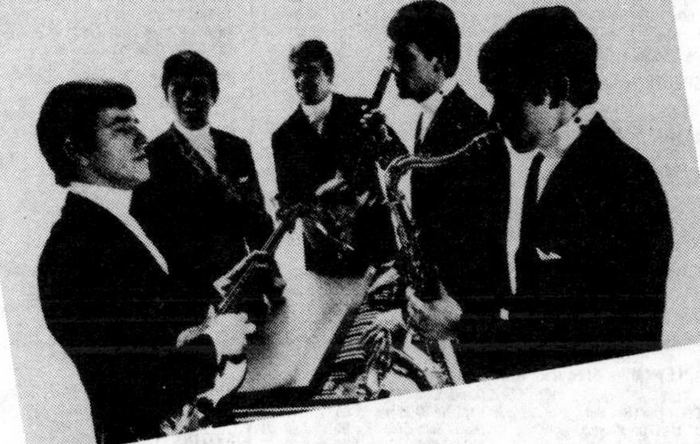

TITLE/FLIP — LABEL & NO. — GOOD — NEAR MINT — YR.

ITCO
RECORDS
E.H. Morris (Blue Seas-JAC) ASCAP
Arr. & Cond. by Phil Bodner
SS 101
SS 101-A
Time: 2:29
PROMOTIONAL NOT FOR SALE
I'LL NEVER FALL IN LOVE
(Bacharach & David)
THE BRASS RING
A PRODUCT OF INTERNATIONAL TAPE CARTRIDGE

BRAUN, Bob (Robert Earl Brown)
- **TILL DEATH DO US PART**/So It Goes (Decca 31355) .75 3.00 62

BREAD (Featuring David Gates)
- **AUBREY**/Don't Even Know Her Name (Elektra 45832) .50 2.00 73
- **BABY I'M-A-WANT YOU**/Truckin' (Elektra 45751) .50 2.00 71
- **COULD I**/You Can't Measure The Cost (Elektra 45668) 1.00 4.00 69
- **DIARY**/Down On My Knees (Elektra 45784) .50 2.00 72
- **DISMAL DAY**/Any Way You Want Me (Elektra 45666) 1.00 4.00 69
- **EVERYTHING I OWN**/I Don't Love You (Elektra 45765) .50 2.00 72
- **GUITAR MAN, THE**/Just Like Yesterday (Elektra 45803) .50 2.00 72
- **HOOKED ON YOU**/Our Lady Of Sorrow (Elektra 54389) .50 2.00 77
- **IF**/Take Comfort (Elektra 45720) .50 2.00 71
- **IT DON'T MATTER TO ME**/Call On Me (Elektra 45701) .50 2.00 70
- **LET YOUR LOVE GO**/Too Much Love (Elektra 45711) .50 2.00 71
- **LOST WITHOUT YOUR LOVE**/Change Of Heart (Elektra 45365) .50 2.00 76
- **MAKE IT WITH YOU**/Why Do You Keep Me Waiting (Elektra 45686) .50 2.00 70
- **MOTHER FREEDOM**/Live In Your Love (Elektra 45740) .50 2.00 71
- **SWEET SURRENDER**/Make It By Yourself (Elektra 45818) .50 2.00 72

Even though David Gates was the featured lead singer on the groups hits, many of the flip sides spotlighted the lead vocals of James Griffin.

BREAKAWAYS, The
- **GRANADA**/The Flipper (Melbourne 1805) .75 3.00 64
- **THAT BOY OF MINE**/Here She Comes (London 10526) .75 3.00 64
- **THAT'S HOW IT GOES**/He Doesn't Love Me (Cameo 323) .75 3.00 64

Also see Carefrees, The
Also see Vernons Girls

BREAKERS, The
- **BALBOA MEMORIES**/Long Way Home (Marsh 206) 1.00 4.00 63
- **JET STREAM**/Beach Head (DJB 116) 1.25 5.00 64
- **SAY YOU'RE MINE**/Once More (Moxie 103) 1.00 4.00 63
- **SUPER JET STREAM**/Beach Head (DJB 116) 1.00 4.00 64
- **SURF BIRD**/Surfin' Tragedy (Impact 14) 1.00 4.00 63
- **SURF BREAKERS**/Kami-Kaze (Brana 1001/2) 1.00 4.00 63

BREAKERS, The
- **ALL MY NIGHTS, ALL MY DAYS**/Better For The Both Of Us (Jerden 789) .75 3.00 66

BREATHLESS
- **TAKIN' IT BACK**/Alibis (EMI American 8020) .50 2.00 79

BRECKER BROTHERS, The (Mike & Randy)
- **DON'T STOP THE MUSIC**/Finger Lickin' Good (Arista 0253) .50 2.00 76
- **IF YOU WANNA BOOGIE... FORGET IT**/ (Arista 0182) .50 2.00 75
- **SNEAKIN' UP BEHIND YOU**/Sponge (Arista 0122) .50 2.00 75

BREMERS, Beverly
- **DON'T SAY YOU DON'T REMEMBER**/Get Smart Girl (Scepter 12315) .50 2.00 71
- **FLIGHT 309 TO TENNESSEE**/ (Columbia 10451) .50 2.00 76
- **I'LL MAKE YOU MUSIC**/I'll Make A Man Out Of You (Scepter 12363) .50 2.00 72
- **WE'RE FREE**/Colors Of Love (Scepter 12348) .50 2.00 72

BRENDON
- **MAKE ME A DOLLAR, MAKE ME A DIME**/ (UK 49027) .50 2.00 72

BRENNAN, Buddy, Quartet
- **CHASE, THE**/Big River (Warwick 517) 1.00 4.00 59

BRENNAN, Rose
- **KISS ME AGAIN**/Bold Black Knight (RCA Victor 47-5916) 1.00 4.00 54

BRENNAN, Walter
- **DUTCHMAN'S GOLD**/Back To The Farm (Dot 16066) .75 3.00 60
- **HENRY HAD A MERRY CHRISTMAS**/White Christmas (Liberty 55518) .75 3.00 62
- **HOUDINI, THE**/Old Kelly Place (Liberty 55477) .75 3.00 62
- **LIFE GETS TEE-JUS DON'T IT?**/Tribute To A Dog (Dot 16348) .75 3.00 62
- **MAMA SANG A SONG**/Who Will Take Gramma (Liberty 55508) .75 3.00 62
- **OLD RIVERS**/The Epic Ride Of John Glenn (Liberty 55436) .75 3.00 62

BRENT & THE SPECTRAS
- **OH DARLING**/Patricia (Spectras) 1.25 5.00

BRENT, Frankie (With The Counts)
- **COLD AS ICE**/ (Vik 0322) 1.00 4.00 58
- **NO ROCK & ROLLIN' HERE**/Lover's Lane (Strand 25014) 1.00 4.00 60

BRENT, Ronnie
- **COWBOYS & INDIANS**/Flow Gently (Colt-45 108) 1.00 4.00
- **MY SWEET VERLENA**/Love (United Artists 108) 6.25 25.00 58

BRENTWOODS, The
- **MIDNIGHT STAR**/As I Live From Day To Day (Dore 559) 2.00 8.00 60

BRET & TERRY
- **BEATLE FEVER**/The Beatle (Prestige 313) 1.50 6.00 64

BREWER & SHIPLEY (Mike Brewer & Tom Shipley)
- **BLACK SKY**/ (Kama Sutra 567) .50 2.00 73
- **KEEPER OF THE KEYS**/I Can't See Her (A&M 905) 1.00 4.00 68
- **ONE TOKE OVER THE LINE**/Oh Mommy (Kama Sutra 516) .50 2.00 71
- **RISE UP EASY RIDER**/Boomerang (Buddah 154) 1.00 4.00 70
- **SHAKE OFF THE DEMON**/Indian Summer (Kama Sutra 539) .75 3.00 72
- **TARKIO ROAD** /Seems Like A Long Time (Kama Sutra 524) .75 3.00 71
- **TIME & CHANGES**/Dreamin' In The Shade (A&M 996) 1.00 4.00 69
- **TRULY RIGHT**/Green Bamboo (A&M 938) 1.00 4.00 68
- **YANKEE LADY**/Natural Child (Kama Sutra 547) .75 3.00 72

TITLE/FLIP — LABEL & NO. — GOOD — NEAR MINT — YR.

BREWER, Teresa
- **AIN'T HAD NO LOVIN'**/Evil On Your Mind (Philips 40389) .75 3.00 66
- **ANYMORE**/That Piano Man (Coral 62219) .75 3.00 60
- **AU REVOIR**/Danger Signs (Coral 61225) 1.25 5.00 54
- **BABY, BABY, BABY**/I Guess It Was You All The Time (Coral 61067) 1.25 5.00 54
- **BELL BOTTOM BLUES**/Our Heartbreaking Waltz (Coral 61066) 1.25 5.00 54
- **BORN TO LIVE**/It's The Same Old Jazz (Momma) (Coral 61878) 1.00 4.00 57
- **BYE BYE BABY GOOD-BYE**/Chain Of Friendship (Coral 62126) 1.00 4.00 59
- **CHOO'N GUM**/Honky Tonkin' (London 678) 1.50 6.00 50
- **COME ON IN**/Simple Things (Philips 40177) .75 3.00 64
- **CRY BABY**/I Hear The Angels Singing (Coral 62428) .75 3.00 64
- **DARN YA (DERN YA)**/Mama Never Told Me (Philips 40227) .75 3.00 64
  (Answer song)
- **EMPTY ARMS**/Ricky Tick Song (Coral 61805) 1.00 4.00 57
- **GOLDFINGER**/Make Room For One More Fool (Philips 40253) .75 3.00 64
- **GONNA GET ALONG WITHOUT YA NOW**/
  Roll Them Roly Poly Eyes (Coral 60676) 1.25 5.00 52
- **GOOD MAN IS HARD TO FIND, A**/It's Siesta Time (Coral 61548) 1.00 4.00 56
- **GRIZZLY BEAR**/Molasses Molasses (London 30290) 1.50 6.00 50
- **HANDLE WITH CARE**/I Can't Remember Ever Loving You (Phillips 40367) .75 3.00 66
- **HE UNDERSTANDS ME**/Just Before We Say Goodbye (Philips 40135) .75 3.00 63
- **HEAVENLY LOVER**/Fair Weather Sweetheart (Coral 62084) 1.00 4.00 59
- **HELLO**/A Penny A Kiss (London 878) 1.50 6.00 50
  (With Snooky Lanson)
- **HONEYMOON**/When You Wore A Tulip (Coral 65581) .75 3.00 64
- **HOW LONELY CAN ONE BE**/I'm Drowning My Sorrows (Coral 61776) 1.00 4.00 57
- **HOW TO BE VERY POPULAR**/The Banjo's Back In Town (Coral 61448) 1.00 4.00 55
- **HULA HOOP SONG, THE**/So Shy (Coral 62033) 1.00 4.00 58
- **I LOVE MICKEY (With Mickey Mantle)**/
  Keep Your Cotton Pickin' Paddies Off Of My Heart (Coral 61700) 1.00 4.00 56
- **IF YOU WANT SOME LOVIN'**/I've Got The Time (London 967) 1.50 6.00 51
- **I WISH I WUZ**/If You Don't Marry Me (London 1085) 1.50 6.00 51
- **I'VE GROWN ACCUSTOMED TO HIS FACE**/
  Supercalifragilisticexpialidocious (Philips 40282) .75 3.00 65
- **JEALOUS HEART**/Walking The Floor Over You (Coral 65569) .75 3.00 63
- **JILTED**/Le Grand Tour de L'Amour (Coral 61152) 1.25 5.00 54
- **KISSES ON PAPER**/I Hear The Bluebells Ring (Coral 60755) 1.25 5.00 52
- **LET ME GO LOVER**/The Moon Is On Fire (Coral 61315) 1.25 5.00 54
- **LONESOME GAL**/Counterfeit Kisses (London 970) 1.50 6.00 51
- **LONGING FOR YOU**/Jazz Me Blues (London 1086) 1.50 6.00 51
- **MUSIC! MUSIC! MUSIC!**/Copenhagen (London 30023) 1.50 6.00 50
- **MUSIC, MUSIC, MUSIC**/Gonna Get Along Without Ya Now (Coral 65520) .75 3.00 63
  (Re-recorded version of "Music, Music, Music" for Coral Records.)
- **MUTUAL ADMIRATION SOCIETY**/Crazy With Love (Coral 61737) 1.00 4.00 56
- **MY SWEETIE WENT AWAY**/Time (Coral 61286) 1.25 5.00 54
- **ONE ROSE, THE**/Satelite (Coral 62057) 1.00 4.00 59
- **PLEDGING MY LOVE**/How Important Can It Be (Coral 61362) 1.00 4.00 55
- **PUNKY PUMPKIN**/ (London 30188) 1.50 6.00 51
- **RHODE ISLAND REDHEAD**/
  En Thuz E Uz E As M (By Eileen Barton) (Coral 60775) 1.50 6.00 52
- **RICOCHET**/Too Young To Tango (Coral 61043) 1.25 5.00 53
- **ROCK LOVE**/Dweedlee Dee (Coral 61366) 1.00 4.00 55
- **SAY SOMETHING SWEET TO YOUR SWEETHEART**/
  What About Time (Philips 40310) .75 3.00 65
- **SECOND HAND ROSE**/Stand In (Philips 40120) .75 3.00 63
- **(SHE'LL NEVER LOVE YOU) LIKE I DO**/Thrill Is Gone (Philips 40095) .75 3.00 63
- **SHOOT IT AGAIN**/You're Telling Our Secrets (Coral 61528) 1.00 4.00 55
- **SILVER DOLLAR**/I Don't Want To Be Lonely Tonight (Coral 61394) 1.00 4.00 55
- **SING SING SING**/I Don't Care (Coral 60591) 1.25 5.00 51
- **SKINNIE MINNIE**/I Had Someone Else Before I Had You (Coral 61197) 1.25 5.00 54
- **SWEET OLD FASHIONED GIRL, A**/Goodbye, John (Coral 61636) 1.00 4.00 56
- **TEARDROPS IN MY HEART**/Lula Rock-A-Hula (Coral 61850) 1.00 4.00 57
- **TEAR FELL, A**/Bo Weevil (Coral 61590) 1.00 4.00 56
- **THING, THE**/I Guess I'll Have To Dream The Rest (London 873) 1.50 6.00 50
- **TIL I WALTZ AGAIN WITH YOU**/Hello Bluebird (Coral 60873) 1.25 5.00 52
- **TOO FAT FOR THE CHIMNEY**/I Just Can't Wait (Coral 61079) 1.25 5.00 54
- **YOU GOT ME CRYING AGAIN**/You Can Come Back (London 795) 1.50 6.00 50
- **YOU SEND ME**/Would I Were (Coral 61898) 1.00 4.00 57
- **YOU'LL NEVER GET AWAY**/
  Hookey Song (With Don Cornell) (Coral 60829) 1.25 5.00 52
- **WANG WANG BLUES**/Oceana Roll (London 1083) 1.50 6.00 51
- **WAY BACK HOME**/Copper Canyon (With Bobby Wayne) (London 30007) 2.00 8.00 49
- **WHIP-POOR-WILL**/Older & Wiser (Coral 62253) .75 3.00 61
- **WHIRLPOOL**/There's Nothing As Lonesome As Saturday Night (Coral 61948) 1.00 4.00 58

BRIANS, Robin Hood
- **DIS A ITTY BIT!**/Without You (Fraternity 803) 18.75 75.00 58

BRIGADIERS, The
- **CRY OF THE WILD GOOSE**/Dixie Brigade (Mala 441) .75 3.00

BRIGATI (Eddie Brigati)
- **GROOVIN'**/ (Elektra 45328) .50 2.00 76

Also see Young Rascals, The

BRIGGS, Lillian
- **EDDIE MY LOVE**/Teen In Jeans From New Orleans (Epic 9151) 1.00 4.00 56
- **I WANT YOU TO BE MY BABY**/Don't Stay Away Too Long (Epic 9115) 1.00 4.00 55
- **ROCK N' ROL-Y POLY SANTA CLAUS**/Can't Stop (Epic 9138) 1.00 4.00 56

BRIGHT, Larry
- **BACON FAT**/Do The Thing (Del Fi 4209) .75 3.00 63
- **GOT MY MOJO WORKING**/I'm A Man (Del Fi 4234) .75 3.00 63
- **MOJO WORKOUT**/I'll Change My Ways (Tide 006) 1.00 4.00 60
- **PLEASE GIVE YOUR LOVE**/It Ain't Right (Edit 2001) 1.00 4.00 62
- **PLEASE GIVE YOUR LOVE**/It Ain't Right (Tide 1083) .75 3.00 61

(The above two records are the same except for the year of release and issue number and the fact that EDIT is TIDE spelled backwards.)

- **SHAKE THAT THING**/
  When I Did The Mashed Potatoes With You (Del Fi 4214) .75 3.00 63
- **SHE BELONGS TO ME**/La Bomba (Bright 0014) .75 3.00 65
- **SHOULD I**/Natural Born Lover (Tide 008) .75 3.00 60
- **SURFIN' QUEEN**/My Hands Are Tied (Del Fi 4204) .75 3.00 63
- **TWINKIE-LEE**/Should I (Highland 1052) 1.25 5.00 61
- **WHEN I'M WITH YOU**/(I'm A) Mojo Man (Tide 0012) .75 3.00 60
- **WAY DOWN HOME**/Bloodhound (Tide 0021) .75 3.00 61

BRIGHTONES, The
- **SWIM, SWIM, SWIM**/Rumors (Warner Bros. 5472) .75 3.00 64

BRILL, Marty
- **BUTTER HEART & CANDY LIPS**/ (Mercury 71009) 1.00 4.00 56
- **JAMES BLONDE**/ (Colpix 790) 1.00 4.00 65
  (With Larry Foster)

BRINKLEY, Jay
- **FORCES OF EVIL**/ (Dot 15371) 1.25 5.00 55

BRINSLEY SCHWARZ (With Nick Lowe & Ian Gomm)
- **HAPPY DOING WHAT WE'RE DOING**/ (United Artists 50976) .50 2.00 72

This band also contained three members of Rumor.

BRISCOE, Johnny, & The Little Beavers
- **WHY DO FOOLS FALL IN LOVE**/ (Atlantic 2822) 1.25 5.00 71

BRISTOL, Bob
- **HUMPTY DUMPTY**/Love Flew Away (Riter 105) 1.25 5.00

BRITINS, The
- **MARIA**/Maria (Nova 457901) .50 2.00 79
- **SHE KNOWS**/I Want To Hold Your Hand (Bananas 1001) .50 2.00 77

BRITISH LIONS, The (Formerly Mott)
- **WILD IN THE STREETS**/Booster (RSO 898) .50 2.00 78

TITLE/FLIP — LABEL & NO. — GOOD — NEAR MINT — YR.

BRITISH ROAD RUNNERS
- **DO SOMETHING TO ME**/Flower Movement (Laurie LR-3426) .75 3.00 68

BRITISH WALKERS, The
- **DIDDLEY DADDY**/I Found You (Try 502) 1.25 5.00 64
- **SHAKE**/That Was Yesterday (Cameo 466) 1.25 5.00 64
- **WATCH YOURSELF**/Bad Lightin' (Manchester 651120) 1.50 6.00

BRITT, Lynn
- **TOO LONG**/Two Times A Stranger (Miki 1117) .75 3.00 61
- **TOO LONG**/Two Times A Stranger (Dot 16203) 1.00 4.00 61

BRITT, Tommy
- **FABULOUS, FANTASTIC & FIFTEEN**/Same Girl (Unison 201) 1.00 4.00 59

BROCK, B., & His Vibratos
- **HANG FIVE**/Fright (La Broc 101) 1.00 4.00

BROCK B. & SULTANS
- **DO THE BEETLE**/ (Crown 5399) 1.25 5.00 64

BROGUES, The
- **BUT NOW I'M FINE**/Someday (Twilight 408) 3.00 12.00
- **DON'T SHOOT ME DOWN**/I Ain't No Miracle Worker (Challenge 59316) 2.00 8.00 65

Also see Quicksilver

BROMBERG, David
- **HOLDUP, THE (With George Harrison)**/Sing The Blues (Columbia 45612) 1.00 4.00 72
- **I WANT TO GO HOME**/ (Fantasy 812) .50 2.00 77
- **SHARON**/Sharon (Columbia 45767) 1.00 4.00 73

BROOD, Herman, & His Wild Romance
- **SATURDAYNIGHT**/Back (In Y'r Love) (Ariola 7754) .50 2.00 79

BROOK BROTHERS, The
- **ONCE IN AWHILE**/Poor Poor Plan (London 9668) 1.00 4.00 64
  (Shown as by the Brooks)
- **ONE LAST KISS**/Ain't Gonna Wash For A Week (London 10501) 1.00 4.00 61
- **TELL TALE**/Too Sacred (London 10515) 1.00 4.00 62
- **WAR PAINT**/Sometimes (London 1987) 1.00 4.00 61

BROOKER, Gary (Of Procol Harum)
- **NO MORE FEAR OF FLYING**/ (Chrysalis 2358) .50 2.00 79
- **SAVANNAH**/ (Chrysalis 2326) .50 2.00 79

BROOKLYN BRIDGE, The (Featuring Johnny Maestro)
- **BLESSED IS THE RAIN**/Welcome Me Love (Buddah 95) .75 3.00 69
- **BRUNO'S PLACE**/ (Buddah 293) 1.00 4.00 72
- **DAY IS DONE**/Opposites (Buddah 193) 1.00 4.00 70
- **DOWN BY THE RIVER**/Look Again (Buddah 179) 1.00 4.00 70
- **FREE AS THE WIND**/He's Not A Happy Man (Buddah 162) 1.00 4.00 70
- **WEDNESDAY IN YOUR GARDEN**/ (Buddah 230) 1.00 4.00 71
- **WORST THAT COULD HAPPEN**/Your Kite, My Kite (Buddah 75) .75 3.00 68
- **YOU'LL NEVER WALK ALONE**/Minstral Sunday (Buddah 139) .50 2.00 69
- **YOUR HUSBAND, MY WIFE**/Everybody's Cookin' (Buddah 126) .75 3.00 69
- **YOUR HUSBAND, MY WIFE**/Upside Down (Inside Out) (Buddah 126) .75 3.00 69

("Upside Down" is the same song as "Everybody Cookin.")
Also see Crests, The

BROOKLYN DREAMS
- **MUSIC, HARMONY & RHYTHM**/Old Fashioned Girl (Millenium 610) .75 3.00 77
- **SAD EYES**/Hollywood Circles (Millenium 606) .75 3.00 77

BROOKS, Albert
- **PARTY FROM OUTER SPACE**/Phone Call To Americans (Asylum 45259) .75 3.00
- **REWRITING THE NATIONAL ANTHEM**/ (ABC 11391) .50 2.00 73

BROOKS & KORNFELD (Joe Brooks)
- **RIDE ON THE RAIN**/
  As I Walk Into The Morning Of Your Life (Epic 10190) .75 3.00 67

BROOKS, Bonnie
- **BRING BACK MY BEATLES TO ME**/
  A Letter From My Love (United Artists 708) 1.25 5.00 64

BROOKS, The: see Brook Brothers, The

BROOKS, Chuck & The Sharpies
- **SPINNING MY WHEELS**/You Make Me Feel Mean (DUB 2844) 25.00 100.00 58

BROOKS, Clinton, & The B's
- **TOM DULEY ROCK**/ (Apache 188) 1.00 4.00 59

BROOKS, Donnie
- **ALL I CAN GIVE**/Wishbone (Era 3049) .75 3.00 61
- **BOOMERANG**/How Long (Era 3052) .75 3.00 61
- **DEVIL AIN'T A MAN, THE**/How Long (Era 3014) .75 3.00 60
- **DOLL HOUSE**/Round Robin (Era 3028) .75 3.00 60
- **GOODNIGHT JUDY**/Up To My Ears In Tears (Era 3063) .75 3.00 61
- **IT'S NOT THAT EASY**/Cries My Heart (Era 3095) .75 3.00 62
- **MISSION BELL**/Do It For Me (Era 3018) .75 3.00 60
- **MEMPHIS**/That's Why (Era 3042) .75 3.00 61
- **MY FAVORITE KIND OF FACE**/He Stole Flo (Era 3071) .75 3.00 62
- **OH, YOU BEAUTIFUL DOLL**/Just A Bystander (Era 3077) .75 3.00 62
- **SWAY & MOVE WITH THE BEAT**/White Orchid (Era 3007) .75 3.00 60
- **UP TO MY EARS IN TEARS**/Sweet Lorraine (Era 3059) .75 3.00 69
- **YOUR LITTLE BOY'S COME HOME**/Goodnight Judy (Era 3063) .75 3.00 61

BROOKS, Elkie
- **HONEY, CAN I PUT YOUR CLOTHES ON**/ (A&M 1968) .50 2.00 77
- **PEARL'S A SINGER**/ (A&M 1935) .50 2.00 77
- **SUNSHINE AFTER THE RAIN**/ (A&M 1953) .50 2.00 77

Elkie Brooks is Billy J. Kramer's sister.

BROTHER NIGEL'S PROXY PARTY
- **LOOK AT THE FLOOR**/Dancing Girl (Fantasy 621) .75 3.00 69

BROTHERS, The
- **GIRLS ALRIGHT, THE**/Love Story (White Whale 255) .75 3.00 67
- **TODAY IS TODAY**/With The Rain (White Whale 250) .75 3.00 67

BROTHERS FOUR, The
- **AND THEN THE SUN GOES DOWN**/All I Need Is You (Columbia 4-43984) .75 3.00 66
- **BLUE WATER LINE**/Summer Days Alone (Columbia 4-42256) .75 3.00 61
- **CHICKA MUCKA HI DI**/Darlin',Won't You Wait (Columbia 4-41461) .75 3.00 59
- **FROGG**/Sweet Rosyanne (Columbia 4-41958) .75 3.00 61
- **GREENFIELDS**/Angelique O (Columbia 4-41571) .75 3.00 60
- **GREENFIELDS**/Angelique O (Columbia S7-30571) 1.50 6.00 60
  (Stereo single)
- **GREEN LEAVES OF SUMMER, THE**/
  Beautiful Brown Eyes (Columbia 4-41808) .75 3.00 60
- **GREEN LEAVES OF SUMMER, THE**/
  Beautiful Brown Eyes (Columbia S7-30808) 1.50 6.00 60
  (Stereo single)
- **HOOTENANNY SATURDAY NIGHT**/Across The Sea (Columbia 4-42927) .75 3.00 63
- **MY TANI**/Ellie Lou (Columbia 4-41692) .75 3.00 60
- **RATMAN & BOBIN IN THE CLIPPER CAPER**/
  Muleskinner (Columbia 4-43547) 1.25 5.00 66
- **TRY TO REMEMBER**/Sakura (Columbia 4-43404) .75 3.00 65

BROTHER SISTERS, The
- **ALONE**/Pass Me The Mustard (Mercury 71195) 1.00 4.00 5

BROWN, Al, & His Tunetoppers
- **MADISON, THE**/Mo Madison (Amy 804) 1.00 4.00 60

TITLE/FLIP	LABEL & NO.	GOOD	NEAR MINT	YR.
BROWN & HARPER				
ASTRONAUGHTS, THE/Zounds	(Crystal)	2.50	10.00	
BROWN, Arthur (The Crazy World of Arthur Brown)				
FIRE/Rest Cure	(Atlantic 2556)	.75	3.00	68
NIGHTMARE/I Put A Spell On You	(Track 2582)	.75	3.00	69
BROWN, B. & THE ROCKIN' McVOUTS				
FANNIE MAE IS BACK/Candied Yams	(Vest 830)	.75,	3.00	60

TITLE/FLIP	LABEL & NO.	GOOD	NEAR MINT	YR.
BROWN, Bill				
TIGHT LEVIS & BOOTS/ The Heart That You've Been Walkin' On	(Custom Sound SC-164)	3.75	15.00	
BROWN, Billy				
FLIP OUT/Echo Mountain	(Columbia 41297)	1.00	4.00	58
I WANTED YOU/Meet Me In The Alley, Sally	(Columbia 41100)	1.00	4.00	58
NEXT/Once In A Lifetime	(Columbia 41174)	1.00	4.00	58
BROWN, Boots				
BLOCK BUSTER/Shortnin' Bread	(RCA Victor 47-5110)	1.25	5.00	53
BLUE FAIRY BOOGIE/Breakfast Ball	(RCA Victor 47-5228)	1.25	5.00	53
CERVEZA/Juicy	(RCA Victor 47-7269)	1.00	4.00	58
TROLLIN'/Jim Twangy	(RCA Victor 47-7399)	1.00	4.00	59
Instrumentals				
BROWN, Brian, Trio				
BLUE'S FOR THE UFO/	(Academy 121)	.75	3.00	
BROWN BROTHERS, The				
BEST YOU CAN, THE/The Best You Can	(Columbia 45774)	.50	2.00	73
BROWN, Capability				
LIAR/	(Charisma 101)	.50	2.00	72
BROWN, Dee				
WATERGATE BLUES/	(Dee 1)	.75	3.00	72
BROWN, Don				
HUG ON A THRILL/	(First American 105)	.50	2.00	78
SITTING IN LIMBO/Romance & Magic	(First American 102)	.50	2.00	77
BROWN, Doug				
T.G.I.F./The First	(Hideout 1008)	1.00	4.00	
BROWN, Jay, & The Jets				
ROCKIN' THE GUITAR/	(Peach 736)	1.00	4.00	
BROWN, Louise				
SON-IN-LAW (Answer Song)/You Gave Me Misery	(Witch 1)	.75	3.00	61
BROWN, Michael (Of The Left Banke)				
CIRCLES/	(Kama Sutra 563)	.50	2.00	73
Also see Stories, The				
BROWN, Stanky, Group				
COALTOWN/Life Beyond	(Sire 745)	.50	2.00	77
CONFIDENT MAN/Free & Easy	(Sire 1007)	.50	2.00	77
DON'T YOU REFUSE/	(Sire 730)	.50	2.00	76
FALLING FAST/She's A Taker	(Sire 1023)	.50	2.00	78
ROCK 'N' ROLL STAR/	(Arista 0104)	.50	2.00	75
STOP IN THE NAME OF LOVE/Faith In The Family	(Sire 739)	.50	2.00	77
YOU'VE COME OVER ME/	(Sire 724)	.50	2.00	76
BROWN, Timmy				
DO THE CROSSFIRE/Love, Love, Love	(Mercury 72175)	.75	3.00	62
RUNNIN' LATE/If I Loved You	(Mercury 72226)	.75	3.00	63
BROWN, Tom, & The Tom Tom's				
TOMAHAWK/	(Jaro 77023)	2.00	8.00	
BROWNE, Duncan				
JOURNEY/	(RAK 4511)	.50	2.00	73
ON THE BOMBSITE/Alfred Bell	(Immediate 5010)	.75	3.00	69
WILD PLACES, THE/Camino Real (Parts 2 & 3)	(Sire 1047)	.50	2.00	79
BROWNE, Jackson				
DOCTOR MY EYES/Looking Into You	(Asylum 11004)	.50	2.00	72
FOUNTAIN OF SORROW/The Late Show	(Asylum 45242)	.50	2.00	75
HERE COME THOSE TEARS AGAIN/Linda Paloma	(Asylum 45379)	.50	2.00	77
PRETENDER, THE/Daddy's Tune	(Asylum 45399)	.50	2.00	77
REDNECK FRIEND/These Times You've Gone	(Asylum 11023)	.50	2.00	73
ROCK ME ON THE WATER/Something Fine	(Asylum 11006)	.50	2.00	72
RUNNING ON EMPTY/Nothing But Time	(Asylum 45460)	.50	2.00	78
STAY/Rosie	(Asylum 45485)	.50	2.00	78
TAKE IT EASY/Ready Or Not	(Asylum 11030)	.50	2.00	74
WALKING SLOW/	(Asylum 45227)	.50	2.00	74
YOU LOVE THE THUNDER/The Road	(Asylum 45543)	.50	2.00	78
BROWNSVILLE STATION				
BE-BOP CONFIDENTIAL/	(Warner Bros. 7441)	.50	2.00	71
I'M THE LEADER OF THE GANG/ Meet Me On The Fourth Floor	(Big Tree 15005)	.50	2.00	74
KINGS OF THE PARTY/Ostrich	(Big Tree 16001)	.50	2.00	74
LADY (PUT THE LIGHT ON ME)/Rockers & Rollers	(Private Stock 45149)	.50	2.00	77
LET YOUR YEAH BE YEAH/Mister Robert	(Big Tree 161)	.50	2.00	73
LOVE STEALER/Fever	(Epic 50695)	.50	2.00	79
MAMA DON'T ALLOW NO PARKIN'/I Got It Bad For You	(Big Tree 16029)	.50	2.00	75
MARTIAN BOOGIE, THE/Mr. Johnson Sez	(Private Stock 45167)	.50	2.00	77
RED BACK SPIDER, THE/Rock With The Music	(Big Tree 156)	.50	2.00	72
ROADRUNNER/Do The Bosco	(Warner Bros. 7456)	.50	2.00	70
SMOKIN' IN THE BOYS ROOM/Barefootin'	(Big Tree 10611)	.50	2.00	73

TITLE/FLIP	LABEL & NO.	GOOD	NEAR MINT	YR.
BRUBECK, Dave				
BOSSA NOVA U.S.A./This Can't Be Love	(Columbia 42651)	.75	3.00	62
TAKE FIVE/Blue Rondo A La Turk	(Columbia 41479)	.75	3.00	61
UNSQUARE DANCE/It's A Raggy Waltz	(Columbia 42228)	.75	3.00	61
Instrumentals				
BRUCE & JERRY				
I SAW HER FIRST/Take This Pearl	(Arwin 1003)	1.00	4.00	59
BRUCE & TERRY (Bruce Johnston & Terry Melcher)				
CARMEN/I Love You Model T	(Columbia 43238)	1.00	4.00	65
COME LOVE/Thank You Baby	(Columbia 43479)	1.00	4.00	65
CUSTOM MACHINE/Makaha At Midnight	(Columbia 42956)	1.00	4.00	64
DON'T RUN AWAY/Girl It's All Right Now	(Columbia 43582)	1.00	4.00	66
RAINING IN MY HEART/Four Strong Winds	(Columbia 43378)	1.00	4.00	65
SUMMER MEANS FUN/Yeah!	(Columbia 43055)	1.00	4.00	64
Also see California Music				
Also see Day, Terry				
Also see Sagittarius				
Also see Rip Chords, The				
BRUCE, Ed				
SEE THE BIG MAN CRY/You Need A New Love	(Wand 140)	.75	3.00	63
BRUCE, Jack (Of Cream)				
KEEP IT DOWN/	(RSO 507)	.50	2.00	75
BRUNO, Bruce				
DEAR JOANNE/Venus In Blue Jeans	(Roulette 4427)	1.50	6.00	62
HEY LITTLE ONE/Same Time Same Place	(Roulette 4386)	1.50	6.00	61
BRUNO & THE GLADIATORS				
ISTAMBUL/Warm Is The Sun	(Vault 901)	.75	3.00	62
BRYAN, Billy: see Pitney, Gene				
BRYAN, Dora				
ALL I WANT FOR CHRISTMAS IS A BEATLE/ If I Were A Fairy	(Fontana 427)	1.25	5.00	64
BRYANT, Anita				
AN ANGEL CRIED/I Can't Do It By Myself	(Carlton 547)	1.00	4.00	61
IN MY LITTLE CORNER OF THE WORLD/ Anyone Would Love You	(Carlton 530)	.75	3.00	60
ONE OF THE LUCKY ONES/Love Look Away	(Carlton 535)	.50	2.00	60
ORANGE BIRD SONG/Orange Tree	(Disneyland 823)	.50	2.00	71
PAPER ROSES/Mixed Emotions	(Carlton 528)	.75	3.00	60
PAPER ROSES/Mixed Emotions (Stereo single)	(Carlton 528)	1.50	6.00	60
PROMISE ME A ROSE/Do-Re-Mi	(Carlton 523)	.75	3.00	59
PROMISE ME A ROSE/Do-Re-Mi (Stereo single)	(Carlton 523)	1.50	6.00	59
SIX BOYS & SEVEN GIRLS/The Blessings Of Love	(Carlton 518)	.75	3.00	59
TEXAN & A GIRL FROM MEXICO, A/He's Not Good Enough	(Carlton 538)	.75	3.00	61
TILL THERE WAS YOU/Little George	(Carlton 512)	.75	3.00	59
TILL THERE WAS YOU/Little George (Stereo single)	(Carlton 512)	1.50	6.00	59
WONDERLAND BY NIGHT/Pictures	(Carlton 537)	.75	3.00	60
WORLD OF LONELY PEOPLE, THE/ It's Better To Cry Today Than Cry Tomorrow	(Columbia 43037)	.75	3.00	64
BRYANT, Laura				
BILLY/Part Time Gal	(Cameo 106)	1.00	4.00	57
BOBBY/Angel Tears	(Cameo 124)	1.00	4.00	58
KISS I NEVER HAD, THE/I Don't Hurt Anymore	(Cameo 112)	1.00	4.00	57
BRYANT, Lillie				
GOOD MORNING BABY/Gambler, The	(Cameo 122)	1.00	4.00	58
BRYANT, Ray				
LITTLE SUSIE (PART 4)/Little Susie (Part 2)	(Signature Records 12026)	.75	3.00	
MADISON TIME, THE/Madison Time, The (Part 2)	(Columbia 41628)	.75	3.00	60
BRYNDLE (Andrew Gold, Karla Bonoff, Wendy Waldman, Kenny Edwards)				
WOKE UP/Let's Go Home	(A&M 1252)	.75	3.00	72
B. T. EXPRESS, The				
FUNKY MUSIC (DON'T LAUGH AT MY FUNK)/ We Got It Together	(Columbia 3-10582)	.50	2.00	77
BUBBLE PUPPY, The				
BEGINNING/If I Had A Reason	(International Artists 133)	1.25	5.00	69
DAY'S OF OUR TIME/Thinking About Thinking	(International Artists 136)	1.25	5.00	69
HOT SMOKE & SASAFRASS/Lonely	(International Artists 128)	1.25	5.00	69
HURRY SUNDOWN/What Do You See	(International Artists 138)	1.25	5.00	70
BUBI & BOB				
MUMMY, THE/Biscayne Beat	(Shinx 1201)	1.25	5.00	59
BUCHANAN & ANCELL (Bill Buchanan & Bob Ancell)				
CREATURE, THE/Meet The Creature (Novelty/Break-in)	(Flying Saucer 501)	2.50	10.00	57
BUCHANAN & CELLA (With Bill Buchanan)				
STRING ALONG WITH PAL-O-MINE/More String Along With Pal-o-mine- Still More String Along With Pal-o-mine ("Paladin" Parody)	(ABC-Paramount 10033)	1.50	6.00	59
BUCHANAN & GOODMAN (Bill Buchanan & Dickie Goodman)				
BACK TO EARTH/Back To Earth (Part 2) (Original Title of "The Flying Saucer")	(Luniverse 101X)	15.00	60.00	
BANANA BOAT STORY, THE/The Mystery (Instrumental)	(Luniverse 103)	2.50	10.00	56
BUCHANAN & GOODMAN ON TRIAL/Crazy	(Luniverse 102)	3.75	15.00	56
FLYING SAUCER/Flying Saucer (Part 2)	(Radioactive 101)	3.75	15.00	
FLYING SAUCER, THE/Flying Saucer (Part 2) (Reissue of "Back To Earth")	(Luniverse 101)	2.00	8.00	56
FLYING SAUCER THE 2ND/Martian Melody (Instrumental)	(Luniverse 105)	2.50	10.00	57
FLYING SAUCER THE 3RD/The Cha Cha Lesson	(Comic 500)	2.50	10.00	59
FLYING SAUCER GOES WEST/ Saucer Serenade (Instrumental)	(Luniverse 108)	2.00	8.00	58
FRANKENSTEIN OF '59/Frankenstein Returns	(Novelty 301)	2.00	8.00	59
PUBLIC OPINION/Public Opinion (Part 2)	(Luniverse 102X)	50.00	200.00	56
SANTA & THE SATELLITE (PART 1)/ Santa & The Satellite (Part 2)	(Luniverse 107)	2.00	8.00	57
Novelties-most are break-ins.				
BUCHANAN & GREENFIELD (Bill Buchanan & Howard Greenfield)				
INVASION, THE/What A Lonely Party (Red Label)	(Novel 711)	2.50	10.00	64
INVASION, THE/What A Lonely Party (Red & White Label)	(Novel 711)	.75	3.00	72
BUCHANAN, Bill				
NIGHT BEFORE HALLOWEEN, THE/Beware	(United Artists 531)	1.25	5.00	62
THING, THE/Oh Happy Day	(Gone 5032)	3.75	15.00	58
BUCHANAN BROTHERS, The (Terry Cashman, Tommy West, Gene Pistilli)				
LAST TIME/The Feeling That I Get	(Event 3307)	.75	3.00	69
MEDICINE MAN/Medicine Man (Part 2)	(Event 3302)	.75	3.00	69
ROSIANNA/A Sad Song With A Happy Soul	(Event 3309)	.75	3.00	70
SON OF A LOVIN' MAN/I'll Never Get Enough	(Event 3305)	.75	3.00	69

TITLE/FLIP	LABEL & NO.	GOOD	NEAR MINT	YR.
BUCHANAN, Roy				
CIRCLE, THE/	(Atlantic 3433)	.50	2.00	77
DOWN BY THE RIVER/Supernova	(Atlantic 3489)	.50	2.00	78
GREEN ONIONS/	(Atlantic 3414)	.50	2.00	77
BUCK, John, & His Blazers				
FORBIDDEN CITY/Chi Chi	(Warner Bros. 5194)	.75	3.00	61
BUCKACRE				
BOUND TO BE BLUE/Love Never Lasts Forever	(MCA 40616)	.50	2.00	76
MORNING COMES/Just Another Night	(MCA 40702)	.50	2.00	77
STAR THAT SHINES/Tear Down The Walls	(MCA 40919)	.50	2.00	78
BUCKEYE				
JUST THE WAY/	(Polydor 2042)	.50	2.00	79
WHERE WILL YOUR HEART TAKE YOU/That Kind Of Man	(Polydor 14578)	.50	2.00	79
BUCKINGHAM-NICKS (Lindsay Buckingham & Stevie Nicks)				
CRYING IN THE NIGHT/Stephanie	(Polydor 14428)	.50	2.00	77
DON'T LET ME DOWN AGAIN/	(Polydor 14335)	.50	2.00	76
Also see Fleetwood Mac				
BUCKINGHAMS, The				
BACK IN LOVE AGAIN/You Misunderstand Me	(Columbia 44533)	.75	3.00	68
DON'T YOU CARE/Why Don't You Love Me	(Columbia 44053)	.75	3.00	67
HEY BABY (THEY'RE PLAYING OUR SONG)/ And Our Love	(Columbia 44254)	.75	3.00	67
I CALL YOUR NAME/Wakin' Up & Breakin' Up	(USA 848)	1.00	4.00	66
I'LL GO CRAZY/Don't Want To Cry	(USA 844)	1.00	4.00	66
I'VE BEEN WRONG/Love Ain't Enough	(USA 853)	1.00	4.00	66
KIND OF A DRAG/You Make Me Feel So Good	(USA 860)	1.00	4.00	66
LAWDY MISS CLAWDY/I Call Your Name	(USA 869)	1.00	4.00	67
MERCY, MERCY, MERCY/You Are Gone	(Columbia 44182)	.75	3.00	67
SONG OF THE BREEZE/Where Did You Come From	(Columbia 44533)	.75	3.00	68
SUMMERTIME/I Don't Want To Cry	(USA 873)	1.00	4.00	67
SUSAN/Foreign Policy	(Columbia 44378)	1.00	4.00	67
SWEETS FOR MY SWEET/Beginners Love	(Spectra-Sound 4618)	2.50	10.00	67
THIS IS HOW MUCH I LOVE YOU/Can't Find The Words	(Columbia 44790)	.75	3.00	69
Also see Centuries, The				
Also see Falling Pebbles, The				
Also see Tufano & Giammerese				

TITLE/FLIP	LABEL & NO.	GOOD	NEAR MINT	YR.
BUCKINGHAMS, The				
GONNA SAY GOODBYE/Many Times	(Laurie 3258)	.75	3.00	64
BUCKINS, Mickey, & The New Breed				
BIG BOY PETE/Reflections Of Charlie Brown	(South Camp 7007)	.75	3.00	67
BUCKLEY, Lord Richard				
GETTYSBURG ADDRESS, THE (Original Version)/ Gettysburg Address (Hip Version)	(Hip-Hi 301)	1.00	4.00	
BUCKLEY, Tim				
AREN'T YOU THE GIRL/Strange Street Affair Under Blue	(Elektra 45612)	.75	3.00	66
MORNING GLORY/Once I Was	(Elektra 45623)	.75	3.00	67
BUCKWHEAT				
HEY LITTLE GIRL/	(London 184)	.50	2.00	72
I GOT TO BOOGIE/I Just Can't Turn My Habit Into Love	(London 189)	.50	2.00	72
SIMPLE SONG OF FREEDOM/I Got To Boogie	(London 176)	.50	2.00	72
BUD & TRAVIS (Bud Dashiel & Travis Edmonson)				
BALLAD OF THE ALAMO/Green Leaves Of Summer	(Liberty 55284)	.75	3.00	60
CLOUDY SUMMER AFTERNOON/E La Bas	(Liberty 55235)	.75	3.00	60
BUDD, Julie				
MUSIC TO MY HEART/	(Tom Cat 10600)	.50	2.00	77
MUSIC TO MY HEART/	(Alston 3730)	.50	2.00	77
OH NO NOT MY BABY/	(RCA 0817)	.50	2.00	73
ONE FINE DAY/Mama Joan (Shown as by Julie)	(Tom Cat 10454)	.50	2.00	76
SEE YOU IN SEPTEMBER/	(RCA 0741)	.50	2.00	73
BUDDIES, The				
MUST BE TRUE LOVE/Holly Gully Mama	(Comet 2143)	1.25	5.00	
BUDDIES, The				
BEATLE, THE/Pulsebeat	(Swan 4170)	1.25	5.00	64
ON THE GO/Only My Friend	(Swing 102)	.75	3.00	64
BUDDY & THE DIMES				
IT'S A SIN TO TELL A LIE/Sweet Heart	(Emi 2440)	1.25	5.00	
BUDDY & THE HEARTS				
THIRTY DAYS/Let It Rock	(Landa 701)	.75	3.00	64
BUDDY & THE WILDCATS				
NIGHT CRAWL/(The Party's) Over Here	(Rust 5060)	.75	3.00	63
BUDGIE				
CRASH COURSE/Nude Disintegrating Parachutist Woman	(Kapp 2152)	.50	2.00	72
WHISKEY RIVER/Stranded	(Kapp 2185)	.50	2.00	72
BUENA VISTAS, The				
FOXY/Filet Of Soul	(Swan 4269)	.75	3.00	66
HERE COME DA JUDGE/Big Red	(Marquee 443)	.75	3.00	68
HOT SHOT/	(Swan 4255)	.75	3.00	66

TITLE/FLIP	LABEL & NO.	GOOD	NEAR MINT	YR.
BUFFALO REBELS, The				
BUFFALO TWIST/	(Mar-Lee 0958)	1.50	6.00	61
DONKEY WALK/Buffalo Blues	(Mar-Lee 0095)	1.50	6.00	61
THEME FROM REBEL/Any Way You Want Me	(Mar-Lee 0096)	1.50	6.00	61
Also see Rebels, The				
Also see Rockin' Rebels, The				
BUFFALO SPRINGFIELD, The				
BLUEBIRD/Mr. Soul	(Atco 6499)	.75	3.00	67
EVERYBODY'S WRONG/Burned	(Atco 6452)	1.00	4.00	66
EXPECTING TO FLY/Everydays	(Atco 6545)	.75	3.00	67
FOR WHAT IT'S WORTH (STOP, HEY WHAT'S THAT SOUND)/ Do I Have To Come Right Out & Say It	(Atco 6459)	.75	3.00	67
NOWADAYS CLANCY CAN'T EVEN SING/Go & Say Goodbye	(Atco 6428)	1.00	4.00	66
ON THE WAY HOME/Four Day's Gone	(Atco 6615)	.75	3.00	67
ROCK 'N' ROLL WOMAN/A Child's Claim To Fame	(Atco 6519)	.75	3.00	67
SPECIAL CARE/Kind Woman	(Atco 6602)	.75	3.00	68
UN-MUNDO/Merry-Go-Round	(Atco 6572)	.75	3.00	68
Group members: Stephen Stills, Neil Young, Richie Furay, Jim Messina, Bruce Palmer, Dewey Martin.				
BUFFETT, Jimmy				
CAPTAIN & THE KID, THE/	(ABC 12175)	.50	2.00	76
CHANGES IN LATITUDES, CHANGES IN ATTITUDES/Landfall	(ABC 12305)	.50	2.00	77
CHEESEBURGER IN PARADISE/African Friend	(ABC 12358)	.50	2.00	78
COME MONDAY/The Wino & I Know	(Dunhill 4385)	.50	2.00	74
GRAPEFRUIT - JUICY FRUIT/	(Dunhill 4359)	.50	2.00	73
GREAT FILLING STATION HOLDUP, THE/ Why Don't We Get Drunk (& Screw)	(Dunhill 4348)	1.00	4.00	73
HAVANA DAYDREAMIN'/	(ABC 12143)	.50	2.00	76
HE WENT TO PARIS/	(ABC 11399)	.50	2.00	73
FINS/Dreamsicle	(MCA 41109)	.50	2.00	79
LIVINGSTON SATURDAY NIGHT/Cowboy In The Jungle	(ABC 12391)	.50	2.00	78
MANANA/Coast Of Marseilles	(ABC 12428)	.50	2.00	78
MARGARITTAVILLE/Miss You Badly	(ABC 12254)	.50	2.00	77
PENCIL THIN MOUSTACHE/	(Dunhill 15011)	.50	2.00	74
PIRATE LOOKS AT FORTY, A/Presents To Send You	(Dunhill 15029)	.50	2.00	74
SAXOPHONES/Ringaling, Ringaling	(Dunhill 4378)	.50	2.00	73
WOMAN GOIN' CRAZY ON CAROLINE STREET/	(ABC 12200)	.50	2.00	76
VOLCANO/Stranded On A Sandbar	(MCA 41161)	.50	2.00	79
BUG COLLECTORS, The				
BEATLE BUG/Thief In The Night	(Catch 103)	1.25	5.00	64
BUG MEN, The				
BEATLES, YOU BUG ME/Bloomin' Bird	(Dot 16592)	1.25	5.00	64
BUGGLES, The				
VIDEO KILLED THE RADIO STAR/Kid Dynamo	(Island 49114)	.50	2.00	79
BUGGS, The				
BUGGS VS. THE BEATLES, THE/She Loves Me	(Soma 1413)	1.50	6.00	64
BUGS, The				
PRETTY GIRL/Slide	(Polaris 0001)	1.25	5.00	
BULAWAYO SWEET RHYTHM BOYS, The				
SKOKIAAN/In The Mood	(London 1491)	1.25	5.00	54
BULLDOG (With Gene Cornish & Dino Danelli)				
ARE YOU REALLY HAPPY TOGETHER/	(MCA 40014)	.50	2.00	73
I TIP MY HAT/	(MCA 40050)	.50	2.00	73
MAN OF CONSTANT SORROW/	(Guyden 5000)	.50	2.00	
NO/Good Times Are Comin'	(Decca 32996)	.50	2.00	72
Also see Young Rascals, The				
Also see Fotomaker				
BULLDOG				
WHEI-LING-TY-LOU (HOW I LOVE YOU)/	(Buddah 299)	.50	2.00	72
BULLDOGS, The				
JOHN, PAUL, GEORGE & RINGO/What Do I See	(Mercury 72262)	1.50	6.00	64
BULLENS, Cindy				
ANXIOUS HEART/Time 'N' Charges	(United Artists-Mainman 1293)	.50	2.00	79
HIGH SCHOOL HISTORY/Mr. Anonymous	(United Artists-Mainman 1248)	.50	2.00	78
SURVIVOR/Finally Rockin'	(United Artists-Mainman 1261)	.50	2.00	79
TRUST ME/	(Casablanca 2217)	.50	2.00	79
BULLET				
LITTLE BIT O' SOUL/Up Your Sleeve	(Big Tree 140)	.50	2.00	72
WHITE LIES, BLUE EYES/Changes Of Mind	(Big Tree 123)	.50	2.00	71
WILL POWER WEAK, TEMPTATION STRONG/	(Big Tree 131)	.50	2.00	72
BUMBLE, B., & The Stingers: see B. Bumble & The Stingers				
BUNGLE & KLEEN				
UFO LANDING, THE/ (Novelty/Break-in)	(Partee 1302)	1.25	5.00	
BUNKER HILL				
HIDE & GO SEEK (PART 1)/Hide & Go Seek (Part 2)	(Mala 451)	.75	3.00	65
BUOYS, The				
GIVE UP YOUR GUNS/	(Scepter 12318)	.50	2.00	71
TIMOTHY/It Feels Good	(Scepter 12275)	.50	2.00	71
BURCHETT, Dave, & Mark Smith				
MONDAY NIGHT FOOTBALL/Howard Nosale (Novelty/Break-in)	(Birdie 9)	1.25	5.00	
BURDON, Eric, & Jimmy Witherspoon				
SOLEDAD/Headin' For Home	(MGM 14296)	.75	3.00	71
BURDON, Eric, & War				
MAGIC MOUNTAIN/Home Dream	(ABC 12244)	.50	2.00	77
REAL ME, THE/Letter From The Country Farm	(Capitol 3997)	.75	3.00	74
SPILL THE WINE/Magic Mountain	(MGM K-14118)	.75	3.00	70
THEY CAN'T TAKE AWAY OUR MUSIC/Home Cookin'	(MGM K-14196)	.75	3.00	70
Also see Animals, The				
BURGESS, Dave (Of The Champs)				
DON'T CRY, FOR YOU I LOVE/Fire In The Eyes (Shown as by Dave Dupre)	(Challenge 1001)	1.00	4.00	57
EVERLOVIN'/Just For Me (With the Chimes)	(Challenge 59045)	1.00	4.00	59
I'M AVAILABLE/Who's Gonna Cry	(Challenge 1008)	1.00	4.00	57
JOB WELL DONE, A/Our Tomorrow (Shown as by Dave Dupre)	(Challenge 1005)	1.00	4.00	57
LOVEY DOVEY BABY/I Hang My Head & Cry	(Challenge 59032)	1.00	4.00	59
LULU/I Don't Want To Know (With the Chimes)	(Challenge 59037)	1.00	4.00	59
MAYBELLE/Take This Love	(Challenge 1018)	1.00	4.00	58
BURK, Tommy, & The Counts				
YOU TOOK MY HEART/She Told A Lie	(Rich-Rose 1003)	6.25	25.00	
BURKE, Keni (Of The Stairsteps)				
KEEP ON SINGING/Day	(Dark Horse 8522)	.50	2.00	77
SHUFFLE/From Me To You	(Dark Horse 8474)	.50	2.00	77
BURNETT, Carol				
I JUST MADE A FOOL OF MYSELF (OVER JOHN FOSTER DULLES)/	(ABC-Paramount 9850)	1.00	4.00	57
MEANTIME/You're So London (With Julie Andrews)	(Columbia 57712/3)	.75	3.00	63
BURNETTE, Billy				
BELIEVE WHAT YOU SAY/Mississippi Line	(Polydor-BGO 14549)	.50	2.00	79
BURNETTE, Billy Joe				
WELCOME HOME ELVIS/Welcome Home Elvis	(Gusto-Starday 167)	.50	2.00	77
BURNETTE, Dorsey				
BE A NAVY MAN/	(No label or number)	1.25	5.00	
BE A NAVY MAN/ (Picture sleeve)	(No label or number)	3.75	15.00	
BERTHA LOU/Til The Law Says Stop	(Cee Jam 16)	1.25	5.00	57
CALL ME LOW DOWN/One Lump Sum	(Happy Tiger 563)	.75	3.00	70
CASTLE IN THE SKY/Boys Kept Hanging Around	(Reprise 20093)	.75	3.00	62
CIRCLE ROCK/House With A Tin Roof Top	(Imperial 5987)	1.00	4.00	63
DARLING JANE/I'm A Waitin' For Ya Baby	(Reprise 20121)	.75	3.00	63
DEVIL'S QUEEN, THE/Let's Fall In Love	(Abbott 188)	1.50	6.00	55
EVER SINCE THE WORLD BEGAN/Long, Long Time Ago	(Melody 118)	1.00	4.00	64
FOUR FOR TEXAS/Foolish Pride	(Reprise 0246)	1.00	4.00	63
GHOST OF BILLY MALLOO, THE/Red Roses	(Era 3025)	.75	3.00	61
GREAT SHAKIN' FEVER/That's Me Without You	(Era 3045)	.75	3.00	61
GREATEST LOVE, THE/Thin Little, Plain Little, Simple Little Girl	(Liberty 56087)	.75	3.00	69
HEY LITTLE ONE/Big Rock Candy Mountain	(Era 3019)	.75	3.00	60
I'LL WALK AWAY/ Son, You've Got To Make It Alone	(Music Factory 417)	.75	3.00	68
IF YOU WANT TO LOVE SOMEBODY/ Teach Me Little Children	(Smash 2039)	.75	3.00	66
IN THE MORNING/To Remember	(Smash 2029)	.75	3.00	66
INVISIBLE CHAINS/Pebbles	(Reprise 20177)	.75	3.00	63
(IT'S NO) SIN/Hard Rock Mine	(Era 3041)	.75	3.00	61
JIMMY BROWN/Everybody's Angel	(Mel-o-dy 116)	.75	3.00	64
LITTLE ACORN/Cold As Usual	(Mel-o-dy 113)	.75	3.00	64
LONELY TRAIN/Misery	(Imperial 5597)	1.00	4.00	59
LUCY DARLIN'/Black Roses	(Merri 206)	.75	3.00	
MAGNIFICENT SANCTUARY BAND/	(Condor 1005)	.50	2.00	70
ONE OF THE LONELY/Where's The Girl	(Reprise 20208)	.75	3.00	63
RAINING IN MY HEART/A Full House	(Dot 16230)	1.00	4.00	61
RIVER & THE MOUNTAIN, THE/This Hotel	(Era 3033)	.75	3.00	61
SAD BOY/The Feminine Touch	(Dot 16265)	.75	3.00	61
TALL OAK TREE/I Just Can't Be Tamed	(Smash 2062)	.75	3.00	66
TALL OAK TREE/Juarez Town	(Era 3012)	.75	3.00	60
TO BE A MAN/Fly Away & Hurry Home	(Happy Tiger 546)	.50	2.00	70
TRY/You Came As A Miracle	(Imperial 5561)	1.00	4.00	59
YOUR LOVE/Way In The Middle Of The Night	(Imperial 5668)	1.00	4.00	60
BURNETTE, Johnny				
ALL WEEK LONG/It Isn't There	(Capitol 5023)	1.00	4.00	63
BIG BIG WORLD/Ballad Of The One Eyed Jacks	(Liberty 55318)	.75	3.00	61
BIGGER MAN/Less Than A Heartache	(Magic Lamp 515)	1.00	4.00	64
CLOWN SHOES/Why I Am	(Liberty 55416)	.75	3.00	62
DAMN THE DEFIANT/Lonesome Waters	(Liberty 55489)	.75	3.00	62
DON'T DO IT/Patrick Henry	(Liberty 55243)	1.00	4.00	60
DREAMIN'/Cincinnatti Fireball	(Liberty 55258)	1.00	4.00	60
FOOL OF THE YEAR, THE/Poorest Boy In Town	(Liberty 55448)	.75	3.00	62
FOUNTAIN OF LOVE/What A Summer Day	(Sahara 512)	1.00	4.00	64
GIRLS/I've Got A Lot Of Things To Do	(Liberty 55345)	.75	3.00	61
GOD, COUNTRY & MY BABY/Honestly I Do	(Liberty 55379)	.75	3.00	61
GUMBO/Me & The Bear	(Freedom 44011)	1.25	5.00	59
I WANNA THANK YOU FOLKS/Giant	(Chancellor 1116)	1.50	6.00	62
I'M RESTLESS/Kiss Me	(Freedom 44001)	1.25	5.00	59
LITTLE BOY SAD/I Go Down To The River	(Liberty 55298)	.75	3.00	61
OPPOSITE, THE/You Taught Me The Way To Love You	(Capitol 5114)	1.25	5.00	64
REMEMBER ME/Time Is Not Enough	(Chancellor 1129)	1.25	5.00	62
SETTIN' THE WOODS ON FIRE/Kentucky Waltz	(Liberty 55222)	1.25	5.00	60
SWEET DOLL BABY/I'll Never Love Again	(Freedom 44017)	1.25	5.00	59
SWEET SUZIE/Walkin' Talkin' Doll	(Capitol 5176)	1.00	4.00	64
TAG-ALONG/Party Girl	(Chancellor 1123)	1.50	6.00	62
YOU'RE SIXTEEN/I Beg Your Pardon	(Liberty 55285)	.75	3.00	60
BURNETTE, Johnny & Dorsey				
HEY SUE/It Don't Take Much	(Reprise 20153)	1.25	5.00	63
WARM LOVE/My Honey (Shown as by the Burnette Brothers)	(Imperial 5509)	3.75	15.00	58
Also see Texans, The				
BURNETTE, Johnny, Trio (Johnny Burnette, Dorsey Burnette, Paul Burlison)				
BLUES, STAY AWAY FROM ME/Midnight Train	(Coral 62190)	6.25	25.00	60
DRINKIN' WINE SPO-DEE-O-DEE/Butterfingers (Shown as by Johnny Burnette)	(Coral 61869)	12.50	50.00	57
DRINKIN' WINE SPO-DEE-O-DEE/Butterfingers (Promotional issue, shown as by Johnny Burnette.)	(Coral 61869)	10.00	40.00	57
EAGER BEAVER BABY/Touch Me (Shown as by Johnny Burnette)	(Coral 61829)	10.00	40.00	57
EAGER BEAVER BABY/Touch Me (Promotional issue, shown as by Johnny Burnette.)	(Coral 61829)	7.50	30.00	57
HONEY HUSH/The Train Kept A Rollin'	(Coral 61719)	15.00	60.00	56
HONEY HUSH/The Train Kept A Rollin' (Promotional issue)	(Coral 61719)	12.50	50.00	56
LONESOME TRAIN (ON A LONESOME TRACK)/ I Just Found Out	(Coral 61758)	10.00	40.00	56
LONESOME TRAIN (ON A LONESOME TRACK)/ I Just Found Out (Promotional issue)	(Coral 61758)	7.50	30.00	56
MIDNIGHT TRAIN/Oh Baby Babe (Shown as by Johnny Burnette & The Rock 'N Roll Trio)	(Coral 61675)	12.50	50.00	56
MIDNIGHT TRAIN/Oh Baby Babe (Promotional issue) (Shown as by Johnny Burnette & The Rock 'N Roll Trio)	(Coral 61675)	10.00	40.00	56
ROCK BILLY BOOGIE/If You Want It Enough (Shown as by Johnny Burnette)	(Coral 61918)	12.50	50.00	57
ROCK BILLY BOOGIE/If You Want It Enough (Promotional issue, shown as by Johnny Burnette.)	(Coral 61918)	10.00	40.00	57
TEAR IT UP/You're Undecided (Shown as by Johnny Burnette & The Rock 'N Roll Trio)	(Coral 61651)	12.50	50.00	56
TEAR IT UP/You're Undecided (Promotional issue) (Shown as by Johnny Burnette & The Rock 'N Roll Trio)	(Coral 61651)	10.00	40.00	56
YOU'RE UNDECIDED/Go Along Mule (Shown as by Johnny Burnette & The Rock 'N Roll Trio)	(Von 1006)	37.50	150.00	54
BURNING SLICKS, The				
MIDNIGHT DRAG/Hard Drivin' Man	(Battle 45926)	1.00	4.00	63
MIDNIGHT DRAG/Hard Drivin' Man	(Riverside 4571)	1.00	4.00	63
BURNS, George				
OLD FOLDS/Mr. Bojangles	(Buddah 338)	.50	2.00	72
BURRELL, Boz (Later of Bad Company)				
PINOCCHIO/The Baby Song	(Epic 10097)	1.25	5.00	66
BURTON, James				
CORN PICKIN'/Texas Waltz (shown as by James Burton & Ralph Mooney)	(Capitol 2140)	1.00	4.00	68
JIMMY'S BLUES/Love Lost (Shown as by Jimmy Burton)	(Miramar 108)	1.50	6.00	
James Burton's lead guitar artistry has been heard on nearly all of the Rick Nelson hits. From 1969 until Elvis Presley's death in 1977, James was the lead guitarist for Elvis, both in the studio and on tour.				
BURTON, Richard				
MARRIED MAN/ Finding Words For Spring (By Richard Hayman)	(MGM 13307)	.75	3.00	64
BURTON, Wendy				
17 MILLION BICYCLES/ Mommy's Daddy, Daddy's Daddy & Santa Claus	(Columbia 42624)	.75	3.00	62
BUSCH, Lou (Joe "Fingers" Carr)				
11TH HOUR MELODY/Charming Mademoiselle	(Capitol 3349)	1.00	4.00	56
ZAMBEZI/Rainbow's End	(Capitol 3272)	1.00	4.00	55
BUSEY, Gary				
CLEAR LAKE MEDLEY: (OH BOY-MAYBE BABY-NOT FADE AWAY)/ Everyday	(Epic-American Intl. 50607)	.50	2.00	78
TRUE LOVE WAYS/Maybe Baby	(Epic-American Intl. 50581)	.50	2.00	78
Gary Busey portrayed Buddy Holly in the film "The Buddy Holly Story."				
BUSH, Kate				
MAN WITH THE CHILD IN HIS EYES, THE/Moving	(EMI America 8006)	.50	2.00	79
WUTHERING HEIGHTS/Kite	(EMI America 8003)	.50	2.00	78
BUSKIN, David (Of Pierce Arrow)				
REST OF THE YEAR, THE/	(Epic 10817)	.50	2.00	72
WHEN I NEED YOU MOST OF ALL/	(Epic 10880)	.50	2.00	72
BUSS				
TOO YOUNG TO UNDERSTAND/Woman	(Onyx 7008)	1.25	5.00	
BUSTERS, The				
ALL AMERICAN SURFER/Pine Tree Hop	(Arlen 740)	1.25	5.00	63
BUST OUT/Astronauts	(Arlen 735)	1.25	5.00	63
TORRID ZONE/ Instrumentals	(Arlen 745)	1.25	5.00	64
BUTANES, The				
DON'T FORGET I LOVE YOU/That's My Desire	(Enrico 1007)	.75	3.00	61
BUTLER, Daws				
RINGO RINGO/Clementine	(Mercury 72262)	1.25	5.00	64
BUTTERFIELD BLUES BAND, The (With Paul Butterfield & Elvin Bishop)				
COME ON IN/I Got A Mind To Give Up Living	(Elektra 45609)	1.25	5.00	67
BUTTERFLYS, The				
GOODNIGHT BABY/The Swim	(Red Bird 009)	.75	3.00	64
BUTTONS, The				
FOOT STOMPIN' U.S.A./Walk Away Girl	(Columbia 42834)	.75	3.00	63
BUTTONS & BEAUS, The				
NEVER LEAVE YOUR SUGAR (STANDING IN THE RAIN)/ Twistin' Blues	(Zen 104)	1.25	5.00	63
BUTTONS, Red				
HO HO SONG, THE/Strange Things Are Happening	(Columbia 39981)	1.00	4.00	53
BUZZ & BUCKY				
TIGER-A-GO-GO/Bay City	(Amy 924)	.75	3.00	65
BUZZ, The				
I'VE GOTTA BUZZ/You're Holding Me Down	(Coral 62492)	1.00	4.00	64
BUZZCOCKS, The				
EVERYBODY'S HAPPY NOWADAYS/ Why Can't I Touch It?	(International R.S. 9001)	.50	2.00	79
BUZZSAW				
LIVE IN THE SPRINGTIME/ I Can Make You Happy	(RCA Victor 47-8000)	1.25	5.00	62
BYE BYES, The				
BLONDE HAIR, BLUE EYES, RUBY LIPS/Do You?	(Mercury 71530)	1.00	4.00	59
BYRD, Charlie				
MEDITATION (MEDITACAO)/O Barquinho (Instrumentals)	(Riverside 4544)	.75	3.00	63
BYRD, Jerry				
(THEME FROM) ADVENTURES IN PARADISE/ Indian Love Call	(Monument 419)	.75	3.00	60
MEMORIES OF MARIA/Invitation Instrumentals	(Monument 449)	.75	3.00	62
BYRD, Russell (Bert Russell)				
YOU'D BETTER COME HOME/Let's Tell Him All About It	(Wand 107)	.75	3.00	61

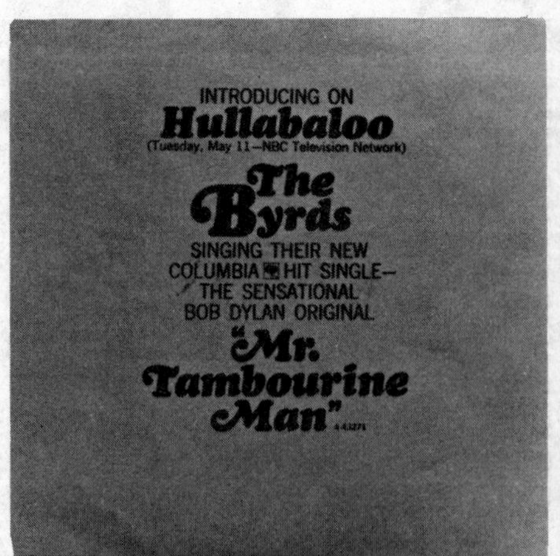

TITLE/FLIP	LABEL & NO.	GOOD	NEAR MINT	YR.
BYRDS, The				
ALL I REALLY WANT TO DO/ All I Really Want To Do (Red plastic promotional issue)	(Columbia 43332)	6.25	25.00	65
ALL I REALLY WANT TO DO/ I'll Feel A Whole Lot Better	(Columbia 43332)	1.00	4.00	65
AMERICA'S GREAT NATIONAL PASTIME/ Farther Along	(Columbia 45514)	.75	3.00	71
BALLAD OF EASY RIDER/Wasn't Born To Follow	(Columbia 44990)	1.00	4.00	69
CHESTNUT MARE/Just A Season	(Columbia 45259)	.75	3.00	70
COWGIRL IN THE SAND/Long Live The King	(Asylum 11019)	.50	2.00	73
DRUG STORE, TRUCK DRIVIN' MAN/ Bad Night At The Whiskey	(Columbia 44746)	.75	3.00	69

TITLE/FLIP	LABEL & NO.	GOOD	NEAR MINT	YR.
EIGHT MILES HIGH/Why	(Columbia 43578)	.75	3.00	66
5 D (FIFTH DIMENSION)/Captain Soul	(Columbia 43702)	1.00	4.00	66
FULL CIRCLE/Long Live The King	(Asylum 11016)	.50	2.00	73
GLORY, GLORY/Citizen Kane	(Columbia 45440)	.75	3.00	71
GOIN' BACK/Change Is Now	(Columbia 44362)	1.00	4.00	67
HAVE YOU SEEN HER FACE/Don't Make Waves	(Columbia 44157)	1.00	4.00	67
JESUS IS JUST ALRIGHT/ It's All Over Now, Baby Blue	(Columbia 45071)	.75	3.00	70
LADY FRIEND/Old John Robertson	(Columbia 44230)	1.00	4.00	67
LAY LADY, LAY/Old Blue	(Columbia 44868)	1.00	4.00	69
LOVER OF THE BAYOU/Goin' Back	(Scholastic 1602)	1.50	6.00	
MR. SPACEMAN/What's Happening	(Columbia 43766)	1.00	4.00	66
MR. TAMBOURINE MAN/I Knew I'd Want You	(Columbia 43271)	1.00	4.00	65
MR. TAMBOURINE MAN/Mr. Tambourine Man (Red plastic promotional issue)	(Columbia 43271)	10.00	40.00	65
MR. TAMBOURINE MAN/Mr. Tambourine Man (Picture sleeve for promotional issue)	(Columbia 43271)	15.00	60.00	65
MY BACK PAGES/Renaissance Fair	(Columbia 44054)	1.00	4.00	67
PRETTY BOY FLOYD/I Am A Pilgrim	(Columbia 44643)	1.00	4.00	68
SET YOU FREE THIS TIME/It Won't Be Wrong	(Columbia 43501)	1.00	4.00	66
SO YOU WANNA BE A ROCK & ROLL STAR/ Everybody's Been Burned	(Columbia 43987)	1.00	4.00	67
TURN, TURN, TURN/She Don't Care About Time	(Columbia 43424)	1.00	4.00	65
TURN, TURN, TURN/Turn, Turn, Turn (Red plastic promotional issue)	(Columbia 43424)	6.25	25.00	65
YOU AIN'T GOIN' NOWHERE/Artificial Energy	(Columbia 44499)	1.00	4.00	68

Group members: Roger McGuinn, David Crosby, Gene Clark, Chris Hillman, Michael Clark.
Also see Battin, Skip
Also see Beefeaters, The
Also see Clark, Gene

BYRNES, Edward

TITLE/FLIP	LABEL & NO.	GOOD	NEAR MINT	YR.
KOOKIE, KOOKIE (LEND ME YOUR COMB) (With Connie Stevens)/ You're The Top	(Warner Bros. 5047)	1.00	4.00	59
KOOKIE'S LOVE SONG (PART 1)/ Kookies Love Song (Part 2) (With the Mary Kaye Trio)	(Warner Bros. 5114)	1.00	4.00	59
LIKE I LOVE YOU (With "Friend")/ Kookie's Mad Pad	(Warner Bros. 5087)	1.00	4.00	59
YULESVILLE/Lonely Christmas	(Warner Bros. 5121)	1.00	4.00	59

BYRON, Jimmy

TITLE/FLIP	LABEL & NO.	GOOD	NEAR MINT	YR.
SIDEWALK ROCK/Screamin' (Instrumentals)	(Teen 113)	1.25	5.00	57

BYRON, Lord Douglas

TITLE/FLIP	LABEL & NO.	GOOD	NEAR MINT	YR.
BIG BAD HO-DAD/Coffee House (By The Continentals)	(Union 505)	1.00	4.00	62
SURFIN' SANTA/The Drink That Makes You Shrink	(Dot 16685)	.75	3.00	65

C

CABBOT, Johnny

TITLE/FLIP	LABEL & NO.	GOOD	NEAR MINT	YR.
NIGHT & DAY/On My Own Again	(Columbia 4-42283)	5.00	20.00	62
NIGHT & DAY/On My Own Again (Promotional issue)	(Columbia 4-42283)	3.00	12.00	62
NIGHT & DAY/On My Own Again (Compact 33 single)	(Columbia 3-42283)	10.00	40.00	62

Also see 4 Seasons, The

CACTUS (With Tim Bogert & Carmine Appice)

TITLE/FLIP	LABEL & NO.	GOOD	NEAR MINT	YR.
ALASKA/Token Chokin'	(Atco 6842)	.75	3.00	71

Also see Vanilla Fudge

CADD, Brian (Of Axiom)

TITLE/FLIP	LABEL & NO.	GOOD	NEAR MINT	YR.
WHITE ON WHITE ELDORADO/Longest Night	(Capitol 4374)	.50	2.00	77

Brian Cadd was also with the group.

CADO BELLE

TITLE/FLIP	LABEL & NO.	GOOD	NEAR MINT	YR.
AIRPORT SHUTDOWN/Paper In The Rain	(Anchor 21005)	.50	2.00	75
GOT TO LOVE/	(Anchor 21007)	.50	2.00	77

CAESAR & CLEO: see Sonny & Cher

CAESAR, Irving

TITLE/FLIP	LABEL & NO.	GOOD	NEAR MINT	YR.
WHAT! NO MICKEY MOUSE/ What Kind Of Party Is This	(Buena Vista 477)	.75	3.00	64

CAESARS, The

TITLE/FLIP	LABEL & NO.	GOOD	NEAR MINT	YR.
(LA LA) I LOVE YOU/Get Yourself Together	(Lanie 2001)	1.00	4.00	

CAFE CREAM

TITLE/FLIP	LABEL & NO.	GOOD	NEAR MINT	YR.
DISCOMANIA (PART 1)/Discomania (Part 2) (Medley; 12" single issue)	(RSP 899)	1.25	5.00	78

Part 1: Hey Jude-Day Tripper-Get Back-Back In The U.S.S.R.-I Want To Hold Your Hand-Yellow Submarine-Ob-La-Di, Ob-La-Da-Lucy In the Sky With Diamonds-Michelle-All My Loving-With A Little Help From My Friends-Penny Lane-Eleanor Rigby-Twistin' In The Sixties.
Part 2: Hey Jude-Twist & Shout-Birthday-Good Day Sunshine-Let It Be-Sgt. Pepper's Lonely Hearts Club Band-Eight Days A Week-Strawberry Fields Forever-Day Tripper-Eleanor Rigby-I Saw Her Standing There-Come Together-From Me To You-I Want You-A Hard Day's Night-Paperback Writer-Something-Hello Goodbye.

CAGLE, Aubrey

TITLE/FLIP	LABEL & NO.	GOOD	NEAR MINT	YR.
BE-BOP BLUES/Just For You	(Glee 100)	3.75	15.00	60

CAHPERONES, The: see Chaperones, The

CAIN, Jeff

TITLE/FLIP	LABEL & NO.	GOOD	NEAR MINT	YR.
LONELY BOY/Oh Tomorrow	(Altera 001)	1.50	6.00	

CAIN, Jonathan

TITLE/FLIP	LABEL & NO.	GOOD	NEAR MINT	YR.
'TIL IT'S TIME TO SAY GOODBYE/Ladies' Night	(October 1001)	.50	2.00	76

CAIOLA, Al

TITLE/FLIP	LABEL & NO.	GOOD	NEAR MINT	YR.
BONANZA/The Bounty Hunter	(United Artists 302)	.75	3.00	61
MAGNIFICENT SEVEN, THE/The Lonely Rebel (Instrumentals)	(United Artists 261)	.75	3.00	60

CAKE

TITLE/FLIP	LABEL & NO.	GOOD	NEAR MINT	YR.
FIRE FLY/Rainbow Wood	(Decca 32235)	1.00	4.00	67
MOCKINGBIRD/Baby, That's Me	(Decca 32179)	1.00	4.00	67
P.T. 280/Have You Heard The News About Miss Molly	(Decca 32347)	1.00	4.00	68
YOU CAN HAVE HIM/I Know	(Decca 32212)	1.00	4.00	67

CAL & IVAN

TITLE/FLIP	LABEL & NO.	GOOD	NEAR MINT	YR.
LAZY (PART 1)/Lazy (Part 2)	(Skoop 1052)	1.00	4.00	60

CALE, J.J.

TITLE/FLIP	LABEL & NO.	GOOD	NEAR MINT	YR.
AFTER MIDNIGHT/Crying Eyes	(Shelter 7321)	.50	2.00	72
CAJUN MOON/Starbound	(Shelter 40238)	.50	2.00	74
CRAZY MAMA/Don't Go To Strangers	(Shelter 7314)	.50	2.00	71
DICK TRACY/It's A Go-Go Place	(Liberty 55840)	.50	2.00	65
GOING DOWN/Louisiana Women	(Shelter 7332)	.50	2.00	73
HEY BABY/	(Shelter 62006)	.50	2.00	77
I'LL BE THERE (IF YOU EVER WANT ME)/ Precious Memories	(Shelter 40290)	.50	2.00	74
LIES/Riding Home	(Shelter 7326)	.50	2.00	72
ROCK & ROLL RECORDS/I Got The Same Old Blues	(Shelter 40366)	.50	2.00	75

CALE, John (Of Velvet Underground)

TITLE/FLIP	LABEL & NO.	GOOD	NEAR MINT	YR.
DAYS OF STEAM/Legs Larry At Television Centre	(Reprise 1108)	.50	2.00	72

CALEN, Frankie

TITLE/FLIP	LABEL & NO.	GOOD	NEAR MINT	YR.
JOANIE/Pa, I Passed My Drivin' Test	(Spark 902)	.75	3.00	61

CALENDAR GIRLS, The

TITLE/FLIP	LABEL & NO.	GOOD	NEAR MINT	YR.
PEOPLE WILL TALK/Sha-Rel-a-Nova	(4 Corners of the World 118)	1.00	4.00	65

CALENDARS, The

TITLE/FLIP	LABEL & NO.	GOOD	NEAR MINT	YR.
I'M GONNA LAUGH AT YOU/You're Too Fast	(Coed 564)	5.00	20.00	61

CALHOON

TITLE/FLIP	LABEL & NO.	GOOD	NEAR MINT	YR.
(DO YOU WANNA) DANCE, DANCE, DANCE/ Rain 2000	(Warner-Spector 0405)	.50	2.00	75
SOUL MAN (PART 1)/Soul Man (Part 2)	(Warner-Spector 0407)	.50	2.00	76

CALIFORNIA

TITLE/FLIP	LABEL & NO.	GOOD	NEAR MINT	YR.
ABRAHAM, MARTIN, & JOHN/Song Of 1000 Voices	(Laurie 3639)	.75	3.00	

CALIFORNIA (With Curt Boetcher)

TITLE/FLIP	LABEL & NO.	GOOD	NEAR MINT	YR.
I CAN HEAR MUSIC/Love's Supposed To Be That Way	(RSO 901)	.50	2.00	78
MUSIC, MUSIC, MUSIC/Happy In Hollywood	(Warner Bros. 8253)	.50	2.00	76

CALIFORNIA MUSIC (Brian Wilson, Bruce Johnston, Terry Melcher)

TITLE/FLIP	LABEL & NO.	GOOD	NEAR MINT	YR.
DON'T WORRY BABY/Ten Years Harmony	(RCA Equinox 10120)	2.00	8.00	74
JAMAICA FAREWELL/California Music	(RCA Equinox 10572)	2.00	8.00	76
WHY DO FOOLS FALL IN LOVE/ Don't Worry Baby	(RCA Equinox 10363)	2.00	8.00	75

CALIFORNIA SUNS, The

TITLE/FLIP	LABEL & NO.	GOOD	NEAR MINT	YR.
MASKED GRANDMA/Little Bit Of Heaven	(Imperial 66179)	1.00	4.00	64

CALLENDER, Bobby

TITLE/FLIP	LABEL & NO.	GOOD	NEAR MINT	YR.
LITTLE STAR/Love & Kisses	(Roulette 4471)	.75	3.00	63

CALLICUTT, Dudley, & The Go Boys

TITLE/FLIP	LABEL & NO.	GOOD	NEAR MINT	YR.
GET READY BABY/Heart Trouble	(DC 0412)	10.00	40.00	

CALLOWAY, Cab

TITLE/FLIP	LABEL & NO.	GOOD	NEAR MINT	YR.
LITTLE CHILD (With Daughter Lael)/Voice	(ABC-Paramount 9671)	1.00	4.00	56
MINNIE THE MOOCHER/ A Chicken Ain't Nothin' But A Bird	(RCA-Hologram 11364)	.50	2.00	78

CALVERT, Eddie

TITLE/FLIP	LABEL & NO.	GOOD	NEAR MINT	YR.
OH MEIN PAPA/Mystery Street	(Essex 336)	1.25	5.00	53

CALVEYS, The

TITLE/FLIP	LABEL & NO.	GOOD	NEAR MINT	YR.
WIND, THE/I Need Love	(Comma 84349)	7.50	30.00	

CAMBRIDGE, STRINGS & SINGERS, The

TITLE/FLIP	LABEL & NO.	GOOD	NEAR MINT	YR.
THEME FROM "TUNES OF GLORY"/ Love Theme From "The World Of Suzie Wong"	(London 1960)	.75	3.00	61

CAMEL

TITLE/FLIP	LABEL & NO.	GOOD	NEAR MINT	YR.
ANOTHER NIGHT/Lunar Sea	(Janus 262)	.50	2.00	76

CAMEL DRIVERS, The

TITLE/FLIP	LABEL & NO.	GOOD	NEAR MINT	YR.
GRASS LOOKS GREENER, THE/It's Gonna Rain	(Top Dog 100)	1.00	4.00	
SUNDAY MORNING 6 O'CLOCK/Give It A Try	(Top Dog 103)	1.00	4.00	
SUNDAY MORNING 6 O'CLOCK/Give It A Try	(Buddah 61)	.75	3.00	68

CAMELOTS, The

TITLE/FLIP	LABEL & NO.	GOOD	NEAR MINT	YR.
DANCE GIRL/That's My Baby (By the Suns)	(Times Square 32)	.75	3.00	
DANCE GIRL/That's My Baby (By the Suns) (Colored plastic)	(Times Square 32)	1.50	6.00	
DON'T LEAVE ME BABY/The Letter	(Crimson 1001)	1.00	4.00	
POCAHONTAS/Searching For My Baby	(Ember 1108)	1.25	5.00	62
SUNDAY KIND OF LOVE/My Imagination	(AAnko 1004)	5.00	20.00	63
YOUR WAY/Don't Leave Me Baby	(AAnko 1001)	5.00	20.00	63
YOUR WAY/I Wonder	(Dream 1001)	1.00	4.00	

Also see Harps, The

CAMEOS, The

TITLE/FLIP	LABEL & NO.	GOOD	NEAR MINT	YR.
BEST OF THE CAN CAN (PART 1)/ Best Of The Can Can (Part 2)	(Cameo 176)	1.00	4.00	58
MERRY CHRISTMAS/New Years Eve (Group Sound)	(Cameo 123)	6.25	25.00	58

CAMEOS, The

TITLE/FLIP	LABEL & NO.	GOOD	NEAR MINT	YR.
CANADIAN SUNSET/Never Before	(Matador 1813)	1.50	6.00	60
WAIT UP/Lost Lover	(Johnson 108)	1.50	6.00	60
WAIT UP/Lost Lover	(Dean 504)	6.25	25.00	60
WE'LL STILL BE TOGETHER/I Remember When	(Matador 1808)	1.50	6.00	60

CAMERONS, The

TITLE/FLIP	LABEL & NO.	GOOD	NEAR MINT	YR.
CHERYL/Boom Chic-a-boom (Although shown as by the Camerons, the actual singers on this release were a different group, previously known as the Jiveliers.)	(Cousins CS1-2)	2.50	10.00	60
GUARDIAN ANGEL/A Girl I Marry	(Cousins 1003)	6.25	25.00	61
GUARDIAN ANGEL/A Girl I Marry	(Felsted 8638)	2.00	8.00	61

Also see Taylor, Mike

CAMILLI, Jim

TITLE/FLIP	LABEL & NO.	GOOD	NEAR MINT	YR.
KING OF ROCK & ROLL/King Of Rock & Roll (Novelty Break-in, gold plastic)	(No Label)	1.25	5.00	77

CAMP, Hamilton

TITLE/FLIP	LABEL & NO.	GOOD	NEAR MINT	YR.
HERE'S TO YOU/Leavin' Anyhow	(Warner Bros. 7165)	.75	3.00	68

CAMPANELLA, David, & The Dellchords

TITLE/FLIP	LABEL & NO.	GOOD	NEAR MINT	YR.
SOMEWHERE OVER THE RAINBOW/Everything's That Way	(Kane 25593)	5.00	20.00	59

CAMPANIONS, The

TITLE/FLIP	LABEL & NO.	GOOD	NEAR MINT	YR.
I WANT A YUL BRYNNER HAIRCUT/Dorthy, My Monster	(Dee-Dee 1047)	2.00	8.00	

Also see Del Satins, The

CAMPBELL, Glen

TITLE/FLIP	LABEL & NO.	GOOD	NEAR MINT	YR.
ALL I HAVE TO DO IS DREAM/Less Of Me (With Bobbie Gentry)	(Capitol 2745)	.50	2.00	70
AMAZING GRACE/God Must Have Blessed America	(Capitol 4515)	.50	2.00	77
AS FAR AS I'M CONCERNED/	(Capitol 5037)	.75	3.00	63
BEAUTIFUL LOVE SONG/Bring Back My Yesterday	(Capitol 3669)	.50	2.00	73
BONAPARTE'S RETREAT/Too Many Mornings	(Capitol 3926)	.50	2.00	74
BURNING BRIDGES/	(Capitol 5773)	.75	3.00	66
BY THE TIME I GET TO PHOENIX/ You've Still Got A Place In My Heart	(Capitol 2015)	.50	2.00	67
CHRISTMAS IS FOR CHILDREN/ There's No Place Like Home	(Capitol 2336)	.75	3.00	68
COUNTRY BOY (YOU GOT YOUR FEET IN L.A.)/ Record Collector's Dream	(Capitol 4155)	.50	2.00	75
DON'T PULL YOUR LOVE-THEN YOU CAN TELL ME GOODBYE/ I Miss You Tonight	(Capitol 4245)	.50	2.00	76
DREAM BABY/Here & Now	(Capitol 3062)	.50	2.00	71
DREAMS OF THE EVERYDAY HOUSEWIFE/Kelli Hoedown	(Capitol 2224)	.50	2.00	68
EVERYTHING A MAN COULD EVER NEED/Norwood	(Capitol 12843)	.50	2.00	70
FOR THE LOVE OF A WOMAN/Smokey Blue Eyes	(Starday 853)	.50	2.00	68
GALVESTON/How Come Every Time I Itch I Wind Up Scratchin' You	(Capitol 2428)	.50	2.00	69
GENTLE ON MY MIND/Just Another Man	(Capitol 5939)	.50	2.00	67
GUESS I'M DUMB/That's All Right (Written, arranged, produced & conducted by Brian Wilson.)	(Capitol 5441)	5.00	20.00	65
HEY LITTLE ONE/My Baby's Gone	(Capitol 2076)	.50	2.00	68
HONEY COME BACK/Where Do You Go	(Capitol 2178)	.50	2.00	70
HOUSTON (I'M COMING TO SEE YOU)/Honestly Love	(Capitol 3808)	.50	2.00	74
I BELIEVE IN CHRISTMAS/New Snow On The Roof	(Capitol 3509)	.50	2.00	72
IF I WERE LOVING YOU/ It's A Sin When You Love Somebody	(Capitol 3988)	.50	2.00	74
I KNEW JESUS (BEFORE HE WAS A STAR)/On This Road	(Capitol 3548)	.50	2.00	73
I SAY A LITTLE PRAYER-BY THE TIME I GET TO PHOENIX/ All Through The Night (With Anne Murray)	(Capitol 3200)	.50	2.00	71
IT'S ONLY MAKE BELIEVE/Pave Your Way Into Tomorrow	(Capitol 2905)	.50	2.00	70
I'VE GOT TO WIN/Dreams For Sale (With the Glen-Aires)	(Ceneco 132)	1.25	5.00	
I WANNA LIVE/That's All That Matters	(Capitol 2146)	.50	2.00	68
I WILL NEVER PASS THIS WAY AGAIN/ We All Pull The Load	(Capitol 3411)	.50	2.00	72
LAST TIME I SAW HER, THE/Bach Talk	(Capitol 3123)	.50	2.00	71
LET IT BE ME/Little Green Apples (With Bobbie Gentry)	(Capitol 2387)	.50	2.00	69
LONG BLACK LIMOUSINE/Here I Am	(Capitol 4856)	1.00	4.00	62
MACARTHUR PARK/My Way	(Capitol 6190)	.50	2.00	72
MANHATTAN, KANSAS/Wayfarin' Stranger	(Capitol 3305)	.50	2.00	72
MIRACLE OF LOVE/Once More	(Crest 1096)	1.25	5.00	62
MORNIN' GLORY/Less Of Me (With Bobbie Gentry)	(Capitol 2314)	.50	2.00	68
OH HAPPY DAY/Someone Above	(Capitol 2787)	.50	2.00	70
OKLAHOMA SUNDAY MORNING/ Everybody's Got To Go There Sometime	(Capitol 3254)	.50	2.00	71
ONE LAST TIME/All My Tomorrows	(Capitol 3483)	.50	2.00	72
PRIMA DONNA/Oh My Darling	(Capitol 4925)	.75	3.00	63
RHINESTONE COWBOY/Lovelight	(Capitol 4095)	.50	2.00	75
SATISFIED MIND/Can't You See I'm Tryin'	(Capitol 5633)	.75	3.00	66
SEE YOU ON SUNDAY/Bloodline	(Capitol 4288)	.50	2.00	76
SOUTHERN NIGHTS/William Tell Overture	(Capitol 4376)	.50	2.00	77
SUMMER, WINTER, SPRING & FALL/Heartaches Can Be Fun	(Capitol 5279)	.75	3.00	64
SUNFLOWER/How High Did We Go	(Capitol 4445)	.50	2.00	77
TOMORROW NEVER COMES/It's A Woman's World	(Capitol 5360)	.75	3.00	65
TOO LATE TO WORRY TOO BLUE TO CRY/ How Do I Tell My Heart Not To Break	(Capitol 4783)	1.00	4.00	62
TRUE GRIT/Hava Nagila	(Capitol 2573)	.50	2.00	69
TRY A LITTLE KINDNESS/Lonely My Lonely Friend	(Capitol 2659)	.50	2.00	69
TURN AROUND, LOOK AT ME/Brenda	(Crest 1087)	1.25	5.00	61
UNIVERSAL SOLDIER, THE/Spanish Shades	(Capitol 5504)	.75	3.00	65
WALK RIGHT IN/Delight, Arkansas	(Everest 2500)	.75	3.00	69
WHEREFORE & WHY/	(Capitol 3735)	.50	2.00	73
WHERE'S THE PLAYGROUND SUSIE/Arkansas	(Capitol 2494)	.50	2.00	69
WICHITA LINEMAN/Fate Of Man	(Capitol 2302)	.50	2.00	68

Also see Capehart, Jerry
Also see Gee Cees, The
Also see Sagittarius

CAMPBELL, Glen & Anne Murray: see Campbell, Glen

CAMPBELL, Glen & Bobbie Gentry: see Campbell, Glen

CAMPBELL, Jo Ann

TITLE/FLIP	LABEL & NO.	GOOD	NEAR MINT	YR.
CRAZY DAISY/But, Maybe This Year	(ABC-Paramount 10172)	1.25	5.00	60
FOREVER YOUNG/Come On Baby	(Eldorado 504)	1.50	6.00	
I AIN'T GOT NO STEADY DATE/Beach-Comber	(Gone 5068)	1.25	5.00	59
I WISH IT WOULD RAIN ALL SUMMER/ Amateur Night	(ABC-Paramount 10335)	1.00	4.00	62
(I'M THE GIRL FROM) WOLVERTON MOUNTAIN (Answer song)/ Sloppy Joe	(Cameo 223)	.75	3.00	62
I'VE CHANGED MY MIND, JACK/ You Made Me Love You	(ABC-Paramount 10300)	1.00	4.00	62
KOOKIE LITTLE PARADISE, A/ Bobby-Bobby-Bobby	(ABC-Paramount 10134)	1.00	4.00	60
KOOKIE LITTLE PARADISE, A/ Bobby-Bobby-Bobby (Stereo single issue)	(ABC-Paramount S-10134)	3.75	15.00	60
LET ME DO IT MY WAY/Mr. Fix-It Man	(Cameo 237)	.75	3.00	63
MAMA (CAN I GO OUT TONIGHT)/Nervous	(Gone 5055)	1.25	5.00	59
MAMA DON'T WANT/Duane	(ABC-Paramount 10258)	1.00	4.00	61
MOTHER, PLEASE!/Waitin' For Love	(Cameo 249)	.75	3.00	63
MOTORCYCLE MICHAEL/Puka, Puka Pants	(ABC-Paramount 10200)	1.00	4.00	61

Also see Jo Ann & Troy

CAMPBELL, Junior (Of Marmalade)

TITLE/FLIP	LABEL & NO.	GOOD	NEAR MINT	YR.
HALLELUJAH FREEDOM/Alright With Me	(Deram 85082)	.50	2.00	72

CAMPERS, The (Sonny Curtis & The Crickets)

TITLE/FLIP	LABEL & NO.	GOOD	NEAR MINT	YR.
BALLAD OF BATMAN/Batmobile	(Parkway 974)	3.75	15.00	65

Also see Camps, The

CAMPS, The (The Campers)

TITLE/FLIP	LABEL & NO.	GOOD	NEAR MINT	YR.
BALLAD OF BATMAN/Batmobile	(Parkway 974)	3.75	15.00	65

This record was also issued as by The Campers.

CAMPLIN, Bill

TITLE/FLIP	LABEL & NO.	GOOD	NEAR MINT	YR.
LUCKY MAN/Honky Tonkin'	(Tool Room 45001)	.50	2.00	76

CAN

TITLE/FLIP	LABEL & NO.	GOOD	NEAR MINT	YR.
MOON SHAKE/Future Days	(United Artists UA-XW446-W)	.50	2.00	74

CANADIAN BEATLES, The

TITLE/FLIP	LABEL & NO.	GOOD	NEAR MINT	YR.
LOVE WALKED AWAY/I'm Coming Home	(Tide 2006)	1.25	5.00	64
THINK I'M GONNA CRY/I'll Show You The Way	(Tide 2003)	1.25	5.00	64

CANADIAN ROGUES, The

TITLE/FLIP	LABEL & NO.	GOOD	NEAR MINT	YR.
OOH-POO-PA-DOO/Deep In Touch	(Palmer 5017)	1.25	5.00	

CANADIAN SQUIRES, The

TITLE/FLIP	LABEL & NO.	GOOD	NEAR MINT	YR.
LEAVE ME ALONE/Uh-Uh-Uh	(Ware 6002)	3.75	15.00	

Also see Band, The

CANADIAN SWEETHEARTS, The (Featuring Lucille Starr)

TITLE/FLIP	LABEL & NO.	GOOD	NEAR MINT	YR.
FREIGHT TRAIN/Out For Fun	(A&M 713)	.75	3.00	63

Also see Bob & Lucille

CANARIES, The

TITLE/FLIP	LABEL & NO.	GOOD	NEAR MINT	YR.
I'M SORRY BABY/	(Dimension 1047)	.75	3.00	63

CANDIDO, Candy

TITLE/FLIP	LABEL & NO.	GOOD	NEAR MINT	YR.
BARNACLE BILL (THE SAILOR)/ You're Nothin' But A Nothin'	(Capitol 3156)	1.00	4.00	55

CANDIES, The

TITLE/FLIP	LABEL & NO.	GOOD	NEAR MINT	YR.
I'M ONLY MAKING IT EASIER FOR YOU/Yes, I Love You	(Ember 1092)	1.00	4.00	63
STOP/If You Wanna Do A Smart Thing	(Fleetwood 7003)	1.25	5.00	

CANDOLI, Pete

TITLE/FLIP	LABEL & NO.	GOOD	NEAR MINT	YR.
BEATLE BUG JUMP/You Made Me Love You	(Nan 3004)	1.00	4.00	64

jubilee
Vocal with Inst. Accomp.
Lollipop Music Corp. (BMI)
Record No. 45-5539 (JB-12523)
Time: 2:20
ADVANCE RELEASE DISC-JOCKEY RECORD NOT FOR SALE
DANCING ON THE BEACH
(T. Martin-E. Miller-J. Dee)
JOEY DEE and THE STARLIGHTERS
Arr. & Cond. by Trade Martin
A Miller-Martin Production

Mac Dav

Alice Cooper

Bing Crosby

Donna Dameron

TITLE/FLIP	LABEL & NO.	GOOD	NEAR MINT	YR.
CARIBBEANS, The				
KEEP HER BY MY SIDE/I Knew	(20th Fox 112)	2.00	8.00	58
CARILLO (Frank Carillo)				
I WANNA LIVE AGAIN/Let's Give It Up	(Atlantic 3492)	.50	2.00	78
SHE TAKES THE NIGHT/	(Atlantic 3589)	.50	2.00	79
WHAT'D YOU LIGHT THE FIRE WITH/	(Atlantic 3520)	.50	2.00	78
CARL & THE COMMANDERS				
FARMER JOHN/Cleanin' Up	(Cameo 197)	.75	3.00	61
CARLIN, George				
11 O'CLOCK NEWS (PART 1)/11 O'Clock News (Part 2)	(Little David 720)	.75	3.00	74
NEW NEWS (PART 1)/New News (Part 2)	(Little David 731)	.75	3.00	75
WONDERFUL WINO/ Al Sleet, Your Hippy Dippy Weatherman	(RCA Victor 47-9110)	1.00	4.00	67
Comedy				
CARLO (Carlo Mastrangelo)				
BABY DOLL/Write Me A Letter	(Laurie 3151)	3.00	12.00	63
CLAUDINE/Fever	(Raftis 110)	1.50	6.00	
FIVE MINUTES MORE/The Story Of My Love	(Laurie 3175)	3.00	12.00	63
LET THERE BE LOVE/	(Raftis 112)	1.25	5.00	
LITTLE ORPHAN GIRL/Mairzy Doats	(Laurie 3157)	3.00	12.00	63
RING-A-LING/Stranger In My Arms	(Laurie 3227)	5.00	20.00	64
Also see Belmonts, The				
Also see Endless Pulse				
Also see Stuart, Glen Chorus				
CARLO & JIMMY (With Carlo Mastrangelo)				
HAPPY TUNE/Rockin' Rocket	(Laurie 3063)	1.50	6.00	60
CARLO & THE SECRETS				
PONY PARTY/100 Pounds Of Potatoes	(Thrown 801)	2.00	8.00	
CARLOS, Barry, & The Night-Caps				
ARE YOU RUNNING AWAY/Don't You Know	(Amber 3537)	.75	3.00	65
CARLOS BROTHERS, The				
COME ON LET'S DANCE/Tonight	(Del Fi 4112)	1.00	4.00	59
LA BAMBA/It's Time To Go	(Del Fi 4145)	1.00	4.00	60
CARLO'S CROWN JEWEL (Featuring Carlo Mastrangelo)				
IT'S ALRIGHT/Shoo-fly Pie & Apple Pan Dowdy	(Tower 497)	1.50	6.00	68
CARLTON THE DOORMAN (Lorenzo Music)				
WHO IS IT?/The Girl In 510	(United Artists 643)	.50	2.00	76
Carlton appeared on TV's "Rhoda"				
CARMEL				
I CAN'T SHAKE THIS FEELING/Let My Child Be Free	(MGM 13869)	2.00	8.00	67
THEY DIDN'T BELIEVE ME/One Day	(MGM 13985)	2.00	8.00	68
Also see Rat Pack, The				
Also see Grape Vine				
CARMEL COVERED POPCORN				
SUZIE Q/Looking For A Place	(Vistone 2055)	.75	3.00	
CARMEL SISTERS, The (Carol & Cheryl)				
GO GO G.T.O./Sunny Winter	(Colpix 767)	1.00	4.00	65
(Shown as by Carol & Cheryl)				
GO GO G.T.O./Sunny Winter	(Colpix 767)	1.00	4.00	65
JOEY'S COMIN' HOME/The Rumor	(Jubilee 5464)	1.00	4.00	63
CARMELETTES, The				
MY FOOLISH HEART/Promise Me A Rose	(Alpine 53)	.75	3.00	59
SOMETHING TELLS ME I'M IN LOVE/Aching For You	(Alpine 61)	.75	3.00	60
CARMEN, Eric (Of The Raspberries)				
ALL BY MYSELF/Everything	(Arista 0165)	.50	2.00	75
BABY, I NEED YOUR LOVIN'/Heaven Can Wait	(Arista 0384)	.50	2.00	79
BOATS AGAINST THE CURRENT/Take It Or Leave It	(Arista 0295)	.50	2.00	77
CHANGE OF HEART/Hey Deanie	(Arista 0354)	.50	2.00	78
MARATHON MAN/I Think I Found Myself	(Arista 0319)	.50	2.00	78
NEVER GONNA FALL IN LOVE AGAIN/No Hard Feelings	(Arista 0184)	.50	2.00	76
SHE DID IT/Someday	(Arista 0266)	.50	2.00	77
SUNRISE/My Girl	(Arista 0200)	.50	2.00	76
SUNRISE (Live)/My Girl	(Arista 0200 SL)	.50	2.00	76
CARMEN, Tony, & The Spitfires				
DON'T RUN TO ME/Spitfire	(Abel 224)	1.00	4.00	
Also see Tony & The Day Dreams				
CARNABY STREET RUNNERS, The				
LIVE & IN PERSON/Dom's Frantic Pandemonium	(Buddah BDA-30)	1.00	4.00	68
WHILE YOU'RE OUT LOOKING FOR SUGAR/ Makin Love In A Tree House	(Super K SK-11)	1.00	4.00	69
CARNATIONS, The				
SLEEPY HOLLOW/Barbary Coast	(Terry Tone 199)	1.00	4.00	
CARNATIONS, The				
FUNNY TIME/Punctuation	(Laurie 3163)	.75	3.00	
SCORPION/Fireball Mail	(Tilt 780)	1.00	4.00	
Instrumentals				
Also see Cosmo				
CARNES, Kim				
BAD SEED/	(A&M 1807)	.50	2.00	76
IT HURTS SO BAD/Lookin' For A Big Night	(EMI America 8011)	.50	2.00	79
LET YOUR LOVE COME EASY/Last Thing You Ever Wanted To Do	(A&M 1902)	.50	2.00	77
SAILIN'/He'll Come Home	(A&M 1943)	.50	2.00	77
TO LOVE SOMEBODY/Fell In Love With A Poet	(Amos 166)	.50	2.00	
WHAT AM I GONNA DO?/Goodnight Moon	(EMI America 8014)	.50	2.00	79
YOU'RE A PART OF ME/	(A&M 1767)	.50	2.00	74
CARNEY, Art				
NEW FACE ON THE BARROOM FLOOR/ A Little Beauty	(Columbia 40623)	1.50	6.00	55
OH BOY (AIN'T IT GREAT TO BE CRAZY)/ The Silly Signs Song	(Columbia 40714)	1.50	6.00	56
SANTA & THE DOODLE-LI-BOOP/ Twas The Night Before Christmas	(Columbia 40400)	1.50	6.00	55
SHEESH, WHAT A GROUCH/ She Never Left The Table	(Columbia 40387)	1.50	6.00	54
SONG OF THE SEWER/Va Va Va Voom	(Columbia 40242)	1.50	6.00	54
Novelties				
CARO, Tony				
CHEMISTRY OF LOVE/Hard To Get	(Crystalette 742)	1.00	4.00	60
CAROL & CHERYL: see Carmel Sisters, The				
CARONATORS, The				
LONG HOT SUMMER/Senorita	(Clock 1045)	1.50	6.00	60
CAROSONE, Renalto				
TORERO/	(Capitol 71080)	1.00	4.00	58
CAROUSELS, The				
BENEATH THE WILLOW/Sail Away	(Autumn 13)	.75	3.00	65
CAROUSELS, The				
IF YOU WANT TO/Pretty Little Thing	(Gone 5118)	1.25	5.00	61
NEVER LET HIM GO/Dirty Tricks	(Gone 5131)	1.25	5.00	62
CARP				
PINE CREEK BRIDGE/Page 258	(Epic 5-10647)	.75	3.00	70
CARPENTER, Carleton, & Debbie Reynolds				
ABA DABA HONEYMOON/Row Row Row	(MGM 30282)	1.50	6.00	51
CARPENTER, Chris				
WATERFALLS/This World	(United Artists 50266)	.75	3.00	68
CARPENTERS, The (Karen & Richard Carpenter)				
ALL YOU GET FROM LOVE IS A LOVE SONG/I Have You	(A&M 1940)	.50	2.00	77
CALLING OCCUPANTS OF INTERPLANETARY CRAFT/ Can't Smile Without You	(A&M 1978)	.50	2.00	77
CLOSE TO YOU/I Kept On Loving You	(A&M 1183)	.50	2.00	70
FOR ALL WE KNOW/Don't Be Afraid	(A&M 1243)	.50	2.00	71
GOODBYE TO LOVE/Crystal Lullaby	(A&M 1367)	.50	2.00	72
GOOFUS/Boat To Sail	(A&M 1859)	.50	2.00	76
HURTING EACH OTHER/Maybe It's You	(A&M 1322)	.50	2.00	72
I BELIEVE YOU/B'wana She No Home	(A&M 2097)	.50	2.00	78
I NEED TO BE IN LOVE/Sandy	(A&M 1828)	.50	2.00	76
IT'S GOING TO TAKE SOME TIME/Flat Baroque	(A&M 1351)	.50	2.00	72
I WON'T LAST A DAY WITHOUT YOU/One Love	(A&M 8566)	.50	2.00	74
MERRY CHRISTMAS DARLING/The Christmas Song	(A&M 1991)	.50	2.00	77
MERRY CHRISTMAS DARLING/Mr. Guder	(A&M 1236)	.50	2.00	70
ONLY YESTERDAY/Happy	(A&M 1677)	.50	2.00	75
PLEASE MR. POSTMAN/This Masquerade	(A&M 1646)	.50	2.00	74
RAINY DAYS & MONDAYS/Saturday	(A&M 1260)	.50	2.00	71
SANTA CLAUS IS COMING TO TOWN/ Merry Christmas Darling	(A&M 1648)	.50	2.00	74
SING/Druscilla Penny	(A&M 1413)	.50	2.00	73
SOLITAIRE/Love Me For What I Am	(A&M 1721)	.50	2.00	75
SUPERSTAR/Bless The Bests & Children	(A&M 1289)	.50	2.00	71
SWEET, SWEET SMILE/I Have You	(A&M 2008)	.50	2.00	78
THERE'S A KIND OF HUSH/Goodbye & I Love You	(A&M 1800)	.50	2.00	76
TICKET TO RIDE/Your Wonderful Parade	(A&M 1142)	.50	2.00	69
TOP OF THE WORLD/Heather	(A&M 1468)	.50	2.00	73
WE'VE ONLY JUST BEGUN/All Of My Life	(A&M 1217)	.50	2.00	70
YESTERDAY ONCE MORE/Road Ode	(A&M 1446)	.50	2.00	73
CARPENTER, Thelma				
YES, I'M LONESOME TONIGHT/Gimmie A Little	(Coral 62241)	.75	3.00	60
CARR, Cathy				
FIRST ANNIVERSARY/With Love	(Roulette 4125)	1.00	4.00	59
HALF-PINT BOOGIE/Heartbroken	(Coral 60907)	1.25	5.00	53
HEART HIDEAWAY/The Boy On Page 35	(Fraternity 743)	1.00	4.00	56
I'LL CRY AT YOUR WEDDING/Cryin' For The Carolines	(Coral 91092)	1.25	5.00	54
I'M GONNA CHANGE HIM/The Little Things You Do	(Roulette 4152)	1.00	4.00	59
I'M GONNA CHANGE HIM/The Little Things You Do	(Roulette SSR-4152)	2.00	8.00	59
(Stereo single issue)				
IVORY TOWER/Please Please Believe Me	(Fraternity 734)	1.00	4.00	56
MORNING NOON & NIGHT/Toward Evening	(Fraternity 718)	1.00	4.00	56
SOMEBODY TOLD YOU A LIE/I Just Can't Get Started	(Coral 60988)	1.25	5.00	53
WARM YOUR HEART/ I Never Really Stopped Loving You	(Fraternity 712)	1.00	4.00	55
CARR, Joe "Fingers" (Lou Busch)				
DOWN YONDER/Ivory Rag	(Capitol 1777)	1.00	4.00	51
PORTUGUESE WASHERWOMEN/Lucky Pierre	(Capitol 3418)	1.00	4.00	56
SAM'S SONG/Ivory Rag	(Capitol 962)	1.00	4.00	50
CARR, Linda, & The Impossibles				
HAPPY TEENAGER/I'll Never Get Married	(Skyla 1052)	1.00	4.00	61
CARR, Pete				
CANADIAN SUNSET/Rings Of Saturn	(Big Tree 16126)	.50	2.00	78
Also see LeBlanc & Carr				
CARR, Timothy				
STOP ALONG THE WAY, A/ Let's Start All Over Again	(Hot Biscuit Disc 1454)	.75	3.00	67
CARR, Valerie				
OVER THE RAINBOW/You're The Greatest	(Roulette 4038)	1.00	4.00	57
WHEN THE BOYS TALK ABOUT THE GIRLS/Padre	(Roulette 4066)	1.00	4.00	58
CARR, Vikki				
HE'S A REBEL/Be My Love	(Liberty 55493)	.75	3.00	62
CARRADINE, Keith				
I'M EASY/2000 Years (By Henry Gibson)	(ABC 12117)	.50	2.00	76
MR. BLUE/	(Asylum 45454)	.50	2.00	77
CARRIBEANS, The				
WONDERFUL GIRL/Oh My Love	(Amy 871)	2.50	10.00	63
CARROLL, Andrea (Andrea Lee DeCapito)				
HEY BEACH BOYS/	(United Artists 50039)	.75	3.00	66
IT HURTS TO BE SIXTEEN/Why Am I So Shy	(Big Top 3156)	1.00	4.00	63
I'VE GOT A DATE WITH FRANKIE/Young & Lonely	(Epic 9438)	.75	3.00	61
MISS HAPPINESS/15 Shades Of Pink	(Epic 9523)	.75	3.00	62
PLEASE DON'T TALK TO THE LIFEGUARD/ Room Of Memories	(Epic 9450)	.75	3.00	61
CARROLL, Bernadette				
MY HEART STOOD STILL/Sweet Sugar Sweet	(Julia 1106)	.75	3.00	62
NICKY/All The Way Home I Cried	(Laurie 3217)	1.25	5.00	63
PARTY GIRL/I Don't Wanna Know	(Laurie 3238)	.75	3.00	64
CARROLL, Bob				
BUTTERFLY/Look What You've Done To Me	(Bally 1028)	1.00	4.00	57
CARROLL BROTHERS, The (With Pete Carroll)				
BO DIDDLEY/Don't Knock The Twist	(Cameo 213)	.75	3.00	62
I FOUND YOU/Movin' Day	(Felsted 8550)	.75	3.00	59
SWEET GEORGIA BROWN/Boot It	(Cameo 221)	.75	3.00	62
CARROLL, Cathy				
JIMMY LOVE/Deep In A Young Boys Heart	(Triodex 110)	1.25	5.00	61
(With The Earls)				
POOR LITTLE PUPPET/Love & Learn	(Warner Bros. 5284)	.75	3.00	62
CARROLL, Corkey, & His Fabulous Corketts				
SKATEBOARD BILL/Pocket Rocket (Blue plastic)	(Jet JT-1001)	.75	3.00	77
TAN PUNKS ON BOARDS/ From Pizza Towers To Defeat	(Pacific Arts 45-1030)	.75	3.00	78
CARROLL, David				
IT'S ALMOST TOMORROW/Rascination	(Mercury 70717)	.75	3.00	55
JACQUELINE & CAROLINE/Little Pixie	(Mercury 72046)	.75	3.00	62
MELODY OF LOVE/La Golondrina	(Mercury 70516)	.75	3.00	54
Instrumentals				
CARROLL, Jimmy				
ANGELINA/Anita	(Carousel 44)	1.50	6.00	59
ANGELINA/Anita	(Carousel S-44)	3.00	12.00	59
(Stereo single issue)				
BIG GREEN CAR/	(Fascination 2000)	10.00	40.00	
CARROLL, Pete (Of The Carroll Brothers)				
YOU'RE A DOG/Fiasco	(Cameo 279)	.75	3.00	63
CARROLL, Ronnie				
SAY WONDERFUL THINGS/Please Tell Me Your Name	(Philips 40110)	.75	3.00	63
CARROLL, Wayne				
CHICKEN OUT/Cindy Lee	(King 5123)	3.00	12.00	57
CARROLL, Yvonne				
GEE WHAT A GUY/Stuck On You	(Domain 1018)	1.00	4.00	63
CARSON, Don & The Whirlaways				
THREE CARBURETORS/Smoke Smoke Smoke	(Crest 1051)	1.00	4.00	60
CARSON, Kit (Liza Morrow)				
BAND OF GOLD/Cast Your Bread	(Mars 1007)	1.50	6.00	55
BAND OF GOLD/Cast Your Bread	(Capitol 3283)	.75	3.00	55
CARSON, Mindy				
MEMORIES ARE MADE OF THIS/ Cryin' For Your Kisses	(Columbia 40573)	1.00	4.00	55
MY FOOLISH HEART/Candy & Cake	(RCA Victor 47-3204)	1.25	5.00	50
SINCE I MET YOU BABY/Goodnight My Love	(Columbia 40789)	1.00	4.00	56
WAKE THE TOWN & TELL THE PEOPLE/ Hold Me Tight	(Columbia 40537)	1.00	4.00	55
CARS, The				
DOUBLE LIFE/	(Elektra 46580)	.50	2.00	79
GOOD TIMES ROLL/All Mixed Up	(Elektra 46014)	.50	2.00	79
IT'S ALL I CAN DO/Got A Lot On My Head	(Elektra 46546)	.50	2.00	79
JUST WHAT I NEEDED/I'm In Touch With Your World	(Elektra 45491)	.50	2.00	78
LET'S GO/That's It	(Elektra 46063)	.50	2.00	79
MY BEST FRIEND'S GIRL/Don't Cha Stop	(Elektra 45537)	.50	2.00	78
CARTER, Joey				
NAME GAME, THE/	(Epic 9393)	1.00	4.00	59
CARTER, Lynda				
ALL NIGHT SONG/Put On A Show	(Epic 50624)	.50	2.00	78
TOTO (DON'T IT FEEL LIKE PARADISE)/Put On A Show	(Epic 50569)	.50	2.00	78
Lynda starred as TV's "Wonder Woman."				
CARTER, Mel				
(ALL OF A SUDDEN) MY HEART SINGS/ When I Hold The Hand Of The One I Love	(Imperial 66138)	.75	3.00	65
BAND OF GOLD/Detour	(Imperial 66165)	.75	3.00	66
DEED I DO/What's On Your Mind	(Imperial 66052)	.75	3.00	64
HIGH NOON/I Just Can't Imagine	(Imperial 66101)	.75	3.00	65
HOLD ME, THRILL ME, KISS ME/A Sweet Little Girl	(Imperial 66113)	.75	3.00	65
I NEED YOU SO/When I Grow Too Old To Dream	(Mercury 71893)	1.00	4.00	62
LOVE IS ALL WE NEED/I Wish I Didn't Love You So	(Imperial 66148)	.75	3.00	66
RICHEST MAN ALIVE/I'll Never Be Free	(Imperial 66078)	.75	3.00	65
TIME OF YOUNG LOVE/Wonderful Love	(Derby 1005)	1.00	4.00	63
WHEN A BOY FALLS IN LOVE/So Wonderful	(Derby 1003)	1.00	4.00	63
WHO DO YOU LOVE/Wrong Side Of Town	(Phillips 40049)	1.00	4.00	62
(With Clydie King)				
WHY I CALL HER MINE/ After The Parting, The Meeting Is Sweeter	(Derby 1008)	1.00	4.00	63
CARTER, Valerie				
DA DOO RENDEZVOUS/	(Columbia-ARC 10881)	.50	2.00	78
OOH CHILD/Heartache	(Columbia 10505)	.50	2.00	77
CARTOON CANDY CARNIVAL, The				
EVERYTHING IS MICKEY MOUSE/ Mickey Mouse Concerto In B Flat	(Metromedia 105)	.75	3.00	69
CARTOONE				
MR. POOR MAN/Knick Knack Man	(Atlantic 2598)	1.00	4.00	69
(With Jimmy Page)				
REFLECTIONS ON A COMMON THEME/ A Penny For The Sun	(Atlantic 2630)	.50	2.00	70
CARTOONS, The				
BIG BAD BATUSI/Batusi	(Tuba 20006)	.75	3.00	66
CARTRIDGE, Flip				
DEAR MRS. APPLEBEE/ Don't Take The Lovers From The World	(Parrot 306)	.75	3.00	66
CARTY, Ric				
YOUNG LOVE/Oooh-eee	(RCA Victor 47-6751)	3.75	15.00	56
CARUSO, Dick				
BLUE DENIM/I'll Tell You In This Song	(MGM 12811)	1.00	4.00	59
TEENAGERS BLUES/Playing The Field	(MGM 12827)	1.00	4.00	59
CARUSO, Marian				
MY FAVORITE SONG/	(Devon 1001)	1.25	5.00	52
CARVELS, The				
SEVENTEEN/Don't Let Him Know	(Twirl 2022)	.75	3.00	66
CASANOVA & THE CHANTS, The				
GERALDINE/I Know You	(Saphire 2254)	1.00	4.00	
CASANOVAS, The				
IN MY LAND OF DREAMS/	(Planet 1027)	6.25	25.00	62
CASCADES, The				
ALL'S FAIR IN LOVE & WAR/Midnight Lace	(Arwin 134)	.75	3.00	66
BIG CITY COUNTRY BOY/Indian River	(Uni 55169)	.75	3.00	69
CHERYL'S GOIN HOME/Trulie Julie's Blues	(Arwin 132)	.75	3.00	66
EVERYONE IS BLOSSOMING/Two Sided Man	(Probe 543)	.75	3.00	68
FLYING ON THE GROUND/Main Street	(Smash 2101)	1.00	4.00	67
(With Neil Young on Guitar)				
FOR YOUR SWEET LOVE/Jeannie	(RCA Victor 47-8268)	.75	3.00	63
HEY LITTLE GIRL OF MINE/Blue Hours	(Smash 2083)	.75	3.00	67
I BET YOU WON'T STAY/She's In Love Again	(Liberty 55822)	.75	3.00	65
LAST LEAF, THE/Shy Girl	(Valiant 6028)	.75	3.00	63
LITTLE BITTY FALLING STAR/ Those Were The Good Old Days	(RCA Victor 47-8321)	.75	3.00	64
LITTLE LIKE LOVIN'/Cinderella	(RCA Victor 47-8206)	.75	3.00	63
MAYBE THE RAIN WILL FALL/Naggin' Cries	(Uni 55152)	.75	3.00	69
MY BEST GIRL/She Was Never Mine (To Lose)	(Charter 1018)	.75	3.00	64
MY FIRST DAY ALONE/I Wanna Be Your Lover	(Valiant 6032)	.75	3.00	63
RHYTHM OF THE RAIN/Let Me Be	(Valiant 6026)	.75	3.00	62
SWEET AMERICA/I Started A Joke	(Canbase 714)	.50	2.00	72
THERE'S A REASON/Second Chance	(Valiant 6021)	.75	3.00	62
Also see Lind, Bob				
CASE, Scot Richard (SRC)				
I'M SO GLAD/Who Is That Girl	(A-Square 301)	1.25	5.00	
CASEY, Al				
CARAVAN (PART 1)/Caravan (Part 2)	(Gregmark 5)	1.00	4.00	61
(Shown as by Duane Eddy)				
CHICKEN FEATHERS/Laughin'	(Stacy 950)	.75	3.00	63
COCOANUT GROVE/Alley Cat	(Challenge 59086)	.75	3.00	60
COOKIN'/Hot Foot	(Stacy 925)	.75	3.00	62
COOKIN'/What Are We Gonna Do In '64	(Stacy 971)	.75	3.00	64
DOIN' IT/Monte Carlo	(Stacy 956)	.75	3.00	63
FUN HOUSE/Indian Love Call	(Stacy 961)	.75	3.00	63

TITLE/FLIP — LABEL & NO. — GOOD — NEAR MINT — YR.

- GUITARS, GUITARS, GUITARS (With the K-C Ettes)/Surfin' Blues (Stacy 964) .75 3.00 63
- JIVIN' AROUND/Doin' The Shotish (Stacy 936) .75 3.00 62
- KEEP TALKING/The Stinger (United Artists 158) .75 3.00 59
- NIGHT BEAT/The Stinger (Highland 1004) .75 3.00 60
- PINK PANTHER/If I Told You (MCI 1004) 1.25 5.00 55
- SURFIN' HOOTENANNY (With the K-C Ettes)/Easy Pickin' (Stacy 962) 1.00 4.00 63

Also see Clark, Sanford
Also see Reynolds, Jody

CASH, Eddie & The Cashiers
- DOING ALL RIGHT/Land Of Promises (Peak 1001) 12.50 50.00 58

CASHMAN & WEST (Terry Cashman & Tommy West)
- AMERICAN CITY SUITE/I Belong To You (Dunhill 4324) .50 2.00 72
- I COULD FEEL THE MORNING/Lifesong (Dunhill 15021) .50 2.00 73
- FRIEND IS DYING, A/American City Suite (Lifesong 45000) .50 2.00 75
- KING OF ROCK & ROLL, THE (Tribute to Chuck Berry)/Somebody Stole The Sun (Dunhill 4349) .75 3.00 73
- SONGMAN/If You Were A Rainbow (Dunhill 4333) .50 2.00 72

Also see Criterions, The

CASHMAN PISTILLI & WEST (Terry Cashman, Gene Pistilli, Tommy West)
- SHE NEVER LOOKED BETTER/Goodbye Jo (Capitol 2747) .75 3.00 71

CASHMERES, The
- EVERYTHING'S GONNA BE ALRIGHT/Four Lonely Nights (Lake 703) 1.25 5.00 61
- I GOTTA GO/Singing Waters (Laurie 3088) 1.25 5.00 61
- POPPA SAID/Life Line (Laurie 3105) 1.25 5.00 61
- VERY SPECIAL BIRTHDAY, A/I Believe In St. Nick (Laurie 3078) 3.00 12.00 60

CASINOS, The
- FOREVER & A NIGHT/ (Fraternity 987) .75 3.00 67
- IT'S ALL OVER NOW/Tailor Made (Fraternity 985) .75 3.00 67
- MOON RIVER/Soul Serenade (Fraternity 306) .75 3.00 66
- PLEASE LOVE ME/When I Stop Dreaming (Fraternity 995) .75 3.00 67
- THEN YOU CAN TELL ME GOODBYE/I Still Love You (Fraternity 977) .75 3.00 67
- TOO GOOD TO BE TRUE/That's The Way (Airtown 886002) 1.25 5.00
- TOO GOOD TO BE TRUE/That's The Way (Terry 116) .75 3.00

CASINOS, The
- DO YOU RECALL/The Suns (ITZY-2) 2.50 10.00

CASLONS, The
- ANNIVERSARY OF LOVE/The Quiet One (Seeco 6078) 1.50 6.00 61
- FOR ALL WE KNOW/Settle Me Down (Amy 836) 1.00 4.00 62

CASSIDY
- JAKARANDA/Same Old Way (Epic 10808) .50 2.00 71

CASSIDY, David (Of The Partridge Family)
- BREAKIN' DOWN AGAIN/On Fire (RCA Equinox PB-10647) .50 2.00 76
- CHERISH/All I Wanna Do Is Touch You (Bell 45150) .50 2.00 71
- COULD IT BE FOREVER/Blind Hope (Bell 45187) .50 2.00 72
- DARLIN'/This Could Be The Night (RCA Equinox PB-10405) .50 2.00 75
- DAYDREAM/Can't Go Home Again (Bell 45386) .50 2.00 73
- GET IT UP FOR LOVE (With Carl Wilson)/Love In Bloom (RCA Equinox PB-10321) 1.25 5.00 75
- HOW CAN I BE SURE/ (Bell 45220) .50 2.00 72
- ROCK ME BABY/Two Time Loser (Bell 45260) .50 2.00 72
- ROSA'S CANTINA/Saying Goodbye Ain't Easy (We'll Have To Go Away) (RCA Equinox PB-10921) .50 2.00 77
- THIS COULD BE THE NIGHT/Darlin' (RCA Equinox PB-10405) .50 2.00 75

CASSIDY, Hopalong: see Boyd, William

CASSIDY, Pam (With Cindy Watson)
- LIFE OF ELVIS, THE/God Can't Lie (Moon 1003) .50 2.00 77

CASSIDY, Shaun
- DA DOO RON RON/Holiday (Warner Bros. 8365) .50 2.00 77
- DO YOU BELIEVE IN MAGIC/Teen Dream (Warner-Curb 8533) .50 2.00 77
- HEY DEANIE/Strange Sensation (Warner-Curb 8488) .50 2.00 77
- MIDNIGHT SUN/She's Right (Warner-Curb 8698) .50 2.00 78
- OUR NIGHT/Right Before Your Skies (Warner-Curb 8634) .50 2.00 78
- THAT'S ROCK 'N' ROLL/I Wanna Be With You (Warner Bros. 8423) .50 2.00 77
- YOU'RE USIN' ME/You Still Surprise Me (Warner-Curb 8859) .50 2.00 79

Shaun is David Cassidy's half-brother.

CASSIDY, Ted
- LURCH, THE/Westley (Capitol 5503) 1.00 4.00 65

CASTALEERS, The
- THAT'S WHY I CRY/My Baby's All Right (Planet 44) 2.50 10.00 60
- THAT'S WHY I CRY/My Baby's All Right (Donna 1349) 1.25 5.00 61

CASTAWAYS, The
- I FOUND YOU/Hey There (Assault 1870) 2.00 8.00

CASTAWAYS, The
- GOODBYE BABE/A Man's Gotta Be A Man (Soma 1442) .75 3.00 65
- LIAR, LIAR/Sam (Soma 1433) .75 3.00 65
- WALKING IN DIFFERENT CIRCLES/Just On High (Fontana 1615) .75 3.00 66
- WHAT KIND OF FACE/Lavender Popcorn (Fontana 1626) .75 3.00 68

CASTELLS, The (Featuring Chuck Girard)
- COULD THIS BE MAGIC/Shinny Up Your Own Side (Warner Bros. 5445) 1.00 4.00 64
- I DO/Teardrops (Warner Bros. 5421) 6.25 25.00 64

("I Do" was arranged, produced & written by Brian Wilson. The song's melody is identical to "County Fair," the flip side of "Ten Little Indians" by The Beach Boys.)

- ETERNAL LOVE, ETERNAL SPRING/Clown Prince (Era 3098) 1.00 4.00 62
- JUST WALK AWAY/An Angel Cried (Decca 31834) 1.25 5.00 65
- LITTLE SAD EYES/Romeo (Era 3038) 1.00 4.00 61
- LITTLE SAD EYES/Initials (Era 3102) 1.00 4.00 63
- LOVE FINDS A WAY/Tell Her If I Could (Warner Bros. 5486) 1.00 4.00 64
- MAKE BELIEVE WEDDING/My Miracle (Era 3057) 1.00 4.00 61
- OH, WHAT IT SEEMED TO BE/Stand There Mountain (Era 3083) 1.00 4.00 62
- ONLY ONE/Echoes In The Night (Era 3089) 1.00 4.00 62
- SACRED/I Get Dreamy (Era 3048) 1.00 4.00 61
- SOME ENCHANTED EVENING/Jerusalem (United Artists 50324) .75 3.00 68
- SO THIS IS LOVE/On The Street Of Tears (Era 3073) 1.00 4.00 62
- VISION OF YOU, THE/Stiki De Boom Boom (Era 3064) 1.00 4.00 61
- WHAT DO LITTLE GIRLS DREAM OF/Some Enchanted Evening (Era 3107) 1.00 4.00 63

CASTLE, David
- LONELIEST MAN ON THE MOON, THE/Pretending (Parachute 505) .50 2.00 78
- TEN TO EIGHT/Finally (Parachute 501) .50 2.00 77

CASTLE, Joey, & The Daddy-O's
- ROCK & ROLL DADDY/Wild Love (Headline 1008) 12.50 50.00 59

CASTLE KINGS, The
- YOU CAN GET HIM FRANKENSTEIN/Loch Lomond (Atlantic 2107) .75 3.00 61

CASTLE SISTERS, The
- GOODBYE DAD/Wishing Star (Terrace 7506) .75 3.00 62
- WILL YOU LOVE ME TOMORROW/Thirteen (Roulette 4220) .75 3.00 60

CASTLE, Tony, & The Raiders
- SALTY/Salty (Gone 5099) 1.00 4.00 60

CASTLE-TONES, The
- WE MET AT A DANCE/At The Hot Dog Stand (Fire Fly 321) 1.25 5.00

CASTRO, Frankie
- STEAMBOAT/Why Baby Why (Wing 90051) 1.00 4.00

CASTRO, Vince
- BONG BONG (I LOVE YOU MADLY)/You're My Girl (Doe 102) 3.00 12.00 59
- BONG BONG (I LOVE YOU MADLY)/You're My Girl (Apt 25007) 1.50 6.00 58
- BONGO TWIST/You're My Girl (Apt 25047) 1.25 5.00 59

CASUALAIRS, The
- AT THE DANCE/Satisfied (Mona-Lee 136) 2.00 8.00
- CRUISING/Bossa Nova Twist (Craig 5001) 1.50 6.00

CASUALEERS, The
- COME BACK TO MY ARMS/When I'm In Your Arms (Laurie 3441) 1.00 4.00 68
- OPEN YOUR EYES/You Better Be Sure (Laurie 3407) 1.00 4.00 68

CASUALS, The
- SO TOUGH/I Love My Darling (Back Beat 503) 1.25 5.00 58

This group was also known as the Original Casuals.

CASUALS, The
- HELLO LOVE/Till You Come Back To Me (Dot 15671) 1.00 4.00 57
- MY LOVE SONG FOR YOU/Somebody Help Me (Dot 15557) 1.00 4.00 57
- WE GO TOGETHER/Pardners (Black Hawk 500) .75 3.00

CASUALS, The
- MONEY/Big Hammer (Minaret 109) .75 3.00
- MUSTANG 2 + 2/Play Me A Sad Song (Sound Stage 7 2534) 1.00 4.00 64

CASUAL THREE The (Featuring Dickie Goodman)
- INVISIBLE THING/Some Other Fellow (Luniverse 109) 1.25 5.00 58

CASUALTONES, The
- BRAND "X"/Stackin' Books (Library 763) 1.25 5.00

Instrumentals

CASULTARS, The
- JUST FOR YOU/This Is A Mean World (Autumn 21) .75 3.00 65

CASWELL, Johnny
- AT THE SHORE/Gotta Dance (Smash 1833) 1.00 4.00 63
- MY GIRL/Hot Dogs (Smash 1879) 1.00 4.00 63

Also see Crystal Mansion

CAT
- LIGHT OF LOVE/Looking Through A Glass Darkly (RCA 74-0279) .75 3.00 69

C.A.T.
- USE WHAT YOU GOT/Please Help Me Feel (Magna-Gilde MGR-333) .75 3.00 77

CAT MOTHER & THE ALL NIGHT NEWSBOYS
- CAN YOU DANCE TO IT/ (Polydor 14007) .75 3.00 69
- GOOD OLD ROCK & ROLL/Bad News (Polydor 14002) .75 3.00 69

CATALANO, Vinny
- PLEASE MR. JUKE BOX MAN/Rags To Riches (Hammer 6312) 1.25 5.00

CATALINAS, The
- CASTLE OF LOVE/Give Me Your Love (Little 812) 5.00 20.00

CATALINAS, The
- BAIL OUT/Bulletin (Dee Jay 1010) 1.25 5.00 63
- BAIL OUT/Bulletin (Sims 134) 1.00 4.00 63
- BANZAI WASHOUT/Beach Walkin' (Ric 113) 1.00 4.00 63
- RING OF STARS/Woolie Woolie Willie (Rita 107) 1.00 4.00 60
- RING OF STARS/Woolie Woolie Willie (Rita 1006) 1.00 4.00 60
- SAFARI/Pretty Little Nashville Girl (20th Fox 299) 1.00 4.00 63
- SURFER BOY/Boss Barracuda (Ric 164) 1.25 5.00
- TICK TOCK/You Haven't The Right (Scepter 12188) 1.00 4.00 67

Even though all of these releases are shown as being by a group using the same name, the possibility exists that they are not all by the same group.

CATE BROTHERS, The
- CAN'T CHANGE MY HEART/Time For Us (Asylum 45326) .50 2.00 76
- IN ON EYE & OUT THE OTHER/Start All Over Again (Asylum 45354) .50 2.00 76
- UNION MAN/Easy Way Out (Asylum 45294) .50 2.00 76
- WHERE CAN WE GO/Start All Over Again (Elektra 45370) .50 2.00 77
- YIELD NOT TO TEMPTATION/You're The Reason (Asylum 45435) .50 2.00 77

CATERPILLARS, The
- CATERPILLAR SONG, THE/Hello Happy Happy Goodbye (Port 70038) 1.00 4.00 64

CATES, George
- MOONGLOW (THEME FROM PICNIC)/Rio Baracuda (Coral 61618) 1.00 4.00 56
- WHERE THERE'S LIFE/One Night In Monte Carlo (Coral 61683) 1.00 4.00 56

Instrumentals
Also see Allen, Steve

CATES, Ronnie, & The Travellers
- OLD MAN RIVER/Long Time (Terrace 7501) 2.00 8.00

CATHY & JOE
- BYE BYE LOVE/A Day At A Time (Smash 1959) .75 3.00 65
- I SEE YOU/It's All Over Now (Smash 1929) .75 3.00 64

CATHY JEAN
- DOUBLE TROUBLE/Believe Me (Philips 40143) .75 3.00 63
- MY HEART BELONGS TO ONLY YOU/I Only Want You (Philips 40106) .75 3.00 63

Also see Cathy Jean & The Roomates

CATHY JEAN & THE ROOMATES
- BELIEVE ME/Double Trouble (Phillips 40014) 2.00 8.00 62
- I ONLY WANT YOU/One Love (Valmor 11) 1.50 6.00 61
- MAKE ME SMILE AGAIN/Sugar Cake (Valmor 009) 1.00 4.00 61
- PLEASE LOVE ME FOREVER/Canadian Sunset (Valmor 007) 1.00 4.00 61
- PLEASE TELL ME/Sugar Cake (Valmor 016) 1.00 4.00 62

CATMAN & TOENAIL
- ELECTION '76/Tap Your Toenail (Fun-e-Bone 4612) 1.00 4.00

(Novelty/Break-in)

CATS, The
- BE MY DAY/Time Machine (Fantasy 727) .75 3.00 74
- COME SUNDAY/Time Machine (MCA 40588) .50 2.00 76
- LET'S DANCE/I've Been In Love Before (Fantasy 685) .75 3.00 73
- LET'S DANCE/Love In Your Eyes (Fantasy 722) .75 3.00 74
- LET'S GO TOGETHER/Time Machine (Fantasy 708) .75 3.00 73

CAUDELL, Lane
- ALABAMA BOY/ (Private Stock 45122) .50 2.00 76
- HANGING ON A STAR/I Love You Girl (MCA 40901) .50 2.00 78
- THOSE EYES/ (MCA 40935) .50 2.00 78

CAVALIERS, The
- TEARS OF HAPPINESS/Summertime (Josie 924) .75 3.00 64

Also see Wilson, J. Frank

CAVALIERS, The
- DANCE DANCE DANCE/Play By The Rules Of Love (Apt 25004) 1.50 6.00 58
- SUNDAY IN MAY/Why Why Why (Apt 25031) 1.50 6.00 59

(With Scott Stevens)

CAVALLERO, Carmen
- MEET MISTER CALLAGHAN/Runnin' Wild Boogie (Decca 28373) 1.25 5.00 52
- MUSIC! MUSIC! MUSIC!/O, Katharina (Decca 24881) 1.25 5.00 50

CAVE DWELLERS, The
- MEDITATION/Night Runner (Bay Town 003) .75 3.00

CAVELL, Marc, & The Classmates
- I DIDN'T LIE/I See It (Candix 329) 3.75 15.00

CAVELLO, Jimmy, & His House Rockers
- FOOT STOMPIN'/Ooh-Wee (Coral 61787) 2.50 10.00 57
- ROCK ROCK ROCK (Film soundtrack)/The Big Beat (Coral 61728) 2.50 10.00 56
- ROCK THE JOINT/Leave Married Women Alone (BSD 1005) 3.75 15.00 51
- SODA SHOPPE ROCK/That's The Groovy Thing (Coral 61689) 2.50 10.00 56

C.C.S. (With Alexis Korner)
- TAP TURNS ON THE WATER/ (RAK 4507) .50 2.00 71
- WHOLE LOTTA LOVE/Boom Boom (RAK 4501) .50 2.00 71

CECILIO & KAPONO
- ABOUT YOU/ (Columbia 10322) .50 2.00 76
- I LOVE YOU/50¢ A Song (Columbia 10530) .50 2.00 76

CELEBRATION (With Mike Love)
- ALMOST SUMMER/Lookin' Good (MCA 40891) .75 3.00 78
- ALMOST SUMMER (KRTH version)/Almost Summer (Reg. version) (MCA S45-1982) 3.00 12.00 78

(Special Los Angeles radio station pressing)

- STARBABY/Gettin' Hungry (Pacific Arts 45104) 2.00 8.00 79

("Gettin' Hungry" is a different recording than was previously issued by the Beach Boys)

- SUMMER IN THE CITY/Island Girl (MCA 40930) .75 3.00 78

CELEBRITIES, The
- I WANT YOU/Mambo Daddy (Music Makers 101) .75 3.00 61

CENICOLA, P. G.
- LOVIE COLETTI/I Got Fired (Pepsi 770) 1.00 4.00

CENTRAL NERVOUS SYSTEM
- ALICE IN WONDERLAND/Something Happened To Me (Laurie 3446) .75 3.00 68

CENTURIES, The
- I LOVE YOU NO MORE/It's Alright (Spectra-Sound 641) 3.00 12.00

Also see Buckinghams, The

CERF, Chris
- CHEERLEADER, THE/In The Middle Of The Night (MGM 13103) .75 3.00 62

CHACKSFIELD, Frank
- EBB TIDE/Waltzing Bugle Boy (London 1358) 1.00 4.00 53
- LIMELIGHT (TERRY'S THEME)/Limelight (Incidental Music) (London 1342) 1.00 4.00 53
- ON THE BEACH/Paris Valentine (London 1901) 1.00 4.00 50

Instrumentals

CHAD & JEREMY (Chad Stuart & Jeremy Clyde)
- BEFORE & AFTER/Fare Thee Well (Columbia 43277) .75 3.00 65
- DISTANT SHORES/Last Night (Columbia 43682) .75 3.00 66
- FAMILY WAY/Rest In Peace (Columbia 44131) .75 3.00 67
- FROM A WINDOW/My Coloring Book (World Artists 1056) .75 3.00 65
- I DON'T WANNA LOSE YOU BABY/Pennies (Columbia 43339) .75 3.00 65
- I HAVE DREAMED/Should I (Columbia 43414) .75 3.00 65
- IF I LOVED YOU/Donna Donna (World Artist 1041) .75 3.00 65
- PAINTED DYNAGLOW SMILE/Editorial (Columbia 44379) .75 3.00 67
- SUMMER SONG, A/No Tears For Johnny (World Artists 1027) .75 3.00 64
- TEENAGE FAILURE/Early Morning Rain (Columbia 43490) .75 3.00 66
- WHAT DO YOU WANT WITH ME/A Very Good Year (World Artists 1052) .75 3.00 65
- WILLOW WEEP FOR ME/If She Were Mine (World Artists 1034) .75 3.00 64
- YESTERDAY'S GONE/Lemon Tree (World Artists 1021) .75 3.00 64
- YOU ARE SHE/I Won't Cry (Columbia 43807) .75 3.00 66

Also see Stuart, Chad & Jill

CHADONS, The (Featuring Chad Allen)
- START ALL OVER AGAIN/ (Chattahoochee 664) 1.00 4.00 65

CHAINS, The
- CAROL'S GOT A COBRA/I Hate To See You Crying (HBR 460) 1.00 4.00 66

CHALETS, The
- FAT FAT MOM-MI-O/Who's Laughing Who's Crying (Tru-Lite 1001) 1.00 4.00 61
- FAT FAT MOM-MI-O/Who's Laughing Who's Crying (Dart 1026) .75 3.00 61

CHALLENGERS, The (With Richard Delvy)
- ASPHALT SPINNER/Pipeline (Triump 1/2) 1.00 4.00
- BUTTERFLY, THE/Who Shot The Hole In My Sombrero (Challenge 1105) 1.00 4.00 62
- CHANNEL NINE/Can't Seem To Get Over You (Vault 918) 1.00 4.00 65
- DEADLINE/Cry Of The Goose (Triodex 107) 1.00 4.00 64
- EVERY DAY/I Hear An Echo (Tri Phi 1020) 1.00 4.00 62
- FOOT TAPPER/On The Move (Vault 904) 1.00 4.00 63
- GOOFUS/Lazy Twist (Tirodex 102) 1.00 4.00 64
- HOT ROD HOOTENANNY/Maybelling (Vault 910) 1.00 4.00 64
- I WANNA HOLD YOU/The Challengers Take A Ride On The Jefferson Airplane (Night Owl 6794) 1.25 5.00 67
- K-39/Hot Rod Show (Vault 913) 1.00 4.00 64
- MOONDOG/Tidal Wave (Vault 902) 1.00 4.00 63
- STAY WITH ME/Honey, Honey, Honey (Tri Phi 1012) 1.00 4.00 62
- TORQUAY/Bulldog (Vault 900) 1.00 4.00 63

Instrumentals
Also see Belairs, The
Also see Good Guys

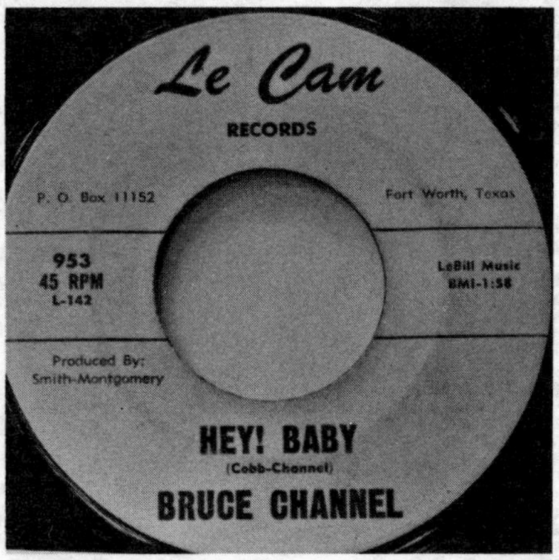

TITLE/FLIP	LABEL & NO.	GOOD	NEAR MINT	YR.

CHAMBERLIN BROTHERS, The

CRY BLUE BABY/My Baby Walked Out On Me	(Porter 1001)	.75	3.00	

CHAMBERLAIN, Richard

ALL I HAVE TO DO IS DREAM/Hi-Lili, Hi-Lo	(MGM 13121)	.75	3.00	63
BLUE GUITAR/(They Long To Be) Close To You	(MGM 13170)	.75	3.00	63
I WILL LOVE YOU/True Love	(MGM 13148)	.75	3.00	63
LOVE ME TENDER/All I Do Is Dream Of You	(MGM 13097)	.75	3.00	62
ROME WILL NEVER LEAVE YOU/ You Always Hurt The One You Love	(MGM 13285)	.75	3.00	64
SECRET KINGDOM/The Slipper & The Rose Waltz	(MCA 40691)	.50	2.00	77
THEME FROM DR. KILDARE (THREE STARS WILL SHINE TONIGHT)/ A Kiss To Build A Dream On	(MGM 13075)	.75	3.00	62

CHAMBERLAIN, Wilt "The Stilt"

BY THE RIVER/That's Easy	(End 1066)	1.00	4.00	60

CHAMPAGNE

OH ME OH MY, GOODBYE/The Last Song	(Ariola America 7668)	.50	2.00	77
ROCK & ROLL STAR/Kiss You Baby	(Ariola America 7658)	.50	2.00	77
VALENTINO/Rock & Roll Star	(Ariola America 7684)	.50	2.00	77

CHAMPAGNES, The

CASH/Crazy	(Skymac 1002)	1.25	5.00	
CASH/Crazy	(Laurie 3189)	.75	3.00	

CHAMP, Billy

HUSH-A-BYE/Believe Me (Group Sound)	(ABC-Paramount 10518)	1.50	6.00	64

CHAMPION

IT'S YOU LIFE/Sweet Mystery	(Epic 50614)	.50	2.00	78

CHAMPLIN, Bill (Of The Sons Of Champlin)

WHAT GOOD IS LOVE/	(Full Moon-Epic 50589)	.50	2.00	78

CHAMPS, The

ALLEY CAT/Coconut Grove	(Challenge 59086)	.75	3.00	60
ANNA/Buckaroo	(Challenge 59322)	.75	3.00	65
BRIGHT LIGHTS, BIG CITY/French '75	(Challenge 59277)	.75	3.00	65
CANTINA/Panic Button	(Challenge 9116)	.75	3.00	61
CHARIOT ROCK/Subway	(Challenge 59018)	.75	3.00	58
EL RANCHO ROCK/Midnighter	(Challenge 59007)	.75	3.00	58
EXPERIMENT IN TERROR/La Cucaracha	(Challenge 9140)	.75	3.00	62
FACE, THE/Tough Train	(Challenge 59097)	.75	3.00	60
GONE TRAIN/Beatnik	(Challenge 59035)	.75	3.00	59
HOKEY POKEY/Jumping Bean	(Challenge 9103)	.75	3.00	61
KAHLUA/Fraternity Waltz	(Challenge 59263)	.75	3.00	64
LA CUCARACHA/Experiment In Terror	(Challenge 9140)	.75	3.00	62
LITTLE MATADOR, THE/Red Eye	(Challenge 59076)	.75	3.00	60
LIMBO DANCE/Latin Limbo	(Challenge 9162)	.75	3.00	62
LIMBO ROCK/Tequila Twist	(Challenge 9131)	.75	3.00	62
MAN FROM DURANGO/Red Pepper	(Challenge 59314)	.75	3.00	65
MOONLIGHT BAY/Caramba	(Challenge 59043)	.75	3.00	59
MR. COOL/3/4 Mash	(Challenge 9180)	.75	3.00	62
NIGHT TRAIN/The Rattler	(Challenge 59049)	.75	3.00	59
NIK NAK/Shades	(Challenge 9189)	.75	3.00	63
ONLY THE YOUNG/Switzerland	(Challenge 59236)	.75	3.00	64
ROOTS/Cactus Juice	(Challenge 9199)	.75	3.00	62
SAN JUAN/Jalisco	(Challenge 59219)	.75	3.00	63
SKY HIGH/Double Eagle Rock	(Challenge 59053)	.75	3.00	59
SOMBRERO/The Shoddy Shoddy	(Challenge 9113)	.75	3.00	61
TEQUILA/Train To Nowhere	(Challenge 1016)	.75	3.00	58
TOO MUCH TEQUILA/Twenty Thousand Leagues	(Challenge 59063)	.75	3.00	59
TOUGH TRAIN/The Face	(Challenge 59097)	.75	3.00	60
TURNPIKE/Rockin' Mary	(Challenge 59026)	.75	3.00	58
VARSITY ROCK/That Did It	(Challenge 9174)	.75	3.00	62
WHAT A COUNTRY/I've Just Seen Her	(Challenge 9143)	.75	3.00	61

Instrumentals
Also see Burgess, Dave
Also see Rio, Chuck
Also see Seals, Jimmy

CHANCE, Larry (Of the Earls)

LET THEM TALK/Promise Her Anything	(Barry 110)	6.25	25.00	64

Also see Barons, The
Also see Crowns, The

CHANGE, Wayne

SEND HER TO ME/Just A Little Bit O' Lovin'	(Whirlybird 2006)	2.00	8.00	

CHANCELLORS, The

TELL ME YOU LOVE ME/There Goes My Girl	(Port 5000)	3.75	15.00	

CHANCELLORS, The

DEAR JOHN/5 Minus 3	(Fenton 2072)	1.00	4.00	
ONCE IN A MILLION/Journey	(Fenton 2066)	1.00	4.00	
YO YO/Little Latin Lupe Lu	(Soma 1421)	1.00	4.00	

CHANCERS, The

SHIRLEY ANN/My One	(Dot 15870)	1.50	6.00	58

CHANDELIERS, The

BLUEBERRY SWEET/One More Step	(Angletone 521)	3.00	12.00	57
DOLLY/Dancin' In The Congo	(Angletone 529)	3.00	12.00	57

CHAN-DELLS, The

SAND SURFER/Louie Louie	(ARC 8101)	1.00	4.00	63

CHANDLER, Bobby

I'M SERIOUS/If You Loved Me	(OJ 1000)	.75	3.00	

CHANDLER, Karen

HIT THE TARGET/Positively No Dancing	(Coral 61137)	1.00	4.00	54
HOLD ME, THRILL ME, KISS ME/One Dream	(Coral 60831)	1.00	4.00	52
MAN IN THE RAINCOAT/Sentimental Fool	(Coral 61433)	1.00	4.00	55

CHANDLER, Kenny

DRUMS/The Magic Ring	(United Artists 342)	1.00	4.00	61
HEART/Wait For Me	(Laurie 3158)	1.00	4.00	63
I CAN'T STAND TEARS AT A PARTY/I Tell Myself	(Laurie 3181)	.75	3.00	63
MAN ON THE RUN/Leave Me If You Want To	(Laurie 3140)	.75	3.00	63
PLEASE MR. MOUNTAIN/ What Kind Of Love Is Yours	(United Artists 384)	.75	3.00	61

CHANEY, Lon

MONSTER HOLIDAY/Yuletide Jerk (Novelty)	(Tower 114)	1.00	4.00	64

CHANGIN' TIMES, The

ALADDIN/All In The Mind Of A Young Girl	(Philips 40401)	.75	3.00	66
GOIN' LOVIN' WITH YOU/ I Should Have Brought Her Home	(Philips 49368)	.75	3.00	66
PIED PIPER, THE/Thank You Babe	(Philips 40320)	.75	3.00	65

CHANGING COLORS (With Jerry Vance)

DA DA DA DA/Gimmie Back	(Tower 492)	1.00	4.00	69
GIRL FOR ALL SEASONS/Want You By My Side	(Tower 457)	1.00	4.00	68

CHANNEL, Bruce

BLUE MONDAY/My Baby	(Le Cam 125)	.75	3.00	64
COME ON BABY/Mine Exclusively	(Smash 1769)	.75	3.00	62
DIPSY DOODLE/Send Her Home	(Smash 1838)	.75	3.00	63
GOING BACK TO LOUISIANA/Forget Me Not	(Le Cam 122)	.75	3.00	64
HEY! BABY/Dream Girl	(Le Cam 953)	2.00	8.00	62
HEY! BABY/Dream Girl	(Smash 1731)	.75	3.00	62
KING IS FREE (LOVE ME), THE (With Major Bill Smith)/ Funky Dude (By Andy & The Dude)	(Le Cam 7277)	.50	2.00	77
MR. BUS DRIVER/It's Me	(Mala 579)	.75	3.00	67
NO OTHER BABY/Night People	(Smash 1826)	.75	3.00	63
NUMBER ONE MAN/If Only I Had Known	(Smash 1752)	.75	3.00	62
OH BABY/Let's Hurt Together	(Smash 1792)	.75	3.00	62
PRESLEY MEDLEY, A/A Man Without A Woman (With Bill, Larry & Gene)	(Le Cam 1117)	.50	2.00	77
RUN ROMANCE RUN/Don't Leave Me	(Manco 1035)	.75	3.00	62
RUN ROMANCE, RUN/Don't Leave Me	(Teenager 601)	1.25	5.00	62
SATISFIED MIND/That's What's Happenin'	(Mel-o-dy 112)	.75	3.00	64
SOMEWHERE IN THIS TOWN/Stand Tough	(Smash 1780)	.75	3.00	62
YOU MAKE ME HAPPY/You Never Looked Better	(Mel-o-dy 114)	.75	3.00	64

CHANTAYS, The

BEYOND/I'll Be Back Someday	(Downey 126)	1.00	4.00	64
GREENZ/Three Coins In The Fountain	(Downey 130)	1.00	4.00	65
MONSOON/Scotch High's	(Downey 108)	1.25	5.00	63
MONSOON/Scotch High's	(Dot 16492)	.75	3.00	63
ONLY IF YOU CARE/Love Can Be Cruel	(Downey 120)	1.00	4.00	64
PIPELINE/Move It	(Downey 104)	1.50	6.00	63
PIPELINE/Move It	(Dot 16440)	.75	3.00	63
SPACE PROBE/Continental Missile	(Downey 116)	1.00	4.00	63

Instrumentals
Also see Ill Winds, The

CHANTEERS, The

I WAITED/Just A Little Boy	(Mercury 72037)	.75	3.00	62
SHE'S COMING HOME/Mr. Zebra	(Mercury 71979)	.75	3.00	62

CHANTELLES, The

OUT OF MY MIND/More To Love	(GNP Crescendo 415)	.75	3.00	68

CHANTIERS, The

PEPPERMINT/Dear Mr. Clock	(DJB 112)	2.00	8.00	64

CHANTONES, The

STORMY WEATHER/Sweet Georgia Brown	(Capitol 4661)	1.25	5.00	61
TANGEROCK/Don't Open That Door	(Top Rank 2066)	.75	3.00	60

CHANTS, The

CLOSE FRIENDS/Lost & Found	(Capitol 3949)	1.00	4.00	58
DICK TRACY/Choo-Choo	(Verve VK-10244)	.75	3.00	
RESPECTABLE/Kiss Me Goodbye	(Eko 3567)	1.50	6.00	61
RESPECTABLE/Kiss Me Goodbye	(MGM 13008)	.75	3.00	61
SURFSIDE/Chicken N' Gravy	(Checker 1209)	.75	3.00	68

Even though all of these releases are shown as being by a group using the same name, the possibility exists that they are not all by the same group.

CHANTS, The

I COULD WRITE A BOOK/A Thousand Stars	(Cameo 297)	1.50	6.00	64
I DON'T CARE/Come Go With Me	(Cameo 277)	1.25	5.00	63
SHE'S MINE/Then I'll Be Home	(Interphon 7703)	1.25	5.00	64

CHAPARRALS, The

BEER BARREL ROCK/Leapin' Guitar (Instrumentals)	(Roulette 4229)	.75	3.00	60

CHAPEL, Jean

HELP STAMP OUT LONELINESS/	(Challenge 59362)	.50	2.00	69
I STARTED LOVING YOU AGAIN/Bluebird Ridge	(Kapp 2034)	.50	2.00	69
I WON'T BE ROCKIN' TONIGHT/Welcome To The Club	(Sun 244)	3.00	12.00	56
I WON'T BE ROCKIN' TONIGHT/Welcome To The Club	(RCA Victor 47-6681)	1.00	4.00	56

CHAPELAIRES, The

GLORIA/Under Hawaiian Skies	(Hac 102)	1.00	4.00	61
I'M STILL IN LOVE WITH YOU/Not Good Enough	(Hac 101)	1.00	4.00	61

CHAPERONES, The

BLUEBERRY SWEET/The Man From The Moon	(Josie 891)	3.00	12.00	61
DANCE WITH ME/Cruise To The Moon (With Label Misprint, showing artist as The Cahperones)	(Josie 880)	2.50	10.00	60
DANCE WITH ME/Cruise To The Moon	(Josie 880)	2.00	8.00	60
SHINING STAR/My Shadow & Me	(Josie 885)	2.50	10.00	61

CHAPIN, Harry

BETTER PLACE TO BE/	(Elektra 45828)	.50	2.00	73
BETTER PLACE TO BE (PART 1)/ Better Place To Be (Part 2)	(Elektra 45327)	.50	2.00	76
CAT'S IN THE CRADLE/Vacancy	(Elektra 45203)	.50	2.00	74
COREY'S COMING/	(Elektra 45368)	.50	2.00	76
COULD YOU PUT YOUR LIGHT ON, PLEASE/ Any Old Kind Of Day	(Elektra 45792)	.50	2.00	72
DANCE BAND ON THE TITANIC/ I Wonder What Happened To Him	(Elektra 45426)	.50	2.00	77
DREAMS GO BY/Sandy	(Elektra 45264)	.50	2.00	75
IF YOU WANT TO FEEL/ I Wonder What Would Happen To This World	(Elektra 45497)	.50	2.00	78
I WANNA LEARN A LOVE SONG/ She Sings Songs Without Words	(Elektra 45236)	.50	2.00	75
MY OLD LADY/I Do It For You, Jane	(Elektra 45445)	.50	2.00	78
SUNDAY MORNING SUNSHINE/Burning Herself	(Elektra 45811)	.50	2.00	72
TANGLED UP PUPPET/ Dirt Gets Under The Fingernails	(Elektra 45285)	.50	2.00	75
TAXI/Empty	(Elektra 45770)	.50	2.00	72
WHAT MADE AMERICA FAMOUS?/Old College Avenue	(Elektra 45893)	.50	2.00	74
WOLD/Short Stories	(Elektra 45874)	.50	2.00	74

CHAPINS The (Tom & Steve Chapin)

OLD TIME MOVIES/Not Your Kind	(Rock-Land 664)	1.25	5.00	
WORKIN' ON MY LIFE/	(Epic 10761)	1.00	4.00	71

CHAPLAIN, Paul

SHORTNIN' BREAD/Nicotine (With The Emeralds)	(Harper 100)	1.00	4.00	60

CHARACTERS, The

WE'RE DEPENDING ON YOU, GENERAL CUSTER/ Columbus, You Big Bag Of Steam (Novelty)	(Pip 100)	1.00	4.00	59

CHARADES, The (Featuring Billy Storm)

CLOSE TO ME/Take A Chance	(Original Sound 47)	2.00	8.00	
FLAMINGO/Someones In The Kitchen With Dinah	(Skylark 502)	1.50	6.00	64
MAKE ME HAPPY BABY/Shang Lang A Ding Dong	(United Artists 132)	1.50	6.00	58
PLEASE BE MY LOVE TONIGHT/Turn Him Down	(AVA 154)	2.00	8.00	63

CHARADES, The

CORRUPTION/Corruption (Instrumental)	(Charade 502)	.75	3.00	76
FOR YOU/Sophia	(Northridge 1002)	1.25	5.00	62
PLEASE BE MY LOVE TONIGHT/Turn Him Down	(Ava 154)	1.00	4.00	63
SURF 'N' STOMP/Christina	(Impact 32)	1.00	4.00	63
TAKE A CHANCE/Close To Me	(Orginial Sound 47)	1.00	4.00	64

One time Charades' member, Tommy Johnston, was later with the Doobie Brothers.

CHARADES, The

KEY TO MY HAPPINESS, THE/	(MGM K-13540)	.75	3.00	67

CHARIOTS, The

GLORIA/A Sunday Morning Love	(Time 1006)	3.75	15.00	59
OPEN HOUSE/Tiger In Your Tank	(RSVP 1105)	.75	3.00	

CHARITY SHAYNE

AIN'T IT, BABE?/Then You Try	(Autumn 22)	1.50	6.00	65

CHARLATANS, The

DATE: MAY 19, 1969/ (Promotional issue)	(Philips 44824)	2.50	10.00	69
HIGH COIN/When I Go Sailin' By	(Philips 40610)	3.00	12.00	69
SHADOW KNOWS, THE/32-20	(Kapp 779)	3.75	15.00	66

Also see Hicks, Don, & His Hot Licks

CHARLES, Jimmy

AGE FOR LOVE, THE/Follow The Swallow	(Promo 1003)	.75	3.00	60
MILLION TO ONE, A/Hop Scotch Hop	(Promo 1002)	.75	3.00	60

CHARLES, Ray, Singers

AL-DI-LA/Till The End Of Time	(Command 4049)	.75	3.00	64
AUTUMN LEAVES/Early Autumn	(MGM 12068)	1.00	4.00	55
LOVE ME WITH ALL YOUR HEART/ Sweet Little Mountain Bird	(Command 4046)	.75	3.00	64
ONE MORE TIME/Bluesette	(Command 4057)	.75	3.00	64
THIS IS MY PRAYER/A Toy For Boy	(Command 4059)	.75	3.00	65

CHARLES, Sonny (& Checkmates Ltd.)

BLACK PEARL/Lazy Susan	(A&M 1053)	1.00	4.00	69
DO THE WALK/Glad For You	(Capitol 5603)	.75	3.00	66
LOVE IS ALL I HAVE TO GIVE/Never Should Have Lied	(A&M 1039)	1.00	4.00	68
PLEASE DON'T TAKE MY WORLD AWAY/ Mastered The Art Of Love	(Capitol 5814)	.75	3.00	67
PROUD MARY/Do You Love Your Baby	(A&M 1127)	1.00	4.00	69
WALK IN THE SUNLIGHT/A & I	(Capitol 5922)	.75	3.00	67

CHARLES, Tommy

AFTER SCHOOL/I'll Wait For Your Call	(Decca 29946)	1.00	4.00	56
OUR LOVE AFFAIR/If You Were Me	(Decca 29717)	1.00	4.00	56

CHARLIE

JOHNNY HOLD BACK/Love Is Alright	(Janus 272)	.50	2.00	77
KILLER CUT/The End Of It All	(Arista 0449)	.50	2.00	79
SHE LOVES TO BE IN LOVE/Life So Cruel	(Janus 276)	.50	2.00	78
TURNING TO YOU/Pressure Point	(Janus 270)	.50	2.00	77
WATCHING T.V./Out Of Control	(Janus 275)	.50	2.00	78

CHARLIE (Charles Reinhart)

BEATLES/Best Ex-Beatle (Novelties: Beatle break-in/Pete Best break-in.)	(C&E 45-101)	.50	2.00	79

CHARLIE & CHAN

MY BOYFRIND'S LEARNING KARATE/Rickshaw Drag Race	(Kapp 582)	.75	3.00	64

CHARLIE & THE PEP BOYS

LARA/Give Me More	(A&M 1849)	.50	2.00	77

CHARMERS, The

I CRIED/Shy Guy	(Laurie 3173)	1.00	4.00	63
JOHNNY/My Kind Of Love	(Laurie 3142)	1.00	4.00	62

CHARMETTES, The

DONNIE/Too Much True Lovin'	(Markey 101)	.75	3.00	62
MY LOVER IS A BOY SCOUT/Mailbox	(Mala 491)	.75	3.00	64
ON A NIGHT LIKE TONIGHT/Why Oh Why	(Tri Disc 103)	.75	3.00	62
PLEASE DON'T KISS ME AGAIN/What Is A Tear	(Kapp 547)	1.00	4.00	63
0021-0021-OOH/He's A Wise Guy	(Kapp 570)	1.00	4.00	64

CHARTBUSTERS, The

LONELY SURFER BOY/New Orleans	(Crusader 118)	1.00	4.00	65
SHE'S THE ONE/Slippin' Thru Your Fingers	(Mutual 502)	.75	3.00	64
WHY (DONCHA BE MY GIRL)/Stop The Music	(Mutual 508)	.75	3.00	64
YOU'RE BREAKIN MY HEART/Can't You Hear Me Calling	(Mutual 511)	.75	3.00	65

CHASE

GET IT ON/River	(Epic 10738)	.50	2.00	71
HANDBAGS & GLADRAGS/Open Up Wide	(Epic 10775)	.50	2.00	71
SO MANY PEOPLE/Paint It Sad	(Epic 10806)	.50	2.00	71

CHASE, Allen

FAME & FORTUNE/All I Want Is You	(Columbia 41538)	1.00	4.00	59
I'M IN LOVE WITH MISS CONNIE FRANCIS/Lonely Heart	(Cinema 108)	1.00	4.00	61

CHASE, Ellison (Of Canyon)

LET'S ROCK/To The Disco	(Big Tree BT-16072)	.50	2.00	76
TOO BAD/Run For The Daylight	(Magna-Gilde 5N-423)	.50	2.00	75
YOU'RE THE ONLY ONE/Hold On	(Big Tree BT-16086)	.50	2.00	77

CHATEAUS, The

BROWN EYES/Satisfied	(Warner Bros. 5023)	2.50	10.00	58
HONEST I WILL/Summer's Here	(Coral 62364)	5.00	20.00	63
LADDER OF LOVE/You'll Reap What You Sow	(Warner Bros. 5071)	2.50	10.00	59
MASQUERADE IS OVER, THE/If I Didn't Care	(Warner Bros. 5043)	2.50	10.00	59

CHATEAUS, The

I'M THE ONE/The Bells Of Ryhmney	(Boss 9912)	1.50	6.00	65
MOANIN'/Seven Come Eleven	(Sound Stage 7 2536)	1.50	6.00	65
SUMMER HAS COME & GONE/Count On Me	(Jam 114)	1.50	6.00	65

Also see Glenwoods, The

TITLE/FLIP — LABEL & NO. — GOOD — NEAR MINT — YR.

CHATER, Kerry (Of The Union Gap)
AIN'T NOTHIN' FOR A HEARTACHE/
Leave Well Enough Alone (Warner-Popcorn 8645) .50 2.00 78
MISTY MARY/ (Warner-Popcorn 8389) .50 2.00 76
PART TIME LOVE/No Love On The Black Keys (Warner-Popcorn 8310) .50 2.00 76
WELL ON MY WAY TO LOVING YOU/
Leave Well Enough Alone (Warner-Popcorn 8591) .50 2.00 77

CHAUNCEY, Sir (Ernie Freeman)
BEAUTIFUL OBSESSION/Tenderfoot (Pattern 603) 1.25 5.00 60
BEAUTIFUL OBSESSION/Tenderfoot (Warner Bros. 5150) .75 3.00 60
Instrumentals

CHAVIS BROTHERS, The
SO TIRED/I Love You (Clock 1025) 1.00 4.00 59

CHAYNS, The
NIGHT TIME/Live With The Moon (International Artists 114) 1.00 4.00 67
THERE'S SOMETHING WRONG/See It Through (International Artists 119) 1.00 4.00 67

CHEAP SKATES
LATIN SKATE/ (Bang B-539) .75 3.00 67

CHEAP TRICK
AIN'T THAT A SHAME/Elo Kiddies (Epic 50743) .50 2.00 79
CALIFORNIA MAN/I Wan You To Want Me (Live) (Epic 50625) .50 2.00 78
DREAM POLICE/Heaven Tonight (Epic 50774) .50 2.00 79
I WANT YOU TO WANT ME/Clock Strikes Ten (Epic 50680) .50 2.00 79
I WANT YOU TO WANT ME/Oh Boy (Instrumental) (Epic 50435) .75 3.00 77
OH, CANDY/Daddy Should Have Stayed In High School (Epic 50375) .75 3.00 77
SOUTHERN GIRLS/You're All Talk (Epic 50485) .75 3.00 77
SURRENDER/Auf Wiedersehen (Epic 50570) .50 2.00 78
VOICES/The House Is Rockin' (With Domestic Problems) (Epic 50814) .50 2.00 79

PARKWAY
Jay & Cee
Arma B.M.I.
Time: 2:32
THE TWIST
CHUBBY CHECKER
811 A
© 1960 PARKWAY RECORDS, INC.

CHECKER, Chubby (Ernest Evans)
BACK IN THE U.S.S.R./Windy Cream (Buddah 100) .50 2.00 69
BIRDLAND/Black Cloud (Parkway 873) .75 3.00 63
CLASS, THE/Schooldays, Oh Schooldays (Parkway 804) 1.50 6.00 59
DANCE THE MESS AROUND/Good, Good Lovin' (Parkway 822) .75 3.00 61
DANCIN' PARTY/Gotta Get Myself Together (Parkway 842) .75 3.00 62
DANCING DINOSAUR/
Those Private Eyes (Keep Watching Me) (Parkway 810) 1.50 6.00 60
EVERYTHING'S WRONG/Cu Ma La Be Stay (Parkway 959) .75 3.00 65
FLY, THE/That's The Way It Goes (Parkway 830) .75 3.00 61
HEY, BOBBA NEEDLE/Spread Joy (Parkway 907) .75 3.00 64
HEY YOU, LITTLE BOO-GA-LOO/Pussy Cat (Parkway 989) .75 3.00 66
HUCKLEBUCK, THE/Whole Lot Of Shakin' Goin' On (Parkway 813) .75 3.00 60
JET, THE/Ray Charles-ton (Parkway 006) .75 3.00
KARATE MONKEY/Her Heart (Parkway 112) .75 3.00 66
LAZY ELSIE MOLLY/Rosie (Parkway 920) .75 3.00 64
LET'S DO THE FREDDIE/At The Discotheque (Parkway 949) .75 3.00 65
LET'S TWIST AGAIN/Everything's Gonna Be All Right (Parkway 824) .75 3.00 61
LIMBO ROCK/Popeye (The Hitchhiker) (Parkway 849) .75 3.00 62
LODDY LO/Hooka Tooka (Parkway 890) .75 3.00 63
LODDY LO/Everything's Gonna Be Alright (Parkway 890) .75 3.00 63
LOVELY, LOVELY/The Weekend's Here (Parkway 936) .75 3.00 64
PONY TIME/Oh Susannah (Parkway 818) .75 3.00 61
SHE WANTS T' SWIM/You Better Believe It (Parkway 922) .75 3.00 64
SLOW TWISTIN' (With Dee Dee Sharp)/La Paloma Twist (Parkway 835) .75 3.00 62
TWENTY MILES/Let's Limbo Some More (Parkway 862) .75 3.00 63
TWIST, THE/Toot (Parkway 811) 1.25 5.00 60
TWIST, THE/Twistin' U.S.A. (Parkway 811) 1.50 6.00 61
(Promotional yellow plastic issue.)
TWIST, THE/Twistin' U.S.A. (Parkway 811) .75 3.00 61
TWIST IT UP/Surf Party (Parkway 879) .75 3.00 63
WHOLE LOTTA LAUGHIN'/Samson & Delilah (Parkway 808) 1.25 5.00 60
YOU GOT THE POWER/Looking At Tomorrow (Parkway 105) .75 3.00 66

CHECKER, Chubby, & Bobby Rydell
JINGLE BELL ROCK/Jingle Bell Imitations (Cameo 205) .75 3.00 61

CHECKERS, The
BLUE SATURDAY/Cascade (Skyla 1120) .75 3.00 62
(Instrumentals)

CHECKMATES LTD: see Charles, Sonny

CHEECH & CHONG (Richard Marin & Thomas Chong)
BASKETBALL JONES (Featuring Tyrone Shoelaces)/
Don't Bug Me (Ode 66038) .50 2.00 73
BLACK LASSIE (Featuring Johnnie Stash)/
Coming Attractions (Ode 66104) .50 2.00 74
BLOAT ON/Just Say Right On (The Bloaters Creed) (Ode 50471) .50 2.00 77
(With the Bloaters)
EARACHE MY EYE/Turn That Thing Down (Ode 66102) .50 2.00 74
(With Alice Bowie)
FRAMED/Pedro's Request (Ode 66124) .50 2.00 76
(HOW I SPENT MY SUMMER VACATION) OR A DAY AT THE
BEACH WITH PEDRO & THE MAN (PART 1)/
(How I Spent My Summer Vacation) Or A Day At The
Beach With Pedro & The Man (Part 2) (Ode 66115) .50 2.00 75
SANTA CLAUS & HIS OLD LADY/Dave (Ode 66021) .50 2.00 72
SISTER MARY ELEPHANT/Wink Dinkerson (Ode 66041) .50 2.00 73
UP IN SMOKE/Rock Fight (Warner Bros. 8666) .50 2.00 78
Also see Taylor, Bobby, & The Vancoovers

CHEE-CHEE & PEPPY
I KNOW I'M IN LOVE/My Love Will Never Fade Away (Buddah 225) 1.50 6.00 71

CHEERIOS, The
DING DONG HONEY MOON/Where Are You Tonight (Infinity 11) 3.00 12.00
DING DONG HONEY MOON/Where Are You Tonight (Oldies 1) 1.50 6.00

CHEERS, The
(BAZOOM) I NEED YOUR LOVIN'/Arivederci (Capitol 2921) 1.25 5.00 54
BIG FEET/Chug Chug Toot Toot (Mercury 71083) 1.00 4.00 57
BLACK DENIM TROUSERS/Some Night In Alaska (Capitol 3219) 1.25 5.00 55
BLUEBERRIES/Can't We Be More Than Friends (Capitol 3075) 1.25 5.00 55
CHICKEN/Don't Do Anything (Capitol 3353) 1.25 5.00 56
HEAVEN ON EARTH/Que Pasa Muchacha (Capitol 3409) 1.25 5.00 56
I MUST BE DREAMING/Fancy Meeting You Here (Capitol 3146) 1.25 5.00 55
TWO HEARTS/You Never Have The Time (Mercury 71100) 1.00 4.00 57
(Shown as by Bert Convy & The Cheers)
WHADAYA WANT/Bernies Tune (Capitol 3019) 1.25 5.00 55

CHEETAHS, The
MECCA/That Goodnight Kiss (Philips 40239) .75 3.00 64

CHELSEA BOYS, The
CHANGING MIND/Boatrider (Keff 4446) 1.00 4.00
MOLLY MALONE/Little Boy Blue (Keff 2664) 1.25 5.00

CHER (Of Sonny & Cher)
ALFIE/She's No Better Than Me (Imperial 66192) .75 3.00 66
ALL I REALLY WANT TO DO/I'm Gonna Love You (Imperial 66114) .75 3.00 65
AM I BLUE/How Long Has This Been Going On (MCA 40039) .50 2.00 73
BABY, I LOVE YOU/A Woman's Story (Warner-Spector 0400) .50 2.00 75
BANG, BANG (MY BABY SHOT ME DOWN)/
Needles & Pins (Imperial 66160) .75 3.00 66
BANG, BANG (MY BABY SHOT ME DOWN)/
Our Day Will Come (Imperial 66160) .75 3.00 66
BEHIND THE DOOR/Magic In The Air (Imperial 66217) .75 3.00 66
BORROWED TIME/Long Distance Love Affair (Warner Bros. 8263) .50 2.00 76
CAROUSEL MAN/ (MCA 40324) .50 2.00 75
CHASTITY'S SONG/Guilded Splinters (Atlantic 6684) .75 3.00 69
CLICK SONG NUMBER ONE, THE/
But I Can't Love You More (Imperial 66282) .75 3.00 68
DARK LADY/Two People Clinging To A Thread (MCA 40161) .50 2.00 73
DON'T HIDE YOUR LOVE/The First Time (Kapp 2184) .50 2.00 72
DON'T PUT IT ON ME/Classified 1A (Kapp 2134) .50 2.00 71
DREAM BABY/Mama (When My Dollies Have Babies) (Imperial 66223) .75 3.00 66
DREAM BABY/Stan Quetzal (Imperial 66081) 2.00 8.00 64
(Shown as by Cherilyn)
GYPSYS, TRAMPS & THIEVES/He'll Never Know (Kapp 2146) .50 2.00 71
HALF-BREED/Melody (MCA 40102) .50 2.00 73
HANGIN' ON/For What It's Worth (Atco 6704) .75 3.00 69
HELL ON WHEELS/Git Down (Guitar Groupie) (Casablanca 2208) .50 2.00 79
HEY JOE/Our Day Will Come (Imperial 66252) .75 3.00 66
HOLDIN' OUT FOR LOVE/Boys & Girls (Casablanca 2228) .50 2.00 79
I SAW A MAN & HE DANCED WITH HIS WIFE/
I Hate To Sleep Alone (MCA 40273) .50 2.00 74
LAY LADY LAY/Hangin' On (Atco 6868) .75 3.00 72
LIVING IN A HOUSE DIVIDED/One Honest Man (Kapp 2171) .50 2.00 72
LOVE LIKE YOURS, A (With Nilsson)/
(Just Enough To Keep Me) Hanging' On (Warner-Spector 0402) .50 2.00 75
OUR DAY WILL COME/Ol' Man River (United Artists 50974) .50 2.00 72
PIRATE/Send The Man Over (Warner Bros. 8311) .50 2.00 77
REASON TO BELIEVE/Will You Love Me Tomorrow (United Artists 50864) .50 2.00 71
RESCUE ME/Dixie Girl (MCA 40375) .50 2.00 75
SUPERSTAR/The First Time (Atco 6793) .75 3.00 70
TAKE ME HOME/My Song (Too Far Gone) (Casablanca 965) .50 2.00 79
TAKE ME HOME/My Song (Too Far Gone) (Casablanca 20150) 1.50 6.00 79
(12" single issue)
THESE DAYS/Geronimo's Cadillac (Warner Bros. 8096) .50 2.00 75
TOO LATE TO LOVE ME NOW/ (Casablanca 20168) 1.25 5.00 80
(12" single issue)
TRAIN OF THOUGHT/Dixie Girl (MCA 40245) .50 2.00 74
WAR PAINT & SOFT FEATHERS/Send The Man Over (Warner Bros. 8366) .50 2.00 77
WASN'T IT GOOD/It's Too Late To Love Me Now (Casablanca 987) .50 2.00 79
WAY OF LOVE, THE/Don't Put It On Me (Kapp 2158) .50 2.00 72
WHERE DO YOU GO/See See Blues (Imperial 66136) .75 3.00 65
YOU BETTER SIT DOWN KIDS/Elusive Butterfly (Imperial 66261) .75 3.00 67
YOU BETTER SIT DOWN KIDS/
Mama (When My Dollies Have Babies) (Imperial 66261) .75 3.00 67
YOU KNOW DARN WELL/ (MCA 40083) .50 2.00 73
YOU MADE ME SO VERY HAPPY/First Time (Atco 6713) .75 3.00 69
YOURS UNTIL TOMORROW/Thought Of Loving You (Atco 6658) .75 3.00 69
Also see Caesar & Cleo
Also see Mason, Bonnie Jo
Also see Allman & Woman

CHERILYN: see Cher

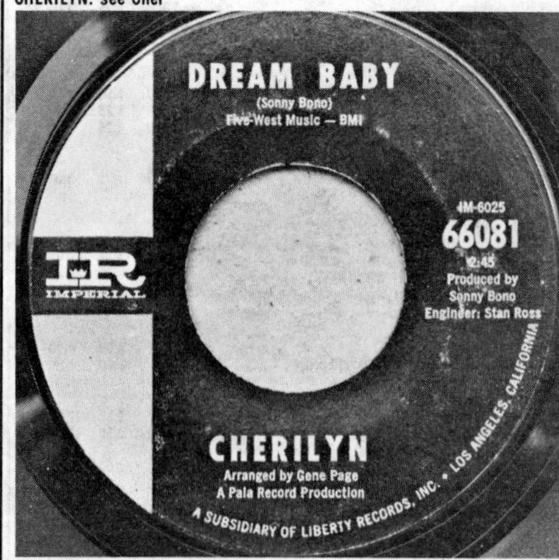

DREAM BABY
(Sonny Bono)
Five-West Music — BMI
4M-6025
66081
2:45
Produced by
Sonny Bono
Engineer: Stan Ross
IMPERIAL
CHERILYN
Arranged by Gene Page
A Pala Record Production
A SUBSIDIARY OF LIBERTY RECORDS, INC. • LOS ANGELES, CALIFORNIA

CHEROKEE (Formerly The Robbs)
GIRL, I'VE GOT NEWS FOR YOU/All The Way Home (ABC 11304) .50 2.00 71

CHEROKEES, The
CHEROKEE STOMP/Uprisin' (Challenge 9135) .75 3.00 61
(Instrumentals)

CHEROKEES, The
DIG A LITTLE DEEPER/Turn My Back On You (MGM 13433) 1.00 4.00 65
SEVEN DAFFODILS/A Wondrous Place (MGM 13334) 1.00 4.00 64

CHERRY, Don
BAND OF GOLD/Rumble Boogie (Columbia 40597) 1.00 4.00 55
GHOST TOWN/I'll Be Around (Columbia 40705) 1.00 4.00 56
NAMELY YOU/If I Had My Druthers (Columbia 40746) 1.00 4.00 56
THINKING OF YOU/Here In My Arms (Decca 27128) 1.25 5.00 50
VANITY/Powder Blue (Decca 27618) 1.25 5.00 51
WILD CHERRY/I'm Still A King To You (Columbia 40665) 1.00 4.00 56

CHERUBS, The
JULIE, JULIE (16 & 23)/They Go Ape (Dore 545) .75 3.00 60

CHESSMAN SQUARE
CIRCLES/Try (Lion 1002) 1.25 5.00

CHESSMEN, The
DO WOP/I Live For You (Mirasonic 1868) 2.00 8.00
KEEPER OF MY LOVE/ (Safari 1011) 1.25 5.00
MR. CUPID/What's To Become Of Me (AMC 101) 1.50 6.00
STORMY DREAMS/Pick It Up (Amy 841) 1.00 4.00 63
VOYAGE/Sorry (G-Clef 707) .75 3.00
Even though all of these releases are shown as being by a group using the same name, the possibility exists that they are not all by the same group.

CHESTERFIELDS, The
THAT IS ROCK & ROLL/Why Do Fools Fall In Love (A&M 2041) .75 3.00 78

CHESTERFIELDS, The (With Al Reno)
I GOT FIRED/Meet Me At The Candy Store (Cub 9008) 1.50 6.00 58

CHESTER, Gary
ROCKIN' DRUMMER/Sing Sing Sing (Coral 62379) .75 3.00 63
(Instrumental)

CHEVELLE FIVE, The
COME BACK BIRD/I'm Sorry Girl (UMI 100) .75 3.00 66
DANGLING LITTLE FRIENDS/Stone & Steel Man (Titan 1737) .75 3.00 67

CHEVELLES, The
GALLOP, THE/
Talking About My Baby (By Gloria Walker) (Flaming Arrow 35) .75 3.00
LET THERE BE SURF/Riptide (Chevelle 101) 1.25 5.00 63
(Instrumentals)

CHEVELS, The
HOOTENANNY HO-DOWN/Hendersonville (Gass 1001) .75 3.00 63
PLAY ME A SAD SONG/Devil's Little Angel (Musicland 20,010) 2.00 8.00

CHEVRONS, The
COME GO WITH ME/I'm In Love Again-All Shook Up (Time 1) 1.00 4.00 61
LITTLE DARLIN'/Little Star (Brent 7015) 1.00 4.00 59
LULLABYE/Day After Forever (Brent 7007) 1.00 4.00 59
MINE FOREVER MORE/In The Depths Of My Soul (Independence IND-94) .75 3.00

CHIC
DANCE, DANCE, DANCE (Yowsah, Yowsah, Yowsah)/
Sao Paulo (Atlantic 3435) .50 2.00 77
EVERYBODY DANCE/ (Atlantic 3469) .50 2.00 78
I WANT YOUR LOVE/ (Atlantic 3557) .50 2.00 79
LE FREAK/ (Atlantic 3519) .50 2.00 78
LE FREAK/ (Atlantic 4700) 1.00 4.00 78
(12" single issue)

CHICAGO
ALIVE AGAIN/Love Was New (Columbia 3-10845) .50 2.00 78
ANOTHER RAINY DAY IN NEW YORK CITY/
Hope For Love (Columbia 3-10360) .50 2.00 76
BABY, WHAT A BIG SURPRISE (With Carl Wilson)/
Takin' It On Uptown (Columbia 3-10620) .75 3.00 77
BEGINNINGS/Poem 58 (Columbia 4-45011) .50 2.00 69
BEGINNINGS/Colour My World (Columbia 4-45417) .50 2.00 71
BRAND NEW LOVE AFFAIR (PART 1 & 2)/Hideaway (Columbia 3-10200) .50 2.00 75
CALL ON ME/Prelude To Aire (Columbia 4-46062) .50 2.00 74
COLOUR MY WORLD/I'm A Man (Columbia 4-45467) .50 2.00 72
DIALOGUE/Now That You've Gone (Columbia 4-45717) .50 2.00 72
DOES ANYBODY REALLY KNOW WHAT TIME IT IS/
Listen (Columbia 45264) .50 2.00 70
FEELIN' STRONGER EVERY DAY/Jenny (Columbia 4-45880) .50 2.00 73
FREE/Free Country (Columbia 4-45331) .50 2.00 71
GONE LONG GONE/The Greatest Love On Earth (Columbia 3-10935) .50 2.00 79
HARRY TRUMAN/Till We Meet Again (Columbia 3-10092) .50 2.00 75
IF YOU LEAVE ME NOW/Together Again (Columbia 3-10390) .50 2.00 76
JUST YOU 'N' ME/Critic's Choice (Columbia 45933) .50 2.00 73
LITTLE ONE/Till The End Of Time (Columbia 10683) .50 2.00 77
LOWDOWN/Loneliness Is Just A Word (Columbia 4-45370) .50 2.00 71
MAKE ME SMILE/Colour My World (Columbia 45127) .50 2.00 69
MUST HAVE BEEN CRAZY/Closer To You (Columbia 1-11061) .50 2.00 79
NO TELL LOVER/Take A Chance (Columbia 3-10879) .50 2.00 79
OLD DAYS/Hideaway (Columbia 3-10131) .50 2.00 75
QUESTIONS 67 & 68/Listen (Columbia 4-44909) .75 3.00 69
QUESTIONS 67 & 68/I'm A Man (Columbia 4-45467) .50 2.00 71
SATURDAY IN THE PARK/Alma Mater (Columbia 4-45657) .50 2.00 72
SEARCHIN' SO LONG/Byblos (Columbia 4-46020) .50 2.00 74
STREET PLAYER/Window Dreamin' (Columbia 1-11124) .50 2.00 79
STREET PLAYER/Window Dreamin' (Columbia 43-11138) 1.25 5.00 80
(12" single issue)
TAKE ME BACK TO CHICAGO/Policeman (Columbia 3-10737) .50 2.00 78
THUNDER & LIGHTNING/ (Columbia 1-11345) .50 2.00 80
25 OR 6 TO 4/Where Do We Go From Here (Columbia 4-45194) .50 2.00 70
WISHING YOU WERE HERE/Life Saver (Columbia 3-10049) .50 2.00 74
("Wishing You Were Here" also features Carl & Dennis Wilson and Al Jardine)
YOU ARE ON MY MIND/Gently I'll Wake You (Columbia 3-10523) .50 2.00 77
Also see Guercio, James William

CHICAGO, Artie From the Bronx (Ernie Maresca with The Tremonts)
WANDERER, THE/Please Don't Play Me A-7 (Laurie 3424) 2.00 8.00 68

CHICAGO FIRE, The
CANDY & ME/Come See What I Got (U.S.A. 898) .75 3.00 68

CHICAGO LOOP, The
CAN'T FIND THE WORDS/Saved (Mercury 72755) .75 3.00 67
RICHARD COREY/Cloudy (Dyno Voice 230) .75 3.00 67
SHE COMES TO ME (WHEN SHE NEEDS GOOD LOVIN')/
This Must Be The Place (Dyno Voice 226) .75 3.00 66
TECHNICOLOR THRUSDAY/Beginning At The End (Mercury 72802) .75 3.00 68

CHICAGO PRHIBITION - 1931
BALLAD OF BONNIE & CLYDE, THE/Rag Time (Buddah BDA 27) .75 3.00 68

CHICK & THE NOBLES
I CRY/Island For Two (U.S.A. 772) 2.00 8.00 65

CHICK & RICK
DEAR MR. T.V. PICTURE EYE/Back To School (Kenco 5018) .75 3.00 61

CHICKEN SHACK (With Stan Webb)
AS TIME GOES PASSING BY/ (Deram 7537) .75 3.00 73
MAUDIE/Diary Of Your Life (Blue Horizon 302) .75 3.00 69
TEARS IN THE WIND/The Things You Put Me Through (Blue Horizon 100) .75 3.00 70
WORRIED ABOUT MY WOMAN/Six Nights In Seven (Epic 10414) 1.00 4.00 68
Christine McVie was formerly with this group.

CHIC-LETS, The
I WANT YOU TO BE MY BOYFRIEND/Don't Goof On Me (Josie 919) .75 3.00 64

CHICORY
GOOD GRIEF CHRISTINA/Move On (Epic 10984) .50 2.00 73
(Shown as by Chicory Tip)
SON OF MY FATHER/Pride Comes Before A Fall (Epic 10837) .50 2.00 72
WHAT'S YOUR NAME/Memory (Epic 10889) .50 2.00 72

CHICORY TIP: see Chicory

CHIEFS, The

Title/Flip	Label & No.	Good	Near Mint	Yr.
APACHE/	(Greenwich 408)	1.00	4.00	
TOM TOM/How!	(Valiant 6038)	1.00	4.00	

CHIFFONS, The (Featuring Judy Craig)

Title/Flip	Label & No.	Good	Near Mint	Yr.
AFTER LAST NIGHT/Doctor Of Hearts	(Reprise 20103)	1.00	4.00	62
HE'S SO FINE/Oh My Lover	(Laurie 3152)	.75	3.00	63
I HAVE A BOY FRIEND/I'm Gonna Dry My Eyes	(Laurie 3212)	.75	3.00	63
IF I KNEW THEN (WHAT I KNOW NOW)/ Keep The Boys Happy	(Laurie 3377)	.75	3.00	67
LOVE ME LIKE YOU'RE GONNA LOSE ME/ Three Dips Of Ice Cream	(Laurie 3497)	.75	3.00	69
LOVE SO FINE, A/Only My Friend	(Laurie 3159)	.75	3.00	63
NEVER NEVER/No More Tomorrows	(Wildcat 601)	1.25	5.00	
NOBODY KNOWS WHAT'S GOIN' ON/ Did You Ever Go Steady	(Laurie 3301)	.75	3.00	65
NOBODY KNOWS WHAT'S GOING ON/The Real Thing	(Laurie 3301)	.75	3.00	
ONE FINE DAY/Why Am I So Shy	(Laurie 3179)	.75	3.00	63
OUT OF THIS WORLD/Just A Boy	(Laurie 3350)	.75	3.00	66
SAILOR BOY/When Summer's Through	(Laurie 3262)	.75	3.00	64
STOP, LOOK & LISTEN/March	(Laurie 3357)	.75	3.00	66
SWEET TALKIN' GUY/Did You Ever Go Steady	(Laurie 3340)	.75	3.00	66
TONIGHT'S THE NIGHT/Do You Know	(Big Deal 6003)	2.50	10.00	60
UP ON THE BRIDGE/March	(Laurie 3460)	.75	3.00	68

Also see Four Pennies, The
Also see Little Jimmy & The Tops

CHILD, Desmond & Rouge

Title/Flip	Label & No.	Good	Near Mint	Yr.
GOODBYE BABY/Imitation Of Love	(Capitol 4791)	.50	2.00	79
MAIN MAN/Givin' In To My Love	(Capitol 4710)	.50	2.00	79
OUR LOVE IS INSANE/City In Heat	(Capitol 4669)	.50	2.00	79
OUR LOVE IS INSANE/City In Heat (12" single issue)	(Capitol 4669)	1.25	5.00	79

CHIYO & THE CRESCENTS: see Crescents, The

CHILLY CHARLIE

Title/Flip	Label & No.	Good	Near Mint	Yr.
CRISIS AT OLE MISS/Crisis At Ole Miss (Part 2) (Novelty/Break-in)	(Band Box 329)	2.00	8.00	

CHILLIWACK

Title/Flip	Label & No.	Good	Near Mint	Yr.
ARMS OF MARY/I Wanna Be The One	(Mushroom 7033)	.50	2.00	78
BABY BLUE/Something Better	(Mushroom 7028)	.50	2.00	78
CALIFORNIA GIRL/Reach	(Mushroom 7022)	.50	2.00	77
CHAIN TRAIN/I Must Have Been Blind	(Parrot 350)	.75	3.00	71
COME ON OVER/	(Sire 718)	.50	2.00	73
CRAZY TALK/In & Out	(Sire 716)	.50	2.00	73
EVERYDAY/Sundown	(Parrot 357)	.75	3.00	71
FLY AT NIGHT/Mary Lou & Me	(Mushroom 7024)	.50	2.00	77
LAST DAY OF DECEMBER/	(Sire 723)	.50	2.00	74
LONESOME MARY/Ridin'	(A&M 1310)	.75	3.00	72
NOTHIN' TO DO/Ground Hog	(A&M 1395)	.75	3.00	72
SOMETHING BETTER/Reach	(Mushroom 7025)	.50	2.00	77
NEVER BE THE SAME/	(Mushroom 7038)	.50	2.00	78

CHIMES, The

Title/Flip	Label & No.	Good	Near Mint	Yr.
DU WAP/Stop Look & Listen	(Limelight 3002)	1.25	5.00	

Also see Lenny & The Chimes
Also see Riffs, The

CHIMES, The

Title/Flip	Label & No.	Good	Near Mint	Yr.
I'M IN THE MOOD FOR LOVE/Only Love	(Tag 445)	1.00	4.00	61
LET'S FALL IN LOVE/Dream Girl	(Tag 447)	1.00	4.00	61
ONCE IN A WHILE/Summer Night	(Tag 444)	1.00	4.00	60
PARADISE/My Love	(Tag 450)	1.00	4.00	62
WHOSE HEART ARE YOU BREAKIN' NOW/ Baby's Comin' Home	(Laurie 3211)	1.00	4.00	60
WHOSE HEART ARE YOU BREAKIN' NOW/ Baby's Coming Home	(Metro 1)	1.00	4.00	63

CHIP & THE QUARTER TONES

Title/Flip	Label & No.	Good	Near Mint	Yr.
SIMPLE SIMON/You Were My Baby	(Carlton 604)	1.50	6.00	62

CHIPMUNKS, The (With David Seville) (Staring Alvin, Theodore & Simon)

Title/Flip	Label & No.	Good	Near Mint	Yr.
ALL MY LOVIN'/Do You Want To Know A Secret	(Liberty 55734)	.75	3.00	64
ALVIN FOR PRESIDENT/Sack Time	(Liberty 55277)	.75	3.00	60
ALVIN TWIST, THE/I Wish I Could Speak French	(Liberty 55424)	.75	3.00	62
ALVIN'S ALL STAR CHIPMUNK BAND/ Old Mac Donald Cha Cha Cha	(Liberty 55544)	.75	3.00	63
ALVIN'S HARMONICA/Mediocre	(Liberty 55179)	.75	3.00	59
ALVIN'S ORCHESTRA/Copyright 1960	(Liberty 55233)	.75	3.00	60
AMERICA THE BEAUTIFUL/My Wild Irish Rose	(Liberty 55452)	.75	3.00	62
CHIPMUNK SONG, THE/Almost Good	(Liberty 55168)	1.00	4.00	58
CHIPMUNK SONG, THE/Alvin's Harmonica	(Liberty 55250)	.75	3.00	59
CHIPMUNK SONG, THE/Alvin's Harmonica (Stereo single issue)	(Liberty S-77250)	2.00	8.00	59
COMIN' ROUND THE MOUNTAIN/Sing A Goofy Song	(Liberty 55246)	.75	3.00	60
EEFIN ALVIN/Flip Side	(Liberty 55632)	.75	3.00	63
I'M HENRY VIII, I AM/What's New Pussycat	(Liberty 55832)	.75	3.00	65
RAGTIME COWBOY JOE/Flip Side	(Liberty 55200)	.75	3.00	59
RAGTIME COWBOY JOE/Flip Side (Stereo single issue)	(Liberty S-77200)	2.00	8.00	59
RUDOLPH THE RED NOSED REINDEER/Spain	(Liberty 55289)	.75	3.00	60
SUPERCALIFRAGILISTICEXPIALIDOUCIOUS/Do-Re-Mi	(Liberty 55773)	.75	3.00	65
WONDERFUL DAY/Night Before Christmas	(Liberty 55635)	.75	3.00	63

"The Chipmunk Song" was reissued each Christmas for many years, but beginning in 1959 the catalog number & flip side was changed. "Rudolph The Red Nosed Reindeer" was also reissued for several years but with the same number & flip.
Also see Canned Heat

CHIPPENDALES, The

Title/Flip	Label & No.	Good	Near Mint	Yr.
DRIP DROP/What A Night	(Andie 5013)	1.50	6.00	59

CHIPS, The (With Joe South)

Title/Flip	Label & No.	Good	Near Mint	Yr.
BYE BYE MY LOVE/What A Lie	(Ember 1077)	1.00	4.00	61
PARTY PEOPLE/Long Lonely Winter	(Tollie 9042)	.75	3.00	65

CHOCOLATE TELEPHONE POLE, The

Title/Flip	Label & No.	Good	Near Mint	Yr.
LET'S TRANQUALIZE WITH COLOR/One By One	(Jack O'Diamonds 1011)	1.25	5.00	67

CHOCOLATE TUNNEL, The

Title/Flip	Label & No.	Good	Near Mint	Yr.
OSTRICH PEOPLE/Highly Successful Young Rupert White	(Era 3185)	1.25	5.00	67

CHOCOLATE WATCH BAND, The

Title/Flip	Label & No.	Good	Near Mint	Yr.
BABY BLUE/Sweet Young Thing	(Uptown 740)	2.50	10.00	67
MISTY LANE/She Weaves A Tender Trap	(Uptown 749)	2.50	10.00	67
NO WAY OUT/Are You Gonna Be There	(Tower 373)	2.50	10.00	67

CHOIR, The

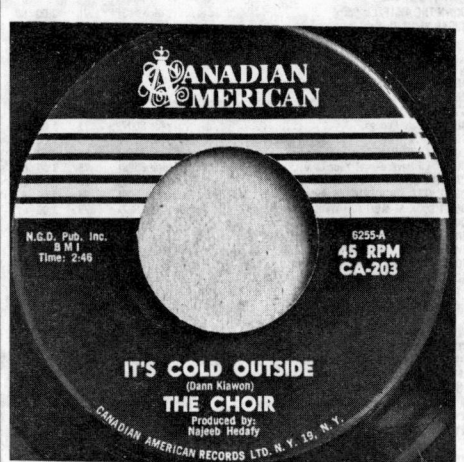

Title/Flip	Label & No.	Good	Near Mint	Yr.
CHANGIN' MY MIND/When You Were With Me	(Roulette 7005)	1.50	6.00	68
IT'S COLD OUTSIDE/I'm Going Home	(Canadian American 203)	5.00	20.00	67
IT'S COLD OUTSIDE/I'm Going Home	(Roulette 4738)	1.25	5.00	67
NO ONE HERE TO PLAY WITH/ Don't You Feel A Little Sorry For Me	(Roulette 4760)	2.00	8.00	67

Also see Carmen, Eric
Also see Cyrus Erie
Also see Quick
Also see Raspberries, The

CHORDETTES, The (With Janet Ertel)

Title/Flip	Label & No.	Good	Near Mint	Yr.
BORN TO BE WITH YOU/Love Never Changes	(Cadence 1291)	1.00	4.00	56
DOWN BY THE OLD MILL STREAM/Oh Joe	(Columbia 38949)	2.00	8.00	50
EDDIE MY LOVE/Whistlin' Willie	(Cadence 1284)	1.00	4.00	56
GIRL'S WORK IS NEVER DONE, A/No Wheels	(Cadence 1366)	1.00	4.00	59
HUMMINGBIRD/I Told A Lie	(Cadence 1267)	1.00	4.00	55
JUST BETWEEN YOU & ME/Soft Sands	(Cadence 1330)	1.00	4.00	57
LAY DOWN YOUR ARMS/Teen Age Goodnight	(Cadence 1299)	1.00	4.00	56
LOLLIPOP/Baby Come-a-back-a	(Cadence 1345)	1.00	4.00	58
LOVELY LIPS/Dudelsack Song	(Cadence 1259)	1.00	4.00	54
MR. SANDMAN/I Don't Wanna See You Crying	(Cadence 1247)	1.00	4.00	54
NEVER ON SUNDAY/Faraway Star	(Cadence 1402)	.75	3.00	61
NO OTHER ARMS, NO OTHER LIPS/ We Should Be Together	(Cadence 1361)	1.00	4.00	59
TRUE LOVE/It's You, It's You I Love	(Cadence 1239)	1.00	4.00	54
TRUE LOVE GOES ON & ON/All My Sorrows	(Cadence 1442)	.75	3.00	64
WEDDING, THE/I Don't Know I Don't Care	(Cadence 1273)	1.00	4.00	55
ZORRO/Love Is A Two-Way Street	(Cadence 1349)	1.00	4.00	58

CHOSEN FEW, The

Title/Flip	Label & No.	Good	Near Mint	Yr.
I THINK IT'S TIME/Nobody But Me	(Autumn 17)	1.25	5.00	65
NOBODY BUT ME/I Think It's Time	(North Beach 1003)	2.00	8.00	66

Also see Flamin' Groovies, The

CHOSEN FEW, The

Title/Flip	Label & No.	Good	Near Mint	Yr.
ANOTHER GOODBYE/Forget About The Past	(Power International)	.75	3.00	66
FOOLIN' AROUND WITH ME/We Walk Together	(Dart 1080)	.75	3.00	67
FOOTSEE/You Never Be Wrong	(Roulette 7015)	.75	3.00	68
HEY JOE/Summer's Love	(Canusa 504)	1.00	4.00	
I'VE HAD IT/Ask Me Baby	(Playboy 106)	1.00	4.00	
LA LA LA LA LA LA/Why Can't I Love You	(Co-op 510)	.75	3.00	
PINK CLOUDS & LEMONADE/Stop In The Name Of Love	(Denim 1092)	.75	3.00	68
SUMMER'S LOVE/Why Can't I Love You (Instrumental)	(Co-op 511)	1.00	4.00	
SYNTHETIC MAN/Last Man Alive	(Liberty 55919)	1.00	4.00	67
TALKING ALL THE LOVE I CAN/Birth Of A Playboy	(Canyon 1000)	1.00	4.00	
YOU'RE A BIG GIRL NOW/ You're A Big Girl Now (Version 2)	(Crystal 1107)	1.25	5.00	

Even though all of these releases are shown as being by a group using the same name, the possibility exists that they are not all by the same group.

CHOSEN LOT, The

Title/Flip	Label & No.	Good	Near Mint	Yr.
TIME WAS/If You Want To	(Sidra 9004)	1.00	4.00	

CHRIS & KATHY (Chris Montez & Kathy Young)

Title/Flip	Label & No.	Good	Near Mint	Yr.
ALL YOU HAD TO DO (WAS TELL ME)/Love Me (Remake of Chris Montez's '61 Hit)	(Monogram 517)	1.00	4.00	64
SHOOT THAT CURL/It Takes Two	(Monogram 520)	1.00	4.00	64

CHRIS BARBER'S JAZZ BAND

Title/Flip	Label & No.	Good	Near Mint	Yr.
PETITE FLEUR/Wild Cat Blues (Instrumentals)	(Laurie 3022)	.75	3.00	58

CHRISTIAN, Bobby

Title/Flip	Label & No.	Good	Near Mint	Yr.
SPIDER & THE FLY, THE/Cha Cha Hop	(Mercury 72102)	1.00	4.00	63

CHRISTIAN, Roger

Title/Flip	Label & No.	Good	Near Mint	Yr.
BIG BAD HO-DAD/The Last Drag	(NBI 100)	1.00	4.00	
LITTLE MARY CHRISTMAS/ The Meaning Of Merry Christmas	(Rendezvous 195)	.75	3.00	62

CHRISTIAN'S CRUSADERS

Title/Flip	Label & No.	Good	Near Mint	Yr.
THAT'S NICE/She's Got The Action	(RCA Victor 47-8828)	.75	3.00	65

CHRISTIE, Dean

Title/Flip	Label & No.	Good	Near Mint	Yr.
GET WITH IT/That's My Girlfriend	(Mercury 72228)	.75	3.00	64
HEART BREAKER/I'm A Loser	(Select 715)	.75	3.00	62
HEART BREAKER/Mashed Potato Twist	(SWL 1607)	.75	3.00	62
MONA/City Boy	(Mercury 72140)	.75	3.00	63
SO MUCH/Oh What A Love (With the Hi Flyers)	(Top Flight 113)	3.00	12.00	
TEENAGE JEZEBEL/Shake	(Select 718)	1.25	5.00	62

CHRISTIE, Gaylon, & The Downbeats

Title/Flip	Label & No.	Good	Near Mint	Yr.
TELL ME WHAT'S ON YOUR MIND/ (With Roy Robinson)	(Capri 504)	1.25	5.00	

CHRISTIE, Lou (Lugee Geno Sacco)

Title/Flip	Label & No.	Good	Near Mint	Yr.
ARE YOU GETTING ANY SUNSHINE/I'll Take Time	(Buddah 149)	1.25	5.00	69
BEYOND THE BLUE HORIZON/Saddle The Wind	(Three Brothers 402)	3.75	15.00	73
BIG TIME/Cryin' On My Knees	(Colpix 799)	1.25	5.00	64
BLUE CANADIAN ROCKY DREAM/ Wilma Lee & Stoney	(Three Brothers 400)	3.75	15.00	73
CANTERBURY ROAD/Saints Of Aquarius	(Buddah 76)	1.25	5.00	68
CLOSE YOUR EYES/Funny Thing (Shown as by the Classics)	(Starr 508)	25.00	100.00	60
CLOSE YOUR EYES/Funny Thing (Reissue of Starr 508, shown as by Lou Christie & the Classics)	(Alcar 207)	3.75	15.00	63
DON'T STOP ME/Back To The Days Of The Romans	(Columbia 4-44338)	2.00	8.00	67
GLORY RIVER/Indian Lady	(Buddah 192)	1.25	5.00	70
GOOD MORING-ZIP-A-DEE DOO DAH/ You Were The One	(Three Brothers 403)	5.00	20.00	74
GYPSY CRIED, THE/Red Sails In The Sunset	(C And C 102)	18.75	75.00	62
GYPSY CRIED, THE/Red Sails In The Sunset	(Roulette 4457)	.75	3.00	63
HAVE I SINNED/Pot Of Gold	(Colpix 753)	1.25	5.00	64
HEY YOU CAJUN/Sunbeam	(Three Brothers 405)	3.00	12.00	75
HOW MANY TEARDROPS/You & I	(Roulette 4504)	.75	3.00	63
I REMEMBER GINA/Escape	(Columbia 4-44240)	2.00	8.00	67
IF MY CAR COULD ONLY TALK/Song Of Lita	(MGM 13576)	1.25	5.00	66
IF MY CAR COULD ONLY TALK/Song Of Lita (Picture sleeve)	(MGM 13576)	2.50	10.00	66
I'M GONNA MAKE YOU MINE/I'm Gonna Get Married	(Buddah 116)	.75	3.00	69
JURY, THE/Little Did I Know	(Robbee R-112)	8.75	35.00	61
JURY, THE/Little Did I Know (Reissue of Robbee R-112, but shown as by Lou Christie)	(World W-1002)	1.50	6.00	
JURY, THE/Little Did I Know (Reissue of World W-1002)	(American Music Makers AMM-006)	1.50	6.00	
LIGHTHOUSE/Waco (Promotional copies that should have featured "Lighthouse" were pressed with "Waco" on both sides, in error)	(Buddah 235)	1.50	6.00	71
LIGHTNIN' STRIKES/Cryin' In The Streets	(MGM 13412)	.75	3.00	65
LOVE IS OVER/She Sold Me Magic	(Buddah 163)	1.25	5.00	70
MAKE SUMMER LAST FOREVER/Why Did You Do It Baby?	(Colpix 770)	1.25	5.00	65
MERRY-GO-ROUND/Guitars & Bongos	(Colpix 735)	1.25	5.00	64
MICKEY'S MONKEY/Wonderful Dream	(Buddah 257)	2.00	8.00	71
OUTSIDE THE GATES OF HEAVEN/ All That Glitters Isn't Gold	(Co & Ce 235)	1.50	6.00	66
PAINTER/Du Rhonda	(MGM 13533)	.75	3.00	66
RAKE UP THE LEAVES/Genesis & The Third Verse	(Buddah 65)	1.25	5.00	68
RHAPSODY IN THE RAIN/Trapeze (With the lyrics "We Were Makin' Out In The Rain," and the matrix number 66-XY-308 in the vinyl trail-off)	(MGM 13473)	7.50	30.00	65
RHAPSODY IN THE RAIN/Trapeze (With the lyrics "We Fell In Love In The Rain," and the matrix number 66-XY-308-1 in the vinyl trail-off)	(MGM 13473)	.75	3.00	65
RHAPSODY IN THE RAIN/Trapeze (Picture sleeve)	(MGM 13473)	1.25	5.00	65
RIDIN' IN MY VAN/Summer In Malibu	(Epic 50244)	.75	3.00	76
SELF EXPRESSION/Back To The Days Of The Romans	(Columbia 4-44177)	2.00	8.00	67
SHAKE HANDS & WALK AWAY CRYING/Escape	(Columbia 4-44062)	1.50	6.00	67
SHUFFLE ON DOWN TO PITTSBURGH/I'm Gonna Get Married	(Buddah 312)	2.50	10.00	73
SHY BOY/It Can Happen	(Roulette 4527)	1.50	6.00	63
SINCE I DON'T HAVE YOU/Wild Life's In Season	(MGM 13623)	1.50	6.00	66
SING ME, SING ME/The Paper Song	(Buddah 285)	2.00	8.00	72
SPANISH WINE/Dancing In The Sand	(Midsong Intl. 10959)	.75	3.00	77
STAY/There They Go	(Roulette 4545)	1.50	6.00	64
SUMMER DAYS/ The One & Only Original Sunshine Kid	(Slipped Disc 45270)	2.50	10.00	76
SWEET LONDON LADY/ Down When It's Up, Up When It's Down (English Release)	(Buddah 2011-016)	3.00	12.00	70
TEENAGER IN LOVE, A/Back Track	(Colpix 778)	1.25	5.00	65
THEME FROM "PEOPLE" (PART 1)/ Theme From "People" (Part 2) (Shown as by Sacco)	(Lifesong ZS8-1175)	.50	2.00	78
THEME FROM "PEOPLE" (PART 1)/ Theme From "People" (Part 2) (12" single issue, shown as by Sacco)	(Lifesong 2Z8-1776)	3.00	12.00	78
TOMORROW WILL COME/You're With It (Shown as by Lou Christie & The Classics)	(Alcar 208)	2.50	10.00	63
TWO FACES HAVE I/All That Glitters Isn't Gold	(Roulette 4481)	.75	3.00	63
WACO/Waco (Promotional issue)	(Buddah 231)	2.50	10.00	71
WHEN YOU DANCE/Maybe You'll Be There	(Roulette 4554)	1.50	6.00	64
WHY DO FOOLS FALL IN LOVE/ I'm Gonna Get Married (English Release)	(Buddah 2011-127)	3.00	12.00	71
YOU'RE GONNA MAKE LOVE TO ME/Fantasies	(Midland Int'l 10848)	.75	3.00	76

Also see Christie, Susan
Also see Christy, Chic
Also see Marcy Joe

CHRISTIE, Susan

Title/Flip	Label & No.	Good	Near Mint	Yr.
I LOVE ONIONS/Take Me As You Find Me	(Columbia 43595)	.75	3.00	66

Susan is the sister of Lou Christie and provided back-up vocals on many of his recordings.
Also see Christy, Chic

CHRISTIE, Tony

Title/Flip	Label & No.	Good	Near Mint	Yr.
AMARILLO/Love Is A Friend Of Mine	(MCA 40749)	.50	2.00	77
AVENUES & ALLEYWAYS (THEME FROM "THE PROTECTORS")/ I Never Was A Child	(Kapp 2190)	.50	2.00	72
DON'T GO DOWN TO RENO/Sunday Morning	(Kapp 2174)	.50	2.00	72
DRIVE SAFELY, DARLIN'/	(MCA 40493)	.50	2.00	76
GIVE ME YOUR LOVE AGAIN/I Did What I Did For Maria	(Kapp 2139)	.50	2.00	71
HAVE YOU EVER BEEN TO GEORGIA/ Smile A Little Smile For Me	(Kapp 2149)	.50	2.00	71
IS THIS THE WAY TO AMARILLO/Love Is A Friend Of Mine	(Kapp 2161)	.50	2.00	72
LAS VEGAS/Let Me Be Turned To Stone	(Kapp 2124)	.50	2.00	71

CHRISTMAS, Johnny, & The Dynamics

Title/Flip	Label & No.	Good	Near Mint	Yr.
SOFT LIPS/Dum Dum (The Lollipop Song)	(PDQ 001)	1.50	6.00	

CHRISTMAS SPIRIT (With Linda Ronstadt)

Title/Flip	Label & No.	Good	Near Mint	Yr.
WILL YOU STILL BELIEVE IN ME/	(White Whale 290)	1.00	4.00	69

CHRISTOPHER & THE CHAPS

Title/Flip	Label & No.	Good	Near Mint	Yr.
IT'S ALRIGHT MA, I'M ONLY BLEEDING/ They Just Don't Care	(Fontana 1530)	1.00	4.00	65

CHRISTY, Charles

Title/Flip	Label & No.	Good	Near Mint	Yr.
CHERRY PIE/Will I Find Her (With the Crystals)	(HBR 455)	.75	3.00	66
YOUNG & BEAUTIFUL/In The Arms Of A Girl	(HBR 473)	.75	3.00	66

CHRISTY, Chic

Title/Flip	Label & No.	Good	Near Mint	Yr.
WITH THIS KISS/My Billet-Doux To You (Lou Christie and his sister Susan Christie are featured on this recording.)	(Hac 103)	2.00	8.00	62

CHRISTY, Don (Sonny Bono)

Title/Flip	Label & No.	Good	Near Mint	Yr.
ONE LITTLE ANSWER/Wearing Black	(Specialty 672)	1.25	5.00	59

CHROMIUM

Title/Flip	Label & No.	Good	Near Mint	Yr.
STAR TO STAR/Castaway	(Infinity 50023)	.50	2.00	79

CHUCK & BETTY

Title/Flip	Label & No.	Good	Near Mint	Yr.
COME BACK LITTLE GIRL/Sissy Britches	(Decca 30985)	.75	3.00	59

CHUCK-A-LUCKS, The

Title/Flip	Label & No.	Good	Near Mint	Yr.
HEAVEN KNOWS/Chuck-a-lucks	(Bow 305)	2.50	10.00	

CHUCKENDOES, The

Title/Flip	Label & No.	Good	Near Mint	Yr.
BUTTER FINGERS/Liebestraum (Instrumentals)	(Toppa 1097)	1.00	4.00	

CHUCKLES, The

Title/Flip	Label & No.	Good	Near Mint	Yr.
ON THE STREET WHERE YOU LIVE/I'll Wait	(West Side 1019)	2.00	8.00	64

Also see Consorts, The

CHUCKLES, The: see Three Chuckles, The

CHUG & DOUG

Title/Flip	Label & No.	Good	Near Mint	Yr.
RINGO COMES TO TOWN/My Girl	(Charger 101)	1.50	6.00	64

CHURCH STREET FIVE, The (Featuring "Daddy G")

Title/Flip	Label & No.	Good	Near Mint	Yr.
EVERYBODY'S HAPPY/Fallen Arches	(Le Grand 1010)	.75	3.00	61
LOOK ALIVE/Ten, Two & Four	(Le Grand 1028)	.75	3.00	63
MOONLIGHT IN VERMONT/Sing A Song Children	(Le Grand 1026)	.75	3.00	63
NIGHT WITH DADDY "G" (PART 1), A/ A Night With Daddy "G" (Part 2)	(Legrande 1004)	.75	3.00	61

(This track was the same music that was later used by Gary "U.S." Bonds on his hit "Quarter To Three," wherein he mentions "A Night With Daddy G.")
Instrumentals

TITLE/FLIP	LABEL & NO.	GOOD	NEAR MINT	YR.

LEGRAND
RECORDS
Distributed by LAURIE RECORDS, INC.
Record No. 1004
Pepe Music (BMI)
Time: 2:38
ZTSP 66761
A NIGHT WITH DADDY "G"
PART 1
(Barge - Guida - Royster)
THE CHURCH STREET FIVE

CICCONE, Don (Of the Critters)

TITLE/FLIP	LABEL & NO.	GOOD	NEAR MINT	YR.
DOWN WHEN IT'S UP, UP WHEN IT'S DOWN/ There's Got To Be A Word	(Kama Sutra 506)	1.00	4.00	70
Also see 4 Seasons				

CIMMERON

TITLE/FLIP	LABEL & NO.	GOOD	NEAR MINT	YR.
ROCK & ROLL THE NIGHT AWAY/My Kind Of Girl	(Hammerhead 22)	.50	2.00	79
WE CAN FLY (PASS AN APPLE)/Changing-Rearranging	(Greentree 1340)	.75	3.00	76
(Shown as by the Cimmeron Show Review)				

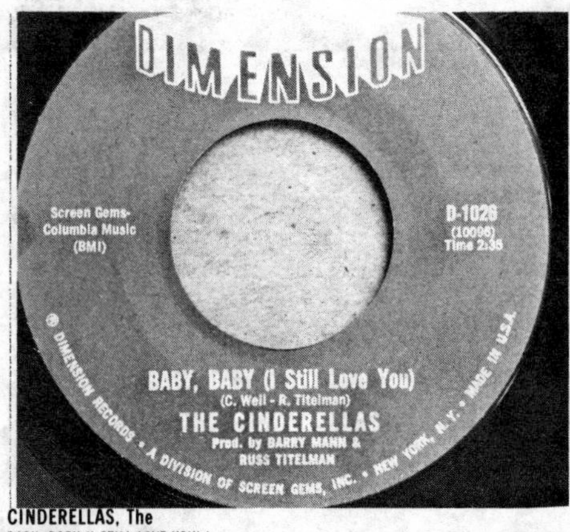

CINDERELLAS, The

TITLE/FLIP	LABEL & NO.	GOOD	NEAR MINT	YR.
BABY, BABY (I STILL LOVE YOU)/ Please Don't Wake Me	(Dimension 1026)	3.75	15.00	64
I WAS ONLY FIFTEEN/You Never Shoulda Gone Away	(Decca 30925)	1.00	4.00	59

CINDERS, The

TITLE/FLIP	LABEL & NO.	GOOD	NEAR MINT	YR.
CINNAMON CINDER (IT'S A VERY NICE DANCE), THE/ C'mon Wobble	(Warner Bros. 5326)	.75	3.00	62

CINDY & LINDY (Cindy Lord & Linda Doherty)

TITLE/FLIP	LABEL & NO.	GOOD	NEAR MINT	YR.
LANGUAGE OF LOVE, THE/Brigette's Song	(ABC-Paramount 9847)	1.00	4.00	57
LET'S GO STEADY/The Wedding Is Over	(Pilgrim 702)	1.50	6.00	60
LET'S GO STEADY/There Are Such Things	(Coral 62165)	.75	3.00	60
LOVIN' & BEING LOVED NOT/Hungry Heart	(Pilgrim 705)	1.25	5.00	60

CINDY & SANDY

TITLE/FLIP	LABEL & NO.	GOOD	NEAR MINT	YR.
MAKE BELIEVE BABY/Why Not	(Tailspin 102)	.75	3.00	60

CINERAMAS, The

TITLE/FLIP	LABEL & NO.	GOOD	NEAR MINT	YR.
CRYING FOR YOU/I'm Sorry Baby	(Rhapsody 71964)	3.00	12.00	
LIFE CAN BE BEAUTIFUL/It Must Be Love	(Champ 103)	2.00	8.00	

CINNAMONS, The

TITLE/FLIP	LABEL & NO.	GOOD	NEAR MINT	YR.
DANCE TO THE MUSIC/Mr. Cupid '65	(B.T. Puppy 508)	.75	3.00	65
STRANGE STRANGE FELLING/I'm Not Gonna Worry	(B.T. Puppy 503)	.75	3.00	65

CITATIONS, The

TITLE/FLIP	LABEL & NO.	GOOD	NEAR MINT	YR.
GIRL NEXT DOOR, THE/Ten Miles From Nowhere	(Vangee 301)	5.00	20.00	
GIRL NEXT DOOR, THE/Ten Miles From Nowhere	(Fraternity 992)	2.50	10.00	

CITATIONS, The

TITLE/FLIP	LABEL & NO.	GOOD	NEAR MINT	YR.
MOON RACE/Slippin' & Sliddin'	(Epic 9603)	1.00	4.00	63
(Instrumental)				

CITATIONS, The (With Nicki North)

TITLE/FLIP	LABEL & NO.	GOOD	NEAR MINT	YR.
MAGIC EYES/Mystery Of Love	(Canadian American 136)	1.50	6.00	61

CITY (Featuring Carole King)

TITLE/FLIP	LABEL & NO.	GOOD	NEAR MINT	YR.
SNOW QUEEN/Paradise Alley	(Ode 113)	1.50	6.00	68
THAT OLD SWEET ROLL (HI-DE-HO)/Why Are You Leaving	(Ode 119)	1.50	6.00	69

CITY BOY

TITLE/FLIP	LABEL & NO.	GOOD	NEAR MINT	YR.
DAY THE EARTH CAUGHT FIRE, THE/	(Atlantic 3612)	.50	2.00	79
5.7.0.5./Bad For Business	(Mercury 73999)	.50	2.00	78
HAYMAKING TIME/	(Mercury 73835)	.50	2.00	76
I'VE BEEN SPUN/Goodbye Blue Monday	(Mercury 73953)	.50	2.00	77
SHE'S GOT STYLE/The Runaround	(Mercury 73968)	.50	2.00	78
VIOLIN, THE/	(Mercury 73900)	.50	2.00	77
WHAT A NIGHT/Goodbye Laurelie	(Mercury 74032)	.50	2.00	78

CITY SURFERS, The

TITLE/FLIP	LABEL & NO.	GOOD	NEAR MINT	YR.
BEACH BALL/Sun Tan Baby	(Capitol 5002)	1.00	4.00	63
POWDER PUFF/50 Miles To Go	(Capitol 5052)	1.00	4.00	64

CLANCY BROTHERS, The

TITLE/FLIP	LABEL & NO.	GOOD	NEAR MINT	YR.
BEER, BEER, BEER/Jennifer Gentle	(Columbia 45014)	.75	3.00	68

CLANTON, Ike

TITLE/FLIP	LABEL & NO.	GOOD	NEAR MINT	YR.
DOWN THE AISLE/I'm Sorry	(Ace 583)	.75	3.00	60
SUGAR PLUM/Guilty	(Mercury 71975)	.75	3.00	62
Ike is Jimmy Clanton's brother.				

CLANTON, Jimmy

TITLE/FLIP	LABEL & NO.	GOOD	NEAR MINT	YR.
ANOTHER SLEEPLESS NIGHT/I'm Gonna Try	(Ace 585)	.75	3.00	60
BECAUSE I DO/Just A Moment	(Ace 655)	.75	3.00	62
C'MON JIM/The Absence Of Lisa	(Imperial 66242)	.75	3.00	67
CINDY/I Care Enough	(Ace 8007)	.75	3.00	63
COME BACK/Wait	(Ace 600)	.75	3.00	60
COOLEST HOT PANTS/	(Spiral 3406)	.75	3.00	71
CURLY/I'll Never Forget Your Love	(Laurie 3508)	.75	3.00	69
DARKEST STREET IN TOWN/Dreams Of A Fool	(Ace 8005)	.75	3.00	62
DON'T KEEP YOUR FRIENDS AWAY/Hurting Each Other	(Mala 500)	.75	3.00	65
DON'T LOOK AT ME/I Just Want To Make Love	(Ace 622)	.75	3.00	61
DOWN THE AISLE/No Longer Blue	(Ace 616)	.75	3.00	61
ENDLESS NIGHTS/Another Day Another Night	(Ace 8006)	.75	3.00	61
EVERYTHING I TOUCH TURNS TO TEARS/That Special Way	(Mala 516)	.75	3.00	65
FOLLOW THE SUN/Lock The Windows	(Philips 40219)	.75	3.00	64
GO, JIMMY, GO/I Trusted You	(Ace 575)	1.00	4.00	59
I TRUSTED YOU/That's You Baby	(Ace 537)	1.25	5.00	57
I WANNA GO HOME/	(Starfire 104)	.75	3.00	78
(Orange plastic)				
I'LL BE LOVING YOU/Calico Junction	(Imperial 66274)	.75	3.00	67
I'LL STEP ASIDE/I Won't Cry Anymore	(Philips 40181)	.75	3.00	64
JUST A DREAM/You Aim To Please	(Ace 546)	1.00	4.00	58
LETTER TO AN ANGEL, A/A Part Of Me	(Ace 551)	1.00	4.00	58
LUCKY IN LOVE WITH YOU/Not Like A Brother	(Ace 634)	.75	3.00	61
MILLION DRUMS, A/If I'm A Fool For Loving You	(Philips 40208)	.75	3.00	64
MY OWN TRUE LOVE/Little Boy In Love	(Ace 567)	1.00	4.00	59
MY OWN TRUE LOVE/Little Boy In Love	(Ace 567)	2.00	8.00	59
(Stereo single)				
MY PRIDE & JOY/Emma Lee	(Drew-Blan 1003)	2.50	10.00	58
(Shown as by Jimmy Dale)				
OLD ROCK'N ROLLER/	(Starcrest 078)	.50	2.00	76
RED DON'T GO WITH BLUE/All The Worlds In The World	(Philips 40161)	.75	3.00	63
SHIP ON A STORMY SEA/My Love Is Strong	(Ace 560)	1.00	4.00	59
TELL ME/I'll Never Forget Your Love	(Laurie 3534)	.75	3.00	69
TWIST ON LITTLE GIRL/Wayward Girl	(Ace 641)	.75	3.00	62
VENUS IN BLUE JEANS/Highway Bound	(Ace 8001)	.75	3.00	62
VENUS IN BLUE JEANS/Highway Bound	(Ace 644)	2.00	8.00	62
(Promotional issue only)				
WHAT AM I GONNA DO/If I	(Ace 607)	.75	3.00	60
WHAT AM I LIVING FOR/Wedding Bells	(Vin 1028)	.75	3.00	

CLAPTON, Eric (Of Cream)

TITLE/FLIP	LABEL & NO.	GOOD	NEAR MINT	YR.
AFTER MIDNIGHT/Easy Now	(Atco 6784)	.75	3.00	70
BELL BOTTOM BLUES/Little Wing	(Polydor 15056)	.75	3.00	73
CARNIVAL/Hungry	(RSO 868)	.50	2.00	77
COCAINE/Tulsa Time	(RSO 928)	.50	2.00	79
HELLO OLD FRIEND/All Our Pastimes	(RSO 861)	.50	2.00	76
I SHOT THE SHERIFF/Give Me Strength	(RSO 409)	.50	2.00	74
I SHOT THE SHERIFF/Give Me Strength	(RSO 500)	.50	2.00	74
(Reissued with a different catalog number)				
KNOCKIN' ON HEAVEN'S DOOR/Someone Like You	(RSO 513)	.50	2.00	75
LAY DOWN SALLY/Next Time You See Her	(RSO 886)	.50	2.00	77
LET IT RAIN/Easy Now	(Polydor 15049)	.75	3.00	72
PROMISES/Watch Out For Lucy	(RSO 910)	.50	2.00	78
SWING LOW SWEET CHARIOT/Pretty Blue Eyes	(RSO 509)	.50	2.00	75
TEASING (With King Curtis)/Souling (By King Curtis)	(Atco 6738)	.75	3.00	71
WILLIE & THE HAND JIVE/Mainline Florida	(RSO 503)	.50	2.00	74
WONDERFUL TONIGHT/Peaches & Diesel	(RSO 895)	.50	2.00	78
Also see Blind Faith				
Also see Delany & Bonnie & Friends				
Also see Derek & The Dominoes				
Also see Mayall, John & Eric Clapton				
Also see Yardbirds, The				

CLARK, Alan

TITLE/FLIP	LABEL & NO.	GOOD	NEAR MINT	YR.
LONG TALL SALLY/Teresa	(Clark 1061)	1.00	4.00	
ROCK & ROLL/What A Heck Of A Mess (With Wildfire)	(Clark 003)	.75	3.00	75

CLARK, Claudine

TITLE/FLIP	LABEL & NO.	GOOD	NEAR MINT	YR.
ANGEL OF HAPPINESS/Teenage Blues	(Herald 521)	1.50	6.00	58
(Group Sound)				
PARTY LIGHTS/Disappointed	(Chancellor 1113)	.75	3.00	62
WALK ME HOME/Who Will You Hurt	(Chancellor 1130)	.75	3.00	63
WALKIN' THROUGH A CEMETERY/Telephone Game	(Chancellor 1124)	.75	3.00	62

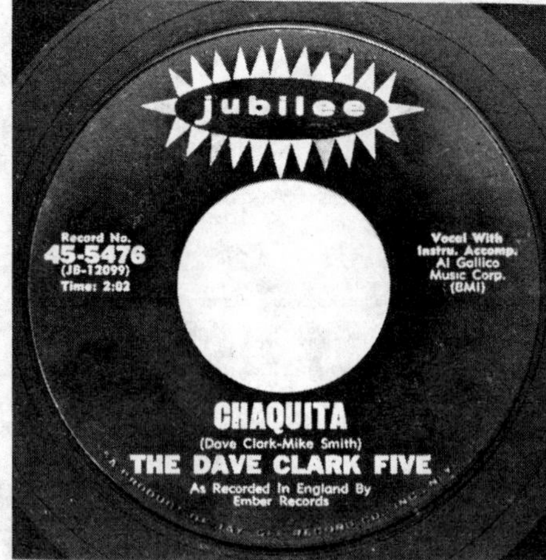

jubilee
Record No. 45-5476 (JB-12099)
Time: 2:02
Vocal With Instru. Accomp. Al Gallico Music Corp. (BMI)
CHAQUITA
(Dave Clark-Mike Smith)
THE DAVE CLARK FIVE
As Recorded In England By Ember Records

CLARK, Dave, Five, The

TITLE/FLIP	LABEL & NO.	GOOD	NEAR MINT	YR.
ANY WAY YOU WANT IT/Crying Over You	(Epic 9739)	.75	3.00	64
AT THE SCENE/I Miss You	(Epic 9882)	.75	3.00	66
BECAUSE/Theme Without A Name	(Epic 9704)	.75	3.00	64
BITS & PIECES/All Of The Time	(Epic 9671)	.75	3.00	64
BRING IT ON HOME TO ME/Darling I Love You	(Epic 10547)	.75	3.00	70
CAN'T YOU SEE THAT SHE'S MINE/No Time To Lose	(Epic 9692)	.75	3.00	64
CATCH US IF YOU CAN/On The Move	(Epic 9833)	.75	3.00	65
CHAQUITA/In Your Heart	(Jubilee 5476)	2.50	10.00	64
COME HOME/Your Turn To Cry	(Epic 9763)	.75	3.00	65
DO YOU LOVE ME/Chaquita	(Epic 9678)	.75	3.00	64
EVERYBODY KNOWS/Inside & Out	(Epic 10265)	.75	3.00	67
EVERYBODY KNOWS (I STILL LOVE YOU)/Ol Sol	(Epic 9722)	.75	3.00	64
GLAD ALL OVER/I Know You	(Epic 9656)	.75	3.00	64
GOOD OLD ROCK 'N' ROLL (Medley)/One Night	(Epic 10684)	.75	3.00	70
GOOD OLD ROCK 'N' ROLL (Medley)/One Night	(Epic 10684)	2.00	8.00	70
(With picture sleeve)				
HERE COMES SUMMER/Five By Five	(Epic 10635)	.75	3.00	70
IF SOMEBODY LOVES YOU/Best Days Work	(Epic 10509)	.75	3.00	69
I KNEW IT ALL THE TIME/That's What I Said	(Congress 212)	2.50	10.00	64
I LIKE IT LIKE THAT/Hurting Inside	(Epic 9811)	.75	3.00	65
I WALK THE LINE/First Love	(Rust 5078)	2.00	8.00	64
(Instrumentals)				
I'VE GOT TO HAVE A REASON/Good Time Woman	(Epic 10114)	.75	3.00	67
LITTLE BIT NOW, A/You Don't Play Me Around	(Epic 10209)	.75	3.00	67
NINETEEN DAYS/Sitting Here Baby	(Epic 10076)	.75	3.00	66
OVER & OVER/I'll Be Yours (My Love)	(Epic 9863)	.75	3.00	65
PARADISE (IS HALF AS NICE)/34-06	(Epic 10474)	.75	3.00	69
PLEASE STAY/Forget	(Epic 10325)	.75	3.00	68
PLEASE TELL ME WHY/Look Before You Leap	(Epic 10031)	.75	3.00	66
RED & BLUE/Concentration Baby	(Epic 10244)	.75	3.00	67
RED BALLOON/Maze Of Love	(Epic 10375)	.75	3.00	69
REELIN' & ROCKIN'/I'm Thinking	(Epic 9786)	.75	3.00	65
RUB IT IN/Break Down & Cry	(Epic 10894)	.75	3.00	72
SATISFIED WITH YOU/Don't Let Me Down	(Epic 10053)	.75	3.00	66
SOUTHERN MAN/If You Wanna See Me Cry	(Epic 10704)	.75	3.00	71
TRY TOO HARD/All Night Long	(Epic 10004)	.75	3.00	66
YOU MUST HAVE BEEN A BEAUTIFUL BABY/ Man In The Pin Stripe Suit	(Epic 10179)	.75	3.00	67
YOU'VE GOT WHAT IT TAKES/Doctor Rhythm	(Epic 10144)	.75	3.00	67
WON'T YOU BE MY LADY/	(Epic 10768)	.75	3.00	71

CLARK, Gene (Of the Byrds)

TITLE/FLIP	LABEL & NO.	GOOD	NEAR MINT	YR.
HOME RUN KING/	(RSO 876)	.50	2.00	77
I FOUND YOU/Echoes	(Columbia 43903)	.75	3.00	66
LIFE'S GREATEST FOOL/	(Asylum 45222)	.50	2.00	74
Also see Dillard & Clark				

CLARK, Lucky

TITLE/FLIP	LABEL & NO.	GOOD	NEAR MINT	YR.
EVERYTIME TWO FOOLS COLLIDE/ Another Honky Tonk Night	(Polydor 14393)	.50	2.00	77
FEELING OF LOVE/Let Me Be The Fool	(Chess 1806)	.75	3.00	61
SO SICK/Two Kinds Of People	(Chess 1782)	1.00	4.00	61

CLARK, Michael

TITLE/FLIP	LABEL & NO.	GOOD	NEAR MINT	YR.
BEST TIMES OF MY LIFE/Wings Meant To Fly	(Capitol 4646)	.50	2.00	78
COME A LITTLE BIT CLOSER/Drinkin' Man's Blues	(Capitol 4474)	.50	2.00	77
IT MUST BE LOVE/Love Is On The Line	(Capitol 4758)	.50	2.00	79
SILVER SADDLE, FADED ROSE/ Wings Meant To Fly	(Capitol 4560)	.50	2.00	78
SWEET SURRENDER/Dancin' Shoes	(Capitol 4670)	.50	2.00	78

CLARK, Petula

TITLE/FLIP	LABEL & NO.	GOOD	NEAR MINT	YR.
AMERICAN BOYS/Look To The Sky	(Warner Bros. 7244)	.75	3.00	68
BABY LOVER/Ever Been In Love	(Imperial 5582)	1.00	4.00	59
CAT IN THE WINDOW, THE/Fancy Dancin' Man	(Warner Bros. 7073)	.75	3.00	67
COLOR MY WORLD/Take Me Home Again	(Warner Bros. 5882)	.75	3.00	66
DON'T GIVE UP/Every Time I See A Rainbow	(Warner Bros. 7216)	.75	3.00	68
DON'T SLEEP IN THE SUBWAY/ Here Comes The Mornin'	(Warner Bros. 7049)	.75	3.00	67
DOWNTOWN/You'd Better Love Me	(Warner Bros. 5494)	.75	3.00	64
HAPPY HEART/Love Is The Only Thing	(Warner Bros. 7275)	.75	3.00	69
I COULDN'T LIVE WITHOUT YOUR LOVE/ Your Way Of Life	(Warner Bros. 5835)	.75	3.00	66
I KNOW A PLACE/Jack & John	(Warner Bros. 5612)	.75	3.00	65
I WILL FOLLOW HIM/Darling Cheri	(Laurie 3156)	1.00	4.00	63
KISS ME GOODBYE/I've Got Love Going For Me	(Warner Bros. 7170)	.75	3.00	68
LITTLE SHOEMAKER, THE/Helpless	(King 1371)	1.25	5.00	54
LOOK AT MINE/You & I	(Warner Bros. 7310)	.75	3.00	69
MY GUY/Little Bit O' Lovin'	(MGM 14392)	.50	2.00	72
MY LOVE/Where Am I Going	(Warner Bros. 5684)	.75	3.00	65
NO ONE BETTER THAN YOU/Things Bright & Beautiful	(Warner Bros. 7343)	.75	3.00	69
NOW THAT I NEED YOU/I Love A Violin	(Imperial 5655)	1.00	4.00	60
OTHER MAN'S GRASS IS ALWAYS GREENER, THE/ At The Crossroads	(Warner Bros. 7079)	.75	3.00	67
ROAD, THE/In Love	(Laurie 3259)	.75	3.00	64
ROAD, THE/Jumble Sale	(Laurie 3143)	1.00	4.00	62
ROMANCE IN ROME/Pendulum Song	(MGM 12049)	1.25	5.00	55
ROMEO/Isn't It A Lovely Day	(Warwick 652)	1.00	4.00	61
ROUND EVERY CORNER/Two Rivers	(Warner Bros. 5661)	.75	3.00	65
SIGN OF THE TIMES, A/Time For Love (No Mi Guardi Mi)	(Warner Bros. 5802)	.75	3.00	66
SONG IS LOVE, THE/Beautiful Sounds	(Warner Bros. 7422)	.75	3.00	70
SONG OF MY LIFE, THE/Couldn't Sleep	(Warner Bros. 7467)	.75	3.00	70
TELL ME TRULY/Song Of A Mermaid	(Coral 60971)	1.25	5.00	53
TENDER LOVE/Whistlin' For The Moon	(London 10516)	1.00	4.00	62
THIS IS MY SONG/High	(Warner Bros. 7002)	.75	3.00	67
WEDDING SONG (THERE IS LOVE)/Song Without End	(MGM 14431)	.50	2.00	72
WHERE DID MY SNOWMAN GO/3 Little Kittens	(Coral 61077)	1.25	5.00	54
WITH ALL MY LOVE/My Friend The Sea	(London 10504)	1.00	4.00	62
WHO AM I/Love Is A Long Journey	(Warner Bros. 5863)	.75	3.00	66
YOU'D BETTER COME HOME/Heart	(Warner Bros. 5643)	.75	3.00	65

CLARK, Sanford

TITLE/FLIP	LABEL & NO.	GOOD	NEAR MINT	YR.
BAD LUCK/My Jealousy	(Jamie 1120)	.75	3.00	59
CHEAT, A/Usta Be My Baby (Maroon label)	(Dot 15516)	2.50	10.00	56
CHEAT, A/Usta Be My Baby (Black label)	(Dot 15516)	1.25	5.00	56
FOOL, THE/Lonesome For A Letter	(MCI 1003)	7.50	30.00	55
FOOL, THE/Lonesome For A Letter (Maroon label)	(Dot 15481)	2.50	10.00	56
FOOL, THE/Lonesome For A Letter (Black label)	(Dot 15481)	1.25	5.00	56
FOOL, THE/Step Aside	(Ramco 1972)	.50	2.00	66
GLORY OF LOVE, THE/Darling Dear	(Dot 15556)	1.00	4.00	57
IT HURTS ME TOO/Guess It's Love	(Trey 3016)	.75	3.00	61
LOU BE DOO/Love Charms	(Dot 15585)	1.00	4.00	57
MODERN ROMANCE/	(Dot 15738)	10.00	40.00	58
9 LB. HAMMER/Ooo Baby	(Dot 15534)	1.00	4.00	57
PLEDGING MY LOVE/Go On Home	(Jamie 1153)	.75	3.00	60
RUN BOY, RUN/New Kind Of Fool	(Jamie 1129)	.75	3.00	59
SING 'EM SOME BLUES (With Duane Eddy)/ Still As The Night (With Al Casey)	(Jamie 1107)	1.25	5.00	58
Al Casey played lead guitar on many of Sanford Clark's early sessions.				

CLARKE, Allan (Of the Hollies)

TITLE/FLIP	LABEL & NO.	GOOD	NEAR MINT	YR.
IF YOU THINK YOU KNOW HOW TO LOVE ME/ Light A Light	(Asylum 45313)	.50	2.00	76
I'M BETTING MY LIFE ON YOU/ Who's Goin' Out The Back Door	(Atlantic 3522)	.50	2.00	78
I WASN'T BORN YESTERDAY/ The Man Who Manufactures Daydreams	(Atlantic 3497)	.50	2.00	78
RUBY/Baby, It's All Right With Me	(Epic 10914)	.50	2.00	72
SLIPSTREAM/	(Elektra 46617)	.50	2.00	80

CLARKE, Michael: see Firefall

CLARKE, Stanley

TITLE/FLIP	LABEL & NO.	GOOD	NEAR MINT	YR.
ROCK 'N' ROLL JELLY/Slow Dance	(Nemperor ZS8-7518)	.50	2.00	78
WE SUPPLY/	(Epic 9-50890)	.50	2.00	80

CLASH, The

TITLE/FLIP	LABEL & NO.	GOOD	NEAR MINT	YR.
GATES OF THE WEST/Groovy Times	(Epic AEM 1178)	.50	2.00	79
I FOUGHT THE LAW/White Man In Hammersmith Palais	(Epic 50738)	.50	2.00	79

CLASS-AIRS, The

TITLE/FLIP	LABEL & NO.	GOOD	NEAR MINT	YR.
TOO OLD TO CRY/My Tears Start To Fall	(Honey Bee)	8.75	35.00	

CLASS MATES, The

TITLE/FLIP	LABEL & NO.	GOOD	NEAR MINT	YR.
HERE COMES SUZY/Homework	(Seg-Way 104)	1.50	6.00	61
HIGH SCHOOL/Don't Make Me Cry	(Marquee 101)	2.50	10.00	60
UNTIL THEN/Pretty Little Pet	(Marquee 102)	3.75	15.00	60

CLASSICS, The: see Christie, Lou

CLASSICS, The (Featuring Emil Stuccio)

TITLE/FLIP	LABEL & NO.	GOOD	NEAR MINT	YR.
ANGEL ANGELA/Eenie Minie & Mo	(Dart 1032)	3.75	15.00	60
CINDERELLA/So In Love	(Dart 1015)	2.50	10.00	60

TITLE/FLIP	LABEL & NO.	GOOD	NEAR MINT	YR.
CANDY & THE KISSES				
81, THE/Two Happy People	(Cameo 336)	.75	3.00	64
LET THE GOOD TIMES ROLL/A Good Cry	(R&L 500)	1.00	4.00	63
SOLDIER BABY/Shakin' Time	(Cameo 355)	.75	3.00	65
CANDY GIRLS, The				
RUNAROUND (BABY-BABY)/Run	(Rotate 5005)	1.25	5.00	
TOMORROW MY LOVE/Run	(Rotate 5001)	1.25	5.00	
CANDYMEN, The				
CANDYMAN/Crowded Room	(ABC 11077)	.75	3.00	68
GEORGIA PINES/Movies In My Mind	(ABC 10995)	.75	3.00	67
HAPPY TONIGHT/Papers	(Liberty 56172)	.75	3.00	70
Also see Atlanta Rhythm Section, The				
Also see Orbison, Roy				
CANE, Gary, & His Friends				
C'MERE BABY DOLL/The Fight	(Shell 717)	1.00	4.00	60
YEN YET SONG, THE/I'll Walk The Earth	(Shell 719)	1.00	4.00	60
CANE, Stacey				
FUNNY FACE/Who Are You	(Jubilee 5500)	.75	3.00	65
CANNED HEAT				
CHRISTMAS BLUES, THE/The Chipmunk Song (With The Chipmunks)	(Liberty 56079)	5.00	20.00	68
GOING UP THE COUNTRY/One Kind Favor	(Liberty 56077)	1.00	4.00	68
GOING UP THE COUNTRY/Future Blues	(Liberty 56180)	.50	2.00	71
LET'S WORK TOGETHER/I'm Her Man	(Liberty 56151)	.75	3.00	70
ON THE ROAD AGAIN/Boogie Music	(Liberty 56038)	.75	3.00	68
ROCKIN' WITH THE KING/ I Don't Care What You Tell Me (With Little Richard)	(United Artists 50892)	.75	3.00	72
ROLLIN' & TUMBLIN'/Bullfrog Blues	(Liberty 55979)	.75	3.00	68
SIC 'EM PIGS/Poor Moon	(Liberty 56127)	.75	3.00	69
TIME WAS/Low Down	(Liberty 56097)	.75	3.00	69
WOOLY BULLY/My Time Ain't Long	(Liberty 56127)	.75	3.00	71
CANNIBAL & THE HEADHUNTERS				
DANCE BY THE LIGHT/Means So Much	(Aires 1001)	1.00	4.00	64
FOLLOW THE MUSIC/I Nee Your Loving	(Rampart 646)	.75	3.00	65
LAND OF 1000 DANCES/I'll Show You How To Love Me	(Rampart 642)	1.00	4.00	65
LAND OF 1000 DANCES/Love Bird	(Date 1525)	.50	2.00	66
MEAN SO MUCH/Get In On Up	(Capitol 2393)	.75	3.00	69
NAU NINNY NAU/Here Comes Love	(Rampart 644)	.75	3.00	65
OUT OF SIGHT/Please Baby Please	(Rampart 654)	1.00	4.00	66
ZULU KING/La Bamba	(Date 1516)	.75	3.00	66
CANNON, Ace				
BIG SHOT/Rest	(Santo 506)	1.00	4.00	62
BLUES (STAY AWAY FROM ME)/Blues In My Heart	(Hi 2051)	.75	3.00	62
COTTONFIELDS/Mildew	(Hi 2065)	.75	3.00	63
SEARCHIN'/Love Letters In The Sand	(Hi 2074)	.75	3.00	64
SUGAR BLUES/38 Special	(Santo 503)	1.00	4.00	62
SUMMERTIME/Hoe Down Rock	(Fernwood 135)	1.00	4.00	60
TUFF/Sittin' Tight	(Hi 2040)	.75	3.00	61
Instrumentals				
CANNON BROTHERS, The				
SURFIN' IN BERMUDA/Look What You've Done	(Ric 107)	1.00	4.00	63
CANNON, Freddy (Fredrick Anthony Picariello)				
ABIGAIL BEECHER/All American Girl	(Warner Bros. 5409)	1.00	4.00	64
ACTION/Beachwood City	(Warner Bros. 5645)	1.00	4.00	65
BEAUTIFUL DOWNTOWN BURBANK/If You Give Me A Title	(Sire 4103)	.75	3.00	69
BUZZ BUZZ A-DIDDLE-IT/Opportunity	(Swan 4071)	1.25	5.00	61
CHARGED UP, TURNED UP, ROCK & ROLL SINGER/ I Ain't Much But I'm Yours	(Royal American 2)	.50	2.00	70
CHATTANOOGA SHOE SHINE BOY/Boston	(Swan 4050)	1.00	4.00	60
CINCINNATI WOMAN/20th Century Fox	(Warner Bros. 7075)	1.00	4.00	67
DEDICATION SONG, THE/Come On Come On	(Warner Bros. 5693)	1.00	4.00	66
DO WHAT THE HIPPIES DO/That's The Way Girls Are	(Swan 4155)	.75	3.00	63
EVERYBODY MONKEY/Oh Gloria	(Swan 4149)	.75	3.00	63
FOR ME & MY GAL/Blue Plate Special	(Swan 4083)	1.00	4.00	61
FOUR LETTER MAN/Come On & Love Me	(Swan 4132)	.75	3.00	63
GOTTA GOOD THING GOIN'/Summertime U.S.A.	(Warner Bros. 5448)	1.00	4.00	64
GREATEST SHOW ON EARTH, THE/Hokie Pokie Girl	(Warner Bros. 5810)	.75	3.00	66
HAPPY CLOWN/In My Wildest Dreams	(Warner Bros. 5876)	.75	3.00	66
HAPPY SHADES OF BLUE/Cuernavaca Choo Choo	(Swan 4057)	1.00	4.00	60
HUMDINGER/My Blue Heaven	(Swan 4061)	1.00	4.00	60
IF YOU WERE A ROCK & ROLL RECORD/The Truth, Ruth	(Swan 4122)	1.00	4.00	62
IF YOU'VE GOT THE TIME/	(Metromedia 262)	.50	2.00	72
IN THE NIGHT/Little Miss A Go Go Go	(Warner Bros. 5615)	1.00	4.00	64
JUMP OVER/The Urge	(Swan 4053)	1.00	4.00	60
LET ME SHOW YOU WHERE IT'S AT/ The Old Rag Man	(Warner Bros. 5666)	1.00	4.00	65
LITTLE AUTOGRAPH SEEKER/ Too Much Monkey Business	(Warner Bros. 5487)	1.00	4.00	64
MAVERICK'S FLAT/Run To The Poet Man	(Warner Bros. 7019)	.75	3.00	67
MUSKRAT RAMBLE/Two Thousand-88	(Swan 4066)	1.00	4.00	60
OK WHEELER, THE USED CAR DEALER/ Odie Cologne	(Warner Bros. 5434)	1.00	4.00	64
OKEFENOKEE/Kookie Hat	(Swan 4038)	1.00	4.00	59
PALISADES PARK/June July & August	(Swan 4106)	.75	3.00	62
PATTY BABY/Betty Jean	(Swan 4139)	.75	3.00	63
ROCK AROUND THE CLOCK/ Sock It To Me Judge	(We Make Rock & Roll Records 1601)	.75	3.00	
SEA CRUISE/ She's A Friday Night Fox	(We Make Rock & Roll Records 1604)	.75	3.00	
STRAWBERRY WINE/Blossom Dear	(Royal American 288)	.75	3.00	69
SUGAR (PART 1)/Sugar (Part 2)	(Claridge 416)	.50	2.00	76
SWEET GEORGIA BROWN/What A Party	(Swan 4168)	1.00	4.00	64
TALLAHASSEE LASSIE/You Know	(Swan 4031)	1.00	4.00	59
TEEN QUEEN OF THE WEEK/Wild Guy	(Swan 4096)	1.00	4.00	62
TRANSISTOR SISTER/Walk To The Moon	(Swan 4078)	1.00	4.00	61
UPS & DOWNS OF LOVE, THE/It's Been Nice	(Swan 4178)	1.00	4.00	64
WAY DOWN YONDER IN NEW ORLEANS/Fractured	(Swan 4043)	1.00	4.00	59
WHAT'S GONNA HAPPEN WHEN SUMMER'S DONE/ Broadway	(Swan 4117)	1.00	4.00	62
CANNONBALLS, The				
TEEN TANGO/Summer Feeling	(Brunswick 55231)	.75	3.00	62
CANO, Eddie				
TASTE OF HONEY, A/Panchita (Instrumentals)	(Reprise 20075)	.75	3.00	63
CANTERBURY FAIR				
DAY'S I LOVE/Song On A May Morning	(Koala 8081)	1.00	4.00	
CANTRELL, Lana				
LIKE A SUNDAY MORNING/Good Times	(Polydor 14261)	.50	2.00	75
CANUCKS, The				
ROCK AROUND THE BARN/Never Before	(Diadon 116)	1.00	4.00	60
CANYON (Featuring Ellison Chase)				
OVERLOADED/Rock N' Roll Sister	(Magna-Glide 5N-327)	.75	3.00	75
TOP OF THE WORLD/Boogie down Broadway	(Magna-Gilde MGN323)	.75	3.00	75
CANYON, Rusty				
BANANA-WHAT A CRAZY FRUITI/The Storyman (With The Banana Boys)	(Teenerama TE-1001)	.75	3.00	58
CAPALDI, Jim (Of Traffic)				
DAUGHTER OF THE NIGHT/I'm Gonna Do It	(RSO 912)	.50	2.00	78
EVE/Going Down Slow All The Way	(Island 1204)	.50	2.00	72
GOOD NIGHT & GOOD MORNING/Short Cut Draw Blood	(Island 067)	.50	2.00	76
IT'S ALL RIGHT/Whale Meat Again	(Island 003)	.50	2.00	75
IT'S ALL UP TO YOU/I've Got So Much Lovin'	(Island 025)	.50	2.00	75
LOVE HURTS/Sugar Honey	(Island 045)	.50	2.00	75
OPEN YOUR HEART/After The Ball	(Island 1205)	.50	2.00	72
TRICKY DICKIE RIDES AGAIN/Love Is All You Can Try	(Island 1216)	.50	2.00	72
CAPEHART, Jerry (Jerry Neal)				
ROLLIN'/Walkin' Stick Boogie (With the Cochran Brothers, Eddie & Hank)	(Cash 1021)	5.00	20.00	56
SONG OF NEW ORLEANS/The Young & Blue (Features Eddie Cochran on guitar. Glen Campbell is said to be on 12 string guitar on this session.)	(Crest 1101)	3.75	15.00	62
CAPES OF GOOD HOPE, The				
SHADES/Lady Margaret	(Round 1001)	.75	3.00	66
CAPITALS, The				
THREE O'CLOCK ROCK/Write Me A Love Letter	(Triumph 601)	1.00	4.00	59
CAPITOLS, The				
ANGEL OF LOVE/Cause I Love You	(Pet 807)	5.00	20.00	58
DAY BY DAY/Little Things	(Gateway 721)	7.50	30.00	
Also see Toliver, Mickey & The Capitols				
CAPP, Joe, & The Starfires				
COMIC STRIP WOBBLE/It's Wobblin' Time	(Roulette 4436)	.75	3.00	62
GROOVY MOVIE/Scooter Booter (With the Countdowns)	(Roulette 4458)	.75	3.00	62
CAPREEZ, The				
IT'S GOOD TO BE HOME AGAIN/ How To Make A Sad Man Glad	(Sound 149)	1.00	4.00	67
ROSANNA/Over You	(Sound 126)	1.00	4.00	66
TIME/Soulsation	(Sound 171)	1.00	4.00	67
TIME/Soulsation	(Tower 370)	.75	3.00	67
CAPRI, Bobby				
NIGHT, THE/I'm Gonna Be Another Man (With the Velvet Satins)	(Johnson 126)	5.00	20.00	61
ONE SIDED LOVE/Charm Bracelet	(Ariste 101)	5.00	20.00	
YOU & I/Cleopatra	(Johnson 124)	1.50	6.00	61
CAPRI, John				
WHEN I'M LONELY/Love For Me (With the Fabulous Fours)	(Bomarc 306)	6.25	25.00	
CAPRIS, The (Featuring Nick Santamaria)				
GIRL IN MY DREAMS/My Island In The Sun	(Old Town 1107)	2.00	8.00	61
LIMBO/From The Vine Came The Grape	(Mr. Peeke 118)	1.00	4.00	63
THERE'S A MOON OUT TONIGHT/Indian Girl (Pink Label)	(Lost Nite 101)	5.00	20.00	
THERE'S A MOON OUT TONIGHT/Indian Girl	(Trommers 101)	3.75	15.00	60
THERE'S A MOON OUT TONIGHT/Indian Girl	(Planet 1010)	18.75	75.00	60
THERE'S A MOON OUT TONIGHT/Indian Girl	(Old Town 1094)	1.50	6.00	60
WHERE I FELL IN LOVE/Some People Think	(Old Town 1099)	1.50	6.00	61
WHY DO I CRY/Tears In My Eyes	(Old Town 1103)	1.50	6.00	61
CAPS, The				
DADDY DEAN/Red Headed Flea	(White Star 102)	1.00	4.00	59
CAPT. GROOVEY & HIS BUBBLEGUM ARMY (Featuring Bobby Bloom)				
CAPT. GROOVEY & HIS BUBBLE GUM ARMY/ Bubblegum March	(Super K SK4)	1.00	4.00	69
CAPTAIN & TENNILE, The (Darryl Dragon & Toni Tennille)				
CAN'T STOP DANCING/Mis Canciones	(A&M 1912)	.50	2.00	77
CIRCLES/1954 Boogie Blues	(A&M 1970)	.50	2.00	77
COMO YO QUIERO SENTIERETE (THE WAY I WANT TO TOUCH YOU)/	(A&M 1725)	.50	2.00	75
COME IN FROM THE RAIN/We Never Really Say Goodbye	(A&M 1944)	.50	2.00	77
DO THAT TO ME ONE MORE TIME/Deep In The Dark	(Casablanca 2215)	.50	2.00	79
I'M ON MY WAY/We Never Really Say Goodbye	(A&M 2063)	.50	2.00	78
LONELY NIGHT (Angel Face)/Smile For Me One More Time	(A&M 1782)	.50	2.00	76
LOVE WILL KEEP US TOGETHER/Broddy Bounce (Por Amor Viviremos)	(A&M 1715)	.50	2.00	75
LOVE WILL KEEP US TOGETHER/Gentle Stranger	(A&M 1672)	.50	2.00	75
MUSKRAT LOVE/Honey Come Love Me	(A&M 1870)	.50	2.00	76
POR AMOR VIVEREMOS (LOVE WILL KEEP UP TOGETHER)/ Broddy Bounce	(A&M 1715)	.50	2.00	75
SHOP AROUND/Butterscotch Castle	(A&M 1817)	.50	2.00	76
SONG OF JOY/Wedding Song (There Is Love)	(A&M 8601)	.50	2.00	77
WAY I WANT TO TOUCH YOU, THE/ Disney Girls	(Butterscotch Castle BC-001)	10.00	40.00	74
WAY I WANT TO TOUCH YOU, THE/Disney Girls	(Joyce 101)	3.75	15.00	74
WAY I WANT TO TOUCH YOU/Disney Girls	(A&M 1624)	.50	2.00	74
WAY I WANT TO TOUCH YOU/Broddy Bounce	(A&M 1725)	.50	2.00	75
YOU NEED A WOMAN TONIGHT/Love Me Like A Baby	(A&M 2106)	.50	2.00	78
YOU NEVER DONE IT LIKE THAT/"D" Keyboard Blues	(A&M 2063)	.50	2.00	78
Also see Dragons, The				
CAPTAIN BEEFHEART				
WHO DO YOU THINK YOU'RE FOOLING/Diddy Wah Diddy	(A&M 794)	.75	3.00	66
YELLOW BRICK ROAD/Abba Dabba	(Buddah 9)	.75	3.00	68
CAPTAIN LOCKHEED & THE STARFIGHTERS				
EJECTION/Catch A Falling Star Fighter	(United Artists 297)	.50	2.00	72
Some members of this band also appeared in Hawkwind.				
CAPT. REDFEATHER				
ELEPHANT BOY, THE/Mumbo Jumbo	(Conte CO-825)	.50	2.00	
CAPTAIN ZAP & HIS MOTORTOWN CUT-UP				
LUNEY LANDING, THE/The Luney Take-Off (Novelty/Break-In)	(Motown 1151)	3.00	12.00	69
CAPTAIN ZOOM & THE ANDROIDS				
CAPTAIN ZOOM (HERE COMES CAPTAIN ZOOM)/ The Zoom	(A&M 781)	.75	3.00	65
LONG TALL TEXAN/I Really Want You	(A&M 785)	.75	3.00	65
CAPTANS, The				
HOMEWORK/Say Yes	(DC 0416)	1.00	4.00	59
CAPTIVATIONS, The				
RED HOT SCRAMBLER/Speedshift	(Garpax 44179)	1.00	4.00	64
CARAMEN, Art "Tink"				
FALLING FOR YOU/Eternity Of Love	(Dasa 101)	2.00	8.00	
CARAVELLES, The				
HAVE YOU EVER BEEN LONELY/Don't Blow Your Cool	(Smash 1869)	.75	3.00	64
HOW CAN I BE SURE/You Are Here	(Smash 1901)	.75	3.00	64
YOU DON'T HAVE TO BE A BABY TO CRY/ Last One To Know	(Smash 1852)	.75	3.00	63
CARAVELLES, The				
ANGRY ANGEL/Pink Lips	(Starmaker 1925)	2.00	8.00	
ONE LITTLE KISS/Twistin' Marie	(Joey 6208)	7.50	30.00	62
CARDBOARD ZEPPELIN, The (The Regents)				
CITY LIGHTS/Ten Story Building	(Laurie LR-3433)	2.00	8.00	68
CARDELL, Nick				
ARLENE/How Can I Help It	(Liberty 55556)	2.00	8.00	63
I STAND ALONE/Everybody Jump	(Amcan 405)	2.00	8.00	
CARDIGAN BROTHERS, The				
EVERYBODY LOVES A GUY NAMED JOHNNY/Say Hello	(Motion 3000)	1.25	5.00	62
I KNOW, I KNOW, I KNOW/Let's Go To The Movies	(Chairman 4400)	1.25	5.00	62
CARDIGANS, The				
MAKE UP YOUR MIND/Half Breed	(Spann 6931)	1.00	4.00	59
YOUR GRADUATION MEANS GOODBYE/ Bo-Weevil On The Mountain Top	(Mercury 71251)	1.00	4.00	58
CARE				
WOUNDED KNEE/Tomorrow Will Come	(Heartland 4183)	.50	2.00	74

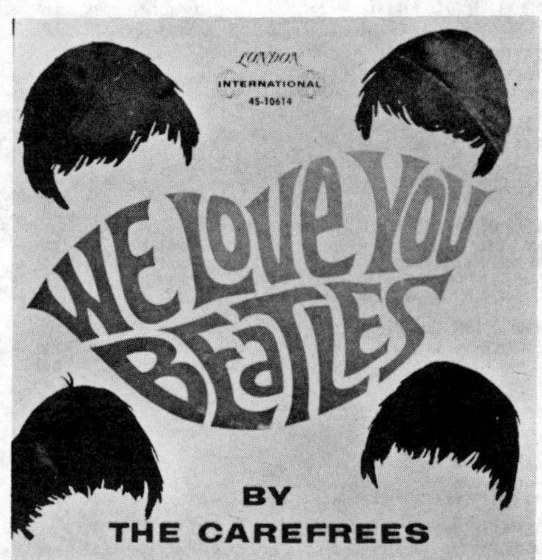

TITLE/FLIP	LABEL & NO.	GOOD	NEAR MINT	YR.
CAREFREES, The				
PADDY WACK/ Aren't You Glad You're You	(London International 10615)	.75	3.00	64
WE LOVE YOU BEATLES/ Hot Blooded Lover	(London International 45-10614)	1.50	6.00	64
WE LOVE YOU BEATLES/ Hot Blooded Lover (Picture sleeve)	(London International 45-10614)	2.00	8.00	64
CARETAKERS, The				
EAST SIDE STORY/Epic	(Rip'Off 1001)	1.50	6.00	
CARIANS, The				
ONLY A DREAM/Girls	(Magenta 04)	2.00	8.00	61
SHE'S GONE/Snooty Friends	(Indigo 136)	3.75	15.00	60
CARI, Eddie				
WISHING TIME/This Love Of Mine (Group Sound)	(Mermaid 104)	1.25	5.00	

TITLE/FLIP	LABEL & NO.	GOOD	NEAR MINT	YR.
I APOLOGIZE/Love For Today	(Piccolo 500)	.75	3.00	65
LIFE IS BUT A DREAM/That's The Way	(Dart 1038)	3.75	15.00	60
LIFE IS BUT A DREAM/That's The Way	(Mercury 71829)	2.00	8.00	61
LIFE IS BUT A DREAM/Nuttin' In The Noggin'	(Stream Line 1028)	.75	3.00	61
P.S. I LOVE YOU/Wrap Your Troubles In A Dream	(Music Note 118)	1.25	5.00	63
TILL THEN/Enie Minie Mo	(Music Note 1116)	1.00	4.00	63
TOO YOUNG/Who's Laughing Who's Crying	(Musictone 6131)	1.25	5.00	
YOU'LL NEVER KNOW/Dancing With You	(Stork 2)	1.00	4.00	64

Even though all of these releases are shown as being by a group using the same name, the possibility exists that they are not all by the same group.

CLASSICS, The (Featuring Herb Lance)

TITLE/FLIP	LABEL & NO.	GOOD	NEAR MINT	YR.
BLUE MOON/Little Boy Lost	(Promo 1010)	1.25	5.00	57

CLASSICS IV, The (Featuring Dennis Yost)

TITLE/FLIP	LABEL & NO.	GOOD	NEAR MINT	YR.
CHANGE OF HEART/Rainy Day	(Imperial 66393)	.75	3.00	69
EVERYDAY WITH YOU GIRL/Sentimental Lady	(Imperial 66378)	.75	3.00	69
FUNNIEST THING, THE/	(Imperial 66439)	.75	3.00	70
GOD KNOWS I LOVED HER/We Miss You	(Liberty 56182)	.50	2.00	70
HEAVENLY BLISS/Please Be Mine	(Twist 1003)	3.00	12.00	
ISLAND OF PARADISE/What Will I Do Without You	(Twist 1001)	3.00	12.00	
IT'S TOO LATE/Don't Make Me Wait	(Arlen 746)	2.00	8.00	
LITTLE DARLING/Nothing To Lose	(Capitol 5816)	2.50	10.00	67
MIDNIGHT/The Comic	(Imperial 66424)	.75	3.00	69
MY FIRST DAY WITHOUT HER/Lovin' Each Other	(MGM 14785)	.50	2.00	75
POLLYANA/Cry Baby (Shown as by the Classics)	(Capitol 5710)	2.50	10.00	66
SOUL TRAIN/Strange Changes	(Imperial 66293)	.75	3.00	68
SPOOKY/Poor People	(Imperial 66259)	.75	3.00	67
STORMY/24 Hours Of Loneliness	(Imperial 66328)	.75	3.00	68
TRACES/Mary, Mary Row Your Boat	(Imperial 66352)	.75	3.00	69
TRUE STORY/What Would I Do	(Algonquin 1651)	2.50	10.00	
WHAT AM I CRYING FOR?/All In Your Mind	(MGM South 7002)	.50	2.00	72
WHERE DID ALL THE GOOD TIMES GO/ Ain't It The Truth	(Liberty 56200)	.50	2.00	70

Also see Atlanta Rhythm Section, The

CLASSICS, The (With Lou Christie): see Christie, Lou

CLASSMATES, The

TITLE/FLIP	LABEL & NO.	GOOD	NEAR MINT	YR.
GOTTA GO & SEE MY BABY/ Washed My Heart Of Love	(Silhouette 509)	1.00	4.00	56
TEENAGE TWISTER/Graduation	(Radar 2624)	.75	3.00	62

CLASSMEN, The

TITLE/FLIP	LABEL & NO.	GOOD	NEAR MINT	YR.
DO YOU WANT TO DANCE/All Time Fool	(Limelight 3016)	.75	3.00	63
MY SPECIAL ANGEL/Love Is Gone	(Limelight 3012)	.75	3.00	63

CLAY, Cassius (Muhammed Ali)

TITLE/FLIP	LABEL & NO.	GOOD	NEAR MINT	YR.
STAND BY ME/I Am The Greatest	(Columbia 43007)	1.50	6.00	64
STAND BY ME/I Am The Greatest (Picture sleeve)	(Columbia 43007)	3.00	12.00	64
WILL THE REAL SONNY LISTON PLEASE FALL DOWN/ The Prediction (Promotional issue only, shown as by Cassius Marcellus Clay Jr.)	(Columbia 75717)	6.25	25.00	64

CLAY, Chris

TITLE/FLIP	LABEL & NO.	GOOD	NEAR MINT	YR.
SANTA UNDER ANALYSIS/Santa Under Analysis (Part 2) (Novelty/Break-In)	(Veltone 111)	3.00	12.00	

CLAY, Tom

TITLE/FLIP	LABEL & NO.	GOOD	NEAR MINT	YR.
MARRY ME/Never Before	(Chant 103)	.75	3.00	
OFFICIAL IBBB INTERVIEW (PART 1)/ Official IBBB Interview (Part 2) (Part 1: Interview with John, Paul & Ringo/Part 2: Interview with Ringo & George)	(ZTSC 9743)	10.00	40.00	64
WHAT THE WORLD NEEDS NOW IS LOVE-ABRAHAM, MARTIN & JOHN/ The Victors	(Mowest-5002)	.50	2.00	71

CLAYTON, Merry

TITLE/FLIP	LABEL & NO.	GOOD	NEAR MINT	YR.
AFTER ALL THIS TIME/Steamroller	(Ode 66020)	.50	2.00	72
AFTER ALL THIS TIME/Whatever	(Ode 66018)	.50	2.00	71
COUNTRY ROAD/Forget It, I Got It	(Ode 66007)	.50	2.00	70
GIMME SHELTER/Good Girls	(Ode 66003)	.50	2.00	70
IT'S IN HIS KISS/Magic Of Romance	(Capitol 4984)	.75	3.00	63
KEEP YOUR EYE ON THE SPARROW (THEME FROM BARETTA)/ Loving Grows Up Slow	(Ode 66110)	.50	2.00	75
KNOCK ON THE DOOR/This Is My Dream	(Capitol 5343)	.75	3.00	65
NOTHING LEFT TO DO BUT CRY/Usher Boy	(Capitol 5100)	.75	3.00	64
ONE MORE RIDE/If I Lose	(Ode 66116)	.50	2.00	76

CLAYTON, Paul

TITLE/FLIP	LABEL & NO.	GOOD	NEAR MINT	YR.
CONVENT AT RONDA, THE/Wings Of A Dove	(Monument 432)	1.00	4.00	60
SAN FRANCISCO BAY BLUES/Green Rocky Road	(Monument 819)	1.00	4.00	63

CLEAR LIGHT

TITLE/FLIP	LABEL & NO.	GOOD	NEAR MINT	YR.
BALCK ROSES/She's Ready To Be Free	(Elektra 45622)	1.00	4.00	67

CLEE SHAYS, The

TITLE/FLIP	LABEL & NO.	GOOD	NEAR MINT	YR.
DYNAMITE/The Man From Uncle	(Triumph 65)	.75	3.00	66

CLEFS OF LAVENDER HILL, The

TITLE/FLIP	LABEL & NO.	GOOD	NEAR MINT	YR.
IT WON'T BE LONG/Play With Fire	(Date 1533)	.75	3.00	66
ONE MORE TIME/So I'll Try	(Date 1530)	.75	3.00	66
STOP! GET A TICKET/First Tell Me Why	(Date 1510)	.75	3.00	66
STOP! GET A TICKET/First Tell Me Why	(Thames)	1.50	6.00	66

CLEMENTINO, Clairette

TITLE/FLIP	LABEL & NO.	GOOD	NEAR MINT	YR.
ADONIS/Bless My Soul	(Capitol 5081)	.75	3.00	61
SEE ME/Ev'ry Where	(Capitol 5003)	.75	3.00	61
TEENAGE FAIR/ I Can't Believe (That You're In Love With Me)	(Encore 1204)	.75	3.00	62
YOU'VE BEEN TELLING OUR SECRETS/ My Reason For Living	(Encore 1201)	.75	3.00	61

CLEMENT, Jack

TITLE/FLIP	LABEL & NO.	GOOD	NEAR MINT	YR.
TEN YEARS/Lover Boy	(Sun 291)	1.00	4.00	58
TIME AFTER TIME AFTER TIME/My Voice Is Changing	(Hall-Way 1796)	.75	3.00	62

CLEMENTS, Jack, & Dale Stevens

TITLE/FLIP	LABEL & NO.	GOOD	NEAR MINT	YR.
DOG DOCTOR, THE/Talking Horses (Novelty)	(Fraternity 911)	1.00	4.00	

CLEMENTS, Vassar, Band

TITLE/FLIP	LABEL & NO.	GOOD	NEAR MINT	YR.
JESSICA/Don't Mess Around With My Funk	(MCA 40776)	.50	2.00	77
YAKETY BOW/Barnyard Boogie	(Mercury 73748)	.50	2.00	75

CLICK CLACKS, The

TITLE/FLIP	LABEL & NO.	GOOD	NEAR MINT	YR.
KISS GOODBYE/Rocket Roll	(Apt 25032)	1.00	4.00	59

CLIENTELLS, The

TITLE/FLIP	LABEL & NO.	GOOD	NEAR MINT	YR.
CHRUCH BELLS MAY RING/My Love	(M.B.S. 7)	3.75	15.00	

CLIFF DWELLERS, The

TITLE/FLIP	LABEL & NO.	GOOD	NEAR MINT	YR.
MIDNIGHT IN CANAVERAL/	(Liza 1962)	1.00	4.00	

CLIFF, Jimmy

TITLE/FLIP	LABEL & NO.	GOOD	NEAR MINT	YR.
COME INTO MY LIFE/Viet Nam	(A&M 1167)	.50	2.00	70
HARDER THEY COME, THE/ You Can Get It If You Really Want	(Mango 7500)	.50	2.00	74
LET'S SEIZE THE TIME/Goodbye Yesterday	(A&M 1270)	.50	2.00	71
WONDERFUL WORLD, BEAUTIFUL PEOPLE/	(A&M 1146)	.50	2.00	69

CLIFFORD, Buzz

TITLE/FLIP	LABEL & NO.	GOOD	NEAR MINT	YR.
BABY SITTER BOOGIE/Driftwood (Original Title)	(Columbia 4-41876)	3.00	12.00	60
BABY SITTIN' BOOGIE/Driftwood	(Columbia 4-41876)	.75	3.00	61
BABY SITTIN' BOOGIE/Driftwood (Stereo single)	(Columbia 4-41876)	1.50	6.00	61
FOREVER/Magic Circle (With the Teenangers)	(Columbia 4-42290)	3.75	15.00	62
FOREVER/Magic Circle (Compact 33 single, with the Teen Angels)	(Columbia 3-42290)	3.75	15.00	62
HELLO MR. MOONLIGHT/Blue Lagoon	(Columbia 4-41774)	.75	3.00	
I'LL NEVER FORGET/The Awakening (With the Teenangers)	(Columbia 4-42019)	5.00	20.00	
I'LL NEVER FORGET/The Awakening (Stereo single) (With the Teenangers)	(Columbia 4-42019)	7.50	30.00	
MORE DEAD THAN ALIVE/ No One Loves Me Like You Do	(Roulette 4451)	1.50	6.00	
MOVING DAY/Loneliness	(Columbia 4-42177)	.75	3.00	61
MY GIRL/Pretend	(Roulette 4500)	1.00	4.00	
THREE LITTLE FISHES/Simply Because	(Columbia 4-41979)	.75	3.00	61
THREE LITTLE FISHES/Simply Because (Stereo single)	(Columbia 4-41979)	1.50	6.00	61

CLIFFORD, Doug "Cosmo" (Of Creedence Clearwater Revival)

TITLE/FLIP	LABEL & NO.	GOOD	NEAR MINT	YR.
LATIN MUSIC/Take A Train	(Fantasy 686)	.50	2.00	73

CLIFFORD, Mike

TITLE/FLIP	LABEL & NO.	GOOD	NEAR MINT	YR.
ALL THE COLORS OF THE RAINBOW/ It Had Better Be Tonight	(United Artists 713)	.75	3.00	64
AT LAST/Pretty Little Girl In The Yellow Dress	(Columbia 4-42029)	.75	3.00	61
BEFORE I LOVED HER/Shirl Girl	(Cameo C-381)	.75	3.00	65
CLOSE TO CATHY/She's Just Another Girl	(United Artists 489)	.75	3.00	62
HOW TO MURDER YOUR WIFE/Here's To My Lover	(United Artists 823)	.75	3.00	65
I DON'T KNOW WHY/I'm Afraid To Say I Love You	(Liberty 55219)	.75	3.00	59
ONE BOY TOO LATE/Danny's Dream	(United Artists 588)	.75	3.00	63
SHOULD I/Whisper, Whisper (With Patience & Prudence)	(Liberty 55207)	1.00	4.00	59
WHAT TO DO WITH LAURIE/That's What They Said	(United Artists 557)	.75	3.00	62

CLIFFTERS, The

TITLE/FLIP	LABEL & NO.	GOOD	NEAR MINT	YR.
DJANGO/Amapola	(Phillips 40050)	1.00	4.00	62

CLIFTON, Bill

TITLE/FLIP	LABEL & NO.	GOOD	NEAR MINT	YR.
BEATLE CRAZY/Little Girl Dressed In Blue (Novelty/Break-in)	(London 9638)	1.50	6.00	64

CLIMAX (With Sonny Geraci)

TITLE/FLIP	LABEL & NO.	GOOD	NEAR MINT	YR.
COMPOSITION OF UNRELATED BIRTHDAYS/ It Hurts Me Too	(Patti Platters 1024)	1.00	4.00	67
HARD ROCK GROUP/	(Carousel 30050)	.50	2.00	71
LIFE & BREATH/If It Feels Good Do It	(Rocky Road 30061)	.50	2.00	72
LOVE WILL FIND A WAY/Together By Myself	(Patti Platters 1025)	1.00	4.00	67
PRECIOUS & FEW/Park Preserve	(Carousel 30055)	.50	2.00	71
PRECIOUS & FEW/Park Preserve	(Rocky Road 30055)	.50	2.00	72
RAINBOW RIDES ARE FREE/	(Bell 904)	.50	2.00	71

Also see Outsiders, The

CLIMAX BLUES BAND, The

TITLE/FLIP	LABEL & NO.	GOOD	NEAR MINT	YR.
CHILDREN OF THE NIGHTTIME/Long Distance Love	(Sire 49012)	.50	2.00	79
COULDN'T GET IT RIGHT/Sav'ry Gravy	(Sire 736)	.50	2.00	77
HEY MAMA/That's All	(Sire 358)	.50	2.00	73
I AM CONSTANT/Goin' To New York	(Sire 712)	.50	2.00	74
MAKIN' LOVE/The Gospel Singer	(Sire 1026)	.50	2.00	78
MISTRESS MOONSHINE/	(Sire 1031)	.50	2.00	78
REACHING OUT/Milwaukee Truckin' Blues (Chipper's Song)	(Sire 715)	.50	2.00	75
SENSE OF DIRECTION/	(Sire 713)	.50	2.00	74
TOGETHER & FREE/Berlin Blues	(Sire 747)	.50	2.00	77
USING THE POWER/Running Out Of Time	(Sire 721)	.50	2.00	76

CLINGER, Peggy

TITLE/FLIP	LABEL & NO.	GOOD	NEAR MINT	YR.
I HATE TO SLEEP ALONE/Dreams Of You	(Chelsea BCBO-0136)	.50	2.00	

Also see Cymbal & Clinger

CLINGER SISTERS, The

TITLE/FLIP	LABEL & NO.	GOOD	NEAR MINT	YR.
GOLLY MOM/Puppet	(Tollie 9035)	.75	3.00	64
SHOOP SHOOP DE DOOP, RAMA LAMA DING DONG, YEAH YEAH YEAH/ Lipstick Song	(Tollie 9020)	1.00	4.00	64
WHAT CAN I GIVE HIM/Jingle Dingle Do	(Tollie 9038)	.75	3.00	64

CLINTONIAN CUBS, The

TITLE/FLIP	LABEL & NO.	GOOD	NEAR MINT	YR.
SHE'S JUST MY SIZE/Confusion	(My Boss 508)	8.75	35.00	

CLIQUE, The

TITLE/FLIP	LABEL & NO.	GOOD	NEAR MINT	YR.
I'LL HOLD OUT MY HAND/Soul Mates	(White Whale 333)	.75	3.00	69
IT'S NOT A VERY PLEASANT DAY TODAY/	(Mercury 72952)	.75	3.00	69
MY DARKEST HOUR/My Darkest Hour	(White Whale 335)	.75	3.00	69
SPARKLE & SHINE/Sparkle & Shine	(White Whale 338)	.75	3.00	70
STAY BY ME/Splash One	(Scepter 12202)	1.00	4.00	67
SUGAR ON SUNDAY/Superman	(White Whale 323)	.75	3.00	69
SUPERMAN/Shadow Of Your Love	(White Whale 312)	.75	3.00	69

CLIQUE, The

TITLE/FLIP	LABEL & NO.	GOOD	NEAR MINT	YR.
SHE AIN'T NO GOOD/Time Time Time	(ABC-Paramount 10655)	1.00	4.00	65

CLOCK-WORK ORANGE

TITLE/FLIP	LABEL & NO.	GOOD	NEAR MINT	YR.
WHAT AM I WITHOUT YOU/Image Of You	(Rust 5126)	1.25	5.00	64

CLOCKWORK ORANGES, The

TITLE/FLIP	LABEL & NO.	GOOD	NEAR MINT	YR.
READY STEADY/After Tonight	(Liberty 55887)	.75	3.00	66

CLOONEY, Rosemary

TITLE/FLIP	LABEL & NO.	GOOD	NEAR MINT	YR.
BE MY LIFE'S COMPANION/Why Don't You Love Me	(Columbia 39631)	1.25	5.00	52
BEAUTIFUL BROWN EYES/Shot Gun Boogie	(Columbia 39212)	1.25	5.00	51
BLUES IN THE NIGHT/Who Kissed Me Last Night	(Columbia 39813)	1.25	5.00	52
BOTCH-A-ME/On The First Warm Day	(Columbia 39767)	1.25	5.00	52
COME ON-A MY HOUSE/Rose Of The Mountain	(Columbia 39467)	1.50	6.00	51
FLATTERY/Love Eyes	(MGM K-12760)	1.00	4.00	59
HALF AS MUCH/Poor Whipoorwill	(Columbia 39710)	1.25	5.00	52
HELLO YOUNG LOVERS/Peachy, Peachy	(Columbia 40723)	1.00	4.00	56
HEY THERE/This Ole House	(Columbia 40266)	1.25	5.00	54
IF TEARDROPS WERE PENNIES/ I'm Waiting Just For You	(Columbia 39535)	1.25	5.00	51
MAMBO ITALIANO/We'll Be Together Again	(Columbia 40361)	1.25	5.00	54
MANDY/The Best Things Happen While Dancing	(Columbia 40356)	1.25	5.00	54
MANGOS/Independent	(Columbia 40835)	1.00	4.00	57
RED GARTERS/Man & Woman	(Columbia 40158)	1.25	5.00	54
SAILOR BOYS HAVE TALK TO ME IN ENGLISH/ Go On By	(Columbia 40534)	1.25	5.00	55
SPOONFUL OF SUGAR/Stay Awake	(Reprise 0327)	.75	3.00	64
SUMMERTIME LOVE/Watermellon Heart (With Perez Prado)	(RCA Victor 47-7707)	.75	3.00	60
TENDERLY/Did Anyone Call	(Columbia 39648)	1.25	5.00	52
TOO OLD TO CUT THE MUSTARD (With Marlene Dietrich)/ Good For Nothing	(Columbia 39812)	1.25	5.00	52
YOU ARE MY SUNSHINE/Nobody's Darling But Mine	(Columbia 40760)	1.00	4.00	56
YOU'RE JUST IN LOVE/ Marrying For Love (With Guy Mitchell)	(Columbia 39052)	1.25	5.00	51

Also see Boyd, Jimmy

CLOUD, Christopher: see Boyce, Tommy

CLOUDS, The (Featuring Bill Medley)

TITLE/FLIP	LABEL & NO.	GOOD	NEAR MINT	YR.
NIGHT OWL/My Tears Will Go Away	(Medley 1001)	1.50	6.00	

CLOUDS, The

TITLE/FLIP	LABEL & NO.	GOOD	NEAR MINT	YR.
DARLING I LOVE YOU/T.V. Mix Up	(Round 1008)	1.00	4.00	

CLOUT

TITLE/FLIP	LABEL & NO.	GOOD	NEAR MINT	YR.
SINCE YOU'VE BEEN GONE/	(Epic 50815)	.50	2.00	79
SUBSTITUTE/When Will You Be Mine	(Epic 50591)	.50	2.00	78
YOU'VE GOT ALL OF ME/Feel My Need	(Epic 50729)	.50	2.00	79

CLOVER

TITLE/FLIP	LABEL & NO.	GOOD	NEAR MINT	YR.
STEEL MARBLE/Tar Baby-Newgene & The Lion	(MCA 40774)	.50	2.00	77
TAKE ANOTHER LOOK/The Storm	(Mercury 73935)	.50	2.00	77
WADE IN THE WATER/Stealin'	(Fantasy 639)	.75	3.00	70

This group was formerly Elvis Costello's back-up band.

CLUSTERS, The

TITLE/FLIP	LABEL & NO.	GOOD	NEAR MINT	YR.
FORECAST OF OUR LOVE/	(Epic 9330)	1.50	6.00	58
PARDON MY HEART/Darling Can't You Tell	(Tee Gee 102)	1.50	6.00	58

C-NOTES, The

TITLE/FLIP	LABEL & NO.	GOOD	NEAR MINT	YR.
FROM NOW ON/On Your Mark	(Everlast 5005)	2.00	8.00	57
WE WERE MEANT FOR EACH OTHER/Last Saturday Nite	(ARC 4447)	2.00	8.00	

COACHMEN, The

TITLE/FLIP	LABEL & NO.	GOOD	NEAR MINT	YR.
GIRL IN THE WIND/The News Is Out	(Target 1001)	.75	3.00	69
MR. MOON/Nothing At All	(MMC 010)	1.50	6.00	65
MR. MOON/Nothing At All	(Bear 1974)	.75	3.00	66
SEASONS IN THE SUN/Garrielle	(Capitol 5896)	1.00	4.00	67
TELL HER NO/Time Won't Change	(MMC 014)	1.00	4.00	67

COACHMEN FIVE, The (Featuring Ray Davis)

TITLE/FLIP	LABEL & NO.	GOOD	NEAR MINT	YR.
OH JOAN/This I Know	(Janson 100)	3.75	15.00	

COALKITCHEN

TITLE/FLIP	LABEL & NO.	GOOD	NEAR MINT	YR.
KEEP ON PUSHIN'/Git It	(Full Moon-Epic 50476)	.50	2.00	77

COASTLINERS, The

TITLE/FLIP	LABEL & NO.	GOOD	NEAR MINT	YR.
ALRIGHT/Wonderful You	(Back Beat 554)	1.00	4.00	60
I SEE ME/California On My Mind	(Dear 1300)	1.25	5.00	
SHE'S MY GIRL/	(Back Beat 566)	1.00	4.00	60

COBRAS, The

TITLE/FLIP	LABEL & NO.	GOOD	NEAR MINT	YR.
CINDY/I Will Return (Previously shown as "Sindy")	(Modern 964)	12.50	50.00	55
LA LA/Goodbye Molly	(Casino 1309)	6.25	25.00	
LA LA/Goodbye Molly	(Swan 4176)	1.25	5.00	64
SINDY/I Will Return	(Modern 964)	15.00	60.00	55

COCHISE (With Mick Grabham)

TITLE/FLIP	LABEL & NO.	GOOD	NEAR MINT	YR.
LOVE'S MADE A FOOL OF YOU/ Words Of A Dying Man	(United Artists 50756)	.50	2.00	71

Also see Procol Harum

COCHRAN BROTHERS, The (Eddie & Hank)

TITLE/FLIP	LABEL & NO.	GOOD	NEAR MINT	YR.
GUILTY CONSCIENCE/Your Tomorrows Never Come	(Ekko 1005)	15.00	60.00	56
TWO BLUE SINGING STARS/Mr. Fiddle	(Ekko 1003)	15.00	60.00	56
TIRED & SLEEPY/Fool's Paradise	(Ekko 3001)	25.00	100.00	56

Eddie Cochran & Hank Cochran, were both successful as solo artists in the years that followed, and despite being billed as "brothers" they were actually not related.

COCHRAN, Eddie

TITLE/FLIP	LABEL & NO.	GOOD	NEAR MINT	YR.
C'MON EVERYBODY/Don't Ever Let Me Go	(Liberty 55166)	2.00	8.00	58
CUT ACROSS SHORTY/Three Steps To Heaven (Green label)	(Liberty 55242)	2.00	8.00	60
CUT ACROSS SHORTY/Three Steps To Heaven (Black label)	(Liberty 55242)	1.00	4.00	61
DRIVE-IN SHOW/Am I Blue	(Liberty 55087)	2.50	10.00	57
HALLELUJAH, I LOVE HER SO/Little Angel	(Liberty 55217)	1.25	5.00	59
JEANNIE, JEANNIE, JEANNIE/Pocketful Of Hearts	(Liberty 55123)	3.75	15.00	58
MEAN WHEN I'M MAD/One Kiss	(Liberty 55070)	1.50	6.00	57
PRETTY GIRL/Teresa	(Liberty 55138)	1.50	6.00	58
SITTIN' IN THE BALCONY/Dark Lonely Street	(Liberty 55056)	1.50	6.00	57
SKINNY JIM/Half Loved	(Crest 1026)	20.00	80.00	56
SOMETHIN' ELSE/Boll Weevil Song (With horizontal silver lines)	(Liberty 55203)	3.00	12.00	59
SOMETHIN' ELSE/Boll Weevil Song (Without horizontal silver lines)	(Liberty 55203)	1.25	5.00	59
SUMMERTIME BLUES/Love Again	(Liberty 55144)	2.00	8.00	58
SWEETIE PIE/Lonely	(Liberty 55278)	1.25	5.00	60
TEENAGE HEAVEN/I Remember	(Liberty 55177)	1.50	6.00	59
TWENTY FLIGHT ROCK/Cradle Baby	(Liberty 55112)	5.00	20.00	58

A top rated session guitarist, Eddie Cochran made many guest appearences on other artists' records. They are cross-referenced here:

Also see Capehart, Jerry
Also see Cochran Brothers, The
Also see Davis, Bo
Also see Denson, Lee
Also see Galaxies, The
Also see Gee Cees, The
Also see Jewel & Eddie
Also see Kelly Four, The
Also see Neal, Jerry
Also see Stanley, Ray

COCHRAN, Wayne (& The C C Riders)

TITLE/FLIP	LABEL & NO.	GOOD	NEAR MINT	YR.
DO YOU LIKE THE SOUND OF MUSIC/ Somebody's Been Cuttin' In On My Groove	(Epic 10859)	.50	2.00	72
GOIN' BACK TO MIAMI/I'm In Trouble	(Mercury 72623)	1.00	4.00	67
HARLEM SHUFFLE/Somebody Please	(Mercury 72507)	1.00	4.00	65
HARLEM SHUFFLE/Somebody Please	(Soft 779)	1.00	4.00	65
LAST KISS/I Dreamed, I Gambled, I Lost	(King 5856)	1.00	4.00	64
LONG, LONG DAY/Sleepless Nights	(Epic 10893)	.50	2.00	72
MY LITTLE GIRL/The Coo	(Scottie 1303)	1.25	5.00	59

TITLE/FLIP	LABEL & NO.	GOOD	NEAR MINT	YR.
COCKER, Joe				
CRY ME A RIVER/Give Peace A Chance	(A&M 1200)	.50	2.00	70
DELTA LADY/She's So Good To Me	(A&M 1112)	.50	2.00	69
FEELING ALRIGHT/Sandpaper Cadillac	(A&M 1063)	.50	2.00	69
FUN TIME/Watching The River Flow	(Asylum 45540)	.50	2.00	78
HIGH TIME WE WENT/Black-Eyed Blues	(A&M 1258)	.50	2.00	71
I CAN STAND A LITTLE RAIN/I Get Mad	(A&M 1626)	.50	2.00	74
IT'S ALL OVER BUT THE SHOUTIN'/Forgive Me Now	(A&M 1758)	.50	2.00	75
JEALOUS KIND, THE/You Came Along	(A&M 1830)	.50	2.00	76
LADY PUT THE LIGHT OUT/	(Asylum 46001)	.50	2.00	79
LETTER, THE/Space Captain	(A&M 1174)	.50	2.00	70
MARJORIE/New Age Of The Lily	(A&M 928)	.75	3.00	68
MIDNIGHT RIDER/Woman To Woman	(A&M 1370)	.50	2.00	72
PARDON ME SIR/St. James Infirmary Blues	(A&M 1407)	.50	2.00	73
PUT OUT THE LIGHT/If I Love You	(A&M 1539)	.50	2.00	74
SHE CAME IN THROUGH THE BATHROOM WINDOW/ Change In Louise	(A&M 1147)	.50	2.00	69
WITH A LITTLE HELP FROM MY FRIENDS/ Something's Coming In	(A&M 991)	.50	2.00	68
YOU ARE SO BEAUTIFUL/It's A Sin When You Love Somebody	(A&M 1641)	.50	2.00	75
YOU CAME ALONG/I Broke Down	(A&M 1855)	.50	2.00	76
Also see Vance, Arnold, & The Avengers				
Also see Grease Band, The				
COCKRELL & SANTOS (Of It's A Beautiful Day) (Cockrell also from Pablo Cruise)				
I WANNA STAY WITH YOU/	(A&M 2077)	.50	2.00	78
CODD, Pat				
HARRY & THE HULAHOOPS/	(UK 49029)	.50	2.00	74
C.O.D.'S, The				
I'M A GOOD GUY/Pretty Baby	(Kellmac 1005)	.75	3.00	66
MICHAEL/Cry No More	(Kellmac 1003)	.75	3.00	65
CODY, Commander, & His Lost Planet Airmen				
BEAT ME DADDY EIGHT TO THE BAR/ Daddy's Gonna Treat You Right	(Paramount 0169)	.75	3.00	72
DADDY'S DRINKING UP OUR CHRISTMAS/ Daddy's Drinking Up Our Christmas	(Dot 17487)	.75	3.00	72
DON'T LET GO/Keep On Lovin' Her	(Warner Bros. 8073)	.75	3.00	74
HOT ROD LINCOLN/My Home In My Hand	(Paramount 0146)	.75	3.00	72
LOST IN THE OZONE/Midnight Shift	(Paramount 0130)	.75	3.00	72
MAMA HATED DIESELS/Truck Stop Rock	(Paramount 0178)	.75	3.00	73
RIOT IN CELL BLOCK #9/Riot In Cell Block #9	(Paramount 0278)	.75	3.00	74
SEVEN-ELEVEN/Snooze You Lose	(Arista 0271)	.50	2.00	77
SMOKE SMOKE SMOKE (THAT CIGARETTE)/ Rock That Boogie	(Paramount 0216)	.75	3.00	72
THANK YOU LONE RANGER/	(Arista 0344)	.50	2.00	78
WATCH MY .38/Semi-Truck	(Paramount 0193)	.75	3.00	73
COE, Jamie, & The Gigolos				
BUT YESTERDAY/Cleopatra	(Big Top 3107)	1.00	4.00	62
DEALER, THE/Close Your Eyes	(Enterprise 5005)	1.25	5.00	64
DEALER, THE/Close Your Eyes	(Reprise 0295)	.75	3.00	64
FOOL, THE/Got That Feeling	(Big Top 3139)	1.00	4.00	63
HOW LOW IS LOW/Little Dear Little Darling	(ABC-Paramount 10267)	1.00	4.00	61
I WAS THE ONE/Good Enough For You	(Enterprise 5055)	1.00	4.00	65
I'M GETTING MARRIED/2 Dozen & A Half	(ABC-Paramount 10203)	1.00	4.00	61
SCHOOL DAY BLUES/I'll Go On Loving You	(Addison 15003)	1.25	5.00	
SUMMERTIME SYMPHONY/There's Gonna Be A Day	(Addison 15001)	.75	3.00	
CO-EDS, The				
LA LA LA/Juke Box	(Cameo 134)	1.00	4.00	58
JUKE BOX/Big Chief	(Cameo 129)	1.00	4.00	57
WHEN IT'S OVER/Annabelle Lee	(Cha Cha 715)	.75	3.00	61
CO-EDS, The (Featuring Gwen Edwards)				
I LOVE AN ANGEL/I'm In Love	(Old Town 1033)	6.25	25.00	57
LOVE YOU BABY ALL THE TIME/I Beg Your Forgiveness	(Old Town 1027)	6.25	25.00	56
COFFEE, Red				
DUCKY CHRISTMAS/Jolly Jingle Bells	(Warner Bros. 5128)	1.00	4.00	59
COHEN, Leonard				
BIRD ON THE WIRE/Seems So Long Ago, Nancy	(Columbia 44827)	.75	3.00	69
PASSING THRU/	(Columbia 45852)	.50	2.00	72
SUZANNE/Hey, That's No Way To Say Goodbye	(Columbia 44439)	.75	3.00	68
SUZANNE/Bird Of The Wire	(Columbia 33192)	.75	3.00	69
(Label error, title should read "Bird On The Wire")				
COLD BLOOD (With Lydia Pense)				
BABY I LOVE YOU/Baby I Love You	(Reprise 1157)	.50	2.00	73
DOWN TO THE BONE/Valdez In The Country	(Reprise 1092)	.50	2.00	72
I GET OFF ON YOU/	(ABC 12173)	.50	2.00	75
I'M A GOOD WOMAN/ I Wish I Knew How It Would Feel To Be Free	(San Francisco 61)	.75	3.00	70
TOO MANY PEOPLE/Too Many People	(San Francisco 62)	.75	3.00	70
UNDERSTANDING/Shop Talk	(San Francisco 66)	.75	3.00	70
YOU GOT ME HUMMIN'/If You Will	(San Francisco 60)	.75	3.00	70
COLDER, Ben				
GOIN' SURFIN'/Still No. 2	(MGM 13147)	1.00	4.00	63
COLE, Bobby				
MR. BOJANGLES/Bus 22 To Bethlehem	(Date 1613)	.75	3.00	68
COLE, Carmen				
BOBBY DARLIN'/I Just Don't Understand	(Groove 0057)	1.25	5.00	
COLE, Cindy				
LONELY CITY BLUE BOY/Just Being Your Baby	(Tower 302)	.75	3.00	66
LOVE LIKE YOURS, A/He's Sure The Boy I Love	(Tower 145)	.75	3.00	65
COLE, Clay				
TWIST AROUND THE CLOCK/ Don't Twist (With Anyone Else But Me)	(Imperial 5804)	.75	3.00	62
COLE, Cozy				
ALA TOPSY (PART 3)/Ala Topsy (Part 4)	(Aristique 602)	.75	3.00	
(EVERYTHING IS) TOPSY TURVY/Bad	(Love 5016)	1.00	4.00	59
LATE & LAZY/Charleston	(Love 5023)	1.00	4.00	59
TOPSY (PART 2)/Topsy (Part 1)	(Love 5004)	1.00	4.00	58
TURVY (PART 2)/Turvy (Part 1)	(Love 5014)	1.00	4.00	58
TURVY (PART 2)/Turvy (Part 1)	(Love 5014)	2.00	8.00	59
(Stereo single issue)				
Instrumentals				
COLE, Don & Allyne				
SOMETHING'S GOT A HOLD ON ME/Poor Fool	(Son Ray 101)	1.00	4.00	65
COLE, Fred E.				
BIG BOOTS/Hey Little Lover	(Lois 101)	1.00	4.00	61
COLE, Jerry				
LIBERATED LADY/In The Pocket	(Warner Bros. 8156)	.50	2.00	75
(With Trinity)				
MEET ME ON THE CORNER/Life Will Go On	(Capitol 5256)	1.00	4.00	64
MIDNIGHT MARY/Land Of Dreams	(Capitol 5056)	1.00	4.00	63
NIGHT RUMBLE/Boss Dance	(Capitol 5141)	1.00	4.00	64
POKEY/One Color Blues	(Capitol 5106)	1.00	4.00	64

TITLE/FLIP	LABEL & NO.	GOOD	NEAR MINT	YR.
SUSANNA'S SONG (IN THE CALIFORNIA MORNING)/ Child Of The Times	(Warner Bros. 8101)	.50	2.00	75
(With Trinity)				
Also see Super Stocks, The				
COLE, Johnny, & The Reptiles				
LIZZARD GIZZARD/Wrap My Heart In Velvet	(Radiant 1503)	1.00	4.00	61
COLE, Lee				
COOL BABY/Suzy Ann	(Mist 1010)	1.25	5.00	59
COLEMAN, Cy				
PLAYBOY'S THEME/You Fascinate Me So	(Playboy 1001)	.75	3.00	60
(Instrumental)				
COLEMAN, Joe				
ROCK ALL NIGHT/Rock All Night (Part 2)	(Rem 304)	1.00	4.00	60
COLEMAN, Lenny				
FOUR SEASONS/Shake It Easy	(Laurie 3290)	3.75	15.00	65
(With Nino & The Ebb Tides)				
COLE, Nat King				
ALL FOR YOU/Vom-Vim-Veedle	(Tampa 134)	1.00	4.00	
ANSWER ME, MY LOVE/Why	(Capitol 2687)	1.25	5.00	53
ASK ME/Nothing Ever Changes My Love For You	(Capitol 3328)	1.00	4.00	56
BALLAD OF CAT BALLOU, THE/They Can't Make Her Cry	(Capitol 5412)	.75	3.00	65
(With Stubby Kaye)				
BALLERINA/You Are My First Love	(Capitol 3619)	1.00	4.00	56
BECAUSE YOU'RE MINE/Never Satisfied	(Capitol 2212)	1.25	5.00	52
BLOSSOM FELL, A/If I May (With the Four Knights)	(Capitol 3095)	1.25	5.00	55
CAN'T I/Blue Gardenia	(Capitol 2389)	1.25	5.00	53
CHRISTMAS SONG, THE (MERRY CHRISTMAS TO YOU)/ My Two Front Teeth	(Capitol 90036)	1.50	6.00	50
(With the King Cole Trio)				
CHRISTMAS SONG, THE (MERRY CHRISTMAS TO YOU)/ My Two Front Teeth	(Capitol 2955)	1.25	5.00	54
(With the King Cole Trio)				
CHRISTMAS SONG, THE (MERRY CHRISTMAS TO YOU)/ The Little Boy That Santa Claus Forgot	(Capitol 3561)	.75	3.00	56
(Originally released in 1946 on 78 rpm, Capitol 311, this perennial favorite was assigned a 45 rpm number in 1950, Capitol 90036. The same two sides were reissued in 1954, Capitol 2955, and in 1956 with a new number, Capitol 3561, and flip side.)				
COME CLOSER TO ME/Nothing In The World	(Capitol 4004)	1.00	4.00	58
DARLING JE VOUS AIME BEAUCOUP/ The Sand & The Sea	(Capitol 3027)	1.00	4.00	55
DEAR LONELY HEARTS/Who's Next In Line	(Capitol 4870)	.75	3.00	62
FORGIVE MY HEART/Someone You Love	(Capitol 3234)	1.00	4.00	55
HAJJI BABA/Unbelievable	(Capitol 2949)	1.25	5.00	54
I DON'T WANT TO BE HURT ANY MORE/People	(Capitol 5155)	.75	3.00	64
IF I KNEW/World In My Arms	(Capitol 4481)	.75	3.00	60
JET/Magic Tree	(Capitol 1365)	1.25	5.00	51
LONG LONG AGO/Open Up The Doghouse	(Capitol 2985)	1.25	5.00	54
(With Dean Martin)				
LOOKING BACK/Do I Like It	(Capitol 3939)	1.00	4.00	58
L-O-V-E/I Don't Want To See Tomorrow	(Capitol 5261)	.75	3.00	65
MIDNIGHT FLYER/Sweet Bird Of Youth	(Capitol 4248)	1.00	4.00	59
MONA LISA/Greatest Inventor	(Capitol 1010)	1.25	5.00	50
MY ONE SIN/Blues (From "Kiss Me Deadly")	(Capitol 3136)	1.00	4.00	55
MY TRUE CARRIE, LOVE/Rag A Bone & A Hank Of Hair	(Capitol 5125)	.75	3.00	64
NIGHT LIGHTS/To The Ends Of The Earth	(Capitol 3551)	1.00	4.00	56
NON DIMENTICAR/Bend A Little My Way	(Capitol 4056)	1.00	4.00	58
ORANGE COLORED SKY/Jambo (with Stan Kenton Trio)	(Capitol 1184)	1.25	5.00	50
PRETEND/Don't Let Your Eyes Go Shopping	(Capitol 2346)	1.25	5.00	52
RAMBLIN' ROSE/The Good Times	(Capitol 4804)	.75	3.00	62
RED SAILS IN THE SUNSET/Little Child	(Capitol 1468)	1.25	5.00	51
RUBY & THE PEARL, THE/Faith Can Move Mountains	(Capitol 2230)	1.25	5.00	52
SEND FOR ME/My Personal Possession	(Capitol 3737)	1.00	4.00	57
SMILE/It's Crazy	(Capitol 2897)	1.25	5.00	54
SOMEWHERE ALONG THE WAY/What Does It Take	(Capitol 2069)	1.25	5.00	52
TAKE ME BACK TO TOYLAND/ I'm Gonna Laugh You Right Out Of My Life	(Capitol 3305)	1.00	4.00	55
THAT SUNDAY, THAT SUMMER/Mr. Wishing Well	(Capitol 5027)	.75	3.00	63
THAT'S ALL THERE IS TO THAT/My Dream Sonata	(Capitol 3456)	1.00	4.00	56
(With the Four Knights)				
THOSE LAZY, HAZY, CRAZY, DAYS OF SUMMER/ In The Cool Of The Day	(Capitol 4965)	.75	3.00	63
TOO YOUNG/That's My Girl	(Capitol 1449)	1.25	5.00	51
TOO YOUNG TO GO STEADY/Never Let Me Go	(Capitol 3390)	1.00	4.00	56
TOYS FOR TOTS/Toys For Tots	(Capitol 17965)	1.25	5.00	
(Public service promotional issue)				
UNFORGETTABLE/You're My First & Last Love	(Capitol 1808)	1.25	5.00	51
WALKIN' MY BABY BACK HOME/Funny	(Capitol 2130)	1.25	5.00	52
WHEN ROCK & ROLL CAME TO TRINIDAD/China Gate	(Capitol 3702)	1.00	4.00	57
WITH YOU ON MY MIND/Raintree County	(Capitol 3782)	1.00	4.00	57
COLE, Sonny, & Rhythm Roamers				
I DREMPT I WAS ELVIS/Curfue Cops	(Roll N' Rock 001)	2.00	8.00	
COLL, Brian, & The Plattermen				
I'M IN LOVE AGAIN/I'll Take You Home Again Kathleen	(Parrot 10818)	.75	3.00	66
COLLAGE				
ANYDAY'S A SUNDAY AFTERNOON/Driftin'	(Smash 2150)	.75	3.00	68
STORY OF ROCK & ROLL, THE/ Virginia Day's Ragtime Stories	(Smash 2170)	.75	3.00	68
COLLAY & HIS SATELLITES				
LAST CHANCE/Little Girl Next Door	(Sho Biz 1002)	.75	3.00	
COLLECTION				
AQUARIOUS/Paper Crown Of Gold	(RCA Victor 47-9463)	1.00	4.00	68
BOTH SIDES NOW/Tomorrow Is A Window	(Hot Biscuit Company 1455)	1.00	4.00	68
COLLECTORS, The				
LYDIA PURPLE/She (Will-o' The Wind)	(Warner Bros. 7194)	.75	3.00	68
COLLEGIANS, The				
I'M READY/Grandma Told Me So	(Post 10002)	.75	3.00	62
RIGHT AROUND THE CORNER/Teenie Weenie Little Bit	(Winley 263)	1.50	6.00	61
TONITE OH TONITE/Oh I Need Your Love	(Winley 261)	1.50	6.00	61
ZOOM ZOOM ZOOM/On Your Merry Way	(Winley 224)	1.50	6.00	57
COLLEGIATES, The				
I HAD A DREAM/Growing Up	(Heritage 105)	2.00	8.00	61
COLLEY, Keith				
ENAMORADO/No Joke	(Unical 3006)	.75	3.00	63
ENAMORADO/Shame Shame Shame	(Columbia 4-44410)	.50	2.00	68
QUERIDITA MIA (LITTLE DARLING)/Ramblin' Bee	(Unical 3011)	.75	3.00	63
SCARLET/Put 'Em Down	(Era 3067)	1.00	4.00	60
ZING, WENT THE STRINGS OF MY HEART/ It's Nice Out Tonight	(Era 3054)	1.00	4.00	61
COLLINS, Dave & Ansell				
DOUBLE BARREL/Double Barrel (Instrumental)	(Big Tree 115)	.50	2.00	
MONKEY SPANNER/Minkey Spanner (Version Two)	(Big Tree 125)	.50	2.00	
COLLINS, Dorothy				
BACIARE BACIARE/In The Good Old Days	(Top Rank 2024)	.75	3.00	59
BANJO BOY/Happy Heart Of Paris	(Top Rank 2052)	.75	3.00	60
MY BOY FLAT TOP/In Love	(Coral 61510)	1.00	4.00	55
SEVEN DAYS/Manuello	(Coral 61562)	1.00	4.00	55

TITLE/FLIP	LABEL & NO.	GOOD	NEAR MINT	YR.
COLLINS, Judy				
AMAZING GRACE/Nightingale 1	(Elektra 45709)	.50	2.00	70
ANGEL SPREAD YOUR WINGS/ The Moon Is A Harsh Mistress	(Elektra 45289)	.50	2.00	75
BOTH SIDE NOW (CLOUDS)/ Who Knows Where The Time Goes	(Elektra 45639)	.75	3.00	68
BREAD & ROSES/Out Of Control	(Elektra 45355)	.50	2.00	76
CHELSEA MORNING/Pretty Polly	(Elektra 45657)	.75	3.00	69
COOK WITH HONEY/So Begins The Task	(Elektra 45831)	.50	2.00	73
EVERYTHING MUST CHANGE/Special Delivery	(Elektra 45372)	.50	2.00	76
HARD LOVIN' LOSER/	(Elektra 45610)	.75	3.00	67
HARD TIMES FOR LOVERS/Happy End	(Elektra 46020)	.50	2.00	79
HOSTAGE, THE/Che	(Elektra JC-3)	.50	2.00	73
I'LL KEEP IT WITH MINE/Thirsty Boots	(Elektra 45601)	.75	3.00	66
IN MY LIFE/Sunny Goodge Street	(Elektra 45813)	.50	2.00	72
OPEN THE DOOR (SONG FOR JUDITH)/Innisfree	(Elektra 45755)	.50	2.00	71
SECRET GARDENS/	(Elektra 45849)	.50	2.00	73
SEND IN THE CLOWNS/Houses	(Elektra 45253)	.50	2.00	75
SOMEDAY SOON/My Father	(Elektra 45649)	.75	3.00	69
SPECIAL DELIVERY/Born To The Bread	(Elektra 45415)	.50	2.00	77
SUZANNE/Someday Soon	(Elektra 45791)	.50	2.00	72
TURN! TURN! TURN! (TO EVERYTHING THERE IS A SEASON)/ Pack Up Your Sorrows	(Elektra 45680)	.75	3.00	69
WHERE OR WHEN/Dorothy	(Elektra 46050)	.50	2.00	79

TITLE/FLIP	LABEL & NO.	GOOD	NEAR MINT	YR.
COLLOM, Tookie				
I COULD LOVE YOU/You Torture Me	(Holiday Inn 101)	.75	3.00	
(With the Roller Coasters)				
COLONIALS, The				
LITTLE MISS MUFFET/Do Pop Si	(Tru-Lite 127)	5.00	20.00	
COLORING BOOK, The				
YOU MAKE ME FEEL SO GOOD/Smoke Stack Lightnin'	(Challenger 118)	1.00	4.00	
COLOURS, The				
BROTHER LOU'S LOVE COLONY/Brother Lou's Love Colony	(Dot 17060)	1.00	4.00	68
GOD PLEASE TAKE MY LIFE/Angie	(Dot 17280)	1.00	4.00	69
HYANNISPORT SOUL/Run Away From Here	(Dot 17181)	1.00	4.00	69
LOVE HEALS/Bad Day At Black Rock Baby	(Dot 17132)	1.00	4.00	68
COLTON, Tony, & The Concords				
GOODBYE CINDY GOODBYE/Tell The World	(Roulette 4475)	1.25	5.00	63
COL. SPLENDID				
EMPEROR HUDSON/Blue-Eyed Blast	(Lucky Token 1003)	1.00	4.00	65
EMPEROR NELSON/Cavendish Caper	(Lucky Token 1006)	1.00	4.00	65
In 1965, Bob Hudson & Gene Nelson were dee jays at KRLA, Los Angeles, & KYA, San Francisco, respectively. Both used the title "Emperor" on their shows. Bob Hudson went on to join Ron Landry both on the air and on record as "Hudson & Landry."				
COLTRANE, Chi				
GO LIKE ELIJAH/It's Really Come To This	(Columbia 4-45749)	.50	2.00	72
THUNDER & LIGHTNING/Time To Come In	(Columbia 4-45640)	.50	2.00	72
YOU WERE MY FRIEND/	(Columbia 4-45802)	.50	2.00	73
WHAT'S HAPPENING TO ME/	(Clouds 10)	.50	2.00	78
COLT, Steve, & The 45's				
DYNAMITE/Take Away	(Big Beat 1006)	1.25	5.00	
HEY GIRL, HOW YA GONNA ACT/I've Been Loving You	(Big Beat 1001)	1.25	5.00	
JUST A LITTLE BIT OF SOUL/So Far Away	(RCA Victor 47-8913)	1.00	4.00	66
COLUMBO, Chris, (Quintet)				
SUMMERTIME/Minerology	(Strand 25056)	.75	3.00	63
YOU CAN'T SIT DOWN/Stranger On The Shore	(Battle 45904)	.75	3.00	63
Instrumentals				
COLUMBUS, Ray, & The Invaders				
I WANNA BE YOUR MAN/Cat's Eye	(Philips 40189)	1.00	4.00	64
I WOULD RATHER BLOW A BAGPIPE/ In The Morning Of Today	(Colstar 1003)	.75	3.00	67
KICK ME/She's A Mod	(Colstar 1001)	.75	3.00	67
SHE'S A MOD/The Cruel Sea	(Philips 40340)	1.00	4.00	64
WHERE HAVE YOU BEEN/She's Back	(Philips 40326)	1.00	4.00	65
COMIC BOOKS, The				
MAUNUEL/Black Magic & Witchcraft	(New Phoenix 6199)	8.75	35.00	
MAUNUEL/Black Magic & Witchcraft	(Citation 5001)	6.25	25.00	
COMICS, The				
CALLING DADDY WARBUCKS/	(Minaret 152)	1.00	4.00	69
COMMANCHES, The				
TOMORROW/Missed Your Lovin'	(Hickory 1264)	.75	3.00	64
COMMITTEE, The				
CALIFORNIA MY WAY/You For Weren't It If	(White Whale 257)	1.50	6.00	67
COMMUNICATION AGGREGATION, The				
FREAK-OUT U.S.A./Off The Wall	(RCA Victor 47-8930)	1.00	4.00	66
COMO, Nicky				
YOUR GUARDIAN ANGEL/Just A Little While	(Tang 1231)	2.00	8.00	
(With The Del Satins)				
COMO, Perry				
ALL AT ONCE YOU LOVE HER/The Rose Tatoo	(RCA Victor 47-6294)	1.00	4.00	55
BIBBIDI-BOBBIDI-BOO/ A Dream Is A Wish Your Heart Makes	(RCA Victor 47-3607)	1.50	6.00	49
(With The Fontane Sisters)				

TITLE/FLIP — LABEL & NO. — GOOD — NEAR MINT — YR.

BUSHEL & A PECK, A/She's Woman (RCA Victor 47-3930) 1.50 6.00 50
(With Betty Hutton)
CATCH A FALLING STAR/Magic Moments (RCA Victor 47-7128) 1.00 4.00 57
CATERINA/Island Of Forgotten Lovers (RCA Victor 47-8004) .75 3.00 62
CHEE CHEE-OO CHEE/Two Lost Souls (RCA Victor 47-6137) 1.00 4.00 55
(With Jaye P. Morgan)
DANCIN'/Marchin Along To The Blues (RCA Victor 47-6991) 1.00 4.00 57
DELAWARE/I Know What God Is (RCA Victor 47-7670) .75 3.00 60
DELAWARE/I Know What God Is (RCA Victor 61-7670) 1.50 6.00 60
(Stereo single issue)
DON'T LET THE STARS GET IN YOUR EYES/Lies (RCA Victor 47-5064) 1.25 5.00 52
GIRL WITH THE GOLDEN BRAIDS, THE/
My Little Baby (RCA Victor 47-6904) 1.00 4.00 57
HIT & RUN AFFAIR/
There Never Was A Night So Beautiful (RCA Victor 47-5749) 1.25 5.00 54
HOME FOR THE HOLIDAYS/
God Rest Ye Merry Gentlemen (RCA Victor 47-5950) 1.25 5.00 54
HOOP-DEE-DOO/On The Outgoing Tide (RCA Victor 47-3747) 1.50 6.00 50
(With The Fontane Sisters)
HOT DIGGITY/Juke Box Baby (RCA Victor 47-6427) 1.00 4.00 56
I CROSS MY FINGERS/If You Were My Girl (RCA Victor 47-3846) 1.50 6.00 50
(With The Fontane Sisters)
I KNOW/You Are In Love (RCA Victor 47-7541) .75 3.00 59
I KNOW/You Are In Love (RCA Victor 61-7541) 1.50 6.00 59
(Stereo single issue)
(I LOVE YOU) DON'T YOU FORGET IT/
One More Mountain (RCA Victor 47-8186) .75 3.00 63
IF/Zing Zing Zoom Zoom (RCA Victor 47-3997) 1.25 5.00 50
IT'S BEGINNING TO LOOK A LOT LIKE CHRISTMAS/
There Is No Christmas (RCA Victor 47-4314) 1.25 5.00 51
(With The Fontane Sisters)
JUST BORN/Ivy Rose (RCA Victor 47-7050) 1.00 4.00 57
KEWPIE DOLL/Dance Only With Me (RCA Victor 47-7202) 1.00 4.00 58
KO KO MO/You'll Always Be My Love (RCA Victor 47-5994) 1.25 5.00 54
LOVE MAKES THE WORLD GO ROUND/
Mandolins In The Moonlight (RCA Victor 47-7353) 1.00 4.00 58
LOVE MAKES THE WORLD GO ROUND/
Mandolins In The Moonlight (RCA Victor 61-7353) 1.50 6.00 58
(Stereo single issue)
MAKE SOMEONE HAPPY/Gone Is My Love (RCA Victor 47-7812) .75 3.00 60
MAYBE/Watermelon Weather (RCA Victor 47-4744) 1.25 5.00 51
(With Eddie Fisher)
MOON TALK/Beats There A Heart So True (RCA Victor 47-7274) 1.00 4.00 58
MOONLIGHT LOVE/Chincherinchee (RCA Victor 47-6670) 1.00 4.00 56
MORE/Glendora (RCA Victor 47-6554) 1.00 4.00 56
MY DAYS OF LOVIN' YOU/Yesterday I Heard The Rain (RCA 74-0518) .50 2.00 71
NO OTHER LOVE/Keep It Gay (RCA Victor 47-5317) 1.25 5.00 53
PAPA LOVES MAMBO/The Things I Didn't Do (RCA Victor 47-5857) 1.25 5.00 54
PATRICIA/Watchin' The Train Go By (RCA Victor 47-3905) 1.50 6.00 50
ROUND & ROUND/Mi Casa, Su Casa (RCA Victor 47-6815) 1.00 4.00 57
SAY YOU'RE MINE AGAIN/My One & Only Heart (RCA Victor 47-5277) 1.25 5.00 53
SEATTLE/Sunshine Wine (RCA 47-9722) .50 2.00 69
SOMEBODY UP THERE LIKES ME/
Dream Along With Me (RCA Victor 47-6590) 1.00 4.00 56
THERE'S A BIG BLUE CLOUD/There's No Boat (RCA Victor 47-4158) 1.25 5.00 51
TINA MARIE/Fooled (RCA Victor 47-6192) 1.00 4.00 55
TOMBOY/Kiss Me & Kiss Me & Kiss Me (RCA Victor 47-7464) 1.00 4.00 59
TOMBOY/Kiss Me & Kiss Me & Kiss Me (RCA Victor 61-7464) 1.50 6.00 59
(Stereo single issue)
TULIPS & HEATHER/Please Mr. Sun (RCA Victor 47-4453) 1.25 5.00 52
WANTED/Look Out The Window (RCA Victor 47-5647) 1.25 5.00 54
WILD HORSES/I Confess (RCA Victor 47-5152) 1.25 5.00 53
YOU ALONE/Pa-Pa-Ya Mama (RCA Victor 47-5447) 1.25 5.00 53
YOU'RE FOLLOWING ME/Especially For The Young (RCA Victor 47-7962) .75 3.00 61
YOU'RE JUST IN LOVE/It's A Lonely Day Today (RCA Victor 47-3945) 1.50 6.00 50
(With The Fontane Sisters)

COMPANIONS, The
I'LL ALWAYS LOVE YOU/A Little Bit Of Blue (Columbia 4-42279) 2.50 10.00 62
IT'S TOO LATE/These Foolish Things (Gina 722) 2.00 8.00 63
ITS TOO LATE/These Foolish Things (Arlen 722) 1.00 4.00 63
NO FOOL AM I/How Could You (Amy 852) 1.50 6.00 63

COMPANIONS, The
I DIDN'T KNOW/Why Oh Why Baby (Brooks 100) 3.75 15.00

COMPETITORS, The
LITTLE STICK NOMAD/Power Shift (Dot 16560) 1.00 4.00 63

COMRADE X
SPACENIK/Theme From Spacenik (Era 3048) 1.25 5.00 61

COMSTOCK, Bobby (With The Counts)
BEATLE BOUNCE, THE/Since You Been Gone (Lawn 229) 1.25 5.00 64
BONY MORONIE/Do That Little Thing (Jubilee 5392) 1.00 4.00 60
EVERYDAY BLUES/The Wayward Wind (Mohawk 124) .75 3.00 61
GARDEN OF EDEN, THE/Just A Piece Of Paper (Festival 25000) 1.00 4.00 61
I CAN'T HELP MYSELF/Run My Heart (Lawn 224) .75 3.00 63
JAMBALAYA/Let's Talk It Over (Atlantic 2051) 1.00 4.00 60
JEALOUS FOOL/Zig Zag (Triumph 602) 1.25 5.00 59
JEZEBEL/Your Big Brown Eyes (Jubilee 5396) 1.00 4.00 60
LET'S STOMP/I Want To Do It (Lawn 202) 1.00 4.00 62
SUNNY/Chicken Back (Lawn 217) 1.00 4.00 63
SUSIE BABY/Take A Walk (Lawn 210) 1.00 4.00 63
TENNESSEE WALTZ/Sweet Talk (Blaze 349) 1.00 4.00 59
YOUR BIG BROWN EYES/Jezebel (Jubilee 5396) 1.00 4.00 61
YOUR BIG FRIEND'S BACK/This Little Love Of Mine (Lawn 219) 1.00 4.00 63

CONCORDS, The
AGAIN/The Boy Most Likely (RCA Victor 47-7911) 1.25 5.00 61
COLD & FROSTY MORNING/Don't Go Now (Herald 578) 2.00 8.00 62
CROSS MY HEART/Our Last Goodbye (Gramercy 304) 1.25 5.00 61
DOWN THE ISLE OF LOVE/I Feel A Love Comin' On (Boom 60021) 2.50 10.00 66
DOWN THE ISLE OF LOVE/I Feel A Love Comin' On (Polydor 14036) 1.25 5.00 70
MARLENE/Our Love Wasn't Meant To Be (Herald 576) 1.25 5.00 62
MY DREAMS/Scarlet Ribbons (Gramercy 305) 1.25 5.00 62
ONE STEP FROM HEAVEN/Away (Rust 5048) 2.00 8.00 62
SHOULD I CRY/It's Our Wedding Day (Epic 9697) 3.75 15.00 64
Also see Lisa & The Lullabies
Also see Lisi, Ricky
Also see Roberts, Wayne
Also see Scott, Neil
Also see Sherwoods, The
Also see Snowmen, The

CONEY ISLAND KIDS, The
POP CORN & CANDY/Not You Pie Face (Josie 809) 1.50 6.00 56

CONFESSIONS, The
BE BOP BABY/Before You Change Your Mind (Epic 9474) 1.00 4.00 61

CONIGLIARO, Tony
POETRY/Midnight In Boston (Magna-Glide 5N-326) .50 2.00 75

CONLAN & THE CRAWLERS (Featuring Chuck Conlan)
I WON'T TELL/ (Marlin 16006) 1.00 4.00
Also see Nightcrawlers, The

CONNELL, Doug, & The Hot Rods
ON OUR WAY FROM SCHOOL/You're My Girl (Alton 600) 1.50 6.00

CONNIE & THE BELLHOPS
BOP STICKS/Shot Rod (Our 505) .75 3.00

CONNIE & THE CONES
I LOVE MY TEDDY BEAR/Lonely Girl's Prayer (Roulette 4223) .75 3.00 60
I SEE THE IMAGE OF YOU/Let Us Pretend (NRC 5006) .75 3.00 59
TAKE ALL THE KISSES/No Time For Tears (Roulette 4313) .75 3.00 61

CONNIFF, Ray, Singers
INVISIBLE TEARS/Singing The Blues (Columbia 4-43061) .75 3.00 64
MIDNIGHT LACE (PART 1)/Midnight Lace (Part 2) (Columbia 4-41800) .75 3.00 60
MIDNIGHT LACE (PART 1)/Midnight Lace (Part 2) (Columbia 3-41800) 1.25 5.00 60
(Compact 33 single)
OKLAHOMA/On The Street Where You Live (Columbia 4-41349) .75 3.00 59
SOMEWHERE MY LOVE/Midsummer In Sweden (Columbia 4-43626) .75 3.00 66
'S WONDERFUL/Say It With Music (Columbia 4-40827) .75 3.00 57

CONNOLY, Robert
COMPLACENT AMERICANS, THE/ (Cee Dee CA-45) .75 3.00

CONNOR, Chris
CIRCUS/Flying Home (Atlantic 2017) .75 3.00 59
I CONCENTRATE ON YOU/A Lot Of Livin' To Do (F.M. 3002) .75 3.00 63
I MISS YOU SO/My Heart Is So Full Of You (Atlantic 1105) .75 3.00 56
MISTY/Senor Blues (Atlantic 2037) .75 3.00 59
THAT'S MY DESIRE/I Only Want Some (Atlantic 2053) .75 3.00 60
THROUGH THE TEENAGE YEARS/Summertime (Atlantic 5014) .75 3.00 61
TRUST IN ME/Mixed Emotions (Atlantic 1138) .75 3.00 57

CONNORS, Carol (Of The Teddy Bears)
I WANNA KNOW/Tommy Go Away (Era 3096) .75 3.00 62
LISTEN TO THE BEAT/My Special Boy (Columbia 4-42155) 1.25 5.00 61
LISTEN TO THE BEAT/My Special Boy (Columbia 3-42155) 2.50 10.00 61
(Compact 33 single)
LONELY LITTLE BEACH GIRL/My Baby (Mira 219) .75 3.00 66
TWO RIVERS/Big, Big Love (Era 3084) .75 3.00 62
WHAT DO YOU SEE IN HIM/That's All It Takes (Columbia 4-42337) 1.25 5.00 62
WHAT DO YOU SEE IN HIM/That's All It Takes (Columbia 3-42337) 2.50 10.00 62
(Compact 33 single)
YOU ARE MY ANSWER/My Diary (Columbia 4-41976) 1.25 5.00 61
YOU ARE MY ANSWER/My Diary (Columbia 3-41976) 2.50 10.00 61
(Compact 33 single)

CONNORS, Gregg
CAUGHT IN THE ACT/Your Love Tears Me Up (Trey 3003) 1.00 4.00 60

CONNOTATIONS, The
TWO HEARTS FALL IN LOVE/Before I Go (Technichord 1000) 2.50 10.00

CONQUERORS, The
BILLY IS MY BOY FRIEND/Duchess Conquers Duke (Lupine 108) 7.50 30.00 62

CONNY
THIS LITTLE GIRL'S GONE ROCKIN'/Midi, Midinette (Capitol 4526) 1.00 4.00 61

CONRAD & HURRICANE STRINGS
HURRICANE/Sweet Love (Daytone 6401) 1.25 5.00 64
HURRICANE/Sweet Love (Era 3130) .75 3.00 64

CONRAD, Bob
BYE, BYE BABY/Love You (Warner Bros. 5242) .75 3.00 61

CONROY, Bert, & The Misfits
DEBBIE/That Old Gang Of Mine (Deb-co 1000) 2.00 8.00

CONSORTS, The (Featuring Bruce Laurent)
PLEASE BE MINE/Time After Time (Cousins 1004) 7.50 30.00 61
PLEASE BE MINE/Time After Time (Apt 25066) 1.50 6.00 61
Also see Chuckles, The
Also see 4 Clefs, The

CONSPIRATORS, The
WATERLOO '73/ (Sunday 1291) 1.00 4.00 73

CONTENDERS, The
DUNE BUGGY, THE/Go Ahead (Chattahoochee 644) 1.00 4.00 64
JOHNNY B. GOODE/Rise & Shine (Chattahoochee 656) 1.00 4.00 64
MR. DEE JAY/Yes I Do (Blue Sky 105) 1.00 4.00 59

CONTINENTAL MINIATURES, The
STAY AWHILE/Glad All Over (London 266) .50 2.00 78

CONTINENTAL ROCKERS, The
FLASHBACK/Heat Wave (Nimbo 1774) 1.00 4.00 64

CONTINENTALS, The
CATHY'S CLOWN/Maybe Baby (Lifetime 1019) .75 3.00 66

CONTINENTELS, The
COFFEE HOUSE/Big Bad Ho-Dad (By Lord Douglas Byron) (Union 505) 1.00 4.00 62

CONTINO, Dick
LADY OF SPAIN/Squeeze Box Boogie (Mercury 70420) 1.25 5.00 54
PLEDGE OF LOVE/Two Loves Have I (Mercury 71079) .75 3.00 57
SILVER BELLS/Jing A Ling (RCA Victor 47-3940) 1.25 5.00 50
TWILIGHT TIME/Mexicali Rose (Mercury 70911) 1.00 4.00 56
YOURS/Adios (Mercury 70455) 1.00 4.00 54

CONTRABAND
EVERYTHING HAS GOT TO BE FREE/Sweet Lady Ms (RCA 0913) .50 2.00 73
GOIN' DOWN/Once Before I Die (RCA 74-0831) .50 2.00 72

CONTRABAND
THAT'S YOUR WAY/Leave The Killing To You (Portrait 70021) .50 2.00 78

CONTRAILS, The
FEEL SO FINE/Make Me Love You (Millage 104) 1.00 4.00
SOMEONE/Mummy Walk (Diamond 213) 1.00 4.00 66

CONVY, Bert, & The Cheers: see Cheers, The

COODER, Ry
AVAILABLE SPACE/ (Reprise 0910) .75 3.00 69
LIFE GAME/1983 (Musicor 1148) 1.00 4.00 66
MONEY HONEY/Billy The Kid (Reprise 1071) .50 2.00 72
MONEY HONEY/Billy The Kid (Reprise Pro-514) 1.00 4.00 72
(Promotional issue only)

COOK E. JARR: see Jarr, Cook E.

COOK, Ira
WHAT IS A BOY?/What Is A Girl? (Imperial 5627) 1.00 4.00 59

COOK, Jack
RUN BOY, RUN BOY/I Got A Book (Ramco 1739) 1.00 4.00 62
WALK ANOTHER MILE/My Evil Mind (Ruby 1) 1.00 4.00 63
WALK ANOTHER MILE/My Evil Mind (Ramco 1721) .75 3.00 62

COOK, Peter, & Dudley Moore
BEDAZZLED/Love Me (Parrot 3016) .75 3.00 68

COOK, Roger (Of David & Jonathan)
IF IT WASN'T FOR THE REASON/ (Kama Sutra 571) .50 2.00 73
SWEET AMERICA/ (Kama Sutra 554) .50 2.00 72
WHAT'S YOUR NAME, WHAT'S YOUR NUMBER/
Blue Day (Capricorn 0274) .50 2.00 77

COOKER
TRY (TRY TO FALL IN LOVE)/The Ah-Ah Song (Scepter 12388) .50 2.00 74

COOKIE MONSTER
"C" IS FOR COOKIE/ (Columbia 4-45943) .50 2.00 73

COOKIE & THE CRUMBS
MY DREAM OF YOU/Someday Baby (Vest 55) .75 3.00 66

COOKIES, The
ALL MY TRIALS/Wounded (Warner Bros. 7025) .75 3.00 67
MRS. CUPID/ (Warner Bros. 7047) .75 3.00 67

COOKIES, The (Featuring Earl-Jean McCree)
CHAINS/Stranger In My Arms (Dimension 1002) .75 3.00 62
DON'T SAY NOTHIN' BAD (ABOUT MY BABY)/
Softly In The Night (Dimension 1008) .75 3.00 63
GIRLS GROW UP FASTER THAN BOYS/
Only To Other People (Dimension 1020) .75 3.00 63
I NEVER DREAMED/The Old Crowd (Dimension 1032) 1.00 4.00 64
WILL POWER/I Want A Boy For My Birthday (Dimension 1012) .75 3.00 63

COOL, Calvin
BEACH BASH/El Tetolote (Charter 7) 1.00 4.00 63

COOLEY, Eddie (& The Dimples)
DRIFTWOOD/A Spark Met A Flame (Royal Roost 626) 1.00 4.00 57
HEY YOU/Pull, Pull (Royal Roost 628) 1.00 4.00 57
LEONA/Be My Steady (Triumph 609) .75 3.00
PRISCILLA/Got A Little Woman (Royal Roost 621) 1.00 4.00 56
PRISCILLA/A Spark Met A Flame (Roulette 4272) .75 3.00 60

COOLIDGE, Rita
CRAZY LOVE/Mountains (A&M 1271) .50 2.00 71
FAMILY FULL OF SOUL/Most Likely You Go Your Way (A&M 1353) .50 2.00 72
FEVER/My Crew (A&M 1398) .50 2.00 72
FROM THE BOTTLE TO THE BOTTOM/Song I'd Like To Sing (A&M 1475) .50 2.00 73
HEAVEN'S DREAM/Love Has No Pride (A&M 1642) .50 2.00 74
HIGHER & HIGHER (YOUR LOVE HAS LIFTED ME)/
Who's To Bless & Who's To Blame (A&M 1922) .50 2.00 77
HOLD AN OLD FRIEND'S HAND/Mama Lou (A&M 1545) .50 2.00 74
I BELIEVE IN YOU/Mud Island (A&M 1256) .50 2.00 71
I'D RATHER LEAVE WHILE I'M IN LOVE/Sweet Emotion (A&M 2199) .50 2.00 79
KEEP THE CANDLE BURNING/Late Again (A&M 1816) .50 2.00 76
NICE FEELIN'/Lay My Burden Down (A&M 1324) .50 2.00 72
ONE FINE DAY/Sweet Emotion (A&M 2169) .50 2.00 79
RAINBOW CHILD/Secret Places, Hiding Faces (Pepper 442) .75 3.00 68
STAR/Am I Blue (A&M 1792) .50 2.00 76
TURN AROUND & LOVE YOU/Walkin' In The Mornin' (Pepper 443) .75 3.00 69
WAY YOU DO THE THINGS YOU DO, THE/
I Feel The Burden (Being Lifted Off My Shoulders) (A&M 2004) .50 2.00 77
WE'RE ALL ALONE/Southern Lady (A&M 1965) .50 2.00 77
WHISKEY, WHISKEY/Donut Man (A&M 1414) .50 2.00 73
YOU/Only You Know & I Know (A&M 2058) .50 2.00 78

COOLIDGE, Rita & Kris Kristofferson
I'M DOWN/Loving Arms (A&M 1498) .50 2.00 74
LOVER PLEASE/Slow Down (Monument ZS8-8636) .50 2.00 75
RAIN/Wat'cha Gonna Do (Monument ZS8-8630) .50 2.00 74
SWEET SUSANNAH/We Must Have Been Out Of Our Minds (ZS8-8646) .50 2.00 75

COOLIDGE-JONES, Priscilla
IF YOU DON'T WANT MY LOVE/You Got Me Spinnin' (Capricorn 0329) .50 2.00 79
Priscilla is Rita Coolidge's sister and the wife of Booker T. Jones.

COOL-TONES, The
DIXIE BLUES, THE/Daylight In Dixie (Radiant 1510) .75 3.00
GINCHY/Movin' Out (Warwick 505) .75 3.00 59
(Instrumentals)

COOPER, Alice
BE MY LOVER/Yeah, Yeah, Yeah (Warner Bros. 7568) .75 3.00 72
BE MY LOVER (Stereo)/Be My Lover (Mono) (Warner Bros. 7568) 1.25 5.00 72
(Promotional issue)
BILLION DOLLAR BABIES/Mary Ann (Warner Bros. 7724) .75 3.00 73
BILLION DOLLAR BABIES (Stereo)/
Billion Dollar Babies (Mono) (Warner Bros. 7724) 1.25 5.00 73
(Promotional issue)
CAUGHT IN A DREAM/Hallowed Be My Name (Warner Bros. 7490) 1.00 4.00 71
CAUGHT IN A DREAM (Stereo)/
Caught In A Dream (Mono) (Warner Bros. 7490) 1.50 6.00 71
(Promotional issue)
CLONES (WE'RE ALL)/Model Citizen (Warner Bros. 49204) .50 2.00 80
CLONES (WE'RE ALL) (Stereo)/
Clones (We're All) (Mono) (Warner Bros. 49204) 1.00 4.00 80
(Promotional issue)
CLONES (WE'RE ALL)/Model Citizen (Warner Bros. PRO-A-864) 2.00 8.00 80
(Promotional 12" single issue)
DEPARTMENT OF YOUTH/Some Folks (Atlantic 3280) .75 3.00 75
DEPARTMENT OF YOUTH (Stereo)/
Department Of Youth (Mono) (Atlantic 3280) 1.25 5.00 75
(Promotional issue)
EIGHTEEN/Body (Warner Bros. 7449) 1.00 4.00 70
EIGHTEEN/Body (Warner Bros. 7449) 1.50 6.00 70
(Promotional issue)
ELECTED/Luney Tune (Warner Bros. 7631) 1.00 4.00 72
ELECTED (Stereo)/Elected (Mono) (Warner Bros. 7631) 1.50 6.00 72
(Promotional issue)
FROM THE INSIDE/Nurse Rozetta (Warner Bros. 8760) .75 3.00 79
FROM THE INSIDE (Stereo)/From The Inside (Mono) (Warner Bros. 8760) 1.25 5.00 79
(Promotional issue)

TITLE/FLIP	LABEL & NO.	GOOD	NEAR MINT	YR.
HELLO HURRAY/Generation Landslide	(Warner Bros. 7673)	.75	3.00	73
HELLO HURRAY (Stereo)/Hello Hurray (Mono)	(Warner Bros. 7673)	1.50	6.00	73
(Promotional issue)				
HOW YOU GONNA SEE ME NOW/ No Tricks (With Betty Wright)	(Warner Bros. 8695)	1.25	5.00	78
("No Tricks" is the only singles' track that is not available on any LP.)				
HOW YOU GONNA SEE ME NOW (Stereo)/ How You Gonna See Me Now (Mono)	(Warner Bros. 8695)	1.50	6.00	78
(Promotional issue)				
I'M EIGHTEEN/Muscle Of Love	(Warner Bros. 8023)	.75	3.00	74
I'M EIGHTEEN (Stereo)/I'm Eighteen (Mono)	(Warner Bros. 8023)	1.00	4.00	74
(Promotional issue)				
I'M FLASH/Trapped (By Elkie Brooks)	(Chrysalis 2069)	3.00	12.00	75
(Promotional release, issued in England only)				
I NEVER CRY/Go To Hell	(Warner Bros. 8228)	.75	3.00	76
I NEVER CRY (Stereo)/I Never Cry (Mono)	(Warner Bros. 8228)	1.00	4.00	76
(Promotional issue)				
MUSCLE OF LOVE/Crazy Little Child	(Warner Bros. 7783)	.75	3.00	74
MUSCLE OF LOVE (Stereo)/Muscle Of Love (Mono)	(Warner Bros. 7783)	1.25	5.00	74
(Promotional issue)				
(NO MORE) LOVE AT YOUR CONVENIENCE/ I Never Wrote Those Songs	(Warner Bros. 8448)	.75	3.00	77
(NO MORE) LOVE AT YOUR CONVENIENCE/ I Never Wrote Those Songs	(Warner Bros. 8448)	1.00	4.00	77
(Promotional issue)				
NO MORE MR. NICE GUY/Raped & Freezin'	(Warner Bros. 7691)	.75	3.00	73
NO MORE MR. NICE GUY (Stereo)/ No More Mr. Nice Guy (Mono)	(Warner Bros. 7691)	1.25	5.00	73
(Promotional issue)				
ONLY WOMEN/Cold Ethyl	(Atlantic 3254)	.75	3.00	75
ONLY WOMEN (Stereo)/Only Women (Mono)	(Atlantic 3254)	1.00	4.00	75
(Promotional issue)				
REFLECTED/Living	(Straight 101)	2.50	10.00	69
SCHOOL'S OUT/Gutter Cat	(Warner Bros. 7596)	.75	3.00	72
SCHOOL'S OUT/Gutter Cat	(Warner Bros. 7596)	1.25	5.00	72
(Picture sleeve)				
SCHOOL'S OUT (Stereo)/School's Out (Mono)	(Warner Bros. 7596)	2.00	8.00	72
(Promotional issue)				
SCHOOL'S OUT (Live Version)/ School's Out (Studio Version)	(Warner Bros. 8607)	1.00	4.00	77
SHOE SALESMAN/Return Of The Spiders	(Straight 7398)	2.00	8.00	70
SHOE SALESMAN/Return Of The Spiders	(Warner Bros. 7398)	1.50	6.00	70
(Promotional issue)				
TALK TALK (Stereo)/Talk Talk (Mono)	(Warner Bros. 49526)	1.00	4.00	80
(As of press time this record was available only as a promotional issue)				
TEENAGE LAMENT '74/Hard Hearted Alice	(Warner Bros. 7762)	.75	3.00	73
TEENAGE LAMENT '74 (Stereo)/ Teenage Lament '74 (Mono)	(Warner Bros. 7762)	1.25	5.00	73
(Promotional issue)				
UNDER MY WHEELS/Desperado	(Warner Bros. 7529)	.75	3.00	71
("Desperado" is a tribute to Jim Morrison of the Doors)				
UNDER MY WHEELS/Desperado	(Warner Bros. 7529)	1.25	5.00	71
(Promotional issue)				
WELCOME TO MY NIGHTMARE/Cold Ethyl	(Atlantic 3298)	.75	3.00	75
WELCOME TO MY NIGHTMARE (Stereo)/ Welcome To My Nightmare (Mono)	(Atlantic 3298)	1.00	4.00	75
(Promotional issue)				
YOU AND ME/It's Hot Tonight	(Warner Bros. 8349)	.75	3.00	77
YOU AND ME (Stereo)/You And Me (Mono)	(Warner Bros. 8349)	1.00	4.00	77
(Promotional issue)				
From 1969 through 1974 releases were shown as by the Alice Cooper Group. After that, Alice Cooper became a solo artist.				
Also see Billion Dollar Babies, The				
Also see Frost				
Also see Nazz, The				
Also see Spiders				
COOPER BROTHERS, The				
AWAY FROM YOU/Portrait	(Capricorn 0315)	.50	2.00	79
DREAM NEVER DIES, THE/Crazy Sundays	(Capricorn 0308)	.50	2.00	78
I'LL KNOW HER WHEN I SEE HER/Heroes	(Capricorn 0325)	.50	2.00	79
ROCK & ROLL COWBOYS/Portrait	(Capricorn 0303)	.50	2.00	78
COOPER, Christine				
HEARTACHES AWAY MY BOY/A Bad Boy	(Parkway P-983)	.75	3.00	66
I MUST HAVE YOU OR NO ONE/Good Looks	(Parkway P-122)	.75	3.00	66
S.O.S. HEART IN DISTRESS/Say What You Feel	(Parkway P-971)	.75	3.00	66
COOPER, Johnny				
FLAME OF LOVE/Oreo	(Ermine E-44)	.75	3.00	63
LITTLE BRIDE/Dumb Dumb Bunny	(Ermine E-38)	.75	3.00	62
RIVALRY/I Found Love With You	(Ermine E-37)	.75	3.00	62
COOPER, Les, & The Soul Rockers				
GONNA HAVE A LOT OF FUN/Thank God For You	(Atco 6644)	.75	3.00	69
WAHOO/Skatin' With Bill	(Samar 114)	.75	3.00	66
WIGGLE WOBBLE/Dig Yourself	(Everlast 5019)	.75	3.00	62
(Instrumental)				
COPELAND, Ken				
PLEDGE OF LOVE/Night Air (By the Mints)	(Lin 5007)	2.00	8.00	57
PLEDGE OF LOVE/Night Air (By the Mints)	(Imperial 5432)	.75	3.00	57
TEENAGE/Bed Of Lies	(Imperial 5453)	.75	3.00	57
COPELAND, Tony				
PASSING OF A KING, THE/Rambler	(Arco 104)	.75	3.00	77
COPESETICS, The				
COLLEGIAN/Believe In Me	(Premium 409)	3.75	15.00	56
COPPERHEAD				
ROLLER DERBY STAR/Chameleon	(Columbia 45810)	.75	3.00	73
Some members of Quicksilver Messenger Service were in this band.				
COPPER PENNY				
DISCO QUEEN/	(Capitol 4090)	.50	2.00	75
SITTING ON A POOR MAN'S THRONE/Bad Manners	(Big Tree 16005)	.50	2.00	76
COPS 'N ROBBERS				
I COULD HAVE DANCED ALL NIGHT/Keep Right On	(Coral 62460)	.75	3.00	65
ST. JAMES INFIRMARY/There's Got To Be A Reason	(Parrot 9716)	.75	3.00	64
COPY CATS, The				
CHIEF SITTING BULL/Abominable Snow Man	(Prince 5061)	1.00	4.00	60
CHIEF SITTIN' BULL/Abominable Snow Man	(Rust 5024)	.75	3.00	60
(Answer song to "Mr. Custer")				
COQUETTES, The				
CREW CUT & BABY BLUE EYES/ That Naughty Waltz	(RCA Victor 47-6143)	1.25	5.00	55
CORALS, The				
MY BEST FRIEND/Dancin' & Cryin'	(Rayna 5010)	1.25	5.00	
CORBETTA, Jerry (Of Sugarloaf)				
BOOGIE MAN/I Got A Song	(Claridge 408)	.50	2.00	75
SENSITIVE SOUL/Caribbean Lady	(Warner Bros. 8672)	.50	2.00	78
YOU SET MY DREAMS TO MUSIC	(Claridge 415)	.50	2.00	78
CORBITT, Jerry (Of the Youngbloods)				
LOVE YOU ALL/Let The Music Come Inside	(Polydor 14016)	.75	3.00	71
CORDEL, Pat & The Crescents				
DARLING COME BACK/My My Tears	(Club 1011)	12.50	50.00	56
DARLING COME BACK/My My Tears	(Michele M-503)	2.50	10.00	59
(Reissue of Club 1011 but shown as by Pat Cordel & The Elegants.)				
DARLING COME BACK/My My Tears (Red plastic)	(Victory 1001)	1.50	6.00	61
(Previously issued on both Club & Michele, this time shown as by "Pat Cordel & The Crescents Later Known As The Elegants." Actually only Vito Picone & Carman Romano later became members of the Elegants.)				
CORDELL, Richie				
GEORGIANA/Better Lovin'	(Amy 882)	.75	3.00	64
I WISH IT COULD BE/Maybe, Baby, I'm Blue	(Street Car 400)	1.00	4.00	
THINKING OF YOU/Raindrops	(Street Car 101)	1.00	4.00	
TICK TOCK/Please Don't Tell Her	(Ron 707)	1.50	6.00	62
Also see Gentry, Bo, & Ritchie Cordell				
Also see Inner Lite, The				
CORDELLS, The				
BEAT OF MY HEART, THE/Laid Off	(Bargain 5004)	1.50	6.00	61
PLEASE DON'T GO/Believe In Me	(Bullseye 1017)	3.75	15.00	58
CORDIALLS, The				
OH HOW I LOVE HER/You Can't Believe In Love	(Liberty 55784)	1.25	5.00	65
CORDIALS, The				
DAWN IS ALMOST HERE/Keep An Eye	(7 Arts 707)	3.00	12.00	61
ETERNAL LOVE/The International Twist	(Reveille 106)	5.00	20.00	62
LISTEN MY HEART/My Heart's Desire	(Whip 276)	6.25	25.00	
ONCE IN A LIFETIME/What Kind Of Fool Am I	(Felsted 8653)	1.25	5.00	62
CORDING, Henry				
ROCK & ROLL MOPS/Hiccough Rock	(Columbia 4-40762)	1.25	5.00	57
(With Big Mike & His Parisian Rockets)				
CORDOVANS, The				
MY HEART/Come On Baby	(Johnson 731)	1.50	6.00	60
CORDUROYS, The				
TICK TOCK/Too Much Of A Woman	(Planet 122)	.75	3.00	67
COREY, Ed				
LINDY HOP/Dingy Dong	(Mala 443)	.75	3.00	62
COREY, Herb				
THIS COULD BE THE NIGHT/Midnight Blues	(Top Rank 2018)	2.00	8.00	59
COREY, Jill				
BIG DADDY/Wherefore Art Thou Romeo	(Columbia 4-41202)	.75	3.00	58
CRY ME A RIVER/Nobody's Heart	(Columbia 4-40596)	1.00	4.00	55
EDWARD/I'm Not At All In Love	(Columbia 4-40410)	1.00	4.00	55
I LOVE MY BABY/Egghead	(Columbia 4-40794)	1.00	4.00	56
LET HIM KNOW/What Am I To Do	(Columbia 4-40743)	1.00	4.00	56
LET IT BE ME/Make Like A Bunny, Honey	(Columbia 4-40878)	.75	3.00	57
LOVE ME TO PIECES/Love	(Columbia 4-40955)	.75	3.00	57
SHOULD I TELL/A Good Kiss Is A Good Night's Work	(Columbia 4-40188)	1.00	4.00	54
WHERE ARE YOU/Number One Boy	(Columbia 4-40327)	1.00	4.00	55

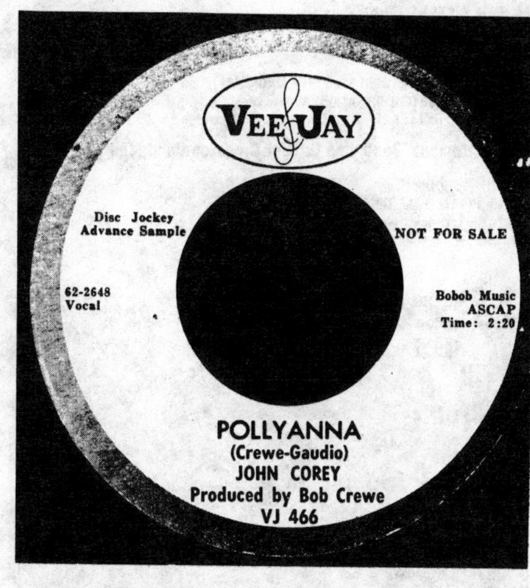

TITLE/FLIP	LABEL & NO.	GOOD	NEAR MINT	YR.
COREY, John				
POLLYANNA/I'll Forget	(Vee Jay 466)	2.50	10.00	62
(With the 4 Seasons)				
CORIN, Terri, & The Mellos				
TRULY, I LOVE YOU TRULY/Why Did You Do It	(Rider 10)	1.50	6.00	
CORLEY, Bob				
JURY DUTY/Income Tax	(RCA Victor 47-6438)	1.00	4.00	56
NUMBER ONE STREET/Number One Street	(Stars 4773)	1.00	4.00	55
CORNBREAD & BISCUITS				
LAST OF THE BIG TIME SPENDERS (PART 1)/ Last Of The Big Time Spenders (Part 2)	(Maske 102)	.75	3.00	60
CORNBREAD & JERRY (With Jerry Smith)				
LIL' OLE ME/Loco Moto	(Liberty 55322)	1.00	4.00	61
ROADHOUSE (PART 1)/Roadhouse (Part 2)	(Southtown 22004)	.75	3.00	64
(Instrumentals)				
Also see Dixiebelles, The				
CORNELL, Don				
BIBLE TELLS ME SO, THE/ Love Is A Many Splendored Thing	(Coral 61467)	1.00	4.00	55
FORT KNOX/But Love Me	(Coral 61631)	1.00	4.00	56
HOLD MY HAND/I'm Blessed	(Coral 61206)	1.00	4.00	54
I/Be Fair	(Coral 60860)	1.00	4.00	52
I'LL WALK ALONE/	(Coral 60659)	1.00	4.00	52
I'M YOURS/My Mother's Pearls	(Coral 60690)	1.00	4.00	52
MAMA GUITAR/Face In The Crowd	(Coral 61819)	1.00	4.00	57
MOST OF ALL/The Door Is Still Open To My Heart	(Coral 61393)	1.00	4.00	55
ROCK ISLAND LINE/Na-Ne Na-Na	(Coral 61613)	1.00	4.00	56
SEE-SAW/From The Bottom Of My Heart	(Coral 61621)	1.00	4.00	56
SIZE TWELVE/Hold Me	(Coral 61125)	1.00	4.00	54
TEENAGE MEETING/I Still Have A Prayer	(Coral 61584)	1.00	4.00	56
THIS IS THE BEGINNING OF THE END/ I Can't Cry Anymore	(Coral 60748)	1.00	4.00	52
UNCHAINED MELODY/All Of You	(Coral 61407)	1.00	4.00	55
YOUNG ABE LINCOLN/Dream World	(Coral 61521)	1.00	4.00	55
Also see Desmond, Johnny, Alan Dale & Don Cornell				
CORNELL, Doug				
HONG KONG ROCK/Toddling	(Deb 1000)	1.00	4.00	59
CORNELLS, The				
BEACHBOUND/Lone Star Stomp	(Garex 201)	1.25	5.00	63
MALIBU SURF/Agua Caliente	(Garex 102)	1.25	5.00	63
SURF FEVER/Do The Slawson	(Garex 206)	1.25	5.00	63
CORNISH, Chuck				
TRIBUTE TO MOHAMMED ALI/Let's Go Steady	(White Cliffs 258)	.75	3.00	67
CORNISH, Gene, & The Unbeatables				
DO THE CAPRI/Lonely I Will Stay	(Dawn 550)	1.50	6.00	64
I WANNA BE A BEETLE/Oh Misery	(Dawn 557)	1.50	6.00	64
Also see Young Rascals, The				
CORONA				
I'D DO ANYTHING FOR YOU/Paula's English	(Regina 106)	1.50	6.00	
CORONADOS, The				
FLORIDA SUN/	(Arlingwood 6467)	1.00	4.00	
CORPORATE IMAGE, The				
NOT FADE AWAY/I'm Not The Same	(MGM 13614)	.75	3.00	66
CORRENTE, Sal (Of The Dials)				
RUN RUN RUN/Love Me	(Roulette 4673)	2.00	8.00	66
CORTEZ, Dave "Baby" (David Clowney)				
CAT NIP/Talk Is Cheap	(Clock 169)	.75	3.00	
DAVE'S SPECIAL/Whisper	(Clock 1016)	.75	3.00	59
DEEP IN THE HEART OF TEXAS/You're Just Right	(Clock 1020)	.75	3.00	60
FIESTA/Hey Hey Hey	(Emit 301)	.75	3.00	62
HAPPY ORGAN, THE/Love Me As I Love You	(Clock 1009)	.75	3.00	59
HAPPY WEEKEND/Fiddle Sticks	(Chess 1834)	.75	3.00	62
HOT CAKES! 1ST SERVING/Hot Cakes! 2nd Serving	(Chess 1850)	.75	3.00	63
HURRICANE/The Shift	(Clock 1031)	.75	3.00	60
IT'S A SIN TO TELL A LIE/Piano Shuffle	(Clock 1014)	.75	3.00	59
JOHN HENRY/The Madison Shuffle	(Fire 1020)	.75	3.00	
ORGAN SHOUT/Precious You	(Chess 1861)	.75	3.00	63
RINKY DINK/Getting Right	(Julia 452)	1.50	6.00	62
RINKY DINK/Getting Right	(Chess 1829)	.75	3.00	62
SCOTTY (PART 1)/Scotty (Part 2)	(Winley 267)	.75	3.00	
TOOTSIE/Second Chance	(Clock 71824)	.75	3.00	61
TWEEDLE DEE/Gift Of Love	(Chess 1842)	.75	3.00	63
WHISTLING ORGAN, THE/I'm Happy	(Clock 1012)	.75	3.00	59
CORVAIRS, The				
SING A SONG OF SIXPENCE/Yeah Yeah	(Cub 9065)	1.00	4.00	60
TRUE TRUE LOVE/Hey Sally Mae	(Comet 2145)	1.00	4.00	62
CORVELLS, The				
BELLS, THE/Don't Forget	(Blast 208)	5.00	20.00	62
JOKE'S ON ME, THE/One (Is Such A Lonely Number)	(Cub 9122)	1.5	6.00	63
TAKE MY LOVE/Daisy	(ABC-Paramount 10324)	5.00	20.00	62
CORVETTES, The				
IN THE CHAPEL/The Swinging Smitty	(Sheraton 201)	3.75	15.00	
CORWINS, The				
LITTLE STAR/When	(Gilmar 222)	2.00	8.00	
COSBY, Bill				
BOOGIE ON YOUR FACE/What's In A Slang	(Capitol 4501)	.50	2.00	77
FUNKY NORTH PHILLY/Stop, Look & Listen	(Warner Bros. 7171)	.75	3.00	68
GROVER HENSON FEELS FORGOTTEN/ Grover Henson Feels Forgotten (Instrumental)	(Uni 55223)	.50	2.00	70
HIKKY BURR (PART 1)/Hikky Burr (Part 2)	(Uni 55184)	.50	2.00	69
HOORY FOR THE SALVATION ARMY BAND (PURPLE HAZE)/Ursalena	(Warner Bros. 7096)	.75	3.00	67
I LUV MYSELF BETTER THAN I LUV MYSELF/ Do It To Me	(Capitol 4299)	.50	2.00	76
LITTLE OLE MAN (UPTIGHT-EVERYTHING'S ALRIGHT)/ Don' Cha Know	(Warner Bros. 7072)	.75	3.00	67
LITTLE OLE MAN (UPTIGHT-EVERYTHING'S ALRIGHT)/ Hush Hush	(Warner Bros. 7072)	.75	3.00	67
MERRY CHRISTMAS MAMA/ Merry Christmas Mama (Instrumental)	(Capitol 4501)	.50	2.00	77
WHEN I MARRY YOU/Stand Still For My Lovin'	(Warner Bros. 5499)	.75	3.00	65
YES, YES, YES/Ben	(Capitol 4258)	.50	2.00	76
COSMO				
I'M A LITTLE MIXED-UP/You Can't Get Kissed	(Tilt 787)	.75	3.00	
(With The Carnations)				
COSMO, Tony				
TEENAGER FOR PRESIDENT, A/Give Me Some	(Roulette 4265)	.75	3.00	60
COSMOS, The				
ANGEL ANGEL/You're Torturing My Heart	(Big "L" 502)	1.25	5.00	
COSTA, Don				
I'LL WALK THE LINE/Catwalk	(United Artists 190)	.75	3.00	59
ILLYA DARLING/Trini's Tune	(Verve 10511)	.50	2.00	66
NEVER ON SUNDAY/Sound Of Love	(United Artists 234)	.75	3.00	60
(THEME FROM) UNFORGIVEN, THE/Streets Of Paris	(United Artists 221)	.75	3.00	60
Instrumentals				
COSTELLO, Elvis				
ACCIDENTS WILL HAPPEN/Sunday's Best	(Columbia 3-10919)	.50	2.00	79
ALISON/Miracle Man	(Columbia 3-10641)	.50	2.00	77
NEW AMSTERDAM/	(Columbia 1-11284)	.50	2.00	80
(With the Attractions)				
THIS YEAR'S GIRL/Big Tears	(Columbia 3-10762)	.50	2.00	78
WATCHING THE DETECTIVES/Alison	(Columbia 3-10705)	.50	2.00	78
Also see Clover				
COTILLIONS, The				
SURF TWIST/Sahara	(Alley 1003)	1.00	4.00	62
(Instrumentals)				
COTTON, Gene				
BEFORE MY HEART FINDS OUT/ Like A Sunday In Salem	(Ariola America 7675)	.50	2.00	77
DAMN IT ALL/Country Spirit	(ABC 12087)	.50	2.00	75
LET YOUR LOVE FLOW/Keepin' It On The Road	(ABC 12137)	.50	2.00	75
LIKE A SUNDAY IN SALEM (THE AMOS & ANDY SONG)/ Shine ON (You Got To Shine On Your Light)	(Ariola 7723)	.50	2.00	78
OCEAN OF LIFE/Michael	(Ariola 7778)	.50	2.00	79
RAIN ON/Song For You	(ABC 12250)	.50	2.00	77
SWEET DESTINY/My Love Comes Alive	(ABC 12282)	.50	2.00	77
SUNSHINE ROSES/Mrs. Oliver	(Myrrh 137)	.50	2.00	74
YOU'RE A PART OF ME (With Kim Carnes)/ Shine On (You GotTo Shine On Your Light)	(Ariola America 7704)	.50	2.00	78
YOU'VE GOT ME RUNNIN'/It's Over Goodbye	(ABC 12227)	.50	2.00	76
COTTON LLOYD & CHRISTIAN (Darryl Cotton, Michael Lloyd, Chris Christian)				
I CAN SING, I CAN DANCE/ (You've Given Me) Sunshine	(20th Century 2253)	.50	2.00	75
I GO TO PIECES/	(20th Century 2217)	.50	2.00	75
COUCHOIS				
DO IT IN DARKNESS/No Longer Needed	(Warner Bros. 8834)	.50	2.00	79
WALKIN' THE FENCE/Cripple	(Warner Bros. 8749)	.50	2.00	79
COUNT & THE COLONY				
CAN'T YOU SEE/That's The Way	(Pa-Go-Go- 121)	1.25	5.00	

TITLE/FLIP	LABEL & NO.	GOOD	NEAR MINT	YR.
COUNT FIVE, The				
CONTRAST/Merry-Go-Round	(Double Shot 115)	1.25	5.00	67
DECLARATION OF INDEPENDENCE/ Revelation In Slow Motion	(Double Shot 125)	1.25	5.00	68
MAILMAN/Pretty Big Mouth	(Double Shot 141)	1.25	5.00	68
PEACE OF MIND/Morning After	(Double Shot 106)	1.25	5.00	66
PSYCHOTIC REACTION/They're Gonna Get You	(Double Shot 104)	1.25	5.00	66
TEENY BOPPER, TEENY BOPPER/ You Must Believe Me	(Double Shot 110)	1.25	5.00	67
COUNT LORRY & THE BITERS				
FRANKENSTEIN STOMP/Groovin' With Drac.	(Dragon 4406)	1.00	4.00	65
COUNTDOWNS, The				
YOU KNOW I DO/	(Bear 1968)	.75	3.00	66
COUNTRY BOYS, The (Featuring David Gates)				
OAKIE SURFER, THE/Blue Surf	(Del Fi 4248)	2.50	10.00	64
COUNTRY COALITION, The				
KEEPIN' FREE/	(ABC 11286)	.50	2.00	73
TAKE ME TO THE MOUNTAINS/Age Of Angels	(ABC 11279)	.50	2.00	72
TIME TO GET TOGETHER/How Do I Love You	(ABC Bluesway 61034)	.50	2.00	70
COUNTRY GAZETTE				
KEEP ON PUSHIN'/Hot Burrito Breakdown	(United Artists 50982)	.75	3.00	70
Some members of this band were later in the Flying Burrito Brothers.				
COUNTRY HAMS, The (Paul McCartney & Wings, Chet Atkins, Floyd Cramer)				
WALKING IN THE PARK WITH ELOISE/ Bridge On The River Suite	(Apple 3977)	.50	2.00	74
WALKING IN THE PARK WITH ELOISE/ Bridge On The River Suite (Picture sleeve)	(Apple 3977)	1.00	4.00	74
COUNTRY JOE & THE FISH (Featuring Country Joe McDonald)				
HERE I GO AGAIN/Baby You're Driving Me Crazy	(Vanguard 35090)	1.25	5.00	69
JANIS/Janis (Part 2)	(Vanguard 35068)	1.25	5.00	68
NOT SO SWEET MATHA LORRAINE/Masked Matauder	(Vanguard 35052)	1.25	5.00	67
ROCK & SOUL MUSIC/Rock & Soul Music (Part 2)	(Vanguard 35059)	1.25	5.00	68
WHO AM I/Thursday	(Vanguard 35061)	1.25	5.00	68
COUNTS, The				
COUNTED OUT/You'll Feel It Too	(Nat 100)	1.50	6.00	62
STORMY WEATHER/True Love's Gone	(Nat 101)	1.25	5.00	63
STORMY WEATHER/True Love's Gone	(Smash 1821)	.75	3.00	63
COUNT YATES				
CHIMPANZEE/The Golden Key	(Regis 1)	.75	3.00	
COURAGE, Alexander				
SURFSIDE 6/That's All (Instrumentals)	(Decca 31194)	.75	3.00	60
COUSIN FESCUE				
HOODS IN MY LITTLE GIRL'S LIFE, THE/ Shuby Duby Dooley (Parodies)	(Fun 10003)	1.00	4.00	66
COUTO & MULLIGAN				
EVERYBODY IS AN ASSHOLE (TO SOMEBODY SOMETIME)/ Long Ago	(Mullco 8082-10)	.75	3.00	80
COVELLE, Buddy				
BILLY BOY/Show Me How (Shown as by Valine Hackert)	(Brunswick 9-55151)	12.50	50.00	59
I'LL GO ON LOVING YOU/Lorraine	(Coral 9-62181)	1.25	5.00	60
COVEN (Featuring Teresa Kelly)				
JAILHOUSE ROCK/Nightingale	(MGM 14348)	.50	2.00	71
ONE TIN SOLDIER (THE LEGEND OF BILLY JACK)/ I Guess It's A Beautiful Day	(MGM 14308)	.50	2.00	71
ONE TIN SOLDIER (THE LEGEND OF BILLY JACK)/ Johnnie (Soundtrack)	(Warner Bros. 7146)	.50	2.00	72
ONE TIN SOLDIER (THE LEGEND OF BILLY JACK)/ Johnnie	(Warner Bros. 7509)	.50	2.00	71
COVERDALE, David: see David Coverdale's Whitesnake				
COVINGTON, Warren: see Dorsey, Tommy				
COWBOY				
I WILL BE THERE (PAT'S SONG)/	(Capricorn 0289)	.50	2.00	78
TAKIN' IT ALL THE WAY/River To The Sea	(Capricorn 0283)	.50	2.00	78
COWSILL, Susan (Of The Cowsills)				
IT MIGHT AS WELL RAIN UNTIL SEPTEMBER/ Mohammed's Radio	(Warner Bros. 8232)	.50	2.00	76
NEXT TIME THAT I SEE YOU, THE/ I Think Of You	(Warner Bros. 8333)	.50	2.00	76
COWSILLS, The				
ALL I REALLY WANT TO BE IS ME/And The Next Day, Too	(Joda 103)	1.25	5.00	65
CANDY KID, THE/Impossible Years	(MGM 14011)	.75	3.00	69
CAPTAIN SAD & HIS SHIP OF FOOLS/ Path Of Love	(MGM 14003)	.75	3.00	68
COVERED WAGON/Blue Road	(London 170)	.50	2.00	72
HAIR/What Is Happy	(MGM 14026)	.75	3.00	69
INDIAN LAKE/Newspaper Blanket	(MGM 13944)	.75	3.00	68
IN NEED OF A FRIEND/Mister Flynn	(MGM 13909)	.75	3.00	68
MOST OF ALL/Siamese Cat	(Philips 40382)	1.00	4.00	66
MOST PECULIAR MAN, A/Could It Be, Let Me Know	(Philips 40437)	1.00	4.00	67
ON MY SIDE/There Is A Child	(London 149)	.50	2.00	71
PARTY GIRL/What's It Gonna Be Like	(Philips 40406)	1.00	4.00	66
POOR BABY/Meet Me At The Wishing Well	(MGM 13981)	.75	3.00	68
PROPHECY OF DANIEL & JOHN THE DEVINE/ Gotta Get Away From It All	(MGM 14063)	.75	3.00	69
RAIN, THE PARK & OTHER THINGS, THE/River Blue	(MGM 13810)	.75	3.00	67
SILVER THREADS & GOLDEN NEEDLES/ Love American Style	(MGM 14084)	.75	3.00	69
II X II/Start To Love	(MGM 14106)	.75	3.00	70
WE CAN FLY/A Time For Rememberance	(MGM 13886)	.75	3.00	68
COX, Jerry				
DEBBIE JEAN/Sherry	(Frantic 751)	1.00	4.00	59
LOVER MAN/Maria	(Buz 100)	1.00	4.00	
COX, Wally				
HEEBEE JEEBES/I Can't Help it	(Arvee 5008)	.75	3.00	60
THERE'S A TAVERN IN THE TOWN/ What A Crazy Girl	(RCA Victor 47-5278)	.75	3.00	53
C-QUENTS, The				
DEAREST ONE/It's You & Me	(Essica 004)	1.50	6.00	
MERRY CHRISTMAS BABY/	(Captown 4027)	1.50	6.00	
C-QUINS, The				
MY ONLY LOVE/You've Been Crying	(Ditto 501)	1.25	5.00	62
MY ONLY LOVE/You've Been Crying	(Chess 1815)	.75	3.00	62
CRABBY APPLETON				
GO BACK/Try	(Elektra 45687)	.50	2.00	70
LOVE CAN CHANGE EVERYTHING/Smokin' In The Morning	(Elektra 45781)	.50	2.00	71

TITLE/FLIP	LABEL & NO.	GOOD	NEAR MINT	YR.
MY LITTLE LUCY/Some Madness	(Elektra 45702)	.50	2.00	70
TOMORROW'S A NEW DAY/It's So Hard	(Elektra 45754)	.50	2.00	71
CRACKERJACK SOCIETY				
WALK IN THE SKY/Listen To This Side	(Columbia 4-44434)	1.00	4.00	67
CRACK THE SKY				
I AM THE WALRUS/Lighten Up McGraw	(Lifesong 1782)	.50	2.00	78
LONG NIGHTS/Give Myself To You	(Lifesong 1764)	.50	2.00	78
(WE DON'T WANT YOUR MONEY) WE WANT MINE/ Invaders From Mars	(Lifesong 45016)	.50	2.00	77
CRADDOCK, Crash (Billy Craddock)				
AH, POOR LITTLE BABY/Lulu Lee	(Date 1007)	1.50	6.00	58
ALL I WANT IS YOU/Letter Of Love	(Columbia 4-41619)	1.00	4.00	60
AM I TO BE THE ONE?/I Miss You So Much	(Columbia 4-41316)	1.00	4.00	59
BETTY, BETTY/Right Around The Corner	(King 5912)	.75	3.00	64
BIRD DOGGIN'/Millionaire	(Colonial CR-721)	1.50	6.00	58
BLABBERMOUTH/Sweetie Pie	(Columbia 4-41367)	1.00	4.00	59
DON'T DESTROY ME/Boom Boom Baby	(Columbia 4-41470)	1.00	4.00	59
GOOD TIME BILLY/Heavenly Love	(Columbia 4-41822)	1.00	4.00	60
MY BABY'S GOT FLAT FEET/ One Heartache Too Many	(King 5924)	.75	3.00	64
ONE LAST KISS/Is It True Or False	(Columbia 4-41677)	1.00	4.00	60
SINCE SHE TURNED SEVENTEEN/I Want That	(Columbia 4-41536)	1.00	4.00	60
TRULY LOVE/How Lonely He Must Be	(Mercury 71811)	1.00	4.00	61
CRAFT, Morty				
ALL MIXED UP/Guessin' Games (Novelty/Break-in)	(Tod 122)	3.75	15.00	57
CRAFTSMEN, The				
GOOFUS/Rock A Long	(Warwick 538)	.75	3.00	60
WHAT'S THE MATTER WITH GROWNUPS/Mc Boing-Boing	(Warwick 678)	.75	3.00	62
CRAFTYS, The				
L-O-V-E/Heart Breaking World	(7 Arts 708)	1.50	6.00	61
ZOOM ZOOM ZOOM/I Went To A Party	(Elmor 310)	3.00	12.00	62
CRAIG & HIS DADDY				
BRING MY DADDY AN ELECTRIC TRAIN/	(Amy 834)	.75	3.00	62
CRAIG, Greer				
LOVE ME/Little Sister	(Trail 1862)	.50	2.00	77
CRAIG, Jimmie				
ALL FOR YOU/Gonna Love My Baby	(Brill 1)	1.00	4.00	59
CRAIG, The				
I MUST BE MAD/Suspense	(Fontana 1579)	.75	3.00	67
CRAIN, Jimmy				
SHING-A-SHAG/	(Spangle 2009)	2.50	10.00	
CRAMPTON SISTERS, The				
I DIDN'T KNOW WHAT TIME IT WAS/ I Cried When I Found You Gone	(DCP 1001)	.75	3.00	64
CRANE, Carol (Mrs. Brown's Lovely Daughter)				
(MOTHER, IT'S A) FRIGHTFUL SITUATION (Answer song)/ What Else Do You Do For Kicks	(Challenge 59292)	1.25	5.00	61
CRANSTON, Lamont, Band: see Lamont Cranston Band, The				
CRAWFORD, Bobby				
MRS. SMITH, PLEASE WAKE UP JOAN/ That Little Ole Lovemaker Me	(Del Fi 4211)	1.00	4.00	63
Bobby is Johnny Crawford's brother.				

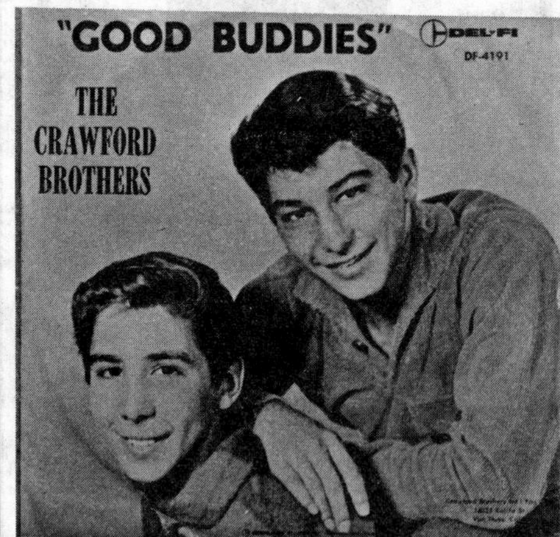

TITLE/FLIP	LABEL & NO.	GOOD	NEAR MINT	YR.
CRAWFORD BROTHERS, The (Johnny & Bobby)				
GOOD BUDDIES/You Gotta Wear Shoes	(Del Fi 4191)	.75	3.00	62
CRAWFORD, Johnny (John Earnest Crawford)				
ASK/Dance With The Dolly	(Wynne 124)	1.50	6.00	60
CINDY'S BIRTHDAY/Something Special	(Del Fi 4178)	.75	3.00	62
CINDY'S GONNA CRY/Debbie	(Del Fi 4221)	.75	3.00	63
CRY ON MY SHOULDER/When I Fall In Love	(Del Fi 4203)	.75	3.00	63
DAYDREAMS/So Goes The Story	(Del Fi 4162)	.75	3.00	61
GIRL NEXT DOOR (ONCE UPON A TIME)/ Sittin & A Watchin'	(Del Fi 4242)	.75	3.00	64
JUDY LOVES ME/Living In The Past	(Del Fi 4231)	.75	3.00	63
PATTI ANN/Donna	(Del Fi 4172)	.75	3.00	62
PROUD/Lonesome Town	(Del Fi 4193)	.75	3.00	62
RUMORS/No One Really Loves A Clown	(Del Fi 4188)	.75	3.00	62
SANDY/Ol' Shorty	(Del Fi 4229)	.75	3.00	64
WHAT HAPPENED TO JANIE/Petite Chanson	(Del Fi 4215)	.75	3.00	63
YOUR LOVE IS GROWING OLD/The Treasure	(Del Fi 4165)	.75	3.00	61
YOUR NOSE IS GONNA GROW/Mr. Blue	(Del Fi 4181)	.75	3.00	62
CRAWLER (Formerly Back Street Crawler)				
HOW WILL YOU BREAK MY HEART/Hold On	(Epic 50628)	.50	2.00	78
STONE COLD SOBER/One Too Many Lovers	(Epic 50492)	.50	2.00	77
WITHOUT YOU BABE/You Are My Savious	(Epic 50628)	.50	2.00	78
CRAYONS, The				
LOVE AT FIRST SIGHT/Pete's Body Shop (By The Rogues)	(Counsel 122)	.75	3.00	63
TEACH ME MAMA/Crazy Dream	(Counsel 121)	.75	3.00	63

TITLE/FLIP	LABEL & NO.	GOOD	NEAR MINT	YR.
CRAZY ELEPHANT				
GIMMIE, GIMMIE GOOD LOVIN'/Hips & Lips	(Bell 763)	.75	3.00	69
GIMME SOME MORE/My Baby (Honey Pie)	(Bell 817)	1.00	4.00	69
SUNSHINE, RED WINE/Pam	(Bell 804)	1.00	4.00	69
THERE AIN'T NO UMBOPO/Land Rover (With 10CC)	(Bell 875)	1.25	5.00	70
THERE'S A BETTER DAY A COMMIN'/Space Buggy	(Bell B-846)	1.00	4.00	70
CRAZY GIRLS, The				
HEY HEY, HA HA/Joe, The Guitar Man (With the Javelins)	(Capitol 5050)	.75	3.00	63

TITLE/FLIP	LABEL & NO.	GOOD	NEAR MINT	YR.
CRAZY HORSE				
ALL ALONE NOW/One Thing I Love	(Reprise 1075)	.50	2.00	72
DANCE, DANCE, DANCE/Dance, Dance, Dance	(Reprise 1025)	.50	2.00	71
DIRTY, DIRTY/Beggars Day	(Reprise 1046)	.50	2.00	71
LOVE/	(M.O.C. 45-671)	.75	3.00	
ROCK & ROLL BAND/	(Epic 10925)	.50	2.00	72
Crazy Horse was Neil Young's Band				
CRAZY JACKS, The				
LISZT STOMP/Paganni Stomp (Instrumentals)	(London 10024)	.75	3.00	63
CRAZY KATS, The				
MAKIN' WHOOPEE/The Candy Stik Twist	(Deauville 1005)	.75	3.00	
CRAZY LUKE				
KARATE/Tea & Rice	(Do Brooks 1)	.75	3.00	63
CRAZY MORLEY				
AS LONG AS WE'RE HAPPY TOGETHER/I Chicken Out	(Cameo 147)	1.00	4.00	58
CRAZY OTTO				
GLAD RAG DOLL/Smiles	(Decca 29403)	1.00	4.00	55
TIN PAN ALLEY MEDLEY/Gaslight Medley Instrumentals	(Decca 29753)	1.00	4.00	55
CREACH, Papa John				
I'M THE FIDDLE MAN/Joyce	(Buddah 509)	.50	2.00	76
OVER THE RAINBOW/The Janitor Drives A Cadillac	(Grunt 0501)	.75	3.00	71
STRING JET ROCK/Papa John's Down Home Blues	(Grunt 0505)	.75	3.00	72
Papa John is a violinist with Jefferson Starship.				
CREAM				
ANYONE FOR TENNIS/Pressed Rat & Warthog	(Atco 6575)	1.00	4.00	68
BADGE (With George Harrison)/What A Bringdown	(Atco 6668)	1.00	4.00	69
CROSSROADS/Passing The Time	(Atco 6646)	.75	3.00	69
I FEEL FREE/N.S.U.	(Atco 6462)	1.00	4.00	67
LAWDY MAMA/Sweet Wine	(Atco 6708)	1.00	4.00	70
SPOONFUL/Spoonful (Part 2)	(Atco 6522)	1.00	4.00	68
STRANGE BREW/Tales Of Brave Ulysses	(Atco 6488)	1.00	4.00	67
SUNSHINE OF YOUR LOVE/Swlabr	(Atco 6544)	.75	3.00	68
WHITE ROOM/Those Were The Days	(Atco 6617)	.75	3.00	68
Also see Baker, Ginger; Also see Bruce, Jack; Also see Clapton, Eric				
CREATION				
HOW DOES IT FEEL?/Life Is Just Beginning	(Decca 32227)	.75	3.00	67
IF I STAY TOO LONG/Nightmares	(Decca 32155)	.75	3.00	67
MAKING TIME/Try & Stop Me	(Planet 116)	1.00	4.00	66
PAINTER MAN/Biff! Bang! Pow!	(Planet 119)	1.00	4.00	66
CREATIONS, The				
BELLS, THE/Shang Shang	(Jamie 1197)	1.25	5.00	61
THERE GOES THE GIRL I LOVE/You Are My Darling	(Lido 501)	2.00	8.00	56
THERE GOES THE GIRL I LOVE/You Are My Darling	(Tip Top 501)	.75	3.00	
THIS IS OUR NIGHT/You're My Inspiration	(Mel-o-dy 101)	1.50	6.00	62
CREATIONS, The				
CRASH/Chickie Darlin' (Instrumental)	(Top Hat 1003)	7.50	30.00	
CREATIONS IV				
DANCE IN THE PARK/Little Girl	(HBR 440)	.75	3.00	65
CREATORS, The				
BOY, HE'S GOT IT/I'll Never, Never Do It Again	(T-Kay 110)	1.00	4.00	63
BOY, HE'S GOT IT/Yeah, He's Got It/Boy, He's Got It	(Philips 40058)	.75	3.00	63
CROSS FIRE/Crazy Love	(Epic 9605)	.75	3.00	63
I'LL STAY HOME (NEW YEAR'S EVE)/Shoom Ba Boom	(Philips 40083)	.75	3.00	63
Even though all of these releases are shown as being by a group using the same name, the possibility exists that they are not all by the same group.				
CREATURES, The				
HURTIN' ALL OVER/Love Is A Funny Little Game	(Columbia 4-44145)	1.00	4.00	67
LOOKING AT TOMORROW/Someone Needs You	(Columbia 4-43884)	1.00	4.00	66
STRING ALONG/The Trip Is Warm	(Columbia 4-43689)	1.00	4.00	66
TURN OUT THE LIGHT/It Must Be Love	(Columbia 4-43480)	1.00	4.00	66
CREDIBILITY GAP (With David L. Lander & Michael McKean)				
COMIN' INTO MY OWN/Bein' Like The Birdies	(Capitol 2246)	.75	3.00	68
Lander & McKean, also known as Lenny & Squiggy, later recorded as Lenny & The Squigtones.				

TITLE/FLIP — LABEL & NO. — GOOD — NEAR MINT — YR.

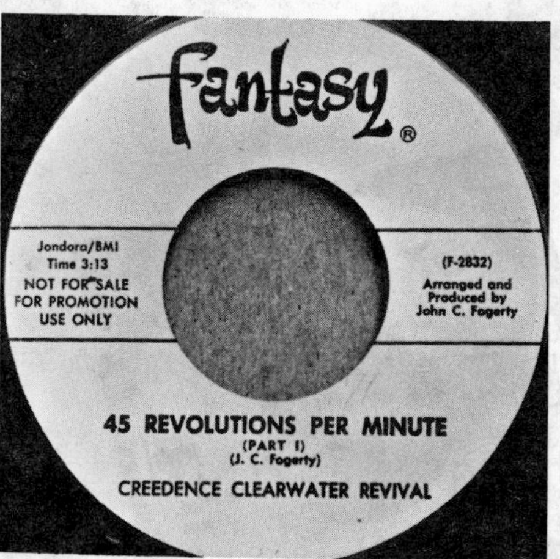

Fantasy
Jondora/BMI
Time 3:13
NOT FOR SALE
FOR PROMOTION
USE ONLY
(F-2832)
Arranged and
Produced by
John C. Fogerty
45 REVOLUTIONS PER MINUTE
(PART I)
(J. C. Fogerty)
CREEDENCE CLEARWATER REVIVAL

CREEDENCE CLEARWATER REVIVAL (Formerly The Golliwogs)

BAD MOON RISING/Lodi (Fantasy 622) .75 3.00 69
BROWN EYED GIRL/You Better Be Careful (Scorpio 404) 3.00 12.00 65
(Shown as by the Golliwogs)
DON'T TELL ME NO LIES/
Little Girl Does Your Mama Know (Fantasy 590) 3.75 15.00 65
(Shown as by the Golliwogs)
DOWN ON THE CORNER/Fortunate Son (Fantasy 634) .75 3.00 69
45 REVOLUTIONS PER MINUTE/ (Fantasy 2838) 3.00 12.00 69
(Promotional issue only)
FRAGILE CHILD/Fight Fire (Scorpio 405) 2.00 8.00 66
(Shown as by the Golliwogs)
GREEN RIVER/Commotion (Fantasy 625) .75 3.00 69
HAVE YOU EVER SEEN THE RAIN/Hey Tonight (Fantasy 655) .75 3.00 71
I HEARD IT THROUGH THE GRAPEVINE/
Good Golly Miss Molly (Fantasy 759) .75 3.00 76
I PUT A SPELL ON YOU/Walk On The Water (Fantasy 617) .75 3.00 68
(Also see "Walking On The Water")
LOOKIN' OUT MY BACK DOOR/Long As I Can See The Light (Fantasy 645) .75 3.00 70
PORTERVILLE/Call It Pretending (Scorpio 412) 2.50 10.00 67
PORTERVILLE/Call It Pretending (Scorpio 412) 3.75 15.00 67
(Promotional issue only, shown as by the Golliwogs.)
PROUD MARY/Born On The Bayou (Fantasy 619) .75 3.00 69
RUN THROUGH THE JUNGLE/Up Around The Bend (Fantasy 641) .75 3.00 70
SOMEDAY NEVER COMES/Tearin' Up The Country (Fantasy 676) .75 3.00 72
SUZIE Q (PART 1)/Suzie Q (Part 2) (Fantasy 616) .75 3.00 68
SWEET HITCH-HIKER/Door To Door (Fantasy 665) .75 3.00 71
TRAVELIN' BAND/(Who'll Stop The Rain) (Fantasy 637) .75 3.00 70
WALKING ON THE WATER/
You Better Get It Before It Gets You (Scorpio 408) 3.75 15.00 66
(This is the same song as "Walk On The Water," but shown as by the Golliwogs.)
YOU GOT NOTHIN' ON ME/You Can't Be True (Fantasy 599) 3.00 12.00 65
(Shown as by the Golliwogs)
YOU CAME WALKING/Where You Been (Fantasy 597) 3.00 12.00 65
(Shown as by the Golliwogs)

CREELS, The
SEE ME ONCE AGAIN/Do You Wanta Jump (Judd J1005) 1.00 4.00

CREEP, The
CONVENTION '76/Revolution '76 (by Hickey Badman) (Nixxxon 1976) .75 3.00 76
(Novelty/Break-in)
HALDERMAN, ERLICHMAN, MITCHELL & DEAN/ (Mr. G 826) 1.25 5.00 73
(Novelty)

CREME, Lol & Kevin Godley (Of 10 CC)
FIVE O'CLOCK IN THE MORNING/The Flood (Mercury 73965) .50 2.00 77

CRESCENDOS, The
I'LL BE SEEING YOU/Sweet Dreams (Atlantic 2014) 1.25 5.00 59
LET'S TAKE A WALK/Strange Love (Scarlet 4007) 1.25 5.00 57
MY HEARTS DESIRE/Take My Heart (Music City 831) 3.00 12.00 57
MY HEARTS DESIRE/Take My Heart (Gone 5100) 1.25 5.00 61
OH JULIE/ (Tap 7027) 1.50 6.00
OH JULIE/My Little Girl (Nasco 6005) 1.00 4.00 57
SCHOOL GIRL/Crazy Hop (Nasco 6009) 1.25 5.00 58
SWEET DREAMS/Finders Keepers (Atlantic 1109) 1.25 5.00 56
YOUNG & IN LOVE/Rainy Sunday (Nasco 6021) 1.25 5.00 58

CRESCENDOS
FELLOW NEEDS A GIRL, A/Black Cat (Domain 1025) 1.50 6.00

CRESCENTS, The
SMOKE GETS IN YOUR EYES/Johnny Won't Run Around (Arlen 743) 1.50 6.00
WHEN YOU WISH UPON A STAR/Hey There (Hamilton 50033) 2.00 8.00

CRESCENTS, The (Featuring Chiyo)
PINK DOMINOS/Devil Surf (Break Out BBM-4) 1.50 6.00 63
(Shown as by Chiyo & The Crescents)
PINK DOMINOS/Break Out (Era 3116) .75 3.00 63
Instrumentals

CRESTERS, The
PUT YOUR ARMS AROUND ME/Do It With Me (Capitol 5238) 1.50 6.00 64

CRESTRIDERS, The
SURF STOMP/Surfin' Fever (Crystalette 756) 1.25 5.00 61
(Instrumentals)

CRESTS, The (Featuring Johnny Maestro)
ACTOR, THE/Three Tears In A Bucket (Trans Atlas 696) 1.50 6.00 62
ANGELS LISTENED IN, THE/I Thank The Moon (Coed 515) 1.25 5.00 59
BABY/I Love You So (Times Square 6) 1.00 4.00 63
DID I REMEMBER/Tears Will Fall (Selma 4000) 2.00 8.00 63
EARTH ANGEL/Tweedle Dee (King Tut 172) 1.00 4.00
16 MILLION HEARTBEATS/Before I Loved Her (United Artists 474) 3.75 15.00 62
FLOWER OF LOVE/Molly Mae (Coed 511) 1.25 5.00 59
GUILTY/Number One With Me (Selma 311) 2.00 8.00 62
I REMEMBER (THE STILL OF THE NIGHT)/
Good Golly Miss Molly (Coed 543) 1.00 4.00 61
ISN'T IT AMAZING/Molly Mae (Coed 537) 1.25 5.00 60
JOURNEY OF LOVE/If My Heart Could Write A Letter (Coed 535) 1.25 5.00 60
LEAN ON ME/Make Up My Mind (Cameo 305) 1.25 5.00 64
LITTLE MIRACLES/Baby I Gotta Know (Coed 561) 1.00 4.00 62
NO ONE TO LOVE/Wish She Was Mine (Joyce 105) 12.50 50.00 57
OVER THE WEEKEND/I'll Be True (Cameo 256) 1.50 6.00 63

PHONE BOOTH ON THE HIGHWAY/She's All Mine Alone (Apt 25075) 1.50 6.00 65
PRETTY LITTLE ANGEL/I Thank The Moon (Coed 501) 5.00 20.00 58
SIX NIGHTS A WEEK/I Do (Coed 509) 1.25 5.00 59
16 CANDLES/Beside You (Coed 506) 1.25 5.00 58
STEP BY STEP/Gee (But I'd Give The World) (Coed 525) 1.25 5.00 60
SWEETEST ONE/My Juanita (Joyce 103) 6.25 25.00 57
(With the large "Y" in the Joyce logo)
SWEETEST ONE/My Juanita (Joyce 103) 2.00 8.00 57
(With all of the letters in the Joyce logo the same size)
SWEETEST ONE/My Juanita (Musictone 1106) 1.00 4.00 62
TROUBLE IN PARADISE/Always You (Coed 531) 1.25 5.00 60
YEAR AGO TONIGHT, A/Paper Clown (Coed 521) 1.25 5.00 59
YOU BLEW OUT THE CANDLES/A Love To Last A Lifetime (Coral 62403) 2.50 10.00 64

CREW, The
FLIGHT 889/Do You Think She'll Call (Yucca 713) 1.25 5.00 59
HOT WIRE/Big Junk (Brass 194) 1.00 4.00 63
(Instrumentals)

CREW CUTS, The
ALL I WANNA DO/The Barking Dog (Mercury 70490) 1.25 5.00 54
ANGELS IN THE SKY/Mostly Martha (Mercury 70741) 1.00 4.00 55
CRAZY 'BOUT YOU BABY/Angela Mia (Mercury 70341) 1.25 5.00 54
DON'T BE ANGRY/Chop Chop Boom (Mercury 70597) 1.00 4.00 55
GUM DROP/Song of a Fool (Mercury 70668) 1.00 4.00 55
KO KO MO/Earth Angel (Mercury 70529) 1.25 5.00 54
MALAGUENA/Why Not (Warwick M-595) .75 3.00 61
OOP-SHOOP/Do Me Good Baby (Mercury 70443) 1.25 5.00 54
SEVEN DAYS/That's Your Mistake (Mercury 70782) 1.00 4.00 55
SH-BOOM/I Spoke Too Soon (Mercury 70404) 1.25 5.00 54
STORY UNTOLD, A/Carmens Boogie (Mercury 70634) 1.00 4.00 55
TELL ME WHY/Rebel In Town (Mercury 70890) 1.00 4.00 56
TWINKLE TOES/Dance Mr. Snowman Dance (Mercury 70491) 1.25 5.00 54
UNCHAINED MELODY/Two Hearts (Mercury 70598) 1.00 4.00 55
YOUNG LOVE/Little By Little (Mercury 71022) 1.00 4.00 56

CREWE, Bob, Generation
AFTER THE BALL/One More Tear (DynoVoice 231) .50 2.00 67
BATTLE HYMN OF THE REPUBLIC '68/ (DynoVoice 915) .50 2.00 68
BIRDS OF BRITAIN/I Will Wait For You (DynoVoice 902) .50 2.00 67
BLACK QUEEN'S BEADS/The Angel Is Love (DynoVoice 928) .50 2.00 68
DAY BY DAY/Dandylion (Crewe 605) .50 2.00 71
LOVER'S CONCERTO, A/You Only Live Twice (DynoVoice 237) .50 2.00 67
MAMMY BLUE/Better Be Gone (Metromedia 229) .50 2.00 71
MINISKIRTS/Theme For A Lazy Girl (DynoVoice 233) .50 2.00 67
MUSIC TO WATCH GIRLS BY/Girls On The Rocks (DynoVoice 229) .50 2.00 66
STREET WALK/ (20th Century 2271) .50 2.00 76
WHIFFENPOOF SONG, THE/Let's Pretend (Warwick 519) .75 3.00 60

CREWNECKS, The
ROCKIN' ZOMBIE/When I First Fall In Love (Rhapsody 71961-2) 1.00 4.00 59

CRIB & BEN
EMILY/ (Decca 32453) .75 3.00 69

CRIBBINS, Bernard
WHEN I'M SIXTY-FOUR/Oh My Word (Capitol 5933) .75 3.00 67

CRICKETS, The
ALL OVER YOU/(They Call Her) La Bamba (Liberty F-55696) 2.00 8.00 64
EV'RYBODY'S GOT A LITTLE PROBLEM/Now Hear This (Liberty F-55767) 2.00 8.00 65
FROM ME TO YOU/Please Please Me (Liberty F-55668) 3.00 12.00 64
HE'S OLD ENOUGH TO KNOW BETTER/
I'm Feeling Better (Liberty F-55392) 2.00 8.00 61
I'M NOT A BAD GUY/Don't Ever Change (Liberty F-55441) 2.00 8.00 62
IT'S SO EASY/Lonesome Tears (Brunswick 9-55094) 2.50 10.00 59
(With Buddy Holly)
IT'S SO EASY/Lonesome Tears (Promotional issue) (Brunswick 9-55094) 20.00 80.00 59
(With Buddy Holly)
LITTLE HOLLYWOOD GIRL/Parisian Girl (Liberty F-55495) 2.00 8.00 62
LOVE'S MADE A FOOL OF YOU/Someone, Someone (Brunswick 9-55124) 3.00 12.00 59
LOVE'S MADE A FOOL OF YOU/Someone, Someone (Brunswick 9-55124) 5.00 20.00 59
(Promotional issue)
MAYBE BABY/Tell Me How (Brunswick 9-55053) 2.50 10.00 58
(With Buddy Holly)
MAYBE BABY/Tell Me How (Promotional issue) (Brunswick 9-55053) 20.00 80.00 58
(With Buddy Holly)
MILLION DOLLAR MOVIE/A Million Miles Apart (Music Factory MU-415) 3.75 15.00 68
MORE THAN I CAN SAY/Baby My Heart (Coral 9-62198) 2.50 10.00 60
MY LITTLE GIRL/Teardrops Fall Like Rain (Liberty F-55540) 2.50 10.00 63
OH, BOY/Not Fade Away (Brunswick 9-50035) 2.50 10.00 57
(With Buddy Holly)
OH, BOY/Not Fade Away (Promotional issue) (Brunswick 9-50035) 15.00 60.00 57
(With Buddy Holly)
PEGGY SUE GOT MARRIED/Don't Cha Know (Coral 62238) 3.75 15.00 60
THAT'LL BE THE DAY/
I'm Looking For Someone To Love (Brunswick 55009) 2.50 10.00 57
(With Buddy Holly)
THAT'LL BE THE DAY/I'm Looking
For Someone To Love (Promotional issue) (Brunswick 55009) 20.00 80.00 57
(With Buddy Holly)
THINK IT OVER/Fool's Paradise (Brunswick 55072) 2.50 10.00 58
(With Buddy Holly)
THINK IT OVER/Fool's Paradise (Promotional issue) (Brunswick 55072) 12.50 50.00 58
(With Buddy Holly)
TRUE LOVE WAYS/Rockin' 50's Rock & Roll (Barnaby ZS7-2061) 2.50 10.00 72
WHEN YOU ASK ABOUT LOVE/Deborah (Brunswick 55153) 3.00 12.00 59

Although not credited on the label, the Picks provided vocal backing on the above Brunswick singles that are shown as being "With Buddy Holly."
Coral and Liberty promotional copies are valued at approximately 20-25% more than commercial issues, which are priced above.
Also see Box, David
Also see Campers, The
Also see Camps, The
Also see Ivan

CRIME
HOT WIRE MY HEART/Baby You're So Repulsive (Crime Music 188) .75 3.00 78

CRITERIONS, The (Featuring Tommy West)
DON'T SAY GOODBYE/Crying The Blues Over Me (Celilia 1010) 1.25 5.00 59
I REMAIN TRULY YOURS/You, Just You (Celilia 1208) 2.00 8.00 59
I REMAIN TRULY YOURS/You, Just You (Laurie 3305) 1.00 4.00 65
MURDER BY GUITAR/Frustration (Crime Music-No Number Given) 1.00 4.00
Also see Cashman & West

CRIMSON TIDE (With Wayne Perkins)
LOVE STOP/Funky Side Of Town (Capitol 4632) .50 2.00 78
RECKLESS LOVE/ (Capitol 4755) .50 2.00 79

CRISTO, Bobby
GOTTA GOOD THING GOING/That's Love (United Artists Int'l 2807) .75 3.00 67

CRITTERS, The (Featuring Don Ciccione)
BAD MISUNDERSTANDING/Forever Or No More (Kapp 793) .75 3.00 66
COOL SUNDAY MORNING/Lisa, But Not The Same (Project 3 1349) .75 3.00 68
DANCING IN THE STREETS/Little Girl (Kapp 858) .75 3.00 67
DON'T LET THE RAIN FALL ON ME/Walk Like A Man Again (Kapp 838) .75 3.00 67
GOOD MORNING SUNSHINE/Moment Of Being With You (Project 3 1326) .75 3.00 67
I JUST WANT TO SIT RIGHT HERE & LOOK AT YOU/
She Said She Loved Him (Project 3 1363) .75 3.00 69
MARRYIN' KIND OF LOVE/New York Bound (Kapp 805) .75 3.00 66
MR. DIEINGLY SAD/It Just Won't Be That Way (Kapp 769) .75 3.00 66
NO ONE BUT YOU/I'm Telling Everyone (Prancer 6001) .75 3.00 68
YOUNGER GIRL/Gone For Awhile (Kapp 752) .75 3.00 66

CROCE, Jim
BAD, BAD LEROY BROWN/
Good Time Man Like Me Ain't Got No Business (ABC 11359) .50 2.00 73
CHAIN GANG MEDLEY: CHAIN GANG-HE DON'T LOVE YOU-SEARCHIN'/Stone Walls (Lifesong 45001) .50 2.00 76
I GOT A NAME/Alabama Rain (ABC 11389) .50 2.00 73
I'LL HAVE TO SAY I LOVE YOU IN A SONG/
Salon & Saloon (ABC 11424) .50 2.00 74
IT DOESN'T HAVE TO BE THAT WAY/
Roller Derby Queen (ABC 11413) .50 2.00 73
MISSISSIPPI LADY/Maybe Tomorrow (Lifesong 45005) .50 2.00 76
ONE LESS SET OF FOOTSTEPS/
It Doesn't Have To Be That Way (ABC 11346) .50 2.00 73
OPERATOR (THAT'S NOT THE WAY IT FEELS)/
Rapid Roy (The Stock Car Boy) (ABC 11335) .50 2.00 72
TIME IN A BOTTLE/Hard Time Losin' Man (ABC 11405) .50 2.00 73
WORKIN' AT THE CAR WASH BLUES/Thursday (ABC 11447) .50 2.00 74
YOU DON'T MESS AROUND WITH JIM/
Photographs & Memories (ABC 11328) .50 2.00 72
Also see Jim & Ingrid

CROCKETT BROTHERS, The
MOTHER, MOTHER CAN I GO SURFIN'/
After You've Been So True (Del Fi 4213) 1.00 4.00 63

CROSBY, Bing
ALL SHE SAID WAS "UMH HUM"/
She's The Sunshine Of Virginia (Decca 29568) 1.00 4.00 55
AND THE BELLS RANG/Time To Be Jolly (Daybreak 1001) .50 2.00 70
ANGEL BELLS/Let's Harmonize (Decca 29636) 1.00 4.00 55
AROUND THE WORLD/
Around The World (By Victor Young & His Orchestra) (Decca 30262) 1.00 4.00 57
CALL OF THE SOUTH/Cornbelt Symphony (Decca 29147) 1.25 5.00 54
(With Gary Crosby)
CHANGING PARTNERS/Y'all Come (Decca 28969) 1.25 5.00 53
CHRISTMAS IS A-COMIN'/Is Christmas Only A Tree (Decca 29790) 1.00 4.00 55
COOL WATER/South Rampart St. Parade (Decca 28419) 1.25 5.00 53
COUNT YOUR BLESSINGS INSTEAD OF SHEEP/
What Can You Do With A General (Decca 29251) 1.25 5.00 54
DOMINO/When The World Was Young (Decca 27830) 1.25 5.00 51
DOWN BY THE RIVERSIDE/
What A Little Moonlight Can Do (Decca 28955) 1.25 5.00 54
FAREWELL/Jim, Johnny & Jonas (Decca 29483) 1.00 4.00 55
GRANADA/It Had To Be You (Decca 28743) 1.25 5.00 53
HEY JUDE/Lonely Street (Amos 111) .50 2.00 69
HUSH A BYE/Mother Darlin' (Decca 28581) 1.25 5.00 53
IDA! SWEET AS APPLE CIDER/
I Can't Believe That You're In Love With Me (Decca 28963) 1.25 5.00 54
(With Carmen Cavallaro)
IF THERE'S ANYBODY HERE (FROM OUT OF TOWN)/
Back In The Old Routine (Decca 29035) 1.25 5.00 54
IN A LITTLE SPANISH TOWN/Ol' Man River (Decca 29850) 1.00 4.00 56
IN THE COOL, COOL, COOL OF THE EVENING/
Misto Christopho Columbo (Decca 27678) 1.25 5.00 51
(With Jane Wyman)
IN THE GOOD OLD SUMMERTIME/Oh' Tell Me Why (Decca 29212) 1.25 5.00 54
IT'S ALL IN THE GAME/More & More (Amos 116) .50 2.00 69
KEEP IT A SECRET/Sleighbell Serenade (Decca 28511) 1.25 5.00 53
MADEMOISELLE DE PAREE/Embrasse Moi Ben-De (Decca 28814) 1.25 5.00 53
MOONLIGHT BAY/When You & I Were Young (Decca 27577) 1.25 5.00 51
(With Gary Crosby)
NOBODY/Silver Moon (Decca 29483) 1.00 4.00 55
NOW YOU HAS JAZZ (With Louis Armstrong)/
High Society Calypso (By Louis Armstrong) (Capitol 3506) 1.00 4.00 56
OPEN UP YOUR HEART/You Don't Know (Decca 28470) 1.25 5.00 53
SAM'S SONG/Play A Simple Melody (Decca 27112) 1.25 5.00 50
(With Gary Brosby)
SEARCH IS THROUGH, THE/The Land Around Us (Decca 29410) 1.00 4.00 55
SECRET LOVE/My Love, My Love (Decca 29024) 1.25 5.00 54
SONG FROM DESIREE/Who Gave You The Rose (Decca 29357) 1.00 5.00 54
(With Alfred Newman & His Orchestra)
SWANEE/Honeysuckle Rose (Decca 29981) 1.00 4.00 56
(With The Buddy Cole Trio)
TENDERFOOT/Walk Me By The River (Decca 28733) 1.25 5.00 53
TRUE LOVE (With Grace Kelly)/
Well Did You Evah? (With Frank Sinatra) (Capitol 3507) 1.00 4.00 56
WHEN YOU'RE IN LOVE/John Barleycorn (Decca 29817) 1.00 4.00 56
YOUNG AT HEART/I Get So Lonely (Decca 29054) 1.25 5.00 54

CROSBY, Bob
PETITE FLEUR/Such A Long Night (Dot 15890) .75 3.00 59
(With the Bob Cats)
Bob is Bing Crosby's Brother.

CROSBY, Chris
LOVE IS A ROSE/Only The Young (Challenge 59282) .75 3.00 65
YOUNG & IN LOVE/Raindrops In My Heart (MGM 13191) .75 3.00 64
Chris is Bob Crosby's son.

CROSBY, David (Of The Byrds)
MUSIC IS LOVE/Laughing (Atlantic 2792) .50 2.00 71
ORLEANS/Traction In The Rain (Atlantic 2809) .50 2.00 71

CROSBY, David, & Graham Nash
CARRY ME/Mama Lion (ABC 12140) .50 2.00 75
IMMIGRATION MAN/Whole Cloth (Atlantic 2873) .50 2.00 72
LOVE WORK OUT/Bittersweet (ABC 12185) .50 2.00 76
OUT OF THE DARKNESS/Broken Bird (ABC 12199) .50 2.00 76
SOUTHBOUND TRAIN/The Wall Song (Atlantic 2892) .50 2.00 72
SPOTLIGHT/Foolish Man (ABC 12217) .50 2.00 77
TAKE THE MONEY & RUN/Bittersweet (ABC 12165) .50 2.00 76

CROSBY, Gary
THAT'S ALRIGHT BABY/Who (Gregmark 11) .75 3.00 63
TRULY DO/His & Hers (Decca 29527) 1.00 4.00 55
(With the Paris Sisters)

CROSBY, STILLS & NASH
(David Crosby, Stephen Stills, Graham Nash)
FAIR GAME/Anything At All (Atlantic 3432) .50 2.00 77
I GIVE YOU GIVE BLIND/Carried Away (Atlantic 3453) .50 2.00 78
JUST A SONG BEFORE I GO/Dark Star (Atlantic 3401) .50 2.00 77
MARRAKESH EXPRESS/Helplessly Hoping (Atlantic 2652) .50 2.00 69
STUIE: JUDY BLUE EYES/Long Time Gone (Atlantic 2676) .50 2.00 69

CROSBY, STILLS, NASH & YOUNG
(David Crosby, Stephen Stills, Graham Nash, Neil Young)
OHIO/Find The Cost Of Freedom (Atlantic 2740) .50 2.00 70
OUR HOUSE/Deja Vu (Atlantic 2760) .50 2.00 70
TEACH YOUR CHILDREN/Carry On (Atlantic 2735) .50 2.00 70
WOODSTOCK/Helpless (Atlantic 2723) .50 2.00 70

CROSS COUNTRY (The Tokens)
IN THE MIDNIGHT HOUR/A Smile Song (Atco 6934) .50 2.00 73
ROCK & ROLL MUSIC/ (Atco 6932) .50 2.00 73
TASTES SO GOOD TO ME/ (Atco 6947) .50 2.00 73

CROSSFIRES, The
FIBERGLASS JUNGLE/Dr. Jekyll & Mr. Hyde (Capco 104) 2.00 8.00
ONE POTATO TWO POTATO/That'll Be The Day (Lucky Token 112) 1.00 4.00
Also see Turtles, The

BOB DYLAN SINGS
"SUBTERRANEAN HOMESICK BLUES"
c/w "SHE BELONGS TO ME" ON COLUMBIA RECORDS
COLUMBIA
Produced by John Hammond
45 RPM
4-42656
MIXED UP CONFUSION
- B. Dylan -
BOB DYLAN
MARCAS REG. PRINTED IN U.S.A.
COLUMBIA
NOT FOR RESALE
45 RPM
RADIO STATION COPY
BOB DYLAN
STEREO
AE 7 1039
JZSS 156319
2:40
Publisher: Big Sky Mus. (ASCAP)
IF NOT FOR YOU
- B. Dylan -
Produced by: Bob Johnston
"COLUMBIA" MARCAS REG PRINTED IN U.S.A.
BOB DYLAN
AE 25
JZSS 154036
3:11
Publisher: Big Sky Music ASCAP
ALL THE TIRED HORSES
- B. Dylan -
From the Columbia Lp "BOB DYLAN SELF PORTRAIT" C2X 30050
Produced by Bob Johnston

Bob Dylan

TITLE/FLIP	LABEL & NO.	GOOD	NEAR MINT	YR.
CROSS, Jimmy				
HEY LITTLE GIRL (PART 1)/Hey Little Girl (Part 2)	(Chicken 101)	1.00	4.00	65
HEY LITTLE GIRL/Super-Duper Man	(Red Bird 10-042)	.75	3.00	65
I WANT MY BABY BACK/Play The Other Side	(Tollie 9039)	1.25	5.00	64
PRETTY GIRLS EVERYWHERE/Suntan Sally	(Recordo 502)	1.25	5.00	61
CROUCH, Dub				
LEGEND OF ELVIS PRESLEY, THE/ Dallas Blues	(Professional Artist 774588)	.50	2.00	77
CROW (With David Wagner)				
CADO QUEEN/If It Feels Good, Do It	(Amaret 148)	.50	2.00	71
COTTAGE CHEESE/Busy Day	(Amaret 119)	.50	2.00	70
COTTAGE CHEESE/Slow Down	(Amaret 119)	.50	2.00	70
DON'T TRY TO LAY NO BOOGIE-WOOGIE ON THE KING OF ROCK & ROLL/Satisfied	(Amaret 125)	.50	2.00	70
EVIL WOMAN DON'T PLAY YOUR GAMES WITH ME/ Gonna Leave A Mark	(Amaret 112)	.50	2.00	69
IF IT FEELS GOOD DO IT/Cado Queen	(Amaret 148)	.50	2.00	72
MOBILE BLUE/Everything Has To Be Free	(Amaret 145)	.50	2.00	72
SOMETHING IN YOUR BLOOD/Yellow Dawg	(Amaret 133)	.50	2.00	71
WATCHING CAN WASTE UP THE TIME/Yellow Dawg	(Amaret 129)	.50	2.00	71
CROWNS, The				
I WONDER WHY/Better Luck Next Time	(Vee Jay 546)	1.25	5.00	63
PARTY TIME/Amazon Basin Pop	(Chordette 1001)	.75	3.00	62
POSSIBILITY/Watch Out (With Larry Chance)	(Old Town 1171)	2.50	10.00	63
CRUISERS, The				
ANOTHER LONELY NIGHT/Please Let Me Be	(Pharaoh 128)	1.25	5.00	
THERE'S A GIRL/Foolish Me	(Zebra 119)	10.00	40.00	
CRUSIERS, The				
BETTY ANN/You Made A Fool Out Of Me	(Coda 3005)	1.00	4.00	59
CRUSIN'/My Mary Lou	(Winston 1033)	1.00	4.00	59
CRYAN' SHAMES, The				
FIRST TRAIN TO CALIFORNIA/A Master's Fool	(Columbia 4-45027)	.75	3.00	68
GREENBURG, GLICKSTEIN, CHARLES, DAVID SMITH & JONES/ The Warm	(Columbia 4-44638)	.75	3.00	68
I WANNA MEET YOU/We Could Be Happy	(Columbia 4-43836)	.75	3.00	66
IT COULD BE WE'RE IN LOVE/I Was Lonely When	(Columbia 4-44191)	.75	3.00	67
MR. UNRELIABLE/Georgia	(Columbia 4-44037)	.75	3.00	67
RAINMAKER/Bits & Pieces	(Columbia 4-45027)	.75	3.00	70
SUGAR & SPICE/Ben Franklin's Almanac	(Destination 624)	.75	3.00	66
UP ON THE ROOF/Sailing Ship	(Columbia 4-44457)	.75	3.00	67
YOUNG BIRDS FLY/Sunshine Psalm	(Columbia 4-44545)	.75	3.00	68
CRYERS, The				
(IT'S GONNA BE) A HEARTBREAKER/ Just A Little Rain	(Mercury 74017)	.50	2.00	78
TALK TO ME (TALK TO ME)/Faith & Hope	(20th Century-Fox 2419)	.50	2.00	79
CRYIN' SHAMES, The				
PLEASE STAY (DON'T GO)/Whats New Pussy Cat	(London 1001)	.75	3.00	68
CRYSTAL, Cathy				
JIMMY/Sing A Song Of Loneliness	(Day Dell 1001)	1.00	4.00	
CRYSTAL GLASS				
LEMME SEE YA GITCHERYER THING OFF, BABY/ Tajmahal	(Private Stock 45082)	1.00	4.00	76
CRYSTAL, Lou				
SHIELA BABY/Dreaming Of An Angel (Group Sound)	(SFAZ 1001)	3.00	12.00	62
CRYSTAL MANSION, The (Featuring Johnny Caswell)				
EVERYTHING'S IN LOVE TODAY/Country	(Capitol 2543)	.75	3.00	69
FOR THE FIRST TIME/I Got Something For You	(Capitol 2424)	.75	3.00	68
THOUGHT OF LOVING YOU/Hallelujah	(Capitol 2275)	.75	3.00	68
CRYSTAL TONES, The				
GIRL I LOVE, A/Debra-Lee	(M.Z. 007)	5.00	20.00	
CRYSTALS, The				
ALL GROWN UP/Irving (Jaggered Sixteenths)	(Philles 122)	1.50	6.00	64
DA DOO RON RON (WHEN HE WALKED ME HOME)/Git It	(Philles 112)	1.00	4.00	63
DREAMS & WISHES/Mr. Brush	(Indigo 114)	1.50	6.00	61
HE HIT ME (& IT FELT LIKE A KISS)/ No One Ever Tells You	(Philles 105)	3.00	12.00	62
HE'S A REBEL/I Love You Eddie	(Philles 106)	1.00	4.00	62
HE'S SURE THE BOY I LOVE/Walkin' Along	(Philles 109)	1.00	4.00	62
LITTLE BOY/Harry (From W. Va.) & Milt	(Philles 119)	1.50	6.00	64
MY PLACE/You Can't Tie A Good Girl Down	(United Artists 927)	1.00	4.00	65
THEN HE KISSED ME/Brother Julius	(Philles 115)	1.00	4.00	63
THERE'S NO OTHER (LIKE MY BABY)/ Oh Yeah Maybe Baby	(Philles 100)	1.25	5.00	61
UPTOWN/What A Nice Way To Turn Seventeen	(Philles 102)	1.25	5.00	62
CUBS, The				
I HEAR WEDDING BELLS/Why Did You Make Me Cry	(Savoy 1502)	1.25	5.00	56
CUFF LINKS, The (Ron Dante)				
RUN, SALLY RUN/I Remember	(Decca 32639)	.50	2.00	70
THANK YOU PRETTY BABY/Kiss	(Decca 32732)	.50	2.00	70
TRACY/Where Do You Go?	(Decca 32533)	.50	2.00	69
WHEN JULIE COMES AROUND/	(Decca 32592)	.50	2.00	69
CUFFLINKS, The				
ONLY ONE LOVE/Next To You	(Gait 1445)	7.50	30.00	
CULOMBO, Joe				
CRAZY FOR YOU/Closer You Are	(Style-no number)	1.50	6.00	
CUMMINGS, Burton (Of Guess Who)				
BREAK IT TO THEM GENTLY/Roll With The Punches	(Portrait 70016)	.50	2.00	78
I'M SCARED/Sugartime Flashback Joys	(Portrait 70002)	.50	2.00	77
MY OWN WAY TO ROCK/A Song For Him	(Portrait 70007)	.50	2.00	77
NEVER HAD A LADY BEFORE/Timeless Love	(Portrait 70003)	.50	2.00	77
STAND TALL/Burch Magic	(Portrait 70001)	.50	2.00	76
TAKES A FOOL TO LOVE A FOOL/I Will Play A Rhapsody	(Portrait 70024)	.50	2.00	78
CUPCAKES, The				
DEUTSCHE ROCK & ROLL/It's Willy	(Time 1011)	1.00	4.00	59
CUPS, The				
GOOD AS GOLD/My Life & Times	(Tetragrammaton 1538)	.75	3.00	69
CURB, Mike, Congregation				
BURNING BRIDGES/	(MGM 14151)	.50	2.00	71
COME TOGETHER-HEY JUDE/ Suspicious Minds-Midnight Special	(Coburt 101)	.75	3.00	70
DO YOU WANNA DANCE/ Fools Rush In (Where Angels Fear To Tread)	(Capitol 4166)	.50	2.00	75
EIGHT YOUNG MEN (DEVIL'S 8 THEME)/	(Tower 480)	.75	3.00	69
FLY ME A PLACE FOR THE SUMMER/Sweet Gingerbread Man	(MGM 14265)	.50	2.00	71
I WAS BORN IN LOVE WITH YOU/	(Air 168)	.75	3.00	71
I WAS BORN IN LOVE WITH YOU/Sweet Gingerbread Man	(MGM 14243)	.50	2.00	71
LONG HAIRED LOVER FROM LIVERPOOL/ Sweet Gingerbread Man	(MGM 14140)	.50	2.00	70
MICKEY MOUSE MARCH/Mickey Mouse Alma Mater	(Buena Vista 499)	.50	2.00	75
MICKEY MOUSE MARCH/You Were On My Mind	(Capitol 4102)	.50	2.00	75
CURLS, The				
HE'S MY HERO/Like A Waterfall	(Everest 19350)	.75	3.00	60
CURRENTS, The				
NIGHT RUN/Riff Raff (Instrumentals)	(Laurie 3205)	1.00	4.00	63
CURRIE, Cherie & Marie (Of The Runaways)				
SINCE YOU'VE BEEN GONE/Longer Than Forever	(Capitol 4754)	.50	2.00	79
CURRY, Tim				
BABY LOVE/Just 14 (With Brian Wilson)	(Ode 66117)	10.00	40.00	
BABY LOVE/Baby Love	(Ode 66117)	.75	3.00	
(As noted above, Brian Wilson appears on "Just 14," the flip side of the commercial issue. Since the promotional issue does not have that song its value is minimal.)				
I DO THE ROCK/Hide This Face	(A&M 2166)	.50	2.00	79
I WILL/	(A&M 2105)	.50	2.00	78
CURTISS, Dave, & The Tremors				
QUE SERA SERA/How I Cry	(Karate 514)	.75	3.00	65
CURTISS, Jimmy				
LET'S DANCE CLOSE/ The Girl From The Land Of A Thousand Dances (With the Regents)	(Laurie 3315)	2.50	10.00	65
CURTIS, Sonny (Of The Crickets)				
ATLANTA GEORGIA STRAY/Day Drinker	(Viva 626)	2.00	8.00	68
BEATLE I WANT TO BE, A/So Used To Loving You	(Dimension 1024)	2.00	8.00	64
BO DIDDLEY BACH/I Pledge My Love To You	(Liberty 55710)	2.50	10.00	64
COWBOY SINGER, THE/Cheatin' Clouds	(Elektra 46526)	.50	2.00	79
DESTINY'S CHILD/The Collector	(Viva 607)	2.00	8.00	66
GIRL OF THE NORTH/Hung Up In Your Eyes	(Viva 636)	2.50	10.00	69
HOLIDAY FOR CLOWNS/Day Gig	(Viva 634)	2.50	10.00	69
I WANNA GO BUMMING AROUND/I'm A Gypsy Man	(Viva 617)	2.00	8.00	67
LOVE IS ALL AROUND/The Clone Song	(Elektra 46663)	.50	2.00	80
LOVE IS ALL AROUND ("MARY TYLER MOORE" THEME)/ Here, There & Everywhere	(Ovation 1006)	4.00	16.00	70
LOVESICK BLUES/It's Only A Question Of Time	(Capitol 4158)	2.00	8.00	75
ROCK & ROLL, I GAVE YOU THE BEST YEARS OF MY LIFE/ My Mama Sure Left Me Some Good Old Days	(Mercury 73438)	2.50	10.00	72
MY WAY OF LIFE/Last Call	(Viva 602)	2.00	8.00	66
REAL BUDDY HOLLY STORY, THE/Ain't Nobody Honest	(Elektra 46616)	.50	2.00	80
RED HEADED STRANGER/Talk About My Baby	(Coral 62207)	5.00	20.00	60
SO USED TO LOVING YOU/ Last Song I'm Ever Gonna Sing	(Dimension 1017)	2.00	8.00	63
STRAIGHT LIFE, THE/How Little Men Care	(Viva 630)	2.00	8.00	68
SUNNY MORNIN'/The Lights Of L.A.	(A&M 1359)	4.00	16.00	72
WALK RIGHT BACK/ Do You Remember "Roll Over Beethoven"	(Elektra 46568)	.50	2.00	79
WHEN IT'S JUST YOU & ME/It's Only A Question Of Time	(Capitol 4227)	2.00	8.00	76
WHERE'S PATRICIA NOW/When It's Just You & Me	(Capitol 4240)	3.00	12.00	76
WILLA MAE JONES/A Pretty Girl	(Dot 15799)	2.50	10.00	58
WRONG AGAIN/Laughing Stock	(Dot 15754)	4.00	16.00	58
YOU DON'T BELONG IN THIS PLACE/Unsaintly Judy	(Ovation 1023)	2.50	10.00	70
YOU DON'T BELONG IN THIS PLACE/Unsaintly Judy	(Dimension 1023)	2.00	8.00	63
CURTOLA, Bobby				
ALADDIN/I Don't Want To Go On Without You	(Del Fi 4185)	1.00	4.00	62
DESTINATION LOVE/Hitchhicker	(Del Fi 4195)	1.00	4.00	63
FORTUNETELLER/Johnny Take Your Time	(Del Fi 4177)	1.00	4.00	62
MY HEART'S TONGUE-TIED/Don't You Sweetheart Me	(Del Fi 4163)	1.00	4.00	61
THREE ROWS OVER/How'm I Gonna Tell You	(Del Fi 4223)	1.00	4.00	63
CURVED AIR				
BACK STREET LUV/Everdance	(Warner Bros. 7519)	.50	2.00	71
IT HAPPENED TODAY/ What Happens When You Blow Yourself Up	(Warner Bros. 7470)	.50	2.00	71
CUSTER & THE SURVIVERS				
I SAW HER WALKING/Flapjacks	(Golden State 657)	1.25	5.00	
CUSTOMS, The				
BECAUSE OF LOVE/Earthquake (Instrumental)	(Arlen 511)	1.00	4.00	63
CUTE TEENS, The				
WHEN MY TEENAGE DAYS ARE OVER/ From This Day Forward	(Aladdin 3458)	1.00	4.00	59
CUTUPS, The				
CUTUPS/Romeo	(Music Makers 301)	.75	3.00	
CYCLONE III				
SURFANNANNY/You've Got A Bomb	(Philips 40258)	1.00	4.00	65
CYCLONES, The (Featuring Bill Taylor)				
BULLWHIP ROCK/Nelda Jane (Instrumental)	(Trophy 500)	2.00	8.00	58
CYMANDE				
BRA/Ras Tafarian Folk Song	(Janus 215)	.75	3.00	73
CYMARRON				
RINGS/Like Children	(Entrance 7500)	.50	2.00	71
VALERIE/	(Entrance 7502)	.50	2.00	71
CYMBAL & CLINGER (Johnny Cymbal & Peggy Clinger)				
DYING RIVER, THE/A Little Bit No, A Little Bit Yes	(Chelsea 78-0112)	.50	2.00	73
MOOKIE MOOKIE MAN, THE/The Pool Shooter	(Marina 502)	.50	2.00	72
CYMBAL, Johnny				
BACHELOR MAN/Growing Up With You	(Kedlen 2001)	2.00	8.00	
BACHELOR MAN/Growing Up With You	(Vee Jay 495)	1.25	5.00	63
BIG RIVER/Girl From Willow County	(Amaret 110)	.75	3.00	69
DUM DUM DEE DUM/Tijuana	(Kapp 539)	.75	3.00	63
GO VW GO/Sorrow & Pain	(DCP 1135)	.75	3.00	65
HURDY GURDY MAN/Marshmallow	(Kapp 556)	.75	3.00	63
IT'LL BE ME/Always	(MGM 12935)	1.00	4.00	60
LITTLE MISS LONELY/Connie	(Kapp 614)	1.25	5.00	64
MR. BASS MAN/Sacred Lovers Vow	(Kapp 503)	.75	3.00	63
("Mr. Bass Man" on this recording was Ronnie Bright, formerly the bass singer for the Valentines.)				
SUMMERTIME'S HERE AT LAST/My Last Day	(DCP 1146)	.75	3.00	65
TEENAGE HEAVEN/Cinderella Baby	(Kapp 524)	1.00	4.00	63
THERE GOES A BAD GIRL/Refreshment Time	(Kapp 576)	.75	3.00	64
WATER WAS RED, THE/Bunny	(MGM 12978)	1.00	4.00	60
Also see Cymbal & Clinger				
Also see Derek				
Also see Taurus				
CYRKLE, The				
CAMARO/SS 396 (By Paul Revere & The Raiders) (Special Chevrolet products issue)	(Columbia 466)	1.50	6.00	
FRIENDS/Reading Her Paper	(Columbia 4-44426)	.75	3.00	68
I WISH YOU COULD BE HERE/ The Visit (She Was Here)	(Columbia 4-43965)	.75	3.00	67
PENNY ARCADE/The Words	(Columbia 4-44224)	.75	3.00	67
PLEASE DON'T EVER LEAVE ME/Money To Burn	(Columbia 4-43871)	.75	3.00	66
RED RUBBER BALL/How Can I Leave Her	(Columbia 4-43589)	.75	3.00	66
RED RUBBER BALL/Red Rubber Ball (Red plastic, promotional issue)	(Columbia 4-43589)	1.00	4.00	65
TURN-DOWN DAY/Big, Little Woman	(Columbia 4-43729)	.75	3.00	66
TURN OF THE CENTURY/ Don't Cry, No Fears, No Tears Comin' Your Way	(Columbia 4-44366)	.75	3.00	67
WE HAD A GOOD THING GOIN'/Two Rooms	(Columbia 4-44108)	.75	3.00	67
CYRUS ERIE (Featuring Eric Carmen)				
SPARROW/Get The Message	(Epic 10451)	2.50	10.00	69
Also see Quick, The				
Also see Choir, The				
Also see Raspberries, The				

TITLE/FLIP	LABEL & NO.	GOOD	NEAR MINT	YR.
D.J. PAUL				
HI YA PIERREPONT/	(Dor 1001)	1.00	4.00	
"D" MEN, The				
DON'T YOU KNOW/No Hope For Me	(Veep 1206)	.75	3.00	66
JUST DON'T CARE/Mousin' Around	(Veep 1209)	.75	3.00	66
D'ABO, Mike (Of Manfred Mann)				
LITTLE MISS UNDERSTOOD/	(A&M 1374)	.50	2.00	73
MISS ME IN THE MORNING/Arabella Cinderella	(Bell 956)	.50	2.00	71
D'ACCORDS, The				
RUNNIN' AROUND/Who's Been Lovin' You	(Don-El 110)	3.75	15.00	
DACHE, Bertell (Tony Orlando)				
NOT JUST TOMORROW, BUT ALWAYS/Love Eyes (With Carole King)	(United Artists 290)	3.75	15.00	61
DADDY BOB (Bob Bertram)				
WELCOME HOME ELVIS/Poppa's Gone	(Bertram-International 1835)	.50	2.00	77
DADDY COOL				
STORY OF DADDY COOL, THE/ Wedding Bells Are Ringing In My Ears	(Blue Sky 107)	2.50	10.00	
TEENAGE HEAVEN/ (Stereo 78rpm, promotional issue only)	(Reprise PRO 522)	3.75	15.00	72
DADDY DEWDROP				
CHANTILLY LACE/Migraine Headaches	(Sunflower 119)	.50	2.00	72
CHICK-A-BOOM (DON'T YA JES' LOVE IT)/ John Jacob Jingleheimer Smith	(Sunflower 105)	.50	2.00	71
DADDY O's, The				
GOT A MATCH/Have A Cigar	(Cabot 122)	1.00	4.00	58
DAE, Tommy, & The High Tensions				
ITSY BITSY TEENIE WEENIE YELLOW POLKA-DOT BIKINI/ Summertime Girl	(Diamond 226)	.75	3.00	67
D'AGOSTIN, Dick				
NANCY LYNNE/Afraid To Take A Chance	(Dot 15773)	3.00	12.00	58
DAHCOTAH				
TOO EASY TO LOVE/	(Cognito 006)	.75	3.00	

TITLE/FLIP	LABEL & NO.	GOOD	NEAR MINT	YR.

DAHILLS, The
DO YOU WANT TO GO STEADY/Please Be My Girlfriend ..... (Clifton 14) .75 3.00
MICHELLE/Why Do We Have To Say Goodnight .... (Musicor 1041) 2.00 8.00 64

DAHL, Dick
UNTRUE/Don't Let The Little Girl Cry .... (Original Sound 53) 1.00 4.00

DAHL, Steve, & The Teenage Radiation
AYATOLLAH/Unhappy New Year .... (Coho 007) .50 2.00 79
DO YOU THINK I'M DISCO/Coho Lip Blues .... (Ovation OV-1132) .50 2.00 79
(Parody)

DAILEY, Jack
LITTLE CHARMER/Please Understand (German) .... (Guyden 2038) .75 3.00 60
LITTLE CHARMER/Please Understand (English) .... (Jamie 1162) .75 3.00 60

DAILY FLASH
FRENCH GIRL/Green Rocky Road .... (Uni 55001) .75 3.00 67
QUEEN JANE APPROXIMATELY/Jack Of Diamonds .... (Parrot 308) .75 3.00 66

DAKIL, Floyd, Combo
DANCE FRANNY DANCE/
Look What You've Gone & Done .... (Guyden 2111) 1.25 5.00 65
DANCE, FRANNY, DANCE/
Look What You've Gone & Done .... (Jetstar 103) 3.75 15.00 64

DAKOTAS, The
CRUEL SEA, THE/The Millionaire .... (Liberty 55618) .75 3.00 63
(Instrumental)
Also see Kramer, Billy J., & the Dakotas

DALE, Alan
CHERRY PINK & APPLE BLOSSOM WHITE/I'm Sincere ..... (Coral 61373) 1.00 4.00 55
SWEET & GENTLE/You Still Mean The Same .... (Coral 61435) 1.00 4.00 55
Also see Desmond, Johnny, Alan Dale & Don Cornell

DALE & GRACE (Dale Houston & Grace Broussard)
I'M LEAVING IT UP TO YOU/Foolin' Around .... (Michelle 921) 1.50 6.00 63
I'M LEAVING IT UP TO YOU/That's What I Like About You .. (Montel 921) .75 3.00 63
LET THEM TALK/I'd Rather Be Free .... (HBR 472) .75 3.00 66
LONELIEST NIGHT, THE/I'm Not Free .... (Michelle 928) 1.50 6.00 64
LONELIEST NIGHT, THE/I'm Not Free .... (Montel 928) .75 3.00 64
SO FINE/It Keeps Right On A Hurtin' .... (Montel 989) .75 3.00 67
STOP & THINK IT OVER/Bad Luck .... (Michelle 923) 1.50 6.00 63
STOP & THINK IT OVER/Bad Luck .... (Montel 922) .75 3.00 63
WHAT AM I LIVING FOR/Something Special .... (Montel 942) .75 3.00 64

DALE, Denny, & The Honeymoons
MR. MOON/Why Did You Leave Me .... (Soma 1447) .75 3.00 66

DALE, Dick (With The Del-tones)
EYES OF A CHILD/Just A Waitin' .... (Accent 1243) .75 3.00 68
GLORY WAVE/Never On Sunday .... (Capitol 5225) 1.00 4.00 64
JESSIE PEARL/St. Louis Blues .... (Deltone 5014) 5.00 20.00 60
KING OF THE SURF GUITAR/Hava Nagilah .... (Capitol 4963) 1.00 4.00 63
KING OF THE SURF GUITAR/Hava Nagilah .... (Capitol 4963) 2.50 10.00 63
(Picture sleeve)
LET'S GO TRIPPIN'/Del-Tone Rock .... (Deltone 5017) 1.00 4.00 61
LET'S GO TRIPPIN'/Those Memories Of You .... (GNP Crescendo 804) .50 2.00 75
LET'S GO TRIPPIN' '65/Watusi Jo .... (Capitol 5389) .75 3.00 65
LOVIN' ON MY BRAIN/Run For Your Life .... (Deltone 5028) 2.50 10.00 63
MISERLOU/Eight Till Midnight .... (Deltone 5019) 1.00 4.00 62
MISERLOU/Eight Till Midnight .... (Capitol 4939) .75 3.00 62
MR. ELIMINATOR/Victor .... (Capitol 5140) 1.00 4.00 64
OH WHEE MARIE/Breaking Heart .... (Deltone 5012) 1.25 5.00 59
PEPPERMINT MAN/Surf Beat .... (Deltone 4940) 1.25 5.00 62
PEPPERMINT MAN/Surf Beat .... (Deltone 5020) 1.00 4.00 62
PEPPERMINT MAN/Surf Beat .... (Capitol 4940) .75 3.00 63
PEPPERMINT MAN/
Open-End Interview-Misirlou .... (Capitol PRO-2320) 3.75 15.00 63
(Compact 33 single)
PEPPERMINT MAN/
Open-End Interview-Misirlou .... (Capitol PRO-2320) 6.25 25.00 63
(Promotional picture sleeve for compact 33 single.)
SCAVENGER, THE/Wild Ideas .... (Capitol 5048) 1.00 4.00 63
SECRET SURFIN' SPOT/Surfin' & A-Swingin' .... (Capitol 5010) 1.00 4.00 63
SHAKE & STOMP/Jungle Fever .... (Deltone 5018) 1.00 4.00 62
STOP TEASING/Without Your Love .... (Deltone 5013) 5.00 20.00 59
TACO WAGON/Spanish Kiss .... (Cougar 712) .50 2.00 67
THUNDER WAVE/Spanish Kiss .... (Capitol PRO-2646) 1.50 6.00 63
(Bonus 45, packaged with "Surf Age" LP)
WE'LL NEVER HEAR THE END OF IT/Fairest Of Them All ... (Cupid 106) 2.00 8.00 60
WE'LL NEVER HEAR THE END OF IT/Fairest Of Them All ... (Saturn 401) 1.25 5.00 63
WE'LL NEVER HEAR THE END OF IT/
Fairest Of Them All .... (Concert Room 371) 1.00 4.00 63
WE'LL NEVER HEAR THE END OF IT/Fairest Of Them All .... (Yes 7014) .75 3.00
WEDGE, THE/Night Rider .... (Capitol 5098) 1.00 4.00 63
WHO CAN HE BE/Oh Marie .... (Capitol 5290) 1.00 4.00 64
WILD, WILD MUSTANG/Grudge Run .... (Capitol 5187) 1.00 4.00 64
Also see Exiles, The

DALE, Jimmy: see Clanton, Jimmy

DALES, The
ROCKIN' NELLIE/Sweet Annie .... (Crest 1069) 1.00 4.00 60

DALLARA, Tony
COME PRIMA (THE FIRST TIME)/Condannami .... (Mercury 71327) 1.00 4.00 58

DALLAS, Jackie
LORRAINE/You Told A Lie .... (Fawn 6002) 1.25 5.00

DALTON BROTHERS, The (Scott Engel & John Stewart)
I ONLY CAME TO DANCE WITH YOU/Without You, Love .. (Martay 2001) 3.75 15.00 64
Also see Walker Brothers, The

DALTON, Danny
WHO'S GONNA HOLD YOUR HAND/Walkin' .... (Teen 505) 1.00 4.00 59

DALTON, Frank
QUICK DRAW MC GRAW/Cruised .... (Mercury 71857) .75 3.00 61

DALTON, James & Sutton
I'VE GOT YOU, YOU'VE GOT ME/ .... (RCA 74-0853) .50 2.00 72
WE CAN CHANGE IT/Esatoria .... (RCA 74-0688) .50 2.00 72

DALTREY, Roger (Of The Who)
AVENGING ANNIE/The Prisoner .... (MCA-Goldhawke 40800) .50 2.00 77
COME & GET YOUR LOVE/Heart-s Right .... (MCA-Goldhawke 40453) .50 2.00 75
DOING IT ALL AGAIN/One Of The Boys .... (MCA 40761) .50 2.00 77
GIVING IT ALL AWAY/Way Of The World .... (Track 40053) .50 2.00 73
I'M FREE/Underture .... (Ode 66040) .50 2.00 72
LEON/The Prisoner .... (MCA—Goldhawke 40862) .50 2.00 77
LOVE'S DREAM/Orpheus Song (With Rick Wakeman) .... (A&M 1779) .50 2.00 76
(Promotional issue only.)
OCEANS AWAY/Feeling .... (MCA-Goldhawke 40512) .50 2.00 76
ONE OF THE BOYS/
Please Don't Say Goodbye (By Steve Gibbons) .... (MCA 1962) 1.00 4.00 77
(12" promotional issue)
SAY IT AIN'T SO, JOE/Satin & Lace .... (MCA-Goldhawke 40765) .50 2.00 77
THINKING/ .... (Track 40084) .50 2.00 73

DAMASCANS, The
GO 'WAY GIRL/ .... (Pyramid 6372) 1.25 5.00

DAMERON, Donna
BOPPER 486609/ 2.50 10.00 59
(Answer song to "Chantilly Lace")

DAMIANO, Joe (Joe DiAngelis)
I CRIED/Sittin' On A Shelf .... (Chancellor 1339) 1.00 4.00 59

DAMITA JO
I'LL BE THERE (Answer song)/
Love Laid Its Hands On Me .... (Mercury 71840) .75 3.00 61
I'LL SAVE THE LAST DANCE FOR YOU (Answer song)/
Forgive .... (Mercury 71690) .75 3.00 60
KEEP YOUR HANDS OFF OF HIM/
Hush Somebody's Calling .... (Mercury 71760) .75 3.00 61

DAMONE, Vic
AN AFFAIR TO REMEMBER/
In The Eyes Of The World .... (Columbia 4-40945) .75 3.00 57
APRIL IN PORTUGAL/I'm Walking Behind You .... (Mercury 70125) 1.00 4.00 53
CALLA CALLA/It's A Long Way .... (Mercury 5698) 1.00 4.00 51
DO I LOVE YOU (BECAUSE YOU'RE BEAUTIFUL)/
Legend Of The Bells .... (Columbia 4-40858) .75 3.00 57
GIGI/On The Street Where You Live .... (Columbia 4-41122) .75 3.00 58
JUST SAY I LOVE HER/Can Anyone Explain .... (Mercury 5474) 1.00 4.00 50
LONGING FOR YOU/Son Of A Sailor .... (Mercury 5655) 1.00 4.00 51
MY HEART CRIES FOR YOU/Music By The Angels .... (Mercury 5563) 1.00 4.00 50
MY TRULY, TRULY FAIR/My Life's Desire .... (Mercury 5646) 1.00 4.00 51
ON THE STREET WHERE YOU LIVE/We All Need Love (Columbia 4-40654) .75 3.00 56
POR FAVOR/Born To Sing The Blues .... (Mercury 70699) 1.00 4.00 55
TZENA, TZENA, TZENA/I Love That Girl .... (Mercury 5454) 1.00 4.00 50
VAGABOND SHOES/I Hadn't Anyone Till You .... (Mercury 5429) 1.00 4.00 50
WAR & PEACE/Speak My Love .... (Columbia 4-40733) .75 3.00 56

DAMON, Liz: see Liz Damon's Orient Express

DAMPHIER, Tom (With The Tokens)
MISTER RADIO MAN/Everybody Tries .... (Kirshner 4264) .50 2.00

DAN & DALE
BATMAN'S THEME/Robin's Theme .... (Tifton 125) 1.00 4.00 66
(Instrumentals)

DANA
ARE YOU STILL MAD AT ME/
There's Nothin' You Can Do To Change My Mind .(Ariola America 7604) .50 2.00 76
FAIRYTALE/Country Girl .... (Ariola America 7647) .50 2.00 77
GIRL IS BACK (IN TOWN), THE/Slip Away .... (Epic 50705) .50 2.00 79
WHO PUT THE LIGHTS OUT/Always A Few Things .... (London 1033) .50 2.00 72

DANA, Jeff
OH GINA/A Boy Can Dream .... (Fleetwood 1011) 2.00 8.00

DANA, Vic
BRING A LITTLE SUNSHINE/That's All .... (Dolton 305) .75 3.00 65
CRYSTAL CHANDELIER/What Now My Love .... (Dolton 313) .75 3.00 65
DANGER/Heart Hand & Teardrop .... (Dolton 73) .75 3.00 63
FRENCHY/It Was Night .... (Dolton 301) .75 3.00 64
GARDEN IN THE RAIN/Stairway To The Stars .... (Dolton 99) .75 3.00 64
I WILL/Proud .... (Dolton 51) .75 3.00 62
LITTLE ALTAR BOY/Hello Roomate .... (Dolton 48) .75 3.00 61
LOVE IS ALL WE NEED/I Need You Now .... (Dolton 95) .75 3.00 64
MOONLIGHT & ROSES/What'll I Do .... (Dolton 309) .75 3.00 65
MORE/That's Why I'm Sorry .... (Dolton 81) .75 3.00 63
PRISONER'S SONG/Voice In The Wind .... (Dolton 87) .75 3.00 63
RED ROSES FOR A BLUE LADY/Blue Ribbons .... (Dolton 304) .75 3.00 65
SHANGRI-LA/Warm & Tender .... (Dolton 92) .75 3.00 64

DANCER PRANCER, & NERVOUS
HAPPY REINDEER, THE/Dancer's Waltz .... (Capitol 4300) 1.00 4.00 59
Also see Summers, Little Davey

DANDELION WINE
SOME KIND OF A SUMMER/Hot Dog .... (Sussex 502) 1.00 4.00

DANDEVILLES, The
THERE'S A REASON/Nasty Breaks .... (Guyden 2014) 1.50 6.00 58

D'ANDREA, Bob
FALLING FROM PARADISE/Ecuador .... (Tribute 216) .75 3.00

DANIEL, Godfrey
HEY JUDE/Shop Around .... (Nostalgia 102) 1.00 4.00

DANIELS, Charlie, Band
BEHIND YOUR EYES/ .... (Epic 50806) .50 2.00 79
BILLY THE KID/ .... (Epic 50322) .50 2.00 76
BIRMINGHAM BLUES/Damn Good Cowboy .... (Kama Sutra 606) .50 2.00 75
DEVIL WENT DOWN TO GEORGIA, THE/Rainbow Ride .... (Epic 50700) .50 2.00 79
GREAT BIG BUNCHES OF LOVE/ .... (Kama Sutra 553) .50 2.00 72
HEAVEN CAN BE ANYWHERE (TWIN PINES THEME)/ .... (Epic 50456) .50 2.00 77
LONG HAIRED COUNTRY BOY/I've Been Down .... (Kama Sutra 601) .50 2.00 75
MARIA TERESA/ .... (Epic 50576) .50 2.00 78
MIDDLE OF A HEARTACHE/Skip It .... (Paula 418) .50 2.00 76
PASSING LANE/Mississippi .... (Epic 50768) .50 2.00 79
SOUTH'S GONNA DO IT AGAIN, THE/
New York City, King Size Rosewood Bed .... (Kama Sutra 598) .50 2.00 75
TEXAS/Everything Is Kinda Alright .... (Kama Sutra 607) .50 2.00 76
UNEASY RIDER/Funky Junky .... (Kama Sutra 576) .50 2.00 73
WICHITA JAIL/It's My Life .... (Epic 50243) .50 2.00 76

DANIELS, Jeff
DADDY-O-ROCK/Hey Woman .... (Meladee 117) 25.00 100.00 58

DANISH LOST & FOUND
NO, NO, NO, NO/The First Cut Is The Deepest .... (Laurie 3492) .75 3.00 69

DANKO, RICK (Of The Band)
JAVA BLUES/ .... (Arista 0320) .50 2.00 78
WHAT A TOWN/Shake It .... (Arista 0306) .50 2.00 78

DANKWORTH, Johnny
EXPERIMENTS WITH MICE/Applecake .... (Capitol 3499) 1.00 4.00 56

D'ANNA, Darin
WE WERE LOVERS/Gonna Feel Alright .... (World Artists 1045) .75 3.00 65
YOUR LOVE IS STRONG/Bimbo .... (World Artists 1046) .75 3.00 65

DANNY & THE CROWNS
STORY OF JACK & JILL, THE/Night Moon .... (Mercury 72096) .75 3.00 62

DANNY & THE DREAMERS
FORGIVE ME/Venus .... (Dream 7) 2.00 8.00

DANNY & THE HITMAKERS
BIMBA ROCK/Orangoutang Roll .... (Cavalcade 1001) .75 3.00 64

DANNY & THE JUNIORS (Featuring Danny Rapp)
AT THE HOP/Sometimes (When I'm All Alone) .... (Singular 711) 7.50 30.00 57
(Blue label)
AT THE HOP/Sometimes (When I'm All Alone) .... (ABC-Paramount 9871) 1.00 4.00 57
BACK TO THE HOP/Charleston Fish .... (Swan 4082) 1.00 4.00 61
CANDY CANE, SUGARY PLUM/O Holy Night .... (Swan 4064) 1.00 4.00 60
CANDY CANE, SUGARY PLUM/O Holy Night .... (Swan 4064) 2.00 8.00 60
(Picture sleeve)
CHA CHA GO GO/Mr. Whisper .... (Swan 4072) 1.00 4.00 61
CRAZY CAVE/A Thief .... (ABC-Paramount 9953) 1.00 4.00 58
DO YOU LOVE ME/Somehow I Can't Forget ..... (ABC-Paramount 10004) 1.00 4.00 59
DOIN' THE CONTINENTAL WALK/Mashed Potatoes .... (Swan 4100) 1.00 4.00 62
DOTTIE/In The Meantime .... (ABC-Paramount 9926) 1.00 4.00 58
MO'REEN/I Can't See Nobody .... (Ronn 24) 1.00 4.00 68
OO-LA-LA-LIMBO/Now & Then .... (Guyden 2076) 1.00 4.00 62
PLAYING HARD TO GET/Of Love .... (ABC-Paramount 10052) 1.00 4.00 59
PONY EXPRESS/Daydreamer .... (Swan 4068) 1.00 4.00 61
ROCK & ROLL IS HERE TO STAY/
School Boy Romance .... (ABC-Paramount 9888) 1.00 4.00 58
ROCK & ROLL IS HERE TO STAY/Sometimes .... (Lub 252) 1.00 4.00 68
SASSY FRAN/I Feel So Lonely .... (ABC-Paramount 9978) 1.00 4.00 59
TWISTIN' ALL NIGHT LONG/Some Kind Of Nut .... (Swan 4092) 1.00 4.00 61
(With Freddy Cannon)
TWISTIN' U.S.A./A Thousand Miles Away .... (Swan 4060) 1.00 4.00 60
WE GOT SOUL/Funny .... (Swan 4113) 1.00 4.00 62

DANNY & THE MEMORIES (Featuring Neil Young)
CAN'T HELP LOVIN' THAT GIRL OF MINE/Don't Go .... (Valiant 6049) 3.75 15.00 64

DANNY & THE SAINTS
BIG LULU/ .... (Fanelle 101) 1.00 4.00

DANNY & THE VELAIRES
I FOUND A LOVE/It's Over .... (Ramco 1983) 3.75 15.00
WHAT AM I LIVIN' FOR/ .... (Brent 7072) 2.50 10.00

DANTE
BYE BYE BABY/That's Why .... (Decca 31268) 1.25 5.00 61
IF YOU DON'T KNOW/Leave Your Tears Behind You ..... (Decca 31178) 1.25 5.00 60
MY ACHING HEART/My Lament .... (Tide 003) 1.25 5.00 60
RING OR WRITE OR CALL/Say It To Me .... (Decca 31319) 1.25 5.00 61
SPEEDOO/Sweet Lover .... (A&M 788) .75 3.00 66

DANTE & HIS FRIENDS
MISS AMERICA/Now I've Got You .... (Imperial 5827) .75 3.00 62
SOMETHING HAPPENS/Are You Just My Friend .... (Imperial 5798) .75 3.00 61

DANTE & THE EVERGREENS
ALLEY-OOP/The Right Time .... (Madison 130) 1.25 5.00 60
THINK SWEET THOUGHTS/Da Doo .... (Madison 154) 1.25 5.00 61
TIME MACHINE/Dream Land .... (Madison 135) 1.25 5.00 60
WHAT ARE YOU DOING NEW YEAR'S EVE/Yeah Baby .... (Madison 143) 1.25 5.00 60
Also see Dante & His Friends

DANTE, Ron (Of the Archies)
CHARMER/Yesterday Dreamin .... (Bell 45610) .50 2.00 74
HOW AM I TO KNOW/ .... (RCA 10898) .50 2.00 77
LET ME BRING YOU UP/How Do You Know .... (Kirshner 63-1010) .50 2.00 70
SUGAR SUGAR/ .... (RCA 10340) .50 2.00 75
Also see Cuff Links, The

DANTES, The
DRAGON WALK/Zebra Shoot .... (Courtney 713) 1.00 4.00 64
(Instrumentals)
TOP DOWN TIME/How Many Times .... (Rotate 5008) 1.50 6.00 64

DANTE'S INFERNOS
MY FIRST TRUE LOVE (THERE SHE GOES)/Teenage Blues .... (Lido 507) 2.00 8.00

DA-PREES
PAYDAY/Sometimes .... (Twist 70913) 6.25 25.00

DARBY SISTERS, The
GO BACK, GO BACK TO YOUR PONTIAC/Misunderstood ...... (Cub 9041) 1.00 4.00 59
THINK OF ALL THE FUN WE'VE HAD/Why Did You Go .(Columbia 41580) 1.00 4.00 60
YA GOTTA/Don't Let It End .... (Musicor 1007) .75 3.00 61

DARDENELLES, The
BABY, DO THE FROG/Alright .... (Cameo 271) .75 3.00 63

DARENSBOURG, Joe, & The Dixie Flyers
OVER THE WAVES/Petite Fleur .... (Lark 4510) .75 3.00 59
SASSY GAL/Snag It .... (Lark 455) .75 3.00 58
YELLOW DOG BLUES/Martinque .... (Lark 452) .75 3.00 57
YELLOW DOG BLUES/Martinque .... (Lark 452) 1.00 4.00 57
(Blue plastic)
Instrumentals

DARIAN, Fred (Of The Balladeers)
BATTLE OF GETTYSBURG, THE/
The Legend Of The Ghost Stage .... (JAF 2020) .75 3.00 61
I GOT PLENTY OF NUTTIN'/Now & Then .... (Okeh 7113) .75 3.00 59
JOHNNY WILLOW/Strong Man .... (JAF 2023) .75 3.00 61

DARIN, Bobby (Robert Walden Cassotto)
ARTIFICIAL FLOWERS/Somebody To Love .... (Atco 6179) .75 3.00 60
AVERAGE PEOPLE/Something In Her Love .... (Motown 1212) .50 2.00 72
BABY FACE/You Know How .... (Atco 6236) .75 3.00 62
BABY MAN/Sweet Reasons .... (Dimension 4001) .50 2.00 70
BE MAD LITTLE GIRL/Since You Been Gone .... (Capitol 5079) .75 3.00 63
BEACHCOMBER (Piano Solo)/Autumn Blues .... (Atco 6173) .75 3.00 60
BEYOND THE SEA/That's The Way Love Is .... (Atco 618) .75 3.00 59
BREAKING POINT/Silver Dollar .... (Atlantic 2317) .75 3.00 66
CHRISTMAS AULD LANG SYNE/Child Of God .... (Atco 6183) .75 3.00 60
CLEMENTINE/Tall Story .... (Atco 6161) .75 3.00 60
COME SEPTEMBER/Walk Back To Me .... (Atco 6200) .75 3.00 61
DARLING BE HOME SOON/Hello Sunshine .... (Atlantic 2420) .75 3.00 67

TITLE/FLIP	LABEL & NO.	GOOD	NEAR MINT	YR.

TITLE/FLIP	LABEL & NO.	GOOD	NEAR MINT	YR.
DEALER IN DREAMS/Help Me	(Decca 30225)	3.75	15.00	57
(With the Jaybirds)				
DEALER IN DREAMS/Help Me	(Decca 30737)	1.00	4.00	59
DISTRACTIONS (PART 1)/Distractions (Part 2)	(Direction 352)	.50	2.00	69
(Shown as by Bob Darin)				
DON'T CALL MY NAME/Pretty Baby	(Atco 6103)	1.25	5.00	57
DREAM LOVER (With Neal Sedaka on piano)/Bullmoose	(Atco 6140)	1.00	4.00	59
EARLY IN THE MORNING/Now We're One	(Brunswick 55073)	10.00	40.00	58
(Shown as by the Ding Dongs)				
EARLY IN THE MORNING/Now We're One	(Atco 6121)	2.50	10.00	58
(Reissue of Brunswick 55073, shown as by the Rinky Dinks)				
EARLY IN THE MORNING/Now We're One	(Atco 6121)	1.00	4.00	58
(Shown as by Bobby Darin with the Rinky Dinks)				
18 YELLOW ROSES/Not For Me	(Capitol 4970)	.75	3.00	63
FUNNY WHAT LOVE CAN DO/ We Didn't Ask To Be Brought Here	(Atlantic 2305)	.75	3.00	65
GIRL THAT STOOD BESIDE ME, THE/Reason To Believe	(Atlantic 2367)	.75	3.00	66
GREATEST BUILDER, THE/Hear Them Bells	(Decca 30031)	2.00	8.00	56
GYP THE CAT/That Funny Feeling	(Capitol 5481)	.75	3.00	64
HAPPY/Something In Her Love	(Motown 1217)	.50	2.00	72
HELLO DOLLY/Goodbye Charlie	(Capitol 5359)	.75	3.00	65
I FOUND A MILLION DOLLAR BABY/Talk To Me	(Atco 6092)	1.00	4.00	57
I FOUND A NEW BABY/Keep A Walkin'	(Atco 6244)	.75	3.00	62
I WONDER WHO'S KISSING HER NOW/ As Long As I'm Singing	(Capitol 5126)	.75	3.00	64
IF A MAN ANSWERS/True True Love	(Capitol 4837)	.75	3.00	62
IF I WERE A CARPENTER/Rainin'	(Atlantic 2350)	.75	3.00	66
IRRESISTIBLE YOU/Multiplication	(Atco 6214)	.75	3.00	61
JUST IN CASE YOU CHANGE YOUR MIND/So Mean	(Atco 6109)	1.00	4.00	58
LADY CAME FROM BALTIMORE, THE/I Am	(Atlantic 2395)	.75	3.00	67
LAZY RIVER/Oo-Ee-Train	(Atco 6188)	.75	3.00	61
LONG LINE RIDER/Change	(Direction 350)	.50	2.00	68
LOVIN' YOU/Amy	(Atlantic 2376)	.75	3.00	67
MACK THE KNIFE/Was There A Call For Me	(Atco 6147)	.75	3.00	59
MAME/Walking In The Shadow Of Love	(Atlantic 2329)	.75	3.00	66
MAYBE WE CAN GET TOGETHER/	(Direction 4002)	.75	3.00	70
(Shown as by Bob Darin)				
ME & MR. HOHNER/Song For A Dollar	(Direction 351)	.50	2.00	68
MIGHTY, MIGHTY MAN/You're Mine	(Atco 6128)	2.50	10.00	58
(Shown as by the Rinky Dinks)				
MIGHTY, MIGHTY MAN/You're Mine	(Atco 6128)	1.00	4.00	58
(Shown as by Bobby Darin with the Rinky Dinks)				
MILORD/Golden Earrings	(Atco 6297)	.75	3.00	64
MINNIE THE MOOCHER/Hard Hearted Hannah	(Atco 6334)	.75	3.00	65
NATURE BOY/Look For My True Love	(Atco 6196)	.75	3.00	61
O COME ALL YE FAITHFUL/Ave Maria	(Atco 6211)	.75	3.00	61
PLAIN JANE/When I'm Gone	(Atco 6133)	1.00	4.00	59
PLAIN JANE/When I'm Gone	(Atco SD-6133)	3.75	15.00	59
(Stereo single issue)				
QUEEN OF THE HOP/Lost Love	(Atco 6127)	1.00	4.00	58
ROCK ISLAND LINE/Timber	(Decca 29883)	3.75	15.00	56
(With the Jaybirds)				
SILLY WILLY/Blue Eyed Mermaid	(Decca 29922)	3.75	15.00	56
(With the Jaybirds)				
SIMPLE SONG OF FREEDOM/I'll Be Your Baby	(Motown 1193)	.50	2.00	71
SOMEDAY WE'LL BE TOGETHER/Melodie	(Motown 1183)	.50	2.00	71
SPLISH SPLASH/Judy, Don't Be Moody	(Atco 6117)	1.00	4.00	58
SWEET REASONS/Baby May	(Direction 4001)	.50	2.00	69
SWING LOW SWEET CHARIOT/Similau	(Atco 6316)	.75	3.00	64
TALK TO THE ANIMALS/She Knows	(Atlantic 2433)	.75	3.00	67
THINGS/Jailer Bring Me Water	(Atco 6229)	.75	3.00	62
THINGS IN THIS HOUSE, THE/Wait By The Water	(Capitol 5257)	.75	3.00	64
TREAT MY BABY GOOD/Down So Long	(Capitol 5019)	.75	3.00	63
WHAT'D I SAY (PART 1)/What'd I Say (Part 2)	(Atco 6221)	.75	3.00	62
WHEN I GET HOME/Lonely Road	(Capitol 5443)	.75	3.00	65
WHO'S AFRAID?/Merci Cherie	(Atlantic 2341)	.75	3.00	66
WON'T YOU COME HOME BILL BAILEY/I'll Be There	(Atco 6167)	.75	3.00	60
YOU MUST HAVE BEEN A BEAUTIFUL BABY/ Sorrow Tomorrow	(Atco 6206)	.75	3.00	61
YOU'RE THE REASON I'M LIVING/Now You're Gone	(Capitol 4897)	.75	3.00	62
DARLENE & THE JOKERS				
FRANKIE/Love Me, Love Me	(Danco 115)	1.00	4.00	60
DARLIN, Florraine				
LONG AS THE ROSE IS RED/I Don't Know	(Epic 9529)	.75	3.00	62
DARLINGS, The				
TWO TIME LOSER/Please Let Me Know	(Mercury 72185)	.75	3.00	63
DARNELL & THE DREAMS				
DAY BEFORE YESTERDAY, THE/I Had A Love	(West Side 1020)	2.00	8.00	
DARNELL, Bill				
CHATTANOOGA SHOE SHINE BOY/Sugarfoot Rag	(Coral 60147)	1.25	5.00	50
KO KO MO/So All Alone	("X" 0087)	1.00	4.00	55
ROCK A BOOGIE BABY/Guilty Lips	(London 1665)	1.00	4.00	56
ROCK & ROLL BABY/A Million Thanks	("X" 0109)	1.00	4.00	55
TELL ME MORE/My Little Mother	(London 1632)	1.00	4.00	56
DARREL & THE OXFORDS (The Tokens)				
CAN'T YOU TELL/Your Mother Said No	(Roulette 4230)	2.50	10.00	60
PICTURE IN MY WALLET/Roses Are Red	(Roulette 4174)	2.50	10.00	59
DARRELL, Guy "Daddy Cool"				
DADDY COOL, DADDY COOL/Nobody Else But You	(Warwick 614)	1.25	5.00	61
DARRELLS, The				
SO TENDERLY/Without Warning	(Lyco 1003)	1.50	6.00	

TITLE/FLIP	LABEL & NO.	GOOD	NEAR MINT	YR.
DARREN, James (James Ercolani)				
ALL/Misty Morning Eyes	(Warner Bros. 5874)	.75	3.00	67
ANGEL FACE/I Don't Wanna Lose Ya	(Colpix 119)	1.00	4.00	59
(Shown as by Jimmy Darren)				
ANGEL FACE/I Don't Wanna Lose Ya	(Colpix SCP-119)	2.00	8.00	59
(Stereo single issue shown as by Jimmy Darren)				
BACK STAGE/Under The Yum Yum Tree	(Colpix 708)	.75	3.00	63
BECAUSE THEY'RE YOUNG/Tears In My Eyes	(Colpix 142)	1.00	4.00	60
(Shown as by Jimmy Darren)				
BECAUSE YOU'RE MINE/Millions Of Roses	(Warner Bros. 5648)	.75	3.00	68
CHERIE/Wait Until Dark	(Warner Bros. 7152)	.75	3.00	67
CONSCIENCE/Dream Big	(Colpix 630)	.75	3.00	62
GEGETTA/Grande Luna, Italiana	(Colpix 696)	.75	3.00	63
GIDGET/You	(Colpix 113)	1.00	4.00	59
(Shown as by Jimmy Darren)				
GIDGET GOES HAWAIIAN/	(Colpix 189)	.75	3.00	60
GOODBYE CRUEL WORLD/Valerie	(Colpix 609)	.75	3.00	61
HAIL TO THE CONQUERING HERO/ Too Young To Go Steady	(Colpix 655)	.75	3.00	62
HEAR WHAT I WANNA HEAR/I'll Be Loving You	(Colpix 664)	.75	3.00	62
HER ROYAL MAJESTY/If I Could Only Tell You	(Colpix 622)	.75	3.00	62
I AIN'T SHARIN' SHARON/Love Among The Young	(Colpix 128)	1.00	4.00	60
(Shown as by Jimmy Darren)				
I WANT TO BE LONELY/Tom Hawk	(Warner Bros. 5689)	.75	3.00	66
JUST THINK OF TONIGHT/Punch & Judy	(Colpix 758)	.75	3.00	64
MAN ABOUT TOWN/Come On My Love	(Colpix 168)	1.00	4.00	60
(Shown as by Jimmy Darren)				
MARRIED MAN, A/Baby, Talk To Me	(Colpix 765)	.75	3.00	64
MARY'S LITTLE LAMB/Life Of The Party	(Colpix 644)	.75	3.00	62
P.S. I LOVE YOU/Love Theme From "La Strada"	(Colpix 145)	1.00	4.00	60
(Shown as by Jimmy Darren)				
PIN A MEDAL ON JOEY/Diamond Head	(Colpix 672)	.75	3.00	63
TEEN AGE TEARS/Let There Be Love	(Colpix 130)	1.00	4.00	59
(Shown as by Jimmy Darren)				
THERE'S NO SUCH THING/Mighty Pretty Territory	(Colpix 102)	1.00	4.00	58
(Shown as by Jimmy Darren)				
THEY DON'T KNOW/Crazy Me	(Warner Bros. 5838)	.75	3.00	66
THEY DON'T KNOW/House Song	(Warner Bros. 7071)	.75	3.00	67
THEY SHOULD HAVE GIVEN YOU THE OSCAR/ Blame It On My Youth	(Colpix 685)	.75	3.00	63
WHERE DID WE GO WRONG/Counting The Cracks	(Warner Bros. 5812)	.75	3.00	66
YOU ARE MY DREAM/Your Smile	(Colpix 138)	1.00	4.00	60
(Shown as by Jimmy Darren)				
DARROW, Jay				
GIRL IN MY DREAMS/I Love That Girl	(Keen 82124)	1.25	5.00	60
D'ARROW, Phillip				
BURN THE DISCO DOWN/Rock & Roll Respectable	(Polydor 14570)	.50	2.00	79
DARTELLS, The (Featuring Doug Philips)				
CLAP YOUR HANDS/Where Do We Stand	(HBR 457)	.75	3.00	66
DANCE, EVERYBODY, DANCE/Scoobie Song	(Arlen 513)	1.25	5.00	63
DANCE, EVERYBODY, DANCE/Scoobie Song	(Dot 16502)	.75	3.00	63
HOT PASTRAMI/Dartell Stomp	(Arlen 509)	1.25	5.00	63
HOT PASTRAMI/Dartell Stomp	(Dot 16453)	.75	3.00	63
SWEET PEA/Convicted	(Dot 16551)	.75	3.00	63
SWISS CHEESE/Dartell Stomp	(Dot 16646)	.75	3.00	64
DARTS, The				
DADDY COOL-THE GIRL CAN'T HELP IT/ Too Hot In The Kitchen	(United Artists 1125)	.75	3.00	77
IT'S RAINING/Naff Off	(Polydor 14518)	.75	3.00	78
DARTS, The				
SWEET LITTLE BABY/Gee-Ver-Men-Nee-Vers	(Dot 15752)	1.25	5.00	58
DARVELL, Barry				
ADAM & EVE/King For Tonight	(Atlantic 2138)	1.00	4.00	62
ALL I NEED IS YOU/Run Little Billy	(Colt 45 301)	.75	3.00	63
BEGGAR'S PARADE/My World Of Make Believe	(Columbia 4-44197)	1.00	4.00	67
BUTTERFLY BABY/Send Me Some Loving	(Colt 45 110)	.75	3.00	60
GERONIMO STOMP/How Will It End	(Colt 45 107)	.75	3.00	59
LITTLE ANGEL LOST/Fountain Of Love	(Cub 9088)	.75	3.00	61
LOST LOVE/Silver Dollar	(Atlantic 2128)	.75	3.00	61
DARVELS, The				
I LOST MY BABY/Gone	(Eddies 69)	1.50	6.00	
DARWIN & THE CUPIDS				
GOODNIGHT MY LOVE/Won't You Give Me A Chance	(Jerden 9)	1.00	4.00	60
HOW LONG?/Chloe	(Jerden 1)	1.00	4.00	60
DARWINS, The				
MONKEE, THE/Monkee Sax (Instrumental)	(Vee Jay 508)	.75	3.00	63
DASHIELL, Bud, & The Kinsmen				
I TALK TO THE TREES/Pom Pa Lom	(Warner Bros. 5231)	.75	3.00	61
Also see Bud & Travis				
DAVANI, Dave, Four				
TOSSIN' & TURNIN'/	(Capitol 5788)	.75	3.00	66
DAVE & BOB				
TWO OLD SPARROWS/Whoa Bessie	(M&F 169)	6.25	25.00	
DAVE & THE CUSTOMS (Dave Zdunich)				
ALI BABA/Shortnin' Bread	(DAC 500)	1.00	4.00	63
(Instrumentals)				
DAVE & THE ORBITS				
CHEETA'S UNCLE/Chili Beans	(American Arts 14)	1.00	4.00	64
DAVE & THE SAINTS				
LEAVING SURF CITY/Fever	(Band Box 341)	1.25	5.00	63
DAVE & THE SHADOWS				
BLUE DOWN/Hereafter	(Check Mate 1011)	1.00	4.00	62
FAITH/Playboy	(Fenton 942)	1.00	4.00	
DAVE & THE STEREOS				
ROAMIN' ROMEO/This Must Be Love	(Pennant 1001)	3.75	15.00	
DAVE, STAN & ROBIN				
DAY TRIPPER/Get Off Of My Cloud	(Startime 106)	1.00	4.00	66
DAVE T. & THE DEL-RAYS: see Del-Rays, The				
DAVID & FREDDIE				
OY VAH/Quackety-Quack (By David Ellin)	(Bullseye 1010)	3.00	12.00	58
(Parodies of "Witch Doctor" & "Yakety-Yak")				
DAVID & GOLIATH				
LIKE STRANGERS/I'm Still Loving You	(Tomaro 101)	2.00	8.00	
DAVID & JONATHAN (Roger Greenaway & Roger Cook)				
MICHELLE/How Bitter The Taste Of Love	(Capitol 5563)	.75	3.00	66
MODESTY/Willie Waltz	(20th Fox 641)	.75	3.00	66
OH, MY WORD/Lovers Of The World Unite	(Capitol 5700)	.75	3.00	66
SOFTLY WHISPERING I LOVE YOU/ Something's Gotten Hold Of My Heart	(Amy 11012)	.75	3.00	68
SPEAK HER NAME/I Know	(Capitol 5625)	.75	3.00	66
TIME/The Magic Book	(Capitol 5777)	.75	3.00	66

TITLE/FLIP	LABEL & NO.	GOOD	NEAR MINT	YR.

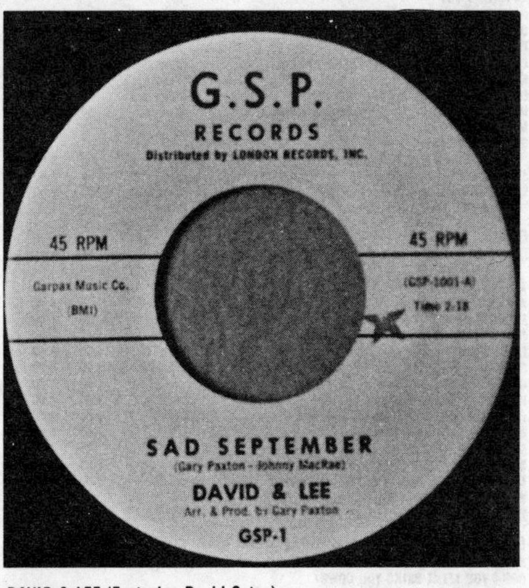

TITLE/FLIP	LABEL & NO.	GOOD	NEAR MINT	YR.
DAVID & LEE (Featuring David Gates)				
SAD SEPTEMBER/	(G.S.P. GSP-1)	3.00	12.00	
DAVID COVERDALE'S WHITESNAKE				
AIN'T NO LOVE IN THE HEART OF THE CITY/	(United Artists 1240)	.50	2.00	78
LONG WAY FROM HOME/	(United Artists 1323)	.50	2.00	79
DAVIDSON, John				
CALIFORNIA BLOODLINES/I Am Now	(Columbia 4-44896)	.50	2.00	69
DAYDREAM/I'll Always Remember	(Columbia 4-44005)	.50	2.00	67
EVERYTIME I SING A LOVE SONG/ Love In The Shadows	(20th Century 2293)	.50	2.00	76
FLAME/Visions Of Sugarplums	(Columbia 4-44478)	.50	2.00	68
GOOD TIMES/	(Columbia 4-45486)	.50	2.00	72
I CAN'T HELP THIS FEELING I FEEL/ I Still Send Her Flowers	(Columbia 4-43531)	.50	2.00	66
IN THE SUNSHINE DAYS/ If You Can Put That In A Bottle	(Columbia 4-44210)	.50	2.00	67
SAVE THE LAST DANCE FOR ME/Patch It Up	(20th Century 2326)	.50	2.00	77
STEAL HER AWAY/I Let You Walk Away	(20th Century 2313)	.50	2.00	76
SUMMER LOVE/I'll Try Lovin' You Less	(Columbia 4-43635)	.50	2.00	66
WHAT IS A WOMAN/ How Come You Do Me Like You Do	(Columbia 4-44334)	.50	2.00	67
WONDER OF YOU, THE/Words	(Columbia 4-444770)	.50	2.00	69
DAVIE, Hutch				
BEGIN THE BEGUINE/The Dipsy Doodle	(Atco 6136)	.75	3.00	59
BUT I DO/Time Was	(Congress 102)	.75	3.00	62
WOODCHOPPER'S BALL/Honky Tonk Train	(Atco 6110)	.75	3.00	58
Instrumentals				
DAVIES, Bob				
ROCK N'ROLL SHOW/With You Tonight	(Click 14)	.75	3.00	63
DAVIES, Dave (Of The Kinks)				
DEATH OF A CLOWN/Leave Me Till The Sun Shines	(Reprise 0614)	.75	3.00	67
SUSANNAH'S STILL ALIVE/Funny Face	(Reprise 0660)	.75	3.00	68
DAVIES, Gwen				
FIRST TRIP TO THE DENTIST (PART 1)/ First Trip To The Dentist (Part 2)	(Mercury 30104)	.75	3.00	62
PETER PONSIL & HIS TONSIL (PART 1)/ Peter Ponsil & His Tonsil (Part 2)	(Mercury 30103)	.75	3.00	62
DA VINCI, Paul				
YOUR BABY AIN'T YOUR BABY ANYMORE/ She'll Only Hurt You	(Mercury 73611)	1.50	6.00	72
DAVIS, Bette				
WHATEVER HAPPENED TO BABY JANE/ I've Written A Letter	(MGM 13107)	.75	3.00	62
DAVIS, Bo				
LET'S COAST AWHILE/Drownin' All My Sorrows	(Crest 1027)	12.50	50.00	56
(Features Eddie Cochran on guitar)				
DAVIS, Ginger, & The Snaps				
GROWING UP IS HARD TO DO/7 Days In September	(MGM 13413)	1.00	4.00	65
I'M NO RUNAROUND/Laughin'	(Swan 4090)	2.00	8.00	61
(Answer song to "Runaround Sue")				
DAVIS, Harley, & The Teen-Aires				
MAD LOVER/My Definition Of You	(Wildcat W0064)	1.00	4.00	
DAVIS, Hayward				
BUBBLE GUM ROCK/Rock My Rockin' Chair	(Christy 103)	1.00	4.00	60
DAVIS, Jan				
BOSS MACHINE/Fugitive	(A&M 733)	.75	3.00	64
SNOW SURFIN' MATADOR/Scramble	(Smash 1863)	.75	3.00	64
UNWANTED/Guitar Star	(A&M 744)	.75	3.00	64
Instrumentals				
DAVIS, Jesse Ed				
ALCATRAZ/Ululu	(Atco 6889)	.50	2.00	72
EXCLUSIVE INTERVIEW (PART 1)/ Exclusive Interview (Part 2)	(Columbia AE7 1067)	1.00	4.00	70
(Promotional issue only)				
SUE ME, SUE YOU BLUES/My Captain	(Atco 6873)	.50	2.00	72
DAVIS, Johnny				
RED CAPRIS/Lazy Guitar	(Smash 1839)	.75	3.00	63
DAVIS, Joyce				
STOP GIVING YOUR MAN AWAY/ When Boy Meets Girl	(United Artists UA-339)	.75	3.00	60
DAVIS, Link				
BEATLE BUG/I Keep Wanting You More	(Kook 1026)	1.00	4.00	64
DAVIS, Lucky				
MIDNIGHT IN JACKSONVILLE/Carol	(Kissin' 42)	1.00	4.00	61
DAVIS, Martha				
GET OUT THOSE OLD RECORDS/Would I Love You	(Coral 61048)	1.00	4.00	53
DAVIS, Myler				
MD TWIST/Let's Twist Again	(Cameo 210)	.75	3.00	62

TITLE/FLIP	LABEL & NO.	GOOD	NEAR MINT	YR.
DAVIS, Paul				
BOOGIE WOOGIE MAN/Johnny Poverty	(Bang 599)	.50	2.00	72
DARLIN'/You're Not Just A Rose	(Bang 736)	.50	2.00	78
I GO CRAZY/	(Bang 733)	.50	2.00	77
I JUST WANNA KEEP IT TOGETHER/Pollyanna	(Bang 579)	.50	2.00	70
KEEP OUR LOVE ALIVE/	(Bang 718)	.50	2.00	76
LITTLE BIT OF SOAP, A/Three Little Words	(Bang 576)	.50	2.00	70
MAKE HER MY BABY/Can't Get Back To Alabama	(Bang 717)	.50	2.00	75
MEDICINE WOMAN/	(Bang 729)	.50	2.00	76
RIDE 'EM COWBOY/ I'm The Only Sinner (In Salt Lake City)	(Bang 712)	.50	2.00	74
SWEET LIFE/Bad Dream	(Bang 738)	.50	2.00	78
SUPERSTAR/Magnolia Blues	(Bang 726)	.50	2.00	76
THINKING OF YOU/Karma Baby	(Bang 724)	.50	2.00	76
DAVIS, Ronny				
LET'S BEETLE IN THE ROCKET/	(Sheridan 573)	1.25	5.00	64
DAVIS, Sammy, Jr.				
ALL OF YOU/Six Bridges To Cross	(Decca 29402)	1.00	4.00	55
BECAUSE OF YOU (PART 1)/Because Of You (Part 2)	(Decca 29200)	1.00	4.00	54
CANDY MAN, THE/I Want To Be Happy	(MGM 14320)	.50	2.00	71
EARTHBOUND/Just One Of Those Things	(Decca 30035)	1.00	4.00	56
FRANKIE & JOHNNY/Circus	(Decca 29795)	1.00	4.00	55
GET OUT OF THE CAR/Without You I'm Nothing	(Decca 29929)	1.00	4.00	56
HEY THERE/This Is My Beloved	(Decca 29199)	1.00	4.00	54
IT'S BIGGER THAN YOU & ME/Back Track	(Decca 29649)	1.00	4.00	55
NEW YORK'S MY HOME/Never Like This	(Decca 30111)	1.00	4.00	56
SHELTER OF YOUR ARMS, THE/This Was My Love	(Reprise 20216)	.75	3.00	63
SOMETHING'S GOTTA GIVE/Love Me Or Leave Me	(Decca 29484)	1.00	4.00	55
THAT OLD BLACK MAGIC/Man With A Dream	(Decca 29541)	1.00	4.00	55
WHAT KIND OF FOOL AM I/Gonna Build A Mountain	(Reprise 20048)	.75	3.00	62
YOU'RE SENSATIONAL/Five Little Fingers	(Decca 29976)	1.00	4.00	56
DAVIS, Spencer, Group (Featuring Steve Winwood)				
AFTER TEA/Looking Back	(United Artists 50286)	.75	3.00	68
DON'T YOU LET IT BRING YOU DOWN/ Today Gluggo, Tomorrow The World	(Vertigo 110)	.50	2.00	73
GIMME SOME LOVIN'/Blues In F	(United Artists 50108)	.75	3.00	66
I CAN'T STAND IT/Midnight Train	(Fontana 1960)	.50	2.00	64
I'M A MAN/Can't Get Enough Of It	(United Artists 50144)	.75	3.00	67
KEEP ON RUNNING/High Time Baby	(Atco 6400)	.50	2.00	66
LIVING IN A BACK STREET/Need A Helping Hand	(Vertigo 112)	.50	2.00	73
RAINY SEASON/Tumble-Down Tenement Row	(United Artists 50993)	.75	3.00	73
SOMEBODY HELP ME/On The Green Light	(United Artists 50162)	.75	3.00	67
SOMEBODY HELP ME/Stevie's Blues	(Atco 6416)	.50	2.00	66
SUNDAY WALK IN THE RAIN/Listen To The Rhythm	(United Artists 50922)	.75	3.00	72
TIME SELLER/Don't Want You No More	(United Artists 50202)	.75	3.00	67
Stevie Winwood left the group in 1967.				
DAWN				
CAN'T GET HIM OFF MY MIND/Two Of A Kind	(Apt 25088)	.75	3.00	65
GIMMIE A GOOD OLD MAMMY SONG/ Little Heads In Bunkbeds	(Arista 0105)	.50	2.00	75
MIDNIGHT LOVE AFFAIR/Selfish One	(Elektra 45319)	.50	2.00	76
SING/Sweet On Candy	(Elektra 45387)	.50	2.00	77
Also see Orlando, Tony				
DAWN (The Five Discs)				
BRING IT ON HOME/Baby I Love You	(Rust 5128)	1.00	4.00	65
DAWN, Billy				
GOTTA FIND MY BABY/Whip It Up	(Coed 516)	1.00	4.00	59
DAWN, Ginger				
ROCKIN' WITH SANTA/Madness	(Lee 1001)	.75	3.00	
DAWNS, The				
IT SEEMS LIKE YESTERDAY/From You, Only You	(Atco 6296)	1.00	4.00	64
DAWSON, Jim (Of New Riders Of The Purple Sage)				
FOUR STRONG WINDS/ The Woman With The Beautiful Eyes	(RCA PB-10040)	.50	2.00	74
L.A. FREEWAY/	(RCA 10213)	.50	2.00	74
LET'S PRETEND/	(Kama Sutra 568)	.50	2.00	73
OH NO, MERCY ME/Whatever Happened	(RCA APBO-0285)	.50	2.00	74
SIMPLE SONG/	(Kama Sutra 537)	.50	2.00	72
WHEN YOU FINALLY COME AROUND/	(Kama Sutra 546)	.50	2.00	72
DAX				
GARDEN OF EDEN1/Bien Venido Amigo	(Dore 877)	.50	2.00	72
DAY BLINDNESS				
HOUSE & A DOG, A/Middle Class Lament	(Studio 10-2494)	1.25	5.00	
DAY BROTHERS,The				
CLEOPATRA BROWN/Wait For Me Steam	(Firebird 103)	1.00	4.00	
DAY, Caroline				
TEENAGE PRAYER/	(Dimension 1025)	.75	3.00	64
DAY, Darlene (With The Imaginations)				
WILL/I Love You So	(Music Makers 106)	5.00	20.00	61
DAY, Dennis				
CHRISTMAS IN KILLARNEY/ I'm Praying To St. Christmas	(RCA Victor 47-3970)	1:25	5.00	50
DEAR HEARTS & GENTLE PEOPLE/ I Must Have Done Something Wonderful	(RCA Victor 47-3102)	1.25	5.00	49
GOODNIGHT, IRENE/All My Love	(RCA Victor 47-3870)	1.25	5.00	50
I'LL STEP ASIDE/Saint Cecilia	(RCA Victor 47-5348)	1.25	5.00	53
IRISHMEN WILL STEAL YOUR HEART AWAY/ His Eye Is On The Sparrow	(RCA Victor 47-5762)	1.25	5.00	54
MR. & MISSISSIPPI/Trinket Of Shiny Gold	(RCA Victor 47-4140)	1.25	5.00	51
MONA LISA/	(RCA Victor 47-3753)	1.25	5.00	50
ST. PATRICK'S DAY PARADE/B'Gilly B'Golly	(RCA Victor 47-4061)	1.25	5.00	51
SILVER MOON/When Hearts Are Young	(RCA Victor 47-4052)	1.25	5.00	51
TAKE MY HEART/Siren Of The Sea	(RCA Victor 47-4784)	1.25	5.00	52
THERE WILL NEVER BE ANOTHER YOU/Beautiful	(RCA Victor 47-3900)	1.25	5.00	50
WONDER BOY FROM PERU, THE/Shrine Of St. Ann	(RCA Victor 47-4592)	1.25	5.00	52
DAY, Doris				
ASK ME/Lonesome & Sorry	(Columbia 4-39490)	1.00	4.00	55
BUSHEL & A PECK, A/The Best Thing For You	(Columbia 6-838)	1.25	5.00	50
BUSHEL & A PECK, A/The Best Thing For You	(Columbia 1-838)	2.50	10.00	50
(Compact 33 single)				
DARN THAT DREAM/I've Forgotten You	(Columbia 6-708)	1.25	5.00	50
DARN THAT DREAM/I've Forgotten You	(Columbia 1-708)	2.50	10.00	50
(Compact 33 single)				
EVERLASTING ARMS, THE/David's Psalm	(Columbia 6-846)	1.25	5.00	51
EVERLASTING ARMS, THE/David's Psalm	(Columbia 1-846)	2.50	10.00	51
(Compact 33 single)				
EVERYBODY LOVES A LOVER/Instant Love	(Columbia 4-41195)	.75	3.00	58
GENTLY JOHNNY/A Little Kiss Goodnight	(Columbia 4-39714)	1.00	4.00	55
GOT HIM OFF MY HANDS/Kiss Me Goodbye	(Columbia 4-39534)	1.00	4.00	55
GUY IS A GUY, A/Who, Who, Who	(Columbia 4-39673)	1.25	5.00	52
I AM LOVED/From This Moment On	(Columbia 6-912)	1.25	5.00	51
I CAN'T GET OVER A BOY LIKE YOU/Pumpernickle	(Columbia 4-39255)	1.25	5.00	51
IF I GIVE MY HEART TO YOU/ Anyone Can Fall In Love	(Columbia 4-40300)	1.25	5.00	54
IF I WERE A BELL/I've Never Been In Love	(Columbia 6-862)	1.25	5.00	51
JULIE/Love In A Home	(Columbia 4-40758)	1.00	4.00	56
OOH BANG-JIGGILY JANG/Jimmy Unknown	(Columbia 4-40581)	1.00	4.00	55
ORANGE COLORED SKY/A Load Of Hay	(Columbia 6-811)	1.25	5.00	50
PARTY'S OVER, THE/Whad-Ja Put In That Kiss	(Columbia 4-40798)	1.00	4.00	56

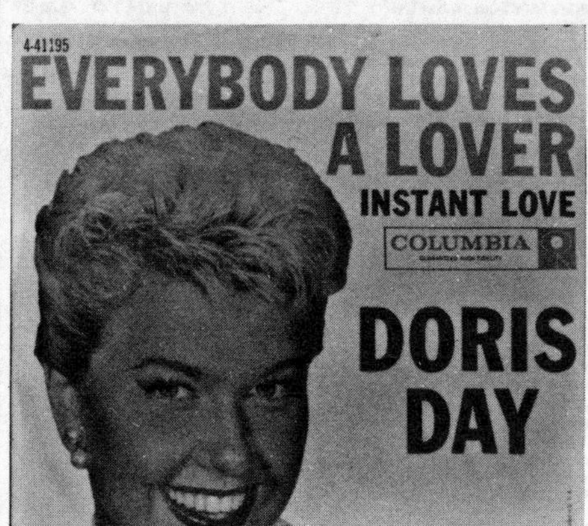

TITLE/FLIP	LABEL & NO.	GOOD	NEAR MINT	YR.
READY, WILLING & ABLE/Hold Me In Your Arms	(Columbia 4-40371)	1.00	4.00	55
SECRET LOVE/The Deadwood Stage	(Columbia 4-40108)	1.25	5.00	53
SHANGHAI/My Life's Desire	(Columbia 4-39423)	1.25	5.00	51
SILVER BELLS/The Christmas Story	(Columbia 6-863)	1.25	5.00	50
SILVER BELLS/The Christmas Story	(Columbia 1-863)	2.50	10.00	50
(Compact 33 single)				
SOMEBODY, SOMEWHERE/We'll Love Again	(Columbia 4-40673)	1.00	4.00	56
SOMETHING WONDERFUL/We Kissed In A Shadow	(Columbia 4-39293)	1.25	5.00	51
TEACHER'S PET/A Very Precious Love	(Columbia 4-41123)	.75	3.00	58
THERE THEY ARE/ Every Now & Then (You Come Around)	(Columbia 4-43606)	.50	2.00	66
TUNNEL OF LOVE/Runaway, Skidaddle, Skidoo	(Columbia 4-41252)	.75	3.00	58
WHATEVER WILL BE, WILL BE (QUE SERA, SERA)/ I've Gotta Sing Away These Blues	(Columbia 4-40704)	1.00	4.00	56

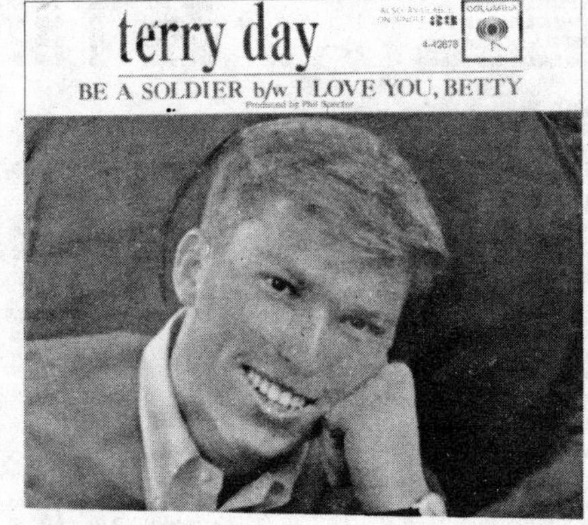

TITLE/FLIP	LABEL & NO.	GOOD	NEAR MINT	YR.
DAY, Terry (Terry Melcher)				
BE A SOLDIER/I Love You Betty	(Columbia 4-42678)	1.50	6.00	63
I WAITED TOO LONG/That's All I Want	(Columbia 4-42427)	1.00	4.00	63
Terry is Doris Day's son. Also see Bruce & Terry				
DAYE, Carolyn				
FRAGILE/Alone At The Prom	(Challenge 9150)	.75	3.00	62
DAYE, Frankie, & The Knights				
DANCE PARTY ROCK/Drag It	(Studio 9904)	1.00	4.00	59
DAYTON, Dan				
IT'S A GAS/It's A Gas (Part 2)	(Jemkl 3291)	1.00	4.00	
SKYLAB/Meanwhile, Back On The Air (By Martian Top)	(Jemkl 3291)	1.00	4.00	
Novelty/Break-ins				
D.C. PLAYBOYS, The				
YOU WERE ALL I NEEDED/Too Much	(Arock 1009)	.75	3.00	
D.D.T. & The Repellents				
FLY SWATTER/Bee Side	(RCA Victor 47-8064)	1.00	4.00	62
DE LORY, Al				
TRAFFIC JAM/	(Phi Dan 5006)	.75	3.00	65
SONG FROM M*A*S*H/Feeling Of Love	(Capitol 2811)	.50	2.00	70
DE LOS, The				
LULABYE SERANADE/Pork & Gravy	(Cedar 302)	1.00	4.00	
DEACON & THE ROCK & ROLLERS				
ROCKIN' ON THE MOON/I Don't Wanna Leave	(Nau-voo 804)	1.25	5.00	59
DEAD BOYS, The				
SONIC REDUCER/Down In Flames	(Sire 1004)	.75	3.00	77
DEAL, Bill, & The Rhondells				
CAN YOU MAKE IT/Sea Of Love	(Polydor 14103)	.50	2.00	73
EVERYBODY'S GOT SOMETHING TO HIDE/	(Buddah 330)	.50	2.00	71
HEY BULDOG/	(Heritage 824)	.50	2.00	70
IT'S TOO LATE/	(Buddah 318)	.50	2.00	71
I'VE BEEN HURT/I've Got My Needs	(Heritage 812)	.50	2.00	69
MAY I/Day By Day My Love Grows Stronger	(Heritage 803)	.50	2.00	68
NOTHING SUCCEEDS LIKE SUCCESS/	(Heritage 821)	.50	2.00	70
SWINGIN' TIGHT/Tuck's Theme	(Heritage 818)	.50	2.00	69
WHAT KIND OF FOOL DO YOU THINK I AM/ Are You Ready For This	(Heritage 817)	.50	2.00	69
DEAL, Don				
MY BLIND DATE/Even Then	(Era 1051)	1.00	4.00	57
SHE WAS HERE, BUT NOW SHE'S GONE/ You'd Look Good With A Tear In Your Eye	(Era 1060)	1.00	4.00	58
UNFAITHFUL DIANE/Devil Of Deceit	(Era 1039)	1.00	4.00	57
DEAL, Harry, & The Galaxies				
YOU'RE ALWAYS IN MY MIND/I Still Love You	(Eclipse 6000)	.75	3.00	70
DEAN, Allan				
HIGH ON A WINDY HILL/Say You Love Me	(MGM 11393)	1.25	5.00	52
LUNA ROSA/I'll Forget You	(MGM 11269)	1.25	5.00	52
MAKE ME YOUR SLAVE/Love Me Love Me	(MGM 11513)	1.25	5.00	53
SO LONG/You Made Me Care	(MGM 12088)	1.00	4.00	55
WITHOUT YOU/Take A Bow	(MGM 12189)	1.00	4.00	56
DEAN & JEAN				
GODDESS OF LOVE/Lovingly Yours	(Rust 5100)	.75	3.00	65
HEY JEAN, HEY DEAN/Please Don't Tell Me Now	(Rust 5075)	.75	3.00	64
I WANNA BE LOVED/Thread Your Needle	(Rust 5081)	.75	3.00	64
NEVER LET OUR LOVE FADE AWAY/Turn It Off	(Ember 1054)	.75	3.00	64
TRA LA LA SUZY/I Love The Summertime	(Rust 5067)	1.00	4.00	63
DEAN & MARC (Dean & Marc Mathis)				
CRY/The Beginning Of Love	(Bullseye 1026)	1.00	4.00	59
TELL HIM NO/Change Of Heart	(Bullseye 1025)	1.00	4.00	59
Also see Newbeats, The				
DEAN, Bobby				
GO MR. DILLON/I'm Ready	(Chess 1710)	2.50	10.00	59
IT'S A FAD, MA/Just Between Teens	(Profile 4006)	3.75	15.00	59

TITLE/FLIP	LABEL & NO.	GOOD	NEAR MINT	YR.
DEAN, Debbie				
EVERYBODY'S TALKING ABOUT MY BABY/ I Cried All Night	(Motown 1025))	1.25	5.00	62
EVERYBODY'S TALKING ABOUT MY BABY/ I Cried All Night	(Motown 1025))	3.75	15.00	62
(Picture sleeve)				
DEAN, Donnie				
MOVIE STAR/Ridin' On A Rainbow	(Apt 25082)	1.25	5.00	60
DEAN, James				
JUNGLE RHYTHM/Dean's Lament	(Romeo 100)	2.50	10.00	
(James Dean on bongos)				
DEAN, Larry				
PONY TAIL/All The Time	(Brunswick 55056)	1.00	4.00	58
DEAN, Wally				
SADDLE UP A SATELLITE/	(Arctic 103)	3.00	12.00	
(Novelty/Break-in)				
DEANE, Janet				
ANOTHER NIGHT ALONE/I'm Glad I Waited	(Gateway 719)	1.50	6.00	
(With the Skyliners)				
DEANS, The				
HUMPTY DUMPTY/La Chaim (Good Luck)	(Mohawk 119)	1.00	4.00	60
IT'S YOU/I Don't Want To Wait	(Mohawk 126)	1.00	4.00	61
LITTLE WHITE GARDENIA/I Don't Want To Wait	(Laurie 3114)	1.25	5.00	61
MY HEART IS LOW/I'll Love You Forever	(Mohawk 114)	1.00	4.00	60
DEARLY BELOVEDS, The				
PEEP PEEP POP POP/It Is Better	(Columbia 4-43797)	.75	3.00	66
DEATON, Frank, & The Mad Lads				
MY LOVE FOR YOU/Just A Little Bit More	(Bally 1042)	12.50	50.00	57
DEBBIE & THE DARNELS				
DADDY/Mr. Johnny Jones	(Columbia 4-42530)	1.00	4.00	62
SANTA, TEACH ME TO DANCE/This Time	(Vernon 101)	1.00	4.00	61
TIME, THE/Why, Why	(Vernon 100)	1.50	6.00	61
This group may also be shown as the Teen Dreams.				
DEBONAIRES, The				
DARLING/Whispering Blues	(Herald 509)	1.00	4.00	57
EVERY ONCE IN A WHILE/Mama Don't Care	(Dore 526)	2.50	10.00	59
EVERY ONCE IN A WHILE/Gert's Skirts	(Dore 592)	1.50	6.00	61
EVERY ONCE IN A WHILE/Gert's Skirts	(Dore 702)	.75	3.00	64
EVERYBODY'S MOVIN'/Mama Don't Care	(Dore 712)	1.00	4.00	64
I WANT TO TALK ABOUT IT (WORLD)/ I Want To Talk About It (World) (Part 2)	(Galaxy 787)	1.00	4.00	67
THIS MUST BE PARADISE/I Need You Darling	(Elmont 1004)	2.00	8.00	
WE'LL WAIT/Make Believe Lover	(Gee 1054)	1.00	4.00	61
DEBREE, Peter, & The Wanderers				
HEY MR PRESLEY/Long Tall You	(Fortune 134)	2.50	10.00	
HEY MR PRESLEY/Honey Won't You Love Me	(Fortune 134)	2.50	10.00	
(Shown as by Jimmy Gartin & the Swingers)				
DEBS, The				
(WE LIKE) CREW CUTS (With the Escorts)/ Swingin' Sam (By the Pastels)	(Josie 833)	1.25	5.00	58
DEB-TONES, The				
GIVE IT UP/Rock A Bye	(RCA Victor 47-7384)	1.00	4.00	58
I'M IN LOVE AGAIN/Knock Knock, Who's There	(RCA Victor 47-7539)	1.00	4.00	59
MISS LONELY HEARTS/Cuddly Baby	(RCA Victor 47-7242)	1.00	4.00	58

TITLE/FLIP — LABEL & NO. — GOOD — NEAR MINT — YR.

DEBUTANTES, The
ON BROADWAY/Little Latin Lupe Lou .... (Gail & Rice 101) 1.00 4.00

DE CASTRO SISTERS, The
SNOWBOUND FOR CHRISTMAS/Christmas Is A-Comin' .... (Abbott 3012) 1.00 4.00 55
TEACH ME TONIGHT/It's Love .... (Abbott 3001) 1.00 4.00 54
TEACH ME TONIGHT CHA CHA/
The Things I Tell My Pillow .... (ABC-Paramount 9988) .75 3.00 58

DECOU, Art
I CRIED A MILLION TEARS/Where Are You? .... (Form 100) .75 3.00 59

DECOYS, The
I WANT ONLY YOU/For You .... (Aanko 1005) 8.75 35.00
I WANT ONLY YOU/For You .... (Time Square) 1.25 5.00

DEDICATIONS, The
SHINING STAR/ .... (C&A 506) 10.00 40.00
TEARDROPS/Teardrops .... (White Whale 340) 2.50 10.00 70
WHY DON'T YOU WRITE ME/Boppin' Around .... (Card 336) 2.50 10.00

DEE, Billy, & The Superchargers
CURB SERVICE/ .... (Westford 101) 1.00 4.00 63
(Instrumental)

DEE, Dave, Dozy, Beaky, Mick & Tich
BEND IT/She's So Good .... (Fontana 1559) .75 3.00 66
BREAKOUT/Mrs. Thursday .... (Imperial 66309) .75 3.00 68
HERE'S A HEART/Hideaway .... (Fontana 1553) .75 3.00 66
HOLD TIGHT/You Know What I Want .... (Fontana 1545) .75 3.00 66
LEGEND OF XANADU/Please .... (Imperial 66287) .75 3.00 68
MASTER LLEWELLYN/Okay .... (Fontana 1591) .75 3.00 67
NO TIME/You Make It Move .... (Fontana 1537) .75 3.00 66
SAVE ME/Shame .... (Fontana 1569) .75 3.00 67
ZABADAK/The Sun Goes Down .... (Imperial 66270) .75 3.00 67
Also see Dozy, Beaky, Mick & Tich

DEE, Jackie: see DeShannon, Jackie

DEE JAY & THE RUNAWAYS
AND I KNOW/Sunshine Morning .... (Sonic 155) .75 3.00 68
PETER RABBIT/Three Steps To Heaven .... (Smash 2034) .75 3.00 66
SHE'S A BIG GIRL NOW/He's Not Your Friend .... (Smash 2049) .75 3.00 66

DEE, Jimmy (& The Offbeats)
HENRIETTA/Don't Cry No More .... (TNT 148) 5.00 20.00 57
HENRIETTA/Don't Cry No More .... (Dot 15664) 1.00 4.00 57
I FEEL LIKE ROCKIN'/Rock Tick Tock .... (TNT 161) 3.75 15.00 59
YOU SAY YOU BEAT ME TO THE PUNCH (Answer Song)/
I've Got A Secret .... (Cutie 1400) .75 3.00 63
YOU'RE LATE MISS KATE/Here I Come .... (Dot 15721) 2.50 10.00 58

DEE, Joe, & His Top Hands
BELIEVE MY HEART/Legend Of Love .... (Pat Riccio 101) 2.00 8.00
(With the Tremonts)
HONKY-TONK GUITAR/Blind Heart .... (Pat Riccio 1105) 1.25 5.00
(Instrumentals)
SOME OF THESE NIGHTS/
I Thought I Heard You Calling My Name .... (Pat Riccio 1107) 1.25 5.00

DEE, Joey, & The Starliters
BABY YOU'RE DRIVING ME CRAZY/
Help Me Pick Up The Pieces .... (Roulette 4467) .75 3.00 63
DANCE, DANCE, DANCE/Let's Have A Party .... (Roulette 4503) .75 3.00 63
DANCING ON THE BEACH/Good Little You .... (Jubilee 5539) 1.00 4.00 65
EVERYTIME (I THINK ABOUT YOU)/
Everytime (I Think About You) (Part 2) .... (Roulette 4431) .75 3.00 63
FACE OF AN ANGEL/Shimmy Baby .... (Scepter 1210) 1.25 5.00 60
FANNIE MAE/Ya Ya .... (Roulette 4525) .75 3.00 63
GETTIN' NEARER/Down By The Riverside .... (Roulette 4539) .75 3.00 63
HEY LET'S TWIST/Roly Poly .... (Roulette 4408) .75 3.00 62
HOT PASTRAMI WITH MASHED POTATOES/
Hot Pastrami With Mashed Potatoes (Part 2) .... (Roulette 4488) .75 3.00 63
I LOST MY BABY/Keep Your Mind On What Your Doin' .. (Roulette 4456) .75 3.00 62
PEPPERMINT TWIST (PART 1)/
Peppermint Twist (Part 2) .... (Roulette 4401) .75 3.00 61
PEPPERMINT TWIST/ .... (Vaseline Hair Tonic R-12) 3.00 12.00 62
(Special products issue. Price includes cover & insert.)
SHE'S SO EXCEPTIONAL/It's Got You .... (Jubilee 5554) 1.00 4.00 65
SHOUT (PART 1)/Shout (Part 2) .... (Roulette 4416) .75 3.00 62
WHAT KIND OF LOVE IS THIS/Wing-Ding .... (Roulette 4438) .75 3.00 62
YAYA TWIST, THE/Runaround Sue (By Dion &
The Belmonts) .... (Monument-No Number Given) 1.25 5.00 61
YOU CAN'T SIT DOWN/Put Your Heart In It .... (Jubilee 5566) 1.00 4.00 65
Also see Hawk

DEE, Johnny: see Loudermilk, John D.

DEE, Kiki
AMOUREUSE/Rest My Head .... (Rocket 40157) .50 2.00 73
CHICAGO/Bad Day Child .... (Rocket 40730) .50 2.00 77
DAY WILL COME/My Whole World Ended .... (Tamla 54193) .75 3.00 70
HOW GLAD I AM/Peter .... (Rocket 40401) .50 2.00 75
I/Stop & Think .... (Liberty 55994) 1.00 4.00 67
I'VE GOT THE MUSIC IN ME/Simple Melody .... (Rocket 40293) .50 2.00 74
LONNIE & JOSIE/Last Good Man In My Life .... (Rocket 40095) .50 2.00 73
LOVE MAKES THE WORLD GO ROUND/Jimmy .... (Rare Earth 5025) .50 2.00 71
LOVING & FREE/Super Cool .... (Rocket 40256) .50 2.00 74
ONCE A FOOL/Someone To Me .... (Rocket 40506) .50 2.00 76
ONE JUMP AHEAD OF THE STORM/Don't Stop Loving Me (Rocket 11490) .50 2.00 79
ONE STEP/ .... (Rocket 11413) .50 2.00 78
SMALL TOWN/I Dig You Baby .... (World Pacific 77820) 1.00 4.00 66
STEP BY STEP/Amourese .... (Rocket 40355) .50 2.00 74
Also see John, Elton

DEE, Lola
PAPER ROSES/Only You .... (Wing 90015) 1.00 4.00 55

DEE, Ricky, & The Embers
WORKOUT (PART 1)/Workout (Part 2) .... (Newtown 5001) .75 3.00 62

DEE, Ronnie
ACTION PACKED/Make The Love .... (Back Beat 522) 2.00 8.00 62

DEE, Sandra
DEAR JOHNNY/When I Fall In Love .... (Decca 30142) .75 3.00 60
DO IT WHILE YOU'RE YOUNG/Questions .... (Decca 31063) .75 3.00 60

DEE, Sonny
HERE I STAND/I'm Not The One For You .... (Kapp 421) 1.00 4.00 61

DEES, Rick, & His Cast Of Idiots
ONE MORE JELLY DOUGHNUT (Elvis Novelty)/
Barely White (Barry White novelty) .... (RSO 860) 1.50 6.00 76

DEE, Tommy, With Carol Kay & The Teen-Aires
MERRY CHRISTMAS, MARY/Angel Of Love .... (Crest 1067) .75 3.00 59
THREE STARS/I'll Never Change .... (Crest 1057) 1.00 4.00 59
(Tribute to Buddy Holly, Richie Valens & the Big Bopper)
THREE STARS/I'll Never Change .... (Crest 1057) 3.75 15.00 59
(Stereo single issue)

DEE, Tony, & The Pageants
MAKE ME YOUR QUEEN/Saturday Romance .... (Du-Well 101) 6.25 25.00
MAKE ME YOUR QUEEN/Saturday Romance .... (Arlen 731) 3.75 15.00

DEEP PURPLE (With Ritchie Blackmore, Jon Lord & Ian Paice)
BLACK NIGHT/Into The Fire .... (Warner Bros. 7504) .75 3.00 70
BURN/Coronarias Redig .... (Warner-Purple 7809) .50 2.00 74
EMMARETTA/The Bird Has Flown .... (Tetragrammaton 1519) 1.00 4.00 69
FIREBALL/I'm Alone .... (Warner Bros. 7528) .75 3.00 71
GETTING TIGHTER/ .... (Warner-Purple 8182) .50 2.00 75
HALLELUJAH (I AM THE PREACHER)/
April (Part 1) .... (Tetragrammaton 1537) 1.00 4.00 69
HIGHWAY STAR (Long Vervion)/
Highway Star (Short Vervion) .... (Warner Bros. 7634) .75 3.00 73
HUSH/One More Rainy Day .... (Tetragrammaton 1503) 1.00 4.00 68
KENTUCKY WOMAN/Hard Road .... (Tetragrammaton 1508) 1.00 4.00 68
LAZY/ .... (Warner Bros. 7595) .75 3.00 72
MIGHT JUST TAKE YOUR LIFE/Coronarias Redig .... (Warner-Purple 7784) .50 2.00 74
NEVER BEFORE/When A Blind Man Cries .... (Warner Bros. 7572) .75 3.00 72
RIVER DEEP-MOUNTAIN HIGH/
Listen, Learn, Read On .... (Tetragrammaton 1514) 1.00 4.00 69
SMOKE ON THE WATER/Smoke On The Water (Live) . (Warner Bros. 7710) .75 3.00 73
STORMBRINGER/Love Don't Mean A Thing .... (Warner-Purple 8069) .50 2.00 75
STRANGE KIND OF WOMAN/I'm Alone .... (Warner Bros. 7595) .75 3.00 72
SUPER TROUPER/Woman From Tokyo .... (Warner Bros. 7737) .75 3.00 73
WOMAN FROM TOKYO/Super Trouper .... (Warner Bros. 7672) .75 3.00 73
YOU CAN'T DO IT RIGHT (WITH THE ONE YOU LOVE)/
High Ball Shooter .... (Warner-Purple 8049) .50 2.00 75
Also see Ashton, Gardner & Dyke
Also see Gillan, Ian, Band
Also see Glover, Roger, & Guests

DEEP SIX, The
COUNTING/When Morning Breaks .... (Liberty 55882) 1.00 4.00 66
IMAGE OF A GIRL/C'mon Baby .... (Liberty 55926) 1.25 5.00 66
LAST TIME AROUND/One & One .... (Soft 960) 1.00 4.00 65
RISING SUN/Strollin' Blues .... (Saw-Man 001) 1.50 6.00 65
RISING SUN/Strollin' Blues .... (Liberty 55380) .75 3.00 65
THINGS WE SAY/I Wanna Shout .... (Liberty 55858) 1.00 4.00 66
WHY SAY GOODBYE/
What Would You Wish From The Golden Fish .... (Liberty 55901) 1.00 4.00 66

DEEPEST BLUE
PRETTY LITTLE THING/Somebody's Girl .... (Blue-Fin 102) 1.25 5.00

DEFENDERS, The
BEATLES, WE WANT OUR GIRLS BACK NOW/ .... (Realm 001) 1.50 6.00 64
I LAUGHED SO HARD/Island Of Love .... (Parkway 926) 1.50 6.00 64

DE-FENDERS, The
(DANCE TO THE) YAKETY SAX/Wild One .... (World Pacific 382) 1.00 4.00 63
LITTLE DEUCE COUPE/Hayburner (By the Deuce Coupes) . (Del Fi 4226) 1.00 4.00 63

DEFIANTS, The
SURFER'S TWIST/Twistin' N Stompin' .... (Baronet 5) 1.00 4.00 62
(Instrumentals)

DE FRANCO FAMILY, The (Featuring Tony DeFranco)
ABRA-CA-DABRA/Same Kind 'A Love .... (20th Century TC-2070) .50 2.00 73
HEARTBEAT, IT'S A LOVEBEAT/
Sweet, Sweet Loretta .... (20th Century TC-2030) .50 2.00 73
SAVE THE LAST DANCE FOR ME/
Because We Both Are Young .... (20th Century TC-2088) .50 2.00 74
WE BELONG TOGETHER/Time Enough For Love .. (20th Century TC-2214) 1.25 5.00 75
WRITE ME A LETTER/Baby Blue .... (20th Century TC-2128) .75 3.00 74

DE JOHN SISTERS, The
C'EST LA VIE/Uninvited Love .... (Epic 9131) 1.00 4.00 55
(MY BABY DON'T LOVE ME) NO MORE/
Theresa (The Little Flower) .... (Epic 9085) 1.00 4.00 54
NEVER, SINCE SCHOOL/The Angel Passed By .... (Okeh 6989) 1.25 5.00 53
STRAIGHTEN UP & FLY RIGHT/Wrong Guy .... (Sunbeam 106) .75 3.00 58

DEKKER, Desmond, & The Aces
ISRAELITES, THE/My Precious World (The Man) .... (Uni 55129) .75 3.00 69
IT MEK/Problems .... (Uni 55150) .75 3.00 69
PERSEVERANCE/You Can Get It If You Really Want .... (Uni 55261) .75 3.00 70

DELACARDOS, The
FORGET ABOUT THE GUY/ .... (Dimension 1040) 1.25 5.00 64
HOLD BACK THE TEARS/Mr. Dillon .... (United Artists 310) 1.25 5.00 61
I GOT IT/Thing-a-ma-jig .... (United Artists 276) 1.25 5.00 60
LETTER TO A SCHOOL GIRL, A/I'll Never Let You Know .... (Elgey 1001) 2.00 8.00 59

DE LYON, Leo, & The Musclemen
SICK MANNY'S GYM/Plunkin' .... (Musicor 1001) 1.25 5.00 60
(Novelty)

DEL & THE ESCORTS
BABY DOLL/Someone To Watch Over Me .... (Rome 103) 2.00 8.00
HAPPY/You're For Me (& I'm For You) .... (Taurus 350) 3.75 15.00
The Escorts were actually the Earls

DEL CADES, The
WORLDS FAIR U.S.A./
It Takes Two To Fall In Love .... (United Sound Associates 175) 2.00 8.00

DEL CAPRIS, The
SPEAK TO ME OF LOVE/Theresa .... (Almont 304) 1.25 5.00

DEL 4'S, The
BEATLE SONG/Dare Me .... (Zenith 250) 1.50 6.00 64

DEL MARS, The
SNACKY POO (PART 1)/Snacky Poo (Part 2) .... (Mercury 72244) 2.00 8.00 64

DEL RAYS, The
AROUND THE CORNER/Have A Heart .... (Moon 110) 10.00 40.00 59
MY DARLING/The One I Adore .... (Warner Bros. 5022) 3.75 15.00 58

DEL RONS, The: see Reparata & The Del Rons

DEL ROYS, The
LOVE ME TENDERLY/Pleasing You .... (Carol 4113) 1.25 5.00 61

DEL SATINS, The
BALLAD OF A D.J./Does My Heart Stand A Chance .... (Laurie 3149) 2.00 8.00 62
COUNTING TEARDROPS/Remember .... (Win 702) 2.00 8.00
FEELIN' NO PAIN/Who Cares .... (Columbia 42802) 1.25 5.00 63
GIRL NAMES ARLENE, A/I'll Do My Crying Tomorrow .. (B.T. Puppy 563) 2.00 8.00 67
HANG AROUND/My Candy Apple Vette .... (B.T. Puppy 506) .75 3.00 65
I'LL PRAY FOR YOU/I Remember The Night .... (End 1096) 2.50 10.00 61
LITTLE RAIN MUST FALL, A/Love, Hate, Revenge .... (Diamond 216) 1.00 4.00 67
RELIEF/Throwaway Song .... (B.T. Puppy 514) 1.00 4.00 65
SWEETS FOR MY SWEET/A Girl Named Arlene .... (B.T. Puppy 509) 1.25 5.00 65
TEARDROPS FOLLOW ME/
Best Wishes, Good Luck, Goodbye .... (Laurie 3132) 1.25 5.00 62
TWO BROKEN HEARTS/Believe In Me .... (Mala 475) 1.25 5.00 64
Also see Como, Nicky
Also see Foreign Intrigue
Also see Maresca, Ernie

DEL SHAYS, The
I'LL LOVE YOU FOREVER/Fake It .... (Charger 102) 3.00 12.00 64

DEL-AIRES, The
ARLENE/I'm Your Baby .... (Coral 62419) 3.75 15.00 64
ELAINE/Just Wigglin' N' Wobblin' .... (Coral 62370) 2.50 10.00 63

IT TOOK A LONG TIME/Ma Ma Marie .... (Delsey 302) 1.25 5.00
MY FUNNY VALENTINE/Drag .... (Coral 62404) 3.75 15.00 64
(Shown as by Ronnie & the Delaires)
WHILE WALKING/Lost My Job .... (MBS 001) 1.25 5.00
WHY DID HE LEAVE/I'm Lonely .... (Arrawak 1003) 1.00 4.00
Even though all of these releases are shown as being by a group using the same name, the possibility exists that they are not all by the same group.

DELANEY & BONNIE (Delaney & Bonnie Bramlet)
CHERRY PIE/Hey, Mr. Weatherman .... (Garpax 4084) 1.50 6.00 64
(Shown as by Lani & Boni)
COMIN' HOME (Featuring Eric Clapton)/Groupie .... (Atco 6725) .75 3.00 70
HARD TO SAY GOODBYE/ .... (Stax 0057) .75 3.00 69
IT'S BEEN A LONG TIME COMING/
We Have Just Been Feeling Bad .... (Stax 0003) .75 3.00 68
MOVE 'EM OUT/Sing My Way Home .... (Atco 6866) .50 2.00 72
NEVER ENDING SONG OF LOVE/
Don't Deceive Me (Please Don't Go) .... (Atco 6804) .50 2.00 71
ONLY YOU KNOW & I KNOW/God Knows I Love You .... (Atco 6838) .50 2.00 71
SING MY WAY HOME/ .... (Atco 6904) .50 2.00 72
SOUL SHAKE/Free The People .... (Atco 6756) .50 2.00 70
WADE IN THE RIVER JORDAN/Country Life .... (Columbia 45608) .50 2.00 73
WHEN THE BATTLE IS OVER/Get Ourselves Together ... (Elektra 45662) .75 3.00 69
WHERE THERE'S A WILL THERE'S A WAY/Lonesome &
A Long Way From Home (With George Harrison) .... (Atco 6883) .50 2.00 72
YOU'VE LOST THAT LOVIN' FEELIN'/ .... (Independence 78) 1.00 4.00 68
Also see Bad Habits, The
Also see Bramlett, Delaney
Also see Shindogs, The

DEL-LARKS, The
LADY LOVE/Remember The Night .... (East West 116) 5.00 20.00

DELBERT & GLEN (With Delbert McClinton)
I RECEIVED A LETTER/ .... (Clean 60003) .50 2.00 72
OLD STANDBY/Everybody's A Holiday .... (Clean 60004) .50 2.00 73

DELEGATES, The
CONVENTION '72/Convention '72 (Part 2) .... (Mainstream 5525) 1.50 6.00 72
CONVENTION '72/Funky Butt .... (Mainstream 5525) 1.25 5.00 72
RICHARD M. NIXON-FACE THE ISSUES/
Richard M. Nixon-Face The Issues (Part 2) .... (Mainstream 5530) 1.25 5.00 72
Novelty/Break-ins

DELFONICS, The
OVER & OVER/There They Go .... (Fling 727) 1.25 5.00

DELICATES, The
TOO YOUNG TO DATE/The Kiss .... (United Artists 228) 1.00 4.00 60

DELICATO, Paul
CARA MIA/ .... (Artists of America 111) .50 2.00 75
IT'S THE SAME OLD SONG/I Can't Make It Alone (Artists of America 120) .50 2.00 76

DELL, Danny, & The Trends
FROGGY (Went A Courting)/ .... (Rockin' RR-160) 1.00 4.00

DELL, Dickey, & The Bing Bongs
DING-A-LING-A-LING/The Cling .... (Dragon 10205) 6.25 25.00

DELL, Don, & The Upstarts
MAKE BELIEVE LOVE/
I Want You, I Need You, I Love You .... (Roman 2963) 1.50 6.00
(Shown as by Don Dell & The Montereys)
SPECIAL LOVE, A/Someone For Me .... (East Coast 105) 2.00 8.00
TIME/May It Be My Fortune .... (East Coast 102) 2.00 8.00

DELL, Jimmy
COOL IT BABY/The Message .... (RCA Victor 47-7194) 2.00 8.00 58
SHE WON'T PET/Teeny Weeny .... (RCA Victor 47-7134) 2.00 8.00 58

DELL, Tony
MY GIRL/Magic Wand .... (King 5766) 6.25 25.00 63
(Group Sound)

DELL-COEDS, The
LOVE IN RETURN/Hey Mr. Banjo .... (Enith 712) 1.25 5.00

DEL-LOURDS, The
ALONE/All Alone .... (Solar 1001) 1.25 5.00 63
(Accappella)
GLORIA/All Alone .... (Solar 1003) 1.25 5.00 63
(Accappella)

DELLWOODS, The
DON'T PUT ONIONS ON YOUR HAMBURGER/
Her Mustache .... (Big Top 3137) 2.00 8.00 63
(Novelty)
(SHE GOT A) NOSE JOB/ .... (Mad) 2.50 10.00 62
(Plastic soundsheet orginally attached to an issue of Mad Magazine. Price is for soundsheet only.)
(SHE GOT A) NOSE JOB/ .... (Mad) 6.25 25.00 62
(Plastic soundsheet still intact with issue of Mad Magazine)

DELMAR, Eddie
GARDEN IN THE RAIN/My Heart Beckons You .... (Vegas 628) 2.00 8.00 65
LOVE BELLS/Blanche .... (Madison 168) 5.00 20.00 61
(With Bob Knight Four)

DELMONICOS, The
THERE THEY GO/You Can Call .... (Aku 6318) 1.25 5.00
UNTIL YOU/Worlds Biggest Fool .... (Musictone 6122) 1.25 5.00

TITLE/FLIP	LABEL & NO.	GOOD	NEAR MINT	YR.
DELONGS, The				
I WANT YOUR LOVE/You're Never Too Young	(Art Flow 3906)	1.50	6.00	
DELRAYS INC., The				
I'M A-LOVIN'/Billy's Beat	(Salen 002)	1.25	5.00	
DEL-RAYS, The (With Dave T.)				
GIRL IN MY HEART/Scooter Town	(Carousel 213)	5.00	20.00	
(Shown as by Dave T. & The Del-Rays)				
LORRAINE/The Bounce	(Planet 52)	3.75	15.00	
DEL-RICOS, The				
BEATLE CRAWL, THE/Beatle Hootenanny	("620" 1008)	1.50	6.00	64
DEL RIOS, The				
VALERIE/Mystery	(Rust 5066)	1.25	5.00	63
VINES OF LOVE, THE/Session	(Big 613)	3.00	12.00	
DELRONS, The: see Reparata & The Delrons				
DELTAS, The				
GOODNIGHT MY LOVE/Give My Love A Chance	(Cambridge 124)	1.00	4.00	
DELTAS, The				
MY OWN TRUE LOVE/Hold Me, Thrill Me, Kiss Me	(Philips 40023)	.75	3.00	62
DEL-TINOS, The				
NIGHTLITE/Pa Pa Ooh Mau Mau	(Conic 1451)	1.25	5.00	
DELUGG, Milton				
HOORAY FOR SANTA CLAUS/Lonely Beach	(4 Corners 114)	.75	3.00	64
THEME FROM "THE MUNSTERS"/Ghost Meets Ghoul	(Epic 9728)	.75	3.00	64
DEL-VETTS, The				
I CALL MY BABY S.T.P./That's The Way It Is	(Dunwich 142)	1.00	4.00	66
LAST TIME AROUND/Everytime	(Dunwich 125)	1.00	4.00	
LITTLE LATIN LUPE LU/Ram Charger	(Seeburg Jukebox 1018)	1.00	4.00	
DELVY, Richard (Of The Challengers)				
ATLANTIS/Steve's Tune	(Triumph 55)	1.00	4.00	63
(Instrumentals)				
Also see Belairs, The				
DEMARCO, Lou				
CARELESS LOVE/My Lady Fair	(Ferris 320)	2.00	8.00	
DE MARCO, Ralph				
MORE THAN RICHES/Old Shep	(Guaranteed 202)	2.00	8.00	59
DE MATTEO, Nicky, & The Sorrows				
I WANNA BE LONELY/Little Red Kitten	(Cameo 407)	1.50	6.00	65
SUDDENLY/More Than Riches	(Guyden 2024)	1.00	4.00	60
DEMENSIONS, The				
AGAIN/Count Your Blessings Instead Of Sheep	(Coral 62277)	1.25	5.00	61
AS TIME GOES BY/My Foolish Heart	(Coral 65611)	1.25	5.00	63
AS TIME GOES BY/Seven Days A Week	(Coral 62293)	1.25	5.00	61
GOD'S CHRISTMAS/Ave Maria	(Mohawk 121)	1.25	5.00	60
MY FOOLISH HEART/Just One More Chance	(Coral 62344)	1.25	5.00	63
OVER THE RAINBOW/Nursery Rhyme Rock	(Mohawk 116)	1.00	4.00	60
OVER THE RAINBOW/Zing Went The Strings Of My Heart	(Coral 65559)	1.25	5.00	62
TEAR FELL, A/Theresa	(Mohawk 123)	1.25	5.00	61
YOUNG AT HEART/Your Cheatin' Heart	(Coral 62323)	1.25	5.00	62
ZING WENT THE STRINGS OF MY HEART/ Don't Take Your Love From Me	(Mohawk 120)	1.25	5.00	60
This group may also be shown as The Dimensions on some releases.				
DEMIAN, Max, Band				
PARADISE/Still Hosed	(RCA PB-11525)	.50	2.00	79
DEMILLES, The (Featuring Carlo Mastrangelo)				
CRY & BE ON YOUR WAY/Lazy Love	(Laurie 3247)	2.50	10.00	64
DONNA LEE/Um Ba Pa	(Laurie 3230)	1.25	5.00	64
DEMOLYRS, The				
RAIN/Hey Little Rosie	(U.W.R. 900)	7.50	30.00	
DEMOTRONS, The				
HOMBRE/Swingin' Soiree	(Radar 2615)	.75	3.00	62
PRETZEL TWIST, THE/Meet Mister Calahan	(Radar 2616)	.75	3.00	62
SLEEP, SLEEP, SLEEP/Take This Love	(Scepter 12148)	1.50	6.00	66
STEEL DRIVING MAN/Frisky	(Dorset 5010)	.75	3.00	
STICKS & STONES/Adventures In Paradise (Theme From)	(Radar 2621)	.75	3.00	62
Also see Mitlo Sisters, The				
DEMOTRONS, The				
BEG, BORROW & STEAL/Midnight In New York	(Cameo 456)	.75	3.00	67
DENELS, The				
HERE COME THE HO-DADS/Massacre Stomp	(Bamboo 517)	1.50	6.00	62
HERE COME THE HO-DADS/Massacre Stomp	(Union 502)	.75	3.00	62
Instrumentals				
DENIMS, The				
SALTY DOG/Salty Dog Man	(Cavort 122333)	1.00	4.00	
(Instrumental)				
DENISON, Homer, Jr.				
CHICKIE RUN/March Slave Boogie	(Brunswick 55150)	1.00	4.00	59
DENNIS, Allen, & The Disco Turkeys				
GREAT DEBATE, THE/Super Stu	(Brown Dog 9016)	.75	3.00	
(Novelty/Break-In)				
DENNIS & THE EXPLORERS				
REMEMBER/Every Road	(Coral 62295)	2.50	10.00	62
VISION OF LOVE/On A Clear Night	(Coral 62147)	3.75	15.00	60
DENNIS & THE SUPERTONES				
DOIN' THE SUPERMAN/Superman	(Smash 1809)	.75	3.00	63
DENNY & THE DEDICATIONS				
LOST LOVE/I'll Show You How To Love	(Susan 1111)	2.00	8.00	
DENNY & THE LP'S				
WHY NOT GIVE ME YOUR HEART/Slide-cha-lypso	(Rock-it 001)	5.00	20.00	
DENNY, Martin				
ENCHANTED SEA, THE/Stranger In Paradise	(Liberty F-55212)	.75	3.00	59
FRANKIE & JOHNNY/Banana Choo Choo	(Liberty F-55236)	.75	3.00	60
MARTINIQUE/Sake Rock	(Liberty F-55199)	.75	3.00	59
MARTINIQUE/Sake Rock	(Liberty S-55199)	1.50	6.00	59
(Stereo single issue)				
PAYOFF, THE/Cast Your Fate To The Wind	(Liberty F-55514)	.75	3.00	63
QUIET VILLAGE/Llama Serenade	(Liberty F-55162)	.75	3.00	59
QUIET VILLAGE/Happy Talk	(Liberty J-77015)	2.00	8.00	59
(Compact 33 stereo single)				
QUIET VILLAGE/Llama Serenade	(Liberty S-77162)	1.50	6.00	59
(Stereo single issue)				
TASTE OF HONEY, A/Brighter Side	(Liberty F-55470)	.75	3.00	62
Instrumentals				
DENNY, Sandy (Of Fairport Convention)				
CRAZY LADY BLUES/Let's Jump The Broomstick	(A&M 1331)	.75	3.00	72
LISTEN LISTEN/Tomorrow Is A Long Time	(A&M 1410)	.75	3.00	73
Also see Strawbs, The				

TITLE/FLIP	LABEL & NO.	GOOD	NEAR MINT	YR.
DENNY-O				
TRIAL OF THE PRESIDENT/ Trial Of The President (Part 2)	(Blind Justice 101)	1.00	4.00	
(Novelty/Break-In)				
DENOTATIONS, The				
LONE STRANGER/Nena	(Lawn 253)	6.25	25.00	65
DENSON, Lee				
NEW SHOES (Features Eddie Cochran on Guitar)/ Climb Love Mountain	(Vik 0281)	5.00	20.00	56
DENTON, Bob				
LOVER'S PLEA/I'll Always Be Yours	(Judd 1013)	1.00	4.00	59
(Shown as by Bobby Denton)				
PLAYBOY/24 Hour Night	(Dot 15833)	2.50	10.00	58
DENTON, Mickey				
STEADY KIND/Now You Can't Give Them Away	(Big Top 3078)	.75	3.00	61
DENVER, BOISE & JOHNSON (John Denver, David Boise, Michael Johnson)				
TAKE ME TO TOMORROW/ '68 Nixon (This Year's Model)	(Reprise 695)	2.00	8.00	68
DENVER, John (Henry John Deutschendorf)				
ANNIE'S SONG/Cool An' Green An' Shady	(RCA APBO-0295)	.75	3.00	74
ANTHEM (REVELATION)/	(RCA 74-0305)	1.00	4.00	70
AUTOGRAPH/The Mountain Song	(RCA PB-11915)	.50	2.00	80
BABY YOU LOOK GOOD TO ME TONIGHT/ Wrangle Mountain Song	(RCA PB-10854)	.75	3.00	76
BACK HOME AGAIN/It's Up To You	(RCA PB-10065)	.75	3.00	74
BET ON THE BLUES/	(RCA JD-11189)	1.50	6.00	77
(One sided promotional 12" issue)				
CHRISTMAS FOR COWBOYS/Silent Night	(RCA PB-10464)	.75	3.00	75
CITY OF NEW ORLEANS/Everyday	(RCA 74-0647)	1.00	4.00	71
DANCING WITH THE MOUNTAINS/American Child	(RCA PB-12017)	.75	3.00	79
DAYDREAM/ I Wish I Knew How It Would Feel To Be Free	(RCA 74-0275)	1.25	5.00	69
DOWNHILL STUFF/Life Is So Good	(RCA PB-11479)	.75	3.00	79
FAREWELL ANDROMEDA (WELCOME TO MY MORNING)/ Whiskey Basin Blues	(RCA APBO-0067)	.75	3.00	73
"Farewell Andromeda (Welcome To My Morning)" was reissued as "Welcome To My Morning (Farewell Andromeda)." See "My Sweet Lady" for that listing.				
FLY AWAY (With Olivia Newton-John)/Two Shots	(RCA PB-10517)	.75	3.00	75
FOLLOW ME/Isabel	(RCA 74-0332)	1.00	4.00	70
FRIENDS WITH YOU/Starwood In Aspen	(RCA 74-0567)	.75	3.00	71
GARDEN SONG/Berkeley Woman	(RCA PB-11637)	.75	3.00	79
GOODBYE AGAIN/The Eagle & The Hawk	(RCA 74-0737)	1.00	4.00	72
HARD LIFE, HARD TIMES (PRISONERS)/ Late Winter, Early Spring	(RCA 74-0801)	1.00	4.00	73
HAVE YOURSELF A MERRY LITTLE CHRISTMAS-WE WISH YOU A MERRY CHRISTMAS/A Baby Just Like You	(RCA PB-11767)	1.25	5.00	79
(With The Muppets, issued on red plastic.)				
HOW CAN I LEAVE YOU AGAIN/To The Wild Country	(RCA PB-11036)	.75	3.00	77
I'D RATHER BE A COWBOY/ Sunshine On My Shoulders (Acoustic version)	(RCA 74-0955)	1.25	5.00	73
I'M SORRY/Calypso	(RCA PB-10353)	.75	3.00	75
IT AMAZES ME/Druthers	(RCA PB-11214)	.75	3.00	78
IT MAKES ME GIGGLE/Spirit	(RCA PB-10687)	.75	3.00	76
I WANT TO LIVE/Tradewinds	(RCA PB-11267)	.75	3.00	78
JIMMY NEWMAN/	(RCA SPS-45-217)	1.50	6.00	70
(Promotional issue)				
LIKE A SAD SONG/Pegasus	(RCA PB-10774)	.75	3.00	76

TITLE/FLIP	LABEL & NO.	GOOD	NEAR MINT	YR.
LOOKING FOR SPACE/Windsong	(RCA PB-10586)	.75	3.00	76
MY SWEET LADY/ Welcome To My Morning (Farewell Andromeda)	(RCA PB-10911)	.75	3.00	77
PLEASE DADDY/Rocky Mountain Suite	(RCA APBO-0182)	.75	3.00	73
RHYMES & REASONS/	(RCA 74-)	1.50	6.00	69
ROCKY MOUNTAIN HIGH/Spring	(RCA 74-0829)	.75	3.00	72
SAIL AWAY HOME/I Wish I Could Have Been There	(RCA 74-0376)	1.25	5.00	70
SUNSHINE ON MY SHOULDERS/Around & Around	(RCA APBO-0213)	.75	3.00	74
SUNSHINE ON MY SHOULDERS (Long version)/ Sunshine On My Shoulders (Short version)	(RCA DJBO-0213)	1.25	5.00	74
(Promotional issue)				
SWEET SURRENDER/Summer	(RCA PB-10148)	.75	3.00	74
TAKE ME HOME, COUNTRY ROADS (With Fat City)/ Poems, Prayers & Promises	(RCA 74-0445)	.75	3.00	71
THANK GOD I'M A COUNTRY BOY/My Sweet Lady	(RCA PB-10239)	.75	3.00	75
WHAT'S ON YOUR MIND/Sweet Melinda	(RCA PB-11535)	.50	2.00	79
WHO'S GARDEN WAS THIS/Mr. Bojangles	(RCA 74-0391)	1.00	4.00	70
Also see Mitchell Trio, The				
DEODATO				
ALSO SPRANCH ZARATHUSTRA (2001)/Spirit Of Summer	(CTI 12)	.50	2.00	73
PETER GUNN/Amani	(MCA 40631)	.50	2.00	76
PINA COLADA/Love Island	(Warner Bros. 8588)	.50	2.00	78
RHAPSODY IN BLUE/Super Strut	(CTI 16)	.50	2.00	73
WATUSI STRUT/CARAVAN/Watusi Strut	(MCA 40469)	.50	2.00	75
WHISTLE BUMP/Love Island	(Warner Bros. 8606)	.50	2.00	78
DE PAUL, Lynsey				
WON'T SOMEBODY DANCE WITH ME/So Good To You	(MAM 3634)	.50	2.00	73
DERBYS, The				
NIGHT AFTER NIGHT/Just Leave Me Alone	(Mercury 71437)	2.00	8.00	59
WIPE OUT/People Say (She's No Good)	(Dawn 303)	.75	3.00	66
DEREK (Johnny Cymbal)				
BACK DOOR MAN/Sell Your Soul	(Bang 566)	.75	3.00	69
CINNAMON/This Is My Story	(Bang 558)	.75	3.00	68
INSIDE OUT-OUTSIDE IN/Sell Your Soul	(Bang 571)	.75	3.00	69
DEREK & RAY				
DRAGNET '67/Interplay	(RCA Victor 47-9111)	.75	3.00	67
DEREK & THE DOMINOES (Featuring Eric Clapton)				
BELL BOTTOM BLUES/	(Atco 6803)	.50	2.00	71
LAYLA (Short version)/I Am Yours	(Atco 6809)	.75	3.00	71
LAYLA (Long version)/I Am Yours	(Atco 6809)	.50	2.00	72
TELL THE TRUTH/Roll It Over	(Atco 6780)	.50	2.00	70
WHY DOES LOVE GOT TO BE SO SAD/ Presence Of The Lord	(RSO 400)	.50	2.00	73
DERRINGER, Rick (Rick Zehringer)				
DON'T EVER SAY GOODBYE/	(Blue Sky 2757)	.50	2.00	75
HANG ON SLOOPY/Skyscraper Blues	(Blue Sky 2755)	.50	2.00	75
IT'S RAINING/	(Blue Sky 2753)	.50	2.00	74
LAWYERS, GUNS & MONEY/Sleepless	(Blue Sky 2770)	.50	2.00	78
LET ME IN/You Can Have Me	(Blue Sky 2765)	.50	2.00	76
MIDNIGHT ROAD/Rocka Rolla	(Blue Sky 2774)	.50	2.00	78
ROCK & ROLL, HOOCHIE KOO/Time Warp (Instrumental)	(Blue Sky 2751)	.50	2.00	74
TEENAGE LOVE AFFAIR/Slide On Over Slinky	(Blue Sky 2752)	.50	2.00	74
Also see McCoys, The				
Also see Winter, Edgar, Group.				
DE SARIO, TERI				
AIN'T NOTHING GONNA KEEP ME FROM YOU/ Sometime Kind Of Thing	(Casablanca 929)	.50	2.00	78
DESDA				
SPLISH SPLASH TWIST/Sittin' In The Corner	(Del Fi 4174)	.75	3.00	62
DE SHANNON, Jackie				
ALL NIGHT DESIRE/Fire In The City	(Columbia 10340)	.75	3.00	76
BABY (WHEN YA' KISS ME)/Ain't That Love	(Liberty F-55387)	1.00	4.00	61
BRIGHTON HILL/You Can Come To Me	(Imperial 66438)	.75	3.00	70
BUDDY/Strolypso Dance	(Liberty F-55148)	2.00	8.00	58
(Shown as by Jackie Dee)				
CHAINS ON MY SOUL/Peaceful In My Soul	(Atlantic 2924)	.50	2.00	72
COME & GET ME/Splendor In The Grass	(Imperial 66171)	.75	3.00	66
COME ON DOWN/Find Me Love	(Imperial 66224)	.75	3.00	67
DIDN'T WANT TO HAVE TO DO IT/ Splendor In The Grass	(Imperial 66312)	.75	3.00	68
DO YOU KNOW HOW CHRISTMAS TREES ARE GROWN/ Christmas	(Imperial 66403)	.75	3.00	70
DON'T LET THE FLAME BURN OUT/ I Don't Think I Can Wait	(Amherst 725)	.50	2.00	78
FADED LOVE/Dancing Silhouettes	(Liberty F-55526)	1.00	4.00	63
HOLLY WOULD/Laurel Canyon	(Imperial 66342)	.75	3.00	68
I CAN MAKE IT WITH YOU/To Be Myself	(Imperial 66202)	.75	3.00	66
I'LL BE TRUE/How Wrong Was I	(Gone 5008)	3.75	15.00	57
(Shown as by Jackie Dee)				
I'LL DROWN IN MY OWN TEARS/The Prince	(Liberty F-55425)	1.00	4.00	62
I WANNA GO HOME/So Warm	(Edison International 416)	1.25	5.00	60
IT'S ALL IN THE GAME/Changin' My Mind	(Imperial 66251)	.75	3.00	67
IT'S LOVE BABY/ He's Got The Whole World In His Hands	(Liberty F-55730)	1.00	4.00	64
IT'S SO NICE/Mediterranean Sky	(Liberty F-56187)	1.00	4.00	70
JIMMIE, JUST SING ME ONE MORE SONG/You've Changed	(Atlantic 3041)	.50	2.00	74
JUST ANOTHER LIE/Cajun Blues	(Sage 290)	3.75	15.00	59
(Shown as by Jackie Shannon & the Cajuns)				
JUST ANOTHER LIE/Cajun Blues	(Fraternity 836)	3.00	12.00	59
(Shown as by Jackie Shannon & the Cajuns)				
JUST ANOTHER LIE/Cajun Blues	(Dot 15928)	1.50	6.00	59
(Shown as by Jackie Shannon & the Cajuns)				
JUST LIKE IN THE MOVIES/Guess Who	(Liberty F-55484)	1.00	4.00	62
KEEP ME WARM/Salinas	(Capitol 3130)	.75	3.00	71
LET THE SAILORS DANCE/Boat To Sail (With Brian Wilson)	(Columbia 10221)	2.50	10.00	76
LIFETIME OF LONELINESS, A/ Don't Turn Your Back On Me	(Imperial 66132)	.75	3.00	65
LITTLE YELLOW ROSES/Oh Sweet Chariot	(Liberty F-55602)	1.00	4.00	63
LITTLE YELLOW ROSES/500 Miles	(Liberty F-55602)	1.00	4.00	63
LOOKING FOR SOMEONE TO LOVE/Oh Boy	(Liberty F-55678)	1.00	4.00	64
LOVE & LEARN/I'm Glad It's You	(MGM 13349)	1.00	4.00	65
LOVE WILL FIND A WAY/(I Let Go) Completely	(Imperial 66419)	.75	3.00	69
ME ABOUT YOU/I Keep Wanting You	(Imperial 66281)	.75	3.00	68
MEDLEY: YOU KEEP ME HANGIN' ON-HURT SO BAD/ What Was Your Day Like	(Imperial 66452)	.75	3.00	70
NEEDLES & PINS/Did He Call Today Mama	(Liberty F-55563)	.75	3.00	63
NOBODY'S HOME TO GO HOME TO/Nicole	(Imperial 66301)	.75	3.00	68
PARADISE/I Wanna Roo You	(Atlantic 2895)	.50	2.00	72
PUT A LITTLE LOVE IN YOUR HEART/ Always Be Together	(Imperial 66385)	.75	3.00	69
PUT MY BABY DOWN/The Foolish One	(Edison International 418)	1.25	5.00	60
SHE DON'T UNDERSTAND HIM LIKE I DO/ Hold Your Head High	(Liberty F-55705)	1.00	4.00	64
STONE COLD SOUL/West Virginia Mine	(Capitol 3185)	.75	3.00	71
SWEET SIXTEEN/Speak Out To Me	(Atlantic 2919)	.75	3.00	72
TEACH ME/Lonely Girl	(Liberty F-55288)	1.00	4.00	61
THINGS WE SAID TODAY/	(Amherst 737)	.50	2.00	78
THINK ABOUT YOU/Heaven Is Being With You	(Liberty F-55342)	1.00	4.00	61
TOO LOVE SOMEBODY/	(Amherst 727)	.50	2.00	78
TROUBLE/Lies	(P.J. 101)	3.00	12.00	59
(Shown as by Jackie Shannon)				
TROUBLE/Lies	(Sand 330)	2.50	10.00	59
(Shown as by Jackie Shannon)				
TROUBLE/Lies	(Dot 15980)	1.50	6.00	59
(Shown as by Jackie Shannon)				

TITLE/FLIP	LABEL & NO.	GOOD	NEAR MINT	YR.
TRUST ME/What is This	(Imperial 66370)	.75	3.00	69
TWENTY-FOUR HOURS A DAY/ He's Got The Whole World In His Hands	(Liberty F-55730)	1.00	4.00	64
VANILLA OLAY/Only Love Can Break Your Heart	(Atlantic 2871)	.75	3.00	72
WEIGHT, THE/Effervescent Blue	(Imperial 66313)	.75	3.00	68
WEIGHT, THE/Splendor In The Grass	(Imperial 66313)	.75	3.00	68
WHAT THE WORLD NEEDS NOW IS LOVE/ I Remember The Boy	(Imperial 66110)	.75	3.00	65
WHEN YOU WALK IN THE ROOM/Over You	(Liberty F-55735)	1.00	4.00	64
WHEN YOU WALK IN THE ROOM/ Till You Say You'll Be Mine	(Liberty F-55645)	1.00	4.00	63
WINDOWS & DOORS/So Long, Johnny	(Imperial 66196)	.75	3.00	66
WISH I COULD FIND A BOY (JUST LIKE YOU)/ I Won't Turn You Down	(Liberty F-55358)	1.00	4.00	61
WISHING DOLL, THE/Where Does The Sun Go	(Imperial 66236)	.75	3.00	67
YOUR BABY IS A LADY/(If You Never Have A Big Hit Record) You're Still Gonna Be A Star	(Atlantic 2994)	.75	3.00	73
YOUR BABY IS A LADY (Stereo)/Your Baby Is A Lady (Mono) (Promotional issue only)	(Atlantic 2994)	1.25	5.00	73
YOU'RE THE ONLY DANCER/ Tonight You're Doin' It Right	(Amherst 733)	.50	2.00	78
YOU WON'T FORGET ME/ I Don't Think So Much Of Myself Now	(Liberty F-55497)	1.00	4.00	62
YOU'RE STILL GONNA BE MY STAR (Stereo)/ You're Still Gonna Be My Star (Mono)	(Atlantic 2994)	1.25	5.00	73
Also see A Date With Soul				
DESIRES, The				
PHYLLIS BELOVED/The Girl For Me	(Dasa 102)	2.50	10.00	
DESIRES, The				
I DON'T KNOW WHY/Longing	(20th Fox 195)	1.50	6.00	60
THERE I GO AGAIN/I Never Loved Like This	(Smash 1763)	1.00	4.00	62
DESIRES, The (The Regents)				
I ASK YOU/Story Of Love	(Seville 118)	2.00	8.00	62
DESMOND, Johnny				
C'EST SI BON/	(MGM 10613)	1.25	5.00	50
HIGH & THE MIGHTY, THE/Got No Time	(Coral 61204)	1.00	4.00	54
PLAY ME HEARTS & FLOWERS/I'm So Ashamed	(Coral 61379)	1.00	4.00	55
SIXTEEN TONS/Ballo Italiano	(Coral 61529)	1.00	4.00	55
WHITE SPORT COAT, A/Just Lookin'	(Coral 61835)	1.00	4.00	57
YELLOW ROSE OF TEXAS, THE/ You're In Love With Someone	(Coral 61476)	1.00	4.00	55
DESMOND, JOHNNY, ALAN DALE & DON CORNELL				
HEART OF MY HEART/I Think I'll Fall In Love Tonight	(Coral 61076)	1.00	4.00	53
DE SOTO, Bobby				
CHEATER, THE/Don't Talk, Just Kiss	(Claro 5914)	1.00	4.00	59
DESTINAIRES, The				
CHAPEL BELLS/It's Better This Way	(Old Timer 610)	.75	3.00	
RAG DOLL/Teardrops	(Old Timer 609)	.75	3.00	
Acappella recordings				
DESTINATIONS, The				
HELLO GIRL/With You	(Destination 638)	.75	3.00	67
DESTINEERS, The				
SO YOUNG/Take A Look	(RCA Victor 47-8049)	.75	3.00	62
DETECTIVE, The				
RECOGNITION/	(Swan Song 70114)	.50	2.00	77
SOMETHING BEAUTIFUL/	(Swan Song 70117)	.50	2.00	78
DETERGENTS, The				
DOUBLE O SEVEN/The Blue Kangaroo	(Roulette 4603)	1.00	4.00	65
I CAN NEVER EAT HOME ANYMORE/	(Kapp 735)	1.00	4.00	66
LEADER OF THE LAUNDROMAT/Ulcers	(Roulette 4590)	1.00	4.00	64
LITTLE DUM-DUM/Soldier Girl	(Roulette 4616)	1.00	4.00	65
MRS. JONES (HOW 'BOUT IT)/Tea & Crumpets	(Roulette 4616)	1.00	4.00	65
Novelties				
DETOURS, The				
BRING BACK MY BEATLES TO ME/Money	(McSherry 1285)	1.50	6.00	64
DETROIT WHEELS, The				
LINDA SUE DIXON/Tally Ho	(Inferno 5002)	.75	3.00	68
THINK/Think (Part 2)	(Inferno 5003)	.75	3.00	68
Also see Ryder, Mitch, & The Detroit Wheels				
DETROIT ROAD RUNNERS, The				
NEW KIND OF LOVE/Swingin' Camels	(ABC 45-11117)	.75	3.00	69
DEUCE COUPES, The				
HAYBURNER/Little Deuce Coupe (By the De-fenders)	(Del Fi 4226)	1.00	4.00	63
DEUCES WILD, The				
I'M IN A WHIRL/The Meaning Of Love	(Specialty 654)	1.00	4.00	59
DEVERONS, The				
ON THE ROAD AGAIN/Unnoticed	(Raynard 1406)	.75	3.00	66
DEVILLES, The				
JOAN OF LOVE/Tell Me So	(Orbit 540)	1.00	4.00	
DEVLIN, Johnny				
STAYIN' UP LATE/Angel Of Love	(Coral 62335)	.75	3.00	62
DEVO				
UNCONTROLLABLE URGE/ (I Can't Get No) Satisfaction	(Warner Bros. 8675)	.50	2.00	78
COME BACK JONEE/Praying Hands	(Warner Bros. 8745)	.50	2.00	79
SECRET AGENT MAN/Red Eye	(Warner Bros. 49028)	.50	2.00	79
DE VOL, Frank				
LA MONTANA/The Key Theme	(Columbia 4-41620)	.75	3.00	60
Instrumentals				
DE VORZON, Barry				
BABY DOLL/Barbara Jean	(RCA Victor 47-7124)	1.00	4.00	57
BLESS THE BEASTS & THE CHILDREN/	(A&M 1890)	1.00	4.00	77
CORA LEE/Blue, Green, & Gold	(RCA Victor 47-7510)	1.25	5.00	59
HONEY BUNNY/Too Soon	(RCA Victor 47-7406)	2.50	10.00	58
ROSEMARY/Hey Little Darlin'	(Columbia 4-41612)	1.00	4.00	60
Also see Barry & The Tamerlanes				
DE VORZON, Barry, & Perry Botkin Jr.				
BLESS THE BEASTS & THE CHILDREN/ Down The Line	(A&M 1890)	.50	2.00	77
NADIA'S THEME (THE YOUNG & THE RESTLESS)/ Down The Line	(A&M 1856)	.50	2.00	76
DEVOTIONS, The				
HOW DO YOU SPEAK TO AN ANGEL/Teardrops Follow Me	(Kape 701)	.75	3.00	
RIP VAN WINKLE/I Love You For Sentimental Reasons	(Delta 1001)	7.50	30.00	61
RIP VAN WINKLE/I Love You For Sentimental Reasons (White label)	(Roulette 4406)	3.75	15.00	61
RIP VAN WINKLE/I Love You For Sentimental Reasons (Orange label)	(Roulette 4541)	.75	3.00	64
SNOW WHITE/Zindy Lou	(Roulette 4580)	2.00	8.00	64
SUNDAY KIND OF LOVE/Tears From A Broken Heart	(Roulette 4556)	1.50	6.00	64
DEWEY, George & Jack				
FLYING SAUCERS HAVE LANDED/ Flying Saucers Have Landed (Part 2) (Novelty/Break-In)	(Raven 700)	5.00	20.00	
DE YOUNG, Cliff (Of Clear Light)				
IF I COULD PUT YOU INTO MY SONG/ You Will Never Know	(MCA 40388)	.50	2.00	75
MY SWEET LADY/Sunshine	(MCA 40156)	.50	2.00	74
DEY, Tracey				
GONNA' GET ALONG WITHOUT YOU NOW/Go Away	(Amy 901)	.75	3.00	64
HANGING ON TO MY BABY/Ska-doo-dee-yah	(Amy 908)	.75	3.00	64
HERE COMES THE BOY/Teddy's The Boy I Love	(Amy 894)	.75	3.00	63
JERRY (I'M YOUR SHERRY) (Answer song)/ Once In A Blue, Blue Moon	(Vee Jay 467)	1.00	4.00	62
TEEN AGE CLEOPATRA/Who's That	(Liberty 55604)	.75	3.00	63
DE ZASTA, Gen.				
SPANISH MARCHING SONG, THE (PART 2) (Novelty vocal)/ The Spanish Marching Song (Part 1) (Serious vocal) (Novelty)	(Roulette 4141)	1.00	4.00	59
Also see Reisman, Joe				
DIALS, The				
MONKEY DANCE/Monkey Walk	(Time 1068)	.75	3.00	63
DIALS, The (Featuring Sal Corrente)				
AT THE START OF A NEW ROMANCE/ These Foolish Things	(Philips 40040)	2.00	8.00	62
Sal Corrente also performed as Sal Anthony				
DIALTONES, The				
TILL I HEARD IT FROM YOU/Johnny	(Goldisc 3005)	1.25	5.00	60
Members of this group were previously with Randy & The Rainbows				
DIALTONES, The				
CHERRY PIE/Again	(Dandy Dan 1)	2.00	8.00	59
SO YOUNG/Chicago Bird	(Lawn 203)	1.00	4.00	63
DIAMOND, Brian, & The Cutters				
BIG BAD WOLF/See If I Care	(Hickory 1321)	.75	3.00	65
DIAMOND, Dave				
DR. DAREKIL/Allergy Novelty	(Vision 1003)	.75	3.00	62
DIAMOND, Gerry				
NANCY/A Little Rock, A Little Roll	(Dwain 811)	.75	3.00	60
DIAMOND, Leo				
MELODY OF LOVE/Phantom Gaucho	(RCA Victor 47-5973)	1.00	4.00	55
DIAMOND, Neil				
BE/Flight Of The Gull (Instrumental)	(Columbia 4-45942)	.50	2.00	73
BEAUTIFUL NOISE/Signs	(Columbia 3-10452)	.50	2.00	76
BROOKLYN ROADS/Holiday Inn Blues	(Uni 55065)	.75	3.00	68
CHERRY CHERRY/Morningside	(MCA 40017)	.50	2.00	73
CLOWN TOWN/At Night	(Columbia 4-42809)	3.75	15.00	63
CRACKLIN' ROSE/Lordy	(Uni 55250)	.50	2.00	70
DESIREE/Once In A While	(Columbia 3-10657)	.50	2.00	78
DO IT/Hanky Panky	(Bang 580)	.75	3.00	70
DON'T THINK. . .FEEL/Home Is A Wounded Heart	(Columbia 3-10405)	.50	2.00	76
FOREVER IN BLUE JEANS/Remember Me	(Columbia 3-10897)	.50	2.00	79
GIRL, YOU'LL BE A WOMAN SOON/You'll Forget	(Bang 542)	.75	3.00	67
HE AIN'T HEAVY, HE'S MY BROTHER/Free Life	(Uni 55264)	.75	3.00	70
HOLLY HOLY/Hurtin' You Don't Come Easy	(Uni 55175)	.75	3.00	69
I AM I SAID/Done Too Soon	(Uni 55278)	.75	3.00	71
IF YOU KNOW WHAT I MEAN/Street Life	(Columbia 3-10366)	.50	2.00	76
I GOT THE FEELING (OH NO NO)/The Boat I Row	(Bang 536)	.75	3.00	66
I'M A BELIEVER/Crooked Street	(Bang 586)	.75	3.00	71
I'VE BEEN THIS WAY BEFORE/Raggae Strut	(Columbia 3-10084)	.50	2.00	75
KENTUCKY WOMAN/Time Is Now	(Bang 551)	.75	3.00	67
LAST PICASSO, THE/The Gift Of Song	(Columbia 3-10138)	.50	2.00	75
LAST THING ON MY MIND, THE/Canta Libra	(MCA 40092)	.50	2.00	73
LONGFELLOW SERENADE/Rosemary's Wine	(Columbia 3-10043)	.50	2.00	74
LONG WAY HOME, THE/Monday, Monday	(Bang 703)	.75	3.00	73
NEW ORLEANS/Hanky Panky	(Bang 554)	.75	3.00	68
PLAY ME/Porcupine Pie	(Uni 55346)	.50	2.00	72
RED RED WINE/Red Rubber Ball	(Bang 556)	.75	3.00	68
SAY MAYBE/Diamond Girls	(Columbia 3-10945)	.50	2.00	79
SEPTEMBER MORN'/I'm A Believer	(Columbia 3-11175)	.50	2.00	79
SHILO/La Bamba	(Bang 561)	.75	3.00	69
SHILO/La Bamba	(Bang 575)	.50	2.00	70
SHOTGUN/Good, Good Lovin	(Atco 6655)	1.00	4.00	69
SKYBIRD/Lonely Looking Sky	(Columbia 4-45998)	.50	2.00	74
SOLITARY MAN/Do It	(Bang 519)	.75	3.00	66
SOLITARY MAN/The Time Is Now	(Bang 578)	.50	2.00	70
SONG SUNG BLUE/Gitchy Goomy	(Uni 55326)	.50	2.00	72
SOOLAIMON (AFRICAN TRILOGY II)/ And The Grass Won't Pay No Mind	(Uni 55224)	.50	2.00	70
STONES/Cruncy Granola Suite	(Uni 55310)	.50	2.00	71
SUNDAY SUN/Honey-Drippin' Times	(Uni 55084)	.50	2.00	68
SWEET CAROLINE (GOOD TIMES NEVER SEEMED SO GOOD)/ Dig In	(Uni 55136)	.50	2.00	69
THANK THE LORD FOR THE NIGHT TIME/ The Long Way Home	(Bang 547)	.75	3.00	67
TWO-BIT MANCHILD/Broad Old Woman (6 AM Insanity)	(Uni 55075)	.50	2.00	68
UNTIL IT'S TIME FOR YOU TO GO/ And The Singer Sings His Song	(Uni 55204)	.50	2.00	70
WALK ON WATER/High Rolling Man	(Uni 55352)	.50	2.00	72
YOU GOT TO ME/Someday Baby	(Bang 540)	.75	3.00	67
DIAMOND REO				
AIN'T THAT PECULIAR/(From Here To) Infinity	(Big Tree 16030)	.50	2.00	75
DIAMONDS, The				
BLACK DENIM TROUSERS & MOTORCYCLE BOOTS/ Nip Sip	(Coral 61502)	1.50	6.00	55
CHURCH BELLS MAY RING, THE/Little Girl Of Mine	(Mercury 70835)	1.00	4.00	56
HIGH SIGN/Chick-Lets	(Mercury 71291)	1.00	4.00	58
KATHY-O/Happy Years	(Mercury 71330)	1.00	4.00	58
LITTLE DARLIN'/Faithful & True	(Mercury 71060)	1.00	4.00	57
LOVE, LOVE, LOVE/Ev'ry Night About This Time	(Mercury 70889)	1.00	4.00	56
MY JUDGE & JURY/Put Your House In Order	(Mercury 70983)	1.00	4.00	56
ONE SUMMER NIGHT/It's A Doggone Shame	(Mercury 71831)	1.00	4.00	61
SHE SAY (OOM DOOBY DOOM)/ From The Bottom Of My Heart	(Mercury 71404)	1.00	4.00	59
SILHOUETTES/Daddy Cool	(Mercury 71197)	1.00	4.00	57
SMOOCH ME/Be My Lovin' Baby	(Coral 61577)	1.25	5.00	55
SOFT SUMMER BREEZE/Ka-Ding-Dong	(Mercury 70934)	1.00	4.00	56
STROLL, THE/Land Of Beauty	(Mercury 71242)	1.00	4.00	57
THOUSAND MILES AWAY, A/Every Minute Of The Day	(Mercury 71021)	1.00	4.00	56
WALKIN' THE STROLL/ Batman, Wolfman, Frankenstein Or Dracula	(Mercury 71534)	1.00	4.00	59
WALKING ALONG/Eternal Lovers	(Mercury 71366)	1.00	4.00	58
WHY DO FOOLS FALL IN LOVE/You Baby You	(Mercury 70790)	1.00	4.00	56
WORDS OF LOVE/Don't Say Goodbye	(Mercury 71128)	1.00	4.00	57
ZIP ZIP/Oh, How I Wish	(Mercury 71165)	1.00	4.00	57
DIAN & THE GREENBRIAR BOYS (With James Dian)				
HE HAS A FRIEND/Brown Ferry Blues	(Elektra 45001)	.75	3.00	63
SALLY LET YOUR BANGS HANG DOWN/If I Were Free	(Elektra 45005)	.75	3.00	63
DIAN, Humorous				
INTERVIEW WITH MR. K/Three Hip Pigs (Novelty/Break-In)	(Veltone 712)	1.50	6.00	
DIANE & THE DARLETTES				
JUST YOU/The Wobble	(Dunes 2016)	1.00	4.00	62
DIATONES, The				
RUBY BE GONE/Oh Baby, Come Dance With Me	(Bandera 2509)	3.75	15.00	

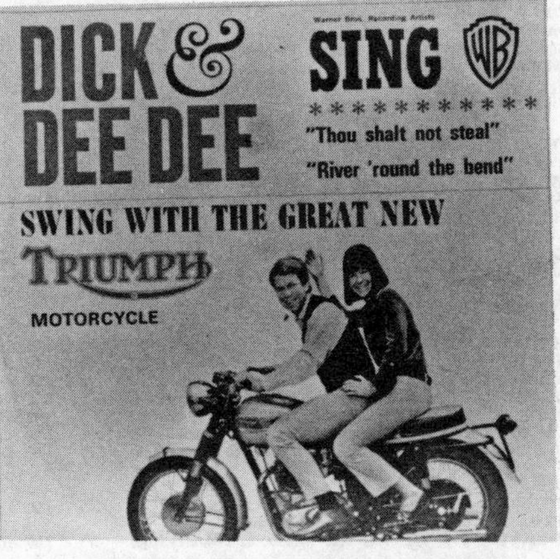

TITLE/FLIP	LABEL & NO.	GOOD	NEAR MINT	YR.
DICK & DEEDEE (Dick St. John & Deedee Sperling)				
ALL MY TRIALS/Don't Think Twice It's All Right	(Warner Bros. 5411)	.75	3.00	64
BE MY BABY/Be My Baby	(Warner Bros. 5608)	.75	3.00	64
DO I LOVE YOU/You Come Back To Haunt Me	(Warner Bros. 17305)	.75	3.00	69
GIFT, THE/Not Fade Away	(Warner Bros. 5426)	.75	3.00	64
GOODBYE TO LOVE/Swing Low	(Lama 7780)	1.50	6.00	61
GOODBYE TO LOVE/Swing Low	(Liberty F-55382)	.75	3.00	61
LIFE IS JUST A PLAY/All I Want	(Liberty F-55478)	.75	3.00	62
LOVE IS A ONCE IN A LIFETIME THING/ Chug-a-chuga Choo Choo	(Warner Bros. 5364)	.75	3.00	63
MOUNTAIN'S HIGH, THE/I Want Someone	(Lama 7778)	2.50	10.00	61
MOUNTAIN'S HIGH, THE/I Want Someone	(Liberty F-55350)	.75	3.00	61
NEW ORLEANS/Tell Me What You've Got	(Warner Bros. 5680)	.75	3.00	65
P.S. 1402 (YOUR LOCAL CHARM SCHOOL)/ Use What You've Got	(Warner Bros. 5671)	.75	3.00	65
REMEMBER WHEN/You Were Mine	(Warner Bros. 5451)	.75	3.00	64
RIVER TOOK MY BABY, THE/My Lonely Self	(Warner Bros. 5320)	.75	3.00	63
SOME THINGS JUST STICK IN YOUR MIND/ When Blue Turns To Grey	(Warner Bros. 5627)	.75	3.00	65
TELL ME/Will You Always Love Me	(Lama 7783)	2.50	10.00	62
TELL ME/Will You Always Love Me	(Liberty F-55412)	.75	3.00	62
THOU SHALT NOT STEAL/ Just 'Round The River Bend	(Warner Bros. 5482)	.75	3.00	64
TURN AROUND/Don't Leave Me	(Warner Bros. 5396)	.75	3.00	63
WE'LL SING IN THE SUNSHINE/In The Season Of Our Love	(Dot 17261)	.75	3.00	69
WHERE DID THE GOOD TIMES GO/ Guess Our Love Must Show	(Warner Bros. 5383)	.75	3.00	63
WORLD IS WAITING, THE/Vini Vini	(Warner Bros. 5652)	.75	3.00	65
YOUNG & IN LOVE/Say To Me	(Warner Bros. 5342)	.75	3.00	63
DICK & RICHARD				
STINKY, THE LITTLE RAINDEER/ Santa Caught A Cold On Christmas Eve	(Capitol 5097)	.75	3.00	63
DICKIE & THE DEBONAIRES				
DEBONAIRE ROCK/The Stomp (Instrumentals)	(Asta 101)	1.00	4.00	61
YO YO GIRL/Please Mr. Disc Jockey	(Valli 302)	3.75	15.00	
DICKSON, Barbara				
ANOTHER SUITCASE IN ANOTHER HALL/	(MCA 40695)	.50	2.00	77
WHO WAS IT STOLE YOUR HEART AWAY/Stolen Love	(RSO 875)	.50	2.00	77
DICTATORS, The				
DISEASE/Hey Boys	(Asylum 45420)	.50	2.00	77
DILL, Danny				
I'M HUNGRY FOR YOU LOVIN'/	(ABC-Paramount 9734)	5.00	20.00	56
DILLARD & CLARK (With Gene Clark)				
DON'T LET ME DOWN/Rocky Top	(A&M 1165)	.75	3.00	70
WHY NOT LET YOUR BABY/	(A&M 1087)	.75	3.00	69
DILLARDS, The				
IT'S ABOUT TIME/One A.M.	(Anthem 101)	.50	2.00	71
LISTEN TO THE SOUND/The Biggest Whatever	(Elektra 45661)	.75	3.00	67
REASON TO BELIEVE/Nobody Knows	(Elektra 45641)	.75	3.00	67
DILLMAN, Daisy, Band				
BORDER BOUND/Flyin' Solo	(United Artists 1128)	.50	2.00	77
DILLON, Zig				
BEETLE BUG/	(R 512)	2.00	8.00	
DIMENSIONS, The				
TREAT ME RIGHT/We're Doing Fine	(Washington Square 2025)	1.25	5.00	
DIMENSIONS, The				
SHE'S BOSS/Penny	(Panorama 25)	1.00	4.00	66
SHE'S BOSS/Penny	(HBR 477)	.75	3.00	66
DIMINISHED 5TH, The				
DOCTOR DEAR/Do You Hear	(Hush 231)	1.50	6.00	
DIMPLES, The				
INVITATION TO A PARTY/My Sister's Beau	(Dore 517)	1.00	4.00	59
DING DONGS, The: see Darin, Bobby				
DINGOES, The				
SMOOTH SAILING/	(A&M 1975)	.50	2.00	77
DINKS, The				
UGLY GIRL/Rocka-mow-mow	(Sully 925)	.75	3.00	66
DINNER, Michael				
PROMISED LAND, THE/Icarus	(Fantasy 750)	.50	2.00	76
SILVER BULLETS/The Swallow	(Fantasy 781)	.50	2.00	76

DINNING, Mark

TITLE/FLIP	LABEL & NO.	GOOD	NEAR MINT	YR.
ANOTHER LONELY GIRL/Can't Forget	(MGM 13007)	.75	3.00	61
CUTIE CUTIE/Life Of Love	(MGM 12775)	1.00	4.00	59
LONELY ISLAND/Turn Me On	(MGM 13024)	.75	3.00	61
LOVIN' TOUCH, THE/Come Back To Me	(MGM 12929)	.75	3.00	60
PICKUP, THE/All Of This For Sally	(MGM 13061)	.75	3.00	62
SHE CRIED ON MY SHOULDER/ The World Is Gettin' Smaller	(MGM 12958)	.75	3.00	60
STAR IS BORN, A (A LOVE HAS DIED)/You Win Again	(MGM 12888)	.75	3.00	60
TEEN ANGEL/Bye Now Baby	(MGM 12845)	.75	3.00	59
TOP FORTY, NEWS, WEATHER & SPORTS/Suddenly	(MGM 12980)	1.00	4.00	61

DINO & THE DIPLOMATS

TITLE/FLIP	LABEL & NO.	GOOD	NEAR MINT	YR.
HOMEWORK/Hush-a-bye My Love	(Vida 100)	2.50	10.00	
I CAN'T BELIEVE/My Dream	(Laurie 3103)	2.00	8.00	61
SOFT WIND/Such A Fool For You	(Vida 102)	2.50	10.00	

DINO, DESI & BILLY (Dino Martin, Jr., Desi Arnaz Jr., Billy Hinsche)

TITLE/FLIP	LABEL & NO.	GOOD	NEAR MINT	YR.
IF YOU'RE THINKIN' WHAT I'M THINKIN'/ Pretty Flamingo	(Reprise 0544)	.75	3.00	67
I HOPE SHE'S THERE TONIGHT/Josephine	(Reprise 0529)	.75	3.00	66
I'M A FOOL/So Many Ways	(Reprise 0367)	.75	3.00	65
IT'S JUST THE WAY YOU ARE/Tie Me Down	(Reprise 0462)	.75	3.00	66
KITTY DOYLE/Without Hurtin' Some	(Reprise 0619)	.75	3.00	67
LADY LOVE/A Certain Sound	(Reprise 0965)	3.75	15.00	70
LOOK OUT GIRLS (HERE WE COME)/ She's So Far Out She's In	(Reprise 0496)	.75	3.00	66
MY WHAT A SHAME/ The Inside Outside Caspar Milquetoast Eskimo Flash	(Reprise 0653)	.75	3.00	68
NOT THE LOVIN' KIND/Chimes Of Freedom	(Reprise 0401)	.75	3.00	65
PLEASE DON'T FIGHT IT/The Rebel Kind	(Reprise 0426)	.75	3.00	65
SINCE YOU BROKE MY HEART/We Know	(Reprise 0324)	.75	3.00	65
SUPERMAN/I Can't Get Her Off My Mind	(Reprise 0444)	.75	3.00	66
TELL SOMEONE YOU LOVE THEM/General Outline	(Reprise 0698)	.75	3.00	68
TIE ME DOWN/It's Just The Way You Are	(Reprise 0462)	.75	3.00	66
TWO IN THE AFTERNOON/Good Luck, Best Wishes To You	(Reprise 0579)	.75	3.00	67

DINO, Kenny

TITLE/FLIP	LABEL & NO.	GOOD	NEAR MINT	YR.
ROSIE, WHY DO YOU WEAR MY RING/What Did I Do	(Musicor 1015)	.75	3.00	62
YOUR MA SAID YOU CRIED IN YOUR SLEEP LAST NIGHT/ Dream A Girl	(Musicor 1013)	.75	3.00	61

DINO, Paul

TITLE/FLIP	LABEL & NO.	GOOD	NEAR MINT	YR.
GINNIE BELL/Bye-Bye	(Promo 2180)	1.00	4.00	60

DINOSAUR

TITLE/FLIP	LABEL & NO.	GOOD	NEAR MINT	YR.
KISS ME AGAIN/Kiss Me Again (Instrumental)	(Sire 1034)	.50	2.00	78

DION (Dion DiMucci)

TITLE/FLIP	LABEL & NO.	GOOD	NEAR MINT	YR.
ABRAHAM, MARTIN & JOHN/Daddy Rollin' (In Your Arms)	(Laurie 3464)	.50	2.00	68
BE CAREFUL OF STONES THAT YOU THROW/ I Can't Believe (That You Don't Love Me Anymore)	(Columbia 4-42810)	.75	3.00	63
BORN TO BE WITH YOU/ Running Close Behind You	(Big Tree-Spector 16063)	.50	2.00	76
BOTH SIDES NOW/	(Laurie 3495)	.75	3.00	69
COME GO WITH ME/King Without A Queen	(Laurie 3171)	.75	3.00	63
CLOSE TO IT ALL/Let It Be	(Warner Bros. 7469)	.75	3.00	71
DOCTOR ROCK & ROLL/Sunshine Lady	(Warner Bros. 7704)	.75	3.00	73
DONNA THE PRIMA DONNA/You're Mine	(Columbia 4-42852)	.75	3.00	63
DRIP DROP/No One's Waiting For Me	(Columbia 4-42917)	.75	3.00	63
HAVIN' FUN/North East End Of The Corner	(Laurie 3081)	1.00	4.00	61
HEY MY LOVE/Lover Boy Supreme	(Warner Bros. 8234)	.75	3.00	76
IF ONLY WE HAVE LOVE/Natural Man	(Warner Bros. 7356)	.75	3.00	69
I'M YOUR HOOCHIE COOCHIE MAN/Gloria	(Columbia 4-42977)	.75	3.00	64
(I USED TO BE A) BROOKLYN DODGER/ Streetheart Theme	(Lifesong 1785)	.50	2.00	79
JOHNNY B. GOODE/Chicago Blues	(Columbia 4-43096)	.75	3.00	64
JOSIE/Sunniland	(Warner Bros. 7491)	.75	3.00	71
KICKIN' CHILD/Spoonful	(Columbia 4-43293)	1.00	4.00	65
KISSIN' GAME/Heaven Help Me	(Laurie 3090)	1.00	4.00	61
LITTLE DIANE/Lost For Sure	(Laurie 3134)	.75	3.00	62
LITTLE GIRL/Shout	(Laurie 3240)	1.00	4.00	63
LONELY TEENAGER/Little Miss Blue	(Laurie 3070)	.75	3.00	60
LONELY WORLD/Tag Along	(Laurie 3187)	1.00	4.00	63
LOVE CAME TO ME/Little Girl	(Laurie 3145)	.75	3.00	62
LOVERS WHO WANDER/(I Was) Born To Cry	(Laurie 3123)	.75	3.00	62
MAKE THE WOMAN LOVE ME/ Running Close Behind You	(Warner-Spector 0403)	.75	3.00	75
MIDTOWN AMERICAN STREET GANG/	(Lifesong 1770)	.50	2.00	78
NEW YORK CITY SONG/Richer Than A Rich Man	(Warner Bros. 7793)	.75	3.00	74
PURPLE HAZE/The Dolphins	(Laurie 3478)	.75	3.00	69
QUEEN OF '59/Oh The Night	(Warner Bros. 8293)	.75	3.00	76
RUBY BABY/He'll Only Hurt You	(Columbia 4-42662)	.75	3.00	62
RUNAROUND SUE/Runaway Girl	(Laurie 3110)	.75	3.00	61
RUNAROUND SUE/Ya Ya Twist, The (By Joey Dee & The Starliters)	(Monument-No number given)	1.25	5.00	61
RUNNING CLOSE BEHIND YOU/Sea Gull	(Warner Bros. 7663)	.75	3.00	72
SANCTUARY/Brand New Morning	(Warner Bros. 7537)	.75	3.00	71
SANDY/Faith	(Laurie 3153)	.75	3.00	63
SOMEBODY NOBODY WANTS/ Could Somebody Take My Place Tonight	(Laurie 3101)	1.00	4.00	61
SWEET, SWEET BABY/Unloved, Unwanted Me	(Columbia 4-43213)	1.00	4.00	65
THEN I'LL BE TIRED OF YOU/After The Dance	(Laurie 3225)	1.00	4.00	63
THIS LITTLE GIRL/Loneliest Man In The World	(Columbia 4-42776)	.75	3.00	63
WANDERER, THE/The Majestic	(Laurie 3115)	.75	3.00	61
WANDERER, THE (Motion picture soundtrack)/ (Promotional issue only)	(Warner Bros. PRO-S-814)	2.50	10.00	79
WAY YOU DO THE THINGS YOU DO, THE/ Lover Boy Supreme	(Warner Bros. 8258)	.75	3.00	76
YOUR OWN BACK YARD/Sit Down, Old Friend	(Warner Bros. 7401)	.75	3.00	70
YOUNG VIRGIN EYES (I'M ALL WRAPPED UP)/ On The Night	(Warner Bros. 8406)	.75	3.00	77

On some Columbia releases, Dion's last name may be shown as DiMuci.
Also see Dion & The Belmonts
Also see Dion & The Timberlanes

DION & THE BELMONTS (Featuring Dion DiMucci)

TITLE/FLIP	LABEL & NO.	GOOD	NEAR MINT	YR.
DON'T PITY ME/Just You	(Laurie 3021)	1.25	5.00	58
FOR BOBBIE/Movin' Man	(ABC 10896)	.75	3.00	67
I WONDER WHY/Teen Angel (Gray label)	(Laurie 3013)	3.75	15.00	58
I WONDER WHY/Teen Angel (Red & white label)	(Laurie 3013)	1.50	6.00	58
IN THE STILL OF THE NIGHT/A Funny Feeling	(Laurie 3059)	1.00	4.00	60
MY GIRL, THE MONTH OF MAY/Berimbau	(ABC 10868)	.75	3.00	66
NO ONE KNOWS/I Can't Go On (Rosalie) (Blue label)	(Laurie 3015)	2.50	10.00	58
NO ONE KNOWS/I Can't Go On (Rosalie) (Red & white label)	(Laurie 3015)	1.00	4.00	58
TAG ALONG/We Went Away	(Mohawk 107)	5.00	20.00	57
TEENAGER IN LOVE, A/I've Cried Before	(Laurie 3027)	1.00	4.00	59
TEENAGER IN LOVE, A/I've Cried Before (Stereo single issue)	(Laurie S-3027)	5.00	20.00	59
WHEN YOU WISH UPON A STAR/Wonderful Girl	(Laurie 3052)	1.00	4.00	60
WHERE OR WHEN/That's My Desire	(Laurie 3044)	1.00	4.00	59

DION & THE TIMBERLANES (Featuring Dion DiMucci)

TITLE/FLIP	LABEL & NO.	GOOD	NEAR MINT	YR.
CHOSEN FEW, THE/Out In Colorado	(Mohawk 105)	6.25	25.00	57
CHOSEN FEW, THE/Out In Colorado	(Jubilee 5294)	2.50	10.00	57

DION & THE WANDERERS

TITLE/FLIP	LABEL & NO.	GOOD	NEAR MINT	YR.
SO MUCH YOUNGER/Two Ton Feather	(Columbia 4-43692)	1.25	5.00	66
TOMORROW WON'T BRING THE RAIN/ You Move Me Baby	(Columbia 4-43423)	1.25	5.00	65
WAKE UP BABY/Time In My Heart For You	(Columbia 4-43483)	1.25	5.00	66

DIPLOMATS, The

TITLE/FLIP	LABEL & NO.	GOOD	NEAR MINT	YR.
HERE'S A HEART/He's Got You Now	(Arock 1004)	.75	3.00	64

DIPLOMETTES, The

TITLE/FLIP	LABEL & NO.	GOOD	NEAR MINT	YR.
MY INTUITION/Sit Yourself Down	(Diplomacy 24)	.75	3.00	

DIRE STRAIGHTS

TITLE/FLIP	LABEL & NO.	GOOD	NEAR MINT	YR.
LADY WRITER/Where Do You Thing You're Goin'?	(Warner Bros. 49006)	.50	2.00	79
ONCE UPON A TIME IN THE WEST/News	(Warner Bros. 49082)	.50	2.00	79
SULTANS OF SWING/Southbound Again	(Warner Bros. 8736)	.50	2.00	79

DIRKSEN, Senator Everett McKinley

TITLE/FLIP	LABEL & NO.	GOOD	NEAR MINT	YR.
FIRST TIME THE CHRISTMAS STORY WAS TOLD/ I Heard The Bells On Christmas Day	(Capitol 2034)	.75	3.00	66
GALLANT MEN/	(Capitol 5805)	.75	3.00	66
MAN IS NOT ALONE/Shepherd & His Flock	(Capitol 5912)	.75	3.00	66

Narrations

DIRT BAND, The (Formerly The Nitty Gritty Dirt Band)

TITLE/FLIP	LABEL & NO.	GOOD	NEAR MINT	YR.
BUY FOR ME THE RAIN/ Mother Earth (Provides For Me)	(United Artists UA-XW936Y)	.50	2.00	77
COSMIC COWBOY/Stars & Stripes Forever	(United Artists UA-XW830Y)	.50	2.00	76

DIRTY FILTHY MUD

TITLE/FLIP	LABEL & NO.	GOOD	NEAR MINT	YR.
FOREST OF BLACK, THE/Morning Sunflower	(Worex 2340)	3.75	15.00	

DIRTY HALF DOZEN, The

TITLE/FLIP	LABEL & NO.	GOOD	NEAR MINT	YR.
DARBY'S RAM/	(Fun 1024)	.75	3.00	

DISCIPLES OF SHAFTESBURY, The

TITLE/FLIP	LABEL & NO.	GOOD	NEAR MINT	YR.
MY CUP IS FULL/Times Gone By	(International Artists 109)	1.25	5.00	66

DISCO CHICKEN, The

TITLE/FLIP	LABEL & NO.	GOOD	NEAR MINT	YR.
ENERGY CRISIS/	(Circus 1)	.75	3.00	

DISENTRI, Turner (Bob Gaudio)

TITLE/FLIP	LABEL & NO.	GOOD	NEAR MINT	YR.
10,000,000 TEARS/Spanish Lace	(Topix 6001)	5.00	20.00	

Also see 4 Seasons, The
Also see Royal Teens, The

DIVOTS, The

TITLE/FLIP	LABEL & NO.	GOOD	NEAR MINT	YR.
DRY CEREAL/	(Mark 3516)	1.25	5.00	

DIXIE CUPS, The (Barbara Hawkins, Rosa Hawkins, Joan Johnson)

TITLE/FLIP	LABEL & NO.	GOOD	NEAR MINT	YR.
CHAPEL OF LOVE/Ain't That Nice	(Red Bird 001)	.75	3.00	64
DADDY SAID NO/Love Ain't So Bad	(ABC 10855)	1.00	4.00	66
GEE THE MOON IS SHINING BRIGHT/Gonna Get You Yet	(Red Bird 032)	1.00	4.00	65
I'M NOT THE KIND OF GIRL (TO MARRY)/ What Goes Up Must Come Down	(ABC 10715)	1.00	4.00	65
IKO IKO/I'm Gonna Get You Yet	(Red Bird 024)	.75	3.00	65
LITTLE BELL/Another Boy Like Mine	(Red Bird 017)	1.00	4.00	64
PEOPLE SAY/Girls Can Tell	(Red Bird 006)	.75	3.00	64
THAT'S WHAT THE KIDS SAID/The ABC Song	(ABC 10755)	1.00	4.00	65
THAT'S WHERE IT'S AT/Two-way-poc-a-way	(ABC 10692)	1.00	4.00	65
YOU SHOULD HAVE SEEN THE WAY HE LOOKED AT ME/ No True Love	(Red Bird 012)	1.00	4.00	64

DIXIE DREGS, The

TITLE/FLIP	LABEL & NO.	GOOD	NEAR MINT	YR.
PUNK SANDWICH/Country House Shuffle	(Capricorn 0327)	.50	2.00	79
TAKE IT OFF THE TOP/Little Kids	(Capricorn 0291)	.50	2.00	77

DIXIEBELLES, The

TITLE/FLIP	LABEL & NO.	GOOD	NEAR MINT	YR.
(DOWN AT) PAPA JOE'S/Rock, Rock, Rock	(Sound Stage 7 2507)	.75	3.00	63
NEW YORK TOWN/Street Dog	(Sound Stage 7 2521)	.75	3.00	64
SOUTHTOWN U.S.A./Why Don't You Set Me Free	(Sound Stage 7 2517)	.75	3.00	63

Jerry Smith's piano accompaniment is heard on the above recordings.
Also see Cornbread & Jerry

DIXON, Billy, & The Topics (Frankie Valli & 4 Seasons)

TITLE/FLIP	LABEL & NO.	GOOD	NEAR MINT	YR.
I AM ALL ALONE/Trance	(Topix 6002)	7.50	30.00	60
LOST LULLABYE/Trance	(Topix 6008)	10.00	40.00	61

DIXON HOUSE BAND, The

TITLE/FLIP	LABEL & NO.	GOOD	NEAR MINT	YR.
RUNNIN' SCARED/Saracen Ride	(Infinity 50014)	.50	2.00	79
SOONER OR LATER/	(Infinity 50022)	.50	2.00	79

DIXON, Webb

TITLE/FLIP	LABEL & NO.	GOOD	NEAR MINT	YR.
ROCK & ROLL ANGEL/Rock Awhile	(Astro 102)	1.00	4.00	59

DOBKINS, Carl, Jr.

TITLE/FLIP	LABEL & NO.	GOOD	NEAR MINT	YR.
CHANCE TO BELONG/Sawdust Dolly	(Decca 31301)	1.00	4.00	61
EXCLUSIVELY YOURS/One Little Girl	(Decca 31088)	1.00	4.00	60
GENIE/A Different Kind Of Love	(Decca 31143)	1.00	4.00	60
IF YOU DON'T WANT MY LOVIN'/Love Is Everything	(Decca 30856)	1.00	4.00	59
IF TEARDROPS WERE DIAMONDS/I'm So Sorry Little Girl	(Atco 6283)	.75	3.00	63
LITTLE BIT LATER DOWN THE LINE, A/ His Loss Is My Gain	(Colpix 762)	.75	3.00	65
LOVE LIGHT/Take Time Out	(Decca 31182)	1.00	4.00	60
LUCKY DEVIL/In My Heart	(Decca 31020)	1.00	4.00	59
MY HEART IS AN OPEN BOOK/My Pledge To You	(Decca 30803)	1.00	4.00	59
PROMISE ME/Ask Me No Questions	(Decca 31353)	1.00	4.00	62
TAKE HOLD OF MY HAND/That's Why I'm Asking	(Fraternity 794)	1.50	6.00	58
THAT'S WHAT I CALL TRUE LOVE/ Pretty Little Girl In The Yellow Dress	(Decca 31260)	1.00	4.00	61

DOBRO, Jimmie

TITLE/FLIP	LABEL & NO.	GOOD	NEAR MINT	YR.
SWAMP SURFER/Everybody Listen To The Dobro	(Philips 40137)	.75	3.00	63

DOBRO, Lon, Combo

TITLE/FLIP	LABEL & NO.	GOOD	NEAR MINT	YR.
MID-NIGHT SURF/ (Instrumental)	(Troy 1003)	1.00	4.00	63

DOCTOR & PATIENT

TITLE/FLIP	LABEL & NO.	GOOD	NEAR MINT	YR.
DORA HE TOLD ME TO TELL YOU THAT HE LOVES YOU, DON'T CRY/Sure It Hurts	(Dore 562)	1.00	4.00	60

DR. HOOK (Dennis Locorriere & Ray Sawyer)

TITLE/FLIP	LABEL & NO.	GOOD	NEAR MINT	YR.
ALL THE TIME IN THE WORLD/Dooley Jones	(Capitol 4677)	.50	2.00	79
BALLAD OF LUCY JORDAN, THE/Make It Easy	(Columbia 3-10032)	.75	3.00	74
BETTER LOVE NEXT TIME/Mountain Mary	(Capitol 4785)	.50	2.00	79
CARRY ME, CARRIE/I Call That True Love	(Columbia 4-45667)	.75	3.00	72
COPS & ROBBERS/	(Columbia 4-46026)	.75	3.00	74
COVER OF "THE ROLLING STONE," THE/ Queen Of The Silver Dollar	(Columbia 4-45732)	.75	3.00	72
IF NOT YOU/Bad Eye Bill	(Capitol 4364)	.50	2.00	76
LIFE AIN'T EASY/The Wonderful Soup Stone	(Columbia 4-45925)	.75	3.00	73
LITTLE BIT MORE, A/A Couple More Years	(Capitol 4280)	.50	2.00	76
MAKING LOVE & MUSIC/Who Dat	(Capitol 4534)	.50	2.00	78
MILLIONAIRE, THE/Cooky & Lila	(Capitol 4104)	.50	2.00	75
ONLY SIXTEEN/Let Me Be Your Lover	(Capitol 4171)	.50	2.00	76
ROLAND THE ROADIE & GERTRUDE THE GROUPIE/ Put A Little Bit On Me	(Columbia 4-45878)	.75	3.00	73
SHARING THE NIGHT TOGETHER/ You Make My Pants Want To Get Up & Dance	(Capitol 4621)	.50	2.00	78
STIMU DOCTOR HOOK: EXCERPTS FROM "BANKRUPT" (PART 1), THE/ The Stimu Doctor Hook: Excerpts From "Bankrupt" (Part 2) (Promotional issue)	(Capitol 8220)	.50	2.00	75
SYLVIA'S MOTHER/Makin' It Natural	(Columbia 4-45562)	.75	3.00	72
WALK RIGHT IN/Sexy Energy	(Capitol 4423)	.50	2.00	77
WHEN YOU'RE IN LOVE WITH A BEAUTIFUL WOMAN/ Knowing She's There	(Capitol 4705)	.50	2.00	79

Also see Beach Boys, The
This group was shown as Dr. Hook & The Medicine Show on the Columbia issues.

DR. JOHN (Mac Rebbena)

TITLE/FLIP	LABEL & NO.	GOOD	NEAR MINT	YR.
DANCE THE NIGHT AWAY WITH YOU/	(Horizon 117)	.50	2.00	79
(EVERYBODY WANNA GET RICH) RITE AWAY/ Mos' Scocious	(Atco 6957)	.75	3.00	74
IKO IKO/Huey Smith Medley: High Blood Pressure/ Don't You Just Know It/I'll Be John Brown	(Atco 6882)	.75	3.00	72
KEEP THAT MUSIC SIMPLE/ I Thought I Heard New Orleans Say	(Horizon 125)	.50	2.00	79
LET THE GOOD TIMES ROLL/	(Atco 6900)	.75	3.00	72
RIGHT PLACE, WRONG TIME/I Been Hoodood	(Atco 6914)	.75	3.00	73
SUCH A NIGHT/Cold Cold Cold	(Atco 6937)	.75	3.00	73
SWEET RIDER/Take Me Higher (By Mickey Thomas)	(RCA 11285)	.50	2.00	78

DR. WEST'S MEDICINE SHOW & JUNK BAND (With Norman Greenbaum)

TITLE/FLIP	LABEL & NO.	GOOD	NEAR MINT	YR.
BULLETS LAVERNE/Jigsaw (Shown as by Dr. West Medicine Band)	(Gregar 00106)	1.00	4.00	68
EGGPLANT THAT ATE CHICAGO, THE/ You Can't Fight City Hall Blues	(Go Go 100)	1.00	4.00	66
YOU CAN FLY/Circus Left Town Today	(Go Go 104)	1.00	4.00	67

DODD, Dick (Of the Standells)

TITLE/FLIP	LABEL & NO.	GOOD	NEAR MINT	YR.
GUILTY/Requiem: 820	(Attarack 102)	1.25	5.00	
LITTLE SISTER/Lonely Weekends	(Tower 447)	1.00	4.00	

DODD, Jimmy: see Annette

DODGERS, The (With Tom Evans)

TITLE/FLIP	LABEL & NO.	GOOD	NEAR MINT	YR.
DON'T LET ME BE WRONG/Get To You	(Island 058)	.50	2.00	76
LOVE ON THE REBOUND/Come Out Fighting	(Polydor 14515)	.50	2.00	78

Also see Badfinger

DODO, Joe, & The Groovers

TITLE/FLIP	LABEL & NO.	GOOD	NEAR MINT	YR.
GOIN' STEADY/Groovy	(RCA Victor 47-7207)	1.00	4.00	58

DODSON, Herb

TITLE/FLIP	LABEL & NO.	GOOD	NEAR MINT	YR.
DISC JOCKEY'S CHRISTMAS EVE/What Is A Disc Jockey	(Stacey 954)	.75	3.00	62

DOGG, Redd

TITLE/FLIP	LABEL & NO.	GOOD	NEAR MINT	YR.
WHO'S LONESOME TONIGHT, ACT 3 (PART 1)/ Who's Lonesome Tonight, Act 3 (Part 2) (Answer Song)	(Del Fi 4152)	1.25	5.00	61

DOHERTY, Denny (Of The Mamas & The Papas)

TITLE/FLIP	LABEL & NO.	GOOD	NEAR MINT	YR.
MY SONG/	(Columbia 4-45866)	.50	2.00	73
YOU'LL NEVER KNOW/Goodnight & Goodmorning	(Ember 0286)	.50	2.00	

DOLENZ, JONES, BOYCE & HART (Mickey Dolenz, Davey Jones, Tommy Boyce, Bobby Hart)

TITLE/FLIP	LABEL & NO.	GOOD	NEAR MINT	YR.
I LOVE YOU (& I'M GLAD THAT I SAID IT)/ Savin' My Love For You	(Capitol 4271)	.75	3.00	76
I REMEMBER THE FEELING/You & I	(Capitol 4180)	.75	3.00	75

Also see Boyce & Hart

DOLENZ, Mickey (Of The Monkees)

TITLE/FLIP	LABEL & NO.	GOOD	NEAR MINT	YR.
BUDDY HOLLY TRIBUTE: PEGGY SUE-EVERYDAY-MAYBE BABY- THAT'LL BE THE DAY/Ooh She's Young	(Romar 715)	.75	3.00	74
DAYBREAK/Love War	(Romar 710)	.75	3.00	73
DON'T DO IT/Plastic Symphony III	(Challenge 59353)	1.25	5.00	67
EASY ON YOU/Oh Someone	(MGM 14309)	1.00	4.00	71
HUFF PUFF/	(Challenge 59372)	1.25	5.00	67
LOVER'S PRAYER, A/Unattended In The Dungeon	(MGM 14395)	1.00	4.00	72

DOLLAR

TITLE/FLIP	LABEL & NO.	GOOD	NEAR MINT	YR.
SHOOTING STAR/Star Control	(Carrere 7208)	.50	2.00	79

DOLLS, The: see New York Dolls, The

DOLPHINS, The

TITLE/FLIP	LABEL & NO.	GOOD	NEAR MINT	YR.
DANCE/Pony Race	(Gemini 501)	1.00	4.00	62
HANG ON/Swingin' Soiree	(Laurie 3202)	1.00	4.00	63
HEY-DA-DA-DOW/I Don't Want To Go On Without You	(Fraternity 937)	1.00	4.00	64
LITTLE DONNA/Beautiful Woman	(Fraternity 940)	1.00	4.00	65
SURFIN' EAST COAST/I Should Have Stayed	(Yorkshire 125)	1.25	5.00	66
TELL-TELL KISSES/I Found True Love	(Shad 5020)	2.50	10.00	60

Even though all of these releases are shown as being by a group using the same name, the possibility exists that they are not all by the same group.

DOMINEERS, The

TITLE/FLIP	LABEL & NO.	GOOD	NEAR MINT	YR.
NOTHING CAN GO WRONG/Richie, Come On Down	(Roulette 4245)	1.00	4.00	60

DON & JUAN (Of The Genies)

TITLE/FLIP	LABEL & NO.	GOOD	NEAR MINT	YR.
COULD THIS BE LOVE/Lonely Man	(Mala 469)	1.00	4.00	63
MAGIC WAND/What I Really Meant To Say	(Big Top 3121)	1.25	5.00	62
TRUE LOVE NEVER RUNS SMOOTH/ Is It Alright If I Love You	(Big Top 3145)	1.00	4.00	63
TWO FOOLS ARE WE/Pot Luck	(Big Top 3106)	1.25	5.00	62
WHAT'S YOUR NAME/Chicken Necks	(Big Top 3079)	1.00	4.00	62

Don is Roland Trone; Juan is Claude Johnson

DON, DICK N' JIMMY (With Don Ralke)

TITLE/FLIP	LABEL & NO.	GOOD	NEAR MINT	YR.
ANGELA MIA/Brand Me With Your Kisses	(Crown 104)	1.25	5.00	54
HAWAIIAN WAR CHANT/Ole Man River	(Crown 116)	1.25	5.00	54
LAST TIME, THE/Piano Players	(Crown 112)	1.25	5.00	54
LOVE IS A MANY SPLENDORED THING/In Madrid	(Crown 158)	1.25	5.00	55
MAKE YOURSELF COMFORTABLE/Song From Desiree	(Crown 138)	1.25	5.00	54
THAT'S WHAT I LIKE/ You Can't Have Your Cake & Eat It Too	(Crown 125)	1.25	5.00	54
TOO YOUNG TO BOP/This Was My Sin	(Dot 15768)	1.25	5.00	54
TOUCH OF YOUR LIPS/I Go To You	(Crown 131)	1.25	5.00	54

DON & THE GALAXIES

TITLE/FLIP	LABEL & NO.	GOOD	NEAR MINT	YR.
SUNDOWN/Avalanche	(Fox-Fidel 3)	1.00	4.00	

DON & THE GOODTIMES

TITLE/FLIP	LABEL & NO.	GOOD	NEAR MINT	YR.
BAMBI/Sally (Studio & At 6 O'clock In The Morning)	(Epic 10241)	.75	3.00	67
BLUE TURNS TO GRAY/I'm Real	(Jerden 805)	1.00	4.00	66
BIG, BIG KNIGHT (ON A BIG WHITE HORSE)/ I'll Be Down Forever	(Dunhill 4015)	1.25	5.00	65
HAPPY & ME/If You Love Her, Cherish Her & Such	(Epic 10199)	.75	3.00	67
I COULD BE SO GOOD TO YOU/And It's So Good	(Epic 10145)	.75	3.00	67
I HATE TO HATE YOU/You Were A Child	(Jerden 251)	1.00	4.00	66
LITTLE GREEN THING/Little Sally Tease	(Dunhill 4008)	1.25	5.00	65
MAY MY HEART BE CAST INTO STONE/Hold Of Fire	(Epic 10280)	.75	3.00	68

DON RAYS, The: see Herman, Cleve

DONALDSON, Bo, & The Heywoods

TITLE/FLIP	LABEL & NO.	GOOD	NEAR MINT	YR.
BILLY, DON'T BE A HERO/Don't Ever Look Back	(ABC 11435)	.75	3.00	74
DA DOO RON RON/	(Family 0923)	.75	3.00	74
GIVE SOME TIME/	(Playboy 5820)	.50	2.00	77
HEARTBREAK KID, THE/Girl Don't Make Me Wait	(ABC 12039)	.75	3.00	74
OH BOY/Tie Me Down	(Capitol 4237)	.50	2.00	76
OUR LAST SONG TOGETHER/ Make The Most Of This World	(ABC 12108)	.75	3.00	75
WHO DO YOU THINK YOU ARE/Fools Way Of Lovin'	(ABC 12006)	.75	3.00	74

DONATO, Mike

TITLE/FLIP	LABEL & NO.	GOOD	NEAR MINT	YR.
DORA/Summertime Love	(PM 101)	1.50	6.00	

DONEGAN, Lonnie

TITLE/FLIP	LABEL & NO.	GOOD	NEAR MINT	YR.
BAD NEWS/Interstate 40	(Hickory 1274)	.75	3.00	64
DOES YOUR CHEWING GUM LOSE IT'S FLAVOR (ON THE BEDPOST OVER NIGHT)/Aunt Rhody	(Dot 15911)	.75	3.00	59
FISHERMAN'S LUCK/There's A Big Wheel	(Hickory 1267)	.75	3.00	64
FORT WORTH JAIL/Whoa Back, Buck	(Dot 15953)	.75	3.00	59
HAVE A DRINK ON ME/Beyond The Sunset	(Atlantic 2108)	.75	3.00	61
JUNCO PARTNER/Lorelei	(Atlantic 2081)	.75	3.00	60
LIGHT FROM THE LIGHTHOUSE/Whoa Back, Buck	(Dot 16263)	.75	3.00	61
LOST JOHN/Stewball	(Mercury 70872)	1.00	4.00	56
MY OLD MAN'S A DUSTMAN/The Golden Vanity	(Atlantic 2058)	.75	3.00	60
ROCK ISLAND LINE/John Henry	(London 1650)	1.25	5.00	56
ROCK ISLAND LINE/John Henry	(Felsted 8630)	.75	3.00	61
TAKE THIS HAMMER/Nobody Understands Me	(Atlantic 2063)	.75	3.00	60
WRECK OF THE JOHN B./Sorry, But I'm Gonna Have To Pass	(Atlantic 2123)	.75	3.00	61

DONLAYS, The

TITLE/FLIP	LABEL & NO.	GOOD	NEAR MINT	YR.
BAD BOY/Devil In His Heart	(Brent 7033)	.75	3.00	62

DONNELL, Doug, & The Hot Rods

TITLE/FLIP	LABEL & NO.	GOOD	NEAR MINT	YR.
ON OUR WAY FROM SCHOOL/You're My Girl	(Alton 602)	1.00	4.00	59

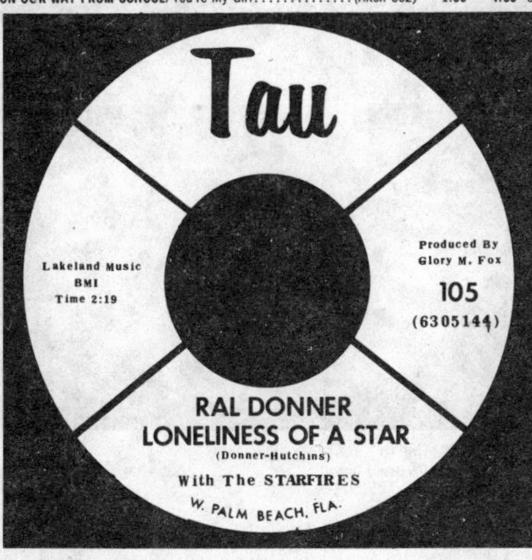

DONNER, Ral (Ralph Donner)

TITLE/FLIP	LABEL & NO.	GOOD	NEAR MINT	YR.
(ALL OF A SUDDEN) MY HEART SINGS/Lovin' Place	(MJ 222)	1.00	4.00	70
(The picture sleeve for this release actually had no picture on it.)				
BEYOND THE HEARTBREAK/Run Little Linda	(Reprise 20192)	5.00	20.00	63
CHRISTMAS DAY/	(Starfire 103)	.75	3.00	78
Issued on green plastic, previously released as "(These Are The Things That Make Up) Christmas Day."				
DAY THE BEAT STOPPED, THE/Rock On Me	(Thunder 7801)	.75	3.00	78
(Elvis tribute, issued on clear plastic)				
GIRL OF MY BEST FRIEND/It's Been A Long Time	(Gone 5102)	3.75	15.00	60
(Black label)				
GIRL OF MY BEST FRIEND/It's Been A Long Time	(Gone 5102)	.75	3.00	61
(Multi-color label)				
GOOD LOVIN'/The Other Side Of Me	(Smash 34774)	5.00	20.00	65
(Smash label issues were for promotional use only)				
GOOD LOVIN'/The Other Side Of Me	(Fontana 1515)	2.00	8.00	65
I GOT BURNED/A Tear In My Eye	(Reprise 20141)	2.00	8.00	63
I GOT BURNED/A Tear In My Eye	(Reprise 20141)	5.00	20.00	63
(Picture sleeve)				
I WISH THIS NIGHT WOULD NEVER END/Don't Put Your Heart In His Hands	(Reprise 20176)	2.50	10.00	63
(IF I HAD MY) LIFE TO LIVE OVER/Lost	(Mid-Eagle 101)	1.00	4.00	68
IF I PROMISE/Just A Little Sunshine In The Rain	(Rising Sons 714)	1.00	4.00	68
LOVELESS LIFE/Bells Of Love	(Gone 5129)	1.25	5.00	62
LONELINESS OF A STAR/And Then	(Tau 105)	3.00	12.00	63
(Recorded in 1960, not released until 1963)				
LOVE ISN'T LIKE THAT/It Will Only Make Me Love You More	(Red Bird 10-057)	3.00	12.00	66
PLEASE DON'T GO/I Didn't Figure On Him	(Gone 5114)	1.00	4.00	61
POISON IVY LEAGUE/You Finally Said Something Good	(Fontana 1502)	2.50	10.00	64
RIP IT UP/Don't Leave Me Now	(Starfire 114)	.75	3.00	79
RIP IT UP/Don't Leave Me Now	(Starfire 114)	2.50	10.00	79
(45rpm picture disc)				
SCHOOL OF HEARTBREAKERS/Because We're Young	(Gone 5119)	5.00	20.00	61
SHE'S EVERYTHING (I WANTED YOU TO BE)/Because We're Young	(Gone 5121)	1.50	6.00	61
SHE'S EVERYTHING (I WANTED YOU TO BE)/Will You Love Me In Heaven	(Gone 5121)	1.00	4.00	61
SO MUCH LOVIN'/Francene (By the Zantees)	(Eva-Tone/Goldmine GM-1)	.50	2.00	79
(Red plastic soundsheet)				
TELL ME WHY/That's All Right With Me	(Scottie 1310)	6.25	25.00	59
(THESE ARE THE THINGS THAT MAKE UP) CHRISTMAS DAY/Second Miracle	(Reprise 20135)	2.50	10.00	62
TO LOVE/And Then	(Gone 5108)	3.75	15.00	61
(Shortly after its release, this single was replaced with "You Don't Know What You've Got"/"So Close To Heaven," which maintained the same catalog number.)				
TO LOVE/Sweetheart	(Gone 5133)	1.25	5.00	62
WAIT A MINUTE NOW/Don't Let It Slip Away	(Sunlight 1006)	1.50	6.00	72
WAIT A MINUTE NOW/Don't Let It Slip Away	(Starfire 100)	1.00	4.00	78
(Issued on white plastic)				
WEDDING SONG, THE/Godfather Per Me'	(Chicago Fire 7402)	1.25	5.00	74
WEDDING SONG, THE/So Much Lovin'	(Mid-Eagle 275)	1.00	4.00	76
WILL YOU LOVE ME IN HEAVEN/(What A Sad Way) To Love Someone	(Gone 5125)	1.50	6.00	62
YOU DON'T KNOW WHAT YOU'VE GOT/So Close To Heaven	(Gone 5108)	1.00	4.00	61
(Gone's 5108 catalog number was originally used for "To Love"/"And Then.")				
YOU DON'T KNOW WHAT YOU'VE GOT/She's Everything	(End GG-19)	3.00	12.00	63
On the Tau and on a couple of the Gone releases the artist was shown as Ral Donner & the Starfires.				

DONNIE & THE COR-VETS

TITLE/FLIP	LABEL & NO.	GOOD	NEAR MINT	YR.
SOME LITTLE SOMEONE/The Skip	(Aertaun 1104)	.75	3.00	65

DONNIE & THE DARLINGTONS

TITLE/FLIP	LABEL & NO.	GOOD	NEAR MINT	YR.
POPPIN' MY CLUTCH/Since Grandpa Got A Rail Job	(ABC-Paramount 10633)	1.00	4.00	65

DONNIE & THE DEL CHORDS (Featuring Donnie Huffman)

TITLE/FLIP	LABEL & NO.	GOOD	NEAR MINT	YR.
I DON'T CARE/I'll Be With You In Apple Blossom Time	(Taurus 357)	1.50	6.00	63
I FOUND HEAVEN/Be With You	(Taurus 363)	3.75	15.00	63
I'M IN THE MOOD FOR LOVE/I've Got A Woman	(Taurus 364)	1.50	6.00	63
THAT OLD FEELING/Transylvania Mist	(Taurus 361)	1.50	6.00	63
WHEN YOU'RE ALONE/So Lonely	(Taurus 352)	2.50	10.00	61
WHEN YOU'RE ALONE/So Lonely	(Epic 9495)	1.25	5.00	61

DONNIE & THE DREAMERS

TITLE/FLIP	LABEL & NO.	GOOD	NEAR MINT	YR.
CAROLE/Ruby My Love	(Decca 31312)	2.50	10.00	61
COUNT EVERY STAR/Dorothy	(Whale 500)	1.50	6.00	61
MY MEMORIES OF YOU/Teenage Love	(Whale 505)	2.00	8.00	61
Also see Kenny & The Whalers				

DONNY & THE BI-LANGOS

TITLE/FLIP	LABEL & NO.	GOOD	NEAR MINT	YR.
I'M NOT A KNOW-IT-ALL/I	(Colton 101)	3.75	15.00	

DONOVAN (Donovan P. Leitch)

TITLE/FLIP	LABEL & NO.	GOOD	NEAR MINT	YR.
ATLANTIS/To Susan On The West Coast Waiting	(Epic 10434)	.75	3.00	69
BARABAJAGAL (LOVE IS HOT)/Trudi	(Epic 10510)	.75	3.00	69
(With the Jeff Beck Group)				
CATCH THE WIND/Why Do You Treat Me Like You Do	(Hickory 1309)	1.00	4.00	65
CELIA OF THE SEALS/The Song Of The Wandering Angels	(Epic 10694)	.75	3.00	71
COLOURS/Josie	(Hickory 1324)	1.00	4.00	65
DARE TO BE DIFFERENT/International Man	(Arista 0280)	.50	2.00	77
EPISTLE TO DIPPY/Preachin' Love	(Epic 10127)	.75	3.00	67
HEY GIP/The Way Drags On	(Hickory 1417)	1.00	4.00	66
HURDY GURDY MAN/Teen Angel	(Epic 10345)	.75	3.00	68
I LIKE YOU/Earth Sign Man	(Epic 10983)	.75	3.00	73
JENNIFER JUNIPER/Poor Cow	(Epic 10300)	.75	3.00	68
LALENA/Aye My Love	(Epic 10393)	.75	3.00	68
LITTLE TIN SOLDIER, THE/You're Gonna Need Somebody On Your Mind	(Hickory 1375)	1.00	4.00	66
MARIA MAGENTA/The Intergalactic Laxative	(Epic 11023)	.75	3.00	73
MELLOW YELLOW/Sunny South Kensington	(Epic 10098)	.75	3.00	66
RIKI TIKI TAVI/Roots Of Oak	(Epic 10649)	.75	3.00	70
ROCK & ROLL SOULJER/How Silly	(Epic 50077)	.75	3.00	75
ROCK 'N' ROLL WITH ME/The Divine Daze Of Deathless Delight	(Epic 50016)	.75	3.00	74
SAILING HOMEWARD/Yellow Star	(Epic 11108)	.75	3.00	74
SUNNY GOODGE STREET/Summer Day Reflection Song	(Hickory 1470)	1.00	4.00	67
SUNSHINE SUPERMAN/The Trip	(Epic 10045)	.75	3.00	66
THERE IS A MOUNTAIN/Sand & Foam	(Epic 10212)	.75	3.00	67
TO TRY FOR THE SUN/Turquoise	(Hickory 1402)	1.00	4.00	66
UNIVERSAL SOLDIER/Do You Hear Me Now	(Hickory 1338)	1.00	4.00	65
WEAR YOUR LOVE LIKE HEAVEN/Oh Gosh	(Epic 10253)	.75	3.00	67
WELL KNOWN HAS-BEEN, A/Dark-Eyed Blue Jean Angel	(Epic 50237)	.75	3.00	76
WHY DO YOU TREAT ME LIKE YOU DO/Do You Hear Me Now	(Hickory 1492)	1.00	4.00	68

DOO, Dickey, & The Don'ts (Gerry Granahan)

TITLE/FLIP	LABEL & NO.	GOOD	NEAR MINT	YR.
CLICK CLACK/Did You Cry	(Swan 4001)	1.00	4.00	58
CLICK CLACK '65/Don't Count Me Out	(Ascot 2178)	.75	3.00	65
JUDGE, THE/A Little Dog Cried	(United Artists 362)	1.00	4.00	61
JUDGE, THE/Doo Plus Two	(Danna 4001)	.75	3.00	67
LEAVE ME ALONE (LET ME CRY)/Wild Party	(Swan 4014)	1.00	4.00	58
NEE NEE NA NA NA NA NU NU/Flip Top Box	(Swan 4006)	1.00	4.00	58
TEARDROPS WILL FALL/Come With Us	(Swan 4025)	1.00	4.00	59
TEEN SCENE/Pity, Pity	(United Artists 238)	.75	3.00	60
WABASH CANNON BALL/Drums Of Richard A. Doo	(Swan 4046)	1.00	4.00	59

DOOBIE BROTHERS, The

TITLE/FLIP	LABEL & NO.	GOOD	NEAR MINT	YR.
ANOTHER PARK, ANOTHER SUNDAY/Black Water	(Warner Bros. 7795)	.50	2.00	74
BEHIVE STATE/Closer Every Day	(Warner Bros. 7544)	.75	3.00	72
BLACK WATER/Song To See You Through	(Warner Bros. 8062)	.50	2.00	74
CHINA GROVE/Evil Woman	(Warner Bros. 7728)	.50	2.00	73
DEPENDIN' ON YOU/How Do The Fools Survive?	(Warner Bros. 49029)	.50	2.00	79
ECHOES OF LOVE/There's A Light	(Warner Bros. 8471)	.50	2.00	77
EYES OF SILVER/You Just Can't Stop It	(Warner Bros. 7832)	.50	2.00	74
FEELIN' DOWN FARTHER/Travelin' Man	(Warner Bros. 7527)	.50	2.00	71
I CHEAT THE HANGMAN/Music Man	(Warner Bros. 8161)	.50	2.00	75
IT KEEPS YOU RUNNIN'/Turn It Loose	(Warner Bros. 8282)	.50	2.00	76
JESUS IS JUST ALRIGHT/Rockin' Down The Highway	(Warner Bros. 7661)	.50	2.00	72
LISTEN TO THE MUSIC/Toulouse Street	(Warner Bros. 7619)	.50	2.00	72
LITTLE DARLING (I NEED YOU)/Losin' End	(Warner Bros. 8408)	.50	2.00	77
LIVIN' ON THE FAULT LINE/Nothin' But A Heartache	(Warner Bros. 8500)	.50	2.00	77
LONG TRAIN RUNNIN'/Without You	(Warner Bros. 7698)	.50	2.00	73
MINUTE BY MINUTE/Sweet Feelin'	(Warner Bros. 8828)	.50	2.00	79
NOBODY/Flying Cloud	(Warner Bros. 8041)	.50	2.00	74
REAL LOVE/Thank You Love	(Warner Bros. 49503)	.50	2.00	80
SWEET MAXINE/Double Dealin' Four-Flusher	(Warner Bros. 8126)	.50	2.00	75
TAKE ME IN YOUR ARMS (ROCK ME)/Slat Key Soquel Rag	(Warner Bros. 8092)	.50	2.00	75
TAKIN' TO THE STREETS/For Someone Special	(Warner Bros. 8196)	.50	2.00	76
WHAT A FOOL BELIEVES/Don't Stop To Watch The Wheels	(Warner Bros. 8725)	.50	2.00	79
WHEELS OF FORTUNE/Slat Key Soquel Rag	(Warner Bros. 8233)	.50	2.00	76
Also see Johnston, Tom				

DOOLEY, Tom

TITLE/FLIP	LABEL & NO.	GOOD	NEAR MINT	YR.
CAN'T TURN YOU LOOSE/You're My Baby	(TRX 5009)	.75	3.00	
HAVE A HAPPY, HAPPY TIME/Bring It On Home	(Hickory 1446)	.75	3.00	66
MY GROOVY BABY/You'd Better Stop	(TRX 5013)	.75	3.00	
SATISFACTION/Don't Leave	(TRX 5018)	.75	3.00	
WINDS OF NEW YORK CITY, THE/Tight Rope	(TRX 5022)	.75	3.00	

DOOR NOBS, The

TITLE/FLIP	LABEL & NO.	GOOD	NEAR MINT	YR.
HI-FI BABY/I Need Your Lovin, Babe	(Viv 4625)	1.00	4.00	

DOORS, The (Featuring Jim Morrison)

TITLE/FLIP	LABEL & NO.	GOOD	NEAR MINT	YR.
BREAK ON THROUGH/End Of The Night	(Elektra 45611)	1.50	6.00	66
GET UP & DANCE/Treetrunk	(Elektra 45793)	1.25	5.00	72
HELLO, I LOVE YOU/Love Street	(Elektra 45635)	.75	3.00	68
LIGHT MY FIRE/Crystal Ship	(Elektra 45615)	.75	3.00	67
LOVE HER MADLY/(You Need Meat) Don't Go No Further	(Elektra 45726)	.75	3.00	71
LOVE ME TWO TIMES/Moolight Drive	(Elektra 45624)	.75	3.00	67
MOSQUITO, THE/It Slipped My Mind	(Elektra 45807)	.75	3.00	72
PEOPLE ARE STRANGE/Unhappy Girl	(Elektra 45621)	.75	3.00	67
PIANO BIRD/	(Elektra 45825)	1.00	4.00	72
RIDERS ON THE STORM/Changeling	(Elektra 45738)	.75	3.00	71
ROADHOUSE BLUES/Albionis Adgio	(Elektra 46005)	.75	3.00	79
RUNNIN' BLUE/Do It	(Elektra 45675)	.75	3.00	69
SHIPS WITH SAILS/	(Elektra 45768)	1.00	4.00	72
TELL ALL THE PEOPLE/Easy Ride	(Elektra 45663)	.75	3.00	69
TIGHTROPE RIDE/Variety Is The Spice Of Life	(Elektra 45757)	.75	3.00	71
TOUCH ME/Wild Child	(Elektra 45646)	.75	3.00	68
UNKNOWN SOLDIER/We Could Be So Good Together	(Elektra 45628)	.75	3.00	68
WISHFUL SINFUL/Who Scared You	(Elektra 45656)	.75	3.00	69
YOU MAKE ME REAL/Roadhouse Blues	(Elektra 45685)	.75	3.00	70
Also see Manzarek, Ray				

DOREN, Van

TITLE/FLIP	LABEL & NO.	GOOD	NEAR MINT	YR.
HUNTINGTON BEACH/Surfin' Liza	(Hickory 45-1262)	.75	3.00	64

DORIES, The

TITLE/FLIP	LABEL & NO.	GOOD	NEAR MINT	YR.
STOMPIN' SH-BOOM/Breakup	(Dore 629)	.75	3.00	62
THEY GO APE/Don't Jump	(Dore 556)	1.00	4.00	60
TRAGEDY OF LOVE/I Loved Him So	(Dore 528)	1.00	4.00	60
Also see Enchanters, The				

DORMAN, Harold

TITLE/FLIP	LABEL & NO.	GOOD	NEAR MINT	YR.
IN THE BEGINNING/Wait 'Til Saturday Night	(Sun 377)	.75	3.00	62
JUST ONE STEP/Uncle Jonah's Place	(Sun 370)	.75	3.00	62
MOUNTAIN OF LOVE/To Be With You	(Rita 1003)	1.00	4.00	60
MOVED TO KANSAS CITY/Take A Chance	(Rita 1012)	1.00	4.00	60
RIVER OF TEARS/I'll Come Running	(Tince 1002)	1.00	4.00	60
RIVER OF TEARS/I'll Come Running	(Rita 1008)	1.00	4.00	60

DORN, Jerry

TITLE/FLIP	LABEL & NO.	GOOD	NEAR MINT	YR.
I'M SO IN LOVE WITH YOU/Nightmare	(King 4968)	1.00	4.00	56
WISHING WELL/Sentimental Heaven	(King 4932)	3.75	15.00	56
(With the Hurricanes)				

DORSEY, Jimmy

TITLE/FLIP	LABEL & NO.	GOOD	NEAR MINT	YR.
ALWAYS IN MY HEART/Yours	(Decca 9-28457)	1.25	5.00	53
BALLERINA/Angela Mia	(MGM K-11739)	1.00	4.00	54
DARKTOWN STRUTTER'S BALL/Dusk	(Coral 9-60000)	1.50	6.00	49
JUMP BACK HONEY/Love Came Back	(Columbia 4-39896)	1.25	5.00	52
JUNE NIGHT/Jay Dee's Boogie Woogie	(Fraternity 777)	.75	3.00	57
MOON OVER MIAMI/Quien Sabe?	(MGM K-11230)	1.25	5.00	52
NO OTHER LOVE BUT YOURS/Confetti	(Columbia 4-39691)	1.25	5.00	52
SO RARE/Sophisticated Swing	(Fraternity 755)	.75	3.00	57
TELL ME TRUE/The Night Is Filled With Echoes	(Columbia 4-39728)	1.25	5.00	52
WIMOWEH/I'll Always Be Following You	(Columbia 4-39651)	1.25	5.00	52

DORSEY, Tommy

TITLE/FLIP	LABEL & NO.	GOOD	NEAR MINT	YR.
BLUE MOON/Liza Jane	(Decca 9-29057)	1.00	4.00	54
GIRL FRIEND/Without A Word Of Warning	(Decca 9-27801)	1.25	5.00	51
I WONDER WHO'S KISSING HER NOW/Falling In Love With Love	(Decca 9-28847)	1.00	4.00	53
I'M GETTING SENTIMENTAL OVER YOU/Sentimental	(Decca 9-28684)	1.00	4.00	53
ISLAND QUEEN/You're The Cause Of It All	(Decca 9-28978)	1.00	4.00	54
MARCHETTA/Don't Take Your Love Away	(Decca 9-27890)	1.25	5.00	52
ONE KISS/The Most Beautiful Girl	(Decca 9-28766)	1.00	4.00	53
SOLITAIRE/With All My Heart & Soul	(Decca 9-27843)	1.25	5.00	51

DORSEY, Tommy, Orchestra (Conducted by Warren Covington)

TITLE/FLIP	LABEL & NO.	GOOD	NEAR MINT	YR.
EXECUTIONER THEME FROM MURDER BY CONTRACT/Oh, To Be Loved Again	(Decca 9-30936)	.75	3.00	59
I WANT TO BE HAPPY CHA CHA/Satan Takes A Holiday	(Decca 9-30790)	.75	3.00	58
TEA FOR TWO CHA CHA/My Baby Just Cares For Me	(Decca 9-30704)	.75	3.00	58

DOUBLE IV

TITLE/FLIP	LABEL & NO.	GOOD	NEAR MINT	YR.
MAGIC STAR (TELSTAR)/Is There Anything I Can Do For You	(Capitol 4902)	.75	3.00	63

DOUCET, Suzanne

TITLE/FLIP	LABEL & NO.	GOOD	NEAR MINT	YR.
SEI MEIN BABY (BE MY BABY)/Das Geht Doch Keinen	(Interphon 7704)	1.50	6.00	64

DOUCETTE (Jerry Doucette)

TITLE/FLIP	LABEL & NO.	GOOD	NEAR MINT	YR.
ALL I WANNA DO/	(Mushroom 7036)	.50	2.00	78
DOWN THE TOAD/Cat Walk	(Mushroom 7029)	.50	2.00	77
MAMA LET HIM PLAY/All Over You	(Mushroom 7030)	.50	2.00	78
NOBODY/All Over Me	(Mushroom 7042)	.50	2.00	79

DOUG & FREDDY

TITLE/FLIP	LABEL & NO.	GOOD	NEAR MINT	YR.
TAKE A CHANCE ON LOVE/I Know You're Lyin'	(Finer Arts 1001)	7.50	30.00	
(With the Pyramids)				

DOUGIE & THE DOLPHINS

TITLE/FLIP	LABEL & NO.	GOOD	NEAR MINT	YR.
YESTERDAYS DREAMS/Double Date	(Angletone 542)	1.00	4.00	

DOUGLAS, Gary

TITLE/FLIP	LABEL & NO.	GOOD	NEAR MINT	YR.
SANTA GOOFED/Santa Caught A Cold	(Antique 0013)	.75	3.00	60

DOUGLAS, Mike

TITLE/FLIP	LABEL & NO.	GOOD	NEAR MINT	YR.
FIRST CHRISTMAS CAROL (STORY OF THE)/Touch Hands On Christmas Morning	(Epic 5-10089)	.75	3.00	66
HIGH ON A HILL/Tonight	(Blue River 220)	.75	3.00	66
HOUSE OF LOVE/Cabaret	(Epic 5-10078)	.75	3.00	66
MEN IN MY LITTLE GIRL'S LIFE, THE/Stranger On The Shore	(Epic 5-9876)	.75	3.00	65
PARENTS OF THE KIDS IN LOVE/Real Love	(Epic 5-10041)	.75	3.00	66
PASS ME BY/Ev'ryone Here Loves Kelly	(Epic 5-9760)	.75	3.00	65

TITLE/FLIP	LABEL & NO.	GOOD	NEAR MINT	YR.
DOUGLAS, Ronny				
CANDY & GUM/You'll Come Back	(Everest 19425)	.75	3.00	61
RUN, RUN, RUN/You Say	(Everest 19413)	.75	3.00	61
SAY DIDD-I-LEE HEY (GONNA SEE MY BABY)/ Worth Waiting For	(Epic 5-9843)	.75	3.00	65
DOUGLAS, Ronny, & Bobby Lonero				
JUBILATION (EXCITATION)/This World	(Columbia 4-45594)	.75	3.00	72
MARY'S PARTY/Baby Take My Hand	(Columbia 4-45504)	.75	3.00	71
DOUGLAS, Scott				
BEATLES' BARBER, THE/The Wall Paper Song	(Apogee 105)	1.50	6.00	64
DOUGLAS, Steve				
YES SIR, THAT'S MY BABY/Lt. Col. Bogey's Parade	(Phillies 104)	.75	3.00	62
DOVAL, Jim (With the Gauchos)				
BARACUDA/The Scrub	(Dot 16571)	.75	3.00	64
BEATLE RULE/Pink Elephants	(Diplomacy 6)	1.25	5.00	64
BONY MARONI/She's A Very Nice Girl	(Diplomacy 7)	.75	3.00	64
DONNA/The Scrub	(Diplomacy 3)	.75	3.00	64
FIRE BALL/Good & Bad	(Dot 16468)	.75	3.00	63
GOOD & THE BAD, THE/Fireballed	(Diplomacy 8)	.75	3.00	65
I KNOW YOU'RE FOOLING AROUND/ Uptown Caballero	(ABC-Paramount 10637)	.75	3.00	65
LOVE ME ONE MORE TIME (PART 1)/ Love Me One More Time (Part 2)	(Diplomacy 1000)	1.00	4.00	64
(Shown as by Jimmy Sandoval & the Gauchos.)				
LOVE ME ONE MORE TIME (PART 1)/ Love Me One More Time (Part 2)	(Dot 16548)	.75	3.00	64
MAMA, KEEP YOUR BIG MOUTH SHUT/ She's So Fine	(Diplomacy 17)	.75	3.00	65
OUT OF SIGHT/Annie Ya Ya	(ABC-Paramount 10621)	.75	3.00	65
STRANDED IN THE POOL/Right Now	(Diplomacy 5)	1.00	4.00	64
DOVALE, Debbie				
HEY LOVER/This World We Live In	(Roulette 4521)	.75	3.00	63
DOVE, Ronnie				
CRY/Autumn Rhapsody	(Diamond 214)	.75	3.00	67
DANCIN' OUT OF MY HEART/Back From Baltimore	(Diamond 233)	.75	3.00	67
HAPPY/(Hey, Hey, Hey) Alright	(Swan 4231)	.75	3.00	63
HELLO PRETTY GIRL/Keep It A Secret	(Diamond 176)	.75	3.00	64
I NEED YOU NOW/	(Diamond 260)	.75	3.00	69
I REALLY DON'T WANT TO KNOW/Years Of Tears	(Diamond 205)	.75	3.00	66
I WANT TO LOVE YOU FOR WHAT YOU ARE/	(Diamond 227)	.75	3.00	67
I'LL MAKE ALL YOUR DREAMS COME TRUE/ I Had To Lose You (To Find I That I Need You)	(Diamond 188)	.75	3.00	65
IN SOME TIME/Livin' For Your Lovin'	(Diamond 240)	.75	3.00	68
KISS AWAY/Where In The World	(Diamond 191)	.75	3.00	65
LET'S START ALL OVER AGAIN/That Empty Feeling	(Diamond 195)	.75	3.00	66
LITTLE BIT OF HEAVEN, A/If I Live To Be A Hundred	(Diamond 184)	.75	3.00	64
MOUNTAIN OF LOVE/ Never Gonna Cry (The Way I'll Cry Tonight)	(Diamond 244)	.75	3.00	68
MY BABE/	(Diamond 221)	.75	3.00	67
ONE KISS FOR OLD TIMES' SAKE/ No Greater Love	(Diamond 179)	.75	3.00	65
ONE MORE MOUNTAIN TO CLIMB/All	(Diamond 217)	.75	3.00	67
PLEASE COME TO NASHVILLE/Pictures On Paper	(Melodyland 6004)	.50	2.00	75
RIGHT OR WRONG/Baby Put Your Arms Around Me	(Diamond 173)	.75	3.00	64
SADDEST SONG (OF THE YEAR)/No Greater Love	(Jalo 1406)	1.50	6.00	62
(With the Beltones)				
SAY YOU/Let Me Stay Today	(Diamond 167)	.75	3.00	64
THINGS/Here We Go Again	(Melodyland 6011)	.50	2.00	75
TOMBOY/Tell Me Tomorrow	(Diamond 249)	.75	3.00	68
WHEN LIKING TURNS TO LOVING/ I'm Learning How To Smile Again	(Diamond 191)	.75	3.00	66
YOUR SWEET LOVE/Drina	(Melodyland 6021)	.50	2.00	75
DOVERS, The				
ALICE MY LOVE/A Lonely Heart	(Valentine 1000)	5.00	20.00	
DOVELLS, The (Featuring Len Barry)				
BE MY GIRL/Dragster On The Prowl	(Parkway 901)	.75	3.00	63
BETTY IN BERMUDAS/Dance The Froog	(Parkway 882)	.75	3.00	63
BRISTOL STOMP, THE/Out In The Cold	(Parkway 827)	1.25	5.00	61
BRISTOL STOMP, THE/Letters Of Love	(Parkway 827)	.75	3.00	61
BRISTOL TWISTIN' ANNIE/The Actor	(Parkway 838)	.75	3.00	62
DO THE NEW CONTINENTAL/Mope-Itty Mope Stomp	(Parkway 833)	.75	3.00	61
HAPPY BIRTHDAY JUST THE SAME/One Potato	(Parkway 911)	.75	3.00	63
HAPPY SUMMER DAYS/Long After	(Diamond 198)	.75	3.00	66
HULLY GULLY BABY/Your Last Chance	(Parkway 845)	.75	3.00	62
JITTERBUG, THE/Kissin' In The Kitchen	(Parkway 855)	.75	3.00	62
KISS THE HURT AWAY/He Cries Like A Baby	(Decca 32919)	.75	3.00	70
NO, NO, NO/Letters Of Love	(Parkway 819)	1.50	6.00	61
STOP MONKEYIN' AROUN'/No, No, No	(Parkway 889)	.75	3.00	63
WATUSI WITH LUCY/What In The Worlds Come Over You	(Parkway 925)	.75	3.00	63
YOU CAN'T RUN AWAY FROM YOURSELF/ Save Me Baby	(Parkway 861)	.75	3.00	63
YOU CAN'T SIT DOWN/Stompin' Everywhere	(Parkway 867)	.75	3.00	63
YOU CAN'T SIT DOWN/Wildwood Days	(Parkway 867)	.75	3.00	63
DOWD, Larry, & The Rockatones				
BLUE SWINGIN' MAMA/Pink Cadillac	(Spinning 6009)	6.25	25.00	59
DOWD, Tommy				
ELECTION YEAR 1964/Election Year 1964 (Part 2)	(Red Bird 10-013)	1.25	5.00	64
(Novelty/Break-In)				

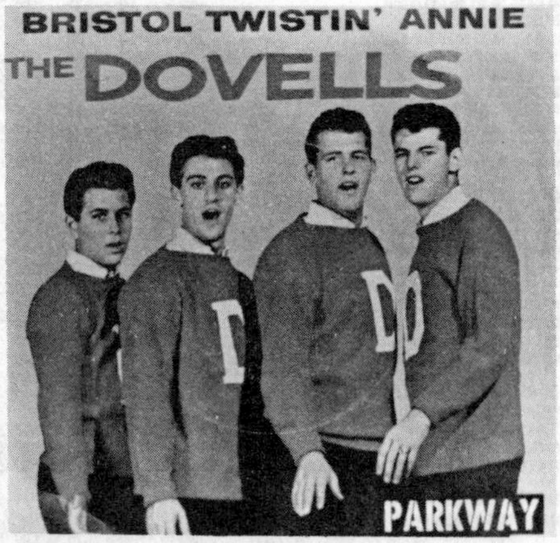

TITLE/FLIP	LABEL & NO.	GOOD	NEAR MINT	YR.
DOWELL, Joe				
BOBBY BLUE LOVES LINDA LOU/ My Darling Wears White Today	(Smash 1816)	.75	3.00	63
BRIDGE OF LOVE, THE/Just Love Me	(Smash 1717)	.75	3.00	61
(I WONDER) WHO'S SPENDING CHRISTMAS WITH YOU/ A Kiss For Christmas (O Tanenbaum)	(Smash 1728)	.75	3.00	
LITTLE RED RENTED ROWBOAT/One I Left For You	(Smash 1759)	.75	3.00	62
OUR SCHOOL DAYS/Bringa-Branga-Brought	(Smash 1799)	.75	3.00	63
POOR LITTLE CUPID/No Secrets	(Smash 1786)	.75	3.00	62
SOUND OF SADNESS/Thorn On The Rose	(Smash 1730)	.75	3.00	62
WOODEN HEART/Little Bo Beep	(Smash 1708)	.75	3.00	61
DOWLANDS, The				
ALL MY LOVING/Hey Sally	(Tollie 9002)	1.00	4.00	64
DOWN BEATS, The				
DEDICATED TO THE ONE I LOVE/Over My Room	(Down Beat 1029)	2.50	10.00	
DOWN CHILDREN, The				
NIGHT TIME GIRL/I Can Tell	(Philips 40441)	.75	3.00	67
DOWNBEATS, The				
ALFALFA/Red X	(Wilco 9)	.75	3.00	
DOWNBEAT/Rug Cuttin'	(Dynamite 1011)	.75	3.00	62
(Instrumentals)				
MY GIRL/China Doll	(Gee 1019)	2.00	8.00	56
YOU GOTTA TELL ME/It Won't Be Easy	(Diamond 243)	.75	3.00	
DOWNERS, Jack E., & His Friends				
SURFIN' WAY OUT/Strictly Drums	(Jedco 5001)	1.00	4.00	
DOWNLINERS SECT				
LITTLE EGYPT/Sect Appeal	(Smash 1954)	.75	3.00	64
DOYLE, Dickie				
MY LITTLE ANGEL/Dreamland Last Night	(Wye 1009)	7.50	30.00	
DOZY, BEAKY, MICK & TICH				
BAD NEWS/Tonight-Today	(Cotillion 44061)	.75	3.00	70
Also see Dee, Dave, Dozy, Beaky, Mick & Tich				
DRABOLIQUES, The				
BUBBLES/Birdland	(Merri 6005)	.75	3.00	
DRAFI				
MARBLE BREAKS & IRON BENDS/Amanda	(London 10825)	.75	3.00	66
DRAG KINGS, The				
NITRO/Bearing Burners	(United Artists 676)	.75	3.00	64
(Instrumentals)				
DRAGON				
APRIL SUN IN CUBA/Mr. Thunder	(Portrait 70019)	.50	2.00	78
ARE YOU OLD ENOUGH/	(Portrait 70023)	.50	2.00	79
IN THE RIGHT DIRECTION/	(Portrait 70013)	.50	2.00	78
DRAGON, Paul				
MEAN WOMAN BLUES/Blue Suede Shoes	(Starfire 109)	.75	3.00	79
DRAGONS, The (With Daryl Dragon)				
TROLL/Elephant Stomp	(Capitol 5278)	1.25	5.00	64
Also see Captain & Tennille, The				
DRAKE, Charlie				
MY BOOMERANG WON'T COME BACK/ She's My Girl	(United Artists 398)	2.00	8.00	61
(Lyric in "My Boomerang Won't Come Back"says "Practiced Till I Was Black In The Face.")				
MY BOOMERANG WON'T COME BACK/ She's My Girl	(United Artists 398)	.75	3.00	61
(Lyric in "My Boomerang Won't Come Back"says "Practiced Till I Was Blue In The Face.")				
TANGLEFOOT/Charlie's Progress	(United Artists 437)	.75	3.00	62
DRAKE, Mann				
HORROR MOVIE/Vampire's Ball	(Bethlehem 3049)	1.00	4.00	62
(Novelties)				
DRAPER, Rusty				
ALL FOR THE LOVE OF FLO/I Get So Jealous	(Mercury 71545)	.75	3.00	59
ARE YOU SATISFIED/Wabash Cannonball	(Mercury 70757)	1.00	4.00	55
BUZZ BUZZ BUZZ/I Get The Blues When It Rains	(Mercury 71221)	1.00	4.00	57
FREIGHT TRAIN/Seven Come Eleven	(Mercury 71102)	1.00	4.00	57
GAMBLERS GUITAR/Free Home Demonstration	(Mercury 70167)	1.00	4.00	53
LADY OF THE HOUSE/I Should Be Easier Now	(Monument 832)	.75	3.00	64
MULE SKINNER BLUES/Please Help Me I'm Falling	(Mercury 30113)	.75	3.00	63
NIGHT LIFE/That's Why I Love You Like I Do	(Monument 823)	.75	3.00	63
NO HELP WANTED/Texarkana Baby	(Mercury 70077)	1.00	4.00	53
PINK CADILLAC/In The Middle Of The House	(Mercury 70921)	1.00	4.00	56
SEVENTEEN/Can't Live Without Them	(Mercury 70651)	1.00	4.00	55
SHIFTING, WHISPERING SANDS, THE/Time	(Mercury 70696)	1.00	4.00	55
TIGER LILY/Confidential	(Mercury 70989)	1.00	4.00	56
DREAM GIRLS, The (With Bobbie Smith)				
DON'T BREAK MY HEART/Oh This Is Why	(Cameo 165)	1.00	4.00	59
DON'T BREAK MY HEART/I Could Write A Book	(Big Top 3059)	.75	3.00	60
DUTCHESS OF EARL/Mine All Mine	(Big Top 3100)	3.75	15.00	61
DREAM MERCHANTS, The				
I'LL BE WITH YOU IN APPLE BLOSSOM TIME/Rattler	(London 1015)	1.25	5.00	51
DREAM POLICE, The				
LIVING IS EASY/I'll Be Home	(Deram 3024)	1.00	4.00	
DREAM WEAVERS, The				
GIVE US THIS DAY/Why I Chose You	(Decca 29990)	1.00	4.00	56
INTO THE NIGHT/You're Mine	(Decca 29819)	1.00	4.00	56
IT'S ALMOST TOMORROW/You've Got Me Wondering	(Decca 29683)	1.00	4.00	55
LITTLE LOVE CAN GO A LONG LONG WAY, A/ Is There Somebody Else	(Decca 29905)	1.00	4.00	56
DREAMERS, The				
CANADIAN SUNSET/Mary Mary	(Guaranteed 219)	1.25	5.00	60
Also see Accents, The				
DREAMERS, The				
BECAUSE OF YOU/Little Girl	(Cousins 1005)	5.00	20.00	61
BECAUSE OF YOU/Little Girl	(May 133)	2.50	10.00	61
TEENAGE VOWS OF LOVE/Natalie	(Goldisc 3015)	1.25	5.00	61
DREAMS, The				
I LOVE YOU/Popeye	(Talent 1004)	2.00	8.00	
MARYANNE/Devil Lady	(Columbia 4-45300)	.75	3.00	71
MEDICATED GOO/New York	(Columbia 4-45524)	.75	3.00	72
TOO LATE/Inexperience	(Smash 1748)	.75	3.00	62
Even though all of these releases are shown as being by a group using the same name, the possibility exists that they are not all by the same group.				
DRESSLER, Len				
CHAIN GANG/These Hands	(Mercury 70774)	1.00	4.00	56
TELL HIM/Just Because	(Capitol 5055)	.75	3.00	63
DRIVER				
(I'VE BEEN LOOKING FOR) A NEW WAY TO SAY I LOVE YOU/ Bring It To Me	(A&M 1966)	.50	2.00	77

TITLE/FLIP	LABEL & NO.	GOOD	NEAR MINT	YR.
DRIVERS, The				
HIGH GEAR/Low Gear	(Comet 2142)	1.25	5.00	61
(Instrumentals)				
DRONGOS, The				
IF YOU WNAT TO KNOW/Under My Thumb	(White Whale 235)	1.50	6.00	66
DRUIDS, The				
DOCTOR FRIEND/	(Thunderbird 505)	1.00	4.00	
DRYSDALE, Don				
ONE LOVE/Give Her Love	(Reprise 20162)	.75	3.00	63
DUAL TONES, The				
BUBBLE GUM BOP/I'll Belong To You	(Sabre 204)	1.00	4.00	60
DUALS, The				
NEAREST TO MY HEART/Bye Bye	(Arc 4446)	1.25	5.00	
STICK SHIFT/Cruisin'	(Star Revue 1031)	2.50	10.00	61
STICK SHIFT/Cruisin'	(Sue 745)	.75	3.00	61
Instrumentals				
DUANE, Dick				
FAME & FORTUNE/Men Don't Cry	(ABC-Paramount 9709)	1.25	5.00	56
DUCANES, The				
I'M SO HAPPY/Little Did I Know	(Gold Disc 3024)	3.75	15.00	61
DUCKS DELUXE				
PLEASE PLEASE PLEASE/	(RCA 0297)	.50	2.00	71
DUDEK, Les (Of Krueger, Finnegan & Dudek)				
GONNA MOVE/Tears Turn Into Diamonds	(Columbia 3-10744)	.50	2.00	78
OLD JUDGE JONES/	(Columbia 3-10537)	.50	2.00	77
DUDES, The				
RUDOLPH THE RED NOSED REINDEER/Jingle Bells	(Sue 723)	1.00	4.00	59
MACK THE KNIFE/Organ Grinder Swing	(Sue 725)	1.00	4.00	60
DUDLEY				
EL PIZZA ("El Paso" parody)/ Lone Prairie Rock (Instrumental)	(Arvee 587)	1.00	4.00	60
DUKE & THE DRIVERS				
ROCK 'N' ROLL HIGH/	(ABC 12152)	.50	2.00	75
WHAT YOU GOT/Like I Want It	(ABC 12110)	.50	2.00	75
DU-KANES, The				
OUR STAR/Shock Treatment	(HSH 501)	.75	3.00	
DUKE, Patty				
DON'T JUST STAND THERE/Everything But Love	(United Artists 875)	.75	3.00	65
SAY SOMETHING FUNNY/Funny Little Butterflies	(United Artists 915)	.75	3.00	65
WHENEVER SHE HOLDS YOU/Nothing But You	(United Artists 978)	.75	3.00	66
DUNCAN, Lesley				
FINE FRIENDS/	(MCA 40635)	.50	2.00	76
HELP ME JESUS/Emma	(Columbia 4-45549)	.50	2.00	73
LOVE SONG/Exactly Who You Are	(Date 1677)	.75	3.00	70
RESCUE ME/	(MCA 40593)	.50	2.00	76
SING CHILDREN SING/	(Columbia 45473)	.50	2.00	72
DUNCAN, Leslie, & The Jokers				
I WANT A STEADY GUY/Moving Away	(Jerden 755)	.50	2.00	65
DUNDAS, David				
ANOTHER FUNNY HONEYMOON/Daisy Star	(Chrysalis 2142)	.50	2.00	77
JEANS ON/Sleepy Serena	(Chrysalis 2094)	.50	2.00	76
DUNE, Lorna				
MIDNIGHT JOEY (Answer song)/I'm Going With Bobby	(Select 730)	1.00	4.00	64
DUNES, The				
LONELY SANDS/Sloppy Jalopy	(Madison M-156)	1.00	4.00	61
(Instrumentals)				
DUNHILLS, The				
SOUND OF THE WIND/Ricochet	(Royal 110)	1.00	4.00	
DUPONTS, The				
SCREAMIN' AT DRACULA'S BALL/Half Past Nothing	(Roulette 4060)	1.00	4.00	58
DUPREE, Simon				
KITES/Like The Sun, Like The Fire	(Tower 377)	.75	3.00	69
Also see Gentle Giant				
DUPREES, The (Featuring Joey Vann)				
AROUND THE CORNER/ They Said It Couldn't Be Done	(Columbia 4-43336)	1.00	4.00	65
BE MY LOVE/I Understand	(Columbia 4-44078)	1.50	6.00	67
GONE WITH THE WIND/Let's Make Love Again	(Coed 576)	1.00	4.00	63
GOODNIGHT MY LOVE/	(Heritage 805)	1.00	4.00	68
HAVE YOU HEARD/Love Eyes	(Coed 584)	1.00	4.00	63
HAVE YOU HEARD/	(Heritage 826)	1.00	4.00	70
I'D RATHER BE HERE IN YOUR ARMS/ I Wish I Could Believe You	(Coed 574)	1.00	4.00	62
I'M YOURS/Wedding Ring	(Coed 596)	1.00	4.00	64
IT ISN'T FAIR/So Little Time	(Coed 595)	1.00	4.00	64
(IT'S NO) SIN/The Sand & The Sea	(Coed 587)	1.00	4.00	63

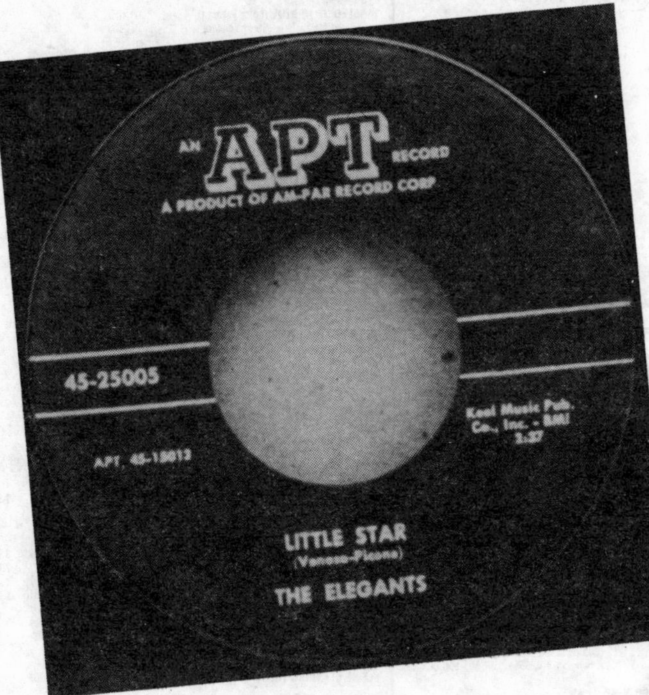

Fabian

Jimmy Ellis

TITLE/FLIP	LABEL & NO.	GOOD	NEAR MINT	YR.
IT'S NOT TIME NOW/Don't Want To Have To Do It	(Columbia 4-43802)	1.50	6.00	66
LET THEM TALK/Exodus Song	(Columbia 4-43577)	1.50	6.00	66
MY LOVE, MY LOVE/The Sky's The Limit	(Heritage 808)	1.00	4.00	69
MY OWN TRUE LOVE/Ginny	(Coed 571)	1.00	4.00	62
MY SPECIAL ANGEL/Ring Of Love	(Heritage 804)	1.00	4.00	68
PLEASE LET HER KNOW/Where Are You?	(Coed 591)	1.00	4.00	64
SHE WAITS FOR HIM/Norma Jean	(Columbia 4-43464)	1.25	5.00	65
SKY'S THE LIMIT, THE/Delecious	(RCA PB-10407)	.75	3.00	75
SO MANY HAVE TOLD ME/Unbelievable	(Coed 593)	1.00	4.00	64
TAKE ME AS I AM/I Gotta Tell Her Now	(Coed 580)	1.00	4.00	63
TWO DIFFERENT WORLDS/Hope	(Heritage 811)	1.00	4.00	69
WHY DON'T YOU BELIEVE ME/My Dearest One	(Coed 584)	1.00	4.00	63
YOU BELONG TO ME/Take Me As I Am	(Coed 569)	1.00	4.00	62

Group members: Joseph Canzano, Mike Arnone, John Salvato, Joe Santollo & Tom Bialaglow.
Also see I.A.P.C.O.

DURANTE, Jimmy

TITLE/FLIP	LABEL & NO.	GOOD	NEAR MINT	YR.
BLACK STRAP MOLASSES/How Do Ye Do	(Decca 9-27748)	1.25	5.00	51
I LOVE YOU, I DO/Swingin' With Rhythm & Blues	(Decca 9-29581)	1.25	5.00	55
ONE OF THOSE SONGS/What Became Of Life	(Warner Bros. 5686)	.75	3.00	65
SEPTEMBER SONG/Young At Heart	(Warner Bros. 5382)	.75	3.00	63
YOU SAY THE NICEST THINGS/If You Catch A Girl	(Decca 9-27865)	1.25	5.00	52

DURDEN, Tom

TITLE/FLIP	LABEL & NO.	GOOD	NEAR MINT	YR.
ELVIS/Elvis	(Westbound 55405)	.50	2.00	77

DURKEE, Ray

TITLE/FLIP	LABEL & NO.	GOOD	NEAR MINT	YR.
COSMONAUT, THE/The Cosmonaut (Part 2) (Novelty/Break-in)	(Jubilee 5422)	1.50	6.00	

DUROCS, The

TITLE/FLIP	LABEL & NO.	GOOD	NEAR MINT	YR.
IT HURTS TO BE IN LOVE/No Fool No Fun	(Capitol 4756)	.50	2.00	79
SAVING IT ALL UP FOR LARRY/	(Capitol 4787)	.50	2.00	79

DURY, Ian, & The Blockheads

TITLE/FLIP	LABEL & NO.	GOOD	NEAR MINT	YR.
HIT ME WITH YOUR RHYTHM STICK/ There Ain't Half Been Some Clever Bastards	(Stiff-Epic 50726)	.50	2.00	79
REASONS TO BE CHEERFUL, (PART 3)/ Hit Me With Your Rhythm Stick (Dance Version)	(Stiff-Epic 50800)	.50	2.00	79

DUSK

TITLE/FLIP	LABEL & NO.	GOOD	NEAR MINT	YR.
ANGEL BABY/	(Bell 961)	.50	2.00	71
I HEAR THOSE CHURCH BELLS RINGING/ I Cannot See To Touch You	(Bell 990)	.50	2.00	71
TREAT ME LIKE A GOOD PIECE OF CANDY/	(Bell 45148)	.50	2.00	72

DUST

TITLE/FLIP	LABEL & NO.	GOOD	NEAR MINT	YR.
LOVE ME HARD/	(Kama Sutra 541)	.50	2.00	73
STONE WOMAN/	(Kama Sutra 534)	.50	2.00	73

Also see Stories

DUVALL, Huelyn

TITLE/FLIP	LABEL & NO.	GOOD	NEAR MINT	YR.
COMIN' OR GOIN'/Teen Queen (Blue label)	(Challenge 1012)	7.50	30.00	58
COMIN' OR GOIN'/Teen Queen (Maroon label)	(Challenge 1012)	3.75	15.00	58
JULIET/Friday Night On A Dollar Bill	(Challenge 59025)	3.75	15.00	58
LITTLE BOY BLUE/Three Months To Kill	(Challenge 59014)	3.75	15.00	59
PUCKER PAINT/Boom Boom Baby	(Challenge 59069)	5.00	20.00	60
YOU KNOCK ME OUT/Humdingers	(Challenge 59002)	3.75	15.00	58

DUVALS, The

TITLE/FLIP	LABEL & NO.	GOOD	NEAR MINT	YR.
LAST SUPPER, THE/Roast	(Prelude 110)	.75	3.00	

DUVELLS, The

TITLE/FLIP	LABEL & NO.	GOOD	NEAR MINT	YR.
DANNY BOY/How Come	(Rust 5045)	1.00	4.00	63

DYLAN, Bob (Robert Zimmerman)

TITLE/FLIP	LABEL & NO.	GOOD	NEAR MINT	YR.
ALL THE TIRED HORSES (Stereo)/ All The Tired Horses (Mono) (Promotional issue only)	(Columbia AE 25)	6.25	25.00	70
BABY STOP CRYING/New Pony	(Columbia 3-10805)	1.25	5.00	78
BABY STOP CRYING (Long Version)/ Baby Stop Crying (Short Version) (Promotional issue)	(Columbia 3-10805)	3.00	12.00	78
BLOWIN' IN THE WIND/ Don't Think Twice, It's All Right	(Columbia 4-42856)	31.25	125.00	63
BLOWIN' IN THE WIND/ Don't Think Twice, It's All Right (Promotional issue)	(Columbia 4-42856)	31.25	125.00	63
BLOWIN' IN THE WIND/ Don't Think Twice, It's All Right (Biographical paper insert, packaged with the promotional issue of this single.)	(Columbia 4-42856)	6.25	25.00	63
CAN YOU PLEASE CRAWL OUT YOUR WINDOW/ Highway 61 Revisited	(Columbia 4-43477)	2.50	10.00	65
CAN YOU PLEASE CRAWL OUT YOUR WINDOW/ Highway 61 Revisited (Promotional issue)	(Columbia 4-43477)	6.25	25.00	65
CAN YOU PLEASE CRAWL OUT YOUR WINDOW/ Highway 61 Revisited (This release was shown on the label as "Positively 4th Street," although it was actually an alternate take of "Can You Please Crawl Out Your Window." This disc is usually referred to as the "Out-take promo" of "Can You Please Crawl Out Your Window.")	(Columbia 4-43389)	15.00	60.00	65
CHANGING OF THE GUARDS/ Senor (Tales Of Yankee Power)	(Columbia 3-10851)	1.50	6.00	78
CHANGING OF THE GUARDS (Long Version)/ Changing Of The Guards (Short Version) (Promotional issue)	(Columbia 3-10851)	2.00	8.00	78
FOOL SUCH AS I, A/Lily Of The West	(Columbia 4-45982)	1.00	4.00	73
FOOL SUCH AS I, A (Stereo)/A Fool Such As I (Mono)	(Columbia 4-45982)	2.50	10.00	73
GEORGE JACKSON (Acoustic Version)/ George Jackson (Big Band Version)	(Columbia 4-45516)	2.00	8.00	71
GEORGE JACKSON (Acoustic Version)/ George Jackson (Big Band Version) (Promotional issue)	(Columbia 4-45516)	3.75	15.00	71
GOTTA SERVE SOMEBODY/Trouble In Mind	(Columbia 1-11072)	.50	2.00	79
GOTTA SERVE SOMEBODY (Long Version)/ Gotta Serve Somebody (Short Version) (Promotional issue)	(Columbia 1-11072)	1.50	6.00	79
HURRICANE (PART 1)/Hurricane (Part 2)	(Columbia 3-10245)	.50	2.00	75
HURRICANE (PART 1) (Stereo)/ Hurricane (Part 1) (Mono) (Promotional issue, edited or "bleeped" version.)	(Columbia 3-10245)	3.00	12.00	75
HURRICANE (Stereo)/Hurricane (Mono) (Promotional compact 33 single, side 1 is the complete "Hurricane," parts 1 & 2. Side 2 is the edited or "bleeped" version.)	(Columbia 3-10245)	5.00	20.00	75
HURRICANE (PART 1)/Mozambique (Columbia "Hall Of Fame" series)	(Columbia 13-33324)	1.25	5.00	76
IF NOT FOR YOU/Tomorrow Is A Long Time (Promotional issue only)	(Columbia AE 7-1039)	6.25	25.00	71
IT AIN'T ME BABE/ All Along The Watchtower (Live, with the Band)	(Asylum E-45212)	2.50	10.00	74
IT AIN'T ME BABE/ All Along The Watchtower (Live, with the Band) (Promotional issue)	(Asylum E-45212)	3.75	15.00	74
I THREW IT ALL AWAY/Drifter's Escape	(Columbia 4-44826)	1.50	6.00	69
I THREW IT ALL AWAY/Drifter's Escape (Promotional issue)	(Columbia 4-44826)	3.75	15.00	69
I WANT YOU/Just Like Tom Thumb's Blues (Live)	(Columbia 4-43683)	1.25	5.00	66
I WANT YOU/I Want You (Red plastic promotional issue.)	(Columbia 4-43683)	6.25	25.00	66
I WANT YOU/Just Like Tom Thumb Blues (Live) (Promotional issue)	(Columbia 4-43683)	5.00	20.00	66
I WANT YOU/Just Like Tom Thumb Blues (Live) (Picture sleeve)	(Columbia 4-43683)	3.75	15.00	66
I WANT YOU/Just Like Tom Thumb Blues (Live) (Titled "Swingin' Party," this was a five record boxed set featuring one Dylan disc. The other four discs were by other Columbia artists, and all came with picture sleeves. The catalog number of the complete set is Columbia Masterworks 437.)	(Columbia 4-43683)	12.50	50.00	66
I WANT YOU/Just Like A Woman (Columbia "Hall Of Fame" series)	(Columbia 13-33108)	1.25	5.00	67
JUST LIKE A WOMAN/Obviously Five Believers	(Columbia 4-43792)	1.25	5.00	66
JUST LIKE A WOMAN/Just Like A Woman (Red plastic promotional issue)	(Columbia 4-43792)	6.25	25.00	66
JUST LIKE A WOMAN/Obviously Five Believers (Promotional issue)	(Columbia 4-43792)	5.00	20.00	66
KNOCKIN' ON HEAVENS DOOR/Turkey Chase	(Columbia 4-45913)	.50	2.00	73
KNOCKIN' ON HEAVENS DOOR (Stereo)/ Knockin' On Heavens Door (Mono) (Promotional issue)	(Columbia 4-45913)	2.50	10.00	73
KNOCKIN' ON HEAVEN'S DOOR/A Fool Such As I (Columbia "Hall Of Fame" series)	(Columbia 13-33259)	1.25	5.00	74
LAY LADY, LAY/Peggy Day	(Columbia 4-44926)	.75	3.00	69
LAY LADY, LAY/Peggy Day (Promotional issue)	(Columbia 4-44926)	3.75	15.00	69
LAY LADY, LAY/I Threw It All Away (Columbia "Hall Of Fame" series)	(Columbia 13-33178)	1.25	5.00	72
LEOPARD-SKIN PILL-BOX HAT/ Most Likely You Go Your Way And I'll Go Mine	(Columbia 4-44069)	2.00	8.00	67
LEOPARD-SKIN PILL-BOX HAT/ Most Likely You Go Your Way And I'll Go Mine (Promotional issue)	(Columbia 4-44069)	5.00	20.00	67
LIKE A ROLLING STONE/Gates Of Eden	(Columbia 4-43346)	1.25	5.00	65
LIKE A ROLLING STONE (PART 1)/ Like A Rolling Stone (Part 2) (Blue plastic promotional issue.)	(Columbia 4-43346)	25.00	100.00	65
LIKE A ROLLING STONE (PART 1)/ Like A Rolling Stone (Part 2) (Red plastic promotional issue.)	(Columbia 4-43346)	6.25	25.00	65
LIKE A ROLLING STONE (PART 1)/ Like A Rolling Stone (Part 2) (Promotional issue)	(Columbia 4-43346)	5.00	20.00	65
LIKE A ROLLING STONE/Rainy Day Women # 12 & 35 (Columbia "Hall Of Fame" series)	(Columbia 13-33100)	1.25	5.00	66
MAN GAVE NAMES TO ALL THE ANIMALS/ When You Gonna Wake Up	(Columbia 1-11168)	.50	2.00	79
MAN GAVE NAMES TO ALL THE ANIMALS/ When You Gonna Wake Up (Promotional issue)	(Columbia 1-11168)	1.50	6.00	79
MILLION DOLLAR BASH/Tears Of Rage	(Columbia 3-10217)	2.00	8.00	76
MILLION DOLLAR BASH (Stereo)/ Million Dollar Bash (Mono) (Promotional issue)	(Columbia 3-10217)	1.25	5.00	76
MIXED UP CONFUSION/Corrina Corrina	(Columbia 4-42656)	37.50	150.00	63
MIXED UP CONFUSION/Corrina Corrina (Promotional issue)	(Columbia 4-42656)	37.50	150.00	63
MOST LIKELY YOU GO YOUR WAY AND I'LL GO MINE (Live)/ Stage Fright (By the Band) (With the Band)	(Asylum AS-11043)	1.50	6.00	74
MOST LIKELY YOU GO YOUR WAY AND I'LL GO MINE (Live)/ Stage Fright (By the Band) (With the Band) (Promotional issue)	(Asylum AS-11043)	2.00	8.00	74
MOZAMBIQUE/Oh Sister	(Columbia 3-10298)	.50	2.00	75
MOZAMBIQUE (Stereo)/Mozambique (Mono) (Promotional issue)	(Columbia 3-10298)	1.25	5.00	75
ON A NIGHT LIKE THIS/You Angel You	(Asylum AS-11033)	.50	2.00	74
ON A NIGHT LIKE THIS/You Angel You (Promotional issue)	(Asylum AS-11033)	2.00	8.00	74
ONE OF US MUST KNOW (SOONER OR LATER)/ Queen Jane Approximately	(Columbia 4-43541)	2.00	8.00	66
ONE OF US MUST KNOW (SOONER OR LATER)/ Queen Jane Approximately (Promotional issue)	(Columbia 4-43541)	5.00	20.00	66
ONE OF US MUST KNOW (SOONER OR LATER) (Long Version)/One Of Us Must Know (Sooner Or Later) (Short Version) (Promotional issue)	(Columbia-No # given)	6.25	25.00	66
POSITIVELY 4TH STREET/From A Buick 6 (Gray label issue)	(Columbia 4-43389)	2.50	10.00	65
POSITIVELY 4TH STREET/From A Buick 6 (Red label issue)	(Columbia 4-43389)	1.25	5.00	65
POSITIVELY 4TH STREET/Positively 4th Street (Red plastic promotional issue.)	(Columbia 4-43389)	6.25	25.00	65
POSITIVELY 4TH STREET/From A Buick 6 (Promotional issue)	(Columbia 4-43389)	5.00	20.00	65
POSITIVELY 4TH STREET/From A Buick 6 (Picture sleeve)	(Columbia 4-43389)	3.75	15.00	65
POSITIVELY 4TH STREET/ Subterranean Homesick Blues (Columbia "Hall Of Fame" series)	(Columbia 13-33221)	1.25	5.00	73
RAINY DAY WOMEN # 12 & 35/Pledging My Time	(Columbia 4-43592)	1.25	5.00	66
RAINY DAY WOMEN # 12 & 35/Pledging My Time (Promotional issue)	(Columbia 4-43592)	5.00	20.00	66
RITA MAY/Stuck Inside Mobile With The Memphis Blues Again (Live)	(Columbia 3-10454)	2.00	8.00	77
RITA MAY/Stuck Inside Mobile With The Memphis Blues Again (Live) (Promotional issue)	(Columbia 3-10454)	3.00	12.00	77
SLOW TRAIN/Do Right To Me Baby (Do Unto Others)	(Columbia 1-11235)	1.25	5.00	80
SLOW TRAIN/Do Right To Me Baby (Do Unto Others) (Picture sleeve)	(Columbia 1-11235)	.75	3.00	80
SLOW TRAIN/Slow Train (Promotional issue)	(Columbia 1-11235)	1.50	6.00	80
SLOW TRAIN/Slow Train (Promotional picture sleeve)	(Columbia 1-11235)	1.00	4.00	80
SOLID ROCK/Covenant Woman	(Columbia 1-11318)	.50	2.00	80
SOLID ROCK/Covenant Woman (Promotional issue)	(Columbia 1-11318)	1.50	6.00	80
SOMETHING THERE IS ABOUT YOU/ Tough Mama	(Asylum AS-11035)	1.50	6.00	74
SOMETHING THERE IS ABOUT YOU/ Tough Mama (Promotional issue)	(Asylum AS-11035)	2.00	8.00	74
SUBTERRANEAN HOMESICK BLUES/ She Belongs To Me (Gray label issue)	(Columbia 4-43242)	2.50	10.00	65
SUBTERRANEAN HOMESICK BLUES/ She Belongs To Me (Red label issue)	(Columbia 4-43242)	1.50	6.00	65
SUBTERRANEAN HOMESICK BLUES/ Subterranean Homesick Blues (Red plastic promotional issue. This was one of three records issued in a Columbia "Hit Pack." This listing is for the Dylan disc only.)	(Columbia 4-43242)	6.25	25.00	65
SUBTERRANEAN HOMESICK BLUES/ Subterranean Homesick Blues (Columbia Records "Hit Pack." This promotional three record set contained the above Dylan record plus one record by Andy Williams and another by Barbra Streisand, all on colored plastic. A special picture sleeve was also issued. Above price is for the complete set.)	(Columbia 4-43242)	12.50	50.00	65
SUBTERRANEAN HOMESICK BLUES/ Subterranean Homesick Blues (Columbia "Hit Pack" special picture sleeve.)	(Columbia 4-43242)	5.00	20.00	65
SUBTERRANEAN HOMESICK BLUES/ She Belongs To Me (Promotional issue)	(Columbia 4-43242)	5.00	20.00	65
SUBTERRANEAN HOMESICK BLUES/ She Belongs To Me (Picture sleeve, orginally issued only with promotional copies of this single.)	(Columbia 4-43242)	50.00	200.00	65
SWINGIN' PARTY: see "I Want You"				
TANGLED UP IN BLUE/If You See Her, Say Hello	(Columbia 3-10106)	2.00	8.00	75
TANGLED UP IN BLUE (Stereo)/ Tangled Up In Blue (Mono) (Promotional issue)	(Columbia 3-10106)	3.00	12.00	75
TANGLED UP IN BLUE (Long Version)/ Tangled Up In Blue (Short Version) (Promotional issue)	(Columbia 3-10106)	3.00	12.00	75
TANGLED UP IN BLUE/If You See Her, Say Hello (Columbia "Hall Of Fame" series)	(Columbia 13-33280)	2.00	8.00	75
TONIGHT I'LL BE STAYING HERE WITH YOU/ Country Pie	(Columbia 4-45004)	1.50	6.00	69
TONIGHT I'LL BE STAYING HERE WITH YOU (Stereo)/ Tonight I'll Be Staying Here With You (Mono) (Promotional issue)	(Columbia 4-45004)	3.75	15.00	69
WATCHING THE RIVER FLOW/ Spanish Is The Loving Tongue	(Columbia 4-45409)	1.25	5.00	71
WATCHING THE RIVER FLOW (Stereo)/ Watching The River Flow (Mono) (Promotional issue)	(Columbia 4-45409)	3.75	15.00	71
WHAT'S IT ALL ABOUT (Bob Dylan)/ What's It All About (David Bowie) (Public service disc, with interviews and song excerpts.)	(Program #509/510)	5.00	20.00	
WIGWAM/Copper Kettle (The Pale Moonlight) (First pressing: solid red Columbia label with black lettering.)	(Columbia 4-45199)	5.00	20.00	70
WIGWAM/Copper Kettle (The Pale Moonlight) (Second pressing: red label with "Columbia Records" in white letters circling label's outer edge.)	(Columbia 4-45199)	5.00	20.00	70
WIGWAM/Copper Kettle (The Pale Moonlight) (Third pressing: "Columbia Records" shown on horizontal lines across entire label.)	(Columbia 4-45199)	2.50	10.00	70
WIGWAM/Copper Kettle (The Pale Moonlight) (Promotional issue)	(Columbia 4-45199)	3.75	15.00	70

Also see Ginsberg, Allen
Also see Sahm, Doug & Bob Dylan

DYNAMICS, The

TITLE/FLIP	LABEL & NO.	GOOD	NEAR MINT	YR.
WHENEVER I'M WITHOUT YOU/Love To A Guy	(Top Ten TT-927)	1.50	6.00	
YES, I LOVE YOU BABY/Soul Sloopy	(Top Ten TT-100)	1.50	6.00	

DYNAMICS, The

TITLE/FLIP	LABEL & NO.	GOOD	NEAR MINT	YR.
GIRL I MET LAST NIGHT, THE/ Nobody's Going Out With Me	(Dynamic Sound 504)	3.00	12.00	
DELSINIA/So Fine	(Reprise 20183)	2.00	8.00	63
ENCHANTED LOVE/Happiness & Love	(Arc 4450)	1.25	5.00	
SEEMS LIKE ONLY YESTERDAY/How Should I Feel	(Decca 9-31046)	1.25	5.00	60
SEEMS LIKE ONLY YESTERDAY/How Should I Feel	(Decca 9-31450)	.75	3.00	62
SOMEONE/Moonlight	(Impala)	3.75	15.00	59
SOMEONE/Moonlight	(Seeco 6008)	2.00	8.00	59

DYNAMICS, The

TITLE/FLIP	LABEL & NO.	GOOD	NEAR MINT	YR.
I'LL BE STANDING THERE/All She Said	(Jerden 800)	.75	3.00	66

DYNAMOS, The

TITLE/FLIP	LABEL & NO.	GOOD	NEAR MINT	YR.
TEEN BLUES/The Harem	(Press 101)	.75	3.00	61

DYNA-SORES, The

TITLE/FLIP	LABEL & NO.	GOOD	NEAR MINT	YR.
ALLEY-OOP/Jungle Walk	(Rendezvous 120)	1.25	5.00	60

DYNATONES, The

TITLE/FLIP	LABEL & NO.	GOOD	NEAR MINT	YR.
SKUNK, THE/The Skunk (Part 2)	(Alto 2020)	.75	3.00	66

DYNATONES, The

TITLE/FLIP	LABEL & NO.	GOOD	NEAR MINT	YR.
FIFE PIPER/And I Always Will	(St. Clair 117)	1.25	5.00	66
FIFE PIPER/And I Always Will	(HBR 494)	.75	3.00	66

DYSON, Ronnie

TITLE/FLIP	LABEL & NO.	GOOD	NEAR MINT	YR.
I DON'T WANT TO CRY/She's Gone	(Columbia 4-45240)	.50	2.00	70
(IF YOU LET ME MAKE LOVE TO YOU THEN) WHY CAN'T I TOUCH YOU?/	(Columbia 4-45110)	.50	2.00	70
JUST DON'T WANT TO BE LONELY/ Point Of No Return	(Columbia 4-45867)	.50	2.00	73
ONE MAN BAND/I Think I'll Tell Her	(Columbia 4-45800)	.50	2.00	73

EAGER, Johnny

TITLE/FLIP	LABEL & NO.	GOOD	NEAR MINT	YR.
I UNDERSTAND/Blessing Of Love	(End 1061)	1.00	4.00	59

EAGLES, The

TITLE/FLIP	LABEL & NO.	GOOD	NEAR MINT	YR.
ALREADY GONE/Is It True?	(Asylum 11036)	.50	2.00	74
BEST OF MY LOVE/Ol' 55	(Asylum 45218)	.50	2.00	74
HEARTACHE TONIGHT/Teenage Jail	(Asylum 46545)	.50	2.00	79
HOTEL CALIFORNIA/Pretty Maids All In A Row	(Asylum 45386)	.50	2.00	77
JAMES DEAN/Good Day In Hell	(Asylum 45202)	.50	2.00	74
LIFE IN THE FAST LANE/TheLast Resort	(Asylum 45403)	.50	2.00	77
LONG RUN, THE/The Disco Strangler	(Asylum 46569)	.50	2.00	79
LYIN EYES/Too Many Hands	(Asylum 45279)	.50	2.00	75
NEW KID IN TOWN/Victim Of Love	(Asylum 45373)	.50	2.00	76
ONE OF THESE NIGHTS/Visions	(Asylum 45257)	.50	2.00	75
OUTLAW MAN/Certain Kind Of Fool	(Asylum 11025)	.50	2.00	73
PEACEFUL EASY FEELING/Trying	(Asylum 11013)	.50	2.00	72
PLEASE COME HOME FOR CHRISTMAS/Funky New Year	(Asylum 45555)	.50	2.00	78
TAKE IT EASY/Get You In The Mood	(Asylum 11005)	.50	2.00	72
TAKE IT TO THE LIMIT/After The Thrill Is Gone	(Asylum 45293)	.50	2.00	75
TEQUILA SUNRISE/Twenty One	(Asylum 11017)	.50	2.00	73
WITCHY WOMAN/Early Bird	(Asylum 11008)	.50	2.00	72

EAGLES, The

TITLE/FLIP	LABEL & NO.	GOOD	NEAR MINT	YR.
I TOLD MYSELF/What A Crazy Feeling	(Mercury 70524)	1.25	5.00	55
SUCH A FOOL/Don't You Wanna Be Mine	(Mercury 70464)	1.25	5.00	54
TRYIN' TO GET TO YOU/Please Please	(Mercury 70391)	1.25	5.00	54

EAGLES, The

TITLE/FLIP	LABEL & NO.	GOOD	NEAR MINT	YR.
CHRISTINE/Stalactite (Instrumentals)	(Smash 1837)	.75	3.00	63

EARL-JEAN (Earl-Jean McCree)

TITLE/FLIP	LABEL & NO.	GOOD	NEAR MINT	YR.
I'M INTO SOMETHIN' GOOD/We Love & Learn	(Colpix 729)	.75	3.00	64
RANDY/They're Jealous of Me	(Colpix 748)	.75	3.00	64

Also see Cookies, The

TITLE/FLIP	LABEL & NO.	GOOD	NEAR MINT	YR.
EARLS, The (Featuring Larry Chance)				
ALL THROUGH OUR TEENS/Whoever You Are	(Rome 114)	1.50	6.00	76
(Colored plastic)				
ALL THROUGH OUR TEENS/Whoever You Are	(Rome 114)	.75	3.00	76
(Reissue of early sixties recordings.)				
DADDY'S HOME/If I Could Do It Once Again	(Bo-P-C 45-100)	.75	3.00	
(Shown as by Jimmy Cee & the Earls)				
EYES/Look My Way	(Old Town 1141)	1.25	5.00	63
GET ON UP & DANCE THE CONTINENTAL/ Love Epidemic	(Woodbury 1000)	2.00	8.00	76
(10" single issue)				
GOIN' UPTOWN/Mrs. Woman	(Columbia 3-10225)	1.00	4.00	76
I BELIEVE/Don't Forget	(Old Town 1149)	3.75	15.00	63
(Solid blue label)				
I BELIEVE/Don't Forget	(Old Town 1149)	2.00	8.00	63
(Multi-colored label)				
I BELIEVE/Don't Forget	(Barry BRY-1021)	.75	3.00	63
IF I COULD DO IT OVER AGAIN/Papa	(Mr. "G" 801)	2.00	8.00	
IT'S BEEN A LONG TIME COMING/My Lonely Lonely Room	(ABC 11109)	2.00	8.00	68
KISSIN'/Cry Cry Cry	(Old Town 1145)	1.25	5.00	63
LIFE IS BUT A DREAM/It's You	(Rome 101)	3.75	15.00	61
LIFE IS BUT A DREAM/Without You	(Rome 101)	2.50	10.00	61
LITTLE BOY & GIRL/Lost Love	(Rome 112)	1.50	6.00	76
(Colored plastic)				
LITTLE BOY & GIRL/Lost Love	(Rome 112)	.75	3.00	76
(Reissue of early sixties recordings.)				
LOOKIN' FOR MY BABY/Cross My Heart	(Rome 102)	2.50	10.00	61
MY HEART'S DESIRE/I'll Never Cry	(Rome R-5117)	3.75	15.00	62
NEVER/I Keep A Telling You	(Old Town 1133)	1.00	4.00	63
OH WHAT A TIME/Ask Anybody	(Old Town 1169)	2.00	8.00	64
REMEMBER ME BABY/Amor	(Old Town 1182)	1.50	6.00	65
REMEMBER ME BABY/Amor	(Old Town 1181)	3.00	12.00	65
(Promotional copy. Label error showed catalog number as 1181.)				
REMEMBER THEN/Let's Waddle	(Old Town 1230)	.75	3.00	63
STORMY WEATHER/ Could This Be Magic (By the Pretenders)	(Rome 111)	.75	3.00	76
(Reissue of early sixties recordings.)				
TONIGHT (COULD BE THE NIGHT)/Meditation	(Woodbury 101)	.75	3.00	77
TONIGHT (COULD BE THE NIGHT)/Meditation	(Woodbury 101)	1.50	6.00	77
(12" single issue)				
EARTH OPERA, The				
COME TO YOU/Alfie Finney	(Elektra 45650)	.75	3.00	67
EARTHQUAKE				
BRIGHT LIGHTS/Bright Lights	(A&M 1365)	1.00	4.00	72
FRIDAY ON MY MIND/Tall Order For A Short Guy	(Beserkley 5737)	1.00	4.00	
I GET THE SWEETEST FEELING/Live & Let Live	(A&M 1338)	1.00	4.00	72
KICKS/Trainride	(Beserkley 5747)	1.00	4.00	
MR. SECURITY/Madness	(Beserkley 5734)	1.00	4.00	72
TICKLER/Guarding You	(A&M 1301)	1.00	4.00	
EASTWOOD, Clint				
COWBOY WEDDING SONG/Rowdy	(Cameo 240)	.75	3.00	62
UNKNOWN GIRL OF MY DREAMS/For All We Know	(Gothic 005)	.75	3.00	
WHEN I LOVED HER/Burning Bridges	(Certron 10010)	.75	3.00	
EASY RIDERS, The: see Gilkyson, Terry				
EASYBEATS, The				
COME IN, YOU'LL GET PNEUMONIA/ Hello, How Are You	(United Artists 50289)	1.00	4.00	68
FALLING OFF THE EDGE OF THE WORLD/ Remember Sam	(United Artists 50187)	1.00	4.00	67
FRIDAY ON MY MIND/ Made My Bed: Gonna Lie In It	(United Artists 50106)	.75	3.00	67
GONNA HAVE A GOOD TIME/Lay Me Down & Die	(United Artists 50488)	1.00	4.00	69
HEAVEN & HELL/Pretty Girl	(United Artists 50187)	1.00	4.00	67
IN MY BOOK/Make You Feel Alright (Woman)	(Ascot 2214)	2.00	8.00	66
ST. LOUIS/Can't Find Love	(Rare Earth 5009)	1.00	4.00	69
Also see Flash In The Pan				
EATON, Sally				
BREATHIN' IS BELIEVIN'/I Can Afford	(Paramount 0114)	.50	2.00	73
EBB TIDES, The				
LOW TIDE/A Ballad Of Jed Clampett	(R & R 303)	.75	3.00	62
EBBS, The				
CARTOONS/Vickie Sue	(Dore 521)	1.00	4.00	59
EBBTIDES, The				
COME ON & CRY/Straightaway	(Monument 520)	.75	3.00	62
EBBTONES, The				
BAM INDUCTION/Rockin' On The Range	(Part 70026)	1.00	4.00	63
SURFING BOOP-BOOP-ADO/King Of Lovers	(Dot 16577)	1.00	4.00	64
EBSEN, Buddy: see Parker, Fess				
ECHOES, The				
ANGEL OF LOVE/Twistin' Town	(Felsted 8614)	1.50	6.00	61
ANGEL OF MY HEART/Gee Oh Gee	(Seg-way 1002)	1.50	6.00	60
BABY BLUE/Boomerang	(SRG 101)	2.50	10.00	61
BABY BLUE/Boomerang	(Seg-way 103)	1.50	6.00	61
BYE-BYE MY BABY/Do I Love You	(Columbia 41549)	1.00	4.00	60
I LOVE CANDY/Paper Roses	(Ascot 2188)	2.50	10.00	61
LOVING & LOSING/Ecstasy	(Columbia 4-41709)	1.00	4.00	60
SAD EYES/It's Rainin'	(Seg-Way 106)	1.50	6.00	61

TITLE/FLIP	LABEL & NO.	GOOD	NEAR MINT	YR.
ECHOES, The				
ANNABELLE LEE/If Love Is	(Smash 1850)	1.00	4.00	63
BLUEBIRDS OVER THE MOUNTAIN/ A Chicken Ain't Nothin' But A Bird	(Smash 1766)	1.00	4.00	62
KEEP AN EYE ON HER/A Million Miles From Nowhere	(Smash 1807)	1.00	4.00	63
ECHOES, The (Don Robertson & Bonnie Guitar)				
BORN TO BE WITH YOU/My Guiding Light	(Dolton 18)	1.00	4.00	60
ECHOES, The: see Innocents, The				
ECHOMORES, The (Featuring Lee Wagoner)				
CUTE CHICK/Little Chick	(Rocket 1042)	2.50	10.00	
ECKSTINE, Billy				
BE MY LOVE/Only A Moment Ago	(MGM 10799)	1.25	5.00	50
BITTER WITH THE SWEET, THE/Grapevine	(RCA Victor 47-6436)	1.00	4.00	56
COUQUETTE/Fool In Love	(MGM 11439)	1.25	5.00	53
DON'T GET AROUND MUCH ANYMORE/Lost In Loveliness	(MGM 11694)	1.25	5.00	53
EVERYTHING I HAVE IS YOURS/Darling, Why Did You	(Mercury 72128)	.75	3.00	63
GATHER YOUR DREAMS/Love Is A Ball	(Mercury 72106)	.75	3.00	63
(With Damita Jo)				
I APOLOGIZE/Bring Back The Thrill	(MGM 10903)	1.25	5.00	51
I WANT TO BE LOVED/Stardust	(MGM 10716)	1.25	5.00	50
IF/When You Return	(MGM 10896)	1.25	5.00	51
IS ANYONE HERE GOIN' MY WAY/Thank You Love	(Motown 1120)	.75	3.00	68
I'M SO CRAZY FOR LOVE/I Guess I'll Have To Go	(MGM 10856)	1.25	5.00	51
JALOUSIE/Strange Interlude	(MGM 11111)	1.25	5.00	51
KISS OF FIRE/Never Like This	(MGM 11225)	1.25	5.00	52
LA DE DO DE DO (THE HONEY BUG SONG)/ Farewell To Romance	(MGM 12105)	1.00	4.00	55
LOVE ME/One Sweet Kiss	(MGM 11855)	1.25	5.00	54
MY FOOLISH HEART/Sure Thing	(MGM 10623)	1.25	5.00	50
MY HEART SAYS NO/Joey, Joey, Joey	(RCA Victor 47-6488)	1.00	4.00	56
ONLY YOU/Love Me Or Leave me	(MGM 11984)	1.00	4.00	55
OUT OF MY MIND/My Fickle Heart	(MGM 12237)	1.00	4.00	56
PEOPLE/Sweet Georgia Brown	(Mercury 72264)	.75	3.00	64
SITTING BY THE WINDOW/Lost In A Dream	(MGM 10602)	1.25	5.00	50
TENNESSEE ROCK 'N ROLL/Condemned For Life	(RCA Victor 47-6524)	1.00	4.00	56
YOU'LL GET YOURS/Lonely Avenue	(MGM 12160)	1.00	4.00	56
ECSTASIES, The				
THAT LUCKY OLD SUN/A Time For Love	(Amy 853)	2.00	8.00	62
ECUADORS, The				
SAY YOU'LL BE MINE/Let Me Sleep, Woman	(Argo 5353)	1.00	4.00	60
EDDIE & BETTY (Eddie & Betty Cole)				
EMBARCADERO BOOGIE/ Give Up Your Twin Pipe Mother	(Warner Bros. 5079)	1.00	4.00	59
SWEET SOMEONE/One Little Dream Of You	(Six Thousand 601)	1.25	5.00	57
SWEET SOMEONE/You Took Your Love From Me	(Lark 4512)	1.00	4.00	59
(With Joe Darensbourg)				
SWEET SOMEONE/Saturday Night Fish Fry	(Warner Bros. 5054)	.75	3.00	59
EDDIE & THE EVERGREENS (Sha Na Na)				
IN THE STILL OF THE NIGHT/	(Kama Sutra 578)	1.00	4.00	73
EDDIE & THE HOT RODS				
DO ANYTHING YOU WANNA DO/ Ignore Them (Always Crashing In The Same Bar)	(Island 093)	.50	2.00	78
GET OUT OF DENVER/Teenage Depression	(Island 082)	.50	2.00	77
EDDIE & THE SHOWMEN				
FAR AWAY PLACES/Lanky Bones	(Liberty 55695)	1.00	4.00	64
MOVIN'/Mr. Rebel	(Liberty 55659)	1.00	4.00	64
SQUAD CAR/Scratch	(Liberty 55608)	1.00	4.00	63
TOES ON THE NOSE/Border Town	(Liberty 55566)	1.00	4.00	63
WE ARE THE YOUNG/Young & The Lonely	(Liberty 55720)	1.00	4.00	64
Instrumentals				
EDDIE, Jason, & The Centermen				
SINGING THE BLUES/True To You	(Capitol 5727)	.75	3.00	66
EDDIE, PAUL & STEVE				
FATTY THE DEALER/I Came To You First	(Crook 101)	1.50	6.00	
EDDY, Duane				
AVENGER, THE/Londonderry Air	(Jamie 1206)	1.00	4.00	61
BALLAD OF PALADIN, THE/The Wild Westerner	(RCA Victor 47-8047)	.75	3.00	61
BECAUSE THEY'RE YOUNG/Rebel Walk	(Jamie 1156)	.75	3.00	60
BECAUSE THEY'RE YOUNG/Rebel Walk	(Jamie 1156)	2.00	8.00	60
(Picture sleeve)				
BONNIE COME BACK/Lost Island	(Jamie 1144)	1.00	4.00	59
BONNIE COME BACK/Lost Island	(Jamie 1144)	2.50	10.00	59
(Picture sleeve)				
BOSS GUITAR/Desert Rat	(RCA Victor 47-8131)	.75	3.00	63
(With the Rebelettes)				
CANNONBALL/Mason-Dixon Line	(Jamie 1111)	1.00	4.00	58
CARAVAN (PART 1)/Caravan (Part 2)	(Gregmark 5)	1.00	4.00	61
(Shown as by Duane Eddy but was actually performed by Al Casey.)				
(DANCE WITH THE) GUITAR MAN/Stretchin' Out	(RCA Victor 47-8087)	.75	3.00	62
(With the Rebelettes)				
DAYDREAM/This Guitar Was Made For Twangin'	(Reprise 0504)	1.00	4.00	66
DEEP IN THE HEART OF TEXAS/Saints & Sinners	(RCA Victor 47-7999)	.75	3.00	62
DON'T THINK TWICE, IT'S ALRIGHT/ House Of The Rising Sun	(Colpix 788)	1.00	4.00	66

TITLE/FLIP	LABEL & NO.	GOOD	NEAR MINT	YR.
DON'T THINK TWICE, IT'S ALRIGHT/ House Of The Rising Sun	(Colpix 788)	5.00	20.00	66
(Picture sleeve)				
DRIVIN' HOME/Tammy	(Jamie 1195)	.75	3.00	61
DRIVIN' HOME/Tammy	(Jamie 1195)	2.50	10.00	61
(Picture sleeve)				
EL RANCHO GRANDE/Poppa's Movin' On	(Colpix 795)	1.00	4.00	66
FIVE-SEVENTEEN, THE/Something	(Uni 55237)	1.00	4.00	70
FORTY MILES OF BAD ROAD/The Quiet Three	(Jamie 1126)	1.00	4.00	59
FORTY MILES OF BAD ROAD/The Quiet Three	(Jamie 1126)	2.50	10.00	59
(Picture sleeve)				
FORTY MILES OF BAD ROAD/The Quiet Three	(Jamie 1126)	3.00	12.00	59
(Stereo single issue)				
FREIGHT TRAIN/Put A Little Love In Your Heart	(Congress 6010)	.75	3.00	70

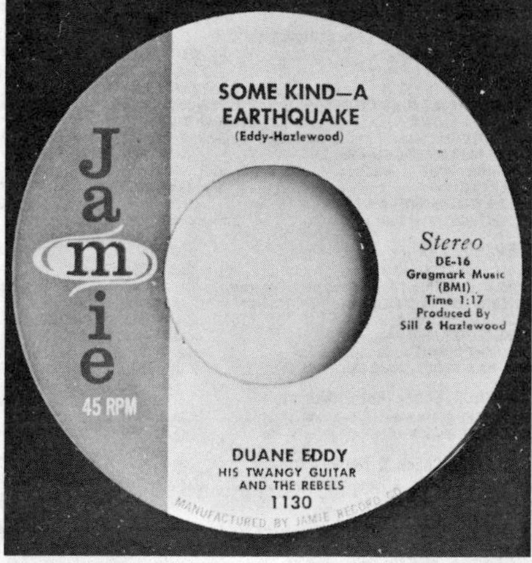

TITLE/FLIP	LABEL & NO.	GOOD	NEAR MINT	YR.
GIRL ON DEATH ROW, THE/Words Mean Nothing	(Jamie 1158)	.75	3.00	60
GUITAR CHILD/Jerky Jalopy	(RCA Victor 47-8335)	1.00	4.00	64
(With the Rebelettes)				
GUITAR ON MY MIND (With Mirriam Eddy)/ Wicked Woman From Wickenburg	(Reprise 0622)	1.00	4.00	67
GUITAR STAR/The Iguana	(RCA Victor 47-8442)	1.00	4.00	64
KOMMOTION/(Theme From) Moon Children	(Jamie 1163)	.75	3.00	60
KOMMOTION/(Theme From) Moon Children	(Jamie 1163)	2.00	8.00	60
(Picture sleeve)				
LONELY BOY, LONELY GUITAR/Joshin'	(RCA Victor 47-8180)	1.00	4.00	63
LONELY ONE, THE/Detour	(Jamie 1117)	1.00	4.00	59
LONELY ONE, THE/Detour	(Jamie 1117)	3.00	12.00	59
(Stereo single issue)				
MONSOON/Roarin'	(Reprise 0557)	1.00	4.00	66
MOONSHOT/Roughneck	(RCA Victor 47-8507)	1.00	4.00	65
MOVIN' & GROOVIN'/Up & Down	(Jamie 1101)	1.25	5.00	58
MY BLUE HEAVEN/Along Came Linda	(Jamie 1200)	.75	3.00	61
NIGHTLY NEWS/Renegade	(Big Tree 157)	1.00	4.00	72
NIKI HOKEY/Velvet Nights (Theme from Elvira Madigan)	(Reprise 0690)	1.00	4.00	68
PEPE/Lost Friend	(Jamie 1175)	.75	3.00	60
PEPE/Lost Friend	(Jamie 1175)	2.50	10.00	60
(Red picture sleeve)				
PEPE/Lost Friend	(Jamie 1175)	2.00	8.00	60
(Yellow picture sleeve)				
PETER GUNN/Along The Navajo Trail	(Jamie 1168)	.75	3.00	60
RAMROD/Caravan	(Ford 500)	5.00	20.00	57
(With the Rock-a-billies)				
RAMROD/The Walker	(Jamie 1109)	1.00	4.00	58
REBEL ROUSER/Stalkin'	(Jamie 1104)	1.00	4.00	58
RENEGADE/Nightly News	(Big Tree 157)	.75	3.00	72
RING OF FIRE/Bobbie	(Jamie 1187)	.75	3.00	61
RING OF FIRE/Bobbie	(Jamie 1187)	2.00	8.00	61
(Picture sleeve)				
RUNAWAY PONY/Just Because	(Jamie 1224)	1.00	4.00	62
SHAZAM!/The Secret Seven	(Jamie 1151)	1.00	4.00	60
SHAZAM!/The Secret Seven	(Jamie 1151)	2.50	10.00	60
(Picture sleeve)				
SOME KIND-A EARTHQUAKE/First Love, First Tears	(Jamie 1130)	1.00	4.00	59
SOME KIND-A EARTHQUAKE/First Love, First Tears	(Jamie 1130)	2.50	10.00	59
(Picture sleeve)				
SOME KIND-A EARTHQUAKE/First Love, First Tears	(Jamie 1130)	3.00	12.00	59
(Stereo single issue)				
SON OF A REBEL 'ROUSER, THE/ The Story Of Three Loves	(RCA Victor 47-8276)	1.00	4.00	63
SOUTH PHOENIX/Trash	(Colpix 779)	1.00	4.00	65
THEME FROM DIXIE/Gidget Goes Hawaiian	(Jamie 1183)	.75	3.00	61
THEME FROM DIXIE/Gidget Goes Hawaiian	(Jamie 1183)	2.00	8.00	61
(Picture sleeve)				
THIS GUITAR WAS MADE FOR TWANGIN'/Daydream	(Reprise 504)	.75	3.00	66
THIS TOWN/There Is A Mountain	(Reprise 0662)	1.00	4.00	68

TITLE/FLIP	LABEL & NO.	GOOD	NEAR MINT	YR.
TRAMBONE/The Battle	(Jamie 1209)	1.00	4.00	61
WATER SKIING/(Theme From) A Summer Place	(RCA Victor 47-8376)	1.00	4.00	64
YEP!/3:30 Blues	(Jamie 1122)	1.00	4.00	59
YEP!/3:30 Blues	(Jamie 1122)	2.50	10.00	59
(Picture sleeve)				
YOU ARE MY SUNSHINE/7 To 8	(Elektra 45359)	.75	3.00	77
(Shown as by "Duane Eddy Featuring Deed & Some Very Good Friends." Deed is Kim Vassy of the Back Portch Majority, and among the "Good Friends" are Waylon Jennings & Willie Nelson.)				
YOUR BABY'S GONE SURFIN'/Shuckin'	(RCA Victor 47-8214)	1.00	4.00	63

Most Duane Eddy releases were instrumentals. On those vocals that are shown as being with the Rebelettes, it should be noted that this group was actually the Blossoms.
Also see Jimmy & Duane

EDDY, Jim

TITLE/FLIP	LABEL & NO.	GOOD	NEAR MINT	YR.
TEEN AGE ANGEL/Everglades	(Dore 537)	1.00	4.00	59

EDE, Dave, & The Rabin Band

TITLE/FLIP	LABEL & NO.	GOOD	NEAR MINT	YR.
TWISTIN' THOSE MEECES TO PIECES/Twistin' The Trad	(Rust 5047)	1.00	4.00	62

EDELMAN, Randy

TITLE/FLIP	LABEL & NO.	GOOD	NEAR MINT	YR.
CAN'T IT ALL BE LOVE/Sentimental Fools	(Arista 0268)	.50	2.00	77
CONCRETE & CLAY/	(20th Century 2274)	.50	2.00	76
EVERYBODY WANTS TO FIND A BLUEBIRD/ Pistol Packin' Melody	(20th Century 2155)	.50	2.00	75
FRESH OUT'A LOVE/Bring The Baby In With The Bacon	(20th Century 2245)	.50	2.00	75
IF THIS IS LOVE/	(Arista 0393)	.50	2.00	79
MEXICO/	(Lion 144)	.75	3.00	73
TAKE MY HAND/Today (June Song)	(Arista 0309)	.50	2.00	77
YOU'RE THE ONE/	(Arista 0434)	.50	2.00	79

EDEN ROCKERS, The

TITLE/FLIP	LABEL & NO.	GOOD	NEAR MINT	YR.
CRUISE, THE/Wasted	(Cannady 100)	1.00	4.00	59

EDEN ROCS, The

TITLE/FLIP	LABEL & NO.	GOOD	NEAR MINT	YR.
EDEN ROCK/Walkin' With Satan	(Nugget 1006)	1.00	4.00	59

EDGE, Graeme (With Graeme Edge & Adrian Gurvitz)

TITLE/FLIP	LABEL & NO.	GOOD	NEAR MINT	YR.
EVERYBODY NEEDS SOMEONE/Be My Eyes	(London 1071)	.50	2.00	77
WE LIKE TO DO IT/Shotgun	(Threshold 67018)	.75	3.00	74

Also see Gun
Also see Moody Blues

EDISON LIGHTHOUSE

TITLE/FLIP	LABEL & NO.	GOOD	NEAR MINT	YR.
IT'S UP TO YOU, PETULA/Lets Make It Up	(Bell 960)	.50	2.00	70
LOVE GROWS (WHERE MY ROSEMARY GOES)/Every Lonely Day	(Bell 868)	.50	2.00	70

EDITORS, The

TITLE/FLIP	LABEL & NO.	GOOD	NEAR MINT	YR.
MY SON THE BED BUG/	(Dexter 101)	2.00	8.00	64
(Beatle novelty)				

EDMUNDS, Dave (Of Love Sculputure)

TITLE/FLIP	LABEL & NO.	GOOD	NEAR MINT	YR.
BABY I LOVE YOU/Maybe	(RCA 74-0882)	1.00	4.00	73
BLUE MONDAY/I'll Get Along	(MAM 3611)	1.00	4.00	71
BORN TO BE WITH YOU/Pick Axe Rag	(RCA APBO-5000)	1.00	4.00	73
CRAWLING FROM THE WRECKAGE/Queen Of Hearts	(Swan Song 71002)	.50	2.00	79
GET OUT OF DENVER/	(Swan Song 70116)	.75	3.00	77
GIRLS TALK/The Creature From The Black Lagoon	(Swan Song 71001)	.50	2.00	79
I HEAR YOU KNOCKING/Black Bill	(MAM 3601)	.75	3.00	70
I'M COMING HOME/Country Roll	(MAM 3608)	1.00	4.00	71
LITTLE DARLIN'/I Knew The Bride	(Swan Song 70113)	.75	3.00	77
NEED A SHOT OF RHYTHM & BLUES/Let It Be Me	(RCA PB-10118)	1.00	4.00	74
TROUBLE BOYS/What Looks Best On You	(Swan Song 70118)	.50	2.00	78

EDWARD BEAR

TITLE/FLIP	LABEL & NO.	GOOD	NEAR MINT	YR.
CLOSE YOUR EYES/Cachet County	(Capitol 3581)	.50	2.00	73
DOES YOUR MOTHER KNOW/Coming Home Christmas	(Capitol 3780)	.50	2.00	73
FREEDOM FOR THE STALLION/Why Won't You Marry Me?	(Capitol 3978)	.50	2.00	74
LAST SONG/Best Friend	(Capitol 3452)	.50	2.00	72
SAME OLE FEELING/Fool	(Capitol 3804)	.50	2.00	74
YOU CAN'T DENY IT/	(Capitol 2955)	.50	2.00	70
YOU, ME & MEXICO/Sinking Ship	(Capitol 2801)	.50	2.00	70

EDWARDS, Bobby (Robert Moncrief)

TITLE/FLIP	LABEL & NO.	GOOD	NEAR MINT	YR.
WHAT'S THE REASON/Walk Away Slowly	(Capitol 4674)	.75	3.00	61
YOU'RE THE REASON/I'm A Fool For Loving You	(Crest 1075)	.75	3.00	61

EDWARDS, Chuck, & The Five Crowns

TITLE/FLIP	LABEL & NO.	GOOD	NEAR MINT	YR.
IF I WERE KING/Lucy & Jimmy Got Married	(Alanna 557)	1.25	5.00	59

EDWARDS, Cliff

TITLE/FLIP	LABEL & NO.	GOOD	NEAR MINT	YR.
WHEN YOU WISH UPON A STAR/Give A Little Whistle	(Decca 9-29487)	2.50	10.00	55

(Known as "Ukulele Ike" in the early days of radio. Edwards was also the voice of Jiminy Cricket, for Walt Disney. This record, done in the voice of Jiminy, was the theme song for the "Wonderful World of Disney" TV show - as well as from the film "Pinocchio.")

EDWARDS, Jimmy (Jimmy Bullington)

TITLE/FLIP	LABEL & NO.	GOOD	NEAR MINT	YR.
LOVE BUG CRAWL/Honey Lovin'	(Mercury 71209)	1.00	4.00	57

EDWARDS, Johnny, & The White Caps

TITLE/FLIP	LABEL & NO.	GOOD	NEAR MINT	YR.
ROCK & ROLL SADDLES/	(Northland 7002)	2.00	8.00	

EDWARDS, Jonathan

TITLE/FLIP	LABEL & NO.	GOOD	NEAR MINT	YR.
CAROLINA CAROLINE/ Never Together (But Close Sometimes)	(Warner Bros. 8364)	.50	2.00	77
EVERYBODY KNOWS HER/Train To Glory	(Atco 6881)	.75	3.00	72
HONKY TONK STARDUST COWBOY/	(Atco 6920)	.75	3.00	73
STOP & START IT ALL AGAIN/	(Atco 6911)	.75	3.00	72
SUNSHINE/Emma	(Capricorn 8021)	.75	3.00	71

EDWARDS, Tom

TITLE/FLIP	LABEL & NO.	GOOD	NEAR MINT	YR.
GOOD NIGHT ROCK & ROLL/Spirit Of Seventeen	(Coral 61938)	1.00	4.00	57
WHAT IS A TEENAGE GIRL?/What Is A Teenage Boy?	(Coral 61773)	1.00	4.00	57

EDWARDS, Tommy

TITLE/FLIP	LABEL & NO.	GOOD	NEAR MINT	YR.
BABY, LET ME TAKE YOU DREAMING/My Sweetheart	(MGM K-12095)	1.00	4.00	55
BEGGER IN LOVE/I'll Never Know Why	(MGM K-10973)	1.25	5.00	51
DON'T FENCE ME IN/I'm Building Castles	(MGM K-12871)	.75	3.00	60
DON'T FENCE ME IN/I'm Building Castles	(MGM SK-12871)	1.50	6.00	60
(Stereo single issue)				
FORGIVE ME/The Bridge	(MGM K-11170)	1.25	5.00	51
FRIEND OF JOHNNY'S/Once There Lived A Fool	(MGM K-10884)	1.25	5.00	51
GYPSY HEART/Operetta	(MGM K-10921)	1.25	5.00	51
HONESTLY & TRULY/(New In) The Ways Of Love	(MGM K-12837)	1.00	4.00	59
HONESTLY & TRULY/(New In) The Ways Of Love	(MGM SK-12837)	2.00	8.00	59
(Stereo single issue)				
HOW HIGH THE MOON/Cowboy Rhumba	(Columbia 4-38950)	2.50	10.00	50
I REALLY DON'T WANT TO KNOW/Unloved	(MGM K-12890)	.75	3.00	60
IT'S CHRISTMAS ONCE AGAIN/Everyday Is Christmas	(MGM K-11624)	1.25	5.00	53
IT'S ALL IN THE GAME/All Over Again	(MGM K-11035)	2.50	10.00	51
IT'S ALL IN THE GAME/Please Love Me Forever	(MGM K-12688)	.75	3.00	58
IT'S NOT THE END OF EVERYTHING/Blue Heartaches	(MGM K-12916)	.75	3.00	60
I'VE BEEN THERE/I Looked At Heaven	(MGM K-12814)	.75	3.00	59
I'VE BEEN THERE/I Looked At Heaven	(MGM SK-12814)	1.50	6.00	59
(Stereo single issue)				
JOKER, THE (IN THE CARD GAME OF LIFE)/ Within My Heart	(MGM K-11718)	1.25	5.00	54
KRIS KRINGLE/Christmas Is For Children	(MGM K-11097)	1.25	5.00	51
LINGER IN MY ARMS/If You Would Love Me Again	(MGM K-11763)	1.25	5.00	54
LOVE IS A CHILD/There Must Be A Way To Your Heart	(MGM K-12248)	1.00	4.00	56
LOVE IS ALL WE NEED/Mr. Music Man	(MGM K-12722)	1.00	4.00	58
LOVE IS ALL WE NEED/Mr. Music Man	(MGM SK-12722)	2.00	8.00	58
(Stereo single issue)				
MORNING SIDE OF THE MOUNTAIN, THE/F'R Instance	(MGM K-10989)	2.00	8.00	51
MY GIRL/Piano, Bass & Drums	(MGM K-11209)	1.25	5.00	52
MY MELANCHOLY BABY/It's Only The Good Times	(MGM K-12794)	.75	3.00	59
MY MELANCHOLY BABY/It's Only The Good Times	(MGM SK-12794)	1.50	6.00	59
(Stereo single issue)				
NOW & THEN THERE'S A FOOL/I Can't Love	(MGM K-11395)	1.25	5.00	53
PLEASE MR. SUN/Where I May Live With You	(MGM K-11134)	2.00	8.00	51
PLEASE MR. SUN/The Morning Side Of The Mountain	(MGM K-12757)	.75	3.00	59
PLEASE MR. SUN/Morning Side Of The Mountain	(MGM SK-50112)	1.50	6.00	59
(Stereo single issue)				
SO LITTLE TIME/Blue Bird	(MGM K-11582)	1.25	5.00	53
TAKE THESE CHAINS FROM MY HEART/Paging Mr. Martin	(MGM K-11485)	1.25	5.00	53
TEARDROP ON A ROSE/To Those Who Wait	(MGM K-12054)	1.00	4.00	55
THAT'S ALL/Secret Love	(MGM K-11604)	1.25	5.00	54
THAT'S THE WAY WITH LOVE/The Golden Chain	(MGM K-13002)	.75	3.00	61
THERE WAS A TIME/Wall Of Ice	(MGM K-11668)	1.25	5.00	53
WELCOME TO MY WORLD/ Spring Never Came Around This Year	(MGM K-11993)	1.00	4.00	55
YOU WALK BY/I Have That Kind Of Heart	(MGM K-11821)	1.25	5.00	54
YOU WIN AGAIN/Sinner & Saint	(MGM K-11326)	1.25	5.00	52

"It's All In The Game," "Please Mr. Sun" and "The Morning Side Of The Mountain" were completely different recordings on the late fifties releases than they were on those from 1951.

EDWARDS, Vern

TITLE/FLIP	LABEL & NO.	GOOD	NEAR MINT	YR.
COOL, COOL BABY/Glenda	(Probe 100)	1.00	4.00	59

EDWARDS, Vince

TITLE/FLIP	LABEL & NO.	GOOD	NEAR MINT	YR.
DON'T WORRY 'BOUT ME/And Now	(Decca 9-31413)	.75	3.00	62
I GOT IT BAD (& THAT AIN'T GOOD)/Say It Isn't So	(Decca 9-31426)	.75	3.00	62
SQUEELIN' PARROT/Oh Babe	(Russ-Fi 1)	1.00	4.00	59
UNCHAINED MELODY/	(Decca 7-34074)	1.25	5.00	
(Stereo compact 33 single)				
WHY DID YOU LEAVE ME/Squeelin' Parrot (Twist)	(Russ-Fi 7001)	.75	3.00	62

EGAN, Joe (Of Stealer's Wheel)

TITLE/FLIP	LABEL & NO.	GOOD	NEAR MINT	YR.
FREEZE/The Last Farewell	(Ariola 7769)	.50	2.00	79

EGAN, Walter

TITLE/FLIP	LABEL & NO.	GOOD	NEAR MINT	YR.
HOT SUMMER NIGHTS/She's So Tough	(Columbia 3-10824)	.50	2.00	78
MAGNET & STEEL/Tunnel O' Love	(Columbia 3-10719)	.50	2.00	78
ONLY THE LUCKY/I'd Rather Have Fun	(Columbia 3-10531)	.50	2.00	77
THAT'S THAT/	(Columbia 1-11116)	.50	2.00	79
UNLOVED/Make It Alone	(Columbia 3-10916)	.50	2.00	79
WHEN I GET MY WHEELS/Waitin'	(Columbia 3-10591)	.50	2.00	77
YOU'RE THE ONE/Like You Do	(Columbia 1-11046)	.50	2.00	79

EGYPTIAN COMBO, The

TITLE/FLIP	LABEL & NO.	GOOD	NEAR MINT	YR.
GALE WINDS/Rockin' Little Egypt	(Norman 549)	.75	3.00	64
(Instrumentals)				

EL CHICANO

TITLE/FLIP	LABEL & NO.	GOOD	NEAR MINT	YR.
BROWN-EYED GIRL/	(Kapp-Gordo 2173)	.75	3.00	71
DANCIN' MAN/	(Shadybrook 45032)	.50	2.00	77
EL CAYUCO/You've Been Wrong So Long	(MCA 40240)	.50	2.00	74
ELEANOR RIGBY/Coming Home Baby	(Kapp-Gordo 2099)	.75	3.00	71
LAST TANGO IN PARIS/	(MCA 40021)	.50	2.00	73
LITTLE BROTHER/	(Shadybrook 1039)	.50	2.00	78
MIGHT AS WELL/Put On A Show	(MCA 40391)	.50	2.00	75
TELL HER SHE'S LOVELY/	(MCA 40164)	.50	2.00	73
VIVA TIRADO (PART 1)/Viva Tirado (Part 2)	(Gordo 703)	1.00	4.00	70
VIVA TORADO (PART 1)/Viva Torado (Part 2)	(Kapp-Gordo 2085)	.75	3.00	70
YOU CAN HAVE THE BEST OF EVERYTHING/ Follow The Apollo	(MCA 40359)	.50	2.00	75

EL CLOD

TITLE/FLIP	LABEL & NO.	GOOD	NEAR MINT	YR.
HE'S NOT A REBEL (Answer song)/Holiday In Havana	(Mercury 72082)	1.00	4.00	63
TIJUANA BORDER/Pedro's Piano Roll Twist	(Challenge 9159)	1.00	4.00	62
("Tijuana Border" is a "Wolverton Mountain" parody.)				
TIJUANA WATUSI/Gringo	(Vee Jay 647)	.75	3.00	65

EL DOMINGOS, The

TITLE/FLIP	LABEL & NO.	GOOD	NEAR MINT	YR.
EVENING BELLS/I'm Not Kidding You	(Kappa Rex 206)	2.00	8.00	
LUCKY ME, I'M IN LOVE/Made In Heaven	(Chelsea 1009)	3.75	15.00	
LUCKY ME, I'M IN LOVE/Made In Heaven	(Candelight 418)	1.00	4.00	

EL REYS, The

TITLE/FLIP	LABEL & NO.	GOOD	NEAR MINT	YR.
BEVERLY/Angalie	(Ideal 95388)	1.25	5.00	
DIAMONDS & PEARLS/Rocket of Love	(Ideal 94706)	1.25	5.00	

EL SIERROS, The

TITLE/FLIP	LABEL & NO.	GOOD	NEAR MINT	YR.
LIFE IS BUT A DREAM/Pretty Little Girl	(Times Square 101)	.75	3.00	
PICTURE OF LOVE/(Flip by the Youngtones)	(Times Square 36)	.75	3.00	
SUNDAY KIND OF LOVE/Daddie's Comin' Home	(Yussels 7702)	.75	3.00	

EL TONES, The

TITLE/FLIP	LABEL & NO.	GOOD	NEAR MINT	YR.
LIKE MATTIE/Lovin' With A Beat	(Cub 9011)	3.00	12.00	58

EL TORROS, The

TITLE/FLIP	LABEL & NO.	GOOD	NEAR MINT	YR.
LOVE IS LOVE/All The Tears Is Gone	(Fraternity 811)	3.75	15.00	

EL VENOS, The

TITLE/FLIP	LABEL & NO.	GOOD	NEAR MINT	YR.
GERALDINE/Now We're Together	(Groove 0170)	2.50	10.00	56
MY HEART BEATS FASTER/You Won't Be True	(Vik 0305)	3.00	12.00	57
MY HEART BEATS FASTER/You Won't Be True	(RCA Victor 47-8303)	1.25	5.00	64

ELASTIC OZ BAND, The

TITLE/FLIP	LABEL & NO.	GOOD	NEAR MINT	YR.
DO THE OZ/God Save Us (By Bill Elliot)	(Apple 1835)	.75	3.00	71

ELCHORDS, The (Featuring Butchy Saunders)

TITLE/FLIP	LABEL & NO.	GOOD	NEAR MINT	YR.
PEPPERMINT STICK/Gee I'm In Love	(Good 544)	3.00	12.00	58
(With horizontal lines)				
PEPPERMINT STICK/Gee I'm In Love	(Good 544)	1.50	6.00	58
(Without horizontal lines)				

Also see Little Butchie

ELDRIDGE, Billy

TITLE/FLIP	LABEL & NO.	GOOD	NEAR MINT	YR.
IT'S OVER/	(Vulco 1580)	1.00	4.00	

ELECTRAS, The

TITLE/FLIP	LABEL & NO.	GOOD	NEAR MINT	YR.
LITTLE GIRL OF MINE/Mary Mary	(Ruby Doo 2)	1.00	4.00	

ELECTRIC FLAG, The (With Buddy Miles)

TITLE/FLIP	LABEL & NO.	GOOD	NEAR MINT	YR.
DOCTOR OH DOCTOR (MASSIVE INFUSION)/	(Atlantic 3237)	.75	3.00	75
GROOVIN' IS EASY/Over Lovin' You	(Columbia 4-44307)	1.50	6.00	67
PETER'S TRIP/Green & Gold	(Sidewalk 929)	2.50	10.00	67
SUNNY/Soul Searchin'	(Columbia 4-44376)	1.25	5.00	67
SWEET SOUL MUSIC/Every Now & Then	(Atlantic 3222)	.75	3.00	74

ELECTRIC INDIAN, The

TITLE/FLIP	LABEL & NO.	GOOD	NEAR MINT	YR.
KEEM-O-SABE/Broad Street	(Marmaduke 4001)	2.00	8.00	69
KEEM-O-SABE/Broad Street	(United Artists 50563)	.75	3.00	69
LAND OF 1000 DANCES/Geronimo	(United Artists 50613)	.75	3.00	69

Instrumentals

ELECTRIC LIGHT ORCHESTRA, The (With Jeff Lynne)

TITLE/FLIP	LABEL & NO.	GOOD	NEAR MINT	YR.
BOY BLUE/Eldorado	(United Artists 634)	.75	3.00	75
CAN'T GET IT OUT OF MY HEAD/Illusions In G Major	(United Artists 573)	.75	3.00	74
CONFUSION/Poker	(Jet 5064)	.50	2.00	79
DAYBREAKER/Ma-Ma-Ma Belle	(United Artists 405)	.1.00	4.00	74
DON'T BRING ME DOWN/Dreaming Of 4000	(Jet 5060)	.50	2.00	79
DO YA/Nightrider	(United Artists 939)	.75	3.00	76
EVIL WOMAN/10538 Overture	(United Artists 729)	.75	3.00	75
IT'S OVER/The Whale	(Jet 5052)	.50	2.00	78
LAST TRAIN TO LONDON/Down Home Town	(Jet 5067)	.50	2.00	79
LIVIN' THING/Ma-Ma-Ma Belle	(United Artists 888)	.75	3.00	76
LIVIN' THING/	(Jet SP-137)	2.50	10.00	78
(Promotional 12" one-sided issue)				
MR. BLUE SKY/One Summer Dream	(Jet 5050)	.50	2.00	78
MR. BLUE SKY/Mr. Blue Sky	(Jet XSS-164392)	2.50	10.00	78
(Promotional 12" issue)				
10538 OVERTURE/Battle Of Marston Moor	(United Artists 50914)	.75	3.00	72
ROLL OVER BEETHOVEN/Queen Of The Hours	(United Artists 173)	.75	3.00	73
SHINE A LITTLE LOVE/Jungle	(Jet 5057)	.50	2.00	79
SHOWDOWN/In An Old England Town	(United Artists 337)	.75	3.00	73
STRANGE MAGIC/New World Rising	(United Artists 770)	.75	3.00	76
SWEET TALKIN' WOMAN/Fire On High	(Jet 1145)	.50	2.00	78
TELEPHONE LINE/Poorboy (The Greenwood)	(United Artists 1000)	.75	3.00	77
TURN TO STONE/Mister Kingdom	(Jet 1099)	.50	2.00	77

Also see Move, The

ELECTRIC PRUNES, The

TITLE/FLIP	LABEL & NO.	GOOD	NEAR MINT	YR.
AIN'T IT HARD/Little Olive	(Reprise 0473)	2.50	10.00	66
DR. DO GOOD/Hideaway	(Reprise 0594)	1.50	6.00	67
FINDERS, KEEPERS, LOSERS, WEEPERS/Love Grows	(Reprise 0858)	1.25	5.00	69
GET ME TO THE WORLD ON TIME/ Are You Lovin' Me More (But Enjoying It Less)	(Reprise 0564)	1.25	5.00	67
GREAT BANANA HOAX/Wind-Up Toys	(Reprise 0607)	1.50	6.00	67
HELP US/The Adoration	(Reprise 0305)	3.00	12.00	65
HEY MR. PRESIDENT/Flowing Smoothly	(Reprise 0805)	1.25	5.00	69
I HAD TOO MUCH TO DREAM (LAST NIGHT)/Luvin	(Reprise 0532)	1.25	5.00	66
SANCTUS/Credo	(Reprise PRO-277)	3.75	15.00	
(Promotional issue only)				
SELL/Violent Rose	(Reprise 0833)	1.25	5.00	69
YOU NEVER HAD IT BETTER/ Everybody Knows You're Not In Love	(Reprise 0652)	1.25	5.00	68

Also see Association, The

ELEGANT 4, The

TITLE/FLIP	LABEL & NO.	GOOD	NEAR MINT	YR.
TIME TO SAY GOODBYE/I'm Tired	(Cousins 1005)	2.00	8.00	61
TIME TO SAY GOODBYE/I'm Tired	(Mercury 72516)	.75	3.00	65

ELEGANT TASTE

TITLE/FLIP	LABEL & NO.	GOOD	NEAR MINT	YR.
CHAMPAGNE & CAVIAR/Elegant Taste	(Magna-Glide 5N-328)	.75	3.00	75

ELEGANTS, The (Featuring Vito Picone)

TITLE/FLIP	LABEL & NO.	GOOD	NEAR MINT	YR.
BELINDA/Lazy Love	(Laurie 3324)	1.25	5.00	65
(Shown as by Vito & the Elegants)				
DRESSIN' UP/A Dream Can Come True	(Photo 2662)	2.00	8.00	
DRESSIN' UP/A Dream Can Come True	(Photo 2662)	2.50	10.00	
(Picture sleeve)				
DRESSIN' UP/A Dream Can Come True	(Photo 2662)	2.00	8.00	
(Photo insert, orginally packaged inside picture sleeve)				
HAPPINESS/Spiral	(United Artists 295)	2.50	10.00	61
LETTER FROM VIET NAM, A/Barbara Beware	(Laurie 3283)	1.25	5.00	65
LET MY PRAYERS BE WITH YOU/Speak Low	(United Artists 230)	2.00	8.00	60
LITTLE BOY BLUE/Get Well Soon	(Hull 732)	5.00	20.00	60
LITTLE STAR/Getting Dizzy	(Apt 25005)	3.75	15.00	58
(Black label with silver letters)				
LITTLE STAR/Getting Dizzy	(Apt 25005)	1.00	4.00	58
(Multi-colored label)				
LONESOME WEEKEND/It's Just A Matter Of Time	(Bim Bam Boom 121)	2.00	8.00	
(Colored plastic)				
LONESOME WEEKEND/It's Just A Matter Of Time	(Bim Bam Boom 121)	.75	3.00	
PAYDAY/True Love Affair	(Apt 25029)	2.00	8.00	5
PLEASE BELIEVE ME/Goodnight	(Apt 25017)	2.00	8.00	5
TINY CLOUD/I've Seen Everything	(ABC-Paramount 10219)	2.00	8.00	6

TITLE/FLIP	LABEL & NO.	GOOD	NEAR MINT	YR.
WAKE UP/Bring Back Wendy	(Laurie 3298)	2.50	10.00	65
Also see Barbarians, The				
Also see Cordell, Pat, & the Crescents				
Also see Picone, Vito				
ELEGANTS, The				
I TRIED/Love Me & Don't Fool Around	(Elegants 101)	1.00	4.00	
ELEKTRAS, The				
ALL I WANT TO DO IS RUN/It Ain't As Easy As That.	(United Artists 594)	1.00	4.00	63
ELEPHANTS MEMORY, The				
CROSSROADS OF THE STEPPING STONES/ Jungle Gym At The Zoo	(Buddah 98)	.75	3.00	69
LIBERATION SPECIAL/Power Boogie	(Apple 1854)	.75	3.00	72
MONGOOSE/I Couldn't Dream	(Metromedia 182)	.75	3.00	70
ROCK 'N' ROLL STREAKER/Angels Forever	(RCA 0268)	.50	2.00	74
SKYSCRAPER COMMANDO/	(Metromedia 210)	.75	3.00	71
ELF				
HOOCHIE KOOCHIE LADY/	(Epic 10933)	.75	3.00	72
L.A. 59/	(MGM 14752)	.75	3.00	71
Also see Blackmore's Rainbow				

TITLE/FLIP	LABEL & NO.	GOOD	NEAR MINT	YR.
ELGART, Les				
BANDSTAND BOOGIE/ When Yuba Plays The Rhumba On The Tuba	(Columbia 40180)	3.75	15.00	54
(This was the instrumental theme for "American Bandstand")				
BANDSTAND TWIST/	(Columbia 56767)	1.25	5.00	62
(Promotional issue only)				
ELGINS, The				
PICTURE OF YOU, A/Mademoiselle	(MGM K-12670)	3.00	12.00	58
ELGINS, The				
HERE IN MY HEART/We're Gonna Have A Good Time	(Congress 225)	2.50	10.00	64
ELIGIBLES, The (With Al Capp)				
CAR TROUBLE/I Wrote A Song	(Capitol 4203)	1.00	4.00	59
SEE WHAT YOU CAN DO FOR ME/Gabie	(Warner Bros. 5344)	.75	3.00	63
WALKIN' WITH MY BABY/Big Day	(Courtney 712)	.75	3.00	63
ELITES, The				
NORTHERN STAR/The Little Chapel	(Abel 225)	1.50	6.00	59
ELITES, The				
YOU MEAN SO MUCH TO ME/	(Hi-lite 106)	1.00	4.00	
ELLEDGE, Jimmy				
BO DIDDLEY/Diamonds	(RCA Victor 47-8042)	.75	3.00	62
FUNNY HOW TIME SLIPS AWAY/ Hey Jimmy, Joe, John, Jim, Jack	(RCA Victor 47-7946)	.75	3.00	61
ELLIMAN, Yvonne				
CAN'T FIND MY WAY HOME/ I Would Have Had A Good Time	(Decca 32949)	.75	3.00	71
COULD WE START AGAIN PLEASE (With Michael Jason)/ Heaven On Their Minds (By Ben Vereen)	(Decca 33018)	.75	3.00	72
EVERYTHING'S ALRIGHT/ Heaven On Their Minds (By various artists)	(Decca 32870)	.75	3.00	71
FROM THE INSIDE/	(RSO 511)	.50	2.00	74
HELLO STRANGER/She'll Be The Home	(RSO 871)	.50	2.00	77
I CAN'T GET YOU OUTTA MY MIND/I Know	(RSO 877)	.50	2.00	77
I DON'T KNOW HOW TO LOVE HIM/ Overture: Jesus Christ Superstar (Orchestra)	(Decca 32785)	.75	3.00	71
IF I CAN'T HAVE YOU/Good Sign	(RSO 884)	.50	2.00	77
LOVE ME/(I Don't Know Why) I Keep Hangin' On	(RSO 858)	.75	3.00	76
LOVE PAINS/Rock Me Slowly	(RSO 1007)	.50	2.00	79
MOMENT BY MOMENT/Sailing Ships	(RSO 915)	.50	2.00	78
SAVANNAH/Up To The Man In You	(RSO 905)	.50	2.00	78
WALK RIGHT IN/Small Town Talk	(RSO 517)	.50	2.00	75
Also see Jesus Christ Superstar				
ELLIN, David: see David & Freddie				
ELLIOT, Bill, & The Elastic Oz Band (With John Lennon)				
GOD SAVE US (With John Lennon)/ Do The Oz (By John Lennon & The Elastic Oz Band)	(Apple 1835)	.75	3.00	71
ELLIOT, Bern, & The Fenmen				
MONEY/Nobody But Me	(London 9722)	.75	3.00	63
ELLIOT, Mama Cass: see Mama Cass				
ELLIOTT, Ramblin' Jack				
ME & BOBBY McGEE/Girl Of The North Country	(Reprise 0900)	.75	3.00	69
ELLIS				
GOOD TO BE ALIVE/	(Epic 10965)	.50	2.00	72
ELLIS, Don, & The Royal Dukes				
PARTY DOLL/A Woman's Love	(Bee 201)	1.50	6.00	
ELLIS, Jimmy				
I'M NOT TRYING TO BE LIKE ELVIS/ Games You've Been Playing	(Boblo 536)	.75	3.00	78
THAT'S ALL RIGHT/Blue Moon Of Kentucky	(Sun 1129)	1.00	4.00	72
(Promotional issue, artists' name is not shown on label.)				
THAT'S ALL RIGHT/Blue Moon Of Kentucky	(Sun 1129)	.50	2.00	72
THAT'S ALL RIGHT-BLUE MOON OF KENTUCKY/ D.O.A. (By Misty)	(Sun 1136)	.75	3.00	77
TUPELO WOMAN/	(Boblo 526)	.75	3.00	77
Also see Orion				
ELLIS, Ray				
LA DOLCE VITA/Parlami Di Me	(RCA Victor 47-7888)	.75	3.00	60
MIDNIGHT LACE/Grand Jury (Theme)	(MGM K-12942)	.75	3.00	61
ELLIS, Shirley				
CLAPPING SONG, THE/This Is Beautiful	(Congress 234)	.75	3.00	65
NAME GAME, THE/Whisper To The Wind	(Congress 230)	.75	3.00	64
NITTY GRITTY, THE/Give Me A List	(Congress 202)	.75	3.00	63
PUZZLE SONG, THE/I See It, I Like It, I Want It	(Congress 238)	.75	3.00	65
SOUL TIME/	(Columbia 44021)	.75	3.00	67
THAT'S WHAT THE NITTY GRITTY IS/Get Out	(Congress 208)	.75	3.00	64
ELMO, Sunnie, & The Minor Chords				
LET ME/Indian Love Call	(Flick 009)	1.25	5.00	
ELO: see Electric Light Orchestra, The				
EL-RICH TRIO, The				
THIS I SWEAR/House Of Blue Lights	(Elco SK-1)	1.25	5.00	
ELY, Jack, & The Courtmen				
LOUIE, GO HOME/Ride Ride Baby	(Bang 534)	.75	3.00	66
Jack Ely was previously the lead singer for the Kingsmen, and was featured on their "Louie Louie."				
EMANONS, The				
DEAR ONE/We Teenagers (Know What We Want)	(Winley 226)	2.50	10.00	58
DEAR ONE/We Teenagers (Know What We Want)	(ABC-Paramount 9913)	1.25	5.00	58
EMBERGLOWS, The				
SACK & CHEMISE GANG FIGHT/ Have You Found Someone New	(Dore 591)	1.25	5.00	61
SENTIMENTAL REASONS/Make Up Your Mind	(Amazon 1005)	1.25	5.00	62
EMBERS, The				
MOONLIGHT SURF/Little "D" Special	(Moonglow 232)	1.00	4.00	64
EMBERS, The				
I WONDER WHY/Little Girl Next Door	(Ara 210)	1.50	6.00	
EMBLEMS, The				
POOR HUMPTY DUMPTY/Would You Still Be Mine	(Bay Front 107)	2.00	8.00	
TOO YOUNG/Bang Bang, Shoot em' Up Daddy	(Bay Front 108)	2.00	8.00	
EMCEES, The				
WINE, WINE, WINE/Hot Rock	(Cimarron 4044)	1.00	4.00	60
EMERALDS, The				
CUSTER'S LAST STAND/I Kneel At Your Throne	(Rex 1013)	1.25	5.00	
ONE I ADORE, THE/You Belong To My Heart	(ABC-Paramount 9889)	2.00	8.00	58
EMERALDS, The				
LITTLE "D" SPECIAL/Search For Love	(Riviera 714)	1.25	5.00	64
SURFIN' 'ROUND THE WORLD/Emerald Surf	(DC 179)	1.25	5.00	64
EMERSON, LAKE & PALMER (Keith Emerson, Greg Lake, Carl Palmer)				
ALL I WANT IS YOU/Tiger In The Spotlight	(Atlantic 3555)	.50	2.00	78
BRAIN SALAD SURGERY/Still... You Turn Me On	(Manticore 2003)	.75	3.00	74
C'EST LA VIE (By Greg Lake)/Jeremy Bender	(Atlantic 3405)	.50	2.00	77
FANFARE FOR THE COMMON MAN/Brain Salad Surgery	(Atlantic 3398)	.50	2.00	77
FROM THE BEGINNING/Living Sin	(Cotillion 44158)	.50	2.00	72
LUCKY MAN/Knife's Edge	(Cotillion 44106)	.50	2.00	71
NUTROCKER/The Great Gates Of Kiev	(Cotillion 44151)	.50	2.00	72
STONE OF YEARS/A Time & A Place	(Cotillion 44131)	.75	3.00	71
EMJAYS, The (Featuring Jimmy Curtis)				
CROSS MY HEART/All My Love, All My Life	(Greenwich 412)	1.25	5.00	59
OVER THE RAINBOW/Cookie Jar	(Paris 538)	1.25	5.00	60
THIS IS MY LOVE/Waitin' (The Pitty Pat Song)	(Greenwich 411)	1.25	5.00	59
EMMERSON, Les (Of The Five Man Electrical Band)				
CONTROL OF ME/Goin' Through The Motions	(Lion 141)	.50	2.00	73
EMOTIONS, The				
BOOMERANG/I Love You Madly	(20th Fox 478)	1.25	5.00	64
(BY THE LIGHT OF THE) SILVERY MOON/Do You Love Me	(Card 600)	3.75	15.00	
ECHO/Come Dance Baby	(Kapp 490)	1.00	4.00	62
HEART STRINGS/Every Time	(20th Fox 623)	1.25	5.00	65
I WONDER/Hey Baby	(Karate 506)	1.00	4.00	64
IT'S LOVE/Candlelight	(Fury 1010)	1.50	6.00	58
L-O-V-E/A Million Reasons	(Kapp 513)	1.25	5.00	63
RAINBOW/Little Miss Blue	(20th Fox 452)	1.25	5.00	63
SHE'S MY BABY/Baby I Need Your Loving	(Calla 122)	1.25	5.00	65
STARLIT NIGHT/Fools Paradise	(Laurie 3167)	2.00	8.00	63
STORY UNTOLD, A/One Life, One Love, One You	(20th Fox 430)	1.50	6.00	63
YOU'RE A BETTER MAN THAN I/Are You Real	(Johnson 746)	1.00	4.00	
EMPEROR, The (Bob Hudson)				
I'M NORMAL (Answer song)/Crossing Game	(Current 111)	1.00	4.00	66
Also see Col. Splendid				
Also see Hudson & Landry				
EMPERORS, The				
SEARCHIN' 'ROUND THE WORLD/	(Wickwire 13003)	1.00	4.00	64
EMPERORS, The				
KARATE/I've Got To Have Her	(Mala 543)	.75	3.00	66
EMPIRES, The				
LOVE IS STRANGE/Have Mercy	(DCP 1116)	1.00	4.00	64
LOVE YOU SO BAD/Come Home Girl	(Chavis 1026)	1.50	6.00	
ONLY IN MY DREAMS/Definition Of Love	(Calico 121)	1.25	5.00	
OVER THE SUMMER VACATION/You're So Popular	(Lake 711)	1.25	5.00	
TEARS IN MY EYES/Single & Free	(Colpix 112)	2.50	10.00	59
THREE LITTLE FISHES/Everybody Knew But Me	(Colpix 680)	1.50	6.00	63
EMPIRES, The (Featuring Jay Black)				
TIME & A PLACE, A/Punch Your Nose	(Epic 9527)	2.00	8.00	62
Also see Jay & The Americans				
ENCHANTERS, The				
I LIED TO MY HEART/Talk While You Walk	(Musitron 1072)	.75	3.00	61
I WANNA THANK YOU/I'm A Good Man	(Warner Bros. 5460)	.75	3.00	64
ENCHANTERS, The				
OH ROSEMARIE/Bewildered	(J.J. & M 1562)	2.50	10.00	
SPELLBOUND BY THE MOON/Know It All	(Stardust 102)	3.00	12.00	
TOUCH OF LOVE/Cafe Bohemian	(Orbit 532)	1.25	5.00	
This group includes members of the Dories and the Safaris				
ENCHANTERS, The				
SURF BLAST/	(Tom Tom 301)	1.25	5.00	
(Instrumental)				
ENCHANTMENTS, The				
I LOVE MY BABY/Pains In My Heart	(Ritz 17003)	6.25	25.00	
I'M IN LOVE WITH YOUR DAUGHTER (PART 1)/ I'm In Love With Your Daughter (Part 2)	(Faro 620)	1.00	4.00	
(I LOVE YOU) SHERRY/Come On Home	(Gone 5130)	1.25	5.00	62
ENCHANTONES, The				
MY PICTURE OF YOU/We Fell In Love	(Popular 116)	3.00	12.00	62
ENCHORDS, The				
ZOOM ZOOM ZOOM/I Need You Baby	(Laurie 3089)	2.50	10.00	61
ENCORES, The				
BARBARA/Thank You	(Bow 302)	3.00	12.00	
ENCOUNTERS, The				
DON'T STOP/A Place In Your Heart	(Swan 4205)	3.00	12.00	65
ENDELLS, The				
VICKY/The Monkey Dance	(Heigh Ho 605)	1.25	5.00	
ENDLESS PULSE (Featuring Carlo Mastrangelo)				
NOWHERE CHICK/Wake Me, Shake Me	(Laurie 3488)	1.00	4.00	69
TIME IS A WASTIN'/Ghost Town	(Laurie 3448)	1.00	4.00	68
YOU TURNED ME OVER/Just You	(Laurie 3468)	1.00	4.00	68
END, The				
I CAN'T GET MY JOY/Hey Little Girl	(Philips 40323)	.75	3.00	65
SHADES OF ORANGE/Loving, Sacred Loving	(London 1016)	.75	3.00	67
ENEMYS, The				
GLITTER & GOLD/Too Much Monkey Business	(MGM 13485)	1.00	4.00	66
HEY JOE/My Dues Have Been Paid	(MGM 13525)	1.00	4.00	66
MO-JO WOMAN/My Dues Have Been Paid	(MGM 13573)	1.00	4.00	66
Also see Hutton, Danny				
ENERGIZERS, The (Magic Triplets)				
(SAVE OUR ENERGY) THAT'S WHAT SIMON SAYS/ Energy Rock	(Kef 4458)	1.50	6.00	
ENGEL, Butch, & The Styx				
I LIKE HER/Going Home	(Loma 2065)	2.00	8.00	66
ENGEL, Joanne				
MIRROR MIRROR ON THE WALL/Set Me Free	(Sabrina 508)	1.00	4.00	63
ENGEL, Scott				
ANYTHING WILL DO/Forevermore	(Liberty F-55428)	2.00	8.00	62
ANYTHING WILL DO/Mr. Jones	(Liberty F-55312)	2.50	10.00	62
BLUEBELL/Paper Doll	(Orbit 512)	1.50	6.00	58
BLUEBELL/Paper Doll	(Orbit 512)	2.50	10.00	58
(Picture sleeve)				
CHARLEY BOP/All I Do Is Dream	(Orbit 511)	2.00	8.00	58
CHARLEY BOP/All I Do Is Dream	(Orbit 511)	6.25	25.00	58
(Picture sleeve)				
COMIN' HOME/I Don't Wanna Know	(Orbit 543)	1.50	6.00	59
DEVIL SURFER/Your Guess	(Martay 2004)	2.50	10.00	63
(Instrumental)				
GOLDEN RULE OF LOVE/Sunday	(Orbit 537)	1.50	6.00	59
GOLDEN RULE OF LOVE/Sunday	(Orbit 537)	2.50	10.00	59
(Picture sleeve)				
LIVIN' END, THE/Good For Nothin'	(Orbit 506)	1.50	6.00	58
LIVIN' END, THE/Good For Nothin'	(Orbit 506)	2.50	10.00	58
(With picture sleeve)				
Also see Walker, Scott				
ENGLAND DAN (Dan Seals) & JOHN FORD COLEY				
CASEY/Simone	(A&M 1354)	1.00	4.00	72
FREE THE PEOPLE/Carolina	(A&M 1369)	1.00	4.00	72
GONE TOO FAR/Where Do I Go From Here	(Big Tree 16102)	.50	2.00	77
HOLLYWOOD HECKLE & JIVE/Rolling Fever	(Big Tree 16135)	.50	2.00	79
I'D REALLY LOVE TO SEE YOU TONIGHT/ It's Not The Same	(Big Tree 16069)	.50	2.00	76
IF THE WORLD RAN OUT OF LOVE TONIGHT/	(Big Tree 16125)	.50	2.00	78
I HEAR THE MUSIC/Miss You Song	(A&M 1465)	.75	3.00	73
I HEAR THE MUSIC/Simone	(A&M 1871)	.75	3.00	77
IT'S SAD TO BELONG/The Time Has Come	(Big Tree 16088)	.50	2.00	77
LOVE IS THE ANSWER/Running After You	(Big Tree 16131)	.50	2.00	79
NEW JERSEY/Tell Her Hello	(A&M 1278)	.75	3.00	71
NIGHTS ARE FOREVER WITHOUT YOU/Showboat Gambler	(Big Tree 16079)	.50	2.00	76
SOMEONE/	(A&M 1871)	.75	3.00	77
WE'LL NEVER HAVE TO SAY GOODBYE AGAIN/ Calling For You Again	(Big Tree 16110)	.50	2.00	77
WESTWARD WIND/Some Things Don't Come Easy	(Big Tree 16130)	.50	2.00	78
WHAT CAN I DO WITH THIS BROKEN HEART/ Caught Up In The Middle	(Big Tree 17000)	.50	2.00	79
YOU CAN'T DANCE/Wanting You Desperately	(Big Tree 16117)	.50	2.00	78
Also see Southwest F.O.B.				
Dan Seals' brother is Jimmy Seals, of Seals & Crofts.				
ENGLISH CONGREGATION, The				
IF I COULD HAVE MY WAY/	(Signpost 7004)	.50	2.00	73
SOFTLY WHISPERING I LOVE YOU/ When Susue Takes The Plane	(Atco 6865)	.50	2.00	72
ENGLISH, Scott				
BRANDY/Lead Me Back	(Janus J-171)	1.25	5.00	71
("Brandy" was later recorded by Barry Manilow as "Mandy.")				
HERE COMES THE PAIN/All I Want Is You	(Spokane 4007)	1.25	5.00	64
(With the Accents)				
HIGH ON A HILL/When	(Sultan 4003)	2.50	10.00	63
(With the Accents)				
HIGH ON A HILL/When	(Spokane 4003)	1.25	5.00	64
(With the Accents)				
RAGS TO RICHES/Where Can I Go	(Sultan 5500)	2.50	10.00	63
(With the Accents)				

TITLE/FLIP	LABEL & NO.	GOOD	NEAR MINT	YR.

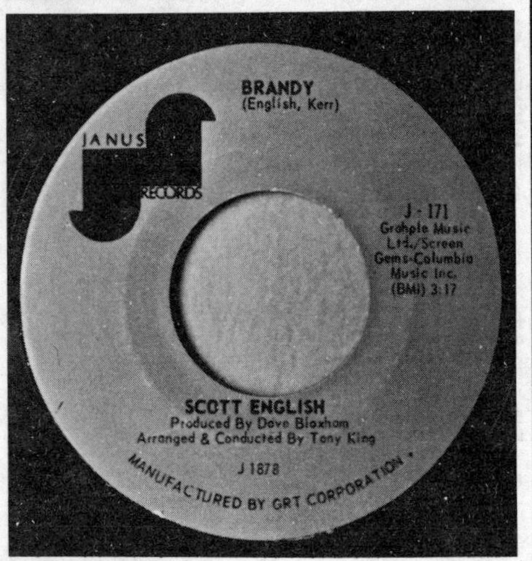

TITLE/FLIP	LABEL & NO.	GOOD	NEAR MINT	YR.
UGLY PILLS (YOU'RE TAKIN')/When	(Joker 777)	1.25	5.00	62
WHITE CLIFFS OF DOVER/4000 Miles Away	(Dot 16099)	2.00	8.00	60
(With the Accents)				
WOMAN IN MY LIFE/Ballad Of The Unloved	(Janus J-192)	.75	3.00	72
ENJOYABLES, The				
PUSH A LITTLE HARDER/We'll Make A Way	(Capitol 5321)	1.00	4.00	64
ENO (Brian Eno)				
LION SLEEPS TONIGHT, THE/	(Island 036)	.50	2.00	72
Also see Roxy Music				
ENTERTAINERS, The				
FUDDY DUDDY WALK/Marianne	(Catch 101)	1.00	4.00	63
HOW MUCH DO YOU LOVE ME/Danny Boy	(Demand 2932)	2.00	8.00	
ENTWHISTLE, John: see John Entwhistle's Rigor Mortis				
EPIC SPLENDOR, The				
LITTLE RAIN MUST FALL, A/Cowboys & Indians	(Hot Biscuit 1450)	.75	3.00	67
SHE'S HIGH ON LIFE/It Could Be Wonderful	(Hot Biscuit 1452)	.75	3.00	68
EPICS, The				
KNOCK ON WOOD/Flea Espanol	(Joni 107)	1.00	4.00	64
THEME FOR JANET/Tite Jaws	(Joni 104)	1.00	4.00	63
WE BELONG TOGETHER/Baltimore	(Joni 101)	1.00	4.00	63
EPIKS, The				
WHEN WE'RE APART/Give Me A Chance	(Process 146)	1.50	6.00	
EPISODE SIX, The				
HERE, THERE & EVERYWHERE/Mighty Morris Ten	(Warner Bros. 5851)	.75	3.00	66
LOVE-HATE-REVENGE/Baby, Baby, Baby	(Elektra 45617)	.75	3.00	67
MORNING DEW/Sunshine Girl	(Compass 7007)	.75	3.00	67
EPISODES, The				
CHRISTMAS TREE/Where Is My Love	("4-Seasons"-no number)	6.25	25.00	
EPPS, Preston				
BONGO BONGO BONGO/Holly Golly Bongo	(Original Sound 9)	.75	3.00	60
BONGO ROCK/Bongo Party	(Original Sound 4)	.75	3.00	59
BONGO ROCK/Bongo Party	(Original Sound ORS-4)	1.50	6.00	59
(Stereo single issue)				
JUNGLE DRUMS/Bongo Rocket	(Original Sound 17)	.75	3.00	61
Instrumentals				
EQUALS, The				
BABY COME BACK/Hold Me Closer	(RCA Victor 47-9583)	.75	3.00	68
FIRE/I Won't Be There	(President 103)	1.00	4.00	67
GIDDY UP A DING DONG/I Get So Excited	(President 108)	1.00	4.00	68
YOU GOT TOO MANY BOY FRIENDS/My Life Ain't Easy	(President 105)	1.00	4.00	67
ERICKSON, Roxy (Of The 13th Floor Elevators)				
BERMUDA/The Interpreter	(Rhino 003)	.50	2.00	77
ERIK & THE VIKINGS				
STEP BY STEP/Heaven In Paradise	(Karate 503)	1.25	5.00	
ERNIE (Jim Henson)				
RUBBER DUCKIE/Sesame Street	(Columbia 4-45207)	.50	2.00	70
Also see Bert				
ERNIE & THE EMPERORS				
MEET ME AT THE CORNER/Got A Lot I Want To Say	(Reprise 0414)	1.00	4.00	65
ERNIE & THE HALOS				
GIRL FROM ACROSS THE SEA (ANGEL MARIE)/ Darling Don't Make Me Cry	(Guyden 2085)	3.00	12.00	65
ERVIN, Frankie				
WHY DID IT END/Try To Care	(Don 202)	3.00	12.00	
(With the Spears)				
ERWIN, Bill, & The 4 Jacks				
TOO YOUNG TO BE BLUE/High School Days	(Pel 501)	2.50	10.00	
TOO YOUNG TO BE BLUE/High School Days	(Fairlane 21020)	2.50	10.00	
ESCORTS, The: see Goldie & The Escorts				
ESCORTS, The				
C'MON HOME BABY/She Gets No Lovin' That Way	(Fontana 1512)	.75	3.00	65
DIZZY MISS LIZZY/All I Want Is You	(Fontana 1912)	.75	3.00	64
ESQUIRE, Kenny, & The Starlites				
PRETTY BROWN EYES/They Call Me A Dreamer	(Ember 1011)	2.00	8.00	56
ESSEX, The (Featuring Anita Humes)				
EASIER SAID THAN DONE/Are You Going My Way	(Roulette 4494)	.75	3.00	63
MOONLIGHT, MUSIC & YOU/The Eagle	(Bang 537)	.75	3.00	66
SHE'S GOT EVERYTHING/Out Of Sight Out Of Mind	(Roulette 4530)	.75	3.00	63
WALKIN' MIRACLE, A/ What I Don't Know Won't Hurt Me	(Roulette 4515)	.75	3.00	63
WHAT DID I DO/Curfew Lover	(Roulette 4542)	.75	3.00	64
ESSEX, David				
AMERICA/Dance Little Girl	(Columbia 10005)	.50	2.00	74
GONNA MAKE YOU A STAR/Window	(Columbia 10039)	.50	2.00	74
HOLD ME CLOSE/	(Columbia 10256)	.50	2.00	76
LAMPLIGHT/We All Insane	(Columbia 46041)	.50	2.00	74
OH WHAT A CIRCUS/Ships That Pass In The Night	(RSO 1006)	.50	2.00	79
ROCK ON/On & On	(Columbia 45940)	.50	2.00	73
ROLLING STONE/Coconut Ice	(Columbia 10183)	.50	2.00	75
SHE'S LEAVING HOME/He's A Better Man Than Me	(Uni 55020)	1.25	5.00	67
E-TYPES, The				
BIG CITY/Back To Me	(Uptown 754)	1.00	4.00	
I CAN'T DO IT/Long Before	(Link E-1)	2.00	8.00	
I CAN'T DO IT/Long Before	(Dot 16864)	1.00	4.00	66
LOVE OF THE LOVED, THE/She Moves Me	(Sunburst 001)	1.25	5.00	
PUT THE CLOCK BACK ON THE WALL/4th Street	(Tower 325)	1.00	4.00	
ETZEL, Jack				
MEANWHILE AT THE CONVENTION, PARTS ONCE/ Meanwhile At The Convention, Parts Twice	(Rat 45)	5.00	20.00	
(Novelty/Break-in)				
EUBANKS, Bob				
HEAVEN OF THE STARS/Heaven Of The Stars	(Tracy 6101)	1.25	5.00	61
EUBANKS, Jack				
SEARCHING/Take A Message	(Monument 451)	.75	3.00	61
EUCLID BEACH BAND, The				
END OF THE WORLD/	(Epic-Cleveland Intl 50782)	.50	2.00	79
I NEED YOU/Hard To Say Goodbye	(Epic-Cleveland Intl. 50676)	.50	2.00	79
THERE'S A MOON OUT TONIGHT/	(Epic-Cleveland Intl. 50741)	.50	2.00	79
THERE'S NO SURF IN CLEVELAND/ Laugh In The Dark	(Epic-Cleveland Intl. 40484)	.75	3.00	78
EUNIQUES, The				
CRY CRY CRY/Chicken (Yeah)	("620" 1006)	10.00	40.00	
PRETTY BABY/	("620" 1003)	2.50	10.00	
EUPHORIA				
NO ME TOMORROW/Hungry Women	(Mainstream 655)	1.25	5.00	68
YOU MUST FORGET/Ride The Magic Carpet	(Heritage 831)	1.00	4.00	69
EVANS, Paul				
AT MY PARTY/Beat Generation	(Atco 6138)	1.00	4.00	59
BRIGADE OF BROKEN HEARTS, THE/Twins	(Guaranteed 210)	.75	3.00	60
CAUGHT/Poor Broken Heart	(RCA Victor 47-6992)	1.25	5.00	57
EVEN TAN/Ten Thousand Years	(Kapp 527)	.75	3.00	63
FEELIN' NO PAIN/Picture Of You	(Kapp 473)	.75	3.00	62
HAPPY-GO-LUCKY-ME/Fish In The Ocean	(Guaranteed 208)	.75	3.00	60
HUSHABYE LITTLE GUITAR/Blind Boy	(Guaranteed 213)	.75	3.00	60
I LOVE TO MAKE LOVE TO YOU/Show Folk	(Carlton 539)	.75	3.00	61
MIDNITE SPECIAL/Since I Met You Baby	(Guaranteed 205)	.75	3.00	59
LONG GONE/Mickey, My Love	(Atco 6170)	1.00	4.00	60
NOT ME/After The Hurricane	(Carlton 543)	.75	3.00	61
OVER THE MOUNTAIN, ACROSS THE SEA/Sisal Twine	(Carlton 558)	.75	3.00	62
SEVEN LITTLE GIRLS SITTING IN THE BACK SEAT/ Worshipping An Idol	(Guaranteed 200)	.75	3.00	59
THIS PULLOVER/Just Because I Love You	(Carlton 554)	.75	3.00	61
WHAT DO YOU KNOW/Dorthy	(RCA Victor 47-6806)	1.25	5.00	57
EVERETTE, Leon				
GOODBYE KING OF ROCK 'N' ROLL/ Where The Daisies Grow Wild	(True 107)	.50	2.00	77
EVERETT, Vince (Marvin Benefield)				
BABY LET'S PLAY HOUSE/Livin' High	(ABC-Paramount 10472)	3.75	15.00	63
BUTTERCUP/Lane Of No Return	(Town 1964)	2.50	10.00	60
I AIN'T GONNA BE YOUR LOW DOWN DOG NO MORE/ Sugar Bee	(ABC-Paramount 10360)	2.50	10.00	62
SUCH A NIGHT/Don't Go	(ABC-Paramount 10313)	3.75	15.00	62
TO HAVE, TO HOLD & LET GO/Big Brother	(ABC-Paramount 10624)	2.50	10.00	65
EVERLY BROTHERS, The (Don & Phil)				
ALL I HAVE TO DO IS DREAM/Claudette	(Cadence 1348)	1.00	4.00	58
(Silver & maroon label)				
BIRD DOG/Devoted To You	(Cadence 1350)	1.00	4.00	58
BOWLING GREEN/I Don't Want To Love You	(Warner Bros. 7020)	.75	3.00	67
BYE BYE LOVE/I Wonder If I Care As Much	(Cadence 1315)	1.00	4.00	57
CAROLINA ON MY MIND/My Little Yellow Bird	(Warner Bros. 7326)	.75	3.00	69
CATHY'S CLOWN/Always It's You	(Warner Bros. 5151)	.75	3.00	60
CATHY'S CLOWN/Always It's You	(Warner Bros. S-5151)	2.50	10.00	60
(Stereo single issue)				
CRYING IN THE RAIN/I'm Not Angry	(Warner Bros. 5250)	.75	3.00	61
DON'T ASK ME TO BE FRIENDS/ No One Can Make My Sunshine Smile	(Warner Bros. 5297)	.75	3.00	62
DON'T BLAME ME/Muskrat	(Warner Bros. 5501)	.75	3.00	61
FERRIS WHEEL, THE/Don't Forget To Cry	(Warner Bros. 5441)	.75	3.00	64
FIFI THE FLEA/Like Everytime Before	(Warner Bros. 5857)	1.00	4.00	67
GONE, GONE, GONE/Torture	(Warner Bros. 5478)	.75	3.00	64
HELLO AMY/Ain't That Lovin' You Baby	(Warner Bros. 5422)	1.00	4.00	64
I WONDER IF I CARE AS MUCH/T For Texas	(Warner Bros. 7262)	1.00	4.00	69
I'LL NEVER GET OVER YOU/Follow Me	(Warner Bros. 5639)	1.00	4.00	65
I'M AFRAID/It's Been Nice	(Warner Bros. 5362)	1.00	4.00	63
I'M HERE TO GET MY BABY OUT OF JAIL/ Lightning Express	(Cadence 1429)	1.00	4.00	62
I'M ON MY WAY HOME AGAIN/Cuckoo Bird	(Warner Bros. 7290)	1.00	4.00	69
IT'S ALL OVER/I Used To Love You	(Warner Bros. 5682)	1.00	4.00	65
IT'S MY TIME/Empty Boxes	(Warner Bros. 7192)	1.00	4.00	68
LADIES LOVE OUTLAWS/Not Fade Away	(RCA 0901)	.75	3.00	73
LAY IT DOWN/Paradise	(RCA 0849)	.75	3.00	72
LET IT BE ME/Since You Broke My Heart	(Cadence 1376)	1.00	4.00	59
LIKE STRANGERS/Brand New Heartache	(Cadence 1388)	1.00	4.00	60
LOVE HER/The Girl Sang The Blues	(Warner Bros. 5389)	.75	3.00	63
LOVE IS STRANGE/Man With Money	(Warner Bros. 5649)	1.00	4.00	65
LOVEY KRAVEZIT/The Doll House Is Empty	(Warner Bros. 5698)	1.00	4.00	66
LOVE OF THE COMMON PEOPLE/Voice Within	(Warner Bros. 7088)	1.00	4.00	67
MARY JANE/Talking To The Flowers	(Warner Bros. 7062)	1.00	4.00	67
MILK TRAIN/Lord Of The Manor	(Warner Bros. 7226)	1.00	4.00	68
PRICE OF LOVE, THE/It Only Costs A Dime	(Warner Bros. 5628)	1.00	4.00	65
PROBLEMS/Love Of My Life	(Cadence 1355)	1.00	4.00	58
RIDIN' HIGH/Stories We Should Tell	(RCA 0717)	.75	3.00	72
SHE NEVER SMILES ANYMORE/Devil's Child	(Warner Bros. 5901)	1.00	4.00	67
(SO IT WAS... SO IT IS) SO IT WILL ALWAYS BE/ Nancy's Minuet	(Warner Bros. 5346)	1.00	4.00	63
SO SAD (TO WATCH GOOD LOVE GO BAD)/ Lucille	(Warner Bros. 5163)	.75	3.00	60
SOMEBODY HELP ME/Hard, Hard Year	(Warner Bros. 5833)	1.00	4.00	66
SUN KEEPS SHINING, THE/Keep A Loving Me	(Columbia 4-21496)	5.00	20.00	56
(Numbered in sequence with Columbia's country music series.)				
TAKE A MESSAGE TO MARY/Poor Jenny	(Cadence 1364)	1.00	4.00	59
TEMPTATION/Stick With Me Baby	(Warner Bros. 5220)	.75	3.00	61
THAT'LL BE THE DAY/Give Me A Sweetheart	(Warner Bros. 5611)	1.00	4.00	65
THAT'S OLD FASHIONED (THAT'S THE WAY LOVE SHOULD BE)/ How Can I Meet Her	(Warner Bros. 5273)	.75	3.00	62
THIS LITTLE GIRL OF MINE/Should We Tell Him	(Cadence 1342)	1.00	4.00	58
TILL I KISSED YOU/Oh What A Feeling	(Cadence 1369)	1.00	4.00	59
WAKE UP LITTLE SUSIE/Maybe Tomorrow	(Cadence 1337)	1.00	4.00	57
WALK RIGHT BACK/Ebony Eyes	(Warner Bros. 5199)	.75	3.00	61
WHEN WILL I BE LOVED/Be Bop A-Lula	(Cadence 1380)	1.00	4.00	60
(YOU GOT) THE POWER OF LOVE/ Leave My Girl Alone	(Warner Bros. 5808)	1.00	4.00	66
YOU'RE MY GIRL/ Don't Let The Whole World Know	(Warner Bros. 5600)	1.00	4.00	65
YOU'RE THE ONE I LOVE/Ring Around My Rosie	(Warner Bros. 5466)	1.00	4.00	64
YVES/Human Race	(Warner Bros. 7425)	1.00	4.00	70
EVERLY, Don (Of The Everly Brothers)				
BROTHER JUKEBOX/Oh, What A Feeling	(ABC-Hickory 54012)	.75	3.00	77
LOVE AT LAST SIGHT/Oh, I'd Like To Go Away	(ABC-Hickory 54002)	.75	3.00	76
ONLY ME/Tumbling Tumbleweeds	(Ode '70 66009)	.75	3.00	70
SINCE YOU BROKE MY HEART/Deep Water	(ABC-Hickory 54005)	.75	3.00	76
WARMIN' UP THE BAND/Evelyn Swing	(Ode 66046)	.75	3.00	73
YESTERDAY JUST PASSED MY WAY AGAIN/ Never Like This	(ABC-Hickory 368)	.75	3.00	75
EVERLY, Phil (Of The Everly Brothers)				
BETTER THAN NOW/	(Pye 71050)	.75	3.00	74
GOD BLESS OLDER LADIES/Sweet Grass Country	(Pye 71056)	.75	3.00	75
LIVING ALONE/I Just Don't Feel Like Dancing	(Elektra 46519)	.50	2.00	79
NEW OLD SONG/Better Than Now	(Pye 71036)	.75	3.00	73
OLD KENTUCKY RIVER/	(Pye 71014)	.75	3.00	73
WORDS IN YOUR EYES/	(Pye 71055)	.75	3.00	75
YOU BROKE IT/	(Elektra 46556)	.50	2.00	79
EVERPRESENT FULLNESS, The				
DOIN' A NUMBER/Wild About My Lovin'	(White Whale 233)	1.25	5.00	
FINE & DANDY/Wild About My Lovin'	(White Whale 233)	1.25	5.00	
YEAH!/Darlin' You Can Count On Me	(White Whale 248)	1.25	5.00	
EVERY FATHERS' TEENAGE SON				
LETTER TO DAD, A (Answer song)/Josephine's Song	(Buddah 25)	.75	3.00	67
EVERY MOTHER'S SON				
COME ON DOWN TO MY BOAT/I Believe In You	(MGM 13733)	.75	3.00	67
NO ONE KNOWS/What Became Of Mary	(MGM 13887)	.75	3.00	68
PONY WITH THE GOLDEN MANE/Doll's In The Clock	(MGM 13844)	.75	3.00	67
PUT YOUR MIND AT EASE/Proper Four Leaf Clover	(MGM 13788)	.75	3.00	67
RAINFLOWERS/For Brandy	(MGM 13987)	.75	3.00	68
EVERYTHING IS EVERYTHING				
WITCHI TAI TO/Oo Baby	(Vanguard Apostolic 35082)	.75	3.00	69
EXCELLENTS, The				
CONEY ISLAND BABY/You Baby You	(Blast 205)	3.00	12.00	62
(Red label with black letters)				
CONEY ISLAND BABY/You Baby You	(Blast 205)	1.00	4.00	62
(Red & white label)				
I HEAR A RHAPSODY/Why Did You Laugh	(Blast 207)	2.00	8.00	63
RED RED ROBIN/Love No One But You	(Mermaid 106)	7.50	30.00	
SUNDAY KIND OF LOVE, A/Helen	(Bobby 601)	2.50	10.00	64
(Shown as by the Excellons)				
SUNDAY KIND OF LOVE, A/Helen	(Old Timer 601)	.75	3.00	
EXCELLONS, The: see Excellents, The				
EXCELS, The				
CAN'T HELP LOVIN' THAT GIRL OF MINE/ Till You Were Gone	(R.S.V.P. 111)	1.50	6.00	61
EXCELS, The				
YOU'RE MINE FOREVER/Baby Doll	(Central 2601)	1.25	5.00	
EXCEPTIONS, The				
GIRL FROM NEW YORK/As Far As I Can See	(Quill 114)	2.00	8.00	67
GIRL FROM NEW YORK/As Far As I Can See	(Capitol 5982)	.75	3.00	67
EXCEPTIONS, The				
DOWN BY THE OCEAN/Pancho's Villa	(Pro 1)	3.00	12.00	
DOWN BY THE OCEAN/Pancho's Villa	(Cameo 378)	1.25	5.00	65
EXCITERS, The				
DO-WAH-DIDDY/If Love Came Your Way	(United Artists 662)	.75	3.00	63
GET HIM/It's So Exciting	(United Artists 604)	.75	3.00	63
HE'S GOT THE POWER/Drama Of Love	(United Artists 572)	.75	3.00	63
I WANT YOU TO BE MY BOY/Tonight, Tonight	(Roulette 4591)	.75	3.00	64
TELL HIM/Hard Way To Go	(United Artists 544)	.75	3.00	62
EXCITING VOICES, The				
DIDN'T IT RAIN/	(Bel Canto 722)	.75	3.00	
EXECS, The				
WALKING IN THE RAIN/Palladium	(Fargo 1005)	15.00	60.00	58
EXILE				
CHURCH ST. SOUL REVIVAL/Your Day Is Comin'	(Columbia 44972)	1.00	4.00	69
(Shown as by the Exiles)				
DEVIL'S BITE/	(Wooden Nickel 0115)	.50	2.00	72
HOW COULD THIS GO WRONG/ Being In Love With You Is Easy	(Warner-Curb 8796)	.50	2.00	79
KISS YOU ALL OVER/Don't Do It	(Warner-Curb 8589)	.50	2.00	78
PART OF ME THAT NEEDS YOU MOST, THE/ Let's Do It Again	(Warner-Curb 8848)	.50	2.00	79
PUT YOUR HANDS TOGETHER/Your Day Is Comin'	(Columbia 45210)	1.00	4.00	70
(Shown as by the Exiles)				
TOO PROUD TO CRY/Destiny	(Warner-Curb 49048)	.50	2.00	79
TRY IT ON/Show Me What You Got	(Atco 7072)	.50	2.00	77
YOU THRILL ME/One Step At A Time	(Warner-Curb 8711)	.50	2.00	78
EXILES, The: see Exile				
EXILES, The (Featuring Dick Dale)				
TAKE IT OFF/Ten Little Indians	(Campus 1111)	5.00	20.00	
(Instrumental)				
EXODUS: see Four Epics				
EXOTICS, The				
LORRAINE/Gee	(Springboard 101)	3.00	12.00	
THAT'S MY DESIRE/Darling I Want To Get Married	(Coral 62268)	1.50	6.00	61
EXPLORERS, The				
DON'T BE A FOOL/ In The Wee Small Hours Of The Morning	(Coral 62175)	1.50	6.00	60
REMEMBER/Every Road	(Coral 62295)	1.50	6.00	61
(Shown as Dennis & the Explorers)				
VISION OF LOVE/On A Clear Night	(Coral 62147)	1.50	6.00	59
EXPRESSIONS, The				
BE BOP A LULA/Skinny Minnie	(Guyden 2122)	.75	3.00	65
KAREN/Thrill	(Smash 1848)	.75	3.00	63
MY LOVE, MY LOVE/The Sign Of Happiness	(Arliss 1012)	2.00	8.00	
NOW THAT YOU'RE GONE/Crazy	(Teen 101)	6.25	25.00	
ON THE CORNER/To Cry	(Parkway 892)	1.25	5.00	66
ONE PLUS ONE/Playboy	(Reprise 0360)	2.50	10.00	65
EXTERMINATORS, The				
BEATLE BOMB/Stomp Em' Out	(Chancellor 1148)	1.00	4.00	64
EXTREMES, The				
EAT HERE, GET GAS/We Are Us	(Golden Circle 5611)	1.50	6.00	64
EXTREMES, The				
BELLS, THE/That's All I Want	(Paro 733)	6.25	25.00	
(With Bobby Sanders)				
LET'S ELOPE/Come Next Spring	(Everlast 5013)	1.50	6.00	5
Also see Bobby & The Velvets				
EXZELS, The				
CANADIAN SUNSET/Hit Talk	(Crossfire 101)	1.00	4.00	
EZRA & THE IVIES				
COMIC BOOK CRAZY/Rockin' Shoes	(United Artists 165)	1.25	5.00	5

F

TITLE/FLIP	LABEL & NO.	GOOD	NEAR MINT	YR.
FABARES, Shelley				
FOOTBALL SEASON'S OVER/He Don't Love Me	(Colpix 721)	1.25	5.00	64
JOHNNY ANGEL/Where's It Gonna Get Me	(Colpix 621)	.75	3.00	62
JOHNNY LOVES ME/I'm Growing Up	(Colpix 636)	.75	3.00	62
LOST SUMMER LOVE/I Know You'll Be There	(Vee Jay 632)	1.00	4.00	64
MY PRAYER/Pretty Please	(Dunhill 4001)	1.00	4.00	65
RONNIE, CALL ME WHEN YOU GET A CHANCE/ I Left A Note To Say Goodbye	(Colpix 682)	1.25	5.00	62
TELEPHONE (WON'T YOU RING)/Big Star	(Colpix 667)	1.25	5.00	62
THINGS WE DID LAST SUMMER, THE/ Breaking Up Is Hard To Do	(Colpix 654)	.75	3.00	62
WELCOME HOME/Billy Boy	(Colpix 705)	1.25	5.00	62
WHERE'S IT GONNA GET ME/It Keeps Right On Hurtin'	(Colpix 140)	1.00	4.00	64
Also see Peterson, Paul, & Shelley Fabares				

TITLE/FLIP	LABEL & NO.	GOOD	NEAR MINT	YR.
FABIAN (Fabian Forte)				
ABOUT THIS THING CALLED LOVE/String Along	(Chancellor C 1047)	1.00	4.00	60
ABOUT THIS THING CALLED LOVE/String Along (Stereo single issue)	(Chancellor SC 1047)	3.00	12.00	60
BE MY STEADY DATE/Lilly Lou	(Chancellor C 1024)	2.50	10.00	58
BREAK DOWN & CRY/She's Stayin' Inside With Me	(Dot 16413)	1.00	4.00	62
COME ON & GET ME/Got The Feeling	(Chancellor C 1041)	1.00	4.00	59
COME ON & GET ME/Got The Feeling (Stereo single issue)	(Chancellor SC 1041)	3.00	12.00	59
DAVID & GOLIATH/Grapevine	(Chancellor C 1072)	1.25	5.00	61
GIRL LIKE YOU, A/Dream Factory	(Chancellor C 1084)	1.25	5.00	61
HOUND DOG MAN/This Friendly World	(Chancellor C 1044)	1.00	4.00	59
HOUND DOG MAN/This Friendly World (Stereo single issue)	(Chancellor SC 1044)	3.00	12.00	59
I'M A MAN/Hypnotized	(Chancellor C 1029)	1.50	6.00	58
I'M A MAN/Hypnotized (Stereo single issue)	(Chancellor SC 1029)	3.75	15.00	58
I'M GONNA SIT RIGHT DOWN & WRITE MYSELF A LETTER/ Strollin' In The Springtime	(Chancellor C 1051)	1.25	5.00	60
I'M IN LOVE/Shivers	(Chancellor C 1020)	2.50	10.00	58
KING OF LOVE/Tomorrow	(Chancellor C 1055)	1.25	5.00	60
KISSIN' & TWISTIN'/Long Before	(Chancellor C 1061)	1.25	5.00	60
TIGER/Mighty Cold	(Chancellor C 1037)	1.00	4.00	59
TIGER/Mighty Cold (Stereo single issue)	(Chancellor SC 1037)	3.00	12.00	59
TONGUE TIED/Kansas City (With the Fabulous Four)	(Chancellor C 1086)	1.50	6.00	61
TURN ME LOOSE/Stop Thief!	(Chancellor C 1033)	1.00	4.00	59
TURN ME LOOSE/Stop Thief! (Stereo single issue)	(Chancellor SC 1033)	3.00	12.00	59
WILD PARTY/Made You (With the Fabulous Four)	(Chancellor C 1092)	1.50	6.00	61
YOU KNOW YOU BELONG TO SOMEONE ELSE/ Hold On	(Chancellor C 1067)	1.25	5.00	60
YOU'RE ONLY YOUNG ONCE/ The Love That I'm Giving To You	(Chancellor C 1079)	1.25	5.00	61
Vocal backing on some of the Chancellor tracks is provided by the 4 Dates.				
FABIO & BRUNO				
WHAT'S WHY/Do You Know	(Vim 509)	.75	3.00	
FABRIC, Bent (Bent Fabricius-Bjerre)				
ALLEY CAT/Markin' Time	(Atco 6226)	.50	2.00	62
CHICKEN FEED/That Certain Party (Instrumentals)	(Atco 6245)	.75	3.00	62
FABULAIRES, The				
WEDDING SONG/Lonely Days, Lonely Nights	(Chelsea 103)	2.50	10.00	63
FABULONS, The				
CONNIE/This Is The End	(Benson Ritco 100)	2.50	10.00	63
CONNIE/This Is The End	(Benson 100)	1.25	5.00	63
FABULOUS CONTINENTALS, The				
UNDERTOW/Return To Me (Instrumental)	(CB 5003)	.75	3.00	
FABULOUS FARQUAHR, The (Barnswallow Farquahr)				
HANGIN' ON BY A THREAD/Start Living	(Elektra 45713)	.75	3.00	71
HOLLYWOOD ENDING/Some Kind Of God	(Verve Forecast 5109)	1.00	4.00	69
KISS THE WIND GOODBYE/Neither Here Nor There	(Warner Bros. 7354)	1.00	4.00	70
MY EGGS DON'T TASTE THE SAME WITHOUT YOU/	(Verve Forecast 5077)	1.25	5.00	68
MY ISLAND/Teddy Bear Days	(Verve Forecast 5085)	1.25	5.00	68
STREETS OF MONTREAL/Much Too Nice A Day	(Elektra 45704)	.50	2.00	71
FABULOUS FIDELS, The				
WESTSIDE BOY, EASTSIDE GIRL/Soul St.	(Jaa Dee 106)	1.00	4.00	
FABULOUS FOUR, The				
BETTY ANN/Prisoner Of Love	(Chancellor 1085)	5.00	20.00	61
FOREVER/It's No Sin	(Chancellor 1102)	1.50	6.00	62
I'M COMIN' HOME/Everybody Knows	(Chancellor 1090)	2.00	8.00	61
PRECIOUS MOMENTS/Let's Try Again	(Chancellor 1062)	1.50	6.00	60
WHY DO FOOLS FALL IN LOVE/The Sound Of Summer	(Chancellor 1078)	3.00	12.00	61
Also see Fabian				
Also see 4-J's, The				
FABULOUS FOUR, The				
HAPPY/Who Could It Be	(Brass 314)	1.25	5.00	64
NOW YOU CRY/Got To Get Her Back	(Brass 311)	1.50	6.00	64
NOW YOU CRY/Got To Get Her Back	(Coral 62479)	.75	3.00	64
WELCOME ME HOME/Oop Shoobee Doop	(Melic 4114)	1.50	6.00	
YOUNG BLOOD/I'm Always Doing Something Wrong	(Brass 316)	1.25	5.00	64
FABULOUS FUTURAS, The				
LA DO DA DA/When You Ask About Love	(Okon-No Number)	1.50	6.00	
FABULOUS IDOLS, The				
BABY/Nellie	(Kenco 5011)	1.25	5.00	
FABULOUS PACK, The (Formerly With Terry Knight)				
HARLEM SHUFFLE/I've Got News	(Lucky Eleven 003)	2.00	8.00	
TEARS COME ROLLIN'/Color Of Our Love	(Wingate 007)	2.50	10.00	
WIDETRACKIN'/Does It Matter To You Girl	(Lucky Eleven 007)	2.00	8.00	
WITHOUT A WOMAN/Next To Your Fire (Shown as by the Pack)	(Capitol 2174)	1.25	5.00	68
FABULOUS PEARL DEVINES, The				
YOU'VE BEEN GONE/So Lonely	(Alco 101)	6.25	25.00	63
FABULOUS PEPS, The				
I CAN'T GET RIGHT/ Why Are You Blowing My Mind	(Premium Stuff #1)	1.50	6.00	
WITH THESE EYES/Love Of My Life	(Wheelsville 109)	1.50	6.00	
FABULOUS PERSIANS, The				
SAVE THE LAST DANCE FOR ME/Ling Ting Tong	(Bobby-O 3123)	1.50	6.00	
FABULOUS POODLES, The				
MAN WITH MONEY/	(Epic-Park Lane 50823)	.50	2.00	79
MIRROR STAR/Tit Photographer Blues	(Epic-Park Lane 50666)	.50	2.00	79
WORK SHY/Toytown People	(Epic-Park Lane 50720)	.50	2.00	79
FABULOUS ROYALS, The				
LAND OF 1000 DANCES/I Only Have Eyes For You	(Aegis 1006)	1.00	4.00	
FABULOUS SILVER CATS, The				
(THEME FROM) DRAWBRIDGE/On The Beach	(Elm 8255)	1.25	5.00	68
FACENDA, Tommy				
HIGH SCHOOL U.S.A./Give Me Another Chance (With Gary U.S. Bonds)	(Legrande 1001)	1.25	5.00	59
HIGH SCHOOL U.S.A./Plea Of Love	(Atlantic 2051-2078)	1.50	6.00	59

The original version of "High School U.S.A." on Legrande was a regional release which included the actual names of high schools in Virginia. It was completely re-recorded for Atlantic records and given a different flip side. The song was recorded with a standard opening on the master that was used for national release, but with different school names edited into 28 different pressings, each for regional release, each mentioning actual high schools in a specific area. The effect was a national release, but unique in that no matter where the listener lived he would hear the mention of local or nearby high schools.

Each of the custom made regional releases had its own Atlantic catalog. In theory, all are of equal value. However any of them could be of much greater value to a collector trying to complete the entire set of 28.

TITLE/FLIP	LABEL & NO.	GOOD	NEAR MINT	YR.
Virginia	(Atlantic 2051)			
New York City Area	(Atlantic 2052)			
North Carolina-South Carolina	(Atlantic 2053)			
Washington D.C.	(Atlantic 2054)			
Philadelphia	(Atlantic 2055)			
Detroit, Michigan	(Atlantic 2056)			
Pittsburgh Area	(Atlantic 2057)			
Minneapolis-St. Paul	(Atlantic 2058)			
Florida	(Atlantic 2059)			
Newark, New Jersey	(Atlantic 2060)			
Boston Area	(Atlantic 2061)			
Cleveland	(Atlantic 2062)			
Buffalo, New York	(Atlantic 2063)			
Hartford Area	(Atlantic 2064)			
Nashville, Tennessee	(Atlantic 2065)			
Indiana	(Atlantic 2066)			
Chicago Area	(Atlantic 2067)			
New Orleans	(Atlantic 2068)			
St. Louis-Kansas City Area	(Atlantic 2069)			
Alabama-Georgia	(Atlantic 2070)			
Cincinnati, Ohio	(Atlantic 2071)			
Memphis	(Atlantic 2072)			
Los Angeles Area	(Atlantic 2073)			
San Francisco Area	(Atlantic 2074)			
Texas	(Atlantic 2075)			
Seattle-Portland	(Atlantic 2076)			
Denver	(Atlantic 2077)			
Oklahoma	(Atlantic 2078)			
FACES (Formerly Small Faces)				
CHRISTMAS/New Years Resolution	(Iguana 101)	1.25	5.00	
CINDY INCIDENTALLY/Skewiff (Mend The Fuse)	(Warner Bros. 7681)	.75	3.00	73
I'LL WALK ALONE/I Didn't Want Her	(Regina 1328)	1.50	6.00	
MAYBE I'M AMAZED/Oh Lord I'm Browned Off	(Warner Bros. 7483)	.75	3.00	71
OOH-LA-LA/Borstal Boys	(Warner Bros. 7711)	.75	3.00	73
SKEETER JONES/What Is This Dream	(Regina 1326)	1.00	4.00	
STAY WITH ME/You're So Rude	(Warner Bros. 7545)	.75	3.00	71
YOU CAN MAKE ME DANCE, SING OR ANYTHING (EVEN TAKE THE DOG FOR A WALK, MEND A FUSE, FOLD AWAY THE IRONING BOARD, OR ANY OTHER DOMESTIC SHORT COMINGS)/ As Long As You Tell Him	(Warner Bros. 8066)	1.25	5.00	74
YOU CAN MAKE ME DANCE, SING OR ANYTHING (EVEN TAKE THE DOG FOR A WALK, MEND A FUSE, FOLD AWAY THE IRONING BOARD, OR ANY OTHER DOMESTIC SHORT COMINGS)/ As Long As You Tell Him (Warner Bros. 8102 is a re-mix of Warner Bros. 8066.)	(Warner Bros. 8102)	.75	3.00	75
Also see Stewart, Rod				
Als see Wood, Ron				
FADS, The				
JUST LIKE A WOMAN/The Problem Is	(Mercury 72542)	.75	3.00	66
FAGAN, Jim				
THAT LAST ENCORE/The Night My Lady Learned To Love	(Webcor 101)	.50	2.00	77
FAIA, Tommy, & The True Blue Facts				
I'M BACK/Who's Got The Right	(A&M 900)	1.00	4.00	68
RAIN, RAIN, RAIN, RAIN/The Boy I Left Behind	(A&M 945)	1.00	4.00	68
YOU'VE GOT MY SOUL/An Exception To The Rule	(A&M 983)	1.00	4.00	68
FAIR, Carlo				
BEETLE BOUNCE/	(Express 801)	1.25	5.00	64
FAIRLANES, The				
SURF TRAIN/Lonely Weekends	(Reprise 20213)	1.00	4.00	63
FAIRLANES, The				
BABY BABY/Tell Me	(Radiant 101)	2.50	10.00	
I'M NOT THE KIND OF GUY/The Dagwood	(Minaret 103)	1.00	4.00	
FAIRMOUNTS, The				
TIMES & PLACES/Lucky Guy	(Planet 53)	2.50	10.00	
FAIRPORT CONVENTION (With Sandy Denny & Ian Matthews)				
SI TU DOIS PARTIRI/Genesis Hall	(A&M 1155)	1.00	4.00	71
TIME IS NEAR, THE/John Lee	(A&M 1348)	1.00	4.00	72
FAITH, Adam				
DON'T THAT BEAT ALL/Mix Me A Person	(Dot 16407)	1.00	4.00	62
FIRST TIME, THE/So Long Baby	(Amy 895)	1.00	4.00	64
I DON'T NEED THAT KIND OF LOVIN'/ I'm Used To Losing You	(Capitol 5543)	1.00	4.00	65
IT'S ALRIGHT/Just Don't Know	(Amy 913)	.75	3.00	64
SO LONG BABY/The First Time	(Amy 895)	1.00	4.00	64
TALK ABOUT LOVE/Stop Feeling Sorry For Yourself	(Amy 922)	1.00	4.00	65
TO MAKE A BIG MAN CRY/Here's Another Day	(Capitol 5699)	1.00	4.00	66
WE ARE IN LOVE/What Now?	(Amy 899)	.75	3.00	64
WHAT DO YOU WANT/From Now Until Forever	(Cub 9061)	1.00	4.00	59
FAITH BAND, The				
DANCIN' SHOES/Desire	(Village 202)	.75	3.00	78
DANCIN' SHOES/Desire	(Mercury-Village 74037)	.50	2.00	78
PARADISE/	(Mercury-Village 76024)	.50	2.00	79
TOUCHY SITUATION/Big City Lights	(Mercury-Village 74090)	.50	2.00	79
YOU'RE MY WEAKNESS/Forever	(Mercury-Village 74068)	.50	2.00	79
FAITH, Percy				
ALL MY LOVE/This Is The Time	(Columbia 1-752)	1.25	5.00	50
DELICADO/Festival	(Columbia 4-39708)	1.25	5.00	52
HOT CANARY, THE/Nervous Gavotte	(Columbia 4-39329)	1.25	5.00	52
I CROSS MY FINGERS/Valencia	(Columbia 1-607)	1.25	5.00	50
IF I HAD A MAGIC CARPET/ They Can't Take Her Love Away From Me	(Columbia 4-38862)	1.25	5.00	50
ON TOP OF OLD SMOKEY (With Burl Ives)/ Syncopated Clock	(Columbia 4-39328)	1.25	5.00	51
(SONG FROM) MOULIN ROUGE (With Felicia Sanders Vocal)/ Swedish Rhapsody	(Columbia 4-39944)	1.25	5.00	53
(THEME FOR) YOUNG LOVERS/Bimini Goombay (Instrumentals)	(Columbia 4-41655)	.75	3.00	60
(THEME FROM) A SUMMER PLACE/Go-Go-Po-Go	(Columbia 4-41490)	.75	3.00	60
(THEME FROM) A SUMMER PLACE/Go-Go-Po-Go (Stereo single issue)	(Columbia S7-41490)	1.50	6.00	60
TIME FOR LOVE IS ANYTIME, THE/ Peppermint Hill & Strawberry Lane	(Columbia 4-45051)	.75	3.00	69
FAITHFULL, Marianne				
AS TEARS GO BY/Greensleeves	(London 9697)	.75	3.00	64
BROKEN ENGLISH/Brain Drain	(Island 49121)	.50	2.00	79
COME & STAY WITH ME/What Have I Done Wrong	(London 9731)	.75	3.00	65
COUNTING/Tomorrow's Calling	(London 20012)	.75	3.00	66
GO AWAY FROM MY WORLD/Oh Look Around You	(London 9802)	.75	3.00	65
IS THIS WHAT I GET (FOR LOVING YOU)/ Tomorrow's Calling	(London 20020)	.75	3.00	72
SISTER MORPHINE/Something Better (With the Rolling Stones)	(London 1022)	12.50	50.00	69
SUMMER NIGHTS/The Sha-La-La Song	(London 9780)	.75	3.00	65
THIS LITTLE BIRD/Morning Sun	(London 9759)	.75	3.00	65
FALANA, Lola				
COCONUT GROVE/Working In The Coal Mine	(Reprise 0553)	.75	3.00	67
FALCONE, Tommy, & The Centuries				
LIKE WEIRD/Ship To Shore (Instrumentals)	(Design DSR-841)	1.00	4.00	59
FALCON, Billy: see Billy Falcon's Burning Rose				
FALCONER, Roderick				
PLAY IT AGAIN/New Nation	(United Artists 900)	.50	2.00	76
ROCK CITY/	(United Artists 1058)	.50	2.00	77
FALLEN ANGELS, The				
BAD WOMAN/Pimples & Braces	(Eceip 1004)	1.00	4.00	
UP ON THE MOUNTAIN/So Young, So Fine	(Tollie 9049)	1.00	4.00	65
FALLING PEBBLES, The (The Buckinghams)				
LAWDY MISS CLAWDY/Virginia Wolf	(Alley Cat 201)	3.00	12.00	
FALLING STARS, The				
BATMAN/Real Batman	(Black 101)	.75	3.00	66
FAME, Georgie				
BALLAD OF BONNIE & CLYDE, THE/Beware Of The Dog	(Epic 10283)	.75	3.00	68
EVERLOVIN' WOMAN/	(Island 035)	.75	3.00	75
FIRE & RAIN/The Movie Star Song	(Epic 10640)	.75	3.00	70
GET AWAY/El Bandido (With the Blue Flames)	(Imperial 66189)	.75	3.00	66
HIDEAWAY/Kentucky Child	(Epic 10347)	.75	3.00	68
IN THE MEANTIME/Let The Sunshine In (With the Blue Flames)	(Imperial 66104)	.75	3.00	65
LAST NIGHT/Funny How The Time Slips Away (With the Blue Flames)	(Imperial 66299)	.75	3.00	67
LIKE WE USED TO BE/Blue Monday (With the Blue Flames)	(Imperial 66125)	.75	3.00	65
SOMEONE TO WATCH OVER ME/For Your Pleasure	(Epic 10402)	.75	3.00	69
YEH, YEH/Preach & Teach (With the Blue Flames)	(Imperial 66086)	.75	3.00	65
FAME & PRICE - PRICE & FAME TOGETHER (Georgie Fame & Alan Price)				
ROSETTA/John & Mary	(Reprise 1014)	.75	3.00	71
FAMILY (With Chapman & Whitney)				
BURLESQUE/The Rockin' R's	(United Artists 50951)	.75	3.00	72
IN MY OWN TIME/Seasons	(United Artists 50832)	.75	3.00	71
IT'S ONLY A MOVIE/	(United Artists 416)	.75	3.00	73
MY FRIEND THE SUN/	(United Artists 171)	.75	3.00	72
FAMILY, The				
FACE THE AUTUMN/So Much To Remember	(USA 886)	1.00	4.00	68
FAMILY AT MAX				
LEARNIN' TO LIVE TOGETHER (SPACE CAPTAIN)/ We Got To Get Together	(Sound Odyssey 5008)	1.00	4.00	73
FAMILY TREE, The				
DO YOU HAVE THE TIME/Keepin' A Secret	(RCA Victor 47-9184)	1.00	4.00	67
ELECTRIC KANGAROO/Terry Tommy	(Paula 329)	1.00	4.00	68
PRINCE OF DREAMS/	(Mira 228)	1.00	4.00	
SLIPPIN' THROUGH MY FINGERS/Miss Butters	(RCA Victor 47-9565)	1.00	4.00	68
SHE HAD TO FLY/He Spins Around	(RCA Victor 47-9671)	1.00	4.00	68
FAMOUS MC LEVERTYS, The				
DON'T BLAME IT ON ELVIS/Tickie Tickie	(Verve 10029)	2.00	8.00	56
FANCY				
TOUCH ME/I Don't Need Your Love	(Big Tree 16026)	.75	3.00	74
WILD THING/Fancy	(Big Tree 15004)	.75	3.00	74

TITLE/FLIP | LABEL & NO. | GOOD | NEAR MINT | YR.

FANDANGO
BLAME IT ON THE NIGHT/ (RCA 11711) .50 2.00 79
HEADLINER/ (RCA 11194) .50 2.00 78
LAST KISS/San Joaquin (RCA 11357) .50 2.00 78
LATE NIGHTS/ (RCA 11639) .50 2.00 79

FANNY
AIN'T THAT PECULIAR/Think About The Children (Reprise 1080) .50 2.00 72
ALL MINE/ (Reprise 1148) .75 3.00 73
BUTTER BOY/Begger Man (Casablanca 814) .50 2.00 75
CHANGING HORSES/Conversation With A Cop (Reprise 0963) .75 3.00 71
CHARITY BALL/Place In The Country (Reprise 1033) .50 2.00 71
I'VE HAD IT/The First Time (Casablanca 0009) .50 2.00 74
KNOCK ON MY DOOR/Young & Dumb (Reprise 1119) .75 3.00 73
LADIES' CHOICE/New Day (Reprise 0901) .75 3.00 70
LAST NIGHT I HAD A DREAM/Beside Myself (Reprise 1162) .75 3.00 73
NOWHERE TO RUN/ (Reprise 0938) .75 3.00 70
WONDERFUL FEELING/Rock Bottom Blues (Reprise 1097) .75 3.00 72
This band backed up Barbra Streisand (Circa 1970) at one time.

FANS, The
I WANT A BEETLE FOR CHRISTMAS/
How Far Should My Heart Go (Dot 16688) 1.25 5.00 64

FANTASTIC BAGGIES, The (Phil Sloan & Steve Barry)
ANYWHERE THE GIRLS ARE/Debbie Be True (Imperial 66072) 2.00 8.00 64
ALONE ON THE BEACH/It Was I (Imperial 66092) 2.50 10.00 65
TELL 'EM I'M SURFIN'/Surfer Boy's Dream (Imperial 66047) 2.00 8.00 64
Also see Philip and Stephen

FANTASTICS, The
DANCE FOR AN UN-NAMED GYPSY QUEEN/Malaguena (Scorpio 407) 1.50 6.00 66

FARAGHER BROTHERS, The
FOLLOW MY HEART/I'm Wakin' Up (ABC 12277) .75 3.00 77
IT'S ALL RIGHT/Give It Up (ABC 12191) .75 3.00 76
NEVER GET YOUR LOVE BEHIND ME/Never Felt Love Before (ABC 12210) .75 3.00 76
OPEN YOUR EYES/ (Polydor 14563) .50 2.00 79
SAY WHEN/ (Polydor 2038) .50 2.00 79
STAY THE NIGHT/That's A Start (Polydor 14533) .50 2.00 79
THANX A LOT/You Know That (ABC 12259) .75 3.00 77

FARDON, Don
DELTA QUEEN/Hometown Baby (Chelsea 0115) .50 2.00 73
(LAMENT OF THE CHEROKEE, THE) INDIAN RESERVATION/
Dreaming Room (GNP Crescendo 405) .75 3.00 68
TAKE A HEART/How Do You Mend A Broken Heart? (GNP Crescendo 418) .75 3.00 68

FARINA, Mini & Richard
ONE WAY TICKET/Reno Nevada (Vanguard 35030) .75 3.00 65
Mini Farina is Joan Baez's sister.

FARLOWE, Chris
HANDBAGS & GLADRAGS/Everyone Makes A Mistake (Immediate 5005) .75 3.00 68
OUT OF TIME/Baby, Make It Soon (MGM 13567) 1.25 5.00 66
PAINT IT, BLACK/You're So Good To Me (Immediate 5002) .75 3.00 67
PAINT IT BLACK/What Have I Been Doing (Immediate 5011) .75 3.00 68
Also see Atomic Rooster

FARMER, Donny
MY BRIDE/A Boy, A Girl & A Breeze (Roulette 4193) 1.00 4.00 59

FARNER, Mark, & Don Brewer
WE GOTTA HAVE LOVE/Harlem Shuffle (Lucky Eleven 74011) 1.25 5.00 68
Farner & Brewer became members of Grand Funk Railroad. They later comprised Monumental Funk.

FARNER, Mark, Band
JUST ONE LOOK/ (Atlantic 3529) .50 2.00 78
WHEN A MAN LOVES A WOMAN/If It Took All Day (Atlantic 3510) .50 2.00 78
YOU & ME BABY/ (Atlantic 3448) .50 2.00 77

FARON'S FLAMINGOS
LET'S STOMP/
I Can Tell (By Rory Storm & The Hurricanes) (Columbia 4-43018) 1.25 5.00 64

FAR-OUT UNDERGROUND ACID ROCK FEET OF HARRY ZONK, The
HEY JUDE/For What It's Worth (Crazy Horse 1314) .75 3.00 69

FARR, Gary, & The T-Bones
GIVE ALL SHE'S GOT/Don't Stop & Stare (Epic 9832) .75 3.00 65

FARR, Little Joey
ROCK & ROLL SANTA/Big White Cadillac (Band Box 286) .75 3.00 61

FARRAR, Tony
BLAST FROM THE PAST, A/Following You (Trans Atlas 001) 1.50 6.00 61
(Begins with a portion of "In The Still Of The Night" by the Five Satins. Tony then begins his recording as the Satins fade out.)

FARREL & THE FLAMES
YOU'LL BE SORRY/Dreams & Memories (Fransil 14) 3.75 15.00

FARRELL, Mickey, & The Dynamics
BABY MINE/I'm Calling On You (Bethlehem 3080) 2.50 10.00

FARRELL, Tony
FLAME IN MY HEART, A/Stumpy Stump (Time 1000) 1.00 4.00 58

FASCINATORS, The
CHAPEL BELLS/I Wonder Who (Capitol 4053) 6.25 25.00 58
CHAPEL BELLS/I Wonder Who (Capitol 4544) 3.75 15.00 61
OH ROSE MARIE/Fried Chicken & Macaroni (Capitol 4247) 6.25 25.00 59
OH ROSE MARIE/Forgive Me My Darling (Bim Bam Boom 110) 1.00 4.00
("Oh Rose Marie" is a different version than issued by Capitol)
WHO DO YOU THINK YOU ARE/Come To Paradise (Capitol 4137) 6.25 25.00 59

FASHION
INNOCENT, THE/Red Green &
Gold-Sodium Pentothal Negative (International R.S. 9502) .50 2.00 79

FASHIONETTES, The
DAYDREAMIN' OF YOU/Only Love (GNP-Crescendo 322) .75 3.00 64

FASHIONS, The
FAIRY TALES/Please Let It Be Me (Elmor 301) 1.00 4.00
SURFER'S MEMORIES/Surfin' Back To School (Felsted 8689) 1.25 5.00 63

FASTEST GROUP ALIVE, The
LULLABYE-5:15 SPORTS/Bad News (Valiant 759) 1.25 5.00 67
(Parody)

FAT
OVER THE HILL/The Shape I'm In (RCA 9913) .75 3.00 70
STILL WATER/Jump Town Girl (RCA 0408) .75 3.00 70

FAT CHANCE
COUNTRY MORNING/Hello Misery (RCA 0706) .75 3.00 72

FAT CITY (Bill & Taffy Danoff)
CITY CAT/Wall Street (Probe 469) 1.00 4.00 69
HEY LORETTA/Workingman's Day (Paramount 0176) 1.00 4.00 72

I GUESS HE'D RATHER BE IN COLORADO/
Morning Go Away (Paramount 0162) 1.00 4.00 72
Also see Bill & Taffy
Aslo see Denver, John
Also see Starland Vocal Band, The

FAT MAN'S MUSIC FESTIVAL (With John Carter)
HIGHWAY OF YOUR DREAMS/Boats Of Angel Bay (Scepter SCE-12274) .75 3.00 69
Also see Ivy League

FAULKNER, Clem, & Robert Oakes Jordan
COUNTDOWN/Russian Countdown (Orbit 516) 1.25 5.00
(Novelties)

FAYE, Boots
TIP TOES/Dreamy Moon (RCA Victor 47-8211) .75 3.00 63
(Instrumentals)

FEATHER
FREINDS/Salli (White Whale 353) .75 3.00 70

FEATHERS, The
TRYIN' TO GET TO YOU/My Baby's Soul Good (Team TM-518) .75 3.00 68

FEATHERBED (Featuring Barry Manilow)
AMY/Morning (Bell 971) 3.00 12.00 71
COULD IT BE MAGIC/ (Bell 5133) 3.00 12.00 71

FEDERALS, The
BUCKET FULL OF LOVE/Leah (Capitol 5526) .75 3.00 65

FEGER, Don
LOOK OUT BABY (Ebony 103) 1.00 4.00
(With the Embers)

FELDER'S ORIOLES
DOWN HOME GIRL/Misty (Mercury 72480) 1.00 4.00 65

FELDMAN, Victor, Quartet
TASTE OF HONEY, A/Valerie (Infinity 020) .75 3.00 62
(Instrumentals)

FELICIANO, Jose
ANGELA/ (Private Stock 45062) .50 2.00 76
CHICO & THE MAN (MAIN THEME)/ (RCA 10145) .75 3.00 75
FELIZ NAVIDAD/The Little Drummer Boy (RCA 0404) .75 3.00 70
HEY! BABY/My World Is Empty Without You (RCA 9715) .75 3.00 69
HI-HEEL SNEAKERS/Hitchcock Railway (RCA Victor 47-9641) .75 3.00 68
I LOVE MAKING LOVE TO YOU/ (Private Stock 45151) .50 2.00 77
LIGHT MY FIRE/California Dreamin' (RCA Victor 47-9550) .75 3.00 68
MARGUERITA/ (Private Stock 45143) .50 2.00 77
MARLEY PURT DRIVE/ (RCA 9739) .75 3.00 69
RAIN/ (RCA 9757) .75 3.00 69
STAR SPANGLED BANNER, THE/And I Love Her (RCA Victor 47-9665) .75 3.00 68
SUSIE-Q/Destiny (RCA 0358) .75 3.00 70
WHERE IS MY WOMAN/One More Mile (RCA 0841) .75 3.00 72
WHY/ (Private Stock 45103) .50 2.00 76

FELIX & THE ESCORTS (With Felix Cavaliere)
SYRACUSE, THE/Save (Jag 685) 5.00 20.00 64
Also see Young Rascals, The

FELIX & THE IDEALS
YOU/Go Ahead & Cry (Fame 1011) 5.00 20.00

FELIX, Julie
CLOTHO'S WEB/Moonlight (RAK 4513) .50 2.00 73

FELTS, Narvel
CRY BABY CRY/Lonesome Feeling (Mercury 71190) 1.25 5.00 57
CUTIE BABY/Three Thousand Miles (Pink 701) 1.00 4.00 59
DREAM WORLD/Rocket Ride (Mercury 71249) 1.25 5.00 57
DREAM WORLD/Rocket Ride Stroll (Mercury 71275) 1.00 4.00 57
HONEY LOVE/Genavee (Pink 702) 1.00 4.00 60
KISS-A-ME BABY/Foolish Thoughts (Mercury 71140) 1.25 5.00 57
MOUNTAIN OF LOVE/End Of My World (Groove 0029) .75 3.00 63

FEMALE BEATLES, The
I WANT YOU/I Don't Want To Cry (20th Fox 531) 1.50 6.00 64

FENCEMEN, The
SOUR GRAPES/Sunday Stranger (Liberty F-55535) 1.00 4.00 63
SWINGIN' GATES/Bach & Roll (Liberty F-55509) 1.00 4.00 62
Instrumentals

FENDER, Freddie
HOLY ONE/Mean Woman (Duncan 1000) 2.00 8.00
HOLY ONE/Mean Woman (Imperial 5659) 1.25 5.00 60
LOVE'S LIGHT IS AN EMBER/The New Stroll (LBL Nocturn 100) 1.00 4.00
MAN CAN CRY, A/You're Something Else (Argo 5375) 2.00 8.00 61
SINCE I MET YOU BABY/Little Mama (Duncan 1004) 2.00 8.00
WASTED DAYS & WASTED NIGHTS/San Antonio Rock (Duncan 1001) 2.50 10.00
WASTED DAYS & WASTED NIGHTS/
I Can't Remember When I Didn't Love You (Imperial 5670) 1.25 5.00 60
WILD SIDE OF LIFE, THE/Crazy Baby (Duncan 1002) 2.00 8.00
"Wasted Days & Wasted Nights" and "Since I Met You Baby" were reissued in 1975 on Dot and on GRT, respectively.

FENDER IV, The
EVERYBODY UP/Malibu Run (Imperial 66098) 1.00 4.00 65
YOU BETTER TELL ME NOW/Mar Gaya (Imperial 66061) 1.00 4.00 64

FENDERMEN, The
CAN'T YOU WAIT/Heartbreakin' Special (Soma 1155) 1.00 4.00 61
DON'T YOU JUST KNOW IT/Beach Party (Soma 1142) 1.00 4.00 60
MULE SKINNER BLUES/Torture (Cuca 1003) 5.00 20.00 60
MULE SKINNER BLUES/Torture (Soma 1137) 1.00 4.00 60
RAIN DROP/"Fas-Nacht-Kuechel" (Dab 102) 1.00 4.00

FENTON, Shane, & The Fentones
DON'T DO THAT/I'll Know (Laurie 3287) .75 3.00 63
DON'T DO THAT/I'll Know (20th Fox 439) .75 3.00 63

FENWAYS, The
BE CAREFUL LITTLE GIRL/Be Careful Little Girl (Part 2) (Beumar 402) 1.25 5.00 64
BE CAREFUL LITTLE GIRL/Be Careful Little Girl (Part 2) (Roulette 4573) .75 3.00 64
HARD ROAD AHEAD/Fight, The (Blue Cat 116) .75 3.00 65
I MOVE AROUND/A Go-Go (Co & Ce 241) .75 3.00 66
I'M A MOVER/Satisfied (Co & Ce 233) .75 3.00 66
I'M YOUR TOY/Theme For Pammy (Co & Ce 243) .75 3.00 66
NOTHING TO OFFER YOU/The #1 Song In The Country (Ricky 106) 1.50 6.00 64
NOTHING TO OFFER YOU/Humpty Dumpty (Beumar 401) 1.25 5.00 64
NOTHING TO OFFER YOU/Humpty Dumpty (Chess 1901) 1.00 4.00 64
WALK/Whip & Jerk (Imperial 66082) .75 3.00 64

FERGUSON, Jay (Of Spirit)
LOSING CONTROL/Happy Birthday, Baby (Asylum 45480) .50 2.00 78
LOSING CONTROL/City Of Angels (Asylum 46041) .50 2.00 79
PAYING TIME/Too Late To Save Your Heart (Asylum 46508) .50 2.00 79
THUNDER ISLAND/Magic Moment (Asylum 45444) .50 2.00 77
Also see Jo Jo Gunne

FERGUSON, Johnny
ANGELA JONES/Blue Serge & White Lace (MGM K-12855) 1.00 4.00 60
I UNDERSTAND JUST HOW YOU FEEL/Flutter Flutter (MGM K-12905) .75 3.00 60
WAITIN' FOR THE SANDMAN/Afterglow (MGM K-12789) 1.00 4.00 59

FERGUSON TRACTOR
12 O'CLOCK HIGH/Desperation Blues (MTA 169) 1.00 4.00

FERIS WHEEL
BEST PART OF BREAKING UP/Woman (Magenda 5653) 1.00 4.00

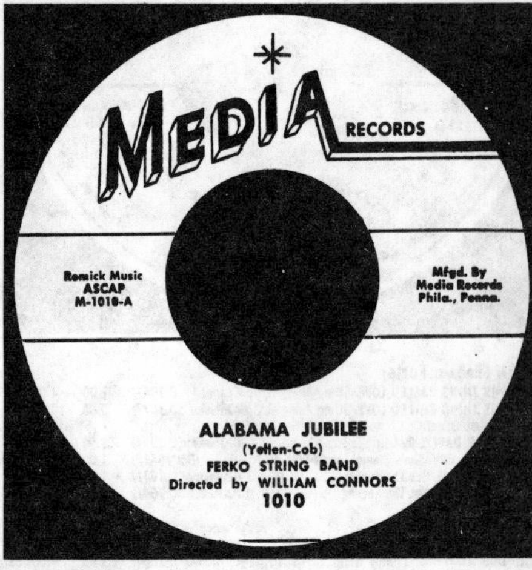

FERKO STRING BAND, The
AULD LANG SYNE/My Little Girl (Palda 1100) 1.00 4.00
ALABAMA JUBILEE/Sing A Little Melody (Media 1010) 1.00 4.00 55
DEEP IN THE HEART OF TEXAS/Happy Days Are Here Again (Media 1016) 1.00 4.00 55
GOLDEN SLIPPERS/Hello (Ferko 4501) 1.00 4.00
YOU ARE MY SUNSHINE/Ma (Media 1013) 1.00 4.00 55

FERNANDEZ, Pepe
C-RATIONS & CORN BREAD/Having Fun (20th Fox 6685) .75 3.00 67

FERN, Bill
BIG GAME/Stolen Bases (Sport 505) 2.50 10.00
(Novelty/Break-in)

FERRANTE & TEICHER (Arthur Ferrante & Louis Teicher)
BEEZWHACKS/That Old Black Magic (Columbia 103) 1.25 5.00 53
EXODUS/Twilight (United Artists 274) .75 3.00 60
EXODUS/Twilight (United Artists 274) 1.50 6.00 60
(Stereo single issue)
LIDA ROSE/Take Me Along (ABC-Paramount 10165) .75 3.00 61
LIDA ROSE/Till There Was You (ABC-Paramount 10347) .75 3.00 62
LOVERS SYMPHONY/Dream Concerto (United Artists 196) .75 3.00 59
MIDNIGHT COWBOY/Popi (United Artists 50554) .50 2.00 69
PIECES OF DREAMS/Magical Connection (United Artists 50711) .50 2.00 70
SIDE SADDLE/Prairie Blues (ABC-Paramount 10017) 1.00 4.00 59
TABU/Semper Fidelis (Columbia 4-40068) 1.25 5.00 53
THEME FROM STAR STEK/Swinging On A Star (United Artists UA-X1173-Y) .50 2.00 78
(THEME FROM) THE APARTMENT/Lonely (United Artists 231) .75 3.00 60
TONIGHT/Dream Of Love (United Artists 373) .75 3.00 61
WHAT MORE CAN I SAY/
I've Grown Acustomed To Her Face (United Artists 770) .75 3.00 64

FERRARA, Peter, & Bobby Pickett
STARDREK/Theme From Star Trek (Pizzeria 1) 1.25 5.00
STARDREK/Godfather's Respect (Pizzeria 1) 1.00 4.00
STARDREK/Godfather's Respect (Pizzeria-Space 1) .75 3.00
STARDREK/Mangy Old Sidewinder (Pizzeria 1) 1.00 4.00
(This issue contains a different take of "Stardrek.")

FERRA, Tina
"R" (IS FOR RINGO)/Modern Youth (Limelight 3027) 1.25 5.00 64

FERRELL, Fancy
CHRIS ANN/Please Hold Me (Centauri 1) 2.00 8.00

FERRER, Jose
WOMAN (UH-HUH)/Man (By Rosemary Clooney) (Columbia 4-40144) 1.25 5.00 53

FERRIER, Garry
RINGO-DEER/Just My Luck (Academy 112) 1.25 5.00 64

FERRIS & THE WHEELS
I WANT TO DANCE (EVERY NIGHT)/Chop Chop (Bambi 801) 1.50 6.00 61
MOMENTS LIKE THIS/He Was A Fortune Teller (United Artists 458) 6.25 25.00 62

TITLE/FLIP	LABEL & NO.	GOOD	NEAR MINT	YR.
FERRY, Bryan (Of Roxy Music)				
HARD RAIN'S A GONNA FALL, A/	(Atlantic 3017)	.50	2.00	74
HEART ON MY SLEEVE/Re-Make Re-Model	(Atlantic 3364)	.50	2.00	77
LET'S STICK TOGETHER (LET'S WORK TOGETHER)/ Sea Breezes	(Atlantic 3351)	.50	2.00	76
SIGN OF THE TIMES/Can't Let Go	(Atlantic 3539)	.50	2.00	79
TOKYO JOE/	(Atlantic 3399)	.50	2.00	77
FEVER TREE, The				
CLANCY (NOWADAYS CLANCY CAN'T EVEN SING)/ The Sun Also Rises	(Uni 55172)	1.25	5.00	69
GIRL, OH GIRL (DON'T PUSH ME)/Steve Lenore	(Mainstream 665)	2.00	8.00	67
HEY MISTER/I Can Beat Your Drum	(Mainstream 661)	2.00	8.00	67
LOVE MAKES THE SUN RISE/Filigree & Shadow	(Uni 55146)	1.25	5.00	69
SAN FRANCISCO GIRLS (RETURN OF THE NATIVE)/ Come With Me (Rainsong)	(Uni 55060)	1.00	4.00	68
SHE COMES IN COLOR/	(Ampex 11013)	1.00	4.00	70
WHAT TIME DID YOU SAY IT WAS IN SALT LAKE CITY/ Where Do You Go	(Uni 55095)	1.25	5.00	68
F.F. & Z				
EVERYBODY GET OUT OF BED/Spaced On Happy	(Epic 5-1-9-6)	.75	3.00	72
FIDELITONES, The				
PLAYBOY/Say Hey Pretty Baby	(Marlo 1518)	1.00	4.00	
Fi-DELLS, The				
NO OTHER LOVE/Come Back To Me	(Warner 1014)	1.00	4.00	
(Female group)				
FI-DELLS				
WHAT IS LOVE/Don't Let Me Love You	(Imperial 5780)	1.00	4.00	61
(Male group)				
FIELD, Jerry, & The Lawyers				
TRIAL, THE/Easy Steppin'	(Parkway 801)	2.50	10.00	59
(Novelty/Break-in, may also be shown as by Jerry Field & the Philadelphia Lawyers.)				
FIELD, Sally				
FELICIDAD/Find Yourself A Rainbow	(Colgems 66-1008)	.75	3.00	67
GOLDEN DAYS/You're A Grand Old Flag	(Colgems 66-1014)	.75	3.00	68
FIELDS, Ernie				
CHARLESTON, THE/12th Street Rag	(Rendezvous 150)	.75	3.00	61
CHATTANOOGA CHOO CHOO/Workin' Out	(Rendezvous 117)	.75	3.00	60
IN THE MOOD/Christopher Columbus	(Rendezvous 110)	.75	3.00	59
TEEN FLIP/Sweet Slumber	(Rendezvous 129)	.75	3.00	60
Instrumentals				
FIELDS, W. C., Memorial Electric String Band				
HIPPY ELEVATOR OPERATOR/Don't Lose The Girl	(HBR 507)	1.50	6.00	66
I'M NOT YOUR STEPPING STONE/Round World	(Mercury 72578)	2.00	8.00	66
FIENDS, The				
THEME FROM "THE ADDAMS FAMILY"/ Quetzal Quake	(GNP-Crescendo 335)	.75	3.00	65
(Instrumentals)				
FIFTH DIMENSION, The (Featuring Marilyn McCoo & Billy Davis Jr.)				
A CHANGE IS GONNA COME-PEOPLE GOTTA BE FREE (MEDLEY)/The Declaration	(Bell 860)	.50	2.00	70
ANOTHER DAY, ANOTHER HEARTACHE/Rosecrans Blvd.	(Soul City 755)	.75	3.00	67
AQUARIUS-LET THE SUNSHINE IN-THE FLESH FAILURES (MEDLEY)/Don'tcha Hear Me	(Soul City 772)	.75	3.00	69
ASHES TO ASHES/The Singer	(Bell 45380)	.50	2.00	73
BLOWING AWAY/Skinny Man	(Soul City 780)	.75	3.00	70
CALIFORNIA SOUL/It'll Never Be The Same	(Soul City 770)	.75	3.00	68
CARPET MAN/The Magic Garden	(Soul City 762)	.75	3.00	68
EVERYTHING'S BEEN CHANGED/There Never Was A Day	(Bell 45338)	.50	2.00	73
GIRL'S SONG, THE/It'll Never Be The Same	(Soul City 781)	.75	3.00	70
GO WHERE YOU WANNA GO/Too Poor To Die	(Soul City 753)	.75	3.00	67
IF I COULD REACH YOU/Tomorrow Belongs To The Children	(Bell 45261)	.50	2.00	72
(LAST NIGHT) I DIDN'T GET TO SLEEP AT ALL/ The River Watch	(Bell 45195)	.50	2.00	72
LIGHT SINGS/Viva Tirado	(Bell 999)	.50	2.00	71
LIVING TOGETHER, GROWING TOGETHER/	(Bell 45310)	.50	2.00	73
LOVE HANGOVER/Will You Be There	(ABC 12181)	.50	2.00	76
LOVE'S LINES, ANGELS & RHYMES/The Singer	(Bell 965)	.50	2.00	71
MAGIC IN MY LIFE/	(ABC 12136)	.50	2.00	75
NEVER MY LOVE/	(Bell 45134)	.50	2.00	71
ON THE BEACH (IN THE SUMMERTIME)/	(Bell 913)	.50	2.00	70
ONE LESS BELL TO ANSWER/Feelin' Alright	(Bell 940)	.50	2.00	70
PAPER CUP/Poor Side Of Town	(Soul City 760)	.75	3.00	68
PUPPET MAN/A Love Like Ours	(Bell 880)	.50	2.00	70
SAVE THE COUNTRY/	(Bell 895)	.50	2.00	70
STONED SOUL PICNIC/The Sailboat Song	(Soul City 766)	.75	3.00	68
SWEET BLINDNESS/ Bobby's Blues (Who Do You Think Of?)	(Soul City 768)	.75	3.00	68
TOGETHER LET'S FIND LOVE/I Just Wanta Be Your Friend	(Bell 45170)	.50	2.00	72
TRAIN, KEEP ON MOVING/I'll Be Loving You Forever	(Soul City 752)	.75	3.00	66
UP, UP & AWAY/Which Way To Nowhere	(Soul City 756)	.75	3.00	67
WEDDING BELL BLUES/Lovin' Stew	(Soul City 779)	.75	3.00	69
WORKIN' ON A GROOVY THING/Broken Wing Bird	(Soul City 779)	.75	3.00	69
Marilyn McCoo & Billy Davis Jr. are not featured on the ABC issues. Also see Versatiles, The				
FIFTH ESTATE, The				
DING DONG THE WITCH IS DEAD/The Rub-a-dub	(Jubilee 5573)	.75	3.00	67
GOFFIN' SONG, THE/Lost Generation	(Jubilee 5588)	.75	3.00	67
HEIGH-HO/It's Waiting There For You	(Jubilee 5595)	.75	3.00	67
MICKEY MOUSE CLUB MARCH/ I Knew You Before I Met You	(Jubilee 5655)	.75	3.00	69
MORNING, MORNING/Tomorrow Is My Turn	(Jubilee 5607)	.75	3.00	67
FINDERS KEEPERS				
FRIDAY KIND OF MONDAY/On The Beach	(Fontana 1609)	.75	3.00	68
FINNEGAN, Larry				
DEAR ONE/Candy Lips	(Old Town 1113)	.75	3.00	62
PRETTY SUZY SUNSHINE/The Walkin' Talkin' Blues	(Old Town 1120)	.75	3.00	63
THERE AIN'T NOTHIN' IN THIS WORLD/I'll Be Back Jack	(Coral 62313)	.75	3.00	62
TRIBUTE TO RINGO STARR (THE OTHER RINGO), A/ When My Love Passes By	(Ric 146)	1.00	4.00	64
FINNEGAN, Mike (Of Krueger, Finnegan & Dudek)				
EXPRESSWAY TO YOUR HEART/ Blood Is Thicker Than Water	(Columbia 10712)	.50	2.00	78
EXPRESSWAY TO YOUR HEART/ Blood Is Thicker Than Water	(Columbia 10741)	.50	2.00	78
SAVED BY THE GRACE OF YOUR LOVE/	(Warner Bros. 8264)	.75	3.00	76
FINN, Mickey, & The Blue Men				
THIS SPORTING LIFE/Night Comes Down	(United Artists 1048)	.75	3.00	65
FIRE				
FLIGHT TO CUBA/Soul On Ice	(Bay Town 014)	1.00	4.00	
FIREBALLS, The (With Jimmy Gilmer)				
BOTTLE OF WINE/Can't You See I'm Trying	(Atco 6491)	.75	3.00	67
BULLDOG/Nearly Sunrise	(Top Rank 2026)	1.00	4.00	59
BULLDOG/Nearly Sunrise	(Top Rank 2026-ST)	2.00	8.00	59
(Stereo single issue)				

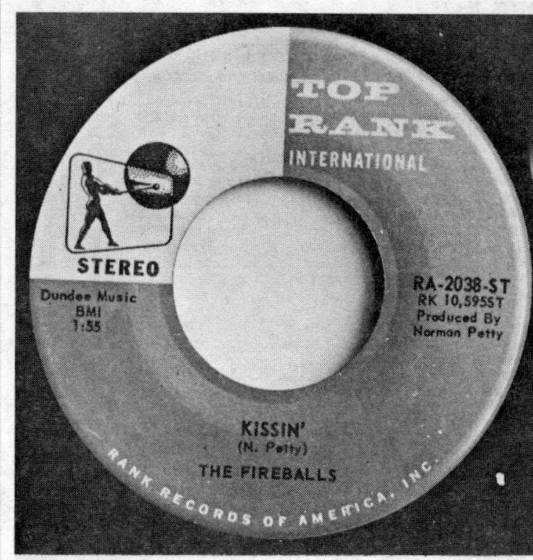

TITLE/FLIP	LABEL & NO.	GOOD	NEAR MINT	YR.
CAMPUSOLOGY/Ahhh, Soul	(Dot 16745)	.75	3.00	65
CHICKEN LITTLE/3 Minutes Time	(Dot 6595)	.75	3.00	68
COME ON, REACT/Woman Help Me	(Atco 6614)	.75	3.00	68
FIREBALL/I Don't Know	(Kapp 248)	1.00	4.00	59
FOOT PATTER/Kissin'	(Top Rank 2038)	1.00	4.00	60
FOOT PATTER/Kissin'	(Top Rank 2038-ST)	2.00	8.00	60
(Stereo single issue, although only "Kissin'" is in true stereo.)				
GOIN' AWAY/Groovy Motions	(Atco 6569)	.75	3.00	68
GOOD MORNING SHAME/Watch Her Walk	(Atco 6678)	.75	3.00	70
I THINK I'LL CATCH A BUS/Shy Girl	(Dot 16992)	.75	3.00	67
LONG GREEN/Light In The Window	(Atco 6651)	.75	3.00	69
MR. REED/Dumbo	(Dot 16661)	.75	3.00	64
MORE THAN I CAN SAY/The Beating Of My Heart	(Dot 16715)	.75	3.00	65
QUITE A PARTY/Gunshot	(Warwick 644)	1.00	4.00	61
RIK-A-TIK/Yacky Doo	(Top Rank 3003)	1.00	4.00	61
RIK-A-TIK/Yacky Doo	(Warwick 630)	.75	3.00	61
SWEET TALK/Almost Paradise	(Top Rank 2081)	1.00	4.00	61
TORQUAY/Cry Baby	(Top Rank 2008)	1.00	4.00	59
TORQUAY TWO/Peg Leg	(Dot 16493)	.75	3.00	63
VAQUERO/Chief Whoopen Koff	(Top Rank 2054)	1.00	4.00	60
Instrumentals				
FIREBIRDS, The				
FIREBIRD/Wheels On Fire	(Super K SK-6)	.75	3.00	68
FIRE ESCAPE				
LOVE SPECIAL DELIVERY/Blood Beat	(GNP Crescendo 384)	.75	3.00	67
FIREFALL (Featuring Rick Roberts)				
CINDERELLA/Dolphin's Lullaby	(Atlantic 3392)	.50	2.00	77
GOODBYE, I LOVE YOU/Baby	(Atlantic 3544)	.50	2.00	78
JUST REMEMBER I LOVE YOU/Just Think	(Atlantic 3420)	.50	2.00	77
LIVIN' AIN'T LIVIN'/Love Isn't All	(Atlantic 3333)	.50	2.00	76
SO LONG/Piece Of Paper	(Atlantic 3452)	.50	2.00	77
STRANGE WAY/Anymore	(Atlantic 3518)	.50	2.00	78
SWEET & SOUR/Wrong Side Of Town	(Atlantic 3566)	.50	2.00	79
YOU ARE THE WOMAN/Sad Ol' Love Song	(Atlantic 3335)	.50	2.00	76
This group also contained Mark Andes (Of Spirit/Jo Jo Gunne) & Michael Clarke (Of The Byrds).				
FIREFLIES, The (Featuring Richie Adams)				
BLACKSMITH BLUES/Tuff-a-nuff	(Hamilton 50036)	1.00	4.00	63
GIVE ALL YOUR LOVE TO ME/Marianne	(Canadian American 117)	1.25	5.00	60
I CAN'T SAY GOODBYE/What Did I Do Wrong	(Ribbon 6904)	1.25	5.00	59
MY GIRL/Because Of My Pride	(Ribbon 6906)	1.25	5.00	60
YOU WERE MINE (FOR AWHILE)/One O'Clock Twist	(Taurus 355)	3.00	12.00	62
YOU WERE MINE/Stella Got A Fella	(Ribbon 6901)	1.00	4.00	59
FIRE OVER GIBRALTAR				
EPITAPH OF TOMORROW/Now He's Gone	(Kim 103)	.75	3.00	70
FIRESIGN THEATRE				
FORWARD INTO THE PAST/Station Break	(Columbia 4-45052)	.75	3.00	69
HOLYGRAM SONG, THE/	(Columbia AE7-1)	1.25	5.00	70
FIRST CLASS				
AIN'T NO LOVE/	(Private Stock-UK 45093)	.50	2.00	76
BEACH BABY/Both Sides Of The Story	(UK 49022)	.50	2.00	74
DREAMS ARE TEN A PENNY/Lavender Man	(UK 49028)	.50	2.00	74
FUNNY HOW LOVE CAN BE/Surfer Queen	(UK 49033)	.50	2.00	75
FIRST EDITION, THE: see Rogers, Kenny, & The First Edition				
FISHBURN, Mack				
GRACELAND KING, THE/Roads	(Sweetwood 8012)	.50	2.00	77
FISHER BROTHERS, The				
GIRLS CRY OVER BOYS/Thunder & Lightnin'	(Columbia 4-42522)	.75	3.00	62
FISHER, Chip				
NO ONE/Poor Me	(Addison 15002)	1.00	4.00	
FISHER, Eddie				
ANY TIME/Never Before	(RCA Victor 47-4359)	1.25	5.00	51
CINDY, OH CINDY/Around The World	(RCA Victor 47-6677)	1.00	4.00	56
COUNT YOUR BLESSINGS/Fanny	(RCA Victor 47-5871)	1.25	5.00	54
DUNGAREE DOLL/Everybody's Got A Home But Me	(RCA Victor 47-6337)	1.00	4.00	55
FORGIVE ME/That's The Chance You Take	(RCA Victor 47-4574)	1.25	5.00	52
HEART/Near To You	(RCA Victor 47-6015)	1.00	4.00	55
I NEED YOU NOW/Heaven Was Never Like This	(RCA Victor 47-5830)	1.25	5.00	54
I'M WALKING BEHIND YOU/Just Another Polka	(RCA Victor 47-5293)	1.25	5.00	53
I'M YOURS/Just A Little Lovin'	(RCA Victor 47-4680)	1.25	5.00	52
LADY OF SPAIN/Outside Of Heaven	(RCA Victor 47-4963)	1.25	5.00	52
MANY TIMES/Just To Be With You	(RCA Victor 47-5453)	1.25	5.00	53
OH! MY PA-PA/Until You Said "Goodbye"	(RCA Victor 47-5552)	1.25	5.00	53
TELL ME WHY/Trust In Me	(RCA Victor 47-4444)	1.25	5.00	51
THINKING OF YOU/If You Should Leave Me	(RCA Victor 47-3901)	1.25	5.00	50
TURN BACK THE HANDS OF TIME/ I Can't Go On Without You	(RCA Victor 47-4257)	1.25	5.00	51
WISH YOU WERE HERE/The Hand Of Fate	(RCA Victor 47-4830)	1.25	5.00	52
WITH THESE HANDS/When I Was Young	(RCA Victor 47-5365)	1.25	5.00	53
FISHER, Gene, & Mystics				
REMEMBER (YOU'RE MY GIRL)/Listen To Me	(Plateau 101)	.75	3.00	
FISHER, Johnny				
TAN DAN/Everytime You Cry	(Park Ave. 102)	1.25	5.00	63
It had once been thought that Johnny Fisher and Johnny Fortune were one in the same. They are two completely different artists.				
FISHER, Mary Ann				
I CAN'T TAKE IT/Forever More	(Seg-Way 1001)	.75	3.00	61
FISHER, Miss Toni				
BIG HURT, THE/Memphis Belle	(Signet 275)	1.00	4.00	59
EVERLASTING LOVE/The Red Sea Of Mars	(Signet 279)	1.00	4.00	60
HOLD ME/Laugh Or Cry	(Smash 1797)	.75	3.00	63
HOW DEEP IS THE OCEAN/Blue, Blue, Blue	(Signet 276)	1.00	4.00	60
MUSIC FROM THE HOUSE NEXT DOOR/Quickly My Love	(Big Top 3124)	.75	3.00	62
TRAIN OF LOVE/Springtime Of Life	(Signet 664)	1.00	4.00	64
WEST OF THE WALL/What Did I Do	(Big Top 3097)	.75	3.00	62
FISHER, Tommy				
ROCK & ROLL ROBIN HOOD/Audrey	(B&D 1314)	.75	3.00	62
FITE, Buddy				
FOR ONCE IN MY LIFE/Glad Rag Doll	(Cyclone 6)	1.00	4.00	69
(12" 33 single issue, shown on the label as being "the world's first 12" single.")				
FITZGERALD, Ella				
GIVE A LITTLE, GET A LITTLE/There Never Was	(Decca 9-27724)	1.50	6.00	51
GUY IS A GUY, A/That Old Feeling	(Decca 9-28049)	1.50	6.00	52
HOT CANARY, THE/Two Little Men	(Decca 9-27578)	1.50	6.00	51
LOVER, COME BACK TO ME/Old Devil Moon	(Decca 9-29580)	1.00	4.00	55
MACK THE KNIFE/Lorelei	(Verve 10209)	.75	3.00	60
MACK THE KNIFE/Lorelei	(Verve VK-10209)	1.50	6.00	60
(Stereo single issue)				
PETE KELLY'S BLUES/Hard Hard Hannah	(Decca 9-29609)	1.00	4.00	55
RINGO BEAT/I'm Falling In Love	(Verve 10340)	1.00	4.00	64
SATISFIED MIND, A/Soldier Boy	(Decca 9-29648)			55
SMOOTH SAILING/Love You Madly	(Decca 9-27693)	1.50	6.00	51
SOMEBODY BAD STOLE DE WEDDING BELL/ Melancholy Me	(Decca 9-29008)	1.25	5.00	53
TENDER TRAP, THE/My One & Only Love	(Decca 9-29746)	1.00	4.00	55
THAT'S MY DESIRE/A Sunday Kind Of Love	(Decca 9-28993)	1.25	5.00	53
FITZHUGH, Sammy				
LINDA BABY/Sadie Mae	(Poplar 115)	1.00	4.00	59
FIVE AMERICANS, The				
EVOL-NOT LOVE/Don't Blame Me	(HBR 468)	.75	3.00	66
EVOL-NOT LOVE/Don't Blame Me	(HBR 468)	2.00	8.00	66
(Picture sleeve)				
GENERATION GAP/The Source	(Abnak 132)	1.00	4.00	68
GOOD TIMES/Losing Game	(HBR 483)	1.00	4.00	66
I SEE THE LIGHT/The Outcast	(Abnak 109)	2.50	10.00	65
I SEE THE LIGHT/The Outcast	(HBR 454)	.75	3.00	65
I'M FEELING O.K./Slippin' & Slidin'	(Jetstar 105)	3.00	12.00	65
I'M GONNA LEAVE YA/It's You Girl	(Jetstar 104)	3.00	12.00	65
LOVE, LOVE, LOVE/Show Me	(ABC 10686)	1.50	6.00	65
LOVIN' IS LOVIN'/Con Man	(Abnak 131)	1.00	4.00	68
NO COMMUNICATION/The Rain Maker	(Abnak 128)	1.00	4.00	68
SCROOGE/Ignery Women	(Abnak 137)	1.00	4.00	68
7:30 GUIDED TOUR/See-Saw-Man	(Abnak 126)	1.00	4.00	68
SHE'S TOO GOOD TO ME/Molly Black	(Abnak 142)	1.25	5.00	69
SOUND OF LOVE/Sympathy	(Abnak 120)	.75	3.00	67
TELL ANN I LOVE HER/Stop Light	(Abnak 125)	1.00	4.00	67
WESTERN UNION/Now That It's Over	(Abnak 118)	.75	3.00	67
ZIP CODE/Sweet Bird Of Youth	(Abnak 123)	.75	3.00	67
Group members: John Durrill, Mike Rabon, Norm Ezell, Jim Grant & Jimmy Wright (whose wife was Robin, of Jon & Robin).				
FIVE & DIME				
RAIN/Penny Candy	(Laurie 3452)	1.25	5.00	68
FIVE BARS, The				
SOMEBODY ELSE'S FOOL/Stormy Weather	(Money 224)	1.25	5.00	
FIVE BLOBS, The (With Bernie Nee)				
BLOB, THE/Night In Tijuana	(Columbia 4-41250)	1.25	5.00	58
ROCKIN' POW WOW/From The Top Of Your Guggle	(Joy 226)	1.00	4.00	59
JULIET/Young & Wild	(Joy 230)	1.00	4.00	59
5 X 5				
AIN'T GONNA BE YOUR FOOL NO MORE/She Digs My Love	(Paula 113)	.75	3.00	68
15 GOING ON 20/Penthouse Pauper	(Paula 326)	.75	3.00	69
GOOD CONNECTION/Never	(Paula 328)	.75	3.00	70
SHAKE A TAIL FEATHER/Tell Me What To Do	(Paula 261)	.75	3.00	67
FIVE CARDS STUD				
BE-BOP-A-LULA/Everybody Needs Somebody	(Red Bird 10-802)	.75	3.00	66
BEG ME/Once	(Smash 2080)	.75	3.00	67
5 CHANELS, The				
REASON, THE/Skiddily Doo	(Deb 500)	1.00	4.00	58
5 CHORDS, The				
LOVE IS LIKE MUSIC/Don't Just Stand There	(Jamie 1110)	2.00	8.00	58
FIVE CLASSICS, The				
LOVE ME/Mississippi Mud	(Pova 6142)	1.50	6.00	
MY IMAGINATION/Come On Baby	("A" Records 317)	1.50	6.00	61
MY IMAGINATION/Come On Baby	(Arc 4454)	1.50	6.00	61
OLD CAPE COD/Magic Star	(Medieval 204)	1.50	6.00	
FIVE COUNTS, The				
GOING AWAY FROM YOU/Shame Shame	(Vistar 1000)	1.00	4.00	
FIVE CRYSTALS, The				
HEY LANDLORD/Good Looking Out	(Kane 25592)	1.50	6.00	
FIVE DISCS, The				
ADIOS/My Baby Loves Me	(Callo 202)	3.00	12.00	
COME ON BABY/I Don't Know What I'll Do	(Yale 243)	7.50	30.00	
I REMEMBER/The World Is A Beautiful Place	(Emge 1004)	7.50	30.00	58
I REMEMBER/The World Is A Beautiful Place	(Vik 0327)	3.75	15.00	58
I REMEMBER/The World Is A Beautiful Place	(Rust 5027)	1.00	4.00	63
NEVER LET YOU GO/That Was The Time	(Cheer 1000)	2.00	8.00	
ROCK & ROLL REVIVAL/Gypsy Women	(Laurie 3601)	1.00	4.00	71
ROSES/My Chinese Girl	(Dwain 6072)	8.75	35.00	
ROSES/My Chinese Girl	(Dwain 803)	6.25	25.00	
ROSES/My Chinese Girl	(Mellomood 1002)	1.00	4.00	
WHEN LOVE COMES KNOCKING/Go-Go	(Yale 240)	3.00	12.00	
(Shown as by Adrian Allen & the Five Discs) Also see Boy Friends, The. Also see Dawn. Also see Gee, Frankie				
FIVE EMPREES, The				
LITTLE MISS SAD/Hey Lover	(Freeport 1001)	1.50	6.00	65
(Shown as by the Five Empressions)				
LITTLE MISS SAD/Hey Lover	(Freeport 1001)	.75	3.00	65
JOHNNY B. GOODE/Hey Lover	(Freeport 1010)	1.00	4.00	66
LITTLE MISS HAPPINESS/Over The Mountain	(Freeport 1007)	1.00	4.00	66
PRETTY FACE (PART 1)/Pretty Face (Part 2)	(Freeport 1009)	1.00	4.00	66
This group was forced to change their name from The Five Empressions to the Five Emprees in order to avoid being confused with the Impressions.				
FIVE EMPRESSIONS, The: see Five Emprees, The				
FIVE GENTS, The				
SANDY/Baby Doll	(Viking 101)	6.25	25.00	
FIVE HUNDREDS, The				
RUN LITTLE RABBIT/Wheel's Last Ride	(Mercury 72291)	.75	3.00	64

TITLE/FLIP	LABEL & NO.	GOOD	NEAR MINT	YR.
FIVE KINGS, The				
HERE COMES MY BABY/Tina	(Yvette 101)	3.00	12.00	
LIGHT BULB/Don't Send Me Away	(Columbia 4-43060)	6.25	25.00	64
LIGHT BULB/Don't Send Me Away	(Columbia 4-43060)	5.00	20.00	64
(Promotional issue)				
FIVE MAN ELECTRICAL BAND, The				
ABSOLUTELY RIGHT/(You & I) Butterfly	(Lionel 3220)	.75	3.00	71
I'M A STRANGER HERE/Doin' The Best We Can Rag	(Lion 149)	.50	2.00	73
MONEY BACK GUARANTEE/	(Lion 127)	.50	2.00	72
RIVERBOAT/Good	(Capitol 2628)	1.25	5.00	69
SIGNS/Hello Melinda Goodbye	(MGM 14182)	1.00	4.00	70
SIGNS/Hello Melinda Goodbye	(Lionel 3213)	.50	2.00	71
SUNRISE TO SUNSET/Little Bit Of Love	(Capitol 2562)	1.25	5.00	69
WEREWOLF/Country Angel	(Polydor 14221)	.50	2.00	74
FIVE OF A KIND				
NEVER AGAIN/	(Vandan 3668)	.75	3.00	
FIVE PENNIES, The				
MR. MOON/Let It Rain	(Savoy 1182)	1.50	6.00	55
MY HEART TREMBLES/Money	(Savoy 1190)	1.50	6.00	55
FIVE PLAYBOYS, The				
SHE'S MY BABY/Mr. Echo	(Petite 504)	2.00	8.00	
WHEN WE WERE YOUNG/Rage Of My Scrapbook	(Fee Bee 213)	3.75	15.00	57
WHEN WE WERE YOUNG/Rage Of My Scrapbook	(Dot 15605)	2.50	10.00	57
WHY BE A FOOL/Time Will Allow	(Mercury 71269)	1.50	6.00	58
FIVE REASONS, The				
GO TO SCHOOL/3 O'clock Rock	(Cub 9006)	6.25	25.00	58
FIVE SECRETS, The				
SEE YOU NEXT YEAR/Queen Bee	(Decca 9-30350)	1.25	5.00	57
FIVE SHADES, The				
VICKIE/I'll Give You Love	(Veep 1208)	1.25	5.00	
FIVE SHARKS, The				
STORMY WEATHER (Long Version)/If You Love Me...	(Times Square 35)	3.75	15.00	
STORMY WEATHER (Short Version)/If You Love Me..	(Times Square 35)	2.50	10.00	
Also see Gold Bugs, The				
Also see Sharks, The				
FIVE SOUNDS, The				
GOOD TIME BABY/That's When I Fell In Love	(Baritone 0941)	2.00	8.00	
FIVE SPARKS, The				
LITTLE BO PEEP/A Million Tears	(Jimbo 1)	2.00	8.00	59
FIVE STARS, The				
BABY BABY/Blabber Mouth	(End 1028)	2.00	8.00	58
BABY BABY/Blabber Mouth	(Columbia 4-42056)	1.25	5.00	61
FIVE SUPERIORS, The				
THERE'S A FOOL BORN EVERY DAY/Big Shot	(Garpax 44170)	2.00	8.00	62
FIVE TEENBEATS, The				
TIME TO ROCK/Autumn Mood	(Big Top 3062)	1.00	4.00	60
FIVE TROJANS, The (Featuring Nicky St. Claire)				
I HEAR THOSE BELLS/Creator Of Love	(Edison International 410)	7.50	30.00	59
LOLA LEE/Little Doll	(Edison International 412)	1.50	6.00	59
FIVE VETS, The				
RIGHT NOW/You're In Love	(Allstar 713)	3.00	12.00	
FIVE WHISPERS, The				
MIDNIGHT SUN/Moon In The Afternoon	(Dolton 61)	1.00	4.00	62
SLEEP WALK/Can't Face The Crowd	(Dolton 90)	1.00	4.00	63
Instrumentals				
FLAGMAN, The				
DRAG STRIP U.S.A./Mary	(Limelight 3014)	1.00	4.00	64
FLAIRS, The				
MEMORY LINGERS ON, THE/Shake Shake Sherry	(Epic 5-9447)	3.75	15.00	61
ROLL OVER BEETHOVEEN /Brazil	(Palms 5961)	1.00	4.00	
FLAME				
ANOTHER DAY LIKE HEAVEN/I'm So Happy	(Brother 3501)	3.00	12.00	71
SEE THE LIGHT/Get Your Mind Made Up	(Brother 3500)	2.00	8.00	70
FLAME				
SHADOW IN THE NIGHT/	(RCA PB-11348)	.50	2.00	78
TOO MANY COOKS/	(RCA PB-11266)	.50	2.00	78
FLAME				
TEENAGER IN LOVE/Hear The Band Play	(Live Wire 4008)	2.00	8.00	
FLAMIN' GROOVIES, The				
HAVE YOU SEEN MY BABY?/Yesterday's Numbers	(Kama Sutra 527)	.75	3.00	71
ROCKIN' PNEUMONIA & THE BOOGIE WOOGIE FLU/ The First One's Free	(Epic 10507)	1.00	4.00	69
SOMETHIN' ELSE/Laurie Did It	(Epic 10564)	1.00	4.00	70
YOU TORE ME DOWN/Him Or Me	(Bomp 101)	.50	2.00	75
Also see Chosen Few, The				
FLANAGAN, Ralph				
HARBOR LIGHTS/Singing Winds	(RCA Victor 47-3911)	1.25	5.00	50
HOT TODDY/Serenade	(RCA Victor 47-5095)	1.25	5.00	52
SLOW POKE/Charmaine	(RCA Victor 47-4373)	1.25	5.00	51
FLANDERS, Tommy (Of The Blues Project)				
MOONSTONE, THE/Between Purple & Blue	(Verve-Folkways 3075)	.75	3.00	69
FLASH				
SMALL BEGINNINGS/Morning Haze	(Capitol 3345)	.50	2.00	72
FLASH & THE PAN				
DOWN AMONG THE DEAD MEN/ The Man Who Knew The Answer	(Epic 50761)	.50	2.00	79
HEY, ST. PETER/Walking In The Rain	(Epic 50715)	.50	2.00	79
Flash & the Pan were Vanda & Young, formerly of the Easybeats				
FLASH CADILLAC & THE CONTINENTAL KIDS				
AT THE HOP/She's So Fine	(Epic 11043)	.75	3.00	73
DANCIN'/The Way I Feel Tonight	(Epic 11102)	.75	3.00	74
DID YOU BOOGIE (WITH YOUR BABY)/ Maybe It's All In My Mind	(Private Stock 45079)	.50	2.00	76
(With Wolfman Jack)				
GOOD TIMES ROCK & ROLL/	(Private Stock 006)	.50	2.00	74
SEE MY BABY JIVE/	(Private Stock 45134)	.50	2.00	77
TIME WILL TELL/Hot Summer Girls	(Private Stock 026)	.50	2.00	75
FLAVOR				
SALLY HAD A PARTY/Shop Around	(Columbia 4-44521)	.75	3.00	68
FLEAS, The				
SCRATCHIN'/Tears	(Challenge 9115)	1.00	4.00	61
(Instrumentals)				
FLEET & FREDDY				
DRAG RACE BOOGIE/Sunset Till Dawn	(Arlen 1002)	1.25	5.00	61
(Instrumentals)				
FLEETS, The				
PLEASE RETURN TO ME/Go Away	(Volt 120)	.75	3.00	64
FLEETWOOD MAC (Mick Fleetwood, Stevie Nicks, Christine McVie, John McVie, Lindsey Buckingham)				
ALBATROSS/Jigsaw Puzzle Blues	(Epic 5-10436)	1.25	5.00	69
ALBATROSS/Black Magic Woman	(Epic 5-11029)	.50	2.00	73
BLACK MAGIC WOMAN/Long Grey Mare	(Epic 5-10351)	1.50	6.00	68
COMING YOUR WAY/Rattlesnake Shake	(Reprise 860)	1.00	4.00	69
DID YOU EVER LOVE ME/Revelation	(Reprise 1172)	.75	3.00	73
DON'T STOP/Never Going Back Again	(Warner Bros. 8413)	.50	2.00	77
DREAMS/Songbird	(Warner Bros. 8371)	.50	2.00	77
FOR YOUR LOVE/	(Reprise 1188)	.75	3.00	73
GO YOUR OWN WAY/Silber Springs	(Warner Bros. 8304)	.50	2.00	77
GREEN MANALISHI, THE/World In Harmony	(Reprise 0925)	1.00	4.00	70
GREEN MANALISHI, THE/Oh Well	(Reprise 0108)	.75	3.00	73
HEROES ARE HARD TO FIND/Born Enchanter	(Reprise 1317)	.75	3.00	74
JEWEL EYED JUDY/Station Man	(Reprise 984)	.75	3.00	71
MAN OF THE WORLD/ Best Girl In The World (By Danny Kirwan)	(DJM 1007)	1.25	5.00	73
NEED YOUR LOVE SO BAD/Stop Messin' Round	(Epic 5-10386)	1.50	6.00	68
OH WELL (PART 1)/Oh Well (Part 2)	(Reprise 0883)	.75	3.00	70
OVER MY HEAD/I'm So Afraid	(Reprise 1339)	.75	3.00	75
RATTLESNAKE SHAKE/Coming Your Way	(Reprise 0860)	1.00	4.00	69
REMEMBER ME/Dissatisfied	(Reprise 1159)	.75	3.00	73
RHIANNON (WILL YOU EVER WIN)/Sugar Daddy	(Reprise 1345)	.50	2.00	76
SANDS OF TIME/Lay It All Down	(Reprise 1057)	.75	3.00	71
SARA/That's Enough For Me	(Warner Bros. 49150)	.50	2.00	79
SAY YOU LOVE ME/Monday Morning	(Reprise 1356)	.50	2.00	76
SENTIMENTAL LADY/Sunny Side Of Heaven	(Reprise 1093)	.75	3.00	72
TUSK/Never Make Me Cry	(Warner Bros. 49077)	.50	2.00	79
WALKIN'/Hungry Country Girl (With Otis Spann)	(Blue Horizon 304)	1.50	6.00	70
YOU MAKE LOVING FUN/Gold Dust Woman	(Warner Bros. 8483)	.50	2.00	77
Also see Buckingham-Nicks				
Also see Kirwan, Danny				
Also see Welch, Bob				

TITLE/FLIP	LABEL & NO.	GOOD	NEAR MINT	YR.
FLEETWOODS, The (Gary Troxel, Barbara Ellis, Gretchen Christopher)				
BEFORE & AFTER (LOSING YOU)/ Lonely Is As Lonely Does	(Dolton 302)	.75	3.00	64
BILLY OLD BUDDY/Trouble	(Dolton 49)	.75	3.00	61
COME SOFTLY TO ME/I Care So Much	(Liberty F-55188)	1.25	5.00	59
COME SOFTLY TO ME/I Care So Much	(Liberty S-77188)	2.50	10.00	59
(Stereo single issue)				
COME SOFTLY TO ME/I Care So Much	(Dolphin 1)	1.00	4.00	59
CONFIDENTIAL/I Love You So	(Dolton 30)	.75	3.00	60
GOODNIGHT MY LOVE/Jimmy Beware	(Dolton 75)	.75	3.00	63
GRADUATION'S HERE/Oh Lord Let It Be	(Dolton 3)	1.00	4.00	59
GRADUATION'S HERE/Oh Lord Let It Be	(Dolton S-3)	2.50	10.00	59
(Stereo single issue)				
GREAT IMPOSTER, THE/Poor Little Girl	(Dolton 45)	.75	3.00	61
LAST ONE TO KNOW, THE/Dormilona	(Dolton 27)	.75	3.00	60
LONESOME TOWN/Ruby Red, Baby Blue	(Dolton 93)	.75	3.00	64
LOVERS BY NIGHT, STRANGERS BY DAY/ They Tell Me It's Summer	(Dolton 62)	.75	3.00	62
MR. BLUE/You Mean Everything To Me	(Dolton 5)	1.00	4.00	59
MR. SANDMAN/This Is My Prayer	(Dolton 98)	.75	3.00	64
OUTSIDE MY WINDOW/Magic Star	(Dolton 15)	.75	3.00	60
RUNAROUND/Truly Do	(Dolton 22)	1.00	4.00	60
TEN TIMES BLUE/Ska Light, Ska Bright	(Dolton 98)	.75	3.00	64
TRAGEDY/Little Miss Sad One	(Dolton 40)	.75	3.00	61
WHAT'LL I DO/Baby Bye-O	(Dolton 86)	.75	3.00	63
YOU SHOULD HAVE BEEN THERE/ Sure Is Lonesome Downtown	(Dolton 74)	.75	3.00	63
FLEISCHMAN, Robert (Of Journey)				
NEVER NEVER LAND/All For You	(Arista 0411)	.50	2.00	79
FLEMING, Frankie Jr.				
ALL BY MYSELF/Blue Heartaches	(Amy 879)	1.50	6.00	63
FLEMONS, Wade				
WHEN IT RAINS IT POURS/Watch Over Her	(Vee Jay 578)	2.50	10.00	64
(With the Four Seasons)				
Wade Flemons' listings would be found in the *Blues-Rhythm & Blues-Soul guide, but we have included this particular recording here because of its interest to 4 Seasons collectors.*				
FLIES, The				
BLOW IN MY EAR (AND I'LL FOLLOW YOU ANYWHERE)/ I Got A Letter Today From The President	(Capitol 2429)	.75	3.00	69
FLINT				
BACK IN MY ARMS AGAIN/Keep Ya Movin' On	(Columbia 3-10870)	.50	2.00	78
This band was made up of three former members of Grand Funk.				
FLINTALES, The				
D-RAIL/Flintales' Rock	(Flick 429)	1.25	5.00	
(Instrumentals)				
FLINT, Shelby				
ANGEL ON MY SHOULDER/Somebody	(Valiant 6001)	.75	3.00	60
BOY I LOVE, THE/Ugly Duckling	(Valiant 6022)	1.00	4.00	63
CAST YOUR FATE TO THE WIND/The Lily	(Valiant 743)	.75	3.00	66
EVERY NIGHT/I Will Love You	(Valiant 6010)	1.00	4.00	61
I LOVE A WANDERER/The Riddle Song	(Valiant 6017)	1.00	4.00	62
I WILL LOVE YOU/Oh, I Miss Him So	(Cadence 1352)	1.25	5.00	58
LITTLE DANCING DOLL/It Really Wouldn't Matter	(Valiant 6031)	1.00	4.00	63
MAGIC WAND/A Broken Vow	(Valiant 6014)	1.00	4.00	61
OUR TOWN/I've Grown Accustomed to Your Face	(Valiant 6060)	1.00	4.00	64
FLINTSTONE, Fred				
QUARRY STONE ROCK/(A Night In) Bedrock Forest	(B-H 001)	.75	3.00	62
STONE AGE ROCK/Bedrock Beat	(Epic 5-9475)	.75	3.00	61
FLIPS, The				
GONE AWAY/It Will Never Be The Same	(Mercury 71426)	1.00	4.00	59
FLIRTATIONS, The				
NOTHING BUT A HEARTACHE/ Christmas Time Is Here Again	(Deram 85036)	.75	3.00	69
FLO & EDDIE (Mark Kaylan & Howard Volman)				
ELENORE/The Love You Gave Away	(Columbia 10425)	.75	3.00	77
KEEP IT WARM/	(Columbia 10458)	.75	3.00	77
LET ME MAKE LOVE TO YOU/Come To My Rescue Webelos	(Columbia 10028)	.75	3.00	74
REBECCA/Illega, Immoral & Fattening	(Columbia 10264)	.75	3.00	76
Also see Turtles, The				
FLOATING BRIDGE				
BROUGHT UP WRONG/	(Vault 947)	1.00	4.00	68
FLOCK, The				
CAN'T YOU SEE/Hold On To My Mind	(Destination 628)	1.50	6.00	67
I LIKE YOU/Are You The Kind	(Destination 631)	1.50	6.00	67
MAGICAL WINGS/What Would You Do If The Sun Died?	(U.S.A. 910)	1.25	5.00	68
TAKE ME BACK/Each Day Is A Lonely Night	(Destination 636)	1.50	6.00	67
TIRED OF WAITING/Store Bought Store Thought	(Columbia 4-45021)	1.00	4.00	70
FLOOD, Dick				
IT'S MY WAY/It Only Costs A Dime	(Monument 414)	1.00	4.00	60
THREE BELLS, THE/Far Away	(Monument 408)	1.00	4.00	59
FLOWER				
MAGIC IS YOU, THE/	(United Artists 1138)	.50	2.00	78
RUN TO ME/You Don't Have To Say It (I Think I Know)	(United Artists 1092)	.50	2.00	77
FLOWER CHILDREN, The				
MINI-SKIRT BLUES/Marching Lovers	(Castil 101)	1.00	4.00	67
FLOWER POT, The				
MR. ZIG ZAG MAN/Black Moto	(Vault 935)	1.25	5.00	67
FLOWER POTS, The				
LET'S GO TO SAN FRANCISCO (PART 1)/ Let's Go To San Francisco (Part 2)	(Deram 7513)	1.25	5.00	67
FLOWER POWER				
TRIVIALITIES/Mr. Olympus	(Tune-Kel 612)	1.50	6.00	69
YOU MAKE ME FLY/Sunshine Day	(Tune-Kel 608)	1.50	6.00	69
FLOWER SHOPPE, The				
YOU'VE COME A LONG WAY BABY/Kill The Monster	(Spring 111)	1.00	4.00	
FLOYD & JERRY & THE COUNTERPOINTS				
GIRL/Believe In Things	(Presta 1003)	.75	3.00	66
FLUFFER, Jive M.				
WATERBLADDER/Waterbladder (Instrumental)	(Blade 001)	1.00	4.00	72
(Novelty/Break-In)				
FLUORESCENTS, The				
FACTS OF LOVE/Shoopy-pop-a-doo	(Hanover 4520)	5.00	20.00	59
FACTS OF LOVE/Shoopy-pop-a-doo	(Candelite 420)	1.00	4.00	59
FLYING BURRITO BROTHERS, The				
BON SOIR BLUES/Hot Burrito #3	(Columbia 3-10287)	.50	2.00	76
BUILDING FIRES/Hot Burrito #3	(Columbia 3-10229)	.50	2.00	76
DOWN IN THE CHURCHYARD/	(A&M 1169)	.75	3.00	70
IF YOU GOTTA GO/Cody, Cody	(A&M 1166)	.75	3.00	70
TRAIN SONG, THE/Hot Burrito #1	(A&M 1167)	.75	3.00	69
WAITIN' FOR LOVE TO BEGIN/Bon Soir Blues	(Columbia 3-10389)	.50	2.00	76
Also see Country Gazette				
Also see Poco				
Also see Byrds, The				
FLYING CIRCUS, The				
I'M GOING/Midnight Highway	(MTA 117)	2.00	8.00	
FLYING GIRAFFE				
BRING BACK HOWDY DOODY/Let's Get To Gettin'	(Bell 801)	1.50	6.00	69
FLYING LIZARDS, The				
MONEY/Money	(Virgin 67003)	.50	2.00	79
FLYING MACHINE, The				
BABY MAKE IT SOON/	(Congress 6012)	.75	3.00	70
SMILE A LITTLE SMILE FOR ME/ Maybe We've Been Loving Too Long	(Congress 6000)	.75	3.00	69
FLYS, The				
GOT TO GET AWAY/Reality Composition No. 1	(Myskatonic 100)	1.00	4.00	66
FOAM, Freddy				
ARTIFICIAL RESPIRATION/Artificial Respiration (Part 2)	(R&R 302)	1.00	4.00	
FOCUS				
HAREM SCAREM/Birth	(Atco 7002)	.50	2.00	75
HOCUS POCUS/Hocus Pocus (Part 2)	(Sire 704)	.50	2.00	73
SYLVIA/	(Sire 708)	.50	2.00	73
FOGELBERG, Dan				
ANYWAY I LOVE YOU/Looking For A Lady	(Columbia 4-45764)	.75	3.00	73
BELOW THE SURFACE/Comes & Goes	(Full Moon-Epic 8-50189)	.50	2.00	76
CAPTURED ANGEL/Next Time	(Full Moon-Epic 8-50165)	.50	2.00	75
CROW/Old Tennessee	(Full Moon-Epic 8-50234)	.50	2.00	76
LONGER/Along The Road	(Full Moon-Epic 50824)	.50	2.00	79
LOVE GONE BY/Scarecrow's Dream	(Full Moon-Epic 50412)	.50	2.00	77
MORNING SKY/Changing Horses	(Epic 8-50108)	.50	2.00	75
NETHERLANDS/False Faces	(Full Moon-Epic 50462)	.50	2.00	77
PART OF THE PLAN/Song From Half Mountain	(Epic 8-50055)	.50	2.00	74
PROMISES MADE/Sketches	(Full Moon-Epic 50536)	.50	2.00	78
THERE PLACE IN THE WORLD FOR A GAMBLER/ Souvenirs	(Full Moon-Epic 50577)	.50	2.00	78
Also see Fool's Gold				
FOGELBERG, Dan & Tim Weisberg				
POWER OF GOLD, THE/Lahaina Luna	(Full Moon-Epic 50606)	.50	2.00	78
TELL ME TO MY FACE/Hurtwood Alley	(Full Moon-Epic 50605)	.50	2.00	79
FOGERTY, John (Of Creedence Clearwater Revival)				
ALMOST SATURDAY NIGHT/Sea Cruise	(Asylum 45291)	.50	2.00	75
COMIN' DOWN THE ROAD/Comin' Down The Road	(Fantasy 717)	.75	3.00	73
ROCKIN' ALL OVER THE WORLD/The Wall	(Asylum 45274)	.50	2.00	75
YOU GOT THE MAGIC/Evil Thing	(Asylum 45309)	.50	2.00	76
Also see Blue Ridge Rangers, The				

Freddie & The Dreamers

Norman Fox & The Rob Roys

Wayne Fontana & The Mindbenders

The Four Seasons

FOGERTY, Tom (Of Creedence Clearwater Revival)

TITLE/FLIP	LABEL & NO.	GOOD	NEAR MINT	YR.
BONITA/	(Orchestra 1010)	3.75	15.00	
(Shown as by Tom Fogerty & The Blue Velvets)				
CAST THE FIRST STONE/Lady Of Fatima	(Fantasy 680)	.75	3.00	72
GOODBYE MEDIA MAN/Goodbye Media Man (Part 2)	(Fantasy 661)	.75	3.00	71
JOYFULL RESURRECTION/Heartbeat	(Fantasy 702)	.75	3.00	73
SWEET THINGS TO COME/	(Fantasy 737)	.75	3.00	73

Also see Ruby

FOGHAT

TITLE/FLIP	LABEL & NO.	GOOD	NEAR MINT	YR.
DRIVIN' WHEEL/Night Shift	(Bearsville 0313)	.50	2.00	76
FOOL FOR THE CITY/Take It Or Leave It	(Bearsville 0307)	.50	2.00	76
HIGH ON LOVE/Sweet Home Chicago	(Bearsville 0329)	.50	2.00	78
I JUST WANNA MAKE LOVE TO YOU/Fool For The City	(Bearsville 0319)	.50	2.00	77
I JUST WANNA MAKE LOVE TO YOU/Hole To Hide In	(Bearsville 0008)	.75	3.00	72
I'LL BE STANDING BY/Take Me To The River	(Bearsville 0315)	.50	2.00	77
RIDE, RIDE, RIDE/It's Too Late	(Bearsville 0016)	.75	3.00	73
RUN, RUN, RUDOLPH/	(Bearsville PRO S-780)	.75	3.00	78
SLOW RIDE/Save Your Loving (For Me)	(Bearsville 0306)	.75	3.00	75
STEP OUTSIDE/	(Bearsville 0021)	.75	3.00	74
STONE BLUE/Chevrolet	(Bearsville 0325)	.50	2.00	78
THAT'LL BE THE DAY/Wild Cherry	(Bearsville 0019)	.75	3.00	74
THIRD TIME LUCKY (FIRST TIME I WAS A FOOL)/ Love In Motion	(Bearsville 49125)	.50	2.00	79
WHAT A SHAME/Helping Hand	(Bearsville 0014)	.50	2.00	73

Also see Savoy Brown
Also see Wishbone Ash

FOLDY, Peter

TITLE/FLIP	LABEL & NO.	GOOD	NEAR MINT	YR.
ROXANNE/Funny	(Polydor 14344)	.50	2.00	76

FONDETTES, The

TITLE/FLIP	LABEL & NO.	GOOD	NEAR MINT	YR.
BEATLES ARE IN TOWN, THE/	(Arhoolie 507)	1.00	4.00	64

FONTAINE, Eddie

TITLE/FLIP	LABEL & NO.	GOOD	NEAR MINT	YR.
NOTHIN' SHAKIN'/Oh Wonderful Night	(Sunbeam 105)	3.00	12.00	59
NOTHIN' SHAKIN'/Oh Wonderful Night	(Argo 5309)	2.00	8.00	59

FONTAINE, Frank

TITLE/FLIP	LABEL & NO.	GOOD	NEAR MINT	YR.
ALOUETTE/R.S.V.P.	(ABC-Paramount 10517)	.75	3.00	63
OH HOW I MISS YOU TONIGHT/Daddy's Little Girl	(ABC-Paramount 10491)	.75	3.00	63
WHEN YOUR HAIR HAS TURNED TO SILVER/ Heart Of My Heart	(ABC-Paramount 10484)	.75	3.00	63

FONTANA, Wayne

TITLE/FLIP	LABEL & NO.	GOOD	NEAR MINT	YR.
COME ON HOME/My Eyes Break Out In Tears	(MGM 13516)	1.00	4.00	66
IT WAS EASIER TO HURT HER/ You Made Me What I Am Today	(MGM 13456)	1.00	4.00	66
PAMELA, PAMELA/Something Keeps Calling Me Back	(MGM 13661)	1.00	4.00	67
SAY GOODBYE TO YESTERDAY/Datyon, Ohio	(Metromedia 133)	1.00	4.00	69
SWEET AMERICA/Interested	(Brut 812)	1.00	4.00	73
24 SYCAMORE/From A Boy To A Man	(MGM 13762)	1.00	4.00	67

FONTANA, Wayne, & The Mindbenders

TITLE/FLIP	LABEL & NO.	GOOD	NEAR MINT	YR.
GAME OF LOVE/Since You've Been Gone	(Fontana 1503)	1.25	5.00	65
GAME OF LOVE/One More Time	(Fontana 1509)	.75	3.00	65
HELLO JOSEPHINE/Road Runner	(Fontana 1917)	1.00	4.00	
IT'S JUST A LITTLE BIT TOO LATE/Long Time Comin'	(Fontana 1514)	.75	3.00	65
SHE NEEDS LOVE/Like I Did	(Fontana 1524)	1.00	4.00	65
UM, UM, UM/First Taste Of Love	(Fontana 1945)	1.00	4.00	

Also see Mindbenders, The

FONTANE SISTERS, The (Geri, Marge, Bea)

TITLE/FLIP	LABEL & NO.	GOOD	NEAR MINT	YR.
DADDY-O/Adorable	(Dot 15428)	1.00	4.00	55
EDDIE MY LOVE/Yum-Yum	(Dot 15450)	1.00	4.00	56
HEARTS OF STONE/Bless Your Heart	(Dot 15265)	1.00	4.00	54
I'M IN LOVE AGAIN/You Always Hurt The One You Love	(Dot 15462)	1.00	4.00	56
KISSING BRIDGE/Silver Bells	(RCA Victor 47-5524)	1.25	5.00	53
MOST OF ALL/Put Me In The Mood	(Dot 15352)	1.00	4.00	55
NUTTIN' FOR CHRISTMAS/Silver Bells	(Dot 15434)	1.00	4.00	55
PLAYMATES/Rollin' Stone	(Dot 15370)	1.00	4.00	55
ROCK LOVE/You're Mine	(Dot 15333)	1.00	4.00	55
SEVENTEEN/If I Could Be With You	(Dot 15386)	1.00	4.00	55
TENNESSEE WALTZ/I Guess I'll Have To	(RCA Victor 47-3979)	1.25	5.00	51
TILL THEN/The Baion	(RCA Victor 47-5612)	1.25	5.00	54
VOICES (With Pat Boone)/Lonesome Lover Blues	(Dot 15480)	1.00	4.00	55

FOOL'S GOLD

TITLE/FLIP	LABEL & NO.	GOOD	NEAR MINT	YR.
ONE BY ONE/Choices	(Morning Sky 701)	.75	3.00	76
RAIN, OH RAIN/One By One	(Morning Sky 700)	.75	3.00	76
RUNNIN' & HIDIN'/Fly Away	(Columbia 10592)	.50	2.00	77
WOULDN'T I LOVE TO LOVE YOU/ Where Did Our Love Go Wrong	(Columbia 10635)	.50	2.00	77

This band was Dan Fogelberg's back-up group.

FORBERT, Steve

TITLE/FLIP	LABEL & NO.	GOOD	NEAR MINT	YR.
GOIN' DOWN TO LAUREL/Steve Forbert's Moon River	(Nemperor 7520)	.50	2.00	79
IT ISN'T GONNA BE THAT WAY/Big City	(Nemperor 7519)	.50	2.00	79
ROMEO'S TUNE/Make It All So Real	(Nemperor 7525)	.50	2.00	79

FORCE FIVE

TITLE/FLIP	LABEL & NO.	GOOD	NEAR MINT	YR.
GEE TOO TIGER/I Want You Babe	(Ascot 2206)	1.00	4.00	66

FORCEP, Bent, & The Patients

TITLE/FLIP	LABEL & NO.	GOOD	NEAR MINT	YR.
MY SON, THE DOCTOR/ I Know What Happened To Baby Jane	(Original Sound 26)	.75	3.00	63

FORD, Danby

TITLE/FLIP	LABEL & NO.	GOOD	NEAR MINT	YR.
LONG TALL TEXAN/Draft Dodger Rag	(Accent 1196)	.75	3.00	66

FORD, Frankie

TITLE/FLIP	LABEL & NO.	GOOD	NEAR MINT	YR.
ALIMONY/Can't Tell My Heart	(Ace 566)	1.25	5.00	59
CHEATIN WOMAN/Last One To Cry	(Ace 549)	1.25	5.00	58
CHINATOWN/What's Going On	(Ace 592)	1.25	5.00	60
I CAN'T FACE TOMORROW/Half A Crown	(Doubloon 101)	.75	3.00	
LET THEM TALK/What Happened To You	(Imperial 5776)	1.00	4.00	61
MY SOUTHERN BELLE/The Groon	(Imperial 5706)	1.00	4.00	60
SATURDAY NIGHT FISH FRY/Love Don't Love Nobody	(Imperial 5749)	1.00	4.00	61
SEA CRUISE/Roberta	(Ace 554)	1.00	4.00	59
SEVENTEEN/Dog House	(Imperial 5735)	1.00	4.00	61
THEY SAID IT COULDN'T BE DONE/A Man Only Does	(Imperial 5819)	1.00	4.00	62
TIME AFTER TIME/I Want To Be Your Man	(Ace 580)	1.25	5.00	59
YOU TALK TOO MUCH/If You've Got Troubles	(Imperial 5686)	1.00	4.00	60

FORD, Jim

TITLE/FLIP	LABEL & NO.	GOOD	NEAR MINT	YR.
LINDA COMES RUNNING/Sing With Linda	(Mustang 3025)	1.25	5.00	67
STORY OF ELVIS PRESLEY, THE/ Desert Walk (With The Starfires)	(Drumfire 1/2)	3.00	12.00	

FORD, Mr., & Goon Bones

TITLE/FLIP	LABEL & NO.	GOOD	NEAR MINT	YR.
AIN'T SHE SWEET/The Shiek Of Araby	(Crystalette 1803)	2.00	8.00	49
AIN'T SHE SWEET/The Shiek Of Araby	(Dot 15920)	1.00	4.00	59

(Instrumentals)
Also see Goon Bones, The

FORD, Neal, & The Fanatics

TITLE/FLIP	LABEL & NO.	GOOD	NEAR MINT	YR.
SHAME ON YOU/Gonna Be My Girl	(Hickory 1433)	.75	3.00	68
THAT GIRL OF MINE/I Have Thoughts Of You	(Hickory 1490)	.75	3.00	68
WAIT FOR ME/Brand New Girl	(Hickory 1450)	.75	3.00	68

FOREIGNER (With Mick Jones & Lou Gramm)

TITLE/FLIP	LABEL & NO.	GOOD	NEAR MINT	YR.
BLUE MORNING, BLUE DAY/I Have Waited So Long	(Atlantic 3543)	.50	2.00	78
COLD AS ICE/I Need You	(Atlantic 3410)	.50	2.00	77
DIRTY WHITE BOY/Rev On The Red Line	(Atlantic 3618)	.50	2.00	79
DOUBLE VISION/Lonely Children	(Atlantic 3514)	.50	2.00	78
FEELS LIKE THE FIRST TIME/Woman Oh Woman	(Atlantic 3394)	.50	2.00	77
HEAD GAMES/Do What You Like	(Atlantic 3633)	.50	2.00	79
HOT BLOODED/Tramontane	(Atlantic 3488)	.50	2.00	78
LONG, LONG WAY FROM HOME/The Damage Is Done	(Atlantic 3439)	.50	2.00	77

Also see Spooky Tooth

FOREIGN INTRIGUE (Ernie Mareesca & The Del Satins)

TITLE/FLIP	LABEL & NO.	GOOD	NEAR MINT	YR.
WANDERER, THE/Blind Date	(E.M. 1001)	1.00	4.00	

FORGE, Val E.

TITLE/FLIP	LABEL & NO.	GOOD	NEAR MINT	YR.
PAUL REVERE/Oh Susanna	(Strand 25022)	.75	3.00	60

FORMATIONS, The

TITLE/FLIP	LABEL & NO.	GOOD	NEAR MINT	YR.
AT THE TOP OF THE STAIRS/Magic Melody	(Bank 1007)	2.00	8.00	68
AT THE TOP OF THE STAIRS/Magic Melody	(MGM 13899)	.75	3.00	68
DON'T GET CLOSE/There's No Room	(MGM 14009)	1.00	4.00	69
LOVE'S NOT ONLY FOR THE HEART/Lonely Voice Of Love	(MGM 13963)	1.00	4.00	68

FORREST, Jimmy

TITLE/FLIP	LABEL & NO.	GOOD	NEAR MINT	YR.
BLUE GROOVE/Hey, Mrs. Jones	(United 130)	1.25	5.00	52
NIGHT TRAIN/Bolo Blues	(United 110)	1.25	5.00	52

Instrumentals

FORREST, Sonny

TITLE/FLIP	LABEL & NO.	GOOD	NEAR MINT	YR.
DIDDY BOP/Knockdown	(Atco 6157)	1.00	4.00	60

FORSAKEN

TITLE/FLIP	LABEL & NO.	GOOD	NEAR MINT	YR.
BABE/She's Alright	(MTA 106)	1.25	5.00	

FORTE FOUR, The

TITLE/FLIP	LABEL & NO.	GOOD	NEAR MINT	YR.
I DON'T WANNA SAY GOODNIGHT/The Climb	(Decca 32029)	1.00	4.00	66

FORTUNE, Diane

TITLE/FLIP	LABEL & NO.	GOOD	NEAR MINT	YR.
HOUSE OF CARDS/Set Me Free	(Brunswick 55074)	1.00	4.00	58

FORTUNE, Johnny (Johnny Suddeta)

TITLE/FLIP	LABEL & NO.	GOOD	NEAR MINT	YR.
DON'T STAY OUT AFTER MIDNIGHT/ Don't You Lie To Me	(United Artists 780)	1.00	4.00	64
GEE BUT I MISS YOU/I'm In Heaven	(Emmy 1002)	2.00	8.00	60
GEE BUT I MISS YOU/I'm A Fool For You	(Arhaven 1001)	1.50	6.00	62
GEE BUT I MISS YOU/I'm A Fool For You	(Arena 102)	1.25	5.00	63
GEE BUT I MISS YOU/If You Love Me	(Crusader 104)	1.00	4.00	64
IF YOU LOVE ME (I WANT YOU TO KNOW TONIGHT)/ Alone & Cryin'	(Emmy 1001)	2.00	8.00	60
I'M LONELY FOR YOU/I'll Never Let You Go	(Current 105)	1.00	4.00	65
I'M TALKIN' ABOUT YOU/My Wandering Love	(Park Ave. 4905)	1.50	6.00	63
(With The Paramours)				
JUAREZ/It Ain't Necessarily So	(United Artists 720)	1.00	4.00	64
NEED YOU/One Less Angel	(Park Ave. 104)	1.00	4.00	63
SAY YOU WILL/Come On & Love Me	(Current 101)	1.00	4.00	65
SIBONEY/Dragster	(Park Ave. 130)	1.00	4.00	63
SOUL SURFER/Midnight Surf	(Park Ave. 110-597)	.75	3.00	63
STAY ONE MORE DAY/I'm Requesting A Love Song	(Beaver 111)	1.00	4.00	66
SURFERS TRIP/Soul Traveler	(Park Ave. 103)	1.00	4.00	63
YOU WANT ME TO BE YOUR BABY/Dan Stole My Girl	(Current 104)	1.00	4.00	65
YOUR TRUE LOVE/Tell Me You Love Me	(Vault 954)	.75	3.00	70

Also see Sweet Souls, The

FORTUNEERS, The

TITLE/FLIP	LABEL & NO.	GOOD	NEAR MINT	YR.
LOOK-A-THERE/Oh, Woh, Baby	(Skytone 1000)	2.00	8.00	

FORTUNES, The

TITLE/FLIP	LABEL & NO.	GOOD	NEAR MINT	YR.
FIRE BRIGADE/Painting A Shadow	(United Artists 50280)	1.00	4.00	68
FREEDOM COMES, FREEDOM GOES/There's A Man	(Capitol 3179)	.75	3.00	72
HERE COMES THAT RAINY DAY FEELING AGAIN/ I Gotta Dream	(Capitol 3086)	.50	2.00	71
HERE IT COMES AGAIN/Things I Should Have Known	(Press 9798)	.75	3.00	65
HIS SMILE WAS A LIE/The Idol	(United Artists 50211)	1.00	4.00	67
THAT SAME OLD FEELING/Lifetime Of Love	(World Pacific 77937)	.75	3.00	70
THIS GOLDEN RING/Someone To Care	(Press 9811)	1.00	4.00	66
YOU'VE GOT YOUR TROUBLES/I've Gotta Go	(Press 9773)	.75	3.00	65
WAIT UNTIL SEPTEMBER/Don't Sing To Me	(Capitol 3445)	.75	3.00	72
WHENEVER IT'S A SUNDAY/Give Me Some Room	(Capitol 3626)	.75	3.00	73

FORTUNES, The

TITLE/FLIP	LABEL & NO.	GOOD	NEAR MINT	YR.
GHOUL IN SCHOOL/You Don't Know (What I've Been Thru)	(Cub 9123)	.75	3.00	63

FORTUNE SEEKERS, The

TITLE/FLIP	LABEL & NO.	GOOD	NEAR MINT	YR.
WHY I CRY/Break Loose	(Trident 9966)	.75	3.00	

FORTUNE TELLERS, The

TITLE/FLIP	LABEL & NO.	GOOD	NEAR MINT	YR.
SCHOOL PROM/Just A Little Bit Of Your Love	(Sheryl 340)	1.25	5.00	
SONG OF THE NAIROBI TRIO/Camel Train	(Music Makers 105)	.75	3.00	

FORUM, The

TITLE/FLIP	LABEL & NO.	GOOD	NEAR MINT	YR.
RIVER IS WIDE, THE/A Girl Without A Boy	(Mira 232)	1.00	4.00	67
RIVER IS WIDE, THE/I Fall In Love	(Mira 232)	.75	3.00	67
RIVER IS WIDE, THE/The River Is Wide (Part 2)	(Penthouse 504)	1.25	5.00	66

FOSTER BROTHERS, The

TITLE/FLIP	LABEL & NO.	GOOD	NEAR MINT	YR.
LAND OF LOVE/	(Diller 101)	.75	3.00	

FOSTER, Bruce

TITLE/FLIP	LABEL & NO.	GOOD	NEAR MINT	YR.
BORN TO BREAK MY HEART/Baby It's Gone	(Millenium 600)	.50	2.00	77
PLATINUM HEROES/I Remember (The Revolution)	(Millenium 602)	.50	2.00	77

FOSTER, John, & Sons Ltd.

TITLE/FLIP	LABEL & NO.	GOOD	NEAR MINT	YR.
THINGUMYBOB/Yellow Submarine	(Apple Corps 1800)	1.25	5.00	68

FOSTER, Reb

TITLE/FLIP	LABEL & NO.	GOOD	NEAR MINT	YR.
SOMETHING YOU GOT/	(Loma 2002)	1.00	4.00	64

FOTO-FI FOUR, The

TITLE/FLIP	LABEL & NO.	GOOD	NEAR MINT	YR.
STAND UP & HOLLER/Isamel	(Foti-Fi 107)	1.25	5.00	64

FOTOMAKER (Gene Cornish, Dino Dannelli, Wally Bryson)

TITLE/FLIP	LABEL & NO.	GOOD	NEAR MINT	YR.
IF I CAN'T BELIEVE IN YOU/	(Atlantic 3561)	.50	2.00	79
LOVE ME FOREVER/Fooled Again	(Atlantic 3621)	.50	2.00	79
MILES AWAY/Snowblind	(Atlantic 3531)	.50	2.00	78
OTHER SIDE, THE (SO WHEN I SEE YOU AGAIN)/Pain	(Atlantic 3485)	.50	2.00	78
WHERE HAVE YOU BEEN ALL MY LIFE/ Say The Same For You	(Atlantic 3471)	.50	2.00	78

Cornish & Dannelli appeared earlier in the Rascals and in Bulldog. Bryson was with the Choir and Raspberries.

FOUNTAIN, Roosevelt

TITLE/FLIP	LABEL & NO.	GOOD	NEAR MINT	YR.
RED PEPPER (PART 1)/Red Pepper (Part 2)	(Prince-Adams 447)	.75	3.00	62

(Instrumentals)

FOUNDATIONS, The

TITLE/FLIP	LABEL & NO.	GOOD	NEAR MINT	YR.
ANY OLD TIME (YOU'RE LONELY & SAD/ We Are Happy People	(Uni 55073)	.75	3.00	68
BABY, NOW THAT I'VE FOUND YOU/Come On Back To Me	(Uni 55038)	.75	3.00	67
BACK ON MY FEET AGAIN/I Can Take Or Leave Your Loving	(Uni 55058)	.75	3.00	68
BUILD ME UP BUTTERCUP/New Direction	(Uni 55051)	.75	3.00	68
IN THE BAD, BAD OLD DAYS (BEFORE YOU LOVED ME)/	(Uni 55117)	.75	3.00	69
MY LITTLE CHICKADEE/	(Uni 55157)	.75	3.00	69
STONEY GROUND/I'll Give You Love	(Uni 55315)	.75	3.00	71

FOUR, The

TITLE/FLIP	LABEL & NO.	GOOD	NEAR MINT	YR.
LONELY SURFER BOY/Now Is The Time	(Clark 225)	1.00	4.00	65

FOUR ACES, The (Featuring Al Alberts)

TITLE/FLIP	LABEL & NO.	GOOD	NEAR MINT	YR.
BAHAMA MAMA/You're Mine	(Decca 9-30242)	1.00	4.00	57
DREAM/It Shall Come To Pass	(Decca 9-29217)	1.25	5.00	54
FALSE LOVE/Don't Forget Me	(Decca 9-28744)	1.25	5.00	53
FRIENDLY PERSUASION/You Can't Run Away From It	(Decca 9-30041)	1.00	4.00	56
HEART/Slue Foot	(Decca 9-29476)	1.25	5.00	55
HEART & SOUL/Just Squeeze Me	(Decca 9-28390)	1.25	5.00	52
I ONLY KNOW I LOVE YOU/Dreamer	(Decca 9-29989)	1.00	4.00	56
I UNDERSTAND/I'm Yours	(Decca 9-28162)	1.25	5.00	52
IF YOU CAN DREAM/The Gal With The Yaller Shoes	(Decca 9-29809)	1.00	4.00	56
IT'S A WOMAN'S WORLD/Cuckoo Bird In The Tree	(Decca 9-29269)	1.25	5.00	54
I'VE BEEN WAITING A LIFETIME/Laughing On The Outside	(Decca 9-28843)	1.25	5.00	53
JINGLE BELLS/The Christmas Song	(Decca 9-29702)	1.25	5.00	55
LOVE IS A MANY SPLENDORED THING/ Shine On Harvest Moon	(Decca 9-29625)	1.25	5.00	55
MELODY OF LOVE/There Is A Tavern In The Town	(Decca 9-29395)	1.25	5.00	54
MISTER SANDMAN/In Apple Blossom Time	(Decca 9-29344)	1.25	5.00	54
MY HERO/Spring Is A Wonderful Thing	(Decca 9-28073)	1.25	5.00	52
NO OTHER ARMS, NO OTHER LIPS/ The Inn Of The Sixth Happiness	(Decca 9-30822)	1.00	4.00	59
O HOLY NIGHT/Silent Night	(Decca 9-29712)	1.25	5.00	55
PERFIDIA/You Brought Me Love	(Decca 9-27987)	1.25	5.00	52
ROCK & ROLL RHAPSODY/	(Decca 9-30575)	1.00	4.00	58
SHOULD I/There's Only Tonight	(Decca 9-28323)	1.25	5.00	52
SIN/Arizona Moon (Red plastic)	(Victoria 101)	5.00	20.00	51
SIN/Arizona Moon	(Victoria 101)	2.50	10.00	51
SO LONG/Amor	(Decca 9-29036)	1.25	5.00	54
SOMEONE TO LOVE/Written On The Wind	(Decca 9-30123)	1.00	4.00	56
STRANGER IN PARADISE/ (The Gang That Sang) "Heart Of My Heart"	(Decca 9-28927)	1.25	5.00	53
TELL ME WHY/Garden In The Rain	(Decca 9-27860)	1.25	5.00	51
THERE GOES MY HEART/You'll Always Be The One	(Decca 9-29435)	1.25	5.00	55
THERE'S A CHRISTMAS TREE IN HEAVEN/ There's A Small Hotel	(Victoria 102)	2.50	10.00	51
THREE COINS IN THE FOUNTAIN/Wedding Bells (Are Breaking Up That Old Gang Of Mine)	(Decca 9-29123)	1.25	5.00	54
TO LOVE AGAIN/Charlie Was A Boxer	(Decca 9-29889)	1.00	4.00	56
WANTED/Too Much In Love	(Merion 104)	2.50	10.00	52
WHO'S TO BLAME/Two Little Kisses	(Flash 103)	2.00	8.00	50
WOMAN IN LOVE, A/Of This I'm Sure	(Decca 9-29725)	1.25	5.00	55
WORLD OUTSIDE, THE/	(Decca 9-30764)	1.00	4.00	58
YOU FOOLED ME/If You Take My Heart Away	(Decca 9-28560)	1.25	5.00	53

4 AFTER 5'S, The

TITLE/FLIP	LABEL & NO.	GOOD	NEAR MINT	YR.
HELLO SCHOOLTEACHER/ I Gotta Have Somebody (Lonely Boy)	(All Time 9076)	3.00	12.00	61

FOUR BLADES, The

TITLE/FLIP	LABEL & NO.	GOOD	NEAR MINT	YR.
CHURCH BELLS MAY RING/Stardust	(Gateway 1174)	10.00	40.00	
I WANT YOU TO BE MY GIRL/Can You Find It In Your Heart	(Gateway 1170)	10.00	40.00	

FOUR BUDDIES, The

TITLE/FLIP	LABEL & NO.	GOOD	NEAR MINT	YR.
I WANT TO BE THE BOY YOU LOVE/ Just Enough Of Your Love	(Imperial 66018)	2.50	10.00	64
SLOW LOCOMOTION/Lonely Summer	(Philips 40122)	.75	3.00	63

FOUR CAL-QUETTES, The

TITLE/FLIP	LABEL & NO.	GOOD	NEAR MINT	YR.
I'LL NEVER COME BACK (SILLY BOY)/Again	(Capitol 4725)	1.00	4.00	62
MOST OF ALL/I'm Gonna Love Him Anyway	(Capitol 4657)	1.00	4.00	61
MOVIE MAGAZINES/I Cried	(Liberty 55549)	1.00	4.00	63
SPARKLE & SHINE/In This World	(Capitol 4534)	1.25	5.00	61
(Shown as by the Four Couquettes)				
STARBRIGHT/Billy, My Billy	(Capitol 4574)	1.00	4.00	61

FOUR CASTS, The

TITLE/FLIP	LABEL & NO.	GOOD	NEAR MINT	YR.
STORMY WEATHER/Working At The Factory	(Atlantic 2228)	1.00	4.00	64

FOUR CHEERS, The

TITLE/FLIP	LABEL & NO.	GOOD	NEAR MINT	YR.
FATAL CHARMS OF LOVE/Perriwinkle Blue	(End 1034)	2.00	8.00	58

FOUR CHEVELLES, The

TITLE/FLIP	LABEL & NO.	GOOD	NEAR MINT	YR.
I KNOW/I Can't Believe	(Band Box 358)	1.50	6.00	57

4 CLEFS, The

TITLE/FLIP	LABEL & NO.	GOOD	NEAR MINT	YR.
PLEASE BE MINE/Time After Time	(BJ 1000)	1.25	5.00	

Also see Consorts, The

FOUR COACHMEN, The

TITLE/FLIP	LABEL & NO.	GOOD	NEAR MINT	YR.
THAT THING CALLED A GIRL/Wintertime	(Adonis A-102)	.75	3.00	

FOUR COINS, The

TITLE/FLIP	LABEL & NO.	GOOD	NEAR MINT	YR.
I LOVE YOU MADLY/Maybe	(Epic 9082)	1.25	5.00	54
MEMORIES OF YOU/Tear Down The Fence	(Epic 9129)	1.25	5.00	55
MY ONE SIN/This Life	(Epic 9229)	1.00	4.00	57
ONCE MORE/We'll Be Married	(Epic 9074)	1.25	5.00	54
SHANGRI-LA/First In Line	(Epic 9213)	1.00	4.00	57
SHOUT SHOUT/People Get Jealous	(Laurie 3360)	1.00	4.00	66
STORY UNTOLD/Magnolia	(Epic 9107)	1.25	5.00	55
WORLD OUTSIDE, THE/Roselle	(Epic 9295)	1.00	4.00	58

FOUR COUNTS, The

TITLE/FLIP	LABEL & NO.	GOOD	NEAR MINT	YR.
YOUNG HEARTS/I'm Gonna Love You	(Dart 1014)	1.50	6.00	

FOUR COUQUETTES: see Four Cal-Quettes, The

FOUR DATES, The

TITLE/FLIP	LABEL & NO.	GOOD	NEAR MINT	YR.
I'M HAPPY/Eloise	(Chancellor 1014)	1.00	4.00	58
TEENAGE NEIGHBOR/I Feel Good	(Chancellor 1027)	2.00	8.00	58

The Four Dates were also featured as the back up group on many of Fabian's records.

4 DIRECTIONS, The

TITLE/FLIP	LABEL & NO.	GOOD	NEAR MINT	YR.
TONIGHT WE LOVE/Arthur	(Coral 62456)	5.00	20.00	64

Also see Themes, The

FOUR DOTS, The (With Jewel Akens)

TITLE/FLIP	LABEL & NO.	GOOD	NEAR MINT	YR.
DON'T WAKE UP THE KIDS/Pleading For Your Love	(Freedom 44005)	3.75	15.00	59

(Features Eddie Cochran on lead guitar)

FOUR EKKOS, The

TITLE/FLIP	LABEL & NO.	GOOD	NEAR MINT	YR.
MY LOVE I GIVE/	(Rip 12558)	1.25	5.00	
SATELITE GIRL/Sputnik	(Brunswick 55037)	5.00	20.00	57

FOUR EPICS, The

TITLE/FLIP	LABEL & NO.	GOOD	NEAR MINT	YR.
AGAIN/I Love You Diane	(Laurie 3155)	1.25	5.00	63
HOW I WISH I WAS SINGLE AGAIN/Dance Joanne	(Laurie 3183)	1.25	5.00	63
I'M ON MY WAY/When The Music Ends	(Heritage 109)	2.00	8.00	62
M&M/Silhouettes-You Cheated	(Wand 11248)	1.00	4.00	72
(Shown as by Exodus)				
MR. CUPID/When I Walk With My Angel	(Swan 4156)	2.00	8.00	64
(Shown as by the Vespers)				

FOUR ESCORTS, The

TITLE/FLIP	LABEL & NO.	GOOD	NEAR MINT	YR.
DON'T YOU REMEMBER/My Special Girl	(Skyla 1113)	1.25	5.00	62

FOUR ESQUIRES, The

TITLE/FLIP	LABEL & NO.	GOOD	NEAR MINT	YR.
CAN'T HELP FALLING IN LOVE/ Merry-Go-Rounds Of Rome	(Terrace 7502)	.75	3.00	61
FOLLOW ME/Summer Vacation	(Pilgrim 717)	1.25	5.00	59
FOLLOW ME/Land Of You & Me	(Paris 526)	1.00	4.00	59
HIDEAWAY/Repeat After Me (With Rosemary June)	(Paris 520)	1.00	4.00	58
JAMES BOND THEME, THE/Summer Vacation	(Terrace 7516)	.75	3.00	63
LOOK HOMEWARD ANGEL/Santo Domingo	(London 1652)	1.00	4.00	56
LOVE ME FOREVER/I Ain't Been Right Since You Left	(Paris 509)	1.00	4.00	57

FOUR FLICKERS, The

TITLE/FLIP	LABEL & NO.	GOOD	NEAR MINT	YR.
IS THERE A WAY/Yo Yo	(Lee 1002)	.75	3.00	
LONG TALL TEXAN/	(Lee 1003)	.75	3.00	

FOUR FRESHMEN, The

TITLE/FLIP	LABEL & NO.	GOOD	NEAR MINT	YR.
ANGEL EYES/Love Is Just Around The Corner	(Capitol 3359)	1.00	4.00	56
CHARMAINE/In This Whole Wide World	(Capitol 3292)	1.25	5.00	55
DAY BY DAY/How Can I Tell Her	(Capitol 3154)	1.25	5.00	55
GRADUATION DAY/Lonely Night In Paris	(Capitol 3410)	1.00	4.00	56
HOLIDAY/It Happened Once Before	(Capitol 2564)	1.25	5.00	53
I WANNA GO WHERE YOU GO/Mr. B's Blues	(Capitol 1293)	1.25	5.00	50
IT'S A BLUE WORLD/Tuxedo Junction	(Capitol 2152)	1.25	5.00	52
MAYALA/It Never Occurred To Me	(Capitol 3070)	1.25	5.00	55
NOW YOU KNOW/Pick Up Your Tears	(Capitol 1377)	1.25	5.00	51
POINCIANA/The Baltimore Oriole	(Capitol 2398)	1.25	5.00	53
STORMY WEATHER/The Day Isn't Long Enough	(Capitol 2286)	1.25	5.00	54

4 GRADUATES, The

TITLE/FLIP	LABEL & NO.	GOOD	NEAR MINT	YR.
CANDY QUEEN/A Boy In Love	(Rust 5084)	3.75	15.00	63
LONELY WAY TO SPEND AN EVENING/Picture Of An Angel	(Rust 5062)	5.00	20.00	63
Also see Happenings, The				

FOUR GUYS, The

TITLE/FLIP	LABEL & NO.	GOOD	NEAR MINT	YR.
YOU DON'T HAVE TO TELL ME/ You Took My Heart By Surprise	(Kent 113)	2.50	10.00	

FOUR HOLIDAYS, The

TITLE/FLIP	LABEL & NO.	GOOD	NEAR MINT	YR.
I DON'T WANNA GO TO SCHOOL/Love Ya	(Verve 10204)	1.00	4.00	60

FOUR HORSEMEN, The

TITLE/FLIP	LABEL & NO.	GOOD	NEAR MINT	YR.
MY HEARTBEAT/A Long Long Time	(United Artists 134)	6.25	25.00	58

FOUR IMPERIALS, The

TITLE/FLIP	LABEL & NO.	GOOD	NEAR MINT	YR.
LAZY BONNIE/Let's Make A Scene	(Dot 15737)	3.75	15.00	58
MY GIRL/Teen Age Fool	(Chant 101)	1.50	6.00	

FOUR JACKS, The

TITLE/FLIP	LABEL & NO.	GOOD	NEAR MINT	YR.
LITTLE DARLIN'/	(Gateway 1211)	1.50	6.00	
ONLY YOU/	(Gateway 1147)	1.50	6.00	
R-O-C-K/Gum Drop	(Gateway 1136)	1.50	6.00	

FOUR JACKS & A JILL

TITLE/FLIP	LABEL & NO.	GOOD	NEAR MINT	YR.
MASTER JACK/I Looked Back	(RCA Victor 47-9473)	.75	3.00	68
MISTER NICO/Hamba Liliwam	(RCA Victor 47-9572)	.75	3.00	68

FOUR JOKERS, The (With Nervous Norvus)

TITLE/FLIP	LABEL & NO.	GOOD	NEAR MINT	YR.
TRANSFUSION/You Did	(Diamond 3004)	3.75	15.00	56
(Jimmy Drake, later known as Nervous Norvus, was a background singer on this release.)				

FOUR J's, The (James, Joseph, Jimmy and Joe)

TITLE/FLIP	LABEL & NO.	GOOD	NEAR MINT	YR.
BY LOVE POSSESSED/My Love, My Love	(Jamie 1274)	1.00	4.00	64
DREAMIN'/Love My Love	(Congress 6003)	1.00	4.00	69
DREAMS ARE A DIME A DOZEN/Kissin' At the Drive-In	(Herald 528)	1.00	4.00	58
HERE I AM BROKEN HEARTED/She Said That She Loved Me	(Jamie 1267)	1.00	4.00	64
NURSERY/Will You Be My Love	(4-J 506)	1.00	4.00	63
ROCK & ROLL AGE/Be Nice, Don't Fight	(United Artists 125)	1.50	6.00	58
Also see Fabulous Four, The				

FOUR KINGS, The

TITLE/FLIP	LABEL & NO.	GOOD	NEAR MINT	YR.
ONE NIGHT/Lonely Lover	(Canadian American 173)	1.25	5.00	64

FOUR KNIGHTS, The

TITLE/FLIP	LABEL & NO.	GOOD	NEAR MINT	YR.
ANNIVERSARY SONG/A Few Kind Words	(Capitol 2403)	2.00	8.00	53
BABY DOLL/Tennessee Train	(Capitol 2517)	2.00	8.00	53
CHARMAINE/Cry	(Capitol 1875)	2.50	10.00	52
DON'T DEPEND ON ME/You're A Honey	(Capitol 3494)	1.50	6.00	56
DON'T SIT UNDER THE APPLE TREE/Believing You	(Capitol 3192)	1.50	6.00	55
EASY STREET/I Ain't Got Nobody: see Four Knights Sing Spotlight Songs				
FOUR KNIGHTS SING SPOTLIGHT SONGS	(Capitol CCF-346)	15.00	60.00	53
(A boxed set of three 45rpm singles)				
FOOLISHLY YOURS/Inside Out	(Capitol 3093)	1.50	6.00	55
GEORGIA ON MY MIND/Sentimental Journey: see Four Knights Sing Spotlight Songs				
GRATEFULLY YOURS (With Pee Wee Hunt)/Me	(Capitol 3155)	1.50	6.00	55
GUILTY/You	(Capitol 3279)	1.50	6.00	55
HE'LL UNDERSTAND AND SAY WELL DONE/ Lead Me To That Rock	(Decca 9-14524)	10.00	40.00	50
(Originally issued on 78rpm, Decca 48018, this first 45rpm issue appeared on Decca's purple label 'Faith' series.)				
HONEY BUNCH/Write Me Baby	(Capitol 3024)	1.50	6.00	55
HOW WRONG CAN YOU BE/Period	(Capitol 2847)	2.00	8.00	54
I DON'T WANNA SEE YOU CRYING/I Saw Your Eyes	(Capitol 2938)	2.00	8.00	54
I GET SO LONELY/I Couldn't Stay Away From You	(Capitol 2654)	2.00	8.00	53
(Reissue of "Oh Baby Mine")				
I GO CRAZY/Got Her Off My Hands	(Capitol 1787)	3.00	12.00	51
I LOVE YOU STILL/Happy Birthday Baby	(Capitol 3339)	1.50	6.00	56
I WAS MEANT FOR YOU/They Tell Me	(Capitol 2782)	1.50	6.00	54
IDA, SWEET AS APPLE CIDER/When My Baby Smiles At Me: see Four Knights Sing Spotlight Songs				
IF YOU EVER CHANGE YOUR MIND/ Yes I Do (The Wedding Song)	(Coral 61981)	1.25	5.00	58
IN THE CHAPEL IN THE MOONLIGHT/I Want To Say Hello	(Capitol 1840)	2.50	10.00	51
IN THE CHAPEL IN THE MOONLIGHT/Easy Street	(Capitol 2894)	1.50	6.00	54
IT'S A SIN TO TELL A LIE/I'm The Worlds Biggest Fool	(Capitol 2087)	3.00	12.00	52
(IT'S NO) SIN/The Glory Of Love	(Capitol 1806)	3.00	12.00	51
MARSHMELLOW MOON/Five Foot Two	(Capitol 1914)	3.75	15.00	52
MISTAKEN/Bottle Up The Moonlight	(Capitol 3386)	1.50	6.00	56
MORE I GO OUT WITH SOMEBODY, THE/Dance With Dolly	(Capitol 1998)	2.00	8.00	52
O' FALLING STAR/Foolish Tears	(Coral 62045)	1.25	5.00	58
OH BABY MINE (I GET SO LONELY)/ I Couldn't Stay Away From You	(Capitol 2654)	3.00	12.00	53
("Oh Baby Mine" was the original title. This song was reissued as "I Get So Lonely")				
OH, HAPPY DAY/A Million Tears	(Capitol 2315)	2.00	8.00	52
ONE WAY KISSES/Lies	(Capitol 2234)	2.00	8.00	52
PERDIDO/After	(Capitol 3250)	1.50	6.00	55
SENTIMENTAL FOOL/I Love The Sunshine	(Capitol 1587)	3.75	15.00	51
THAT'S THE WAY IT'S GONNA BE/Say No More	(Capitol 2195)	2.00	8.00	52
WALKING IN THE SUNSHINE/There Are Two Sides	(Capitol 1971)	3.00	12.00	52
WHEN YOUR LOVER HAS GONE/Four Minute Mile	(Coral 61936)	1.25	5.00	58
WHERE IS THE LOVE/Things To Do Today	(Coral 62110)	1.25	5.00	59
WHO AM I/Walking & Whistling Blues	(Capitol 1707)	3.00	12.00	51
WIN OR LOSE/Doo Wacka Doo	(Capitol 2127)	2.00	8.00	52
WISH I HAD A GIRL/The Way I Feel	(Capitol 1930)	3.00	12.00	52

FOUR LABELS, The

TITLE/FLIP	LABEL & NO.	GOOD	NEAR MINT	YR.
LOOKIN'/Susie	(Gralow 5524)	1.50	6.00	

FOUR LADS, The

TITLE/FLIP	LABEL & NO.	GOOD	NEAR MINT	YR.
BUS STOP SONG, THE (A PAPER OF PINS)/ A House With Love In It	(Columbia 4-40736)	1.00	4.00	56
DOWN BY THE RIVER SIDE/Take Me Back	(Columbia 4-40005)	1.25	5.00	53
ENCHANTED ISLAND/Guess What The Neighbors'll Say	(Columbia 4-41194)	1.00	4.00	58
FOUNTAIN OF YOUTH/Meet Me Tonight In Dreamland	(Columbia 4-41365)	1.00	4.00	59
GILLY GILLY OSSENFEFFER KATZENELLEN BOGEN BY THE SEA/ I Hear It Everywhere	(Columbia 4-40236)	1.25	5.00	54
GIRL ON PAGE 44, THE/Sunday	(Columbia 4-41310)	1.00	4.00	59
HEAVENLY FATHER/Rocks In My Bed (With Dolores Hawkins)	(Okeh 6880)	2.00	8.00	
I JUST DON'T KNOW/Golly	(Columbia 4-40914)	1.00	4.00	57
ISTANBUL/I Should Have Told You Long Ago	(Columbia 4-40082)	1.25	5.00	53
MOCKING BIRD, THE/ Won' Cha (Few Me Something in Return)	(Columbia 4-41266)	1.00	4.00	58
MOCKING BIRD, THE/I May Hate Myself In The Morning	(Okeh 6885)	2.00	8.00	52
MOCKING BIRD, THE/I May Hate Myself In The Morning	(Epic 9150)	1.00	4.00	56
MOMENTS TO REMEMBER/Dream On Love, Dream	(Columbia 4-40539)	1.00	4.00	55
NO, NOT MUCH/I'll Never Know	(Columbia 4-40629)	1.00	4.00	56
PLEDGING MY LOVE/I've Been Thinking	(Columbia 4-40436)	1.25	5.00	55
PUT A LIGHT IN THE WINDOW/ The Things We Did Last Summer	(Columbia 4-41058)	1.00	4.00	57
SKOKIAAN/Why Should I Love You	(Columbia 4-40306)	1.25	5.00	54
STANDING ON THE CORNER/My Little Angel	(Columbia 4-40674)	1.00	4.00	56
THERE'S ONLY ONE OF YOU/Blue Tattoo	(Columbia 4-41136)	1.00	4.00	58
TIRED OF LOVING YOU/Turn Back	(Okeh 6860)	2.00	8.00	52
WHO NEEDS YOU/It's So Easy To Forget	(Columbia 4-40811)	1.00	4.00	56

FOURLANES, The

TITLE/FLIP	LABEL & NO.	GOOD	NEAR MINT	YR.
SURF TRAIN/Lonely Weekends	(Reprise 20213)	1.00	4.00	63

FOUR LARKS, The

TITLE/FLIP	LABEL & NO.	GOOD	NEAR MINT	YR.
GROOVIN' AT THE GO-GO/ I Still Love (From The Bottom Of My Heart)	(Tower 402)	.75	3.00	68

FOUR LOVERS, The (Frankie Valli, Tom Devito, Nick Devito, Hank Majewski)

TITLE/FLIP	LABEL & NO.	GOOD	NEAR MINT	YR.
HAPPY AM I/Never Never	(RCA Victor 47-6768)	3.75	15.00	56
HONEY LOVE/Please Don't Leave Me	(RCA Victor 47-6519)	3.75	15.00	56
JAMBALAYA/Be Lovey Dovey	(RCA Victor 47-6646)	3.75	15.00	56
MY LIFE FOR YOUR LOVE/Pucker Up	(Epic 5-9255)	37.50	150.00	57
REAL (THIS IS REAL)/Com Se Bella	(Cindy 3012)	18.75	75.00	59
(Shown as by Frankie Valle & the Romans)				
SHAKE A HAND/The Stranger	(RCA Victor 47-6812)	3.75	15.00	57
YOU'RE THE APPLE OF MY EYE/The Girl In My Dreams	(RCA Victor 47-6518)	3.75	15.00	56

FOUR MINTS, The

TITLE/FLIP	LABEL & NO.	GOOD	NEAR MINT	YR.
TEENAGE WONDERLAND/Hey Little Neil	(NRC 003)	1.25	5.00	58
TOMORROW NIGHT/Pina Colada	(NRC 037)	1.25	5.00	59
YOU BELONG TO MY HEART/	(NRC 011)	1.25	5.00	58

FOUR MOST, The

TITLE/FLIP	LABEL & NO.	GOOD	NEAR MINT	YR.
BREEZE & I, THE/I Love You	(Milo 107)	2.50	10.00	
BREEZE & I, THE/I Love You (Blue plastic)	(Milo 107)	1.25	5.00	
BREEZE & I, THE/I Love You	(Relic 501)	.75	3.00	

FOUR NATURALS, The

TITLE/FLIP	LABEL & NO.	GOOD	NEAR MINT	YR.
THOUGHT OF YOU DARLING, THE/Long Long Ago	(Red Top 125)	3.75	15.00	

FOUR OF A KIND

TITLE/FLIP	LABEL & NO.	GOOD	NEAR MINT	YR.
YOU WERE MADE TO LOVE/Love Every Moment	(Cameo 154)	1.00	4.00	58

4 OF US

TITLE/FLIP	LABEL & NO.	GOOD	NEAR MINT	YR.
I FEEL A WHOLE LOT BETTER/ I Can't Live Without Your Love	(Hideout 1012)	1.50	6.00	66
YOU'RE GONNA BE MINE/Batman	(Hideout 1003)	1.50	6.00	65
YOU'RE GONNA BE MINE/Free Fall	(Hideout 1003)	1.50	6.00	65
("Free Fall" & "Batman" are the same recording. Another version of this same song, titled "Fugitive," was recorded by the Fugitives.)				

FOUR PAGES, The

TITLE/FLIP	LABEL & NO.	GOOD	NEAR MINT	YR.
AUTOGRAPH BOOK/Much As I Do	(Plateau 101)	1.25	5.00	62

FOUR PALS, The

TITLE/FLIP	LABEL & NO.	GOOD	NEAR MINT	YR.
IF I CAN'T HAVE THE ONE I LOVE/I Flipped	(Royal Roost 610)	1.00	4.00	56
LONG BLACK STOCKINGS/Yours To Posses	(Roulette 4127)	1.00	4.00	59
NO ONE EVER LOVED ME/Can't Stand It Any Longer	(Royal Roost 616)	1.00	4.00	56

FOUR PENNIES, The (The Chiffons)

TITLE/FLIP	LABEL & NO.	GOOD	NEAR MINT	YR.
MY BLOCK/Dry Your Eyes	(Rust 5071)	1.25	5.00	63
WHEN THE BOY'S HAPPY/Hockaday (Part 1)	(Rust 5070)	1.25	5.00	63

FOUR PREPS, The

TITLE/FLIP	LABEL & NO.	GOOD	NEAR MINT	YR.
BALBOA/I've Already Started In	(Capitol 4478)	.75	3.00	61
BAND OF ANGELS/How About That	(Capitol 3775)	1.00	4.00	57
BIG DRAFT, THE/Suzy Cockroach	(Capitol 4716)	1.00	4.00	62
BIG MAN/Stop, Baby	(Capitol 3960)	1.00	4.00	58
BIG SURPRISE/Try My Arms	(Capitol 4218)	1.00	4.00	59
CINDERELLA/Gidget	(Capitol 4078)	1.00	4.00	58
DOWN BY THE STATION/Listen Honey	(Capitol 4312)	1.00	4.00	59
DREAMY EYES/Fools Will Be Fools	(Capitol 3576)	1.00	4.00	56
GIRL IN THE SHADE OF A STRIPED UMBRELLA/ Let's Call It A Day Girl	(Capitol 5687)	.75	3.00	66
GOT A GIRL/(Wait Till You) Hear It From Me	(Capitol 4362)	1.00	4.00	60
GREATEST SURFER COUPLE/ I'm Falling In Love With A Girl	(Capitol 5074)	1.00	4.00	63
KAW-LIGA/The Sand & The Sea	(Capitol 4435)	.75	3.00	60
LAZY SUMMER NIGHT/Summertime Lies	(Capitol 4023)	1.00	4.00	58
LETTER TO THE BEATLES, A/Collage Cannonball	(Capitol 5143)	1.25	5.00	64
MADELINA/Sentimental Kid	(Capitol 4400)	.75	3.00	60
MOONSTRUCK IN MADRID/I Cried A Million Tears	(Capitol 3621)	1.00	4.00	57
MORE MONEY FOR YOU & ME MEDLEY/ Swing Down Chariot	(Capitol 4599)	1.00	4.00	61
SHE WAS 5 & HE WAS 10/Riddle Of Love	(Capitol 4126)	1.00	4.00	59
26 MILES/It's You	(Capitol 3845)	1.00	4.00	57
WHAT KIND OF BIRD IS THAT/I've Known You All My Life	(Capitol 5178)	.75	3.00	64
Group members: Bruce Belland, Don Clarke, Glen Larson, Ed Cobb.				

FOUR QUEENS, The

TITLE/FLIP	LABEL & NO.	GOOD	NEAR MINT	YR.
BLACK STOCKINGS/It's Too Late	(ABC-Paramount 10409)	1.00	4.00	63

4 SEASONS, The (Featuring Frankie Valli)

TITLE/FLIP	LABEL & NO.	GOOD	NEAR MINT	YR.
AIN'T THAT A SHAME/Soon (I'll Be Home Again)	(Vee Jay 512)	1.00	4.00	63
ALONE/Long Lonely Nights (Yellow label)	(Vee Jay 597)	2.50	10.00	64
ALONE/Long Lonely Nights (Black & silver label)	(Vee Jay 597)	1.50	6.00	64
ALONE/Long Lonely Nights (Rainbow label)	(Vee Jay 597)	1.00	4.00	64
ALONE/Long Lonely Nights	(Vee Jay 597)	1.50	6.00	64
(Picture sleeve)				
AND THAT REMINDS ME (MY HEART REMINDS ME)/ The Singles Game	(Crewe 333)	.75	3.00	69
BEGGIN'/Dody	(Philips 40433)	.75	3.00	67
BEGGIN'/Dody	(Philips 40433)	1.25	5.00	67
(Picture sleeve)				
BIG GIRLS DON'T CRY/Connie-O (Black & silver label)	(Vee Jay 465)	1.50	6.00	62
BIG GIRLS DON'T CRY/Connie-O (Rainbow label)	(Vee Jay 465)	1.00	4.00	62
BIG GIRLS DON'T CRY/Connie-O	(Oldies 45 OL-47)	.75	3.00	62
BIG MAN IN TOWN/Little Angel	(Philips 40238)	.75	3.00	64
BIG MAN IN TOWN/Little Angel	(Philips 40238)	2.00	8.00	64
(Picture sleeve)				
BIG MAN'S WORLD/(Flip not by 4 Seasons)	(Columbia M-6675)	5.00	20.00	64
(Special products cardboard soundsheet.)				
BYE BYE BABY/Searching Wind	(Philips 40260)	.75	3.00	64
BYE BYE BABY/Searching Wind	(Philips 40260)	1.50	6.00	64
(Picture sleeve)				
CANDY GIRL/Marlena	(Vee Jay 539)	1.00	4.00	63
CANDY GIRL/Dear One (By the Scarlets)	(Oldies 45 OL-115)	2.00	8.00	63
CANDY GIRL/Marlena	(Oldies 45 OL-116)	.75	3.00	63
C'MON MARIANNE/Let's Ride Again	(Philips 40460)	.75	3.00	67
C'MON MARIANNE/Let's Ride Again	(Philips 40460)	1.00	4.00	67
(Picture sleeve)				
COUSIN BRUCIE GO GO (THEME)/	(WABC Radio 77)	12.50	50.00	64
(Custom pressing, yellow plastic)				
DAWN (GO AWAY)/No Surfin' Today	(Philips 40166)	.75	3.00	64
DECEMBER, 1963 (OH, WHAT A NIGHT)/Slip Away	(Warner Bros. 8168)	.50	2.00	75
DON'T THINK TWICE/Sassy	(Philips 40324)	.75	3.00	66
DOWN THE HALL/I Believe In You	(Warner Bros. 8407)	.75	3.00	77
ELECTRIC STORIES/Pity	(Philips 40577)	1.00	4.00	68
GIRL COME RUNNING/Cry Myself To Sleep	(Philips 40305)	.75	3.00	65
GIRL COME RUNNING/Cry Myself To Sleep	(Philips 40305)	1.00	4.00	65
(Picture sleeve)				
GIRL IN MY DREAMS, THE/	(Perri 1007)	6.25	25.00	61
(One-sided disc, shown as by the Topics)				
HAPPY HAPPY BIRTHDAY BABY/Apple Of My Eye	(Vee Jay 618)	1.50	6.00	65
HICKORY/Charisma	(Motown 1288F)	2.00	8.00	73
HICKORY (Stereo)/Hickory (Mono)	(Motown 1288F)	1.00	4.00	73
(Promotional issue)				
HOW COME/Life & Breath	(Motown 1255F)	2.00	8.00	73
HOW COME (Stereo)/How Come (Mono)	(Motown 1255F)	1.50	6.00	73
(Promotional issue)				
IDAHO/Something's On Her Mind	(Philips 40597)	1.00	4.00	69
I SAW MOMMY KISSING SANTA CLAUS/Christmas Tears	(Vee Jay 626)	1.50	6.00	64
I'VE GOT YOU UNDER MY SKIN/Huggin' My Pillow	(Philips 40393)	.75	3.00	66
I'VE GOT YOU UNDER MY SKIN/Huggin' My Pillow	(Philips 40393)	1.00	4.00	66
(Picture sleeve)				
JOEY REYNOLDS' THEME/	(WXYZ-Detroit 121003)	6.25	25.00	65
(Custom pressing done to the tune of "Big Girls Don't Cry")				
JOEY REYNOLDS' THEME/	(Wibbage, WIBG-Philadelphia)	6.25	25.00	65
(Custom pressing done to the tune of "Big Girls Don't Cry")				
LAY ME DOWN (WAKE ME UP)/Heartaches & Raindrops	(Philips 40688)	3.75	15.00	70
LAY ME DOWN (WAKE ME UP) (Stereo)/ Lay Me Down (Wake Me Up) (Mono)	(Bob Crew Presents DJP-71)	2.50	10.00	70
(Promotional issue)				
LAY ME DOWN (WAKE ME UP) (Stereo)/ Lay Me Down (Wake Me Up) (Mono)	(Philips 40688)	1.50	6.00	70
(Promotional issue)				
LET'S HANG ON/On Broadway Tonight	(Philips 40317)	.75	3.00	65
LITTLE BOY (IN GROWN UP CLOTHES)/Silver Wings	(Vee Jay 713)	2.00	8.00	65
(Maroon label)				
LITTLE BOY (IN GROWN UP CLOTHES)/Silver Wings	(Vee Jay 713)	1.00	4.00	65
(Black label)				
LONESOME ROAD/Around & Around	(Philips 40471)	1.00	4.00	66
(Shown as by the Wonder Who?)				
LOST LULLBYE/Trance	(Topix 6008)	7.50	30.00	61
(Shown as by Billy Dixon & the Topics)				
MY MOTHER'S EYES/Stay	(Vee Jay 719)	2.00	8.00	66
NEVER ON SUNDAY/Connie-O	(Vee Jay 639)	1.50	6.00	65
NEW MEXICAN ROSE/That's The Only Way	(Vee Jay 562)	1.00	4.00	63
NEW MEXICAN ROSE/That's The Only Way	(Vee Jay 562)	2.50	10.00	63
(Promotional issue, reads "That's The Way It Is.")				
NEW MEXICAN ROSE/That's The Only Way	(Vee Jay 562)	1.50	6.00	63
(Promotional issue, does not read "That's The Way It Is.")				
ON THE GOOD SHIP LOLLIPOP/ Your Nobody Till Somebody Loves You	(Philips 40380)	1.00	4.00	66
(Shown as by the Wonder Who?)				
OPUS 17 (DON'T YOU WORRY 'BOUT ME)/Beggar's Parade	(Philips 40370)	.75	3.00	66
OPUS 17 (DON'T YOU WORRY 'BOUT ME)/Beggar's Parade	(Philips 40370)	1.00	4.00	66
(Picture sleeve)				
PATCH OF BLUE/She Gives Me Light	(Philips 40662)	.75	3.00	71
PATCH OF BLUE/She Gives Me Light	(Philips 40662)	1.00	4.00	71
(Picture sleeve)				
PEANUTS/My Sugar	(Vee Jay 717)	3.00	12.00	64
(Shown as by the Wonder Who?)				
PEANUTS/My Sugar	(Vee Jay 1-901)	3.75	15.00	64
(Promotional issue only)				
RAG DOLL/Silence Is Golden	(Philips 40211)	.75	3.00	64
RAG DOLL/Jealous (By Little Royal)	(Gorda 500)	1.25	5.00	65
RED LIPS/ To Young To Start (Yellow & black label)	(Topix 6000)	6.25	25.00	60
(Shown as by the Village Voices)				
RED LIPS/ To Young To Start (Yellow, black & white label)	(Topix 6000)	5.00	20.00	60
(Shown as by the Village Voices)				
RONNIE/Born To Wander	(Philips 40185)	.75	3.00	64
RONNIE/Born To Wander	(Philips 40185)	1.00	4.00	64
(Picture sleeve)				
SANTA CLAUS IS COMING TO TOWN/Christmas Tears	(Vee Jay 478)	1.25	5.00	62
SATURDAY'S FATHER/Good-Bye Girl	(Philips 40542)	1.00	4.00	68
SATURDAY'S FATHER/Good-Bye Girl	(Philips 40542)	3.75	15.00	68
(Fold-out picture sleeve)				
SATURDAY'S FATHER/Good-Bye Girl	(Philips 40542)	1.00	4.00	68
(Regular picture sleeve)				
SAVE IT FOR ME/Funny Face	(Philips 40225)	.75	3.00	64
SHERRY/I've Cried Before (Black & silver label)	(Vee Jay 456)	1.50	6.00	62
SHERRY/I've Cried Before	(Rainbow 456)	1.00	4.00	62
SHERRY/I've Cried Before	(Oldies 45 OL-18)	.75	3.00	62
SILVER STAR/Mystic Mr. Sun	(Warner Bros. 8203)	.75	3.00	76
SINCE I DON'T HAVE YOU/Tonight Tonight	(Vee Jay 664)	2.00	8.00	65
SINCERELY/One Song	(Vee Jay 608)	1.25	5.00	64
SLEEPING MAN/Whatever You Say	(Warner Bros. K-16107)	12.50	50.00	71
(Released in England only.)				
SPANISH LACE/Bermuda	(Gone 5122)	5.00	20.00	61
STAY/Peanuts	(Vee Jay 576)	12.50	50.00	64
STAY/Goodnight My Love	(Vee Jay 582)	1.00	4.00	64
STAY/Please Please Me (By the Beatles)	(Vee Jay 581/582)	6.25	25.00	64
(Label error showed Beatles' flip side.)				
TELL IT TO THE RAIN/Show Girl	(Philips 40412)	.75	3.00	66
TELL IT TO THE RAIN/Show Girl	(Philips 40412)	1.50	6.00	66
(Picture sleeve)				
TOY SOLDIER/Betrayed	(Philips 40278)	1.00	4.00	65
TOY SOLDIER/Betrayed	(Philips 40278)	1.25	5.00	65
(Picture sleeve)				
TRANCE/I Am All Alone	(Topix 6002)	5.00	20.00	60
(Shown as by Billy Dixon & the Topics)				
TRANCE/I Am All Alone	(Seasons 4 Ever 777)	1.25	5.00	71
TRANCE/I Am All Alone (Colored plastic)	(Seasons 4 Ever 777)	2.50	10.00	71
WALK LIKE A MAN/Lucky Ladybug	(Vee Jay 485)	1.00	4.00	63
WALK LIKE A MAN/Lucky Ladybug	(Oldies 45 OL-60)	.75	3.00	63
WALK LIKE A MAN/Lucky Ladybug	(Oldies 45 OL-60)	2.00	8.00	63
(Flip side is a selection by Ray Stevens.)				
WALK ON, DON'T LOOK BACK/Sun County	(Mowest 5026F)	2.00	8.00	72
WALK ON, DON'T LOOK BACK (Stereo)/ Walk On Don't Look Back (Mono)	(Mowest 5026F)	1.25	5.00	72
(Promotional issue)				

TITLE/FLIP — LABEL & NO. — GOOD — NEAR MINT — YR.

WATCH THE FLOWERS GROW/Raven (Philips 40490) .75 3.00 67
WATCH THE FLOWERS GROW/Raven (Philips 40490) 1.00 4.00 67
(Picture sleeve)
WHERE ARE MY DREAMS/
Medley: Any Day Now-Happy Day (Philips 40694) 6.25 25.00 71
WHERE ARE MY DREAMS (Stereo)/
Where Are My Dreams (Mono) (Philips DJP-74) 2.50 10.00 71
(Promotional issue)
WHO LOVES YOU/Who Loves You (Disco version) (Warner Bros. 8122) .50 2.00 75
WILL YOU LOVE ME TOMORROW/Around & Around (and-aroundandaroundandaroundandaround) (Philips 40523) .75 3.00 68
WORKING MY WAY BACK TO YOU/Too Many Memories (Philips 40350) .75 3.00 66

The 4 Seasons evolved from the remnants of the Four Lovers (1954-1960). The early 4 Seasons consisted of Frankie Valli, keyboardist Bob Gaudio, bassists Nick Massi (1960-1965) and Joey Long (1965-1975), and lead guitarists Tommy DeVito (1960-1970) and Dimitri Callas (1971-1973). In the early seventies, they permanently expanded to a six man format in order to add a drummer and allow Gaudio to limit his involvement to recordings only. The five touring members perform as "Frankie Valli and the 4 Seasons". This format initially required several temporary non-recording members, of no significance today to collectors. since January 1974, the six group members are: Frankie Valli, bob Gaudio, Gerri Polci, Don Ciccone, formerly of the Critters, Joey Long (replaced by John Paiva in 1975 and larry Lingle in 1980) and Lee Shapiro (replaced by Sugarloaf's jerry Corbetta in 1979).

Also see Alda, Alex
Also see Corey, John
Also see Felmons, Wade
Also see Four Lovers
Also see Halo, Johnny
Also see Hayes, Tommy
Also see Kokomos
Also see Larry & The Legends
Also see Mathews, Shirley
Also see Mitchell, Evan
Also see Santos, Larry
Also see Tyler, Frankie
Also see Valli, Frankie
Also see Victorians, The
Also see Village Voices, The

FOUR SEASONS, The
DON'T SWEAT IT BABY/That's The Way The Ball Bounces (Alanna 555) 2.00 8.00 59
("Don't Sweat It Baby" was also issued as "I'm Still In Love With You.")
I'M STILL IN LOVE WITH YOU/
That's The Way The Ball Bounces (Alanna 555) 2.00 8.00 59
("I'm Still In Love With You" was also issued as "Don't Sweat It Baby.")
LOVE KNOWS NO SEASON/Hot Water Bottle (Alanna 558) 2.00 8.00 60
This group should not be confused with the 4 Seasons, featuring Frankie Valli.

FOUR SPEEDS, The (With Gary Usher)
FOUR ON THE FLOOR/Cheater Slicks (Challenge 9202) 1.50 6.00 63
R.P.M./My Sting Ray (Challenge 9187) 1.50 6.00 63

FOUR STARS, The
BLUE DAWN/The Frog (Era 3021) .75 3.00 60

FOUR TEMPTATIONS, The: see Temptations, The

FOUR TEENS, The
GO LITTLE GO CAT/Spark Plug (Challenge 59021) 10.00 40.00 58

FOUR TOPHATTERS, The
45 MEN IN A TELEPHONE BOOTH/Wild Rosie (Cadence 1268) 1.25 5.00 55

FOUR TOWNSMEN, The
IT WASN'T SO LONG BEFORE/Sometimes (Artflow 145) 3.75 15.00

FOUR UNIQUES, The
LOOKING FOR A LOVE/Too Young (Adam 9002) 5.00 20.00 61
SHE'S THE ONLY GIRL/Twistin' Around (Adam 9004) 3.75 15.00 62

FOUR UPSETTERS, The
SURFIN' CALLIOPE/Wabash Cannonball (Sun 386) 1.00 4.00 63

FOUR VOICES, The
ANGEL OF LOVE/Such A Shame (Columbia 4-40933) 1.00 4.00 57
DANCING WITH MY SHADOW/Bon Bon (Columbia 4-41076) 1.00 4.00 57
DARLING, THANKS TO YOU/The Big Eye (Columbia 4-40582) 1.00 4.00 55
HONEST, DARLING/Hey Honey (Columbia 4-40516) 1.00 4.00 55
I LOVE YOU STILL/Sentimental (Columbia 4-40838) 1.00 4.00 57
I'M DREAMIN' OF WEDDING BELLS/
The Ties That Bind (Columbia 4-40749) 1.00 4.00 56
LET'S WRITE OUR OWN LOVE STORY/Bim Bam Baby (Columbia 4-40699) 1.00 4.00 56
LOVELY ONE/Geronimo (Columbia 4-40643) 1.00 4.00 56
LOVELY ONE/Geronimo (Mr. Peacock 106) .75 3.00 62
SIDEWALK BOP/ (Columbia 4-40983) 1.00 4.00 57
YOU KNOW I DO/Ev'ry Hour, Ev'ry Day Of My Life (Columbia 4-41167) 1.00 4.00 58

FOUR WHEELS, The
CENTRAL HIGH PLAYMATE/Cold 45 (Soma 1428) 1.25 5.00 65
SNEAKY LITTLE SLEEPER/Ratchet (Deleware 1803) 2.00 8.00 64

FOUR WINDS, The
DADDY'S HOME/Bull Moose Stomp (Warwick 633) 2.50 10.00 61
FIND SOMEONE NEW/Colorado Moon (Vik 221) 1.25 5.00 56
PLAYGIRL/Jennifer (Derby 10022) 2.50 10.00
REMEMBER LAST SUMMER/Strange Feelings (Swing 100) 1.25 5.00 64
SHORT SHORTS/Five Minutes More (Decor 175) 1.25 5.00 57
(With Their Teenage Friends)
Even though all of these releases are shown as being by a group using the same name, the possibility exists that they are not all by the same group.

FOUR WINDS, The (The Tokens)
ONE FACE IN THE CROWD/Let It Ride (B.T. Puppy 555) 1.00 4.00 69

FOUR YOUNG MEN, The
YOU BEEN TORTURING ME/See Them Laugh (Crest 1076) .75 3.00 61

FOUR-EVERS, The
BE MY GIRL/If I Were A Magician (Smash 1887) .75 3.00 64
(Reissue of "Please Be Mine.")
COME UP IN THE WORLD/Colors (Chattahoochee 630) .75 3.00 64
DOO BE DUM/Everlasting (Smash 1921) 1.00 4.00 64
LOVELY WAY TO SPEND AN EVENING, A/
The Girl I Want (Columbia 4-43886) 1.00 4.00 66
LOVER COME BACK TO ME/It's Love (Smash 1853) .75 3.00 63
ONE MORE TIME/Everybody South Street (Jamie 1247) 1.50 6.00 63
PLEASE BE MINE/If I Were A Magician (Smash 1887) 1.50 6.00 64
(Original issue, also see "Be My Girl.")
STORMY/I'm Walkin' (Into The Crowd) (Constellation 151) 3.00 12.00 65
WHAT A SCENE/You Never Had It So Good (Red Bird 10-078) 2.00 8.00 66
YOU BELONG TO ME/
Such A Good Night For Dreaming (Columbia 4-42303) 5.00 20.00 62
YOU BELONG TO ME/
Such A Good Night For Dreaming (Columbia 3-42303) 8.75 35.00 62
(Compact 33 single)
Also see Candy Girls, The

FOUR-FIFTHS, The
AFTER GRADUATION/Come On Girl (Hudson 8101) 5.00 20.00
IF YOU STILL WANT ME/Have You Ever Loved A Girl (Columbia 4-43913) 1.25 5.00 66

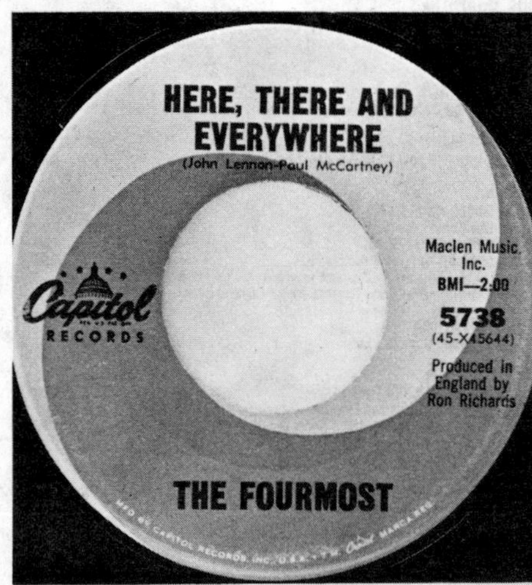

FOURMOST, The
HELLO LITTLE GIRL/Just In Case (Atco 6280) 2.00 8.00 63
HERE THERE & EVERYWHERE/You've Changed (Capitol 5738) 2.50 10.00 66
HOW CAN I TELL HER/You Got That Way (Atco 6317) 1.50 6.00 64
IF YOU CRY/Little Bit Of Loving (Atco 6307) 1.50 6.00 64
RESPECTABLE/I'm In Love (Atco 6285) 1.50 6.00 64
WHY DO FOOLS FALL IN LOVE/Girls, Girls, Girls (Capitol 5591) 1.50 6.00 66

FOURMOST AUTHORITY, The
DANCE, DANCE/Left Hand Lawyer (Crescendo 386) .75 3.00 67
CHILDHOOD FRIENDS/Woe Is Me (Crescendo 403) .75 3.00 68
GO FOR WHAT YOU KNOW/I Can't Get By (Crescendo 416) .75 3.00 68

FOURTH DIMENSION, The
RAINY DAY/Land Of Make Believe (Columbia 4-43778) .75 3.00 66

FOURTH ST. EXIT, The
LOVE LIKE THIS, A/Strange One (Rowena 792) 1.00 4.00

FOURTH WAY, The
BUCKLEHUGGIN/Clouds (Capitol 2619) 1.00 4.00 69
FAR SIDE OF YOUR MOON/Pink Cloud (Soul City 765) 1.25 5.00 68

FOWLER, Jimmy
LET'S ROCK & ROLL/Please Answer My Call (Dart 118) 1.00 4.00 59

FOWLER, Wally
NEW STAR IN HEAVEN, A/A Wonderful Time Up There (Dove 100) .50 2.00 77
PRICILLA/He'll Never Be Lonely Again (Dove 2177) .50 2.00 77

FOWLEY, Kim
AMERICAN DREAM/The Statue (Mira 209) 1.25 5.00 65
BIG BAD CADILLAC/A Man Without A Country (Original Sound 99) .75 3.00 75
(Shown as by King Lizard)
BIG SUR (BEAR MOUNTAIN, CIROS, FLIP SIDE, PROTEST SONG)/
The Trip (Corby 216) 2.00 8.00 65
BORN DANCER/Something New (Capitol 3662) .75 3.00 73
BORN TO BE WILD/Space Odyssey (Imperial 66326) .75 3.00 68
DON'T BE CRUEL/Strangers From The Sky (Reprise 0569) 1.00 4.00 67
E.S.P. READER/International Heroes (Capitol 3534) .75 3.00 73
FORBIDDEN LOVE/I'm Bad (Capitol 3403) .75 3.00 72
LIGHTS/Something New & Different (Loma 2064) 1.00 4.00 66
LOVE IS ALIVE & WELL/Reincarnation (Tower 342) 1.00 4.00 67
MR. RESPONSIBILITY/My Foolish Heart (Living Legend 721) 2.00 8.00 65
UNDERGROUND LADY/Pop Art '66 (Living Legend 725) 2.00 8.00 66
WILDFIRE/Bubble Gum (Imperial 66349) 1.25 5.00

FOWLS, The
YANKS ARE THE CHAMPS, THE/The Yanks Are Back (Rotten Rat 1018) 1.50 6.00

FOX
IMAGINE ME, IMAGINE YOU/If I Point At The Moon (Ariola-GTO 7608) .50 2.00 75
ONLY YOU CAN/Out Of My Body (GTO 1003) .75 3.00 74
ONLY YOU CAN/Out Of My Body (Ariola-GTO 7601) .50 2.00 75

FOX
SUN CITY (PART 1)/Sun City (Part 2) (Studio 107) 1.25 5.00
SUN CITY (PART 1)/Sun City (Part 2) (San Francisco Session 107) 1.00 4.00

FOX, Norman, & The Rob-Roys
DANCE GIRL DANCE/My Dearest One (Back Beat 508) 3.00 12.00 58
PIZZA PIE/Dream Girl (Capitol 4128) 8.75 35.00 59
TELL ME WHY/Audrey (Back Beat 501) 2.00 8.00 57

FOXES, The
GET 'EM WITH A WINK/The Sassy One (Pickwick City) 1.25 5.00
SOUL CITY/Those Days Are Gone Forever (Bridgeview 7000) 1.50 6.00
WHO FONDLED YOU AS FONDLY AS I/Thrilled (Titanic 101) 1.25 5.00 63

FRAGILE LIME
SHE'S GOT ME SHAKIN'/ (Metromedia 266) .50 2.00 72

FRAMPTON, Peter (Of The Herd)
ALL NIGHT LONG/Don't Fade Away (A&M 1456) 1.50 6.00 73
(Shown as by Frampton's Camel)
BABY, I LOVE YOUR WAY/Money (I'll Give You) (A&M 1738) 1.00 4.00 75
BABY, I LOVE YOUR WAY/It's A Plain Shame (A&M 1832) .50 2.00 76
(BABY) SOMETHING'S HAPPENING/
I Wanna Go To The Sun (A&M 1506) 1.25 5.00 74
DO YOU FEEL LIKE WE DO/Penny For Your Thoughts (A&M 1867) .50 2.00 76
I CAN'T STAND IT NO MORE/May I Baby (A&M 2148) .50 2.00 79
(I'LL GIVE YOU) MONEY/ (A&M 1763) 1.00 4.00 75
I'M IN YOU/St. Thomas (Know How I Feel) (A&M 1941) .50 2.00 77
JUMPING JACK FLASH/Oh For Another Day (A&M 1379) 1.50 6.00 72
(Shown as by Pete Frampton)
SHE DON'T REPLY/St. Thomas (Don't You Know
How I Feel) (A&M 2174) .50 2.00 79
SHOW ME THE WAY/Crying Clown (A&M 1693) 1.00 4.00 75
SHOW ME THE WAY/Shine On (A&M 1795) .50 2.00 76
SIGNED, SEALED, DELIVERED (I'M YOURS)/
Rocky's Hot Club (A&M 1972) .50 2.00 77
TRIED TO LOVE/You Don't Have To Worry (A&M 1988) .50 2.00 77
WHICH WAY THE WIND BLOWS/I Believe (A&M 1470) 1.50 6.00 73
(Shown as by Frampton's Camel)
Also see Humble Pie

FRAMPTON'S CAMEL: see Frampton, Peter

FRANCE, Larry
LAST KISS/Germ City (Landa 700) .75 3.00 64

FRANCIS, Connie (Constance Franconero)
ADDIO MI 'AMORE (GOODBYE MY LOVE)/
Say Goodbye (A Comme Amour) (MGM K-13923) .75 3.00 71
ALL THE LOVE IN THE WORLD/So Nice (Summer Samba) (MGM K-13578) .75 3.00 66
AMONG MY SOUVENIRS/God Bless America (MGM K-12841) 1.00 4.00 59
ANOTHER PAGE/Souvenir D'Italie (MGM K-13665) .75 3.00 67
ANSWER, THE (SHOULD I TIE A YELLOW RIBBON 'ROUND THE
OLE OAK TREE)/Paint The Rain (GSF 6901) .75 3.00 73
ARE YOU SATISFIED/My Treasure (MGM K-12122) 3.00 12.00 55
BE ANYTHING (BUT BE MINE)/Tommy (MGM K-13237) .75 3.00 64
BLUE WINTER/You Know You Don't Want Me (MGM K-13214) .75 3.00 64
BREAKIN' IN A BRAND NEW BROKEN HEART/
Someone Else's Boy (MGM K-12995) .75 3.00 61
DON'T BREAK THE HEART THAT LOVES YOU/Drop It Joe (MGM K-13059) .75 3.00 62
DON'T EVER LEAVE ME/We Have Something More (MGM K-13287) .75 3.00 64
DROWNIN' MY SORROWS/Mala Femmena (MGM K-13160) .75 3.00 63
EVERYBODY'S SOMEBODY'S FOOL/Jealous Of You (MGM K-12899) .75 3.00 60
FADED ORCHID/Eighteen (MGM K-12490) 2.00 8.00 57
FALLIN'/Happy Days & Lonely Nights (MGM K-12713) 1.00 4.00 58
FOLLOW THE BOYS/Waiting For Billy (MGM K-13127) .75 3.00 63
FOR MAMA/She'll Be Comin' Round The Mountain (MGM K-13325) .75 3.00 65
FORGET DOMANI/No One Sends Me Roses (MGM K-13363) .75 3.00 65
FORGETTING/Send For My Baby (MGM K-12251) 2.50 10.00 56
FREDDY/Didn't I Love You Enough (MGM K-12015) 3.00 12.00 55
GONE LIKE THE WIND/Am I Blue (MGM K-14058) .75 3.00 69
HEARTACHES/I Miss You So (MGM K-12669) 1.50 6.00 58
(HE'S MY) DREAMBOAT/Hollywood (MGM K-13039) .75 3.00 61

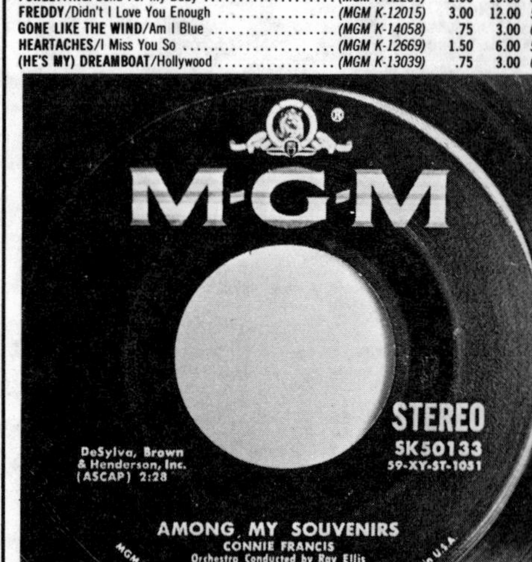

M-G-M
STEREO
5K50133
59-XY-ST-1051
DeSylva, Brown & Henderson, Inc. (ASCAP) 2:28
AMONG MY SOUVENIRS
CONNIE FRANCIS
Orchestra Conducted by Ray Ellis
Comps.—Leslie-Nicholls
MGM RECORDS—A DIVISION OF LOEW'S INCORPORATED—Made in U.S.A.

I ALMOST LOST MY MIND/Come Back To Sorrento (MGM SB-10) 3.75 15.00 60
(Stereo single issue)
I DON'T WANNA WALK WITHOUT YOU/Don't Turn Around (Ivanhoe 508) .75 3.00 76
I NEVER HAD A SWEETHEART/Little Blue Wren (MGM K-12375) 2.00 8.00 56
I WAS SUCH A FOOL/He Thinks I Still Care (MGM K-13096) .75 3.00 62
IF I DIDN'T CARE/Toward The End Of The Day (MGM K-12769) 1.00 4.00 59
IF MY PILLOW COULD TALK/
You're The Only One Who Can Hurt Me (MGM K-13143) .75 3.00 63
I'M GONNA BE WARM THIS WINTER/Al Di La (MGM K-13116) .75 3.00 62
I'M SORRY I MADE YOU CRY/Lock Up Your Heart (MGM K-12647) 1.00 4.00 58
IN THE SUMMER OF HIS YEARS/My Buddy (MGM K-13203) .75 3.00 63
INVIERNO TRISTES/Noches Espanolas Y Tu (MGM K-14089) .75 3.00 70
IT'S A DIFFERENT WORLD/Empty Chapel (MGM K-13505) .75 3.00 66
JEALOUS HEART/Can I Rely On You (MGM K-13420) .75 3.00 65
LETTER FROM A SOLDIER, A/Somewhere My Love (MGM K-13545) .75 3.00 66
LIPSTICK ON YOUR COLLAR/Frankie (MGM K-12793) 1.00 4.00 59
LONELY AGAIN/When You Care A Lot For Someone (MGM K-13814) .75 3.00 68
LOOKING FOR LOVE/This Is My Happiest Moment (MGM K-13256) .75 3.00 64
MAJESTY OF LOVE (With Marvin Rainwater)/
You My Darling, You (MGM K-12555) 2.00 8.00 57
MAMA/Teddy (MGM K-12878) .75 3.00 60
MANY TEARS AGO/Senza Mamma (MGM K-12964) 1.00 4.00 60
MY FIRST REAL LOVE/Believe In Me (MGM K-12191) 2.50 10.00 56
(With the Jaybirds)
MY HAPPINESS/Never Before (MGM K-12738) 1.00 4.00 58
MY HAPPINESS/Never Before (MGM SK-50117) 3.75 15.00 59
(Stereo single issue)
MY HEART CRIES FOR YOU/
Someone Took The Sweetness Out Of Sweetheart (MGM K-13773) .75 3.00 67
MY HEART HAS A MIND OF IT'S OWN/Malaguena (MGM K-12923) .75 3.00 60
MY SAILOR BOY/Everyone Needs Someone (MGM K-12335) 2.50 10.00 56
MY WORLD IS SLIPPING AWAY/Till We're Together (MGM K-13876) .75 3.00 68
NO OTHER ONE/I Leaned On A Man (MGM K-12440) 2.00 8.00 57
OH PLEASE MAKE HIM JEALOUS/Goody Goodbye (MGM K-12056) 2.50 10.00 55

TITLE/FLIP — LABEL & NO. — GOOD — NEAR MINT — YR.

ROCK-A-BYE YOUR BABY WITH A DIXIE MELODY/
Ciao Ciao Bambina (MGM SB-9) 3.75 15.00 60
(Stereo single issue)
ROUNDABOUT/Bossa Nova Hand Dance (MGM K-13389) .75 3.00 65
SECOND HAND LOVE/Gonna Git That Man (MGM K-13074) .75 3.00 62
SOMEBODY ELSE IS TAKING MY PLACE/
Brother Can You Spare A Dime (MGM K-13948) .75 3.00 68
SPANISH NIGHTS & YOU/Games Lovers Play (MGM K-13610) .75 3.00 66
STUPID CUPID/Carolina Moon (MGM K-12683) 1.00 4.00 58
SWANEE/Atashi No (MGM K-13005) .75 3.00 61
TIME ALONE WILL TELL (NON PENSARE)/Born Free (MGM K-13718) .75 3.00 67
TOGETHER/Too Many Rules (MGM K-13019) .75 3.00 61
VACATION/Biggest Sin Of All (MGM K-13087) .75 3.00 62
WEDDING CAKE, THE/Over Hill Underground (MGM K-14034) .75 3.00 69
WELFARE CHECK, THE/I Don't Wanna Play House (MGM K-14004) .75 3.00 69
WHEN THE BOY IN YOUR ARMS/Baby's First Christmas (MGM K-13051) .75 3.00 61
WHERE THE BOYS ARE/No One (MGM K-12971) .75 3.00 61
WHOSE HEART ARE YOU BREAKING TONIGHT/C'mon Jerry (MGM K-13303) .75 3.00 64
WHO'S SORRY NOW/You Were Only Fooling (MGM K-12588) 1.00 4.00 58
WHY SAY GOODBYE/Addio Me Amore (MGM K-13923) .75 3.00 68
WISHING IT WAS YOU/
You're Mine (Just When You're Lonely) (MGM K-13331) .75 3.00 64
YOUR OTHER LOVE/Whatever Happened To Rose Marie (MGM K-13176) .75 3.00 63
YOU'RE GONNA MISS ME/Plenty Good Lovin' (MGM 12824) 1.00 4.00 59
ZINGARA (GYPSY)/Mr. Love (MGM K-14091) .75 3.00 70

FRANCOIS & THE ANGELOS
MIMI/City Farm (Romulus 3004) 1.00 4.00

FRANK & JACK
TWAS THE NIGHT BEFORE CHRISTMAS/Jingle Bells (Bergen 100) 2.00 8.00
TWAS THE NIGHT BEFORE CHRISTMAS/Jingle Bells (Joz 827) 1.50 6.00

FRANKIE & JOHNNY
PLEASE BE MY LOVE TONIGHT/Picadilly Rose (Blast Off 100) 1.00 4.00

FRANKIE & THE ECHOES
COME BACK BABY/Until We Meet Again (Savoy 1544) 1.00 4.00 58

FRANKIE & THE FLIPS
DEVIL DOG ROCK/
Popeye Twist (Popeye The Sailor Man) (Savoy 1602) .75 3.00 61

FRANKIE & THE TIMEBREAKERS
I'LL BE HOME/Is There Anybody (Mercury 72837) 1.25 5.00 68

FRANKLIN, Doug
I WONDER WHO'S KISSING HER NOW/
I Used To Wonder (Colonial 8888) 1.00 4.00 58
MY LUCKY LOVE/Drizzlin' Rain (Colonial 7777) 1.00 4.00 58

FRANKLIN, Gene, & The Spacemen
ITCHIN' & TWISTIN'/ (Kay Dee 5001) .75 3.00

FRANKLYN CIRCLE
MIDNIGHT MAGIC MAN/Theme From Midnight Magic Man (Laurie 3559) 1.25 5.00

FRANKS, Michael
LADY WANTS TO KNOW, THE/ (Warner Bros. 8368) .50 2.00 77
POPSICLE TOES/I Don't Know Why I'm So Happy I'm Sad (Reprise 1360) .75 3.00 76
WHEN THE COOKIE JAR IS EMPTY/ (Warner Bros. 8583) .50 2.00 78

FRANTICS, The
FOG CUTTER/Black Sapphire (Dolton 6) 1.00 4.00 59
STRAIGHT FLUSH/Young Blues (Dolton 2) 1.00 4.00 59
WEREWOLF/No Werewolf (Dolton 16) 1.00 4.00 60
(Werewolf sounds by Bob Reisdorf)
WHIP, THE/Delilah (Dolton 24) 1.00 4.00 60

FRATERNITY BROTHERS, The
BIG TOWN/Sad Little Boy (Date 1528) 1.50 6.00 60

FREBERG, Stan
BA BA BALL & CHAIN/Abe Snake For President (Capitol 2125) 2.50 10.00 52
BANANA BOAT (DAY-O)/Tele-Vee-Shun (Capitol 3687) 1.50 6.00 57
C'EST SI BON (IT'S SO GOOD)/
A Dear John & Martha Letter (Capitol 2677) 1.50 6.00 57
CHRISTMAS DRAGNET (PART 1)/Christmas Dragnet (Part 2) (Capitol 2671) 3.00 12.00 53
(Reissued the following year using the title "Yulenet")
COMMENTS FOR OUR TIME (PART 1)/
Comments For Our Time (Part 2) (Capitol 4433) 1.00 4.00 60
ELDERLY MAN RIVER/
The Zazzaloph Family-Puffed Grass Commercial (Capitol PRO 732) 5.00 20.00
GREAT PRETENDER, THE/The Quest For Bridey Murphy (Capitol 3396) 2.00 8.00 56
GREEN CHRITMA (PART 1)/Green Christmas (Part 2) (Capitol 3503) 2.00 8.00 56
GREEN CHRITMA/The Meaning Of Christmas (Capitol 4097) 1.50 6.00 58
HEARTBREAK HOTEL/Rock Island Line (Capitol 3480) 3.00 12.00 56
I'VE GOT YOU UNDER MY SKIN/That's My Boy (Capitol 1711) 2.50 10.00 51
JOHN & MARSHA/Ragtime Dan (Capitol 1356) 2.50 10.00 51
LONE PSYCHIATRIST, THE/The Honeyearthers (Capitol 3138) 3.00 12.00 55
MUSIC TO BUBBLE-UP BY/ (Coca-Cola Bottling Co. 2227) 5.00 20.00
NUTTIN' FOR CHRISTMAS/Night Before Christmas (Capitol 3280) 1.50 6.00 55
OLD PAYOLA ROLL BLUES, THE (PART 1)/
The Old Payola Roll Blues (Part 2) (Capitol 4329) 1.50 6.00 60
POINT OF ORDER/Person To Person (Capitol 2838) 2.00 8.00 54
SH-BOOM/Wide Screen Mama Blues (Capitol 2929) 2.00 8.00 54
ST. GEORGE & THE DRAGONET/Little Blue Riding Hood (Capitol 2596) 2.00 8.00 53
STAN FREEBERG...ON COMMERCIALS/ (No Label or Number Known) 5.00 20.00
(Promotional issue)
SWIMSUITSMANSHIP/Swimsuitsmanship (Rose Marie-no number) 3.75 15.00
(Special products release)

TELE VEE SHUN/Maggie (Capitol 1962) 2.00 8.00 52
TRY/Pass Under The Udder (Capitol 2029) 2.50 10.00 52
WORLD IS WAITING FOR THE SUNRISE, THE/
The Boogie-Woogie Banjo Man From Birmingham (Capitol 2279) 2.00 8.00 52
WUNERFUL, WUNERFUL (PART 1)/
Wunerful, Wunerful (Part 2) (Capitol 3815) 2.50 10.00 57
YA GOT TROUBLE/Gary, Indiana (Capitol 3892) 1.25 5.00 58
YELLOW ROSE OF TEXAS, THE/Rock Around Stephen Foster (Capitol 3249) 2.00 8.00 55
YULENET (PART 1)/Yulenet (Part 2) (Capitol 2986) 2.00 8.00 54
(Reissue of "Christmas Dragnet")

FRECKLES, The
LITTLE STAR/Freckle Face (Madison 158) 1.50 6.00 61

FREDDIE & LOU
YOU'LL BE MINE TONIGHT/Rosalie (Thunder T-2150) 1.25 5.00

FREDDIE & THE DREAMERS (Featuring Freddie Garrity)
DO THE FREDDIE/Tell Me When (Mercury 72428) .75 3.00 65
I DON'T KNOW/Windmill In Old Amsterdam (Mercury 72487) 1.00 4.00 65
I'M TELLING YOU NOW/What Have I Done To You (Capitol 5053) 2.50 10.00 63
I'M TELLING YOU NOW/What Have I Done To You (Tower 125) .75 3.00 65
I UNDERSTAND (JUST HOW YOU FEEL)/I Will (Mercury 72377) .75 3.00 65
JUST FOR YOU/Don't Do That To Me (Mercury 72327) 1.00 4.00 64
LITTLE YOU, A/Things I'd Like To Say (Mercury 72462) .75 3.00 65
SEND A LETTER TO ME/
There's Not One Thing (By Just Four Men) (Tower 163) 1.00 4.00 65
SUSANS TUBA/She Needs Me (Super K SK-146) .75 3.00 70
YOU WERE MADE FOR ME/Send A Letter To Me (Capitol 5137) 2.50 10.00 64
YOU WERE MADE FOR ME/So Fine (By The Beat Merchants) (Tower 127) .75 3.00 65

FREDDIE & THE PARLIAMENTS
DARLENE/That Girl (Twirl 1003) 1.00 4.00 59
(Features Johnny Paris on saxophone.)
Also see Johnny & the Hurricanes

FREDDIE THE FLEA
SHALL WE WALK OR TAKE A DOG/Hexorcist World Premier (Nik 74) 1.25 5.00

FREDDY & CLAIRE
AFTER SCHOOL/Love Is A Game (Reprise 2049) 2.00 8.00 62

FREDDY & THE FAT BOYS
WHY DO FOOLS FALL IN LOVE/Ballad Of Freddie & Rich (Fat Man 101) 5.00 20.00

FREDDY & THE KINFOLK
GOAT, THE/ (Dade 217) 1.00 4.00 68

FRED, John (& His Playboy Band)
AGNES ENGLISH/Sad Story (Paula 273) .75 3.00 67
BACK IN THE U.S.S.R./
Silly Sarah Carter (Eating On A Moonpipe) (Uni 55135) .75 3.00 69
CAN'T I GET (A WORD IN)/Sun City (Paula 234) .75 3.00 66
DIAL 101/There Goes That Train (Jewel 730) 1.00 4.00 64
DOIN' THE BEST I CAN/Leave Her Never (Paula 244) .75 3.00 66
DOWN IN NEW ORLEANS/I Love You (Montel 904) 1.50 6.00 61
GOOD LOVIN'/You Know You Made Me Cry (Montel 1007) 1.25 5.00 60
HEY, HEY BUNNY/No Letter Today (Paula 294) .75 3.00 68
JUDY IN DISGUISE (WITH GLASSES)/
When The Lights Go Out (Paula 282) .75 3.00 67
JULIA, JULIA/Love My Soul (Uni 55187) .75 3.00 69
LITTLE DUM DUM/ (Paula 310) .75 3.00 69
LOVE COMES IN TIME/Outta My Head (Paula 247) .75 3.00 66
MIRROR MIRROR (ON THE WALL)/To Have & To Hold (Montel 2001) 1.50 6.00 62
MY FIRST LOVE/Boogie Children (Jewel 737) 1.00 4.00 65
(Shown as by the Playboys)
MY FIRST LOVE/Boogie Children (N-Joy 1005) 1.25 5.00
SHIRLEY/My Love For You (Montel 1002) 2.00 8.00 59
THREE DEEP IN A FEELING/Open Doors (Uni 55160) .75 3.00 70
WE PLAYED GAMES/ (Paula 303) .75 3.00 69
WRONG TO ME/How Can I Prove (Jewel 743) 1.00 4.00 65
YOU'RE MAD AT ME/Lenne (Jewel 736) 1.00 4.00 64

FREE
WHAT MAKES YOU/ (Marque 448) 1.00 4.00

FREE (With Paul Rodgers, Simon Kirke & Paul Kosoff)
ALL RIGHT NOW/Mouthful Of Grass (A&M 1206) .50 2.00 70
LITTLE BIT OF LOVE/Sail On (A&M 1352) .75 3.00 71
STEALER/Broad Daylight (A&M 1230) .50 2.00 70
WISHING WELL/ (Island 1212) .75 3.00 72
Rodgers & Kirke were with Bad Company, Kosoff was in Back Street Crawler.

FREE BEER
QUEEN OF THE PURPLE SAGE/California (RCA PB-10881) .50 2.00 77
UPTOWN LOVER/ (RCA PB-10719) .50 2.00 76

FREED, Alan, Band
CAMEL ROCK, THE/I Don't Need Lottsa Money (Coral 9-61660) 2.00 8.00 56
RIGHT NOW, RIGHT NOW/Tina's Canteen (Coral 9-61626) 2.00 8.00 56
ROCK & ROLL BOOGIE/ (Coral 9-61749) 2.00 8.00 56
SENTIMENTAL JOURNEY/Stop! Look! & Run! (Coral 9-61818) 1.50 6.00 58
Also see Williams, Billy

FREED, Alan, Steve Allen, Al "Jazzbo" Collins & The Modernaires
SPACE MAN, THE/
Jazzbo's Theory (By Al "Jazzbo" Collins) (Coral 9-61693) 3.00 12.00 56
(Novelty/Break-in.)

FREEMAN, Bobby
ELVIS, GOODBYE/Impressions (Kimray 81677) .75 3.00 77
(Blue plastic)

FREEMAN, Ernie
DUMPLIN'S/Beautiful Weekend (Imperial 5461) 1.00 4.00 57
HEARTBREAK HOTEL/Hawaiian Eye (Imperial 5716) .75 3.00 60
INDIAN LOVE CALL/Summer Serenade (Imperial 5518) 1.00 4.00 58
JIVIN' AROUND (PART 1)/Jivin' Around (Part 2) (Cash 1017) 1.25 5.00 55
OUR LOVE/The Shuck (With Bobby Relf) (Cash 1019) 1.25 5.00 55
POOR FOOL/Somehow This Is Love (Mambo 107) 1.50 6.00 54
RAINY DAY/Funny Face (Imperial 5391) 1.00 4.00 56
RAUNCHY/Puddin' (Imperial 5474) 1.00 4.00 57
ROCKIN' AROUND/Lost Dreams (Imperial 5381) 1.00 4.00 56
SCHOOL ROOM ROCK/Blues After Hours (Imperial 5551) 1.00 4.00 58
(THEME FROM) DARK AT THE TOP OF THE STAIRS, THE/
Come On Home (Imperial 5693) .75 3.00 60
TUTTLE, THE/Leaps & Bounds (Imperial 5486) 1.00 4.00 57
TWIST, THE/Shine On Harvest Moon (Imperial 5793) .75 3.00 61
WALKING THE BEAT/Spring Fever (Imperial 5403) 1.00 4.00 56
Instrumentals
Also see Sir Chauncey

FREE, Scott
LOVE'S LOST/You're My Girl (Alanna 559) 1.25 5.00 60

FREE SPIRITS, The
GIRL OF THE MOUNTAIN/Tattoo Man (ABC 10872) 1.00 4.00 66

FREEWAYS, The
GOFFIN GOFFIN/I Need Love (Hiback 107) .75 3.00 66

FREEWHEELERS, The
BEACH BOY/Annie (Epic 9725) 1.00 4.00 64

FREHLEY, Ace (Of Kiss)
NEW YORK GROOVE/Snow Blind (Casablanca 941) .50 2.00 78

FRENCH, Don
LITTLE BLONDE GIRL/I Look Into My Heart (Lancer 105) 3.75 15.00 59
LONELY SATURDAY NIGHT/Goldilocks (Lancer 104) 1.25 5.00 59

FRENCHY & CHESSMEN
BEETLE BEBOP/El Tacos (Temple 2081) 1.25 5.00 64

FRESH
JUST HOW DOES IT FEEL/ (Prodigal 0639) .50 2.00 78
SUMMERTIME/ (Prodigal 0642) .50 2.00 78

FRESH AIRE
FLYING OVER AMERICA/Living In The Space Age (Atlantic 3482) .50 2.00 78

FRIAR TUCK (Curt Boetcher)
ALLEY OOP/Sweet Pea (Mercury 72684) 1.00 4.00 67
RETURN OF ROBIN HOOD/ (Banshee 100) 2.50 10.00

FRIEDMAN, Dean
ARIEL/Funny Papers (Lifesong 45022) .50 2.00 77
LUCKY STARS/ (Lifesong 1767) .50 2.00 78
ROCKING CHAIR (IT'S GONNA BE ALL RIGHT)/
Shopping Bag Ladies (Lifesong 1774) .50 2.00 78
WOMAN OF MINE/ (Lifesong 1756) .50 2.00 77

FRIEND & LOVER (James & Cathy Post)
IF LOVE IS IN YOUR HEART/ (Verve-Forecast 5091) .75 3.00 68
I WANT TO BE FREE/Circus (Verve Forecast 5100) .75 3.00 68
REACH OUT IN THE DARKNESS/Time Is On Your Side
(You're Only 15 Years Old) (Verve-Forecast 5069) .75 3.00 68
TOWN CALLED LOVE/If Tomorrow (ABC 10910) .75 3.00 67

FRIENDS OF WHITNEY SUNDAY, The
BALLAD OF THUNDER ROAD/Love Will Conquer All (Capitol 2714) .75 3.00 69

FRIJID PINK
GOD GAVE ME YOU/Drivin' Blues (Parrot 340) .75 3.00 70
HEARTBREAK HOTEL/Bye Bye Blues (Parrot 352) .50 2.00 70
HOUSE OF THE RISING SUN/Drivin' Blues (Parrot 341) .50 2.00 70
I LOVE HER/Lost Son (Parrot 360) .75 3.00 71
LAZY DAY/Earth Omen (Lion 115) 1.00 4.00 72
MUSIC FOR THE PEOPLE/ (Parrot 355) .75 3.00 71
SING A SONG FOR FREEDOM/End Of The Line (Parrot 349) .75 3.00 70
TELL ME WHY/Cryin' Shame (Parrot 334) 1.00 4.00 69
WE'RE GONNA BE THERE/Shorty Kline (Parrot 358) .75 3.00 71

FRINGE BENEFIT
ALL IN VAIN/ (Capricorn 0271) .50 2.00 78
WANNA BE WITH YOU/Darling (Capricorn 0277) .50 2.00 78

FROGATT, Raymond
ALL BECAUSE OF YOU/Me & My Ideas (Jet 5062) .50 2.00 79

FROGMEN, The
BEWARE BELOW/Tioga (Candix 326) .75 3.00 61
BEWARE BELOW/Tioga (Scott 102) 1.50 6.00 61
SEA HUNT/Diamond Back (Tee Jay 131) 1.25 5.00
SEAHORSE FLATS/Tioga (Scott 101) 1.50 6.00 61
UNDERWATER/Mad Rush, The (Astra 1009) 1.25 5.00 61
UNDERWATER/Mad Rush, The (Candix 314) .75 3.00 61
Instrumentals

FROMAN, Jane
I BELIEVE/Ghost Of A Rose (Capitol 2332) 1.25 5.00 53
I'LL WALK ALONE/With A Song In My Heart (Capitol 2044) 1.25 5.00 52

FRONT END, The
BEVERLY/Go On Home (Smash 2172) 1.00 4.00 68
REMEMBER WALKING IN THE SAND/The Real Thing (Smash 2199) 1.25 5.00 68

FRONTIERS, The
DING DONG DOO/Why Pretend (King 5481) 1.00 4.00 61
EACH NIGHT I PRAY/ (King 5609) 1.00 4.00 62
NEAREST THING TO HEAVEN/Oh Nurse (King 5534) 1.00 4.00 61

FRONTIERS, The (Featuring Roger Koob)
I JUST WANT YOU/I'm Still Loving You (Philips 40148) 1.50 6.00 63
I ONLY HAVE EYES FOR YOU/Don't Come Crying (Philips 40113) 1.50 6.00 63
YOU/When I See You (MGM 13722) 1.50 6.00 67

FRONT LINE, The
I DON'T CARE/Got Love (York 9000) 1.00 4.00 66
I DON'T CARE/Got Love (Atlantic 4057) .75 3.00 65
SAIGON GIRL/Three Day Pass (Titan 2001) .75 3.00 67

FROST (With Dick Wagner)
MYSTERY MAN/Stand In The Shadows (Vanguard 35089) .75 3.00 69
ROCK & ROLL MUSIC/Donny's Blues (Vanguard 35111) .75 3.00 69
Dick Wagner was with the Alice Cooper group.

FROST, Max, & The Troupers
SHAPE OF THINGS TO COME/Free Lovin' (Tower 419) .75 3.00 68
STOMPER'S RIDE/There Is A Party Going On (Sidewalk 938) .75 3.00 68

FROST, Thomas & Richard
SHE'S GOT LOVE/The Word Is Love (Imperial 66405) .75 3.00 69

FRUGAL SOUND, The
NORWEGIAN WOOD/Cruel To Be Kind (Red Bird 10-052) 1.00 4.00 66

FRUIT OF THE LOOM
ONE HAND IN DARKNESS/A Little Bit Of Bach (Loom 101) 1.25 5.00

FRUMMOX
THERE YOU GO/Mary Martin (ABC-Probe 470) .75 3.00 70

FRYE, David
MY WAY/ (Elektra 45722) .75 3.00 71
(Richard Nixon impersonation)

FUGITIVES, The
FUGITIVE, A (Vocal)/A Fugitive (Instrumental) (D-Town 1034) 1.25 5.00
I DON'T WANT TO TALK/ (Westchester 1002) 1.25 5.00
I'LL BE A MAN/Mean Woman (Columbia 4-43261) 1.00 4.00 65
ON TRIAL/Let's Get On With It (D-Town 1044) 1.25 5.00
YOU CAN'T MAKE ME LONELY/I Don't Wanna Talk (Westchester 1002) 1.25 5.00
Also see 4 Of Us

FUGITIVES, The
FREEWAY/Fugitive (Sims 115) 1.50 6.00 60
FREEWAY/Fugitive (Arvee 5014) .75 3.00 60
GOLDENROD/ 5.00 20.00 65
Instrumentals

FUGS
FRENZY/I Want To Know (ESP 4507) .75 3.00 66

FULLER, Bobby, Four
EVERY MOMENT/Once In This World (Hi-Tone 310) 1.00 4.00
FOOL OF LOVE/Shakedown (Exeter 126) 2.50 10.00 64
I FOUGHT THE LAW/ (Exeter 124) 7.50 30.00 64
I FOUGHT THE LAW/Little Annie Lou (Mustang 3014) .75 3.00 65

TITLE/FLIP	LABEL & NO.	GOOD	NEAR MINT	YR.
LET HER DANCE/Another Sad & Lonely Night	(Liberty 55812)	1.25	5.00	65
LET HER DANCE/Another Sad & Lonely Night	(Mustang 3006)	1.00	4.00	65
LET HER DANCE/Another Sad & Lonely Night	(Mustang 3012)	1.00	4.00	
LOVE'S MADE A FOOL OF YOU/Don't Ever Let Me Know	(Mustang 3016)	.75	3.00	66
MY HEART JUMPED/Gently, My Love	(Yucca 144)	2.50	10.00	62
MY TRUE LOVE/The Magic Touch	(Mustang 3018)	1.00	4.00	66
NEVER TO BE FORGOTTEN/You Kiss Me	(Mustang 3011)	1.00	4.00	65
NOT FADE AWAY/Nervous Breakdown	(Eastwood 0345)	3.00	12.00	62
SATURDAY NIGHT/The Stinger	(Todd 1090)	2.50	10.00	
TAKE MY WORD/She's My Girl	(Mustang 3004)	1.00	4.00	65
THOSE MEMORIES OF YOU/ Our Favorite Martian (Instrumental)	(Donna 1403)	1.25	5.00	63
WINE WINE WINE/King Of The Beach	(Exeter 122)	2.50	10.00	64
YOU'RE IN LOVE/Guess We'll Fall In Love	(Yucca 141)	5.00	20.00	
Also see Fuller, Randy				
Also see Shindigs, The				
FULLER BROTHERS, The				
WHY DO FOOLS FALL IN LOVE/ Judge Me With Your Heart	(Monument 925)	.75	3.00	66
FULLER BROTHERS, The (Featuring Jerry Fuller)				
BALLAD OF THE MIDNIGHT SPECIAL/The Gallow Tree	(Challenge 9145)	.75	3.00	62
FRAMED, CONVICTED & CONDEMNED/Moon River	(Challenge 9119)	.75	3.00	61
FULLER, Craig & Eric Kaz (Of American Flyer)				
ANNABELLA/Let The Fire Burn All Night	(Columbia 45209)	.50	2.00	78
FULLER, Jerry				
ABOVE & BEYOND/One Heart	(Challenge 59074)	1.00	4.00	60
(With Diane Fuller)				
ANGEL FROM ABOVE/A Certain Smile	(Lin 5015)	1.50	6.00	59
BETTY MY ANGEL/Memories Of You	(Challenge 59052)	2.50	10.00	59
BLUE MEMORIES/I Found A New Love	(Lin 5011)	1.50	6.00	58
DEAR TERESA/Give My Love To Christy	(Challenge 9284)	.75	3.00	63
DOUBLE LIFE/Turn To Me	(Challenge 59329)	.75	3.00	66
FANNY BROWN/Chaser Of Hearts	(Lin 5017)	1.50	6.00	59
GONE FOR THE SUMMER/Anna From Louisiana	(Challenge 59085)	1.00	4.00	60
GUILTY OF LOVING YOU/First Love Never Dies	(Challenge 9114)	.75	3.00	61
HOLLYWOOD STAR/Footprints In The Snow	(Challenge 59235)	.75	3.00	64
I DREAMED ABOUT MY LOVER/Two Loves Have I	(Challenge 59068)	1.00	4.00	60
I GET CARRIED AWAY/Am I That Easy To Forget	(Challenge 59279)	.75	3.00	65
I ONLY CAME TO DANCE WITH YOU/Young Land	(Challenge 59217)	.75	3.00	63
IF I HAD A MIND TO/Go	(Columbia 45209)	.50	2.00	70
LIPSTICK & ROUGE/Mother Goose At The Bandstand	(Lin 5019)	2.00	8.00	59
POOR LITTLE HEART/A Place Where I Cry	(Challenge 9128)	1.00	4.00	61
ROSES LOVE SUNSHINE/Don't Let Go	(Challenge 59252)	.75	3.00	64
SHY AWAY/Heavenly	(Challenge 59104)	.75	3.00	61
TEENAGE LOVE/Do You Love Me	(Lin 5012)	2.00	8.00	58
TENNESSEE WALTZ/Charlene	(Challenge 59057)	1.00	4.00	59
WAKE UP SLEEPING BEAUTY/Trust Me	(Challenge 9132)	.75	3.00	62
WHY DO THEY SAY GOODBYE/Let Me Be With You	(Challenge 9161)	.75	3.00	62
WILLINGLY/Too Many People	(Challenge 9148)	.75	3.00	62
FULLER, Randy				
WOLFMAN/It's Love, Come What May	(Mustang 3020)	1.00	4.00	66
Randy is Bobby Fuller's brother.				
Also see Shindigs				
FULLER, Ronnie				
DO THE DIVE/Big Hurt Of All	(Joli 074)	.75	3.00	65
FUN & GAMES				
ELEPHANT CANDY/Way She Smiles	(Uni 55086)	.75	3.00	68
GROOVIEST GIRL IN THE WORLD, THE/ It Must Of Been The Wind	(Uni 55098)	.75	3.00	68
FUNKY COMMUNICATION COMMITTEE, The (FCC)				
BABY I WANT YOU/That Didn't Hurt Too Bad	(Free Flight 11595)	.50	2.00	79
IT TOOK A WOMAN LIKE YOU/	(Free Flight 11744)	.50	2.00	79
FUNKY KINGS (With Jack Tempchin & Jules Shear)				
SLOW DANCING/Nothing Was Exchanged	(Arista 0209)	.50	2.00	76
FUNNY BUNNIES, The				
MIDNIGHT SUN/Sick Song	(Dore 542)	.75	3.00	60
FUNZONE				
BACK TO HAVANA/	(First Artists 41001)	.50	2.00	77
FURAY, Richie (Of Poco)				
DANCE A LITTLE LIGHT/Someone Who Cares	(Asylum 45520)	.50	2.00	78
LONELY TOO LONG/I Still Have Dreams	(Asylum 46534)	.50	2.00	79
STILL ROLLING STONES/	(Asylum 45331)	.50	2.00	77
THIS MAGIC MOMENT/Bittersweet Love	(Asylum 45487)	.50	2.00	78
Also see Souther, Hillman & Furay				
FURE, Tret				
CATALINA/	(MCA 40029)	.50	2.00	72
FURTER, Frank				
GREEN WEENIE, THE/Imitation	(Uptown 738)	.75	3.00	60
FURY, Billy				
BABY, HOW I CRIED/Colette	(London 1925)	.75	3.00	60
GO AHEAD & ASK HER/I'm Lost Without You	(London 9740)	.75	3.00	65
IT'S ONLY MAKE BELIEVE/ Baby, What Do You Want Me To Do	(Parrot 9682)	.75	3.00	64
LIKE I'VE NEVER BEEN GONE/Because Of Love	(London 9594)	.75	3.00	64

TITLE/FLIP	LABEL & NO.	GOOD	NEAR MINT	YR.
MAYBE TOMORROW/Gonna Type A Letter	(London 1857)	1.00	4.00	59
FURYS, The				
BEACHIN/	(Lavender 1805)	.75	3.00	
FUT (Steve Kipner & Maurice Gibb)				
HAVE YOU HEARD THE WORD/Futting	(Beacon 160)	1.00	4.00	70
HAVE YOU HEARD THE WORD/Futting	(Fut 160)	.75	3.00	76
Also see Tin Tin				
Also see Bee Gees, The				
FYREBIRDS, The				
I'M ALIVE/	(Great Lakes 2528)	1.00	4.00	

G

TITLE/FLIP	LABEL & NO.	GOOD	NEAR MINT	YR.
GABRIEL				
BE MY WOMAN/	(ABC 12151)	.75	3.00	76
LOVE'S DISGUISE/	(ABC 12245)	.75	3.00	77
MARTHA (YOUR LOVERS COME & GO)/ Didn't I Love You	(Epic-Sweet City 50594)	.50	2.00	78
OOO WEE BABY/For Quite Awhile	(Epic-Sweet City 50649)	.50	2.00	79
GABRIEL & THE ANGELS				
ALL WORK, NO PLAY/Peanut Butter Song	(Swan 4133)	1.00	4.00	63
I'M GABRIEL/Ginza	(Norman 506)	1.00	4.00	61
THAT'S LIFE (THAT'S TOUGH)/Don't Wanna Twist	(Swan 4118)	1.00	4.00	62
ZING WENT THE STRINGS OF MY HEART/The Rooster	(Amy 823)	6.25	25.00	61
GABRIEL & THE TEENAGE CHOIR				
CHOCOLATE ON SUNDAY/Christmas Is Love	(Dunhill 4058)	.75	3.00	66
TWEEDLEE DUM'S DRIVE-IN (PART 1)/ Tweedlee Dum's Drive-In (Part 2)	(Dunhill 4039)	.75	3.00	66
GABRIEL, Peter (Of Genesis)				
DO IT YOURSELF (D.I.Y.)/Mother Of Violence	(Atlantic 3479)	.50	2.00	78
SOLSBURY HILL/Moribund The Burgermeister	(Atco 7079)	.50	2.00	77
GADABOUTS, The				
BUSY BODY ROCK/All My Love Belongs To You	(Mercury 70823)	1.00	4.00	56
BY THE WATERS OF MINNETONKA/ Giuseppe Mandolino	(Mercury 70495)	1.00	4.00	54
GO BOOM BOOM/Oochi Pachi	(Mercury 70581)	1.00	4.00	55
STRANDED IN THE JUNGLE/Blues Train	(Mercury 70898)	1.00	4.00	56
TEEN AGE ROCK/If You Only Had A Heart	(Wing 90043)	1.25	5.00	
TWO THINGS I LOVE/Glass Heart	(Wing 90008)	1.25	5.00	
GADSON, Mel				
COMIN' DOWN WITH LOVE/ I'm Getting Sentimental Over You	(Big Top 3034)	1.00	4.00	60
GAIL TONES, The				
LOVER BOY/Please Don't Go	(Decca 9-30726)	5.00	20.00	58
GAINORS, The				
I'M IN LOVE WITH YOU/Nothing Means More To Me	(Mercury 71632)	1.00	4.00	60
SHE'S GONE/Please Consider	(Mercury 71569)	1.00	4.00	60
SECRET, THE/Gonna Rock Tonite	(Cameo 151)	2.00	8.00	
THIS IS A PERFECT MOMENT/Where I Want To Be	(Tally-Ho 102)	1.00	4.00	61
YOU MUST BE AN ANGEL/Follow Me	(Cameo 156)	1.00	4.00	59
GALAHAD, Johnny				
'29 MODEL-A/Movin' Free	(Decca 31564)	1.00	4.00	63
GALAXIES, The				
BIG TRIANGLE, THE/Until The Next Time	(Capitol 4427)	1.00	4.00	60
DEAR SOMEONE/The Leopard	(Richie 458)	1.00	4.00	
JUST ANOTHER DATE/Little Man	(Ronnie 201)	1.00	4.00	
MY BLUE HEAVEN/Tremble	(Dot 16212)	.75	3.00	61
TREMBLE/My Blue Heaven	(Dot 16212)	.75	3.00	61
GALAXIES, The				
MY TATTLE TALE/Love Has It's Ways	(Guaranteed 216)	2.50	10.00	60
(Features Eddie Cochran on guitar)				
GALENS, The				
BABY I DO LOVE YOU/Love Bells	(Challenge 9212)	.75	3.00	63
STRANGER IN PARADISE/Chinese Lanterns	(Challenge 59253)	.75	3.00	64
GALES, The				
I LOVE YOU/Squeeze Me	(Winn 916)	3.75	15.00	
GALE, Sunny				
C'EST LA VIE/Looking Glass	(RCA Victor 47-6286)	1.00	4.00	55
GOODNIGHT, SWEETHEART, GOODNIGHT/ Call Off The Wedding	(RCA Victor 47-5746)	1.00	4.00	54
ROCK & ROLL WEDDING/Winner Take All	(RCA Victor 47-6479)	1.00	4.00	56
GALLAGHER & LYLE (Benny Gallagher & Graham Lyle)				
EVERY LITTLE TEARDROP/Street Boys	(A&M 1904)	.50	2.00	77
GIVE A BOY A BREAK/Harmonium	(A&M 1428)	.75	3.00	73
HEARTBREAKER/	(A&M 2017)	.50	2.00	78
HEART ON MY SLEEVE/Storm In My Soul	(A&M 1850)	.50	2.00	76
I WANT TO STAY WITH YOU/Fifteen Summers	(A&M 1778)	.50	2.00	76
RUNAWAY, THE/Street Boys	(A&M 1932)	.50	2.00	77
SEEDS OF CHANGE/Shine A Light	(A&M 1518)	.50	2.00	74
SHOWDOWN/Golden Boy	(A&M 2042)	.50	2.00	78
Also see McGuiness-Flint				
GALLAHADS, The (Featuring James Pipkin)				
FOOL, THE/Morning Mail	(Jubilee 5252)	1.00	4.00	56
GONE/So Long	(Night Owl 20)	2.00	8.00	61
I'M WITHOUT A GIRL FRIEND/Be Fair	(Del Fi 4148)	1.00	4.00	60
KEEPER OF DREAMS/Sad Girl	(Starla 15)	2.50	10.00	60
LONELY GUY/Jo Jo The Big Wheel	(Donna 1322)	2.50	10.00	60
LONELY GUY/JoJo The Big Wheel	(Del Fi 4137)	1.00	4.00	60
THIS LETTER TO YOU/The Answer To Love	(Donna 1361)	1.25	5.00	62
WHY DO FOOLS FALL IN LOVE/Gone	(Rendezvous 153)	3.75	15.00	61
GALLANT, Billy (Of the Roulettes)				
THINKING, HOPING, WISHING/Scribbling On The Wall	(Dee Dee 501)	2.00	8.00	
THINKING, HOPING, WISHING/Scribbling On The Wall	(Gold Disc 1012)	1.50	6.00	
GALLANTS, The				
BATMAN THEME/Robin's Theme	(Capitol 5586)	.75	3.00	66
MAN FROM U.N.C.L.E./The Vagabond	(Capitol 5376)	.75	3.00	65
GALLERY, The				
BIG CITY MISS RUTH ANN/	(Sussex 248)	.50	2.00	72
I BELIEVE IN MUSIC/Someone	(Sussex 239)	.50	2.00	72
NICE TO BE WITH YOU/Ginger Haired Man	(Sussex 232)	.50	2.00	72

TITLE/FLIP	LABEL & NO.	GOOD	NEAR MINT	YR.
GALLOP, Frank				
BALLAD OF IRVING/	(Kapp 745)	.75	3.00	66
(Novelty)				
GOT A MATCH?/Beg Your Pardon	(ABC-Paramount 9931)	1.00	4.00	58
SON OF IRVING/The One Love I'll Never Forget	(Musicor 1191)	.75	3.00	66
GALLO, Robert John				
SIMPLE SONG/I Lost My Way	(Mandala 2510)	.75	3.00	72
GAMBLERS, The				
MOON DAWG/LSD 25	(World Pacific 815)	1.00	4.00	60
TEEN MACHINE/Tonky	(Last Chance 2)	.75	3.00	61
TONKY/Teen Machine	(Last Chance 108)	.75	3.00	62
GAMMA (With Ronnie Montrose)				
I'M ALIVE/	(Elektra 46555)	.50	2.00	79
GANTS, The				
DR. FEELGOOD/Crackin' Up	(Liberty 55844)	.75	3.00	66
LITTLE BOY SAD/Smoke Rings (You Can't Blow)	(Liberty 55853)	.75	3.00	66
ROAD RUNNER/My Baby Don't Care	(Liberty 55829)	.75	3.00	65
GARABEDIAN, George, Players				
DONALD'S TUNE/	(Mark 56 809)	1.00	4.00	59
MR. GRILLON/The Crope	(Mark '56 801)	1.00	4.00	58
THOMAS DOOLEY CHA-CHA-CHA/Two Hearts To Sing	(Mark '56 804)	1.00	4.00	59
Novelties				
GARCIA, Jerry (Of the Grateful Dead)				
DEAL/The Wheel	(Warner Bros. 7551)	1.00	4.00	72
DEAL/The Wheel	(Warner Bros. 514)	1.50	6.00	72
(Promotional issue only)				
LET IT ROCK/	(Round 4504)	.75	3.00	74
SOUTH SIDE STRUT/Uncle Martin's	(Douglas 7 6501)	1.00	4.00	73
(With Howard Wales)				
SUGAREE/Eep Hour	(Warner Bros. 7569)	.75	3.00	72
GARDENIAS, The				
WHAT'S THE MATTER WITH ME/ Darling It's You You You	(Fairland 21019)	.75	3.00	
GARDEN OF EDEN, The				
FLOWER MAN/Samantha	(Verve 10541)	1.25	5.00	67
GARDNER, Dave				
WHITE SILVER SANDS/Fat Charlie	(OJ 1002)	1.00	4.00	57
GARDNER, J.				
99 PLUS 1/Mustard Greens	(Blue Rock 4026)	.75	3.00	65
GARFIELD				
ALL ALONE AGAIN/Mississippi Jimmie	(Capricorn 0299)	.50	2.00	78
GARFUNKEL, Art (Of Simon & Garfunkle)				
ALL I KNOW/Mary Was An Only Child	(Columbia 4-45926)	.50	2.00	73
BEAT LOVE/Dream Alone	(Warwick 515)	3.75	15.00	59
(Shown as by Artie Garr)				
BREAK AWAY/Disney Girls	(Columbia 3-10273)	.50	2.00	75
BRIGHT EYES/Sail On A Rainbow	(Columbia 3-11050)	.50	2.00	79
CRYING IN MY SLEEP/Mr. Shuck 'N' Jive	(Columbia 3-10608)	.50	2.00	78
IN A LITTLE WHILE (I'LL BE ON MY WAY)/And I Know	(Columbia 3-10933)	.50	2.00	79
I ONLY HAVE EYES FOR YOU/ Looking For The Right One	(Columbia 3-10190)	.50	2.00	75
I SHALL SING/Feuilles-Oh/Do Space Men Pass Dead Souls On Their Way To The Moon?	(Columbia 4-45983)	.50	2.00	73
PRIVATE WORLD/Forgive Me	(Octavia 8002)	3.00	12.00	61
(Shown as by Artie Garr)				
RAG DOLL/	(Columbia 3-10230)	.75	3.00	75
SECOND AVENUE/Woyaya	(Columbia 3-10020)	.50	2.00	74
SINCE I DON'T HAVE YOU/ When Someone Doesn't Want You	(Columbia 3-10999)	.50	2.00	79
TRAVELING BOY/	(Columbia 4-46030)	.75	3.00	74
(WHAT A) WONDERFUL WORLD/Wooden Planes	(Columbia 3-10676)	.50	2.00	78
(With James Taylor & Paul Simon)				
Also see Garr, Artie				
Also see Simon & Garfunkle				
GARI, Frank				
LULLABY OF LOVE/Tonight Is Our Last Night	(Crusade 1021)	.75	3.00	61
PRINCESS/Last Bus Left At Midnight	(Crusade 1022)	.75	3.00	61
UTOPIA/I Ain't Got A Girl	(Crusade 1020)	.75	3.00	60
YOU BETTER KEEP RUNNIN'/ There's Lots More Where This Came From	(Crusade 1024)	.75	3.00	62
YOU'RE ONLY LOVE/Lil' Girl	(Ribbon 6903)	1.00	4.00	59
GARLAND, Judy (Francis Gumm)				
HEARTBROKEN/Go Home Joe	(Columbia 4-40023)	2.00	8.00	53
I COULD GO ON SINGING/Hello Bluebird	(Capitol 4938)	1.00	4.00	60
IT'S A GREAT DAY FOR THE IRISH/Pretty Girl	(Decca 9-25043)	2.50	10.00	50
MAN THAT GOT AWAY/Here's What I'm Here For	(Columbia 4-40270)	1.50	6.00	54
SEND MY BABY BACK TO ME/Without A Memory	(Columbia 4-40010)	2.00	8.00	53
SMILIN' THROUGH/The Boy Next Door	(Decca 9-29296)	1.50	6.00	54
YOU'LL NEVER WALK ALONE/ Have Yourself A Merry Little Christmas	(Decca 9-29295)	1.50	6.00	54
YOU'VE GOT ME WHERE YOU WANT ME/Mine	(Decca 9-28210)	2.00	8.00	53
GARNER, Johnny				
DIDI DIDI/Fool	(Imperial 5548)	10.00	40.00	58
KISS ME SWEET/	(Imperial 5536)	3.00	12.00	58
GARNETT, Gale				
I'LL CRY ALONE/Where Do You Go To Go Away	(RCA Victor 47-8549)	.75	3.00	65
I'M GONNA SIT RIGHT DOWN & WRITE MYSELF A LETTER/ Why Am I Standing At The Window	(RCA Victor 47-8668)	.75	3.00	65
LOVIN' PLACE/I Used To Live Here	(RCA Victor 47-8472)	.75	3.00	64
WE'LL SING IN THE SUNSHINE/Prism Song	(RCA Victor 47-8388)	.75	3.00	64
GARR, Artie: see Garfunkle, Art				
GARRET, Scott				
DAY I DIED, THE/In My Heart	(Okeh 7104)	1.00	4.00	60
GARRETT, Johnny, & The Rising Signs				
GET AROUND DOWNTOWN GIRL/Good People	(Uni 55179)	1.25	5.00	69
GARRETT, Kelly				
LEAVIN' ON YOUR MIND/	(RCA PB-10624)	.50	2.00	76
GARRETT, Lee				
YOU'RE MY EVERYTHING/Love Enough For Two	(Chrysalis 2112)	.50	2.00	76
GARRETT, Robin				
RINGO'S REVENGE/You Run Around	(Mutual 510)	1.25	5.00	64
GARRETT, Scott				
HOUSE OF LOVE, A/So Far So Good	(Laurie 3023)	1.00	4.00	59
LOVE STORY/Graduation Souvenirs	(Laurie 3029)	3.00	12.00	59
(With the Mystics)				
SO FAR, SO GOOD/A House Of Love	(Laurie 3023)	1.00	4.00	59
GARSON, Mort				
(BUBBLES BURLESQUE) THE STRIPPER'S SISTER/ Bowl-A-Rama Stomp	(G-Note G-2001)	.75	3.00	

TITLE/FLIP	LABEL & NO.	GOOD	NEAR MINT	YR.
ARTHWAITE, Terry (Of The Joy Of Cooking)				
NGEL OF LOVE/	(Arista 0164)	.50	2.00	75
WANT TO BE THE ONE/	(Capitol 3547)	.75	3.00	73
(With Tony Brown)				
LENDER THREAD/	(Arista 0176)	.50	2.00	76
ARTIN, Jimmy, & The Swingers: see Debree, Peter, & The Wanderers				
ARY & CLYDE (Gary Paxton & Clyde Batton)				
WHY NOT CONFESS/Johnny Risk	(Rev 3523)	3.00	12.00	59
Also see Skip & Flip				
ARY & GREEN				
LL AROUND THE WORLD/				
Baby Doll (With the Rhythm Aces Band)	(Capri 101)	1.00	4.00	
ARY & THE HORNETS				
ABY IT'S YOU/Tell Tale	(Smash 2090)	.75	3.00	67
I HI HAZEL/Patty Girl	(Smash 2061)	.75	3.00	66
IND OF HUSH, A/That's All For Now, Sugar Baby	(Smash 2078)	.75	3.00	67
URN THE WORLD ON/Holdin' Back	(Smash 2145)	.75	3.00	68
ARY & THE KNIGHT LITES				
CAN'T LOVE YOU ANYMORE/Will You Go Steady	(Prima 1016)	3.75	15.00	
ONELY SOLDIER'S PLEDGE/So Far Away From Home	(Bell 643)	2.00	8.00	66
ARY & THE NITE LITES				
ONY MORONIE/Glad You're Mine	(Seeburg Jukebox 3017)	2.50	10.00	65
DON'T NEED YOUR HELP/Big Bad Wolf	(U.S.A. 833)	2.00	8.00	66
WEET LITTLE 16/Take Me Back	(Seeburg Jukebox 3016)	2.50	10.00	65
Also see American Breed, The				
ARY & THE WOMBATS				
O TOUGH/Winter Dream	(Regina 297)	1.00	4.00	63
UMMER'S OVER/Squidgy Bod	(Regina 291)	1.00	4.00	63
ARY, PHIL & THE ROCK & ROLL ZOO				
OCK & ROLL IS BACK TO STAY/Forgive Me Tonight	(Bravo 1303)	1.50	6.00	
AS COMPANY, The				
LOW YOUR MIND/Your Time's Up	(Mirwood 5501)	1.00	4.00	65
ET OUT OF MY LIFE/We Need A Lot More Of Jesus	(Reprise 0512)	1.00	4.00	66
OU'RE ALL ALONE/You'll Need Love	(Reprise 0464)	1.00	4.00	66
ATES, David				
AN I CALL YOU/Chingo	(Elektra 46646)	.50	2.00	80
LOUDS/I Use The Soap	(Elektra 45857)	.50	2.00	73
OODBYE GIRL/Sunday Rider	(Elektra 45450)	.50	2.00	78
APPIEST MAN ALIVE/The Road Leads To Love	(Mala 418)	2.50	10.00	60
O BABY/Lovin' At Night	(Robbins 1008)	2.00	8.00	61
(With the Accents)				
ITTLE MISS STUCK-UP/The Brighter Side	(Planetary 103)	2.50	10.00	65
(Shown as by Del Ashley)				
EVER LET HER GO/Watch Out	(Elektra 45223)	.50	2.00	75
O ONE REALLY LOVES A CLOWN/				
You Had It Comin' To You	(Del Fi 4206)	2.00	8.00	63
NCE UPON A TIME/Let You Go	(Planetary 108)	1.50	6.00	65
AIL AROUND THE WORLD/	(Elektra 45868)	.50	2.00	73
WINGIN' BABY DOLL/Walkin' & Talkin'	(East West 123)	2.50	10.00	59
EARDROPS IN MY HEART/Jo Baby	(Mala 427)	2.50	10.00	61
OOK THE LAST TRAIN/Ann	(Elektra 45500)	.50	2.00	78
WHERE DOES THE LOVIN' GO/Starship Ride	(Elektra 46588)	.50	2.00	79
OU'LL BY MY BABY/What's This I Hear	(Mala 413)	2.50	10.00	60
Also see Bread				
Also see Country Boys, The				
Also see Dave & Lee				
Also see Gary & Dave				
Also see Manchesters, The				
ATURS, The				
OOGER MAN/Cold Bear	(Atco 6870)	.50	2.00	72
AVIN, Jimmy				
SIT IN MY WINDOW/Lonely Chair	(Cameo 113)	1.00	4.00	57
AY, Ben, & The Silly Savages				
ALLAD OF BEN GAY, THE/Silly Savage Serenade	(Elm 103)	1.00	4.00	
(Novelty)				
AYLADS, The				
OPEYE THE SAILOR MAN/Ah So	(Audan 120)	1.00	4.00	61
AYLE, Melvin				
KRUSCHEV TWIST/You're In Love	(Castle 1604)	1.00	4.00	62
AYLORD & HOLIDAY (Ronnie Gaylord & Burt Holiday)				
EH! CUMPARI/The Little Shoemaker	(Prodigal 0622)	.50	2.00	76
LACE TO HIDEAWAY, A/Love (Where Have You Gone?)	(Palmer 5022)	.75	3.00	
Also see Gaylords, The				
AYLORDS, The (Featuring Ronnie Gaylord)				
ROM THE VINE CAME THE GRAPE/Stolen Moments	(Mercury 70296)	1.25	5.00	54
ROM THE VINE CAME THE GRAPE/Patzo For Pizza	(Mercury 70308)	1.25	5.00	54
OW ABOUT ME/Again	(Mercury 71399)	1.00	4.00	59
OW ABOUT ME/Again	(Mercury SS-10000)	1.00	4.00	59
(Stereo single issue)				
SLE OF CAPRI/Love I You	(Mercury 70350)	1.25	5.00	54
ITTLE SHOEMAKER, THE/Mecque, Mecque	(Mercury 70403)	1.25	5.00	54
O ARMS CAN EVER HOLD YOU/Bring Me A Bluebird	(Mercury 70706)	1.25	5.00	55
SPINNING A WEB/Ramona	(Mercury 70112)	1.25	5.00	53
ELL ME YOU'RE MINE/Cuban Love Song	(Mercury 70030)	1.50	6.00	52
ELL ME YOU'RE MINE/Aye Aye Aye	(Mercury 70067)	1.25	5.00	53
AYS, The				
LONE AT THE HARBOR/Command My Heart	(Decca 9-30988)	.75	3.00	60
AYTEN, Paul				
EATNIK BEAT/Scratch Back	(Anna 1112)	1.00	4.00	60
E MY BABY/The Music Goes Round & Round	(Argo 5257)	1.00	4.00	57
UNCH, THE/Hot Cross Buns	(Anna 1106)	1.00	4.00	59
ERVOUS BOOGIE/Flat Foot Sam	(Argo 5277)	1.00	4.00	57
OH BOO/Cow Cow Blues	(Okeh 6982)	1.50	6.00	53
INDY/Tickle Toe	(Argo 5300)	1.00	4.00	58
-CLEFS, The				
NGEL, LISTEN TO ME/Nobody But Betty	(Regina 1319)	.75	3.00	64
IG RAIN/All My Trials	(Terrace 7514)	1.00	4.00	63
IRL HAS TO KNOW, A/Lad	(Terrace 7503)	1.00	4.00	62
UNDERSTAND (JUST HOW YOU FEEL)/				
Little Girl I Love You	(Terrace 7500)	.75	3.00	61
S THIS THE WAY/Zing Zang Zoo	(Paris 506)	1.25	5.00	57
A-DING DONG/Darla, My Darlin'	(Pilgrim 715)	1.25	5.00	56
ITTLE LONELY BOY/Party '66	(Loma 2034)	.75	3.00	66
AKE UP YOUR MIND/They'll Call Me Away	(Terrace 7507)	1.00	4.00	62
N THE OTHER SIDE OF TOWN/I Have	(Veep 1218)	.75	3.00	65
LEASE WRITE WHILE I'M AWAY/Cause You're Mine	(Pilgrim 720)	1.25	5.00	56
ITTING IN THE MOONLIGHT/				
Lover's Prayer (All Through The Night)	(Terrace 7510)	1.00	4.00	62
YMBOL OF LOVE/				
Love Her In The Morning & Love Her In The Night Time	(Paris 502)	1.25	5.00	57
EDDINS & SONS				
PACE MOON/Irma Special	(Jumping 50001)	3.75	15.00	

TITLE/FLIP	LABEL & NO.	GOOD	NEAR MINT	YR.
GEE, Bobby, & The Celestials				
BLUE JEAN/Julie Is Mine	(Stacy 922)	1.50	6.00	59
LITTLE MISS FANTASY/Sealed With A Kiss	(XYZ 611)	1.50	6.00	60
GEE CEES, The				
BUZZSAW/Annie Had A Party	(Crest 1088)	5.00	20.00	61
Glen Campbell, whose initials inspired this group's name, is featured on "Buzzsaw" and Eddie Cochran plays lead guitar on "Annie Had a Party." "Annie Had a Party" was first issued in 1959 by the Kelly Four and was titled "Annie Has a Party."				
GEE, Frankie				
BE MY BABY/Be My Baby (Disco Version)	(Lipstick 101)	.75	3.00	
DATE WITH THE RAIN/Ya Ya	(Claridge 410)	1.25	5.00	
(With the Five Discs)				
GEE SISTERS, The				
(HELP ME) TELSTAR/Andy	(Palette 5101)	.75	3.00	63
GEE, Sonny, & The Standels				
TIDAL WAVE/Ingrid	(Arlen 506)	1.00	4.00	63
GEILS, J., Band				
(AIN'T NOTHIN' BUT A) HOUSEPARTY/Give It To Me	(Atlantic 3350)	.50	2.00	76
CRUSIN' FOR A LOVE/Wait	(Atlantic 2802)	.75	3.00	71
DID YOU NO WRONG/That's Why I'm Thinking Of You	(Atlantic 3007)	.75	3.00	73
GIVIN' IT ALL UP/Gettin' Out	(Atlantic 3251)	.75	3.00	75
GIVE IT TO ME/Hold Your Loving	(Atlantic 2953)	.50	2.00	73
HOMEWORK (AIN'T GONNA DO IT BABY)/				
First I Look At The Purse	(Atlantic 2784)	.75	3.00	71
I DO/	(Atlantic 3658)	.50	2.00	78
(Shown as by Geils)				
I DON'T NEED YOU NO MORE/Dead Presidents	(Atlantic 2843)	.75	3.00	71
LOOKING FOR A LOVE/Whammer Jammer	(Atlantic 2844)	.75	3.00	71
LOVE-ITIS/Think It Over	(Atlantic 3301)	.75	3.00	76
MAKE UP YOUR MIND/Southside Shuffle	(Atlantic 2974)	.75	3.00	73
MUST OF GOT LOST/Funky Judge	(Atlantic 3214)	.50	2.00	74
ONE LAST KISS/Revenge	(EMI America 8007)	.50	2.00	78
PEANUT BUTTER/	(Atlantic 3378)	.75	3.00	76
SURRENDER/	(Atlantic 3438)	.50	2.00	77
(Shown as by Geils)				
TAKE IT BACK/I Can't Believe You	(EMI America 8012)	.50	2.00	79
WHERE DID OUR LOVE GO/What's Your Hurry	(Atlantic 3320)	.50	2.00	76
WILD MAN/Jus' Can't Stop Me	(EMI America 8016)	.50	2.00	79
YOU'RE THE ONLY ONE/Wreckage	(Atlantic 3411)	.50	2.00	77
(Shown as by Geils)				
GEMS, The				
CRAZY CHICKEN/Hippy Dippy	(Mercury 71819)	1.00	4.00	61
NURSERY RHYMES/The Night Is Over	(Win 701)	3.00	12.00	
PUNCH HAPPY/	(Vergelle 711)	1.00	4.00	61
SCHOOL ROCK/There's No One Like My Love	(Pat 101)	1.00	4.00	61
WAITING/Please Change Your Mind	(Recorte 407)	2.50	10.00	58
GENE & DEBBIE (Gene Thomas & Debbie Nevills)				
GO WITH ME/Torch I Carry	(TRX 5002)	.75	3.00	67
LOVIN' SEASON/Love Will Give Us Wings	(TRX 5010)	.75	3.00	68
MAKING NOISE LIKE LOVE/Rings Of Gold	(TRX 5014)	.75	3.00	68
PLAYBOY/I'll Come Running	(TRX 5006)	.75	3.00	68
GENE & THE ESQUIRES				
RAVE ON/Space Race	(GNP-Crescendo 345)	1.00	4.00	65
GENE & TOMMY				
RICHARD & ME/Can't Get To Stoppin'	(ABC 10981)	.75	3.00	67
GENE THE HAT				
(PASS) THE BUG (PART 1)/(Pass) The Bug (Part 2)	(Deauville 1007)	.75	3.00	62
GENELLS, The				
RAINY NIGHT/Linda Please Wait	(Dewey 101)	2.00	8.00	
GENESIS				
ANGELINE/Suzanne	(Mercury 72806)	3.75	15.00	68
ENTANGLED/Ripples	(Atco 7050)	.50	2.00	77
FOLLOW YOU, FOLLOW ME/Inside & Out	(Atlantic 3474)	.50	2.00	78
GO WEST YOUNG MAN (IN THE MOTHERLODE)/				
Scenes From A Night's Dream	(Atlantic 3511)	.50	2.00	78
I KNOW WHAT I LIKE/	(Charisma 26002)	1.00	4.00	73
LAMB LIES DOWN ON BROADWAY, THE/	(Atco 7013)	.75	3.00	76
WATCHER OF THE SKIES/	(Charisma 103)	1.00	4.00	73
YOUR OWN SPECIAL WAY/...In That Quiet Earth	(Atco 7076)	.50	2.00	77
Also see Hackett, Steve				
GENEVIEVE				
I'M NEVER GONNA KISS YOU/Cherie, Cherie	(Cadence 1354)	1.25	5.00	58
(With Johnny Tillotson.)				
GENOA, Tommy, & The Precisions				
WHAT HAS HAPPENED TO YOU/The Lover	(Bella 606)	2.50	10.00	
GENOTONES, The				
CITY LIGHTS/Counting Stars	(Casino 52261)	2.50	10.00	
RITA MY TEENAGE BRIDE/Midnight Walk	(WGW 3003)	2.50	10.00	
GENTEELS, The				
TAKE IT OFF/Hitchhiker	(Sage 2930)	1.25	5.00	62
TAKE IT OFF/Hitchhiker	(Capitol 4798)	.75	3.00	62
GENTLE GIANT (Simon Dupree)				
WORDS FROM THE WISE/	(Capitol 4652)	.50	2.00	78
GENTRY, Bo, & Ritchie Cordell				
LOVE IS HERE/Daylong	(Columbia 4-44635)	.75	3.00	69
GENTRY, Bobbie				
APARTMENT 21/Seasons Come, Seasons Go	(Capitol 2849)	.75	3.00	70
BUT I CAN'T GET BACK/Marigolds & Tangerines	(Capitol 3071)	.75	3.00	71
FANCY/Courtyard	(Capitol 2675)	.75	3.00	69
HE MADE A WOMAN OUT OF ME/Billy The Kid	(Capitol 2788)	.75	3.00	70
LOUISIANA MAN/Courtyard	(Capitol 2147)	.75	3.00	68
ODE TO BILLIE JOE/Mississippi Delta	(Capitol 5950)	.75	3.00	67
ODE TO BILLIE JOE (MAIN TITLE)/	(Warner-Curb 8210)	.50	2.00	76
(From the orginial soundtrack)				
OKOLONA RIVER BOTTOM BAND/Penduli Pendulum	(Capitol 2044)	.75	3.00	67
PAPPA, WONCHA YOU LET ME GO TO TOWN WITH YOU/				
I Saw An Angel Die	(Capitol 5992)	.75	3.00	67
GENTRYS, The				
WILD/Moments	(Kado 0074)	1.50	6.00	
GENTRYS, The (With Larry Raspberry)				
CHANGIN'/Let Me Put This Ring On Your Finger	(Capitol 3459)	.75	3.00	72
CINNAMON GIRL/I Just Got The News	(Sun 1114)	.50	2.00	70
EVERYDAY I HAVE TO CRY/Don't Let It Be (This Time)	(MGM 13495)	.75	3.00	66
GODDESS OF LOVE/Friends	(Sun 1120)	.75	3.00	70
HIGH FLYER/Little Gold Band	(Stax 0242)	.50	2.00	74
I CAN SEE/90 Pound Weakling	(MGM 13749)	.75	3.00	67
KEEP ON DANCING/Make Up Your Mind	(Youngstown 601)	2.50	10.00	65
KEEP ON DANCING/Make Up Your Mind	(MGM 13379)	.75	3.00	65
LITTLE GOLD BAND/All Hung Up On You	(Stax 0223)	.50	2.00	74
LITTLE DROPS OF WATER/Sometimes	(Youngstown 600)	2.50	10.00	65
LOVE YOU ALL MY LIFE/God Save Our Country	(Sun 1126)	.75	3.00	71
SPREAD IT ON THICK/Brown Paper Sack	(MGM 13432)	.75	3.00	65

TITLE/FLIP	LABEL & NO.	GOOD	NEAR MINT	YR.
WHY SHOULD I CRY/I Need Love	(Sun 1108)	.50	2.00	70
WILD WORLD/Sunshine	(Sun 1122)	.75	3.00	71
WOMAN OF THE WORLD, A/				
There Are Two Sides To Every Story	(MGM 13561)	.75	3.00	66
GENTS, The				
I'LL NEVER LET YOU GO/				
Darling I Love You (By the Teen 5)	(Times Square 99)	1.00	4.00	64
ISLAND OF LOVE/Till The End Of Time (By the Teen 5)	(Times Square 98)	1.00	4.00	64
Accapella recordings				
GENTS, The				
MOONLIGHT SURF/Lazy Day	(Nite Owl 10)	1.00	4.00	60
GEORGE & CO.				
WHEN THE LOVELIGHT STARTS SHINING THROUGH HER EYES/				
Layers & Layers	(Veep 1271)	.75	3.00	67
GEORGE & GENE: see Pitney, Gene				
GEORGE & LOUIS (With George Kline)				
RETURN OF JERRY LEE (Novelty/Break-in)/				
Lewis Boogie (By Jerry Lee Lewis)	(Sun 301)	1.25	5.00	58
RETURN OF JERRY LEE (PART 1)/Return Of Jerry Lee (Part 2)	(Sun 301)	1.00	4.00	58
(Novelty/Break-in)				
GEORGE, Barbara				
I KNOW (YOU DON'T LOVE ME NO MORE)/				
Love (Is Just A Chance You Take)	(AFO 302)	.75	3.00	61
YOU TALK ABOUT LOVE/Whip O Will	(AFO 304)	.75	3.00	62
GEORGE, Johnny				
FIDDLE & A BOW, A/Flying Blues Angels (With the Pilots)	(Coed 555)	.75	3.00	61
GEORGE, Lowell				
WHAT DO YOU WANT THE GIRL TO DO/				
20 Million Things	(Warner Bros. 8847)	.50	2.00	79
GEORGIE PORGIE & THE CRY BABIES				
SAD KID/Hurt	(Georgie Porgie 96281)	1.25	5.00	
GERARD, Danyel				
BUTTERFLY/Let's Love	(Columbia 4-45468)	.75	3.00	72
BUTTERFLY/Let's Love	(MGM-Verve 10670)	.50	2.00	72
GERARDI, Bob, & The Classic 4				
NOBODY WANTS YOU ANYMORE/You're Everything To Me	(Recorte 441)	1.00	4.00	
Also see Rockin' Chairs, The				
GERMZ (With Carole King)				
BOY-GIRL LOVE/No Easy Way Down	(Vertigo 8001)	2.50	10.00	
GERRARD, Donny (Of Skylark)				
(BABY) DON'T LET IT MESS YOUR MIND/				
A Woman, A Lover, A Friend	(Rocket 40405)	.50	2.00	76
GERRI & SHERRI				
JELLYBEAN/Gotta Make It Grow	(RCA Victor 47-8096)	1.00	4.00	62
GERRY & THE PACEMAKERS (Featuring Gerry Marsden)				
DON'T LET THE SUN CATCH YOU CRYING/I'm The One	(Laurie 3251)	1.00	4.00	64
DON'T LET THE SUN CATCH YOU CRYING/Away From You	(Laurie 3251)	.75	3.00	64
FERRY ACROSS THE MERSEY/Pretend	(Laurie 3284)	.75	3.00	65
GIRL ON A SWING/The Way You Look Tonight	(Laurie 3354)	.75	3.00	66
GIVE ALL YOUR LOVE TO ME/You're The Reason	(Laurie 3313)	.75	3.00	65
HOW DO YOU DO IT/I'm The One	(Laurie 3233)	1.00	4.00	64
HOW DO YOU DO IT/You'll Never Walk Alone	(Laurie 3261)	.75	3.00	64
I LIKE IT/It's Happened To Me	(Laurie 3196)	1.25	5.00	63
I LIKE IT/Jambalaya	(Laurie 3271)	.75	3.00	64
I'LL BE THERE/You You You	(Laurie 3279)	.75	3.00	64
IT'S GONNA BE ALRIGHT/Skinny Minnie	(Laurie 3293)	.75	3.00	65
LA LA LA/Without You	(Laurie 3337)	.75	3.00	66
LOOKING FOR MY LIFE/Big Bright Green Pleasure Machine	(Laurie 3370)	.75	3.00	67
WALK HAND IN HAND/Dreams	(Laurie 3323)	1.00	4.00	65
YOU'LL NEVER WALK ALONE/It's All Right	(Laurie 3218)	1.00	4.00	64
YOU'LL NEVER WALK ALONE/Away From You	(Laurie 3302)	.75	3.00	65
GESTICS, The				
INVASION/Rockin' Fury	(Surfer 114)	1.25	5.00	63
LET'S GO TRIPPIN'/Kahuna	(Surfer 106)	1.25	5.00	63
GESTURES, The				
DON'T MESS AROUND/Candlelight	(Soma 1426)	.75	3.00	
RUN RUN RUN/It Seems To Me	(Soma 1417)	.75	3.00	64
GETZ, Stan				
DESAFINADO/Theme From Dr. Kildare	(Verve 10260)	.75	3.00	62
(With Charlie Byrd)				
GIRL FROM IPANEMA, THE/Blowin' In The Wind	(Verve 10323)	.75	3.00	64
(Vocal by Astrud Gilberto)				
GHETTO-PACIFIC				
LEAPARD SKIN PILL BOX HAT/				
You Can't Judge A Book By The Cover	(Challenger 121)	1.00	4.00	
GHIGGS, Ray				
MONKEY'S DISGRACE, THE/The Persian Cat	(Amber 4086)	.75	3.00	
GIANOTTA, Sonny				
LAST BLAST OF THE BLASTED BUGLER, THE/				
Pain Set To Music (By Phil Carrametta)	(ABC-Paramount 10308)	2.00	8.00	
(Novelty)				
GIANT JELLYBEAN COPOUT, The				
AWAKE IN A DREAM/Look At The Girls	(Poppy 504)	1.00	4.00	68
GIANT SUNFLOWER, The				
FEBRUARY SUNSHINE/Big Apple	(Ode 102)	.75	3.00	67
FEBRUARY SUNSHINE/More Sunshine	(Take 6 1000)	.75	3.00	67
WHAT'S SO GOOD ABOUT GOODBYE/Mark Twain	(Ode 104)	.75	3.00	67
GIBBONS, Steve, Band				
CHELITA/	(Polydor 14516)	.50	2.00	78
HE GAVE HIS LIFE FOR ROCK 'N' ROLL/				
You Gotta Pay	(MCA-Gold Hawke 40946)	.50	2.00	78
JOHNNY COOL/Strange World	(MCA-Gold Hawke 40551)	.50	2.00	76
NO SPITTING ON THE BUS/When You Get Outside	(Polydor 14501)	.50	2.00	78
PLEASE DON'T SAY GOODBYE/	(MCA-Gold Hawke 40751)	.50	2.00	77
SPARK OF LOVE/Speed Kills	(MCA-Gold Hawke 40597)	.50	2.00	76
TULANE/	(MCA-Gold Hawke 40712)	.50	2.00	77
GIBB, Andy				
AN EVERLASTING LOVE/Flowing Rivers	(RSO 904)	.50	2.00	78
I JUST WANT TO BE YOUR EVERYTHING/In The End	(RSO 872)	.50	2.00	77
(LOVE IS) THICKER THAN WATER/Words & Music	(RSO 883)	.50	2.00	77
(OUR LOVE) DON'T THROW IT ALL AWAY/				
One More Look At The Night	(RSO 911)	.50	2.00	78
SHADOW DANCING/Let It Be Me	(RSO 893)	.50	2.00	77
Andy's three older brothers, Barry, Robin and Maurice Gibb (the Bee Gees), are featured on many of his recordings.				
GIBB, Robin (Of The Bee Gees)				
OH! DARLING/She's Leaving Home	(RSO 907)	.50	2.00	78
(By the Bee Gees, Jay McIntosh & John Wheeler)				
SAVED BY THE BELL/Mother & Jack	(Atco 6698)	.75	3.00	71
SESAME STREET FEVER/Trash	(Sesame Street 199070)	.50	2.00	78

TITLE/FLIP	LABEL & NO.	GOOD	NEAR MINT	YR.
GIBBS, Georgia (Fredda Lipson)				
DANCE WITH ME HENRY/Ballin' The Jack	(Mercury 70572)	1.00	4.00	55
GOODBYE TO ROME/24 Hours A Day	(Mercury 70743)	1.00	4.00	55
HAPPINESS STREET/Happiness, A Thing Called Joe	(Mercury 70920)	1.00	4.00	56
HULA HOOP SONG, THE/Keep In Touch	(Roulette 4106)	1.00	4.00	58
I STILL FEEL THE SAME ABOUT YOU/ Get Out Those Old Records	(Coral 60353)	1.25	5.00	51
I WANT YOU TO BE MY BABY/ Come Rain Or Come Shine	(Mercury 70685)	1.00	4.00	55
IF I KNEW YOU WERE COMIN' I'D'VE BAKED A CAKE/ Stay With The Happy People	(Coral 60169)	1.50	6.00	50
KISS ME ANOTHER/Fool Of The Year	(Mercury 70850)	1.00	4.00	56
KISS OF FIRE/A Lasting Thing	(Mercury 5823)	1.25	5.00	52
ROCK RIGHT/The Greatest Thing	(Mercury 70811)	1.00	4.00	56
SEVEN LONELY DAYS/If You Take	(Mercury 70095)	1.25	5.00	53
TRA LA LA/Morning Noon & Night	(Mercury 70998)	1.00	4.00	56
TWEEDLE DEE/You're Wrong, All Wrong	(Mercury 70517)	1.00	4.00	54
WHILE YOU DANCED, DANCED, DANCED/ While We're Young	(Mercury 5681)	1.25	5.00	51
GIBSON, Bobby				
SAMOA/B-52	(Gibson 6003)	1.00	4.00	
GIBSON, Ginny				
MIRACLE OF LOVE/Two Innocent Hearts	(ABC-Paramount 9739)	1.00	4.00	56
GIBSON, Harry "The Hipster"				
KEEP VENICE NUDE/Putzi-Putzi	(Mile M-102)	.50	2.00	76
GIBSON, Jill				
IT'S AS EASY AS 1, 2, 3/Jilly's Flip Side	(Imperial 66068)	1.25	5.00	
Jill Gibson was a girlfriend of Jan Berry and was closely involved in the career of Jan & Dean.				
GIBSON, Johnny				
MIDNIGHT/Chuck-A-Luck (Instrumentals)	(Big Top 3088)	.75	3.00	62
GIBSON, Steve (With The Red Caps)				
IT HURTS ME BUT I LIKE IT/Ouch!	(Jay Dee 796)	2.50	10.00	
ROCK & ROLL STOMP/Love Me Tenderly	(ABC-Paramount 9702)	1.25	5.00	57
SAN ANTONIO ROSE/Where Are You?	(Hunt 330)	1.25	5.00	59
SILHOUETTES/Flamingo	(ABC-Paramount 9856)	1.25	5.00	57
GIFTS, The				
GOODBYE MY LOVE/Soul Dust	(Ballad 6002)	.75	3.00	66
LOVIN' YOU/Rock My Soul	(Ballad 6001)	.75	3.00	66
YOU CAN'T KEEP LOVE IN A BROKEN HEART/	(Ballad 6003)	.75	3.00	66
GIGI				
THIS TIME NEXT SUMMER/Little Bit Of Lovin'	(Seg Way 1010)	2.00	8.00	
GIGOLOS, The				
BLACK & BLUE/	(Broadway 1000)	2.50	10.00	
DON'T YOU JUST KNOW IT/Movin' Out	(Enterprise 5000)	1.50	6.00	
GIGOLO'S, The				
SWINGIN' SAINTS/Night Creature (Instrumentals)	(Daynite 1)	2.50	10.00	60
GILBERTO, Astrud				
TIME FOR US, A/The Thought Of Loving You	(Verve 10643)	.75	3.00	69
Also see Getz, Stan				
GILDER, Nick (Of Sweeny Todd)				
ELECTRIC LOVE/World's Collide	(Chrysalis 2357)	.50	2.00	79
HERE COMES THE NIGHT/Rockaway	(Chrysalis 2264)	.50	2.00	78
HOT CHILD IN THE CITY/Backstreet Noise	(Chrysalis 2226)	.50	2.00	78
ROCK ME/Got To Get Out	(Chrysalis 2332)	.50	2.00	79
ROXY ROLLER/Prophet's Tale	(Chrysalis 2115)	.50	2.00	76
RUNAWAYS IN THE NIGHT/	(Chrysalis 2161)	.50	2.00	77
GILDO, Rex				
DEVIL IN DESGUISE/Say Wonderful Things (Sung in German)	(Capitol 5076)	1.00	4.00	63
GILKYSON, Terry, & The Easy Riders				
MARIANNE/Goodbye Chaquita	(Columbia 4-40817)	1.00	4.00	57
TINA/Strollin' Blues	(Columbia 4-40910)	1.00	4.00	57
GILL, Ronnie & The Pastel Keys				
STANDING ON THE MOUNTAIN/Geraldine	(Rio 129)	10.00	40.00	58
GILLAN, Ian, Band				
DOWN THE ROAD/	(Oyster 703)	.75	3.00	76
Also see Deep Purple				
GILLESPIE, Wesley				
WORLD LOVES YOU ELVIS, THE/Early Sunday Morning	(Rome 1017)	.50	2.00	77
GILMER, Jimmy (With The Fireballs)				
AIN'T GONNA TELL ANYBODY/Young Am I	(Dot 16583)	.75	3.00	64
ALL I DO IS DREAM OF YOU/Ain't That Rain	(Dot 16881)	1.00	4.00	66
BECAUSE I NEED YOU/Look Alive	(Decca 30942)	1.50	6.00	59
BORN TO BE WITH YOU/Lonesome Tears	(Dot 16714)	1.00	4.00	65
BREAK HIS HEART FOR ME/Cinnamon Cindy	(Dot 16687)	1.00	4.00	65
COME TO ME/Codine	(Dot 16768)	1.00	4.00	65
CRY BABY/Thunder & Lightnin'	(Dot 16666)	1.00	4.00	64
DAISY PETAL PICKIN'/When My Tears Have Dried	(Dot 16539)	.75	3.00	63
FOOL, THE/Somebody Stole My Watermelon	(Dot 16743)	1.00	4.00	65
GOOD GOOD LOVIN'/Do You Think	(Warwick 592)	1.25	5.00	60
HUNGRY, HUNGRY, HUNGRY/White Roses	(Dot 16833)	1.00	4.00	66
I'M GONNA GO WALKING/Won't Be Long	(Hamilton 50037)	1.25	5.00	63
LOOK AT ME/I'll Send For You	(Dot 16609)	1.00	4.00	64
SUGAR SHACK/My Heart Is Free	(Dot 16487)	.75	3.00	63
THREE SQUARES (& A PLACE TO LAY YOUR HEAD)/Baby	(Atco 6583)	.75	3.00	68
TRUE LOVE WAYS/Wishing	(Warwick 547)	1.50	6.00	60
WHAT KINDA LOVE/Wishing	(Dot 16642)	1.00	4.00	64
Also see Jim & Monica				
GILREATH, James				
LITTLE BAND OF GOLD/I'll Walk With You	(Joy 274)	.75	3.00	63
GINGER & THE CHIFFONS				
WHERE WERE YOU LAST NIGHT/She	(Groove 0003)	1.00	4.00	61
GINO				
GROUCH/She Looks So Tough	(Parnaso 102)	2.50	10.00	
GINO & GINA				
(IT'S BEEN A LONG LONG TIME) PRETTY BABY/ Love's A Carousel	(Mercury 71283)	1.00	4.00	58
GINSBERG, Alen				
SEPTEMBER ON JESSORE ROAD/	(Sing Out/Eva-Tone)	6.25	25.00	72
(The January-February, 1972, issue of "Sing Out" magazine was packaged with this plastic soundsheet. Bob Dylan provides backup vocals on this track. Price here is for magazine and soundsheet still intact.)				
SEPTEMBER ON JESSORE ROAD/ (Price is for soundsheet only.)	(Eva-Tone soundsheet)	3.00	12.00	72
GIORDANO, Lou				
STAY CLOSE TO ME/Don't Cha Know	(Brunswick 9-55115)	68.75	275.00	59
(Features Buddy Holly on guitar. Price range is for maroon label issue.)				
GIORGIO (Moroder)				
BORN TO DIE/	(London 212)	.75	3.00	74
MOODY TRUDY/Stop	(Atco 6731)	.75	3.00	71
SON OF MY FATHER/Underdog	(Dunhill 4304)	.75	3.00	72
GIRLFRIENDS, The				
BABY DON'T CRY/I Don't Believe In You	(Colpix 744)	1.00	4.00	64
MY ONE & ONLY, JIMMY BOY/For My Sake	(Colpix 712)	1.00	4.00	63
NO MORE TEARS/I Want To Be Happy	(Melic 4125)	1.00	4.00	63
GIRLFRIENDS, The				
FOUR SHY GIRLS (IN THEIR ITSY BITSY TEENIE WEENIE YELLOW POLKA-DOT BIKINIS)/Jackie (Answer song)	(Pioneer 71833)	1.00	4.00	60
GIRLS FROM SYRACUSE, The				
LOVE IS HAPPENING TO ME NOW/ You Could Have Had Me All Along	(Palmer 5001)	2.00	8.00	
GLAHE, Will				
LIECHTENSTEINER POLKA/Schweizer Kanton-Polka	(London 1755)	1.00	4.00	57
SWEET ELIZABETH/Tavern In The Town	(London 1788)	1.00	4.00	58
GLANOTTA, Sunny				
LAST BLAST OF THE BLASTED BUGLER/	(ABC-Paramount 10308)	.75	3.00	62
GLASS MANAGERIE, The				
END OF THE LINE/Troubled Mind	(Revolvo 208)	1.50	6.00	
GLAZER, Tom, & The Children's Chorus				
IT'S A MAD MAD MAD MAD WORLD/Dance With A Dolly	(Kapp 559)	.75	3.00	63
ON TOP OF SPAGHETTI/Battle Hymn Of The Children	(Kapp 526)	.75	3.00	63
GLEAMS, The				
I DON'T KNOW WHY YOU SENT FOR ME/ You Broke My Heart	(Kip 237)	1.00	4.00	
MR. MAGIC MOON/Pile Driver	(Kapp 565)	1.00	4.00	63
GLEAVES, Cliff				
LONG BLACK HEARSE/You & Your Kind	(Liberty 55263)	1.00	4.00	61
GLEASON, Jackie				
ALONE TOGETHER/Body & Soul	(Capitol 2473)	1.25	5.00	53
CASEY AT THE BAT/I Had But 50¢ (Shown as by Reginald Van Gleason II)	(Capitol 5420)	1.00	4.00	65
MELANCHOLY SERNADE/You're Getting To Be	(Capitol 2361)	1.25	5.00	53
MY FUNNY VALENTINE/Love Is Here To Stay	(Capitol 2438)	1.25	5.00	53
THEME FROM LIMELIGHT/Peg O' My Heart	(Capitol 2507)	1.25	5.00	53
WHAT IS A BOY/What Is A Girl	(Decca 9-27684)	1.50	6.00	51
GLEASON, Reginald Van, II: see Gleason, Jackie				
GLEEMS, The				
SANDRA BABY/Are You The One	(Parkway 893)	1.00	4.00	63
GLENCOVES, The				
DON'T KNOCK/Ginny's Come Home	(Select 726)	.75	3.00	63
HOOTENANNY/It's Sister Ginny's Turn	(Select 724)	.75	3.00	63
GLENDOWN, Cerf				
HEY NIGHT OWL/There's Love	(Pioneer 1784)	.75	3.00	
GLENN, Darrell				
CRYING IN THE CHAPEL/Hang Up That Telephone	(Valley 105)	1.25	5.00	53
GLENN, Tyree				
SWEET & LOVELY/All Of Me (Stereo single issue)	(Roulette SSR-8008)	1.25	5.00	59
TEACH ME TONIGHT/ There Will Never Be Another You (Stereo single issue)	(Roulette SSR-8002)	1.25	5.00	59
GLENS, The				
IMAGE OF LOVE/I Feel So Blue	(Ro-Nan 1002)	1.00	4.00	
GLENWOODS, The				
ELAINE/That's The Way It'll Be	(Jubilee 5402)	2.00	8.00	60
Also see Chateaus, The				
GLITTER BAND, The				
GOODBYE MY LOVE/	(Arista 0107)	.50	2.00	75
MAKES YOU BLIND/People Like You & People Like Me	(Arista 0207)	.50	2.00	76
Also see Glitter, Gary				
GLITTER, Gary (With The Glitter Band)				
BABY PLEASE DON'T GO/	(Bell 45345)	.75	3.00	73
DO YOU WANNA TOUCH ME/	(Bell 45326)	.75	3.00	73
HAPPY BIRTHDAY/	(Bell 45375)	.75	3.00	73
I DIDN'T KNOW I LOVED YOU (TILL I SAW YOU ROCK & ROLL)/Shakey Sue	(Bell 45276)	.50	2.00	72
I LOVE YOU LOVE ME LOVE/	(Arista 0173)	.75	3.00	75
I LOVE YOU LOVE ME LOVE/	(Bell 45438)	.75	3.00	74
I'M THE LEADER OF THE GANG/	(Bell 45398)	.75	3.00	74
ROCK & ROLL (PART 2)/Rock & Roll (Part 1)	(Bell 45237)	.50	2.00	72
GLITTERS, The				
CHAINS/	(Power 16)	1.50	6.00	
WALK LIKE A MAN/Mama Didn't Lie	(Big C-23)	1.50	6.00	
WHAT ARE BOYS MADE OF/	(Big C-28)	1.50	6.00	
Also see Songspinners, The				
GLOBETROTTERS, The				
CHEER ME UP/Gravy	(Kirshner 5006)	.75	3.00	70
DUKE OF EARL/Everybody's Got Hot Pants	(Kirshner 5012)	1.25	5.00	71
EVERYBODY NEEDS LOVE/ESP	(Kirshner 5016)	.75	3.00	71
RAINY DAY BELLS/Meadowlark	(Kirshner 5008)	1.25	5.00	70
GLOVER, Roger, & Guests				
LOVE IS ALL/	(UK 2800)	.75	3.00	75
Also see Deep Purple				
GLOWTONES, The				
GIRL I LOVE, THE/Ping Pong	(East West 101)	1.50	6.00	57
GIRL I LOVE, THE/Ping Pong	(Atlantic 1156)	1.00	4.00	57
GLYNN, Richard				
HIGH SCHOOL FOOL/It Seems To Me	(Dot 15927)	1.00	4.00	59
G-MEN, The				
JOHNNY & THE MERMAID/Raunchy Twist	(Groove 0009)	.75	3.00	61
G-NOTES, The				
I WOULD/Ronnie	(Tender 510)	1.25	5.00	58
I WOULD/Ronnie	(Jackpot 48000)	1.00	4.00	58
JOHNNY, JOHNNY, JOHNNY/Broken Down Merry-Go-Round	(Guyden 2012)	1.00	4.00	59
GOBEL, George				
BIRDS & THE BEES, THE/Bright Red Convertible	(RCA Victor 47-6483)	1.00	4.00	56
GO BOYS, The				
FLIPPIN'/Ramble	(DC 0418)	1.00	4.00	59
GO-CARTS, The				
BLUE MOON OF KENTUCKY/Rockin' Liza	(Hope 1003)	1.00	4.00	61
GODFATHER, The				
FAVOR, THE/	(Columbia 4-45639)	.75	3.00	72
GODFREY, Arthur				
BUSYBODY/Can You Whistle Johanna	(Columbia 4-39755)	1.25	5.00	52
CANDY & CAKE/The Thousand Islands Song	(Columbia 4-38721)	1.25	5.00	50
DANCE ME LOOSE/Slow Poke	(Columbia 4-39632)	1.25	5.00	51
I LIKE THE WIDE OPEN SPACES/Love Is The Reason	(Columbia 4-39404)	1.25	5.00	51
I LOVE GIRLS/Honey	(Columbia 4-39792)	1.25	5.00	52
THING, THE/Yea-Boo	(Columbia 4-39068)	1.25	5.00	51
WHAT IS A BOY/What Is A Girl	(Columbia 4-39487)	1.25	5.00	51
Also see Martin, Mary & Arthur Godfrey				
GODZ, The (Formerly The Capitol City Rockets)				
GOTTA KEEP A RUNNIN'/Go Away	(Millenium 614)	.50	2.00	78
GOFFIN, Gerry				
IT'S NOT THE SPOTLIGHT/Down On The Street	(Adelphi 452)	.50	2.00	
Also see Goffin, Louise				
GOFFIN, Louise				
JIMMY & THE TOUGH KIDS/Trapeze	(Elektra 46505)	.50	2.00	79
KID BLUE/	(Elektra 46561)	.50	2.00	79
REMEMBER (WALKING IN THE SAND)/Trapeze	(Elektra 46521)	.50	2.00	79
Louise is the daughter of Carole King & Gerry Goffin.				
GO GO's, The				
WILD ONE/Saturday's Hero	(RCA Victor 47-8435)	.75	3.00	64
GOINS, Herbie, & The Nightriders				
INCREDIBLE MISS BROWN, THE/Comin' Home To You	(Capitol 5978)	.75	3.00	67
GOLD				
LOVIN' YOU IS A GROOVE/I Was Gonna Leave Today	(Paramount 0013)	1.25	5.00	
SUMMERTIME/No Parking	(Golden State 501)	1.25	5.00	
GOLD, Andrew (Of Bryndle)				
GO BACK HOME AGAIN/Firefly	(Asylum 45439)	.50	2.00	77
HEARTACHES IN HEARTACHES/Endless Flight	(Asylum 45307)	.50	2.00	76
HOW CAN THIS BE LOVE/Looking For My Love	(Asylum 45521)	.50	2.00	78
I'M ON MY WAY/	(Asylum 45522)	.50	2.00	78
LONELY BOY/Must Be Crazy	(Asylum 45384)	.50	2.00	77
NEVER LET HER SLIP AWAY/Genevieve	(Asylum 45489)	.50	2.00	78
ONE OF THEM IS ME/Passing Thing	(Asylum 45417)	.50	2.00	77
STAY/Firefly	(Asylum 45339)	.50	2.00	76
THANK YOU FOR BEING A FRIEND/ Still You Linger On	(Asylum 45456)	.50	2.00	78
THAT'S WHY I LOVE YOU/A Note From You	(Asylum 45286)	.50	2.00	76
Andrew Gold was once a member of Linda Ronstadt's Band.				
GOLDBERG, Barry				
HOLE IN MY POCKET/Sittin' In Circles (Shown as by the Barry Goldberg Reunion)	(Buddah 59)	.75	3.00	68
YOU GOT ME CRYING/Aunt Lilly	(TMP-Ting 117)	1.00	4.00	
GOLDBERG-MILLER BLUES BAND, The (Barry Goldberg-Steve Miller)				
MOTHER SONG, THE/More Soul Than Soulful (Blue plastic)	(Epic 9865)	3.75	15.00	65
MOTHER SONG, THE/More Soul Than Soulful	(Epic 9865)	1.00	4.00	65
WHOLE LOTTA SHAKIN GOIN' ON/Ginger Man	(Epic 10033)	1.00	4.00	66
GOLD BUGS, The				
STOP THAT WEDDING/It's So Nice	(Coral 62453)	1.00	4.00	65
Also see Five Sharks, The				
GOLDE, Frannie				
HERE I GO (I'M FALLING IN LOVE AGAIN)/ Tell Me What's Going On	(Portrait 70031)	.50	2.00	79
I'M HYPNOTIZED/	(Atlantic 3386)	.75	3.00	77
SAVE ME (I'M FALLING IN LOVE AGAIN)/	(Big Tree 16058)	.75	3.00	76
GOLDEN EARRING				
CANDY'S GOING BAD/She Flies On Strange Wings	(Track 40309)	.50	2.00	74
CE SOIR/Lucky Numbers	(Track 40369)	.50	2.00	75
EIGHT MILES HIGH/One Huge Road	(Atlantic 2710)	.50	2.00	70
RADAR LOVE/Just Like Vince Taylor	(Track 40202)	.50	2.00	74
RADAR LOVE (LIVE)/Radar Love	(MCA 40802)	.50	2.00	78
SLEEP WALKIN'/Babylon	(MCA 40513)	.50	2.00	76
SWITCH, THE/The Lomesome D.J.	(Track 40412)	.50	2.00	75
WEEKEND LOVE/Tiger Bay	(Polydor 2004)	.50	2.00	79
This group may also be shown as Golden Earrings.				
GOLDEN HORIZON				
DEAR EMILY/Love Is The Only Answer	(Fontana 1666)	.75	3.00	69
GOLDIE & THE ESCORTS				
AS I LOVE YOU/Gaudamaus (Blue Label)	(Coral 62317)	3.75	15.00	62
AS I LOVE YOU/Gaudamaus (Orange Label)	(Coral 62317)	3.00	12.00	62
BACK HOME AGAIN/Something Has Changed Him	(Coral 62372)	1.25	5.00	63
GLORIA/Seven Wonders Of The World	(Coral 62302)	1.25	5.00	62
MY HEART CRIES FOR YOU/Give Me Tomorrow	(Coral 62385)	1.50	6.00	63
ONE HAND, ONE HEART/I Can't Be Free	(Coral 62349)	1.25	5.00	63
SUBMARINE RACE WATCHING/Womewhere	(Coral 62336)	1.25	5.00	62
GOLDIE & THE GINGERBREADS				
THAT'S WHY I LOVE YOU/What Kind Of Man Are You	(Atco 6354)	.75	3.00	65
WALKING IN DIFFERENT CIRCLES/Song Of The Moon	(Atco 6475)	.75	3.00	67
GOLDSBORO, Bobby				
BLUE AUTUMN/I Just Don't Love You Anymore	(United Artists 50087)	.75	3.00	66
BROOMSTICK COWBOY/Ain't Got Time For Happy	(United Artists 925)	.75	3.00	65
I DON'T KNOW YOU ANYMORE/Little Drops Of Water	(United Artists 781)	.75	3.00	64
I KNOW YOU BETTER THAN THAT/ When Your Love Has Gone	(United Artists 50018)	.75	3.00	66
IF YOU'VE GOT A HEART/If You Wait For Love	(United Artists 908)	.75	3.00	65
IT HURTS ME/Pity The Fool	(United Artists 50056)	.75	3.00	66
IT'S TOO LATE/I'm Going Home	(United Artists 980)	.75	3.00	66
LITTLE THINGS/I Can't Go On Pretending	(United Artists 810)	.75	3.00	64
LONELY TRAVELER/You Better Go Home	(Laurie 3130)	1.00	4.00	62
LONGER THAN FOREVER/Take Your Love	(United Artists 50044)	.75	3.00	66
LOOK AROUND YOU (IT'S CHRISTMAS TIME)/ Christmas Wish	(United Artists 50470)	.75	3.00	68
ME JAPANESE BOY, I LOVE YOU/Everyone But Me	(United Artists 742)	.75	3.00	64
MOLLY/Honey Baby	(Laurie 3148)	1.00	4.00	62
RUNAROUND, THE/The Letter	(Laurie 3159)	1.00	4.00	63
SEE THE FUNNY LITTLE CLOWN/Hello Loser	(United Artists 672)	.75	3.00	63
TAKE A LITTLE GOOD WILL HOME/ She Thinks I Still Care (With Del Reeves)	(United Artists 50591)	.75	3.00	62
THAT'S WHAT LOVE WILL DO/ Light The Candles (Throw The Rice)	(Laurie 3168)	1.00	4.00	63
VOODOO WOMAN/It Breaks My Heart	(United Artists 862)	.75	3.00	65
WHENEVER HE HOLDS YOU/If She Was Mine	(United Artists 710)	.75	3.00	64
GOLLIWOGS, The: see Creedence Clearwater Revival				
GOMM, Ian (Of Brinsley Schwartz)				
HOLD ON/Another Year	(Stiff-Epic 50747)	.50	2.00	79
HOOKED ON LOVE/	(Stiff-Epic 50802)	.50	2.00	79
GONE ALL STARS, The				
"7-11"/Down Yonder Rock (Instrumentals)	(Gone 5016)	1.00	4.00	58

TITLE/FLIP	LABEL & NO.	GOOD	NEAR MINT	YR.
GONGETTES, The				
GONG GONG-I'M BLUE/Trouble	(Original Sound 21)	.75	3.00	62
GONZALES, Ziggy				
LET ME WALK YOU HOME/Cherokee	(Pop Side 5)	1.00	4.00	61
GOOBERS, The				
HAWAIIAN HOLIDAY/Buyer Beware	(Surf 1001)	.75	3.00	63
(Instrumentals)				
GOOD, BAD & SISTER UGLY, The				
BEHIND THE THEATRE DOOR & THE RESURRECTION OF PORNO/ B.C.	(Sister Ugly's 2)	1.25	5.00	
(Novelty/Break-in)				
GOODEES, The				
ONDITION RED/Didn't Know Love Was So Good	(Hip 8005)	1.00	4.00	68
ILTED/	(Hip 8010)	.75	3.00	69
GOOD GUYS, The				
SPHALT WIPE-OUT/Scratch	(GNP-Crescendo 326)	1.00	4.00	64
(Instrumental)				
Also see Challengers				
GOODHAND-TALT, Phillip				
LMOST KILLED A MAN/	(20th Fox 2100)	.50	2.00	74
ESUS DIDN'T ONLY LOVE THE COWBOYS/	(20th Fox 2149)	.50	2.00	74
UGAR TRAIN/Forever Kind Of Love	(20th Fox 2059)	.50	2.00	73
GOODIES, The				
UM DUM DITTY, THE/Sophisticated Boom Boom	(Blue Cat 117)	.75	3.00	64
GOODMAN, Dickie				
ATMAN & HIS GRANDMOTHER/Suspense	(Red Bird 10-058)	1.00	4.00	66
EN CRAZY/Flip Side	(J.M.D. 001)	3.00	12.00	
EN CRAZY/Flip Side	(Diamond 119)	1.00	4.00	62
ERLIN TOP TEN/Little Tiger	(Rori 602)	1.25	5.00	61
ONSTITUTION, THE/The End	(Rainy Wednesday 205)	1.50	6.00	74
NERGY CRISIS '74/The Mistake	(Rainy Wednesday 206)	1.00	4.00	74
NERGY CRISIS '74/Ruthie's Theme	(Rainy Wednesday 206)	1.00	4.00	74
ERRY FORD-A-SPECIAL REPORT/	(Rainy Wednesday 208)	1.00	4.00	75
ORROR MOVIES/Whoa Mule	(Rori 601)	2.00	8.00	61
NFLATION IN THE NATION/Jon & Jed's Theme	(Rainy Wednesday 209)	1.00	4.00	74
AMES BOMB/Seventh Theme	(Twirl 2015)	2.50	10.00	
ONG/Ed's Tune	(Shock 6)	.75	3.00	77
UNA TRIP/My Victrola (By Joey Pastrana)	(Cotique 173)	1.00	4.00	69
R. JAWS/Irv's Theme	(Cash 451)	.75	3.00	75
R. PRESIDENT/Popularity	(Rainy Wednesday 207)	1.00	4.00	74
N CAMPUS/Mambo Suzie (By Johnny Colon)	(Cotique 158)	1.00	4.00	69
RESIDENTIAL INTERVIEW (FLYING SAUCER '64)/	(Audio Spectrum 75)	2.00	8.00	64
URPLE PEOPLE EATER/Ruthie's Socks	(Rainy Wednesday 204)	2.00	8.00	73
ANTA & THE TOUCHABLES/North Pole Rock	(Rori 701)	2.00	8.00	61
ENATE HEARING/Lock Up	(20TH Fox 443)	1.25	5.00	63
HMONANZA/Backwards Theme	(M.D. 101)	2.00	8.00	
PEAKING OF ECOLOGY/Dayton's Theme	(Rampo 501)	2.00	8.00	
OUCHABLES, THE/Martian Melody	(Mark-X 8009)	1.50	6.00	61
OUCHABLES, THE/Martian Melodies	(Mark-X 8009)	1.50	6.00	61
(Issued with "Martian Melody" shown as "Martian Melodies")				
OUCHABLES IN BROOKLYN, THE/Mystery	(Mark-X 8010)	1.50	6.00	61
ATERGRATE/Friends	(Rainy Wednesday 202)	1.00	4.00	73
Most of the above are novelty/break-ins, with the exceptions usually found n the flip sides.				
Also see Buchanan & Goodman				
Also see Casual Three, The				
OODMAN, Steve				
AN'T GO BACK/Between The Lines	(Asylum 45331)	.50	2.00	76
UTCHMAN, THE/	(Buddah 348)	.75	3.00	73
'S A SIN TO TELL A LIE/	(Asylum 45284)	.50	2.00	76
NE THAT GOT AWAY, THE/Luxury's Lap	(Asylum 46012)	.50	2.00	79
DEO TAPE/My Old Man	(Asylum 45481)	.50	2.00	78
OOD RATS, The				
UST FOUND A LADY/Coo Coo Coo Blues	(Passport 7912)	.50	2.00	79
OOD SHIP LOLLIPOP, The				
AXWELL'S SILVER HAMMER/How Does It Feel	(Ember 701)	.75	3.00	69
OODTIME WASHBOARD THREE, The				
ON'T BLAME P.G. & E., PAL/Oakland	(Fantasy 582)	1.25	5.00	67

TITLE/FLIP	LABEL & NO.	GOOD	NEAR MINT	YR.
OOD TONE BANJO BOYS, The				
UCKS YAS YAS/Beautiful Missouri Waltz	(Good Tone 001)	1.25	5.00	72
(Stereo 78 issue, with special sleeve containing artwork by Robert Crumb.)				
OODWIN, Ron				
WINGING SWEETHEARTS/I'll Find You	(Capitol 3748)	1.00	4.00	57
HEME FROM LIMELIGHT/When I Fall In Love	(Coral 9-61006)	1.25	5.00	53
OOFERS, The				
EARTS OF STONE/You're The One	(Coral 9-61305)	1.00	4.00	54
IP FLOP & FLY/My Babe	(Coral 9-61383)	1.00	4.00	55
OOFY DRY BONE/Nare	(Coral 9-61431)	1.00	4.00	55
EE-DO, DEE-DO/What Does That Dream Mean	(Coral 9-61480)	1.00	4.00	55
CK SICK SICK/Twenty-one	(Coral 9-61545)	1.00	4.00	55
RAVE ME/Oh How I Miss You Tonight	(Coral 9-61593)	1.00	4.00	56
EARDROP MOTEL/Tennessee Rock & Roll	(Coral 9-61650)	1.00	4.00	56
M GONNA ROCK & ROLL 'TIL I DIE/Our Miss Brooks	(Coral 9-61664)	1.00	4.00	56

TITLE/FLIP	LABEL & NO.	GOOD	NEAR MINT	YR.
GOOGY & JOE'S WORKSHOP				
TO FERNANDA WITH LUV (PART 1)/ To Fernanda With Luv (Part 2)	(Parkway 154)	.75	3.00	67
GOON BONES, The (Trio)				
AIN'T SHE SWEET/Mary Lou (By Muzzy Marcellino)	(Crest 706)	1.25	5.00	55
CRAZY BONE RAG/I'm Forever Blowing Bubbles	(Mercury 5498)	1.50	6.00	50
DIESEL RAG/Goofus	(Mercury 5482)	1.50	6.00	50
FAST FREIGHT BLUES/A Smile Will Go A Long Way	(Mercury 5472)	1.50	6.00	50
MONKEYSHINES/That's The One For Me	(Mercury 5632)	1.25	5.00	51
PROFESSOR SPOONS/Should I	(Mercury 5591)	1.25	5.00	51
SMILES/When You Were A Tulip	(Mercury 5561)	1.25	5.00	51
Also see Ford, Mr., & Goon Bones				
GOON, Peter				
WHISTLER/Song Titles (By Bab Boon)	(Poleese 100)	7.50	30.00	
GOOSE CREEK SYMPHONY				
CHARLIE'S TUNE/No News Is Good News	(Capitol 2853)	.75	3.00	70
BIG TIME SATURDAY NITE/Beautiful Bertha	(Capitol 2729)	.75	3.00	70
MERCEDEZ BENZ/Rush On Love	(Capitol 3246)	.75	3.00	70
GORDON & SUE				
SURFIN' SAL & CHARMIN' WILLY/Surfin' Sax	(Carlton 595)	1.00	4.00	63
GORDON, Barry				
I CAN'T WHISTLE/The Milkman's Polka	(MGM K-12222)	1.00	4.00	56
HOW DO WE LOOK TO THE MONKEYS/Ten Years To Go	(MGM K-12276)	1.00	4.00	56
NUTTIN' FOR CHRISTMAS/ Santa Claus Looks Just Like Daddy	(MGM K-12092)	1.00	4.00	55
ROCK AROUND MOTHER GOOSE/Seven	(MGM K-12166)	1.00	4.00	56
YOU CAN'T LIE TO A LIAR/You Can't See The Trees	(Cadence 1431)	.75	3.00	62
GORDON, Mike, & The Agates				
RUMBLE AT NEWPORT BEACH/Last Call For Supper	(Dore 681)	1.00	4.00	63
GORDON, Robert (With Link Wray)				
BLACK SLACKS/Walk On By	(RCA PB-11608)	.50	2.00	79
FIRE/If This Is Wrong	(Private Stock 45203)	.50	2.00	78
IT'S ONLY MAKE BELIEVE/Rock Bill Boogie	(RCA PB-11471)	.50	2.00	79
RED HOT/Sweet Surrender	(Private Stock 45156)	.50	2.00	77
SEA CRUISE/If This Is Wrong	(Private Stock 45191)	.50	2.00	78
GORE, Lesley				
ALL OF MY LIFE/I Cannot Hope For Anyone	(Mercury 72412)	.75	3.00	65
BACK TOGETHER/Quiet Love	(Crewe 601)	1.00	4.00	71
BRINK OF DISASTER/On A Day Like Today	(Mercury 72726)	1.00	4.00	67
CALIFORNIA NIGHTS/I'm Going Out (The Same Way I Came In)	(Mercury 72649)	.75	3.00	66
HE GIVES ME LOVE (LA LA LA)/Brand New Me	(Mercury 72817)	1.00	4.00	68
HEY NOW/Sometimes I Wish I Were A Boy	(Mercury 72352)	.75	3.00	64
I DON'T WANNA BE A LOSER/It's Gotta Be You	(Mercury 72270)	.75	3.00	64
I'LL BE STANDING BY/Look The Other Way	(Mercury 72867)	1.00	4.00	68
IMMORTALITY/Give It To Me, Sweet Thing	(A&M 1710)	1.00	4.00	75
IT'S A HAPPENING WORLD/Magic Colors	(Mercury 72759)	1.00	4.00	67
IT'S MY PARTY/Danny	(Mercury 72119)	.75	3.00	63
I WON'T LOVE YOU ANYMORE (SORRY)/ No Matter What You Do	(Mercury 72513)	1.00	4.00	65
JE NE SAIS PLUS/Je N'ose Pas	(Mercury 72245)	1.25	5.00	64
(French language version of "You Don't Own Me"/"Run Bobby Run")				
JUDY'S TURN TO CRY/Just Let Me Cry	(Mercury 72143)	.75	3.00	63
LOOK OF LOVE, THE/Little Girl Go Home	(Mercury 72372)	.75	3.00	64
MAYBE I KNOW/Wonder Boy	(Mercury 72309)	.75	3.00	64
MY TOWN, MY GUY & ME/A Girl In Love	(Mercury 72475)	.75	3.00	65
OFF & RUNNING/I Don't Care	(Mercury 72580)	1.00	4.00	66
ROAD I WALK, THE/She Said That	(Mowest 5029)	1.00	4.00	72
SHE'S A FOOL/The Old Crowd	(Mercury 72180)	.75	3.00	63
SMALL TALK/Say What You See	(Mercury 72787)	1.00	4.00	68
SOMETIMES/Give It To Me, Sweet Thing	(A&M 1829)	1.00	4.00	76
SUMMER & SANDY/I'm Falling Down	(Mercury 72683)	.75	3.00	67
SUMMER SYMPHONY/98.6-Lazy Day	(Mercury 72931)	1.00	4.00	69
SUNSHINE, LOLLIPOPS & RAINBOWS/ You've Come Back	(Mercury 72433)	.75	3.00	65
TAKE GOOD CARE OF MY HEART/ You Sent Me Silver Bells	(Mercury 72892)	1.00	4.00	69
THAT'S THE WAY BOYS ARE/ That's The Way The Ball Bounces	(Mercury 72259)	.75	3.00	64
TREAT ME LIKE A LADY/Maybe Now	(Mercury 72611)	1.00	4.00	66
WE KNOW WERE IN LOVE/That's What I'll Do	(Mercury 72530)	1.00	4.00	66
WEDDING BELL BLUES/One By One	(Mercury 72969)	1.00	4.00	69
WHEN YESTERDAY WAS TOMORROW/	(Crewe 344)	1.00	4.00	70
WHERE CAN I GO/I Can't Make It Without You	(Mercury 72842)	.75	3.00	68
WHY DOESN'T LOVE MAKE ME HAPPY/Tomorrow's Children	(Crewe 338)	1.00	4.00	70
YOU DON'T OWN ME/Run Bobby Run	(Mercury 72206)	.75	3.00	63
YOUNG LOVE/I Just Don't Know If I Can	(Mercury 72553)	.75	3.00	66
Also see Billy & Sue				
GORGONI, Martin, & Taylor (With Chip Taylor)				
I CAN'T LET GO/	(Buddah 295)	.50	2.00	72
GORME, Eydie				
BLAME IT ON THE BOSSA NOVA/ Guess I Should Have Loved Him More	(Columbia 4-42661)	.75	3.00	62
DON'T TRY TO FIGHT IT, BABY/Light Fantastic	(Columbia 4-42790)	.75	3.00	63
I'LL TAKE ROMANCE/First Impression	(ABC-Paramount 9780)	1.00	4.00	57
I'M YOURS/Don't Take Your Love From Me	(ABC-Paramount 10006)	1.00	4.00	59
I'M YOURS/Don't Take Your Love From Me	(ABC-Paramount S-10006)	1.25	5.00	59
(Stereo single issue)				
MAMA, TEACH ME TO DANCE/ You Bring Out The Lover In Me	(ABC-Paramount 9722)	1.00	4.00	56
TOO CLOSE FOR COMFORT/That's How	(ABC-Paramount 9684)	1.00	4.00	56
YOU NEED HANDS/Dormi, Dormi, Dormi	(ABC-Paramount 9825)	1.00	4.00	58
Also see Lawrence, Steve, & Eydie Gorme				
GORSHIN, Frank				
RIDDLER, THE/Never Let Her Go	(A&M 804)	.75	3.00	66
GOSSERT, Gus				
RETURN OF THE SAUCER (1972)/ Return Of The Saucer (1972) (Part 2)	(Penny Arcade 100)	2.00	8.00	
(Novelty/Break-in)				
GOTHAM CITY CRIME FIGHTERS, The				
THAT'S LIFE/	(Batwing 1001)	1.50	6.00	
GOTHAM CITY TEENS, The				
(HOLY HOLY) RAVIOLI/Ravioli	(RMT 1000)	1.25	5.00	66
GOTHICS, The				
MY DREAM/Love You Too Much	(Carol 4115)	6.25	25.00	
GO TOGETHERS, The				
TRAIN/Time After Time	(Coast 100)	1.25	5.00	
GOULET, Robert				
MY LOVE FORGIVE ME/I'd Rather Be Rich	(Columbia 4-43131)	.75	3.00	64
SUMMER SOUNDS/The More I See of Mimi	(Columbia 4-43301)	.75	3.00	65
WHAT KIND OF FOOL AM I/Where Do I Go From Here	(Columbia 4-42519)	.75	3.00	62
GOULD, Sandra				
HELLO MELVIN (Answer song)/My Son The Surfer	(Philips 40138)	1.00	4.00	63
GOWANS, Sammy				
ROCKIN BY MYSELF/Kissin' At The Drive-In	(United Artists 114)	10.00	40.00	57

TITLE/FLIP	LABEL & NO.	GOOD	NEAR MINT	YR.
GO ZOO BAND, The				
OH BABY MINE (I GET SO LONELY)/Sid's Lid	(Go Go 101)	.75	3.00	66
GRABEAU, Bobby				
BACK TO SCHOOL, BACK TO YOU/Don't Ever Let Me Go	(Crest 1064)	1.00	4.00	59
OLITA/There's Something About Your Kiss	(Crest 1059)	1.00	4.00	59
GRACIE, Charlie				
ANGEL OF LOVE/I'm A Fool, That's Why	(Coral 9-62115)	1.25	5.00	59
BUTTERFLY/Ninety-Nine Ways	(Cameo 105)	1.00	4.00	57
COOL BABY/You've Got A Heart Like A Rock	(Cameo 118)	1.25	5.00	57
CRAZY GIRL/Dressin' Up	(Cameo 127)	1.25	5.00	58
DOODLEBUG/Hurry Up Buttercup	(Coral 9-62073)	1.25	5.00	59
FABULOUS/Just Lookin'	(Cameo 107)	1.00	4.00	57
HE'LL NEVER LOVE YOU LIKE I DO/ Keep My Love Next To Your Heart	(Diamond 178)	.75	3.00	65
I LOVE YOU SO MUCH IT HURTS/Wanderin' Eyes	(Cameo 111)	1.00	4.00	57
LOVE BIRD/Trying	(Cameo 141)	1.25	5.00	58
MY BABY LOVES ME/Head Home, Honey	(20th Fox 5033)	.75	3.00	65
NIGHT & DAY U.S.A./Pretty Baby	(President 825)	1.00	4.00	62
OH-WELL-A/Because I Love You So	(Coral 9-62141)	1.25	5.00	59
RACE, THE/I Look For You	(Roulette 4255)	1.00	4.00	59
SORRY FOR YOU/Scenery	(Roulette 4312)	1.00	4.00	61
W-WOW/Makin' Whoopie	(Felsted 8629)	1.00	4.00	61
GRADDY, Bob				
GONNA BE AT THE STATION/	(Old Town 1119)	1.25	5.00	62
GRADS, The				
EVERYTHING IN THE GARDEN/Stage Door	(A&M 797)	.75	3.00	66
IT HAPPENED ONCE BEFORE/ Their Heart Were Full Of Spring	(MGM 13216)	1.00	4.00	63
ONCE AGAIN/White Steeple	(Valiant 6023)	1.00	4.00	62
Also see Sandpipers, The				
GRADUATES, The				
BALLAD OF A GIRL & BOY/Care	(Shan-Todd 0055)	1.50	6.00	59
WHAT GOOD IS GRADUATION/Lonely	(Corsican 0058)	1.50	6.00	59
GRADUATES, The				
SHAPE OF THINGS TO COME, THE/Listen To The Music	(Crescendo 404)	1.00	4.00	
GRADY & BRADY: see Sneed, Brady & Grady				
GRADY, Leigh				
BLUE CHRISTMAS/How Great Thou Art	(Appaloosa 112)	1.00	4.00	77
GRANAHAN, Gerry (Of Dickie Doo & The Don'ts)				
DANCE GIRL, DANCE/Too Big For Her Bikini	(Caprice 108)	5.00	20.00	61
(With the Wildwoods, who were actually the Five Satins)				
IN MY HEART/When Irish Eyes Are Smiling	(Canadian American 116)	1.25	5.00	60
KING SIZE/I'm Afraid You'll Never Know	(Sunbeam 122)	1.25	5.00	59
LET THE RUMORS FLY/Put Me Anywhere	(Gone 5065)	1.25	5.00	59
LOOK FOR ME/It Hurts	(Gone 5081)	1.25	5.00	60
NO CHEMISE, PLEASE/Girl Of My Dreams	(Sunbeam 102)	1.00	4.00	58
RING, A BRACELET, A HEART, A/"A" You're Adorable	(Sunbeam 127)	1.25	5.00	59
UNCHAINED MELODY/Dancing Man	(Caprice 106)	1.25	5.00	61
YOU'LL NEVER WALK ALONE/Where's The Girl	(Canadian American 119)	1.25	5.00	60
GRAND CANYON, The				
EVIL BOOL-WEEVIL/Got To Find My Way Back	(Bang 713)	.75	3.00	
UNIVERSAL PERSON/Range Rider	(Faithful Virtue 7004)	.75	3.00	70
GRAND FUNK RAILROAD (Grand Funk)				
BAD TIME/Good & Evil	(Capitol 4046)	.50	2.00	75
CAN YOU DO IT/1976	(MCA 40590)	.50	2.00	76
CLOSER TO HOME/Aimless Lady	(Capitol 2877)	.50	2.00	70
FEELIN' ALRIGHT/I Want Freedom	(Capitol 3095)	.50	2.00	71
FOOTSTOMPIN' MUSIC/I Come Tumblin'	(Capitol 3255)	.50	2.00	71
GIMME SHELTER/I Can Feel Him In The Morning	(Capitol 3160)	.75	3.00	71
HEARTBREAKER/	(Capitol 2732)	.75	3.00	70
JUST COULDN'T WAIT/Out To Get You	(MCA 40641)	.75	3.00	77
LOCO-MOTION, THE/Destitute & Losin'	(Capitol 3840)	.50	2.00	74
MEAN MISTREATER (Live)/Mark Says Alright	(Capitol 2996)	.50	2.00	70
MR. LIMOUSINE DRIVER/	(Capitol 2691)	1.00	4.00	69
NOTHING IS THE SAME/Sin's A Good Man's Brother	(Capitol 2816)	.75	3.00	70
ROCK 'N' ROLL SOUL/Flight Of The Phoenix	(Capitol 3363)	.50	2.00	72
SALLY/Love Is Dyin'	(Capitol 4235)	.50	2.00	76
SAVE THE LAND/People, Let's Stop The War	(Capitol 3217)	.75	3.00	71
SHININ' ON/Mr. Pretty Boy	(Capitol 3917)	.50	2.00	74
SOME KIND OF WONDERFUL/Wild	(Capitol 4002)	.50	2.00	74
TAKE ME/Genevieve	(Capitol 4199)	.50	2.00	75
TIME MACHINE/High On A Horse	(Capitol 2567)	.50	2.00	69
UPSETTER/No Lies	(Capitol 3316)	.75	3.00	72
WALK LIKE A MAN/The Railroad	(Capitol 3760)	.50	2.00	73
WE'RE AN AMERICAN BAND/Creepin'	(Capitol 3660)	.50	2.00	73
Also see Flint				
Also see Farner, Mark, & Don Brewer				
Also see Knight, Terry, & The Pack				
GRAND, K.C., & The Shades				
LOOKIE LOOKIE LOOKIE/	(Matt 0003)	2.00	8.00	
GRAND PREES, The				
ALONE/I'm Gone	(Haral 780)	3.00	12.00	
GRAND PRIX, The				
CANDY APPLE BUGGY/'41 Ford	(Vault 906)	1.00	4.00	63
GRAND PRIX MACHINE, The				
CYNTHIA/Theme From Cynthia	(Laurie 3512)	1.00	4.00	69
GRANT, Carrie, & The Grandeors				
THERE'LL COME A TIME/Take All Of My Life	(New Art 1003)	.75	3.00	
GRANT, Earl				
END, THE/Hunky Dunky Doo	(Decca 9-30719)	1.00	4.00	58
EVENING RAIN/	(Decca 9-30819)	1.00	4.00	59
LAST NIGHT/Imitation Of Life	(Decca 9-30856)	1.00	4.00	59
LITTLE GIRL LOST/One Way Street	(Progressive 1201)	1.25	5.00	59
NOT ONE MINUTE MORE/All For The Best	(Decca 9-30983)	1.00	4.00	59
SWINGIN' CHRISTMAS/Christmas Card	(Decca 9-31022)	1.00	4.00	59
SWINGIN' GENTLY/Beyond The Reef	(Decca 9-25560)	.75	3.00	62
(Instrumentals)				
WISH/Don't Point Your Finger At Somebody Else	(Decca 9-30908)	1.00	4.00	59
GRANT, Gogi (Audrey Brown)				
GOIN' HOME/All God's Children Got Shoes	(Liberty 55229)	.75	3.00	60
I'LL NEVER SMILE AGAIN/If & When	(Liberty 55214)	.75	3.00	59
RESTLESS PAIR/The Ride Back From Boot Hill	(RCA Victor 47-7492)	.75	3.00	59
RESTLESS PAIR/The Ride Back From Boot Hill	(RCA Victor 61-7492)	1.25	5.00	59
(Stereo single issue)				
STAY HERE WITH ME/I Never Meant To Fall In Love	(Liberty 55252)	.75	3.00	60
SUDDENLY THERE'S A VALLEY/Love Is	(Era 1003)	1.00	4.00	55
TENDER IS THE NIGHT/Magic Music	(20th Fox 297)	.75	3.00	62
TWO DREAMS/Honey, Honey	(RCA Victor 47-7438)	.75	3.00	59
WAYWARD WIND, THE/No More Than Forever	(Era 1013)	1.00	4.00	56
WHO ARE WE/We Believe In Love	(Era 1008)	1.00	4.00	55
YOU'RE IN LOVE/When The Tide Is High	(Era 1019)	1.00	4.00	56
GRANT, Janie				
OH JOHNNY/Oh My Love	(Caprice 113)	.75	3.00	62
ROMEO/Roller Coaster	(Caprice 109)	.75	3.00	61
TELL ME MAMA/Who's Heart Are You Breaking Now	(United Artists 616)	.75	3.00	63

The Fontane Sisters

Gerry & The Pacemakers

Lt. Garcias Magic Music Box

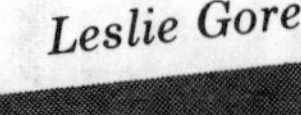

Leslie Gore

TITLE/FLIP	LABEL & NO.	GOOD	NEAR MINT	YR.
THAT GREASY KID STUFF (With James Ray)/ Trying To Forget You	(Caprice 115)	.75	3.00	62
THAT KIND OF BOY/Priceless Possession	(United Artists 649)	.75	3.00	63
TRIANGLE/She's Going Steady With You	(Caprice 104)	.75	3.00	61
TWO IS COMPANY & THREE'S A CROWD/	(Caprice 119)	.75	3.00	62
UNHAPPY BIRTHDAY/I Wonder Who's Kissing Him Now	(Caprice 111)	.75	3.00	61
GRANTS, Little Guy				
SO YOUNG/It's You	(Lawn 103)	10.00	40.00	59
GRAPEFRUIT				
DEAR DELILAH/Dead Boot	(Equinox 70000)	.75	3.00	68
YES/Elevator	(Equinox 70005)	.75	3.00	68
GRAPEVINE				
I CAN'T GET ENOUGH OF YOU/Independent Me	(MGM K-13933)	1.25	5.00	68
Also see Carmel				
GRASS, Dick, & The Hoppers				
MR. JOHN LAW/Please Dear	(Arrow 738)	.75	3.00	
GRASS ROOTS, The				
ANYWAY THE WIND BLOWS/Monday Love	(Dunhill 4325)	.75	3.00	73
BABY HOLD ON/Get It Together	(Dunhill 4237)	.50	2.00	70
BELLA LINDA/Hot Bright Lights	(Dunhill 4162)	.50	2.00	68
COME ON & SAY IT/	(Dunhill 4248)	.75	3.00	70
GLORY BOUND/Only Love	(Dunhill 4302)	.50	2.00	72
HEAVEN KNOWS/Don't Remind Me	(Dunhill 4217)	.50	2.00	69
I'D WAIT A MILLION YEARS/Fly Me To Havana	(Dunhill 4198)	.50	2.00	69
LET'S LIVE FOR TODAY/Depressed Feeling	(Dunhill 4084)	.75	3.00	67
LOVE IS WHAT YOU MAKE IT/Someone To Love	(Dunhill 4335)	.50	2.00	73
LOVIN' THINGS/You & Love Are The Same	(Dunhill 4180)	.50	2.00	69
MAMACITA/The Last Time Around	(Haven 7015)	.50	2.00	75
MELODY FOR YOU, A/Hey Friend	(Dunhill 4122)	.75	3.00	68
MIDNIGHT CONFESSIONS/Who Will You Be Tomorrow	(Dunhill 4144)	.50	2.00	68
MR. JONES (A BALLAD OF A THIN MAN)/ You're A Lonely Girl	(Dunhill 4013)	.75	3.00	65
ONLY WHEN YOU'RE LONELY/ This Is What I Was Made For	(Dunhill 4043)	1.00	4.00	66
OUT IN THE OPEN/	(Haven 802)	.50	2.00	76
RIVER IS WIDE, THE/(You Gotta) Live For Love	(Dunhill 4187)	.50	2.00	69
RUNAWAY, THE/Move Along	(Dunhill 4316)	.50	2.00	72
SOONER OR LATER/I Can Turn Off The Rain	(Dunhill 4279)	.50	2.00	71
TEMPTATION EYES/Keepin' Me Down	(Dunhill 4263)	.50	2.00	70
THINGS I SHOULD'VE SAID/Tip Of My Tongue	(Dunhill 4094)	.75	3.00	67
TWO DIVIDED BY LOVE/Let It Go	(Dunhill 4289)	.50	2.00	71
WAKE UP, WAKE UP/No Exit	(Dunhill 4105)	.75	3.00	67
WALKING THROUGH THE COUNTRY/Truck Drivin' Man	(Dunhill 4227)	.50	2.00	70
WE ALMOST MADE IT TOGETHER/Stealin' Love	(Dunhill 15006)	.75	3.00	74
WHERE'S THERE'S SMOKE THERE'S FIRE/	(Dunhill 4345)	.75	3.00	73
WHERE WERE YOU WHEN I NEEDED YOU/ (These Are) Bad Times	(Dunhill 4029)	.75	3.00	66
GRATEFUL DEAD, The (Featuring Jerry Garcia)				
DANCIN' IN THE STREETS/Terrapin Station	(Arista 0276)	.50	2.00	77
DARK STAR/Born Cross-eyed	(Warner Bros. 7186)	1.50	6.00	68
DON'T EASE ME IN/Stealin'	(Scorpio 201)	10.00	40.00	66
DUPREE'S DIAMOND BLUES/Cosmic Charlie	(Warner Bros. 7324)	1.50	6.00	69
EYES OF THE WORLD/Weather Report	(Grateful Dead 02)	1.25	5.00	74
FRANKLIN'S TOWER/Help On The Way	(Grateful Dead 762)	1.00	4.00	76
GOLDEN ROAD, THE (TO UNLIMITED DEVOTION)/ Cream Puff War	(Warner Bros. 7016)	1.25	5.00	67
GOOD LOVIN'/Stagger Lee	(Arista 0383)	.50	2.00	78
HELP ON THE WAY/Music Never Stopped	(Grateful Dead 718)	1.00	4.00	75
JOHNNY B. GOODE/ So Fine (By The Elvin Bishop Group)	(Warner/Fillmore 7627)	2.00	8.00	72
(Promotional issue only)				
JOHNNY B. GOODE/Johnny B. Goode	(Warner Bros. 7627)	1.25	5.00	72
(Promotional issue only)				
JOHNNY B. GOODE/Truckin'	(Warner Bros. 7653)	1.00	4.00	72
LET ME SING YOUR BLUES AWAY/ Here Comes Sunshine	(Grateful Dead 01)	1.00	4.00	74
MUSIC NEVER STOPPED, THE/Help On The Way	(Grateful Dead 718)	1.00	4.00	75
PASSENGER/Terrapin Station	(Arista 0291)	.50	2.00	77
SUGAR MAGNOLIA/Mr. Charlie	(Warner Bros. 7667)	1.25	5.00	73
TRUCKIN'/Ripple	(Warner Bros. 7464)	1.00	4.00	71
U.S. BLUES/Loose Lucy	(Grateful Dead 03)	1.00	4.00	74
UNCLE JOHN'S BAND/New Speedway Boogie	(Warner Bros. 7410)	1.50	6.00	70
Also see Hart, Mickey				
Also see Hunter, Robert				
Also see Weir, Bob				
GRAVES, Billy				
LONG JOURNEY HOME/Midnight Bus	(Monument 404)	1.00	4.00	59
MIDNIGHT BUS/Long Journey Home	(Monument 404)	1.00	4.00	59
SHAG, THE (IS TOTALLY COOL)/Uncertain	(Monument 401)	1.00	4.00	59
GRAVES, Carl (Of Skylark)				
BABY, HANG UP THE PHONE/	(A&M 1620)	.50	2.00	74
SAD GIRL/Walk In Love	(Ariola America 7660)	.50	2.00	75
GRAVES, Joe				
SEE SAW/Beautiful Girl	(Parkway 964)	1.00	4.00	65
GRAY, Dobie				
BE A MAN/Inka Dinka Doo	(Jaf 2504)	1.00	4.00	63
BOY & A GIRL IN LOVE, A/Kissin' Doll	(Stripe 832)	1.25	5.00	61
DRIFT AWAY/City Stars	(Decca 33057)	.75	3.00	73
FEELIN' IN MY HEART/That's How You Treat A Cheater	(Cordak 1605)	1.00	4.00	63
FIND 'EM, FOOL 'EM & FORGET 'EM/	(Capricorn 0259)	.50	2.00	76
HONEY, YOU CAN'T TAKE IT BACK/	(White Whale 342)	.75	3.00	70

TITLE/FLIP	LABEL & NO.	GOOD	NEAR MINT	YR.
IF LOVE MUST GO/	(Capricorn 0249)	.50	2.00	76
"IN" CROWD, THE/Be A Man	(Charger 105)	.75	3.00	64
IN HOLLYWOOD/Mr. Engineer	(Charger 109)	.75	3.00	65
LET GO/	(Capricorn 0267)	.50	2.00	77
LOOK AT ME/Walkin' & Whistlin'	(Cordak 1602)	.75	3.00	62
LOVE HAS A WAY/Delia	(Stripe 829)	1.25	5.00	60
LOVE HAS A WAY/Young Boy	(Stripe 831)	1.00	4.00	61
LOVING ARMS/Now That I'm Without You	(MCA 40100)	.75	3.00	73
MONKEY JERK/My Baby	(Charger 113)	.75	3.00	65
MY SHOES KEEP WALKIN' BACK TO YOU/Funny Feelin'	(Cordak 1701)	1.00	4.00	64
OUT ON THE FLOOR/No Room To Cry	(Charger 115)	.75	3.00	66
RAGS TO RICHES/I Can Hardly Wait	(Stripe 828)	1.25	5.00	60
RIVER DEEP MOUNTAIN HIGH/Tennessee Waltz	(Capitol 5853)	1.00	4.00	67
ROLL ON SWEET MISSISSIPPI/	(MCA 40315)	.75	3.00	75
ROSE GARDEN/	(White Whale 300)	.75	3.00	69
SEE YOU AT THE "GO-GO"/Walk With Love	(Charger 107)	.75	3.00	65
SPENDING TIME, MAKING LOVE & GOING CRAZY/	(Infinity 50020)	.50	2.00	79
TEARS FALLING FROM MY TEARS/Love Has A Way	(Real Fine 835)	1.00	4.00	61
'TO BE WANTED/Hearts Are Wild	(Stripe 827)	1.25	5.00	60
WHAT A WAY TO GO/Do You Really Have A Heart	(White Whale 330)	.75	3.00	69
WHO'S LOVIN' YOU/Thank You For Tonight	(Infinity 50010)	.50	2.00	79
YOU CAN DO IT/Sharing The Night Together	(Infinity 50003)	.50	2.00	78
GRAY, Dolores				
SHRIMP BOATS/More, More, More	(Decca 9-27832)	1.00	4.00	51
GRAY, Gene, & The Stingrays				
SURF BUNNY/Surfer's Mood	(Linda 110)	1.25	5.00	63
SURF BUNNY/Surfer's Mood	(Dot 16478)	.75	3.00	63
GRAY, Maureen				
CRAZY OVER YOU/Today's The Day	(Chancellor 1082)	1.00	4.00	61
DANCIN' THE STRAND/Oh My	(Landa 689)	.75	3.00	62
PEOPLE ARE TALKING/Oh My	(Landa 692)	.75	3.00	62
THERE IS A BOY/I'm So Young	(Chancellor 1100)	.75	3.00	62
GREASE				
ALONE AT A DRIVE-IN MOVIE/Beauty School Dropout	(Lion 142)	.75	3.00	73
WE GO TOGETHER/	(Lion 133)	.75	3.00	72
The above releases are from the orginal cast recording.				
GREASE BAND, The (With Henry McCullough)				
LAUGHED AT THE JUDGE/Let It Be Gone	(Shelter 7304)	.75	3.00	71
Members of this group were previously with Joe Cocker's Band.				
Also see Wings				
GREAT!! SOCIETY!!, The (Featuring Grace Slick)				
SALLY GO 'ROUND THE ROSES/Didn't Think So	(Columbia 4-44583)	1.50	6.00	68
SOMEONE TO LOVE/Free Advice	(Northbeach 1001)	7.50	30.00	
("Someone To Love" was later issued as "Somebody To Love," and released by the Jefferson Airplane.)				
GREAT TRAIN ROBBERY, The (Featuring Chuck Trois)				
HEARTLESS HURDY GURDY/Wasted	(ABC 45-11205)	.75	3.00	69
(Chuck Trois was previously with the 1910 Fruitgum Co. and with the Soul Survivors.)				
GREATS, The				
MARCHING ELVIS/Fiddler's Rock	(Ebb 145)	3.00	12.00	58
GREAT SPECKLED BIRD, The (Featuring Ian Tyson & Sylvia Fricker)				
TRUCKER'S CAFE/Smiling Wine	(Ampex 11006)	.75	3.00	70
WE SAIL/Disappearing Woman	(Ampex 11003)	.75	3.00	70
GRECCO, Cyndi				
HELLO AGAIN/	(Private Stock 45132)	.50	2.00	76
I THINK I CAN MAKE IT/Dancing, Dancing	(Private Stock 45110)	.50	2.00	76
MAKING OUR DREAMS COME TRUE (THEME FROM "LAVERNE & SHIRLEY")/Watching You	(Private Stock 45086)	.50	2.00	76
THIS TIME (I'M IN IT FOR LOVE)/	(Private Stock 45162)	.50	2.00	77
GRECO, Buddy				
AROUND THE WORLD/Hey, There	(Epic 9451)	.75	3.00	61
I RAN ALL THE WAY HOME/Glory Of Love	(Coral 9-60573)	1.25	5.00	51
LADY IS A TRAMP, THE/Like Young	(Epic 9387)	.75	3.00	60
MR. LONELY/Sentimental Fool	(Epic 9536)	.75	3.00	62
GRECO, Johnny, & The Davies				
HIGH SCHOOL DANCE/Hogwalk	(Sonic 813)	1.25	5.00	59
ROCKET RIDE/Why Don't You Love Me	(Pageant 602)	5.00	20.00	
GREEK FOUNTAINS, The				
BLUE JEAN/Countin' The Steps	(Philips 40355)	1.00	4.00	66
GREENBAUM, Norman (Of Dr. West's Medicine Show & Junk Band)				
CALIFORNIA EARTHQUAKE/Rhode Island Red	(Reprise 1008)	1.00	4.00	71
CANNED HAM/Junior Cadillac	(Reprise 0919)	1.00	4.00	70
I.J. FOXX/Rhode Island Red	(Reprise 0956)	1.00	4.00	70
SPIRIT IN THE SKY/Milk Cow	(Reprise 0885)	.75	3.00	70
TWENTIETH CENTURY FOX/Nancy Whiskey	(Gregar 0107)	1.25	5.00	69
GREEN BEANS, The				
KNOCK ON MY DOOR/Who Needs You	(Tower 237)	.75	3.00	66
GREENBERG, Steve				
BIG BRUCE/Run To You	(Trip 3000)	.75	3.00	69
(Novelty)				
GREENE, Lorne				
AN OLD TIN CUP/Sand	(RCA Victor 47-8554)	.75	3.00	65
MAN, THE/Pop Goes The Hammer	(RCA Victor 47-8490)	.75	3.00	64
RINGO/Bonanza	(RCA Victor 47-8444)	.75	3.00	64
WACO/All But Remembering	(RCA Victor 47-8901)	.75	3.00	66
GREEN, Darren				
LOVE DOESN'T GROW ON TREES/Checkin' On You	(RCA PB-10050)	.50	2.00	74
WHY DO FOOLS FALL IN LOVE/Dream World	(RCA APBO-0294)	.75	3.00	74
GREEN, De Roy, & The Cool Gents				
BEGGAR TO A QUEEN/At The Teen Center	(Cee-Jay 584)	1.25	5.00	
GREEN, Larry				
BEWITCHED/If I Had You On A Desert Island	(RCA Victor 47-3726)	1.25	5.00	50
I'LL GET BY/Western Melody	(RCA Victor 47-3990)	1.25	5.00	50
I'M IN THE MIDDLE/I Don't Mind	(RCA Victor 47-3957)	1.25	5.00	50
TENDERLY/Legend Of The Glass Mountain	(RCA Victor 47-4064)	1.25	5.00	51
GREENLEE, Lee				
STARLIGHT/Cherry, I'm In Love With You Baby	(Brent 7003)	1.25	5.00	59
GREENSTREET				
MOON SHOT/Locust Raid	(Corsair 400)	.75	3.00	64
GREENWICH, Ellie (Of the Raindrops)				
AIN'T THAT PECULIAR/I Don't Wanna Be Left Outside	(Bell 855)	.75	3.00	69
I WANT YOU TO BE MY BABY/ Goodnight, Goodnight	(United Artists 50151)	.75	3.00	67
MAYBE I KNOW/	(Verve 10719)	.75	3.00	
YOU DON'T KNOW/Baby	(Red-Bird 10-034)	.75	3.00	65
GREENWOOD COUNTY SINGERS, The: see Greenwoods, The				

TITLE/FLIP	LABEL & NO.	GOOD	NEAR MINT	YR.
GREENWOODS, The				
FRANKIE & JOHNNY/Climb Up Sunshine Mountain	(Kapp 591)	.75	3.00	64
(Shown as by the Greenwood Country Singers)				
PLEASE DON'T SELL MY DADDY NO MORE WINE/ Southbound	(Kapp 742)	.75	3.00	66
GREG & PAUL (Greg Evigan & Paul Shaefer)				
SHE'S A REBEL/	(Casablanca 893)	.50	2.00	77
GREGG, Bobby (& His Friends)				
DRUMMER MAN/Walk On	(Epic 9579)	.75	3.00	66
JAM, THE (PART 1)/Jam, The (Part 2)	(Cotton 1003)	.75	3.00	62
KANGAROO (PART 2) (TIE ME KANGAROO DOWN SPORT)/ Kootanda	(Epic 9616)	.75	3.00	63
LET'S JAM AGAIN/	(Epic 9541)	.75	3.00	62
POTATO PEELER/Sweet Georgia Brown	(Cotton 1006)	.75	3.00	62
TAKE ME OUT TO THE BALL GAME/Scarlet O'Hara	(Epic 9601)	.75	3.00	63
Instrumentals				
GREGORY, Harrison				
TWISTIN' RAINDROPS/I'm Alone	(Cordella 047)	5.00	20.00	
(With Paul Simon)				
GREGORY, Ivan, & The Bluenotes				
ELVIS PRESLEY BLUES/Kathy	(G & G 110)	5.00	20.00	56
GREGORY, Steve				
YOU'RE MY KINDA GIRL/Don't Ever Let Me Go	(Kenco 5008)	1.50	6.00	
GREY, Al				
TACOS & GRITS/Smile	(Argo 5461)	.75	3.00	64
GREYHOUND, The				
MOON RIVER/	(A&M 1342)	.50	2.00	72
GREY, Joel				
MOONLIGHT SWIM/Everytime I Ask My Heart	(Capitol 3777)	1.00	4.00	57
1941/Don't Remind Me Now Of Time	(Columbia 4-44907)	.75	3.00	69
GRIEVES, Grant				
FOUR IN THE FLOOR/Married Woman	(Big K 1002)	1.00	4.00	
FOUR IN THE FLOOR/M1 Automatic	(Injun 106)	1.00	4.00	
GOODTIME GIRL/I've Got You	(Cracker Box 10075)	1.00	4.00	
HONKY TONK FEVER/Drinkin' & Drivin'	(Big K 1003)	1.00	4.00	
I'LL GET TO YOU/From 9 To 5	(Cracker Box 10076)	1.00	4.00	
SHAKE IT BABY/If I Ever Stop Laughing	(Big K 1007)	1.25	5.00	
Also see Strangers, The				

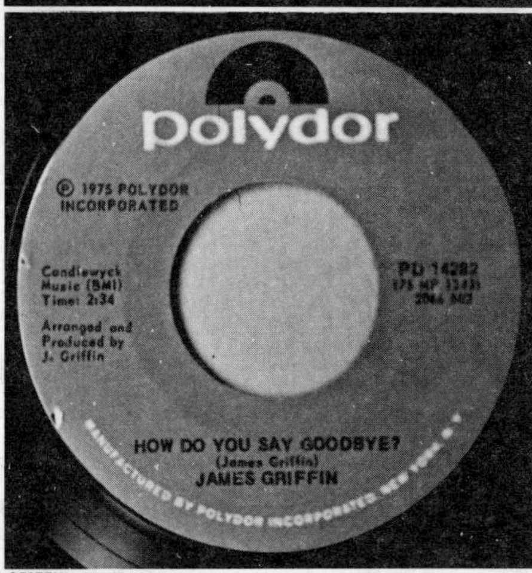

TITLE/FLIP	LABEL & NO.	GOOD	NEAR MINT	YR.
GRIFFIN, James (Of Bread)				
BREAKIN' UP IS EASY/Melody Maker	(Polydor PD-14213)	.75	3.00	73
GIRLS GROW UP FASTER THAN BOYS/ It's A Free Country	(Reprise R-20,114)	1.25	5.00	63
HARD ROW TO HOE/He Will Break Your Heart	(Imperial 66152)	1.00	4.00	66
HOW DO YOU SAY GOODBYE/Treat Her Right	(Polydor PD-14282)	.75	3.00	75
LITTLE MISS COOL/Marie Is Moving	(Reprise R-20,221)	1.25	5.00	63
MIRACLE WORKER, THE/Lookin' So Much Better	(Viva 611)	1.00	4.00	67
(Shown as by James Arthur Griffin)				
MIRACLE WORKER, THE/Thank You Love	(Viva 642)	.75	3.00	70
MY BABY MADE ME CRY/All My Loving	(Reprise 0268)	1.25	5.00	64
RUNNING TO YOU/Gotta Lotta Love (Ciribiribin)	(Reprise 0280)	1.25	5.00	64
SUMMER HOLIDAY/Love Letters In The Sand	(Reprise R-20178)	1.25	5.00	63
THANK YOU LOVE/The Light Of Your Mind	(Viva 627)	1.00	4.00	68
THESE ARE THE TIMES/Walking To New Orleans	(Imperial 66108)	1.00	4.00	65
TRY/You're Nobody Till Somebody Loves You	(Reprise 0304)	1.25	5.00	64
WHAT KIND OF GIRL ARE YOU/ A Little Like Lovin' You	(Reprise R-20,161)	1.25	5.00	63
GRIFFIN, James Arthur: see Griffin, James				

TITLE/FLIP — LABEL & NO. — GOOD — NEAR MINT — YR.

GRIFFIN, Ken
FLIRTATION WALTZ/Lonesome (Columbia 4-40153) 1.25 5.00 54
HARBOR LIGHTS/Josephine (Columbia 4-38889) 1.50 6.00 50
IT HAD TO BE YOU/I Know Why (Columbia 4-40101) 1.25 5.00 53
SEPTEMBER IN THE RAIN/
Somebody Else Is Taking My Place (Columbia 4-40416) 1.25 5.00 54
SMILE/I Need You Now (Columbia 4-40346) 1.25 5.00 54

GRIFFIN, Merv
ALL THE LIVELONG DAY/Hey Garcon (Columbia 4-40141) 1.25 5.00 54
ALWAYS/Hey Pretty Baby (Cameo 266) .75 3.00 63
BAND IN BOSTON/The World We Love In (Carlton 540) .75 3.00 61
BOBBY SOX BOUNCE, THE/Love Is On A Holiday (Cavalcade 803) 1.50 6.00
CHARANGA, THE/Along Came Joe (Carlton 545) .75 3.00 61
DO YOU REMEMBER ME/The Story Of Tina (Columbia 4-40328) 1.25 5.00 54
HAVE I TOLD YOU LATELY THAT I LOVE YOU/
I'm Sorry I Made You Cry (Cameo 298) .75 3.00 64
HOUSE OF HORRORS/Pretty Girl (Mercury 71993) 1.00 4.00 62
I'VE GOT A LOVELY BUNCH OF COCONUTS/Bluebird On
Your Windowsill (With Freddy Martin) (RCA 3047) 1.50 6.00 49
JOEY, JOEY, JOEY/Ginny (Columbia 4-40685) 1.25 5.00 55
MUCH TO YOUNG TO DIE/
The Girl With A Figure Like An Hour Glass (Columbia 4-40274) 1.25 5.00 54

GRIFFITH, Andy
ANDY & CLEOPATRA (PART 1)/
Andy & Cleopatra (Part 2) (Capitol 5073) 1.00 4.00 63
CARMEN (PART 1)/Carmen (Part 2) (Capitol 3402) 1.25 5.00 56
HAMLET/Hamlet (Part 2) (Capitol 4157) 1.00 4.00 59
MAKE YOURSELF COMFORTABLE/Ko Ko Mo (Capitol 3057) 1.25 5.00 55
POOL TABLE/Whistling Ping Pong Game (Capitol 4848) 1.00 4.00 62
ROMEO & JULIET (PART 1)/Romeo & Juliet (Part 2) (Capitol 2698) 1.50 6.00 54
SILHOUETTES/Conversation With A Mule (Capitol 3872) 1.00 4.00 58
STANDING ON THE CORNER/No Time For Sergeants (Capitol 3498) 1.25 5.00 56
SWAN LAKE (PART 1)/Swan Lake (Part 2) (Capitol 2855) 1.50 6.00 54
WHAT IT WAS, WAS FOOTBALL/
Romeo & Juliet (Colonial-no number given) 3.00 12.00 53
(When Capitol issued "What It Was, Was Football" (2693), it divided the track into 2 parts, using both sides of the single. The Colonial flip side, "Romeo & Juliet," was also issued on Capitol the following year.)
WHAT IT WAS, WAS FOOTBALL (PART 1)/
What It Was, Was Football (Part 2) (Capitol 2693) 1.50 6.00 53
On some releases, this artist was shown as "Deacon" Andy Griffith.

GRILL, Rob (Of The Grass Roots)
ROCK SUGAR/Have Mercy (Mercury 76009) .50 2.00 79

GRIMMS, The
BACK BREAKER/ (DJM 1001) 1.50 6.00 73
This band contained members of the Bonzo Dog Band & the Scaffold (but did not include Mike McGear.)

GRIN (With Nils Lofgren)
END UNKIND/Slippery Fingers (Spindizzy 4006) .75 3.00 72
EVERYBODY'S MISSING THE SUN/18-Faced Lover (Spindizzy 4002) .75 3.00 71
IF I WERE A SONG/See What A Love Can Do (Spindizzy 4001) .75 3.00 71
WHITE LIES/Just To Have You (Spindizzy 4005) .75 3.00 72
YOU'RE THE WEIGHT/ (A&M 1502) .50 2.00 74

GRINDER SWITCH
REDWING/ (Atco-Rabbit 7087) .50 2.00 77
YOU & ME/ (Atco-Rabbit 7089) .50 2.00 78

GROCE, Larry
JUNK FOOD JUNKIE/
The Little Old Lady In Cowboy Boots (Peaceable 45003) 1.00 4.00 75
JUNK FOOD JUNKIE/Muddy Boggy Banjo Man (Warner Bros. 8165) .50 2.00 75

GRODES, The
GIVE ME SOME TIME/
Give Me Some Time (Instrumental) (Splitsound 4-1) .75 3.00

GROGAN, Toby
ANGEL/Just A Friend (Vee Jay 560) .75 3.00 63

GROOTNA
FULL TIME WOMAN/Full Time Woman (Columbia 4-45461) 1.00 4.00 71
WAITIN' FOR MY SHIP/Waitin' For My Ship (Columbia 4-45538) 1.00 4.00 72

GROOVE, The
LOVE IS GETTING BETTER/The Light Of Love (20th Fox 45-6671) 1.00 4.00 66
LOVE IS GETTING BETTER/The Light Of Love (Wand 1163) .75 3.00 67

GROOVIE GOOLIES, The
FIRST ANNUAL SEMI-FORMAL COMBINATION CELEBRATION MEET-THE-MONSTER POPULATION PARTY/Save Your Good
Lovin' For Me (RCA 74-0383) 1.25 5.00 70

GROPUS CACKUS
GIMMIN SOME LOVIN'/Music Maker (Jaguar 106) 1.25 5.00
LOVE, LOVE, LOVE/Rhyme & Reason (Bell 45162) 1.00 4.00 72

GROSS, Henry (Of Sha Na Na)
COME ON SAY IT/The Ever Lovin' Days (A&M 1534) .75 3.00 74
MEET ME ON THE CORNER/With The Sleep In My Eyes (A&M 1613) .75 3.00 75
ONE MORE TOMORROW/Evergreen (A&M 1682) .75 3.00 75
ONLY THE BEAUTIFUL/Creepin' Jenny (Lifesong 1761) .50 2.00 78
PAINTING MY LOVE SONG/String Of Hearts (Lifesong 45023) .50 2.00 77
SOMEDAY (I DON'T WANT TO HAVE TO BE THE ONE)/
Lincoln Road (Lifesong 45014) .50 2.00 76
SPRINGTIME MAMA/Overton Square (Lifesong 45008) .50 2.00 76
SHANNON/Pokey (Lifesong 45002) .50 2.00 76
WHAT A SOUND/ (Lifesong 45024) .50 2.00 77

GROUNDHOGS, The
ROCK ME/Shake It (Interphon 7715) 1.00 4.00 65

GROUNDSPEED
L-12 EAST/In A Dream (Decca 32344) .75 3.00 68

GROUP "B"
I NEVER REALLY KNEW/I Know Your Name Girl (Scorpio 406) 2.00 8.00
STOP CALLING ME/She's Gone (Scorpio 402) 2.00 8.00

GROUP WITH NO NAME, The
BABY LOVE (HOW COULD YOU LEAVE ME)/All I Need (Casablanca 860) .50 2.00 77
GET OUT IN THE SUNSHINE/ (Casablanca 868) .50 2.00 77
ROLL ON BROTHER/ (Elektra 45451) .50 2.00 77

GROVE, Harry, Trio
FATHER'S DOING FINE/Pagan In The Parlour (London 1293) 1.25 5.00 52
LITTLE RED MONKEY/Music Box Magic (London 1316) 1.25 5.00 53
MEET MR. CALLAGHAN/Intermezzo (London 1248) 1.25 5.00 52

GRUMP
HEARTBREAK HOTEL/I'll Give You Love (Magic Carpet 901) .75 3.00 69

GTO'S, The
GIRL FROM NEW YORK CITY/Missing Out On The Fun (Parkway 108) 1.25 5.00 66
SHE RIDES WITH ME/Rudy Vadoo (Claridge 312) 1.25 5.00 66
(These tracks were previously issued on Claridge 304 but shown as by Joey & the Continentals. Both releases contain the exact same recordings.)

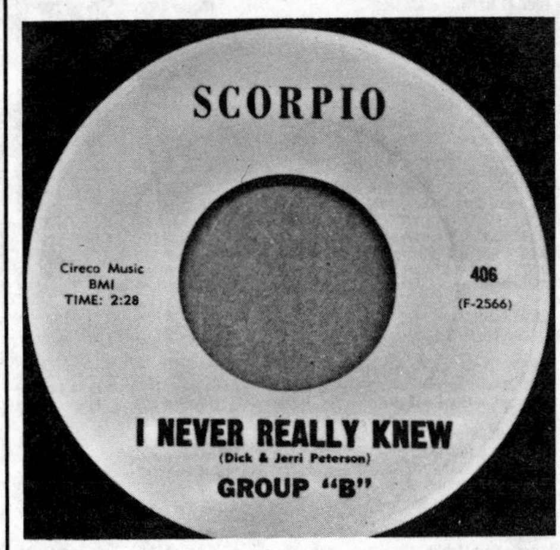

SCORPIO
Cireco Music
BMI
TIME: 2:28
406
(F-2566)
I NEVER REALLY KNEW
(Dick & Jerri Peterson)
GROUP "B"

GUARALDI, Vince, Trio
CAST YOUR FATE TO THE WIND/Samba De Orpheus (Fantasy 563) .75 3.00 62

GUERCIO, James William (Featuring Robert Lamm)
TELL ME/ (Columbia 4-45886) .75 3.00 70
Also see Chicago

GUERRERO, Lalo
ELVIS PEREZ/Lola (L&M 1001) 3.75 15.00 56
POUND DOG/Pancho Claus (L&M 1000) 3.75 15.00 56

GUESS WHO, The (Featuring Burton Cummings)
ALBERT FLASHER/Broken (RCA 74-0458) .75 3.00 71
AMERICAN WOMAN/No Sugar Tonight (RCA 74-0325) .75 3.00 70
AND SHE'S MINE/All Right (Amy 967) 2.00 8.00 67
BELIEVE ME/Baby Feelin' (Scepter 12131) 1.50 6.00 66
CLAP FOR THE WOLFMAN/Road Food (RCA APBO-0324) .50 2.00 74
CLOCK ON THE WALL/One Day (Scepter 12144) 1.50 6.00 66
C'MON LITTLE MAMA/Moon Wave Maker (Hilltak 7803) .50 2.00 78
DANCIN' FOOL/Seems Like I Can't Live With You, But
I Can't Live Without You (RCA PB-10075) .50 2.00 74
FOLLOW YOUR DAUGHTER HOME/Bye Bye Babe (RCA 74-0880) .75 3.00 73
GLAMOUR BOY/Lie Down (RCA 74-0977) 1.00 4.00 73
GOODNIGHT, GOODNIGHT/Hey Ho What You Do To Me (Scepter 12018) 1.50 6.00 65
GUNS, GUNS, GUNS/Heaven Only Moved Once Yesterday (RCA 74-0708) .75 3.00 72
HAND ME DOWN WORLD/Runnin' Down The Street (RCA 74-0367) .50 2.00 70
HANG ON TO YOUR LIFE/Do You Miss Me Darlin' (RCA 74-0414) .75 3.00 71
HEARTBROKEN BOPPER/Arrivederci Girl (RCA 74-0659) .75 3.00 72
HURTING EACH OTHER/Baby's Birthday (Scepter 12118) 1.50 6.00 65
IT'S MY PRIDE/His Girl (Amy 976) 2.00 8.00 67
LAUGHING/Undun (RCA 74-0195) .75 3.00 69
LOVES ME LIKE A BROTHER/Hoe Down Time (RCA PB-10216) .75 3.00 75
NO TIME/Proper Stranger (RCA 74-0300) .75 3.00 69
ORLY/Watcher, The (RCA 74-0926) 1.00 4.00 73
RAIN DANCE/One Divided (RCA 74-0522) .50 2.00 71
ROSEANNE/Dreams (RCA PB-10306) .75 3.00 75
RUNNIN' BACK TO SASKATOON/New Mother Nature (RCA 74-0803) .75 3.00 72
SHAKIN' ALL OVER/
Monkey In A Cage (By the Discotays) (Scepter SCE-1295) 2.00 8.00 65
SHAKIN' ALL OVER/Till We Kissed (Scepter 5-1295) 1.25 5.00 65
SHARE THE LAND/Bus Rider (RCA 74-0388) .50 2.00 70
SILVER BIRD/Runnin' Down The Street (RCA PB-10716) .75 3.00 76
SOUR SUITE/Life In The Bloodstream (RCA 74-0578) .75 3.00 71
STAR BABY/Musicione (RCA 74-0217) .75 3.00 74
SWEET YOUNG THING/ (Hilltak 7807) .50 2.00 79
THERE'S NO GETTING AWAY FROM YOU/
This Time Long Ago (Fontana 1597) 2.00 8.00 69
THESE EYES/Lightfoot (RCA 74-0102) .75 3.00 69
WHEN THE BAND WAS SINGIN' "SHAKIN' ALL OVER"/
Woman (RCA PB-10410) .75 3.00 75
Chad Allen, the group's orginal lead singer, left the group before they signed with RCA. Beginning in 1969, Burton Cummings was their lead voice. Cummings departed for a solo career in 1976. During their peak years, Randy Bachman was also with the band.
Also see Allen, Chad, & The Reflections.

GUEST, Chris
THOSE FABULOUS 60's/ (Banana 218) 1.25 5.00
(Bob Dylan impersonation)

GUEVARA, Rubin
STAR SPANGLE BANNER/America The Beautiful (Big 7) 1.50 6.00

GUILD, The
WHAT AM I GONNA DO/ (Elektra 45823) .50 2.00 72

GUILLOTEENS, The
FOR MY OWN/Don't Let The Rain Get You Down (HBR 451) 1.00 4.00 65
I DON'T BELIEVE/Hey You (HBR 446) 1.00 4.00 65
I SIT & CRY/Crying All Over My Time (HBR 486) 1.00 4.00 66
WILD CHILD/You Think You're Happy (Columbia 4-43852) 1.25 5.00 66

GUITAR, Billy, & The Night Hawks
HERE COMES THE NIGHT/
You Should Have Loved Her More (Decca 30634) 15.00 60.00 58

GUM DROPS, The
CHAPEL OF HEARTS/Natural Born Lover (King 4963) 1.00 4.00 56
DON'T TAKE IT SO HARD/I'll Wait For One More Train (King 1499) 1.00 4.00 55
GUM DROP/Don't Take It So Hard (King 1496) 1.00 4.00 55
IT HAPPENS EVERY DAY/They Wake Me (Coral 62138) 1.00 4.00 59
I'LL FOLLOW YOU/I Wonder & Wonder (King 4913) 1.00 4.00 56
MY OWN TRUE LOVE/On The Wings Of The Wind (Coral 62003) 1.00 4.00 58
YOU'RE THE ONE/
Gum Drop Shoes & Bells In Her Hair (Decca 30584) 1.00 4.00 58
Also see Allen, Ray, Trio

GUN (Featuring Adrian & Ben Gurvitz)
LONG HAIR WILDMAN/Drown Yourself In The River (Epic 10593) .75 3.00 70
RACE WITH THE DEVIL/Sunshine (Epic 10413) .75 3.00 69

GUNHILL ROAD
BACK WHEN MY HAIR WAS SHORT/We Can't Hide The
Roller Coaster Anymore (Kama Sutra 569) .75 3.00 73
42ND STREET/ (Mercury 73232) .75 3.00 72

GURUS, The
BLUE SNOW NIGHT/Come Girl (United Artists 50089) .75 3.00 66
IT JUST WON'T BE THAT WAY/
Everybody's Got To Be Alone Sometime (United Artists 50140) .75 3.00 67

GURVITZ, Adrian (Of Gun)
UNTOUCHABLE & FREE/Drifting Star (Jet 5058) .50 2.00 79
Also see Edge, Graeme, Band
Also see Parrish & Gurvitz
Also see Baker-Burvitz Army

GUTHRIE, Arlo
ALICE'S ROCK & ROLL RESTAURANT/
Coming In To Los Angeles (Reprise 0877) .75 3.00 69
BALLAD OF TRICKY FRED/Shackles & Chains (Reprise 0994) .75 3.00 70
CITY OF NEW ORLEANS, THE/Days Are Short (Reprise 1103) .50 2.00 72
GABRIEL'S MOTHER'S HIWAY BALLAD #16 BLUES/
Valley To Pray (Reprise 0951) .75 3.00 70
GYPSY DAVY/Week On The Rag (Reprise 1158) .75 3.00 73
MASSACHUSETTS/ (Reprise 1388) .75 3.00 75
MOTORCYCLE SONG, THE (PART 1)/
The Motorcycle Song (Part 2) (Reprise 0793) .75 3.00 68
MOTORCYCLE SONG, THE/Now & Then (Reprise 0644) .75 3.00 67
NOSTALGIA RAG/Presidential Rag (Reprise 1121) .75 3.00 73
PAUSE OF MR. CLAUS, THE/The Motorcycle Song (Reprise PRO 304) 1.25 5.00 68
(Promotional issue)
PROLOGUE/Wedding Song (With Shenandoah) (Warner Bros. 49037) .50 2.00 79
UKELELE LADY/Cooper's Lament (Reprise 1137) .75 3.00 73
Arlo is the son of Woody Guthrie.

GUY, Bob: see Zappa, Frank

GYPSY
DAY AFTER DAY/Lean On Me (RCA 74-0862) .75 3.00 72
GYPSY QUEEN (Part 2)/Dead & Gone (Metromedia 202) .50 2.00 70

HACKERT, Veline: see Covelle, Buddy

HACKETT, Buddy
CHINESE ROCK & EGG ROLL/Ting Me A Tong (Coral 9-61594) 1.25 5.00 56
CHINESE WAITER/Diet (Coral 61105) 1.25 5.00 54

HACKETT, Steve (Of Genesis)
NARNIA/ (Chrysalis 2237) .50 2.00 78

HAGAN, Sammy, & The Viscounts
TAIL LIGHT/Snuggle Bunny (Capitol 3885) 2.00 8.00 56
OUT OF YOUR HEART/Smoochie Poochie (Capitol 3772) 5.00 20.00 57

HAGAR, Sammy (Of Montrose)
CATCH THE WIND/Red (Capitol 4388) .50 2.00 76
CRUSIN' & BOOZIN'/ (Capitol 4411) .50 2.00 77
FLAMINGOS FLY/Urban Guerrilla (Capitol 4261) .50 2.00 76
I'VE DONE EVERYTHING FOR YOU/Someone Out There (Capitol 4596) .50 2.00 78
PLAIN JANE/Wounded In Love (Capitol 4757) .50 2.00 79
(SITTIN' ON) THE DOCK OF THE BAY/
I've Done Everything For You (Capitol 4669) .50 2.00 79
TURN UP THE MUSIC/Hey Boys (Capitol 4550) .50 2.00 78
YOU MAKE ME CRAZY/Reckless (Capitol 4502) .50 2.00 77

HA HA'S, The
DING-A-LING/Why Not (Dino 327) .75 3.00 70

HAHN, Joyce
GONNA FIND ME A BLUEBIRD/I Saw You (Cadence 1318) 1.00 4.00 57

HAIG, Ronnie
DON'T YOU HEAR ME CALLING BABY/
Traveler Of Love (Note 10010) 5.00 20.00 58
DON'T YOU HEAR ME CALLING BABY/
Traveler Of Love (ABC-Paramount 9912) 3.00 12.00 58
DON'T YOU HEAR ME CALLING BABY/
Traveler Of Love (ABC-Paramount 10209) 1.00 4.00 61
ROCKIN' WITH RHYTHM & BLUES/
Money Is A Thing Of The Past (Note 10014) 5.00 20.00 58

HAINES, Gary, & The Five Sequins
ANOTHER GIRL LIKE YOU/Tse Tse Fly (Kapp 383) 1.00 4.00 61

HAIR
EASY TO BE HARD (By Cheryl Barnes)/
Good Morning Starshine (RCA PB-11548) .50 2.00 79
(From the orginial soundtrack recording.)

HAIRCUTS, The
SHE LOVES YOU/Love Me Do (Parkway 899) 1.50 6.00 64

HAIRPOWER
ROYAL INTERNATIONAL LOVE-IN/Dead End (Epic 10627) .75 3.00 70

HAL & JEAN
HEY YOU STANDING THERE/Don't Tell Me Lies (Capitol 5041) .75 3.00 63

HALE & THE HUSHABYES
YES SIR, THAT'S MY BABY/900 Quetzals (Apogee 104) 6.25 25.00 65
YES SIR, THAT'S MY BABY/Jack's Theme (Reprise 0299) 5.00 20.00 64
Hale & The Hushabyes was the name given a star studded group, assembled by Jack Nitzsche, featuring: Brian Wilson, Sonny & Cher, the Blossoms, Darlene Love, Jackie DeShannon, Edna Wright of the Honey Cone and Albert Stone of the Shaklefords. This same recording was later issued, but shown as by A Date With Soul.

HALEY, Bill & His Comets
A.B.C. BOOGIE, THE/ (Kasey 7006) 1.00 4.00 61
BURN THAT CANDLE/Stop, Look, & Listen (Apt 25081) 2.50 10.00 65
BURN THAT CANDLE/Rock-a-Beatin' Boogie (Decca 9-29713) 1.00 4.00 55
CALDONIA/Shaky (Decca 9-30926) 1.00 4.00 59
CANDY KISSES/Tamiami (Warner Bros. 5145) 1.25 5.00 60
CHARMAINE/I Got A Woman (Decca 9-30844) 1.00 4.00 59
CHICK SAFARI/Hawk (Warner Bros. 5154) 1.25 5.00 60
CHIQUITA LINDA (UN POQUITO DE TU AMOR?)/
Whoa Mabel (Decca 9-30741) 1.00 4.00 58
CORRINE, CORRINA/B.B. Betty (Decca 9-30781) 1.00 4.00 58
CORRINE CORRINA/The Green Door (Decca 725751) .75 3.00 69
CRAZY MAN, CRAZY/Whatcha Gonna Do (Essex 321) 6.25 25.00 53

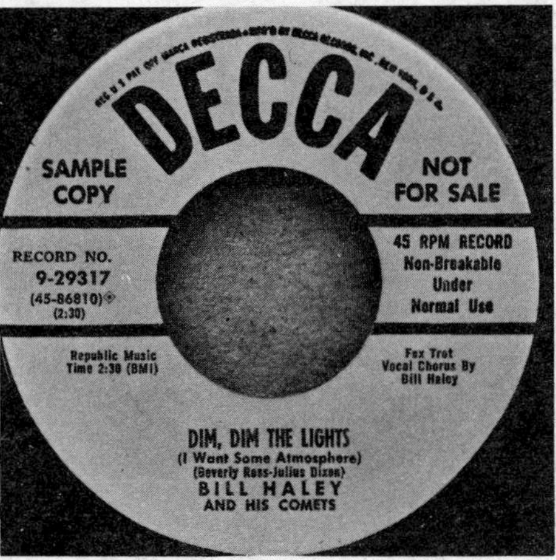

TITLE/FLIP	LABEL & NO.	GOOD	NEAR MINT	YR.
DANCE AROUND THE CLOCK/ What Can I Say After I Say I'm Sorry	(Newtown 5024)	1.00	4.00	63
DIM, DIM THE LIGHTS/Happy Baby	(Decca 9-29317)	1.25	5.00	54
DIM, DIM THE LIGHTS/Happy Baby (Promotional issue)	(Decca 9-29317)	2.00	8.00	54
DIPSY DOODLE, THE/Miss You	(Decca 9-30394)	1.00	4.00	57
DON'T KNOCK THE ROCK/Choo Choo Ch 'Boogie	(Decca 9-30148)	1.00	4.00	56
FLIP, FLOP & FLY/Honky Tonk	(Warner Bros. 5228)	2.00	8.00	60
FORTY CUPS OF COFFEE/Line & Sinker	(Decca 9-30214)	1.00	4.00	57
GREEN DOOR, THE/Yeah! She! Evil	(Decca 9-31650)	.75	3.00	64
GREEN TREE BOOGIE/Down Deep In My Heart	(Holiday 108)	37.50	150.00	51
HALEY A GO-GO/Tongue Tied Tony	(Apt 25087)	2.50	10.00	65
HOT DOG BUDDY BUDDY/Rockin' Through The Eye	(Decca 9-29948)	1.00	4.00	56
I'LL BE TRUE/Ten Little Indians	(Essex 340)	6.25	25.00	53
I'M CRYING/Pretty Baby	(Holiday 110)	37.50	150.00	51
JOEY'S SONG/Ooh! Look-A-There, Ain't She Pretty	(Decca 9-30956)	1.00	4.00	59
JUKEBOX CANNONBALL/Sundown Boogie	(Holiday 113)	37.50	150.00	52
JUKEBOX CANNONBALL/Sundown Boogie	(Essex 374)	7.50	30.00	54
LEAN JEAN/Don't Nobody Move	(Decca 9-30681)	1.00	4.00	58
LITTLE PIECE AT A TIME/Traveling Band	(Janus 162)	2.00	8.00	71
LIVE IT UP/Farewell So Long Goodbye	(Essex 332)	3.00	12.00	53
MAMBO ROCK/Birth Of The Boogie	(Decca 9-29418)	1.25	5.00	55
MARY, MARY LOU/It's A Sin	(Decca 9-30530)	1.00	4.00	58
MIDNIGHT IN WASHINGTON/White Parakeet	(Newtown 5014)	1.00	4.00	63
(NOW & THEN THERE'S) A FOOL SUCH AS I/ Where'd You Go Last Night	(Decca 9-30873)	1.00	4.00	59
PAT-A CAKE/Fractured	(Essex 327)	6.25	25.00	53
(PUT ANOTHER NICKEL IN) MUSIC, MUSIC, MUSIC!/ Strictly Instrumental	(Decca 9-31080)	1.00	4.00	60
RAZZLE-DAZZLE/Two Hound Dogs	(Decca 9-29552)	1.25	5.00	55
REAL ROCK DRIVE/ Stop Beatin' Round The Mulberry Bush	(Essex 310)	6.25	25.00	52
RIP IT UP/Teenager's Mother (Are You Right?)	(Decca 9-30028)	1.25	5.00	56
RIVIERA/War Paint	(Gone 5116)	2.00	8.00	61
R-O-C-K/The Saints Rock 'N Roll	(Decca 9-29870)	1.25	5.00	56
ROCK AROUND THE CLOCK (WE'RE GONNA)/ Thirteen Women (& Only One Man In Town)	(Decca 9-29124)	1.25	5.00	55
ROCK AROUND THE CLOCK (WE'RE GONNA)/ Thirteen Women (& Only One Man In Town) (Promotional issue) (Just prior to press time, we have been informed of the possible discovery of an earlier version of "Rock Around The Clock," backed with "Crazy, Man, Crazy," released on Essex 102A/B. This 1952 78rpm could have extraordinary value, perhaps greater than any other recording.)	(Decca 9-29124)	6.25	25.00	55
ROCK THE JOINT/Icy Heart (Red plastic issue, shown as by Bill Haley & the Saddlemen.)	(Essex 303)	37.50	150.00	52
ROCK THE JOINT/Icy Heart (Label name in block print, artist shown as Bill Haley & the Saddlemen.)	(Essex 303)	12.50	50.00	52
ROCK THE JOINT/Farewell, So Long, Goodbye (Label name in script print, artist shown as Bill Haley & His Comets.)	(Essex 399)	5.00	20.00	54
ROCK THE JOINT/How Many	(Decca 9-30461)	1.00	4.00	57
ROCKET 88/Tearstains On My Heart	(Holiday 105)	37.50	150.00	51
ROCKET 88/Green Tree Boogie	(Essex 381)	18.75	75.00	54
ROCKET 88/Green Tree Boogie	(Transworld 381)	12.50	50.00	54
ROCKING CHAIR ON THE MOON/ Dance With The Dolly (With A Hole In Her Stocking)	(Essex 305)	12.50	50.00	52
RUDY'S ROCK/Blue Comet Blues	(Decca 9-30085)	1.25	5.00	56
SEE YOU LATER ALLIGATOR/ The Paper Boy (On Main Street, U.S.A.)	(Decca 9-29791)	1.25	5.00	55
SHAKE, RATTLE & ROLL/A.B.C. Boogie	(Decca 9-29204)	1.25	5.00	54
SKINNY MINNIE/Sway With Me	(Decca 9-30592)	1.00	4.00	58
SKOKIAAN/Puerto Rican Peddler	(Decca 9-31030)	1.00	4.00	59
SO RIGHT TONIGHT/ Let The Good Times Roll, Creole	(Warner Bros. 5171)	1.25	5.00	60
SPANISH TWIST, THE/My Kind Of Woman	(Gone 5111)	2.00	8.00	61
STRAIGHT JACKET/Chattanooga Choo Choo	(Essex 348)	7.50	30.00	53

TITLE/FLIP	LABEL & NO.	GOOD	NEAR MINT	YR.
TANDY/You Call Everybody Darling	(Newtown 5025)	1.00	4.00	63
TENOR MAN/Up Goes My Love	(Newtown 5013)	1.00	4.00	63
THAT'S HOW I GOT TO MEMPHIS/ Ain't Love Funny, Ha Ha Ha	(United Artists 50483)	.75	3.00	69
YAKETY SAX/	(Logo 7005)	1.00	4.00	61
YEAR AGO THIS CHRISTMAS, A/ Don't Want To Be Alone This Christmas	(Holiday 111)	37.50	150.00	51
YES INDEED/Real Rock Drive	(Transworld 718)	6.25	25.00	53
(YOU HIT THE WRONG NOTE) BILLY GOAT/ Rockin' Rollin' Rover	(Decca 30314)	1.00	4.00	57

On some releases, the artists is shown as Bill Haley & His Comets. On others, only as Bill Haley. Some of the Essex releases are shown as by Bill Haley & the Saddlemen.)

HALF A SIXPENCE

TITLE/FLIP	LABEL & NO.	GOOD	NEAR MINT	YR.
MR. ZERO/Can It Be	(Mike 4005)	.75	3.00	66

HALF DOZEN, The

TITLE/FLIP	LABEL & NO.	GOOD	NEAR MINT	YR.
ANGELS LISTENED IN, THE/Another Day	(Dunwich 134)	1.00	4.00	66
ANGELS LISTENED IN, THE/Heat Wave	(Soma 1453)	1.00	4.00	66

HALL, Brenda

TITLE/FLIP	LABEL & NO.	GOOD	NEAR MINT	YR.
SOLDIER BABY OF MINE/Oh Eddy, My Baby	(Loma 2020)	1.25	5.00	65

HALL BROTHERS, The

TITLE/FLIP	LABEL & NO.	GOOD	NEAR MINT	YR.
MY WHITE CONVERTABLE/Now You Say We Are Thru	(Arc 4444)	1.00	4.00	

HALL, Daryl, & John Oates

TITLE/FLIP	LABEL & NO.	GOOD	NEAR MINT	YR.
BACK TOGETHER AGAIN/Room To Breathe	(RCA PB-10970)	.50	2.00	77
DON'T CHANGE/The Emptyness	(RCA PB-11181)	.50	2.00	77
DO WHAT YOU WANT, BE WHAT YOU ARE/ You'll Never Learn	(RCA PB-10808)	.50	2.00	76
GOODNIGHT & GOOD MORNING/ (Shown as by Whole Oates)	(Atlantic 2922)	1.00	4.00	72
I DON'T WANNA LOSE YOU/August Day	(RCA PB-11424)	.50	2.00	78
I'M SORRY/	(Atlantic 2939)	.75	3.00	73
IT'S A LAUGH/Serious Music	(RCA PB-11371)	.50	2.00	78
IT'S UNCANNY/Lilly (Are You Happy)	(Atlantic 3397)	.75	3.00	77
RICH GIRL/London, Luck & Love	(RCA PB-10860)	.50	2.00	77
SARA SMILE/Soldering	(RCA PB-10530)	.50	2.00	76
SHE'S GONE/I'm Just Like A Kid (Don't Make Me Feel Like A Man)	(Atlantic 2993)	.75	3.00	74
SHE'S GONE/I'm Just Like A Kid (Don't Make Me Feel Like A Man)	(Atlantic 3332)	.75	3.00	76
WAIT FOR ME/No Brain No Pain	(RCA PB-11747)	.50	2.00	79
WHY DO LOVERS (BREAK EACH OTHER'S HEART)/ The Girl Who Used To Be	(RCA PB-11132)	.50	2.00	77

HALLDAY, Chance

TITLE/FLIP	LABEL & NO.	GOOD	NEAR MINT	YR.
DEEP SLEEP/	(Buldog 193)	.75	3.00	

HALLEY, Bob

TITLE/FLIP	LABEL & NO.	GOOD	NEAR MINT	YR.
DOESN'T ANYBODY MAKE SHORT MOVIES ANYMORE/ Key To Room	(Columbia 4-42354)	.75	3.00	62
THAT TWISTIN' GIRL OF MINE/ Tonight You Belong To Me	(Columbia 4-42524)	.75	3.00	62

HALL, John (Of Orleans)

TITLE/FLIP	LABEL & NO.	GOOD	NEAR MINT	YR.
HOME AT LAST/	(Columbia-ARC 1105)	.50	2.00	79
NIGHT/	(Asylum 45499)	.50	2.00	78
RUN AWAY WITH ME/Cocaine Drain	(Columbia-ARC 11078)	.50	2.00	79

HALL, Lani (Of Sergio Mendes & Brasil '66)

TITLE/FLIP	LABEL & NO.	GOOD	NEAR MINT	YR.
BANQUET/	(A&M 1433)	.50	2.00	73
DOUBLE OR NOTHING/	(A&M 2144)	.50	2.00	79
HOW CAN I TELL YOU/	(A&M 1633)	.50	2.00	74
LOVE SONG/How Can I Tell You	(A&M 1385)	.50	2.00	73
NOBODY GETS THIS CLOSE TO ME/Magic Garden	(A&M 2177)	.50	2.00	79
TOO MANY MORNINGS/	(A&M 1903)	.50	2.00	77

Lani Hall was married to Herb Alpert.

HALL, Larry

TITLE/FLIP	LABEL & NO.	GOOD	NEAR MINT	YR.
FOR EVERY BOY/I'll Stay Single	(Strand 25016)	1.00	4.00	60
GIRL LIKE YOU, A/Rosemary	(Strand 25013)	1.00	4.00	60
LIPS OF WINE/Rebel Heart (Also see "Sweet Lips")	(Strand 25029)	1.00	4.00	60
SANDY/Lovin' Tree	(Hot 1)	1.25	5.00	59
SANDY/Lovin' Tree	(Strand 25007)	1.00	4.00	59
SWEET LIPS/Rebel Heart (Also released as "Lips Of Wine." They are identical recordings.)	(Strand 25029)	1.25	5.00	62

HALL, Linda

TITLE/FLIP	LABEL & NO.	GOOD	NEAR MINT	YR.
ALL SUMMER LONG/Beach Boys	(Artcraft 007)	1.50	6.00	65
ALMOST ALWAYS TRUE/G.I. Guy	(Cuca 1070)	1.50	6.00	62
YOU DON'T HAVE A WOODEN HEART/Treat Me Nice	(Cuca 1044)	1.50	6.00	61

HALLORAN, Jack, Singers

TITLE/FLIP	LABEL & NO.	GOOD	NEAR MINT	YR.
LITTLE DRUMMER BOY, THE/	(Dot 16275)	.75	3.00	63

HALLOWAY, Larry

TITLE/FLIP	LABEL & NO.	GOOD	NEAR MINT	YR.
BEATLE TEEN BEAT/Going Up	(Parkway 903)	1.25	5.00	64

HALL, Reggie

TITLE/FLIP	LABEL & NO.	GOOD	NEAR MINT	YR.
JOKE, THE/You Can Think What You Want	(Rip-Chess 1816)	.75	3.00	62

HALL, Roy

TITLE/FLIP	LABEL & NO.	GOOD	NEAR MINT	YR.
BLUE SUEDE SHOES/Luscious	(Decca 9-29880)	3.75	15.00	56
SEE YOU LATER ALLIGATOR/Don't Stop Now	(Decca 9-29786)	3.75	15.00	56
THREE ALLEY CATS/Diggin' The Boogie (Conterfeit copies exist of this release.)	(Decca 9-30060)	7.50	30.00	56
WHOLE LOT OF SHAKIN' GOIN' ON/All By Myself (Conterfeit copies exist of this release.)	(Decca 9-29697)	3.75	15.00	55

HALLYDAY, Johnny

TITLE/FLIP	LABEL & NO.	GOOD	NEAR MINT	YR.
BE BOP A LULA/I Got A Woman	(Philips 40024)	.75	3.00	62
HEY LITTLE GIRL/Caravan Of Lonely Men	(Philips 40043)	.75	3.00	62

HALO, Johnny

TITLE/FLIP	LABEL & NO.	GOOD	NEAR MINT	YR.
BETTY JEAN/More Lovin', Less Talkin' (With the 4 Seasons)	(Topix 6004)	3.75	15.00	62
ERRAND BOY/Babby Sitter (By Andri Prince)	(Southern Sound 109)	1.50	6.00	62

HAMILTON, Bobby

TITLE/FLIP	LABEL & NO.	GOOD	NEAR MINT	YR.
CRAZY EYES FOR YOU/While Walking Together	(Apt 25002)	1.00	4.00	58
UH-HUH/Lonesome Blues	(Diana 100)	1.00	4.00	59

HAMILTON, Dave

TITLE/FLIP	LABEL & NO.	GOOD	NEAR MINT	YR.
BEATLE WALK/The Argentina	(Fortune 861)	1.25	5.00	64

HAMILTON, George, IV

TITLE/FLIP	LABEL & NO.	GOOD	NEAR MINT	YR.
GEE/I Know Your Sweetheart	(ABC-Paramount 10028)	1.00	4.00	59
HIGH SCHOOL ROMANCE/Everybody's Boby	(ABC-Paramount 9838)	1.00	4.00	57
I KNOW WHERE I'M GOING/ Who's Taking You To The Prom	(ABC-Paramount 9924)	1.00	4.00	58
NOW & FOR ALWAYS/One Heart	(ABC-Paramount 9898)	1.00	4.00	58
ONLY ONE LOVE/If I Possessed A Printing Press	(ABC-Paramount 9782)	1.00	4.00	57
ROSE & A BABY RUTH, A/If You Don't Know	(Colonial 420)	3.75	15.00	56
ROSE & A BABY RUTH, A/If You Don't Know	(ABC-Paramount 9765)	1.00	4.00	56
STEADY GAME/Can You Blame Us	(ABC-Paramount 10009)	1.00	4.00	59
TWO OF US, THE/Lucy, Lucy	(ABC-Paramount 9966)	1.00	4.00	59
WHEN WILL I KNOW/Your Cheatin' Heart	(ABC-Paramount 9946)	1.00	4.00	58
WHY DON'T THEY UNDERSTAND/Even Tho'	(ABC-Paramount 9862)	1.00	4.00	57

HAMILTON, Joe Frank & Dennison (Dan Hamilton, Joe Frank Carollo, Alan Dennison)

TITLE/FLIP	LABEL & NO.	GOOD	NEAR MINT	YR.
DON'T FIGHT THE HANDS (THAT NEED YOU)/ Get On The Bus	(Playboy 6088)	.50	2.00	76
LIGHT UP THE WORLD WITH SUNSHINE/Houdini	(Playboy 6077)	.50	2.00	76
NOW THAT I'VE GOT YOU/Get On The Bus	(Playboy 5801)	.50	2.00	77

Also see Hamilton, Joe Frank & Reynolds

HAMILTON, Joe Frank & Reynolds

TITLE/FLIP	LABEL & NO.	GOOD	NEAR MINT	YR.
ANNABELLA/Goin' Down	(Dunhill 4287)	.75	3.00	71
DAISY MAE/	(Dunhill 4296)	.75	3.00	71
DON'T PULL YOUR LOVE/Funk-In-Wagnal	(Dunhill 4276)	.75	3.00	71
EVERYDAY WITHOUT YOU/Badman	(Playboy 6068)	.50	2.00	76
FALLIN' IN LOVE/So Good At Lovin' You	(Playboy 6024)	.50	2.00	75
WINNERS & LOSERS/Barroom Blues	(Playboy 6054)	.50	2.00	75

Although (Tom) Reynolds is credited, actually it is Alan Dennison who appeares on these Playboy issues.

HAMILTON, Roy

TITLE/FLIP	LABEL & NO.	GOOD	NEAR MINT	YR.
ALL OF A SUDDEN MY HEART SINGS/ I'm Gonna Lock You In My Heart	(Epic 5-9232)	1.00	4.00	57
CLIMB EV'RY MOUNTAIN/I'll Come Running Back To You	(Epic 5-9520)	.75	3.00	62
CLOCK, THE/I Get The Blues When It Rains	(Epic 5-9390)	1.00	4.00	60
CRAZY FEELIN'/In A Dream	(Epic 5-9268)	1.00	4.00	58
DON'T COME CRYIN' TO ME/If Only I Had Known	(Epic 5-9492)	.75	3.00	62
DON'T LET GO/The Right To Love	(Epic 5-9257)	1.00	4.00	58
EBB TIDE/Beware	(Epic 5-9068)	1.25	5.00	54
EVERYBODY'S GOT A HOME/Take Me With You	(Epic 5-9132)	1.25	5.00	55
FORGIVE THIS FOOL/You Wanted To Change Me	(Epic 5-9111)	1.00	4.00	55
GREAT ROMANCE, A/On My Way Home	(Epic 5-9342)	1.00	4.00	59
HURT/Star Of Love	(Epic 5-9086)	1.25	5.00	54
I AM/Earthquake	(Epic 5-9538)	.75	3.00	62
I BELIEVE/If You Are But A Dream	(Epic 5-9092)	1.25	5.00	55
I NEED YOUR LOVIN'/Blue Prelude	(Epic 5-9307)	1.00	4.00	59
I TAUGHT HER EVERYTHING SHE KNOWS/Lament	(RCA Victor 47-9061)	.75	3.00	67
I TOOK MY GRIEF TO HIM/Chained	(Epic 5-9180)	1.00	4.00	56
IF/There We Were	(Epic 5-9466)	.75	3.00	61
IF I LOVED YOU/So Let There Be Love	(Epic 5-9047)	1.25	5.00	54
IMPOSSIBLE DREAM, THE/She's Got A Heart	(RCA Victor 47-8813)	.75	3.00	66
IT'S ONLY MAKE BELIEVE	(AGP 125)	.75	3.00	69
LIPS/Jungle Fever	(Epic 5-9274)	1.00	4.00	58
LITTLE VOICE, A/All This Is Mine	(Epic 5-9118)	1.00	4.00	55
LONELY HANDS/Your Love	(Epic 5-9407)	1.00	4.00	60
LOVER'S PRAYER, A/Never Let Me Go	(Epic 5-9398)	1.00	4.00	60
MY FAITH, MY HOPE, MY LOVE/So Long	(Epic 5-9212)	1.00	4.00	57
PLEASE LOUISE/No Substitute For Love	(Epic 5-9449)	.75	3.00	61
PLEDGING MY LOVE/My One & Only Love	(Epic 5-9294)	1.00	4.00	58
SIMPLE PRAYER, A/A Mother's Love	(Epic 5-9203)	1.00	4.00	57
SINCE I FELL FOR YOU/Somebody Somewhere	(Epic 5-9160)	1.00	4.00	56
SOMEWHERE ALONG THE WAY/It's Never To Late	(Epic 5-9301)	1.00	4.00	59
SWEET VIOLET/A Thousand Tears Ago	(MGM K-13315)	.75	3.00	65
THAT OLD FEELING/The Aisle	(Epic 5-9224)	1.00	4.00	57
THERE GOES MY HEART/Walk Along	(Epic 5-9147)	1.00	4.00	56
THERE SHE IS/Panic Is On	(MGM K-13217)	.75	3.00	64
TIME MARCHES ON/Take It Easy, Joe	(Epic 5-9323)	1.00	4.00	59
TO THE ONE I LOVE/You're Gonna Need Magic	(Epic 5-9443)	.75	3.00	61
YOU'LL NEVER WALK ALONE/ I'm Gonna Sit Right Down & Cry (Over You)	(Epic 5-9015)	1.25	5.00	54
UNCHAINED MELODY/From Here To Eternity	(Epic 5-9102)	1.00	4.00	55
WAIT FOR ME/Everything	(Epic 5-9282)	1.00	4.00	58
WALK HAND IN HAND/Crackin' Up	(RCA Victor 47-8960)	.75	3.00	66
WITHOUT A SONG/Cuban Love Song	(Epic 5-9125)	1.00	4.00	55
YOU CAN HAVE HER/Abide With Me	(Epic 5-9434)	.75	3.00	61

HAMILTON, Russ

TITLE/FLIP	LABEL & NO.	GOOD	NEAR MINT	YR.
RAINBOW/We Will Make Love	(Kapp 184)	1.00	4.00	57
WEDDING RING/I Still Belong To You	(Kapp 194)	1.00	4.00	57

HAMLET

TITLE/FLIP	LABEL & NO.	GOOD	NEAR MINT	YR.
I FEEL LIKE SMILING (TONIGHT)/Voodoo Man	(Capitol 3716)	.50	2.00	73

HAMMEL, Karl, Jr.

TITLE/FLIP	LABEL & NO.	GOOD	NEAR MINT	YR.
SUMMER SOUVENIRS/The Magic Of Summer	(Arliss 1007)	.75	3.00	61

HAMMER, Jan, Group

TITLE/FLIP	LABEL & NO.	GOOD	NEAR MINT	YR.
OH, PRETTY WOMAN/	(Asylum 46548)	.50	2.00	79
TOO MUCH TO LOSE/What It Is	(Nemperor 7516)	.50	2.00	78
WINDOW OF LOVE/Don't You Know	(Nemperor 7515)	.50	2.00	77

HAMMOND, Albert (Of The Magic Lanterns)

TITLE/FLIP	LABEL & NO.	GOOD	NEAR MINT	YR.
AIR DISASTER/Candle Light, Sweet Candle Light	(Mums 6030)	.50	2.00	74
DOWN BY THE RIVER/The Last One To Know	(Mums 6009)	.50	2.00	72
FREE ELECTRIC BAND, THE/You Taught Me To Sing The Blues	(Mums 6018)	.50	2.00	73
HALF A MILLION MILES FROM HOME/ I Think I'll Go That Way	(Mums 6024)	.50	2.00	73
IF YOU GOTTA BREAK ANOTHR.R HEART/ That Old Merican Dream	(Mums 6015)	.50	2.00	73
I'M A TRAIN/Brand New Day	(Mums 6026)	.50	2.00	74
IT NEVER RAINS IN SOUTHERN CALIFORNIA/ Anyone Here In The Audience	(Mums 6011)	.50	2.00	72
MOONLIGHT LADY/Cry Baby	(Epic 50277)	.50	2.00	76
NAMES, TAGS, NUMBERS & LABELS/Fountain Avenue	(Mums 6032)	.50	2.00	74
99 MILES FROM L.A./Rivers Are For Boats	(Mums 6037)	.50	2.00	75
PEACEMAKER, THE/Who's For Lunch Today?	(Mums 6021)	.50	2.00	73

Also see Hammond-Hazlewood

HAMMOND, Wayne, & The Starfires

TITLE/FLIP	LABEL & NO.	GOOD	NEAR MINT	YR.
CAN'T SEE WHY/Carolyn	(Gala 105)	3.00	12.00	

HAMPSHIRE, Keith

TITLE/FLIP	LABEL & NO.	GOOD	NEAR MINT	YR.
BIG TIME OPERATOR/	(A&M 1486)	.75	3.00	73
DAYTIME NIGHT-TIME/	(A&M 1396)	.75	3.00	72
DAYTIME NIGHT-TIME/	(A&M 1403)	.75	3.00	72
FIRST CUT IS THE DEEPEST/You Can't Hear The Song I Sing	(A&M 1432)	.75	3.00	73

TITLE/FLIP	LABEL & NO.	GOOD	NEAR MINT	YR.
HAMPTON, Johnny				
BEATLE DANCE/I Can't Get Along With You	(Rose 003)	1.00	4.00	64
HAMPTON, Paul				
LIVE A LIFE OF LOVE/Slam Bam, Thank You Ma'am	(Columbia 4-41145)	2.00	8.00	58
HANDY, Wayne				
SAY YEAH/Could It Be	(Renown 102)	.75	3.00	
HANEY, Bill				
CAUSE YOU WERE THERE/City Days & Country Nights	(Rav CAL-13)	.75	3.00	77
HANSEN BROTHERS, The (Paul, Dale, Tom, Ray)				
IF IT WASN'T FOR ELVIS/ Dancin' At The Disco	(Paul, Dale, Tom & Ray 001)	.75	3.00	77
(With Deke Rivers)				
MY FRIEND ELVIS/Tonite's The Time	(AAA-Aron 001)	.50	2.00	77
YOU'RE MEMORY IN MY MIND/ My Friend Elvis-If It Wasn't For Elvis	(Starfire 102)	.75	3.00	78
YOU'RE MINE ANITA/	(Jazzy Be Bopper 001)	.75	3.00	78
HANSON				
MODERN DAY RELIGION/	(Manticore 2004)	.50	2.00	73
HANSON, Bo				
BLACK RIDERS, THE/Flight To The Ford	(Charisma 104)	.50	2.00	73
HANSON, Jerry				
COOL MAN!/Why Not Cha Cha Cha	(Colpix 137)	1.00	4.00	61
HAPPENINGS, The (Featuring Bob Miranda)				
ANSWER ME MY LOVE/I Need A Woman	(Jubilee 5686)	.75	3.00	70
BREAKING UP IS HARD TO DO/Anyway	(BT Puppy 543)	.75	3.00	68
CRAZY LOVE/Chain Of Hands	(Jubilee 5702)	.75	3.00	70
CRAZY RHYTHM/Love Song Of Mommy & Daddy	(BT Puppy 545)	1.00	4.00	68
EL PASO COUNTY JAIL/Won't Anybody Listen	(Jubilee 5677)	.75	3.00	69
EVERYBODY IS A STAR/Evergreen (By Bob Miranda)	(BT Puppy 5709)	.75	3.00	69
GIRL ON A SWING/When I Lock My Door (By Bob Mirandaer)	(BT Puppy 544)	1.25	5.00	68
GIRLS ON THE GO/Go Go	(BT Puppy 517)	1.00	4.00	66
GO AWAY LITTLE GIRL/Tea Time	(BT Puppy 522)	.75	3.00	66
GOODNIGHT MY LOVE/Lillies By Monet	(BT Puppy 523)	.75	3.00	66
I GOT RHYTHM/You're In A Bad Way	(BT Puppy 527)	.75	3.00	67
HAVE YOURSELF A MERRY CHRISTMAS/	(BT Puppy 181)	1.25	5.00	66
(Promotional issue)				
LULLABY IN THE RAIN/I Wish You Could Know Me	(BT Puppy 5712)	.75	3.00	69
MAKE YOUR OWN KIND OF MUSIC/	(Jubilee 5721)	1.00	4.00	69
ME WITHOUT YOU/God Bless JoAnna	(Big Tree 153)	1.00	4.00	72
MUSIC MUSIC MUSIC/When I Lock My Door	(BT Puppy 538)	.75	3.00	68
MY MAMMY/I Believe In Nothing	(BT Puppy 527)	.75	3.00	67
RANDY/Love Song Of Mommy & Daddy	(BT Puppy 540)	.75	3.00	68
SEALED WITH A KISS/Anyway	(BT Puppy 542)	.75	3.00	68
SEE YOU IN SEPTEMBER/He Thinks He's A Hero	(BT Puppy 520)	.75	3.00	66
SWEET SEPTEMBER/Condition Red	(Jubilee 5703)	1.25	5.00	70
(Shown as by the Honor Society)				
THAT'S ALL I WANT FROM YOU/He Thinks He's A Hero	(BT Puppy 549)	1.25	5.00	69
THAT'S WHY I LOVE YOU/	(Midland Intl. 10897)	.75	3.00	77
(Shown as by Bob Miranda & the Happenings)				
TOMORROW; TODAY WILL BE YESTERDAY/Chain Of Hands	(Jubilee 5698)	.75	3.00	70
WE'RE ALMOST HOME/	(Musicore 1482)	1.25	5.00	72
(Shown as by Sun Dog)				
WHERE DO I GO-BE IN (HARE KRISHNA)/ New Day Comin'	(Jubilee 5666)	.75	3.00	69
WHY DO FOOLS FALL IN LOVE/ When The Summer Is Through	(BT Puppy 532)	.75	3.00	67
WORKING MY WAY BACK TO YOU/Strawberry Morning	(Big Tree 146)	1.25	5.00	72
Also see 4 Graduates, The				
HAPPY JESTERS, The				
JUST BECAUSE/Heart Of My Heart	(Dot 15566)	1.25	5.00	57
HAPPYTONES, The				
SUMMERTIME NIGHTS/Papa Shame	(Colpix 693)	1.00	4.00	63
HARBINGER COMPLEX, The				
I THINK I'M DOWN/My Dear & Kind Sir	(Brent 7056)	1.25	5.00	66
HARBOR LIGHTS, The (With Jay Black)				
ANGEL OF LOVE/Tick-a Tick-a-tock	(Mala 422)	2.50	10.00	60
WHAT WOULD I DO WITHOUT YOU/ Is That Too Much To Ask	(Jaro 77020)	2.50	10.00	60
(Shown as by the Harbor Lites)				
Also see Jay & The Americans				
HARDLY WORTHIT PLAYERS: see Senator Bobby				
HARDIN, Tim				
DON'T MAKE PROMISES/ Lady Came From Baltimore	(Verve Forecast 3078)	.75	3.00	68
DO THE DO/Sweet Lady	(Columbia 4-45695)	.75	3.00	70
SIMPLE SONG OF FREEDOM/Question Of Birth	(Columbia 4-44920)	.75	3.00	69
HARDSELL, Harold				
INSTANT REPLAY/	(Decca 32892)	.75	3.00	71
SPEAKING OF STREAKING/Streak Easy	(Dunhill 4384)	.75	3.00	74
HARLAN, Billy				
SCHOOL HOUSE ROCK/I Wanna Bop	(Brunswick 9-55066)	15.00	60.00	58
HARLEY & THE NIGHT RIDERS				
WILD ANGELS RIDE TONIGHT/Won't You Help Me	(Manhattan 806)	.75	3.00	67
SEBASTIAN/	(EMI 3846)	.50	2.00	74
TUMBLING DOWN/	(EMI 4023)	.50	2.00	75
HARMONICATS, The				
BYE BYE BLUES/Willow Weep For Me	(London 769)	1.50	6.00	50
CHERRY PINK & APPLE BLOSSOM WHITE/ Lonely Love	(Columbia 4-41816)	.75	3.00	60
(Shown as by Jerry Murad's Harmonicats)				
HARBOR LIGHTS/At Sundown	(Mercury 5461)	1.25	5.00	50
NIGHT TRAIN/Hootin'	(Mercury 5869)	1.25	5.00	52
PEG O' MY HEART/Fantasy Impromptu	(London 512)	2.00	8.00	49
PETITE WALTZ/Warsaw Waltz	(Mercury 5493)	1.25	5.00	50
Instrumentals				
HARMONY GRITS, The				
AM I TO BE THE ONE/I Could Have Told You	(End 1051)	1.00	4.00	59
SANTA CLAUS IS COMIN' TO TOWN/Gee	(End 1063)	1.00	4.00	59
HARNELL, Joe				
DIANE/The Walking Song	(Kapp 521)	.75	3.00	63
FLY ME TO THE MOON, BOSSA NOVA/Harlem Nocturne	(Kapp 497)	.75	3.00	62
MIDNIGHT COWBOY/	(Motown 1154)	.50	2.00	73
MY CHERIE AMOUR/	(Motown 1161)	.50	2.00	73
MY ONE & ONLY LOVE/Our Day Will Come	(Kapp 528)	.75	3.00	63
THEME FROM "THE INCREDIBLE HULK"/ Love Theme From "The Incredible Hulk"	(MCA 40953)	.50	2.00	79
Instrumentals				
HARPER, Chuck (Chuck Fassett)				
SUMMER IS THRU/Call On Me	(Felsted 8658)	2.00	8.00	62
Also see Regents, The				
HARPER, Janice				
BON VOYAGE/Tell Me That You Love Me	(Prep 111)	1.00	4.00	57
CRY ME A RIVER/Just Say I Love Him	(Capitol 4324)	1.00	4.00	59
DEVOTION/Hands Across The Sea	(Capitol 3984)	1.00	4.00	58
THAT'S WHY I WAS BORN/Moonlit Sea	(Prep 123)	1.00	4.00	57
HARPER, Reed				
OH ELVIS!/O' Sole Mia-Rock & Roll	(Pyramid 4012)	2.50	10.00	
HARPER'S BIZARRE (Featuring Ted Templeman)				
ANYTHING GOES/Malibu U.	(Warner Bros. 7063)	.75	3.00	67
ANYTHING GOES/Virginia City	(Warner Bros. 7388)	.75	3.00	69
BATTLE OF NEW ORLEANS/Green Apple Tree	(Warner Bros. 7223)	.75	3.00	68
BOTH SIDES NOW/Small Talk	(Warner Bros. 7200)	.75	3.00	68
CHATTANOOGA CHOO CHOO/Hey You In The Crowd	(Warner Bros. 7090)	.75	3.00	67
COME TO THE SUNSHINE/The Debutantes Ball	(Warner Bros. 7028)	.75	3.00	67
COTTON CANDY SANDMAN/Virginia City	(Warner Bros. 7172)	.75	3.00	68
59TH STREET BRIDGE SONG (FEELIN' GROOVY)/ Lost My Love Today	(Warner Bros. 5890)	.75	3.00	67
I LOVE YOU, ALICE B. TOKLAS/ Look To The Rainbow	(Warner Bros. 7238)	.75	3.00	68
IF WE EVER NEEDED THE LORD BEFORE/Mad	(Warner Bros. 7399)	.75	3.00	70
POLY HIGH/Knock On Wood	(Warner Bros. 7647)	.75	3.00	72
POLY HIGH/Soft Soundin' Music	(Warner Bros. 7377)	.75	3.00	69
WITCHI TAI TO/Knock On Wood	(Warner Bros. 7296)	.75	3.00	69
YOU GOTTA MAKE YOUR OWN SUNSHINE/	(Forest Bay Co. 7547)	.50	2.00	75
HARPS, The				
MARIE/Daddy's Going Away Again	(Laurie 3239)	1.50	6.00	64
Also see Camelots, The				
HARRIS, Dave				
ELVIS & UNMENTIONABLES/ The Mad 40 Show By The Mad D.J.	(Town 2004)	3.75	15.00	

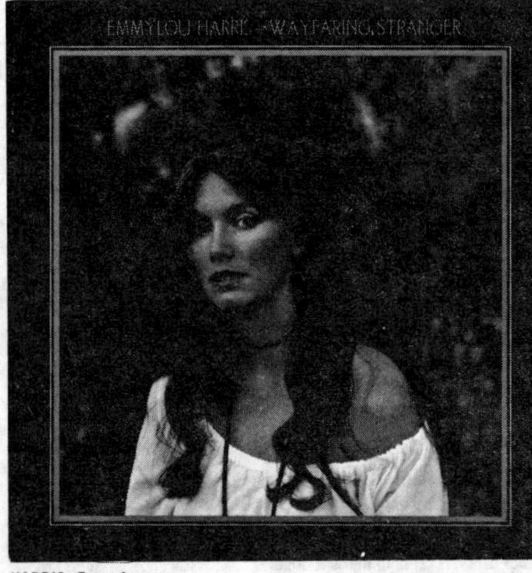

TITLE/FLIP	LABEL & NO.	GOOD	NEAR MINT	YR.
HARRIS, Emmylou				
BLUE KENTUCKY GIRL/Leaving Louisiana In The Broad Daylight	(Warner Bros. 49056)	.50	2.00	79
EASY FROM NOW ON/ You're Supposed To Be Feeling Good	(Warner Bros. 8623)	.50	2.00	78
HERE, THERE & EVERYWHERE/Together Again	(Reprise 1346)	.75	3.00	76
IF I COULD ONLY WIN YOUR LOVE/ Boulder To Birmingham	(Reprise 1332)	.75	3.00	75
I'LL BE YOUR BABY TONIGHT/I'll Never Fall In Love	(Jubilee 5679)	2.00	8.00	69
LIGHT OF THE STABLE/Bluebird Wine	(Reprise 1341)	1.25	5.00	75
LIGHT OF THE STABLE/Bluebird Wine	(Reprise 1341)	2.00	8.00	75
(Picture sleeve)				
LIGHT OF THE STABLE/Boulder To Birmingham	(Reprise 1379)	.75	3.00	77
LOVE DOESN'T CARE WHOSE HOUSE IT LIVES IN/ Little Darlin'	(Asylum 7922)	.50	2.00	76
MAKING BELIEVE/I'll Be Your San Antonio Rose	(Warner Bros. 8388)	.50	2.00	77
ONE OF THESE DAYS/Till I Gain Control Again	(Reprise 1353)	.75	3.00	76
PADDY/Fugue For The Ox	(Jubilee 5697)	1.50	6.00	70
SAVE THE LAST DANCE FOR ME/ Even Cowgirls Get The Blues	(Warner Bros. 8815)	.50	2.00	79
SWEET DREAMS/Amarillo	(Reprise 1371)	.75	3.00	76
TO DADDY/Tulsa Queen	(Warner Bros. 8498)	.50	2.00	77
TOO FAR GONE/Boulder To Birmingham	(Reprise 1326)	.75	3.00	75
TOO FAR GONE/Tulsa Queen	(Warner Bros. 8732)	.50	2.00	78
TWO MORE BOTTLES OF WINE/ I Ain't Living Long Like This	(Warner Bros. 8553)	.50	2.00	78
(YOU NEVER CAN TELL) C'EST LA VIE/ You're Supposed To Be Feeling Good	(Warner Bros. 8329)	.50	2.00	77
WAYFARING STRANGER/Green Pastures	(Warner Bros. 49239)	.50	2.00	80
Also see Orbison, Roy & Emmylou Harris				
HARRIS, Eddie				
EXODUS/Alicia	(Vee Jay 378)	.75	3.00	61
(Instrumentals)				
HARRIS, Frosty				
BIG NOISE FROM L.A./That's All	(Dot 16171)	.75	3.00	60
(Instrumentals)				
HARRIS, Genee				
BYE BYE ELVIS/You're Like A Jumpin' Jack	(ABC-Paramount 9900)	3.00	12.00	58
HARRIS, Leslie				
COME ON LITTLE SARAH/I Hung My Head & Cried	(Shad 5006)	1.00	4.00	60
HARRIS, Nick, & The Soundbarriers				
MUSIC MUSIC/Big Nick	(Northwest Sound 10)	1.00	4.00	
HARRISON, Bob 'Lil Elvis"				
ELVIS IS GONE (BUT HIS SPIRIT LIVES ON)/ Yellow Moon	(Lil Elvis World Inc. 114)	.50	2.00	77
HARRISON, Danny				
SPEAK OF THE DEVIL/I'm A Rollin' Stone	(Coral 62450)	.75	3.00	64
HARRISON, George				
BANGLA-DESH (WE'VE GOT TO RELIEVE)/Deep Blue	(Apple 1836)	.50	2.00	71
BANGLA-DESH (WE'VE GOT TO RELIEVE)/Deep Blue	(Apple 1836)	1.50	6.00	71
(Picture sleeve)				
BLOW AWAY/Soft-Hearted Hana	(Dark Horse DRC-8763)	.50	2.00	79
BLOW AWAY/Blow Away	(Dark Horse DRC-8763)	1.25	5.00	79
(Promotional issue)				
BLOW AWAY/Soft-Hearted Hana	(Dark Horse DRC-8763)	1.00	4.00	79
(Picture sleeve)				
CRACKERBOX PALACE/Learning How To Love You	(Dark Horse DRC-8313)	.50	2.00	77
CRACKERBOX PALACE/Learning How To Love You	(Dark Horse DRC-8313)	1.25	5.00	77
(Promotional issue)				
DARK HORSE/I Don't Care Anymore	(Apple 1877)	.50	2.00	74
DARK HORSE/Dark Horse	(Apple 1877)	1.25	5.00	74
(Promotional issue)				
DARK HORSE/I Don't Care Anymore	(Apple 1877)	1.00	4.00	74
(Picture sleeve)				
DARK HORSE/You (Capitol's round logo)	(Capitol Starline 6245)	.50	2.00	77
DARK HORSE/You (Capitol's dome logo)	(Capitol Starline 6245)	.50	2.00	77
DING DONG, DING DONG/Hari's On Tour (Express)	(Apple 1879)	.50	2.00	75
DING DONG, DING DONG/Hari's On Tour (Express)	(Apple 1879)	1.25	5.00	75
(Promotional issue)				
DING DONG, DING DONG/Hari's On Tour (Express)	(Apple 1879)	1.00	4.00	75
(Picture sleeve)				
GIVE ME LOVE (GIVE ME PEACE ON EARTH)/Miss O'Dell	(Apple 1862)	.50	2.00	73
GIVE ME LOVE (GIVE ME PEACE ON EARTH)/Miss O'Dell	(Apple 1862)	1.25	5.00	73
(Promotional issue)				
LOVE COMES TO EVERYONE/Soft Touch	(Dark Horse DRC-8844)	.50	2.00	79
LOVE COMES TO EVERYONE/Soft Touch	(Dark Horse DRC-8844)	1.25	5.00	79
(Promotional issue)				
MY SWEET LORD/Isn't It A Pity	(Apple 2995)	.50	2.00	70
MY SWEET LORD/My Sweet Lord	(Apple 2995)	1.25	5.00	70
(Promotional issue)				
MY SWEET LORD/Isn't It A Pity	(Apple 2995)	2.50	10.00	70
(Picture sleeve)				
THIS GUITAR (CAN'T KEEP FROM CRYING)/Maya Love	(Apple 1885)	.50	2.00	75
THIS GUITAR (CAN'T KEEP FROM CRYING)/ This Guitar (Can't Keep From Crying)	(Apple 1885)	1.25	5.00	75
(Promotional issue)				
THIS SONG/Learning How To Love You	(Dark Horse DRC-8294)	.50	2.00	76
THIS SONG/This Song	(Dark Horse DRC-8294)	1.25	5.00	76
(Promotional issue)				
THIS SONG/Learning How To Love You	(Dark Horse DRC-8294)	1.50	6.00	76
(Promotional picture sleeve)				
WHAT IS LIFE/Apple Scruffs	(Apple 1828)	.50	2.00	71
WHAT IS LIFE/What Is Life	(Apple 1828)	1.50	6.00	71
(Promotional issue)				
WHAT IS LIFE/Apple Scruffs	(Apple 1828)	2.50	10.00	71
(Picture sleeve)				
YOU/World Of Stone	(Apple 1884)	.50	2.00	75
YOU/You	(Apple 1884)	1.25	5.00	75
(Promotional issue)				
YOU/World Of Stone	(Apple 1884)	1.00	4.00	75
(Picture sleeve)				
Also see Hopkins, Nicky				
Also see Hosford, Larry				
HARRISON, Jim & Bob				
LITTLE SCHOOLGIRL/Baby I Love You	(Smash 1803)	.75	3.00	63
HARRISON, Mike (Of Spooky Tooth)				
SOMEWHERE OVER THE RAINBOW/Okay Lay Lady Lay	(Island 052)	.50	2.00	75
HARRISON, Noel				
ANOTHER VIRGIN SPRING/Tin Wedding	(Reprise 0914)	.75	3.00	70
CHERYL'S GOING HOME/In A Dusty Old Room	(London 20017)	.75	3.00	66
GREAT ELECTRIC EXPERIMENT IS OVER, THE/ I'll Be Your Baby Tonight	(Reprise 0795)	.75	3.00	68
IT'S ALL OVER NOW, BABY BLUE/Much As I Love You	(London 9815)	.75	3.00	66
MAN BEHIND THE RED BALLOON/Marieke	(London 20011)	.75	3.00	66
ONE TOO MANY MORNINGS/Barbara Allen	(London 9755)	.75	3.00	65
OUT FOR THE DAY/Fly Sing Song	(London 20021)	.75	3.00	67
SUZANNE/Life Is A Dream	(Reprise 0615)	.75	3.00	67
WINDMILLS OF YOUR MIND, THE/Leitch On The Beach	(Reprise 0758)	.75	3.00	68
YOUNG GIRL, A/The Future Mr. 'Awkins	(London 9795)	.75	3.00	65
HARRIS, Phil				
CHATTANOOGIE SHOE SHINE BOY/That's A Plenty	(RCA Victor 47-3692)	2.00	8.00	50
DIG FOR YOUR DINNER/I've Been Floating	(RCA Victor 47-3825)	2.00	8.00	50
EVERYBODY WANTS TO BE A CAT/Thomas O'Malley Cat	(Buena Vista 478)	.75	3.00	64
GOLDEN TRAIN/Hillbilly Ghost	(RCA Victor 47-4224)	2.00	8.00	51
HAMBONE/Mama's On The Warpath	(RCA Victor 47-4584)	2.00	8.00	52
HOW DO'YE DO AN SHAKE HANDS/	(RCA Victor 47-4225)	2.00	8.00	51
LETTER, THE/Possibilities	(RCA Victor 47-4124)	2.00	8.00	51
OLD MASTER PAINTER, THE/	(RCA Victor 47-3114)	2.50	10.00	49
PIECE OF PUDDIN'/Hi Diddle Diddle	(RCA Victor 47-4993)	.75	3.00	52
POTATO CHIPS/Under The Lamp Post	(RCA Victor 47-4750)	2.00	8.00	52
RUGGED BUT RIGHT/Where The Blues Were	(RCA Victor 47-4342)	2.00	8.00	51
RUN RED RUN/Old Man Time	(Reprise 20117)	.75	3.00	61
SIX WHITE BOOMERS/Lost Little Boy	(Epic 9641)	.75	3.00	63
SOUTHERN FRIED BOOGIE/Oh What A Face	(RCA Victor 47-4070)	2.00	8.00	51
THAT'S WHAT I LIKE ABOUT THE SOUTH/ Dark Town Poker Club	(RCA Victor 47-2471)	2.50	10.00	49
THING, THE/Goofus	(RCA Victor 47-3968)	2.50	10.00	50
WINE, WOMEN & SONG/8th Street Association	(RCA Victor 47-4450)	2.00	8.00	52
HARRIS, Richard				
DIDN'T WE/Paper Chase	(Dunhill 4194)	.75	3.00	69
HOW TO HANDLE A WOMAN/ I Wonder What The King Is Doing Tonight	(Warner Bros. 7215)	.75	3.00	67
MACARTHUR PARK/Didn't We	(Dunhill 4132)	.75	3.00	68
MACARTHUR PARK/Didn't We	(Dunhill 4132)	1.00	4.00	68
(Promotional issue)				
MACARTHUR PARK/Didn't We	(Dunhill 4132)	1.25	5.00	68
(Picture sleeve for promotional issue)				
MY BOY/Why Did You Leave Me	(Dunhill 4293)	.75	3.00	71
THAT'S THE WAY IT WAS/The Hive	(Dunhill 4175)	.75	3.00	68
THERE ARE TOO MANY SAVIORS ON MY CROSS/	(Dunhill 4322)	.75	3.00	72
YARD WENT ON FOREVER, THE/Lucky Me	(Dunhill 4170)	.75	3.00	68
HARRIS, Rolf				
BIG DOG/Jake The Peg	(Epic 10037)	.75	3.00	66
BIG BLACK HAT, THE/Lost Little Boy	(20th Fox 230)	1.00	4.00	61
COURT OF KING CARACTUS/Two Buffalos	(Epic 9682)	.75	3.00	64
LOST LITTLE BOY/Six White Boomers	(Epic 9641)	.75	3.00	63
NICK TEEN & AL K. HALL/I Know A Man	(Epic 9615)	.75	3.00	63
RINGO FOR PRESIDENT/Click Go The Shears	(Epic 9721)	1.25	5.00	64
SUN ARISE/Someone's Pinched My Winkles	(Epic 9567)	.75	3.00	63
THING, THE/Wild Colonial Boy	(Epic 9756)	.75	3.00	65
TIE MY HUNTING DOG DOWN, JED/Five Young Apprentices	(Epic 9780)	.75	3.00	65
TIE ME KANGAROO DOWN SPORT/Nick Teen & Al K. Hall	(20th Fox 207)	1.25	5.00	60
TIE ME KANGAROO DOWN SPORT/Big Black Hat	(Epic 9596)	.75	3.00	63
TWO LITTLE BOYS/I Love My Love	(MGM 14103)	.75	3.00	70
HARRIS, Shawn (Of The West Coast Pop Arts Experimental Band)				
I'LL CRY OUT/Color Of Your Eyes	(Capitol 3697)	.75	3.00	73
HARRIS, Slim, & His Sterophonixs				
FRANKIE & JOHNNY/Secret Lover	(Fran 102)	.75	3.00	
HARRIS, Tony				
CHICKEN, BABY, CHICKEN/I'll Forever Love You	(Ebb 104)	1.25	5.00	56
HARRIS, Tony, & The Woodies				
GO GO LITTLE SCRAMBLER/Poor Boy	(Triumph 60)	1.25	5.00	
HARRY & THE CROCO-DILES				
CHEETA/Jungle Hootenanny	(RCA Victor 47-8244)	.75	3.00	63
HARSHMAN, Robert Luke: see Hart, Bobby				
HART, Billy & Don				
BLABBERMOUTH/Checkmated & Bingoed	(Roulette 4172)	1.00	4.00	59
HART, Bob & Margie				
EATER, THE/Conversation	(Twi-Lite 1007)	.75	3.00	
(Comedy)				

The Hilltoppers

The Hullaballoos

Herman's Hermits

TITLE/FLIP	LABEL & NO.	GOOD	NEAR MINT	YR.
HART, Bobby (Robert L Harshman)				
AROUND THE CORNER/Cry My Eyes Out	(DCP 1152)	.75	3.00	66
EASY EVIL/California	(Chelsea 0026)	.75	3.00	72
GIRL I USED TO KNOW/The Spider & The Fly	(Bamboo 507)	2.50	10.00	61
GIRL IN THE WINDOW/Journey Of Love	(Reel 100)	1.25	5.00	60
GIRL IN THE WINDOW/Journey Of Love	(Reel 100)	1.00	4.00	61
HARD CORE MAN (THEME FROM "FREEBIE & THE BEAN")/ To Keep From Crying	(Warner Bros. 8058)	.75	3.00	74
IS YOU IS OR IS YOU AIN'T MY BABY/Girl Of My Dreams	(Guyden 2022)	3.75	15.00	59
(Shown as by Robert Luke Harshman)				
JEALOUS FEELING/Baby, Let Your Hair Down	(DCP 1142)	2.00	8.00	65
LONELIEST NIGHT, THE/	(Warner-Curb 49079)	.50	2.00	79
LOVE WHATCHA DOIN' TO ME/Stop Talkin', Start Lovin'	(Radio 122)	5.00	20.00	60
(Shown as by Robert Luke Harshman)				
LOVESICK BLUES/I Think It's Called A Heartache	(Infinity 022)	1.00	4.00	62
THAT'LL BE THE DAY/Turn On Your Lovelight	(DCP 1113)	.75	3.00	64
TOO MANY TEARDROPS/The People Next Door	(Infinity 017)	1.00	4.00	62
Also see Boyce & Heart				
HART, Judy				
THAT'S ENOUGH/Didn't He Ramble	(Staccatto 101)	.75	3.00	62
HARTFORD, John				
ONE TOO MANY MORNINGS/	(Ampex 11019)	.75	3.00	70
HARTFORD, Ken				
JAY WALKER/Little Joe, Go Lightly	(Southern Sound 119)	2.50	10.00	63
(With Frankie Valli)				
HARTMAN, Dan (Of The Edgar Winter Group)				
BOOGIE ALL SUMMER/Love Is A Natural	(Blue Sky 2776)	.50	2.00	79
HANDS DOWN/Hands Down (Hands Up)	(Blue Sky 2782)	.50	2.00	79
HIGH SIGN/	(Blue Sky 2760)	.50	2.00	76
INSTANT REPLAY/Instant Replay (Replayed)	(Blue Sky 2772)	.50	2.00	78
RELIGHT MY FIRE/Vertigo	(Blue Sky 2784)	.50	2.00	79
THIS IS IT/Countdown	(Blue Sky 2775)	.50	2.00	79
HARTMAN, Lisa				
KENTUCKY RAINBOW/	(Kirshner 4265)	.50	2.00	77
NOBODY LIKES LOVIN' MORE THAN I DO (A DREAMER OF DREAMS)/	(Kirshner 4275)	.50	2.00	78
PICKIN' UP THE PIECES/	(Kirshner 4260)	.50	2.00	76
SAYING HELLO, SAYING I LOVE YOU, SAYING GOODBYE/	(Kirshner 4262)	.50	2.00	77
WALK AWAY/	(Kirshner 4283)	.50	2.00	79
HART, Mickey (Of The Grateful Dead)				
BLIND JOHN/Pump Man	(Warner Bros. 7644)	1.00	4.00	71
HART, Richie				
GREAT DUANE (EDDY), THE/I'm Hyptnotized	(Felsted 8593)	2.00	8.00	59
HART, Rocky (With The Passions)				
CRYING/	(Big Top 3069)	2.00	8.00	61
EVERY DAY/Come With Me	(Cub 9052)	2.00	8.00	60
I PLAY THE PART OF A FOOL/ Someone Stole My Baby While Doing The Twist	(Glo 216)	6.25	25.00	61
HART, Ron				
CALHOUN THE ELEPHANT/Ghost Of Glory	(Columbia 4-42866)	.75	3.00	63
HARVEY & DOC & THE DWELLERS				
UNCLE KEN/Oh Baby	(Annette 1002)	2.00	8.00	
HARVEY BOYS, The				
NOTHING IS TOO GOOD FOR YOU/Marina Girl	(Cadence 1306)	1.00	4.00	56
HARVEY, Phil (Phil Harvey Spector)				
BUMBERSHOOT/Willy Boy	(Imperial 5583)	2.00	8.00	59
(Instrumentals)				
HARVEY, Tina				
HAVE YOU SEEN YOUR MOTHER, BABY, STANDING IN THE SHADOWS?/Lifetime Of Loneliness	(UK 49016)	.75	3.00	73
WORKING MY WAY BACK TO YOU/Tina's Song	(UK 49006)	.75	3.00	72
HASKELL, Jimmy				
I'M ALL WOKE UP/	(Imperial 5491)	1.00	4.00	58
HASSAN, Ali				
MALAGUENA/Chop Sticks	(Phillies 103)	1.00	4.00	62
HASSELS, The (With Billy Joel)				
EVERY STEP I TAKE (EVERY MOVE I MAKE)/ I Hear Voices	(United Artists 50258)	1.25	5.00	67
GREAT BALLS OF FIRE/Traveling Band	(United Artists 50586)	1.25	5.00	69
HATFIELD, Bobby (Of The Righteous Brothers)				
ANSWER ME MY LOVE/I Only Have Eyes For You	(Verve 10641)	.75	3.00	69
BROTHER/What's The Matter Baby	(Verve 10621)	.75	3.00	68
HANG UPS/Soul Cafe	(Verve 10598)	.75	3.00	68
I NEED A GIRL/Hot Tamale	(Moonglow 220)	1.00	4.00	63
MY PRAYER/Wish I Didn't Love You So	(Verve 10639)	.75	3.00	69
ONLY YOU/Wonder Of You	(Verve 10634)	.75	3.00	69
OO WE BABY, I LOVE YOU/Rock 'N' Roll Woman	(Warner Bros. 7566)	.75	3.00	72
HATFUL OF RAIN				
PECULIAR SITUATION/Have You Ever Loved Somebody	(Sentar 1208)	1.00	4.00	67
HAVENS, The				
ONLY ONCE/Want You	(Poplar 123)	1.50	6.00	
HAVENS, Richie				
EYESIGHT TO THE BLIND/Underture	(Ode 66032)	.75	3.00	72
FREEDOM/Handsome Johnny	(Stormy Forest 666)	.75	3.00	71
HERE COMES THE SUN/Younger Men Get Older	(Stormy Forest 656)	.75	3.00	71
I'M NOT IN LOVE/Dreaming As One	(A&M 1882)	.50	2.00	77
IT WAS A VERY GOOD YEAR/I Know I Won't Be There	(Stormy Forest 671)	.75	3.00	71
JUST ABOVE MY HOBBY HORSE'S HEAD/ Indian Rope Man	(Verve Forecast 5092)	.75	3.00	68
ROCKY RACCOON/	(Stormy Forest 650)	.50	2.00	70
WE ALL WANNA BOGGIE/Nobody Left To Crown	(A&M 1984)	.75	3.00	77
HAWK (Featuring Joey Dee)				
WASN'T IT A HEAVY SUMMER/	(Sunburst 521)	1.25	5.00	
HAWK, The (Jerry Lee Lewis)				
I GET THE BLUES WHEN IT RAINS/ In The Mood	(Phillips International 3559)	2.00	8.00	60
(Instrumentals)				
HAWKINS, Dale				
AIN'T THAT LOVIN' YOU BABY/My Dream	(Checker 923)	1.00	4.00	59
BABY BABY/Mrs. Merguitory's Daughter	(Checker 876)	2.50	10.00	57
BABY WE HAD IT/Johnny Be Good	(Lincoln 002)	1.00	4.00	
BACK TO SCHOOL BLUES/Liza Jane	(Checker 934)	1.00	4.00	59
CLASS CUTTER (YEAH YEAH)/Lonely Nights	(Checker 916)	1.00	4.00	59
GOTTA DANCE/	(Zonk 1002)	1.00	4.00	
HOT DOG/Don't Break Your Promise To Me	(Checker 940)	1.00	4.00	60
HOUSE, A CAR & A WEDDING RING, A/My Babe	(Checker 906)	1.00	4.00	58
I WANT TO LOVE YOU/Grandma's House	(Checker 970)	1.00	4.00	61
LA LA SONG, THE/I'll Fly High	(ABC-Paramount 10668)	1.00	4.00	65
LA-DO-DA-DA/Crossties	(Checker 900)	1.00	4.00	58
LINDA/Who	(Checker 962)	1.00	4.00	61
LITTLE RAIN CLOUD/Back Street	(Bell 807)	1.00	4.00	69

TITLE/FLIP	LABEL & NO.	GOOD	NEAR MINT	YR.
OUR TURN/Lifeguard Man	(Checker 929)	1.00	4.00	59
PEACHES/Gotta Dance	(Atlantic 1002)	1.00	4.00	
POOR LITTLE RHODE ISLAND/Every Little Girl	(Checker 944)	1.00	4.00	62
SAME OLD WAY, THE/Money Honey	(Tilt 781)	1.00	4.00	62
SEE YOU SOON BABOON/Four Letter Word	(Checker 843)	2.50	10.00	56
STAY AT HOME LULU/ I Can't Erase You (Out Of My Heart)	(Atlantic 2126)	.75	3.00	61
SUSIE-Q/Don't Treat Me This Way	(Checker 863)	2.50	10.00	57
(Web design on label)				
SUSIE-Q/Don't Treat Me This Way	(Checker 863)	1.00	4.00	57
TAKE MY HEART/Someday One Day	(Checker 914)	1.00	4.00	59
TORNADO/Little Pig	(Checker 892)	1.00	4.00	58
WISH I HADN'T CALLED HOME/Forbidden Love	(Tilt 783)	1.00	4.00	
WITH A FEELING/Women-That's What's Happening	(Atlantic 2150)	.75	3.00	62
HAWKINS, Jimmy				
SURE DO/Back To School Blues (Red plastic)	(Kem 2751)	1.00	4.00	57
HAWKINS, Ronnie				
BALLAD OF CARYL CHESSMAN/Tale Of Floyd Collins	(Roulette 4231)	1.00	4.00	60
BO DIDDLEY/Who Do You Love	(Roulette 4483)	1.00	4.00	63
CLARA/Lonely Hours	(Roulette 4228)	1.00	4.00	60
COLD COLD HEART/Nobody's Lonesome For Me	(Roulette 4311)	1.00	4.00	61
CORA MAE/Lawdy Miss Clawdy	(Monument 8548)	.75	3.00	72
DOWN IN THE ALLEY/	(Cotillion 44060)	.75	3.00	70
FORTY DAYS/One Of These Days	(Roulette 4154)	1.25	5.00	59
FORTY DAYS/One Of These Days	(Roulette SSR-4154)	5.00	20.00	59
(Stereo single issue)				
FORTY DAYS/Bitter Green	(Cotillion 44067)	.75	3.00	70
HIGH BLOOD PRESSURE/There's A Screw Loose	(Roulette 4502)	1.00	4.00	63
I FEEL GOOD/Come Love	(Roulette 4400)	1.00	4.00	61
LONESOME TOWN/Kinky	(Monument 8561)	.75	3.00	72
MARY LOU/Need Your Lovin'	(Roulette 4177)	1.00	4.00	59
MARY LOU/Need Your Lovin'	(Roulette SSR-4177)	3.75	15.00	59
(Stereo single issue)				
ONE MORE NIGHT/	(Cotillion 44076)	.75	3.00	71
RUBY BABY/Hay Ride	(Roulette 4249)	1.00	4.00	60
SOUTHERN LOVE/Love Me Like You Can	(Roulette 4209)	1.00	4.00	59
SUMMERTIME/Mister & Mississippi	(Roulette 4267)	1.00	4.00	60
Ronnie Hawkins' backup band on the Roulette issues was the Hawks. In 1968, members of the Hawks began to record as the Band. Also see Lennon, John, & Ronnie Hawkins				
HAWKINS, Walter & Selah				
IT PAYS/Where Will You Run?	(Fantasy 688)	.50	2.00	72
HAWKS, The				
GRASSHOPPER/The Grissle	(ABC-Paramount 10116)	.75	3.00	60
HAWKS, Mickey				
BIP BOP BOOM/Rock & Roll Rhythm	(Profile 4002)	5.00	20.00	
(With Moon Mullins & His Knight Riders)				
HAWKWIND				
KINGS OF SPEED/	(Atco 7017)	.50	2.00	75
SILVER MACHINE/Seven By Seven	(United Artists 50949)	.50	2.00	71
URBAN GUERRILLA/Brainbox Pollution	(United Artists 314)	.50	2.00	73
HAWLEY, Deane				
LIKE A FOOL/Stay At Home Blues	(Dore 569)	.75	3.00	60
LOOK FOR A STAR/Bossman	(Dore 554)	.75	3.00	60
LOVE OF THE COMMON PEOPLE/I Hate To See Me Go	(Sundown 111)	1.25	5.00	
MUMMY'S BRACELET, THE/Don't Keep Me Guessing	(Valor 45-VA-005)	.75	3.00	
(With the Crystals)				
POCKETFUL OF RAINBOWS/That Dream Could	(Liberty 55359)	.75	3.00	61
RAINBOW/Hey There	(Dore 577)	.75	3.00	61
HAWTHORNE, Jim "Specs"				
WALKIN' TO NEW ORLEANS/Gaucho	(Bingo 1001)	1.00	4.00	58
HAYDOCK, Ron				
BE-BOP-A JEAN/99 Chicks (White label)	(Cha Cha 701)	12.50	50.00	59
BE-BOP-A JEAN/99 Chicks (Red label)	(Cha Cha 701)	2.00	8.00	59
HAYES & HEALY (Peter Lind Hayes & Mary Healy)				
REMEMB'RING/I Wish I Was A Car	(Columbia 4-40547)	1.00	4.00	55
HAYES, Bill				
BALLAD OF DAVY CROCKETT, THE/Farewell	(Cadence 1256)	1.00	4.00	55
BERRY TREE, THE/	(Cadence 1261)	1.00	4.00	55
I KNOW AN OLD LADY/Das Ist Musik	(Cadence 1294)	1.00	4.00	56
LEGEND OF WYATT EARP/White Buffalo	(Cadence 1275)	1.00	4.00	55
MESSAGE FROM JAMES DEAN, A/Trails' End	(Cadence 1301)	1.00	4.00	56
THAT DO MAKE IT NICE/Kwela Kwela	(Cadence 1274)	1.00	4.00	55
WANDERIN'/You're Nearer	(MGM 12004)	1.00	4.00	55
WRINGLE WRANGLE/Westward Ho The Wagons	(ABC-Paramount 9785)	1.00	4.00	56
HAYES, Jerry				
MAGIC OF YOUR SMILE, THE/Spend Some Time With Me	(Capitol 2679)	.50	2.00	69
HAYES, Jimmy, & Soul Surfers				
SUMMER SURFIN'/Down To The Beach	(Imperial 5987)	1.00	4.00	63
HAYES, Richard				
ABA DABA HONEYMOON, THE/I Don't Want To Love	(Mercury 5586)	1.25	5.00	51
(With Kitty Kallen)				
JUNCO PARTNER/Summertime	(Mercury 5833)	1.25	5.00	52
OUR LADY OF FATIMA (With Kitty Kallen)/ Honestly I Love You	(Mercury 5466)	1.25	5.00	50
OUT IN THE COLD AGAIN/Once	(Mercury 5724)	1.25	5.00	51
HAYES, Tommy				
TRANCE/Glistening Lights	(Philips 40259)	3.00	12.00	65
(With the 4 Seasons)				
HAYES, Peter Lind				
COOL ALASKA ROCK & ROLL/ Cool Alaska Rock & Roll (By Mary Healy)	(Dot 15881)	1.00	4.00	59
Also see Hayes & Healy				
HAYMAN & AUGUST (Richard Hayman & Jan August)				
(THEME FROM) 3 PENNY OPERA, THE/ In Apple Blossom Time	(Mercury 70781)	1.00	4.00	56
(Instrumental)				
HAYMAN, Richard				
APRIL IN PORTUGAL/Anna	(Mercury 70114)	1.00	4.00	53
RUBY/Love Mood	(Mercury 70115)	1.00	4.00	53
HAYMES, Dick				
ANYTIME/Bouquet Of Roses	(Decca 9-27885)	1.25	5.00	51
CAN ANYONE EXPLAIN/If I Had A Magic Carpet	(Decca 9-27161)	1.25	5.00	50
COUNT EVERY STAR/If You Were Only Mine	(Decca 27042)	1.25	5.00	50
HERE IN MY HEART/I'm Sorry	(Decca 9-28213)	1.25	5.00	52
HOME/Could Be	(Decca 9-27217)	1.25	5.00	50
LOVE IS A GREAT BIG NOTHIN'/I Never Get Enough Of You	(Capitol 3531)	1.00	4.00	56
MY PRAYER/Too Late Now	(Decca 9-27565)	1.25	5.00	51
MY SILENT LOVE/Don't Be Afarid	(Decca 9-27175)	1.25	5.00	50
TELL ME/Who'll Take My Place	(Decca 9-27646)	1.25	5.00	51
TWO DIFFERENT WORLDS/Never Leave Me	(Capitol 3565)	1.00	4.00	56
HAY, Timothy				
THAT'S WHAT GIRLS ARE MADE FOR/Breakaway	(RCA Victor 47-7945)	.75	3.00	61

TITLE/FLIP	LABEL & NO.	GOOD	NEAR MINT	YR.
HAYWARD, Justin (Of The Moody Blues)				
COUNTRY GIRL/Songwriter (Part 2)	(Deram 7542)	.50	2.00	77
FOREVER AUTUMN (With Jeff Wayne)/ The Fighting Machine (Instrumental by Jeff Wayne)	(Columbia 10799)	.50	2.00	78
Also see Hayward, Justin, & John Lodge				
HAYWARD, Justin, & John Lodge (Of The Moody Blues)				
BLUE GUITAR/When You Wake Up	(Threshold 67021)	.75	3.00	75
I DREAMED LAST NIGHT/Remember Me, My Friend	(Threshold 67019)	.75	3.00	75
HAZELWOOD, Lee				
DELLA/Don't Cry	(Smash 1734)	1.00	4.00	61
DOLLY PARTON'S GUITAR/A Taste Of You	(MCA 41003)	.50	2.00	79
FOUR KINDS OF LONELY/By The Way (I Still Love You)	(Reprise PRO 211)	1.00	4.00	64
NANCY & ME/	(Capitol 3611)	.50	2.00	72
TROUBLE MAKER/Greyhound Bus Depot	(LHI 20)	.75	3.00	68
RAINBOW WOMAN/I Am, You Are	(Reprise 0667)	.75	3.00	68
Also see Shacklefords, The				
HAZZARD, Tony				
BLUE MOVIE MAN/Abbot Of The Vale	(Uni 55316)	.50	2.00	73
WOMAN IN THE WEST/Hangover Blues	(Uni 55312)	.50	2.00	73
HEAD EAST				
GETTIN' LUCKY/Sands Of Time	(A&M 1930)	.50	2.00	77
LOVE ME TONIGHT/Fly By Night Lady	(A&M 1784)	.50	2.00	75
NEVER BEEN ANY REASON/One Against The Other	(A&M 1718)	.75	3.00	75
NEVER BEEN ANY REASON/I'm Feelin' Fine	(A&M 2122)	.50	2.00	79
SINCE YOU BEEN GONE/Pictures	(A&M 2026)	.50	2.00	78
HEAD, HANDS & FEET (With Albert Lee)				
ONE WOMAN/	(Atco 6923)	.50	2.00	73
HEAD, Murray				
SAY IT AIN'T SO HEAD/	(A&M 1796)	.75	3.00	76
SUPERSTAR/John Nineteen Forty-One	(Decca 732603)	.75	3.00	70
SUPERSTAR/John Nineteen Forty-One (Reissue)	(Decca 32603)	.50	2.00	71
HEAD, Roy (& The Traits)				
AIN'T GOIN' DOWN RIGHT/Lovin' Man On Your Hands	(Mercury 72848)	.75	3.00	68
APPLE OF MY EYE/I Pass The Day	(Back Beat 555)	.75	3.00	65
BIT BY BIT/Wait Till I Arrive	(TMI 9010)	.75	3.00	73
GET BACK (PART 1)/Get Back (Part 2)	(Scepter 12124)	.75	3.00	66
JUST A LITTLE BIT/Treat Me Right	(Scepter 12116)	.75	3.00	65
MY BABE/Pain	(Back Beat 560)	.75	3.00	66
NOBODY BUT ME/A Good Man Is Hard To Find	(Back Beat 582)	.75	3.00	67
ONE MORE TIME/Don't Be Blue	(TNT 194)	1.25	5.00	60
PUFF OF SMOKE/	(TMI 9000)	.75	3.00	72
TEEN-AGE LETTER/Pain	(Back Beat 543)	.75	3.00	65
TO MAKE A BIG MAN CRY/Don't Cry No More	(Back Beat 571)	.75	3.00	66
TREAT HER RIGHT/So Long, My Love	(Back Beat 546)	.75	3.00	65
TURN OUT THE LIGHTS/Broadway Walk	(Mercury 72799)	.75	3.00	68
WHY DON'T WE GO SOMEWHERE & LOVE/	(TMI 0106)	.75	3.00	73
YOU'RE (ALMOST) TUFF/Tush Hog	(Back Beat 576)	.75	3.00	66
WIGGLIN' & GIGGLIN'/Driving Wheel	(Back Beat 563)	.75	3.00	66
HEADBOYS, The				
SHAPE OF THINGS TO COME, THE/The Mood I'm In	(RSO 1005)	.50	2.00	79
HEADHUNTERS, The				
TIMES WE SHARE/Think What You've Done	(Fenton 2518)	1.00	4.00	
HEALY, Mary: see Hayes, Peter Lind				
HEAP, Jimmy				
BUTTER NUT/It Takes A Heap Of Lovin'	(Capitol 3333)	1.00	4.00	55
HEARD, Lonnie				
SUNDAY KIND OF LOVE, A/Romance In The Dark	(Ariliss 1006)	1.50	6.00	
HEART				
GIVE ME A HAPPY HEART/Now	(Look 5023)	.75	3.00	69
I LOVE YOU/Love	(Look 5029)	.75	3.00	70
HEART (Ann & Nancy Wilson)				
BARRACUDA/Cry To Me	(Portrait 70004)	.50	2.00	77
CRAZY ON YOU/Dreamboat Annie	(Mushroom 7021)	.50	2.00	76
DOG & BUTTERFLY/Mistral Wind	(Portrait 70025)	.50	2.00	79
DREAMBOAT ANNIE/Sing Child	(Mushroom 7023)	.50	2.00	76
GO ON CRY/Kick It Out	(Portrait 70010)	.50	2.00	77
HEARTLESS/Just The Wine	(Mushroom 7031)	.50	2.00	78
KICK IT OUT/Go On Cry	(Portrait 70010)	.50	2.00	77
LITTLE QUEEN/Treat Me Well	(Portrait 70008)	.50	2.00	77
MAGAZINE/Devil Delight	(Mushroom 7043)	.50	2.00	79
MAGIC MAN/How Deep It Goes	(Mushroom 7011)	.50	2.00	76
STRAIGHT ON/Lighter Touch	(Portrait 70020)	.50	2.00	78
STRAIGHT ON/Straight On	(Portrait XSS-16445)	2.00	8.00	78
(12" promotional single)				
WITHOUT YOU/Here Song	(Mushroom 7035)	.50	2.00	78
Also see Wilson, Ann & The Daybreaks				
HEART-ATTACKS, The				
BABBA DIDDY BABY/I'm Angry Baby	(Remus 5000)	1.50	6.00	
HEART BREAKERS, The				
LOVE YOU TILL.../My Love	(Vik 299)	1.25	5.00	57
1, 2, I LOVE YOU/Without A Cause	(Vik 261)	5.00	20.00	57
HEARTBREAKERS, The				
IT'S HARD BEING A GIRL/Special Occasions	(MGM 13129)	.75	3.00	63
YOU HAD TIME/Willow Wept	(Atco 6258)	.75	3.00	63
HEARTS & FLOWERS, The				
PLEASE/View From Ward 3	(Capitol 5897)	1.00	4.00	67
ROCK & ROLL GYPSIES/Road To Nowhere	(Capitol 5829)	1.25	5.00	67
TIN ANGEL (WILL YOU EVER COME DOWN)/ She Sang Hymns Out Of Tune	(Capitol 2167)	1.00	4.00	68
HEATH, Joyce				
HONOR ROLL OF LOVE/The Bunny Tale	(Agon 1003)	1.50	6.00	
(Shown as by Joyce & the Priviteers)				
JOHNNY FAIR/Rain On The River	(Laurie 3062)	1.00	4.00	60
OUR FIRST KISS/A Letter To A Disc Jockey	(Dragon 412)	1.00	4.00	60
HEATHERTON, Joey				
CRAZY/	(MGM 14499)	.50	2.00	73
GONE/The Road I Took To You (Pieces)	(MGM 14387)	.50	2.00	72
I'M CRAZY/	(MGM 14434)	.50	2.00	72
HEATWAVES, The (Featuring Billy Carl)				
BAD GIRL/So Much About My Baby	(Philtown 40001)	2.00	8.00	
I'LL DO MY CRYING TOMORROW/No Where To Go	(Josie 941)	1.50	6.00	65
Also see Billy & the Essentials				
HEAVEN BOUND				
HE'D RATHER HAVE THE RAIN/Come Run With Me	(MGM 14284)	.50	2.00	71
HEAVY CRUISER (With Neil Merryweather)				
LOUIE LOUIE/Outlaw	(Family 0909)	.75	3.00	72
HEBEL, Ray				
(ELVIS) HIS LEGEND'S STILL ALIVE OR IT'S GREAT TO HAVE AN IDOL (PART 1)/(Elvis) His Legend's Still Alive Or It's Great To Have An Idol (Part 2)	(Encore 1775)	.50	2.00	77

TITLE/FLIP — LABEL & NO. — GOOD — NEAR MINT — YR.

HEDGEHOPPERS ANONYMOUS
BABY (YOU'RE MY EVERYTHING)/Remember (Parrot 3002) 1.00 4.00 66
DON'T PUSH ME/Please Don't Hurt (Parrot 9817) 1.00 4.00 65
IT'S GOOD NEWS WEEK/Afraid Of Love (Parrot 9800) 1.00 4.00 65

HEFTI, Neal
BATMAN THEME/Batman Chase (RCA Victor 47-8755) .75 3.00 66
BEN CASEY (THEME)/Andy Griffith (Theme) (Reprise 20080) .75 3.00 63
MOOD INDIGO/One O'Clock Jump (Epic 9042) .75 3.00 56
X-15 (THEME)/ (Reprise 20039) .75 3.00 61

HEGGENESS & WEST
DOCTOR GORRIE'S LABORATORY/
You'll Be Sorry-If You Play This Side (Clowd 7302) .75 3.00 73
DOCTOR GORRIE'S PRESS CONFERENCE/Casey At The Bat (Clowd 7403) 1.00 4.00 69
Novelty/Break-ins

HEIGHT, Ronnie
COME SOFTLY TO ME/So Young, So Wise (Dore 516) 1.00 4.00 59
I'M CONFESSIN'/Dolores (Bamboo 500) .75 3.00 61
IT'S NOT THAT EASY/Portrait Of Linda (Era 3000) .75 3.00 59
KISS TO BUILD A DREAM ON, A/Maybe Tomorrow (Era 3009) .75 3.00 59
MEM'RIES & HABITS/One Finger Symphony (Era 3017) .75 3.00 60
MR. BLUES, I PRESUME/Juvenile (Era 3005) .75 3.00 59
NO DATE/Mr. Blues I Presume (Era 3031) .75 3.00 61

HEIGHTSMEN, The
KRETCHMA (KHRUSHCHEV'S WEAKNESS)/Johnny Reb (Imperial 5848) .75 3.00 62

HEINDORF, Ray
GIANT/There's Been Anyone Else But You (Columbia 4-40761) 1.00 4.00 56

HEINZ
DON'T WORRY BABY/Heart Full Of Sorrow (Tower 195) .75 3.00 65

HELLO PEOPLE, The
BOOK OF LOVE/How High Is The Moon (ABC 12160) .75 3.00 76
FUTURE SHOCK/ (Dunhill 15023) .75 3.00 75
IT'S A MONDAY KIND OF TUESDAY/
(As I Went Down To) Jerusalem (Philips 40531) .75 3.00 68
STRANGER AT THE DOOR/Paisley Teddy Bear (Philips 40522) .75 3.00 68

HELL, Richard, & The Voidoids (Of Television)
BLANK GENERATION/Love Comes In Spurts (Sire 1003) .50 2.00 77

HELM, Levon (Of The Band)
AIN'T NO WAY TO FORGET YOU/
Standing On A Mountaintop (ABC 12416) .50 2.00 78
MILK COW BOOGIE/ (ABC 12336) .50 2.00 78

HELMS, Jimmie
SENIOR CLASS RING/It Was Ours (East West 114) 1.00 4.00

HENDERSON, Joe
BIG LOVE/After Loving You (Todd 1077) .75 3.00 62
SEARCHING IS OVER, THE/Three Steps (Todd 1079) .75 3.00 62
SNAP YOUR FINGERS/If You See Me, Cry (Todd 1072) .75 3.00 62

HENDRICKS, James (Of The Mugwumps)
LONG LONESOME HIGHWAY/ (Starcrest 060) .50 2.00 76

HENDRIX, Al
RHONDA LEE/Go, Daddy, Rock (Tally 119) 3.75 15.00 57
(With Jolly Jody & His Go Daddies)
RHONDA LEE/Go, Daddy, Rock (ABC-Paramount) 2.00 8.00 57
(With Jolly Jody & His Go Daddies)

HENRIX, Jimi, & Little Richard
GOODNIGHT IRENE/Why Don't You Love Me (Alanna 1175) .75 3.00

HENDRIX, Jimi, Experience
ALL ALONG THE WATCHTOWER/
Burning Of The Midnight Lamp (Reprise 0767) .75 3.00 68
CROSSTOWN TRAFFIC/Gypsy Eyes (Reprise 0792) .75 3.00 68
DOLLY DAGGER/Star Spangled Banner (Reprise 1044) 1.00 4.00 71
DOLLY DAGGER (Stereo)/Dolly Dagger (Mono) (Reprise 1044) 1.50 6.00 71
(Promotional issue)
FOXEY LADY/Hey Joe (Reprise 0641) .75 3.00 67
FREEDOM/Angel (Reprise 1000) .75 3.00 71
HEY JOE/51st. Anniversary (Reprise 0572) 3.75 15.00 67
JOHNNY B. GOODE/Lover Man (Reprise 1082) 1.50 6.00 72
LITTLE WING/The Wind Cries Mary (Reprise 1118) 1.50 6.00 72
NO SUCH ANIMAL/No Such Animal (Part 2) (Audio Fidelity 167) 2.50 10.00
PURPLE HAZE/The Wind Cries Mary (Reprise 0597) .75 3.00 67
STEPPING STONE/Izhbella (Reprise 0905) 2.00 8.00 70
STONE FREE/If 6 Was 9 (Reprise 0853) 2.00 8.00 69
SUSPICIOUS/Hot Trigger (Trip 3002) 1.00 4.00 72
UP FROM THE SKIES/One Rainy Wish (Reprise 0665) 2.50 10.00 68

HENHOUSE FIVE PLUS TWO, The (With Ray Stevens)
IN THE MOOD/Classical Cluck (Warner-Ahab 8301) .50 2.00 77

HENKE, Mel
"77" SUNSET STRIP/Oliver's Twist (Warner Bros. 5295) .75 3.00 62
(Instrumentals)

HENLEY, Larry (Of The Newbeats)
HIS GIRL/Eastman Prison Farm (Hickory 1298) .75 3.00 66
I'D BE A-LYIN'/I Wouldn't Trade It For The World (Hickory 1354) .75 3.00 65
MY REASONS FOR LIVING/Stickin' Up For My Baby (Hickory 1272) .75 3.00 66

HENN, Rick (Of The Sunrays)
I LIVE FOR THE SUN/Girl On The Beach (Epic 11086) 1.00 4.00 74
Also see Joy

HENSLEY, Ken (Of Uriah Heep)
FORTUNE/When Evening Comes (Mercury 73410) .50 2.00 73
FROM TIME TO TIME/ (Mercury 73382) .50 2.00 73

HENSON
GOD ONLY KNOWS/Do Me Wrong, But Do Me (Fame 385) .75 3.00

HENSON, Jim: see Ernie

HEPCAT, Harry, & The Boogie Woogie Band
STREAKIN' U.S.A./Little Darlin (Graffiti 101) .75 3.00 72

HEP STARS, The (With Benny Andersson)
CADILLAC/Farmer John (Cameo 376) 2.50 10.00 65
MUSTY DUSTY/It's Now Winter's Day (Chartmaker 414) 1.50 6.00 69
NO RESPONSE/Sunny Girl (Dunhill 4040) 2.00 8.00 66
Also see Abba
Also see Bjorn & Benny

HERB B. LOU (Herb Alpert & Lou Adler)
TRIAL, THE/Kiss Me (By the Legal Eagles) (Arch 1607) 1.50 6.00 59
(Novelty/Break-ins)

HERBIE & THE CLASS CUTTERS
JUST A SUMMER KICK/Like Those Ivy Walls (RCA 7649) 1.00 4.00 59

TITLE/FLIP — LABEL & NO. — GOOD — NEAR MINT — YR.

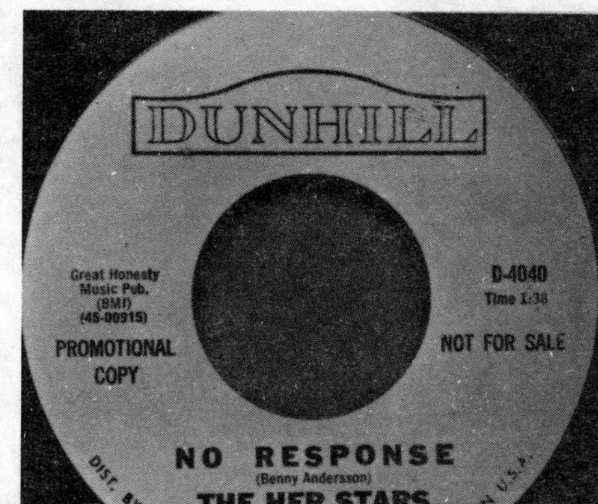

HERD, The (Featuring Peter Frampton)
BEAUTY QUEEN/The Game (Fontana 1646) 1.00 4.00 68
COME ON, BELIEVE ME/Paradise Lost (Fontana 1610) 1.00 4.00 67
FROM THE UNDERWORLD/Sweet William (Fontana 1602) 1.00 4.00 67
I CAN FLY/Understand Me (Fontana 1588) 1.00 4.00 67
I DON'T WANT OUR LOVING TO DIE/Our Fairy Tale (Fontana 1618) 1.00 4.00 68

HERD, The
THINGS WON'T CHANGE/The Sun Has Gone (Octopus 257) .75 3.00

HERMAN, Cleve
IN THIS CORNER/
Pacific Honky Tonk (By the Don Rays) (Capco 103) 2.00 8.00
(Novelty/Break-in)

HERMANN, Bernard
DIARY OF A TAXI DRIVER/Theme From Taxi Driver (Arista 0186) .50 2.00 76
(With dialogue by Robert DeNiro)

HERMAN'S HERMITS (Featuring Peter Noone)
CAN'T YOU HEAR MY HEARTBEAT/I Know Why (MGM K-13310) .75 3.00 65
DANDY/My Reservation's Been Confirmed (MGM K-13603) .75 3.00 66
DON'T GO OUT INTO THE RAIN (YOU'RE GOING TO
MELT)/Moonshine Man (MGM K-13761) .75 3.00 67
EAST WEST/What is Wrong, What Is Right (MGM K-13639) .75 3.00 66
GINNY GO SOFTLY/Blond-Haired Blue-Eyed Boy (Private Stock 45019) .75 3.00 75
I CAN TAKE OR LEAVE YOUR LOVIN/Marcel's (MGM K-13885) .75 3.00 68
I'M IN A LONELY SITUATION (LOVE IS ALL I NEED)/
Blond-Haired Blue-Eyed Boy (Buddah 576) .75 3.00 74
I'M HENRY VIII, I AM/The End Of The World (MGM K-13367) .75 3.00 65
I'M INTO SOMETHING GOOD/Your Hand In Mine (MGM K-13280) .75 3.00 64
IT'S ALRIGHT NOW/Star, The (Here Comes) (MGM K-14100) .75 3.00 69
JUST A LITTLE BIT BETTER/Sea Cruise (MGM K-13398) .75 3.00 65
LEANING ON THE LAMP POST/Hold On (MGM K-13500) .75 3.00 66
LISTEN PEOPLE/Got A Feeling (MGM K-13462) .75 3.00 66
MRS. BROWN YOU'VE GOT A LOVELY DAUGHTER/
I Gotta Dream On (MGM K-13341) .75 3.00 65
MOST BEAUTIFUL THING IN MY LIFE/
Ooh She's Done It Again (MGM K-13994) .75 3.00 68
MUSEUM/Last Bus Home (MGM K-13787) .75 3.00 67
MUST TO AVOID, A/The Man With The Cigar (MGM K-13437) .75 3.00 65
MY SENTIMENTAL FRIEND/My Lady (MGM K-14060) .75 3.00 69
SILHOUETTES/Walkin With My Angel (MGM K-13332) .75 3.00 65
SLEEPY JOE/Just One Girl (MGM K-13934) .75 3.00 68
SOMETHING'S HAPPENING/
Little Miss Sorrow Child Of Tomorrow (MGM K-14035) .75 3.00 69
SUNSHINE GIRL/Nobody Needs To Know (MGM K-13973) .75 3.00 68
THERE'S A KIND OF HUSH (ALL OVER THE WORLD)/
No Milk Today (MGM K-13681) .75 3.00 67
THIS DOOR SWINGS BOTH WAYS/For Love (MGM K-13548) .75 3.00 66
WONDERFUL WORLD/Traveling Light (MGM K-13354) .75 3.00 65

HERO
BOYS WILL BE BOYS/ (20th Fox 2394) .50 2.00 78
SPICER-MAN/ (Lifesong 45004) .50 2.00 75

HERSHEY, Bill, & The Almonds
IS THERE A DOCTOR IN THE HOUSE/Yogi Man's Bikini (Gulf 027) 1.00 4.00 60

HEWITT, Ben
FOR QUITE A WHILE/Patricia June (Mercury 71472) 2.00 8.00 59
I AIN'T GIVIN' UP NOTHIN' (IF I CAN'T GET SOMETHING FROM YOU)/
You Break Me Up (Mercury 71413) 1.50 6.00 59

HEYBURNERS, The
BIRD WALK/Speedway (Titanic 5009) 1.00 4.00 63

HEYWOOD, Eddie
SOFT SUMMER BREEZE/Heywood's Bounce (Mercury 70863) 1.00 4.00 56
(Instrumentals)

HIATT, John
RADIO GIRL/Sharon's Got A Drugstore (MCA 41019) .50 2.00 79

HIBBLER, Al
AFTER THE LIGHTS GO DOWN LOW/Tell Me (Orginial 1006) 2.50 10.00 54
AFTER THE LIGHTS GO DOWN LOW/
I Was Telling Her About You (Decca 9-29982) 1.00 4.00 56
ANNE/You & I (Norgran 100) 1.50 6.00 55
AS TIME GOES BY/I'm Getting Sentimental (Clef 89095) 2.00 8.00 54
AUTUMN WINDS/You Will Be Mine (Orginial 1008) 2.50 10.00 54
BLUES CAME FALLING DOWN, THE/Old Folks (Atlantic 925) 5.00 20.00 50
DANNY BOY/Song Of The Wanderer (Atlantic 911) 5.00 20.00 50
DANNY BOY/Now I Lay Me Down (Atlantic 1071) 1.50 6.00 55
DON'T TAKE YOUR LOVE FROM ME/
I Got It Bad, & That Ain't Good (Aladin 3328) 1.50 6.00 56
HE/Breeze, Blow My Baby Back To Me (Decca 9-29660) 1.00 4.00 55
11TH HOUR MELODY/Let's Try Again (Decca 9-29789) 1.00 4.00 56
FLAMINGO/I Let A Song Go Out Of My Heart (Norgran 105) 1.50 6.00 55
GOIN' TO CHICAGO/Sent For You Yesterday (Clef 89028) 2.00 8.00 54
GOIN' TO CHICAGO/Sent For You Yesterday (Mercury 89028) 1.00 4.00 56
LITTLE BROWN JUG/I'm Just A Lucky So & So (Norgran 114) 1.50 6.00 55
NEVER TURN BACK/Away All Boats (Decca 9-29950) 1.00 4.00 56
NOW I LAY ME DOWN TO DREAM/This Is Always (Atlantic 945) 3.75 15.00 51
PLEASE/Believe It Beloved (Clef 89011) 2.00 8.00 54
PLEASE/Believe It Beloved (Mercury 89011) 1.00 4.00 56
THEY SAY YOUR LAUGHING AT ME/
I Can't Put My Arms Around A Memory (Decca 9-29543) 1.00 4.00 55
THERE IS NO GREATER LOVE/It Must Be True (Clef 89046) 2.00 8.00 54

TITLE/FLIP — LABEL & NO. — GOOD — NEAR MINT — YR.

THERE IS NO GREATER LOVE/It Must Be True (Mercury 89046) 1.00 4.00 56
THIS LOVE OF MINE/Every Hour On The Hour (Norgran 143) 1.50 6.00 55
TRAVELIN' LIGHT/If I Knew You Were There (Atlantic 932) 3.75 15.00 51
TREES/The Town Crier (Decca 9-30176) 1.00 4.00 57
UNCHAINED MELODY/Daybreak (Decca 9-29441) 1.00 4.00 55
WORLD IS WAITING FOR SUNRISE, THE/ (Columbia 4-30195) 3.75 15.00 51

HICKEY, Ersel
BLUEBIRDS OVER THE MOUNTAIN/Hangin' Around (Epic 9263) 1.00 4.00 58
BLUEBIRDS OVER THE MOUNTAIN/Self Made Man (Janus 151) .50 2.00 71
LOVER'S LAND/Goin' Down That Road (Epic 9278) 1.25 5.00 58
YOU NEVER CAN TELL/Wedding Day (Epic 9298) 1.00 4.00 58
YOU THREW A DART/Don't Be Afraid Of Love (Epic 9309) 1.00 4.00 58
WHAT DO YOU WANT/Love In Bloom (Epic 9357) 1.00 4.00 59

HICKMAN, Duane
PRETTY BABY-O/ (ABC-Paramount) 1.25 5.00

HICKOX, Jack
WE'RE SURE GONNA MISS YOU OLD FRIEND/
Your Memory Sure Does Get Around (Constellation 001) .50 2.00 77

HICKS, Bob
ROCK, BABY ROCK/Baby Sittin' All The Time (Mirasonic 1001) 1.25 5.00 59

HICKS, Don, & His Hot Licks
I'M AN OLD COWHAND/Woe, The Luck (Blue Thumb 213) 1.00 4.00 73
MOODY RICHARD/ (Blue Thumb 211) 1.00 4.00 73
MY OLD TIMEY BABY/Cheaters Don't Win (Blue Thumb 235) 1.00 4.00 74
Also see Charlatans, The

HI-FI FOUR, The
BAND OF GOLD/Davy You Upset My Life (King 4856) 1.00 4.00 56

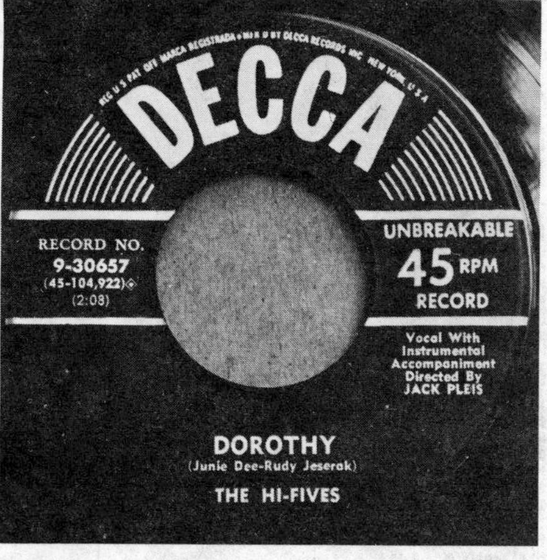

HI-FIVES, The
DOROTHY/Just A Shoulder To Cry On (Decca 9-30657) 2.50 10.00 58
DOROTHY/Just A Shoulder To Cry On (Decca 9-30657) 2.00 8.00 58
(Promotional issue)
FELICIA/Windy City Special (Bingo 1006) 1.00 4.00 60
MY FRIEND/How Can I Win (Decca 9-30576) 3.00 12.00 58
MY FRIEND/How Can I Win (Decca 9-30576) 2.00 8.00 58
(Promotional issue)
WHAT'S NEW, WHAT'S NEW/Lonely (Decca 9-30744) 1.50 6.00 58
WHAT'S NEW, WHAT'S NEW/Lonely (Decca 9-30744) 1.00 4.00 58
(Promotional issue)

HIGH & MIGHTY, The
TRYIN' TO STOP CRYIN'/Escape From Cuba (ABC 10821) 1.00 4.00 66
Also see Reflections, The

HIGH NUMBERS, The
ZOOT SUIT/I'm The Face (Fontana TF-480) 37.50 150.00 64
(English release)
This group evolved into the Who.

HIGH SEAS, The
SUNDAY KIND OF LOVE/We Go Together (D-M-G 4000) 2.50 10.00 60

HIGHLIGHTS, The
ALL THE WAY WITH L.B.J./Hot To Trot (Arcade 190) .75 3.00 64

HIGHLIGHTS, The
CITY OF ANGELS/Listen My Love (Bally 1016) 1.25 5.00 56
INDIANA STYLE/Turn Around Shoes (Bally 1044) 1.25 5.00 58
TO BE WITH YOU/Will I Ever Know (Bally 1027) 1.25 5.00 57

HIGHSCHOOL CHANTERS, The
HOODOO THE VOODOO/Teenage Chant (Fashion 001) 1.00 4.00 59

HIGHWAY (Formerly Sherbet)
YOU MADE A FOOL/Cheatin' Eyes (RSO 923) .50 2.00 79

HIGHWAY 101
EVERY MOMENT/I Want You Again (Rocket 40739) .50 2.00 77

HIGHWAYMEN, The
BIRD MAN, THE/Cindy Oh Cindy (United Artists 475) .75 3.00 62
COTTON FIELDS/The Gypsy Rover (United Artists 370) .75 3.00 61
I'M ON MY WAY/Whiskey In The Jar (United Artists 439) .75 3.00 62
MICHAEL/Santiano (United Artists 258) .75 3.00 61
MICHAEL '65/Puttin' On The Style (United Artists 801) .75 3.00 65
Group members: Steve Butts, Chan Daniels, Bobby Burnett, Gil Robbins, Dave Fisher.

HI-JACKS, The
WONDERFUL ONE/Letter I Wrote Today (ABC-Paramount 9742) 1.25 5.00 56

HI-LITES, The
FOR SENTIMENTAL REASONS/For Your Precious Love (Record Fair 501) 1.00 4.00 62
4,000 MILES AWAY/Woke Up This Morning (Jet 502) 1.00 4.00 61
GIRLS/ (Seg-Way 105) 1.50 6.00 61
GROOVY/Hey Baby (Wassel 701) .75 3.00 65
PONY, THE (PART 1)/The Pony (Part 2) (Jet 501) 1.00 4.00 61
WALKING MY BABY BACK HOME/I'm Falling In Love (Record Fair 500) 1.00 4.00 61

HILL
SYLVIE/Fourth Annual Convention Of The Buttery
Hen Farmer's Association (Part 2) (Immediate 5016) .75 3.00 69

HILL, Bunker
HIDE & GO SEEK (PART 1)/Hide & Go Seek (Part 2) (Mala 451) .75 3.00 62

TITLE/FLIP	LABEL & NO.	GOOD	NEAR MINT	YR.

HILL, Dan
ALL I SEE IS YOUR FACE/Longer Fuse (20th Century-Fox 2378) .50 2.00 78
GROWN' UP/People (20th Century 2254) .50 2.00 76
HOLD ON TO THE NIGHT/ (20th Century-Fox 2425) .50 2.00 79
LET THE SONG LAST FOREVER/Indian Woman (20th Century-Fox 2392) .50 2.00 78
PHONE CALL/ (20th Century 2334) .50 2.00 77
SOMETIMES WHEN WE TOUCH/Still Not Used To (20th Century 2355) .50 2.00 77

HILL, Dave
ONLY BOY ON THE BEACH/New Orleans (Apogee 106) .75 3.00 64

HILL, David
LIVING DOLL/ (Kapp 293) 1.00 4.00 59
TWO BROTHERS/Deep Goes My Love (Kapp 266) 1.00 4.00 59

HILL, Jackie
WON'T YOU COME CLOSER/My Man, He's Everything (Mar-Brit 301) 1.50 6.00

HILL, Joel (Joel Scott Hill)
LITTLE LOVER/I Thought It Over (Trans-American 519) 6.25 25.00 61
LOOK OUT/Sticks & Stones (Monogram 521) 1.50 6.00 64
(With the Invaders)
MONKEY BUSINESS/Hannibal's Hundred (Monogram 615) 1.00 4.00 65
(Instrumental)
Also see Canned Heat
Also see Strangers, The

HILL, John, & The Piemen
SUNDAY MORNING SOFTBALL/Second Base Blues (Otty 101) 1.25 5.00

HILL, Tiny
BATTLE OF THE BOTTLE/It Must Have Been (Mercury 5726) 1.25 5.00 51
DON'T DO IT DARLING/On The Uppermost Branch (Mercury 70395) 1.00 4.00 54
FIVE FOOT TWO/Move It On Over (Mercury 70029) 1.00 4.00 53
HOT ROD RACE/Love Bug Itch (Mercury 5547) 1.25 5.00 50
HOT ROD RACE NO. 2/Let's Live A Little (Mercury 5598) 1.25 5.00 51
I GET THE BLUES/Someday You'll Be Sorry (Mercury 70448) 1.00 4.00 54
I'LL SAIL MY SHIP ALONE/Back In Your Own Backyard (Mercury 5508) 1.25 5.00 50
I'M MOVIN' ON/Just A Girl That Men Forget (Mercury 5524) 1.25 5.00 50
SLOW POKE/Don't Put A Tax On Love (Mercury 5740) 1.25 5.00 52
TWO TON TESSIE/Don't Bring Lulu (Mercury 90249) 1.00 4.00 53

HILLMAN, Chris (Of The Byrds)
HEARTBREAKER/ (Asylum 45428) .50 2.00 77
LOVE IS THE SWEETEST AMNESTY/ (Asylum 45350) .50 2.00 76
STEP ON OUT/Take It On The Run (Asylum 45330) .50 2.00 76
Also see Souther, Hillman & Furay

HILLTOPPERS, The (Featuring Jimmy Sacca)
DO THE BOP/When You're Alone (Dot 15451) 1.00 4.00 56
EYES OF FIRE, LIPS OF WINE/I'm Walking Through Heaven (Dot 15468) 1.00 4.00 56
FALLEN STAR, A/Footsteps (Dot 15594) 1.00 4.00 57
FROM THE VINE CAME THE GRAPE/Time Will Tell (Dot 15127) 1.00 4.00 54
I LOVE MY GIRL/I'm Serious (Dot 15560) 1.00 4.00 57
IF I WERE KING/I Can't Lie To Myself (Dot 15055) 1.25 5.00 53
I'D RATHER DIE YOUNG/Welcome To My Heart (Dot 15085) 1.25 5.00 53
JOKER, THE/ (Dot 15662) 1.00 4.00 57
KA-DING-DONG/Into Each Life Some Rain Must Fall (Dot 15489) 1.00 4.00 56
MARIANNE/You're Wasting Your Time (Dot 15479) 1.00 4.00 57
MUST I CRY AGAIN/I Keep Telling Myself (Dot 15034) 1.50 6.00 52
MY TREASURE/The Last Word In Love (Dot 15437) 1.00 4.00 55
ONLY YOU (& YOU ALONE)/Until The Real Thing Comes Along (Dot 15423) 1.00 4.00 55
P.S.: I LOVE YOU/I'd Rather Die Young (Dot 15085) 1.25 5.00 53
POOR BUTTERFLY/Wrapped In A Dream (Dot 15156) 1.00 4.00 54
SEARCHING/All I Need Is You (Dot 15415) 1.00 4.00 55
SO TIRED/Faded Rose (Dot 15459) 1.00 4.00 56
TILL THEN/I Found Your Letter (Dot 15132) 1.00 4.00 54
TO BE ALONE/Love Walked In (Dot 15105) 1.25 5.00 53
TRYING/You Made Up (Dot 15018) 1.50 6.00 52
(Shown as by the Hill Toppers)

HINDUS, The
FRENZY/Theme Of Etiquette (Dardeu 1011) .75 3.00

HINES, Earl "Fatha"
RON THE KNIFE/
The Medi-Cal Blues (SF Orig. Gold Seal-No number given) 1.25 5.00
("Ron The Knife," a "Mack The Knife" parody, told the story of former California governor Ronald Reagan's university budget cuts.A compact 33 single.)

HINSON, Don & The Rigamorticians
MONSTER JERK/Riboflavin-flavored, Non-carbonated, Polyunsaturated Blood (Capitol 5314) 1.25 5.00 64

HIPPIES, The: see Tams, The

HI-ROLLERS, The
SLAVE CHAIN/Runaway (Van 03165) .75 3.00

HIRT, Al
AL'S PLACE/Mister Sandman (RCA Victor 47-8542) .75 3.00 65
COTTON CANDY/Walkin' (RCA Victor 47-8346) .75 3.00 64
FANCY PANTS/Star Dust (RCA Victor 47-8487) .75 3.00 65
FEELIN' FRUGGY/Louisiana Lullaby (RCA Victor 47-8684) .75 3.00 65
FEUDING PIPERS (FEUDIN' BANJOS)/
Southern Scramble (Monument ZS8-8652) .50 2.00 75
(With Boots Randolph)
GREEN HORNET THEME/Strawberry Jam (RCA Victor 47-8925) .75 3.00 66
HOORAY FOR SANTA CLAUS/White Christmas (RCA Victor 47-8478) .75 3.00 64
JAVA/Al Di La (RCA Victor 47-8280) .75 3.00 64
KEEP THE BALL ROLLIN'/ (RCA Victor 47-9417) .75 3.00 68
SANTA CLAUS IS COMIN' TO TOWN/Nutty Jingle Bells (RCA Victor 47-8706) .75 3.00 65
SILENCE, THE/Love Theme From "The Sandpiper" (RCA Victor 47-8653) .75 3.00 65
SUGAR LIPS/Poupee Brisee (RCA Victor 47-8391) .75 3.00 64
YESTERDAY/Arena, The (RCA Victor 47-8736) .75 3.00 65
UP ABOVE MY HEAD/September Song (RCA Victor 47-8439) .75 3.00 64
Also see Ann-Margret

HITMAKERS, The
CHAPEL OF LOVE/Cool School (Original Sound 1) 1.25 5.00
HOW TO MAKE A HIT RECORD/Buttermilk (Dore 738) .75 3.00 65

HI-TONES, The
LOVER'S QUARREL/Just For You (Fonsca 201) 2.00 8.00 61
NO MORE PAIN/I Don't Know Why (Fonsca 202) 2.00 8.00 61
Also see Shytones, The
Also see Trentons, The

HIX, Chuck, & The Count Downs
BALLAD OF A BADMAN/Is You Is (Verve 10190) 1.00 4.00 59
LORETTA/Cookie Duster (Flair 101) 1.00 4.00 61
SANDY/Sixteen (Verve 10169) 1.00 4.00 59

H. M. SUBJECTS
DON'T PUT ME DOWN (Uncensored)/
Don't Put Me Down (Censored) (Blue Saint 1001) 1.25 5.00

HO, Don, & The Aliis
TINY BUBBLES/Born Free (Reprise 0507) .75 3.00 66

HOBBITS, The
STRAWBERRY CHILDREN/Pretty Young Thing (Decca 32270) .75 3.00 68
SUNNY DAY GIRL/Daffodil Days (Decca 32226) .75 3.00 68

HO-DADS, The
HONKY/Legends (Imperial 66001) 1.00 4.00 63
SPACE RACE/After Dark (Imperial 66023) 1.00 4.00 63

HODGE, Chris
BEAUTIFUL LOVE/Sweet Lady From The Sky (RCA APBO-0289) .50 2.00 74
GOODBYE SWEET LORRAINE/Constant Love (Apple 1858) .75 3.00 73
MY LINDA/ (RCA 5003) .50 2.00 75
WE'RE ON OUR WAY/Supersoul (Apple 1850) .75 3.00 72

HODGES, Eddie
ACROSS THE STREET (IS A MILLION MILES AWAY)/ (Aurora 150) .75 3.00 65
BANDIT OF MY DREAMS/Mugmates (Cadence 1410) .75 3.00 62
HITCH HIKE/Old Rag Man (Aurora 161) .75 3.00 66
I'M GONNA KNOCK ON YOUR DOOR/
Ain't Gonna Wash For A Week (Cadence 1397) 1.00 4.00 61
JUST A KID IN LOVE/Avalanche (MGM 13219) .75 3.00 64
LOVE MINUS ZERO/
The Water Is Over My Head (With "Crazy Horse") (Aurora 156) .75 3.00 65
MADE TO LOVE (GIRLS, GIRLS, GIRLS)/
I Make Believe It's You (Cadence 1421) .75 3.00 62
NEW ORLEANS/Hard Times For Young Lovers (Aurora 153) .75 3.00 65
RAININ' IN MY HEART/Halfway (Columbia 4-42811) .75 3.00 63
SEEIN' IS BELIEVIN'/Secret (Columbia 4-42649) .75 3.00 62
WOULD YOU COME BACK/Too Soon To Know (Columbia 4-52697) .75 3.00 63

HODGES, Eddie, & Haley Mills
BEAUTIFUL BEAULAH/Flitterin' (Buena Vista 420) .75 3.00 63

HODGES, Johnny
BLUES SERNADE/Jitterbug's Line Lullabye (Columbia 4-40233) 1.50 6.00 54
CASTLE ROCK/Jeep's Blues (Mercury 8944) 1.50 6.00 51
GLOBETROTTER/Gentle Breeze (Mercury 8954) 1.50 6.00 51
GLOBETROTTER/You Blew Out The Flame (Mercury 8958) 1.25 5.00 51
TIRED SOCKS/Jeep Is Jumpin' (Mercury 6824) 1.50 6.00 51

HOFFAR, Gary
HANK'S 715TH/Memories Of Yesterday (By Ellison Pinder) (Jemkl 3294) 1.25 5.00 76
(Novelty/Break-in)

HOG HEAVEN
HAPPY/Prayer (Roulette 7101) .50 2.00 71

HOGS, The
LOOSE LIP SYNC SHIP/Blues Theme (HBR 481) 2.00 8.00 66
(With Frank Zappa)

HOLBROOK, Tom
OH YES HE'S GONE/A New Beginning (Hillside 08) .50 2.00 77

HOLDEN, Ron
BIG SHOE, THE/Let No One Tell You (Donna 1335) .75 3.00 61
GEE BUT I'M LONESOME/Susie Jane (Donna 1324) 1.00 4.00 60
I'LL BE HAPPY/I'll Always Have You (Eldo 117) .75 3.00 61
LOVE YOU SO/My Babe (Nite Owl 10) 3.75 15.00 60
LOVE YOU SO/My Babe (Donna 1315) 1.00 4.00 60
TRUE LOVE CAN BE/Everything's Gonna Be Allright (Donna 1328) 1.00 4.00 60
WHO SAYS THERE AINT NO SANTA CLAUS/
Your Line Is Busy (Donna 1331) 1.00 4.00 60

HOLIDAY, Chico
LONESOME STRANGER/Please Don't Touch (RCA Victor 47-7574) 1.00 4.00 59
LULU HAD A BABY/Your Kid Sister (RCA Victor 47-7545) 1.00 4.00 59
YOUNG IDEAS/Cuckoo Girl (RCA Victor 47-7499) 1.00 4.00 59
YOUNG IDEAS/Cuckoo Girl (RCA Victor 61-7499) 2.00 8.00 59
(Stereo single issue)

HOLIDAY, Connie
MRS. JAMES I'M MRS. BROWN'S DAUGHTER/
Old Friend (Answer song) (Capitol 5447) .75 3.00 65
WHO'LL BE THE BOY THIS SUMMER/
I'll Be At Your Command (Smash 1764) .75 3.00 62

HOLIDAY, Johnny
BALLAD OF A GIRL & BOY, THE/Goodbye My Love (Lawn 208) 1.50 6.00 63

HOLIDAYS, The
IMA-LIKA-YOU (I'M LIKA PIZZA PIE)/Rolling River (King 1217) 2.50 10.00 51
ONE LITTLE KISS/My Girl (Nix 537) 1.50 6.00
PATTY ANN/Big Brown Eyes (Track 87479) 1.50 6.00
STARS WILL REMEMBER/Who Knows, Who Cares (Andie 5019) 1.50 6.00
Even though all of these releases are shown as being by a group using the same name, the possibility exists that they are not all by the same group.

HOLIEN, Danny
COLORADO/ (Tumbleweed 1004) .50 2.00 72

HOLLAND, Ray
SURFBOARD STAG/My Summer Baby (Margo 101) 1.00 4.00 63

HOLLER, Dick, & His Rockets
UH-UH-BABY/Livin' By The Gun (Ace 540) 1.25 5.00 58

HOLLERS, Wayne
DANCE IN THE SAND/Why (Del Fi 4121) 1.00 4.00 59

HOLLIES, The (Featuring Allan Clarke)
AFTER THE FOX (With Peter Sellers)/
Fox Trot (Instrumental) (United Artists 50079) 2.00 8.00 65
AIR THAT I BREATHE, THE/No More Riders (Epic 11100) .50 2.00 74
ANOTHER NIGHT/Time Machine Jive (Epic 50110) .50 2.00 75
BABY, THE/Oh Granny (Epic 10842) 1.00 4.00 72
BUS STOP/Don't Run & Hide (Imperial 66186) .75 3.00 66
CARRIE-ANNE/Signs That Will Never Change (Epic 10180) .75 3.00 67
COME ON BACK/We're Through (Imperial 66070) 2.00 8.00 64
DAY THAT CURLY BILLY SHOT DOWN CRAZY SAM MCGEE, THE/
Born A Man (Epic 11051) 1.00 4.00 73
DEAR ELOISE/When Your Lights Turned On (Epic 10251) .75 3.00 67
DO THE BEST YOU CAN/Elevated Observations (Epic 10361) 1.25 5.00 68
DON'T LET ME DOWN/Lay Into The Music (Epic 50029) 1.00 4.00 74
DRAGGIN' MY HEELS/I Won't Move Over (Epic 50422) .75 3.00 77
HE AIN'T HEAVY, HE'S BROTHER/
Cos You Like To Love Me (Epic 10532) .75 3.00 69
HERE I GO AGAIN/Lucille (Imperial 66044) 2.00 8.00 64
HEY WILLY/Row The Boat Together (Epic 10754) 1.00 4.00 71
I CAN'T LET GO/I've Got A Way Of My Own (Imperial 66158) 1.25 5.00 66
I CAN'T TELL THE BOTTOM FROM THE TOP/
Mad Professor Blyth (Epic 10613) 1.00 4.00 70
I'M ALIVE/You Know He Did (Imperial 66119) 1.50 6.00 65
I'M DOWN/Look Out Johnny (There's A Monkey On Your Back) (Epic 50144) 1.00 4.00 75
IF I NEED SOMEONE/I'll Be True To You (Yes I Will) (Imperial 66271) 2.00 8.00 68
JENNIFER ECCLES/Try It (Epic 10298) 1.00 4.00 68
JESUS WAS A CROSSMAKER/I Had A Dream (Epic 10989) 1.00 4.00 73
JUST ONE LOOK/Keep Off That Friend Of Mine (Imperial 66026) 1.50 6.00 64
JUST ONE LOOK/Running Through The Night (Imperial 66258) 1.00 4.00 67
KING MIDAS IN REVERSE/Water On The Brain (Epic 10234) 1.00 4.00 67
LISTEN TO ME/Everything Is Sunshine (Epic 10400) 1.25 5.00 68
LONG COOL WOMAN (IN A BLACK DRESS)/
Look What We've Got (Epic 10871) .50 2.00 72
LONG DARK ROAD/Indian Girl (Epic 10920) .50 2.00 72
LOOK THROUGH ANY WINDOW/So Lonely (Imperial 66134) 1.25 5.00 65
MAGIC WOMAN TOUCH/Blue In The Morning (Epic 10951) .75 3.00 73
ON A CAROUSEL/All The World Is Love (Imperial 66231) .75 3.00 67
PAY YOU BACK WITH INTEREST/
Whatcha Gonna Do 'Bout It (Imperial 66240) 1.00 4.00 67
SANDY/Second Hand Hangups (Epic 50086) 1.00 4.00 75
SLOW DOWN/Won't We Feel Good (Epic 11025) 1.00 4.00 73
SORRY SUZANNE/Not That Way At All (Epic 10454) .75 3.00 69
STAY/Now's The Time (Liberty 55674) 5.00 20.00 64
STOP, STOP, STOP/It's You (Imperial 66214) .75 3.00 66
SURVIVAL OF THE FITTEST/Man Without A Heart (Epic 10716) 1.50 6.00 71
WRITE ON/Crocodile Woman (She Bites) (Epic 50204) .75 3.00 76
WRITING ON THE WALL/Burn Out (Epic 50523) .50 2.00 78
YES I WILL/Nobody (Imperial 66099) 2.00 8.00 65
Also see Clarke, Allan
Also see Nash, Graham
Graham Nash was a member of the Hollies until late 1968.

HOLLOWAY, Bobby
FUNKY LITTLE DRUMMER BOY/
Cornbread, Hog Maw & Chitterlin's (Smash 2137) .75 3.00 67

HOLLY, Buddy (Charles Hardin Holley)
BLUE DAYS, BLACK NIGHTS/Love Me (Decca 9-29854) 15.00 60.00 56
BLUE DAYS, BLACK NIGHTS/Love Me (Decca 9-29854) 12.50 50.00 56
(Promotional issue)
BROWN EYED HANDSOME MAN/Wishing (Coral 62369) 3.75 15.00 63
EARLY IN THE MORNING/Now We're One (Coral 9-62006) 2.50 10.00 58
GIRL ON MY MIND/Ting-A-Ling (Decca 9-30650) 10.00 40.00 58
(With the Three Tunes)
HEARTBEAT/Well... All Right (Coral 9-62051) 2.50 10.00 58
I'M GONNA LOVE YOU TOO/Listen To Me (Coral 9-61947) 2.50 10.00 57
IT DOESN'T MATTER ANYMORE/Raining In My Heart (Coral 9-62074) 2.50 10.00 59
LOVE IS STRANGE/You're The One (Coral 62558) 2.50 10.00 69
LOVE ME/You Are My One Desire (Decca 9-30543) 7.50 30.00 58
(With the Three Tunes)
MAYBE BABY/Not Fade Away (Coral 62407) 3.75 15.00 64
MODERN DON JUAN/You Are My One Desire (Decca 9-30166) 10.00 40.00 56
(With the Three Tunes)
PEGGY SUE/Everyday (Coral 9-61885) 2.00 8.00 57
(Copies exist both with and without the "9" prefix.)
PEGGY SUE GOT MARRIED/Crying, Waiting, Hoping (Coral 9-62134) 6.25 25.00 60
RAVE ON/Early In The Morning (Coral 62554) 3.75 15.00 58
RAVE ON/Take Your Time (Coral 9-61985) 2.50 10.00 58
REMINISCING/Wait Till The Sun Shines Nellie (Coral 62329) 3.75 15.00 63
ROCK AROUND WITH OLLIE VEE/I'm Gonna Love You Too (Coral 62390) 3.75 15.00 64
SLIPPIN' & SLIDIN'/What To Do (Coral 62448) 7.50 30.00 65
THAT'LL BE THE DAY/I'm Lookin' For Someone To Love (Coral 65618) 3.00 12.00 71
THAT'LL BE THE DAY/Rock Around With Olive Vee (Decca 9-30434) 15.00 60.00 58
(With the Three Tunes)
TRUE LOVE WAYS/Bo Diddley (Coral 62352) 3.75 15.00 63
TRUE LOVE WAYS/That Makes It Tough (Coral 9-62210) 5.00 20.00 60
WORDS OF LOVE/Mailman, Bring Me No More Blues (Coral 9-61852) 25.00 100.00 57
WORDS OF LOVE/Mailman, Bring Me No More Blues (Coral 9-61852) 20.00 80.00 57
(Promotional issue)
Decca issues with the stars on the label are valued at approximately 20-25% less than those with the parallel silver lines, which are priced above.
Decca and Coral promotional issues, not seperately listed above, are valued at approximately 20-25% more than commercial issues, which are priced above.
Also see Giordano, Lou
Also see Ivan
Also see Jennings, Waylon
Also see Petty, Norman, Trio

HOLLYHAWKS, The (Niki Sullivan & Gene Evans)
WHEN CAME THE FALL/I Cry All The Time (Jubilee 5441) 5.00 20.00 63

HOLLYHOCKS, The
DON'T SAY TOMORROW/You For Me (Nasco 6001) 1.00 4.00 57

HOLLYRIDGE STRINGS, The
ALL MY LOVING/Love Me Do (Capitol 5207) .75 3.00 64
SANTA'S GOT A BRAND NEW BAG/
Have Yourself A Merry Little Christmas (Capitol 5533) .75 3.00 65
THEME FROM "THE SEVEN FACES OF DR. LAO"/
The Fall Of Love (Capitol 5165) .75 3.00 64
THOSE LAZY-HAZY-CRAZY DAYS OF SUMMER/L-o-v-e (Capitol 5432) .75 3.00 65
Instrumentals

HOLLY TWINS, The
I WANT ELVIS FOR CHRISTMAS/Tender Age, The (Liberty 55048) 2.50 10.00 56

HOLLYWOOD ARGYLES, The (With Gary Paxton)
ALLEY-OOP/Sho Know A Lot About Love (Lute 5905) .75 3.00 60
ALLEY OOP '66/Do The Funky Foot (Kammy 105) .75 3.00 66
(Shown as by the New Hollywood Argyles)
HULLY GULLY/So Fine (Lute 6002) 1.00 4.00 60
LONGHAIR, UNSQUARE DUDE CALLED JACK/Ole (Chattahoochee 691) .75 3.00 65
YOU BEEN TORTURING ME/The Grubble (Paxley 752) 1.00 4.00 61
Also see Argyles, The

HOLLYWOOD PERSUADERS, The
DRUMS-A-GO-GO/Agua Caliente (Original Sound 50) .75 3.00 64
GRUNION RUN/Tijuana (Original Sound 39) 1.00 4.00 63
Instrumentals

HOLLYWOOD PLAYBOYS, The (Featuring Nick Massi)
TALK TO AUDREY/Ding Dong, School Is Out (Sure 105) 2.00 8.00
Also see 4 Seasons, The

HOLLYWOOD STARS, The
ALL THE KIDS ON THE STREET/All For Love (Arista 0241) .50 2.00 77
STAY THE WAY YOU ARE/ (Arista 0262) 1.00 4.00 77

TITLE/FLIP	LABEL & NO.	GOOD	NEAR MINT	YR.
HOLLYWOOD TORNADOES, The (Formerly The Tornadoes)				
BUSTIN' SURFBOARDS/Beyond The Surf (Shown as by the Tornadoes)	(Aertaun 100)	1.00	4.00	62
GREMMIE, THE (PART 1)/Gremmie, The (Part 2) (Instrumental)	(Aertaun 101)	1.00	4.00	62
MOON DAWG/Inebriated Surfer, The	(Aertaun 102)	1.00	4.00	63
PERSUASION/Juarez	(Original Sound 44)	1.00	4.00	64
PHANTOM SURFER/Shootin' Beavers	(Aertaun 103)	1.00	4.00	63
This group changed their name from the Tornadoes to the Hollywood Tornadoes to set them apart from the English group the Toranadoes that recorded for London Records.				
HOLMES, Leroy				
HIGH & THE MIGHTY, THE/Lisa	(MGM K-11761)	1.00	4.00	54
(THEME FROM) PROUD ONES, THE/ Wouldn't It Be Loverly	(MGM K-12275)	1.00	4.00	56
WHEN THE WHITE LILACS BLOOM AGAIN/Last Wagon	(MGM K-12317)	1.00	4.00	56
Instrumentals				
HOLMES, Rupert				
ESCAPE (THE PINA COLADA SONG)/Drop It	(Infinity 50035)	.50	2.00	79
HIM/Get Outta Yourself	(MCA 41173)	.50	2.00	80
I DON'T WANT TO HOLD YOUR HAND/ Man Behind The Woman	(Epic 8-50096)	.75	3.00	75
LET'S GET CRAZY TONIGHT/The Long Way Home	(Private Stock 45199)	.50	2.00	78
OUR NATIONAL PASTIME/Phantom Of The Opera	(Epic 5-11117)	.75	3.00	74
TERMINAL/Bagdad	(Epic 8-50013)	1.00	4.00	74
TERMINAL/Deco Lady	(Epic 8-50161)	.75	3.00	75
WEEKEND LOVER (PART 1)/Weekend Lover (Part 2)	(Epic 8-50223)	.75	3.00	76
WHO, WHAT, WHEN, WHERE, WHY/You Make Me Real	(Epic 8-50292)	.75	3.00	76
HOLT, Davey, & The Hubcaps				
PITTERY PAT/You Move Me	(United Artists 110X)	1.00	4.00	58
HOLY MODAL ROUNDERS, The				
BOOBS A LOT/Love Is The Closest Thing	(Metromedia 223)	1.00	4.00	71
HOMBRES, The				
IT'S A GAS/Am I High	(Verve Forecast 5076)	.75	3.00	68
LET IT OUT (LET IT ALL HANG OUT)/ Go Girl Go	(Verve Forcast 5058)	.75	3.00	67
PRODIGAL, THE/Mau Mau Mau	(Verve Forecast 5083)	.75	3.00	68
TAKE MY OVERWHELMING LOVE/Pumpkin Man	(Verve Forecast 5093)	.75	3.00	68
HOME (With Mike Stubbs)				
GREEN-EYED LADY/Sister Rosalie	(Epic 20003)	.75	3.00	72
SOMEONE IN YOUR LIFE/Happy Song	(Columbia 4-45490)	.75	3.00	71
HOMEMADE THEATER, The				
SANTA JAWS (PART 1)/Santa Jaws (Part 2)	(A&M 1776)	1.00	4.00	
HOMETOWNERS, The				
DING DONG/I Wanna Go Home	(Fraternity 842)	1.00	4.00	59
HONDAS, The				
SEND IT/Twelve Feet High	(Eden 4)	.75	3.00	62
HONDELLS, The (With Gary Usher)				
ATLANTA GEORGIA STRAY/Another Woman	(Columbia 4-44557)	1.00	4.00	68
FOLLOW THE BOUNCING BALL/	(Amos 131)	1.00	4.00	69
HOT ROD HIGH/Little Honda (With Brian Wilson) (Promotional issue, designating "Hot Rod High" as the "plug" side.)	(Mercury 72324)	2.00	8.00	64
KISSIN' MY LIFE AWAY/A Country Love	(Mercury 72605)	1.00	4.00	67
LEGEND OF FRANKIE & JOHNNY/Shine On Ruby Mountain	(Amos 150)	1.00	4.00	70
LITTLE HONDA (With Brian Wilson)/Hot Rod High	(Mercury 72324)	1.50	6.00	64
LITTLE SIDEWALK SURFER GIRL/Come On (Pack It On)	(Mercury 72405)	1.25	5.00	65
MY BUDDY SEAT (With Brian Wilson)/ You're Gonna Ride With Me	(Mercury 72366)	1.50	6.00	64
SEA OF LOVE/Do As I Say	(Mercury 72443)	1.25	5.00	65
YOU MEET THE NICEST PEOPLE ON A HONDA/ Sea Cruise	(Mercury 72479)	1.50	6.00	65
YOUNGER GIRL/All American Girl	(Mercury 72563)	1.00	4.00	67
HONEY CONE, The (With Edna Wright)				
DAY I FOUND MYSELF, THE/When Will It End	(Hot Wax 7113)	.50	2.00	71
GIRLS, IT AIN'T EASY/The Feeling's Gone	(Hot Wax 6903)	.75	3.00	69
ONE MONKEY DON'T STOP NO SHOW (PART 1)/ One Monkey don't Stop No Show (Part 2)	(Hot Wax 7110)	.50	2.00	71
SITTIN' ON A TIME BOMB/ It's Better To Have Loved Than Lost	(Hot Wax 7205)	.50	2.00	72
STICK UP/V.I.P.	(Hot Wax 7106)	.50	2.00	71
TAKE ME WITH YOU/	(Hot Wax 7001)	1.00	4.00	70
WHEN WILL IT END/	(Hot Wax 7005)	1.00	4.00	70
WANT ADS/We Belong Together	(Hot Wax 7011)	.50	2.00	71
WHILE YOU'RE OUT LOOKING FOR SUGAR/ The Feeling's Gone	(Hot Wax 6901)	.75	3.00	69
Also see Hale & the Hushabyes				
HONEYCOMBS, The				
CAN'T GET THROUGH TO YOU/That's The Way	(Warner Bros. 5655)	1.00	4.00	65
HAVE I THE RIGHT/Please Don't Pretend Again	(Interphon 7707)	1.00	4.00	64
HOW WILL I KNOW/Who Is Sylvia	(Warner Bros. 5803)	1.00	4.00	66
I CAN'T STOP/I'll Cry Tomorrow	(Interphon 7713)	1.00	4.00	64
I'LL SEE YOU TOMORROW/ Something Better Beginning	(Warner Bros. 5634)	1.00	4.00	65
THAT'S THE WAY/Color Slide	(Interphon 7716)	1.00	4.00	65
HONEYCONES, The				
OP/Vision Of You	(Ember 1036)	1.00	4.00	58
HONEYMAN				
BROTHER BILL (THE LAST CLEAN SHIRT)/ James Junior	(Red-Bird 10-007)	1.00	4.00	68
HONEYS, The				
HE'S A DOLL/Love Of A Boy & Girl	(Warner Bros. 5430)	10.00	40.00	64
ONE YOU CAN'T HAVE, THE/From Jimmy, With Tears	(Capitol 5093)	17.50	70.00	63
PRAY FOR SURF/Hide Go Seek	(Capitol 5034)	12.50	50.00	63
SURFIN' DOWN THE SWANEE RIVER/Shoot The Curl	(Capitol 4952)	12.50	50.00	63
SURFIN' DOWN THE SWANEE RIVER/Shoot The Curl (Picture sleeve)	(Capitol 4952)	25.00	100.00	63
TONIGHT YOU BELONG TO ME/Goodnight My Love	(Capitol 2454)	7.50	30.00	69
The Honeys consisted of Ginger Blake, also known as Saundra Glantz, Diane Rovell & Marilyn Rovell (Marilyn later married Brian Wilson...thus Marilyn Wilson.)				
All of their records had Brian Wilson involvement and the Beach Boys actually sang a solo part on "Surfin' Down the Swanee River."				
Also see Beach Boys, The				
Also see Jan & Dean				
Also see Sharon Marie				
Also see Spring				
Also see Surfaris, The				
Also see Usher, Gary				
HONG KONG WHITE SOX, The				
CHOLLEY-OOP (Parody)/He'd Better Go	(Trans-World 6906)	1.00	4.00	60
HONG KONGS, The				
SURFIN' IN THE CHINA SEA/Popeye	(Melody Mill 303)	1.00	4.00	63
HONORABLES, The				
CASTLE IN THE SKY/	(Honor Records 100)	5.00	20.00	
HONOR SOCIETY, The: see Happenings, The				
HOODOO RHYTHM DEVILS, The				
HOODOO BEAT/Uncle Joe's Homemade Brew (Shown as by Joe Crane & His Hoodoo Rhythm Devils)	(Capitol 3166)	.75	3.00	71
SEA OF LOVE/	(Blue Thumb 224)	.75	3.00	74
WORKING IN A COAL MINE/	(Fantasy 815)	.75	3.00	78
HOOK, Marcus, Roll Band				
NATURAL MAN/Boogalooing Is For Wooing	(Capitol 3505)	2.50	10.00	73
HOPE, Bob				
AIN'T WE GOT FUN/Lucky Us (With Margaret Whiting)	(Capitol 783)	2.00	8.00	49
BLIND DATE/Home Cookin' (With Margaret Whiting)	(Capitol 1042)	1.25	5.00	50
FOUR-LEGGED FRIEND, A/There's A Cloud	(Capitol 2161)	1.25	5.00	52
PARIS HOLIDAY/Nothing In Common (With Bing Crosby)	(United Artists 109)	1.00	4.00	58
THAT CERTAIN FEELING/ Zing Went The Strings Of My Heart	(RCA Victor 47-6577)	1.00	4.00	56
WING DING/Am I In Love (With Jane Russell)	(Capitol 2109)	1.25	5.00	52
HOPEFUL, The				
6 O'CLOCK NEWS-SILENT NIGHT/ 6 O'clock News-America The Beautiful	(Mercury 72637)	1.00	4.00	66
HOPKIN, Mary				
GOODBYE/Sparrow	(Apple 1806)	.75	3.00	69
IF YOU LOVE ME (REALLY LOVE ME)/Tell Me How	(RCA PB-10694)	.50	2.00	76
KNOCK KNOCK WHO'S THERE/International	(Apple 1855)	.75	3.00	72
QUE SERA SERA/Fields Of St. Etienne	(Apple 1823)	.75	3.00	70
TEMMA HARBOUR/Lontano Dagli Occhi	(Apple 1816)	.75	3.00	70
THINK ABOUT YOUR CHILDREN/Heritage	(Apple 1825)	.75	3.00	70
THOSE WERE THE DAYS/Turn, Turn, Turn	(Apple 1801)	.75	3.00	68
WATER, PAPER, & CLAY/Streets Of London	(Apple 1843)	.75	3.00	71
HOPKINS, Nicky (Of Quicksilver Messenger Service)				
SPEED ON/Sundown In Mexico (With George Harrison on guitar)	(Columbia 4-45869)	1.00	4.00	72
Also see Night				
HORIZON, The				
SHE'S A RAINBOW/Tell Me, My Lady	(Capitol 3339)	.75	3.00	72
HORIZONS, The				
HEY NOW BABY/Strange Oh Strange	(Regina 1321)	1.00	4.00	
HORNELS, The				
RUNT/Breakfast In Bed	(Emerald 5014)	.75	3.00	
HORNETS, The				
ON THE TRACK/Motorcycles U.S.A.	(Liberty 55688)	1.00	4.00	64
HORN, Paul				
WITCH DOCTOR/	(Mushroom 7037)	.50	2.00	78
HORSLIPS				
LONELINESS/Homesick	(DJM 1105)	.50	2.00	79
NIGHTTOWN BOY/	(RCA PB-10123)	.75	3.00	75
RESCUE ME/Soap Opera	(Mercury 76030)	.50	2.00	79
SURE THE BOY WAS GREEN/Exiles (Pressed on green vinyl)	(DJM 1036)	.50	2.00	78
WARM SWEET BREATH OF LOVE/	(DJM 1026)	.50	2.00	77
HORTON, Jamie				
MY LITTLE MARINE/Missin'	(Joy 234)	1.00	4.00	60
ROBOT MAN/We're Through-We're Finished	(Joy 241)	1.00	4.00	60
THEY'RE PLAYING OUR SONG ("16 CANDLES")/ Going, Going, Gone	(Joy 258)	1.00	4.00	61
HOSFORD, Larry				
EVERYTHING'S BROKEN DOWN/Long Line To Chicago	(Shelter 40381)	.50	2.00	74
WISHING I COULD/Nobody Remembers The Losers (With George Harrison on guitar)	(Shelter 62001)	.50	2.00	76
HOSS, Charley, & The Ponies				
MADISON TWIST/Raunchy Twist	(Columbia 4-41855)	.75	3.00	60
HOT				
ANGEL IN YOUR ARMS/Just 'Cause I'm Guilty	(Big Tree 16085)	.50	2.00	77
I DON'T WANNA BE THE REASON THAT YOU LEAVE HER/	(Big Tree 16127)	.50	2.00	78
IF THAT'S THE WAY THAT YOU WANT IT/	(Big Tree 16118)	.50	2.00	78
RIGHT FEELING AT THE WRONG TIME, THE/ Why Don't You Believe In Your Man	(Big Tree 16099)	.50	2.00	77
TAKE MY LOVE FOR GRANTED/	(Big Tree 16134)	.50	2.00	79
YOU BROUGHT THE WOMAN OUT OF ME/If You Don't Love Her (When You Gonna Leave Her?)	(Big Tree 16108)	.50	2.00	78
YOU CAN DO IT/If You Don't Love Her (When You Gonna Leave Her?)	(Big Tree 16104)	.50	2.00	77
HOT CHOCOLATE				
BROTHER LOUIE/I Want To Be Free	(RAK 4515)	.50	2.00	73
CAVEMAN BILLY/I Believe (In Love)	(RAK 4506)	.50	2.00	73
DISCO QUEEN/Makin' Music	(Big Tree 16038)	.50	2.00	75
DON'T STOP IT NOW/Beautiful Lady	(Big Tree 16060)	.50	2.00	76
EMMA/A Love Like Yours	(Big Tree 16031)	.50	2.00	75
EVERY 1'S A WINNER/Power Of Love	(Infinity 50002)	.50	2.00	78
GIVE PEACE A CHANCE/Living Without Tomorrow (Shown as by the Hot Chocolate Band)	(Apple 1812)	1.00	4.00	69
GOING THROUGH THE MOTIONS/Don't Turn It Off	(Infinity 50016)	.50	2.00	79
HEAVEN IS IN THE BACK SEAT OF MY CADILLAC/	(Big Tree 16078)	.50	2.00	76
I JUST LOVE WHAT YOU'RE DOING/	(Infinity 50033)	.50	2.00	79
MAN TO MAN/	(Big Tree 16101)	.50	2.00	77
SO YOU WIN AGAIN/A Part Of Being With You	(Big Tree 16096)	.50	2.00	77
YOU COULD HAVE BEEN A LADY/Everybody's Laughing	(RAK 4503)	.50	2.00	72
YOU SEXY THING/Amazing Skin Song	(Big Tree 16047)	.50	2.00	75
HOT KNIVES, The				
HEY GRANDMA/I Hear The Wind Blow	(K.O. 0002)	.75	3.00	
LOVIN' YOU/Around The World	(K.O. 0001)	.75	3.00	
HOT PEPPERS, The				
SURFIN' WITH THE MONKEY/New Orleans Surf	(Sea Horn 101)	1.00	4.00	63
HOT TAMALES, The				
MEXICAN TWIST/The Pony	(Alpine 68)	.75	3.00	60
HOT TUNA (With Paul Cassady & Jorma Kaukonen)				
BEEN SO LONG/Candy Man	(Grunt 0528)	1.25	5.00	71
HOT JELLY ROLL BLUES/Surphase Tension	(Grunt 10443)	1.00	4.00	75
IT'S SO EASY/I Can't Be Satisfied	(Grunt 10776)	1.00	4.00	76
WATER SONG/Keep On Truckin'	(Grunt 0502)	1.25	5.00	71
Cassady & Kaukonen were previously with Jefferson Airplane.				
HOTEL				
HOLD ON THE THE NIGHT/Losing My Mind	(MCA 41113)	.50	2.00	79
YOU'LL LOVE AGAIN/Take A Chance	(Mercury 73979)	.50	2.00	78
YOU'VE GOT ANOTHER THING COMING/One Time Too Many	(MCA 41050)	.50	2.00	79
HOTLEGS (Eric Stewart, Kevin Godley & Lol Cream)				
NEANDERTHAL MAN/ You Didn't Like It Because You Didn't Think Of It	(Capitol 2886)	1.25	5.00	70
HOW MANY TIMES/Run Baby Run	(Capitol 3043)	3.75	15.00	71
Also see Mindbenders, The				
Also see 10CC				
HOT-TODDYS, The				
HOE DOWN/Nan-je-di	(Strand 25011)	1.00	4.00	59
ROCKIN' CRICKETS/Shakin' & Stompin'	(Shan-Todd 0056)	1.25	5.00	59
ROCKIN' CRICKETS/Shakin' & Stompin'	(Corsican 0056)	1.00	4.00	59
("Rockin' Crickets" was reissued in 1963 and shown as by the Rockin' Rebels.)				
HOUNDS, The				
DOO WAH DIDDY DIDDY/Angel Of Fire	(Columbia 11114)	.50	2.00	79
UNDER MY THUMB/The Moth & The Fire	(Columbia 11159)	.50	2.00	79
HOUR GLASS, The: see Allman Brothers, The				
HOWARD, Don				
OH HAPPY DAY/You Went Away	(Triple-A 2503)	2.00	8.00	52
OH HAPPY DAY/You Went Away	(Essex 311)	1.25	5.00	52
HOWARD, Eddy				
AUF WIEDERSEH'N SWEETHEART/I Don't Want To Take	(Mercury 5871)	1.25	5.00	52
BE ANYTHING (BUT BE MINE)/She Took	(Mercury 5815)	1.25	5.00	52
SIN/My Wife & I	(Mercury 5711)	1.25	5.00	51
STOLEN LOVE/Wishin'	(Mercury 5784)	1.25	5.00	52
TEEN-AGER'S WALTZ, THE/Choo-Choo-Cha-Cha	(Mercury 70700)	1.00	4.00	55
TO THINK YOU'VE CHOSEN ME/The One Rose	(Mercury 5517)	1.25	5.00	50
HOWARD, Gregory				
WHEN IN LOVE (DO AS LOVERS DO)/Sweet Pea (Promotional issue only, vocal backing by the Cadillacs)	(Kapp 536)	12.50	50.00	63
(A bootleg version of this recording is on Gee 1013, and is shown as by the Gee Tones.)				
HOWARD, Jerry				
SNAKE IN THE GARDEN/My Every Heartbeat	(Imperial 5632)	2.00	8.00	59
HOWDY DOODY (With Bob Smith)				
HOWDY DOODY SANTA CLAUS/ Howdy Doody & Mother Goose	(RCA Victor 47-4017)	2.50	10.00	51
IT'S HOWDY DOODY TIME/Howdy Doody's Do's & Don'ts	(RCA 0499)	.75	3.00	71
H.P. LOVECRAFT				
ANYWAY THAT YOU WANT ME/It's All Over For You	(Philips 40464)	.75	3.00	
KEEPER OF THE KEYS/Blue Jack Of Diamonds	(Philips 40578)	.75	3.00	
WAYFARING STRANGER/The Time Machine	(Philips 40491)	.75	3.00	67
WHITE SHIP/	(Philips 40506)	.75	3.00	
HUB				
SWEET MUSIC/Think About It	(Capitol 4268)	.50	2.00	76
WHERE THERE'S SMOKE, THERE'S FIRE/	(Capitol 4310)	.50	2.00	76
Some members of Hub were previously with Rare Earth.				
HUB KAPP & THE WHEELS (Featuring Pat McMahan)				
LET'S REALLY HEAR IT (FOR HUB KAPP)/Work, Work	(Take Five 631)	1.25	5.00	63
LITTLE VOLKS/What You're Doin To Me	(Framagratz)	1.25	5.00	63
SIGH, CRY, ALMOST DIE/Bony Marony	(Capitol 5215)	1.25	5.00	64
SIGH, CRY, ALMOST DIE/Bony Marony (Picture sleeve)	(Capitol 5215)	2.50	10.00	64
HUBBARD, Muvva "Guitar"				
PONYTAIL/Congo Mambo	(ABC-Paramount 9774)	1.00	4.00	56
RAUNCHY/The Other Side	(ABC-Paramount 9869)	1.00	4.00	57
WHIRLPOOL/Ponytail	(ABC-Paramount 9982)	1.25	5.00	58
HUBBELL, Frank, & The Hubb-Caps				
BROKEN DATE/	(Topix 6005)	1.25	5.00	58
HUBBELS, The				
HIPPY DIPPY FUNKY MONKEY DOUBLE BUBBLE SITAR MAN/ City Woman	(Audio Fidelity 150)	.75	3.00	69
HUBCAPS, The (Ernie Maresca & Tom Bogdany)				
HOT ROD CITY/Hot Rod City (Instrumental)	(Laurie 3219)	1.25	5.00	65
HUCKLEBERRY HOUND				
BINGO RINGO/	(Merri 6011)	1.50	6.00	64
HUDDERSFIELD TRANSIT AUTHORITY, The				
RUNAWAY/Bayou Farm	(Decca 32956)	.75	3.00	71
HUDSON: see Hudson Brothers				
HUDSON & COMPANY				
SUPER ROCK/State Of Mind	(G.M. 156)	.75	3.00	
HUDSON & JUDSON				
WHO'S ON FIRST/The Pits (Comedy)	(Cream 7824)	.50	2.00	78
HUDSON & LANDRY (Bob Hudson & Ron Landry)				
AJAX AIRLINES/Bruiser LaRue	(Dore 868)	.75	3.00	72
AJAX LIQUOR STORE/Hippie & The Redneck	(Dore 855)	.75	3.00	71
AJAX MORTUARY/Ajax Pet Store	(Dore 881)	.75	3.00	73
FRONTIER CHRISTMAS/Soul Bowl	(Dore 879)	.75	3.00	72
HIPPIE & THE REDNECK/Top 40 D.J.'s	(Dore 852)	.75	3.00	71
WEIRD KINGDOM, THE/Montague For Governor (Comedy)	(Dore 898)	.75	3.00	74
HUDSON, Bob (Of Hudson & Landry)				
WHAT IS A BLIND DATE/Last Dance At The Prom	(Dore 814)	1.00	4.00	
Also see Emperor, The				
HUDSON BROTHERS, The (Bill, Bret, Mark)				
BE A MAN/Sunday Driver	(Rocket 40317)	.50	2.00	74
COOCHIE COOCHIE COO/Me & My Guitar	(Casablanca 816)	.50	2.00	74
HELP WANTED/The Last Time I Looked	(Arista 0208)	.50	2.00	76
I DON'T WANNA BE LONELY/Pauline	(Arista 0286)	.50	2.00	77
IF YOU REALLY NEED ME/America/Fight Back (Shown as by Hudson)	(Rocket 40141)	.50	2.00	73
LEAVIN' IT'S OVER/ (Shown as by Hudson)	(Playboy 60001)	.50	2.00	73
LONELY SCHOOL YEAR/If You Really Need Me	(Rocket 40464)	.50	2.00	75
RENDEZVOUS/Medley: a) These Things We Do, b) Home, c) Out Of The Rainbow, d) Find Me A Woman, e) Little Brown Box, f) One & The Same	(Rocket 40417)	.50	2.00	75
RUNAWAY, THE/You Can't Make Me Cry	(Arista 0371)	.50	2.00	78
SO YOU ARE A STAR/Ma Ma Ma Baby	(Casablanca 0108)	.50	2.00	74
SO YOU ARE A STAR/Ma Ma Ma Baby	(Casablanca 801)	.50	2.00	74
SPINNING THE WHEEL (WITH THE GIRL YOU LOVE)/ Bernie Was A Friend Of Ours	(Rocket 40508)	.50	2.00	76
WORLD WOULD BE A LITTLE BETTER, THE/ (Shown as by Hudson)	(Lionel 3211)	1.00	4.00	
HUDSON, Rock				
PILLOW TALK/Roly Poly	(Decca 9-30966)	1.00	4.00	59
HUFFMAN, Donnie (Of Donnie & Delchords)				
PINK CADILLAC/This Is The Last Time	(Taurus 3542)	1.00	4.00	
HUGHES, Lynne (Of The Charlatans)				
FREEWAY GYPSY/Never Stop A Dream	(Mercury 73059)	1.50	6.00	70
Also see Tongue & Groove				
HUGHES, Marvin				
BLAST OFF/Nashville Bossa Nova	(Capitol 4950)	.75	3.00	63

TITLE/FLIP — LABEL & NO. — GOOD — NEAR MINT — YR.

HUGHLEY, George
DO THE BEATLE/My Love Is True (Gaye 004) 1.25 5.00 64

HUGO & LUIGI (Hugo Peretti & Luigi Creatore)
YOUNG ABE LINCOLN/
Two Thirds Of The Tennessee River (Mercury 70721) 1.00 4.00 55

HUHN, Billy, & The Catalinas
BALTIMORE/Freshman Queen (Lesley 1923) 5.00 20.00

HULIN, T.K.
I'M NOT A FOOL ANYMORE/Teardrops, More Teardrops (LK 1112) 1.00 4.00 63
I'M NOT A FOOL ANYMORE/Teardrops, More Teardrops (Smash 1830) .75 3.00 63

HULLABALLOOS, The
DID YOU EVER/Beware (Roulette 4593) 1.00 4.00 65
I WON'T TURN AWAY NOW/My Heart Keeps Telling Me (Roulette 4622) 1.00 4.00 65
I'M GONNA LOVE YOU TOO/Party Doll (Roulette 4587) 1.00 4.00 64
LEARNING THE GAME/Don't Stop (Roulette 4612) 1.00 4.00 65

HUMAN BEINGS, The
BECAUSE I LOVE HER/Ain't That Lovin' You Baby (Warner Bros. 5622) 1.25 5.00 65
I CAN'T TELL/Yessir, That's My Baby (Impact 1022) 1.50 6.00 65

HUMAN BEINZ, The
EVERY TIME WOMAN/The Face (Capitol 2198) 1.00 4.00 68
NOBODY BUT ME/Sueno (Capitol 5990) 1.00 4.00 67
PIED PIPER/You Can't Make Me Cry (Gateway 838) 1.25 5.00 67
THIS LITTLE GIRL OF MINE/I've Got To Keep On Pushin' (Capitol 2431) 1.00 4.00 69
TIMES THEY ARE A CHANGING, THE/Gloria (Gateway 828) 1.25 5.00 66
TURN ON YOUR LOVE LIGHT/It's Fun To Be Clean (Capitol 2119) 1.00 4.00 68

HUMAN EXPRESSION, The
EVERY NIGHT/Love At Psychedelic Velocity (Accent 1214) .75 3.00 67

HUMAN INSTINCT, The
PINK DAWN/Renaissance Fair (Time 503) .75 3.00 69

HUMAN JUNGLE, The
GORILLA MILK/World's Tallest Pigmy (Double Shot 112) 1.25 5.00 67

HUMBLEBUMS, The (With Gerry Rafferty & Billy Conally)
ALL THE BEST PEOPLE DO IT/Crusin' (United Artists 50711) 1.00 4.00 71

HUMBLE PIE (With Steve Marriott & Peter Frampton)
BLACK COFFEE/Say No More (A&M 1406) .75 3.00 72
GET DOWN TO IT/Honky Tonk Woman (A&M 1440) .75 3.00 73
HOT 'N' NASTY/You're So Good For Me (A&M 1349) .75 3.00 72
I DON'T NEED NO DOCTOR/A Song For Jenny (A&M 1282) 1.25 5.00 71
NATURAL BORN WOMAN/I'll Go Alone (Immediate 001) 1.50 6.00 69
NINETY-NINE POUNDS/Rally With Ali (A&M 1530) .75 3.00 74
ROCK & ROLL MUSIC/Road Hog (A&M 1711) .75 3.00 75
30 DAYS IN THE HOLE/Sweet Peace & Time (A&M 1366) .75 3.00 72
Also see Herd
Also see Small Faces

HUMDINGERS, The
NECKLACE OF TEAR DROPS/The Clock In Lovers Lane (Dale 106) 1.00 4.00 57

HUMMINGBIRD
SHE IS MY LADY/ (A&M 1993) .50 2.00 77
TROUBLE MAKER/Gypsy Skys (A&M 1874) .50 2.00 76

HUMPERDINCK, Englebert (Gerry Dorsey)
AFTER THE LOVIN'/Let's Remember The Good Times (Epic 50270) .50 2.00 76
AM I THAT EASY TO FORGET/ (Parrot 40023) .75 3.00 67
ANOTHER TIME, ANOTHER PLACE/ (Parrot 40065) .75 3.00 71
GOODBYE MY FRIEND/I Believe In Miracles (Epic 50365) .50 2.00 76
I'M A BETTER MAN/Cafe (Cosa Hai Messo Nel Caffe) (Parrot 40040) .75 3.00 69
I'M LEAVING YOU/ (Parrot 40075) .75 3.00 73
I NEVER SAID GOODBYE/Time After Time (Parrot 40072) .75 3.00 73
IN TIME/How Does It Feel (Parrot 40071) .75 3.00 72
LAST WALTZ, THE/That Promise (Parrot 40019) .75 3.00 67
LES BICYCLETTES DE BELSIZE/Three Little Words (Parrot 40032) .75 3.00 68
LOVE IS ALL (Parrot 40076) .75 3.00 73
MAN WITHOUT LOVE, A (QUANDO M'INNAMORO)/
Call On Me (Parrot 40027) .75 3.00 68
MISTY BLUE/Quando, Quando, Quando (London 20093) .50 2.00 76
MY MARIE/ (Parrot 40049) .75 3.00 70
RELEASE ME (& LET ME LOVE AGAIN)/Ten Guitars (Parrot 40011) .75 3.00 67
SWEETHEART/Born To Be Wanted (Parrot 40054) .75 3.00 70
THIS IS WHAT YOU MEAN TO ME/World Without Music (Parrot 40085) .75 3.00 74
TOO BEAUTIFUL TO LAST/A Hundred Times A Day (Parrot 40069) .75 3.00 72
THERE GOES MY EVERYTHING/You Love (Parrot 40015) .75 3.00 67
WAY IT USED TO BE, THE/A Good Thing Going (Parrot 40036) .75 3.00 69
WHEN THERE'S NO YOU/ (Parrot 40059) .75 3.00 71
WINTER WORLD OF LOVE/Take My Heart (Parrot 40044) .75 3.00 69

HUNG JURY, The
BUSES/Let The Good Times In (Colgems 1010) 1.00 4.00 67

HUNGRY TIGER
FE FI FO FUM/Fum Fi Fo Fee (White-Whale WW-313) .75 3.00 69
TEN MILES LONG/Can't Stop Breathing (Magna-Glide MGR-331) .50 2.00 77

HUNT, Pee Wee
MUSKRAT RAMBLE/Royal Garden Blues (Capitol 1141) 1.50 6.00 50
OH!/Darktown Strutters' Ball (Capitol 1691) 1.25 5.00 51
OH!/San (Capitol 2442) 1.00 4.00 53
(Instrumental)
Also see Blanc, Mel
Also see Four Knights, The

HUNT SISTERS, The
ELVIS IS ROCKIN' AGAIN/Teardrops (Fortune 210) 2.50 10.00 60

HUNTER, Christine
SANTA BRING ME RINGO/Where Were You Daddy (Roulette 4589) 1.25 5.00 64

HUNTER, Ian (Of Mott The Hoople)
JUST ANOTHER NIGHT/Cleveland Rocks (Chrysalis 2352) .50 2.00 79
ONCE BITTEN TWICE SHY/3,000 Miles From Home (Columbia 10161) .75 3.00
WHEN THE DAYLIGHT COMES/Life After Death (Columbia 10161) .75 3.00 75

HUNTER, Robert (Of The Grateful Dead)
RUM RUNNERS/ (Round 4505) .50 2.00 74

HUNTER, Rod
APACHE/Dear Miss Christie (London 1044) .50 2.00 72
(Instrumental)

HUNTER, Tab (Arthur Andrew Kelm)
I'LL BE WITH YOU IN APPLE BLOSSOM TIME/
My Only Love (Warner Bros. 5032) .75 3.00 59
I'LL BE WITH YOU IN APPLE BLOSSOM TIME/
My Only Love (Warner Bros. 5032) 1.50 6.00 59
(Stereo single issue)
I'M ALONE BECAUSE I LOVE YOU/Don't Let It Get Around (Dot 15657) 1.00 4.00 57
JEALOUS HEART/Lonesome Road (Warner Bros. 5008) .75 3.00 58
NINETY-NINE WAYS/Don't Get Around Much Anymore (Dot 15548) 1.00 4.00 57
THERE'S NO FOOL LIKE A YOUNG FOOL/
I'll Never Smile Again (Warner Bros. 5051) .75 3.00 59

TITLE/FLIP — LABEL & NO. — GOOD — NEAR MINT — YR.

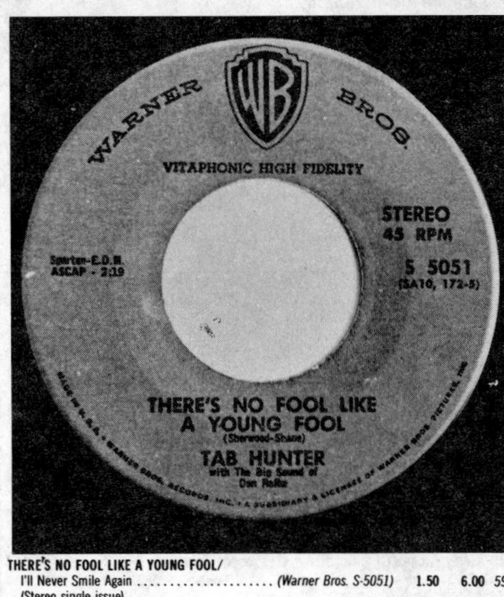

THERE'S NO FOOL LIKE A YOUNG FOOL/
I'll Never Smile Again (Warner Bros. S-5051) 1.50 6.00 59
(Stereo single issue)
YOUNG LOVE/Red Sails In The Sunset (Dot 15533) 1.00 4.00 56

HUSHLEY, George
DO THE BEATLE/ (Gaye 004) 1.25 5.00 64

HUTCH, Billy
EEFIN-NANNY STOMP/Eefin-nanny Monkey (Time 1067) 1.00 4.00 63

HUTTON, Danny
BIG BRIGHT EYES/Monster Shindig (Part 2) (HBR 453) 1.00 4.00 65
FUNNY HOW LOVE CAN BE/Dreamin' Isn't Good For You (MGM 13502) 1.00 4.00 66
ROSES & RAINBOWS/Monster Shindig (HBR 447) 1.00 4.00 65
Also see Three Dog Night
Also see Enemys, The

HYLAND, Brian
COME WITH ME/Delilah (Dot 17078) .75 3.00 68
DREAMY EYES/Gonna Make A Woman Of You (Dot 17291) .75 3.00 69
FOUR LITTLE HEELS (THE CLICKITY CLACK SONG)/
That's How Much (Kapp 352) 1.00 4.00 60
GET THE MESSAGE/Kinda Groovy (Philips 40472) .75 3.00 67
GINNY COME LATELY/I Should Be Gettin' Better (ABC-Paramount 10294) .75 3.00 62
GYPSY WOMAN/You & ME (Uni 55240) .50 2.00 70
HE DON'T UNDERSTAND YOU/Love Will Find A Way (Philips 40263) .75 3.00 65
HERE'S TO OUR LOVE/Two Kinds Of Girls (Philips 40179) .75 3.00 64
HOLIDAY FOR CLOWNS/Yesterday I Had A Girl (Philips 40444) .75 3.00 67
HUNG UP IN YOUR EYES/Why Mine (Philips 40424) .75 3.00 67
I LOVE EVERY LITTLE THING ABOUT YOU/
With My Eyes Wide Open (Uni 55323) .50 2.00 72
I MAY NOT LIVE TO SEE TOMORROW/
It Ain't That Way At All (ABC-Paramount 10374) 1.00 4.00 62
I WISH TODAY WAS YESTERDAY/
Somewhere In The Night (ABC-Paramount 10427) 1.00 4.00 63
IF MARY'S THERE/Remember Me (ABC-Paramount 10400) 1.00 4.00 63
IF YOU COME BACK/Out Of The Blue (Uni 55306) .50 2.00 71
I'LL NEVER STOP WANTING YOU/Night I Cried (ABC-Paramount 10262) 1.00 4.00 61
I'M AFRAID TO GO HOME/
Save Your Heart For Me (ABC-Paramount 10452) 1.00 4.00 63
ITSY BITSY TEENIE WEENIE YELLOW POLKADOT BIKINI/
Don't Dilly Dally Sally (Leader 805) 1.50 6.00 60
ITSY BITSY TEENIE WEENIE YELLOW POLKADOT BIKINI/
Don't Dilly Dally, Sally (Kapp 342) 1.00 4.00 60
JOKER WENT WILD, THE/I Can Hear The Rain (Philips 40377) .75 3.00 66
LET ME BELONG TO YOU/Let It Die (ABC-Paramount 10236) 1.00 4.00 61
LET US MAKE OUR OWN MISTAKES/
Nothing Matters But You (ABC-Paramount 10494) 1.00 4.00 63
LIBRARY LOVE AFFAIR/Rosemary (Leader 801) 2.00 8.00 60
LIPSTICK ON YOUR LIPS/When Will I Know (Kapp 401) 1.00 4.00 61
LONELY TEARDROPS/ (Uni 55272) .50 2.00 71
LOP SIDED OVER LOADED (& IT WIGGLED WHEN WE ROAD IT)/
I Gotta Go (Because I Love You) (Kapp 363) 1.25 5.00 61
MILLION TO ONE, A/It Could All Begin Again (Dot 17222) .75 3.00 69
ONLY WANNA TO MAKE YOU HAPPY/ (Uni 55334) .50 2.00 72
OUT OF SIGHT, OUT OF MIND/Act Naturally (ABC-Paramount 10549) 1.00 4.00 64
PLEDGING MY LOVE/Devoted To You (Philips 40203) .75 3.00 64
RUN, RUN, LOOK & SEE/Why Did You do It (Philips 40405) .75 3.00 66
SEALED WITH A KISS/Summer Job (ABC-Paramount 10336) .75 3.00 62
SHE'S MY ALL AMERICAN GIRL/The Night I Cried (Kapp 429) 1.25 5.00 61
SO LONG, MARIANNE/ (Uni 55287) .50 2.00 71
SOMETIMES THEY DO, SOMETIMES THEY DON'T/ (Philips 40354) .75 3.00 66
SPRINGFIELD, ILLINOIS/The Lover (Dot 17109) .75 3.00 68
STAY & LOVE ME ALL SUMMER/Rainy April Morning (Dot 17258) .75 3.00 69
STAY AWAY FROM HER/I Can't Keep A Secret (Philips 40306) .75 3.00 65
TRAGEDY/You Better Stop & Think It Over (Dot 17176) .75 3.00 68
WARMED OVER KISSES/Walk A Lonely Mile (ABC-Paramount 10359) 1.00 4.00 62
WORDS ON PAPER/Apologize (Dot 17050) .75 3.00 67
WORDS ON PAPER/It's Christmas Time Once Again (Dot 17061) .75 3.00 67
YOU & ME/Could You Dig It (Uni 55193) .75 3.00 70

HYMAN, Dick, Trio
HI-LILI, HI-LO/Junglero (MGM K-12207) 1.00 4.00 56
(THEME FROM) THREE PENNY OPERA/
Baubles, Bangles & Beads (MGM K-12149) 1.00 4.00 56

HYPO DERMICS, The
BLUES TILL NEWS/Operation Twisted (Titanic 5002) .75 3.00 62

The transition to a country music style has been made by several pop & rock singers of the fifties and sixties. The pop & rock releases by these artists will appear in this guide, while the country music releases will be listed in our guides covering that field of music.

Likewise, your favorite soul and rhythm & blues artists that are not covered in this guide are—or will soon be—included in our Blues-Rhythm & Blues-Soul Price Guide.

TITLE/FLIP — LABEL & NO. — GOOD — NEAR MINT — YR.

I.A.& P. CO., The (Italian Asphalt & Pavement Company)
CHECK YOURSELF/ (Colossus 110) 1.00 4.00 70
Also see Duprees, The

IAN & SYLVIA (Ian Tyson & Sylvia Fricker)
CREATORS OF RAIN/Summer Wages (Columbia 4-45430) .75 3.00 71
FOUR STRONG WINDS/C.C. Rider (Vanguard 35021) 1.25 5.00 63
HOUSE OF CARDS/90 Degrees X 90 Degrees (Vanguard 35062) 1.00 4.00 68
LOVIN' SOUND/Pilgrimage To Paradise (MGM K-13686) .75 3.00 66
MORE OFTEN THAN NOT/Some Kind Of Fool (Columbia 4-45475) .75 3.00 71
YOU WERE ON MY MIND/Someday Soon (Vanguard 35025) 1.25 5.00 64
YOU WERE ON MY MIND/Salmon In The Sea (Columbia 4-45680) .75 3.00 72
Also see Great Speckled Bird

IAN & THE ZODIACS
CRYIN' GAME/Lovin' Wreck (Philips 40244) 1.00 4.00 64
MESSAGE TO MARTHE/Good Morning Little School Girl (Philips 40277) 1.00 4.00 65
NO MONEY, NO HONEY/Where Were You (Philips 40369) 1.00 4.00 66
SO MUCH IN LOVE WITH YOU/This Empty Place (Philips 40291) 1.00 4.00 65
WHY CAN'T IT BE ME/Leave It To Me (Philips 40343) 1.00 4.00 66

IAN, Janis
AT SEVENTEEN/Stars (Columbia 10154) .50 2.00 75
BOY I REALLY TIED ONE ON/Aftertones (Columbia 10297) .50 2.00 76
BRIDGE, THE/Do You Wanna Dance (Columbia 10864) .50 2.00 78
EVERYBODY KNOWS/Janey's Blues (Verve Forecast 5099) 1.00 4.00 68
FLY TOO HIGH/Night Rains (Columbia 11111) .50 2.00 79
FRIENDS AGAIN/Lady Of The Night (Verve Forecast 5059) 1.00 4.00 68
HERE COMES THE NIGHT (THEME FROM "THE BELL JAR")/
Tonight Will Last Forever (Columbia 10979) .50 2.00 79
HE'S A RAINBOW/Here In Spain (Capitol 3107) .75 3.00 71
I WANT TO MAKE YOU LOVE ME/ (Columbia 10526) .50 2.00 77
I WOULD LIKE TO DANCE/Goodbye To Morning (Columbia 10331) .50 2.00 76
IN THE WINTER/Thankyous (Columbia 10228) .50 2.00 75
I'LL GIVE YOU A STONE IF YOU'LL THROW IT/
Younger Generation Blues (Verve Forecast 5041) 1.00 4.00 67
INSANITY COMES QUIETLY TO THE STRUCTURED MIND/
Sunflakes Fall, Snowrays Call (Verve Forecast 5072) 1.00 4.00 67
LONELY ONE/
Song For All The Seasons Of Your Mind (Verve Forecast 5079) 1.00 4.00 68
MAN YOU ARE IN ME, THE/Jesse (Columbia 46034) .50 2.00 74
MIRACLE ROW/ (Columbia 10484) .50 2.00 77
ROSES/Love Is Blind (Columbia 10391) .50 2.00 76
SOCIETY'S CHILD (BABY I'VE BEEN THINKING)/
Letter To Jon (Verve Folkways 5027) 1.00 4.00 66
THAT GRAND ILLUSION/Jopper Painting (Columbia 10813) .50 2.00 78

ICE CREAM
CHEWING GUM KID/Epitaph To Marie (Capitol 2321) .75 3.00 68

ICEMEN
HOW CAN I GET OVER A FOX LIKE YOU/
Loogaboo (Choice Is Yours) (ABC 11038) .75 3.00 68

ICHABOD & THE CRANES
TURTLE, THE/Supermarket Of Love (Coral 62401) .75 3.00 64

ID
SHORT CIRCUIT/Boil The Kettle, Mother (RCA Victor 47-9136) 1.00 4.00 67
WILD TIMES/The Take (RCA Victor 47-9195) 1.00 4.00 67

IDAHO, Ken
SCHOOL OF LOVE/From Loving You (Fame 506) 1.00 4.00 59

IDEALS
DO I HAVE THE RIGHT/You Won't Like It (Cool 108) 12.50 50.00
Also see Ovations, The

IDEALS, The
IVY LEAGUE LOVER/Don't Be A Baby, Baby (Decca 9-30800) 1.00 4.00 59
PLEASE JAN/Always Yours (Stars Of Hollywood 1001) 3.00 12.00 59
MY GIRL/Annie Was A Stroller (Decca 9-30720) 1.25 5.00 58
TEENS/Magic (Paso 6402) 1.00 4.00 61
TRANS ZIZSTOR/The Duchess (Fargo 1024) .75 3.00 62
Even though all of these releases are shown as being by a group using the same name, the possibility exists that they are not all by the same group.

IDES OF MARCH, The (With Jim Peterik)
FRIENDS OF FEELING/Tie-Dye Princess (Warner Bros. 7507) 1.00 4.00 71
GIDDY-UP RIDE ME/Freedom Sweet (Warner Bros. 7526) 1.00 4.00 71
GIVE YOUR MIND WINGS/My Foolish Pride (Parrot 321) 1.50 6.00 67
HOLE IN MY SOUL/Girls Don't Grow On Trees (Parrot 326) 1.25 5.00 67
HOT WATER/Heavy On The Country (RCA 0052) .75 3.00 73
L.A. GOODBYE/Mrs. Grayson's Farm (Warner Bros. 7466) 1.00 4.00 71
MELODY/The Sky Is Falling (Warner Bros. 7426) 1.00 4.00 70
MOTHER AMERICA/Landlady (RCA 0850) .75 3.00 72
ONE WOMAN MAN/High On A Hillside (Warner Bros. 7334) 1.00 4.00 69
ROLLER COASTER/Things Aren't Always What They Seem (Parrot 310) 1.50 6.00 66
SHA-LA-LA-LA-LEE/You Need Love (Parrot 312) 1.50 6.00 66
STRAWBERRY SUNDAY/Nobody Loves Me (Kapp 992) 1.25 5.00 69
SUPERMAN/Home (Warner Bros. 7403) .75 3.00 70
VEHICLE/Lead Me Home, Gently (Warner Bros. 7378) .50 2.00 70
YOU WOULDN'T LISTEN/I'll Keep Searching (Parrot 304) 2.00 8.00 66

IDIOTS, The (Sascha Burland & Mason Adams)
SCHOOL FOR AIRPLANE PIRATES/The Sportscaster (Riverside 4505) 1.00 4.00 61
SCHOOL FOR AIRPLANE PIRATES/The Sportscaster (Riverside 4505) .75 3.00 61
(Shown as by the Idiots & Co.)

IDIOTS & CO., The: see Idiots, The

IDLE RACE (Featuring Jeff Lynne)
HERE WE GO AROUND THE LEMON TREE/
My Fathers Son (Liberty 55997) 3.75 15.00 67
Also see Electric Light Orchestra
Also see Move, The

IDLERS, The
CHASE, THE/Ja-Da (Audio Spectrum 68) .75 3.00 64
(Instrumentals)

IDOLS, The
JEANNINE/Can't Tag Along (E-Z 1) 1.50 6.00
WHY MUST I CRY/Just A Little Bit More (Dot 16210) .75 3.00 61

IDYLLS, The
ANNETTE/Love Me Again (Spinning 6012) 2.50 10.00 60

TITLE/FLIP	LABEL & NO.	GOOD	NEAR MINT	YR.
IF				
I BELIEVE IN ROCK & ROLL/Still Alive	(Capitol 3932)	.75	3.00	73
PROMISED LAND/I'm Reaching Out On All Sides	(Capitol 2909)	.75	3.00	70
WATERFALL/	(Metromedia 258)	.75	3.00	72
WHAT DID I SAY ABOUT THE BOX, JACK/ Raise The Level Of Your Conscious Mind	(Capitol 2090)	.75	3.00	70
YOUR CITY IS FALLING/Woman Can't You See	(Capitol 3068)	.75	3.00	71
IFIELD, Frank				
I REMEMBER YOU/I Listen To My Heart	(Vee Jay 457)	.75	3.00	62
I'M CONFESSIN'/Waltzing Matilda	(Capitol 5032)	.75	3.00	63
LONESOME JUBILEE/Teach Me Little Children	(MAM 3612)	.50	2.00	72
LOVESICK BLUES/Anytime	(Vee Jay 477)	.75	3.00	63
NOBODY'S DARLIN' BUT MINE/Unchained Melody	(Vee Jay 525)	.75	3.00	63
OUT OF NOWHERE/Kaw-Liga	(Hickory 1454)	.75	3.00	67
PLEASE/Mule Train	(Capitol 5089)	.75	3.00	63
WAYWARD WIND, THE/I'm Smiling Now	(Vee Jay 499)	.75	3.00	63
IGGY & THE STOOGES: see Pop, Iggy				
IGUANAS, The				
DIANA/This Is What I Was Made For	(Dunhill 4056)	1.25	5.00	66
MICHELLE/Meet Me Tonight Little Girl	(Dunhill 3001)	1.25	5.00	
THIS IS WHAT I WAS MADE FOR/ Don't Come Running To Me	(Dunhill 4004)	1.25	5.00	65
ILFORD SUBWAY				
NEW SONG/3rd Prophecy	(Equinox 70001)	1.00	4.00	67
ILL WIND				
IN MY DARK WORLD/Walkin' & Singin'	(ABC 11107)	.75	3.00	68
ILL WINDS, The (The Chantays)				
I IDOLIZE YOU/A Letter	(Reprise 492)	1.25	5.00	66
SO BE ON YOUR WAY (I WON'T CRY)/Fear Of The Rain	(Reprise 423)	1.25	5.00	65
ILLINOIS SPEED PRESS, The (With Paul Cotton)				
GET IN THE WIND/Get In The Wind (Part 2)	(Columbia 4-44564)	.75	3.00	68
SADLY OUT OF PLACE/Country Dumplin'	(Columbia 4-45166)	.75	3.00	70
Also see Poco				
ILLUSION, The				
DID YOU SEE HER EYES/Falling In Love	(Steed 718)	.75	3.00	69
HOW DOES IT FEEL/Once In A Lifetime	(Steed 721)	.75	3.00	69
LET'S MAKE EACH OTHER HAPPY/Beside You	(Steed 726)	.75	3.00	70
TOGETHER/Don't Push It	(Steed 722)	.75	3.00	69
WAIT A MINUTE/Collection	(Steed 732)	.75	3.00	71
ILLUSIONS, The				
CAN'T WE FALL IN LOVE/How High Is The Mountain	(Ember 1071)	1.50	6.00	61
CLOSER YOU ARE, THE/For Sentimental Reasons	(Kape 1001)	.75	3.00	
HEY BOY/Lonely Soldier	(Mali 104)	1.50	6.00	62
HEY BOY/Lonely Soldier	(Sheraton 104)	1.25	5.00	62
I KNOW/Take My Heart	(Columbia 4-43700)	.75	3.00	66
IN THE BEGINNING/Maybe	(Laurie 3245)	1.50	6.00	64
LETTER, THE/Henry & Henrietta	(Coral 62173)	2.00	8.00	60
IMAGINATIONS, The				
GOODNIGHT BABY/The Search Is Over	(Music Makers 103)	2.00	8.00	61
GUARDIAN ANGEL/Hey You	(Music Makers 108)	1.50	6.00	61
GUARDIAN ANGEL/Hey You	(Duel 507)	1.25	5.00	
GUARDIAN ANGEL/Hey You	(Bo Marc 301)	.75	3.00	
I WANT A GIRL/I Love You More (Than Anyone)	(Bacon Fat BF-101)	.75	3.00	
Also see Bloom, Bobby				
Also see Day, Darleen				
IMAGINATIONS, The (Phil Sloan & Steve Barri)				
SUMMER IN NEW YORK/I Love You When You're Mad	(Dunhill 4092)	.75	3.00	67
IMPACS, The				
DON'T CRY BABY/Ain't That The Way Life Is	(King 5910)	1.00	4.00	64
JO-ANN/Two Strangers	(King 5851)	2.00	8.00	64
SHE DIDN'T EVEN SAY HELLO/Kool It	(King 5891)	1.00	4.00	64
SHIMMY SHIMMY/Zot	(King 5851)	1.00	4.00	64
TEARS IN MY HEART/I'm Gonna Make You Cry	(Parkway 865)	1.50	6.00	63
YOUR MAMA PUT THE HURT ON ME/Cape Kennedy, Florida	(King 5965)	1.00	4.00	65
IMPACTS, The				
CANADIAN SUNSET/They Say	(Watts 5600)	6.25	25.00	59
CANADIAN SUNSET/They Say	(RCA Victor 47-7609)	3.75	15.00	59
CROC-O-DOLL/Bobby Sox Squaw	(RCA Victor 47-7583)	1.00	4.00	59
DARLING, NOW YOU'RE MINE/Help Me Somebody	(Carlton 548)	1.25	5.00	61
NOW IS THE TIME/Soup	(Watts 5599)	1.25	5.00	59
SUMMER/Lindae	(Anderson 104)	2.00	8.00	
IMPACTS, The				
DON'T YOU DARE/	(Lavender 2005)	1.25	5.00	
JUST BECAUSE/Pigtails	(DCP 1150)	1.00	4.00	66
YOU GET YOUR KICKS/	(Lavender 2006)	1.25	5.00	
(Shown as by the Impact Express)				
IMPACT EXPRESS, The: see Impacts, The				
IMPAKS, The				
MAKE UP YOUR MIND/Climb Upon Your Rockin' Chair	(Express 716)	2.00	8.00	
IMPALAS, The				
I NEED YOU SO MUCH/For The Love Of Mike	(Checker 999)	.75	3.00	61
I STILL LOVE YOU/Whip It On Me	(Bunky 7762)	1.00	4.00	
LONELY ONE, THE/Lost Boogie	(Sundown 115)	1.00	4.00	59
IMPALAS, The				
I CAN'T SEE ME WITHOUT YOU/Old Man Mose	(Rite-On 101)	.75	3.00	
WHEN YOU DANCE/I Can't See Me Without You	(Steady 044)	2.00	8.00	
(Reissue of Red Boy 113)				
WHEN YOU DANCE/I Can't See Me Without You	(Red Boy 113)	1.00	4.00	

The above group featured Dave Rick (Of Vito & The Salutations) as producer and Eddie (Of The Five Discs) on vocals. One member of the original Impalas (listed directly below) is thought to be a member of this group; thus the same group name.

TITLE/FLIP	LABEL & NO.	GOOD	NEAR MINT	YR.
IMPALAS, The (Featuring Joe "Speedo" Frazier)				
FIRST DATE/I Was A Fool	(Hamilton 50026)	1.50	6.00	
OH, WHAT A FOOL/Sandy Went Away	(Cub K-9033)	1.00	4.00	59
PEGGY DARLING/Bye Everybody	(Cub K-9053)	1.00	4.00	59
SORRY (I RAN ALL THE WAY HOME)/Fool Fool Fool	(Cub K-9022)	1.00	4.00	59
WHEN MY HEART DOES ALL THE TALKING/All Alone	(Cub K-9066)	1.00	4.00	60
(Shown as by Speedo & The Impalas)				
IMPAX, The				
BABY, YOU'RE MY LOVE/Cool Breeze	(Warner Bros. 5153)	1.00	4.00	60
IMPERIAL GENTS, The				
LITTLE DARLIN'/The Imperial Gents Stomp	(Laurie 3540)	2.50	10.00	70
IMPERIAL WORKERS, The				
WHEN I FALL IN LOVE/Trying To Get To You	(Black Prince 317)	.75	3.00	
IMPERIALITES, The				
HAVE LOVE, WILL TRAVEL/Let's Get One	(Imperial 66015)	1.00	4.00	64
IMPERIALS, The				
I'M STILL DANCING/Bermuda Wonderful	(Capitol 4924)	.75	3.00	63
IMPI				
DEEP RIVER/Herd Boy	(Epic 10721)	.75	3.00	71
IMPOSSIBLES, The				
CHAPEL BELLS/Little By Little	(Blanche 29)	5.00	20.00	
EVERYWHERE I GO/Well It's Alright '66	(RMP 500)	1.50	6.00	66
MR. MAESTRO/Well, It's Alright	(RMP 1030)	2.50	10.00	
PAINT ME A PRETTY PICTURE/Lonely Bluebird	(Reprise 0305)	1.25	5.00	64
IMPRESSORS, The				
DO YOU LOVE HER/Loneliness	(Cub 9010)	1.25	5.00	58
IS IT TOO LATE/No No No	(Onyx 514)	2.00	8.00	57
IMPROPER BOSTONIANS, The				
GEE I'M GONNA MISS YOU/Victim Of Environment	(Coral 62543)	1.25	5.00	67
HOW MANY TEARS/I Still Love You	(Minuteman 207)	1.50	6.00	66
OUT OF MY MIND/You Made Me A Giant	(Minuteman 209)	1.50	6.00	67
SET YOU FREE THIS TIME/Come To Me My Baby	(Minuteman 208)	1.50	6.00	67
IMUS IN THE MORNING (Don Imus)				
BALLAD OF RICK (DON'T CALL ME RICKY CAUSE I'M A VETERAN)/ From Adam's Rib To Women's Lib	(Happy Tiger 576)	1.25	5.00	71
1200 HAMBURGERS TO GO/Reverend Billy Sol Hargis	(RCA 1031)	1.00	4.00	72
RENT-A-CAR PHONE CALL/Holyland Record Package	(RCA 0789)	1.00	4.00	72
SON OF CHECKERS (THE WATERGATE CASE)/ Oh Billy Sol, Please Heal Us All	(RCA 0982)	1.00	4.00	73
(Shown as by Don Imus)				
Comedy-Novelties				
IMUS, Jay Jay, & Freddy Ford				
I'M A HOT RODDER/The Boogala	(Challange 59248)	1.00	4.00	63
IN BETWEEN SET, The				
WALKIN' IN THE RAIN/The One Who Really Loves You	(Rust 5125)	1.50	6.00	65
IN CROWD, The: see Jon & Robin				
IN CROWD, The				
CAT DANCE/Grapevine	(Brent 7046)	.75	3.00	65
GIRL IN THE BLACK BIKINI/Do The Surfer Jerk	(Musicor 11111)	1.25	5.00	65
IF I KNEW A MAGIC WORD/Never Ending Symphony	(Viva 610)	.75	3.00	67
QUESTIONS & ANSWERS/Happiness In My Heart	(Viva 604)	.75	3.00	66
THAT'S HOW STRONG MY LOVE IS/Things She Says	(Tower 147)	.75	3.00	65
WHY MUST THEY CRITICIZE/I Don't Mind	(Tower 196)	.75	3.00	65
INCIDENTALS, The				
BARBARA/Where's My True Love	(Gar-lo 1000)	1.50	6.00	61
DRIVING GUITARS/All Night	(Ford 134)	1.00	4.00	64
LUCILLE/Fireside	(Ford 138)	1.00	4.00	65
INCOGNITOS, The				
DEE JAY'S DILEMMA/Forget It	(Zee 001)	5.00	20.00	61
INCONCEIVABLES, The				
HAMBURGER PATTI/Patti's Theme	(Columbia 4-43894)	1.00	4.00	66
INCREDABLES, The				
IF YOU GAVE A PARTY/Little Bitty Bandit	(Kelrich 851)	2.00	8.00	
INCREDIBLE BONGO BAND, The				
BONGO ROCK/Bongolia	(Pride 1015)	.75	3.00	72
BONGO ROCK/Bongolia	(MGM 14588)	.50	2.00	73
INCREDIBLE INVADERS, The				
THIS TIME/Boy Is Gone	(Prophonics 2028)	1.25	5.00	
INDIGOS, The				
GIRL BY THE WAYSIDE/Ho-hum, Deedle-dum	(Image 5001)	1.25	5.00	
HE'S COMING HOME/ What Good Am I Without You	(Cor 6581)	1.00	4.00	65
HE'S COMING HOME/ What Good Am I Without You	(Verve Folkways 5002)	.75	3.00	65
WOO WOO PRETTY GIRL/Servant Of Love	(Cornel 3001)	12.50	50.00	58
INDUSTRIAL IMAGE, The				
LIVING IN THE MIDDLE AGES/Put My Mind At Ease	(Epic 10096)	.75	3.00	66
INELIGIBLES, The				
TIGER PAWS/	(Anderson 109)	1.00	4.00	
INFASCINATIONS, The				
ONE CHANCE/I'm So In Love	(Clauwell 003)	1.25	5.00	
INFATUATORS, The				
I FOUND MY LOVE/Where Are You	(Destiny 504)	2.50	10.00	61
I FOUND MY LOVE/Where Are You	(Vee Jay 395)	2.00	8.00	61
INFERNOS, The				
GOIN' CRUISIN'/	(Hawk 13500)	1.00	4.00	63
(Instrumental)				
INGMANN, Jorgen				
ANNA/Cherokee	(Atco 6195)	.75	3.00	61
APACHE/Echo Boogie	(Atco 6184)	.75	3.00	61
TOKYO MELODY/Sunrise Serenade	(Parrot 45006)	.50	2.00	
Instrumentals				
INITIALS, The				
SCHOOL DAY/This Song Is Number One	(Congress 207)	1.00	4.00	64
SEVENTEEN GUYS ON A BLANKET AT THE BEACH/ Dancing On The Sand	(Congress 219)	1.00	4.00	64
YOU/Bells Of Joy	(Dee 1001)	1.50	6.00	
YOU/Bells Of Joy	(Sherry 667)	1.25	5.00	
INMAN, Jimmy				
LOVED HER THE WHOLE WEEK THROUGH/Saving My Love	(NRC 5004)	1.50	6.00	59
INMATES, The				
DIRTY WATER/I Can't Sleep	(Polydor-Radar 2032)	.50	2.00	79
INNER CIRCLE, The (Phil Sloan & Steve Barri)				
SO LONG MARIANNE/Goes To Show You	(Dunhill 4128)	1.25	5.00	68
INNER CITY MISSION, The				
GET BACK JOHN/	(Kama Sutra 510)	2.00	8.00	70
(Refers to John Lennon)				
INNER LITE, The (With Ritchie Cordell)				
HOLD ON TO HIM/Tabula Rasa	(Ssexx 666)	1.50	6.00	
INNES, Dixie Lee (Of The Original Caste)				
DOLPHINS, THE/Black Paper Roses	(Bell 45230)	.50	2.00	72
INNOCENCE, The (Pete Anders & Vinnie Poncia)				
ALL I DO IS THINK ABOUT YOU/ Whence I Make Thee Mine	(Kama Sutra 228)	1.00	4.00	67
DAY TURNS ME ON, THE/ It's Not Gonna Take Too Long	(Kama Sutra 237)	1.00	4.00	67
MAIRZY DOATS/A Lifetime Loving You	(Kama Sutra 222)	1.00	4.00	67
THERE'S GOT TO BE A WORD/ I Don't Want To Be Around You	(Kama Sutra 214)	1.00	4.00	66
SOMEONE GOT CAUGHT IN MY EYE/ Your Show Is Over	(Kama Sutra 232)	1.00	4.00	67
INNOCENTS, The (Darron Stankey, Al Candaleria, Jim West)				
BEWARE/Because I Love You So	(Indigo 124)	1.00	4.00	61
COME ON LOVER/Don't Cry	(Decca 31519)	1.00	4.00	63
DEE DEE DI OH/Time	(Andex 22102)	1.50	6.00	59
(Shown as by the Echoes)				
DEE DEE DI OH/Time	(Indigo 141)	1.00	4.00	62
DONNA/You Got Me Goin'	(Indigo 128)	1.25	5.00	61
GEE WHIZ/Please Mr. Sun	(Indigo 111)	1.00	4.00	60
HONEST I DO/My Baby Hully Gullys	(Indigo 105)	1.00	4.00	60
KATHY (Kathy Young)/In The Beginning	(Indigo 116)	1.25	5.00	61
MY HEART STOOD STILL/ Don't Call Me Lonely Anymore	(Warner Bros. 5450)	1.50	6.00	64
OH HOW I MISS MY BABY/Be Mine	(Reprise 20112)	1.25	5.00	62
OH HOW I MISS MY BABY/You're Never Satisfied	(Reprise 20125)	1.25	5.00	63
PAINS IN MY HEART/When I Become A Man	(Indigo 132)	1.25	5.00	62
TICK TOCK/The Rat (Instrumental)	(Trans World 7001)	1.00	4.00	60
Also see Kenjolairs, The				
Also see Sugar Beats, The				
Also see Young, Kathy				
INRHODES, The				
HOLD THE HIGH GROUND/Looking Around	(Dunhill 4055)	.75	3.00	66
TRY & STOP ME/Looking Around	(Dunhill 4078)	.75	3.00	67
INSECT TRUST				
BEEN HERE & GONE/The INvasion Is Coming	(Dynamic Sound 2004)	.75	3.00	67
INSECTS, The				
LET'S BUG THE BEATLES/ Dear Beatles (By The Little Lady Beatles)	(Applause 1002)	1.25	5.00	64
INSIDE-OUTS, The				
GUNFRED GOON/My Love (I'll Be True To You)	(Palmer 5012)	1.50	6.00	
INSIDERS, The				
CHAPEL BELLS ARE CALLING/I'm Stuck On You	(Red Bird 10-055)	1.00	4.00	66
INSPIRATIONS, The				
ANGEL IN DISGUISE/Stool Pigeon	(Al-Brite 1651)	3.75	15.00	60
ANGEL IN DISGUISE/Stool Pigeon	(Sparkle 102)	3.00	12.00	60
ANGEL IN DISGUISE/Stool Pigeon	(Gone 5097)	2.00	8.00	61
DRY YOUR EYES/Good Bye (Black label)	(Jamie 1212)	5.00	20.00	61
DRY YOUR EYES/Good Bye (Multi-color label)	(Jamie 1212)	2.00	8.00	61
GENIE, THE/Feeling Of Her Kiss	(Sultan 111)	1.25	5.00	
INTENTIONS, The				
I'M IN LOVE WITH A GO' GO GIRL/Wonderful Girl	(Melron 5014)	6.25	25.00	
NIGHT RIDER/Don't Forget That I Love You	(Philips 40428)	.75	3.00	67
SUMMERTIME ANGEL/Mr. Misery	(Jamie 1253)	15.00	60.00	63
TIME/Cool Summer Night	(Uptown 710)	1.25	5.00	65
WHAT AM I GONNA DO WITH YOU/Hey Baby	(Black Pearl 100)	1.00	4.00	

Even though all of these releases are shown as being by a group using the same name, the possibility exists that they are not all by the same group. Any information on this would be appreciated.

TITLE/FLIP	LABEL & NO.	GOOD	NEAR MINT	YR.
INTERIORS, The				
DARLING LITTLE ANGEL/Voodoo Doll	(Worthy 1008)	1.50	6.00	61
INTERLUDES, The				
DARLING I'LL BE TRUE/Wilted Rose Bud	(King 5633)	1.25	5.00	62
I SHED A MILLION TEARS/Oo-wee	(RCA Victor 47-7281)	1.25	5.00	58
NUMBER ONE IN THE NATION/ Beautiful, Wonderful, Heavenly You	(ABC-Paramount 10213)	1.00	4.00	61
INTERNATIONALS, The				
GOIN' TO A PARTY/I Love You So	(ABC-Paramount 9964)	1.50	6.00	58
INTERPRETERS, The				
I GET THE MESSAGE/Stop That Man	(Gemini 100)	.75	3.00	65
INTERVALS, The				
HERE'S THAT RAINY DAY/Wish I Could Change My Mind	(Class 304)	2.50	10.00	
SIDE STREET/I Still Love That Man	(Ad 104)	2.00	8.00	59
SIDE STREET/I Still Love That Man	(Apt 25019)	1.50	6.00	59
INTIMATES, The				
GOT YOU WHERE I WANT YOU/	(Amcan 402)	2.00	8.00	
SMART...TOO LATE/I've Got A Tiger In My Tank	(Epic 9743)	2.50	10.00	64
INTREPIDES, The				
GOLASH/Donna	(Mascio 120)	1.50	6.00	65
INTRUDERS, The				
CAMPTOWN ROCK/Morse Code	(Beltone 1009)	1.00	4.00	61
CREEPIN'/Frankfurters & Sauerkraut	(Fame 313)	1.25	5.00	59
FRIED EGGS/Jeffrie's Rock	(Fame 101)	1.25	5.00	59
I'M SOLD/Come Home Soon	(Gowen 1401)	1.00	4.00	
ROCK-A-MA-ROLE/Cha-rock-a	(Fame 616)	1.25	5.00	59
WILD GOOSE/Trambone	(Sahara 101)	1.00	4.00	63
INVADERS, The				
CALIFORNIA SUN/Love & Hate	(Capitol 2292)	1.00	4.00	68
FLOWER SONG/With A Tear	(U.S.A. 902)	1.00	4.00	68
I WANNA BE YOUR MAN/Cat's Eyes	(Philips 40189)	1.25	5.00	64
ID, THE/One Step Into Darkness	(Mohawk 139)	1.25	5.00	
INVASION/Pam	(Instro 1000)	1.25	5.00	
STORMY MONDAY BLUES/	(OO 301)	1.25	5.00	
INVASION				
I WANT TO THANK YOU/The Invasion Is Coming	(Dynamic Sound 2004)	.75	3.00	67
INVICTAS, The				
BREAKOUT/Missing	(20th Fox 493)	1.00	4.00	64
GONE SO LONG/Nellie	(Jack Bee 1003)	1.00	4.00	59
IRENE & THE SCOTTS				
WHY DO YOU TREAT ME LIKE YOU DO/ I'm Stuck On My Baby	(Smash 2138)	.75	3.00	67
IRIDESCENTS, The				
THREE COINS IN THE FOUNTAIN/Strong Love	(Hudson 8102)	2.00	8.00	63
IRISH ROVERS, The				
BIPLANE EVER MORE, THE/Liverpool Lou	(Decca 32371)	.75	3.00	68
LILY THE PINK/Mrs. Crandall's Boardinghouse	(Decca 32444)	.75	3.00	69
UNICORN, THE/Black Velvet Band	(Decca 32254)	.75	3.00	68
WHISKEY ON A SUNDAY (THE PUPPET SONG)/ The Orange & The Green	(Decca 32333)	.75	3.00	68
IRON BUTTERFLY, The (With Doug Ingle)				
EASY RIDER (LET THE WIND PAY THE WAY)/ Soldier In Our Town	(Atco 6782)	1.00	4.00	70
GET IT OUT/Beyond The Milky Way	(MCA 40493)	.75	3.00	75
I CAN'T HELP BUT DECEIVE YOU LITTLE GIRL/ To Be Alone	(Atco 6712)	1.00	4.00	69
IN-A-GADDA-DA-VIDA/Iron Butterfly Theme	(Atco 6606)	.75	3.00	68
IN THE TIME OF OUR LIVES/It Must Be Love	(Atco 6676)	1.00	4.00	69
SEARCHIN' CIRCLES/Pearly Gates	(MCA 40379)	.75	3.00	75
SILLY SALLY/Stone Believer	(Atco 6818)	1.00	4.00	71
SOUL EXPERIENCE/In The Crowds	(Atco 6647)	1.00	4.00	69
UNCONSCIOUS POWER/Possession	(Atco 6573)	1.00	4.00	68
IRON GATE, The				
YOU MUST BELIEVE ME/Get Ready	(Mobie 3429)	1.00	4.00	68

Ivan

Elton John

The Kasenetz-Katz Singing Orchestral Circ

TITLE/FLIP — LABEL & NO. — GOOD — NEAR MINT — YR.

IRONHORSE (With Randy Bachman)
SWEET LUI-LOUISE/Watch Me Fly (Scotti Bros. 406) .50 2.00 79

IRRIDESCENTS, The
SWAMP SURFER/Beli Ha'i (Hawk 4001) 1.50 6.00 63
Also see Sixpence

IRWIN, Big Dee (Of The Pastells)
I WISH YOU A MERRY CHRISTMAS/
The Christmas Song (Dimension 1021) .75 3.00 63
(With Little Eva)
SWINGING ON A STAR/Another Night With The Boys (Dimension 1010) .75 3.00 63
(With Little Eva)

IRWIN, Big Dee, & Little Eva: see Irwin, Big Dee

ISABELL, Rusty
FIREWATER/The Blast (Brent 7001) 1.25 5.00 59
MANHUNT/I Give Up (Brent 7006) 1.25 5.00 59

ISIS
AIN'T NO BACKIN' UP NOW/ (Buddah 475) .75 3.00 75
BOBBI & MARIA (PART 1)/Bobbi & Maria (Part 2) (Buddah 446) .75 3.00 74
ICY WINDS/ (Buddah 511) .75 3.00 75
RUBBER BOY/Do The Football (Buddah 428) .75 3.00 74

ISLANDERS, The (With Randy Starr)
AUTUMN LEAVES/Kon-tiki (Mayflower 19) 1.00 4.00 60
BLUE RAIN/Tornado (Mayflower 18) 1.00 4.00 60
ENCHANTED SEA, THE/Pollyanna (Mayflower 16) 1.00 4.00 59
FORBIDDEN ISLAND/City Under The Sea (Mayflower 22) 1.00 4.00 60

ISLE, Jimmy
BABY-O/Hassie (Bally 1034) 1.00 4.00 57
BILLY BOY/Oh Judy (Everest 19320) 1.00 4.00 59
GOING WILD/You & Johnny Smith (Roulette 4065) 1.00 4.00 58

ITELS, The
STAR OF PARADISE/
Chubby Isn't Chubby Anymore (Magnifico 101) 2.50 10.00 61

IT'S A BEAUTIFUL DAY (Featuring David LaFlamme)
AIN'T THAT LOVIN' YOU BABY/Time (Columbia 4-45853) 1.25 5.00 73
ANYTIME/Oranges & Apples (Columbia 4-45536) 1.25 5.00 72
BULGARIA/Aquarian Dream (San Francisco Sound S7A/B-11680) 2.50 10.00
(A completely different song, using the same title, appeared on this group's first Columbia LP.)
DOLPHINS, THE/Do You Remember The Sun (Columbia 4-45309) 1.25 5.00 71
SOAPSTONE MOUNTAIN/Do You Remember The Sun (Columbia 4-45152) 1.25 5.00 70
WHITE BIRD/Wasted Union Blues (Columbia 4-44928) 1.00 4.00 69
WHITE BIRD/Wasted Union Blues (Columbia 4-45788) .75 3.00 73

I.V. LEAGUERS, The
RING CHIMES/The Story (Porter 1003) 2.50 10.00 57
RING CHIMES/The Story (Dot 15677) 1.50 6.00 57
TOLD BY THE STARS/Jim Jam (Nau-Voo 803) 1.00 4.00 59

IVAN (Jerry Ivan Allison)
FRANKIE FRANKENSTEIN/That'll Be Alright (Coral 62081) 12.50 50.00 59
REAL WILD CHILD/Oh You Beautiful Doll (Coral 62017) 10.00 40.00 59
(With Buddy Holly on guitar)
REAL WILD CHILD/That'll Be Alright (Coral 65607) 5.00 20.00 67
Also see Crickets, The

IVES, Jimmy
MY TUMBLING HEART/Settle Down (Comet 21) 3.75 15.00

IVEYS, The
MAYBE TOMORROW/Daddy's A Millionaire (Apple 1803) 1.00 4.00 69

IVIES, The
I REALLY WANT TO KNOW/Voodoo (Roulette 4183) 1.00 4.00 59

IVOLEERS, The
LOVER'S QUARREL/Come With Me (Buzz 101) 3.00 12.00 59

IVORIES, The
ME & YOU/I'm In Love (Mercury 71239) 3.00 12.00 57

IVORYS, The
WHY DON'T YOU WRITE ME/Deep Freeze (Sparta 001) 1.00 4.00 62

IVY JIVES, The
MILLION DOLLAR GIRL/Knockout (Jaro 77036) 1.00 4.00 60

IVY LEAGUE, The (Featuring John Carter)
FUNNY HOW LOVE CAN BE/Lonely Room (Cameo 356) .75 3.00 65
GIRL LIKE YOU, A/That's Why I'm Crying (Cameo 365) .75 3.00 65
I COULD MAKE YOU FALL IN LOVE/
Our Love Is Slipping Away (Cameo 388) .75 3.00 66
MY WORLD FELL DOWN/When You're Young (Cameo 449) .75 3.00 66
TOSSIN' & TURNIN'/Graduation Day (Cameo 377) .75 3.00 65
WHAT MORE DO YOU WANT/Your Love Is All I Want (Cameo 343) .75 3.00 65
Also see Fat Man's Music Festival

IVY THREE, The
BAGOO/Suicide (Shell 306) 1.00 4.00 61
HUSH LITTLE BABY/Alone In the Chapel (Shell 723) 2.50 10.00 60
NINE OUT OF TEN/I've Cried Enough For Two (Shell 302) 1.00 4.00 61
YOGI/Was Judy There (Shell 720) 1.00 4.00 60

IVY TONES, The
OO-WEE BABY/Each Time (Red Top 105) 2.00 8.00 58

IVYS, The
ALL I WANT/Lost Without You (Coed 518) 1.25 5.00 59

J

J. & THE SABERS
TWIST MARY SUE/Little One (Vav Ray 1003) .75 3.00 62

JACK & JILL
LAURIE'S LOVE/Very Few Heartaches (Arlen 26) .75 3.00 63
VERY FEW HEARTACHES/Laurie's Love (Smash 1824) .75 3.00 63

JACK & JIM
TARZAN & JANE/Midnight Monsters Hop (Brunswick 9-55141) 1.00 4.00 59

JACK, Robin (Jonathan King)
HAPPY PEOPLE SONG/I've Never Seen (UK-Midland Intl. 10583) .75 3.00 75

JACKIE & JILL
I WANT THE BEATLES FOR CHRISTMAS/
Jingle Bells (USA 791) 1.50 6.00 64

JACKS & JILLS, The
I CAN'T FORGET/Red Dog (MGM K-12671) 1.00 4.00 58
I HEAR A MELODY/Roses Never Fade (Empire 101) 1.00 4.00 56

JACKS, Susan (Of The Poppy Family)
YOU'RE A PART OF ME/I'd Rather Know You (Mercury 73649) .50 2.00 75

JACKS, Terry (Of The Poppy Family)
CONCRETE SEA/She Even Took The Cat (London 181) .50 2.00 73
IF YOU GO AWAY/Me & You (Bell 45467) .50 2.00 74
SEASONS IN THE SUN/Put The Bone In (Bell 45432) .50 2.00 74

JACKS, Warren
LEGEND OF A KING, THE/Dream Only Dream (Paper Dragon 5083) .75 3.00 77

JACKSON BROTHERS, The
BABY, BABY/Troubles (Candy 002) 1.00 4.00 59
LOVE ME/Tell Him No (Atlantic 1034) 1.25 5.00 54

JACKSON JILLS, The
PRETTY LITTLE DUTCH GIRL/Mommie's Little Baby (Dot 16541) .75 3.00 63

JACKSON, J.J.
BUT IT'S ALL RIGHT/Boogaloo Baby (Calla 119) .75 3.00 66
BUT IT'S ALL RIGHT/Ain't Too Proud To Beg (Warner Bros. 7276) .50 2.00 69
I DIG GIRLS/That Ain't Right (Calla 125) .75 3.00 67
LET ME TRY AGAIN/When Love Meets Love (Magna-Glide SN-325) .50 2.00 75

JACKSON, Joe
I'M THE MAN/ (A&M 2186) .50 2.00 79
IS SHE REALLY GOING OUT WITH HIM/
(Do The) Instant Mash (A&M 2132) .50 2.00 79
IT'S DIFFERENT FOR GIRLS/ (A&M 2186) .50 2.00 79

JACKSON, Python Lee: see Python Lee Jackson

JACKSON, Ray
TEXAS-ALASKA/Alaska (D 1012) 2.00 8.00 59

JACKSON, Sammy
TEEN AGE MISS/Single & Searchin' (Orbit 583) 1.25 5.00 59

JACOBS, Dick
BALLAD OF JAMES DEAN, THE/
A Boy Named Jimmy Dean (Coral 61705) 1.00 4.00 56
EAST OF EDEN (THEME)/Seven Wonders Of The World (Coral 61692) 1.00 4.00 56
MAIN TITLE & MOLLY-O (FROM "MAN WITH THE GOLDEN ARM")/
Butternut (Coral 61606) 1.00 4.00 56
Instrumentals

JACOBS, Hank
SO FAR AWAY/Monkey Hips & Rice (Sue 795) .75 3.00 64
(Instrumentals)

JADES, The
FLOWER POWER/The Glide (Uni 55019) 1.00 4.00 67
I'M ALRIGHT/ (Ector 101) 1.00 4.00

JADES, The
HOLD BACK THE DAWN/When They Ask About You (Dore 687) 1.50 6.00 63

JAGGERZ, The
I CALL MY BABY CANDY/ (Kama Sutra 509) .75 3.00 70
RAPPER, THE/Born Poor (Kama Sutra 502) .75 3.00 70
2+2/ (Wooden Nickel 10194) .75 3.00 75
WHAT A BUMMER/ (Kama Sutra 513) .75 3.00 70

JAGUARS, The
ANOTHER LONELY NIGHT/Night People Make It (Jaguar 102) 1.00 4.00
ST. JAMES INFIRMARY/Good Time (Jaguar 104) 1.00 4.00
YOU'LL TURN AWAY/The Gorilla (Jaguar 101) 1.00 4.00

JAIM
SHIP OF TIME/Running Behind (Ethereal 101) 1.25 5.00

J.A.K.E. (Just Another Kind of Energy)
FOREVER ON MY MIND (Featuring Cheree)/
Meeting Of Chance (Featuring Peter Jay) (Sphyr a mid FF-4179) 1.00 4.00 80

JAM
I NEED YOU (FOR SOMEONE)/ (Polydor 14462) .50 2.00 78
IN THE CITY/Takin' My Love (Polydor 14442) .50 2.00 78
MR. CLEAN/Down In The Tube Station At Midnight (Polydor 14566) .50 2.00 79
STRANGE TOWN/The Butterfly Collector (Yellow plastic) (Polydor 14553) .50 2.00 79

JAMES, Bill
SCHOOL'S OUT/Voo-doo Queen & The Medicine Man (Mun-Rab 104) 1.00 4.00 59

JAMES, Bob
(ANGELA) THEME FROM "TAXI"/Caribbean Nights (Tappan Zee 10896) .50 2.00 79
HEADS/We're All Alone (Tappan Zee 10668) .50 2.00 78
NIGHT CRAWLER/You Are So Beautiful (Tappan Zee 10715) .50 2.00 78
TOUCHDOWN/Sun Runner (Tappan Zee 10969) .50 2.00 79
WINCHESTER LADY (PART 1)/ (CTI 31) .50 2.00 76

JAMES, Brian
AIN'T THAT A SHAME/Living In Sin/I Can
Make You Cry (Int'l. Record Synd. 9501) .50 2.00 79

JAMES, Deviny (Jim Pewter)
LITTLE GIRL/Blue, Blue Denims (Beta 45-1006) 2.00 8.00 59
THAT'S ALL RIGHT MAMA/Baby Child (Studio City SC-1002) 1.50 6.00 61

JAMES, Dian, & The Satisfactions
SATISFACTION (I GET LOTS OF)/Angry Desert (Radiant 1515) 1.25 5.00 65
(Answer song)

JAMES GANG, The
EVERYBODY KNOWS (BUT HER)/Ladies Man (Ascot 2168) .75 3.00 64

JAMES GANG, The (With Joe Walsh, Tommy Bolin & Dominic Troiano)
FUNK #49/Thanks (ABC 11272) .75 3.00 70
HAD ENOUGH/Kick Back Man (ABC 11336) .75 3.00 72
I NEED LOVE/Feelin' Alright (Atco 7067) .75 3.00 75
LOOKING FOR MY LADY/Hairy Hypochondriac (ABC 11325) .75 3.00 72
MIDNIGHT MAN/White Man/Black Man (ABC 11312) .75 3.00 71
MUST BE LOVE/Got No Time For Trouble (Atco 6953) .75 3.00 74
STANDING IN THE RAIN/From Another Time (Atco 6966) .75 3.00 74
WALK AWAY/Yadig? (ABC 11301) .75 3.00 71

JAMES, Jimmy, & The Candy Canes
TEEN-AGE BEAUTY/Marjolaine (Columbia 4-41192) 1.00 4.00 58

JAMES, Jimmy, & The Vagabonds
COME TO ME SOFTLY/ (Atco 6551) .75 3.00 67

JAMES, Joni (Joan Carmella Babbo)
DON'T TELL ME NOT TO LOVE YOU/
Somewhere Someone Is Lonely (MGM K-12175) 1.00 4.00 56
GIVE US THIS DAY/How Lucky You Are (MGM K-12288) 1.00 4.00 56
HAVE YOU HEARD/Wishing Ring (MGM K-11390) 1.25 5.00 52
HOW IMPORTANT CAN IT BE/This Is My Confession (MGM K-11919) 1.25 5.00 55
I NEED YOU NOW/You Belong To Me (MGM K-12885) .75 3.00 60
I STILL GET A THRILL/Perhaps (MGM K-12779) 1.00 4.00 59
I STILL GET A THRILL/Perhaps (MGM SK-12779) 2.00 8.00 59
(Stereo single issue)
I STILL GET JEALOUS/My Prayer Of Love (MGM K-12807) 1.00 4.00 59
I STILL GET JEALOUS/My Prayer Of Love (MGM SK-12807) 2.00 8.00 59
(Stereo single issue)
I WOKE UP CRYING/Maverick Queen, The (MGM K-12213) 1.00 4.00 56
IS IT ANY WONDER/Almost Always (MGM K-11470) 1.25 5.00 53
LITTLE THINGS MEAN A LOT/I Laughed At Love (MGM K-12849) 1.00 4.00 59
LITTLE THINGS MEAN A LOT/I Laughed At Love (MGM SK-12849) 2.00 8.00 59
(Stereo single issue)
MY BELIEVING HEART/You Never Fall In Love Again (MGM K-12126) 1.25 5.00 55
MY LAST DATE (WITH YOU)/I Can't Give You Anything (MGM K-12933) .75 3.00 60
MY LOVE, MY LOVE/You Are Fooling Someone (MGM K-11543) 1.25 5.00 53
SUMMER LOVE/Sorry For You My Friend (MGM K-12480) 1.00 4.00 57
THERE GOES MY HEART/Funny (MGM K-12706) 1.00 4.00 58
THERE GOES MY HEART/Funny (MGM SK-12706) 2.00 8.00 58
(Stereo single issue)
THERE MUST BE A WAY/Sorry For Myself (MGM K-12746) 1.00 4.00 59
THERE MUST BE A WAY/Sorry For Myself (MGM SK-50111) 2.00 8.00 59
(Stereo single issue)
WHY DON'T YOU BELIEVE ME/Purple Shades (MGM K-11333) 1.25 5.00 52
YOU ARE MY LOVE/I Lay Me Down To Sleep (MGM K-12066) 1.25 5.00 55
YOUR CHEATIN' HEART/I'll Be Waiting For You (MGM K-11426) 1.25 5.00 53

JAMES, Mark
EVERYBODY LOVES A RAIN SONG/
If I'm Where You Want To Be Tonight (Private Stock 45179) .50 2.00 78
IT'S NO LAUGHING MATTER/ (New Design 1002) .75 3.00 71

JAMES, Roland
GUITARVILLE/Patriotic Guitar (Judd 1012) 1.50 6.00 59

JAMES T. & THE WORKERS
LET ME SEE YOU CRYING/I Can't Stop (Prophonics 2026) 1.25 5.00

JAMES, Tommy (Of The Shondells)
ADRIENNE/Light Of Day (Roulette 7100) .50 2.00 71
BALL & CHAIN/Candy Maker (Roulette 7084) .50 2.00 70
BOO, BOO, DON'T 'CHA BE BLUE/Rings & Things (Roulette 7140) .50 2.00 73
CALICO/Hey, My Lady (Roulette 7147) .75 3.00 73
CAT'S EYE IN THE WINDOW/Dark Is The Night (Roulette 7126) .75 3.00 72
CELEBRATION/Last One To Know (Roulette 7135) .75 3.00 72
DRAGGIN' THE LINE/Bits & Pieces (Roulette 7103) .50 2.00 71
I LOVE YOU LOVE ME LOVE/Devil Gate Drive (Fantasy 761) .50 2.00 76
I'M COMIN' HOME/Sing, Sing, Sing (Roulette 7110) .50 2.00 71
LOVE IS GONNA FIND A WAY/I Don't Love You Anymore (Fantasy 811) .50 2.00 78
LOVE SONG/Kingston Highway (Roulette 7130) .50 2.00 72
NOTHING TO HIDE/Walk A Country Mile (Roulette 7114) .50 2.00 71
TELL 'EM WILLIE BOY'S A-COMIN'/ (Roulette 7119) .75 3.00 72
TIGHTER, TIGHTER/ (Fantasy 776) .50 2.00 76
THREE TIMES IN LOVE/
I Just Wanna Play The Music (Millennium YB-11785) .50 2.00 79

JAMES, Tommy, & The Shondells
BALL OF FIRE/Makin' Good Time (Roulette 7060) .75 3.00 69
CHURCH STREET SOUL REVIVAL/Draggin' The Line (Roulette 7093) 1.00 4.00 70
COME TO ME/Talkin' & Signifyin' (Roulette 7076) 1.00 4.00 70
CRIMSON & CLOVER/Some Kind Of Love (Roulette 7028) .50 2.00 68
CRYSTAL BLUE PERSUASION/I'm Alive (Roulette 7050) .50 2.00 69
DO SOMETHING TO ME/Ginger Bread Man (Roulette 7024) .75 3.00 68
GET OUT NOW/Wish It Were You (Roulette 7000) .75 3.00 68
GETTIN' TOGETHER/Real Girl (Roulette 4762) .75 3.00 67
GOTTA GET BACK TO YOU/Red Rover (Roulette 7071) .75 3.00 70
HANKY PANKY/Thunderbold (Red Fox 110) 3.75 15.00 66
(Shown as by the Shondells)
HANKY PANKY/Thunderbolt (Snap 102) 2.00 8.00 65
(Shown as by the Shondells)
HANKY PANKY/Thunderbolt (Roulette 4686) .50 2.00 66
I LIKE THE WAY/(Baby) Baby I Can't Take It No More (Roulette 4756) .75 3.00 67
I THINK WE'RE ALONE NOW/Gone, Gone, Gone (Roulette 4720) .75 3.00 67
IT'S ONLY LOVE/Ya! Ya! (Roulette 4710) .75 3.00 66
MIRAGE/Run, Run, Baby, Run (Roulette 4736) .75 3.00 67
MONY MONY/One Two Three & I Fell (Roulette 7008) .75 3.00 68
OUT OF THE BLUE/Love's Closin' In On Me (Roulette 4775) .75 3.00 67
SAY I AM (WHAT I AM)/Lots Of Pretty Girls (Roulette 4695) .75 3.00 66
SHE/Loved One (Roulette 7066) .75 3.00 69
SOMEBODY CARES/Do Unto Me (Roulette 7016) .75 3.00 68
SWEET CHERRY WINE/Breakaway (Roulette 7039) .75 3.00 69
WHY DO FOOLS FALL IN LOVE/
Upsetter Of Her Heart (Selsom 102) 1.50 6.00 65
(Shown as by The Shondells)

JAMESON, Bobby
EACH & EVERYDAY/All I Want Is My Baby (London 9730) 3.75 15.00 64
(The backing track used on "Each & Everyday" is identical to the one used on the Rolling Stones' version of the same song, heard on their "Metamorphosis" LP.)

JAMESTOWN MASSACRE, The
SUMMER SUN/Words & Rhymes (Warner Bros. 7603) .50 2.00 72

JAMIE & JANE (Gene Pitney & Ginny Arnell)
FAITHFUL OUR LOVE/Classical Rock & Roll/ (Decca 9-30934) 2.50 10.00 59

JAMIES, The
DON'T DARKEN MY DOOR/The Evening Star (United Artists 193) .75 3.00 59
SNOW TRAIN/When The Sun Goes Down (Epic 9299) 1.00 4.00 58
SNOW TRAIN/When The Sun Goes Down (Epic 9565) .75 3.00 62
SUMMERTIME, SUMMERTIME/Searching For You (Epic 9281) .75 3.00 58
(With the same number & flip side.)

JAN & ARNIE (Jan Berry & Arnie Ginsburg)
BABY TALK/Jeanette Get Your Hair Done (Dore 522) 25.00 100.00 59
(First pressings showed the artists as Jan & Arnie. The record was quickly reissued, correctly shown as by Jan & Dean.)
GAS MONEY/Bonnie Lou (Arwin 111) 1.50 6.00 58
GAS MONEY/Gotta Get A Date (Dot 16116) 1.50 6.00 60
I LOVE LINDA/The Beat That Can't Be Beat (Arwin 113) 2.00 8.00 58
JENNIE LEE/Gotta Get A Date (Arwin 108) 1.50 6.00 58
Also see Rituals, The

JAN & DEAN (Jan Berry & Dean Torrence)
BABY TALK/Jeanette Get Your Hair Done (Dore 522) 1.00 4.00 59
(Previously issued with the label showing the artists as Jan & Arnie.)
BAGGY PANTS/Judy's An Angel (Dore 583) 1.50 6.00 61
BATMAN/Bucket "T" (Liberty 55860) .75 3.00 66
CALIFORNIA LULLABY/Summertime (J&D 401) 6.25 25.00 66
CALIFORNIA LULLABY/Summertime (Magic Lamp 401) 5.00 20.00 66
CLEMENTINE/You're On My Mind (Dore 539) 1.25 5.00 60
CLEMENTINE/You're On My Mind (Dore 539) 5.00 20.00 60
(Picture sleeve)
DEAD MAN'S CURVE/The New Girl In School (Liberty 55672) .75 3.00 64
DRAG CITY/Schlock Rod (Part 1) (Liberty 55641) .75 3.00 63
DRAG CITY/Schlock Rod (Part 1) (Liberty 55641) 2.50 10.00 63
(Picture sleeve)
FAN TAN/Love & Hate (Jan & Dean 11) 12.50 50.00 66

TITLE/FLIP — LABEL & NO. — GOOD — NEAR MINT — YR.

FIDDLE AROUND/A Surfer's Dream (Liberty 55905) 1.25 5.00 66
FOLK CITY/A Beginning From An End (Liberty 55849) 1.50 6.00 65
FOLK CITY/A Beginning From An End (Liberty 55849) 6.25 25.00 65
(Picture sleeve)
FUN CITY/Totally Wild (Ode 66111) 6.25 25.00 75
GEE/Such A Good Night For Dreaming (Dore 576) 1.25 5.00 60
HAWAII/Tijuana (Jan & Dean 10) 10.00 40.00 66
HEART & SOUL/Those Words (Challenge 9111) 5.00 20.00 61
HEART & SOUL/Midsummer Night's Dream (Challenge 59111) 2.00 8.00 61
HEART & SOUL/Midsummer Night's Dream (Challenge 9111) 1.00 4.00 61
(HERE THEY COME) FROM ALL OVER THE WORLD/
Freeway Flyer (Liberty 55766) .75 3.00 65
HONOLULU LULU/Someday (You'll Go Walking By) (Liberty 55613) .75 3.00 63
HONOLULU LULU/Someday (You'll Go Walking By) (Liberty 55613) 2.50 10.00 63
(Picture sleeve)
I FOUND A GIRL/It's A Shame To Say Goodbye (Liberty 55833) .75 3.00 65
I KNOW MY MIND/Laurel & Hardy (Warner Bros. 7219) 7.50 30.00 68
IN THE STILL OF THE NIGHT/
Girl, You're Blowing My Mind (Warner Bros. 7240) 12.50 50.00 68
(Promotional issue only)
JENNIE LEE (By Jan & Arnie)/
Vegetables (With Brian Wilson & Spring) (United Artists 50859) 2.00 8.00 72
JENNIE LEE (By Jan & Arnie)/
Vegetables (With Brian Wilson & Spring) (United Artists 50859) 3.00 12.00 72
(Picture sleeve)
JULIE/Don't Fly Away (Dore 610) 1.50 6.00 61
LIKE A SUMMER RAIN/Louisiana Man (J&D 402) 5.00 20.00 66
(With the Quacks)
LINDA/When I Learn How To Cry (Liberty 55531) .75 3.00 63
LITTLE OLD LADY FROM PASADENA, THE/
My Mighty G.T.O. (Liberty 55704) .75 3.00 64
LITTLE OLD LADY FROM PASADENA, THE/
My Mighty G.T.O. (Liberty 55704) 2.50 10.00 64
(Picture sleeve)
NEW GIRL IN SCHOOL, THE/School Day (Liberty 55923) .75 3.00 66
ONLY A BOY/Love & Hate (Warner Bros. 7151) 7.50 30.00 67
POPSICLE/Norwegian Wood (This Bird Has Flown) (Liberty 55866) .75 3.00 66
RIDE THE WILD SURF/The Anaheim, Azusa & Cucamonga Sewing
Circle Book Review & Timing Association (Liberty 55724) .75 3.00 64
RIDE THE WILD SURF/The Anaheim, Azusa & Cucamonga Sewing
Circle Book Review & Timing Association (Liberty 55724) 2.50 10.00 64
(Picture sleeve)
SHE'S STILL TALKIN' BABY TALK/Frosty The Snowman (Liberty 55522) 7.50 30.00 62
SIDEWALK SURFIN'/Gonna Hustle You (United Artists 670) 2.00 8.00 76
SIDEWALK SURFIN'/When It's Over (Liberty 55727) .75 3.00 64
("Sidewalk Surfin" is the music of "Catch A Wave," by the Beach Boys, with different lyrics.)
SIDEWALK SURFIN'/When It's Over (Liberty 55727) 2.50 10.00 64
(Picture sleeve)
SUNDAY KIND OF LOVE, A/Poor Little Puppet (Liberty 55397) 1.00 4.00 62
SURF CITY (With Brian Wilson)/She's My Summer Girl (Liberty 55580) .75 3.00 63
SURF CITY (With Brian Wilson)/She's My Summer Girl (Liberty 55580) 2.50 10.00 63
(Picture sleeve)
TENNESSEE/Your Heart Has Changed It's Mind (Liberty 55454) 1.00 4.00 62
THERE'S A GIRL/My Heart Sings (Dore 531) 1.50 6.00 59
VEGETABLES/Snowflakes (White Whale 261) 3.75 15.00 67
(Shown as by Laughing Gravy)
WANTED: ONE GIRL/Something A Little Bit Different (Challenge 9120) 1.25 5.00 61
WE GO TOGETHER/Rosilane (Dore 555) 1.25 5.00 60
WE GO TOGETHER/Rosilane (Dore 555) 5.00 20.00 60
(Picture sleeve)
WHITE TENNIS SNEAKERS/Cindy (Dore 548) 1.50 6.00 60
WHO PUT THE BOMP/My Favorite Dream (Liberty 55496) 1.25 5.00 62
YELLOW BALLOON/Taste Of Rain (Columbia 4-44036) 3.75 15.00 67
YOU REALLY KNOW HOW TO HURT A GUY/
It's As Easy As 1-2-3 (Liberty 55792) .75 3.00 65
YOU REALLY KNOW HOW TO HURT A GUY/
It's As Easy As 1-2-3 (Liberty 55792) 2.50 10.00 65
(Picture sleeve)
Also see Jan & Arnie
Also see Laughing Gravy
Also see Legendary Masked Surfers, The
Also see Our Gang
Also see Rally Packs, The

JAN & JERRY
BANDSTAND BABY/Nellie Sits O'Waitin' (Metro 20024) 1.00 4.00 59

JAN & KJELD
BANJO BOY/
Don't Raise A Storm (Mach Doch Nicht So Viel Wind) (Kapp 335) .75 3.00 60
PENNY MELODY/
Ting-a-ling (My Banjo Sings) (Jaro International 77032) .75 3.00

JAN & PHIL
DON'T YOU WEEP/ (Crusader 106) .75 3.00 64

JAN & THE RADIANTS
IF YOU LOVE ME/Is It True (Queen 24007) 1.50 6.00

JANIS, Johnny
LATER BABY/All The Time (ABC-Paramount 9840) 1.25 5.00 57
MOVE IT OR LOSE IT/I'm Throwing Rice (Coral 61552) 1.50 6.00 55
PLEDGE OF LOVE/I Played The Field (ABC-Paramount 9800) 1.25 5.00 57

KAPP
K-335X
BANJO BOY
JAN AND KJELD
MANUFACTURED BY KAPP RECORDS, INC. NEW YORK

JANKOWSKI, Horst
BLACK FOREST HOLIDAY/Elmer's Tune (Mercury 72567) .75 3.00 66
SIMPLE GIMPLE/Charming Vienna (Mercury 72465) .75 3.00 65
WALK IN THE BLACK FOREST, A/Nola (Mercury 72425) .75 3.00 65
WALK IN THE BLACK FOREST, A/Blue Spring (Beverly Hills 4116) .50 2.00 72
Instrumentals

JANSSEN, Danny
MIRROR ON THE WALL/Blue Moon (Stephany 1841) 1.25 5.00

JANS, Tom
WHY DON'T YOU LOVE ME/Fineline (Columbia 10470) .50 2.00 77

JAPANESE BEATLES, The
BEATLE SONG (JAPANESE STYLE)/
Beatle Song (Japanese Style) (Part 2) (Golden Crest 584) 1.50 6.00 64

JARETT, Peter, & The Fifth Circle
RUN, RUN, BABY RUN/Let's Dance Close (MGM K-13768) 3.00 12.00 67

JARMELS, The
COME ON GIRL/Keep Your Mind On Me (Laurie 3174) 1.00 4.00 63
GEE OH GOSH/I'll Follow You (Laurie 3116) 1.00 4.00 61
LITTLE BIT OF SOAP, A/The Way You Look Tonight (Laurie 3098) 1.00 4.00 61
LITTLE BUG/One By One (Laurie 3141) 1.00 4.00 62
LITTLE LONELY ONE/She Loves To Dance (Laurie 3085) 1.00 4.00 61
RED SAILS IN THE SUNSET/Loneliness (Laurie 3124) 1.00 4.00 62

JARRARD, Rick
HIGH COIN/Time Is Tomorrow (Chattahoochee 700) 2.00 8.00 67
IF I ONLY HAD A GIRL/Tell Me Not (Plebe 101) 2.50 10.00 62

JARR, Cook E.
DARLING BE HOME SOON/Red Balloon (RCA 47-9708) .75 3.00 69
PLEDGING MY LOVE/If I Were A Carpenter (RCA 74-0119) .75 3.00 69
REASON TO BELIEVE/Do You Believe In Magic (RCA 74-0182) 1.00 4.00 69
WHO WEARS HOT PANTS/Cookie's Bag (Epic 5-10735) .75 3.00 71

JARRE, Jean-Michael
OXYGENE (PART 4)/Oxygene (Part 6) (Polydor 14425) .50 2.00 78

JARVIS, Carol
GOLDEN BOY/Acorn (Dot 15679) 1.00 4.00 57
REBEL/Whirlpool Of Love (Dot 15586) 1.00 4.00 57

JARVIS, Felton
DIMPLES/Little Wheel (Thunder Int'l. 1030) 1.00 4.00 60
DON'T KNOCK ELVIS/Honest John (Viva 1001) 3.75 15.00 59
SKI KING/Be-I-by (ABC-Paramount 10570) .75 3.00 64
TOO MANY TIGERS/Knuckie Knuckie (ABC-Paramount 1064) .75 3.00 64
Felton Jarvis was the producer of most of Elvis Presley's post-1965 recordings.

JASON GARFIELD (Group)
BLESSED ARE THE PROTESTERS/Ship Of Freedom (Kef 4451) 1.50 6.00
PICTURE OF LILLI, A/Where Did I Lose My Way (Kef 4445) 2.00 8.00

JAVALONS, The
TOOK A CHANCE (I TOOK A CHANCE)/
That Is Why (I Love You) (Eko 6901) 2.50 10.00 61

JAXON, Bob
BEACH PARTY/I Hanging Around (RCA Victor 47-6945) 1.50 6.00 57

JAY & THE AMERICANS (Featuring Jay Black)
CAPTURE THE MOMENT/
Do You Ever Think Of Me? (United Artists 50654) .75 3.00 70
CARA MIA/When It's All Over (United Artists 881) .75 3.00 65
COME A LITTLE BIT CLOSER/
Goodbye Boys Goodbye (Ciao Bagazzi Ciao) (United Artists 759) .75 3.00 64
COME DANCE WITH ME/
Look In My Eyes Marie (United Artists 669) 1.00 4.00 63
CRYING/I Don't Need A Friend (United Artists 50016) .75 3.00 66
DO I LOVE YOU?/Tricia (Tell Your Daddy) (United Artists 50683) .75 3.00 70
GOT HUNG UP ALONG THE WAY/
(We'll Meet In The) Yellow Forest (United Artists 50196) .75 3.00 67
HE'S RAINING IN MY SUNSHINE/
The Reason For Living (United Artists 50094) .75 3.00 66
HUSHABYE/Gypsy Woman (United Artists 50535) .75 3.00 69
(I'D KILL) FOR THE LOVE OF A LADY/
Learnin' How To Fly (United Artists 50567) .75 3.00 69
LET'S LOCK THE DOOR (& THROW AWAY THE KEY)/
I'll Remember You (United Artists 805) .75 3.00 64
LIVIN' ABOVE YOUR HEAD/
Look At Me-What Do You See (United Artists 50046) .75 3.00 66
ONLY IN AMERICA/My Clair De Lune (United Artists 626) .75 3.00 63
SHANGHAI NOODLE FACTORY/French Provincial (United Artists 50222) .75 3.00 67
SHE CRIED/Dawning (United Artists 415) .75 3.00 62
SOME ENCHANTED EVENING/Girl (United Artists 919) .75 3.00 65
STRANGERS TOMORROW/What's The Use (United Artists 566) .75 3.00 62
SUNDAY & ME/Through This Doorway (United Artists 948) .75 3.00 65
THINK OF THE GOOD TIMES/If You Were Mine Girl (United Artists 845) .75 3.00 65
THIS IS IT/It's Your Turn To Cry (United Artists 479) 1.00 4.00 62
THIS MAGIC MOMENT/Since I Don't Have You (United Artists 50475) .75 3.00 68
TOMORROW/Yes (United Artists 504) .75 3.00 62
TONIGHT/Other Girls, The (United Artists 353) .75 3.00 61
TO WAIT FOR LOVE/Friday (United Artists 693) .75 3.00 64
WALKING IN THE RAIN/(I'd Kill) For The
Love Of A Lady (United Artists 50605) .75 3.00 69

WHEN YOU DANCE/No, I Don't Know Her (United Artists 50510) .75 3.00 69
WHY CAN'T YOU BRING ME HOME/
Baby Stop Your Crying (United Artists 992) .75 3.00 66
YOU AIN'T AS HIP AS ALL THAT BABY/
Nature Boy (United Artists 50139) .75 3.00 67
YOU AIN'T GONNA WAKE UP CRYING/Gemini (United Artists 50448) .75 3.00 68
Although Jay Black was the group's famous lead singer, Jay Taylor was featured on their first few recordings. Other group members were: Sandy Yaguda, Kenny Rosenberg & Howard Kirschenbaum.
Also see Harbor Lights

JAY & THE DELTAS
BELLS ARE RINGING/Super Hawk (Warner Bros. 5404) 3.00 12.00 64

JAY & THE TECHNIQUES (Featuring Jay Proctor)
APPLES, PEACHES, PUMPKIN PIE/Stronger Than Dirt (Smash 2086) .75 3.00 67
BABY MAKE YOUR OWN SWEET MUSIC/ (Smash 2154) .75 3.00 68
KEEP THE BALL ROLLIN'/Here We Go Again (Smash 2124) .75 3.00 67
STRAWBERRY SHORTCAKE/Still (In Love With You) (Smash 2142) .75 3.00 68

JAY, Dale
SHAKEN ALL OVER/Our Love Is For Real (Raven 001) .75 3.00

JAY, Jerry: see Osborne, Jerry

JAY, Jimmy
DON'T LET THE STARS GET IN YOUR EYES/
300 Miles Of Steel (Philips 40115) .75 3.00 63
FAIRY TALES DON'T EVER COME TRUE/
I Know That Feeling (Philips 40155) .75 3.00 63

JAY, Jimmy, & The Blue Falcons
TURBINE DRIVE/Take Ten (Belmont 4006) 1.00 4.00 62

JAY, Johnny
SUGAR DOLL/Tears (Mercury 71232) 2.00 8.00 57

JAY, Morty, & The Surferin' Cats
SALTWATER TAFFY/What Is Surfin' All About (Legend 124) .75 3.00 63

JAY WALKERS, The
I GOT MY OWN THING GOIN'/I Do (Selsom 109) 1.25 5.00

JAYE, Jerry
COTTAGE FOR SALE/Going To The River (Label 2020) 1.00 4.00 59
I STARTED LOVING YOU AGAIN/Long Black Veil (Hi 2150) .75 3.00 68
LET THE FOUR WINDS BLOW/Singing The Blues (Hi 2128) .75 3.00 67
MY GIRL JOSEPHINE/Five Miles From Home (Hi 2120) .75 3.00 67

JAYHAWKERS
CERTAIN GIRL, A/Come On (Lucky Eleven 232) 1.00 4.00

JAYNE, Betty, & The Teenettes
I'M NO LONGER JIMMY'S GIRL (Answer song)/
Tag Along (Carellen 107) 1.25 5.00 61
LONELY TEENAGER/Time Will Tell (Mona Lee 139) 1.50 6.00

JAYNELLS, The
I'LL STAY HOME NEW YEARS EVE/Down Home (Cameo 286) .75 3.00 63

JAYNETTS, The
KEEP AN EYE ON HER/Keep An Eye On Her (Instrumental) (Tuff 371) .75 3.00 63
NO LOVE AT ALL/Johnny, Don't You Cry (Tuff 377) .75 3.00 64
SALLY, GO ROUND THE ROSES/
Sally, Go Round The Roses (Instrumental) (Tuff 369) .75 3.00 63
SNOWMAN SNOWMAN SWEET POTATO NOSE/
Snowman Snowman Sweet Potato Nose (Instrumental) (Tuff 374) .75 3.00 63
WE BELONG TO EACH OTHER/He's Crying Inside (Goldie 1102) 1.00 4.00 62

JAYTONES, The
MY ONLY LOVE/Absolutely Right (Cub 9057) 3.75 15.00 60

JAYWALKER & THE PEDESTRIANS (Featuring Pete Antell)
HEY NOW/Never Happen (Amy 848) 1.50 6.00 62

JEAN, Bobbie
HOMEWORK/I Don't Want A Bunny Or A Dolly (Blue Ribbon 304) 1.00 4.00 59

JEANIE & THE BOY FRIENDS
IT'S ME KNOCKING/Baby (Warwick 508) 2.00 8.00 59

JEANNE & JANIE: see Black, Jeanne

JEFF & THE GINOS
ONE SUMMER IN A MILLION/Let Me Out (Mercury 72138) .75 3.00 63

JEFFERSON
BABY TAKE ME IN YOUR ARMS/I Fell Flat On My Face (Janus 106) .75 3.00 69
COLOUR OF MY LOVE, THE/Look No Further (Decca 32501) .75 3.00 69

RCA VICTOR
JEFFERSON AIRPLANE
47-8769
PLUG SIDE
NOT FOR SALE
Producers: Matthew Katz & Tommy Olive
IT'S NO SECRET
(Marty Balin)

JEFFERSON AIRPLANE
(With Grace Slick, Paul Kantner & Marty Balin)
BALLAD OF YOU & ME & POONEIL/Two Heads (RCA Victor 47-9297) 1.00 4.00 67
BRINGING ME DOWN/Let Me In (RCA Victor 47-8967) 2.00 8.00 66
COME UP THE YEARS/Blues From An Airplane (RCA Victor 47-8848) 2.50 10.00 66
CROWN OF CREATION/Lather (RCA Victor 47-9644) 1.00 4.00 68
GREASY HEART/Share A Little Joke (With The World) (RCA Victor 47-9496) 1.00 4.00 68
HAVE YOU SEEN THE SAUCERS/Mexico (RCA 74-0343) 1.25 5.00 70
IT'S NO SECRET/Runnin' 'Round This World (RCA Victor 47-8769) 2.00 8.00 66

TITLE/FLIP	LABEL & NO.	GOOD	NEAR MINT	YR.
MILK TRAIN/Long John Silver	(Grunt 0506)	.75	3.00	71
MY BEST FRIEND/How Do You Feel	(RCA Victor 47-9063)	1.25	5.00	67
PLASTIC FANTASTIC LOVER/Other Side Of This Life	(RCA 74-0150)	1.25	5.00	69
PRETTY AS YOU FEEL/Wild Turkey	(Grunt 0500)	.75	3.00	71
SOMEBODY TO LOVE/She Has Funny Cars	(RCA Victor 47-9140)	.75	3.00	67
TWILIGHT DOUBLE LEADER/Trial By Fire	(Grunt 0511)	1.25	5.00	72
VOLUNTEERS/We Can Be Together	(RCA Victor 47-0245)	1.00	4.00	69
WATCH HER RIDE/Martha	(RCA Victor 47-9389)	1.00	4.00	67
WHITE RABBIT/Plastic Fantastic Lover	(RCA Victor 47-9248)	.75	3.00	67

Also see Great!! Society!!, The
Also see Hot Tuna
Also see Jefferson Starship

JEFFERSON COUNTY

CITY BILLY/	(De Gee 3016)	.75	3.00	

JEFFERSON HANDKERCHIEF

I'M ALLERGIC TO FLOWERS/The Little Matador	(Challenge 59371)	1.50	6.00	67

JEFFERSON STARSHIP (Formerly Jefferson Airplane)

CAROLINE/Be Young You	(Grunt 10206)	.75	3.00	75
CHILD IS COMING, A/Let's Go Together (Shown as by Paul Kantner & Jefferson Starship)	(RCA 74-0426)	1.00	4.00	71
COUNT ON ME/Show Yourself	(Grunt 11196)	.50	2.00	78
CRAZY FEELIN'/Love Too Good	(Grunt 11374)	.50	2.00	78
JANE/Freedom At Point Zero	(Grunt 11750)	.50	2.00	79
LIGHT THE SKY ON FIRE/Hyperdrive	(Grunt 11426)	.50	2.00	78
MIRACLES/Ai Garimsu (There Is Love)	(Grunt 10367)	.50	2.00	75
PLAY ON LOVE/I Want To See Another World	(Grunt 10456)	.50	2.00	75
RIDE THE TIGER/Devils Den	(Grunt 10080)	.75	3.00	74
RUNAWAY/Hot Water	(Grunt 11274)	.50	2.00	78
ST. CHARLES/Love Lovely Love	(Grunt 10791)	.50	2.00	76
WITH YOUR LOVE/Switchblade	(Grunt 10746)	.50	2.00	76

JEFFREYS, Garland

COOL DOWN BOY/New York Skyline	(A&M 1952)	.50	2.00	77
DISCO KID, THE (PART 1)/The Disco Kid (Part 2)	(Arista 0119)	.50	2.00	75
REELIN' (With Phoebe Snow)/One-Eyed Jack	(A&M 2030)	.50	2.00	78
SHE DIDN'T LIE/Scream In The Night	(Atlantic 2948)	.75	3.00	73
SHE DIDN'T LIE/Scream In The Night	(A&M 2074)	.50	2.00	78
WILD IN THE STREETS/	(Atlantic 2981)	.75	3.00	73
WILD IN THE STREETS/Ghost Writer	(A&M 1934)	.50	2.00	77

JEKYLL & HYDE

FRANKENSTEIN MEETS THE BEATLES/Dracula Drag	(DCP 1126)	1.50	6.00	64

JELLY

I WANT YOU TO DANCE/	(Asylum 45449)	.50	2.00	77
NO ONE LIKE MY BABY/Broken Man	(Asylum 45388)	.50	2.00	77

JELLY BEANS, The

BABY BE MINE/The Kind Of Boy You Can't Forget	(Red Bird 10-011)	.75	3.00	64
I WANNA LOVE HIM SO BAD/So Long	(Red Bird 10-003)	.75	3.00	64
YOU DON'T MEAN NO GOOD TO ME/I'm Hip To You	(Eskee 001)	.75	3.00	65

JENKINS, Donald & The Delighters

ELEPHANT WALK/Wang Dang Dula	(Cortland 109)	1.00	4.00	63
ELEPHANT WALK/Wang Dang Dula	(Cortland 3045)	.75	3.00	63
SOMEBODY HELP ME/Adios (My Secret Love)	(Cortland 112)	1.00	4.00	63

JENKINS, Gordon

BEWITCHED/Where In The World	(Decca 9-24983)	1.25	5.00	50
CHARMAINE/When A Man Is Free	(Decca 9-27859)	1.25	5.00	51
GOODNIGHT IRENE/Tzena, Tzena, Tzena (With the Weavers)	(Decca 9-27077)	1.25	5.00	50
I'M FOREVER BLOWING BUBBLES/You're Mine (With Artie Shaw)	(Decca 9-27186)	1.25	5.00	50
MY FOOLISH HEART/Don't Do Something To Someone	(Decca 9-24830)	1.25	5.00	50
ROSE, ROSE, I LOVE YOU/Unless	(Decca 9-27594)	1.25	5.00	51
SO LONG/Lonesome Traveler (With the Weavers)	(Decca 9-27376)	1.25	5.00	50
WHISPERING/Song Of The Bayou	(Decca 9-27585)	1.25	5.00	51

JENKINS, Jimmy

FARWELL TO THE KING/Only Myself (Novelty/Break-in)	(Seatbelts Fastened? EP-60 Ohio 102675)	.75	3.00	77

JENNINGS, Waylon

ANOTHER BLUE DAY/Never Again	(Trend 102)	3.75	15.00	61
DREAM BABY/Crying	(Bat 121639)	3.00	12.00	62
FOUR STRONG WINDS/Just To Satisfy You	(A&M 739)	1.25	5.00	64
JOLE BLON/When Sin Stops (Maroon label) (With Buddy Holly on Guitar and King Curtis on Sax.)	(Brunswick 55130)	25.00	100.00	59
JOLE BLON/When Sin Stops (Promotional issue with Buddy Holly on Guitar and King Curtis on Sax.)	(Brunswick 55130)	18.75	75.00	59
RAVE ON/Love Denied	(A&M 722)	1.25	5.00	63
STAGE, THE/My Baby Walks All Over Me	(Trend '63 106-45)	7.50	30.00	63

Also see Eddy, Duane

JENSEN, Dick

SURFIN' IN HAWAII/Doin' The Tamure	(Mahalo 1012)	1.00	4.00	63

JENSEN, Kris

JACKIE LOOK, THE/Tender Hearted Baby	(Kapp 393)	.75	3.00	61
PLEASE LET ME LOVE YOU TONIGHT/Your Daddy Don't Like Me	(Leader 813)	1.25	5.00	60
THREE VANILLA, TWO CHOCOLATE, ONE PISTACHIO ICE CREAM CONES/Danny's Dreams	(Kapp 410)	.75	3.00	61
TORTURE/Let's Sit Down	(Hickory 1173)	.75	3.00	62

JERICHO

MAKE IT BETTER/Cheater Man	(Bearsville 31003)	.50	2.00	72

JERICHO HARP

IS IT REALLY LOVE AT ALL/If I Were A Captain	(United Artists 1121)	.50	2.00	78
OH SARAH/	(United Artists 1049)	.50	2.00	77

JERRY & JEFF (Jerry Kasenetz & Jeff Katz)

SWEET CHARITY/Voodoo Medicine Man (Vocal by Neil Bogart, also known as Neil Scott.)	(Super K SK-7)	1.25	5.00	68
SWEET SWEET LOVIN' YOU/(Poor Old) Mr. Jensen (Vocal by Tony Orlando)	(Super K SK-101)	1.00	4.00	69

JERRY & MEL

DOUBLE WHAMMY/Confessions Of A North Beach Poet	(Warner Bros. 5195)	.75	3.00	61

JERRY & THE ATTACHES

MESSING WITH THE KID (PART 1)/Messing With The Kid (Part 2)	(Crash 1002)	.75	3.00	64

JERRY & THE LANDSLIDES

GET OFF OF MY ROOF/Green Fire	(PPX 441)	1.00	4.00	66

JERRY & THE RADIANTS

CALIFORNIA SUN/Trash	(Jox 016)	.75	3.00	64

JERRY & THE UPBEATS

CROW, THE/Sour Apples	(United Artists 547)	1.00	4.00	62

JERRY B.

DOUBLE-O SOUL IN ACTION/Soul Bag (Novelty/Break-in)	(Double Check 4002)	1.25	5.00	

JERRY MURAD'S HARMONICATS, The: see Harmonicats, The

JESSIE & JAMES

G.I. ROCK/Number Please	(Epic 9331)	1.00	4.00	59

JESTERS, The

DIESEL/Jamaican Holiday	(RIO-B10)	1.25	5.00	

JESTERS, The: see Messina, Jim, & The Jesters

JESUS CHRIST SUPERSTAR (London Stage Original Cast)

I DON'T KNOW HOW TO LOVE HIM (By Yvonne Elliman)/	(Decca 34801)	.50	2.00	72
LAST SUPPER (EXCERPT) (LOOKING AT ALL MY TRIALS & TRIBULATIONS) (By the Apostles)/Gethsemane (I Only Want To Say)(By Ian Gillan)	(Decca 34802)	.50	2.00	72
SUPERSTAR (By Murray Head)/King Herod's Song (By Mike D'Abo)	(Decca 34803)	.50	2.00	72

JETHRO TULL (Featuring Ian Anderson)

BUNGLE IN THE JUNGLE/Back-Door Angel	(Chrysalis 2101)	.50	2.00	74
HOME/Warm Sporran	(Chrysalis 2387)	.50	2.00	79
HYMN 43/Mother Goose	(Chrysalis-Reprise 1024)	.75	3.00	71
INSIDE/Time For Everything	(Chrysalis-Reprise 0927)	1.00	4.00	70
LIVING IN THE PAST/Driving Song	(Chrysalis-Reprise 0845)	1.00	4.00	72
LIVING IN THE PAST/Christmas Song	(Chrysalis 2006)	.50	2.00	72
LOCOMOTIVE BREATH/Wind-Up	(Chrysalis-Reprise 1054)	.75	3.00	72
LOCOMOTIVE BREATH/Fat Man	(Chrysalis 2110)	.50	2.00	76
LOVE STORY/Song For Jefferey	(Chrysalis-Reprise 0815)	1.00	4.00	70
MINSTREL IN THE GALLERY/Summer Day Sand	(Chrysalis 2106)	.50	2.00	75
PASSION PLAY, A (Edit No. 10)/A Passion Play (Edit No. 6)	(Chrysalis 2017)	.75	3.00	73
PASSION PLAY, A (Edit No. 8)/A Passion Play (Edit No. 9)	(Chrysalis 2012)	.50	2.00	73
REASONS FOR WAITING/Sweet Dream	(Chrysalis-Reprise 0886)	1.00	4.00	69
SKATING AWAY (ON THE THIN ICE OF THE NEW DAY)/Sealion	(Chrysalis 2103)	.75	3.00	75
TEACHER/Witch's Promise	(Chrysalis-Reprise 0899)	1.00	4.00	70
TOO YOUNG TO ROCK & ROLL: TOO YOUNG TO DIE/Bad Eyed & Loveless	(Chrysalis 2114)	.75	3.00	76
WHISTLER, THE/Strip Cartoon	(Chrysalis 2135)	.50	2.00	77

JET STREAM

QUIET ON WEST 23rd/Crazy Me All's	(Smash 2095)	.75	3.00	67
READY TO LEAVE/Silky Tonight	(Smash 2113)	.75	3.00	67

JEWEL & EDDIE (Jewel Akens & Eddie Daniels)

DOIN' THE MONSTER MASH/13 Steps (To Room Blue)	(Drandell 001)	1.00	4.00	63
DOIN' THE HULLY GULLY/Opportunity	(Silver 1004)	1.25	5.00	60
OPPORTUNITY/Strollin' Guitar	(Silver 1004)	1.25	5.00	60
SIXTEEN TONS/My Eyes Are Crying For You	(Silver 1008)	1.25	5.00	60

Speculation persists as to the theory that Eddie Cochran plays guitar on the Silver releases.

JEWELL & THE RUBIES

KIDNAPPER/Thrill	(ABC-Paramount 10485)	.75	3.00	63

JEWELL, Leonard

DOIN' THE MONSTER MASH/13 Steps (To Room Blue)	(Drandell 001)	.75	3.00	63

JEWELL, Nancy

WE DIDN'T GET ENOUGH OF YOU/Marriage A 50-50 Deal	(Pickin' Post 8830)	.50	2.00	77

JEWELS, The

BUT I DO/Smokey Joe	(Dimension 1048)	.75	3.00	65
OPPORTUNITY/Gotta Find A Way	(Dimension 1034)	.75	3.00	64

JIGSAW

BRAND NEW LOVE AFFAIR/Have You Heard The News	(Chelsea 3043)	.50	2.00	76
IF I HAVE TO GO AWAY/One More Time For Love	(20th Century 2347)	.50	2.00	77
LOVE FIRE/Mystic Harmony	(Chelsea 3037)	.50	2.00	76
ONLY WHEN I'M LONELY/	(20th Century 2369)	.50	2.00	78
SKY HIGH/Brand New Love Affair	(Chelsea 3022)	.50	2.00	75

JILL & RAY: see Paul & Paula

JILLETTES

WHY DID I CRY/Can't Play A Playgirl	(Philips 40140)	.75	3.00	63

JIM & BILL

WOODPECKER, THE/	(Quartercash 73)	1.00	4.00	

JIM & INGRID (Jim & Ingrid Croce)

WASTING OUR TIME/	(Capitol)	3.75	15.00	69

JIM & JEAN

PEOPLE WORLD/Time Goes Backwards	(Verve Forecast 5073)	.75	3.00	68

JIM & MONICA (With Jimmy Gilmer)

KEEP A KNOCKING/What A Sad Thing That Was	(Betty 1209)	1.25	5.00	64
REELIN' & ROCKIN'/It's Summer	(Betty 1210)	1.25	5.00	64
SLIPPIN' & SLIDIN'/Slippin' & Slidin' (Instrumental)	(Betty 1207)	1.25	5.00	64

JIM DANDIES, The

MACKEY'S TWIST (MACK THE KNIFE)/My Kisses For Your Thoughts	(Empress 105)	.75	3.00	62

JIM, JEFF & JAN

I KNOW WHERE I'M GOING/Star Bright	(Capitol 5059)	.75	3.00	63

JIMENEZ, Jose (Bill Dana)

ASTRONAUT, THE (PART 1)/The Astronaut (Part 2)	(Kapp 409)	.75	3.00	61
JOSE & CLEOPATRA (PART 1)/Jose & Cleopatra (Part 2)	(Kapp 540)	.75	3.00	62
SHINE ON HARVEST MOON/Jingle Bells	(Kapp 434)	.75	3.00	61

Comedy

JIMMY & DUANE (Jimmy Delbridge & Duane Eddy)

SODA FOUNTAIN GIRL/ (With Buddy Long & the Western Melody Boys)	(EB X. Preston 212)	25.00	100.00	

JIMMY & ILLUSIONS

UNDERTOW/Karen	(Julynn 36)	.75	3.00	63

JIMMY & THE REBELS

SHIEK OF ARABY/You Are My Sunshine	(Roulette 4201)	1.00	4.00	59

JIMMY & THE ROADRUNNERS

RUNAWAY/It's Only Make Believe	(Varmint 101)	.75	3.00	66

JIMMY J. & THE J'S

GIRLFRIEND (PLEASE BE MY)/I've Lost	(Salco 647)	1.25	5.00	61

JINKINS, Gus

SO WHAT/Spark Plug	(Flash 116)	1.00	4.00	57
TRICKY/You Told Me	(Flash 115)	1.00	4.00	56

Instrumentals

JIVA

SOMETHIN'S GOIN' ON INSIDE L.A./Take My Love	(Dark Horse 10006)	.50	2.00	76
TAKE MY LOVE/Love Is The Feeling	(Polydor 14506)	.50	2.00	78
THAT SCENE AGAIN/	(Polydor 14526)	.50	2.00	79

JIVELIERS, The: see Camerons, The

JIVETONES, The

DING DING DONG/Geraldine	(Apt 25020)	3.75	15.00	58

JIVING JUNIORS, The

MOONLIGHT LOVER/Sweet As An Angel	(Asnes 103)	1.50	6.00	

JO

DON'T WANNA BE ANOTHER GOOD LUCK CHARM/She Can Have You (Answer song)	(Capitol 4745)	1.25	5.00	62

JO ANN & TROY (Jo Ann Campbell & Troy Seals)

I FOUND A LOVE, OH WHAT A LOVE/Who Do You Love	(Atlantic 2256)	2.50	10.00	64

JO, Damita: see Damita Jo

JO JO GUNNE (Featuring Jay Ferguson)

RUN, RUN, RUN/Take It Easy	(Asylum 11003)	.50	2.00	72

JOAN & JOY

MY BABY HAS LEFT ME/You're My Prescription	(Hull 725)	1.00	4.00	58

JODIMARS, The

LET'S ROCK/Now Dig This	(Capitol 3285)	1.25	5.00	55

Also see Haley, Bill, & His Comets

JOE & ANN

GEE BABY/Wherever You May Be	(Ace 577)	1.00	4.00	59

JOE & EDDIE

SWING DOWN CHARIOT/Wild Is The Wind	(GNP Crescendo 316)	.75	3.00	64
THERE'S A MEETIN' HERE TONIGHT/Lonesome Traveler	(GNP Crescendo 195)	.75	3.00	63

JOE, Marcy

JUMPING JACK/Take A Word	(Robbee 117)	.75	3.00	61
RONNIE/My First Mistake	(Robbee 110)	.75	3.00	61
WHAT I DID THIS SUMMER/Since Gary Went In The Navy (With Lou Christie.)	(Robbee 115)	1.25	5.00	61

JOEL, Billy

BIG SHOT/Root Beer Rag	(Columbia-Family 10913)	.50	2.00	79
DON'T ASK ME WHY/	(Columbia 1-11331)	.50	2.00	80
ENTERTAINER, THE/The Mexican Connection	(Columbia-Family 10064)	.75	3.00	74
EVERYBODY LOVES YOU NOW/She's Got A Way	(Family 0900)	1.25	5.00	73
HONESTY/The Mexican Connection	(Columbia-Family 10959)	.50	2.00	79
IT'S STILL ROCK & ROLL TO ME/	(Columbia 1-11276)	.50	2.00	80
JUST THE WAY YOU ARE/Get It Right The First Time	(Columbia-Family 10646)	.50	2.00	77
MOVIN' OUT (ANTHONY'S SONG)/She's Always A Woman	(Columbia-Family 10624)	.75	3.00	77
MOVIN' OUT (ANTHONY'S SONG)/Everybody Has A Dream	(Columbia-Family 10708)	.50	2.00	78
MY LIFE/52nd Street	(Columbia-Family 10853)	.50	2.00	78
ONLY THE GOOD DIE YOUNG/Get It Right The First Time	(Columbia-Family 10750)	.50	2.00	78
PIANO MAN/You're My Home	(Columbia-Family 45963)	.75	3.00	74
SAY GOODBYE TO HOLLYWOOD/I've Loved These Days	(Columbia-Family 10562)	.50	2.00	77
SHE'S ALWAYS A WOMAN/Vienna	(Columbia-Family 10788)	.50	2.00	78
SOUVENIR/All For Leyna	(Columbia 1-11229)	.50	2.00	80
SUMMER, HIGHLAND FALLS/James	(Columbia-Family 10412)	.75	3.00	76
TOMORROW IS TODAY/Everybody Loves You Now	(Family 0906)	1.25	5.00	73
TRAVELIN' PRAYER/	(Columbia-Family 10015)	.75	3.00	74
WORSE COMES TO WORST/Somewhere Along The Line	(Columbia-Family 46055)	.75	3.00	74

JOEY

PLACE IN YOUR HEART, A/I Got Feelings	(Taurus 353)	2.50	10.00	62

JOEY & DANNY

UNDERWATER SURFERS/I Got Rid Of The Rats	(Swan 4157)	1.00	4.00	63

JOEY & THE CONTINENTALS

LYNDA/Will Love Ever Come My Way	(Komet 1001)	1.50	6.00	
SAD GIRL/Baby	(Laurie 3294)	3.00	12.00	65
SHE RIDES WITH ME/Rudy Vadoo (Reissued on Claridge 312, but shown as by the GTO's.)	(Claridge 304)	1.50	6.00	65

JOEY & THE LEXINGTONS

BOBBIE/Tears From My Eyes	(Dunes 2029)	3.75	15.00	63
HEAVEN/The Girl I Love	(Comet 2154)	5.00	20.00	

JOEY & THE TEENAGERS

WHAT'S ON YOUR MIND/The Draw	(Columbia 4-42054)	8.75	35.00	61
WHAT'S ON YOUR MIND/The Draw (Compact 33 single)	(Columbia 3-42054)	15.00	60.00	61

The Teenagers on this release were previously back-up singers for Frankie Lymon.

JOEY & THE TWISTERS

BONY MORONIE/Mumblin'	(Dual 505)	1.00	4.00	62
DO YOU WANT TO DANCE/Last Dance	(Dual 509)	1.00	4.00	62

JOHANSEN, David (Of The New York Dolls)

FUNKY BUT CHIC/The Rope (The Let Go Song)	(Blue Sky 2771)	.50	2.00	78
MELODY/Wreckless Crazy	(Blue Sky 2781)	.50	2.00	79
SWAHETO WOMAN/	(Blue Sky 2789)	.50	2.00	80

JOHN & ERNEST

SOUL PRESIDENT NUMBER ONE/Crossover	(Rainy Wednesday 203)	.75	3.00	73
SUPERFLY MEETS SHAFT/Problems	(Rainy Wednesday 201)	.75	3.00	73

JOHN & PAUL

PEOPLE SAY/I'm Walkin' (Beatle novelty, not actually performed by Lennon & McCartney)	(Tip 1021)	2.50	10.00	64

JOHN, Billy, & The Continentals

OOH POOH PAH DOO/Does Someone Care (For Me)	(N-Joy 1012)	.75	3.00	62
LOVER BOY BLUE/Put The Hurt On You	(N-Joy 1014)	.75	3.00	62

JOHN, Elton

BENNIE & THE JETS/Harmony	(MCA 40198)	.50	2.00	74
BITCH IS BACK, THE/Cold Highway	(MCA 40297)	.50	2.00	74
BITE YOUR LIP (GET UP & DANCE)/Chameleon	(MCA-Rocket 40677)	.50	2.00	77
BORDER SONG/Bad Side Of The Moon	(Congress 6022)	3.00	12.00	
BORDER SONG/Bad Side Of The Moon	(Uni 55246)	1.25	5.00	
BORDER SONG/Bad Side Of The Moon	(MCA 60161)	.50	2.00	
CROCODILE ROCK/Elderberry Wine	(MCA 40000)	.50	2.00	72
DANIEL/Skyline Pidgeon	(MCA 40046)	.50	2.00	73
DON'T GO BREAKING MY HEART/Snow Queen (With Kiki Dee)	(Rocket 40585)	.50	2.00	76
DON'T LET THE SUN GO DOWN ON ME/Sick City	(MCA 40259)	.50	2.00	74
FRIENDS/Honey Roll	(Uni 55277)	1.00	4.00	71
FRIENDS/Honey Roll	(MCA 60162)	.50	2.00	75
FROM DENVER TO L.A./(Flip-side not by Elton John)	(Viking 1010)	5.00	20.00	69
GOODBYE YELLOW BRICK ROAD/Young Man's Blues	(MCA 40148)	.50	2.00	73
GROW SOME FUNK OF YOUR OWN/I Feel Like A Bullet (In The Gun Of Robert Ford)	(MCA 40505)	.50	2.00	76
HONKY CAT/Slave	(Uni 55343)	1.00	4.00	72
HONKY CAT/Slave	(MCA 60166)	.50	2.00	75
ISLAND GIRL/Sugar On The Floor	(MCA 40461)	.50	2.00	75
JOHNNY B. GOODE/Georgia	(MCA 41159)	.50	2.00	79
LADY SAMANTHA/All Across The Havens	(DJM 70008)	3.75	15.00	69
LADY SAMANTHA/It's Me That You Need	(Congress 6017)	3.75	15.00	69
LADY SAMANTHA/It's Me That You Need	(MCA 60172)	.50	2.00	75
LEVON/Goodbye	(Uni 55314)	1.00	4.00	71
LEVON/Goodbye	(MCA 60163)	.50	2.00	75

TITLE/FLIP — LABEL & NO. — GOOD — NEAR MINT — YR.

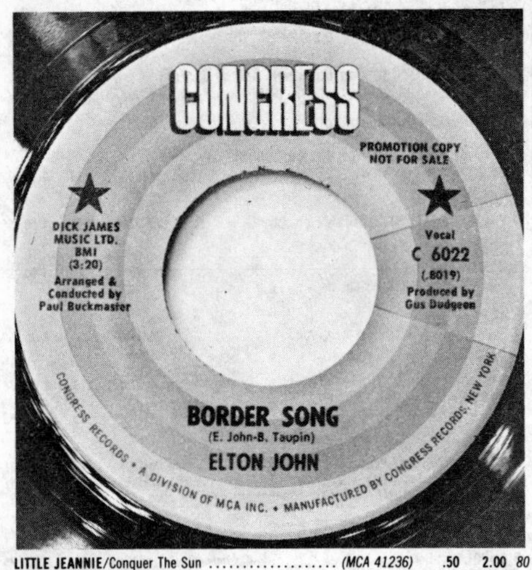

LITTLE JEANNIE/Conquer The Sun (MCA 41236) .50 2.00 80
LOVE SONG (With Lesley Duncan)/ (MCA 1938) 3.00 12.00
(Promotional issue only)
LUCY IN THE SKY WITH DIAMONDS/One Day At A Time (MCA 40344) .50 2.00 74
MAMA CAN'T BUY YOU LOVE/Three Way Love Affair (MCA 41042) .50 2.00 79
PART-TIME LOVE/I Cry At Night (MCA 40973) .50 2.00 78
PHILADELPHIA FREEDOM/I Saw Her Standing There (With John Lennon) (MCA 40364) .75 3.00 75
PHILADELPHIA FREEDOM/I Saw Her Standing There (MCA 40364) 7.50 30.00 75
(Custom WFIL, Philadelphia, picture sleeve)
PINBALL WIZARD/Acid Queen (By Tina Turner) (Polydor 002) 6.25 25.00 75
(Promotional issue only)
ROCKET MAN/Suzie (Dramas) (Uni 55328) 1.00 4.00 72
ROCKET MAN/Suzie (Dramas) (MCA 60165) .50 2.00 75
SATURDAY NIGHT'S ALRIGHT FOR FIGHTING/Jack Rabbit-Whenever You're Ready (We'll Go Steady Again) (MCA 40105) .50 2.00 73
SOMEONE SAVED MY LIFE TONIGHT/House Of Cards (MCA 40421) .50 2.00 75
SONG FOR GUY/Lovesick (MCA 40993) .50 2.00 79
SORRY SEEMS TO BE THE HARDEST WORD/Shoulder Holster (MCA-Rocket 40645) .50 2.00 76
STEP INTO CHRISTMAS/Ho Ho Ho (Who'd Be A Turkey At Christmas) (MCA 65018) .50 2.00 73
TINY DANCER/Razor Face (Uni 55318) 1.00 4.00 72
TINY DANCER/Razor Face (MCA 60164) .50 2.00 75
VICTIM OF LOVE/Strangers (MCA 41126) .50 2.00 79
YOUR SONG/Take Me To The Pilot (Uni 55265) 1.00 4.00 70
YOUR SONG/Take Me To The Pilot (MCA 60047) .50 2.00 73
Also see China

JOHN ENTWHISTLE'S RIGOR MORTIS (Of The Who)
I WONDER/ (Decca 33052) .75 3.00 72
MADE IN JAPAN/Roller Skate Kate (Track 40066) .75 3.00 73

JOHN, Robby
TEENAGE BILL OF RIGHTS/ (Del Fi 4115) 1.00 4.00 59

JOHN, Robert
GIVE A LITTLE MORE/Poor Side Of Town (Ariola 7963) .50 2.00 78
HUSHABYE/ (Atlantic 2884) .50 2.00 72
I DON'T WANT TO MAKE YOU LOVE ME/I'm Gonna Be Strong (A&M 1341) .75 3.00 71
IF YOU DON'T WANT MY LOVE/Don't Go (Columbia 4-44435) .75 3.00 68
LION SLEEPS TONIGHT (WIMOWEH)(MBUBE)/Janet (Atlantic 2846) .50 2.00 72
LONELY EYES/Dance The Night Away (EMI America 8030) .50 2.00 79
ONLY TIME/Stay A Little Longer (EMI America 8023) .50 2.00 79
SAD EYES/Am I Ever Gonna Hold You Again (EMI America 8015) .50 2.00 79
WHEN THE PARTY IS OVER/Raindrops, Love & Sunshine (A&M 1210) .75 3.00 70
YOU DON'T NEED A GYPSY/ (Atlantic 2930) .50 2.00 72

JOHNNIE & JOE
ACROSS THE SEA/You Said It & Don't Forget It (Chess 1769) 1.00 4.00 60
I ADORE YOU/I Want You Here Beside Me (ABC-Paramount 10079) 1.00 4.00 60
OVER THE MOUNTAIN, CROSS THE SEA/My Baby's Gone, On, On (J & S 1664) 6.25 25.00 57
OVER THE MOUNTAIN; CROSS THE SEA/My Baby's Gone, On, On (Chess 1654) 1.25 5.00 57
(Blue & silver label)
OVER THE MOUNTAIN, CROSS THE SEA/My Baby's Gone On, On (Chess 1654) .75 3.00 60
(Red & yellow label)

JOHNNY & JACKEY
LONELY & BLUE/Let's Go To A Movie Baby (Anna 1108) 1.25 5.00 59

JOHNNY & THE DREAMS
YOU'RE TOO YOUNG FOR ME/Are You With That (Richie 457) 2.00 8.00

JOHNNY & THE HURRICANES (Featuring Johnny Paris)
BEATNIK FLY/Sand Storm (Warwick 520) 1.00 4.00 60
COME ON TRAIN/San Antonio Rose (Big Top 3113) .75 3.00 62
CROSSFIRE/Lazy (Twirl 1001) 2.50 10.00 59
CROSSFIRE/Lazy (Warwick 502) .75 3.00 59
DOWN YONDER/Sheba (Big Top 3036) 1.00 4.00 60
HIGH VOLTAGE/Old Smokie (Big Top 3076) 1.00 4.00 61
I LOVE YOU/Judy's Moody (Atila 214) .75 3.00
IT'S A MAD, MAD, MAD, MAD WORLD/Shadows (Mala 470) 1.00 4.00 65
JA-DAMr. Lonely (Big Top 3063) 1.00 4.00 61
KAW-LIGA/Rough Road (Big Top 3159) 1.00 4.00 63
MONEY HONEY/That's All (Mala 483) 1.00 4.00 65
OLD SMOKIE/High Voltage (Big Top 3076) 1.00 4.00 61
PSYCHEDELIC WORM/Red River Rock '67 (Atila A-216) .75 3.00
RED RIVER ROCK/Buckeye (Warwick 509) 1.00 4.00 59
RED RIVER ROCK/Buckeye (Warwick S-509) 3.00 12.00 59
(Stereo single issue)
RENE/Saga Of The Beatles (Atila A-211) .75 3.00
REVEILLE ROCK/Time Bomb (Warwick 513) 1.25 5.00 59
REVEILLE ROCK/Time Bomb (Warwick S-513) 3.00 12.00 59
(Stereo single issue)
ROCKING GOOSE/Revival (Big Top 3051) 1.00 4.00 60
SAGA OF THE BEATLES/Rene (Jeff 211) 1.25 5.00 64
SAGA OF THE BEATLES/Rene (Atilla 211) .75 3.00 64
SALVATION/Misirlou (Big Top 3103) 1.00 4.00 62
SAN ANTONIO ROSE/Come On Train (Big Top 3113) 1.00 4.00 62
SHIEK OF ARABY/Minnesota Fats (Big Top 3125) 1.00 4.00 62
TRAFFIC JAM/Farewell, Farewell (Big Top 3090) 1.00 4.00 61
WHATEVER HAPPENED TO BABY JANE/Greens & Beans (Big Top 3132) 1.00 4.00 62
WHAT YOU KNOW ABOUT LOVE/Yes It's You (Atila A-221) .75 3.00
WISDOM'S FIFTH TAKE/Because I Love Her (Atila A-215) .75 3.00
YOU ARE MY SUNSHINE/Molly-O (Big Top 3056) 1.00 4.00 60
Instrumentals
Also see Freddie & The Parliaments

JOHNNY & THE JAMMERS
SCHOOL DAY BLUES/You Know I Love You (Dart 131) 1.00 4.00 60

JOHNNY & THE JOKERS
DO-RE-MI ROCK/Why Must It Be (Harvard 804) 2.00 8.00

JOHNNY & THE TOKENS
TASTE OF A TEAR/Never Till Now (Warwick 658) 1.25 5.00 61
Also see Tokens, The

JOHNNY & THE VIBRATONES
BIRD STOMPIN'/Movin' The Bird (Warner Bros. 5372) 1.00 4.00 63

JOHNNY Z.
MIDNIGHT BEACH PARTY/Beach Bum (Dore 667) .75 3.00 63

JOHN'S CHILDREN
SMASHED! BLOCKED!/Strange Affair (White Whale 239) 2.00 8.00 66

JOHNS, Johnny
STOMPIN' USA/Someone (Hi Mar 1001) 1.00 4.00 62

JOHNS, Sammy
BLESS MY SOUL/ (Warner-Curb 8270) .50 2.00 76
CHEVY VAN/Hang My Head & Moan (GRC 2046) .50 2.00 75
EARLY MORNING LOVE/Holy Mother, Aging Father (GRC 2021) .50 2.00 74
PEAS IN A POD/Friends Of Mine (Warner-Curb 8224) .50 2.00 76
RAG DOLL/Friends Of Mine (GRC 2062) .50 2.00 75

JOHNSON, Betty
CLAY IDOL/Why Do You Cry (Bally 1013) 1.00 4.00 56
DOES YOUR HEART BEAT FOR ME/You & Only You (Atlantic 2019) 1.00 4.00 59
DREAM/How Much (Atlantic 1186) 1.00 4.00 58
HONKY TONK ROCK/Say It Isn't So, Joe (Bally 105) 1.00 4.00 56
HOOPA HOOLA/One More Time (Atlantic 2002) 1.00 4.00 58
I DON'T WANT TO GO TO SLEEP TONIGHT/Depend On Me (Republic 2011) .75 3.00 61
I DREAMED/If It's Wrong To Love You (Bally 1020) 1.00 4.00 56
I'LL WAIT/Please Tell Me Why (Bally 1000) 1.00 4.00 56
LITTLE BLUE MAN, THE/Winter In Miami (Atlantic 1169) 1.00 4.00 58
LITTLE WHITE LIES/1492 (Bally 1033) 1.00 4.00 57
MY KIND OF GUY (Answer Song)/A Gal's Best Friend Is Her Make-up (Republic 2021) .75 3.00 61
SLIPPING AROUND/One Has My Name (Dot 16127) .75 3.00 60
SONG YOU HEARD WHEN YOU FELL IN LOVE, THE/I'm Beginning To Wonder (Bally 1041) 1.00 4.00 57
THERE'S A STAR SPANGLED BANNER WAVING SOMEWHERE/Take A Little Luck (Coed 532) 1.00 4.00 60
THERE'S NEVER BEEN A NIGHT/Mr. Brown Is Out Of Town (Atlantic 1193) 1.00 4.00 58
YOU CAN'T GET TO HEAVEN ON ROLLER SKATES/I Want A Good Home For My Cat (Atlantic 2009) 1.00 4.00 58

JOHNSON BROTHERS, The
CASTIN' MY SPELL/Zombie Lou (Valor 2006) 1.00 4.00 59

JOHNSON, Buddy
I DON'T WANT NOBODY/I'm Just Your Fool (Mercury 71723) .75 3.00 60
IT'S OBDACIOUS/Save Your Love For Me (Mercury 70695) 1.00 4.00 55

JOHNSON, Candy, Show
HOUND DOG/ (Canjo 102) 1.00 4.00 64

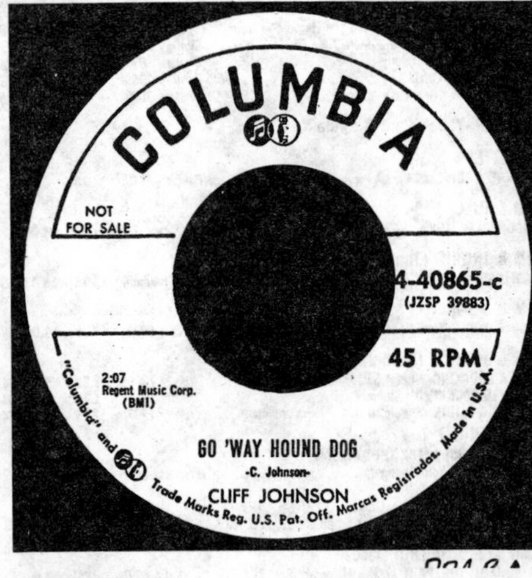

JOHNSON, Cliff
GO 'WAY HOUND DOG (Answer song)/Twenty-Four Hours A Day (Columbia 4-40865) 3.00 12.00 57

JOHNSON, Dee
BACK TO SCHOOL/I'm Your Guy (Dixie 2022) 1.00 4.00 59

JOHNSON, Howard
SLIDE/That Magic Touch Can Send You Flying (Shout S-237) .75 3.00 70

JOHNSON, Jackie
STAR LIGHT, STAR BRIGHT/ (Williamette 102) .75 3.00

JOHNSON, Joe
COOL LOVE/Gila Monster (Cascade 5909) 1.00 4.00 59

JOHNSON, Johnny, & The Bandwagon
LET'S HANG ON/I Ain't Lying (Direction 4180) 2.00 8.00

JOHNSON, Larry
WATCH YOUR STEP/Can You Monkey (Zorro 418) 1.25 5.00

JOHNSON, Michael
ALMOST LIKE BEING IN LOVE/Ridin' In The Sky (EMI America 8004) .50 2.00 78
BLUER THAN BLUE/Two In Love (EMI America 8001) .50 2.00 78
ROOTY TOOT TOOT FOR THE MOON/ (Atco 6942) .75 3.00 73
SAILING WITHOUT A SAIL/When You Come Home (EMI America 8008) .50 2.00 78
THIS NIGHT WON'T LAST FOREVER/I Just Can't Say No To You (EMI America 8019) .50 2.00 79
Also see Denver, Boise & Johnson

JOHNSON, Ray
SHEIK OF ARABY, THE/Deep Are The Roots (Of A Happy Home) (RCA Victor 47-7737) 1.00 4.00 60

JOHNSON, Robert
I'LL BE WAITING/Tell Me About It, "Slim" (Infinity 50000) .50 2.00 78

JOHNSTON, Bruce
DO THE SURFER STOMP (PART 1)/Do The Surfer Stomp (Part 2) (Ronda 1003) 1.50 6.00 62
DO THE SURFER STOMP (PART 1)/Do The Surfer Stomp (Part 2) (Donna 1354) 1.50 6.00 62
ORIGINAL SURFER STOMP, THE/Pajama Party (Del Fi 4202) 1.25 5.00 63

JOINER, ARKANSAS JR. HIGH SCHOOL BAND, The
ARKANSAS TRAVELER/Hot Time In The Old Town (Liberty 55276) .75 3.00 60
NATIONAL CITY/Big Ben (Liberty 55244) .75 3.00 60
Instrumentals

JOINER, ARKANSAS STATE COLLEGE BAND
HIGHLAND ROCK/Hop-Scotch (Liberty 55341) .75 3.00 61
Instrumentals

JOLAIRS, The
COUNTY LINE/Ralphie's June (Delmar 101) .75 3.00

JOLLY, Pete
LITTLE BIRD/Falling In Love With Love (Ava 116) .75 3.00 63
(Instrumentals)

JOLLY ROCKERS, The
SLOP, THE/Freddie's Blues (Mark X 8003) .75 3.00 60

JON & ROBIN, & The In Crowd (Jon Abdnor & Robin Wright)
DO IT AGAIN, A LITTLE BIT SLOWER/If I Need Someone It's You (Abnak 119) .75 3.00 67
DO IT AGAIN, A LITTLE BIT SLOWER/If I Need Someone It's You (Abnak 119) 1.25 5.00 67
(Gold plastic)
DR. JON (THE MEDICINE MAN)/Love Me Baby (Abnak 127) .75 3.00 68
DRUMS/You Don't Care (Abnak 122) .75 3.00 67
I WANT SOME MORE/Love Me Baby (Abnak 124) .75 3.00 67
INSIDE OUT/Big Cities (Abnak 121) .75 3.00 67
(Shown as by the In Crowd)
YOU GOT STYLE/Thursday Morning (Abnak 130) .75 3.00

JONES, Billy, & The Teenettes
SHOPPIN' 'ROUND FOR LOVE/I Would Never Dare (Net 101) .75 3.00 61

JONES BOYS, The
BEATLEMANIA/Honky (Sabra 555) 1.50 6.00 64
IF I EVER FIND THE TIME/Could This Be The Start (Atco 6460) .75 3.00 67
IMPRESSIONS/I Remember Barbara (Atco 6426) .75 3.00 66
WHY DID HE HAVE TO BRING HER/Seashore Dreamin' (Atco 6506) .75 3.00 67

JONES, Carl
ROCK & ROLL KING/Same Flip (C.J. 675) .75 3.00 77

JONES, David
LET'S DO IT/I'm In Pain (Apt 25064) 1.25 5.00 62
LOVE IS STRANGE/Velvet Waters (Audicon 117) 1.25 5.00 62
LOVE YOUR WAY/ (Apt 25013) 1.25 5.00 61
NO MORE TEARS/Tootsie Wootsie (Glades 601) 2.50 10.00 59

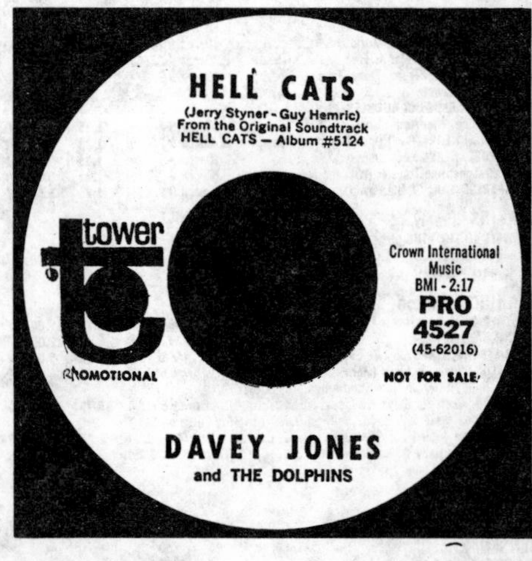

JONES, Davey, & The Dolphins
DANCE DANCE, LITTLE GIRL DANCE/Annabelle-Lee (Sinclair 1005) 1.25 5.00 61
HELL CATS/The Only Way To Fly (Tower 4527) 1.00 4.00

JONES, Davy (Of The Monkees)
DREAM GIRL/Take Me To Paradise (Colpix 764) 1.50 6.00 65
(Shown as by David Jones)
GIRL FROM CHELSEA/Theme For A New Love (Colpix 789) 1.50 6.00 65
(Shown as by David Jones)
RAINY JANE/Welcome To My Love (Bell 45111) .75 3.00 71
RUBBERENE/ (MGM 14524) .75 3.00 73
SITTING IN THE APPLE TREE/I Really Love You (Bell 45136) .75 3.00 71
WHAT ARE WE GOING TO DO/This Bouquet (Colpix 784) 1.50 6.00 65
(Shown as by David Jones)
WHAT ARE WE GOING TO DO/This Bouquet (Colpix 784) 2.50 10.00 65
(Picture sleeve, shown as by David Jones)
WHO WAS IT?/You're A Lady (MGM 14458) .75 3.00 72

JONES, Dean
PROUD DON'T CRY, THE/What Do I Do With My New Tattoo Of You (Liberty F-55502) .75 3.00 62

JONES, Gary
SCIENCE FICTION/What In The World (Tyfilms 122879) .50 2.00 79

JONES, Jack
CALL ME IRRESPONSIBLE/Mutiny On The Bounty (Kapp 516) .75 3.00 63
DEAR HEART/Emily (Kapp 635) .75 3.00 64
FIRST NIGHT OF THE FULL MOON, THE/Far Away (Kapp 589) .75 3.00 64
LOLLIPOPS & ROSES/Julie (Kapp 435) .75 3.00 62
RACE IS ON, THE/I Can't Believe I'm Losing You (Kapp 651) .75 3.00 65
WIVES & LOVERS/Toys In The Attic (Kapp 551) .75 3.00 63

JONES, Janie
DEAR DIARY/My First Romance (Jama 501) .75 3.00

JONES, Johnny, & The Catalinas
RUN LITTLE RABBIT/The Queen (RI 133) 1.25 5.00

JONES, Kay Cee
JAPANESE FARWELL SONG, THE/I Wore Dark Glasses (Marquee 1031) 1.00 4.00 55

TITLE/FLIP	LABEL & NO.	GOOD	NEAR MINT	YR.
JONES, Paul (Of Manfred Mann)				
I'VE BEEN A BAD, BAD BOY/Sonny Boy Williamson	Capitol 5857	.75	3.00	68
LOVE ENOUGH/	Private Stock 45004	.50	2.00	75
MIGHTY SHIP/17	London 168	.50	2.00	72
POD THAT CAME BACK, THE/Construction Worker's Song	London 178	.50	2.00	72
PRIVILEGE/Free Me	Capitol 5970	.75	3.00	68
JONES, Rickie Lee				
CHUCK E'S IN LOVE/ On Saturday Afternoons In 1963	Warner Bros. 8825	.50	2.00	79
YOUNG BLOOD/Coolsville	Warner Bros. 49018	.50	2.00	79
JONES, Rodney E., & Friends				
SOUL HEAVEN/Soul Heaven (By Friends)	Twinight 5002	1.00	4.00	
JONES, Romeo				
ETERNAL LOVE/How 'Bout That (Instrumental)	Little Star 119	.75	3.00	
JONES, Ronnie, & The Classmates				
LITTLE GIRL NEXT DOOR/Teenage Rock	End 1125	3.75	15.00	62
LONELY BOY/My Baby Cries	End 1014	3.75	15.00	58
JONES, Ruby (Ruby Starr)				
46th STREET/	Curtom 1969	.50	2.00	73
JONES, Spike (& His City Slickers)				
BLACK BOTTOM/Doin' The New Racoon	RCA Victory 47-3676	3.75	15.00	50
BOTTOMS UP/	RCA Victory 47-4228	3.00	12.00	51
CHARLESTON, THE/Charleston-Mio	RCA Victory 47-3675	3.75	15.00	50
CHEERIO/	RCA Victory 47-4728	3.00	12.00	51
CHINESE MULE TRAIN/Riders In The Sky	RCA Victor 47-3741	3.75	15.00	50
COCKTAILS FOR TWO/Chloe	RCA Victor 42-0030	3.75	15.00	49
DANCE OF THE HOURS/None But The Lonely Hearts	RCA Victor 47-3516	3.75	15.00	49
DEEP PURPLE/It Never Rains In Sunny California	RCA Victor 47-4546	3.00	12.00	51
DOWN SOUTH/I've Turned A Gadabout	RCA Victor 47-4568	3.00	12.00	51
DRAGNET/Pal Yat Chee	RCA Victor 47-5472	3.00	12.00	52
DRINK TO THE BONNIE LASSIES/	RCA Victory 47-4730	3.00	12.00	51
GESUNDHEIT POLKA/A Din Skay, A Min Skal	RCA Victory 47-4731	3.00	12.00	51
GREEN GREEN/Ballad Of Jed Clampett	Liberty 55649	.75	3.00	63
HI MISTER/This Song Is For The Birds	RCA Victor 47-6064	2.00	8.00	55
HOT LIPS/Hotter Than A Pistol	RCA Victor 47-4875	3.00	12.00	51
I JUST LOVE MY MOMMY/God Bless Us All	RCA Victor 47-5413	3.00	12.00	52
I KISS YOUR HAND, MADAME/ I'm Getting Sentimental Over You	RCA Victory 47-2949	3.75	15.00	49
I KNOW A SECRET/Charleston-Mio	RCA Victor 47-3827	3.75	15.00	50
I SAW MOMMY KISSING SANTA CLAUS!/Winter	RCA Victor 47-5067	3.00	12.00	51
I WANT EDDIE FISHER FOR XMAS/ Japanese Skokiaan	RCA Victor 47-5920	2.00	8.00	54
I WENT TO YOUR WEDDING/I'll Never Work There	RCA Victor 47-5107	3.00	12.00	52
I WONDER WHERE MY BABY IS TONIGHT?Varsity	RCA Victory 47-3677	3.75	15.00	50
I'M IN THE MOOD FOR LOVE/Secret Love	RCA Victor 47-5742	3.00	12.00	52
LATE, LATE, LATE MOVIES (PART 1)/ Late, Late, Late Movies (Part 2)	Liberty 55191	1.00	4.00	59
LULU HAD A BABY/The Boys In The Back Room	RCA Victor 47-5239	3.00	12.00	52
MEMORIES ARE MADE OF THIS/Sixteen Tons	Verve 2003	1.50	6.00	56
MOLASSES, MOLASSES/Baby Buggie Boogie	RCA Victor 47-3939	3.75	15.00	50
MOMMY, WON'T YOU BUY A BABY BROTHER/ Ruldoph The Red-Nosed Reindeer	RCA Victor 47-3934	3.75	15.00	50
MONSTER MOVIE BABE/Teenage Brain Surgeon	Warner Bros. 5116	1.00	4.00	59
MY DADDY IS A GENERAL TO ME/I'll Barkio	RCA Victor 47-4125	3.00	12.00	51
MY TWO FRONT TEETH (ALL I WANT FOR CHRISTMAS)/ Rudolph The Raindeer	RCA Victor 47-3177	3.75	15.00	49
PETER COTTONTAIL/Rhapsody From Hunger(y)	RCA Victor 47-4055	3.00	12.00	51
SOCKO THE SMALLEST SNOWBALL/Barnyard Xmas	RCA Victor 47-5015	3.00	12.00	52
STOP YOUR GAMBLIN'/ There's A Blue Sky Way Out Yonder	RCA Victor 47-4669	3.00	12.00	51
TENNESSEE WALTZ/ I Haven't Been Home For Three Whole Weeks	RCA Victor 47-4011	3.00	12.00	50
THREE LITTLE FISHES/A Din Skal A Min Skal-Vi	RCA Victor 47-5320	3.00	12.00	52
TOO YOUNG/So 'Elp Me	RCA Victor 47-4209	3.00	12.00	51
WHERE DID MY SNOWMAN GO/ Santa Brought Me Choo Choo Trains	RCA Victor 47-5497	3.00	12.00	52
WILD BILL HICCUP/Morpheus	RCA Victor 47-3620	3.75	15.00	49
YA WANNA BUY A BUNNY?/ Knock, Knock (Who's There?)	RCA Victory 47-3359	3.75	15.00	49
YES! WE HAVE NO BANANAS/ Yaaka Dula Hickey Dula	RCA Victor 47-3912	3.75	15.00	50
Comedy				
JONES, Spike, Jr.				
HOORAY FOR HAZEL/Song With A Peel	Viva 618	.75	3.00	67
JONES, Tom				
AIN'T NO LOVE/	Parrot 40083	.50	2.00	74
BABY I'M IN LOVE/Chills & Fever	Tower 190	1.00	4.00	66
CAN'T STOP LOVING YOU/Never Give Away Love	Parrot 40056	.75	3.00	70
DAUGHTER OF DARKNESS/Tupelo Mississippi Flash	Parrot 40048	.75	3.00	70
DELILAH/Smile Away Your Blues	Parrot 40025	.75	3.00	68
DETROIT CITY/Ten Guitars	Parrot 40012	.75	3.00	67
FUNNY FAMILIAR FORGOTTEN FEELINGS/	Parrot 40014	.75	3.00	67
GREEN, GREEN GRASS OF HOME/	Parrot 40009	.75	3.00	66
HELP YOURSELF (GLI OCCHI MIEI)Day By Day	Parrot 40029	.75	3.00	68
I'LL NEVER FALL IN LOVE AGAIN/Once Upon A Time	Parrot 40018	.75	3.00	67
I'M COMING HOME	Parrot 40024	.75	3.00	67
IT'S NOT UNUSUAL/To Wait For Love	Parrot 9737	.75	3.00	65
I'VE GOT YOUR NUMBER/	Parrot 40084	.50	2.00	74
I (WHO HAVE NOTHING)/Stop Breaking My Heart	Parrot 40051	.75	3.00	70
LETTER TO LUCILLE, A/	Parrot 40074	.50	2.00	73
LITTLE LONELY ONE/That's What We'll All Do	Tower 126	1.00	4.00	65
LONELY JOE/I Was A Fool	Tower 176	1.00	4.00	65
LOVE, LOVE, LOVE/	Parrot 40078	.50	2.00	73
LOVE ME TONIGHT/Hide & Seek	Parrot 40038	.75	3.00	69
MINUTE OF YOUR TIME, A/Looking Out My Window	Parrot	.75	3.00	68
MR. HELPING HAND/	Parrot 40086	.50	2.00	75
NOT RESPONSIBLE/Once There Was A Time	Parrot 40006	.75	3.00	66
PLEDGING MY LOVE/	Parrot 40081	.50	2.00	73
PROMISE HER ANYTHING/	Parrot 9809	.75	3.00	66
PUPPET MAN/Every Mile	Parrot 40062	.75	3.00	71
RESURRECTION SHUFFLE/	Parrot 40064	.75	3.00	71
SAY YOU'LL STAY UNTIL TOMORROW/Lady Lay	Epic 50308	.50	2.00	77
SHE'S A LADY/My Way	Parrot 40058	.75	3.00	71
SIXTEEN TONS/Things I Wanna Do	Parrot 40016	.75	3.00	67
THUNDERBALL/Key To My Heart	Parrot 9801	.75	3.00	65
TILL/One Day Soon	Parrot 40067	.75	3.00	71
WHAT'S NEW PUSSYCAT/Once Upon A Time	Parrot 9765	.75	3.00	65
WITHOUT LOVE (THERE IS NOTHING)/ The Man Who Knows Too Much	Parrot 40045	.75	3.00	69
WITH THESE HANDS/Some Other Guy	Parrot 9787	.75	3.00	65
YOUNG NEW MEXICAN PUPPETEER, THE/ All That I Need Is Some Time	Parrot 40070	.50	2.00	72
JONES, Toni				
DEAR (HERE COMES MY BABY)/Love Is Strange	Smash 1814	.75	3.00	63
JOPLIN, Janis (Of Big Brother & The Holding Company)				
CRY BABY/Mercedes Benz	Columbia 4-45379	1.00	4.00	71
DOWN ON ME/Bye Bye Baby	Columbia 4-45630	2.00	8.00	72
(Recorded during live concert)				
GET IT WHILE YOU CAN/Move Over	Columbia 4-45433	1.00	4.00	71
KOSMIC BLUES/Little Girl Blue	Columbia 4-45023	1.00	4.00	69
MAYBE/Work Me, Lord	Columbia 4-45128	1.50	6.00	70
ME & BOBBY McGEE/Half Moon	Columbia 4-45314	.75	3.00	70
ONE GOOD MAN/Try A (Little Bit Harder)	Columbia 4-45080	1.50	6.00	70
JORDAN				
GIVE ME YOUR LOVE/Once Upon A Time	Carol 4116	3.00	12.00	62
IF YOU REALLY LOVE ME/I'm Goin' Home	Josie 895	3.75	15.00	62
(With the Fascinations)				
LOVE WILL MAKE YOUR MIND GO WILD/ My Baby Doesn't Smile Anymore	Dapt 207	3.75	15.00	61
MY IMAGINATION/I'll Be Forever Loving You	Dapt 203	2.50	10.00	61
JORDAN BROTHERS, The				
GOOD LOVE GOES BAD/Break Down & Cry	Cameo 370	.75	3.00	65
JORDAN, Lonnie (Of War)				
GREY RAINY DAYS/Best Way I Can	United Artists-Far Out 873	.50	2.00	77
JUNKIE TO MY MUSIC/ He Used To Be A Friend Of Mine	MCA-Far Out 40882	.50	2.00	78
NASTY/Grey Rainy Days	MCA-Far Out 40921	.50	2.00	78
JOSEPH CONSORTIUM, The				
JACOB & SONS/Any Dream Will Do	Scepter 12308	.75	3.00	71
JOSEPHINE XIII				
DOWN ON THE FUNNY FARM/	Cameo 427	2.00	8.00	66
(Answer song)				
JOSIE & THE PUSSYCATS (With Cheryl Ladd)				
JOSIE/With Every Beat Of My Heart	Capitol Creative Products 59-2	1.00	4.00	70
JOURNEY (With Neal Schon)				
ANYTIME/Can Do	Columbia 10757	.50	2.00	78
JUST THE SAME WAY/Somethin' To Hide	Columbia 10928	.50	2.00	79
KAHOUTEK/Topaz	Columbia 128	1.00	4.00	74
(Compact 33 single)				
LIGHTS/Somethin' To Hide	Columbia 10800	.50	2.00	78
LOOK INTO THE FUTURE/ On A Saturday Night/All Too Much	Columbia AE7 1098	.75	3.00	74
LOVIN', TOUCHIN', SQUEEZIN'/Daydream	Columbia 11036	.50	2.00	79
ON A SATURDAY NIGHT/To Play Some Music	Columbia 10324	.50	2.00	76
SPACEMAN/	Columbia 10522	.50	2.00	76
TOO LATE/Do You Recall	Columbia 11143	.50	2.00	79
TO PLAY SOME MUSIC/	Columbia 10137	.50	2.00	75
WHEEL IN THE SKY/Can Do	Columbia 10700	.50	2.00	78
JO-VALS, The				
BALLERINA/I Want You To Be My Girl	Alwil 101	2.00	8.00	
SOMETIMES I'M HAPPY/You You My Love	Laurie 3229	2.00	8.00	63
JOVATIONS, The				
TAKE YOU BACK AGAIN/My Dreams	Taurus 36	1.25	5.00	63
JOY (With Rick Henn)				
FOXY, I LOVE YOU/Hancock Pk.	Phillips 40617	1.00	4.00	70
SO LOVELY/	Philips 40555	1.00	4.00	69
JOY, Barbara				
TWISTIN' & STOMPIN'/Do This, Do That	Tar-Get 1001	.75	3.00	62
JOY OF COOKING, The				
BEGINNING TOMORROW/	Fantasy 808	.50	2.00	77
(Shown as by Joy)				
BROWNSVILLE/Only Time Will Tell Me	Capitol 3075	.75	3.00	71
CLOSER TO THE GROUND/Pilot	Capitol 3224	.75	3.00	72
DON'T THE MOON LOOK FAT & LONESOME/ All Around The Sun & The Moon	Capitol 3396	.75	3.00	72
HUSH/Red Wine At Noon	Capitol 3132	.75	3.00	71
I WANT TO BE THE ONE/	Capitol 3547	.75	3.00	73
LET LOVE CARRY YOU ALONG/Home Town Man	Capitol 3330	.75	3.00	72
MORNING MAN/	Fantasy 817	.50	2.00	78
(Shown as by Joy)				
JOY, Roddie				
COME BACK BABY/Love Me With A Wallop	Red Bird 10-021	.75	3.00	65
HE'S EASY TO LOVE/La La Song	Red-Bird 10-031	.75	3.00	65
JOYCE & THE PRIVITEERS: see Heath, Joyce				
J.T.S. BAND, The				
STAY WITH ME/Time To Be Flyin'	Mercury 73896	.50	2.00	77
JUDAS PRIEST				
DIAMONDS & RUST/Starbreaker	Columbia 11135	.50	2.00	79
GREEN MANALISHI (WITH THE TWO-PRONGED CROWN), THE/ Rock Forever	Columbia 11000	.50	2.00	79
JUDGE DREAD				
BIG SEVEN/Dread	20th Century 2037	.50	2.00	73
BIG SIX/One Armed Bandit	20th Century 2014	.50	2.00	73
JUDY & THE DUETS				
CHRISTMAS WITH THE BEATLES/Blind Boy, The	Ware 6000	1.50	6.00	64
JUJUS, The				
YOU TREAT ME BAD/Hey Little Girl	Fenton 1004	1.25	5.00	
JULES & THE POLAR BEARS (With Jules Shear)				
YOU JUST DON'T WANNA KNOW/	Columbia 10850	.50	2.00	79
Also see Funky Kings, The				
JUMPIN' TONES, The				
GRANDMA'S HEARING AID/That Angel Is You	Raven 8005	5.00	20.00	64
I HAD A DREAM/I Wonder	Raven 8004	5.00	20.00	64
Also see Raindrops, The				
JUMPING JUDGE & HIS COURT, The				
TRIAL, THE/Cockroach Run	Jumping 5000	7.50	30.00	
JUNE & JOY				
DEDICATED TO THE ONE I LOVE/Lindy Lou	Dot 16134	.75	3.00	60
JUNIE'S JIVIN' FIVE				
OODABEGGA WOW/Yankee Rouser	Ad 2067	.75	3.00	60
J.R. & THE ATTRACTIONS				
BRISTOL STOMP/I'm Yours	Hunch 928	5.00	20.00	65
JUNIOR & HIS FRIENDS				
WHO'S OUR PET, ANNETTE/A B C's Of Love	ABC-Paramount 10089	2.00	8.00	60
JUNS, Jimmy				
RING BELLS, RING/	Vulcan 1001	1.00	4.00	
JUST FOUR MEN: see Freddie & The Dreamers				
JUST US				
I CAN'T GROW PEACHES ON A CHERRY TREE/ I Can Save You	Minuteman 203	1.25	5.00	65
I CAN'T GROW PEACHES ON A CHERRY TREE/I Can Save You	Colpix 803	.75	3.00	65
I KEEP CHANGING MY MIND/Listen To The Drummer	Kapp 768	.75	3.00	66
RUN, BOY, RUN/Sorry	Kapp 785	.75	3.00	66
JUST US GIRLS (Featuring Dick Wagner)				
TIME WARP/By The Fire	Epic-Cleveland Intl. 50733	.50	2.00	79
JUST WATER				
KING KONG/Play It Loud	Just 2072	.50	2.00	
JUSTICE DEPARTMENT, The				
LET JOHN & YOKO STAY IN THE U.S.A./	New Design 1008	3.00	12.00	
LET JOHN & YOKO STAY IN THE U.S.A./	New Design 1008	3.75	15.00	
(Paper insert containing the lyrics.)				
JUSTIS, Bill (& His Orchestra)				
BOP TRAIN/ String Of Pearls-Cha Hot Cha	Phillips International 3535	1.00	4.00	59
CATTYWAMPUS/Summer Holiday	Phillips International 3529	1.00	4.00	58
COLLEGE MAN/The Stranger	Phillips International 3522	1.00	4.00	58
FLEA CIRCUS/Cloud Nine	Phillips International 3544	1.00	4.00	59
RAUNCHY/Midnight Man	Phillips International 3519	1.00	4.00	57
WILD RICE/Scrougie	Phillips International 3525	1.00	4.00	58
JUVENILES, The				
BABY BABY/I've Searched	Jerden 795	.75	3.00	66
BEAT IN MY HEART/I've Lied	Mode 1	1.25	5.00	65
BO DIDDLEY/Yes I Believe	Jerden 770	.75	3.00	65
J-WALKERS, The				
ROCK BOTTOM/Harvey's Theme	Tidal 1005	1.00	4.00	61
(Instrumental)				

K

TITLE/FLIP	LABEL & NO.	GOOD	NEAR MINT	YR.
KACHER, Del				
NIGHTMIST OVER HIGHWAY NO. 2/	Merri 201	.75	3.00	60
KAC-TIES, The				
OH WHAT A NIGHT/Let Me In Your Life	Shelly 165	1.50	6.00	64
OH WHAT A NIGHT/Let Me In Your Life	Atco 6299	1.25	5.00	64
GIRL IN MY HEART/Happy Birthday	Kape 501	1.00	4.00	
KAEMPFERT, Bert				
RED ROSES FOR A BLUE LADY/Lonely Nightingale	Decca 31722	.75	3.00	64
WONDERLAND BY NIGHT/Dreaming The Blues	Decca 31141	.75	3.00	60
Instrumentals				
KAHANE, Jackie				
REQUIEM FOR ELVIS/Requiem For Elvis (Theme)	Raintree 2206	.50	2.00	77
KAJANUS PICKET				
MOVIN' ON/	MCA 40047	.50	2.00	73
KAK				
I'VE GOT THE TIME/Disbelievin'	Epic 10446	1.25	5.00	69
KALEIDOSCOPE				
TEMPE, ARIZONA/Lie To Me	Epic 10500	.75	3.00	69
KALIN TWINS, The				
COOL/When I Look In The Mirror	Decca 9-30868	1.00	4.00	59
FORGET ME NOT/Dream Of Me	Decca 9-30745	1.00	4.00	58
IT'S ONLY THE BEGINNING/Oh! My Goodness	Decca 9-30807	1.00	4.00	59
JUMPIN' JACK/Walkin' To School	Decca 9-30552	1.00	4.00	58
SWEET SUGAR LIPS/Moody	Decca 9-30911	1.00	4.00	60
WHEN/Three O'Clock Thrill	Decca 9-30642	1.00	4.00	58
KALLEN, Kitty				
ABA DABA HONEYMOON/I Don't Want To Love You	Mercury 5586	1.25	5.00	51
BUSHEL & A PECK, A/Silver Bells	Mercury 5501	1.25	5.00	50
DREAM AWHILE/Halls Of Ivy	Mercury 5499	1.25	5.00	50
GO ON WITH THE WEDDING (With Georgie Shaw)/ The Second Greatest Sex	Decca 9-29776	1.00	4.00	55
HONESTLY I LOVE YOU/Our Lady Of Fatima	Mercury 5466	1.25	5.00	50
I GOT TOOKIN'/If You Smile At The Sun	Mercury 5452	1.25	5.00	50
IF I GIVE MY HEART TO YOU/ The Door That Won't Open	Columbia 4-41473	.75	3.00	59
IN THE CHAPEL IN THE MOONLIGHT/ Take Everything But You	Decca 9-29130	1.00	4.00	54
IT IS NO SECRET/Get Out Those Old Records	Mercury 5564	1.25	5.00	51
LIKE THE MOON ABOVE YOU/	Columbia 4-39765	1.25	5.00	52
LITTLE THINGS MEAN A LOT/ I Don't Think You Love Me Anymore	Decca 9-29037	1.00	4.00	54
MY COLORING BOOK/Here's To Us	RCA Victor 47-8124	.75	3.00	62
THAT OLD FEELING/Need Me	Columbia 4-41546	.75	3.00	60
KALLMANN, Gunter, Chorus				
WISH ME A RAINBOW/The Day The Rains Came	4 Corners 138	.75	3.00	66
KALLUM, Johnny				
BIG DEBATE, THE/	Bang 730	1.00	4.00	
KAN DELLS, The				
CLOUDBURST/Cry Girl	Boss 6501	1.25	5.00	
KANE, Bernie, & The Rockin' Rhythm's				
HIGH TIDE/Pink Lady	Tabb 9133	.75	3.00	66
KANE, Eden				
GET LOST/I'm Telling You	London 9508	.75	3.00	61
WELL I ASK YOU/Before I Lost My Mind	London 1993	.75	3.00	61
KANE, Paul: see Simon, Paul				
KANE'S COUSINS				
TAKE YOUR LOVE & SHOVE IT/National Anthem	Shove Love 0069	1.00	4.00	
(Shown as by the Cousins)				
TAKE YOUR LOVE & SHOVE IT/National Anthem	Shove Love 0069	.50	2.00	
KANNON, Jackie				
BOBBY BABY YA YA/I Will Follow You	Stage 518	1.00	4.00	
KANNON, Sandy (Of The Ovations)				
SWEET DOTTIE DOODLE/Mr. Hitmaker	Kef 4444	2.50	10.00	
KANSAS				
CAN I TELL YOU/The Pilgrimmage	Kirshner 4253	.75	3.00	75
CARRY ON MY WAYWARD SON/Questions Of Childhood	Kirshner 4267	.50	2.00	76
DUST IN THE WIND/Paradox	Kirshner 4274	.50	2.00	78
IT TAKES A WOMAN'S LOVE (TO MAKE A MAN)/It's You	Kirshner 4259	.75	3.00	76
LONELY WIND/Song For America	Kirshner 4280	.50	2.00	78
PEOPLE OF THE SOUTH WIND/Stay Out Of Trouble	Kirshner 4284	.50	2.00	79
POINT OF KNOW RETURN/Closet Chronicles	Kirshner 4273	.50	2.00	77
PORTRAIT (HE KNEW)/Lightning's Hand	Kirshner 4276	.50	2.00	78
REASON TO BE/How My Soul Cries Out For You	Kirshner 4285	.50	2.00	79
SONG FOR AMERICA/Song For America (Instrumental)	Kirshner 4258	.75	3.00	76
WHAT'S ON MY MIND/Lonely Street	Kirshner 4270	.75	3.00	77
KANTNER, Paul, & Grace Slick (Of Jefferson Airplane)				
CHINA/Sunfighter	Grunt 0503	1.00	4.00	72

TITLE/FLIP	LABEL & NO.	GOOD	NEAR MINT	YR.
KAPLAN, Gabriel				
DE AMERIKANS/Ed Sullivan, Ed Sullivan	(ABC 12027)	.50	2.00	76
UP YOUR NOSE/Bye Centennial Minutes	(Elektra 45369)	.50	2.00	77
Comedy				
"KAPT. KOPTER" RANDY CALIFORNIA (Of Spirit)				
WALKIN' THE DOG/Live For The Day	(Epic 10927)	.75	3.00	73
KAPTAIN KOOL & THE KONGS				
AND I NEVER DREAMED/Crazy Girl	(Epic 50627)	.50	2.00	78
KAPTIONS, The				
DREAMING OF YOU/I Know Somewhere	(Ham-Mil 1520)	1.50	6.00	
Also see Contenders, The				
KARAS, Anton				
THIRD MAN THEME, THE/The Cafe Mozart Waltz	(London 536)	1.25	5.00	50
(Instrumentals)				
KARLOFF, Boris				
COME MY LAURIE, WITH ME/He Is There	(MOL 52)	.75	3.00	67
KARPETBAGGERS, The				
FIRE I FEEL, THE/	(Trig 202)	1.25	5.00	
KARR, Eddie				
ELVIS/Elvis	(Memory 38656)	.50	2.00	77
KARTUNES (With Teddy Randazzo)				
DEDICATED TO LOVE/Willie The Weeper	(MGM K-12680)	1.00	4.00	58
RAINDROPS/Will You Marry Me	(MGM K-12598)	3.75	15.00	58
KASEM, Casey				
LETTER FROM ELAINA, A (Beatle novelty)/ Theme For Elaina (Instrumental)	(Warner Bros. 5474)	1.50	6.00	64
KASENETZ-KATZ SINGING ORCHESTRAL CIRCUS, The				
DONG DONG DIKI DONG/Bubblegum March	(Super K SK-9)	.75	3.00	69
(Shown as by the Kasenetz-Katz Super Cirkus)				
DOWN IN TENNESSEE/Mrs. Green	(Buddah BDA-52)	.75	3.00	68
EMBRASSER/Mrs. Green	(Buddah BDA-90)	.75	3.00	68
(Shown as by the Kasenetz-Katz Super Cirkus)				
HEART GET READY FOR LOVE/Jungle Junk	(Epic 8-50443)	.50	2.00	77
(Shown as by the Kasenetz-Katz Super Cirkus)				
I'M IN LOVE WITH YOU/To You With Love	(Buddah BDA-82)	.75	3.00	68
(Shown as by the Kasenetz-Katz Super Cirkus)				
MAMA LU/Collide	(Magna-Glide 5N-327)	.50	2.00	75
(Shown as by the Kasenetz-Katz Super Cirkus)				
PICKIN' UP STICKS/All Fall Down	(Super K SK-14825)	.75	3.00	71
(Shown as by the Kasenetz-Katz Fighter Squadron)				
QUICK JOEY SMALL (RUN JOEY RUN)/ (Poor Old) Mr. Jensen	(Buddah BDA-64)	.75	3.00	68
SYMPHONY NO. 9/Blue Danube Waltz	(Super K SK-14657)	.75	3.00	69
WHEN HE COMES/Ah La	(Bell B-966)	2.00	8.00	71
(Shown as by the Kasenetz-Katz Fighter Squadron; vocals by members of 10CC.)				
YUMMY YUMMY YUMMY/ Pop Goes The Weasel-Mother Goose-Simon Says	(Buddah SP 1)	1.25	5.00	68
(Promotional issue only)				
Recordings by this group were actually done by members of: the 1910 Fruitgum Co., the Ohio Express, the Music Explosion, the Teri Nelson group, the 1981 Musical Marching Zoo, the St. Louis Invisible Marching Band, Lt. Garcia's Magic Music Box, the J.C.W. Rat Finks, as well as other, sometimes prominent, guest artists.				
KATFISH				
DEAR PRUDENCE/Street Walkin'	(Big Tree 16045)	.50	2.00	75
KAUKONEN, Peter				
PRISONERDynamo Snackbar	(Grunt 0507)	.75	3.00	72
UP OR DOWN/That's A Good Question	(Grunt 0510)	.75	3.00	73
Peter Kaukonen is the brother of Jorma Kaukonen, of the Jefferson Airplane.				
KAVANOVICH, Ivan				
DEAR JIMMY/	(Elko 1)	1.00	4.00	62
(Answer song)				
KAY, Jerry				
LOVE ME/See See Rider	(Press-ley 103)	1.50	6.00	
KAY, John (Of Steppenwolf)				
GIVE ME SOME NEWS I CAN USE/Say You Will	(Mercury 74004)	.50	2.00	78
I'M MOVIN' ON/Walk Beside Me	(Dunhill 4309)	.75	3.00	72
SOMEBODY/You Win Again	(Dunhill 4319)	.75	3.00	72
KAYAK				
KEEP THE CHANGE/Ivory Dence	(Janus 278)	.50	2.00	78
I WANT YOU TO BE MINE/Irene	(Janus 274)	.50	2.00	78
KAYE, Danny				
D-O-D-G-E-R-S SONG, THE/Myti Kaysi At The Bat	(Reprise 20105)	.75	3.00	62
EAT, EAT, EAT/Santa Claus Looks Like My Daddy	(Decca 9-27829)	1.25	5.00	51
I'VE GOT A LOVELY BUNCH OF COCONUTS/Penny Bush	(Decca 9-24784)	1.25	5.00	50
LEFT MY HAT IN HAITI/How Could You Believe	(Decca 9-27463)	1.25	5.00	51
LOVE ME DO/Ciu Ciu Bella	(Capitol 3603)	1.00	4.00	57
THING, THE/The Little White Duck	(Decca 9-27350)	1.25	5.00	51
THUMBELINA/No Two People	(Decca 9-28380)	1.25	5.00	52
TONGUE TWISTERS/Riley's Daughter	(Decca 9-27822)	1.25	5.00	51
Novelties				
KAYE, Mary, Trio				
DID HE ASK ABOUT ME/One More Kiss	(MGM K-11518)	1.00	4.00	53
DO YOU BELIEVE IN DREAMS/Toreador	(RCA Victor 47-5586)	1.00	4.00	53
SOME OF THESE DAYS/Watching & Waiting	(Capitol 1412)	1.25	5.00	51
YOU CAN'T BE TRUE DEAR/Because Of You	(Warner Bros. 5050)	.75	3.00	59
YOU CAN'T BE TRUE DEAR/Because Of You	(Warner Bros. 5050)	1.50	6.00	59
(Stereo single issue)				
KAYE, Sammy				
HARBOR LIGHTS/Sugar Sweet	(Columbia 6-784)	.75	3.00	50
IN THE MISSION OF ST. AUGUSTINE/ No Stone Unturned	(Columbia 4-40061)	1.25	5.00	53
LONGING FOR YOU/Mary Rose	(Columbia 4-39499)	1.25	5.00	51
OBJECT OF MY AFFECTION/I Thought She Was A Local	(RCA Victor 47-3828)	1.50	6.00	50
TENNESSEE WALTZ/Get Out Those Old Records	(Columbia 4-39113)	1.25	5.00	50
YOU/Oh How I Miss You Tonight	(Columbia 4-39724)	1.25	5.00	52
WALKIN' TO MISSOURI/One For The Wonder	(Columbia 4-39769)	1.25	5.00	52
KAYLI, Bob (Robert Gordy)				
EVERYONE WAS THERE/I Took A Dare	(Carlton 482)	1.25	5.00	58
Robert is Barry Gordy Jr.'s brother.				
KAYNINES, The				
ANGEL EYES/That Ain't Right	(Amber 3352)	1.25	5.00	
KAYO & THE TRINITIES				
KATHY JO/Walking To School With My Love	(Souvenir 1004)	.75	3.00	
KAZ, Eric Justin (Of The Blues Magoos)				
CRUEL WIND/	(Atlantic 2936)	.50	2.00	73
KC & THE SUNSHINE BAND (Featuring Harry W. Casey)				
BLOW YOUR WHISTLE/I'm Gonna Do Something Good To You	(TK 1001)	.50	2.00	73
KEEP IT COMIN' LOVE/	(TK 1023)	.50	2.00	77
SHAKE YOUR BOOTY (SHAKE, SHAKE, SHAKE)/ Boogie Shoes	(TK 1019)	.50	2.00	76
KEEN, Speedy (Of Thunderclap Newman)				
AIRES LADY/Let Us In	(Track 40062)	.50	2.00	73
KEENE, Bob				
TEEN TALK/Toughest Theme	(Del Fi 4144)	.75	3.00	60
KEENE, Bobby				
MOVE OVER ANGELS/Listen Little Girl	(Coral 62260)	1.50	6.00	61
KEITH (James Barry Keefer)				
AIN'T GONNA LIE/Our Love Started All Over Again	(Mercury 72596)	.75	3.00	66
CANDY, CANDY/I'm So Proud	(Mercury 72746)	.75	3.00	67
DAYLIGHT SAVIN' TIME/Happy Walking Around	(Mercury 72695)	.75	3.00	67
EASY AS PIE/Sugar Man	(Mercury 72715)	.75	3.00	67
IN & OUT OF LOVE/	(DiscReet 1193)	.75	3.00	71
98.6/Tenny Bopper Song	(Mercury 72639)	.75	3.00	66
PLEASURE OF YOUR COMPANY/Hurry	(Mercury 72794)	.75	3.00	68
TELL ME TO MY FACE/Pretty Little Shy One	(Mercury 72652)	.75	3.00	67
KEITH, Bryan				
HOUND DOG/Cute Little Frown	(Dot 16532)	.75	3.00	63
KELLER, Jerry				
AMERICAN BEAUTY ROSE/Lonesome Lullaby	(Kapp 322)	1.00	4.00	60
HERE COMES SUMMER/Time Has A Way	(Kapp 277)	1.00	4.00	59
THERE ARE SUCH THINGS/Now, Now, Now	(Kapp 310)	1.00	4.00	59
WHAT MORE CAN I SAY/Whole Heartedly	(Kapp 353)	1.00	4.00	60
WHITE FOR YOU & BLUES FOR ME/My Name Ain't Joe	(Kapp 337)	1.00	4.00	60
KELLERMAN, Sally				
ROLL WITH THE FEELIN'/Child Of Mine	(Decca 33024)	.50	2.00	73
KELLUM, Murry				
I DREAMED I WAS A BEATLE/Oh How Sweet It Could Be	(MOC 658)	1.25	5.00	64
LONG TALL TEXAN/I Gotta Leave This Town	(MOC 653)	.75	3.00	63
RED RIDER/Texas Lil	(MOC 657)	.75	3.00	64
KELLY, Casey				
POOR BOY/You'll Never Leave My Mind	(Elektra 45804)	.50	2.00	72
YOU CAN'T GET THERE FROM HERE/	(Elektra 45826)	.50	2.00	73
WHERE YOU BEEN/	(Private Stock 45145)	.50	2.00	77
KELLY FOUR, The				
ANNIE HAS A PARTY/So Fine Be Mine	(Silver 1006)	2.00	8.00	59
ANNIE HAD A PARTY/Sweet Angelina	(Candix 325)	1.25	5.00	63
("Annie Has A Party" and "Annie Had A Party" are different takes of the same song.)				
STROLLIN' GUITAR/Guybo	(Silver 1001)	1.25	5.00	59
Featuring Eddie Cochran on guitar				
KELLY, Monty				
SUMMER SET/Analia (Queli)	(Carlton 527)	.75	3.00	60
KELLY, Peter				
HARD ROAD/	(RSO 403)	.50	2.00	73
KELLOGS, The				
SNAP, CRACKLE & POP/Like A Mad Fool	(Laurie 3476)	3.75	15.00	69
KELSO, Jackie, & The Orch.				
BLUE MOON/	(Mambo 108)	.75	3.00	
KENDALL SISTERS, The				
I'M AVAILABLE/Don't Bother Me	(Argo 5278)	1.00	4.00	57
YEA, YEA/Won't You Be My Baby	(Argo 5291)	1.00	4.00	58
KENJOLAIRS, The (Ken, Joe & Larry)				
LITTLE WHITE LIES/Story Of An Evergreen Tree	(A&M 704)	.75	3.00	62
Larry Knew, of this group, was previously with the Echoes on Andex. The other members of the Echoes later became the Innocents.				
KENNEDY, Dave, & The Ambassadors				
KISS ME QUICK/Peepin' & Hidin'	(Cuca 1107)	1.00	4.00	62
KENNEDY, Jerry				
WILLIE & THE HAND JIVE/Willie & The Hand Jive	(Smash 1815)	1.00	4.00	63
Jerry was previously with Tom & Jerry, the Mercury recording artists.				
KENNEDY, President John F.				
VOICE OF THE PRESIDENT/ Inaugural Address, January 20, 1961	(Golden 766)	.75	3.00	
VOICE OF THE PRESIDENT/ Inaugural Address, January 20, 1961	(Golden 766)	2.00	8.00	
(Picture sleeve)				
Side one contains President Kennedy's acceptance (July 15, 1960) and oath of office (January 20, 1961) speeches.				
KENNY				
BUMP, THE/	(UK 49032)	.50	2.00	74
JULIE ANE/The Sound Of Super K	(Mercury 73721)	.50	2.00	76
TAKE AWAY HER HEART OF STONE/	(Atco 6921)	.50	2.00	72
KENNY & CORKY				
NUTTIN' FOR CHRISTMAS/Suzy Snowflake	(Big Top 3031)	1.00	4.00	59
KENNY & THE CADETS: see Beach Boys, The				
KENNY & THE CASUALS				
JOURNEY TO TYME/	(Mark 1006)	3.75	15.00	
IT'S ALL RIGHT/You Make Me	(Mark 1003)	3.75	15.00	
NOTHIN' BETTER TO DO/Floatin'	(Mark 911)	3.75	15.00	
KENNY & THE FIENDS				
HOUSE ON HAUNTED HILL (PART 1)/ House On Haunted Hill (Part 2)	(Princess 51)	1.50	6.00	63
HOUSE ON HAUNTED HILL (PART 1)/ House On Haunted Hill (Part 2)	(Dot 15668)	.75	3.00	63
KENNY & THE MODADS				
MAGIC LAMP/Magic Lamp	(Baytown 24-1)	1.00	4.00	
KENNY & THE SOCIALITES				
I'LL HAVE TO DECIDE/The King Tut Rock	(Crosstown 001)	3.75	15.00	
KENNY & THE WHALERS				
LIFE IS BUT A DREAM/	(Whale 504)	3.75	15.00	61
KENNY, Frank & Ray				
EVERYBODY LOVES SATURDAY NIGHT/I'm Going Away	(Cameo 144)	1.00	4.00	58
KENNY, G.W.				
EVERYBODY BUT ME/404 (Carry On)	(Kama-Sutra KA-581)	.50	2.00	73
KENNY, Gerrard, & The New York Band				
GET BACK BEATLES/	(Int'l. Committee To Reunite The Beatles 001)	2.00	8.00	
KENNY & THE SHEPHERDS				
RUNAWAY/Just A Taste	(Kapp 792)	.75	3.00	67
KENTONES, The				
MARIE/Please Make Up Your Mind	(Siroc 202)	1.00	4.00	
KENTS, The				
I LOVE YOU SO/Happy Beat	(Dome 501)	3.75	15.00	
KERR, Anita, Singers				
WAITIN' FOR THE EVENING TRAIN/ Guitar Country (With Chet Atkins)	(RCA Victor 47-8246)	.75	3.00	63
Also see Anita & The So So's				
Also see Little Dippers, The				
KERR, Richard				
I KNOW I'LL NEVER LOVE THIS WAY AGAIN/	(A&M 2099)	.50	2.00	78
KESTRELS, The				
IN THE CHAPEL IN THE MOONLIGHT/There Comes A Time	(Laurie 3053)	3.00	12.00	60
KEVIN & GREGG				
BOY YOU OUGHTA' SEE HER NOW/Sparkle	(Associated Artists 116)	.75	3.00	63
I KNOW JUST HOW YOU FEEL/ You're Still On My Mind	(Associated Artists 464)	.75	3.00	64
KEVIN, Chris, & The Comics				
HERE HE COMES, THERE THEY GO/Haunted House	(Colt 45 103)	.75	3.00	
KEY, Scott				
TOWN CRYER/Town Cryer (Part 2)	(Pyramid 8002)	.75	3.00	
KEYHOLE PEEPERS, The				
KEYHOLE PEEPERS INTERVIEWS BATMAN & ROBIN/ One More Time	(Triad 501)	2.00	8.00	
KEYS, Bobby				
GIMME THE KEY/Honky Tonk (Parts 1 & 2)	(Ring O' 4129)	.50	2.00	75
KGB (Mike Bloomfield, Barry Goldberg, Rick Gretch, Carmine Appice, Ray Kennedy)				
MAGIC IN YOUR TOUCH, THE/Midnight Traveler	(MCA 40544)	.75	3.00	76
KHAN, Steve				
DARLIN' DARLIN' BABY (SWEET TENDER LOVE)/ Soft Summer Breeze	(Tappan Zee 10669)	.50	2.00	78
Steve Khan was a guitarist in Billy Joel's Band.				
KICKS & COMPANY				
FOLLOW THE LEADER/Puppy Love	(RCA 74-0165)	.75	3.00	70
("Follow The Leader" is actually sung by Paul Anka)				
KICKSTANDS, The				
SHE RIDES ALONE/Sincerely	(China 612)	1.25	5.00	63
KID BROTHER				
TELL ME ANOTHER ONE/Rock 'N' Roller	(MCA-Montage 41111)	.50	2.00	79
KIDD, Johnny, & The Pirates				
I'LL NEVER GET OVER YOU/Then I Got Everything	(Capitol 5065)	1.00	4.00	63
KIDDS, The				
STRAIGHTEN UP & FLY RIGHT/ See What My Love Means	(Big Beat 1017)	1.00	4.00	
KIDS FROM C.A.P.E.R., The				
WHEN IT HIT ME (THE HURRICANE SONG)/	(Kirshner 4266)	.50	2.00	76
KIDS NEXT DOOR, The				
INKY DINKY SPIDER (THE SPIDER SONG)/ Goodbye, Don't Cry	(4 Corners Of The World 129)	.75	3.00	65
KIHN, Greg, Band				
BESIDE MYSELF/Getting Away With Murder	(Beserkley 46517)	.50	2.00	79
REMEMBER/	(Beserkley 5794)	.50	2.00	78
ROAD RUNNER/	(Beserkley 46542)	.50	2.00	79
KIM, Andy				
BABY, I LOVE YOU/Gee Girl	(Steed 716)	.75	3.00	69
BE MY BABY/Love That Little Woman	(Steed 729)	.75	3.00	70
ESSENCE OF JOAN (AIN'T IT FUNNY HOW LOVE CAN OWN YOU), THE/	(Capitol 4032)	.75	3.00	75
FIRE, BABY I'M ON FIRE/Here Comes The Mornin'	(Capitol 3962)	.50	2.00	74
FOUNDATION OF MY SOUL/Tricia Tell Your Daddy	(Steed 715)	.75	3.00	69
FRIEND IN THE CITY, A/You	(Steed 723)	.75	3.00	70
GIVE ME YOUR LOVE/Lil' Liz (I Love You)	(TCF 5)	1.25	5.00	64
GIVE ME YOUR LOVE/That Girl	(20th Fox 6709)	.75	3.00	68
HOW'D WE EVER GET THIS WAY/Are You Ever Comin' Home	(Steed 707)	.75	3.00	68
I BEEN MOVED/If I Had You	(Steed 734)	.75	3.00	71
I HEAR YOU SAY (I LOVE YOU)/Falling In Love	(Red-Bird 10-040)	1.00	4.00	65
I LOVED YOU ONCE/Love Me, Love Me	(United Artists 591)	.75	3.00	63
I WISH I WERE/Walkin' My La De Da	(Steed 731)	.75	3.00	71
IT'S YOUR LIFE/To Be Continued	(Steed 727)	.75	3.00	70
OH, WHAT A DAY/	(Uni 55356)	.75	3.00	72
RAINBOW RIDE/Resurrection	(Steed 711)	.75	3.00	68
ROCK ME GENTLY/Rock Me Gently (Part 2)	(Capitol 3895)	.50	2.00	74
SHOOT 'EM UP BABY/Ordinary Kind Of Girl	(Steed 710)	.75	3.00	68
SO GOOD TOGETHER/I Got To Know	(Steed 720)	.75	3.00	69
WHO HAS THE ANSWERS?/	(Uni 55332)	.75	3.00	72
KIMBERLY, Adrian				
DRAGGIN' DRAGON/When You Wish Upon A Star	(Calliope 6504)	.75	3.00	61
POMP & CIRCUMSTANCE/Black Mountain Stomp	(Calliope 6501)	.75	3.00	61
Instrumentals				
KING BEES, The (With Danny Kortchmar)				
I WANT MY BABY/	(Pyramid 6217)	1.50	6.00	
RHYTHM & BLUES/On Your Way Down The Drain	(RCA Victor 47-8787)	.75	3.00	65
KING BISCUIT BOY				
NEW ORLEANS/I'm Writing You A Letter	(Epic 50129)	.50	2.00	75
KING BROTHERS, The				
I'M OLD FASHIONED/My Mother's Eyes	(Bell 706)	1.00	4.00	67
I'M OLD FASHIONED/My Mother's Eyes	(Dunhill 4114)	.75	3.00	67
KING, Buzzy				
SCHOOL BOY BLUES/Your Picture	(Top Rank 2027)	1.00	4.00	59
KING, Carole (Carole Klein)				
BABY SITTIN'/Under The Stars	(ABC-Paramount 9986)	7.50	30.00	59
CORAZON/That's How Things Go Down	(Ode 66039)	.50	2.00	73
BEEN TO CANAAN/Bitter With The Sweet	(Ode 66031)	.50	2.00	72
GOIN' WILD/The Right Girl	(ABC-Paramount 9921)	7.50	30.00	58
HARD ROCK CAFE/To Know That I Love You	(Avatar 4455)	.50	2.00	77
HE'S A BAD BOY/We Grew Up Together	(Dimension 1009)	2.50	10.00	63
HIGH OUT OF TIME/I'd Like To Know You Better	(Ode 66123)	.50	2.00	76
IT MIGHT AS WELL RAIN UNTIL SEPTEMBER/ Nobody's Perfect	(Companion 2000)	6.25	25.00	62
IT MIGHT AS WELL RAIN UNTIL SEPTEMBER/ Nobody's Perfect	(Dimension 2000)	1.00	4.00	62
IT'S GOING TO TAKE SOME TIME/	(Ode 66027)	.75	3.00	72
IT'S TOO LATE/I Feel The Earth Move	(Ode 66015)	.50	2.00	71
JAZZMAN/You Go Your Way, I'll Go Mine	(Ode 66101)	.50	2.00	74
MAIN STREET SATURDAY NIGHT/Changes	(Avatar 4593)	.50	2.00	78
MORNING SUN/Sunbird	(Avatar 4649)	.50	2.00	78
MOVE LIGHTLY/Whiskey	(Capitol 4718)	.50	2.00	79
NIGHTINGALE/You're Something New	(Ode 66106)	.50	2.00	75
OH, NEIL (Answer song)/A Very Special Boy	(Alpine 57)	10.00	40.00	60
ONLY LOVE IS REAL/Still Here Thinking Of You	(Ode 66119)	.50	2.00	76

TITLE/FLIP	LABEL & NO.	GOOD	NEAR MINT	YR.
ROAD TO NOWHERE, A/Some Of Your Lovin'	(Tomorrow 7502)	2.50	10.00	66
SCHOOL BELLS ARE RINGING/ I Didn't Have Any Summer Romance	(Dimension 1004)	2.50	10.00	63
SHORT MORT (Answer song)/Queen Of The Beach	(RCA Victor 47-7560)	6.25	25.00	59
SIMPLE THINGS/Hold On	(Avatar 4497)	.50	2.00	77
SO FAR AWAY/Smackwater Jack	(Ode 66019)	.50	2.00	71
SWEET SEASONS/Pocket Money	(Ode 66022)	.50	2.00	72
TIME GOES BY/Dreamlike I Wander	(Capitol 4766)	.50	2.00	79
UP ON THE ROOF/Eventually	(Ode 66006)	.75	3.00	71
YOU LIGHT UP MY LIFE/Believe In Humanity	(Ode 66035)	.50	2.00	73
Also see Bertell Dache				
Also see City				
Also see Germz				
KING Crimson (With Greg Lake & Robert Fripp)				
IN THE COURT OF THE CRIMSON KING/	(Atlantic 2703)	.75	3.00	70
NIGHT WATCH, THE/	(Atlantic 3016)	.75	3.00	74
KING COLEMAN				
BULLDOG/Black Bottom Blues	(Columbia 4-41927)	.75	3.00	61
KING CROONERS, The				
NOW THAT SHE'S GONE/Won't You Let Me Know	(Excello 2168)	3.75	15.00	60
SCHOOL DAZE/Memories	(Excello 2187)	3.75	15.00	60
KING, Dave				
BEATLE WALK, THE/	(Teia 1004)	1.25	5.00	64
KING FLASH				
ZOMBIE JAMBOREE/Mama Looks Boo Boo	(Columbia 4-40866)	1.25	5.00	57
KING GEORGE & THE CHECKMATES				
YO YO/	(Jerden 790)	1.00	4.00	66
KING GUION				
MOTHER FLETCHER'S INSTANT CHA-CHA/Arriba	(Romar RO-45-100)	1.00	4.00	
KING HARVEST				
DANCING IN THE MOONLIGHT/Marty & The Captain	(Perception 515)	.50	2.00	72
HARD TO LOVE SOMEBODY/	(A&M 1761)	.50	2.00	76
LITTLE BIT LIKE MAGIC, A/	(Perception 527)	.50	2.00	73
VAEA/A Little Bit Like Magic	(A&M 1728)	2.50	10.00	75
(With Carl Wilson & Mike Love)				
KING, Hial				
MALIBU SUNSET/War-Path	(MBK 104)	.75	3.00	63
KING, Johnny				
ROCK MEETING/Forsake Me Not	(Dot 15784)	1.25	5.00	58
KING, Jonathan				
EVERYONE'S GONE TO THE MOON/Summer's Coming	(Parrot 9774)	.75	3.00	65
FLIRT/Hey Jim	(Parrot 3030)	.75	3.00	72
HOOKED ON A FEELING/I Don't Want To Be Gay	(Parrot 3029)	.75	3.00	71
ICICLES (FELL FROM THE HEART OF A BLUEBIRD)/ In A Hundred Years From Now	(Parrot 3008)	1.00	4.00	66
JUST LIKE A WOMAN/Land Of The Golden Tree	(Parrot 3005)	1.00	4.00	66
KUNG-FU ANTHEM, THE/A Little Bit Left Of Right	(UK 49018)	.50	2.00	74
LAZYBONES/I Just Want To Say "Thank You"	(Parrot 3027)	.75	3.00	70
MARY, MY LOVE/A Little Bit Left Of Right	(UK 49014)	.75	3.00	73
(MESSAGE TO THE POLITICAL CANDITATES) 1968/ Colloquial Sex	(Parrot 3021)	1.25	5.00	68
PALOMA BLANCA (WHITE DOVE)/	(UK-Big Tree 16046)	.75	3.00	75
ROUND ROUND/Time & Motion	(Parrot 3011)	1.00	4.00	67
TALL ORDER FOR A SHORT GUY, A/Learned Tax Council	(UK 49002)	.75	3.00	73
WAY YOU LOOK TONIGHT, THE/The True Story Of Molly Malone	(UK 49034)	.75	3.00	74
WHERE THE SUN HAS NEVER SHONE/Green Is The Grass	(Parrot 9804)	1.00	4.00	65
Also see Jack, Robin				
KING, Lenore, & Tommy Anderson				
BEATLES IS BACK, YEA YEA, THE/Ye Old Lion & His Feudin' Cousins (By Tommy Anderson)	(Her Majesty 101)	1.50	6.00	65
KING LIZARD: see Fowley, Kim				
KING OF HEARTS				
STAY WITH ME/	(Capitol 4634)	.50	2.00	78
KING, Peggy				
MAKE YOURSELF COMFORTABLE/ The Gentleman In The Next Apartment	(Columbia 4-40363)	1.00	4.00	55
KING, Ramona				
IT'S IN HIS KISS (THE SHOOP SHOOP SONG)/ It Couldn't Happen To A Nicer Guy	(Warner Bros. 5416)	1.00	4.00	64
ORIENTAL GARDEN/Soul-mate	(Eden 3)	1.00	4.00	62
RUN JOHNNY, RUN/ It Couldn't Happen To A Nicer Guy	(Warner Bros. 5452)	1.00	4.00	64
KING, Teddi				
MARRIED I CAN ALWAYS GET/La Strada	(RCA Victor 47-6660)	1.00	4.00	56
MR. WONDERFUL/ Are You Slipping Through My Fingers	(RCA Victor 47-6392)	1.00	4.00	56
KING TUT				
TWISTIN' AT LITTLE BIG HORN/Shorter Hours At School	(Starline 1001)	.75	3.00	62
KING, Victor				
BOPPIN' BOBBIE JEAN/Bohemian Baby	(Madison 110)	1.25	5.00	59

TITLE/FLIP	LABEL & NO.	GOOD	NEAR MINT	YR.
KINGFISH				
HARD TO LOVE SOMEBODY/	(Jet 5053)	.50	2.00	78
HYPNOTIZE/	(Round 794)	.50	2.00	76
Bob Weir, of the Grateful Dead, was orginally with this band.				
KINGS, The				
COME ON LITTLE BABY/Angel (Red plastic)	(Jalo 203)	1.50	6.00	
KINGS KOUNTY KARNIVAL, The				
PROOF OF THE PUDDING/ Don't Vote For Luke McCabe	(United Artists 50479)	1.25	5.00	69
(With Jay & The Americans)				
KINGSMEN, The				
CAT WALK, THE/Conga Rock	(East West 120)	1.00	4.00	58
WEEKEND/Better Believe It	(East West 115)	1.00	4.00	58
This group includes members of Bill Haley's Comets.				
KINGSMEN, The (With Jack Ely & Lynn Easton)				
ANNIE FANNY/Give Her Lovin'	(Wand 189)	.75	3.00	65
CLIMB, THE/The Waiting	(Wand 183)	.75	3.00	65
DEATH OF AN ANGEL/Searching For Love	(Wand 164)	.75	3.00	64
DIG THIS/Lady's Choice	(Jalynne 108)	3.00	12.00	61
FEED ME/Just A B Side	(Earth 104)	1.00	4.00	
GET OUT OF MY LIFE WOMAN/Since You've Been Gone	(Wand 1174)	1.00	4.00	68
IF I NEEDED SOMEONE/Grass Is Green	(Wand 1137)	1.00	4.00	66
IT'S ONLY THE DOG/(You Got) The Gamma Goochee	(Wand 1107)	1.00	4.00	65
JOLLY GREEN GIANT, THE/Long Green	(Wand 172)	.75	3.00	64
KILLER JOE/Little Green Thing	(Wand 1115)	.75	3.00	66
LITTLE LATIN LUPE LU/David's Moon	(Wand 157)	.75	3.00	64
LOUIE LOUIE/Haunted Castle	(Jerden 712)	3.75	15.00	63
LOUIE LOUIE/Haunted Castle	(Wand 143)	.75	3.00	63
LOUIE LOUIE 64-65-66.../Haunted Castle (Reissue)	(Wand 143)	.50	2.00	66
MONEY/Bent Scepter	(Wand 150)	.75	3.00	64
MY WIFE CAN'T COOK/Little Sally Tease	(Wand 1127)	1.00	4.00	66
TROUBLE/Daytime Shadows	(Wand 1147)	1.00	4.00	67
WOLF OF MANHATTAN/Children's Caretaker	(Wand 1154)	1.00	4.00	67
YOU BETTER DO RIGHT/Today	(Capitol 3576)	1.00	4.00	72
KINGSTON TRIO, The				
ALLY ALLY OXEN FREE/Marcelle Vahine	(Capitol 5078)	.75	3.00	63
BAD MAN BLUNDER/The Escape Of Old John Webb	(Capitol 4379)	.75	3.00	60
BIG SHIP GLORY/	(Mountain Creek 301)	.50	2.00	78
COMING FROM THE MOUNTAINS/ Nothing More To Look Forward To	(Capitol 4642)	.75	3.00	61
COO COO-U/Green Grasses	(Capitol 4303)	.75	3.00	59
C'MON HOME BETTY/Old Joe Clark	(Capitol 4808)	.75	3.00	61
DESERT PETE/Ballad Of The Thresher	(Capitol 5005)	.75	3.00	63
EL MATADOR/Home From The Hill	(Capitol 4338)	.75	3.00	60
EVERGLADES/This Mornin', This Evenin', So Soon	(Capitol 4441)	.75	3.00	60
GOODNIGHT MY BABY/Somerset Gloucestershire Wassail	(Capitol 4475)	.75	3.00	60
GREENBACK DOLLAR (Uncensored)/ Reverend Mr. Black	(Capitol Starline 6071)	.75	3.00	
GREENBACK DOLLAR/New Frontier	(Capitol 4898)	.75	3.00	63
HOPE YOU UNDERSTAND/My Ramblin' Boy	(Decca 31702)	.75	3.00	64
I'M GOING HOME/Little Play Soldiers	(Capitol 31730)	.75	3.00	65
LAST NIGHT I HAD THE STRANGEST DREAM/ Patriot Game	(Capitol 5132)	.75	3.00	64
M.T.A./All My Sorrows	(Capitol 4221)	.75	3.00	59
ONE MORE TOWN/She Was Too Good To Me	(Capitol 4842)	.75	3.00	62
RASPBERRIES, STRAWBERRIES/Sally	(Capitol 4114)	1.00	4.00	58
REVEREND MR. BLACK/One More Round	(Capitol 4951)	.75	3.00	63
RUNAWAY SONG/Parchment Farm (Blues)	(Decca 31806)	.75	3.00	65
SCARLET RIBBONS/Thirteen Jolly Coachmen	(Capitol 3970)	1.00	4.00	58
SCOTCH & SODA/Jane, Jane, Jane	(Capitol 4740)	.75	3.00	62
SEASONS IN THE SUN/If You Don't Look Around	(Capitol 5166)	.75	3.00	64
STAY AWHILE/Yes, I Can Feel It	(Capitol 31790)	.75	3.00	65
TIJUANA JAIL, THE/Oh Cindy	(Capitol 4167)	.75	3.00	59
TIJUANA JAIL, THE/Oh Cindy	(Capitol 4167)	2.00	8.00	59
(Stereo single issue)				
TOM DOOLEY/Ruby Red	(Capitol 4049)	.75	3.00	58
WHERE HAVE ALL THE FLOWERS GONE/Oken Karanga	(Capitol 4671)	.75	3.00	62
WORRIED MAN, A/San Miguel	(Capitol 4271)	.75	3.00	59
YOU'RE GONNA MISS ME/En El Agua	(Capitol 4536)	.75	3.00	61
Original group members were Dave Guard, Nick Reynolds & Bob Shane. In 1967 John Stewart joined the trio, replacing Dave Guard.				
KINGTONES, The				
TWINS/Have Good Faith	(Derry 101)	1.00	4.00	
KINGTONES, The				
GOODNIGHT BABY/Like A Cast-off	(Atco 6673)	.75	3.00	69
KINKS, The (Featuring Ray Davies)				
ALL DAY & ALL OF THE NIGHT/I Gotta Move	(Reprise 0334)	1.25	5.00	65
APEMAN/Rats	(Reprise 0979)	1.00	4.00	70
AUTUMN ALMANAC/David Watts	(Reprise 0647)	1.50	6.00	67
CATCH ME NOW, I'M FALLING/	(Arista 0458)	.50	2.00	79
CELLULOID HEROES/	(RCA 0852)	1.00	4.00	73
DAYS/She's Got Everything	(Reprise 0762)	1.50	6.00	68
DEADEND STREET/Big Black Smoke	(Reprise 0540)	1.25	5.00	66
DEDICATED FOLLOWER OF FASHION/Sittin' On My Sofa	(Reprise 0417)	1.25	5.00	66
FATHER CHRISTMAS/Prince Of The Punks	(Arista 0296)	.75	3.00	77
GALLON OF GAS, A/Low Budget	(Arista 0448)	.50	2.00	79
GOD'S CHILDREN/The Way Love Used To Be	(Reprise 1017)	1.25	5.00	71
HERE COMES FLASH/	(RCA 0275)	1.00	4.00	74
I'M IN DISGRACE/The Hard Way	(RCA 10551)	1.00	4.00	76
JUKE BOX MUSIC/Life Goes On	(Arista 0247)	.75	3.00	77
LIVE LIFE/Black Messiah	(Arista 0372)	.50	2.00	78
LOLA/Mindless Child Of Motherhood	(Reprise 0930)	1.00	4.00	70

TITLE/FLIP	LABEL & NO.	GOOD	NEAR MINT	YR.
LONG TALL SALLY/I Took My Baby Home	(Cameo 308)	12.50	50.00	64
LONG TALL SALLY/I Took My Baby Home	(Cameo 345)	7.50	30.00	
MIRROR OF LOVE/He's Evil	(RCA 10019)	1.00	4.00	74
MR. PLEASANT/Harry Rag	(Reprise 0587)	1.25	5.00	67
NEVER MET A GIRL LIKE YOU BEFORE/See My Friends	(Reprise 0409)	2.00	8.00	65
ONE OF THE SURVIVORS/	(RCA 0940)	1.00	4.00	73
POLLY/Wonderboy	(Reprise 0691)	1.50	6.00	68
ROCK 'N' ROLL FANTASY, A/Live Life	(Arista 0342)	.50	2.00	78
SALVATION ROAD/Preservation	(RCA 10121)	1.00	4.00	74
SET ME FREE/I Need You	(Reprise 0379)	1.25	5.00	65
SITTING IN THE MIDDAY SUN/Sweet Lady Genevieve	(RCA 5001)	1.00	4.00	74
SLEEPWALKER/Full Moon	(Arista 0240)	.50	2.00	77
STARMAKER/Ordinary People	(RCA 10251)	1.00	4.00	75
STARSTRUCK/Picture Book	(Reprise 0806)	1.25	5.00	69
SUNNY AFTERNOON/I'm Not Like Everybody Else	(Reprise 0497)	1.25	5.00	66
TILL THE END OF THE DAY/ Where Have All The Good Times Gone	(Reprise 0454)	1.25	5.00	66
TIRED OF WAITING FOR YOU/Come On Down	(Reprise 0347)	1.25	5.00	65
20TH CENTURY MAN/Skin & Bone	(RCA 0620)	1.00	4.00	72
VICTORIA/Brainwashed	(Reprise 0863)	1.25	5.00	69
VILLAGE GREEN PRESERVATION SOCIETY/ Do You Remember Walter	(Reprise 0847)	1.25	5.00	69
WATERLOO SUNSET/Two Sisters	(Reprise 0612)	1.50	6.00	67
WELL RESPECTED MAN, A/Such A Shame	(Reprise 0420)	1.25	5.00	65
WHO'LL BE THE NEXT IN LINE/ Everybody's Gonna Be Happy	(Reprise 0366)	1.25	5.00	65
(WISH I COULD FLY LIKE) SUPERMAN/Low Budget	(Arista 0409)	.50	2.00	79
YOU DON'T KNOW MY NAME/Supersonic Rocketship	(RCA 0807)	1.00	4.00	72
YOU REALLY GOT ME/It's All Right	(Reprise 0306)	1.25	5.00	64
YOU STILL WANT ME/You Do Something To Me	(Cameo 348)	20.00	80.00	65
Reprise promotional issues, which were pressed on vinyl, can bring twice the value of the commercial copies, which were pressed on polystyrene.				
KIP & KEN				
NO ROOM TO CRY/Love! Say Yea Yea Yea	(Crusader 126)	.75	3.00	65
TROUBLE WITH A WOMAN/It's Nice To Be Alive	(Crusader 119)	.75	3.00	65
KIPNER, Steve (Of Tin Tin)				
KNOCK THE WALLS DOWN/	(Elektra 46504)	.50	2.00	79
LOVE IS IT'S OWN REWARD/ Love Is It's Own Reward (Instrumental)	(RSO 902)	.50	2.00	78
Also see Fut, The				
KIPPER & THE EXCITERS				
DRUM TWIST (PART 1)/Drum Twist (Part 2) (Instrumental)	(Torchlite 501)	.75	3.00	62
KIRBY, Buzz				
SPEEDOO/She's My Girl	(Parkway 906)	1.00	4.00	64
KIRBY, Kathy				
(HE'S A) BIG MAN/Slowly	(London 9572)	.75	3.00	62
I'LL TRY NOT TO CRY/I Belong	(London 9750)	.75	3.00	65
WAY OF LOVE, THE/Oh Darling How I Miss You	(Parrot 9775)	.75	3.00	65
KIRBY STONE FOUR, The				
BAUBLES, BANGLES & BEADS/Medley: In The Good Old Summertime-Take The Lady	(Columbia 4-41183)	.75	3.00	58
EVERYTHING'S COMING UP ROSES/Red Shoes	(Columbia 4-41385)	.75	3.00	59
ZING! WENT THE STRINGS OF MY HEART/Let's Do It	(Columbia 4-41229)	.75	3.00	58
KIRBY, Ted, & The Starliters				
PINK PETTICOAT/An Empty House	(Gala 104)	.75	3.00	
KIRK, Lisa, & Fran Warren				
DEARIE/Just A Girl That Men Forget	(RCA Victor 47-3696)	1.25	5.00	50
KIRKLAND, Jimmy				
I WONDER IF YOU WONDER/Come On Baby	(Fox 918)	1.00	4.00	
(With Stan Getz & the Tom Cats)				
KIRWAN, Danny (Of Fleetwood Mac)				
BEST GIRL IN THE WORLD/Man Of The World	(DJM 1007)	.50	2.00	76
RAM JAM CITY/	(DJM 1004)	.50	2.00	75
SECOND CHAPTER/Skip A Dee Doo	(DJM 1005)	.50	2.00	76
KISS (Gene Simmons, Ace Frehley, Paul Stanley, Peter Criss)				
BETH/Detroit Rock City	(Casablanca 863)	.50	2.00	76
(Also see "Detroit Rock City")				
CALLING DR. LOVE/Take Me	(Casablanca 880)	.50	2.00	77
CHRISTINE SIXTEEN/Shock Me	(Casablanca 889)	.50	2.00	77
C'MON & LOVE ME/	(Casablanca 841)	.75	3.00	75
DETROIT ROCK CITY/Beth	(Casablanca 863A)	.75	3.00	76
(First issues had "Detroit Rock City" as the plug side. Note the "A" as part of the catalog number, not used when second pressings pluged "Beth" as the top side.)				
FLAMING YOUTH/God Of Thunder	(Casablanca 858)	.50	2.00	76
HARD LUCK WOMAN/Mr. Speed	(Casablanca 863)	.50	2.00	76
I WAS MADE FOR LOVIN' YOU/Hard Times	(Casablanca 983)	.50	2.00	79
KISSIN' TIME/Nothin' To Lose	(Casablanca 0011)	.50	2.00	74
LET ME GO, ROCK 'N' ROLL/Hotter Than Hell	(Casablanca 823)	.75	3.00	74
LOVE GUN/Hooligan	(Casablanca 895)	.50	2.00	77
LOVE THEME FROM KISS/Nothin' To Lose	(Casablanca 0004)	.75	3.00	74
ROCK & ROLL ALL NITE/Getaway	(Casablanca 829)	.50	2.00	75
ROCK & ROLL ALL NITE/Rock & Roll All Nite (Live)	(Casablanca 850)	.50	2.00	75
ROCKET RIDE/Tomorrow & Tonight	(Casablanca 915)	.50	2.00	78
SHOUT IT OUT LOUD (Live)/Nothin' To Lose (Live)	(Casablanca 906)	.50	2.00	77
SHOUT IT OUT LOUD/Sweet Pain	(Casablanca 854)	.50	2.00	76
STRUTTER/100,000 Years	(Casablanca 0015)	.75	3.00	74
STRUTTER '78/Shock Me	(Casablanca 928)	.50	2.00	78
SURE KNOW SOMETHING/Dirty Livin'	(Casablanca 2205)	.50	2.00	79
KISSOON, Mac & Katie				
CHIRPY CHIRPY CHEEP CHEEP Walking Around	(ABC 11306)	.75	3.00	71
LIKE A BUTTERFLY/A Beautiful Day	(MCA-State 40482)	.50	2.00	75
LOVE WILL KEEP US TOGETHER/	(Bell 45436)	.75	3.00	72
SUGAR CANDY KISSES/Black Rose	(MCA-State 40409)	.50	2.00	75
TWO OF US, THE/	(MCA-State 40550)	.50	2.00	76
WHERE WOULD OUR LOVE BE/	(MCA-State 40609)	.50	2.00	76
KIT & THE OUTLAWS				
MIDNIGHT HOUR/Don't Tred On Me	(Philips 40420)	1.00	4.00	67
KITCHEN CINQ, The				
GOOD LOVIN'/For Never We Meet	(Decca 32262)	.75	3.00	68
RIDE THE WIND/If You Think	(L.H.I. 17005)	1.00	4.00	67
RIDE THE WIND/Still In Love With You Baby	(L.H.I. 17010)	1.00	4.00	67
STREET SONG/When The Rainbow Disappears	(L.H.I. 17015)	1.00	4.00	67
YOU'LL BE SORRY SOMEDAY/Determination	(L.H.I. 17000)	1.00	4.00	66
KITT, Eartha				
C'EST SI BON/African Lullaby	(RCA Victor 47-5358)	1.00	4.00	53
SANTA BABY/Under The Bridges Of Paris	(RCA Victor 47-5502)	1.00	4.00	53
SOMEBODY BAD STOLE DE WEDDING BELL/ Lovin' Spree	(RCA Victor 47-5610)	1.00	4.00	54
KITTENS, The				
COUNT EVERY STAR/I'm Worried	(Chestnut 203)	3.00	12.00	
I NEED YOUR LOVE TONIGHT/Johnny's Place	(Don El 205)	1.00	4.00	63
ITSY BITSY, TEENIE WEENIE, YELLOW POLKA DOT BIKINI/ Dark, Dark Sunglasses	(Alpine 64)	1.00	4.00	60
LETTER ON HIS SWEATER/Broken Dreams	(Alpine 67)	1.00	4.00	60
LETTER TO DONNA/It's All Over Now	(Unart 2010)	1.00	4.00	59
SHINDIG/I Got To Know Him	(ABC-Paramount 10619)	1.00	4.00	65
YOU CHEATED/Wedding Bells	(Imperial 5728)	1.00	4.00	61

TITLE/FLIP	LABEL & NO.	GOOD	NEAR MINT	YR.
KLAATU				
CALIFORNIA JAM/Doctor Marvello	(Island 011)	.75	3.00	75
CALLING OCCUPANTS/Sub-Rosa Subway	(Capitol 4412)	.50	2.00	77
DEAR CHRISTINE/Older	(Capitol 4627)	.50	2.00	78
WE'RE OFF YOU KNOW/Around The Universe In Eighty Days	(Capitol 4516)	.50	2.00	77
KLEIN, George				
U.T. PARTY/U.T. Party (Part 2)	(Sun 358)	1.00	4.00	61
Also see George & Louis				
KLEIN, Mo				
HOT SAKI/Japanese Kid, The	(Crystalette 727)	1.25	5.00	59
KLEIN, Robert				
FABULOUS '50S/	(Brut 802)	.75	3.00	73
FALLIN'/Fill In The Words	(Casablanca 972)	.50	2.00	79
IF HE REALLY KNEW ME/Workin' It Out	(Casablanca 971)	.50	2.00	79
(With Lucie Arnaz)				
KLINE, Mo, & Sergeants				
ALL RIGHT PRIVATE (PRESLEY)/Flying Lox Box	(Crystalette 722)	3.00	12.00	54
KLOWNS, The				
I DON'T BELIEVE IN MAGIC/	(RCA 0274)	.75	3.00	70
LADY LOVE/If You Can't Be A Clown	(RCA 0393)	.75	3.00	70
KNACK, The				
BANANA MAN/Pretty Daisy	(Capitol 5940)	.75	3.00	67
FREEDOM NOW/Lady In The Window	(Capitol 2075)	.75	3.00	68
SOFTLY SOFTLY/The Spell	(Capitol 5889)	.75	3.00	67
TIME WAITS FOR NO ONE/I'm Aware	(Capitol 5774)	.75	3.00	67
KNACK, The				
GOOD GIRLS DON'T/Frustration	(Capitol 4771)	.50	2.00	79
MY SHARONA/Let Me Out	(Capitol 4731)	.50	2.00	79
MY SHARONA (Stereo)/My Sharona (Mono)	(Capitol P-4731)	.50	2.00	79
(Promotional issue)				
MY SHARONA (Stereo)/My Sharona (Mono)	(Capitol P-4731)	.75	3.00	79
(Picture sleeve for promotional issue.)				
KNAVES, The				
INSIDE OUTSIDE/Your Stuff	(Dunwich 164)	.75	3.00	67
LEAVE ME ALONE/The Girl I Threw Away	(Dunwich 147)	.75	3.00	67
KNICKERBOCKERS, The (Featuring Buddy Randell)				
ALL I NEED IS YOU/Bite Bite Barracuda	(Challenge 59268)	1.00	4.00	65
AS A MATTER OF FACT/They Ran For Their Lives	(Challenge 59384)	1.00	4.00	67
CHAPEL IN THE FIELDS/Just One Girl	(Challenge 59335)	1.00	4.00	66
COME & GET IT/Wishful Thinking	(Challenge 59366)	1.00	4.00	67
HIGH ON LOVE/Stick With Me	(Challenge 59332)	1.00	4.00	66
I CAN DO IT BETTER/You'll Never Walk Alone	(Challenge 59380)	1.00	4.00	67
JERKTOWN/Room For One More	(Challenge 59293)	1.00	4.00	65
LIES/The Coming Generation	(Challenge 59321)	1.00	4.00	65
LOVE IS A BIRD/Rumors, Gossip, Words Unture	(Challenge 59341)	1.00	4.00	66
ONE TRACK MIND/I Must Be Doing Something Right	(Challenge 59326)	1.00	4.00	66
PLEASE DON'T LOVE HIM/Can You Help Me	(Challenge 59348)	1.00	4.00	66
WHAT DOES THAT MAKE YOU/Sweet Green Fields	(Challenge 59359)	1.00	4.00	67
Also see Royal Teens, The				
KNIGHT, Baker, & His Knightmares				
BRING MY CADILLAC BACK/	(Decca 9-30135)	3.75	15.00	57
KNIGHT, Bob, Four				
I'M SELLING MY HEART/The Lazy Piano (Instrumental)	(Taurus 356)	1.50	6.00	62
MEMORIES/Somewhere	(Josie 899)	1.25	5.00	62
SO SO LONG/You Tease Me	(Taurus 100)	1.50	6.00	61
("So So Long" may be shown on some labels as "Good Good Bye")				
TOMORROW WE'LL BE MARRIED/Willingly	(Goal 4)	1.00	4.00	64
TWO FRIENDS/Crazy Love	(Jubilee 5451)	1.00	4.00	63
KNIGHT BROTHERS, The				
TEMPTATION 'BOUT TO GET ME/Sinking Low	(Checker 1107)	.75	3.00	65
KNIGHT, Jimmy				
CRANKSHAFT KID/Teenage Retirement	(Kangaroo 27)	.75	3.00	64
KNIGHT, Johnny, & The Kingsmen				
SECRET HEART/Push A Little Button	(Chance 568)	1.50	6.00	
KNIGHT RAIDERS, The (Featuring Mickey Hawks)				
SCREAMING MINI JEANNIE/I'm Lost	(Profile 4010)	10.00	40.00	
KNIGHT, Ted				
MAN WHO USED TO BE, THE/Birds Of Paradise	(Ranwood 1045)	.50	2.00	75
KNIGHT, Terry & The Pack				
BETTER MAN THAN I/Got Love	(Lucky Eleven 226)	1.25	5.00	66
CHANGE ON THE WAY, A/What's On Your Mind	(Lucky Eleven 229)	1.25	5.00	66
FOREVER & A DAY/Lizbeth Peach	(Cameo 482)	.75	3.00	67
HOW LONG HAS IT BEEN/	(Fraternity 987)	.75	3.00	67
(I) WHO HAVE NOTHING/Numbers	(Lucky Eleven 230)	1.25	5.00	66
(I) WHO HAVE NOTHING/Lizabeth Peach	(Abkco 4005)	.50	2.00	75
I'VE BEEN TOLD/How Much More	(Lucky Eleven 225)	1.25	5.00	66
LADY JANE/	(Lucky Eleven 227)	1.25	5.00	66
LIZABETH PEACH/Forever & A Day	(Cameo 482)	.75	3.00	67
LOVE LOVE LOVE LOVE LOVE/This Precious Time	(Lucky Eleven 235)	1.25	5.00	67
ONE MONKEY DON'T STOP NO SHOW/The Train	(Lucky Eleven 236)	1.25	5.00	67
ST. PAUL (THE LEGEND OF)/Legend Of William & Mary	(Capitol 2506)	1.00	4.00	69
SUCH A LOVELY LIFE/Lullaby	(Capitol 2409)	1.00	4.00	69
Also see Grand Funk Railroad				

TITLE/FLIP	LABEL & NO.	GOOD	NEAR MINT	YR.
KNIGHT, Vicki				
TO ELVIS IN HEAVEN/Learning To Love Again	(American Sound 3096)	.50	2.00	77
KNIGHTLY, John				
GREAT SPACE FLIGHT/Great Space Flight (Part 2)	(Spar 103)	3.75	15.00	
KNIGHTON, Reggie				
CLONE IN LOVE/Magnum Sally	(Columbia-ARC 10917)	.50	2.00	79
KNIGHTS, The				
HOT ROD HIGH/Theme For Teen Love	(Capitol 5302)	1.50	6.00	64
KNIGHTSBRIDGE STRINGS, The				
CRY/My Prayer	(Top Rank 2006)	.75	3.00	59
WHEEL OF FORTUNE/Cow Cow Boogie	(Top Rank 2014)	.75	3.00	59
Instrumentals				
KNOCKOUTS, The				
DARLING LORRAINE/Riot In Room 3C	(Shad 5013)	1.00	4.00	60
RICH BOY POOR BOY/Please Be Mine	(Shad 5018)	1.00	4.00	60
WHAT'S ON YOUR MIND/Tweet-Tweet	(Tribute 201)	.75	3.00	64
KNOX, Buddy				
ALL BY MYSELF/Three Eyed Man	(Liberty 55366)	1.00	4.00	62
CHI-HUA-HUA/Open	(Liberty 55411)	1.00	4.00	62
DEAR ABBY/Three Way Love Affair	(Liberty 55503)	1.00	4.00	62
GOOD TIME GIRL/Livin' In A House Full Of Love	(Reprise 0395)	.75	3.00	65
HULA LOVE/Devil Woman	(Roulette 4018)	1.00	4.00	57
I AIN'T SHARIN' SHARON/Taste Of The Blues	(Roulette 4179)	1.00	4.00	59
I THINK I'M GONNA KILL MYSELF/To Be With You	(Roulette 4140)	1.00	4.00	59
JO-ANN/Don't Make a Ripple	(Ruff 1001)	1.00	4.00	65
LING-TING-TONG/The Kisses	(Liberty 55305)	1.00	4.00	61
LONG LONELY KNIGHTS/Storm Clouds	(Roulette 4262)	1.00	4.00	60
LOVER'S QUESTION, A/You Said Goodbye	(Reprise 0431)	.75	3.00	65
LOVEY DOVEY/I Got You	(Liberty 55290)	.75	3.00	60
PARTY DOLL/I'm Stickin' With You (by Jimmy Bowen)	(Triple D 797)	37.50	150.00	57
(Shown as by Buddy Knox with the Orchids)				
PARTY DOLL/My Baby's Gone	(Roulette 4002)	1.50	6.00	57
(On "roulette wheel" label)				
PARTY DOLL/My Baby's Gone	(Roulette 4002)	1.00	4.00	57
ROCK YOUR LITTLE BABY TO SLEEP/ Don't Make Me Cry	(Roulette 4009)	1.50	6.00	57
(On "roulette wheel" label)				
ROCK YOUR LITTLE BABY TO SLEEP/ Don't Make Me Cry	(Roulette 4009)	1.00	4.00	57
SHE'S GONE/Now There's Only Me	(Liberty 55473)	1.00	4.00	62
SOMEBODY TOUCHED ME/C'mon Baby	(Roulette 4082)	1.00	4.00	58
SWINGIN' DADDY/Whenever I'm Lonely	(Roulette 4042)	1.00	4.00	58
TEASABLE, PLEASABLE YOU/That's Why I Cry	(Roulette 4120)	1.00	4.00	59
THANKS A LOT/Hitch-hike Back To Georgia	(Liberty 55650)	1.00	4.00	63
TOMORROW IS A COMIN'/Shadaroom	(Liberty 55592)	1.00	4.00	63
TRAVELIN' LIGHT/Come Softly To Me	(United Artists 50789)	.75	3.00	71
WHITE SPORT COAT, A/That Don't Do Me No Good	(Reprise 0463)	.75	3.00	61
Many of the Roulette issues showed the artist as Buddy Knox With The Rhythm Orchids, of which Jimmy Bowen was the bass player.				
KOEMPEL, Doug				
ROCK ON & ON & ON/Cold, Cold Ground	(Chart Action 114)	.50	2.00	77
KOFFMAN, Moe				
LITTLE PIXIE/Koko-Mamey	(Jubilee 5324)	.75	3.00	58
SWINGIN' SHEPHERD BLUES, THE/Hambourg Bound	(Jubilee 5311)	.75	3.00	58
Instrumentals				
KOKOMO				
ASIA MINOR/Roy's Tune	(Future 1023)	1.25	5.00	61
ASIA MINOR/Roy's Tune	(Felsted 8612)	.75	3.00	61
THEME FROM A SILENT MOVIES/Humorous	(Felsted 8622)	.75	3.00	61
Instrumentals				
KOKOMOS, The				
OPEN HOUSE PARTY/No Lies	(Josie 906)	1.50	6.00	62
YOURS TRULY/Mamma's Boy	(Gone 5134)	1.50	6.00	62
(With the 4 Seasons)				
KOLBY, Diane				
DEATH OF THE SUN/	(Columbia 4-45712)	.75	3.00	71
HOLY MAN/	(Columbia 4-45169)	.75	3.00	70
JUJU WOMAN/Nivey Klaine	(Columbia 4-45290)	.75	3.00	71
KOLE, Kenny, & The Huskies				
SORRY/Who	(Klick 8205)	1.00	4.00	
KOLOC, Bonnie				
SUNDAY MORNING MOVIES/Mama's Blues	(Ovation 1041)	.50	2.00	75
KONGOS, John				
HE'S GONNA STEP ON YOU AGAIN/	(Elektra 45729)	.50	2.00	71
JUBILEE CLOUD/I Would Have Had A Good Time	(Elektra 45779)	.50	2.00	72
TOKOLOSHE MAN/ Can Someone Please Direct Me Back To Earth	(Elektra 45760)	.50	2.00	72
KOOB, Roger				
GIVE ME THE LOVE I'M NEEDING/You'll Be Alone	(Birth 102)	.75	3.00	70
(Shown as by Roger K.)				
Also see the Frontiers				
Also see the Premiers				
Also see Roger & the Travelers				
KOOKIE BEAVERS, The				
DOGGIE IN THE WINDOW/Three Little Fishes	(Gone 5086)	.75	3.00	60
KOOKIE KAT				
I WUV YOU/Neow, Not Neow	(Atco 6156)	1.00	4.00	59
KOOL GENTS, The				
PICTURE ON THE WALL/Come To Me	(Bethlehem 3061)	3.75	15.00	
KOOPER, Al (Of The Blues Project)				
JOLIE/John The Baptist	(Columbia 4-45412)	.75	3.00	71
SAM STONE/	(Columbia 4-45691)	.75	3.00	71
Also see Blood, Sweat & Tears				
Also see Bloomfield, Mike				
KORMAN, Jerry				
BLIND DAIT BAIT/Hurry Back	(ABC-Paramount 10024)	1.00	4.00	59
KORNER, Alexis				
GET OFF MY CLOUD/	(Columbia 3-10166)	.75	3.00	75
(With Keith Richards on guitar)				
KORNFELD, Arnie				
ISLAND SONG/Feel	(Neighborhood 4206)	.50	2.00	73
K-OTICS, The				
DOUBLE SHOT (OF MY BABY'S LOVE)/I'm Leaving Here	(Bang 521)	1.00	4.00	66
KOTTKE, Leo				
POWER FAILURE/Can't Quite Put It Into Words	(Capitol 4177)	.50	2.00	75
KRAFTONES, The				
MEMORIES/Everybody's Got A Home But Me	(Medieval 206)	1.00	4.00	

TITLE/FLIP	LABEL & NO.	GOOD	NEAR MINT	YR.
KRAFTWERK				
AUTOBAHN/Morganspaziergang (Morning Walk)	(Vertigo 203)	.50	2.00	75
COMET MELODY 2/	(Vertigo 204)	.75	3.00	75
RADIOACTIVITY/Antenna	(Capitol 4211)	.75	3.00	76
TRANS-EUROPE EXPRESS/Franz Schubert	(Capitol 4460)	.75	3.00	77
KRAMER, Billy J., & The Dakotas				
BAD TO ME/I Call Your Name	(Liberty 55626)	1.25	5.00	63
DO YOU WANT TO KNOW A SECRET/I'll Be On My Way	(Liberty 55586)	2.00	8.00	63
DO YOU WANT TO KNOW A SECRET/Bad To Me	(Liberty 55667)	1.00	4.00	64
FROM A WINDOW/I'll Be On My Way	(Imperial 66051)	.75	3.00	64
I'LL BE DOGGONE/Neon City	(Imperial 66143)	1.00	4.00	65
I'LL KEEP YOU SATISFIED/I Know	(Liberty 55643)	1.25	5.00	63
I'LL KEEP YOU SATISFIED/I Know	(Imperial 66048)	.75	3.00	64
IT'S GOTTA LAST FOREVER/They Remind Me Of You	(Imperial 66085)	.75	3.00	64
LITTLE CHILDREN/Bad To Me	(Imperial 66027)	.75	3.00	64
TAKE MY HAND/You Make Me Feel Like Someone	(Imperial 66210)	1.00	4.00	66
TRAINS & BOATS & PLANES/I'll Be On My Way	(Imperial 66115)	.75	3.00	65
TRAINS & BOATS & PLANES/That's The Way I Feel	(Imperial 66115)	.75	3.00	65
TWLIGHT TIME/Irresistible You	(Imperial 66135)	1.00	4.00	65
KREKEL, Tim				
LITTLE BITTY PRETTY ONE/The Way Lover Move	(Capricorn 0324)	.50	2.00	79
KIRS & RITA (Kris Kristofferson & Rita Coolidge)				
LOVER PLEASE/	(Monument 8636)	.50	2.00	75
LOVING ARMS/I'm Down (But I Keep Falling)	(A&M 1498)	.50	2.00	74
RAIN/	(Monument 8630)	.50	2.00	75
SONG I'D LIKE TO SING, A/From The Bottle To The Bottom	(A&M 1475)	.50	2.00	73
KRISTOFFERSON, Kris				
EASY, COME ON/Rocket To Stardom	(Monument 8658)	.50	2.00	74
FOREVER IN YOUR LOVE/The Fighter	(Columbia 10731)	.50	2.00	78
I MAY SMOKE TOO MUCH/The Lights Of Magdala	(Monument 8618)	.50	2.00	74
IT'S NEVER GONNA BE THE SAME AGAIN/	(Monument 8707)	.50	2.00	75
JESSE YOUNGER/Give It Time To Be Tender	(Monument 8564)	.50	2.00	73
JESUS WAS A CAPRICORN/	(Monument 8558)	.50	2.00	72
JOSIE/Border Lord	(Monument 8536)	.50	2.00	72
LOVING HER WAS EASIER (THAN ANYTHING I'LL EVER DO AGAIN)/Epitaph (Black & White)	(Monument 8525)	.50	2.00	71
PILGRIM, CHAPTER 33, THE/	(Monument 8531)	.50	2.00	71
PROVE IT TO YOU ONE MORE TIME AGAIN/	(Columbia 11160)	.50	2.00	79
WATCH CLOSELY NOW/Crippled Crow	(Columbia 10525)	.50	2.00	77
WHY ME/Help Me	(Monument 8571)	.50	2.00	73
YEAR 2000 MINUS 25, THE/	(Monument 8679)	.50	2.00	75
KUBAN, Bob, & The In-Men				
BATMAN THEME/ You Better Run - You Better Hide	(Musicland U.S.A. 20017)	.75	3.00	67
CHEATER, THE/Try Me Baby	(Musicland U.S.A. 20001)	.75	3.00	66
DRIVE MY CAR/The Pretzel	(Musicland U.S.A. 20007)	.75	3.00	66
HARLEM SHUFFLE/Theme From Virginia Wolfe	(Musicland U.S.A. 20013)	.75	3.00	67
JERKIN' TIME/Turn On Your Love Light	(Norman 558)	1.00	4.00	65
SOUL MAN/Hard To Handle	(Reprise 0937)	.75	3.00	70
TEASER, THE/All I Want	(Musicland U.S.A. 20006)	.75	3.00	66
TURN ON YOUR LOVELIGHT/Jerkin' Time	(Norman 558)	1.00	4.00	66
(Shown as by the Bob Kuban Band.)				

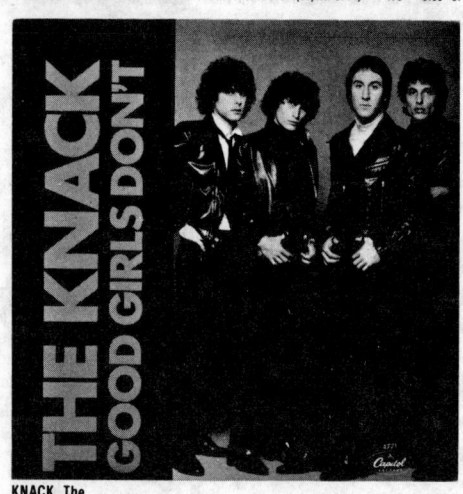

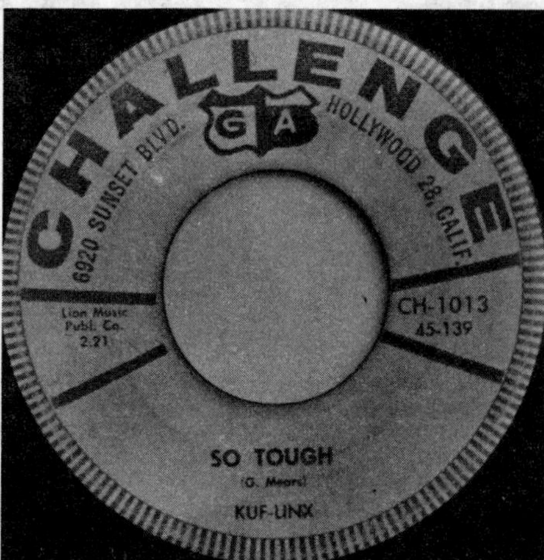

TITLE/FLIP	LABEL & NO.	GOOD	NEAR MINT	YR.
KUF-LINX, The				
CLIMB LOVE'S MOUNTAIN/All That Good	(Challenge 59015)	1.25	5.00	58
EYEBALLIN'/Service With A Smile	(Challenge 59004)	1.25	5.00	58
SO TOUGH/What Cha Gonna Do (White label)	(Challenge 1013)	2.00	8.00	58
SO TOUGH/What Cha Gonna Do (Maroon label)	(Challenge 1013)	1.00	4.00	58
KUKLA, FRAN & OLLIE				
TOOIE TALK/The Cuckoo	(RCA Victor 47-4289)	1.50	6.00	51
KULIS, Charlie				
RUNAWAY/When I See Her	(Playboy 6023)	.50	2.00	75
KUNKEL, Leah				
STEP RIGHT UP/	(Columbia 10926)	.50	2.00	79
Leah was the sister of "Mama" Cass Elliot.				
KUSIK/ADAMS				
CRAZY LIKE A FOX/Shock Me	(Hollywood 1107)	1.25	5.00	
KUSTOM KINGS, The				
CLUTCH RIDER/In My '40 Ford	(Smash 1883)	1.50	6.00	64
KWESKIN, Jim, Jug Band				
SHEIK OF ARABY, THE/Minglewood	(Reprise 0624)	1.00	4.00	67

L

TITLE/FLIP	LABEL & NO.	GOOD	NEAR MINT	YR.
LA LUPE				
CARLOS DOMINGUEZ/	*(Roulette 7141)*	.75	3.00	*72*
LA RAYS, The				
WOMAN LIKE YOU, A/Yesterday & You Around	*(Arlen 517)*	1.25	5.00	*63*
LA RELLS, The				
EVERYBODY KNEW/Please Be Fair	*(Robbee 109)*	1.50	6.00	*61*
L.A. EXPRESS, The (Formerly Tom Scott's L.A. Express)				
DANCE THE NIGHT AWAY/Double Your Pleasure	*(Caribou 9018)*	.50	2.00	*78*
L.A. JETS, The (Formerly Goodthunder)				
DANCIN' THRU THE NIGHT/Money Money	*(RCA 10668)*	.50	2.00	*76*
PRISONER (CAPTURED BY YOUR EYES)/ I'll Get Along Somehow	*(RCA PB-10826)*	.50	2.00	*76*
LABOE, Art				
PICKWICK TWIST/Mexican Midnight	*(Original Sound 23)*	.75	3.00	*62*
LA BOUNTY, Bill				
IN 25 WORDS OR LESS/	*(Warner Bros. 8642)*	.50	2.00	*78*
LIE TO ME/	*(20th Century 2290)*	.50	2.00	*76*
TAKE A STEP (YESTERDAY WALTZ)/	*(20th Century 2268)*	.50	2.00	*75*
THIS NIGHT WON'T LAST FOREVER/I Hope You'll Be Very Unhappy Without Me	*(Warner Bros. 8529)*	.50	2.00	*78*
LACE, Patty, & The Petticoats				
NEW BOY, A/Say One (Is A Lonely Number)	*(Kapp 667)*	.75	3.00	*65*
SNEAKY SUE/The Back	*(Kapp 563)*	.75	3.00	*63*
LADD, Cheryl (Of Josie & The Pussycats)				
GOOD GOOD LOVIN'/Skinnydippin'	*(Capitol 4650)*	.50	2.00	*78*
THINK IT OVER/Here Is A Song	*(Capitol 4599)*	.50	2.00	*78*
LADDINS, The				
NOW YOU'RE GONE/Did It	*(Central 2602)*	1.25	5.00	*57*
NOW YOU'RE GONE/Did It	*(Times Square 3)*	1.00	4.00	*57*
YES, OH BABY YES/Light A Candle	*(Grey Cliff 721)*	1.25	5.00	*59*
LADY BUGS, The				
HOW DO YOU DO IT/Liver-Pool	*(Chattahoochee 637)*	1.25	5.00	*64*
LADY JANE & VERITY				
JUNIOR AT THE SENIOR PROM, A/Slow Rock	*(Palette 5031)*	1.00	4.00	*59*
LADY JEAN				
TEENIE JEANIE/It's Been So Long	*(CJ 616)*	1.00	4.00	*60*
LAFAYETTE & THE LASABRES				
CURE FOR LOVE/Free Way	*(Port 70036)*	.75	3.00	
LA FLAMME, David (Of It's A Beautiful Day)				
EASY WOMAN/	*(Amherst 721)*	.50	2.00	*77*
WHITE BIRD/Spirit Of America	*(Amherst 717)*	.50	2.00	*77*
LAFORGE, Jack				
GOLDFINGER/Zelda's Theme	*(Regina 1323)*	.75	3.00	*65*
(Instrumentals)				
LAINE, Denny (Of The Moody Blues)				
IT'S SO EASY-LISTEN TO ME/ Lookin' For Someone To Love	*(Capitol-MPL 4340)*	.75	3.00	*76*
MOONDREAMS/Heartbeat	*(Capitol-MPL 4425)*	.50	2.00	*77*
SAY YOU DON'T MIND/Ask The People	*(Deram 7509)*	.75	3.00	*67*
Also see Wings				
LAINE, Frankie (Frank LoVecchio)				
CRY OF THE WILD GOOSE, THE/Black Lace	*(Mercury 5363)*	2.00	8.00	*50*
DON'T MAKE MY BABY BLUE/The Moment Of Truth	*(Columbia 4-42767)*	.75	3.00	*63*
GANDY DANCERS' BALL, THE/When You're In Love	*(Columbia 4-39665)*	1.50	6.00	*52*
GANG THAT SANG HEART OF MY HEART, THE/ You Left Me Out	*(Mercury 5656)*	2.00	8.00	*51*
GIRL IN THE WOODS, THE/Wonderful, Wasn't It?	*(Columbia 4-39489)*	1.50	6.00	*51*
GOD BLESS THE CHILD/Don't Cry Little Children	*(Mercury 5355)*	2.00	8.00	*50*
HEY JOE!/Sittin In The Sun	*(Columbia 4-40036)*	1.25	5.00	*53*
HIGH NOON/The Rock Of Gibraltar	*(Columbia 4-39770)*	1.50	6.00	*52*
I BELIEVE/Your Cheating Heart	*(Columbia 4-39938)*	1.25	5.00	*53*
I LOVE YOU FOR THAT/If I Were You, Baby	*(Mercury 5442)*	2.00	8.00	*50*
JEALOUSY (JALOUSIE)/Flamenco	*(Columbia 4-39585)*	1.50	6.00	*51*
JEZEBEL/Rose, Rose, I Love You	*(Columbia 4-39367)*	1.50	6.00	*51*
LET'S GO FISHIN'/Little Child	*(Columbia 4-40650)*	1.00	4.00	*56*
(With Jimmy Boyd)				
LOVE IS A GOLDEN RING/ There's Not A Moment To Spare	*(Columbia 4-40856)*	1.00	4.00	*57*
MERMAID, THE/Ruby & The Pearl	*(Columbia 4-39862)*	1.50	6.00	*52*
METRO POLKA/Jalopy Song	*(Mercury 5581)*	2.00	8.00	*51*
MOONLIGHT GAMBLER/Lotus Land	*(Columbia 4-40780)*	1.00	4.00	*56*
MULE TRAIN/Carry Me Back To Old Virginney	*(Mercury 5343)*	2.00	8.00	*49*
MUSIC MAESTRO, PLEASE/ Dream A Little Dream Of Me	*(Mercury 5458)*	2.00	8.00	*50*
NEVERTHELESS/I Was Dancing With Someone	*(Mercury 5495)*	2.00	8.00	*50*
RAIN, RAIN, RAIN/Your Heart, My Heart	*(Columbia 4-40295)*	1.25	5.00	*54*
RAWHIDE/The Hanging Tree	*(Columbia 4-41230)*	1.00	4.00	*58*
RAWHIDE/Magnificent Obsession	*(Columbia 4-41230)*	1.00	4.00	*58*
SEPTEMBER IN THE RAIN/Ain't That Just Like Me	*(Mercury 5003)*	2.00	8.00	*50*
SHINE/We'll Be Together Again	*(Mercury 5091)*	2.00	8.00	*49*
SLEEPY OL' RIVER/If I Were A Bell	*(Mercury 5500)*	2.00	8.00	*50*
SOME DAY/There Must Be A Reason	*(Columbia 4-40235)*	1.25	5.00	*54*
STARS & STRIPES FOREVER/Thanks For Your Kisses	*(Mercury 5421)*	2.00	8.00	*50*
SWAMP GIRL/A Kiss For Tomorrow	*(Mercury 5390)*	2.00	8.00	*50*
TELL ME A STORY/The Little Boy & The Old Man	*(Columbia 4-39945)*	1.25	5.00	*53*
(With Jimmy Boyd)				
THAT LUCKY OLD SUN/I Get Sentimental	*(Mercury 5316)*	2.00	8.00	*49*
LAINE, Frankie & Jimmy Boyd: see Laine, Frankie				
LAING, Corky (Of Mountain)				
MAKIN' IT ON THE STREETS/Somebody Told Me	*(Elektra 45423)*	.50	2.00	*77*
SEE ME THROUGH/	*(Elektra 45393)*	.50	2.00	*77*
Also see West, Bruce & Laing				
LAKE				
ON THE RUN/	*(Columbia 10580)*	.50	2.00	*77*
PARADISE WAY/Hard Road	*(Columbia 11010)*	.50	2.00	*79*
SEE THEM GLOW/	*(Columbia 10818)*	.50	2.00	*78*
TIME BOMB/Chasing Colours	*(Columbia 10614)*	.50	2.00	*77*
LAKE, Greg (Of Emerson, Lake & Palmer)				
I BELIEVE IN FATHER CHRISTMAS/Humbug	*(Atlantic 3305)*	.50	2.00	*76*
LAMB, Kevin				
ON THE WRONG TRACK/When My Love	*(Arista 0316)*	.50	2.00	*78*
LAMBERT, Dave (Of The Strawbs)				
TAKE A LITTLE BIT OF MY LIFE/ This Is My Neighborhood	*(Polydor 14554)*	.50	2.00	*79*
LAMEGO, Danny, & The Jumpin' Jacks				
HICKORY DICKORY ROCK/Chicken Feed	*(Andrea 101)*	1.00	4.00	
LAMM, Robert (Of Chicago)				
WHERE DO YOU THINK YOU'RE GOING/	*(Columbia AE7-1054)*	.75	3.00	*72*
LAMONT CRANSTON BAND, The				
TAKIN' A CHANCE/E Jam	*(Waterhouse 15002)*	.50	2.00	*79*
LAMONT, Paula				
BEATLE MEETS A LADY BUG/ Greatest Lover Under The Sun	*(Loadstone 1605)*	1.25	5.00	*64*
LAMP OF CHILDHOOD, The				
TWO O'CLOCK MORNING/No More Running Around	*(Dunhill 4089)*	1.00	4.00	*67*
LANCASTERS, The				
EARTHSHAKER/Satan's Holiday	*(Titan 1730)*	1.00	4.00	
LANCE, Herb, & The Classics				
BLUE MOON/Little Boy Lost	*(Promo 1010)*	1.00	4.00	*61*
LANCELO & THE TEERS				
WHISPERING BELLS/It's Not For Me To Say	*(Promenade 12)*	1.00	4.00	
LANCERS, The				
OH LITTLE GIRL/You're The Right One	*(Lawn 205)*	1.00	4.00	*63*
WARMTH OF THE SUN, THE/Hushabye	*(Vee Jay 654)*	1.50	6.00	*65*
LAND, Billy				
FOUR WHEELS/Shimmy Shake	*(Esco 4710)*	1.25	5.00	*59*
FOUR WHEELS/Shimmy Shake	*(Warner Bros. 5083)*	.75	3.00	*59*
LAND, Eddie				
EASY ROCKIN'/On My Way	*(Ron 320)*	1.25	5.00	*59*
SHE'S MINE, ALL MINE/Troubles, Troubles	*(Ron 324)*	1.25	5.00	*59*
LANDIS, Jerry: see Simon, Paul				
LANDON, Michael				
GIMME A LITTLE KISS (WILL "YA" HUH)/ Be Patient With Me	*(Fono Graf FG-1240)*	1.25	5.00	*60*
GIMME A LITTLE KISS (WILL "YA" HUH)/ Be Patient With Me	*(Fono Graf FG-1240)*	2.50	10.00	*60*
(Picture sleeve)				
LANE BROTHERS, The				
MARIANNE/Sogno D'oro	*(RCA Victor 47-6810)*	1.00	4.00	*57*
LANE, Ronnie (Of Small Faces)				
HOW COME?/	*(A&M 1524)*	.50	2.00	*73*
LANE, Mickey Lee				
HEY SAH-LO-NEY/Yesterday	*(Swan 4222)*	.75	3.00	*65*
LITTLE GIRL (I WAS WRONG)/ When You're In Love (That's How You'll Know)	*(Swan 4210)*	.75	3.00	*65*
SENIOR CLASS (THEY'RE ALL IN THE)/The Zoo	*(Swan 4199)*	.75	3.00	*65*
SHAGGY DOG/Oo-oo	*(Swan 4183)*	.75	3.00	*64*
LANGFORD, Gerry				
STILL OF THE NIGHT, THE/Tell Me	*(Del Fi 4113)*	1.00	4.00	*59*
LANHAM, Richard				
DAY I MET YOU, THE/Wishing All The Time	*(Acme 722)*	5.00	20.00	*57*
DON'T BELIEVE HIM/Have A Little Faith	*(Josie 985)*	1.00	4.00	*65*
ON YOUR RADIO/Dance Of Love	*(Acme 712)*	3.00	12.00	*57*
LANI & BONI: see Delaney & Bonnie				
LANSON, Snooky				
AFTER SCHOOL/I'm Tired Of Everyone But You	*(Dot 15475)*	1.00	4.00	*56*
IT'S ALMOST TOMORROW/Stop! Let Me Off The Bus	*(Dot 15424)*	1.00	4.00	*55*
SEVEN DAYS/Tippity Top	*(Dot 15445)*	1.00	4.00	*56*
WALK RIGHT IN/By The Light Of The Silvery Moon	*(Dot 15455)*	1.00	4.00	*56*
WHY DON'T YOU WRITE ME/Last Minute Love	*)Dot 15385)*	1.00	4.00	*55*
LANZA, Mario				
ARRIVEDERCI ROMA/Younger Than Springtime	*(RCA Victor 47-7164)*	1.00	4.00	*58*
AVE MARIA/I'll Walk With God	*(RCA Victor 47-6334)*	1.00	4.00	*55*
BE MY LOVE/I'll Never Love You	*(RCA Victor 47-1561)*	2.00	8.00	*50*
BECAUSE/For You Alone	*(RCA Victor 47-3207)*	1.50	6.00	*51*
BECAUSE YOU'RE MINE/Song The Angels Sing	*(RCA Victor 47-3914)*	1.50	6.00	*52*
EARTHBOUND/This Land	*(RCA Victor 47-6644)*	1.00	4.00	*56*
LOVELIEST NIGHT OF THE YEAR, THE/ La Donna E Mobile	*(RCA Victor 47-3300)*	1.50	6.00	*51*
SERNADE/My Destiny	*(RCA Victor 47-6478)*	1.00	4.00	*56*
VESTI LA GIUBBA/Ave Maria	*(RCA Victor 47-3228)*	1.50	6.00	*51*
LAPELS, The				
SNEAKIN' AROUND/Sneaky Blues	*(Melker 103)*	1.50	6.00	*60*
SNEAKIN' AROUND/Sneaky Blues	*(Dot 16129)*	.75	3.00	*60*
LARKS, The				
THERE IS A GIRL/Let's Drink A Toast	*(Sheryl 338)*	1.00	4.00	
LARKTONES, The				
NOSY NEIGHBORS/Why Are You Tearing Us Apart	*(Riki 140)*	2.00	8.00	
LAROCCA, Pat				
MY HEART BELONGS TO ONLY YOU/Cathy	*(Jan ell 1)*	.75	3.00	*60*
MY HEART BELONGS TO ONLY YOU/Cathy	*(Jan ell 6)*	.75	3.00	*60*
LA ROC, Dallan				
BEGINNING OF LOVE/	*(Arteen 711)*	.75	3.00	*61*
UNTIL/Margo	*(Arteen 102)*	.75	3.00	*61*

TITLE/FLIP	LABEL & NO.	GOOD	NEAR MINT	YR.
LA ROSA, Julius				
ANYWHERE I WONDER/This Is Heaven	*(Cadence 1230)*	1.25	5.00	*53*
DOMANI/Mama Rosa	*(Cadence 1265)*	1.00	4.00	*55*
EH CUMPARI/Till They've All Gone Home	*(Cadence 1232)*	1.25	5.00	*53*
GOOD LIFE, THE/	*(RCA 0938)*	.50	2.00	*73*
LIPSTICK & CANDY & RUBBER SOLE SHOES/ Winter In New England	*(RCA Victor 47-6416)*	1.00	4.00	*56*
SUDDENLY THERE'S A VALLEY/ Everytime That I Kiss Carrie	*(Cadence 1270)*	1.00	4.00	*55*
THIS IS ALL I HAD/Where Do I Go	*(Crewe 335)*	.50	2.00	*69*
LARRY & JOHNNY				
BEATLE TIME (PART 1)/Beatle Time (Part 2)	*(Jola 1000)*	1.25	5.00	*64*
LARRY & MIKE				
QUEEN OF THE STARLIGHT DANCE/We Fell In Love	*(Picadilly 500)*	1.25	5.00	
SO LONG LITTLE BUDDY/Little Ol' Love-Maker Me	*(Era 3135)*	.75	3.00	*64*
LARRY & THE LEGENDS				
DON'T PICK ON ME, BABY/The Creep	*(Atlantic 2220)*	2.00	8.00	*64*
(With the 4 Seasons)				
LARRY & THE STANDARDS				
MY LUCKY NIGHT/Where Is She	*(Laurie 3119)*	2.00	8.00	*62*
LARSON, Nicolette				
GIVE A LITTLE/Mexican Divorce	*(Warner Bros. 8851)*	.50	2.00	*79*
LET ME GO, LOVE/Trouble	*(Warner Bros. 49130)*	.50	2.00	*79*
LOTTA LOVE/Angels Rejoiced	*(Warner Bros. 8664)*	.50	2.00	*78*
RUHMBA GIRL/Last In Love	*(Warner Bros. 8795)*	.50	2.00	*79*
LAS VEGAS NIGHTS				
WHERE DO WE GO FROM HERE/ Free As The Wind	*(Magna-Gilde MGR-337)*	.50	2.00	*77*
LASSIES, The				
I LOOK AT YOU/Sleepy Head	*(Decca 9-29868)*	1.00	4.00	*56*
LAST WORD, The				
CAN'T STOP LOVING YOU/Don't Fight It	*(Atco 6498)*	.75	3.00	*67*
LATIN LADS, The				
NUNCA/School Is Over (By the Clif-Tones)	*(Clifton 15)*	.75	3.00	
LATONS, The				
SO IN LOVE/Love Me	*(Port 70030)*	1.00	4.00	*62*
LAUGHING DOGS, The				
GET 'EM OUT OF TOWN/Get Outa My Way	*(Columbia 11059)*	.50	2.00	*79*
REASON FOR LOVE/	*(Columbia 11108)*	.50	2.00	*79*
LAUGHING GRAVY: see Jan & Dean				
LAUGHING WIND				
DON'T TAKE VERY MUCH TO SEE TOMORROW/ Good To Be Around	*(Tower 266)*	.75	3.00	*66*
LAUREL & HARDY (Stan Laurel & Oliver Hardy)				
TRAIL OF THE LONESOME PINE, THE/Honolulu Baby	*(Mark 56 303)*	.50	2.00	*76*
LAURELS, The				
BABY TALK/You Left Me	*(Spring 1112)*	1.50	6.00	*60*
PICTURE OF LOVE/	*(ABC-Paramount 10048)*	2.00	8.00	*59*
LAUREN, Rod				
IF I HAD A GIRL/No Wonder	*(RCA Victor 47-7645)*	.75	3.00	*59*
LISTEN MY LOVE/This I Know	*(RCA Victor 47-7720)*	.75	3.00	*60*
LISTEN MY LOVE/This I Know	*(RCA Victor 47-7720)*	1.50	6.00	*60*
(Stereo single issue)				
LAURIE, Linda				
AMBROSE (PART 5)/Ooh! What A Lover	*(Glory 294)*	1.00	4.00	*59*
FOREVER AMBROSE/Wherever He Goes, I Go	*(Glory 294)*	1.50	6.00	*59*
PRINCE CHARMING/Soupin' Up Your Motor	*(Rust 5022)*	1.00	4.00	*62*
STAY AT HOME SUE (Answer song)/	*(Rust 5042)*	1.50	6.00	*62*
(With the Del-Satins)				
LAURIE SISTERS, The				
DIXIE DANNY/No Chance	*(Mercury 70548)*	1.00	4.00	*55*
GIVE ME ONE KISS/Shame On You Georgie	*(Vik 4X-0247)*	1.00	4.00	*56*
LAVELLS, The				
MIXED UP GIRL/Mama's Boy	*(Mercury 72186)*	.75	3.00	*63*

LAVENDERS, The

TITLE/FLIP	LABEL & NO.	GOOD	NEAR MINT	YR.
ANGEL/The Slide	(C.R. 103)	1.25	5.00	61
BELLS, THE/I Said Cook	(Lake 706)	1.50	6.00	61
ONE MORE TIME/One More Once	(Mercury 72126)	1.00	4.00	63

LAVERNE & SHIRLEY (Penny Marshall & Cindy Williams)

TITLE/FLIP	LABEL & NO.	GOOD	NEAR MINT	YR.
DA DO RON RON/Five Years ON	(Atlantic 3383)	.50	2.00	77
GRADUATION DAY/	(Atlantic 3406)	.50	2.00	77
SIXTEEN REASONS/Chapel Of Love	(Atlantic 3367)	.50	2.00	76

LAW

TITLE/FLIP	LABEL & NO.	GOOD	NEAR MINT	YR.
HOLD ON TO IT/Sun Won't Shine	(MCA 40807)	.50	2.00	77

LAW, Johnny, Four

TITLE/FLIP	LABEL & NO.	GOOD	NEAR MINT	YR.
CALL ON ME/There Ought To Be A Law	(Providence 419)	3.75	15.00	
SINCE I DON'T HAVE YOU/Underdog	(Providence 421)	3.75	15.00	

LAWRENCE, Bernie

TITLE/FLIP	LABEL & NO.	GOOD	NEAR MINT	YR.
COLLECTING GIRLS/That Was Yesterday	(United Artists UA-388)	1.50	6.00	61
Bernie is Steve Lawrence's brother.				

LAWRENCE, Bob

TITLE/FLIP	LABEL & NO.	GOOD	NEAR MINT	YR.
COME MY LITTLE BABY/Honey Dew	(Mark-X 7005)	1.00	4.00	

LAWRENCE, Eddie

TITLE/FLIP	LABEL & NO.	GOOD	NEAR MINT	YR.
DOCTOR'S PHILOSOPHER/Blackout Of 1984	(Signature 12010)	1.00	4.00	
OLD, OLD VIENNA (PART 1)/Old, Old Vienna (Part 2)	(Coral 61168)	1.25	5.00	54
OLD PHILOSOPHER, THE/King Arthur's Mines	(Coral 61671)	1.25	5.00	56

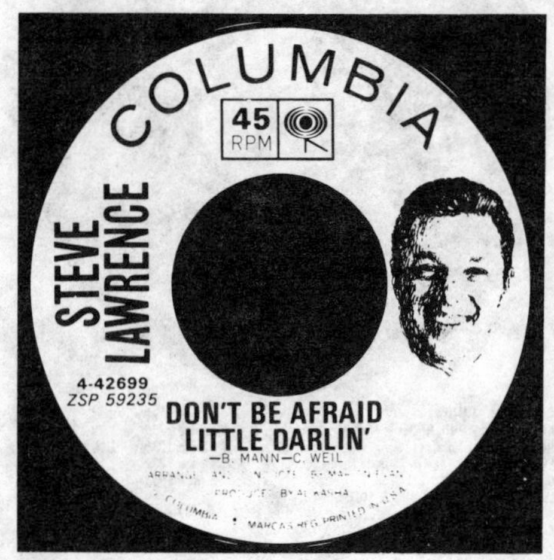

LAWRENCE, Steve (Steve Leibowitz)

TITLE/FLIP	LABEL & NO.	GOOD	NEAR MINT	YR.
BANANA BOAT SONG, THE/Long Before I Knew You	(Coral 61761)	1.00	4.00	57
CAN'T WAIT FOR SUMMER/Fabulous	(Coral 61834)	1.00	4.00	57
DON'T BE AFRAID, LITTLE DARLIN'/ Don't Come Running	(Columbia 4-42699)	.75	3.00	63
EVERYTHING WONDERFUL/ There'll Be Some Changes Made	(ABC-Paramount 10031)	.75	3.00	59
FOOTSTEPS/You Don't Know	(ABC-Paramount 10085)	.75	3.00	59
FRAULEIN/Blue Rememberin' You	(Coral 61876)	1.00	4.00	57
GO AWAY LITTLE GIRL/If You Love Her Tell Her So	(Columbia 4-42601)	.75	3.00	62
GIRLS, GIRLS, GIRLS/Little Boy Blue	(United Artists 233)	.75	3.00	60
GOING STEADY/Come Back Silly Girl	(ABC-Paramount 10146)	.75	3.00	60
HANSEL & GRETEL/Tears From Heaven	(United Artists 240)	.75	3.00	60
MANY A TIME/All About Love	(Coral 62025)	1.00	3.00	58
MY CLAIRE DE LUNE/In Time	(United Artists 335)	.75	3.00	61
PARTY DOLL/Pum-Pa-Lum	(Coral 61792)	1.00	4.00	57
POINCIANA/Never Leave Me	(King 15185)	.75	3.00	52
POOR LITTLE RICH GIRL/More	(Columbia 4-42795)	.75	3.00	63
PORTRAIT OF MY LOVE/Oh How You Lied	(United Artists 291)	.75	3.00	61
PRETTY BLUE EYES/You're Nearer	(ABC-Paramount 10058)	.75	3.00	59
SENTIMENTAL ME/You Can't Be True Dear	(ABC-Paramount 10008)	.75	3.00	59
SOMEWHERE ALONG THE WAY/ While There's Still Time	(United Artists 364)	.75	3.00	61
TEARS FROM HEAVEN/Hansel & Gretel	(United Artists 240)	.75	3.00	60

LAWRENCE, Steve, & Eydie Gorme

TITLE/FLIP	LABEL & NO.	GOOD	NEAR MINT	YR.
I CAN'T STOP TALKING ABOUT YOU/ To The Movies We Go	(Columbia 4-42932)	.75	3.00	63
I WANT TO STAY HERE/Ain't Love	(Columbia 4-42815)	.75	3.00	63
SENTIMENTAL ME/You Can't Be True Dear	(ABC-Paramount 10008)	.75	3.00	59
SENTIMENTAL ME/You Can't Be True Dear	(ABC-Paramount S-10008)	1.50	6.00	59
(Stereo single issue)				

LAWRENCE, Syd

TITLE/FLIP	LABEL & NO.	GOOD	NEAR MINT	YR.
ANSWER TO THE FLYING SAUCER, THE (Novelty)/ Haunted Guitar (Instrumental, by Billy Mure)	(Cosmic 1001/2)	1.50	6.00	

LAWRENCE, Vicki

TITLE/FLIP	LABEL & NO.	GOOD	NEAR MINT	YR.
HE DID WITH ME/	(Bell 45362)	.50	2.00	73
NIGHT THE LIGHTS WENT OUT IN GEORGIA, THE/ Dime A Dance	(Bell 45303)	.50	2.00	73
OTHER WOMAN, THE/Cameo	(Private Stock 45036)	.50	2.00	75
THERE'S A GUN STILL SMOKIN' IN NASHVILLE/	(Private Stock 45067)	.50	2.00	76

LAYMEN, The

TITLE/FLIP	LABEL & NO.	GOOD	NEAR MINT	YR.
PRACTICE WHAT YOU PREACH/Hey Joe	(Rise 101)	1.25	5.00	

LAYNE, Joy

TITLE/FLIP	LABEL & NO.	GOOD	NEAR MINT	YR.
YOUR WILD HEART/Dum-Dum	(Mercury 71038)	1.00	4.00	57

LAZY EGGS, The

TITLE/FLIP	LABEL & NO.	GOOD	NEAR MINT	YR.
I'M GONNA LOVE YOU/As Long as I Have You	(Enterprise 5060)	1.00	4.00	

LAZY RACER

TITLE/FLIP	LABEL & NO.	GOOD	NEAR MINT	YR.
KEEP ON RUNNING AWAY/Every Other Day	(A&M 2152)	.50	2.00	79

LAZY SUSANS, The

TITLE/FLIP	LABEL & NO.	GOOD	NEAR MINT	YR.
IF YOU LOVE ME/I Give In	(Kapp 741)	.75	3.00	66

L.B.J. & THE BIRDS

TITLE/FLIP	LABEL & NO.	GOOD	NEAR MINT	YR.
HELLO HELLO/Beat Bam	(Era 3180)	.75	3.00	67

L'CAPTANS

TITLE/FLIP	LABEL & NO.	GOOD	NEAR MINT	YR.
SAY YES/Home Work	(Savoy 1567)	1.00	4.00	59

LEACH, Billy

TITLE/FLIP	LABEL & NO.	GOOD	NEAR MINT	YR.
SONG OF THE BAREFOOT MAILMAN/Lils' Grill	(Bally 1039)	1.00	4.00	57

LEADON, BERNIE, MICHAEL GEORGIADES BAND, The

TITLE/FLIP	LABEL & NO.	GOOD	NEAR MINT	YR.
YOU'RE THE SINGER/As Time Goes On	(Asylum 45433)	.50	2.00	77
Bernie Leadon was also with the Eagles				

LEAPING FERNS, The

TITLE/FLIP	LABEL & NO.	GOOD	NEAR MINT	YR.
IT NEVER WORKS OUT FOR ME/Maybe Baby	(X-P-A-N-D-E-D Sound 103)	1.00	4.00	64

LEAPY LEE

TITLE/FLIP	LABEL & NO.	GOOD	NEAR MINT	YR.
I'LL BE YOUR BABY TONIGHT/Best To Forget	(Decca 32808)	.75	3.00	71
JUST ANOTHER NIGHT/My Advice To You	(MAM 3618)	.75	3.00	72
LITTLE ARROWS/Time Will Tell	(Decca 32380)	.75	3.00	68
LITTLE YELLOW AEROPLANE/ Boom Boom (That's How My Heart Beats)	(Decca 32492)	.75	3.00	70
SOMEONE'S IN LOVE/Best To Forget	(Decca 32584)	.75	3.00	69

LEASEBREAKERS, The

TITLE/FLIP	LABEL & NO.	GOOD	NEAR MINT	YR.
HELP/Gabrielle	(United Artists 937)	.75	3.00	65

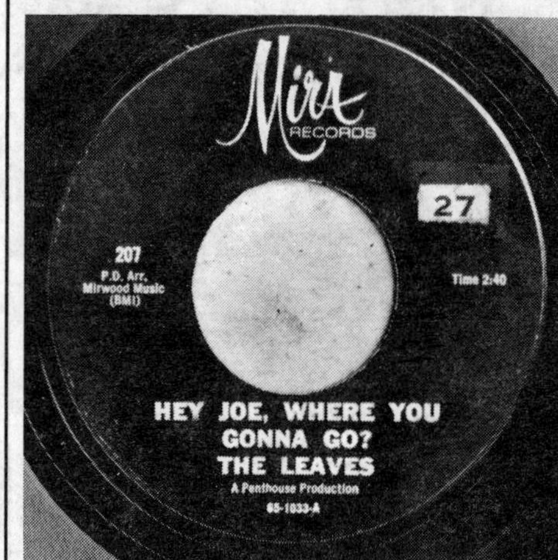

LEAVES, The

TITLE/FLIP	LABEL & NO.	GOOD	NEAR MINT	YR.
GET OUT OF MY LIFE WOMAN/Girl From The East	(Mira 231)	1.25	5.00	66
HEY JOE/Funny Little World	(Mira 222)	1.00	4.00	66
HEY JOE/Girl From The East	(Mira 222)	1.00	4.00	66
HEY JOE, WHERE YOU GONNA GO/Be With You	(Mira 207)	2.50	10.00	65
(Reissued on Mira 222 using the shorter title, "Hey Joe.")				
LEMON PRINCESS/Twilight Sanctuary	(Capitol 5799)	1.25	5.00	66
TOO MANY PEOPLE/Love Minus Zero	(Mira 202)	2.00	8.00	65
TOO MANY PEOPLE/Girl From The East	(Mira 227)	1.00	4.00	66
YOU BETTER MOVE ON/A Different Story	(Mira 213)	1.50	6.00	66
YOU BETTER MOVE ON/Be With You	(Mira 234)	1.25	5.00	66

LE BLANC & CARR (Lenny LeBlanc & Pete Carr)

TITLE/FLIP	LABEL & NO.	GOOD	NEAR MINT	YR.
FALLING/I Believe That We	(Big Tree 16100)	.50	2.00	77
MIDNIGHT LIGHT/How Does It Feel (To Be In Love)	(Big Tree 16114)	.50	2.00	78
SOMETHING ABOUT YOU/Coming & Going	(Big Tree 16092)	.50	2.00	77

LE BLANC, Lenny

TITLE/FLIP	LABEL & NO.	GOOD	NEAR MINT	YR.
AIN'T IT FUNNY/	(Big Tree 16073)	.50	2.00	76
HOUND DOG MAN (PLAY IT AGAIN)/ Sharing The Night Together	(Big Tree 16062)	.50	2.00	77
LADY SINGER/	(Big Tree 16077)	.50	2.00	76

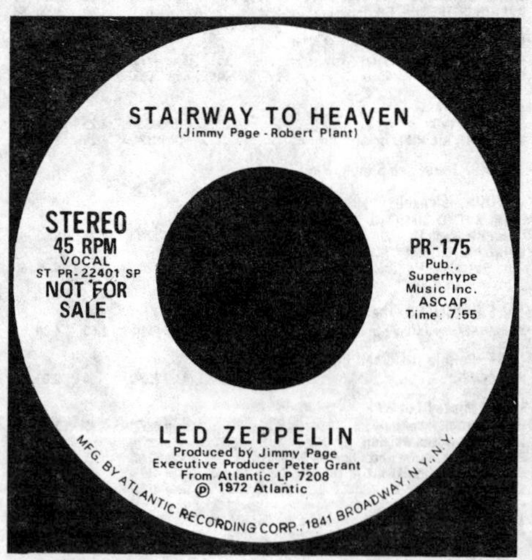

LED ZEPPELIN (Featuring Robert Plant & Jimmy Page)

TITLE/FLIP	LABEL & NO.	GOOD	NEAR MINT	YR.
BLACK DOG/Misty Mountain Hop	(Atlantic 2849)	.75	3.00	71
DAZED & CONFUSED/	(Atlantic 1019)	3.75	15.00	
D'YER MAK'ER/The Crunge	(Atlantic 2986)	.75	3.00	73
FOOL IN THE RAIN/Hot Dog	(Swan Song 71003)	.50	2.00	79
GOOD TIMES BAD TIMES/Communication Breakdown	(Atlantic 2613)	1.00	4.00	69
IMMIGRANT SONG/Hey, Hey, What Can I Do	(Atlantic 2777)	.75	3.00	70
OVER THE HILLS & FAR AWAY/Dancing Days	(Atlantic 2970)	.75	3.00	73
OVER THE HILLS & FAR AWAY (Stereo)/ Over The Hills & Far Away (Mono)	(Atlantic 2970)	1.25	5.00	73
(Promotional issue)				
ROCK & ROLL/Four Sticks	(Atlantic 2865)	.75	3.00	72
ROCK & ROLL (Stereo)/Rock & Roll (Mono)	(Atlantic 2865)	1.25	5.00	72
(Promotional issue)				
ROYAL ORLEANS/Candy Store Rock	(Swan Song 70110)	.50	2.00	77
STAIRWAY TO HEAVEN (Stereo)/ Stairway To Heaven (Mono)	(Atlantic PR-175)	7.50	30.00	72
(Promotional issue only. Atlantic sampler with the 7:55 version on both sides.)				
STAIRWAY TO HEAVEN (Stereo)/ Stairway To Heaven (Mono)	(Atlantic PR-175)	12.50	50.00	72
(Promotional sleeve for the Atlantic sampler.)				
STAIRWAY TO HEAVEN (Stereo)/ Stairway To Heaven (Mono)	(Atlantic PR-269)	6.25	25.00	72
(Promotional issue only, with 7:55 version.)				
TRAMPLED UNDERFOOT/Black Country Woman	(Swan Song 70102)	.50	2.00	74
WHOLE LOTTA LOVE/ Living Loving Maid (She's Just A Woman)	(Atlantic 2690)	.75	3.00	69
WHOLE LOTTA LOVE (Long version)/ Whole Lotta Love (Short version)	(Atlantic 2690)	1.25	5.00	69
(Promotional issue)				

LEDO, Les

TITLE/FLIP	LABEL & NO.	GOOD	NEAR MINT	YR.
SCARLET ANGEL/Don't Fight	(Shell 721)	7.50	30.00	60

LEE, Albert (Of Head, Hands & Feet)

TITLE/FLIP	LABEL & NO.	GOOD	NEAR MINT	YR.
COUNTRY BOY/Setting Me Up	(A&M 2150)	.50	2.00	79
Also see Crickets, The				

LEE, Alvin & Mylon LeFevre

TITLE/FLIP	LABEL & NO.	GOOD	NEAR MINT	YR.
SO SAD (NO LOVE OF HIS OWN)/Riffin	(Columbia 4-45987)	.50	2.00	74
(With George Harrison on guitar)				

LEE, Alvin, & Ten Years Later (Formerly Ten Years After)

TITLE/FLIP	LABEL & NO.	GOOD	NEAR MINT	YR.
RIDE ON COWBOY/Can't Sleep At Nite	(RSO 936)	.50	2.00	79
Also see Lee, Alvin & Mylon LeFevre				

LEE & LOWE

TITLE/FLIP	LABEL & NO.	GOOD	NEAR MINT	YR.
HOUND DOG MAN'S GONE HOME/Living Without You	(Music Mill 1011)	.50	2.00	77

LEE & PAUL (Lee Pockriss & Paul Vance)

TITLE/FLIP	LABEL & NO.	GOOD	NEAR MINT	YR.
CHICK, THE/Valentina, My Valentina	(Columbia 4-41337)	.75	3.00	59

LEE, Arthur

TITLE/FLIP	LABEL & NO.	GOOD	NEAR MINT	YR.
NINTH WAVE, THE/Rumble-Still-Skins	(Capitol 4980)	1.00	4.00	63
(Instrumental)				

LEE, Arthur (Of Love)

TITLE/FLIP	LABEL & NO.	GOOD	NEAR MINT	YR.
EVERYBODY'S GOTTA LIVE/ Love Jumped Through My Window	(A&M 1361)	.50	2.00	72
SAD SONG/You Want Change For Your Rerun	(A&M 1381)	.50	2.00	72

LEE, Brenda (Brenda Mae Tarpley)

TITLE/FLIP	LABEL & NO.	GOOD	NEAR MINT	YR.
AIN'T GONNA CRY NO MORE/It Takes One To Know One	(Decca 31970)	.75	3.00	66
ALL ALONE AM I/Save All Your Lovin' For Me	(Decca 31424)	.75	3.00	63
ALONE WITH YOU/My Dreams	(Decca 31628)	.75	3.00	64
ALWAYS ON MY MIND/That Ain't Right	(Decca 32975)	.75	3.00	72
AS USUAL/Lonely Lonely Lonely Me	(Decca 31570)	.75	3.00	63
BILL BAILEY, WON'T YOU PLEASE COME HOME/ Hummin' The Blues Over You	(Decca 30806)	1.25	5.00	59
BREAK IT TO ME GENTLY/So Deep	(Decca 31348)	.75	3.00	62
CABARET/Mood Indigo	(Decca 32299)	.75	3.00	68
(With Pete Fountain)				
COMING ON STRONG/You Keep Coming Back To Me	(Decca 32018)	.75	3.00	66
DO RIGHT WOMAN, DO RIGHT MAN/Sisters In Sorrow	(Decca 32734)	.75	3.00	70
DUM DUM/Eventually	(Decca 31272)	.75	3.00	61
DYNAMITE/Love You Till I Die	(Decca 30333)	1.50	6.00	57
EACH DAY IS A RAINBOW/Kansas City	(Decca 32330)	.75	3.00	68
EMOTIONS/I'm Learning About Love	(Decca 31195)	.75	3.00	60
EVERYBODY LOVES ME BUT YOU/ Here Comes That Feeling	(Decca 31379)	.75	3.00	62
FOOL #1/Anybody But Me	(Decca 31309)	.75	3.00	61
GRASS IS GREENER, THE/Sweet Impossible You	(Decca 31539)	.75	3.00	63
HEART IN HAND/It Started All Over Again	(Decca 31407)	.75	3.00	62
I WANT TO BE WANTED/Just A Little	(Decca 31149)	.75	3.00	60
IF THIS IS OUR LAST TIME/ Everybody's Reaching Out For Someone	(Decca 32848)	.75	3.00	71
I'M GONNA LASSO SANTA CLAUS/Christy Christmas	(Decca 88215)	2.50	10.00	56
(Issued in Decca's Children's Series, Shown as by "Little Brenda Lee, 9 Years Old.")				
I'M GONNA LASSO SANTA CLAUS/Christy Christmas	(Decca 30107)	1.25	5.00	56
I'M SORRY/That's All You Gotta Do	(Decca 31093)	.75	3.00	60
IS IT TRUE/Just Behind The Rainbow	(Decca 31690)	.75	3.00	64
I THINK I LOVE YOU AGAIN/Hello Love	(Decca 32675)	.75	3.00	70
JAMBALAYA/Bigelow 6-200 (Black label)	(Decca 30050)	5.00	20.00	56
JAMBALAYA/Bigelow 6-200 (Multi-color label)	(Decca 30050)	1.50	6.00	60
JINGLE BELL ROCK/Winter Wonderland	(Decca 31687)	1.00	4.00	64
JOHNNY ONE TIME/I Must Have Been Out Of My Mind	(Decca 32428)	.75	3.00	69
LET IT BE ME/You Better Move On	(Decca 32560)	.75	3.00	69
LET'S JUMP THE BROOMSTICK/Some Of These Days	(Decca 30885)	2.50	10.00	59
LOSING YOU/He's So Heavenly	(Decca 31478)	.75	3.00	63
MY WHOLE WORLD IS FALLING DOWN/I Wonder	(Decca 31510)	.75	3.00	63
ONE STEP AT A TIME/Fairyland	(Decca 30198)	1.25	5.00	57
ONE TEENAGER TO ANOTHER/Ain't That Love	(Decca 30411)	1.25	5.00	57
OPEN-END INTERVIEW WITH BRENDA LEE (PART 1)/ Open-End Interview With Brenda Lee (Part 2)	(Decca 34370)	1.25	5.00	72
(Promotional issue only)				
RIDE, RIDE, RIDE/Lonely People Do Foolish Things	(Decca 32079)	.75	3.00	67
RING-A MY PHONE/ Little Jonah (Rock On Your Steel Guitar)	(Decca 30673)	1.50	6.00	58
(Side 1: with the Jordanaires. Side 2: with the Anita Kerr Singers)				
ROCK-A-BYE-BABY BLUES/Dance The Bop	(Decca 30535)	2.50	10.00	58
ROCK-A-BYE-BABY BLUES/Dance The Bop	(Decca 30535)	3.75	15.00	58
(Green label promotional issue)				
ROCKIN' AROUND THE CHRISTMAS TREE/Papa Noel	(Decca 30776)	.75	3.00	60
RUSTY BELLS/If You Don't	(Decca 31849)	.75	3.00	65
SWEET NOTHIN'S/Weep No More My Baby	(Decca 30967)	1.50	6.00	59
SWEET NOTHIN'S/Weep No More My Baby	(Decca 30967)	5.00	20.00	59
(Picture sleeve)				
TAKE ME/Born To Be By Your Side	(Decca 32119)	.75	3.00	67
THANKS A LOT/Crying Game, The	(Decca 31728)	.75	3.00	64
THAT'S ALL RIGHT/Fantasy	(Decca 32248)	.75	3.00	68
THINK/Waiting Game, The	(Decca 31599)	.75	3.00	64
THIS TIME OF THE YEAR/ Christmas Will Be Just Another Lonely Day	(Decca 31688)	.75	3.00	64
TOO LITTLE TIME/Time & Time Again	(Decca 31917)	.75	3.00	66

Jamie Lyons

John Lennon

(Just Like) Starting Over

Produced by John Lennon, Yoko Ono and Jack Douglas

John Lennon & Yoko Ono

MICHAEL LANDON

STAR OF TELEVISION AND MOTION PICTURES

"GIMME A LITTLE KISS" (Will "Ya" Huh)

"BE PATIENT WITH ME"

FG-1240

FONO GRAF RECORDS INC.

Trini Lopez

TITLE/FLIP	LABEL & NO.	GOOD	NEAR MINT	YR.
TOO MANY RIVERS/No One	(Decca 31792)	.75	3.00	65
TRULY TRULY TRUE/I Still Miss Someone	(Decca 31762)	.75	3.00	65
WHEN YOU LOVED ME/He's Sure To Remember Me	(Decca 31654)	.75	3.00	64
WHERE LOVE IS/My Heart Keeps Hanging On	(Decca 32161)	.75	3.00	67
WHERE'S IS THE MELODY/Save Me For A Rainy Day	(Decca 32213)	.75	3.00	67
YOU CAN DEPEND ON ME/It's Never Too Late	(Decca 31231)	.75	3.00	61
YOU DON'T NEED ME FOR ANYTHING ANYMORE/ Bring Me Sunshine	(Decca 32491)	.75	3.00	69
YOUR USED TO BE/She'll Never Know	(Decca 31454)	.75	3.00	63

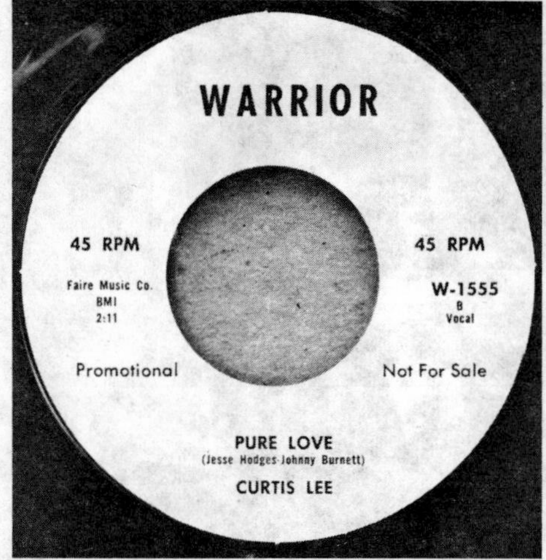

LEE, Curtis

TITLE/FLIP	LABEL & NO.	GOOD	NEAR MINT	YR.
AFRAID/Mary Go Round	(Dunes 2017)	1.00	4.00	62
CALIFORNIA GL-903/Then I'll Know	(Dunes 801)	2.00	8.00	60
I NEVER KNEW WHAT LOVE COULD DO/Gotta Have You	(Hot 7)	3.75	15.00	60
I'M SORRY/That's What's Happening	(Dunes 2023)	1.00	4.00	63
JUST ANOTHER FOOL/A Night At Daddy Gee's	(Dunes 2012)	1.00	4.00	62
LET'S TAKE A RIDE/I'm Asking Forgiveness	(Sabra 517)	2.50	10.00	61
LET'S TAKE A RIDE/I'm Asking Forgiveness	(Dunes 2010)	1.25	5.00	61
LONELY WEEKENDS/Better Him Than Me	(Dunes 2020)	1.00	4.00	63
PICKIN' UP THE PIECES OF MY HEART/Mr. Mistaker	(Dunes 2021)	1.00	4.00	63
PLEDGE OF LOVE/Then I'll Know	(Dunes 2003)	1.00	4.00	61
PRETTY LITTLE ANGEL EYES/Gee How I Wish	(Dunes 2007)	1.00	4.00	61
SPECIAL LOVE/D-in Love	(Dunes 2001)	1.25	5.00	60
UNDER THE MOON OF LOVE/Beverly Jean	(Dunes 2008)	1.00	4.00	61
WITH ALL MY HEART/Pure Love	(Warrior 1555)	3.75	15.00	60
WOBBLE, THE/Does He Mean That Much To You	(Dunes 2015)	1.00	4.00	62

LEE, Dick

TITLE/FLIP	LABEL & NO.	GOOD	NEAR MINT	YR.
OH MEIN PAPA/There's No Forgetting You	(Blue Bell 503)	.75	3.00	61

LEE, Dickie

TITLE/FLIP	LABEL & NO.	GOOD	NEAR MINT	YR.
BIG BROTHER/She's Walking Away	(TCF Hall 1924)	.75	3.00	64
DICKIE LEE STORY, THE (PART 1)/ The Dickie Lee Story (Part 2) (Probably a promotional release only, although no information is given on the label. Contains an excerpt of Elvis Presley's "She Thinks I Still Care" which was written by Dickie Lee.)	(No label or number given)	2.50	10.00	76
DON'T WANNA THINK ABOUT PAULA/Just A Friend	(Smash 1808)	.75	3.00	63
GIRL FROM PEYTON PLACE, THE/ The Girl I Used To Know	(TCF Hall 111)	.75	3.00	65
GOOD GIRL GOIN' BAD/Pretty White Dress	(TCF 118)	.75	3.00	65
GOOD LOVIN'/Memories Never Grow Old	(Sun 280)	1.25	5.00	57
I GET LONELY/Ten Million Faces	(Smash 1822)	.75	3.00	63
I SAW LINDA YESTERDAY/Girl I Can't Forget	(Smash 1791)	.75	3.00	62
LAURIE (STRANGE THINGS HAPPEN)/Party Doll	(TCF Hall 102)	1.00	4.00	65
LIFE IN A TEENAGE WORLD/Why Don't You Write Me	(Dot 16087)	1.25	5.00	60
ME & MY TEARDROPS/Only Trust In Me	(Smash 1913)	.75	3.00	64
MOTHER NATURE/To The Aisle	(Smash 1871)	.75	3.00	64
PATCHES/More Or Less	(Smash 1758)	.75	3.00	62
RED, GREEN, YELLOW & BLUE/Run Right Back	(Atco 6546)	.75	3.00	68
SHE WANTS TO BE BOBBY'S GIRL/ Day The Sawmill Closed Down	(Smash 1844)	.75	3.00	63
STAY TRUE BABY/Dream Boy	(Tampa 45-TP 131)	3.75	15.00	
TRUTH FROM MY EYES/Walk	(Tracie 2002)	.75	3.00	
YOU'RE YOUNG & YOU'LL FORGET/ Waitin' For Love To Come My Way	(Atco 6609)	.75	3.00	68

LEE, James Washington

TITLE/FLIP	LABEL & NO.	GOOD	NEAR MINT	YR.
I NEED SOMEBODY/Don't Ask Me	(L&M 1003)	1.00	4.00	

LEE, Jimmy, & The Earls

TITLE/FLIP	LABEL & NO.	GOOD	NEAR MINT	YR.
IF I COULD DO IT ONCE AGAIN/Daddy's Home	(Bo-P-C 100)	1.00	4.00	

LEE, Kui

TITLE/FLIP	LABEL & NO.	GOOD	NEAR MINT	YR.
I'LL REMEMBER YOU/Rain Rain Go Away	(Columbia 4-43776)	.75	3.00	66

LEE, Larry

TITLE/FLIP	LABEL & NO.	GOOD	NEAR MINT	YR.
LITTLE LANA/Stood Up (With Frankie Valli)	(Genius 2100)	1.50	6.00	

LEE, Leapy: see Leapy Lee

LEE, Michelle

TITLE/FLIP	LABEL & NO.	GOOD	NEAR MINT	YR.
I CAN'T BELIEVE I'M LOSING YOU/I Didn't Come To New York To Meet A Guy From My Home Town	(Columbia 4-44554)	.75	3.00	69
L. DAVID SLOANE/Everybody Loves My Baby (But My Baby Don't Love Nobody But Me)	(Columbia 4-44413)	.75	3.00	68

LEE, Myron

TITLE/FLIP	LABEL & NO.	GOOD	NEAR MINT	YR.
BABY SITTIN'/Come Back Baby	(Keen 82104)	1.00	4.00	59

LEE, Peggy

TITLE/FLIP	LABEL & NO.	GOOD	NEAR MINT	YR.
ALRIGHT, OKAY, YOU WIN/My Man	(Capitol 4115)	1.00	4.00	59
FEVER/You Don't Know	(Capitol 3998)	1.00	4.00	58
IS THAT ALL THERE IS/Me & My Shadow	(Capitol 2602)	.50	2.00	69
LET'S LOVE/Always	(Atlantic 3215)	.50	2.00	74
LOVER/You Go To My Head (With Gordon Jenkins)	(Decca 28215)	1.25	5.00	52
MR. WONDERFUL/Crazy In The Heart	(Decca 29834)	1.25	5.00	56

LEE, Perk

TITLE/FLIP	LABEL & NO.	GOOD	NEAR MINT	YR.
PEANUT BUTTER SANDWICH/The Docks	(Boss 2125)	1.25	5.00	

LEE, Randy

TITLE/FLIP	LABEL & NO.	GOOD	NEAR MINT	YR.
GOODBYE MARY ANN/ Like The Feller & The Girl On The Late Show	(Philips 40006)	.75	3.00	61
IGMOO/It Could Have Been Me	(Philips 40063)	.75	3.00	62
LA DO DA DA/Keep The Hall Light Burning	(Philips 40089)	.75	3.00	63

LEE, Terri, & The Swinging 7 Colossal Cimmunicators Chorus

TITLE/FLIP	LABEL & NO.	GOOD	NEAR MINT	YR.
PHOENIX, MY HOME TOWN/Funlovin' Phoenix	(Shamrock 7777777)	.75	3.00	

LEE, Veronica, & The Moniques

TITLE/FLIP	LABEL & NO.	GOOD	NEAR MINT	YR.
RINGO DID IT/Foreign Boy	(Centaur 106)	1.25	5.00	64

LEE, Wally, & The Storms

TITLE/FLIP	LABEL & NO.	GOOD	NEAR MINT	YR.
EENY MEENY/I Never Felt This Way	(Sundown 122)	1.25	5.00	59

LEEN TEENS, The

TITLE/FLIP	LABEL & NO.	GOOD	NEAR MINT	YR.
SO SHY/Dream Around You	(Imperial 5593)	1.00	4.00	59

LEERICS, The

TITLE/FLIP	LABEL & NO.	GOOD	NEAR MINT	YR.
ISLAND OF LOVE/Hey Patty	(Un-Released Gold 799)	1.00	4.00	

LE FEVRE, Mylon

TITLE/FLIP	LABEL & NO.	GOOD	NEAR MINT	YR.
BETTER COME BACK/	(Warner Bros. 8764)	.50	2.00	78
MAMA, YOU BEEN ON MY MIND/Kickin'	(Columbia 4-45671)	1.00	4.00	70
ROWENA/	(Warner Bros. 8673)	.50	2.00	78
SECOND HAND LADY/	(Warner Bros. 8468)	.50	2.00	77

LE FEVRE, Raymond, & His Orchestra

TITLE/FLIP	LABEL & NO.	GOOD	NEAR MINT	YR.
DAY THE RAINS CAME, THE/Butterfingers	(Kapp 231)	.75	3.00	58
SOUL COAXING (AME CALINE)/ If I Were A Carpenter (Instrumentals)	(Four Corners of the World 147)	.50	2.00	68

LEFT BANKE, The (Featuring Michael Brown)

TITLE/FLIP	LABEL & NO.	GOOD	NEAR MINT	YR.
AND SUDDENLY/Ivy, Ivy	(Smash 2089)	.75	3.00	67
BARTENDERS & THEIR WIVES/ She May Call You Up Tonight	(Smash 2197)	.75	3.00	67
DESIREE/I've Got Something On My Mind	(Smash 2119)	.75	3.00	67
PRETTY BALLERINA/Lazy Day	(Smash 2074)	.75	3.00	66
WALK AWAY RENEE/I Haven't Got The Nerve	(Smash 2041)	.75	3.00	66

LEGEND, Tom

TITLE/FLIP	LABEL & NO.	GOOD	NEAR MINT	YR.
WHERE I BELONG/I'm Always Chasing Rainbows	(Colpix 619)	1.00	4.00	62

LEGENDARY MASKED SURFERS, The

TITLE/FLIP	LABEL & NO.	GOOD	NEAR MINT	YR.
SUMMER MEANS FUN/Gonna Hustle You	(United Artists 270)	2.00	8.00	73
SUMMER MEANS FUN/Gonna Hustle You (Picture sleeve)	(United Artists 270)	5.00	20.00	73
SUMMERTIME SUMMERTIME/Gonne Hustle You	(United Artists 50958)	2.50	10.00	72

Also see Beach Boys, The
Also see Jan & Dean

LEGENDARY STARDUST COWBOY, The

TITLE/FLIP	LABEL & NO.	GOOD	NEAR MINT	YR.
DOWN IN THE WRECKING YARD/ I Took A Trip On A Gemini Spaceship	(Mercury 72891)	1.25	5.00	69
EVERYTHING'S GETTIN' BIGGER BUT OUR LOVE/ Kiss & Run	(Mercury 72912)	1.25	5.00	69
WHO'S KNOCKING ON MY DOOR/Paralyzed	(Psycho-Sauve' PS-1033)	2.50	10.00	68
WHO'S KNOCKING ON MY DOOR/Paralyzed	(Mercury 72862)	1.25	5.00	68

LEGENDS, The

TITLE/FLIP	LABEL & NO.	GOOD	NEAR MINT	YR.
I'M JUST A GUY/	(Fenton 2512)	1.00	4.00	

LEGENDS, The

TITLE/FLIP	LABEL & NO.	GOOD	NEAR MINT	YR.
SURF'S UP/Dance With The Drummer Man	(Doc Holiday 107)	1.00	4.00	63

LEGENDS, The

TITLE/FLIP	LABEL & NO.	GOOD	NEAR MINT	YR.
ROCK & ROLL WOMAN/	(Epic 10937)	.50	2.00	73

LEGGERIORS, The

TITLE/FLIP	LABEL & NO.	GOOD	NEAR MINT	YR.
FLAME OF LOVE/Justine	(Goliath 1351)	.75	3.00	63

LEGS DIAMOND

TITLE/FLIP	LABEL & NO.	GOOD	NEAR MINT	YR.
HELP WANTED/	(Cream 7937)	.50	2.00	79
YOU'VE LOST THAT LOVIN' FEELIN'/	(Cream 7831)	.50	2.00	78

LEHMAN, Billy, & The Penn-Man

TITLE/FLIP	LABEL & NO.	GOOD	NEAR MINT	YR.
FIRST SIGN OF LOVE/Audrey	(Arp 14)	1.25	5.00	

LEHMAN, John

TITLE/FLIP	LABEL & NO.	GOOD	NEAR MINT	YR.
ROSY/Be All Your Own	(Mercury 73352)	.50	2.00	72

Lehman was a back-up singer on Linda Ronstadt's "Living In The U.S.A." LP.

LEHMANN, Frankie

TITLE/FLIP	LABEL & NO.	GOOD	NEAR MINT	YR.
LONG DAY'S FIGHT, A/Nickita's Lament	(VJM 4424)	2.00	8.00	

LEIBER-STOLLER ORCH., The (Jerry Leiber & Mike Stoller)

TITLE/FLIP	LABEL & NO.	GOOD	NEAR MINT	YR.
CAFE ESPRESSO/Blue Baion	(United Artists 441)	.75	3.00	61

LEIGH BELL & THE CHIMES

TITLE/FLIP	LABEL & NO.	GOOD	NEAR MINT	YR.
TERRY/Eternity	(Rust 5031)	.75	3.00	62

LEIGHTON, Bernie

TITLE/FLIP	LABEL & NO.	GOOD	NEAR MINT	YR.
DON'T BREAK THE HEART THAT LOVES YOU/ Till You Return (Instrumental)	(Colpix 645)	.75	3.00	62

LEISURE LADS, The

TITLE/FLIP	LABEL & NO.	GOOD	NEAR MINT	YR.
BABY, I'M ALL ALONE/A Teenage Memory	(Delco 801)	1.50	6.00	

LEMAIRE, Eddie

TITLE/FLIP	LABEL & NO.	GOOD	NEAR MINT	YR.
YOU & I AGAINST THE WORLD/I Want You	(MCI 103)	1.00	4.00	60

LEMON DROPS, The

TITLE/FLIP	LABEL & NO.	GOOD	NEAR MINT	YR.
CUTE LITTLE WIGGLE/Lo-o-ve	(Coral 62145)	1.00	4.00	59

LEMON PIPERS, The (Featuring Ivan Browne)

TITLE/FLIP	LABEL & NO.	GOOD	NEAR MINT	YR.
BLUEBERRY BLUE/Blueberry Blue (Promotional issue only)	(Buddah 31)	1.00	4.00	68
GREEN TAMBOURINE/No Help From Me	(Buddah 23)	.75	3.00	67
JELLY JUNGLE (OF ORANGE MARMALADE)/ Here I Go	(Buddah 41)	.75	3.00	68
LONELY ATMOSPHERE/Wine & Violet	(Buddah 63)	.75	3.00	69
RICE IS NICE/Blueberry Blue	(Buddah 31)	.75	3.00	68
TURN AROUND & TAKE A LOOK/Danger	(Buddah 11)	.75	3.00	67

LENDELLS, The (The Lydells)

TITLE/FLIP	LABEL & NO.	GOOD	NEAR MINT	YR.
(DON'T BE A) LITTERBUG/Maryann	(Reach 2)	18.75	75.00	

LENNON, Freddie

TITLE/FLIP	LABEL & NO.	GOOD	NEAR MINT	YR.
THAT'S MY LIFE (MY LOVE & MY HOME)/ The Next Time You Feel Important	(Jerden 792)	2.00	8.00	65

Freddie is John Lennon's father.

LENNON, John, (Of The Beatles)

TITLE/FLIP	LABEL & NO.	GOOD	NEAR MINT	YR.
AIN'T THAT A SHAME/Ain't That A Shame (Promotional issue only)	(Apple 1883)	15.00	60.00	
COLD TURKEY/Don't Worry Kyoko (Mummy's Only Looking For A Hand In The Snow)	(Apple 1813)	.75	3.00	69
COLD TURKEY/Cold Turkey (Promotional issue)	(Apple 1813)	2.00	8.00	69
COLD TURKEY/Don't Worry Kyoko (Mummy's Only Looking For A Hand In The Snow) (Picture sleeve)	(Apple 1813)	15.00	60.00	69
GIVE PEACE A CHANCE/Remember Love	(Apple 1809)	.75	3.00	69
GIVE PEACE A CHANCE/Give Peace A Chance (Promotional issue)	(Apple 1809)	2.00	8.00	69
GIVE PEACE A CHANCE/Remember Love (Picture sleeve)	(Apple 1809)	5.00	20.00	69
HAPPY XMAS (WAR IS OVER)/Listen, The Snow Is Falling	(Apple 1842)	.75	3.00	71
HAPPY XMAS (WAR IS OVER)/Listen, The Snow Is Falling (With "faces" label)	(Apple 1842)	.50	2.00	71
HAPPY XMAS (WAR IS OVER)/Happy Xmas (War Is Over) (Promotional issue)	(Apple 1842)	1.50	6.00	71
HAPPY XMAS (WAR IS OVER)/Listen, The Snow Is Falling (Picture sleeve)	(Apple 1842)	2.00	8.00	71
IMAGINE/It's So Hard (Green label)	(Apple 1840)	.75	3.00	71
IMAGINE/It's So Hard (Brown label)	(Apple 1840)	1.50	6.00	71
IMAGINE/It's So Hard (Promotional issue)	(Apple 1840)	1.50	6.00	71
INSTANT KARMA (WE ALL SHINE ON)/ Who Has Seen The Wind	(Apple 1818)	.75	3.00	70
INSTANT KARMA (WE ALL SHINE ON)/ Instant Karma (We All Shine On) (Promotional issue)	(Apple 1818)	2.00	8.00	70
INSTANT KARMA (WE ALL SHINE ON)/ (One-sided promotional issue)	(Apple 1818)	50.00	200.00	70
INSTANT KARMA (WE ALL SHINE ON)/ Who Has Seen The Wind (Picture sleeve)	(Apple 1818)	3.75	15.00	70
(JUST LIKE) STARTING OVER/Kiss Kiss Kiss	(Geffen 49604)	.50	2.00	80
(JUST LIKE) STARTING OVER/(Just Like) Starting Over (Promotional issue)	(Geffen 49604)	2.50	10.00	80
(JUST LIKE) STARTING OVER/Kiss Kiss Kiss (Picture sleeve)	(Geffen 49604)	.50	2.00	80
MIND GAMES/Meat City	(Apple 1868)	.50	2.00	73
MIND GAMES/Mind Games (Promotional issue)	(Apple 1868)	1.00	4.00	73
MIND GAMES/Meat City (Picture sleeve)	(Apple 1868)	.75	3.00	73
MOTHER/Why	(Apple 1827)	1.25	5.00	70
MOTHER/Mother (Promotional issue)	(Apple 1827)	2.50	10.00	70
MOTHER/Why (Picture sleeve)	(Apple 1827)	3.75	15.00	70
#9 DREAM/What You Got	(Apple 1878)	.50	2.00	74
#9 DREAM/#9 Dream (Promotional issue)	(Apple 1878)	.75	3.00	74
POWER TO THE PEOPLE/Touch Me	(Apple 1830)	.75	3.00	71
POWER TO THE PEOPLE/Power To The People (Promotional issue)	(Apple 1830)	2.00	8.00	71
POWER TO THE PEOPLE/Touch Me (Picture sleeve)	(Apple 1830)	2.50	10.00	71
SLIPPIN & SLIDIN/Slippin & Slidin (Promotional issue only)	(Apple 1883)	15.00	60.00	74
STAND BY ME/More Over Ms. L	(Apple 1881)	.50	2.00	75
STAND BY ME/Stand By Me (Promotional issue)	(Apple 1881)	.75	3.00	75
STAND BY ME/Woman Is The Nigger Of The World	(Capitol 6244)	.50	2.00	77
WHATEVER GETS YOU THROUGH THE NIGHT/ Beef Jerky	(Apple 1874)	.50	2.00	74
WHATEVER GETS YOU THROUGH THE NIGHT/ Whatever Gets You Through The Night (Promotional issue)	(Apple 1874)	1.50	6.00	74
WOMAN IS THE NIGGER OF THE WORLD/ Sisters O Sisters	(Apple 1848)	.50	2.00	72
WOMAN IS THE NIGGER OF THE WORLD/ Woman Is The Nigger Of The World (Promotional issue)	(Apple 1848)	1.50	6.00	72
WOMAN IS THE NIGGER OF THE WORLD/ Sisters O Sisters (Picture sleeve)	(Apple 1848)	.75	3.00	72

Also see John, Elton
Also see Elliot, Bill & The Elastic Oz Band
Also see Ono, Yoko, & The Plastic Ono Band

ITLE/FLIP	LABEL & NO.	GOOD	NEAR MINT	YR.
ENNON, John & Ronnie Hawkins				
OHN LENNON ON RONNIE HAWKINS, THE LONG RAP/John Lennon On Ronnie Hawkins, The Short Rap & Down The Alley	(Cotillion 105)	5.00	20.00	70
(Promotional issue only. This record has now been conterfeited.)				
ENNON, Kipp				
ONG FROM "BUCK ROGERS" (SUSPENSION)/ Cloudy Morning	(MCA 41026)	.50	2.00	79
Kipp is a brother of the Lennon Sisters.				
ENNON SISTERS (Peggy, Kathy, Janet, Dianne)				
AD MOVIES (MAKE ME CRY)/I Don't Know Why	(Dot 16255)	.75	3.00	61
ONIGHT YOU BELONG TO ME/ When The Lilacs Bloom Again	(Coral 61701)	1.00	4.00	56
(With Lawrence Welk & his orchestra)				
ENNY & THE CHIMES				
ARADISE/My Love	(Tag 450)	1.00	4.00	61
WO TIMES TWO/Only Forever	(Vee Jay 605)	.75	3.00	64
Also see Chimes, The				
ENNY & THE CONTINENTALS				
ITTLE JOE & LINDA LEE/The Shuck	(Tribute 119)	.75	3.00	63
EO & THE DUETS				
OWN THE AISLE/Goodnight Sweetheart	(Co-op 514)	.75	3.00	
EOLA & LOVEJOYS				
E AIN'T NO ANGEL/Wait Round The Corner	(Tiger 101)	.75	3.00	
EON & THE METRONOMES				
UY THIS RECORD FOR ME/ I'll Catch You On The Rebound	(Carnival 515)	1.00	4.00	66
EONARD, Ben				
ONGO BONGO/Little Girl	(Reo 1458)	.75	3.00	
EONARD, Bobby, & The Explorers				
ROJECT VENUS/Rockin' Ship	(Unity 2114)	2.50	10.00	
(Novelty/Break-in)				
EONETTI, Tommy				
REE/It's Wild	(Capitol 3442)	1.00	4.00	56
EARTLESS/Sometime	(Capitol 3274)	1.00	4.00	55
OUL DANCE/Somebody Loves You	(RCA Victor 47-8251)	.75	3.00	63
WITHOUT LOVE/Blue Bird Of Happiness	(Atlantic 45-2065)	.75	3.00	60
EROUX, Kelly				
MY LITTLE GIRL'S PRAYER (FOR ELVIS)/ Wallisville County Jail	(King's International 5099)	.50	2.00	77
EROY & THE ROCKY FELLERS				
NFINISHED FIFTH/River Wide	(Cameo 194)	.75	3.00	61
EROY & WALLY				
OCK-A-DOODLE REVEILLE/It's Paris	(Carlton 500)	1.00	4.00	59
ES COMPAGNONS DE LA CHANSON				
OWN BY THE RIVERSIDE/Margoton	(Capitol 4342)	.75	3.00	60
HREE BELLS, THE/Whirlwind	(Columbia 4-39657)	1.00	4.00	52
ESLEY, Tom				
ASHVILLE REPORTER/Rockin' Banjo	(Enola 314)	2.50	10.00	
ESTER, Jerry				
ORANGE COLORED SKY/Time Takes Care Of Everything	(Coral 9-60325)	1.25	5.00	50
ESTER, Ketty				
BUT NOT FOR ME/Once Upon A Time	(Era 3080)	.75	3.00	62
OVE LETTERS/I'm A Fool To Want You	(Era 3068)	.75	3.00	62
ULLABY FOR LOVERS/Fallen Angel	(Era 3103)	.75	3.00	63
HIS LAND IS YOUR LAND/Love Is For Everyone	(Era 3094)	.75	3.00	62
OU CAN'T LIE TO A LIAR/River Of Salt	(Era 3088)	.75	3.00	62
LETTERMEN, The				
ADY OF SPAIN/Stand In	(Moonglow 5138)	1.50	6.00	
This group changed their name to the Rhythm Rockers to avoid being confused with the Lettermen, whose section follows.)				
LETTERMEN, The (Jim Pike, Tony Dutalo, Bob Engmann)				
AGAIN/Tree In The Meadow	(Capitol 4851)	.75	3.00	62
ANYONE WHO HAD A HEART/All The Grey Haired Men	(Capitol 2196)	.75	3.00	68
COME BACK SILLY GIRL/A Song For Young Love	(Capitol 4699)	.75	3.00	62
EVERYTHING IS GOOD ABOUT YOU/	(Capitol 3020)	.50	2.00	71
GOIN' OUT OF MY HEAD-CAN'T TAKE MY EYES OFF YOU/ I Believe	(Capitol 2054)	.75	3.00	67
HANG ON SLOOPY/	(Capitol 2774)	.50	2.00	70
HEARTACHE ON HEARTACHE/No Other Love	(Capitol 4914)	.75	3.00	63
HEY, BIG BRAIN/Guiro	(Liberty 55141)	1.25	5.00	58
HOW IS JULIE?/Turn Around, Look At Me	(Capitol 4746)	.75	3.00	62
HURT SO BAD/Catch The Wind	(Capitol 2482)	.75	3.00	69
I ONLY HAVE EYES FOR YOU/	(Capitol 5649)	.75	3.00	66
ISN'T IT A SHAME/	(Capitol 3912)	.50	2.00	75
LOVE/	(Capitol 3192)	.50	2.00	71
MAKE A TIME FOR LOVIN'/You Are My Sunshine Girl	(Capitol 4096)	.50	2.00	75
MAYBE WE SHOULD/	(Capitol 3449)	.50	2.00	72
OH MY LOVE/	(Capitol 3285)	.50	2.00	72
OUR WINTER LOVE/	(Capitol 5813)	.75	3.00	67
PUT YOUR HEAD ON MY SHOULDER/	(Capitol 2324)	.75	3.00	68
SECRETLY/The Things We Did Last Summer	(Capitol 5499)	.75	3.00	62
SHANGRI-LA/	(Capitol 2643)	.75	3.00	69
SHE CRIED/	(Capitol 2820)	.50	2.00	70
SHERRY DON'T GO/	(Capitol 2132)	.75	3.00	68
SILLY BOY/I Told The Stars	(Capitol 4810)	.75	3.00	62
SUMMER SONG/	(Capitol 3617)	.75	3.00	74
THEIR HEARTS WERE FULL OF SPRING/ When	(Warner Bros. 5152)	1.00	4.00	60
(THEME FROM) A SUMMER PLACE/ Sealed With A Kiss	(Capitol 5437)	.75	3.00	65
TRACES-MEMORIES MEDLEY/	(Capitol 2697)	.75	3.00	69
TWO HEARTS/Magic Sound	(Warner Bros. 5178)	.75	3.00	60
WAY YOU LOOK TONIGHT, THE/That's My Desire	(Capitol 4586)	.75	3.00	61
WHEN I FALL IN LOVE/Smile	(Capitol 4658)	.75	3.00	61
WHERE OR WHEN/Be My Girl	(Capitol 5091)	.75	3.00	63
Bob Engemann was replaced by Gary Pike in 1968.				
LEVEES, The				
OUR LOVE IS A VOW/Walkie Talkie Baby	(Karen 1004)	3.75	15.00	
LEVINE, Jeff				
AN ECONOMY PACKAGE/ Still More With Gerald Bored	(Question Mark 301)	.75	3.00	
LEVINE, Hank				
IMAGE (PART 1)/Image (Part 2)	(ABC-Paramount 10256)	.75	3.00	61
(Instrumentals)				
LEVINSKY & SINCLAIR				
ONLY FEEL THIS WAY/Home Is Where The Heart Is	(Charisma 702)	.50	2.00	79
LEVON & THE HAWKS (Featuring Levon Helm)				
GO GO LISA JANE/He Don't Love You	(Atco 6625)	1.50	6.00	68
STONES I THROW, THE/He Don't Love You	(Atco 6383)	1.50	6.00	65
Also see Band, The				
Also see Hawkins, Ronnie				

TITLE/FLIP	LABEL & NO.	GOOD	NEAR MINT	YR.
LEVONS, The				
COME TO ME/Everytime	(Columbia 4-42506)	.75	3.00	62
WE'RE JUST FRIENDS NOW/Love Is Better Than Ever	(Columbia 4-42798)	.75	3.00	63
LEWIS & CLARKE EXPEDITION, The (Travis Lewis & Boomer Clarke)				
CHAIN AROUND THE FLOWERS/ Why Need They Pretend	(Colgems 66-1022)	1.00	4.00	68
DESTINATION UNKNOWN/Freedom Bird	(Colgems 66-1011)	1.00	4.00	67
EXPEDITION WEST/For Your Freedom Tonight	(Chartmaker 402)	1.00	4.00	66
(Shown as by Lewis & Clarke)				
I FEEL GOOD (I FEEL BAD)/Blue Revelations	(Colgems 66-1006)	1.00	4.00	67
Travis Lewis was Michael Murphey; Boomer Clarke was Boomer Castleman.				
LEWIS, Dave				
TREES/Dave's Fifth Avenue	(Jerden 785)	.75	3.00	66
LEWIS, Donna				
SURFER BOY BLUE/Call Him Back	(Decca 9-31554)	1.00	4.00	63
LEWIS, Gary, & The Playboys				
COUNT ME IN/Little Miss Go Go	(Liberty 55778)	.75	3.00	65
EVERYBODY LOVES A CLOWN/Time Stands Still	(Liberty 55818)	.75	3.00	65
GIRLS IN LOVE/Let's Be More Than Friends	(Liberty 55971)	.75	3.00	67
GREEN GRASS/I Can Read Between The Lines	(Liberty 55880)	.75	3.00	66
HAPPINESS/Has She Got The Nicest Eyes	(Liberty 56011)	.75	3.00	67
HAYRIDE/Gary's Groove	(Liberty 56121)	.75	3.00	69
I SAW ELVIS PRESLEY LAST NIGHT/ Something Is Wrong	(Liberty 56144)	2.00	8.00	69
JILL/New In Town	(Liberty 55985)	.75	3.00	67
LOSER, THE (WITH A BROKEN HEART)/ Ice Melts In The Sun	(Liberty 55949)	.75	3.00	67
MAIN STREET/See See Rider	(Liberty 56075)	.75	3.00	68
MY HEART'S SYMPHONY/Tina	(Liberty 55898)	.75	3.00	66
SAVE YOUR HEART FOR ME/Without A Word Of Warning	(Liberty 55809)	.75	3.00	65
SEALED WITH A KISS/Sara Jane	(Liberty 56037)	.75	3.00	68
SHE'S JUST MY STYLE/I Won't Make That Mistake Again	(Liberty 55846)	.75	3.00	65
SURE GONNA MISS HER/I Don't Wanna Say Goodnight	(Liberty 55865)	.75	3.00	66
THIS DIAMOND RING/Hard To Find	(Liberty 55756)	.75	3.00	64
WHERE WILL THE WORDS COME FROM/ May The Best Man Win	(Liberty 55933)	.75	3.00	66
Gary is Jerry Leiws' son.				
Also see Attitudes, The				
LEWIS, Happy (With Mae Queste)				
DREGNET (PART 1)/Dregnet (Part 2)	(Jubilee 3525)	1.25	5.00	
ROMEO & JULIET (PART 1)/Romeo & Juliet (Part 2)	(Jubilee 3526)	1.25	5.00	
LEWIS, Jerry				
I LIKE IT, I LIKE IT/I'll Tell A Policeman On You	(Capitol 1740)	1.50	6.00	51
IT ALL DEPENDS ON YOU/	(Decca 9-30263)	1.00	4.00	57
I'M A LITTLE BUSY BODY/Sunday Driving	(Capitol 1045)	1.50	6.00	50
NAVY GETS THE GRAVY, THE/Pa Pa Pa Pa Polka	(Capitol 1385)	1.50	6.00	51
NEVER BEEN KISSED/A Hunting We Will Go	(Capitol 1482)	1.50	6.00	51
ROCK-A-BYE YOUR BABY WITH A DIXIE MELODY/ Come Rain Or Come Shine	(Decca 9-30124)	1.00	4.00	56
LEWIS, Jerry Lee				
BABY BABY BYE BYE/Old Black Joe	(Sun 337)	.75	3.00	60
BALLAD OF BILLY JOE, THE/Let's Talk About Us	(Sun 324)	.75	3.00	59
BREAK-UP/I'll Make It All Up To You	(Sun 303)	1.00	4.00	58
BREATHLESS/Down The Line	(Sun 288)	1.00	4.00	58
CARRY ME BACK TO OLD VIRGINIA/I Know What It Means	(Sun 396)	.75	3.00	64
CRAZY ARMS/End Of The Road	(Sun 267)	2.50	10.00	57
GOOD GOLLY MISS MOLLY/I Can't Trust Me	(Sun 382)	.75	3.00	63
GREAT BALLS OF FIRE/You Win Again	(Sun 281)	1.00	4.00	57
GREEN GRASS OF HOME/ Baby (You Got What It Takes) (With Linda Gail Lewis)	(Smash 2006)	.75	3.00	65
HANG UP MY ROCK & ROLL SHOES/John Henry	(Sun 344)	.75	3.00	60
HIGH HEEL SNEAKERS/You Went Back On Your Word	(Smash 1930)	.75	3.00	64
HIGH SCHOOL CONFIDENTIAL/Fools Like Me	(Sun 296)	2.50	10.00	58
(Picture sleeve)				
I BELIEVE IN YOU/Baby Hold Me Close	(Smash 1969)	1.00	4.00	65
I'LL SAIL MY SHIP ALONE/It Hurt Me So	(Sun 312)	.75	3.00	59
I'M ON FIRE/Bread & Butter Man	(Smash 1886)	.75	3.00	64
IT WON'T HAPPEN WITH ME/Cold Cold Heart	(Sun 364)	.75	3.00	62
I'VE BEEN TWISTIN'/Ramblin' Rose	(Sun 374)	.75	3.00	62
LEWIS BOOGIE/Return Of Jerry Lee (By George & Lewis)	(Sun 301)	1.25	5.00	58
(Novelty/Break-in about Jerry Lee, using cut-ins from his recordings.)				
LITTLE QUEENIE/I Could Never Be Ashamed Of You	(Sun 330)	.75	3.00	59
LOVIN' UP A STORM/Big Blon' Baby	(Sun 317)	1.00	4.00	59
MEMPHIS BEAT/If I Had It All To Do Over	(Smash 2053)	.75	3.00	66
MONEY/Bonnie B	(Sun 371)	.75	3.00	62
PEN & PAPER/Hit The Road Jack	(Smash 1857)	.75	3.00	63
ROCKIN' PNEUMONIA & BOOGIE WOOGIE FLU/ This Must Be The Place	(Smash 1992)	.75	3.00	65
SAVE THE LAST DANCE FOR ME/As Long As I Live	(Sun 367)	.75	3.00	63
SWEET LITTLE SIXTEEN/How's My Ex Treating You	(Sun 379)	.75	3.00	62
TEENAGE LETTER/Seasons Of My Heart	(Sun 384)	.75	3.00	63
WHAT'D I SAY/Livin' Lovin' Wreck	(Sun 356)	.75	3.00	61
WHEN I GET PAID/Love Made A Fool Of Me	(Sun 352)	.75	3.00	60
WHOLE LOT OF SHAKIN' GOING ON/It'll Be Me	(Sun 267)	1.00	4.00	57
Also see Hawk, The				
LEWIS, Jona				
GOD BLESS WHOEVER MADE YOU/Hallelujah Europa	(Stiff-Epic 50826)	.50	2.00	79
LEWIS, Jon Jon				
I'M A NUT/World Full Of Sadness	(World Pacific 77810)	.75	3.00	66
LEWIS, Linda				
CAN'T WE JUST SIT DOWN & TALK IT OVER/ Never Been Done Before	(Arista 0307)	.50	2.00	78
IT'S IN HIS KISS (THE SHOOP SHOOP SONG)/	(Arista 0129)	.50	2.00	75
OLD SCHOOLYARD, THE/	(Arista 0109)	.50	2.00	75
REACH FOR THE TRUTH/Rock A Doodle Doo	(Reprise 1168)	.50	2.00	73
THIS TIME I'LL BE SWEETER/	(Arista 0151)	.50	2.00	75
LEWIS, Ramsey, Trio				
HANG ON SLOOPY/Movin' Easy	(Cadet 5522)	.75	3.00	65
"IN" CROWD, THE/Since I Fell For You	(Argo 5506)	.75	3.00	65
SOMETHING YOU GOT/My Babe	(Argo 5481)	.75	3.00	64
LEWIS, Shari				
MR. SANTA/Som Things For Xmas (A Snake, Some Mice, Some Glue & A Hole Too)	(Musicor 1140)	.75	3.00	65
LEWIS, Wally				
EVERY DAY/That's The Way It Goes	(Liberty 55178)	.75	3.00	59
KATHLEEN/Donna	(Tally 117)	2.00	8.00	58
KATHLEEN/Donna	(Dot 15705)	1.00	4.00	58
SALLY GREEN/Arms Of Jo-Ann	(Liberty 55196)	.75	3.00	59
WHITE BOBBY SOX/I'm With You	(Dot 15763)	1.00	4.00	58
LEXINGTONS, The				
MY HONEY LOVES ANOTHER GIRL/Ba Ba Doo	(International 500)	2.00	8.00	
LEYDEN, Jimmy				
MARIANNE/Wringle, Wrangle (By Jimmy Carroll)	(Bell 26)	.75	3.00	
LIA, Orsa				
I CAN'T HOLD ON/	(Infinity 50032)	.50	2.00	79
I NEVER SAID I LOVE YOU/ No Walls, No Ceilings, No Floors	(Infinity 50004)	.50	2.00	79

TITLE/FLIP	LABEL & NO.	GOOD	NEAR MINT	YR.
LIAR				
FRUSTRATION/	(Bearsville 0333)	.50	2.00	78
SET THE WORLD ON FIRE/High On Love	(Bearsville 0328)	.50	2.00	78
LIEBERMAN, Lori				
AND THE FEELING'S GOOD/	(Capitol 3577)	.50	2.00	72
LET ME DOWN EASY/Boston	(Millenium 622)	.50	2.00	78
RAISE UP OFF OF ME/	(Capitol 4020)	.50	2.00	75
LIFE GUARDS, The (Phil Sloan & Steve Barri)				
STATE BEACH/Big Swim	(Catch 104)	1.00	4.00	64
SWIMTIME U.S.A./Swim Party	(Reprise 277)	1.25	5.00	64
LIFEGUARDS, The				
EVERYBODY OUT 'A THE POOL/Teenage Tango	(ABC-Paramount 10021)	1.50	6.00	59
EVERYBODY OUT 'A THE POOL/Teenage Tango	(DR 69)	.75	3.00	65
This group includes former members of Bill Haley's Comets.				
LIGHT				
BACK UP/Music Box	(A&M 873)	1.00	4.00	67
LIGHTFOOT, Gordon				
BEAUTIFUL/Don Quixote	(Reprise 1088)	.75	3.00	72
CAN'T DEPEND ON LOVE/It's Worth Believin'	(Reprise 1145)	.75	3.00	73
CAREFREE HIGHWAY/Seven Island Suite	(Reprise 1309)	.75	3.00	74
CIRCLE IS SMALL, THE/Sweet Guinevere	(Warner Bros. 8518)	.50	2.00	78
DAYLIGHT KATY/Hangdog Hotel Room	(Warner Bros. 8579)	.50	2.00	78
DREAMLAND/Songs The Mistrel Song	(Warner Bros. 8644)	.50	2.00	78
IF I COULD/	(United Artists 50765)	.75	3.00	72
IF YOU COULD READ MY MIND/Poor Little Allison	(Reprise 0974)	.75	3.00	70
I'LL BE ALRIGHT/Go Go Round	(United Artists 50114)	.75	3.00	67
IT'S TOO LATE, HE WINS/Negotiations	(ABC-Paramount 45-10373)	1.25	5.00	62
JUST LIKE TOM THUMB'S BLUES/Ribbon Of Darkness	(United Artists 929)	.50	2.00	77
ME & BOBBY MCGEE/The Pony Man	(Reprise 0926)	.75	3.00	70
PEACEFUL WATERS/The Way I Feel	(United Artists 50152)	.75	3.00	67
RACE AMONG THE RUINS/Protocol	(Reprise 1380)	.75	3.00	77
RAINY DAY PEOPLE/Cherokee Bend	(Reprise 1328)	.75	3.00	75
(REMEMBER ME) I'M THE ONE/Daisy-Doo	(ABC-Paramount 45-10352)	1.50	6.00	62
(Shown as by Gord Lightfoot)				
SUMMER SIDE OF LIFE/Love & Maple Syrup	(Reprise 1035)	.75	3.00	71
SUNDOWN/Too Late For Prayin'	(Reprise 1194)	.75	3.00	74
TALKING IN YOUR SLEEP/Nous Vivons Ensemble	(Reprise 1020)	.75	3.00	71
YOU ARE WHAT I AM/The Same Old Obsession	(Reprise 1128)	.75	3.00	73
WRECK OF THE EDMOND FITZGERALD, THE/ The House You Live In	(Reprise 1369)	.75	3.00	76
LIGHTHOUSE				
GOOD DAY/	(Polydor 14246)	.50	2.00	74
HATS OFF (TO THE STRANGER)/Sing, Sing, Sing	(Evolution 1041)	.75	3.00	71
IF THERE EVER WAS A TIME/Eight Miles High	(RCA 74-0224)	.75	3.00	69
I JUST WANNA BE YOUR FRIEND/	(Evolution 1058)	.75	3.00	72
ONE FINE MORNING/Little Kind Words	(Evolution 1048)	.75	3.00	71
PRETTY LADY/Bright Side	(Polydor 14198)	.50	2.00	73
SUNNY DAYS/Lonely Places	(Evolution 1069)	.75	3.00	72
TAKE IT SLOW (OUT IN THE COUNTRY)/	(Evolution 1052)	.75	3.00	71
LILA & RONNIE				
MY STEADY/My Imagination	(Secco 6009)	2.00	8.00	
LIL' BOYS BLUE				
I'M NOT THERE/Take You Away	(Bat Wing 2003)	1.50	6.00	
LILE, Bobby				
BOOK WORM/A Labor Of Love	(4 Star 1723)	1.00	4.00	58
BOOK WORM/Lighthouse	(Trill 641)	.75	3.00	
KATHY/All The Time	(4 Star 1734)	1.00	4.00	59
MY BIG MISTAKE/A Little Bit	(Imperial 5690)	.75	3.00	60
LILLEY, Carol J.				
TRIBUTE TO WOODY (Woody Hayes)/ I Wish I Was A Kid Again	(Starr SF-1219)	.50	2.00	79
LIL' WALLY & THE VENTURES				
WELCOME BEATLES/My Happiness	(Drum Boy 108)	1.25	5.00	65
LIMELITERS, The (Glenn Yarbrough, Lou Gottliev & Alex Hassilev)				
CHARLIE, THE MIDNIGHT MARAUDER/The Hammer Song	(Elektra 8)	1.00	4.00	60
DOLLAR DOWN, A/ When Twice The Moon Has Come & Gone	(RCA Victor 47-7859)	.75	3.00	61
HUNDRED YEARS AGO, A/Paco Peco	(RCA Victor 47-7913)	.75	3.00	61
I HAD A MULE/The Riddle Song	(RCA Victor 47-8069)	.75	3.00	62
JUST AN HONEST MISTAKE/Jonah	(RCA Victor 47-7966)	.75	3.00	61
MIDNIGHT SPECIAL/Mc Lintock's Theme	(RCA Victor 47-8255)	.75	3.00	63
RED ROSES & WHITE WINE/Milk & Honey	(RCA Victor 47-7942)	.75	3.00	61
WHO WILL BUY/Funk	(RCA Victor 47-8094)	.75	3.00	62
LINCOLN FIG & THE DATES				
WAY UP/Kiss Me Tenderly	(Worthy 1006)	2.50	10.00	
LINCOLN PARK ZOO, The				
LOVE THEME FROM HAIGHT ST./If You Gotta Go	(Mercury 72708)	1.00	4.00	67
LINCOLNS, The				
COME ALONG & DREAM/Smile Baby Smile	(Tripp 1000)	1.00	4.00	
LIND, Bob (Of The Cascades)				
BLACK NIGHT/White Snow	(Verve Folkways 5029)	.75	3.00	
ELUSIVE BUTTERFLY/Cheryl's Goin' Home	(World Pacific 77808)	.75	3.00	65
I JUST LET IT TAKE ME/We've Never Spoken	(World Pacific 77830)	.75	3.00	67
REMEMBER THE RAIN/Truly Julie's Blues	(World Pacific 77822)	.75	3.00	66
SAN FRANCISCO WOMAN/Oh Babe Take Me Home	(World Pacific 77839)	.75	3.00	67
LINDEN, Kathy				
BILLY/If I Could Hold You In My Arms	(Felsted 8510)	1.00	4.00	58
GOODBYE, JIMMY, GOODBYE/Heartaches At Sweet 16	(Felsted 8571)	1.00	4.00	59
SOMEBODY LOVES YOU/You Walked Into My Life	(Felsted 8554)	1.00	4.00	59
TOUCH OF LOVE, THE/It's Just My Luck To Be Fifteen	(National 106)	1.00	4.00	
YOU DON'T KNOW GIRLS/So Close To My Heart	(Felsted 8587)	1.00	4.00	59
YOU'D BE SURPRISED/Why Oh Why	(Felsted 8521)	1.00	4.00	58
LINDISFARNE				
COURT IN THE ACT/	(Elektra 45835)	.75	3.00	73
DON'T ASK ME/	(Elektra 45819)	.75	3.00	72
LADY ELEANOR/Down	(Elektra 45744)	.75	3.00	72
RUN FOR HOME/Stick Together	(Atco 7093)	.50	2.00	78
LINDSAY, Mark (Of Paul Revere & The Raiders)				
AND THE GRASS WON'T PAY NO MIND/ Funny How Little Men Care	(Columbia 4-45229)	.75	3.00	70
ARE YOU OLD ENOUGH/	(Columbia 4-45462)	.75	3.00	71
ARIZONA/Man From Houston	(Columbia 4-45037)	.75	3.00	69
BEEN TOO LONG ON THE ROAD/	(Columbia 4-45385)	.75	3.00	71
FIRST HYMN FROM GRAND TERRACE/ Old Man At The Fair	(Columbia 4-44875)	.75	3.00	69
MISS AMERICA/Small Town Woman	(Columbia 4-45125)	.75	3.00	70
SILVER BIRD/So Hard To Leave You	(Columbia 4-45180)	.75	3.00	70
SING ME HIGH (SING ME LOW)/	(Warner Bros. 8359)	.50	2.00	77
SING YOUR OWN SONG/	(Greedy 106)	.50	2.00	76
PROBLEM CHILD/	(Columbia 4-45286)	.75	3.00	71
LINDSAY, Merle				
TIGHT SLACKS/Born To Lose	(Shasta 117)	1.25	5.00	59

TITLE/FLIP	LABEL & NO.	GOOD	NEAR MINT	YR.
LINER				
STRANGE FASCINATION/	(Atco 7200)	.50	2.00	79
YOU & ME/Ship On The Ocean	(Atco 7097)	.50	2.00	79
LINHART, Buzzy				
IF YOU GOTTA BREAK ANOTHER HEART/	(Buddah 561)	.50	2.00	73
YOU GOT WHAT IT TAKES/	(Buddah 548)	.50	2.00	72
LINKLETTER, Art				
WE LOVE YOU, CALL COLLECT/Dear Mom & Dad	(Capitol 2678)	.75	3.00	69
LINN COUNTY				
CAVE SONG/Think	(Mercury 72852)	1.00	4.00	
FEVER SHOT/Girl Can't Help It	(Mercury 72907)	1.00	4.00	
LET THE MUSIC BEGIN/Wine Take Me Away	(Philips 40644)	2.00	8.00	
LOWER LEMONS/Fast Days	(Mercury 72882)	1.00	4.00	
LINNETTES, The				
SOMEDAY/Big Eyed Baby	(Palette 5112)	1.25	5.00	60
LINSEY, Bill				
BLUE/Winter Love	(Dot 16452)	.75	3.00	63
LIONS, The				
NO ONE (NO ONE BUT YOU)/Giggles	(Everest 19388)	2.00	8.00	
LIPSCOMB, Max K.				
GIRL NEXT DOOR WENT 'A WALKING/ (You're So Square) Baby I Don't Care	(Dot 16324)	2.00	8.00	
LIPTON, Peggy				
RED CLAY COUNTY LINE/ Just A Little Lovin' (Early In The Morning)	(Ode 118)	.75	3.00	69
WEAR YOUR LOVE LIKE HEAVEN/Honey Won't Let Me	(Ode 66001)	.75	3.00	69
LISA & THE LULLABIES, (The Concords)				
WHY DO I CRY/He's So Good	(Coed 589)	1.50	6.00	
LISI, Ricky				
DON'T GO NOW/The River	(Roulette 4511)	1.50	6.00	
(With the Concords)				
LISTENING				
HELLO YOU/Life Stories	(Vanguard 35094)	1.00	4.00	71
LITTERBUGS, The				
VALERIE/Calypso	(Okeh 7164)	3.75	15.00	60
LITTLE ANGEL				
COME ON & ROCK/Help Me Baby	(Award 126)	1.00	4.00	59
LITTLE AUGGIE AUSTIN				
MY LOVE FOR YOU/I Thank My Lucky Star	(Pontiac 101)	1.25	5.00	
LITTLE BEATS, The				
SOMEONE FOR ME/Love Is True	(Mercury 71155)	5.00	20.00	59
LITTLE BERNIE				
WADDLE, THE/Lonely Soldier	(Jove 100)	.75	3.00	62
LITTLE BERNIE & THE CAVALIERS				
DO YOU/Poor Town	(Ascot 2183)	1.00	4.00	65
LITTLE BILL & THE BLUENOTES				
BYE BYE BABY/I Love An Angel	(Dolton 4)	1.00	4.00	59
LITTLE BILLY MASON				
MAKE ME YOUR OWN/I Love My Baby	(Rama 212)	1.00	4.00	
LITTLE BITS, The (Featuring Karyl Mann)				
SUN AIN'T GONNA SHINE (ANYMORE), THE/ The Feeling Of Love	(DynoVoice 919)	1.00	4.00	
LITTLE BOB & THE LOLLIPOPS				
TWISTING HOME/You Don't Have To Cry	(Decca 9-31412)	.75	3.00	62
LITTLE BOBBY RIVERA				
CORALEE/Joys Of Love	(Jury 1004)	6.25	25.00	
LITTLE BONES, The				
YA YA/What'd I Say	(Prann 5001)	1.25	5.00	61
LITTLE BOY BLUES, The				
I CAN ONLY GIVE YOU EVERYTHING/You Don't Love Me	(Irc 6939)	1.25	5.00	
I'M READY/Little Boy Blues' Blues	(Irc 6936)	1.25	5.00	
IT'S ONLY YOU/Is Love?	(Fontana 1623)	1.00	4.00	67
LOOK AT THE SUN/Love For A Day	(Irc 6928)	1.25	5.00	
LITTLE BUTCHIE & The Vells: see Saunders, Little Butchie & His Buddies.				
LITTLE CHERYL				
CAN'T WE JUST BE FRIENDS/Heaven Only Knows	(Cameo 270)	.75	3.00	63
HEAVEN ONLY KNOWS/	(Cameo 270)	.75	3.00	63
I LOVE YOU, CONRAD/Come Home	(Cameo 292)	.75	3.00	64
JIM/Pocketful Of Money	(Reprise 20109)	.75	3.00	62
MAMA, LET THE PHONE BELL RING/ Can't We Just Be Friends	(Cameo 276)	.75	3.00	63
YEH YEH WE LOVE 'EM ALL/Nick & Joe	(Cameo 307)	.75	3.00	64
LITTLE CLYDIE & THE TEENS				
CASUAL LOOK, A/Oh Me	(RPM 462)	3.75	15.00	56
LITTLE DAVID (The Regents)				
CALL ON ME/I Want The Good Life	(Symphony 40)	3.00	12.00	
LITTLE DIPPERS, The				
BE SINCERE/Tonight	(University 630)	.75	3.00	60
FOREVER/Two By Four	(University 210)	.75	3.00	60
("Forever" was actually performed by the Anita Kerr Singers. Other releases by the Little Dippers were by studio singers whose identity is not yet known.)				
LONELY/I Wonder, I Wonder, I Wonder	(University 608)	.75	3.00	60
LITTLE DOUG: see Sahm, Doug				
LITTLE DUCK & THE QUACKERS				
OUT OF SIGHT/Excuse Me	(Ronn 19)	.75	3.00	
LITTLE "E" & THE MELLO TONE 3				
CANDY APPLE RED IMPALA/Bye Bye Pretty Baby	(Falco 302)	1.00	4.00	
LITTLE EVA (Eva Boyd)				
BEND IT/Just One Word Ain't Enough	(Verve 10459)	.75	3.00	66
CONGA (WITH A LITTLE BIT OF ROCK & ROLL)/ Makin' With The Magilla	(Dimension 1035)	.75	3.00	64
KEEP YOUR HANDS OFF MY BABY/Where Do I Go	(Dimension 1003)	.75	3.00	62
LET'S START THE PARTY AGAIN/Please Hurt Me	(Dimension 1019)	.75	3.00	64
LET'S TURKEY TROT/Down Home	(Dimension 1006)	.75	3.00	63
LOCO-MOTION, THE/He Is The Boy	(Dimension 1000)	.75	3.00	62
OLD SMOKEY LOCOMOTION/Just A Little Girl	(Dimension 1011)	.75	3.00	63
STAND BY ME/That's My Man	(Amy 943)	.75	3.00	66
WAKE UP JOHN/Takin' Back What I Said	(Dimension 1042)	.75	3.00	65
WHAT I GOTTA DO (TO MAKE YOU JEALOUS)/ Trouble With Boys	(Dimension 1013)	.75	3.00	63
Also see Irwin, Big Dee				
LITTLE FAY				
I DON'T CARE WHAT THE PEOPLE SAY/ Joey Won't You Ask Me	(Top Pop 260)	.75	3.00	66
LITTLE FEAT (Featuring Lowell George)				
HAMBURGER MIDNIGHT/Strawberry Flats	(Warner Bros. 7431)	.50	2.00	70
LONG DISTANCE LOVE/	(Warner Bros. 8174)	.50	2.00	76
OH ATLANTA/Down The Road	(Warner Bros. 8054)	.50	2.00	75
OH ATLANTA/Willin'	(Warner Bros. 8566)	.50	2.00	78
TIME LOVES A HERO/Sailin' Shoes	(Warner Bros. 8420)	.50	2.00	77
LITTLE GRACIE				
SIXTEEN TEENS/You're My Tarzan	(Band Box 268)	1.00	4.00	61
LITTLE GUY & THE GIANTS				
SO YOUNG/It's You	(Lawn 103)	5.00	20.00	
LITTLE JAN & THE RADIANTS				
HEART & SOUL/If You Love Me	(Vim 507)	3.75	15.00	60
IF YOU LOVE ME/Now Is The Hour	(Goldisc 15)	3.00	12.00	
LITTLE JIMMY & THE TOPS				
PUPPY LOVE/Say You Love Me	(Len 1011)	1.50	6.00	
PUPPY LOVE/Say You Love Me	(V-Tone 102)	1.25	5.00	
PUPPY LOVE/Say You Love Me	(Swan 4091)	1.00	4.00	
(Shown as by Little Jimmy Rivers & The Tops)				
Also see Chiffons, The				
LITTLE JO ANN				
MY DADDY IS PRESIDENT/ Macaroni (Harmony Jones Orchestra)	(Kapp 467)	.75	3.00	62
LITTLE JOE & THE MORROCOS				
BUBBLE GUM/	(Bumble Bee 500)	.75	3.00	
LITTLE JOE & THE MUSTANGS				
I DIG YOU BABY/Love Me One More Time	(Challenge 59258)	1.00	4.00	64
LITTLE JOEY & THE FLIPS				
BONGO GULLY/It Was Like Heaven	(Joy 268)	.75	3.00	62
BONGO STOMP/Lost Love	(Joy 262)	.75	3.00	62
Also see Joey & The Flips				
LITTLE JOHN & SHERWOODS				
RAG BAG/Long Hair	(Fleetwood 001)	1.50	6.00	
LITTLE JOSEPH				
STORY OF CHRISTMAS/Christmas Jingle	(Blue Cat 103)	.75	3.00	65
LITTLE LADY BEATLES, The				
DEAR BEATLES/	(Applause 1002)	1.00	4.00	64
LITTLE LAMBSIE PENN				
I WANT TO SPEND XMAS WITH ELVIS/ Painted Lips & Pig Tails	(Atco 6082)	2.00	8.00	56
LITTLE LARRY				
I'M CONFESSIN'/I'm Lonesome	(Agon 1000)	.75	3.00	61
LITTLE LISA				
PUPPET ON A STRING/Hang On Bill	(V.I.P. 25023)	.75	3.00	65
LITTLE LOUIE & THE LOVERS				
SOMEDAY YOU'LL PAY/Nothing But The Two Step	(Viscount 102)	2.50	10.00	
LITTLE MAN & THE VICTORS				
KING OF THE MOUNTAIN/I Need An Angel	(Tarheel 064)	1.50	6.00	
LITTLE MARCUS & THE DEVOTIONS				
LONE STRANGER WENT MAD, THE/ I'll Always Remember	(Gordie 1001)	5.00	20.00	
LITTLE PETE & THE YOUNGSTERS				
YOU TOLD ANOTHER LIE/I'll Never Leave You Again	(Lesley 1925)	5.00	20.00	
LITTLE, Rich				
ONE BO-DILLION YEARS/I Catch Myself Crying	(Sound Stage 7 2567)	.75	3.00	66
LITTLE RIVER BAND, The				
COOL CHANGE/Middle Man	(Capitol 4789)	.50	2.00	79
HAPPY ANNIVERSARY/Changed & Different	(Harvest 4524)	.50	2.00	77
HELP IS ON THE WAY/The Inner Light	(Harvest 4428)	.50	2.00	77
I'LL ALWAYS CALL YOUR NAME/The Man In Black	(Harvest 4380)	.50	2.00	77
IT'S A LONG WAY THERE/Meanwhile	(Harvest 4318)	.50	2.00	76
LADY/Take Me Home	(Harvest 4667)	.50	2.00	78
LONESOME LOSER/Shut Down Turn Off	(Capitol 4748)	.50	2.00	79
REMINISCING/So Many Paths	(Harvest 4605)	.50	2.00	78
LITTLE ROMEO & THE CASANOVAS				
REMEMBER LORI/That's How Little Girls Get Boys	(Ascot 2192)	2.00	8.00	
Also see Ovations, The				
LITTLE RONNIE & THE CHROMATICS				
CAN YOU FORGIVE, CAN YOU FORGET/ Get To Stepping	(Early Bird 49660)	.75	3.00	
SPEAK WHAT'S ON YOUR MIND/What A Day This Has Been	(His 1004)	.75	3.00	
LITTLE SAMMY ROZZI & THE GUYS				
OVER THE RAINBOW/Christine	(Pelham 722)	5.00	20.00	
OVER THE RAINBOW/Christine	(Jaclyn 1161)	2.00	8.00	
(Shown as by Little Sammy & The Tones)				
LITTLE SISTER				
SOMEBODY'S WATCHING YOU/Stanga	(Stone Flower 9001)	1.50	6.00	
YOU'RE THE ONE/You're The One (Part 2)	(Stone Flower 9000)	1.50	6.00	
LITTLE SISTERS, The				
TWIST, THE/The Pony	(Parkway 815)	.75	3.00	60
LITTLE SUNNY DAY & THE CLOUDS				
LOU-ANN/Baby Doll	(Tandem 7001)	2.50	10.00	
LITTLE SUSIE				
(WHY DOES EVERYBODY IMITATE) MY DADDY/	(Roulette 4466)	.75	3.00	62
LITTLE TED & THE NOVAS				
ALL YOUR LOVIN'/Baby Baby Baby	(Kay-Gee 440)	2.00	8.00	
LITTLE THUMPERS, The				
BUCK DANCE/Baja	(RCA Victor 47-7440)	1.00	4.00	59
BUCK DANCE/Baja	(RCA Victor 61-7440)	2.00	8.00	59
(Stero single)				
LITTLE TOM & THE VALENTINES				
SCHOOL GIRL/Letter From My Darling	(Mr. Big 222)	1.00	4.00	61
LITTLE TOMMY & THE ELGINS				
NEVER LOVE AGAIN/I Walk On	(Elmar 1084)	3.75	15.00	62
NEVER LOVE AGAIN/I Walk On	(ABC-Paramount 10358)	2.00	8.00	62
LITTLE VICTOR & THE VISTAS				
NO MORE/Love Marches On	(Rendezvous 183)	3.00	12.00	
LITTLE WHEELS				
FOUR WHEELED BALL BEARING SURFING BOARD/ The Bumper	(Dot 16676)	1.00	4.00	64
LITTLE WILLIE & THE ADOLESCENTS				
GET OUT OF MY LIFE/	(Tener 1009)	.75	3.00	
LIVELY ONES, The				
HIGH TIDE/Goofy Foot	(Del Fi 4210)	1.00	4.00	63
MISERLOU/Livin'	(Del Fi 4219)	1.00	4.00	64
NIGHT & DAY/Hey Scrounge	(Smash 1880)	1.00	4.00	64
RIC-A-TIC/Surfer Boogie	(Del Fi 4205)	1.00	4.00	63
SURF RIDER/Surfers Lament	(Del Fi 4196)	1.00	4.00	63
TELSTAR SURF/Surf City	(Del Fi 4217)	1.00	4.00	63
Instrumentals				
Also see Surfmen, The				
LIVERBIRDS, The				
WHY DO YOU HANG AROUND ME/Didley Daddy	(Philips 40288)	1.00	4.00	65
LIVERPOOL EXPRESS, The				
EVERY MAN MUST HAVE A DREAM/	(Atco 7075)	.50	2.00	77
YOU ARE MY LOVE/Never Be The Same Boy	(Atco 7058)	.50	2.00	77
LIVERPOOL FIVE, The				
ANY WAY THAT YOU WANT ME/The Snake	(RCA Victor 47-8968)	.75	3.00	66
CLOUDY/She's (Got Plenty Of Love)	(RCA Victor 47-9158)	.75	3.00	67
IF YOU GOTTA GO, GO NOW/Too Far Out	(RCA Victor 47-8660)	.75	3.00	65
NEW DIRECTIONS/ What A Crazy World (We're Living In)	(RCA Victor 47-8906)	.75	3.00	66
SISTER LOVE/She's Mine	(RCA Victor 47-8816)	.75	3.00	66
LIVERPOOL SET, The				
OH GEE GIRL/Walking The Dog	(Columbia 4-43512)	.75	3.00	66
LIVERS, The				
BEATLE TIME/This Is The Night	(Constellation 118)	1.25	5.00	64
LIVINGSTON, Patty				
I'VE GOT MY BABY/	(Dimension 1044)	.75	3.00	64
LIZ DAMON'S ORIENT EXPRESS				
LONINESS REMEMBERS/The Quiet Sound	(Anthem 51005)	.50	2.00	71
1900 YESTERDAY/You're Falling In Love	(Makaha 503)	1.00	4.00	70
1900 YESTERDAY/You're Falling In Love	(White Whale 368)	.50	2.00	70
LIZARDS, The				
HOT ROD/Sweet Young Thing	(20th Fox 519)	1.00	4.00	64
LLOYD, Adrian				
JUSTINE/She Treats Me Better Than You	(Sunset 603)	1.00	4.00	
LLOYD, Ian (Of Stories)				
NEVER BEEN A MAN/Silver Chains	(Polydor 14319)	.50	2.00	76
OH LET ME IN/	(Polydor 14351)	.50	2.00	76
SHE BROKE YOUR HEART/Easy Money	(Scotti Bros. 501)	.50	2.00	79
SLIP AWAY/Easy Money	(Scotti Bros. 505)	.50	2.00	79
LLOYD, Jackie				
WARM LOVE/Come & Get Me	(Hero 342)	7.50	30.00	
LLOYD, Melody				
FORGET ME NEVER/Elvis, A legendary Angel	(Star 9277)	.50	2.00	77
LLOYD, Michael (Of Cotton, Lloyd & Christian)				
HEY ROCK & ROLLER/	(Warner Bros. 8621)	.50	2.00	78
LOADING ZONE, The				
DON'T LOSE CONTROL/ Danger, Heartbreak Dead Ahead	(RCA Victor 47-9538)	1.25	5.00	68
NO MORE TEARS/Can I Dedicate	(RCA Victor 47-9620)	1.25	5.00	68
ONE FOR ALL/Time Stops	(Umbrells 1001)	1.50	6.00	
TIMES ARE GONNA BE DIFFERENT/ I Couldn't Care Less	(Columbia 4-43938)	1.50	6.00	66
LOBO				
AFTERGLOW/Our Best Time	(Warner Bros. 8493)	.50	2.00	76
CALIFORNIA DID & REEMO/A Little Different	(Big Tree 119)	.50	2.00	71
DON'T EXPECT ME TO BE YOUR FRIEND/A Big Red Kite	(Big Tree 158)	.50	2.00	72
DON'T TELL ME GOODNIGHT/My Momma Had A Soul	(Big Tree 15033)	.50	2.00	75
HOLDIN' ON FOR DEAR LOVE/Gus, The Dancing Dog	(MCA 41152)	.50	2.00	79
HOW CAN I TELL HER/Hope You're Proud Of Me Girl	(Big Tree 16004)	.50	2.00	73
I'D LOVE YOU TO WANT ME/Am I True To Myself	(Big Tree 147)	.50	2.00	72
IT SURE TOOK A LONG, LONG TIME/Running Deer	(Big Tree 16001)	.50	2.00	73
ME & YOU & A DOG NAMED BOO/Walk Away From It All	(Big Tree 112)	.50	2.00	71
RINGS/I'm, Only Sleeping	(Big Tree 15008)	.50	2.00	74
SHE DIDN'T DO MAGIC/I'm The Only One	(Big Tree 116)	.50	2.00	71
SIMPLE MAN, A/Don't Expect Me To Be Your Friend	(Big Tree 141)	.50	2.00	72
STANDING AT THE END OF THE LINE/Stoney	(Big Tree 15001)	.50	2.00	74
THERE AIN'T NO WAY/Love Me For What I Am	(Big Tree 16012)	.50	2.00	73
WHERE WERE YOU WHEN I WAS FALLING IN LOVE/ I Don't Wanna Make Love Anymore	(MCA 41065)	.50	2.00	79
WOULD I STILL HAVE YOU/Morning Sun	(Big Tree 15040)	.50	2.00	75
YOU ARE ALL I'LL EVER NEED/	(Warner Bros. 8537)	.50	2.00	78
LOCKETTES, The				
GEE I'D SWEAR I WAS FALLING IN LOVE/ I Love The Boy Who Lives Next Door	(ABC 10882)	.75	3.00	66
LOCOMOTIONS, The				
LITTLE EVA/Adios My Love	(Gone 5142)	1.00	4.00	62
MAKE IT SATURDAY NIGHT/Weekend Workout	(Swan 4237)	.75	3.00	65
LODGE, John (Of The Moody Blues)				
NATURAL AVENUE/Say You Love Me	(London 1069)	.50	2.00	77
LOFGREN, Nils (Of Grin)				
BACK IT UP/	(A&M 1692)	.50	2.00	75
CRY TOUGH/Share A Little	(A&M 1812)	.50	2.00	76
I CAME TO DANCE/Code Of The Road	(A&M 1927)	.50	2.00	77
IT'S NOT A CRIME/	(A&M 1839)	.50	2.00	76
LOGGINS & MESSINA (Kenny Loggins & Jim Messina)				
ANGRY EYES/	(Columbia 10444)	.50	2.00	76
CHANGES/Get A Hold	(Columbia 10077)	.50	2.00	75
GROWIN'/Keep Me In Mind	(Columbia 10118)	.50	2.00	75
HOUSE AT POOH CORNER/Peace Of Mind	(Columbia 45664)	.50	2.00	72
I LIKE IT LIKE THAT/Angry Eyes	(Columbia 10188)	.50	2.00	75
JUST BEFORE THE NEWS/	(Columbia AE7 1060)	.50	2.00	72
LOVER'S QUESTION, A/Angry Eyes	(Columbia 10222)	.50	2.00	75
LOVE SONG/My Music	(Columbia 45952)	.50	2.00	73
MY MUSIC/A Love Song	(Columbia 45952)	.50	2.00	73
NOBODY BUT YOU/Danny's Song	(Columbia 45617)	.50	2.00	73
PEACEMAKER/When I Was A Child	(Columbia 10311)	.50	2.00	76
PRETTY PRINCESS/Native Son	(Columbia 10376)	.50	2.00	76
THINKING OF YOU/Till The Ends Meet	(Columbia 45815)	.50	2.00	73
VAHEVELLA/Same Old Wind	(Columbia 45550)	.50	2.00	72
WATCHING THE RIVER RUN/Travelin' Blues	(Columbia 46010)	.50	2.00	74
YOUR MAMA DON'T DANCE/Golden Ribbons	(Columbia 45719)	.50	2.00	72
LOGGINS, Dave				
BUILDING CONDEMNED/	(Vanguard 35177)	.50	2.00	73
ONE WAY TICKET TO PARADISE/Crowd Of Lonely People	(Epic 50509)	.50	2.00	78
PIECES OF APRIL/Color Of The Mood	(Epic 50711)	.50	2.00	79
PLEASE COME TO BOSTON/Let Me Go Now	(Epic 50035)	.50	2.00	74
SHIP IN A BOTTLE/The Ballad Of Cowboy Twenty	(Epic 50491)	.50	2.00	77
SO MUCH FOR DREAMS/You Found It Now	(Epic 50578)	.50	2.00	78
THREE LITTLE WORDS (I LOVE YOU)/ Don't Treat Me Like A Stranger	(Epic 50326)	.50	2.00	77
YOU'VE GOT ME TO HOLD ON TO/Savior Of My Natural Life	(Epic 50246)	.50	2.00	76

TITLE/FLIP	LABEL & NO.	GOOD	NEAR MINT	YR.
LOGGINS, Kenny (Of Loggins & Messina)				
CELEBRATE ME HOME/Why Do People Live	(Columbia 10652)	.50	2.00	77
EASY DRIVER/Somebody Knows	(Columbia 10866)	.50	2.00	78
I BELIEVE IN LOVE/Enter My Dream	(Columbia 10569)	.50	2.00	77
THIS IS IT/Will It Last	(Columbia 11109)	.50	2.00	79
WHENEVER I CALL YOU FRIEND (With Stevie Nicks)/ Angelique	(Columbia 10794)	.50	2.00	78
LOKO				
WATER-GATE REPORT/Loko Music	(Fun-e-bone 99)	1.00	4.00	73
(Novelty)				
LOLITA (Lolita Ditta)				
COWBOY JIMMY JOE (DIE STERNE DER PRARIE)/ Theme From "A Summer Place" (Wen Der Sommer Kommt)	(Kapp 370)	.75	3.00	61
SAILOR/La Luna	(Kapp 349)	.75	3.00	60
LOLLIPOP TREE, The				
HEY JUDE/Peace	(BTP 546)	1.00	4.00	
LOLLIPOPS, The				
MISTER SANTA/Little Donkey	(Warner Bros. 5122)	1.00	4.00	59
LOLLIPOPS, The				
PEGGY GOT ENGAGED/I'll Set My Love To Music	(RCA Victor 47-8344)	.75	3.00	64
LOLLYPOPS, The				
BELIEVE IN ME/My Love Is Real	(Holland 7420)	3.00	12.00	
LOMAX, Jackie				
HOW THE WEB WAS WOVEN/(I) Fall Inside Your Eyes	(Apple 1819)	.75	3.00	70
LAVENDER DREAM/Lost	(Warner Bros. 7564)	.75	3.00	72
LET THE PLAY BEGIN/Lavender Dream	(Warner Bros. 514-3)	1.00	4.00	72
(Promotional issue)				
NEW DAY/Thumbin' A Ride	(Apple 1807)	.75	3.00	69
ROLL ON/Hellfire, Night-Crier	(Warner Bros. 7589)	.75	3.00	73
SOUR MILK SEA/The Eagle Laughs At You	(Apple 1802)	.75	3.00	68
SOUR MILK SEA/(I) Fall Inside Your Eyes	(Apple 1834)	.50	2.00	71
LOMBARDO, John				
SING, SING, SING/Lady Jane	(Paramount 0105)	.50	2.00	72
LONDON & THE BRIDGES				
IT JUST AIN'T RIGHT/Leave Her Alone	(Date 1502)	1.25	5.00	
LONDONAIRS, The				
DEAREST EMMA/Bugles A Go-Go	(London 1002)	.75	3.00	68
(Reference is to the Avengers' Emma Peel.)				
LONDON BRIDGE				
SUN DON'T SHINE, THE/Don't Worry Baby	(Capitol 3629)	.50	2.00	73
LONDON, Julie				
CRY ME A RIVER/S'Wonderful	(Liberty 55006)	1.00	4.00	55
I'M COMING BACK TO YOU/ When Snow Flakes Fall In The Summer	(Liberty 55605)	.75	3.00	63
SLIGHTLY OUT OF TUNE (DESAFINADO)/ Where Did The Gentleman Go	(Liberty 55512)	.75	3.00	63
LONDON, Laurie				
HE'S GOT THE WHOLE WORLD (IN HIS HANDS)/ Handed Down	(Capitol 3891)	1.00	4.00	58
MY MOTHER/Three O'Clock	(Capitol 4133)	1.00	4.00	59
LONELY BOYS, The				
SPOKEN LETTER, A/My Girl	(NuWay 555)	2.00	8.00	
LONELY ONE, The				
LETTER TO MY LOVE, A/Buddys Beat	(Carol 103)	2.50	10.00	
LONERO, Bobby				
LITTLE BIT/The Girl That I Marry	(Liberty 55180)	7.50	30.00	58
LONG, Bobby				
NIGHT TO REMEMBER, A/Why You Left Me	(Zip 102)	3.00	12.00	
LONGBRANCH PENNYWHISTLE				
DON'T TALK NOW/	(Amos 121)	1.25	5.00	69
LUCKY LOVE/Rebecca	(Amos 129)	1.25	5.00	69
Also see Eagles, The				
LONGET, Claudine				
GOOD DAY SUNSHINE/	(A&M 864)	.50	2.00	67
HELLO, HELLO/	(A&M 846)	.50	2.00	67
HERE, THERE & EVERYWHERE/A Man & A Woman (Un Homme Et Une Femme)	(A&M 832)	.50	2.00	67
LAZY SUMMER NIGHTS/Shadows Of The Night	(A&M 1098)	.50	2.00	69
LOVE IS BLUE/	(A&M 909)	.50	2.00	68
MEDITATION/	(A&M 817)	.50	2.00	66
LONG, Huey				
ELVIS STOLE MY GAL/Ballad Of John Glenn	(Fidelity 4055)	2.50	10.00	
LONNIE & THE CARROLLONS				
BEELINE/Need Your Lovin'	(Mohawk 122)	.75	3.00	61
(Shown as by Lonnie)				
CHAPEL OF TEARS/My Heart (Green label)	(Mohawk 108)	5.00	20.00	60
CHAPEL OF TEARS/My Heart (Red label)	(Mohawk 108)	1.25	5.00	60
CHAPEL OF TEARS/Wild Weekend (By the Barons)	(Mohawk 902)	2.00	8.00	
TRUDY/Hold Me Close	(Mohawk 111)	1.25	5.00	60
YOU SAY/Backyard Rock	(Mohawk 112)	1.25	5.00	60

TITLE/FLIP	LABEL & NO.	GOOD	NEAR MINT	YR.
LONNIE & THE CRISIS				
BELLS IN THE CHAPEL/Santa Town U.S.A.	(Universal 103)	3.75	15.00	
LONNIE & THE LEGENDS				
PENGUIN WALK/Carzy Penguin	(Rev 1005)	1.00	4.00	
LOOKING GLASS, The				
IF I NEVER LOVE AGAIN/ Silver & Sunshine (How Wonderful Is Our Love)	(Valiant 750)	.75	3.00	66
LOVE IS NOT EVERYTHING/Lonely Stranger	(Warner Bros. 7050)	.75	3.00	67
TONGUE TWISTERS/B Side Blues	(Sunny 105)	.75	3.00	69
WHAT AM I DOING CRYING/ Virginia Day's Ragtime Memories	(Uni 55034)	.75	3.00	67
LOOKING GLASS, The				
BRANDY (YOU'RE A FINE GIRL)/One By One	(Epic 5-10874)	.50	2.00	72
DON'T IT MAKE YOU FEEL GOOD/Catherine Street	(Epic 5-10834)	.50	2.00	72
GOLDEN RAINBOW/Jenny-Lynne	(Epic 5-10900)	.50	2.00	72
JIMMY LOVES MARY-ANNE/Wooly Eyes	(Epic 5-10953)	.50	2.00	73
SWEET SOMETHIN'/Rainbow Man	(Epic 5-10953)	.50	2.00	73
LOOSE GRAVEL				
FRISCO BAND/Waiting in Line	(Kelly 26945)	1.00	4.00	
LOPEZ, Trini				
A-M-E-R-I-C-A/Let It Be Known	(Reprise 20168)	.75	3.00	63
ARE YOU SINCERE/You'll Be Sorry	(Reprise 0376)	.75	3.00	65
GONNA GET ALONG WITHOUT YA' NOW/	(Reprise 0547)	.75	3.00	67
IF I HAD A HAMMER/Unchain My Heart	(Reprise 20198)	.75	3.00	63
I'M COMIN' HOME, CINDY/The 32nd Of May	(Reprise 0455)	.75	3.00	66
JAILER, BRING ME WATER/You Can't Say Goodbye	(Reprise 0260)	.75	3.00	64
KANSAS CITY/Lonesome Traveler	(Reprise 20236)	.75	3.00	63
LA BAMBA, (PART 1)/Trini's Tune	(Reprise 0480)	.75	3.00	66
LEMON TREE/Pretty Eyes	(Reprise 0336)	.75	3.00	65
MICHAEL/San Francisco De Assisi	(Reprise 0300)	.75	3.00	64
ROCK ON/Since I Don't Have	(King 5187)	1.00	4.00	59
SAD TOMORROWS/I've Lost My Love For You	(Reprise 0328)	.75	3.00	65
SALLY WAS A GOOD OLD GIRL/	(Reprise 0659)	.75	3.00	68
SINNER MAN/Double Trouble	(Reprise 0405)	.75	3.00	65
SINNER NOT A SAINT/If	(Ultra Modern 106)	1.00	4.00	64
WHAT HAVE I GOT OF MY OWN/Ya Ya	(Reprise 0276)	.75	3.00	64
LOR, Denise				
IF I GIVE MY HEART TO YOU/Hello Darling	(Major 27)	1.25	5.00	54
LORD & THE FLIES				
COME WHAT MAY/Echoes	(USA 857)	.75	3.00	66
LORD, Brian				
BIG SURFER/Not Another One	(Capitol 4981)	1.00	4.00	63
LORD, Dick				
LIKE RINGO/The Name On The Wall	(Atco 6331)	1.25	5.00	64
LORD ROCKINGHAM'S XI				
FRIED ONIONS/The Squelch	(London 1810)	1.00	4.00	58
LORELEIS				
YOU'RE SO NICE TO BE NEAR/Wildsville	(Spotlight 390)	1.25	5.00	55
LOREN, Donna				
DANNY/I Can't Make My Heart Say Goodbye	(Challenge 59222)	.75	3.00	63
I'M IN LOVE WITH THE TICKET TAKER AT THE BIJOU MOVIE/ I'm Gonna Be All Right	(Challenge 9173)	.75	3.00	62
ON THE GOOD SHIP LOLLIPOP/If You Love Me	(Challenge 9190)	.75	3.00	63
LOREN, Frankie				
SOON THE SCHOOL YEAR WILL BE OVER/ Hey Little Girl	(Mercury 71444)	1.00	4.00	59
LOREN, Sophia				
WOMAN OF THE RIVER (MAMBO)/ Nyves (Mambo Suby)	(RCA Victor 47-6385)	1.00	4.00	55
LORIN, Terry				
DREAM DATE/Sick Sick Sick	(Colony 110)	1.25	5.00	
(With & The Boyfriends)				
TRULY, I LOVE YOU TRULY/Why Did You Do It	(Rider 108)	1.25	5.00	
(Shown as by Terry & The Mellows)				
LORING, Gloria				
CHELSEA MORNING/	(MGM 13942)	.50	2.00	72
LORIS & SCHULMAN				
BROAD STREET BULLIES/	(So-Char 101)	1.25	5.00	
LORNETTES, The				
HIS WAY WITH THE GIRLS/Down The Block & Up To Heaven	(Gallo 110)	.75	3.00	
LOS BRAVOS (Featuring Mike Kennedy)				
BLACK IS BLACK/I Want A Name	(Press 60002)	.75	3.00	66
BRING A LITTLE LOVIN'/Make It Last	(Press 3020)	.75	3.00	68
GOING NOWHERE/Brand New Baby	(Press 60003)	.75	3.00	66
I'M ALL EARS/You'll Never Get The Chance Again	(Press 60004)	.75	3.00	67
LOSERS, The				
BALBOA PARTY/Snake Eyes	(Party 711)	1.00	4.00	62
LOS INDIOS TABAJARAS				
ALWAYS IN MY HEART/Moonlight & Shadows	(RCA Victor 47-8313)	.75	3.00	64
MARIA ELENA/Jungle Dream	(RCA Victor 47-8216)	.75	3.00	63
Instrumentals				
LOST				
I SHALL BE RELEASED/	(Janus 109)	1.25	5.00	66
KEROUAC/Mass. Ave.	(Garage 505)	1.25	5.00	66
MAYBE MORE THAN YOU/Back Door Blues	(Capitol 5519)	1.25	5.00	65
VIOLET GOWN/Mean Motorcycle	(Capitol 5708)	1.25	5.00	66
VIOLET GOWN/No Reason Why	(Capitol 5725)	1.25	5.00	66
LOST & FOUND				
FOREVER LASTING PLASTIC/Everybody's Here	(International Artists 120)	1.25	5.00	67
PROFESSOR BLACK/ When Will You Come Through	(International Artists 125)	1.25	5.00	67
LOST SOULS, The				
ARTIFICIAL ROSE/Sad Little Girl	(Liberty 56024)	1.50	6.00	
LOTHAR & THE HAND PEOPLE				
EVERY SINGLE WORD/Comic Strip	(Capitol 5945)	2.00	8.00	67
HAVE MERCY/Let The Boy Pretend	(Capitol 2008)	1.50	6.00	67
L-O-V-E/Rose Colored Glasses	(Capitol 5874)	2.00	8.00	67
MACHINES/Milkweed Love	(Capitol 2376)	1.25	5.00	69
MIDNIGHT RANGER/Yes, I Love You	(Capitol 2556)	1.25	5.00	69
LOU, Bonnie				
DADDY-O/Dancin' In My Socks	(King 4835)	1.00	4.00	55
LOUDERMILK, John D.				
ANGELA JONES/Road Hog	(RCA Victor 47-8101)	.75	3.00	62
BLUE TRAIN (OF THE HEARTBREAK LINE)/ Rhythm & Blues	(RCA Victor 47-8308)	.75	3.00	64
CALLIN' DOCTOR CASEY/Oh How Sad	(RCA Victor 47-8054)	.75	3.00	62
EVERY DAY I LEARN A LITTLE MORE ABOUT LOVE/ What Would It Take	(Music Is Medicine 002)	.50	2.00	78

TITLE/FLIP	LABEL & NO.	GOOD	NEAR MINT	YR.
GOIN' AWAY TO SCHOOL/This Cold War With You	(Columbia 41247)	2.00	8.00	58
GUITAR PLAYER/Bad News	(RCA Victor 47-8154)	.75	3.00	63
LANGUAGE OF LOVE/Darling Jane	(RCA Victor 47-7938)	.75	3.00	61
LOVER'S LANE/Yo Yo	(Columbia 41209)	2.00	8.00	58
ROAD HOG/Angela Jones	(RCA Victor 47-8101)	.75	3.00	62
SITTIN' IN THE BALCONY/A-Plus In Love	(Colonial 430)	1.00	4.00	57
(Shown as by Johnny Dee)				
SOMEBODY SWEET/They Were Right	(Dot 15699)	1.00	4.00	58
(Shown as by Johnny Dee)				
TEENAGE QUEEN/It's Gotta Be You	(Colonial 433)	1.25	5.00	57
(Shown as by Johnny Dee)				
TH' WIFE/Nothing To Gain	(RCA Victor 47-8389)	.75	3.00	64
THOU SHALT NOT STEAL/Mister Jones	(RCA Victor 47-7993)	.75	3.00	62
YEARBOOK/Susie's House	(Columbia 41165)	2.00	8.00	58
Also see Sneezer, Ebe				
LOU, Herb B: see Herb B. Lou				
LOUISIANA'S LE ROUX				
FEEL IT/Thunder N' Lightnin'	(Capitol 4736)	.50	2.00	79
NEW ORLEANS LADIES/Love Abductor	(Capitol 4586)	.50	2.00	78
TAKE A RIDE ON A RIVER BOAT/	(Capitol 4651)	.50	2.00	78
LOUNGERS, The				
CATHY'S CLOWN/Girls	(Beachwood 4422)	.75	3.00	64
LOUSY LOVERS, The				
GYPSY GOOD TIME, A/Scraping The Bottom	(Pooch 1020)	1.25	5.00	67
LOVE (Featuring Arthur Lee)				
ALONE AGAIN OR/A House Is Not A Motel	(Elektra 45629)	1.25	5.00	68
ALONE AGAIN OR/A House Is Not A Motel	(Elektra 45700)	.75	3.00	70
I'LL PRAY FOR YOU/Stand Out	(Blue Thumb 106)	1.00	4.00	
KEEP ON SHINING/The Everlasting First	(Blue Thumb 7116)	1.00	4.00	
MY LITTLE RED BOOK/Message To Pretty	(Elektra 45603)	1.00	4.00	66
ORANGE SKIES/She Comes In Colors	(Elektra 45608)	1.25	5.00	66
QUE VIDA/Revelation	(Elektra 45613)	1.25	5.00	67
7 & 7 IS/No. Fourteen	(Elektra 45605)	1.25	5.00	66
TIME IS LIKE A RIVER/With A Little Energy	(RSO 502)	1.00	4.00	74
YOU SAID YOU WOULD	(RSO 506)	1.00	4.00	75
YOUR MIND & WE BELONG TOGETHER/ Laughing Stock	(Elektra 45633)	1.25	5.00	
Also see Lee, Arthur				
LOVE AFFAIR, The				
BRINGING ON BACK THE GOOD TIMES/Another Day	(Date 1652)	.75	3.00	69
EVERLASTING LOVE/Gone Are The Songs Of Yesterday	(Date 1591)	.75	3.00	68
I'M HAPPY/A Day Without Love	(Date 1627)	.75	3.00	68
LET ME KNOW/One Road	(Date 1646)	.75	3.00	69
SOMEONE LIKE ME/Rainbow Valley	(Date 1608)	.75	3.00	68
LOVE, Billy, & The Lovers				
LEGEND OF LOVE/Hold Me Close	(Dragon 4403)	2.50	10.00	
LOVE, Darlene (Of The Blossoms)				
CHRISTMAS (BABY, PLEASE COME HOME)/ Harry & Milt Meet Hal B.	(Phillies 119)	1.25	5.00	63
CHRISTMAS/Winter Blues	(Phillies 125)	1.50	6.00	64
CHRISTMAS (BABY, PLEASE COME HOME)/ Winter Blues	(Phillies X125)	2.00	8.00	65
CHRISTMAS (BABY, PLEASE COME HOME)/ Winter Wonderland	(Warner-Spector 0401)	.50	2.00	74
FINE FINE BOY, A/Nino & Sonny	(Phillies 117)	1.25	5.00	63
HE'S A QUIET GUY/Stumble & Fall	(Phillies 123)	6.25	25.00	64
IF/Too Late To Say You're Sorry	(Reprise 534)	1.00	4.00	66
(TODAY I MET) BOY I'M GONNA MARRY, THE/ My Heart Beat A Little Bit	(Philles 111)	2.00	8.00	63
(TODAY I MET) THE BOY I'M GONNA MARRY/ Playing For Keeps	(Philles 111)	1.00	4.00	63
WAIT 'TILL MY BOBBY GETS HOME/Take It From Me	(Philles 114)	1.00	4.00	63
Also see Bob B. Soxx & The Blue Jeans				
Also see Moose & The Pelicans				
LOVE EXCHANGE, The				
SWALLOW THE SUN/	(Uptown)	1.25	5.00	
LOVE, Frankie				
FIRST STAR/Save Her Love For Me	(LaRosa 101)	1.00	4.00	
LOVE, Honey, & The Love Notes				
WE BELONG TOGETHER/Mary Ann	(Cameo 380)	1.00	4.00	65
WE BELONG TOGETHER/Mary Ann	(Cameo 380)	.75	3.00	66
LOVEJAYS, The				
IT'S MIGHTY NICE/Payin' (For The Wrong I've Done)	(Red-Bird 10-003)	.75	3.00	64
LOVELESS, Bobby				
NIGHT OWL/You Are Doing Me Wrong	(Michelle 932)	.75	3.00	
LOVE NOTES, The				
GLORIA/Mathematics Of Love	(Wilshire 203)	2.00	8.00	63
OUR SONGS OF LOVE/Nancy	(Wilshire 200)	2.00	8.00	63
LOVERS, The				
SOMEONE/Do This For Me	(Philips 40353)	1.00	4.00	66
LOVERS, The				
DARLING IT'S WONDERFUL/ Gotta Whole Lot Of Lovin To Do	(Lamp 2005)	1.00	4.00	57
LOVERS, The				
CARAVAN OF LONELY MEN/In My Tenement	(Agon 1011)	2.50	10.00	
LOVE SCULPTURE (Featuring Dave Edmunds)				
IN THE LAND OF THE FEW/Farandole	(Parrot 342)	2.00	8.00	70
SABRE DANCE/I Think Of Love	(Parrot 335)	2.50	10.00	68
LOVE SOCIETY, The				
DON'T WORRY BABY/You Know How I Feel	(RCA 0257)	1.25	5.00	74
TOBACCO ROAD/Drops Of Rain	(Scepter 12236)	1.00	4.00	68
LOVETTE, Eddie				
BY-OOH-PAOOH-PA-YA/You're My Girl	(Steady 122)	.75	3.00	69
LITTLE BLUE BIRD/	(Steady 002)	.75	3.00	69
TOO EXPERIENCED/	(Steady 124)	.75	3.00	69
LOVICH, Lene				
HOME/	(Stiff-Epic 50767)	.50	2.00	79
LUCKY NUMBER/Lucky Number (Slavic Dance Version)	(Stiff-Epic 50725)	.50	2.00	79
LOVIN' COHENS, The				
NOSHVILLE KATZ/Shoily Klein	(MGM 13700)	.75	3.00	67
LOVIN' SPOONFUL, The (Featuring John Sebastian)				
DARLING BE HOME SOON/Darling Companion	(Kama Sutra 220)	.75	3.00	67
DAYDREAM/Night Owl Blues	(Kama Sutra 208)	.75	3.00	66
DID YOU EVER HAVE TO MAKE UP YOUR MIND/ Didn't Want To Have To Do It	(Kama Sutra 209)	.75	3.00	66
DO YOU BELIEVE IN MAGIC/On The Road Again	(Kama Sutra 201)	.75	3.00	65
LONELY (AMY'S THEME)/You're A Big Boy Now	(Kama Sutra 231)	.75	3.00	67
ME ABOUT YOU/Amazing Air	(Kama Sutra 255)	.75	3.00	69
MONEY/Close Your Eyes	(Kama Sutra 241)	.75	3.00	68
NASHVILLE CATS/Full Measure	(Kama Sutra 219)	.75	3.00	66
NEVER GOING BACK/Forever	(Kama Sutra 250)	.75	3.00	68
RAIN ON THE ROOF/Pow	(Kama Sutra 216)	.75	3.00	66

TITLE/FLIP	LABEL & NO.	GOOD	NEAR MINT	YR.
REVELATION: REVOLUTION '69/Run With You (Till I)	(Kama Sutra 251)	.75	3.00	68
SHE IS STILL A MYSTERY/Only Pretty, What A Pity	(Kama Sutra 239)	.75	3.00	67
SIX O'CLOCK/You're A Big Boy Now (Finale)	(Kama Sutra 225)	.75	3.00	67
SUMMER IN THE CITY/Butchie's Tune	(Kama Sutra 211)	.75	3.00	66
(TIL I) RUN WITH YOU/Revelation: Revolution '69	(Kama Sutra 251)	.75	3.00	68
YOU DIDN'T HAVE TO BE SO NICE/My Gal	(Kama Sutra 205)	.75	3.00	65
LOW, Andy Fairweather (Of Amen Corner)				
LA BOOGA ROOGA/Half Way To Everything	(A&M 1752)	.50	2.00	76
SPIDER JIVING/The Light Is Within	(A&M 1649)	.50	2.00	75
WIDE EYED & LEGLESS/	(A&M 1788)	.50	2.00	76
WIDE EYED & LEGLESS/Grease It Up	(A&M 1831)	.50	2.00	77
LOWE, Bernie				
SING SING SING/Intermission Riff (Instrumentals)	(Cameo 153)	.75	3.00	58
LOWE, Jim				
BLUE SUEDE SHOES/Sixty-Four Thousand Dollar Question	(Dot 15456)	1.00	4.00	56
BY YOU, BY YOU, BY YOU/I Feel The Beat	(Dot 15525)	1.00	4.00	56
FOUR WALLS/Talkin' To The Blues	(Dot 15569)	1.00	4.00	57
GAMBLERS & THE GUITAR/Martins & Coys	(Mercury 70168)	1.25	5.00	53
GO & LEAVE ME/Pretty Fickle Darling	(Mercury 70208)	1.25	5.00	53
GREEN DOOR, THE/Little Man In Chinatown	(Dot 15486)	1.00	4.00	56
JOHN JACOB JINGLEHEIMER SMITH/St. James Avenue	(Dot 15429)	1.00	4.00	55
MAYBELLENE/Rene La Rue	(Dot 15407)	1.00	4.00	55
NUEVO LORADO/Close The Door	(Dot 15381)	1.00	4.00	55
RIVERBOAT/Goodbye Little Sweetheart	(Mercury 70319)	1.25	5.00	54
SANTA CLAUS RIDES A STRAWBERRY ROAN/Look In Both Directions	(Mercury 70265)	1.25	5.00	53
LOWE, Nick, & Rockpile				
CRUEL TO BE KIND/Endless Grey Ribbon	(Columbia 11018)	.50	2.00	79
(I LOVE THE SOUND OF) BREAKING GLASS/Endless Sleep	(Columbia 10844)	.50	2.00	78
SO IT GOES/Heart Of The City (Live)	(Columbia 10734)	.50	2.00	78
SWITCHBOARD SUSAN/Basing Street	(Columbia 11131)	.50	2.00	79
Nick Lowe was previously with Brinsley Schwartz.				
LOWE, Virginia				
I'M IN LOVE WITH ELVIS PRESLEY/Empty Feeling	(Melba 107)	2.50	10.00	56
LOYE, Bobby, Jr.				
I JUST STAND HERE/One Of The Lonely Ones	(Ember 1111)	1.25	5.00	61
I'M STARTIN' TONIGHT/Another Mr. Blue	(Laurie 3222)	3.75	15.00	63
LOVING TREE/Another Mr. Blue	(Wilshire 202)	2.00	8.00	
LP'S, The (Featuring Denny)				
WHY NOT GIVE ME YOUR HEART/Slide Calypso	(Rock-It 001)	3.75	15.00	
LUCIA & JOHNNY				
NO MORE/Marriage Talk	(Jet 165)	1.00	4.00	60
NO MORE/Marriage Talk	(Roulette 4278)	.75	3.00	60
LUCKY STARS, The				
MY SURFIN' CITY SWEETHEART/The Strut	(Guyden 2097)	1.00	4.00	63
LUGEE & THE LIONS: see Christie, Lou				
LUKE, Robin				
BAD BOY/School Bus Love Affair	(Dot 16040)	.75	3.00	60
EVERLOVIN'/Well Oh, Well Oh	(Dot 16096)	.75	3.00	60
FIVE MINUTES MORE/Won't You Please Be Mine	(International 212)	2.50	10.00	59
FIVE MINUTES MORE/Who's Gonna Hold Your Hand	(Dot 15959)	.75	3.00	59
MAKE ME A DREAMER/Walkin In The Moonlight	(Dot 16001)	.75	3.00	59
MY GIRL/Chicka Chicka Honey	(International 208)	2.50	10.00	58
MY GIRL/Chicka Chicka Honey	(Dot 15839)	1.00	4.00	58
PART OF A FOOL/Poor Little Rich Boy	(Dot 16229)	.75	3.00	61
STROLLIN' BLUES/You Can't Stop Me From Dreamin'	(International 210)	2.50	10.00	58
STROLLIN' BLUES/You Can't Stop Me From Dreaming	(Dot 15899)	.75	3.00	59
SUSIE DARLIN'/Living's Loving You	(Dot 15781)	1.00	4.00	58
SUSIE DARLIN'/Living's Loving You	(International 206)	5.00	20.00	58
SUSIE DARLIN'/Living's Loving You (Picture Sleeve)	(International 206)	7.50	30.00	58
LUKE, Robin, & Roberta Shore				
FOGGIN' UP THE WINDOWS/Wound Time	(Dot 16366)	.75	3.00	62
LULLABYES, The				
MY HEART CRIES FOR YOU/	(Dimension 1039)	1.00	4.00	64
LULU (Marie Lawrie)				
AFTER THE FEELING IS GONE/Good Day Sunshine	(Atco 6761)	.75	3.00	70
BEST OF BOTH WORLDS/Love Loves To Love Love	(Epic 10260)	.75	3.00	67
BOAT THAT I ROW/Dreary Nights & Days	(Epic 10187)	.75	3.00	67
BOY/Sad Memories	(Epic 10346)	.75	3.00	68
DREARY NIGHTS & DAYS/Let's Pretend	(Epic 10210)	.75	3.00	67
HEAVEN & EARTH & THE STARS/	(Chelsea 3038)	.50	2.00	73
HUM A SONG (FROM YOUR HEART)/Where's Eddie	(Atco 6749)	.75	3.00	70
I'LL COME RUNNING/Here Comes The Night	(Parrot 9714)	1.00	4.00	65
I'M A TIGER/Rattler	(Epic 10420)	.75	3.00	68
IT TAKES A REAL MAN (TO BRING THE WOMAN OUT OF ME)/	(Atco 6885)	.75	3.00	72
LEAVE A LITTLE LOVE/He Don't Want Your Love Anymore	(Parrot 9778)	1.00	4.00	65
LOVE IS THE GREATEST MISTAKE/Don't Take Love For Granted	(Rocket 11355)	.50	2.00	78
MAKE BELIEVE WORLD/Help Me Help You	(Chelsea 0121)	.50	2.00	73
MAN WHO SOLD THE WORLD, THE/	(Chelsea 3001)	.50	2.00	73
ME, THE PEACEFUL HEART/Look Out	(Epic 10302)	.75	3.00	68
MORNING DEW/You & I	(Epic 10367)	.75	3.00	68
OH ME OH MY (I'M A FOOL FOR YOU BABY)/Sweep Around Your Own Back Door	(Atco 6722)	.75	3.00	69
SHOUT/Forget Me Baby	(Parrot 9678)	1.00	4.00	64
SHOUT/When He Touches Me	(Parrot 40021)	.75	3.00	67
TO SIR WITH LOVE/The Boat That I Row	(Epic 10187)	.75	3.00	67
TRY TO UNDERSTAND/Not In This Whole World	(Parrot 9791)	1.00	4.00	65
WITHOUT HIM/This Time (Bistro)	(Epic 10403)	.75	3.00	68
LUMAN, Bob				
ALL NIGHT LONG/Red Cadillac & A Black Moustache (Maroon label)	(Imperial 8311)	3.75	15.00	59
ALL NIGHT LONG/Red Cadillac & A Black Moustache (Black label)	(Imperial 8311)	1.25	5.00	59
BUTTERCUP/Dreamy Doll	(Warner Bros. 5105)	.75	3.00	59
BIG RIVER ROSE/Belonging To You	(Warner Bros. 5272)	.75	3.00	62
BOSTON ROCKER/Old Friends	(Warner Bros. 5506)	.75	3.00	61
CLASS OF '59/My Baby Walks All Over Me	(Warner Bros. 5081)	.75	3.00	59
CHRISTMAS TRIBUTE, A/Give Someone You Love	(Polydor 1444)	.50	2.00	77
GREAT SNOWMAN, THE/The Pig Latin Song	(Warner Bros. 5204)	.75	3.00	61
HEY JOE/Fool	(Warner Bros. 5299)	.75	3.00	62
LET'S THINK ABOUT LIVING/You've Got Everything	(Warner Bros. 5172)	.75	3.00	60
LOUISIANA MAN/Rocks Of Reno	(Warner Bros. 5272)	.75	3.00	62
OH, LONESOME ME/Why, Bye, Bye	(Warner Bros. 5184)	.75	3.00	61
PRIVATE EYE/You've Turned Down The Light	(Warner Bros. 5233)	.75	3.00	61
RED HOT/Whenever You're Ready (Maroon label)	(Imperial 8313)	7.50	30.00	55
RED HOT/Whenever You're Ready (Black label)	(Imperial 8313)	2.50	10.00	59
SVENGALI/Precious	(Capitol 4059)	2.00	8.00	58
YOU'RE EVERYTHING/Envy	(Warner Bros. 5321)	.75	3.00	63
YOUR LOVE/Make Up Your Mind Baby (Maroon label)	(Imperial 8315)	3.75	15.00	56
YOUR LOVE/Make Up Your Mind Baby (Black label)	(Imperial 8315)	1.25	5.00	59
LUND, Art				
MONA LISA/When My Stage Coach Reaches Heaven	(MGM 10689)	1.25	5.00	50
PHILADELPHIA U.S.A./Mam'selle	(Coral 62054)	1.00	4.00	58

TITLE/FLIP	LABEL & NO.	GOOD	NEAR MINT	YR.
LUNDBERG, Victor				
AN OPEN LETTER TO MY TEENAGE SON/My Buddy Carl.	(Liberty 55996)	.75	3.00	67
AN OPEN LETTER TO MY TEENAGE SON/My Buddy Carl.	(Liberty 54567)	.75	3.00	68
LUREX, Larry				
I CAN HEAR MUSIC/Goin' Back	(Anthem 204)	2.50	10.00	
Also see Queen				
LURIE, Elliot				
RICH GIRL/	(Arista 0251)	.50	2.00	76
LUV'D ONES, The				
DANCE KID, DANCE/I'm Leaving You	(Dunwich 136)	.75	3.00	66
I'M LEAVING YOU/Walking The Dog	(Dunwich 117)	.75	3.00	66
STAND TALL/Come Back	(Dunwich 130)	.75	3.00	66
LY-DELLS, The				
GENIE OF THE LAMP/Teenage Tears	(Master 111)	6.25	25.00	
THERE GOES THE BOY/Talking To Myself	(Parkway 897)	1.50	6.00	64
3 LITTLE MONKEYS/Playing Hide & Seek	(Southern Sound 122)	1.25	5.00	65
WIZARD OF LOVE/Let This Night Last	(Master 251)	3.00	12.00	61
LYMAN, Arthur				
LOVE FOR SALE/Love	(Hi Fi 5066)	.75	3.00	63
TABOO/Dahil Sayo	(Hi Fi 550)	.75	3.00	59
YELLOW BIRD/Havah Nagilah (Instrumentals)	(Hi Fi 5024)	.75	3.00	61
LYME & CYBELLE				
FOLLOW ME/Like The Seasons	(White Whale 228)	.75	3.00	66
IF YOU GOT TO GO, GO NOW/I'll Go On	(White Whale 232)	.75	3.00	66
WRITE IF YOU GET WORK/Song #7	(White Whale 245)	.75	3.00	67
LYNAM, Mike, & The Little People				
MESSAGE TO PRETTY/I Need You	(Emanon 101)	1.00	4.00	
LYN & THE INVADERS				
SECRETLY/Boy Is Gone	(Fenton 2040)	1.25	5.00	
LYNDON, Frank (Of The Belmonts)				
DON'T GO AWAY BABY/Lisa	(Uptown 758)	2.50	10.00	
EARTH ANGEL/Don't Look At Me	(Bang 531)	3.75	15.00	66
EARTH ANGEL/Don't Look At Me	(Sabina 520)	3.75	15.00	65
FONZIE MEETS THE SWEAT HOGS/	(Strawberry 101)	.75	3.00	76
SANTA'S JET/Sing Along With Santa's Jet	(Laurie 3322)	3.00	12.00	65
TONIGHT WE WAIL/Cry Cry Cry (With the Regents)	(Jab 1004)	2.00	8.00	
LYNN & THE MERSEY MAIDS				
MRS. JONES YOUR SON GIVES UP TOO EASY/	(Ric 161)	.75	3.00	65
LYNN, Donna				
DONNA LOVES JERRY/Oh, I'm In Love	(Epic 9580)	.75	3.00	63
JAVA (JAVA JONES)/Things I Feel	(Capitol 5156)	.75	3.00	64
MY BOY FRIEND GOT A BEATLE HAIRCUT/That Winter Weekend	(Capitol 5127)	1.50	6.00	64
RONNIE/That's Me I'm The Brother	(Capitol 5087)	.75	3.00	63
LYNNE, Connie				
TRIBUTE TO ELVIS, MEMORIES OF YOU, A/A Tribute To Elvis, Memories Of You	(American Sound 3102)	.50	2.00	77
LYNNE, Gloria				
I WISH YOU LOVE/Through A Long & Sleepless Night	(Everest 2036)	.75	3.00	63
IMPOSSIBLE/This Little Boy Of Mine	(Everest 19418)	.75	3.00	61
WATERMELON MAN/All Alone	(Fontana 1511)	.75	3.00	65
YOU DON'T HAVE TO BE A TOWER OF STRENGTH/I Will Follow You	(Everest 19428)	.75	3.00	61
LYNNE, Jeff (Of The Move)				
DOIN' THAT CRAZY THING/Goin' Down To Rio	(Jet 1060)	.50	2.00	77
DOIN' THAT CRAZY THING/Goin' Down To Rio (12" single issue)	(Jet 1072)	1.00	4.00	77
Also see Electric Light Orchestra, The				
Also see Idle Race				
LYNN, Vera				
AUF WIEDERSEH'N SWEETHEART/Parting Song	(London 1227)	1.00	4.00	52
DON'T CRY MY LOVE/By The Fountains Of Rome	(London 1729)	1.00	4.00	57
IF YOU LOVE ME (REALLY LOVE ME)/C'Est La Vie	(London 1412)	1.00	4.00	54
SUCH A DAY/Unfaithful You	(London 1642)	1.00	4.00	56
YOURS/Love Of My Life	(London 1261)	1.00	4.00	52
LYNYRD SKYNYRD (Featuring Ronnie Van Zant)				
DOUBLE TROUBLE/Roll Gypsy Roll	(MCA 40532)	.50	2.00	76
DOWN SOUTH JUNKIN'/Wino	(MCA 40957)	.50	2.00	78
FREE BIRD/Down South Junkin'	(MCA 40328)	.50	2.00	74
FREE BIRD/Searching	(MCA 40665)	.50	2.00	76
GIMME BACK MY BULLETS/All I Can Do Is Write About It	(MCA 40565)	.50	2.00	76
GIMME THREE STEPS/Travelin' Man	(MCA 40647)	.50	2.00	77
I KNOW A LITTLE/What's Your Name	(MCA 40819)	.50	2.00	77
NEED ALL MY FRIENDS/Michelle	(Atnia 129)	.75	3.00	78
SATURDAY NIGHT SPECIAL/	(MCA 40416)	.50	2.00	75
SWEET HOME ALABAMA/Take YOUR Time	(MCA 40258)	.50	2.00	74
WHAT'S YOUR NAME/I Know A Little	(MCA 40819)	.50	2.00	77
YOU GOT THAT RIGHT/Ain't No Good Life	(MCA 40888)	.50	2.00	78
LYONS, Jamie, Group				
GONNA HAVE A GOOD TIME/Heart Full O' Soul II	(Laurie LR-3427)	.75	3.00	68
LITTLE BLACK EGG/Stay By My Side	(Laurie LR-3409)	.75	3.00	67
SOUL STRUTTIN'/Flowers To Sunshine	(Laurie LR-3422)	.75	3.00	68
STONEY/Rhapsody In F Major	(Laurie LR-3465)	.75	3.00	69
Also see Music Machine, The				
LYRICS, The				
MO SON/So Glad	(Crescendo 381)	.75	3.00	
WAIT/Mr. Man	(Crescendo 393)	.75	3.00	
LYTLE, Johnny				
LOOP, THE/Hot Sauce	(Tuba 2004)	.75	3.00	66

The transition to a country music style has been made by several pop & rock singers of the fifties and sixties. The pop & rock releases by these artists will appear in this guide, while the country music releases will be listed in our guides covering that field of music.

Likewise, your favorite soul and rhythm & blues artists that are not covered in this guide are—or will soon be—included in our Blues-Rhythm & Blues-Soul Price Guide.

TITLE/FLIP	LABEL & NO.	GOOD	NEAR MINT	YR.
M				
MOONLIGHT & MUZAK/	(Sire 49136)	.50	2.00	79
POP MUZIK/M Factor	(Sire 49033)	.50	2.00	79
MAC, Johnny				
EMOTIONAL STORM/Save Me	(Studio 108)	1.00	4.00	
MAC GREGOR, Mary				
FOR A WHILE/The Lady I Am	(Ariola America 7668)	.50	2.00	77
GOOD FRIEND/Rudy & Tripper (Instrumental)	(RSO 938)	.50	2.00	79
I'VE NEVER BEEN TO ME/In Your Eyes	(Ariola 7677)	.50	2.00	78
MEMORIES/	(Ariola 7708)	.50	2.00	78
THIS GIRL HAS JUST TURNED INTO A WOMAN/Good Together	(Ariola America 7662)	.50	2.00	77
TORN BETWEEN TWO LOVERS/I Just Want To Love You	(Ariola America 7638)	.50	2.00	76
WEDDING SONG (THERE IS LOVE), THE/Benjamin	(Ariola 7726)	.50	2.00	78
MACH, Leon				
YOU HURT ME SO/	(Lavender 1554)	.75	3.00	
MAC KENZIE, Gisele				
HARD TO GET/Boston Fancy	("X" 0137)	1.00	4.00	55
PEPPER-HOT BABY/That's The Chance I Have To Take	("X" 0172)	1.00	4.00	55
STAR YOU WISHED UPON LAST NIGHT, THE/It's Delightful To Be Married	(Vik 0233)	1.00	4.00	56
MACK, Lonnie				
BABY, WHAT'S WRONG/Where There's A Will	(Fraternity 918)	.75	3.00	63
COASTIN'/Crying Over You	(Fraternity 942)	.75	3.00	65
HONKY TONK '65/Chicken Pickin'	(Fraternity 951)	.75	3.00	65
I'VE HAD IT/Nashville	(Fraternity 925)	.75	3.00	64
LONNIE ON THE MOVE/Say Something Nice To Me	(Fraternity 920)	.75	3.00	64
MEMPHIS/Down In The Dumps	(Fraternity 906)	.75	3.00	63
TONKY-GO-GO/When I'm Alone	(Fraternity 946)	.75	3.00	64
WHAM!/Suzie-Q	(Fraternity 912)	.75	3.00	63
MACRAE, Meredith				
IMAGE OF A BOY/Time Stands Still	(Canjo 103)	.75	3.00	64
MADDIN, Jimmy				
DON'T STOP NOW/Tongue Tied	(American International 542)	1.25	5.00	
MADDOX, Johnny				
CRAZY OTTO (MEDLEY), THE/Humoresque	(Dot 15325)	1.00	4.00	55
HEART & SOUL/Dixieland Band	(Dot 15488)	1.00	4.00	56
YELLOW DOG BLUES/Sugar Train (Instrumentals)	(Dot 15683)	1.00	4.00	58
MAD ENGLISHMEN & THE FURYS, The				
BEETLE MANIA/Janice	(Vee Six 1023)	2.00	8.00	64
MAD HATTERS, The				
I'LL COME RUNNING/Hello Girl	(Fontana 1582)	.75	3.00	67
MAD LADS, The				
DON'T HAVE TO SHOP AROUND/Tear Maker	(Volt 127)	1.25	5.00	65
WHY/Hey Man	(Mark-Fi 342)	2.50	10.00	
MAD MARTIANS, The				
OUTER SPACE LOOTERS NO. 1/Outer Space Looters No. 2 (Novelty/Break-in)	(Satellite 33617)	5.00	20.00	
MAD MIKE & THE MANIACS				
QUARTER TO FOUR/The Hunch	(Hunch 345)	1.00	4.00	61
MAD MILO				
ELVIS FOR XMAS/Happy New Year	(Million $ 20018)	5.00	20.00	
MAD RIVER				
COPPER PLATES/Harfy Magnum	(Capitol 2559)	1.50	6.00	69
HIGH ALL THE TIME/A Gazelle	(Capitol 2310)	2.00	8.00	68
MADARA, Johnny				
HEAVENLY/Save It	(Landa 687)	1.00	4.00	
LOVESICK/Be My Girl	(Prep 110)	1.25	5.00	57
STORY UNTOLD, A/Vacation Time	(Bamboo 511)	1.25	5.00	
MADIGAN, Betty				
DANCE EVERYONE DANCE/My Symphony Of Love	(Coral 62007)	1.00	4.00	58
JOEY/And So I Walked Alone	(MGM 11716)	1.00	4.00	54
THERE SHOULD BE RULES/Strangers	(MGM 12094)	1.00	4.00	55
TONIGHT, TONIGHT/Just As I Am	(Coral 62139)	1.00	4.00	60
MADISON, Ronnie				
LINDA/Here I Stand	(Storm 987)	5.00	20.00	
TRUE LOVE GONE/Lovely Night	(Coral 61812)	1.25	5.00	57
MADISONS, The				
CAN YOU IMAGINE IT/The Wind & The Rain	(Lawn 240)	2.50	10.00	64
MADISONS, The (Featuring Larry Santos)				
CHERYL ANNE/Looking For True Love	(MGM 13312)	3.00	12.00	65
ONLY A FOOL/Stagger	(Jumaca 601)	1.25	5.00	65
MADISON STREET (Vinny Corella With Randy & The Rainbows)				
MINSTREL MAN/King Of Love	(Millenium 605)	.75	3.00	
Also see Triangle				
MADMAN JONES, The				
JESS' ONE MO' TIME/Oh Henry	(Cameo 146)	1.00	4.00	58

TITLE/FLIP	LABEL & NO.	GOOD	NEAR MINT	YR.
MADURI, Carl				
MISS TEENAGE AMERICA/What A Night	(Cameo 202)	.75	3.00	61
MAESTRO, Johnny (Johnny Mastroangelo)				
ESAME BABY/It Must Be Love	(Coed 562)	10.00	40.00	61
IFTY MILLION HEARTBEATS/Before I Loved Her	(United Artists 474)	2.50	10.00	62
LL BE TRUE/Over The Weekend	(Cameo 256)	2.00	8.00	63
.O.U./The Way You Look Tonight	(Coed 557)	1.00	4.00	61
S IT YOU/My Time	(Parkway 118)	1.00	4.00	67
IODEL GIRL/We've Got To Tell Them	(Coed 545)	1.00	4.00	61
EAN ON ME/Make Up My Mind	(Cameo 305)	1.00	4.00	64
IR. HAPPINESS/Test Of Love	(Coed 552)	1.00	4.00	61
HONE BOOTH ON THE HIGHWAY/She's All Mine Alone	(Apt 25075)	1.50	6.00	65
AIN CAME, THE/Never Knew This Kind Of Hurt Before	(Buddah 201)	1.25	5.00	71
NOW/	(Buddah 289)	1.25	5.00	72
RY ME/Heartburn	(Parkway 987)	1.00	4.00	66
VHAT A SURPRISE/Warning Voice	(Coed 549)	1.00	4.00	61
Johnny Maestro was the voice of both the Crests and the Brooklyn Bridge groups. He also recorded as Johnny Masters.				
MAGIC				
THINK I LOVE YOU/That's How Strong My Love Is	(Monster 0001)	1.00	4.00	
MAGIC CHRISTIANS, The (With Trevor Burton)				
OME & GET IT/Nats	(Commonwealth United 3006)	.75	3.00	70
Trevor Burton was also in the Move.				
MAGIC FERN				
WONDER WHY/Maggie	(Jerden 813)	.75	3.00	67
MAGICIANS, The				
N INVITATION TO CRY/ Rain Don't Fall On Me No More	(Columbia 43435)	1.00	4.00	65
ND I'LL TELL THE WORLD/I'd Like To Know	(Columbia 43725)	1.00	4.00	65
MAGIC LANTERN				
OUNTRY WOMAN/	(Charisma 100)	.50	2.00	72
MAGIC LANTERNS, The (With Albert Hammond & Mike Hazlewood)				
BOSSA NOVA 1940-HELLO YOU LOVERS/ Melt All Your Troubles Away	(Atlantic 2626)	.75	3.00	69
GIVE ME LOVE/Biding My Time	(Atlantic 2600)	.75	3.00	69
GREEDY GIRL/Excuse Me, Baby	(Epic 10062)	.75	3.00	66
KNIGHT IN RUSTY ARMOUR/Simple Things	(Epic 10111)	.75	3.00	66
LET THE SUN SHINE IN/	(Big Tree 113)	.50	2.00	71
ONE NIGHT STAND/Frisco Annie	(Atlantic 2715)	.75	3.00	70
ONE NIGHT STAND/Frisco Annie	(Big Tree 109)	.50	2.00	71
SHAME, SHAME/Baby, I Got To Go	(Atlantic 2560)	.75	3.00	68
MAGIC MUSHROOMS, The				
CRY BABY/I'm Gone	(Warner Bros. 5846)	.75	3.00	66
T'S-A-HAPPENING/Never More	(A&M 815)	.75	3.00	66
LOOK IN MY FACE/Never Let Go	(Philips 40483)	.75	3.00	67
MUNICIPAL WATER MAINTENANCE MAN/ Let The Rain Be Me	(East Coast 1001)	1.25	5.00	
MAGIC RING, The				
LITTLE MARY SUNSHINE/Do I Love You	(Music Factory 404)	.75	3.00	68
MAGIC SHIP, The				
NIGHT TIME MUSIC/Green Plant	(BT Puppy 548)	1.00	4.00	66
NIGHT TIME MUSIC/To Love Somebody	(Crazy Horse 1322)	1.00	4.00	66
MAGIC TOUCH, The (Vito & The Salutaions)				
BABY YOU BELONG TO ME/Lost & Lonely Boy	(Roulette 7143)	1.50	6.00	73
MAGIC TRIPLETS, The				
PHONEY BALONEY/Tic Tac Toe	(Decca 32478)	2.50	10.00	69
RATED X/Don't Need A Love To Tie Me Down	(Keff 4447)	2.00	8.00	
STOP LOOK & LISTEN/Stormy Weather	(Keff 4452)	2.00	8.00	
Also see Energizers, The				
MAGICS, The				
CHAPEL BELLS/She Can't Stop Dancing	(Debra 1003)	1.50	6.00	63
MAGISTRATES, The				
HERE COMES THE JUDGE/Girl	(MGM 13946)	1.25	5.00	69
This group includes some former members of the Dovells.				
MAGNETICS, The				
WHERE ARE YOU/The Train	(Allrite 620)	1.00	4.00	
MAGNETS, The				
DRAG RACE/Joker	(London 10036)	.75	3.00	63
MAGNETS, The				
YOU JUST SAY THE WORD/Surprise	(Groove 0058)	3.75	15.00	55
WHEN THE SCHOOL BELLS RING/ Don't Tarry Little Mary	(RCA Victor 47-7391)	3.00	12.00	58
MAGNIFICENT FOUR, The				
LOSER YOU ARE, THE/Uncle Sam	(Blast 210)	2.00	8.00	63
LOSER YOU ARE, THE/Uncle Sam	(Whale 506)	2.00	8.00	63
MAGNIFICENT MEN				
BABE, I'M CRAZY ABOUT YOU/Forever Together	(Capitol 2062)	.75	3.00	67
COULD BE SO HAPPY/You Changed My Life	(Capitol 5905)	.75	3.00	67
MUCH MUCH MORE OF YOUR LOVE/Stormy Weather	(Capitol 5812)	.75	3.00	67
SWEET SOUL MEDLEY (PART 1)/ Sweet Soul Medley (Part 2)	(Capitol 5976)	.75	3.00	67
MAGNIFICENT VII, The				
SHOW ME/Boogidy	(Dimension 1050)	.75	3.00	65
MAHARIS, George				
ABY HAS GONE BYE BYE/After One Kiss	(Epic 9555)	.75	3.00	62
OVE ME AS I LOVE YOU/They Knew About You	(Epic 9522)	.75	3.00	62
EACH ME TONIGHT/After The Lights Go Down Low	(Epic 9504)	.75	3.00	62
WHERE CAN YOU GO/Kiss Me	(Epic 9600)	.75	3.00	63
MAHOGANY RUSH (Featuring Frank Marino)				
LL ALONG THE WATCHTOWER/Down, Down, Down	(Columbia 11077)	.50	2.00	79
EW ROCK & ROLL, A/Child Of The Novelty	(20th Century 2111)	.50	2.00	74
ATISFY YOUR SOUL/	(20th Century 2166)	.50	2.00	75
MAJESTICS, The				
OSS WALK (PART 1)/Boss Walk (Part 2)	(Dunes 2014)	.75	3.00	
IRL OF MY DREAMS/It Hurts Me	(Linda 121)	1.00	4.00	
ONELY HEART/Gwendolyn	(Chex 1006)	2.50	10.00	
EARCHING FOR A NEW LOVE/Angel Of Love	(Jordan 123)	1.25	5.00	61
EARCHING FOR A NEW LOVE/Angel Of Love	(Nu-Tone 123)	1.25	5.00	61
EARCHING FOR A NEW LOVE/Angel Of Love	(Pixie 6901)	1.25	5.00	61
MAJESTICS, The				
ONE STRANGER, THE/Sweet One (With the Nightwinds)	(20th Fox 171)	1.50	6.00	59
ONE STRANGER, THE/Sweet One (With the Nightwinds)	(Sioux 91459)	2.00	8.00	59
COWBOYS/So You Want To Rock	(Faro 592)	1.50	6.00	59
MAJORETTES, The				
ET'S DO THE KANGAROO/Dance With Me	(Troy 1004)	1.00	4.00	
WHITE LEVIS/Please Come Back	(Troy 1000)	2.00	8.00	63
(Picture sleeve)				

TITLE/FLIP	LABEL & NO.	GOOD	NEAR MINT	YR.
MAJORS, The				
ANYTHING YOU CAN DO/What In The World	(Imperial 5914)	.75	3.00	63
I'LL BE THERE/Ooh Wee Baby	(Imperial 6009)	.75	3.00	63
LITTLE BIT NOW, A/She's A Troublemaker	(Imperial 5879)	.75	3.00	62
TRA-LA-LA/What Have You Been Doin'	(Imperial 5936)	.75	3.00	63
WHICH WAY DID SHE GO/Your Life Begins	(Imperial 5991)	.75	3.00	63
WONDERFUL DREAM, A/Time Will Tell	(Imperial 5855)	.75	3.00	62
Group members: Ricky Cordo, Idella Morris, Frank Troutt, Ronald Gathers, Eugene Glass.				
MAJORS, Farrah Fawcett				
YOU/Let Me Get To Know You (With Jean-Paul Vignon)	(NBR 7902)	.50	2.00	
MALIBUS, The				
LEAVE ME ALONE/Cry	(Planet 58)	1.25	5.00	
MALIBU'S				
BROKEN MAN, A/It's All Over But The Shouting	(White Whale 289)	.75	3.00	69
MALMKVIST, Siw, & Umberto Marcato				
SOLE SOLE SOLE/Sabato Sera	(Jubilee 5479)	.75	3.00	64
MALO (Featuring Jorge Santana)				
CAFE/Peace	(Warner Bros. 7605)	.50	2.00	72
MIDNIGHT THOUGHTS/Latin Bugaloo	(Warner Bros. 7677)	.50	2.00	73
PYE MANA/I'm For Real	(Warner Bros. 7668)	.50	2.00	72
SUAVECITO/Nena	(Warner Bros. 7559)	.50	2.00	72
MALOMEN, The				
SHE MEANS THE WORLD TO ME/	(P.H. 2455)	.75	3.00	
MALTBY, Richard				
RAT RACE, THE/Walkie Talkie	(Roulette 4270)	.75	3.00	60
ST. LOUIS BLUES MAMBO/Beloved, Be True	("X" 0042)	1.00	4.00	54
THEME FROM "THE MAN WITH THE GOLDEN ARM"/Hearts	(Vik 0196)	1.00	4.00	56
Instrumentals				
MAMA CASS (Cass Elliot of the Mamas & Papas)				
BABY I'M YOURS/Cherries Jubilee	(RCA 0644)	.75	3.00	72
CALIFORNIA EARTHQUAKE/Talkin' To Your Toothbrush	(Dunhill 4166)	.75	3.00	68
DON'T LET THE GOOD LIFE PASS YOU BY/ Song That Never Comes	(Dunhill 4264)	.75	3.00	70
DREAM A LITTLE DREAM OF ME/Midnight Voyage	(Dunhill 4145)	.75	3.00	68
GOOD TIMES ARE COMING/Welcome To The World	(Dunhill 4253)	.75	3.00	70
(IF YOU'RE GONNA) BREAK ANOTHER HEART/Disney Girls	(RCA 0764)	.75	3.00	72
IT'S GETTING BETTER/Who's To Blame	(Dunhill 4195)	.75	3.00	69
LISTEN TO THE WORLD/I Think A Lot About You	(RCA 0957)	.75	3.00	73
MAKE YOUR OWN KIND OF MUSIC/Lady Love	(Dunhill 4214)	.75	3.00	69
MOVE IN A LITTLE CLOSER, BABY/All For Me	(Dunhill 4184)	.75	3.00	69
NEW WORLD COMING/Blow Me A Kiss	(Dunhill 4225)	.75	3.00	69
SOMETHING TO MAKE YOU HAPPY/Next To You	(Dunhill 4226)	.75	3.00	71
(With Dave Mason)				
SONG THAT NEVER COMES, A/I Can Dream, Can't I	(Dunhill 4244)	.75	3.00	70
TOO MUCH TRUTH, TOO MUCH LOVE/Walk To The Point	(Dunhill 4271)	.75	3.00	71
(With Dave Mason)				
MAMA CATS, The				
MISS YOU/My Boy	(Hideout 1225)	1.25	5.00	
MAMAS & PAPAS, The (John Phillips, "Mama" Cass Elliot, Denny Doherty, Michelle Gilliam)				
CALIFORNIA DREAMIN'/Somebody Groovy	(Dunhill 4020)	.75	3.00	65
CREEQUE ALLEY/Did You Ever Want To Cry	(Dunhill 4083)	.75	3.00	67
DANCING BEAR/John's Music Box	(Dunhill 4113)	.75	3.00	67
DEDICATED TO THE ONE I LOVE/Free Advice	(Dunhill 4077)	.75	3.00	67
DO YOU WANNA DANCE/My Girl	(Dunhill 4171)	.75	3.00	68
FOR THE LOVE OF IVY/Strange Young Girl	(Dunhill 4150)	.75	3.00	68
GLAD TO BE UNHAPPY/Hey Girl	(Dunhill 4107)	.75	3.00	67
I SAW HER AGAIN/Even If I Could	(Dunhill 4031)	.75	3.00	66
LOOK THROUGH MY WINDOW/Once Was A Time I Thought	(Dunhill 4026)	.75	3.00	66
LOOK THROUGH ANY WINDOW/Once Was A Time I Thought	(Dunhill 4050)	.75	3.00	66
MONDAY MONDAY/Got A Feelin'	(Dunhill 4026)	.75	3.00	66
SAFE IN MY GARDEN/Too Late	(Dunhill 4125)	.75	3.00	68
STEP OUT/Shooting Star	(Dunhill 4301)	.75	3.00	72
TWELVE THIRTY (YOUNG GIRLS ARE COMING TO THE CANYON)/ Straight Shooter	(Dunhill 4099)	.75	3.00	67
WORDS OF LOVE/Dancing In The Street	(Dunhill 4057)	.75	3.00	66
Also see Mugwumps, The				
MAMA'S PRIDE				
SHE'S A STRANGER TO ME NOW/	(Atco 7081)	.50	2.00	78
MAN				
OUT OF YOUR HEAD/(I'm A) Love-Taker	(MCA 40539)	.50	2.00	76
MAN (With Richard Supa)				
GIRL OF THE NORTH COUNTRY/	(Columbia 44953)	.75	3.00	69
MANCHESTER, Melissa				
BETTER DAYS/Sing, Sing, Sing	(Arista 0183)	.50	2.00	76
DIRTY WORK/Be Somebody	(Arista 0237)	.50	2.00	77
DON'T CRY OUT LOUD/We Had This Time	(Arista 0373)	.50	2.00	78
I WANNA BE WHERE YOU ARE/No One's Ever Seen The Sight Of Me	(Arista 0267)	.50	2.00	77
JUST TOO MANY PEOPLE/This Lady's Not Home	(Arista 0146)	.50	2.00	75
JUST YOU & I/My Sweet Thing	(Arista 0168)	.50	2.00	76
O HEAVEN (HOW YOU'VE CHANGED TO ME)/	(Bell 45465)	.50	2.00	74
MIDNIGHT BLUE/I Got Eyes	(Arista 0116)	.50	2.00	75
MONKEY SEE, MONKEY DO/So's My Old Man	(Arista 0218)	.50	2.00	77
PRETTY GIRLS/It's All In The Sky Above	(Arista 0456)	.50	2.00	79
RESCUE ME/Happy Endings	(Arista 0196)	.50	2.00	76
TELLIN' THE WORLD (TO GET OUT & VOTE)/	(RCA 366)	.75	3.00	72
THEME FROM ICE CASTLES (THROUGH THE EYES OF LOVE)/ Such A Morning	(Arista 0405)	.50	2.00	79
MANCHESTERS, The (Featuring David Gates)				
I DON'T COME FROM ENGLAND/Dragonfly	(Vee Jay VJ-700)	1.25	5.00	65
MANCINI, Henry				
BANZAI PIPELINE/Rhapsody In Blue	(RCA Victor 47-8184)	.75	3.00	63
CHARADE/Orange Tamoure	(RCA Victor 47-8256)	.75	3.00	63
DAYS OF WINE & ROSES/76 Trombones	(RCA Victor 47-8120)	.75	3.00	63
FALLOUT/Dreamsville	(RCA Victor 47-7442)	.75	3.00	59
FALLOUT/Dreamsville	(RCA Victor 61-7442)	1.50	6.00	59
(Stereo single)				
MR. LUCKY/Floating Pad	(RCA Victor 47-7705)	.75	3.00	60
MOON RIVER/Breakfast At Tiffany's	(RCA Victor 47-7916)	.75	3.00	61
PETER GUNN THEME/The Brothers Go To Mother's	(RCA Victor 47-7460)	.75	3.00	59
PINK PANTHER THEME, THE/It Had Better Be Tonight	(RCA Victor 47-8286)	.75	3.00	64
POW!/Cha Cha For Gia	(Liberty F-55184)	1.00	4.00	59
RAVEL'S BOLERO/It's Easy To Say (With Julie Andrews & Dudley Moore)	(Warner Bros. 49139)	.50	2.00	79
SHOT IN THE DARK, A/The Shadows Of Paris	(RCA Victor 47-8381)	.75	3.00	64
(THEME FROM) GREAT IMPOSTER, THE/ Love Music	(RCA Victor 47-7830)	.75	3.00	61
MANDERINS, The				
GOING AWAY/Let The Bells Ring	(Band Box 236)	1.50	6.00	

TITLE/FLIP	LABEL & NO.	GOOD	NEAR MINT	YR.
MANFRED MANN (With Mike D'Abo)				
BLINDED BY THE LIGHT/Starbird No. 2	(Warner Bros. 8252)	.50	2.00	76
COME TOMORROW/What Did I Do Wrong	(Ascot 2170)	1.00	4.00	65
DO WAH DIDDY DIDDY/What You Gonna Do	(Ascot 2157)	.75	3.00	64
FEELING SO GOOD/Ha, Ha Said The Clown	(Mercury 72675)	.75	3.00	67
5-4-3-2-1/Without You	(Prestige 312)	1.50	6.00	64
FOX ON THE RUN/Too Many People	(Mercury 72879)	.75	3.00	68
HI LILI, HI LO/She Needs Company	(Ascot 2210)	1.00	4.00	66
I CAN'T BELIEVE WHAT YOU SAY/ My Little Red Bood (All I Do Is Talk About You)	(Ascot 2241)	1.00	4.00	68
IF YOU GOTTA GO, GO NOW/One In The Middle	(Ascot 2194)	1.00	4.00	65
I'M UP & I'M LEAVING/	(Polydor 14130)	.50	2.00	72
IT'S ALL OVER NOW BABY BLUE/	(Polydor 14164)	.50	2.00	73
JUST LIKE A WOMAN/I Wanna Be Rich	(Mercury 72607)	.75	3.00	66
MIGHTY QUINN (QUINN THE ESKIMO)/ By Request-Edwin Garvey	(Mercury 72770)	.75	3.00	68
(Reissue of "Quinn The Eskimo," with different title)				
MY LITTLE RED BOOK/What Am I Doing Wrong	(Ascot 2184)	1.25	5.00	65
MY NAME IS JACK/There Is A Man	(Mercury 72882)	.75	3.00	68
PLEASE MRS. HENRY/Prayer	(Polydor 14097)	.50	2.00	71
QUINN THE ESKIMO/By Request-Edwin Garvey	(Mercury 72770)	1.25	5.00	68
(Second pressings used the title "The Mighty Quinn")				
RAGMUFFIN MAN/'B' Side	(Mercury 72921)	.75	3.00	69
SEMI-DETACHED SUBURBAN MR. JONES/ Each & Every Day	(Mercury 72629)	.75	3.00	66
SHA LA LA/John Hardy	(Ascot 2165)	1.00	4.00	64
SPIRIT IN THE NIGHT/Questions	(Warner Bros. 8355)	.50	2.00	77
WHEN WILL I BE LOVED/Do You Have To Do That	(United Artists 55066)	1.00	4.00	66
MANFRED MANN'S EARTH BAND (Formerly Manfred Mann)				
CALIFORNIA/Bouillabaisse	(Warner Bros. 8574)	.50	2.00	78
DAVY'S ON THE ROAD AGAIN/Bouillabaisse	(Warner Bros. 8620)	.50	2.00	78
FATHER OF NIGHT/	(Polydor 14225)	.50	2.00	74
GET YOUR ROCKS OFF/Wind	(Polydor 14191)	.50	2.00	73
JOYBRINGER/Cloudy Eyes	(Polydor 14205)	.50	2.00	73
LIVING WITHOUT YOU/Tribute	(Polydor 14113)	.50	2.00	72
MARDI GRAS DAY/	(Polydor 14173)	.50	2.00	72
SPIRIT IN THE NIGHT/As Above So Below	(Warner Bros. 8152)	.50	2.00	76
YOU ANGEL YOU/"Belle" Of The Earth	(Warner Bros. 8850)	.50	2.00	79
MANGANO, Silvana				
ANNA/I Loved You	(MGM 11457)	1.00	4.00	53
MANGIONE, Chuck				
BELLAVIA/	(A&M 1773)	.50	2.00	76
BELLAVIA (BELLA VEEYA)/Lullabye	(A&M 2118)	.50	2.00	79
CHASE THE CLOUDS AWAY/Soft	(A&M 1707)	.50	2.00	75
CHILDREN OF SANCHEZ/Doin' Everything With You	(A&M 2088)	.50	2.00	78
FEEL OF A VISION, THE/And In The Beginning	(Mercury 73238)	.50	2.00	72
FEELS SO GOOD/Maui-Waui	(A&M 2001)	.50	2.00	78
HILL WHERE THE LORD HIDES/Friends & Love	(Mercury 73208)	.50	2.00	72
HILL WHERE THE LORD HIDES/Land Of Make Believe	(Mercury 74016)	.50	2.00	78
LAND OF MAKE BELIEVE/Legend Of The One-Eyed Sailor	(Mercury 73432)	.50	2.00	73
LAST TANGO IN PARIS/Legend Of The One-Eyed Sailor	(Mercury 73371)	.50	2.00	72
LOOK TO THE CHILDREN/Freddie's Walkin'	(Mercury 73262)	.50	2.00	72
MAIN SQUEEZE/Come Take A Ride With Me	(A&M 1886)	.50	2.00	76
Instrumentals				
MANHATTAN TRANSFER				
BIRDLAND/	(Atlantic 3636)	.50	2.00	79
HELPLESS/	(Atlantic 3349)	.50	2.00	76
IT'S NOT THE SPOTLIGHT/	(Atlantic 3491)	.50	2.00	78
OPERATOR/Tuxedo Junction	(Atlantic 3292)	.50	2.00	75
POPSICLE TOES/Chanson D'Amour	(Atlantic 3374)	.50	2.00	76

TITLE/FLIP	LABEL & NO.	GOOD	NEAR MINT	YR.
MANILOW, Barry				
CAN'T SMILE WITHOUT YOU/Sunrise	(Arista 0305)	.50	2.00	78
COPACABANA (AT THE COPA)/Copacabana (At The Copa)	(Arista 0339)	.50	2.00	78
COULD IT BE MAGIC/Cloudburst	(Bell 45-422)	1.00	4.00	74
COULD IT BE MAGIC/I Am Your Child	(Arista 0126)	.50	2.00	75
DAYBREAK/Jump Shout Boogie	(Arista 0273)	.50	2.00	77
EVEN NOW/I Was A Fool (To Let You Go)	(Arista 0330)	.50	2.00	78
IT'S A MIRACLE/One Of These Days	(Arista 0108)	.50	2.00	75
I WRITE THE SONGS/A Nice Boy Like Me	(Arista 0157)	.50	2.00	75
LET'S TAKE SOME TIME TO SAY GOODBYE/	(Bell 45-443)	1.00	4.00	
LOOKS LIKE WE MADE IT/New York City Rhythm	(Arista 0244)	.50	2.00	77
MANDY/Somethin's Comin' Up	(Bell 45-613)	.50	2.00	74
READY TO TAKE A CHANCE AGAIN/Sweet Life	(Arista 0357)	.50	2.00	78
SHIPS/	(Arista 0464)	.50	2.00	79
SOMEWHERE IN THE NIGHT/Leavin' In The Morning	(Arista 0382)	.50	2.00	78
SWEET WATER JONES/One Of These Days	(Bell 45-357)	1.00	4.00	73
THIS ONE'S FOR YOU/Riders To The Stars	(Arista 0206)	.50	2.00	76
TRYIN' TO GET THE FEELING AGAIN/Beautiful Music	(Arista 0172)	.50	2.00	76
WEEKEND IN NEW ENGLAND/Say The Words	(Arista 0212)	.50	2.00	76
WHEN I WANTED YOU/	(Arista 0481)	.50	2.00	79
Also see Featherbed				
MANIN BROTHERS, The				
HOT ROD SUSIE/Uhm De Ahde	(Apt 25033)	1.25	5.00	59
MANIS, Georgie				
HIGH SCHOOL LOVE/Oriental Rock	(Gizmo 66347)	1.00	4.00	61
MANN, Barry				
ALMOST GONE/For No Reason At All	(Warner Bros. 8752)	.50	2.00	79
ANGELICA/Looking At Tomorrow	(Capitol 5695)	.75	3.00	66
BEST THAT I KNOW HOW, THE/	(United Artists 1021)	.50	2.00	78
BLESS YOU/Teenage Has-Been	(ABC-Paramount 10380)	1.00	4.00	62
DON'T GIVE UP ON ME/	(New Design 1005)	.50	2.00	72
FEELINGS/	(Scepter 12281)	.50	2.00	70
HAPPY BIRTHDAY BROKEN HEART/ The Millionaire	(ABC-Paramount 10180)	1.00	4.00	61
HEY BABY I'M DANCIN'/Like I Don't Love You	(ABC-Paramount 10356)	1.00	4.00	62
I'M A SURVIVOR/Don't Seem Right	(RCA 10319)	.50	2.00	76
JOHNNY SURFBOARD/Graduation Time	(Colpix 691)	.75	3.00	63
LAY IT ALL OUT	(New Design 1006)	.50	2.00	72
LITTLE MISS U.S.A./Find Another Fool	(ABC-Paramount 10263)	1.00	4.00	61
LOVE TO LAST A LIFETIME, A/All The Things You Are	(JDS 5002)	1.25	5.00	59
NOBODY BUT YOU/	(RCA 10104)	.50	2.00	74
NOTHING GOOD COMES EASY/Woman Woman Woman	(RCA 10230)	.50	2.00	75
PRINCESS & THE PUNK, THE/Jennifer	(Arista 0194)	.50	2.00	76
TALK TO ME BABY/Amy	(Red Bird 10-015)	.75	3.00	64
WAR PAINT/Counting Teardrops	(ABC-Paramount 10143)	1.00	4.00	60
WHERE DO I GO FROM HERE/She Is Today	(Capitol 5894)	.75	3.00	67
WHO PUT THE BOMP (IN THE BOMP, BOMP, BOMP)/ Love True Love	(ABC-Paramount 10237)	1.00	4.00	61
YOUNG ELECTRIC PSYCHEDELIC HIPPY FLIPPY/ Take Your Love	(Capitol 2082)	1.00	4.00	68
MANN, Bobby (Bobby Bloom)				
HEART OF TOWN/Make The Radio A Little Louder	(Kama Sutra 210)	1.00	4.00	66
MANN, Carl				
GONNA ROCK & ROLL TONIGHT/Rockin' Love	(Jaxon 502)	8.75	35.00	
I AIN'T GOT NO HOME/If I Could Change You	(Phillips International 3569)	1.00	4.00	60
MONA LISA/Foolish One	(Phillips International 3539)	1.00	4.00	59
MOUNTAIN DEW/ When I Grow Too Old To Dream	(Phillips International 3579)	1.00	4.00	60
PRETEND/Rockin' Love	(Phillips International 3546)	1.00	4.00	
SOME ENCHANTED EVENING/I Can't Forget	(Phillips International 3550)	1.00	4.00	60
WAYWARD WIND/Born To Be Bad	(Phillips International 3564)	1.00	4.00	60
MANN, Gloria				
EARTH ANGEL/I Love You Yes I Do	(Sound 109)	1.25	5.00	55
TEEN AGE PRAYER/Gypsy Lady	(Sound 126)	1.25	5.00	55
WHY DO FOOLS FALL IN LOVE?/Partners For Life	(Decca 29832)	1.00	4.00	56
MANNING, Linda				
OUR WORLD OF ROCK & ROLL/Sweeter Than Sweet	(Bulletin 1000)	.75	3.00	61
MANN, Johnny				
TOO YOUNG TO CRY/Wouldn't Be Going Steady	(Tiara 6118)	3.75	15.00	
MANN, Johnny, Singers				
UP, UP & AWAY/Joey Is The Name	(Liberty 55972)	.75	3.00	67
MANNO, Tommy				
TOO GOOD TO BE TRUE/That's For Me To Know	(Atlantic 2149)	.75	3.00	62
TOO GOOD TO BE TRUE/That's For Me To Know	(Flippin' 311)	1.25	5.00	62
MANONE, Wingy				
PARTY DOLL/Real Gone	(Decca 30211)	1.00	4.00	57
MANSFIELD, Jayne				
LITTLE THINGS MEAN A LOT/That Makes It	(Original Sound 51)	1.00	4.00	64
MANSHIP, Jimmy & Judy				
TEENAGE SWEETIE/Blue, Blue Love	(Blue Hen 118)	1.00	4.00	59
MANTOVANI (Annunzio Mantovani)				
AROUND THE WORLD IN 80 DAYS/Road To Ballingarry	(London 1746)	1.00	4.00	57
CHARMAINE/Just For A Little While	(London 1020)	1.00	4.00	51
LET ME BE LOVED/Call Of The West	(London 1761)	1.00	4.00	57
MOULIN ROUGE, THE (THEME)/Cola Colomba	(London 1328)	1.00	4.00	53
MANUEL & THE RENEGADES				
REV-UP/Trans-Miss-Yen	(Piper 7001)	1.00	4.00	63
SURF WALK/Woody Wagon	(Piper 7000)	1.00	4.00	63
MANZAREK, RAY (Of The Doors)				
DOWNBOUND TRAIN/Choose Up & Choose Off	(Mercury 73601)	.50	2.00	74
SOLAR BOAT/	(Mercury 73477)	.50	2.00	73
WHOLE THING STARTED WITH ROCK & ROLL & NOW IT'S OUT OF CONTROL, THE/	(Mercury 73664)	.50	2.00	74
MARA, Tommy				
WHERE THE BLUE OF THE NIGHT/ What Makes You So Lovely	(Felsted 8532)	.75	3.00	58
MARAUDERS, The				
JUGBAND MUSIC/Out Of Sight, Out Of Mind	(Laurie 3356)	1.25	5.00	
SINCE I MET YOU/I Don't Know How	(Skyview 001)	2.00	8.00	
MARBLES, The				
BREAKING UP IS HARD TO DO/Little Laughing Girl	(Cotillion 44046)	.75	3.00	70
WALLS FALL DOWN/Love You	(Cotillion 44029)	.75	3.00	69
MARCELLE, Lydia				
GIRL HE NEEDS, THE/Come On & Get It	(Manhattan 805)	.75	3.00	
MARCEL, Pete				
SLOPPY TWIST A FISH/Sloppy Twist A Fish (Part 2)	(Futura 104)	.75	3.00	61
MARCH, Little Peggy				
BOOM BANG-A-BANG/Lilac Skies	(RCA 74-0136)	.75	3.00	71
EVERY LITTLE MOVE YOU MAKE/After You	(RCA Victor 47-8302)	.75	3.00	64
HEAVEN FOR LOVERS/He Couldn't Care Less	(RCA Victor 47-8710)	.75	3.00	65
HELLO HEARTACHE, GOODBYE LOVE/Boy Crazy	(RCA Victor 47-8221)	.75	3.00	63
IMPOSSIBLE HAPPENED, THE/Waterfall	(RCA Victor 47-8267)	.75	3.00	63
I WILL FOLLOW HIM/Wind-Up Doll	(RCA Victor 47-8139)	.75	3.00	63
I WISH I WERE A PRINCESS/ My Teenage Castle (Is Tumblin' Down)	(RCA Victor 47-8189)	.75	3.00	63
LEAVE ME ALONE/Takin' The Long Way Home	(RCA Victor 47-8357)	.75	3.00	64
LITTLE ME/Pagan Love Song	(RCA Victor 47-8107)	.75	3.00	62
OH MY WHAT A GUY/ Only You Could Do That To My Heart	(RCA Victor 47-8418)	.75	3.00	64
WATCH WHAT YOU DO WITH MY BABY/ Can't Stop Thinking About Him	(RCA Victor 47-8460)	.75	3.00	64
WHY CAN'T HE BE YOU/Losin' My Touch	(RCA Victor 47-8534)	.75	3.00	65
YOUR GIRL/Let Her Go	(RCA Victor 47-8605)	.75	3.00	65
Shown on some records as Peggy March				
MARCO, Nick, & The Venetians				
LITTLE BOY LOST/Would It Hurt You	(Dwain 813)	2.00	8.00	
MARCUS HOOK ROLL BAND, The (With Vanda & Young)				
LOUISIANA LADY/Hoochie Coochie	(EMI 3560)	.75	3.00	73
Also see Easybeats, The				
Also see Flash In The Pan				
MARCUS, Jonathan				
WHAT ABOUT ME/Mad About You Baby	(MGM 13580)	1.25	5.00	66
MARCY JO & EDDIE RAMBEAU				
CAR HOP & THE HARD TOP, THE/	(Swan 4145)	.75	3.00	63
TAKE A WORD/Jumping Jack	(Robbee 117)	.75	3.00	62
THOSE GOLDEN OLDIES/When You Wore A Tulip	(Swan 4136)	1.00	4.00	63
MARDIN, Arif				
GLASS ONION/Sympathy For The Devil (Instrumentals)	(Atlantic 2658)	.50	2.00	72
MARDONES, Benny				
ALL FOR A REASON/Susquehanna Lady	(Private Stock 45205)	.50	2.00	78
MARENO, Lee (With the Regents)				
GODDESS OF LOVE/He's Gone (Lonely Summer)	(New Art 103)	2.50	10.00	
GODDESS OF LOVE/He's Gone (Lonely Summer)	(Scepter 1222)	2.00	8.00	
(Shown as by Lee)				
MARESCA, Ernie				
BEETLE DANCE, THE/Theme From Lilly Lilly	(Rust 5076)	1.25	5.00	64
DOWN ON THE BEACH/Mary Jane	(Seville 119)	1.00	4.00	62
I CAN'T DANCE/It's Their World	(Seville 138)	1.00	4.00	63
I DON'T KNOW WHY/Lonesome Blues	(Seville 107)	1.00	4.00	61
LORELEI/Love Express	(Seville 125)	1.00	4.00	63
ROVIN' KIND/Please Be Fair	(Seville 129)	1.25	5.00	63
SHOUT! SHOUT! (KNOCK YOURSELF OUT)/ Crying Like A Baby	(Seville 117)	.75	3.00	62
SOMETHING TO SHOUT ABOUT/How Many Times	(Seville 122)	1.00	4.00	62
Ernie Maresca occasionally used the Del-Satins for backup.				
Also see Chicago, Artie				
Also see Desires, The				
Also see Foreign Intrigue				
Also see Hubcaps, The				
MARESCO, Tony, & The Dynamics (Anthony & The Sophmores)				
BETTY MY OWN/Forever Love	(Herald 569)	10.00	40.00	
MARIDIAN				
SAN FRANCISCO WOMAN/San Francisco Woman	(Mercury 73076)	1.00	4.00	69
MARIE & REX (Marie Knight & Rex Garvin)				
I CAN'T SIT DOWN/Miracles	(Carlton 502)	1.00	4.00	59
MARIE & THE DECCORS				
QUEEN OF FOOLS/I'm The One	(Cub 9115)	1.50	6.00	62
MARIE, Ann				
(I KNOW THAT) YOUR HEART'S NOT MADE OF WOOD (Answer Song)/ Dear Teddy	(Epic 9465)	1.00	4.00	61
RUNAROUND/There Must Be A Reason	(Jubilee 5490)	1.00	4.00	64
MARIE, Donna				
EDDIE WASN'T THERE/Mankiller	(Coral 62445)	.75	3.00	65
MARIE, Rose: see Rose Marie				
MARIMBA CHIAPAS, The				
MARIMBA CHARLESTON/La Marimba	(Capitol 3447)	1.00	4.00	56
MARINERS, The				
I SEE THE MOON/I Just Want You	(Columbia 40047)	1.25	5.00	53
SOMETIME/Stars	(Columbia 1-600)	2.00	8.00	50
(This was Columbia's first 45 RPM release)				
MARIO & THE FLIPS				
TWISTIN' TRAIN/You Made Me Love You	(Decca 31252)	.75	3.00	61
MARION & HERBIE				
GOIN' STEADY BY THE NUMBERS/School Days	(Ultra-sonic 1717)	.75	3.00	60
MARK (Of the 1910 Fruitgum Co.)				
GOOD N' PLENTY/It Could Set You Back A Month	(Super K SK-103)	.75	3.00	69
GOODNIGHT/Good Morning	(Team TM-521)	.75	3.00	69
MARK & CLARK BAND, The				
JIGSAW WOMAN/	(Columbia 10500)	.50	2.00	77
WHEN IT COMES TO LOVE/	(Columbia 10594)	.50	2.00	77
MARK & ESCORTS				
DANCE WITH ME/Silly Putty	(GNP-Crescendo 358)	.75	3.00	6
GET YOUR BABY/Tuff Stuff	(GNP-Crescendo 350)	.75	3.00	6
MARK FOUR, The				
GO AWAY NOW/Forget It Baby	(Pacific Challenger 1004)	.75	3.00	
JUST MY DREAM/Swingin' Hangout	(Pacific Challenger 1002)	.75	3.00	
MARK OF KINGS, The				
DON'T WALK OUT ON ME/	(Flip Top 2192)	1.25	5.00	
MARK II, The				
AND A ROBIN CRIED/Blue Fantasy	(WYE 1004)	.75	3.00	6
NIGHT THEME/Confusion	(WYE 1001)	.75	3.00	6
MARK III, The				
VALERIE/The Man	(ABC-Paramount 10280)	.75	3.00	6
VALERIE/The Man	(BRB 100)	1.00	4.00	6
MARK IV, The				
DANTE'S INFERNO/Move Over Rover	(Mercury 71445)	1.00	4.00	5
I GOT A WIFE/Ah-OOO-Gah	(Mercury 71403)	1.00	4.00	5
(MAKE WITH) THE SHAKE/45 RPM	(Cosmic 704)	1.00	4.00	5
MARK-ALMOND (Jon Mark & Johnny Almond)				
LONELY GIRL/	(Columbia 45951)	.50	2.00	
ONE WAY SUNDAY/The Bay	(Blue Thumb 206)	.50	2.00	
NEW YORK STATE OF MIND/Return To The City	(ABC 12221)	.50	2.00	
WHAT AM I LIVING FOR/	(Columbia 45745)	.50	2.00	
MAR-KETS, The				
BALBOA BLUE/Stompede	(Union 504)	1.00	4.00	6
BALBOA BLUE/Stompede	(Liberty 55443)	.75	3.00	6
CALIFORNIA SUMMER/Groovin' Time	(World Pacific 77899)	.75	3.00	6
CANADIAN SUNSET/Stompin Room Only	(Union 507)	1.00	4.00	6
LADY IN THE CAGE/Ready, Steady, Go	(Warner Bros. 5670)	.75	3.00	6
LOOK FOR A STAR/Come See Come Ska	(Warner Bros. 5468)	.75	3.00	6
MIAMI BLUES/Napoleon's Solo	(Warner Bros. 5641)	.75	3.00	6
OUTER LIMITS/Bella Dalena	(Warner Bros. 5391)	1.25	5.00	6
(Reissued using the title "Out Of Limits")				
OUT OF LIMITS/Bella Dalena	(Warner Bros. 5391)	.75	3.00	6
(First released as "Outer Limits".)				
SURFER'S STOMP/Start	(Union 501)	1.00	4.00	6
SURFER'S STOMP/Start	(Liberty 55401)	.75	3.00	6
VANISHING POINT/Borealis	(Warner Bros. 5423)	.75	3.00	6
WOODY WAGON/Cobra	(Warner Bros. 5365)	.75	3.00	6
Instrumentals				
MARK-ETTES, The				
BATMAN THEME/Richie's Theme	(Warner Bros. 5696)	.75	3.00	6
MYSTERY MOVIE THEME/Sister Candy	(Mercury 73433)	.50	2.00	
TAKE ME OUT TO THE BALL GAME/The Hut Sut Song	(Big 20 869)	.75	3.00	
MAR-KEYS, The				
BEACH BASH/Bush Bash	(Stax 156)	.75	3.00	6
DRIBBLE, THE/Bo-time	(Stax 133)	.75	3.00	6
GRAB THIS THING/Grab This Thing (Part 2)	(Stax 181)	.75	3.00	6
LAST NIGHT/Night Before	(Satellite 107)	1.00	4.00	6
MORNING AFTER/Diana	(Stax 112)	.75	3.00	6
POP-EYE STROLL/Po-Dunk	(Stax 121)	.75	3.00	6
SAILOR MAN/Sack Of Woe	(Stax 129)	.75	3.00	6
Instrumentals				
MARKS, David (Of The Beach Boys)				
CRUSIN'/Kustom Kar Show	(A&M 730)	3.75	15.00	6
(Shown as by Dave & the Marksmen)				
DO YOU KNOW WHAT LOVERS SAY/Food Fair	(A&M 745)	3.75	15.00	6
(Shown as by Dave & the Marksmen)				
I WANNA CRY/I Could Make You Mine	(Warner Bros. 5485)	2.50	10.00	6
(Shown as by Dave & the Marksmen)				
JOHN AUTOMATION/Faces	(Imperial 66330)	2.50	10.00	6
(Shown as by the Moon)				
MOTHERS & FATHERS/Someday Girl	(Imperial 66285)	2.50	10.00	6
(Shown as by the Moon)				
PIRATE/Not To Know	(Imperial 66415)	2.50	10.00	6
(Shown as by the Moon)				
MARKS, Guy				
HOW THE WEST WAS WON-VOLARE/This Is Forever	(ABC 11148)	.75	3.00	6
LOVING YOU HAS MADE ME BANANAS/ Forgive Me My Love	(ABC 11055)	.75	3.00	6
MEET ME TONIGHT BY THE POSTAGE MACHINE/ This Is Forever	(ABC 11099)	.75	3.00	6
Comedy				
MARKSMEN, The: see Ventures, The				
MARLINS, The				
EVERYBODY DO THE SWIM (PART 1)/ Everybody Do The Swim (Part 2)	(Cameo 333)	.75	3.00	6
MARLO, Micki				
LITTLE BY LITTLE/It All Started	(ABC-Paramount 9762)	1.00	4.00	5
MARMALADE (Featuring Junior Campbell)				
COUSIN NORMAN/Lonely Man	(London 20068)	.75	3.00	7
FALLING APART AT THE SEAMS/Fly Fly Fly	(Ariola America 7619)	.50	2.00	7
LOVIN' THINGS/Hey Joe	(Epic 10340)	.75	3.00	6
MAN IN A SHOP/Cry (The Shoob Dorooie Song)	(Epic 10284)	.75	3.00	6
MY LITTLE ONE/Is Your Life Your Own	(London 20066)	1.00	4.00	
RAINBOW/The Ballad Of Cherry Flavar	(London 20059)	1.00	4.00	7
REFLECTIONS OF MY LIFE/Rollin' My Thing	(London 20058)	1.00	4.00	7
RADANCER/Just One Woman	(London 20072)	1.00	4.00	
TIME IS ON MY SIDE/Baby, Make It Soon	(Epic 10493)	.75	3.00	6
WALKING A TIGHTROPE/	(Ariola America 7631)	.50	2.00	7
WISHING WELL/Engine Driver	(EMI 3676)	.50	2.00	7
Also see Blue				
MAROONS, The				
DON'T LEAVE ME BABY, DON'T/Someday I'll Be The One	(Queen 24012)	1.50	6.00	6
MARREN, Howard				
PHANTOM STRIKES AGAIN, THE/ I'm Getting To Be A Big Boy Now	(Fargo 1006)	2.00	8.00	5
MARRIOTT, Steve (Of Small Faces)				
STAR IN MY LIFE/	(A&M 1825)	.50	2.00	7
Also see Humble Pie				
MARS BONFIRE (With Dennis Edmonton)				
FASTER THAN THE SPEED OF LIFE/She	(Columbia 44772)	.75	3.00	6
LADY MOON WALKER/In Christina's Arms	(Columbia 44888)	.75	3.00	6
Also see Steppenwolf				
MARSDEN, Gerry (Of Gerry & The Pacemakers)				
GILBERT GREEN/Please Let Them Be	(Columbia 44309)	.75	3.00	6
MARSHALL ARTS, The				
GOT TO GET YOU OUT OF MY LIFE/In The Pines	(Kickapoo 6301)	1.00	4.00	6
MARSHALL, Jack				
THEME FROM "THE MUNSTERS"/The Ghoul (Instrumentals)	(Capitol 5288)	.75	3.00	6

THE
MERSEY
MONSTERS
Parchment
records
UNCENSORED
COPY
STEREO
DJ COPY
Produced by
Thomas
Williams
Arranged by
Steve Meisburg
& John Walters
℗ 1976
Parchment
Records
PR0413769
Time 2:14
Intro: 0:04
Southern
Music-ASCAP
Parchment
Music-ASCAP
GRADUATION DAY
(John Walters)
MEISBURG &
WALTERS
Mfg. & Dist. by Parchment Records, P.O. Box 22106, Greensboro, N.C. 27420 USA

Haley Mills

The Mersey Monsters

The Merseybeats

Professor Morrison's Lollipop

Janis Martin

Nervous Norvus

Terry Noland

The 1910 Fruitgum Company

TITLE/FLIP	LABEL & NO.	GOOD	NEAR MINT	YR.
MARSHALL TUCKER BAND, The (With Doug Gray & Toy Caldwell)				
ANOTHER CRUEL LOVE/Blue Ridge Mountain Sky	(Capricorn 0049)	.50	2.00	74
CAN'T YOU SEE/Fly Like An Eagle	(Capricorn 0278)	.50	2.00	77
CAN'T YOU SEE/See You Later, I'm Gone	(Capricorn 1163)	.75	3.00	73
DREAM LOVER/Change Is Gonna Come	(Capricorn 0300)	.50	2.00	78
FIRE ON THE MOUNTAIN/Bob Away My Blues	(Capricorn 0244)	.50	2.00	75
HEARD IT IN A LOVE SONG/Life In A Song	(Capricorn 0270)	.50	2.00	77
I'LL BE LOVING YOU/Everybody Needs Somebody	(Capricorn 0307)	.50	2.00	78
LAST OF THE SINGING COWBOYS/Pass It On	(Warner Bros. 8841)	.50	2.00	79
LONG HARD RIDE/Windy City Blues	(Capricorn 0258)	.50	2.00	76
MY JESUS TOLD ME SO/Take The Highway	(Capricorn 0030)	.50	2.00	73
RUNNING LIKE THE WIND/Answer To Love	(Warner Bros. 49068)	.50	2.00	79
SEARCHIN' FOR A RAINBOW/Walkin' & Talkin'	(Capricorn 0251)	.50	2.00	76
THIS OL' COWBOY/Try One More Time	(Capricorn 0228)	.50	2.00	75
MARSHMALLOW HIGHWAY				
I DON'T WANNA LIVE THIS WAY/Loving You	(Kapp 904)	1.00	4.00	68
MARSHMALLOW WAY (Featuring Billy Carl)				
C'MON KITTY KITTY/	(V.A. 50545)	1.25	5.00	69
MUSIC MUSIC/Good Day	(V.A. 50611)	1.25	5.00	69
Also see Billy & The Essentials				
MARSHON, Chris				
GOD CALLED ELVIS HOME/Elvis For Just An Hour Or Two	(NIF 1001)	.50	2.00	77
GOD CALLED ELVIS HOME/Elvis For Just An Hour Or Two	(Phono 2657)	.50	2.00	77
MARSH, Richie (Sky Saxon)				
BABY BABY BABY/Half Angel	(Acama 125)	1.25	5.00	61
CRYING INSIDE MY HEART/Goodbye	(Ava 122)	1.25	5.00	63
THERE'S ONLY ONE GIRL/What Chance Have I	(Rosco 412)	1.50	6.00	60
(Shown also as by Dick Marsh)				
THEY SAY/Darling, I Swear That It's True	(Shepherd 2203)	2.00	8.00	
MARTELLS, The				
FORGOTTEN SPRING/Va Va Voom	(Cessna 477)	2.50	10.00	61
MARTELS, The				
ROCKIN' SANTA CLAUS/	(Bella 20)	1.00	4.00	59
MARTIN, Al, Six				
BABY BEATLE WALK/Prego	(Bell 605)	1.25	5.00	
MARTIN, Angela				
DIP DA DIP/Take Me To The Fair	(Atco 6327)	1.00	4.00	65
MARTIN, Aston, & Moon Discs				
FALLOUT/Moonbeat	(Del Rio 230)	1.25	5.00	
MARTIN, Bobbi				
DON'T FORGET I STILL LOVE YOU/On The Outside	(Coral 62426)	.75	3.00	64
MARTIN CIRCUS, The				
MA-RY-LEWE/Loiw D'e	(Roulette 7177)	1.50	6.00	71
MARTINDALE, Wink (Winston Conrad)				
BLACK LAND FARMER/Make Him Happy	(Dot 16243)	.75	3.00	61
DECK OF CARDS/Now You Know How It Feels	(Dot 15968)	.75	3.00	59
NEVERTHELESS/I Heard The Bluebirds Sing	(Dot 16531)	.75	3.00	63
NEXT TIME, THE/Violet & Rose	(Dot 18130)	.75	3.00	63
OUR LOVE AFFAIR (With Robin Ward)/The First Kiss	(Dot 16555)	.75	3.00	63
MARTIN, Danny				
ROCKIN' MEMPHIS MAMA/Pool Cue	(Riot 431)	1.25	5.00	57
MARTIN, Dean				
ALL IN A NIGHT'S WORK/	(Capitol 4551)	1.00	4.00	61
ANGEL BABY/I'll Gladly Make The Same Mistake Again	(Capitol 3988)	1.00	4.00	58
APRIL AGAIN/That Old Time Feelin'	(Reprise 0761)	.75	3.00	68
COME RUNNING BACK/Bouquet Of Roses	(Reprise 0466)	.75	3.00	66
DOOR IS STILL OPEN TO MY HEART, THE/ Every Minute Every Hour	(Reprise 0307)	.75	3.00	64
EVERYBODY LOVES SOMEBODY/A Little Voice	(Reprise 0281)	.75	3.00	64
FROM THE BOTTOM OF MY HEART/	(Reprise 20116)	.75	3.00	62
GOOD MORNIN' LIFE/	(Capitol 3841)	1.00	4.00	57
HEY BROTHER, POUR THE WINE/I'd Cry Like A Baby	(Capitol 2749)	1.25	5.00	54
HOUSTON/Bumming Around	(Reprise 0393)	.75	3.00	65
I'LL ALWAYS LOVE YOU/Baby, Obey Me	(Capitol 1028)	1.50	6.00	50
IF/I Love The Way	(Capitol 1342)	1.25	5.00	51
IN NAPOLI/I Like Them All	(Capitol 3238)	1.25	5.00	55
INNAMORATA/Lady With The Big Umbrella	(Capitol 3352)	1.25	5.00	56
IN THE CHAPEL IN THE MOONLIGHT/Welcome To My World	(Reprise 0601)	.75	3.00	67
IN THE MISTY MOONLIGHT/	(Reprise 0640)	.75	3.00	67
I TAKE A LOT OF PRIDE IN WHAT I AM/ Drowning In My Tears	(Reprise 0841)	.75	3.00	69
I WILL/You're The Reason I'm In Love	(Reprise 0415)	.75	3.00	65
LAY SOME HAPPINESS ON ME/Think About Me	(Reprise 0571)	.75	3.00	67
LITTLE OLE WINE DRINKER, ME/ I Can't Help Remembering You	(Reprise 0608)	.75	3.00	67
MEMORIES ARE MADE OF THIS/Change Of Heart	(Capitol 3295)	1.00	4.00	55
MILLION & ONE, A/Shades	(Reprise 0500)	.75	3.00	66
MY RIFLE, MY PONY, & ME/Rio Bravo	(Capitol 4174)	1.25	5.00	59
NOBODY'S BABY AGAIN/It Just Happened That Way	(Reprise 0516)	.75	3.00	66
NOT ENOUGH INDIANS/	(Reprise 0780)	.75	3.00	68
ON AN EVENING IN ROMA/	(Capitol 4222)	1.00	4.00	59
ONCE UPON A TIME/The Magician	(Capitol 4065)	1.00	4.00	58
ONLY TRUST YOUR HEART/	(Capitol 3680)	1.00	4.00	57
(OPEN UP YOUR DOOR &) LET THE GOOD TIMES IN/ I'm Not The Marryin' Kind	(Reprise 0538)	.75	3.00	66
REMEMBER ME (I'M THE ONE WHO LOVES YOU)/	(Reprise 0369)	.75	3.00	65
RETURN TO ME/Forgetting You	(Capitol 3894)	1.00	4.00	58
SANTA LUCIA/Hold Me	(Apollo 1116)	2.50	10.00	50
SEND ME THE PILLOW YOU DREAM ON/	(Reprise 0344)	.75	3.00	65
SOMEWHERE THERE'S A SOMEONE/ That Old Clock On The Wall	(Reprise 0443)	.75	3.00	66
STANDING ON THE CORNER/Watching The World Go By	(Capitol 3414)	1.25	5.00	56
STREET OF LOVE/	(Capitol 3468)	1.25	5.00	56
SWAY/Money Burns A Hole In My Pocket	(Capitol 2818)	1.25	5.00	54
THAT'S AMORE/You're The Right One	(Capitol 2589)	1.25	5.00	53
TRICHE TRACHE, THE/	(Capitol 3787)	1.00	4.00	57
VOLARE/Outta My Mind	(Capitol 4028)	1.00	4.00	58
WALKING MY BABY BACK HOME/Oh Marie	(Apollo 1088)	2.50	10.00	50
YOU BELONG TO ME/Hominy Grits	(Capitol 2165)	1.25	5.00	52
YOU'RE NOBODY TILL SOMEBODY LOVES YOU/ You'll Always Be The One I Love	(Reprise 0333)	.75	3.00	64
YOU'VE STILL GOT A PLACE IN MY HEART/	(Reprise 0627)	.75	3.00	68
MARTIN, Derek				
YOU BETTER GO/You Know	(Roulette 4631)	.75	3.00	65
MARTIN, Dewey, & Medicine Ball				
CARESS ME PRETTY MUSIC/There Must Be A Reason	(RCA 0489)	1.50	6.00	71
INDIAN CHILD/I Do Believe	(UNI 55245)	1.00	4.00	70
MARTIN, Dino, Jr. (Of Dino, Desi & Billy)				
SITTING IN LIMBO/Sitting In Limbo (Instrumental)	(Reprise 1129)	.50	2.00	72
MARTINE, Layng, Jr.				
CRAZY DAISY/Love Comes & Goes	(Date 1511)	.75	3.00	66
PICK ALL THE FLOWERS THAT YOU CAN/ Surabian Lament	(General International 351)	.75	3.00	66
MARTIN, Freddy With Merv Griffin: see Merv Griffin				
MARTIN, George				
ALL QUIET ON THE MERSEY FRONT/ Cast Your Fate To The Wind	(United Artists 831)	.75	3.00	65
HARD DAY'S NIGHT, A/I Should Have Known Better	(United Artists 750)	1.00	4.00	64
LOVE IN THE OPEN AIR/Bahama Sound	(United Artists 50148)	.75	3.00	66
RINGO'S THEME (THIS BOY)/And I Love Her	(United Artists 745)	1.00	4.00	64
Instrumentals				
MARTIN, Janis				
ALL RIGHT BABY/Billy Boy, Billy Boy	(RCA Victor 47-7104)	5.00	20.00	58
BANG BANG/Please Be My Love	(RCA Victor 47-7318)	3.00	12.00	58
(With the Boyfriends)				
LOVE & KISSES/I'll Never Be Free	(RCA Victor 47-6983)	1.50	6.00	57
MY BOY ELVIS/Little Bit	(RCA Victor 47-6652)	3.75	15.00	56
OOBY DOOBY/One More Year To Go	(RCA Victor 47-6560)	3.75	15.00	56
WILL YOU WILLYUM/Drug Store Rock & Roll	(RCA Victor 47-6491)	3.00	12.00	56
MARTIN, Jimmy				
ROCK HEARTS/I'll Never Take No For An Answer	(Decca 30703)	1.00	4.00	58
MARTIN, Kenny Lee				
ROCK KEEPS ON ROLLIN', THE/The Shape I'm In	(Decca 30754)	1.25	5.00	59
MARTIN, Marty				
HOOTENANNY SANTA/ All I Got For Christmas Was A Broken Heart	(Anvil 1001)	1.00	4.00	63
MARTIN, Mary, & Arthur Godfrey				
GO TO SLEEP, GO TO SLEEP, GO TO SLEEP/ But Me I Love You	(Columbia 38744)	1.25	5.00	50
MARTIN, Moon				
HOT NITE IN DALLAS/	(Capitol 4639)	.50	2.00	78
NO CHANCE/Gun Shy	(Capitol 4794)	.50	2.00	79
ROLENE/Dangerous	(Capitol 4765)	.50	2.00	79
MARTINO, Al (Alfred Cini)				
ALWAYS TOGETHER/Thank You For Loving Me	(Capitol 5239)	.75	3.00	64
DARLING, I LOVE YOU/Memory Of You	(20th Fox 153)	1.00	4.00	59
HERE IN MY HEART/I Cried Myself To Sleep	(BBS 101)	1.50	6.00	52
HERE IN MY HEART/Granada	(Capitol 4593)	.75	3.00	61
I CAN'T GET YOU OUT OF MY HEART/ Two Hearts Are Better Than One	(20th Fox 132)	1.00	4.00	59
I CAN'T GET YOU OUT OF MY HEART/ Two Hearts Are Better Than One	(20th Fox 530)	.75	3.00	64
I LOVE YOU BECAUSE/Merry-Go-Round	(Capitol 4930)	.75	3.00	63
I LOVE YOU MORE & MORE EVERY DAY/ I'm Living My Heaven With You	(Capitol 5108)	.75	3.00	64
LIVING A LIE/I Love You Truly	(Capitol 5060)	.75	3.00	63
PAINTED, TAINTED ROSE/ That's The Way Its Got To Be	(Capitol 5000)	.75	3.00	63
SPANISH EYES/Melody Of Love	(Capitol 5542)	.75	3.00	65
TAKE MY HEART/I Never Cared	(Capitol 2122)	.75	3.00	52
TEARS & ROSES/A Year Ago Tonight	(Capitol 5183)	.75	3.00	64
MARTIN, Ricci				
STOP LOOK AROUND/I Had A Dream	(Capitol 4164)	.50	2.00	76
Ricci is another of Dean Martin's sons.				
MARTIN, Steve				
CRUEL SHOES/Drop-Thumb Medley	(Warner Bros. 49122)	.50	2.00	79
GRANTMOTHER'S SONG/Let's Get Small	(Warner Bros. 8503)	.50	2.00	77
KING TUT/Sally Goodin/Hoedown At Alice's	(Warner Bros. 8577)	.50	2.00	78
Comedy				
MARTIN, Tony				
HERE/Philosophy	(RCA Victor 47-5665)	1.00	4.00	54
I GET IDEAS/Tahiti My Island	(RCA Victor 47-4141)	1.25	5.00	51
I SAID MY PAJAMAS (& PUT ON MY PRAYERS)/ Have I Told You Lately That I Love You	(RCA Victor 47-3119)	1.25	5.00	50
(With Fran Warren)				
KISS OF FIRE/For The Very First Time	(RCA Victor 47-4671)	1.00	4.00	52
STRANGER IN PARADISE/I Love Paris	(RCA Victor 47-5535)	1.00	4.00	53
WALK HAND IN HAND/Flamenco Love	(RCA Victor 47-6493)	1.00	4.00	56
MARTIN, Trade				
HOT DIGGITY/Lovability	(Coed 579)	.75	3.00	63
IF I WERE A RICH MAN/	(Toot 606)	.75	3.00	67
JOANNE/Liverpool Baby	(Coed 594)	1.25	5.00	63
POMP & CIRCUMSTANCE/My Song Of Love	(Roulette 4258)	.75	3.00	60
SHE PUT THE HURT ON ME/Son Of A Millionaire	(Stallion 1003)	1.00	4.00	
STRATEGY/Lucky Boy Happy Girl Lonely Me	(Coed 575)	.75	3.00	63
THAT STRANGER USED TO BE MY GIRL/ We'll Be Dancin' On The Moon	(Coed 570)	.75	3.00	62
YOU'RE THE CAUSE/	(Toot 610)	1.00	4.00	67
MARTIN, Vince				
CINDY, OH CINDY/Only If You Praise The Lord	(Glory 247)	1.00	4.00	56
(With the Tarriers)				
1-2-3-4 ANYPLACE ROAD/Katie-O	(Glory 252)	1.00	4.00	57
MARTY				
MARTY ON PLANET MARS (PART 1)/ Marty On Planet Mars (Part 2)	(Novelty 101)	2.50	10.00	56
(Novelty/Break-in)				
MARTY				
SINCE YOU'RE MINE/Dear Mom & Dad	(Di Venus 103)	1.25	5.00	
(Some members of the Regents are heard on this recording.)				
MARTY & MONKS				
MRS. SCHWARTZ YOU'VE GOT AN UGLY DAUGHTER/	(Associated Artists 3065)	1.00	4.00	65
(Parody)				
MARTY & THE MELLOW YELLOW BUNCH				
TWO BANANAS IN LOVE (PART 1)/ Two Bananas In Love (Part 2)	(Megaphone 101)	1.00	4.00	67
MARTY & THE SYMBOLS				
YOU'RE THE ONE/Rip Van Winkle (By Mr. Bassman)	(Graphic Arts 1000)	3.00	12.00	63
MARTYN, John				
DON'T WANT TO KNOW ABOUT EVIL/May You Never	(Island 1213)	.50	2.00	72
MARVELOWS, The				
I DO/My Heart	(ABC-Paramount 10629)	.75	3.00	65
SHIM SHAM, THE/Your Little Sister	(ABC-Paramount 10708)	.75	3.00	65
MARVELS, The				
FOR SENTIMENTAL REASONS/Come Back	(Winn 1916)	3.75	15.00	
SO YOUNG, SO SWEET/I Shed So Many Tears	(Laurie 3016)	2.50	10.00	58
MAR-VELS, The				
GO ON & HAVE YOURSELF A BALL/ How Do I Keep The Girls Away	(Angie 1005)	1.00	4.00	
MARVELS FIVE, The				
DON'T PLAY THAT SONG (YOU LIED)/Forgive Me	(Uptown 722)	.75	3.00	66
MARX				
ONE MINUTE MORE/You Are My Love	(Dahlia 1002)	3.75	15.00	
MARX, Dick				
COOL/All Of You	(Omega Disk OSRS-137)	1.50	6.00	59
(Stereo single issue)				
MICKEY MOUSE THEME, THE/Joey, Joey	(Omega Disk OSRS-135)	1.50	6.00	59
(Stereo single issue)				
MARX, Groucho				
LYDIA/Show Me A Rose	(A&M 1412)	.50	2.00	73
MARX, Melinda				
EAST SIDE OF TOWN, THE/How I Wish You Came	(Vee Jay 657)	.75	3.00	64
MAS, Carolyn				
STILLSANE/Baby Please	(Mercury 76004)	.50	2.00	79
QUOTE GOODBYE QUOTE/	(Mercury 76019)	.50	2.00	79
MASCOTS, The				
BLUE BIRDS OVER THE MOUNTAIN/Timberlands	(Mermaid 107)	5.00	20.00	
ONCE UPON A LOVE/Hey Little Angel (Red label)	(Blast 206)	3.00	12.00	62
ONCE UPON A LOVE/Hey Little Angel (White label)	(Blast 206)	1.00	4.00	62
MASHMAKAN				
AS THE YEARS GO BY/Days When We Are Free	(Epic 10634)	.75	3.00	70
DANCE A LITTLE STEP/One Night Stand	(Jamie 1418)	.75	3.00	69
MASKED DEMONS, The				
HI SURFIN'/Way Out	(R.R.E. 1016)	1.25	5.00	63
MASKED MARAUDERS, The				
COW PIE/I Can't Get No Nookie	(Deity 0870)	1.00	4.00	69
MASON, Bonnie Jo (Cher)				
RINGO I LOVE YOU/Beatle Blues	(Annette 1001)	3.75	15.00	64
MASON, Dave (Of Traffic)				
ALL ALONG THE WATCHTOWER/Sad & Deep As You	(Columbia 10469)	.50	2.00	76
BABY...PLEASE/Side Tracked	(Columbia 45947)	.50	2.00	73
BRING IT ON HOME TO ME/Harmony & Melody	(Columbia 10174)	.50	2.00	74
DON'T IT MAKE YOU WONDER/Warm Desire	(Columbia 10819)	.50	2.00	78
EVERY WOMAN/Relationships	(Columbia 10104)	.50	2.00	75
HEARTACHE, A SHADOW, A LIFETIME, A/ Can't Stop Worrying	(Blue Thumb 205)	.75	3.00	72
LET IT GO, LET IT FLOW/Takin' The Time To Find	(Columbia 10662)	.50	2.00	77
ONLY YOU KNOW & I KNOW/Sad & Deep As You	(Blue Thumb 114)	.75	3.00	70
ONLY YOU KNOW & I KNOW/Sad & Deep As You	(Blue Thumb 276)	.50	2.00	78
SATIN RED & BLACK VELVET WOMAN/ Shouldn't Have Took More Than You Gave	(Blue Thumb 7117)	.75	3.00	70
SHOW ME SOME AFFECTION/Get Ahold On Love	(Columbia 10162)	.50	2.00	75
SO HIGH (ROCK ME BABY & ROLL ME AWAY)/ You Just Have To Wait Now	(Columbia 10509)	.50	2.00	77
TO BE FREE/Pearly Queen	(Blue Thumb 209)	.75	3.00	72
WAITIN' ON YOU/Just A Song	(Blue Thumb 7122)	.75	3.00	71
WE JUST DISAGREE/Mystic Traveler	(Columbia 10575)	.50	2.00	77
WILL YOU STILL LOVE ME TOMORROW/Mystic Traveler	(Columbia 10749)	.50	2.00	78
WORLD IN CHANGES/ Can't Stop Worrying, Can't Stop Loving	(Blue Thumb 112)	.75	3.00	70
Also see Blind Faith				
Also see Elliot, Mama Cass				
MASON PROFFIT				
HOPE/Jewel	(Ampex 11048)	.75	3.00	71
TWO HANGMEN/Sweet Lady Love	(Happy Tiger 552)	.75	3.00	70
MASSI, Nick (Nicholas Macioci)				
BALLAD OF MR. NIXON, THE/Little Pony	(One Way 244)	.75	3.00	
Also see 4 Seasons, The				
MASTERS, The				
LOVELY WAY TO SPEND AN EVENING, A/Dores Blues	(Bingo 1008)	3.75	15.00	60
MASTERS, Johnny (Johnny Maestro)				
SAY IT ISN'T SO/The Great Physician	(Coed 527)	2.00	8.00	60
MASTERS, Sammy				
CHAROLETTE (IN THE PINK CORVETTE)/Golden Slippers	(Lode 109)	1.50	6.00	60
CHAROLETTE (IN THE PINK CORVETTE)/Golden Slippers	(Dot 16123)	.75	3.00	60
PINK CADILLAC/Some Like It Hot	(4 Star 1695)	3.75	15.00	
ROCKIN' RED WING/Lonely Weekend	(Lode 108)	1.50	6.00	60
ROCKIN' RED WING/Lonely Weekend	(Warner Bros. 5102)	.75	3.00	60
MATADORS				
C'MON LET YOURSELF GO (PART 1)/ C'mon Let Yourself Go (Part 2)	(Colpix 741)	1.25	5.00	64
I'VE GOTTA DRIVE/La Corrida	(Colpix 718)	1.25	5.00	64
PERFIDIA/Ace Of Hearts	(Colpix 698)	1.25	5.00	63
MATADORS, The				
YOU'D BE CRYING TOO/My Foolish Heart	(Keith 45-6504)	.75	3.00	
MATERO, Ricky				
SPIN SPIN THE RECORD/	(Hillside 500)	.75	3.00	
MATHERS, Jerry "Beaver"				
DON'T CHA CRY/	(Atlantic 2156)	.75	3.00	62
MATHEWS BROTHERS, The				
STUPID/Mora Dora	(ABC-Paramount 10473)	3.75	15.00	63
MATHEWS, Dino				
GIRL THAT I LOVE, THE/Lenore	(Dot 16365)	5.00	20.00	62
MATHEWS, Ronnie				
LONESOME TEENAGER/The Week Is Over	(Dayhill 2004)	3.00	12.00	
MATHEWS, Shirley				
BIG TOWN BOY/Count On That	(Tamarac 602)	1.50	6.00	63
BIG TOWN BOY/Count On That	(Atlantic 2210)	1.00	4.00	63
IS HE REALLY MINE/He Makes Me Feel So Pretty	(Amy 910)	1.00	4.00	64
PRIVATE PROPERTY/Wise Guys	(Atlantic 2224)	1.00	4.00	64
STOP THE CLOCK/If I Had It All To Do Again	(Amy 921)	1.00	4.00	65
MATHEWS, Tobin				
RUBY DUBY DU/Leatherjacket Cowboy	(Chief 7022)	.75	3.00	60
MATHIESON, Muir				
LOLA'S THEME/Mike & Lola's Love Theme	(Columbia 40725)	1.00	4.00	56
MATHIS & HILLYER				
STASH CITY HIGH SCHOOL/Mr. Gums	(96X 9600)	1.00	4.00	
MATHIS, Bobby, & Sevilles				
GOING TO THE CITY/	(Sioux 51860)	2.50	10.00	
MATHIS, Johnny				
BYE BYE BARBARA/Great Night For Crying	(Mercury 7222)	.75	3.00	63
CALL ME/Stairway To The Sea	(Columbia 41253)	.75	3.00	58
CERTAIN SMILE, A/Let It Rain	(Columbia 41193)	.75	3.00	58
CHANCES ARE/The Twelfth Of Never	(Columbia 40993)	1.00	4.00	57
GINA/I Love Her That's Why	(Columbia 42582)	.75	3.00	62
HOW TO HANDLE A WOMAN/While You're Young	(Columbia 41866)	.75	3.00	60
HOW TO HANDLE A WOMAN/While You're Young	(Columbia 3-41866)	1.25	5.00	60
(Compact 33 single)				

Title/Flip	Label & No.	Good	Near Mint	Yr.

4-40993

CHANCES ARE
THE TWELFTH OF NEVER
JOHNNY MATHIS
COLUMBIA

Title/Flip	Label & No.	Good	Near Mint	Yr.
IT'S NOT FOR ME TO SAY/Warm & Tender	(Columbia 40851)	1.00	4.00	57
LET'S LOVE/You Are Beautiful	(Columbia 41304)	.75	3.00	59
MARIA/Hey Love	(Columbia 41684)	.75	3.00	60
MISTY/The Story Of Our Love	(Columbia 41483)	.75	3.00	59
MISTY/The Story Of Our Love	(Columbia 7-30483)	1.25	5.00	59
(Compact 33 single)				
MY LOVE FOR YOU/Oh That Feeling	(Columbia 41764)	.75	3.00	60
MY LOVE FOR YOU/Oh That Feeling	(Columbia 3-41764)	1.25	5.00	60
(Compact 33 single)				
SMALL WORLD/You Are Everything To Me	(Columbia 41410)	.75	3.00	59
SMALL WORLD/You Are Everything To Me	(Columbia 7-30410)	1.25	5.00	59
(Compact 33 single)				
SOMEONE/Very Much In Love	(Columbia 41355)	.75	3.00	59
WONDERFUL! WONDERFUL!/When Sunny Gets Blue	(Columbia 40784)	1.00	4.00	57

MATTHEWS, Ian (Of Fairport Convention)

Title/Flip	Label & No.	Good	Near Mint	Yr.
BROWN-EYED GIRL/	(Columbia 10374)	.50	2.00	76
DO DOO RON RON (WHEN HE WALKED ME HOME)/	(Vertigo 103)	.50	2.00	72
DON'T HANG UP YOUR DANCING SHOES/Slip Away	(Mushroom 7041)	.50	2.00	79
GIVE ME AN INCH/Let There Be Blues	(Mushroom 7040)	.50	2.00	79
HEARTS/If You Saw Thro' My Eyes	(Vertigo 101)	.75	3.00	71
7 BRIDGES ROAD/	(Elektra 45871)	.50	2.00	73
SHAKE IT/Stealin' Home	(Mushroom 7039)	.50	2.00	78
TIGERS WILL SURVIVE/	(Columbia 10533)	.50	2.00	77
Also See Matthews' Southern Comfort				

MATTHEWS, Jim, M.D. ("The Singing Surgeon")

Title/Flip	Label & No.	Good	Near Mint	Yr.
WE'LL HAVE A BLUE CHRISTMAS, ELVIS/ Gone The Old, Come The New	(Music Emporium 7030)	.50	2.00	77

MATTHEWS' SOUTHERN COMFORT (With Ian Matthews)

Title/Flip	Label & No.	Good	Near Mint	Yr.
MARE, TAKE ME HOME/	(Decca 32845)	.50	2.00	71
TELL ME WHY/To Love	(Decca 32874)	.50	2.00	71
WOODSTOCK/Ballad Of Obray Ramsey	(Decca 32774)	.50	2.00	71

MAUDS, The

Title/Flip	Label & No.	Good	Near Mint	Yr.
HOLD ON/C'mon & Move	(Dunwich 160)	1.00	4.00	67
HOLD ON/C'mon & Move	(Mercury 72694)	.75	3.00	67
MAN WITHOUT A DREAM/Forget It, I've Got It	(RCA 74-0377)	1.00	4.00	70
ONLY LOVE CAN SAVE YOU NOW/Sergeant Sunshine	(Mercury 72877)	1.25	5.00	69
SATISFY MY HUNGER/Brother Chickee	(Mercury 72919)	1.25	5.00	69
SOUL DRIPPIN'/Forever Gone	(Mercury 72832)	1.00	4.00	68
YOU MADE ME FEEL SO BAD/ When Something Is Wrong	(Mercury 72720)	1.25	5.00	67

MAURIAT, Paul

Title/Flip	Label & No.	Good	Near Mint	Yr.
CHITTY CHITTY BANG BANG/ Comme Un Garcon (What A Guy)	(Philips 40574)	.50	2.00	68
HEY JUDE/Those Were The Days	(Philips 40594)	.50	2.00	69
LOVE IN EVERY ROOM/	(Philips 40530)	.50	2.00	68
LOVE IS BLUE (L'AMOUR EST BLEU)/ Alone In The World (Seuls Au Monde)	(Philips 40495)	.50	2.00	68
LOVE IS BLUE (L'AMOUR EST BLEU)/Sunny	(Philips 40495)	.50	2.00	68
SWEET CHARITY/Irresistiblement (Irresistibly)	(Philips 40595)	.50	2.00	69

MAVRICKS, The

Title/Flip	Label & No.	Good	Near Mint	Yr.
ANGEL WITH A HEARTACHE/Sugar Babe	(Capitol 4507)	1.25	5.00	61
GOING TO THE RIVER/Just To Hear Ole Cotton Sing	(Capitol 4560)	1.25	5.00	61

MAX DEMIAN BAND: see Demian, Max, Band

MAXIMILLIAN

Title/Flip	Label & No.	Good	Near Mint	Yr.
TWISTIN' GHOST, THE/ The Breeze & Theme From Peter Gunn	(Big Top 3095)	.75	3.00	61
Maximillian was the organist on Del Shannon's Big Top recordings.				

MAXIMUS & HIS PROJECTORS

Title/Flip	Label & No.	Good	Near Mint	Yr.
BANG BANG LOU LOU/Limericks (Part 1)	(MBM 1945)	.75	3.00	
(Novelty)				

MAXWELL, Bobby

Title/Flip	Label & No.	Good	Near Mint	Yr.
CHINATOWN, MY CHINATOWN/Shuffle Off To Buffalo	(Mercury 5773)	1.00	4.00	52
Also see Mozart, Mickey				

MAXWELL, Bobby, & The Exploits

Title/Flip	Label & No.	Good	Near Mint	Yr.
YOU'RE LAUGHING AT ME/Stay With Me	(Fargo 1010)	3.75	15.00	58

MAXWELL, Diane

Title/Flip	Label & No.	Good	Near Mint	Yr.
DATE BAIT/Jimmy Kiss & Run	(Challenge 59039)	1.00	4.00	59

MAXWELL, Len

Title/Flip	Label & No.	Good	Near Mint	Yr.
MERRY MONSTER CHRISTMAS/Sounds Of Christmas	(20th Fox 551)	.75	3.00	64

MAYALL, John

Title/Flip	Label & No.	Good	Near Mint	Yr.
BROKEN WINGS/Sonny Boy Blow	(London 20039)	.75	3.00	68
DON'T WASTE MY TIME/	(Polydor 14004)	.75	3.00	69
KEY TO LOVE/Parchman Farm	(London 20016)	.75	3.00	66
LET ME GIVE/	(Polydor 14253)	.75	3.00	74
LIVING ALONE/Walking On Sunset	(London 20042)	.75	3.00	68
NATURE'S DISAPPEARING/	(Polydor 14051)	.75	3.00	70
TELEPHONE BLUES/I'm Your Witchdoctor	(Immediate 502)	1.00	4.00	67

MAYALL, John With Eric Clapton & The Blues Breakers

Title/Flip	Label & No.	Good	Near Mint	Yr.
ALL YOUR LOVE/Hideaway	(London 20024)	1.00	4.00	68

MAY, Billy

Title/Flip	Label & No.	Good	Near Mint	Yr.
MAIN TITLE-THE MAN WITH THE GOLDEN ARM/ The Phonograph Song	(Capitol 3372)	1.00	4.00	56

MC ANNALLY, Mac

Title/Flip	Label & No.	Good	Near Mint	Yr.
BAD BOY/Let Him Go	(Ariola America 7671)	.50	2.00	77
OPINION/	(Ariola 7688)	.50	2.00	78
IT'S A CRAZY WORLD/We Can Be Strong	(Ariola America 7665)	.50	2.00	77

MC BRIDE, Bob (Of Lighthouse)

Title/Flip	Label & No.	Good	Near Mint	Yr.
MY WORLD IS EMPTY WITHOUT YOU/Quiet Moments	(MCA 40853)	.50	2.00	78

MC CABE, Chuck

Title/Flip	Label & No.	Good	Near Mint	Yr.
LIVE AT THE PET ROCK SHOW/That Old Pet Rock Of Mine	(GRT 044)	.75	3.00	75

MC CAFFERTY (Of Nazareth)

Title/Flip	Label & No.	Good	Near Mint	Yr.
OUT OF TIME/Cinnamon Girl	(A&M 1753)	.50	2.00	75

MC CANN, Peter

Title/Flip	Label & No.	Good	Near Mint	Yr.
DON'T TAKE IT OUT ON ME/	(Columbia 10989)	.50	2.00	79
DO YOU WANNA MAKE LOVE/Right Time Of The Night	(20th Century 2335)	.50	2.00	77
JUST ONE WOMAN/Come By Here	(Columbia 10899)	.50	2.00	79
SAVE ME YOUR LOVE/It's Easy	(20th Century 2335)	.50	2.00	77

MC CARTNEY, Paul (Of The Beatles)

Title/Flip	Label & No.	Good	Near Mint	Yr.
ANOTHER DAY/Oh Woman Oh Why	(Apple 1829)	.75	3.00	71
ANOTHER DAY/Another Day	(Apple 1829)	2.00	8.00	71
(Promotional issue)				
ANOTHER DAY/Oh Woman Oh Why	(Capitol 1829)	.50	2.00	
ARROW THROUGH ME/Old Siam Sir	(Columbia 1-11070)	.50	2.00	79
ARROW THROUGH ME/Arrow Through Me	(Columbia 1-11070)	1.25	5.00	79
(Promotional issue)				
BAND ON THE RUN/Nineteen Hundred & Eighty Five	(Apple 1873)	.50	2.00	74
BAND ON THE RUN/Band On The Run	(Apple 1873)	2.00	8.00	74
(Promotional issue)				
BAND ON THE RUN/Nineteen Hundred & Eighty Five	(Capitol 1873)	.50	2.00	
COMING UP/Coming Up (Live)-Lunchbox-Oddsox	(Columbia 1-11263)	.50	2.00	80
COMING UP/Coming Up	(Columbia 1-11263)	1.25	5.00	80
(Promotional issue)				
COMING UP (LIVE)/	(Columbia 1-11263)	.75	3.00	80
(One-sided promotional issue, included with "McCartney II" LP)				
COMING UP (LIVE)/	(Columbia 1-11263)	2.50	10.00	80
(One-sided promotional issue, distributed to the media)				
GETTING CLOSER/Spin It On	(Columbia 3-11020)	.50	2.00	79
GETTING CLOSER/Getting Closer	(Columbia 3-11020)	1.25	5.00	79
(Promotional issue)				
GETTING CLOSER/Spin It On	(Columbia 3-11020)	5.00	20.00	79
(Picture sleeve)				
GIVE IRELAND BACK TO THE IRISH/ Give Ireland Back To The Irish (Version)	(Apple 1847)	.50	2.00	72
GIVE IRELAND BACK TO THE IRISH/ Give Ireland Back To The Irish	(Apple 1847)	2.00	8.00	72
(Promotional issue)				
GIVE IRELAND BACK TO THE IRISH/ Give Ireland Back To The Irish (Version)	(Apple 1847)	1.00	4.00	72
(Picture sleeve)				
GIVE IRELAND BACK TO THE IRISH/ Give Ireland Back To The Irish (Version)	(Capitol 1847)	.50	2.00	
GOODNIGHT TONIGHT/Daytime Nightime Suffering	(Columbia 3-10939)	.50	2.00	79
GOODNIGHT TONIGHT/Goodnight Tonight	(Columbia 3-10939)	1.25	5.00	79
(Promotional issue)				
GOODNIGHT TONIGHT/Daytime Nightime Suffering	(Columbia 10940)	1.50	6.00	79
(12" single issue)				
HELEN WHEELS/Country Dreamer	(Apple 1869)	.50	2.00	73
HELEN WHEELS/Helen Wheels	(Apple 1869)	2.00	8.00	73
(Promotional issue)				
HELEN WHEELS/Helen Wheels	(Capitol 1869)	.50	2.00	
HI HI HI/C Moon	(Apple 1857)	.50	2.00	72
HI HI HI/Hi Hi Hi	(Apple 1857)	2.00	8.00	72
(Promotional issue)				
HI HI HI/C Moon	(Capitol 1857)	.50	2.00	
I'VE HAD ENOUGH/Deliver Your Children	(Capitol-MPL 4594)	.50	2.00	78
I'VE HAD ENOUGH/I've Had Enough	(Capitol-MPL 4594)	1.25	5.00	78
(Promotional issue)				
JET/Let Me Roll It	(Apple 1871)	1.50	6.00	74
JET/Jet	(Apple 1871)	2.00	8.00	74
(Promotional issue)				
JET/Mamunia	(Apple 1871)	.50	2.00	74
JET/Mamunia	(Capitol 1871)	.50	2.00	
JUNIOR'S FARM/Sally G	(Apple 1875)	.50	2.00	74
JUNIOR'S FARM/Junior's Farm	(Apple 1875)	2.00	8.00	74
(Promotional issue)				
JUNIOR'S FARM/Sally G	(Capitol 1875)	.50	2.00	
LET EM IN/Beware My Love	(Capitol 4293)	.50	2.00	76
LET EM IN/Let Em In	(Capitol 4293)	2.00	8.00	76
(Promotional Copy)				
LETTING GO/You Gave Me The Answer	(Capitol 4145)	.50	2.00	75
LETTING GO/Letting Go	(Capitol 4145)	2.00	8.00	75
(Promotional Copy)				
LISTEN TO WHAT THE MAN SAID/Love In Song	(Capitol 4091)	.50	2.00	75
LISTEN TO WHAT THE MAN SAID/ Listen To What The Man Said	(Capitol 4091)	2.00	8.00	75
(Promotional issue)				
LISTEN TO WHAT THE MAN SAID/Love In Song	(Capitol 4091)	.75	3.00	75
(Picture sleeve)				
LIVE & LET DIE/I Lie Around (By Denny Laine)	(Apple 1863)	.50	2.00	73
LIVE & LET DIE/Live & Let Die	(Apple 1863)	2.00	8.00	73
(Promotional issue)				
LIVE & LET DIE/I Lie Around (By Denny Laine)	(Capitol 1863)	.50	2.00	73
LONDON TOWN/I'm Carrying	(Capitol-MPL 4625)	.50	2.00	78
LONDON TOWN/London Town	(Capitol-MPL 4625)	1.25	5.00	78
(Promotional issue)				
MARY HAD A LITTLE LAMB/Little Woman Love	(Apple 1851)	.50	2.00	72
MARY HAD A LITTLE LAMB/Mary Had A Little Lamb	(Apple 1851)	2.00	8.00	72
(Promotional issue)				
MARY HAD A LITTLE LAMB/Little Woman Love	(Apple 1851)	5.00	20.00	72
(Picture sleeve. Both song titles are shown on sleeve.)				
MARY HAD A LITTLE LAMB/Little Woman Love	(Apple 1851)	1.00	4.00	72
(Picture sleeve. "Little Woman Love" title is not shown on sleeve.)				
MARY HAD A LITTLE LAMB/Little Woman Love	(Capitol 1851)	.50	2.00	
MAYBE I'M AMAZED/Maybe I'm Amazed	(Capitol PRO-8574-F2)	7.50	30.00	77
(Promotional 12" single issue)				
MAYBE I'M AMAZED/Soily	(Capitol 4385)	.50	2.00	76
MAYBE I'M AMAZED/Maybe I-m Amazed	(Capitol 4385)	1.25	5.00	76
(Promotional Copy)				
MULL OF KINTYRE/Girl's School	(Capitol-MPL 4504)	.50	2.00	77
MULL OF KINTYRE/Mull Of Kintyre	(Capitol-MPL 4504)	1.25	5.00	77
(Promotional issue)				
MY LOVE/The Mess	(Apple 1861)	.50	2.00	73
MY LOVE/My Love	(Apple 1861)	1.25	5.00	73
(Promotional issue)				
MY LOVE/The Mess	(Capitol 1861)	.50	2.00	
SILLY LOVE SONGS/Cook Of The House	(Capitol 4256)	.50	2.00	76
SILLY LOVE SONGS/Silly Love Songs	(Capitol 4256)	1.25	5.00	76
(Promotional Copy)				
UNCLE ALBERT-ADMIRAL HALSEY/Too Many People	(Apple 1839)	.75	3.00	71
UNCLE ALBERT-ADMIRAL HALSEY/ Uncle Albert-Admiral Halsey	(Apple 1839)	1.25	5.00	71
(Promotional issue)				
UNCLE ALBERT-ADMIRAL HALSEY/Too Many People	(Capitol 1839)	.50	2.00	
VENUS & MARS ROCK SHOW/ Magneto & Titanium Man	(Capitol 4175)	.50	2.00	75
VENUS & MARS ROCK SHOW/ Venus & Mars Rock Show	(Capitol 4175)	1.25	5.00	75
(Promotional Copy)				
WATERFALLS/Check The Machine	(Columbia 1-11335)	.50	2.00	80
WATERFALLS/Waterfalls	(Columbia 1-11335)	1.25	5.00	80
(Promotional issue)				
WITH A LITTLE LUCK/Backwards Traveller-Cuff Link	(Capitol-MPL 4559)	.50	2.00	78
WITH A LITTLE LUCK/Backwards Traveller-Cuff Link	(Capitol-MPL 4559)	1.25	5.00	78
(Promotional issue)				
WONDERFUL CHRISTMASTIME/ Rudolph The Red-Nosed Reggae	(Columbia 11162)	.50	2.00	79
WONDERFUL CHRISTMASTIME/ Wonderful Christmastime	(Columbia 11162)	1.25	5.00	79
(Promotional issue)				

Columbia & Capitol's most recent single issues with picture sleeves are not given seperate listings in this edition because the values given for the records themselves should include the sleeves.

MC CLINTON, Delbert

Title/Flip	Label & No.	Good	Near Mint	Yr.
TAKE IT EASY/	(Capricorn 0303)	.50	2.00	78
Also see Delbert & Glen				

MC COO, Marilyn, & Billy Davis (Of The Fifth Dimension)

Title/Flip	Label & No.	Good	Near Mint	Yr.
I HOPE WE GET TO LOVE IN TIME/	(ABC 12170)	.50	2.00	76
LOOK WHAT YOU'VE DONE TO MY HEART/In My Lifetime	(ABC 12298)	.50	2.00	77
YOU DON'T HAVE TO BE A STAR (TO BE IN MY SHOW)/ We've Got To Get It On Again	(ABC 12208)	.50	2.00	76
YOUR LOVE/My Love For You (Will Always Be The Same)	(ABC 12262)	.50	2.00	77

MC CORMICK, Gayle (Of Smith)

Title/Flip	Label & No.	Good	Near Mint	Yr.
GONNA BE ALRIGHT NOW/	(Dunhill 4281)	.50	2.00	71
IT'S A CRYING SHAME/If Only You Believe	(Dunhill 4288)	.50	2.00	71
NEAR YOU/Take Me Back	(Decca 33030)	.50	2.00	72
SWEET FEELING (THAT OLD TIME FEELING)/	(MCA 40007)	.50	2.00	73
YOU REALLY GOT A HOLD ON ME/	(Dunhill 4298)	.50	2.00	72

MC COY BOYS, The (Gil Garfield, Perry Botkin, Ray Campi)

Title/Flip	Label & No.	Good	Near Mint	Yr.
OUR MAN IN HAVANA/Reprieve Of Love	(Verve 10208)	1.25	5.00	60

MC COY, Charley

Title/Flip	Label & No.	Good	Near Mint	Yr.
CHERRY BERRY WINE/My Little Woman	(Cadence 1390)	.75	3.00	61

MC COY, Patty, & The Renegades

Title/Flip	Label & No.	Good	Near Mint	Yr.
GOODBYE/Stranger	(Counsel 116)	1.25	5.00	

MC COYS, The (With Rich Zehringer)

Title/Flip	Label & No.	Good	Near Mint	Yr.
BEAT THE CLOCK/Like You Do To Me	(Bang 543)	.75	3.00	67
FEVER/Sorrow	(Bang 511)	.75	3.00	65
HANG ON SLOOPY/I Can't Explain It	(Bang 506)	.75	3.00	65
JESSE BRADY/Resurrection	(Mercury 72843)	.75	3.00	68
ONLY HUMAN/Love Don't Stop	(Mercury 72917)	.75	3.00	68
Rich Zehringer is now known as Rick Derringer.				

MC COYS, The

Title/Flip	Label & No.	Good	Near Mint	Yr.
FULL GROWN CAT/Throwing Kisses	(RCA Victor 47-7354)	1.00	4.00	58

MC COY, Van

Title/Flip	Label & No.	Good	Near Mint	Yr.
GIRL'S ARE SENTIMENTAL/Baby Don't Tease Me	(Rock 'N 1012)	1.00	4.00	61
HUSTLE, THE/Hey Girl, Come & Get It	(Avco 4653)	.50	2.00	75
MR. D.J./Never Trust A Friend	(Rock 'N 101)	1.00	4.00	61

MC CREA, Jody

Title/Flip	Label & No.	Good	Near Mint	Yr.
CHICKEN SURFER/	(Canjo 106)	1.25	5.00	64

MC CREARY, Mary

Title/Flip	Label & No.	Good	Near Mint	Yr.
BROTHER/Singing The Blues (Reggae)	(Shelter 40327)	.50	2.00	75
EVERYBODY'S HAVING PROBLEMS/Singing The Blues	(Shelter 40365)	.50	2.00	75
SINGIN' THE BLUES/	(Shelter 40217)	.50	2.00	74

MC CREE, Earl-Jean: see Earl-Jean

MC CURN, George

Title/Flip	Label & No.	Good	Near Mint	Yr.
I'M JUST A COUNTRY BOY/ In My Little Corner Of The World	(A&M 705)	.75	3.00	63
WHEN THE WIND BLOWS IN CHICAGO/Georgia Town	(A&M 726)	.75	3.00	63

MC DANIELS, Gene

Title/Flip	Label & No.	Good	Near Mint	Yr.
CHIP CHIP/Another Tear Falls	(Liberty 55405)	.75	3.00	62
CRY BABY CRY/The Puzzle	(Liberty 55541)	.75	3.00	63
FUNNY/Chapel Of Tears	(Liberty 55444)	.75	3.00	62
HUNDRED POUNDS OF CLAY, A/Come On Take A Chance	(Liberty 55308)	.75	3.00	61
IT'S A LONELY TOWN/False Friends	(Liberty 55597)	.75	3.00	63
POINT OF NO RETURN/Warmer Than A Whisper	(Liberty 55480)	.75	3.00	62
SPANISH LACE/Somebody's Waiting	(Liberty 55510)	.75	3.00	62
TEAR, A/She's Come Back	(Liberty 55344)	.75	3.00	61
TOWER OF STRENGTH/Secret	(Liberty 55371)	.75	3.00	61

MC DEVITT, Charles, Skiffle Group

Title/Flip	Label & No.	Good	Near Mint	Yr.
FREIGHT TRAIN/Cotton Song (With Nancy Whiskey)	(Chic 1008)	1.00	4.00	57

MC DONALD, Country Joe

Title/Flip	Label & No.	Good	Near Mint	Yr.
BREAKFAST FOR TWO/Lost My Connection	(Fantasy 758)	.50	2.00	75
BRING BACK THE '60s, MAN/	(Fantasy 822)	.50	2.00	78
COYOTE/	(Fantasy 814)	.50	2.00	78
DR. HIP/Dr. Hip	(Vanguard 35181)	1.00	4.00	72
HOLD ON, IT'S COMING/Playing With Fire	(Vanguard 35133)	1.00	4.00	71
SAVE THE WHALES/Save The Whales	(Fantasy 814)	.50	2.00	78
SAVE THE WHALES/Save The Whales	(Fantasy 765)	.75	3.00	75

MC DONOUGH, Megan

Title/Flip	Label & No.	Good	Near Mint	Yr.
NO RETURN/	(Wooden Nickel 0112)	.50	2.00	71

MC5, The (The Motor City Five)

Title/Flip	Label & No.	Good	Near Mint	Yr.
AMERICAN RUSE, THE/Shakin' Street	(Atlantic 2724)	1.25	5.00	69
I CAN ONLY GIVE YOU EVERYTHING/I Just Don't Know	(AMG 1000)	2.50	10.00	66
I CAN ONLY GIVE YOU EVERYTHING/One Of The Guys	(AMG 1001)	2.50	10.00	66
KICK OUT THE JAMS/Motor City Is Burning	(Elektra 45648)	2.00	8.00	69
LOOKING AT YOU/Borderline	(A^2 333)	3.75	15.00	67
LOOKING AT YOU/Borderline	(A^2 333)	8.75	35.00	67
(Picture sleeve)				
TONIGHT/Looking At You	(Atlantic 2678)	1.25	5.00	69
Group members: Mike Davis, Dennis Thompson, Fred Smith, Wayne Kramer, Rob Tyner.				

MC DOWELL, Ronnie

Title/Flip	Label & No.	Good	Near Mint	Yr.
HERE COMES THE REASON I LIVE/ Travlin' Wanderin' Man	(Scorpion 159)	.50	2.00	78
I JUST WANTED YOU TO KNOW/Animal	(Scorpion 0553)	.50	2.00	78
(With the Jordanaires)				
I LOVE YOU, I LOVE YOU, I LOVE YOU/	(Scorpion 149)	.50	2.00	77
KING IS GONE, THE/Walking Through Georgia In The Rain	(Scorpion 135)	.50	2.00	77

MC DOWELL, Roger

Title/Flip	Label & No.	Good	Near Mint	Yr.
STATUE OF A KING/Teach Me Not To Cry	(Compass 009)	.50	2.00	77

MC FADDEN, Bob, & Dor (Rod McKuen)

Title/Flip	Label & No.	Good	Near Mint	Yr.
FRANKIE & IGOR AT A ROCK & ROLL PARTY/ Children Cross The Bridge	(Brunswick 55120)	1.25	5.00	59
MUMMY, THE/The Beat Generation	(Brunswick 55140)	1.00	4.00	59

MC FARLAND, Gary

Title/Flip	Label & No.	Good	Near Mint	Yr.
HARD DAY'S NIGHT/And I Love Her	(Verve 10342)	.75	3.00	65

MC GEAR, Mike (Of Scaffold)

Title/Flip	Label & No.	Good	Near Mint	Yr.
LEAVE IT/Sweet Baby	(Warner Bros. 8037)	.50	2.00	74
Mike McGear is Paul McCartney's brother.				

MC GEE, Gerry

Title/Flip	Label & No.	Good	Near Mint	Yr.
MOONLIGHT SURFIN'/Cajun Guitar	(A&M 771)	1.00	4.00	65

TITLE/FLIP	LABEL & NO.	GOOD	NEAR MINT	YR.
MC GEE, Parker				
BOY NEEDS GIRL/	(Big Tree 16098)	.50	2.00	77
I JUST CAN'T SAY NO TO YOU/Talk About Lovin' You	(Big Tree 16082)	.50	2.00	77
LITTLE LOVE & UNDERSTANDING, A/	(Big Tree 16091)	.50	2.00	77
MC GILL				
PEOPLE ARE TALKIN' (PART 1)/People Are Talkin' (Part 2)	(Cameo 119)	1.00	4.00	57
MC GOVERN, Maureen				
CAN YOU READ MY MIND (LOVE THEME FROM SUPERMAN)/ You Love Me Too Late	(Warner-Curb 8750)	.50	2.00	79
CAN'T TAKE MY EYES OFF YOU/	(Warner-Curb 49129)	.50	2.00	79
DIFFERENT WORLDS (THEME FROM THE PARAMOUNT TV SERIES "ANGIE")/Carolina Moon	(Warner-Curb 8835)	.50	2.00	79
EVEN BETTER THAN I KNOW MYSELF/	(20th Century 2213)	.50	2.00	75
GIVE ME A REASON TO BE GONE/	(20th Century 2109)	.50	2.00	74
I WON'T LAST A DAY WITHOUT YOU/	(20th Century 2051)	.50	2.00	73
LOVE SONGS ARE GETTING HARDER TO SING/ Stop Me (If You've Heard This Song Before)	(20th Century 2234)	.50	2.00	75
MORNING AFTER, THE/Midnight Storm	(20th Century 2010)	.50	2.00	73
WE'LL NEVER HAVE TO SAY GOODBYE AGAIN/ I Thought You Might Like To Know	(Epic 50515)	.50	2.00	78
WE MAY NEVER LOVE THIS WAY AGAIN/	(20th Century 2158)	.50	2.00	75
MC GUINN, Clark & Hillman (Of The Byrds)				
BACKSTAGE PASS/Bye Bye Baby	(Capitol 4763)	.50	2.00	79
DON'T YOU WRITE HER OFF/Sad Boy	(Capitol 4693)	.50	2.00	79
SURRENDER TO ME/Little Mama	(Capitol 4739)	.50	2.00	79
MC GUINN, Roger (Of The Byrds)				
AMERICAN GIRL/I'm Not Lonely Anymore (Shown as by Roger McGuinn & Thunderbyrd)	(Columbia 10543)	.50	2.00	77
DRAGGIN'/Time Cube	(Columbia 45931)	.50	2.00	73
LOVER OF THE BAYOU/	(Columbia 10201)	.50	2.00	76
PEACE ON YOU/	(Columbia 10044)	.50	2.00	75
SAME OLD SOUND/	(Columbia 10019)	.50	2.00	74
TAKE ME BACK/	(Columbia 10385)	.50	2.00	76
MC GUIRE, Barry				
ANOTHER MAN/Bull 'gine Run	(Horizon 354)	.75	3.00	62
CHILD OF OUR TIMES/Upon A Painted Ocean	(Dunhill 4014)	.75	3.00	65
CINDY & JOHNNY/I've Got A Secret	(Mosiac 1004)	.75	3.00	62
CLOUDY SUMMER AFTERNOON RAINDROPS/ I'd Have To Be Outta My Mind	(Dunhill 4028)	.75	3.00	66
DON'T YOU WONDER WHERE IT'S AT/This Precious Time	(Dunhill 4019)	.75	3.00	65
EVE OF DESTRUCTION/ What Exactly's The Matter With Me	(Dunhill 4009)	.75	3.00	65
ONE BY ONE/Town & Country	(Horizon 4)	1.00	4.00	62
MC GUIRE SISTERS, The (Phyllis, Dorothy, Christine)				
GOODNIGHT MY LOVE, PLEASANT DREAMS/Mommy	(Coral 61748)	1.00	4.00	56
GOODNIGHT, SWEETHEART, GOODNIGHT/Heavenly Feeling	(Coral 61187)	1.00	4.00	54
HE/If You Believe	(Coral 61501)	1.00	4.00	55
JUST FOR OLD TIMES SAKE/Really Neat	(Coral 62249)	1.00	4.00	61
MAY YOU ALWAYS/Achoo-Cha-Cha	(Coral 62059)	1.00	4.00	58
MUSKRAT RAMBLE/Lonesome Polecat	(Coral 61278)	1.00	4.00	54
PICNIC/Delilah Jones	(Coral 61627)	1.00	4.00	56
SINCERELY/No More	(Coral 61323)	1.00	4.00	54
SOMETHING'S GOTTA GIVE/Rhythm 'N' Blues	(Coral 61423)	1.00	4.00	55
SUGARTIME/Banana Split	(Coral 61924)	1.00	4.00	57
MC KEE, Ron				
ELVIS, WE MISS YOU TONIGHT/Be-Bop-A-Lula	(American Sound 3090)	.50	2.00	77
MC KEE, Ron, & The Rivieres				
JAILHOUSE ROCK/Summertime Fun	(Lincoln 710)	1.00	4.00	64
MC KENDREE SPRING				
GOD BLESS THE CONSPIRACY/Flying Dutchman	(Decca 33000)	.50	2.00	72
TOO YOUNG TO FEEL THIS OLD/ I'm Gonna Lose That Game Again	(Pye 71060)	.50	2.00	76
UNDERGROUND RAILROAD/	(MCA 40024)	.50	2.00	73
MC KENZIE, Scott (Scott MacKenzie)				
ALL I WANT IS YOU/Look In Your Eyes	(Capitol 5961)	.75	3.00	67
GOING HOME AGAIN/Take A Moment	(Ode 70 66012)	.75	3.00	70
LIKE AN OLD TIME MOVIE/What's The Difference, Chapter 11	(Ode 105)	.75	3.00	67
NO, NO, NO, NO, NO/	(Epic 10124)	.75	3.00	67
SAN FRANCISCO (BE SURE TO WEAR SOME FLOWERS IN YOUR HAIR)/ What's The Difference	(Ode 103)	.75	3.00	67
MC KUEN, Rod				
OLIVER TWIST/Celebrity Twist	(Spiral 1407)	1.25	5.00	62
OLIVER TWIST MEETS THE DUKE OF OIL/ Steel Men	(Jubilee 5420)	1.25	5.00	62
Also see McFadden, Bob, & Dor				
MC LAIN, Tommy				
I CAN'T TAKE IT NO MORE/Think It Over	(MSL 209)	.75	3.00	66
SWEET DREAMS/I Need You So	(Jin 197)	1.25	5.00	66
SWEET DREAMS/I Need You So	(MSL 197)	.75	3.00	66
MC LAURIN, Bette				
I MAY HATE MYSELF IN THE MORNING/I Hear A Rhapsody	(Derby 790)	1.25	5.00	52
MC LEAN, Don				
AMERICAN PIE (PART 1)/American Pie (Part 2)	(United Artists 50856)	.50	2.00	71
DREIDEL/Bronco Bill's Lament	(United Artists 51100)	.50	2.00	73
IF WE TRY/The More You Pay (The More It's Worth)	(United Artists 206)	.50	2.00	73
IT DOESN'T MATTER ANYMORE/If We Try	(Arista 0379)	.50	2.00	78
LA LA LOVE YOU/Homeless Brother	(United Artists 579)	.50	2.00	74
MULE SKINNER BLUES/Sitting On Top Of The World	(United Artists 541)	.50	2.00	74
PRIME TIME/The Statue	(Arista 0284)	.50	2.00	77
VINCENT/Castles In The Air	(United Artists 50887)	.50	2.00	72
WONDERFUL BABY/Birthday Song	(United Artists 614)	.50	2.00	75
MC LEAN, Phil				
SMALL SAD SAM/Chicken	(Versatile 107)	.75	3.00	61
MC NAMARA, Robin				
GOT TO BELIEVE IN LOVE/	(Steed 728)	.50	2.00	70
HANG IN THERE BABY/Together Forever	(Steed 730)	.50	2.00	71
LAY A LITTLE LOVIN' ON ME/I'll Tell You Tomorrow	(Steed 724)	.50	2.00	70
MARY, JANEY & ME/Beer Drinkin' Man	(Steed 736)	.50	2.00	71
MC NAUGHTON & HIS ALL-NEWS ORCHESTRA				
RIGHT FROM THE SHARK'S JAWS/Jaws Jam	(Jamie 1427)	.75	3.00	
MC NICHOL, KIRSTY & JIMMY				
HE'S SO FINE/He's A Dancer	(RCA 11271)	.50	2.00	78
PAGE BY PAGE/	(RCA 11385)	.50	2.00	78
MC RAE, Carmen				
NEXT TIME IT HAPPENS/Come On Come In	(Decca 29749)	1.00	4.00	56
MC TELL, Ralph				
STREETS OF LONDON/	(Paramount 0096)	.50	2.00	73
MC VOY, Carl				
TOOTSIE/You Are My Sunshine	(Phillips International 3526)	1.25	5.00	
ME & DEM GUYS				
BLACK CLOUD/Don't You Just Know It	(Dearborn 550)	1.50	6.00	
BLACK CLOUD/Come On Little Sweetheart	(Palmer 5007)	1.25	5.00	

TITLE/FLIP	LABEL & NO.	GOOD	NEAR MINT	YR.
ME & THEM				
EVERYTHING I DO IS WRONG/Show You Mean It to Me	(U.S. songs 601)	1.25	5.00	
MEADER, Vaughn				
NO HIDING PLACE/Elephant Song	(MGM 13169)	.75	3.00	63
TWAS THE NIGHT BEFORE CHRISTMAS/ St. Nick Visits The White House (Comedy)	(Verve 10309)	1.25	5.00	63
MEADOWS, Audrey & Jane				
DEAR RALPH/Dungaree Dan & Chino Sue	(RCA Victor 47-6447)	1.25	5.00	56
MEADOWS, Larry				
PHYLLIS/We're Through	(Stratolite 969)	3.75	15.00	
MEAD, Sister Janet				
LORD'S PRAYER, THE/Brother Sun & Sister Moon	(A&M 1491)	.50	2.00	74
TAKE MY HAND/	(A&M 1611)	.50	2.00	74
MEANS, Kieth, & The Knighters				
SHAM-BAM (PART 1)/Sham-Bam (Part 2)	(Rena 3001)	.75	3.00	61
MEANTIME (With Ellie Greenwich)				
FRIDAY KIND OF MONDAY/Right Back	(Atco 6524)	.75	3.00	67
MEAT LOAF (Marvin Lee Aday)				
MORE THAN YOU DESERVE/Presence Of The Lord	(RSO 407)	.50	2.00	74
PARADISE BY THE DASHBOARD LIGHT: I. PARADISE II. LET ME SLEEP ON IT III. PRAYING FOR THE END OF TIME/ "Bat" Overture	(Epic-Cleveland Intl. 50588)	.50	2.00	78
TWO OUT OF THREE AIN'T BAD/ For Crying Out Loud	(Epic-Cleveland Intl. 50513)	.50	2.00	78
YOU TOOK THE WORDS RIGHT OUT OF MY MOUTH (HOT SUMMER NIGHT)/For Crying Out Loud	(Epic-Cleveland Intl. 50467)	.50	2.00	77
YOU TOOK THE WORDS RIGHT OUT OF MY MOUTH/Paradise By The Dashboard Light: I. Paraidse II. Let me Sleep On It III. Praying For The End Of Time	(Epic-Cleveland Intl. 50634)	.50	2.00	78
MEDALLIONS, The				
LOVE THAT GIRL/Carachi	(Sultan 1004)	1.00	4.00	
MEDICINE HEAD				
(AND THE) PICTURES IN THE SKY/Natural Sight	(Elektra 45741)	.50	2.00	71
RISING SUN/	(Polydor 15083)	.50	2.00	70
MEDLEY, Bill (Of The Righteous Brothers)				
BROWN EYED WOMAN/Let The Good Times Roll	(MGM 13959)	.75	3.00	68
FREEDOM FOR THE STALLION/	(A&M 1350)	.75	3.00	72
I CAN'T MAKE IT ALONE/One Day Girl	(MGM 13931)	.75	3.00	68
LAY A LITTLE LOVIN' ON ME/	(United Artists 1256)	.75	3.00	78
LEAVIN' TOWN/I Surrender (To Your Touch)	(Reprise 0413)	.75	3.00	64
PEACE BROTHER, PEACE/Winter Won't Come This Year	(MGM 14000)	.75	3.00	68
STATUE OF A FOOL	(United Artists 1270)	.75	3.00	79
THAT LUCKY OLD SUN/My Darling Clementine	(Verve 10569)	.75	3.00	67
WE'VE ONLY JUST BEGUN/A Song For You	(A&M 1311)	.75	3.00	71
Also see Clouds, The				
MEDLIN, Joe				
I KNEEL AT YOUR THRONE/Out Of Sight, Out Of Mind	(Mercury 71415)	1.00	4.00	59
MEEHAN, Don				
AN OPEN LETTER TO MR. KHRUSHCHEV/ Beautiful Lady In White	(Joy 246)	1.00	4.00	60
MEEP MEEP & THE ROADRUNNERS				
JUSTINE/A-flat Blues	(Boomerang 651)	.75	3.00	
MEGATONS, The				
SHIMMY, SHIMMY WALK (PART 1)/ Shimmy, Shimmy Walk (Part 2)	(Dodge 808)	1.00	4.00	62
SHIMMY SHIMMY WALK (PART 1)/	(Checker 1002)	.75	3.00	62
MEGATRONS, The				
VELVET WATERS/The Merry Piper (Instrumentals)	(Acousticon 101)	1.00	4.00	59
MEISBURG & WALTERS (Steven Meisburg & John Walters)				
GRADUATION DAY (Uncensored)/ Graduation Day (Censored)	(Parchment PRO-413769)	.75	3.00	76
MEISNER, Randy (Of The Eagles)				
I REALLY WANT YOU HERE TONIGHT/Heartsong	(Asylum 45502)	.50	2.00	78
Also see Poco				
MELANIE (Melanie Safka)				
BITTER BAD/Do You Believe	(Neighborhood 4210)	.50	2.00	73
BRAND NEW KEY/Some Say (I Got The Devil)	(Neighborhood 4201)	.50	2.00	71
CYCLONE/If I Needed You	(Atlantic 3380)	.50	2.00	77
GOOD BOOK, THE/We Don't Know Where We're Going	(Buddah 224)	.50	2.00	71
I'D RATHER LEAVE WHILE I'M IN LOVE/ Record People	(Midsong Intl. 40858)	.50	2.00	78
I'M BACK IN TOWN/Johnny Boy	(Buddah 304)	.50	2.00	72
KNOCK ON WOOD/Record People	(Midsong Intl. 40903)	.50	2.00	78
LAY DOWN (CANDLES IN THE RAIN)/Candles In The Rain	(Buddah 167)	.50	2.00	70
LOVE TO LOSE AGAIN/Pine & Feather	(Neighborhood 4214)	.50	2.00	74
NICKEL SONG, THE/What Have They Done To My Song Ma	(Buddah 268)	.50	2.00	71
PEACE WILL COME (ACCORDING TO PLAN)/Stop! I Don't Wanna Hear It Anymore	(Buddah 186)	.50	2.00	70
RING THE LIVING BELL/Railroad	(Neighborhood 4202)	.50	2.00	72
RUBY TUESDAY/Merry Christmas	(Buddah 202)	.50	2.00	70
RUNNING AFTER LOVE/Holding Out	(Tomato 10007)	.50	2.00	78
SEEDS/Some Say (I Got The Devil)	(Neighborhood 4212)	.50	2.00	73
SOME DAY I'LL BE A FARMER/Steppin'	(Neighborhood 4204)	.50	2.00	72
SWEET MISERY/	(Neighborhood 10001)	.50	2.00	75
TOGETHER ALONE/Center Of The Circle	(Neighborhood 4207)	.50	2.00	72
WILL YOU LOVE ME TOMORROW?/Here I Am	(Neighborhood 4213)	.50	2.00	73
YOU'RE NOT A BAD GHOST JUST AN OLD SONG/ Eyes Of Man	(Neighborhood 10000)	.50	2.00	75
MELCHER, Terry (Terry Day)				
FIRE IN A RAINSTORM/So Right Tonight	(RCA-Equinox 10587)	.50	2.00	76
MELCHER, Terry, & Bruce Johnston				
TAKE IT TO MEXICO/Rebecca	(RCA-Equinox 10238)	.50	2.00	75
Also see Bruce & Terry				
MELLODEERS, The				
LETTER, THE/Nairna Nairna	(Shelley 127)	1.50	6.00	61
SUMMER ROMANCE/Charock	(Gone 5033)	1.25	5.00	58
THREE DEUCES & TWIN PIPES/Born To Be Mine	(Shelley 161)	1.00	4.00	62
WISHING IS FOR FOOLS/Rudolph The Red Nosed Reindeer	(Studio 9908)	2.00	8.00	60
MELLO-HARPS, The				
GUMMA GUMMA/No Good	(Casino 104)	5.00	20.00	58
MELLO-KINGS, The				
BABY TELL ME (WHY, WHY, WHY)/ The Only Girl (I'll Ever Love)	(Herald 511)	2.00	8.00	57
CHAPEL ON THE HILL/Sassafras	(Herald 507)	1.50	6.00	57
KID STUFF/I Promise	(Herald 554)	1.50	6.00	60
PENNY/Till There Was None	(Herald 561)	1.50	6.00	60
TONITE, TONITE/Do Baby Do	(Herald 502)	1.50	6.00	57
TONITE, TONITE/Do Baby Do (Shown as by the Mellotones on first pressing.)	(Herald 502)	6.25	25.00	57
VALERIE/She's Real Cool	(Herald 518)	1.50	6.00	57

TITLE/FLIP	LABEL & NO.	GOOD	NEAR MINT	YR.
MELLOTONES see: Mello-Kings, The				
MELODY MAKERS, The				
LET'S MAKE LOVE WORTHWHILE/	(Hollis 1001)	2.00	8.00	
MELO GENTS, The				
BABY BE MINE/Get Off My Back	(Warner Bros. 5056)	3.75	15.00	59
MELTON, Levy, & The Dey Brothers				
I STILL LOVE YOU ANYWAY/Runaway Child	(Mercury 73170)	.75	3.00	69
S.O.S./S.O.S	(Mercury 72860)	1.00	4.00	68
THEM CHANGERS/Spot On The Wall	(Mercury 73008)	.75	3.00	69
WE GOT LOVE/We Got Love	(Columbia 10030)	.50	2.00	75
WHOLESALE LOVE/Wholesale Love	(Mercury 73205)	.75	3.00	69
MEMBERS, The				
JENNY-JENNY/	(Label 101)	.75	3.00	
MEMORIES, The				
LOVE BELLS/I Promise	(Way-Lin 101)	7.50	30.00	
MEMPHIS MILL				
ELVIS IS THE KING/Elvis Is The King (Instrumental)	(W.B. Sound 1621)	.75	3.00	77
MENAGERIE, The				
TELEPHONE SONG/Love The Thing	(Vision 1003)	1.00	4.00	
MENDES, Sergio, & Brasil '66 (With Lani Hall)				
CONSTANT RAIN/	(A&M 825)	.50	2.00	66
FOOL ON THE HILL, THE/So Many Stars	(A&M 961)	.50	2.00	68
FOR ME/	(A&M 836)	.50	2.00	67
LOOK OF LOVE, THE/Like A Lover	(A&M 924)	.50	2.00	68
MAS QUE NADA/	(A&M 807)	.50	2.00	66
NIGHT & DAY/	(A&M 853)	.50	2.00	67
PRETTY WORLD/	(A&M 1049)	.50	2.00	69
REAL THING, THE/ (Solo by Sergio Mendes)	(Elektra 45360)	.50	2.00	76
SCARBOROUGH FAIR/Canto Triste	(A&M 986)	.50	2.00	68
(SITTIN' ON) THE DOCK OF THE BAY/Song Of No Regrets	(A&M 1073)	.50	2.00	69
WICHITA LINEMAN/	(A&M 1132)	.50	2.00	69
MENG, Jimmy				
TRUE & FAITHFUL/Don't Be Blue	(Jay Em 1000)	1.25	5.00	61
TRUE & FAITHFUL/Don't Be Blue	(Liberty 55346)	.75	3.00	61
MERCED BLUE NOTES, The				
MIDNIGHT SESSION/Midnight Session	(Tri-Phi 1011)	1.00	4.00	64
WHOLE LOTTA NOTHIN'/Whole Lot Of Nothing	(Tri-Phi 1023)	1.25	5.00	64
RUFUS JR./Thompin' (Instrumentals)	(Galaxy 738)	.75	3.00	65
MERCEEDEES, The (With The Individuals)				
PLEASE BABY, BE MINE/Not Me	(Gold Seal 1000)	2.00	8.00	
MERCER, Wally				
ROCK AROUND THE CLOCK/Don't Wait Till Tomorrow	(Dot 1099)	1.25	5.00	
MERCY				
FOREVER/The Morning's Come	(Warner Bros. 7297)	.75	3.00	69
HELLO BABY/Heard You Went Away	(Warner Bros. 7331)	.75	3.00	69
LOVE (CAN MAKE YOU HAPPY)/Fire Ball	(Sundi 6811)	.75	3.00	69
MERLIN, Jack				
GIRL OF MY DREAMS/I Beat The Blues	(Dot 16332)	1.00	4.00	62
MERMAN, Ethel & Dick Haymes				
YOU'RE JUST IN LOVE/Something To Dance About	(Decca 27317)	1.25	5.00	51
MERRY ELVES, The (Milton, Sleepy & Ringo)				
ROCK & ROLL AROUND THE CHRISTMAS TREE/ I Love Christmas	(Argus 250)	1.25	5.00	64
MERRY-GO-ROUND, The (Featuring Emitt Rhodes)				
COME RIDE, COME RIDE/She Laughed Loud	(A&M 899)	.75	3.00	67
GONNA LEAVE YOU ALONE/Listen, Listen	(A&M 920)	.75	3.00	67
LIVE/Time Will Show The Wiser	(A&M 834)	.75	3.00	67
WE'RE IN LOVE/Gonna Fight The War	(A&M 857)	.75	3.00	67
YOU'RE A VERY LOVELY WOMAN/ Where Have You Been All My Life	(A&M 863)	.75	3.00	67
MERSEYBEATS, The				
DON'T TURN AROUND/Really Mystified	(Fontana 1905)	1.00	4.00	64
I LOVE YOU, YES I DO/See Me Back	(Fontana 1532)	1.00	4.00	65
I THINK OF YOU/Mister Moonlight	(Fontana 1882)	1.00	4.00	64
SEE ME BACK/Last Night	(Fontana 1950)	1.00	4.00	64
MERSEY LADS, The				
WHATCHA' GONNA DO BABY/Johnny No Love	(MGM 13481)	.75	3.00	66
MERSEY MONSTERS, The				
BURIED ACROSS THE MERSEY/I Feel Mine (Parodies)	(Fright'n 1011)	3.75	15.00	65
MERSEY SOUNDS, The				
GET ON YOUR HONDA & RIDE/Honda Holiday	(Montel 966)	.75	3.00	66
MESA				
SAILING SHIPS/City Lights	(Ariola America 7654)	.50	2.00	77
MESSINGERS, The				
MIDNIGHT HOUR/Up Til News (Shown as by Michael & the Messengers)	(USA 866)	.75	3.00	67
THAT'S THE WAY A WOMAN IS/In The Jungle	(Rare Earth 5032)	.75	3.00	71
WINDOW SHOPPING/California Soul	(Soul 35037)	.75	3.00	67
This group should not be confused with the Michael & the Messengers listed elsewhere in this section. Although both groups recorded for USA, they are competely different bands.				
Also see Movies, The				
MESSENGERS, The (Michael & The Messengers)				
GOTTA TAKE IT EASY/I Need Her Here	(U.S.A. 897)	.75	3.00	68
IN THE MIDNIGHT HOUR/Hard Hard Year	(U.S.A. 866)	.75	3.00	67
ROMEO & JULIET/Life (Don't Mean Nothing)	(U.S.A. 874)	.75	3.00	67
RUN & HIDE/She Was The Girl	(U.S.A. 889)	.75	3.00	67
MESSINA, Jim, & The Jesters				
BREEZE & I/Strange Man	(Audo Fidelity 98)	1.25	5.00	64
DRAG BIKE BOOGIE/A-rab	(Ultima U-705)	1.50	6.00	64
PANTHER POUNCE/Tiger Tail	(Feature 101)	1.50	6.00	64
Also see Loggins & Messina				
METIS, Frank				
WIGGLE, THE/Sweet Perfume	(Mayflower M-20)	1.00	4.00	59
METROS, The				
LOOKIN'/All Of My Life	(Just 1502)	3.75	15.00	
MGM STUDIO ORCHESTRA, The				
ROCK AROUND THE CLOCK/Blackboard Jungle (Instrumentals)	(MGM 12028)	1.25	5.00	55
MICHAEL & THE CONTINENTALS				
LITTLE SCHOOL GIRL/Rain In My Eyes	(Audio Fidelity 139)	1.00	4.00	65
MICHAEL & THE MESSENGERS: see Messengers				

TITLE/FLIP	LABEL & NO.	GOOD	NEAR MINT	YR.

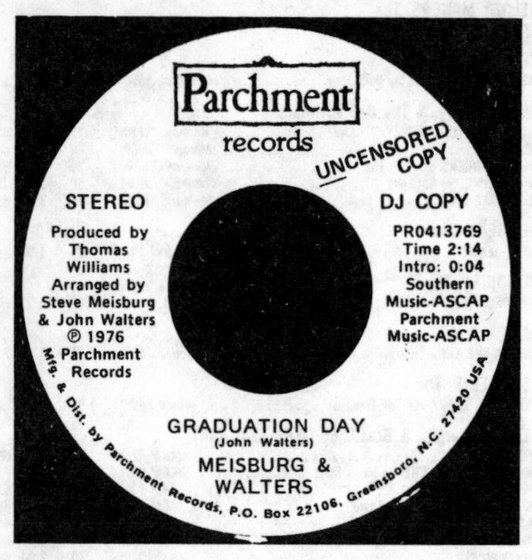

Parchment
records
UNCENSORED COPY
STEREO
DJ COPY
Produced by Thomas Williams Arranged by Steve Meisburg & John Walters ℗ 1976 Parchment Records
PR0413769 Time 2:14 Intro: 0:04 Southern Music-ASCAP Parchment Music-ASCAP
GRADUATION DAY
(John Walters)
MEISBURG & WALTERS
Mfg. & Dist. by Parchment Records, P.O. Box 22106, Greensboro, N.C. 27420 USA

MICHAEL, George
FANTASTIC PHILADELPHIA FLYERS/ Fantastic Philadelphia Flyers (WFIL 84514) .75 3.00

MICHAELS, Lee
CAN I GET A WITNESS/You Are What You Do (A&M 1303) .75 3.00 71
DO YOU KNOW WHAT I MEAN/Keep The Circle Turning (A&M 1262) .75 3.00 71
GOODBYE, GOODBYE/The War (A&M 1048) .75 3.00 69
HEIGHTY HI/Heighty Hi (A&M 1095) .75 3.00 69
HELLO/Love (A&M 911) 1.25 5.00 68
SAME OLD SONG/Rock & Roll Community (Columbia 45874) .50 2.00 73
TOMORROW/Sounding The Sleeping (A&M 912) 1.25 5.00

MICHEL, Tiffany
DIXIE/Come Closer (MGM 13624) 1.50 6.00 66

MICKEY & KITTY
OOH-SH-LALA/The Kid Brother (Atlantic 2024) 1.00 4.00 59

MIDDLE OF THE ROAD
ON THIS LAND/The Talk Of All (RCA 0732) .50 2.00 72
SOLEY SOLEY/To Remind Me (RCA 0612) .50 2.00 72
TWEEDLE DEE TWEEDLE DUM/Give It Time (RCA 0539) .50 2.00 71

MIDDLETON, Tom
ONE NIGHT LOVERS/O'Rosey (Columbia 10231) .50 2.00 76

MIDLER, Bette
BIG NOISE FROM WINNETKA/Rain (Atlantic 3628) .50 2.00 79
BOOGIE WOOGIE BUGLE BOY/Delta Dawn (Atlantic 2964) .50 2.00 73
DO YOU WANT TO DANCE?/Superstar (Atlantic 2928) .50 2.00 72
FRIENDS/Chapel Of Love (Atlantic 2980) .50 2.00 73
HANG ON IN THERE BABY/Cradle Days (Atlantic 3616) .50 2.00 79
IN THE MOOD/ (Atlantic 3004) .50 2.00 74
MARRIED MEN/Bang, You're Dead (Atlantic 3582) .50 2.00 79
OLD CAPE COD/Tragedy (Atlantic 3325) .50 2.00 76
PARADISE/Red (Atlantic 3475) .50 2.00 77
STORYBOOK CHILDREN (DAYBREAK)/Empty Bed Blues (Atlantic 3431) .50 2.00 77
STRANGERS IN THE NIGHT/Samedi Et Vendredi (Atlantic 3319) .50 2.00 76
YOU'RE MOVIN' OUT TODAY/Let Me Just Follow Behind (Atlantic 3379) .50 2.00 77
WHEN A MAN LOVES A WOMAN/ (Atlantic 3643) .50 2.00 79

MIDNIGHT ANGELS, The
I'M SUFFERIN'/In The Moonlight (Apex 77073) 1.25 5.00

MIDNIGHTERS, The
BIG SURFER/Not Another One (Capitol 4981) 1.00 4.00 63

MIDNIGHTERS, Thee: see Thee Midniters

MIGHTY AVENGERS, The
WHEN BLUE TURNS TO GRAY/I'm Lost Without You (Press 9746) .75 3.00 65

MIGIL 5, The
MOCKIN' BIRD HILL/Long Ago & Far Away (Cameo 316) .75 3.00 64

MIKE & LULU
BABY TALK/Baby's Lullaby (Top Rank 2036) 1.00 4.00 60

MIKE & THE RAVENS
I'VE TAKEN ALL I CAN/Mr. Heartbreak (Empire 1) .75 3.00

MIKE & THE UTOPIANS (With Mike Lasman)
ERLENE/I Found A Penny (Cee-Jay 574) 7.50 30.00
ERLENE/ I Wish (This is the same song as "I Found A Penny.") (Cee-Jay 574) 7.50 30.00

MIKKELSEN, Don, & The Birds
CHAPEL OF LOVE/Where I Came In (Deck 600) 1.50 6.00

MILES, Buddy, Express
DOWN BY THE RIVER/Heart's Delight (Mercury 73086) .75 3.00 70
DREAMS/ (Mercury 73119) .75 3.00 70
MEMPHIS TRAIN/ (Mercury 72945) .75 3.00 69
ROCKIN' & ROLLIN' ON THE STREETS OF HOLLYWOOD/ Livin' In The Right Space (Casablanca 839) .50 2.00 75
69 FREEDOM SPECIAL/Miss Lady (Mercury 72903) .75 3.00 68
THEM CHANGES/ (Mercury 73008) .75 3.00 70
THEM CHANGES/ (Mercury 73228) .75 3.00 71
WE GOT TO LIVE TOGETHER/ (Mercury 73159) .75 3.00 70
WHERE ARE YOU GONNA RUN TO LADY/ (Casablanca 859) .50 2.00 76
WHOLESALE LOVE/ (Mercury 73205) .75 3.00 71
Also see Electric Flag

MILES, Garry (Of The Statues)
DREAM GIRL/Wishing Well (Liberty 55279) .75 3.00 60
LOVE AT FIRST SIGHT/Commandments Of Love (Liberty 55363) .75 3.00 61
LOOK FOR A STAR/Afraid Of Love (Liberty 55261) .75 3.00 60
LOOK FOR A STAR/Afraid Of Love (Liberty 55261) 1.50 6.00 60
(Picture sleeve)

MILES, John
HIGHFLY/There's A Man Behind The Guitar (London 20084) .50 2.00 76
I HAVE NEVER BEEN IN LOVE BEFORE/ (Arista 0331) .50 2.00 78
MANHATTAN SKYLINE/ (London 20094) .50 2.00 77
MUSIC/When You Lose Someone So Young (London 20086) .50 2.00 76
REMEMBER YESTERDAY/ (London 20089) .50 2.00 76
SLOWDOWN/Stand Up (& Give Me A Reason) (London 20092) .50 2.00 77
SLOWDOWN/Stranger In The City (London 3002) 1.00 4.00 77
(12" single issue)

MILES, Lenny
DON'T BELIEVE HIM, DONNA/Invisible (Secpter 1212) .75 3.00 61
IN BETWEEN TEARS/I Know Love (Secpter 1218) .75 3.00 61

MILK (With Johnny Cymbal)
ANGELA JONES/Ochiltree (Buddah 80) .75 3.00 68

MILKY WAY, The
SUNSHINE DAFFODILS/Your Love Comes Shinin' Through (Capitol 2453) 1.25 5.00 69

MILKY WAYS, The
TEENAGE ISLAND/My Love (Liberty 55255) 1.00 4.00 60

MILLENNIUM
5 AM/Prelude (Columbia 44607) .75 3.00 68
IT'S YOU/I Just Want To Be Your Friend (Columbia 44546) .75 3.00 68

MILLER, Chuck
AFTER ALL/The Pucker-nut Tree (Capitol 2700) 1.00 4.00 54
AUCTIONEER, THE/Baby Doll (Mercury 71001) 1.00 4.00 56
BOOGIE BLUES/Lookout Mountain (Mercury 70767) 1.00 4.00 55
BRIGHT RED CONVERTIBLE/Baltimore Jones (Mercury 70842) 1.00 4.00 56
COOL IT BABY/Vim Vam Vamoose (Mercury 70942) 1.00 4.00 56
HAWK-EYE/Something To Live For (Mercury 70697) 1.00 4.00 55
HOPAHULA BOOGIE/I'll Know My Love (Capitol 2841) 1.00 4.00 54
HOUSE OF BLUE LIGHTS, THE/Can't Help Wonderin' (Mercury 70627) 1.00 4.00 55
ROGUE RIVER VALLEY/No Baby Like You (Capitol 3187) 1.00 4.00 55

MILLER, Clint
BERTHA LOU/Doggone It Baby, I'm In Love (ABC-Paramount 9878) 1.50 6.00 58
LOVER'S PRAYER, A/No Never My Love (ABC-Paramount 9979) 1.25 5.00 58

MILLER, Frankie
BE GOOD TO YOURSELF/Down The Honky Tonk (Chrysalis 2147) .50 2.00 77
DARLIN'/Drunken Nights In The City (Chrysalis 2255) .50 2.00 78
DOODLE SONG, THE/(I'll Never) Live In Vain (Chrysalis 2145) .50 2.00 77
FOOL IN LOVE, A/ (Chrysalis 2108) .50 2.00 76
LOVE LETTERS/ (Chrysalis 2166) .50 2.00 77
SOMETHING ABOUT YOU/ (Chrysalis 2351) .50 2.00 79
STUBBORN KIND OF FELLOW/Good Time Love (Chrysalis 2223) .50 2.00 78
WHEN I'M AWAY FROM YOU/Ain't Got No Money (Chrysalis 2273) .50 2.00 79

MILLER, Hal, & The Rays
AN ANGEL CRIED/Hope Faith & Dreams (Topix 6003) 3.75 15.00 61
(With the 4 Seasons)
Hal Miller was formerly a lead singer with the Mellows

MILLER, Jody
BE MY MAN/Never Let Him Go (Capitol 5353) .75 3.00 65
FEVER, THE/In My Room (Capitol 5192) .75 3.00 64
HE WALKS LIKE A MAN/ Looking At The World Through A Tear (Capitol 5090) .75 3.00 63
HOME OF THE BRAVE/This Is The Life (Capitol 5483) .75 3.00 65
LONELY QUEEN/Magic Town (Capitol 5541) .75 3.00 65
MY BABY'S GONE/Warm Is The Love (Capitol 5269) .75 3.00 64
QUEEN OF THE HOUSE (Answer song)/Greatest Actor (Capitol 5402) .75 3.00 65
SILVER THREADS & GOLDEN NEEDLES/ Melody For Robin (Capitol 5429) .75 3.00 65
THEY CALL MY GUY A TIGER/ Wonderful Round Of Indifference (Capitol 5162) .75 3.00 64

MILLER, Mike, & Jack Casey
DON'T MESS UP MY HAIR/I Need You (Cameo 137) 1.00 4.00 57

MILLER, Mitch (With Chorus)
CHILDREN'S MARCHING SONG, THE/ Carolina In The Morning (Columbia 41317) .75 3.00 59
MARCH FROM THE RIVER KWAI & COLONEL BOGEY/ Hey Little Baby (Columbia 41066) .75 3.00 57
(THEME SONG FROM) SONG FOR A SUMMER NIGHT (PART 1)/ Theme Song From Song For A Summer Night (Part 2) (Columbia 40730) .75 3.00 56
TZENA, TZENA, TZENA/The Sleigh (Columbia 38885) 1.00 4.00 50
YELLOW ROSE OF TEXAS, THE/Blackberry Winter (Columbia 40540) .75 3.00 55

MILLER, Steve, Band
DON'T LET NOBODY TURN YOU AROUND/Little Girl (Capitol 2638) 1.25 5.00 69
FANDANGO/Love's Riddle (Capitol 3344) .75 3.00 72
FLY LIKE AN EAGLE/Lovin' Cup (Capitol 4372) .50 2.00 76
GOING TO THE COUNTRY/Never Kill Another Man (Capitol 2878) 1.00 4.00 70
JET AIRLINER/Babes In The Wood (Capitol 4424) .50 2.00 77
JOKER, THE/Something To Believe In (Capitol 3732) .50 2.00 73
JUNGLE LOVE/Wish Upon A Star (Capitol 4466) .50 2.00 77
LIVING IN THE U.S.A./Quicksilver Girl (Capitol 2287) 2.50 10.00 68
LIVING IN THE U.S.A./Kow Kow Calqulator (Capitol 3884) .50 2.00 74
MY DARK HOUR (With Paul McCartney)/ Song For Our Ancestors (Capitol 2520) 1.25 5.00 69
ROCK 'N ME/Living In The U.S.A. (Capitol 4323) .50 2.00 76
ROCK LOVE/Let Me Serve You (Capitol 3228) .75 3.00 71
ROCK LOVE/Let Me Serve You (Capitol 2447) 1.00 4.00 69
SITTIN' IN CIRCLES/Dear Mary (Capitol 2520) 1.00 4.00 68
SITTIN' IN CIRCLES/Roll With It (Capitol 2156) 2.50 10.00 67
STEVE MILLER'S MIDNIGHT TANGO/Going To Mexico (Capitol 2945) .75 3.00 70
SWINGTOWN/Winter Song (Capitol 4496) .50 2.00 77
TAKE THE MONEY & RUN/Sweet Maree (Capitol 4260) .50 2.00 76
YOUR CASH AIN'T NOTHIN' BUT TRASH/Evil (Capitol 3837) .50 2.00 74

MILLINGTON (Jean & June Millington)
LADIES ON THE STAGE/ (United Artists 1143) .50 2.00 78
LOVE BROUGHT US TOGETHER/Young & In Love (United Artists 1045) .50 2.00 77
Jean & June were previously with Fanny.

MILLIONAIRES, The
IF I HAD YOU BABE/ (Philips 40477) .75 3.00 67

MILLS BROTHERS, The
BE MY LIFE'S COMPANION/Love Lies (Decca 27889) 1.25 5.00 52
CAN'T YOU HEAR ME CALLING CAROLINE/ Meet Me Tonight In Dreamland (Decca 24763) 1.50 6.00 49
DADDY'S LITTLE GIRL/If I Lived To Be A Hundred (Decca 24872) 1.25 5.00 50
DADDY'S LITTLE GIRL/Daddy's Little Boy (Decca 29564) 1.00 4.00 55
GLOW WORM/After All (Decca 28384) 1.25 5.00 52
GOT HER OFF MY HANDS/I Ran All The Way Home (Decca 27762) 1.50 6.00 51
JONES BOY, THE/She Was Five & He Was Ten (Decca 28945) 1.00 4.00 54
NEVERTHELESS/Thirsty For Your Kisses (Decca 27253) 1.25 5.00 50
QUEEN OF THE SENIOR PROM/My Troubled Mind (Decca 30299) 1.00 4.00 57
STANDING ON THE CORNER/King Porter Stomp (Decca 29897) 1.00 4.00 56
SUDDENLY THERE'S A VALLEY/Gum Drop (Decca 29686) 1.00 4.00 56
YELLOW BIRD/Baby Clementine (Dot 15858) .75 3.00 59
YOU DON'T HAVE TO DROP A HEART TO BREAK IT/ Around The World (Decca 27400) 3.00 12.00 51

MILLS, Frank (Of The Bells)
LOVE ME, LOVE ME, LOVE/Windsong (Sunflower 118) .50 2.00 72
MUSIC BOX DANCER/The Poet & I (Polydor 14517) .50 2.00 79
PETER PIPER/Interlude (Polydor 2002) .50 2.00 79
POOR LITTLE FOOL/What Do You Think Of Love (Sunflower 122) .50 2.00 72

MILLS, Gary
LOOK FOR A STAR (PART 1)/Look For A Star (Part 2) (Imperial 5674) .75 3.00 60
(Part 2 is identical to part 1)

HAYLEY MILLS sings "LET'S GET TOGETHER"
from "The PARENT TRAP"
....also "Cobbler, Cobbler"

MILLS, Hayley (Haley Catherine Rose Vivian Mills)
CASTAWAY/Sweet River (Buena Vista 408) .75 3.00 62
ENJOY IT (With Maurice Chevalier)/Let's Climb (Buena Vista 409) .75 3.00 62
FLITTERIN'/Beautiful Beaulah (Buena Vista 420) .75 3.00 63
(With Eddie Hodges)
JOHNNY JINGO/Jeepers, Creepers (Buena Vista 395) .75 3.00 62
JOHNNY JINGO/Jeepers, Creepers (Buena Vista 395) 1.50 6.00 62
(Picture sleeve)
LET'S GET TOGETHER/Cobbler, Cobbler (Buena Vista 385) .75 3.00 61
LET'S GET TOGETHER/Cobbler, Cobbler (Buena Vista 385) 1.50 6.00 61
(Picture sleeve)
SIDE BY SIDE/Ding Ding Ding (Buena Vista 401) .75 3.00 62

MILLS, Hayley, & Burl Ives
SUMMER MAGIC/ (Buena Vista 4023) .75 3.00 64
(Alcoa Wrap special products release, with Eddie Hodges & Deborah Walley)
SUMMER MAGIC/ (Buena Vista 4023) 1.50 6.00 64
(Picture sleeve)

MILSAP, Ronnie
AIN'T NO SOLE IN THESE OLD SHOES/ Another Branch From The Old Tree (Scepter 12161) 1.00 4.00 66
DENVER/Nothing Is As Good As It Used To Be (Scepter 12246) 1.00 4.00 69
DO WHAT YOU GOTTA DO/Mr. Mailman (Scepter 12228) 1.00 4.00 68
END OF THE WORLD/I Saw Pity In The Face Of A Friend (Scepter 12145) 1.00 4.00 66
IT WENT TO YOUR HEAD/Total Disaster (Warner Bros. 5405) 1.25 5.00 64
LOVING YOU IS A NATURAL THING/So Hung Up On Sylvia (Chips 2889) .75 3.00 70
NEVER HAD IT SO GOOD/Lets Go Get Stoned (Scepter 12109) 1.00 4.00 65
ROSE BY ANY OTHER NAME (IS STILL A ROSE), A/ Sermonette (Chips 2987) .75 3.00 70
WHAT'S YOUR NAME/Love Will Never Pass Us By (Scepter 12272) 1.00 4.00 69
WHEN IT COMES TO MY BABY/ Thousand Miles From Nowhere (Scepter 12127) 1.00 4.00 66

MINA
WORLD WE LOVE IN, THE/You're Tired Of Me (Time 1030) .75 3.00

MINDBENDERS, The (With Eric Stewart)
ASHES TO ASHES/You Don't Know About Love (Fontana 1555) 1.00 4.00 66
GROOVY KIND OF LOVE, A/Love Is Good (Fontana 1541) .75 3.00 66
I WANT HER, SHE WANTS ME/The Morning After (Fontana 1571) 1.00 4.00 67
OFF & RUNNING/It's Getting Harder All The Time (Fontana 1595) 1.00 4.00 67
YELLOW BRICK ROAD/Blessed Are The Lonely (Fontana 1620) 1.00 4.00
Also see Fontana, Wayne, & The Mindbenders
Also see 10CC

MINEO, Sal
I'LL NEVER BE MYSELF AGAIN/Words That I Whisper (Epic 9345) 1.00 4.00 59
LASTING LOVE/You Shouldn't Do That (Epic 9227) 1.00 4.00 57
LITTLE PIGEON/Cuttin' In (Epic 9260) 1.00 4.00 58
MAKE BELIEVE BABY/Young As We Are (Epic 9327) 1.00 4.00 59
PARTY TIME/The Words That I Whisper (Epic 9246) 1.00 4.00 57
START MOVIN'/Love Affair (Epic 9216) 1.00 4.00 57

MINETS, The
SECRET OF LOVE/Together (Rock-it 200054) 1.25 5.00

MINETS OF ENGLAND, The
WAKE UP/My Love Is Yours (DCP 1129) 1.00 4.00 65

MINIATURE MEN, The
BABY ELEPHANT WALK/Bool-Ya-Base (Dolton 57) .75 3.00 62
(Instrumentals)

MINK DE VILLE
GUARDIAN ANGEL/Easy Slider (Capitol 4607) .50 2.00 78
MIXED UP, SHOOK UP GIRL/Spanish Stroll (Capitol 4461) .50 2.00 77

MINNELLI, Liza
RING THEM BELLS/It Was A Good Time (Columbia 45715) .50 2.00 71
Lisa Minnelli is Judy Garland's daughter.

MINTS, The
BUSY BODY ROCK/Alone (Lin 5001) 1.00 4.00 57
Also see Copeland, Ken

MINT TATTOO, The
I'M TALKING ABOUT YOU/Mark Of The Beast (Dot 17242) 1.50 6.00 69

MINUTE MEN, The
PLEASE KEEP THE BEATLES IN ENGLAND/ (Argo 5469) 1.25 5.00

MINUTE-MEN, The
YANKEE DIDDLE/Blue Pearl (Capitol 4458) 1.00 4.00 61
SMOKIN' IN THE BOYS' ROOM/Rollin In Money (Rust 5103) 1.25 5.00 64

MINUTEMEN, The
THINKING OF YOU/Remember (Keltone International 1003) 1.00 4.00

MIRANDA, Bob: see Happenings

MIRROR, Danny
I REMEMBER ELVIS PRESLEY/I'm Gonna Love You (Redwood 1001) .50 2.00 78

MISFITS, The
NAUGHTY ROOSTER/Chicago Confidential (Joey 117) .75 3.00 61
Instrumentals

TITLE/FLIP — LABEL & NO. — GOOD — NEAR MINT — YR.

KELTONE
INTERNATIONAL
FREBON PUBLISHING CO. B.M.I. TIME 2:22
45-1003 (GRA-109) PRODUCED BY FRED BONAMICI
THINKING OF YOU
G. CRAIG – E. CRAIG
THE MINUTEMEN
A PRODUCT OF KELTONE RECORDS, VAN NUYS, CALIFORNIA, U.S.A., A DIVISION OF KELTONE INTERNATIONAL

MISFITS, The
MIDNIGHT STAR/I Don't Know .... (Aries 7-10) 5.00 20.00

MISSLES, The
SPACE SHIP/We Belong Together .... (Novel 200) 2.50 10.00 60
(Novelty/Break-in)

MISSOURI
MOVIN' ON/Can't Stop .... (Panama 2202) .50 2.00 78
MOVIN' ON/Can't Stop .... (Polydor 14571) .50 2.00 79

MISTAKES, The
CHAPEL BELLS/I Got Fired .... (Lo-Fi 2312) 2.00 8.00

MR. BIG
ROMEO/Ain't Bin A Man .... (Arista 0229) .50 2.00 77

MISTICS, The
MEMORIES/Without Love .... (Capri 631) 2.00 8.00

MISTRESS
MISTRUSTED LOVE/ .... (RSO 1009) .50 2.00 79

MISTY
D.O.A./That's All Right-Blue
Moon Of Kentucky (By Jimmy Ellis) .... (Sun 1136) .75 3.00 77

MITCHELL, Chad, Trio
BALLAD OF HERBIE SPEAR/Sally Ann .... (May 116) 1.00 4.00 62
JOHN BIRCH SOCIETY, THE/The Golden Vanity .... (Kapp 457) .75 3.00 62
LIZZIE BORDEN/Super Skier .... (Kapp 439) .75 3.00 62
VAYA CON DIOS/Sally Ann .... (Colpix 133) 1.25 5.00 60
WHAT'S THAT GOTTA DO WITH ME/The Bus Song .... (Amy 054) .75 3.00 63

MITCHELL, Guy (Al Cernik)
BELLE, BELLE, MY LIBERTY BELLE/
Sweetheart Of Yesterday .... (Columbia 39512) 1.00 4.00 51
DON'T ROB ANOTHER MAN'S CASTLE/
Why Should I Go Home .... (Columbia 39886) 1.00 4.00 53
GUILTY HEART/Half As Much .... (Columbia 41311) 1.00 4.00 58
HEARTACHES BY THE NUMBER/Two .... (Columbia 41476) 1.00 4.00 59
I'D LIKE TO SAY A FEW WORDS ABOUT TEXAS/
Finders Keepers .... (Columbia 40724) 1.00 4.00 56
KNEE DEEP IN THE BLUES/Take Me Back Baby .... (Columbia 40820) 1.00 4.00 56
MY HEART CRIES FOR YOU/The Roving Kind .... (Columbia 918) 1.25 5.00 50
MY HEART CRIES FOR YOU/Under A Rainbow .... (Columbia 41274) .75 3.00 58
MY SHOES KEEP WALKING BACK TO YOU/
Silver Moon .... (Columbia 41725) .75 3.00 60
MY TRULY, TRULY FAIR/Who Knows Love .... (Columbia 39415) 1.00 4.00 51
PITTSBURGH, PENNSYLVANIA/Doll With The Saw .... (Columbia 39663) 1.00 4.00 51
ROCK-A-BILLY/Hoot Owl .... (Columbia 40877) 1.00 4.00 57
SINGING THE BLUES/Crazy With Love .... (Columbia 40769) 1.00 4.00 56
SPARROW IN THE TREE TOP/Christopher Columbus .... (Columbia 39190) 1.00 4.00 51

MITCHELL, Jock
WORK WITH ME ANNIE/You May Lose The One You Love (Impact 1004) 1.00 4.00

MITCHELL, Joni
BIG YELLOW TAXI/Woodstock .... (Reprise 0906) .75 3.00 70
BIG YELLOW TAXI/Rainy Night House .... (Asylum 54221) .50 2.00 74
BOTH SIDES NOW/Chelsea Morning .... (Reprise 1154) .75 3.00 73
CALIFORNIA/Case Of You .... (Reprise 1049) .75 3.00 71
CAREY/Jericho .... (Asylum 45244) .50 2.00 75
COYOTE/Blue Motel Room .... (Asylum 45377) .50 2.00 77
DRY CLEANER FROM DES MOINES, THE/
God Must Be A Boogie Man .... (Asylum 46506) .50 2.00 79
FREE MAN IN PARIS/People's Parties .... (Asylum 11041) .50 2.00 74
HELP ME/Just Like This Train .... (Asylum 11034) .50 2.00 74
IN FRANCE THEY KISS ON MAIN STREET/
The Boho Dance .... (Asylum 45298) .50 2.00 76
JERICHO/Dreamland .... (Asylum 45467) .50 2.00 78
RAISED ON ROBBERY/Court & Spark .... (Asylum 11029) .50 2.00 73
YOU TURN ME ON, I'M A RADIO/Urge For Going .... (Asylum 11010) .50 2.00 72

MITCHELL, Lee
FROG, THE/A Little Bird Told Me .... (Phillips International 3530) 1.25 5.00 59
(With the Curley Money Combo)
ROOTIE TOOTIE BABY/Who's That Big Man .... (Sharp 0862) 1.25 5.00 59

MITCHELL, Marlon
ICE COLD BABY/Bermuda Shorts .... (Vena 100) .75 3.00

MITCHELL, Tony
CANDLE IN THE WIND/A Million Drums .... (Canadian-American 157) 1.00 4.00 63
CANDLE IN THE WIND/Write Me A Letter .... (Canadian-American 143) 1.25 5.00 63
PONCHINELLO/Write Me A Letter .... (Canadian-American 162) 1.50 6.00 64
Also see Tony & The Twilights

MITCHUM, Robert
BALLAD OF THUNDER ROAD, THE/
My Honey's Loving Arms (Purple label) .... (Capitol 3986) 1.25 5.00 58
BALLAD OF THUNDER ROAD, THE/
My Honey's Loving Arms (Orange/yellow swirl label) .... (Capitol 3986) .75 3.00 62

MITLO SISTERS, The
LET ME TELL YOU/Lonely Sea .... (Klik 8405) 2.00 8.00
(With the Demotrons)

MIXTURES, The
CANADIAN SUNSET/Olive Oyl .... (Linda 108) .75 3.00 63
CHINESE CHECKERS/Dig These Blues .... (Linda 113) .75 3.00 64
JAWBONE/It's Gonna Work Out Fine .... (Linda 106) .75 3.00 62
RAINBOW STOMP (PART 1)/Rainbow Stomp (Part 2) .... (Linda 104) .75 3.00 62
SEN-SA-SHUN/Last Minute .... (Linda 115) .75 3.00 64
TIKI/Poochum .... (Linda 109) .75 3.00 63
Instrumentals

MIXTURES, The
PUSHBIKE SONG/Who Loves Ya .... (Sire 350) .75 3.00 71

MIZZY, Vic
MAIN THEME FROM THE ADDAMS FAMILY/
Main Theme From Kentucky Jones .... (RCA Victor 47-8477) .75 3.00 65
(Instrumentals)

MOB, The
DON'T LET IT GET YOU DOWN/ .... (Private Stock 45084) .50 2.00 76
GIVE IT TO ME/ .... (Colossus 134) .75 3.00 71
I DIG EVERYTHING ABOUT YOU/
Love Has Got A Hold On Me .... (Colossus 130) .75 3.00 71
LOVE CONNECTION/ .... (Private Stock 45159) .50 2.00 77
MONEY (THAT'S WHAT I WANT)/
Once A Man, Twice A Child .... (Colossus 145) .75 3.00 72
Also See Blue

MOBY GRAPE
CAN'T BE SO BAD/Bitter Wind .... (Columbia 44567) 1.00 4.00 69
CHANGES/Fall On You .... (Columbia 44170) 1.00 4.00 67
COME IN THE MORNING/Hey Grandma .... (Columbia 44174) 1.00 4.00 67
8:05/Mister Blues .... (Columbia 44172) 1.00 4.00 67
HEY GRANDMA/Omaha .... (Columbia 44175) 1.00 4.00 67
INDIFFERENCE/Sitting By the Window .... (Columbia 44171) 1.00 4.00 67
IT'S A BEAUTIFUL DAY TODAY/Ooh Mama Ooh .... (Columbia 44885) 1.00 4.00 69
OMAHA/Someday .... (Columbia 44173) 1.00 4.00 67
TRUCKING MAN/If You Can't Learn
From My Mistakes .... (Columbia 44789) 1.00 4.00 69
(Columbia 44170, 71, 72, 73, 74 and 75 were issued simultaneously)

MOCEDADES
ERES TU (TOUCH THE WIND)/Touch The Wind (Eres Tu) .... (Tara 100) .50 2.00 74

MOCKINGBIRDS, The (With Graham Gouldman & Kevin Godley)
THAT'S HOW (IT'S GONNA STAY)/
I Never Should've Kissed You .... (ABC-Paramount 10653) 2.00 8.00 65
Also see 10CC

MOD ROCKERS, The
STOP & SMELL THE FLOWERS/Lover's Lane .... (Dot 16907) .75 3.00 66

MODERNAIRES, The
APRIL IN PARIS/Hi-Diddle-I-Di .... (Coral 61599) 1.00 4.00 56

MODINE, Jerry
BLUE DENIM/Stranger To Me .... (Mercury 72066) .75 3.00 62

MODUGNO, Domenico
NEL BLU DIPINTO DI BLU (VOLARE)/Mariti In Citta .... (Decca 30677) 1.00 4.00 58

MOHAWKS, The
BEWITCHED (BOTHERED & BEWILDERED)/I Got A Girl .... (Val-ue 211) 1.50 6.00 60

MOJO MEN, The
CANDLE TO BURN/Make You At Home .... (GRT 8) .75 3.00
DANCE WITH ME/Loneliest Boy In Town .... (Autumn 19) 1.25 5.00 65
DON'T BE CRUEL/Let It Be Him .... (Reprise 0759) 1.00 4.00 68
(Shown as by Mojo)
EVERYDAY LOVE/There Goes My Mind .... (GRT 16) .75 3.00
I CAN'T LET GO/Flower Of Love .... (GRT 5) .75 3.00
ME ABOUT YOU/When You're In Love .... (Reprise 0580) 1.00 4.00 67
NEW YORK CITY/Not Too Old To Start Crying .... (Reprise 0661) 1.00 4.00 68
SHE'S MY BABY/Fire In My Heart .... (Autumn 27) 2.50 10.00
OFF THE HOOK/Mama's Little Baby .... (Autumn 11) 1.50 6.00 66
SHOULD I CRY/You To Me .... (Reprise 0689) 1.25 5.00 68
(Shown as by Mojo)
SIT DOWN, I THINK I LOVE YOU/
Don't Leave Me Crying Like Before .... (Reprise 0539) 1.00 4.00 67
WHAT EVER HAPPENED TO HAPPY/Make You At Home .... (Reprise 0617) 1.00 4.00 67

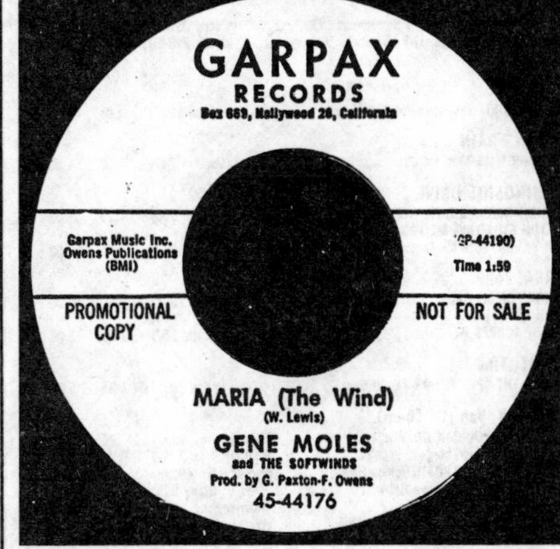

GARPAX
RECORDS
Box 689, Hollywood 28, California
Garpax Music Inc. Owens Publications (BMI)
GP-44190
Time 1:59
PROMOTIONAL COPY
NOT FOR SALE
MARIA (The Wind)
(W. Lewis)
GENE MOLES
and THE SOFTWINDS
Prod. by G. Paxton-F. Owens
45-44176

MOLES, Gene, & The Softwinds
BURNING RUBBER/Twin Pipes .... (Challenge 59249) 1.00 4.00 64
(Shown as by Gene Moles "The Draggin' King.")
KAHA HUNA (GODDESS OF SURFING)/
Maria (The Wind) .... (Garpax 45-44176) 1.00 4.00 63

MOLITTERI, Pat
U.S.A., THE/Say That You Love Me .... (Teen 414) 6.25 25.00 61

MOLLY HATCHET
DREAMS I'LL NEVER SEE/The Creeper .... (Epic 50669) .50 2.00 79
FLIRTIN' WITH DISASTER/Gunsmoke .... (Epic 50822) .50 2.00 79
IT'S ALL OVER NOW/ .... (Epic 50809) .50 2.00 79
JUNKIN' CITY/Gunsmoke .... (Epic 50773) .50 2.00 79

MOMENTS, The
HOMEWORK/Big Round Wheel .... (Era 3104) .75 3.00 63
SURFIN' TISTAN/Mamu Zey .... (Era 3114) .75 3.00 63
WALK RIGHT IN/Walk Right In (Instrumental) .... (Era 3099) .75 3.00 62
Also see Shacklefords, The

MONARCHS, The
PRETTY LITTLE GIRL/In My Younger Days .... (Neil 101) 3.00 12.00 56
PRETTY LITTLE GIRL/In My Younger Days .... (Melba 101) 1.50 6.00 56

MONARCHS, The
LOOK HOMEWARD ANGEL/
What Made You Change Your Mind .... (Sound Stage 7 2516) .75 3.00 64

MONARCS, The
FRIDAY NIGHT/El-Bandito .... (Zone 1067) 1.00 4.00 63
(Instrumental)

MONDO, Joe
LAST SUMMER LOVE/Doin' The Thing .... (EPI 1003) 1.50 6.00

MONEY, Eddie
CAN'T KEEP A GOOD MAN DOWN/Nightmare (Columbia-Wolfgang 10981) .50 2.00 79
GET A MOVE ON/Don't You Ever
Say No (By Zane Buzby) .... (Columbia-Wolfgang-Lorimar 11064) .50 2.00 79
MAUREEN/Love The Way You Love Me .... (Columbia-Wolfgang 11030) .50 2.00 79
MAYBE I'M A FOOL/Life For The Taking .... (Columbia-Wolfgang 10900) .50 2.00 79
TWO TICKETS TO PARADISE/Don't Worry .... (Columbia-Wolfgang 10765) .50 2.00 78
YOU'VE REALLY GOT A HOLD ON ME/
Jealousys .... (Columbia-Wolfgang 10842) .50 2.00 78

MONGO SANTA MARIA: see Santa Maria, Mongo

MONIQUES, The
ALL THE WAY NOW/Rock Pretty Baby .... (Centaur 105) 1.00 4.00
HALO/Don't Throw Stones .... (Centaur 104) 1.00 4.00

MONKEES, The
(Michael Nesmith, Mickey Dolenz, David Jones, Peter Tork)
DAYDREAM BELIEVER/Goin' Down .... (Colgems 1012) 1.00 4.00 67
DAYDREAM BELIEVER/Monkees' Theme .... (Arista 0201) .50 2.00 76
D.W. WASHBURN/It's Nice To Be With You .... (Colgems 1023) 1.00 4.00 68
GIRL I KNEW SOMEWHERE/Little Bit Me, Little Bit You .... (Colgems 1006) 1.00 4.00 67
GOOD CLEAN FUN/Mommy & Daddy .... (Colgems 5005) 1.00 4.00 69
I'M A BELIEVER/(I'm Not Your) Stepping Stone .... (Colgems 1002) 1.00 4.00 66
LAST TRAIN TO CLARKSVILLE/Take A Giant Step .... (Colgems 1001) 1.00 4.00 66
LISTEN TO THE BAND/Someday Man .... (Colgems 5004) .75 3.00 69
LITTLE BIT ME, A LITTLE BIT YOU, A/
The Girl I Knew Somewhere .... (Colgems 1004) 1.00 4.00 67
OH MY MY/I Love You Better .... (Colgems 5011) 1.25 5.00 70
PLEASANT VALLEY SUNDAY/Words .... (Colgems 1007) 1.00 4.00 67
PORPOISE SONG/As We Go Along .... (Colgems 1031) 1.00 4.00 68
TEAR DROP CITY/A Man Without A Dream .... (Colgems 5000) 1.00 4.00 69
VALLERI/Tapioca Tundra .... (Colgems 1019) 1.00 4.00 68

MONOCHROME SETS
HE'S FRANK/Alphaville .... (IRS-Rough Trade 9002) .50 2.00 79

MONOGRAMS, The
BABY BLUE EYES/Little Suzie .... (Rust 5036) 1.50 6.00 62
MY BABY DEAREST DARLING/Please Baby Please .... (Saga 1000) 3.75 15.00

MONORAYS, The (With Tony March)
5 MINUTES TO LOVE YOU/Guardian Angel .... (Tammy 1005) 5.00 20.00 59
5 MINUTES TO LOVE YOU/Guardian Angel .... (Red Rocket 476) 1.25 5.00 59

MONROE, Larry
WHAT IS A DISC JOCKEY/What Is A Secretary .... (Lin 5003) 1.00 4.00 57

MONROE, Marilyn (Norma Jean Baker)
HEAT WAVE/After You Get What You Want .... (RCA Victor 47-6033) 2.00 8.00 55
RIVER OF NO RETURN, THE/
I'm Gonna File My Claim .... (RCA Victor 47-5745) 3.75 15.00 54
RIVER OF NO RETURN/One Silver Dollar .... (20th Fox 311) .75 3.00 62

MONROE, Vaughn
BLACK DENIM TROUSERS & MOTORCYCLE
BOOTS/All By Myself .... (RCA Victor 47-6260) 1.00 4.00 55
MULE TRAIN/ .... (RCA Victor 47-3106) 1.25 5.00 49
OLD SOLDIERS NEVER DIE/Love & Devotion .... (RCA Victor 47-4146) 1.25 5.00 51
ON TOP OF OLD SMOKY/Shall We Dance .... (RCA Victor 47-4114) 1.25 5.00 51
RIDERS IN THE SKY/Single Saddle .... (RCA Victor 47-2902) 3.00 12.00 49
SOMEDAY/And It Still Goes .... (RCA Victor 47-2986) 1.25 5.00 49
SOUND OFF/Oh Marry Marry Me .... (RCA Victor 47-4113) 1.25 5.00 51
THEY WERE DOIN' THE MAMBO/Mister Sandman .... (RCA Victor 47-5767) 1.00 4.00 54

MONRO, Matt
GIRL I KNOW/Leave Me Now .... (Liberty 55573) .75 3.00 63
MY KIND OF GIRL/This Time .... (Warwick 636) .75 3.00 61
SOFTLY AS I LEAVE YOU/Is There Anything I Can Do .... (Liberty 55449) .75 3.00 62
WALK AWAY/April Fool .... (Liberty 55745) .75 3.00 64

MONTANAS, The
CIAO BABY/Anyone There .... (Warner Bros. 7021) 1.00 4.00 67
CIAO BABY/Anyone There .... (Warner Bros. 7208) .75 3.00 68
GOODBYE LITTLE GIRL/
That's When Happiness Began .... (Warner Bros. 5871) .75 3.00 66
I'M GONNA CHANGE/A Step In The Right Direction .... (Independence 87) 1.00 4.00 68
RUN TO ME/Your Making A Big Mistake .... (Independence 89) 1.00 4.00 68
TAKE MY HAND/Top Hat .... (Independence 79) 1.00 4.00 67
YOU'VE GOT TO BE LOVED/Difference Of Opinion .... (Independance 83) 1.00 4.00 68

MONTCLAIRS, The
GOODNIGHT, WELL IT'S TIME TO GO/Broken Promise .... (Audicon 111) 2.50 10.00 60
LISA/Tap Tap Daisy .... (United International 1007) 1.50 6.00

TITLE/FLIP	LABEL & NO.	GOOD	NEAR MINT	YR.
MONTELLS, The				
GEE BABY/My Prince Will Come	(Golden Crest 585)	1.00	4.00	
MONTE, Lou				
AT THE DARK TOWN STRUTTERS' BALL/ I Know How You Feel	(RCA Victor 47-5611)	1.25	5.00	54
ELVIS PRESLEY FOR PRESIDENT/ If I Was A Millionaire	(RCA Victor 47-6704)	2.50	10.00	56
I WANT TO HOLD YOUR HAND (ITALIAN STYLE)/ My Paisan's Across The Way	(Reprise 326)	1.25	5.00	64
LAZY MARY/Angelique	(RCA Victor 47-7160)	1.25	5.00	58
PEPINO THE ITALIAN MOUSE/ What Did Washington Say	(Reprise 20106)	.75	3.00	62
PEPINO'S FRIEND PASQUAL/ I Like You, You Like Me, Eh Paisan	(Reprise 20146)	.75	3.00	63
PIZZA BOY U.S.A./Italian Cowboy Song	(RCA Victor 47-7467)	1.00	4.00	59
SHEIK OF ARABY, THE/Eh, Marie! Eh, Marie!	(RCA Victor 47-7265)	1.00	4.00	58
MONTENEGRO, Hugo				
GOOD, THE BAD & THE UGLY, THE/ March With Hope	(RCA Victor 47-9423)	.50	2.00	68
GOOD VIBRATIONS/Tony's Theme	(RCA 47-9712)	1.00	4.00	69
HANG 'EM HIGH/Tomorrow's Love	(RCA Victor 47-9554)	.50	2.00	68
HAVE I TOLD YOU LATELY THAT I LOVE YOU/ Mom & Dad's Waltz	(Time 1065)	.75	3.00	63
I AIN'T DOWN YET/If I Knew	(Time 1035)	.75	3.00	61
SHERRY/Get Off The Moon	(Time 1058)	.75	3.00	62
TARANTELLA TWIST/Nenella Bella	(Time 1048)	.75	3.00	62
YOUNG SAVAGES/Majorca	(Time 1040)	.75	3.00	62
MONTERAYS, The				
BLAST OFF/You Never Cared	(Planet 57)	1.25	5.00	
MONTEREYS, The				
FACE IN THE CROWD/	(Blast 219)	8.75	35.00	63
GOODBYE MY LOVE/It Hurts Me So	(Arwin 130)	5.00	20.00	59
I STILL LOVE YOU/For Sentimental Reasons	(Crescendo 314)	1.50	6.00	
I'LL LOVE YOU AGAIN/The American Teens	(East West 121)	1.50	6.00	58
MY GIRL/With You	(Saturn 1002)	1.00	4.00	
WITHOUT A GIRL/So Deep	(Impala 213)	7.50	30.00	
Even though all of these releases are shown as being by a group using the same name, the possibility exists that they are not all by the same group.				
MONTE, Vinnie				
HEY LOOK AT THE WINTER SNOW/What's The Matter	(TCF 7)	3.75	15.00	
I WALK ALONE/I Don't Have The Heart To Tell Her	(RCA Victor 47-8611)	1.00	4.00	65
NAUGHTY NAUGHTY BABY/	(Fargo 1000)	1.00	4.00	58
ONE OF THE GUYS/The Year May Be Over (But The Heartaches Are Just Beginning)	(Jubilee 5419)	1.50	6.00	62
YOUR CUTE LITTLE WAYS/ Without Your Love (With the Jay Birds)	(Josie 793)	1.50	6.00	56
MONTEZ, Chris				
ALL YOU HAD TO DO/Love Me	(Monogram 500)	1.00	4.00	62
(May have been issued promotionally on the Indigo label.)				
CALL ME/Go Head On	(A&M 780)	.75	3.00	65
END OF THE LINE, THE/We Can Make The World A Whole Lot Brighter	(Paramount 0109)	.75	3.00	73
JUST FRIENDS/Foolin' Around	(A&M 855)	.75	3.00	67
JUST FRIENDS/Twiggy	(A&M 852)	.75	3.00	67
LET'S DANCE/You're The One	(Monogram 505)	1.00	4.00	62
MORE I SEE YOU/You, I Love You	(A&M 796)	.75	3.00	66
MY BABY LOVES TO DANCE/In An English Towne	(Monogram 513)	1.00	4.00	63
ONCE IN AWHILE/Te Face I Love	(A&M 906)	.75	3.00	68
OUR LOVE IS HERE TO STAY/Nothing To Hide	(A&M 958)	.75	3.00	68
SOME KINDA FUN/Tell Me	(Monogram 507)	1.00	4.00	62
THERE WILL NEVER BE ANOTHER YOU/ You Can Hurt The One You Love	(A&M 810)	.75	3.00	66
TIME AFTER TIME/Keep Talkin'	(A&M 822)	.75	3.00	66
Also see Chris & Kathy				
MONTGOMERYS, The				
PROMISE OF LOVE/Gotta Make A Hit Record	(Amy 883)	7.50	30.00	
MONTGOMERY, Tammy				
I CRIED/If You Don't Think	(Try Me 28001)	.75	3.00	
MONTIONE, "Banana Joe"				
CAKEWALK TO THE CUP 3:30/4:32	(WFIL WC 1001)	.75	3.00	
MONTROSE (With Sammy Hagar & Ronnie Montrose)				
LET'S GO/	(Warner Bros. 8351)	.50	2.00	77
MAGIC MAN/	(Warner Bros. 8281)	.50	2.00	76
MAKE IT LAST/Space Station #5	(Warner Bros. 7814)	.50	2.00	74
MATRIARCH/Clown Woman	(Warner Bros. 8172)	.50	2.00	75
PAPER MONEY/The Dreamer	(Warner Bros. 8063)	.50	2.00	75
MONTROSE, Ronnie (Of Montrose)				
TOWN WITHOUT PITY/No Beginning/No End	(Warner Bros. 8544)	.50	2.00	78
MONTY PYTHON				
SINGLE, THE (Side-B Stereo)/ The Single (Side B-Mono)	(Arista 0130)	.75	3.00	75
(Promotional issue)				
MOOD MAKERS, The				
DOLORES/Dream A Dream	(Bambi 800)	2.00	8.00	
MOODY & THE DELTAS				
MONKEY CLIMB/Come Clap Your Hands	(Daisy 504)	.75	3.00	63
MOODY BLUES, The				
BOULEVARD DE LA MADELEINE/ This Is My House (But Nobody Calls)	(London 1005)	1.00	4.00	67
DRIFTWOOD/I'm Your Man	(London 273)	.50	2.00	78
EV'RY DAY/You Don't	(London 9799)	1.00	4.00	65
FROM THE BOTTOM OF MY HEART/And My Baby's Gone	(London 9764)	1.00	4.00	65
GO NOW/Lose Your Money	(London 9726)	1.00	4.00	65
I'M JUST A SINGER (IN A ROCK & ROLL BAND)/ For My Lady	(Threshold 67012)	.50	2.00	73
I REALLY HAVEN'T GOT THE TIME/Fly Me High	(London 20030)	1.00	4.00	67
ISN'T LIFE STRANGE/After You Came	(Threshold 67009)	.50	2.00	72
NEVER COMES THE DAY/So Deep Within You	(Deram 85044)	.75	3.00	69
NIGHTS IN WHITE SATIN/Cities	(Deram 85023)	.50	2.00	68
QUESTION/Candle Of Life	(Threshold 67004)	.50	2.00	70
RIDE MY SEE SAW/Voices In The Sky	(Deram 85033)	.75	3.00	68
STEPPIN' IN A SLIDE ZONE/I'll Be Level With You	(London 270)	.50	2.00	78
STOP/Bye Bye Bird	(London 9810)	1.00	4.00	65
STORY IN YOUR EYES, THE/Melancholy Man	(Threshold 67006)	.50	2.00	71
TUESDAY AFTERNOON (FOREVER AFTERNOON)/ Another Morning	(Deram 85028)	.75	3.00	68
Also see Edge, Graeme, Band				
Also see Hayward, Justin				
MOON BEAMS, The				
DON'T GO AWAY/A Lover's Plea	(Great 100)	2.00	8.00	
MOONEY, Art				
GIANT/Rock & Roll Tumbleweed	(MGM 12320)	1.00	4.00	56
HONEY-BABE/No Regrets	(MGM 11900)	1.00	4.00	55
THEME FROM "REBEL WITHOUT A CAUSE"/ Theme From "East Of Eden"	(MGM 13212)	1.00	4.00	64
(James Dean Tribute)				
MOONGOONERS, The (Scott Engel & John Stewart)				
MOONGOON STOMP/Long Trip, The	(Candix 335)	1.25	5.00	62
MOONGOON TWIST/Willie & The Hand Jive	(Donna 1373)	1.25	5.00	62
MOONGOON TWIST/Willie & Hand Jive	(Esar 1007)	1.25	5.00	62
Instrumentals				
MOON, Keith (Of The Who)				
CRAZY LIKE A FOX/In My Life	(Track 40433)	.75	3.00	75
DON'T WORRY BABY/Teenage Idol	(Track 40316)	.75	3.00	75
SOLID GOLD/Move Over Ms. L	(Track 40387)	.75	3.00	75
MOON RAKERS, The				
BABY, PLEASE DON'T GO/I Don't Believe	(Tower 239)	1.00	4.00	66
I'M ALL RIGHT/Come On, Let's Move	(Tower 180)	1.00	4.00	65
This group was previously known as the Surfin' Classics.				
MOONSHINE (With The Americans)				
WHISTLING IN THE WIND/Out A Hand	(United Artists 50658)	1.25	5.00	70
Also see Jay & the Americans				
MOON STARS BAND, The				
HOT FOOTSIE (PART 1)/Hot Footsie (Part 2)	(Good Sound 108)	.75	3.00	62
MOORE, Bernie				
45RPM'S/I'll Never Begin To Forget	(Burdett 1911)	.75	3.00	66
MOORE, Bob				
MEXICO/Hot Spot	(Monument 446)	.75	3.00	61
(Instrumentals)				
MOORE, Cecil				
DIAMOND BACK/Rise & Shine	(Sary 206)	1.25	5.00	
DIAMOND BACK/Rise & Shine	(Atco 6309)	.75	3.00	
DUCK WALK/Stormy	(Sary 211)	1.25	5.00	
MOORE, Harv				
INTERVIEW OF THE FAB FOUR/I Feel So Fine	(American Arts 20)	7.50	30.00	64
MOORE, Matthew				
SAVANNAH/Moon Dew	(Caribou-Shelter 9025)	.50	2.00	78
MOORE, Steve				
FORTY DAYS/Pledging My Love	(Scott 002)	.75	3.00	
MOORE, Tim				
CHARMER/I'll Be Your Time	(Asylum 45214)	.50	2.00	75
FALLEN ANGEL/	(Asylum 46047)	.50	2.00	79
FOOL LIKE YOU, A/	(Dunhill 4337)	.50	2.00	73
IN THE MIDDLE/To Cry For Love	(Asylum 45394)	.50	2.00	77
SECOND AVENUE/	(Asylum 45208)	.50	2.00	74
SECOND AVENUE/Strengthen My Love	(Asylum 45427)	.50	2.00	77
MOORPARK INTERSECTION				
I THINK I'LL JUST GO & FIND ME A FLOWER/ Yesterday—Holds On	(Capitol 2115)	1.25	5.00	68
MOOSE & THE PELICANS (With Darlene Love)				
HE'S A REBEL/	(Vanguard 35129)	3.75	15.00	71
WE'RE ROCKIN'/	(Vanguard 35110)	1.25	5.00	71
MORAN				
BEATLES THING, THE/Lady Loves Me	(Epic 10987)	1.00	4.00	71
MORGAN				
HIGH SCHOOL STEADY/Oh, Hey There You	(Laurie 1013)	1.00	4.00	60
MORGAN, Jane				
DAY THE RAINS CAME, THE/ Le Jour ou la Pluie Viendra (The Day The Rains Came)	(Kapp 235)	1.00	4.00	58
FASCINATION/Fascination (Instrumental)	(Kapp 191)	1.00	4.00	57
WITH OPEN ARMS/I Can't Begin To Tell You	(Kapp 284)	.75	3.00	59
MORGAN, Jaye P.				
ARE YOU LONESOME TONIGHT/Miss You	(MGM 12752)	.75	3.00	59
ARE YOU LONESOME TONIGHT/Miss You	(MGM SK-50113)	1.50	6.00	59
(Stereo single issue)				
I WALK THE LINE/Wondering Where You Are	(MGM 12924)	.75	3.00	60
LOST IN THE SHUFFLE/Play For Keeps	(RCA Victor 47-6505)	1.00	4.00	56
PEPPER-HOT BABY/If You Don't Want My Love	(RCA Victor 47-6282)	1.00	4.00	55
THAT'S ALL I WANT FROM YOU/Dawn	(RCA Victor 47-5896)	1.00	4.00	54
MORGAN, Russ				
DOGFACE SOLDIER/Don't Cry Sweetheart	(Decca 29703)	1.00	4.00	55
POOR PEOPLE OF PARIS, THE/Annabelle	(Decca 29835)	1.00	4.00	56
Instrumentals				
MORLEY, Cozy				
I LOVE MY GIRL/Why Don't You Fall In Love	(ABC-Paramount 9811)	1.00	4.00	57
MORNING RAIN				
TAKE YOUR TIME/Most Peculiar	(Buddah 247)	1.00	4.00	71
MORNINGSIDE DRIVE				
SUN AIN'T GONNA SHINE, THE/Morningside Theme	(Copperfield 200)	.75	3.00	
WILL YOU STILL LOVE ME TOMORROW/ Will You Still Love Me Tomorrow (Disco version)	(Copperfield 1)	.75	3.00	
MORRA, Tony				
LOOKING FOR MY BABY/I Can't Believe	(Du-Well 1005)	2.50	10.00	
(With the Do-Wells)				
MY BABY SCARES ME/Claire	(Arcade 152)	1.25	5.00	
MORRIE, Tiny				
BEETLE & THE SPIDER/Let's Talk It Over	(Hurricane 1937)	1.25	5.00	64
MORRISON, Van (Of Them)				
AIN'T NOTHIN' YOU CAN DO/Wild Children	(Warner Bros. 7797)	.75	3.00	74
BLUE MONEY/Sweet Thing	(Warner Bros. 7462)	.75	3.00	71
BRIGHT SIDE OF THE ROAD/Rolling Hills	(Warner Bros. 49086)	.75	3.00	79
BROWN EYED GIRL/Goodbye Baby	(Bang 545)	1.00	4.00	67
BULBS/	(Warner Bros. 8029)	.75	3.00	74
CALL ME UP IN DREAMLAND/Street Choir	(Warner Bros. 7488)	.75	3.00	71
CHECKIN' IT OUT/Kindgom Hall	(Warner Bros. 8805)	.75	3.00	79
CHICK-A-BOOM/Ro Ro Rosey	(Bang 552)	1.00	4.00	67
COME RUNNING/Crazy Love	(Warner Bros. 7383)	.75	3.00	70
DOMINO/Sweet Jannie	(Warner Bros. 7434)	.75	3.00	70
JACKIE WILSON SAID (I'M IN HEAVEN WHEN YOU SMILE)/ You've Got The Power	(Warner Bros. 7616)	.75	3.00	72
JOYOUS SOUND/Mechanical Bliss	(Warner Bros. 8411)	.75	3.00	77
MOONDANCE/Cold Wind In August	(Warner Bros. 8450)	.75	3.00	77
NATALIA/Lifetimes	(Warner Bros. 8743)	.75	3.00	79
OLD OLD WOODSTOCK/(Straight To Your Heart) Like A Cannonball	(Warner Bros. 7573)	.75	3.00	72
REDWOOD TREE/Saint Dominic's Preview	(Warner Bros. 7638)	.75	3.00	72
SAINT DOMINIC'S PREVIEW/Gypsy	(Warner Bros. 7638)	.75	3.00	73
SPANISH ROSE/Midnight Special	(Bang 585)	1.00	4.00	68
TUPELO HONEY/Starting A New Life	(Warner Bros. 7543)	.75	3.00	72
WARM LOVE/Will Be There	(Warner Bros. 7706)	.75	3.00	73
WAVELENGTH/Checkin' It Out	(Warner Bros. 8661)	.75	3.00	78
WILD NIGHT/When That Evening Sun Goes Down	(Warner Bros. 7518)	.75	3.00	71
MORROW, Buddy				
(MAIN TITLE FROM) MAN WITH THE GOLDEN ARM, THE/ I Should Care	(Wing 90063)	1.00	4.00	56
(Instrumental)				
MORSE, Ella Mae				
AN OCCASIONAL MAN/Birmingham	(Capitol 3210)	1.00	4.00	55
BLACKSMITH BLUES/Love Me Or Leave Me	(Capitol 1922)	1.25	5.00	52
COFFEE DATE/I'm Gonna Walk	(Capitol 3458)	1.00	4.00	56
COW COW BOOGIE/Shoo Shoo Baby	(Capitol 1561)	1.25	5.00	51
40 CUPS OF COFFEE/Oh! You Crazy Moon	(Capitol 2539)	1.00	4.00	54
GIVE ME LOVE/Won't You Listen To Me Baby	(Capitol 3320)	1.00	4.00	56
GOODNIGHT, SWEETHEART, GOODNIGHT/Happy Habit	(Capitol 2800)	1.00	4.00	54
GUY WHO INVENTED KISSIN, THE/Good	(Capitol 2343)	1.00	4.00	53
HEART FULL OF HOPE/Livin', Livin', Livin'	(Capitol 3167)	1.00	4.00	55
I LOVE YOU, YES I DO/Money Honey	(Capitol 2882)	1.00	4.00	54
IS IT ANY WONDER/Big Mamou	(Capitol 2441)	1.00	4.00	53
LOVEY DOVEY/Bring Back My Baby To Me	(Capitol 2992)	1.00	4.00	55
MISTER MEMORY MAKER/What Good'll It Do Me	(Capitol 3688)	1.00	4.00	57
OAKIE BOOGIE/Love Ya' Like Mad	(Capitol 2072)	1.25	5.00	52
POINT OF NO RETURN, THE/Give A Little Time	(Capitol 2959)	1.00	4.00	54
PUT YOUR ARMS AROUND ME, HONEY/A Long Time Ago	(Capitol 3638)	1.00	4.00	57
ROCK & ROLL WEDDING/Down In Mexico	(Capitol 3387)	1.00	4.00	56
SEVENTEEN/Razzle-Dazzle	(Capitol 3199)	1.00	4.00	55
SMACK DAB IN THE MIDDLE/Yes, Yes I Do	(Capitol 3105)	1.00	4.00	55
SWAY ME/I'm Gone	(Capitol 3759)	1.00	4.00	57
WHEN BOY KISS GIRL/Sing-Ing-Ing-Ing	(Capitol 3263)	1.00	4.00	55
Many of Ella's original recordings from the Big Band Era were reissued on 45rpm in the early fifties. These are all valued about the same as the above listings, which were issued originally on 45rpm.				
MORTIMER				
DEDICATED MUSIC MAN/	(Philips 40524)	.75	3.00	68
MOSES, Rick				
BABY, YOU MOVE ME/Part Of The Game	(20th Century-Fox 2398)	.50	2.00	79
MOSS, Gene				
I WANT TO BITE YOUR HAND/	(RCA 8438)	1.25	5.00	64
Beatle novelty				
MOST, Donny				
ALL ROADS (LEAD BACK TO YOU)/ Better To Forget Him	(United Artists 871)	.50	2.00	77
HERE'S SOME LOVE/	(Venture 101)	.50	2.00	78
MOTELS, The				
LOVE DON'T HELP/Total Control	(Capitol 4796)	.50	2.00	79
MOTHER EARTH				
BRING ME HOME/I'll Be Long Gone	(Reprise 1041)	.75	3.00	
REVOLUTION/Stranger In My Own Home Town	(United Artists 50303)	1.00	4.00	68
SATISFIED/Andy's Song	(Mercury 73116)	.75	3.00	69
WAIT, WAIT, WAIT/I Wanna Be Your Mama Again	(Mercury 72943)	1.00	4.00	69
MOTHER EARTH (With Tracy Nelson & Eric Kaz)				
DOWN SO LOW/Good Night Grebe, The Telephone Company Has Cut Us Off	(Mercury 72878)	1.00	4.00	68
TEMPTATION TOOK CONTROL OF ME & I FELL/ Soul Of Sadness	(Reprise 1019)	.75	3.00	70
MOTHERLODE				
MEMORIES OF A BROKEN PROMISE/What Does It Take	(Buddah 144)	.75	3.00	69
WHEN I DIE/Hard Life	(Buddah 131)	.75	3.00	69
MOTHERS OF INVENTION: see Zappa, Frank				
MOTHER'S WORRY				
YESTERDAY WHERE'S MY MIND/It's A Long Way Back	(Look 5013)	.75	3.00	
MOTIONS, The				
BEATLE DRUMS/Long Hair	(Mercury 72297)	1.00	4.00	64
WHERE IS YOUR HEART/Big Chief	(ABC-Paramount 10529)	1.00	4.00	64
MOTLEY, Frank				
EVERYBODY WANTS A FLAT TOP/Space Age	(DC 0415)	1.00	4.00	
MOTLEYS, The				
MY RACE IS RUN/You	(Valiant 739)	.75	3.00	66
MOTORS, The (With Bram Tchaikovsky)				
AIRPORT/Mamma Rock 'N' Roller	(Virgin 9519)	.50	2.00	78
DANCING THE NIGHT AWAY/Whisky & Wine	(Virgin 9515)	.50	2.00	77
FORGET ABOUT YOU/Breathless	(Virgin 9520)	.50	2.00	78
TODAY/The Hustler	(Virgin 9521)	.50	2.00	78
MOTT THE HOOPLE (Featuring Ian Hunter)				
ALL THE WAY FROM MEMPHIS/Ballad Of Mott The Hopple (March 26 1972-Zurich)	(Columbia 45920)	.75	3.00	73
ALL THE YOUNG DUDES (Live Version)/ Rose (Live Version)	(Columbia 10091)	.75	3.00	75
ALL THE YOUNG DUDES/One Of The Boys	(Columbia 45673)	.50	2.00	72
GOLDEN AGE OF ROCK 'N' ROLL, THE/ Rest In Peace	(Columbia 46035)	.75	3.00	74
GOLDEN AGE OF ROCK N ROLL (Stereo)/ Golden Age Of Rock N Roll (Mono)	(Columbia 46035)	1.00	4.00	
(Promotional issue)				
HONALOOCHIE BOOGIE/Rose	(Columbia 45882)	.75	3.00	73
ONE OF THE BOYS/	(Columbia 45754)	.75	3.00	72
ONE OF THE BOYS (Stereo)/ One Of The Boys (Mono)	(Columbia 45754)	1.00	4.00	
(Promotional issue)				
ROCK & ROLL QUEEN/	(Atlantic 2749)	1.00	4.00	70
ROLL AWAY THE STONE/Looking Glass	(Columbia 46076)	.75	3.00	74
ROLL AWAY THE STONE (Stereo)/ Roll Away The Stone (Mono)	(Columbia 46076)	1.00	4.00	74
(Promotional issue)				
SWEET JANE/	(Columbia 45784)	.75	3.00	73
Also see Bad Company				
MOUNTAIN (Featuring Leslie West & Corky Laing)				
ANIMAL TRAINER & THE TOAD, THE/ Tired Angels (For J.M.H.)	(Windfall 534)	.75	3.00	71
FOR YASGUR'S FARM/To My Friend	(Windfall 533)	.75	3.00	70
MISSISSIPPI QUEEN/The Laird	(Windfall 532)	.75	3.00	70
MOUNT RUSHMORE				
STONE FREE/She's So Good To Me	(Dot 17158)	.75	3.00	68
MOURNING REIGN				
EVIL HEARTED YOU/Get Out Of My Life Woman	(Contour 601)	2.50	10.00	
EVIL HEARTED YOU/Get Out Of My Life Woman	(Link MR-2)	3.00	12.00	
SATISFACTION GUARANTEED/Our Fate	(Link MR-1)	3.00	12.00	
MOUSE				
MOUSE/Streets Of Dusty Town	(Capitol 2460)	1.00	4.00	69
PUBLIC EXECUTION, A/All For You	(Fraternity 956)	1.25	5.00	65
WOULD YOU BELIEVE/Like I Know You Do	(Fraternity 971)	1.25	5.00	66
MOUSE & THE TRAPS				
SOMETIMES YOU JUST CAN'T WIN/ Beg, Borrow & Steal	(Fraternity 1005)	.75	3.00	66
MOUSKOURI, Nana				
I LOVE MY MAN/Half A Crown	(Fontana 1517)	.75	3.00	66
MOUTH & MAC NEAL				
HEY, YOU LOVE/Why Did You, Why?	(Philips 40717)	.50	2.00	72
HOW DO YOU DO?/Land Of Milk & Honey	(Philips 40715)	.50	2.00	72

TITLE/FLIP	LABEL & NO.	GOOD	NEAR MINT	YR.
MOVE, The (Featuring Jeff Lynne & Roy Wood)				
BLACKBERRY WAY/Something	(A&M 1020)	.75	3.00	69
BRONTOSAURUS/	(A&M 1197)	.75	3.00	69
CALIFORNIA MAN/Do Ya	(United Artists 50928)	.50	2.00	72
CHINATOWN/Down On The Bay	(MGM 14332)	2.00	8.00	72
CHINATOWN/Down On The Bay	(United Artists 50876)	.50	2.00	72
CURLY/This Time Tomorrow	(A&M 1119)	.75	3.00	69
FIRE BRIGADE/Walk Upon The Water	(A&M 914)	.75	3.00	68
FLOWERS IN THE RAIN/ Lemon Tree (Here We Go 'Round The)	(A&M 884)	.75	3.00	67
I CAN HEAR THE GRASS GROW/ Wave The Flag & Stop The Train	(Deram 7506)	1.00	4.00	67
NIGHT OF FEAR/The Disturbance	(Deram 7504)	1.00	4.00	67
SOMETHING/Yellow Rainbow	(A&M 966)	.75	3.00	68
TONIGHT/Don't Mess Me Up	(Capitol 3126)	2.50	10.00	70
TONIGHT/My Marge	(United Artists 202)	.50	2.00	
MOVIES, The				
DANCIN' ON ICE/American Beauty Rose	(Arista 0202)	.50	2.00	77
HELLO, HELLO YOUNG LOVERS/	(Arista 0261)	.50	2.00	77
SATELLITE TOUCHDOWN/Ahead Of The Game	(Arista 0235)	.50	2.00	77
This group contained some members of the Messengers.				
MOVING SIDEWALKS, The				
99TH FLOOR/What Are You Going To Do?	(Tantara)	3.00	12.00	
99TH FLOOR/What Are You Going To Do?	(Wand 1156)	1.00	4.00	67
Also see Z.Z. Top				
MOZART, Mickey, Quintet (Robert Maxwell)				
LITTLE DIPPER/Mexican Hop	(Roulette 4148)	.75	3.00	59
M.P.D. LIMITED				
WENDY (DON'T GO)/Little Boy Sad	(LTD 400)	1.00	4.00	65
MR. BASSMAN				
RIP VAN WINKLE/ You're The One (By Marty & The Symbols)	(Graphic Arts 1000)	3.00	12.00	63
Also see Devotions, The				
MR. MILLER				
MRS. BROWN YOU'VE GOT A LOVELY DAUGHTER/ I'm Henry VIII, I Am	(Swan 4256)	1.00	4.00	65
MRS. MILLER (Elva Miller)				
I'VE GOTTA BE ME/Renaissance Of Smut	(Amaret 114)	.75	3.00	69
LOVER'S CONCERTO, A/Downtown	(Capitol 5640)	1.00	4.00	66
UP UP & AWAY/Green Thumb	(Amaret 101)	.75	3.00	69
MRS. MILLS				
BOOBIKINS/Popcorn	(Capitol 4758)	.75	3.00	62
MU				
BALLAD OF BROTHER LEW/Nobody Wants To Shine	(Mantra 101)	1.00	4.00	
MUDCRUTCH (With Tom Petty)				
DEPOT STREET/Wild Eyes	(Shelter 40357)	.75	3.00	75
Also see Petty, Tom, & The Heartbreakers				
MUGWUMPS, The (Cass Elliot, Denny Doherty, John Sebastian, Zal Yanovsky, James Hendricks)				
I'LL REMEMBER TONIGHT/I Don't Wanna Know	(Warner Bros. 5471)	1.25	5.00	64
JUG BAND MUSIC/Bald Headed Woman	(Sidewalk 900)	1.00	4.00	66
SEARCHIN'/Here It Is Another Day	(Warner Bros. 7018)	1.00	4.00	67
SEASON OF THE WITCH/My Gal	(Sidewalk 909)	1.00	4.00	67
Also see Mamas & The Papas, The				
Also see Lovin' Spoonful, The				
MULBERRY FRUIT BAND, The (Peter Anders & Vinnie Poncia)				
YES, WE HAVE NO BANANAS/The Audition	(Buddah 1)	1.00	4.00	67
MULDAUR, Geoff, & Bonnie Raitt				
SINCE I'VE BEEN WITH YOU BABY/	(Reprise 1370)	.50	2.00	76
Geoff Muldaur was previously with Jim Kweskin's Jug Band.				
MULDAUR, Maria (Of Jim Kweskin's Jug Band)				
BIRDS FLY SOUTH (WHEN WINTER COMES)/	(Warner Bros. 49058)	.50	2.00	79
GRINGO EN MEXICO/Oh Papa	(Reprise 1331)	.50	2.00	75
I'M A WOMAN/Cool River	(Reprise 1319)	.50	2.00	74
MAKE LOVE TO THE MUSIC/ I'll Keep My Light In The Window	(Warner Bros. 8580)	.50	2.00	78
MIDNIGHT AT THE OASIS/Any Old Time	(Reprise 1183)	.50	2.00	74
SWEET HARMONY/Jon The Generator	(Reprise 1362)	.50	2.00	76
MULL, Martin				
BOOGIE MAN/	(ABC 12251)	.50	2.00	77
BERNIE DON'T DISCO/Bun & Run (No. 1) ("Daddy's Back") /Bun & Run (No. 3) ("Happy Cows")	(Elektra 46057)	.50	2.00	79
DO THE DOG/	(Capricorn 0241)	.50	2.00	76
DUELING TUBAS/	(Capricorn 0019)	.50	2.00	73
GET UP, GET DOWN/	(ABC 12304)	.50	2.00	77
PIG IN A BLANKET/The Fruit Song	(Elektra 46056)	.50	2.00	79
SANTA DOESN'T COP OUT ON DOPE/ (Promotional issue)	(Capricorn 554)	.75	3.00	75
SANTAFLY/Santa Doesn't Cop Out On Dope	(Capricorn 0282)	.50	2.00	77
MUNGO JERRY				
IN THE SUMMERTIME/Mighty Man	(Janus 125)	.50	2.00	70
JOHNNY B. BADDE/My Friend	(Janus 128)	.50	2.00	70
MUNSTERS, The				
MUNSTER CREEP/Make It Go Away	(Decca 31670)	.75	3.00	64
MUPPETS, The (With Jim Henson & Frank Oz)				
MAHNA MAHNA/Mr. Bass Man	(Arista 0290)	.50	2.00	77
RAINBOW CONNECTION/ I Hope That Somethin' Better Comes Along	(Atlantic 3610)	.50	2.00	79
Also see Denver, John				
MURAD Jerry: see Jerry Murad's Harmonicats				
MURALS, The				
SEE YOU IN SEPTEMBER/Ambush	(Climax 110)	1.00	4.00	59
MURE, Billy				
STRING OF GUITARS/Diamonds (With the Karats)	(Riverside 4547)	.75	3.00	
STRING OF TRUMPETS, A/Tea & Trumpets (With the Trumpeteers) Instrumentals	(Splash 800)	1.00	4.00	59
MURE, Sal				
MORSE CODE/Desire	(United Artists 153)	3.75	15.00	59
MURMAIDS, The (With Cathy Brasher)				
GO AWAY/Little Boys	(Chattahoochee 711)	.75	3.00	67
HEARTBREAK AHEAD/He's Good To Me	(Chattahoochee 636)	.75	3.00	64
PAPER SUN/Song Through Perception	(Liberty 56078)	.75	3.00	68
POPSICLES & ICICLES/Blue Dress	(Chattahoochee 628)	.75	3.00	63
POPSICLES & ICICLES/Huntington Flats	(Chattahoochee 628)	.75	3.00	63
WILD & WONDERFUL/Bull Talk	(Chattahoochee 650)	.75	3.00	65

TITLE/FLIP	LABEL & NO.	GOOD	NEAR MINT	YR.
MURPHEY, Michael (Of Lewis & Clarke Expedition)				
BACKSLIDER'S WINE/	(Epic 50739)	.50	2.00	79
CAROLINA IN THE PINES/Without My Lady There	(Epic 50131)	.50	2.00	75
CHAIN GANG/Lightning	(Epic 50686)	.50	2.00	79
CHEROKEE FIDDLE/Running Wide Open	(Epic 50319)	.50	2.00	77
GERONIMO'S CADILLAC/Boy From The Country	(A&M 1368)	.50	2.00	72
HOLY ROLLER/Rye-By-The Sea	(Epic 11130)	.50	2.00	74
NOTHING IS YOUR OWN/Song Dog	(Epic 50540)	.50	2.00	78
PARADISE TONIGHT/Song Dog	(Epic 50572)	.50	2.00	78
RENEGADE/A Mansion On The Hill	(Epic 50184)	.50	2.00	76
SWANS AGAINST THE SUN/Rhythm Of The Road	(Epic 50214)	.50	2.00	76
WILDFIRE/Night Thunder	(Epic 50084)	.50	2.00	75
YOU CAN ONLY SAY SO MUCH/Fort Worth I Love You	(Epic 50014)	.50	2.00	75
MURPHY, Elliott				
DRIVE ALL NIGHT/Rock Ballad	(Columbia 10547)	.50	2.00	77
MURPHY, Rose				
CECILIA/I Can't Give You Anything But Love	(Decca 29674)	1.25	5.00	55
LINDY LOU/Mean To Me	(Decca 29542)	1.25	5.00	55
MURRAY, Anne				
BROKEN HEARTED ME/Why Don't You Stick Around	(Capitol 4773)	.50	2.00	79
CALL, THE/Lady Bug	(Capitol 4207)	.50	2.00	76
COTTON JENNY/Destiny	(Capitol 3260)	.50	2.00	72
DANNY'S SONG/Drown Me	(Capitol 3481)	.50	2.00	73
DAYDREAMER BELIEVER/	(Capitol 4813)	.50	2.00	79
DAY TRIPPER/Lullaby	(Capitol 4000)	.50	2.00	74
DREAM LOVER/A Stranger In My Place	(Capitol 4072)	.50	2.00	75
GOLDEN OLDIE/Together	(Capitol 4265)	.50	2.00	76
I JUST FALL IN LOVE AGAIN/ Just To Feel This Love From You	(Capitol 4675)	.50	2.00	79
JUST ONE LOOK/Son Of A Rotten Gambler	(Capitol 3955)	.50	2.00	74
LOVE SONG/You Can't Go Back	(Capitol 3776)	.50	2.00	73
PUT YOUR HAND IN THE HAND/It Takes Time	(Capitol 3082)	.50	2.00	71
ROBBIE'S SONG FOR JESUS/You Can't Have A Hand On Me	(Capitol 3352)	.50	2.00	72
SEND A LITTLE LOVE MY WAY/Head Above The Water	(Capitol 3648)	.50	2.00	73
SHADOWS IN THE MOONLIGHT/Yucatan Cafe	(Capitol 4716)	.50	2.00	79
SING HIGH - SING LOW/Days Of The Looking Glass	(Capitol 2988)	.50	2.00	70
SNOWBIRD/Just Bidin' My Time	(Capitol 2738)	.50	2.00	70
STRANGER IN MY PLACE, A/Sycamore Slick	(Capitol 3059)	.50	2.00	71
SUNDAY SCHOOL TO BROADWAY/Dancin' All Night Long	(Capitol 4375)	.50	2.00	77
SUNDAY SUNRISE/Out On The Road Again	(Capitol 4142)	.50	2.00	75
TALK IT OVER IN THE MORNING/Head Above The Water	(Capitol 3159)	.50	2.00	71
THINGS/Caress Me Pretty Music	(Capitol 4329)	.50	2.00	76
UPROAR/Lift Your Hearts To The Sun	(Capitol 4025)	.50	2.00	75
WALK RIGHT BACK/A Million More	(Capitol 4527)	.50	2.00	78
WHAT ABOUT ME/Let Sunshine Have Its Day	(Capitol 3600)	.50	2.00	73
YOU NEEDED ME/I Still Wish The Very Best For You	(Capitol 4574)	.50	2.00	78
YOU WON'T SEE ME/He Thinks I Still Care	(Capitol 3867)	.50	2.00	74
MURRAY, Ray, & The Dynamics				
WITH ALL MY LOVE/Baby What You Want Me To Do	(Arbo 222)	2.50	10.00	
MURRAY THE "K" (Murray Kaufman)				
IT'S WHAT'S HAPPENING BABY/Sins Of A Family	(Red-Bird 10-045)	.75	3.00	65
MUSHROOMS, The				
SUCH A LOVELY CHILD/Burned	(Hideout 1121)	1.00	4.00	
MUSIC EXPLOSION, The (Featuring Jamie Lyons)				
LITTLE BIT O' SOUL/I See The Light	(Laurie LR-3380)	.75	3.00	67
LITTLE BLACK EGG/Stay By My Side	(Attack A-1404)	1.50	6.00	66
SUNSHINE GAMES/Can't Stop Now	(Laurie LR-3400)	.75	3.00	67
WE GOTTA GO HOME/Hearts & Flowers	(Laurie LR-3414)	.75	3.00	67
WHAT YOU WANT/Road Runner	(Laurie LR-3429)	.75	3.00	68
WHAT'S YOUR NAME/Calling Me Anything	(Laurie LR-3479)	.75	3.00	69
WHERE ARE WE GOING/Flash	(Laurie LR-3440)	.75	3.00	67
(Lead vocal on "Where Are We Going" is by Bobby Bloom.)				
YES SIR/Dazzling	(Laurie LR-3454)	.75	3.00	69
MUSIC MACHINE, The				
ADVISE & CONSENT/Mother Nature, Father Earth	(Bell 764)	1.50	6.00	
DOUBLE YELLOW LINE/Absolutely Positively	(Original Sound 71)	1.00	4.00	67
EAGLE NEVER HUNTS THE FLY, THE/	(Original Sound 75)	1.00	4.00	67
HEY JOE/	(Original Sound 82)	1.00	4.00	67
PEOPLE IN ME, THE/Masculine Intution	(Original Sound 67)	1.00	4.00	67
TALK TALK/Come On In	(Original Sound 61)	1.00	4.00	66
YOU'LL LOVE ME AGAIN/To The Light	(Warner Bros. 7199)	1.00	4.00	68
MUSIL, Jim, Combo				
GRUNION RUN/North Beach (Instrumentals)	(Jay Emm 423)	.75	3.00	62
MUSSIES, The				
LOUIE GO HOME/12 O'clock July	(Fenton 2508)	1.25	5.00	
MUSTANGS, The				
BABY, LET ME TAKE YOU HOME/Davie Was A Bad Boy	(Keetch 6002)	1.00	4.00	
DARTELL STOMP/Lazy Love	(Providence 401)	1.00	4.00	63
FIRST LOVE/A Change	(Sure Shot 5004)	1.00	4.00	64
OVER THE RAINBOW/Look	(Vest 51)	1.00	4.00	
TOPSY '65/Rumpus	(Providence 407)	1.00	4.00	64
MUS-TWANGS, The				
MARIE/Rock Lomond	(Smash 1700)	.75	3.00	61
MYCHAEL				
STAY/Neon Dreams	(Free Flight 11475)	.50	2.00	79
MYDDLE CLASS, The				
DON'T LOOK BACK/Wind Chime Laughter	(Tomorrow 912)	1.25	5.00	67
GATES OF EDEN/Free As The Wind	(Tomorrow 7501)	1.25	5.00	65
I HAPPEN TO LOVE YOU/Don't Let Me Sleep Too Long	(Buddah 150)	1.00	4.00	69
I HAPPEN TO LOVE YOU/Don't Let Me Sleep Too Long	(Tomorrow 7503)	1.25	5.00	66
MYERS, Dave, & Surftones				
LET THE GOOD TIMES ROLL/Gearl	(Wickwire 13008)	1.00	4.00	64
MYLON: see LeFevre, Mylon				
MYRON & THE VAN DELLS				
HEARTACHES/Crazy Little Mama	(Flo Roe 531)	2.00	8.00	
MYSTERIONS, The				
IS IT A LIE/Why Should I Love You	(Jox 040)	1.50	6.00	
Also see (Question Mark)? & The Mysterions				
MYSTERIONS, The				
JERICO ROCK/Bite (Instrumental)	(BRS 1011)	1.00	4.00	
MYSTERY TOUR, The				
BALLAD OF PAUL (Paul McCartney)/Same	(MGM 14097)	1.50	6.00	69
MYSTERY TREND, The				
JOHNNY WAS A GOOD BOY/A House On The Hill	(Verve 10499)	2.00	8.00	67
MYSTICS, The				
ALL THROUGH THE NIGHT/To Think Again Of You	(Laurie 3047)	2.00	8.00	60
BLUE STAR/White Cliffs Of Dover	(Laurie 3058)	1.50	6.00	60
DON'T TAKE THE STARS/So Tenderly	(Laurie 3038)	1.50	6.00	59
HUSHABYE/Adam & Eve	(Laurie 3028)	1.25	5.00	59
STAR CROSSED LOVERS/Goodbye Me Blues	(Laurie 3086)	1.50	6.00	
SUNDAY KIND OF LOVE/Darling I Know How	(Laurie 3104)	2.00	8.00	
Also see Garrett, Scott				

TITLE/FLIP	LABEL & NO.	GOOD	NEAR MINT	YR.
NAN & JAN				
BEATLE BOG/Believe It Or Not	(Debby 069)	1.25	5.00	64
NANTUCKET				
GIRL, YOU BLEW A GOOD THING/Quite Like You	(Epic 50622)	.50	2.00	78
HEARTBREAKER/She's No Good	(Epic 50556)	.50	2.00	78
NAPOLEON XIV (Jerry Samuels)				
DOIN' THE NAPOLEON/ I'm In Love With My Little Red Tricycle	(Warner Bros. 5853)	1.50	6.00	66
THEY'RE COMING TO TAKE ME AWAY, HA-HAAA/ Aaah-Ah, Yawa Em Ekat Ot Gnimoc Er' Yeht	(Warner Bros. 5831)	1.00	4.00	66
THEY'RE COMING TO TAKE ME AWAY, HA-HAAA/ !aaaH-aH, yawA eM ekaT oT gnimoC er'yehT	(Warner Bros. 7726)	1.00	4.00	73
THEY'RE COMING TO TAKE ME AWAY, HA-HAAA/ Photogenic, Schizophrenic You	(Eric 195)	1.00	4.00	76
NARTICALS, The				
CASTAWAY/	(Polo 210)	1.00	4.00	
NASEY, Ron Cameron				
PANIC, THE/The Stop (Novelty/Break-in)	(Rendezvous 137)	2.50	10.00	60
NASH, Graham (Of The Hollies)				
CHICAGO/Simple Man	(Atlantic 2804)	.75	3.00	71
IN THE '80S/	(Capitol 4812)	.50	2.00	79
MILITARY MADNESS/Sleep Song	(Atlantic 2827)	.75	3.00	71
USED TO BA A KING/Wounded Bird	(Atlantic 2840)	.75	3.00	71
Also see Crosby, Stills & Nash				
NASH, Johnny				
ALMOST IN YOUR ARMS/Midnight Moonlight	(ABC-Paramount 9960)	1.00	4.00	58
AS TIME GOES BY/The Voice Of Love	(ABC-Paramount 9996)	1.00	4.00	59
BIG CITY/	(Joda 106)	.75	3.00	65
CLOSER/Mr. Sea	(Epic 50737)	.50	2.00	79
CUPID/	(JAD 220)	.50	2.00	69
FALLING IN & OUT OF LOVE/	(Janus 136)	.50	2.00	70
HOLD ME TIGHT/Cupid	(JAD 207)	.50	2.00	68
I CAN SEE CLEARLY NOW/How Good It Is	(Epic 10902)	.50	2.00	72
I'LL WALK ALONE/The Ladder Of Love	(ABC-Paramount 9844)	1.00	4.00	57
I LOST MY LOVE LAST NIGHT/	(ABC-Paramount 9927)	1.00	4.00	58
LET'S MOVE & GROOVE TOGETHER/Understanding	(Joda 102)	.75	3.00	65
LOVE I LOVE, THE/	(ABC-Paramount 10095)	1.00	4.00	59
LOVING YOU/	(Epic 11070)	.50	2.00	73
MY MERRY-GO-ROUND/Loving You	(Epic 11003)	.50	2.00	73
MY PLEDGE TO YOU/	(ABC-Paramount 9894)	1.00	4.00	57
MY TIME/	(Babylon 1001)	.50	2.00	
ONE MORE TIME/Tryin' To Find Her	(Joda 105)	.75	3.00	65
OOH WHAT A FEELING/Yellow House	(Epic 11034)	.50	2.00	73
STIR IT UP/Ooh Baby You've Been Good To Me	(Epic 10949)	.50	2.00	73
TAKE A GIANT STEP/But Not For Me	(ABC-Paramount 10046)	1.00	4.00	59
THEN YOU CAN TELL ME GOODBYE/Always	(Argo 5479)	1.00	4.00	64
THOUSAND MILES AWAY, A/	(ABC-Paramount 10212)	1.00	4.00	60
VERY SPECIAL LOVE, A/ Won't You Let Me Share My Love With You	(ABC-Paramount 9874)	1.00	4.00	57
WE KISSED/	(ABC-Paramount 10137)	1.00	4.00	59
(WHAT A) WONDERFUL FEELING/Rock It Baby (Baby We've Got A Date)	(Epic 50219)	.50	2.00	76
YOU GOT SOUL/Don't Cry	(JAD 209)	.75	3.00	68
NASHVILLE TEENS, The				
ELLA JAMES/	(United Artists 50880)	1.00	4.00	72
FIND MY WAY BACK HOME/Devil-in-law	(London 9736)	1.00	4.00	65
GOOGLE EYE/T.N.T.	(London 9712)	1.00	4.00	64
HARD WAY, THE/Upside Down	(MGM 13483)	1.00	4.00	66
I KNOW HOW IT FEELS TO BE LOVED/Soon Forgotten	(MGM 13406)	1.00	4.00	65
LITTLE BIRD, THE/Whatcha You Gonna Do	(MGM 13357)	1.00	4.00	65
THAT'S MY WOMAN/Words	(MGM 13678)	1.00	4.00	67
TOBACCO ROAD/I Like It Like That	(London 9689)	1.00	4.00	64
NATIONAL LAMPOON				
DETERIORATA (Answer song)/	(Banana 218)	.75	3.00	72
NATURAL GAS (Featuring Joey Molland)				
ONCE AGAIN, A LOVE SONG/	(Private Stock 45116)	.50	2.00	76
RIGHT TIME, THE/	(Private Stock 45100)	.50	2.00	76
Also see Badfinger				
NATURALS, The				
BLUE MOON/How Strange	(Hunt 325)	1.00	4.00	59
NAUGHTON, David				
MAKIN' IT/Still Makin' It	(RSO 916)	.50	2.00	78
NAVIGATORS, The				
SPACE COUP/The Westener	(Monument 934)	.75	3.00	66
NAYLOR, Jerry				
BUT FOR LOVE/	(Columbia 45106)	.50	2.00	70
I'M TIRED/	(Skyla 1123)	1.00	4.00	62
STOP YOUR CRYING/You're Thirteen	(Skyla 1118)	1.00	4.00	62
Also see Crickets				
NAZARETH				
BROKEN DOWN ANGEL/Hard Living	(A&M 1453)	.50	2.00	73
CARRY OUT FEELINGS/Lift The Lid	(A&M 1819)	.50	2.00	76
GONE DEAD TRAIN/Kentucky Fried Blues	(A&M 2029)	.50	2.00	78
LORETTA/Lift The Lid	(A&M 1854)	.50	2.00	76
LOVE HURTS/Hair Of The Dog	(A&M 1671)	.50	2.00	75
MORNING DEW/	(Warner Bros. 7598)	.75	3.00	71
RAZMANAZ/	(A&M 1469)	.50	2.00	73
SHOT ME DOWN/Kentucky Fried Blues	(A&M 2009)	.50	2.00	78
STAR/Expect No Mercy	(A&M 2158)	.50	2.00	79
THIS FLIGHT TONIGHT/Somebody To Roll	(A&M 1936)	.50	2.00	77
NAZY, Ron Cameron				
GREAT DEBATE, THE: MR. ICKSON/Mr. Benady (Novelty/Break-in)	(Trey 3013)	2.00	8.00	60

TITLE/FLIP — LABEL & NO. — GOOD — NEAR MINT — YR.

VERY RECORD
1110 E. Turney, Phoenix, Ariz. 85014
S-001
1:58
Produced by
D. Phillips
LAY DOWN AND DIE, GOODBYE
NAZZ
(M. Bruce, G. Buxton, D. Dunaway,
V. Furnier, T. Speer)

NAZZ (Featuring Alice Cooper)
LAY DOWN & DIE, GOODBYE/
Wonder Who's Loving Her Now (Very Record S-001) 37.50 150.00 67
"Lay Down & Die, Goodbye" is an earlier version than was later released by Alice Cooper. Except for drummer, Tom Speer, this band was the same as the Alice Cooper Group.

NAZZ (Featuring Todd Rundgren)
HELLO IT'S ME/Open My Eyes (SGC 001) 1.00 4.00 69
MAGIC ME/Some People (SGC 009) 1.25 5.00 69
UNDER THE ICE/Not Wrong Long (SGC 006) 1.25 5.00 69

NBC'S SATURDAY NIGHT LIVE (Featuring Jane Curtin, Laraine Newman & Gilda Radner)
CHEVY'S GIRLS/ (Arista 0224) .50 2.00 76

NEAL & THE NEWCOMBERS
REELING & ROCKING/Rocking Pneumonia (Hall Way 1206) .75 3.00 64

NEAL, Jerry (Jerry Capehart)
I HATES RABBITS/Scratchin' (Instrumental) (Dot 15810) 2.00 8.00 58
(Features Eddie Cochran on guitar)

NECESSARIES, The
YOU CAN BORROW MY CAR/
Runaway Child (Minors Beware) (International R.S.-Spy 9003) .50 2.00 79

NEE, Bernie
HEY JANIE/Hey Liley, Liley Lo (Columbia 40906) 1.00 4.00 57

NEGLIGEES, The
NO CHEMISE '65/ (Lancer 3333) .75 3.00 65

NEIGHBORHOOD, The
BIG YELLOW TAXI/You Could Be Born Again (Big Tree 102) .75 3.00 70

NEIGHB'RHOOD CHILDR'N, The
BEHOLD THE LILIES/I Want Action (Acta 828) 1.00 4.00 68
MAINTAIN/Just No Way (Acta 813) 1.00 4.00 68
PLEASE LEAVE ME ALONE/Happy Child (Acta 823) 1.00 4.00 68
WOMAN THINK/On Our Way (Dot 17238) 1.00 4.00 69

NEKTAR
ASTRAL MAN/Nelly The Elephant (Passport 7904) .75 3.00 75
REMEMBER THE FUTURE/ (Passport 7902) .75 3.00 74

DUEL
A Division of Allied Entertainment Corp. Of America
Saxon Music Corp.
B.M.I.
508
N9OW 1434
Time: 2:09
YOU ARE MY LOVE AT LAST
(Neil Diamond)
NEIL & JACK

NEIL & JACK (With Neil Diamond)
YOU ARE MY LOVE AT LAST/What Will I Do (Duel 508) 3.00 12.00

NELSON, Rick
BE-BOP BABY/Have I Told You Lately That I Love You (Imperial 5463) 1.25 5.00 57
BELIEVE WHAT YOU SAY/My Bucket's Got A Hole In It (Imperial 5503) 1.00 4.00 58
CONGRATULATIONS/One Minute To One (Imperial 66017) .75 3.00 64
DON'T BLAME IT ON YOUR WIFE/Promenade In Green (Decca 32284) .75 3.00 68
DON'T MAKE PROMISES/Barefoot Boy (Decca 32298) .75 3.00 68
DOWN ALONG THE BAYOU COUNTRY/How Long (Decca 32739) .75 3.00 70
DREAM LOVER/That Ain't The Way Love's Supposed To Be (Epic 50674) .50 2.00 79
DREAM WEAVER/Baby Close It's Eyes (Decca 32222) .75 3.00 67
EASY TO BE FREE/Come On In (Decca 32635) .75 3.00 70
EVERYBODY BUT ME/Lucky Star (Imperial 66039) .75 3.00 64
FOOLS RUSH IN/Down Home (Decca 31533) .75 3.00 63
FOR YOU/That's All She Wrote (Decca 31574) .75 3.00 63
GARDEN PARTY/So Long Mama (Decca 32980) .75 3.00 72
GIMME A LITTLE SIGN/ (Epic 50501) .50 2.00 78
HAPPY GUY, A/Don't Breathe A Word (Decca 31703) .75 3.00 64
I SHALL BE RELEASED/If You Gotta Go, Go Now (Decca 32676) .75 3.00 70
I WANNA BE LOVED/Mighty Good (Imperial 5614) 1.00 4.00 59
I'M NOT AFRAID/Yes Sir, That's My Baby (Imperial 5685) 1.00 4.00 60
IT'S UP TO YOU/I Need You (Imperial 5901) .75 3.00 62
LIFE/California (Decca 32779) .75 3.00 71
LIFESTREAM/Evil Woman Child (MCA 40130) .75 3.00 73
LONESOME TOWN/I Got A Feeling (Imperial 5545) 1.00 4.00 58
LONG VACATION, A/Mad Mad World (Imperial 5958) .75 3.00 63
LOUISIANA MAN/You Just Can't Quit (Decca 31956) .75 3.00 66
LOVE & KISSES/Say You Love Me (Decca 31845) .75 3.00 65
LOVE MINUS ZERO-NO LIMIT/Gypsy Pilot (Decca 32906) .75 3.00 72
MEAN OLD WORLD/When The Chips Are Down (Decca 31756) .75 3.00 65
NEVER BE ANYONE ELSE BUT YOU/It's Late (Imperial 5565) 1.00 4.00 59
OLD ENOUGH TO LOVE/If You Can't Rock Me (Imperial 5935) .75 3.00 63
ONE NIGHT STAND/Lifestream (MCA 40214) .75 3.00 74
PALACE GUARD/A Flower Opens Gently (MCA 40001) .75 3.00 72
POOR LITTLE FOOL/Don't Leave Me This Way (Imperial 5528) 1.00 4.00 58
PROMENADE IN GREEN/Don't Make Promises (Decca 32284) .75 3.00 68
ROCK & ROLL LADY/Fade Away (MCA 40458) .75 3.00 75
SHE BELONGS TO ME/Promises (Decca 32550) .75 3.00 69
STOOD UP/Waitin' In School (Imperial 5483) 1.25 5.00 57
STRING ALONG/Gypsy Woman (Decca 31495) .75 3.00 63
SUZANNE ON A SUNDAY MORNING/Moonshine (Decca 32176) .75 3.00 67
SWEETER THAN YOU/Just A Little Too Much (Imperial 5595) 1.00 4.00 59
TAKE A BROKEN HEART/
They Don't Give Medals (To Yesterday's Heros) (Decca 32055) .75 3.00 66
TAKE A CITY BRIDE/I'm Called Lonely (Decca 32120) .75 3.00 67
TEEN AGE IDOL/I've Got My Eyes On You
(& I Like What I See) (Imperial 5864) .75 3.00 62
TEENAGER'S ROMANCE, A/I'm Walking (Verve 10047) 1.50 6.00 57
THANK YOU LORD/Sing Me A Song (Decca 32860) .75 3.00 71
THAT'S ALL/I'm In Love Again (Imperial 5910) .75 3.00 63
THERE'S NOTHING I CAN SAY/Lonely Corner (Decca 31656) .75 3.00 64
THINGS YOU GAVE ME/Alone (Decca 32026) .75 3.00 66
TIME AFTER TIME/There's Not A Minute (Imperial 5985) .75 3.00 63
TODAY'S TEARDROPS/Thank You Darlin' (Imperial 66004) .75 3.00 63
TRAVELIN' MAN/Hello Mary Lou (Imperial 5741) .75 3.00 61
TRY (TRY TO FALL IN LOVE)/Louisiana Belle (MCA 40392) .75 3.00 75
VERY THOUGHT OF YOU, THE/I Wonder (If Your Love
Will Ever Belong To Me) (Decca 31612) .75 3.00 64
WE GOT SUCH A LONG WAY TO GO/Look At Mary (Decca 32711) .75 3.00 70
WINDFALL/Legacy (MCA 40187) .75 3.00 74
YESTERDAY'S LOVE/Come Out Dancin' (Decca 31800) .75 3.00 65
YOU ARE THE ONLY ONE/Milk Cow Blues (Imperial 5707) 1.00 4.00 60
YOU CAN'T DANCE/It's Another Day (Epic 50458) .75 3.00 77
YOU DON'T LOVE ME ANYMORE/I Got A Woman (Decca 31475) .75 3.00 63
YOU'RE MY ONE & ONLY LOVE/
Honey Rock (Instrumental by Barney Kessell) (Verve 10070) 1.50 6.00 57
YOUNG EMOTIONS/Right By My Side (Imperial 5663) 1.00 4.00 60
YOUNG WORLD/Summertime (Imperial 5805) .75 3.00 62
YOUR KIND OF LOVIN'/Fire Breathin' Dragon (Decca 31900) .75 3.00 66
WONDER LIKE YOU, A/Everlovin' (Imperial 5770) .75 3.00 61
Releases after "Hello Mary Lou"/"Traveling Man" (1961) were shown as by Rick Nelson.

NELSON, Sandy
ALEXES/You Name It (Imperial 5940) .75 3.00 63
ALL NIGHT LONG/Rompin' & Stompin' (Imperial 5860) .75 3.00 62
AND THEN THERE WERE DRUMS/Live It Up (Imperial 5870) .75 3.00 62
CARAVAN/Sandy (Imperial 5988) .75 3.00 63
CASTLE ROCK/You Don't Say (Imperial 66034) .75 3.00 64
CHOP CHOP/Reach For a Star (Imperial 66093) .75 3.00 65
(Instrumental)
COOL OPERATOR/Jive Talk (Imperial 5708) .75 3.00 61
DAY TRAIN/Teenage House Party (Imperial 5884) .75 3.00 62
DRUM SHACK/Kitty's Theme (Imperial 66019) .75 3.00 64
DRUMMIN' UP A STORM/Drum Stomp (Imperial 5829) .75 3.00 62
DRUMS A GO-GO/Casbah (Imperial 66127) .75 3.00 65
DRUMS ARE MY BEAT/The Birth Of The Beat (Imperial 5809) .75 3.00 62
DRUMS GO ON, THE/Lawdy Miss Clawdy (Imperial 66246) .75 3.00 67
GET WITH IT/Big Noise From The Jungle (Imperial 5745) .75 3.00 61
HERE WE GO/Just Bull (Imperial 5965) .75 3.00 63
LET THE FOUR WINDS BLOW/Be Bop Baby (Imperial 5904) .75 3.00 62
LET THERE BE DRUMS/Quite A Beat (Imperial 5775) .75 3.00 61
LET THERE BE DRUMS '66/Land of 1000 Dances (Imperial 66107) .75 3.00 65
LET'S GO TRIPPIN'/Pipeline (Imperial 66209) .75 3.00 66
LOST DREAMS/Bouncy (Imperial 5672) .75 3.00 60
LOVER'S CONCERTO, A/Treat Her Right (Imperial 66146) .75 3.00 65
MANHATTAN SPIRITUAL/The Stripper (Imperial 66375) .75 3.00 69
OOH POO PAH DOO/Feel So Good (Imperial 5932) .75 3.00 63
PARTY TIME/The Wiggle (Imperial 5648) .75 3.00 60
SOCK IT TO EM J.B./The Charge (Imperial 66193) .75 3.00 66
TEEN BEAT/Big Jump (Original Sound 5) 1.00 4.00 59
TEEN BEAT '65/Kitty's Theme (Imperial 66060) .75 3.00 64
Instrumentals
Also see Teddy Bears, The

NELSON, Teri, Group
SWEET TALKIN' WILLIE/Backside (Kama Sutra KA-245) .75 3.00 68

NELSON, Tracy (Of Mother Earth)
IT TAKES A LOT TO LAUGH, IT TAKES A TRAIN TO CRY/ (Atlantic 3235) .75 3.00 75
SWEET SOUL MUSIC/Nothing I Can't Handle (MCA 40479) .75 3.00 75

NEMETZ, Shelley
FAMILY, THE/The Family (Fantasy 674) .75 3.00 72

NEON
MOVIN'/Darling Before I Go (Paramount 0121) .50 2.00 73

NEON LEON
HEART OF STONE/Rock & Roll Is Alive-Noh Time (Big Deal 777) .75 3.00
("Heart of Stone" has vocal backing by Mick Jagger)
HEART OF STONE/Rock & Roll Is Alive-Noh Time (Big Deal 777) 1.25 5.00
(Picture sleeve)

NEON PHILHARMONIC, The
CLOUDS/Snow (Warner Bros. 7355) .75 3.00 69
FLOWERS FOR YOUR PILLOW/ (Warner Bros.) .75 3.00 70
HEIGHDY-HO PRINCESS/ (Warner Bros. 7380) .75 3.00 70
MORNING GIRL/Brilliant Colors (Warner Bros. 7261) .75 3.00 69
NO ONE IS GOING TO HURT YOU/You Lied (Warner Bros. 7311) .75 3.00 69
SO GLAD YOU'RE A WOMAN/Making Out The Best I Can (MCA 40518) .50 2.00 76
SOMETHING TO BELIEVE IN/A Little Love (Warner Bros. 7457) .75 3.00 71

NEONS, The
ANGEL FACE/Kiss Me Quickly (Tetra 444) 3.75 15.00 56
ROAD TO ROMANCE/My Chickadee (Tetra 4449) 6.25 25.00 57

NEONS, The
FAT GIRLS/Magic Moment (Challenge 9147) 3.75 15.00 61

NEPTUNES, The
I'VE GOT PLANS/Shame Girl (Warner Bros. 5453) 1.50 6.00 64

NERVOUS NORVUS (Jimmy Drake)
APE CALL (With Red Blanchard)/Wild Dog Of Kentucky (Dot 15485) 2.00 8.00 56
FANG, THE/The Bullfrog Hop (Dot 15500) 2.50 10.00 56
I LIKE GIRLS/Stoneage Woo (Embee 117) 3.00 12.00 59
PURE GOLD/Let's Worship God Each Sunday (Big Ben 101) 2.50 10.00
(Shown as by Nervous Norvous & His Guitar)
TRANSFUSION/Dig (Dot 15470) 1.50 6.00 56
Novelties
Also see Four Jokers, The

NERVOUS SYSTEM, The
MAKE LOVE, NOT WAR/Bones (Jambee 1002) 1.00 4.00

NESBITT, Jim
HUSBAND-IN-LAW/New Frontier (Rush 2003) 1.25 5.00 62
HUSBAND-IN-LAW/New Frontier (Smash 1746) .75 3.00 62
I'M A MARRIED MAN/Livin' Offa Credit (Rally 569) 1.25 5.00 62
I'M A MARRIED MAN/Livin' Offa Credit (Dot 16424) .75 3.00 62
PLEASE MR. KENNEDY/Horse Race (Country Jubilee 549) 1.25 5.00 61
PLEASE MR. KENNEDY/Horse Race (Ace 621) 1.00 4.00 61
PLEASE MR. KENNEDY/Horse Race (Dot 16197) .75 3.00 61

NESMITH, Michael
CRUSIN' (LUCY & RAMONA & SUNSET SAM)/ (Pacific Arts 108) .50 2.00 79
I'VE JUST BEGUN TO CARE (PROPINQUITY)/Only Bound (RCA 0540) .75 3.00 72
JUST A LITTLE LOVE/Curson Terrace (Edan 1001) 1.25 5.00
MAGIC (THIS NIGHT IS MAGIC)/ (Pacific Arts 106) .50 2.00 79
MAMA ROCKER/Lazy Lady (RCA 0629) .75 3.00 72
NEVADA FIGHTER/Here I Am (RCA 0453) .75 3.00 71
RIO/Casablanca Moonlight (Pacific Arts 104) .50 2.00 79
RIO/Life, The Unsuspecting Captive (Pacific Arts 84) .75 3.00 75
ROLL WITH THE FLOW/I've Just Begun To Care (Pacific Arts 101) .75 3.00 78
ROLL WITH THE FLOW/Keep On (RCA 0804) .75 3.00 72
SILVER MOON/Lady Of The Valley (RCA 0399) .75 3.00 70
TEXAS MORNING/Tumbling Tumbleweeds (RCA 0491) .75 3.00 71
TEXAS MORNING-TUMBLING TUMBLEWEEDS/
Tumbling Tumbleweeds (RCA 0263) 1.00 4.00 71
(Promotional issue only)
On some issues the artist may be shown as with the First National Band, or with the Second National Band.
Also see Monkees, The

NETWORK
SAVE ME, SAVE ME/Holly (Epic 50489) .50 2.00 78
YOU LIED/Fly Away (Epic 50449) .50 2.00 78

NEUMAN, Alfred E., & The Furshlugginer 5
WHAT...ME WORRY?/Portzebie (ABC-Paramount 10013) 1.50 6.00 59
(Novelties)

NEW ARRIVALS, The
JUST OUTSIDE MY WINDOW/Let's Get With It (Southbay 104) 1.25 5.00
JUST OUTSIDE MY WINDOW/Let's Get With It (Macy's 104) 1.50 6.00
SCRATCH YOUR NAME/Just Outside My Window (Southbay 103) 1.25 5.00
TAKE ME FOR WHAT I AM/
You Know You're Gonna Be Mine (Southbay 102) 1.25 5.00

NEW BREED, The
DON'T JIVE/Unlock Your Mind (New Breed 13635) 2.00 8.00
FINE WITH ME/The Sound Of The Music (World United 003) 2.00 8.00
GREEN EYED WOMAN/I'm In Love (Diplomacy 22) 1.25 5.00
LEAVE ME BE/I've Been Wrong Before (Mercury 72556) 1.25 5.00 66
WANT AD READER/One More For The Good Guys (HBR 508) 1.00 4.00 66
WANT AD READER/One More For The Good Guys (World United 001) 2.00 8.00

NEW CHRISTY MINSTRELS, The
BEAUTIFUL, BEAUTIFUL WORLD/A Corner In The Sun (Columbia 43822) .75 3.00 66
BROTHER/I Still Do (Gregar 0106) .75 3.00 69
CHIM, CHIM, CHEREE/
They Gotta Quit Kickin' My Dog Around (Columbia 43215) .75 3.00 65
DENVER/Liza Lee (Columbia 42673) .75 3.00 63
GREEN, GREEN/The Banjo (Columbia 42805) .75 3.00 63
GREEN, GREEN/The Banjo (Columbia 42805) 1.25 5.00 63
(Green plastic promotional issue)
IT SHOULD HAVE BEEN YOU/Sleep Comes Easy (Columbia 43961) .75 3.00 66
SATURDAY NIGHT/The Wheeler Dealers (Columbia 42887) .75 3.00 63
SILLY OL' SUMMERTIME/The Far Side Of The Hill (Columbia 43092) .75 3.00 64
THIS LAND IS YOUR LAND/Don't Cry, Suzanne (Columbia 42592) .75 3.00 62
TODAY/Miss Katy Cruel (Columbia 43000) .75 3.00 64
Also see Rogers, Kenny, & the First Edition
Also see McGuire, Barry
Also see Sparks, Randy

NEW COLONY SIX, The
BARBARA, I LOVE YOU/Prarie Grey (Mercury 73004) .75 3.00 70
CAN'T YOU SEE ME CRY/
Summertime's Another Name For Love (Mercury 72817) .75 3.00 68
CLOSE YOUR EYES LITTLE GIRL/ (Mercury 73093) .75 3.00 70
COME ON DOWN/Someone, Sometime (Sunlight 1005) .75 3.00 72
I CONFESS/Dawn Is Breaking (Centaur 1201) 1.00 4.00 66
I COULD NEVER LIE TO YOU/Just Feel Worse (Mercury 72920) .75 3.00 69
I LIE AWAKE/At The River's Edge (Centaur 1202) 1.00 4.00 66
I WANT YOU TO KNOW/Free (Mercury 72961) .75 3.00 69
I WILL ALWAYS THINK ABOUT YOU/
Hold Me With Your Eyes (Mercury 72775) .75 3.00 68
I'M JUST WAITING ANTICIPATING HER TO SHOW UP/
Hello Lonely (Sentar 1207) 1.00 4.00 67
LONG TIME TO BE ALONE/Never Be Lonely (Sunlight 1004) .75 3.00 71
LOVE YOU SO MUCH/Let Me Love You (Sentar 1205) 1.00 4.00 67
NEVER BE LONELY/Long Time To Be Alone (MCA 40215) .75 3.00 74
PEOPLE & ME/ (Mercury 73063) .75 3.00 70
POWER OF LOVE/(Ballad Of The) Wingbat Marmaduke (Sentar 1204) 1.00 4.00 66
ROLL ON/If You Could See (Sunlight 1001) .75 3.00 71
SUNSHINE/Cadillac (Sentar 1203) 1.00 4.00 66
THINGS I'D LIKE TO SAY/
Come & Give Your Love To Me (Mercury 72858) .75 3.00 68
TREAT HER GROOVY/Rap-A-Tap (Mercury 72737) .75 3.00 67
YOU'RE GONNA BE MINE/Woman (Sentar 1206) 1.00 4.00 67
Ronnie Rice is featured as lead singer on the Mercury releases.

NEW DAY
NIGHT AFTER DAY/Ada Lane (Kef 4457) .75 3.00

NEW ENGLAND
DON'T EVER WANNA LOSE YA/Shoot (Infinity 50013) .50 2.00 79
HELLO, HELLO, HELLO/Encore (Infinity 50021) .50 2.00 79

NEW ERA, The
WE AIN'T GOT TIME/Won't You Please Be My Friend (Great Lakes 2532) 1.50 6.00

NEW ESTABLISHMENT, The
SUNDAY'S GONNA COME ON TUESDAY/
Baby The Rain Must Fall (Colgems 5006) .75 3.00 69

NEW HAPPINESS (Featuring Smooth Lundull)
ODE TO LARSEN WHIPSWADE/Dear Chester (Columbia 44612) 1.00 4.00 68
WINCHESTER CATHEDRAL/I'm Gonna Spoil You Baby (Columbia 43851) 1.00 4.00 66

NEW HOPE
LOOK WAY/Money Game (Jamie 1388) .75 3.00 70
RAIN/ (Jamie 1385) .75 3.00 70
WON'T FIND BETTER (THAN ME)/They Call It Love (Jamie 1381) .75 3.00 69

NEW LEGION ROCK SPECTACULAR, The
WILD ONE/Second Cousin (Spectacular 11075) .50 2.00 75

TITLE/FLIP	LABEL & NO.	GOOD	NEAR MINT	YR.
NEW PHOENIX				
GIVE TO ME YOUR LOVE/Thanks	(World Pacific 77884)	1.00	4.00	
NEW RIDERS OF THE PURPLE SAGE, The				
DEAD FLOWERS/She's Looking Better Every Beer	(MCA 40591)	.50	2.00	76
DON'T PUT HER DOWN/Fifteen Days Under The Hood	(MCA 40564)	.50	2.00	76
GROUPIE/Groupie	(Columbia 45763)	1.00	4.00	72
I DON'T KNOW YOU/Garden Of Eden	(Columbia 45526)	1.00	4.00	72
I DON'T NEED NO DOCTOR/Runnin' Back To You	(Columbia 45607)	1.00	4.00	72
(JUST) ANOTHER NIGHT IN RENO/	(MCA 40715)	.50	2.00	77
LOUISIANA LADY/Last Lonely Eagle	(Columbia 45469)	1.00	4.00	71
LOVE HAS STRANGE WAYS/	(MCA 40686)	.50	2.00	77
PANAMA RED/Cement, Clay & Grass	(Columbia 45976)	1.00	4.00	73
RAINBOW/Rainbow	(Columbia 45682)	1.00	4.00	72
YOU ANGEL YOU/Parson Brown	(Columbia 10067)	1.00	4.00	74
NEW SEEKERS, The (Featuring Eve Graham)				
BEAUTIFUL PEOPLE/When There's No Love Left	(Elektra 45710)	.50	2.00	71
BEG, STEAL OR BORROW/	(Elektra 45780)	.50	2.00	72
BUY THE WORLD A COKE/ Little Bit Of Sunshine-It's The Real Thing	(Coca Cola)	.75	3.00	
(Special products release)				
CIRCLES/	(Elektra 45787)	.50	2.00	72
COME SOFTLY TO ME/	(Verve 10698)	.50	2.00	73
DANCE, DANCE, DANCE/	(Elektra 45805)	.50	2.00	72
GIVE ME LOVE YOUR WAY/	(Columbia 10559)	.50	2.00	77
I'D LIKE TO TEACH THE WORLD TO SING (IN PERFECT HARMONY)/Boom-Town	(Elektra 45762)	.50	2.00	71
LOOK WHAT THEY'VE DONE TO MY SONG, MA/ It's A Beautiful Day	(Elektra 45699)	.50	2.00	70
NICKEL SONG/Cincinnati	(Elektra 45719)	.50	2.00	71
PINBALL WIZARS/SEE ME FEEL ME/	(Verve 10709)	.50	2.00	73
Also see Seekers, The				
NEW SOCIETY, The				
DAWN OF SORROW/We Have So Little Time	(RCA Victor 47-8958)	.75	3.00	66
DO NOT ASK FOR LOVE/Buttermilk	(RCA Victor 47-8807)	.75	3.00	66
NEWBEATS, The (Featuring Larry Henley)				
AIN'T THAT LOVIN' YOU/Girls & The Boys	(Hickory 1522)	.75	3.00	68
BAD DREAMS/The Swinger	(Hickory 1496)	.75	3.00	68
BIRD DOG/Evil Eva	(Hickory 1408)	.75	3.00	66
BIRDS ARE FOR THE BEES, THE/ Better Watch Your Step	(Hickory 1305)	.75	3.00	65
BREAD & BUTTER/Tough Little Buggy	(Hickory 1269)	.75	3.00	54
BREAK AWAY (FROM THAT BOY)/Hey-O-Daddy-O	(Hickory 1290)	.75	3.00	65
EVERYTHING'S ALRIGHT/Pink Dally Rue	(Hickory 1282)	.75	3.00	64
GROOVIN' (OUT ON LIFE)/Bread & Butter	(Hickory 1552)	.75	3.00	69
HIDE THE MOON/It's Really Goodbye	(Hickory 1467)	.75	3.00	67
I'VE BEEN A LONG TIME LOVING YOU/	(Hickory 1510)	.75	3.00	68
PATENT ON LOVE/My Yesterday Love	(Hickory 1422)	.75	3.00	66
RUN, BABY, RUN/Mean Wolly Willie	(Hickory 1332)	.75	3.00	65
SHAKE HANDS & COME OUT CRYING/ Too Sweet To Be Forgotten	(Hickory 1366)	.75	3.00	66
SHE WON'T HANG HER LOVE OUT/I'm A Teardrop	(Hickory 1569)	.75	3.00	70
THOU SHALT NOT STEAL/Great Balls Of Fire	(Hickory 1539)	.75	3.00	69
TOP SECRET/So Fine	(Hickory 1436)	.75	3.00	67
Also see Dean & Marc				
NEWLEY, Anthony				
I SAW HER STANDING THERE/ I Love Everything About You	(London 5202)	1.00	4.00	63
POP GOES THE WEASEL/	(London 9501)	.75	3.00	61
WHAT KIND OF FOOL AM I/Gonna Build A Mountain	(London 9546)	.75	3.00	62
NEWLOOK				
EAST OF THE DAWN (IN THE YEAR OF OUR LOVE)/ What Did You Take Me For	(TRX 5011)	1.00	4.00	68
NEWMAN, Carl				
ETHEL/Tom Tom	(Trio 849)	.75	3.00	
NEWMAN, Lionel				
(THEME FROM) THE PROUD ONES/ Who Gave You The Roses	(Columbia 40717)	1.00	4.00	56
(Instrumental)				

TITLE/FLIP	LABEL & NO.	GOOD	NEAR MINT	YR.
NEWMAN, Randy				
BALTIMORE/You Can't Fool The Fat Man	(Warner Bros. 8550)	.50	2.00	78
I THINK IT'S GOING TO RAIN TODAY/The Beehive State	(Reprise 0284)	1.00	4.00	78
(Promotional 78rpm "Speed Series" issue)				
IT'S MONEY THAT I LOVE/Ghosts	(Warner Bros. 49088)	.50	2.00	79
LAST NIGHT I HAD A DREAM/Old Man On The Farm	(Reprise 0771)	.75	3.00	68
LOUISIANA 1927/	(Reprise 1387)	.50	2.00	74
RIDER IN THE RAIN/Sigmund Freud's Impersonation Of Albert Einstein In America	(Warner Bros. 8630)	.50	2.00	78
SAIL AWAY/Political Science	(Reprise 1102)	.50	2.00	70
SHORT PEOPLE/Old Man On The Farm	(Warner Bros. 8492)	.50	2.00	77
STORY OF A ROCK & ROLL BAND, THE/	(Warner Bros. 49149)	.50	2.00	79
NEWMAN, Ted				
I DOUBLE DARE YOU/None Of Your Tears	(Rev 3511)	1.00	4.00	57
PLAYTHING/Unlucky Me	(Rev 3505)	1.00	4.00	57
NEWPORTERS, The				
LOOSE BOARD/Adventures In Paradise	(Scotchtown 500)	1.00	4.00	
NEWPORT NOMADS, The				
BLUE MALLARD/Harem Belles	(Prince 6304)	1.00	4.00	62
(Instrumental)				
NEWPORTS, The				
IF I COULD TONIGHT/A Fellow Needs A Girl	(Guyden 2067)	3.75	15.00	61
NEWPORTS, The				
LISTEN (TO YOUR BIG BROTHER)/Party Night	(Parrot 40008)	2.50	10.00	66
NEWPORTS, The				
WISHING STAR/Hands	(Image 45-501)	.50	2.00	78

TITLE/FLIP	LABEL & NO.	GOOD	NEAR MINT	YR.
NEWTON BROTHERS, The (Wayne & Jerry)				
I SPY/The Real Thing	(Capitol 4236)	1.00	4.00	59
IF THE EASTER BUNNY KNEW THE FUN HE'D HAVE ON XMAS/ Rascal Boogie	(Ranger 45-401)	2.50	10.00	58
(Shown as by the Newton Rascals)				
IF THE EASTER BUNNY KNEW THE FUN HE'D HAVE ON XMAS/ Rascal Boogie	(Ranger 45-401)	3.75	15.00	58
(Paper insert showing Wayne Newton, age 12, and Jerry Newton, age 14 as the "Rascals In Rhythm.")				
LITTLE JUKEBOX/Wild	(George 7778)	2.00	8.00	61
(Shown as by the Newton Brothers featuring Wayne)				
LITTLE WHITE CLOUD THAT CRIED/Calorie Date	(George 7777)	1.50	6.00	61
YOU'RE MUCH TO LOVELY TO CRY/I Still Love You	(George 7780)	1.50	6.00	61
NEWTON, Holder				
LOST ON THE RIVER NILE/Oh Safari	(Capitol 4601)	.75	3.00	61
NEWTON-JOHN, Olivia				
BANKS OF THE OHIO/It's So Hard To Say Goodbye	(Uni 55304)	.75	3.00	71
COME ON OVER/Small Talk & Pride	(MCA 40525)	.50	2.00	76
DEEPER THAN THE NIGHT/Please Don't Keep Me Waiting	(MCA 41009)	.50	2.00	79
DON'T STOP BELIEVIN'/Greensleeves	(MCA 40600)	.50	2.00	76
EVERY FACE TELLS A STORY/Love You Hold The Key	(MCA 40642)	.50	2.00	76
GOIN' BACK/Your My Baby Now	(Kirshner 5005)	1.25	5.00	70
HAVE YOU NEVER BEEN MELLOW/Water Under The Bridge	(MCA 40349)	.50	2.00	75
HOPELESSLY DEVOTED TO YOU/ Love Is A Many Splendored Thing (Instrumental)	(RSO 903)	.50	2.00	78
IF NOT FOR YOU/The Bigger Clown	(Uni 55281)	1.00	4.00	71
IF YOU LOVE ME (LET ME KNOW)/Brotherly Love	(MCA 40209)	.50	2.00	74
I HONESTLY LOVE YOU/Don't Cry For Me Argentian	(MCA 40811)	.50	2.00	77
I HONESTLY LOVE YOU/Home Ain't Home Anymore	(MCA 40280)	.50	2.00	74
JUST A LITTLE TOO MUCH/My Old Man's Got A Gun	(Uni 55348)	1.50	6.00	72
LET ME BE THERE/Maybe Then I'll Think Of You	(MCA 40101)	.50	2.00	73
LET IS SHINE/He Ain't Heavy... He's My Brother	(MCA 40495)	.50	2.00	75
LITTLE MORE LOVE, A/Borrowed Time	(MCA 40975)	.50	2.00	78
MAGIC/Fool Country	(MCA 41247)	.50	2.00	80
MAKING A GOOD THING BETTER/I Think I'll Say Goodbye	(MCA 40737)	.50	2.00	77
PLEASE MR. PLEASE/And In The Morning	(MCA 40418)	.50	2.00	75
SAM/I'll Bet You A Kangaroo	(MCA 40670)	.50	2.00	77
SOMETHING BETTER TO DO/He's My Rock	(MCA 40459)	.50	2.00	75
TAKE ME HOME, COUNTRY ROADS/	(MCA 40043)	.50	2.00	73
TOTALLY HOT/Dancin' 'Round & 'Round	(MCA 41074)	.50	2.00	79
WHAT IS LIFE/	(Uni 55317)	1.00	4.00	72
XANADU/	(MCA 41285)	.50	2.00	80
(With the Electric Light Orchestra)				
NEWTON, Johnny, & The Tags				
SORRY, SORRY (I RAN ALL THE WAY HOME)/ A Teenager In Love	(Bell 114)	2.00	8.00	59
NEWTON, Juice				
ANYWAY THAT YOU WANT ME/	(Capitol 4768)	.50	2.00	79
COME TO ME/	(Capitol 4499)	.50	2.00	77
HEY BABY/It's Not Impossible	(Capitol 4611)	.50	2.00	78
IF I EVER/Bye, Bye Baby	(RCA PB-10828)	.50	2.00	76
(With Silver Spur)				
IT'S A HEARTACHE/Wouldn't Mind The Rain	(Capitol 4552)	.50	2.00	78
LAY BACK IN THE ARMS OF SOMEONE/	(Capitol 4714)	.50	2.00	79
LOVE IS A WORD/Sweetest Thing (I've Ever Known)	(RCA PB-10538)	.50	2.00	76
(With Silver Spur)				
TELL MY BABY GOODBYE/Let's Keep It That Way	(Capitol 4679)	.50	2.00	79
UNTIL TONIGHT/	(Capitol 4793)	.50	2.00	79

TITLE/FLIP	LABEL & NO.	GOOD	NEAR MINT	YR.
NEWTON, Wayne				
CAN'T YOU HEAR THE SONG/	(Chelsea 0105)	.50	2.00	72
COMING ON TOO STRONG/Looking Through A Tear	(Capitol 5338)	3.75	15.00	65
(With Terry Melcher & Bruce Johnson)				
DADDY DON'T YOU WALK SO FAST/	(Chelsea 0100)	.50	2.00	72
DANKE SCHOEN/Better Now Than Later	(Capitol 4989)	.75	3.00	63
HEART/So Long Lucy	(Capitol 4920)	.75	3.00	63
I'LL BE WITH YOU IN APPLE BLOSSOM TIME/Laura Lee	(Capitol 5419)	.75	3.00	65
LITTLE WHITE CLOUD THAT CRIED, THE/ Born When You Kissed Me	(Challenge 59238)	.75	3.00	64
(Previously issued as by the Newton Brothers)				
RED ROSES FOR A BLUE LADY/One More Memory	(Capitol 5366)	.75	3.00	65
REMEMBER WHEN/Keep The Lovin' Feelin'	(Capitol 5514)	.75	3.00	65
SHIRL GIRL/Someone's Ahead Of You	(Capitol 5058)	.75	3.00	63
SUMMER WIND/I'll Be Standing By	(Capitol 5470)	.75	3.00	65
TOO LATE TO MEET/Only You	(Capitol 5203)	.75	3.00	64
NEW TRADITION, The				
STREETS IN THE CITY/I'm Happy Again	(United Artists 50608)	1.25	5.00	69
NEW VAUDEVILLE BAND, The (Featuring Tristam VII)				
FINCHLY CENTRAL/Sadie Moonshine	(Fontana 1589)	.75	3.00	67
PEEK-A-BOO/Amy	(Fontana 1573)	.75	3.00	67
WINCHESTER CATHEDRAL/Wait For Me Baby	(Fontana 1589)	.75	3.00	67
NEW WORLD				
LIVING NEXT DOOR TO ALICE/Something To Say	(RAK 4514)	.50	2.00	73
TOM TOM TURNAROUND/Lay Me Down	(RAK 4505)	.50	2.00	72
NEW YORK CITY BAND, The				
BO DIDDLEY/Sometimes	(American Int'l. 4101)	.50	2.00	79
NEW YORK DOLLS, The				
SLOW MOTION/	(Mercury 73807)	.75	3.00	76
(Shown as by the Dolls)				
STRANDED IN THE JUNGLE/Who Are The Mystery Girls?	(Mercury 73478)	1.00	4.00	74
TRASH/Bad Girl	(Mercury 73414)	1.00	4.00	73
Also see Johansen, David				
NEW YORKERS, The				
DO WAH DIDDY/ I Guess The Lord Must Be In New York City	(Decca 32569)	.75	3.00	69
SEEDS OF SPRING/Mr. Kirby	(Scepter 12199)	1.00	4.00	67
NEW YORK ROCK EXCHANGE, The				
HEY BABY/Harmonica Man	(United Artists 50326)	1.00	4.00	68
NEW YORK THRUWAY, The				
DAPHNE/Jack B. Nimble	(MGM 14071)	1.50	6.00	69
NEXT EXIT, The				
SOULFUL CHILD/Know	(Spirit 0004)	1.00	4.00	
NICE (Featuring Keith Emerson)				
AMERICA-2ND AMENDMENT/Diamond Hard Apples Of The Moon	(Immediate 5008)	.75	3.00	68
COUNTRY PIE-BRANDENBURG CONCERTO #6 (PART 1)/ Country Pie-Brandenburg Concerto #6 (Part 2)	(Mercury 73114)	.75	3.00	70
THOUGHTS OF AMERLIST DAUJACK/ Azrael (Angel Of Death)	(Immediate 5004)	.75	3.00	68
Also see Emerson, Lake & Palmer				
NICHOLAS, Jenny				
ELVIS/Daddy' Gone Bye-Bye	(Blue Candle 1525)	.50	2.00	77
NICHOLAS, Paul				
HEAVEN ON THE 7TH FLOOR/Do You Want My Love	(RSO 878)	.50	2.00	77
ON THE STRIP/Beauty Queen	(RSO 887)	.50	2.00	78
NICHOLS, Pamela				
DON'T CRY LISA/Don't Think It's Wrong	(Heartsong 458)	.50	2.00	77
NICHOLS, Roger, Trio				
SNOW QUEEN/Love Song Love Song	(A&M 830)	.75	3.00	
NICKIE & THE NITELITES (Featuring Nick Massi)				
I'M LONELY/Tell Me You Care	(Brunswick 55155)	5.00	20.00	59
Also see 4 Seasons, The				
NICKY & THE NACKS				
NIGHT, THE/That Old Black Magic	(Barry 108)	7.50	30.00	
NICKY & THE NOBLES				
POOR ROCK & ROLL/Ting-A-Ling	(Lost Nite 153)	.75	3.00	
SCHOOL DAY CRUSH/School Bells (Black label)	(Gone 5039)	3.00	12.00	58
SCHOOL DAY CRUSH/School Bells (Multi-color label)	(Gone 5039)	1.00	4.00	58
NIC NACKS, The				
JOLENE/Since You Came	(Ovation 6201)	.75	3.00	63
NIGHT (With Chris Thompson)				
COLD WIND ACROSS MY HEART/ Come Around (If You Want Me)	(Planet 45903)	.50	2.00	79
HOT SUMMER NIGHTS/Party Shuffle	(Planet 45903)	.50	2.00	79
Chris Thompson was previously in Manfred Mann's Earth Band.				
Also see Hopkins, Nicky				
NIGHTCAPS, The				
NEXT TIME YOU SEE ME/	(Vandan 4280)	.75	3.00	66
WINE, WINE, WINE/Nightcap Rock	(Vandan 7491)	1.00	4.00	60
WINE WINE WINE #2/Walking The Dog	(Vandan 4733)	.75	3.00	65
NIGHTCRAWLERS, The				
BASKET OF FLOWERS/Washboard	(Kapp 746)	1.00	4.00	66
LITTLE BLACK EGG/If I Were You	(Lee 1012)	2.00	8.00	66
LITTLE BLACK EGG/If I Were You	(Kapp 709)	1.00	4.00	66
MY BUTTERFLY/Today I'm Happy	(Kapp 826)	1.00	4.00	67

TITLE/FLIP	LABEL & NO.	GOOD	NEAR MINT	YR.
NIGHT HAWKS, The				
YOU'RE MY BABY/	(Stars 550)	3.75	15.00	
NIGHT OWLS, The				
BELLS RING/Let's Go Again	(Bethlehem 3087)	1.50	6.00	
NIGHT PEOPLE, The				
SO DEEP/Nothing	(Berma 1311)	1.00	4.00	
NIGHT RAIDERS, The				
COTTONPICKIN'/Hidi Hidi Hidi	(Profile 4007)	2.50	10.00	
NIGHT RIDERS, The				
PRETTY PLAID SKIRT/I'll Never Change	(Sue 713)	1.00	4.00	59
NIGHTRANES, The				
ROCKIN' ABE/Hangover	(Cuca 0444)	1.00	4.00	60
NIKITA THE K				
GO GO RADIO MOSCOW/The Spoiler (Novelty/Break-in)	(Warner Bros. 7005)	1.50	6.00	67
NILSSON (Harry Nilsson)				
AIN'T IT KINDA WONDERFUL/I'm A Bringing A Red Rose (Soundtrack)	(RCA 11193)	.50	2.00	78
AS TIME GOES BY/Lullaby In Ragtime	(RCA 0039)	.50	2.00	73
CAROLINE/Yellow Man	(RCA 0336)	.50	2.00	70
COCONUT/Down	(RCA 0718)	.50	2.00	72
DAYBREAK/Down	(RCA 0246)	.50	2.00	74
DON'T FORGET ME/Loop De Loop	(RCA 10139)	.50	2.00	75
DOWN TO THE VALLEY/Buy My Album	(RCA 0362)	.50	2.00	70
EVERYBODY'S TALKIN'/Don't Leave Me	(RCA Victor 47-9544)	.75	3.00	68
EVERYBODY'S TALKIN'/Rainmaker	(RCA 0161)	.50	2.00	69
GOOD TIMES/Growin' Up	(Tower 518)	.75	3.00	
GROWIN' UP/She's Yours	(Tower 244)	.75	3.00	66
I GUESS THE LORD MUST BE IN NEW YORK CITY/Maybe	(RCA 0261)	.50	2.00	69
JUMP INTO THE FIRE/The Moonbeam Song	(RCA 0673)	.50	2.00	72
JUST ONE LOOK-BABY I'M YOURS/That Is All (With Lynda Laurence)	(RCA 10759)	.50	2.00	77
KOJAK COLUMBO/Turn Out The Light	(RCA 10183)	.50	2.00	75
LIFE LINE/Poli High/ Me & My Arrow/Think about Your Trouble (Promotional issue)	(RCA SP-248)	.75	3.00	71
MANY RIVERS TO CROSS/Don't Forget Me	(RCA 10001)	.50	2.00	74
MATCHIN' DOWN BROADWAY/Maybe	(RCA 0207)	.50	2.00	69
ME & MY ARROW/Are You Sleeping?	(RCA 0443)	.50	2.00	71
ME & MY ARROW/The Town (Narration) Me & My Arrow (Promotional issue)	(RCA SP-258)	.75	3.00	71
ONE/Sister Marie	(RCA Victor 47-9462)	.75	3.00	68
RAINMAKER/I Will Take You There	(RCA Victor 47-9675)	.75	3.00	68
REMEMBER (CHRISTMAS)/The Lottery Song	(RCA 0855)	.50	2.00	72
SAIL AWAY/Moonshine Bandit	(RCA 10634)	.50	2.00	76
SIXTEEN TONS/	(Tower 103)	1.00	4.00	64
SPACEMAN/Turn On Your Radio	(RCA 0788)	.50	2.00	72
SUBTERRANEAN HOMESICK BLUES/Mucho Mungo-Mt. Elga	(RCA 10078)	.50	2.00	74
WAITING/I'll Be Home	(RCA 0310)	.50	2.00	70
WHO DONE IT?/Perfect Day	(RCA 11059)	.50	2.00	77
WITHOUT HER/Freckles	(RCA Victor 47-9206)	.75	3.00	67
WITHOUT HER/Gold Old Desk	(RCA 0524)	.50	2.00	71
WITHOUT YOU/Gotta Get Up	(RCA 0604)	.50	2.00	71
YOU CAN'T DO THAT/Ten Little Indians	(RCA Victor 47-9298)	1.50	6.00	67
YOU CAN'T TAKE YOUR LOVE AWAY FROM ME/ Born In Grenada	(Tower 136)	1.00	4.00	66
NIMBLE, Jack B., & The Quicks				
NUT ROCKER/Never On Sunday	(Del Rio 2305)	1.25	5.00	62
NUT ROCKER/Never On Sunday (Instrumentals)	(Dot 16319)	.75	3.00	62
NIMOY, Leonard				
COTTON CANDY/Ballad Of Billbo Baggins	(Dot 17028)	.75	3.00	67
I'D LOVE MAKING LOVE TO YOU/ Please Don't Try To Change My Mind	(Dot 17125)	.75	3.00	68
VISIT TO A SAD PLANET, A/Them From Star Trek	(Dot 17038)	.75	3.00	67
1910 FRUITGUM CO., The (Featuring Mark Gutkowski)				
GO AWAY/The Track	(Super K SK-15)	.75	3.00	70
GOODY, GOODY GUMDROPS/Candy Kisses	(Buddah BDA-71)	.75	3.00	68
INDIAN GIVER/Pow Wow	(Buddah BDA-91)	.75	3.00	69
LAWDY, LAWDY/The Clock	(Attack 10293AT)	.75	3.00	70
MAY I TAKE A GIANT STEP (INTO YOUR HEART)/ (Poor Old) Mr. Jensen	(Buddah BDA-39)	.75	3.00	68
1, 2, 3, RED LIGHT/Sticky, Sticky	(Buddah BDA-54)	.75	3.00	68
SIMON SAYS/Reflections From The Looking Glass	(Buddah BDA-24)	.75	3.00	67
SPECIAL DELIVERY/No Good Annie	(Buddah BDA-114)	.75	3.00	69
TRAIN, THE/Eternal Light	(Buddah BDA-130)	.75	3.00	69
WHEN WE GET MARRIED/Baby Bret	(Buddah BDA-146)	.75	3.00	69
Also see Great Train Robbery, The				
1929 DEPRESSION, The (The Regents)				
CHILD OF CLAY/You've Been Cheatin' On Me Baby	(Providence 422)	2.50	10.00	
1994				
DON'T BREAK IT UP/	(A&M 2194)	.50	2.00	79
NINO & THE EBB TIDES (Featuring Nino Aiello)				
AUTOMATIC REACTION/Linda Lou Garrett (Likes 24 Karat)	(Mala 480)	2.00	8.00	64
FRANNY FRANNY/Darling I'll Love Only You	(Acme 720)	5.00	20.00	57
HAPPY GUY, A/Wished I Was Home	(Mr. Peacock 102)	2.50	10.00	61
I LOVE GIRLS/Don't Look Around	(Recorte 413)	5.00	20.00	
I'M CONFESSIN'/Tell The World I Do	(Recorte 409)	5.00	20.00	59
JUKE BOX SATURDAY NIGHT/ (Someday) I'll Fall In Love	(Madison 166)	1.50	6.00	61
LITTLE MISS BLUE/Someday	(Marco 105)	2.00	8.00	61
PUPPY LOVE/You Make Me Want To Rock & Roll	(Recorte 405)	5.00	20.00	58
REAL MEANING OF CHRISTMAS, THE/Purple Shadows	(Recorte 408)	8.75	35.00	58
STAMPS BABY STAMPS/Lovin' Time	(Mr. Peacock 117)	2.00	8.00	62
THOSE OLDIES BUT GOODIES (REMIND ME OF YOU)/ Don't Run Away	(Madison 162)	2.00	8.00	61
TONIGHT/Nursery Rhymes	(Mr. Peeke 123)	2.50	10.00	63
WEEK FROM SUNDAY, A/Say No More (By Miss Frankie Nolan with the Ebbtides	(Madison 151)	2.00	8.00	61
Also see Coleman, Lenny				
Also see Nolan, Miss Frankie				
Also see Winchell, Danny				
NIPTONES, The				
ANGIE/It's Gonna Be Too Late	(Lorraine 1001)	1.50	6.00	65
NITEBEATS, The				
SCRAMBLED EGGS/I Think It's Love	(Tide 1088)	1.00	4.00	63
NITE CITY (Featuring Ray Manzarek)				
MIDNIGHT QUEEN/	(20th Century 2336)	.50	2.00	77
Ray Manzarek was previously with the Doors.				
NITE-NIKS, The				
HORN SHAKIN'/Shawnee	(Lawn 207)	.75	3.00	63
NITE WALKERS, The				
HIGH CLASS/You've Got Me	(Russell 43107)	.75	3.00	
NITRO EXPRESS, The				
HOME IN LINCOLN COUNTY/Train 99	(Buffalo 200)	1.00	4.00	

TITLE/FLIP	LABEL & NO.	GOOD	NEAR MINT	YR.
NITTY GRITTY DIRT BAND, The				
(ALL I HAVE TO DO IS) DREAM/ Raleigh-Durham Reel	(United Artists 655)	.50	2.00	75
AN AMERICAN DREAM/Take Me Back (With Linda Ronstadt)	(United Artists 1330)	.50	2.00	79
BALTIMORE/	(United Artists 50921)	.50	2.00	72
BATTLE OF NEW ORLEANS/	(United Artists 544)	.50	2.00	74
BUY FOR ME THE RAIN/Candy Man	(Liberty 55948)	.75	3.00	67
BUY FOR ME THE RAIN/ Mother Earth (Provides For Me)	(United Artists 936)	.50	2.00	77
COLLEGIANA/These Days	(Liberty 56045)	.75	3.00	68
COSMIC COWBOY (PART 1)/Fish Song	(United Artists 263)	.50	2.00	73
COSMIC COWBOY/Stars & Stripes Forever	(United Artists 830)	.50	2.00	76
FOR A LITTLE WHILE/	(United Artists 1268)	.50	2.00	79
HOUSE ON POOH CORNER/	(United Artists 50769)	.50	2.00	71
IN FOR THE NIGHT/Wild Nights	(United Artists 1228)	.50	2.00	78
IN HER EYES/Jas' Moon	(United Artists 1312)	.50	2.00	79
I SAW THE LIGHT (With Roy Acuff)/ The Precious Jewel	(United Artists 50849)	.50	2.00	71
JAMBALAYA (ON THE BAYOU)/Hoping To Say	(United Artists 50890)	.50	2.00	72
MR. BOJANGLES/Mr. Bojangles	(Liberty 56197)	.75	3.00	70
MOTHER OF LOVE/	(United Artists 741)	.50	2.00	75
RAVE ON/The Cure	(Liberty 56159)	.75	3.00	70
SOME OF SHELLY'S BLUES/The Cure	(United Artists 50817)	.50	2.00	71
SOME OF SHELLY'S BLUES/Yukon Railroad	(Liberty 56134)	.75	3.00	69
TEDDY BEAR'S PICNIC/Truly Right	(Liberty 55982)	.75	3.00	67
WILL THE CIRCLE BE UNBROKEN/	(United Artists 177)	.50	2.00	73
Beginning in 1976, this group was shown as the Dirt Band.				
NITZSCHE, Jack				
HARD WORKIN' MAN/Coke Machine (With Captain Beefheart)	(MCA 40897)	.50	2.00	78
LAST RACE/The Man With The Golden Arm	(Reprise 0262)	.75	3.00	64
LONELY SURFER, THE/Song For A Summer Night	(Reprise 20,202)	1.00	4.00	63
PUERTA VALLARTA/Senorita From Detroit	(Reprise 0364)	.75	3.00	65
RUMBLE/Theme For A Broken Heart	(Reprise 20,225)	.75	3.00	63
THEME FROM ONE FLEW OVER THE CUCKOO'S NEST/ The Last Dance (Instrumentals)	(Fantasy 760)	.50	2.00	76
Also see Hale & the Hushabyes				
NIX, Ford, & The Moonshiners				
NINE TIMES OUT OF TEN/	(Clix 813)	15.00	60.00	
NOBELLS, The				
SEARCHIN' FOR MY LOVE/Crying Over You	(Mar 101)	6.25	25.00	62
NOBLE, Beverly				
WHY MUST I CRY/You Cheated	(Sparrow 100)	1.00	4.00	
NOBLE, Nick				
BIBLE TELLS ME SO, THE/Army Of The Lord	(Wing 90003)	1.00	4.00	55
MOONLIGHT SWIM/Lucy Lau	(Mercury 71169)	1.00	4.00	57
TO YOU, MY LOVE/You Are My Only Love	(Mercury 70821)	1.25	5.00	56
TO YOU, MY LOVE/You Are My Only Love	(Wing 90045)	1.00	4.00	56
NOBLEMEN, The				
DRAGON WALK/Thunder Wagon (Instrumentals)	(U.S.A. 1213)	1.50	6.00	63
NOBLES, The				
POOR ROCK & ROLL/Ting A Ling	(Klik 305)	6.25	25.00	58
POOR ROCK & ROLL/Ting A Ling	(Times Square 1)	.75	3.00	62
NOBLES, The				
MARLENE/That Special One	(U.S.A. 788)	2.50	10.00	65
NOBLETONES, The				
I'M CRYING/Mambo Boogie	(C&M 438)	5.00	20.00	58
I'M REALLY TOO YOUNG/I Love You	(C&M 182)	5.00	20.00	58
NO DEPOSIT NO RETURN				
I'VE GOT MY NEEDS/Your Love Is My Love	(Philips 40451)	.75	3.00	67
NO DICE				
WHY SUGAR/Down 'N' Dry	(Capitol 4579)	.50	2.00	78
NOEL, Sid				
FLYING SAUCER/Flying Saucer (Part 2) (Novelty/Break-in)	(Aladdin 3331)	3.75	15.00	56
NOGUEZ, Jacky				
CIAO, CIAO BAMBINA/De Serait Dommage	(Jamie 1127)	.75	3.00	59
CIAO, CIAO BAMBINA/De Serait Dommage (Stereo single issue)	(Jamie 1127)	1.50	6.00	59
MARINA/Adonis (Instrumentals)	(Jamie 1137)	.75	3.00	59

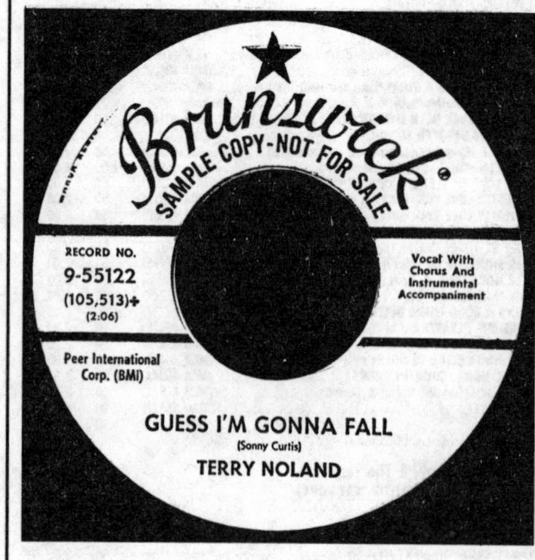

TITLE/FLIP	LABEL & NO.	GOOD	NEAR MINT	YR.
NOLAND, Terry				
GUESS I'M GONNA FALL/Teenage Teardrops	(Brunswick 55122)	1.50	6.00	59
HYPONTIZED/Ten Little Women	(Brunswick 55010)	7.50	30.00	57
LONG GONE BABY/There Goes A Girl	(Apt 25065)	1.25	5.00	60
PATTY BABY/	(Brunswick 55036)	1.50	6.00	57
PUPPY LOVE/Look At Me	(Brunswick 55054)	1.50	6.00	58

TITLE/FLIP	LABEL & NO.	GOOD	NEAR MINT	YR.
NOLAN, Kenny				
BUT LOVE ME/	(Polydor 14502)	.50	2.00	78
I LIKE DREAMIN'/Time Ain't Time Enough	(20th Century 2287)	.50	2.00	77
LOVE'S GROWN DEEP/ Today I Met The Girl I'm Gonna Marry	(20th Century 2331)	.50	2.00	77
MY EYE'S GET BLURRY/	(20th Century 2352)	.50	2.00	77
SONG BETWEEN US, A/	(Polydor 14486)	.50	2.00	78
NOLAN, Miss Frankie				
I STILL CARE/ I Wish It Were Summer All Year Round (With Frankie Valli)	(ABC-Paramount 10231)	6.25	25.00	61
Also see Nino & The Ebbtides				
NOMADS, The				
BOUNTY HUNTER/Desert Tramp	(Rust 5028)	1.00	4.00	61
I'M POPEYE, THE SAILOR MAN/ On The Atchison, Topeka & The Sante Fe	(ABC-Paramount 10191)	1.00	4.00	61
POPEYE THE SAILOR/Sante Fe Rock	(Genie 7817)	1.00	4.00	61
SAN FRANCISCO BAY BLUES/Oh Jennie	(Pharos 101)	1.00	4.00	
NO NAMES, The				
LOVE/Jam (Instrumental)	(Guyden 2114)	1.50	6.00	59
NOONE, Peter (Of Herman's Hermits)				
GETTING OVER YOU/All Sing Together	(Philips 40730)	.50	2.00	71
MEET ME ON THE CORNER DOWN AT JOE'S CAFE/ (Blame It) On The Pony Express	(Casablanca 0017)	.50	2.00	73
MEET ME ON THE CORNER DOWN AT JOE'S CAFE/ (Blame It) On The Pony Express	(Casablanca 0106)	.50	2.00	74
SOMETHING OLD, SOMETHING NEW/	(Casablanca 824)	.50	2.00	75
NORDINE, Ken				
BACHMAN/Crimson & Olive	(Dunwich 123)	.75	3.00	66
I USED TO THINK MY RIGHT HAND WAS UGLIER THAN MY LEFT/ My Baby	(Dot 16000)	2.00	8.00	59
Also see Vaughn, Billy				
NORELL, Jerry				
COMIC BOOK HOP/The Freshman	(Hamilton 50022)	1.50	6.00	59
COMIC BOOK HOP/The Freshman	(Brunswick 55148)	1.00	4.00	59
WHAT IS SURFIN' ALL ABOUT/ (With the Beach Girls)	(Legent 124)	1.00	4.00	63
NORMAL, The				
T.V.O.D./Warm Leatherette	(Sire 1044)	.50	2.00	79
NORMAN, Gene, & The Rockin' Rockets				
SNAGGLE TOOTH ANN/Long Gone Night Train	(Snag 101)	37.50	150.00	58
NORMAN, Jimmy, & The Hollywood Teeners				
BOY & A GIRL, A/A Bride	(Fun 101)	.75	3.00	60
MY THANKS/Para Siempre	(Fun 102)	.75	3.00	60
NORMAN, Val				
BALLAD OF BARBARA GRAHAM, THE/ The Sweetest Words I've Ever Heard	(Valor 2005)	1.25	5.00	58
NORM N. NITE & THE FABULOUS FOURTUNES				
LET'S TRY IT AGAIN/Good Old Rock & Roll Music	(Globe 107)	1.25	5.00	71
NORRIS, Bobby				
I WENT ROCKIN'/Rock-a-bye Me Mama	(Capitol 3945)	1.25	5.00	58
NORTH, Angelmaye				
PRESLEY THE KING "CADILLAC MAN"/ Presley The King "Cadillac Man"	(High Country 108)	.75	3.00	77
NORTH ATLANTIC INVASION FORCE, The				
BLACK IN WHITE/The Orange Patch	(Mr. G 808)	1.00	4.00	
BLUE & GREEN GOWN/Fire, Wind & Rain	(Congressional 999)	1.25	5.00	
NORTHCOTT, Tom				
GIRL FROM THE NORTH COUNTRY/ Landscape Grown Cold	(Warner Bros. 7212)	.75	3.00	69
1941/Other Times	(Warner Bros. 7160)	.75	3.00	68
SUNNY GOODGE STREET/ Who Planted Thorns In Miss Alice's Garden	(Warner Bros. 7051)	.75	3.00	67
NORTHERN LIGHT				
MINNESOTA/Theme From Minnesota (Instrumental)	(Glacier 4501)	.75	3.00	75
MINNESOTA/Theme From Minnesota (Instrumental)	(Columbia 10136)	.50	2.00	75
THINK SNOW/Etude (Think Snow)	(Glacier 4502)	.75	3.00	77
NORTONES, The				
BOY/Smile Just Smile	(Warner Bros. 5115)	2.00	8.00	59
COOKIE MON/I'm Gonna Find You	(Stack 502)	1.00	4.00	60
SUSIE JONES/That's The Way The Cookie Crumbles	(Warner Bros. 5065)	2.00	8.00	59
NOTABLES, The				
SURFSIDE/Lisa Maree (Instrumental)	(Big Top 3141)	1.00	4.00	63
NOTATIONS, The				
WHAT A NIGHT FOR LOVE/Chapel Doors	(Wonder 100)	18.75	75.00	
NOTATIONS, The				
YOU SHOULD KNOW/Eleven O'Clock	(Sue 5)	.75	3.00	69
NOTE TORIALS, The				
MY VALERIE/Loved & Lost	(Sunbeam 119)	7.50	30.00	59
NOTES FROM THE UNDERGROUND				
DOWN IN THE BASEMENT/I Wish I Was A Punk	(Vanguard 35073)	1.25	5.00	69
NOVAS, The				
CRUSHER, THE/Take 7 (Instrumentals)	(Parrot 45005)	1.00	4.00	64
NRBQ				
GET THAT GASOLINE/	(Buddah 546)	.50	2.00	74
I LOVE HER, SHE LOVES ME/Green Light	(Mercury 73991)	.50	2.00	78
MAGNET/	(Kama Sutra 549)	.50	2.00	73
STOMP/I Didn't Know Myself	(Columbia 44865)	.75	3.00	69
NUGENT, Ted (Of The Amboy Dukes)				
CAT SCRATCH FEVER/Wang Dang Sweet Poontang	(Epic 50425)	.50	2.00	77
DOG EAT DOG/Light My Way	(Epic 50301)	.50	2.00	76
FREE-FOR-ALL/Street Rats	(Epic 50363)	.50	2.00	77
HEY BABY/Stormtroopin'	(Epic 50197)	.50	2.00	76
HOME BOUND/Death By Misadventure	(Epic 50493)	.50	2.00	77
I WANT TO TELL YOU/Bite Down Hard	(Epic 50713)	.50	2.00	79
NEED YOU BAD/I Got The Feelin'	(Epic 50648)	.50	2.00	78
WHERE HAVE YOU BEEN ALL MY LIFE/	(Epic 50172)	.50	2.00	76
YANK ME, CRANK ME (Live Version)/ Cat Scratch Fever (Live Version)	(Epic 50533)	.50	2.00	78
NUMBERS, The				
MY PILLOW/Big Red	(Bonneville 101)	3.75	15.00	62
MY PILLOW/Big Red	(Dore 641)	.75	3.00	62
NU TORNADOS, The				
'OLE MUMMER'S STRUT, THE/Let's Have A Party	(Carlton 497)	1.00	4.00	59
PHILADELPHIA U.S.A./Magic Record	(Carlton 492)	1.00	4.00	58

TITLE/FLIP	LABEL & NO.	GOOD	NEAR MINT	YR.
NUTTY NED & MARVIN				
BIG TRIAL, THE/Comin' Down The Track	(Arch 1812)	1.50	6.00	
(Novelty/Break-in)				
NUTTY SQUIRRELS, The				
EAGER BEAVER/Zowee	(Hanover 4551)	1.00	4.00	60
HELLO AGAIN/Bluesette	(RCA Victor 47-8287)	1.00	4.00	63
PLEASE DON'T TAKE OUR TREE FOR CHRISTMAS/ Nuttty Noel	(Columbia 41818)	1.00	4.00	60
UH! OH! (PART 2)/Uh! Oh! (Part 1)	(Hanover 4540)	1.00	4.00	59
Novelties				
NYE, Louis				
HI-HO STEVE-O/I Gotta Run	(Coral 61836)	1.25	5.00	57
ROLAND ROCKOFF/Teenage Beatnik	(Wig 103)	1.00	4.00	59
NYLONS, The: see Rumblers, The				
N.Y. ROCK & ROLL ENSEMBLE				
KISS HER ONCE/	(Atco 6501)	.75	3.00	67
NYRO, Laura				
AND WHEN I DIE/Flim Flam Man	(Verve Forecast 5051)	.75	3.00	67
ELI'S COMIN'/Sweet Blindness	(Columbia 44531)	.50	2.00	68
GOODBYE JOE/Billie's Blues	(Verve Forecast 5038)	.75	3.00	67
IT'S GONNA TAKE A MIRACLE/Desiree	(Columbia 45537)	.50	2.00	72
SAVE THE COUNTRY/Timer	(Columbia 44592)	.50	2.00	68
STONEY END/Wedding Bell Blues	(Verve Folkways 5024)	.75	3.00	66
UP ON THE ROOF/	(Columbia 45230)	.50	2.00	70

O

TITLE/FLIP	LABEL & NO.	GOOD	NEAR MINT	YR.
OBERLE, Scott				
CUPIDS' POISON DART/You're My Dream Girl	(Atco 6293)	2.00	8.00	64
OCEAN, Billy				
AMERICAN HEARTS/	(Epic 50810)	.50	2.00	79
L.O.D. (LOVE ON DELIVERY)/ Mr. Businessman	(Ariola America-GTO 7630)	.50	2.00	76
LOVE REALLY HURTS WITHOUT YOU/ You're Running Outa Fools	(Ariola America-GTO 7621)	.50	2.00	76
OCHS, Phil				
FLOWER LADY/Cross My Heart	(A&M 881)	.75	3.00	67
HARDER THEY FALL, THE/The War Is Over	(A&M 891)	.75	3.00	67
MY LIFE/The World Began In Eden & Ended In Los Angeles	(A&M 1070)	.75	3.00	69
OUTSIDE OF A SMALL CIRCLE OF FRIENDS/Miranda	(A&M 891)	.75	3.00	67
OCTOPUS				
RED WHITE & BLUE/Heroes	(Buddah BDA-346)	.50	2.00	73
O'CONNELL, Helen				
BE ANYTHING (BUT BE MINE)/Right Or Wrong	(Capitol 2011)	1.25	5.00	52
SLOW POKE/I Wanna Play House With You	(Capitol 1837)	1.25	5.00	51
O'CONNOR, Carroll & Jean Stapleton (As "The Bunkers")				
OH BABE, WHAT WOULD YOU SAY?/They Can't Take That Away From Me/Moments To Remember	(RCA 0962)	.75	3.00	73
(Shown as by Archie & Edith)				
THOSE WERE THE DAYS/Those Were The Days	(Atlantic 2847)	.75	3.00	71
("All In The Family" theme)				
O'CONNOR, Donald				
BIGGEST BLOOMIN' BUMBERSHOOT/Love Is In The Air	(Decca 28816)	1.25	5.00	53
I'M WALKING BEHIND YOU/Crash	(Decca 28692)	1.25	5.00	54
NO TWO PEOPLE/You Can't Love Me	(Columbia 39863)	1.25	5.00	53
(With Doris Day)				
OCTAVES, The				
YOU'RE TOO YOUNG/Mombo Carolyn	(Val 1001)	3.75	15.00	
OCTOBER COUNTRY				
MY GIRL FRIEND IS A WITCH/I Just Don't Know	(Epic 10320)	.75	3.00	69
OCTOBER COUNTRY/Baby What I Mean	(Epic 10252)	.75	3.00	68
OCTOBER, Johnny (Of the 4 Dates)				
FIRST TIME/You're My Girl	(First 106)	1.25	5.00	
GROWIN' PRETTIER/Young & In Love	(Capitol 4267)	1.25	5.00	59
OCTOBERS, The				
STOP IT LITTLE GIRL/I Should'a Listened To Mama	(Chairman 4402)	1.25	5.00	
(Answer song)				
O'DAY, Alan				
OH JOHNNY/People Who Talk To Themselves	(Pacific 100)	.50	2.00	79
SATISFIED/	(Pacific 004)	.50	2.00	78
SOLDIER OF FORTUNE/	(Pacific 003)	.50	2.00	78
STARTED OUT DANCING, ENDED UP MAKING LOVE/ Angie Baby	(Pacific 002)	.50	2.00	77
UNDERCOVER ANGEL/Just You	(Pacific 001)	.50	2.00	77
O'DAY, Anita				
TENNESSEE WALTZ/Yea Boo	(London 867)	1.25	5.00	51
ODDIS, Ray				
HAPPY GHOULTIDE/	(VIP 25012)	.75	3.00	65
ODDS & ENDS, The				
YOU DON'T LOVE ME/Be Happy Baby	(Southbay 102)	.75	3.00	
O'DELL, Kenny				
BEAUTIFUL PEOPLE/Flower Girl	(Vegas 718)	.75	3.00	67
HAPPY WITH YOU/I Could Love You	(Vegas 724)	.75	3.00	68
OLD TIME LOVIN'/Take Another Look	(Mar-Kay 3696)	1.00	4.00	
SPRINGFIELD PLANE/I'm Gonna Take It	(Vegas 722)	.75	3.00	68
OFARIM, Esther & Abi				
CINDERELLA ROCKEFELLA/ Your Heart Is Free Just Like The Wind	(Philips 40526)	.75	3.00	68
OFF-BEATS, The				
YOU TELL ME/Mary	(Tower 205)	.75	3.00	66
OFF KEYS, The				
OUR WEDDING DAY/Singing Bells	(Technichord 1001)	2.50	10.00	62
OUR WEDDING DAY/Singing Bells	(Rowe 003)	2.00	8.00	62

TITLE/FLIP	LABEL & NO.	GOOD	NEAR MINT	YR.
O'HENRY, Lenny				
ACROSS THE STREET/Saturday Angel	(Atco 6525)	2.00	8.00	67
CHEATED HEART/Billy, The Continental Kid (With The Short Stores)	(ABC-Paramount 10222)	1.25	5.00	61
SWEET YOUNG LOVE/Savin' All My Love	(Atco 6312)	1.25	5.00	65
TOUCH OF YOU, THE/Goin' To A Party	(ABC-Paramount 10272)	2.00	8.00	61
Also see 4 Seasons, The				
OHIO EXPRESS, The (Featuring Joey Levine)				
BEG, BORROW OR STEAL/Maybe	(Cameo C-483)	.75	3.00	67
BEG, BORROW OR STEAL/Maybe	(Attack 1401)	1.25	5.00	66
(Shown as by the Rare Breed)				
CHEWY CHEWY/Firebird	(Buddah BDA-70)	.75	3.00	68
COWBOY CONVENTION/The Race	(Buddah BDA-147)	.75	3.00	69
(Vocals by Carter & Lewis, of the Ivy League.)				
DOWN AT LULU'S/She's Not Comin' Home	(Buddah BDA-56)	.75	3.00	68
HOT DOG/Ooh La La	(Super K SK-14)	.75	3.00	69
LET ME KISS YOU WITH A DREAM/	(Crewe 337)	.75	3.00	69
LOVE EQUALS LOVE/Peanuts	(Buddah BDA-160)	.75	3.00	70
(Vocals by Carter & Lewis, of the Ivy League.)				
MERCY/Roll It Up	(Buddah BDA-102)	.75	3.00	69
PINCH ME/Peanuts	(Buddah BDA-117)	.75	3.00	69
SAUSALITO/Make Love Not War	(Buddah BDA-129)	.75	3.00	69
(Lead vocal by Graham Gouldman, later of 10CC.)				
SWEETER THAN SUGAR/Bitter Lemon	(Buddah BDA-92)	.75	3.00	69
THAT'S THE WAY A WOMAN IS/Talkin' Bout You	(Attack 10043AT)	.75	3.00	70
TRY IT/Soul Struttin'	(Cameo KC-2001)	.75	3.00	67
WHAM BAM/	(Buddah BDA-386)	.75	3.00	72
(Shown as by Ohio LTD.)				
YUMMY, YUMMY, YUMMY/Zig Zag	(Buddah BDA-38)	.75	3.00	68
Also see Reunion				
OHIO LTD.				
WHAM BAM/Slow & Steady	(Buddah BDA-386)	.75	3.00	73
O.K'S, The				
SUGAR BOWL BLUES/Don't Leave Me Now	(Summer 290)	1.25	5.00	57
O'KEEFE, Danny (Of Calliope)				
GOOD TIME CHARLIE'S GOT THE BLUES/ The Valentine Pieces	(Signpost 70006)	.50	2.00	72
QUITS/	(Atlantic 3267)	.50	2.00	75
RUNAWAY, THE/Just Jones	(Warner Bros. 8489)	.50	2.00	78
YOU LOOK JUST LIKE A GIRL AGAIN/ On Discovering A Missing Person	(Warner Bros. 8435)	.50	2.00	77
OLA & THE JANGLERS				
CALIFORNIA SUN/Baby, Baby, Baby	(Crescendo 432)	.75	3.00	68
I CAN WAIT/	(London 29934)	.75	3.00	68
LET'S DANCE/Strolling Along	(GNP Crescendo 423)	.75	3.00	69
THAT'S WHY I CRY/What A Way To Die	(GNP Crescendo 427)	.75	3.00	69
OLDFIELD, Mike				
HERGEST RIDGE/	(Virgin 223)	.50	2.00	75
ON HORSEBACK/Theme From Ommadawn	(Virgin 9505)	.50	2.00	77
TUBULAR BELLS/Tubular Bells	(Virgin 55100)	.75	3.00	74
(Different versions of the theme from "The Exorcist")				
OLENN, Johnny				
BORN RECKLESS/You Loveable You	(Antler 1105)	1.00	4.00	
(With the Blockbusters)				
SMILE/My Sweetie Pie	(Antler 4009)	1.00	4.00	59
OLIVER (William Oliver Swofford)				
ANGELICA/Anna	(Crewe 341)	.50	2.00	70
GOOD MORNING STARSHINE/Can't You See	(Jubilee 5659)	.50	2.00	69
I CAN REMEMBER/Where There's A Heartache There Must Be A Heart	(Crewe 346)	.50	2.00	70
JEAN/The Arrangement	(Crewe 334)	.50	2.00	69
SUNDAY MORNIN'/Letmekissyouwithadream	(Crewe 337)	.50	2.00	69
Also see Billy & Sue				
OLIVER & THE TWISTERS				
LOCOMOTION TWIST/Mother Goose Twist	(Colpix 615)	.75	3.00	61
OLIVER, O. Jay, & The Crackerjacks				
REAL LOVE & AFFECTION/Good Gravey	(Coed 500)	1.50	6.00	58
OLSSON, Nigel				
DANCIN' SHOES/Living In A Fantasy	(Bang 740)	.50	2.00	78
GIRL LIKE YOU, A/	(Rocket 40491)	.50	2.00	75
LITTLE BIT OF SOAP/Thinking Of You	(Bang 4800)	.50	2.00	79
ONLY ONE WOMAN/In Good Time	(Rocket 40337)	.50	2.00	75
PART OF THE CHOSEN FEW/All It Takes	(Bang 4803)	.50	2.00	79
RAINY DAY/	(Columbia 10733)	.50	2.00	78
SOMETHING LACKING IN ME/Songs I Sing	(Rocket 40455)	.50	2.00	75
SOME SWEET DAY/Weirdhouse	(Uni 55291)	.50	2.00	71
SUNSHINE LOOKS LIKE RAIN/And I Know In My Heart	(Uni 55308)	.50	2.00	72
Nigel Olsson was also a member of Elton John's Band.				
OMAR & THE VILLAGE IDIOTS				
DEEP INSIDE/Liz	(Pacific Challenger 105)	1.00	4.00	
OMEGAS, The				
MIDNIGHT RUN/I Wanna Go Home	(Groove G4-4)	1.00	4.00	
STUDY HALL/So How Come (No One Loves You)	(Decca 31094)	1.00	4.00	60
O'NEAL, Fluke				
BILLY'S BACK/	(Te Ma 1014)	.75	3.00	78
O'NEILL, Jim				
FACE ON THE PENNY/Happy Town	(Del Fi 4141)	.75	3.00	60
ONES, The				
DON'T LET ME LOSE THIS DREAM/ I've Been Good To You	(Motown 1130)	.75	3.00	
YOU HAVEN'T SEEN MY LOVE/Happy Day	(Fenton 2514)	1.25	5.00	
YOU HAVEN'T SEEN MY LOVE/Happy Day	(Spirit 0001)	1.25	5.00	
ONO, Yoko, & The Plastic Ono Band				
DEATH OF SAMANTHA/Yang Yang	(Apple 1859)	.75	3.00	73
MRS. LENNON/Midsummer New York	(Apple 1839)	.75	3.00	71
NOW OR NEVER/Move On Fast	(Apple 1853)	.75	3.00	72
WOMAN POWER/Men, Men, Men	(Apple 1867)	.75	3.00	73
Also see Lennon, John				
OP BIRDS, The				
OP SONG/Dreamy Dolls Of Duesseldorf	(Epic 9582)	.75	3.00	63
OPALS, The				
NO, NO, NEVER AGAIN/Just Like A Little Bitty Baby	(Laurie 3288)	.75	3.00	65
ORBISON, Don				
TIME/	(Lavender 2040)	.75	3.00	
ORBISON, Roy (Of The Teen Kings)				
ALMOST EIGHTEEN/Jolie	(RCA Victor 47-7447)	2.50	10.00	59
BELINDA/No Chain At All	(Monument 8690)	.50	2.00	76
BLUE ANGEL/Today's Teardrops	(Monument 425)	1.00	4.00	60
BORN TO BE LOVED BY YOU/Shy Away	(MGM 13889)	.75	3.00	68
BREAKIN' UP IS BREAKIN MY HEART/Wait	(MGM 13446)	.75	3.00	66
CHICKEN HEARTED/I Like Love	(Sun 284)	1.50	6.00	58
COMMUNICATION BREAKDOWN/Going Back To Gloria	(MGM 13634)	.75	3.00	66
CRAWLING BACK/If You Can't Say Something Nice	(MGM 13410)	.75	3.00	65

TITLE/FLIP	LABEL & NO.	GOOD	NEAR MINT	YR.
CROWD, THE/Mama	(Monument 461)	.75	3.00	62
CRY SOFTLY LONELY ONE/Pistolero	(MGM 13764)	.75	3.00	67
CRYING/Candy Man	(Monument 447)	.75	3.00	61
CRYING/Candy Man	(Monument 447)	1.25	5.00	61
(Picture sleeve)				
DREAM BABY (HOW LONG MUST I DREAM)/The Actress	(Monument 456)	.75	3.00	62
EASY WAY OUT/Tears	(Asylum 46048)	.50	2.00	79
FALLING/Distant Drums	(Monument 815)	.75	3.00	63
GOODNIGHT/Only With You	(Monument 873)	.75	3.00	65
HEARTACHE/Sugar Man	(MGM 13991)	.75	3.00	68
HERE COMES THE RAIN BABY/She	(MGM 13817)	.75	3.00	67
(I'M A) SOUTHERN MAN/Born To Love Me	(Monument 200)	.75	3.00	77
I'M HURTIN'/I Can't Stop Loving You	(Monument 433)	1.00	4.00	60
IN DREAMS/Shahdaroba	(Monument 806)	.75	3.00	63
IT'S OVER/Indian Wedding	(Monument 837)	.75	3.00	64
LANA/Our Summer Song	(Monument 939)	.75	3.00	62
LEAH/Workin' For The Man	(Monument 467)	.75	3.00	
LET THE GOOD TIMES ROLL/Distant Drums	(Monument 906)	.75	3.00	65
MEAN WOMAN BLUES/Blue Bayou	(Monument 824)	.75	3.00	63
OH PRETTY WOMAN/Yo Te Amo Maria	(Monument 851)	.75	3.00	64
ONLY THE LONELY (KNOW THE WAY I FEEL)/ Here Comes That Song Again	(Monument 421)	1.00	4.00	60
OOBY DOOBY/Go Go Go	(Sun 242)	2.50	10.00	56
(With the Teen Kings)				
PAPER BOY/With The Bug	(Monument 409)	1.25	5.00	
PENNY ARCADE/Tennessee Owns My Soul	(MGM 14079)	.75	3.00	69
PRETTY PAPER/Beautiful Dreamer	(Monument 830)	.75	3.00	63
RIDE AWAY/Wondering	(MGM 13386)	.75	3.00	65
ROCKHOUSE/You're My Baby	(Sun 251)	2.00	8.00	56
(With the Teen Kings)				
ROY ORBISON—MGM CELEBRITY SCENE (Box Set Of Five Singles)/	(MGM CS9-5)	7.50	30.00	66
(Includes the following singles: "Ride Away," "Communication Breakdown," "Breakin' Up Is Breakin' My Heart," "Sweet Dreams," "You'll Never Be Sixteen Again." Set also includes biography insert on Orbison and juke box title strips for each of the singles.)				
RUNNING SCARED/Love Hurts	(Monument 438)	.75	3.00	61
(SAY YOU'RE) MY GIRL/Sleepy Hollow	(Monument 891)	.75	3.00	65
SHE CHEATS ON ME/How Do You Start Over	(MGM 14105)	.75	3.00	68
SOUTHBOUND JERICHO PARKWAY/My Friend	(MGM 14039)	.75	3.00	69
SWEET & EASY/Devil Doll	(Sun 265)	2.00	8.00	57
SWEET & EASY/Devil Doll	(Sun 353)	.75	3.00	61
SWEET & INNOCENT/Seems To Me	(RCA Victor 47-7381)	2.50	10.00	58
TOO SOON TO KNOW/You'll Never Be Sixteen Again	(MGM 13549)	.75	3.00	66
TWINKLE TOES/Communication Breakdown	(MGM 13758)	.75	3.00	67
TWINKLE TOES/Where Is Tomorrow	(MGM 13498)	.75	3.00	66
UPTOWN/Pretty One	(Monument 412)	1.00	4.00	60
WALK ON/Flowers	(MGM 13950)	.75	3.00	68
ORBISON, Roy & Emmylou Harris				
THAT LOVIN' YOU FEELING AGAIN/	(Warner Bros. 49262)	.50	2.00	80
ORBIT ROCKERS, The				
ROCK IT/	(Williamette 107)	1.00	4.00	
ORBITS, The				
MESSAGE OF LOVE/I Really Do	(Flair-X 5000)	1.50	6.00	56
ORCHIDS, The				
TELL ME A STORY/From Bad To Worse	(Columbia 43066)	1.25	5.00	64
THAT BOY IS MESSIN' UP MY MIND/Harlem Tango	(Columbia 42913)	1.25	5.00	63
ORIENTALS, The				
PLEASE COME BACK HOME/	(Kayo 927)	1.25	5.00	
ORIENTS, The				
QUEEN OF THE ANGELS/Shouldn't I	(Laurie 3232)	3.75	15.00	64
ORIGINAL CASTE, The				
MR. MONDAY/Highway	(TA 192)	.50	2.00	70
ONE TIN SOLDIER/Live For Tomorrow	(TA 186)	.50	2.00	69
Also see Innes, Dixie Lee				
ORIGINAL HAUNTED, The				
I'M GONNA BLOW MY LITTLE MIND TO BITS/Mona	(Jet 4002)	.75	3.00	67
ORIGINAL SAFARIS, The				
GUM DIPPED SLICKS/High Time	(Safari 301)	.75	3.00	64
ORIGINALS, The				
LET ME HEAR YOU SAY YEAH/Wishing Star	(Original Sound 10)	.75	3.00	60
ORLANDO, Tony				
BEAUTIFUL DREAMER/Loneliest	(Epic 9562)	1.00	4.00	62
BLESS YOU/Am I The Guy	(Epic 9452)	1.00	4.00	61
CANDIDA/Look At	(Bell 903)	.50	2.00	70
(Shown as by Dawn)				
CHILLS/At The Edge Of Tears	(Epic 9519)	1.00	4.00	62
CUPID/You're Growin' On Me	(Elektra 45302)	.50	2.00	76
DING DONG/You & Only You	(Mile 101)	7.50	30.00	59
HALFWAY TO PARADISE/Lonely Tomorrows	(Epic 9441)	1.00	4.00	61
HAPPY TIMES ARE HERE TO STAY/ Will You Love Me Tomorrow	(Epic 55299)	1.25	5.00	61
(Promotional issue only)				
HAPPY TIMES ARE HERE TO STAY/Lonely Am I	(Epic 9476)	1.00	4.00	61
HE DON'T LOVE YOU (LIKE I LOVE YOU)/ Pick It Up	(Elektra 45240)	.50	2.00	75
I'D NEVER FIND ANOTHER YOU/Love On Your Lips	(Epic 9502)	1.00	4.00	62
I'LL BE THERE/What Am I Gonna Do	(Epic 9622)	1.00	4.00	63

TITLE/FLIP	LABEL & NO.	GOOD	NEAR MINT	YR.
I PLAY & SING/Get Out From Where We Are	(Bell 970)	.50	2.00	71
(With Dawn)				
IT ONLY HURTS WHEN I TRY TO SMILE/	(Bell 45,450)	.50	2.00	74
KNOCK THREE TIMES/Home	(Bell 938)	.50	2.00	70
(Shown as by Dawn)				
LOOK IN MY EYES PRETTY WOMAN/My Love Has No Pride	(Bell 45,620)	.50	2.00	74
MORNIN' BEAUTIFUL/	(Elektra 45260)	.50	2.00	75
MY BABY'S A STRANGER/Talkin About You	(Epic 9491)	1.00	4.00	62
RUNAWAY-HAPPY TOGETHER (Medley)/	(Bell 45,175)	.50	2.00	72
(Shown as by Dawn)				
SAY, HAS ANYBODY SEEN MY SWEET GYPSY ROSE/	(Bell 45,374)	.50	2.00	73
(Shown as by Dawn)				
SHE DOESN'T KNOW IT/Tell Me What I Can Do	(Epic 9668)	1.00	4.00	64
SHE LOVES ME/Think Before You Act	(Atco 6376)	1.00	4.00	65
SHIRLEY/Joanie	(Epic 9570)	1.00	4.00	63
SKYBIRD/That's The Way A Wallflower Feels	(Arista 0156)	.50	2.00	75
STEPPIN' OUT (GONNA BOOGIE TONIGHT)/	(Bell 45,601)	.50	2.00	74
(With Dawn)				
SUMMER SAND/	(Bell 45,107)	.50	2.00	71
(With Dawn)				
SWEETS FOR MY SWEET/High Steppin'	(Casablanca 991)	.50	2.00	79
SWEET SWEET/Manuelito (Little Manuel)	(Cameo 471)	.75	3.00	67
TIE A YELLOW RIBBON 'ROUND THE OLE OAK TREE/ I Can't Believe How Much I Love You	(Bell 45,318)	.50	2.00	73
(With Dawn)				
TO WAIT FOR LOVE/Accept It	(Epic 9715)	1.00	4.00	64
VAYA CON DIOS/	(Bell 45,225)	.50	2.00	72
(With Dawn)				
WHAT ARE YOU DOING SUNDAY/ Sweet Soft Sounds Of Love	(Bell 45,151)	.50	2.00	71
(With Dawn)				
WHO'S IN THE STRAWBERRY PATCH WITH SALLY/ Ukelele Man	(Bell 45,424)	.50	2.00	73
(With Dawn)				
YOU'RE A LADY/	(Bell 45,285)	.50	2.00	72
(With Dawn)				
YOU'RE ALL I NEED TO GET BY/ I Know You Like A Book	(Elektra 45275)	.50	2.00	75

Also see Dache, Bertell
Also see Jerry & Jeff
Also see Shields, Billy
Also see Wind
Also see Dawn

ORLEANS

TITLE/FLIP	LABEL & NO.	GOOD	NEAR MINT	YR.
BUSINESS AS USUAL/Time Passes On	(Asylum 45447)	.50	2.00	77
DANCE WITH ME/Ending Of A Song	(Asylum 45261)	.50	2.00	75
DON'T THROW OUR LOVE AWAY/ The Flame & The Moth	(Infinity 50017)	.50	2.00	79
FOREVER/Keep On Rollin'	(Infinity 50036)	.50	2.00	79
LET THERE BE MUSIC/Give One Heart	(Asylum 45243)	.50	2.00	75
LOVE TAKES TIME/Isn't It Easy	(Infinity 50006)	.50	2.00	79
REACH/Sweet Destiny	(Asylum 45375)	.50	2.00	77
SPRING FEVER/The Bum	(Asylum 45391)	.50	2.00	77
STILL THE ONE/Siam Sam	(Asylum 45336)	.50	2.00	76

Also see Hall, John

ORLIE & THE SAINTS

TITLE/FLIP	LABEL & NO.	GOOD	NEAR MINT	YR.
BOSTON TWIST & FREEZE/King Kong	(Band Box 253)	.75	3.00	

ORLONS, The (Featuring Shirley Brickley)

TITLE/FLIP	LABEL & NO.	GOOD	NEAR MINT	YR.
ANYONE WHO HAD A HEART/Spinnin' Top	(Calla 113)	.75	3.00	66
BON-DOO-WAH/Don't Throw Your Love Away	(Cameo 287)	.75	3.00	63
COME ON DOWN BABY/I Ain't Comin' Back	(Cameo 352)	.75	3.00	65
CROSS FIRE/It's No Big Thing	(Cameo 273)	.75	3.00	63
DON'T HANG UP/The Conservative	(Cameo 231)	.75	3.00	62
DON'T YOU WANT MY LOVIN'/I Can't Take It	(Cameo 372)	.75	3.00	65
I AIN'T COMIN' BACK/Envy (In My Eyes)	(Cameo 346)	.75	3.00	64
I'LL BE TRUE/Heart Darling Angel	(Cameo 198)	1.00	4.00	62
KNOCK KNOCK (WHO'S THERE)/Goin' Places	(Cameo 332)	.75	3.00	64
MR. 21/Please Let It Be Me	(Cameo 211)	1.00	4.00	62
NO LOVE BUT YOUR LOVE/Envy	(Cameo 384)	.75	3.00	65
NOT ME/My Best Friend	(Cameo 257)	.75	3.00	63
RULES OF LOVE/Heartbreak Hotel	(Cameo 319)	.75	3.00	64
SHIMMY SHIMMY/Everything Nice	(Cameo 295)	.75	3.00	64
SOUTH STREET/Them Terrible Boots	(Cameo 243)	.75	3.00	63
WAH WATUSI, THE/Holiday Hill	(Cameo 218)	.75	3.00	62

ORPHANS, The

TITLE/FLIP	LABEL & NO.	GOOD	NEAR MINT	YR.
THERE'S NO FLOWERS IN MY GARDEN/One Spoken Word	(Epic 10288)	1.25	5.00	
THIS IS THE TIME/Deserted	(Epic 10348)	1.25	5.00	

ORPHENS, The

TITLE/FLIP	LABEL & NO.	GOOD	NEAR MINT	YR.
MY LIFE/Music Minus Orphens	(Red Bird 10-041)	.75	3.00	65

ORPHEUS, The

TITLE/FLIP	LABEL & NO.	GOOD	NEAR MINT	YR.
BROWN ARMS IN HOUSTON/I Can Make The Sun Rise	(MGM 14022)	.75	3.00	69
CAN'T FIND THE TIME/Lesley's World	(MGM 13882)	.75	3.00	68
I'VE NEVER SEEN LOVE LIKE THIS/Congress Alley	(MGM 13947)	.75	3.00	68

ORRISON, Bob

TITLE/FLIP	LABEL & NO.	GOOD	NEAR MINT	YR.
SARAH LEE/Florecita	(Liberty 55257)	1.00	4.00	60

ORSI, Phil, & The Little Kings

TITLE/FLIP	LABEL & NO.	GOOD	NEAR MINT	YR.
COME ON EVERYBODY/Oh My Darling	(Lucky 1009)	3.00	12.00	63
DON'T YOU JUST KNOW IT/	(Lucky 1015)	2.00	8.00	63
SORRY, I RAN ALL THE WAY HOME/ Who Ever He May Be	(U.S.A. 847)	1.25	5.00	66
STAY/Who Ever He May Be	(U.S.A. 841)	1.25	5.00	66

O'RYAN, Jack, & Al Tercek

TITLE/FLIP	LABEL & NO.	GOOD	NEAR MINT	YR.
POLITICAL CIRCUS (PART 1)/Political Circus (Part 2)	(Nocturne P-8)	6.25	25.00	56
(The theory that Eddie Cochran was featured on this release is, as of yet, unproven.)				
(Novelty/Break-in)				

OSBORN, Bobby

TITLE/FLIP	LABEL & NO.	GOOD	NEAR MINT	YR.
I DON'T CARE IF THE SUN DON'T SHINE/	(Knickerbocker 1312)	1.00	4.00	

OSBORNE, Arthur

TITLE/FLIP	LABEL & NO.	GOOD	NEAR MINT	YR.
HEY RUBY/Don't Give Me Heartaches	(Brunswick 55068)	5.00	20.00	58

OSBORNE, Jerry

TITLE/FLIP	LABEL & NO.	GOOD	NEAR MINT	YR.
COUNTRY SIDE OF '76, THE/The Country Side of '76	(Jellyroll 10676)	.75	3.00	76
(With Bruce Hamilton)				
KINGS COUNTRY, THE (WORLD PREMIER)/ Merry Christmas To You	(Quality 201)	6.25	25.00	66
(Shown as by Jerry Jay)				
PLANE CRAZY/Political Circus '72	(Jellyroll 69)	.75	3.00	75
(Shown as by Ratmore Slinky)				
Novelty/Break-ins				

OSHINS, Milt

TITLE/FLIP	LABEL & NO.	GOOD	NEAR MINT	YR.
ALL ABOUT ELVIS (PART 1)/All About Elvis (Part 2)	(Pelvis 169)	5.00	20.00	56

OSKAR, Lee (Of War)

TITLE/FLIP	LABEL & NO.	GOOD	NEAR MINT	YR.
BLT/I Remember Home (A Peasant's Symphony) The Immigrant	(United Artists-Far Out 807)	.50	2.00	76

OSMOND BROTHERS, The

TITLE/FLIP	LABEL & NO.	GOOD	NEAR MINT	YR.
BE MY LITTLE BABY BUMBLE BEE/ I Wouldn't Trade The Silver In My Mother's Hair	(MGM 13162)	.75	3.00	63
I CAN'T STOP/Flower Music	(Uni 55015)	.75	3.00	67
I'VE GOT LOVING ON MY MIND/Mollie A	(Barnaby 2004)	.75	3.00	68
MARY ELIZABETH/Speak Like A Child	(Barnaby 2002)	.75	3.00	68
MISTER SANDMAN/My Mom	(MGM 13281)	.75	3.00	64
MOVIN' ALONG/	(MGM 14159)	.75	3.00	70
TAKING A CHANCE ON LOVE/ Groove With What You Got	(Barnaby 2005)	.75	3.00	69
TRAVELS OF JAMIE McPHEETERS/Aura Lee	(MGM 13174)	.75	3.00	63

OSMOND, Donny (Of The Osmonds)

TITLE/FLIP	LABEL & NO.	GOOD	NEAR MINT	YR.
ARE YOU LONESOME TONIGHT/When I Fall In Love	(MGM-Kolob 14677)	.50	2.00	73
C'MON MARIANNE/	(Polydor-Kolob 14320)	.50	2.00	76
GO AWAY LITTLE GIRL/	(MGM-Kolob 14285)	.50	2.00	71
HEY GIRL/I Knew You When	(MGM-Kolob 14322)	.50	2.00	71
I HAVE A DREAM/	(MGM-Kolob 14781)	.50	2.00	75
LONELY BOY/Why	(MGM-Kolob 14424)	.50	2.00	72
MILLION TO ONE, A/Young Love	(MGM-Kolob 14583)	.50	2.00	73
PUPPY LOVE/	(MGM-Kolob 14367)	.50	2.00	72
SWEET & INNOCENT/	(MGM-Kolob 14227)	.50	2.00	71
TOO YOUNG/Love Me	(MGM-Kolob 14407)	.50	2.00	72
TWELFTH OF NEVER, THE/ Life Is Just What You Make It	(MGM-Kolob 14503)	.50	2.00	73

OSMOND, Donny & Marie

TITLE/FLIP	LABEL & NO.	GOOD	NEAR MINT	YR.
DEEP PURPLE/	(MGM-Kolob 14840)	.50	2.00	75
I'M LEAVIN' IT UP TO YOU/	(MGM-Kolob 14735)	.50	2.00	73
MAKE THE WORLD GO AWAY/	(MGM-Kolob 14807)	.50	2.00	75
MORNING SIDE OF THE MOUNTAIN/	(MGM-Kolob 14765)	.50	2.00	73

OSMOND, Little Jimmy (Of The Osmonds)

TITLE/FLIP	LABEL & NO.	GOOD	NEAR MINT	YR.
LONG HAIRED LOVER FROM LIVERPOOL/	(MGM-Kolob 14376)	.50	2.00	72
TWEEDLE DEE/	(MGM-Kolob 14468)	.50	2.00	73

OSMOND, Marie (Of The Osmonds)

TITLE/FLIP	LABEL & NO.	GOOD	NEAR MINT	YR.
IN MY LITTLE CORNER OF THE WORLD/	(MGM-Kolob 14694)	.50	2.00	73
PAPER ROSES/Least Of All You	(MGM-Kolob 14609)	.50	2.00	73
THIS IS THE WAY I FEEL/	(Polydor-Kolob 14385)	.50	2.00	77
WEEPING WILLOW/	(Polydor-Kolob 14303)	.50	2.00	76
WHO'S SORRY NOW/	(MGM-Kolob 14785)	.50	2.00	73

OSMONDS, The (Formerly The Osmond Brothers)

TITLE/FLIP	LABEL & NO.	GOOD	NEAR MINT	YR.
CRAZY HORSES/That's My Girl	(MGM-Kolob 14450)	.50	2.00	72
DOUBLE LOVIN'/Chilly Winds	(MGM-Kolob 14259)	.50	2.00	71
DOWN BY THE LAZY RIVER/He's The Light Of The World	(MGM-Kolob 14323)	.50	2.00	72
GOIN' HOME/Are You Up There?	(MGM-Kolob 14562)	.50	2.00	73
HOLD HER TIGHT/Love Is	(MGM-Kolob 14405)	.50	2.00	72
I CAN'T LIVE A DREAM/Check It Out	(Polydor-Kolob 14348)	.50	2.00	76
I CAN'T STOP/	(Uni 55276)	.50	2.00	71
I'M STILL GONNA NEED YOU/	(MGM-Kolob 14831)	.50	2.00	75
LET ME IN/	(MGM-Kolob 14617)	.50	2.00	73
LOVE ME FOR A REASON/Fever	(MGM-Kolob 14746)	.50	2.00	74
ONE BAD APPLE/	(MGM-Kolob 14193)	.50	2.00	71
PROUD ONE, THE/	(MGM-Kolob 14791)	.50	2.00	75
WE CAN MAKE IT TOGETHER/	(MGM-Kolob 14383)	.50	2.00	72
(With Steve Lawrence & Eydie Gorme)				
YO-YO/Keep On My Side	(MGM-Kolob 14295)	.50	2.00	71

O'SULLIVAN, Gilbert

TITLE/FLIP	LABEL & NO.	GOOD	NEAR MINT	YR.
ALONE AGAIN, (NATURALLY)/Save It	(MAM 3619)	.50	2.00	72
CLAIR/Ooh-Wakka-Doo-Wakka-Day	(MAM 3626)	.50	2.00	72
GET DOWN/A Very Extraordinary Sort Of Girl	(MAM 3629)	.50	2.00	73
HAPPINESS IS ME & YOU/Breakfast Dinner & Tea	(MAM 3636)	.50	2.00	74
I DON'T LOVE YOU BUT I THINK I LIKE YOU/	(MAM 3644)	.50	2.00	75
MARRIAGE MACHINE/Tell Me Why	(MAM 3643)	.50	2.00	75
NOTHING RHYMED/Everybody Knows	(MAM 3602)	.50	2.00	71
OOH BABY/Good Company	(MAM 3633)	.50	2.00	73
OUT OF THE QUESTION/Everybody Knows	(MAM 3628)	.50	2.00	73
TO CUT A LONG STORY SHORT/You Are You	(MAM 3642)	.50	2.00	74
UNDERNEATH THE BLANKET GO/	(MAM 3607)	.50	2.00	71
WE WILL/I Didn't Know What To Do	(MAM 3613)	.50	2.00	72
WOMAN'S PLACE, A/	(MAM 3641)	.50	2.00	74

OTHER HALF, The

TITLE/FLIP	LABEL & NO.	GOOD	NEAR MINT	YR.
I NEED YOU/No Doubt About It	(Acta 806)	1.25	5.00	67
OZ LEEK EAVES DROPS/Morning Fire	(Atco 825)	1.25	5.00	68
MR. PHARMACIST/I've Come So Far	(GNP Crescendo 378)	1.25	5.00	67
WONDERFUL DAY/Flight Of The Dragon Lady	(Atco 801)	1.25	5.00	67

OTHER SIDE, The

TITLE/FLIP	LABEL & NO.	GOOD	NEAR MINT	YR.
WALKING DOWN THE ROAD/Streetcar	(Brent 7061)	1.25	5.00	64

OTHERS, The

TITLE/FLIP	LABEL & NO.	GOOD	NEAR MINT	YR.
OH YEAH!/I'm Taking Her Home	(Fontana 1944)	.75	3.00	64

OTHER TIKIS, The

TITLE/FLIP	LABEL & NO.	GOOD	NEAR MINT	YR.
LOST MY LOVE TODAY/Bye Bye Bye	(Autumn 28)	1.00	4.00	66

Also see Tikis
Also see Harpers Bizzare

OTTO & THE ELEVATORS

TITLE/FLIP	LABEL & NO.	GOOD	NEAR MINT	YR.
LADY JANE/Suicide's No Fun Gimme That Gun	(Vera 5076)	.50	2.00	76

OUR GANG (Jan Berry & Dean Torrance)

TITLE/FLIP	LABEL & NO.	GOOD	NEAR MINT	YR.
SUMMERTIME SUMMERTIME/ Theme From Leon's Garage	(Br'er Bird 001)	12.50	50.00	66

OUTCASTS, The

TITLE/FLIP	LABEL & NO.	GOOD	NEAR MINT	YR.
I'M IN PITTSBURGH (& IT'S RAINING)/ Price Of Glory	(Askel 102)	.75	3.00	

OUTLAWS, The

TITLE/FLIP	LABEL & NO.	GOOD	NEAR MINT	YR.
BREAKER - BREAKER/South Carolina	(Arista 0188)	.50	2.00	75
GREEN GRASS & HIGH TIDES/Holiday	(Arista 0338)	.50	2.00	78
GREEN GRASS & HIGH TIDES/Prisoner	(Arista 0213)	.50	2.00	76
HEARIN' MY HEART TALKIN'/Holiday	(Arista 0282)	.50	2.00	77
HURRY SUNDOWN/So Afraid	(Arista 0258)	.50	2.00	77
IF DREAMS CAME TRUE/	(Arista 0397)	.50	2.00	79
TAKE IT AWAY YOU WANT IT/Cry Some More	(Arista 0378)	.50	2.00	78
THERE GOES ANOTHER LOVE SONG/Keep Prayin'	(Arista 0150)	.50	2.00	75

OUTRAGE

TITLE/FLIP	LABEL & NO.	GOOD	NEAR MINT	YR.
BE MY BABY/The City	(Kama Sutra 252)	1.50	6.00	68
LETTER, THE/The Letter (Edited version)	(Kama Sutra 259)	1.50	6.00	69

OUTSIDERS, The (Featuring Sonny Geraci)

TITLE/FLIP	LABEL & NO.	GOOD	NEAR MINT	YR.
CHANGES/Lost In My World	(Bell 904)	.75	3.00	70
GIRL IN LOVE/What Makes You So Bad, You Weren't Brough Up That Way	(Capitol 5646)	1.00	4.00	66
GUY WITH THE LONG LIVERPOOL HAIR, THE/Outsider	(Karate 505)	1.00	4.00	64
HELP ME GIRL/You Gotta Look	(Capitol 5759)	1.00	4.00	66
I JUST CAN'T SEE YOU ANYMORE/Gotta Leave Us Alone	(Capitol 5892)	1.00	4.00	67
I WILL LOVE YOU/Little Bit of Lovin'	(Capitol 2055)	1.00	4.00	67
I'LL GIVE YOU TIME/I'm Not Tryin' to Hurt You	(Capitol 5843)	1.00	4.00	67
I'LL SEE YOU IN THE SUMMERTIME/ And Now You Want My Sympathy	(Capitol 5955)	1.00	4.00	67
OH HOW IT HURTS/We Ain't Gonna Make It	(Capitol 2216)	1.00	4.00	68
RESPECTABLE/Lost In My World	(Capitol 5701)	1.00	4.00	66
RICKITY-BOOM-BAL-AYE/The Bird Battle	(Ellen 503)	2.00	8.00	
TIME WON'T LET ME/Was It Really Real	(Capitol 5573)	1.00	4.00	66
TINKER TAILOR/You're Not So Pretty	(Kapp 2104)	1.00	4.00	

OVATIONS, The

TITLE/FLIP	LABEL & NO.	GOOD	NEAR MINT	YR.
DAY WE FELL IN LOVE/My Lullabye	(Barry 101)	3.00	12.00	62
("Day We Fell In Love" is the same song as "Oh What A Day.")				
I DON'T WANNA CRY/Loneliness	(Capitol 5082)	2.50	10.00	63
OH WHAT A DAY/Real True Love	(Epic 9470)	3.75	15.00	61
(Reissued using the title "Day We Fell In Love")				
WHOLE WIDE WORLD/My Lullabye	(Andie 5017)	3.75	15.00	60

OVATIONS, The

TITLE/FLIP	LABEL & NO.	GOOD	NEAR MINT	YR.
REMEMBERING/Who Needs Love	(Josie 916)	3.00	12.00	64

Also see Kannon, Sandy
Also see Little Romeo & The Casanovas

OVATIONS, The

TITLE/FLIP	LABEL & NO.	GOOD	NEAR MINT	YR.
RUNAROUND/I Still Love You	(Hawk 153)	3.00	12.00	

OVERLANDERS, The

TITLE/FLIP	LABEL & NO.	GOOD	NEAR MINT	YR.
DON'T MAKE YOU FEEL GOOD/Movin'	(Hickory 1275)	1.00	4.00	64
LEAVES ARE FALLING/January	(Hickory 1295)	1.00	4.00	65
MICHELLE/Cradle of Love	(Hickory 1362)	1.00	4.00	65
MY LIFE/Girl From Indiana	(Hickory 1384)	1.25	5.00	66
YESTERDAY'S GONE/Over The Rainbow	(Hickory 1258)	1.00	4.00	64

OVERTONES, The

TITLE/FLIP	LABEL & NO.	GOOD	NEAR MINT	YR.
FROM MY HEART/Sally Put Your Red Dress On	(Ajax 174)	1.50	6.00	
LA-LA-LA-LA-LA/Please Let Me Know	(Ajax 173)	1.00	4.00	
THIS OLD LOVE OF MINE/	(Slate 4013)	1.00	4.00	

OWEN, B.

TITLE/FLIP	LABEL & NO.	GOOD	NEAR MINT	YR.
MISSISSIPPI MAMA/Nowhere To Run	(Janus 107)	.75	3.00	70

OWEN, Reg

TITLE/FLIP	LABEL & NO.	GOOD	NEAR MINT	YR.
DOWN BY THE RIVERSIDE/Ambush	(Palette 5015)	.75	3.00	59
MANHATTAN SPIRITUAL/Ritual Blues	(Palette 5005)	.75	3.00	58
Instrumentals				

OWENS, Donnie

TITLE/FLIP	LABEL & NO.	GOOD	NEAR MINT	YR.
BETWEEN MIDNIGHT & DAWN/Ask Me Anything	(Guyden 2013)	1.00	4.00	59
MY WORLD/Soldiers Last Letter	(ARA 1966)	1.00	4.00	
NEED YOU/If I'm Wrong	(Guyden 2001)	1.00	4.00	58
STORMY/What A Dream	(Trey 124)	1.00	4.00	60
TOMORROW/	(Guyden 2006)	1.00	4.00	59

OX-BOW INCIDENT, The

TITLE/FLIP	LABEL & NO.	GOOD	NEAR MINT	YR.
REACH OUT/Harmonica Man	(Smash 2189)	1.00	4.00	68

OXFORD CIRCLE, The

TITLE/FLIP	LABEL & NO.	GOOD	NEAR MINT	YR.
MIND DESTRUCTION/Foolish Woman	(World United 002)	7.50	30.00	

OZARK MOUNTAIN DAREDEVILS, The

TITLE/FLIP	LABEL & NO.	GOOD	NEAR MINT	YR.
CHICKEN TRAIN STOMP/	(A&M 1842)	.50	2.00	76
CRAZY LOVIN'/Stinghead	(A&M 1989)	.50	2.00	77
FOLLOWING THE WAY I FEEL/Snowbound	(A&M 2016)	.50	2.00	78
IF I ONLY KNEW/Dreams	(A&M 1772)	.50	2.00	76
IF YOU WANNA GET TO HEAVEN/Spaceship Orion	(A&M 1515)	.50	2.00	74
JACKIE BLUE/Better Days	(A&M 1654)	.50	2.00	75
KEEP ON CHURNIN'/Time Warp	(A&M 1808)	.50	2.00	76
NOAH (LET IT RAIN)/	(A&M 1880)	.50	2.00	76
THIN ICE/Colorado Song	(A&M 1709)	.50	2.00	75
YOU KNOW LIKE I KNOW/Arroyo	(A&M 1888)	.50	2.00	77
YOU MADE IT RIGHT/Dreams	(A&M 1809)	.50	2.00	76

OZO

TITLE/FLIP	LABEL & NO.	GOOD	NEAR MINT	YR.
LISTEN TO THE BUDDAH/Kites	(DJM 1012)	.50	2.00	76

PAAR, Jack

TITLE/FLIP	LABEL & NO.	GOOD	NEAR MINT	YR.
BLUE WIGGLE/	(RCA Victor 47-7306)	1.00	4.00	58
I-M-4-U/	(Columbia 4-40628)	1.25	5.00	55

PABLO CRUISE (Cory Lerios, Steve Price, Dave Jenkins, Bud Cockrell)

TITLE/FLIP	LABEL & NO.	GOOD	NEAR MINT	YR.
DON'T WANT TO LIVE WITHOUT IT/Raging Fire	(A&M 2076)	.50	2.00	78
I GO TO RIO/Raging Fire	(A&M 2112)	.50	2.00	79
I WANT YOU TONIGHT/Family Man	(A&M 2195)	.50	2.00	79
LOVE WILL FIND A WAY/Always Be Together	(A&M 2048)	.50	2.00	78
NEVER HAD A LOVE/Atlanta June	(A&M 1999)	.50	2.00	77
PLACE IN THE SUN, A/El Verano	(A&M 1976)	.50	2.00	77
WHATCHA GONNA DO?/Atlanta June	(A&M 1920)	.50	2.00	77
WHAT DOES IT TAKE/	(A&M 1742)	.50	2.00	75

Lerios, Price & Jenkins were previously with Stoneground, Bud Cockrell was formerly in It's A Beautiful Day.

PACERS, The

TITLE/FLIP	LABEL & NO.	GOOD	NEAR MINT	YR.
HOW SWEET/	(Guyden 2064)	10.00	40.00	61

PACERS, The

TITLE/FLIP	LABEL & NO.	GOOD	NEAR MINT	YR.
YOU GOT ME BUGGED/Sassy Sue	(Coral 62398)	.75	3.00	63

PACE-SETTERS, The

TITLE/FLIP	LABEL & NO.	GOOD	NEAR MINT	YR.
MUSTANG/Heads Up	(Ava 161)	.75	3.00	64

PACETTES, The

TITLE/FLIP	LABEL & NO.	GOOD	NEAR MINT	YR.
DON'T READ THE LETTER/You Don't Know Baby	(Regina 306)	.75	3.00	63

PACIFIC GAS & ELECTRIC (P G & E)

TITLE/FLIP	LABEL & NO.	GOOD	NEAR MINT	YR.
ARE YOU READY/Staggolee	(Columbia 45158)	.75	3.00	70
FATHER COME ON HOME/Elvira	(Columbia 45221)	.75	3.00	70
(LOVE IS LIKE A) HEAT WAVE/	(Columbia 45621)	.75	3.00	72
THANK GOD FOR YOU BABY/See The Monkey Run	(Columbia 45519)	.75	3.00	72
WADE IN THE WATER/Live Love	(Power 1701)	1.25	5.00	

PACKERS, The

TITLE/FLIP	LABEL & NO.	GOOD	NEAR MINT	YR.
HOLE IN THE WALL/Go 'Head On	(Pure Soul Music 1107)	.75	3.00	65
(Instrumentals)				

PAGE, Allen

TITLE/FLIP	LABEL & NO.	GOOD	NEAR MINT	YR.
DATELESS NIGHT/	(Moon 302)	3.00	12.00	
HONEYSUCKLE/	(Moon 301)	3.00	12.00	
SHE'S THE ONE THAT'S GOT IT/	(Moon 303)	3.00	12.00	

PAGE BOYS, The

TITLE/FLIP	LABEL & NO.	GOOD	NEAR MINT	YR.
IF TEARS COULD SPEAK/Old Buttermilk Sky	(Decca 3105)	1.25	5.00	
WAITING/This I Give To You	(Prep 117)	1.25	5.00	57

PAGE, Jimmy

TITLE/FLIP	LABEL & NO.	GOOD	NEAR MINT	YR.
SHE JUST SATISFIES/Keep Moving	(Fontana 533)	25.00	100.00	65
(English release)				

Also see Led Zepplin
Also see Yardbirds, The

PAGE, Patti (Clara Ann Fowler)

TITLE/FLIP	LABEL & NO.	GOOD	NEAR MINT	YR.
ALL MY LOVE/Roses Remind Me Of You	(Mercury 5455)	1.50	6.00	50
ALLEGHENY MOON/The Strangest Romance	(Mercury 70878)	1.00	4.00	56
AND SO TO SLEEP AGAIN/One Sweet Letter	(Mercury 5706)	1.25	5.00	51

TITLE/FLIP	LABEL & NO.	GOOD	NEAR MINT	YR.
ARFIE, THE DOGGIE IN THE WINDOW/ Arfie Goes To School	(Mercury 70190)	1.50	6.00	53
BOY'S NIGHT OUT, THE/Three Fools	(Mercury 72013)	.75	3.00	62
CHANGING PARTNERS/Where Did My Snowman Go	(Mercury 70260)	1.25	5.00	53
CHANGING PARTNERS/Don't Get Around Much Anymore	(Mercury 70295)	1.25	5.00	53
COME WHAT MAY/Retreat	(Mercury 5772)	1.25	5.00	52
CROCE DI ORO/Search My Heart	(Mercury 70713)	1.25	5.00	55
CROSS OVER THE BRIDGE/Johnny Guitar	(Mercury 70302)	1.25	5.00	54
CROSS OVER THE BRIDGE/My Restless Lover	(Mercury 70302)	1.25	5.00	54
DETOUR/Who's Gonna Shoe My Pretty Little Feet	(Mercury 5682)	1.25	5.00	51
DOGGIE IN THE WINDOW, THE/My Jealous Eyes	(Mercury 70070)	1.25	5.00	53
GO ON WITH THE WEDDING/The Voice Inside	(Mercury 70766)	1.25	5.00	55
HUSH, HUSH, SWEET CHARLOTTE/ Longing To Hold You Again	(Columbia 43251)	.75	3.00	65
I WENT TO YOUR WEDDING/You Belong To Me	(Mercury 5899)	1.25	5.00	52
I'M WALKIN'/Invitation To The Blues	(Mercury 72123)	.75	3.00	62
LEFT RIGHT OUT OF YOUR HEART/ Longing To Hold You Again	(Mercury 71331)	1.00	4.00	58
MAMA FROM THE TRAIN/Every Time (I Feel His Spirit)	(Mercury 70971)	1.00	4.00	56
MISTER & MISSISSIPPI/These Things I Offer You	(Mercury 5645)	1.25	5.00	51
MOCKIN' BIRD HILL/I Love You Because	(Mercury 5595)	1.25	5.00	51
MOST PEOPLE GET MARRIED/You Don't Know Me	(Mercury 71950)	.75	3.00	62
OLD CAPE COD/Wondering	(Mercury 71101)	1.00	4.00	57
ONE OF US (WILL WEEP TONIGHT)/ What Will My Future Be	(Mercury 71639)	1.00	4.00	60
TENNESSEE WALTZ, THE/ Boogie Woogie Santa Claus	(Mercury 5534)	1.50	6.00	50
WHAT A DREAM/I Cried	(Mercury 70416)	1.25	5.00	54
WITH MY EYES WIDE OPEN I'M DREAMING/ My Mother's Eyes	(Mercury 71469)	1.00	4.00	59
WITH MY EYES WIDE OPEN I'M DREAMING/ Oklahoma Blues	(Mercury 5344)	2.00	8.00	49
WOULD I LOVE YOU (LOVE YOU, LOVE YOU)/ Sentimental Music	(Mercury 5571)	1.25	5.00	51
PAGEBOYS, The				
WHEN I MEET A GIRL LIKE YOU/I Have Love	(Seville 135)	.75	3.00	63
PAGE-BOYS, The				
TWIST ENOS TWIST/I Got The Blues Again (With the Starfires)	(Whirl 126)	.75	3.00	
PAGEANTS, The				
SATURDAY ROMANCE/Make You My Queen	(Arlen 731)	3.00	12.00	62
SATURDAY ROMANCE/Make You My Queen (With Tony Dee)	(Du-Well 101)	6.25	25.00	62
PAGEANTS, The				
HAPPY TOGETHER/Why Did You Go	(Goldisc 3013)	7.50	30.00	60
PAGENTS, The				
ENCHANTED SURF/Big Daddy (Instrumental)	(Ike 631)	1.25	5.00	63
PAGES				
I DO BELIEVE IN YOU/Two People	(Epic 50769)	.50	2.00	79
PAIGE, Joey				
SURFER FROM TENNESSEE/ Such Wonderful Dreams	(Warner Bros. 5377)	1.00	4.00	63
PAINTER				
WEST COAST WOMAN/Space Truck	(Elektra 45862)	.50	2.00	73
PAKALAMEREDITH				
THANK YOU BABY/Better Days	(Elektra 45408)	.50	2.00	77
PALACE GUARD, The (Featuring Don Grady)				
ALL NIGHT LONG/Playgirl	(Orange Empire 331)	1.00	4.00	65
FALLING SUGAR/Oh Blue	(Orange Empire 400)	1.00	4.00	66
FALLING SUGAR/Oh Blue	(Verve 10410)	.75	3.00	66
GIRL YOU CAN DEPEND ON, A/If You Need Me	(Orange Empire 332)	1.00	4.00	65
SATURDAY'S CHILD/Party Lights	(Parkway 111)	1.00	4.00	66
SUMMERTIME GAME/Little People	(Orange Empire 9164)	1.00	4.00	67
Also see Yellow Balloon, The				
PALEY BROTHERS,The (With Andy Paley)				
ECSTASY/Hide 'N' Seek	(Sire 1001)	.50	2.00	77
TELL ME TONIGHT/Turn The Tide	(Sire 1033)	.50	2.00	78
YOU'RE THE BEST/Magic Power	(Sire 1021)	.50	2.00	78
PALISADES, The				
CLOSE YOUR EYES/I Can't Quit	(Calico 113)	1.25	5.00	60
DEAR JOAN/The Shrine	(Leader 806)	1.25	5.00	60
MAKE THE NIGHT A LITTLE LONGER/ Heaven Being With You (With Carole King)	(Chairman 4401)	2.00	8.00	63
THIS IS THE NITE/Relic Rock	(Medieval 205)	1.50	6.00	62
PALMER, Odie				
LETTER TO ELVIS, A/All I Can See Is You	(Little Gem 1020)	.50	2.00	77
PALMER, Robert				
BAD CASE OF LOVING YOU (DOCTOR DOCTOR)/ Love Can Run Faster	(Island 49016)	.50	2.00	79
CAN WE STILL BE FRIENDS/Remember To Remember	(Island 29137)	.50	2.00	79
EVERY KINDA PEOPLE/How Much Fun	(Island 100)	.50	2.00	78
GIVE ME AN INCH, GIRL/Pressure Drop	(Island 049)	.50	2.00	76
JEALOUS/In Walks Love Again	(Island 49094)	.50	2.00	79
MAN SMART, WOMAN SMARTER/Keep In Touch	(Island 075)	.50	2.00	76
ONE LAST LOOK/Some People Can Do What They Like	(Island 081)	.50	2.00	77
SNEAKIN' SALLY THROUGH THE ALLEY/Epidemic	(Island 006)	.50	2.00	75
WHICH ONE OF US IS THE FOOL/	(Island 042)	.50	2.00	76
YOU OVERWHELM ME/Come Over	(Island 105)	.50	2.00	78
YOU'RE GONNA GET WHAT'S COMING/Where Can It Go?	(Island 8696)	.50	2.00	78
Also see Bown, Allan				
PALS, The				
MY BABY LIKES TO ROCK/Summer Is Here	(Turf 1000/1)	3.00	12.00	58
MY BABY LIKES TO ROCK/Summer Is Here	(Guyden 2019)	1.50	6.00	59
PAN (With Ron Elliott)				
LADY HONEY/Lady Honey	(Columbia 45806)	1.00	4.00	73
MORE THAN MY GUITAR/More Than My Guitar	(Columbia 45870)	1.00	4.00	73
Also see Beau Brummels, The				
PANDORAS, The				
ABOUT MY BABY/New Day	(Liberty 55945)	1.00	4.00	67
GAMES/Don't Bother	(Liberty 55999)	1.00	4.00	67
PANICS (With Sonny Richards)				
BONY MORONIE/Panicsville	(Chancellor 1109)	.75	3.00	62
KANGAROO, THE/It Ain't What You Got	(Phillips 40230)	1.00	4.00	64
SKINNIE MINNIE OLIVE OIL/Voodoo Walk	(Chancellor 1127)	.75	3.00	62
PAONE, Nicola				
BLAH, BLAH, BLAH/ Ciao, Bellezza (So Long, Beautiful)	(ABC-Paramount 9993)	1.00	4.00	59
HOLD YOUR HORSES/Poor Man's Polka	(ABC-Paramount 10025)	1.00	4.00	59
PRETTY LADY/La Cafettera	(Cadence 1363)	1.00	4.00	59
PAPA DOO RUN RUN				
DISNEY GIRLS/Be True To Your School	(RCA 10404)	1.00	4.00	

TITLE/FLIP	LABEL & NO.	GOOD	NEAR MINT	YR.
PAPER DOLLS, The				
CAUSE I LOVE YOU/You're The Boy I Want To Marry	(MGM 13766)	1.00	4.00	67
PAPER DOLLS, The				
SOMETHING HERE IN MY HEART/ All The Time In The World	(Warner Bros. 7191)	.75	3.00	68
PAPER LACE				
BILLY, DON'T BE A HERO/	(Mercury-Bus Stop 73429)	.50	2.00	74
BLACK-EYED BOYS, THE/Jean	(Mercury-Bus Stop 73694)	.50	2.00	75
NIGHT CHICAGO DIED, THE/Can You Get It When You Want It	(Mercury-Bus Stop 73492)	.50	2.00	74
SO WHAT IF I AM/Himalayan Lullabye	(Merucry-Bus Stop 73694)	.50	2.00	75
PAPER TRAIN, The				
BROTHER/Time Waits For No One	(Capitol 2464)	1.25	5.00	69
PAPPAS, Peter				
SOUND OF ANGELS/The Dive	(RuVal 4503)	1.50	6.00	
PARADE, The				
A.C./D.C./She Sleeps Alone	(A&M 950)	.75	3.00	68
FROG PRINCE/Hallelujah Rocket	(A&M 887)	.75	3.00	67
HALLELUJAH ROCKET/Laughing Lady	(A&M 970)	.75	3.00	67
RADIO SONG, THE/I Can See Love	(A&M 904)	.75	3.00	68
SUNSHINE GIRL/This Old Melody	(A&M 841)	.75	3.00	67
PARADOX				
FUSION/Lost Horizons	(Magna-Glide MGR-332)	.50	2.00	77
PARAKEETS, The				
SHANGRI-LA/Come Back	(Jubilee 5407)	2.00	8.00	61
PARALLELS, The				
SURF-A-NOVA/Da Dipty	(Twilight 405)	1.00	4.00	
SURF-A-NOVA/Da Dipty (Shown as by the Tri-Tones)	(Twilight 405)	1.00	4.00	
PARAMOUNTS, The				
CHRISTOPHER COLUMBUS/I Know You'll Be My Love	(Fleetwood 1014)	2.00	8.00	
GIRL FRIEND/Trying	(Carlton 524)	1.25	5.00	60
JUST TO BE WITH YOU/One More For The Road	(Laurie 3201)	2.00	8.00	63
WHEN YOU DANCE/You're 17	(Dot 16201)	2.00	8.00	60
WHERE'S CAROLYN TONIGHT/When I Dream	(Centaur 103)	1.50	6.00	
PARAMOUNTS, The				
POISON IVY/I Feel Good All Over	(Liverpool Sound 903)	2.50	10.00	64
Also see Procol Harum				

TITLE/FLIP	LABEL & NO.	GOOD	NEAR MINT	YR.
PARAMOURS, The (Bill Medley & Bobby Hatfield)				
CUTIE CUTIE/Miss Social Climber	(Smash 1718)	2.00	8.00	61
THAT'S ALL I WANT TONIGHT/ There She Goes (She's Walking)	(Moonglow 214)	2.00	8.00	62
THAT'S ALL I WANT TONIGHT/ There She Goes (She's Walking) (Red plastic)	(Moonglow 214)	3.00	12.00	62
THAT'S THE WAY WE LOVE/Prison Break	(Smash 1701)	2.00	8.00	61
Also see Righteous Brothers, The				
PARIS (Featuring Bob Welch)				
BIG TOWNE, 2061/	(Capitol 4356)	.75	3.00	76
PARISIANS, The				
WHY/On The Sunny Side Of The Street	(Pova 1004)	1.50	6.00	62
PARISIAN SEXTET, The				
POOR PEOPLE OF PARIS, THE/Don't Let The Stars Get In Your Eyes	(Challenge 9137)	.75	3.00	61
PARIS SISTERS, The (Priscilla, Sherrell, Albeth)				
BE MY BOY/I'll Be Crying Tomorrow	(Gregmark 2)	1.00	4.00	61
DREAM LOVER/Lonely Girl	(MGM 13236)	.75	3.00	64
HE KNOWS I LOVE HIM TOO MUCH/Lonely Girl's Prayer	(Gregmark 10)	1.00	4.00	62
I LOVE HOW YOU LOVE ME/All Through The Night	(Gregmark 6)	1.00	4.00	61
LET ME BE THE ONE/What Am I To Do	(Gregmark 12)	1.00	4.00	62
MY GOOD FRIEND/It's My Party	(Reprise 05111)	.75	3.00	66
OLD ENOUGH TO CRY/Tell Me More	(Imperial 5465)	1.25	5.00	57
SING EVERYTHING UNDER THE SUN/	(Reprise 6259)	.75	3.00	67
SOME OF YOUR LOVIN/	(Reprise 0548)	.75	3.00	67
YES I LOVE YOU/Once Upon A While Ago	(Gregmark 13)	1.00	4.00	62
Also see Crosby, Gary				
PARKAYS, The				
LATE DATE/Get It	(ABC-Paramount 10242)	.75	3.00	61
PARKER, Bobby				
WATCH YOUR STEP/Steal Your Heart Away	(V-Tone 223)	.75	3.00	61
PARKER, Fess				
BALLAD OF DAVY CROCKETT, THE/I Give My Love	(Columbia 40449)	1.25	5.00	55
BALLAD OF DAVY CROCKETT, THE/Farewell	(Disneyland DBR-21)	1.00	4.00	55
BALLAD OF JOHN COLTER/Pioneer's Prayer	(Disneyland 45)	1.00	4.00	57
BE SURE YOU'RE RIGHT (THEN GO AHEAD)/ Old Betsy (With Buddy Ebsen)	(Columbia 40510)	1.25	5.00	55
FAREWELL (From "Davy Crockett")/ I'm Lonely My Darling	(Columbia 40450)	1.25	5.00	55
KING OF THE RIVER/Yaller Yaller Gold	(Columbia 40568)	1.25	5.00	55
WRINGLE WRANGLE/The Ballad Of John Colter	(Disneyland 43)	1.00	4.00	57

TITLE/FLIP	LABEL & NO.	GOOD	NEAR MINT	YR.
PARKER, Gigi, & The Lovelies				
BEATLES PLEASE COME BACK/In This Room	(MGM 13225)	1.25	5.00	64
PARKER, Graham & The Rumor				
HEAT IN HARLEM, THE/Stick To Me	(Mercury 73970)	.50	2.00	77
HEAT TREATMENT/Back Door Love	(Mercury 73876)	.50	2.00	76
HOLD BACK THE NIGHT/(Let Me Get) Sweet On You- White Honey (Live)-Soul Shoes (Live)	(Mercury 74000)	.50	2.00	77
LOCAL GIRLS/I Want You Back	(Arista 0420)	.50	2.00	79
SOUL SHOES/	(Mercury 73834)	.50	2.00	76
PARKER, Richard				
MONKEY ALL OVER/Welcome To Paradise	(Philips 40133)	.75	3.00	63
PARK, Jan, Band				
RUNNIN' AFTER LOVE (MAKIN' IT EASY THIS TIME)/	(Columbia 10942)	.50	2.00	79
PARKS, Michael				
LONG LONESOME HIGHWAY/Mountain High	(MGM 14104)	.75	3.00	70
SALLY (WAS A GENTLE WOMAN)/Say A Little, Spend A Little (Give A Little Away)	(MGM 14154)	.75	3.00	70
TIE ME TO YOUR APRON STRINGS AGAIN/Won't You Ride In My Little Red Wagon	(MGM 14092)	.75	3.00	69
PARKS, Van Dyke				
OCCAPELLA/	(Warner Bros. 7609)	.50	2.00	72
PARKTOWNS, The				
STOP, LOOK & LISTEN/You Hurt Me Inside	(Impels 214)	7.50	30.00	
STOP, LOOK & LISTEN/You Hurt Me Inside	(Thor 3258)	5.00	20.00	
THAT DAY WILL NEVER COME/You Hurt Me Inside	(Crimson 1006)	5.00	20.00	
PARLETTES, The				
TONIGHT I MET AN ANGEL/Because We're Very Young	(Jubilee 5467)	1.50	6.00	63
PARLIAMENTS, The				
YOU'RE CUTE/I'll Get You Yet	(Symbol 917)	2.00	8.00	63
PARRISH & GURVITZ (With Adrian Gurvitz)				
JANINE/I've Got Time	(Decca 32967)	.75	3.00	72
PARSONS, Alan, Project (With Allan Clarke)				
DAMNED IF I DO/If I Could Change Your Mind	(Arista 0454)	.50	2.00	79
DAY AFTER DAY (THE SHOW MUST GO ON)/Breakdown	(Arista 03100)	.50	2.00	78
DON'T LET IT SHOW/I Robot	(Arista 0288)	.50	2.00	77
I WOULDN'T WANT TO BE LIKE YOU/Nucleus	(Arista 0260)	.50	2.00	77
RAVEN, THE/ Prelude To The Fall Of The House Of Usher	(20th Century 2308)	.50	2.00	76
(SYSTEM OF, THE) DOCTOR TARR & PROFESSOR FETHER/ A Dream Within A Dream	(20th Century 2297)	.50	2.00	76
TO ONE IN PARADISE/	(20th Century 2333)	.50	2.00	76
WHAT GOES UP/In The Lap Of The Gods	(Arista 0352)	.50	2.00	78
This band also included former members of Pilot & of Cockney Rebel.				
PARSONS, Bill (Bobby Bare)				
ALL AMERICAN BOY, THE/Rubber Dolly	(Fraternity 835)	2.00	8.00	58
EDUCATED ROCK & ROLL/The Carefree Wanderer	(Fraternity 838)	1.00	4.00	59
PARSONS, Gram				
SHE/That's All It Took	(Reprise 1139)	.75	3.00	73
PARTON, David				
ISN'T SHE LOVELY/Love & Peace Of Mind	(Private Stock 45139)	.50	2.00	77
PARTRIDGE FAMILY, The (Featuring David Cassidy)				
AM I LOSING YOU/If You Ever Go	(Bell 45,200)	.75	3.00	72
BREAKING UP IS HARD TO DO/I'm Here, You're Here	(Bell 45,235)	.75	3.00	72
DOESN'T SOMEBODY WANT TO BE WANTED/ You Are Always On My Mind	(Bell 963)	.75	3.00	71
FRIEND & A LOVER/	(Bell 45,336)	.75	3.00	73
I'LL MEET YOU HALFWAY/Morning Rider On The Road	(Bell 996)	.75	3.00	71
I THINK I LOVE YOU/Somebody Wants To Love You	(Bell 910)	.75	3.00	70
I WOKE UP IN LOVE THIS MORNING/Twenty-Four Hours A Day	(Bell 45,130)	.75	3.00	71
IT'S ONE OF THOSE NIGHTS (YES LOVE)/One Night Stand	(Bell 45,160)	.75	3.00	71
LOOKING THROUGH THE EYES OF LOVE/Storybook Love	(Bell 45,301)	.75	3.00	72
PARTY FAVORS, The				
CHANGED DISPOSITION/You're Not The Marrying Kind	(R.S.V.P. 1109)	2.00	8.00	
PASS, Tony				
SPRING FEVER/True True Love	(Atco 6421)	1.50	6.00	66
PASSIONS, The				
ADHRODITE/I've Gotta Know	(Octavia 8005)	6.25	25.00	62
BEAUTIFUL DREAMER/One Look Is All It Took	(Audicon 108)	2.50	10.00	60
BULLY, THE/The Empty Seat	(ABC-Paramount 10436)	2.50	10.00	63
BULLY, THE/The Empty Seat (Promotional issue)	(ABC-Paramount 10436)	2.00	8.00	63
GLORIA/Jungle Drums	(Audicon 106)	2.00	8.00	60
I ONLY WANT YOU/This Is My Love	(Audicon 105)	2.00	8.00	60
JUST TO BE WITH YOU/Oh Melancholy Me	(Audicon 102)	2.00	8.00	59
LONELY ROAD/One Look	(Jubilee 5406)	2.00	8.00	61
MADE FOR LOVERS/Don't Love Me Any More	(Audicon 112)	2.00	8.00	61
16 CANDLES/The Third Floor	(Diamond 146)	1.50	6.00	63
Also see Saber, Johnny				
PASSIONS, The				
JACKIE BROWN/My Aching Heart	(Capitol 3963)	2.50	10.00	58
PASSPORT				
JU JU MAN/Infinity Machine	(Atco 7054)	.75	3.00	76
MANDRAKE/Loco-Motive	(Atlantic 3487)	.75	3.00	78
PASTEL SIX, The				
BRAHM'S NIGHTMARE/Open House	(Downey 102)	.75	3.00	62
CINNAMON CINDER (IT'S A VERY NICE DANCE)/ Bandido	(Zen 102)	.75	3.00	62
OPEN HOUSE AT THE CINDER/Twitchin'	(Downey 101)	.75	3.00	63
SING-A-LONG SONG, A/The Strange Ghost	(Zenith 105)	.75	3.00	63
TWITCHIN'/Wino Stomp	(Downey 101)	.75	3.00	63
Also see Patterson, Sonny, & the Pastel Six				
PASTRANA, Joey				
MY VICTROLA/Afro Azul	(Cotique 158)	1.00	4.00	
PAT & THE SATELLITES				
JUPITER-C/Oh! Oh! Darlin'	(Atco 6131)	1.00	4.00	59
PAT & THE WILDCATS				
GIGGLER, THE/Green Tomatoes	(Crusader 100)	.75	3.00	64
PATE, Johnnie				
STAY IN THE KNOW/Don't Worry About Me	(Gig 225)	1.25	5.00	56
PATE, Johnny, Quintet				
SWINGING SHEPHERD BLUES/The Elder (Instrumental)	(Federal 12312)	1.00	4.00	57
PATENTS, The				
BLUE SURF/Jumpin' In (Instrumentals)	(Hart-Van 127)	1.00	4.00	63
PATEY BROTHERS, The				
HEY DOLL BABY/Jeanie	(Ron Mar 1004)	1.00	4.00	59

Gene Pitney

Fess Parker

Bobby Pickett

Patti Page

Peter & Gordon

TITLE/FLIP	LABEL & NO.	GOOD	NEAR MINT	YR.

PATIENCE & PRUDENCE (Patience & Prudence McIntyre)
TONIGHT YOU BELONG TO ME (New Version)/
How Can I Tell Him (Chattahoochee 665) .75 3.00 65
TONIGHT YOU BELONG TO ME/Smile & A Ribbon (Liberty 55022) 1.00 4.00 56
GONNA GET ALONG WITHOUT YA NOW/Money Tree, The (Liberty 55040) 1.00 4.00 56
Also see Clifford, Mike

PATRICK, Butch
GYPSY RAINBOW/ (Metromedia 0106) .75 3.00 69

PATTERSON, Mike, & The Fugitives
JERKY/Cookin' Beans (Imperial 66083) .75 3.00 64

PATTERSON, Sonny, & The Pastel Six
TROUBLES/Gone So Long (Vault 903) .75 3.00 63

PATTON, Jimmy
TEEN-AGE HEART/ (Sims 104) .75 3.00 63

PATTON, Robbie
DARLIN'/Never Comin' Down (Backstreet 41105) .50 2.00 79

PATTY & THE EMBLEMS
MIXED-UP, SHOOK-UP GIRL/Ordinary Guy (Herald 590) .75 3.00 64

PATTY CAKES, The
I UNDERSTAND THEM/I Understand Them (Instrumental) (Tuff 378) .75 3.00 64

PATTY FLABBIES COUGHED ENGINE
BILLY'S GOT A GOAT/Tin Can Eater (Diamond D-252) .75 3.00 68

PAUL (Ray Hildebrand)
HEY YOU, WALK WITH ME/Happy Music (Charay 48) 1.00 4.00 66
HEY YOU, WALK WITH ME/Happy Music (Dot 16936) .75 3.00 66
PAPER CLOWN/Patsy (Tower 304) .75 3.00 67
Also see Paul & Paula

PAUL & PAULA (Ray Hildebrand & Jill Jackson)
ALL THESE THINGS/The Wedding (Uni 55052) .75 3.00 68
ANYWAY YOU WANT ME (THAT'S HOW I WILL BE)/
True Love (Philips 40268) .75 3.00 65
BEGINNING OF LOVE/All I Want Is You (LeCam 99) 2.50 10.00 63
CRAZY LITTLE THINGS/We'll Never Break Up For Good (Philips 40168) .75 3.00 64
DEAR PAULA/All The Love (Philips 40296) .75 3.00 65
FIRST DAY BACK AT SCHOOL/Perfect Pair (Philips 40142) .75 3.00 63
FIRST QUARREL/School Is Thru (Philips 40114) .75 3.00 63
HEY PAULA/Bobbie Is The One (Le Cam 979) 3.00 12.00 62
(Shown as by Jill & Ray)
HAY PAULA/Bobby Is The One (Philips 40084) .75 3.00 76
HOLIDAY FOR TEENS/Holiday Hootenanny (Philips 40158) .75 3.00 63
NO OTHER BABY/Too Dark To See (Philips 40234) .75 3.00 64
SOMETHING OLD, SOMETHING NEW/Flipped Over You (Philips 40130) .75 3.00 63
YOUNG LOVERS/Ba-Hey-Be (Philips 40096) .75 3.00 63
YOUNG LOVERS/Ba-Hey-Be (Philips 40096) 1.25 5.00 63
(Picture sleeve)
YOUNG YEARS/Darlin' (Philips 40209) .75 3.00 64

PAULA, Marlene
I WANT TO SPEND CHRISTMAS WITH ELVIS/
Once More It's Xmas (Regent 7506) 2.00 8.00 56

PAULETTE SISTERS, The
YOU WIN AGAIN/Mama El Baion (Capitol 3186) 1.00 4.00 55

PAUL, Henry, Band
CROSSFIRE/ (Atlantic 3578) .50 2.00 79
SO LONG/ (Atlantic 3607) .50 2.00 79
Also see Outlaws, The

PAUL, Les, & Mary Ford
AMUKIRIKI/Magic Melody (Capitol 3248) 1.00 4.00 55
CINCO ROBLES/Ro-Ro-Robinson (Capitol 3612) 1.00 4.00 56
DRY MY TEARS/Cryin' (Capitol 1088) 1.50 6.00 50
(Shown as by Les Paul)
HOW HIGH THE MOON/Walkin' & Whistling (Capitol 1451) 1.25 5.00 51
HUMMINGBIRD/Goodbye, My Love (Capitol 3165) 1.00 4.00 55
I'M A FOOL TO CARE/Auctioneer (Capitol 2839) 1.25 5.00 54
I'M SITTING ON TOP OF THE WORLD/Sleep (Capitol 2400) 1.25 5.00 53
JUST ONE MORE CHANCE/Jazz Me Blues (Capitol 1825) 1.25 5.00 51
MOCKIN' BIRD HILL/Chicken Reel (Capitol 1373) 1.25 5.00 51
MY BABY'S COMING HOME/Lady Of Spain (Capitol 2265) 1.25 5.00 52
NO LETTER TODAY/Genuine Love (With Mary Ford) (Capitol 3108) 1.00 4.00 54
PUT A RING ON MY FINGER/Fantasy (Columbia 41222) 1.00 4.00 58
SMOKE RINGS/In The Good Old Summertime (Capitol 2123) 1.25 5.00 52
STROLLIN' BLUES/I Don't Want You No More (Capitol 3776) 1.00 4.00 57
(Shown as by Les Paul)
TENNESSEE WALTZ/Little Rock Getaway (Capitol 1316) 1.50 6.00 50
VAYA CON DIOS/Johnny (Capitol 2486) 1.25 5.00 53
WORLD IS WAITING FOR THE SUNRISE, THE/Whispering (Capitol 1748) 1.25 5.00 51

PAVLOV'S DOG
JULIA/Episode (Columbia 10152) .50 2.00 76

PAVONE, Rita
BALLO DEL MATTONE/Cuore (RCA Victor 47-8212) .75 3.00 63
HEART/The Man Who Made Music (RCA Victor 47-9051) .75 3.00 66
I DON'T WANT TO BE HURT/Eyes Of Mine (RCA Victor 47-8538) .75 3.00 65
REMEMBER ME/Just Once More (RCA Victor 47-8365) .75 3.00 64
RIGHT NOW/Oh My Mama (RCA Victor 47-8612) .75 3.00 65
WAIT FOR ME/It's Not Easy (RCA Victor 47-8420) .75 3.00 64

PAXTON, Gary (Of Skip & Flip)
BAKERSFIELD/ (Bakersfield Centennial 1001) .75 3.00
CUTE LITTLE COLT/Super Torque (London 5208) 1.00 4.00 64
(With the Road Runners)
DUAL BUMP CAMEL NAMED ROBERT E. LEE/
Your Past Is Back Again (Garpax 44108) .75 3.00 64
IT'S MY WAY (OF LOVING YOU)/
My Heart Won't Let My Lips Say Goodbye (Capitol 5467) .75 3.00 65
KANSAS CITY/Sweet Senorita From Santa Fe (Felsted 8691) .75 3.00 63
SCAVENGER, THE/
How To Be A Fool (In Six Easy Lessons) (Garpax 44177) .75 3.00 63
SPOOKIE MOVIES/Spookie Movies (Part 2) (Liberty 55584) .75 3.00 63
Also see Salles, Jessie, & the Crypt-Kickers
Also see Robbins & Paxton
Also see Hollywood Argyles, The

PAXTON, Tom
JESUS CHRIST, S.R.O./ (Reprise 1110) .50 2.00 71
WHOSE GARDEN WAS THIS/Annie's Going To Sing Her Song (Asylum 45703) .50 2.00 70

PAYNE, Tommy
GO APE/Trouble & Pain (Felsted 8531) 1.50 6.00 58
MY STEADY GIRL/Crusin' Around (XYZ 603) 1.00 4.00 59
SHY BOY/Fire Engine Red Bandanna (Motorcycle Queen) (XYZ 601) 1.00 4.00 59

PEANUT BUTTER CONSPIRACY, The
CAPTAIN SANDWICH/Turn On A Friend (Columbia 44356) 1.00 4.00 67
BARK ON YOU NOW/Then Came Love (Columbia 44063) 1.00 4.00 67
IT'S A HAPPENING THING/Twice Is Life (Columbia 43985) 1.00 4.00 67
TIME IS AFTER YOU/Floating Dream (Vault 933) 1.25 5.00 66

PEARSON, Randy
FLY, JONATHAN, FLY/ (A&M 1383) .50 2.00 73
FLY, JONATHAN, FLY/ (Polydor 14172) .50 2.00 72

PEBBLES & BAMM BAMM
DADDY/The World Is Full Of Joys (For Little Girls & Boys) (HBR 484) .75 3.00 65
OPEN UP YOUR HEART/The Lord Is Counting On You (HBR 449) .75 3.00 65

PEDICIN, Mike
LARGE LARGE HOUSE/Hotter Then A Pistol (RCA Victor 47-6369) 1.00 4.00 56
SHAKE A HAND/Dickie Doo, The (Cameo 125) 1.00 4.00 57

PEDRICK, Bobby, Jr.
COME OUT COME OUT/School Crush (Shell 722) 2.50 10.00 58
DINING & DANCING/Two Ton Tessie (Duel 516) 1.25 5.00
DON'T TRY TO CHANGE MY WAYS/
Teach Myself How To Cry (MGM 13384) 1.25 5.00
I'M SCARED/That Girl Is You (Duel 504) 1.25 5.00
IF MARY ONLY KNEW/If I Had My Life To Live Over (Duel 525) 1.25 5.00
KARINE/Maybe (Verve 10402) 3.75 15.00 66
PAJAMA PARTY/Betty Blue Eyes (Big Top 3008) 1.25 5.00 59
SUMMER NIGHTS/My Private Joy (Big Top 3024) 1.25 5.00 60
WHITE BUCKS & SADDLE SHOES/Stranded (Big Top 3004) 1.00 4.00 58
Also see Bobby & the Consoles

PEEK, Dan (Of America)
ALL THINGS ARE POSSIBLE/Hometown (Lamb & Lion 814) .50 2.00 79
ALL THINGS ARE POSSIBLE/Hometown (Songbird-Firewind 41123) .50 2.00 79
READY FOR LOVE/ (Songbird-Firewind 41160) .50 2.00 79

PEEK, Paul
BROTHER-IN-LAW (HE'S A MOOCHER)/
Through The Teenage Years (Fairlane 702) 1.00 4.00 61
HURTIN' INSIDE/Walking The Floor Over You (NRC 048) 1.00 4.00 60
I'M A HAPPY MAN/Where There's A Will (NRC 059) 1.00 4.00 60
I'M NOT YOUR FOOL ANYMORE/Oldsmo William (NRC 008) 2.50 10.00 58
PIN THE TAIL ON THE DONKEY/
Rockin' Pheumonia & Boogie Woogie Flu (Columbia 43527) .75 3.00 66
ROCK AROUND, THE/Sweet Skinny Jenny (NRC 001) 1.25 5.00 58
SHADOW KNOWS, THE/I'm Moving Uptown (Columbia 43771) .75 3.00 66
SWEET LORRAINE/Out Went The Lights Of My World ("1-2-3" 1714) .75 3.00 69
WAIKIKI BEACH/Gee But I Miss That Girl (NRC 033) 1.00 4.00 59

PEELS, The
JUANITA BANANA/Fun (Karate 522) .75 3.00 66

PEEPS, The
GOT PLENTY OF LOVE/Now Is The Time (Philips 40315) .75 3.00 65

PEERCE, Jan
WHAT IS A BOY?/Because Of You (RCA Victory 47-3425) 1.25 5.00 51

PENDELTONS, The
BAREFOOT ADVENTURE/Board Party (Dot 16511) 1.00 4.00 63

PENDULUM
NOW I'LL CRY/Dead Dog (Kama Sutra 257) 1.25 5.00
SILLY SALLY SUNDAY/I Do You (Kama Sutra 253) 1.25 3.00

PENN, Tonny
I DON'T WANT TO STAY HOME/A King Or Fool (PRI 7016) .75 3.00

PENN, William, & The Quakers
BLOW MY MIND/Swami (Thunderbird 502) 1.25 5.00
(Shown as by the William Penn Fyve)
COMING UP MY WAY/Care Free (Duane 104) 1.25 5.00
GHOST OF THE MONKS/Goodbye My Love (Twilight 410) 1.25 5.00
LITTLE GIRL/Somebody's Dum Dum (Hush 230) 1.25 5.00
PHILLY/Santa Needs Ear Muffs On His Nose (Melron 5024) 1.25 5.00
SWEET CAROLINE/Santa Needs Ear Muffs On His Nose (Melron 5024) 1.25 5.00

PENNA, D.R., The Mississippi Jook Band
MYSTERY TRAIN/Pledging My Love (P&M 392) 2.00 8.00

PENNSYLVANIA PLAYERS, The
WASHINGTON UPTIGHT/The Cat (Oron 101) 1.25 5.00

PENNY ARCADE, The
FRANCINE/Me & My Piano (Weil Levenson with
Anders & Poncia) (United Artists 50221) 2.00 8.00 68
TEARS IN MY HEART/The Bubble Gum Tree (Smash 2190) 1.00 4.00 68

PENNY, Paul
CHANGE IN PLANS/True Fine Mama (Jam 108) .75 3.00

PENTAGONS, The
I LIKE THE WAY YOU LOOK (AT ME)/
For A Love That Is Mine (Donna 1344) 1.00 4.00 61
I WONDER/She's Mine (Jamie 1201) 1.00 4.00 61
I'M IN LOVE/Until Then (Jamie 1210) 1.00 4.00 62
TO BE LOVED (FOREVER)/Down At The Beach (Donna 1337) 1.00 4.00 61
TO BE LOVED (FOREVER)/Down At The Beach (Fleet Int'l 100) 2.00 8.00 61

PENTANGLE
LET NO MAN STEAL YOUR TYME/Way Behind The Sun (Reprise 0784) .75 3.00 68
SALLY GO ROUND THE ROSES/Light Flight (Reprise PRO 391) 1.00 4.00 68
(Promotional issue only)

PEOPLE (With Larry Norman)
APPLE CIDER/Ashes Of Me (Capitol 2251) 1.00 4.00 68
CHANT FOR PEACE/I Don't Carry No Guns (Polydor 14087) 1.00 4.00 71
FOR WHAT IT'S WORTH/Maple Street (Paramount 0019) 1.00 4.00 70
I LOVE YOU/Somebody Tell Me My Name (Capitol 2078) 1.00 4.00 68
LOVE WILL TAKE US HIGHER & HIGHER/Livin' It Up (Paramount 0005) 1.00 4.00 69
ONE CHAIN DON'T MAKE NO PRISON/Keep It Alive (Paramount 0028) 1.00 4.00 70
ORGAN GRINDER/Riding High (Capitol 5920) 2.00 8.00 67
SUNSHINE LADY/Crosstown Bus (Paramount 0011) 1.00 4.00 69
TURNIN' ME IN/Ulla (Capitol 2499) 1.00 4.00 69
ULLA/Turnin' Me In (Capitol 2449) 1.00 4.00 69

PEPE & THE ASTROS
JUDY, MY LOVE/Now, Ain't That A Shame (Swami 554) 6.25 25.00

PEPPER POTS, The
RUBY DUBY DU/Leatherjacket Cowboy (Panlin 7320) .75 3.00 60

PEPPERMINT, Danny, & The Jumping Jacks (With Danny Lamego)
PEPPERMINT TWIST, THE/
Somebody Else Is Taking My Place (Carlton 565) .75 3.00 61

PEPPERMINT RAINBOW, The
DON'T WAKE ME UP IN THE MORNING, MICHAEL/
Rosemary (Decca 32498) .75 3.00 69
PINK LEMONADE/Walking In Different Circles (Decca 32316) .75 3.00 68
WILL YOU BE STAYING AFTER SUNDAY/
And I'll Be There (Decca 32410) .75 3.00 68

PEPPERMINTS, The
PEPPERMINT JERK/We All Warned You (RSVP 1112) .75 3.00 65
TEEN AGE IDOL/Believe Me (House of Beauty 1) 1.00 4.00 59

PEPPERMINT TROLLEY COMPANY, The
BABY, YOU COME ROLLING ACROSS MY MIND/
9 O'Clock Business Man (Acta 815) .75 3.00 68
BEAUTIFUL SUN/I've Got To Be Going (Acta 813) .75 3.00 68
LOLLIPOP TRAIN/Bored To Tears (Valiant 752) 1.00 4.00
TRUST/I Remember Long Ago (Acta 829) .75 3.00 68

PERCELLS, The
I STAND ALONE/The Greatest (ABC-Paramount 10516) .75 3.00 63
LOOK AT THAT GUY/Boy Friends (ABC-Paramount 10449) .75 3.00 63
MY GUY/Hully Gully Guitar (ABC-Paramount 10476) .75 3.00 63
WHAT ARE BOYS MADE OF/Cheek To Cheek (ABC-Paramount 10401) .75 3.00 63

PERFECTIONS, The
AM I GONNA LOSE YOU/I Love You, My Love (SVR 1005) 1.00 4.00
HEY GIRL/My Baby (Yellow plastic) (Lost Nite 111) 1.25 5.00

PERFECT STRANGERS, The
TAKE A CHANCE/I Will Always Wait For You (Capitol 5607) 1.50 6.00 66

PERFIDIANS, The
WHIPLASH/La Paz (Husky 1) 1.00 4.00 62
(Instrumentals)

PERICOLI, Emilio
AL DI LA/Sassi (Warner Bros. 5259) .75 3.00 62

PERIDOTS, The
HULLY GULLY ALL NITE LONG/It's The Bomp (Deauville 100) .75 3.00 61

PERISCOPES, The
BEAVER SHOT/I'm Happy To Be (W.D.R. 2274) 1.00 4.00 65

PERKINS, Joe
LITTLE EEFIN ANNIE/Uncle Eeef (Sound Stage 7 2511) .75 3.00 63

PERKINS, Reggie
DATE BAIT BABY/High School Caesar (Note 9) 1.00 4.00 59

PERKINS, Tony
MOONLIGHT SWIM/She Used To Be My Girl (RCA Victor 47-7020) 1.00 4.00 57
WHEN SCHOOL STARTS AGAIN/Rocket To The Moon (RCA Victor 47-7078) 1.00 4.00 57

PERMANENTS, The
LET ME BE BABY/Oh Dear, What Can The Matter Be (Chairman 4405) 1.00 4.00 63

PERPETUAL MOTION WORK SHOP, The
INFILTRATE YOUR MIND/Won't Come Down (Rally 66506) 1.00 4.00

PERRY, Frank
SANTA'S CAUGHT ON THE FREEWAY/Young & Innocent (Belle 251) 1.00 4.00 59

PERRY SISTERS, The
FABIN/Willie Boy (Decca 30910) 1.00 4.00 60
PLAYBOY/Blue Highway (Decca 31006) 1.00 4.00 59

PERSIANS, The
GET A HOLD OF YOURSELF/Steady Kind (Pageant P-601) 1.00 4.00 63
(LET'S MONKEY) AT THE PARTY/Let's Get Married (Goldisc 17) 1.00 4.00 63
(LET'S MONKEY) AT THE PARTY/Let's Get Married (Music World MW-102) 1.25 5.00 63
SUNDAY KIND OF LOVE/When We Get Married (RTO 100) 1.00 4.00 62
TEARS OF LOVE/Dance Now (RSVP 114) 2.00 8.00 62
VAULT OF MEMORIES/Teardrops Are Falling (Goldisc 1) 1.50 6.00 63

PERSONALITIES, The
WOE WOE BABY/Yours To Command (Safari 1002) 7.50 30.00 57

PERSUADERS, The (The Hollywood Persuaders)
TIJUANA SURF/Grunion Run (Original Sound 39) .75 3.00 63
(Instrumentals)

PERSUADERS, The (Featuring Chuck "Tequila" Rio)
SURFING STRIP/Hanging Ten (Saturn 404) 1.50 6.00 63
(Instrumentals)

PERSUASIONS, The
BIG BROTHER/Deep Down Love (Tower 197) 1.00 4.00 66

PETE & VINNIE (Pete Anders & Vinnie Poncia)
HAND CLAPPIN' TIME (PART 1)/
Hand Clappin' Time (Part 2) (Big Top 3155) 1.25 5.00 63

PETER & GORDON (Peter Asher & Gordon Waller)
DON'T PITY ME/Crying In The Rain (Capitol 5532) .75 3.00 65
I CAN REMEMBER (NOT TOO LONG AGO)/
Hard Time, Rainy Day (Capitol 2544) .75 3.00 69
I DON'T WANT TO SEE YOU AGAIN/
I Would Buy You Presents (Capitol 5272) .75 3.00 64
I DON'T WANT TO SEE YOU AGAIN/Woman (Capitol 6155) .75 3.00 70
I GO TO PIECES/Love Me, Baby (Capitol 5335) .75 3.00 65
JOKERS, THE/Red, Cream & Velvet (Capitol 5919) .75 3.00 67
KNIGHT IN RUSTY ARMOUR/Flower Lady (Capitol 5808) .75 3.00 66
LADY GODIVA/Morning's Call (Capitol 5740) .75 3.00 66
NEVER EVER/Greener Days (Capitol 2071) .75 3.00 68
NOBODY I KNOW/You Don't Have To Tell Me (Capitol 5211) .75 3.00 64
NOBODY I KNOW/World Without Love (Capitol 6076) .75 3.00 74
SUNDAY FOR TEA/Hurtin' Is Lovin' (Capitol 5864) .75 3.00 67
THERE'S NO LIVIN' WITHOUT YOUR LOVIN'/
Stranger With A Black Dove (Capitol 5650) .75 3.00 66
TO KNOW YOU IS TO LOVE YOU/I Told You So (Capitol 5461) .75 3.00 65
TO SHOW I LOVE YOU/Start Trying Someone Else (Capitol 5684) .75 3.00 66
TRUE LOVE WAYS/If You Wish (Capitol 5406) .75 3.00 65
WOMAN/Wrong From The Start (Capitol 5579) .75 3.00 66
WORLD WITHOUT LOVE, A/If I Were You (Capitol 5175) .75 3.00 64
WRONG FROM THE START/You've Lost That Lovin'
Feelin' (By The Lettermen) (Capitol Creative Prod. 51) 1.00 4.00 66
(Special products, Fritos giveaway item)
YOU'VE HAD BETTER TIMES/Sippin' My Wine (Capitol 2214) .75 3.00 68

PETER G. & PATTY
WHISTLER, THE/Peter Good Private Eye (Shirley 105) 3.00 12.00

PETERIK, Jim (Of The Ides Of March)
CLOSEST THING TO MY MIND/ (Epic 50406) .50 2.00 76

PETER, PAUL & MARY (Peter Yarrow, Paul Stookey & Mary Travers)
A' SOALIN'/Hush-A-Bye (Warner Bros. 5402) .75 3.00 63
BIG BOAT/Tiny Sparrow (Warner Bros. 5325) .75 3.00 62
BLOWIN' IN THE WIND/Flora (Warner Bros. 5368) .75 3.00 63
CRUEL WAR, THE/Mon Vrai Destin (Warner Bros. 5809) .75 3.00 66
DAY IS DONE/Make Believe Town (Warner Bros. 7279) .75 3.00 69
DON'T THINK TWICE, IT'S ALL RIGHT/
Autumn To May (Warner Bros. 5385) .75 3.00 63
DON'T THINK TWICE, IT'S ALL RIGHT/
For Lovin' Me (Warner Bros. 7142) .75 3.00 72
EARLY MORNING RAIN/The Rising Of The Moon (Warner Bros. 5659) .75 3.00 65
FOR BABY (FOR BOBBIE)/Hurry Sundown (Warner Bros. 5883) .75 3.00 66
FOREVER YOUNG/Best Of Friends (Warner Bros. 8728) .75 3.00 78
FOR LOVIN' ME/Monday Morning (Warner Bros. 5496) .75 3.00 65
I DIG ROCK & ROLL MUSIC/
Great Mandella (Wheel Of Life) (Warner Bros. 7067) .75 3.00 67
IF I HAD A HAMMER/Gone The Rainbow (Warner Bros. 5296) .75 3.00 62
LEAVING ON A JET PLANE/The House Song (Warner Bros. 7340) .75 3.00 69

TITLE/FLIP	LABEL & NO.	GOOD	NEAR MINT	YR.
LEMON TREE/Early In The Morning	(Warner Bros. 5274)	.75	3.00	62
LEAVING ON A JET PLANE/Day Is Done	(Warner Bros. 7132)	.75	3.00	70
LIKE THE FIRST TIME/Best Of Friends	(Warner Bros. 8684)	.75	3.00	78
OH, ROCK MY SOUL (PART 1)/ Oh, Rock My Soul (Part 2)	(Warner Bros. 5442)	.75	3.00	64
OTHER SIDE OF THIS LIFE, THE/Sometime Lovin'	(Warner Bros. 5849)	.75	3.00	66
PUFF (THE MAGIC DRAGON)/Pretty Mary	(Warner Bros. 5348)	.75	3.00	63
SETTLE DOWN/500 Miles	(Warner Bros. 5334)	.75	3.00	63
STEWBALL/Cruel War	(Warner Bros. 5399)	.75	3.00	63
TELL IT ON THE MOUNTAIN/Old Coat	(Warner Bros. 5418)	.75	3.00	64
TOO MUCH OF NOTHING/House Song	(Warner Bros. 7092)	.75	3.00	67
WHEN THE SHIP COMES IN/ The Times, They Are A Changing	(Warner Bros. 5625)	.75	3.00	65
YESTERDAY'S TOMORROW/ Love City (Postcard To Duluth)	(Warner Bros. 7232)	.75	3.00	68
PETERS, Bernadette				
GEE WHIZ (LOOK AT HIS EYES)/	(MCA 41210)	.50	2.00	80
WHEN I HEAR OUR SONG/ And The Trouble With You Is Me	(ABC 10726)	.75	3.00	65
YOU'RE TAKIN' ME FOR GRANTED/ Will You Care What's Hap'nin' To Me	(Columbia 44106)	.75	3.00	67
PETERSON, Bobby, Quintet				
HUNCH, THE/Love You Pretty Baby	(V-Tone 205)	1.00	4.00	59
IRRESISTABLE YOU/Piano Rock	(V-Tone 214)	1.00	4.00	60
PETERSON, Paul				
AMY/Goody Goody	(Colpix 676)	.75	3.00	63
CHEER LEADER, THE/Polka Dots & Moonbeams	(Colpix 707)	.75	3.00	63
GIRLS IN THE SUMMERTIME/Mama Your Little Boy Fell	(Colpix 697)	.75	3.00	63
HEY THERE BEAUTIFUL/Where Is She	(Colpix 730)	.75	3.00	64
KEEP YOUR LOVE LOCKED (DEEP IN YOUR HEART)/ Be Everything To Anyone	(Colpix 632)	.75	3.00	62
LITTLE BIT FOR SANDY, A/ Our Love's Got Me Burnin' Alive	(Motown 1129)	.75	3.00	68
LITTLE DREAMER/Happy	(Colpix 763)	.75	3.00	65
LOLLIPOPS & ROSES/Please Mr. Sun	(Colpix 649)	.75	3.00	62
MY DAD/Little Boy Sad	(Colpix 663)	.75	3.00	62
RING, THE/	(Colpix 785)	.75	3.00	65
SHE CAN'T FIND HER KEYS/Very Unlikely	(Colpix 620)	.75	3.00	62
SHE RIDES WITH ME/Poorest Boy In Town (With the Beach Boys)	(Colpix 720)	3.75	15.00	64
PETERSON, Paul, & Shelly Fabares				
WHAT DID THEY DO BEFORE ROCK & ROLL/Very Unlikely	(Colpix 631)	1.00	4.00	62
PETERSON, Ray				
ACROSS THE STREET/When I Stop Dreaming	(MGM 13299)	.75	3.00	64
CORINNA, CORINNA/Be My Girl	(Dunes 2002)	1.00	4.00	60
GOODNIGHT MY LOVE/Till Then	(RCA Victor 47-7635)	1.00	4.00	59
GIVE US YOUR BLESSING/Without Love	(Dunes 2025)	1.00	4.00	63
HOUSE WITHOUT WINDOWS, A/ Wish I Could Say No To You	(MGM 13336)	.75	3.00	65
I COULD HAVE LOVED YOU SO WELL/ Why Don't You Write Me	(Dunes 2009)	1.00	4.00	61
I FORGOT WHAT IT WAS LIKE/Be My Girl	(Dunes 2027)	1.00	4.00	63
I'M NOT JIMMY/A Love To Remember	(Dunes 2022)	1.00	4.00	63
I'M ONLY HUMAN/Oh Lonesome Rose	(MGM 13388)	.75	3.00	65
IF ONLY TOMORROW/You Didn't Care	(Dunes 2018)	1.00	4.00	62
IF YOU WERE HERE/Oh No	(MGM 13269)	.75	3.00	64
LOVE RULES THE WORLD/Together	(Reprise 0811)	.75	3.00	69
LET'S TRY ROMANCE/Shirley Purley	(RCA Victor 47-7165)	1.00	4.00	58
MISSING YOU/You Thrill Me	(Dunes 2006)	1.00	4.00	61
MY BLUE ANGEL/Come & Get It	(RCA Victor 47-7578)	1.00	4.00	59
MY BLUE ANGEL/I'm Tired	(RCA Victor 47-7845)	.75	3.00	61
OH NO/If You Were Here	(MGM 13269)	.75	3.00	64
PROMISES/Sweet Little Kathy	(Dunes 2030)	1.00	4.00	63
RICHER THAN I/Love Is A Woman	(RCA Victor 47-7404)	.75	3.00	63
SWEET LITTLE KATHY/You Didn't Care	(Dunes 2004)	1.00	4.00	61
TEENAGE HEARTACHE/I'll Always Want You Near	(RCA Victor 47-7779)	1.00	4.00	60
TELL LAURA I LOVE HER/Wedding Day	(RCA Victor 47-7745)	1.00	4.00	60
TELL LAURA I LOVE HER/Wedding Day (Stereo single issue)	(RCA Victor 47-7745)	2.00	8.00	60
UNCHAINED MELODY/That's All	(MGM 13330)	.75	3.00	65
WHERE ARE YOU/Deep Are The Roots	(Dunes 2024)	1.00	4.00	63
WONDER OF YOU, THE/I'm Gone	(RCA Victor 47-7513)	1.00	4.00	59
WONDER OF YOU, THE/Goodnight My Love	(RCA Victor 47-8333)	.75	3.00	64
YOU KNOW ME MUCH TOO WELL/You Didn't Care	(Dunes 2013)	1.00	4.00	62
PETITE TEENS, The				
MY SINGING IDOL & POOR LITTLE FOOL/ We're In Our Teens	(Brunswick 55119)	1.25	5.00	59
PETITES, The				
GET YOUR DADDY'S CAR TONIGHT/Sun Showers	(Columbia 41662)	1.00	4.00	60
I'M GONNA LOVE HIM/Is 13 Too Young To Fall In Love	(Ascot 2166)	1.50	6.00	64
MARGUERITE/	(Spinning 6003)	1.25	5.00	58
SWEETIE PIE/Who Kicked The Light Plug Out Of The Socket	(Spinning 6005)	1.25	5.00	58
PETRICOIN, Barry, & The Belairs				
PRETTY LITTLE ANGEL/Come Back To Sorrento	(Al-Stan 103)	1.50	6.00	
PETRIFIED FOREST				
SO MYSTIFYING/ She's The Only Thing That Keeps Me Going	(Fontana 1596)	.75	3.00	67
PETS, The				
CHA-HUA-HUA/Cha-Kow-Ski	(Arwin 109)	1.00	4.00	58
PETTICOATS, The				
SURFIN' SALLY/Why Does Billy Play in Your Yard	(Challenge 9211)	1.00	4.00	63
PETTY, Frank, Trio				
DOWN YONDER/Precious	(MGM 11057)	1.25	5.00	51
RAIN/A Precious Little Thing Called Love	(MGM 8016)	1.25	5.00	50
PETTY, Norman, Trio				
ALMOST PARADISE/It's Been A Long Long	(Nor-Va-Jak 1316)	1.50	6.00	57
ALMOST PARADISE/It's Been A Long Long	(ABC-Paramount 9787)	1.00	4.00	57
CANDLES IN THE WIND/Little Black Samba	(Nor-Va-Jak 1322)	1.25	5.00	58
FIND ME A GOLDEN STREET/Weird	(Norman 500)	1.25	5.00	60
FIRST KISS, THE/The First Kiss	(Columbia 40929)	1.00	4.00	57
HEY! GOOD LOOKIN'/Oh You Pretty Woman	("X" 130)	1.25	5.00	55
MOOD INDIGO/On The Alamo (Featuring Vi Petty, wife of Norman)	(Felsted 8647)	.75	3.00	61
MOOD INDIGO/Petty's Little Polka	("X" 0040)	1.50	6.00	54
MOONDREAMS/ (With Buddy Holly on guitar)	(Columbia 41039)	5.00	20.00	57
SOLITUDE/Darkness On The Delta	("X" 0167)	1.25	5.00	55
THREE LITTLE KISSES/Wonder Why	("X" 0104)	1.25	5.00	55
PETTY, Tom, & The Heartbreakers				
AMERICAN GIRL/	(Shelter 62007)	.50	2.00	77
BREAKDOWN/Fooled Again (I Don't Like It)	(Shelter 62008)	.50	2.00	77
DON'T DO ME LIKE THAT/Casa Dega	(Backstreet 41138)	.50	2.00	79
I NEED TO KNOW/No Second Thoughts	(Shelter 62010)	.50	2.00	78
LISTEN TO HER HEART/I Don't Know What To Say To You	(Shelter 62011)	.50	2.00	78
Also see Mudcrutch				
PEWTER, Jim: see James, Deviny				
PEYTON, Dori				
RINGO BOY/In The Spring Of The Year	(Ohio 101)	1.25	5.00	64
PEZBAND				
BABY IT'S COLD OUTSIDE/Princess Mary	(Passport 7909)	.50	2.00	77
P.F.M. (PREMIATA FORNERIA MARCONI)				
CELEBRATION/	(Manticore 2002)	.75	3.00	73
CELEBRATION/	(Manticore 7003)	.50	2.00	75
PHAETONS, The (With Dean Torrance)				
BEATLE WALK, THE/ Frantic (Instrumental by the Premiers)	(Sahara 103)	1.50	6.00	
PHANTOM, The				
CALM BEFORE THE STORM/Black Magic, White Magic	(Hideout 1080)	1.25	5.00	
WHISPERING/Five Foot Two, Eyes Of Blue	(Capitol 45-4055)	1.25	5.00	58
PHANTOM OF ROCK, The (Wayne Stierle)				
ROCK ERA, THE (PART 1)/Rock Era (Part 2)	(Patti 1000)	1.25	5.00	70
PHANTOMS, The				
NIGHT THEME/Night Beat	(Original Sound 11)	.75	3.00	60
PHARAOS				
TENDER TOUCH/Heads Up, High Hopes Over You	(Donna 1327)	1.25	5.00	60
PHAROS, The				
RHYTHM SURFER/Pintor	(Del Fi 4208)	1.00	4.00	63
PHASE THREE				
LISSY/His Song	(Karmil 2500)	1.00	4.00	
PHEASANTS, The				
OUT OF THE MIST/Hot Biscuits	(Throne 802)	1.50	6.00	
PHILADELPHIANS, The				
COMING HOME TO YOU/Church Bells	(Campus 103)	1.00	4.00	62
DEAR/The Love That I Lost	(Campus 101)	1.00	4.00	62
VOW, THE/I Missed Her	(Cameo 216)	1.00	4.00	62
PHIL & DEL				
MY GIRL/Don't Play With Love	(Linda 105)	.75	3.00	62
PHIL & THE FRANTICS				
I MUST RUN/Pain	(Rabbitt 1219)	1.00	4.00	
SAY THAT YOU WILL/Till You Get What You Want	(ARA 1968)	1.00	4.00	
SHE'S MY GAL/Koko Joe	(La Mar 100)	1.00	4.00	
PHILIP & STEPHAN (Phil Sloan & Steve Barri)				
MEET ME TONIGHT LITTLE GIRL/When You're Near	(Interphon 7711)	1.25	5.00	64
PHILIPS, Terry				
HANDS OF A FOOL/My Foolish Ways	(V.A. 351)	12.50	50.00	
PHILLIPS, John (Of The Mamas & The Papas)				
GREEN-EYED LADY/	(Atco 6960)	.50	2.00	74
MISSISSIPPI/April Anne	(Dunhill 4236)	.50	2.00	70
REVOLUTION ON VACATION/	(Columbia 45737)	.50	2.00	73
PHILLIPS, Michelle (Of The Mamas & The Papas)				
ACHING KIND/Lady Of Fantasy	(A&M 1996)	.50	2.00	78
ALOHA LOUIE/	(A&M 1740)	.50	2.00	75
NO LOVE TODAY/Aloha Louie	(A&M 1824)	.50	2.00	76
VICTIM OF ROMANCE/	(A&M 2012)	.50	2.00	78
PHILLIPS, Phil				
DON'T LEAVE ME/Providing	(Mercury 71550)	1.00	4.00	60
NOBODY KNOWS & NOBODY CARES/ Come Back My Darling	(Mercury 71657)	1.00	4.00	60
SEA OF LOVE/Juella (With the Twilights)	(Khourys 711)	12.50	50.00	59
SEA OF LOVE/Juella (With the Twilights)	(Mercury 71465)	1.00	4.00	59
VERDIE MAE/Take This Heart	(Mercury 71531)	1.00	4.00	59
WHAT WILL I TELL MY HEART/ Your True Love Once More	(Mercury 71611)	1.00	4.00	60
PHILLIPS, Shawn				
DO YOU WONDER/Summer Vignette	(A&M 1750)	.50	2.00	75
LOST HORIZON/Landscape	(A&M 1405)	.50	2.00	73
NEW FRANKIE & JOHNNIE SONG, THE/Cloudy Summer	(Ascot 2152)	.50	2.00	64
WE/	(A&M 1402)	.75	3.00	73
PIAF, Edith				
LA VIE EN ROSE/The Three Bells (Not by Piaf)	(Columbia 776)	1.25	5.00	50
LA VIE EN ROSE/Un Refrain Courait Dans La Rue	(Columbia 743)	1.25	5.00	50
MILORD/	(Capitol 4493)	1.00	4.00	61
PICARDY				
5:30 PLANE/In The Name Of You	(Dunhill 4140)	.75	3.00	68
PICKARD, George				
ELVIS THE MAN FROM TUPELO/ Elvis The Man From Tupelo	(Bar-Tone 77169)	.75	3.00	77
PICKETT, Bobby "Boris"				
GRADUATION DAY/The Humpty Dumpty	(Garpax 44175)	1.00	4.00	63
I'M DOWN TO MY LAST HEARTBREAK/I Can't Stop	(Garpax 724)	1.00	4.00	
ME & MY MUMMY/ It's Not The Same Without You (With Joan Payne)	(Metromedia 0089)	.75	3.00	68
ME & MY MUMMY/ It's Not The Same Without You (With Joan Payne)	(Metromedia 9989)	.50	2.00	73
MONSTER CONCERT/	(Anthem 205)	1.00	4.00	
MONSTER MASH/Monster's Mash Party (With the Crypt-Kickers)	(Garpax 1)	1.50	6.00	62
MONSTER MASH/Monsters' Mash Party (With the Crypt-Kickers)	(Garpax 44167)	.75	3.00	62
MONSTER MASH/Monsters' Mash Party (With the Crypt-Kickers)	(Parrot 348)	.50	2.00	73
MONSTER SWIM/Werewolf Watusi	(RCA Victor 47-8312)	1.00	4.00	64
MONSTERS' HOLIDAY/Monster Motion	(Garpax 44175)	1.00	4.00	62
SIMON THE SENSIBLE SURFER/Simon Says "So What"	(Capitol 5063)	1.25	5.00	63
SMOKE SMOKE SMOKE/Gotta Leave This Town	(RCA Victor 47-8312)	1.00	4.00	64
Also see Ferrara, Peter & Bobby Pickett				
PICKETTYWITCH				
THAT SAME OLD FEELING/Maybe We've Loved Too Long	(Janus 118)	.50	2.00	70
PICKLEDISH, Thorndike: see Thorndike Pickledish				
PICONE, Vito (Of The Elegants)				
PATH IN THE WILDERNESS/Get On The Right Track	(IPG 1016)	1.00	4.00	63
SONG FROM THE MOULIN ROUGE/I Like To Run	(Admiral 103)	2.00	8.00	63
STILL WATERS RUN DEEP/Bolt Of Lightning (Shown as by Vito)	(Admiral 302)	3.00	12.00	63
PIECES OF EIGHT, The (Formerly The Swingin' Medallions)				
COME BACK GIRL/T.N.T.	(A&M 879)	.75	3.00	67
I'D PAY THE PRICE (PART 1)/I'd Pay The Price (Part 2)	(Mala 12024)	.75	3.00	68
LONELY DRIFTER/Who's Afraid Of Virginia Woolf	(A&M 854)	.75	3.00	67
PIERCE, Alan				
SWAMPWATER/The Growl	(Challenge 59093)	1.00	4.00	60
PIERCE ARROW (With David Buskin & David Batteaux)				
CAN'T BREAK THE HABIT/Everyday, Everynight	(Columbia 10833)	.50	2.00	78
IF I COULD BE WITH YOU/Take This Heart	(Columbia 10581)	.50	2.00	77
I LOVE YOU MORE EACH DAY/	(Columbia 10639)	.50	2.00	77
PIERMEN, The				
PIERMEN STOMP, THE/Nancy (Instrumental)	(Jesse 1000)	1.00	4.00	62
PIERSOL, Jeannie				
GLADYS/With Your Love	(Cadet Concept 7003)	1.00	4.00	
NEST, THE/Your Sweet Inner Self	(Cadet Concept 7012)	1.00	4.00	
PIERSON, Con, & The Ekhoes				
I HEARD THOSE BELLS/Six Pretty Gals	(Le Mans 007)	2.00	8.00	
PIGLETS, THE (With Jonathan King)				
THIS IS REGGAE/Blanket Coverage	(UK 49001)	.75	3.00	72
PILLAR, Dick, & The Orchestra				
BEATLE SONG/Johnny's Polka	(Steljo 602)	1.25	5.00	
PILOT				
RIDER/	(RCA 0770)	.50	2.00	72
PILOT				
CANADA/	(EMI 4305)	.50	2.00	76
GET UP & GO/One Good Reason Why	(Arista 0259)	.50	2.00	77
JANUARY/Do Me Good	(EMI 4202)	.50	2.00	76
JUST A SMILE/Don't Speak Loudly	(EMI 4135)	.50	2.00	75
MAGIC/Just Let Me Be	(EMI 3992)	.50	2.00	75
PILTDOWN MEN, The				
BRONTOSAURUS STOMP/McDonald's Cave	(Capitol 4414)	.75	3.00	60
FOSSIL ROCK/Gargantua	(Capitol 4581)	.75	3.00	61
GOODNIGHT MRS. FLINTSTONE/The Great Imposter	(Capitol 4501)	.75	3.00	61
NIGHT SURFIN'/Tequila Bossa Nova	(Capitol 4875)	.75	3.00	62
PILTDOWN RIDES AGAIN/Bubbles In The Tar	(Capitol 4460)	.75	3.00	60
PRETTY GIRL IS LIKE A MELODY/Big Lizzard (Instrumentals)	(Capitol 4703)	.75	3.00	62
PINAFORES, The				
I DON'T CARE WHAT ANYONE SAYS/ It Only Happens In The Movies	(Capitol 4818)	.75	3.00	62
PINA, Johnny				
GOODBYE TO HILLSIDE HIGH/	(Dimension 1030)	.75	3.00	64
PINARD, Henry & The Three Ds: see Three Ds, The				
PINERA, Mike (Of Thee Image)				
ALONE WITH YOU/	(Capricorn 0288)	.50	2.00	78
CAN'T YOU BELIEVE/I Am The Bubble	(SRI 00002)	.50	2.00	79
PINETOPPERS, The				
MOCKIN' BIRD HILL/Flying Eagle Polka	(Coral 64061)	1.25	5.00	51
PINK FLOYD				
FEARLESS/One Of These Days	(Capitol 3240)	.75	3.00	71
FLAMING/The Gnome	(Tower 378)	1.25	5.00	67
FREE FOUR/Stay	(Captiol 3391)	.75	3.00	72
HAVE A CIGAR/Welcome to The Machine	(Columbia 10248)	.50	2.00	75
LET THERE BE MORE LIGHT/Remember A Day	(Tower 440)	1.25	5.00	68
MONEY/Any Colour You Like	(Harvest 3609)	.50	2.00	73
SEE EMILY PLAY/Scarecrow	(Tower 356)	1.25	5.00	67
TIME/Us & Them	(Harvest 3832)	.50	2.00	74
PINK LADY (Mie & Kei)				
DANCING IN THE HALLS OF LOVE/	(Elektra-Curb 46524)	.50	2.00	79
KISS IN THE DARK/Walk Away Renee	(Elektra-Curb 46040)	.50	2.00	79
PINKERTON'S (ASSORTED) COLOURS				
MIRROR, MIRROR/She Don't Care	(Parrot 9820)	.75	3.00	65
PIN UPS, The				
KENNY/Lookin For Boys	(Stork 1)	1.25	5.00	
PIPER				
CAN'T WAIT/	(A&M 1969)	.50	2.00	77
PIPKINS, The				
GIMME DAT DING/To Love You	(Capitol 2819)	.50	2.00	70
SUGAR'N'SPICE/Yakety Yak	(Capitol 2874)	.75	3.00	70
PIRATES, The				
SHAKIN' ALL OVER/Saturday Night Shoot Out	(Warner Bros. 8718)	.50	2.00	78
Also see Kidd, Johnny, & the Pirates				
PITCH PIKES, The				
ZING ZING/Never Never Land	(Mercury 71099)	2.50	10.00	57
PITMAN, Barbara				
EVERLASTING LOVE/Cold, Cold Heart	(Phillips Int'l 3527)	1.50	6.00	59
TWO YOUNG FOOLS IN LOVE/ I'm Getting Better All The Time	(Phillips Int'l. 3518)	1.50	6.00	58
PITNEY, Gene				
BABY AIN'T THAT FINE/Everybody Knows But You & Me (With Melba Montgomery)	(Musicor 1135)	.75	3.00	65
BABY, YOUR MY KIND OF WOMAN/Hate	(Musicor 1348)	.75	3.00	69
BACKSTAGE/Blue Color	(Musicor 1171)	.75	3.00	66
BIG JOB/Your Old Standby (With George Jones)	(Musicor 1115)	.75	3.00	65
BILLY, YOU'RE MY FRIEND/Lonely Drifter	(Musicor 1331)	.75	3.00	68
CALIFORNIA/Playing Games Of Love	(Musicor 1361)	.75	3.00	69
CLASSICAL ROCK & ROLL/Faithful Our Love (Duet with Ginny Arnell, shown as by Jamie & Jane.)	(Decca 30934)	2.50	10.00	59
COLD LIGHT OF DAY/Bosses Daughter	(Musicor 1200)	.75	3.00	66
DEDICATION (THIS SONG I WANT TO DEDICATE TO YOU)/	(Epic 50332)	.50	2.00	77
DON'T MEAN TO BE A PREACHER/ Animal Crackers In My Soup	(Musicor 1235)	.75	3.00	67
EVERY BREATH I TAKE/Mr. Moon Mr. Cupid & I	(Musicor 1011)	.75	3.00	61
GOING BACK TO MY LOVE/Cradle Of My Arms (Shown as by Billy Bryan)	(Blaze 351)	2.50	10.00	60
HALF HEAVEN-HALF HEARTACHE/Tower Tall	(Musicor 1026)	.75	3.00	62
I'M GONNA BE STRONG/Aladdin's Lamp	(Musicor 1045)	.75	3.00	64
I'M GONNA BE STRONG/E Se Domani	(Musicor 1045)	.75	3.00	64
I'M GONNA LISTEN TO ME/For Me This Is Happy	(Musicor 1233)	.75	3.00	67
I MUST BE SEEING THINGS/Marianne	(Musicor 1070)	.75	3.00	65
IT HURTS TO BE IN LOVE/Hawaii	(Musicor 1040)	.75	3.00	64
IT'S OVER IT'S OVER (MEDLEY)/Walkin' In The Sun (A medley of two completely "It's Over" songs)	(Epic 50461)	.50	2.00	77
I'VE GOT A NEW HEARTACHE/ My Shoes Keep Walking Back To You (With George Jones)	(Musicor 1071)	.75	3.00	65
I'VE GOT FIVE DOLLARS & IT'S SATURDAY NIGHT/ Wreck On The Highway (With George Jones)	(Musicor 1066)	.75	3.00	65
(I WANNA) LOVE MY LIFE AWAY/ I Laughed So Hard I Cried	(Musicor 1002)	.75	3.00	61
JUST ONE SMILE/Innamorato	(Musicor 1219)	.75	3.00	66
LAST CHANCE TO TURN AROUND/Save Your Love	(Musicor 1093)	.75	3.00	65
LONELY DRIFTER/Somewhere In The Country	(Musicor 1308)	.75	3.00	68
LOOKING THROUGH THE EYES OF LOVE/ There's No Livin Without Your Lovin'	(Musicor 1103)	.75	3.00	65

TITLE/FLIP	LABEL & NO.	GOOD	NEAR MINT	YR.
LOUISIANA MAN/I'm A Fool To Care (With George Jones)	(Musicor 1097)	.75	3.00	65
(MAN WHO SHOT, THE) LIBERTY VALANCE/ Take It Like A Man	(Musicor 1020)	.75	3.00	62
MECCA/Teardrop By Teardrop	(Musicor 1028)	.75	3.00	63
ONLY LOVE CAN BREAK A HEART/If I Didn't Have A Dime (To Play The Jukebox)	(Musicor 1022)	.75	3.00	62
PLEASE COME BACK BABY/I'll Find You	(Festival 25002)	1.50	6.00	60
PRINCESS IN RAGS/Amore Mio	(Musicor 1130)	.75	3.00	65
SHE LETS HER HAIR DOWN (EARLY IN THE MORNING)/ I Remember	(Musicor 1384)	.75	3.00	69
SHE'S A HEARTBREAKER/Conquistador	(Musicor 1306)	.75	3.00	68
SOMETHING'S GOTTEN HOLD OF MY HEART/ Building Up My Dream World	(Musicor 1252)	.75	3.00	67
STROLLING (THRU' THE PARK)/Snuggle Up Baby (Duet with Ginny Arnell, shown as by Jamie & Jane.)	(Decca 30862)	2.50	10.00	59
TAKE ME TONIGHT/Louisiana Mama	(Musicor 1006)	.75	3.00	61
THAT GIRL BELONGS TO YESTERDAY/Who Needs It?	(Musicor 1036)	.75	3.00	64
TOWN WITHOUT PITY/Air Mail Special Delivery	(Musicor 1009)	.75	3.00	61
TRUE LOVE NEVER RUNS SMOOTH/ Donna Means Heartbreak	(Musicor 1032)	.75	3.00	63
TWENTY FOUR HOURS FROM TULSA/Lonely Night Dreams (Of Far Away Arms)	(Musicor 1034)	.75	3.00	63
WHERE DID THE MAGIC GO/Tremblin'	(Musicor 1245)	.75	3.00	67
WON'T TAKE LONG/The More I Saw Of Her	(Musicor 1299)	.75	3.00	68
YESTERDAY'S HERO/Cornflower Blue	(Musicor 1038)	.75	3.00	64
Y'ALL COME/That's All It Took (With George Jones)	(Musicor 1165)	.75	3.00	66
PITTS, Clyde				
SHAKIN' LIKE A LEAF/Just A Reminder	(Toppa 1018)	1.00	4.00	
PIXIES, The				
GEISHA GIRL/He's Got You	(Autumn 12)	1.00	4.00	65
PIXIES THREE, The				
BIRTHDAY PARTY/Our Love	(Mercury 72130)	.75	3.00	63
COLD COLD WINTER/442 Glenwood Avenue	(Mercury 72208)	.75	3.00	63
GEE/After The Party	(Mercury 72250)	.75	3.00	64
PIZANI, Frank (Of The Highlights)				
ANGRY/Every Time	(Bally 1040)	1.00	4.00	57
P.K. LIMITED				
SHADES OF GRAY/My Imagination	(Colgems 5014)	.75	3.00	70
PLAGUES, The				
I'VE BEEN THROUGH IT BEFORE/Tears From My Eyes	(Fenton 2070)	1.25	5.00	
WHY CAN'T YOU BE TRUE/Through This World	(Quarantined 2020)	1.25	5.00	
PLAIDS, The				
AROUND THE CORNER/He Stole Flo	(Era 3002)	.75	3.00	63
PLAIN BROWN WRAPPER				
JUNIOR SAW IT HAPPEN/Real Person	(Monster 0002)	1.25	5.00	
STRETCH OUT YOU HAND/Stretch Out You Hand (Part 2)	(Spirit 0010)	1.25	5.00	
PLANT LIFE				
FLOWER GIRL/Say It Over Again	(Date 1572)	1.00	4.00	67
PLANET, Richard				
GOIN' TO CALIFORNIA/All Thru The Day	(Capitol-Sovereign 3482)	.50	2.00	73
PLANETS, The				
MR. MOON/You Are My Sunshine	(Roulette 4551)	3.75	15.00	64
PLASTIC BERTRAND				
CA PLANE POUR MOI/Pogo Pogo	(Sire 1020)	.50	2.00	78
PLASTIC ONO BAND, The: see Lennon, John				
PLATT, Eddie				
CHA-HUA-HUA/Vodka	(Gone 5031)	1.00	4.00	58
TEQUILA/Popcorn Instrumentals	(ABC-Paramount 9899)	1.00	4.00	58
PLAYBOYS, The				
SHORTNIN' BREAD/Cheater Stomp	(Catalina 1069)	1.00	4.00	
PLAYBOYS, The				
BOSTON HOP/	(Chancellor 1074)	1.00	4.00	61
CRAZY DAISY/Sweet Talk	(Imperial 5586)	1.00	4.00	59
DUCK WALK/If I Had My Way	(Chancellor 1106)	1.00	4.00	62
MEMORIES/You're All I See	(ABC-Paramount 10070)	1.00	4.00	59
OVER THE WEEKEND/Double Talk	(Cameo 142)	1.00	4.00	58
OVER THE WEEKEND/Double Talk	(Martinique 101)	2.00	8.00	58
PLEASE FORGIVE ME/Sing Along	(Martinique 400)	1.50	6.00	59
PLAYBOYS, The				
CAREFUL WITH MY HEART/Girl Of My Dreams	(Cotton 1008)	1.25	5.00	62
PLAYBOYS OF EDINBURG, The				
DREAM WORLD/One Way Ticket	(Columbia 43933)	.75	3.00	66
LET'S GET BACK TO ROCK & ROLL/Homemade Cookin	("1-2-3" 1722)	1.00	4.00	69
LOOK AT ME GIRL/News Sure Travels Fast	(Columbia 43716)	.75	3.00	66
MICKEY'S MONKEY/Sanford Ringleton I Of Abernathy	(Columbia 44093)	.75	3.00	67
PLAYER (Formerly Bandana)				
BABY COME BACK/Love Is Where You Find It	(RSO 879)	.50	2.00	77
PRISONER OF YOUR LOVE/Join In The Dance	(RSO 908)	.50	2.00	78
SILVER LINING/Forever	(RSO 914)	.50	2.00	78
THIS TIME I'M IN IT FOR LOVE/Every Which Way	(RSO 890)	.50	2.00	78
PLAYERS, The				
MEMORIES OF A HIGH SCHOOL BRIDE/The Rebel	(Artemis 101)	1.50	6.00	
PLAYGIRLS, The				
GEE, BUT I'M LONESOME/Sugar Beat	(RCA Victor 47-7719)	1.00	4.00	60
PLAYMATES, The (Donny Conn, Morey Carr, Chic Hetti)				
BEEP BEEP/Your Love	(Roulette 4115)	1.00	4.00	58
COWBOY'S NEVER CRY/Tell Me What She Said	(Roulette 4370)	.75	3.00	61
DAY I DIED, THE/While The Record Goes Around	(Roulette 4100)	1.00	4.00	58
DON'T GO HOME/Can't Get It Through Your Head	(Roulette 4072)	1.00	4.00	54
FIRST LOVE/A Ciu-e	(Roulette 4200)	1.00	4.00	59
JO-ANN/You Can't Stop Me From Dreaming	(Roulette 4037)	1.00	4.00	58
KEEP YOUR HANDS IN YOUR POCKETS/ Cop On The Beat	(Roulette 4432)	.75	3.00	62
LET'S BE LOVERS/Give Me Another Chance	(Roulette 4056)	1.00	4.00	58
LITTLE MISS STUCK UP/Real Life	(Roulette 4322)	1.00	4.00	61
ON THE BEACH/The Song Everybody's Singing	(Roulette 4211)	1.00	4.00	59
OUR WEDDING DAY/Parade Of Pretty Girls	(Roulette 4252)	1.00	4.00	60
SECOND CHANCE/These Things I Offer You	(Roulette 4227)	1.00	4.00	60
STAR LOVE/Thing-A-Ma-Jig, The	(Roulette 4136)	1.00	4.00	59
WAIT FOR ME/Eyes Of An Angel	(Roulette 4276)	1.00	4.00	60
WHAT A FUNNY WAY TO SHOW IT/Petticoats Fly	(Roulette 4464)	.75	3.00	63
WHAT IS LOVE?/I Am	(Roulette 4160)	1.00	4.00	59
PLEASE, Bobby				
MONSTER, THE/	(Jamie 1118)	1.00	4.00	59
YOUR DRIVER'S LICENSE, PLEASE/Heartache Street	(Era 3044)	1.00	4.00	61
PLEASURE FAIR, The (Featuring Robb Royer)				
I'M GONNA HAVTA LET YOU GO/Today	(Uni 55078)	.75	3.00	68
MORNING GLORY DAYS/Fade In, Fade Out (Also see Bread)	(Uni 55016)	.75	3.00	67
PLEASURE SEEKERS, The				
GOOD KIND OF HURT/Light Of Love	(Mercury 72800)	1.00	4.00	68
NEVER THOUGHT YOU'D LEAVE ME/What A Way To Die	(Hideout 1006)	1.25	5.00	
PLEDGES (Clyde Batton & Gary Paxton)				
BETTY JEAN/Bermuda Shorts (Also see Skip & Flip)	(Rev 3517)	2.00	8.00	57
PLEIS, Jack				
GIANT/Lonesome Without You	(Decca 30055)	1.00	4.00	56
I'LL ALWAYS BE IN LOVE WITH YOU/The Waltz Of Tears	(Decca 30086)	1.00	4.00	56
THAT'S LIFE/Goodnight Waltz	(Decca 30303)	1.00	4.00	57
PLUM RUN				
MY BOY LILLIPOP, LOLLIPOP/Little Miss Inside	(Avco Embassy 4511)	.75	3.00	69
PLUNDERERS, The				
BATMAN/Boss	(Roulette 4665)	.75	3.00	66
PLURALS, The				
GOOD NIGHT/I'm Sold	(Wanger 188)	1.00	4.00	
PLUSHTONES, The				
RAINDROPS/Penny Loafers	(Plush 601)	.75	3.00	60
PLYMOUTH ROCKERS, The				
BROWN EYED HANDSOME MAN/Around & Around	(Warner Bros. 5475)	1.25	5.00	64
DON'T SAY WHY/Walk A Lonely Mile	(Valiant 737)	.75	3.00	66
P-NUT BUTTER				
WHAT AM I DOIN' HERE WITH YOU/Still In Love With You	(Tower 265)	1.00	4.00	66
P-NUT GALLERY, The				
DO YOU KNOW WHAT TIME IT IS/Lanny's Tune	(Buddah 239)	1.25	5.00	71
POCO				
C'MON/I Guess You Made It	(Epic 10714)	.75	3.00	71
CRAZY LOVE/Barbados	(ABC 12439)	.50	2.00	79
FAITH IN THE FAMILIES/Rocky Mountain Breakdown	(Epic 11141)	.75	3.00	74
FOOL'S GOLD/Here We Go Again	(Epic 11055)	.75	3.00	73
GO & SAY GOODBYE/	(Epic 10958)	.75	3.00	73
HEART OF THE NIGHT/The Last Goodbye	(MCA 41023)	.50	2.00	79
HIGH & DRY/	(Epic 50076)	.75	3.00	75
INDIAN SUMMER/Me & You	(ABC 12295)	.50	2.00	77
JUST FOR ME & YOU/Ol' Forgiver	(Epic 10804)	.75	3.00	71
KEEP ON TRYIN'/Georgia, Bind My Ties	(ABC 12126)	.50	2.00	75
LEGEND/Indian Summer	(MCA 41103)	.50	2.00	79
MAGNOLIA/	(Epic 11092)	.75	3.00	74
MAKIN' LOVE/	(ABC 12159)	.50	2.00	75
ROSE OF CIMARRON/Tulan Turnaround	(ABC 12204)	.50	2.00	76
YOU ARE THE ONE/Railroad Days	(Epic 10816)	.75	3.00	71
YOU BETTER THINK TWICE/Anyway Bye Bye	(Epic 10636)	.75	3.00	70
Also see Boenzee Cryque				
Also see Buffalo Springfield				
Also see Eagles, The				
Also see Furay, Richie				
Also see Illinois Speed Press				
Also see Meisner, Randy				
Also see Messina, Jim				
POINT BLANK				
BEAUTIFUL LOSER/	(Arista 0298)	.50	2.00	77
MEAN TO YOUR QUEENIE/Changed My Mind	(MCA 41119)	.50	2.00	79
MOVING/Bad Bees	(Arista)	.50	2.00	76
POINTER, Bonnie (Of The Pointer Sisters)				
FREE ME FROM MY FREEDOM TIE ME TO A TREE (HANDCUFF ME)/ Free Me From My Freedom Tie Me To A Tree (Handcuff Me) (Instrumental)	(Motown 1415)	.50	2.00	78
HEAVEN MUST HAVE SENT YOU (LP Version)/Heaven Must Have Sent You	(Motown 1459)	.50	2.00	79
POINTER SISTERS, The				
BLIND FAITH/The Shape I'm In	(Planet 45906)	.50	2.00	79
FAIRYTALE/Love In Them Thar Hills	(Blue Thumb 254)	.50	2.00	74
FIRE/Love Is Like A Rolling Stone	(Planet 45901)	.50	2.00	78
GOING DOWN SLOWLY/Sleeping Alone	(Blue Thumb 268)	.50	2.00	75
HAPPINESS/Lay It On The Line	(Planet 45902)	.50	2.00	79
HAVING A PARTY/Lonely Gal	(Blue Thumb 275)	.50	2.00	77
HOW LONG (BETCHA' GOT A CHICK ON THE SIDE)/ Easy Days	(Blue Thumb 265)	.50	2.00	75
LIVE YOUR LIFE BEFORE YOU DIE/Shaky Flat Blues	(Blue Thumb 262)	.50	2.00	75
STEAM HEAT/Shaky Flat Blues	(Blue Thumb 248)	.50	2.00	74
WANG DANG DOODLE/Cloudburst	(Blue Thumb 243)	.50	2.00	73
WHO DO YOU LOVE/	(Planet 45908)	.50	2.00	79
YES WE CAN CAN/Jada	(Blue Thumb 229)	.50	2.00	73
YOU GOTTA BELIEVE/Shaky Flat Blues	(Blue Thumb 271)	.50	2.00	76
POLARAS, The				
BREAKER/Cricket (Instrumentals)	(Pharos 100)	.75	3.00	63
POLICE				
CAN'T STAND LOSING YOU/No Time This Time	(A&M 2147)	.50	2.00	79
MESSAGE IN A BOTTLE/Landlord	(A&M 2190)	.50	2.00	79
ROXANNE/Dead End Job	(A&M 2096)	.50	2.00	79
POLNAREFF, Michael				
COME ON LADY BLUE/	(Atlantic 3327)	.50	2.00	76
IF YOU ONLY BELIEVE (JESUS FOR TONIGHT)/ Since I Saw You	(Atlantic 3314)	.50	2.00	76
LIPSTICK/	(Atlantic 3330)	.50	2.00	76
POMERANZ, David				
FINE WOMAN, A/Dagger	(Decca 32947)	.50	2.00	72
MISSIN' SONG/Brenda, Please	(Decca 32847)	.50	2.00	72
PONDIROSAS, The				
EVERYBODY'S SURFIN'/High Country	(Co & Ce 236)	.75	3.00	66
PONI-TAILS, The				
BORN TOO LATE/Come On Joey, Dance With Me	(ABC-Paramount 9934)	1.00	4.00	58
CAN I BE SURE/Still In Your Teens	(Marc 1001)	1.50	6.00	57
EARLY TO BED/Father Time	(ABC-Paramount 9995)	1.00	4.00	59
I'LL KEEP TRYIN'/I'll Be Seeing You	(ABC-Paramount 10047)	1.00	4.00	59
JUST MY LUCK TO BE FIFTEEN/ Wild Eyes & Tender Lips	(ABC-Paramount 9846)	1.00	4.00	58
OH, MY, YOU/Who, When, & Why	(ABC-Paramount 10114)	1.00	4.00	60
SEVEN MINUTES IN HEAVEN/Close Friends	(ABC-Paramount 9969)	1.00	4.00	58
YOUR WILD HEART/Que La Bozena	(Point 8)	1.50	6.00	57
POOH & THE HEFFALUMPHS				
LADY GODIVA/Rooty Toot	(Laurie 3281)	1.25	5.00	66
POOLE, Brian, & The Tremelos				
AFTER A WHILE/Don't Cry	(Monument 882)	1.00	4.00	65
CANDY MAN/I Can Dance	(Monument 840)	1.00	4.00	64
I NEED HER TONIGHT/Everything I Touch Turns to Tears	(Date 1539)	.75	3.00	66
KEEP ON DANCING/Blue	(London 9600)	1.00	4.00	63
SOMEONE, SOMEONE/ (Meet Me) Where We Used To Meet	(Monument 846)	1.00	4.00	64
POP, Iggy (Of Iggy & The Stooges)				
DOWN ON THE STREET/ (Shown as by The Stooges)	(Elektra 45695)	1.00	4.00	70
I GOT A RIGHT/Gimme Some Skin (With James Williamson)	(Siamese 001)	.50	2.00	77
I WANNA BE YOUR DOG/ I Wanna Be Your Dog (Part 2) (Shown as by The Stooges)	(Elektra 45664)	1.25	5.00	69
SEARCH & DESTROY/Penetration (Also see Bowie, David)	(Columbia 45877)	1.00	4.00	71
POP, The				
WAITING FOR THE NIGHT/	(Arista 0475)	.50	2.00	79
POP TOPS, The				
VOICE OF A DYING MAN/Oh, Lord, Why Lord	(Calla 154)	.75	3.00	68
POP UPS, The				
CANDY ROCK/Lurking	(HBR 459)	.75	3.00	66
POPPIES, The				
DO IT WITH SOUL/He Means So Much To Me	(Epic 10059)	.75	3.00	66
HE'S GOT REAL LOVE/He's Ready	(Epic 10019)	.75	3.00	66
LULLABY OF LOVE/I Wonder Why	(Epic 9893)	.75	3.00	66
MY LOVE & I/There's A Pain In My Heart	(Epic 10086)	.75	3.00	66
POPPY FAMILY, The (With Susan & Terry Jacks)				
GOOD FRIENDS?/Tryin'	(London 172)	.50	2.00	72
NO GOOD TO CRY/	(London 164)	.50	2.00	71
THAT'S WHERE I WENT WRONG/Shadows On My Wall	(London 139)	.50	2.00	70
WHERE EVIL GROWS/I Was Wondering	(London 148)	.50	2.00	71
WHICH WAY YOU GOIN' BILLY/	(London 129)	.50	2.00	70
POPSICLES, The				
I DON'T WANT TO BE YOUR BABY ANYMORE/ Baby I Miss You	(GNP-Crescendo 336)	.75	3.00	65
THUMB PRINT/This Is The End	(Knight 2002)	1.50	6.00	
PORTRAITS, The				
MILLION TO ONE, A/Let's Tell The World	(Sidewalk 928)	2.50	10.00	
OVER THE RAINBOW/Runaround Girl	(Sidewalk 935)	2.50	10.00	
THREE BLIND MICE/We're Gonna Party	(Tri-Disc 109)	1.00	4.00	63
PORTSMOUTH SINFONIA				
WILLIAM TELL OVERTURE/Also Sprach Zarathustra	(Columbia 10057)	.50	2.00	75
POSITIVELY 13 O'CLOCK				
PSYCHOTIC REACTION/13 O'clock Theme For Psychotics	(HBR 500)	1.50	6.00	66
POSSESIONS, The				
NO MORE LOVE/You & Your Lies (Blue plastic)	(Britton 1003)	2.50	10.00	64
NO MORE LOVE/You & Your Lies	(Britton 1003)	2.00	8.00	64
NO MORE LOVE/You & Your Lies	(Parkway 930)	1.25	5.00	64
POSSUM				
COCKROACH THAT ATE CINCINNATI, THE/Chula Vista (Parody)	(Highland 10)	1.25	5.00	66
POST, Mike				
FOR MY HOME/Long Time Alone	(Reprise 0406)	.75	3.00	65
MANHATTAN SPIRITUAL/	(MGM 14829)	.50	2.00	75
ROCKFORD FILES, THE/Dixie Lullabye	(MGM 14722)	.50	2.00	75
THEME FROM "BAA BAA BLACK SHEEP"/Southbound	(Epic 50325)	.50	2.00	77
POTLIQUOR				
CHEER/Chattanooga	(Janus 179)	.50	2.00	72
POTTER, Danny				
STANDING IN THE SUNSHINE/	(Warner-Spector 0408)	.50	2.00	76
POURCEL, Franck				
ONLY YOU/Rainy Night In Paris (Instrumentals)	(Capitol 4165)	.75	3.00	59
POUSETTE-DART BAND, The (With Jon Pousette-Dart)				
FALL ON ME/	(Capitol 4420)	.50	2.00	77
SHE FOUNT OUT/For Love	(Capitol 4764)	.50	2.00	79
STAND BY ME/So In Love	(Capitol 4590)	.50	2.00	78
WHAT CAN I SAY/	(Capitol 4278)	.50	2.00	76
POWDER PUFFS, The				
MY BOYFRIEND'S WOODY (YOU CAN'T TAKE)/ Woody Wagon	(Imperial 66014)	1.25	5.00	64
POWDRILL, Pat				
HAPPY ANNIVERSARY/ I Forgot More Than You'll Ever Know	(Reprise 20204)	.75	3.00	63
I ONLY CAME TO DANCE WITH YOU/ Fell By The Wayside	(Reprise 20166)	.75	3.00	63
POWELL, Cozy (Of Jeff Beck Group)				
DANCE WITH THE DEVIL/And Then There Was Skin (Also see Blackmore's Rainbow)	(Chrysalis 2029)	.50	2.00	74
POWELL, Jane				
TRUE LOVE/Mind If I Make Love To You	(Verve 2018)	1.00	4.00	56
POWELL, Sandy				
BON BON/Pistol Packin' Mama	(Herald 557)	10.00	40.00	
POWER				
CHILDREN ASK (IF HE IS DEAD)/ She Is The Color Of	(MGM K-13815)	.75	3.00	67
POWER, Duffy (Of Blues Inc.)				
HELLHOUND/Hummingbird	(Epic 10650)	.50	2.00	70
POWER, Johnny				
TEENAGER'S PRAYER, A/Young Boy's Heart	(Triodex 103)	1.00	4.00	60
POWERFUL PEOPLE				
(LITTLE GIRL) SAY YES/Can't Shake My Love	(Epic 8-50390)	.50	2.00	77
(LITTLE GIRL) SAY YES/(Little Girl) Say Yes (12" single issue)	(Epic ASD-356)	1.00	4.00	77
POWERS, Joey				
BILLY OLD BUDDY/In The Morning Gloria	(Amy 898)	.75	3.00	63
MIDNIGHT MARY/Where Do You Want The World Delivered	(Amy 892)	.75	3.00	63
TEARS KEEP FALLING/Where Did The Summer Go	(Amy 914)	.75	3.00	64
YOU COMB HER HAIR/Love Is A Reason	(Amy 903)	.75	3.00	64
POWERS, Johnny				
BE MINE, ALL MINE/With Your Love, With Your Kiss	(Sun 327)	1.00	4.00	59
HONEY LET'S GO (TO A ROCK & ROLL SHOW)/Your Love (With Stan Getz on guitar)	(Fortune 199)	1.00	4.00	55
ROCK ROCK/Long Blond Hair, Red Rose Lips (With Stan Getz on guitar)	(Fox 916)	1.00	4.00	57
POWERS OF BLUE, The				
(I CAN'T GET NO) SATISFACTION/Good Lovin'	(MTA 113)	.75	3.00	66
(I CAN'T GET NO) SATISFACTION/Good Lovin'	(MTA 5025)	.75	3.00	66
POWERS, Tina				
MAKING UP IS FUN TO DO (Answer song)/ Back To School	(Parkway 847)	1.00	4.00	62
POWERS, Wayne				
MY LOVE SONG/Point Of View	(Phillips Int'l. 3523)	2.00	8.00	58

TITLE/FLIP	LABEL & NO.	GOOD	NEAR MINT	YR.
POZO SECO SINGERS, The (With Don Williams)				
I BELIEVED IT ALL/	(Columbia 44041)	.75	3.00	67
I CAN MAKE IT WITH YOU/Come A Little Bit Closer	(Columbia 43784)	.75	3.00	66
I'LL BE GONE/	(Columbia 43646)	.75	3.00	66
LOOK WHAT YOU'VE DONE/Almost Persuaded	(Columbia 43929)	.75	3.00	66
LOUISIANA MAN/	(Columbia 44263)	.75	3.00	67
TIME/Down The Road I Go	(Columbia 43437)	.75	3.00	66
TIME/Down The Road I Go	(Edmark 10017)	1.50	6.00	66
PRADO, Perez				
CHERRY PINK & APPLE BLOSSOM WHITE/ St. Louis Blues Mambo	(RCA Victor 47-5965)	1.00	4.00	55
PATRICIA/Why Wait	(RCA Victor 47-7245)	1.00	4.00	58
Instrumentals				
PRAIRIE MADNESS				
SHAME THE CHILDREN/Shame The Children	(Columbia 45645)	.75	3.00	72
PRANCERS, The				
RUDOLPH THE RED NOSED RAINDEER/ Short Short'nin	(Guaranteed 204)	1.00	4.00	59
PRATT & McCLAIN (Truett Pratt & Jerry McClain)				
DEVIL WITH A BLUE DRESS/ Tonight We're Gonna Fall In Love	(Reprise 1361)	.50	2.00	76
HAPPY DAYS/Cruisin' With The Fonz	(Reprise 1351)	.50	2.00	76
ONE WAY OR THE OTHER/	(Reprise 1367)	.50	2.00	76
WACHERSIGN/	(Reprise 1373)	.50	2.00	77
PRATT, Andy				
ALL I WANT IS YOU/	(Nemperor 013)	.50	2.00	77
AVENGING ANNIE/So Fine (It's Frightening)	(Columbia 45804)	.75	3.00	73
IF YOU COULD SEE YOURSELF (THROUGH MY EYES)/	(Nemperor 007)	.50	2.00	76
SOME THINGS GO ON FOREVER/ That's When Miracles Occur	(Nemperor 008)	.50	2.00	76
PRECISIONS, The				
IF THIS IS LOVE/You'll Soon Be Gone	(Drew 1003)	1.00	4.00	67
INSTANT HEARTBREAK/Dream Girl	(Drew 1004)	1.00	4.00	68
LOVER'S PLEA/Such Misery	(Drew 1001)	1.00	4.00	66
NEVER LET HER GO/A Place	(Drew 1005)	1.00	4.00	68
WHAT I WANT/Why Girl	(Drew 1002)	1.00	4.00	67
PRELUDE				
AFTER THE GOLDRUSH/Johnson Boy	(Island 002)	.50	2.00	74
FOR A DANCER/Best Of A Bad Time	(Pye 71045)	.50	2.00	75
PRELUDES FIVE, The				
STARLIGHT/Don't You Know Love	(Pik 231)	.75	3.00	61
PREMEERS, The				
DIARY OF OUR LOVE/Gee Oh Gee	(Herald 577)	1.50	6.00	62
PREMIERE, Ronnie, & The Royal Lancers				
SO LOVED AM I/	(Sara 1020)	.75	3.00	
PREMIERES, The				
FIREWATER/Younger Than You	(Nu-Phi 429)	.75	3.00	
PREMIERS, The				
FARMER JOHN/Duffy's Blues	(Warner Bros. 5443)	.75	3.00	64
FARMER JOHN/Duffy's Blues	(Faro 605)	1.00	4.00	64
PREMIERS, The				
EVENING STAR/Last Of The Real Smart Guys	(Dore 603)	1.00	4.00	61
RED LIGHT BANDIT (Caryl Chessmen)/True Deep Love	(Dore 547)	1.25	5.00	60
SHE GOES OONKA CHICKA/What Makes Little Girls Cry	(Dore 614)	1.00	4.00	61

TITLE/FLIP	LABEL & NO.	GOOD	NEAR MINT	YR.
PREMIERS, The (With Roger Koob)				
FALLING STAR/She Gives Me Fever	(Rust 5032)	1.50	6.00	60
JOLENE/Oh Theresa	(Alert 706)	2.50	10.00	59
PIGTAILS EYES ARE BLUE/I Pray	(Fury 1029)	2.50	10.00	60
Also see Roger & the Travelers				
PREMIERS, The				
I THINK I LOVE YOU/Tonight	(Mink 021)	3.00	12.00	59
I THINK I LOVE YOU/Tonight	(Parkway 807)	1.50	6.00	61
PREPS, The				
IT AIN'T GREEN CHEESE/	(Southbay 001)	1.25	5.00	
NIGHT THEME/	(Warped 5000)	1.25	5.00	

The enormous output of Elvis Presley's recordings, coupled with the hundreds of variations and oddities available, has necessitated a separate price guide and collector's workbook. For more information on this massive volume, *Presleyana*, see the following page.

TITLE/FLIP	LABEL & NO.	GOOD	NEAR MINT	YR.
PRESTON, Billy				
ALL THAT I'VE GOT (I'M GONNA GIVE IT TO YOU)/ As I Get Older	(Apple 1817)	.75	3.00	70
DO IT WHILE YOU CAN/Song Of Joy	(A&M 1892)	.50	2.00	77
DON'T LET THE SUN CATCH YOU CRYIN'/Billy's Bag	(Vee Jay 653)	1.25	5.00	64
EVERYTHING'S ALL RIGHT/I Want To Thank You	(Apple 1814)	.75	3.00	69
FANCY LADY/Song Of Joy	(A&M 1735)	.50	2.00	75
GET BACK/Space Race	(A&M 2071)	.50	2.00	78
GIRL/Ecstasy	(A&M 1925)	.50	2.00	77
GIRL'S GOT "IT", THE/The Night	(Capitol 5611)	1.00	4.00	66
HEY BROTHER (Vocal)/Hey Brother (Instrumental)	(Capitol 2309)	1.00	4.00	69
I'M REALLY GONNA MISS YOU/Attitudes	(A&M 2012)	.50	2.00	78
IN THE MIDNIGHT HOUR/Advice	(Capitol 5660)	1.00	4.00	66
I'VE GOT THE SPIRIT/	(A&M 1892)	.50	2.00	77
LOG CABIN/	(Vee Jay 692)	1.25	5.00	65
MY KIND OF MUSIC/	(Contract 5101)	2.00	8.00	61
MY SWEET LORD/Little Girl	(Apple 1826)	.75	3.00	70
NOTHING FROM NOTHING/My Soul Is A Witness	(A&M 1544)	.50	2.00	74
OUTA-SPACE/I Wrote A Simple Song	(A&M 1320)	.50	2.00	72
SLAUGHTER/God Loves You	(A&M 1380)	.50	2.00	72
SPACE RACE/We're Gonna Make It	(A&M 1463)	.50	2.00	73
STRUTTIN'/You Are So Beautiful	(A&M 1644)	.50	2.00	74
SUNNY/Let The Music Play	(Capitol 5730)	1.00	4.00	66
THAT'S THE WAY GOD PLANNED IT/What About You	(Apple 1808)	.75	3.00	69
WIDE STRIDE/Whole New Thing	(A&M 1980)	.50	2.00	77
WILL IT GO ROUND IN CIRLCES/Blackbird	(A&M 1411)	.50	2.00	73
YOU'RE SO UNIQUE/How Long Has The Train Been Gone	(A&M 1492)	.50	2.00	74
PRESTON, Johnny				
ALL AROUND THE WORLD/Just Plain Hurt	(Hall Way 1201)	.75	3.00	64
CRADLE OF LOVE/City Of Tears	(Mercury 71598)	1.00	4.00	60
FEEL SO FINE/I'm Starting to Go Steady	(Mercury 71651)	1.00	4.00	60
GOOD GOOD LOVIN'/I'm Asking Forgiveness	(TCF 120)	.75	3.00	65
I WANT A ROCK & ROLL GUITAR/ New Baby For Christmas	(Mercury 71728)	2.50	10.00	60
KISSIN' TREE/Free Me	(Mercury 71908)	1.00	4.00	61
LEAVE MY KITTEN ALONE/Token Of Love	(Mercury 71761)	1.00	4.00	61
LET THEM TALK/She Once Belonged To Me	(Mercury 71865)	1.00	4.00	61
RUNNING BEAR/My Heart Knows	(Mercury 71474)	1.00	4.00	59
RUNNING BEAR '65/Dedicated To The One I Love	(Hall Way 1927)	.75	3.00	65
WILLIE & THE HAND JIVE/I've Got My Eyes On You	(Hall Way 1204)	.75	3.00	64
YOU CAN MAKE IT IF YOU TRY/Sounds Like Trouble	(TCF 101)	.75	3.00	65
PRESTON, Mike				
HOUSE, A CAR & A WEDDING RING, A/ My Lucky Love	(London 1834)	1.00	4.00	58
PRETENDERS, The				
COULD THIS BE MAGIC/ A Very Precious Love	(Power-Martin 1006/1007)	.75	3.00	76
COULD THIS BE MAGIC/ Stormy Weather (By the Earls)	(Power-Martin 1005)	.75	3.00	76
SMILE/I'm So Happy	(Power-Martin 1001)	5.00	20.00	61
PRETTY THINGS, The				
BIG BOSS MAN/Rosalyn	(Fontana 1916)	1.00	4.00	64
COME & SEE ME/Judgement Day	(Fontana 1550)	1.00	4.00	66
CRY TO ME/I Can Never Say	(Fontana 1518)	1.00	4.00	65
I CAN NEVER SAY/Honey, I Need You	(Fontana 1508)	1.00	4.00	65
IT ISN'T ROCK 'N' ROLL/Remember That Boy	(Swan Song 70107)	.50	2.00	76
JOEY/	(Swan Song 70104)	.50	2.00	75
MIDNIGHT TO SIX MAN/Can't Stand The Pain	(Fontana 1540)	1.00	4.00	66
PREVIN, Andre, & David Rose				
LIKE YOUNG/Young Man's Lament	(MGM 12792)	.75	3.00	59
(Instrumental)				
PRICE, Alan, Set				
HI-LILI, HI-LO/Take Me Home	(Parrot 3007)	1.00	4.00	66
I PUT A SPELL ON YOU/Iechyd-Da	(Parrot 3001)	1.00	4.00	66
I WANNA DANCE/Just For You	(Jet 1119)	.50	2.00	77
NOT BORN TO FOLLOW/To Romona	(Parrot 3019)	1.00	4.00	66
O LUCKY MAN/Poor People	(Warner Bros. 7717)	.75	3.00	72
THIS IS YOUR LUCKY DAY (THE GIRL WON'T GET UNDER)/ Mama Don't Go Home	(Jet 5056)	.50	2.00	79
Alan Price was originally a member of the Animals				
Also see Fame & Price, Price & Fame Together				
PRICE, David				
LOVE HIM TENDER, SWEET JESUS/ Love Him Tender, Sweet Jesus	(Rice 5075)	.50	2.00	77
PRICE, Ronnie, & The Velvets				
WHITE BUCKS/Look At Me	(Carousel 1001)	1.00	4.00	
PRIDE & JOY				
GIRL/If You're Ready	(Dunwich 152)	1.00	4.00	67
THAT'S THE WAY IT IS/We Got A Long Way To Go	(Acta 817)	1.00	4.00	67
PRIMA, Louis				
OH, BABE!/Piccolina Lena	(Robin Hood 101)	1.25	5.00	50
WONDERLAND BY NIGHT/Ol' Man Mose	(Dot 16151)	.75	3.00	60
Instrumentals				
PRIMA, Louis, & Keely Smith				
THAT OLD BLACK MAGIC/Are You My Love	(Capitol 4063)	1.00	4.00	58
PRIMITIVES, The (Jerry Vance & Lou Reed)				
SNEAKY PETE/The Ostrich	(Pickwick 1001)	1.50	6.00	
PRINCE & THE PAUPERS				
DON'T WAKE UP/No Shame To Hide	(Clarity 115)	1.25	5.00	
PRINCE CHARLES				
GOOD LUCK CHARM/Twistin' At The Pool	(Class 301)	.75	3.00	62
PRINCE LA LA				
GETTIN' MARRIED SOON/Come Back To Me	(AFO 303)	1.00	4.00	61
SHE PUT THE HURT ON ME/Don't You Know Little Girl	(AFO 301)	1.00	4.00	61
PRINCE, Rod				
RAINBOW OF LOVE/My Star All Alone	(Comet 2140)	3.75	15.00	
PRINE, John				
COMMON SENSE/Come Back To Us Barbara Lewis Hare Krishna Beauregard	(Atlantic 3297)	.50	2.00	75
EVERYBODY/	(Atlantic 2925)	.50	2.00	72
FISH & WHISTLE/Sabu Visits The Twin Cities Alone	(Asylum 45509)	.50	2.00	78
ILLEGAL SMILE/	(Atlantic 3218)	.50	2.00	74
SADDLE IN THE RAIN/Middle Man	(Atlantic 3276)	.50	2.00	75
SAM STONE/	(Atlantic 2815)	.50	2.00	71
THERE SHE GOES/That's The Way The World Goes 'Round	(Asylum 45550)	.50	2.00	78
PRISM				
FLYIN'/Crime Wave	(Ariola 7714)	.50	2.00	78
IT'S OVER/Julie	(Ariola America 7691)	.50	2.00	78
SEE FOREVER EYES/	(Ariola 7724)	.50	2.00	78
SPACESHIP SUPERSTAR/Julie	(Ariola America 7672)	.50	2.00	77
TAKE ME TO THE KAPTAIN/I Ain't Lookin' Anymore	(Ariola America 7678)	.50	2.00	77
VIRGINIA/Armegeddon	(Ariola 7759)	.50	2.00	79
PRISONER				
FOOL (IF YOU THINK IT'S OVER)/	(Warner-Curb 8601)	.50	2.00	78
HOT SUMMER NIGHT/I Wanna Be The One	(Warner-Curb 8635)	.50	2.00	78
TRY A LITTLE TENDERNESS/I Wanna Be The One	(Warner-Curb 8702)	.50	2.00	78

TITLE/FLIP	LABEL & NO.	GOOD	NEAR MINT	YR.
PROBY, P.J. (James Smith)				
BUTTERFLY HIGH/Just Holding On	(Liberty 55989)	.75	3.00	67
HOLD ME/The Tip Of My Fingers	(London 9688)	1.00	4.00	64
I APOLOGIZE BABY/It's Your Turn Today	(Liberty 56031)	.75	3.00	68
I CAN'T MAKE IT ALONE/If I Ruled The World	(Liberty 55915)	.75	3.00	66
I CAN'T TAKE IT LIKE YOU CAN/So Do I	(Liberty 55588)	.75	3.00	63
MARIA/Good Things Are Coming My Way	(Liberty 55850)	.75	3.00	66
MY PRAYER/Wicked Woman	(Liberty 55875)	.75	3.00	66
NIKI HOEKY/Good Things Are Coming My Way	(Liberty 55936)	.75	3.00	67
ROCKIN' PNEUMONIA/Just Call, I'll Be There	(Liberty 66079)	.75	3.00	64
ROCKIN' PNEUMONIA/I Apologize	(Liberty 55777)	.75	3.00	65
SOMEWHERE/Just Like Him	(Liberty 55757)	.75	3.00	65
STAGGER LEE/Mission Bell	(Liberty 55791)	.75	3.00	65
THAT MEANS A LOT/Let The Water Run Down	(Liberty 55806)	.75	3.00	65
TOGETHER/Sweet & Tender Romance	(London 9705)	1.00	4.00	64
TRY TO FORGET HER/There Stands The One	(Liberty 55367)	.75	3.00	61
WATCH ME WALK AWAY/The Other Side Of Town	(Liberty 55505)	.75	3.00	62
WHAT'S WRONG WITH MY WORLD/Turn Her Away	(Liberty 56051)	.75	3.00	68
YOU CAN'T COME HOME AGAIN (IF YOU LEAVE ME NOW)/ Work With Me Annie	(Liberty 55974)	.75	3.00	67
YOU GOT ME CRYING/I Need Love	(Surfside 714)	1.00	4.00	65
PROCOL HARUM (Featuring Gary Brooker)				
CONQUISTADOR/A Salty Dog	(A&M 1347)	.75	3.00	72
HOMBURG/Good Captain Clark	(A&M 885)	1.00	4.00	67
IN THE WEE SMALL HOURS OF SIXPENCE/Quite Rightly So	(A&M 927)	1.25	5.00	68
NOTHING BUT THE TRUTH/Drunk Again	(Chrysalis 2032)	.75	3.00	74
PANDORA'S BOX/The Piper's Tune	(Chrysalis 2109)	.75	3.00	75
SALTY DOG, A/	(A&M 1069)	1.00	4.00	69
WHITER SHADE OF PALE, A/Lime St. Blues	(Deram 7507)	1.00	4.00	67
WIZARD MAN/Something Magic	(Warner-Chrysalis 2115)	.75	3.00	77
Also see Paramounts, The				
PROFESSOR BUG				
BEATLEMANIA/Beatlemania (Part 2)	(Beetle 1600)	2.50	10.00	64
PROFESSOR MORRISON'S LOLLIPOP				
ANGELA/Duba Duba Do	(White Whale WW-288)	1.00	4.00	69
OO-POO-PAH SUSIE/You Take It	(White Whale WW-293)	1.00	4.00	69
(Vocal by Lange Martine Jr.)				
YOU GOT THE LOVE/Gypsy Lady	(White Whale WW-275)	1.00	4.00	68
PROFILES, The				
RIGHT BY HER SIDE/Never	(Gait 1444)	10.00	40.00	
PROMISES, The				
I DON'T WANT TO TALK ABOUT IT/Try It Again	(Ascot 2201)	1.25	5.00	66
PROPHETS, The				
LITTLE MISS DREAMER/	(Jairick 201)	2.50	10.00	
PROPHETS, Thee: See The Prophets				
PROTHROE, Brian				
PINBALL/Money Love	(Chrysalis 2104)	.50	2.00	75
PSYCHOS, The				
MACK THE KNIFE/Tragedy	(Fernwood 126)	.75	3.00	60
PUCKETT, Gary (Of The Union Gap)				
GENTLE WOMAN/	(Columbia 4-45438)	.75	3.00	71
I CAN'T HOLD ON/Hello Morning	(Columbia 4-45509)	.75	3.00	72
I JUST DON'T KNOW WHAT TO DO WITH MYSELF/ All That Matters	(Columbia 4-45249)	.75	3.00	70
KEEP THE CUSTOMER SATISFIED/ No One Really Knows	(Columbia 4-45303)	.75	3.00	71
LEAVIN' IN THE MORNING/Bless The Child	(Columbia 4-45678)	.75	3.00	72
LIFE HAS IT'S LITTLE UPS & DOWNS/Shimmering Eyes	(Columbia 4-45358)	.75	3.00	71
PUCKETT, Gary, & The Union Gap				
DON'T GIVE IN TO HIM/Could I	(Columbia 4-44788)	.75	3.00	69
LADY WILLPOWER/Daylight Stranger	(Columbia 4-44547)	.75	3.00	68
LET'S GIVE ADAM & EVE ANOTHER CHANCE/ The Begger	(Columbia 4-45097)	.75	3.00	70
OVER YOU/If The Day Would Come	(Columbia 4-44644)	.75	3.00	68
THIS GIRL IS A WOMAN NOW/His Other Woman	(Columbia 4-44788)	.75	3.00	69
WOMAN WOMAN/Don't Make Promises	(Columbia 4-44297)	1.00	4.00	67
(Shown as by the Union Gap)				
YOUNG GIRL/I'm Losing You	(Columbia 4-44450)	.75	3.00	68
PUDDING				
MAGIC BUS/It's Too Late	(Press 5010)	.75	3.00	68
PUFF, Ray, & The Checkmates				
BEATLE MANIAS/Took A Liking To You	(Lin 5034)	1.25	5.00	64
PUFFS, The				
MOON OUT THERE/I Only Cry Once A Day Now	(Dore 757)	1.00	4.00	68
PULLEN, Dwight				
SUNGLASSES AFTER DARK/Teenage Bug	(Carlton 455)	18.75	75.00	61
PULLINS, Leroy				
I'M A NUT/Knee Deep	(Kapp 758)	.75	3.00	66
TATERVILLE WOMEN'S AUXILIARY SEWING CIRCLE/ Tickled Pink	(Kapp 775)	.75	3.00	66
PULSE				
CAN CAN GIRL/Burritt Bradley	(Atco 6530)	1.00	4.00	67
PUPPET, Polly				
PUPPETEER, THE/Puppet Serenade	(Challenge 9126)	.75	3.00	61
PUPPETS, The				
LOVE IS A BEAUTIFUL THING/ I Ain't Gonna Eat Out My Heart	(Red Rooster 311)	1.25	5.00	
PURE PRAIRIE LEAGUE				
AMIE/Memories	(RCA 10184)	.50	2.00	75
DANCE/	(RCA 10829)	.50	2.00	77
FADE AWAY/	(RCA 10880)	.50	2.00	77
I CAN'T HOLD BACK/	(RCA 11678)	.50	2.00	79
LOVE WILL GROW/	(RCA 11282)	.50	2.00	78
SUN SHONE BRIGHTLY/	(RCA 11148)	.50	2.00	77
THAT'LL BE THE DAY/I Can Only Think Of You	(RCA 10679)	.50	2.00	76
TWO LANE HIGHWAY/Sister's Keeper	(RCA 10302)	.50	2.00	75
WORKING IN THE COAL MINE/Bad Dream	(RCA 11260)	.50	2.00	78
YOU'RE BETWEEN ME/Tears	(RCA 1028)	.50	2.00	72
Also see American Flyer				
PURPLE GANG, The				
BRING YOUR OWN SELF DOWN/One Of The Bunch	(MGM 13607)	.75	3.00	66
I KNOW WHAT I AM/Answer The Phone	(Jerden 794)	1.00	4.00	66
PURPLE REIGN				
THIS OLD MAN/This Old Man	(Private Stock 45052)	.50	2.00	75
THIS OLD MAN/This Old Man	(Go-Rilla 4594)	.75	3.00	75
PURSELL, Bill				
OUR WINTER LOVE/A Wound Time Can't Erase	(Columbia 42619)	.75	3.00	63
(Instrumentals)				
PUSSYCATS, The				
ANNIVERSARY OF LOVE/Mickey Mouse March	(Keyman 6000)	1.50	6.00	

PRESLEYANA

More than a PRICE GUIDE!

304 pages of information Presleyana serves as a handbook, a checklist and a workbook, as well as providing fascinating insights into the recording career of the greatest entertainer of them all.

ELVIS' SINGLE RELEASES

ELVIS' SINGLES

A

A BIG HUNK O' LOVE/MY WISH CAME TRUE

☐ *RCA Victor 47-7600* (45)	1.50	6.00
☐ *RCA Victor 47-7600* (Picture sleeve)	4.00	16.00

A FOOL SUCH AS I/I NEED YOUR LOVE TONIGHT

☐ *RCA Victor 47-7506* (45)	1.50	6.00
☐☐ *RCA Victor 47-7506* (Picture sleeve)	4.00	16.00

NOTE: Two variations are known to exist for this picture sleeve. One has an ad for the EP "Elvis Sails" on the back, the other carries a listing of available Elvis records on the back. No difference in value has yet been established.

MORE of ELVIS on any of these RCA VICTOR RECORDS

One of the back cover versions of the 47-7506 sleeve.

andy
hecklist
oxes
rovided

A LITTLE LESS CONVERSATION/ALMOST IN LOVE

☐ *RCA Victor 47-9610* (45)	—	3.00
☐ *RCA Victor 47-9610* (Promo 45)	2.00	8.00
☐ *RCA Victor 47-9610* (Picture sleeve)	2.00	8.00

AIN'T THAT LOVING YOU BABY/ASK ME

☐ *RCA Victor 47-8440* (45)	1.00	4.00
☐ *RCA Victor 47-8440* (Promo 45)	4.00	16.00
☐☐ *RCA Victor 47-8440* (Picture sleeve)	3.00	12.00

NOTE: Two variations are known to exist for this picture sleeve. First issue reads "Coming Soon!" whereas second issue reads "Ask For!" with regard to "Roustabout" LP promotional announcement at bottom of sleeve. No difference in value has yet been established.

ALL SHOOK UP/THAT'S WHEN YOUR HEARTACHES BEGIN

☐ *RCA Victor 20-6870* (78)	8.00	32.00
☐ *RCA Victor 47-6870* (45)	1.50	6.00
☐ *RCA Victor 47-6870* (Picture sleeve)	7.00	28.00

AN AMERICAN TRILOGY/THE FIRST TIME EVER I SAW YOUR FACE

☐ *RCA 74-0672* (45)	1.00	4.00
☐ *RCA 74-0672* (Promo 45)	2.50	10.00
☐ *RCA 74-0672* (Picture sleeve)	2.50	10.00

NOTE: Do not be confused by the promotional announcement at the bottom of this sleeve refering to Elvis' "Standing Room Only" LP. There was never an Elvis album issued by RCA using this title. The idea was simply scrapped, but after the sleeves for this single were already printed.

ARE YOU LONESOME TO-NIGHT?/I GOTTA KNOW

☐ *RCA Victor 47-7810* (45)	1.00	4.00
☐ *RCA Victor 47-7810* (Picture sleeve)	3.00	12.00
☐ *RCA Victor 61-7810* (Living Stereo 45)	60.00	240.00

ARE YOU SINCERE/SOLITAIRE

☐ *RCA PB-11533* (45)	—	2.00
☐ *RCA PB-11533* (Promo 45)	1.50	6.00
☐ *RCA PB-11533* (Picture sleeve)	1.00	4.00

B

BABY LET'S PLAY HOUSE/I'M LEFT, YOU'RE RIGHT, SHE'S GONE

☐ *Sun 217* (78)	25.00	100.00
☐ *Sun 217* (45)	60.00	240.00
☐ *RCA Victor 20-6383* (78)	9.00	36.00
☐ *RCA Victor 47-6383* (45)	4.00	16.00

NOTE: No RCA original picture sleeve exists for this release. Any 47-6383 sleeve you may find is a bootleg.

1

Prices for 45 & 78rpm singles, picture sleeves and promotional issues for "Good" to "Near Mint" condition copies.

Hundreds of photos of Elvis and His Recordings

Detailed explanations, making PRESLEYANA a valuable reference source.

PRESLEYANA SEQUENCE OF CONTENTS

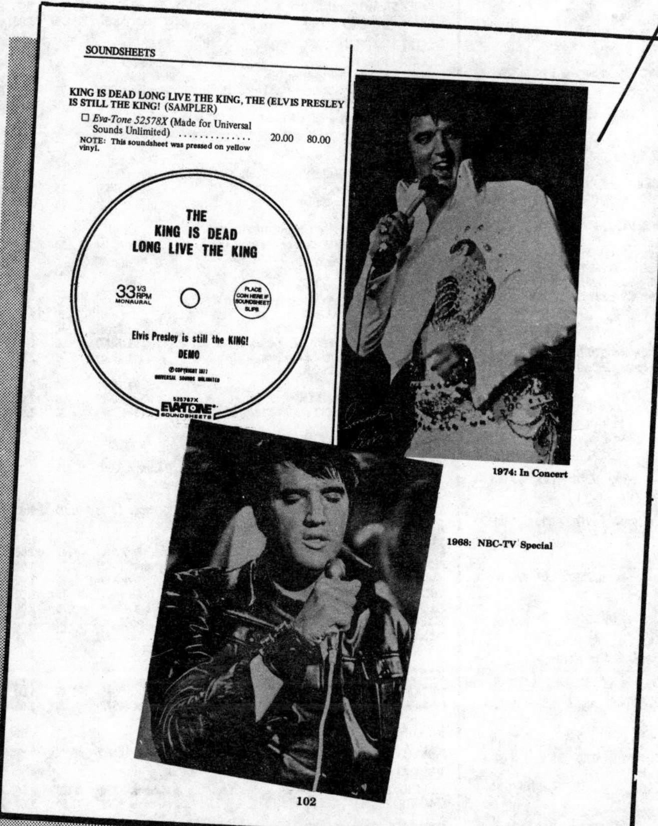

SOUNDSHEETS

KING IS DEAD LONG LIVE THE KING, THE (ELVIS PRESLEY IS STILL THE KING! (SAMPLER)

☐ *Eva-Tone 52578X* (Made for Universal Sounds Unlimited)	20.00	80.00

NOTE: This soundsheet was pressed on yellow vinyl.

1974: In Concert

1968: NBC-TV Special

102

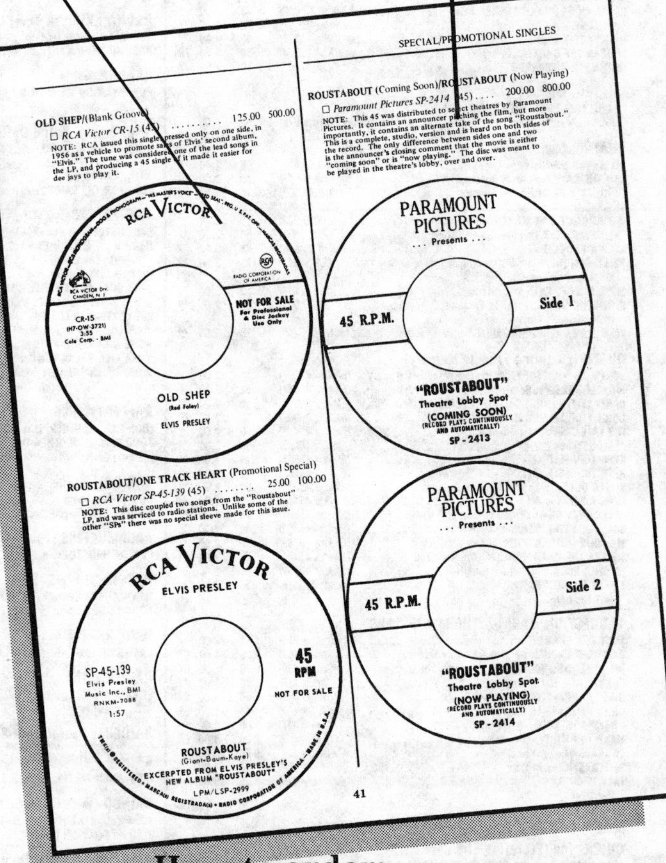

SPECIAL/PROMOTIONAL SINGLES

OLD SHEP/(Blank Groove)

☐ *RCA Victor CR-15* (45)	125.00	500.00

NOTE: RCA issued this single pressed only on one side, in 1956 as a vehicle to promote sales of Elvis' second album, "Elvis." The tune was considered one of the lead songs in the LP, and producing a 45 single of it made it easier for dee jays to play it.

ROUSTABOUT/ONE TRACK HEART (Promotional Special)

☐ *RCA Victor SP-45-139* (45)	25.00	100.00

NOTE: This disc coupled two songs from the "Roustabout" LP, and was serviced to radio stations. Unlike some of the other "SPs" there was no special sleeve made for this issue.

ROUSTABOUT (Coming Soon)/**ROUSTABOUT** (Now Playing)

☐ *Paramount Pictures SP-2414* (45)	200.00	800.00

NOTE: This 45 was distributed to select theatres by Paramount Pictures. It contains an announcer pitching the film, but more importantly, it contains an alternate take of the song "Roustabout." This is a complete, studio, version and is heard on both sides of the record. The only difference between sides one and two is the announcer's closing comment that the movie is either "coming soon" or is "now playing." The disc was meant to be played in the theatre's lobby, over and over.

41

How to order:
There is a handy order form on page 184 of this book!

TITLE/FLIP	LABEL & NO.	GOOD	NEAR MINT	YR.
PYRAMIDS				
CONTACT/Pressure	(Cedwicke 13006)	1.00	4.00	64
MIDNIGHT RUN/Custom Caravan	(Cedwicke 13005)	1.00	4.00	64
PENETRATION/Here Comes Marsha	(Best 102)	2.00	8.00	64
(Label does not read "Distributed by London")				
PENETRATION/Here Comes Marsha	(Best 13002)	1.00	4.00	64
(Label reads "Distributed by London")				
PYRAMID STOMP/Paul	(Best 101)	2.00	8.00	63
(Label does not read "Distributed by London")				
PYRAMID STOMP/Paul	(Best 13001)	1.00	4.00	63
(Label reads "Distributed by London")				
PYRAMIDS, The				
ANKLE BRACELET/Hot Dog Dooly Wah	(Shell 711)	3.00	12.00	59
(With two sea shells logo on label.)				
ANKLE BRACELET/Hot Dog Dooly Wah	(Shell 711)	1.25	5.00	59
(Without sea shell logo.)				
CRYIN'/I'm The Playboy	(Cub 9112)	1.00	4.00	62
SHAKIN' FIT/What Is Love	(Vee Jay 489)	1.00	4.00	63
PYTHON LEE JACKSON: see Stewart, Rod				

Q

TITLE/FLIP	LABEL & NO.	GOOD	NEAR MINT	YR.
Q (With Robert Peckman & Don Garvin)				
DANCIN' MAN/Love Pollution	(Epic 50335)	.50	2.00	77
FEEL IT IN YOUR BACKBONE, GOT IT IN YOUR FEET/	(Epic 50440)	.50	2.00	77
Peckman & Garvin were previously with the Jaggerz.				
QUADS, The				
SURFIN' HEARSE/Little Queenie	(Vault 907)	1.00	4.00	63
(Instrumental)				
QUAITE, Christine				
TELL ME MAMMA/In The Middle Of The Floor	(World Artists 1022)	.75	3.00	64
QUAKER CITY BOYS, The				
EVERYWHERE YOU GO/Love Me Tonight	(Swan 4026)	1.00	4.00	59
GOODBYE 50's, HELLO 60's/You Call Everybody	(Swan 4045)	1.00	4.00	59
TEASIN'/Won't Cha Come Out Tonight	(Swan 4023)	1.00	4.00	59
QUARRY, The				
MOCKINGBIRD HILL/We're All Going To Leave This World Someday	(Berkshire Hamony 0001)	1.00	4.00	
QUARTER NOTES, The				
I'VE BEEN LOVED/Hey Little Girl	(Boom 018)	1.00	4.00	
LIKE YOU BUG ME/Please Come Home	(Dot 15685)	1.00	4.00	57
PRETTY PRETTY EYES/I Don't Want To Go Home	(Guyden 2083)	1.00	4.00	63
PUNKANILLA/The Interview	(RCA Victor 47-7327)	1.00	4.00	58
RECORD HOP BLUES/Suki-Yaki-Rocki	(Wizz 715)	1.00	4.00	59
QUATEMAN, Bill				
GET IT RIGHT ON OUT THERE/Circles	(Columbia AE7 1062)	.75	3.00	72
ONLY LOVE/Keep Dreaming	(Columbia 45792)	.75	3.00	73
NIGHT AFTER NIGHT/	(RCA 10912)	.50	2.00	77
SHOT IN THE DARK/All Over Now	(RCA 11254)	.50	2.00	78
WAIT UNTIL TOMORROW/	(RCA 11180)	.50	2.00	77
QUATRO, Michael				
IN COLLABORATION WITH THE GODS/Neptune's Nicromea	(United Artists 672)	.50	2.00	75
QUATRO, Suzi				
ALL SHOOK UP/Glycerine Queen	(Bell 45,477)	.50	2.00	74
CAN THE CAN/Don't Mess Around	(Big Tree 16053)	.50	2.00	76
DEVIL GATE DRIVE/In The Morning	(Bell 45,609)	.75	3.00	74
48 CRASH/	(Bell 45,401)	.75	3.00	73
IF YOU CAN'T GIVE ME LOVE/Non-Citizen	(RSO 929)	.50	2.00	79
I'VE NEVER BEEN IN LOVE/Space Cadets	(RSO 1001)	.50	2.00	79
KEEP A KNOCKIN'/	(Bell 45,615)	.75	3.00	74
ROLLING STONE/Brain Confusion (For All The Lonely People)	(RAK 4512)	.75	3.00	72
(Shown as by Susie Quatro)				
SHE'S IN LOVE WITH YOU/Starlight Lady	(RSO 1014)	.50	2.00	79
STUMBLIN' IN/A Stranger To Paradise	(RSO 917)	.50	2.00	79
(With Smokie's Chris Norman)				
YOUR MAMA WON'T LIKE ME/Peter Peter	(Arista 0106)	.75	3.00	75
QUEEN (Featuring Freddie Mercury)				
BOHEMIAN RHAPSODY/I'm In Love With My Car	(Elektra 45297)	.50	2.00	75
BICYCLE RACE/Fat Bottomed Girls	(Elektra 45541)	.50	2.00	78
CRAZY LITTLE THING CALLED LOVE/Spread Your Wings	(Elektra 46579)	.50	2.00	79
DON'T STOP ME NOW/More Of That Jazz	(Elektra 46008)	.50	2.00	79
IT'S LATE/Sheer Heart Attack	(Elektra 45478)	.50	2.00	78
JEALOUSY/Fun It	(Elektra 46039)	.50	2.00	79
KEEP YOURSELF ALIVE/	(Elektra 45863)	.75	3.00	74
KEEP YOURSELF ALIVE/Lily Of The Valley	(Elektra 45268)	.75	3.00	75
KILLER QUEEN/Flick Of The Wrist	(Elektra 45226)	.50	2.00	75
LONG AWAY/You & I	(Elektra 45412)	.75	3.00	77
SEVEN SEAS OF RHYE/See What A Fool I Am	(Elektra 45891)	.75	3.00	74
SOMEBODY TO LOVE/White Man	(Elektra 45362)	.50	2.00	76
TIE YOUR MOTHER DOWN/Drowse	(Elektra 45385)	.50	2.00	77
WE ARE THE CHAMPIONS/We Will Rock You	(Elektra 45441)	.50	2.00	77
WE WILL ROCK YOU/Let Me Entertain You	(Elektra 46532)	.50	2.00	79
YOU'RE MY BEST FRIEND/'39	(Elektra 45318)	.50	2.00	76
Also see Smile				
? (QUESTION MARK) & THE MYSTERIANS				
AIN'T IT A SHAME/Turn Around Baby	(Tangerine 989)	1.50	6.00	
CAN'T GET ENOUGH OF YOU BABY/Smokes	(Cameo 467)	1.00	4.00	67
DO SOMETHING TO ME/Love Me Baby	(Cameo 496)	1.00	4.00	67
FUNKY LADY/Hot N' Groovin'	(Lub 159)	1.50	6.00	73
GIRL (YOU CAPTIVATE ME)/Got To	(Cameo 479)	1.00	4.00	67
HANG IN/Sha La La (Instrumental)	(Super K SK-102)	.75	3.00	69
I NEED SOMEBODY/"8" Teen	(Cameo 441)	1.00	4.00	66
MAKE YOU MINE/I Love You Baby	(Capitol 2162)	2.00	8.00	68
96 TEARS/Midnight Hour	(Pa-Go-Go 102)	10.00	40.00	66
96 TEARS/Midnight Hour	(Cameo 428)	.75	3.00	66
TALK IS CHEAP/	(Chicory 410)	3.75	15.00	67
QUESTS, The				
SCREAM LOUD/Psychic	(Fenton 2032)	1.25	5.00	
QUICK, The (Featuring Eric Carmen)				
AIN'T NOTHING GONNA STOP ME/Southern Comfort	(Epic 10516)	3.00	12.00	69
QUICKLY, Tommy				
WILD SIDE OF LIFE/Forget The Other Guy	(Liberty 55753)	1.00	4.00	64
YOU MIGHT AS WELL FORGET HIM/It's As Simple As That	(Liberty 55732)	1.00	4.00	64
QUICKSILVER MESSENGER SERVICE, The				
DOIN' TIME IN THE U.S.A./Changes	(Capitol 3349)	.75	3.00	72
FRESH AIR/Freeway Flyer	(Capitol 2920)	.75	3.00	70
GYPSY LIGHTS/Witches' Moon	(Capitol 4206)	.75	3.00	76
HOLY MOLY/Words Can't Say	(Capitol 2670)	.75	3.00	69
HOPE/I Found Love	(Capitol 3233)	.75	3.00	71
PRIDE OF MAN/Dino's Song	(Capitol 2194)	1.00	4.00	68
SHADY GROVE/Three Or Four Feet From Home	(Capitol 2800)	1.00	4.00	70
STAND BY ME/Bears	(Capitol 2320)	1.00	4.00	69
WHAT ABOUT ME/Good Old Rock & Roll	(Capitol 3046)	.75	3.00	71
WHO DO YOU LOVE/Which Do You Love	(Capitol 2557)	.75	3.00	69
Also see Hopkins, Nicky				
QUINN, Carole				
WHAT'S SO SWEET ABOUT SWEET 16/Good Boy, Bad Boy	(MGM 13265)	1.25	5.00	64
QUINTEROS, Eddie				
COME DANCE WITH ME/Vivian	(Brent 7009)	1.00	4.00	60
LOOKIN' FOR MY BABY/Please Don't Go	(Brent 7012)	1.00	4.00	60
SLOW DOWN SANDY/Linda Lou	(Brent 7014)	1.00	4.00	60
QUOTATIONS, The				
IMAGINATION/Ala-Men-Sa-Aye	(Verve 10245)	2.00	8.00	61
IT CAN HAPPEN TO YOU/I Don't Have To Worry	(DeVenus 107)	1.00	4.00	
NIGHT/Why Do You Do Me Like You Do	(Downstairs 1003)	.75	3.00	74
SEE YOU IN SEPTEMBER/Summer Time Goodbyes	(Verve 10261)	3.00	12.00	62
THIS LOVE OF MINE/Will Reach Heaven Together	(Verve 10252)	3.00	12.00	62

R

TITLE/FLIP	LABEL & NO.	GOOD	NEAR MINT	YR.
RABIN, Mike, & The Demons				
I'M LEAVING YOU/Head Over Heels	(Tower 109)	.75	3.00	64
RABON, Michael, & Choctaw				
LET YOUR LIGHT SHINE ON/Texas Sparrow	(Uni-Abnak 55305)	.75	3.00	71
MARY MILES/Carolina, Hollywood	(Uni-Abnak 55289)	.75	3.00	70
Also see Five Americans, The				
RACEY				
LAY YOUR LOVE ON ME/I Believed You	(Infinity 50007)	.50	2.00	79
SOME GIRLS/Fighting Change	(Infinity 50030)	.50	2.00	79
RACHEL & THE REVOLVERS				
REVOLUTION, THE/Number One	(Dot 16392)	12.50	50.00	62
RACING CARS, The				
BRING ON THE NIGHT/	(Chrysalis 2279)	.50	2.00	78
THEY SHOOT HORSES DON'T THEY/Four Wheel Drive	(Chrysalis 2129)	.50	2.00	77
RADER, Quantrell				
I LOSE MORE GIRLS THAT WAY/The Special Way	(RCA Victor 47-8317)	.75	3.00	64
RADHA KRISHNA TEMPLE, The				
GOVINDA/Govinda Jai Jai	(Apple 1821)	.75	3.00	70
HARE KRISHNA MANTRA/Prayer To The Spiritual Masters	(Apple 1810)	.75	3.00	69
RADNER, Gilda				
HONEY (TOUCH ME WITH MY CLOTHES ON)/The Audition-I Love To Be Unhappy	(Warner Bros 49133)	.50	2.00	79
RAE, Donny, & The Defiants				
BEATLE MANIA/Hold On	(Arlen 521)	1.25	5.00	64
RAE, Linda				
LOOK FOR THE RAINBOW/Teenager	(Mike 4002)	.75	3.00	
RAFFERTY, Gerry (Of Stealer's Wheel)				
BAKER STREET/Big Change In The Weather	(United Artists UA-X1192-Y)	.50	2.00	78
CAN I HAVE MY MONEY BACK/Sign On The Dotted Line	(Blue Thumb 231)	.75	3.00	72
CITY TO CITY/Mattie's Rag	(United Artists UA-XW1098)	.50	2.00	77
DAYS GONE DOWN (STILL GOT THE LIGHT IN YOUR EYES)/Why Won't You Talk To Me?	(United Artists UA-X1298-Y)	.50	2.00	79
GET IT RIGHT NEXT TIME/It's Gonna Be A Long Night	(United Artists UA-X1316Y)	.50	2.00	79
HOME & DRY/Mattie's Rag	(United Artists UA-X1266-Y)	.50	2.00	78
MAKE YOU, BREAK YOU/	(Signpost 70001)	.75	3.00	72
RIGHT DOWN THE LINE/Waiting For The Day	(United Artists UA-X1233-Y)	.50	2.00	78
Also see Humblebums, The				
RAFFERTY, Jim				
(DON'T LET ANOTHER) DAY GO BY/	(London 20077)	.50	2.00	78
TOMORROW IS ANOTHER DAY/	(London 20098)	.50	2.00	78
Jim is Gerry Rafferty's brother.				
RAG DOLLS, The				
DUSTY/Hey, Hoagy	(Mala 493)	.75	3.00	65
SOCIETY GIRL/Ragen (Society Girl Bossa Nova)	(Parkway 921)	.75	3.00	64
RAGAMUFFINS, The				
FUN WE HAD, THE/Don't Be Gone Long	(Tollie 9027)	1.25	5.00	64
RAGING STORMS, The				
DOWN AT THE CORNER/So Hard To Take	(Tran Atlas 691)	1.00	4.00	62
HOUND DOG/Dribble Twist	(Warwick 677)	.75	3.00	62
RAIDERS, The				
CASTLE OF LOVE, THE/Raiders From Outer Space	(Atco 6125)	5.00	20.00	
RAIDERS, The				
STICK SHIFT/Skipping Around	(Vee Jay 504)	.75	3.00	63
(Instrumentals)				
RAIDERS, Paul Revere & The: see Revere, Paul, & The Raiders				
RAIN				
E.S.P./Outta My Life	(A.P.I. 336)	1.50	6.00	
RAINBO (With Cissy Spacek)				
JOHN YOU WENT TOO FAR THIS TIME/C'mon Teach Me To Live	(Roulette 7030)	1.00	4.00	68
RAINBOW: see Blackmore's Rainbow				
RAINBOWS, The				
JU JU HAND/Balla Balla	(Epic 9900)	.75	3.00	66
ONLY A PICTURE/I Know	(Dave 908)	1.25	5.00	63
TILL TOMORROW/Mama Take Your Daughter Back	(Gramo 5508)	1.50	6.00	
RAINBOWS, The				
MY RINGO/He's Hooked On J's	(Dot 16612)	1.25	5.00	64
RAINBOW'S END, The				
I'VE BEEN MISUSED/I Can't Get Enough Of You	(Kef 4454)	.75	3.00	
RAINDROPS, The (Jeff Barry & Ellie Greenwich)				
DON'T LET GO/My Mama Don't Like Him	(Jubilee 5497)	.75	3.00	64
BOOK OF LOVE/I Won't Cry	(Jubilee 5469)	.75	3.00	64
KIND OF BOY YOU CAN'T FORGET, THE/Even Though You Can't Dance	(Jubilee 5455)	.75	3.00	63
LET'S GET TOGETHER/You Got What I Like	(Jubilee 5475)	.75	3.00	64
ONE MORE TEAR/Another Boy Like Mine	(Jubilee 5487)	.75	3.00	64
THAT BOY JOHN/Hanky Panky	(Jubilee 5466)	.75	3.00	63
WHAT A GUY/It's So Wonderful	(Jubilee 5444)	.75	3.00	63
RAINDROPS, The				
LOVE IS LIKE A MOUNTAIN/Maybe	(Corsair 104)	1.00	4.00	60
LOVE IS LIKE A MOUNTAIN/Maybe	(Dore 561)	.75	3.00	60
RAINDROPS, The				
I REMEMBER IN THE STILL OF THE NIGHT/The Sweetheart Song	(Imperial 5785)	3.00	12.00	61
Also see Jumpin' Tones, The				
RAINES, Rita				
SUCH A DAY/Old Devil Moon	(Deed 1010)	1.00	4.00	56
RAINMAKERS, The				
DON'T BE AFRAID/I Won't Turn Away Now	(Discotheque 875)	1.25	5.00	
TELL HER NO/You're Not The Only One	(Phalanx 1029)	1.25	5.00	
RAINY DAYS, The				
TURN ON YOUR LOVELIGHT/Go On & Cry	(Panik 7542)	1.25	5.00	
RAINY DAZE, The				
BLOOD OF OBLIVION/Stop Sign	(Uni 55026)	1.00	4.00	67
DISCOUNT CITY/Good Morning, Mr. Smith	(Uni 55011)	1.00	4.00	67
MAKE ME LAUGH/My Door Is Always Open	(White Whale 279)	1.00	4.00	68
THAT ACAPULCO GOLD/In My Mind Lives A Forest	(Chicory 404)	1.50	6.00	67
THAT ACAPULCO GOLD/In My Mind Lives A Forest	(Uni 55002)	.75	3.00	67
RAITT, Bonnie				
GAMBLIN' MAN/About To Make Me Leave Home	(Warner Bros. 8485)	.50	2.00	77
GOOD ENOUGH/My First Night Alone Without You	(Warner Bros. 8166)	.50	2.00	75
RUNAWAY/Louise	(Warner Bros. 8382)	.50	2.00	77
RUN LIKE A THIEF/Walk Out The Front Door	(Warner Bros. 8189)	.50	2.00	76
TOO LONG AT THE FAIR/Under The Falling Sky	(Warner Bros. 7645)	.50	2.00	72
TWO LIVES/	(Warner Bros. 8430)	.50	2.00	77
YOU GOT TO BE READY FOR LOVE (IF YOU WANNA BE MINE)/	(Warner Bros. 8044)	.50	2.00	75
YOU'RE GONNA GET WHAT'S COMING/The Glow	(Warner Bros. 49116)	.50	2.00	79
RALKE, Don				
TEEN BEAT/Four Paces East	(Warner Bros. 5104)	.75	3.00	59
77 SUNSET STRIP/Sebastian	(Warner Bros. 5025)	.75	3.00	59
Instrumentals				
RALLY PACKS, The (With Jan Berry & Dean Torrance)				
MOVE OUT LITTLE MUSTANG/Bucket Seats	(Imperial 66036)	2.00	8.00	64
RAM JAM				
BLACK BETTY/I Should Have Known	(Epic 8-50357)	.50	2.00	77
(Vocal by Bill Bartlett, of the Lemon Pipers.)				
BLACK BETTY/Black Betty	(Epic ASF-321)	1.00	4.00	77
(12" single issue)				
KEEP YOUR HANDS ON THE WHEEL/Right On The Money	(Epic 8-50451)	.50	2.00	77
PRETTY POISON/Runway Runaway	(Epic 8-50587)	.50	2.00	78
Also see August				
RAMADAS, The				
SUMMER STEADY/Lonely Tears	(Philips 40117)	.75	3.00	63
TEENAGE DREAM/My Angel Eyes	(Philips 40097)	.75	3.00	63
RAMBEAU, Eddie				
CLOCK/If I Were You	(Dyno Voice 225)	.75	3.00	66
CONCRETE & CLAY/Don't Believe Him	(Dyno Voice 204)	.75	3.00	65
MY NAME IS MUD/I Just Need Your Love	(Dyno Voice 207)	.75	3.00	65
YESTERDAY'S NEWSPAPERS/The Train	(Dyno Voice 211)	.75	3.00	65
Also see Joe, Marcy & Eddie Rambeau				
RAMBLERS, The				
BIRDLAND BABY/School Girl	(Almont 313)	.75	3.00	64
FATHER SEBASTIAN/Barbara (I Love You)	(Almont 311)	.75	3.00	64
RAMBLING/Devil Train	(Addit 1257)	.75	3.00	60
SURFIN' SANTA/Silly Little Boy	(Almont 315)	.75	3.00	64
RAMBLES, Renee, & The Rhinestone				
BACKSTAGE WITH RENEE/Renee's Theme Song	(RCA 0846)	.50	2.00	72
RAMONES, The				
BLITZKREIG BOP/Havana Affair	(Sire 725)	.50	2.00	76
CALIFORNIA SUN/I Don't Wanna Walk Around With You-I Wanna Be Your Boyfriend	(Sire 734)	.50	2.00	76
DON'T COME CLOSE/I Don't Want You	(Sire 1025)	.50	2.00	78
DO YOU WANNA DANCE?/Baby Sitter	(Sire 1017)	.50	2.00	78
NEEDLES & PINS/I Wanted Everything	(Sire 1045)	.50	2.00	79
ROCK 'N' ROLL HIGH SCHOOL/Do You Wanna Dance? (Live Version)	(Sire 1051)	.50	2.00	79
ROCKAWAY BEACH/Locket Love	(Sire 1008)	.50	2.00	77
SHEENA IS A PUNK ROCKER/I Don't Care	(Sire 746)	.50	2.00	77
RAMOS, Juan, Y Los Principes				
ELVIS PRESLEY: EL REY DEL ROCK 'N' ROLL/Te Vas Angel Mio	(Teardrop 3397)	.75	3.00	77
RAMPAGES, The				
ALLIGATOR STOMP/My Dear Heart	(Wedge 1011)	1.00	4.00	64
RAMRODS, The				
BOING/War Cry	(Amy 846)	.75	3.00	62
FLOWERS IN MY MIND/	(Plymouth 2965)	.75	3.00	
(GHOST) RIDERS IN THE SKY/Zig Zag	(Amy 813)	.75	3.00	60
MOONLIGHT SURF/Night Ride	(R&H 1001)	.75	3.00	
SLEE-ZEE/Slouch-ee	(Queen 24014)	.75	3.00	62
TAKE ME BACK TO MY BOOTS & SADDLE/Loch Lomond Rock	(Amy 817)	.75	3.00	61
(Instrumentals)				
RANCHEROS, The				
LINDA'S TUNE/Little Linda	(Lonnie 5005)	1.25	5.00	63
LINDA'S TUNE/Little Linda	(Dot 16572)	.75	3.00	63
RANDAL, Ted				
WHAT IS A HIT/What Is A Disc Jockey	(Verve 10119)	1.00	4.00	59
RANDALL, Elliott				
I GIVE UP/High On Love	(Kirshner 4269)	.50	2.00	77
SAMANTHA/	(Kirshner 4271)	.50	2.00	77
RANDALL, Tony				
BYRD (YOU'RE THE BIRD OF THEM ALL)/Annie Doesn't Live Here Anymore	(Mercury 72671)	.75	3.00	67

TITLE/FLIP	LABEL & NO.	GOOD	NEAR MINT	YR.
RANDAZZO, Teddy (Of The Three Chuckles)				
AWKWARD AGE/Laughing On The Outside	(ABC-Paramount 10014)	1.00	4.00	59
BIG WIDE WORLD/Be Sure My Love	(Colpix 662)	.75	3.00	62
BROKEN BELL/Let The Sunshine In	(ABC-Paramount 10228)	1.00	4.00	61
CHERIE/The Way Of A Clown (In Italian)	(ABC-Paramount 10103)	1.00	4.00	60
COTTON FIELDS/Dance To The Locomotion	(ABC-Paramount 10350)	1.00	4.00	62
DEAR HEART/Just Hold My Hand	(Colpix 684)	.75	3.00	63
DON'T GO AWAY/One More Chance	(ABC-Paramount 10247)	1.00	4.00	61
DOO DAH/Pretty Blue Eyes	(DCP 1003)	.75	3.00	63
I'M ON A MERRY-GO-ROUND/Lies	(ABC-Paramount 10043)	1.00	4.00	59
IT WASN'T A DREAM/Echoes	(ABC-Paramount 10377)	1.00	4.00	62
JOURNEY TO LOVE/Misery	(ABC-Paramount 10131)	1.00	4.00	60
LITTLE SERENADE/Be My Kitten Little Chicken	(Vik 0330)	1.25	5.00	58
NEXT STOP PARADISE/How Could You Know	(Vik 0277)	1.25	5.00	58
TEENAGE SENORITA/Blue Hawaiian Moon	(ABC-Paramount 10312)	1.00	4.00	62
WAY OF A CLOWN, THE/Cherie	(ABC-Paramount 10088)	1.00	4.00	60
YOU ARE ALWAYS IN MY HEART/Pepito	(ABC-Paramount 9998)	1.00	4.00	59
YOU DON'T CARE ANYMORE/How I Need You	(ABC-Paramount 10068)	1.00	4.00	59
Also see Kartunes, The				
RAND, Bobby				
DON'T MAKE MY POOR HEART WEEP/Talking To Myself	(Dot 15580)	1.00	4.00	57
RANDELL, Buddy				
BE MY BABY/Randi, Randi	(Uni 55209)	.75	3.00	70
Also see Knickerbockers, The				
RANDELL, Denny				
HEY CHICKIE BABY/There's Gonna Be A Showdown	(Cameo 255)	1.00	4.00	63
I'M BACK BABY (Answer song)/ Blues For A 4-string Guitar	(Ascot 2137)	1.25	5.00	63
LONELY MELODY/Limbo Lou	(Jamie 1241)	1.25	5.00	62
RAN-DELLS, The				
BEYOND THE STARS/Wintertime	(RSVP 1104)	1.50	6.00	64
MARTIAN HOP, THE/Forgive Me Darling	(Chairman 4403)	1.25	5.00	64
SOUND OF THE SUN/Come On & Love Me Too	(Chairman 4407)	1.25	5.00	63
RANDLE, Dell				
INTRODUCING THE BEATLES TO MONEY LAND/ The Monkey & The Beatles	(Shakari 101)	1.50	6.00	64
RANDOLPH, Boots				
YAKETY SAX/I Really Don't Want To Know	(Monument 804)	.75	3.00	63
YAKETY SAX/Percolator	(RCA Victor 47-7395)	1.25	5.00	58
(Shown as by Randy Randolph)				
RANDOLPH, Dean				
GIRL IN THE WHITE CONVERTIBLE/False Love	(Chancellor 1138)	.75	3.00	63
HOW ABOUT THAT/Come With Me	(Chancellor 1122)	.75	3.00	63
RANDOLPH, Randy: see Randolph, Boots				
RANDY & RALPH				
DON'T LEAVE ME LONELY TONIGHT/Hungry	(United Artists 146)	1.00	4.00	58
RANDY & THE RAINBOWS (Featuring Dominick Safuto)				
BONNIE'S PART OF TOWN/Can It Be	(Mike 4008)	2.00	8.00	66
DENISE/Come Back (Blue label)	(Rust 5059)	2.50	10.00	63
DENISE/Come Back (Rust & white label)	(Rust 5059)	.75	3.00	63
HAPPY TEENAGER/Dry Your Eyes	(Rust 5080)	1.00	4.00	64
I'LL BE SEEING YOU/Oh To Get Away	(B.T. Puppy 535)	1.50	6.00	67
JOYRIDE/Little Hot Rod Susie	(Rust 5101)	1.25	5.00	64
LITTLE STAR/Sharin'	(Rust 5091)	1.25	5.00	64
LOVELY LIES/I'll Forget Her Tomorrow	(Mike 4001)	1.50	6.00	66
QUARTER TO THREE/He's A Fugitive	(Mike 4004)	1.50	6.00	66
WHY DO KIDS GROW UP/She's My Angel	(Rust 5073)	1.00	4.00	63
Also see Dialtones, The				
Also see Madison Street				
RANDY & THE ROCKETS				
GENEVIEVE/If You Really Care	(Viking 1000)	1.00	4.00	59
LET'S DO THE CAJUN TWIST/	(Jin 161)	.75	3.00	62
RANDY PIE				
BACK STREET BOY/	(Polydor 14424)	.50	2.00	77
RANEY, Zyndall				
GOT THAT LONESOME FEELIN'/	(Rimrock 243)	.75	3.00	
RANGERS, The				
JUSTINE/Reputation	(Challenge 59239)	.75	3.00	64
MOGUL MONSTER/Snow Skiing	(Challenge 9196)	.75	3.00	64
RIDERS IN THE SKY/Four On The Floor	(FTP 404)	.75	3.00	61
RANKIN, Kenny				
COMIN' DOWN/	(Little David 725)	.50	2.00	75
CREEPIN'/	(Little David 733)	.50	2.00	76
ON & ON/	(Little David 735)	.50	2.00	77
SUNDAY KIND OF LOVE/Inside	(Little David 732)	.50	2.00	76
THERE'LL BE NO OTHER LOVE (FOR ME)/ Knowing I Won't Go Back There	(Columbia 43201)	1.00	4.00	65
WHEN SUNNY GETS BLUE/I Love You	(Little David 737)	.50	2.00	77
WHERE DID MY LITTLE GIRL GO/U.S. Mail	(Columbia 43036)	1.00	4.00	64
RANK, Ken				
TWIN CITY SAUCER/Ken's Thing (By the Jades)	(Fenton 2194)	5.00	20.00	
RARE BREED, The				
COME & TAKE A RIDE IN MY BOAT/ Take Me To This World Of Yours	(Attack A-1403)	1.00	4.00	66
Also see Ohio Express, The				
RARE EARTH				
BORN TO WANDER/Here Comes The Night	(Rare Earth 5021)	.50	2.00	70
CHAINED/Fresh From The Can	(Rare Earth 5057)	.50	2.00	73
GET READY/Magic Key	(Rare Earth 5012)	.50	2.00	70
GOOD TIME SALLY/	(Rare Earth 5048)	.50	2.00	72
HEY BIG BROTHER/	(Rare Earth 5038)	.50	2.00	71
I CAN FEEL MY LOVE RISING/S.O.S. (Stop Her On Sight)	(Prodigal 0643)	.50	2.00	78
I JUST WANT TO CELEBRATE/	(Rare Earth 5031)	.50	2.00	71
(I KNOW) I'M LOSING YOU/When Joanie Smiles	(Rare Earth 5017)	.50	2.00	70
IT MAKES YOU HAPPY (BUT IT AIN'T GONNA LAST TOO LONG)/	(Rare Earth 5058)	.50	2.00	75
MIDNIGHT LADY/	(Rare Earth 5060)	.50	2.00	76
STOP-WHERE DID OUR LOVE GO/Mother's Oats	(Verve 10622)	.75	3.00	68
WARM RIDE/Would You Like To Come Along	(Prodigal 0640)	.50	2.00	78
WE'RE GONNA HAVE A GOOD TIME/	(Rare Earth 5052)	.50	2.00	73
WHAT'D I SAY/	(Rare Earth 5043)	.50	2.00	72
RASCALS, The: see Young Rascals				
RASPBERRIES, The (With Eric Carmen)				
CRUSIN' MUSIC/Party's Over	(Capitol 4001)	1.00	4.00	74
DON'T WANT TO SAY GOODBYE/Rock & Roll Mama	(Capitol 3280)	1.00	4.00	72
DON'T WANT TO SAY GOODBYE/Ecstacy	(Capitol 3826)	.75	3.00	74
DRIVIN' AROUND/Might As Well	(Capitol 3885)	1.00	4.00	74
GO ALL THE WAY/With You In My Life	(Capitol 3348)	1.00	4.00	72
HANDS ON YOU/Overnight Sensation	(Capitol 3946)	1.00	4.00	74
I'M A ROCKER/Money Down	(Capitol 3765)	1.00	4.00	73
I WANNA BE WITH YOU/Goin' Nowhere Tonight	(Capitol 3473)	1.00	4.00	72
LET'S PRETEND/Every Way I Can	(Capitol 3546)	1.00	4.00	73
OVERNIGHT SENSATION (HIT RECORD)/Hands On You	(Capitol 3946)	1.00	4.00	74
TONIGHT/Hard To Get Over A Heartbreak	(Capitol 3610)	1.00	4.00	73
Also see Choir, The				
Also see Cyrus Erie				
Also see Quick, The				
RASPBERRY, Larry, & The Highsteppers				
PLEASE FORGIVE A FOOL (SONG FOR MISSY)/	(Mercury 76028)	.50	2.00	79
Also see Gentrys, The				
RATCHELL				
LAZY LADY/Problems	(Decca 32893)	.50	2.00	72
RAT PACK				
I CAN DO THE MOUSE NOW/Crazy Crazy Love	(DCP 1145)	2.00	8.00	65
Also see Carmel				
RATFINKS, J.C.W. (Featuring Mark Gutkowski)				
POP GOES THE WEASEL/Magic Windmill	(Buddah BDA-40)	.75	3.00	68
Also see 1910 Fruitgum Co. The				
RATIONALS, The				
FEELIN' LOST/Little Girls Cry	(A^2 103)	1.50	6.00	66
GUITAR ARMY/Sunset	(Genesis 1)	1.50	6.00	
HANDBAGS & GLADRAGS/	(Crewe 340)	1.00	4.00	69
I NEED YOU/Out In The Streets	(A^2 107)	1.50	6.00	66
LEAVIN' HERE/Respect	(A^2 104)	1.50	6.00	66
LOOK WHAT YOU'RE DOIN'/Gave My Love	(A^2 101)	1.50	6.00	66
RESPECT/Feelin Lost	(A^2 104/103)	1.50	6.00	66
RESPECT/Feelin' Lost	(Cameo 437)	1.00	4.00	66
RATNER, Marc				
DON'T GO LOOKING/Go Ahead	(RSO 1004)	.50	2.00	79
RATTLES, The				
DEVIL'S ON THE LOOSE/I Know You Don't Know	(London 1037)	1.00	4.00	
SHA LA LA LA LEE/Dance	(Mercury 72554)	.75	3.00	66
WITCH, THE/Geraldine	(Probe 480)	.75	3.00	70
RAVAN, Genya (Of Ten Wheel Drive)				
BACK IN MY ARMS AGAIN/Do It Just For Me	(20th Century-Fox 2374)	.50	2.00	78
JERRY'S PIGEONS/Cornered	(20th Century-Fox 2384)	.50	2.00	78
KEEP ON GROWING/	(ABC-Dunhill 4530)	.50	2.00	73
STEVE/It's Me	(20th Century-Fox 2430)	.50	2.00	79
RAVEL, Joe				
HOUSE OF COOL, THE/The Bronx Blues	(Goal 701)	1.00	4.00	
RAVELLES, The				
PSYCHEDELIC MOVEMENT/She's Forever On My Mind	(Mobie 3430)	1.25	5.00	68
RAVEN				
CHILDREN AT OUR FEET/Here Come A Truck	(Columbia 45163)	1.00	4.00	70
FEELIN' GOOD/Green Mountain Dream	(Columbia 44988)	1.00	4.00	69
RAVEN				
CALAMITY JANE/Now She's Gone	(Rust 5123)	1.00	4.00	63
RAVENAIRS, The				
TOGETHER FOREVER/A Night To Remember	(Algonquin 718)	2.00	8.00	
RAVENSCROFT, Thurl				
DR. GEEK/I'll Pay As I Go	(Aardell 105)	1.25	5.00	
RAVONS, The				
TEEN-AGE IDOL/I'm A Fugitive	(Davis 464)	1.00	4.00	59
RAWLS, Lou				
IN MY HEART/That Lucky Old Sun	(Capitol 4622)	.75	3.00	61
IN MY LITTLE BLACK BOOK/ Just Thought You'd Like To Know	(Candix 305)	1.00	4.00	60
KIDDIO/Walkin' (For Miles)	(Shar-Dee 705)	1.00	4.00	60
LOVE LOVE LOVE/My Heart Belongs To You	(Shar-Dee 702)	1.00	4.00	60
THREE O'CLOCK IN THE MORNING/ Nothing Really Feels The Same	(Capitol 5424)	.75	3.00	65
TOBACCO ROAD/Blues For A Four String Guitar	(Capitol 5049)	.75	3.00	63
WHEN WE GET OLD/80 Ways	(Candix 312)	1.00	4.00	61
RAY, Annita, & The Nature Boys				
ELVIS PRESLEY BLUES, THE/Frankies Song	(Dream 1300)	3.00	12.00	56
RAY & THE DARCHAES				
CAROL/Little Girl So Fine	(Aljon 1249/1250)	1.25	5.00	62
DARLING FOREVER/There Will Always Be	(Buzzy 202)	3.75	15.00	
RAY, Bobby, & Cadillacs				
I SAW YOU/La Bomba	(Capitol 4935)	.75	3.00	63
RAY, Diane				
PLEASE DON'T TALK TO THE LIFEGUARD/ That's All I Want From You	(Mercury 72117)	.75	3.00	63
RAY, Johnnie				
ALL OF ME/Sinner Am I	(Columbia 39788)	1.25	5.00	52
BUILD YOUR LOVE (ON A STRONG FOUNDATION)/ Street Of Memories	(Columbia 40942)	1.00	4.00	57
CRY/Little White Cloud That Cried	(Okeh 6840)	1.50	6.00	51
HERNANDO'S HIDEAWAY/Hey There	(Columbia 40224)	1.25	5.00	54
I'VE WAITED SO LONG/You Gotta Pet Me Baby	(Okeh 18030)	1.50	6.00	53
JOHNNIE'S COMIN' HOME/Love, Love, Love	(Columbia 40578)	1.25	5.00	55
JUST WALKING IN THE RAIN/In The Candlelight	(Columbia 40729)	1.00	4.00	56
LET'S FORGET IT NOW/In The Heart Of A Fool	(Cadence 1387)	1.00	4.00	59
LOVE ME (BABY CAN'T YOU LOVE ME)/ Faith Can Move Mountains	(Columbia 39837)	1.00	4.00	52
PLEASE, MR. SUN/Here Am I Brokenhearted	(Columbia 39636)	1.00	4.00	52
SOMEBODY STOLE MY GAL/Glad Rag Doll	(Columbia 39961)	1.00	4.00	53
TANGO OF LOVE/Mirage	(Standard 183)	1.25	5.00	
WALKIN' MY BABY BACK HOME/Give Me Time	(Columbia 39750)	1.00	4.00	52
WHAT'S THE USE/Mountains In The Moonlight	(Columbia 39698)	1.00	4.00	52
YES TONIGHT JOSEPHINE/No Wedding Today	(Columbia 40893)	1.00	4.00	57
YOU DON'T OWE ME A THING/Look Homeward Angel	(Columbia 40803)	1.00	4.00	56
RAY, Leda				
CRY, CRY A FEW TEARS FOR ELVIS/ Think I'm Gonna Love You	(Allied Artists 008)	.50	2.00	77
RAY, Ritchie				
COME BACK TO ME/The Twirl	(Imperial 5981)	.75	3.00	63
RAYBURN, Margie				
BOY & A GIRL, A/Tell Him No	(Liberty 55183)	1.00	4.00	59
EVERY MINUTE OF THE DAY/Take A Gamble On Me	(Liberty 55043)	1.00	4.00	56
HERE I AM/Cast A Little Spell On Me	(Challenge 9110)	.75	3.00	61
INCLOSED ARE MY TEARS/The Boy From The Hills	(Alma 81)	1.25	5.00	54
I'M AVAILABLE/If You Were	(Liberty 55102)	1.00	4.00	57
MAKE ME A QUEEN AGAIN/Wait	(Liberty 55174)	1.00	4.00	59
THEY ALL SAY I'M LUCKY/I'm The One For You	(S&G 5005)	1.25	5.00	54
RAYE, Cal				
YOU'RE MY LOVIN BABY/My Tears Start To Fall	(Super 101)	1.00	4.00	
RAYE, Patsy, & The Beatniks				
BEATNIK'S BLUES/Beatnik's Wish	(Roulette 4208)	1.00	4.00	59
RAYMARKS, The				
DR. FEELGOOD/I Believed	(Jerden 774)	.75	3.00	66
RAYNOR, Wilguis J.C.				
MY CHRISTMAS CAME EARLY/A Christmas Letter To Daddy (With Donna Jo)	(RTF 101)	.50	2.00	77
MY HEART'S CONTENT (GOODBYE FROM THE KING)/ Just Before Dawn	(RTF 100)	.50	2.00	77

TITLE/FLIP	LABEL & NO.	GOOD	NEAR MINT	YR.
RAYS, The (With Hal Miller & Frankie Valli)				
ARE YOU HAPPY NOW/Bright Brown Eyes	(Perri 1004)	1.50	6.00	62
RAY-VONS, The				
JUDY/Regina	(Laurie 3248)	3.75	15.00	64
RAZOR'S EDGE, The				
DON'T LET ME CATCH YOU IN HIS ARMS/Night & Day	(Pow 415)	1.00	4.00	66
LET'S CALL IT A DAY GIRL/Avril (April)	(Pow 101)	1.00	4.00	66
R.C. & THE TAMBORINES				
TAMBORINE/Quirk	(Ikon 169)	.75	3.00	
REA, Chris				
DON'T WANT YOUR BEST FRIEND/ No Qualifications	(United Artists-Magnet 1301)	.50	2.00	79
DIAMONDS/Cleveland Calling	(United Artists-Magnet 1285)	.50	2.00	79
FOOL (IF YOU THINK IT'S OVER)/ Midnight Love	(United Artists-Magnet 1198)	.50	2.00	78
WHATEVER HAPPENED TO BENNY SANTINI/ Three Angels	(United Artists-Magnet 1252)	.50	2.00	78
REACTIONS				
JUST A LITTLE LOVE/Let Me Hang Around You	(Cool Sound 701)	1.00	4.00	
THAT GIRL/Our Wonderful Love	(Mutual 509)	1.25	5.00	
READ, John Dawson				
FRIEND OF MINE IS GOING BLIND, A/ Superficial Things	(Chrysalis 2105)	.50	2.00	75
REAL ORIGINAL BEATLES, The				
BEATLE STORY, THE/The Beatle Story (Part 2)	(Dot 16655)	1.50	6.00	64
REASONS, The				
WINDOW SHOPPING/Then Came Heartbreak	(United Artists 961)	1.25	5.00	65
REBEL ROUSERS, The				
NIGHT SURFIN'/Thunder	(Memphis 107)	1.00	4.00	64
REBELS, The				
WILD WEEKEND/Wild Weekend Cha Cha	(Marlee 0094)	2.50	10.00	60
Also see Buffalo Rebels, The				
Also see Rockin Rebels, The				
REBENACK, Mac (Dr. John)				
GOOD TIMES/Sahara	(Ace 611)	2.00	8.00	61
STORM WARNING/	(Rex 1008)	2.00	8.00	
REBOUNDS, The				
(I'M NOT YOUR) STEPPING STONE/Since I Fell For You	(Tower 288)	1.25	5.00	66

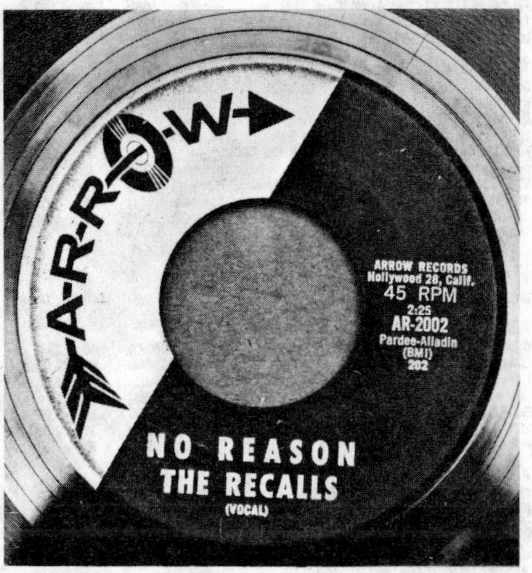

TITLE/FLIP	LABEL & NO.	GOOD	NEAR MINT	YR.
RECALLS, The				
NO REASON/	(Arrow 2002)	1.25	5.00	
NOBODY'S GUY/	(Arrow 2003)	1.25	5.00	
RECORDS				
STARRY EYES/Paint Her Face	(Virgin 67000)	.50	2.00	79
TEENARAMA/Held Up High	(Virgin 67002)	.50	2.00	79

TITLE/FLIP	LABEL & NO.	GOOD	NEAR MINT	YR.
REDBONE (Featuring Pat & Lolly Vegas)				
COME & GET YOUR LOVE/Day To Day Life	(Epic 11035)	.50	2.00	74
CONDITION YOUR CONDITION/Poison Ivy	(Epic 10946)	.50	2.00	72
FIAS DO/	(Epic 10910)	.50	2.00	72
GIVE OUR LOVE ANOTHER TRY/Funky Silk	(RCA 11096)	.50	2.00	78
MAGGIE/New Blue Sermonette	(Epic 10670)	.50	2.00	71
SUZIE GIRL/Interstate Highway 101	(Epic 50015)	.50	2.00	74
WE WERE ALL WOUNDED AT WOUNDED KNEE/	(Epic 10979)	.50	2.00	73
WITCH QUEEN OF NEW ORLEANS, THE/Chant: 13th Hour	(Epic 10979)	.50	2.00	73
Also see Avantis, The				
REDBONE, Leon				
CHAMPAGNE CHARLIE/Please Don't Talk About Me When I'm Gone	(Warner Bros. 8706)	.50	2.00	78
SHINE ON HARVEST MOON/Crazy Blues	(Warner Bros. 8336)	.50	2.00	77
REDDING, Dexter				
GOD BLESS/Love Is Bigger Than Baseball	(Capricorn 0033)	1.00	4.00	
REDD, Sharon, Ula Hedwig & Charlotte Crossley				
AIN'T NO MAN WORTH IT/Put It Where You Want It	(Columbia 10713)	.50	2.00	78
DOES YOU MAMA KNOW ABOUT ME/Maiden Voyage	(Columbia 10665)	.50	2.00	77
These girls were previously backup singers with Bette Midler's group, known as the Harlettes				
REDDY, Helen				
AIN'T NO WAY TO TREAT A LADY/Long Time Looking	(Capitol 4128)	.50	2.00	75
ANGIE BABY/I Think I'll Write A Song	(Capitol 3972)	.50	2.00	74
BLUEBIRD/You Don't Need A Reason	(Capitol 4108)	.50	2.00	75
CANDLE ON THE WATER/	(Capitol 4521)	.50	2.00	77
CRAZY LOVE/Best Friend	(Capitol 3128)	.50	2.00	71
DELTA DAWN/If We Could Still Be Friends	(Capitol 3645)	.50	2.00	73
EMOTION/I've Been Wanting You So Long	(Capitol 4021)	.50	2.00	75
GLADIOLA/You Make It So Easy	(Capitol 4350)	.50	2.00	76
HAPPY GIRLS, THE/	(Capitol 4487)	.50	2.00	77
I AM WOMAN/More Than You Could Take	(Capitol 3350)	.50	2.00	72
I CAN'T HEAR YOU NO MORE/Music Is My Life	(Capitol 4312)	.50	2.00	76
I DON'T KNOW HOW TO LOVE HIM/I Believe In Music	(Capitol 3027)	.50	2.00	71
KEEP ON SINGING/You're My Home	(Capitol 3845)	.50	2.00	74
LEAVE ME ALONE (RUBY RED DRESS)/ The Old Fashioned Way	(Capitol 3768)	.50	2.00	73
LET ME BE YOUR WOMAN/	(Capitol 4786)	.50	2.00	79
MAKE LOVE TO ME/	(Capitol 4712)	.50	2.00	79
NO SAD SONG/	(Capitol 2131)	.50	2.00	71
PEACEFUL/What Would They Say	(Capitol 3527)	.50	2.00	73
READY OR NOT/	(Capitol 4582)	.50	2.00	78
SOMEWHERE IN THE NIGHT/Ten To Eight	(Capitol 4192)	.50	2.00	75
WE'LL SING IN THE SUNSHINE/	(Capitol 4555)	.50	2.00	78
YOU & ME AGAINST THE WORLD/Love Song For Jeffrey	(Capitol 3897)	.50	2.00	74
YOU'RE MY WORLD/Thank You	(Capitol 4418)	.50	2.00	77
REDELL, Teddy				
JUDY/Can't You See	(Atco 6162)	.75	3.00	60
PIPELINER/I Want To Hold You	(Vaden 117)	1.25	5.00	60
PIPELINER/I Want To Hold You	(Hi 2024)	.75	3.00	60
REDEYE				
GAMES/Collections Of Yesterday & Now	(Pentagram 204)	.50	2.00	70
RED EYE BLUES/The Making Of A Hero	(Pentagram 206)	.50	2.00	71
REDJACKS, The				
BIG BROWN EYES/To Make You Mine	(Oklahoma 5005)	2.50	10.00	58
BIG BROWN EYES/To Make You Mine	(Apt 25006)	1.00	4.00	58
REDS				
VICTIMS/Not You	(A&M 2175)	.50	2.00	79
REDWAY, Mike				
JOHN KENNEDY/Come Summer	(London 10613)	.75	3.00	64
REDWING				
BONNIE BONES/I'm Your Lover Man	(Fantasy 670)	.75	3.00	71
CALIFORNIA BLUES/Dark Thursday	(Fantasy 657)	.75	3.00	71
FOXFIRE/Foxfire	(Fantasy 730)	.75	3.00	73
SOUL THEFT/Reaching Out	(Fantasy 682)	.75	3.00	72
REDWOODS, The (With Jeff Barry)				
NEVER TAKE IT AWAY/Unemployment Insurance	(Epic 9473)	2.50	10.00	62
SHAKE SHAKE SHERRY/The Memory Lingers On	(Epic 9447)	2.50	10.00	62
WHERE YOU USE TO BE/Please Mr. Scientist	(Epic 9505)	2.50	10.00	62
REED, Chuck				
JUST PLAIN HURT/Talkin' No Trash	(Choctaw 101)	.75	3.00	62
JUST PLAIN HURT/Talkin' No Trash	(Hit 101)	.75	3.00	62
REED, Dean				
FEMALE HERCULES/La Novia	(Capitol 4608)	1.00	4.00	61
SEARCH, THE/Anabelle	(Capitol 4121)	1.00	4.00	59
REED, Denny				
TEENAGER FEELS IT TOO, A/Hot Water	(MCI 1024)	3.00	12.00	60
TEENAGER FEELS IT TOO, A/Hot Water	(Trey 3007)	1.00	4.00	60
LONELY LITTLE BLUEBIRD/No One Cares	(Trey 3014)	1.00	4.00	61
REED, Jerry				
GOODNIGHT, IRENE/I'm Movin' On	(Columbia 42417)	.75	3.00	62
HULLY GULLY GUITARS/Twist-A-Roo	(Columbia 42533)	.75	3.00	62
IT SURE IS BLUE OUT TONIGHT/Hit & Run	(Columbia 42183)	.75	3.00	61
LET'S GET READY FOR THE SUMMER/The Shock	(Columbia 42808)	.75	3.00	63
LOVE & WAR (AIN'T MUCH DIFFERENCE IN THE TWO)/ Love Is The Cause Of It All	(Columbia 42047)	.75	3.00	61
LOVE DON'T GROW ON TREES/The Mountain Man	(Columbia 42863)	.75	3.00	63
PITY THE FOOL/I've Got Everybody Fooled But Me	(Columbia 42311)	.75	3.00	62
SOLDIER'S JOY/Little Lovin Liza	(NRC 5008)	1.00	4.00	59
TOO OLD TO CUT THE MUSTARD/ Overlooked & Underloved	(Columbia 42639)	.75	3.00	62
REED, Larry, The & Shados				
LITTLE MISS SURFER/Bread N' Butler	(Arlen 515)	1.00	4.00	63
REED, Lou (Of The Velvet Underground)				
CHARLEY'S GIRL/Nowhere At All	(RCA 10573)	.50	2.00	76
CRAZY FEELING/Nowhere At All	(RCA 10648)	.50	2.00	76
I BELIEVE IN LOVE/Senselessly Cruel	(Arista 0215)	.50	2.00	76
SALLY CAN'T DANCE/	(RCA 10081)	.50	2.00	74
SATELLITE OF LOVE/Walk & Talk It	(RCA 0964)	.50	2.00	73
VICIOUS/	(RCA 0054)	.50	2.00	73
WALK ON THE WILD SIDE/Perfect Day	(RCA 0887)	.50	2.00	73
REESE, Della				
AND THAT REMINDS ME/I Cried For You	(Jubilee 5292)	1.00	4.00	57
DON'T YOU KNOW/Soldier, Won't You Marry Me	(RCA Victor 47-7591)	.75	3.00	59
NOT ONE MINUTE MORE/You're My Love	(RCA Victor 47-7644)	.75	3.00	59
SOMEDAY/Faraway Boy	(RCA Victor 47-7706)	.75	3.00	60
REFLECTIONS, The				
GIRL IN THE CANDY STORE/Your Kind Of Love	(Golden World 29)	.75	3.00	66
HENPECKED GUY, A/Don't Do That To Me	(Golden World 16)	.75	3.00	64
I REALLY MUST KNOW/Maybe Tomorrow	(Cross Roads 401)	3.75	15.00	61
IN THE STILL OF THE NIGHT/Tic Toc	(Tigre 602)	2.50	10.00	
(JUST LIKE) ROMEO & JULIET/ Can't You Tell By The Look In My Eyes	(Golden World 8/9)	.75	3.00	64
LIKE ADAM & EVE/Vito's House	(ABC 10794)	.75	3.00	66
LIKE COLUMBUS DID/Lonely Girl	(Golden World 12)	.75	3.00	64

TITLE/FLIP	LABEL & NO.	GOOD	NEAR MINT	YR.
OOWEE NOW/Talkin Bout My Girl	(Golden World 15)	.75	3.00	64
OUT OF THE PICTURE/June Bride	(Golden World 24)	.75	3.00	66
POOR MAN'S SON/Comin' At You	(Golden World 20)	.75	3.00	65
ROCKET TO THE MOON/Because Of You	(Cross Roads 402)	3.75	15.00	62
SHABBY LITTLE HUT/You're My Baby	(Golden World 19)	.75	3.00	64
THREE STEPS FROM TRUE LOVE/	(Capitol 4072)	.75	3.00	75
UNBORN MAN/She's Running Away	(Flax 1001)	.75	3.00	
WHEELIN' & DEALIN/Deborah Ann	(Golden World 22)	.75	3.00	65
WHEELIN DEALIN/Deborah Ann	(Golden World 22)	.75	3.00	65
YOU'RE GONNA FIND OUT YOU NEED ME/Long Cigarette	(ABC 10822)	.75	3.00	66
Even though all of these releases are shown as being by a group using the same name, the possibility exists that they are not all by the same group.				
Also see High & Mighty				
REGAL, Mike				
TOO YOUNG/Is It True What They Say About Barbara	(Kapp 506)	2.00	8.00	63
REGALS, The				
SEE YOU IN THE MORNING/Yes, My Love	(Lavender 1452)	1.00	4.00	
REGAN, Bob				
TARANTULA/Highland Lassie	(Challenge 59244)	.75	3.00	64
REGAN, Eddie				
TALK ABOUT HEARTACHES/Playin' Hide & Seek	(ABC-Paramount 10795)	1.25	5.00	66
REGAN, Joan				
CROCE DI ORO/Evermore	(London 1605)	1.25	5.00	55
REGAN, Tex, & Jim Myers				
PRETTY BABY ROCK/J & D Hop	(Fortune 211)	1.00	4.00	60
REGAN, Tommy				
I ADORE YOU/Nine To Five	(World Artists 1049)	1.00	4.00	65
NEVER STOP LOVING YOU/ This Time I'm Losing You (With the Marcels)	(Colpix 725)	6.25	25.00	64
REGENTS, The				
BARBARA-ANN/I'm So Lonely	(Cousins 1002)	10.00	40.00	61
BARBARA ANN/I'm So Lonely	(Gee 1065)	1.00	4.00	61
LIAR/Don't Be A Fool	(Gee 1073)	1.25	5.00	61
RUNAROUND/Laura My Darling	(Gee 1071)	1.25	5.00	61
Also see Cardboard Zeppelin				
Also see Curtis, Jimmy				
Also see Desires				
Also see Harper, Chuck				
Also see Law, Johnny Four				
Also see Little David				
Also see Mareno, Lee				
Also see 1929 Depression				
Also see Runarounds, The				
Also see Villari, Guy				
REGENTS, The				
ME & YOU/Playmates	(Blue Cat 110)	1.00	4.00	65
SUMMERTIME BLUES/	(Peoria 0008)	1.50	6.00	
THAT'S WHAT I CALL A GOOD TIME/	(Kayo 101)	1.50	6.00	
REID, Mathew				
CRY MYSELF TO SLEEP/Lollypops Went Out Of Style	(Topix 6006)	3.75	15.00	61
FADED ROSES "THE TOP 40 SONG"/Tomorrow	(Sceptre 1238)	3.75	15.00	
JANE/Why Start	(ABC-Paramount 10259)	3.75	15.00	61
THROUGH MY TEARS/The Tarzan Twist (Bwana Ungava)	(ABC 10305)	3.75	15.00	62
Also see Valli, Frankie				
REISMAN, Joe				
ARMEN'S THEME/I'll Take You Dancing	(RCA Victor 47-6740)	1.00	4.00	56
PAMELA THROWS A PARTY/Navajo Nocturne	(RCA Victor 47-6826)	1.00	4.00	57
SPANISH MARCHING SONG, THE/The French Cadets (Instrumentals.)	(Roulette 4137)	1.00	4.00	59
Also see De Zasta, Gen.				
REJOICE				
GOLDEN GATE PARK/Sonora	(Dunhill 4158)	.75	3.00	68
QUICK DRAW MAN/November Snow	(Dunhill 4176)	.75	3.00	68
RELATIONS, The				
BACK TO THE BEACH/ Too Proud To Let You know	(Davy Jones Presents 664)	1.50	6.00	
BACK TO THE BEACH/Too Proud To Let You Know	(Demand 501)	1.25	5.00	
CROWD WITH THE PHONY TATOO/Say You Love Me	(Zell's 712)	1.00	4.00	
WHAT DID I DO WRONG/Too Proud To Let You Know	(Kape 703)	.75	3.00	
RELF, Keith (Of The Yardbirds)				
MR. ZERO/Knowing	(Epic 10044)	1.25	5.00	66
SHAPES IN MY MIND/Blue Sands	(Epic 10110)	1.25	5.00	67
RELLA, Cinda				
BRING ME A BEATLE FOR XMAS/Cla-Wence	(Drum Boy 112)	2.00	8.00	64
REMAINS, The				
DIDDY WAH DIDDY/Once Before	(Epic 10001)	1.00	4.00	66
DON'T LOOK BACK/Me About You	(Epic 10060)	1.00	4.00	66
I CANT GET AWAY/But I Ain't Got You	(Epic 9842)	1.00	4.00	65
WHY DO I CRY/My Babe	(Epic 9783)	1.00	4.00	65
REMINISCENTS, The				
CARDS OF LOVE/Flames	(Marcel 1000)	3.00	12.00	
ZOOM ZOOM ZOOM/Oh Let Me Dream	(Day 1000)	3.00	12.00	
RENAISSANCE				
CARPET OF THE SUN/	(Capitol-Sovereign 3715)	.75	3.00	73
CARPET OF THE SUN/Kiev	(Sire 728)	.50	2.00	76
MIDAS MAN/The Captive Heart	(Sire 740)	.50	2.00	77
MOTHER RUSSIA/I Think Of You	(Sire 714)	.50	2.00	76
NORTHERN LIGHTS/Opening Out	(Sire 1022)	.50	2.00	78
SPARE SOME LOVE/Prologue	(Capitol-Sovereign 3487)	.75	3.00	72
RENAY, Diane				
BILLY BLUE EYES/Watch Out Sally	(MGM 13296)	.75	3.00	64
KISS ME SAILOR/Soft Spoken Guy	(20th Fox 477)	.75	3.00	64
NAVY BLUE/Unbelievable Guy	(20th Fox 456)	.75	3.00	64
PRESENT FROM EDDIE/It's In Your Tears	(20th Fox 533)	.75	3.00	64
WAITIN' FOR JOEY/Growin' Up Too Fast	(20th Fox 514)	.75	3.00	64
RENDELLS, The				
HOT LICKS/Oh It Hurts	(Carmax 101)	1.00	4.00	63
RENDEZVOUS, The				
CONGRATULATIONS BABY/Faithfully	(Reprise 20089)	1.25	5.00	62
IT BREAKS MY HEART/Take A Break	(Rust 5041)	1.25	5.00	63
RENDEZVOUS STOMPERS, The				
GREMMIES UNITE/Rock Me Gently	(Dore 626)	1.00	4.00	62
RENE & RAY				
QUEEN OF MY HEART/Do What You Feel	(Donna 1360)	.75	3.00	62
RENE & RENE				
ANGELITO/Write Me Soon	(Jox 17)	1.25	5.00	64
ANGELITO/Write Me Soon	(Columbia 43045)	.75	3.00	64
LAS COSAS/You Will Cry (Lloraras)	(White Whale 298)	.75	3.00	69
LO MUCHO QUE TE QUIERO (THE MORE I LOVE YOU)/Mornin'	(White Whale 287)	.75	3.00	68

TITLE/FLIP	LABEL & NO.	GOOD	NEAR MINT	YR.
YO TE LO DIJE (I COULD HAVE TOLD YOU)/ Pretty Flowers Fade Away	(Columbia 43140)	.75	3.00	64
YO TE LO DIJE (I COULD HAVE TOLD YOU)/ Pretty Flowers Fade Away	(Aru 5011)	1.00	4.00	
RENE, Henri				
HAPPY WANDERER, THE/My Impossible Love	(RCA Victor 47-5715)	1.00	4.00	54
LOVE ME TENDER/Little White Horse	(RCA Victor 47-6728)	1.00	4.00	56
RENEGAIDS, The (Featuring Bob Vaught)				
SURFIN' TRAGEDY/Exotic	(GNP Crescendo 193)	1.00	4.00	63
RENO, Al				
CHERYL/Congratulations	(Kapp 432)	2.00	8.00	61
Also see Selections, The				
RENO, Nick				
I HAD A DREAM/My Darling	(Ges 100)	3.75	15.00	
RENOVATIONS, The				
THANKS TO HIM/As We Danced	(Angel Town 101)	1.00	4.00	
RENOWNS, The				
MY MIND'S MADE UP/Wild One	(Everest 19396)	2.50	10.00	61
R.E.O. SPEEDWAGON (Featuring Kevin Kronin)				
I NEED YOU TONIGHT/Easy Money	(Epic 50764)	.50	2.00	79
KEEP PUSHIN/Flying Turkey Trot	(Epic 50459)	.50	2.00	77
KEEP PUSHIN/Tonight	(Epic 50254)	.50	2.00	76
LAY ME DOWN/	(Epic 10892)	.50	2.00	72
LITTLE QUEENIE/Golden Country	(Epic 10975)	.50	2.00	73
157 RIVERSIDE AVENUE/	(Epic 10847)	.50	2.00	72
ONLY THE STRONG SURVIVE/Drop It (An Old Disguise)	(Epic 50790)	.50	2.00	79
OPEN UP/Start A New Life	(Epic 11132)	.50	2.00	74
OUT OF CONTROL/Running Blind	(Epic 50120)	.50	2.00	75
REELIN'/Headed For A Fall	(Epic 50180)	.50	2.00	76
RIDIN' THE STORM OUT/Being Kind (Can Hurt Sometimes)	(Epic 50367)	.50	2.00	77
RIDIN' THE STORM OUT/Whiskey Night	(Epic 11078)	.50	2.00	73
ROLL WITH THE CHANGES/ The Unidentified Flying Tuna Trot	(Epic 50545)	.50	2.00	78
SOPHISTICATED LADY/Prison Women	(Epic 10827)	.50	2.00	72
TIME FOR ME TO FLY/Runnin' Blind	(Epic 50582)	.50	2.00	78
THROW THE CHAINS AWAY/	(Epic 50059)	.50	2.00	75
REPARATA & THE DELRONS (Featuring Mary Aiese)				
CAPTAIN OF YOUR SHIP/Toom Toom (Is A Little Boy)	(Mala 589)	1.00	4.00	68
HE'S THE GREATEST/Summer Thought (Shown as by Reparata)	(World Artists 1075)	1.00	4.00	65
I BELIEVE/It's Waiting There For You	(Mala 573)	1.00	4.00	67
I CAN TELL/Take A Look Around You	(RCA Victor 47-8721)	1.00	4.00	65
I CAN HEAR THE RAIN/Alway's Waitin'	(RCA Victor 47-9185)	1.00	4.00	67
I FOUND MY PLACE/The Boy I Love (Shown as by Reparata)	(World Artists 1062)	1.00	4.00	65
I'M NOBODY'S BABY NOW/Lonliest Girl In Town	(RCA Victor 47-4820)	1.00	4.00	66
KIND OF TROUBLE I LOVE, THE/Boys & Girls	(RCA Victor 47-9123)	1.00	4.00	67
MAMA'S LITTLE GIRL/He Don't Want You	(RCA Victor 47-8921)	1.00	4.00	66
OCTOPUS' GARDEN/Your Life Is Gone (Incorrectly labeled as "Octopus's Garden," shown as by Reparata.)	(Laurie 3589)	.75	3.00	72
(THAT'S WHAT SENDS MEN TO THE) BOWERY/ I've Got An Awful Lot Of Losing To Do	(Kapp 989)	1.25	5.00	69
TOMMY/Mama Don't Allow	(World Artists 1051)	1.00	4.00	65
WALKING IN THE RAIN/ I've Got An Awful Lot Of Losing To Do	(Kapp 2050)	1.00	4.00	70
WHENEVER A TEENAGER CRIES/He's My Guy	(World Artists 1036)	.75	3.00	64•
YOUR BIG MISTAKE/Leave Us Alone (Shown as by the Del-Rons)	(Laurie 3252)	2.00	8.00	64
REED, Tommy, & The Runaways				
SWAMP RIDER/Durango	(Token 103)	1.00	4.00	63
RESNICK, Artie				
BALLOON MAN/Here We Go	(White Whale WW-294)	.75	3.00	69
RESONSICS, The				
I'M REALLY IN LOVE/Think Right	(Lucky Token 108)	.75	3.00	
RESTIVO, Johnny				
DOCTOR LOVE/Magic Age Is Seventeen	(20th Fox 279)	.75	3.00	61
SHAPE I'M IN, THE/Ya Ya	(RCA Victor 47-7559)	1.00	4.00	59
SHAPE I'M IN, THE/Ya Ya (Stereo single issue)	(RCA Victor 61-7559)	2.50	10.00	59
REUNION				
LIFE IS A ROCK (BUT THE RADIO ROLLED ME)/ Are You Ready To Believe	(RCA 10056)	.50	2.00	74
THEY DON'T MAKE 'EM LIKE THAT ANYMORE/Goodstuff	(RCA 10252)	.50	2.00	75
Also see Ohio Express, The				
REVALONS, The				
DREAMS ARE FOR FOOLS/This Is The Moment	(Pet 802)	2.00	8.00	58
REVELLES, The				
ONE MORE DAY/You Love Me No More	(Freeport 1005)	.75	3.00	
RE'VELLS				
LET IT PLEASE BE YOU/Love Walked In	(Roman Press 201)	3.00	12.00	
REVELS, The				
DEAD MAN'S STROLL/Talking To My Heart	(Norgolde 103)	3.75	15.00	59
MIDNIGHT STROLL/Talking To My Heart ("Midnight Stroll" is "Dead Man's Stroll" retitled.)	(Norgolde 103)	1.00	4.00	59
REVELS, The (With Sam Eddy)				
CHURCH KEY/Vesuvius	(Impact 1)	.75	3.00	61
INTOXICA/Commanche	(Downey 123)	1.00	4.00	64
INTOXICA/(Like) Tequila	(Impact 3)	.75	3.00	61
PLEASE/Two Little Monkeys (In A Banana Tree)	(Andie 5077)	1.00	4.00	60
REVELLION/Conga Twist	(Impact 22)	.75	3.00	62
SKIP TO MY LOU/Lonely Walk (Instrumentals)	(Dayco 702)	.75	3.00	
REVERE, Paul & The Raiders				
ALL NIGHT LONG/Groovy	(Gardena 124)	2.00	8.00	62
ALL OVER YOU/Seaboard Line Boogie	(Columbia 4-45898)	.75	3.00	73
BEATNICK STICKS/Orbit (The Spy) (Instrumentals)	(Gardena 106)	2.50	10.00	60
BIRDS OF A FEATHER/The Turkey	(Columbia 4-45453)	.50	2.00	71
BRITISH ARE COMING, THE/	(20th Century 2281)	.75	3.00	76
CINDERELLA SUNSHINE/It's Happening	(Columbia 4-44655)	.75	3.00	68
COUNTRY WINE/It's So Hard Getting Up Today	(Columbia 4-45535)	.75	3.00	72
DON'T TAKE IT SO HARD/ Observation From Flight 285 (In 3/4 Time)	(Columbia 4-44553)	.75	3.00	68
GONE MOVIN' ON/Interlude (To Be Forgotten)	(Columbia 4-45150)	1.00	4.00	70
GONNA HAVE A GOOD TIME/Your Love	(Columbia 3-10126)	.75	3.00	75
GOOD THING/Undecided Man	(Columbia 4-43907)	.75	3.00	66
GREAT AIRPLANE STRIKE, THE/In My Community	(Columbia 4-43810)	.75	3.00	66
HIM OR ME, WHAT'S IT GONNA BE/ The Legend Of Paul Revere	(Columbia 4-44094)	.75	3.00	67
HUNGRY/There She Goes	(Columbia 4-43678)	.75	3.00	66
I HAD A DREAM (LAMENT OF THE CHEROKEE)/ Upon Your Leaving	(Columbia 4-44227)	.75	3.00	67
INDIAN RESERVATION (THE LAMENT OF THE CHEROKEE)/ Terry's Tune	(Columbia 4-45332)	.75	3.00	71
JUST LIKE ME/B.F.D.R.F. Blues	(Columbia 4-43461)	.75	3.00	65

JUST SEVENTEEN/Sorceress With Blue Eyes (Columbia 4-45082) .75 3.00 70
KICKS/Shake It Up (Columbia 4-43556) .75 3.00 66
KICKS/Kicks (Columbia 4-43556) 2.50 10.00 66
(Red plastic promotional issue)
LET ME/I Don't Know (Columbia 4-44854) .75 3.00 69
LIKE BLUEGRASS/Leatherneck (Gardena 127) 2.00 8.00 62
LIKE CHARLESTON/Midnite Ride (Gardena 118) 2.50 10.00 61
(Instrumentals)
LIKE LONG HAIR/Sharon (Gardena 116) 2.50 10.00 61
LOUIE GO HOME/Have Love Will Travel (Columbia 4-43008) 1.00 4.00 64
LOUIE LOUIE/Night Train (Columbia 4-42814) 1.00 4.00 63
LOUIE LOUIE/Night Train (Sande 101) 2.00 8.00 63
LOVE MUSIC/ (Columbia 4-45759) .75 3.00 73
MR. SUN, MR. MOON/Without You (Columbia 4-44744) .75 3.00 69
OH POO PAH DOO/Sometimes (Columbia 4-43273) 1.00 4.00 64
OVER YOU/Swim (Columbia 4-43114) 1.00 4.00 64
PAUL REVERE'S RIDE/Unfinished Fifth (Gardena 115) 2.50 10.00 61
PEACE OF MIND/Do Unto Others (Columbia 4-44335) .75 3.00 67
POWDER BLUE MERCEDES QUEEN/
Golden Girls Sometimes (Columbia 4-45601) .75 3.00 72
SS 396/Camaro (By the Cyrcle)
(Special products issue for Chevrolet) (Columbia 466) 1.50 6.00
SHAKE IT UP (PART 1)/Shake It Up (Part 2) (Gardena 131) 2.00 8.00 62
SIMPLE SONG/Song Seller (Columbia 4-45688) .75 3.00 72
SO FINE/Blues Stay Away (Jerden 807) 2.50 10.00 63
STEPPIN' OUT/Blue Fox (Columbia 4-43375) .75 3.00 62
TALL COOL ONE/Road Runner (Gardena 137) 2.00 8.00 62
TOO MUCH TALK/Happening '68 (Columbia 4-44444) .75 3.00 68
UPS & DOWNS/Leslie (Columbia 4-44018) .75 3.00 67
WE GOTTA ALL GET TOGETHER/Frankfort Side Street (Columbia 4-44970) .75 3.00 69
Also see Association, The

REVERES, The
BEYOND THE SEA/The Show Must Go On (Jubilee 5463) 2.00 8.00 63
ME & MY SPYDER/Big T. (Valiant 6041) 1.50 6.00 64

REV-LONS, The
GIVE ME ONE MORE CHANCE/Boy Trouble (Garpax 44168) .75 3.00 62

REVLONS, The
DRY YOUR EYES/She'll Come To Me (Capitol 4739) .75 3.00 63

REVOLTING 3, The
REVOLUTION/William Tell Rock (Que Pasa 100) 2.50 10.00

REX: see Smith, Rex

REY, Little Bobby
ROCKIN' "J" BELLS/Corrido De Auld (Original Sound 08) 1.00 4.00 59
(Black & silver label)
Instrumentals

REYNOLDS, Allen
HERE COMES RAGEDY ANN/She Really Lied (RCA Victor 47-8190) .75 3.00 63

REYNOLDS, Debbie
AM I THAT EASY TO FORGET/Ask Me To Go Steady (Dot 15985) .75 3.00 60
CAROLINA IN THE MORNING/
Never Mind The Noise In The Market (MGM 11939) 1.00 4.00 55
TAMMY/French Heels (Coral 61851) 1.00 4.00 57
TENDER TRAP, THE/Canoodlin Rag (MGM 12086) 1.00 4.00 55
VERY SPECIAL LOVE, A/I Saw A Country Boy (Coral 61897) 1.00 4.00 58
Also see Carpenter, Carlton

REYNOLDS, Jody
ELOPE WITH ME/Closin' In (Demon 1511) 1.00 4.00 58
ENDLESS SLEEP/Tight Capris (Demon 1507) 1.00 4.00 58
FIRE OF LOVE/Daisy Mae (Demon 1509) 1.00 4.00 58
GOLDEN IDOL/Beaulah Lee (Demon 1515) 3.75 15.00 59
STONE COLD/(The Girl With The) Raven Hair (Demon 1524) 1.25 5.00 59
STORM, THE/Please Remember (Demon 1519) 1.00 4.00 59
WHIPPING POST, THE/I Wanna Be With You Tonight (Demon 1523) 1.00 4.00 59
Some Demon tracks feature Al Casey on guitar.

REYNOLDS, Joey: see 4 Seasons, The

RHINOCEROUS
APRICOT BRANDY/ (Elketra 45647) .75 3.00 69
YOU'RE MY GIRL (I DON'T WANT TO DISCUSS IT)/
I Will Serenade You (Elektra 45640) .75 3.00 68

RHODES, Emitt (Of The Merry-Go-Round)
FRESH AS A DAISY/You Take The Dark Out Of The Night. (Dunhill 4267) .75 3.00 71
REALLY WANTED YOU/ (Dunhill 4295) .75 3.00 71
WITH MY FACE ON THE FLOOR/Lullabye (Dunhill 4280) .75 3.00 71

RHYTHM ACES, The
MOHAWK ROCK/It'll Do (Roulette 4268) .75 3.00 60
RAUNCHY TWIST/Mocking Bird Twist (Roulette 4426) .75 3.00 62

RHYTHM HERITAGE (With Bill Conti)
BARETTA'S THEME (KEEP YOUR EYES ON THE SPARROW)/
My Cherie Amour (ABC 12177) .50 2.00 76
THEME FROM ROCKY (GONNA FLY NOW)/
Last Night On Earth (ABC 12243) .50 2.00 77
THEME FROM S.W.A.T./Wouldn't Trust A Dog (ABC 12135) .50 2.00 75

RHYTHM ROCKERS, The (With Mike Patterson)
WE BELONG TOGETHER/Oh, Boy (Satin 921) 1.00 4.00 60

RHYTHM ROCKETS, The (Formerly The Lettermen)
FOOT CRUISING/Get It On (Wipeout 102) 1.00 4.00 63
PACHUKO HOP/Stranger (Moonglow 2002) 1.00 4.00 63
RENDEVOUS STOMP/The Slide (Challenge 9196) 1.00 4.00 64
Instrumentals

RHYTHM STARS, The
OH MOON/Lynn (Clock 1007) 3.75 15.00 59

RHYTHM SURFERS, The
BIG CITY SURF/501 (Daytone 6301) 1.00 4.00 63

RHYTHMERES, The
ELAINE/Bow Legged Baby (Brunswick 55083) 2.50 10.00 58

RHYTHMETTES, The
HIGH SCHOOL LOVERS/Snow Queen (Coral 62186) .75 3.00 60

RIA & THE REASONS
MEMORIES LINGER ON/Sorry I Lied (Amy 888) .75 3.00 64

RIA & THE REVELLONS
SHE FELL IN LOVE/He's Not There (RSVP 1110) 1.50 6.00 64

RIBBONS, The
AFTER LAST NIGHT/This Is Our Melody (Marsh 35) .75 3.00 63
AIN'T GONNA KISS YA/My Baby Said (Marsh 202) .75 3.00 63

RIC-A-SHAYS, The
GROOVY/Turn On (Lola 002) .75 3.00

RICE, Ronnie
COME BACK LITTLE GIRL/Who's The New Girl (IRC 6917) 1.00 4.00
OVER THE MOUNTAIN/T.N.T. (IRC 6910) 1.00 4.00
TELL HER/I Want You, I Need You (IRC 6931) 1.00 4.00
WARM BABY/La-Do-Da-Da (Quill 106) 1.50 6.00
(Shown as by Ronnie Rice & the Gents)
Also see New Colony Six, The

RICE, Tony
LITTLE SCHOOL GIRL/Blue Bird Of Happiness (Rae Cox 106) 1.50 6.00 61
(With the Overtones)
MY DARLING Y-O-U/I Thank You Baby (Action 100) 1.00 4.00

RICH & THE BAGS
PLEASE BE MY FRIEND/Fat Boy's Back In Town (Dirt Bag 100) 2.00 8.00

RICH & THE RAYS
MY HEART/The Way You Look Tonight (Richly 101) .75 3.00

RICH, Charlie
BIG BOSS MAN/Let Me Go My Merry Way (Groove 0025) 1.00 4.00 63
BIG MAN/Rebound (Phillips International 3542) 1.25 5.00 59
DANCE OF LOVE/I Can't Go On (Smash 2012) 1.00 4.00 65
EASY MONEY/Midnite Blues (Phillips International 3576) 1.25 5.00 62
GONNA BE WAITIN'/School Days (Phillips International 3560) 1.25 5.00 60
JUST A LITTLE BIT SWEET/It's Too Late (Phillips International 3572) 1.25 5.00 61
LONELY WEEKENDS/
Everything I Do Is Wrong (Phillips International 3552) 1.25 5.00 60
MOHAIR SAM/I Washed My Hands In Muddy Water (Smash 1993) 1.00 4.00 65
NO HOME/Tears Ago (Smash 2038) 1.00 4.00 66
RED MAN/Sad News (Sun 354) 1.50 6.00 61
(Shown as by Bobby Sheridan)
SHE LOVED EVERYBODY BUT ME/
The Grass Is Always Greener (RCA Victor 47-0020) 1.00 4.00 64
SITTIN' & THINKIN'/Finally Found Out (Phillips International 3582) 1.25 5.00 62
SOMETHING JUST CAME OVER ME/Hawg Jaw (Smash 2022) 1.00 4.00 66
STAY/On My Knees (Phillips International 3562) 1.25 5.00 60
THERE'S ANOTHER PLACE I CAN'T GO/
I Need Your Love (Phillips International 3584) 1.25 5.00 63
WHIRLWIND/Philadelphia Baby (Phillips International 3532) 2.00 8.00 59
WHO WILL THE NEXT FOOL BE/
Caught In The Middle (Phillips International 3566) 1.25 5.00 61

RICH, Frankie, & Nashville East
FOR ELVIS/Lori (Texas Records 1004) .50 2.00 77

RICHARD & THE YOUNG LIONS
LOST & FOUND/Nasty (Philips 40414) .75 3.00 66
OPEN UP YOUR DOOR/Once Upon Your Smile (Philips 40381) .75 3.00 66

RICHARD, Cliff
BACHELOR BOY/True True Lovin' (Epic 9691) .75 3.00 64
BLUE TURNS TO GREY/I'll Walk Alone (Epic 10018) .75 3.00 62
CATCH ME, I'M FALLING/"D" In Love (ABC-Paramount 10175) 1.00 4.00 61
CONGRATULATIONS/ (Uni 55069) .75 3.00 68
DAY I MET MARIE, THE/Sweet Little Jesus Boy (Uni 55145) .75 3.00 69
DEVIL WOMAN/Love ON (Shine On) (Rocket 40574) .50 2.00 76
DON'T BE MAD AT ME/
A Voice In The Wilderness (ABC-Paramount 10093) 1.00 4.00 60
DON'T TURN THE LIGHT OFF/
Nothing Left For Me To Say (Rocket 40724) .50 2.00 77
DYNAMITE/Traveling Light (ABC-Paramount 10066) 1.50 6.00 59
FALL IN LOVE WITH YOU/Choppin' & Changin' (ABC-Paramount 10109) 1.00 4.00 60
GREEN LIGHT/ (Rocket 11463) .50 2.00 79
I AIN'T GOT TIME ANYMORE/Monday Comes Too Soon. (Monument 1229) .75 3.00 72
I CAN'T ASK FOR ANYMORE THAN YOU/Junior Cowboy (Rocket 40652) .50 2.00 76
I DON'T WANNA LOVE YOU/Look In My Eyes (Epic 9737) .75 3.00 64
I ONLY HAVE EYES FOR YOU/I'm The Lonely One (Epic 9670) .75 3.00 64
IT'S ALL IN THE GAME/I'm Looking Out Of The Window (Epic 9633) .75 3.00 63
LIVING IN HARMONY/ (Sire 703) .75 3.00 73
LIVIN' LOVIN' DOLL/Steady With You (Capitol 4154) 1.25 5.00 59
LIVING DOLL/Apron Strings (ABC-Paramount 10042) 1.25 5.00 59
LUCKY LIPS/Next Time (Epic 9597) .75 3.00 63
MINUTE YOU'RE GONE, THE/Again (Epic 9757) .75 3.00 65
MISS YOU NIGHTS/Love Enough (Rocket 40531) .50 2.00 76
ON MY WORD/I Could Easily Fall In Love With You (Epic 9810) .75 3.00 65
POWER TO ALL OUR FRIENDS/Come Back Billie Jo (Sire 707) .75 3.00 73
REFLECTIONS/Throw Down A Line (Warner Bros. 7344) .75 3.00 69
THEME FOR A DREAM/Mumblin' Mosie (ABC-Paramount 10195) 1.00 4.00 61
TRY A SMILE/You've Got Me Wondering (Rocket 40771) .50 2.00 77
TWELFTH OF NEVER/Paradise Lost (Epic 9839) .75 3.00 65
VISIONS/Quando Quando Quando (Epic 10070) .75 3.00 66
WE DON'T TALK ANYMORE/Count Me Out (EMI America 8025) .50 2.00 79
WHERE IS MY HEART/Please Don't Teach (ABC-Paramount 10136) 1.00 4.00 60
WIND ME UP (& LET ME GO)/Eye Of A Needle (Epic 9867) .75 3.00 65
YOUNG ONES/We Say Yeah (Big Top 3101) .75 3.00 62
Backing is by the Drifters (English instrumental group) on ABC-Paramount and by the Shadows on Epic.

RICHARD, Scott Case
I'M SO GLAD/Who Is That Girl (A^2 301) 1.50 6.00

RICHARDS, Cal
LET HIM GET HIS OWN GIRL/Small Town Girl (Vitose 100) 2.00 8.00

RICHARDS, Jay
HIGH SCHOOL SWEETHEART/Gosh Dog Baby (Hollywood 1099) 1.00 4.00 59

RICHARDS, Jimmy (Ray Conniff)
COOL AS A MOOSE/Strollin' & Boppin' (Columbia 4-41083) 1.00 4.00 58

RICHARDS, Keith (Of The Rolling Stones)
RUN RUDOLPH RUN/The Harder They Come (Rolling Stones 10311) .50 2.00 79

RICHARDS, Marty
EVALINE/I'll Speak Now (Music Makers 102) .75 3.00

RICHARDS, Sonny
SKINNIE MINNIE OLIVE OIL/The Voodoo Walk (Chancellor 1127) .75 3.00 62

RICHARDS, Tony, & The Twilights
PLEASE BELIEVE IN ME/Paper Boy (Colpix 178) 3.00 12.00 60
Also see Fascinators, The

RICHARDSON, Jape (The Big Bopper)
BEGGAR TO A KING/Crazy Blues (Mercury 71219) 2.00 8.00 57
TEENAGE MOON/Monkey Song (Mercury 71312) 2.00 8.00 58

RICHARDSON, Rudi
FOOL'S HALL OF FAME/Why Should I Cry (Sun 271) 1.25 5.00 57

RICHIE & SAXONS
BOTTOM OF THE BARREL/Easy Now (Tip 1020) .75 3.00

RICHIE & THE ROYALS
AND WHEN I'M NEAR YOU/Goody Goody (Rello 1) 3.75 15.00 61
BE MY GIRL/We're Strollin' (Rello 3) 3.75 15.00 62

RICHIE'S RENEGADES
BABY IT'S ME/ (Polaris 65) 1.25 5.00

RICK & EDDY
JEANNIE (WITH THE LIGHT BROWN HAIR)/
I Never Loved (Hit-Teen 877) .75 3.00

RICK & THE KEENS
DARLA/Someone New (Le Cam 113) 1.50 6.00 64
DARLA/Someone New (Tollie 9016) .75 3.00 64
MAYBE/Popcorn (Smash 1722) 1.00 4.00 61
PEANUTS/I'll Be Home (Austin) 5.00 20.00 61
PEANUTS/I'll Be Home (Le Cam 721) 3.00 12.00 61
PEANUTS/I'll Be Home (Smash 1705) .75 3.00 61
YOUR TURN TO CRY/Tender Years (Jamie 1219) 1.00 4.00 62

RICK & THE LEGENDS
I WONDER WHY/Love Me Like I Know You Can (United Artists 50093) 1.00 4.00 63

RICK & THE MASTERS
BEWITCHED BOTHERED & BEWILDERED/
A Kissin' Friend (Haral 778) 2.50 10.00 62
FLAME OF LOVE/Here Comes Nancy (Cameo 226) 2.00 8.00 62
FLAME OF LOVE/Here Comes Nancy (Taba 101) 3.75 15.00 62
LET IT PLEASE BE YOU/I Don't Want Your Love (Cameo 247) 2.00 8.00 63

RICK & THE RAIDERS
I KNOW THAT I LOVE YOU/What Can I Do (Sonic 76234) 1.50 6.00

RICK & THE RANDELLS
LET IT BE YOU/Honey Doll (ABC-Paramount 10055) 1.00 4.00 59

RICK & THE RICK-A-SHAYS
DRAG, THE/Running Bear (Reprise 20226) 1.00 4.00 63

RICKIE & THE HALLMARKS (With Ricki Lisi)
WHEREVER YOU ARE/Joanie Don't You Cry (Amy 877) 2.00 8.00 63

RICKY & ROBBY
PURPLE PEDAL PUSHERS/Suzanne (Golden Crest 530) 1.00 4.00 59

RICKY & THE SAINTS
WHEN THE SAINTS TWIST/My Special Angel (7 Teen 101) .75 3.00 62

RICKY & THE VACELS
HIS GIRL/Don't Want Your Love No More (Fargo 1050) 1.25 5.00 60
LORRAINE/Bubble Gum (Express 711) 1.25 5.00
Also see Shaggy Boys, The

RICO & THE RAVENS
DON'T YOU KNOW/In My Heart (Autumn 6) 1.00 4.00 65
DON'T YOU KNOW/In My Heart (Rally 1601) 1.50 6.00 65

RICOCHETTES
FIND ANOTHER BOY/I Don't Want You (Destination 629) .75 3.00 67

RIDDELL, Don, Four
GIRL OF MY BEST FRIEND/Don't Be Cruel (General 723) 2.00 8.00

RIDDLE, Nelson
LISBON ANTIGUA/Robin Hood (Capitol 3287) 1.00 4.00 55
NAKED CITY THEME/Defenders Theme (Capitol 4843) .75 3.00 62
PORT AU PRINCE/Midnight Blues (Capitol 3374) 1.00 4.00 56
ROUTE 66 THEME/Lolita Ya Ya (Capitol 4741) .75 3.00 62
SONG FROM CAINE MUTINY/Vilia (Capitol 2893) 1.25 5.00 54
THOROUGHLY MODERN MILLIE/See The Cheetah (Liberty 55952) .50 2.00 67
Instrumentals

RIDDLES, The
SWEETS FOR MY SWEET/ (Mercury 72669) .75 3.00 67

RIELS, The
LET HIM GO/Paul (Laurie 3237) 1.00 4.00 64

TITLE/FLIP	LABEL & NO.	GOOD	NEAR MINT	YR.
RIFFS, The				
LITTLE GIRL/Why Are The Nights So Cold	(Sunny 22)	3.75	15.00	
TELL HER/I Been Thinkin'	(Jamie 1296)	1.50	6.00	64
TELL TALE FRIENDS/Why Are The Nights So Cold	(Old Town 1179)	2.50	10.00	
Also see Chimes, The				
RIGHTEOUS BROTHERS The (Bob Hatfield & Bill Medley)				
ALONG CAME JONES/Jimmy's Blues	(Verve 10479)	.75	3.00	67
AND THE PARTY GOES ON/Woman, Man Needs Ya	(Verve 10648)	.75	3.00	68
BRING YOUR LOVE TO ME/Fannie Mae	(Moonglow 238)	1.00	4.00	65
BRING YOUR LOVE TO ME/I Need A Girl	(Moonglow 245)	1.00	4.00	66
DREAM ON/Dr. Rock & Roll	(Haven 7006)	.50	2.00	74
EBB TIDE/(I Love You) For Sentimental Reasons	(Philles 130)	1.00	4.00	65
FOR YOU LOVE/Gotta Tell You How I Feel	(Moonglow 243)	1.00	4.00	65
GEORGIA ON MY MIND/My Tears Will Go Away	(Moonglow 244)	1.00	4.00	65
GIVE IT TO THE PEOPLE/Love Is Not A Dirty Work	(Haven 7004)	.50	2.00	74
GO AHEAD & CRY/Things Didn't Go Your Way	(Verve 10430)	.75	3.00	66
HE/He Will Break Your Heart	(Verve 10406)	.75	3.00	66
HERE I AM/So Many Lonely Nights Ahead	(Verve 10577)	.75	3.00	68
HOLD ON (TO WHAT YOU GOT)/Let Me Make The Music	(Haven 800)	.50	2.00	76
JUSTINE/In That Great Gettin Up Mornin	(Moonglow 242)	1.00	4.00	65
JUST ONCE IN MY LIFE/The Blues	(Philles 127)	1.00	4.00	65
KOKO JOE/B Flat Blues	(Moonglow 224)	1.00	4.00	63
LITTLE LATIN LUPE LU/I'm So Lonely	(Moonglow 215)	1.00	4.00	63
MELANCHOLY MUSIC MAN/Don't Give Up On Me	(Verve 10507)	.75	3.00	67
MY BABE/Fee-Fi-Fidily-I-Oh	(Moonglow 223)	1.00	4.00	63
NEVER SAY I LOVE YOU/High Blood Pressure	(Haven 7011)	.50	2.00	75
ON THIS SIDE OF GOODBYE/Man Without A Dream	(Verve 10449)	.75	3.00	66
ROCK & ROLL HEAVEN/I Just Wanna Be Me	(Haven 7002)	.50	2.00	74
RAT RACE/Green Onions	(Verve 10403)	.75	3.00	66
SOUL & INSPIRATION/B Side Blues	(Verve 10383)	.75	3.00	65
STRANDED IN THE MIDDLE OF NO PLACE/Been So Nice	(Verve 10551)	.75	3.00	67
THAT LUCKY OLD SUN/My Darling Clementine	(Verve 10569)	.75	3.00	67
THIS LITTLE GIRL OF MINE/ If Your Lying, You'll Be Crying	(Moonglow 235)	1.00	4.00	64
TRY TO FIND ANOTHER MAN/I Still Love You	(Moonglow 231)	1.25	5.00	64
UNCHAINED MELODY/Hung On You	(Philles 129)	1.00	4.00	65
WHITE CLIFFS OF DOVER/She's Mine, All Mine	(Philles 132)	1.25	5.00	66
YOU CAN HAVE HER/Love Or Magic	(Moonglow 239)	1.00	4.00	65
YOU'VE LOST THAT LOVIN' FEELIN'/There's A Woman	(Philles 124)	1.00	4.00	64
Also see Paramours, The				
RILEY, Allan				
TRUE STORY OF TOM DOOLEY/Ballad Of Ma Dooley	(Prospect 701)	.75	3.00	59
RILEY, Bob				
WEEDEND VACATION/Memories Of Home	(Tibor 4500)	1.25	5.00	
RINCON SURFSIDE BAND, The				
SURFER GIRL-HONOLULU LULU- LITTLE DEUCE COUPE (MEDLEY)/	(Dunhill D1)	1.50	6.00	63
RING-A-DINGS, The				
OUR MAN FLINT/ Theme From "The Spy Who Came In From The Cold"	(Reprise 0445)	.75	3.00	66
RINGO, Ron				
RINGO'S JERK/Queen Of The Jerk	(Juggy 701)	1.50	6.00	64
RINKY DINKS, The				
HOT POTATO/Hot Potato (Part 2)	(Enjoy 1010)	.75	3.00	63
RINKY-DINKS, The: see Darin, Bobby				
RIO				
GOIN' HOME/Where Can You Run	(Zero 602117)	.75	3.00	76
RIO, Bobby				
DON DIDDLY/I Got You	(Lenox 5569)	1.00	4.00	63
RIO, Bobby, & The Revelles				
BOY MEETS GIRL/ Don't Break My Heart & Run Away	(ABC-Paramount 10656)	1.00	4.00	65
RIO, Chuck "Tequila"				
BAD BOY/Denise	(Challenge 59019)	1.00	4.00	58
BIG BOY/You Don't Have To Be A Baby To Cry	(Flair 103)	.75	3.00	62
KRESHENDO STOMP/Rock-A-Nova	(Saturn 402)	1.00	4.00	62
MARGARITA/C'est La Vie	(Jackpot 48016)	1.00	4.00	59
(With The Originals)				
Also see Persuaders, the				
RIO, Jerry, & The Stompmen				
DOIN' THE EMPIRE STOMP (PART 1)/ Doin' The Empire Stomp (Part 2)	(PNR 1)	1.00	4.00	62
RIOS, Augie				
DONDE ESTA SANTA CLAUS/Ol' Fatso	(Metro 20010)	1.00	4.00	58
DONDE ESTA SANTA CLAUS/Ol' Fatso	(MGM 13292)	.75	3.00	64
HOP, SKIP & JUMP/Run Rattler Run	(Metro 20016)	1.00	4.00	59
I'VE GOT A GIRL/There's A Girl Down The Way	(Shelley 181)	2.50	10.00	
(With the Notations)				
TEACH ME TO-NIGHT/Linda Lou	(Shelly 192)	1.25	5.00	
RIOS, Miguel				
SONG OF JOY (HIMNO A LA ALEGRIA), A/El Rio	(A&M 1193)	.50	2.00	70
RIOT SQUAD, The				
CRY, CRY, CRY/How Is It Done	(Reprise 0457)	.75	3.00	66
I TAKE IT THAT WE'RE THROUGH/Working Man	(HBR 485)	.75	3.00	67
RIP CHORDS, The (Featuring Bruce Johnston & Terry Melcher)				
DON'T BE SCARED/Bunny Hill	(Columbia 4-43221)	1.00	4.00	65
GONE/She Thinks I Still Care	(Columbia 4-42812)	1.00	4.00	63
GONE/Gone	(Columbia 4-42812)	3.00	12.00	63
(Promotional blue plastic issue)				
GONE/Gone	(Columbia 4-42812)	3.75	15.00	63
(Promotional picture sleeve)				
HERE I STAND/Karen	(Columbia 4-42687)	1.00	4.00	63
HEY LITTLE COBRA/Hey Little Cobra	(Columbia 4-42921)	3.00	12.00	64
(Promotional yellow plastic issue)				
HEY LITTLE COBRA/The Queen	(Columbia 4-42921)	1.00	4.00	63
ONE PIECE TOPLESS BATHING SUIT/Wah-Wahini	(Columbia 43093)	1.00	4.00	64
THREE WINDOW COUPE/Hot Rod U.S.A	(Columbia 4-43035)	1.00	4.00	64
THREE WINDOW COUPE/Three Window Coupe	(Columbia 4-43035)	3.75	15.00	64
(Promotional red plastic issue)				
RIP TIDES, The				
SALLY ANN/April	(Sidewalk 904)	2.00	8.00	
RIP TIDES, The				
HANKY PANKY/	(Challenge 9062)	.75	3.00	61
LOVER & FRIEND/Return To Forever	(Capitol 4761)	.50	2.00	79
MACHINE GUN/Deep Blue	(Challenge 59058)	.75	3.00	59
MEMORY LANE/I'm A Woman	(Capitol 4706)	.50	2.00	79
WOULDN'T MATTER WHERE YOU ARE/ Gettin' Ready For Your Love	(Epic 50394)	.50	2.00	77
RIPERTON, Minnie (Of The Rotary Connection)				
ADVENTURES IN PARADISE/When It Comes Down To It	(Epic 50190)	.50	2.00	76
INSIDE MY LOVE/Don't Let Anyone Bring You Down	(Epic 50128)	.50	2.00	75
LES FLEUR/OH! By The Way	(GRT 42)	.75	3.00	72
LOVIN' YOU/The Edge Of A Dream	(Epic 50057)	.50	2.00	75
REASONS/	(Epic 11139)	.50	2.00	74
SEEING YOU THIS WAY/	(Epic 50020)	.50	2.00	74
SIMPLE THINGS/Minnie's Lament	(Epic 50166)	.50	2.00	75
STICK TOGETHER (PART 1)/Stick Together (Part 2)	(Epic 50377)	.50	2.00	77
RISING SONS, The				
TALK TO ME BABY/Try To Be A Man	(Amy 931)	1.00	4.00	65
RISING SUNS, The				
CANDY MAN/The Devil's Got My Woman	(Columbia 4-43534)	.75	3.00	66
RIS-KAYS				
TOPLESS BATHING SUIT/Salt Crackers	(Hi-g Lo-c 3109)	1.00	4.00	64
RITUALS, The (Featuring Arnie Ginsburg)				
GIRL IN ZANZIBAR/Guitarro	(Arwin 120)	1.25	5.00	59
SURFERS RULE/Gone	(Arwin 128)	1.25	5.00	60
THIS IS PARADISE/Gone	(Arwin 127)	1.25	5.00	60
RIVALS, The				
I MUST SEE YOU AGAIN/Rigelty Tick	(Darryl 722)	1.50	6.00	
RIVERA, Scarlet				
SCARLET FEVER/Morning Glories	(Warner Bros. 8587)	.50	2.00	78
Scarlet Rivera is also Bob Dylans's violinist.				
RIVERS, Derk: see Hansen Brothers, The				
RIVERS, Little Jimmy & The Tops: See Little Jimmy & The Tops				
RIVERS, Johnny				
ANSWER ME, MY LOVE/Customary Thing	(Cub 9058)	1.25	5.00	60
ANSWER ME MY LOVE/Customary Thing	(MGM 13266)	.75	3.00	64
ASHES & SAND/Outside help	(Soul City 007)	.50	2.00	77
BABY COME BACK/Long Long Walk	(Gone 5026)	2.50	10.00	64
BABY COME BACK/Long Long Walk	(Roulette 4565)	1.25	5.00	64
("Baby Come Back" is similar in music and arrangement to "Santa Bring My Baby Back To Me," as recorded by Elvis Presley.)				
BABY I NEED YOUR LOVIN'/ Gettin' Ready For Tomorrow	(Imperial 66227)	.75	3.00	67
BLUE SKIES/That Someone Should Be Me	(Chancellor 1096)	1.00	4.00	62
BLUE SUEDE SHOES/Stories To A Child	(United Artists 198)	.50	2.00	73
CALL ME/Andersonville	(Era 3037)	1.00	4.00	61
CAN I CHANGE MY MIND/John Lee Hooker	(Epic-Soul City 50150)	.50	2.00	75
CURIOUS MIND (UM, UM, UM, UM, UM, UM)/ Ashes & Sand	(Big Tree-Soul City 16106)	.50	2.00	77
EVERYDAY/Darling Talk To Me	(Cub 9047)	1.25	5.00	59
FIRE & RAIN/Apple Tree	(Imperial 66453)	.75	3.00	70
GET IT UP FOR LOVE/John Lee Hooker '74	(Atlantic 3230)	.75	3.00	74
HELP ME RHONDA (With Brian Wilson)/ New Lovers & Old Friends	(Epic 50121)	1.00	4.00	75
HELP ME RHONDA (With Brian Wilson)/ New Lovers & Old Friends	(Epic-Soul City 50121)	.75	3.00	75
IF YOU WANT IT I'VE GOT IT/My Heart Is In Your Hands	(Capitol 4913)	1.00	4.00	63
I'LL FEEL A WHOLE LOT BETTER/Over The Line	(United Artists 310)	.50	2.00	73
INTO THE MYSTIC/Jesus Is A Soul Man	(Imperial 66448)	.75	3.00	70
KNOCK THREE TIMES/I Get So Doggone Lonesome	(Chancellor 1070)	1.00	4.00	61
KNOCK THREE TIMES/Oh What A Kiss	(United Artists 741)	.75	3.00	64
LINDA LU/	(Epic-Soul City 50248)	.50	2.00	76
LONG BLACK VEIL/This Could Be The One	(Capitol 4850)	1.00	4.00	62
LONG BLACK VEIL/Don't Look Now	(Capitol 5232)	.75	3.00	64
LOOK TO YOUR SOUL/Something Strange	(Imperial 66286)	.75	3.00	68
MAYBELLINE/Walk Myself On Home	(Imperial 66056)	.75	3.00	64
MEDLEY: SEARCHIN'-SO FINE/New York City Dues	(United Artists 226)	.50	2.00	73
MEMPHIS/It Wouldn't Happen With Me	(Imperial 66032)	.75	3.00	64
MIDNIGHT SPECIAL/Cupid	(Imperial 66087)	.75	3.00	65
MOUNTAIN OF LOVE/Moody River	(Imperial 66075)	.75	3.00	64
MUDDY RIVER/Resurrection	(Imperial 66386)	.75	3.00	69
MUDDY WATER (I WASHED MY HANDS IN)/ Roogalator	(Imperial 66175)	.75	3.00	66
ONE WOMAN/	(Imperial 66418)	.75	3.00	69
OUTSIDE HELP/Welcome Home	(Epic-Soul City 50208)	.50	2.00	76
POOR SIDE OF TOWN/A Man Can Cry	(Imperial 66205)	.75	3.00	66
RIGHT RELATIONS/A Better Life	(Imperial 66335)	.75	3.00	68
ROCKIN' PNEUMONIA-BOOGIE WOOGIE FLU/ Come Home America	(United Artists 50960)	.50	2.00	72
SEA CRUISE/	(United Artists 50778)	.50	2.00	71
SECRET AGENT MAN/You Dig	(Imperial 66159)	.75	3.00	66
SEVENTH SON/Un-Square Dance	(Imperial 66112)	.75	3.00	65
SIX DAYS ON THE ROAD/Artists & Poets	(Atlantic 3028)	.75	3.00	74
SUMMER RAIN/Memory Of The Coming Good	(Imperial 66267)	.75	3.00	67
SWAYIN' TO THE MUSIC (SLOW DANCIN')/ Outside Help	(Big Tree-Soul City 16094)	.50	2.00	77
THAT'S MY BABY/Your First & Last Love	(Coral 62425)	1.25	5.00	64
THESE ARE NOT MY PEOPLE/	(Imperial 66360)	.75	3.00	69
THINK HIS NAME/Permanent Change	(United Artists 50822)	.50	2.00	71
TO BE LOVED/Dream Doll	(United Artists 769)	.50	2.00	64
TO BE LOVED/Too Good To Last	(Chancellor 1108)	1.00	4.00	62
TRACKS OF MY TEARS/Rewind Melody	(Imperial 66244)	.75	3.00	67
UNDER YOUR SPELL AGAIN/Long Time Man	(Imperial 66144)	.75	3.00	65
WHERE HAVE ALL THE FLOWERS GONE/ Love Me While You Can	(Imperial 66133)	.75	3.00	65
YOUR FIRST & LAST LOVE/(There'll Be Blue Birds Over) The White Cliffs Of Dover	(Dee Dee 239)	2.00	8.00	59
YOU'RE THE ONE/A Hole In The Ground	(Guyden 2003)	1.50	6.00	58
YOU'RE THE ONE/A Hole In The Ground	(Guyden 2110)	.75	3.00	62
RIVIERAS, The				
CALIFORNIA SUN/H.B. Goose Step	(Riviera 1401)	1.00	4.00	64
LET'S GO TO HAWAII/Lakeview Lane	(Riviera 1406)	1.00	4.00	65
LITTLE DONNA/Let's Have A Party	(Riviera 1402)	1.00	4.00	64
("Little Donna" is nearly the same music & arrangement as "Rock & Roll Music," as recorded by Chuck Berry and others.)				
RIP IT UP/Whole Lotta Shakin'	(Riviera 1405)	1.00	4.00	64
ROCKIN' ROBIN/Battle Line	(Riviera 1403)	1.00	4.00	64
ROACHES, The				
BEATLEMANIA BLUES/Angel Of Angels	(Crossway 447)	1.25	5.00	64
ROAD				
IF I EVER NEEDED A WOMAN/Alone	(Kama Sutra 531)	.75	3.00	71
SHE'S NOT THERE/A Bummer	(Kama Sutra 256)	.75	3.00	69
ROAD HOG & THE NEON CACTUS				
PRESIDENTIAL DEBATE, THE/Suitcase	(Epic 50305)	1.25	5.00	76
(Novelty Break-in)				
Also see Imus, Don				
ROADMASTER				
CIRCLE OF LOVE/You Come See Me	(Mercury 74038)	.50	2.00	79
ROAD RUNNERS, The				
DEAD MAN/Pretty Girls	(Challenge 9197)	1.00	4.00	63
GOODBYE/Tell Her You Love Her	(Morocco 001)	1.00	4.00	66
I'LL MAKE IT UP TO YOU/Take Me	(Miramar 116)	1.00	4.00	65
QUASIMOTO/Road Runner	(Felsted 8692)	1.00	4.00	63
ROADSTERS, The				
DRAG/Joy Ride	(20th Fox 486)	.75	3.00	64
MAG RIMS/Candymatic	(Donna 1390)	1.00	4.00	63
ROBB, Dee				
HE'S GOT THE WHOLE WORLD IN HIS HANDS/ Say That Thing	(Score 1006)	.75	3.00	64
(With the Robbins)				
PROM, THE/Bye Bye Baby	(Argo 5439)	1.25	5.00	63
Also see Robbs, The				
ROBBINS & PAXTON (With Gary Paxton)				
STRANGE RAIN/Teen Angel	(Rori 704)	.75	3.00	62
ROBBINS, Eddie				
GIRL LIKE YOU, A/Dear Parents	(Power 214)	3.75	15.00	58
JANICE/It Was Fun	(David 1001)	3.00	12.00	
ROBBS, The (With Dee Robb)				
BITTERSWEET/End Of The Week	(Mercury 72641)	.75	3.00	66
CHANGIN' WINDS/A Good Time Song	(Atlantic 2578)	.75	3.00	68
GIRLS, GIRLS/Violets Of Dawn	(Mercury 72730)	.75	3.00	67
LAST OF THE WINE/Written In The Dust	(Dunhill 4233)	.75	3.00	70
NEXT TIME YOU SEE ME/I Don't Feel Alone	(Mercury 72616)	.75	3.00	66
RACE WITH THE WIND/In A Funny Sort Of Way	(Mercury 72579)	.75	3.00	66
RAPID TRANSIT/Cynthia Loves	(Mercury 72678)	.75	3.00	67
Also see Cherokee				
ROBBY & THE ROBBINS				
SHE CRIED/Surfer's Life	(Todd 1089)	1.50	6.00	63
ROBERTS, Austin				
BALTIMORE/Sarah	(Philips 40649)	.75	3.00	71
DON'T STOP ME BABY (I'M ON FIRE)/	(Arista 0335)	.50	2.00	78
JUST TO MAKE YOU MIND/	(Private Stock 45061)	.50	2.00	76
KEEP ON SINGING/	(Chelsea 0110)	.50	2.00	75
MARY & ME/I'll Smile	(Philips 40560)	.75	3.00	68
ROCKY/You Got The Power	(Private Stock 45020)	.50	2.00	75
RUNAWAY-JUST A LITTLE/Sarah	(Philips 40638)	.75	3.00	70
SOMETHING'S WRONG WITH ME/	(Chelsea 0101)	.50	2.00	72
ROBERTS, Bruce				
STARMAKER/	(Elektra 45455)	.50	2.00	78
ROBERTS, Buddy, & The Hi Liters				
DING DONG/Black & Blue	(Bonanza 689)	2.00	8.00	
ROBERTS, Lea				
ALL RIGHT NOW/	(United Artists 626)	.50	2.00	75
LAUGHTER IN THE RAIN/She Will Break Your Heart	(United Artists 539)	.50	2.00	74
ROBERTS, Rick (Of Firefall)				
DELIVER ME/	(A&M 1399)	.50	2.00	73
Also see Dillard & Clark				
Also see Flying Burrito Brothers, The				
ROBERTS, Stan				
DREAM TIME/Hold on Baby	(Deb-Lyn 102)	1.25	5.00	
ROBERTS, Wayne (Neil Scott-Bogart)				
LITTLE GIRL/One Piece Bathing Suit	(20th Fox 644)	2.00	8.00	
(With The Concords)				
ROBERTSON, Don				
BORN TO BE WITH YOU/Ninety Miles An Hour	(RCA Victor 47-8584)	.75	3.00	65
HAPPY WHISTLER, THE/You're Free To Go	(Capitol 3391)	1.00	4.00	56
ROBERTSON, Doug				
DESIREE/Drivin' Home	(Jerden 739)	1.25	5.00	
ROBIC, Ivo				
EIN GANZES LEBEN LANG (I CAN'T STOP LOVING YOU)/ Ich Denk' Nur An's Wiederseh'	(Philips 40078)	.75	3.00	62
HAPPY MULETEER, THE/Rhondaly	(Laurie 3045)	.75	3.00	60
MORGEN/Ay Ay Ay Paloma	(Laurie 3033)	.75	3.00	59
ROBIN & THE THREE HOODS				
I WANNA DO IT/	(Hollywood 1110)	.75	3.00	
ROBIN HOOD & HIS MERRY MEN				
SANTA, BRING ME A DOLL/Ellen	(Mohawk 130)	.75	3.00	60
ROBIN, Tina				
EVERYDAY/Believe Me	(Coral 9-61935)	1.50	6.00	57
LITTLE BIRD TOLD ME, A/ We've All Gotta Live In This House	(Coral 9-62015)	1.50	6.00	58
NO SCHOOL TOMORROW/Sugar Blues	(Coral 9-61977)	1.50	6.00	58
PLAY IT AGAIN/Nothing Is Impossible	(Mercury 71852)	1.50	6.00	61
TOO YOUNG/River Of Tears	(Coral 9-62121)	1.50	6.00	59
ROBINS, The				
BATMAN/Batarang	(Ardent 106)	.75	3.00	66
QUARTER TO 12, A/Pretty Little Dolly	(Knight 2001)	1.00	4.00	
ROBINS, The				
JOHNNY/Doing The Popeye	(Sweet Taffy 400)	.75	3.00	
ROBINSON, Claude				
COTTON PICKIN' MAMA/	(Studio 1002)	1.00	4.00	
ROBINSON, Floyd				
MAKIN' LOVE/My Girl	(RCA Victor 47-7529)	1.00	4.00	59
MOTORCYCLE MAN/Sidewalk Surf Board	(United Artists 986)	2.00	8.00	66
TONIGHT YOU BELONG TO ME/Let It Be Me	(RCA Victor 47-7637)	1.00	4.00	59
ROBINSON, Matt				
MOBITY MOSLEY'S MONTHS/The Safety Boy Blues	(Columbia 45378)	.75	3.00	72
ROBINSON, Stan				
BOOM-A-DIP-DIP/My Heart Beats	(Monument 402)	1.00	4.00	59
ROBINSON, Tom, Band				
BULLY FOR YOU/Our People	(Harvest 4726)	.50	2.00	79
2-4-6-8 MOTORWAY/I Shall Be Released	(Harvest 4533)	.50	2.00	78
ROBISON, Chris				
I'M GONNA STAY WITH MY BABY TONIGHT/ (With The Rockaways)	(Buddah 406)	1.25	5.00	
ROCK & ROLL DUBBLE BUBBLE TRADING CARD CO. OF PHILADELPHIA 19141				
BUBBLE GUM MUSIC/On A Summer Night	(Buddah 78)	.75	3.00	68
ROCK & ROLL SCHOOLTEACHER, The				
LESSON 1 (GEOGRAPHY)/Lesson 2 (Earp Burped)	(Okeh 7117)	1.00	4.00	59
ROCK BROTHERS, The				
DUNGAREE DOLL/Livin' It Up	(King 4851)	1.00	4.00	55
I GOTTA GET BACK/Oh Didn't I Ramble	(King 4882)	1.00	4.00	55
ROCK FLOWERS, The				
DOUBLE SCOOP/	(Wheel 0039)	.50	2.00	72
NUMBER WONDERFUL/	(Wheel 0032)	.50	2.00	72
PUT A LITTLE LOVE AWAY/	(Wheel 0042)	.50	2.00	73
ROCK GARDEN, The				
JOY OF GIVING/Sweet Pajamas	(BT Puppy 536)	.75	3.00	68
ROCK-A-TEENS, The				
TWANGY/Doggone It Baby	(Roulette 4217)	.75	3.00	60
WOO-HOO/Untrue	(Doran 3515)	3.75	15.00	
WOO HOO/Untrue	(Roulette 4192)	1.00	4.00	59

Bobby Hatfield (Of The Righteous Bros.)

Bill Medley (Of The Righteous Bros.)

Linda Ronstadt

From her new album "Mad Love"

PERFECT WOMAN

(Steve Kosoff)

Caddy Music

& Cousins, Inc.

5644

Produced by

45-9725 LONDON

THE ROLLING STONES

HEART OF STONE

Produced by Andrew Loog Oldham

Golden West

BMI

Vocal

U-252

FOOL'S HALL OF FAME

(Danny Wolf)

RUDI RICHARDSON

271

MEMPHIS, TENNESSEE

ROCKAWAYS, The

TITLE/FLIP	LABEL & NO.	GOOD	NEAR MINT	YR.
TOP DOWN TIME/ Don't Cry (Tomorrow's Tears Tonight)	Red-Bird 10-005)	1.50	6.00	64
Also see Robison, Chris				

ROCKBUSTERS, The

TITLE/FLIP	LABEL & NO.	GOOD	NEAR MINT	YR.
TOUGH CHICK/Chico	(Cadence 1371)	1.00	4.00	59

ROCKETEERS, The

TITLE/FLIP	LABEL & NO.	GOOD	NEAR MINT	YR.
DRAGSTRIP/Summertime	(Glad Hamp 2017)	1.00	4.00	63
RIPPIN' & ROCKIN'/Downtown	(Val-ue 1002)	1.00	4.00	60

ROCKET, Robin

TITLE/FLIP	LABEL & NO.	GOOD	NEAR MINT	YR.
CHANGING SCHOOLS/You Hold The Key	(Lode 107)	1.00	4.00	60

ROCKETS, The

TITLE/FLIP	LABEL & NO.	GOOD	NEAR MINT	YR.
HOLE IN MY POCKET/Hole In My Pocket	(White Whale 270)	1.00	4.00	68
Also see Crazy Horse				

ROCKETS, The

TITLE/FLIP	LABEL & NO.	GOOD	NEAR MINT	YR.
GIBRALTAR ROCK/Walkin' Home	(Columbia 41512)	1.00	4.00	59

ROCKETS, The (Formerly The Detroit Wheels)

TITLE/FLIP	LABEL & NO.	GOOD	NEAR MINT	YR.
CAN'T SLEEP/Something Ain't Right	(RSO 926)	.50	2.00	79
OH WELL/Love Me Once Again	(RSO 935)	.50	2.00	79
SHE'S A PRETTY ONE/	(Tortoise 11207)	.50	2.00	78
Also see Ryder, Mitch & The Detroit Wheels				

ROCKIN' BERRIES, The

TITLE/FLIP	LABEL & NO.	GOOD	NEAR MINT	YR.
DOESN'T TIME FLY/The Water Is Over My Head	(Reprise 0442)	1.00	4.00	66
HE'S IN TOWN/Flashback	(Reprise 0329)	1.00	4.00	64
POOR MAN'S SON/Follow Me	(Reprise 0377)	1.00	4.00	65
WHAT IN THE WORLD'S COME OVER YOU/ You Don't Know What To Do	(Reprise 0355)	1.00	4.00	65
YOUR MY GIRL/Brother Bill (Last Clean Shirt)	(Reprise 0400).	1.00	4.00	65

ROCKIN' CHAIRS, The

TITLE/FLIP	LABEL & NO.	GOOD	NEAR MINT	YR.
COME ON BABY/Please Mary Lou	(Recorte 404)	3.00	12.00	
KISS IS A KISS, A/Rockin' Chair Boogie	(Recorte 402)	2.50	10.00	
MEMORIES OF LOVE/Girl Of Mine	(Recorte 412)	3.00	12.00	
Also see Gerardi, Bob, & The Classic 4				

ROCKIN' FOO

TITLE/FLIP	LABEL & NO.	GOOD	NEAR MINT	YR.
ROCHESTER RIVER/	(Hobbit 42001)	.75	3.00	69

ROCKING GHOSTS, The

TITLE/FLIP	LABEL & NO.	GOOD	NEAR MINT	YR.
BELINDA/Ghost Walk	(Mod 1001)	1.00	4.00	66

ROCKINGHAM, David, Trio

TITLE/FLIP	LABEL & NO.	GOOD	NEAR MINT	YR.
DAWN/That's All	(Josie 913)	.75	3.00	63
(Instrumentals)				

ROCKIN' G'S, The

TITLE/FLIP	LABEL & NO.	GOOD	NEAR MINT	YR.
CYCLONE/Lani-Town	(Town 1967)	.75	3.00	60

ROCKIN' R'S, The

TITLE/FLIP	LABEL & NO.	GOOD	NEAR MINT	YR.
BEAT, THE/Crazy Baby	(Tempus 7541)	1.50	6.00	59
HUM BUG/Mix	(Vee Jay 346)	1.00	4.00	60
MUSTANG /I'm Still In Love	(Vee Jay 334)	.75	3.00	
MUSTANG/I'm Still In Love With You	(Tempus 1515)	1.50	6.00	60
NAMELESS/Heat	(Tempus 1507)	1.50	6.00	59
WALKIN' YOU TO SCHOOL/ Bewitched (Bothered & Bewildered)	(Stepheny 1842)	1.25	5.00	60
Instrumentals				

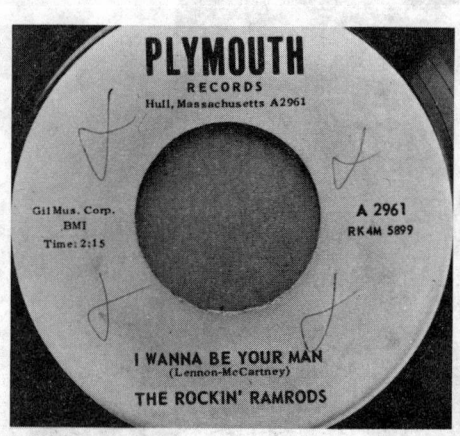

ROCKIN' RAMRODS, The

TITLE/FLIP	LABEL & NO.	GOOD	NEAR MINT	YR.
BRIGHT LIT, BLUE SKIES/Mister Wind	(Plymouth 2963)	1.00	4.00	66
(Shown as by the Ramrods)				
DON'T FOOL WITH FUMANCHU/Tears	(Claridge 301)	1.00	4.00	65
FLOWERS IN MY MIND/Mary, Mary	(Plymouth 2965)	1.00	4.00	66
(Shown as by The Ramrods)				
I WANNA BE YOUR MAN/I'll Be On My Way	(Plymouth 2961)	1.00	4.00	64
PLAY IT/Got My Mojo Working	(Claridge 317)	1.00	4.00	66
SHE LIED/Girl Can't Help It	(Bon-Bon 1315)	1.00	4.00	64
WILD ABOUT YOU/Cry In My Room	(Southern Sound 205)	1.00	4.00	65

ROCKIN' REBELS, The

TITLE/FLIP	LABEL & NO.	GOOD	NEAR MINT	YR.
ANOTHER WILD WEEKEND/Happy Popcorn	(Swan 4150)	.75	3.00	63
BONGO BLUE BEAT/Burn Baby Burn	(Stork 3)	1.00	4.00	64
MONDAY MORNING/Flibbity Jibbit	(Swan 4161)	.75	3.00	63
ROCKIN' CRICKETS/Hully Gully Rock	(Swan 4140)	.75	3.00	63
WILD WEEKEND/Wild Weekend Cha Cha	(Swan 4125)	.75	3.00	62
Instrumentals				
Also see Buffalo Rebels, The				
Also see Rebels, The				

ROCKIN' SAINTS, The

TITLE/FLIP	LABEL & NO.	GOOD	NEAR MINT	YR.
HALF & HALF/Cheat On Me	(Decca 31144)	1.00	4.00	60
SAINTS ROCK, THE/Alright Baby	(Decca 30990)	1.00	4.00	59

ROCKIN' SIDNEY

TITLE/FLIP	LABEL & NO.	GOOD	NEAR MINT	YR.
ACTIONS SPEAK LOUDER THAN WORDS/ Lias Per Le Patate	(Goldband 1158)	.75	3.00	63
CORPUS CHRISTI/	(Goldband 1177)	.75	3.00	63
DON'T LET ME CROSS OVER/You Don't Have To Go	(Jin 170)	1.00	4.00	62
DON'T SAY GOODBYE/My Little Girl	(Jin 110)	1.00	4.00	59
NO GOOD WOMAN/You Ain't Nothin But Fine	(Jin 156)	1.00	4.00	62
SOMETHING'S WRONG/	(Jin 174)	1.00	4.00	62

ROCKIN' STOCKINGS, The

TITLE/FLIP	LABEL & NO.	GOOD	NEAR MINT	YR.
YULEVILLE U.S.A./Rockin' Lang Syne	(Sun 1960)	1.00	4.00	60

ROCKIN' VICKERS

TITLE/FLIP	LABEL & NO.	GOOD	NEAR MINT	YR.
DANDY/I Don't Need Your Kind	(Columbia 43818)	.75	3.00	66

ROCKITE, Walter

TITLE/FLIP	LABEL & NO.	GOOD	NEAR MINT	YR.
PET ROCKS ARE COMING, THE/Rocky Road	(Westbound 5022)	.75	3.00	75
(Novelty)				

ROCK, Jimmy

TITLE/FLIP	LABEL & NO.	GOOD	NEAR MINT	YR.
DRAG, THE/We Two	(Todd 1024)	1.00	4.00	59

ROCKY & HIS FRIENDS

TITLE/FLIP	LABEL & NO.	GOOD	NEAR MINT	YR.
RIOT CITY/You're Not Wrong	(Tower 178)	.75	3.00	65

ROCKY FELLERS, The

TITLE/FLIP	LABEL & NO.	GOOD	NEAR MINT	YR.
BEACHCOMBER SONG, THE/Don't Sit Down	(Donna 1383)	1.00	4.00	63
CHING-A-LING BABY/Hey Little Donkey	(Scepter 1258)	.75	3.00	63
DON'T THROW MY TOYS AWAY/ The Man With The Blue Guitar	(Warner Bros. 5497)	.75	3.00	65
KILLER JOE/Lonely Teardrops	(Scepter 1246)	.75	3.00	63
LIKE THE BIG GUYS DO/Great Big World	(Scepter 1254)	.75	3.00	63
RENTED TUXEDO/ Two Steps Downstairs In The Basement	(Warner Bros. 5613)	.75	3.00	65
SANTA SANTA/Great Big World	(Scepter 1245)	.75	3.00	62
SHE MAKES ME WANNA DANCE/Bye Bye Baby	(Scepter 1263)	.75	3.00	63
TIGER (EVERYBODY WANTS TO BE A)/ Jeannie Memsah	(Warner Bros. 5440)	.75	3.00	64

RODEO

TITLE/FLIP	LABEL & NO.	GOOD	NEAR MINT	YR.
MILLIE THE PRO/Felicia-Jo	(St. Peter 101)	1.00	4.00	

RODGERS, Eileen

TITLE/FLIP	LABEL & NO.	GOOD	NEAR MINT	YR.
MIRACLE OF LOVE/Unwanted Heart	(Columbia 40708)	1.00	4.00	56
TREASURE OF YOUR LOVE/A Little Bit Bluer	(Columbia 41214)	1.00	4.00	58
WALL, THE/This Day	(Columbia 40850)	1.00	4.00	57

RODGERS, Jimmie

TITLE/FLIP	LABEL & NO.	GOOD	NEAR MINT	YR.
ARE YOU REALLY MINE/The Wizard	(Roulette 4090)	1.00	4.00	58
BIMBOMBEY/You Understand Me	(Roulette 4116)	1.00	4.00	58
BO DIDDLEY/Soldier, Won't You Marry Me	(Roulette SSR-8001)	1.50	6.00	59
(Stereo single issue)				
CHILD OF CLAY/Turnaround	(A&M 871)	.75	3.00	67
EASY TO LOVE (With Michelle Rodgers)/Easy	(Scrimshaw 1319/20)	.50	2.00	79
EVERYTIME I SING A LOVE SONG/	(Scrimshaw 1314)	.50	2.00	78
EVERYTIME MY HEART SINGS/I'm On My Way	(Roulette 4349)	.75	3.00	61
FACE IN A CROWD/Lonely Tears	(Dot 16450)	.75	3.00	63
FROGGY WENT A-COURTIN'/Because You're Young	(Roulette 4129)	.75	3.00	59
FROGGY WENA A-COURTIN'/Liza	(Roulette SSR-8007)	1.50	6.00	59
(Stereo single issue)				
GOOD WOMAN LIKES TO DRINK WITH THE BOYS, A/ Everybody Needs Love	(Scrimshaw 1313)	.50	2.00	77
HONEYCOMB/Their Hearts Were Full Of Spring	(Roulette 4015)	1.00	4.00	57
I'LL NEVER STAND IN YOUR WAY/Afraid	(Dot 16428)	.75	3.00	63
I'M NEVER GONNA TELL/Because You're Young	(Roulette 4129)	.75	3.00	59
IT'S CHRISTMAS ONCE AGAIN/Wistful Willie	(Roulette 4205)	1.00	4.00	59
IT'S OVER/Anita, You're Dreaming	(Dot 16821)	.75	3.00	66
JOHN BROWN'S BABY/I'm Goin' Home	(Roulette 4371)	.75	3.00	61
JUST A CLOSER WALK WITH THEE/ Joshua Fit The Battle O' Jerico	(Roulette 4234)	.75	3.00	60
JUST A LITTLE TIME/	(Scrimshaw 1313)	.50	2.00	77
KISSES SWEETER THAN WINE/ Better Loved You'll Never Be	(Roulette 4031)	1.00	4.00	57
LITTLE DOG CRIED/English Country Garden	(Roulette 4384)	.75	3.00	61
NO ONE WILL EVER KNOW/Because	(Dot 16378)	.75	3.00	62
OH-OH I'M FALLING IN LOVE AGAIN/ The Long Hot Summer	(Roulette 4045)	1.00	4.00	58
RAINBOW AT MIDNIGHT/Rhumba Boogie	(Dot 16407)	.75	3.00	62
RING-A-LING-A-LARIO/Wonderful You	(Roulette 4158)	.75	3.00	59
RING-A-LING-A-LARIO/Wonderful You	(Roulette SSR-4158)	1.50	6.00	59
(Stereo single issue)				
SECRETLY/	(Scrimshaw 1318)	.50	2.00	78
SECRETLY/Make Me A Miracle	(Roulette 4070)	1.00	4.00	58
T.L.C. (TENDER LOVE & CARE)/Waltzing Matilda	(Roulette 4218)	.75	3.00	60
T.L.C. (TENDER LOVE & CARE)/Waltzing Matilda	(Roulette SSR-4218)	1.50	6.00	60
(Stereo single issue)				
TUCUMCARI/The Night You Became Seventeen	(Roulette 4191)	.75	3.00	59
TWO-TEN, SIX-EIGHTEEN/Banana Boat Song	(Dot 16527)	.75	3.00	63
WHEN OUR LOVE BEGAN (COWBOYS & INDIANS)/	(Scrimshaw 1316)	.50	2.00	78
WOMAN FROM LIBERIA/Come Along Julie	(Roulette 4293)	.75	3.00	60
WORLD I USED TO KNOW, THE/ I Forgot More Than You'll Ever Know	(Dot 16595)	.75	3.00	64
WRECK OF THE "JOHN B", THE/ Four Little Girls In Boston	(Roulette 4260)	.75	3.00	60

RODGERS, Jimmie

TITLE/FLIP	LABEL & NO.	GOOD	NEAR MINT	YR.
I WON'T SING ROCK & ROLL/I Always Knew	(Zig-Zag 2072)	1.00	4.00	
(With Frankie Bell)				

RODNEY & THE BLAZERS

TITLE/FLIP	LABEL & NO.	GOOD	NEAR MINT	YR.
SNOW WHITE/Tell Me Baby	(Dore 588)	.75	3.00	61
TEENAGE CINDERELA/Summertime	(Kampus 100)	1.50	6.00	60
TEENAGE CINDERELLA/Stone	(Dore 572)	.75	3.00	60

ROE, Tommy (Thomas David Roe)

TITLE/FLIP	LABEL & NO.	GOOD	NEAR MINT	YR.
BRUSH A LITTLE SUNSHINE/King Of Fools	(ABC 11281)	.75	3.00	70
CAROL/Be A Good Little Girl	(ABC-Paramount 10543)	.75	3.00	64
CAVEMAN/I Gotta Girl	(Trumpet 1401)	5.00	20.00	60
(With the Satins & the Flamingos)				
CAVEMAN/I Gotta Girl	(Judd 1018)	3.75	15.00	60
(With the Satins & the Flamingos)				
CAVEMAN/I Gotta Girl	(Mark IV 001)	2.50	10.00	60
(With the Satins & the Flamingos)				
COME ON/There Will Be Better Years	(ABC-Paramount 10515)	.75	3.00	64
DIANE FROM MANCHESTER SQUARE/ Love Me Love Me	(ABC-Paramount 10623)	.75	3.00	65
DIZZY/The You I Need	(ABC 11164)	.75	3.00	68
DON'T CRY DONNA/Gonna Take A Chance	(ABC-Paramount 10389)	.75	3.00	63
DOTTIE, I LIKE IT/Soft Words	(ABC 11039)	.75	3.00	68
DREAMIN' AGAIN/Love The Way You Love Me Up	(Warner-Curb 8660)	.50	2.00	78
EVERYBODY/Sorry I'm Late, Lisa	(ABC-Paramount 10478)	.75	3.00	63
EVERY TIME A BLUEBIRD CRIES/ Doesn't Anybody Know My Name	(ABC-Paramount 10738)	.75	3.00	65
FOLK SINGER, THE/Count On Me	(ABC-Paramount 10423)	.75	3.00	62
FOURTEEN PAIRS OF SHOES/Combo Music	(ABC-Paramount 10665)	.75	3.00	65
GLITTER & GLEAM/Bad News	(Monument 8644)	.50	2.00	72
GOTTA KEEP ROLLIN' ALONG/It's Gonna Hurt Me	(ABC 11140)	.75	3.00	68
HEATHER HONEY/Money Is My Pay	(ABC 11211)	.75	3.00	69
HOORAY FOR HAZEL/Need Your Love	(ABC 10852)	.75	3.00	66
I KEEP REMEMBERING/ Wish You Didn't Have To Go	(ABC-Paramount 10706)	.75	3.00	65
I'M A RAMBLER, I'M A RAMBLER/Gunfighter	(ABC-Paramount 10696)	.75	3.00	65
IT'S NOW WINTER'S DAY/Kick Me Charlie	(ABC 10888)	.75	3.00	
JACK & JILL/Tip Toe Tina	(ABC 11229)	.75	3.00	69
JAM UP JELLY TIGHT/Moontalk	(ABC 11247)	.75	3.00	69
KISS & RUN/What Makes The Blues	(ABC-Paramount 10454)	.75	3.00	63
LITTLE MISS GOODIE TWO SHOES/Traffic Jam	(ABC 11287)	.75	3.00	70
LITTLE MISS SUNSHINE/The You I Need	(ABC 10945)	.75	3.00	67
MASSACHUSETTS/Just Look At Me	(Warner-Curb 8800)	.50	2.00	79
MEAN LITTLE WOMAN, ROSALIE/	(MGM-South 7001)	.50	2.00	72
MELANCHOLY MOOD/Paisley Dreams	(ABC 10989)	.75	3.00	67
OH SO RIGHT/I Think I Love You	(ABC-Paramount 10579)	.75	3.00	64
OLDIE BUT GOODIE/Sugar Cane	(ABC 11076)	.75	3.00	68
PARTY GIRL/Oh How I Could Love You	(ABC-Paramount 10604)	.75	3.00	64
PEARL/Dollars Worth Of Pennies	(ABC 11266)	.75	3.00	70
RITA & HER BAND/Snowing Me Under	(Monument 8662)	.50	2.00	74
SHEILA/Pretty Girl	(Judd 1022)	7.50	30.00	62
SHEILA/Save Your Kisses	(ABC-Paramount 10329)	.75	3.00	62
SING ALONG WITH ME/Nightime	(ABC 10908)	.75	3.00	67
STAGGER LEE/Back Streets & Alleys	(ABC 11307)	.75	3.00	71
STIR IT UP & SERVE IT/Firefly	(ABC 11258)	.75	3.00	70
SUSIE DARLIN'/Piddle De Pat	(ABC-Paramount 10362)	.75	3.00	62
SWEET PEA/Much More Love	(ABC 10762)	.75	3.00	66
SWEET SOUNDS/Moon Talk	(ABC 10933)	.75	3.00	67
TOWN CRIER/Rainbow	(ABC-Paramount 10379)	.75	3.00	62
WE CAN MAKE MUSIC/Gotta Keep Rollin' Along	(ABC 11273)	.75	3.00	70
WORKING CLASS HERO/	(MGM-South 701)	.50	2.00	73
YOU BETTER MOVE ON/	(Warner-Curb 49085)	.50	2.00	79
YOUR LOVE WILL SEE ME THROUGH/	(Monument 45228)	.50	2.00	77

ROGER & THE TRAVELERS (Featuring Roger Koob)

TITLE/FLIP	LABEL & NO.	GOOD	NEAR MINT	YR.
YOU'RE DADDY'S LITTLE GIRL/Just Gotta Be That Way	(Ember 1079)	2.50	10.00	62

ROGERS, Dann

TITLE/FLIP	LABEL & NO.	GOOD	NEAR MINT	YR.
LOOKS LIKE LOVE AGAIN/Lucy	(IA 500)	.50	2.00	79

ROGERS, Julie

TITLE/FLIP	LABEL & NO.	GOOD	NEAR MINT	YR.
LIKE A CHILD/The Love Of A Boy	(Mercury 72380)	.75	3.00	65
WEDDING, THE/Without Your Love	(Mercury 72332)	.75	3.00	64

ROGERS, Kenny

TITLE/FLIP	LABEL & NO.	GOOD	NEAR MINT	YR.
FOR YOU ALONE/I've Got A Lot To Learn	(Carlton 468)	2.00	8.00	58
JOLE BLON/Lonely	(Ken-Lee 102)	2.50	10.00	
TAKE LIFE IN STRIDE/Here's That Rainy Day	(Mercury 72545)	1.00	4.00	66
THAT CRAZY FEELING/We'll Always Have Each Other	(Carlton 454)	2.00	8.00	58

ROGERS, Kenny & The First Edition

TITLE/FLIP	LABEL & NO.	GOOD	NEAR MINT	YR.
ARE MY THOUGHTS WITH YOU/ If I Could Only change Your Love	(Reprise 0773)	1.25	5.00	68
BUT YOU KNOW I LOVE YOU/Homemade Lies	(Reprise 0799)	.75	3.00	68
DREAM ON/Only Me	(Reprise 0683)	1.00	4.00	68
HEED THE CALL/A Stranger In My Place	(Reprise 0953)	.75	3.00	70
I FOUND A REASON/Ticket To Nowhere	(Reprise 0628)	1.50	6.00	67
(Shown as by the First Edition)				
JUST DROPPED IN (TO SEE WHAT CONDITION MY CONDITION WAS IN)/Shadow In The Corner Of Your Mind	(Reprise 0655)	.75	3.00	68
LOOK AROUND, I'LL BE THERE/Charlie The Fer' De Lance	(Reprise 0693)	1.00	4.00	68
ONCE AGAIN SHE'S ALL ALONE/Good Time Liberator	(Reprise 0822)	1.00	4.00	69
REUBEN JAMES/Sunshine	(Reprise 0854)	.75	3.00	69
RUBY, DON'T TAKE YOUR LOVE TO TOWN/ Girl Get A Hold Of Yourself	(Reprise 0829)	.75	3.00	69
SCHOOL TEACHER/	(Reprise 1069)	1.00	4.00	72
SOMEONE WHO CARES/	(Reprise 0999)	1.00	4.00	71
SOMETHING'S BURNING/Momma's Waiting	(Reprise 0888)	.75	3.00	70
TAKE MY HAND/	(Reprise 1018)	1.00	4.00	71
TELL IT ALL BROTHER/ Just Remember You're My Sunshine	(Reprise 0923)	.75	3.00	70
WHAT AM I GONNA DO/Where Does Rosie Go	(Reprise 1053)	1.00	4.00	71

ROGERS, Timmie "Oh Yeah"

TITLE/FLIP	LABEL & NO.	GOOD	NEAR MINT	YR.
BACK TO SCHOOL AGAIN/I've Got A Dog Who Loves Me	(Cameo 116)	1.00	4.00	57
TAKE ME TO YOUR LEADER/Fla-Ga-La-Pa	(Cameo 131)	1.00	4.00	58

ROGUES, The

TITLE/FLIP	LABEL & NO.	GOOD	NEAR MINT	YR.
BARRACUDA/Jezebel	(Bing 4900)	1.00	4.00	64
EVERYDAY/Roger's Reef	(Columbia 43190)	1.00	4.00	65

ROGUES, The

TITLE/FLIP	LABEL & NO.	GOOD	NEAR MINT	YR.
SAY YOU LOVE ME/Secondary Man	(Thunderbird 507)	.75	3.00	

ROKES, The

TITLE/FLIP	LABEL & NO.	GOOD	NEAR MINT	YR.
LET'S LIVE FOR TODAY/I'll Change My Papers	(RCA Victor 47-9199)	.75	3.00	67

ROLLERS, The (Formerly The Bay City Rollers)

TITLE/FLIP	LABEL & NO.	GOOD	NEAR MINT	YR.
TURN ON THE RADIO/Hello & Welcome Home	(Arista 0476)	.50	2.00	79

ROLLING STONES, The (Featuring Mick Jagger)

TITLE/FLIP	LABEL & NO.	GOOD	NEAR MINT	YR.
AIN'T TOO PROUD TO BEG/Dance Little Sister	(Rolling Stones RS-19302)	.50	2.00	74
ANGIE/Silver Train	(Rolling Stones RS-19105)	.50	2.00	73
AS TEARS GO BY/Gotta Get Away	(London 9808)	1.00	4.00	65
AS TEARS GO BY/Gotta Get Away	(London 9808)	2.50	10.00	65
(Promotional issue)				
BEAST OF BURDEN/When The Whip Comes Down	(Rolling Stones RS-19309)	.50	2.00	78
BEAST OF BURDEN/When The Whip Comes Down	(Rolling Stones RS-19309)	12.50	50.00	78
(Picture sleeve)				
BEFORE THEY MAKE ME RUN (Stereo)/ Before They Make Me Run (Mono)	(Rolling Stones PR-316)	2.50	10.00	78
(Promotional issue)				
BEFORE THEY MAKE ME RUN (Stereo)/ Before They Make Me Run (Mono)(Picture sleeve)	(Rolling Stones PR-316)	3.00	12.00	78
(This sleeve has been counterfeited, however originals can best be detected by the clarity of Keith Richard's right eye, especially the pupil. The pupil is not clear or visable on the fakes.)				
BROWN SUGAR/Bitch	(Rolling Stones RS-19100)	.50	2.00	71
CON LE MIE LACRIME (AS TEARS GO BY)/ Heart Of Stone	(Decca F-22270)	3.00	12.00	65
(Listed because "As Tears Go By" is sung in Italian; the only instance of the group performing in another language on record.)				
DANDELION/We Love You	(London 905)	.75	3.00	67
DANDELION/We Love You	(London 905)	2.50	10.00	67
(Promotional issue)				
DANDELION/We Love You	(London 905)	12.50	50.00	67
(Picture sleeve)				

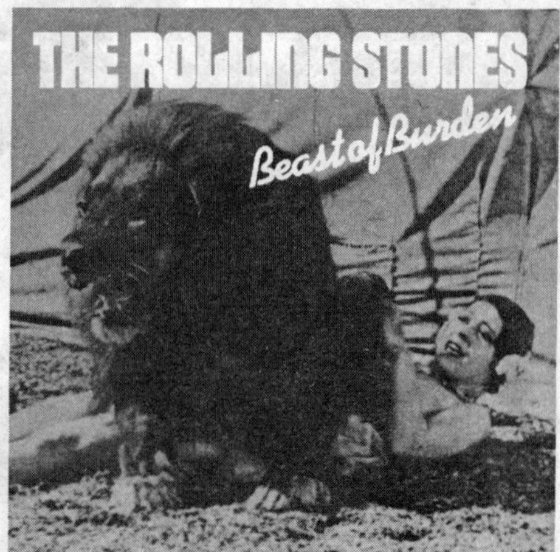

TITLE/FLIP	LABEL & NO.	GOOD	NEAR MINT	YR.
DOO DOO DOO DOO DOO (HEARTBREAKER)/ Dancing With Mr. D	(Rolling Stones RS-19109)	.50	2.00	74
EMOTIONAL RESCUE/Down In The Hole	(Rolling Stones RS-20001)	.50	2.00	80
EMOTIONAL RESCUE/Down In The Hole (12" single issue)	(Rolling Stones PR-367)	3.75	15.00	80
FOOL TO CRY/Hot Stuff (Also see "Hot Stuff"/"Crazy Mama")	(Rolling Stone RS-19304)	.75	3.00	76
GET OFF OF MY CLOUD/I'm Free	(London 9792)	1.00	4.00	65
GET OFF OF MY CLOUD/I'm Free (Promotional issue)	(London 9792)	2.50	12.00	65
HAPPY/All Down The Line	(Rolling Stones RS-19104)	.50	2.00	72
HAVE YOU SEEN YOUR MOTHER BABY, STANDING IN THE SHADOW?/Who's Driving My Plane	(London 903)	.75	3.00	66
HAVE YOU SEEN YOUR MOTHER BABY, STANDING IN THE SHADOW?/Who's Driving My Plane (Promotional issue)	(London 903)	2.50	10.00	66
HAVE YOU SEEN YOUR MOTHER BABY, STANDING IN THE SHADOW?/Who's Driving My Plane (Picture sleeve)	(London 903)	2.00	8.00	66
HEART OF STONE/What A Shame (Blue swirl label)	(London 9725)	1.00	4.00	64
HEART OF STONE/What A Shame (Purple & white label)	(London 9725)	2.50	10.00	64
HEART OF STONE/What A Shame (Promotional issue)	(London 9725)	3.00	12.00	64
HEART OF STONE/What A Shame (Picture sleeve)	(London 9725)	10.00	40.00	64
HONKY TONK WOMEN/ You Can't Always Get What You Want	(London 910)	.75	3.00	69
HONKY TONK WOMEN/ You Can't Always Get What You Want (Promotional issue)	(London 910)	1.50	6.00	69
HONKY TONK WOMEN/ You Can't Always Get What You Want (Picture sleeve)	(London 910)	1.50	6.00	69

TITLE/FLIP	LABEL & NO.	GOOD	NEAR MINT	YR.
HOT STUFF/Crazy Mama (12" single issue) (This disc was orginally issued on blue & black vinyl with the black coloring in sort of a weave pattern across the disc. Counterfeit copies have the black in 'blobs' rather than evenly distributed in the pattern.)	(Rolling Stones PR-70)	10.00	40.00	76
(I CAN'T GET NO) SATISFACTION/ Under Assistant West Coast Promotion Man	(London 9766)	1.25	5.00	65
(I CAN'T GET NO) SATISFACTION/ Under Assistant West Coast Promotion Man (Promotional issue)	(London 9766)	3.00	12.00	65
(I CAN'T GET NO) SATISFACTION/ Under Assistant West Coast Promotion Man (Picture sleeve)	(London 9766)	6.25	25.00	65
I DON'T KNOW WHY/Try A Little Harder	(ABKCO 4701)	.75	3.00	75
IT'S ALL OVER NOW/Good Times Bad Times (Blue swirl label)	(London 9687)	1.00	4.00	64
IT'S ALL OVER NOW/Good Times Bad Times (Purple & white label)	(London 9687)	2.50	10.00	64
IT'S ALL OVER NOW/Good Times Bad Times (Promotional issue)	(London 9687)	3.00	12.00	64
IT'S ALL OVER NOW/Good Times Bad Times (Picture sleeve)	(London 9687)	3.75	15.00	64
IT'S ONLY ROCK 'N' ROLL (BUT I LIKE IT)/ Through The Lonely Nights	(Rolling Stones RS-19301)	.50	2.00	74
IT'S ONLY ROCK 'N' ROLL (BUT I LIKE IT)/ Through The Lonely Nights (Promotional issue, edited version.)	(Rolling Stones RS-19301)	1.50	6.00	74
JUMPIN' JACK FLASH/Child Of The Moon	(London 908)	.75	3.00	68
JUMPIN' JACK FLASH/Child Of The Moon (Promotional issue)	(London 908)	2.00	8.00	68

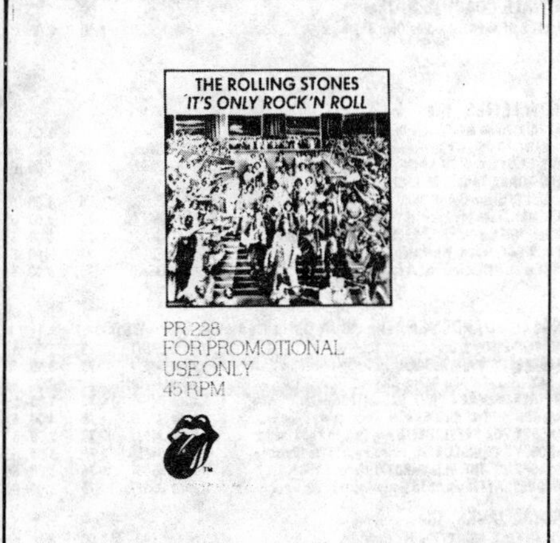

THE ROLLING STONES
IT'S ONLY ROCK'N ROLL
PR 228
FOR PROMOTIONAL
USE ONLY
45 RPM

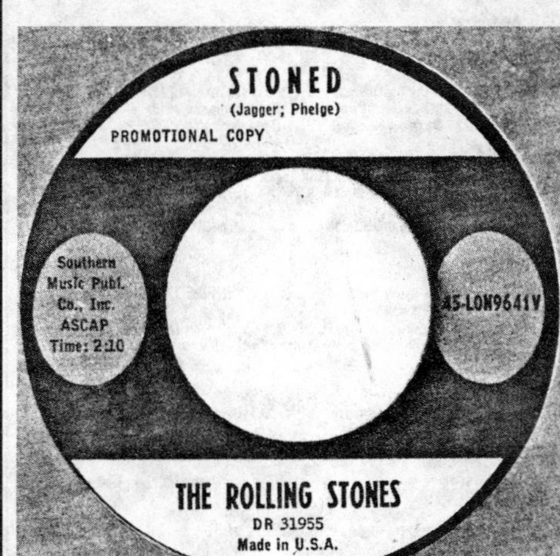

TITLE/FLIP	LABEL & NO.	GOOD	NEAR MINT	YR.
JUMPIN' JACK FLASH/Child Of The Moon (Picture sleeve)	(London 908)	1.50	6.00	68
LAST TIME, THE/Play With Fire (London logo in white letters)	(London 9741)	1.50	6.00	65
LAST TIME, THE/Play With Fire (Promotional issue)	(London 9741)	3.00	12.00	65
LAST TIME, THE/Play With Fire (Picture sleeve) (When compared to originals, counterfeit issues of this sleeve show many of the strands of the group's hair clearly, whereas originals picture more of a 'solid' head of hair, with less definition of the strands.)	(London 9741)	1.50	6.00	65
MISS YOU/Far Away Eyes (Promotional 12" issue)	(Rolling Stones PR-119)	3.75	15.00	78
MISS YOU/Far Away Eyes (12" single issue, with blue "no tongue" cover)	(Rolling Stones RS-4609)	1.50	6.00	78
MISS YOU/Far Away Eyes (12" single issue, with white "tongue" cover)	(Rolling Stones RS-4609)	2.00	8.00	78
MISS YOU/Far Away Eyes	(Rolling Stones RS-19307)	.50	2.00	78
MISS YOU/Hot Stuff (Reissue series)	(Atco 4616)	1.50	6.00	79
MOTHER'S LITTLE HELPER/Lady Jane	(London 902)	1.00	4.00	66
MOTHER'S LITTLE HELPER/Lady Jane (Promotional issue)	(London 902)	2.50	10.00	66
MOTHER'S LITTLE HELPER/Lady Jane (Picture sleeve)	(London 902)	2.00	8.00	66
19TH NERVOUS BREAKDOWN/Sad Day	(London 9823)	1.00	4.00	66
19TH NERVOUS BREAKDOWN/Sad Day (Promotional issue)	(London 9823)	2.50	10.00	66
19TH NERVOUS BREAKDOWN/Sad Day (Picture sleeve)	(London 9823)	2.50	10.00	66
NOT FADE AWAY/I Wanna Be Your Man (Blue swirl label)	(London 9657)	1.00	4.00	64
NOT FADE AWAY/I Wanna Be Your Man (Purple & white label)	(London 9657)	2.50	10.00	64
NOT FADE AWAY/I Wanna Be Your Man (Promotional issue)	(London 9657)	3.75	15.00	64

TITLE/FLIP	LABEL & NO.	GOOD	NEAR MINT	YR.
NOT FADE AWAY/I Wanna Be Your Man (Picture sleeve)	(London 9657)	12.50	50.00	64
OUT OF TIME/Jiving Sister Fanny	(ABKCO 5N-4702)	.75	3.00	75
PAINT IT BLACK/Stupid Girl	(London 901)	1.00	4.00	66
PAINT IT BLACK/Stupid Girl (Promotional issue)	(London 901)	2.50	10.00	66
PAINT IT BLACK/Stupid Girl (Picture sleeve)	(London 901)	1.50	6.00	66
RUBY TUESDAY/Let's Spend The Night Together	(London 904)	.75	3.00	67
RUBY TUESDAY/Let's Spend The Night Together (Promotional issue)	(London 904)	2.50	10.00	67
RUBY TUESDAY/Let's Spend The Night Together (Picture sleeve)	(London 904)	1.50	6.00	67
SHATTERED/Everything Is Turning To Gold	(Rolling Stones RS-19310)	.50	2.00	78
SHE'S A RAINBOW/2,000 Light Years From Home	(London 906)	.75	3.00	68
SHE'S A RAINBOW/2,000 Light Years From Home (Promotional issue)	(London 906)	2.50	10.00	68
SHE'S A RAINBOW/2,000 Light Years From Home (Picture sleeve)	(London 906)	1.50	6.00	68
SHE'S SO COLD/Send It To Me	(Rolling Stones RS-21001)	.50	2.00	80
SHE'S SO COLD ("GOD DAMN" VERSION)/ She's So Cold ("Cleaned Up" Version) (Promotional issue only)	(Rolling Stones RS-21001)	1.25	5.00	80
STONED/I Wanna Be Your Man (Promotional issue)	(London 9641)	37.50	150.00	64
STREET FIGHTING MAN/No Expectations	(London 909)	.75	2.00	68
STREET FIGHTING MAN/No Expectations (Promotional issue)	(London 909)	2.00	8.00	68
STREET FIGHTING MAN/ No Expectations (Picture sleeve) (Prices may vary widely on this sleeve. Offers of $1000.00 have been made but, as of press time, there has been no sale at that figure. Certainly, a near mint copy would bring $750.00.)	(London 909)	187.50	750.00	68

TITLE/FLIP	LABEL & NO.	GOOD	NEAR MINT	YR.
TELL ME (YOU'RE COMING BACK)/ I Just Want To Make Love To You (Blue swirl label)	(London 9682)	1.00	4.00	64
TELL ME (YOU'RE COMING BACK)/ I Just Want To Make Love To You (Purple & white label)	(London 9682)	2.50	10.00	64
TELL ME (YOU'RE COMING BACK)/ I Just Want To Make Love To You (Promotional issue)	(London 9682)	3.00	12.00	64
TELL ME (YOU'RE COMING BACK)/ I Just Want To Make Love To You (Picture sleeve)	(London 9682)	5.00	20.00	64
TIME IS ON MY SIDE/Congratulations (Blue swirl label)	(London 9708)	1.00	4.00	64
TIME IS ON MY SIDE/Congratulations (Purple & white label)	(London 9708)	2.50	10.00	64
TIME IS ON MY SIDE/Congratulations (Promotional issue)	(London 9708)	3.00	12.00	64
TIME IS ON MY SIDE/Congratulations (Picture sleeve)	(London 9708)	3.75	15.00	64
TIME WAITS FOR NO ONE (Stereo)/ Time Waits For No One (Mono) (Promotional issue only)	(Rolling Stones RS-228)	1.00	4.00	76
TUMBLING DICE/Sweet Black Angel	(Rolling Stones RS-19103)	.50	2.00	72
WHAT'S IT ALL ABOUT (The Rolling Stones)/ What's It All About (The Beach Boys) (Public service disc, with interviews by Bill Huie)	(Program #507/508)	5.00	20.00	
WILD HORSES/Sway	(Rolling Stones RS-19101)	.50	2.00	71

Also see Faces
Also see Wyman, Bill
Also see Tosh, Peter
Also see Jameson, Bobby
Also see Simon, Carly
Also see Neon Leon
Also see Faithful, Marianne

ROMAN, Dick

TITLE/FLIP	LABEL & NO.	GOOD	NEAR MINT	YR.
THEME FROM A SUMMER PLACE/Butterfly	(Harmon 1004)	.75	3.00	62

ROMANCERS, The

TITLE/FLIP	LABEL & NO.	GOOD	NEAR MINT	YR.
NO GREATER LOVE/You'll Never Know	(Celebrity 701)	1.50	6.00	61

ROME & PARIS

TITLE/FLIP	LABEL & NO.	GOOD	NEAR MINT	YR.
BECAUSE OF YOU/Why Oh Why	(Roulette 4681)	1.50	6.00	66

ROMEO, Al

TITLE/FLIP	LABEL & NO.	GOOD	NEAR MINT	YR.
MOONLIGHT BECOMES YOU/Hot Fudge Sundae	(Laurie 3177)	2.00	8.00	63

ROMEOS, The

TITLE/FLIP	LABEL & NO.	GOOD	NEAR MINT	YR.
PRECIOUS MEMORIES/Juicy Lucy	(Mark II 101)	.75	3.00	67

ROMEOS, The

TITLE/FLIP	LABEL & NO.	GOOD	NEAR MINT	YR.
TIGER'S WIDE AWAKE, THE (Answer song)/ Hitch Hikin'	(Amy 840)	.75	3.00	62

ROMERO, Chan

TITLE/FLIP	LABEL & NO.	GOOD	NEAR MINT	YR.
HIPPY HIPPY SHAKE, THE/If I Had A Way	(Del Fi 4119)	2.50	10.00	59

ROMERO, Rudy

TITLE/FLIP	LABEL & NO.	GOOD	NEAR MINT	YR.
TO THE WORLD/	(Tumbleweed 1012)	.50	2.00	72

RON & JON (With Ron Jacobs)

TITLE/FLIP	LABEL & NO.	GOOD	NEAR MINT	YR.
HAWAII STRIKES BACK/Yeah (Novelty/Break-in)	(Sick 45-50th)	5.00	20.00	

RON & JOE & THE CREW

TITLE/FLIP	LABEL & NO.	GOOD	NEAR MINT	YR.
RIOT IN CELL BLOCK #9/Ain't Love Grand	(Strand 25001)	1.00	4.00	59

RONALD & RUBY

TITLE/FLIP	LABEL & NO.	GOOD	NEAR MINT	YR.
LOLLIPOP/Fickle Baby	(RCA Victor 47-7174)	1.00	4.00	58

RONDELLS, The

TITLE/FLIP	LABEL & NO.	GOOD	NEAR MINT	YR.
EVERYBODY TO & FRO/Have A Real Good Time	(Xpress 203)	.75	3.00	
MATILDA/Tina	(Shalimar 104)	1.00	4.00	63
MATILDA/Tina	(Dot 17323)	.50	2.00	70

RONDELS, The

TITLE/FLIP	LABEL & NO.	GOOD	NEAR MINT	YR.
BACK BEAT NO. 1/Shades Of Green	(Amy 825)	.75	3.00	61
C'MON LET'S GO SWEETHEART/	(Nota 4001)	.75	3.00	
CALDONIA/110 Lbs. Of Drums	(Amy 839)	.75	3.00	62
COVER CHARGE/Meet Us At The Peppermint Lounge	(Amy 857)	.75	3.00	62
MY PRAYER/Satan's Theme	(Amy 830)	.75	3.00	61

RON-DELS, The

TITLE/FLIP	LABEL & NO.	GOOD	NEAR MINT	YR.
IF YOU REALLY WANT ME TO, I'LL GO/Walk About	(Smash 1986)	.75	3.00	65

RONDO, Don

TITLE/FLIP	LABEL & NO.	GOOD	NEAR MINT	YR.
THERE'S ONLY YOU/Forsaking All Others	(Jubilee 5297)	1.00	4.00	57
TWO DIFFERENT WORLDS/He Made You Mine	(Jubilee 5256)	1.00	4.00	56
WHITE SILVER SANDS/Stars Fell On Alabama	(Jubilee 5288)	1.00	4.00	57

RONETTES (Featuring Veronica Bennett-Spector)

TITLE/FLIP	LABEL & NO.	GOOD	NEAR MINT	YR.
BABY I LOVE YOU/Miss Joan & Mr. Sam (Instrumental)	(Philles 118)	1.00	4.00	63
BE MY BABY/Tedesco & Pitman (Instrumental)	(Philles 116)	1.00	4.00	63
(BEST PART OF) BREAKIN' UP, THE/Big Red (Instrumental)	(Philles 120)	1.00	4.00	64
BORN TO BE TOGETHER/Blues For Baby	(Philles 126)	1.00	4.00	64
DO I LOVE YOU/Bebe & Susu (Instrumental)	(Philles 121)	1.00	4.00	64
GOOD GIRLS/Memory	(May 138)	2.50	10.00	63
HE DID IT/Recipe For Love	(Dimension 1046)	7.50	30.00	64
I CAN HEAR MUSIC/When I Saw You	(Philles 133)	1.00	4.00	66

TITLE/FLIP	LABEL & NO.	GOOD	NEAR MINT	YR.
I WANT A BOY/Sweet Sixteen	(Colpix 601)	5.00	20.00	61
(Shown as by Ronnie & the Relatives)				
I WISH I NEVER SAW THE SUNSHINE/ I Wonder What He's Doing	(Buddah 408)	1.00	4.00	74
I'M ON THE WAGON/I'm Gonna Quit While I'm Ahead	(Colpix 646)	3.75	15.00	62
IS THIS WHAT I GET FOR LOVING YOU/Oh I Love You	(Philles 128)	1.00	4.00	65
LOVER LOVER/Go Out & Get It	(Buddah 384)	1.00	4.00	73
MY GUIDING LIGHT/I'm Gonna Quit While I'm Ahead	(May 111)	5.00	20.00	62
(Shown as by Ronnie & the Relatives)				
SILHOUETTES/You Bet I Would	(May 114)	2.50	10.00	62
WALKIN' IN THE RAIN/How Does It Feel	(Philles 123)	1.00	4.00	64
YOU CAME, YOU SAW, YOU CONQUERED/Oh, I Love You	(A&M 1040)	1.00	4.00	69
Also see Bonnie & The Treasures				
Also see Veronica				
RONNIE & JOEY				
FROZEN DINNERS/I Want	(Little Star 106)	.75	3.00	61
RONNIE & THE CRAYONS				
AM I IN LOVE/Birchard's Bread	(Domain 1402)	.75	3.00	64
RONNIE & THE DELAIRES				
DRAG, THE/My Funny Valentine	(Coral 62404)	3.75	15.00	64
RONNIE & THE DIRT RIDERS (With Ron Dante)				
YELLOW VAN/Love Will Never Hurt You	(RCA 10651)	1.25	5.00	76
Also see Cuff Links, The				
RONNIE & THE MANHATTANS				
COME ON BACK/Long Time No See	(Enjoy 2008)	.75	3.00	
RONNIE & THE POMONA CASUALS				
I WANNA DO THE JERK/Sloopy	(Donna 1402)	1.00	4.00	65
SWIMMING AT THE RAINBOW/Casual Blues	(Donna 1400)	1.00	4.00	64
RONNIE & THE PREMIERS				
SHARON/Cha Cha Rock	(Hightland 1014)	1.00	4.00	61
RONNIE & THE RELATIVES: see Ronettes, The				
RONNIE & THE SCHOOLMATES				
DON'T, DON'T, DON'T (DROP OUT)/ Just Born (To Be Your Baby)	(Coed 605)	.75	3.00	65
RONNY & THE DAYTONAS (Featuring Bucky Wilkin)				
ALFIE/The Girls & The Boys	(RCA Victor 47-9435)	1.00	4.00	68
ALL AMERICAN GIRL/Dianne, Dianne	(RCA Victor 47-8896)	1.00	4.00	66
ANTIQUE '32 STUDEBAKER DICTATOR COUPE/ Then The Rains Came	(Mala 531)	1.00	4.00	66
BEACH BOY/No Wheels	(Mala 503)	1.00	4.00	65
BRAVE NEW WORLD/Hold Onto Your Heart	(RCA Victor 47-9253)	1.00	4.00	67
BUCKET "T"/Little Rail Job	(Mala 492)	1.00	4.00	64
CALIFORNIA BOUND/Hey Little Girl	(Mala 490)	1.00	4.00	64
G.T.O./Hot Rod Baby	(Mala 481)	1.00	4.00	64
LITTLE SCRAMBLER/I'll Think Of Summer	(Mala 542)	1.00	4.00	66
LITTLE SCRAMBLER/Teenage Years	(Mala 497)	1.00	4.00	65
SANDY/Sandy (Instrumental)	(Mala 513)	1.00	4.00	65
SOMEBODY TO LOVE ME/Goodbye Baby	(Mala 525)	1.00	4.00	66
WALK WITH THE SUN/Last Letter	(RCA Victor 47-9107)	1.00	4.00	67
WINTER WEATHER/Young	(RCA Victor 47-9022)	1.00	4.00	66
RONSTADT, Linda (Of The Stone Poneys)				
ALISON/Mohammed's Radio	(Asylum 46034)	.50	2.00	79
ALL THE BEAUTIFUL THINGS/Sweet Summer & Gold	(Capitol 5838)	1.25	5.00	67
BACK IN THE U.S.A./White Rhythm & Blues	(Asylum 45519)	.50	2.00	78
BLUE BAYOU/Old Paint	(Asylum 45431)	.50	2.00	77
DIFFERENT DRUM/I've Got To Know	(Capitol 2004)	1.00	4.00	67
(Shown as by the Stone Poneys)				
DOLPHINS/The Long Way Around	(Capitol 2438)	1.00	4.00	69
EVERGREEN/One For All	(Capitol 5910)	1.00	4.00	67
HEAT WAVE/Love Is A Rose	(Asylum 45282)	.50	2.00	75
HOW DO I MAKE YOU/Rambler Gambler	(Asylum 46602)	.50	2.00	80
HURT SO BAD/	(Asylum 46624)	.50	2.00	80
I FALL TO PIECES/Can It Be True	(Capitol 3210)	.75	3.00	72
IT'S SO EASY/Lo Siento Mi vida	(Asylum 45438)	.50	2.00	77
JUST ONE LOOK/Love Me Tender	(Asylum 46011)	.50	2.00	79
LAGO AZUL (BLUE BAYOU)/Lo Siento Mi vida	(Asylum 45464)	.50	2.00	78
LONG LONG TIME/Nobodys	(Capitol 2864)	.50	2.00	70
LOSE AGAIN/Lo Siento Mi Vida	(Asylum 45402)	.50	2.00	77
LOVE HAS NO PRIDE/I Can Almost See It	(Asylum 11026)	.50	2.00	73
LOVE IS A ROSE/Silver Blue	(Asylum 45271)	.50	2.00	75
OOH BABY BABY/Blowing Away	(Asylum 45546)	.50	2.00	78
POOR POOR PITIFUL ME/Simple Man, Simple Dream	(Asylum 45462)	.50	2.00	78
ROCK ME ON THE WATER/Crazy Arms	(Capitol 3273)	.75	3.00	72
(SHE'S A) VERY LOVELY WOMAN/The Long Way Around	(Capitol 3021)	.75	3.00	71
SILVER THREADS & GOLDEN NEEDLES/ Don't Cry For Now	(Asylum 11032)	.50	2.00	74
SO FINE/Everybody Has Their Own Ideas	(Sidewalk 937)	3.00	12.00	66
SOME OF SHELLY'S BLUES/Hobo (Morning Glory)	(Capitol 2195)	1.25	5.00	68
(Shown as by Linda Ronstadt & the Stone Poneys)				
SOMEONE TO LAY DOWN BESIDE ME/Crazy	(Asylum 45361)	.50	2.00	76
THAT'LL BE THE DAY/Try Me Again	(Asylum 45340)	.50	2.00	76
TRACKS OF MY TEARS/ The Sweetest Gift (With Emmylou Harris)	(Asylum 45295)	.50	2.00	75
TUMBLING DICE/I Never Will Marry	(Asylum 45479)	.50	2.00	78
UP TO MY NECK IN HIGH MUDDY WATER/Carnival Bear	(Capitol 2110)	1.25	5.00	68
(Shown as by Linda Rondstadt & the Stone Poneys)				
WHEN WILL I BE LOVED/Crazy Arms	(Captiol 4050)	.75	3.00	75
WHEN WILL I BE LOVED/It Doesn't Matter Any More	(Capitol 4050)	.75	3.00	75
WILL YOU LOVE ME TOMORROW/Lovesick Blues	(Capitol 2767)	1.00	4.00	70
YOU'RE NO GOOD/I Can't Help It (If I'm Still In Love With You)	(Capitol 3990)	.50	2.00	74
YOU'RE NO GOOD/When Will I Be Loved	(Capitol 3990)	1.00	4.00	74
(Promotional issue only)				
ROOFTOP SINGERS, The (Eric Darling, Lynne Taylor, Bill Svanoe)				
MAMA DON'T ALLOW/It Don't Mean A Thing	(Vanguard 35020)	.75	3.00	63
TOM CAT/Shoes	(Vanguard 35019)	.75	3.00	63
WALK RIGHT IN/Cool Water	(Vanguard 35017)	.75	3.00	63
Also see Tarriers, The				
ROOKS, Wayne				
FRATERNITY PIN/Postcard From Paris	(Capitol 4866)	.75	3.00	63
WHERE DOES THE CLOWN GO/Chi Chico Teek	(Capitol 4772)	.75	3.00	62
ROOMATES, The				
ANSWER ME MY LOVE/Gee	(Philips 40105)	1.00	4.00	63
GEE/Answer Me My Love	(Philips 40105)	1.00	4.00	63
GLORY OF LOVE/Never Knew	(Valmor 008)	1.00	4.00	61
I WANT A LITTLE GIRL/Making Believe	(Promo 2211)	1.50	6.00	60
MY FOOLISH HEART/My Kisses For Your Thoughts	(Valmor 13)	1.00	4.00	62
MY HEART/Just For Tonight	(Canadian American 166)	1.50	6.00	64
NEARNESS OF YOU, THE/Please Don't Cheat On Me	(Philips 40161)	1.50	6.00	64
NEARNESS OF YOU, THE/Please Don't Cheat On Me	(Philips 40153)	1.00	4.00	63
SUNDAY KIND OF LOVE/ A Lovely Way To Spend An Evening	(Cameo 233)	.75	3.00	62
Also see Cathy Jean & the Roommates				
ROOSTERS, The				
FUN HOUSE/Chicken Hop	(Felsted 8642)	.75	3.00	62
FUN HOUSE/Chicken Hop	(Shar-dee 704)	1.25	5.00	59
PRETTY GIRL/Let's Try Again	(Epic 9487)	.75	3.00	62

TITLE/FLIP	LABEL & NO.	GOOD	NEAR MINT	YR.
ROSE, Andy				
JUST YOUNG/Lov-A Lov-A Love	(Aamco 100)	1.00	4.00	58
ROSE, Biff				
I FORGOT TO TELL YOU/The Captain	(Buddah 218)	.75	3.00	71
TAKE CARE OF MY BROTHER/Myrtle's Pies	(Tetragrammaton 1543)	.75	3.00	70
WHAT'S GNAWING AT ME/Molly	(Tetragrammaton 1506)	.75	3.00	68
ROSE, David				
CALYPSO MELODY/Theme From "The Wings Of Eagles"	(MGM 12430)	.75	3.00	57
LOVE IS A MANY-SPLENDORED THING/You & You Alone	(MGM 30883)	.75	3.00	55
STRIPPER, THE/Ebb Tide	(MGM 13064)	.75	3.00	62
SWINGING SHEPHERD BLUES/Rock Fiddle	(MGM 12608)	.75	3.00	58
Instrumentals				
ROS, Edmundo				
COLONEL BOGEY/Spanish Gypsy Dance	(London 1779)	.75	3.00	58
MARCH FROM THE RIVER KWAI/ I Talk To The Trees Cha Cha	(London 1831)	.75	3.00	58
WEDDING SAMBA/Too Much Tempo In My Rhumba Beat	(London 499)	.75	3.00	50
Instrumentals				
ROSE GARDEN, The				
HERE'S TODAY/If My World Falls Through	(Atco 6564)	1.00	4.00	68
NEXT PLANE TO LONDON/Flower Town	(Atco 6510)	1.00	4.00	67
ROSELLA, Carmella				
OH, IT WAS ELVIS/Where	(Nancy 1004)	1.50	6.00	56
ROSE MARIE				
CHENALUNA ROCK & ROLL/Two Dollars Please	(Mercury 71144)	1.00	4.00	57
ROSE, Tim				
HEY JOE (YOU SHOT YOUR WOMAN DOWN)/ King Lonely The Blue	(Columbia 43648)	.75	3.00	66
I GOTTA DO THINGS MY WAY/Where Was I	(Columbia 43722)	.75	3.00	66
I'M BRINGING IT HOME/ Mother, Father, Where Are You	(Columbia 43563)	.75	3.00	66
I'M GONNA BE STRONG/I Got A Loneliness	(Columbia 43958)	.75	3.00	67
LONG TIME MAN/Come Away Melinda	(Columbia 44387)	.75	3.00	67
MORNING DEW/You're Slipping Away From Me	(Columbia 44031)	.75	3.00	67
ROSIE (Rosie Hamlin)				
ANGEL BABY/Give Me Love	(Highland 1011)	.75	3.00	60
(With the Originals)				
ANGEL FROM ABOVE/Why Did You Leave Me	(Highland 1025)	1.00	4.00	61
LONELY BLUE NIGHTS/We'll Have A Chance	(Highland)	2.50	10.00	61
LONELY BLUE NIGHTS/We'll Have A Chance	(Brunswick 55205)	.75	3.00	61
MY DARLIN' FOREVER/The Time Is Near	(Brunswick 55213)	1.50	6.00	61
ROSIE & RON (Rosie Hamlin & Ron Holden)				
SO DEAR/	(Donna 1338)	.75	3.00	61
ROSS, Jack				
CINDERELLA/Magarita	(Dot 16333)	.75	3.00	62
(Comedy)				
HAPPY JOSE/Sweet Georgia Brown	(Dot 16302)	.75	3.00	61
(Instrumentals)				
HAPPY JOSE/Sweet Georgia Brown	(Romal 770)	1.00	4.00	61
(Instrumentals)				
ROSS, Jerry, Symposium				
FIRST LOVE/Hope For The Best (Except The Worst)	(Colossum 133)	.50	2.00	71
MA BELLE AMIE/	(Colossum 113)	.50	2.00	70
ROSS, Joe E.				
HELLO DOLLY/Are You Lonesome Tonight	(Roulette 4584)	.75	3.00	63
ROSS, Spencer, Orchestra				
THEME OF A LONELY EVENING/Bobby's Blues	(Big Top 45-3035)	.75	3.00	60
TRACY'S THEME/Thanksgiving Day Parade	(Columbia 41532)	.75	3.00	60
(Instrumentals)				
ROSS, Stan				
AHAB THE ARAB (TEN YEARS LATER ON)/ Drowning In The Surf	(Reprise 20119)	1.00	4.00	62
50 MILE HIKE (PART 1)/50 Mile Hike (Part 2)	(Del Fi 4200)	1.00	4.00	63
(Novelties)				
ROSSI, Frankie, & The Dreams				
DREAM BOY/Around The Corner	(Mark 7001)	2.50	10.00	
ROSSI, Kenny				
BUT I DO/Watch Your P's & Q's	(Gee 1050)	.75	3.00	61
ROTARY CONNECTION, The (Featuring Minnie Riperton)				
LADY JANE/Amen	(Cadet Concept 1)	1.00	4.00	68
PAPER CASTLE/	(Cadet Concept 7007)	.75	3.00	69
RUBY TUESDAY/Soul Man	(Cadet Concept 7002)	.75	3.00	68
RUBY TUESDAY/Soul Man	(Cadet Concept DJ-2)	1.00	4.00	68
(Promotional issue)				
SILENT NIGHT CHANT/	(Cadet Concept 7009)	.75	3.00	69
TEACH ME HOW TO FLY/Stormy Monday Blues	(Cadet Concept 7027)	.75	3.00	70
WANT YOU TO KNOW/	(Cadet Concept 7018)	.75	3.00	70
Also see Aliotta, Haynes & Jeremiah				
ROTATORS, The				
DOUBLE EXPOSURE (PART 1)/ Double Exposure (Part 2)	(Felsted 8632)	.75	3.00	61
ROTH, Linda				
TEENAGE DIARY/Right As Rain	(Intrastate 42)	1.00	4.00	59
ROTINJAIL, Blink				
CUDDLES COMMERCIAL/A Pair Of Dice	(Ditto 127)	1.00	4.00	60
ROTTEN KIDS, The				
LET'S STOMP/Twelve Months Later	(Mercury 72558)	.75	3.00	66
ROTTENCROTCH, Rosie				
FRAGILE (PLEASE HANDLE WITH CARE)/ Where Is The Boy	(Jay Gee 001)	1.25	5.00	62
ROUBIAN, Bob				
BLUE SUEDE SHOES /Candy Coated Kisses	(Capitol 3373)	1.00	4.00	56
CRACKER STACKER/	(Prep 109)	.75	3.00	
ROCKET TO THE MOON/	(Prep 101)	.75	3.00	
ROUGH DIAMOND (With David Byron & Geoff Britton)				
ROCK 'N' ROLL/	(Island 087)	.50	2.00	77
Also see Uriah Heep				
Also see Wings				
ROULETTES, The				
HASTEN JASON/Wouldn't Be Going Steady	(Scepter 1204)	6.25	25.00	60
I SEE A STAR/Come On Baby	(Champ 102)	2.00	8.00	59
ROULETTES, The				
JUNK/Long Cigarette	(United Artists 990)	1.00	4.00	66
SURFER'S CHARGE/The Archibald II (Duke Of Nothing)	(Angle 1001)	1.00	4.00	63
ROULETTES, The				
CAN YOU GO/Soon You'll Be Leaving Me	(United Artists 718)	.75	3.00	64
Also see Faith, Adam				

TITLE/FLIP	LABEL & NO.	GOOD	NEAR MINT	YR.
ROUND ROBIN				
DO THE SLAUSON/Slauson Shuffletime	(Domain 1400)	.75	3.00	63
GIDDYAP KICK/I Know	(Domain 1406)	.75	3.00	64
KICK THAT LITTLE FOOT SALLY ANN/Slausan Party	(Domain 1404)	.75	3.00	64
SIT & DANCE/I'm The Wolfman	(Domain 1009)	.75	3.00	65
SLAUSON TOWN/Malloy, The Engineer	(Domain 1401)	.75	3.00	64
ROUSSOS, Demis (Of Aphrodite's Child)				
L.O.V.E. GOT A HOLD ON ME/Hey Friend	(Mercury 74018)	.50	2.00	78
THAT ONCE IN A LIFETIME/This Song	(Mercury 73992)	.50	2.00	78
ROUTERS, The				
HALF TIME/Make It Snappy	(Warner Bros. 5332)	.75	3.00	63
LET'S GO/Mashy	(Warner Bros. 5283)	.75	3.00	62
STING RAY/Snap Happy	(Warner Bros. 5349)	.75	3.00	63
Instrumentals				
Also see Walker Brothers, The				
ROVER BOYS, The				
FROM A SCHOOL RING TO A WEDDING RING/ Young Love	(ABC-Paramount 9732)	1.00	4.00	56
GRADUATION DAY/I Hear Music	(ABC-Paramount 9700)	1.00	4.00	56
LOVE ME AGAIN/Come To Me	(ABC-Paramount 9659)	1.00	4.00	56
MY QUEEN/Sixteen Teens	(ABC-Paramount 9678)	1.00	4.00	56
SHOW ME/You've Got It	(Coral 61271)	1.25	5.00	54
ROVIN' FLAMES, The				
GLORIA/J.J.J.P.	(Fuller 2627)	.75	3.00	65
ROVIN' KIND, The				
MY GENERATION/Girl	(Dunwich 146)	.75	3.00	67
SHE/Didn't Wanta Have To Do It	(Dunwich 154)	.75	3.00	67
ROWAN & MARTIN (Dan Rowan & Dick Martin)				
HANG ON THE BELL, NELLIE/Birds Do It	(Epic 10354)	.75	3.00	66
ROWAN BROTHERS: see Rowans, The				
ROWANS, The (Lorin, Peter, Chris)				
ALL TOGETHER/	(Columbia 45728)	.75	3.00	72
HICKORY DAY/	(Columbia 45856)	.75	3.00	73
IF I ONLY COULD/Tired Hands	(Asylum 45347)	.50	2.00	76
OOH MY LOVE/Mongolian Swamp-All The Kings Men	(Asylum 45376)	.50	2.00	76
TAKE IT AS IT COMES/	(Asylum 45281)	.50	2.00	75
Also see Earth Opera				
ROWLAND, Steve, & The Ring Leaders				
OUT-RIDIN'/Here Kum The Karts	(Cross Country 1-1818)	1.00	4.00	
ROXY (With Bob Segarini)				
NEW YORK CITY/Love Love Love	(Elektra 45682)	.75	3.00	69
ROXY & THE DAYCHORDS				
I'M SO IN LOVE/Mary Lou	(Candlelite 430)	1.00	4.00	
I'M SO IN LOVE/Mary Lou	(Donel 46)	7.50	30.00	
ROXY MUSIC (Featuring Bryan Ferry)				
ANGEL EYES/My Little Girl	(Atco 7204)	.50	2.00	79
DANCE AWAY/Trash 2	(Atco 7100)	.50	2.00	79
LOVE IS THE DRUG/Both Ends Burning	(Atco 7042)	.50	2.00	75
THRILL OF IT ALL, THE/	(Atco 7018)	.50	2.00	75
ROY, Bobby, & The Chord-A-Roys				
GIRLS WERE MADE FOR BOYS/Little Girl Lost	(J.D.D. 5001)	2.00	8.00	
ROYAL, Billy Joe				
ALL NIGHT RAIN/	(Scepter 12419)	.50	2.00	76
CAMPFIRE GIRLS/Should I Come Back	(Columbia 43740)	.75	3.00	66
CHERRY HILL PARK/Helping Hand	(Columbia 44902)	.75	3.00	69
CHILD OF OUR TIME/	(Columbia 45620)	.75	3.00	72
DARK GLASSES/Perhaps	(Fairlane 21013)	1.25	5.00	62
DOWN IN THE BOONDOCKS/Oh What A Night	(Columbia 43305)	.75	3.00	65
EVERY NIGHT/Burning A Hole	(Columbia 45220)	.75	3.00	70
FAMILY, THE/	(Columbia 45557)	.75	3.00	71
HEART'S DESIRE/Deep Inside Me	(Columbia 43622)	.75	3.00	66
HUSH/Watching From The Bandstand	(Columbia 44277)	.75	3.00	67
I KNEW YOU WHEN/Steal Away	(Columbia 43390)	.75	3.00	65
I'VE GOT TO BE SOMEBODY/ You Make Me Feel Like A Man	(Columbia 43465)	.75	3.00	65
IF IT WASN'T FOR A WOMAN/Wait For Me Baby	(All Wood 401)	1.25	5.00	62
MAMA DIDN'T RAISE NO FOOLS/Get Behind Me, Devil	(Tollie 9011)	1.00	4.00	63
NEVER IN A HUNDRED YEARS/ We Haven't A Moment To Lose	(Atlantic 2328)	.75	3.00	66
NEVER IN A HUNDRED YEARS/ We Haven't A Moment To Lose	(Fairlane 21009)	1.25	5.00	61
REALLY YOU/I'm Specialized	(Player's 1)	1.00	4.00	65
STORYBOOK CHILDREN/Just Between You & Me	(Columbia 44574)	.75	3.00	68
THIS MAGIC MOMENT/Mountain Woman	(MGM-South 7011)	.50	2.00	73
TULSA/Pick Up The Pieces	(Columbia 45289)	.75	3.00	71
UNDER THE BOARDWALK/Precious Time	(Private Stock 45192)	.50	2.00	78
WISDOM OF A FOOL/Everything Turned Blue	(Columbia 44003)	.75	3.00	67
YO YO/We Tried	(Columbia 43883)	.75	3.00	66
ROYAL DEBS, The				
JERRY/I Do	(Tifco 826)	.75	3.00	62
ROYAL DRIFTERS, The				
LITTLE LINDA/S' Why Hard	('Teen 506)	6.25	25.00	
ROYALE COACHMEN, The				
KILLER OF MEN/Standing Over There	(Jowar 103)	1.50	6.00	
ROYALETTES, The				
AFFAIR TO REMEMBER/I Don't Want To Be The One	(MGM K-13544)	.75	3.00	66
I WANT TO MEET HIM/Never Again	(MGM K-13405)	.75	3.00	65
IT'S BETTER NOT TO KNOW/It's A Big Mistake	(MGM K-13507)	.75	3.00	66
IT'S GONNA TAKE A MIRACLE/ Out Of Sight, Out Of Mind	(MGM K-13366)	.75	3.00	65
MY MAN/Take My Love	(MGM K-13627)	.75	3.00	66
ONLY WHEN YOU'RE LONELY/You Bring Me Down	(MGM K-13451)	.75	3.00	66
POOR BOY/Watch What Happens	(MGM K-13327)	.75	3.00	65
WHEN SUMMER'S GONE/Love Without An End	(MGM K-13588)	.75	3.00	66
ROYAL GUARDSMEN, The (With Chris Nunley & Barry Winslow)				
AIRPLANE SONG/Om	(Laurie 3391)	.75	3.00	67
BABY, LET'S WAIT/So Right (To Be In Love)	(Laurie 3461)	.75	3.00	68
I SAY LOVE/I'm Not Gonna Stay	(Laurie 3428)	.75	3.00	68
MOTHER, WHERE'S YOUR DAUGHTER/Magic Window	(Laurie 3494)	.75	3.00	69
RETURN OF THE RED BARON/Sweetmeats Slide	(Laurie 3379)	.75	3.00	67
SNOOPY FOR PRESIDENT/Down Behind The Lines	(Laurie 3451)	.75	3.00	68
SNOOPY'S CHRISTMAS/It Kinda Looks Like Christmas	(Laurie 3416)	.75	3.00	68
SNOOPY VS. THE RED BARON/I Needed You	(Laurie 3366)	.75	3.00	66
WEDNESDAY/So Right To Be In Love	(Laurie 3397)	.75	3.00	67
ROYAL JACKS, The				
I'M IN LOVE AGAIN/The Big Ring	(20th Fox 100)	2.00	8.00	58
NIGHT AFTER NIGHT/Who, What, Where, When & Why	(Studio 9903)	2.00	8.00	59
TAM-O-SHANTER/Anticipation	(Amy 865)	.75	3.00	62

TITLE/FLIP	LABEL & NO.	GOOD	NEAR MINT	YR.
OYAL KINGS, The				
ETER PETER/Keep It To Yourself	(Forlin 502)	5.00	20.00	
OYAL LANCERS, The				
NGEL IN MY EYES/Baby I Don't Care (With Paul Stefen)	(Citation 5004)	2.50	10.00	63
OOD, GOOD LOVIN'/This Time	(Hi Mar HM-501)	1.00	4.00	
OYAL MONARCHS, The				
URF'S UP/My Babe	(Dell-Star 102)	1.00	4.00	63
OYAL PLAYBOYS, The				
OODBYE BO/	(Dodo 101)	.75	3.00	
OYAL ROCKERS, The				
ET 11/Swinging Mambo	(Bee 1113)	1.00	4.00	59
OYALS, The				
HRISTMAS PARTY/White Xmas	(Vagabond 134)	.75	3.00	62
URFIN' LEGOON/Wild Safari	(Vagabond 444)	.75	3.00	63
OYAL TEENS (With Bob Gaudio, Al Kooper, & Buddy Randell)				
ELIEVE ME/Little Cricket	(Capitol 4261)	1.25	5.00	59
G NAME BUTTON/Sham Rock	(ABC-Paramount 9918)	1.00	4.00	58
AVE MAN/Wounded Heart	(Mighty 112)	2.50	10.00	59
ARVEY'S GOT A GIRL FRIEND/Hangin Around	(ABC-Paramount 9945)	1.00	4.00	58
LL LOVE YOU TILL THE END OF TIME (PART 1)/ I'll Love You Till The End Of Time (Part 2) (Instrumental)	(Swan 4200)	2.00	8.00	65
EOTARDS/Royal Blue	(Mighty 111)	1.00	4.00	58
OON'S NOT MEANT FOR LOVERS (ANYMORE), THE/ Was It A Dream	(Capitol 4335)	1.25	5.00	60
Y KIND OF DREAM/I Forgot My Key	(ABC-Paramount 9955)	1.00	4.00	58
Y MEMORIES OF YOU/Little Trixie	(Mighty 200)	1.00	4.00	61
HORT SHORT TWIST/Royal Twist	(Allnew 1415)	.75	3.00	62
HORT SHORTS/Planet Rock	(ABC-Paramount 9882)	1.00	4.00	57
HORT SHORTS/Planet Rock	(Power 215)	6.25	25.00	57
MILE A LITTLE SMILE FOR ME/Hey Jude	(Musicor 139)	.75	3.00	69
ITH YOU/It's The Talk Of The Town	(Capitol 4402)	1.25	5.00	60
OYALTONES, The				
UTTERSCOTCH/Dixie Cup	(Goldisc 3016)	.75	3.00	60
IXIE ROCK/Royal Whirl	(Goldisc 3017)	.75	3.00	60
O THE EARLY BIRD/Scotch & Soda	(Goldisc 3028)	.75	3.00	61
LAMINGO EXPRESS/Tacos	(Goldisc 3011)	.75	3.00	61
TTLE BO/Seesaw	(Jubilee 5362)	.75	3.00	59
UR FADED LOVE/Holy Smokes	(Mala 473)	.75	3.00	64
OOR BOY/Wail	(Jubilee 5338)	.75	3.00	58
HORT LINE/Big Wheel	(Goldisc 3004)	.75	3.00	60
COTCH & SODA/Peppermint Twist	(Goldisc 3026)	.75	3.00	61
IE FLIP/Secret Love	(Goldisc 3011)	.75	3.00	60
EA YEA SONG/Misty Sea	(Mala 487)	.75	3.00	63
OYALTON, The				
M A COOL TEENAGER/Solid Rock	(Federal 12383)	.75	3.00	60
OYCE				
ABY I JUST WANT TO BE WITH YOU/	(UK 49026)	.50	2.00	74
PM'S, The				
EMPHIS BEAT/You Can Love Me	(Mala 508)	.75	3.00	65
TREET SCENE/Love Me	(Port 70032)	.75	3.00	63
.T. POTLICKERS, The				
IGHT WALKER/Sticky Pig Feet	(Hooks 1001)	1.00	4.00	
UBEN & THE JETS: see Zappa, Frank				
UBETTES				
CAN DO IT/If You've Got The Time	(Polydor 15103)	.50	2.00	75
UBICON				
MERICA DREAMS/Higher & Higher	(20th Century-Fox 2397)	.50	2.00	79
HEATIN'/	(20th Century-Fox 2372)	.50	2.00	78
M GONNA TAKE CARE OF EVERYTHING/ That's The Way Things Are	(20th Century-Fox 2362)	.50	2.00	78
UBIES				
E WAS AN ANGEL/He's Mine	(Empress 103)	1.25	5.00	
PANISH BOY/Deeper	(Vee Jay 596)	.75	3.00	64
UBINOOS, The (Featuring Jon Rubin)				
THINK WE'RE ALONE NOW/As Long As I'm With You	(Beserkley 5741)	.50	2.00	77
WANNA BE YOUR BOYFRIEND/Lightning Love Affair	(Beserkley 46518)	.50	2.00	79
OTHING A LITTLE LOVE WON'T CURE/ Leave My Heart Alone	(Beserkley 5810)	.50	2.00	77
UBY (With Tom Fogerty)				
FE IS BUT A DREAM/	(PBR 507)	.50	2.00	77
UBY & THE ROMANTICS (Featuring Ruby Nash)				
ABY COME HOME/Everyday's A Holiday	(Kapp 601)	.75	3.00	64
OES HE REALLY CARE FOR ME/ Nevertheless (I'm In Love With You)	(Kapp 646)	.75	3.00	65
EY THERE LONELY BOY/Not A Moment Too Soon	(Kapp 544)	.75	3.00	63
URTING EACH OTHER/ Baby I Could Be So Good At Lovin' You	(A&M 1042)	.75	3.00	69
IY SUMMER LOVE/Sweet Love & Sweet Forgiveness	(Kapp 525)	.75	3.00	63
OBODY BUT MY BABY/Imagination	(Kapp 702)	.75	3.00	65
UR DAY WILL COME/Moonlight & Music	(Kapp 501)	.75	3.00	63
UR EVERLASTING LOVE/ Much Better Off Than I've Ever Been	(Kapp 578)	.75	3.00	64
E CAN MAKE IT/Remember Me	(Kapp 759)	.75	3.00	66
HEN YOU'RE YOUNG & IN LOVE/I Cry Alone	(Kapp 615)	.75	3.00	64
OUNG WINGS CAN FLY/Day Dreaming	(Kapp 557)	.75	3.00	63
OUR BABY DOESN'T LOVE YOU ANYMORE/We'll Meet Again	(Kapp 665)	.75	3.00	65
UE-TEENS, The				
UCKY BOY/I Don't Cry Over Girls	(Louis 6805)	1.50	6.00	
UFF & REDDY				
ENRY GOES TO THE MOON/ Henry Goes To The Moon (Part 2)	(Cavalier 876)	1.50	6.00	
UFF, Ray				
EATLEMANIA/Took A Liking To You (With The Checkmates)	(Lin 5034)	1.25	5.00	64
ALF-PINT BABY/I Need Someone	(Norman N-503)	.75	3.00	
UFUS				
NCE YOU GET STARTED/Rufusized	(ABC 12066)	.50	2.00	75
LEASE PARDON ME (YOU REMIND ME OF A FREIND)/ Somebody's Watching You (With Chaka Khan)	(ABC 12099)	.50	2.00	75
WEET THING/Circles (With Chaka Khan)	(ABC 12149)	.50	2.00	75
ELL ME SOMETHING GOOD/Smokin' Room	(ABC 12010)	.75	3.00	74
ELL ME SOMETHING GOOD/Smokin' Room	(ABC 11427)	.50	2.00	74
Also see American Breed, The				
UGBYS, The				
OCKIN' ALL OVER AGAIN/	(Amazon 6)	.75	3.00	70
IL THE DAY I DIE/James Is The Name	(Smash 1997)	.75	3.00	65
ALKING IN THE STREETS TONIGHT/Endlessly	(Top Dog 2315)	1.25	5.00	
INDEGAHL THE WARLOCK/	(Amazon 4)	.75	3.00	69
OU, I/Stay With Me	(Amazon 1)	.75	3.00	69

TITLE/FLIP	LABEL & NO.	GOOD	NEAR MINT	YR.
RUMBLERS, The (With Adrian Lloyd)				
ANGRY SEA (WAIMEA)/Bugged	(Downey 107)	1.25	5.00	63
ANGRY SEA (WAIMEA)/Bugged	(Dot 16480)	.75	3.00	63
BOSS/I Don't Need You No More	(Downey 103)	1.25	5.00	63
BOSS/I Don't Need You No More	(Dot 16421)	.75	3.00	63
BOSS SOUL/Till Always	(Downey 133)	1.25	5.00	65
BOSS STRIKES BACK/Sorry	(Downey 106)	1.25	5.00	63
BOSS STRIKES BACK/Sorry	(Dot 16455)	.75	3.00	63
IT'S A GASS/Tootenanny	(Downey 111)	1.25	5.00	64
IT'S A GASS/Tootenanny	(Dot 18292)	.75	3.00	64
MAID-N-JAPAN/Gospell Truth (Shown as by the Nylons)	(Downey 109)	1.00	4.00	63
NIGHT SCENE/High Octane	(Downey 114)	1.25	5.00	64
SOULFUL JERK/Hey-Did-A-Da-Da	(Downey 127)	1.25	5.00	64
Also see Adrian & the Sunsets				
RUMBLES LTD., The				
JEZEBEL/	(Mercury 72723)	.75	3.00	67
99% SURE/Everyday Kind Of Love	(Mercury 72815)	.75	3.00	68
OUT OF HARMONY/It'll Be Alright	(Mercury 72690)	.75	3.00	67
SANTA CLAUS IS COMING TO TOWN/The Wildest Christmas	(Dad's 103)	1.50	6.00	
TRY A LITTLE HARDER/California My Way	(GNP Crescendo 430)	.75	3.00	68
RUMOR, The				
EMOTIONAL TRAFFIC/	(Arista 0451)	.50	2.00	79
I'M SO GLAD/This Town	(Mercury 73949)	.50	2.00	78
This band was made up of Graham Parker's backup group plus former members of Brinsley-Schwartz.				
RUMORS, The				
HOLD ME NOW/Without Her	(Gemcor 5002)	1.00	4.00	
RUNAROUNDS, The (Guy Villari, Chuck Fassert, Ronnie Lapinsky)				
CARRIE, (YOU'RE AN ANGEL)/Send Her Back	(Felsted 8704)	1.50	6.00	64
LET THEM TALK/Are You Looking For A Sweetheart (Shown as by the Run-a-rounds)	(Tarheel 65)	1.50	6.00	63
PERFECT WOMAN/You're A Drag	(Capitol 5644)	1.50	6.00	66
UNBELIEVABLE/Hooray For Love (Brown plastic) (Shown as by the Run-a-rounds)	(KC 116)	2.00	8.00	63
UNBELIEVABLE/Hooray For Love (Shown as by the Run-a-rounds)	(KC 116)	2.00	8.00	63
YOU LIED/My Little Girl (With Tommy Cosgrove & the Elegant Four)	(MGM 13763)	2.00	8.00	67
Also see Regents, The				
Also see Traces, The				
RUNAWAYS, The				
CHERRY BOMB/Blackmail	(Mercury 73819)	1.00	4.00	76
HEARTBEAT/Neon Angels On The Road To Run	(Mercury 73890)	1.00	4.00	77
RUNAWAYS, The				
18TH FLOOR GIRL/Your Foolish Ways	(Alamo 105)	.75	3.00	
KANGAROO HOP/Teenage Style	(Teensound 1924)	2.00	8.00	
PACHUKO HOP/The Stinger	(Moonglow 202)	.75	3.00	61
RUNDGREN, Todd (Of Nazz)				
BLACK & WHITE/Love Of The Common Man	(Bearsville 0310)	.50	2.00	76
BREATHLESS/Wolfman Jack	(Bearsville 0301)	.50	2.00	74
CAN WE STILL BE FRIENDS/Determination	(Bearsville 0324)	.50	2.00	78
COMMUNION WITH THE SUN/Sunburst Finish	(Bearsville 0317)	.50	2.00	77
COULDN'T I JUST TELL YOU/Wolfman Jack	(Bearsville 0007)	.75	3.00	72
DOES ANYBODY LOVE YOU/ Sometimes I Don't Know What To Feel	(Bearsville 0015)	.75	3.00	73
DREAM GOES ON FOREVER, A/Heavy Metal Kids	(Bearsville 0020)	.75	3.00	74
GOOD VIBRATIONS/When I Pray	(Bearsville 0309)	.50	2.00	76
HELLO IT'S ME/Cold Morning Light	(Bearsville 0009)	.50	2.00	72
I SAW THE LIGHT/Marlene	(Bearsville 0003)	.50	2.00	72
I SAW THE LIGHT/Marlene (Blue plastic. Conterfeit copies exist of this release.)	(Bearsville 0003)	3.00	12.00	72
IT WOULDN'T HAVE MADE ANY DIFFERENCE/ Don't You Ever Learn?	(Bearsville 0335)	.50	2.00	79
LOVE IS THE ANSWER/Marriage Of Heaven & Hell	(Bearsville 0321)	.50	2.00	77
REAL MAN/Prana	(Bearsville 0304)	.50	2.00	75
YOU CRIED WOLF/Onomatopoeia	(Bearsville 0330)	.50	2.00	78
Also see Runt				
RUNNER				
FOOLING MYSELF/Living Is Loving You	(Island 49007)	.50	2.00	79
RUNT (Featuring Todd Rundgren)				
BE NICE TO ME/Broke Down & Busted	(Bearsville 31002)	.75	3.00	71
LONG TIME, A LONG WAY TO GO, A/Parole	(Bearsville 31004)	.75	3.00	71
WE GOTTA GET YOU A WOMAN/Baby Let's Swing-The Last Thing You Said-Don't Tie My Hands	(Ampex 31001)	.75	3.00	70
RUSH				
LIFE IN THE BIG CITY/Summer For Bonnie Jean	(Ducal 0)	1.25	5.00	
RUSH				
BASTILLE DAY/Lakeside Park	(Mercury 73737)	.50	2.00	76
CLOSER TO THE HEART/Madrigal	(Mercury 73958)	.50	2.00	77
FLY BY NIGHT/Anthem	(Mercury 73681)	.50	2.00	75
FLY BY NIGHT/Anthem	(Mercury 73990)	.50	2.00	78
FLY BY NIGHT-IN THE MOOD/ Something For Nothing	(Mercury 73873)	.50	2.00	76
MAKING MEMORIES/ The Temples Of Syrinx (2112-Band 2)	(Mercury 73912)	.50	2.00	77
LESSONS/The Twilight Zone	(Mercury 73803)	.50	2.00	76
TREES, THE/Circumstances	(Mercury 74051)	.50	2.00	79
RUSH, Merrilee				
ANGEL OF THE MORNING/Reap What You Sow (With the Turnabouts)	(Bell 705)	.75	3.00	68
COULD IT BE I FOUND TONIGHT/	(United Artists 930)	.50	2.00	77
LOVERS NEVER SAY GOODBYE/Tell Me The Truth	(Merrilin 5301)	1.00	4.00	
RAINSTORM/	(United Artists 1103)	.50	2.00	77
REACH OUT/Love Street	(AGP 107)	.75	3.00	68
ME/Easy, Soft & Slow	(United Artists 993)	.50	2.00	77
THAT KIND OF WOMAN/Sunshine & Roses (With the Turnabouts)	(Bell 738)	.75	3.00	68
RUSH, Tom				
KIDS THESE DAYS/Seems The Songs	(Columbia 45669)	.50	2.00	73
LADIES LOVE OUTLAWS/	(Columbia 10021)	.50	2.00	74
NO REGRETS/	(Columbia 10087)	.50	2.00	74
NO REGRETS/Shadow Dream Song	(Elektra 45630)	.75	3.00	68
MOTHER EARTH/Wind On The Water	(Columbia 45584)	.50	2.00	72
WHO DO YOU LOVE/Something In The Way She Moves	(Elektra 45718)	.50	2.00	70
RUSSELL, Brenda (Of Brian & Brenda Russell)				
SO GOOD, SO RIGHT/You're Free	(Horizon 123)	.50	2.00	79
WAY BACK WHEN/God Bless You	(A&M 2207)	.50	2.00	79
RUSSELL, Brian & Brenda				
DON'T LET LOVE GO/Toronto	(Rocket 40777)	.50	2.00	77
GONNA DO MY BEST TO LOVE YOU (Long version)/ Gonna Do My Best To Love You (Short version)	(Rocket 40602)	.50	2.00	76
HIGHLY PRIZED POSSESION/You'll Never Rock Alone	(Rocket 40521)	.50	2.00	76
THAT'S ALL RIGHT TOO/Who Loves You	(Rocket 40809)	.50	2.00	77
RUSSELL, Kurt				
BABY BELIEVE ME/Hey Baby I Love You	(Capitol 3032)	.50	2.00	70
RUSSELL, Lee: see Russell, Leon				

TITLE/FLIP	LABEL & NO.	GOOD	NEAR MINT	YR.
RUSSELL, Leon				
BACK TO THE ISLAND/Little Hideaway	(Shelter 40483)	.50	2.00	76
BLUEBIRD/Back To The Island	(Shelter 62004)	.50	2.00	76
EASY LOVE/Hold On To This Feeling (With Mary Russell)	(Paradise 8438)	.50	2.00	77
ELVIS & MARILYN/Anita Bryant	(Paradise 8667)	.50	2.00	78
FROM MAINE TO MEXICO/Midnight Lover	(Paradise 8719)	.50	2.00	78
IF I WERE A CARPENTER.../Wild Horses	(Shelter 40210)	.50	2.00	74
LADY BLUE/Laying Right Here In Heaven	(Shelter 40378)	.50	2.00	75
LEAVING WHIPPORWILL/Time For Love	(Shelter 40277)	.50	2.00	74
LOVE CRAZY/Say You Will (With Mary Russell)	(Paradise 8369)	.50	2.00	77
QUEEN OF THE ROLLER DERBY/Roll Away The Stone	(Shelter 7337)	.50	2.00	73
RAINBOW AT MIDNIGHT/Honky Tonk Woman (Shown as by Lee Russell)	(Roulette 4049)	1.50	6.00	58
RAINBOW IN YOUR EYES/ Love's Supposed To Be That Way (With Mary Russell)	(Paradise 8208)	.50	2.00	76
SATISFY YOU/Windsong (With Mary Russell)	(Paradise 8274)	.50	2.00	76
SLIPPING INTO CHRISTMAS/Christmas In Chicago	(Shelter 7328)	.75	3.00	72
SLIPPING INTO CHRISTMAS/Christmas In Chicago	(Shelter 65033)	.50	2.00	75
TIGHT ROPE/This Masquerade	(Shelter 7325)	.50	2.00	72
Leon's wife Mary was formerly Mary McCreary.				
RUSSELL, Leon & Mary: see Russell, Leon				
RUSSELL, Todd				
DON'T TWOW WOCKS AT A RABBIT/	(Pyramid 4029)	1.00	4.00	
RUSSO BROTHERS, The				
VELVET EYES/There's More	(Era 3011)	.75	3.00	60
RUSSO, Charlie				
PREACHERMAN/Teresa (Instrumentals)	(Diamond 131)	.75	3.00	63
RUSTIX				
WHEN I GET HOME/	(Cadet 5628)	.75	3.00	68
RUSTY & DUSTY				
GOODBYE TWELVE, HELLO TEENS/Boys Will Be Boys	(Caprice 0061)	1.00	4.00	60
RU TEENS, The				
HAPPY TEENAGER/Come A Little Bit Closer (Acappella)	(Old Timer 612)	1.00	4.00	
RYAN, Barry (Of Paul & Barry Ryan)				
CAN'T LET YOU GO/L.A. Woman	(Pride 1032)	.50	2.00	71
ELOISE/	(MGM 14010)	.75	3.00	68
RYAN, Jamie				
21 INCHES OF HEAVEN/ The Worst Of The Hurt Is Over	(Columbia 44045)	1.00	4.00	67
RYAN, Paul & Barry				
DON'T BRING ME NO HEARTACHES/To Remind Me	(MGM 13422)	.75	3.00	65
PICTURES OF TODAY/Madrigal	(MGM 13911)	.75	3.00	68
RYAN, Peter				
IF WE TRY/I Can Hear The Music (Beatle novelty)	(Aardvark 101)	2.50	10.00	
RYDELL, Bobby (Robert Lewis Ridarelli)				
ALL I WANT IS YOU/For You, For You	(Cameo 164)	3.75	15.00	59
BUTTERFLY BABY/Love Is Blind	(Cameo 242)	.75	3.00	63
CHA-CHA-CHA, THE/The Best Man Cried	(Cameo 228)	.75	3.00	62
CHAPEL ON THE HILL/It Must Be Love	(RCA 47-9892)	.75	3.00	70
CIAO CIAO BAMBINO/Voce De La Norte	(Cameo 361)	.75	3.00	65
DIANA/Stranger In The World	(Capitol 5352)	.75	3.00	65
EVERY LITTLE BIT HURTS/Time & Changes	(Reprise 0751)	.75	3.00	68
FATTY FATTY/Happy Happy	(Venise 201)	3.75	15.00	58
FATTY FATTY/Dream Age	(Veko 731)	2.50	10.00	58
FISH, THE/The Third House	(Cameo 192)	.75	3.00	61
FORGET HIM/A Message From Bobby	(Cameo 1070)	1.25	5.00	63
FORGET HIM/Love Love Go Away	(Cameo 280)	.75	3.00	63
GOOD TIME BABY/Cherie	(Cameo 186)	.75	3.00	61
I JUST CAN'T SAY GOODBYE/Two Is The Lonliest Number	(Capitol 5305)	.75	3.00	64
I WANT TO THANK YOU/Door To Paradise, The	(Cameo 201)	.75	3.00	61
I'LL NEVER DANCE AGAIN/Gee It's Wonderful	(Cameo 2171)	.75	3.00	62
I'VE GOT BONNIE/Lose Her	(Cameo 209)	.75	3.00	62
KISSIN' TIME/You'll Never Tame Me	(Cameo 167)	1.00	4.00	59
LET'S MAKE LOVE TONIGHT/Childhood Sweetheart	(Cameo 272)	.75	3.00	63
LITTLE QUEENIE/The Woodpecker Song	(Cameo 265)	.75	3.00	63
LOVIN' THINGS, THE/That's What I Call Lovin'	(Reprise 0656)	.75	3.00	67
MAKE ME FORGET/Little Girl You've Had A Busy Day	(Cameo 309)	.75	3.00	64
OPEN FOR BUSINESS AS USUAL/You Gotta Enjoy Joy	(Capitol 5780)	.75	3.00	66
RIVER IS WIDE/Absence Makes The Heart Grow Fonder	(Reprise 0684)	.75	3.00	68
ROSES IN THE SNOW/Word For Today	(Capitol 5556)	.75	3.00	66
SIDE SHOW/The Joker	(Capitol 5438)	1.00	4.00	65
STEEL PIER/ (One-sided promotional issue only.)	(Cameo-No number given)	1.50	6.00	
SWAY/Groovy Tonight	(Cameo 182)	.75	3.00	60
SWINGING SCHOOL/Ding-A-Ling	(Cameo 175)	.75	3.00	60
THAT OLD BLACK MAGIC/Don't Be Afraid	(Cameo 190)	.75	3.00	61
VOLARE/I'll Do It Again	(Cameo 179)	.75	3.00	60
WE GOT LOVE/I Dig Girls	(Cameo 169)	1.00	4.00	59
WE GOT LOVE/I Dig Girls	(Time 1006)	1.25	5.00	59
WILD ONE/Little Bitty Girl	(Cameo 171)	.75	3.00	59
WILDWOOD DAYS/Will You Be My Baby	(Cameo 252)	.75	3.00	63
WORLD WITHOUT LOVE, A/Our Faded Love	(Cameo 320)	.75	3.00	64
Also see Checker, Chubby & Bobby Rydell				
RYDER, John & Anne				
I STILL BELIEVE IN TOMORROW/Daffodil Rain	(Decca 732506)	.75	3.00	69
RYDER, Mitch, & The Detroit Wheels				
BABY I NEED YOUR LOVIN' & THEME FOR MITCH/ Ring Your Bell	(Dyno Voice 934)	.75	3.00	68
BREAK OUT/I Need Help	(New Voice 811)	.75	3.00	66
COME SEE ABOUT ME/Take The Time	(New Voice 828)	.75	3.00	67
DEVIL WITH THE BLUE DRESS ON & GOOD GOLLY MISS MOLLY/ I Had It Made	(New Voice 817)	.75	3.00	66
I NEED HELP (Help Help)/I Hope	(New Voice 801)	.75	3.00	65
I NEED YOUR LOVIN'/The Lights Of Night	(Dyno Voice 916)	.75	3.00	68
IT'S BEEN A LONG LONG LONG TIME/Direct Me	(Dot 17325)	.75	3.00	69
JENNY TAKE A RIDE/Baby Jane (Mo-Mo Jane)	(New Voice 806)	.75	3.00	65
JOY/I'd Rather Go To Jail	(New Voice 824)	.75	3.00	67
LITTLE LATIN LUPE LU/I Hope	(New Voice 808)	.75	3.00	66
RUBY BABY/You Get Your Kicks	(New Voice 830)	.75	3.00	68
SOCK IT TO ME BABY/I Never Had It Better	(New Voice 820)	1.25	5.00	67
Two versions of this song were released. On this first issue, Mitch sang the line "Everytime You Kiss Me, Feels Like A Punch" in such a way that it sounded more like he was saying "Feels Like A Fuck!" After meeting with some resistance from radio stations, the song was recut. The second issue clearly says "Everytime You Kiss Me, It Hits Me Like A PUNCH."				
SOCK IT TO ME BABY/I Never Had It Better	(New Voice 820)	.75	3.00	67
SUGAR BEE (WE THREE)/ I Believe (There Must Be Someone)	(Dot 17290)	.75	3.00	69
TAKIN' ALL I CAN/You Get Your Kicks	(New Voice 814)	.75	3.00	66
TOO MANY FISH IN THE SEA & THREE LITTLE FISHES/ One Grain Of Sand	(New Voice 822)	.75	3.00	67
WHAT NOW MY LOVE/Blessing in Desguise	(Dyno Voice 901)	.75	3.00	67
YOU ARE MY SUNSHINE/Wild Child	(New Voice 826)	.75	3.00	67
(YOU'VE GOT) PERSONALITY & CHANTILLY LACE/ I Make A Fool Of Myself	(Dyno Voice 905)	.75	3.00	68
Also see Detroit Wheels, The				
Also See Rockets, The				

S

TITLE/FLIP	LABEL & NO.	GOOD	NEAR MINT	YR.
SABER, Johnny, & The Passions				
WISH IT COULD BE ME/Dolly In A Toy Shop	(Adonis 103)	6.25	25.00	
SAD CAFE				
BLACK ROSE/Feel Like Dying	(A&M 2134)	.50	2.00	79
EMPTINESS/Cottage Love	(A&M 2181)	.50	2.00	79
RUN HOME GIRL/Black Rose	(A&M 2108)	.50	2.00	78
STRANGE LITTLE GIRL/	(A&M 2200)	.50	2.00	79
SADISTIC MIKA BAND, The				
SUKI SUKI SUKI/Jumi No Kuni	(Harvest 4060)	.75	3.00	65
SADLER, SSGT. Barry				
"A" TEAM, THE/	(RCA Victor 47-8804)	.75	3.00	66
BALLAD OF THE GREEN BERETS, THE/ Letter From Vietnam	(RCA Victor 47-8739)	.75	3.00	66
SAFARIS, The (Featuring Jimmy Stephens)				
GIRL WITH THE STORY IN HER EYES/Summer Nights	(Eldo 105)	1.00	4.00	60
IMAGE OF A GIRL/4 Steps To Love	(Eldo 101)	1.00	4.00	60
IN THE STILL OF THE NIGHT/Shadows	(Eldo 110)	1.50	6.00	61
SOLDIER OF FORTUNE/Garden Of Love	(Eldo 113)	2.00	8.00	61
With The Phantom's Band				
Also see Angels, The				
Also see Dories, The				
Also see Enchanters, The				
Also see Suddens, The				
SAGER, Carole Bayer (Carole Bayer)				
IT'S THE FALLING IN LOVE/ There's Something About You	(Elektra 45507)	.50	2.00	78
SWEET ALIBIS/Aces	(Elektra 45395)	.50	2.00	77
WHERE I WANT TO BE/	(Metromedia 245)	.50	2.00	72
YOU'RE MOVING OUT TODAY/Shy As A Violet	(Elektra 45422)	.50	2.00	77
SAGITTARIUS				
ANOTHER TIME/Pisces	(Columbia 44398)	.75	3.00	67
HOTEL INDISCREET/Virgo	(Columbia 44289)	.75	3.00	67
I GUESS THE LORD MUST BE IN NEW YORK CITY/ I Can Still See Your Face	(Together 122)	1.00	4.00	69
I'M NOT LIVING HERE/Keeper Of The Games	(Columbia 44613)	.75	3.00	68
IN MY ROOM/Navajo Girl	(Together 105)	1.00	4.00	68
MY WORLD FELL DOWN/Libra	(Columbia 44163)	.75	3.00	69
TRUTH IS NOT REAL/You Know I've Found A Way	(Columbia 44503)	.75	3.00	67
Group members: Gary Usher, Glen Campbell, Bruce Johnston, Terry Melcher, Curt Boechter.				
SAHARAS, The				
I'M FREE/The Mornin'	(Fenton 2016)	1.25	5.00	

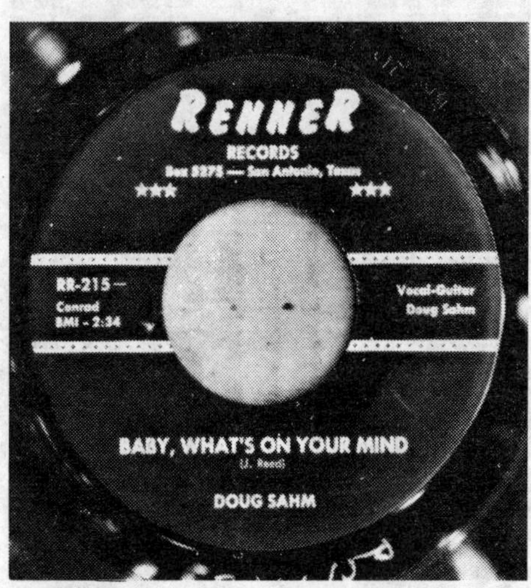

TITLE/FLIP	LABEL & NO.	GOOD	NEAR MINT	YR.
SAHM, Doug (Of The Sir Douglas Quintet)				
BABY TELL ME/Sapphire	(Harlem 108)	2.50	10.00	60
BIG HAT/Makes No Difference	(Renner 212)	2.50	10.00	
COWBOY PEYTON PLACE/I Love The Way You Love (The Way I Love You)	(Dot 17656)	.50	2.00	76
CRAZY CRAZY FEELING/Baby What's On Your Mind	(Personality 3505)	3.00	12.00	
CRAZY CRAZY FEELING/Baby What's On Your Mind	(Renner 215)	2.50	10.00	
CRAZY DAISY/	(Satin 100)	1.50	6.00	
CRY/	(Soft 1031)	2.00	8.00	
CRYIN' INSIDE/SOMETIMES/	(Dot 17674)	.50	2.00	76
GROOVER'S PARADISE/	(Warner Bros. 7819)	.75	3.00	74
(With the Mex Trip)				
HENRIETTA/	(Texas Record 108)	2.00	8.00	
(IS ANYBODY GOING TO) SAN ANTONE/	(Atlantic 2946)	2.50	10.00	73
(With Bob Dylan)				
JUST A MOMENT/	(Harlem 116)	2.50	10.00	60
JUST BECAUSE/Two Hearts In Love	(Renner 226)	2.50	10.00	
LUCKY ME/A Year Ago Today	(Renner 240)	2.50	10.00	
MR. KOOL/	(Renner 247)	2.50	10.00	
ROLLIN' ROLLIN'/	(Sarg 113)	2.50	10.00	
(Shown as by Little Doug)				
SUGAR BEE/	(Pacemaker 260)	2.50	10.00	
(Shown as by Sir Douglas)				
WHY, WHY, WHY/If You Ever Need Me	(Harlem 107)	2.50	10.00	60
SAILCAT				
BABY RUTH/	(Elektra 45817)	.50	2.00	72
MOTORCYCLE MAMA/Rainbow Road	(Elektra 45782)	.50	2.00	72
SHE SHOWED ME/	(Elektra 45844)	.50	2.00	73

TITLE/FLIP	LABEL & NO.	GOOD	NEAR MINT	YR.
SAILOR (Formerly Kajanvs Picket)				
GIRLS, GIRLS, GIRLS/Jacaranda	(Epic 50229)	.50	2.00	76
GLASS OF CHAMPAGNE/Panama	(Epic 50194)	.50	2.00	75
RUNAWAY/Put Your Mouth Where Your Money Is	(Epic 50557)	.50	2.00	78
TRAFFIC JAM/Josephine Baker	(Epic 50094)	.50	2.00	75
SAINTE-MARIE, Buffy				
CAN'T BELIEVE THE FEELING WHEN YOU'RE GONE/Waves	(MCA 40193)	.50	2.00	74
CIRCLE GAME, THE/	(Vanguard 35108)	.75	3.00	69
HE'S AN INDIAN COWBOY IN THE RODEO/	(Vanguard 35156)	.75	3.00	72
FREE THE LADY/Starwalker - For The American Indian Movement	(ABC 12183)	.50	2.00	76
GENERATION/	(MCA 40347)	.50	2.00	75
I CAN'T TAKE IT NO MORE/Star Boy	(MCA 40286)	.50	2.00	74
I'M GONNA BE A COUNTRY GIRL AGAIN/	(Vanguard 35143)	.75	3.00	71
I WANNA HOLD YOUR HAND FOREVER/	(Vanguard 35172)	.75	3.00	73
LOVE'S GOT TO BREATHE & FLY/ Nobody Will Ever Know It's Real But You	(MCA 40368)	.50	2.00	75
MISTER CAN'T YOU SEE/Moonshot	(Vanguard 35151)	.75	3.00	72
UNTIL IT'S TIME FOR YOU TO GO/	(Vanguard 35116)	.75	3.00	69
ST. JOHN, Dick (Of Dick & DeeDee)				
CHILDHOOD/Lady Of The Burning Green Jade	(Dot 17080)	.75	3.00	68
HEY LITTLE GAL/	(Rona 1001)	1.25	5.00	61
SHA-TA/Gonna Stick By You	(Liberty 55380)	.75	3.00	61
SHA-TA/Gonna STick By You	(Pom Pom 4156)	1.25	5.00	61
YOU KNOW WHAT I MEAN/Swanee River	(Philips 40325)	.75	3.00	65
ST. LOUIS UNION				
GIRL/Respect	(Parrot 9812)	.75	3.00	66
ST. PETERS, Crispian				
AT THIS MOMENT/No No No	(Jamie 1309)	.75	3.00	66
BUT SHE'S UNTRUE/Your Ever Changin' Mind	(Jamie 1328)	.75	3.00	67
CHANGES/My Little Brown Eyes	(Jamie 1324)	.75	3.00	66
FREE SPIRITS/I'm Always Crying	(Jamie 1344)	.75	3.00	67
PIED PIPER, THE/Sweet Dawn My True Love	(Jamie 1320)	.75	3.00	66
YOU WERE ON MY MIND/What I'm Gonna Be	(Jamie 1310)	.75	3.00	66
ST. ROMAIN, Kirby				
SUMMER'S COMIN'/Walk On	(Inette 103)	.75	3.00	63
SAINTS, The				
(I'M) STRANDED/No Time	(Sire 1005)	.50	2.00	77
SAKAMOTO, Kyu				
CHINA NIGHTS/Benkyo No Cha Cha Cha	(Capitol 5016)	.75	3.00	63
SUKIYAKI/Anoko No Namaewa Nantenkana	(Capitol 4945)	.75	3.00	63
TANKOBUSHI/Olympics Song	(Capitol 5080)	.75	3.00	64
SAL & THE WATCHERS				
SPOOKY/The Watchers	(Pio 106)	1.50	6.00	
SALAS BROTHERS, The				
DARLING (PLEASE BRING YOUR LOVE)/Leaving You	(Faro 614)	1.00	4.00	64
RETURN OF FARMER JOHN, THE/Love Is Strange	(Faro 619)	1.00	4.00	64
(With the Jaguars)				
SALEMS, The				
MARIA/Ol Man River	(EPK 9480)	.75	3.00	
SALESMEN, The				
SOUPY'S MOUSE/Don't Go Steady With Freddy	(N.Y. Skyline 507)	.75	3.00	65
(Novelty)				
SALES, Soupy				
HILLY BILLY DING DONG CHOO CHOO/ And That's A Shame	(Reprise 20189)	.75	3.00	63
MOUSE, THE/Pachalafaka	(ABC-Paramount 10646)	.75	3.00	65
MUCK-ARTY PARK/Green Grow The Lilacs	(Motown 1141)	.75	3.00	69
MY BABY'S GOT A CRUSH ON FRANKENSTEIN/ Doggone Doggie	(Reprise 20108)	.75	3.00	62
SANTA CLAUS IS SURFIN' TO TOWN/ Santa Claus Is Comin' To Town	(Reprise 244)	.75	3.00	63
SOUPY'S THEME/Because Of Black Tooth	(Reprise 20064)	.75	3.00	62
THAT WASN'T NO GIRL/Spanish Flea	(Capitol 5752)	.75	3.00	66
WHITE FANG/Hippy's Cha Cha Hips	(Reprise 20041)	.75	3.00	61
(Novelties)				
SALLES, Jessie, & The Crypt-Kickers				
JOG, THE/Gary's Theme (Gary Paxton)	(Garpax 44169)	1.00	4.00	62
SALLY & THE ROSES				
CHICKEN BACK/Usher Boy	(Columbia 42895)	.75	3.00	63
SALLY & THE SALLYCATS				
BREAD FRED/Depending On You	(Rendezvous 105)	1.00	4.00	59
SALMA, Doug, & The Highlanders				
SCAVENGER/	(Philips 40131)	1.00	4.00	63
SALT WATER TAFFY				
SUMMERTIME GIRL/Spend The Sunshine	(Metromedia 220)	1.00	4.00	71
SALUGA, Bill (Of The Ace Trucking Co.)				
DANCIN' JOHNSON (PART 1)/Dancin' Johnson (Part 2)	(A&M 2140)	.50	2.00	79
SALVATION				
THINK TWICE/Love Comes In Funny Packages	(ABC-Paramount 11025)	1.00	4.00	59
SALVIN, Dick				
DR. FINKENSTEIN'S CASTLE/	(Graveyard 3000)	3.00	12.00	
(Novelty/Break-in)				
SALVO, Sammy				
OH JULIE/Say Yeah	(RCA Victor 47-7097)	1.00	4.00	57
WOLF BOY/My Perfect Love	(RCA Victor 47-7516)	1.00	4.00	59
SAM THE SHAM & THE PHARAOHS (Featuring "Sam" Samudio)				
BANNED IN BOSTON/Money's My Problem	(MGM 13803)	.75	3.00	69
(Shown as by the Sam The Sham Revue)				
BETTY & DUPREE/Man Child	(Tupelo 2982)	.75	3.00	63
BLACK SHEEP/My Day's Gonna Come	(MGM 13747)	.75	3.00	67
HAIR ON MY CHINNY CHIN CHIN/ Out Crowd (I'm In With The)	(MGM 13581)	.75	3.00	66
HAUNTED HOUSE/How Does A Cheating Woman Feel	(Dingo 001)	1.25	5.00	64
HOW DO YOU CATCH A GIRL/Love You Left Behind	(MGM 13649)	.75	3.00	66
I COULDN'T SPELL !!*@!/The Down Home Strut	(MGM 13972)	.75	3.00	68
JU JU HAND/Big City Lights	(MGM 13364)	.75	3.00	65
LIL' RED RIDING HOOD/Love Me Like Before	(MGM 13506)	.75	3.00	66
OH THAT'S GOOD, NO THAT'S BAD/ Take What You Can Get	(MGM 13713)	.75	3.00	67
OLD MAC DONALD HAD A BOOGALOO FARM/ I Never Had No One	(MGM 13920)	.75	3.00	68
RED HOT/Long Long Way	(MGM 13452)	.75	3.00	66
RING DANG DOO/Don't Try It	(MGM 13397)	.75	3.00	65
SIGNIFYIN' MONKEY, THE/Juimonos	(XL 905)	2.50	10.00	64
WOOLY BULLY/Ain't Gonna Move	(MGM 13322)	.75	3.00	65
WOLLY BULLY/Ain't Gonna Move	(XL 906)	3.75	15.00	65
YAKETY YAK/Let Our Love Light Shine	(MGM 13863)	.75	3.00	69
(Shown as by the Sam The Sham Revue)				
SAMMY & THE DEL-LANDS				
LITTLE DARLING/Sleep Walk	(Stop 101)	1.25	5.00	

TITLE/FLIP	LABEL & NO.	GOOD	NEAR MINT	YR.
SAMMY & THE 5 NOTES				
LION IS AWAKE, THE/Doodle Bug Twist	(Lucky Four 1019)	1.00	4.00	
(Answer song)				
SAMMY & THE TEASERS				
AS I REMEMBER YOU/Penny In A Wishing Well	(Airport 101)	1.00	4.00	
SAMPSON, Jean				
TROUBADOUR FROM MEMPHIS, THE/Do You Believe	(Lighthouse 3000)	.75	3.00	
(Blue plastic)				
SAMUELS, Jerry				
I OWE A LOT TO IOWA POT/Who Are You To Tell Me Not To Smoke Marijuana	(J.E.P. IP-1175)	1.25	5.00	
(Novelty)				
Also see Napoleon XIV				
SANBORN, David				
SMILE/	(Warner Bros. 8272)	.50	2.00	
(Instrumental)				
SAND				
LADY OF MINE/	(Barnaby 5017)	.50	2.00	
SLEEP/	(Dicto 1004)	1.00	4.00	
SANDALS, The				
6 PAK/Endless Summer	(World Pacific 415)	.75	3.00	
CLOUDY/House Of Painted Glass	(World Pacific 77867)	.75	3.00	
SCRAMBLER/Out Front	(World Pacific 405)	.75	3.00	
SANDERS, Arlen				
LETTER TO PAUL, A/Hopped Up Mustang	(Faro 616)	1.50	6.00	
SANDERS, Bobby				
I'M ON MY WAY/It Was You	(Kaybo 618)	3.75	15.00	
LOVER/The Way I Feel	(Pick-A-Hit 100)	1.50	6.00	
Also see Bobby & The Velvets				
SANDERS, Felicia				
BLUE STAR ("MEDIC" THEME)/ My Love's A Gentle Man	(Columbia 40508)	1.00	4.00	
Also see Faith, Percy				
SANDERS, Gary				
AIN'T NO BEATLE/Ain't I Good To You	(Warner Bros. 5676)	1.25	5.00	6
SANDOVAL, Jimmy, & The Gauchos: see Doval, Jim (With The Gauchos				
SANDI & THE STYLERS				
SANDI'S EDDIE'S GIRL/Mixed Up Mommy	(Rachel 101)	3.00	12.00	
SANDPAPERS				
AIN'T GONNA KISS YA/My Baby Said	(Charger 114)	.75	3.00	6
SANDPIPERS, The				
ALL OVER BUT THE CRYING/Ballad To A Missing Lover	(A&M 1004)	.75	3.00	6
CHOTTO MATTE KUDASAI (NEVER SAY GOODBYE)/ Free To Carry On	(A&M 1280)	.75	3.00	7
COME SATURDAY MORNING/	(A&M 1134)	.75	3.00	6
FREE TO CARRY ON/ (He's Got The) Whole World In His Hands	(A&M 1227)	.75	3.00	7
GLASS/It's Over	(A&M 851)	.75	3.00	6
GUANTANAMERA/What Makes You Dream Pretty Girl	(A&M 806)	.75	3.00	6
LOUIE LOUIE/Things We Said Today	(A&M 819)	.75	3.00	6
SANDS, Evie				
ANGEL OF THE MORNING/Dear John	(Cameo 475)	.75	3.00	6
ANYWAY YOU WANT ME/I'll Never Be Alone	(A&M 1090)	.50	2.00	6
BILLY SUNSHINE/It Makes Me Laugh	(Cameo 2002)	.75	3.00	6
BUT YOU KNOW I LOVE YOU/Maybe Tomorrow	(A&M 1175)	.50	2.00	7
CRAZY ANNIE/Maybe Tomorrow	(A&M 1157)	.50	2.00	7
I CAN'T LET GO/You've Got Me Uptight	(Blue Cat 122)	1.00	4.00	6
I LOVE MAKIN' LOVE TO YOU/One Thing On My Mind	(Haven 7013)	.50	2.00	7
KEEP MY LOVE LIGHT BURNIN'/I Can't Wait For You	(RCA 11541)	.50	2.00	7
LOVE OF A BOY, THE/We Know Better	(Cameo 436)	.75	3.00	6
PICTURE ME GONE/It Makes Me Laugh	(Cameo 413)	.75	3.00	6
ROLL/My Dog	(ABC-Paramount 10458)	1.00	4.00	6
TAKE ME FOR A LITTLE WHILE/It's This I Am, I Find	(A&M 1192)	.50	2.00	7
TAKE ME FOR A LITTLE WHILE/Run Home To Your Mama	(Blue Cat 118)	1.00	4.00	6
UNTIL IT'S TIME FOR YOU TO GO/Shadow Of The Evening	(A&M 980)	.50	2.00	6
YESTERDAY CAN'T HURT ME/(Am I) Crazy 'Cause I Believe	(Haven 7020)	.50	2.00	7
YOU BROUGHT THE WOMAN OUT OF ME/ Early Morning Sunshine	(Haven 7010)	.50	2.00	7
YOU SHO' LOOK GOOD TO ME/Brain Damage	(RCA 11653)	.50	2.00	7
WAY YOU DO THE THINGS YOU DO, THE/	(Haven 806)	.50	2.00	7
SANDS, Jodie				
HOLD ME/What Does It Mater	(Thor 101)	1.00	4.00	5
IF YOU'RE NOT COMPLETELY SATISFIED/Sayonara	(Chancellor 1005)	1.00	4.00	5
LOVE ME ALWAYS/Everybody Needs Somebody	(Teen 109)	1.25	5.00	5
LOVE ME ALWAYS/Everybody Needs Somebody	(Bernlo 1003)	1.00	4.00	5
SOMEDAY/Always In My Heart	(Chancellor 1023)	1.00	4.00	5
WITH ALL MY HEART/More Than Only Friends	(Chancellor 1003)	1.00	4.00	5
SANDS OF TIME, The: see Tokens, The				
SANDS, Tommy				
BIG DATE/After The Senior Prom	(Capitol 3985)	1.00	4.00	58
BLUE RIBBON BABY/I Love You Because	(Capitol 4036)	2.50	10.00	58
(With the Raiders)				
DOCTOR HEARTACHE/On & On	(Capitol 4470)	1.00	4.00	6
GOIN' STEADY/Ring My Phone	(Capitol 3723)	1.00	4.00	57
I GOTTA HAVE YOU/You Hold The Future	(Capitol 4316)	1.00	4.00	59
I'LL BE SEEING YOU/That's The Way I Am	(Capitol 4259)	1.00	4.00	59
LET ME BE LOVED/Fantastically Foolish	(Capitol 3743)	1.00	4.00	57
OLD OAKEN BUCKET, THE/ These Are The Things You Are	(Capitol 4405)	1.00	4.00	60
RING-A-DING-A-DING/My Love Song	(Capitol 3690)	1.00	4.00	57
SING BOY SING/Crazy 'Cause I Love You	(Capitol 3867)	1.00	4.00	58
SINNER MAN/Bring Me Your Love	(Capitol 4321)	1.00	4.00	59
TEEN-AGE CRUSH/Hep Dee Hootie	(Capitol 3639)	1.00	4.00	57
TEENAGE DOLL/Hawaiian Rock	(Capitol 3953)	1.00	4.00	58
THAT'S LOVE/Crossroads	(Capitol 4366)	1.00	4.00	60
WORRYIN' KIND, THE/Bigger Than Texas	(Capitol 4082)	1.00	4.00	58
YOUNG MAN'S FANCY/Connie	(ABC-Paramount 10466)	.75	3.00	63
Prior to his signing with Capitol Records, Tommy Sands was a Country/Western singer for RCA Victor.				
SANDY & THE CUPIDS				
REBEL/I Didn't Know Him	(Charter C-2)	.75	3.00	
SANDY, Frank, & The Jackals				
LET'S GO ROCK'N ROLL/	(MGM 12678)	1.00	4.00	58
SANFORD & TOWNSEND BAND, The				
DOES IT HAVE TO BE YOU/ Sunshine In My Heart Again	(Warner Bros. 8476)	.50	2.00	77
EYE OF THE STORM (OH WOMAN)/ Cryin' Like A Child	(Warner Bros. 8539)	.50	2.00	78
GOPHER BROKE/	(Warner Bros. 49053)	.50	2.00	79
PARADISE/Cryin' Like A Child	(Warner Bros. 8565)	.50	2.00	78
SHAKE IT TO THE RIGHT/Rainbows Colored In Blue	(Warner Bros. 8302)	.50	2.00	77
SMOKE FROM A DISTANT FIRE/Lou	(Warner Bros. 8270)	.50	2.00	77
SAN FRANCISCO COMMITTEE OF CORRESPONDENCE, The				
WATERGATE BLUES/Never Before	(Congressional 122)	1.25	5.00	73

Frank Sinatra

Niki Sullivan

Gene Summers

Gene Simmons (Of Kiss)

Dusty Springfield

Sha-Na-Na

Bruce Springsteen

Bobby Sherman

TITLE/FLIP	LABEL & NO.	GOOD	NEAR MINT	YR.
SAN FRANCISCO EARTHQUAKE, The				
DAY LORRAINE CAME HOME/Everybody Laughed	(Smash 2218)	1.00	4.00	69
FAIRY TALES CAN COME TRUE/Su Su	(Smash 2157)	1.00	4.00	68
I FEEL LOVED/That Same Old Fat Man	(Smash 2117)	1.00	4.00	67
MARCH OF THE JINGLE JANGLE PEOPLE/Bring Me Back	(Smash 2179)	1.00	4.00	68
SAN REMO GOLDEN STRINGS, The				
HUNGRY FOR LOVE/All Turned On	(Ric-Tic 104)	.75	3.00	65
I'M SATISFIED/Blueberry Hill	(Ric-Tic 108)	.75	3.00	65
Instrumentals				
SANG, Samantha				
EMOTION (With the Bee Gees)/ When Love Is Gone	(Private Stock 45178)	.50	2.00	77
FROM DANCE TO LOVE/ I'll Never Get Enough Of You	(United Artists 1297)	.50	2.00	79
IN THE MIDNIGHT HOUR/Now	(United Artists 1313)	.50	2.00	79
YOU KEEP ME DANCING/Change Of Heart	(Private Stock 45188)	.50	2.00	78
SANTA ESMERALDA				
DON'T LET ME BE MISUNDERSTOOD/ You're My Everything	(Casablanca 902)	.50	2.00	77
LEARNING THE GAME (EPILOGUE)/ The Wages Of Sin (Part 1)	(Casablanca 948)	.50	2.00	78
HOUSE OF THE RISING SUN, THE/Nothing Else Matters	(Casablanca 913)	.50	2.00	78
SANTAMARIA, Mongo				
EL PUSSY CAT/	(Columbia 43171)	.75	3.00	65
CLOUD NINE/	(Columbia 44740)	.75	3.00	69
FEELIN' ALRIGHT/	(Atlantic 2689)	.50	2.00	69
HIPPO WALK/Tell It	(Atlantic 2794)	.50	2.00	70
OLD CLOTHES/Mongo's Boogaloo	(Columbia 43962)	.75	3.00	66
WATERMELON MAN/Don't Bother Me No More	(Battle 45909)	.75	3.00	63
YEH, YEH/Get The Money	(Battle 45917)	.75	3.00	63
(Instrumentals)				
SANTANA (Featuring Carlos Santana)				
BLACK MAGIC WOMAN/I'll Be Waiting	(Columbia 10677)	.50	2.00	78
BLACK MAGIC WOMAN/ Hope You're Feeling Better	(Columbia 45270)	.75	3.00	70
DANCE SISTER DANCE (BAILA MI HERMANA)/ Let Me	(Columbia 10353)	.50	2.00	76
EUROPA (EARTH'S CRY HEAVEN'S SMILE)/ Take Me With You	(Columbia 10421)	.50	2.00	76
EVERYBODY'S EVERYTHING/Guajira	(Columbia 45772)	.50	2.00	71
EVIL WAYS/Waiting	(Columbia 45069)	.75	3.00	70
EVIL WAYS/Them Changes	(Columbia 45666)	.50	2.00	72
FLOR DE CANELA/Mirage	(Columbia 10073)	.50	2.00	74
GIVE & TAKE/Life Is Anew	(Columbia 10088)	.50	2.00	75
GIVE ME LOVE/Revelations	(Columbia 10524)	.50	2.00	77
INCIDENT AT NESHABUR/Samba Pa' Ti	(Columbia 46067)	.50	2.00	74
JIN-GO-LO-BA/Persuasion	(Columbia 45010)	.75	3.00	69
LET IT SHINE/Tell Me Are You Tired	(Columbia 10336)	.50	2.00	76
LET THE CHILDREN PLAY/Carnaval	(Columbia 10481)	.50	2.00	77
NO ONE TO DEPEND ON/Taboo	(Columbia 45552)	.50	2.00	72
ONE CHAIN (DON'T MAKE NO PRISON)/ Life Is A Lady-Holiday	(Columbia 10938)	.50	2.00	79
OYE COMO VA/Samba Pa Ti	(Columbia 45330)	.50	2.00	71
SAMBA DE SAUSALITO/ When I Look Into Your Eyes	(Columbia 45999)	.50	2.00	74
SHE'S NOT HERE/Zulu	(Columbia 10616)	.50	2.00	77
STORMY/Move On	(Columbia 10873)	.50	2.00	78
WELL ALL RIGHT/Wham!	(Columbia 10839)	.50	2.00	78
YOU KNOW THAT I LOVE YOU/Aqua Marine	(Columbia 11144)	.50	2.00	79
SANTANA, Jorge (Of Malo)				
LOVE THE WAY/Sandy	(Tomato 10006)	.50	2.00	78
Jorge is Carlos Santana's brother				
SANTO & JOHNNY (Santo & Johnny Farina)				
BREEZE & I, THE/Lazy Day	(Canadian American 115)	.75	3.00	60
CARAVAN/Summertime	(Canadian American 111)	.75	3.00	60
HOP SCOTCH/Sea Shells	(Canadian American 124)	.75	3.00	61
I'LL REMEMBER (IN THE STILL OF THE NIGHT)/ Song For Rosemary	(Canadian American 164)	.75	3.00	64
LOVE LOST/Annie	(Canadian American 118)	.75	3.00	60
MANHATTAN SPIRITUAL/Wandering Sea	(Canadian American 155)	.75	3.00	62
MISERLOU/Tokoyo Twilight	(Canadian American 144)	.75	3.00	62
MOUSE, THE/Birmingham	(Canadian American 131)	.75	3.00	61
ON YOUR MARK/Manhattan	(Canadian American 151)	.75	3.00	63
SLEEP WALK/All Night Diner	(Canadian American 103)	1.00	4.00	59
SLEEPWALK/Goldfinger	(Canadian American 182)	.75	3.00	64
SPANISH HARLEM/Stage To Cimarron	(Canadian American 137)	.75	3.00	62
TEAR DROP/The Long Walk Home	(Canadian American 107)	1.00	4.00	59
THEME FROM "COME SEPTEMBER"/ The Long Walk Home	(Canadian American 128)	.75	3.00	61
THOUSAND MILES AWAY, A/Road Block	(Canadian American 167)	.75	3.00	64
THREE CABALLEROS/Step Aside	(Canadian American 141)	.75	3.00	62
TWISTIN' BELLS/Bullseye	(Canadian American 120)	.75	3.00	60
TWISTIN' BELLS/Christmas Day (Vocal by Linda Scott)	(Canadian American 132)	1.00	4.00	61
Instrumentals				
SANTOS, Larry (Of The Madisons)				
DON'T LET THE MUSIC STOP/	(Casablanca 881)	.50	2.00	77
LONG, LONG TIME/You Are Everything I Need	(Casablanca 869)	.50	2.00	76
WE CAN'T HIDE IT ANYMORE/ Can't Get You Off My Mind	(Casablanca 844)	.50	2.00	76
SANTOS, Larry (Of The Tones)				
3 LITTLE LOVERS/We Belong Together	(Baton 265)	2.50	10.00	
SOMEDAY (WHEN I'M GONE)/True	(Atlantic 2250)	1.25	5.00	64
(With the 4 Seasons)				
SAPPHIRES, The				
GOTTA BE MORE THAN FRIENDS/Song From Moulin Rouge	(Swan 4184)	1.00	4.00	64
GOTTA HAVE YOUR LOVE/Gee I'm Sorry Baby	(ABC-Paramount 10639)	.75	3.00	65
HEARTS ARE MADE TO BE BROKEN/ Let's Break Up For Awhile	(ABC-Paramount 10559)	.75	3.00	64
HOW COULD I SAY GOODBYE/Evil One	(ABC-Paramount 10693)	.75	3.00	65
I'VE GOT MINE, YOU BETTER GET YOURS/ I Found Out Too Late	(Swan 4177)	1.00	4.00	64
THANK YOU FOR LOVING ME/ Our Love Is Everywhere	(ABC-Paramount 10590)	.75	3.00	64
WHERE IS JOHNNY NOW/Your True Love	(Swan 4143)	1.00	4.00	63
WHO DO YOU LOVE/Oh So Soon	(Swan 4162)	1.00	4.00	64
YOU'LL NEVER STOP ME FROM LOVING YOU/ Gonna Be A Big Thing	(ABC-Paramount 10753)	.75	3.00	65
SARDO, Frank				
CLASS ROOM/Fake Out	(ABC-Paramount 9963)	1.00	4.00	59
KISS & MAKE UP/The Girl I'm Gonna Dream About	(Lido 602)	1.00	4.00	
OH LINDA/No Love Like Mine	(ABC-Paramount 10003)	1.00	4.00	59
SARDO, Johnny				
LATE, LATE, LATE TO SCHOOL/New Kid In Town	(Warner Bros. 5044)	1.00	4.00	59
TAKE A RIDE WITH ME/Hip Hop	(Chock 104)	1.00	4.00	
SARIDIS, Saverio				
LOVE IS THE SWEETEST THING/ Here's Where I Belong	(Warner Bros. 5243)	.75	3.00	62
LOVE IS THE SWEETEST THING/ Here's Where I Belong	(Warner Bros. 5243)	1.00	4.00	62
(Picture sleeve)				
SARNE, Mike				
MY BABY'S CRAZY 'BOUT ELVIS/ Just For Kicks	(Capitol Of Canada 72071)	3.75	15.00	57
SARSTEDT, Peter				
BERUIT/Hollywood Sign	(Sire 1028)	.50	2.00	78
FROZEN ORANGE JUICE/Aretusa Loser	(World Pacific 77919)	.75	3.00	69
WHERE DO YOU GO TO (MY LOVELY)/ I Am A Cathedral	(World Pacific 77911)	.75	3.00	69
SA-SHAYS, The				
BOO HOO HOO/You Got Love	(Alfi 1)	1.00	4.00	61
SATANS, The				
MAKING DEALS/Lines & Squares	(Manhattan 801)	.75	3.00	66
SATANS 4, The				
OH KATHY/Can't Find The Girl On My Mind	(B.T. Puppy 515)	1.00	4.00	66
SATELLITES, The				
LINDA JEAN/Rockateen	(ABC-Paramount 10038)	2.50	10.00	59
SATISFACTIONS, The				
DADDY YOU JUST GOTTA LET HIM IN/ Bring It All Down	(Imperial 66170)	.75	3.00	66
SATO, Steve				
THERE GOES THE ONE/On The Way To Say I Do	(U.W. Records 1011)	.75	3.00	
SATURDAY KNIGHTS, The				
TICONDEROGA/Tiger Lily	(Swan 4075)	1.50	6.00	61
SATURDAY, Patty				
LOVE IS A BEAUTIFUL THING/Ladies Choice	(Swan 4022)	1.00	4.00	59
SATURDAY'S CHILDREN				
DECK FIVE/The Christmas Song	(Dunwich 144)	1.00	4.00	67
LEAVE THAT BABY ALONE/I Hardly Know Her	(Dunwich 156)	1.00	4.00	67
YOU DON'T KNOW BETTER/Born On Saturday	(Dunwich 139)	1.00	4.00	66
SAUCEDO, Rick				
KING OF BLUE SUEDE SOUL, THE/Jailhouse Rock	(Eclipse 1732)	.50	2.00	77
LEGEND LIVES ON, THE/How Great Thou Art	(Fraternity 3416)	.75	3.00	78
(With the Jordanaires)				
SAUCERS, The				
FLOSSIE MAE/Hi-Oom	(Kixk 100)	6.25	25.00	
SAUNDERS, Little Butchie, & His Buddies				
GREAT BIG HEART/I Wanna Holler	(Herald 491)	2.00	8.00	56
LINDY LOU/Rock & Roll Indian Dance	(Herald 485)	2.00	8.00	56
OVER THE RAINBOW/Sometimes Little Girl	(Angeltone 535)	2.00	8.00	
(Shown as by Little Butchie & The Vells)				
Also see Elchords, The				
SAUNDERS, Red				
HAMBONE/Boot 'Em Up	(Okeh 6862)	1.25	5.00	52
SAVAGE, Lee				
RIDERS IN THE SKY/Teen Age World	(Merri 101)	.75	3.00	60
SAVAGE RESURRECTION				
THING IN "E"/Fox Is Sick	(Mercury 72778)	.75	3.00	68
SAVAGE ROSE				
SUNDAY MORNING/Speak Softly	(Gregar 0104)	.75	3.00	
SAVONICS, The				
SOUL GROOVE/I Had A Girl	(MTA 145)	1.00	4.00	
SAVOY BROWN (With Kim Simmons & Dave Peverett)				
COMING DOWN YOUR WAY/I Can't Find You	(Parrot 40075)	.50	2.00	72
EVERYBODY LOVES A DRINKING MAN/Ride On Babe	(London 206)	.50	2.00	74
GRITS AIN'T GROCERIES/She's Got A Ring	(Parrot 40037)	.75	3.00	69
HARD WAY TO GO, A/The Incredible Gnome meets Jaxman	(Parrot 40046)	.50	2.00	70
I'M TIRED/	(Parrot 40042)	.75	3.00	69
LOST & LONELY CHILD/If I Could See An End	(Parrot 362)	.50	2.00	73
TELL MAMA/	(Parrot 40066)	.50	2.00	71
WALKIN' & TALKIN'/Stranger Blues	(London 234)	.50	2.00	75
Also see Anderson, Miller				
SAVOY, Ronnie				
AND THE HEAVENS CRIED/Big Chain	(MGM 12950)	1.00	4.00	60
SAWBUCK				
THERE WILL BE LOVE/Bible Burning	(Fillmore 7007)	1.00	4.00	
SAWYER, Ray (Of Dr. Hook)				
DANCING FOOL, THE/	(Capitol 4592)	.50	2.00	78
I WANT JOHNNY'S JOB/	(Capitol 4747)	.50	2.00	79
(ONE MORE YEAR OF) DAVY'S LITTLE GIRL/I Need The High	(Capitol 4344)	.50	2.00	76
RED-WINGED BLACKBIRD/	(Capitol 4386)	.50	2.00	77
SAWYER, Tommy, & The Twains				
HOW DEEP IS THE OCEAN/15th Row Down	(Diamond 112)	1.00	4.00	62
SAXON, Sky (Of The Seeds)				
GOODBYE/Crying Inside My Heart	(Ava 122)	3.00	12.00	
(Shown as by Ritchie Marsh)				
THEY SAY/Go Ahead & Cry	(Conquest 777)	2.00	8.00	
THEY SAY/Darling, I Swear It's True	(Shepherd 2203)	3.00	12.00	
(Shown as by Ritchie Marsh)				
SAXTON, Anglo				
RUBY/You Better Leave Me Alone	(Lucky Eleven 009)	1.00	4.00	
SAXTONS, The				
BEATLE DANCE, THE/Sittin' On Top Of The World	(Regina 305)	1.25	5.00	64
SAYER, Leo				
DON'T LOOK AWAY/No Looking Back	(Warner Bros. 8738)	.50	2.00	78
EASY TO LOVE/Haunting Me	(Warner Bros. 8502)	.50	2.00	77
HOW MUCH LOVE/I Hear The Laughter	(Warner Bros. 8319)	.50	2.00	77
LONG TALL GLASSES/In My Life	(Warner Bros. 8043)	.50	2.00	75
(Later issues read "Long Tall Glasses (I Can Dance")				
MOONLIGHTING/Streets Of Your Town	(Warner Bros. 8153)	.50	2.00	75
OH GIRL/An Englishman In The U.S.A.	(Warner Bros. 49134)	.50	2.00	79
ONE MAN BAND/Telepath	(Warner Bros. 8097)	.50	2.00	75
RAINING IN MY HEART/No Looking Back	(Warner Bros. 8682)	.50	2.00	78
SHOW MUST GO ON, THE/	(Warner Bros. 7768)	.50	2.00	73
THUNDER IN MY HEART/Get The Girl	(Warner Bros. 8465)	.50	2.00	77
WHEN I NEED YOU/I Think We Fell In Love Too Fast	(Warner Bros. 8332)	.50	2.00	77
YOU MAKE ME FEEL LIKE DANCING/Magdalena	(Warner Bros. 8283)	.50	2.00	76
SCAFFOLD, The (Featuring Mike McGear)				
DO YOU REMEMBER/Carry On Krow	(Bell 724)	1.00	4.00	68
LILY THE PINK/Buttons Of Your Mind	(Bell 747)	1.00	4.00	68
LIVERPOOL LOU/Ten Years After On Strawberry Jam	(Warner Bros. 8001)	.75	3.00	74
THANK U VERY MUCH/Ide B The First	(Bell 701)	1.00	4.00	68
Mike McGear is Paul McCartney's brother.				
SCAGGS, Boz (Of The Steve Miller Band)				
DINAH FLO/	(Columbia 45670)	.50	2.00	72
HARD TIMES/We're Waiting	(Columbia 10606)	.50	2.00	77
HOLLYWOOD/A Clue	(Columbia 10679)	.50	2.00	78
I'LL BE LONG GONE/I'm Easy	(Atlantic 2692)	.75	3.00	69
IT'S OVER/Harbor Lights	(Columbia 10319)	.50	2.00	76
LIDO SHUFFLE/We're All Alone	(Columbia 10491)	.50	2.00	77
LOWDOWN/Harbor Lights	(Columbia 10367)	.50	2.00	76
NEAR YOU/	(Columbia 45408)	.50	2.00	71
WHAT CAN I SAY/We're All Alone	(Columbia 10440)	.50	2.00	76
YOU MAKE IT SO HARD (TO SAY NO)/ There Is Someone Else	(Columbia 46025)	.50	2.00	73
WE WERE ALWAYS SWEETHEARTS/Painted Bells	(Columbia 45353)	.50	2.00	71
SCANDLIN, Billy, & The Embers				
YOU'LL ALWAYS HAVE SOMEONE/I Keep On Walking	(Viking 1002)	2.00	8.00	
SCARLETS, The				
STAMPEDE/Park Avenue	(Prince 1207)	1.50	6.00	
SCAVENGERS, The				
ANGELS LISTENED IN, THE/My Love Waits For Me	(Mobile Fidelity 1005)	1.00	4.00	63
CURFEW/Oasis	(Fenton 987)	1.00	4.00	64
(Instrumentals)				
DEVIL'S REEF/Little Annie	(Mobile Fidelity 1212)	1.00	4.00	64
(Instrumentals)				
DEVIL'S REEF/Little Annie	(Stars Of Hollywood 1212)	.75	3.00	63
(Instrumentals)				
SCENE, The				
YOU'RE IN A BAD WAY/Scenes From Another World	(B.T. Puppy 533)	.75	3.00	67
SCHIFRIN, Lalo				
AMITYVILLE FRENZY/Amityville (End Title)	(American Intl. 4102)	.50	2.00	79
MISSION IMPOSSIBLE/Jim On The Move	(Dot 17059)	.75	3.00	68
SCHILLING, Johnny, & The Sherwoods				
KING OF THE WORLD/Marcelle	(C&A 507)	3.75	15.00	
SCHOOL BELLES, The				
DON'T BELIEVE HIM/Valley High	(Crest 1104)	.75	3.00	62
SCHRAEDER, John, Orchestra				
FUGITIVE THEME, THE/Don't Break The Heart Of Kimble	(Cameo 366)	.75	3.00	65
SCHUMANN, Walter				
BALLAD OF DAVY CROCKETT, THE/Let's Make Up	(RCA Victor 47-6041)	1.00	4.00	55
SCOGGINS, Jerry				
BALLAD OF JED CLAMPETT/Willow Tree	(Ava 130)	.75	3.00	62
SCOOP				
PATTY/Treehouse	(Essar 7602)	1.00	4.00	
SCORPIONS, The				
LOVING YOU SUNDAY MORNING/Coast To Coast	(Mercury 76008)	.50	2.00	79
SCOTT, Billy				
CAROLE (Carole King)/Stairways To The Stars	(Everest 19315)	2.00	8.00	59
MILLION BOYS, A/Town Of Never Worry, The	(Cameo 143)	1.00	4.00	58
YOU'RE THE GREATEST/That's Why I Was Born	(Cameo 121)	1.00	4.00	57
SCOTT, Bobby				
CHAIN GANG/Shadrack	(ABC-Paramount 9658)	1.00	4.00	55
SCOTT BROTHERS, The				
LOST LOVE/Only Then	(Ribbon 6911)	1.50	6.00	59
PART OF YOU/Kingdom Of Love	(Skyline 502)	2.00	8.00	
YUGGI GUGGI/Our Tune	(Fabor 117)	1.00	4.00	63
SCOTT, Freddie				
HEY, GIRL/Slide	(Colpix 692)	.75	3.00	63
I GOT A WOMAN/Brand New World	(Colpix 709)	.75	3.00	63
LOVING YOU IS KILLING ME/Eillen	(Shout S-238)	.50	2.00	70
WHERE DOES LOVE GO/Where Have All The Flowers Gone	(Colpix 724)	.75	3.00	64

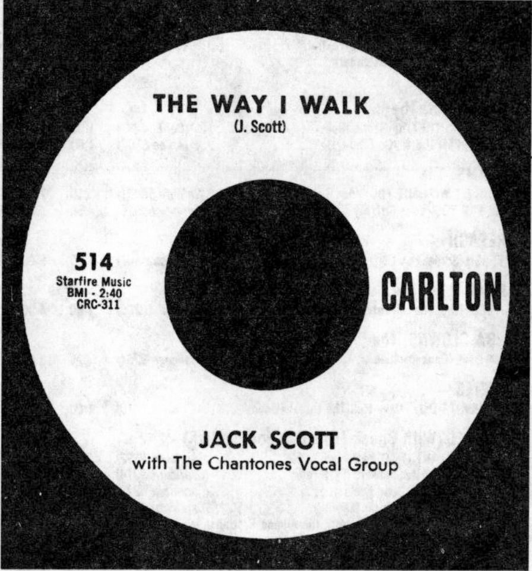

TITLE/FLIP	LABEL & NO.	GOOD	NEAR MINT	YR.
SCOTT, Jack (Jack Scafone)				
ALL I SEE IS BLUE/Meo Myo	(Capitol 4955)	1.50	6.00	63
BABY, SHE'S GONE/ You Can Bet Your Bottom Dollar	(ABC-Paramount 9818)	8.75	35.00	57
BEFORE THE BIRD FLIES/Insane	(ABC-Paramount 10843)	1.25	5.00	66
BURNING BRIDGES/Oh, Little One	(Top Rank 2041)	1.00	4.00	60
CRY CRY CRY/Grizzly Bear	(Capitol 4689)	1.50	6.00	62
DON'T HUSH THE LAUGHTER/ Let's Learn To Live & Love Again	(RCA Victor 47-8724)	1.25	5.00	65
GO WILD LITTLE SADIE/No One Will Ever Know	(Guaranteed 211)	2.50	10.00	60
GOODBYE BABY/Save My Soul	(Carlton 493)	1.25	5.00	58
I CAN'T HOLD YOUR LETTERS (IN MY ARMS)/ Sad Story	(Capitol 4796)	1.50	6.00	62
I DON'T BELIEVE IN TEA LEAVES/ Separation's Now Granted	(RCA Victor 47-8505)	1.25	5.00	65
I KNEW YOU FIRST/Blue Skies (Moving In On Me)	(Groove 0031)	1.25	5.00	64
I NEVER FELT LIKE THIS/Bella	(Carlton 504)	1.25	5.00	59
IF ONLY/Green Green Valley	(Capitol 4855)	1.50	6.00	62
IS THERE SOMETHING ON YOUR MIND/Found A Woman	(Top Rank 2093)	1.25	5.00	61
IT ONLY HAPPENED YESTERDAY/Cool Water	(Top Rank 2055)	1.25	5.00	60
JINGLE BELLS SLIDE/There's Trouble Brewin'	(Groove 0027)	1.25	5.00	63
LAUGH & THE WORLD LAUGHS WITH YOU/Strangers	(Capitol 4903)	1.50	6.00	63
LITTLE FEELING, A/Now That I	(Capitol 4554)	1.50	6.00	61
LOOKING FOR LINDA/I Hope, I Think, I Wish	(RCA Victor 47-8685)	1.25	5.00	65
MY DREAM COME TRUE/Strange Desire	(Capitol 4597)	1.50	6.00	61
MY SPECIAL ANGEL/I Keep Changing My Mind	(Jubilee 5606)	1.50	6.00	67
MY TRUE LOVE/Leroy	(Carlton 462)	1.25	5.00	58

TITLE/FLIP	LABEL & NO.	GOOD	NEAR MINT	YR.
PART WHERE I CRY, THE/You Only See What You Wanna See	(Capitol 4738)	1.50	6.00	62
PATSY/Old Time Religion	(Top Rank 2075)	1.00	4.00	60
STEPS 1 & 2/One Of These Days	(Capitol 4637)	2.00	8.00	61
TALL TALES/Flakey John	(Groove 0049)	2.00	8.00	64
(Shown as by Jack Scott)				
THERE COMES A TIME/Baby Marie	(Carlton 519)	1.25	5.00	59
THOU SHALT NOT STEAL/I Prayed For An Angel	(Groove 0042)	1.25	5.00	64
TWO TIMIN' WOMAN/I Need Your Love	(ABC-Paramount 9860)	12.50	50.00	57
WAY I WALK, THE/Midge	(Carlton 514)	1.25	5.00	59
WHAT A WONDERFUL NIGHT OUT/Wiggle On Out	(Groove 0037)	1.25	5.00	64
WHAT AM I LIVING FOR/Indian Waltz	(Guaranteed 209)	1.50	6.00	60
WHAT IN THE WORLD'S COME OVER YOU/Baby, Baby	(Top Rank 2028)	1.00	4.00	60
WITH YOUR LOVE/Geraldine	(Carlton 483)	1.25	5.00	58
SCOTT, Joel				
HERE I STAND/You're My Only Love	(Philles 101)	1.00	4.00	62
SCOTT, Judy				
TENDER WORD, A/The Parlor Piano	(Decca 30395)	1.00	4.00	59
WITH ALL MY HEART/Game Of Love	(Decca 30324)	1.00	4.00	57
SCOTT, Linda (Linda Joy Sampson)				
AIN'T THAT FUN/Sit Right Down & Write Myself A Letter	(Congress 110)	1.00	4.00	63
BERMUDA/Lonely For You	(Canadian-American 134)	1.00	4.00	62
CHRISTMAS DAY/Twistin' Bells (By Santo & Johnny)	(Canadian American 132)	1.00	4.00	61
COUNT EVERY STAR/Land Of Stars	(Canadian-American 133)	1.00	4.00	62
DON'T BET MONEY HONEY/Starlight, Starbright	(Canadian-American 127)	1.00	4.00	61
DON'T LOSE YOUR HEAD/I'll See You In My Dreams	(Kapp 677)	1.00	4.00	65
I DON'T KNOW WHY/It's All Because	(Canadian-American 129)	1.00	4.00	61
I ENVY YOU/Everybody Stopped	(Congress 209)	1.00	4.00	64
I LEFT MY HEART IN THE BALCONY/Lopsided Love Affair	(Congress 106)	1.00	4.00	62
I'M SO AFRAID OF LOSING YOU/Loneliest Girl In Town	(Congress 108)	1.00	4.00	62
I'VE TOLD EVERY LITTLE STAR/Three Guesses	(Canadian-American 123)	1.00	4.00	61
LET'S FALL IN LOVE/I Know It You Know It	(Congress 200)	1.00	4.00	63
NEVER IN A MILLION YEARS/Through The Summer	(Congress 1101)	1.00	4.00	62
PATCH IT UP/If I Love Again	(Kapp 641)	1.00	4.00	65
THIS IS MY PRAYER/That Old Feeling	(Kapp 610)	1.00	4.00	64
WHO'S BEEN SLEEPING IN MY BED/My Heart	(Congress 204)	1.00	4.00	64
YESSIREE/Town Crier	(Congress 101)	1.00	4.00	62
YOU BABY/I Can't Get Through To You	(Kapp 713)	1.00	4.00	65
SCOTT, Neal (Neil Bogart)				
BOBBY/I Haven't Found It With Another	(Portrait 102)	1.25	5.00	61
LET ME THINK IT OVER/I Don't Stand A Ghost Of A Chance	(Cameo 476)	.75	3.00	67
OH GENIE/Go Bohemian	(Clown 3011)	.75	3.00	
ONE PIECE BATHING SUIT/Little Girl	(Herald 581)	2.00	8.00	63
(With the Concords)				
TOMBOY/Run To Me	(Comet 2151)	1.50	6.00	
(With the Concords)				
Also see Jerry & Jeff				
Also see Beck, Bogart & Appice				
SCOTT, Rodney				
GRANNY WENT ROCKIN'/Bitter Tears	(Cannon 225)	43.75	175.00	
YOU'RE SO SQUARE/	(Mr. Peeke 119)	2.50	10.00	
SCOTT, Sherree				
FASCINATING BABY/You & I	(Rocket 1036)	7.50	30.00	
FASCINATING BABY/You & I	(Rocket 1036)	2.50	10.00	
(Paper insert)				
SCOTT, Simon				
MIDNIGHT/My Baby's Got Soul	(Imperial 66089)	.75	3.00	65
MOVE IT BABY/What Kind Of Woman	(Imperial 66066)	.75	3.00	64
SCOTT, Tom				
BEAUTIFUL MUSIC/Lost Inside The Love Of You	(Columbia 10914)	.50	2.00	79
GOTCHA (THEME FROM "STARSKY & HUTCH")/	(Ode 50433)	.50	2.00	79
LOOKIN' OUT FOR NUMBER SEVEN/Boss Walk	(A&M 1345)	.50	2.00	72
TOM CAT/Keep On Doin' It	(Ode 66105)	.50	2.00	75
UPTOWN & COUNTRY/Appolina (Foxtrata)	(Ode 66118)	.50	2.00	76
(With George Harrison on guitar)				
Instrumentals.				
SCRAMBLERS, The				
BEETLE WALK, THE/The Beetle Blues	(Del Fi 4237)	1.00	4.00	64
SUPER SURFER U.S.A./Go Gilera, Go	(Arvee 6502)	1.00	4.00	65
SCREAMS, The				
IMAGINE ME WITHOUT YOU/Your Girl, My Girl	(Infinity 50031)	.50	2.00	79
I PLAY FOR YOU/Your Girl, My Girl	(Infinity 50025)	.50	2.00	79
SCREEAGH				
SCREEAGH/Screeagh's Gone	(Astra 301)	1.25	5.00	63
SCREWBALLS, The				
JUST BECAUSE/The Screwball March	(Columbia 42209)	1.00	4.00	61
SCUBA CLOWNS, The				
SCUBA DIVE/Concentration	(Challenge 9204)	.75	3.00	64
SCUZZIES				
OUR FAVORITE D.J. /Dave Hull The Hullabalooer	(CRS 1110)	1.00	4.00	64
SEA LEVEL (With Chuck Leavall & Joe English)				
IT HURTS TO WANT IT SO BAD/Had To Fall	(Capricorn 0292)	.50	2.00	78
LIVING IN A DREAM/Sneakers (Fifty-Four)	(Capricorn 0314)	.50	2.00	79
SHAKE A LEG/Just A Good Feeling	(Capricorn 0272)	.50	2.00	77
THAT'S YOUR SECRET/Storm Warning	(Capricorn 0287)	.50	2.00	78
Chuck Leavall was previously with the Allman Brothers; Joe English also appeared in Wings.				
SEALS & CROFTS (Jimmy Seals & Dash Crofts)				
BABY BLUE/Goodbye Old Buddies	(Warner Bros. 8330)	.50	2.00	77
BABY, I'LL GIVE IT TO YOU/Advance Guards	(Warner Bros. 8277)	.50	2.00	76
CASTLES IN THE SAND/Golden Rainbow	(Warner Bros. 8130)	.50	2.00	75
DIAMOND GIRL/Wisdom	(Warner Bros. 7708)	.50	2.00	73
GABRIEL GO ON HOME/Robin	(T.A. 210)	.75	3.00	71
GET CLOSER/Don't Fail	(Warner Bros. 8190)	.50	2.00	76
HUMMINGBIRD/Say	(Warner Bros. 7671)	.50	2.00	73
I'LL PLAY FOR YOU/Truth Is But A Woman	(Warner Bros. 8075)	.50	2.00	75
IRISH LINEN/When I Meet Them	(Warner Bros. 7536)	.50	2.00	71
KING OF NOTHING/Follow Me	(Warner Bros. 7810)	.50	2.00	74
MY FAIR SHARE (LOVE THEME FROM "ONE ON ONE")/East Of Ginger Trees	(Warner Bros. 8405)	.50	2.00	77
RIDIN' THUMB/	(T.A. 208)	.75	3.00	70
SUMMER BREEZE/East Of Ginger Trees	(Warner Bros. 7606)	.75	3.00	72
TAKIN' IT EASY/	(Warner Bros. 8639)	.50	2.00	78
UNBORN CHILD/Ledges	(Warner Bros. 7771)	.50	2.00	74
UNBORN CHILD (Stereo)/Unborn Child (Mono)	(Warner Bros. 0329)	.75	3.00	75
(Promotional issue)				
WE MAY NEVER PASS THIS WAY (AGAIN)/Jessica	(Warner Bros. 7740)	.50	2.00	73
YOU'RE THE LOVE/	(Warner Bros. 8551)	.50	2.00	78
Also see Champs, The				
SEALS, Jimmy				
EVERYBODY'S DOIN' THE JERK/Wa-Hoo	(Challenge 59270)	1.25	5.00	64
LADY HEARTBREAK/Grounded	(Challenge 9200)	1.50	6.00	64
WISH FOR, WANT FOR YOU, WAIT FOR YOU/Runaway Heart	(Challenge 9153)	1.25	5.00	62
Also see Seals & Crofts				
SEAN & THE SHEAS				
SPIDERS/Hi Diddle	(Yorkshire 004)	1.00	4.00	
SEARCHERS, The				
AIN'T THAT JUST LIKE ME/Ain't Gonna Kiss Ya	(Kapp 584)	1.00	4.00	64
AIN'T THAT JUST LIKE ME/I Can Tell	(Mercury 72390)	1.25	5.00	65
BUMBLE BEE/Everything You Do	(Kapp 49)	1.00	4.00	65
DESDEMONA/The World Is Waiting For Tomorrow	(RCA 0484)	.75	3.00	71
DON'T THROW YOUR LOVE AWAY/I Pretend I'm With You	(Kapp 593)	1.00	4.00	64
GOODBYE MY LOVER GOODBYE/'Til I Meet You	(Kapp 658)	1.00	4.00	65
HAVE YOU EVER LOVED SOMEBODY/It's Just The Way (Love Will Come & Go)	(Kapp 783)	1.00	4.00	66
HE'S GOT NO LOVE/So Far Away	(Kapp 686)	1.00	4.00	65
LOVE IS EVERYWHERE/And A Button	(RCA 0652)	.75	3.00	72
LOVE POTION NUMBER NINE/Hi-Heel Sneakers	(Kapp 27)	1.00	4.00	64
NEEDLES & PINS/Saturday Night Out	(Kapp 577)	1.00	4.00	64
NEEDLES & PINS/Ain't That Just Like Me	(Kapp 577)	1.00	4.00	64
POPCORN DOUBLE FEATURE/Lovers	(Kapp 811)	1.00	4.00	67
SOMEDAY WE'RE GONNA LOVE AGAIN/No One Else Could Love Me	(Kapp 609)	1.00	4.00	64
SUGAR & SPICE/Saints & Searchers	(Liberty 55646)	2.00	8.00	63
SUGAR & SPICE/Saints & Searchers	(Liberty 55646)	1.50	6.00	63
(Promotional issue)				
SUGAR & SPICE/Saints & Searchers	(Liberty 55689)	1.00	4.00	64
SWEETS FOR MY SWEET/It's All Been A Dream	(Mercury 72172)	1.25	5.00	65
TAKE ME FOR WHAT I'M WORTH/Too Many Miles	(Kapp 729)	1.00	4.00	66
WHAT HAVE THEY DONE TO THE RAIN/This Feeling Inside	(Kapp 644)	1.00	4.00	65
WHEN YOU WALK IN THE ROOM/I'll Be Missing You	(Kapp 618)	1.00	4.00	65
YOU CAN'T LIE TO A LIAR/Don't You Know Why	(Kapp 706)	1.00	4.00	66
SEASHELLS, The				
LOVE THOSE BEACH BOYS/Close To Jimmy	(Goliath 1357)	1.25	5.00	63
SEASHELLS, The				
(THE BEST PART OF) BREAKING UP/	(Columbia 45760)	.50	2.00	71
SEATRAIN				
CAROLINE, CAROLINE/Suite For Almond	(A&M 1106)	1.25	5.00	68
GRAMERCY/How Sweet Thy Song	(Capitol 3275)	.75	3.00	71
I'M WILLING/	(Capitol 3421)	.75	3.00	72
LET THE DUTCHESS KNOW/As I Lay Losing	(A&M 994)	1.25	5.00	68
PACK OF FOOLS/Abbeville Fair	(Warner Bros. PRO-562)	1.25	5.00	
(Promotional issue)				
SONG OF JOB/Waiting For Elisa	(Capitol 3140)	.75	3.00	71
13 QUESTIONS/Oh My Love-Sally Goodin'	(Capitol 3067)	.75	3.00	71
SEBASTIAN				
ELAINE/Now That It's Over	(Decca 32655)	1.25	5.00	70
TOO YOUNG/Darlin' I Do	(Mr. Maestro 801)	2.00	8.00	
SEBASTIAN, John (Of Lovin' Spoonful)				
HIDEAWAY/One Step Forward, Two Steps Back	(Reprise 1355)	.50	2.00	76
I DON'T WANT NOBODY ELSE/Sweet Muse	(Reprise 1026)	.50	2.00	71
I DON'T WANT NOBODY ELSE-SWEET MUSE/	(Reprise EL-A7277125 XT)	1.00	4.00	71
(Plastic soundsheet with both songs on one side.)				
MAGICAL CONNECTION/Fa-Fana-Fa	(Reprise 0902)	.50	2.00	70
SHE'S A LADY/The Room Nobody Lives In	(Kama Sutra 254)	.75	3.00	68
SHE'S A LADY/The Room Nobody Lives In	(MGM 14122)	1.00	4.00	68
(The MGM and Kama Sutra were simultaneous releases of the same tracks.)				
WELCOME BACK KOTTER/Warm Baby	(Reprise 1349)	.75	3.00	76
WELCOME BACK/Warm Baby	(Reprise 1349)	.50	2.00	76
(Second pressing, dropping "Kotter" from title.)				
WELL, WELL, WELL/	(Reprise 1050)	.50	2.00	71
WHAT SHE THINKS ABOUT/Red-Eye Express	(Reprise 0918)	.50	2.00	70
SECOND COMING, The				
I FEEL FREE/She Has Funny Cars	(Steady 001)	1.00	4.00	
"747"/Take Me Home	(Mercury 73184)	1.00	4.00	70
SECRET AGENTS, The				
I SAW SLOOPY/Things Happen	(Jerden 784)	.75	3.00	66
SECRETS, The				
BOY NEXT DOOR, THE/Learnin' To Forget	(Philips 40146)	.75	3.00	63
HE'S THE BOY/He Doesn't Want You	(Philips 40222)	.75	3.00	64
HERE HE COMES NOW/Oh Donnie	(Philips 40196)	.75	3.00	64
HEY, BIG BOY/The Other Side Of Town	(Philips 40173)	.75	3.00	64
SECRETS, The				
TWIN EXHAUST/Hot Toddy	(Swan 4097)	1.00	4.00	62
SECRETS, The				
SEE YOU NEXT YEAR/Queen Bee	(Decca 30350)	1.00	4.00	57
SECTION, The				
BAD SHOES/	(Capitol 4482)	.50	2.00	77
SEDAKA, Dara				
MY GUY/Beautiful You	(RSO 892)	.50	2.00	78
Dara is Neil Sedaka's daughter.				
SEDAKA, Neil				
ALICE IN WONDERLAND/Circulate	(RCA Victor 47-8137)	.75	3.00	63
ALL YOU NEED IS THE MUSIC/	(Elektra 45525)	.50	2.00	78
ALONE AT LAST/Sleazy Love	(Elektra 45421)	.50	2.00	77
ANSWER LIES WITHIN, THE/Grown Up Games	(RCA Victor 47-8844)	1.00	4.00	66
ANSWER TO MY PRAYER, THE/Blue Boy	(RCA Victor 47-8737)	1.00	4.00	66
AMARILLO/The Leaving Game	(Elektra 45406)	.50	2.00	77
BAD BLOOD (With Elton John)/Your Favorite Entertainer	(Rocket 40460)	.50	2.00	75
BAD GIRL/Wait 'Til You See My Baby	(RCA Victor 47-8254)	.75	3.00	63
BREAKING UP IS HARD TO DO/As Long As I Live	(RCA Victor 47-8046)	.75	3.00	62
BREAKING UP IS HARD TO DO/Nana's Song	(Rocket 40500)	.50	2.00	75
CALENDAR GIRL/The Same Old Fool	(RCA Victor 47-7829)	1.00	4.00	60
CALENDAR GIRL/The Same Old Fool	(RCA Victor 61-7829)	2.50	10.00	60
(Stereo single issue)				
CALENDAR GIRL/The Same Old Fool	(RCA Victor 37-7829)	3.75	15.00	60
(Compact 33 single)				
CLOSEST THING TO HEAVEN, THE/Without A Song	(RCA Victor 47-8341)	.75	3.00	64
DIARY, THE/No Vacancy	(RCA Victor 47-7408)	1.00	4.00	58
DIARY, THE/No Vacancy	(RCA Victor 47-7408)	2.00	8.00	58
(Promotional issue)				
DREAMER, THE/Look Inside Your Heart	(RCA Victor 47-8209)	.75	3.00	63
HAPPY BIRTHDAY SWEET SIXTEEN/Don't Lead Me On	(RCA Victor 47-7957)	.75	3.00	61
HAPPY BIRTHDAY SWEET SIXTEEN/Don't Lead Me On	(RCA Victor 37-7957)	3.75	15.00	61
(Compact 33 single)				
I GO APE/Moon Of Gold	(RCA Victor 47-7473)	1.25	5.00	59
I'M A SONG (SING ME)/	(Kirshner 291)	.75	3.00	72
IMMIGRANT, THE/Hey Mister Sunshine	(Rocket 40370)	.50	2.00	75
KING OF CLOWNS/Walk With Me	(RCA Victor 47-8007)	.75	3.00	62
KING OF CLOWNS/Walk With Me	(RCA Victor 37-8007)	3.75	15.00	62
(Compact 33 single)				
LAUGHTER IN THE RAIN/Endlessly	(Rocket 40313)	.50	2.00	74
LAURA LEE/Snowtime	(Decca 30520)	5.00	20.00	58
LET'S GO STEADY AGAIN/Waiting For Never (La Terza Luna)	(RCA Victor 47-8169)	.75	3.00	63
LET THE PEOPLE TALK/In The Chapel With You	(RCA Victor 47-8511)	1.00	4.00	65
LITTLE DEVIL/I Must Be Dreaming	(RCA Victor 47-7874)	.75	3.00	61
LITTLE DEVIL/I Must Be Dreaming	(RCA Victor 37-7874)	3.75	15.00	61
(Compact 33 single)				
LOVE IS THE SHADOWS/(Baby) Don't Let It Mess Your Mind	(Rocket 40543)	.50	2.00	76
NEXT DOOR TO AN ANGEL/I Belong To You	(RCA Victor 47-8086)	.75	3.00	62
OH! CAROL/One Way Ticket	(RCA Victor 47-7595)	1.00	4.00	59
OH! CAROL/One Way Ticket	(RCA Victor 61-7595)	2.50	10.00	59
(Stereo single issue)				
OH DELILAH/Neil's Twist	(Pyramid 623)	2.00	8.00	62
RAINY JANE/Jeannine	(S.G.C. 008)	1.50	6.00	
RING A ROCKIN'/Fly Don't Fly On Me	(Guyden 2004)	5.00	20.00	58
RING-A-ROCKIN'/Fly Don't Fly On Me	(Legion 133)	8.75	35.00	58
SAD, SAD STORY/	(Elektra 46017)	.50	2.00	78
STAIRWAY TO HEAVEN/Forty Winks Away	(RCA Victor 47-7709)	1.00	4.00	60
STAIRWAY TO HEAVEN/Forty Winks Away	(RCA Victor 61-7709)	2.50	10.00	60
(Stereo single issue)				
STAR CROSSED LOVERS/We Had A Good Thing Goin'	(S.G.C. 005)	1.50	6.00	
STEPPIN' OUT (With Elton John)/I Let You Walk Away	(Rocket 40582)	.50	2.00	76
SUNNY/She'll Never Be You	(RCA Victor 47-8282)	1.00	4.00	64
SWEET LITTLE YOU/I Found My World In You	(RCA Victor 47-7922)	.75	3.00	61
SWEET LITTLE YOU/I Found My World In You	(RCA Victor 37-7922)	3.75	15.00	61
(Compact 33 single)				
THAT'S WHEN THE MUSIC TAKES ME/Standing On The Inside	(Rocket 40426)	.50	2.00	75
TOO LATE/I Hope He Breaks Your Heart	(RCA Victor 47-8453)	1.00	4.00	64
WORLD THROUGH A TEAR, THE/High On A Mountain (Deep In A Valley)	(RCA Victor 47-8637)	1.00	4.00	65
YOU GOTTA LEARN YOUR RHYTHM & BLUES/Crying My Heart Out For You	(RCA Victor 47-7530)	1.25	5.00	59
YOU GOTTA MAKE YOUR OWN SUNSHINE/Perfect Strangers	(Rocket 40614)	.50	2.00	76
YOU MEAN EVERYTHING TO ME/Run Samson Run	(RCA Victor 47-7781)	.75	3.00	60
YOU MEAN EVERYTHING TO ME/Run Samson Run	(RCA Victor 61-7781)	2.50	10.00	60
(Stereo single issue)				
Also see Tokens, The				
SEDAKA, Neil & Dara				
SHOULD'VE NEVER LET YOU GO/	(Elektra 46615)	.50	2.00	80
SEEDS, The (Featuring Sky Saxon)				
BAD PART OF TOWN/Wish Me Up	(MGM K-14163)	1.00	4.00	69
CAN'T SEEM TO MAKE YOU MINE/Daisy Mae	(GNP Crescendo 354)	2.00	8.00	65
CAN'T SEEM TO MAKE YOU MINE/I Tell Myself	(GNP Crescendo 354)	1.00	4.00	67
DID HE DIE/Love Is A Summer Basket	(MGM K-14190)	1.00	4.00	70
MR. FARMER/No Escape	(GNP Crescendo 383)	1.25	5.00	67
MR. FARMER/Up In Her Room	(GNP Crescendo 383)	1.25	5.00	67
900 MILLION DAILY/Satisfy You	(GNP Crescendo 408)	1.25	5.00	68
OTHER PLACE, THE/Try To Understand	(GNP Crescendo 370)	1.50	6.00	65
PUSHIN' TOO HARD/Try To Understand	(GNP Crescendo 372)	1.00	4.00	66
("Pushin' Too Hard" was originally issued as "You're Pushing Too Hard")				
THOUSAND SHADOWS, A/March Of The Flower Children	(GNP Crescendo 394)	1.25	5.00	67
WILD BLOOD/Fallin' Off The Edge Of The World	(GNP Crescendo 422)	1.25	5.00	69
WIND BLOWS YOUR HAIR, THE/Six Dreams	(GNP Crescendo 398)	1.25	5.00	67
YOU'RE PUSHING TOO HARD/Out Of The Question	(GNP Crescendo 364)	2.00	8.00	65
SEEGER, Pete (Of The Weavers)				
LITTLE BOXES/Mail Myself To You	(Columbia 4-42940)	.75	3.00	63
SEEKERS, The (Featuring Judy Durham)				
CARNIVAL IS OVER, THE/We Shall Not Be Moved	(Capitol 5531)	.75	3.00	65
GEORGY GIRL/When The Stars Begin To Fall	(Capitol 5756)	.75	3.00	66
I'LL NEVER FIND ANOTHER YOU/Open Up Them Pearly Gates	(Capitol 5383)	.75	3.00	65
LIGHT FROM THE LIGHTHOUSE/Chilly Wind	(Marvel 1060)	1.00	4.00	65
LOVE IS KIND, LOVE IS WINE/All I Can Remember	(Capitol 2122)	.75	3.00	68
MORNING TOWN RIDE/Walk With Me	(Capitol 5787)	.75	3.00	67
MYRA (SHAKE UP THE PARTY)/Wild Rover	(Amos 711)	.75	3.00	69
ON THE OTHER SIDE/I Wish You Could Be Here	(Capitol 5974)	.75	3.00	67
SOME DAY, ONE DAY/Nobody Knows The Trouble I've Seen	(Capitol 5622)	.75	3.00	66
WHEN THE GOOD APPLES FALL/Myra	(Capitol 2013)	.75	3.00	67
WORLD OF OUR OWN, A/Sinner Man	(Capitol 5430)	.75	3.00	65
Also see New Seekers, The				
SEGER, Bob				
BEAUTIFUL LOSER/Fine Memory	(Capitol 4062)	.75	3.00	75
BEAUTIFUL LOSER/Travelin' Man	(Capitol 4300)	.50	2.00	76
EAST SIDE STORY/East Side Sound	(Cameo 438)	1.00	4.00	66
EAST SIDE STORY/East Side Sound	(Hideout 1013)	3.00	12.00	
GET OUT OF DENVER/Long Song Comin'	(Palladium 1205)	.50	2.00	74
HEAVY MUSIC (PART 1)/Heavy Music (Part 2)	(Ankco 4017)	.50	2.00	72
HEAVY MUSIC (PART 1)/Heavy Music (Part 2)	(Cameo 494)	1.00	4.00	67
HOLLYWOOD NIGHTS/Brave Strangers	(Capitol 4618)	.50	2.00	78
IF I WERE A CARPENTER/Jesse James	(Palladium 1079)	.50	2.00	72
IVORY/The Lost Song (Love Needs To Be Loved)	(Capitol 2480)	.50	2.00	69
KATMANDU/Black Night	(Capitol 4116)	.50	2.00	75
LONELY MAN/Innervenus Eyes	(Capitol 2640)	.75	3.00	70
LOOKIN' BACK/Highway Child	(Capitol 3187)	.75	3.00	71
LUCIFER/Big River	(Capitol 2748)	.75	3.00	70
MAINSTREET/Jody Girl	(Capitol 4422)	.50	2.00	77
MIDNIGHT RIDER/	(Palladium 571)	.75	3.00	71
NEED YA/Seen Alot Of Floors	(Palladium 1171)	.75	3.00	73
NIGHT MOVES/Ship Of Fools	(Capitol 4369)	.50	2.00	76
NOAH/Lennie Johnson	(Capitol 2576)	.75	3.00	69
NUTBUSH CITY LIMITS/Lookin' Back	(Capitol 4269)	.50	2.00	76
NUTBUSH CITY LIMITS/Travelin' Man	(Capitol 4183)	.75	3.00	75
OLD TIME ROCK & ROLL/Sunspot Baby	(Capitol 4702)	.50	2.00	79
PERSECUTION SMITH/Chain' Smokin'	(Abkco 4016)	.50	2.00	75
PERSECUTION SMITH/Chain' Smokin'	(Hideout 1014)	3.00	12.00	68
RAMBLIN' GAMBLIN' MAN/Tales Of Lucy Blue	(Capitol 2297)	.75	3.00	68
ROCK & ROLL NEVER FORGETS/The Fire Down Below	(Capitol 4449)	.50	2.00	77
ROSALIE/Neon Sky	(Palladium 1143)	.75	3.00	73
SOCK IT TO ME SANTA/Florida Time	(Cameo 444)	1.00	4.00	66
STILL THE SAME/Feel Like A Number	(Capitol 4581)	.50	2.00	78
TURN ON YOUR LOVE LIGHT/Who Do You Love	(Reprise 1117)	.75	3.00	72

TITLE/FLIP — LABEL & NO. — GOOD — NEAR MINT — YR.

2 + 2=?/Death Row (Capitol 2143) .75 3.00 68
UMC/This Old House (Palladium 1316) .75 3.00 74
WE'VE GOT TONIGHT/Ain't Got No Money (Capitol 4653) .50 2.00 78
This artists' releases may also be shown as by The Bob Seger System, Bob Seger & The Last Heard, or Bob Seger & The Silver Bullet Band.

SELECTIONS, The (Featuring Al Reno)
GUARDIAN ANGEL/Soft & Sweet (Antone 101) 2.50 10.00
GUARDIAN ANGEL/Soft & Sweet (Mona Lee 129) 2.00 8.00
Also see Fields, Chester

SELF, Ronnie
AIN'T I'M A DOG/Rocky Road Blues (Columbia 4-40989) 2.50 10.00 57
BIG BLON' BABY/Date Bait (Columbia 4-41166) 2.50 10.00 58
BLESS MY BROKEN HEART/Houdini (Kapp 546) 1.00 4.00 63
BOP-A-LENA/I Ain't Goin' Nowhere (Columbia 4-41101) 2.50 10.00 58
HIGH ON SELF/The Road Keeps Winding (Amy 11009) .75 3.00 68
I'VE BEEN THERE/So High (Decca 31131) 1.00 4.00 60
INSTANT MAN/Some Things You Can't Change (Decca 31351) 1.00 4.00 62
OH ME OH MY/Past, Present & Future (Decca 31431) 1.00 4.00 62
THIS MUST BE THE PLACE/Big Town (Decca 30958) 1.00 4.00 59

SELLERS, Peter
AFTER THE FOX (With the Hollies)/
Fox Trot (Instrumental) (United Artists 50079) 2.50 10.00 65
BANGERS & MASH/Goodness Gracious Me (Capitol 4505) 1.25 5.00 61
(With Sophia Loren)
DROP OF THE HARD STUFF/I'm So Ashamed (Capitol 4159) 1.25 5.00 59
HARD DAY'S NIGHT, A/Help! (Capitol 5580) 1.00 4.00 66

SENA, Tommy, & The Val-Monts
ONIONS (REMIND ME OF YOU)/The Wobble (Valmont 905) 5.00 20.00

SENATOR BOBBY (Bill Minkin)
CONGRESSIONAL RECORD/Hardly-Worthit Melody (Parkway 150) 1.00 4.00 67
(Shown as by The Hardly Worthit Players)
MELLOW YELLOW/White Christmas-3:00 Weather Report (Parkway 137) 1.25 5.00 67
(With Senator McKinley)
WILD THING/Wild Thing (By Senator McKinley) (Parkway 127) 1.00 4.00 66

SENATOR BOLLIVAR E. GASSAWAY
SENATOR BOLLIVAR E. GASSAWAY
FOR PRESIDENT/ (RCA Victor 47-7743) 1.00 4.00 60

SENATOR MC KINLEY: see Senator Bobby

SENIORS, The
CINDY/No Surfin' Round Here (ABC-Paramount 10736) 1.25 5.00 65

SENSATIONAL ALEX HARVEY BAND, The
DELILAH/ (Atlantic 3293) .50 2.00 74
GANG BANG/Swamp Snake (Vertigo 113) .50 2.00 74
SGT. FURY/Tomahawk Kid (Vertigo 200) .50 2.00 75

SENTINALS, The
BIG SURF/Sunset Beach (Del Fi 4197) 1.00 4.00 63
COPY CAT WALK/Roughshod (Admiral 900) 1.00 4.00 63
INFINITY/Encineda (Era 3117) 1.00 4.00 63
(Shown as by the Sentinal Six)
LATIN SOUL/Christmas Eve (Era 3097) 1.00 4.00 62
TELL ME/Hit The Road (Westco 14) 1.00 4.00 63
Instrumentals

SEQUINS, The
TO BE YOUNG/Mountains, The (Cameo 161) 1.00 4.00 59

SERENDIPITY SINGERS, The
ANOTHER SIDE TO THIS LIFE/Maybe, Baby (Philips 40385) .75 3.00 66
AUTUMN WIND/Same Old Reason (Philips 40236) .75 3.00 64
BEANS IN MY EARS/Sailin' Away (Philips 40198) .75 3.00 64
DON'T LET THE RAIN COME DOWN (CROOKED LITTLE MAN)/
Freedom's Star (Philips 40175) .75 3.00 64
FRANKIE & JOHNNY (New)/
Down Where The Four Winds Blow (Philips 40215) .75 3.00 64
LITTLE BROTHER/Bells Of Rhymney (Philips 40309) .75 3.00 65
LITTLE BROWN JUG/High North Star (Philips 40246) .75 3.00 64
MY HEART KEEPS FOLLOWING YOU/Rider (Philips 40273) .75 3.00 65
WE BELONG TOGETHER/Run, Run Chicken Run (Philips 40292) .75 3.00 65
WHEN PEACHES GROW ON LILAC TREES/Plastic (Philips 40331) .75 3.00 65

SERINO, Al
ALONE AM I/Mabel (Al-Fred 1005) 1.00 4.00

SESSIONS, Little Ronnie
KEEP A KNOCKIN'/Lot On My Mind (Pike 5908) 1.00 4.00 61

SETTLE, Mike (Of The First Edition)
IF YOU REALLY LOVE ME/ (Uni 55333) .75 3.00 72
SATURDAY'S ONLY/The Nights Of Your Life (Uni 55309) .75 3.00 71

SEVENTEENS, The
STEADY GUY/Bug Out (Golden Crest 503) 2.00 8.00

7TH COURT, The
ONE EYED WITCH/Shake (Prophonics 2027) 1.25 5.00

SEVILLE, David (Ross Bagdasarian)
ARMEN'S THEME/Carousel In Rome (Liberty 55041) 1.00 4.00 56
BIRD ON MY HEAD, THE/Hey There Moon (Liberty 55140) 1.00 4.00 58
FREDDY, FREDDY/
Oh Judge, Your Honor, Dear Sir, Sweet-Heart (Liberty 55314) 1.00 4.00 61
GOTTA GET TO YOUR HOUSE/Camel Rock (Liberty 55079) 1.00 4.00 57
GOTTA GET TO YOUR HOUSE/Camel Rock (Liberty 55079) 1.25 5.00 57
(Picture sleeve)
JUDY/Maria From Madrid (Liberty 55193) 1.00 4.00 59
LITTLE BRASS BAND/Take Five (Liberty 55153) 1.00 4.00 58
WITCH DOCTOR/Don't Whistle At Me (Liberty 55132) 1.00 4.00 58
Also see Alfi & Harry
Also see Chipmunks, The

SEX PISTOLS, The
PRETTY VACANT/Sub-mission (Warner Bros. 8516) .50 2.00 78

SEXTON, Patsy
CHRISTMAS WITHOUT ELVIS/Christmas Card For Elvis (Delta 1151) .50 2.00 77

SHACKLEFORDS, The
STRANGER IN YOUR TOWN, A/Big River (Mercury 72112) .75 3.00 63
Group members: Lee Hazelwood, Marty Cooper, Albert Stone & Garcia Nitzsche, wife of Jack Nitzsche.
Also see A Date With Soul
Also see Moments, The

SHADDEN & THE KING LEARS
ALL I WANT IS YOU/ (Arbel 1061) .75 3.00

SHADES, The
SPLASHIN'/ (Scottie 1309) .75 3.00

SHADES OF BLUE, The
HAPPINESS/The Night (Impact 1015) .75 3.00 66
HOW DO YOU SAVE A DYING LOVE/ (Impact 1026) .75 3.00 67
LONELY SUMMER/With This Ring (Impact 1014) .75 3.00 66
OH HOW HAPPY/Little Orphan Boy (Impact 1007) .75 3.00 66

SHADES OF JOY, The
BYE, BYE, LOVE/Andy's Dream (Fontana 1637) 1.00 4.00 69
FLUTE IN A QUARRY/Together (Douglas 6505) 1.00 4.00
SOUL TRUTH/I Do Like Rock (Fontana 1659) 1.00 4.00 69

SHADOWS, The
UNDER THE STARS OF LOVE/Jungle Fever (Del Fi 4109) 1.25 5.00 58

SHADOWS, The
DANCE ON/The Rumble (Atlantic 2177) .75 3.00 62
DON'T MAKE MY BABY BLUE/My Grandfathers Clock (Epic 9848) .75 3.00 65
FRIGHTENED CITY, THE/FBI (Atlantic 2111) .75 3.00 61
GUITAR TANGO/What A Lovely Tune (Atlantic 2166) .75 3.00 62
KON-TIKI/Man Of Mystery (Atlantic 2135) .75 3.00 62
MARY ANNE/Chu Chi (Epic 9793) .75 3.00 65
RHYTHM & GREENS/The Miracle (Atlantic 2257) .75 3.00 64
RISE & FALL OF FLINGEL BLUNT, THE/
Theme For Young Lovers (Atlantic 2235) .75 3.00 64
SATURDAY DANCE/Lonesome Fella (ABC Paramount 10073) 1.00 4.00 60
SINGRAY/Alice In Sunderland (Epic 9826) .75 3.00 65
STARS FELL ON STOCKTON/Wonderful Land (Atlantic 2146) .75 3.00 62
Also see Richard, Cliff

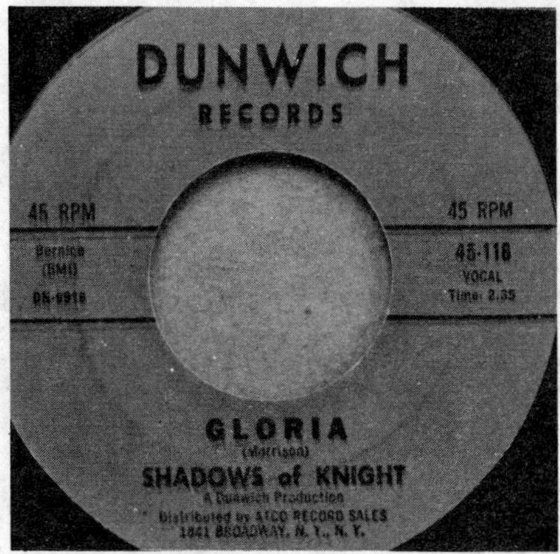

SHADOWS OF KNIGHT, The
BAD LITTLE WOMAN/Gospel Zone (Dunwich 128) 1.25 5.00 66
BEHEMOTH, THE/Willie Jean (Dunwich 151) 1.25 5.00 67
GLORIA/Dark Side (Dunwich 116) 1.25 5.00 66
(Label does not read "Distributed by Atco")
GLORIA/Dark Side (Dunwich 116) 1.00 4.00 66
(Label reads "Distributed by Atco")
GLORIA '69/Spaniard At My Door (Atco 6634) 1.25 5.00 69
I AM THE HUNTER/Warwick Court Affair (Atco 6676) 1.25 5.00 69
I'M GONNA MAKE YOU MINE/I'll Make You Sorry (Dunwich 141) 1.25 5.00 66
MY FIRE DEPARTMENT NEEDS A FIREMAN/Run, Run (Super K SK-10) 1.00 4.00 69
OH YEAH/Light Bulb Blues (Dunwich 122) 1.00 4.00 66
SHAKE/From Way Out To Way Under (Team TM-520) 1.00 4.00 68
SOMEONE LIKE ME/Three For Love (Dunwich 167) 1.25 5.00 67

SHAFTO, Bobby
SHE'S MY GIRL/Wonderful You (Rust 5082) .75 3.00 64

SHAGGY BOYS, The
BEHIND THOSE STAINED GLASS WINDOWS/
That's The Only Way (United Artists 50135) 1.50 6.00 67
IN THE MORNING/Stop The Clock (Red Bird 10-074) 1.50 6.00 66
YOU & ME/Joy In The Morning (United Artists 50100) 1.50 6.00 66
Also see Ricky & The Vacels

SHAG, The
STOP & LISTEN/Melissa (Capitol 5995) .75 3.00 68

SHAGNASTY, Boliver
TAPPING THAT THING/Yo Yo (Fun 10000) .75 3.00

SHAGS, The
AS LONG AS I HAVE YOU/Tell Me (Cameo 470) .75 3.00 67
AS LONG AS I HAVE YOU/Tell Me (Kayden 407) 1.25 5.00 67
BREATHE IN MY EAR/Easy Street (Kayden 408) 1.25 5.00 67
CRYING/You're A Loser (Jo-Jo 101) 1.25 5.00
I CALL YOUR NAME/Hideaway (Laurie 3353) 1.00 4.00 67
WAY I CARE, THE/Ring Around The Rosie (Palmer 5010) 1.00 4.00

SHAKERS, The
ONE WONDERFUL MOMENT/Love, Love, Love (ABC 10960) 1.00 4.00 67
TICKET TO RIDE/Break It All (Audio Fidelity 119) 1.00 4.00 66

SHALONS, The
ANGEL/True Love Came My Way (Ronnie 203) 1.00 4.00

SHA NA NA
JUST LIKE ROMEO & JULIET/ (Kama Sutra 602) .75 3.00 73
MAYBE I'M OLD FASHIONED/Stroll All Night (Kama Sutra 592) .75 3.00 72
ONLY ONE SONG/Yakety Yak (Kama Sutra 522) .75 3.00 71
PAY DAY/ (Kama Sutra 507) .75 3.00 70
ROCK 'N' ROLL IS HERE TO STAY/
Greased Lightnin' (By John Travolta) (RSO 909) .50 2.00 78
TOP FORTY/I Wonder Why (Kama Sutra 528) .75 3.00 71
Also see Eddie & The Evergreens
Also see Gross, Henry

SHANES, The
CHRIS CRAFT #9/Time (Capitol 5963) .75 3.00 67

SHANGO
COWBOYS & INDIANS/Sunshine Superman (A&M 1086) .75 3.00 69
DAY AFTER DAY (IT'S SLIPPIN' AWAY)/Mescalito (A&M 1014) .75 3.00 69
GOOMGAY/Hi-Way Song (Crescendo 407) .75 3.00 69
LET'S GET DRUNK & TRUCK/Gunji (A&M 1129) .75 3.00 69
LJUBA LJUBA/Mama Lion (A&M 1060) .75 3.00 69

SHANGRI-LAS, The
GIVE HIM A GREAT BIG KISS/Twist & Shout (Red Bird 10-018) .75 3.00 64
GIVE US YOUR BLESSINGS/Heaven Only Knows (Red Bird 10-030) .75 3.00 65
HATE TO SAY I TOLD YOU SO/Wishing Well (Scepter 1291) 1.00 4.00 65
HATE TO SAY I TOLD YOU SO/Wishing Well (Spokane 4006) 1.50 6.00 64
HE CRIED/Dressed In Black (Red Bird 10-053) 1.25 5.00 66
I CAN NEVER GO HOME ANYMORE/Bull Dog (Red Bird 10-043) .75 3.00 65
LEADER OF THE PACK/What Is Love (Red Bird 10-014) .75 3.00 64
LONG LIVE OUR LOVE/Sophisticated Boom Boom (Red Bird 10-048) 1.00 4.00 66
MAYBE/Shout (Red Bird 10-019) 1.00 4.00 64
OUT IN THE STREETS/Boy, The (Red Bird 10-025) .75 3.00 65
PAST, PRESENT & FUTURE/
Love You More Than Yesterday (Red Bird 10-068) .75 3.00 66
PAST, PRESENT & FUTURE/Paradise (Red Bird 10-068) .75 3.00 66
REMEMBER (WALKIN' IN THE SAND)/It's Easier (Red Bird 10-008) .75 3.00 64
RIGHT NOW & NOT LATER/Train From Kansas City (Red-Bird 10-036) 1.25 5.00 65
SIMON SAYS/Simon Speaks (Smash 1866) 1.00 4.00 63
SWEET SOUND OF SUMMER/I'll Never Learn (Mercury 72645) 1.00 4.00 66
TAKE THE TIME/Footsteps On The Roof (Mercury 72670) 1.00 4.00 67

SHANKAR, Ravi
GET KIRWANI/Pather Panchelli (World Pacific 77871) .50 2.00 70
I AM MISSING YOU/Lust (Dark Horse 10001) .50 2.00 74
(Shown as by Shankar, Family & Friends)
JOI BANGLA/Oh Bhaugowan Raga Mishra-Jhinjhoti (Apple 1838) .75 3.00 71
(Shown as by Ravi Shankar & Chorus)
TRANSMIGRATION/ (Spark 07) .50 2.00 72

SHANNON (Marty Wilde)
ABERGAVENNY/Alice In Blue (Heritage 814) .75 3.00 69
COME BACK & LOVE ME/ (Epic-Magnet 50191) .50 2.00 75
JESAMINE/Lullabye (Heritage 819) .75 3.00 69

SHANNON, Del (Charles Westover)
BIG HURT, THE/I Got It Bad (Liberty 55866) .75 3.00 66
BREAK UP/Why Don't You Tell Him (Amy 925) .75 3.00 65
COMIN' BACK TO ME/Sweet Mary Lou (Dunhill 4193) .75 3.00 69
CRY, BABY, CRY/In My Arms Again (Island 038) .75 3.00 75
CRY MYSELF TO SLEEP/I'm Gonna Move On (Big Top 3112) .75 3.00 62
DO YOU WANT TO DANCE?/This Is All I Have To Give (Amy 911) .75 3.00 64
FROM ME TO YOU/Two Silhouettes (Big Top 3152) 1.25 5.00 63
GEMINI/Magical Musical Box (Liberty 56036) .75 3.00 68
HANDY MAN/Give Her Lots Of Lovin' (Amy 905) .75 3.00 64
HATS OFF TO LARRY/Don't Gild The Lily Lily (Big Top 3075) .75 3.00 61
HEY LITTLE GIRL/I Don't Care Anymore (Big Top 3091) .75 3.00 61
HEY LITTLE STAR/For A Little While (Liberty 55889) .75 3.00 66
I WON'T BE THERE/Ginny In The Mirror (Big Top 3098) .75 3.00 62
KEEP SEARCHIN' (WE'LL FOLLOW THE SUN)/Broken Promises (Amy 915) .75 3.00 64
LED ALONG/I Can't Be True (Liberty 55961) .75 3.00 67
LITTLE TOWN FLIRT/The Wamboo (Big Top 3131) .75 3.00 62
MARY JANE/Stains On My Letter (Amy 897) .75 3.00 64
MOVE IT ON OVER/She Still Remembers Tony (Amy 937) .75 3.00 65
RAIN DROPS/You Don't Love Me (Liberty 56070) .75 3.00 68
RUNAWAY/He Cheated (Liberty 55993) .75 3.00 67
(Recorded live)
RUNAWAY/Jody (Big Top 3067) .75 3.00 61
RUNNIN' ON BACK/Thinkin' It Over (Liberty 56018) .75 3.00 68
SHE/What Makes You Run (Liberty 55939) .75 3.00 67
SISTER ISABELLE/Colorado Rain (Dunhill 4224) .75 3.00 69
SHOW ME/Never Thought I Could (Liberty 55894) .75 3.00 66
SUE'S GOTTA BE MINE/Now That She's Gone (Berlee 501) 1.00 4.00 63
SO LONG BABY/The Answer To Everything (Big Top 3083) .75 3.00 61
STRANGER IN TOWN/Over You (Amy 919) .75 3.00 65
SWISS MAID, THE/You Never Talked About Me (Big Top 3117) .75 3.00 62
TELL HER NO/Restless (Island 021) .75 3.00 75
THAT'S THE WAY LOVE IS/Time Of The Day (Berlee 502) 1.00 4.00
TWO KINDS OF TEARDROPS/Kelly (Big Top 3143) .75 3.00 63
UNDER MY THUMB/She Was Mine (Liberty 55904) .75 3.00 66
Also see Maximillian

SHANNON, Jackie: see De Shannon, Jackie

SHANNON, Pat
BACK TO DREAMIN' AGAIN/Moody (Uni 55191) .50 2.00
SHE SLEEPS ALONE/Candy Apple & Cotton Candy (Warner Bros. 7210) .75 3.00 68
SNAKE & THE BOOKWORM/Summertime's Coming (Decca 30905) .75 3.00 59

SHAPIRO, Helen
WALKIN' BACK TO HAPPINESS/Kiss 'N Run (Capitol 4662) .75 3.00 61

SHARELL, Jerry
EVERYBODY KNOWS/That's My Business (Alanna 560) 1.50 6.00 59

SHARKS, The
BIG SURF/Spookareno (Sapien 1003) 1.00 4.00 63
(Instrumental)

SHARKS, The
BLUEBERRY HILL/I Love You For Sentimental Reasons (Clifton 10) .50 2.00
SHIRLEY/I'll Be Home (Broadcast 1128) 1.00 4.00
YOU BELONG TO ME/The Glory Of Love (Broadcast 1132) 1.00 4.00
Also see Five Sharks, The
Also see Goldbugs, The

SHARMETTES, The
ANSWER ME/My Dream (King 5648) 1.25 5.00 62

SHARON MARIE (Of The Honeys)
RUNAROUND LOVER/Summertime (Capitol 5064) 10.00 40.00 63
THINKIN' BOUT YOU BABY/Story Of My Life (Capitol 5195) 10.00 40.00 64

SHARP, Dee Dee (Dione LaRue)
DO THE BIRD/Lover Boy (Cameo 244) .75 3.00 63
GRAVY/Baby Cakes (Cameo 219) .75 3.00 62
I REALLY LOVE YOU/Standing In The Need Of Love (Cameo 375) .75 3.00 65
IT'S A SUNNY SITUATION MASHED POTATO TIME/
Set My Heart At Ease (Cameo 212) .75 3.00 62
RIDE/Night (Cameo 230) .75 3.00 62
ROCK ME IN THE CRADLE OF LOVE/You'll Never Be Mine (Cameo 260) .75 3.00 63
WHERE DID I GO WRONG/Willyam, Willyam (Cameo 296) .75 3.00 64
WILD/Why Doncha Ask Me (Cameo 274) .75 3.00 63

SHARPE & KERLIN
BIG GOOF, THE/Canaveral Rock By The Blast (Cape 1999) 2.50 10.00
(Novelty/Break-in)

SHARPE, Ray
BERMUDA/Gonna Let It Go This Time (Jamie 1149) .75 3.00 60
JUSTINE/On The Street Where You Live (Trey 3011) .75 3.00 61
KEWPIE DOLL/Givin' Up (Jamie 1164) .75 3.00 60
LINDA LU/The Bus Song (Gregmark 14) .75 3.00 62
LINDA LU/Monkey's Uncle (Jamie 1128) 1.25 5.00 59
LINDA LU/Red Sails In The Sunset (Jamie 1128) 1.00 4.00 59
RED SAILS IN THE SUNSET/For You My Love (Jamie 1155) .75 3.00 60
T.A. (TEEN AGE) BLUES/Long John (Jamie 1138) 1.00 4.00 58
THAT'S THE WAY I FEEL/Oh, My Baby's Gone (Dot 15974) 1.00 4.00 59

SHARPEES, The
TIRED OF BEING LONELY/ (One-derful 4839) .75 3.00 63

SHARPLES, Bob (Robert Frederick Standish Sharples)
SADIE'S SHAWL/Hurricane Boogie (London 1661) 1.00 4.00 56

SHARPS, The
DOUBLE CLUTCH/If Love Is What You Want (Star-Hi 10406) 1.00 4.00 60
GIG-A-LENE/Here's My Heart (Jamie 1114) 1.00 4.00 59
TEENAGE GIRL/We Three (Win 702) 1.00 4.00

SHAW, Georgie
TILL WE TWO ARE ONE/Honeycomb (Decca 28937) 1.00 4.00 54

TITLE/FLIP	LABEL & NO.	GOOD	NEAR MINT	YR.
SHAW, Sandie				
GIRL DON'T COME/I'd Be Far Better Off Without You	(Reprise 0342)	.75	3.00	65
HOW CAN YOU TELL/If You Ever Need Me	(Reprise 0427)	.75	3.00	65
I'LL STOP AT NOTHING/Stop Feeling Sorry For Yourself	(Reprise 0394)	.75	3.00	65
LONG LIVE LOVE/I've Heard About Him	(Reprise 0375)	.75	3.00	65
LOVE IS FOR THE TWO OF US/Wight Is Wight	(RCA 74-0370)	.75	3.00	69
MONSIEUR DUPONT/Voice In The Crowd	(RCA 74-0118)	.75	3.00	69
NOTHING COMES EASY/Stop Before You Start	(Reprise 0488)	.75	3.00	66
(THERE'S) ALWAYS SOMETHING THERE TO REMIND ME/ Don't You Know	(Reprise 0320)	.75	3.00	64
TOMORROW/Hurting You	(Reprise 0449)	.75	3.00	66
SHAW, Timmy				
GONNA SEND YOU BACK TO GEORGIA/I'm A Lonely Guy	(Wand 146)	.75	3.00	64
SHAYNE, Charity				
AIN'T IT BABE/Then You Try	(Autumn 22)	1.25	5.00	65
SHEAN & JENKYNS				
GOOFY FOOTER HO-DAD/Do The Commercial	(GNP Crescendo 197)	1.00	4.00	63
SHEARS, Billy, & The All Americans				
BROTHER PAUL/Message To Seymour	(Silver Fox 121)	1.25	5.00	
SHEEN, Bobby (Of Bob B. Soxx & The Blue Jeans)				
HOW MANY NIGHTS-HOW MANY DAYS/ How Can We Ever	(Liberty 55459)	1.25	5.00	62
MY SHOES KEEP WALKING BACK TO YOU/ I Want You For My Sweetheart	(Dimension 1043)	1.00	4.00	65
SHEEP				
DYNAMITE/I Feel Good	(Boom 60007)	2.50	10.00	66
HIDE & SEEK/Twelve Months Later	(Boom 60000)	2.50	10.00	65
Also see Strangeloves, The				
SHELBY, Ernie				
TONIGHT YOU BELONG TO ME/That I'm In Love With You	(Capitol 4879)	.75	3.00	62
SHELDON (With the Overland Swingin' Top Brass)				
ENLISTMENT TWIST, THE/Dream Girl Waltz	(Crow Music 1301)	.75	3.00	
SHELTON, Anne				
LAY DOWN YOUR ARMS/Madonna In Blue	(Columbia 40759)	1.00	4.00	56
SHELTON, Gary				
GOODBYE LITTLE DARLIN' GOODBYE/Stop The World	(Mark 143)	20.00	80.00	60
KISSIN' AT THE DRIVE-IN/Yours Till I Die	(Mercury 71310)	3.00	12.00	58
SHENENDOAH 3, The				
BALLAD OF MARILYN MONROE, THE/Sundown	(Goal 501)	1.25	5.00	62
SHEPHERD, Johnny				
HOW BLUE MY HEART/Boom Boom Boomerang	(Tilden 3001)	1.25	5.00	
SHEPHERD SISTERS, The				
ALONE (ORIGINAL VERSION)/Alone (New Version) (Promotional issue)	(York 50002)	.75	3.00	65
ALONE/Congratulations To Someone	(Lance 125)	1.00	4.00	57
DON'T MENTION MY NAME/What Makes Little Girls Cry	(Atlantic 2176)	.75	3.00	63
GETTIN' READY FOR FREDDY/The Best Thing There Is (Shown as by the Sheppard Sisters)	(Mercury 71244)	1.00	4.00	57
HERE COMES HEAVEN AGAIN/I Think It's Time	(Warwick 511)	1.00	4.00	59
HEART & SOUL/(It's No) Sin	(MGM 12766)	1.00	4.00	59
LOLITA YA YA/	(United Artists 456)	.75	3.00	62
REMEMBER THAT CRAZY ROCK 'N' ROLL TUNE/ I Walked Beside The Sea	(Melba 108)	1.00	4.00	57
ROCK & ROLL CHA CHA/Gone With The Wind	(Capitol 2706)	1.25	5.00	54
ROCK & ROLL CHA CHA/Gone With The Wind	(Melba 101)	1.00	4.00	57
TALK IS CHEAP/ (Take A Look At My Guy) The Greatest Lover	(Atlantic 2195)	.75	3.00	63
SHEPARD, Red, & The Flock				
SHE'S A GRABBER/I Can't Hold On	(Philips 40398)	.75	3.00	66
SHEPPARD, Buddy, & The Holidays (The Belmonts)				
BRAHMS LULLABYE/(Time To Dream) My Love Is Real	(Sabina 506)	2.50	10.00	62
NOW IT'S ALL OVER/That Back Sound	(Sabina 510)	3.00	12.00	63
Also see Tony & The Holidays				
SHEPPARD, Neil				
YOU CAN'T GO FAR WITHOUT A GUITAR (UNLESS YOU'RE RINGO STARR)/Betty Is The Girl For You	(Almont 314)	1.50	6.00	64
SHERBET				
GIMME LOVE/	(MCA 40720)	.50	2.00	77
HIGH ROLLIN'/Rock Me Gently	(MCA 40821)	.50	2.00	77
HOWZAT/Motor Of Love	(MCA 40610)	.50	2.00	76
IF I HAD MY WAY/	(MCA 40653)	.50	2.00	76
MIDSUMMER MADNESS/	(MCA 40785)	.50	2.00	77
Also see Highway				
SHERIDAN, Bobby: see Rich, Charlie				
SHERIDAN, Mike, & The Nightriders				
PLEASE MR. POSTMAN/In Love	(Liverpool Sound 902)	11.25	45.00	
SHERIDAN, Tony & The Beat Brothers: see Beatles, The				
SHERIFF & THE RAVELS				
SHOMBALOR/Lonely One	(Vee Jay 306)	2.00	8.00	59
SHERMAN, Allan				
CRAZY DOWNTOWN/The Drop-Outs March	(Warner Bros. 5614)	1.00	4.00	65
DRINKING MAN'S DIET, THE/ The Laarge Daark Aard-Vark Song	(Warner Bros. 5672)	1.00	4.00	65
END OF A SYMPHONY (PART 1)/ End Of A Symphony (Part 2)	(RCA Victor 47-8412)	1.00	4.00	64
HELLO MUDDUH, HELLO FADDUH/ Here's To The Crabgrass	(Warner Bros. 5378)	1.25	5.00	63
HELLO MUDDUH, HELLO FADDUH/Rat Fink	(Warner Bros. 5378)	.75	3.00	63
HELLO MUDDUH, HELLO FADDUH! (1964 VERSION)/ Hello Muddah, Hello Fadduh (1963 Version)	(Warner Bros. 5449)	1.00	4.00	64
I HATE THE BEATLES/Grow Mrs. Goldfarb	(Warner Bros. 5490)	1.50	6.00	64
MY SON, THE VAMPIRE/I Can't Dance	(Warner Bros. 5419)	1.00	4.00	64
ODD BALL/His Own Little Island	(Warner Bros. 5806)	1.00	4.00	66
SKIN (HEART)/The Drop-Outs March	(Warner Bros. 5435)	1.00	4.00	64
12 GIFTS OF CHRISTMAS/ You Went The Wrong Way Old King Louie	(Warner Bros. 5406)	1.00	4.00	63
SHERMAN, Bobby				
ANYTHING YOUR LITTLE HEART DESIRES/ Goody Galum-Shus	(Parkway 967)	1.00	4.00	65
COLD GIRL/Think Of Rain	(Epic 10181)	.75	3.00	67
CRIED LIKE A BABY/Is Anybody There	(Metromedia 206)	.50	2.00	71
DRUM, THE/Free Now To Roam	(Metromedia 217)	.50	2.00	71
EARLY IN THE MORNING/	(Metromedia 0100)	.50	2.00	72
EASY COME, EASY GO/Sounds Along The Way	(Metromedia 177)	.50	2.00	70
GETTING TOGETHER/Jennifer	(Metromedia 227)	.50	2.00	71
GOIN' HOME (SING A SONG OF CHRISTMAS CHEER)/ Love's What You're Gettin' For Christmas	(Metromedia 204)	.50	2.00	71
HEY LITTLE GIRL/Well All Right	(Decca 31779)	1.00	4.00	65
HEY MISTER SUN/Two Blind Minds	(Metromedia 188)	.50	2.00	70
IT HURTS ME/Give Me Your Word	(Decca 31741)	1.00	4.00	65
IT HURTS ME/Give Me Your Word (Picture sleeve)	(Decca 31741)	1.50	6.00	65
JULIE, DO YA LOVE ME/Spend Some Time Lovin' Me	(Metromedia 194)	.50	2.00	70
LA LA LA (IF I HAD YOU)/Time	(Metromedia 150)	.50	2.00	69
LITTLE WOMAN/One Too Many Mornings	(Metromedia 121)	.50	2.00	69
TELEGRAMS/I'll Never Tell You	(Condor 1002)	1.00	4.00	
TOGETHER AGAIN/	(Metromedia 240)	.50	2.00	72
WAITING AT THE BUS STOP/Run Away	(Metromedia 222)	.50	2.00	71
YOU MAKE ME HAPPY/Man Overboard	(Decca 31672)	1.00	4.00	64
SHERMAN, Joe				
TOYS IN THE ATTIC/Too Much Heartache (Instrumentals)	(World Artists 1008)	.75	3.00	63
SHERRIL, Billy				
DRAG RACE/Tipsy	(ABC-Paramount 10465)	1.00	4.00	63
THEME FROM "THE INCREDIBLE HULK"/Last Kiss	(Epic 50527)	.50	2.00	78
SHERRYS, The				
POP POP POP-PIE/Your Hand In Mine	(Guyden 2068)	.75	3.00	62
SATURDAY NIGHT/I've Got No One	(Guyden 2084)	.75	3.00	62
SLOP TIME/Let's Stomp Again	(Guyden 2077)	.75	3.00	63
THAT BOY OF MINE/Monk Monk Monkey	(Guyden 2098)	.75	3.00	63
SHERWOOD, Roberta				
LAZY RIVER/This Train	(Decca 29911)	1.00	4.00	56
SHERWOODS, The				
COLD & FROSTY MORNING/ True Love Was Born (With Our Last Goodbye)	(Dot 16540)	3.75	15.00	63
SHEVELLES, The				
I COULD CONQUER THE WORLD/ How Would You Like Me To Love You	(World Artists 1025)	.75	3.00	64
LIKE I LOVE YOU/Ooh Poo Pah Doo	(World Artists 1023)	.75	3.00	64
SHEVETON, Tony				
MILLION DRUMS, A/Dance With Me	(Parrot 40016)	1.00	4.00	67
SHIEKS, The				
BAGHDAD ROCK (PART 1)/Baghdad Rock (Part 2)	(MGM 12876)	.75	3.00	60
BAGHDAD ROCK (PART 1)/Baghdad Rock (Part 2)	(Trine 1101)	1.00	4.00	59
SHIELDS, Billy (Tony Orlando)				
I WAS A BOY (WHEN YOU NEEDED A MAN)/ Moments From Now, Tomorrow	(Harbour 304)	1.50	6.00	
SHILLINGS, The				
IT WAS MY MISTAKE/Not The Least Bit True	(Fantasy 594)	1.25	5.00	67
JUST FOR YOU BABY/Laugh	(Fontana 1543)	1.25	5.00	66
SHILOH				
GOD BROUGHT THE CURTAIN DOWN/Midnight Music	(Shane 001)	.50	2.00	77
SHIN-DIGGERS, The				
SHINDIG/Station Break	(ABC-Paramount 10612)	.75	3.00	64
SHINDIGS, The (The Bobby Fuller Four)				
WOLFMAN/Thunder Reef (Instrumental)	(Mustang 3003)	1.50	6.00	65
SHINDOGS, The (With Delanny & Bonnie Bramlett)				
WHO DO YOU THINK YOU ARE/Yes, I'm Going Home	(Viva 601)	1.00	4.00	66
SHIPLEY, Ellen				
I SURRENDER/Little Sister	(New York Int'l. 11686)	.50	2.00	79
MAN OF THE WORLD/	(New York Int'l. 11775)	.50	2.00	79
SHIRLEY, Don, Trio				
DROWN IN MY OWN TEARS/Lonesome Road	(Cadence 1408)	.75	3.00	61
WATER BOY/Freedom Instrumentals	(Cadence 1392)	.75	3.00	61
SHIRTS, The				
CAN'T CRY ANYMORE/I'm In Love Again	(Capitol 4750)	.50	2.00	79
SHIVA'S HEAD BAND				
COUNTRY BOY/Such A Joy	(Armadillo 811)	2.50	10.00	
DON'T BLAME ME/Extension	(Armadillo 6)	1.50	6.00	76
KALEIDESCOPTIC/Song For Peace	(Ignite 681)	3.75	15.00	67
TAKE ME TO THE MOUNTAINS/	(Armadillo 3)	2.50	10.00	71
SHOCK				
WE WERE THAT NOISE/Gone For Good (Blue plastic)	(Downtown DT-502)	.75	3.00	78
SHOCKING BLUE				
BOOL WEEVIL/	(Colossus 141)	.75	3.00	71
INKPOT/Oh Lord	(MGM 14543)	.75	3.00	73
LONG & LONESOME ROAD/	(Colossus 116)	.75	3.00	70
MIGHTY JOE/I'm A Woman	(Colossus 111)	.75	3.00	70
NEVER MARRY A RAILROAD MAN/	(Colossus 123)	.75	3.00	70
SERENADE/	(Buddah 258)	.75	3.00	71
VENUS/Hot Sand	(Colossus 108)	.75	3.00	69
WHEN I WAS A GIRL/Eve & The Apple	(MGM 14481)	.75	3.00	72
SHOES				
TOO LATE/Now Or Never	(Elektra 46557)	.50	2.00	79
SHOESTRING				
CANDY ANDY/Sloop-De-Hoop-Twine	(20th Century Fox 6706)	1.00	4.00	
SHONDELL, Troy				
GONE/Some People Never Learn	(Everest 2015)	.75	3.00	63
JUST A DREAM/Just Like Me	(Ric 174)	.75	3.00	
LET'S GO ALL THE WAY/Let Me Love You	(TRX 5015)	.75	3.00	69
NA-NE-NO/Just Because	(Liberty 55445)	1.00	4.00	62
SOMETHING'S WRONG IN INDIANA/	(TRX 5019)	.75	3.00	69
TEARS FROM AN ANGEL/Island In The Sky	(Liberty 55398)	1.00	4.00	61
THIS TIME/I Catch Myself Crying (Shown as by Troy Shundell.)	(Gaye 2010)	3.75	15.00	61
THIS TIME/Girl After Girl (Label does not read "Distributed by Liberty Records Sales Corp." Note unusual spelling of label name.)	(Goldcrest 161-A)	2.50	10.00	61
THIS TIME/Girl After Girl (Label does not read "Distributed by Liberty Records Sales Corp.")	(Goldcrest 161)	1.50	6.00	61
THIS TIME/Girl After Girl (Label reads "Distributed by Liberty Records Sales Corp.")	(Goldcrest 161-A)	1.25	5.00	61
THIS TIME/Girl After Girl	(Liberty 55353)	.75	3.00	61
SHORE, Dinah				
BLUES IN ADVANCE/Bella Musica	(RCA Victor 47-4926)	1.00	4.00	52
CHANTEZ-CHANTEZ/Honky Tonk Heart	(RCA Victor 47-6792)	1.00	4.00	57
COME BACK TO MY ARMS/This Must Be The Place	(RCA Victor 47-5725)	1.00	4.00	54
HI-LILI, HI-LO/Keep It A Secret	(RCA Victor 47-4992)	1.00	4.00	52
I COULD HAVE DANCED ALL NIGHT/ What A Heavenly Lover	(RCA Victor 47-6469)	1.00	4.00	56
IF I GIVE MY HEART TO YOU/Tempting	(RCA Victor 47-5838)	1.00	4.00	54
IF I HAVE TO TELL YOU/Never Underestimate	(RCA Victor 47-5863)	1.00	4.00	54
IT'S SO NICE TO HAVE A MAN AROUND THE HOUSE/	(Columbia 38689)	1.25	5.00	50
LOVE & MARRIAGE/Compare	(RCA Victor 47-6266)	1.00	4.00	55
MELODY OF LOVE/ You're Getting To Be A Habit With Me	(RCA Victor 47-5975)	1.00	4.00	55
MY HEART CRIES FOR YOU/Nobody's Chasing Me	(RCA Victor 47-3978)	1.00	4.00	50
PENNY A KISS, A/In Your Arms (With Tony Martin)	(RCA Victor 47-4019)	1.00	4.00	51
STOLEN LOVE/That's All There Is To That	(RCA Victor 47-6360)	1.00	4.00	55
SWEET VIOLETS/If You Turn Me Down	(RCA Victor 47-4174)	1.00	4.00	51
THREE COINS IN THE FOUNTAIN/Pakistan	(RCA Victor 47-5755)	1.00	4.00	54
WHATEVER LOLA WANTS/Church Twice On Sunday	(RCA Victor 47-6077)	1.00	4.00	55
SHORR, Mickey, & The Cutups				
DR. BEN BASEY (Novelty/Break-in)/ Roaring 20's Rag (Instrumental)	(Tuba 8001)	1.00	4.00	62
SHORR'S STREAKERS				
STREAKIN' '74 (Novelty Break/in)/Virgil	(Eastbound 625)	1.00	4.00	74
SHORT STUFF				
EVERYDAY/Merry Christmas Baby	(Third Coast 5127)	.50	2.00	77
TALK IS CHEAP/Bread & Butter Woman	(Age of Aquarius 1547)	.50	2.00	74
SHORT TWINS, The				
TAKE A LOOK/I'm Gonna Love You More & More	(Eagle 1005)	.75	3.00	
SHORTCUTS, The				
DON'T SAY HE'S GONE/I'll Hide My Love	(Carlton 513)	1.00	4.00	59
SHOW STOPPERS, The				
AIN'T NOTHIN' BUT A HOUSE PARTY/ What Can A Man Do	(Heritage 800)	.75	3.00	68
SHUNDEL, Troy: see Shondell, Troy				
SHU-SHU & THE SPACE JOCKEYS				
VISIT TO PLANET EARTH/ Visit To Planet Earth (Part 2) (Novelty/Break-in)	(King of Music 11081)	1.25	5.00	
SHUT DOWNS, The				
BEACH BUGGY/Four On The Floor	(Dimension 1016)	1.00	4.00	63
SHY GUYS, The				
BURGER SONG, THE/	(Burger 5004)	1.25	5.00	
FEEL A WHOLE LOT BETTER/Without You	(Canusa 503)	1.25	5.00	
WE GOTTA GO/Lay It On The Line	(Panik 511)	1.25	5.00	
WHERE YOU BELONG/A Love So True	(Palmer 5003)	1.25	5.00	
SHY-TONES, The				
LOVER'S QUARREL, A/Just For You	(1 Goodspin 401)	2.00	8.00	
Also see Hi-Tones, The				
Also see Trentons, The				
SICKNIKS, The				
PRESIDENTIAL PRESS CONFERENCE (PART 1)/ Presidential Press Conference (Part 2)	(Amy 824)	1.25	5.00	61
WADJA SAY MR. K./Wadja Say Mr. K. (Part 2)	(Amy 831)	1.25	5.00	61
SIDEKICKS, The				
FIFI THE FLEA/Not Now	(RCA Victor 47-8969)	1.00	4.00	66
SUSPICIONS/Up On The Roof	(RCA Victor 47-8864)	1.00	4.00	66
SIDE OF THE ROAD GANG				
SITTIN' BY THE SIDE OF THE ROAD/Suitcase Life	(Capitol 4298)	.50	2.00	76
WHAT AM I DOIN' HANGIN' ROUND/People In Dallas Got Hair	(Capitol 4338)	.50	2.00	76
SIDEWALK SKIPPER BAND, The				
STRAWBERRY TUESDAY/Cynthia At The Garden	(Capitol 2127)	.75	3.00	68
SIDEWALK SURFERS, The				
SKATEBOARD/Fun Last Summer	(Jubilee 5496)	1.25	5.00	65
SIDEWINDERS, The				
SIDEWINDER/Gulley Washer	(Imperial 5572)	1.00	4.00	59
SIDRAN, Ben (Of The Steve Miller Band)				
HEY HEY BABY/	(Blue Thumb 250)	.50	2.00	74
POOR GIRL/Feel Your Groove	(Capitol 3178)	.50	2.00	71
SONG FOR A SUCKER LIKE YOU/	(Arista 0251)	.50	2.00	77
SPACE COWBOY/Think Twice	(Blue Thumb 236)	.50	2.00	73
SIEGEL-SCHWALL BAND, The				
ALWAYS THINKIN' OF YOU DARLIN'/	(Wooden Nickel 0104)	.50	2.00	73
I THINK IT WAS THE WINE/	(Wooden Nickel 0190)	.50	2.00	74
OLD TIME SHIMMY/	(Wooden Nickel 0066)	.50	2.00	73
SIERRA				
STRANGE HERE IN THE NIGHT/	(Mercury 73966)	.50	2.00	77
SIGLER, Bunny				
LET THE GOOD TIMES ROLL & FEEL SO GOOD/ There's No Love Left	(Parkway 153)	.75	3.00	67
LET THEM TALK/Will You Love Me Tomorrow	(Decca 32183)	.75	3.00	67
SILBERMAN, Benedict				
CHIPMUNK SONG, THE/Lovers Of Paris	(Palette 5037)	.75	3.00	59
SILKIE, The				
BORN TO BE WITH YOU/I'm So Sorry	(Fontana 1551)	.75	3.00	66
LEAVE ME TO CRY/Keys To My Soul	(Fontana 1536)	.75	3.00	66
YOU'VE GOT TO HIDE YOUR LOVE AWAY/City Winds	(Fontana 1525)	.75	3.00	65
SILLY SAVAGES, The				
ARE YOU OLD ENOUGH TO LOVE/Moon Dog	(Dore 772)	.75	3.00	66
SILVA-TONES, The				
THAT'S ALL I WANT FROM YOU/Roses Are Blooming	(Argo 5281)	1.00	4.00	57
THAT'S ALL I WANT FROM YOU/Roses Are Blooming	(Monarch 5281)	1.50	6.00	57
SILVER (With John Batdorf)				
MEMORY/So Much For The Past	(Arista 0210)	.50	2.00	76
MUSICIAN (IT'S NOT AN EASY LIFE)/Goodbye, So Long	(Arista 0227)	.50	2.00	77
WHAM-BAM/Right On Time ("Wham-Bam" is a reissue of "Wham-Bam Shang-A-Lang.")	(Arista 0189)	.50	2.00	76
WHAM-BAM SHANG-A-LANG/Right On Time	(Arista 0189)	.75	3.00	76
Also see Batdorf & Rodney				
SILVERA, Silvio				
BRIGITTE BARDOT/Tumba LeLe	(Barclay 300)	1.00	4.00	
SILVER FLEET (10 CC)				
COME ON PLANE/Look Out World	(Uni 55271)	.75	3.00	71
SILVER LAUGHTER				
LOVER/Rock & Roll Game	(Fanfare 4072)	.50	2.00	77
SILVER METRE, The				
BALLAD OF A WELL-KNOWN GUN/ Compromising Situation	(National General 010)	.75	3.00	72
SUPERSTAR/Now They'ze Found Me (With incorrect spelling of "They've")	(National General 001)	1.50	6.00	72
SUPERSTAR/Now They've Found Me (Reissue, with correct spelling of "They've")	(National General 001)	1.00	4.00	72
SILVERBIRD				
GETTING TOGETHER/You	(Columbia 45625)	.50	2.00	72
I SEE THE WRITING ON THE WALL/	(Columbia 45752)	.50	2.00	72
SILVERSTEIN, Shel				
FRONT ROW SEAT TO HEAR OLE JOHNNY SING, A/ 26 Second Song	(Columbia 45450)	.50	2.00	72
SAHRA CYNTHIA SYLVIA STOUT (WOULD NOT TAKE THE GARBAGE OUT)/	(Columbia 45772)	.50	2.00	72
SILVERTONES, The				
CANADIAN SUNSET/Thinking Of You	(Joey 302)	7.50	30.00	

SILVERTONES, The

TITLE/FLIP	LABEL & NO.	GOOD	NEAR MINT	YR.
GET IT/Bathsheba	(Goliath 1355)	.75	3.00	63

SIMMONS, Gene (Of Kiss)

TITLE/FLIP	LABEL & NO.	GOOD	NEAR MINT	YR.
RADIOACTIVE/See You In Your Dreams	(Casablanca 951)	.50	2.00	79

SIMMONS, Jumpin' Gene

TITLE/FLIP	LABEL & NO.	GOOD	NEAR MINT	YR.
BATMAN/	(Hi 2102)	.75	3.00	67
CALDONIA/Be Her #1	(Hi 2050)	1.00	4.00	62
DODO, THE/The Jump	(Hi 2080)	.75	3.00	64
DON'T WORRY 'BOUT ME/Back Home Again	(AGP 119)	.75	3.00	
FOLSOM PRISON BLUES/Mattie Rea	(Hi 9092)	.75	3.00	65
HAUNTED HOUSE/Hey, Hey Little Girl	(Hi 2076)	.75	3.00	64
HOP SCOTCH/Little Rag Doll	(Tupelo)	.75	3.00	
I'M JUST A LOSER/Lila (Don't Worry)	(Mala 12012)	.75	3.00	68
MAGNOLIA STREET/She's There When I Come Home	(Epic 10601)	.75	3.00	70
SKINNY MINNY/I'm a Ramblin' Man	(Hi 2086)	.75	3.00	65
TEDDY BEAR/Your True Love	(Hi 2034)	.75	3.00	64
WAITING GAME, THE/Shenandoah Waltz (Shown as by Morris Gene Simmons)	(Sandy 1027)	1.25	5.00	

SIMMS, Johnny

TITLE/FLIP	LABEL & NO.	GOOD	NEAR MINT	YR.
TALK TO ME/This Is The Moment	(Alite 101)	1.50	6.00	

SIMON & GARFUNKEL (Paul Simon & Art Garfunkle)

TITLE/FLIP	LABEL & NO.	GOOD	NEAR MINT	YR.
AMERICA/For Emily, Whenever I May Find Her	(Columbia 45663)	.50	2.00	72
AT THE ZOO/59th Street Bridge Song (Feelin' Groovy)	(Columbia 44046)	.75	3.00	67
BABY TALK/ I'm Gonna Get Married (By Ronnie Lawrence) (Shown as by Tom & Jerry)	(Bell 45,120)	6.25	25.00	71
BABY TALK/Two Teenagers (Shown as by Tom & Jerry)	(Big 621)	8.75	35.00	58
BOXER, THE/Baby Driver	(Columbia 44785)	.75	3.00	69
BRIDGE OVER TROUBLED WATER/ Keep The Customer Satisfied	(Columbia 45079)	.50	2.00	70
CECILA/Only Living Boy In New York	(Columbia 45133)	.50	2.00	70
DANGLING CONVERSATION, THE/ Big Bright Green Pleasure Machine	(Columbia 43728)	.75	3.00	66
DON'T SAY GOODBYE/That's My Story (Shown as by Tom & Jerry)	(Big 618)	3.00	12.00	58
DON'T SAY GOODBYE/That's My Story (Shown as by Tom & Jerry)	(Hunt 319)	5.00	20.00	58
EL CONDOR PASA/Why Don't Your Write Me	(Columbia 45237)	.50	2.00	70
FAKIN' IT/You Don't Know Where Your Interest Lies	(Columbia 44232)	.75	3.00	67
HAZY SHADE OF WINTER, A/ For Emily, Whenever I May Find Her	(Columbia 43873)	.75	3.00	66
HEY SCHOOLGIRL/Dancin' Wild (Shown as by Tom & Jerry)	(Big 613)	2.50	10.00	57
HOMEWARD BOUND/Leaves That Are Green	(Columbia 43511)	.75	3.00	66
I AM A ROCK/Flowers Never Bend With The Rainfall	(Columbia 43617)	.75	3.00	66
I AM A ROCK/I Am A Rock (Promotional red plastic issue)	(Columbia 4-43617)	3.75	15.00	65
I'M LONESOME/Looking At You (Shown as by Tom & Jerry)	(Ember 1094)	7.50	30.00	59
MRS. ROBINSON/Old Friends-Bookends	(Columbia 44511)	.75	3.00	68
MY LITTLE TOWN/Rag Doll You're Kind	(Columbia 10230)	.50	2.00	75
OUR SONG/Two Teenagers (Shown as by Tom & Jerry)	(Big 616)	3.00	12.00	58
SCARBOROUGH FAIR (CANTICLE)/April, Come She Will	(Columbia 44465)	.75	3.00	68
SEVEN O'CLOCK NEWS-SILENT NIGHT/	(Columbia 11669)	1.50	6.00	66
SOUNDS OF SILENCE, THE/ We've Got A Groovey Thing Goin'	(Columbia 43396)	.75	3.00	65
SOUNDS OF SILENCE, THE/ We've Got A Groovey Thing Goin' (Promotional red plastic issue)	(Columbia 43396)	5.00	20.00	65
SURRENCER, PLEASE SURRENDER/ Fighting Mad (Shown as by Tom & Jerry)	(ABC-Paramount 10363)	5.00	20.00	62
THIS IS MY STORY/Tia-Juana	(ABC-Paramount 10788)	1.25	5.00	66

SIMON, Carly

TITLE/FLIP	LABEL & NO.	GOOD	NEAR MINT	YR.
ANTICIPATION/The Garden	(Elektra 45759)	.50	2.00	71
ATTITUDE DANCING/Are You Ticklish	(Elektra 45246)	.50	2.00	75
DEVOTED TO YOU (With James Taylor)/Boys In The Trees	(Elektra 45506)	.50	2.00	78
GIRL YOU THINK YOU SEE/Share The End	(Elektra 45796)	.75	3.00	72
HALF A CHANCE/Libby	(Elektra 45341)	.50	2.00	76
HAVEN'T GOT TIME FOR THE PAIN/Mind On My Man	(Elektra 45887)	.50	2.00	74
IT KEEPS YOU RUNNIN'/Be With Me	(Elektra 45323)	.50	2.00	76
IT KEEPS YOU RUNNIN'/Look Me In The Eyes	(Elektra 45323)	.50	2.00	76
LEGEND IN YOUR OWN TIME/Julie Through The Glass	(Elektra 45774)	.50	2.00	72
LOOK ME IN THE EYES/Slave	(Elektra 45248)	.50	2.00	75
MOCKINGBIRD/Grownup (With James Taylor)	(Elektra 45880)	.50	2.00	74
MORE & MORE Love Out In The Street	(Elektra 45278)	.50	2.00	75
NOBODY DOES IT BETTER/After The Storm	(Elektra 45413)	.50	2.00	77
RED, RED ROSE/ Lobster Quadrille (By Lucy & Carly Simon)	(Columbia 45840)	.75	3.00	73
RIGHT THING TO DO, THE/We Have No Secrets	(Elektra 45843)	.75	3.00	73
SPY/Pure Sin	(Elektra 46514)	.50	2.00	79
THAT'S THE WAY I'VE ALWAYS HEARD IT SHOULD BE/ Alone	(Elektra 45724)	.50	2.00	71
TRANQUILLO (MELT MY HEART)/Back Down To Earth	(Elektra 45544)	.50	2.00	78
VENGEANCE/Love You By Heart	(Elektra 46051)	.50	2.00	79
WATERFALL/After The Storm	(Elektra 45263)	.50	2.00	75
YOU BELONG TO ME/In A Small Moment	(Elektra 45477)	.50	2.00	78
YOU'RE SO VAIN/ His Friends Are More Than Fond Of Robin	(Elektra 45824)	.50	2.00	72

Also see Simon Sisters, The

SIMON, Lucy (Of The Simon Sisters)

TITLE/FLIP	LABEL & NO.	GOOD	NEAR MINT	YR.
IF YOU EVER BELIEVED/	(RCA PB-10985)	.50	2.00	76

SIMON, Paul

TITLE/FLIP	LABEL & NO.	GOOD	NEAR MINT	YR.
AMERICAN TUNE/One Man's Ceiling Is Another Man's Floor	(Columbia 45900)	.50	2.00	73
ANNA BELLE/Loneliness (Shown as by Jerry Landis)	(MGM 12822)	3.75	15.00	59
CARLOS DOMINGUEZ/He Was My Brother (Shown as by Paul Kane even though performed by Paul Simon. Any copies showing Paul Simon as the artist are bootleg issues.)	(Tribute 128)	6.25	25.00	
DUNCAN/Run That Body Down	(Columbia 45638)	.50	2.00	72
FIFTY WAYS TO LEAVE YOUR LOVER/ Some Folks Lives Roll Easy	(Columbia 10270)	.50	2.00	75
GONE AT LAST (With Phoebe Snow)/ Take Me To The Mardi Gras	(Columbia 10197)	.50	2.00	75
I WISH I WEREN'T IN LOVE/I'm Lonely (Shown as by Jerry Landis)	(Canadian American 130)	3.00	12.00	61
IT MEANS A LOT TO THEM/Play Me A Sad Song (Shown as by Jerry Landis)	(Warwick 619)	2.50	10.00	61
JUST A BOY/I'd Like To Be (The Lipstick On Your Lips) (Shown as by Jerry Landis)	(Warwick 588)	3.00	12.00	60
JUST A BOY/Shy	(Warwick 552)	3.00	12.00	60
KODACHORME/Tenderness	(Columbia 45859)	.50	2.00	73
LONE TEEN RANGER/Lisa (Shown as by Jerry Landis)	(Amy 875)	3.75	15.00	62
LOVES ME LIKE A ROCK/Learn How To Fall	(Columbia 45907)	.50	2.00	73
ME & JULIO DOWN BY THE SCHOOLYARD/ Congratulations	(Columbia 45585)	.50	2.00	72
MOTHER & CHILD REUNION/Paranoia Blues	(Columbia 45547)	.50	2.00	72
SLIP SLIDIN' AWAY/Something So Right	(Columbia 10630)	.50	2.00	77
STILL CRAZY AFTER ALL THESE YEARS/ I Do It For Your Love	(Columbia 10332)	.50	2.00	76

TITLE/FLIP	LABEL & NO.	GOOD	NEAR MINT	YR.
STRANDED IN A LIMOUSINE/Have A Good Time	(Columbia 10711)	.50	2.00	77
TEENAGE FOOL/True Or False (Shown as by True Taylor)	(Big 614)	3.75	15.00	58

Also see Gregory, Harrison
Also see Simon & Garfunkle
Also see Tico & The Triumphs

SIMON SISTERS (Lucy & Carly Simon)

TITLE/FLIP	LABEL & NO.	GOOD	NEAR MINT	YR.
CUDDLE BUG/No One To Talk My Troubles To	(Kapp 624)	1.00	4.00	64
WINKIN' BLINKIN' & NOD/So Glad I'm Here	(Kapp 586)	1.00	4.00	64

SINATRA, Frank (Francis Albert Sinatra)

TITLE/FLIP	LABEL & NO.	GOOD	NEAR MINT	YR.
ACCIDENTS WILL HAPPEN/One Finger Melody	(Columbia 4-39014)	1.25	5.00	51
ACCIDENTS WILL HAPPEN/One Finger Melody (Microgroove 33 single)	(Columbia 1-845)	1.50	6.00	
ALL OF ME/I Went Down To Virginia	(Columbia 4-38163)	1.25	5.00	49
ALL THE WAY/Chicago	(Capitol 3793)	1.00	4.00	57
AMERICAN BEAUTY ROSE/Dream	(Columbia 4-40522)	1.00	4.00	55
AMERICAN BEAUTY ROSE/Sentimental Journey	(Capitol 4615)	.75	3.00	61
AMONG MY SOUVENIRS/September Song	(Columbia 4-37161)	1.25	5.00	49
AMONG MY SOUVENIRS/September Song	(Columbia 4-50003)	.75	3.00	
ANY TIME (I'LL BE THERE)/The Hurt Doesn't Go Away	(Reprise 1327)	.50	2.00	75
ANYTIME ANYWHERE/From Here To Eternity	(Capitol 2560)	1.00	4.00	53
ANYTIME AT ALL/Available	(Reprise 0350)	.75	3.00	65
BABY JUST LIKE YOU, A/Christmas Mem'ries	(Reprise 1342)	.75	3.00	75
BABY JUST LIKE YOU, A/Christmas Mem'ries (Picture sleeve)	(Reprise 1342)	1.00	4.00	75
BAD BAD LEROY BROWN/ I'm Gonna Make It All The Way	(Reprise 1196)	.75	3.00	74
BAD BAD LEROY BROWN/ Let Me Try Again (Laisse Moi Le Temps)	(Reprise 0113)	.75	3.00	73
BIM BAM BABY/Azure-Te (Paris Blues)	(Columbia 4-39814)	1.25	5.00	52
BIRTH OF THE BLUES/Why Try To Change Me Now	(Columbia 39882)	1.75	3.50	
BYE BYE BABY/Just A Kiss Apart (Microgroove 33 single)	(Columbia 1-316)	1.50	6.00	
CALIFORNIA/America	(Reprise 20157)	6.25	25.00	63
CALL ME IRRESPONSIBLE/Tina	(Reprise 20151)	.75	3.00	63
CAN I STEAL A LITTLE LOVE/Your Love For Me	(Capitol 3608)	1.00	4.00	57
CASTLE ROCK/Deep Night	(Columbia 39527)	1.50	3.00	51
CHATTANOOGIE SHOE SHINE BOY/ God's Country (With the Jeff Alexander Choir)	(Columbia 4-38708)	1.25	5.00	50
CHATTANOOGIE SHOE SHINE BOY/ God's Country (Microgroove 33 single, with the Jeff Alexander Choir)	(Columbia 1-496)	1.50	6.00	
CHRISTMAS WALTZ, THE/White Christmas	(Capitol 2954)	1.00	4.00	54
CHRISTMAS WALTZ, THE/Mistletoe & Holly (With the Ralph Brewster Singers)	(Capitol 3900)	.75	3.00	58
COME BACK TO SORRENTO/Take My Love	(Columbia 4-39118)	1.25	5.00	51
COME BLOW YOUR HORN/I Have Dreamed	(Reprise 20184)	.75	3.00	63
COMME CI COMME CA/While The Angelus Was Ringing (Microgroove 33 single)	(Columbia 1-130)	1.50	6.00	
COULD 'JA/That Lucky Old Sun (Microgroove 33 single)	(Columbia 1-372)	1.50	6.00	
CRAZY LOVE/So Long My Love	(Capitol 3703)	1.00	4.00	57
CYCLES/My Way Of Life	(Reprise 0764)	.50	2.00	68
DAYBREAK/Take Me	(Reprise 20028)	.75	3.00	61
DAY BY DAY/Shelia	(Columbia 4-40565)	1.00	4.00	55
DEAR LITTLE BOY OF MINE/ Life Is So Peculiar (With Helen Carroll) (Microgroove 33 single)	(Columbia 1-780)	1.50	6.00	
DEEP NIGHT/Castle Rock	(Columbia 4-39527)	1.25	5.00	51
DON'T CRY JOE/The Wedding Of Lilli Marlene (Microgroove 33 single)	(Columbia 1-315)	1.50	6.00	
DON'T WORRY 'BOUT ME/I Could Have Told You	(Capitol 2787)	1.00	4.00	54
EAST OF THE SUN/I'm Getting Sentimental Over You	(Reprise 20025)	.75	3.00	61
EVERYBODY HAS THE RIGHT TO BE WRONG/ I'll Only Miss Her When I Think	(Reprise 0410)	.75	3.00	65
EVERYBODY OUGHT TO BE IN LOVE/Night & Day	(Reprise 1368)	.50	2.00	76
EVERYBODY'S TWISTIN'/Nothing But The Best	(Reprise 20063)	1.50	6.00	62
FAITHFUL/Your The One (With Stan Freeman)	(Columbia 4-39213)	1.25	5.00	51
FEELIN' KINDA SUNDAY (With Nancy Sinatra)/ Kids (By Nancy Sinatra)	(Reprise 0980)	1.00	4.00	71
FEET OF CLAY/Don't Ever Be Afraid To Go Home	(Columbia 4-39687)	1.25	5.00	51
FIVE MINUTES MORE/I'll Remember April	(Capitol 4729)	.75	3.00	62
FLOWERS MEAN FORGIVENESS/You'll Get Yours	(Capitol 3350)	1.00	4.00	56
FORGET DOMANI/Can't Believe I'm Losing You	(Reprise 0380)	.75	3.00	65
FRENCH FOREIGN LEGION/Time After Time	(Capitol 4155)	1.00	4.00	59
GOIN' OUT OF MY HEAD/Forget To Remember	(Reprise 0865)	.50	2.00	69
GOODY GOODY/Love Is Just Around The Corner	(Reprise 20092)	.75	3.00	62
GOODNIGHT IRENE/My Blue Heaven	(Columbia 4-38892)	1.25	5.00	50
GRANADA/The Curse Of An Aching Heart	(Reprise 20010)	.75	3.00	61
GUNGA DIN/Gunga Din (Promotional issue only, monologue)	(Reprise PRO-45)	6.25	25.00	66
HALF AS LOVELY/The Gal That Got Away	(Capitol 2864)	1.00	4.00	54
HAVE YOURSELF A MERRY LITTLE CHRISTMAS/ Santa Claus Is Comin' To Town	(Columbia 4-38259)	1.25	5.00	49
HAVE YOURSELF A MERRY LITTLE CHRISTMAS/ Medley Of Carols (By Les Baxter)	(Reprise 0243)	1.25	5.00	63
HEY JEALOUS LOVER/You Forgot All The Words	(Capitol 3552)	1.00	4.00	56
HIGH HOPES/All My Tomorrows (With Eddie Hodges & A Bunch Of Kids)	(Capitol 4214)	1.00	4.00	59
HOW COULD YOU DO A THING LIKE THAT TO ME/ Not As A Stranger	(Capitol 3130)	1.00	4.00	55
HOW LITTLE WE KNOW/Five Hundred Guys	(Capitol 3423)	1.00	4.00	56
HUCKLEBUCK, THE/It Happens Every Spring (Microgroove 33 single)	(Columbia 1-222)	1.50	6.00	
I AM LOVED/You Don't Remind Me	(Columbia 6-936)	1.25	5.00	49
I BELIEVE I'M GONNA LOVE YOU/ The Only Couple On The Floor	(Reprise 1335)	.50	2.00	75
I CAN'T BELIEVE I'M LOSING YOU/How Old Am I?	(Reprise 0677)	.50	2.00	68
I COULD WRITE A BOOK/I Hear A Rhapsody (With the Jeff Alexander Choir)	(Columbia 4-39652)	1.25	5.00	51
I FALL IN LOVE WITH YOU EV'RY DAY/ It's A Long Way From Your House	(Columbia 4-39493)	1.25	5.00	51
I LOVE MY WIFE/ Send In The Clowns (Sinatra dialogue, Bill Miller piano)	(Reprise 1382)	.50	2.00	76
I LOVE PARIS/Hidden Persuasion	(Capitol 4815)	.75	3.00	62
I LOVE YOU/South Of The Border	(Capitol 2638)	1.00	4.00	54
I ONLY HAVE EYES FOR YOU/It All Depends On You (Microgroove 33 single)	(Columbia 1-307)	1.50	6.00	
I SING THE SONGS/Empty Tables (With Bill Miller)	(Reprise 1347)	.75	3.00	76
I WOULD BE IN LOVE ANYWAY/Watertown	(Reprise 0895)	.50	2.00	70
IF I EVER LOVE AGAIN/Every Man Should Marry (Microgroove 33 single)	(Columbia 1-326)	1.50	6.00	
IF I FORGET YOU/I'm A Fool To Want You	(Columbia 4-41133)	1.00	4.00	58
IF I LOVED YOU/You'll Never Walk Alone	(Columbia 36825)	1.00	4.00	
IF YOU ARE BUT A DREAM/Put Your Dreams Away	(Columbia 4-36814)	1.25	5.00	49
I'LL BE SEEING YOU/ The One I Love Belongs To Somebody Else	(Reprise 20023)	.75	3.00	61
I'M GLAD THERE IS YOU/ You Can Take My Word For It Baby	(Columbia 40229)	1.00	4.00	51
I'M NOT AFRAID/ Life's A Trippy Thing (With Nancy Sinatra)	(Reprise 1011)	.75	3.00	71
IMAGINATION/It's Always You	(Reprise 20024)	.75	3.00	61
IT WAS A VERY GOOD YEAR/Moment To Moment	(Reprise 0429)	.50	2.00	65
I'VE GOT A CRUSH ON YOU/Ever Homeward	(Columbia 4-38151)	1.25	5.00	49
I'VE GOT A CRUSH ON YOU/The Birth Of The Blues	(Columbia 4-50028)	.75	3.00	
I'VE GOT THE WORLD ON A STRING/My One & Only Love	(Capitol 2505)	1.00	4.00	53
JUST AN OLD STONE HOUSE/American Beauty Rose (Microgroove 33 single)	(Columbia 1-624)	1.50	6.00	
KISSES & TEARS (With Jane Russell)/ When The Sun Goes Down	(Columbia 4-38790)	1.25	5.00	50
KISSES & TEARS (With Jane Russell)/ When The Sun Goes Down (Microgroove 33 single)	(Columbia 1-611)	1.50	6.00	
LADY DAY/Song Of The Sabia	(Reprise 0970)	.50	2.00	70
LEAN BABY/I'm Walking Behind You	(Capitol 2450)	1.00	4.00	53
LEARNIN' THE BLUES/If I Had Three Wishes	(Capitol 3102)	1.00	4.00	55
LET'S TAKE AN OLD FASHIONED WALK/ Just One Way To Say I Love You ("A" side with Doris Day & the Ken Lane Singers)	(Columbia 4-39513)	1.25	5.00	49
LET'S TAKE AN OLD FASHIONED WALK/ Just One Way To Say I Love You ("A" side with Doris Day & the Ken Lane Singers) (Microgroove 33 single)	(Columbia 1-260)	1.50	6.00	
LIKE A SAD SONG/Dry Your Eyes	(Reprise 1377)	.50	2.00	76
LONDON BY NIGHT/April In Paris	(Columbia 4-39592)	1.25	5.00	51
LOOK OF LOVE, THE/I Left My Heart In San Francisco	(Reprise 20107)	.75	3.00	62
LOST IN THE STARS/The Old Master Painter (Microgroove 33 single)	(Columbia 1-427)	1.50	6.00	
LOVE & MARRIAGE/Impatient Years	(Capitol 3260)	1.00	4.00	55
LOVE ISN'T JUST FOR THE YOUNG/ You Brought A New Kind Of Love To Me	(Reprise 20209)	.75	3.00	63
LOVE MEANS LOVE/Cherry Pies Ought To Be You (With Rosemary Clooney)	(Columbia 4-39141)	1.25	5.00	51
LOVE'S BEEN GOOD TO ME/A Man Alone	(Reprise 0852)	.50	2.00	69
LUNA ROSSA (With the Norman Luboff Choir)/ Tennessee Newsboy	(Columbia 4-39787)	1.25	5.00	52
MAD ABOUT YOU/Stromboli (Microgroove 33 single)	(Columbia 1-380)	1.50	6.00	
MAMA WILL BARK (With Dagmar)/ I'm A Fool To Want You (With imitations by Donald Bain)	(Columbia 4-39425)	1.25	5.00	51
ME & MY SHADOW (With Sammy Davis Jr.)/ Sam's Song (By Sammy Davis Jr. & Dean Martin)	(Reprise 20128)	1.25	5.00	63
ME & MY SHADOW (With Sammy Davis Jr.)/ Sam's Song (By Sammy Davis Jr. & Dean Martin) (Picture sleeve)	(Reprise 20128)	1.50	6.00	63
MELODY OF LOVE/I'm Gonna Live Till I Die	(Capitol 3018)	1.00	4.00	55
MIND IF I MAKE LOVE TO YOU/ Who Wants To Be A Millionaire (With Celeste Holm)	(Capitol 3508)	1.00	4.00	56
MR. SUCCESS/Sleep Warm	(Capitol 4070)	1.00	4.00	58
MOON WAS YELLOW, THE/The Music Stopped	(Columbia 4-38683)	1.25	5.00	50
MOON WAS YELLOW, THE/ I Gotta Right To Sing The Blues	(Capitol 4677)	.75	3.00	62
MY BLUE HEAVEN/Goodnight Irene	(Columbia 6-718)	1.25	5.00	49
MY BLUE HEAVEN/Sentimental Baby	(Capitol 4546)	.75	3.00	61
MY KIND OF TOWN/I Like To Lead When I Dance	(Reprise 0279)	.75	3.00	64
MY WAY/Blue Lace	(Reprise 0817)	.50	2.00	69
NANCY/Ol' Man River	(Columbia 4-43011)	1.25	5.00	64
NEW YORK, NEW YORK/What God Looks Like To Me	(Reprise 49233)	.50	2.00	79
NICE 'N' EASY/This Was My Love	(Capitol 4408)	.75	3.00	60
NO ONE EVER TELLS YOU/To Love & Be Loved	(Capitol 4103)	1.00	4.00	58
NOTHING IN COMMON/How Are Ya Fixed For Love (With Keely Smith)	(Capitol 3952)	1.00	4.00	58
OL' MACDONALD/You'll Always Be The One I Love	(Capitol 4466)	.75	3.00	60
OLDEST ESTABLISHED (PERMANENT FLOATING CRAP GAME IN NEW YORK, THE/Fugue For Tinhorns (With Bing Crosby & Dean Martin)	(Reprise 20217)	1.00	4.00	63
ONCE IN LOVE WITH AMY/Sunflower (Microgroove 33 single)	(Columbia 1-106)	1.50	6.00	
POCKETFUL OF MIRACLES/Name It & It's Yours	(Reprise 20040)	1.00	4.00	61
POCKETFUL OF MIRACLES/Name It & It's Yours (Picture sleeve)	(Reprise 20040)	1.50	6.00	61
POINCIANA/There's No Business Like Show Business (Microgroove 33 single)	(Columbia 1-650)	1.50	6.00	
RAIN IN MY HEART/Star	(Reprise 0798)	.50	2.00	69
REMEMBER ME IN YOUR DREAMS/ Let It Snow, Let It Snow, Let It Snow	(Columbia 6-924)	1.25	5.00	49
REMEMBER ME IN YOUR DREAMS/ Let It Snow, Let It Snow, Let It Snow (Microgroove 33 single)	(Columbia 1-924)	1.50	6.00	49
RIGHT GIRL FOR ME/Night After Night (Microgroove 33 single)	(Columbia 1-191)	1.50	6.00	
RIVER STAY 'WAY FROM MY DOOR/ It's Over, It's Over, It's Over	(Capitol 4376)	.75	3.00	60
SADEST THING OF ALL, THE/Empty Tables (Instrumentals)	(Reprise 1343)	.50	2.00	75
SAME OLD SATURDAY NIGHT/Fairy Tale	(Capitol 3218)	1.00	4.00	55
SAME OLD SONG & DANCE/Monique	(Capitol 4003)	1.00	4.00	58
SATISFY ME ONE MORE TIME/You Turned My World Around	(Reprise 1208)	.50	2.00	74
SATURDAY NIGHT/Five Minutes More	(Columbia 4-50069)	.75	3.00	
SECOND TIME AROUND, THE/Tina	(Reprise 20001)	.75	3.00	61
SEND IN THE CLOWNS/ Let Me Try Again (Laisse Moi Le Temps)	(Reprise 1181)	.50	2.00	73
SHE'S FUNNY THAT WAY/Embraceable You	(Columbia 4-37259)	1.25	5.00	49
SHOULD I/You Do Something To Me	(Columbia 4-38998)	1.25	5.00	51
SOFTLY, AS I LEAVE YOU/Then Suddenly	(Reprise 0301)	.50	2.00	64
SOME ENCHANTED EVENING/Bali Ha'i	(Columbia 4-38446)	1.25	5.00	49
SOME ENCHANTED EVENING/Bali Ha'i (Microgroove 33 single)	(Columbia 1-174)	1.50	6.00	
SOMEONE TO WATCH OVER ME/You My Love	(Capitol 2993)	1.00	4.00	54
SOMETHIN' STUPID (With Nancy Sinatra)/ I Will Wait For You	(Reprise 0561)	.50	2.00	67
SOMETHIN' STUPID (With Nancy Sinatra)/ Give Her Love	(Reprise 0561)	.50	2.00	67
SOMETHING/Bein' Green	(Reprise 0981)	.50	2.00	71
SOMETHING WONDERFUL HAPPENS IN SUMMER/ You're Cheatin' Yourself (If You're Cheatin' On Me	(Capitol 3744)	1.00	4.00	57
SOMEWHERE IN YOUR HEART/Emily	(Reprise 3002)	.75	3.00	64
STARDUST/Come Rain Or Come Shine	(Reprise 20059)	.75	3.00	62
STARGAZER/The Best I Ever Had (With sax by Sam Butera)	(Reprise 1364)	.50	2.00	76
STAY WITH ME/Talk To Me Baby	(Reprise 0249)	.75	3.00	64
STRANGE MUSIC/I Love You	(Columbia 4-38684)	1.25	5.00	50
STRANGERS IN THE NIGHT/Oh, You Crazy Moon	(Reprise 0470)	.50	2.00	66
SUMMER WIND/You Make Me Feel So Young	(Reprise 0509)	.50	2.00	66
SUNSHINE CAKE (With Paula Kelly)/ Sure Thing (With the Modernaires)	(Columbia 4-38705)	1.25	5.00	50
SUNSHINE CAKE (With Paula Kelly)/ Sure Thing (With the Modernaires) (Microgroove 33 single)	(Columbia 1-491)	1.50	6.00	50
TALK TO ME/They Came To Cordura	(Capitol 4284)	1.00	4.00	59
TELL HER YOU LOVE HER EACH DAY/Here's To The Losers	(Reprise 0373)	.75	3.00	65
TENDER TRAP, THE/Weep They Will	(Capitol 3290)	1.00	4.00	55
THAT OLD BLACK MAGIC/How Deep Is The Ocean	(Columbia 4-37257)	1.25	5.00	49
THAT'S LIFE/The September Of My Years	(Reprise 0531)	.50	2.00	66
THERE ARE SUCH THINGS/Polka Dots & Moonbeams	(Reprise 20026)	.75	3.00	61
THIS IS THE NIGHT/ Peach Tree Street (With Rosemary Clooney) (Microgroove 33 single)	(Columbia 1-669)	1.50	6.00	
THIS TOWN/This Is My Love	(Reprise 0631)	.50	2.00	67
THREE COINS IN THE FOUNTAIN/ Rain (Falling From The Skies)	(Capitol 2816)	1.00	4.00	54
TRY A LITTLE TENDERNESS/It Never Entered My Mind	(Columbia 4-39498)	1.25	5.00	51
TWO HEARTS, TWO KISSES/ From The Bottom To The Top (With the Nuggets)	(Capitol 3084)	1.00	4.00	55
WALKIN' IN THE SUNSHINE/My Girl	(Columbia 4-39726)	1.00	4.00	52
WELL DID YOU EVAH (With Bing Crosby)/ True Love (By Bing Crosby & Grace Kelly)	(Capitol 3507)	1.00	4.00	56
WHATEVER HAPPENED TO CHRISTMAS/I Wouldn't Trade Christmas (With Frank Jr., Nancy & Tina Sinatra)	(Reprise 0790)	1.00	4.00	68

TITLE/FLIP	LABEL & NO.	GOOD	NEAR MINT	YR.
WHAT'S NOW IS NOW/The Train	(Reprise 0920)	.50	2.00	70
WHEN I STOP LOVING YOU/It Worries Me	(Capitol 2922)	1.00	4.00	54
WHEN IS SOMETIME/If You Stub Your Toe On The Moon	(Columbia 1-144)	1.50	6.00	
(Microgroove 33 single)				
WHEN SOMEBODY LOVES YOU/When I'm Not Near The Girl I Love	(Reprise 0398)	.75	3.00	65
WHERE IS THE ONE/Bop Goes My Heart	(Columbia 1-154)	1.50	6.00	
(Microgroove 33 single)				
WHERE OR WHEN/None But The Lonely Heart	(Columbia 4-38685)	1.25	5.00	50
WHY CAN'T YOU BEHAVE/No Orchids For My Lady	(Columbia 1-112)	1.50	6.00	
(Microgroove 33 single)				
WHY REMIND ME/Sorry	(Columbia 1-440)	1.50	6.00	
(Microgroove 33 single)				
WHY SHOULD I CRY OVER YOU/Don't Change Your Mind About Me	(Capitol 3050)	1.00	4.00	55
WHY TRY TO CHANGE ME NOW/The Birth Of The Blues	(Columbia 4-39882)	1.25	5.00	52
WITCHCRAFT/Tell Her You Love Her	(Capitol 3859)	1.00	4.00	58
WITHOUT A SONG/It Started All Over Again	(Reprise 20027)	.75	3.00	61
WITHOUT A SONG/I'll Be Seeing You	(Reprise 20053)	.75	3.00	62
WORLD WE KNEW (OVER & OVER), THE/You Are There	(Reprise 0610)	.50	2.00	67
YOU & ME/I've Been There	(Reprise 49517)	.50	2.00	80
YOU CAN TAKE MY WORD FOR IT BABY/I'm Glad There Is You	(Columbia 4-40229)	1.00	4.00	54
YOU WILL BE MY MUSIC/Winners	(Reprise 1190)	.75	3.00	73
YOUNG AT HEART/Take A Chance	(Capitol 2703)	1.00	4.00	54
YOU'LL NEVER WALK ALONE/If I Loved You	(Columbia 4-36825)	1.25	5.00	49
YOU'LL NEVER WALK ALONE/If I Loved You	(Columbia 4-50066)	.75	3.00	
YOU'LL NEVER WALK ALONE/Begin The Beguine	(Columbia 1-508)	1.25	5.00	
YOU'RE SENSATIONAL/Wait For Me (Johnny Concho Theme)	(Capitol 3469)	1.00	4.00	56

As thoroughly as the Sinatra section was researched for this edition, the possibility does exist that some of the early Columbia catalog numbers picked up were 78rpm numbers. It is, nevertheless, believed that all of these singles were on 45rpm.

SINATRA, Nancy

TITLE/FLIP	LABEL & NO.	GOOD	NEAR MINT	YR.
CRUEL WAR/One Way	(Reprise 20118)	1.00	4.00	63
DID YOU EVER/Back On The Road	(Reprise 1021)	.50	2.00	71
(With Lee Hazlewood)				
DRUMMER MAN/	(Reprise 0851)	.50	2.00	69
FRIDAY'S CHILD/Hutchinson Jail	(Reprise 0491)	.50	2.00	66
GENTLE MAN LIKE YOU, A/	(Private Stock 45158)	.50	2.00	77
GOD KNOWS I LOVE YOU/Just Being Plain Old Me	(Reprise 0813)	.50	2.00	69
GOOD TIME GIRL/Old Devil Moon	(Reprise 0789)	.50	2.00	68
HAPPY/Nice 'N' Easy	(Reprise 0756)	.50	2.00	68
HELLO L.A., BYE BYE BIRMINGHAM/White Tattoo	(Reprise 0932)	.50	2.00	70
HERE WE GO AGAIN/Memories	(Reprise 0821)	.50	2.00	69
HOOK & LADDER/Is Anybody Goin' To San Antone	(Reprise 0991)	.50	2.00	71
HOW ARE THINGS IN CALIFORNIA/I'm Not A Girl Anymore	(Reprise 0960)	.50	2.00	70
HOW DOES THAT GRAB YOU, DARLIN'?/The Last Of The Secret Agents	(Reprise 0461)	.50	2.00	66
INDIAN SUMMER/	(Private Stock 45108)	.50	2.00	76
(With Lee Hazlewood)				
IN OUR TIME/Leave My Dog Alone	(Reprise 0514)	.50	2.00	66
JACKSON (With Lee Hazlewood)/You Only Live Twice	(Reprise 0595)	.50	2.00	67
JUNE, JULY & AUGUST/Think Of Me	(Reprise 20097)	1.00	4.00	62
KIND OF A WOMAN/It's The Love (That Keeps It All Together)	(RCA 74-0864)	.50	2.00	72
LADY BIRD (With Lee Hazlewood)/Sand	(Reprise 0629)	.50	2.00	67
LIGHTNING'S GIRL/Until It's Time For You To Go	(Reprise 0620)	.50	2.00	67
LOVE EYES/Coastin'	(Reprise 0559)	.50	2.00	67
LOVE THEM ALL (THE BOYS IN THE BAND)/Home	(Reprise 0890)	.50	2.00	70
100 YEARS/See The Little Children	(Reprise 0670)	.50	2.00	68
SO LONG BABE/If He'd Love Me	(Reprise 0407)	.75	3.00	65
SOME VELVET MORNING/Oh Lonesome Me	(Reprise 0651)	.50	2.00	68
(With Lee Hazlewood)				
SUGAR TOWN/Summer Wine (With Lee Hazlewood)	(Reprise 0527)	.50	2.00	66
THESE BOOTS ARE MADE FOR WALKIN'/The City Never Sleeps At Night	(Reprise 0432)	.50	2.00	65
TONY ROME/	(Reprise 0636)	.50	2.00	67

Nancy is Frank Sinatra's daughter.

SINBAD, Paul

TITLE/FLIP	LABEL & NO.	GOOD	NEAR MINT	YR.
SINCE I MET YOU/	(Hype 104)	2.00	8.00	

SINCERES, The

TITLE/FLIP	LABEL & NO.	GOOD	NEAR MINT	YR.
DARLING/Do You Remember	(Sigma 1004)	7.50	30.00	60
MAGIC OF LOVE, THE/Tell Her	(Taurus 377)	6.25	25.00	66
OUR WINTER LOVE/Kookie Ookie	(Epic 9583)	.75	3.00	63
PLEASE DON'T CHEAT ON ME/If You Should Leave Me	(Richie 545)	6.25	25.00	61
SINCERELY/Snap Your Fingers	(Columbia 43110)	1.00	4.00	64
YOU'RE TOO YOUNG/Forbidden Love	(Jordan 117)	5.00	20.00	60

SINCEROS

TITLE/FLIP	LABEL & NO.	GOOD	NEAR MINT	YR.
TAKE ME TO YOUR LEADER/	(Columbia 11115)	.50	2.00	79
WORLDS APART/	(Columbia 11178)	.50	2.00	79

SINGING ANTS: see Summers, Davey

SINGING BELLS, The

TITLE/FLIP	LABEL & NO.	GOOD	NEAR MINT	YR.
SOMEONE LOVES YOU JOE/The Empty Mailbox	(Madison 126)	.75	3.00	60

SINGING DOGS, The (Don Charles Presents...)

TITLE/FLIP	LABEL & NO.	GOOD	NEAR MINT	YR.
HOT DOG ROCK & ROLL/Hot Dog Boogie	(RCA Victor 47-6432)	1.25	5.00	56
OH! SUSANNA/Jingle Bells	(RCA 1020)	.50	2.00	71
OH! SUSANNA/Jingle Bells	(RCA Victor 47-6344)	1.25	5.00	55

SINGING NUN, The (Sister Soeur Sourire)

TITLE/FLIP	LABEL & NO.	GOOD	NEAR MINT	YR.
AVEC TOI (WITH YOU)/Une Fleur (A Flower)	(Philips 40195)	.75	3.00	63
DOMINIQUE/Les Pieds Des Missionnaiies	(Philips 40163)	.75	3.00	63
DOMINIQUE/Entre Les Etoiles (Among The Stars)	(Philips 40152)	.75	3.00	63
DOMINIQUE/Entre Les Etoiles (Among The Stars)	(Philips 40152)	1.00	4.00	63
(Picture sleeve)				
TOUS LES CHENINS/Frere Tout L' Monde'	(Philips 50165)	.75	3.00	64

SINGING REINDEER, The

TITLE/FLIP	LABEL & NO.	GOOD	NEAR MINT	YR.
HAPPY RAINDEER, THE/Dancer's Waltz	(Capitol 4300)	1.00	4.00	59

SIOUXSIE & THE BANSHEES

TITLE/FLIP	LABEL & NO.	GOOD	NEAR MINT	YR.
HONG KONG GARDEN/Overground	(Polydor 14561)	.50	2.00	79

SIR CHAUNCEY (Ernie Freeman)

TITLE/FLIP	LABEL & NO.	GOOD	NEAR MINT	YR.
BEAUTIFUL OBSESSION/Tenderfoot	(Pattern 603)	1.25	5.00	60
BEAUTIFUL OBSESSION/Tenderfoot	(Warner Bros. 5150)	.75	3.00	60
BEYOND OUR LOVE/Midi Midinette	(Warner Bros. 5185)	.75	3.00	61
Instrumentals				

SIR DOUGLAS QUINTET, The (Featuring Doug Sahm)

TITLE/FLIP	LABEL & NO.	GOOD	NEAR MINT	YR.
ARE INLAWS REALLY OUTLAWS/Sell A Song	(Smash 2169)	.75	3.00	68
BEGINNING OF THE END/Love Don't Treat Me Fair	(Tribe 8318)	1.00	4.00	66
DYNAMITE WOMAN/Too Many Dociled Minds	(Smash 2233)	.75	3.00	69
HANG LOOSE/I'm Sorry	(Tribe 8323)	1.00	4.00	67
IT DIDN'T EVEN BRING ME DOWN/Law, I'm Just A Country Boy In This Great Big Freaky City	(Smash 2222)	.75	3.00	69
MENDOCINO/I Wanna Be Your Mama Again	(Smash 2191)	.75	3.00	69
QUARTER TO THREE/She's Got To Be Boss	(Tribe 8317)	1.00	4.00	66
RAINS CAME, THE/Bacon Fat	(Tribe 8314)	1.00	4.00	66
ROLL WITH THE PUNCHES/	(Casablanca 828)	.50	2.00	74
SHE DIGS MY LOVE/When I Sing The Blues	(Tribe 8321)	1.00	4.00	66
SHE'S ABOUT A MOVER/We'll Take Our Last Walk Tonight	(Tribe 8308)	1.00	4.00	65
STORY OF JOHN HARDY, THE/In Time	(Tribe 8312)	1.00	4.00	65
TEXAS TORNADO (With Bob Dylan)/	(Atlantic 2985)	2.00	8.00	73
TRACKER, THE/Blue Norther	(Tribe 8310)	1.00	4.00	65
WHAT ABOUT TOMORROW?/A Nice Song	(Philips 40676)	.75	3.00	71

SIR JOE & THE MAIDENS

TITLE/FLIP	LABEL & NO.	GOOD	NEAR MINT	YR.
JIVIN' JEAN/Pen Pal	(Lenox 5563)	1.00	4.00	63

SIR WALTER RALEIGH (With Dewey Martin)

TITLE/FLIP	LABEL & NO.	GOOD	NEAR MINT	YR.
IF YOU NEED ME/Tell Her Tonight	(Tower 156)	.75	3.00	65

Also see Buffalo Springfield

SIXPENCE (Formerly The Irridescents)

TITLE/FLIP	LABEL & NO.	GOOD	NEAR MINT	YR.
YOU'RE THE LOVE/What To Do	(Impact 1025)	2.00	8.00	

Also see Strawberry Alarm Clock, The

SKA KINGS, The

TITLE/FLIP	LABEL & NO.	GOOD	NEAR MINT	YR.
JAMAICA SKA/Oil In My Lamp	(Atlantic 2232)	.75	3.00	64

SKARLETTONES, The

TITLE/FLIP	LABEL & NO.	GOOD	NEAR MINT	YR.
DO YOU REMEMBER/Will You Dream	(Ember 1053)	6.25	25.00	59

SKEL, Bobby

TITLE/FLIP	LABEL & NO.	GOOD	NEAR MINT	YR.
KISS & RUN/Say It Now	(Soft 826)	.75	3.00	64

SKELLERN, Peter

TITLE/FLIP	LABEL & NO.	GOOD	NEAR MINT	YR.
HARD TIMES/	(Private Stock 45054)	.50	2.00	75
HOLD ON TO LOVE/	(Private Stock 45028)	.50	2.00	75
YOU'RE A LADY/	(London 20075)	.50	2.00	72

SKELTON, Red

TITLE/FLIP	LABEL & NO.	GOOD	NEAR MINT	YR.
I PLEDGE ALLEGIANCE/	(C.B.S.-Columbia No Number Given)	1.00	4.00	69
(One-sided paper giveaway record.)				
PLEDGE OF ALLEGIANCE/The Circus	(Columbia 44798)	.75	3.00	69

SKEPTICS, The

TITLE/FLIP	LABEL & NO.	GOOD	NEAR MINT	YR.
RIDE CHILD/Apple Candy	(Kampus 814)	.75	3.00	

SKHY, A.B.

TITLE/FLIP	LABEL & NO.	GOOD	NEAR MINT	YR.
CAMEL BACK/Just What I Need	(MGM 14086)	1.00	4.00	69

SKIDMORE, Bill

TITLE/FLIP	LABEL & NO.	GOOD	NEAR MINT	YR.
DATE BAIT/I'm Out Of My Mind	(Crest 1040)	1.25	5.00	60

SKI-KING & THE LIFE BUOYS

TITLE/FLIP	LABEL & NO.	GOOD	NEAR MINT	YR.
THIS GREAT SOCIETY/	(Dixie 1109)	1.00	4.00	

SKIP & FLIP (Clyde Batton & Gary Paxton)

TITLE/FLIP	LABEL & NO.	GOOD	NEAR MINT	YR.
BETTY JEAN/Doubt	(Time 1031)	2.50	10.00	60
CHERRY PIE/Cryin' Over You	(Brent 7010)	.75	3.00	60
EVERYDAY I HAVE TO CRY/Tossin' & Turnin'	(California 2325)	.75	3.00	63
FANCY NANCY/It Could Be	(Brent 7005)	1.00	4.00	59
GREEN DOOR/Willow Tree	(Brent 7017)	1.00	4.00	61
IT WAS I/Lunch Hour	(Brent 7002)	1.00	4.00	59
TEENAGE HONEYMOON/Hully Gully Cha Cha Cha	(Brent 7013)	1.00	4.00	60

Also see Gary & Clyde
Also see Pledges, The

SKIPPY & THE HI LITES

TITLE/FLIP	LABEL & NO.	GOOD	NEAR MINT	YR.
OLD MAN RIVER/Waiting To Take (You Home)	(Elmor)	6.25	25.00	
OLD MAN RIVER/Waiting To Take (You Home)	(Stream-Lite 1027)	3.75	15.00	

SKUNKS, The

TITLE/FLIP	LABEL & NO.	GOOD	NEAR MINT	YR.
SMITTY'S TOY PIANO/Smitty's Christmas Toy Piano	(Arvee 585)	1.00	4.00	59

SKUNKS, The

TITLE/FLIP	LABEL & NO.	GOOD	NEAR MINT	YR.
DOING NOTHING/Listen To The News Today	(Teen Town 110)	1.00	4.00	69
ELVIRA/The Journey	U.S.A. 865)	1.00	4.00	67
I RECOMMEND HER/I Need No One	(World Pacific 77889)	.75	3.00	69
I RECOMMEND HER/I Need No One	(Teen Town 103)	1.00	4.00	68
SMALL TOWN GIRL/You Better Hold On To Me	(Teen Town 106)	1.00	4.00	68

SKY (With Doug Fieger)

TITLE/FLIP	LABEL & NO.	GOOD	NEAR MINT	YR.
GOODIE TWO SHOES/Make It In Time	(RCA 74-0419)	.75	3.00	71
LET IT LIE LOW/Taking The Long Way Home	(RCA 74-0611)	.75	3.00	72

Also see Knack, The

SKYHOOKS

TITLE/FLIP	LABEL & NO.	GOOD	NEAR MINT	YR.
ALL MY FRIENDS ARE GETTING MARRIED/Love On The Radio	(Mercury 73792)	.50	2.00	76
MERCEDES LADIES/You Just Like Me 'Cos I'm Good In Bed	(Mercury 73776)	.50	2.00	76

SKYLARK (With Donny Gerrard & Carl Graves)

TITLE/FLIP	LABEL & NO.	GOOD	NEAR MINT	YR.
I'LL HAVE TO GO AWAY/Twenty-Six Years	(Capitol 3661)	.50	2.00	73
WILDFLOWER/The Writing's On The Wall	(Capitol 3511)	.50	2.00	73

Also see Attitudes, The

SKYLINE DRIVE

TITLE/FLIP	LABEL & NO.	GOOD	NEAR MINT	YR.
TONIGHT COULD BE THE NIGHT-LITTLE DARLIN'/Make It To Spain	(Revve 11043)	2.00	8.00	

SKYLINERS, The (Featuring Jimmy Beaumont)

TITLE/FLIP	LABEL & NO.	GOOD	NEAR MINT	YR.
BELIEVE ME/Happy Time	(Calico 120)	1.25	5.00	60
CLOSE YOUR EYES/Our Love Will Last	(Colpix 613)	1.00	4.00	61
COMES LOVE/Tell Me	(Viscount 104)	1.25	5.00	62
DON'T HURT ME BABY/I Run To You	(Jubilee 5520)	1.00	4.00	66
DOOR IS STILL OPEN, THE/I'll Close My Eyes	(Colpix 188)	1.00	4.00	60
EVERYONE BUT YOU/Three Coins In The Fountain	(Cameo 215)	1.25	5.00	60
GET YOURSELF A BABY/Who Do You Love	(Jubilee 5512)	1.00	4.00	66
HOW MUCH/Lorraine From Spain	(Calico 114)	1.00	4.00	60
IT HAPPENED TODAY/Lonely Way	(Calico 109)	1.00	4.00	59
LOSER, THE/Everything Is Fine	(Jubilee 5506)	.75	3.00	65
OH HOW HAPPY/We've Got Love On Our Side	(Tortoise Int'l. 11343)	.75	3.00	78
PENNIES FROM HEAVEN/I'll Be Seeing You	(Calico 117)	1.00	4.00	60
SINCE I DON'T HAVE YOU/One Night, One Night	(Calico 103/104)	1.00	4.00	59
SINCE I FELL FOR YOU/I'd Die	(Atco 6270)	1.00	4.00	63
THIS I SWEAR/Tomorrow	(Calico 106)	1.00	4.00	59
WHERE HAVE THEY GONE/I Could Have Loved You So Well	(Capitol 3979)	.75	3.00	75

SKYLINERS, The

TITLE/FLIP	LABEL & NO.	GOOD	NEAR MINT	YR.
ROCK N' ROLL RUBY/I Do All Right	(Double AA 1045)	1.25	5.00	

SKYLITERS, The

TITLE/FLIP	LABEL & NO.	GOOD	NEAR MINT	YR.
TIDAL WAVE/Schroeder Walk	(Scoffe 2666)	1.00	4.00	63
(Instrumentals)				

SKYLITES, The

TITLE/FLIP	LABEL & NO.	GOOD	NEAR MINT	YR.
OH HAPPY DAY/My Only Girl	(Ta-Rah 101)	2.00	8.00	61

SLADE

TITLE/FLIP	LABEL & NO.	GOOD	NEAR MINT	YR.
COZ I LOVE YOU/	(Cotillion 44139)	.75	3.00	71
CUM ON FEEL THE NOIZE/I'm Mee, I'm Now An' That's Orl	(Polydor 15069)	.50	2.00	73
GET DOWN & GET WITH IT/	(Cotillion 44128)	.75	3.00	71
GOOD TIME GALS/We're Really Gonna Raise The Roof	(Warner Bros. 7777)	.50	2.00	74
GUDBUY T' JANE/I Won't Let It 'Appen Agen	(Polydor 15060)	.50	2.00	73
HOW DOES IT FEEL/O.K. Yesterday Was Yesterday	(Warner Bros. 8134)	.50	2.00	75
LET THE GOOD TIMES ROLL/Feel So Fine/I Don' Mine	(Polydor 15080)	.50	2.00	73
LOOK WOT YOU DUN/	(Cotillion 44150)	.75	3.00	72
MAMA WEER ALL CRAZEE NOW/Man Who Speeks Evil	(Polydor 15053)	.50	2.00	72
NOBODY'S FOOL/When The Chips Are Down	(Warner Bros. 8185)	.50	2.00	76
SKWEEZE ME, PLEEZE ME/	(Reprise 1182)	.50	2.00	73
TAKE ME BACK 'OME/Wonderin' Y	(Polydor 15046)	.50	2.00	72
WHEN THE LIGHTS ARE OUT/	(Warner Bros. 7808)	.50	2.00	74

SLADES, The

TITLE/FLIP	LABEL & NO.	GOOD	NEAR MINT	YR.
YOU CHEATED/The Waddle	(Domino 500)	2.00	8.00	58
YOU MEAN EVERYTHING TO ME/Baby	(Liberty 55118)	1.50	6.00	59
(Label error shows the artists as the Spades)				
YOU MEAN EVERYTHING TO ME/Baby	(Liberty 55118)	1.00	4.00	59
YOU MUST TRY/Summertime	(Domino 1000)	1.25	5.00	59

SLATKIN, Felix

TITLE/FLIP	LABEL & NO.	GOOD	NEAR MINT	YR.
HAPPY HOBO, THE/Turkish Bath	(Liberty 55232)	.75	3.00	60
THEME FROM THE SUNDOWNERS/Gaythers Gone	(Liberty 55282)	.75	3.00	60
Instrumentals				

SLAY, Frank

TITLE/FLIP	LABEL & NO.	GOOD	NEAR MINT	YR.
FLYING CIRCLE/Cincinnati	(Swan 4085)	.75	3.00	61

Frank Slay's orchestra provided backing for many of Freddy Cannon's Swan recordings.

SLED, Bob & The Tobbogons

TITLE/FLIP	LABEL & NO.	GOOD	NEAR MINT	YR.
HERE WE GO (THE SURFER BOYS ARE GOING SKIING)/Sea & Ski	(Cameo 400)	1.00	4.00	66

SLEEPY KING

TITLE/FLIP	LABEL & NO.	GOOD	NEAR MINT	YR.
PUSHIN' YOUR LUCK/The King Steps Out	(Joy 257)	.75	3.00	61

SLICK, Grace (Of The Jefferson Airplane)

TITLE/FLIP	LABEL & NO.	GOOD	NEAR MINT	YR.
COME AGAIN? TOUCAN/Theme From The Movie Manhole	(Grunt 0183)	.75	3.00	74

Also see Great!! Society!!, The

SLIK

TITLE/FLIP	LABEL & NO.	GOOD	NEAR MINT	YR.
BOOGIEST BAND IN TOWN/	(Polydor 15096)	.50	2.00	74
FOREVER & EVER/Again My Love	(Arista 0179)	.50	2.00	76

SLINKY, Ratmore: see Osborne Jerry

SLIPPERY ROCK STRING BAND, The

TITLE/FLIP	LABEL & NO.	GOOD	NEAR MINT	YR.
TULE FOG/Sally Brought Him Home	(Bummer 6996)	1.00	4.00	
TULE FOG/Sally Brought Him Home	(Dome 504)	1.25	5.00	

SLOAN, P.F. (Phil Sloan)

TITLE/FLIP	LABEL & NO.	GOOD	NEAR MINT	YR.
HALLOWEEN MARY/I'd Have To Be Out Of My Mind	(Dunhill 4016)	1.00	4.00	65
I FOUND A GIRL/A Melody For You	(Dunhill 4054)	1.00	4.00	66
SHE'S MY GIRL/If You Believe In Me	(Mart 802)	1.25	5.00	
SINS OF A FAMILY, THE/This Mornin	(Dunhill 4007)	.75	3.00	65
SUNFLOWER, SUNFLOWER/The Man Behind The Red Ballon	(Dunhill 4064)	1.00	4.00	67
SUNFLOWER, SUNFLOWER/The Man Behind The Red Ballon	(Dunhill 4064)	1.50	6.00	67
(With Picture sleeve)				

Also see Fantastic Baggies, The
Also see Imaginations, The
Also see Inner Circle, The
Also see Street Cleaners, The

SMALL FACES, The (With Steve Marriott)

TITLE/FLIP	LABEL & NO.	GOOD	NEAR MINT	YR.
AFTERGLOW/Wham Bam, Thank You Mam	(Immediate 5014)	1.00	4.00	68
ALL OR NOTHING/Understanding	(RCA Victor 47-8949)	2.00	8.00	66
DONKEY RIDES, A PENNY A GLASS/The Universal	(Immediate 5009)	1.00	4.00	68
GROW YOUR OWN/Sha-La-La-La-Lee	(Press 9826)	1.50	6.00	66
HAD ME A REAL GOOD TIME/	(Warner Bros. 7442)	.75	3.00	70
HERE COMES THE NICE/Talk To Me	(Immediate 1902)	1.00	4.00	67
HEY GIRL/Almost Grown	(Press 5007)	2.00	8.00	68
ITCHYCOO PARK/I'm Only Dreaming	(Immediate 501)	.75	3.00	67
JOURNEY, THE/Mad John	(Immediate 5012)	1.00	4.00	68
LAZY SUNDAY/Rollin' Over	(Immediate 5007)	1.00	4.00	68
MY MIND'S EYE/I Can't Dance With You	(RCA Victor 47-9055)	2.00	8.00	66
TIN SOLDIER/I Feel Much Better	(Immediate 5003)	1.00	4.00	68
WHATCHA' GONNA DO ABOUT IT/What's A Matter Baby	(Press 9794)	2.00	8.00	65

Also see Faces, The
Also see Humble Pie
Also see Lane, Ronnie

SMALL, Millie

TITLE/FLIP	LABEL & NO.	GOOD	NEAR MINT	YR.
DON'T YOU KNOW/Tom Hark	(Smash 1946)	.75	3.00	64
I'VE FALLEN IN LOVE WITH A SNOWMAN/Bring It On Home	(Atlantic 2266)	.75	3.00	64
MY BOY LOLLIPOP/Something's Gotta Be Done	(Smash 1893)	.75	3.00	64
SWEET WILLIAM/What Am I Living For	(Smash 1920)	.75	3.00	64

SMALL WONDER

TITLE/FLIP	LABEL & NO.	GOOD	NEAR MINT	YR.
IT WAS MEANT TO BE/	(Columbia 10364)	.50	2.00	75
WHY WALK WHEN YOU CAN DANCE/	(Columbia 10427)	.50	2.00	76
WILL YOU BE A PART OF ME/	(Columbia 10519)	.50	2.00	77

SMART TONES, The

TITLE/FLIP	LABEL & NO.	GOOD	NEAR MINT	YR.
GINNY/Bob O Link	(Herald 529)	1.00	4.00	58

SMILE

TITLE/FLIP	LABEL & NO.	GOOD	NEAR MINT	YR.
EARTH/Step On Me	(Mercury 72977)	5.00	20.00	68

Also see Queen

SMITH (Featuring Gayle McCormack)

TITLE/FLIP	LABEL & NO.	GOOD	NEAR MINT	YR.
BABY IT'S YOU/I Don't Believe (I Believe)	(Dunhill 4206)	.50	2.00	69
COMIN' BACK TO ME/Minus- Plus-	(Dunhill 4246)	.50	2.00	70
TAKE A LOOK AROUND/Mojalesky Ridge	(Dunhill 4228)	.50	2.00	70
WHAT AM I GONNA DO/Born In Boston	(Dunhill 4238)	.50	2.00	70

SMITH, Betty, Group

TITLE/FLIP	LABEL & NO.	GOOD	NEAR MINT	YR.
BEWITCHED!/Hand Jive	(London 1787)	1.00	4.00	58

SMITH, Bobbie, & The Dream Girls

TITLE/FLIP	LABEL & NO.	GOOD	NEAR MINT	YR.
DUTCHES OF EARL/Mine All Mine	(Big Top 3100)	2.50	10.00	61
MR. FINE/Wanted	(Big Top 3085)	1.00	4.00	61

SMITH, Hurricane

TITLE/FLIP	LABEL & NO.	GOOD	NEAR MINT	YR.
OH BABE, WHAT WOULD YOU SAY?/Getting To Know You	(Capitol 3383)	.50	2.00	72
SAM/Beautiful Day, Beautiful Night	(EMI 3809)	.50	2.00	74
WHO WAS IT?/Take Suki Home	(Capitol 3455)	.50	2.00	73

SMITH, Jennie

TITLE/FLIP	LABEL & NO.	GOOD	NEAR MINT	YR.
(I WON'T) GO AWAY LITTLE BOY (Answer song)/Let It Be Me	(Canadian American 150)	1.25	5.00	63

SMITH, Leon

TITLE/FLIP	LABEL & NO.	GOOD	NEAR MINT	YR.
BASIC SURF/	(Lavender 1851)	1.00	4.00	
DYNAMIC/	(Williamette 106)	1.00	4.00	
FLIP FLOP & FLY/	(Williamette 109)	1.00	4.00	
HONEY HONEY/	(Williamette 105)	1.00	4.00	
LITTLE FORTY FORD/Once I Had A Heart	(Epic 9326)	1.00	4.00	59

SMITH, Melvin

TITLE/FLIP	LABEL & NO.	GOOD	NEAR MINT	YR.
OPEN THE DOOR RICHARD/Zaki Sue	(Cameo 135)	1.00	4.00	58
UGLY GEORGE/Nobody's Fault	(Smash 1775)	.75	3.00	62

SMITH, Ocie (O.C. Smith)

TITLE/FLIP	LABEL & NO.	GOOD	NEAR MINT	YR.
BAD MAN OF MISSOURI/If You Don't Love Me	(Cadence 1312)	1.00	4.00	57
LITTLE GREEN APPLES/Long Black Limousine	(Columbia 4-44616)	.75	3.00	68
MAIN STREET MISSION/Gas, Food, Lodging	(Columbia 4-44555)	.75	3.00	68
SLOW WALK/Forbidden Fruit	(Cadence 1304)	1.00	4.00	56
SON OF HICKORY HOLLER'S TRAMP, THE/Best Man	(Columbia 4-44425)	.75	3.00	68
SONG OF THE DREAMER/Hey There	(Citation 1042)	1.00	4.00	59
THAT'S LIFE/The Season	(Columbia 4-33129)	.75	3.00	68
TRY A LITTLE TENDERNESS/How Times Have Changed	(Citation 1034)	1.00	4.00	59
YOU ARE MY SUNSHINE/Well, I'm Dancing	(Big Top 3039)	1.00	4.00	60
YOU'VE CHANGED/Why Do I Feel So Enchanted	(Citation 1037)	1.00	4.00	59

SMITH, Patti

TITLE/FLIP	LABEL & NO.	GOOD	NEAR MINT	YR.
BECAUSE THE NIGHT/God Speed	(Arista 0318)	.50	2.00	78
FREDERICK/Frederick Live	(Arista 0427)	.50	2.00	79
GLORIA: IN EXCELSIS DEO-GLORIA/My Generation	(Arista 0171)	.50	2.00	77
HEY JOE (VERSION)/Piss Factory	(Mercury 601)	8.75	35.00	74
(Limited pressing of 1600 copies)				
HEY JOE (VERSION)/Piss Factory	(Sire 1009)	.75	3.00	77
SO YOU WANT TO BE (A ROCK 'N' ROLL STAR)/	(Arista 0453)	.50	2.00	79

TITLE/FLIP	LABEL & NO.	GOOD	NEAR MINT	YR.
SMITH, Ray (Raymond Eugene Smith)				
AFTER THIS NIGHT IS THROUGH/Turn On The Moonlight	(Infinity 003)	.75	3.00	62
ALMOST ALONE/A Place Within My Heart	(Toppa 1071)	.75	3.00	62
BLONDE HAIR, BLUE EYES/You Don't Want Me	(Judd 1021)	1.50	6.00	61
CANDY DOLL/Hey Boss Man	(Sun 375)	1.25	5.00	62
DEEP IN MY HEART/She's Mine	(Nu-Tone 1182)	.75	3.00	64
DID WE HAVE A PARTY/Here Comes My Baby Back Again	(Tollie 9029)	2.50	10.00	64
EVERYBODY'S GOIN' SOMEWHERE/Au Go Go Go	(Diamond 193)	.75	3.00	65
I WALK THE LINE/Fool Number One	(Celebrity Circle 6901)	.75	3.00	64
I'M SNOWED/Turn Over A New Leaf	(Warner Bros. 5371)	.75	3.00	63
LET YOURSELF GO/Johnny The Hummer	(Infinity 007)	.75	3.00	62
ONE WONDERFUL LOVE/Makes Me Feel Good	(Judd 1019)	1.25	5.00	60
PUT YOUR ARMS AROUND ME HONEY/Maria Elena	(Judd 1017)	1.25	5.00	60
ROBBIN' THE CRADLE/Rockin' Robin	(Vee Jay 579)	1.00	4.00	64
ROCKIN' BANDIT/Sail Away	(Sun 319)	2.00	8.00	59
ROCKIN' LITTLE ANGEL/That's All Right	(Judd 1016)	1.00	4.00	60
RIGHT BEHIND YOU BABY/So Young	(Sun 298)	2.50	10.00	58
THOSE FOUR PRECIOUS YEARS/Room 503	(Smash 1787)	.75	3.00	62
TRAVELING SALESMAN/Won't Miss You	(Sun 372)	1.25	5.00	62
WHY, WHY, WHY/You Made A Hit	(Sun 308)	1.50	6.00	59
SMITH, Rex (Formerly Rex)				
FOREVER/	(Columbia 11163)	.50	2.00	79
SIMPLY JESSIE/Burn Your Bridges	(Columbia 11032)	.50	2.00	79
SOONER OR LATER/Never Gonna Give You Up	(Columbia 11105)	.50	2.00	79
YOU'RE NEVER TO OLD TO ROCK & ROLL/	(Columbia 10658)	.50	2.00	77
(Shown as by Rex)				
YOU TAKE MY BREATH AWAY/ Better Than It's Ever Been Before	(Columbia 10908)	.50	2.00	79
SMITH, Roger				
BEACH TIME/Cuddle Up A Little Closer	(Warner Bros. 5068)	1.00	4.00	59
LOVE OF TWO/Tick, Tick, Tick	(Warner Bros. 5106)	1.00	4.00	59
SMITH, Ronnie				
I HEAR YOU KNOCKING/I Started Out Walkin'	(Imperial 5679)	.75	3.00	60
SMITH, Shelby				
ROCKIN' MAMA/Since My Baby Said Goodbye	(Rebel 201)	1.00	4.00	62
SMITH, Somethin', & The Redheads				
HEARTACHES/Cecilia	(Epic 9179)	1.00	4.00	56
IN A SHANTY IN OLD SHANTY TOWN/ Coal Dust On The Fiddle	(Epic 9168)	1.00	4.00	56
IT'S A SIN TO TELL A LIE/My Baby Just Cares For Me	(Epic 9093)	1.00	4.00	55
SCHOOL BUS ROCK/I Thank You Mr. Moon	(Epic 9264)	1.00	4.00	58
WHEN ALL THE STREETS ARE DARK/Pretty Baby	(Epic 9119)	1.00	4.00	55
SMITH, Snuffy, & The Hootin Holler Twisters				
SHUFFY TWISTER/Buffalo Twister	(Tempwood 1035)	.75	3.00	62
SMITH, Susan				
LETTER FROM SUSAN, A/ Will You Love Me When I'm Old	(Dynamic Sound 502)	3.00	12.00	62
(Novelty/Break-In)				
SMITH, Tab				
BECAUSE OF YOU/Dee Jay Special	(United 104)	1.00	4.00	51
PRETEND/Crazy Walk	(United 205)	.75	3.00	57
SMITH, Verdelle				
IN MY ROOM (EL LAMOR)/Walk Tall	(Capitol 5567)	.75	3.00	66
TAR & CEMENT/Piece Of The Sky	(Capitol 5632)	.75	3.00	66
SMITH, Whistling Jack				
I WAS KAISER BILL'S BATMAN/British Grin 'N Bear	(Deram 85005)	.75	3.00	67
(Instrumentals)				
SMITHS, The				
NOW I TASTE THE TEARS/I Can't Stop	(Columbia 44494)	1.25	5.00	68
NOW I TASTE THE TEARS/I Can't Stop	(Columbia 44494)	1.00	4.00	68
(Promotional issue)				
SMOKE RING				
NO NOT MUCH/How Did You Get To Be So Wonderful	(Buddah 77)	.75	3.00	69
SMOKESTACK (The Earls)				
THERE'S A WORLD BETWEEN US/Take A Look	(Daisy 1010)	1.25	5.00	
THERE'S A WORLD BETWEEN US/Take A Look	(Dakar 4503)	.75	3.00	
SMOKESTACK LIGHTNIN'				
BABY DON'T GET CRAZY/The Blue Albino Shuffle	(Bell 836)	1.00	4.00	69
HELLO L.A., BYE BYE BIRMINGHAM/Well Tuesday	(Bell 861)	1.00	4.00	70
LIGHT IN MY WINDOW/Long Stemmed Eyes	(Bell 755)	1.00	4.00	68
LOOK WHAT YOU'VE DONE/Got A Good Love	(White Whale 256)	1.50	6.00	67
NADINE/Crossroads Blues	(White Whale 243)	1.50	6.00	67
SOMETHING'S GOT A HOLD ON ME/I Idolize You	(Bell 777)	1.00	4.00	69
SMOKEY: see Smokie				
SMOKEY & HIS SISTER				
CREATORS OF RAIN/In A Dream Of Silent Seas	(Columbia 43995)	.75	3.00	67
SMOKEY VINCE LA SPADA				
THERE'S A HOLE IN MY CIGARETTE (PART 1)/ There's A Hole In My Cigarette (Part 2)	(Cameo 254)	.75	3.00	63
SMOKIE (Featuring Chris Norman)				
DON'T PLAY YOUR ROCK N' ROLL TO ME/	(MCA 40471)	.50	2.00	75
FOR A FEW DOLLARS MORE/I Can't Stay Here Tonight	(RSO 900)	.50	2.00	78
IF YOU THINK YOU KNOW HOW TO LOVE ME/ Make Ya Boogie	(RSO 874)	.50	2.00	77
IF YOU THINK YOU KNOW HOW TO LOVE ME/ 'Tis Me	(MCA 40429)	.50	2.00	75
(Shown as by Smokey)				
LIVING NEXT TO ALICE/ When My Back Was AgainstThe Wall	(RSO 860)	.50	2.00	76
NEEDLES & PINS/No One Could Ever Love You More	(RSO 881)	.50	2.00	77
OH CAROL/No More Letters	(RSO 934)	.50	2.00	79
Also see Quatro, Suzie				
SMOTHERS BROTHERS, The (Tom & Dick)				
FLY EZEKIEL/They Call The Wind Maria	(Mercury 72027)	.75	3.00	62
JENNY BROWN/You Go Thisaway	(Mercury 72182)	.75	3.00	63
SLITHERY DEE/Coo Coo	(Mercury 72323)	.75	3.00	64
TOY SONG, THE/Little Sacka Sugar	(Mercury 72519)	.75	3.00	64
Comedy				
SNAIL				
CATCH ME (GIVE ME A SIGN, SHOW ME A REASON)/	(Cream 7830)	.50	2.00	78
JOKER, THE/Childhood Dreams	(Cream 7827)	.50	2.00	78
TONIGHT/Forever	(Cream 7838)	.50	2.00	79
SNEAKERS, The				
MARY LOU/	(Delta 1868)	.75	3.00	
SNEAKERS & LACE				
SKATEBOARDIN'/	(Pip 6526)	1.00	4.00	
SNEED, Brady & Grady				
LITTLE BITTY HEART/Leavin' It All Up To You	(Dolton 38)	.75	3.00	61
STAR OF THE SHOW/Sad September	(Planetary 107)	.75	3.00	65
(Shown as by Grady & Brady)				
SNEED, Leslie				
OH, BABY DOLL/	(Cascade 103)	.75	3.00	
SNEEKERS, The				
SOUL SNEAKER/Sneaker Talk	(Columbia 43438)	1.00	4.00	65
SNEEZER, Ebe, & The Epidemics (Featuring John D. Loudermilk)				
ASIATIC FLU/That's All I've Got	(Colonial 436)	1.25	5.00	57
SNIDER, Len, & The Jokers				
EVERYONE KNOWS/I'll Be Coming Home Tonight	(All Boy 45-8507)	.75	3.00	
SNIFF 'N' THE TEARS				
DRIVER'S SEAT/Slide Away	(Atlantic 3604)	.50	2.00	79
NEW LINES ON LOVE/Fight For Love	(Atlantic 3626)	.50	2.00	79
SNO-FLAKES, The				
JOEY THE SNOWY SNOWFLAKE/Jingle Bells	(Hi Note 183)	.75	3.00	
SNOW, B.F.				
ELVIS IS A LEGEND/Lisa Is Her Name	(Dee Bee 20)	.50	2.00	77
SNOW MEN, The (The Concords)				
COLD & FROSTY MORNING/You Started It	(Herald 597)	2.50	10.00	63
SNOW, Phoebe				
ALL OVER/No Regrets	(Columbia 10351)	.50	2.00	76
AUTOBIOGRAPHY (SHINE, SHINE, SHINE)/ Teach Me Tonight	(Columbia 10504)	.50	2.00	77
EVERY NIGHT/Random Time	(Columbia 10856)	.50	2.00	78
GOOD TIMES (LET THE GOOD TIMES ROLL)/Harpo's Blues	(Shelter 40278)	.50	2.00	74
LOVE MAKES A WOMAN/Electra	(Columbia 10654)	.50	2.00	77
NEVER LETTING GO/The Middle Of The Night	(Columbia 10626)	.50	2.00	77
POETRY MAN/Either Or Both	(Shelter 40353)	.50	2.00	75
SHAKEY GROUND/Don't Sleep With Your Eyes Closed	(Columbia 10463)	.50	2.00	77
TWO FISTED LOVE/Inspired Insanity	(Columbia 10315)	.50	2.00	76
Also see Simon, Paul				
SNYDER, Bill				
BEWITCHED/Drifting Sands	(Tower 1473)	1.50	6.00	50
BEWITCHED/Drifting Sands	(London 868)	1.00	4.00	51
RIDIN' THE OFFBEAT/Dream Concerto	(Tower 1474)	1.50	6.00	50
RIDIN' THE OFFBEAT/Dream Concerto	(London 869)	1.00	4.00	51
SOCIETY GIRLS, The				
S.P.C.L.G. (SOCIETY FOR THE PREVENTION OF CRUELTY TO LITTLE GIRLS)/You Better Stay Home	(Vee Jay 524)	1.00	4.00	63
SOCIETY'S CHILDREN				
I'LL LET YOU KNOW/Live For Today	(Atco 6597)	.75	3.00	68
TRIBUTE TO THE 4 SEASONS, A/Golden Child	(Atco 6618)	3.75	15.00	68
WHITE CHRISTMAS/I'll Let You Know	(Atco 6538)	.75	3.00	67
SOFFICI, Piero				
THAT'S THE WAY WITH LOVE/Valley Of My Heart	(Kip 224)	.75	3.00	61
SOFT MACHINE				
WHY ARE WE SLEEPING/Joy Of A Toy	(Probe 452)	.75	3.00	70
SOFTWINDS				
CROSS MY HEART/Oh Baby	(Hac 105)	1.00	4.00	61
SOLOMON, Ed				
BEATLE FLYING SAUCER/Whistling Drifter	(Diamond 160)	1.50	6.00	64
(Novelty/Break-in)				
SOMETHING WILD				
TRIPPIN' OUT/She's Kinda Weird	(Psychedelic 1691)	5.00	20.00	
SOMMER, Bert				
SONG'S IN ME, THE/I Got A Woman	(Capitol 4602)	.50	2.00	78
SOMMERS, Joanie				
JOHNNY GET ANGRY/Summer Place, Theme	(Warner Bros. 5275)	.75	3.00	62
ONE BOY/June Is Bustin' Out All Over	(Warner Bros. 5361)	.75	3.00	63
ONE BOY/I'll Never Be Free	(Warner Bros. 5157)	.75	3.00	60
PIANO BOY/Serenade Of The Bells	(Warner Bros. 5226)	.75	3.00	62
WHEN THE BOYS GET TOGETHER/Passing Strangers	(Warner Bros. 5308)	.75	3.00	62
SOMMERS, Ronny: see Sonny				
SONG (With Curt Boettcher)				
LIKE WE WERE BEFORE/Sugar Lady	(MGM 14151)	.75	3.00	70
SONG SPINNERS, The				
DIDDLE DE DUM/	(Power 16)	.75	3.00	
SOUTH STREET/	(Big 28)	.75	3.00	
Also see Glitters, The				
SONGWRITERS, The				
CRYING 'BOUT ELVIS/No Night In Heaven	(Adam's Rib 1112)	.50	2.00	77
SONICS, The				
YOU GOT YOUR HEAD ON BACKWARDS/	(Jerden 809)	1.00	4.00	
WITCH, THE/Keep A Knockin'	(Etiquette ET-11)	1.00	4.00	
SONNY (Salvatore Phillip "Sonny" Bono)				
AS LONG AS YOU LOVE ME/I'll Always Be Grateful	(Go GO-1001)	1.50	6.00	60
(Shown as by Don Christy)				
AS LONG AS YOU LOVE ME/I'll Always Be Grateful	(Name 3)	1.25	5.00	60
(Shown as by Don Christy)				
DON'T SHAKE MY TREE/(Mama) Come Get Your Baby Boy	(Swami 1001)	1.50	6.00	61
(Shown as by Ronny Sommers)				
LAUGH AT ME/Tony	(Atco 6369)	.75	3.00	65
MY BEST FRIEND'S GIRL IS OUT OF SIGHT/ Pammie's On A Bummer	(Atco 6531)	.75	3.00	67
ONE LITTLE ANSWER/Wearing Black	(Speciality 672)	1.25	5.00	59
(Shown as by Don Christy)				
ONE LITTLE ANSWER/ Comin' Down The Chimney (With Little Tootsie)	(Speciality 733)	.75	3.00	65
(Shown as by Sonny Bono)				
REVOLUTION KIND, THE/Georgia & John Quetzel	(Atco 6386)	.75	3.00	65
TRY IT OUT ON ME/	(Highland 1160)	1.25	5.00	63
WEARING BLACK/Don't Have To Tell Me	(Fidelity 3020)	1.25	5.00	60
(Shown as by Don Christy)				

TITLE/FLIP	LABEL & NO.	GOOD	NEAR MINT	YR.
SONNY & CHER (Salvatore Bono & Cher La Piere)				
ALL I EVER NEED IS YOU/I Got You Babe	(Kapp 2151)	.50	2.00	71
BABY DON'T GO/Walkin' The Quetzel	(Reprise 0309)	1.00	4.00	64
BABY DON'T GO/Walkin' The Quetzel	(Reprise 0392)	.75	3.00	65
BEAT GOES ON, THE/Love Don't Come	(Atco 6461)	.75	3.00	67
BEAUTIFUL STORY, A/Podunk	(Atco 6480)	.75	3.00	67
BUT YOU'RE MINE/Hello	(Atco 6381)	.75	3.00	65
COWBOY'S WORK IS NEVER DONE, A/Somebody	(Kapp 2163)	.50	2.00	72
GOOD COMBINATION/You & Me	(Atco 6541)	.75	3.00	67
GREATEST SHOW ON EARTH, THE/You Know Darn Well	(MCA 40083)	.50	2.00	73
HAVE I STAYED TOO LONG/Leave Me Be	(Atco 6420)	.75	3.00	66
I GOT YOU BABE/It's Gonna Rain	(Atco 6359)	.75	3.00	65
IT'S THE LITTLE THINGS/Don't Talk To Strangers	(Atco 6507)	.75	3.00	67
I WOULD MARRY YOU TODAY/Circus	(Atco 6555)	.75	3.00	67
JUST YOU/Sing C'est La Vie	(Atco 6345)	.75	3.00	65
LET THE GOOD TIMES ROLL/Love Is Strange	(Reprise 0419)	1.50	6.00	65
(Shown as by Caesar & Cleo)				
LET THE GOOD TIMES ROLL/Love Is Strange	(Reprise 0419)	3.00	12.00	65
(Picture sleeve. Sonny and Cher are shown on this picture sleeve as "Salvatore Bono and Cher La Piere also known as Caesar & Cleo.")				
LETTER, THE/Spring Fever	(Vault 916)	1.50	6.00	65
LETTER, THE/Spring Fever	(Vault 916)	1.50	6.00	63
(Shown as by Caesar & Cleo)				
LITTLE MAN/Monday	(Atco 6440)	.75	3.00	66
LIVING FOR YOU/Love Don't Come	(Atco 6449)	.75	3.00	66
LOVE IS STRANGE/Do You Want To Dance	(Reprise 0308)	1.50	6.00	64
(Shown as by Caesar & Cleo)				
MAMA WAS A ROCK & ROLL SINGER, PAPA USED TO WRITE ALL HER SONGS/	(MCA 40026)	.50	2.00	73
PLASTIC MAN/It's The Little Things	(Atco 6486)	.75	3.00	67
REAL PEOPLE/Somebody	(Kapp 2141)	.50	2.00	71
WHAT NOW MY LOVE/I Look For You	(Atco 6395)	.75	3.00	66
WHEN YOU SAY LOVE/Crystal Clear-Muddy Water	(Kapp 2176)	.50	2.00	72
YOU'RE A FRIEND OF MINE/I Would Marry You Today	(Atco 6683)	.75	3.00	69
YOU'RE NOT RIGHT FOR ME/	(Warner Bros. 8341)	.50	2.00	77
SONNY & JOYCE				
MISTER FROGGIE/You Keep Doggin' Me	(Ember 1034)	1.00	4.00	58
SON OF PETE				
MANKIND/Ms. Nell Tied To The Tracks & Saved	(Beserkley 5739)	.50	2.00	74
SONS OF ADAM, The				
BROWN EYED WOMAN/I Need Love	(Pentacle 104)	1.00	4.00	
FEATURED FISH/Baby Show The World	(Alamo 5473)	2.00	8.00	
TAKE MY HAND/Tomorrow's Gonna Be Another Day	(Alamo 5473)	2.00	8.00	
THINKING ANIMAL, THE/My Petite	(Pentacle 101)	1.00	4.00	
YOU'RE A BETTER MAN THAN I/Saturday's Son	(Decca 31887)	1.25	5.00	66
SONS OF CHAMPLIN, The				
FREEDOM/Hello Sunlight	(Capitol 2534)	1.25	5.00	69
HERE IS WHERE YOUR LOVE BELONGS/ Follow Your Heart	(Ariola America 7653)	.50	2.00	76
HOLD ON/Still In Love With You	(Ariola America 7626)	.50	2.00	76
IMAGINATION'S SAKE/You	(Ariola America 7633)	.50	2.00	76
IT'S TIME/Why Do People Run	(Capitol 2663)	1.25	5.00	69
LOOKOUT/Lookout	(Goldmine 101)	1.00	4.00	
LOOKOUT/	(Ariola America 7606)	.50	2.00	75
1982-A/Black & Blue Rainbow	(Capitol 2437)	2.00	8.00	69
SAVED BY THE GRACE OF YOUR LOVE/	(Ariola America 7664)	.50	2.00	77
SING ME A RAINBOW/Fat City	(Verve 10500)	1.25	5.00	67
WELCOME TO THE DANCE/Welcome To The Dance	(Columbia 45873)	1.00	4.00	73
YOU CAN FLY/Terry's Tune	(Capitol 2786)	1.50	6.00	70
SOOTZ, Manny				
CAPE CANAVERAL (PART 1)/Cape Canaveral (Part 2)	(Pirate 841)	2.00	8.00	57
(Novelty/Break-in)				
SOPHISTICATES, The				
WHEN ELVIS MARCHES HOME AGAIN/Woody's Places	(Viva 61)	2.50	10.00	60
SOPWITH CAMEL, The				
HELLO HELLO/Treadin'	(Kama Sutra 217)	1.00	4.00	66
POSTCARD FROM JAMAICA/Little Orphan Annie	(Kama Sutra 224)	1.00	4.00	67
SAGA OF THE LOWDOWN LET DOWN/ The Great Morpheum	(Kama Sutra 236)	2.00	8.00	67

TITLE/FLIP	LABEL & NO.	GOOD	NEAR MINT	YR.
SOUL, David				
DON'T GIVE UP ON US/Black Bean Soup	(Private Stock 45129)	.50	2.00	77
GOING IN WITH MY EYES OPEN/Topanga	(Private Stock 45150)	.50	2.00	77
I WILL WARM YOUR HEART/Covered Man	(MGM 13510)	.75	3.00	66
NO ONE'S GONNA CRY/Quiet Kind Of Hate	(MGM 13842)	.75	3.00	67
SILVER LADY/	(Private Stock 45163)	.50	2.00	77
WAS I EVER SO YOUNG/Before	(MGM 13589)	.75	3.00	66
SOUL 4, The				
YOU'RE THE ANGEL/Misery	(Ringo 4321)	.75	3.00	
SOUL POTION				
CIRCLE FULL OF LOVE/Soul Baby	(Sunburst 524)	3.00	12.00	
Also see Vito & the Salutations				
SOUL SURFERS, The				
CANNON BALL/Home From Camp	(Challange 9209)	.75	3.00	64
HOME FROM CAMP/I Want To Get Married	(Challenge 59267)	.75	3.00	65
SOUL SURVIVORS, The (Gene Chalk, Pat Shanahan, Allen Kemp, Bob Webber)				
CAN'T STAND TO BE IN LOVE WITH YOU/Look At Me	(Dot 16793)	1.00	4.00	66
SNOW MAN/Hung Up On Losing	(Dot 16830)	1.00	4.00	66
Pat Shanahan & Allen Kemp later joined Rick Nelson's Stone Canyon Band. Bob Webber became a member of Sugarloaf.				
SOUL SURVIVORS, The				
DEVIL WITH A BLUE DRESS ON/Shakin' With Linda	(Decca 32080)	1.00	4.00	67
EXPLOSION IN YOUR SOUL/Dathon's Theme	(Crimson 1012)	.75	3.00	67
EXPRESSWAY TO YOUR HEART/Hey Gyp	(Crimson 1010)	.75	3.00	67
IMPOSSIBLE MISSION (MISSION IMPOSSIBLE)/Poor Man's Dream	(Crimson 1016)	.75	3.00	68
TURN OUT THE FIRE/Go Out Walking	(Atco 6627)	.75	3.00	68
SOULOSOPHY				
FRIENDS & LOVERS/Take Me To The Pilot	(Epic 10717)	.75	3.00	71
LIVE YOUR LIFE WITH SOMEONE/Mama's Book	(Epic 10658)	.75	3.00	70
OUTRAGE/Dream World	(ABC 11204)	1.00	4.00	69
SOUND MACHINE, The				
GOTTA EASE MY MIND/Spanish Flash	(Canterbury 511)	1.00	4.00	67
SOUND 77				
THERE IS NO REASON/Seven Day Fool	(Mijji 3002)	1.00	4.00	
SOUND 9418 (Jonathan King)				
IN THE MOOD/	(UK-Big Tree 16057)	.50	2.00	76
SOUNDS INCORPORATED, The				
IN THE HALL OF THE MOUNTAIN KING/Time For You	(Liberty 55789)	1.00	4.00	65
(Instrumentals)				
SOUNDS ORCHESTRAL, The				
CANADIAN SUNSET/Have Faith In Your Love	(Parkway 958)	.75	3.00	65
CAST YOUR FATE TO THE WIND/To Wendy With Love	(Parkway 942)	.75	3.00	65
Instrumentals				
SOUR TONES, The				
DESAFINADO (COMPLETELY OUT OF TUNE)/Sour Georgia Brown	(Terri Ann 100)	1.25	5.00	62
(Parody)				
SOUTH				
DAYBREAK/Got Me In The Middle	(A&M 984)	.75	3.00	68
GIRL LIKE YOU, A/	(Silver Fox 7)	.75	3.00	68
SOUTHBOUND FREEWAY, The				
PSYCHEDELIC USED CAR LOT/Southbound Freeway	(Roulette 4739)	1.25	5.00	67
SOUTHER, John David (Of Souther, Hillman & Furay)				
BLACK ROSE/Silver Blue	(Asylum 45332)	.50	2.00	76
HOW LONG/The Fast One	(Asylum 11009)	.50	2.00	74
YOU'RE ONLY LONELY/Songs Of Love	(Columbia 11079)	.50	2.00	79
This artist is sometimes shown as J.D. Souther.				
SOUTHER HILLMAN & FURAY (John David Souther, Chris Hillman, Richie Furay)				
FALLIN' IN LOVE/Heavenly Fire	(Asylum 45201)	.50	2.00	74
FOR SOMEONE I LOVE/	(Asylum 45280)	.50	2.00	75
MEXICO/Move Me Real Slow	(Asylum 45251)	.50	2.00	75
SAFE AT HOME/Border Town	(Asylum 45217)	.50	2.00	74
Also see Byrds, The				
Also see Poco				
SOUTHERN COMFORT (Formerly Matthews' Southern Comfort)				
DON'T TAKE YOUR SWEET LOVE AWAY/Milk & Honey	(Cotillion 44043)	1.00	4.00	69
I SURE LIKE YOUR SMILE/Return To Frog City	(Capitol 3133)	.75	3.00	71
RIVER WOMAN/	(Capitol 3271)	.75	3.00	72
SOUTHERN, Jeri				
AN OCCASIONAL MAN/What Do You See In Her	(Decca 29647)	1.00	4.00	55
SOUTHERN, Johnny				
IN THE MIDDLE OF A LONELY, LONELY NIGHT/I Will Get By	(Liberty 55482)	1.00	4.00	62
SOUTH, Joe				
BACKFIELD IN MOTION/I'll Come Back To You	(Columbia 43893)	.75	3.00	67
BIRDS OF A FEATHER/It Got Away	(Capitol 2060)	.75	3.00	67
BIRDS OF A FEATHER/These Are Not My People	(Capitol 2532)	.50	2.00	69
CHILDREN/Clock Up On The Wall	(Capitol 2755)	.50	2.00	70
CONCRETE JUNGLE/Last One To Know	(MGM 13196)	1.00	4.00	63
DON'T IT MAKE YOU WANT TO GO HOME/Hearts Desire	(Capitol 2592)	.50	2.00	69
DON'T THROW YOUR LOVE TO THE WIND/Redneck	(Capitol 2284)	.75	3.00	68
FOOL IN LOVE/Great Day	(Columbia 44218)	.75	3.00	67
FOOL ME/Devil May Care	(Capitol 3204)	.50	2.00	71
GAMES PEOPLE PLAY/Mirror Of Your Mind	(Capitol 2248)	.50	2.00	68
HOW CAN I UNLOVE YOU/She's Almost You	(Capitol 2169)	.75	3.00	68
I'M A STAR/Misunderstanding	(Capitol 3497)	.50	2.00	72
I'M SNOWED/It's Only You	(NRC 002)	1.25	5.00	58
I'M SORRY FOR YOU/The Masquerade	(Fairlane 21010)	1.00	4.00	61
I'VE GOT TO BE SOMEBODY/Deep Inside Me	(Apt 25084)	1.00	4.00	65
JUST REMEMBER YOU'RE MINE/Silly Me	(Allwood 402)	1.00	4.00	62
LEANIN' ON YOU/Don't You Be Ashamed	(Capitol 2491)	.75	3.00	69
LITTLE BLUEBIRD/Play It Cool	(NRC 041)	1.25	5.00	60
LITTLE QUEENIE/Naughty Claudie	(MGM 13276)	1.00	4.00	64
ONE FOOL TO ANOTHER/Texas Ain't The Biggest Anymore	(NRC 5001)	1.25	5.00	58
PURPLE PEOPLE EATER MEETS THE WITCH DOCTOR, THE/My Fondest Memories	(NRC 5000)	1.25	5.00	58
RIVERDOG/It Hurts Me Too	(Capitol 3717)	.50	2.00	73
SAME OLD SONG/Standing Invitation	(MGM 13145)	1.00	4.00	63
SAVE YOUR BEST/Real Thing	(Capitol 3554)	.50	2.00	73
SLIPPIN' AROUND/Just To Be With You Again	(Fairlane 21015)	1.00	4.00	61
TO HAVE, TO HOLD & LET GO/Midnight Rainbow	(Capitol 4034)	.50	2.00	75
WALK A MILE IN MY SHOES/Shelter	(Capitol 2704)	.50	2.00	70
WHY DOES A MAN DO WHAT HE HAS TO DO/Be A Believer	(Capitol 2916)	.50	2.00	70
YO YO/Naughty Claudie	(A&M 922)	.75	3.00	68
YOU'RE THE REASON/Jukebox	(Fairlane 21006)	1.00	4.00	61
Also see Chips, The				
SOUTHSIDE JOHNNY & THE ASBURY JUKES				
I DON'T WANT TO GO HOME/The Fever	(Epic 50238)	.50	2.00	77
I'M SO ANXIOUS/Your Reply	(Mercury 76007)	.50	2.00	79
LIVING IN THE REAL WORLD/Wait In Vain	(Mercury 76023)	.50	2.00	79
LOVE ON THE WRONG SIDE OF TOWN/Some Things Don't Change	(Epic 50466)	.50	2.00	78
TRAPPED AGAIN/This Time Baby's Gone For Good	(Epic 50646)	.50	2.00	78
WITHOUT LOVE/First Night	(Epic 50393)	.50	2.00	77
SOUTHWEST F.O.B. (Dan Seals & John Ford Coley)				
ALL ONE BIG GAME/Nadine	(Hip 8009)	1.00	4.00	68
FELLIN' GROOVEY/Begger Man	(Hip 8022)	1.00	4.00	69
FELLIN' GROOVEY (Stereo)/Begger Man (Mono)	(Hip 8022)	1.25	5.00	69
(Promotional issue)				
SMELL OF INCENSE/Green Skies	(GPC 1945)	1.00	4.00	68
SMELL OF INCENSE/Green Skies	(Hip 8002)	1.00	4.00	68
Also see England Dan & John Ford Coley				
SOUVENIRS, The				
I COULD HAVE DANCED ALL NIGHT/It's Too Bad	(Inferno 2001)	3.00	12.00	
SAILOR BOY/Never Camp Alone Joe	(Pro 3)	1.00	4.00	
WORM, THE/The Bump	(Reprise 20065)	.75	3.00	62
SPACE MAN & THE SATELLITES				
MAN IN ORBIT/Blast Off	(Chess 1789)	1.50	6.00	61
SPACE, Sam, & The Cadets				
TAKE ME TO YOUR LEADER, CHA CHA/Man With The Green Mustache	(Cabot 127)	1.00	4.00	59
SPACEMEN, The				
BLAST OFF/Jersey Bounce	(Felsted 8578)	1.00	4.00	59
CLOUDS, THE/The Lonely Jet Pilot	(Alton 254)	1.00	4.00	59
ROUND UP/Cinderella's Parade	(Jubilee 5368)	1.00	4.00	59
VENUS TWIST/Oribital Twist	(Markey 100)	.75	3.00	62
Instrumentals				
SPADES, The: see Slades, The				
SPADES, The: see 13th Floor Elevators				
SPAGHETTI HEAD				
BIG NOISE FROM WINNETKA/Funky Axe	(Private Stock 45014)	.50	2.00	75
(Instrumentals)				
SPANDELLS, The				
SAY NO GIRL/The Boy Next Door	(Dimension 1041)	.75	3.00	65
SPANKY & OUR GANG (Featuring Spanky McFarlane)				
AND SHE'S MINE/Leopard Skin Phones	(Mercury 72926)	.75	3.00	69
ANYTHING YOU CHOOSE/Mecca Flats Blues	(Mercury 72890)	.75	3.00	69
EVERYBODY'S TALKIN'/	(Mercury 72982)	.75	3.00	69
GIVE A DAMN/Swinging Gate	(Mercury 72831)	.75	3.00	68
I WON'T BRAND YOU/	(Epic 50170)	.50	2.00	75
L.A. FREEWAY/	(Epic 50206)	.50	2.00	75
LAZY DAY/Byrd Avenue (It Ain't Necessarily)	(Mercury 72732)	.75	3.00	67
LIKE TO GET TO KNOW YOU/Three Ways From Tomorrow	(Mercury 72795)	.75	3.00	68
MAKING EVERY MINUTE COUNT/If You Could Only Be Me	(Mercury 72714)	.75	3.00	67
SUNDAY MORNING/Echoes (Everybody's Talkin')	(Mercury 72765)	.75	3.00	67
SUNDAY WILL NEVER BE THE SAME/Distance	(Mercury 72679)	.75	3.00	67
YESTERDAY'S RAIN/Without Rhyme Or Reason	(Mercury 72871)	.75	3.00	68
SPARKIE				
HOME/It's A Long Way To Tipperary	(Mercury 5494)	1.25	5.00	50
SWEET GEORGIA BROWN/Feather Brain	(Mercury 5460)	1.25	5.00	50
SPARKLES, The				
HIPSVILLE 29 BC (I NEED HELP)/I Want To Be Free	(Hickory 1474)	.75	3.00	67
NO FRIEND OF MIND/First Forget (What Has Made You Blue)	(Hickory 1443)	.75	3.00	67
SPARKLETONES, The: see Bennett, Joe & The Sparkletones				
SPARKS, The				
ACHOO/Something For The Girl With Everything	(Island 023)	1.00	4.00	75
HOLD YOUR HAND/England	(Island 8282)	1.25	5.00	73
LOOKS, LOOKS, LOOKS/Wedding Of Jackie	(Island 043)	1.00	4.00	76
OVER THE SUMMER/	(Columbia 10579)	.50	2.00	78
THIS TOWN AIN'T BIG ENOUGH FOR BOTH OF US/Barbecutie	(Island 001)	1.00	4.00	75
TRYOUTS FOR THE HUMAN RACE/The No. 1 Song In Heaven	(Elektra 46045)	.50	2.00	79
WONDER GIRL/(No More) Mr. Nice Guys	(Bearsville 0006)	1.25	5.00	72
SPARKS, Randy (Of The New Christy Minstrels)				
AT THE END OF THE RAINBOW/Julie Knows	(Columbia 43138)	.75	3.00	65
Also see Back Porch Majority				
SPARROW (With W.D. Sparrow)				
I'M COMING BACK/Dream Song	(Spark 06)	.75	3.00	72
SPARROW				
DREAM ON DREAMER/I'll Be The Boy	(Capitol of Canada 72210)	3.00	12.00	
GREEN BOTTLE LOVER/Down Goes Your Love Life	(Columbia 43960)	1.50	6.00	67
HARD TIMES WITH THE LAW/Meet Me After Four	(Capitol of Canada 72257)	3.75	15.00	
IF YOU DON'T WANT MY LOVE/It's Been One Of Those Days Today	(Capitol of Canada 72203)	3.00	12.00	
SPARROWS & DAISIES/Our Love Has Passed	(Capitol of Canada 72229)	3.00	12.00	
TOMORROWS SHIP/Isn't It Strange	(Columbia 43755)	2.50	10.00	66
Also see Steppenwolf				
SPARTANS, The				
CAN YOU WADDLE (PART 1)/Can You Waddle (Part 2)	(Web 1)	.75	3.00	62
SPATS, The				
GATOR TAILS & MONKEY RIBS/The Roach	(ABC-Paramount 10585)	.75	3.00	64
GATOR TAILS & MONKEY RIBS/The Roach	(Enith 1268)	1.25	5.00	64
SCOOBEE DOO/She Done Moved	(ABC-Paramount 10790)	.75	3.00	66
THERE'S A PARTY IN THE PAD DOWN BELOW/She Kissed Me Last Night	(ABC-Paramount 10600)	.75	3.00	64
SPEARMINTS, The				
JO-ANN/Little One	(Autumn 7)	1.00	4.00	65
SPECTOR, Ronnie (Of The Ronettes)				
IT'S A HEARTACHE/I Wanna Come Over (Is That What Time It Is)	(Alston 3738)	.75	3.00	78
PARADISE/When I Saw You	(Warner-Spector 0409)	.75	3.00	76
SAY GOODBYE TO HOLLYWOOD/Baby Please Don't Go	(Epic-Cleveland Int'l. 50374)	.75	3.00	77
(Shown as by Ronnie Spector & The "E" Street Band.)				
TRY SOME, BUY SOME/Tandoori Chicken	(Apple 1832)	.75	3.00	71
YOU'D BE GOOD FOR ME/	(Tom Cat 10380)	.75	3.00	76
Also see Bonnie & the Treasures				
Also see Veronica				
SPECTORS THREE, The (With Phil Spector)				
I REALLY DO/I Know Why	(Trey 3001)	1.50	6.00	60
MR. ROBIN/My Heart Stood Still	(Trey 3005)	1.50	6.00	64
Also see Teddy Bears, The				
SPEEDWAY BLVD.				
SPEEDWAY BOULEVARD/Out Of The Fire	(Epic 9-50936)	.50	2.00	80
(THINK I BETTER) HOLD ON/Speedway Boulevard	(Epic 9-50879)	.50	2.00	80
(THINK I BETTER) HOLD ON/Out Of The Fire	(Epic 9-50879)	.50	2.00	80
(Reissue, with different flip side.)				

TITLE/FLIP	LABEL & NO.	GOOD	NEAR MINT	YR.
SPEEDY & THE REVERBS				
100 PROOF/Gas Chamber	(Reverb RR-51)	1.00	4.00	
SPEIDELS, The				
DEAR JOAN/No	(Crosley 201)	1.25	5.00	
SPEKTRUMS, The				
SUNDOWN/	(Impact 5)	.75	3.00	61
SPELLBINDERS, The				
CHAIN REACTION/Little On The Blue Side	(Columbia 43522)	.75	3.00	66
FOR YOU/Stone In Love	(Columbia 43384)	.75	3.00	65
HELP ME/Danny Boy	(Columbia 43830)	.75	3.00	66
LONG LOST LOVE/We're Acting Like Lovers	(Columbia 43611)	.75	3.00	66
SPELLBOUND				
RUMOR AT THE HONKY TONK/A Taste Of The Devil	(EMI America 8002)	.50	2.00	78
SPENCER & SPENCER				
RUSSIAN BANDSTAND (Novelty/Break-in)/Brass Wail (Instrumental)	(Argo 5331)	1.50	6.00	59
STAGGER LAWRENCE (Novelty/Break-in)/Stroganoff Cha Cha (Instrumental)	(Gone 5053)	1.50	6.00	59
SPENCER, Jim, & Son Rize				
BLUES ARE OUT TO GET ME, THE/Love Star	(Armada 101)	.50	2.00	79
SPENCER, Jeremy Group				
COOL BREEZE/	(Atlantic 3588)	.50	2.00	79
COOL BREEZE/	(Atlantic 3601)	.50	2.00	79
TRAVELLIN'/	(Atlantic 3648)	.50	2.00	79
Also see Fleetwood Mac				
SPENCER, Sonny				
GILEE/Oh Boy	(Memo 17984)	1.00	4.00	59
HOLD MY HAND/	(Music Hall 2400)	1.00	4.00	
SPERRY, Steve				
FLAME/Comin' Through To You	(Mercury 73905)	.50	2.00	77
SPHEERIS, Jimmy				
I AM THE MERCURY/	(Columbia 45646)	.50	2.00	72
SPICE OF LIFE				
DEDICATIONS/The Spice Of Life	(Poppy P-503)	1.50	6.00	68
SPI-DELLS, The				
GEE BUT I WISH/Never Ever	(Spi-Dells-Little Town 575)	1.00	4.00	
SPIDERS, The (Featuring Alice Cooper)				
DON'T BLOW YOUR MIND/No Price Tag	(Santa Cruz 003)	18.75	75.00	66
WHY DON'T YOU LOVE ME/Hitch Hike	(Nascot N-112)	20.00	80.00	65
SPIDERS FROM MARS				
I DON'T WANT TO DO NO LIMBO/	(Pye 71063)	.50	2.00	76
(This group was David Bowie's backup band)				
SPIKE DRIVERS, The				
HIGH TIME/Baby Won't You Let Me Tell You How I Lost My Mind	(Reprise 0535)	1.00	4.00	66
STRANGE MYSTERIOUS SOUNDS/Break Out The Wine	(Reprise 0558)	1.00	4.00	67
SPIN				
GRASSHOPPER/Spinning	(Ariola America 7932)	.50	2.00	76
SPIRAL STARECASE, The				
MORE THAN YESTERDAY/Broken-hearted Man	(Columbia 44741)	.75	3.00	69
NO ONE FOR ME TO TURN TO/Sweet Little Thing	(Columbia 44924)	.75	3.00	69
SHE'S READY/Judas To The Love We Knew	(Columbia 45048)	.75	3.00	70
SPIRALS, The				
PLEASE BE MY LOVE/Forever & A Day	(Smash 1719)	5.00	20.00	61
SPIRIT				
ANIMAL ZOO/Red Light Roll On	(Epic 10648)	.75	3.00	70
CADILLAC COWBOYS/Darkness	(Epic 10849)	.75	3.00	72
DARK EYED WOMAN/New Dope In Town	(Ode 122)	1.00	4.00	70
FARTHER ALONG/Atomic Boogie	(Mercury 73837)	.50	2.00	76
HOLY MAN/Looking Into Darkness	(Mercury 73722)	.50	2.00	75
I GOT A LINE ON YOU/She Smiles	(Ode 115)	1.00	4.00	68
MAN ENOUGH FOR YOU/No Time To Rhyme	(Roulette 4757)	1.25	5.00	67
MECHANICAL WORLD/Uncle Jack	(Ode 108)	1.00	4.00	68
(Reissued in 1970 using the same number & flip side.)				
MR. SKIN/	(Epic 10701)	.75	3.00	73
NATURE'S WAY/Soldier	(Epic 10685)	.75	3.00	70
1984/Sweet Stella Baby	(Ode 128)	1.00	4.00	70
SPIRITS OF BLUE LIGHTNING				
LOVE MUSCLE/	(Lavender 2009)	.75	3.00	
SPITALNY, Phil				
OUR LADY OF FATIMA/Ave Maria	(RCA Victor 47-3920)	1.25	5.00	50
SPLINTER				
AFTER FIVE YEARS/Half Way There	(Dark Horse 10010)	.75	3.00	76
CHINA LIGHT/Haven't Got Time	(Dark Horse 10003)	.75	3.00	75
COSTAFINE TOWN/Elly-May	(Dark Horse 10002)	.75	3.00	74

SPOELSTRA, Mark (preceded by continuation)

TITLE/FLIP	LABEL & NO.	GOOD	NEAR MINT	YR.
MOTIONS OF LOVE/	(Dark Horse 8523)	.75	3.00	77
ROUND & ROUND/I'll Bend For You	(Dark Horse 8439)	.75	3.00	77
WHICH WAY WILL I GET HOME/ What Is It (If You Never Tried It Yourself)	(Dark Horse 10007)	.75	3.00	76
Also see Elliot, Bill, & The Elastic Oz Band				

SPOELSTRA, Mark

TITLE/FLIP	LABEL & NO.	GOOD	NEAR MINT	YR.
WORKIN' WITH A WOMAN/Tonight's For Lovin'	(Fantasy 664)	1.00	4.00	71

SPOKESMEN, The (David White & Johnny Madara)

TITLE/FLIP	LABEL & NO.	GOOD	NEAR MINT	YR.
BETTER DAYS ARE YET TO COME/Michelle	(Decca 31895)	.75	3.00	66
DAWN OF CORRECTION, THE/For You Babe	(Decca 31844)	.75	3.00	65
FLASHBACK/Mary Jane	(Winchester 1001)	.75	3.00	67
HAVE COURAGE, BE CAREFUL/It Ain't Fair	(Decca 31874)	.75	3.00	65
I LOVE HOW YOU LOVE ME/Beautiful Girl	(Decca 32049)	.75	3.00	66
TODAY'S THE DAY/Enchante	(Decca 31949)	.75	3.00	66

SPONGY & THE DOLLS

TITLE/FLIP	LABEL & NO.	GOOD	NEAR MINT	YR.
IT LOOKS LIKE LOVE/Really, Really, Really Love	(Bridgeview 7001)	1.50	6.00	

SPONTANEOUS COMBUSTION

TITLE/FLIP	LABEL & NO.	GOOD	NEAR MINT	YR.
CHESSBOARD/Rainy Day	(Harvest 3558)	.50	2.00	72

SPOOKY TOOTH (With Gary Wright, Mike Harrison, & Mick Jones)

TITLE/FLIP	LABEL & NO.	GOOD	NEAR MINT	YR.
FEELIN' BAD/	(A&M 1110)	.75	3.00	69
SPOOKY BLOW/Love Really Changed Me	(Mala 12013)	1.00	4.00	68
SUNSHINE HELP ME/Weird	(Mala 587)	1.00	4.00	68
THINGS CHANGE/All Sewn Up	(Island 1219)	.50	2.00	72
Also see Foreigner				

SPORTS

TITLE/FLIP	LABEL & NO.	GOOD	NEAR MINT	YR.
DON'T THROW STONES/	(Arista 0482)	.50	2.00	79
WHO LISTENS TO THE RADIO/Hit Single	(Arista 0468)	.50	2.00	79

SPOTLIGHTS, The

TITLE/FLIP	LABEL & NO.	GOOD	NEAR MINT	YR.
BATMAN & ROBIN/Dayflower	(Smash 2020)	.75	3.00	66

SPRING

TITLE/FLIP	LABEL & NO.	GOOD	NEAR MINT	YR.
GOOD TIME/Sweet Mountain	(United Artists 50907)	7.50	30.00	72
(Commercial copies are not yet known to exist of this release. Price is for promotional issue.)				
NOW THAT EVERYTHING'S BEEN SAID/Awake	(United Artists 50848)	2.50	10.00	71
Also see American Spring				
Also see Honeys, The				

SPRINGERS

TITLE/FLIP	LABEL & NO.	GOOD	NEAR MINT	YR.
I KNOW MY BABY LOVES ME SO/I Know Why	(Way Out 2699)	2.00	8.00	

SPRINGFIELD, Dusty (Of The Springfields)

TITLE/FLIP	LABEL & NO.	GOOD	NEAR MINT	YR.
ALL CRIED OUT/I Wish I'd Never Loved You	(Philips 40229)	.75	3.00	64
ALL I SEE IS YOU/I'm Gonna Leave You	(Philips 40396)	.75	3.00	66
BRAND NEW ME, A/Bad Case Of The Blues	(Atlantic 2685)	.50	2.00	69
DON'T FORGET ABOUT ME/Breakfast In Bed	(Atlantic 2606)	.50	2.00	69
GIVE ME THE NIGHT/Checkmate	(United Artists 1225)	.50	2.00	78
GUESS WHO/Live It Up	(Philips 40245)	.75	3.00	64
HAUNTED/Nothing Is Forever	(Atlantic 2825)	.50	2.00	71
IN THE MIDDLE OF NOWHERE/Baby Don't You Know	(Philips 40303)	.75	3.00	65
I ONLY WANT TO BE WITH YOU/Once Upon A Time	(Philips 40162)	.75	3.00	64
I'LL TRY ANYTHING/Corrupt Ones	(Philips 40439)	.75	3.00	67
I WANNA BE A FREE GIRL/Let Me In Your Way	(Atlantic 2729)	.50	2.00	70
LEARN TO SAY GOODBYE/Mama's Little Girl	(Dunhill 4344)	.50	2.00	73
LET ME LOVE YOU ONCE BEFORE I GO/	(United Artists 1006)	.50	2.00	77
LIVING WITHOUT YOUR LOVE/Get Yourself To Love	(United Artists 1255)	.50	2.00	79
LOOK OF LOVE, THE/Give Me Time (L'Amore Se Ne Va)	(Philips 40465)	.75	3.00	67
LOSING YOU/Here She Comes	(Philips 40270)	.75	3.00	65
LOST/Never Love Again	(Atlantic 2739)	.50	2.00	70
SILLY, SILLY, FOOL/Joe	(Atlantic 2705)	.50	2.00	70
SO MUCH LOVE/In The Land Of Make Believe	(Atlantic 2673)	.50	2.00	69
SON-OF-A-PREACHER MAN/Just A Little Lovin' (Early In The Mornin')	(Atlantic 2580)	.50	2.00	68
STAY AWHILE/Something Special	(Philips 40180)	.75	3.00	64
WHAT'S IT GONNA BE/Small Town Girl	(Philips 40498)	.75	3.00	67
WHO GETS YOUR LOVE/Of All The Things	(Dunhill 4341)	.50	2.00	73
WINDMILLS OF YOUR MIND, THE/ I Don't Want To Hear It Anymore	(Atlantic 2623)	.50	2.00	69
WILLIE & LAURA MAE JONES/ That Old Sweet Roll (Hi-De-Ho)	(Atlantic 2647)	.50	2.00	69
WISHIN' & HOPIN'/Do Re Me (Forget About The Do & Think About Me)	(Philips 40207)	.75	3.00	64
YOU DON'T HAVE TO LOVE ME/Little By Little	(Philips 40371)	.75	3.00	66

SPRINGFIELD REVIVAL

TITLE/FLIP	LABEL & NO.	GOOD	NEAR MINT	YR.
COME FOLLOW, FOLLOW ME/Someone	(Verve-GTO 10717)	.50	2.00	72

SPRINGFIELD, Rick

TITLE/FLIP	LABEL & NO.	GOOD	NEAR MINT	YR.
AMERICAN GIRLS/	(Columbia 46059)	.50	2.00	74
SPEAK TO THE SKY/Why?	(Capitol 3340)	.75	3.00	72
TAKE A HAND/Archangel	(Chelsea 3051)	.50	2.00	76
WHAT WOULD THE CHILDREN THINK/	(Capitol 3466)	.75	3.00	72

SPRINGFIELD RIFLES, The

TITLE/FLIP	LABEL & NO.	GOOD	NEAR MINT	YR.
STOP & TAKE A LOOK AROUND/100 Or Two	(Jerden 812)	.50	2.00	67

SPRINGFIELDS, The (Dusty Springfield, Tom Springfield, Tim Field, Clive Westlake)

TITLE/FLIP	LABEL & NO.	GOOD	NEAR MINT	YR.
DEAR HEARTS & GENTLE PEOPLE/Gotta Travel On	(Philips 40072)	.75	3.00	62
ISLAND OF DREAMS/Foggy Mountain Top	(Philips 40099)	.75	3.00	63
LITTLE BOAT/Say I Won't Be There	(Philips 40121)	.75	3.00	63
SILVER THREADS & GOLDEN NEEDLES/Aunt Rhody	(Philips 40038)	.75	3.00	62
WAF-WOOF/Little By Little	(Philips 40162)	.75	3.00	63

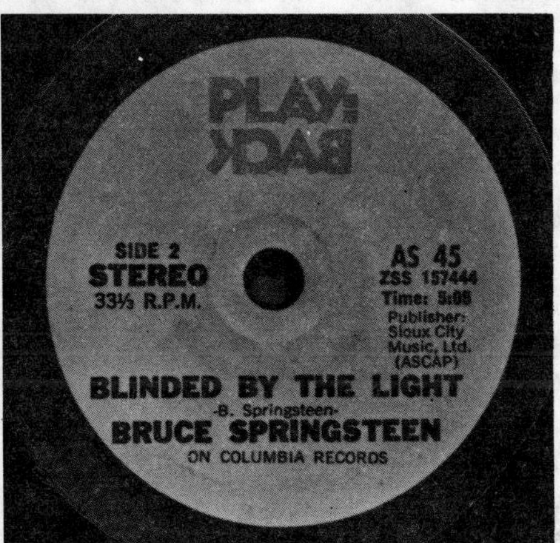

SPRINGSTEEN, Bruce

TITLE/FLIP	LABEL & NO.	GOOD	NEAR MINT	YR.
BADLANDS/Streets Of Fire	(Columbia 3-10801)	.50	2.00	78
BADLANDS/Badlands	(Columbia 3-10801)	1.25	5.00	78
(Promotional issue)				
BLINDED BY THE LIGHT/ Avenging Annie (By Andy Pratt)	(Columbia-Playback 45)	3.75	15.00	72
(Promotional issue, Columbia special products.)				
BLINDED BY THE LIGHT/The Angel	(Columbia 4-45805)	12.50	50.00	73
BLINDED BY THE LIGHT/ Blinded By The Light	(Columbia 4-45805)	3.75	15.00	73
(Promotional issue)				
BLINDED BY THE LIGHT/The Angel	(Columbia 4-45805)	12.50	50.00	73
(Picture sleeve)				
BORN TO RUN/Meeting Across The River	(Columbia 3-10209)	1.00	4.00	75
BORN TO RUN/Born To Run	(Columbia 3-10209)	1.50	6.00	75
(Promotional issue)				
BORN TO RUN/Spirit In The Night	(Columbia 13-33323)	1.00	4.00	76
(Columbia's Hall of Fame reissue series.)				
HUNGRY HEART/Held Up Without A Gun	(Columbia 11-11391)	.50	2.00	80
PROVE IT ALL NIGHT/Factory	(Columbia 3-10763)	.50	2.00	78
PROVE IT ALL NIGHT/Prove It All Night	(Columbia 3-10763)	1.50	6.00	78
(Promotional issue)				
SPIRIT IN THE NIGHT/For You	(Columbia 4-45864)	12.00	50.00	73
SPIRIT IN THE NIGHT/Spirit In The Night	(Columbia 4-45864)	3.75	15.00	73
(Promotional issue)				
TENTH AVENUE FREEZE-OUT/She's The One	(Columbia 3-10274)	.75	3.00	75
TENTH AVENUE FREEZE-OUT/ Tenth Avenue Freeze-Out	(Columbia 3-10274)	2.50	10.00	75
(Promotional issue)				

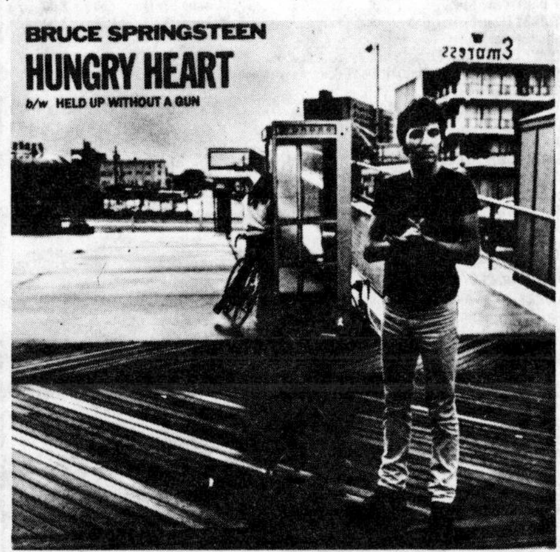

SPROUTS, The

TITLE/FLIP	LABEL & NO.	GOOD	NEAR MINT	YR.
GOODBYE SHE'S GONE/Teen Billy Baby	(Spangle 2002)	3.75	15.00	57
GOODBYE SHE'S GONE/Teen Billy Baby	(RCA Victor 47-7080)	2.00	8.00	57

SPUDD, Bud, & The Sprouts

TITLE/FLIP	LABEL & NO.	GOOD	NEAR MINT	YR.
MASH, THE/Slow Jam	(EM 1001)	.75	3.00	62

SPYDELS, The

TITLE/FLIP	LABEL & NO.	GOOD	NEAR MINT	YR.
CHANGE YOUR MIND/Peace Of Mind	(Assault 1860)	1.25	5.00	
NO MORE TEASING/Wanted Dead Or Alive	(MZ 103)	2.50	10.00	

SPYRO GYRA (With Chet Catallo & Jay Beckenstein)

TITLE/FLIP	LABEL & NO.	GOOD	NEAR MINT	YR.
HELLIOPOLIS-JUBILEE/Morning Dance	(Infinity 1011)	.75	3.00	79
(Promotional issue)				
JUBILEE/Shaker Song	(Infinity 50041)	.50	2.00	79
MORNING SONG/For Lorraine	(Infinity 50011)	.50	2.00	79
SHAKER SONG/Paw Prints	(Amherst 730)	.50	2.00	78
Instrumentals				

SQUEEZE (Formerly U.K. Squeeze)

TITLE/FLIP	LABEL & NO.	GOOD	NEAR MINT	YR.
COOL FOR CATS/	(A&M 2146)	.50	2.00	79
GOODBYE GIRL/Slightly Drunk	(A&M 2168)	.50	2.00	79

SQUIRE, Chris (Of Yes)

TITLE/FLIP	LABEL & NO.	GOOD	NEAR MINT	YR.
LUCKY SEVEN/	(Atlantic 3317)	.50	2.00	76

SQUIRES, The

TITLE/FLIP	LABEL & NO.	GOOD	NEAR MINT	YR.
MOVIN' OUT/Our Theme	(Chan 102)	1.25	5.00	61
MOVIN' OUT/Our Theme	(MGM 13044)	.75	3.00	61

SQUIRES, The

TITLE/FLIP	LABEL & NO.	GOOD	NEAR MINT	YR.
CAN'T BELIEVE YOU'VE GROWN UP/Joyce	(Congress 223)	6.25	25.00	64

SQUIRES, The

TITLE/FLIP	LABEL & NO.	GOOD	NEAR MINT	YR.
SO MANY TEARS AGO/Don't Accuse Me	(Gee 1082)	2.50	10.00	62
WHY SHOULD I SUFFER/Walkin'	(Herald 580)	1.50	6.00	63

STACCATOS, The (The Five Man Electrical Band)

TITLE/FLIP	LABEL & NO.	GOOD	NEAR MINT	YR.
DIDN'T KNOW THE TIME/We Go Together Well	(Capitol 2260)	.75	3.00	68
FACE TO FACE/Let's Run Away	(Tower 277)	1.00	4.00	66

STACKRIDGE (Featuring Mutter Slater)

TITLE/FLIP	LABEL & NO.	GOOD	NEAR MINT	YR.
DORA THE FEMALE EXPLORER/Grande Piano	(Decca 32923)	.50	2.00	72

STACY, Clyde

TITLE/FLIP	LABEL & NO.	GOOD	NEAR MINT	YR.
BABY SHAME/Nobody's Darlin'	(G&H 101)	2.00	8.00	58
BABY SHAME/Nobody's Darlin'	(Bullseye 1004)	1.50	6.00	58
DREAM BOY/A Broken Heart	(Candlelight 1018)	1.50	6.00	57
SO YOUNG/Hoy Hoy	(Candlelight 1015)	3.75	15.00	57
SO YOUNG/Hoy Hoy	(Argyle 1001)	1.00	4.00	59

STAFFORD, Jim

TITLE/FLIP	LABEL & NO.	GOOD	NEAR MINT	YR.
I GOT STONED & I MISSED IT/	(MGM 14819)	.50	2.00	75
JASPER/	(Polydor 14309)	.50	2.00	76
MY GIRL BILL/L.A. Mamma	(MGM 14718)	.50	2.00	74
SPIDERS & SNAKES/Undecided	(MGM 14648)	.50	2.00	73
SWAMP WITCH/	(MGM 14496)	.50	2.00	73
TURN LOOSE OF MY LEG/	(Warner Bros. 8229)	.50	2.00	77
WILDWOOD WEED/The Last Chant	(MGM 14737)	.50	2.00	74
YOUR BULLDOG DRINKS CHAMPAGNE/A Real Good Time	(MGM 14775)	.50	2.00	74

STAFFORD, Jo

TITLE/FLIP	LABEL & NO.	GOOD	NEAR MINT	YR.
BIG D/Warm All Over	(Columbia 40697)	1.00	4.00	56
DEARIE/Monday, Tuesday, Wednesday	(Capitol 858)	1.25	5.00	50
(With Gordon MacRae)				
DON'T GET AROUND MUCH ANYMORE/ Darling, Darling, Darling	(Columbia 40406)	1.00	4.00	55
FOOL SUCH AS I, A/Just Because You're You	(Columbia 39930)	1.00	4.00	53
GOODNIGHT IRENE/Our Very Own	(Capitol 1142)	1.25	5.00	50
HAMBONE/Let's Have A Party	(Columbia 39672)	1.00	4.00	52
(With Frankie Laine)				
HEY, GOOD LOOKIN'/Gambella	(Columbia 39570)	1.00	4.00	51
(With Frankie Laine)				
IT'S ALMOST TOMORROW/If You Want To Love	(Columbia 40595)	1.00	4.00	55
JAMBALAYA/Early Autumn	(Columbia 39838)	1.00	4.00	52
MAKE LOVE TO ME/Adi-Adios Amigo	(Columbia 40143)	1.00	4.00	54
NO OTHER LOVE/Sometime	(Columbia 1053)	1.25	5.00	50
ON LONDON BRIDGE/Bells Are Ringing	(Columbia 40782)	1.00	4.00	56
ST. LOUIS BLUES/Ain'tcha Comin' Out Tonight	(Columbia 40538)	1.00	4.00	55
SHRIMP BOATS/Love, Mystery & Adventure	(Columbia 39581)	1.00	4.00	51
SUDDENLY THERE'S A VALLEY/The Night Watch	(Columbia 40559)	1.00	4.00	55
TEACH ME TONIGHT/Suddenly	(Columbia 40351)	1.00	4.00	54
TENNESSEE WALTZ!/If You've Got The Money	(Columbia 916)	1.00	4.00	51
TENNESSEE WALTZ/Goodnight Pillow	(Columbia 39129)	1.00	4.00	51
THANK YOU FOR CALLING/Where Are You	(Columbia 40250)	1.00	4.00	54
TONIGHT WE'RE SETTING THE WOODS ON FIRE/ Piece A Puddin'	(Columbia 39867)	1.00	4.00	52
(With Frankie Laine)				
YOU BELONG TO ME/Pretty Boy	(Columbia 39811)	1.00	4.00	52

STAFFORD, Terry

TITLE/FLIP	LABEL & NO.	GOOD	NEAR MINT	YR.
FOLLOW THE RAINBOW/Are You A Fool Like Me	(Crusader 109)	1.00	4.00	64
HOPING/A Little Bit Better	(Crusader 110)	1.00	4.00	64
I'LL TOUCH A STAR/Playing With Fire	(Crusader 105)	1.00	4.00	64
MEAN WOMAN BLUES/Candy Man	(MGM 14232)	.75	3.00	71
SUSPICION/Judy	(Crusader 101)	.75	3.00	64
WHEN SIN STOPS, LOVE BEGINS/	(Sidewalk 902)	.75	3.00	65

STAGEHANDS, The

TITLE/FLIP	LABEL & NO.	GOOD	NEAR MINT	YR.
HELLO DOLLY/You Started It	(T.A. 101)	2.00	8.00	

STAGG, Tommy

TITLE/FLIP	LABEL & NO.	GOOD	NEAR MINT	YR.
MEMORIES OF LOVE/Four In Love	(Bambi 802)	3.75	15.00	

STAINED GLASS

TITLE/FLIP	LABEL & NO.	GOOD	NEAR MINT	YR.
FAHRENHEIT/Twiddle My Thumbs	(Capitol 2372)	1.00	4.00	68
GETTIN' ON'S GETTIN' ROUGH/The Necromancer	(Capitol 2521)	1.00	4.00	69
MY BUDDY SIN/Vanity Fair	(RCA Victor 47-8952)	1.25	5.00	66
SCENE IN BETWEEN, A/Mediocre Me	(RCA Victor 47-9354)	1.25	5.00	67
WE GOT A LONG WAY TO GO/Corduroy Joy	(RCA Victor 47-9166)	1.25	5.00	67

STAIRSTEPS, The

TITLE/FLIP	LABEL & NO.	GOOD	NEAR MINT	YR.
FROM US TO YOU/Time	(Dark Horse 10005)	.50	2.00	75
TELL ME WHY/Salaam	(Dark Horse 10009)	.50	2.00	75

STALLION

TITLE/FLIP	LABEL & NO.	GOOD	NEAR MINT	YR.
ATLANTA/	(Casablanca 918)	.50	2.00	78
MAGIC OF THE MUSIC/	(Casablanca 886)	.50	2.00	77
OLD FASHIONED BOY (YOU'RE THE ONE)/Woman	(Casablanca 877)	.50	2.00	77

STAMPEDERS, The

TITLE/FLIP	LABEL & NO.	GOOD	NEAR MINT	YR.
DEVIL YOU/Giant In The Streets	(Bell 45,154)	.50	2.00	71
HIT THE ROAD JACK/Hard Lovin' Woman	(Quality 501)	.50	2.00	76
ME & MY STONE/	(Capitol 3868)	.50	2.00	73
SWEET CITY WOMAN/Gator Road	(Bell 45,120)	.50	2.00	71
SWEET LOVE BANDIT/	(Quality 505)	.50	2.00	76

STANDARDS, The

TITLE/FLIP	LABEL & NO.	GOOD	NEAR MINT	YR.
HELLO LOVE/My Heart Belongs To Only You	(Chess 1869)	1.25	5.00	63
HELLO LOVE/My Heart Belongs To Only You	(Magna 1314)	1.50	6.00	63
IT ISN'T FAIR/Everybody Knows	(Magna 1315)	1.25	5.00	63
TEARS BRING HEARTACHES/No No No	(Debro 3178)	5.00	20.00	63
TEARS BRING HEARTACHES/No No No	(Roulette 4487)	1.50	6.00	63
WHEN YOU WISH UPON A STAR/ When You Wish Upon A Star (Instrumental)	(Amos 134)	.75	3.00	69

TITLE/FLIP	LABEL & NO.	GOOD	NEAR MINT	YR.
STANDELLS, The				
ANIMAL GIRL/Soul Drippin'	(Tower 398)	1.50	6.00	68
BOY NEXT DOOR, THE/B.J. Quezal	(Vee Jay 643)	1.25	5.00	65
DIRTY WATER/Rari	(Tower 185)	.75	3.00	66
DON'T SAY GOODBYE/Big Boss Man	(Vee Jay 679)	1.25	5.00	65
DON'T TELL ME WHAT TO DO/When I Was A Cowboy (Shown as by the Sllednats)	(Tower 312)	2.00	8.00	67
HELP YOURSELF/I'll Go Crazy	(Liberty 55722)	1.50	6.00	64
LINDA LOU/So Fine	(Liberty 55743)	2.00	8.00	64
NINETY-NINE & A HALF/Can't Help But Love You	(Tower 348)	1.50	6.00	68
OOH POO PAH DOO/Help Yourself	(Sunset 61000)	2.50	10.00	
PEPPERMINT BEATLES/The Shake	(Liberty 55680)	2.00	8.00	64
RIOT ON SUNSET STRIP/Black Hearted Woman	(Tower 314)	1.25	5.00	67
SOMETIMES GOOD GUYS DON'T WEAR WHITE/ Why Did You Hurt Me	(Tower 257)	1.00	4.00	66
TRY IT/Poor Shell Of A Man	(Tower 310)	1.50	6.00	67
WHY PICK ON ME/Mr. Nobody	(Tower 282)	1.00	4.00	66
ZEBRA IN THE KITCHEN/Someday You'll Cry	(MGM 13350)	2.50	10.00	65
Also see Dodd, Dick				
Also see Tamblyn, Larry				
Also see Walker Brothers, The				
STANDLEY, Johnny				
GET OUT & VOTE (PART 1)/Get Out & Vote (Part 2)	(Capitol 3544)	1.00	4.00	56
IT'S IN THE BOOK (PART 1)/It's In The Book (Part 2)	(Capitol 2249)	1.25	5.00	52
PROUD NEW FATHER/Clap Your Hands	(Capitol 2569)	1.00	4.00	56
ROCK & ROLL MUST GO/Who'll It Be?	(Magnolia 1003)	1.00	4.00	60
Comedy				
STANLEY, Michael, Band				
BABY IF YOU WANNA DANCE/	(Arista 0368)	.50	2.00	78
LADIES' CHOICE/Sweet Refrain	(Epic 50242)	.50	2.00	77
LAST NIGHT/	(Arista 0436)	.50	2.00	79
NOTHING'S GONNA CHANGE MY MIND/ Love Hasn't Been Here	(Epic 50416)	.50	2.00	77
ROCK & ROLL MAN/Denver Rain	(Tumbleweed 1010)	.50	2.00	72
STANLEY, Paul (Of Kiss)				
HOLD ME, TOUCH ME/Goodbye	(Casablanca 940)	.50	2.00	78
STANLEY, Ray				
MARKET PLACE/Pushin'	(Zephyr 011)	2.50	10.00	56
MY LOVIN' BABY/Love Charms	(Zephyr 012)	2.50	10.00	56
With Eddie Cochran				
STAPLETON, Cyril				
CHILDREN'S MARCHING SONG, THE/ Inn Of Sixth Happiness	(London 1851)	.75	3.00	59
ITALIAN THEME, THE/Tiger Tango	(London 1672)	1.00	4.00	56
STAR DRIFTS, The				
SHE'S GONE/An Eye For An Eye	(Goldisc 63)	1.25	5.00	
STAR FIRES, The				
EACH NIGHT AT NIGHT/What Good Is Money	(Haral 777)	.75	3.00	
FOOLS FALL IN LOVE/Under The Stars	(Duel 518)	3.75	15.00	
LOVE IS HERE TO STAY/Tomorrow	(Decca 30916)	2.50	10.00	59
I HAVE SOMEONE/Three Roses	(Decca 30730)	2.50	10.00	58
THESE FOOLISH THINGS/Let's Do The Pony	(D&H 200)	.75	3.00	
YOU DONE ME WRONG/Like Socks & Shoes	(Laurie 3332)	1.00	4.00	66
STARBREAKER				
SOUND OF SUMMER, THE/Arizona Lost & Gone	(Chrysalis 2133)	.50	2.00	77
STARBUCK				
EVERYBODY BE DANCIN'/Gimme A Break	(Private Stock 45144)	.50	2.00	77
I (WHO HAVE NOTHING)/Let Your Hair Hang Down	(Valiant 744)	1.00	4.00	66
I GOT TO KNOW/ The Slower You Go (The Longer It Last)	(Private Stock 45104)	.50	2.00	76
IT FEELS GOOD/	(United Artists 1263)	.50	2.00	79
(IT'S JUST A) MATTER OF TIME/Steamboat	(Elektra 45706)	.75	3.00	71
LUCKY MAN/So The Night Goes	(Private Stock 45125)	.50	2.00	76
MOONLIGHT FEELS RIGHT/Lash LaRue	(Private Stock 45039)	.50	2.00	76
ONE OF THESE MORNINGS/	(Private Stock 45173)	.50	2.00	77
SEARCHING FOR A THRILL/	(United Artists 1245)	.50	2.00	78
WOULDN'T YOU LIKE IT/	(Atco 6936)	.75	3.00	73
STARCASTLE				
COULD THIS BE LOVE/	(Epic 50486)	.50	2.00	77
DIAMOND SONG (DEEP IS THE LIGHT)/Silver Winds	(Epic 50348)	.50	2.00	77
HALF A MIND TO LEAVE YA/Song For Alaya	(Epic 50630)	.50	2.00	78
LADY OF THE LAKE/Nova	(Epic 50226)	.50	2.00	76
SHINE ON BRIGHTLY/	(Epic 50518)	.50	2.00	78
STARDUST, Alvin				
GROWIN' UP/	(United Artists 992)	.50	2.00	77
MY COO CA CHOO/	(Bell-Magnet 45454)	.50	2.00	73
STARDUSTERS, The				
ROCKIN' THE BOAT/Percussion Twist	(Jo-Ray-Me !)	.75	3.00	62
STARFIRES, The				
BILLY'S BLUES/Chartreuse Caboose	(Pama 117)	.75	3.00	
CAMEL WALK/Fender Bender	(Apt 25030)	.75	3.00	59
SPACE NEEDLE/Jordan Stomp	(Round 1016)	.75	3.00	
Instrumentals				
STARLAND VOCAL BAND, The (Featuring Bill & Taffy Danoff)				
AFTERNOON DELIGHT/Starland	(Windsong 10588)	.50	2.00	76
CALIFORNIA DAY/War Surplus Baby	(Windsong 10785)	.50	2.00	76
HAIL! HAIL! ROCK & ROLL/Ain't It The Fall	(Windsong 10855)	.50	2.00	77
LATE NIGHT RADIO/	(Windsong 11261)	.50	2.00	78
LIBERATED WOMAN/Fallin' In A Deep Hole	(Windsong 10992)	.50	2.00	77
LIGHT OF MY LIFE, THE/Prism	(Windsong 11067)	.50	2.00	77
Also see Fat City				
STARLETS, The				
BETTER TELL HIM NO/You Are The One	(Pam 1003)	.75	3.00	61
MY LAST CRY/Money Hungry	(Pam 1004)	.75	3.00	61
RINGO/All Dressed Up	(Siana 717)	1.25	5.00	64
STARLETS, The				
P.S. I LOVE YOU/Where Is My Love Tonight	(Astro 202)	1.50	6.00	
ROMEO & JULIET/Listen For A Lonely Tambourine	(Astro 204)	1.50	6.00	
Also see Angels, The				
STARLIGHTERS, The				
I CRIED/You're The One To Blame	(End 1049)	2.00	8.00	59
STARR, Karen				
BIG MAN/Get Off The Stage	(RSVP 1106)	1.00	4.00	
STARR, Kay				
ANGRY/Don't Tell Him What Happened	(Capitol 1796)	1.25	5.00	51
BONAPARTE'S RETREAT/Someday Sweetheart	(Capitol 936)	1.50	6.00	50
CHANGING PARTNERS/I'll Always Be In Love With You	(Capitol 2657)	1.25	5.00	53
COME ON-A MY HOUSE/Hold Me, Hold Me, Hold Me	(Capitol 1710)	1.25	5.00	51
COMES ALONG A LOVE/Three Loves	(Capitol 2213)	1.25	5.00	52
FOOL, FOOL, FOOL/Kay's Lament	(Capitol 2151)	1.25	5.00	52
FOOLIN' AROUND/Kay's Lament	(Capitol 4542)	1.25	5.00	61
FOOLISHLY YOURS/For Better Or Worse	(RCA Victor 47-6079)	1.25	5.00	55
FORTUNE IN DREAMS, A/Toy Or Treasure	(Capitol 2887)	1.25	5.00	54
HALF A PHOTOGRAPH/Allez-Vous-En	(Capitol 2464)	1.25	5.00	53
HOLD ME, HOLD ME, HOLD ME/So Help Me	(Capitol 1902)	1.25	5.00	52
HONEYMOON/Nobody's Sweetheart	(Capitol 1194)	1.25	5.00	50
HOOP-DEE-DOO/	(Capitol 980)	1.50	6.00	50
I WAITED A LITTLE TOO LONG/Me Too	(Capitol 2062)	1.25	5.00	52
IF YOU LOVE ME (REALLY LOVE ME)/The Man Upstairs	(Capitol 2769)	1.25	5.00	54
I'LL NEVER BE FREE/Ain't Nobody's Business	(Capitol 1124)	1.25	5.00	50
JAMIE BOY/A Little Loneliness	(RCA Victor 47-6864)	1.00	4.00	57
LOVESICK BLUES/Evenin'	(Capitol 1357)	1.25	5.00	51
MAN WITH THE BAG, THE/Christopher Robin	(Capitol 1256)	1.25	5.00	50
MY HEART REMINDS ME/Flim, Flam, Floo	(RCA Victor 47-6981)	1.00	4.00	57
OCEANS OF TEARS/You're My Sugar	(Capitol 1567)	1.25	5.00	51
OH, BABE/Everybody's Somebody's Baby	(Capitol 1278)	1.25	5.00	50
ON A HONKY TONK HARDWOOD FLOOR/Two Brothers	(Capitol 1856)	1.25	5.00	51
ROCK & ROLL WALTZ/ I've Changed My Mind A Thousand Times	(RCA Victor 47-6359)	1.00	4.00	55
SECOND FIDDLE/Love Ain't Right	(RCA Victor 47-6541)	1.00	4.00	56
SIDE BY SIDE/Noah	(Capitol 2334)	1.25	5.00	53
SO TIRED/Wabash Cannonball	(Capitol 1660)	1.25	5.00	51
THINGS I NEVER HAD, THE/The Good Book	(RCA Victor 47-6617)	1.00	4.00	56
WHEEL OF FORTUNE/I Wanna Love You	(Capitol 1964)	1.25	5.00	52
WHEN MY DREAMBOAT COMES HOME/Swamp Fire	(Capitol 2596)	1.25	5.00	53
WHERE, WHAT OR WHEN/Good & Lonesome	(RCA Victor 47-6146)	1.00	4.00	55
WITHOUT A SONG/Home Sweet Home On The Range	(RCA Victor 47-6247)	1.00	4.00	55
STARR, Lucille (Of The Canadian Sweethearts)				
FRENCH SONG, THE/Sit Down & Write A Letter To Me	(Almo 204)	.75	3.00	64
STARR, Randy				
AFTER SCHOOL/Heaven High	(Dale 100)	1.00	4.00	57
ALL ABOUT ME/Golden Key	(Dale 110)	1.00	4.00	59
DOUBLEDATE/A Dance, A Kiss & A Promise	(Dale 102)	1.00	4.00	57
PINK LEMONADE/Count On Me	(Dale 104)	1.00	4.00	57
YOU'RE GROWING UP/Workin' On The Santa Fe	(Mayflower 17)	1.00	4.00	59
Also see Islanders, The				

TITLE/FLIP	LABEL & NO.	GOOD	NEAR MINT	YR.
STARR, Ringo (Richard Starkey)				
BACK OFF BOOGALOO/Blindman	(Apple 1849)	.50	2.00	72
BACK OFF BOOGALOO (Stereo)/ Back Off Boogaloo (Mono) (Promotional issue)	(Apple 1849)	1.50	6.00	72
BACK OFF BOOGALOO/Blindman (Picture sleeve)	(Apple 1849)	.75	3.00	72
BEAUCOUPS OF BLUES/Coochy Coochy	(Apple 2969)	.50	2.00	70
BEAUCOUPS OF BLUES/Coochy Coochy (With Capitol logo).	(Apple 2969)	1.25	5.00	70
BEAUCOUPS OF BLUES (Stereo)/ Beaucoups Of Blues (Mono) (Promotional issue)	(Apple 2969)	1.50	6.00	70
BEAUCOUPS OF BLUES/Coochy Coochy (Picture sleeve. Some picture sleeves for this issue incorrectly give the catalog number as Apple 1826.)	(Apple 2969)	1.00	4.00	70
DOSE OF ROCK & ROLL, A/Cryin'	(Atlantic 3361)	.50	2.00	76
DOSE OF ROCK & ROLL, A (Stereo)/ A Dose Of Rock & Roll (Mono) (Promotional issue)	(Atlantic 3361)	.75	3.00	76
DROWNING IN THE SEA OF LOVE/Just A Dream	(Atlantic 3412)	.50	2.00	77
DROWNING IN THE SEA OF LOVE (Stereo)/ Drowning In The Sea Of Love (Mono) (Promotional issue)	(Atlantic 3412)	.75	3.00	77
DROWNING IN THE SEA OF LOVE/ Drowning In The Sea Of Love (Promotional 12" single issue)	(Atlantic DSKO-33775 PR)	3.75	15.00	77
HEART ON MY SLEEVE/Who Needs A Heart	(Portrait 70018)	.50	2.00	78
HEART ON MY SLEEVE (Stereo)/Heart On My Sleeve (Mono) (Promotional issue)	(Portrait 70018)	1.00	4.00	78
HEY BABY/Lady Gaye	(Atlantic 3371)	.50	2.00	77
HEY BABY (Stereo)/Hey Baby (Mono) (Promotional issue)	(Atlantic 3371)	.75	3.00	77
IT DON'T COME EASY/Early 1970	(Apple 1831)	.50	2.00	71
IT DON'T COME EASY (Stereo)/It Don't Come Easy (Mono) (Promotional issue)	(Apple 1831)	1.50	6.00	71
IT DON'T COME EASY/Early 1970 (Picture sleeve)	(Apple 1831)	.75	3.00	71
IT'S ALL DOWN TO GOODNIGHT VIENNA/Ooh-Wee	(Apple 1882)	.50	2.00	75
IT'S ALL DOWN TO GOODNIGHT VIENNA (Stereo)/ It's All Down To Goodnight Vienna (Mono) (Promotional issue)	(Apple 1882)	1.50	6.00	75
IT'S ALL DOWN TO GOODNIGHT VIENNA/Ooh-Wee (Picture sleeve)	(Apple 1882)	.75	3.00	75
LIPSTICK TRACES (ON A CIGARETTE)/ Old Time Relovin'	(Portrait 70015)	.50	2.00	78
LIPSTICK TRACES (ON A CIGARETTE) (Stereo)/ Lipstick Traces (On A Cigarette) (Mono) (Promotional issue)	(Portrait 70015)	1.00	4.00	78
NO NO SONG/Snookeroo	(Apple 1880)	.50	2.00	75
NO NO SONG (Stereo)/No No Song (Mono) (Promotional issue)	(Apple 1880)	1.50	6.00	75
NO NO SONG/Snookeroo (Picture sleeve)	(Apple 1880)	.75	3.00	75
OH MY MY/Step Lightly	(Apple 1872)	.50	2.00	74
OH MY MY (Stereo)/Oh My My (Mono) (Promotional issue)	(Apple 1872)	1.50	6.00	74
OH MY MY/Step Lightly (Picture sleeve)	(Apple 1872)	.75	3.00	74
ONLY YOU/Call Me	(Apple 1876)	.50	2.00	74
ONLY YOU (Stereo)/Only You (Mono) (Promotional issue)	(Apple 1876)	1.50	6.00	74
ONLY YOU/Call Me (Picture sleeve)	(Apple 1876)	.75	3.00	74

TITLE/FLIP	LABEL & NO.	GOOD	NEAR MINT	YR.
PHOTOGRAPH/Down & Out	(Apple 1865)	.50	2.00	73
PHOTOGRAPH/Down & Out (Promotional issue)	(Apple 1865)	1.50	6.00	73
PHOTOGRAPH/Down & Out (Picture sleeve)	(Apple 1865)	.75	3.00	73
SNOOKEROO (Stereo)/Snookeroo (Mono) (Promotional issue)	(Apple 1880)	1.25	5.00	75
WINGS/Just A Dream	(Atlantic 3429)	.50	2.00	77
WINGS (Stereo)/Wings (Mono) (Promotional issue)	(Atlantic 3429)	1.00	4.00	77
YOU'RE SIXTEEN/Devil Woman	(Apple 1870)	.50	2.00	73
YOU'RE SIXTEEN (Stereo)/You're Sixteen (Mono) (Promotional issue)	(Apple 1870)	1.50	6.00	73
YOU'RE SIXTEEN/Devil Woman (Picture sleeve)	(Apple 1870)	.75	3.00	73
Also see Beatles, The				
STARR, Ruby (Of Black Oak Arkansas)				
MAYBE I'M AMAZED/Who's Who	(Capitol 4301)	.50	2.00	76
STARR, Sally				
ROCKY, THE ROCKIN' RABBIT/Sing A Song Of Happiness	(Arcade 157)	.75	3.00	60
STAR STEPPERS, The				
FIRST SIGNS OF LOVE, THE/You're Gone	(Amy 801)	2.50	10.00	60
STAR-TREKS, The				
GONNA NEED MAGIC/Dreamin'	(Veep 1254)	1.00	4.00	67
STARZ				
(ANY WAY YOU WANT IT) I'LL BE THERE/Texas	(Capitol-Starz 4546)	.50	2.00	78
CHERRY BABY/Rock Six Times	(Capitol-Starz 4399)	.50	2.00	77
HOLD ON TO THE NIGHT/Texas	(Capitol-Starz 4566)	.50	2.00	78
LAST NIGHT I WROTE A LETTER/Coliseum Rock	(Capitol-Starz 4671)	.50	2.00	79
(SHE'S JUST A) FALLEN ANGEL/Monkey Business	(Capitol-Starz 4343)	.50	2.00	76
SING IT, SHOUT IT/Subway Terror	(Capitol-Starz 4434)	.50	2.00	77
SO YOUNG, SO BAD/Coliseum Rock	(Capitol-Starz 4637)	.50	2.00	79
STATENS, The				
SUMMERTIME IS TIME FOR LOVE/That Certain Kind	(Mark-X 8011)	5.00	20.00	61
STATES				
MY LATEST GIRL/	(Chrysalis 2381)	.50	2.00	79
STATESMEN, The				
RAMPAGE/Forever	(Bradley 200)	.75	3.00	
STATUES, The (Featuring Gary Miles)				
BLUE VELVET/Keep The Hall Light Burning	(Liberty 55245)	1.00	4.00	60
WHITE CHRISTMAS/Jeanie With The Light Brown Hair	(Liberty 55292)	1.25	5.00	60
STATUS QUO, The				
CAROLINE/	(A&M 1510)	.75	3.00	74
DON'T WASTE MY TIME/All The Reasons	(A&M 1425)	.75	3.00	73
DOWN DOWN/By Bye Johnny	(Capitol 4125)	.75	3.00	75
DOWN DOWN/Nightride	(Capitol 4039)	.75	3.00	75
GERUNDULA/In My Chair	(Janus 141)	1.00	4.00	72
ICE IN THE SUN/When My Mind Is Not Live	(Cadet-Concept 7006)	1.00	4.00	68
MEAN GIRL/	(Pye 65017)	.75	3.00	75
PAPER PLANE/All The Reasons	(A&M 1445)	.75	3.00	73
PICTURES OF MATCHSTICK MEN/ Gentleman Joe's Sidewalk Cafe	(Cadet-Concept 7001)	1.00	4.00	68
TECHNICOLOR DREAMS/Spicks & Specks	(Cadet-Concept 7010)	1.00	4.00	69
TUNE TO THE MUSIC/Good Thinking	(Pye 65000)	.75	3.00	75
WILD SIDE OF LIFE/	(Capitol 4407)	.75	3.00	77
STAVELY MAKEPEACE				
RUNAROUND SUE/There's A Wall Between Us	(London 1060)	1.00	4.00	
STEALER'S WHEEL (With Gerry Rafferty & Joe Egan)				
EVERYONE'S AGREED THAT EVERYTHING WILL TURN OUT FINE/ Next To Me	(A&M 1450)	.50	2.00	73
EVERYTHING WILL TURN OUT FINE/ (Shown as by Gerry Rafferty & Joe Egan)	(A&M 2075)	.50	2.00	78
FOUND MY WAY TO YOU/This Morning	(A&M 1675)	.50	2.00	75
STAR/What More Could You Want	(A&M 1483)	.50	2.00	74
STUCK IN THE MIDDLE WITH YOU/Jose	(A&M 1416)	.50	2.00	73
YOU PUT SOMETHING BETTER INSIDE OF ME/Wheelin'	(A&M 1529)	.50	2.00	74
STEAM				
DO UNTO OTHERS/Don't Stop Loving Me	(Mercury 73117)	.75	3.00	70
I'VE GOTTA MAKE YOU LOVE ME/One Good Woman	(Mercury 73020)	.75	3.00	70
NA NA HEY HEY KISS HIM GOODBYE/ It's The Magic In You Girl	(Fontana 1667)	.75	3.00	69
NA NA HEY HEY KISS HIM GOODBYE/ Don't Stop Lovin' Me	(Mercury 30160)	.50	2.00	72
NA NA HEY HEY KISS HIM GOODBYE/ Don't Stop Lovin' Me (Special Chicago White Sox picture sleeve)	(Mercury 30160)	2.00	8.00	76
WHAT I'M SAYING IS TRUE/	(Mercury 73053)	.75	3.00	70
STEEL, Don				
TINA DEGADO IS ALIVE/Hole In My Soul	(Cameo 399)	1.00	4.00	66
STEELERS, The				
GET IT FROM THE BOTTON/	(Date 1642)	.75	3.00	69
YOU'RE WHAT'S BEEN MISSING FROM MY LIFE/ You Got Me Callin'	(Epic 10773)	.75	3.00	71

TITLE/FLIP	LABEL & NO.	GOOD	NEAR MINT	YR.
STEELE, Tracy				
LETTER TO PAUL, A/Your Ring	(Delaware 1705)	1.50	6.00	
STEELEYE SPAN				
GAUDETTE/Royal Forester	(Chrysalis 2008)	.75	3.00	72
GAUDETTE/Royal Forester	(Chrysalis 2102)	.75	3.00	74
RAG DOLL/Hunting The Wren	(Chrysalis 2262)	.50	2.00	78
STEEL, Jake & Jeff				
IMPEACHMENT STORY/Heavy Steppin'	(Peach-Mint 6065)	.75	3.00	
STEEL, Tommy				
HALF A SIXPENCE/If The Rain's Got To Fall	(RCA Victor 47-8602)	.75	3.00	65
HAPPY GO LUCKY BLUES/She's My Baby	(London 1950)	1.00	4.00	60
NEON SIGN/	(London 1795)	1.00	4.00	58
TRIAL,THE/Give, Give, Give	(London 1878)	1.00	4.00	59
STEELY DAN				
BAD SNEAKERS/Chain Lightning	(ABC 12128)	.50	2.00	75
BLACK FIRDAY/Throw Back The Little Ones	(ABC 12101)	.50	2.00	75
DALLAS/Sail The Waterway	(ABC 11323)	.50	2.00	72
DEACON BLUES/Home At Last	(ABC 12355)	.50	2.00	78
DO IT AGAIN/Fire In The Hole	(ABC 11338)	.50	2.00	72
FEZ, THE/Sign In Stranger	(ABC 12222)	.50	2.00	76
FM (NO STATIC AT ALL)/FM (No Static At All Reprise)	(MCA 40894)	.50	2.00	78
I GOT THE NEWS/Peg	(ABC 12320)	.50	2.00	77
JOSIE/Black Cow	(ABC 12404)	.50	2.00	78
KID CHARLEMAGNE/Green Earrings	(ABC 12195)	.50	2.00	76
MY OLD SCHOOL/Pearl Of The Quarter	(ABC 11396)	.50	2.00	73
PEG/I Got The News	(ABC 12320)	.50	2.00	77
PRETZEL LOGIC/Through With Buzz	(ABC 12033)	.50	2.00	74
REELING IN THE YEARS/Only A Fool Would Say That	(ABC 11352)	.50	2.00	73
RIKKI DON'T LOSE THAT NUMBER/ Any Major Dude Will Tell You	(ABC 11439)	.50	2.00	74
SHOW BIZ KIDS/Razor Boy	(ABC 11382)	.50	2.00	73
STEFEN, Paul, & The Apollos				
YOU/Cry Angel Cry	(Cite 5008)	1.50	6.00	
STEIN, Frankie, & The Ghouls				
GOON RIVER/Weerdo The Wolf (Novelties)	(Power 338)	1.00	4.00	64
STEPHENS, Julie, & The Premiers				
ANGEL LOVE/False Love	(Best 1004)	1.50	6.00	62
EVENING STAR/Last Of The Real Smart Guys	(Dore 603)	2.50	10.00	61
STEPPENWOLF				
BORN TO BE WILD/Everybody's Next One	(Dunhill 4138)	.75	3.00	68
CAROLINE (ARE YOU READY FOR THE OUTLAW WORLD)/ Angeldrawers	(Mums 6040)	.50	2.00	75
FOR LADIES ONLY/Sparkle Eyes	(Dunhill 4292)	.75	3.00	71
GET INTO THE WIND/Morning Blue	(Mums 6034)	.50	2.00	74
GIRL I KNEW/The Ostrich	(Dunhill 4109)	.75	3.00	67
HEY LAWDY MAMA/Twisted	(Dunhill 4234)	.75	3.00	70
IT'S NEVER TOO LATE/Happy Birthday	(Dunhill 4192)	.75	3.00	69
MAGIC CARPET RIDE/Sookie Sookie	(Dunhill 4161)	.75	3.00	68
MONSTER/Berry Rides Again	(Dunhill 4221)	.75	3.00	69
MOVE OVER/Power Play	(Dunhill 4205)	.75	3.00	69
OSTRICH, THE/A Girl I Knew	(Dunhill 4109)	.75	3.00	68
RIDE WITH ME/For Madmen Only	(Dunhill 4283)	.75	3.00	71
ROCK ME/Jupiter Child	(Dunhill 4182)	.75	3.00	69
SCREAMING NIGHT HOG/Spiritual Fantasy	(Dunhill 4248)	.75	3.00	70
SMOKEY FACTORY BLUES/A Fool's Fantasy	(Mums 6036)	.50	2.00	75
SNOW BLIND FRIEND/Hippo Stomp	(Dunhill 4269)	.75	3.00	71
SOOKIE SOOKIE/Take What You Need	(Dunhill 4123)	.75	3.00	68
STRAIGHT SHOOTIN' WOMAN/ Justive Don't Be Slow	(Mums 6031)	.50	2.00	74
TELEPHONE BLUES/	(Immediate 502)	1.00	4.00	67
WHO NEEDS YA/Earschplittenloudenboomer	(Dunhill 4261)	.75	3.00	70
Also see Sparrows, The				
STEPPING STONES, The				
I GOT THE JOB THROUGH THE NEW YORK TIMES/ Nearness Of You	(Philips 40108)	.75	3.00	63
LITTLE GIRL OF MINE/	(Diplomacy 15)	1.25	5.00	
PILLS/So Tough	(Diplomacy 21)	1.25	5.00	
STEREOPHONICS, The				
LOVE IS SO WONDERFUL/No More Heartaches	(Apt 25003)	1.00	4.00	58
STEREOS, The				
MEMORY LANE/Teenage Kids	(Mink 22)	3.00	12.00	59
MEMORY LANE/Teenage Kids (Shown as by the Tams)	(Mink 22)	2.00	8.00	59
MEMORY LANE/Teenage Kids (Shown as by the Tams)	(Cameo 863)	1.25	5.00	63
MEMORY LANE/Lonely (Shown as by the Hippies)	(Cameo 863)	.75	3.00	63
STEVE & DONNA				
EVER SINCE THE WORLD BEGAN/ All The Better To Love You	(Liberty 55192)	1.00	4.00	59
STEVE & EYDIE: see Lawrence, Steve, & Eydie Gorme				
STEVE & THE EMPERORS				
GREAT BALLS OF FIRE/The Breeze & I	(Best 103)	1.00	4.00	
STEVENS, April				
GIMMIE A LITTLE KISS, WILL YA HUH?/ Dreamy Melody	(RCA Victor 47-4208)	1.25	5.00	51
I'M IN LOVE AGAIN/Roller Coaster (With Henri Rene)	(RCA Victor 47-4148)	1.25	5.00	51
TEACH ME TIGER/That Warm Afternoon (With Henri Rene)	(Imperial 5626)	1.00	4.00	59
Also see Tempo, Nino, & April Stevens				
STEVENS, Cat				
ANOTHER SATURDAY NIGHT/Home In The Sky	(A&M 1602)	.50	2.00	74
BAD BREAKS/Nascimento	(A&M 2109)	.50	2.00	78
BAD NIGHT/Laughing Apple	(Deram 85015)	1.00	4.00	67
BANAPPLE GAS/Ghost Town	(A&M 1785)	.50	2.00	76
HURT, THE/Silent Sunlight	(A&M 1418)	.50	2.00	73
I LOVE MY DOG/Portobello Road	(Deram 5872)	1.00	4.00	66
I LOVE MY DOG/Portobello Road	(Deram 7501)	.75	3.00	67
KITTY/Where Are You	(Deram 85079)	.75	3.00	71
LADY D' ARBANVILLE/Time/Fill My Eyes	(A&M 1211)	.50	2.00	70
MATTHEW & SON/Granny	(Deram 7505)	.75	3.00	67
MOON SHADOW/I Think I See The Light	(A&M 1265)	.50	2.00	71
MORNING HAS BROKEN/I Want To Live In A Wigwam	(A&M 1335)	.50	2.00	72
OH VERY YOUNG/100 I Dream	(A&M 1503)	.50	2.00	74
PEACE TRAIN/Where Do The Children Play	(A&M 1291)	.50	2.00	71
RANDY/Nasciemento	(A&M 2126)	.50	2.00	79
READY/I Think I See The Light	(A&M 1645)	.50	2.00	74
(REMEMBER THE DAYS OF THE) OLD SCHOOLYARD/ Land O' Freelove & Goodbye	(A&M 1948)	.50	2.00	77
SCHOOL IS OUT/I'm Gonna Get Me A Gun	(Deram 85006)	1.00	4.00	67
SITTING/Crab Dance	(A&M 1396)	.50	2.00	72
TWO FINE APPLE/A Bad Penny	(A&M 1700)	.50	2.00	75
WAS DOG A DOUGHNUT/Sweet Jamaica	(A&M 1971)	.50	2.00	77
WAS DOG A DOUGHNUT/Was Dog A Doughnut (Promotional 12" issue)	(A&M 8440)	1.25	5.00	77
WILD WORLD/Miles From Nowhere	(A&M 1231)	.50	2.00	71
STEVENS, Connie (Concetta Ann Ingolia)				
ALL OF MY LIFE/That's All I Want From You	(Warner Bros. 5804)	.75	3.00	66
HEY GOOD LOOKIN'/Nobody's Lonesome For Me	(Warner Bros. 5318)	.75	3.00	62
LITTLE MISS-UNDERSTOOD/There Goes Your Guy	(Warner Bros. 5380)	.75	3.00	63
MAKE-BELIEVE LOVER/And This Is Mine	(Warner Bros. 5217)	.75	3.00	61
MR. SONGWRITER/I Couldn't Say No	(Warner Bros. 5289)	.75	3.00	62
NOW THAT YOU'VE GONE/Lost In Wonderland	(Warner Bros. 5610)	.75	3.00	65
SIXTEEN REASONS/Little Sister	(Warner Bros. 5137)	.75	3.00	60
TOO YOUNG TO GO STEADY/Little Kiss	(Warner Bros. 5159)	.75	3.00	60
WHY DO I CRY FOR JOEY/Apollo	(Warner Bros. 5092)	1.00	4.00	59
WHY'D YOU WANNA MAKE ME CRY/Just One Kiss	(Warner Bros. 5265)	.75	3.00	62
Also see Byrnes, Ed				
STEVENS, Debbie				
IF YOU CAN'T ROCK ME/What Will I Tell My Heart	(Apt 25027)	1.00	4.00	59
STEVENS, Dodie (Geraldine Ann Pasquale)				
AM I TOO YOUNG/So, Let's Dance	(Dot 16139)	.75	3.00	60
AMIGO'S GUITAR/Candy Store Blues	(Dot 16067)	.75	3.00	60
DANCING ON MY CEILING/I Cried	(Dot 16339)	.75	3.00	62
DOES GOODNIGHT MEAN GOODBYE/Sailor Boy	(Dolton 88)	.75	3.00	63
FOR A LITTLE WHILE/Hello Stranger	(Imperial 5930)	.75	3.00	63
I FALL TO PIECES/Turn Around	(Dot 16200)	.75	3.00	61
I WORE OUT OUR RECORD/ You Don't Have To Prove A Thing To Me	(Dolton 83)	.75	3.00	63
LET ME TELL YOU ABOUT JOHNNY/You Are The Only One	(Dot 16259)	.75	3.00	61
MAIRZY DOATS/Steady Eddy	(Dot 16002)	.75	3.00	59
MERRY CHRISTMAS BABY/Merry Christmas Baby	(Dot 16166)	1.00	4.00	60
MISS LONELY HEARTS/Poor Butterfly	(Dot 15975)	.75	3.00	59
NO/A-Tisket A-Tasket	(Dot 16103)	.75	3.00	60
PINK SHOE LACES/Coming Of Age	(Crystalette 724)	1.00	4.00	59
TRADE WINDS, TRADE WINDS/ In Between Years (Story Of The)	(Dot 16279)	.75	3.00	61
YES, I'M LONESOME TONIGHT/Too Young	(Dot 16167)	.75	3.00	60
YES-SIR-EE/The Five Pennies	(Crystalette 728)	1.00	4.00	59
STEVENS, Jimmy				
HIGH HEEL BLUES/	(RSO 402)	.50	2.00	74
STEVENS, Mark, & The Charmers				
COME BACK TO MY HEART/Magic Rose	(Allison 921)	2.00	8.00	
STEVENS, Neil, & The Temptations				
BALLAD OF LOVE/Tonight My Heart, She Is Crying	(Goldisc 3019)	3.00	12.00	61
STEVENSON, B.W.				
DOWN TO THE STATION/ May You Find Yourself In Heaven	(Warner Bros. 8343)	.50	2.00	78
HOLDIN' ON FOR DEAR LOVE/	(Private Stock 45208)	.50	2.00	78
MY MARIA/August Evening Lady	(RCA 0030)	.50	2.00	73
ON MY OWN/	(RCA 0778)	.50	2.00	73
RIVER OF LOVE/The Lucky Touch	(RCA 0171)	.50	2.00	73
SHAMBALA/My Feet Are So Weary	(RCA 0952)	.50	2.00	73
STEVENS, Randy				
SWEET SHOP/All My Love	(Loma 301)	1.00	4.00	59
STEVENS, Ray				
AHAB, THE ARAB/It's Been So Long	(Mercury 71966)	.75	3.00	62
ALL MY TRIALS/	(Barnaby 2039)	.50	2.00	71
ALONG CAME JONES/Yakety Yak	(Monument 1163)	.50	2.00	69
AMERICA, COMMUNICATE WITH ME/	(Barnaby 2016)	.50	2.00	70
ANSWER ME, MY LOVE/Mary, My Secretary	(Monument 1001)	.75	3.00	67
BE YOUR OWN BEST FRIEND/With A Smile	(Warner-Ahab 8603)	.50	2.00	78
BRIDGET THE MIDGET (QUEEN OF THE BLUES)/ Night People	(Barnaby 2024)	.50	2.00	70
BUBBLE GUM, THE BUBBLE DANCER/ Laughing Over My Grave	(Mercury 72307)	1.00	4.00	64
BUTCH BARBARIAN/Don't Say Anything	(Mercury 72255)	1.00	4.00	64
CAT PANTS/Love Goes On Forever	(Capitol 4030)	1.50	6.00	58
CHICKIE CHICKIE WAH WAH/Crying Goodbye	(Capitol 3967)	1.25	5.00	58
DIXIE HUMMINGBIRD/	(Warner-Ahab 8393)	.50	2.00	77
EVERYBODY NEEDS A RAINBOW/Inside	(Barnaby 610)	.50	2.00	74
EVERYTHING IS BEAUTIFUL/A Brighter Day	(Barnaby 2011)	.50	2.00	70
FEELING'S NOT RIGHT AGAIN, THE/ Get Crazy With Me	(Warner-Ahab 8849)	.50	2.00	79
FIVE MORE STEPS/Tingle	(Prep 122)	1.25	5.00	
FREDDIE FEELGOOD/There's One In Every Crowd	(Monument 946)	.75	3.00	66
FUNNY MAN/Just One Of Life's Little Tragedies	(Mercury 72098)	1.00	4.00	63
FUNNY MAN/Just One Of Life's Little Tragedies	(Mercury 72816)	.75	3.00	68
FURTHER MORE/Saturday Night At The Movies	(Mercury 72039)	1.00	4.00	62
GET CRAZY WITH ME/	(Warner-Ahab 8318)	.50	2.00	77
GITARZAN/Bagpipes-That's My Bag	(Monument 1131)	.50	2.00	69
GREAT ESCAPE, THE/	(Monument 1099)	.75	3.00	68
HARRY THE HAIRY APE/Little Stone Statue	(Mercury 72125)	.75	3.00	63
HAVE A LITTLE TALK WITH MYSELF/Little Woman	(Monument 1171)	.75	3.00	69
HIGH SCHOOL YEARBOOK/Truly True	(NRC 031)	1.25	5.00	59
HONKY TONK WALTZ/	(Warner-Ahab 8237)	.50	2.00	77
I NEED YOUR HELP BARRY MANILOW/ Daydream Romance	(Warner-Ahab 8785)	.50	2.00	79
INDIAN LOVE CALL/Piece Of Paradise	(Barnaby 616)	.50	2.00	75
JEREMIAH PEABODY'S POLY-UNSATURATED, QUICK-DISSOLVING, FAST-ACTING, PLEASANT-TASTING, GREEN & PURPLE PILLS/ Teen Years	(Mercury 71843)	1.00	4.00	61
LADY OF SPAIN/	(Barnaby 619)	.50	2.00	76
LOSING STREAK/	(Barnaby 2065)	.50	2.00	72
MAKE A FEW MEMORIES/Devil-May Care	(Monument 927)	.75	3.00	66
MAMA & A PAPA, A/	(Barnaby 2029)	.50	2.00	71
MR. BAKER, THE UNDERTAKER/The Old English Surfer	(Mercury 72430)	.75	3.00	65
MR. BUSINESSMAN/Face The Music	(Monument 1083)	.50	2.00	68
MISTY/Sunshine	(Barnaby 614)	.50	2.00	75
MOONLIGHT SPECIAL/	(Barnaby 604)	.50	2.00	74
MY HEART CRIES FOR YOU/What Would I Do Without You	(NRC 042)	1.25	5.00	60
PARTY PEOPLE/A-B-C	(Monument 911)	.75	3.00	65
RANG TANG DING DONG/Silver Bracelet	(Prep 108)	1.25	5.00	
ROCKIN' TEENAGE MUMMIES/ It Only Hurts When I Love	(Mercury 72382)	.75	3.00	65
SANTA CLAUS IS WATCHING YOU/Loved & Lost	(Mercury 72058)	.75	3.00	62
SCHOOL/The Clown	(Capitol 4101)	1.00	4.00	59
SCRATCH MY BACK/When You Wish Upon A Star	(Mercury 71888)	1.25	5.00	61
SERGENT PRESTON OF THE YUKON/Who Do You Love	(NRC 057)	1.25	5.00	60
SPEEDBALL/It's Party Time	(Mercury 72189)	.75	3.00	63
STREAK, THE/You've Got The Music Inside	(Barnaby 600)	.50	2.00	74
SUNDAY MORNING COMING DOWN/The Minority	(Monument 1163)	.75	3.00	69
SUNSET STRIP/	(Barnaby 2021)	.50	2.00	70
TURN YOUR RADIO ON/	(Barnaby 2048)	.50	2.00	71
UNWIND/For He's A Jolly Good Fellow	(Monument 1048)	.50	2.00	68
YOU ARE SO BEAUTIFUL/One Man Band	(Warner-Ahab 8198)	.50	2.00	76
YOUNG LOVE/Deep Purple	(Barnaby 618)	.50	2.00	76
STEVENS, Scott				
I LIKE GIRLS & GIRLS LIKE ME/ I Found a Girl	(ABC-Paramount 10054)	1.00	4.00	59
SUNDAY IN MAY/Why, Why, Why	(Apt 25031)	1.25	5.00	59
STEVENS, Tari				
FALSE ALARM/A Bad Boy	(Fairmont F-1001)	.75	3.00	66
Tari Stevens is Christine Cooper's sister.				
STEWART, Al				
CAROL/Sirens of Titen	(Janus 250)	.75	3.00	75
NOSTRADAMUS/Terminal Eyes	(Janus 243)	.75	3.00	74
ON THE BORDER/Flying Sorcery	(Janus 267)	.50	2.00	77
SONG ON THE RADIO/A Man For All Seasons	(Arista 0389)	.50	2.00	79
TIME PASSAGES/Almost Lucy	(Arista 0362)	.50	2.00	78
YEAR OF THE CAT/Broadway Hotel	(Janus 266)	.50	2.00	76
STEWART, Andy				
DONALD, WHERE'S YOUR TROUSERS/The Battles Over	(Warwick 665)	1.00	4.00	61
SCOTTISH SOLDIER (GREEN HILLS OF TYROL), A/ The Muckin 'O' Geordie's Byre	(Warwick 627)	.75	3.00	61
SCOTTISH SOLDIER (GREEN HILLS OF TYROL), A/ The Muckin 'O' Geordie's Byre	(Top Rank 2088)	1.00	4.00	60
STEWART, Jimm, & The Sirs				
16 CANDLES/	(Uni 55090)	1.00	4.00	68
STEWART, John (Of The Kingston Trio)				
ARMSTRONG/Anna On A Memory	(Capitol 2605)	.75	3.00	69
BAD OLD DAYS, THE/Just An Old Love Song	(Warner Bros. 504)	.50	2.00	71
GOLD/Comin' Out Of Nowhere	(RSO 931)	.50	2.00	79
JULY, YOU'RE A WOMAN/She Believes In Me	(Capitol 2538)	.75	3.00	69
LADY & THE OUTLAW/Earth Rider	(Capitol 2711)	.75	3.00	69
LOST HER IN THE SUN/Heart Of The Dream	(RSO 1016)	.50	2.00	79
MIDNIGHT WIND/Somewhere Down The Line	(RSO 1000)	.50	2.00	79
MOTHER COUNTRY/Shackels & Chains	(Capitol 2469)	.75	3.00	69
PROMISE THE WIND/Morning Thunder	(RSO 894)	.50	2.00	78
SURVIVORS/Josie	(RCA 10227)	.50	2.00	75
SURVIVORS/	(RCA 10268)	.50	2.00	75
This singer should not be confused with the John Stewart of the Dalton Brothers.				
STEWART, Johnny				
ROCKIN' ANNA/	(Vita 169)	3.75	15.00	58
STEWART, Judy, & Her Beatle Buddies				
WHO CAN I BELIEVE/I'll Take You Back Again	(Diplomat 0101)	1.25	5.00	
STEWART, Mario				
SKY SURFIN'/Rip Tide (Instrumentals)	(Souvenir 102)	1.00	4.00	63
STEWART, Rod (Of Faces)				
AIN'T LOVE A BITCH/Last Summer	(Warner Bros. 8810)	.50	2.00	79
AN OLD RAINCOAT WON'T EVER LET YOU DOWN/ Handbags & Gladrags	(Mercury 73009)	.75	3.00	70
ANGEL/Lost Paraguayos	(Mercury 73344)	.75	3.00	72
AS LONG AS YOU TELL HIM/ You Can Make Me Dance, Sing Or Anything	(Warner Bros. 8066)	.50	2.00	75
AS LONG AS YOU TELL HIM/ You Can Make Me Dance, Sing Or Anything	(Warner Bros. 8102)	.50	2.00	75
CLOUD NINE/Rod's Blues (With Python Lee Jackson)	(Crescendo 462)	.75	3.00	73
COUNTRY COMFORT/Gasoline Alley	(Mercury 73196)	.75	3.00	71
CUT ACROSS SHORTY/Gasoline Alley	(Mercury 73156)	.75	3.00	70
DA YA THINK I'M SEXY?/Scarred & Scared	(Warner Bros. 8724)	.50	2.00	78
FIRST CUT IS THE DEEPEST/Balltrap	(Warner Bros. 8321)	.50	2.00	77
GOOD MORNING LITTLE SCHOOLGIRL/ I'm Gonna Move To The Outskirts Of Town	(Press 8722)	2.50	10.00	65
HANDBAGS & GLADRAGS/Man Of Constant Sorrow	(Mercury 73031)	.50	2.00	72
HOT LEGS/You're Insane	(Warner Bros. 8535)	.50	2.00	78
I DON'T WANT TO TALK ABOUT IT/ The Best Days Of My Life	(Warner Bros. 49138)	.50	2.00	79
(I KNOW) I'M LOSING YOU/Mandolin Wind	(Mercury 73244)	.50	2.00	71
I WAS ONLY JOKING/Born Loose	(Warner Bros. 8568)	.50	2.00	78
IT'S ALL OVER NOW/	(Mercury 73095)	.75	3.00	70
KILLING OF GEORGIE (PART 1 & 2), THE/Rosie	(Warner Bros. 8396)	.50	2.00	77
LET ME BE YOUR CAR/Sailor	(Mercury 73660)	.50	2.00	75
MAGGIE MAY/Reason To Believe	(Mercury 73224)	.50	2.00	71
MINE FOR ME/Farewell	(Mercury 73636)	.75	3.00	74
MY WAY OF GIVING/	(Mercury 73175)	.75	3.00	71
OH! NO NOT MY BABY/Jodie	(Mercury 73426)	.75	3.00	73
OH! NO NOT MY BABY/Jodie (Picture sleeve)	(Mercury 73426)	1.00	4.00	73
ONLY A HOBO/	(Mercury 73115)	.75	3.00	70
SAILING/All In The Name Of Rock N' Roll	(Warner Bros. 8146)	.50	2.00	75
SHAKE/Shake	(Private Stock 45130)	1.00	4.00	76
THIS OLD HEART OF MINE/Still Love You	(Warner Bros. 8170)	.50	2.00	76
TONIGHT'S THE NIGHT (GONNA BE ALRIGHT)/ Fool For You	(Warner Bros. 8262)	.50	2.00	76
TWISTING THE NIGHT AWAY/True Blue-Lady Day	(Mercury 73412)	.75	3.00	73
WHAT'S MADE MILWAUKEE FAMOUS (HAS MADE A LOSER OUT OF ME)/ Every Picture Tells A Story	(Mercury 73802)	.75	3.00	76
YOU'RE IN MY HEART (THE FINAL ACCLAIM)/ You Got A Nerve	(Warner Bros. 8475)	.50	2.00	77
YOU WEAR IT WELL/True Blue	(Mercury 73330)	.50	2.00	72
YOU WEAR IT WELL/True Blue (Picture sleeve)	(Mercury 73330)	1.00	4.00	72
STEWART, Sandy (Sandra Ester Galitz)				
MY COLORING BOOK/I Heard You Cried Last Night	(Colpix 669)	.75	3.00	62
STEWART, Ty, & The Jokers				
YOUNG GIRL/Here I Am	(Amy 828)	1.25	5.00	62
STICKS & STONES, The				
TRY/Live To Be Free	(Coral 62524)	1.00	4.00	58
STILLS, Stephen (Of Buffalo Springfield)				
BUYIN' TIME/Soldier	(Columbia 10369)	.50	2.00	76
CAN'T GET NO BOOTY/Lowdown	(Columbia 10804)	.50	2.00	78
CHANGE PARTNERS/Relaxing Town	(Atlantic 2806)	.50	2.00	71
DOWN THE ROAD/Guaguanco De Vero (With Manassas)	(Atlantic 2917)	.75	3.00	72
ISN'T IT ABOUT TIME/So Many Times (With Manassas)	(Atlantic 2959)	.50	2.00	73
IT DOESN'T MATTER/Rock & Roll Crazies Medley	(Atlantic 2876)	.50	2.00	72
LOVE THE ONE YOU'RE WITH/To A Flame	(Atlantic 2778)	.50	2.00	70
MARIANNE/Nothin' To Do But Today	(Atlantic 2820)	.50	2.00	71
ROCK & ROLL CRAZIES/Colorado (With Manassas)	(Atlantic 2888)	.50	2.00	72
SHUFFLE JUST AS BAD/Turn Back The Pages	(Columbia 10179)	.50	2.00	75
SIT YOURSELF DOWN/We Are Not Helpless	(Atlantic 2790)	.50	2.00	71
THOROUGHFARE GAP/Lowdown	(Columbia 10872)	.50	2.00	78
TURN BACK THE PAGES/Shuffle Just As Bad	(Columbia 10179)	.50	2.00	75
Also see Crosby, Stills & Nash				
Also see Bloomfield, Mike				
STILLS-YOUNG BAND, The (Stephen Stills & Neil Young)				
LONG MAY YOU RUN/12-8 Blues (All The Same)	(Reprise 1365)	.50	2.00	77
MIDNIGHT ON THE BAY/Black Coral	(Reprise 1378)	.50	2.00	77
STILLWATER				
I RESERVE THE RIGHT/Fair Warning	(Capricorn 0310)	.50	2.00	78
MIND BENDER/Sunshine Blues	(Capricorn 0280)	.50	2.00	77
STINGLEY, Roy				
LONG LIVE THE QUEEN/11:45	(Jerden 801)	.75	3.00	66
STITES, Gary				
GIRL LIKE YOU, A/Hey Little Girl	(Carlton 516)	1.00	4.00	59
HONEY GIRL/Little Lonely One	(Madison 155)	1.00	4.00	61
LAWDY MISS CLAWDY/Don't Wanna Say Goodbye	(Carlton 525)	1.00	4.00	60
LONELY FOR YOU/Shine That Ring	(Carlton 508)	1.00	4.00	59
STARRY EYED/Without Your Love	(Carlton 521)	1.00	4.00	59
YOUNG LOVE/Little Tiger	(Madison 138)	1.00	4.00	60
STOKES, The				
WHIPPED CREAM/	(Alon 9010)	.75	3.00	

TITLE/FLIP	LABEL & NO.	GOOD	NEAR MINT	YR.
STOKES, Simon, & The Nighthawks				
VOO DOO WOMAN/Voo Doo Woman (Part 2)	(Elektra 45670)	.75	3.00	70
STOLLER, Mike, & The Stoller System				
PERFECT WAVE, THE/Numero Uno	(Amy 11039)	.75	3.00	69
STOLOFF, Morris				
MOONGLOW & THEME FROM "PICNIC"/ Theme From "Picnic"	(Decca 29888)	1.00	4.00	56
(George Duning conducting the Columbia Pictures Orchestra)				
STOMPERS, The				
FRUMP/Blacksmith Blues	(Mercury 72111)	.75	3.00	63
QUARTER TO FOUR STOMP/Foolish One	(Landa 684)	.75	3.00	62
STOMPIN' ROUND THE CHRISTMAS TREE/ Stompin' Round The Christmas Tree (Part 2)	(Gone 5120)	1.25	5.00	61
Instrumentals				
STONEBOLT				
I WILL STILL LOVE YOU/Stay In Line	(Parachute 512)	.50	2.00	78
LOVE STRUCK/Was It You	(Parachute 522)	.50	2.00	79
QUEEN OF THE NIGHT/Sail On	(Parachute 507)	.50	2.00	78
STONE, Cliffie				
POPCORN SONG, THE/Barracuda	(Capitol 3131)	1.00	4.00	55
STONE CRUSHERS, The				
CRAWFISH (From "King Creole")/Tadpole Wiggle	(RCA Victor 47-7309)	1.00	4.00	58
STONE, Rosetta (With Ian Mitchell)				
SUNSHINE OF YOUR LOVE/Steal Willie	(Private Stock 45170)	.50	2.00	77
Also see Bay City Rollers, The				
STONEGROUND				
LOOKING FOR YOU/ Added Attraction (Come & See Me)	(Warner Bros. 7496)	.50	2.00	71
PROVE IT/Lead Me Down	(Warner-Curb 8676)	.50	2.00	78
TOTAL DESTRUCTION/Queen Street Dreams	(Warner Bros. 7452)	.50	2.00	71
WAY BACK/	(Flat-Out 002)	.50	2.00	76
YOU MUST BE ONE OF US/Corrina	(Warner Bros. 7535)	.50	2.00	72
Also see Pablo Cruise				
STONEMEN, The				
NO MORE/Where Did Our Love Go	(Big Topper 107)	1.50	6.00	
STONE PONEYS, The: see Rondstadt, Linda				
STONES, The				
SHE SAID YEAH/Watch Me	(Sully 928)	1.25	5.00	66
SHE SAID YEAH/Watch Me	(Sully 928)	1.00	4.00	66
(Shown as by the Tracers)				
STOOGES, The: see Pop, Iggy				
STOOKEY, Paul (Of Peter, Paul & Mary)				
WEDDING SONG (THERE IS LOVE)/Give A Damn	(Warner Bros. 7511)	.50	2.00	71
STOP, Dickie				
CLASS CUTTER/Ruth Ann	(B.E.A.T. 1007)	1.00	4.00	59
STOREY SISTERS, The				
BAD MOTORCYCLE/Sweet Daddy	(Cameo 126)	1.00	4.00	58
LOST LOVE/Lover How I Miss You	(Mercury 71457)	1.00	4.00	59
WHICH WAY DID MY HEART GO/Cha Cha Boom	(Baton 255)	1.00	4.00	58
STORIES, The (Featuring Michael Brown & Ian Lloyd)				
BROTHER LOUIE/What Comes After	(Kama Sutra 577)	.50	2.00	73
DARLING/Take Cover	(Kama Sutra 566)	.50	2.00	73
IF IT FEELS GOOD, DO IT/Circles	(Kama Sutra 588)	.50	2.00	74
I'M COMING HOME/Top Of The City	(Radioactive Gold 85)	.50	2.00	74
MAMMY BLUE/Traveling Underground	(Kama Sutra 584)	.50	2.00	73
TOP OF THE CITY/	(Kama Sutra 558)	.50	2.00	72
Also see Dust				
Also see Left Banke, The				
STORM, Billy (Of The Valiants)				
CHAPEL IN THE MOONLIGHT/Sure As You're Born	(Atlantic 2076)	.75	3.00	60
DEAR ONE/When You Dance	(Atlantic 2098)	.75	3.00	61
DOUBLE DATE/Good Girl	(Buena Vista 415)	.75	3.00	63
EMOTION/I Can't Stop Crying For You	(Columbia 41494)	1.00	4.00	59
ENCHANTED/When The Whole World Smiles Again	(Columbia 41545)	1.00	4.00	59
GOLDFINGER/Debbie & Mitch	(Loma 2009)	.75	3.00	65
HE KNOWS HOW MUCH WE CAN BEAR/Motherless Child	(Buena Vista 424)	.75	3.00	63
HONEY LOVE/A Kiss From Your Lips	(Atlantic 2112)	.75	3.00	61
I NEVER WANT TO DREAM AGAIN/Baby, Don't Look Down	(Loma 2001)	.75	3.00	64
I'VE COME OF AGE/This Is Always	(Columbia 41356)	1.00	4.00	59
LONELY PEOPLE DO FOOLISH THINGS/Deed I Do	(Buena Vista 418)	.75	3.00	63
LOVE THEME FROM "EL CID"/Don't Let Go	(Infinity 013)	.75	3.00	63
LOVE THEME FROM "EL CID"/Cee Cee Rider	(Buena Vista 413)	.75	3.00	63
MILLION MILES FROM NOWHERE/Since I Fell For You	(Infinity 018)	.75	3.00	62
SINCE I FELL FOR YOU/Body & Soul	(Buena Vista 429)	.75	3.00	63
WE KNEW/Walkin' Girl	(Ensign 34035)	.75	3.00	
YOU JUST CAN'T PLAN THESE THINGS/Easy Chair	(Columbia 41431)	1.00	4.00	59
Also see Charades, The				
STORM, Gale				
CASUAL LOOK, A/Cotton Pickin' Kisses	(Dot 15493)	1.00	4.00	56
DARK MOON/A Little Too Late	(Dot 15558)	1.00	4.00	57
I HEAR YOU KNOCKING/Never Leave Me	(Dot 15412)	1.00	4.00	55
IVORY TOWER/I Ain't Gonna Worry	(Dot 15458)	1.00	4.00	56
LOVE BY THE JUKEBOX LIGHT/On My Mind Again	(Dot 15606)	1.00	4.00	57
NOW IS THE HOUR/A Heart Without A Sweetheart	(Dot 15492)	1.00	4.00	56
ON TREASURE ISLAND/Lucky Lips	(Dot 15539)	1.00	4.00	57
TEEN AGE PRAYER/Memories Are Made Of This	(Dot 15436)	1.00	4.00	55
TELL ME WHY/Don't Be That Way	(Dot 15474)	1.00	4.00	56
WHY DO FOOLS FALL IN LOVE/I Walk Alone	(Dot 15448)	1.00	4.00	56
STORM, Rory, & The Hurricanes				
I CAN TELL/Let's Stomp (By Faron's Flamingos)	(Columbia 4-43018)	1.00	4.00	64
STORM, Warren				
GOTTA GO BACK TO SCHOOL/I Can't Love You	(Dot 16272)	1.00	4.00	61
PRISONER SONG, THE/Mama, Mama, Mama	(Nasco 6015)	1.00	4.00	58
THEY WON'T LET ME IN/Sitting Here On The Ceiling	(Kingfish 525)	1.00	4.00	
TROUBLES TROUBLES/My Moments Of Sorrow	(Nasco 6025)	1.00	4.00	59
STORMS, The				
THUNDER/Tarantula	(Sundown 114)	1.00	4.00	59
(Instrumentals)				
STORYTELLERS, The (With Steve Barri)				
I DON'T WANT AN ANGEL/Down In The Valley	(Capitol 5042)	1.50	6.00	63
WHEN TWO PEOPLE/Time Will Tell	(Dimension 1014)	1.50	6.00	63
WHEN TWO PEOPLE/Time Will Tell	(Ramarca 501)	2.50	10.00	63
Also see Fantastic Baggies, The				
Also see Street Cleaners, The				
STORYTELLERS, The				
HEY BABY/You Played Me A Fool	(Stack 500)	3.75	15.00	59
STORYTELLERS, The				
ENGAGEMENT PARTY/The Blue Grass Of Kentucky	(Columbia 42930)	.75	3.00	63
STRAIGHT JACKETS, The				
GIGOLO & I AIN'T GOT NOBODY, A/That Cat	(United Artists 453)	.75	3.00	62
STRANGE, Billy				
GOLDFINGER/The Munsters	(GNP Crescendo 334)	.75	3.00	65
JAMES BOND THEME, THE/007 Theme	(GNP Crescendo 320)	.75	3.00	64
Instrumentals				
STRANGE BROTHERS SHOW, The				
SHAKEY JAKES/Right On	(Sire 4120)	2.50	10.00	
Also see Belmonts, The				
Also see Angels, The				
STRANGELOVES, The (Formerly The Sheep)				
CARA-LIN/(Roll On) Mississippi	(Bang 508)	.75	3.00	65
HONEY DO/I Wanna Do It	(Sire 4102)	.75	3.00	70
I GOTTA DANCE/Hand Jive	(Bang 524)	1.00	4.00	66
I WANT CANDY/It's About My Baby	(Bang 501)	.75	3.00	65
I'M ON FIRE/Love, Love (That's All I Want From You)	(Swan 4192)	1.25	5.00	64
NIGHT TIME/Rhythm Of Love	(Bang 514)	.75	3.00	66
QUARTER TO THREE/Just The Way You Are	(Bang 544)	1.25	5.00	66
STRANGERS, The (With Joel Hill)				
CATERPILLAR CRAWL, THE/Rockin' Rebel	(Titan 1701)	1.25	5.00	59
HILL STOMP/	(Titan 1702)	1.25	5.00	59
Instrumentals				
STRANGERS, The				
CRAB LOUIE/We're In Love, We're In Love, We're In Love	(Christy 107)	.75	3.00	
(Instrumental)				
STRANGERS, The				
BART MAVERICK/Brot Maverick	(Choice 5)	1.00	4.00	60
STRANGLERS, The				
SOMETHING BETTER CHANGE-STRAIGHTEN OUT/ (Get A) Grip (On Yourself)-Hanging Around	(A&M 1973)	.75	3.00	77
(Marble colored plastic)				
STRASSMAN, Marcia				
FLOWER CHILDREN, THE/Out Of The Picture	(Uni 55006)	1.25	5.00	67
FLOWER SHOP, THE/Groovy World Of Jack & Jill	(Uni 55023)	1.25	5.00	67
STRATOJACS, The				
SUNSET SURFER/Hot Toddy	(Parrot 45003)	1.00	4.00	64

TITLE/FLIP	LABEL & NO.	GOOD	NEAR MINT	YR.
STRAWBERRY ALARM CLOCK, The				
BAREFOOT IN BALTIMORE/Angry Young Men	(Uni 55076)	.75	3.00	68
DESIREE/	(Uni 55158)	1.00	4.00	69
GOOD MORNING STARSHINE/Me & The Township	(Uni 55125)	.75	3.00	69
I CLIMBED THE MOUNTAIN/Three	(Uni 55190)	1.00	4.00	70
INCENSE & PEPPERMINTS/The Birdman Of Alcatrash	(All American 373)	1.50	6.00	67
INCENSE & PEPPERMINTS/The Birdman Of Alcatrash	(Uni 55018)	.75	3.00	67
MISS ATTRACTION/Stand By	(Uni 55113)	1.00	4.00	69
PAXTON'S BACK STREET CARNIVAL/Sea Shell	(Uni 55093)	1.00	4.00	68
SIT WITH THE GURU/Pretty Song From Psych-Out	(Uni 55055)	.75	3.00	68
TOMORROW/Birds In My Trees	(Uni 55046)	.75	3.00	67
Also see Sixpense				
Also see Iridescents, The				
STRAWBS, The				
BENEDICTUS/Heavy Disguise	(A&M 1364)	.75	3.00	72
BURNING FOR ME/Heartbreaker	(Oyster 705)	.50	2.00	77
I DON'T WANT TO TALK ABOUT IT/Words Of Wisdom	(Arista 0327)	.50	2.00	78
I ONLY WANT MY LOVE TO GROW IN YOU/ (Wasting My Time) Thinking Of You	(Oyster 702)	.50	2.00	76
LEMON PIE/Where Do You Go (When You Need A Hole To Crawl In)	(A&M 1687)	.75	3.00	74
LITTLE SLEEPY/	(A&M 1747)	.75	3.00	75
OH HOW SHE CHANGED/Or Am I Dreaming	(A&M 944)	.75	3.00	68
POOR JIMMY WILSON/The Man Who Called Himself Jesus	(A&M 998)	.75	3.00	68
ROUND & ROUND/Heroine's Theme	(A&M 1519)	.75	3.00	74
SO CLOSE & YET SO FAR AWAY/	(Oyster 704)	.50	2.00	77
Also see Lambert, Dave				
STREAK				
GONNA HAVE A GOOD TIME/	(A&M 1375)	.50	2.00	72
STREET CLEANERS, The (Phil Sloan & Steve Barri)				
GARBAGE CITY/That's Cool, That's Trash	(Amy 916)	2.00	8.00	64
STREET PEOPLE, The				
I REMEMBER/I Wonder What Happened To Sally	(Musicor 1412)	.75	3.00	70
JENNIFER TOMKINS/All Night Long	(Musicor 1365)	.75	3.00	69
THANK YOU GIRL/World Doesn't Matter Anymore	(Musicor 1401)	.75	3.00	70
STREISAND, Barbra (Barbra Joan Streisand)				
ALL IN LOVE IS FAIR/ Medley: My Buddy-How About Me	(Columbia 46024)	.50	2.00	74
BEFORE THE PARADE PASSES ME BY/ Love Is Only Love	(Columbia 45072)	.50	2.00	70
DIDN'T WE/	(Columbia 45739)	.50	2.00	72
FLIM FLAM MAN/	(Columbia 45384)	.50	2.00	71
FRANK MILLS/Punky's Dilemma	(Columbia 44775)	.50	2.00	69
FREE AGAIN/I've Been Here	(Columbia 43808)	.75	3.00	66
FUNNY GIRL/Absent Minded Me	(Columbia 43127)	.75	3.00	64
HE TOUCHED ME/I Like Him	(Columbia 43403)	.75	3.00	65
HOW LUCKY CAN YOU GET/More Than You Know	(Arista 0123)	.50	2.00	75
IF I CLOSE MY EYES (THEME FROM "UP THE SANDBOX")/	(Columbia 45780)	.50	2.00	73
KISS ME IN THE RAIN/ I Ain't Gonna Cry Tonight	(Columbia 11179)	.50	2.00	79

TITLE/FLIP	LABEL & NO.	GOOD	NEAR MINT	YR.
LITTLE TIN SOLDIER/Honey Pie	(Columbia 44921)	.75	3.00	69
LOVE THEME FROM "A STAR IS BORN" (EVERGREEN)/ I Believe In Love	(Columbia 10450)	.50	2.00	76
LOVE THEME FROM "EYES OF LAURA MARS" (PRISONER)/ Laura & Neville (Instrumental)	(Columbia 10777)	.50	2.00	78
MAIN EVENT-FIGHT, THE/ The Main Event-Fight (Instrumental)	(Columbia 11008)	.50	2.00	79
MOTHER/	(Columbia 45471)	.50	2.00	71
MY COLORING BOOK/Lover Come Back To Me	(Columbia 42648)	1.00	4.00	63
MY MAN/Where Is The Wonder	(Columbia 43323)	.75	3.00	65
NO MORE TEARS (ENOUGH IS ENOUGH) (With Donna Summer)/ Wet	(Columbia 11125)	.50	2.00	79
NO MORE TEARS (ENOUGH IS ENOUGH)/ (With Donna Summer)	(Columbia-Casa Blanca NBD-20199-DJ)	1.25	5.00	79
(Promotional 12" one-sided single. Price includes special jacket.)				
OUR CORNER OF THE NIGHT/He Could Show Me	(Columbia 44474)	.75	3.00	68
PEOPLE/I Am Woman	(Columbia 42965)	.75	3.00	64
SAM, YOU MADE THE PANTS TOO LONG/ The Minute Waltz	(Columbia 43612)	.75	3.00	66
SECOND HAND ROSE/ The Kind Of Man A Woman Needs	(Columbia 43469)	.75	3.00	65
SHAKE ME, WAKE ME (WHEN IT'S OVER)/Widescreen	(Columbia 10272)	.50	2.00	75
SING A SONG-MAKE YOUR OWN KIND OF MUSIC/ Starting Here, Starting Now	(Columbia 45686)	.50	2.00	72
SLEEP IN HEAVENLY PEACE (SILENT NIGHT)/ Gounod's Ave Maria	(Columbia 43896)	.75	3.00	66
SONGBIRD/Honey Can I Put On Your Clothes	(Columbia 10756)	.50	2.00	78
SPACE CAPTAIN (With Fanny)/One Less Bell To Answer/ A House Is Not A Home	(Columbia 45511)	.50	2.00	72
STONEY END/I'll Be Home	(Columbia 45236)	.50	2.00	70
STOUT-HEARTED MEN/Look	(Columbia 44225)	.75	3.00	67
SUPERMAN/A Man I Loved	(Columbia 10931)	.50	2.00	79
SWEET INSPIRATION-WHERE YOU LEAD/Didn't We	(Columbia 45626)	.50	2.00	72
TIME & LOVE/No Easy Way Down	(Columbia 45341)	.50	2.00	71
WAY WE WERE, THE/What Are You Doing The Rest Of Your Life?	(Columbia 45944)	.50	2.00	73
WHEN THE SUN COMES OUT/ Happy Days Are Here Again	(Columbia 42631)	1.00	4.00	62
WHERE AM I GOING?/You Wanna Bet	(Columbia 43518)	.75	3.00	66
WHERE YOU LEAD/Since I Fell For You	(Columbia 45414)	.50	2.00	71
WHY DID I CHOOSE YOU/My Love	(Columbia 43248)	.75	3.00	65
YOU DON'T BRING ME FLOWERS/ You Don't Bring Me Flowers (Part 2)	(Columbia 10840)	.50	2.00	78
(With Neil Diamond)				
Also see Fanny				
STRETCH				
WHY DID YOU DO IT?/Write Me A Note	(Anchor 21003)	.50	2.00	75
STRICKLAND, Johnny				
I'VE HEARD THAT LINE BEFORE/Don't Leave Me Lonely	(Roulette 4147)	1.00	4.00	59
SHE'S MINE/You've Got What It Takes	(Roulette 4119)	5.00	20.00	59
STRIKER				
BY YOUR SIDE/	(Arista 0341)	.50	2.00	78
MORE THAN ENOUGH/	(Arista 0321)	.50	2.00	78
STRING-A-LONGS, The				
BRASS BUTTONS/Panic Button	(Warwick 625)	.75	3.00	61
HAPPY MELODY/Heartaches	(Dot 16448)	.75	3.00	63
MATHILDA/Caravan	(Dot 16708)	.75	3.00	64
MATILDA/Replica	(Dot 16393)	.75	3.00	62
MY BLUE HEAVEN/Spinnin' My Wheels	(Dot 16379)	.75	3.00	62
MYNA BIRD/Scottie	(Dot 16575)	.75	3.00	63
NEARLY SUNRISE/Theme for Twisters	(Warwick 675)	.75	3.00	62
SCOTTIE/Mina Bird	(Warwick 668)	.75	3.00	61

TITLE/FLIP	LABEL & NO.	GOOD	NEAR MINT	YR.
SHOULD I/Take A Minute	(Warwick 654)	.75	3.00	61
TELL THE WORLD/For My Angel	(Warwick 606)	.75	3.00	61
THEME FOR TWISTERS/Nearly Sunrise	(Warwick 675)	.75	3.00	62
TWISTWATCH/Sunday	(Dot 16331)	.75	3.00	62
WHEELS/Am I Asking Too Much	(Warwick 603)	.75	3.00	61
Instrumentals				
STRING DRIVEN THING				
CIRCUS/	(Charisma 102)	.50	2.00	73
CRUEL TO FOOL/	(20th Century 2300)	.50	2.00	75
STROLLERS, The				
COME ON OVER/There's No One But You	(Carlton 546)	.75	3.00	61
SWINGING YELLOW ROSE OF TEXAS/ Jumping With Symphony Sid	(Aladdin 3417)	.75	3.00	58
Instrumentals				
STROLLS, The				
MADISONVILLE/Madisonville (Part 2)	(Sky Rocket)	.75	3.00	60
STEWART, Chad & Jill				
CRUEL WAR, THE/I Can't Talk To You	(Columbia 43467)	.75	3.00	66
Also see Chad & Jeremy				
STUART, Glen, Chorus				
DRIP DROP/Ruby Baby	(Abel 235)	2.50	10.00	
Also see Belmonts, The				
STUBBLEFIELD, Bill				
WHISTLIN' ROCK & ROLL/	(Imperial 5447)	1.00	4.00	57
STUDIO "A"				
DON'T FORGET ABOUT ME/	(Kapp 849)	.75	3.00	67
STUMBLEBUNNY				
TONITE/Young Stuff	(Mercury 74061)	.50	2.00	79
STYLE KINGS, The				
KISSING BEHIND THE MOON/	(Sotoplay 0011)	2.00	8.00	
STYLERS, The				
CONFESSION OF A SINNER/Gonna Tell Em	(Jubilee 5253)	1.00	4.00	56
STYLES, The				
I LOVE YOU FOR SENTIMENTAL REASONS/ School Bells To Chapel Bells	(Josie 920)	3.75	15.00	64
SCARLET ANGEL/Gotta Go, Go, Go	(Serene 1501)	5.00	20.00	
STYLES, Donnie				
CHAPEL OF LOVE/	(Time Square 106)	1.00	4.00	
STYX				
BABE/I'm O.K.	(A&M 2188)	.50	2.00	79
BEST THING/What Has Come Between Us	(Wooden Nickel 0106)	.50	2.00	72
BEST THING/Havin' A Ball	(Wooden Nickel 10329)	.50	2.00	75
BEST THING/Winner Take All	(Wooden Nickel 11205)	.50	2.00	78
BLUE COLLAR MAN (LONG NIGHTS)/Superstars	(A&M 2087)	.50	2.00	78
COME SAIL AWAY/Put Me On	(A&M 1977)	.50	2.00	77
CRYSTAL BALL/Put Me On	(A&M 1931)	.50	2.00	77
FOOLING YOURSELF/The Grand Finale	(A&M 2007)	.50	2.00	78
I'M GONNA MAKE YOU FEEL IT/	(Wooden Nickel 0111)	.75	3.00	73
JENNIFER/Shooz	(A&M 1900)	.50	2.00	77
LADY/	(Wooden Nickel 0116)	.50	2.00	73
LADY/Children Of The Land	(Wooden Nickel 10102)	.50	2.00	74
LIGHT UP/Born For Adventure	(A&M 1818)	.50	2.00	76
LORELEI/Midnight Ride	(A&M 1786)	.50	2.00	76
MADEMOISELLE/Light Up	(A&M 1877)	.50	2.00	76
PUPPETMASTER/	(Onyx 2200)	.50	2.00	
RENEGADE/Sing For The Day	(A&M 2110)	.50	2.00	79
SING FOR THE DAY/Queen Of Spades	(A&M 2110)	.50	2.00	79
WHY ME/Lights	(A&M 2206)	.50	2.00	79
YOU NEED LOVE/You Better Ask	(Wooden Nickel 10272)	.50	2.00	75
STYX				
SOUL FLOW/Promised Land	(Paramount 0104)	.50	2.00	72
SUADES, The				
EVERYBODY'S TRYING TO BE MY BABY/Wrong Yo Yo	(Spinning 6011)	.75	3.00	61
SUBURBANS, The				
ALPHABET OF LOVE/Sweet Diane Cha Cha	(Port 70011)	1.50	6.00	
SUDDENS, The (The Safaris)				
CHILDISH WAYS/Garden Of Love	(Sudden 103)	2.00	8.00	61
SUGAR BUNS, The				
PAJAMA PARTY/Nails & Snails	(Warner Bros. 5046)	1.00	4.00	59
SUGAR CANES, The				
POOR BOY/Sioux Rock	(King 5157)	1.00	4.00	58
(Instrumentals)				
SUGAR BEATS, The (Al Candaleria, Darron Stankey, Larry Knew)				
FIRST LOVE/Begin-Give In-A	(A&M 795)	.75	3.00	66
Also see Innocents, The				
SUGARLOAF (Featuring Jerry Corbetta)				
DON'T CALL US, WE'LL CALL YOU/Texas Two-Lane	(Claridge 402)	.50	2.00	74
GREEN-EYED LADY/West Of Tomorrow	(Liberty 56183)	.50	2.00	70
MOTHER NATURE'S WINE/ Medley: Bach Doors Man/Chest Fever	(United Artists 50784)	.50	2.00	71
ROUND & ROUND/Colorado Jones	(Brut 805)	.50	2.00	73
STARS IN MY EYES/	(Claridge 405)	.50	2.00	75
TONGUE IN CHEEK/Woman	(Liberty 56218)	.50	2.00	71
Also see Soul Survivors, The				
SUGGS, Brad				
ELEPHANT WALK/Like Catchin' Up	(Phillips International 3571)	.75	3.00	59
SULLIVAN, Carolyn				
DEAD/Wow	(Philips 40507)	.75	3.00	68
SULLIVAN, Niki (Of The Crickets)				
DOIN' THE DIVE/My Lost Dream (Vocal by Ronnie Fuller, Niki Sullivan on lead guitar.)	(Joli 073)	5.00	20.00	
IT REALLY DOESN'T MATTER/You Better Get A Move On	(Joli 075)	10.00	40.00	
IT'S ALL OVER/Three Steps To Heaven	(Dot 15751)	10.00	40.00	58
Also see Hollyhawks, The				
SULLIVAN, Tom				
FOOLS RUSH IN/	(ABC 12233)	.50	2.00	77
SINCE I FELL FOR YOU/You're Gonna Find Love	(Warner Bros. 8449)	.50	2.00	78
YES I'M READY/	(ABC 12174)	.50	2.00	75
SULTANS, The				
CHRISTINA/Someone You Can Trust	(Guyden 2079)	2.00	8.00	63
GLORIA/I Wanna Know	(Ascot 2228)	2.00	8.00	64
IT'LL BE EASY/You Got Me Goin' (Yellow label)	(Tilt 782)	5.00	20.00	61
IT'LL BE EASY/You Got Me Goin' (Black label)	(Tilt 782)	1.25	5.00	61
MARY, MARY/How Far Does A Friendship Go	(Jam 107)	1.00	4.00	
SUMMER, FALL, WINTER, SPRING				
FOR A MOMENT/Please Don't Forget Tonight	(United Artists 50112)	1.25	5.00	67

TITLE/FLIP	LABEL & NO.	GOOD	NEAR MINT	YR.
SUMMERS, Bob				
HONDA HAWK/Organization	(Crusader 107)	.75	3.00	64
SUMMERS, Bobby				
BACK BEAT/Comin' 'Round The Mountain	(Capitol 4404)	.75	3.00	60
JINGLE JANGLE JINGLE/Teeter Totter	(Uni 1900)	.75	3.00	61
PARADE ROCK/Pad	(Capitol 4143)	.75	3.00	59
SUMMERS, Little Davey (Russ Regan)				
CALLING ALL CARS/Good Ship Love	(Vim 101)	1.00	4.00	63
GONNA CLIMB THAT BIG OLE HILL/Doin' The Davey Drag (With the Singing Ants)	(Dore 684)	.75	3.00	63
Also see Dancer, Prancer & Nervous				
SUMMERS, Gene				
GOODBYE PRICILLA (BYE BYE BABY BLUE)/	(Teardrop 3405)	.75	3.00	77
GREEN-EYED MONSTER/The Clown	(Mercury 72606)	.75	3.00	66
NERVOUS/Gotta Lotta That	(Jan 102)	3.00	12.00	
SCHOOL OF ROCK 'N ROLL/Straight Skirt	(Jan 100)	5.00	20.00	
SUMMER WINE				
WHY DO FOOLS FALL IN LOVE/	(Sire 701)	.50	2.00	73
SUMMITS, The				
HE'S AN ANGEL/Hanky Panky	(Harmon 1017)	1.50	6.00	63
HE'S AN ANGEL/Hanky Panky	(Rust 5072)	1.00	4.00	63
SUMNER, J.D.				
ELVIS HAS LEFT THE BUILDING/Sweet, Sweet Spirit	(QCA 461)	.50	2.00	77
ELVIS HAS LEFT THE BUILDING/Sweet, Sweet Spirit (Picture sleeve)	(QCA 461)	.75	3.00	77
SUNDAY FUNNIES, The				
WONDER WOMAN/She's Not At All Like You	(Mercury 72571)	.75	3.00	66
SUN DOG: see Happenings, The				
SUNDIALS, The				
WHETHER TO RESIST/Chapel Of Love	(Guyden 2065)	6.25	25.00	62
SUNDOWN PLAYBOYS, The				
SATURDAY NIGHT SPECIAL/ Valse De Soleil Coucher (Sundown Waltz)	(Apple 1852)	.50	2.00	72
SUNGLOWS, The (Featuring Sonny Ozuna)				
GOLLY GEE/Touring	(Sunglow 104)	1.00	4.00	62
GOLLY GEE/Touring	(Okeh 7143)	1.00	4.00	62
IT'S TOO LATE/You Gave Me A True Love	(Tear Drop 3034)	.75	3.00	64
OUT OF SIGHT-OUT OF MIND/No One Else Will Do (Shown as by Sunny & the Sunliners)	(Tear Drop 3027)	.75	3.00	64
PEANUTS (LA CACAHUTA)/Happy Hippo (Instrumentals)	(Disco Grande 1021)	1.00	4.00	65
PEANUTS (LA CACAHUTA)/Happy Hippo (Instrumentals)	(Sunglow 107)	.75	3.00	65
RAGS TO RICHES/Not Even Judgement Day (Shown as by Sunny & the Sunliners)	(Tear Drop 3022)	.75	3.00	63
RAGS TO RICHES/Not Even Judgement Day (Shown as by Sunny & the Sunglows)	(Sunglow 111)	.75	3.00	65
TALK TO ME/Every Week Every Month Every Year (Shown as by Sunny & the Sunglows)	(Tear Drop 3014)	.75	3.00	63
TALK TO ME/Every Week Every Month Every Year (Shown as by Sunny & the Sunglows)	(Sunglow 110)	.75	3.00	63
YOU SEND ME/His Greatest Creation	(Tear Drop 3040)	.75	3.00	64
First Tear Drop pressings are on a red label and do not read "Distributed by Jamie Guyden."				
SUNNY & THE HORIZONS				
NATURE'S CREATION/Because They Tell Me	(Luxor 1013)	7.50	30.00	
SUNNY & THE SUNGLOWS: see Sunglows, The				
SUNNY & THE SUNLINERS: see Sunglows, The				
SUNNY BOYS, The				
CHAPEL BELLS/My Friend Sam	(Mr. Maestro 806)	1.50	6.00	
FOR THE REST OF MY LIFE/Chapel Bells	(Take 3 2001)	1.50	6.00	
FOR THE REST OF MY LIFE/My Friend Sam	(Mr. Maestro 805)	2.00	8.00	
SUNRAYS, The				
ANDREA/You Don't Phase Me	(Tower 191)	.75	3.00	66
CAR PARTY/Out Of Gas	(Tower 101)	.75	3.00	64
GIDEON/Talk To Him	(Warner Bros. 5253)	1.00	4.00	63
HI, HOW ARE YOU/Just Round The River Bend	(Tower 290)	.75	3.00	66
I LIVE FOR THE SUN/Bye Baby Bye	(Tower 148)	.75	3.00	66
I LOOK BABY-I CAN'T SEE/Don't Take Yourself Too Seriously	(Tower 256)	.75	3.00	67
STILL/When You're Not Here	(Tower 224)	.75	3.00	66
TIME (A SPECIAL THING)/Loaded With Love	(Tower 340)	.75	3.00	67
Also see Henn, Rick				
SUNSET BOMBERS (With Doug Fieger)				
I CAN'T CONTROL MYSELF/High Cotton	(Zombie 7676)	.50	2.00	78
Also see Knack, The				
SUNSETS, The				
LONELY SURFER BOY/Playmate Of The Year	(Challange 9198)	1.00	4.00	64
MY LITTLE BEACH BUNNY/My Little Surfin' Woodie	(Challenge 9208)	1.00	4.00	63
ONLY YOU, ONLY ME/Lydia	(Petal 1040)	1.00	4.00	63
SUNSHINE				
I JUST CAN'T HELP BUT YOU/Is There Anybody Else	(Capitol 3051)	1.00	4.00	71

TITLE/FLIP	LABEL & NO.	GOOD	NEAR MINT	YR.
SUNSHINE COMPANY, The				
BACK ON THE STREET AGAIN/ A Year Of Janie's Time	(Imperial 66260)	.75	3.00	67
HAPPY/Blue May	(Imperial 66247)	.75	3.00	67
LOOK, HERE COMES THE SUN/It's Sunday	(Imperial 66280)	.75	3.00	68
LOVE POEM/Willie Jean	(Imperial 66324)	.75	3.00	68
SUNSHYNE				
DANCE LIKE AN ANIMAL/Mighty Rough Road	(PN 500)	1.25	5.00	
SUPA, Richard				
AT EVERY END THERE'S A BEGINNING/	(Arista 0120)	.50	2.00	75
FORGETTING SOMEONE/	(Epic 50287)	.50	2.00	76
GANGSTER ON THE LOOSE/Small Talk	(Polydor-Silver Cloud 14520)	.50	2.00	79
LI'L JESSIE/Burned	(Paramount 0119)	.50	2.00	72
SISTER SALVATION/Goshen Road	(Paramount 0171)	.50	2.00	72
SUITCASE LIFE/Lucrecia	(Polydor-Silver Cloud 14490)	.50	2.00	78
TRACKS OF MY TEARS/Heap-A-Trouble	(Paramount 0182)	.50	2.00	73
SUPER K GENERATION				
HEART FULL O'SOUL (PART 1)/ Heart Full O'Soul (Part 2)	(Laurie LR-3413)	.75	3.00	67
SUPER STOCKS, The (Featuring Gary Usher & Jerry Cole)				
MIDNIGHT RUN/Santa Barbara	(Capitol 2113)	1.00	4.00	68
THUNDER ROAD/Wheel Stands	(Capitol 5153)	1.00	4.00	64
SUPER STU, Allen, Dennis & The Disco Turkeys				
GREAT DEBATE, THE/Lonely Lady	(Brown Dog 9016)	.75	3.00	
SUPERBS, The				
BABY, BABY ALL THE TIME/ Raindrops, Memories & Tears (Instrumental)	(Dore 715)	.75	3.00	64
BABY'S GONE AWAY/Twine & Slide	(Dore 731)	.75	3.00	65
BIG HURT, THE/I Was Blind	(Dore 727)	.75	3.00	65
GODDESS OF LOVE/He Broke A Young Girl's Heart	(Dore 748)	.75	3.00	65
MY HEART ISN'T IN IT/Sad Sad Day	(Dore 722)	.75	3.00	64
STORY BOOK OF LOVE, THE/Better Get Your Own Buddy	(Dore 704)	.75	3.00	64
SUPER-PHONICS, The				
TEEN-AGE PARTNER/	(Lindy 102)	2.00	8.00	
SUPERTONES, The				
SLIPPIN' & STOPPIN' (PART 1)/ Slippin' & Stoppin' (Part 2)	(Everest 19325)	.75	3.00	60
SUPERTRAMP				
AIN'T NOBODY BUT ME/Sister Moonshine	(A&M 1814)	.50	2.00	76
BLOODY WELL RIGHT/Dreamer	(A&M 1660)	.50	2.00	75
DREAMER/From Now On	(A&M 1981)	.50	2.00	77
GIVE A LITTLE BIT/Downstream	(A&M 1938)	.50	2.00	77
GOODBYE STRANGER/Even In The Quietest Moments	(A&M 2162)	.50	2.00	79
LADY/Laughing When I Held You In My Arms	(A&M 1793)	.50	2.00	76
LOGICAL SONG, THE/Just Another Nervous Wreck	(A&M 2128)	.50	2.00	79
TAKE THE LONG WAY HOME/Rudy	(A&M 2193)	.50	2.00	79
SURF, Adam, & The Pebble Beach Band				
FUN FUN FUN/Blue Surf	(Paladin 3)	1.25	5.00	
SURF BOYS, The				
DA DOO RON RON/Hurt	(Karate 526)	.75	3.00	66
SURF BUNNIES, The				
OUR SURFER BOYS/Surf Bunny Beach	(Dot 16523)	.75	3.00	63
OUR SURFER BOYS/Surf Bunny Beach	(Goliath 1352)	1.50	6.00	63
SURF CITY HIGH/Met The Boy I Adore	(Goliath 1353)	1.50	6.00	63
SURF MEN, The				
MALIBU RUN/El Torn	(Titan 1727)	1.00	4.00	63
PARADISE COVE/Ghost Hop	(Titan 1723)	1.00	4.00	62
Instrumentals				
Also see Lively Ones, The				
SURF RIDERS, The				
BLUES FOR THE BIRDS/Birds (Instrumental)	(Decca 31477)	.75	3.00	63
SURF TEENS, The				
MOONSHINE/Moment Of Truth	(Westco 9)	.75	3.00	63
SURFARIS, The				
BEAT '65/Black Denim	(Decca 31731)	1.00	4.00	65
BOSS BEAT/Surfin' '63	(Regano 201)	1.25	5.00	63
CHICAGO GREEN/Show Biz	(Dot 16966)	1.00	4.00	66
DON'T HURT MY LITTLE SISTER/ Catch A Little Ride With Me	(Decca 31835)	1.00	4.00	65
DUNE BUGGY/Boss Barracuda	(Decca 31641)	1.00	4.00	64
HEY JOE, WHERE ARE YOU GOING/So Get Out	(Decca 31954)	1.00	4.00	66
HOT ROD HIGH/Karen	(Decca 31682)	1.00	4.00	64
MIDNIGHT SURF/Psyche-out	(Chancellor 1143)	1.00	4.00	63
MOMENT OF TRUTH/Church Key (By the Biscaynes)	(Northridge 1001)	1.25	5.00	63
MOMENT OF TRUTH/Church Key (By the Biscaynes)	(Reprise 20180)	1.00	4.00	63
MURPHY THE SURFIE/Go, Go, Go For Louie's Place	(Decca 31605)	1.00	4.00	64
POINT PANIC/Waikiki Run	(Decca 31538)	1.00	4.00	63
PSYCHE-OUT/Tor-Chula	(Felsted 8688)	.75	3.00	64
SCATTER SHIELD/ I Wanna Take A Trip To The Islands (With the Honeys)	(Decca 31581)	1.50	6.00	63
SEARCH/Shake	(Dot 17008)	1.00	4.00	67
SOMETHIN' ELSE/Theme Of The Battle Maiden	(Decca 31784)	1.00	4.00	65
SURFARI/Bombara	(Del Fi 4219)	1.25	5.00	63
SURFER JOE/Early In The Evening	(Dot 16757)	1.00	4.00	65
SURFER'S CHRISTMAS LIST/Santa's Speed Shop	(Decca 31561)	1.25	5.00	63
WIPE OUT/I'm A Hog For You	(Decca 32003)	1.00	4.00	63
WIPE OUT/Surfer Joe	(Princess 50)	3.75	15.00	63
WIPE OUT/Surfer Joe	(Dot 16479)	.75	3.00	63
WIPE OUT/Surfer Joe (Containing two additional verses not on the Dot & Princess issues)	(DFS-11/12)	12.50	50.00	63
WIPE OUT/Wipe Out (Promotional red plastic issue. Some copies, though labeled "Wipe Out" on both sides, actually contain "Surfer Joe" on both sides.)	(Dot 144)	5.00	20.00	66
Even though all of these releases are shown as being by a group using the same name, the possibility exists that they are not all by the same group.				
SURFER GIRLS, The				
DRAGGIN' WAGON/One Boy Tells Another	(Columbia 43001)	1.00	4.00	64
SURFERS, The				
STOMPIN' AT THE SURFSIDE/Widget	(DRA 318)	1.00	4.00	62
TAHITI/Ulilie	(Hi-Fi 574)	.75	3.00	61
SURFETTES, The				
SAMMY THE SIDEWALK SURFER/	(Mustang 3001)	1.00	4.00	65
SURPRISE				
DENISE/Blue Moon	(Kare 102)	1.50	6.00	
SURVIVORS, The: see Beach Boys, The				
SUSAN				
THINK IT OVER/	(RCA 11580)	.50	2.00	79
SUSIE & THE 4 TRUMPETS				
STARRY EYES/Blue Little Girl	(United Artists 471)	2.50	10.00	62

TITLE/FLIP	LABEL & NO.	GOOD	NEAR MINT	YR.
SUTCH, Screaming Lord				
SHE'S FALLEN IN LOVE WITH THE MONSTER MAN/ Bye, Bye Baby	(Cameo 341)	.75	3.00	65
SUTHERLAND BROTHERS & QUIVER				
ARMS OF MARY/Love On The Moon	(Columbia 10284)	.50	2.00	75
AS LONG AS I'VE GOT YOU/On The Rocks	(Columbia 11004)	.50	2.00	79
DREAM KID/	(Island 1220)	.50	2.00	73
(I DON'T WANT TO LOVE YOU BUT) YOU GOT ME ANYWAY/ Rock & Roll Show	(Island 1217)	.50	2.00	73
ONE MORE NIGHT WITH YOU/ When I Say I Love You (The Pie)	(Columbia 10758)	.50	2.00	78
(Shown as by the Sutherland Brothers)				
SECRETS/Something's Burning	(Columbia 10460)	.50	2.00	76
WHEN THE TRAIN COMES/	(Columbia 10362)	.50	2.00	76
SUZY & THE RED STRIPES (Featuring Linda McCartney)				
SEASIDE WOMAN/B-Side To Seaside	(Epic 50403)	.50	2.00	77
SEASIDE WOMAN/B-Side To Seaside	(Epic 50403)	2.50	10.00	77
(Red plastic promotional issue.)				
SWAGS, The				
ROCKIN' MATILDA/Blowin' The Blues	(Del Fi 4143)	1.00	4.00	60
SWALLOW				
YES I'LL SAY IT/Aches & Pains	(Warner Bros. 7613)	.75	3.00	72
SWAMP DOGG				
MY HEART JUST CAN'T STOP DANCING/	(Musicor 6306)	.50	2.00	77
SAM STONE/Knowing I'm Pleasing Me & You	(Cream 1021)	.50	2.00	73
SWAMP RATS, The				
IN THE MIDNIGHT HOUR/It's Not Easy	(Co & Ce 245)	.75	3.00	67
SWAN, Billy				
EVERYTHING'S THE SAME (AIN'T NOTHING CHANGED)/ Overnight Thing (Usually)	(Monument 8661)	.50	2.00	75
HELLO! REMEMBER ME/Never Go Lookin' Again	(A&M 2046)	.50	2.00	78
I CAN HELP/Ways Of A Woman In Love	(Monument 8621)	.50	2.00	74
I'M HER FOOL/	(Monument 8641)	.50	2.00	75
JUST WANT TO TASTE YOUR WINE/	(Monument 8682)	.50	2.00	76
(With the Jordanaires)				
NO WAY AROUND IT (IT'S LOVE)/Forever In Your Love	(A&M 2103)	.50	2.00	79
NUMBER ONE/Vanessa	(Monument 8697)	.50	2.00	76
SHAKE, RATTLE & ROLL/	(Columbia 10443)	.50	2.00	77
SWEPT AWAY/	(Columbia 10486)	.50	2.00	77
YOU'RE THE ONE/	(Monument 8706)	.50	2.00	76
SWAN, Mary				
MY GIRL FRIEND BETTY/Prisoner Of Love	(Swan 4028)	1.00	4.00	59
SWANS, The				
BOY WITH THE BEATLE HAIR, THE/Please Hurry Home	(Cameo 302)	2.00	8.00	64
(First known Beatle novelty recording)				
SWANSON, Bobby				
ROCKIN' LITTLE ESKIMO/Ballad Of Angel	(Igloo 1003)	1.00	4.00	59
(With the Sonics)				
TOM & SUZIE/China Doll	(Donna 1326)	.75	3.00	60
SWAWN, Dick, & His Little People				
HAMBONE/La Plume De Ma Tante	(20th Century-Fox 461)	.75	3.00	64
YOU MUSN'T FEEL DISCOURAGED/ Fade Out-Fade In	(20th Century-Fox 522)	.75	3.00	65
SWEATHOG				
HALLELUJAH/Still On The Road	(Columbia 45492)	.50	2.00	71
SWEDEN HEAVEN & HELL (From the Soundtrack)				
MAH-NA-MAH-NA/You Tried To Warn Me	(Ariel 500)	.50	2.00	69
(No artist is actually credited on the label.)				
SWEENY TODD				
ROXY ROLLER/Rue De Chance	(London 240)	.50	2.00	76
(Formerly with Nick Gilder, this is the original instrumental track with Gilder's vocal replaced by another group member.)				
SWEET				
ACTION/Medussa	(Capitol 4220)	.50	2.00	76
BALLROOM BLITZ/Restless	(Capitol 4055)	.50	2.00	75
BLOCKBUSTER/Need A Lot Of Lovin'	(Bell 45,361)	.50	2.00	73
CALIFORNIA NIGHTS/	(Capitol 4610)	.50	2.00	78
CO'CO/	(Bell 45,126)	.50	2.00	71
FEVER OF LOVE/Heartbreak Today	(Capitol 4429)	.50	2.00	77
FOX ON THE RUN/Burn On The Flame	(Capitol 4157)	.50	2.00	75
FUNK IT UP (DAVID'S SONG)/Stairway To The Stary	(Capitol 4454)	.50	2.00	77
LITTLE WILLY/Man From Mecca	(Bell 45,251)	.50	2.00	73
LOVE IS LIKE OXYGEN/Cover Girl	(Capitol 4549)	.50	2.00	78
MOTHER EARTH/Why Don't You	(Capitol 4730)	.50	2.00	79
POPPA JOE/Jeanie	(Bell 45,184)	.50	2.00	72
WIG-WAM BAM/New York connection	(Bell 45,408)	.50	2.00	74
SWEET LINDA DIVINE				
GOOD DAY SUNSHINE/Same Time Same Place	(Columbia 44954)	1.00	4.00	69
SWEET, Rachel				
B-A-B-Y/Wildwood Saloon	(Stiff-Columbia 11100)	.50	2.00	79
I GO TO PIECES/Suspended Animation	(Stiff-Columbia 11052)	.50	2.00	79
WE LIVE IN TWO DIFFERENT WORLDS/	(Derrick 10000)	.50	2.00	76
SWEET SENSATION				
SAD SWEET DREAMER/Surething, Yes I Down	(Pye 71002)	.50	2.00	75
SWEET SICK TEENS, The				
PRETZEL, THE/Agnes, The Teenage Russian Spy	(RCA Victor 47-7940)	1.25	5.00	62
PRETZEL, THE/Agnes, The Teenage Russian Spy	(RCA Victor 37-7940)	2.50	10.00	62
(Compact 33 single)				
SWEET SMOKE				
MORNING DEW/Mary Jane Is To Love	(Jan-Gi 101)	1.25	5.00	
SWEET SOULS, The (Featuring Johnny Fortune)				
I WANT TO MAKE IT WITH YOU/Your Baby	(RPR 112)	.75	3.00	66
SWEET THURSDAY (With Jon Mark)				
DEALER/Jenny	(Great Western 5023)	.50	2.00	72
Also see Mark-Almond				
SWIFT, Allen				
ARE YOU LONESOME TONIGHT/Look Out Below	(Leader 815)	1.50	6.00	61
(Novelty/parody)				
SWINGING BLUE JEANS, The				
DON'T MAKE ME OVER/What Can I Do Today	(Imperial 66154)	1.00	4.00	66
GOOD GOLLY MISS MOLLY/Shaking Feeling	(Imperial 66030)	1.00	4.00	64
HIPPY HIPPY SHAKE/Now I Must Go	(Imperial 66021)	1.00	4.00	64
NOW THE SUMMER'S GONE/ Rumors, Gossip, Words Untrue	(Imperial 66225)	1.00	4.00	67
SOMETHINGS COMING ALONG/Tremblin'	(Imperial 66255)	1.00	4.00	67
TUTTI FRUTTI/Promise You'll Tell Her	(Imperial 66059)	1.00	4.00	64
YOU'RE NO GOOD/Shake, Rattle & Roll	(Imperial 66049)	1.00	4.00	64
SWINGING VYNE, The				
TARZAN (TARZAN'S MARCH)/Sleepwalk	(Epic 10068)	.75	3.00	66
SWINGIN' MEDALLIONS, The				
DOUBLE SHOT/Here It Comes Again	(4 Sale 002)	3.00	12.00	66
DOUBLE SHOT/Here It Comes Again	(Smash 2033)	.75	3.00	66
SHE DRIVES ME OUT OF MY MIND/ You Gotta To Have Faith	(Smash 2050)	.75	3.00	66
SWINGIN' ROCKS, The				
SATELLITE ROCK/Satellite Rock (Part 2)	(Esta 1001)	1.00	4.00	59
SWISHER, Debra				
YOU'RE SO GOOD TO ME/Thank You & Goodnight	(Boom 60001)	1.50	6.00	
SYLVESTER, Terry (Of The Hollies)				
REALISTIC SITUATION/Silver & Gold	(Epic 50532)	.50	2.00	78
FOR THE PEACE OF ALL MANKIND/	(Epic 20002)	.50	2.00	74
SYMBOLS, The				
AGAIN/The Best Part Of Breaking Up	(Laurie 3435)	1.50	6.00	68
BYE BYE BABY/The Things You Do To Me	(Laurie 3401)	1.50	6.00	67
SYMPHONICS, The				
COME ON HONEY/A Blessing To You	(Enrica 1002)	1.50	6.00	64
OUR LOVE WILL GROW/Way Down Low	(Tru-Lite 116)	2.50	10.00	63
SYMS, Sylvia				
DANCING CHANDELIER/Each Day	(Decca 30143)	1.00	4.00	56
ENGLISH MUFFINS & IRISH STEW/Walk Sweet	(Decca 29969)	1.00	4.00	56
I COULD HAVE DANCED ALL NIGHT/World In My Corner	(Decca 29903)	1.00	4.00	56
SYNDICATE OF SOUND, The				
BROWN PAPER BAG/Reverb Beat	(Buddah 156)	.75	3.00	70
GOOD TIME MUSIC/Keep It Up	(Bell 655)	1.00	4.00	66
LITTLE GIRL/You	(Bell 640)	1.00	4.00	66
LITTLE GIRL/You	(Hush 228)	1.25	5.00	66
MEXICO/First To Love You	(Buddah 183)	.75	3.00	70
PREPARE FOR LOVE/Tell The World	(Del Fi 4304)	1.00	4.00	66
PREPARE FOR LOVE/Tell The World	(Scarlet 503)	1.50	6.00	66
RUMORS/The Upper Hand	(Bell 646)	1.00	4.00	66
THAT KIND OF MAN/Mary	(Bell 666)	1.00	4.00	67
YOU'RE LOOKING FINE/Change The World	(Capitol 2426)	.75	3.00	69

T

TITLE/FLIP	LABEL & NO.	GOOD	NEAR MINT	YR.
TABBYS, The				
MY DARLING/Yes I Do	(Time 1008)	1.25	5.00	59
TABS, The				
FIRST STAR/Avenue Of Tears	(Dot 15887)	1.00	4.00	59
ROCK & ROLL HOLIDAY/Never Forget	(Gardena 110)	1.00	4.00	60
ROCK & ROLL HOLIDAY/Never Forget	(Noble 719)	1.25	5.00	59
TAGES, The				
HALCYON DAYS/I Read You Like An Open Book	(Verve 10626)	.75	3.00	68
TAILSMEN, The				
VINTAGE N.S.U./Taxman	(Hideout 1221)	1.50	6.00	
TAKE OFFS, The				
KNOCK DOWN THE DOOR/Take 3 Plus One	(Ford 142)	1.50	6.00	
TALENTS, The				
THREE LITTLE FISHES/My Favorite Things	(Twink 1215)	.75	3.00	
TALISMAN, The				
CASTING MY SPELL/Masters Of War	(American Arts 22)	1.50	6.00	65
OFF TO THE SEA/Tears	(Prestige 357)	1.50	6.00	65
SURFIN' MAN/Jailbreak	(Dot 16068)	1.25	5.00	60
TALKING HEADS				
LIFE DURING WARTIME (THIS AIN'T NO PARTY...THIS AIN'T NO DISCO...THIS AIN'T NO FOOLIN' AROUND)/	(Sire 49075)	.50	2.00	79
LOVE GOES TO BUILDING ON FIRE/New Feeling	(Sire 737)	.50	2.00	77
PSYCHO KILLER/Psycho Killer	(Sire 1013)	.50	2.00	78
TAKE ME TO THE RIVER/ Thank You For Sending Me An Angel	(Sire 1032)	.50	2.00	78
UH-OH, LOVE COMES TO TOWN/ I Wish You Wouldn't Say That	(Sire 1002)	.50	2.00	77
TALKING JUKE BOX, The				
TALKING JUKEBOX,THE/The Talking Jukebox (Part 2)	(Republican 1974)	.75	3.00	
TAMBLYN, Larry				
LIE, THE/My Bridge To Be	(Faro 603)	1.50	6.00	65
PATTY ANN/Dearest	(Faro 601)	1.50	6.00	65
THIS IS THE NIGHT/Destiny	(Faro 612)	1.50	6.00	65
YOU'LL BE MINE SOMEDAY/Girl In My Heart	(Linda 112)	1.50	6.00	65
(Shown as by Larry Tamblyn & the Standells)				
Also see Standells, The				
TAMMYS, The				
EGYPTIAN SHUMBA/ What's So Sweet About Sweet 16	(United Artists 678)	1.00	4.00	64
GYPSY/Hold Back The Light Of Dawn	(Veep 1210)	1.00	4.00	66
TAMS, The: see Stereos, The				
TAN, Roy				
ISABELLA/I Don't Like It	(Tan 3002)	2.00	8.00	57
ISABELLA/I Don't Like It	(Dot 15551)	1.00	4.00	57
TANDI & THE TEAMATES				
TRAMPOLINE QUEEN/Week-end Lover	(Ember 1068)	.75	3.00	60
TANEGA, Norma				
BREAD/Waves	(New Voice 815)	.75	3.00	66
STREET THAT RHYMES AT SIX A.M./Treat Me Right	(New Voice 810)	.75	3.00	66
WALKIN' MY CAT NAMED DOG/I'm The Sky	(New Voice 807)	.75	3.00	66
TANGENTS, The				
SEND ME SOMETHING/I Can't Live Alone	(Fresh 1)	1.50	6.00	
TANGERINE DREAM				
MOONLIGHT (PART 2)/Coldwater Canyon (Part 2)	(Virgin 9516)	.50	2.00	77
PHAEDRA/Mysterious Semblence	(Virgin 214)	.50	2.00	75
TANGIERS, The				
PING PONG/Don't Stop The Music	(Strand 25039)	5.00	20.00	60
TANNER, Marc, Band				
ELENA/Lady In Blue	(Elektra 46003)	.50	2.00	79
SHE'S SO HIGH/Never Again	(Elektra 46043)	.50	2.00	79
TANNO, Marc				
ANGEL/Dear Abby	(Whale 501)	3.75	15.00	61
TANTRUM				
HOW LONG/You Need Me	(Ovation 1135)	.50	2.00	79
YOU CAME TO ME/Kidnapped	(Ovation 1115)	.50	2.00	79
TARANTULAS, The				
TARANTULA/Black Widow	(Atlantic 2102)	.75	3.00	61
Instrumentals				
TARNEY-SPENCER BAND, The				
I'M YOUR ROCK 'N' ROLL MAN/Guitar Slinger	(Private Stock 45088)	.50	2.00	76
IT'S REALLY YOU/Set The Minstrel Free	(A&M 2049)	.50	2.00	78
NO TIME TO LOSE/Live Again	(A&M 2124)	.50	2.00	79
TAKIN' ME BACK/Capital Shame	(A&M 2084)	.50	2.00	78
WON'TCHA TELL ME/The Race Is Almost Run	(A&M 2170)	.50	2.00	79
TARRIERS, The (Bob Carey, Alan Arkin, Erik Darling)				
BANANA BOAT SONG, THE/No Hidin' Place	(Glory 249)	1.00	4.00	56
I KNOW WHERE I'M GOING/Pretty Boy	(Glory 255)	1.00	4.00	57
Also see Martin, Vince				
Also see Rooftop Singers, The				
TARRYTONS, The				
ROUGH SURFIN'/Mansion On The Hill	(Dot 16537)	1.00	4.00	63
TARTANS, The				
I NEED YOU/Nothing But Love	(Impact 1010)	.75	3.00	
TASSELS, The				
MY GUY & I/To A Young Lover	(Madison 121)	1.00	4.00	59
TO A SOLDIER BOY/The Boy For Me	(Madison 117)	1.00	4.00	59
TATTLETALES, The				
DOUBLE TROUBLE/Magic Wand	(Warner Bros. 5066)	1.00	4.00	59
TAURUS (With Johnny Cymbal)				
BLESS YOU/Hey Jane	(Tower 487)	1.25	5.00	
TAYLOR, Alex				
BABY RUTH/	(Capricorn 8016)	.50	2.00	71
DON'T LOOK AT ME THAT WAY/Sunny Day To Rain	(Bang 739)	.50	2.00	79
HIGHWAY SONG/C Song	(Capricorn 8013)	.50	2.00	71
NOGHT OWL/	(Capricorn 8019)	.50	2.00	71
Alex is James Taylor's brother.				
TAYLOR, Austin				
PUSH PUSH/Heart That's True	(Laurie 3068)	1.00	4.00	60
TAYLOR, Billy				
INCOME TAXES & YOU/Lullaby To Carolyn	(Citation 5002)	3.00	12.00	
WOMBIE ZOMBIE/I'm Young	(Felco 101)	1.00	4.00	59
TAYLOR, Bobby				
7 STEPS TO AN ANGEL/Ubangi Stomp	(Hour 102)	2.00	8.00	
TAYLOR, Bobby & The Vancouvers				
DOES YOUR MAMA KNOW ABOUT ME/Fading Away	(Gordy 7069)	.75	3.00	68
I AM YOUR MAN/	(Gordy 7073)	.75	3.00	68
MALINDA/	(Gordy 7079)	.75	3.00	69
Tommy Chong, of Cheech & Chong, was a member of this group.				
TAYLOR BROTHERS, The				
YOUR LAST CHANCE/Show Down	(United 98)	2.00	8.00	
TAYLOR, Chip				
ANGEL OF THE MORNING/Swear To God, Your Honor	(Mala 476)	.75	3.00	66
HELLO ATLANTA (With Ghost Train)/	(Columbia 10446)	.50	2.00	76
IT'S SUCH A LONELY TIME OF YEAR/It's Such A Lonely Time Of Year (Instrumental)	(Columbia 44736)	.50	2.00	69
NOTHIN' LIKE YOU GIRL/	(Columbia 10520)	.50	2.00	77
(THE LIKES OF) LOUISE/	(Warner Bros. 7750)	.50	2.00	73
TAYLOR, Felice				
IT MAY BE WINTER OUTSIDE/Winter Again	(Mustang 3024)	.75	3.00	67
I'M UNDER THE INFLUENCE OF LOVE/Love Theme	(Mustang 3026)	.75	3.00	67
TAYLOR, James				
BRIGHTEN YOUR DAY WITH MY DAY/ Knocking Round The Zoo	(Euphoria 201)	.75	3.00	71
(With the Original Flying Machine)				
CAROLINA IN MY MIND/Something's Wrong	(Apple 1805)	.75	3.00	70
COUNTRY ROAD/Sunny Skies	(Warner Bros. 7460)	.50	2.00	71
DON'T LET ME BE LONELY TONIGHT/ Woh, Don't You Know	(Warner Bros. 7655)	.50	2.00	72
FIRE & RAIN/Anywhere Like Heaven	(Warner Bros. 7423)	.50	2.00	70
HANDY MAN/Bartender's Blues	(Columbia 10557)	.50	2.00	77
HONEY DON'T LEAVE L.A./Another Crazy Morning	(Columbia 10689)	.50	2.00	78
HOW SWEET IT IS (TO BE LOVED BY YOU)/ Sarah Maria	(Warner Bros. 8109)	.50	2.00	75
HYMN/Fanfare	(Warner Bros. 7695)	.50	2.00	73
LET IT ALL FALL DOWN/Daddy's Baby	(Warner Bros. 8015)	.50	2.00	74
LONG AGO & FAR AWAY/Let Me Ride	(Warner Bros. 7521)	.50	2.00	71
LONG AGO & FAR AWAY/Sweet Baby James	(Warner Bros. 7135)	.50	2.00	72
MEXICO/Gorilla	(Warner Bros. 8137)	.50	2.00	75
MOCKINGBIRD/Grownup	(Elektra 45880)	.50	2.00	74
(With Carly Simon)				
ONE MAN PARADE/Nobody But You	(Warner Bros. 7682)	.50	2.00	73
SHOWER THE PEOPLE/I Can Dream Of You	(Warner Bros. 8222)	.50	2.00	76
SWEET BABY JAMES/Suite For 20G	(Warner Bros. 7387)	.50	2.00	70
UP ON THE ROOF/Chanson Francaise	(Columbia 11005)	.50	2.00	79
WALKING MAN/Daddy's Baby	(Warner Bros. 8028)	.50	2.00	74
WOMAN'S GOTTA HAVE IT/You Make It Easy	(Warner Bros. 8278)	.50	2.00	76
YOUR SMILING FACE/If I Keep My Heart Out Of Sight	(Columbia 10602)	.50	2.00	77
YOU'VE GOT A FRIEND/You Can Close Your Eyes	(Warner Bros. 7498)	.50	2.00	71
Also see Attitudes, The				
TAYLOR, Kate				
HOME AGAIN/Lo & Behold.Jesus Is Just Alright	(Cotillion 44124)	.50	2.00	71
IT'S GROWIN'/Slow & Steady	(Columbia 10787)	.50	2.00	78
IT'S IN HIS KISS (THE SHOOP SHOOP SONG)/ Jason & Ida	(Columbia 10596)	.50	2.00	77
Kate is James Taylor's sister.				
TAYLOR, Livingston				
CAROLINA DAY/Sit On It	(Capricorn 8012)	.50	2.00	71
GET OUT OF BED/	(Capricorn 8025)	.50	2.00	72
I'LL COME RUNNING/No Thank You Skycap	(Epic 50667)	.50	2.00	78
I WILL BE IN LOVE WITH YOU/ How Much Your Sweet Love Means To Me	(Epic 50604)	.50	2.00	78
LOVING BE MY NEW HORIZON/I Can Dream Of You	(Capricorn 0045)	.50	2.00	73
Livingston is James Taylor's brother.				
TAYLOR, Mick (Of The Rolling Stones)				
LEATHER JACKET/Slow Blues	(Columbia 11065)	.50	2.00	79
TAYLOR, R. Dean				
AIN'T IT A SAD THING/Back Street	(Rare Earth 5023)	.50	2.00	71
FIRE & RAIN/	(Rare Earth 500)	.50	2.00	70
GOTTA SEE JANE/Back Street	(Rare Earth 5026)	.50	2.00	71

TITLE/FLIP	LABEL & NO.	GOOD	NEAR MINT	YR.
IDIANA WANTS ME/	(Rare Earth 5013)	.50	2.00	70
S A LONG WAY TO ST. LOUIS/I'll Remember	(Mala 444)	5.00	20.00	64
IOS, NEW MEXICO/	(Rare Earth 5041)	.50	2.00	72
AYLOR, True: see Simon, Paul				
AXPAYERS, The				
IPED OUT/	(Poverty 1)	5.00	20.00	
-BIRDS, The				
ILD STOMP/Soft Smoke	(Gone 5141)	.75	3.00	63
-BONES, The				
RAGGIN'/Rail-vette	(Liberty 55677)	1.00	4.00	64
) MATTER WHAT SHAPE (YOUR STOMACH'S IN)/ Feelin' Fine	(Liberty 55836)	.75	3.00	65
PPIN' & CHIPPIN'/Moment Of Softness	(Liberty 55867)	.75	3.00	66
HEREVER YOU LOOK/Underwater	(Liberty 55885)	.75	3.00	66
Also see Hamilton, Joe Frank & Reynolds				
CHAIKOVSKY, Bram (Of The Motors)				
RL OF MY DREAMS/Sarah Smiles	(Polydor-Radar 14575)	.50	2.00	79
ADY FROM THE U.S.A./Turn On The Light	(Polydor-Radar 2016)	.50	2.00	79
EACHERS, The				
VE WALKED IN/Sound Of Music	(PTA 101)	1.50	6.00	
EAMATES, The				
ALENDAR OF LOVE/I Say Goodbye	(LeMans 005)	2.00	8.00	
E'VE BELIEVED IN LOVE/Once There Was A Time	(Phillips 40029)	2.00	8.00	62
EARDROPS, The (Tony & Paul)				
RIDGE OF LOVE/Jellyfish	(Dot 15669)	1.00	4.00	57
EARDROPS, The				
OODNIGHT ELVIS/Hey Gingerbread	(Laurie 3660)	.50	2.00	77
EARS, The				
EATERMAN/Read All About It	(Scorpio 409)	1.00	4.00	67
ECHNIQUES, The				
EY! LITTLE GIRL/In A Round About Way	(Stars 551)	2.00	8.00	57
EY! LITTLE GIRL/In A Round About Way	(Roulette 4030)	1.00	4.00	57
T HER GO/Marindy	(Roulette 4048)	1.00	4.00	58
EDDY & HIS PATCHES				
AIGHT ASHBURY/It Ain't Nothin'	(Chance 669)	2.00	8.00	67
IZY CREAMCHEESE/From Day To Day	(Chance 101)	2.00	8.00	67
EDDY & THE CONTINENTALS				
RYING OVER YOU/Crossfire With My Baby	(Richie 453)	1.50	6.00	
) YOU/Tighten Up	(Richie 445)	1.50	6.00	
EDDY & THE PANDAS				
ILDHOOD FRIENDS/68 Days Til' Sept.	(Tower 433)	1.25	5.00	68
IVELIGHT, THE/Day In The City	(Timbri 101)	1.25	5.00	66
ICE UPON A TIME/Out The Window	(Coristine 574)	1.50	6.00	66
ARCHIN' FOR THE GOOD TIMES/Sunnyside Up	(Musicor 1212)	1.25	5.00	66
E CAN'T GO ON THIS WAY/Smokey Fire	(Musicor 1190)	1.25	5.00	66
EDDY & THE TWILIGHTS				
I JUST YOUR CLOWN/Bimini Bimbo	(Swan 4126)	1.00	4.00	62
OMAN IS A MAN'S BEST FRIEND/Goodbye To Love	(Swan 4102)	1.00	4.00	62
EDDY BEARS (Phil Spector, Annette Klienbard, Marshall Leib)				
ON'T GO AWAY/Seven Lonely Days	(Imperial 5594)	2.00	8.00	59
YOU ONLY KNEW/You Said Goodbye	(Imperial 5581)	2.00	8.00	59
I WHY/I Don't Need You Any More	(Imperial 5562)	2.00	8.00	59
I KNOW HIM, IS TO LOVE HIM/ Don't You Worry My Little Pet	(Dore 503)	1.00	4.00	58
ONDERFUL LOVEABLE YOU/You Said Goodbye	(Dore 520)	1.50	6.00	59
Also see Carol Connors, who was actually Annette Klienbard. She also corded as Annette Bard.				
Also see Nelson, Sandy				
EDDY BOYS, The				
ONA/Good Morning Blues	(Cameo 448)	.75	3.00	67
EE SET, The				
YOU DO BELIEVE IN LOVE/	(Colossus 114)	.75	3.00	70
A BEELE AMIE/Angels Coming In The Holy Night	(Colossus 107)	.75	3.00	70
E LIKES WEEDS/	(Colossus 139)	.75	3.00	71
EEGARDEN & VAN WINKLE				
ERYTHING IS GOING TO BE ALRIGHT/	(Westbound 171)	.75	3.00	70
ID, LOVE & ROCK & ROLL/Work Me Tomorrow	(Westbound 170)	.75	3.00	70
Some members of Bob Seger's Silver Bullet Band were formerly in this oup.				
EEN-BEATS, The				
G BAD BOSS BEAT/Down Below	(Original Sound 46)	.75	3.00	64
GHT SURFIN'/Clair De Lune Rock	(Original Sound 16)	.75	3.00	61
OP BEAT/Calif Boogie	(Original Sound 07)	.75	3.00	60
IMMIN'/Swimmin' (Part 2)	(Original Sound 49)	.75	3.00	64
EEN BUGS, The				
S YOU CAN HOLD MY HAND/Teenitis	(Blue River 208)	1.50	6.00	64
(Answer song)				
EEN DREAMS, The: see Debbie & The Darnels				
EEN 5, The: see Gents, The				
EEN KINGS, The (Featuring Roy Orbison)				
OBY DOOBY/Trying To Get To You	(Jewel JE-101)	62.50	250.00	56
(This is a completely different version than the Sun issue of "Ooby Dooby," ich was shown as by Roy Orbison & The Teen Kings.)				
EEN KINGS, The				
GREATEST WISH/Don't Just Stand There	(Willett 118)	1.50	6.00	
EEN NOTES, The				
CO IN THE COCO/My Precious Jewel	(Deb 121)	.75	3.00	60
EEN ROCKERS, The				
NKY DINK BLUES/	(Deltone 5015)	.75	3.00	60
EEN, Sandra				
IGEL BABY/Stranger In Love	(Impact 4)	.75	3.00	60
EEN TONES, The				
ARLING I LOVE YOU/My Sweet	(Dandy Dan 2)	2.50	10.00	59
) YOU WANNA DANCE/Long Cold Winter Ahead	(T&T 2488)	.75	3.00	65
ON'T CALL ME BABY, I'LL CALL YOU/Yes You May	(Decca 30895)	1.00	4.00	69
ADED LOVE/Gypsy Boogie	(Wynne 107)	1.25	5.00	59
I SO HAPPY/Shoutin' Twist	(Tri Disc 102)	2.00	8.00	61
ISAN ANN/Cuckoo	(Deb 132)	1.00	4.00	60
Even though all of these releases are shown as being by a group using the me name, the possibility exists that they are not all by the same group.				
EENANGELS, The				
LL ME MY LOVE/Ain't Gonna Let You (Break My Heart)	(Sun 388)	5.00	20.00	63
(Promotional issue only)				
EENBEATS, The				
GHTSPOT/Only The Stars	(Myrl 407)	1.00	4.00	61

TITLE/FLIP	LABEL & NO.	GOOD	NEAR MINT	YR.
TEENETTES, The				
I WANT A BOY WITH A HI-FI SUPERSONIC STEREOPHONIC BLOOP BLEEP/From The Word Go	(Brunswick 55125)	1.00	4.00	59
LET ME BE THE ONE/Bye Bye Baby	(Sandy 250)	.75	3.00	63
TEEN-KINGS, The				
THAT'S A TEEN-AGE LOVE/Tell Me If You Know	(Bee 1115)	1.00	4.00	59
TEENOS, The				
LOVE ONLY ONE/Alrightee	(Dub 2839)	1.50	6.00	58
TEIG, Dave				
SPLISH SPLASH/Tutti Frutti	(Signature 12042)	1.00	4.00	60
TELEVISION				
AIN'T THAT NOTHIN'/Glory	(Elektra 45516)	.50	2.00	78
LITTLE JOHNNY JEWEL (PART 1)/Little Johnny Jewel (Part 2)	(Ork 81975)	.50	2.00	75
Also see Hell, Richard, & The Voidoids				
TELLERS, The				
TEARS FELL FROM MY EYES/I Wanna Run To You	(Fire 1038)	2.50	10.00	60
TELSTARS, The				
POW-WOW/	(Teen 513)	1.00	4.00	62
STOMP HAPPY/Continental Mash	(Imperial 5903)	.75	3.00	63
STOMP HAPPY/Continental Mash	(Teen 510)	1.00	4.00	62
TEMKIN, Gary				
I'M THE FALL GUY/	(ABC-Paramount 10271)	.75	3.00	61
TEMPESTS, The				
WHAT YOU GONNA DO/Can't Get You Out Of My Mind	(Smash S-2126)	.75	3.00	67
TEMPO, Nino, & April Stevens				
ALL STRUNG OUT/I Can't Go On Living Baby Without You	(White Whale 236)	.75	3.00	66
BABY WEEMUS/Together	(Atco 6264)	.75	3.00	63
DEEP PURPLE/I've Been Carrying A Torch For You So Long That I Burned A Great Big Hole In My Heart	(Atco 6273)	.75	3.00	63
I CAN'T GO ON LIVING WITHOUT YOU BABY/	(White Whale 252)	.75	3.00	67
LET IT BE ME/Wings Of Love	(White Whale 268)	.75	3.00	67
LOVE STORY/Hoochy-Coochy-Wing Dang Doo	(A&M 1394)	.75	3.00	72
PARADISE/Indian Love Call	(Atco 6248)	.75	3.00	62
STARDUST/I-45	(Atco 6286)	.75	3.00	64
SWEET & LOVELY/True Love	(Atco 6224)	.75	3.00	62
TEA FOR TWO/I'm Confessin'	(Atco 6294)	.75	3.00	64
WHISPERING/Tweedle Dee	(Atco 6281)	.75	3.00	63
TEMPO, Nino, & The 5th Ave. Sax				
DON'T STOP NOW/Gettin' Off	(A&M 1625)	.50	2.00	74
SISTER JAMES/Clair De Lune (In Jazz)	(A&M 1461)	.50	2.00	73
TEMPOS, The				
CROSSROADS OF LOVE/Whatever Happens	(Climax 105)	1.00	4.00	59
I GOT A JOB/Strollin' With My Baby	(Kapp 213)	1.25	5.00	58
KINGDOM OF LOVE/That's What You Do To Me	(Kapp 178)	1.25	5.00	57
LOOK HOMEWARD ANGEL/Under Ten Flags	(Paris 550)	1.00	4.00	59
MY BARBARA ANN/When You Loved Me	(Ascot 2167)	1.50	6.00	65
MY BARBARA ANN/I Wish It Were Summer	(Ascot 2173)	1.50	6.00	65
PRETTIEST GIRL IN SCHOOL, THE/Never You Mind	(Kapp 199)	1.25	5.00	57
SEE YOU IN SEPTEMBER/Bless You My Love	(Climax 102)	1.00	4.00	59
TEMPOS, The				
IT'S TOUGH/Sham-Rock	(Hi-Q 100)	1.25	5.00	59
MONKEY DO/Oh Play That Thing	(Fairmount 611)	1.50	6.00	63
MY DREAM ISLAND/My Love Goes Deep	(Vee Jay 580)	1.50	6.00	64
TEMPOS, The				
WHY DON'T YOU WRITE ME/A Thief In The Night	(U.S.A. 810)	3.00	12.00	64
TEMPTATIONS, The				
BARBARA/Someday (Multi-color label)	(Goldisc 3001)	1.50	6.00	60
BARBARA/Someday (Black label)	(Goldisc 3001)	.75	3.00	60
CATHY/Rock & Roll Baby	(ABC-Paramount 9920)	2.00	8.00	58
(Shown as by the Four Temptations)				
FICKLE LITTLE GIRL/Letter Of Devotion	(Goldisc 3007)	1.50	6.00	60
TEMPTATIONS, The				
BLUE SURF/Egyptian Surf	(P&L 1001)	.75	3.00	63
(Instrumentals)				
TEMPTONES, The				
GIRL, I LOVE YOU/Good-Bye	(Arctic 130)	.75	3.00	
10CC				
ART FOR ART'S SAKE/Get It While You Can	(Mercury 73725)	.50	2.00	75
ART FOR ART'S SAKE/Get It While You Can	(Mercury 73725 DJ-441)	.75	3.00	75
(Promotional issue)				
ART FOR ART'S SAKE/Get It While You Can	(Mercury 73725 DJ-441)	1.50	6.00	75
(Picture sleeve for promotional issue.)				
DONNA/Hot Sun Rock	(UK 49005)	.75	3.00	72
DREADLOCK HOLIDAY/Nothing Can Move Me	(Polydor-Man-Ken 14511)	.50	2.00	78
FOR YOU & I/Take These Chains	(Polydor-Man-Ken 14528)	.50	2.00	78
GOOD MORNING JUDGE/I'm So Laid Back I'm Laid Out	(Mercury 73943)	.50	2.00	77
HEADLINE HUSTLER/Speed Kills	(UK 49019)	.75	3.00	73
I'M MANDY FLY ME/How Dare You	(Mercury 73779)	.50	2.00	76
I'M NOT IN LOVE/Channel Swimmer	(Mercury 73678)	.50	2.00	75
I'M NOT IN LOVE/Channel Swimmer	(Mercury 73678)	.75	3.00	75
(Promotional issue)				
I'M NOT IN LOVE/Channel Swimmer	(Mercury 73678)	1.50	6.00	75
(Picture sleeve for promotional issue.)				

TITLE/FLIP	LABEL & NO.	GOOD	NEAR MINT	YR.
LIFE IS A MINESTRONE/Lazy Ways	(Mercury 73805)	.50	2.00	76
PEOPLE IN LOVE/Don't Squeeze Me Like Toothpaste	(Mercury 73917)	.50	2.00	77
RUBBER BULLETS/Waterfall	(UK 49015)	.75	3.00	73
THINGS WE DO FOR LOVE, THE/Hot To Trot	(Mercury 73875)	.50	2.00	77
WALL STREET SHUFFLE, THE/Gismo My Way	(UK 49023)	.75	3.00	74
WALL STREET SHUFFLE, THE/You've Got A Cold	(Mercury 73980)	.50	2.00	77
(Recorded live)				
Also see Silver Fleet				
Also see Cream, Lol, & Kevin Godley				
Also see Hotlegs				
Also see Crazy Elephant				
Also see Kasenetz-Katz Singing Orchestral Circus				
TEN WHEEL DRIVE (With Genya Ravan)				
MORNING MUCH BETTER/Stay With Me	(Polydor 14037)	.50	2.00	71
TEN YEARS AFTER (With Alvin Lee)				
BABY WON'T YOU LET ME ROCK 'N' ROLL YOU/ Once There Was A Time	(Columbia 45530)	.50	2.00	72
CHOO CHOO MAMA/You Can't Win Them All	(Columbia 45736)	.50	2.00	72
I'D LOVE TO CHANGE THE WORLD/	(Columbia 45457)	.50	2.00	71
IT'S GETTING HARDER/	(Columbia 46061)	.50	2.00	73
LOVE LIKE A MAN/If You Should Love Me	(Deram 7529)	.75	3.00	70
PORTABLE PEOPLE/The Sounds	(Deram 85027)	.75	3.00	68
TENDER SLIM				
TEENAGE HAYRIDE/Hey Joe!	(Grey Cliff 723)	.75	3.00	
TENDERTONES, The				
I LOVE YOU SO/Just For A Little While	(Ducky 713)	6.25	25.00	59
TENNANT, Jimmy				
HEARTBREAK AVENUE/You're The Beat Within My Heart	(Amp 790)	1.00	4.00	59
SALUTE/Big Retreat, The	(Warwick 533)	2.50	10.00	60
(Novelty/break-in)				
TEO, Roy				
MAMA DOLL/Please My Love	(Nasco 6027)	1.00	4.00	59
TERMITES, The				
CARRIE LOU/Give Me Your Heart	(See 1825)	.75	3.00	
TERRACE TONES, The				
RIDE OF PAUL REVERE/Words Of Wisdom	(Apt 25016)	6.25	25.00	58
TERRI & THE KITTENS				
WEDDING BELLS/You Cheated	(Imperial 5728)	1.25	5.00	61
TERRI & THE VELVETEENS				
YOU'VE BROKEN MY HEART/Bells Of Love	(Kerwood 711)	2.00	8.00	
TERRI, Darlene				
RINGO RINGO/A Real Live Boy	(Columbia 43042)	1.25	5.00	64
TERRY & JERRY				
PEOPLE ARE DOING IT EVERYDAY/Mama Julie	(Class 226)	1.00	4.00	58
TERRY & THE CHAIN REACTION				
KEEP YOUR COOL/Stop Stopping Me	(United Artists 50199)	.75	3.00	67
TERRY & THE TAGS				
RAMPAGE/The Twomp	(Sylvester 100)	1.00	4.00	62
TERRY & THE MELLOWS: see Lorin, Terry				
TERRY & THE TUNISIANS				
STREET, THE/Tom-Tom	(Seville 131)	2.00	8.00	63
TERRY & THE TYRANTS				
WEEP NO MORE/Yea, Yea, Yea, Yea	(Kent 399)	.75	3.00	64
TERRY, Maureen				
WHO EVER YOU ARE/There's A Boy	(Maria 102)	2.50	10.00	
TERRYTONES, The (With Claire Charles & Gayle Fortune)				
I BEG YOUR PARDON/Three Steps To The Phone	(Wye 1010)	1.00	4.00	61
TEENAGE NIGHT THEME/I Cry The Blues	(Wye 1003)	1.00	4.00	60
YOU'RE MY IDEAL/Ah Do Me Kitchie	(Wye 1002)	1.00	4.00	60
TEX & THE CHEX				
I DO LOVE YOU/My Love	(Atlantic 2116)	5.00	20.00	61
TEXANS, The (Dorsey & Johnny Burnette)				
GREEN GRASS OF TEXAS/Bloody River	(Infinity 001)	1.50	6.00	61
GREEN GRASS OF TEXAS/Bloody River	(Vee Jay 658)	.75	3.00	65
ROCKIN' JOHNNY HOME/Old Reb	(Jox 001)	1.00	4.00	
Instrumentals				
THARP, Chuck, & The Fireballs				
LET THERE BE LOVE/Long, Long Ponytail	(Jaro 77029)	5.00	20.00	60
LET THERE BE LOVE/Long, Long Ponytail	(Lucky 0012)	6.25	25.00	60
THAXTON, Lloyd				
IMAGE OF A SURFER/My Name Is Lloyd Thaxton	(Capitol 4982)	1.00	4.00	63
THEE IMAGE (Formerly Cactus)				
IT HAPPENS ALL THE TIME/	(Manticore 7001)	.50	2.00	74
THEE MIDNITERS				
LAND OF A THOUSAND DANCES (PART 1)/ Land Of A Thousand Dances (Part 2)	(Chattahoochee 666)	.75	3.00	65
SAD GIRL/Heat Wave	(Chattahoochee 674)	.75	3.00	65
YOU'RE GONNA MAKE ME CRY/Make Ends Meet	(Chattahoochee 511)	.75	3.00	64
THEE PROPHETS				
PLAYGIRL/	(Kapp 962)	.75	3.00	69
THEM (Featuring Van Morrison)				
BUT IT'S ALRIGHT/Square Room	(Tower 407)	.75	3.00	68
CALL MY NAME/Bring 'em On In	(Parrot 9819)	1.25	5.00	66
CORINNA/Dark Are The Shadows	(Tower 493)	.75	3.00	69
DIRTY OLD MAN/	(Sully 1021)	5.00	20.00	
DON'T LOOK NOW/A Girl Like You	(King 5697)	2.00	8.00	65
DON'T START CRYING NOW/ I Can Only Give You Everything	(Parrot 3006)	1.25	5.00	66
DON'T YOU WANNA DANCE/One, Two, Brown Eyes	(Parrot 9702)	2.00	8.00	64
DON'T YOU KNOW/Richard Cory	(Parrot 3008)	1.25	5.00	66
GLORIA'S DREAM/Secret Police	(Loma 2051)	1.50	6.00	66
GLORIA/If You & I Could Be As Two	(Parrot 365)	3.00	12.00	65
GLORIA/Baby Please Don't Go	(Parrot 9727)	.75	3.00	65
GONNA DRESS IN BLACK/(It Won't Hurt) Half As Much	(Parrot 9784)	1.25	5.00	65
HERE COMES THE NIGHT/All For Myself	(Parrot 9749)	1.00	4.00	65
LONELY WEEKENDS/I Am Waiting	(Happy Tiger 525)	.75	3.00	69
MYSTIC EYES/If You & I Could Be As Two	(Parrot 9796)	1.00	4.00	65
WALKING IN THE QUEENS GARDEN/I Happen To Love You	(Tower 384)	.75	3.00	67
WE'VE ALL AGREED TO HELP/Waltz Of The Flies	(Tower 461)	.75	3.00	69
THEM FEATURING HIM				
I'M SORRY NOW/Shattered Dreams	(HEG 501)	2.00	8.00	
THEMES				
MARNIE/There's No Moon Tonight	(Stork 001)	2.00	8.00	
Also see Four Directions				

TITLE/FLIP	LABEL & NO.	GOOD	NEAR MINT	YR.
THEODORE, Donna				
THERE'S NO HOLDING YOU/	(Uni 55331)	.50	2.00	72
WHAT AM I GONNA DO/You Can Make Me Feel Good	(Uni 55300)	.50	2.00	72
THIEVES, The				
400 DRAGONS/Headlights	(Arista 0423)	.50	2.00	79
THINGS TO COME				
I'M NOT TALKIN'/Til' The End	(Dunwich 124)	.75	3.00	66
THINK (Featuring Lou Stallman)				
ONCE YOU UNDERSTAND/Gather	(Big Tree 15000)	.50	2.00	74
ONCE YOU UNDERSTAND/Gather	(Laurie 3583)	.75	3.00	71
THIN LIZZY				
BAD REPUTATION/Dancing In The Moonlight (It's Caught Me In It's Spotlight)	(Mercury 73945)	.50	2.00	77
BOYS ARE BACK IN TOWN/Jailbreak	(Mercury 30174)	.50	2.00	77
BOYS ARE BACK IN TOWN/Jailbreak	(Mercury 73786)	.50	2.00	76
COWBOY SONG/Angel From The Coast	(Mercury 73841)	.50	2.00	76
COWBOY SONG/ Johnny The Fox Meets Jimmy The Weed	(Warner Bros. 8648)	.50	2.00	78
DANCING IN THE MOONLIGHT (IT'S CAUGHT ME IN ITS SPOTLIGHT)/Bad Reputation	(Mercury 73945)	.50	2.00	77
DO ANYTHING YOU WANT TO/S & M	(Warner Bros. 49019)	.50	2.00	79
DON'T BELIEVE A WORD/Boogie Woogie Dance	(Mercury 73892)	.50	2.00	77
JOHNNY THE FOX MEETS JIMMY THE WEED/Old Flame	(Mercury 73882)	.50	2.00	77
LITTLE DARLING/	(London 20082)	.75	3.00	73
ROCKY/Half-Caste	(Mercury 73867)	.50	2.00	76
SHOWDOWN/Night Life	(Vertigo 202)	.50	2.00	75
WHISKEY IN THE JAR/Black Boys On The Corner	(London 20076)	.75	3.00	73
WILD ONE/Freedom Song	(Vertigo 205)	.50	2.00	75
THIRD BOOTH, The				
I NEED LOVE/Mysteries	(Independence 86)	.75	3.00	68
THIRD RAIL, The				
BEGGING ME TO STAY/Ballad Of General Humpty	(Epic 10457)	.75	3.00	69
BOPPA DO DOWN DOWN/Invisible Man	(Epic 10240)	.75	3.00	67
IT'S TIME TO SAY GOODBYE/Overdose Of Love	(Epic 10285)	.75	3.00	68
R SUBWAY TRAIN THAT CAME TO LIFE/Rush Hour Stomp	(Cameo 445)	1.00	4.00	66
RUN, RUN, RUN/No Return	(Epic 10191)	.75	3.00	67
SHAPE OF THINGS TO COME/She Aint't No Choir Girl	(Epic 10323)	.75	3.00	68
THIRTEENTH COMMITTEE, The				
SHA LA LA/You Really Got A Hold On Me	(Manhattan 810)	.75	3.00	67
THIRTEENTH FLOOR ELEVATORS (Featuring Roky Erickson)				
I'VE GOT LEVITATION/Before You Accuse Me	(International Artists 113)	2.50	10.00	67
LIVIN' ON/Scarlet & Gold	(International Artists 130)	2.50	10.00	68
MAY THE CIRCLE REMAIN UNBROKEN/ I'm Gonna Love You Too	(International Artists 126)	2.50	10.00	67
REVERBERATION (DOUBT)/Fire Engine	(International Artists 111)	2.50	10.00	66
SHE LIVES (IN A TIME OF HER OWN)/ Baby Blue	(International Artists 121)	2.50	10.00	67
SLIP INSIDE THIS HOUSE/Splash 1	(International Artists 122)	2.50	10.00	67
SPLASH/	(International Artists 122)	2.50	10.00	67
YOU'RE GONNA MISS ME/Tried To Hide	(International Artists 107)	2.50	10.00	66
YOU'RE GONNA MISS ME/Tried To Hide	(Contact 5269)	6.25	25.00	66
YOU'RE GONNA MISS ME/Tried To Hide	(HBR 492)	12.50	50.00	66
YOU'RE GONNA MISS ME/We Sell Soul	(Zero 10002)	25.00	100.00	66
(Shown as by the Spades)				
13TH POWER, The				
I SEE A CHANGE IS GONNA COME/Captain Hassel	(Sidewalk 927)	1.25	5.00	67
31ST OF FEBRUARY, The (The Allman Brothers Band)				
SANDCASTLES/Pick A Gripe	(Vanguard 35066)	1.00	4.00	68
38 SPECIAL (With Dave Van Zandt)				
I'M A FOOL FOR YOU/	(A&M 2051)	.50	2.00	78
TELL EVERYBODY/	(A&M 1964)	.50	2.00	77
Dave is the brother of Ronnie Van Zandt, of Lynyrd Skynyrd.				
THOMAS, B.J. (Billy Joe Thomas)				
BABY CRIED/I'm Not A Fool Anymore	(Pacemaker 253)	1.00	4.00	65
BILLY & SUE/Never Tell	(Bragg 103)	2.50	10.00	64
BILLY & SUE/Never Tell	(Warner Bros. 5491)	1.25	5.00	64
BILLY & SUE/Never Tell	(Hickory 1395)	.75	3.00	66
BRING BACK THE TIME/	(Pacemaker 234)	1.00	4.00	65
BRING BACK THE TIME/	(Scepter 12154)	.75	3.00	66
DON'T WORRY BABY/My Love	(MCA 40735)	.50	2.00	77
EVERYBODY LOVES A RAIN SONG/Dusty Roads	(MCA 40854)	.50	2.00	78
EVERYBODY'S OUT OF TOWN/Living Again	(Scepter 12277)	.50	2.00	70
EYES OF A NEW YORK WOMAN/ I May Never Get To Heaven	(Scepter 12219)	.50	2.00	68
GOD BLESS THE CHILDREN/ On This Christmas Night	(MCA-Songbird 41134)	.50	2.00	79
HAPPIER THAN THE MORNING SUN/	(Scepter 12364)	.50	2.00	72
HELP ME MAKE IT (TO MY ROCKIN' CHAIR)/ We Are Happy Together	(ABC 12121)	.50	2.00	75
(HEY WON'T YOU PLAY) ANOTHER SOMEBODY DONE SOMEBODY WRONG SONG/City Boys	(ABC 12054)	.50	2.00	75
HOME WHERE I BELONG/	(Myrrh 166)	.50	2.00	77
HOOKED ON A FEELING/ I've Been Down This Road Before	(Scepter 12230)	.50	2.00	68
I CAN'T HELP IT (IF I'M STILL IN LOVE WITH YOU)/ /Baby Cried	(Pacemaker 256)	1.00	4.00	65
I CAN'T HELP IT (IF I'M STILL IN LOVE WITH YOU)/ Baby Cried	(Scepter 12194)	.75	3.00	67
I GOT A FEELING/Hey Judy	(Valerie 226)	1.25	5.00	
I JUST CAN'T HELP BELIEVING/ Send My Picture To Scranton, PA	(Scepter 12283)	.50	2.00	70
I KNOW IT'S WRONG/Lazy Man	(Dante 3002)	3.00	12.00	62
(Shown as by the Triumphs)				
I KNOW IT'S WRONG/Lazy Man	(Dante 1788)	2.50	10.00	62
(Shown as by the Triumphs)				
I'M NOT A FOOL ANYMORE/Baby Cried	(Pacemaker 253)	1.00	4.00	65
I'M SO LONESOME I COULD CRY/Candy Baby	(Pacemaker 227)	1.00	4.00	64
I'M SO LONESOME I COULD CRY/Candy Baby	(Scepter 12129)	.75	3.00	66
IT'S ONLY LOVE/ You Don't Love Me Anymore (The Train Song)	(Scepter 12244)	.50	2.00	69
KEEP IT UP/Vietnam	(Joed 119)	2.00	8.00	
LONG AGO TOMORROW/	(Scepter 12335)	.50	2.00	71
MAMA/Wendy	(Pacemaker 231)	1.00	4.00	
MAMA/Wendy	(Scepter 12139)	.75	3.00	66
MIGHTY CLOUDS OF JOY/Life	(Scepter 12320)	.50	2.00	71
MOST OF ALL/The Mask	(Scepter 12299)	.50	2.00	70
MY HOME TOWN/Plain Jane	(Scepter 12179)	.75	3.00	66
NO LOVE AT ALL/Have A Heart	(Scepter 12307)	.50	2.00	71
PASS THE APPLE EVE/Fairy Tale Of Time	(Scepter 12255)	.75	3.00	69
PLAIN JANE/	(Pacemaker 247)	1.00	4.00	65
RAINDROPS KEEP FALLING ON MY HEAD/ Never Had It So Good	(Scepter 12265)	.50	2.00	69
ROCK & ROLL LULLABYE/Are We Losing Touch	(Scepter 12344)	.75	3.00	72
STILL THE LOVIN' IS FUN/ Play Me A Little Travelin' Music	(MCA 40812)	.50	2.00	77
SWEET YOUNG AMERICAN/Aloha	(MCA 40914)	.50	2.00	78
THAT'S WHAT FRIENDS ARE FOR/	(Scepter 12354)	.50	2.00	72
TOMORROW NEVER COMES/	(Pacemaker 239)	1.00	4.00	65
TOMORROW NEVER COMES/	(Scepter 12165)	.75	3.00	66
WE COULD HAVE BEEN THE CLOSEST OF FRIENDS/ In My Heart	(MCA 40986)	.50	2.00	79

TITLE/FLIP	LABEL & NO.	GOOD	NEAR MINT	YR.
WISDOM OF A FOOL/Treasure Of Love	(Scepter 12200)	1.25	5.00	68
(Promotional issue)				
WITHOUT A DOUBT/	(Myrrh 176)	.50	2.00	78
YOU'LL NEVER WALK ALONE/Chains Of Love	(Hickory 1415)	.75	3.00	66
YOUR MINE TONIGHT/People Sure Act Funny	(Dante 3011)	2.50	10.00	62
(Shown as by the Triumphs)				
THOMAS, Cliff				
SORRY I LIED/Leave It To Me	(Phillips International 3531)	1.00	4.00	59
TREAT ME RIGHT/I'm On The Way Home	(Phillips International 3521)	1.00	4.00	59
THOMAS, David Clayton (Of Blood, Sweat & Tears)				
BORN WITH THE BLUES/Brain Washed	(Tower 263)	1.50	6.00	66
HEY, HEY, HEY/	(Atco 6347)	2.50	10.00	65
NO NO NO/Monopoly	(Roulette 7048)	1.00	4.00	69
SAY BOSS MAN/Done Somebody Wrong	(Decca 7-32556)	1.00	4.00	69
SING A SONG/We're All Meat From The Same Bone	(Columbia 45569)	.75	3.00	71
THOMAS, Gene				
BABY'S GONE/Stand By Love	(United Artists 640)	.75	3.00	63
IT'S MAKE BELIEVE/So Wrong	(United Artists 501)	.75	3.00	62
LAMP OF LOVE/Two Lips	(Venus 1441)	1.00	4.00	62
LAST SONG/Bobby & The Boys	(United Artists 725)	.75	3.00	64
PEACE OF MIND/The Puppet	(United Artists 583)	.75	3.00	63
SOMETIME/Every Night	(United Artists 338)	.75	3.00	61
SOMETIME/Every Night	(Venus 1439)	1.25	5.00	61
THAT'S WHAT YOU ARE TO ME/Mysteries Of Love	(United Artists 418)	.75	3.00	62
Also see Gene & Debbie				
THOMAS GROUP, The				
DON'T START ME TALKIN' 'BOUT MY BABY/Autumn	(Dunhill 4030)	1.25	5.00	66
PENNY ARCADE/Ordinary Girl	(Dunhill 4027)	1.50	6.00	66
THOMAS, Ian				
COMING HOME/	(Atlantic 3470)	.50	2.00	78
LIARS/	(Chrysalis 2116)	.50	2.00	75
LONG LONG WAY/Count Your Blessings	(Janus 242)	.50	2.00	74
PAINTED LADIES/Will You Still Love Me	(Janus 224)	.50	2.00	73
SALLY/	(Atlantic 3505)	.50	2.00	78
THOMAS, Jamo				
I SPY/Snake Hip Mama	(Thomas 303)	.75	3.00	66
THOMAS, Judy				
DON'T FEEL LIKE THE LONE RANGER/Golden Records	(Tollie 9021)	.75	3.00	64
THOMAS, Marlo, & Friends				
FREE TO BE... YOU & ME/Boy Meets Girl-My Dog Is A Plumber-When We Grow Up-Housework	(Bell 12345)	.50	2.00	71
THOMAS, Mickey				
CAN YOU FOOL/	(MCA 40767)	.50	2.00	77
SOMEBODY TO LOVE/Where Are We	(MCA 40767)	.50	2.00	77
TAKE ME HIGHER/Sweet Rider (By Dr. John)	(RCA 12285)	.50	2.00	78
Also see Bishop, Elvin				
THOMAS, Pat				
DESAFINADO/One Note Samba	(MGM 13102)	.75	3.00	62
THOMAS, Ray (Of The Moody Blues)				
ONE NIGHT STAND/Carousel	(Threshold 67023)	.50	2.00	76
LOVE IS THE KEY/High Above My Head	(Threshold 67020)	.50	2.00	75
THOMAS, Susan & Richard				
THOUGHT, A/The Heart, The Desperado	(Blue Hour 1014)	.50	2.00	73
THOMAS, Timmy				
PEOPLE ARE CHANGIN'/Rainbow Power	(Glades 1709)	.50	2.00	73
WHY CAN'T WE LIVE TOGETHER/Funky Me	(Glades 1703)	.50	2.00	72
THOMAS, Vic (With The 4-Evers)				
MARIANNE/Napoleon Bonaparte	(Phillips 40183)	6.25	25.00	64
VILLAGE OF LOVE/Down The Stream To The River	(Phillips 40228)	1.25	5.00	64
THOME, Henry				
SCOTCH & SODA/	(VIV 3)	1.00	4.00	62
THOMPSON, Bob				
CORA'S MELODY/Theme From "The Sundowners"	(RCA Victor 47-7795)	.75	3.00	60
CORA'S MELODY/Theme From "The Sundowners"	(RCA Victor 47-7795)	1.50	6.00	60
(Stereo single issue)				
Instrumentals				
THOMPSON, Claudia				
GLOOMY SUNDAY/Goodnight My Pet	(Edison International 408)	.75	3.00	59
THOMPSON, Chris (Of Manfred Mann's Earth Band)				
IF YOU REMEMBER ME/Theme From "The Champ"	(Planet 45904)	.50	2.00	79
Also see Night				

TITLE/FLIP	LABEL & NO.	GOOD	NEAR MINT	YR.
THOMPSON, Hayden				
WHATCHA GONNA DO/	(Profile 4015)	1.50	6.00	
THOMPSON, Loretta				
BUDDY-BIG-BOPPER-RITCHIE/Square From Nowhere	(Skoop 1050)	3.00	12.00	59
THOMPSON, Robbin				
BOY FROM BOSTON/	(Nemperor 010)	.50	2.00	76
DREAM ON MELINDA/	(Nemperor 011)	.50	2.00	77

TITLE/FLIP	LABEL & NO.	GOOD	NEAR MINT	YR.
THOMPSON, Sue (Eva Sue McKee)				
HAVE A GOOD TIME/If The Boy Only Knew	(Hickory 1174)	.75	3.00	62
JAMES (HOLD THE LADDER STEADY)/My Hero	(Hickory 1183)	.75	3.00	62
NORMAN/Never Love Again	(Hickory 1159)	.75	3.00	61
PAPER TIGER/Mama Don't Cry At My Wedding	(Hickory 1284)	.75	3.00	64
SAD MOVIES (MAKE ME CRY)/Nine Little Teardrops	(Hickory 1153)	.75	3.00	61
TWO OF A KIND/It Has To Be	(Hickory 1166)	.75	3.00	62
WILLIE CAN/Too Much In Love	(Hickory 1196)	.75	3.00	62
THORINSHIELD				
LIFE IS A DREAM/The Best Of It	(Philips 40492)	.75	3.00	67
LONELY MOUNTAIN AGAIN/Family Of Man	(Philips 40521)	.75	3.00	68
THORNDIKE PICKLEDISH (Robert O. Smith)				
BALLAD OF WALTER WART(BRRRIGGETT), THE/ It's Warts On The Flip Side That Counts	(MTA 114)	1.00	4.00	66
(Shown as by the Thorndike Pickledish Pacifist Choir)				
IMPERIAL GRAND MOTHER, THE/S.F. Bound-Paranoia	(Piccadilly 247)	1.25	5.00	67
INTERVIEW WITH MRS. MALOOKA, THE/ Poetry Readings In The Bathroom	(Yonah 2003)	2.50	10.00	63
(Shown as by Bob Smith)				
LENNY FROG/D.J. At The End Of The World	(Lo-Fi 1)	1.25	5.00	67
(Shown as by the Thorndike Pickledish Pacifist Choir)				
LONELY BULL (FROG)/Wart Now My Love	(MTA 126)	1.50	6.00	66
(Shown as by the Thorndike Pickledish Choir)				
SINISTER LUNCHMEAT/Twilight Gallery 2176	(Huggaboom 451)	.75	3.00	76
(Shown as by Dr. zinGRR)				
SLEEPY STONEWALL'S BROTHERHOOD BOOGIE/ Excerpt: Robt. O. Smut	(Lo-Fi 1A)	1.25	5.00	68
WALTER WART THE FREAKY FROG/Viet Nama Mama	(Absurd 303)	1.50	6.00	66
(Shown as by the Thorndike Pickledish Pacifist Choir)				
THORNTON, Fradkin & Unger				
GOD BLESS CALIFORNIA/Sometimes	(ESP-Disk 63019)	.75	3.00	71
(With Paul McCartney on bass and backup vocals)				
THORNTON, Les				
WHAT'S HOLDING UP HER BIKINI/Cindy B.	(Du-well 1009)	.75	3.00	61
THOROGOOD, George, & The Destroyers				
MOVE IT ON OVER/	(Rounder 4518)	.50	2.00	78
MY WAY/You're Gonna Miss Me	(MCA 41117)	.50	2.00	79
IN THE NIGHT TIME/Nadine	(MCA 41136)	.50	2.00	79
WHO DO YOU LOVE?/I'll Change My Style	(Rounder 4519)	.50	2.00	79
THORPE, Billy				
CHILDREN OF THE SUN/ Wrapped In The Chains Of Your Love	(Capricorn 0321)	.50	2.00	79
CHILDREN OF THE SUN/ Wrapped In The Chains Of Your Love	(Polydor 2018)	.50	2.00	79
DREAM-MAKER/The Beginning	(Polydor 2025)	.50	2.00	79
THORPE, Billy, & The Aztecs				
OVER THE RAINBOW/That I Love	(GNP-Crescendo 340)	.75	3.00	65
TWILIGHT TIME/My Girl Josephine	(GNP-Crescendo 359)	.75	3.00	65
THOSE FIVE GUYS				
YOU-EFF-OH/You-Eff-Oh (Part 2)	(Quill 103)	1.50	6.00	
THREE BLOND MICE				
RINGO BELLS/Twelve Days Of Christmas, The	(Atco 6324)	2.00	8.00	64
THREE CHIMES, The				
TEARS & PAIN/Show Me The Way	(Crossway 444)	1.50	6.00	
THREE CHUCKLES, The (Features Teddy Randazzo)				
AND THE ANGELS SING/Tell Me	(Vik 0194)	1.00	4.00	56
ANYWAY/Funny Little Things We Used To Do	("X" 0186)	1.25	5.00	56
ANYWAY/The Funny Little Things We Used To Do	(Vik 0186)	1.00	4.00	56
FOOLISHLY/If You Should Love Again	("X" 095)	1.50	6.00	55
GYPSY IN MY SOUL/We're Still Holding Hands	("X" 0216)	1.25	5.00	56
MIDNIGHT TIL' DAWN/Fallen Out Of Love	(Vik 0232)	1.00	4.00	57
REALIZE/Blue Lover	("X" 0150)	1.50	6.00	55
RUNAROUND/At Last You Understand	(Boulevard 100)	7.50	30.00	53
RUNAROUND/You Lied	(Cloud 507)	.75	3.00	66
RUNAROUND/Lonely Traveler	(ABC-Paramount 10276)	1.00	4.00	61
(Shown as by the Chuckles)				
RUNAROUND/At Last You Understand	("X" 0066)	2.00	8.00	54
SO LONG/You Should Have Told Me	("X" 0134)	1.50	6.00	55
TIMES TWO, I LOVE YOU/Still Thinking Of You	("X" 0162)	1.50	6.00	55
WON'T YOU GIVE ME A CHANCE/We're Gonna Rock Tonight	(Vik 0244)	1.25	5.00	57
THREE DEES, The				
BROKEN HEARTED/I Love You So	(Dean 521)	1.00	4.00	
THREE DEGREES, The				
CLOSE YOUR EYES/Gotta Draw The Line	(Swan 4224)	1.00	4.00	65
GEE BABY (I'M SORRY)/ Do What You're Supposed To Do	(Swan 4197)	1.00	4.00	65
I DO TAKE YOU/You're The Fool	(Roulette 7088)	.75	3.00	70
I WON'T LET YOU GO/Through Misty Eyes	(Roulette 7137)	.75	3.00	73
I'M GONNA NEED YOU/Just Right For Love	(Swan 4214)	1.00	4.00	65
LOOK IN MY EYES/Drivin' Me Mad	(Swan 4235)	1.00	4.00	66
LOVE IS THE MESSAGE/My One & Only Love	(Philadelphia Int'l. 3547)	.50	2.00	74
LOWDOWN/Ebb Tide	(Roulette 7105)	.75	3.00	71
MAYBE/Sugar On Sunday	(Roulette 7079)	.75	3.00	70
THERE'S SO MUCH LOVE ALL AROUND ME/Yours	(Roulette 7102)	.75	3.00	71
TRADE WINDS/I Turn To You	(Roulette 7117)	.75	3.00	72
TSOP (THE SOUND OF PHILADELPHIA)/ Something For Nothing	(Philadelphia Int'l 3540)	.50	2.00	74
WHEN WILL I SEE YOU AGAIN/Years Of Decision	(Philadelphia Int'l. 3550)	.50	2.00	74
YOU'RE THE ONE/Stardust	(Roulette 7097)	.75	3.00	71
THREE DOG NIGHT				
AN OLD FASHIONED LOVE SONG/Jam	(Dunhill 4294)	.50	2.00	71
BLACK & WHITE/Freedom For The Stallion	(Dunhill 4317)	.50	2.00	72
CELEBRATE/Feeling Alright	(Dunhill 4229)	.50	2.00	70
EASY TO BE HARD/Dreaming Isn't Good For You	(Dunhill 4203)	.50	2.00	69
ELI'S COMING/Circle For A Landing	(Dunhill 4215)	.50	2.00	69
EVERYBODY IS A MASTERPIECE/Drive On, Ride On	(ABC 12192)	.50	2.00	76
FAMILY OF MAN/Going In Circles	(Dunhill 4306)	.50	2.00	72
FAMILY OF MAN/Going In Circles	(ABC 1465)	.50	2.00	72
JOY TO THE WORLD/I Can Hear You Calling	(Dunhill 4272)	.50	2.00	71
LET ME SERENADE YOU/Storybook Feeling	(Dunhill 4370)	.50	2.00	73
LIAR/Can't Get Enough Of It	(Dunhill 4282)	.50	2.00	71
MAMA TOLD ME (NOT TO COME)/Rock & Roll Widow	(Dunhill 4239)	.50	2.00	70
NEVER BEEN TO SPAIN/Peace Of Mind	(Dunhill 4299)	.50	2.00	71
NOBODY/It's For You	(Dunhill 4168)	1.00	4.00	68
ONE/Chest Fever	(Dunhill 4191)	.50	2.00	69
ONE MAN BAND/It' Ain't Easy	(Dunhill 4262)	.50	2.00	70
OUT IN THE COUNTRY/Good Time Living	(Dunhill 4250)	.50	2.00	70
PIECES OF APRIL/The Writing's On The Wall	(Dunhill 4331)	.50	2.00	72
PLAY SOMETHING SWEET (BRICKYARD BLUES)/ I'd Be So Happy	(Dunhill 15013)	.50	2.00	74
SHAMBALA/Our "B" Side	(Dunhill 4352)	.50	2.00	73
SHOW MUST GO ON, THE/On The Way Back Home	(Dunhill 15010)	.50	2.00	74
SURE AS I'M SITTIN' HERE/Anytime Babe	(Dunhill 15001)	.50	2.00	74
'TIL THE WORLD ENDS/ Yo Te Quiero Hablar (Take You Down)	(ABC 12114)	.50	2.00	75
TRY A LITTLE TENDERNESS/ That No One Ever Hurt This Bad	(Dunhill 4177)	.75	3.00	69
Also see Hutton, Danny				
Also see Wells, Cory				

TITLE/FLIP	LABEL & NO.	GOOD	NEAR MINT	YR.
THREE Ds, The				
BIRTH OF AN ANGEL/Never Let You Go	(Paris 508)	1.25	5.00	57
CRAZY LITTLE WOMAN/Baby Doll	(Paris 511)	1.25	5.00	58
I NEVER SEE MY BABY ALONE/Jumpin' Jack	(Paris 514)	1.25	5.00	58
MY FRATERNITY DANCE/Summertime Sweetheart	(Lowell 212)	1.25	5.00	
(Shown as by Henry Pinard & The Three Ds.)				
SQUEEZE/Graveyard Cha-Cha	(Square 502)	1.00	4.00	
TELL ME THAT YOU LOVE ME/Broken Dreams	(Pilgrim 719)	1.25	5.00	56
3 FRIENDS, The				
BLANCHE/Baby I'll Cry	(Lido 500)	1.25	5.00	56
I'M ONLY A BOY/Jinx	(Lido 502)	1.25	5.00	57
NOW THAT YOU'RE GONE/Chinese Tea Room	(Lido 504)	1.25	5.00	57
THREE G'S, The				
BARBARA/Don't Cry Katy	(Columbia 41513)	1.00	4.00	59
LET'S GO STEADY FOR THE SUMMER/Love Call	(Columbia 41678)	.75	3.00	60
LET'S GO STEADY FOR THE SUMMER/Wild Man	(Columbia 41175)	1.00	4.00	58
THESE ARE THE LITTLE THINGS/Wonder	(Columbia 41292)	1.00	4.00	58
THREE KITTENS, The				
SAD, SENTIMENTAL & SORRY/Wedding Cake Polka	(Coral 9-61551)	1.25	5.00	55
3 PENNIES, The				
I WAS A FOOL (JUST A FOOL)/ I've Got Bells On My Heart	(Golden Crest 1312)	1.00	4.00	
THREE PROPHETS, The				
RAG DOLL BOY/	(Kapp 617)	3.00	12.00	64
(Answer song)				
THREE STOOGES, The				
SINKIN' THE ROBERT E. LEE/You Are My Girl	(Spinit 105)	1.25	5.00	60
SINKIN' THE ROBERT E. LEE/You Are My Girl	(Epic 9402)	.75	3.00	60
THREE WISHES, The				
GUIDING LIGHT/It's All Said & Done	(Dolton 72)	1.00	4.00	63
THREETEENS, The				
DEAR 53310769 (Elvis' U.S. Army serial number)/ Doowaddie	(Rev 3516)	2.50	10.00	58
FOR THE LOVE OF MIKE/X Plus Y Equals Z	(Rev 3522)	1.25	5.00	59
THRILLS, The				
BRING IT ON HOME TO ME/Here's A Heart	(Capitol 5719)	.75	3.00	66
NO ONE/What Can Go Wrong	(Capitol 5631)	.75	3.00	66
THUMB, Tom, & The Casuals				
I SHOULD KNOW/I Don't Want Much	(Panorama 21)	1.25	5.00	
THUNDER & ROSES				
COUNTRY LIFE/I Love A Woman	(United Artists 50536)	.75	3.00	69
THUNDERBIRDS, The				
YOUR MA SAID YOU CRIED (IN YOUR SLEEP LAST NIGHT)/ Before It's Too Late	(Delaware 1710)	.75	3.00	65
THUNDERBOLTS, The				
LOST PLANET/March Of The Spacemen	(Dot 16496)	.75	3.00	64
THUNDERCLAP NEWMAN (Featuring Seppdy Keen, Jimmy McCulloch & Andy Newman)				
ACCIDENTS/I See It All	(Track 2718)	1.25	5.00	70
SOMETHING IN THE AIR/Wilhelmina	(Track 2656)	1.00	4.00	69
SOMETHING IN THE AIR/Wilhelmina	(Track 2769)	1.00	4.00	70
SOMETHING IN THE AIR/Hollywood #1	(Track 60132)	.75	3.00	75
Also see Wings				
THUNDERGRIN				
WOMEN IN THE STREET/Mr. Simms	(Epic 10215)	1.00	4.00	67
THUNDERMUG				
AFRICA/	(Big Tree 154)	.50	2.00	72
I WANNA BE WITH YOU/	(Epic 11126)	.50	2.00	74
ORBIT/	(Epic 11082)	.50	2.00	73
THUNDERTONES, The				
JUNGLE FEVER/Hot Ice	(Dot 16137)	.75	3.00	60
THUNDPUCKER, Jimmy				
GINNY'S SONG/Ginny's Song (Disco Version)	(Warner Bros. 8245)	.50	2.00	77
TAKE YOUR LIFE/You Can't Fight It	(Windsong 11230)	.50	2.00	78
THURSDAY'S CHILDREN				
AIR CONDITIONED MAN/Dominoes	(International Artists 110)	1.00	4.00	66
THYME				
LOVE TO LOVE/Very Last Day	(Bang 546)	1.00	4.00	67
SOMEHOW/Shame, Shame	(A^2 201)	1.25	5.00	
TIME OF THE SEASON/I Found A Love	(A^2 202)	1.25	5.00	
TICKLERS, The				
MILLIE THE GHOUL/Don't Tickle My Feet	(Mustang 3007)	1.00	4.00	65
(Novelty)				
TICO & THE TRIUMPHS (With Paul Simon)				
CARDS OF LOVE/Noise	(Amy 876)	5.00	20.00	62
CRY LITTLE BOY CRY/Get Up & Do The Wobble	(Amy 860)	1.50	6.00	62
MOTORCYCLE/I Don't Believe Them	(Amy 835)	1.50	6.00	62
MOTORCYCLE/I Don't Believe Them	(Madison 169)	3.00	12.00	62
WILD FLOWER/Express Train	(Amy 845)	1.50	6.00	62
TIDAL WAVE				
SINBAD THE SAILOR/Searching For Love	(Buddah 46)	1.00	4.00	68
TIDAL WAVES, The				
BOOMA SHOOMA ROCK/The Clock	(Tide 0020)	1.00	4.00	61
YOU NAME IT/So I Guess	(Strafford 6503)	1.25	5.00	
TIDAL WAVES, The				
ACTION!/Hot Stuff!	(HBR 515)	1.00	4.00	67
FARMER JOHN/She Left Me Alone	(HBR 482)	1.00	4.00	66
FARMER JOHN/She Left Me Alone	(SVR 1007)	1.50	6.00	66
I DON'T NEED LOVE/Big Boy Pete	(HBR 501)	1.00	4.00	66
TIDES, The				
BANANA BOAT SONG/Patricia	(Mercury 72045)	.75	3.00	62
CHICKEN SPACEMAN/Ring A Ding Ding	(Dore 618)	1.00	4.00	61
DEAR MR. PRESIDENT/Ring A Ding Ding	(Dore 611)	1.00	4.00	61
LIMBO ROCK/Midnight Limbo	(Mercury 71990)	.75	3.00	62
ROCK ME GENTLY/Stoned	(Dore 529)	1.00	4.00	59
SAY YOU'RE MINE/Follow Me	(Dore 579)	1.00	4.00	61
TIFFANYS, The				
HE'S GOOD FOR ME/It's Got To Be A Great Song	(RKO 120)	.75	3.00	
PLEASURE OF LOVE, THE/Atlanta	(Swan 4104)	.75	3.00	62
TAKE ANOTHER LOOK AT ME/Heaven on Earth	(Josie 952)	1.25	5.00	65
TIFFIN, Barry				
CANDY BARS FOR ELVIS/ I Dreamed Elvis Sang My Song	(Tiffin International 8684)	.50	2.00	77
TIGERS, The				
GEE TO TIGER/The Prowl	(Colpix 773)	1.00	4.00	65

TITLE/FLIP	LABEL & NO.	GOOD	NEAR MINT	YR.
TIGRE, Terry				
ELVIS, WE LOVE YOU/Elvis, We Love You	(Gusto-Starday 166)	1.00	4.00	77
(Promotional issue only)				
TIJUANA BRATS, The				
YAKETY BRATS/Karate Chop	(RCA Victor 47-9666)	.75	3.00	68
TIKIS, The				
BYE BYE BYE/Lost My Love Today	(Autumn 28)	2.00	8.00	66
BYE BYE BYE/Lost My Love Today	(Warner Bros. 5818)	1.25	5.00	66
IF I'VE BEEN DREAMING/Pay Attention To Me	(Autumn 18)	2.00	8.00	65
LOST MY LOVE TODAY/Bye Bye Bye	(Warner Bros. 5828)	1.25	5.00	66
Also see Other Tikis				
Also see Harpers Bizarre				
TILLIS, Mel				
HEARTS OF STONE/That's Where The Hurt Comes In	(Columbia 41026)	2.50	10.00	57
TEEN AGE WEDDING/Lonely Street	(Columbia 41115)	2.50	10.00	57
TILLMAN, Mickey				
DEAR MOM & DAD/I Have Chosen You	(Vee Jay 296)	2.50	10.00	58
TILLOTSON, Johnny				
ANGEL/Little Boy	(MGM 13316)	.75	3.00	65
DREAMY EYES/Well, I'm Your Man	(Cadence 1353)	1.25	5.00	58
DREAMY EYES/Well, I'm Your Man	(Cadence 1409)	.75	3.00	61
EARTH ANGEL/Pledging My Love	(Cadence 1377)	1.00	4.00	60
FUNNY HOW TIME SLIPS AWAY/A Very Good Year For Girls	(Cadence 1441)	.75	3.00	63
HEARTACHES BY THE NUMBERS/ Your Mem'ry Comes Along	(MGM 13376)	.75	3.00	65
I CAN'T HELP IT (IF I'M STILL IN LOVE WITH YOU)/ I'm So Lonesome I Could Cry	(Cadence 1432)	.75	3.00	62
I RISE, I FALL/I'm Watching My Watch	(MGM 13232)	.75	3.00	64
IT KEEPS RIGHT ON A-HURTING/ She Gave Sweet Love To Me	(Cadence 1418)	.75	3.00	62
JIMMY'S GIRL/His True Love Said Goodbye	(Cadence 1391)	.75	3.00	61
OUT OF MY MIND/Empty Feelin'	(Cadence 1434)	.75	3.00	63
OUR WORLD/(Wait Till You See) My Gidget	(MGM 13408)	.75	3.00	65
POETRY IN MOTION/Princess, Princess	(Cadence 1384)	.75	3.00	60
SEND ME THE PILLOW YOU DREAM ON/What'll I Do	(Cadence 1424)	.75	3.00	62
SHE UNDERSTANDS ME/Tomorrow	(MGM 13284)	.75	3.00	64
TALK BACK TREMBLING LIPS/Another You	(MGM 13181)	.75	3.00	63
TEARS ON MY PILLOW/Remember When	(Amos 117)	.75	3.00	69
THEN I'LL COUNT AGAIN/One's Yours, One's Mine	(MGM 13344)	.75	3.00	65
TRUE TRUE HAPPINESS/Love Is Blind	(Cadence 1365)	1.00	4.00	59
WHY DO I LOVE YOU SO/Never Let Me Go	(Cadence 1372)	1.00	4.00	60
WITHOUT YOU/Cutie Pie	(Cadence 1404)	.75	3.00	61
WORRIED GUY/Please Don't Go Away	(MGM 13193)	.75	3.00	64
WORRY/Sufferin' From A Heartache	(MGM 13255)	.75	3.00	64
YOU CAN NEVER STOP ME LOVING YOU/ Judy, Judy, Judy	(Cadence 1437)	.75	3.00	63
YOU LOVE'S BEEN A LONG TIME COMIN'/	(Buddah 311)	.75	3.00	73
Also see Genevieve				
TIMEBOX				
BEGGIN'/A Woman That's Waiting	(Deram 85031)	1.00	4.00	68
T.I.M.E.				
TAKE ME ALONG/Make It Alright	(Liberty 56020)	1.25	5.00	68
TAKE ME ALONG/Make It Alright	(Liberty 56020)	2.00	8.00	68
(Picture sleeve)				
WHAT WOULD LIFE BE WITHOUT IT/Trip Into Sunshine	(Liberty 56060)	1.25	5.00	68
TIME TONES, The				
PRETTY PRETTY GIRL/I've Got A Feeling	(Atco 6201)	.75	3.00	61
TIMERS, The				
NO GO SHOWBOAT/Competition Coupe	(Reprise 231)	3.75	15.00	63
(With Brian Wilson)				
TIMON				
AND NOW SHE SAYS SHE IS YOUNG/	(Threshold 67003)	.50	2.00	70
TIM TAM & THE TURN-ONS				
CHERYL ANN/Seal It With A Kiss	(Palmer 5003)	3.00	12.00	66
DON'T SAY HI/Don't Say Hi (Instrumental)	(Palmer 5014)	1.25	5.00	67
KIMBERLY/I Leave You In Tears	(Palmer 5006)	5.00	20.00	66
WAIT A MINUTE/Opella	(Palmer 5002)	1.50	6.00	66
TINKERS, The				
YOU'RE JUST LIKE ALL THE REST/Love Lights	(Stop 106)	1.25	5.00	
YOU'RE MAKING ME SAD/My Lost Love	(Stop 107)	1.25	5.00	
TINO & THE REVLONS				
LAZY MARY MEMPHIS/I'm Coming Home	(Dearborn 530)	1.00	4.00	
LITTLE GIRL, LITTLE GIRL/Rave On	(Dearborn 525)	1.00	4.00	
STORY OF OUR LOVE/Black Bermudas & Knee-Socks	(Mark 154)	2.00	8.00	
WEDDING BELLS WILL RING/Heidi	(Pip 4000)	1.00	4.00	
TIN HUEY				
I'M A BELIEVER/ New York's Finest Dining Experience	(Warner Bros. 49001)	.50	2.00	79
TIN TIN (Featuring Steve Kipner)				
IS THAT THE WAY/	(Atco 6821)	.50	2.00	71
TOAST & MARMALADE FOR TEA/Manhattan Woman	(Atco 6794)	.50	2.00	71
TINY TIM (Herb Khaury)				
BRING BACK THOSE ROCKABYE BABY DAYS/ This Is All I Ask	(Reprise 0760)	.75	3.00	68
GREAT BALLS OF FIRE/As Time Goes By	(Reprise 0802)	1.00	4.00	69
I'M GONNA BE A COUNTRY QUEEN/ I Ain't No Cowboy (I Just Found This Hat)	(True 109)	.50	2.00	71
ON THE GOOD SHIP LOLLIPOP/America I Love You	(Reprise 0837)	.75	3.00	69
THIS IS ALL I ASK/Be My Love	(Reprise 0769)	.75	3.00	69
TIP-TOE THRU THE TULIPS WITH ME/Fill Your Heart	(Reprise 0679)	.75	3.00	68
TINY TIP & THE TIP TOPS				
MATRIMONY/Say It	(Chess 1822)	2.00	8.00	62
TITANS, The				
ARLENE/Love Is A Wonderful Thing	(Specialty 632)	2.00	8.00	58
NO TIME/Tootin' Tutor	(Class 244)	1.00	4.00	59
TITANS, The				
NO PLACE SPECIAL/Reveille Rock	(Soma 1411)	.75	3.00	64
TITONES, The				
SYMBOL OF LOVE/The Movies	(Scepter 1206)	1.50	6.00	59
TJADER, Cal				
SOUL SAUCE/Somewhere In The Night	(Verve 10345)	.75	3.00	65
(Instrumentals)				
TKO				
AIN'T NO WAY TO BE/Bad Sister	(Infinity 50012)	.50	2.00	79
LET IT ROLL/Kill The Pain	(Infinity 50024)	.50	2.00	79
T.M.G.				
HEART OF STONE/	(Atco 7201)	.50	2.00	79
LAZY EYES/Distrubing The Peace	(Atco 7096)	.50	2.00	79

TITLE/FLIP	LABEL & NO.	GOOD	NEAR MINT	YR.
TOADS, The				
BABE, WHILE THE WIND BLOWS GOODBYE/ Leaving It All Behind	(Decca 31847)	.75	3.00	65
BACKARUDA/Modernistic (By the Golden Boys)	(Brent 7050)	1.00	4.00	63
TOBY & RAY				
BOM DO WA/Just Waiting For You	(Blue Moon 411)	1.00	4.00	59
TOBY BEAU				
INTO THE NIGHT/Wink Of An Eye	(RCA 11388)	.50	2.00	78
MY ANGEL BABY/California	(RCA 11250)	.50	2.00	78
THEN YOU CAN TELL ME GOODBYE/Boogie Woogie Melody	(RCA 11670)	.50	2.00	79
TODAY				
WE'VE BEEN A BAD, BAD BOY/That's What I'm For	(Burdette 488)	.75	3.00	
TODAY & TOMORROW				
DOOLEY SWINGS/Dooley Swings (Part 2)	(Noose 812)	5.00	20.00	59
TODD, Art & Dotty				
BOOMPI PA-DEEDLE/Come Josephine In A Flying Machine	(Theme 142)	.75	3.00	
BROKEN WINGS/Heavenly, Heavenly	(RCA Victor 47-5029)	1.50	6.00	52
BUSY SIGNAL, THE/Oh Honey, Why Don't Ya	(Abbott 3006)	1.25	5.00	55
BUT ONLY FOR ME/Kadey Song, The	(Diamond 3003)	.75	3.00	
CHANSON D'AMOUR/Along The Trail With You	(Era 1064)	1.00	4.00	58
DON'T YOU WORRY MY LITTLE PET/Pray	(Era 1087)	1.00	4.00	59
DRIFTING & DREAMING/Ca C'est La Vie	(Decca 31227)	.75	3.00	61
PARADISE/Ayuh Ayuh	(Era 3001)	1.00	4.00	59
SAY YOU/Chop Chop	(Dart 405)	.75	3.00	60
STRAIGHT AS AN ARROW/Stand There, Mountain	(Era 1088)	1.00	4.00	59
SWEET SOMEONE/Ring-A-Ding	(Capitol 4778)	.75	3.00	63
TWELFTH STREET RAG/Button Up Your Overcoat	(Diamond 3002)	.75	3.00	
YOUR CHEATING HEART/Sweet Cha Cha Chariot	(Decca 31329)	.75	3.00	61
TODD, Dick				
DADDY'S LITTLE GIRL/Who'll Be The Next One	(Rainbow 80080)	1.25	5.00	50
TODD, Don				
ELVIS DREAMED & IT CAME TRUE/ I Dreamed Elvis Sang My Song	(Dale 437)	.50	2.00	77
TODD, Dylan				
BALLAD OF JAMES DEAN, THE/	(RCA Victor 47-6463)	1.25	5.00	56
TODD, Nick				
AT THE HOP/I Do	(Dot 15675)	1.00	4.00	57
PLAYTHING/Honey Song, The	(Dot 15643)	1.00	4.00	57
RED ROSES FOR A BLUE LADY/Little Rosey Red	(Dot 15893)	1.00	4.00	59
Nick is Pat Boone's younger brother				
TODDS, The				
POPSICLE/Sugar Hill	(Todd 1076)	1.00	4.00	62
TENNESSEE/May We Always	(Todd 1064)	1.00	4.00	62
TOGETHER				
CONVENTION '72/	(American Worm)	2.50	10.00	
(Novelty/Break-in)				
TOGGERTY FIVE, The				
I'M GONNA JUMP/Bye Bye Bird	(Tower 119)	.75	3.00	
TOKAYS, The				
FATTY FATTY BOOM A LATTY/Lost & Found	(Bonnie 102)	5.00	20.00	
NOW/Ask Me No Questions	(Scorpio 403)	1.50	6.00	69

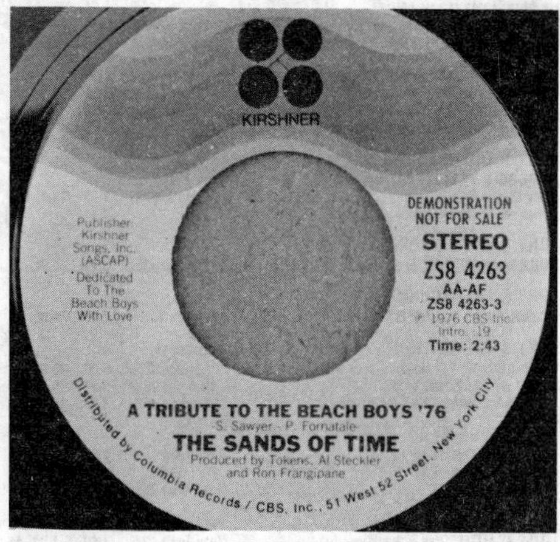

TITLE/FLIP	LABEL & NO.	GOOD	NEAR MINT	YR.
TOKENS, The (Featuring Jay Siegel)				
BANANA BOAT SONG/Grandfather	(Warner Bros. 7233)	.75	3.00	68
BATHROOM WALL/Animal	(Warner Bros. 7202)	.75	3.00	68
BELLS OF ST. MARY'S, THE/Just One Smile	(B.T. Puppy 513)	.75	3.00	64
BIRD FLIES OUT OF SIGHT, A/Wishing	(RCA Victor 47-8114)	1.00	4.00	62
BOTH SIDES NOW/I Can See Me Dancing With You	(Buddah 174)	.75	3.00	70
B'WA NINA/Weeping River	(RCA Victor 47-7991)	1.00	4.00	62
BYE, BYE, BYE/Ain't That Peculiar	(Warner Bros. 7099)	.75	3.00	67
DON'T WORRY BABY/Some People Sleep	(Buddah 159)	.75	3.00	70
GIRL NAMED ARLENE, A/Swing	(B.T. Puppy 500)	1.00	4.00	64
GO AWAY LITTLE GIRL-YOUNG GIRL/ I Want To Make Love To You	(Warner Bros. 7280)	.75	3.00	69
GREATEST MOMENTS IN A GIRLS LIFE, THE/Breezy	(B.T. Puppy 519)	.75	3.00	66
GREEN PLANT/Saloogy	(B.T. Puppy 525)	.75	3.00	67
GROOVIN' ON THE SUNSHINE SESAME STREET/ Listen To The Words (Listen To The Music)	(Buddah 187)	.75	3.00	70
HEAR THE BELLS/A-B-C 1-2-3	(RCA Victor 47-8210)	1.00	4.00	63
HE'S IN TOWN/Oh Cathy	(B.T. Puppy 502)	.75	3.00	64
I HEAR TRUMPETS BLOW/ Don't Cry, Sing Along With The Music	(B.T. Puppy 518)	.75	3.00	66
I'LL DO MY CRYING TOMORROW/ Dream Angel, Goodnight	(RCA Victor 47-8089)	1.00	4.00	62
IT'S A HAPPENING WORLD/How Nice	(Warner Bros. 7056)	1.00	4.00	67
LA BOMBA/A Token Of Love	(RCA Victor 47-8052)	1.00	4.00	62
LET'S GO TO THE DRAG STRIP/2 Cars	(RCA Victor 47-8309)	1.00	4.00	64
LION SLEEPS TONIGHT, THE/Tine	(RCA Victor 47-7954)	.75	3.00	61
NOBODY BUT YOU/Mr. Cupid	(B.T. Puppy 505)	.75	3.00	65
ONLY MY FRIEND/Cattle Call	(B.T. Puppy 512)	.75	3.00	65
PLEASE SAY YOU WANT ME/Get A Job	(B.T. Puppy 522)	1.50	6.00	
PLEASE WRITE/I'll Always Love You	(Laurie 3180)	1.25	5.00	63
PORTRAIT OF MY LOVE/She Comes & Goes	(Warner Bros. 5900)	1.00	4.00	67
RIDDLE, THE/Big Boat	(RCA Victor 47-8018)	1.00	4.00	62
SHE LET'S HER HAIR DOWN (EARLY IN THE MORNING)/ Oh To Get Away	(Buddah 151)	.75	3.00	70
SYLVIE SLEEPIN'/A Message To The World	(B.T. Puppy 507)	.75	3.00	65

TITLE/FLIP	LABEL & NO.	GOOD	NEAR MINT	YR.
TRIBUTE TO THE BEACH BOYS '76, A/Benjis Cincinnati	(Kirshner 4263)	1.00	4.00	76
(Shown as by the Sands Of Time)				
THREE BELLS, THE/A Message To The World	(B.T. Puppy 516)	.75	3.00	66
THROW MY HEAD BACK/You & Me	(Bell 45,190)	.50	2.00	72
TILL/Poor Man	(Warner Bros. 7169)	1.00	4.00	68
TONIGHT I FELL IN LOVE/I'll Always Love You	(Warwick 615)	1.00	4.00	61
TONIGHT I MET AN ANGEL/Hindi Lullabye	(RCA Victor 47-8148)	1.00	4.00	65
WHEN I GO TO SLEEP AT NIGHT/Dry Your Eyes	(RCA Victor 47-7896)	1.25	5.00	61
WHEN THE SUMMER IS THROUGH/Sincerely	(RCA Victor 47-7925)	1.25	5.00	61
WHILE I DREAM/I Love My Baby	(Melba 104)	2.00	8.00	58
(With Neil Sedaka as lead vocalist. This group contained only half of the members who recorded later for RCA Victor.)				
WORLD IS FULL OF WONDERFUL THINGS/ Some People Sleep	(Warner Bros. 7255)	1.00	4.00	68
YOU'RE MY GIRL/Havin' Fun	(B.T. Puppy 504)	.75	3.00	64
Also see Cross Country				
Also see Damphier, Tom				
Also see Darrel & The Oxfords				
Also see Four Winds, The				
Also see Johnny & The Tokens				
Also see Sands Of Time, The				
TOKENS, The				
DOON-LANG/Come Dance With Me	(Gary 1006)	1.50	6.00	
OH WHAT A NIGHT/Juanita	(Date 2737)	1.00	4.00	61
TOLIVER, Mickey, & The Capitols				
DAY BY DAY/Little Things	(Gateway 721)	10.00	40.00	
(Shown as by the Capitols)				
ROSE-MARIE/Millie	(Cindy 3002)	6.25	25.00	
TOLLISON, Johnny				
DARK CLOUD OVER MEMPHIS/Dark Cloud Over Memphis	(Klub 5515)	.75	3.00	77
TOM & JERRY: see Simon & Garfunkel				
TOM SCOTT'S L.A. EXPRESS: see L.A. Express				
TOM THUMB & THE CASUALS				
I DON'T WANT MUCH/	(Verve 10478)	1.25	5.00	67
TONETTES, The				
HE LOVES ME NOT, HE LOVES ME/Uh-Oh	(Doe 103)	2.50	10.00	
OH WHAT A BABY/Howie	(ABC-Paramount 9905)	1.25	5.00	58
TONGUE				
KEEP ON TRUCIN'/Jazz On The Rag	(Hemisphere 101)	.75	3.00	70
TONGUE & GROOVE				
CHERRY BALL/Devil	(Fontana 1640)	1.50	6.00	69
COME ON IN MY KITCHEN/Mailman's Sack	(Fontana 1653)	1.50	6.00	69
TONIO K.				
BETTER LATE THAN NEVER/Willie & The Pigman	(Full Moon-Epic 50681)	.50	2.00	79
TONTO & THE RENEGADES				
EASY WAY OUT/	(Sound Of Screen 2178)	.75	3.00	
TONY & JOE				
FREEZE, THE/Gonna Get A Little Kissin' Tonight	(Dore 688)	.75	3.00	62
FREEZE, THE/Gonna Get A Little Kissin' Tonight	(Era 1075)	1.00	4.00	58
TWIST & FREEZE/Long Black Stockings	(Dore 619)	.75	3.00	61
TONY, BOB & JIMMY (The Lettermen)				
OLD RIVERS/Dutchman's Gold	(Capitol 4760)	1.00	4.00	62
TONY & THE BANDITS				
I'M GOIN' AWAY (FROM YOU)/ The Sun Don't Shine Now That You're Gone	(Coral 62473)	.75	3.00	65
IT'S A BIT OF ALRIGHT/(Oh No!) I Can't Lose	(Coral 62461)	.75	3.00	65
TONY & THE DAY DREAMS				
CHRISTMAS LULLABY/Handin' Hand	(Planet 1054)	1.50	6.00	58
I'LL NEVER TELL/Why Don't You Be Nice	(Planet 1009)	1.50	6.00	58
Also see Carmen, Tony, & The Spitfires				
TONY & THE HOLIDAYS				
THERE GOES MY HEART AGAIN/ My Love Is Real	(ABC-Paramount 10029)	3.75	15.00	59
Also see Sheppard, Buddy, & Holidays				
TONY & THE RAINDROPS				
WHILE WALKING/Our Love Is Over	(Chesapeake 609)	3.75	15.00	
TONY & THE TECHNICS				
WORKOUT WITH YOU PRETTY GIRL/Ha Ha He Told On You	(Chex 1010)	2.00	8.00	62
TONY & THE TWILIGHTS (Anthony & The Sophmores)				
BE MY GIRL/Did You Make Up Your Mind	(Jalynne 106)	5.00	20.00	
KEY TO MY HEART/Yes or No	(Red Top 127)	5.00	20.00	
SUMMER'S COMING/Shout My Name	(Colpix 199)	3.75	15.00	61
TONY'S TYGERS				
CAN'T BELIEVE/Still Love Her	(Teen Town 105)	1.00	4.00	68
(Shown as by the Tygers)				
DEBBIE ON MY MINS/	(Teen Town 103)	1.00	4.00	68
(Shown as by the Tygers)				
LITTLE BY LITTLE/Days & Nights	(A&M 921)	.75	3.00	68
LITTLE BY LITTLE/Days & Nights	(Teen Town 104)	1.00	4.00	68
TOOMORROW (Featuring Olivia Newton-John)				
GOING BACK/You're My Baby Now	(Kirshner 5005)	1.25	5.00	71
TOPICS, The: see Four Seasons, The				
TOP NOTES, The				
ALWAYS LATE (WHY LEAD ME ON)/Twist & Shout	(Atlantic 2115)	1.00	4.00	61
TOP SIX, The				
HANGING OF RAUNCHY REYNOLDS/ Hanging Of Raunchy Reynolds (Part 2)	(P.D.Q. 500)	3.75	15.00	
TOPSIDERS, The				
YOU CAN'T BE HAPPY BY YOURSELF/Baby Of Mine	(Atlantic 2215)	.75	3.00	64
TORKAYS, The				
KARATE/I Don't Like It (But What Can I Do)	(Stacy 960)	.75	3.00	63
TORME, Mel (Melvin Howard)				
COMIN' HOME BABY/Right Now	(Atlantic 2165)	.75	3.00	62
TORNADOES, The				
ICE CREAM MAN/Scales Of Justice (Theme)	(London 9614)	.75	3.00	63
LIKE LOCOMOTION/Globetrottin'	(London 9579)	.75	3.00	63
RIDIN' THE WIND/The Breeze & I	(London 9581)	.75	3.00	63
ROBOT/Life On Venus (Telstar I)	(London 9599)	.75	3.00	62
STINGRAY/Aqua Marina	(Tower 171)	.75	3.00	65
STOMPIN' THROUGH THE RYE/Early Bird	(Tower 152)	.75	3.00	65
TELSTAR/Jungle Fever	(London 9561)	.75	3.00	62
TORNADOES, The: see The Hollywood Tornadoes				
TORQUAYS, The				
ESCONDIDO/Surfer's Cry	(Gee Gee Cee 1009)	1.00	4.00	
HARMONICA MAN/Stoked On Her	(Rock-It 1005)	1.00	4.00	
IMAGE OF A GIRL/Stolen Moments	(Colpix 782)	1.50	6.00	65
IMAGE OF A GIRL/Stolen Moments	(Rock-It 1004)	1.00	4.00	
SHAKE A TAIL FEATHER/Temptation	(Punch 1007)	1.00	4.00	
TORRANCE, Richard				
BE BOP 'N' HOLLA/Let's Call It A Night	(Capitol 4644)	.50	2.00	79
DON'T LET ME DOWN AGAIN/	(Shelter 40374)	.50	2.00	75
(Shown as by Richard Torrance & Eureka)				
I CAN'T ASK FOR ANYMORE THAN YOU/ Long Lonely Nights	(Capitol 4554)	.50	2.00	78
RIO DE JANEIRO BLUES/Leave My Love Behind	(Capitol 4417)	.50	2.00	77
SOUTHERN BELLES/	(Shelter 40419)	.50	2.00	75
TORRES, Liz				
HUSTLE LATION/Hurt	(RCA 10519)	.50	2.00	76
TOSH, Peter (Of Bob Marley & The Wailers)				
BUK-IN-HAMM PALACE/Recruiting Soldiers	(Rolling Stones 20000)	.50	2.00	79
(YOU GOT TO WALK &) DON'T LOOK BACK (With Mick Jagger)/ Soon Come	(Rolling Stones 19308)	1.00	4.00	78
(With "Rolling Stones" at label's top)				
(YOU GOT TO WALK &) DON'T LOOK BACK (With Mick Jagger)/ Soon Come	(Rolling Stones 19308)	.50	2.00	78
(YOU GOT TO WALK &) DON'T LOOK BACK (With Mick Jagger)/ Soon Come	(Rolling Stones 7500)	1.50	6.00	78
(YOU GOT TO WALK &) DON'T LOOK BACK/ (You Got To Walk &) Don't Look Back	(Rolling Stones PR-130)	3.00	12.00	78
(Promotional issue)				
TOTO				
HOLD THE LINE/Takin' It Back	(Columbia 10830)	.50	2.00	78
GEORGY PORGY/Child's Anthem	(Columbia 10944)	.50	2.00	79
I'LL SUPPLY THE LOVE/You Are The Flower	(Columbia 10898)	.50	2.00	79
99/Hydra	(Columbia 11173)	.50	2.00	79
TOUCH (Featuring Don Galucci)				
MISS TEACH/We Feel Fire	(Coliseum 2712)	.75	3.00	
Also see Don & The Goodtimes				
TOW-AWAY ZONE				
SEARCHIN'/Shabd	(Epic 10369)	1.50	6.00	68
TOWER OF POWER				
BACK ON THE STREETS AGAIN/Sparkling In The Sand	(San Francisco)	1.25	5.00	64
DON'T CHANGE HORSES (IN THE MIDDLE OF A STREAM)/ I Got The Chop	(Warner Bros. 7828)	.50	2.00	74
DOWN TO THE NIGHTCLUB/ What Happened To The World That Day	(Warner Bros. 7635)	.75	3.00	72
SO VERY HARD TO GO/	(Warner Bros. 7687)	.50	2.00	73
THIS TIME IT'S REAL/Soul Vacation	(Warner Bros. 7733)	.50	2.00	73
TIME WILL TELL/Oakland Stroll	(Warner Bros. 7796)	.75	3.00	74
WHAT IS HIP?/What Is Hip?	(Warner Bros. 7748)	.75	3.00	73
WHEN I GROW TOO OLD TO DREAM/	(Warner Bros. 7635)	.75	3.00	72
YOU OUGHT TO BE HAVIN' FUN/	(Columbia 10409)	.50	2.00	76
YOU'RE STILL A YOUNG MAN/	(Warner Bros. 7612)	.75	3.00	72
TOWNSEND, Ed				
AND THEN CAME LOVE/Little Bitty Dave	(Challenge 9129)	.75	3.00	61
BE MY LOVE/With No One To Love	(Capitol 4314)	1.00	4.00	59
DREAM WORLD/Cherrigale	(Warner Bros. 5200)	.75	3.00	61
FOR YOUR LOVE/Over & Over Again	(Capitol 3926)	1.00	4.00	58
HOLD ON/This Little Love Of Mine	(Capitol 4240)	1.00	4.00	59
I CAN'T LEAVE YOU ALONE/I Want To Go To Your House	(Dynasty 643)	1.00	4.00	60
I LOVE EVERYTHING ABOUT YOU/ Stay With Me (A Little While Longer)	(Warner Bros. 5174)	.75	3.00	60
I LOVE TO HEAR THAT BEAT/You Walked In	(Challenge 9144)	.75	3.00	62
LOVER COME BACK TO ME/Don't Ever Leave Me	(Capitol 4171)	1.00	4.00	59
WHAT SHALL I DO/Please Never Change	(Capitol 3994)	1.00	4.00	58
WHEN I GROW TOO OLD TO DREAM/ You Are My Everything	(Capitol 4048)	1.00	4.00	58
TOWSHEND, Pete, & Ronnie Land				
KEEP ME TURNING/Nowhere To Run	(MCA 40878)	.50	2.00	78
MY BABY GIVES IT AWAY/April Fool	(MCA 40818)	.50	2.00	77
Also see Angie				
Also see Small Faces				
Also see Who, The				
TOWNSMEN, The				
IS IT ALL OVER/Just A Little Bit	(Herald 585)	1.25	5.00	63
MOONLIGHT WAS MADE FOR LOVERS/ I'm In The Mood For Love	(Joey 6202)	3.75	15.00	63
THAT'S ALL I'LL EVER NEED/I Can't Go (By Louie Lymon)	(P.J. 1340)	6.25	25.00	63
TOYS, The				
ATTACK!/See How They Run	(Dyno Voice 214)	.75	3.00	65
BABY TOYS/Happy Birthday Broken Heart	(Dyno Voice 222)	.75	3.00	66
CAN'T GET ENOUGH OF YOU BABY/Silver Spoon	(Dyno Voice 219)	.75	3.00	66
CIAO BABY/I Got Carried Away	(Philips 40432)	.75	3.00	67
I CLOSE MY EYES/My Love Sonata	(Philips 40456)	.75	3.00	67
LOVER'S CONCERTO, A/This Night	(Dyno Voice 209)	.75	3.00	65
MAY MY HEART BE CAST INTO STONE/On Backstreet	(Dyno Voice 218)	.75	3.00	66
TRACE, Al				
PRETTY EYED BABY/That's One For Me	(Mercury 5609)	.75	3.00	63
TRACERS, The: see Stones, The				
TRACES, The (With Sal Corrente)				
RUNAROUND SUE/Nothing Matter Now	(Laurie 3515)	2.00	8.00	69
WHAT AM I TO DO/Love Me Forever	(Laurie 3493)	2.00	8.00	69
Also see Runarounds, The				
TRADEMARKS, The				
BAHA REE BA (PART 1)/Baha Ree Ba (Part 2) (Instrumental)	(Jubal 91)	1.00	4.00	63
I NEED YOU/If I Was Gone	(Palmer 5018)	1.25	5.00	
TRADE WINDS, The (Pete Anders & Vinnie Poncia)				
CATCH ME IN THE MEADOW/I Believe In Her	(Kama Sutra 218)	.75	3.00	66
GIRL FROM GREENWICH VILLAGE/ Rock & Roll Show In Town	(Red Bird 028)	1.00	4.00	65
MIND EXCURSION/Little Susan's Dreamin'	(Kama Sutra 212)	.75	3.00	66
MIND EXCURSION/Only When I'm Dreamin'	(Kama Sutra 234)	.75	3.00	67
NEW YORK'S A LONELY TOWN/Club Seventeen	(Red Bird 020)	.75	3.00	65
SUMMERTIME GIRL/Party Starts At Nine	(Red Bird 033)	1.00	4.00	65
Also see Innocence, The				
Also see Treasures, The				
Also see Videls, The				
TRADEWINDS, The				
FURRY MURRAY/Crossroads	(RCA Victor 47-7553)	1.00	4.00	59
TWINS/Toni	(RCA Victor 47-7511)	1.00	4.00	59
TRAFFIC				
COLOURED RAIN/ Here We Go Around The Mulberry Bush	(United Artists 50232)	.75	3.00	68
EMPTY PAGES/Stranger To Myself	(United Artists 50692)	.75	3.00	70
FEELIN' ALRIGHT/Withering Tree	(United Artists 50460)	.75	3.00	68
GIMME SOME LOVIN' (PART 1)/ Gimme Some Lovin' (Part 2)	(United Artists 50841)	.75	3.00	71
HOLE IN MY SHOE/Smiling Phases	(United Artists 50218)	.75	3.00	67
MEDICATED GOO/Pearly Queen	(United Artists 50500)	.75	3.00	69
PAPER SUN/Giving To You	(United Artists 50195)	.75	3.00	67
ROCK & ROLL STEW (PART 1)/Rock & Roll Stew (Part 2)	(Island 1201)	.50	2.00	72
WALKING IN THE WIND/ Walking In The Wind (Instrumental)	(Asylum 45027)	.50	2.00	74
TRAINS, The				
14 & GETTING OLDER/The Beware Song	(Swan 4203)	1.25	5.00	65
PLAN, THE/We Two	(Swan 4196)	1.25	5.00	65
TRAITS, The				
HARLEM SHUFFLE/Somewhere	(Universal 30494)	1.25	5.00	66
HARLEM SHUFFLE/Somewhere	(Scepter 12169)	.75	3.00	66
LINDA LOU/Little Mama	(Renner 221)	.75	3.00	
TRAKSTOD				
CAROLINA TRAIN/Say Hello	(Philips 40655)	1.00	4.00	70
TRAMPS, The				
RIDE ON/You're A Square	(Arvee 548)	2.00	8.00	59
YOUR LOVE/Midnight Flyer	(Arvee 570)	2.00	8.00	59
T.R. & THE YARDSMEN				
I TRIED/Movin' Up	(Hideout 1005)	1.25	5.00	
TRANSATLANTIC WINKHAM CHIKEN NO. 5				
CRYSTAL MOUNTING, THE/You'll Never Find Her	(Silverado 101)	3.00	12.00	
TRAN-SISTERS, The				
LET IT IN/Tomorrow The World Will Know	(Pickwick City 1003)	1.25	5.00	
TRAPESE				
COAST TO COAST/Your Love Is Alright	(Threshold 67011)	.50	2.00	72
TRASH				
GOLDEN SLUMBERS-CARRY THAT WEIGHT/Trash Can	(Apple 1811)	.75	3.00	69
ROAD TO NOWHERE/Illusions	(Apple 1804)	.75	3.00	69

TITLE/FLIP	LABEL & NO.	GOOD	NEAR MINT	YR.
TRASHMEN, The				
BAD NEWS/On The Move	(Garrett 4005)	1.00	4.00	64
BIRD DANCE BEAT/A-Bone	(Garrett 4003)	1.00	4.00	64
GREEN GREEN BACKS OF HOME/Address Enclosed	(Metromedia 7927)	.75	3.00	68
NEW GENERATION/Peppermint Man	(Garrett 4010)	1.25	5.00	64
REAL LIVE DOLL/Dancing With Santa	(Garrett 4013)	1.25	5.00	64
SAME LINES/Hanging On Me	(Tribe 8315)	2.00	8.00	66
SURFIN' BIRD/King Of The Surf	(Garrett 4002)	1.00	4.00	63
WHOA DAD/Walkin' My Baby	(Garrett 4012)	1.25	5.00	64
TRAVEL AGENCY				
WHAT'S A MAN/	(Viva 348)	.75	3.00	
TRAVELERS, The				
JUNE, JULY, AUGUST & SEPTEMBER/ What A Weekend	(ABC-Paramount 10119)	1.00	4.00	60
MALIBU SUNSET/Hang On	(Yellow Sand 452)	.75	3.00	65
ROCK ME BABY/Girl In The Bikini	(MGM 928)	.75	3.00	59
SEVEN MINUTES TILL FOUR/Traveler	(Don Ray 5965)	.75	3.00	62
SHE'S GOT THE BLUES/Spanish Moon	(Princess 52)	1.00	4.00	63
SHE'S GOT THE BLUES/Spanish Moon	(Vault 911)	.75	3.00	63
TIE ME SURFER BOARD DOWN, SPORT/In The Pines	(Gass 1000)	1.00	4.00	63
TRAVELERS, The				
OH MY LOVE/White Rose	(Decca 31282)	1.25	5.00	61
WHY/Teen Age Machine Age	(Andex 4006)	2.00	8.00	
TRAVELERS, The (Featuring Frank Lopez)				
LENORA/Betty Jean	(Atlas 1086)	2.00	8.00	57
TRAVELERS IV, The				
MESSAGE FOR YOU, A/This Happens To Me	(Rox 1001)	1.50	6.00	
TRAVERS, Mary (Of Peter, Paul & Mary)				
AIR THAT I BREATHE, THE/You Turn Me Around	(Chrysalis 2202)	.50	2.00	78
FOLLOW ME/I Guess I'd Rather Be In Colorado	(Warner Bros. 7481)	.75	3.00	71
FREEDOM/	(Chrysalis 2367)	.50	2.00	79
SONG IS LOVE, THE/Erika With The Windy Yellow Hair-Rhymes & Reasons	(Warner Bros. 7517)	.75	3.00	71
TRAVERS, Pat				
BOOM BOOM (OUT GO THE LIGHTS)/Go All Night	(Polydor 2003)	.50	2.00	79
GO ALL NIGHT/Hammerhead	(Polydor 14529)	.50	2.00	78
STEVIE/What You Mean To Be (Instrumental)	(Polydor 14416)	.50	2.00	77
TRAVIS & BOB (Travis Pritchett & Bob Weaver)				
LITTLE BITTY JOHNNY/Teenage Vision	(Sandy 1019)	1.00	4.00	59
OH YEAH/Lover's Rendezvous	(Sandy 1024)	1.00	4.00	59
POCAHANTAS/Day Dreams	(Big Top 3054)	.75	3.00	60
TELL HIM NO/We're Too Young	(Sandy 1017)	.75	3.00	59
(Label reads "Distributed by Dot")				
TELL HIM NO/We're Too Young	(Sandy 1017)	1.25	5.00	59
(Label does not read "Distributed by Dot")				
WAKE UP & CRY/That's How Long	(Sandy 1029)	1.00	4.00	59
TRAVIS & PRENTISS				
PEGGIE SUE/	(Ara 206)	1.00	4.00	
TRAVIS, Tony				
LOVE IS THE $64,000 QUESTION/Drummer Boy	(RCA Victor 47-6476)	1.00	4.00	56

TITLE/FLIP	LABEL & NO.	GOOD	NEAR MINT	YR.
TRAVOLTA, Joey				
I DON'T WANNA GO/Big Trouble	(Millenium 615)	.50	2.00	78
IF THIS IS LOVE/	(Millenium 623)	.50	2.00	78
Joey is John Travolta's brother.				
TRAVOLTA, John				
ALL STRUNG OUT ON YOU/Easy Evil	(Midland Int'l. 10907)	.50	2.00	77
(FEEL SO GOOD) SLOW DANCING/	(Midland Int'l. 10977)	.50	2.00	77
GREASED LIGHTNING/Rock & Roll Is Here To Stay (By Sha Na Na)	(RSO 909)	.50	2.00	78
LET HER IN/Big Trouble	(Midland Int'l. 10623)	.50	2.00	76
LET HER IN/Big Trouble (Promotional picture sleeve)	(Midland Int'l. 10623)	1.00	4.00	76
RAZZMATAZZ/What Would They Say	(Midland Int'l. 11206)	.50	2.00	78
SANDY/	(RSO 930)	.50	2.00	79
WHENEVER I'M AWAY FROM YOU/	(Midland Int'l. 10780)	.75	3.00	76
TRAVOLTA, John, & Olivia Newton-John				
SUMMER NIGHTS/Rock 'N' Roll Party Queen (By Louis St. Louis of Sha Na Na)	(RSO 906)	.50	2.00	78
YOU'RE THE ONE THAT I WANT/ Alone At a Drive-In Movie (Instrumental)	(RSO 891)	.50	2.00	78
TRAYLOR, Jack, & Steelwind				
CHILD OF NATURE/Time To Be Happy	(Grunt 0057)	.75	3.00	
TREASURE (With Felix Cavaliere)				
I WANNA LOVE YOU/	(Epic 50519)	.50	2.00	78
TREASURES (Pete Anders & Vinnie Poncia)				
HOLD ME TIGHT/Pete Meets Vinnie	(Shirley 500)	3.75	15.00	64
HOLD ME TIGHT/Pete Meets Vinnie (Promotional issue)	(Shirley 500)	3.00	12.00	64
Also see Tradewinds, The				
TREBLE CHORDS, The				
TERESA/My Little Girl	(Decca 31015)	6.25	25.00	59
TREBLE TONES, The				
CRAWL, THE/Treble Rock	(Atlas 260)	1.00	4.00	60
TREE MENDOUS STUMPS, The				
LISTEN TO LOVE/Jennie Lee	(Record 20013)	2.00	8.00	
TREE SWINGERS, The				
KOOKIE LITTLE PARADISE/ Teaching The Natives To Sing	(Guyden 2036)	1.00	4.00	60
TREMELOES, The				
(CALL ME) NUMBER ONE/Instand Whip	(Epic 10548)	.75	3.00	69
BLUE SUEDE TIE/	(Epic 10996)	.75	3.00	70
EVEN THE BAD TIMES ARE GOOD/Jenny's All Right	(Epic 10233)	.75	3.00	67
GOOD DAY SUNSHINE/What A State I'm In	(Epic 10075)	.75	3.00	66
HARD WOMAN/	(DJM 1008)	.50	2.00	74
HELULE HELULE/Girl From Nowhere	(Epic 10328)	.75	3.00	68
HERE COMES MY BABY/Gentleman Of Pleasure	(Epic 10139)	.75	3.00	67
I SHALL BE RELEASED/I Miss My Baby	(Epic 10437)	.75	3.00	69
MY LITTLE LADY/All The World To Me	(Epic 10376)	.75	3.00	68
SEPTEMBER, NOVEMBER, DECEMBER/	(DJM 1016)	.50	2.00	75
SILENCE IS GOLDEN/Let Your Hair Hang Down	(Epic 10184)	.75	3.00	67
SUDDENLY YOU LOVE ME/Suddenly Winter	(Epic 10293)	.75	3.00	68
TREMONT, Jimmy, & The Bronx Dukes				
I NEVER TELL HER I LOVE HER/ Submarine Races (Part 2)	(Street Corner SC-113)	.50	2.00	79
TREMONTS, The (With Joe Dee)				
BELIEVE MY HEART/Legend Of Love	(Brunswick 9-55217)	1.50	6.00	61
Also see Dee, Joe, & the Top Hands				
TREN-DELLS, The				
MOMENTS LIKE THIS/I Miss You So	(Tilt 788)	2.00	8.00	
NIGHT OWL/Hully Gully Jones	(Capitol 4852)	1.00	4.00	62
NITE OWL/Hully Gully Jones	(Jam J1100)	1.50	6.00	62
TREND-TONES, The				
THIS IS LOVE/Never Again	(Superb 100)	2.00	8.00	
TREN-TEENS, The				
MY BABY'S GONE/Your Yah Yah Is Gone	(Carnival 501)	1.50	6.00	
TRENTONS, The				
ALL ALONE/Star Bright	(Shepherd 2204)	2.50	10.00	62
Also see Hi Tones, The				
Also see Shy Tones, The				
TRETONES, The				
BLIND DATE/Cool Baby	(B-W 604)	.75	3.00	60
TREVOR, Van				
C'MON NOW BABY/A Fling Of The Past (With the 4 Seasons)	(Vivid 1004)	3.75	15.00	
I WANT TO CRY/Tuesday Girl	(Atlantic 2175)	1.25	5.00	62
T-REX (Featuring Marc Bolan)				
BANG A GONG (GET IT ON)/Raw Ramp	(Reprise 1032)	.50	2.00	71
BY THE LIGHT OF THE MAGICAL MOON/ Find A Little Wood	(Blue Thumb 212)	1.00	4.00	72
CHILD STAR/Debora (Shown as by Tyrannosaurus Rex)	(A&M 955)	1.50	6.00	68
GROOVER, THE/Born To Boogie	(Reprise 1161)	1.00	4.00	74
HOT LOVE/Rip Off	(Reprise 1170)	.75	3.00	74
HOT LOVE/One Inch Rock-Seagull Woman	(Reprise 1006)	.75	3.00	71
JEEPSTER/Rip Off	(Reprise 1056)	.75	3.00	71
METAL GURU/Lady	(Reprise 1095)	1.00	4.00	73
PRECIOUS STAR/	(Casablanca 810)	.75	3.00	75
RIDE A WHITE SWAN/Summertime Blues (Shown as by Tyrannosaurus Rex)	(Blue Thumb 7121)	1.00	4.00	71
TELEGRAM SAM/Cadillac	(Reprise 1078)	.75	3.00	72
TRIANGLE (Featuring Vinny Corella)				
JACQUELINE/Your Love Comes Shinin' Through	(Paramount 0055)	2.50	10.00	
JUDGE & JURY/Midnight Magic Man	(Paramount 0123)	2.50	10.00	
(Also see Randy & the Rainbows)				
TRIANGLES, The				
MY OH MY/Really I Do	(Fifo 107)	2.00	8.00	
TRIBE, The				
FICKLE LITTLE GIRL/Try Try	(Fenton 2088)	1.00	4.00	
TRIBUNES, The				
CODE OF LOVE, THE/Now That You're One	(Derrick 502)	1.25	5.00	
TRIBUTES, The				
RINGO DINGO/Here Comes Ringo	(Donna 1391)	1.25	5.00	64
TRICKELS, The				
WITH EACH STEP A TEAR/Outside The Chapel Door	(Gone 5078)	1.50	6.00	60
WITH EACH STEP A TEAR/When I Fall In Love	(Gone 5075)	1.50	6.00	60
TRICKSTER				
IF THAT'S THE WAY THE FEELING TAKES YOU/Goodbye '65	(Jet 5051)	.50	2.00	78
TRIDELS, The				
LAND OF LOVE/Image Of My Love	(San-Dee 1009)	3.75	15.00	
TRIGGER				
SOMEBODY LIKE YOU/	(Casablanca 920)	.50	2.00	78
TRI-LADS, The				
CHERRY PIE/Alway's Be True	(Bullseye 1003)	1.00	4.00	59
TRI-LITES, The				
WILL TO-MORROW BE JUST ANOTHER DAY/ Hot Dog Here He Comes	(Enith 721)	2.00	8.00	
TRILLION				
GIVE ME YOUR MONEY, HONEY/Fancy Action	(Epic 50707)	.50	2.00	79
HOLD OUT/Big Boy	(Epic 50670)	.50	2.00	79
TRILOGY				
I'M BEGINNING TO FEEL IT/Goodbye Flying	(Mercury 73154)	.75	3.00	70
TRIPLETS, The				
GENTLY MY LOVE/Bagdad Beat	(Dore 574)	1.25	5.00	60
TRIPPERS, The				
TAKING CARE OF BUSINESS/Charlena	(Ruby-Doo 5)	1.50	6.00	
TAKING CARE OF BUSINESS/Charlena	(Crescendo 387)	.75	3.00	67
TRIPSICHORD MUSIC BOX, The				
TIMES & SEASONS/Sunday The Third	(San Francisco Sound 115)	1.50	6.00	
TRI-TONES, The				
TEARDROPS/Every Time I Think Of You	(Miss Julie No # given)	3.75	15.00	
Also see Parallels, The				
TRIUMPH				
HOLD ON/Just A Game	(RCA 11569)	.50	2.00	79
LAY IT ON THE LINE/American Girls	(RCA 11690)	.50	2.00	79
ROCKY MOUNTAIN WAY/Bringing It On Home	(RCA 11440)	.50	2.00	78
TRIUMPHS, The: see Thomas, B.J.				
TRIUMPHS, The				
BURNT BISCUITS/Raw Dough	(Volt 100)	.75	3.00	61
TRIUMVIRAT				
WATERFALL/Jo Ann Walker	(Capitol 4700)	.50	2.00	79
TROGGS, The				
ANY WAY YOU WANT ME/66-5-4-3-2-1	(Fontana 1585)	1.00	4.00	67
EASY LOVIN'/Give Me Something	(Page One 21030)	.75	3.00	70
EVERYTHING'S FUNNY/	(Pye 71011)	.50	2.00	75
EVIL WOMAN/Heads Or Tails	(Page One 21026)	.75	3.00	69
GIRL IN BLACK/Night Of The Long Grass	(Fontana 1593)	1.00	4.00	67
GIVE IT TO ME/You're Lying	(Fontana 1576)	1.00	4.00	67
GOOD VIBRATIONS/Push It Up To Me	(Pye 71015)	.50	2.00	75
HIP HIP HOORAY/Say Darlin'	(Fontana 1634)	1.00	4.00	69
I CAN'T CONTROL MYSELF/Gonna Make You	(Atco 6444)	1.25	5.00	66
I CAN'T CONTROL MYSELF/Gonna Make You	(Fontana 1557)	.75	3.00	66
LOVE IS ALL AROUND/When Will The Rain Come	(Fontana 1605)	.75	3.00	68
ROLLING STONE/	(Private Stock 45102)	.50	2.00	77
SATISFACTION/	(Pye 71054)	.50	2.00	76
SUMMERTIME/	(Pye 71035)	.50	2.00	76
SURPRISE, SURPRISE (I NEED YOU)/Cousin Jane	(Fontana 1630)	1.00	4.00	68
WILD THING/With A Girl Like You	(Atco 6415)	1.25	5.00	66
WILD THING/From Home	(Fontana 1548)	.75	3.00	66
WITH A GIRL LIKE YOU/Wild Thing	(Atco 6415)	1.00	4.00	67
WITH A GIRL LIKE YOU/I Want You	(Atco 6415)	1.25	5.00	66
WITH A GIRL LIKE YOU/I Want You	(Fontana 1552)	.75	3.00	66
YOU/The Raver	(Page One 21035)	.75	3.00	70
YOU CAN CRY IF YOU WANT TO/ There's Something About You	(Fontana 1622)	1.00	4.00	68
TROIANO, Dominic (Of The Guess Who)				
WE ALL NEED LOVE/Ambush	(Capitol 4709)	.50	2.00	79
TROJANS, The				
ALL NIGHT LONG/I Wanted You So Long	(Triangle 51317)	1.25	5.00	60
TALK TO ME/We Belong Together	(Air Town 003)	1.25	5.00	
TROLLS, The				
EVERY DAY & EVERY NIGHT/Are You The One?	(ABC 10820)	.75	3.00	66
I GOT TO HAVE YOU/Don't Come Around	(USA 905)	.75	3.00	68
LAUGHING ALL THE WAY/Something Here Inside	(ABC 10884)	.75	3.00	66
STUPID GIRL/I Don't Recall	(Warrior 173)	1.50	6.00	
THERE WAS A TIME/They Don't Know	(ABC 10916)	.75	3.00	67
WHO WAS THAT BOY/Baby, What You Ain't Got	(ABC 10952)	.75	3.00	67
TRONICS, The				
BIG SCROUNGY, THE/South American Sunset	(Landa 680)	.75	3.00	61
PICKIN' & STOMPIN'/Cantina	(Landa 676)	.75	3.00	61
TROOPER				
GENERAL HAND GRENADE/	(Legend 40480)	.75	3.00	75
(IT'S BEEN A) LONG TIME/Oh, Pretty Lady	(MCA 40799)	.50	2.00	77
LIVE FROM THE MOON/The Moment That It Takes	(MCA 40968)	.50	2.00	78
RAISE A LITTLE HELL/A Fine Mess (You've Gotten Us Into)	(MCA 40924)	.50	2.00	78
ROLLER RINK/Baby Woncha Please Come Home	(Legend 40447)	.75	3.00	75
SANTA MARIA/Whatcha Gonna Do About Me	(Legend 40685)	.75	3.00	77
TWO FOR TWO SHOW/	(Legend 40583)	.75	3.00	76
WE'RE HERE FOR A GOOD TIME/Loretta	(MCA 40738)	.50	2.00	77
TROPHIES, The				
DESIRE/Doggone It	(Challenge 9133)	6.25	25.00	62
FELICIA/That's All I Want From You	(Challenge 9170)	2.00	8.00	62
PEG O' MY HEART/I Laughed So Hard I Cried	(Challenge 9149)	2.50	10.00	62
WALKIN' THE DOG/Somethin' Else	(Nork 79907)	1.25	5.00	
TROPICS, The				
FOR A LONG TIME/	(Thames 103)	.75	3.00	
TROWER, Robin (Of Procol Harum)				
CALEDONIA/Messin' The Blues	(Chrysalis 2122)	.50	2.00	76
IT'S FOR YOU/Birthday Boy	(Chrysalis 2272)	.50	2.00	78
MAN OF THE WORLD/Take A Fast Train	(Chrysalis 2009)	.50	2.00	72
MY LOVE (BURNING LOVE)/Sail On	(Chrysalis 2238)	.50	2.00	78
SOMEBODY CALLING/Bluebird	(Chrysalis 2206)	.50	2.00	78
SWEET WINE OF LOVE/In City Dreams	(Chrysalis 2172)	.50	2.00	77
TOO ROLLING STONED/Too Rolling Stoned (Part 2)	(Chrysalis 2113)	.50	2.00	76
TROY				
AND TOMORROW MEANS ANOTHER DAY WE'RE APART/	(Columbia 45748)	1.25	5.00	73
PLEASE SAY YOU WANT ME/It's Just Not The Same	(Columbia 45616)	1.50	6.00	72
TROY, Benny, & Maze				
I DON'T KNOW YOU ANYMORE/ Things Are Lookin' Better	(20th Century 6699)	.75	3.00	
TROY, Doris				
AIN'T THAT CUTE/Vaya Con Dios (With George Harrison)	(Apple 1820)	.75	3.00	70
JACOB'S LADDER/Get Back (With George Harrison)	(Apple 1824)	.75	3.00	70
JUST ONE LOOK/Bossa Nova Blues	(Atlantic 2188)	.75	3.00	63
LYIN' EYES/	(Midland Int'l. 10806)	.50	2.00	76
TRUANTS, The				
TRUANT, THE/Sunset Surf	(Rock-It 1002)	.75	3.00	
TRUC				
THERE'S A MOON OUT TONIGHT/ Me My Baby & My 57 Chevy	(United Artists XW-393)	.75	3.00	73
THERE'S A MOON OUT TONIGHT/ Me, My Baby & My 57 Chevy	(Zero 002)	1.25	5.00	72
TRUSTIN HOWARD				
DIS JOCKEY MEETING/Aladin's Lamp	(Reprise 20139)	3.75	15.00	62
TUBES, The				
DON'T TOUCH ME THERE/Proud To Be An American	(A&M 1826)	.50	2.00	76
PRIME TIME/No Way Out	(A&M 2120)	.50	2.00	78
SHOW ME A REASON/	(A&M 2037)	.50	2.00	78
WHAT DO YOU WANT FROM LIFE/	(A&M 1755)	.50	2.00	76
WHITE PUNKS ON DOPE/ (Promotional issue)	(A&M 11864)	.75	3.00	75
WHITE PUNKS ON DOPE/ (Promotional picture sleeve)	(A&M 11864)	1.00	4.00	75
TUCKER, Mark, & Beach				
SULTRY SUMMER SIREN-MORE THAN JUST FRIENDS/ Kotzebue (Orange plastic)	(Tetrapod Spools 99752)	.75	3.00	79
TUCKER, Marshall, Band: see Marshall Tucker Band, The				
TUCKY BUZZARD				
GOLD MEDALLIONS/	(Passport 7901)	.50	2.00	74
TUFANO & GIAMMERESE (Of The Buckinghams)				
MUSIC EVERYWHERE/Just A Dream Away	(Ode 66033)	.50	2.00	73
TIME CHANGE/Let In The Light	(Ode 66122)	.50	2.00	76
TUFF RATS, The				
(I WANNA KNOW) WHO'S BEEN SLEEPING HERE?/Rats	(Sire 1015)	.50	2.00	78
TUFFS, The: see Bell, Kay, & The Tuffs				
TULLY, Lee, With Milt Moss				
AROUND THE WORLD WITH ELWOOD PRETZEL/ Around The World With Elwood Pretzel (Part 2) (Novelty/Break-in)	(Flair-X 3007)	3.00	12.00	56
TUNE ROCKERS, The				
GREEN MOSQUITO, THE/Warm Up (Instrumental)	(United Artists 139)	1.00	4.00	58
TUNES, The				
LIE, THE/Only Time Will Tell	(Pel 345)	.75	3.00	
TURBO-JETS, The				
BINGO/In Reverse	(Federal 45-12349)	1.00	4.00	60
TURKS, The				
BAJA/Dianne	(P.B.D. 112)	1.00	4.00	
HULLY GULLY/Rockville U.S.A.	(Class 256)	1.00	4.00	59
TURNBOW, Jeanne				
BEATTLE BUG/Summertime	(Ben-Ron 1393)	1.25	5.00	64
TURNER & KIRWAN OF WEXFORD				
GIRL NEXT DOOR, THE/Warts 'N All	(Peters Int'l. 900)	.50	2.00	77

TITLE/FLIP — LABEL & NO. — GOOD — NEAR MINT — YR.

TURNER, Jesse Lee
BABY PLEASE DON'T TEASE/Thinkin' .... (Carlton 509) 1.00 4.00 59
BALLAD OF BILLIE SOL ESTES/Shotgun Boogie.... (GNP-Crescendo 188) .75 3.00 63
DO I WORRY (YES I DO)/All Right, Be That Way ...... (Top Rank 2064) .75 3.00 60
ELOPERS, THE/Together .... (Sudden 105) .75 3.00
LITTLE SPACE GIRL'S FATHER, THE/
Valley Of Lost Soldiers .... (Imperial 5649) .75 3.00 60
LITTLE SPACE GIRL, THE/Shake, Baby, Shake .... (Carlton 496) 1.00 4.00 59
TEEN-AGE MISERY/That's My Girl .... (Fraternity 855) 1.00 4.00 59
VOICE CHANGING SONG, THE/All You Gotta Do ... (GNP-Crescendo 184) .75 3.00 63

TURNER, Sammy (With The Twisters)
ALWAYS/Symphony .... (Big Top 3029) .75 3.00 59
ALWAYS/Symphony .... (Big Top 3029) 2.00 8.00 59
(Stereo single issue)
FALLING/Raincoat In The River .... (Big Top 3089) .75 3.00 61
FOOLS FALL IN LOVE/Stay My Love .... (Big Top 3049) .75 3.00 60
GOODNIGHT IRENE/I Want To Be Loved .... (Big Top 3038) .75 3.00 60
LAVENDER BLUE/Wrapped Up In A Dream .... (Pacific 3016) 2.50 10.00 59
LAVENDER BLUE/Wrapped Up In A Dream .... (Big Top 3016) .75 3.00 59
LAVENDER BLUE/Wrapped Up In A Dream .... (Big Top 3016) 1.00 4.00 59
(Stereo single issue)
PARADISE/I'd Be A Fool Again .... (Big Top 3032) .75 3.00 60
SWEET ANNIE LAURIE/Thunderbolt .... (Big Top 3007) .75 3.00 59
"Lavender Blue" was in reprocessed stereo on the stereo single issue. "Always"/"Symphony" was in true stereo on the single but reprocessed on the Big Top LP.

TURTLES, The (With Mark Volman & Howard Kaylan)
AIN'T GONNA PARTY NO MORE/Who Would Ever Think
That I Would Marry Margaret .... (White Whale 341) .75 3.00 70
CAN I GET TO KNOW YOU BETTER/Like The Seasons .... (White Whale 238) .75 3.00 66
ELENORE/Surfer Dan .... (White Whale 276) .75 3.00 68
EVE OF DESTRUCTION/Wanderin' Kind .... (White Whale 355) .75 3.00 70
GRIM REAPER OF LOVE/Come Back .... (White Whale 231) .75 3.00 66
GUIDE FOR THE MARRIED MAN/Think I'll Run Away . (White Whale 251) .75 3.00 67
HAPPY TOGETHER/Like The Seasons .... (White Whale 244) .75 3.00 67
IS IT ANY WONDER/Wanderin' Kind .... (White Whale 350) .75 3.00 70
IT AIN'T ME BABE/Almost There .... (White Whale 222) .75 3.00 65
LADY-O/Somewhere Friday Night .... (White Whale 334) .75 3.00 69
LET ME BE/Your Maw Said You Cried .... (White Whale 224) .75 3.00 65
LOVE IN THE CITY/Bachelor Mother .... (White Whale 326) .75 3.00 69
ME ABOUT YOU/Think I'll Run Away .... (White Whale 364) .75 3.00 70
OUTSIDE CHANCE/We'll Meet Again .... (White Whale 234) .75 3.00 66
SHE'D RATHER BE WITH ME/Walking Song .... (White Whale 249) .75 3.00 67
SHE'S MY GIRL/Chicken Little Was Right .... (White Whale 260) .75 3.00 67
SOUND ASLEEP/Umbassa & The Dragon .... (White Whale 264) .75 3.00 68
STORY OF ROCK & ROLL/Can't You Hear The Cows.... (White Whale 273) .75 3.00 68
WHO WOULD THINK THAT I WOULD EVER MARRY MARGARET/
We Ain't Gonna Party No More .... (White Whale 341) .75 3.00 70
YOU BABY/Wanderin' Kind .... (White Whale 227) .75 3.00 66
YOU DON'T HAVE TO WALK IN THE RAIN/Come Over. (White Whale 308) .75 3.00 69
YOU KNOW WHAT I MEAN/Rugs Of Wood & Flowers .. (White Whale 254) .75 3.00 67
YOU SHOWED ME/Buzz Saw .... (White Whale 292) .75 3.00 69
Also see Crossfires, The
Also see Flo & Eddie

TWITTY, Conway (Harold Jenkins)
C'EST SI BON/Don't You Dare Let Me Down .... (MGM K-12969) .75 3.00 61
COMFY 'N COZY/A Little Piece Of My Heart .... (MGM K-13072) .75 3.00 62
DANNY BOY/Halfway To Heaven .... (MGM K-12826) .75 3.00 59
DANNY BOY/Halfway To Heaven .... (MGM SK-50130) 2.00 8.00 59
(Stereo single issue)
DOUBLE TALK BABY/Why Can't I Get Through To You . (Mercury 71384) 3.75 15.00 58
GO ON & CRY/She Loves Me .... (ABC-Paramount 10507) .75 3.00 63
GOT MY MOJO WORKING/She Ain't No Angel .... (MGM K-13149) 1.00 4.00 61
HEY LITTLE LUCY/When I'm Not With You .... (MGM K-12785) 1.00 4.00 59
I NEED YOU SO/Teasin' .... (MGM K-12943) 1.00 4.00 60
I NEED YOUR LOVIN'/Born To Sing The Blues .... (Mercury 71086) 3.00 12.00 57
IS A BLUE BIRD BLUE/She's Mine .... (MGM K-12911) .75 3.00 60
IT'S ONLY MAKE BELIEVE/I'll Try .... (MGM K-12677) .75 3.00 58
IT'S ONLY MAKE BELIEVE/I'll Try .... (MGM SK-50107) 2.00 8.00 58
(Stereo single issue)
LONELY BLUE BOY/Star Spangled Heaven .... (MGM K-12857) .75 3.00 59
MILLION TEARDROPS, A/I'm In A Blue, Blue Mood .... (MGM K-13011) 1.00 4.00 61
MONA LISA/Heavenly .... (MGM K-12804) .75 3.00 59
MY BABY LEFT ME/Such A Night .... (ABC-Paramount 10550) 2.00 8.00 64
NEXT KISS (IS THE LAST GOODBYE), THE/Man Alone .. (MGM K-12998) 1.00 4.00 61
PICKUP, THE/I Hope, I Think, I Wish .... (MGM K-13112) 1.00 4.00 62
PORTRAIT OF A FOOL/Tower Of Tears .... (MGM K-13050) 1.00 4.00 62
SHAKE IT UP/Maybe Baby .... (Mercury 71148) 3.75 15.00 57
STORY OF MY LOVE, THE/Make Me Know You're Mine .. (MGM K-12748) .75 3.00 59
SWEET SORROW/It's Drivin' Me Wild .... (MGM K-13034) 1.00 4.00 61
UNCHAINED MELODY/There's Something On Your Mind . (MGM K-13089) 1.00 4.00 62
WHAT A DREAM/Tell Me One More Time .... (MGM K-12918) 1.00 4.00 60
WHAT AM I LIVING FOR/The Hurt In My Heart .... (MGM K-12886) .75 3.00 60
WHOLE LOT OF SHAKIN' GOING ON/The Flame .... (MGM K-12962) .75 3.00 60

TWO CHAPS, The (Featuring Jay Black)
FORGIVE ME/No More .... (Atlantic 1195) 2.50 10.00 59

TWO DOLLAR QUESTION, The
AUNT MATILDA'S DOUBLE YUMMY BROWNIE/
Cincinnati Love Song .... (Intrepid 75001) 1.25 5.00

2 OF CLUBS, The
HEART/My First Heartbreak .... (Fraternity 972) .75 3.00 66
YOU LOVE ME/Let Me Walk With You .... (Fraternity 990) .75 3.00 67
YOU LOVE ME/River Deep Mountain High .... (Fraternity 994) .75 3.00 67
WALK TALL/So Blue Is Fall .... (Fraternity 975) .75 3.00 67

TYANNOSAURUS REX: see T-Rex

TYCOON
SLOW DOWN BOY/Don't Worry .... (Arista 0437) .50 2.00 79
SUCH A WOMAN/How Long (Can We Go On) .... (Arista 0398) .50 2.00 79

TURZY, Jane
GOOD MORNING, MR. ECHO/Be Doggone Sure .... (Decca 27622) 1.25 5.00 51
SWEET VIOLETS/Lonely Little Robin .... (Decca 27668) 1.25 5.00 51

TU-TONES, The
SACCHARIN SALLY/Still In Love With You .... (Lin 5021) 2.50 10.00 59

TWANGY REBELS, The
REBEL ROUSER '65/Lazy Rebel .... (General American 719) 1.00 4.00 65

TWEEDS, The
I WANT HER TO KNOW/We Got Time .... (Coral 62551) .75 3.00 68
THING OF THE PAST, A/What's Your Name .... (Coral 62542) .75 3.00 67

TWEENS, The
WITCHES CREW, THE/17 Little Kisses .... (DC 0429) .75 3.00

TWENTIETH CENTURY ZOO, The
ONLY THING THAT'S WRONG/Stallion Of Fate .... (Vault 961) 1.00 4.00 67

20/20
CHERI/Backyard Guys .... (Portrait 70035) .50 2.00 79
TELL ME WHY (CAN'T UNDERSTAND YOU)/ .... (Portrait 70038) .50 2.00 79

TWICE AS MUCH
SITTIN' ON A FENCE/Baby I Want You .... (MGM K-13530) 1.00 4.00 66
SITTIN' ON A FENCE/Baby I Want You .... (MGM K-13530) 1.50 6.00 66
(Picture sleeve)

TWIGGY
HERE I GO AGAIN/Everything Comes In Time .... (Mercury 73832) .50 2.00 76
OVER & OVER/When I Think Of You .... (Capitol 5903) .75 3.00 67
VANILLA O'LAY/ .... (Mercury 73863) .50 2.00 76
WOMAN IN LOVE, A/I Lie Awake & Dream Of You..... (Mercury 73923) .50 2.00 77

TWIGS, The
DOWN THE ROAD APIECE/I Need Your Love Babe .... (Dot 16830) .75 3.00 66

TWILIGHTS, The
BOHEMIAN/Little Richard .... (6 Star 1001) 3.00 12.00
IT COULD BE TRUE/Sum'pin Else .... (Twilight 1028) 2.00 8.00

TWILITERS, The
HEY THERE/Caused By You .... (Nix 102) 2.00 8.00 61
LOVE BANDIT/Back To School .... (Nix 103) 1.50 6.00 61
MY BEATLE HAIRCUT/Sweet Lips .... (Roulette 4546) 1.50 6.00 64
MY SILENT PRAYER/Little Bitty Bed Bug .... (Bubble 1334) 2.00 8.00

TWILLEY, Dwight, Band
COULD BE LOVE/ .... (Shelter 62003) .50 2.00 76
I'M ON FIRE/Did You See What Happened? .... (Shelter 40380) .50 2.00 75
OUT OF MY HANDS/Nothing's Ever Gonna Change So Fast . (Arista 0415) .50 2.00 79
RUNAWAY/ .... (Arista 0433) .50 2.00 79
SOMEBODY TO LOVE/ .... (Arista 0478) .50 2.00 79
TRYING TO FIND MY BABY/Here She Comes .... (Arista 0299) .50 2.00 78
TWILLEY DON'T MIND/Rock & Roll 47 .... (Arista 0278) .50 2.00 77
YOU WERE SO WARM/Sincerely .... (Shelter 40450) .50 2.00 75

TWINKLE
BOY OF MY DREAMS/Terry .... (Tollie 9040) .75 3.00 65
WHAT AM I DOING HERE WITH YOU/The End Of The World (Aurora 163) .75 3.00

TWINKLES, The
BAD MOTORCYCLE/Sweet Daddy .... (Peak 5001) 1.50 6.00 58

TWINS, The (Jim & John)
JO-ANN'S SISTER/Who Knows The Secret .... (RCA Victor 47-7235) 1.00 4.00 58
This duo was also known as The Twin Tones.

TWISTERS, The
COME GO WITH ME/Pretty Little Girl Next Door .... (Apt 25045) .75 3.00 60
COUNT DOWN 1 2 3/Speed Limit .... (Felco 103) .75 3.00 59
DANCING LITTLE CLOWN/Turn The Page .... (Capitol 4451) .75 3.00 60
ELVIS LEAVES SORRENTO/Street Dance .... (Campus 125) .75 3.00 61
PEPPERMINT TWIST/Silly Chili .... (Dual 502) .75 3.00 61
PLEASE COME BACK/This Is The End .... (Sun-set 501) .75 3.00 61

TYGH & THE CRITERIONS
TO BE MINE/Do What You Wanna .... (Flite 101) 1.00 4.00

TYLER, Bonnie
I BELIEVE IN YOUR SWEET LOVE/ .... (RCA 11763) .50 2.00 79
IF I SING YOU A LOVE SONG/Heaven .... (RCA 11349) .50 2.00 78
IT'S A HEARTACHE/It's About Time .... (RCA 11249) .50 2.00 78
MARRIED MEN/If You Ever Need Me Again .... (RCA 11630) .50 2.00 79
MY GUNS ARE LOADED/Baby I Just Love You .... (RCA 11468) .50 2.00 79

TYLER, Frankie: see Valli, Frankie

TYLER, Kip
SHE GOT EYES/Shadow Street .... (Challenge 1014) 2.00 8.00

TYLER, Terry
THOUSAND FEET BELOW, A/Answer Me .... (Landa 679) .75 3.00 61

TYMES, The
BABY/What Would I So .... (MGM 13631) .75 3.00 66
HERE SHE COMES/Malibu .... (Parkway 924) .75 3.00 64
IT'S COOL/ .... (RCA 10561) .50 2.00 76
MAGIC OF OUR SUMMER LOVE, THE/With All My Heart .. (Parkway 919) .75 3.00 64
MS. GRACE/ .... (RCA 10128) .50 2.00 74
PEOPLE/For Love of Ivy .... (Columbia 44630) .75 3.00 68
PRETEND/Street Talk .... (MGM 13536) .75 3.00 66
SO IN LOVE/Roscoe James McClain .... (Parkway 871A) 1.25 5.00 63
(Reissued as "So Much In Love" using the number 871C.)
SO MUCH IN LOVE/Roscoe James McClain .... (Parkway 871C) .75 3.00 63
(Reissue of "So In Love")
SOMEWHERE/View From My Window .... (Parkway 891) .75 3.00 63
THESE FOOLISH THINGS/This Time It's Love .... (Winchester 1002) .75 3.00 67
TO EACH HIS OWN/Wonderland Of Love .... (Parkway 908) .75 3.00 64
WONDERFUL WONDERFUL/Come With Me To The Sea ... (Parkway 884) .75 3.00 63
YOU LITTLE TRUSTMAKER/ .... (RCA 10022) .50 2.00 74

TYRELL, Steve
YOUNG BOY BLUES/A Boy Without A Girl .... (Philips 40150) .75 3.00 63

TYRONE & THE NU PORTS
FEEL LIKE A MILLION/On A Saturday Night .... (Darrow DS-20) 1.50 6.00

TYSON, Roy
I WANT TO BE YOUR BOYFRIEND/The Girl I Love .... (Double L 733) 2.00 8.00 64
OH WHAT A NIGHT FOR LOVE/Not Too Young .... (Double L 723) 1.25 5.00 63

TZUKE, Judie
STAY WITH ME TILL DAWN/New Friends Again .... (Rocket 41133) .50 2.00 79

U

U & I
REPORT TO THE PEOPLE/There She Blows .... (Black Patch 1) 1.00 4.00

UFO
CHERRY/ .... (Chrysalis 2239) .50 2.00 78
DOCTOR DOCTOR/ .... (Chrysalis 2040) .75 3.00 73
DOCTOR DOCTOR/Lipstick Traces .... (Chrysalis 2100) .50 2.00 74
ONLY YOU CAN ROCK ME/Ain't No Baby .... (Chrysalis 2263) .50 2.00 78
TOO HOT TO HANDLE/Electric Phase .... (Chrysalis 2157) .50 2.00 77
TRY ME/Gettin' Ready .... (Chrysalis 2178) .50 2.00 77

U.K. (With Bill Bruford & John Wetton)
IN THE DEAD OF THE NIGHT/Mental Medication ...... (Polydor 14491) .50 2.00 78
NOTHING TO LOSE/In The Dead Of The Night .... (Polydor 14551) .50 2.00 79
Also see Yes
Also see King Crimson
Also see Uriah Heep

U.K. BABY
HEARTBREAKER/Michael's Blues .... (Imperial 66409) .75 3.00 69
Also see Sutherland Brothers, The

ULTIMATES, The
I CAN TELL YOU LOVE ME TOO/Lonely Nights .... (Enjoy 2302) 2.00 8.00

ULTRATONES, The
LOCOMOTION/Sister Of The Girl I Once Loved .... (Cary 2001) .75 3.00 62
RESTLESS/Chain Reaction .... (San Tana 101) .75 3.00

UNBELIEVABLE UGLIES, The
GET STRAIGHT/Sorry .... (Liberty 55935) .75 3.00 67

UNCHAINED MYNDS
EVERY DAY/ .... (Buddah 119) .75 3.00 69
WE CAN'T GO ON THIS WAY/Going Back To Miami .... (Buddah 111) .75 3.00 69

UNCLE DOG
RIVER ROAD/ .... (MCA 40005) .50 2.00 73

UNCLE SAM
BICENTENNIAL BALL/Bicentennial Ball .... (Jamie 1428) 1.00 4.00 76
(Novelty/Break-in)

UNCLE SOUND (With Jim Seals)
BEVERLY HILLS/I'm Gonna Ask Him .... (Warner Bros. 7197) .75 3.00 68
Also see Seals & Crofts

UNDERBEATS, The
BOOK OF LOVE/Darling Lorraine .... (Soma 1449) 2.00 8.00 65
FOOT STOMPIN'/Route 66) .... (Garrett 4004) 1.00 4.00 64

UNDERDOGS, The
LITTLE GIRL/Don't Pretend .... (Hideout 1004) 1.25 5.00
LOVE'S GONE BAD/Mo Jo Hanna .... (Vip 25040) 1.25 5.00
MAN IN THE GLASS, THE/Judy Be Mine .... (Hideout 1001) 1.25 5.00
SURPRISE/Get Down On Your Knees .... (Hideout 1011) 1.25 5.00

UNDERGROUND SUNSHINE, The
BIRTHDAY/All I Want is You .... (Intrepid 75002) 1.25 5.00 69
DON'T SHUT ME OUT/Take Me, Break Me .... (Intrepid 75012) 1.50 6.00 69

UNDERTAKERS, The
SEARCHING/ .... (PH 110) .75 3.00

UNION GAP, The: see Puckett, Gary & The Union Gap

UNIQUE ECHOS, The
ZOOM/Italian Twist .... (Southern Sound 108) 1.50 6.00

UNIQUES, The (Featuring Joe Stampley)
ALL THESE THINGS/Tell Me What to Do .... (Paula 238) .75 3.00 66
EVERY NOW & THEN/Love Is A Precious Thing .... (Paula 275) .75 3.00 67
GO ON & LEAVE/ .... (Paula 289) .75 3.00 67
GOOD BYE, SO LONG/Run & Hide .... (Paula 245) .75 3.00 66
GROOVIN' OUT (ON YOUR GOOD, GOOD LOVIN')/Areba ..... (Paula 264) .75 3.00 66
I SURE FEEL MORE (LIKE I DO THAN I DID WHEN
I GOT HERE)/It Hurts Me To Remember .... (Paula 307) .75 3.00 68
LADY'S MAN/Bolivar .... (Paula 227) .75 3.00 65
LUCILLE/One Night With You .... (Paramount 0116) .50 2.00 72
NOT TOO LONG AGO/Fast Way Of Living .... (Paula 219) .75 3.00 65
PLEASE COME HOME FOR CHRISTMAS (PART 1)/
Please Come Home For Christmas (Part 2) .... (Paula 255) .75 3.00 66
STRANGE/You Ain't Tuff .... (Paula 231) .75 3.00 65
TOO GOOD TO BE TRUE/Never Been In Love .... (Paula 222) .75 3.00 65

UNIQUES, The
DO YOU REMEMBER/Come Marry Me .... (Flippin 202) 2.00 8.00
I'M SO UNHAPPY/It's Got To Come From Your Heart ...... (Gone 5113) 1.00 4.00 61
I'M SO UNHAPPY/It's Got To Come From Your Heart .... (Pride 4) 2.00 8.00 61
ONE MILLION MILES AWAY/All At Once .... (Tee Kay 112) 6.25 25.00
Also see Addeo, Nicky, & The Uniques

UNIQUES, The
MERRY CHRISTMAS DARLING/Rockin' Rudolph .... (Demand 2396) 1.50 6.00
MERRY CHRISTMAS DARLING/Times Change .... (Dot 16533) .75 3.00
TIMES CHANGE/Allright Okay You Win .... (Demand 2940) 1.50 6.00

UNIQUE TEENS, The
AT THE BALL/Jeannie .... (Hanover 4510) 1.50 6.00 58
AT THE BALL/Jeannie .... (Ivy 112) 3.75 15.00 58
WATCHA KNOW NEW/Run Fast .... (Dynamic 110) 2.00 8.00

UNITED FRUIT CO., The
ON THE GOOD SHIP LOLLIPOP/Sunshine Street .... (Laurie 3408) 1.00 4.00 68

UNIT FOUR PLUS TWO, The (With Russ Ballard)
CONCRETE & CLAY/When I Fall In Love .... (London 9751) .75 3.00 65
CONCRETE & CLAY/Wild As The Wind .... (London 9751) .75 3.00 65
HARK/Stop Wasting Your Time .... (London 9790) .75 3.00 65
I WON'T LET YOU DOWN/I Was Only Playing Games ...... (London 1009) .75 3.00 66
SORROW & PAIN/Woman From Liberia .... (London 9732) .75 3.00 65
YOU'VE NEVER BEEN IN LOVE LIKE THIS BEFORE/
Tell Somebody You Know .... (London 9761) .75 3.00 65

UNKNOWN, The
I HAVE RETURNED (Elvis novelty)/Keep Talking Baby .. (Autograph 206) 2.50 10.00 60

UNKNOWNS, The (With Keith Allison)
MELODY FOR AN UNKNOWN GIRL/Peith's Song .... (Parrot 307) .75 3.00 66
ONE MORE CHANCE/You & Me .... (Shield 7101) 1.00 4.00
Also see Revere, Paul, & the Raiders

TITLE/FLIP	LABEL & NO.	GOOD	NEAR MINT	YR.
UNRELEATED SEGMENTS, The				
CRY, CRY, CRY/It's Not Fair	(Liberty 56052)	.75	3.00	68
STORY OF MY LIFE/It's Unfair	(HBR 514)	.75	3.00	66
WHERE YOU GONNA GO/It's Gonna Rain	(Liberty 55992)	.75	3.00	67
UNTAMED, The				
IT'S NOT TRUE/Gimmie, Gimmie Some Shade	(Planet 117)	.75	3.00	66
UP RISING, The				
JUST LIKE AN ABIRIGINE/Hassan I Sabbah	(Sundance 22190)	1.25	5.00	
UPBEATS, The				
JUST LIKE IN THE MOVIES/My Foolish Heart	(Swan 4010)	1.00	4.00	58
TEENIE WEENIE BIKINI/Satin Shoes	(Joy 229)	1.00	4.00	59
UPCHURCH, Philip, Combo				
THAT'S WHERE IT IS/The Hog	(United Artists 385)	.75	3.00	61
YOU CAN'T SIT DOWN (PART 1)/You Can't Sit Down (Part 2)	(Boyd 329)	1.00	4.00	61
YOU CAN'T SIT DOWN (PART 1)/ You Can't Sit Down (Part 2)	(United Artists 329)	.75	3.00	61
Instrumentals				
UPFRONTS, The				
BABY, FOR YOUR LOVE/It Took Time	(Lummtone 108)	1.00	4.00	
DO THE BEATLE/Most Of The Pretty Girls	(Lummtone 114)	1.25	5.00	64
UPSETTERS, The				
DRAGGIN' THE MAIN/Autumn's Here	(Autumn 4)	1.25	5.00	
UPSTAIRS, The				
BE MY BABY/Operator Please	(Cuca 130)	1.00	4.00	
UPTONES, The				
BE MINE/Dreamin'	(Lute 6229)	2.00	8.00	62
I'LL BE THERE/No More	(Lute 6225)	1.50	8.00	62
UPTOWN GIRLS, The				
CRAZY TALK/Summer Story	(Pickwick City 1004)	1.00	4.00	
URBAN RENEWAL, The				
LOVE EYES/People	(St. George Int'l. 702271)	1.50	6.00	
URIAH HEEP (Featuring Ken Hensley)				
COME BACK TO ME/Love Or Nothing	(Chrysalis-Bronze 2274)	.50	2.00	78
EASY LIVIN'/All My Life	(Mercury 73307)	.75	3.00	72
FREE ME/Masquerade	(Warner Bros. 8581)	.50	2.00	78
GYPSY/Real Turned On	(Mercury 73103)	.75	3.00	70
JULY MORNING/Tears In My Eyes	(Mercury 73406)	.75	3.00	73
PRIMA DONNA/Stealin'	(Warner Bros. 8132)	.50	2.00	75
SALISBURY/	(Mercury 320)	1.00	4.00	72
(Promotional issue)				
SOMETHING OR NOTHING/	(Warner Bros. 7836)	.50	2.00	74
STEALIN'/Sunshine	(Warner Bros. 7738)	.50	2.00	73
SWEET LORRAINE/Blind Eye	(Mercury 73349)	.75	3.00	73
WAKE UP (SET YOUR SIGHTS)/Come Away Melinda	(Mercury 73145)	.75	3.00	70
WIZARD, THE/Why	(Mercury 73271)	.75	3.00	71
URSA MAJOR (With Dick Wagner)				
LET THE MUSIC PLAY/	(RCA 0874)	.50	2.00	72
LIBERTY & JUSTICE/	(RCA 0791)	.50	2.00	72
U.S. BEATLEWIGS, The				
SHE'S SO INNOCENT (OH YEAH)/ Finger Poppin' Girl	(Orbit 531)	1.25	5.00	64
U.S. BONDS: see Bonds, U.S.				
U.S. DOUBLE QUINTET, The (The Tokens & The Kirby Stone Four)				
LIFE IS GROOVY/Split	(B.T. Puppy 524)	1.00	4.00	67
U.S. RADIO BAND, The				
LET ME IN YOUR LIFE/	(ABC 12212)	.50	2.00	76
US				
PROMISE ME/American Girl & Liverpool Boy	(Patty 1373)	2.00	8.00	
US FOUR				
ALLIGATOR, THE/By My Side	(Rising Sons 701)	.75	3.00	
US GROUP, The				
LITTLE BIT OF SOMETHING/Just A Year Ago Today	(Uptown 736)	1.25	5.00	
USHER, Gary				
JODY/Beetle, The	(Capitol 5128)	2.00	8.00	64
JODY/It's A Lie	(Capitol 5403)	1.50	6.00	65
MILKY WAY/Three Surfer Boys	(Dot 16518)	5.00	20.00	63
(With the Usherettes; also known as the Honeys)				
SACRAMENTO/That's The Way I Feel	(Capitol 5193)	6.25	25.00	64
TOMORROW/Lies	(Lan-cet 144)	2.00	8.00	
YOU'RE THE GIRL/Driven Insane	(Titan 1716)	2.00	8.00	
Also see Four Speeds, The				
Also see Hondells, The				
Also see L.A. Teens, The				
Also see Sagittarius				
Also see Super Stocks, The				
Also see Wheele Men, The				
UTOPIA (Featuring Todd Rundgren)				
LOVE IS THE ANSWER/The Marriage Of Heaven & Hell	(Bearsville 0321)	.50	2.00	77
SET ME FREE/Umbrella Man	(Bearsville 49180)	.50	2.00	80
SUNBURST FINISH/Communion With The Sun	(Bearsville 0317)	.50	2.00	76
VERY LAST TIME, THE/Love Alone	(Bearsville 49247)	.50	2.00	80
UTOPIANS, The				
ALONG MY LONELY WAY/Hurry To Your Date	(Imperial 5876)	2.00	8.00	62
DUTCH TREAT/Ain't No Such Thing	(Imperial 5861)	2.00	8.00	62

The transition to a country music style has been made by several pop & rock singers of the fifties and sixties. The pop & rock releases by these artists will appear in this guide, while the country music releases will be listed in our guides covering that field of music.

Likewise, your favorite soul and rhythm & blues artists that are not covered in this guide are—or will soon be—included in our Blues-Rhythm & Blues-Soul Price Guide.

V

TITLE/FLIP	LABEL & NO.	GOOD	NEAR MINT	YR.
VACELS, The				
CAN YOU PLEASE CRAWL OUT YOUR WINDOW/ I'm Just A Poor Boy	(Kama Sutra 204)	1.00	4.00	65
YOU'RE MY BABY/Hey Girl, Stop Leading Me On	(Kama Sutra 200)	1.00	4.00	65
Also see Ricky & the Vacels				
Also see Shaggy Boys, The				
VAGABONDS, The				
NIGHT DRAG/Baby Face McCall	(Abco 1001)	1.00	4.00	64
VAGRANTS, The				
BESIDE THE SEA/A Sunny Summer Rain	(Atco 6513)	.75	3.00	67
I DON'T NEED YOUR LOVING/And When It's Over	(Atco 6552)	.75	3.00	68
RESPECT/I Love, Love You	(Atco 6473)	.75	3.00	67
VALADIERS, The				
GREETINGS (THIS IS UNCLE SAM)/Take A Chance	(Miracle 6)	1.50	6.00	61
VAL-AIRES, The				
LAURIE, MY LOVE/Which One Will It Be	(Coral 62177)	3.75	15.00	59
Also see Vogues, The				
VALAQUONS, The				
JOLLY GREEN GIANT/Diddy Bop	(Rayco 516)	6.25	25.00	
MADELAINE/Teardrops	(Laguna 102)	6.25	25.00	
VAL-CHORDS, The				
CANDY STORE LOVE/You're Laughing At Me	(Gametime 104)	3.75	15.00	57
VALDY				
PETER & LOU/	(A&M 1863)	.50	2.00	76
SIMPLE LIFE (ODE TO L.A.)/Landscapes	(A&M 1764)	.50	2.00	75
YES I CAN/	(A&M 1863)	.50	2.00	76
VALE, Bobby				
MISS HIGH SCHOOL U.S.A./Two Fast Guns	(Lawn 209)	.75	3.00	63
VALE, Jerry				
ADELAIDE/Miracle In The Rain	(Columbia 4-40584)	1.00	4.00	56
ASK ME/A Tear, A Kiss, A Smile	(Columbia 4-40058)	1.25	5.00	53
FOR ME/Tired Of Dreaming	(Columbia 4-39990)	1.25	5.00	53
HAVE YOU LOOKED INTO YOUR HEART/Andiamo	(Columbia 4-43181)	.75	3.00	64
INNAMORATA (SWEETHEART)/Second Ending	(Columbia 4-40634)	1.00	4.00	56
YOU CAN NEVER GIVE ME/And No One Knows	(Columbia 4-39929)	1.25	5.00	53
YOU DON'T KNOW ME/Enchanted	(Columbia 4-40710)	1.00	4.00	56

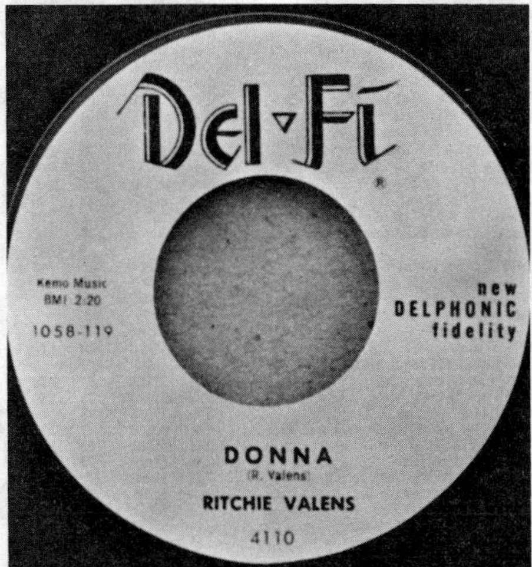

TITLE/FLIP	LABEL & NO.	GOOD	NEAR MINT	YR.
VALENS, Ritchie (Richard Valenzuela)				
COME ON, LET'S GO/Framed	(Del Fi 4106)	1.00	4.00	58
DONNA/La Bamba	(Del Fi 4110)	1.50	6.00	58
(Green label, black print)				
DONNA/La Bamba	(Del Fi 4110)	1.00	4.00	58
("Circles" label "Del Fi" in white)				
FAST FREIGHT/Big Baby Blues	(Del Fi 4111)	2.00	8.00	59
FAST FREIGHT/Big Baby Blues	(Del Fi 4111)	1.50	6.00	59
(Shown as by Arvee Allens)				
LITTLE GIRL/We Belong Together	(Del Fi 4117)	1.00	4.00	59
LITTLE GIRL/We Belong Together	(Del Fi 4117)	2.00	8.00	59
(Picture sleeve)				
PADDIWACK SONG/Cry, Cry, Cry	(Del Fi 4133)	1.25	5.00	60
STAY BESIDE ME/Big Baby Blues	(Del Fi 4128)	1.25	5.00	60
THAT'S MY LITTLE SUZIE/In A Turkish Town	(Del Fi 4114)	1.00	4.00	59
VALENTE, Caterina				
BREEZE & I, THE/Jalousie	(Decca 29467)	1.00	4.00	55
VALENTI, Dino				
DON'T LET IT DOWN/	(Elektra 45612)	1.25	5.00	67
Also see Quicksilver Messenger Service				
VALENTI, John				
ANYTHING YOU WANT/That's The Way Life Goes	(Ariola America 7625)	.50	2.00	76
I LOVE HER TOO/	(Ariola America 7663)	.50	2.00	77
I WROTE THIS SONG FOR YOU/Morning Song	(Ariola America 7656)	.50	2.00	76
VALENTINE & THE LOVERS				
I'M GONNA LOVE/One Teardrop Too Late	(Donna 1345)	1.00	4.00	62
VALENTINE, Jimmy				
JUST KEEP WALKIN' (AMBROSE)/Rockin' Hula	(Cub 9024)	1.00	4.00	59
VALENTINE, Penny				
I WANT TO KISS RINGO GOODBYE/ Show Me The Way To Love You	(Liberty 55774)	1.50	6.00	65

TITLE/FLIP	LABEL & NO.	GOOD	NEAR MINT	YR.
VALENTINES, The				
SOCK, THE/Sixteen Senoritas	(Iona 1003)	.75	3.00	
VALENTINO, Danny				
BIOLOGY/A Million Years	(MGM 12881)	.75	3.00	60
VALENTINO, Mark (Anthony Busillo)				
PUSH & KICK, THE/Walking Alone	(Swan 4121)	.75	3.00	62
VALENTINO, Sal (Of the Beau Brummels)				
ALLIGATOR MAN/An Added Attraction	(Warner Bros. 7268)	1.25	5.00	69
I WANNA TWIST/	(Falco 306)	3.75	15.00	
SILKIE/Song For Rochelle	(Warner Bros. 7368)	1.25	5.00	70
VALERY, Dana				
HAVING YOU AROUND/ You Don't Know Where Your Interest Lies	(Columbia 44004)	2.00	8.00	67
(With Paul Simon)				
I'D LOVE YOU TO LOVE ME/I Never Had It So Good	(Phantom 10316)	.50	2.00	75
I DON'T WANT TO BE LONELY/	(Scotti Bros. 509)	.50	2.00	79
VALIANTS, The				
ARE YOU READY/Frankie's Angel	(KC 108)	1.00	4.00	
JOHNNY LONELY/	(Roulette 4551)	.75	3.00	64
LIVING IN PARADISE/I'm In A World Of My Own	(Imperial 5915)	1.50	6.00	63
YOU ARE SWEETER THAN WINE/ Love Comes In Many Ways	(Imperial 5843)	1.00	4.00	62
VALIANTS, The (Featuring Billy Storm)				
THIS IS THE NIGHT/Good Golly Miss Molly	(Keen 34004)	1.25	5.00	57
VALIDS, The				
BARBARA ANN/Congratulations	(Amber 855)	.75	3.00	66
VALINO, Joe				
GARDEN OF EDEN/Caravan	(Vik 0226)	1.00	4.00	56
VALJEAN (Valjean Johns)				
TILL THERE WAS YOU/The Eighteenth Variation	(Carlton 576)	.75	3.00	62
THEME FROM BEN CASEY/Theme From Dr. Kildare	(Carlton 573)	.75	3.00	62
Instrumentals				
VALLEY, Frankie: see Valli, Frankie				
VALLEY, Frankie & The Travelers: see Valli, Frankie				
VALLI				
HURRY HOME TO ME (SOLDIER BOY)/ Jimmy's In A Hurry	(Scepter 1233)	1.50	6.00	62
(Answer song; has "Soldier Boy" by the Shirelles playing in the background.)				
VALLIE, Frankie & The Romans: see Four Lovers, The				
VALLI, Frankie (Frank Castelluccio)				
BOOMERANG/Look At The World It's Changing	(Private Stock 45109)	.75	3.00	76
BOOMERANG (Long Version)/ Boomerang (Short Version)	(Private Stock 45109)	2.00	8.00	76
(Promotional issue)				
CAN'T TAKE MY EYES OFF YOU/The Trouble With Me	(Philips 40446)	.75	3.00	67
CAN'T TAKE MY EYES OFF YOU/The Trouble With Me	(Philips 40446)	2.50	10.00	67
(Picture sleeve)				
CIRCLES IN THE SAND/My Mother's Eyes	(Philips 40680)	2.00	8.00	70
EASILY/What Good Am I Without You	(Private Stock 45141)	.75	3.00	77
FALLEN ANGEL/Carrie (I Would Marry You)	(Private Stock 45074)	.50	2.00	76
FANCY DANCER/Needing You	(Warner-Curb 8734)	.75	3.00	79
FORGIVE & FORGET/Somebody Else Took Her Home	(Mercury 70381)	15.00	60.00	54
(Red label, shown as by Frankie Valley & the Travelers)				
FORGIVE & FORGET/Somebody Else Took Her Home	(Mercury 70381)	7.50	30.00	54
(Black label, shown as by Frankie Valley & the Travelers)				
GIRL I'LL NEVER KNOW, THE (ANGELS NEVER FLY THIS LOW)/ A Face Without A Name	(Philips 40622)	.75	3.00	69
GIRL I'LL NEVER KNOW, THE (ANGELS NEVER FLY THIS LOW)/ A Face Without A Name	(Philips 40622)	2.00	8.00	69
(Picture sleeve)				
GIRL I'LL NEVER KNOW, THE ANGELS NEVER FLY THIS LOW/ A Face Without A Name	(Bob Crewe Presents CGC1B)	6.25	25.00	69
(Promotional issue)				
GREASE/Grease (Instrumental)	(RSO 897)	.50	2.00	78
I GO APE/If You Care	(Okeh 4-7103)	12.50	50.00	58
(Shown as by Frankie Tyler)				
I GO APE/If You Care	(Okeh 4-7103)	7.50	30.00	58
(Promotional issue, shown as by Frankie Tyler)				
I MAKE A FOOL OF MYSELF/ September Rain (Here Comes The Rain)	(Philips 40484)	.75	3.00	67
I NEED YOU/I'm Gonna Love You	(Private Stock 45169)	.75	3.00	77
JUST LOOK WHAT YOU HAVE DONE/ Just Look What You Have Done	(Motown 124 PR-10)	2.50	10.00	73
(10" single issue)				
LOVE ISN'T HERE/Poor Fool	(Mowest 5011F)	1.25	5.00	71
MY EYES ADORED YOU/Watch Where You Walk	(Private Stock 45003)	.50	2.00	74
MY MOTHERS EYES/The Laugh's On Me	(Corona 1234)	50.00	200.00	53
(Shown as by Frankie Valley)				
NIGHT, THE/The Night	(Mowest 5025)	3.00	12.00	71
(Promotional issue only)				
OUR DAY WILL COME/ You Can Bet (I Ain't Goin' Nowhere)	(Private Stock 45043)	.50	2.00	75
OUR DAY WILL COME (Long Version)/ Our Day Will Come (Short Version)	(Private Stock 45043)	2.50	10.00	75
(Promotional issue)				
PLEASE TAKE A CHANCE/It May Be Wrong	(Decca 9-30994)	12.50	50.00	59
(Shown as by Frankie Vally)				
PLEASE TAKE A CHANCE/It May Be Wrong	(Decca 9-30994)	6.25	25.00	59
(Promotional issue, shown as by Frankie Vally)				
PROUD ONE, THE/Ivy	(Philips 40407)	1.00	4.00	66
PROUD ONE, THE/Ivy	(Philips 40407)	1.25	5.00	66
(Picture sleeve)				
RAINSTORM/I Could Have Loved You	(Private Stock 45180)	.75	3.00	78
SAVE ME, SAVE ME/No Love At All	(Warner-Curb 8670)	.50	2.00	78
SCALAWAG SONG, THE/Listen To Yesterday	(Motown 1279)	2.00	8.00	73
SECOND THOUGHTS/So She Says	(Private Stock 45154)	.75	3.00	77
SUN AIN'T GONNA SHINE (ANYMORE), THE/This Is Goodbye	(Smash 1995)	1.50	6.00	65
SWEARIN' TO GOD/Why	(Private Stock 45021)	.50	2.00	75
SWEARIN' TO GOD (Long Version)/ Swearin' To God (Short Version)	(Private Stock 45021)	2.50	10.00	75
(Promotional issue)				
SWEARIN' TO GOD/ Can't Get You Off My Mind-Boomerang	(Private Stock 5101)	2.00	8.00	77
(12" single issue)				
TO GIVE (THE REASON I LIVE)/Watch Where You Walk	(Philips 40510)	1.00	4.00	67
TO GIVE (THE REASON I LIVE)/Watch Where You Walk	(Philips 40510)	1.25	5.00	67
(Picture sleeve)				
WE'RE ALL ALONE/You To Me Are Everything	(Private Stock 45098)	1.00	4.00	76
WHERE DID WE GO WRONG (With Chris Forde)/Doctor Dance	(MCA 41253)	1.00	4.00	80
(YOU'RE GONNA) HURT YOURSELF/Night Hawk	(Smash 2015)	.75	3.00	65
YOU'RE READY NOW/Cry For Me	(Smash 2037)	1.00	4.00	66
YOU'VE GOT YOUR TROUBLES/Listen To Yesterday	(Motown 1251)	2.00	8.00	73
YOU'VE GOT YOUR TROUBLES/The Dream Of Kings	(Philips 40661)	2.50	10.00	69
Also see Hartford, Ken				
Also see 4 Seasons, The				
VALLI, June				
ANSWER TO A MAIDEN'S PRAYER, THE/In His Arms	(Mercury 71422)	.75	3.00	59
APPLE GREEN/Oh Why	(Mercury 71588)	.75	3.00	60
CRYING IN THE CHAPEL/Love Every Moment	(RCA Victor 47-5368)	1.00	4.00	53

TITLE/FLIP	LABEL & NO.	GOOD	NEAR MINT	YR.
I UNDERSTAND/Love, Tears & Kisses	(RCA Victor 47-5740)	1.00	4.00	54
UNCHAINED MELODY/Tomorrow	(RCA Victor 47-6078)	1.00	4.00	55
WEDDING, THE/Lunch Hour	(Mercury 71382)	.75	3.00	58
VALLY, Frankie: see Valli, Frankie				
VALOR, Tony				
THERE'S A STORY IN MY HEART/So Tenderly	(Musictone 1119)	6.25	25.00	63
VALRAYS, The				
GET A BOARD/Pee Wee	(Parkway 880)	.75	3.00	63
I ASK MYSELF/Tonky	(Parkway 904)	.75	3.00	64
VALS, The				
TOO LATE/I'm Stepping Out With My Memories	(Ascot 2163)	.75	3.00	64
VAN DYKE, Dick				
THREE WHEELS ON MY WAGON/	(Jamie 1178)	.75	3.00	60
THREE WHEELS ON MY WAGON/	(Jamie 1256)	.75	3.00	62
VAN DYKE FIVE, The (The Van Dykes)				
ONLY IF I HAD YOUR LOVE/Bring Back My Life	(Corner Closet 101)	1.50	6.00	
VAN EATON, Lon & Derrek (Of Jacob's Creek)				
LOVING YOU/Baby It's You	(A&M 1845)	.50	2.00	77
MUSIC LOVER/Wildfire	(A&M 1643)	.50	2.00	75
SWEET MUSIC/Song Of Songs	(Apple 1845)	.75	3.00	72
WHO DO YOU OUT DO/	(A&M 1662)	.50	2.00	75
VAN HALEN				
AIN'T TALKIN' 'BOUT LOVE/Feel Your Love Tonight	(Warner Bros. 8707)	.50	2.00	78
BEAUTIFUL GIRLS/D.O.A.	(Warner Bros. 49035)	.50	2.00	79
DANCE THE NIGHT AWAY/Outta Love Again	(Warner Bros. 8823)	.50	2.00	79
JAMIE'S CRYIN'/I'm The One	(Warner Bros. 8631)	.50	2.00	78
RUNNIN' WITH THE DEVIL/Eruption	(Warner Bros. 8556)	.50	2.00	78
YOU REALLY GOT ME/Atomic Funk	(Warner Bros. 8515)	.50	2.00	78
VAN RONK, Dave				
CLOUDS (FROM BOTH SIDES NOW)/ Romping Through The Swamp	(Verve Forecast 5080)	.75	3.00	67
HEAD INSPECTOR/Dink's Song	(Verve Forecast 5070)	1.25	5.00	67
(With the Hudson Dusters)				
VAN ZANDT, Townes				
FRAULEIN/Don't Let The Sunshine Fool You	(Poppy 170)	.50	2.00	71
NO PLACE TO FALL/	(Tomato 10005)	.50	2.00	78
PONCHO & LEFTY/	(Poppy 238)	.50	2.00	72
WAITIN' AROUND TO DIE/Talking Karate Blues	(Poppy 506)	.50	2.00	73
WHO DO YOU LOVE/	(Tomato 10003)	.50	2.00	78
VANCE, Billy (Billy Galenti)				
I WON'T TAKE A CHANCE/ She Wore The Coolest Hot Pants	(August 2585)	2.00	8.00	
VANCE, Kenny (Of Jay & The Americans)				
LOOKING FOR AN ECHO/Each Others Arms	(Atlantic 3259)	.75	3.00	75
VANCE, Paul				
DOMMAGE, DOMMAGE/Sexy	(Scepter 12164)	.75	3.00	66
IT HAPPENS EVERY DAY/My Vie	(Scepter 12175)	.75	3.00	66
VANDALS, The				
WET & WILD/It's Like Now Baby Plus 1 More	(Golden Gate 0011)	1.00	4.00	
VANGELIS (Of Aphrodite's Child)				
SO LONG AGO, SO CLEAR/	(RCA 10733)	.50	2.00	76
VANGUARDS, The				
BABY DOLL/My Friend Mary Ann	(Dot 15791)	1.25	5.00	58
I'M MOVIN'/Moonlight	(Ivy 103)	3.00	12.00	58
VANILLA FUDGE				
I CAN'T MAKE IT ALONE/Need Love	(Atco 6703)	.75	3.00	69
PEOPLE/Some Velvet Morning	(Atco 6679)	.75	3.00	69
SEASON OF THE WITCH (PART 1)/ Season Of The Witch (Part 2)	(Atco 6632)	.75	3.00	68
SHOTGUN/Good, Good Lovin'	(Atco 6655)	.75	3.00	69
TAKE ME FOR A LITTLE WHILE/Thoughts	(Atco 6616)	.75	3.00	68
WHERE IS MY MIND/Look Of Love	(Atco 6554)	.75	3.00	68
YOU KEEP ME HANGIN' ON/ Take Me For A Little While	(Atco 6495)	1.00	4.00	67
YOU KEEP ME HANGIN' ON/ Come By Day, Come By Night	(Atco 6590)	.75	3.00	68
VANITY FARE				
BIG PARADE, THE/Nowhere To Go	(DJM 70029,	.50	2.00	75
EARLY IN THE MORNING/You Made Me Love You	(Page One 21027)	.75	3.00	69
HITCHIN' A RIDE/Man Child	(Page One 21029)	.75	3.00	70
I LIVE FOR THE SUN/On The Other Side	(Page One 21007)	.75	3.00	69
(I REMEMBER) SUMMER MORNING/ Megowd (Something Tells Me)	(Page One 21033)	.75	3.00	70
ROCK & ROLL IS BACK/Making For The Sun	(20th Century 2012)	.50	2.00	73
SALT WATER BABIES/Peter Who?	(Brent 7067)	.50	2.00	67
TAKE IT, SHAKE IT, BREAK MY HEART/Down Home	(20th Century 2036)	.50	2.00	73
WHERE DID ALL THE GOOD TIMES GO/Stand	(DJM 70024)	.50	2.00	75
VANN, Joey (Of the Duprees)				
TRY TO REMEMBER/My Love, My Love	(Coed 606)	1.50	6.00	64
VANN, Teddy				
CINDY/I'm Waiting	(Triple-X 101)	1.00	4.00	60
LONELY CROWD/I Was Born To Love You	(Columbia 41996)	.75	3.00	61
VANN, Tommy, & The Echoes				
TOO YOUNG/Give A Little Bit	(Academy 118)	1.00	4.00	
VANNELLI, Gino				
FEEL THE FIRE (VALLEYS OF VALHALIA)/Black & Blue	(A&M 2002)	.50	2.00	78
FLY INTO THIS NIGHT/Ugly Man	(A&M 1911)	.50	2.00	77
I JUST WANNA STOP/The Surest Things Change	(A&M 2072)	.50	2.00	78
KEEP ON WALKING/Love Is A Night?	(A&M 1790)	.50	2.00	76
LOVE ME NOW/Father & Son	(A&M 1732)	.50	2.00	75
LOVE OF MY LIFE/Omens Of Love	(A&M 1861)	.50	2.00	76
MAMA COCO/Gettin' High	(A&M 1760)	.50	2.00	75
ONE NIGHT WITH YOU/Black & Blue	(A&M 2025)	.50	2.00	78
PEOPLE GOTTA MOVE/Son Of A New York Gun	(A&M 1614)	.50	2.00	74
RIVER MUST FLOW, THE/Mardi Gras	(A&M 2133)	.50	2.00	79
SUMMERS OF MY LIFE/	(A&M 1879)	.50	2.00	76
WHEELS OF LIFE/Mardi Gras	(A&M 2114)	.50	2.00	79
VANWARMER, Randy				
CALL ME/Forever Loving You	(Bearsville 49071)	.50	2.00	79
GOTTA GET OUT OF HERE/Convincing Lies	(Bearsville 49004)	.50	2.00	79
JUST WHEN I NEEDED YOU MOST/Your Light	(Bearsville 0334)	.50	2.00	79
VARE, Ronnie, & The Inspirations				
LET'S ROCK LITTLE GIRL/Love Is Just For Two	(Dell 5203)	1.25	5.00	59
VAREEATIONS, The				
FOOLISH ONE/It's The Loving Season	(Dionn 510)	2.50	10.00	
TIME, THE/Ssab-bbrom	(Dionn 506)	2.50	10.00	

TITLE/FLIP	LABEL & NO.	GOOD	NEAR MINT	YR.
VARNELLS, The				
DAY IN COURT/All Because	(Arnold 1006)	3.75	15.00	61
RAINDROPS/Why Can't You Be True	(Rulu 6753)	20.00	80.00	
(Shown as by the Vernalls)				
WHO CREATED LOVE/Street Time	(Arnold 1003)	3.75	15.00	61
VASEL, Marianne, & Erich Storz				
LITTLE TRAIN, THE/Am I Wasting My Time On You	(Mercury 71286)	1.00	4.00	58
VAUGHAN, Frankie				
JUDY/Am I Wasting My Time On You	(Epic 9273)	1.00	4.00	58
VAUGHAN, Sarah				
BROKEN-HEARTED MELODY/Misty	(Mercury 71477)	.75	3.00	59
C'EST LA VIE/Never	(Mercury 70727)	1.00	4.00	55
ETERNALLY/You're My Baby	(Mercury 71562)	.75	3.00	60
FABULOUS CHARACTER/The Other Woman	(Mercury 70885)	1.00	4.00	56
HOW IMPORTANT CAN IT BE/Waltzing Down The Aisle	(Mercury 70534)	1.00	4.00	55
I COVER THE WATERFRONT/Don't Worry Bout Me	(MGM 10819)	1.25	5.00	50
I'LL KNOW/De Gas Pipe, She's Leaking Joe	(Columbia 39124)	1.25	5.00	51
MAKE YOURSELF COMFORTABLE/Idle Gossip	(Mercury 70469)	1.00	4.00	54
SERENATA/Let's	(Roulette 4285)	.75	3.00	60
SMOOTH OPERATOR/Maybe It's Because	(Mercury 71519)	.75	3.00	59
THESE THINGS I OFFER YOU/Deep Purple	(Columbia 39370)	1.25	5.00	51
THINKING OF YOU/I Love The Guy	(Columbia 38925)	1.25	5.00	51
WHAT A DIFFERENCE A DAY MAKES/I Can't Get Started	(MGM 10762)	1.25	5.00	50
WHATEVER LOLA WANTS/Oh Yeah	(Mercury 70595)	1.00	4.00	55
VAUGHN, Billy (Of The Hilltoppers)				
BLUE HAWAII/Tico Tico	(Dot 15879)	.75	3.00	58
BLUE HAWAII/Tico Tico	(Dot S-201)	1.00	4.00	59
(Stereo single issue)				
HAWAIIAN WAR CHANT/	(Dot 15900)	.75	3.00	59
HAWAIIAN WAR CHANT/	(Dot S-202)	1.00	4.00	59
(Stereo single issue)				
LA PALOMA/Here Is My Love	(Dot 15795)	.75	3.00	58
LOOK FOR A STAR/He'll Have To Go	(Dot 16106)	.75	3.00	60
MELODY OF LOVE/Joy Ride	(Dot 15247)	1.00	4.00	54
SAIL ALONG SILVERY MOON/Raunchy	(Dot 15661)	1.00	4.00	57
SHIFTING WHISPERING SANDS, THE (PART 1)/ The Shifting Whispering Sands (Part 2)	(Dot 15409)	1.00	4.00	
(With narration by Ken Nordine)				
SWINGIN' SAFARI, A/Indian Love Call	(Dot 16374)	.75	3.00	62
THEME FROM (THE THREE PENNY OPERA) MORITAT, A/ Little Boy Blue	(Dot 15444)	1.00	4.00	56
WHEELS/Orange Blossom Special	(Dot 16174)	.75	3.00	61
WHEN THE WHITE LILACS BLOOM AGAIN/Spanish Diary	(Dot 15491)	1.00	4.00	56
YOUR CHEATIN' HEART/Lights Out	(Dot 15936)	.75	3.00	59
YOUR CHEATIN' HEART/Lights Out	(Dot S-205)	1.00	4.00	59
(Stereo single issue)				
VEE, Bobby (Robert Thomas Velline)				
BE TRUE TO YOURSELF/A Letter From Betty	(Liberty 55581)	.75	3.00	63
BEAUTIFUL PEOPLE/I May Be Gone	(Liberty 56009)	.75	3.00	67
BEFORE YOU GO/Here Today	(Liberty 55921)	.75	3.00	66
CHARMS/Bobby Tomorrow	(Liberty 55530)	.75	3.00	63
COME BACK WHEN YOU GROW UP/Swahili Serenade	(Liberty 55964)	.75	3.00	67
CROSS MY HEART/This Is The End	(Liberty 55761)	.75	3.00	65
DEVIL OR ANGEL/Since I Met You Baby	(Liberty 55270)	1.00	4.00	60
DO WHAT YOU GOTTA DO/Thank You	(Liberty 56057)	.75	3.00	68
ELECTRIC TRAINS & YOU/In & Out Of Love	(Liberty 56149)	.75	3.00	69
EV'RY LITTLE BIT HURTS/Pretend You Don't See Her	(Liberty 55751)	.75	3.00	64
GIRL I USED TO KNOW, A/Gone	(Liberty 55854)	.75	3.00	66
HICKORY, DICK & DOC/I Wish You Were Mine Again	(Liberty 55700)	.75	3.00	64
HOW MANY TEARS/Baby Face	(Liberty 55325)	1.00	4.00	61
HOW MANY TEARS/Bashful Bob	(Liberty 3331)	2.00	8.00	61
(Compact 33 stereo single)				
HOW TO MAKE A FAREWELL/Where Is She	(Liberty 55726)	.75	3.00	64
I'LL MAKE YOU MINE/She's Sorry	(Liberty 55670)	.75	3.00	64
IT'S GOOD TO BE HERE/	(Shadybrook 030)	.50	2.00	77
KEEP ON TRYING/You Won't Forget Me	(Liberty 55790)	.75	3.00	65
LET'S CALL IT A DAY GIRL/Gonna Make It Up	(Liberty 56124)	.75	3.00	69
LOOK AT ME GIRL/Save A Love	(Liberty 55877)	.75	3.00	66
LOVIN' YOU/	(Shadybrook 013)	.50	2.00	76
MAYBE JUST TODAY/You're A Big Girl Now	(Liberty 56014)	.75	3.00	68
(MEDLEY) MY GIRL-HEY GIRL/ Just Keep It Up (And See What Happens)	(Liberty 55033)	.75	3.00	68
NIGHT HAS A THOUSAND EYES, THE/ Anonymous Phone Call	(Liberty 55521)	.75	3.00	62
ONE LAST KISS/Laurie	(Liberty 55251)	1.00	4.00	60
PLEASE DON'T ASK ABOUT BARBARA/ I Can't Say Goodbye	(Liberty 55419)	.75	3.00	62
PUNISH HER/Someday (When I'm Gone From You)	(Liberty 55479)	.75	3.00	62
RUBBER BALL/Every Day	(Liberty 55287)	.75	3.00	60
RUN LIKE THE DEVIL/Take A Look Around Me	(Liberty 55828)	.75	3.00	65
RUN TO HIM/Walkin' With My Angel	(Liberty 55388)	.75	3.00	61
SHARING YOU/In My Baby's Eyes	(Liberty 55451)	.75	3.00	62
SOMEONE TO LOVE ME/Thank You	(Liberty 56080)	.75	3.00	68
STAYIN' IN/More Than I Can Say	(Liberty 55296)	.75	3.00	61
STORY OF MY LIFE/High Coin	(Liberty 55843)	.75	3.00	65
STRANGER IN YOUR ARMS/1963	(Liberty 55654)	.75	3.00	64
SUZIE BABY/Flyin' High (Instrumental)	(Soma 1110)	2.50	10.00	
(With the Shadows)				
SUZIE BABY/Flyin' High (Instrumental)	(Liberty 55208)	1.25	5.00	59
(With the Shadows)				
SWEET SWEETHEART/Rock & Roll Music & You	(Liberty 56208)	.50	2.00	70
TAKE GOOD CARE OF MY BABY/Bashful Bob	(Liberty 55354)	.75	3.00	61
TAKE GOOD CARE OF MY BABY/	(United Artists 199)	.50	2.00	71
(Shown as by Robert Thomas Velline)				
WHAT DO YOU WANT/My Love Loves Me	(Liberty 55234)	1.00	4.00	60
WOMAN IN MY LIFE/	(Liberty 56178)	.50	2.00	70
YESTERDAY & YOU (ARMEN'S THEME)/ Never Love A Robin	(Liberty 55636)	.75	3.00	63
YOU'RE NEVER GONNA FIND SOMEONE LIKE ME/	(Shadybrook 026)	.50	2.00	76
VEGAS, Lolly				
I'M GONNA SAY WE'RE THROUGH/It's Love	(Audio International 101)	1.00	4.00	61
VEGAS, Pat & Lolly				
BOOM BOOM (RADDA-DADDA-DA)/ Two Figures (On The Wedding Cake)	(Reprise 20199)	.75	3.00	63
LET'S GET IT ON/Walk On (Right Out Of My Life)	(Mercury 72509)	.75	3.00	65
ROBOT WALK, THE/Don't You Remember	(Apogee 101)	1.00	4.00	64
Also see Redbone				
V-EIGHTS, The				
MY HEART/Papa's Yellow Tie	(ABC-Paramount 10201)	.75	3.00	61
MY HEART/Papa's Yellow Tie	(Vibro 4005)	1.25	5.00	61
VEJTABLES, The				
FEEL THE MUSIC/Shadows	(Uptown 741)	1.50	6.00	
I STILL LOVE YOU/Anything	(Autumn 15)	1.00	4.00	65
LAST THING ON MY MIND, THE/Mansion Of Tears	(Autumn 23)	1.25	5.00	65
VELAIRES, The				
DREAM/Sticks & Stones	(Jamie 1203)	1.00	4.00	61
ROLL OVER BEETHOVEN/Brazil	(Jamie 1198)	1.00	4.00	61
ROLL OVER BEETHOVEN/Frankie & Johnny	(Jamie 1198)	1.00	4.00	61
UBANGI STOMP/It's Almost Tomorrow	(Jamie 1211)	1.00	4.00	62
VELEZ, Martha				
DISCO NIGHT/	(Sire 727)	.50	2.00	76
MAGIC IN HIS HANDS/	(Polydor 14158)	.50	2.00	73
UP TO YOU/	(Sire 1010)	.50	2.00	75

TITLE/FLIP	LABEL & NO.	GOOD	NEAR MINT	YR.
VELONS, The				
SHELLY/From The Chapel	(Blast 216)	6.25	25.00	63
VELS, The				
IN-LAWS/Do The Walk	(Amy 881)	3.00	12.00	63
VEL-TONES, The				
NOW/I Need You So	(Zara 901)	2.50	10.00	
NOW/I Need You So	(Lost Nite 103)	1.25	5.00	
VELTONES, The				
SOMEDAY/Foolin' Love	(Satellite 109)	2.50	10.00	59
VELVET ANGELS, The				
I'M IN LOVE/Let Me Come Back	(Medieval 201)	1.00	4.00	
VELVETEENS, The				
BABY BABY/Teen Prayer	(Stark 101/102)	.75	3.00	61
I THANK YOU/Meant To Be	(Laurie 3126)	.75	3.00	62
VELVET, Jimmy				
BOUQUET OF FLOWERS/When I Needed You	(Cub 9111)	.75	3.00	62
I WON'T BE BACK THIS YEAR/Young Hearts	(Philips 40314)	.75	3.00	65
IT'S ALMOST TOMORROW/Blue Eyes (Don't Run Away)	(Philips 40285)	.75	3.00	65
IT'S ALMOST TOMORROW/Young Hearts	(Velvet Tone 102)	1.00	4.00	65
LOOK AT ME/Sometimes At Night	(Division 102)	1.25	5.00	61
(Shown as by Jimmy Velvit)				
LOOK AT ME/Sometimes At Night	(Cub 9100)	.75	3.00	61
TEEN ANGEL/Mission Bell	(Tollie 9037)	.75	3.00	64
TO THE AISLE/Lonely Lonely Night	(ABC-Paramount 10528)	.75	3.00	64
WE BELONG TOGETHER/ I'm Gonna Try (To Forget The Une I Love)	(Velvet 201)	1.50	6.00	61
(Shown as by Jimmy Velvit)				
WE BELONG TOGETHER/ I'm Gonna Try (To Forget The One I Love)	(Cub 9105)	1.00	4.00	62
WE BELONG TOGETHER/History Of Love	(ABC-Paramount 10488)	.75	3.00	63
VELVET KEYS, The				
DONT TAKE MY PICTURE, TAKE ME/The Truth About Youth	(King 5109)	3.75	15.00	58
LET'S STAY AFTER SCHOOL/My Baby's Gone	(King 5090)	3.75	15.00	57
VELVET NIGHT				
VELVET NIGHT/I'm Sure He'll Come	(Metromedia 110)	.75	3.00	69
VELVETS, The				
DAWN/Crying In The Chapel	(Monument 810)	1.00	4.00	63
EVERYBODY KNOWS/Hand Jivin' Baby	(Plaid 101)	1.00	4.00	59
HAPPY DAYS ARE HERE AGAIN/If I Could Be With You	(20th Fox 165)	1.25	5.00	59
HERE COMES THAT SONG AGAIN/Nightmare	(Monument 836)	1.00	4.00	64
IF/Let The Fool Kiss You	(Monument 861)	1.25	5.00	64
LAUGH/Lana	(Monument 448)	1.50	6.00	62
LET THE GOOD TIMES ROLL/ The Lights Go On, The Lights Go Off	(Monument 464)	1.00	4.00	61
LOVE EXPRESS/Don't Let Him Take My Baby	(Monument 458)	1.00	4.00	62
THAT LUCKY OLD SUN/Time & Again	(Monument 512)	2.00	8.00	62
TONIGHT (COULD BE THE NIGHT)/Spring Fever	(Monument 441)	1.50	6.00	61
VELVET SATINS, The				
AN ANGEL LIKE YOU/Cherry	(General American 716)	3.00	12.00	
ANGEL ADORABLE/Heading For The Rooftop	(General American 720)	3.00	12.00	
VELVET SEED, The				
SHARON PATTERSON/Flim Flan Man	(MAI 201)	1.00	4.00	
VELVET UNDERGROUND, The (With Lou Reed & John Cale)				
I HEARD HER CALL MY NAME/Here She Comes Now	(Verve 10560)	1.25	5.00	67
JESUS/What Goes On	(MGM 14057)	1.25	5.00	69
SUNDAY MORNING/Female Fatale	(Verve 10466)	1.25	5.00	66
(Shown as by Nico & The Velvet Underground)				
WHO LOVES THE SUN/	(Cotillion 44107)	1.00	4.00	71
VENNY & MELVIN (Neil Levenson & Billy Carl)				
DIP DIP DOODLE/Doodle Dip Dance	(Laurie 3574)	1.50	6.00	71
VENTRILLS, The				
CONFUSION/Alone In The Night	(Ivanhoe 5000)	2.00	8.00	67
CONFUSION/Alone In The Night	(Parkway 141)	1.25	5.00	67
VENTURAS, The				
HIGH NOON RUMBLE/Corrido Twist	(Donna 1352)	1.00	4.00	62
RAM CHARGER/Apache	(Drum Boy 107)	1.00	4.00	64
WELCOME BEATLES/My Happiness (Featuring Lil' Wally)	(Drum Boy 108)	1.25	5.00	64
VENTURES, The (Featuring Don Wilson & Bob Bogle)				
ARABESQUE/Ginza Lights	(Dolton 321)	.75	3.00	66
BEETHOVAN'S SONATA/Peter & The Wolf	(United Artists 50903)	.50	2.00	72
BIRD ROCKERS/Ten Seconds To Heaven	(Dolton 308)	.75	3.00	65
BLUE MOON/Lady Of Spain	(Dolton 47)	.75	3.00	61
BLUE STAR/Comin' Home Baby	(Dolton 320)	.75	3.00	66
CHASE, THE/Savage	(Dolton 85)	.75	3.00	63
CISCO KID, THE/	(United Artists 333)	.50	2.00	74
COOKIES & COKE/The Real McCoy	(Blue Horizon 100)	1.50	6.00	60
DIAMOND HEAD/Lonely Girl	(Dolton 303)	.75	3.00	65
FUGITIVE/Scratchin'	(Dolton 94)	.75	3.00	64
GREEN HORNET THEME/Fuzzy & Wild	(Dolton 323)	.75	3.00	66
HAWAII FIVE-O/Soul Breeze	(Liberty 56068)	.75	3.00	69
INSTANT MASHED/My Bonnie Lies	(Dolton 55)	.75	3.00	62
JOURNEY TO THE STARS/Walkin' With Pluto	(Dolton 91)	.75	3.00	64
KICKSTAND/(Theme From) "The Wild Angels"	(Dolton 327)	.75	3.00	66
LA BAMBA/Gemini	(Dolton 311)	.75	3.00	65
LAST TANGO IN PARIS/	(United Artists 207)	.50	2.00	73
LOLITA YA YA/Lucille	(Dolton 60)	.75	3.00	62
LULLABY OF THE LEAVES/Ginchy	(Dolton 41)	.75	3.00	61
MOONLIGHT SERENADE/	(United Artists 784)	.50	2.00	76
(Shown as by the New Ventures)				
NIGHT RUN/Scratch	(Blue Horizon 6052)	1.50	6.00	60
(Shown as by the Marksmen)				
NINTH WAVE, THE/Damaged Goods	(Dolton 78)	.75	3.00	63
ON THE ROAD/Mirrors & Shadow	(Liberty 56007)	.75	3.00	67
PENETRATION/Wild Thing	(Dolton 325)	.75	3.00	66
PERFIDIA/No Trespassing	(Dolton 28)	.75	3.00	60
RAM-BUNK-SHUSH/Lonely Heart	(Dolton 32)	.75	3.00	61
SECRET AGENT MAN/007-11	(Dolton 316)	.75	3.00	66
(THEME FROM) SILVER CITY/Bluer Than Blue	(Dolton 44)	.75	3.00	61
SKIP TO M' LIMBO/El Cumbanchero	(Dolton 68)	.75	3.00	63
SKYLAB (PASSPORT TO THE FUTURE)/	(United Artists 277)	.50	2.00	73
SLAUGHTER ON TENTH AVENUE/Rap City	(Dolton 300)	.75	3.00	64
SLEIGH RIDE/Snow Flakes	(Dolton 312)	1.00	4.00	65
STRAWBERRY FIELDS FOREVER/ (Theme From) "Endless Summer"	(Liberty 55977)	.75	3.00	67
SUPERSTAR REVUE/	(United Artists 687)	.50	2.00	75
SWINGIN' CREEPER/Pedal Pusher	(Dolton 306)	.75	3.00	65
THEME FROM A SUMMER PLACE/A Summer Love	(Liberty 56115)	.75	3.00	69
THEME FROM "CHARLIE'S ANGELS"/	(United Artists 942)	.50	2.00	77
(Shown as by the New Ventures)				
THEME FROM SHAFT/	(United Artists 50851)	.50	2.00	72
2,000 POUND BEE, THE (PART 1)/ 2,000 Pound Bee, The (Part 2)	(Dolton 67)	.75	3.00	62
WALK DON'T RUN/Home	(Blue Horizon 101)	2.50	10.00	60
WALK DON'T RUN/Home	(Dolton 25)	1.00	4.00	60
WALK DON'T RUN/The McCoy	(Dolton 25)	1.00	4.00	60
WALK DON'T RUN '64/Cruel Sea	(Dolton 96)	.75	3.00	64
YELLOW JACKET/Genesis	(Dolton 50)	.75	3.00	61
Instrumentals				

TITLE/FLIP	LABEL & NO.	GOOD	NEAR MINT	YR.
VENUS FLYTRAP				
HAVE YOU EVER/The Note	(Jaguar 103)	1.25	5.00	
VENUS, Vic				
MOONFLIGHT/Everybody's On Strike	(Buddah 118)	.75	3.00	69
(Novelty/Break-in)				
VERA, Billy				
ALL MY LOVE/My Heart Cries	(Rust 5051)	1.00	4.00	62
(With The Contrasts)				
ARE YOU COMING TO MY PARTY/ I've Been Loving You Too Long	(Atlantic 2555)	.75	3.00	68
BIBLE SALESMAN, THE/Are You Coming To My Party	(Atlantic 2628)	.75	3.00	69
JULIE/Time Doesn't Matter Anymore	(Atlantic 2586)	.75	3.00	68
REACHING FOR THE MOON/Tell It Like It Is	(Atlantic 2654)	.75	3.00	69
WITH PEN IN HAND/Good Morning Blues	(Atlantic 2526)	.75	3.00	68
Also see Blue Eyed Soul				
VERA, Billy, & Judy Clay				
COUNTRY GIRL-CITY BOY/So Good	(Atlantic 2480)	.75	3.00	68
STORYBOOK CHILDREN/Really Together	(Atlantic 2445)	.75	3.00	67
VERDICTS, The				
MY LIFE'S DESIRE/The Mummy's Ball	(East Coast 103/104)	3.00	12.00	61
VERNALLS, The: see Varnells, The				
VERNE, Larry				
ABDUL'S PARTY/Tubby Tilly	(Era 3044)	.75	3.00	61
BEATNIK/The Speck	(Era 3065)	.75	3.00	61
CHARLIE AT THE BAT/Pow, Right In The Kisser	(Era 3051)	.75	3.00	61
COWARD THAT WON THE WEST, THE/Porcupine Patrol	(Era 3091)	.75	3.00	62
I'M A BRAVE LITTLE SOLDIER/Hoo Ha	(Era 3075)	.75	3.00	62
MISTER LIVINGSTON/Roller Coaster	(Era 3034)	.75	3.00	60
MR. CUSTER/Okeefenokee Two Step	(Era 3024)	.75	3.00	60
RETURN OF MR. CUSTER, THE/Running Through The Forest	(Era 3139)	.75	3.00	64
Comedy				
VERNON, Ray (Vernon Wray)				
EVIL ANGEL/Remember You're Mine	(Cameo 109)	1.00	4.00	57
EVIL ANGEL/I'll Take Tomorrow Today	(Cameo 109)	1.00	4.00	57
(Reissue)				
IT'S SO EASY/Two Teenage Hearts	(Mark 614)	1.25	5.00	58
TERRY (YOU'RE ASKING TO MUCH)/I'm Countin' On You	(Cameo 115)	1.00	4.00	58
WINDOW SHOPPING/I'll Be So Good To You	(Cameo 136)	1.00	4.00	58
VERNON'S GIRLS				
WE LOVE THE BEATLES/Hey Lover Boy	(Challenge 59234)	1.25	5.00	64
Also see Carefrees, The				
Also see Breakaways, The				

TITLE/FLIP	LABEL & NO.	GOOD	NEAR MINT	YR.
VERONICA (Of the Ronettes)				
SO YOUNG/Larry L	(Phil Spector 1)	1.00	4.00	64
WHY DON'T THEY LET US FALL IN LOVE/ Chubby Danny D	(Phil Spector 2)	1.00	4.00	64
VERSAILLES, The				
LITTLE GIRL OF MINE/Teenagers Dream	(Harlequin 401)	1.00	4.00	
VERSATILES, The				
BYE BYE BABY/You're Good Enough For Me	(Bronco 2050)	1.00	4.00	66
EASY TO SAY/Seven Steps To Love	(Rich Tone 18643)	1.00	4.00	67
Also see Fifth Dimension				
VERSATILES, The				
BLUE FEELING/Just Pretending	(Ramco 3717)	.75	3.00	62
VERSATILES, The				
LUNDEE DUNDEE/Whisper In Your Ear	(Ro-cal 1002)	3.00	12.00	60
VESPERS, The: see Four Epics, The				
VESTEE, Russ				
TEARDROPS/Well All Right	(Amy 833)	2.50	10.00	61
VESTELLES, The				
DITTA WA DO/Come Home	(Decca 30733)	2.00	8.00	58
VETTES, The				
LITTLE FORD RAGTOP/Happy Holiday	(MGM 13186)	1.00	4.00	63
VIBRA-SONICS, The				
DRAG RACE/Thunder Storm	(Ideal 94874)	1.00	4.00	
Instrumentals				
VIBES, The				
YOU GOT ME CRYING/A Killer Came To Town	(Rayna 103)	1.50	6.00	
VIBRANTS, The				
FUEL INJECTION/The Breeze & I	(Bay Towne 409)	1.00	4.00	63
WILDFIRE/Scorpion	(Triumph 101)	1.00	4.00	62
Instrumentals				
VIBRATORS, The				
BABY BABY/London Girls	(Columbia 10685)	.50	2.00	77
VIC & THE CATALINAS				
TALKIN' ABOUT MY GIRL/Hello Girl	(Bar Clay 1967)	1.25	5.00	

TITLE/FLIP	LABEL & NO.	GOOD	NEAR MINT	YR.
VICEROYS, The				
BUZZ BOMB/Joshin'	(Bethlehem 45-3070)	1.00	4.00	63
DARTELL STOMP/Granny Medley	(Bolo 743)	1.00	4.00	63
DON'T LET GO/Down Beat Blues	(E'Den 9001)	1.00	4.00	62
GRANNY'S PAD/Blues	(Dot 16456)	1.00	4.00	63
I'M SO SORRY/Uncle Sam Needs You	(Little Star 1008)	1.00	4.00	61
I'M SO SORRY/Uncle Sam Needs You	(Smash 1716)	.75	3.00	61
SEAGRAMS/Moasin'	(Bethlehem 45-3045)	1.00	4.00	62
("Seagrams" was reissued using the title "Seagreen")				
SEAGREEN/Moasin'	(Bethlehem 45-3045)	.75	3.00	62
VICKI				
JOHNNY HAD A YO YO/	(Parktowne 63)	.75	3.00	
VICTORIANS, The (Featuring Nick Massi)				
BABY TOYS/I Saw My Girl	(Reprise 0434)	3.00	12.00	66
MERRY-GO-ROUND/Wasn't The Summer Short	(Bang 550)	2.50	10.00	66
VICTORIANS, The				
HAPPY BIRTHDAY BLUE/Oh What A Night For Love	(Liberty 55693)	1.00	4.00	63
IF I LOVED YOU/Monkey Stroll	(Liberty 55728)	1.00	4.00	64
MOVE IN A LITTLE CLOSER/Lovin'	(Arnold 571)	1.00	4.00	
WHAT MAKES LITTLE GIRLS CRY/Climb Every Mountain	(Liberty 55574)	1.00	4.00	63
VIDALTONES, The				
FOREVER/Someone To Love	(Josie 900)	2.50	10.00	61
VIDELS, The (With Pete Anders & Vinnie Poncia)				
BE MY GIRL/Place In My Heart	(Medieval 203)	1.00	4.00	59
BE MY GIRL/Place In My Heart	(Rhody 2000)	2.50	10.00	59
I WISH/	(Dusty Disc 473)	1.50	6.00	
LETTER FROM ANN, A/This Year's Mister New	(Kapp 405)	2.00	8.00	61
MISTER LONELY/I'll Forget You	(JDS 5004)	1.25	5.00	60
NOW THAT SUMMER IS HERE/She's Not Coming Home	(JDS 5005)	1.50	6.00	60
STREETS OF LOVE/I'll Keep On Waiting	(Kapp 361)	1.50	6.00	61
WE BELONG TOGETHER/It's All Over	(Musicnote 117)	2.00	8.00	63
Also see Trade Winds, The				
Also see Treasurers, The				
VIDONE, Bob				
WEIRD/Don't Worry	(Fleetwood 1003)	1.00	4.00	
VIGRASS & OSBORNE (Paul Vigrass & Gary Osborne)				
GYPSY WOMAN/	(Epic 50044)	.50	2.00	74
MEN OF LEARNING/Forever Autumn	(Uni 55330)	.50	2.00	72
MISTER DEADLINE/Remember Pearl Harbour	(Uni 55355)	.50	2.00	72
VIRGINIA/Bellerina	(Uni 55344)	.50	2.00	72
VI-KINGS, The				
ROCK A LITTLE BIT/Desert Boots	(Del-Mann 545)	1.00	4.00	60
VIKINGS, The				
SNEAKY SURFIN'/Nicotine	(Athens 201)	1.00	4.00	
VILLAGE STOMPERS, The				
FIDDLER ON THE ROOF/	(Epic 9740)	.75	3.00	64
FROM RUSSIA WITH LOVE/The Bridges Of Budapest	(Epic 9674)	.75	3.00	64
WASHINGTON SQUARE/Turkish Delight	(Epic 9617)	.75	3.00	63
Instrumentals				
VILLAGE VOICES, The: see 4 Seasons, The				
VILLA, Joey (Of the Royal Teens)				
ALL-AMERICAN GIRL/Mickey Mouse Got A Girl Friend	(Capitol 4484)	1.25	5.00	61
BLANCHE/Mona Lisa	(PMFI 2002)	3.75	15.00	
BLANCHE/The Oriental	(Chevron 500)	1.00	4.00	
HONEST DARLING/Chloe	(De-Lite 501)	1.25	5.00	
VILLARI, Guy (Of the Regents)				
MASH POTATO MARY/I'm All Alone	(Cousins 1004)	1.50	6.00	
Also see Runarounds, The				
VINA, Joe				
MARINA/That's Alright	(Allied 7778)	.75	3.00	
VINCE & THE WAIKIKI RUMBLERS				
WAIKIKI RUMBLE/Pacifica	(Big Ben 1003)	1.00	4.00	
(Instrumentals)				
VINCENT, Danny				
CAROLYN/The Days Are Long	(Roulette 4334)	1.00	4.00	61

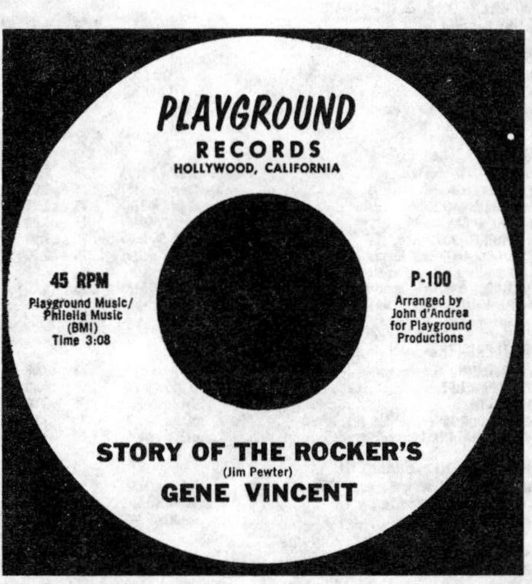

TITLE/FLIP	LABEL & NO.	GOOD	NEAR MINT	YR.
VINCENT, Gene (Vincent Eugene Craddock)				
AIN'T THAT TOO MUCH/Bird Doggin'	(Challenge 59337)	.75	3.00	65
BE-BOP-A-LULA/Woman Love	(Capitol 3450)	1.50	6.00	56
BI-BICKEY BI-BO-BO-GO/Five Days, Five Days	(Capitol 3678)	3.00	12.00	57
BLUEJEAN BOP/Who Slapped John	(Capitol 3558)	1.50	6.00	56
BORN TO BE A ROLLING STONE/Hurtin' For You Baby	(Challenge 59365)	.75	3.00	65
CRAZY LEGS/Important Words	(Capitol 3617)	1.50	6.00	57
DANCE TO THE BOP/I Got It	(Capitol 3839)	1.50	6.00	57
I GOT A BABY/Walkin' Home From School	(Capitol 3874)	1.50	6.00	58
IF YOU WANT MY LOVIN'/Mister Loneliness	(Capitol 4525)	1.25	5.00	61
LITTLE LOVER/Git It	(Capitol 4051)	1.50	6.00	58
LONELY STREET/I've Got My Eyes On You	(Challenge 59347)	.75	3.00	65
LOTTA LOVIN'/Wear My Ring	(Capitol 3763)	1.25	5.00	57
LUCKY STAR/Baby Don't Believe Him	(Capitol 4665)	1.25	5.00	61
PISTOL PACKIN' MAMA/Anna-Annabelle	(Capitol 4442)	1.50	6.00	60
RACE WITH THE DEVIL/Gonna Back Up Baby	(Capitol 3530)	2.00	8.00	56
RIGHT NOW/The Night Is So Lonely	(Capitol 4237)	1.25	5.00	60
RIGHT NOW/The Night Is So Lonely	(Capitol 4237)	8.75	35.00	60
(Picture sleeve)				
ROCKY ROAD BLUES/Yes, I Love You Blue	(Capitol 4010)	2.50	10.00	58
SAY MAMA/Be Bop Boogie Boy	(Capitol 4105)	2.00	8.00	59
STORY OF THE ROCKERS/Pickin' Poppies	(Forever 6001)	1.25	5.00	69
STORY OF THE ROCKER'S/Pickin' Poppies	(Playground P-100)	18.75	75.00	68
(This original label issue contains a different recording of the song than is heard on the Forever release.)				
TRUE TO YOU/Baby Blue	(Capitol 3959)	1.50	6.00	58
WAY THE WORLD TURNED BLUE, THE/ How I Love Them Old Songs	(Kama Sutra 518)	.75	3.00	73
WHO'S PUSHIN' YOUR SWING/Over The Rainbow	(Capitol 4153)	1.50	6.00	59
WILD CAT/Right Here On Earth	(Capitol 4313)	2.00	8.00	60
May be shown as Gene Vincent & the Blue Caps on some issues. Capitol promotional singles may bring slightly more than the prices shown here for commercial releases.				
VINCENT, Rudy				
ROCKIN' CRICKETS/Five Points	(End 1042)	1.00	4.00	59
VINCENT, Stan				
ANGEL BY YOUR SIDE/Little Teardrops	(Marlu 7003)	2.50	10.00	
HI-LI-LI HI LO/Miami	(MGM 13220)	1.00	4.00	64
HOT FUDGE SUNDAES & PIZZA PIES/World Is Round	(Felie 711)	1.25	5.00	
RUNNIN' SCARED/You're Everything I Love	(Gold 101)	2.00	8.00	
VINNY & KENNY				
WHO (IS THE GIRL)/School Time	(Fire 1005)	1.25	5.00	59
VINTON, Bobby (Stanley Robert Vinton)				
BLUE ON BLUE/Those Little Things	(Epic 9593)	.75	3.00	63
BLUE VELVET/Is There A Place (Where I Can Go)	(Epic 9614)	.75	3.00	63
CLINGING VINE/Imagination Is A Magic Dream	(Epic 9705)	.75	3.00	64
CLINGING VINE/Clinging Vine	(Epic 9705)	1.25	5.00	64
(Promotional red plastic issue)				
COMING HOME SOLDIER/Don't Let My Mary Go Around	(Epic 10090)	.75	3.00	66
DEAREST SANTA/The Bell That Couldn't Jingle	(Epic 9741)	.75	3.00	64
DUM-DE-DA/Blue Clarinet	(Epic 10014)	.75	3.00	66
FRESHMAN, & A SOPHOMORE, THE/The Sheik	(Alpine 59)	1.25	5.00	60
I LOVE HOW YOU LOVE ME/Little Barefoot Boy	(Epic 10397)	.75	3.00	68
I LOVE YOU THE WAY YOU ARE/ You're My Girl (By Chuck & Johnny)	(Diamond 121)	1.00	4.00	62
JUST AS MUCH AS EVER/ Petticoat White (Summer Sky Blue)	(Epic 10048)	.75	3.00	66
LITTLE LONELY ONE/Corrina, Corrina	(Epic 9440)	.75	3.00	61
L-O-N-E-L-Y/Graduation Tears	(Epic 9791)	.75	3.00	65
LONG LONELY NIGHTS/Satin	(Epic 9768)	.75	3.00	65
MR. LONELY/It's Better To Have Loved	(Epic 9730)	.75	3.00	64
MR. LONELY/Mr. Lonely	(Epic 9730)	1.25	5.00	64
(Promotional red plastic issue)				
MY HEART BELONGS TO ONLY YOU/Warm & Tender	(Epic 9662)	.75	3.00	64
OVER THE MOUNTAIN (ACROSS THE SEA)/Faded Pictures	(Epic 9577)	.75	3.00	63
RAIN RAIN GO AWAY/Over & Over	(Epic 9532)	.75	3.00	62
ROSES ARE RED (MY LOVE)/You & I	(Epic 9509)	.75	3.00	62
SATIN PILLOWS/Careless	(Epic 9869)	.75	3.00	65
TEARS/Go Away	(Epic 9894)	.75	3.00	66
TELL MY WHY/Remembering	(Epic 9687)	.75	3.00	64
THEME FROM "HARLOW"/If I Should Lose Your Love	(Epic 9814)	.75	3.00	65
THERE! I'VE SAID IT AGAIN/Girl With The Bow In Her Hair	(Epic 9638)	.75	3.00	63
TORNADO/Posin'	(Epic 9417)	.75	3.00	60
TROUBLE IS MY MIDDLE NAME/Let's Kiss & Make Up	(Epic 9561)	.75	3.00	62
WELL, I ASK YA/ Hip-Swinging, High-Stepping Drum Majorette	(Epic 9469)	.75	3.00	61
WHAT COLOR (IS A MAN)/	(Epic 9846)	.75	3.00	65
YOU'LL NEVER FORGET/First Impression	(Alpine 50)	1.25	5.00	59
VIOLINSKI (With Mik Kominski)				
CLOG DANCE/Time To Live	(Jet 5063)	.50	2.00	79
Also see Electric Light Orchestra, The				
VIRGOS, The				
YOU'RE A STRANGER/Humptydumpty	(Pioneer 6621)	2.00	8.00	

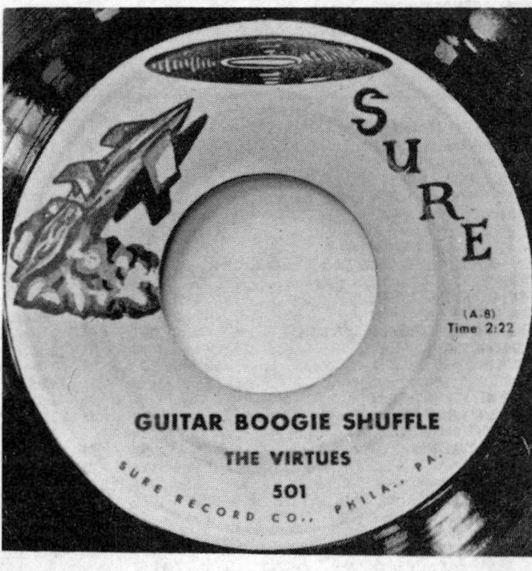

TITLE/FLIP	LABEL & NO.	GOOD	NEAR MINT	YR.
VIRTUES, The (Featuring Frank Virtue)				
BYE BYE BLUES/Happy Guitar	(Highland 2505)	.75	3.00	60
FLIPPIN' IN/Shufflin' Along	(Hunt 327)	1.00	4.00	59
GUITAR BOOGIE SHUFFLE/Guitar In Orbit	(Sure 501)	2.50	10.00	59
GUITAR BOOGIE SHUFFLE/Guitar In Orbit	(Hunt 324)	1.00	4.00	59
GUITAR BOOGIE SHUFFLE '65/Moon Maid	(Fayette 1626)	.75	3.00	65
GUITAR BOOGIE SHUFFLE TWIST/Guitar Boogie Stomp	(Sure 1733)	.75	3.00	62
GUITAR BOOGIE TWIST/Guitar Shimmy	(Virnon 603)	.75	3.00	60
GUITAR ON THE WILD SIDE/Meditation Of The Soul	(Virtue 2503)	.75	3.00	69
HIGHLAND GUITAR/Pickin' Plankin' Boogie	(Wynne 123)	.75	3.00	60
TEL-STAR GUITAR/Jersey Bounce	(Sure 1779)	.75	3.00	62
VAYA CON DIOS/Blues In The Cellar	(Hunt 331)	1.00	4.00	59
VAYA CON DIOS/Blues In The Cellar	(ABC-Paramount 10071)	.75	3.00	60
VIRTUE'S BOOGIE WOOGIE/Pickin' The Stroll	(Hunt 328)	1.00	4.00	59
Instrumentals				
VISAS, The				
MARRIAGE IS A BAG (& I CAN'T PUNCH MY WAY OUT)/ Night Train (Instrumental)	(Dot 16591	.75	3.00	64
MARRIAGE IS A BAG (& I CAN'T PUNCH MY WAY OUT)/ Night Train (Instrumental)	(Timely 904)	1.50	6.00	64

TITLE/FLIP	LABEL & NO.	GOOD	NEAR MINT	YR.
VISCOUNTS, The				
HARLEM NOCTURNE/Dig	(Amy 940)	.75	3.00	65
HARLEM NOCTURNE/Dig	(Madison 123)	1.00	4.00	59
LITTLE BROWN JUG/Opus #1	(Madison 159)	1.00	4.00	61
NIGHT FOR LOVE/Ballin' The Jack	(Mr. Peeke 125)	.75	3.00	62
NIGHT TRAIN/Summertime	(Madison 133)	1.00	4.00	60
NIGHT TRAIN/When The Saints Go Marching In	(Amy 949)	.75	3.00	66
PASSION/Take Me To Your Leader	(Donick 100)	1.00	4.00	59
THIS PLACE/Shadrach	(Madison 152)	1.00	4.00	61
TOUCH, THE/Chug-A-Lug	(Madison 129)	1.00	4.00	60
WABASH BLUES/So Slow	(Madison 140)	1.00	4.00	60
WHEN JOHNNY COMES MARCHING HOME/ Mark's Mood	(Mr. Peacock 101)	.75	3.00	61
Instrumentals				
VISIONS, The				
ALL THROUGH THE NIGHT/Tell Me You're Mine	(Big Top 3092)	1.00	4.00	61
DOWN IN MY HEART/	(Co-Ed 598)	.75	3.00	65
SWINGIN' WEDDING/Secret World (Of Tears)	(Big Top 3119)	1.00	4.00	62
TEENAGER'S LIFE/Little Moon	(Elgey 1003)	1.50	6.00	60
TEENAGER'S LIFE/Little Moon (Pink label)	(Lost Night 102)	2.00	8.00	
TOMMY'S GIRL/Oh Boy, What A Girl	(Mercury 72188)	1.00	4.00	63
VISITORS, The				
THEME FROM "THE WILD ANGELS"/Is It Them Or Me	(Tower 268)	.75	3.00	66
VISTAS, The				
GHOST WAVE/Surfer's Minuet	(Venpro 101)	1.00	4.00	63
(Instrumentals)				
VISUALS, The				
MY JUANITA/Boy, Girl & Dream	(Poplar 117)	3.75	15.00	63
PLEASE DON'T BE MAD AT ME/Blue (Enough To Cry)	(Poplar 121)	6.25	25.00	63
SUBMARINE RACE, THE/Maybe You	(Poplar 115)	3.75	15.00	62
VITALE, Jo Jo				
MY LITTLE CINDERELLA/One Million To One	(May 127)	1.25	5.00	63
VITA-MEN, The				
FROG LEGS/I Can't Help Myself	(Challenge 59327)	.75	3.00	65
VITO: see Elegants, The				
VITO & THE HANDS				
WHERE IT'S AT/Vito & The Hand	(Living Legend 69)	1.50	6.00	
VITO & THE SALUTATIONS				
DAY-O (BANANA BOAT SONG)/Don't Count On Me	(Wells 1010)	1.25	5.00	64
EXTRAORDINARY GIRL/Eenie Meenie	(Herald 586)	1.25	5.00	63
GET A JOB/Girls I Know	(Regina R-1320)	1.00	4.00	
GLORIA/Let's Untwist The Twist	(Rayna 5009)	2.00	8.00	62
GLORIA/Let's Untwist The Twist	(Red Boy 5009)	.75	3.00	
HELLO DOLLY/Can I Depend On You	(Rust R-5106)	.75	3.00	64
HIGH NOON/Walkin'	(Apt 25079)	1.00	4.00	
I WANT YOU TO BE MY BABY/Bring Back Yesterday	(Boom BM-60020)	1.25	5.00	
I'D BEST BE GOING/So Wonderful (My Love)	(Sandbag 103)	1.00	4.00	
LIVERPOOL BOUND/Can I Depend On You	(Wells 1008)	1.50	6.00	64
LIVERPOOL BOUND/Can I Depend On You (Yellow plastic)	(Wells 1008)	3.00	12.00	64
UNCHAINED MELODY/Hey Hey Baby	(Herald 583)	1.25	5.00	63
YOUR WAY/Hey Hey Baby	(Kram 1202)	5.00	20.00	62
VITO, Sonny				
CAMEO RING/Teenage Blues	(ABC-Paramount 9958)	1.25	5.00	58
PUT 'EM DOWN JOE/I Remember The Night	(Chancellor 1112)	2.00	8.00	62
(Answer Song)				
VOCAL LORDS, The				
GIRL OF MINE/At Seventeen	(Able-No number given)	6.25	25.00	59
GIRL OF MINE/At Seventeen	(Tauras-No number given)	5.00	20.00	59
VOCAL-AIRES, The				
DREAM SHIP/(Flip by a different group)	(Ronnie 200)	.75	3.00	
THESE EMPTY ARMS/Dance Dance	(Herald 573)	1.50	6.00	62
Also see Accents, The				
VOCAL-TEENS, The				
TILL THEN/Be A Slave	(Downstairs 1000)	.75	3.00	
Also see Duprees, The				
VOGT, Les				
BLAMERS, THE/Moon Rocketin'	(Apt 25042)	1.00	4.00	
VOGUES, The (Formerly The Val-Aires)				
BIG MAN/Golden Locket	(ABC-Paramount 10672)	.75	3.00	65
EARTH ANGEL/P.S. I Love You	(Reprise 0820)	.75	3.00	69
EV'RY DAY, EV'RY NIGHT/Now I Lay Me Down To Cry	(Cascade 5908)	1.00	4.00	59
FIVE O'CLOCK WORLD/Nothing To Offer You	(Co & Ce 232)	.75	3.00	65
GOD ONLY KNOWS/Moody	(Reprise 0887)	.75	3.00	69
GREEN FIELDS/	(Reprise 0844)	.75	3.00	69
LAND OF MILK & HONEY/True Lovers	(Co & Ce 238)	.75	3.00	66
LOVE IS A FUNNY LITTLE GAME/Which Witch Doctor	(Dot 15798)	1.25	5.00	58
LOVERS OF THE WORLD UNITE/Brighter Days	(Co & Ce 246)	.75	3.00	67
LOVERS OF THE WORLD UNITE/Brighter Days	(MGM 13813)	.75	3.00	67
MAGIC TOWN/Humpty Dumpty	(Co & Ce 234)	.75	3.00	66
MOMENTS TO REMEMBER/Once In A While	(Reprise 0831)	.75	3.00	69
MY SPECIAL ANGEL/	(Reprise 0766)	.75	3.00	68
NEED YOU/	(Mainstream 5524)	.50	2.00	72
NO, NOT MUCH/Woman Helping Man	(Reprise 0803)	.75	3.00	69
PLEASE MR. SUN/Don't Blame The Rain	(Co & Ce 240)	.75	3.00	66
SINCE I DON'T HAVE YOU/I Know You As A Woman	(Reprise 0969)	.75	3.00	70
SUMMER AFTERNOON/Take A Chance On Me Baby	(Co & Ce 244)	.75	3.00	67
THAT'S THE TUNE/Midnight Dreams	(Co & Ce 242)	.75	3.00	66
TILL/	(Reprise 0788)	.75	3.00	68
TRY BABY TRY/Falling Star	(Dot 15859)	1.00	4.00	59
TURN AROUND, LOOK AT ME/Then	(Reprise 0686)	.75	3.00	68
YOU'RE THE ONE/Some Words	(Blue Star 229)	2.00	8.00	65
YOU'RE THE ONE/Some Words	(Co & Ce 229)	.75	3.00	65
YOU'RE THE ONE/Goodnight My Love	(Astra 1029)	.50	2.00	73
VOKSWAGONS, The				
ASTRONAUT/Blues For My Baby	(Do-Re-Mi 201)	2.00	8.00	
VOLCHORDS, The				
BONGO LOVE/Peek-A-Boo Love	(Regatta 2004)	2.00	8.00	
VOLUMES, The				
TROUBLE I'VE SEEN/That Same Old Feeling	(Impact 1017)	1.00	4.00	
VON GAYELS, The				
CRAZY DANCE/The Twirl	(Dore 544)	.75	3.00	60
VOUDOURIS, Roger				
DON'T TURN MY MUSIC DOWN/	(Warner Bros. 8562)	.50	2.00	78
GET USED TO IT/The Next Time Around	(Warner Bros. 8762)	.50	2.00	79
WE CAN'T STAY LIKE THIS FOREVER/ Anything From Anyone	(Warner Bros. 49021)	.50	2.00	79
VOXPOPPERS, The				
LOVE TO LAST A LIFETIME, A/Come Back Little Girl	(Poplar 107)	1.00	4.00	58
PONY TAIL/Ping Pong Baby	(Mercury 71315)	1.00	4.00	58
WISHING FOR YOUR LOVE/The Last Drag	(Amp 3 1004)	1.50	6.00	58
WISHING FOR YOUR LOVE/The Last Drag	(Mercury 71282)	.75	3.00	58
VOYAGER				
HALFWAY HOTEL/Maybe Not Tonight	(Elektra-Mountain 46055)	.50	2.00	79
VULCAINES, The: see Vulcanes, The				
VULCANES, The				
COZIMOTTO/The Last Prom (Shown as by the Vulcaines)	(Goliath 1350)	1.00	4.00	63
LIVERPOOL/The Outrage	(Capitol 5285)	.75	3.00	64
MOON PROBE/Twilight City	(Capitol 5199)	.75	3.00	64
STOMP SIGN/Public Record #1	(Goliath 1348)	1.00	4.00	62
STOMP SIGN/Public Record #1	(Goliath 800)	1.00	4.00	63
VULCANS, The				
POISON IVY/My Heart Won't Believe It	(Capitol 5423)	.75	3.00	65

W

TITLE/FLIP	LABEL & NO.	GOOD	NEAR MINT	YR.
WACKERS, The				
DAY & NIGHT/Last Dance	(Elektra 45816)	.50	2.00	72
HEY LAWDY MAMA/	(Elektra 45841)	.50	2.00	73
I HARLY KNEW HER NAME/Do You Know The Reason	(Elektra 45783)	.50	2.00	72
OH MY LOVE/	(Elektra 45772)	.50	2.00	71
WADE, Adam				
AS IF I DIDN'T KNOW/Playin Around	(Coed 553)	.75	3.00	61
BLACKOUT OF THE MOON/Speaking Of Her	(Coed 536)	.75	3.00	60
FOR THE WANT OF YOUR LOVE/Pursuit Of Happiness	(Coed 539)	.75	3.00	60
PRISONER'S SONG/Them There Eyes	(Coed 566)	.75	3.00	62
RUBY/Too Far	(Coed 526)	.75	3.00	60
TAKE GOOD CARE OF HER/Sleepy Time Girl	(Coed 546)	.75	3.00	61
TAKE GOOD CARE OF HER/Too Far	(Coed 546)	.75	3.00	61
TEENAGE MONA LISA/Why Do We Have To Wait So Long (With the Angels)	(Epic 9590)	.75	3.00	63
TELL HER FOR ME/Don't Cry My Love	(Coed 520)	.75	3.00	60
THERE'LL BE NO TEARDROPS TONIGHT/ Here Comes The Pain	(Epic 9557)	.75	3.00	62
THEY DIDN'T BELIEVE ME/I'm Climbing (The Wall)	(Epic 9521)	.75	3.00	62
WRITING ON THE WALL, THE/Point Of No Return	(Coed 550)	.75	3.00	61
WADE, Brandon				
LETTER FROM A TEENAGE SON (Stereo)/ Letter From A Teenage Son (Mono)	(Philips 40503)	.75	3.00	67
(Answer song)				
WADE, Elvis				
MEMORIES OF THE KING/Memories Of The King	(Memory 244)	.50	2.00	77
WADE, Ronny				
ALL I WANT/A Ring & A Vow	(King 5112)	1.00	4.00	57
GOTTA MAKE HER MINE/Let Me Cry	(King 5061)	1.00	4.00	57
I'LL NEVER FALL IN LOVE AGAIN/ I Know But I'll Never Tell	(King 5078)	1.25	5.00	57
WADSWORTH MANSION				
SWEET MARY/What's On Tonight	(Sussex 209)	.50	2.00	70
WAGNER, Cliff				
WHEN YOU'RE DANCIN'/Something's Got A Hold On Me	(Jolum 2510)	1.25	5.00	
WAGNER, Dick, & The Frosts				
RAINY DAY/Bad Girl	(Date 1577)	1.50	6.00	67
WAIKIKIS, The				
HAWAII HONEYMOON/Remember Boa-Boa	(Kapp 52)	.75	3.00	65
HAWAII TATOO/Tahiti Tamoure	(Kapp 30)	.75	3.00	64
HAWAII TATOO/Tahiti Tamoure	(Palette 5091)	1.00	4.00	64
Instrumentals				
WAILERS, The				
BEAT GUITAR/Mau Mau	(Golden Crest CR-591)	.75	3.00	64
LUCILLE/Scratchin'	(Golden Crest CR-545)	.75	3.00	60
MAU-MAU/Dirty Robber	(Golden Crest CR-526)	.75	3.00	59
ON THE ROCKS/Mashi	(Imperial 66045)	.75	3.00	64
SHANGHIED/Wallin'	(Golden Crest CR-532)	.75	3.00	60
TALL COOL ONE/Road Runner (No picture of group on label.)	(Golden Crest CR-518)	.75	3.00	59
TALL COOL ONE/Road Runner (Picture of group on label.)	(Golden Crest CR-518)	1.25	5.00	64
Instrumentals				
WAILERS, The				
I'M DETERMINED/I Don't Want To Follow You	(Viva 614)	.75	3.00	66
IT'S YOU ALONE/	(Etiquette 24)	1.00	4.00	66
MASHI/Vela	(Etiquette 2)	.75	3.00	63
OUT OF OUR TREE/I Got Me	(Etiquette 21)	.75	3.00	66
WE'RE GOIN' SURFIN'/Shakedown	(Etiquette 6)	1.00	4.00	63
WAINWRIGHT, Loudon, III				
BICENTENNIAL/Talking Big Apple '75	(Arista 0174)	.50	2.00	76
DEAD SKUNK/Needless To Say	(Columbia 45726)	.50	2.00	73
FINAL EXAM/	(Arista 0340)	.50	2.00	78
WAITS, Tom				
BLUE SKIES/	(Asylum 45223)	.50	2.00	74
WAKEMAN, Rick (Of Yes)				
ANNE/Catherine	(A&M 1430)	.50	2.00	73
Also see Daltrey, Roger				
WALDMAN, Wendy				
LIVING IS GOOD/The Main Refrain	(Warner Bros. 8303)	.50	2.00	77
LONG HOT SUMMER NIGHTS/You'll See	(Warner Bros. 8617)	.50	2.00	78
WALDO, Dudley & Dora				
GRAYSON GOOFED/	(Awful 1)	1.00	4.00	59
(Answer song)				
WALDROOP, Les				
WATERGATE BUGS/	(Me Too 27483)	.75	3.00	72
(Novelty)				
WALE, Steve				
BOY MEETS GIRL/	(Lute 6007)	1.00	4.00	61
WALES, Howard, & Jerry Garcia (Of the Greatful Dead)				
SOUTH SIDE STRUT/Uncle Martin's	(Douglas 76501)	.75	3.00	71
WALKER, Boots				
THEY'RE HERE/Bum Can't Cry	(Rust 5115)	.75	3.00	67
WALKER BROTHERS, The				
BEAUTIFUL BROWN EYES/Ninety-Seven	(Kay-y 66785)	.75	3.00	60
WALKER BROTHERS, The (Featuring Scott Engel)				
(BABY) YOU DON'T HAVE TO TELL ME/ The Young Man Cried	(Smash 2048)	.75	3.00	66
I ONLY CAME TO DANCE WITH YOU/Greens (Shown as by "John Stewart & Scott Engel, Now Known As The Walker Brothers.")	(Tower 218)	1.50	6.00	66
LOVE HER/Seventh Dawn	(Smash 1976)	1.00	4.00	65
MAKE IT EASY ON YOURSELF/But I Do	(Smash 2000)	1.00	4.00	65
MAKE IT EASY ON YOURSELF/Doin' The Jerk	(Smash 2009)	.75	3.00	65
MAKE IT EASY ON YOURSELF/Doin' The Jerk (Picture sleeve)	(Smash 2009)	1.25	5.00	65
MY SHIP IS COMIN' IN/You're All Around Me	(Smash 2016)	.75	3.00	66
MY SHIP IS COMIN' IN/You're All Around Me (Picture sleeve)	(Smash 2016)	1.25	5.00	66
PRETTY GIRLS EVERYWHERE/Doin' The Jerk	(Smash 1952)	1.00	4.00	64
SADDEST NIGHT IN THE WORLD/Another Tear Falls	(Smash 2063)	.75	3.00	66
SUN AIN'T GONNA SHINE (ANYMORE)/ After The Lights Go Out	(Smash 2032)	.75	3.00	66
SUN AIN'T GONNA SHINE (ANYMORE)/ After The Lights Go Out (Picture sleeve)	(Smash 2032)	1.25	5.00	66

The John Stewart named above performed with Scott Engel as the Dalton Brothers and as the Moongooners. He should not be confused with the former Kingston Trio member of the same name.

Cross referenced below are some of the other groups that members Scott, Gary and John Walker appeared in, either collectively or individually:

Also see Biscaynes, The
Also see Routers, The
Also see Standells, The
Also see Dalton Brothers, The
Also see Moongooners, The
Also see Walker, Gary
Also see Walker, John
Also see Walker, Scott

TITLE/FLIP	LABEL & NO.	GOOD	NEAR MINT	YR.
WALKER, Gary (Of The Walker Brothers)				
YOU DON'T LOVE ME/Get It Right	(Date 1506)	.75	3.00	66
WALKER, Jackie				
ONLY TEENAGERS ALLOWED/Oh Lonesome Me	(Imperial 5490)	2.00	8.00	58
WALKER, John (Of The Walker Brothers)				
ANNABELLA/You Don't Understand Me	(Smash 2108)	.75	3.00	67
GOOD DAYS/Midnight Morning (Bill Wyman involvement-Rare!)	(Green Mountain 416)	.50	2.00	73
WOMAN/A Dream	(Smash 2213)	.75	3.00	68
WALKER, Robert, & The Night Riders				
KEEP ON RUNNIN'/Everything's Alright	(Detroit Sound 224)	1.00	4.00	
WALKER, Scott (Scott Engel)				
I DON'T WANT TO HEAR IT ANYMORE/ You're All Around Me (These tracks are identical to previously issued versions by The Walker Brothers.)	(Smash 2156)	.75	3.00	68
I STILL SEE YOU/My Way Home	(Philips 40713)	.75	3.00	71
LIGHTS OF CINCINNATI/Two Weeks Since You've Gone	(Smash 2228)	.75	3.00	69
Also see Walker Brothers, The				
WALKER, Wilmar				
STOMPIN' ROACHES/Somebody Will	(Philips 40030)	.75	3.00	62
WALLACE, Jerry				
AUF WIEDERSEHEN/If I Make It Through Today	(Challenge 59223)	.75	3.00	63
AUTUMN HAS COME & GONE/Taj Mahal	(Mercury 70684)	1.00	4.00	55
AUTUMN HAS COME & GONE/Taj Mahal	(Class 502)	1.00	4.00	
BLUE JEAN BABY/Fool's Hall Of Fame	(Challenge 1003)	1.25	5.00	58
CARELESS HANDS/St. Francisco De Assissi	(Mercury 72365)	1.00	4.00	64
DIAMOND RING/All My Love Belongs To You	(Challenge 59027)	1.25	5.00	58
EVEN THE BAD TIMES ARE GOOD/Butterfly	(Challenge 59246)	.75	3.00	64
EYES OF FIRE, LIPS OF WINE/Monkey See, Monkey Do	(Wing 90065)	1.00	4.00	
GEE, BUT I HATE TO GO HOME/ That's What A Woman Can Do To A Man	(Allied 5019)	1.00	4.00	
GLORIA/On A Night When Flowers Were Dancing	(Mercury 70812)	1.00	4.00	56
GOOD & BAD/The Other Me	(Challenge 59072)	.75	3.00	60
HELPLESS/You're Driving Me Out Of My Mind	(Challenge 59278)	.75	3.00	65
HOW THE TIME FLIES/With This Ring	(Challenge 59013)	1.00	4.00	58
IN THE MISTY MOONLIGHT/Cannon Ball	(Challenge 59246)	.75	3.00	64
LIFE'S A HOLIDAY/I Can See An Angel Walking	(Challenge 9107)	.75	3.00	61
LITTLE COCO PALM/Mission Bell Blues	(Challenge 59060)	1.00	4.00	59
LITTLE MISS ONE/Petrillo	(Allied 5015)	1.00	4.00	
LITTLE MISS TEASE/Mr. Lonely	(Challenge 9139)	.75	3.00	62
P.S. I LOVE YOU/ (Flip side is not by Jerry Wallace)	(Tops 369)	1.50	6.00	53
PRIMROSE LANE/By Your Side	(Challenge 59047)	1.00	4.00	59
RAINBOW/Time	(Mercury 72406)	1.00	4.00	65
RUNNIN' AFTER LOVE/Dixie Anna	(Allied 5023)	1.00	4.00	
SHUTTERS & BOARDS/Am I That Easy To Forget	(Challenge 9171)	.75	3.00	62
SPANISH GUITARS/Even The Bad Times Are Good	(Challenge 59265)	.75	3.00	64
SWINGIN' DOWN THE LANE/Teardrop In The Rain	(Challenge 59082)	.75	3.00	60
THERE SHE GOES/Angel On My Shoulder	(Challenge 59098)	.75	3.00	60
THERE'LL BE SOME CHANGES MADE/Mis'rable Blues	(Vogue 1006)	2.00	8.00	52
TOUCH OF PINK, A/Off Stage	(Challenge 59040)	1.00	4.00	59
YOU'RE SINGING OUR LOVE SONG TO SOMEBODY ELSE/ King Of The Mountain	(Challenge 59072)	.75	3.00	60
WALKING IN THE RAIN/Greatest Magic Of Them All	(Mercury 70758)	1.00	4.00	55
WALLER, Gordon (Of Peter & Gordon)				
EVERYDAY/Because Of A Woman	(Capitol 2346)	.75	3.00	68
SPEAK FOR ME/Little Nonie	(Capitol 5886)	.75	3.00	67
WALLER, Jim, & The Deltas				
SURFIN' WILD, A/Church Key	(Arvee 5072)	1.00	4.00	64
WALSH, James, Gypsy Band				
CUZ IT'S YOU, GIRL/Bring Yourself Around	(RCA 11403)	.50	2.00	78
LOVE IS FOR THE BEST IN US/	(RCA 11480)	.50	2.00	79
WALSH, Joe (Of The Eagles)				
LIFE'S BEEN GOOD/Theme From Boat Weirdos	(Asylum 45493)	.50	2.00	78
MEADOWS/Book Ends	(Dunhill 4373)	.50	2.00	74
OVER & OVER/At The Station	(Asylum 45536)	.50	2.00	78
ROCKY MOUNTAIN WAY/(Day Dream) Prayer	(Dunhill 4361)	.50	2.00	73
TIME OUT/Help Me Thru The Night	(ABC 12115)	.50	2.00	75
TURN TO STONE/	(ABC 12246)	.50	2.00	78
TURN TO STONE/All Night Laundry Mat Blues Seulb Tam Yrdnual Thgin Lla	(Dunhill 15026)	.50	2.00	75
WALK AWAY/Help Me Thru The Night	(ABC 12187)	.50	2.00	76
Also see James Gang, The				
WALSH, Johnny				
GIRL MACHINE/	(Warner Bros. 5196)	.75	3.00	61

TITLE/FLIP	LABEL & NO.	GOOD	NEAR MINT	YR.
WALTER & FANCY (Walter Crankcase & Fancy Flickerson)				
CAMPAIGN TRAIN/Campaign Train (Part 2) (Novelty/Break-in)	(Magic Lamp 612)	1.00	4.00	64
WAMMACK, Travis				
SCRATCHY/Fire Fly (Instrumental)	(Ara 204)	.75	3.00	64
WANDERLEY, Walter				
CHEGANCA/Amanha	(Verve 10456)	.75	3.00	66
SUMMER SAMBA/Call Me	(Verve 10421)	.75	3.00	66
Instrumentals				
WANTED				
DON'T WORRY BABY/Big Town Girl	(A&M 856)	1.25	5.00	67
IN THE MIDNIGHT HOUR/Here To Stay	(Detroit Sound 222)	1.25	5.00	67
KNOCK ON WOOD/ Lots More Where They Came From	(Detroit Sound 230)	1.25	5.00	67
WAR				
ALL DAY MUSIC/Get Down	(United Artists 50815)	.50	2.00	71
BALLERO/Slippin' Into Darkness	(United Artists 432)	.50	2.00	74
CISCO KID, THE/Beetles In The Bog	(United Artists 163)	.50	2.00	73
CORNS & CALLOUSES (HEY DR. SHOALS)/ I'm The One Who Understands	(MCA-Far Out 41061)	.50	2.00	79
GALAXY/Galaxy (Part 2)	(MCA-Far Out 40820)	.50	2.00	77
GOOD GOOD FEELIN'/ Baby Face (She Said Do Do Do Do)	(MCA-Far Out 40995)	.50	2.00	79
GYPSY MAN/Deliver The Word	(United Artists 281)	.50	2.00	73
HEY SENORITA/Sweet Fighting Lady	(MCA-Far Out 40833)	.50	2.00	78
L.A. SUNSHINE/Slowly We Walk Together	(Far Out-Blue Note 1009)	.50	2.00	77
LOW RIDER/So	(United Artists 706)	.50	2.00	75
ME & BABY BROTHER/In Your Eyes	(United Artists 350)	.50	2.00	73
SING A HAPPY SONG/ This Funky Music Makes You Feel Good	(United Artists-FO 1247)	.50	2.00	78
SLIPPIN' INTO DARKNESS/Nappy Head	(United Artists 50867)	.50	2.00	72
SUMMER/All Day Music	(United Artists 834)	.50	2.00	76
WHY CAN'T WE BE FRIENDS?/In Mazatlan	(United Artists 629)	.50	2.00	75
WORLD IS A GHETTO, THE/Four Cornered Room	(United Artists 50975)	.50	2.00	72
YOUNGBLOOD (LIVIN' IN THE STREETS)/Youngblood (Livin' In The Streets) (Part 2)	(United Artists-Far Out 1213)	.50	2.00	78
Also see Jordan, Lonnie				
WARD, Burt				
BOY WONDER, I LOVE YOU/	(MGM 13623)	2.50	10.00	67
WARD, Dale				
BIG DALE TWIST/Here's Your Hat	(Boyd 118)	1.00	4.00	64
CRYING FOR LAURA/I've Got A Girl Friend	(Dot 16590)	.75	3.00	64
I TRIED/Living On Coal	(Boyd 152)	1.25	5.00	64
I'LL NEVER LOVE AGAIN (AFTER LOVING YOU)/ Young Lovers After Midnight	(Dot 16632)	.75	3.00	64
LETTER FROM SHERRY, A (With Robin Ward)/Oh Julie	(Dot 16520)	.75	3.00	63
ONE LAST KISS CHERIE/The Fortune	(Dot 16672)	.75	3.00	64
RIVER BOAT ANNIE/I Want The Best For You	(Big Way 001)	1.00	4.00	
SHAKE RATTLE & ROLL/You Gotta Let Me Know	(Boyd 150)	1.50	6.00	64
WARD, Dart, & The Cut-Ups				
Q-T-CUTE/Misery	(Rip 134)	.75	3.00	
WARD, Joe				
NUTTIN' FOR CHRISTMAS/Christmas Questions	(King 4854)	1.00	4.00	55
WARD, Richard, & The Hustlers				
WELL OF LONELINESS, THE/Topless Bathing Suit	(Downey 121)	2.00	8.00	64
WARD, Robin				
IN HIS CAR/Wishing	(Dot 16624)	.75	3.00	64
JOHNNY COME & GET ME/ Where The Blue Meets The Gold	(Dot 16599)	.75	3.00	64
LOSER'S LULLABY/Lolly Too Dum	(Song Unlimited 37)	1.00	4.00	63
TOP FORTY BLUES/Bluegrass Blue (Instrumental)	(Dot 16519)	1.25	5.00	63
(Shown as by Robin)				
WINTER'S HERE/Bobby	(Dot 16578)	.75	3.00	64
WONDERFUL SUMMER/Dream Boy	(Dot 16530)	.75	3.00	63
Also see Martindale, Wink				
Also see Ward, Dale				
WARLOCKS, The				
GIRL/Hey Jo	(Washington Square 2023)	1.25	5.00	
WARMER, Faron				
CRUSIN' CENTRAL/The Switch (Novelty)	(Jo-Ree 501)	2.50	10.00	59
WARNES, Jennifer				
CAJUN TRAIN/	(Parrot 346)	.75	3.00	70
(Shown as by Jennifer)				
DON'T MAKE ME OVER/I'm Restless	(Arista 0455)	.50	2.00	79
EASY TO BE HARD/ Let The Sunshine In (The Flesh Failures)	(Parrot 336)	.75	3.00	69
(Shown as by Jennifer)				
I AM WAITING/The Leaves	(Parrot 333)	.75	3.00	69
(Shown as by Jennifer)				
I KNOW A HEARTACHE WHEN I SEE ONE/ Frankie In The Rain	(Arista 0430)	.50	2.00	79
I'M DREAMING/Don't Lead Me On	(Arista 0252)	.50	2.00	77
PARK, THE/Chelsea Morning	(Parrot 328)	.75	3.00	69
(Shown as by Jennifer)				
RIGHT TIME OF THE NIGHT/Daddy Don't Go	(Arista 0223)	.50	2.00	77
SUNNY DAY BLUE/Here, There & Everywhere	(Parrot 324)	.75	3.00	68
(Shown as by Jennifer)				
WE'RE NOT GONNA TAKE IT/Weather's Better	(Parrot 343)	.75	3.00	70
(Shown as by Jennifer)				
WARREN, Beverly				
HE'S SO FINE/March	(B.T. Puppy 526)	.75	3.00	66
WARWICK, Dionne				
ALFIE/The Beginning Of Loneliness	(Scepter 12187)	.75	3.00	67
AMANDA/He's Moving On	(Scepter 12326)	.50	2.00	71
(Shown as by Dionne Warwicke)				
ANOTHER NIGHT/	(Scepter 12181)	.75	3.00	66
ANYONE WHO HAD A HEART/The Love Of A Boy	(Scepter 1262)	.75	3.00	63
APRIL FOOLS, THE/Slaves	(Scepter 12249)	.75	3.00	69
ARE YOU THERE (WITH ANOTHER GIRL)/ If I Ever Make You Cry	(Scepter 12122)	.75	3.00	65
DEJA VU/All The Time	(Arista 0459)	.50	2.00	79
DON'T EVER TAKE YOUR LOVE AWAY/	(Warner Bros. 8530)	.50	2.00	78
DON'T MAKE ME OVER/	(Scepter 1239)	.75	3.00	62
DO YOU BELIEVE IN LOVE AT FIRST SIGHT/ Do I Have To Cry	(Warner Bros. 8419)	.50	2.00	77
DO YOU KNOW THE WAY TO SAN JOSE/ Let Me Be Lonely	(Scepter 12216)	.75	3.00	68
GOOD LIFE, THE/ Medley: Reach Out & Touch All Kinds Of People	(Scepter 12383)	.50	2.00	73
(Shown as by Dionne Warwicke)				
GREEN GRASS STARTS TO GROW, THE/ They Don't Give Medals To Yesterday's Heroes	(Scepter 12300)	.50	2.00	70
HERE I AM/	(Scepter 12104)	.75	3.00	65
I DIDN'T MEAN TO LOVE YOU/He's Not For You	(Warner Bros. 8280)	.50	2.00	76
I JUST DON'T KNOW WHAT TO DO WITH MYSELF/ In Between The Heartaches	(Scepter 12167)	.75	3.00	66
I THINK YOU NEED LOVE/ Don't Let My Teardrops Bother You	(Warner Bros. 7669)	.50	2.00	73
(Shown as by Dionne Warwicke)				
IF WE ONLY HAVE LOVE/Close To You	(Warner Bros. 7560)	.50	2.00	72
(Shown as by Dionne Warwicke)				
I'LL NEVER FALL IN LOVE AGAIN/ What The World Needs Now Is Love	(Scepter 12273)	.75	3.00	69
I'LL NEVER LOVE THIS WAY AGAIN/In Your Eyes	(Arista 0419)	.50	2.00	79
I'M YOUR PUPPET/Don't Make Me Over	(Scepter 12352)	.50	2.00	72
(Shown as by Dionne Warwicke)				
(I'M) JUST BEING MYSELF/You're Gonna Need Me	(Warner Bros. 7693)	.50	2.00	73
(Shown as by Dionne Warwicke)				
KEEPIN' MY HEAD ABOVE WATER/	(Warner Bros. 8501)	.50	2.00	77
LET ME GO TO HIM/ Loneliness Remembers What Happiness Forgets	(Scepter 12276)	.50	2.00	70
LOOKING WITH MY EYES/ Only The Strong, Only The Brave	(Scepter 12111)	.75	3.00	65
LOVE OF MY MAN, THE/Hurts So Bad	(Scepter 12336)	.50	2.00	72
(Shown as by Dionne Warwicke)				
MAKE IT EASY ON YOURSELF/Knowing When To Leave	(Scepter 12294)	.50	2.00	70
MAKE THE MUSIC PLAY/Please Make Him Love Me	(Scepter 1253)	.75	3.00	63
MESSAGE TO MICHAEL/Here Where There Is Love	(Scepter 12133)	.75	3.00	66
ODDS & ENDS/As Long As There's An Apple Tree	(Scepter 12256)	.75	3.00	69
ONCE YOU HIT THE ROAD/World Of My Dreams	(Warner Bros. 8154)	.50	2.00	75
ONLY LOVE CAN BREAK A HEART/If I Ruled The World	(Musicor 6303)	.50	2.00	77
PAPER MACHE/The Wine Is Young	(Scepter 12285)	.50	2.00	70
PROMISES, PROMISES/Whoever You Are, I Love You	(Scepter 12231)	.75	3.00	68
REACH OUT FOR ME/How Many Days Of Sadness	(Scepter 1285)	.75	3.00	64
SURE THING/Who Knows	(Warner Bros. 8026)	.50	2.00	74
(Shown as by Dionne Warwicke)				
TAKE IT FROM ME/It's Magic	(Warner Bros. 8088)	.50	2.00	74
(Shown as by Dionne Warwicke)				
THEN CAME YOU/Just As Long As We Have Love	(Atlantic 3029)	.50	2.00	74
(With the Spinners)				
THEN CAME YOU/Just As Long As We Have Love	(Atlantic 3202)	.50	2.00	74
(With the Spinners)				
THIS EMPTY PLACE/Wishin' & Hopin'	(Scepter 1247)	.75	3.00	63
THIS GIRL'S IN LOVE WITH YOU/Dream Sweet Dreamer	(Scepter 12241)	.75	3.00	69
TRAINS & BOATS & PLANES/ Don't Go Breaking My Heart	(Scepter 12153)	.75	3.00	66
(THEME FROM) VALLEY OF THE DOLLS/ I Say A Little Prayer	(Scepter 12203)	.75	3.00	67
WALK ON BY/Any Old Time Of Day	(Scepter 1274)	.75	3.00	64
WINDOWS OF THE WORLD, THE/Walk Little Dolly	(Scepter 12196)	.75	3.00	67
WHO CAN I TURN TO/Don't Say I Didn't Tell You So	(Scepter 1298)	.75	3.00	65
WHO GETS THE GUY/	(Scepter 12309)	.50	2.00	71
WHO IS GONNA LOVE ME?/ (There's) Always Something There To Remind Me	(Scepter 12226)	.75	3.00	68
YOU CAN HAVE HIM/Is There Another Way To Love Him	(Scepter 1294)	.75	3.00	65
YOU'LL NEVER GET TO HEAVEN/A House Is Not A Home	(Scepter 1282)	.75	3.00	64
YOU'VE LOST THAT LOVIN' FEELING/Window Wishing	(Scepter 12262)	.75	3.00	69
WASHER WINDSHIELD				
KATHY YOUNG FINDS THE INNOCENTS GUILTY/ (Novelty/Break-in)	(Indigo no number given)	10.00	40.00	61
WASHINGTON, Gino				
GINO IS A COWARD/Puppet On A String	(Ric Tic 100)	.75	3.00	64
GINO IS A COWARD/Puppet On A String	(Son Bert 3770)	1.25	5.00	64
WATERPROOF TINKERTOY				
GROOVY GIRL/This & That	(Laurie 3457)	.75	3.00	68
WATERS, Junior				
ROCKIN' THAT HISTORY/I'll See You In My Dreams	(MGM 13004)	1.00	4.00	61
WATTS, Noble "Thin Man"				
FROG HOP, THE/The Beaver	(Cub K-9078)	.75	3.00	60
HARD TIMES (THE SLOP)/I'm Walkin The Floor Over You (Instrumental)	(Baton 249)	1.00	4.00	57
WAVES, The				
TAKE ME THERE/Summer Sunday	(Polydor 14402)	.50	2.00	77
WAYNE & THE EXCEPTIONS				
HAVE FAITH BABY/Have Faith Baby (Part 2)	(Laurie 3376)	1.00	4.00	67
WAYNE, Artie				
WHERE DOES A ROCK & ROLL SINGER GO/ I Hurt That Girl	(Liberty 55625)	.75	3.00	63
WAYNE, Bobby				
MOTHER AT YOUR FEET IS KNEELING/Immaculate Mother	(London 968)	1.25	5.00	51
WHEEL OF FORTUNE/If I Had The Heart Of A Clown	(Mercury 5779)	1.25	5.00	52
WAYNE, Jeff				
FOREVER AUTUMN (Featuring Justin Hayward)/ The Fighting Machine	(Columbia 10799)	.50	2.00	78
WAYNE, John				
WALK WITH HIM/I Have Faith	(Liberty 55399)	.75	3.00	61
WAYNE, Susan				
RIDING ON A RAINBOW/You Don't Do What I Say	(Columbia 43148)	.75	3.00	64
THAT'S WHAT I LOVE ABOUT YOU/Think Summer	(Columbia 43237)	.75	3.00	65
WAYNE, Thomas (Thomas Wayne Perkins)				
ETERNALLY/Scandalizing My Name	(Fernwood 111)	1.00	4.00	59
GIRL NEXT DOOR/Because Of You	(Fernwood 122)	1.00	4.00	59
GONNA BE WAITIN'/Just Beyond	(Fernwood 113)	1.00	4.00	59
GUILTY OF LOVE/Poncho Villa	(Fernwood 120)	1.00	4.00	59
STOP THE RIVER/Eighth Wonder Of The World	(Santo 9053)	.75	3.00	62
THIS TIME/You're The One That Done It	(Mercury 71454)	.75	3.00	59
THIS TIME/You're The One That Done It	(Fernwood 106)	1.00	4.00	59
TRAGEDY/No More, No More	(Capehart 5009)	1.00	3.00	61
TRAGEDY/Saturday Date	(Fernwood 109)	1.00	4.00	59
TRAGEDY/You're Gonna Be Waiting	(Eric 160)	.50	2.00	
WE FIVE				
CATCH THE WIND/Oh Lonesome Me	(Vault 969)	.75	3.00	67
HIGH FLYING BIRD/What Do I Do Now	(A&M 820)	1.00	4.00	66
LET'S GET TOGETHER/Cast Your Fate To The Wind	(A&M 784)	1.00	4.00	65
NEVER GOIN' BACK/Here Comes The Sun	(Vault 964)	.75	3.00	67
REJOICE/Bandstand Dancer	(Verve 10716)	1.00	4.00	68
SOMEWHERE/There Stands The Door	(A&M 800)	1.00	4.00	66
WALK ON BY/It Really Doesn't Matter	(A&M 1072)	1.00	4.00	69
YOU LET A LOVE BURN OUT/Somewhere Beyond The Sea	(A&M 793)	1.00	4.00	66
YOU WERE ON MY MIND/Small World	(A&M 770)	1.00	4.00	65
WE UGLY DOGS				
FIRST SPRING RAIN/	(BT Puppy 537)	.75	3.00	68
WEATHERLY, Jim				
ALL THAT KEEPS ME GOING/	(ABC 12288)	.50	2.00	77
I'LL STILL LOVE YOU/	(Buddah 444)	.50	2.00	75
NEED TO BE, THE/Like Old Times Again	(Buddah 420)	.50	2.00	74
PEOPLE SOME PEOPLE CHOOSE TO LOVE, THE/	(ABC 12213)	.50	2.00	76
SMOOTH SAILIN'/	(Elektra 46547)	.50	2.00	79
STORMS OF TROUBLED TIMES	(ABC 12252)	.50	2.00	77
WEAVER, Dennis				
APES, THE/Chicken Mash	(Eva 103)	.75	3.00	
GENESIS THROUGH EXODUS/ The Sinking Of The Rebuen James	(Warner Bros. 5352)	.75	3.00	63
WEAVERS, The (Featuring Pete Seeger)				
KISSES SWEETER THAN WINE/ When The Saints Go Marching In	(Decca 27670)	1.25	5.00	51
ON TOP OF OLD SMOKY/Across The Wide Missouri	(Decca 27515)	1.25	5.00	51
ROVING KIND, THE/John B	(Decca 27332)	1.25	5.00	51
WIMOWEH/Old Paint	(Decca 27928)	1.25	5.00	52
(With Gordon Jenkins)				
WEBB, Gary				
DRUM CITY/Drum City (Part 2) (Instrumentals)	(Donna 1321)	.75	3.00	60
WEBB, Jimmy				
CRYING IN MY SLEEP/Ocean In His Eyes	(Asylum 11027)	.50	2.00	72
FEET IN THE SUNSHINE/	(Asylum 11042)	.50	2.00	72
HIGHWAYMAN, THE/	(Atlantic 3426)	.50	2.00	77
LOVE HURTS/	(Reprise 1116)	.50	2.00	71
WEBB, Roger, Trio				
SHE LOVES YOU/Do You Want To Know A Secret	(Swan 4188)	1.00	4.00	64
WEBB, Spider, & The Insects				
BIG NOISE FROM WINNETKA/Maggie	(Lugar 100)	.75	3.00	63
WEBBER, Andrew, Lloyd				
THEME & VARIATIONS/Variation 16	(MCA 40866)	.50	2.00	78
WEBER, Joan				
LET ME GO LOVER/Marionette	(Columbia 40366)	1.00	4.00	54
WEBS, The				
BLUE SKIES/	(Heart 333)	.75	3.00	
LOST (CRICKET IN MY EAR)/	(Lite 9004)	1.00	4.00	
(With Bobby Goldsboro doing cricket sounds)				
WEDLAW, Frankie				
HAVE YOU GOT A CRUSH ON ME/Run, Buddy Run	(Skyla 1054)	1.00	4.00	62
WEDNESDAY				
LAST KISS/Without You	(Sussex 507)	.50	2.00	73
LOVING YOU BABY/Don't Let Me Wait Too Long	(Celebration 1001)	.50	2.00	76
WEED, Gene				
POOR POOR BILLIE/Just For Tonight	(20th Fox 416)	.75	3.00	63
WEEDS, The				
NO GOOD NEWS/Stop	(NWI 2745)	1.25	5.00	
WEEKENDS, The				
CANADIAN SUNSET/You're Number 1 With Me	(Columbia 43597)	1.00	4.00	66
RINGO/I Want You	(Le-Mans 001)	1.00	4.00	64
WEEKS, Christopher, & Fran Stacey				
MY SON THE PRESIDENT/	(Clan 1)	.75	3.00	
WEHBA, Dale				
RUSSIAN ROULETTE/The Screwdriver	(Kings X 3364)	1.00	4.00	
WEIGAND, Jack				
SHANGI-LA/Stairway To The Stars	(Cameo 178)	.75	3.00	60
16 CANDLES/Prisoner Of Love	(Cameo 185)	.75	3.00	60
Instrumentals				
WEIR, Bob (Of the Grateful Dead)				
BOMBS AWAY/Easy To Slip	(Arista 0336)	.50	2.00	78
CASSIDY/One More Saturday Night	(Warner Bros. 7611)	1.00	4.00	72
I'LL BE DOGGONE/Shade Of Grey	(Arista 0336)	.50	2.00	78
WEIR, Frank				
HAPPY WANDERER, THE/From Your Lips	(London 1448)	1.00	4.00	54
WEIRDOS, The				
E.S.P./Shape Of Mind	(Lan-cet 145)	.75	3.00	61
WELCH, Bob (Of Fleetwood Mac)				
CHURCH/Here Comes The Night	(Capitol 4719)	.50	2.00	79
EBONY EYES/Outskirts	(Capitol 4543)	.50	2.00	78
HOT LOVE, COLD WORLD/Danchiva	(Capitol 4588)	.50	2.00	78
PRECIOUS LOVE/Something Strong	(Capitol 4685)	.50	2.00	79
REBEL ROUSER/	(Capitol 4790)	.50	2.00	79
SENTIMENTAL LADY/Hot Love Cold World	(Capitol 4479)	.50	2.00	77
3 HEARTS/Oh Jenny	(Capitol 4745)	.50	2.00	79
Also see Paris				
WELCH, Bruce (Of the Shadows)				
PLEASE MR., PLEASE/	(EMI 3948)	.50	2.00	74
WELCH, Lenny				
BLESSING OF LOVE/Last Star Of The Evening	(Decca 30829)	1.00	4.00	59
BREAKING UP IS HARD TO DO/ Get Mommy To Come Back Home	(Commonwealth United 3004)	.50	2.00	70
CHANGA ROCK/Boogie Cha Cha	(Cadence 1399)	.75	3.00	61
CORONET BLUE/I'm Over You	(Kapp 854)	.75	3.00	66
DARLIN'/I'd Like To Know	(Cadence 1394)	.75	3.00	61
DARLING TAKE ME BACK/	(Kapp 682)	.75	3.00	65
EBB TIDE/Congratulations Baby	(Cadence 1422)	1.00	4.00	64
IF YOU SEE MY LOVE/Father Sebastion	(Cadence 1446)	.75	3.00	64
IT'S JUST NOT THAT EASY/Mama, Don't You Hit That Boy	(Cadence 1316)	.75	3.00	62
RUN TO MY LOVIN' ARMS/	(Kapp 712)	.75	3.00	65
SINCE I FELL FOR YOU/Are You Sincere	(Cadence 1439)	.75	3.00	63
SUNDAY KIND OF LOVE, A/	(Atco 6894)	.75	3.00	72
TASTE OF HONEY, A/The Old Cathedral	(Cadence 1438)	.75	3.00	62
TWO DIFFERENT WORLDS/	(Kapp 689)	.75	3.00	65
YOU DON'T KNOW ME/I Need Someone	(Cadence 1373)	1.00	4.00	60
WELD, Tuesday				
ALL THROUGH SPRING & SUMMER/Are You The Boy	(Plaza 508)	.75	3.00	
WELK, Lawrence				
BABY ELEPHANT WALK/Brothers Grim	(Dot 16364)	.75	3.00	62
CALCUTTA/My Grandfathers Clock	(Dot 16161)	.75	3.00	60
LAST DATE/Remember Lolita	(Dot 16145)	.75	3.00	60
MORITAT (A THEME FROM THE THREE PENNY OPERA)/ Stompin' At The Savoy	(Coral 61574)	1.00	4.00	56
OH, HAPPY DAY/Your Mother & Mine	(Coral 60893)	1.00	4.00	53
POOR PEOPLE OF PARIS, THE/ Nobody Knows But The Lord	(Coral 61592)	1.00	4.00	56
RUNAWAY/Happy Love	(Dot 16336)	.75	3.00	62
SCARLET O'HARA/Breakwater	(Dot 16488)	.75	3.00	63
SWINGIN' BUGLER/Bell Boogie	(Dot 15924)	.75	3.00	59
SWINGIN' BUGLER/Bell Boogie	(Dot S-204)	1.00	4.00	59
(Stereo single issue)				
THEME FROM "MY THREE SONS"/Out Of A Clear Blue Sky	(Dot 16198)	.75	3.00	61
YELLOW BIRD/Cruising Down The River	(Dot 16222)	.75	3.00	61
Instrumentals				
WELLER, Freddy				
MARY, I'M GALD TO SEE YOU/No One To Love	(Dore 595)	1.00	4.00	61
Also see Revere, Paul, & The Raiders				
WELLS, Cory				
MIDNIGHT LADY/	(A&M 2035)	.50	2.00	78
SAY GOODBYE TO DONNA/Sinner Man	(Valiant 714)	1.00	4.00	65
STARLIGHT/I Know You're Willin' Darlin'	(A&M 2013)	.50	2.00	78
Also see Three Dog Night				

TITLE/FLIP	LABEL & NO.	GOOD	NEAR MINT	YR.
WELZ, Joey				
BOPPIN' THE STROLL/Shore Party	(Bat 1001)	1.00	4.00	59
WENDIGO				
GIMMIE SOME LOVIN' (PART 1)/ Gimmie Some Lovin' (Part 2)	(Cousins 1010)	2.50	10.00	68
GIMMIE SOME LOVIN' (PART 1)/ Gimmie Some Lovin' (Part 2)	(Scepter 12211)	1.25	5.00	68
WEREWOLVES, The				
HOLLYWOOD MILLIONAIRE/City By The Sea	(RCA 11283)	.50	2.00	78
WERNER, David				
BALLAD OF TRIXIE SILVER/	(RCA 10006)	.50	2.00	74
COLD SHIVERS/Imagination Quata	(RCA 10535)	.50	2.00	76
WHAT'S RIGHT/Eye To Eye	(Epic 50756)	.50	2.00	79
WHIZZ KID/	(RCA 0253)	.50	2.00	74
WERTH, Howard, & The Moonbeams				
DEAR JOAN/Midnight Flyer	(Rocket 40555)	.50	2.00	76
Howard Werth was also a member of Audience.				
WESLEY, Gate				
DO THE BATMAN/Do The Thing	(Atlantic 2319)	.75	3.00	66
WEST				
JUST LIKE TOM THUMB'S BLUES/ Baby You Been On My Mind	(Epic 10335)	1.00	4.00	68
STEP BY STEP/Summer Flower	(Epic 10387)	1.00	4.00	68
WEST BRUCE & LAING (Leslie West, Corky Laing, Jack Bruce)				
DOCTOR, THE/	(Columbia 45751)	.50	2.00	73
WHY DON'TCHA/Mississippi Queen (By Mountain)	(Columbia 45829)	.50	2.00	73
West & Laing were previously in Mountain; Jack Bruce was with Cream.				
WEST COAST 5, The				
STILL IN LOVE WITH YOU BABY/Good Golly Miss Molly	(Boom 1)	1.50	6.00	
WEST COAST POP ART EXPERIMENTAL BAND, The				
1906/Shifting Sands	(Reprise 0552)	1.00	4.00	66
SMELL OF INCENSE/Unfree Child	(Reprise 0776)	1.00	4.00	68
WEST, Keith				
EXCERPTS FROM A TEENAGE OPERA (PART 1)/ Excerpts From A Teenage Opera (Part 2)	(New Voice 825)	.75	3.00	67
EXCERPTS FROM A TEENAGE OPERA (LONG VERSION)/ Excerpts From A Teenage Opera (Short Version) (Promotional issue)	(New Voice 825)	1.00	4.00	67
WEST, Leslie, Band				
DON'T BURN ME/ESP	(Phantom)	.50	2.00	76
WE GOTTA GET OUT OF THIS PLACE/By The River	(Phantom 10522)	.50	2.00	76
Also see West, Bruce & Laing				
Also see Mountain				
WESTLEY, Tarry				
HE LIVES/You Don't Know Me (Issued with insert)	(Chapman 1118)	.50	2.00	77
WEST, Mae				
DAY TRIPPER/Treat Him Right	(Tower 260)	1.00	4.00	66
SHAKIN' ALL OVER/If You Gotta Go	(Tower 261)	1.00	4.00	66
WEST, Red				
AIN'T NOBODY GONNA TAKE MY PLACE/ My Thanks To You	(Sonnet 2960)	.75	3.00	
F.B.I. STORY/What Must I Do?	(Jaro 77031)	1.00	4.00	60
MIDNIGHT RIDE/Unforgiven (Instrumentals)	(Loma 2005)	1.00	4.00	65
MIDNIGHT RIDE/Unforgiven (Instrumentals)	(Dot 16268)	.75	3.00	61
MY BABE/Bossa Nova Momza	(Santo 9006)	.75	3.00	63
WEST, Rudy				
JUST TO BE WITH YOU/You Were Mine	(King 5276)	2.00	8.00	59
WEST SIDERS, The				
DON'T YOU KNOW/No Tears Left For Crying	(Leopard 5004)	2.00	8.00	63
WEST, Tommy (Of the Buchanan Brothers)				
I KNOW/	(Lifesong 45017)	.50	2.00	77
I'M READY FOR YOU/	(Lifesong 45009)	.50	2.00	76
MAMAS DON'T LET YOUR BABYS GROW UP TO BE COWBOYS/ Nightingale	(Lifesong 45028)	.50	2.00	77
Also see Cashman & West				
WESTON, George				
SHELLEY, SHELLEY/My Foolish Pride	(Jackpot 48017)	.75	3.00	
WESTON, Paul				
NEVERTHELESS/Beloved, Be Faithful	(Columbia 38982)	1.25	5.00	50
WET WILLIE				
COUNTRY SIDE OF LIFE/	(Capricorn 0212)	.50	2.00	74
DIXIE ROCK/	(Capricorn 0231)	.50	2.00	75
EVERYTHING THAT 'CHA DO (WILL COME BACK TO YOU)/ Walkin' By Myself	(Capricorn 0254)	.50	2.00	76
KEEP ON SMILIN'/Soul Jones	(Capricorn 0043)	.50	2.00	74
LEONA/	(Capricorn 0224)	.50	2.00	75
MAKE YOU FEEL LOVE AGAIN/Let It Shine	(Epic 50528)	.50	2.00	78
RAMONA/The Hard Way	(Epic 50760)	.50	2.00	79
STREET CORNER SERENADE/We Got Lovin'	(Epic 50478)	.50	2.00	77
WEEKEND/Mr. Streamline	(Epic 50714)	.50	2.00	79
WETBACKS, The				
JOSE JIMENEZ/Jose Jimenez (Part 2)	(Wildcat 0047)	1.00	4.00	60
WHA-KOO				
DON'T SAY YOU LOVE ME/	(Epic 50772)	.50	2.00	79
LOVE'S BEEN KNOWN/ (Shown as by Big Wha-Koo)	(ABC 12290)	.50	2.00	77
WHISKEY VOICES/ (Shown as by Big Wha-Koo)	(ABC 12271)	.50	2.00	77
(YOU'RE SUCH A) FABULOUS DANCER/Fat Love	(ABC 12354)	.50	2.00	78
Also see Steely Dan				
WHAT FOUR				
NIGHT SURF/Gemini 4	(Reprise 0387)	1.00	4.00	65
WHAT-NOTS, The				
NOBODY ELSE BUT YOU/Look Down	(Amber 101)	.75	3.00	
WHEAT, Peter, & The Breadmen				
ALL THE TIME/Baby, What's New	(Amber 6657)	1.25	5.00	
WHEELER, Mary, & The Knights				
FALLING TEAR, A/I Feel In My Heart	(Atom 701)	2.50	10.00	
WHEELERS, The				
ONCE I HAD A GIRL/Shine 'Em On	(Cenco 107)	5.00	20.00	
WHEELMEN, The (With Gary Usher)				
HON-DA BEACH/School Is A Gas	(Warner Bros. 5480)	1.50	6.00	64
WHEELS, The				
CLAP YOUR HANDS/Clap Your Hands (Part 2)	(Folly 800)	1.00	4.00	59
SKATEBOARD U.S.A./Skateboard U.S.A. (Instrumental)	(Atco 6207)	1.00	4.00	61
WHEELS/Chain Fight	(Sidewalk 946)	.75	3.00	
WHEELS, Helen				
HERE COMES THE DERBY (OFFICIAL THEME SONG OF THE ROLLER DERBY)/Put You Out Of My Misery	(Filmore 7006)	1.00	4.00	72
WHIPPETS, The				
GO GO GO WITH RINGO/I Want To Talk With You	(Josie 921)	1.25	5.00	64
WHIRLWINDS, The				
ANGEL LOVE/The Mountain	(Guyden 2052)	2.00	8.00	62
HEARTBEAT/After The Party	(Phillips 40139)	3.75	15.00	63
HEARTBEAT/After The Party (Promotional issue)	(Phillips 40139)	6.25	25.00	63
WHISKEY RIVER				
HEARTACHES IN HEARTACHES/ Makin' Music For Money	(Northland 31759)	.50	2.00	78
WHISPERS, The				
HERE COMES SUMMER/If You Don't Care	(Laurie 3344)	1.00	4.00	66
WHITCOMB, Ian				
BE MY BABY/No Tears For Johnny	(Tower 189)	.75	3.00	66
18 WHITCOMB STREET/Fizz	(Tower 170)	.75	3.00	65
HIGH BLOOD PRESSURE/Good Hard Rock	(Tower 192)	.75	3.00	65
N-E-R-V-O-U-S/The End	(Tower 155)	.75	3.00	65
SALLY SAILS THE SKY/Groovy Day	(Tower 385)	.75	3.00	68
THEY GO WILD, SIMPLY WILD OVER ME/ Yaaka Hula Hickey	(United Artists 162)	.50	2.00	73
THIS SPORTING LIFE/Fizz	(Tower 120)	.75	3.00	65
WHERE DID ROBINSON CRUSO GO WITH FRIDAY ON SATURDAY NIGHT/Poor Little Bird	(Tower 274)	.75	3.00	66
YOU REALLY BENT ME OUT OF SHAPE/ Rolling Home Georgeanne	(Tower 355)	.75	3.00	67
YOU TURN ME ON (TURN ON SONG)/Poor But Honest	(Tower 134)	.75	3.00	65
YOU WON'T SEE ME/Please Don't Leave Me On the Shelf	(Tower 251)	.75	3.00	66
WHITE, Alan (Of Yes)				
OOOH BABY (GOIN' TO PIECES)/	(Atlantic 3340)	.50	2.00	76
WHITE, Bergen				
COME GO WITH ME/Take Time To Love	(Private Stock 103)	1.00	4.00	76
DUKE OF EARL/	(Private Stock 105)	1.00	4.00	76
WHITE, Bobby				
OUR LAST GOODBYE/No Need To Worry	(End 1097)	2.00	8.00	61
WHITE CAPS, The				
FENDER VENDER/Hi Roll (Instrumentals)	(Blue Roll 201)	1.00	4.00	
WHITE CLOUD				
PAPER CAPER/	(Tammy Jo 2)	2.00	8.00	
WHITE, Kitty				
TEEN AGE PRAYER, A/ I'm Gonna Be A Fool Next Monday	(Mercury 70750)	1.00	4.00	55
WHITE LIE				
CHEAP LOVE-EASY MONEY/Scott's Boogie	(White Lie 11078)	.50	2.00	79
WHITE LIGHTING				
OF PAUPERS & POETS/William	(Atco 6660)	1.25	5.00	69
WHITE, Paul				
ELVIS, CHRISTMAS WON'T BE CHRISTMAS/ Midnight Girl	(Country Jubilee 0101)	.50	2.00	77
WHITE PLAINS				
I CAN'T STOP/Julie Anne	(Deram 85080)	.50	2.00	71
LOVIN' YOU BABY/Noises	(Deram 85066)	.50	2.00	70
MY BABY LOVES LOVIN'/Show Me Your Hand	(Deram 85058)	.50	2.00	70
STEP INTO A DREAM/Look To See	(Deram 85086)	.50	2.00	71
WHITE, Tony Joe				
IT MUST BE LOVE/	(20th Century 2276)	.50	2.00	76
IT MUST BE LOVE/	(Arista 0395)	.50	2.00	79
POLK SALAD ANNIE/Aspen Colorado	(Monument 1104)	.75	3.00	69
ROOSEVELT & IRA LEE/Migrant, The	(Monument 1169)	.75	3.00	69
SAVE YOUR SUGAR FOR ME/My Friend	(Monument 1206)	.75	3.00	70
WHITEFACE				
LOVE CAME/Got To Find The Groove	(Mercury 74075)	.50	2.00	79
WHITESIDE, Bobby				
WENDY/I'm Goin' Your Way	(U.S.A. 775)	1.00	4.00	64
WHITESNAKE: see David Coverdale's Whitesnake				
WHITFIELD, David				
CARA MIA/How, When Or Where	(London 1486)	1.00	4.00	54
SANTO NATALE/Adeste Fideles	(London 1508)	1.00	4.00	54
WHEN YOU LOSE THE ONE YOU LOVE/Angelus	(London 1617)	1.00	4.00	56
WHITING, Margaret				
BLIND DATE (With Bob Hope)/Home Cookin'	(Capitol 1042)	1.25	5.00	50
BROKEN DOWN MERRY-GO-ROUND/ The Gods Were Angry With Me (With Jimmy Wakely)	(Capitol 800)	1.25	5.00	50
BUSHEL & A PECK, A/Beyond The Reef (With Jimmy Wakely)	(Capitol 1234)	1.25	5.00	50
HELLO YOUNG LOVERS/When You & I Were One	(Capitol 1491)	1.25	5.00	51
I SAID MY PAJAMAS & PUT ON MY PRAY'RS/Be Mine	(Capitol 841)	1.25	5.00	50
I CAN'T HELP IT/That's Why I Was Born	(Dot 15680)	1.00	4.00	58
LET'S GO TO CHURCH (NEXT SUNDAY MORNING)/ Why Do You Say Those Things (That Hurt Me So) (With Jimmy Wakely)	(Capitol 960)	1.25	5.00	50
MONEY TREE, THE/Maybe I Love Him	(Capitol 3586)	1.00	4.00	56
SLIPPING AROUND/Wedding Bells (With Jimmy Wakely)	(Capitol 1634)	1.25	5.00	51
WHY DON'T YOU BELIEVE ME/Come Back To Me	(Capitol 2292)	1.25	5.00	52
WHITLEY, Ray				
DEEPER IN LOVE/	(Vee Jay VJ-448)	1.00	4.00	62
YESSIREE-YESSIREE/A Love We Can Have & Hold	(Vee Jay VJ-433)	1.00	4.00	62
WHITTINGTON, Jim				
GOODBYE ELVIS/ Will The Circle Be Unbroken	(Lew Breyer Productions 82977)	.50	2.00	77
WHO, The (Featuring Roger Daltrey)				
ANYWAY ANYHOW ANYWHERE/Anytime You Want Me	(Decca 31801)	3.75	15.00	65
BEHIND BLUE EYES/My Wife	(Decca 32888)	1.00	4.00	71
CALL ME LIGHTNING/Dr. Jekyll & Mr. Hyde	(Decca 32288)	1.50	6.00	68
5:15/I'm One	(Polydor 2022)	.50	2.00	79
HAPPY JACK/Whiskey Man	(Decca 32114)	1.25	5.00	67
I CAN SEE FOR MILES/Mary-Anne With The Shaky Hands	(Decca 32206)	.75	3.00	67
I CAN'T EXPLAIN/Bald Headed Woman	(Decca 31725)	1.50	6.00	65
I CAN'T EXPLAIN/Bald Headed Woman	(Track 60110)	.75	3.00	73
I CAN'T EXPLAIN/Bald Headed Woman	(MCA 60110)	.50	2.00	73
I'M A BOY/In The City	(Decca 32058)	2.00	8.00	66

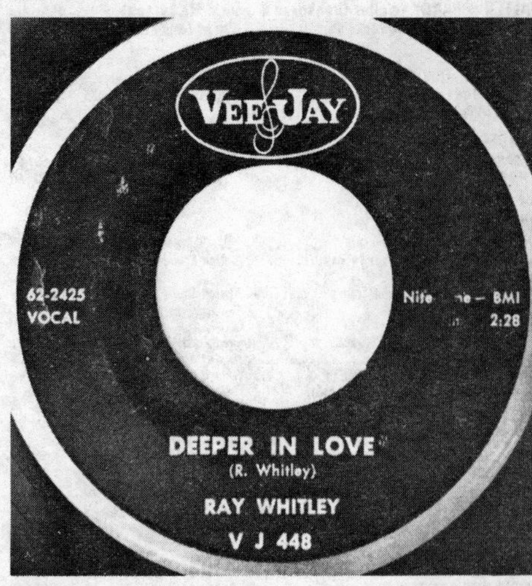

TITLE/FLIP	LABEL & NO.	GOOD	NEAR MINT	YR.
I'M FREE/We're Not Gonna Take It	(Decca 32519)	.75	3.00	69
JOIN TOGETHER/Baby, Don't You Do It	(Decca 32983)	.75	3.00	72
KIDS ARE ALRIGHT, THE/Legal Matter	(Decca 31988)	2.50	10.00	66
LISTENING TO YOU-SEE ME, FEEL ME Overture From Tommy (By Pete Townshend) (The "A" side is shown as by Roger Daltrey & Chorus)	(Polydor 15098)	.50	2.00	75
LONG LIVE ROCK/My Wife	(MCA 41053)	.50	2.00	79
LOVE REIGN O'ER ME/Water	(Track 40152)	.75	3.00	73
MAGIC BUS/Someone's Coming	(Decca 32362)	.75	3.00	68
MY GENERATION/ Out In The Street (You're Going To Know Me)	(Decca 31877)	1.25	5.00	65
PICTURES OF LILY/Doctor Doctor	(Decca 32156)	1.25	5.00	67
PINBALL WIZZARD/Dogs (Part 2)	(Decca 32465)	.75	3.00	69
PINBALL WIZARD/Dogs (Part 2)	(Track 60174)	.75	3.00	74
PINBALL WIZARD/Dogs (Part 2)	(MCA 60174)	.50	2.00	76
POSTCARD/Put The Money Down	(Track 40330)	.75	3.00	74
REAL ME, THE/I'm One	(Track 40182)	.75	3.00	74
RELAY, THE/Waspman	(Track 33041)	.75	3.00	72
SEEKER, THE/Here For More	(Decca 32670)	.75	3.00	70
SEE ME FEEL ME/Overture From Tommy	(Decca 32729)	.75	3.00	70
SEE ME FEEL ME (EXCERPT FROM THE TOMMY FINALE-WE'RE NOT GONNA TAKE IT)/Overture From Tommy (Instrumental)	(Track 60106)	.75	3.00	73
SLIP KID/Dreaming From The Waist	(MCA 40603)	.50	2.00	76
SQUEEZE BOX/Success Story	(MCA 40475)	.50	2.00	75
SUBSTITUTE/Waltz For A Pig	(Atco 6409)	3.00	12.00	67
SUBSTITUTE/Young Man	(Decca 32737)	2.50	10.00	70
SUMMERTIME BLUES/Heaven & Hell	(Decca 32708)	.75	3.00	70
TRICK OF THE LIGHT/905	(MCA 40978)	.50	2.00	78
WHO ARE YOU/Had Enough	(MCA 40948)	.50	2.00	78
WON'T GET FOOLED AGAIN/Don't Even Know Myself	(Decca 32846)	.75	3.00	71
Also see High Numbers				
WHYTE BOOTS				
NIGHTMARE/Let No One Come Between Us	(Phillips 40422)	6.25	25.00	67
WIDOWMAKER (With Aerial Bender)				
LEAVE THE KIDS ALONE/	(Jet 892)	.50	2.00	76
TOO LATE TO CRY/	(Jet 1043)	.50	2.00	77
Aerial Bender, also of Mott The Hoople, was known as Luther Grosvenor when he was with Spooky Tooth.				
WIG				
CRACKIN' UP/Bluescene	(Black Knight 903)	2.00	8.00	
WIGGINS, Jay				
SAD GIRL/No Not Me	(I.P.G. 1008)	.75	3.00	
WILCOX, Eddie, & Sunny Gale				
WHEEL OF FORTUNE/You Showed Me The Way	(Derby 787)	1.25	5.00	52
WILCOX, Harlow				
GROOVY GRUBWORM/ (Instrumentals)	(Plantation 28)	.50	2.00	69
WILD MAN REPORTER RALPH				
BIG RACE/Big Race (Part 2) (Novelty/Break-in)	(Sister Ugly's 1)	1.00	4.00	
WILD ONES, The				
CAUGHT IN THE COOKIE JAR/Super Fox	(Mainline 500)	.75	3.00	65
LORD LOVE A DUCK/My Love	(United Artists 971)	.75	3.00	66
NEVER GIVIN' UP/For Your Love	(United Artists 50043)	.75	3.00	66
VALERIE/Heigh Ho (With Pete Antel)	(Mala 564)	1.25	5.00	67
WILD THING/Just Can't Cry Anymore	(United Artists 947)	.75	3.00	65

Sue Thompson

John Travolta

Lawrence Welk

The Teddy Bears (Phil Spector on Right)

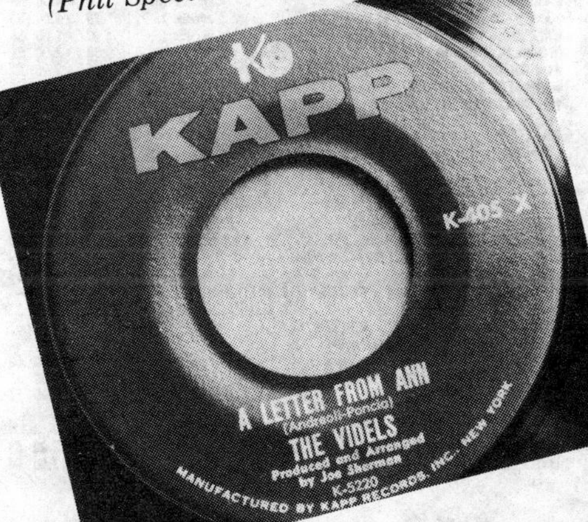

TITLE/FLIP	LABEL & NO.	GOOD	NEAR MINT	YR.
WILD THING				
NEXT TO ME/Old Lady	(Elektra 45672)	1.00	4.00	70
WEIRD HOT NIGHTS (SUFFER BABY)/ Don't Fool With My Girl	(SPQR 1003)	1.00	4.00	
WILD UNCERTAINTY				
MAN WITH MONEY, A/Broken Truth	(Planet 120)	.75	3.00	66
WILD-CATS, The (With Billy Mure)				
GAZACHSTAHAGEN/Billy's Cha Cha (Instrumentals)	(United Artists 154)	1.00	4.00	59
WILDCATS, The (The Blossoms)				
WHAT ARE WE GONNA DO IN '64/3625 Groovy Street	(Reprise 02531)	1.00	4.00	64
WILDCATS, The				
SWIM, THE/Up Stream	(Counsel 1301)	.75	3.00	
WILDE, Jimmy				
CRAZY EYES FOR YOU/Bonnie, Bonnie	(Chelsea 1006)	2.00	8.00	
WILDE, Marty				
ALL NIGHT GIRL/	(Bell 45603)	.50	2.00	74
BAD BOY/Teenage Tears	(Epic 9356)	1.00	4.00	60
MY LUCKY LOVE/Misery's Child	(Epic 9291)	1.00	4.00	59
Also see Shannon				
WILDE, Ricky				
APRIL LOVE/Round & Round	(UK 49013)	.50	2.00	72
I AM AN ASTRONAUT/The Hertfordshire Rock	(UK 49008)	.50	2.00	72
I WANNA GO TO A DISCO/	(UK 49024)	.50	2.00	74
TEEN WAVE/	(UK 49021)	.50	2.00	74
Ricky is Marty Wilde's son.				
WILDFIRE				
HERE COMES SUMMER/Weekend Love	(Casablanca 885)	.50	2.00	77
WILDFLOWER				
BABY DEAR/Wind Dream	(Mainstream 659)	1.25	5.00	68
BUTTERFLY/Holly	(United Artists 50504)	1.00	4.00	69
WILDING, Bobby				
I WANT TO BE A BEATLE/ Since I've Been Wearing My Hair Like A Beatle	(DCP 1009)	2.00	8.00	64
WILDWEEDS, The				
AND WHEN SHE SMILES/And When She Smiles	(Vanguard 35134)	.75	3.00	71
C'MON IF YOU'RE COMIN'/C'mon If You're Comin'	(Vanguard 35155)	.75	3.00	71
I'M DREAMING/Happiness Is Just An Illusion	(Cadet Concept 7004)	1.00	4.00	68
IT WAS FUN/Sorrow's Anthem	(Cadet 5586)	1.00	4.00	68
NO GOOD TO CRY/Never Mind	(Cadet 5561)	1.00	4.00	67
SOMEDAY MORNING/Can't You See That I'm Lonely	(Cadet 5572)	1.00	4.00	67
WILDWOOD				
PLASTIC PEOPLE/Swimming	(Magnum 420)	1.25	5.00	
WILDWOOD COUNTRY/Free Ride	(Magnum 421)	1.25	5.00	
WILKINSON, John				
MAKE IT RAIN/ (You've Got) Nothing To Be Ashamed Of	(RCA Victor 47-9744)	.75	3.00	69
WILLANS, Richard, & The Flame Tones				
OLDIES BUT GOODIES/Little Sister Nell	(Bell 192)	1.25	5.00	72
WILLIAMS, Andy				
AIN'T IT TRUE/	(Columbia 43358)	.50	2.00	65
AND ROSES & ROSES/	(Columbia 43257)	.50	2.00	65
ARE YOU IN THERE?/	(Columbia 10473)	.50	2.00	77
ARE YOU SINCERE/Be Mine Tonight	(Cadence 1340)	1.00	4.00	58
BABY DOLL/Since I've Found My Baby	(Cadence 1303)	1.00	4.00	56
BATTLE HYMN OF THE REPUBLIC/	(Columbia 44650)	.50	2.00	68
BILBAO SONG, THE/How Wonderful To Know	(Cadence 2398)	.75	3.00	61
BUTTERFLY/It Doesn't Take Very Long	(Cadence 1308)	1.00	4.00	57
CANADIAN SUNSET/High Upon A Mountain	(Cadence 1297)	1.00	4.00	56
CAN'T GET USED TO LOSING YOU/ Days Of Wine & Roses	(Columbia 42674)	.75	3.00	63
CAN'T HELP FALLING IN LOVE/	(Columbia 45094)	.50	2.00	70
DANNY BOY/Fly By Night	(Columbia 42199)	.75	3.00	61
DEAR HEART/	(Columbia 43180)	.50	2.00	64
DON'T YOU BELIEVE IT/Summertime	(Columbia 42523)	.75	3.00	62
DO YOU MIND/Dreamsville	(Cadence 1381)	.75	3.00	60
FOOL NEVER LEARNS, A/Charade	(Columbia 42950)	.50	2.00	64
HAPPY HEART/Our Last Goodbye	(Columbia 44818)	.50	2.00	69
HAWAIIAN WEDDING SONG, THE/House Of Bamboo	(Cadence 1358)	1.00	4.00	58
HOME LOVIN' MAN/Who Was It?	(Columbia 45716)	.50	2.00	72
HOPELESS/Peking Theme (So Little Time)	(Columbia 42784)	.75	3.00	63
I LIKE YOUR KIND OF LOVE/Stop Teasin' Me	(Cadence 1323)	1.00	4.00	57
IN THE ARMS OF LOVE/	(Columbia 43737)	.50	2.00	66
LAST TANGO IN PARIS/	(Columbia 45814)	.50	2.00	73
LIPS OF WINE/Straight From My Heart	(Cadence 1336)	1.00	4.00	57
LONELY STREET/Summer Love	(Cadence 1370)	1.00	4.00	59
LOVE IS ALL/	(Columbia 45494)	.50	2.00	71
LOVE THEME FROM "THE GODFATHER"/	(Columbia 45579)	.50	2.00	72
MARMALADE, MOLASSES & HONEY/	(Columbia 45757)	.50	2.00	72
MORE & MORE/	(Columbia 44202)	.50	2.00	67
MUSIC TO WATCH GIRLS BY/	(Columbia 44065)	.50	2.00	67
ONE DAY OF YOUR LIFE/	(Columbia 45175)	.50	2.00	70
ON THE STREET WHERE YOU LIVE/Almost There	(Columbia 43128)	.50	2.00	64
PROMISE ME, LOVE/Your Hand, Your Heart, Your Love	(Cadence 1351)	1.00	4.00	58
QUIET NIGHTS OF QUIET STARS/	(Columbia 43456)	.50	2.00	65
SAD EYES/	(Columbia 10208)	.50	2.00	75
SONG FOR YOU, A/	(Columbia 45434)	.50	2.00	71
STRANGER ON THE SHORE/	(Columbia 42451)	.75	3.00	62
SWEET MEMORIES/	(Columbia 44527)	.50	2.00	68
TELL IT LIKE IT IS/Goin' Through The Motions	(Columbia 10263)	.50	2.00	76
TWILIGHT TIME/So Rare	(Cadence 1433)	.75	3.00	62
VILLAGE OF ST. BERNADETTE, THE/ I'm So Lonesome I Could Cry	(Cadence 1374)	1.00	4.00	59
WAKE ME WHEN IT'S OVER/We Have A Date	(Cadence 1378)	.75	3.00	60
WALK HAND IN HAND/Not Any More	(Cadence 1288)	1.00	4.00	56
(WHERE DO I BEGIN) LOVE STORY/	(Columbia 45317)	.50	2.00	71
WONDERFUL WORLD OF THE YOUNG, THE/	(Columbia 42265)	.75	3.00	62
WRONG FOR EACH OTHER/Madrigal	(Columbia 43015)	.50	2.00	64
YOU DON'T WANT MY LOVE/Don't Go To Strangers	(Cadence 1389)	.75	3.00	60
WILLIAMS, Anson				
DEEPLY/I Want To Believe In This One	(Chelsea 3061)	.50	2.00	77
WILLIAMS, Billy, Quartet				
BABY, BABY/Don't Let Go	(Coral 61932)	1.00	4.00	58
CRAZY LITTLE PALACE, A/Cry Baby	(Coral 61576)	1.00	4.00	56
GOODNIGHT IRENE/Red Hot Love	(Coral 62101)	1.00	4.00	59
GOT A DATE WITH AN ANGEL/The Lord Will Understand	(Coral 61886)	1.00	4.00	57
I'LL GET BY/It's Prayin' Time	(Coral 61999)	1.00	4.00	58
I'M GONNA SIT RIGHT DOWN & WRITE MYSELF A LETTER/ Date With The Blues	(Coral 61830)	1.00	4.00	57
I WANNA HUG YOU, KISS YOU, SQUEEZE YOU/ (With vocal introduction by Alan Freed)	(Coral 9-61363)	1.00	4.00	55
NOLA/Tied To The Strings Of Your Heart	(Coral 9-62069)	1.00	4.00	59
PIED PIPER, THE/Butterfly	(Coral 9-61795)	1.25	5.00	57
SHANGHAI/Wonderous Word, The	(MGM 10998)	1.25	5.00	51
WILLIAMS, Danny				
BLUE ON WHITE/It's Not For Me To Say	(United Artists 50020)	.75	3.00	66
LITTLE TOY BALLOON, A/The Truth Hurts	(United Artists 729)	.75	3.00	64
MORE/Rhapsody	(United Artists 601)	.75	3.00	64
WHITE ON WHITE/Comedy Is Ended	(United Artists 685)	.75	3.00	64
WILLIAMS, Diana				
GOODBYE, BING, ELVIS, & GUY/One More Christmas	(Little Gem 1023)	.50	2.00	77
WILLIAMS, Jerry				
RUNAROUND SUE/The Wanderer	(Laurie 3339)	1.25	5.00	66
WILLIAMS, John				
MAIN TITLE (STAR WARS)/Cantina Band	(20th Century 2345)	.50	2.00	77
THEME FROM "CLOSE ENCOUNTERS OF THE THIRD KIND"/ Nocturnal Pursuit	(Arista 0300)	.50	2.00	77
THEME FROM SUPERMAN (MAIN TITLE)/ Love Theme From Superman	(Warner Bros. 8729)	.50	2.00	79
THEME FROM THE UNIVERSAL MOTION PICTURE SOUNDTRACK "JAWS"/ Instrumentals	(MCA 40439)	.50	2.00	75
WILLIAMS, Lee, & The Moonrays				
I'M SO IN LOVE/(No) I Won't Cry Anymore	(King 5409)	1.25	5.00	60
WILLIAMS, Little Jerry				
I'M THE LOVER MAN/Push, Push, Push	(Southern Sound 118)	1.00	4.00	64
I'M THE LOVER MAN/Push, Push, Push	(Loma 2005)	.75	3.00	64
WILLIAMS, Mason				
BAROQUE-A-NOVA/Wanderlove	(Warner Bros. 7235)	.75	3.00	68
CLASSICAL GAS/Long Time Blues	(Warner Bros. 7190)	.75	3.00	68
GREENSLEEVES/$13 Stella	(Warner Bros. 7272)	.75	3.00	69
SATURDAY NIGHT AT THE WORLD/	(Warner Bros. 7248)	.75	3.00	69
WILLIAMS, Mike				
LONELY SOLDIER/	(Atlantic 2339)	.75	3.00	66
WILLIAMS, Paul				
I WON'T LAST A DAY WITHOUT YOU/	(A&M 1409)	.50	2.00	72
SUMMERTIME LOVE/I Need You	(Astra 3002)	1.00	4.00	
WAKING UP ALONE/	(A&M 1325)	.50	2.00	72
WILLIAMS, Roger				
ALMOST PARADISE/For The First Time	(Kapp 175)	.75	3.00	57
AUTUMN LEAVES/Take Care	(Kapp 116)	.75	3.00	55
AUTUMN LEAVES 1965/Autumn Leaves 1955	(Kapp 707)	.75	3.00	65
LA MER (BEYOND THE SEA/Song Of Devotion	(Kapp 138)	.75	3.00	56
NEAR YOU/Merry Widow Waltz	(Kapp 233)	.75	3.00	58
Instrumentals				
WILLIAMS, Roy				
I REMEMBER ELVIS/ The Fire Of Love Has Gone Out	(WM Country Sound 7700)	.50	2.00	77
WILLIAMS, Tom B.				
WISHING WELL/Come Back	(Topix 6009)	5.00	20.00	62
WILLIE & THE WHEELS				
SKATEBOARD CRAZE/Do What You Did	(Dunhill 4002)	1.25	5.00	65
WILLIS, Billy Jack				
THERE'S GOOD ROCKIN' TONIGHT/	(MGM 11966)	5.00	20.00	55
WILLIS, Hal				
BOP-A-DEE, BOP-A-DOO/My Pink Cadillac	(Atlantic 1114)	15.00	60.00	57
WILLIS, Rod				
SOMEBODY'S BEEN ROCKIN' MY BABY/Old Man Mose	(Chic 1010)	1.00	4.00	59
WILL-O-BEES, The				
IT'S NOT EASY/	(Date 1583)	.75	3.00	68
MAKE YOUR OWN KIND OF MUSIC/Listen To The Music	(SGC 002)	1.25	5.00	69
SHADES OF GREY/If You're Ready	(Date 1543)	.75	3.00	68
UGLIEST GIRL IN TOWN/I Can't Quit Loving You	(SGC 004)	1.25	5.00	69
WILLS, Maury				
BALLAD OF MAURY WILLS, THE/	(Dot 16529)	.75	3.00	64
WILLS, Tommy				
HONKY TONK 66'/Night Train '66 (Instrumentals)	(Air Town 001)	.75	3.00	66
WILSON, Ann, & The Daybreaks				
I'M GONNA DRINK MY HURT AWAY/ Through Eyes & Glass	(Topaz T-1312)	1.25	5.00	67
STANDIN' WATCHIN' YOU/Wonder How I Managed	(Topaz T-1311)	1.25	5.00	67
Also see Heart				
WILSON, Andy				
LITTLE MAMA/Tonite Tonite	(Athens 700)	1.25	5.00	
WILSON, Brian: see Beach Boys, The				
WILSON BROTHERS, The				
ANOTHER NIGHT/	(Atco 7205)	.50	2.00	79
WILSON, Dennis (Of The Beach Boys)				
YOU & I/Friday Night	(Caribou 9023)	.75	3.00	77
WILSON, Hank (Leon Russell)				
ROLL IN MY SWEET BABY'S ARMS/ I'm So Lonesome I Could Cry	(Shelter 7336)	.50	2.00	73
SIX PACK TO GO, A/Uncle Pen	(Shelter 7338)	.50	2.00	74
WILSON, J. Frank, (& The Cavaliers)				
CLOWN, THE/Cool	(Charay 80)	.75	3.00	69
DREAMS OF A FOOL/Open Your Eyes	(Josie 931)	.75	3.00	65
HEY LITTLE ONE/Speak To Me	(Josie 926)	.75	3.00	64
KISS & RUN/Teardrops In My Heart	(Le Cam 1015)	1.00	4.00	65
LAST KISS/Carla ("Last Kiss" is a different recording than was later issued by Tamara.)	(Le Cam 722)	2.50	10.00	64
LAST KISS/That's How Much I Love You	(Tamara 761)	1.50	6.00	64
LAST KISS/That's How Much I Love You (Reissue of Tamara version)	(Josie 923)	.75	3.00	64
LAST KISS/	(Virgo 506)	.50	2.00	73
LAST KISS '69/Kiss & Run	(Charay 13)	.75	3.00	69
SIX BOYS/Say It Now	(Josie 929)	.75	3.00	65
TELL LAURA I LOVE HER/	(April 1)	1.00	4.00	
UNMARKED & UNCOVERED WITH SAND/Me & My Teardrops	(Sully 927)	1.00	4.00	65
WHITE SPORT COAT & A PINK CARNATION/	(Josie 938)	.75	3.00	65
WILSON, Murry				
LEAVES/Plumber's Tune	(Capitol 2063)	2.50	10.00	67
Murry's sons, Brian, Dennis & Carl, are members of The Beach Boys.				
WILSON, Peanuts				
CAST IRON ARM/	(Brunswick 55039)	8.75	35.00	58
Also see Crickets, The				
WILSON, Phill				
WISHIN' ON A RAINBOW/Just Me	(Huron 22000)	.75	3.00	61
WILSON, Ron				
I'LL KEEP ON LOVING YOU/As Tears Go By	(Columbia 44636)	3.00	12.00	68
WILSON, Tony (Of Hot Chocolate)				
I LIKE YOUR STYLE/	(Bearsville 0316)	.50	2.00	77
WINCHELL, Danny (With Nino & The Ebbtides)				
COME BACK BABY/	(Recorte 415)	3.00	12.00	59
JEANNIE/Beware You're Falling In Love	(Recorte 406)	2.00	8.00	59
WE'RE GONNA HAVE A ROCKIN' PARTY/ Don't Say You're Sorry	(Recorte 410)	2.00	8.00	59
WINCHESTER, Jesse				
BRAND NEW TENNESSEE WALTZ/Rough Side Drag	(Bearsville 0311)	.50	2.00	76
EVERYBODY KNOWS BUT ME/	(Bearsville 0314)	.50	2.00	77
NOTHING BUT A BREEZE/Twigs & Seeds	(Bearsville 0318)	.50	2.00	77
RHUMBA MAN/Twigs & Seeds	(Bearsville 0320)	.50	2.00	77
SASSY/Wintry Feeling	(Bearsville 0332)	.50	2.00	78
YANKEE LADY/That's The Touch I Like	(Ampex 11004)	.50	2.00	70
WIND (Featuring Tony Orlando)				
MAKE BELIEVE/Groovin' With Mr. Bloe (Instrumental)	(Life 200)	1.25	5.00	69
TEENY BOPPER/I'll Hold Out My Hand	(Life 202)	1.50	6.00	69
WINDING, Kai				
MORE/Comin Home Baby (Instrumentals)	(Verve 10295)	.75	3.00	63
WINDSORS, The				
CAROL ANN/Keep Me From Crying	(Wig-Wag 203)	7.50	30.00	
WINGS: see McCartney, Paul				
WINGFIELD, Pete				
EIGHTEEN WITH A BULLET/Shadow Of A Doubt	(Island 026)	.50	2.00	75
LOVIN' AS YOU WANNA BE/	(Island 051)	.50	2.00	76
SCRATCHY 45s/	(Island 065)	.50	2.00	77
WINKLE PICKERS, The				
(MY NAME IS) GRANNY GOOSE/I Havn't Got You	(Colpix 796)	1.00	4.00	66
WINKLY & NUTLEY				
REPORT TO THE NATION (PART 1)/ Report To The Nation (Part 2) (Novelty/Break-in)	(MK 101)	1.00	4.00	60
WINSLOW, Barry (Of The Royal Guardsmen)				
SMALLEST ASTRONAUT (A RACE TO THE MOON WITH THE RED BARON), THE/Quality Woman	(Laurie 3509)	.75	3.00	69
WINTER, Edgar, Group (Featuring Dan Hartman)				
DIAMOND EYES/Infinite Peace In Rhythm	(Blue Sky 2763)	.50	2.00	76
EASY STREET/Do Like Me	(Epic 50034)	.50	2.00	74
FRANKENSTEIN/Undercover Man	(Epic 10967)	.50	2.00	73
FREE RIDE/When It Comes	(Epic 11024)	.50	2.00	73
GIVE IT EVERYTHING YOU GOT/You Were My Light (Shown as by Edgar Winter's White Trash)	(Epic 10762)	.75	3.00	71
HANGIN' AROUND/We All Had A Real Good Time	(Epic 11069)	.50	2.00	73
HANGING AROUND/Frankenstein	(Epic 10945)	.50	2.00	73
I ALWAYS WANTED YOU/Outa Control	(Blue Sky 2761)	.50	2.00	76
I CAN'T TURN YOU LOOSE/Cool Fool (Shown as by Edgar Winter's White Trash)	(Epic 10855)	.75	3.00	72
IT'S YOUR LIFE TO LIVE/Forever In Love	(Blue Sky 2780)	.50	2.00	79
KEEP PLAYIN' THAT ROCK 'N' ROLL/Dying To Live (Shown as by Edgar Winter's White Trash)	(Epic 10788)	.75	3.00	71
ONE DAY TOMORROW/Jasmine Nightdream	(Blue Sky 2758)	.50	2.00	75
PEOPLE MUSIC/Cool Dance	(Blue Sky 2762)	.50	2.00	76
RIVER'S RISIN'/Animal	(Epic 11143)	.50	2.00	74
ROUND & ROUND/Catchin' Up	(Epic 10922)	.50	2.00	72
SOMEONE TAKE MY HEART AWAY/Miracle Of Love	(Epic 50060)	.50	2.00	74
STICKIN' IT OUT/Puttin' It Back	(Blue Sky 2769)	.50	2.00	78
TOBACCO ROAD/ (Shown as by Edgar Winter's White Trash)	(Epic 10618)	.75	3.00	70
WHERE WOULD I BE/Good Morning Music (Shown as by Edgar Winter's White Trash)	(Epic 10740)	.75	3.00	71
Also see Derringer, Rick				
Also see Winter, Johnny & Edgar				
WINTER, Jimmy				
ETERNALLY/	(Frolic 1017)	.75	3.00	
WINTER, Johnny				
BONEY MARONEY/Hurting So Bad	(Columbia 46036)	.50	2.00	74
CAN'T YOU FEEL IT/	(Columbia 45899)	.50	2.00	73
GANGSTER OF LOVE/Eternally	(Atlantic 2248)	1.00	4.00	64
GOLDEN OLDEN DAYS OF ROCK & ROLL/	(Blue Sky 2756)	.50	2.00	75
GUY YOU LEFT BEHIND, THE/Road Runner	(Todd 1084)	1.50	6.00	63
JOHNNY B. GOODE/	(Columbia 45058)	.50	2.00	70
JUMPIN' JACK FLASH/Good Morning Little Schoolgirl	(Columbia 45368)	.50	2.00	71
RAISED ON ROCK/Pick Up On My Mind	(Blue Sky 2754)	.50	2.00	75
ROLLIN' & TUMBLIN'/	(Sonobeat 107)	2.50	10.00	
SILVER TRAIN/Rock & Roll	(Columbia 45869)	.50	2.00	73
STONE COUNTY/Bad Luck Situation	(Columbia 46006)	.50	2.00	74
WINTER, Johnny & Edgar				
LET THE GOOD TIMES ROLL/Soul Man	(Blue Sky 2764)	.50	2.00	76
Johnny & Edgar Winter are brothers				
WINTER, Paul, & Winter Consort				
ICARUS/Minuit	(Epic 10928)	.75	3.00	73
ICARUS/Minuit	(A&M 1986)	.50	2.00	77
WINTERHALTER, Hugo (& His Orchestra)				
CANADIAN SUNSET/This Is Real (We're In Love, We're In Love, We're In Love) (With Eddie Heywood)	(RCA Victor 47-6537)	.75	3.00	56
WINTERS BROTHERS BAND, The				
I CAN'T HELP IT/Sweet Dream Lady	(Atco-Rabbit 7082)	.50	2.00	77
SANG HER LOVE SONGS/	(Atco-Rabbit 7077)	.50	2.00	77
SMOKEY MOUNTAIN LOG CABIN/	(Atco-Rabbit 7085)	.50	2.00	77
WINTERS, David				
BYE BYE/Dori Anne	(Rori 703)	2.00	8.00	62
SUNDAY KIND OF LOVE/Princess	(Addicon 15004)	3.75	15.00	
WINTERS, Jonathan				
NEE NEE NA NA NA NU NU/Take Me To Your Leader (With the Martians) (Novelty)	(Coral 61988)	1.50	6.00	58
WINWOOD, Steve (Of the Spencer Davis Group)				
TIME IS RUNNING OUT/Hold On	(Island 091)	.50	2.00	77
Also see Traffic				
WISDOMS, The				
TWO HEARTS MAKE ONE LOVE/Lost In Dreams	(Gaity 169)	2.50	10.00	59
WISHBONE ASH				
BLIND EYE/Queen Of Torture	(Decca 32826)	.50	2.00	71
GOODBYE BABY HELLO FRIEND/Front Page News	(MCA 40829)	.50	2.00	77
JAIL BAIT/Vas Dis	(Decca 32906)	.50	2.00	72
LORELEI/Outward Bound	(Atlantic 3381)	.50	2.00	77
NO EASY ROAD/Rock 'N' Roll Widow	(MCA 40041)	.50	2.00	73
SILVER SHOES/	(MCA 40362)	.50	2.00	75
Some members of this group appeared in Foghat.				

ITLE/FLIP	LABEL & NO.	GOOD	NEAR MINT	YR.
VITCHES & WARLOCK				
EHIND LOCKED DOORS/Behind Locked Doors (Part 2)	(Sew City 103)	1.00	4.00	66
DON'T WANT TO LIVE MY LIFE ALONE/Let Them Talk	(Sew City 61167)	1.00	4.00	67
'ANDERER, THE/Nowhere To Run, Nowhere To Hide	(Sew City 106)	1.00	4.00	68
'HAT WILL I DO NOW/Which Way Did He Go	(Sew City 105)	1.00	4.00	68
VOBBLERS, The				
'OBBLE, THE/Blow Out	(King 5585)	.75	3.00	62
VOLFE, Danny				
RETTY BLUE JEAN BABY/	(Dot 15591)	1.00	4.00	57
VOLFMAN JACK (Bob Smith)				
AIN'T NEVER SEEN A WHITE MAN/	(Wooden Nickel 0108)	.50	2.00	72
ING, TING, TONG/	(Wooden Nickel 0117)	.50	2.00	73
HERE'S AN OLD MAN IN OUR TOWN/	(Wooden Nickel 0110)	.50	2.00	72
VOMB, The				
'ANG ON/My Baby Thinks About The Good Things	(Dot 17250)	1.00	4.00	69
VOMBLES, The (Featuring Mike Batt)				
EMEMBER YOU'RE A WOMBLE/Wellington Womble	(Columbia 10033)	.50	2.00	75
VOMBLING SUMMER PARTY/	(Columbia 10013)	.50	2.00	75
VOMENFOLK, The				
ITTLE BOXES/Love Come A-Tricklin Down	(RCA Victor 47-8301)	.75	3.00	64
VONDERS, The				
AY THERE/Marilyn	(Colpix 699)	1.25	5.00	63
VONDER WHO?, The: see 4 Seasons, The				
VOOD, Bill				
OCK & ROLL HEAVEN/Wicken Women Never Win	(Audan 119)	1.00	4.00	61
VOOD, Del				
OWN YONDER/Dreamy Eyes	(Tennessee 775)	1.25	5.00	51
VOOD, Lauren				
LEASE DON'T LEAVE/Where Di I Get These Tears	(Warner Bros. 49043)	.50	2.00	79
VOOD, Ron (Of The Jeff Beck Group)				
CAN FEEL THE FIRE/Breathe On Me	(Warner Bros. 8036)	.50	2.00	75
YOU DON'T WANT MY LOVE/	(Warner Bros. 8131)	.50	2.00	76
EVEN DAYS/Breakin' My Heart	(Columbia 11014)	.50	2.00	79
Also see Rolling Stones, The				
Also see Faces				
VOOD, Roy (Of The Electric Light Orchestra)				
NY OLD TIME WILL DO/	(United Artists 792)	.50	2.00	76
ALL PARK INCIDENT/The Carlsberg Special (Pianos Demolished: Phone 021 373 4472)	(United Artists 160)	.50	2.00	73
OREVER/Woodbe	(United Artists 394)	.50	2.00	74
EE MY BABY JIVE/Got A Crush On You	(United Artists 272)	.50	2.00	73
VOOD, Scott				
HICKEN ROCK/Three Friends	(Beat 1008)	1.00	4.00	59
VOODS, Little Eddie				
UG KILLER/Is It So Wrong	(Comet 2165)	1.50	6.00	64
VOODYS, The				
AINTS, THE (GO SURFIN' IN)/Red River Valley	(California 304)	1.00	4.00	63
VOOL				
'S ALRIGHT/Take Me To The Pilot	(Columbia 45452)	.50	2.00	72
VOOLIES, The				
RING IT WITH YOU WHEN YOU COME/ We Love You B.B. King	(Spirit 0003)	1.25	5.00	
UNCAN & BRANDY/Love Words	(Dunhill 4088)	.75	3.00	67
OOTCHIE COOTCHIE MAN IS BACK, THE/ Can't Get That Stuff	(Spirit 0014)	1.25	5.00	
IDE RIDE RIDE/We Love You JB Lenoir	(Spirit 0009)	1.25	5.00	
UPER BALL/Back For More	(Spirit 0008)	1.25	5.00	
-WAY WISHES/Chucks Chunk	(Spirit 0006)	1.25	5.00	
ANDEGRAF'S BLUES/Vandegraf's Blahs	(Spirit 0007)	1.25	5.00	
VHO DO YOU LOVE/Hey Girl	(Dunhill 4052)	.75	3.00	66
VHO DO YOU LOVE/Feelin' Good	(Spirit 0013)	1.25	5.00	
VORLD OF OZ, The				
ACK/King Croesus	(Deram 85034)	.75	3.00	68
VORLD OF TEARS, The				
HILDREN OF THE NIGHT/	(Bella 101)	.75	3.00	
VORTH, Stan				
OMAN HOLIDAY/Wiggle Wobble Walkers	(Enith 719)	.75	3.00	63
(Instrumentals)				
VOW WOWS, The				
CHMOND RALLY/Countdown	(Challenge 59046)	1.00	4.00	59
(Instrumentals)				
VRAY BROTHERS, The (Doug, Vernon & Link)				
'OU'RE SWEETER THAN SUGAR/99 Years To Go	(Infinity INX-033)	1.00	4.00	62
Also see Vernon, Ray				
VRAY, Doug				
CHOOL GIRL/Goose Bumps	(Epic 9322)	1.00	4.00	59
VRAY, Link				
CE OF SPADES/The Fuzz	(Swan 4239)	1.00	4.00	65
CE OF SPADES/Hidden Charms	(Swan 4261)	.75	3.00	66
IN'T THAT LOVIN' YOU BABY/Mary Ann	(Epic 9419)	1.00	4.00	60
ABY (WHAT CHA WAN ME TO DO)/Walkin' Down The Street	(Diamond 186)	1.00	4.00	65
(Shown as by the Raymen)				
ATMAN THEME/Alone	(Swan 4244)	.75	3.00	66
IG CITY STOMP/Poppin' Popeye	(Atlas 687)	1.00	4.00	62
OMANCHE/Lillian	(Epic 9321)	1.00	4.00	59
EUCES WILD/Summer Dream	(Swan 4187)	1.00	4.00	64
IRL FROM THE NORTH COUNTRY/You Hurt Me So	(Swan 4232)	1.00	4.00	65
OLDEN STRINGS/Trail Of The Lonesome Pine	(Epic 9361)	1.00	4.00	60
OOD ROCKIN' TONIGHT/I'll Do Anything For You	(Swan 4201)	1.00	4.00	65
OT ANOTHER BABY/What Cha Say Honey	(Starday 575)	3.00	12.00	57
(Shown as by Lucky Wray)				
GOT TO RAMBLE/	(Polydor 14256)	.50	2.00	74
'M BRANDED/Hang On	(Swan 4211)	1.00	4.00	65
T'S MUSIC SHE SAYS/Sick & Tired	(Starday 552)	3.00	12.00	56
(Shown as by Lucky Wray)				
ACK THE RIPPER/The Stranger	(Rumble 1000)	1.50	6.00	61
ACK THE RIPPER/Black Widow	(Swan 4137)	1.00	4.00	63
ACK THE RIPPER/I'll Do Anything For You	(Swan 4282)	.75	3.00	67
UKE BOX MAMA/Fire & Brimstone	(Polydor 14084)	.50	2.00	70
UKE BOX MAMA/Fallin' Rain	(Polydor 14096)	.50	2.00	70
ET THE GOOD TIMES ROLL/Soul Train	(Swan 4273)	.75	3.00	66
AW HIDE/Dixie-Doodle	(Epic 9300)	1.00	4.00	59
UMBLE/The Swag	(Cadence 1347)	1.50	6.00	58
UMBLE MAMBO/Hambone (By Red Saunders)	(Okeh 7166)	1.00	4.00	63
UMBLE MAMBO/Hambone (By Red Saunders)	(Okeh 7282)	.75	3.00	67
UMBLE '68/Blow Your Mind	(Heavy 101)	.75	3.00	68
UMBLE '69/Mind Blower	(Mr. G. 820)	.75	3.00	69
UN CHICKEN RUN/Sweeper	(Swan 4163)	1.00	4.00	63
HADOW KNOWS, THE/My Alberta	(Swan 4171)	1.00	4.00	64
LINKY/Rendezvous	(Epic 9343)	1.00	4.00	59

TITLE/FLIP	LABEL & NO.	GOOD	NEAR MINT	YR.
SLINKY/Rendezvous	(Epic 9343)	3.75	15.00	59
(Picture sleeve)				
TEENAGE CUTIE/Your My Song	(Starday 608)	3.00	12.00	57
(Shown as by Lucky Wray)				
TIJUANA/El Toro	(Epic 9454)	1.00	4.00	61
WEEK END/Turnpike, U.S.A.	(Swan 4154)	1.00	4.00	63
Shown on some releases as Link Wray & His Ray Men. May also be shown as with his Wray Men.				
WRIGHT, Charles, & The Malibus				
LATINIA/Runky	(Titanic 5003)	.75	3.50	
(Instrumentals)				
WRIGHT, Dale				
PLEASE DON'T DO IT/	(Fraternity 818)	1.25	5.00	58
SHE'S NEAT/Say That You Care	(Fraternity 792)	1.25	5.00	58
(With the Rock-Its)				
WRIGHT, Gary				
DREAM WEAVER/Let It Out	(Warner Bros. 8167)	.50	2.00	75
FASCINATING THINGS/Love To Survive	(A&M 1319)	.50	2.00	71
GET ON THE RIGHT ROAD/Over You Now	(A&M 1228)	.50	2.00	70
I CAN'T SEE THE REASON/Stand For Our Rights	(A&M 1267)	.50	2.00	71
I KNOW/Two Faced Man	(A&M 1344)	.50	2.00	72
I'M THE ONE WHO'LL BE BY YOUR SIDE/ Follow Next To You	(Warner Bros. 8809)	.50	2.00	79
LIGHT OF SMILES/Silent Fury	(Warner Bros. 8426)	.50	2.00	77
LOVE IS ALIVE/Much Higher	(Warner Bros. 9143)	.50	2.00	75
MADE TO LOVE YOU/Power Of Love	(Warner Bros. 8240)	.50	2.00	76
PHANTOM WRITER/Child Of Light	(Warner Bros. 8331)	.50	2.00	77
SOMETHING VERY SPECIAL/Sky Eyes	(Warner Bros. 8548)	.50	2.00	78
STARRY EYED/Can't Get Above Losing You	(Warner Bros. 8598)	.50	2.00	78
TOUCH & GONE/Lost In My Emotions	(Warner Bros. 8494)	.50	2.00	77
WATER SIGN/Empty Inside	(Warner Bros. 8383)	.50	2.00	77
Also see Wright's Wonderland				
WRIGHT, Lorna				
NIGHT MUSIC/	(Rocket 11307)	.50	2.00	78
SLOW DANCING/	(Rocket 40750)	.50	2.00	77
Lorna is Gary Wright's sister				
WRIGHT, Priscilla				
MAN IN THE RAINCOAT, THE/Please Have Mercy	(Unique 303)	1.00	4.00	55
WRIGHT, Ruby				
LET'S LIGHT THE CHRISTMAS TREE/ Merry, Merry Christmas	(Fraternity 787)	1.00	4.00	57
THREE STARS/I Only Have One Lifetime	(King 5192)	2.50	10.00	59
(With Dick Pike)				
WRIGHT, Steve				
WILD, WILD WOMAN/Love You	(Lin 5022)	1.00	4.00	59
WRIGHT'S WONDERLAND (Gary Wright)				
I KNOW/	(A&M 1344)	.75	3.00	72
WYATT, Robert (Of the Soft Machine)				
I'M A BELIEVER/	(Virgin 56000)	.50	2.00	74
WYMAN, Bill (Of the Rolling Stones)				
APACHE WOMAN/Soul Satisfying	(Rolling Stones 19303)	1.25	5.00	75
IN ANOTHER LAND/ The Lantern (By the Rolling Stones)	(London 907)	.75	3.00	67
WHITE LIGHTNIN'/I Wanna Get Me A Gun	(Rolling Stones 19111)	1.25	5.00	74
(The Rolling Stones group does not appear on this release, despite label credits that indicate they do.)				
Also see Walker, John				
WYMAN, Karen				
BEAUTIFUL/	(Columbia 45484)	.50	2.00	72
SOMETHING TELLS ME (SOMETHING'S GONNA HAPPEN TONIGHT)/	(Columbia 45700)	.50	2.00	73

X-Y

TITLE/FLIP	LABEL & NO.	GOOD	NEAR MINT	YR.
YACHTS, The				
YACHTING TYPE/	(Polydor-Radar 2027)	.50	2.00	79
YANOVSKY, Zalmon (Of the Lovin' Spoonful)				
AS LONG AS YOU'RE HERE/Ereh Er'uoy Sa Gnol Sa	(Buddah 12)	.75	3.00	68
YARBROUGH, Glenn (Of the Limeliters)				
BABY THE RAIN MUST FALL/I've Been to Town	(RCA Victor 47-8498)	.75	3.00	65
HONEY WIND BLOWS, THE/ San Francisco Bay Blues, The	(RCA Victor 47-8366)	.75	3.00	64
IT'S GONNA BE FINE/She	(RCA Victor 47-8619)	.75	3.00	65
YARDBIRDS, The (Featuring Eric Clapton, Keith Relf, Jeff Beck & Jimmy Page)				
FOR YOUR LOVE/Got To Hurry	(Epic 9790)	1.00	4.00	65
HA HA SAID THE CLOWN/Tinker, Tailor, Soldier, Sailor	(Epic 10204)	.75	3.00	67
HAPPENINGS TEN YEARS TIME AGO/Nazz Are Blue	(Epic 10094)	1.00	4.00	66
HEART FULL OF SOUL/Steeled Blues	(Epic 9823)	1.00	4.00	65
I WISH YOU COULD/A Certain Girl	(Epic 9709)	3.75	15.00	64
I'M A MAN/Still I'm Sad	(Epic 9857)	1.00	4.00	65
LITTLE GAMES/Puzzles	(Epic 10156)	1.25	5.00	67
OVER, UNDER, SIDEWAYS DOWN/Jeff's Boogie	(Epic 10035)	1.00	4.00	66
SHAPES OF THINGS/I'm Not Talking	(Epic 9891)	2.00	8.00	66
SHAPES OF THINGS/New York City Blues	(Epic 10006)	1.00	4.00	66
TEN LITTLE INDIANS/Drinking Muddy Water	(Epic 10248)	3.00	12.00	67
THINK ABOUT IT/Goodnight Sweet Josephine	(Epic 10303)	2.50	10.00	68
YARROW, Peter (Of Peter, Paul & Mary)				
ANOTHER CHAIN UNBOUND/Wanderin'	(Warner Bros. 8114)	.50	2.00	75
DON'T EVER TAKE AWAY MY FREEDOM/Greenwood	(Warner Bros. 7567)	.50	2.00	72
YATES, Little Sammy				
COMIC BOOK CRAZY/Dodge City Baby	(Genie 104)	1.25	5.00	59
(Novelty)				
YELLOW BALLOON, The (Featuring Don Grady)				
CAN'T GET ENOUGH OF YOUR LOVE/ Stained Glass Window	(Canterbury 516)	1.00	4.00	68
GOOD FEELIN' TIME/I've Got A Feeling For Love	(Canterbury 513)	1.00	4.00	67
YELLOW BALLOON/Noollab Wolley	(Canterbury 508)	1.00	4.00	67

TITLE/FLIP	LABEL & NO.	GOOD	NEAR MINT	YR.
YELLOW HAIR (With Scott McCarl)				
SOMEWHERE/Talent For Lovin	(Pacific Avenue 457)	1.50	6.00	
Also see Raspberries, The				
YELLOW JACKETS				
HI BOY/When I First Saw Her Face	(Smash 2180)	.75	3.00	69
YELLOW PAYGES, The				
JEZEBEL/We Got A Love In The Makin'	(Showplace 217)	.50	2.00	70
YES (Featuring Jon Anderson & Rick Wakeman)				
AMERICA/Total Mass Retain	(Atlantic 2899)	.50	2.00	72
AND YOU & I (PART 1)/And You & I (Part 2)	(Atlantic 2920)	.50	2.00	72
EVERY LITTLE THING/Sweetness	(Atlantic 2709)	.50	2.00	70
RELEASE, RELEASE/Don't Kill The Whale	(Atlantic 3534)	.50	2.00	78
ROUNDABOUT/Long Distance Run Around	(Atlantic 2854)	.50	2.00	72
SOON/Sound Chaser	(Atlantic 3242)	.50	2.00	75
WONDROUS STORIES/Awaken (Part 1)	(Atlantic 3416)	.50	2.00	77
YOUR MOVE/Clap	(Atlantic 2819)	.50	2.00	71
YESTER, Jerry (Of the Lovin' Spoonful)				
SOUND OF SUMMER SHOWERS/Ashes Have Turned	(Dunhill 4042)	.75	3.00	66
YIPES				
EAST SIDE KIDS/Hangin' Around	(Millenium 11780)	.50	2.00	79
YOLANDA & THE NATURALS				
MY MEMORIES OF YOU/Jawbone	(Kimley 923)	1.25	5.00	
YORGESSON, Yogi				
CHRISTMAS PARTY, THE/I Was Santa Claus	(Capitol 1831)	1.25	5.00	51
MOTHER-IN-LAW/Ya Ya Ya	(Capitol 2643)	1.00	4.00	54
SOMEONE SPIKED THE PUNCH/My Little Old Shack	(Capitol 1216)	1.25	5.00	50
YINGLE BELLS/I Yust Go Nuts At Christmas	(Capitol 57-781)	1.25	5.00	49
Novelties				
YORK, Dave, & The Beachcombers				
BEACH PARTY/I Wanna Go Surfin	(P-K-M 6700)	1.00	4.00	62
YORK, Rusty				
LOVE STRUCK/ Goodnight Cincinnati, Good Morning Tennessee	(King 5511)	.75	3.00	61
SALLY WAS A GOOD OLD GIRL/ I Might Just Walk Right Back Again	(Gaylord 6428)	.75	3.00	62
SUGAREE/Red Rooster	(P.J. 100)	3.75	15.00	59
SUGAREE/Red Rooster	(Note 10021)	2.50	10.00	59
SUGAREE/Red Rooster	(Chess 1730)	2.00	8.00	59
TORE UP OVER YOU/Tremblin'	(King 5587)	1.50	3.00	61
YORKSHIRES, The				
AND YOU'RE MINE/Tossed Aside	(Westchester 1000)	1.25	5.00	
YOU KNOW WHO GROUP, The				
DON'T PLAY IT (NO MORE)/Run (I Wanna Be Free)	(Casual 94725)	.75	3.00	65
MY LOVE (ROSES ARE RED)/Playboy	(Four Corners 113)	.75	3.00	64
YOUNG, Barry				
ONE HAS MY NAME/Show Me The Way	(Dot 16756)	.75	3.00	65
YOUNG, Colin				
ANY TIME AT ALL/You're No Good	(Uni 55286)	.75	3.00	72
YOUNG, Don				
SHE LET HER HAIR DOWN (EARLY IN THE MORNING)/ Movin'	(Bang 574)	.75	3.00	69
YOUNG ENTERPRISES, The				
LITTLE IMOGENE THE WALKING TALKING MACHINE/ Watchout For The Other Guy	(Fontana 1631)	1.00	4.00	68
YOUNG, Georgie				
CAN'T STOP ME/Come Back To Me	(Mercury 71259)	12.50	50.00	58
NINE MORE MILES/Sneak	(Cameo 150)	1.00	4.00	58
YOUNG, Gordon				
SHE FILLS HER SKIRT/Who's Fooling Who?	(Felsted 8567)	1.00	4.00	59
YOUNG, Jerry				
DEBRA/I Can't See It From Here	(Callender 2276)	.75	3.00	61
YOUNG, Jesse Colin (Of the Youngbloods)				
GOOD TIMES/Peace Song	(Warner Bros. 7581)	.75	3.00	72
HIGH & HIGHER/	(Warner Bros. 8398)	.50	2.00	77
IT'S A LOVELY DAY/It's A Lovely Day	(Warner Bros. 7618)	.75	3.00	72
LAST TRIP TO TULSA/Time Fades Away	(Reprise 1184)	.75	3.00	73
LIGHT SHINE/Light Shine	(Warner Bros. 7816)	.75	3.00	73
LIGHT SHINE/Cuckoo, The	(Warner Bros. 7816)	.75	3.00	74
LOVE ON THE WING/California Cowboy	(Warner Bros. 8352)	.50	2.00	77
MOTORHOME/Sugar Babe	(Warner Bros. 8129)	.50	2.00	75
PEACE SONG/Pretty In The Fair	(Warner Bros. 7404)	.75	3.00	70
PEACE SONG/Peace Song	(Warner Bros. 7404)	.75	3.00	71
PEACE SONG/Sunlight	(Warner Bros. 8225)	.50	2.00	76
RAVE ON/Maui Sunrise	(Elektra 45530)	.50	2.00	78
SONGBIRD/'Til You Come Back Home	(Warner Bros. 8106)	.50	2.00	75
SUSAN/Barbados	(Warner Bros. 8053)	.75	3.00	73
Also see Banana & The Bunch				
YOUNG, John Paul				
I HATE THE MUSIC/St. Louis	(Ariola America 7624)	.50	2.00	76
LOST IN YOUR LOVE/ The Day That My Heart Caught Fire	(Scotti Bros. 405)	.50	2.00	78
LOVE IS IN THE AIR/Where The Action Is	(Scotti Bros. 402)	.50	2.00	78
YESTERDAY'S HERO/The Next Time	(Ariola America 7607)	.50	2.00	75
YOUNG, Kathy (With the Innocents)				
BABY OH BABY/Great Pretender	(Indigo 127)	1.00	4.00	61
DREAM AWHILE/Send Her Away	(Indigo 147)	1.00	4.00	62
DREAM BOY/I'll Love That Man	(Monogram 506)	.75	3.00	62
HAPPY BIRTHDAY BLUES/Someone To Love	(Indigo 115)	.75	3.00	61
LONELY BLUE NIGHTS/I'll Hang My Letters Out To Dry	(Indigo 146)	1.00	4.00	
MAGIC IS THE NIGHT/Du Du'nt Du	(Indigo 125)	1.00	4.00	61
OUR PARENTS TALKED IT OVER/Just As	(Indigo 121)	1.00	4.00	61
THOUSAND STARS, A/Eddie My Darling	(Indigo 108)	1.00	4.00	60
Also see Chris & Kathy				
Also see Washer Windshield				
YOUNG, Kenneth, & The English Muffins				
FREDDY'S STREET/(Mrs. Green's) Ugly Daughter	(Diamond 183)	1.00	4.00	65
YOUNG LADS, The				
NIGHT AFTER NIGHT/Graduation Kiss	(Felice 712)	5.00	20.00	
YOUNG, Lester				
WOBBLE TIME/You'll Miss Me	(Chase 1200)	.75	3.00	
YOUNG LIONS, The				
LITTLE GIRL/It Would Be	(Dot 16172)	5.00	20.00	61
YOUNG, Neil (Of Buffalo Springfield)				
CINNAMON GIRL/	(Reprise 0911)	.50	2.00	70
COMES A TIME/Motorcycle Mama	(Reprise 1395)	.50	2.00	78
DRIVE BACK/Stupid Girl	(Reprise 1350)	.50	2.00	76
FOUR STRONG WINDS/Human Highway	(Reprise 1396)	.50	2.00	79
HEART OF GOLD/Sugar Mountain	(Reprise 1065)	.50	2.00	72
HEY BABE/Homegrown	(Reprise 1390)	.50	2.00	77

TITLE/FLIP	LABEL & NO.	GOOD	NEAR MINT	YR.
LAST TRIP TO TULSA/Time Fades Away	(Reprise 1184)	.50	2.00	73
LIKE A HURRICANE/Hold Back The Tears	(Reprise 1391)	.50	2.00	77
LOOKIN' FOR A LOVE/Sugar Mountain	(Reprise 1344)	.50	2.00	76
OH, LONESOME ME/I've Been Waiting For You	(Reprise 0898)	.75	3.00	69
OLD MAN/Needle & The Damage Done	(Reprise 1084)	.50	2.00	72
ONLY LOVE CAN BREAK YOUR HEART/Birds	(Reprise 0958)	.50	2.00	70
RUST NEVER SLEEPS (HEY HEY, MY MY-INTO THE BLACK)/ Rust Never Sleeps (My My, Hey Hey-Out Of The Blue)	(Reprise 49031)	.50	2.00	79
SUGAR MOUNTAIN/The Loner	(Reprise 0785)	.75	3.00	68
SUGAR MOUNTAIN/The Needle & The Damage Done	(Reprise 1393)	.50	2.00	78
WALK ON/For The Turnstiles	(Reprise 1209)	.50	2.00	74
WAR SONG (With Graham Nash)/ Needle & The Damage Done	(Reprise 1099)	.50	2.00	72
WHEN YOU DANCE I CAN REALLY LOVE/ Sugar Mountain	(Reprise 0992)	.50	2.00	71
Also see Crosby, Stills, Nash & Young				
Also see Danny & The Memories				
YOUNG ONES, The				
DIAMONDS & PEARLS/Three Coins In The Fountain	(Yussels 7704)	1.00	4.00	
I ONLY WANT YOU/Over The Rainbow	(Times Square 104)	1.00	4.00	
I'M IN THE MOOD FOR LOVE/No No Don't Cry	(Yussels 7703)	1.00	4.00	
MARIE/Those Precious Love Letters	(Yussels 7701)	1.00	4.00	
YOUNG RASCALS, The (With Felix Cavaliere & Gene Cornish)				
BEAUTIFUL MORNING, A/Rainy Day	(Atlantic 2493)	.75	3.00	68
BROTHER TREE/Saga Of New York	(Columbia 45568)	.50	2.00	72
CARRY ME BACK/Real Thing	(Atlantic 2664)	.75	3.00	69
COME ON UP/What's The Reason	(Atlantic 2353)	.75	3.00	66
ECHOES/Hummin' Song	(Columbia 45600)	.50	2.00	72
GIRL LIKE YOU, A/It's Love	(Atlantic 2424)	.75	3.00	67
GLORY GLORY/You Don't Know	(Atlantic 2743)	.75	3.00	70
GOOD LOVIN'/Mustang Sally	(Atlantic 2321)	.75	3.00	66
GROOVIN/Sueno	(Atlantic 2401)	.75	3.00	67
GROOVIN (Spanish version)/Groovin' (Italian Version)	(Atlantic 2428)	1.00	4.00	67
HEAVEN/Baby I'm Blue	(Atlantic 2599)	.75	3.00	69
HOLD ON/I Believe	(Atlantic 2695)	.75	3.00	69
HOW CAN I BE SURE/I'm So Happy Now	(Atlantic 2438)	.75	3.00	67
I AIN'T GONNA EAT OUT MY HEART ANYMORE/ Slow Down	(Atlantic 2312)	.75	3.00	65
I'VE BEEN LONELY TOO LONG/If You Knew	(Atlantic 2377)	.75	3.00	67
IT'S WONDERFUL/Of Course	(Atlantic 2463)	.75	3.00	67
LONELY TOO LONG/If You Knew	(Atlantic 2377)	.75	3.00	67
LOVE ME/Happy Song	(Columbia 45400)	.50	2.00	71
LUCKY DAY/Love Letter	(Columbia 45491)	.50	2.00	71
PEOPLE GOT TO BE FREE/My World	(Atlantic 2537)	.75	3.00	68
RAY OF HOPE, A/Any Dance'll Do	(Atlantic 2584)	.75	3.00	68
RIGHT ON/Almost Home	(Atlantic 2773)	.75	3.00	70
SEE/Away Away	(Atlantic 2634)	.75	3.00	69
YOU BETTER RUN/Love Is A Beautiful Thing	(Atlantic 2338)	.75	3.00	66
Also see Felix & The Escorts				
YOUNG SISTERS, The				
JERRY BOY/She Took His Love Away	(Mala 467)	.75	3.00	65
YOUNG, Steve				
DON'T THINK TWICE, IT'S ALL RIGHT/ Montgomery In The Rain	(RCA 11233)	.50	2.00	78
IT'S NOT SUPPOSED TO BE THAT WAY/	(RCA 10868)	.50	2.00	77
RENEGADE PICKER/	(RCA 10769)	.50	2.00	76
YOUNG, Victor				
AROUND THE WORLD/ Around The World (By Bing Crosby)	(Decca 30262)	1.00	4.00	57
HIGH & THE MIGHTY, THE/Moonlight & Roses	(Decca 29203)	1.00	4.00	54
LA VIE EN ROSE/	(Decca 24816)	1.00	4.00	50
MONA LISA/Third Man Theme, The	(Decca 27048)	1.00	4.00	50
YOUNGBLOOD, Edison				
SUMMERTIME FOOL/Big Bad Betty	(Comet 101)	1.50	6.00	
YOUNGBLOODS, The (Featuring Jesse Colin Young)				
DARKNESS, DARKNESS/On Sir Frances Drake	(RCA 0129)	.75	3.00	69
DARKNESS, DARKNESS/On Sir Francis Drake	(RCA 0360)	.75	3.00	70
DREAMBOAT/Dreamboat (Promotional issue)	(Warner-Raccoon 7639)	.75	3.00	72
DREAMER'S DREAM/Quicksand	(RCA Victor 47-9422)	1.00	4.00	68
EUPHORIA/Wine Song	(RCA Victor 47-9222)	1.00	4.00	67
FOOLIN' AROUND (THE WALTZ)/Merry-Go-Round	(RCA Victor 47-9142)	1.00	4.00	67
FOOL ME/I Can Tell	(RCA Victor 47-9360)	1.00	4.00	67
GET TOGETHER/All My Dreams Blue	(RCA Victor 47-9264)	1.00	4.00	67
GET TOGETHER/Beautiful	(RCA 9752)	.75	3.00	69
GRIZZLY BEAR/Tears Are Falling	(RCA Victor 47-9015)	1.25	5.00	66
HIPPIE FROM OLEMA/Misty Roses	(Warner-Raccoon 7445)	.75	3.00	70
IT'S A LOVELY DAY/Ice Bag	(Warner-Raccoon 7499)	.75	3.00	
KIND HEARTED WOMAN/Running Bear	(Warner-Raccoon 7660)	.75	3.00	72
LIGHT SHINE/Will The Circle Be Unbroken	(Warner-Raccoon 7563)	.75	3.00	72
SOMETIMES/Sometimes (Promo Copy)	(Mercury 73068)	1.50	6.00	69
SUNLIGHT/Trillium	(RCA 0270)	.75	3.00	69
SUNLIGHT/Reason To Believe	(RCA 0465)	.50	2.00	71
YO-YOZ, The				
LEAVE ME ALONE/Stay With Me	(Ikon 517)	1.25	5.00	
YUM YUMS, The				
GONNA BE A BIG THING/ Looky Looky (What I Got)	(ABC-Paramount 10697)	.75	3.00	65
YURO, Timi (Rosemarie Yuro)				
BIG MISTAKE/Teardrops 'Till Dawn	(Mercury 72478)	.75	3.00	65
COUNT EVERYTHING/I Know	(Liberty 55432)	.75	3.00	62
GET OUT OF MY LIFE/Can't Stop Running Away	(Mercury 72431)	.75	3.00	65
GOTTA TRAVEL ON/Down In The Valley	(Liberty 55634)	.75	3.00	63
HURT/I Apologize	(Liberty 55343)	.75	3.00	61
I GOT IT BAD & THAT AIN'T GOOD/Johnny	(Mercury 72355)	.75	3.00	64
IF/(I'm Afraid) The Masquerade Is Over	(Mercury 72316)	.75	3.00	64
I'M MOVIN' ON/I'm Movin' On (Part 2)	(Liberty 55747)	.75	3.00	64
INSULT TO INJURY/Just About The Time	(Liberty 55552)	.75	3.00	63
LEGEND IN MY TIME, A/Should I Ever Love Again	(Liberty 55701)	.75	3.00	64
LET ME CALL YOU SWEETHEART/Satan Never Sleeps	(Liberty 55410)	.75	3.00	62
LOVE OF A BOY, THE/I Ain't Gonna Cry No More	(Liberty 55519)	.75	3.00	62
MAKE THE WORLD GO AWAY/Look Down	(Liberty 55587)	.75	3.00	63
PERMANENTLY LONELY/Call Me	(Liberty 55665)	.75	3.00	63
SMILE/She Really Loves You	(Liberty 55375)	.75	3.00	61
SOUTHERN LADY/Lovin' You Is All I Ever Had	(Playboy 6050)	.50	2.00	75
WHAT'S A MATTER BABY/Thirteenth Hour	(Liberty 55469)	.75	3.00	62
YOU CAN HAVE HIM/Could This Be Magic	(Mercury 72391)	.75	3.00	65

The transition to a country music style has been made by several pop & rock singers of the fifties and sixties. The pop & rock releases by these artists will appear in this guide, while the country music releases will be listed in our guides covering that field of music.

Likewise, your favorite soul and rhythm & blues artists that are not covered in this guide are—or will soon be—included in our Blues-Rhythm & Blues-Soul Price Guide.

Z

TITLE/FLIP	LABEL & NO.	GOOD	NEAR MINT	YR.
ZABACH, Florian				
HOT CANARY, THE/Jalousie	(Decca 27509)	1.00	4.00	51
WHEN THE WHITE LILACS BLOOM AGAIN/ Fiddlers Boogie	(Mercury 70936)	.75	3.00	56
ZABE, Dick				
SENIOR PROM/Deep Down In The Well Of Love	(Pio 103)	1.00	4.00	
ZACHARIAS, Helmut				
WHEN THE WHITE LILACS BLOOM AGAIN/Blue Blues	(Decca 30039)	1.00	4.00	56
ZACHERLE, John (The "Cool Ghoul")				
DINNER WITH DRAC/Igor	(Cameo 130)	1.25	5.00	58
DINNER WITH DRAC/Dinner With Drac (Part 2)	(Cameo 130)	1.00	4.00	58
DINNER WITH DRAC/Hurry Bury Hurry	(Parkway 853)	.75	3.00	62
HELLO DOLLY/Monsters Have Problems Too	(Colpix 743)	.75	3.00	64
I WAS A TEENAGE CAVEMAN/Dummy Doll	(Cameo 145)	1.50	6.00	58
LUNCH WITH MOTHER GOOSE/82 Tombstones	(Cameo 139)	2.00	8.00	58
RING-A-DING ORANGOUTANG/Coolest Little Moster	(Elektra 13)	1.25	5.00	60
(Some releases may be shown as by Zacherley)				
Novelties				
ZAGER & EVANS (Denny Zager & Rick Evans)				
HELP ONE MAN TODAY/Yeah 3,2	(RCA 9816)	.75	3.00	70
HYDRA 15,000/	(Vanguard 35125)	.75	3.00	71
IN THE YEAR 2525 (EXORDIUM & TERMINUS)/Little Kids	(RCA 0174)	.75	3.00	69
IN THE YEAR 2525 (EXORDIUM & TREMINUS)/Little Kid's	(Truth 8082)	2.00	8.00	69
LISTEN TO THE PEOPLE/She Never Sleeps Beside Me	(Truth 0299)	1.25	5.00	69
MR. TURNKEY/Cary Lynn Javes	(RCA 0246)	.75	3.00	69
MR. TURNKEY/Cary Lynn Javes	(Truth 0246)	1.50	6.00	69
ZAHND, Ricky				
NUTTIN' FOR CHRISTMAS/ Something Barked Christmas Morning	(Columbia 40576)	1.00	4.00	55
ZANIES, The				
BLOB, THE/Do You Dig Me, Mr. Pigmy	(Dore 509)	1.00	4.00	58
BLOB, THE/Do You Dig Me, Mr. Pigmy	(Era 1080)	2.50	10.00	58
CHICKEN SURFER/London Rock	(Dore 683)	1.25	5.00	63
MR. PRESIDENT-TO-BE/Do The 1-2-3	(Dore 875)	1.50	6.00	72
WILL THE REAL DR. FRANKENSTEIN PLEASE STAND UP/ Frankenstein's Laboratory	(Dore 853)	2.50	10.00	71

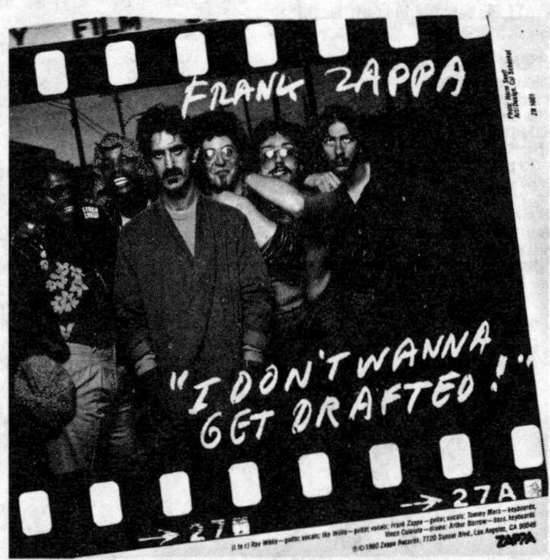

TITLE/FLIP	LABEL & NO.	GOOD	NEAR MINT	YR.
ZAPPA, Frank (Of the Mothers Of Invention)				
ANYWAY THE WIND BLOWS/Jelly Roll Gum Drop	(Verve 10632)	2.00	8.00	68
(Shown as by Ruben & the Jets)				
BIG LEG EMMA/Why Don't You Do Me Right?	(Verve 10513)	3.00	12.00	67
(Shown as by the Mothers Of Invention)				
CLETUS AWREETUS-AWRIGHTUS/Eat That Question	(Bizarre-Reprise 1127)	3.00	12.00	72
(Shown as by the Mothers)				
CLETUS AWREETUS-AWRIGHTUS/Eat That Question	(Bizarre-Reprise 1127)	1.00	4.00	72
(Promotional issue, shown as by the Mothers)				
COSMIK DEBRIS/Don't Eat The Yellow Snow	(DiscReet 1312)	1.00	4.00	74
COSMIK DEBRIS/Uncle Remus	(DiscReet PRO-586)	2.50	10.00	74
(Promotional issue only)				
DANCIN' FOOL/Baby Snakes	(Zappa 10)	.75	3.00	79
DESERI/Jelly Roll Gum Drop	(Verve 10632)	2.00	8.00	68
(Shown as by Ruben & the Jets)				
DISCO BOY/Ms. Pinky	(Warner Bros. 8352)	1.25	5.00	77
FIND HERE FINER/Zoot Allures	(Warner Bros. 8342)	1.25	5.00	76
HOW COULD I BE SUCH A FOOL/Help I'm A Rock	(Verve 10418)	2.00	8.00	66
I DON'T WANT TO GET DRAFTED/Ancient Armaments	(Zappa 1001)	.75	3.00	80
I'M THE SLIME/Montana	(DiscReet 1180)	1.25	5.00	73
(Shown as by the Mothers)				
JOE'S GARAGE/Central Scrutinizer	(Zappa 31)	.75	3.00	79
LONELY LITTLE GIRL/Mother People	(Verve 10570)	3.00	12.00	67
MAGIC FINGERS/Daddy Daddy Daddy	(United Artists 50857)	1.50	6.00	71
MY GUITAR/Dog Breath	(Reprise 0840)	3.00	12.00	69
PEACHES EN REGALIA/Little Umbrellas	(Bizarre-Reprise 0889)	3.75	15.00	69
TEARS BEGAN TO FALL/Junier Mintz Boogie	(Bizarre-Reprise 1052)	2.50	10.00	71
(Shown as by Frank Zappa & the Mothers Of Invention)				
TEARS BEGAN TO FALL/Same	(Straight-Reprise 1027)	3.00	12.00	71
(Shown as by Junier Mintz)				
TELL ME YOU LOVE ME/Would You Go All The Way?	(Bizarre-Reprise 0967)	1.50	6.00	70
TROUBLE COMIN' EVERYDAY/Who Are The Brain Police	(Verve 10458)	2.00	8.00	66
(Shown as by the Mothers Of Invention)				
WPLJ/My Guitar	(Reprise 0892)	2.00	8.00	70
(Shown as by the Mothers Of Invention)				
Also see Baby Ray & the Ferns				
Also see Bob Guy				
Also see Hogs, The				
ZARA, Michael, & The Compliments				
ANGELS OF MERCY/Nobody Knows	(Shell 313)	1.50	6.00	
ZEBRA				
BRING ME TO MY KNEES/Too Hot To Handle	(White Whale WW-305)	.75	3.00	69
CHRISTMAS MORNING/Christmas Morning (Part 2)	(Blue Thumb 109)	1.25	5.00	70

TITLE/FLIP	LABEL & NO.	GOOD	NEAR MINT	YR.
ZEBULONS, The				
FALLING WATER/Wo-Ho-La-Tee-Da	(Cub 9069)	5.00	20.00	60
ZELLA, Danny				
SAPPHIRE/You Made Me Blue	(Dial 100)	1.00	4.00	
(With The Larados)				
WICKED RUBY/Black Saxs	(Fox 10057)	1.00	4.00	59
(With The Zell Rocks)				
ZENTNER, Si				
UP A LAZY RIVER/Shufflin' Blues	(Liberty 55374)	.75	3.00	61
(Instrumentals)				
ZEPHYRS, The				
DON'T MISS THE BOAT/Yes, My Love	(Amber 215)	1.25	5.00	66
HEAR HIM/Pink Rhapsody	(Amber 213)	1.25	5.00	64
SHE'S LOST YOU/There's Something About You	(Rotate 5006)	1.50	6.00	65
SHE'S MINE/Bicycle Ride	(Amber 214)	1.25	5.00	65
WONDER WHAT I'M GONNA DO/Let Me Love You Baby	(Rotate 5009)	1.25	5.00	65
ZEPPA, Ben, & The 4 Jacks				
WHY DO FOOLS FALL IN LOVE/	(Tops 278)	3.75	15.00	
(With The 4 Jacks)				
YOUNG HEARTACHES/Ridin' Herd	(Hush 1000)	1.25	5.00	
(Shown as by Ben Joe Zeppa)				
ZEVON, Warren				
HASTEN DOWN THE WIND/	(Asylum 45356)	.50	2.00	77
JOHNNY STRIKES UP THE BAND/ Nighttime In The Switching Yard	(Asylum 45526)	.50	2.00	78
LAWYERS, GUNS & MONEY/Veracruz	(Asylum 45498)	.50	2.00	78
WEREWOLVES OF LONDON/ Roland The Headless Thompson Gunner	(Asylum 45472)	.50	2.00	78

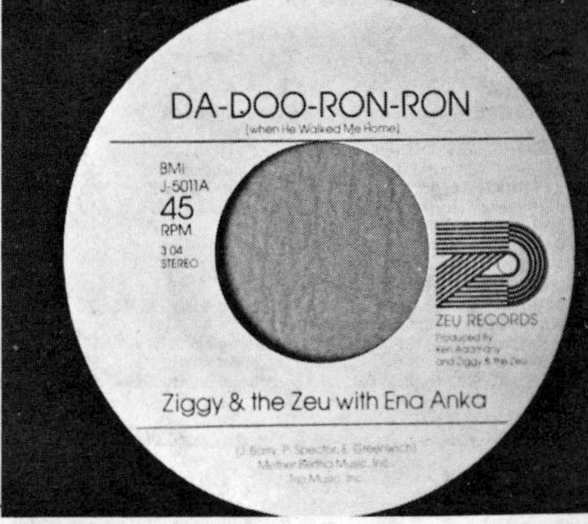

TITLE/FLIP	LABEL & NO.	GOOD	NEAR MINT	YR.
ZIGGY & THE ZEU REVIEW				
DO-DOO-RON-RON (WHEN HE WALKED ME HOME)/	(Zeu 5011)	5.00	20.00	
(With Ena Anka)				
LITTLE STAR/Come Go With Me	(Zeu 5011)	5.00	20.00	
ZILL, Pat				
PICK ME UP ON YOUR WAY DOWN/La Mirada	(Sand 336)	1.25	5.00	61
PICK ME UP ON YOUR WAY DOWN/La Mirada	(Indigo 119)	.75	3.00	61
ZIP & THE ZIPPERS				
WHERE ARE YOU GOING LITTLE BOY/Gig	(Pagent 607)	.75	3.00	63
ZIP CODES, The				
RUN LITTLE MUSTANG/Fancy Filly From Detroit City	(Liberty 55703)	.75	3.00	64
ZIP, Danny				
HEY HEY GIRL/Please Listen To Me	(MGM 13254)	2.00	8.00	64
ZIRCONS, The				
GET UP & GO TO SCHOOL/Mr. Jones	(Federal 12478)	.75	3.00	62
LONELY WAY/Your Way	(Mellomood 1000)	1.00	4.00	
NO TWISTIN' ON SUNDAY/Mama Wants To Drive	(Federal 12452)	.75	3.00	62
SURFIN' IN THE SUNSET/Going Places	(Bagdad 1007)	1.00	4.00	63
WHERE THERE'S A WILL/Don't Put Off for Tomorrow	(Heigh-Ho 607)	1.00	4.00	
ZISKA, Stosh (Of the Del-Satins)				
LITTLE LOVE, A/	(Avco 4542)	1.25	5.00	
ZODIAC				
"X" RATED/Then Goodbye	(Uni 55138)	.75	3.00	69
ZOMBIES, The (Featuring Colin Blunstone & Rod Argent)				
CONVERSATION OF FLORAL STREET/Imagine The Swan	(Date 1644)	.75	3.00	69
DON'T GO AWAY/Is This The Dream	(Parrot 9821)	1.00	4.00	66
IF IT DON'T WORK OUT/Don't Cry For Me	(Date 1648)	.75	3.00	69
I LOVE YOU/Whenever You're Ready	(Parrot 9786)	1.00	4.00	65
IMAGINE THE SWAN/Conversation Of Floral Street	(Date 1644)	.75	3.00	69
INDICATION/How Were We Before	(Parrot 3004)	1.00	4.00	66
ONCE UPON A TIME/I Want You Back Again	(Parrot 9769)	1.00	4.00	65
REMEMBER YOU/Just Out Of Reach	(Parrot 9797)	1.00	4.00	65
SHE'S COMING HOME/I Must Move	(Parrot 9747)	1.00	4.00	65
SHE'S NOT THERE/You Make Me Feel So Good	(Parrot 9695)	1.00	4.00	64
TELL HER NO/Leave Me Be	(Parrot 9723)	1.00	4.00	65
TIME OF THE SEASON/Friends Of Mine	(Date 1628)	.75	3.00	68
TIME OF THE SEASON/I'll Call You Mine	(Date 1604)	.75	3.00	68
TIME OF THE SEASON/Imagine The Swan	(Epic 11145)	.50	2.00	72
THIS WILL BE OUR YEAR/Butcher's Tale (Western Front 1914)	(Date 1612)	.75	3.00	68
ZOO				
GONNA MISS ME/Sometimes	(PKC 1013)	.75	3.00	66
GOOD DAY SUNSHINE/ Where Have All The Good Times Gone	(Parkway 147)	.75	3.00	67
SUNSET STRIP/One Night Man	(Sunburst 775)	.75	3.00	68
ZORRO, Johnny				
CHOKE, THE/Reuben's Nightmare	(Warner Bros. 5162)	.75	3.00	60
ROAD HOG/Camel Train	(Bravo 123)	1.00	4.00	59
ROAD HOG/Coesville	(Warner Bros. 5111)	.75	3.00	59
ZWOL (Walter Zwol)				
CALL OUT MY NAME/It's So Real	(EMI America 8009)	.50	2.00	78
NEW YORK CITY/A Little Bit Crazy	(EMI America 8005)	.50	2.00	78
SHAKA SHAKA/It's A Wonder	(EMI America 8021)	.50	2.00	79
Z Z TOP				
ARRESTED FOR DRIVING WHILE BLIND/It's Only Love	(London 251)	.50	2.00	77
ENJOY & GET IT ON/El Diablo	(London 252)	.50	2.00	77
FRANCENE/	(London 179)	.50	2.00	72
IT'S ONLY LOVE/Asleep In The Desert	(London 241)	.50	2.00	76
LA GRANGE/Just Got Paid	(London 203)	.50	2.00	75
SALT LICK/Miller's Farm	(Scat 500)	1.50	6.00	
TUSH/Blue Jean Blues	(London 220)	.50	2.00	75
Also see Moving Sidewalks, The				

COLLECTOR'S DIRECTORY

ALABAMA

aul Hayes
. O. Box 32, Shannon 35142

harles B. Johnson
704 Roseland Dr., Birmingham 35209

ayne Kelley Enterprises
. O. Box 1337, Clanton 35045
Mail order Elvis items, hard-to-find records, tapes, etc. Many other stars.

ALASKA

ick Levitt/John Farnan (Dixie J Records)
ox 275, Juneau 99802
Buy/sell/trade r&r, r&b, 45s, 78s, LPs, 1950 to present, especially 1955-65. (907) 789-7494.

aker J. Smith
. O. Box 29, Kenai 99611
Collect r&b, blues, rock through early 70s, especially 60s punk and psychedelia. (907) 262-4765.

ARIZONA

ndy Davis
118 West Evans Drive, Glendale 85306

ruce Hamilton
ox 998, Scottsdale 85252
Have many rare #1 magazines from 50s, 60s featuring Elvis, Beatles, etc., $5 to $50 depending on rarity. Write, SASE.

eatrice M. Jones
238 East Portland St., Phoenix 85006

erry Osborne
. O. Box 28312, Tempe 85282
Elvis collector, particularly want 12-inch samplers, boxed sets, any SP or SDS records/sleeves. Will pay top dollar.

illiam Schuh
. O. Box 1572, Scottsdale 85252
Collect anything on Cheryl Ladd, promos, test pressings, etc. Also r&r 45s, LPs, promos, picture discs.

ARKANSAS

red Dalsle
8 Covewood Dr., Conway 72032
I collect 1954-1968 rock & roll and rhythm & blues. Especially interested in Gene Pitney and Jackie Wilson.

CALIFORNIA

reg Aiken
4029 Mira Montana Dr., Del Mar 92014
Collect Blondie domestic/import records, live recordings, magazine covers, posters, photos. Wish to correspond with all Blondie fans.

cott R. S. Bartlett
365 Wishon, Apt. 12, Fresno 93728

he Book Treasury (John Polifronio)
707 Hollywood Blvd., Hollywood 90028
Deal in records of all types, rock to classical. Send inquiries or call. (213) 466-6527.

ernie Borenstein
254 Ladoga Ave., Lakewood 90713
Collect live tapes, picture sleeves, articles and unusual items by the Yardbirds, Buffalo Springfield and Byrds.

ip Brown
925 Mason Ave., Winnetka 91306
Collect surfing 45s, LPs, James Dean items, Pete Best info, etc. (213) 998-9337.

rank F. Campa
5824 East Arrow Highway, Irwindale 91706
Collect anything on Elvis. Also rock and roll 78s and 45s. Must be vg+ or better.

apricorn Music
75 Drakeley, Atwater 95301
Collect country, jazz, rock, soundtracks, colored vinyl. Also interested in books and encyclopedias of music.

rank Cardinal
202 Riderwood Ave., Hacienda Heights 91745
Collect 12" and 7" picture discs, colored vinyl. Buy/sell-/trade. (213) 961-5339.

nn Carter
0718 Louise Ave., Granada Hills 91344
Elvis collector.

ob Cattaneo
. O. Box 720, Daly City 94017
Selling soul, r&b, r&r, disco. We've got it all. Send your want list.

hris Chatman (Full Moon Records)
400½ J St., Sacramento 95814
Collector/dealer specializing in hard to find Elvis, Beatles, r&b, blues, r&r, movie memorabilia (especially promotional). (916) 446-6026.

Jim Clawer
3118 Linkslead Ct., San Jose 95122
Collect 45s, 33s from 50s and 60s. Soundtrack rockers, rhythm & blues. (408) 274-1934.

Jean Cosby
1020 N. Mariposa St., Apt. H, Burbank 91506
Elvis collector.

Lee Cotten
806 K Street, Sacramento 95814
Have retail store dealing in out-of-print records of all types, Elvis, Beatles, etc. (916) 446-3973.

Dan Craven
9737 Turtledove Ave., Fountain Valley 92708

Mike Czapkay
640 Calero Ave., San Jose 95123
Wanted: any Elvis records or memorabilia. Buy/sell/trade. Call between 2:30-9pm. (408) 224-0381.

Bob Daily
759 Central Ave., #7, Napa 94558
Collect all oldies, c/w, Faron Young, Billy Walker, Charles Walker, Ray Price, Lynn Anderson. (707) 226-8194.

Robert Dalley
6209 Oakbank Dr., Azusa 91702
Collect instrumental surf rock 45s, LPs, EPs. (213) 914-1148.

Stephen Howell Delso
4355 Texas St., San Diego 92104

Sandra K. Durrin
106 Montana, Vandenberg, A.F.B. 93437
Collect disco, r&r 1958-80s. Country 45s, LPs. Would like to buy or hear from collectors. (805) 734-1317.

John E. Eby
P. O. Box 2983, San Diego 92112
Will trade or sell, but mainly want to buy obscure, hard-to-find 45s meaning a lot to me.

Greg Estrada
1060 Bernal, Stockton 95203
Collect and sell 45s, rhythm & blues, rock, Beatles, Elvis, 50s and 60s groups.

Ear Wax
P. O. Box 46067, Los Angeles 90046
Sell LPs, 45s, mostly rock & roll, folk, comedy, jazz, rhythm & blues, blues, soundtrack, classical, colored vinyl. Collect progressive.

Dixie Lee Gonzalez
724 W. Bard Road, Oxnard 93030
Collect all Cliff Richard recordings from any country. Buy /trade tapes. (805) 487-0558.

Ethel M. Grimes
4218 Columbus Ave., Apt. B, Bakersfield 93306
Collect David Seville & Chipmunks records & sleeves. Will correspond with Chipmunk maniacs.

John Grimes
6904 Beckett St., Tujunca 91042
Collect late 50s, early 60s rhythm & blues, Johnny Cash, Jerry Lee Lewis. Sell late 60s, early 70s r&r.

Boy Guy
P. O. Box 97, Lakewood 90712
Collect 40s and 50 rhythm & blues, colored vinyl, blues, Elvis, Ricky Nelson, foreign releases.

Paul Hansen
59 Mission Lane, Walnut Creek 94596
Collect r&b 50s, groups 50s and 60s, Drifters, Flamingos, Beach Boys, Beatles, Tokens, doo wop sounds, Elvis, Darin, Holly, Orbison.

Tom Haydon
1083 El Camino Real, Menlo Park 94025
Buy, sell, trade blues on LP pre-war, electric and acoustic, country and city.

Gary Hoffman
18753 Malden St., Northridge 91324

Kathy Keifer
2745 Barbour Dr., Fairfield 94533
Elvis collector of records, photos, menus, post cards, buttons, etc.

J. Kennedy
3223 Ramons St., Pinole 94564
Collect and sell 78s, 45s, LPs from 40s and 50s (some 30s).

Leon Leavitt
P. O. Box 38395, Los Angeles 90038
Conduct American jazz and pop LP auctions.

Chic Leslie
59 Mission Lane, Walnut Creek 94596
Collect Ricky Nelson, Kinks, Jan & Dean, 50s and 60s vocal groups, Bee Gees, early Atlantic label, good doo wop.

Lee C. McDonald, Jr.
2429 East 26th St., Oakland 94601
Interested in early jazz guitarists Cal Farrell, George Benson, Wes Montgomery, Kenny Burrel, Pat Martino.

Johnnie Louise Mills
9420 Sabre Lane, Westminster 92683
Elvis collector.

Ralph O'Tier
1396 Lindsay Way, San Jose 95118
Buy/sell/trade Bill Black, Fats Domino, Beatles, Elvis, Cash, Rolling Stones, others.

Lou Perlberg
c/o Newton Glass, 4 N. 2nd St., Alhambra 91801

Larry J. Prioste
3025 Balmoral Dr., San Jose 95132
Elvis collector. (408) 923-8344.

Rowe's Rare Records & Collectibles
54 West Santa Clara St. San Jose 95113
Specializing in rare out-of-print records. 78 rpm, 33 1/3, 45's with picture covers, picture records and movie memorabilia.

Lynn Saches
5090 Yucca, Edwards 93523
Elvis collector.

Richard Stash
1828 18th St., #E, Santa Monica 90404

C. J. Stevens
P. O. Box 1092, Chino 91710
Collect Waylon Jennings, George "Thumper" Jones, Jerry Lee Lewis.

Ron Sylvester
2675 Fletcher Parkway, #209, El Cajon 92020
Buy/sell/trade commercial/promo/import c/w 45s, picture discs, colored vinyl. Also special Elvis issues.

Pete Tauscher
212 Wheeler Ave., Redwood City 94061
Collect Elvis picture sleeves, 45s by Buddy Holly, Eddie Cochran, G. Vincent, Beatles, bootlegs and 8-tracks.

Robb Warner
126-B Central Ave., San Francisco 94117
Elvis records, articles, Presleyana; 50s groups; Hot 100 singles, novelties, Billboard magazines, colored vinyl.

Terence Wong
231 Curry St., Richmond 94801
Collect all types jazz LPs, specialize in RCA vintage series LPs. Put my name on your price or auction list!

Bobbi Van Zant
P. O. Box 387, Phelan 92371
Collect 45s, LPs of Elvis, also buttons and photos.

Cliff Yamasaki (Let It Be Records)
2434 Judah St., San Francisco 94122
Deal in Beatle records, memorabilia & rarities. Rare & out of print records a specialty. (415) 681-2113.

David Zimmerman
103 N. Kenmore Ave., Los Angeles 90029
Collect pre-recorded reel-to-reel tapes of Sinatra, D. Martin, Presley, Crosby, Annette, Al Jolson, big bands.

Sandra Zoeller
10837 Damond Ave., Bloomington 92316
Collect Elvis.

COLORADO

Dennis Chiesa
2109 Perry St., Denver 80211

Jeff Erickson
13665 West 71st Place, Arvada 80004
I collect all Beatle and Beatle-related products. Also Rolling Stones and Cars records and memorabilia.

G.A.P. Records
P. O. Box 12131, Denver 80212
Specialize in 50s and 60s soul, rhythm & blues, and blues.

E. T. Hobbs (Elvis Presley Record Service)
P. O. Box 33106, Northglenn 80233
Send me your Elvis sales or want list. I will send you names /addresses of specific buyers/sellers. $2.00.

CONNECTICUT

Jim Celon
26 Patmar Dr., Monroe 06468
Elvis collector looking for anything on the King.

Dave Cook
121 Oak St., Southington 06489
Monthly auction list sent to anyone who mentions collecting 45s, 33s or 78s country/bluegrass, from 40s to 60s only.

Gershom Foster
University of Connecticut, Torrington 06790
Collect 50s and 60s rhythm & blues, rock & roll, doo-wop sound, jazz LPs/soundtrack LPs.

Anthony Giustian
398 Celia Dr., Wolcott 06705
Collect Chicago blues Chess label, Little Walter, Sonny Boy Williamson, etc.

Bill Griggs
Buddy Holly Memorial Society
75 Belcher Road, Wethersfield 06109
All records, materials pertaining to Buddy Holly, buy /sell-/trade, including cover records. Write to join society.

Dale Kroop
Box 3291, New Haven 06515
Collect jazz, 60s rock, r&b groups.

Jerry Landrey
191 Oak St., Bridgeport
Collect rhythm & blues, rock & roll, Lenny Bruce, Bee Gees. Have many and various wants in 45s and LPs.

Bob Siani (Night of the Turntable)
17 Cornell St., Plainville 06062
Collect all Chuck Berry records. Buy/sell/trade various artists.

Robb Warner
Gilead Street, Gilead 06248
Collect Elvis records, articles, Presleyana, 50s groups, Hot 100 singles, novelties, Billboard magazines, colored vinyl.

DELAWARE

Kenneth A. Wyatt
228 Ingram St., Glasglow Ct., Newark 19702

FLORIDA

Don Beede
2905 Sequoia Lane, Sarasota 33577
Collect jazz and 50s rock, member IAJRC. Trade cassette tapes. Big Kenton fan. Answer all mail from collectors.

Ed Bittman
4243 2nd Ave., South, St. Petersburg 33711

Robert Brennan
P. O. Box 118, Elkton 32033
Sell 20s and 30s blues and hillbilly, rhythm and blues, rock & roll. Send several large lists per year.

Don Cleary
Box 16265, Ft. Lauderdale 33318

Scott R. Cohen
P. O. Box 16792, Plantation 33318
Collect 45s from 1955 to 1978.

Ray Edwards
1650 N. Hermitage, Ft. Myers 33907
Elvis collector.

Ross Ferguson (R & N Enterprises)
Rt. 1, Box 780 G, Big Pine Key 33043

David Libert
3017 N. W. 43rd. Ave., Gainesville 32605
Collect rock, country/western from 50s, 60s, 70s. Will buy, sell or trade.

Eric G. Mauk
2255 Lake Rudy Rd., Deland 32720

Vincent Miscione
5840 N.E. 22nd Way, Ft. Lauderdale 33308
Collect any unusual Elvis or Beatles items, political or political/novelty, baseball or related novelty items.

Mr. 45 (Rene Cabrera)
240 N.E. Sanchez, Apt. 7, Ocala 32670
Buy/sell/trade all 45s. Specialize in Elvis, Beatles, Beach Boys. Want hard rock, disco. Send want/sell lists.

John A. Morency
235 Orchis Rd., St. Augustine 32084

Richard D. Morrison
706 E. Lake Shore Dr., Ocoee 32761
Collect anything by Elvis and Lefty Frizzell, records, films, etc.

David Perkins
2809 S.W. 14th St., Ocala 32670

Arthur Romano
230 North Halifax, Daytona Beach 32018

Mary Jo Truttschel
2122 Gamma Court, Orange Park 32073
Collect 50s, 60s folk, Elvis, Beatles 45s, LPs. Wish to correspond with Elvis/Beatles fans.

Abe Ziadie, Jr.
3180 65th Way, N., St. Petersburg 33710
Collect Elvis, Cliff Richard, 50s and 60s rock & roll, rockabilly.

GEORGIA

Daddy G's Memory Music
P. O. Box 84, Union City 30291
Nostalgic disc jockey has over 50,000 singles and LPs. Will make custom tapes of all types.

Paul Coggin
4544 Glade Forest Park 30050

Craig Elliott
704 Rosalyn Dr., Marietta 30062
Buy/trade 45s, bootlegs, concert tapes, posters, photos, concert programs, movie/video cassettes, and anything else collectible about Jimi Hendrix.

R. W. Guard
1750 Shady Hill Dr., Marietta 30067
Collect 78s on blues, rhythm & blues, swing, show tunes. Broadway movie. 33s on swing and show tunes.

B. V. Rainwater (Collector's Exchange)
300 West Peachtree 3E, Atlanta 30308
Specialize in all Elvis collectibles and collectible records. Buy/sell. (404) 524-4669.

Earl P. Ross
919 Crosby St., Savannah 31401

HAWAII

Goin' Back Enterprises
P. O. Box 7161, Honolulu 96821
Worldwide mail order retail/wholesale in rock LPs, 60s photo-puzzles, buttons, memorabilia. Elvis, Monkees, Beatles, etc. Introductory catalog.

Daniel McGovern
P. O. Box 1826, Kahului, Maui 96732

ILLINOIS

Dave Becvar
8224 Smith Lane, River Grove 60171
Collect Beatles, Kinks, American & British rock of 60s and 70s. Buy/sell/trade, especially Beatles. Send for LP list.

Frank Black
108 Webster Apts., Clinton 61727
Selling collection 1951-79, dj copies, Chess, Checker, Argo, Excello, RCA, Sun (Presley), r&r, r&b. Send wants. (217) 935-8603.

Bwana Disc Records
1921 N. Keystone, Chicago 60639
Buy/sell rare and original Elvis, Beatles, r&r, r&b, rockabilly, 45s w/ps, LPs. See our ad in Presleyana. (312) 384-2350.

Lew Claussen
606 Wicker Ave., Streamwood 60603
Buy/sell/trade Beatles 45s, picture sleeves, promos, cover singles, Apple Dark Horse. Ringo 45s foreign/American.

Donald Confiliano
813 Pearson Dr., Joliet 60435
Selling collection of 45s from 50s and 60s. Thousands of records.

Wayne Cutshaw, Jr.
326 Bellevue, Round Lake 60073
Elvis collector.

Richard Dean
714 Forest Dr., Gages Lake 60030
Elvis collector.(312) 223-6076.

The Elvis Warehouse
323 Franklin Blvd., South, Suite 804, Box E-33, Chicago 60606
Presley collector records, memorabilia, etc. Send for free catalog.

The Emporium
P. O. Box 158, 629 S. Poplar, Centralis 62801

Patricia Johnson
1120 McCarthy Rd., Lemont 60439
Collect Neil Diamond live concert tapes & other material, songs by Diamond recorded by others. Write if you have any.

R. H. Johnson
18642 Homewood Ave., Homewood 60450

Skip Klowpfer (Full Cyrkle Records)
68 Grant St., Crystal Lake 60014
Buy/sell/trade rock & roll 50s to present. Appreciate collectors who visit store to talk music.

Gregory Larsen
901 East Lake St., Aurora 60506
Collect Elvis, Beatles.

William R. Nicholson
P. O. Box 398, Kirkland 60146
Have store in Rockford. Buy/sell Elvis, uptemp doo wop, 50s-60s r&r, r&b, pop. Holly, Domino, Lewis, etc.

Steve Polwort
787 Portland, Collinsville 62234
50s, 60s, 70s rock & roll, rockabilly, Waylon, Elvis, Neil Diamond, Buddy Holly, Olivia Newton-John.

Ron and Barb Sinclair
1339 S. Clarence, Berwyn 60402
Collect rhythm & blues, rockabilly, Elvis, 45s, LPs. (312) 795-8551.

John E. Swank
3501 N. Olcott St., Chicago 60634

Matt Swanson
2149 Hartrey Ave., Evanston 60201
Buy/sell Elvis films, video tapes of concerts, bootlegs.

Lynn Wietlispach
P. O. Box 1001, Moline 61265
Collect 50s, early 60s, Buddy Holly, Beatles. Will buy often, please put me on your mailing list!

INDIANA

Bygone Stamps & Records
P. O. Box 50081, Indianapolis 46250
Collecting "Top 10" singles for forty years. Specialize in big band and show albums. Would like to correspond.

Carl Kubik
5855 Bonnie Brae St., Indianapolis
Collect Elvis, rock & roll, rockabilly. (317) 257-3691.

Bob LaVergne, Jr.
Rt. #1, South Whitley 46787
New Elvis collector on LPs, 45s, 78s. Also Monkees, Abba, Beach Boys, Boyce & Hart, comedy, modern country. (219) 723-5521.

Mark Lawyer
15821 Coldwater Rd., Ft. Wayne 46825
Interests include Beach Boys, Beatles, Jan & Dean, most any 60s and early 70s LPs.

Martin Nosko
418 E. Iowa St., Evansville 47711
Collect Elvis EPs, 45s, Buddy Holly, Ricky Nelson 45s, LPs, EPs, and all old r&r. Buy/sell/trade.

Thomas Patterson
2028 W. 41st Ave., Gary 46408
Collect Elvis EPs, 45s. Buy/sell, have mint 45s and 78s, never been played.

Phillip W. Paulson
2715 Station St., Indianapolis 46218
Selling Elvis items. Send want list, SASE.

Danny and Diann Taitec
1633 E. Kelly, Indianapolis 46203
Collect Elvis, rock & roll. (317) 783-4431.

Brian Tetreault
101 S.E. 3rd. St., Washington 47501
Interested in all rare items, picture discs, colored vinyl, Elvis, Beatles, Stones, Dylan. Have 4,000 albums, want more.

IOWA

The Haunted Bookshop
227 S. Johnson St., Iowa City 52240
Semi-private walk-in shop specializing in pre-1970 albums of jazz and blues. Shop hours or appointment. (319) 337-2996.

Steve Parrott
525 Terrace Rd., Iowa City 52240
Collect rock & roll 45s from 50s and 60s, especially Beatles and Elvis.

KANSAS

Carolyn Stier
4560 S. Hydraulic, Lot 424, Wichita 67216

KENTUCKY

James Elliott, Jr.
2208 W. Ormsby, Louisville 40210

Adriaan J. Sturm
7750 St. Anthony Church Rd., Louisville 40214
Collect Elvis.

LOUISIANA

Al Bell (B&B Sales)
1014 Joseph St., P. O. Box 7038, Shreveport 71107
Wholesale distributor of Elvis albums, souvenirs, memorabilia. Toll free (800) 551-8997. Local (318) 226-0105.

Donald Breland
641 Keed Ave., Baton Rouge 60806
Collect/trade rhythm & blues, rock from early 60s to present, Beatles memorabilia, novelties and picture discs. Want list available.

Dennis Dans
3026 Lone Oak Dr., Shreveport 71118
Collect anything on Elvis. Please send lists. Buy/sell/trade r&r. Want lists welcome.

The Elvis Store
P. O. Box 7143, Shreveport 71107
Elvis collector records, souvenirs, memorabilia. Free catalog. (318) 226-0105.

Gary Shannon
c/o KROF Radio, Box 610, Abbeville 70510

MAINE

Ed Bangs
P. O. Box 305, Charlestown 02129
Collect local 1960s 45s and LPs, P.F. Sloan related records.

Charles W. Eames
216 Adams, Dedham 02026
I like any rock LPs from the 50s and 60s.

Joan Foley
P. O. Box 513, Scarborough 06074
Elvis collector.

Nelson Gardner
Box 1082, Portland 04104
Buy/sell/collect pop, r&r, rockabilly, Elvis, Beatles, Rolling Stones, new wave, c&w, rare, out-of-print. Imports. Free lists.

George Neumann, Jr.
84 Payson St., Portland 04102
Collect/buy/sell/trade Elvis LPs, country/western, rockabilly, Gene Vincent, Eddie Cochran. (207) 774-2834.

MARYLAND

William Mark Cox
Rt. 2, Box 360, Federalsburg 21632
Collect rock & roll, rhythm & blues, blues of 50s, 60s, 70s. Also doo wop, early soul, disco.

Louis Howard
3821 Ingleside St., Olney 20832
Collect Elvis 45s, LPs, rock & roll, c/w from 50s, 60s. (301) 774-7912.

Martin Levitt
10026 Stedwick Rd., #101, Gaithersburg 20764

Dick O'Brien
Society Record Collectors of Baltimore, Md.
2303 Pentland Dr., Apt. 308, Baltimore 21234

MASSACHUSETTS

Elisabeth E. Ames
9 Overlook Dr., Bedford 01730
Elvis collector.

Barbara Ayscough
21-A Summer St., Wakefield 01880
Collect/sell/trade r&b, r&r from 50s, 60s. 45s, LPs, EPs, picture sleeves.

David Baker
60 Thayer Circle, Randolph 02368
Collect imports, originals and colored vinyl, picture discs, promo, oddities. Send wants and lists of what you have.

Peter M. Ciccone
364 K Street, South Boston 02127
Collect Monkees, Jan & Dean, soundtracks and comedy. (617) 268-8387.

Jim Gavin (Candy Man)
87 Whites Ave., Watertown 02172
Disc-jockey services, need lists of available 45s. Collect 45s 1950-1965, no boots.

Robert Gray
74 Country Club Blvd., Worcester 01605
Collect anything on Elvis, including novelty and tribute records. Send lists.

Chuck Gregory
17 Charenson St., Fall River 02723
Buy/sell r&r, r&b, pop 1945-69, 78s, 45s, EPs, LPs. Fats Domino a specialty. 78 lists welcome.

Thomas J. Hopkinson
45 Breed St., Lynn 01902

Frank Lodato
P. O. Box 272, Arlington 02174
Collect all types original Elvis memorabilia and records. Must be close to mint.

R & M Records
Box 29, Linwood 01525

Thomas Salem
Box 921, Framington 01701
Buy/sell/trade Elvis records from around the world. Send want list for originals.

Omer Tremblay
185 Moody St., Apt. B, Lowell 01854
Collect Elvis, Beatles, early English. Also trade/sell. Have promos by various artists.

Jim Vieira (Memory Lane Records)
P. O. Box L-34, New Bedford 02745
Buy/sell/trade all types records, especially picture sleeves, r&r, r&b. (617) 995-6550.

MICHIGAN

Tom Goforth
15359 Beech Daly, Taylor 48180
Collect Annette, Beach soundtracks, movie posters, Jan Barry, Shelly Fabares, Philles/Motown/Colpix labels, disco, r&r, c/w, surf, Billboard magazines.

Julie Gron
12510 Scott Rd., Davisburgh 48019
Buy/trade rare Beatles, good or better. Want oddities, memorabilia, foreign, picture sleeves, picture discs, promos, pre-Beatle recordings.

Mrs. Victor Kowachek
35420 Hatherly Place, Sterling Heights 48077
Collect soundtracks, original casts, Elvis.

Greg Nicksich
2647 12th St., Wyandotte 48192

Steven Norman
1846 Chamberlain, S.E., Grand Rapids 49506
Collect Elvis Sun and RCA, 45s, 78s, LPs, EPs. Linda Ronstadt records, tapes, live recordings.

R & N Enterprises
P. O. Box 1520, Grand Rapids 49503
We buy/sell/trade rhythm & blues, rock & roll and country/western, 1950-1976.

Record Recovery Room
Box 181, Hazel Park 48030
45s from the 50s, 60s, 70s. Novelties, punk, Detroit sound, Spector Productions.

Nancy Rose
7590 46th St., Rt. #1, Box 144E, Augusta 49012
Elvis collector.

Paul Tournier
14976 Archdale, Detroit 48227
Collect Neil Sedaka, Dion, Freddie Cannon, Kathy Young, Belmonts, Emotions, Jimmy Clanton, anything as long as it's a record.

Jim Vanhollebeke
19367 Poinciana, Redford Township 48240
Collect Elvis.

Cap Wortman (Cappy's Records)
12575 Gratiot Ave., Detroit 48205
Buy sell 45s, 78s, LPs, r&r, r&b, hillbilly, jazz, swing, pop. Open Mon. & Thu.-Sun. (313) 527-4000.

MINNESOTA

Randall N.K. Bennett
Box 52, Amboy 56010
Buy sell/trade Elvis records, memorabilia. Looking for RCA gold standards, promos, and Sun labels. (507) 674-3745.

Robert L. Broz
6820 46th Ave. N., Crystal 55428
Collect 50s, 60s, 70s rockabilly, Elvis. Buy/sell/trade 45s, LPs, EPs, Billboard, Cashbox and radio survey charts. (612) 537-4467.

Fred Heggeness
1027 Summit Ave. Detroit Lakes 56501
Collect Elvis, Beatles, rockabilly, import pop, novelty, original c/w r&b.

David J. Roper
8406 Beverly St., Duluth 55808
Buy/sell/exchange 1950-1965 rock & roll, rhythm & blues. Songs that later came out as cover versions.

Donald Stephans
Minnesota City 55959
Collect 45s from 1954-1978, especially Elvis. Buy/sell all types. (507) 689-2267.

MISSISSIPPI

Jim Bost, Jr.
313 Shumate Dr., Cleveland 38732
Collect LPs; 45s by Elvis and Carl Perkins on Sun. Have 78s, LPs from 1900-60 for sale. (601) 846-6716.

Paul Burlison
5332 Highway 301 N., Walls 38680.
Original member of rock & roll trio, buying/selling the best 50s, 60s rock records.

MISSOURI

Robert W. Bay
1426 Jaywood Dr., St. Louis 63141
Elvis collector.

Collectibles
4547 Gravois, St. Louis 62234
50s, 60s, 70s rock & roll, rockabilly, Waylon, Elvis, Ne[il] Diamond, Buddy Holly, Olivia Newton-John.

Thomas Griffin
P. O. Box 953, Blue Springs 64015
Collect Elvis, Beatles and any 45s from 1960 to 1970.

Richard A. Porter
8004 Brooklyn, Kansas City 64132
Elvis collector.

Ben Schabelski
2419 Menard St., St. Louis 63104

Gary Songer
1702 Westminster, Mexico 65265
Collect Elvis, limited dealing.

MONTANA

Clinton C. Whitmer
Box 86, Wolf Point 59201
Collect 60s British rock, Waylon, Elvis, Apple Records, 50 rock & roll.

NEBRASKA

Lynn Weaver
P. O. Box 803, Grand Island 68801
Buy/trade late 50s 45s, LPs, pop, c/w, r&b, Little Richard Chuck Berry, Elvis, Buddy Holly, Bill Haley, etc.

W. Fred Heille
1604 East Ave., Worthington 56187
Collect early rock, country/western, 45s and 78s.

Ron Kusek
2418 Hickory St., Omaha 68105

Chris Morrison
The Crosiers, Box 789, Hastings 68092
Collect 78s, 45s, LPs from early 20s through the 70s, especially Johnny Mercer. Will trade or sell.

Kenneth R. Stanfield
4724 Davenport, #8, Omaha 68132

NEW HAMPSHIRE

Jim Burnett (House of Oldies)
33 Bonair Ave., Hampton 03842
Dealer in 50s, 60s r&r, r&b, rockabilly, Elvis, Beatles, Hol[ly] thousands of 45s in stock. Lists. Send wants. (603) 926-412

Rick Cunningham (Sounds Unlimited)
P. O. Box 661, Somerworth 03878
Sell/collect most 45s, specializing in 60s, 70s pop hits, c/[w] Some 50s, pop LPs. 20,000 records. Send wants.

Bill Daniels
5 Bailey Rd., Salem 03079
Want discographies on 50s rock & roll, rhythm & blues, mo[st] labels, groups, single artists. Recording and relea[se] information.

NEW JERSEY

Norman P. Anderson
105 Lighthouse Dr., Manahawkin 08050
1920 and earlier, musical and spoken.

Christine Broghers
Ave. "D", Atlantic Highlands 07716
Any type of obsolete 45s, psychedelic LPs from the 60s, som[e] 78s. Appreciate receiving for sale lists.

Lees Browne, Jr.
1465 East Putnam Ave., #623, Old Greenwich 06870
Collect Lou Christie, Tommy James, Chubby Checker, Jo[ey] Dee & Starliters, Tommy Roe, Johnny Rivers, Jan & Dean

S/Sgt. Robert A. Brower
1319 7th Ave., Neptune 00753
Selling LPs movie soundtracks, r&r, single artists, group[s] various artists 50s, 60s, 70s. Send 25¢ for monthly update list.

Richard Castellano
734 Thiele Rd., Brick 08723
I collect all rock records and rock albums.

L. F. Chelson
17 Shadow Lawn Dr., Livingston 07039
Collect rockabilly, British rock, heavy metal, punk.

Frank M. Clark
353 Lincoln Ave., Orange 07050

Bruce Drouin
332 Terrace Ave., Hasbrouck Heights 07604
Collect Elvis items, records, memorabilia.

Donald D. Dunn
170 Beech St., Paterson 07501
Collect Elvis 45s, EPs, LPs and other collectible Buy/sell/trade.

Ross Ens
2023 Polbos Parkway, Oakhurst 07755
Selling all types of 45s and 78s. Send want list.

Robert P. Geden
830-D Berkley St., New Milford 07646
Collect rock instrumentals, surf/hot rod, Dick Dale, Dua[ne] Eddy, Link Wray and Lee Hazelwood related. (201) 265-91

Joe Gerulski
15 Drummond Ave., Fords 08863
Collect records, tapes, photos of Dion, Dion & The Belmon[ts] Carlo, Delsations. Also head Dion Fan Club. (201) 738-812

Raymond B. Homiski
151 Shelley Ave., Elizabeth 07208
Collect all types Elvis, Beatles. Many other artists for trade sale.

Frank Kisko
75 East 25th St., Bayonne 07002
Buying/trading Jan & Dean, Jan & Arnie, U.S., foreign, [D] tapes, sheet music, promos, pictures, magazines, etc.

Joe Lordi
1118 Wooley Ave., Union 07083

Sammie Marrone, Jr.
66 Clinton St., Bloomfield 07003
Elvis collector.

Never Gone Records
926 Grandview Ave., Union 07083
Send for free list of set sale 45s, LPs. Want Bobby Fuller 45s on Donna, Todd, Exeter, Eastwood, Hi-Tone, Mustang.

Alex R. Pierces (Record Finders)
335 Wayland Rd., Cherryhill 08034
Personally collect Elvis. Deal in area searching originals and reissues of rare records.

Barbara Rau
200 3rd Avenue, Hawthorne 07506

Joe Robinette
Box 11, Richwood 08074
Collect soundtracks/original casts, other recordings pertaining to the theatre.

Joe Russo
161 Haase Ave., Paramus 07652
Will trade for or buy absolutely anything on the Monkees. Can trade many rare records.

Richard P. Russo, Jr.
22 Columbia Ave., Kenilworth 07033
Will trade Elvis black label EPs, 45s, w/ps for orange labels. Also want pre-'57 black label 45s.

Estes C. Slade, Jr.
117 Atkins Ave., Neptune 07753

Philip G. Urgola
327 Davis Ave., Apt. 1, Kearny 07032
Fan of music of 50s and bandstand sock hop days. Favorites: Joni James, Como, Laine, Martin, etc. Also country, rockabilly.

Ray B. Van Dyke
80 Garden Rd., Pompton Lakes 07442
Collect anything by the Stones, boots, imports, 45s, EPs, will buy/sell/trade.

Walsh Records & Tapes
Box 635, Moorestown 08057

NEW MEXICO

Lynda Christenson
11612 Mocho Place, N.E., Albuquerque 87123
Collect/sell/trade early to present rock & roll, rhythm & blues, country/western 45s, 78s.

Platter-Wax Museum
1504A Wyoming Blvd., NE, Albuqueruqe 87112
Call (505) 293-4757.

Mrs. T. E. Turpen
327 La Vega Dr., S.W., Albuquerque 87105
Elvis collector.

NEW YORK

Bobby Bank
3025 Ocean Ave., Brooklyn 11235
Collect Barry Manilow, Ron Dante, 45s, LPs, related material. Selling professional photos of r&b, r&r, groups, personalities. Send for catalog.

Burt Belknap
180 Palmdale Dr., Apt. 4, Williamsville 14221
Collect r&r, r&b, c/w rockabilly, Elvis, Everly Brothers, Waylon Jennings, Buddy Holly, picture sleeves, 50s, 60s, LPs. (716) 634-8147.

Bill Bram
2 Spruce St., Great Neck 11021
Elvis collector, LPs, 45s, original and boot.

Sam Buchman
1 Valpage St., Farmingdale 11735
Selling my collection of all types of records, all speeds.

Frank Cassi
548 Seaford Ave., Massapequa 11758

Bill and Jeff Collins
98-25 65th Ave., Rego Park 11374
Collect/want Neil Diamond Columbia recordings, dual 45 open end radio special with Diamond.

Tony Dee (Golden Groove Records)
P. O. Box 432, East Elmhurst 11369
Buy/sell/trade Elvis, picture discs, color vinyl discs, Elvis and Beatles imports. (212)699-7116 (evenings).

Kathy De Marco
529-62nd St., Brooklyn 11220
Interested in anything related to Four Seasons, Four Lovers, Frankie Valle, the Romans. Any pre-Sesons recordings and memorabilia.

F. De Poalo
30 S. Cole Ave., Spring Valley 10977
Collect 50s and early 60s r&r, r&b, rockabilly, doo wop and Elvis.

Philip Evans
7 Ralph Ave., Falconer 14733
Interested in 1960s British beat and surf music.

Steven Feinberg
3815 Atlantic Ave., Seagate 11224
Collect only EPs of pre-1964 rock & roll, rhythm & blues, harmony groups.

Stephen Fisch
998 East Broadway, Woodmere 11598
Collect Stones, Led Zepplin, Who, Pink Floyd, Clash, 45s, 33s, rarities, bootlegs, EPs, imports. Send lists of what you have.

Helen R. From
910 Stuart Ave., Mamaroneck 10543
Elvis collector.

James Gibson
247 Parkview Ave., Bronxville 10708
Buy/sell/trade British rock (no punk) and Bob Dylan. Send out free auction/want lists. Send your wants.

James B. Gilmartin
24 W. 18th Rd., Broad Channel 11693
Beginning collector looking for information books, records, boots, 50s, 60s rock & roll, punk/new wave. Will correspond.

William Guarneri
317 Furman St., Schenectady 12304
Collect/trade all U.S. records.

Martin Karp
2245 Bronxwood Ave., Bronx 10469
Collect 10" LPs and EPs, except classical or c/w. Must have covers in vg or better.

Anna Labbate
P. O. Box 1233, Church St. Station, New York 10008
Elvis collector.

Mike Maione, Jr.
47-23 164th St., Flushing 11358
Collecting Elvis since pre-teens in '60. Buy/sell/trade.

Patricia Marsolais
6 North Pine Ave., Albany 12203
Collect Elvis, Dolly Parton, Tom Jones and Abba.

Ray McDonaugh
8 Walter Ct., Old Bethpage 11804

Jeff Nunes
26 Erie Drive, Fairport 14450
Trade/sell/buy mostly 45s of rock, r&b, c/w, 50s-present. Professional broadcaster, can get obscure demos. (716) 377-4241.

Richie Pandolfo
P. O. Box 171, Bronx 10466
Collect 60s rock, would like to correspond with 60s fans. Willing to pay $25 for Nazz and Nazz Nazz albums.

Stephen J. Tokash
G.P.O. Box 2302, New York 10001
Collect anything on Elvis Presley. Have periodic sale/trade lists on Elvis from all over the world. Send request.

Barry Weisfield
Box 773, Hickville 11802

NORTH CAROLINA

G. W. Anderson, Jr.
111 Erik Dr., Dudley 28333
Collect 45s only, any 50s oldies. Especially interested in Elvis, Buddy Holly, Marty Robbins.

Larry E. Beck
P. O. Box 611, High Point 27261
Elvis collector.

Chauncey Edwards
5630 Kildare Drive, Charlotte 28215

Sheila Icard
Box 187, Rutherford College 28671
Collect all kinds of 50s, 60s records, especially Elvis.

Edward Lebrun
303 N. Holden Rd., Greensboro 27410
Want modern collectibles. Rock picture discs, displays, posters, special promos, etc.

B. Massengill
1000 Washington St., Cary 27511
Collect import 45s, LPs of Heintje on Ariola, Polydor, MGM. Also 60s photos/pictures of Johnny Crawford. VG or better.

OHIO

John P. Arthur
6721 Oak Field Dr., Dayton 45415

T. A. Barker
P. O. Box 152, Duncan Falls 43734
Buy/sell original cast and soundtrack recordings, comedy LPS, any live performance LPs.

Don Berkey
226 Greenwood Heights, Bellevue 44811
Collect rock & roll 50s-60s 45s, picture sleeves, LPs. Penguins, Ricky Nelson, Crystals, Jan & Dean, Gary Lewis, etc.

Brian Bukovey
3418 Ridgewood Road, Akron 44313
Most 60s Beatles and influenced (Badfinger, Emitt Rhodes, Big Star), Kinks, Zombies, some 50s. Mint 60s fan/music mags wanted.

Rich Doran
1408 Dill Rd., S. Euclid 44121

Dusty Disc Records
P. O. Box 310, Middleton 45042
Call (513) 424-5508.

Aladdin J. Feriani (A. J.'s Record-Go-Round)
2240 16th St., N.E., Canton 44705
Specialize in early rock, Beatles, Presley, Beach Boys, early children's records. Buying Beatles imports, rare LPs, bootlegs, posters. (216) 453-5500.

Charles J. Ford
2804 Chinook Lane, Dayton 45420
Collect rhythm & blues vocal groups, preferably black, 50s to early 60s, originals only. (513) 299-8779.

James Franks
1311 West Sandusky St., Findsay 45840

Jerry Geiser
5883 Sterwerf Drive, Cleves 45002
Elvis collector.

Ed Heinzman
14204 Terminal Ave., Cleveland 44135
Collect anything on Elvis, Bee Gees, Springsteen, Manilow, Heart. Buy/trade.

Scott Johnson
1531 Burlington Ave., Columbus 43227

L. David Jones
597 Cedar Dr., Cortland 44410
Collect rhythm & blues, rock & roll, blues 45s from 1950 to 1965.

Gary R. Judeck
3136 Englewood, Cuyahoga Falls 44224
Collect Beatles, Beach Boys, Jan & Dean, Monkees, comedy /novelty, 60s and 70s rock and roll.

Jane Kline
44 North St., Box 56, North Lewisbury 43060
Elvis collector.

Walter O. Koenig, III
1782 Carriage Lane, Apt. 301, Alliance 44601
Collect 60s, 70s r&r, c/w LPs only. Also imports. Especially looking for early 70s country rock: Dillards, Hillmen, Parsons, etc.

Gene Kotecki
4548 East 77th St., Cleveland 44105

Jerry Ladd
7255 Jethve Lane, Cincinnati 45243
Collect Elvis 45s w/picture sleeves, albums and novelty records.

John N. Marsh
435½ Second St., Toledo 43605
Collect rockabilly, Freddy Cannon, break-ins, surf and hot rod music, 45s and LPs.

Donald McCollister
Rt. 32, Box 181-C1, Nelsonville 45764

Ken McPeck
2090 Shady Lane, Zanesville 43701
Collect rock records, books, magazines; Ricky Nelson, Jan & Dean, Fabian, Rydell, Avalon, etc. Also want artist/label discographies. (614) 454-0347.

Diane Pothast
312 Jackson, Delphos 45833
Interested in buying anything to do with Pat Shannon, especially "Moody," "She Sleeps Alone," and "Awaiting Love."

Peter Wilgus
2024 Summ , St., Columbus 43201

OKLAHOMA

James R. Cole
1320 S.W. 23rd. St., Oklahoma City 73108
Buy/sell old 78s, 45s. 1000's in stock.

Brian Gray
5711 S. Gary Place, Tulsa 75105
Collect 60s groups, Beatles, Dave Clark 5, Donovan; new wave, Blondie, Talking Heads; and soundtracks.

Jim Hannaford
RR #2, Box 3, Alva 73717
Exclusively Elvis collector.

Richard Hluchan
P. O. Box 249, Jones 73049
Buy/sell/trade all speeds records/reel to reel tapes. Holly, Haley, Hamilton, etc. Send Sun wants, all mail answered.

Mrs. W. W. Jennings
Rt. #2, Box 97, Blackwell 74631
Collect 45s, 78s, EPs, LPs and anything by/of Marty Robbins. Pay top price for fan club journals. (405) 363-3467.

Debbie Jones
823 S. Seneca, Bartlesville 74003
Collect most anything about, by or related to Elvis.

Fran Stimson
404 N Gladys St., Picher 74360

OREGON

Ken Costello
2840 River Rd., Eugene 97404
Deal in all records in all speeds and categories.

Bob Eager
1424 E. 9th., Minnville 97128
Collect 50s and early 60s rhythm & blues, doo wop, rock & roll 45s.

Bernie Greene
1833 S.E. 7th Ave., Portland 97214
Big free catalog, rock, pop, soul and personality. Please state your interest.

Frank K. Mott, Jr.
2280 S.E. 35th St., Portland 97214
Call (503) 238-4735.

Richard L. Reese
11403 S.E. Stanley, Milwaukie 97222
Collect r&r 1954-70, Rick Nelson, Elvis, Beach Boys, Jan & Dean, Beatles, Frankie Avalon.

Mike Simonson
220 Daniels St., McMinville 97128
Collect Jan & Dean LPs, surfer music, Safaris.

PENNSYLVANIA

Paul Ashwood
P. O. Box 376, Bloomsburg 17815
Buy/sell originals/reissues 50s, 60s, 70s rock 45s, 78s, LPs. R&b, doo wop, Crosby, Sinatra, Presley, etc. Send wants.

C. Allen Baird (Cab's Collections)
R.D. 5, Box 240, Duncansville 16635
Collect albums, 45s, 78s, r&r, soul, disco, folk, classical, soundtracks, some children's albums and 45s. Send lists.

Botchy Press
320 East New St., Lancaster 17602
We sell all types and speeds of records, and collect folk records.

Robert Bower
533 Westminster Ave., Swarthmore 19081

Lane E. Carpenter
110 S. Fraser St., State College 16801
Collect early rock & roll, rhythm & blues, surf and drag, bubble gum, any top ten.

David Cigic
P. O. Box 121, Camp Hill 17011
Collect 45s and some 33s. (717) 761-2724.

Collectors Records
P. O. Box 158, Warrington 18976
Buy/sell records all years, types, sounds. Wants and sale list invited. Search system available. (215) 343-3606.

Steve Curtis
322 East Rockland ST., Philadelphia 19120
Collect Beatles, various artists albums, 60s rock. Sell 45s, LPs, surveys. Send wants.

D.R.T. Enterprises
P. O. Box 261, Lebanon 17042

Edward J. Deem, Jr.
P. O. Box 73, Industry 15052
Collect 60s, 70s rock & roll, rhythm & blues 45s; Beatles custom cassettes; buy/sell/trade early John Lennon.

Lawrence R. Echert
28 Elmwood St., Pittsburgh 15205
Selling rock & roll, Buddy Holly, Fats Domino, etc., 50s and 60s LPs only and some country and western.

Lou Fanty
1504 Wolf St., Philadelphia 19145
Collect Elvis Presley 45s, EPs, LPs, promos, domestic and foreign.

Walt Fisch
712 Picnic Lane, Selingsgrove 17870
Collect Beatles, rhythm & blues vocal groups.

John George (George's Song Shop)
128 Market St., Johnstown 15901
We buy/sell 1950s rhythm & blues.

James Goldbach
740 Darlington RD, Carnegie 15106
Collect/buy/sell/trade all Elvis Presley items. Also want Beatles, Monkees, Stones. (412) 279-6465.

Thomas R. Grosh
P. O. Box 241, Ephrata 17522
Elvis collector/dealer.

Vince Habel, Jr.
R.D. #3, Box 72, Columbia 17512
Collect rockabilly, Elvis, Gene Vincent and 50s rock & roll. (717) 684-5816.

Robert E. Hosie
139 Cranbrooke Dr., Corapolis 15108
Collect LPs, 45 of Easy Listening. (415) 695-7074.

R. E. Janosko
5127 Glenhurst Rd., 2nd Fl., Pittsburgh 15207
Collect rock & roll and pop from 1950 to date, especially British invasion, soul, jazz, some big band.

The Juke Box
Union Deposit Mall, Harrisburg 17111
Deal in original and reissue oldies from the 50s, 60s, 70s. Send us your want lists.

Ted Kacmarik
1523 Oneida Dr., Clairton 15025
Collect r&r, r&b 45s, EPs, LPs.

Stan Komorowski
P. O. Box 2254, Warminster 18974
Collect Frank Sinatra, exclusively.

Rube Leasher
Dawson House, Dawson 15428

Dennis Marakovits
Smith Gap Woodlands, Kunkletown 18058
Collect oldies but goodies, custom cassettes, late 50s-60s, instrumentals, vocals.

John H. McCarthy
115 S. Franklin St., Fleetwood 19522
Collect rock, pop, r&b, reggae, funk, comedy, imports. Send wants/sales lists/catalogs. All inquiries answered, including foreign. (215) 944-0363.

Joseph G. Pcolinsky
126 Mark Rd., Birch Hill Estates, Hazelton 18201
Collect any Elvis items, will buy/trade. Looking for 45s, EPs, LPs, tapes, boots. (717) 459-0877.

Sheldon R. Rupert
24 Slate Ridge Dr., York 17404
Elvis collector.

Lillian R. Salineter
25 Riverview Ave., Pittsburgh 15214
Elvis collector.

Philip J. Schwartz
P. O. Box 1516, Lancaster 17604
Collect all types 45s, LPs, 78s, especially 50s black r&b. Buy/sell/trade.

Barry Selcovitz
7142 Kindred St., Philadelphia 19149
Collect Beatles and Wings buttons and promo items, i.e., pictures, tour books, etc.

Max H. Shenk
304 Glendale St., Carlisle 17013
Edit "Revolver," a newsletter for 60s, 70s rock fans. Send a SASE for sample copy. (717) 243-4361.

Spencer Smith
Box 139, RD #4, Mountain Top 18707
Collect Buddy Holly, Elvis, Johnny Maestro (Crests), Ray Peterson.

RHODE ISLAND

Edward Leonardo
P. O. Box 86, Tiverton 02878
Elvis collector.

Dick J. Vittorioso
R.F.D. Wendy Lane, Carolina 02812
Collect Buddy Holly, radio outtakes, local R.I. artists. Comedy by Spike Jones, Stan Freberg, Bob & Ray.

SOUTH CAROLINA

Donald Gore
Rt. 7, Box 281, Conway 29526
Collect Beatles, Dylan, anything on E.L.O. Buy/sell/trade. (803) 356-2515.

Ronnie Poore
Route 10, Box 64, Anderson 29621
Collect Judy Garland records and memorabilia. Welcome any correspondence from Garland fans.

James V. Wheeler
P. O. Box 1552, Summerville 29483
Collector only.

TENNESSEE

Stan Bazemare
No. 3, Mason Drive, Chattanooga 37415

Jerry M. and Susan M. Dodson
Columbia Garden Apts., #H-68, Columbia 38401
Collect Elvis, Rolling Stones, LPs, 45s, picture sleeves, EPs. Send lists. (615) 388-3683.

Mark Duboise
3096 Rosevay Lane, Bartlett 38134

Karen Furnage
4663 Cedar Rose Dr., Millington 38053

General S. Gentry
Rt. 1, Norris Freeway, Powell 37849

Joe Hodge
3701 Anderson Ave., Chattanooga 37412
Elvis collector.

Randy's Record Shop
321 West Main, P. O. Box 61, Gallatin 37066

Jack W. Scott
512 Amalie Ct., Nashville 37211

TEXAS

Joe Avioli
8403 Concho, Houston 77036
Collect anything on Billy Joel, The Hassles, Attila. Will buy or trade.

Leigh Brown
434 Avant, San Antonio 78210
Buy large collections, have thousands of rare items, 1900-1970. Occasional mail auctions. Send for lists, specify interests.

Collectors Musuem and Market
113 Green Ave., Taft 78390
Thousands of antiques, books, collectibles, records, paintings, jewelry items, rocks, fossils, plants, etc.

Danny Cowan
227 McDougal, San Antonio 78223
Collect/trade rare concert, interview, studio outtake and FM tapes of blues, rock fusion and hard rock.

Denise M. Gregoire
5834 Dean Martin, San Antonio 78240
Collect Bill Haley items and sell records from Mexico and oldies (50s). Send SASE for lists.

Andy Kern (Elvis Unlimited)
2323 San Jacinto, Houston 77002
Collect/buy/sell all Elvis material.

Randy Light
3611 Fleetwood, Amarillo 79109
Serious collector of Beatles before and after split. Will pay top dollar for butcher album. American and British boxed sets.

Evelyn Wray
925 Beachum, Arlington 76011
Collect/buy/sell/trade country and rock 45s. Elvis collector. Have several thousand old juke box records. Wants lists welcome.

UTAH

Ron Steinke
11325 High Mesa Dr., Sandy 84077
Collect 50s rhythm & blues albums. Knox, Holly, J.L. Lewis, Orbison, Valens, Shannon, Perkins, Vincent, Domino, Cochran, Nelson, etc.

VERMONT

David J. Field
R.F.D., Post Mills 05058
WVPR disc jockey will buy r&r, r&b 1953-68 Buy/sell/trade professional recordings of above materials (802) 333-9591.

Violetta A. Goodrich
Townline Rd., Rutland 05701

VIRGINIA

Robert Mike Arbogast
P. O. Box 483, Covington 24426
Collect Buddy Holly, Elvis, r&r, rockabilly, doo wop, Eddie Cochran, Ritchie Valens, Earls.

Ed Caffey, III
1830 Banning Rd., Norfolk 23518
Buddy Holly records wanted, 50s, 60s New York white group doo wops, r&b groups, early country & western. (804) 855-5839.

Mike Callahan
Box 384, Vienna 22180
50s, 60s true stereo, stereo 45s, British invasion, Chicago Top 40 1956-67, Billboard Hot 100. Trade tapes.

Mike S. Cooke (Revived Record Co.)
1130 Sparrow Rd., #28, Chesapeake 23325

Jack Garrett
153 Hawthorne Dr., Danville 24541
Collect 60s beat groups (especially import LPs): Hollies, The Who, Yardbirds, Easybeats, Searchers, Zombies, Kinks, etc.

Tim McManus
2308 Galley Ct., Woodbridge 22192
Elvis collector.

R. A. Palmieri
3404 Richards Blvd., S.W. Roanoke 24018
Collect/sell 50s, 60s, 70s rock, folk, r&b records/tapes. Also soundtracks. Send list or 50¢ for mine.

Pete Petrovich
5748 Heming Ave., Springfield 22151
Collector.

James F. Thompson
214 Randolph St., #39, Ashland 23005

Tracy N. Thore
3200 Jackson, Hopewell 23860

Rick Turner
359 Averett Place, Danville 24541
Collect and deal, especially Elvis.

Dennis W. West
P. O. Box 489, Salem 24153
Call (703) 387-2510.

WASHINGTON

George L. Carter
P. O. Box 42, Woodinville 98072
A hard core Beatle freak with early Sinatra risings. Buy/sell/trade.

Discs Over The Rainbow
4604 Wall Street North, Spokane 99205
You can't find it? We will. Specializing in 1960-80 r&r collectibles, especially Springsteen, Rundgren, Zeppelin.

Wayne Eberhart
P. O. Box 610, North Bend 98045
Collect rock & roll hits and bubble gum to bubble puppy, mid-60s acid rock.

R. C. Fleischmann
P. O. Box 567, Tacoma 98401

Trevor Ford
1718 W. Jackson, Spokane 99205
Collect northwest rock, 60s British invasion, U.S. retaliation psychedelic from 60s, 70s. Trapeze, Deep Purple, bootlegs, LPs, tapes, etc.

Rick Gasperecz
11519 Golden Given Rd., E., Tacoma 98445
Collect Ventures, Duane Eddy, Roy Orbison, early rock 1950-65. Buy/sell/trade northwest sound. Send 45s, LPs wants.

Golden Oldies Records
4538 Roosevelt Way, N.E., Seattle 98105
Selling original label 45s and EPs only (no albums).

Doyle D. Haskett
2104 E. Nebraska, Spokane 99207
Deal in 78s, LPs, 45s, r&b, rock, promos, soundtracks, tapes and recent. Send want list or for my auction file.

Rick Koch
6034 S. Cheyenne, Tacoma 98409
Collect 50s and early 60s rock and pop LPs. Will pay top dollar for American and foreign LPs.

Rick Luther
29047 220th Pl., S.E., Kent 98031
Collect Elvis, 45s, 78s, EPs, LPs. Willing to pay good price for good material. (206) 631-3180.

Timothy D. Moore
3017 N. 25th, Tacoma 98406

The Old Curiosity Shop
N-711 Monroe St., Spokane 99201
50s, 60s rock & roll, Presley, Beatles, movie soundtracks, country/western 45s, LPs.

Ric Towe
19401 Edgecliff Dr., SW, Seattle 98166
Collect all Alice Cooper, Spiders; colored vinyl, interviews, boots, foreign sleeves, unusual LPs. (206) 878-8683.

Jay A. Williams
19720 48th W., Apt. Q14, Lynwood 98036

Del Worrell
4102 McLean Dr., Yakima 98908
Collect 1950s rock and rockabilly LPs, especially G. Vincent, B. Knox, J. Scott and Anka.

WEST VIRGINIA

Patty Caldwell
R. D. #4, Box 41-A, Wheeling 26003

William "Bill" Kovalski
209 N. Broadway St., Wheeling 26003
Collect jazz and rock & roll LP, 45s, also group and single artists of the 50s and 70s.

WISCONSIN

Richard R. Botz
4592 Monches Rd., Colgate 53017
Walt Disney record collector, including soundtracks and the older Park Attraction albums.

Scott Carome
317 E. Kohler St., Sun Prairie 53590
Collect 45s, pictures, etc., of "The Who" and individual members of the band. Would like to correspond with fans.

Rob Edwards
105 S. Main St., Greenwood 54437
Collect/sell new wave/punk, anything on the Stiff label, Bowie items, bootlegs.

Jeff Everson
106 N. Main St., Clintonville 54929
Collect 50s, 60s rock singles, LPs and some imports, soundtracks, Beatles memorabilia.

Jerry Fenske
919 N. 8th Ave., Wausau 54401
Elvis collector.

Joe Fischer
Rt. #2, Box 337, Mukwonago 53149
Collect Elvis, Holly, Valens, Big Bopper.

Buck Hafeman
1603 W. College Ave., Appleton 54911
Collect old rock & roll 45s, 1955-70, especially Elvis.

Dennis R. Hendley
c/o Dietz's Jazz Inn, 4260 N. 49th St., Milwaukee 53216
Elvis collector/dealer.

Steve Johnson
Box 843, Milwaukee 53201
Selling imports Presley, Stones, Beatles, others. 20 different countries. Catalog $1.00.

Doug MacDonald
Box 84, Gordon 54838
Collect Elvis, (715) 376-2218.

Tom Mentch
3325 20th St., Racine 53405
Collect Elvis, Holly, all 50s. (414) 634-1461.

Greg Shriver
Rt. 1, Coloma 54930
Collect Beatles together or alone.

Jack Sprecher
N91 W17582 St. Regis Dr., Menomonee Falls 53051
Collect blues, rhythm & blues.

Herb Stusse
145 N. 91st Pl., Milwaukee 53226
Collect Elvis, rhythm & blues, oldies picture sleeves. (414) 774-3170.

Terry Wachsmuth
2659-B North Weil St., Milwaukee 53212
Deal in all collector records. Send 15¢ stamp for current list. (414) 264-8516.

AUSTRIA

Fritz Schalk
Triesterstrasse 82/10/23, Neunkirchen A-2620
All about Elvis. Buy/trade. (02635) 38194.

CANADA

Ted G. Abel
137 Jarvis St., Toronto, Ontario M5C 2H6

Leach Alden
32430 Diamond Ave., Mission, B.C. V2V 1M2
Collect Elvis, rockabilly, rock & roll, rhythm & blues, and most any other kinds of records except classical. (416) 826-9805.

William Austin
760 Glen Eagles Dr., Kamloops, B.C. V2E 1J8
Interested in 50s and early 60s rock & roll and rhythm & blues.

Phillip Boucher
128 Treeview Dr., Toronto, Ontario M8W 4C3
Collect Elvis, Beatles, 50s, 60s, r&r, r&b, 45s, LPs. Anxious to trade, especially for novelty. (416) 251-8223.

R. G. Budd
110 W. 10th Ave., Apt. 310, Vancouver, B.C. V5Y 1R8
Collect 60s Liverpool, punk, psychedelic, ESP, Chocolate Watch Band LPs.

Marshall Burton
Box 464, Angus, Ontario LOM 1BO

R. Danell
10 Woodstock Lane, Winnipeg, Manitoba R2R 2X4
Collect rock & roll, rhythm & blues, jazz, swing, folk, all sizes and speeds.

Henry M. Dmyterko
222 Coach Hill Dr., Kitchener, Ontario N2E 1P4
Collect records from the 50s and early 60s.

Barry T. Greig
55 Chester Ave., Toronto, Ontario M4K 2Z8
Specialize in collecting Elvis. Interested in any music familiar to me, that's mellow and that has investment potential.

Marlow Harrowby
Warren, Manitoba ROC 3EO
Interested in hard rock, 50s-date. Want to buy/correspond fans/fan clubs/dealers. Presley, Stones, Queen, B.T.O., Beatles, etc.

Tom McCallum
527 Griffith ST., London, Ontario N6K 2S5
Collect/trade/buy sheet music, books, 50s-60s records by Ronnettes, Crystals, Beatles, Holly, Valens, Orbison, Everly Borthers, Jack Scott.

M. S. Lebow
6616 Parkview Rd., Cole St. Lue, Montreal H4V 1E3
Anything written or sung by Neil Sedaka, U.S. or foreign, buy/sell/trade. Want Snowtime/Laura Lee.

Derwyn Powell
P. O. Box 7781, Saskatoon, Saskatoon S7K 4R5
Collect Stones, British invasion, 60s groups, rock buttons, promo items. Buy/sell/trade. Have store at 47 Grosvenor Park. (306) 477-1511.

Leo Roy
244 Des Lilas Ouest, Apt. 6, Quebec, P.Q. G1L 1B3
Collect 45s, EPs, LPs 50s groups, Elvis, Vincent, Cochran, Haley, McPhatter, etc., magazines, pics, films, live shows, books.

Arnold Rutzer
5 Valley Woods Rd., #136, Don Mills, Ontario M3A 2R4

ENGLAND

Anthony Rayner
100, Rectory Grove, Hampton, Middlesex, TW12 1EF
Collect promo picture discs, colored vinyl rarities, live concerts, Ricky Nelson and Ventures.

FRANCE

Marc Labat
14 Rempart St. Vincent, 71100-Chalon sur, Saone
Collect Merseybeat, Beatles, rockabilly, doo wop and 60s punk, mostly LPs.

Jean Claude Roozenbrouck
2 Rue Voltaire, 59790 Ronchin
Collect 45s, LPs of 60s. Buy/sell/trade. Send me your set sale, auction, want lists.

GERMANY

Collector's Service
Verlags-Und Vertriebs-GMBH
Postfach 1228, D-8600, Bamberg 1
Specializing in Elvis.

Andreas Eichel
FredericlastraBe 13, 1000 Berlin 19
Collect 50s, early 60s, r&r and pop, especially Elvis, Everly Brothers and Dion. Please send lists. Telefon 030/3026408.

Karla Feuser
Spangenberger Str. 21, D-3500 Kassel-B
Collecting posters, articles, autographs, etc., from Elvis and Sweet. Same from German sources available for trade.

IRELAND

John Dwyer
5 Seminary Place, Farranree, Cork
Cliff Richard records worldwide. Books, mags, catalogs, discographies of all music but classical. Interested in million selling research.

JAPAN

Kazuo Akimoto
Mena Co-op 1-13-18 Gohtokuji, Setagaya-Ku, Tokyo 154
Want deep soul, vocal groups 60s, 70s minority label 45s, LPs: South Camp, Lawton, Amy, Jubilee, Atco, Minit, etc.

Tetsuro Arai
43-13 Kita-Minemachi, Ota-Ku, Tokyo 145

Charley Hashimito
3-32-1 Sekimachikita, Nerima-Ku, Tokyo 177
Collect Bech Boys, Phil Spector, "Greatest Hits" LPs of 50s and 60s pop artists.

Isao Imahashi
6181 Goi Ichihara City, Chiba-Ken 290
Collect modern jazz, big band, vintage vocal jazz of 50s, 60s, first pressings.

Norihisa Oguchi
1-2-14, Kyonancho, Musashino City, Tokyo 180
Anything and everything that has to do with Elvis. Elvis and r&r on 16mm sound films and video tapes.

SWEDEN

Jorn Wounlund
Brsewitzg. 6, Gothenburg 411 40
Collect anything on Elvis, rockabilly, Sun Records, Buddy Holly, Eddie Cochran, Jerry Lee Lewis, Carl Perkins, Conway Twitty, Wanda Jackson.

WEST GERMANY

Peter Bushoff
Gerhart-Hauptmann-St. 42, 44 Muenster
Collect Dylan and Springsteen bootlegs.

Claus Jacke
Angerstrasse 20, 4300 Essen-Stadtwald
Collect 50s r&r, Merseybeat, west coast, country/rock. Please send your set sale list.

RICHARD MINOR
PO DRAWER AH
PORT SALERNO, FL 33492
PHONE (305) 287-0594

We now accept Visa and Mastercharge Include full number & expiration date.

Mint warehouse originals. Bought out inventory of a large record distributor These have been in warehouse storage all are mint

Our no-hassle guarantee: You must be delighted or your money cheerfully refunded! This means there is never a hassle any purchase may be returned promptly for any reason whatsoever for refund or exchange as you prefer

Postage and handling: Within the USA please add $1 50 for postage and handling $2 50 for first class air mail Canada please add $3 00 to all orders for first class air mail AIR OVERSEAS Great Britain Europe Scandinavia etc $3 00 first record Add $2 00 for each additional LP (2 record sets count as 2 records) and 50s for each additional 45 Australia Japan S Africa etc $3 00 first record $3 00 each additional LP and 75c each additional 45

Send payment with order: We always have everything we advertise In the rare occasion that we run out of an item we are happy to refund send an alternate or send credit slip at your discretion Orders with payment go out immediately Correspondence takes up our time and delays your order We will accept paper currency from any major FREE foreign country Please check your exchange rates and add ten percent which covers our cost for exchange

A SMALL SELECTION FROM OUR EVER EXPANDING INVENTORY!

Original 45's, Mint Warehouse Stock

Apple 1815	Badfinger, Come And Get It	$2.00
Apple 1832	Ronnie Spector, Try Some Buy Some (w/pic sleeve	$3.00
Apple 1835	Elastic Oz Band, God Save Us (w/pic sleeve)	$3.00
Arcadia 110	Curley Langley, Linda Lou	$60.00
Astro 102	Mickey Gilley, Lonely Wine	$10.00
Bang 528	Neil Diamond, Cherry, Cherry	$2.00
C.T.I.-12	Deodato, 2001	$2.00
Gordie 7025	Martha & The Vandellas, Quicksand	$2.00
H.B.R. 449	Pebbles And Bam Bam, Open Up Your Heart (w/pic sleeve)	$5.00
Imperial 5895	Fats Domino, Your Cheatin' Heart	$2.00
Imperial 5935	Ricky Nelson, Old Enough To Love (w/pic sleeve)	$3.00
Instant 3269	Polka Dot Slim, Ain't Broke, Ain't Hungry	$3.00
Kane 007	Newports, A Fellow Needs A Girl	$18.00
Lancer 104	Don French, Baby Love	$2.00
Lancer 104	Don French, Lonely Saturday Night	$3.00
Motown 1066	The Supremes, Baby Love	$2.00
Phillips 3519	Bill Justis, Raunchy	$2.00
Reprise 0894	Beach Boys, Add Some Music	$5.00
Reprise 0929	Beach Boys, Slip On Through	$5.00
Sun 211	Malcolm Yelvington, Drinkin' Wine	$20.00
Sun 265	Roy Orbison, Devil Doll	$6.00
Sun 287	Carl Perkins, Lend Me Your Comb	$4.00
Vista 440	Annette (w/Beach Boys), Monkey's Uncle (w/pic sleeve)	$5.00
Westbound 222	Byron McGregor, Americans	$2.00

Mint LP's — Unopened Warehouse Stock

Vee-Jay LP 104	Gene Chandler, Duke Of Earl	$10.00
Laurie SLP-2047	Dion DiMucci, Dion	$13.00
MGM-SE 4478	Herman's Hermits, Blaze	$10.00

Originals, Imports, And The Hard-To-Find Collector's Items

DO YOU KNOW IF YOUR RECORD COLLECTION IS ADEQUATELY PROTECTED AGAINST LOSS?

LIST YOUR RECORD COLLECTION UNDER A GENERAL HOMEOWNERS POLICY

If you do not have your record collection listed separately in your general homeowners policy, in the event of a loss, you would be paid only a fraction of your collection's actual value.

For example, if a record worth $300.00 in mint condition, is destroyed in a fire, the insurance company would only be able to give you 10% of the ORIGINAL COST of the Record. Since this record may have been released in 1955 and sold for 89¢, you would receive 9¢ for your record!

OBTAIN COMPLETE COVERAGE FOR YOUR COLLECTION

Getting FULL coverage for your record valuables is SIMPLE. It can be accomplished in two easy steps:

1. Make a list of your records. Using the Osborne/Hamilton Price Guide for Collectible Records, write down:

*

1. Name of artist
2. Title of record
3. Label and number
4. Price value

2. Call your insurance agent and tell him you have an itemized list of records that you want protected with your household goods on your homeowners or renters policy or highlight your record collection in the Osborne/Hamilton Guide and turn the guide in to your agent.

* If you do not have all the information listed above, simply inform your insurance agent that you have records which need to be listed with your general household goods. Many insurance companies are currently using the Record Collector's Price Guides to appraise collections.

IS YOUR COLLECTION COMPLETE?

HARDCOVERS & FIRST EDITIONS

AVAILABLE EXCLUSIVELY FROM JELLYROLL PRODUCTIONS

Record Collector's Price Guide

Soft Cover: $11 postpaid
(Limited supply)
Hard Cover: SOLD OUT

Country/Western/Rockabilly Guide

Hard Cover: $13.95 postpaid
(Limited supply)

Record Albums & EP Price Guide
First Edition

Soft Cover: $11 postpaid
(Limited supply)
Hard Cover: $21 postpaid
(Limited supply)

Pop/Rock Singles Price Guide
Second Edition

Hard Cover: $18.95 postpaid
(Limited supply)

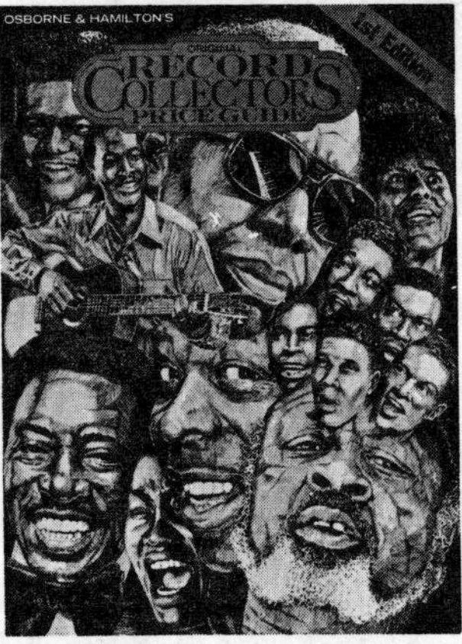

Blues/Rhythm & Blues/Soul Price Guide

Hard Cover: $20 postpaid
(Limited supply)

Record Albums & EP Price Guide
Second Edition

Soft Cover: $10.95
Hard Cover: $18.95 (Limited Qty.)

jellyroll productions
box 3017
scottsdale, arizona 85257

All postpaid offers are for U.S. delivery only. Foreign orders must include sufficient postage. You may use your Visa or Mastercharge. Include card number, expiration date and your signature.

KARAVAN RECORDS
BOX 40927
GARLAND, TEXAS 75040
(214) 495-0996
Karavan
TERRI AND BILL BERRY
WE HAVE ORIGINALS AND REISSUES TO FILL YOUR EVERY RECORD NEED.
WE SERVICE WANT LISTS, SEND YOURS AND TRY US.
LOOK FOR OUR ADS IN MUSIC WORLD AND GOLDMINE. WE SHIP WORLDWIDE. MOST ORDERS SHIP WITHIN 24 HOURS.
10 AM TO 9 PM
CST SEVEN DAYS.
WE PAY TOP PRICES FOR RARE AND SCARCE ROCK-A-BILLY, ROCK AND ROLL, R & B AND PROMOS IN VG+ OR BETTER CONDITION. CALL OR WRITE US.
WE BUY COLLECTIONS OF ONE RECORD OR 1000'S. LET US HEAR FROM YOU.
ELVIS
BEATLES
FATS DOMINO
JAN AND DEAN
RICK NELSON
RAL DONNER
GENE VINCENT
THE CLOVERS
FEATHERS
DION
GENE SUMMERS
THE SPANIELS
BUDDY HOLLY
RICHIE VALENS
BIG BOPPER
JERRY LEE
THE PLATTERS
CHUCK BERRY
ANNETTE
EVERLY BROS.
BEACH BOYS
1000'S MORE
"WE ACCEPT MASTER CARD AND VISA"

SPECIAL ELVIS COLLECTIBLES FROM JELLYROLL

THE LOVE OF ELVIS is the great magazine that documents rare, early and authentic Elvis memorabilia in color, including many Presley collectibles you've never heard of. Some so rare that only one copy is known! Many appearing in print and documented for the first time.
$3.00 (per copy, postpaid in the U.S.)

THE COMPLETE ELVIS is the perfect companion for your PRESLEYANA book! This 98-page, full-color, magazine was, until PRESLEYANA, the most respected and comprehensive Elvis discography ever. You'll even find dozens of photographs of rare Elvis records that do not appear in any other of our publications. Now out of print and a collector's item. . . so order today!
$3.00 (per copy, postpaid in the U.S.)

ELVIS IN UNIFORM is still available while supplies last. This giant 18 X 30-inch, full color, Elvis poster is a must for every fan.
$3.00 (per poster, postpaid in the U.S.)

SPECIAL PACKAGE OFFER:

ORDER BOTH ELVIS MAGAZINES, BOTH NOVELTY RECORDS AND THE ELVIS POSTER – A $14.00 TOTAL VALUE– FOR ONLY $11.00. SAVE $3.00! (PRICE INCLUDES POSTAGE IN THE U.S.

OUR BEST TO YOU is the outstanding feature book published by Jerry Osborne's legendary Record Digest service. A giant 272 page volume crammed with fascinating stories about Elvis, record collecting and much more! Only 500 signed, numbered, copies were printed and we have less than 100 left. Order soon, before they're all gone! Each copy is shipped with the limited edition Elvis novelty/break-in soundsheet, "The Graceland Tour," pressed on red vinyl, included as a bonus. Satisfaction guaranteed!
$14.95 (per copy, postpaid in the U.S.)

THE COUNTRY SIDE OF '76 and PLANE CRAZY/POLITICAL CIRCUS '72 are two hilarious novelty/break-in records that Elvis fans love. All feature cut-ins from the "King's" hits (and are listed in the Elvis Novelty section of this book). Each record was pressed in the limited quantity of 500 copies, and the remainder of the inventory is now being offered. Be sure to add these to your collection!
$5.00 for both records (per pair, postpaid in the U.S.)

ON ALL FOREIGN ORDERS. . . PLEASE REMEMBER TO ADD SUFFICIENT POSTAGE!

The brightest star on earth has now become the brightest star in Heaven, and left us with a love...still burning.

Jerry Osborne
Author-Publisher

"To Elvis: Love Still Burning"

THIS IS THE PICTURE DISC THAT PAVED THE WAY FOR THE DOZENS THAT FOLLOWED!

"TO ELVIS: LOVE STILL BURNING" WAS THE FIRST COMMERCIALLY RELEASED PICTURE DISC ALBUM, BUT ITS PRESS RUN WAS MICROSCOPIC COMPARED TO MANY OTHER PICTURE DISC RELEASES. IT WAS A "LIMITED EDITION" THAT TRULY WAS LIMITED!

WE ARE NOW OFFERING, WHILE THEY LAST, THE REMAINING MANUFACTURER'S INVENTORY OF THIS HISTORIC RELEASE. THESE ARE ALL MINT COPIES AND ARE STILL SEALED. WHEN THEY'RE GONE. . . THEY'RE GONE FOREVER! THEN YOU'LL SEE THIS LP SELLING FOR BIG BUCKS ON THE COLLECTOR'S MARKET.

"TO ELVIS: LOVE STILL BURNING" OFFERS THE COLLECTOR-INVESTOR AN UNBEATABLE COMBINATION:

- THIS LP IS CONSIDERED A "MUST" FOR ELVIS COLLECTORS, AND COLLECTING ELVIS IS THE FASTEST GROWING AREA OF RECORD COLLECTING!
- "LOVE STILL BURNING" WAS THE WORLD'S FIRST ELVIS PRESLEY PICTURE DISC. . . OF ANY TYPE. THERE ARE NO EXCEPTIONS!
- ITS SOUND QUALITY IS SUPERB. NOT LIKE MANY OF THE PICTURE DISCS THAT HAD POOR AUDIO QUALITY.

THE RECENT (1978-1979) PICTURE DISC CRAZE WAS SHORT-LIVED AND NOW ALMOST ANY PICTURE DISC FROM THAT PERIOD IS VALUABLE. ESPECIALLY THE FIRST ONE! ORDER YOUR COPY NOW!

TO ORDER: SEND JUST $12 FOR ONE COPY, PLUS POSTAGE, TO: LARRY HILBURN, P.O. BOX 308, WEST PLAINS, MO 65775 U.S.A.

SPECIAL OFFER! TAKE TWO COPIES FOR ONLY $20. SAVE $4
(Please remember to add sufficient postage)

POSTAGE RATES (For 1 or 2 copies)

U.S. by surface - add $1 to purchase price
U.S. by air - add $3 to purchase price
Foreign by surface - add $2 to purchase price
Foreign by air - add $4 to purchase price

QUANTITY DISCOUNTS BEGIN AT 10 PIECES - WRITE FOR DETAILS

FLEUR DE LIES
Larry Hilburn
P.O. Box 308
West Plains, MO 6577